MORE HELP ONLINE

The Student Center for
The Bedford Introduction to Literature
bedfordstmartins.com/meyerlit

Check out our **FREE and open** visual tutorials, reference materials, and support for working with sources.

- *VirtuaLit* Tutorials for close reading
- *AuthorLinks* for research
- *LitGloss* for literary terms
- *LitQuizzes* for self-testing
- *Sample Papers* for MLA-style
- *Research & Documentation Online* for research
- *The Bedford Bibliographer* for research

VideoCentral: Literature
bedfordstmartins.com/videolit

Explore our growing collection of video interviews with today's writers — on what they read, where they get their ideas, and how they refine their craft. Featured authors include T. Coraghessan Boyle, Chitra Banerjee Divakaruni, Ha Jin, and Anne Rice.

THE BEDFORD INTRODUCTION TO LITERATURE

Reading · Thinking · Writing

NINTH EDITION

THE BEDFORD INTRODUCTION TO LITERATURE

Reading · Thinking · Writing

Michael Meyer

University of Connecticut

BEDFORD/ST. MARTIN'S Boston ◆ New York

For Bedford/St. Martin's

Senior Executive Editor: Stephen A. Scipione
Executive Editor: Ellen Thibault
Developmental Editor: Christina Gerogiannis
Production Editor: Annette Pagliaro Sweeney
Production Supervisor: Jennifer Peterson
Marketing Manager: Adrienne Petsick
Editorial Assistant: Sophia Snyder
Production Assistants: David Ayers and Lidia MacDonald-Carr
Copyeditor: Lisa Wehrle
Senior Art Director: Anna Palchik
Text Design: Claire Seng-Niemoeller
Cover Design: Donna Lee Dennison
Cover Art: Wisconsin and N Street, by Joseph Craig English. Used with permission of the artist.
Composition: Glyph International
Printing and Binding: Worldcolor/Taunton

President: Joan E. Feinberg
Editorial Director: Denise B. Wydra
Editor in Chief: Karen S. Henry
Director of Marketing: Karen R. Soeltz
Director of Editing, Design, and Production: Marcia Cohen
Assistant Director of Editing, Design, and Production: Elise S. Kaiser
Managing Editor: Elizabeth M. Schaaf

Library of Congress Control Number: 2009941478

For information, write: Bedford/St. Martin's, 75 Arlington Street, Boston, MA 02116 (617-399-4000)

ISBN-10: 0-312-53921-5   ISBN-13: 978-0-312-53921-4   (College Edition)
ISBN-10: 0-312-60101-8   ISBN-13: 978-0-312-60101-0   (High School Edition)

Acknowledgments

FICTION

Margaret Atwood. "Happy Endings" from *Good Bones and Simple Murders* by Margaret Atwood. Copyright © 1983, 1992, 1994 by O. W. Toad Ltd. A Nan A. Talese Book. Used by permission of Doubleday, a division of Random House, Inc., and McClelland & Stewart Ltd.

John Barth. "On Minimalist Fiction" from "A Few Words about Minimalism" by John Barth, originally published in the *New York Times.* Copyright © 1986 by John Barth. Reprinted with permission of the Wylie Agency LLC.

Acknowledgments and copyrights are continued at the back of the book on pages 2148–60, which constitute an extension of the copyright page. It is a violation of the law to reproduce these selections by any means whatsoever without the written permission of the copyright holder.

For My Wife
Regina Barreca

About Michael Meyer

Michael Meyer has taught writing and literature courses for more than thirty years — since 1981 at the University of Connecticut and before that at the University of North Carolina at Charlotte and the College of William and Mary. In addition to being an experienced teacher, Meyer is a highly regarded literary scholar. His scholarly articles have appeared in distinguished journals such as *American Literature, Studies in the American Renaissance,* and *Virginia Quarterly Review.* An internationally recognized authority on Henry David Thoreau, Meyer is a former president of the Thoreau Society and co-author (with Walter Harding) of *The New Thoreau Handbook,* a standard reference source. His first book, *Several More Lives to Live: Thoreau's Political Reputation in America,* was awarded the Ralph Henry Gabriel Prize by the American Studies Association. He is also the editor of *Frederick Douglass: The Narrative and Selected Writings.* He has lectured on a variety of American literary topics from Cambridge University to Peking University. His other books for Bedford/St. Martin's include *The Compact Bedford Introduction to Literature,* Eighth Edition; *Poetry: An Introduction,* Sixth Edition; and *Thinking and Writing about Literature,* Second Edition.

Preface for Instructors

Like its predecessors, the ninth edition of *The Bedford Introduction to Literature* assumes that reading and understanding literature offers a valuable means of apprehending life in its richness and diversity. This book also reflects the hope that its selections will inspire students to become lifelong readers of imaginative literature, as well as more thoughtful and skillful writers.

As before, the text is flexibly organized into four parts focusing on fiction, poetry, drama, and critical thinking and writing. The first three parts explain the literary elements of each genre and how to write about them. These three parts also explore several additional approaches to reading literature and conclude with an anthology of literary works. The fourth part provides detailed instruction on thinking, reading, and writing about literature that can be assigned selectively throughout the course. Sample student papers and more than 2,000 assignments appear in the text, offering students the support they need to read and write about literature.

Class-tested in thousands of literature courses, *The Bedford Introduction to Literature* accommodates many different teaching styles. The ninth edition features a new in-depth chapter created with poet Billy Collins and three new case studies on short-short fiction, the natural world, and life's milestones. Two new online resources — a book-specific **Student Center** with lots of help for reading and writing about literature, and *VideoCentral: Literature,* a growing collection of exclusive interviews with today's authors — offer even more options for teaching, learning, and enjoying literature.

FEATURES OF *THE BEDFORD INTRODUCTION TO LITERATURE,* NINTH EDITION

A description of the features and content that have long made *The Bedford Introduction to Literature* a favorite of students and teachers follows. What is new to this edition is described starting on page xi.

A wide and well-balanced selection of literature

77 stories, 466 poems, and 21 plays represent a variety of periods, nationalities, cultures, styles, and voices — from the serious to the humorous, and

from the traditional to the contemporary. Each selection has been chosen for its appeal to students and for its effectiveness in demonstrating the elements, significance, and pleasures of literature. As in previous editions, canonical works by Ernest Hemingway, John Keats, Susan Glaspell, and many others are generously represented. In addition, there are many contemporary selections from writers such as John Patrick Shanley, Lee Smith, Z. Z. Packer, and Junot Díaz, as well as a rich sampling of works by writers from other cultures, such as Naguib Mahfouz (Egypt), Bessie Head (Botswana), Gabriel García Márquez (Colombia), and Yousif al-Sa'igh (Iraq). Recent and international selections appear throughout the anthology and are also conveniently collected in chapters designated as *Albums of Contemporary Literature* and *Albums of World Literature*.

Many options for teaching and learning about literature

Over nine editions, in its continuing effort to make literature come to life for students, and the course a pleasure to teach for instructors, *The Bedford Introduction to Literature* has developed and refined these innovative features:

PERSPECTIVES ON LITERATURE   More than one hundred intriguing documents — including personal journals, letters, critical essays, interviews, and contextual images — appear throughout the book to stimulate class discussion and writing.

CONNECTIONS BETWEEN "POPULAR" AND "LITERARY" CULTURE   The fiction, poetry, and drama introductions incorporate examples from popular culture, effectively introducing students to the literary elements of a given genre through what they already know. For example, students are introduced to the elements of fiction through excerpts from a romance novel and from *Tarzan of the Apes;* to the elements of poetry through greeting card verse and song lyrics by Bruce Springsteen; and to elements of drama through a television script from *Seinfeld.* Unique visual portfolios, Encountering Fiction, Encountering Poetry, and Encountering Drama, present images that demonstrate how literature is woven into the fabric of popular culture and art. Students encounter **fiction** through comics and graphic novels; **poetry** through advertisements, posters, and cartoons; and **drama** through popular images of *Hamlet* in art and performance. These images help students recognize the imprint of literature on their everyday lives.

From "Encountering Poetry."

ENHANCED TREATMENT OF AUTHORS IN DEPTH   Each genre section includes chapters that focus closely on two or more major figures. There are three stories each by Nathaniel Hawthorne and Flannery O'Connor; an extensive

From Chapter 13: A Critical Case Study: William Faulkner's "Barn Burning."

selection of poems by Emily Dickinson, Robert Frost, and Langston Hughes; and two plays each by Sophocles and Shakespeare. Complementing the literature in these chapters are biographical introductions (with author photographs); chronologies; critical perspectives (including complementary critical readings where writers argue for different interpretations of the same texts); cultural documents (such as letters and draft manuscript pages); and a generous collection of images that serve to contextualize the works. A variety of critical thinking and writing questions follow the selections to stimulate student responses. All these supplementary materials engage students more fully with the writers and their works.

CULTURAL, CRITICAL, AND THEMATIC CASE STUDIES   Each *Cultural Case Study* presents a literary work together with documents and images to help students understand the work in its cultural context. For example, James Joyce's "Eveline" is accompanied by a facsimile of its first appearance in an Irish periodical, photographs, a poster, a letter, and an excerpt from a temperance almanac. Each *Critical Case Study* gathers four or more critical analyses of a single work — for example, Henrik Ibsen's *A Doll House* — to illustrate a variety of contemporary critical approaches. Each *Thematic Case Study* invites students to explore literature through a particular topic, such as "Remarkably Short-Short Stories" in fiction, and "Love and Longing" in poetry. In addition, two generously illustrated Case Studies explore intercultural themes and the influence of the South on literature. "Crossing Boundaries," a unique full-color unit, pairs six poems with visual texts on the theme of crossing racial, class-based, and geographical borders.

From "Crossing Boundaries."

Chapter 15, "The Literature of the South," reprints major statements about southern literature and a collection of images — including paintings, an etching, and documentary photographs — that offer contexts for the many works by southern writers included in the anthology.

ACCESSIBLE COVERAGE OF LITERARY THEORY   For instructors who wish to incorporate literary theory into their courses, Chapter 53, "Critical Strategies for Reading," introduces students to a variety of critical strategies, ranging from formalism to cultural criticism. In brief examples the approaches are applied in analyzing Kate Chopin's "The Story of an Hour" as well as other works, so that students will develop a sense of how to use these strategies in their own reading and writing.

Plenty of help with reading, writing, and research

CRITICAL READING*   Advice on how to read literature appears at the beginning of each genre section. Sample Close Readings of selections including Kate Chopin's "Story of an Hour" (Fiction), William Hathaway's "Oh, Oh" (Poetry), and Susan Glaspell's *Trifles* (Drama) provide analyses of the language, images, and other literary elements at work in these selections. Interpretive annotations clearly show students the process of close reading and provide examples of the kind of critical thinking that leads to strong academic writing.

A Sample Close Reading

KATE CHOPIN (1851–1904)
The Story of an Hour   1894

Knowing that Mrs. Mallard was afflicted with a heart trouble, great care was taken to break to her as gently as possible the news of her husband's death.

It was her sister Josephine who told her, in broken sentences; veiled hints that revealed in half concealing. Her husband's friend Richards was there, too, near her. It was he who had been in the newspaper office when intelligence of the railroad disaster was received, with Brently Mallard's name leading the list of "killed." He had only taken the time to assure himself of its truth by a second telegram, and had hastened to forestall any less careful, less tender friend in bearing the sad message.

Later in the book, Chapter 54, "Reading and the Writing Process," provides more instruction on how to read a work closely, annotate a text, take notes, keep a reading journal, and develop a topic into a thesis, with a section on arguing persuasively about literature. An Index of Terms appears at the back of the book, and a glossary provides thorough explanations of more than two hundred terms central to the study of literature.

THE WRITING AND RESEARCH PROCESS   Seven chapters (2, 10, 22, 31, 46, 54, 55) cover every step of the writing process — from generating topics to documenting sources — while sample student papers model the results.

Of these chapters, three — "Writing about Fiction" (2), "Writing about Poetry: From Inquiry to Final Paper" (22), and "Writing about Drama" (46) — focus on genre-specific writing assignments. Another, "Reading and the Writing Process" (54), offers models of the types of papers most frequently assigned in the introductory course.

Thirty sample student papers — all with MLA-style documentation — model how to analyze and argue about literature and how to support ideas by citing examples. The papers are

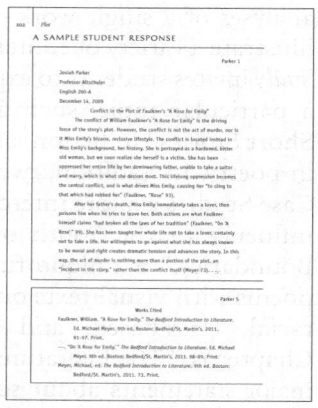

A sample student paper on William Faulkner's "A Rose for Emily" makes an argument about the story and includes parenthetical citations and a Works Cited page.

---

*A reference chart on the book's inside front cover outlines all of the book's help for reading and writing about literature.

integrated throughout the book, as are nine "Questions for Writing" units that guide students through particular writing tasks: reading and writing responsively; developing a topic into a revised thesis; incorporating secondary sources; applying a critical approach to a work; and writing about multiple works by an author.

Two unique chapters, "Combining the Elements of Fiction: A Writing Process" (10) and "Combining the Elements of Poetry: A Writing Process" (31) help students understand how literary elements work together, and how to write papers on the interplay of elements. For fiction, the emphasis is on how to develop a thesis and write an analysis paper, and for poetry, the focus is on writing an explication of a poem.

Chapter 55, "The Literary Research Paper," offers detailed advice for finding, evaluating, and incorporating sources in a paper and includes current, detailed MLA documentation guidelines.

QUESTIONS FOR CRITICAL READING AND WRITING   More than two thousand questions and assignments — "Considerations for Critical Thinking and Writing," "Connections to Other Selections," "First Response" prompts, "Critical Strategies," questions, and "Creative Response" assignments — spark students' interest, sharpen their thinking, and improve their reading, discussion, and writing skills.

NEW TO THIS EDITION

120 fresh selections

21 STORIES, 93 POEMS, AND 6 PLAYS representing canonical, multicultural, contemporary, and popular literature are new to this edition. Complementing the addition of several classic literary works that have long made classroom discussion come alive are numerous stories, poems, and plays that appear for the first time in an introduction to literature anthology. These new works include stories by Rick Moody, David Foster Wallace, and Jhumpa Lahiri; poems by Kay Ryan, Louise Glück, and Alberto Ríos; and plays by Christopher Durang and Josefina Lopez.

Jhumpa Lahiri, author of "Hell-Heaven."

Rick Moody, author of "Boys."

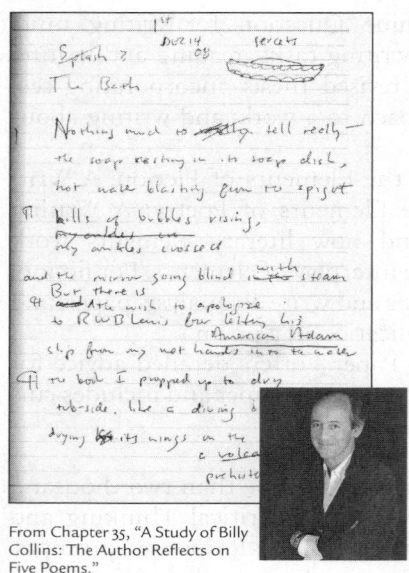

From Chapter 35, "A Study of Billy Collins: The Author Reflects on Five Poems."

An in-depth chapter on Billy Collins — created with Billy Collins

Collins presents five of his own poems in Chapter 35 alongside his own insights — written specifically for Michael Meyer's anthologies — into each work, and shares photographs and pages from his notebooks. Like its sister chapter created with Julia Alvarez (Ch. 36), this new case study continues Meyer's emphasis on poetry as a living, changing art form. Once again, students will enjoy the opportunity to have a major poet speak directly to them, this time in Collins's one-of-a-kind style, about how he writes, why he writes, and the kinds of surprises that occur along the way.

Three new case studies

Chapter 17, "A Thematic Case Study: Remarkably Short-Short Stories," presents captivating stories by writers including Sandra Cisneros, David Foster Wallace, and Margaret Atwood. In a new chapter on **formative experiences and coming-of-age** (Ch. 40), poets such as Charles Simic, Anne Carson, and Yusef Komunyakaa get to the heart of many of life's important milestones with memorable poems that students will relate to. A new chapter on **our relationship with the environment** (Ch. 41) offers literature that is as varied, rich, and personal as the subject itself — with such works as Maxine Kumin's "Though He Tarry" (on the urgency of protecting the earth) and Gail White's "Dead Armadillos" (on beauty, scarcity, and what we choose to save).

YOU GET MORE DIGITAL CHOICES FOR *THE BEDFORD INTRODUCTION TO LITERATURE*

The Bedford Introduction to Literature doesn't stop with a book. Online, you'll find both free and affordable premium resources to help students get even more out of the book and your course. You'll also find convenient instructor resources, and even a nationwide community of teachers. To learn more about or order any of the products below, contact your Bedford/St. Martin's sales representative, e-mail sales support (sales_support@bfwpub.com), or visit the Web site at **bedfordstmartins.com/meyerlit/catalog.**

New! The Student Center for the Bedford Introduction to Literature
bedfordstmartins.com/meyerlit

Send students to free and open resources, choose flexible premium resources to supplement your print text, or upgrade to an expanding collection of innovative digital content.

FREE AND OPEN RESOURCES FOR *THE BEDFORD INTRODUCTION TO LITERATURE* provide students with easy-to-access visual tutorials, reference materials, and support for working with sources.

- *VirtuaLit* Tutorials for Close Reading (Fiction, Poetry, and Drama)
- *AuthorLinks* and Biographies
- Quizzes on Literary Works
- A Glossary of Literary Terms
- MLA-style sample student papers
- Help for finding and citing sources, including Diana Hacker's *Researching and Documentation* online

NEW! *VIDEOCENTRAL: LITERATURE VideoCentral: Literature* — a Bedford/St. Martin's production created with writer and teacher Peter Berkow — is a growing collection of video interviews with today's writers, talking about their craft. Your students can hear from Ha Jin on how he uses humor and tension in his writing, Anne Rice on how she advances plot through

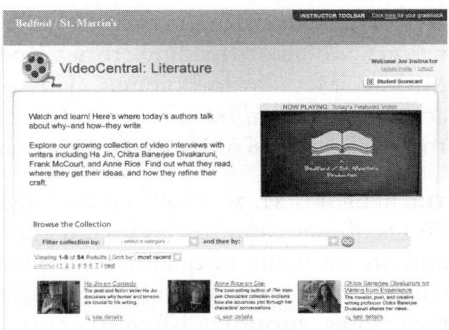

dialogue, Chitra Banerjee Divakaruni on how she writes from experience, and T. C. Boyle on how he creates memorable voices. Related assignments and activities help students get the most out of these instructive videos and apply what they learn to their own thinking and writing.

For a list of authors and topics and a sample video, visit **bedford stmartins.com/videolit**. *VideoCentral: Literature* can be packaged free with new student editions of the book. An activation code is required. To order *VideoCentral: Literature* with the print book, use **ISBN-10: 0-312-64361-6** or **ISBN-13: 978-0-312-64361-4**.

Instructor Resources: bedfordstmartins.com/meyerlit/catalog

You have a lot to do in your course. Bedford/St. Martin's wants to make it easy for you to find the support you need — and to get it quickly.

RESOURCES FOR TEACHING THE BEDFORD INTRODUCTION TO LITERATURE is available as a spiral-bound print manual or as a PDF that can be downloaded from the Bedford/St. Martin's online catalog or *The Student Center*. This 544-page manual supports every selection in the book and has something to offer new and experienced instructors. Resources include commentary, biographical information, additional writing assignments, further connections among the selections, and tips from instructors who have taught with the book. For the PDF, go to **bedfordstmartins.com/meyerlit/catalog.** To order the print edition, use **ISBN-10: 0-312-60102-6** or **ISBN-13: 978-0-312-60102-7**.

TEACHING CENTRAL offers the entire list of Bedford/St. Martin's print and online professional resources in one place. You'll find landmark reference works, sourcebooks on pedagogical issues, award-winning collections, and practical advice for the classroom — all free for instructors and available through the Student Center or at **bedfordstmartins.com/meyerlit/catalog.**

LITERATURE ALOUD is a two-CD set of audio recordings featuring celebrated writers and actors reading stories, poems, and selected scenes included in Michael Meyer's anthologies. This resource is free to instructors who adopt *The Bedford Introduction to Literature*. To order the CD set, use **ISBN-10: 0-312-43011-6** or **ISBN-13: 978-0-312-43011-5**.

THE BEDFORD/ST. MARTIN'S VIDEO & DVD LIBRARY offers selected videos and DVDs of plays and stories included in *The Bedford Introduction to Literature*, and are available to qualified adopters of the anthology. To learn more, contact your Bedford/St. Martin's sales representative or e-mail sales support (**sales_support@bfwpub.com**).

CONTENT FOR COURSE MANAGEMENT SYSTEMS — including Blackboard, WebCT, Angel, and Desire2Learn — allows you to easily download Bedford/ St. Martin's digital materials for your course. For more information, visit **bedfordstmartins.com/cms.**

LITERARY REPRINTS   Titles in the Case Studies in Contemporary Criticism series, Bedford Cultural Edition series, and the Bedford Shakespeare series can be shrink-wrapped with *The Bedford Introduction to Literature* for instructors who want to teach longer works in conjunction with the anthology. (For a complete list of available titles, visit **bedfordstmartins .com/meyerlit/catalog.**)

TRADEUP

ACKNOWLEDGMENTS

This book has benefited from the ideas, suggestions, and corrections of scores of careful readers who helped transform various stages of an evolving manuscript into a finished book and into subsequent editions. I remain grateful to those I have thanked in previous prefaces, particularly the late Robert Wallace of Case Western Reserve University. In addition, many instructors who used the eighth edition of *The Bedford Introduction to Literature* responded to a questionnaire for the book. For their valuable comments and advice I am grateful to Sandra Allen-Kearney, Lincoln Park Academy; Jon W. Brooks, Okaloosa-Walton College; David Brumbley, Salisbury University; Robert Caughey, Torrey Pines High School; S. Elaine Craghead, Massachusetts Maritime Academy; Robert W. Croft, Gainesville State College; Allen Culpepper, Manatee Community College; Samir Dayal, Bentley College; Cheryl DeLacretaz, Dripping Springs High School; Janice Forgione,

Salisbury University; Bernadette Gambino, University of North Florida; Sinceree Renee Gunn, University of Alabama in Huntsville; Cathy Henrichs, Pikes Peak Community College; Susan Hopkirk, Middle Tennessee State University; Mary Lee Stephenson Huffer, Lake Sumter Community College; Michelle Green Jimmerson, Louisiana Tech University; Sharon Johnston, Spokane Virtual Learning/Spokane Public Schools; Tamara Kuzmenkov, Tacoma Community College; Catherine Shanon Lawson, Pikes Peak Community College; Manuel Martinez, Santa Fe Community College; Sarah McIntosh, Santa Fe Community College; Jim McKeown, McLennan Community College; Julie Moore, Green River Community College; Larry Moss, Young Men's Academy for Academic and Civic Development at MacArthur South; Angelina Northrip-Rivera, Missouri State University; David Pink, Rock Valley College; Deidre D. Price, Okaloosa-Walton College; Katharine Purcell, Trident Technical College; Karin Russell, Keiser University; Holly Schoenecker, Milwaukee Area Technical College; Beth Shelton, Paris Junior College; Karen Stewart, Norwich University; John A. Stoler, University of Texas at San Antonio; James D. Suderman, Okaloosa-Walton College; Becky Talk; Gregory J. Underwood, Pearl River Community College — Forrest County Center; Marva Webb, Clinton High School.

I would also like to give special thanks to the following instructors who contributed teaching tips to *Resources for Teaching* THE BEDFORD INTRODUCTION TO LITERATURE: Sandra Adickes, Winona State University; Helen J. Aling, Northwestern College; Sr. Anne Denise Brenann, College of Mt. St. Vincent; Robin Calitri, Merced College; James H. Clemmer, Austin Peay State University; Robert Croft, Gainesville College; Thomas Edwards, Westbrook College; Elizabeth Kleinfeld, Red Rocks Community College; Olga Lyles, University of Nevada; Timothy Peters, Boston University, Catherine Rusco, Muskegon Community College; Robert M. St. John, DePaul University; Richard Stoner, Broome Community College; Nancy Veiga, Modesto Junior College; Karla Walters, University of New Mexico; and Joseph Zeppetello, Ulster Community College.

I am also indebted to those who cheerfully answered questions and generously provided miscellaneous bits of information. What might have seemed to them like inconsequential conversations turned out to be important leads. Among these friends and colleagues are Raymond Anselment, Barbara Campbell, Ann Charters, Karen Chow, John Christie, Eleni Coundouriotis, Irving Cummings, William Curtin, Patrick Hogan, Lee Jacobus, Thomas Jambeck, Bonnie Januszewski-Ytuarte, Greta Little, George Monteiro, Brenda Murphy, Joel Myerson, Rose Quiello, Thomas Recchio, William Sheidley, Stephanie Smith, Milton Stern, Kenneth Wilson, and the dedicated reference librarians at the Homer Babbidge Library, University of Connecticut. I am particularly happy to acknowledge the tactful help of Roxanne Cody, owner of R. J. Julia Booksellers in Madison, Connecticut, whose passion for books authorizes her as the consummate matchmaker for writers, readers, and titles. It's a wonder that somebody doesn't call the cops.

I continue to be grateful for what I have learned from teaching my students and for the many student papers I have received over the years that I have used in various forms to serve as good and accessible models of student writing. I am also indebted to Stefanie Wortman for her extensive work on the ninth edition of *Resources for Teaching* THE BEDFORD INTRODUCTION TO LITERATURE.

At Bedford/St. Martin's, my debts once again require more time to acknowledge than the deadline allows. Charles H. Christensen and Joan E. Feinberg initiated this project and launched it with their intelligence, energy, and sound advice. This book has also benefited from the savvy insights of Denise Wydra and Steve Scipione. Earlier editions of the book were shaped by editors Karen Henry, Kathy Retan, Alanya Harter, Aron Keesbury, and Ellen Thibault; their work was as first rate as it was essential. As development editor for the ninth edition, Christina Gerogiannis expertly kept the book on track and made the journey a pleasure to the end; her valuable contributions richly remind me of how fortunate I am to be a Bedford/St. Martin's author. Stephanie Naudin, associate editor, energetically developed the book's instructor's manual, and Sophia Snyder, editorial assistant, gracefully handled a variety of editorial tasks. Permissions were deftly arranged by Arthur Johnson, Martha Friedman, and Susan Doheny. The difficult tasks of production were skillfully managed by Annette Pagliaro Sweeney, whose attention to details and deadlines was essential to the completion of this project. Lisa Wehrle provided careful copyediting, and Janet Cocker and Linda McLatchie did meticulous proofreading. I thank all of the people at Bedford/St. Martin's — including Donna Dennison, who designed the cover, and Adrienne Petsick, the marketing manager — who helped to make this formidable project a manageable one.

Finally, I am grateful to my sons Timothy and Matthew for all kinds of help, but mostly I'm just grateful they're my sons. And for making all the difference, I thank my wife, Regina Barreca.

Brief Contents

POETRY

DRAMA

Contents

To seek the source, the impulse of a story is like tearing a flower to pieces for wantonness.

— KATE CHOPIN

Writing permits me to experience life as any number of strange creations.

— ALICE WALKER

I put a group of characters in some sort of predicament, and then watch them try to work themselves free.

— STEPHEN KING

It is not necessary to portray many characters. The center of gravity should be in two persons: him and her.
— ANTON CHEKHOV

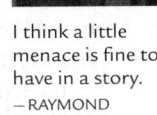

I think a little menace is fine to have in a story.

— RAYMOND CARVER

10. Combining the Elements of Fiction: A Writing Process *378*

Approaches to Fiction 393

11. A Study of Nathaniel Hawthorne 395

My book, if you would see anything in it, requires to be read in the clear, brown, twilight atmosphere in which it was written . . .
—NATHANIEL HAWTHORNE

12. A Study of Flannery O'Connor *442*

13. A Critical Case Study: William Faulkner's "Barn Burning" *499*

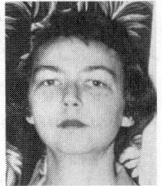

Every time a story of mine appears in a Freshman anthology, I have a vision of it, with its little organs laid open, like a frog in a bottle.
— FLANNERY O'CONNOR

Cartoon by Flannery O'Connor.

It is the writer's privilege to help man endure by lifting his heart.
—WILLIAM FAULKNER

Rowan Oak,
William
Faulkner's home.

14. A Cultural Case Study: James Joyce's "Eveline"   529

15. A Thematic Case Study: The Literature of the South   548

16. A Thematic Case Study: Humor and Satire   566

17. A Thematic Case Study: Remarkably Short-Short Stories   608

A Collection of Stories   629

Writers lie. So
do tape
recorders and
video cameras.
So does mem-
ory. As a fiction
writer this
doesn't bother
me at all.

—AMY BLOOM

POETRY 739

The Elements of Poetry 741

There is no happiness like mine. I have been eating poetry.

—MARK STRAND

A poet has a duty
to words . . .
words can do
wonderful
things.
—GWENDOLYN
BROOKS

Between my
finger and my
thumb / The
squat pen rests. /
I'll dig with it.
— SEAMUS HEANEY

Like a piece of ice
on a hot stove
the poem must
ride on its own
melting.
— ROBERT FROST

25. Figures of Speech 864

Simile and Metaphor 866

Other Figures 869

Poems for Further Study 874

26. Symbol, Allegory, and Irony *888*

Symbol *888*

Allegory *891*

Irony *893*

Poems for Further Study *898*

Literature is
the apparatus
through which
the world tries to
keep intact its
important ideas
and feelings.
— MARY OLIVER

27. Sounds *916*

28. Patterns of Rhythm *946*

I would define, in brief, the Poetry of words as the Rhythmical Creation of Beauty. Its sole arbiter is Taste.
—EDGAR ALLAN POE

A short poem
need not be
small.
— MARVIN BELL

30. Open Form   1000

In poetry you
have a form
looking for a
subject and a
subject look-
ing for a form.
When they come
together success-
fully you have a
poem.
— W. H. AUDEN

31. Combining the Elements of Poetry: A Writing Process   1028

The Elements Together   1028

Mapping the Poem   1029

Asking Questions about the Elements   1031

A SAMPLE CLOSE READING
   An Annotated Version of "Death Be Not Proud"   *1031*

A SAMPLE FIRST RESPONSE   1032

Organizing Your Thoughts   1033

A SAMPLE INFORMAL OUTLINE   1033

The Elements and Theme   1034

A SAMPLE EXPLICATION
   The Use of Conventional Metaphors for Death in John Donne's
   "Death Be Not Proud"   *1034*

Approaches to Poetry   1039

32. A Study of Emily Dickinson   1041

A Brief Biography   1042

An Introduction to Her Work   1047

My business is circumference.

— EMILY DICKINSON

A cartoon from a letter from Emily Dickinson to William Cowper Dickinson.

A poem . . . begins as a lump in the throat, a sense of wrong, a homesickness, a love-sickness. . . .
— ROBERT FROST

A manuscript page from "Neither Out Far nor In Deep."

34. A Study of Langston Hughes 1129

I believe that
poetry
should be
direct,
comprehen-
sible, and the
epitome of
simplicity.
— LANGSTON
HUGHES

Genuine poetry can communicate before it is understood.
— T. S. ELIOT

For a man to become a poet . . . he must be in love or miserable.
— LORD BYRON

An Anthology of Poems 1285

Poetry has become a kind of tool for knowing the world in a particular way.
—JANE HIRSHFIELD

If there were no poetry on any day in the world, poetry would be invented that day. For there would be an intolerable hunger.
—MURIEL RUKEYSER

44. A Collection of Poems *1315*

— LUCILLE CLIFTON

l | *Contents*

—WILLIAM
WORDSWORTH

DRAMA 1359

The Study of Drama 1361

In order to create the universal, you must pay very great attention to the specific.
— LORRAINE HANSBERRY

Plays in Performance

Photos of scenes from:

Oedipus the King

Antigone

A Midsummer Night's Dream

Hamlet

A Doll House

Real Women Have Curves

Doubt

Rodeo

Fences

Between pages 1412 and 1413

A scene from *Antigone.*

I depict men
as they ought
to be . . .
—SOPHOCLES

All the world's a
stage, / And all
the men and
women merely
players: / They
have their exits
and their en-
trances; / And
one man in his
time plays many
parts . . .
—WILLIAM
SHAKESPEARE

Encountering Drama: A Visual Portfolio:
Hamlet in Popular Culture and Performance 1698

49. Modern Drama 1704

50. A Critical Case Study:
Henrik Ibsen's *A Doll House* 1764

The catastrophe
approaches,
inexorably,
inevitably. De-
spair, conflict,
and destruction.
— HENRIK IBSEN

51. A Thematic Case Study: An Album of Contemporary Humor and Satire   1781

A Collection of Plays   1821

52. Plays for Further Reading   1823

All my work
in some sense
confronts the
issue of fluidity
of identity.
— DAVID HENRY
HWANG

My plays are
about love,
honor, duty,
betrayal — things
humans have
written about
since the begin-
ning of time.
— AUGUST WILSON

CRITICAL THINKING
AND WRITING

2039

The answers you
get from litera-
ture depend
upon the ques-
tions you pose.
—MARGARET
ATWOOD

I can't write five
words but that
I change seven.
—DOROTHY
PARKER

Great literature
is simply lan-
guage charged
with meaning to
the utmost pos-
sible degree.
— EZRA POUND

THE BEDFORD
INTRODUCTION TO
LITERATURE

Reading · Thinking · Writing

INTRODUCTION

Reading
Imaginative Literature

Literature has been the salvation of the
damned; literature has inspired and
guided lovers, routed despair, and can
perhaps . . . save the world.
—JOHN CHEEVER

© Jerry Bauer.

THE NATURE OF LITERATURE

Literature does not lend itself to a single tidy definition because the making of it over the centuries has been as complex, unwieldy, and natural as life itself. Is literature everything that has been written, from ancient prayers to graffiti? Does it include songs and stories that were not written down until many years after they were recited? Does literature include the television scripts from *Seinfeld* as well as Shakespeare's *King Lear*? Is literature only writing that has permanent value and continues to move people? Must literature be true or beautiful or moral? Should it be socially useful?

Although these kinds of questions are not conclusively answered in this book, they are implicitly raised by the stories, poems, and plays included here. No definition of literature, particularly a brief one, is likely to satisfy everyone because definitions tend to weaken and require qualification when confronted by the uniqueness of individual works. In this context it is worth recalling Herman Melville's humorous use of a definition of a whale in *Moby-Dick* (1851). In the course of the novel Melville presents his imaginative and symbolic whale as inscrutable, but he begins with a quotation from Georges Cuvier, a French naturalist who defines a whale in his nineteenth-century study *The Animal Kingdom* this way: "The whale is a mammiferous animal without hind feet." Cuvier's description is technically correct, of course, but there is little wisdom in it. Melville understood that the reality of the whale (which he describes as the "ungraspable phantom of life") cannot be caught by isolated facts. If the full meaning of the whale is to be understood, it must be sought on the open sea of experience, where the whale itself is, rather than in exclusionary definitions. Facts and definitions are helpful; however, they do not always reveal the whole truth.

Despite Melville's reminder that a definition can be too limiting and even comical, it is useful for our purposes to describe literature as a fiction consisting of carefully arranged words designed to stir the imagination. Stories, poems, and plays are fictional. They are made up — imagined — even when based on actual historic events. Such imaginative writing differs from other kinds of writing because its purpose is not primarily to transmit facts or ideas. Imaginative literature is a source more of pleasure than of information, and we read it for basically the same reasons we listen to music or view a dance: enjoyment, delight, and satisfaction. Like other art forms, imaginative literature offers pleasure and usually attempts to convey a perspective, mood, feeling, or experience. Writers transform the facts the world provides — people, places, and objects — into experiences that suggest meanings.

Consider, for example, the difference between the following factual description of a snake and a poem on the same subject. Here is *Webster's Eleventh New Collegiate Dictionary*'s definition:

> any of numerous limbless scaled reptiles (suborder Serpentes syn. Ophidia) with a long tapering body and with salivary glands often modified to produce venom which is injected through grooved or tubular fangs.

Contrast this matter-of-fact definition with Emily Dickinson's poetic evocation of a snake in "A narrow Fellow in the Grass":

A narrow Fellow in the Grass
Occasionally rides —
You may have met Him — did you not
His notice sudden is —

The Grass divides as with a Comb —   5
A spotted shaft is seen —
And then it closes at your feet
And opens further on —

He likes a Boggy Acre
A floor too cool for Corn —   10
Yet when a Boy, and Barefoot —
I more than once at Noon

Have passed, I thought, a Whip lash
Unbraiding in the Sun
When stooping to secure it   15
It wrinkled, and was gone —

Several of Nature's People
I know, and they know me —
I feel for them a transport
Of cordiality —   20

But never met this Fellow
Attended, or alone
Without a tighter breathing
And Zero at the Bone —

The dictionary provides a succinct, anatomical description of what a snake is, while Dickinson's poem suggests what a snake can mean. The definition offers facts; the poem offers an experience. The dictionary would probably allow someone who had never seen a snake to sketch one with reasonable accuracy. The poem also provides some vivid subjective descriptions — for example, the snake dividing the grass "as with a Comb" — yet it offers more than a picture of serpentine movements. The poem conveys the ambivalence many people have about snakes — the kind of feeling, for example, so evident on the faces of visitors viewing the snakes at a zoo. In the poem there is both a fascination with and a horror of what might be called snakehood; this combination of feelings has been coiled in most of us since Adam and Eve.

That "narrow Fellow" so cordially introduced by way of a riddle (the word *snake* is never used in the poem) is, by the final stanza, revealed as a snake in the grass. In between, Dickinson uses language expressively to convey her meaning. For instance, in the line "His notice sudden is," listen to the *s* sound in each word and note how the verb *is* unexpectedly appears at the end, making the snake's hissing presence all the more "sudden." And anyone who has ever been surprised by a snake knows the "tighter breathing / And Zero at the Bone" that Dickinson evokes so successfully by the rhythm of her word choices and line breaks. Perhaps even more significant, Dickinson's poem allows those who have never encountered a snake to imagine such an experience.

A good deal more could be said about the numbing fear that undercuts the affection for nature at the beginning of this poem, but the point here is that imaginative literature gives us not so much the full, factual proportions of the world as some of its experiences and meanings. Instead of defining the world, literature encourages us to try it out in our imaginations.

THE VALUE OF LITERATURE

Mark Twain once shrewdly observed that a person who chooses not to read has no advantage over a person who is unable to read. In industrialized societies today, however, the question is not who reads, because nearly everyone can and does, but what is read. Why should anyone spend precious time with literature when there is so much reading material available that provides useful information about everything from the daily news to personal computers? Why should a literary artist's imagination compete for attention that could be spent on the firm realities that constitute everyday life? In fact, national best-seller lists much less often include collections of stories, poems, or plays than they do cookbooks and, not surprisingly, diet books. Although such fare may be filling, it doesn't stay with you. Most people have other appetites too.

Certainly one of the most important values of literature is that it nourishes our emotional lives. An effective literary work may seem to speak directly to us, especially if we are ripe for it. The inner life that good writers reveal in their characters often gives us glimpses of some portion of ourselves. We can be moved to laugh, cry, tremble, dream, ponder, shriek, or rage with a character by simply turning a page instead of turning our lives upside down. Although the experience itself is imagined, the emotion is real. That's why the final chapters of a good adventure novel can make a reader's heart race as much as a 100-yard dash or why the repressed love of Hester Prynne in *The Scarlet Letter* by Nathaniel Hawthorne is painful to a sympathetic reader. Human emotions speak a universal language regardless of when or where a work was written.

In addition to appealing to our emotions, literature broadens our perspectives on the world. Most of the people we meet are pretty much like ourselves, and what we can see of the world even in a lifetime is astonishingly limited. Literature allows us to move beyond the inevitable boundaries of our own lives and culture because it introduces us to people different from ourselves, places remote from our neighborhoods, and times other than our own. Reading makes us more aware of life's possibilities as well as its subtleties and ambiguities. Put simply, people who read literature experience more life and have a keener sense of a common human identity than those who do not. It is true, of course, that many people go through life without reading imaginative literature, but that is a loss rather than a gain. They may find themselves troubled by the same kinds of questions that reveal Daisy Buchanan's restless, vague discontentment in F. Scott Fitzgerald's *The Great Gatsby:* "What'll we do with ourselves this afternoon?" cried Daisy, "and the day after that, and the next thirty years?"

Sometimes students mistakenly associate literature more with school than with life. Accustomed to reading it in order to write a paper or pass an examination, students may perceive such reading as a chore instead of a pleasurable opportunity, something considerably less important than studying for the "practical" courses that prepare them for a career. The study of literature, however, is also practical because it engages you in the kinds of problem solving important in a variety of fields, from philosophy to science and technology. The interpretation of literary texts requires you to deal with uncertainties, value judgments, and emotions; these are unavoidable aspects of life.

People who make the most significant contributions to their professions — whether in business, engineering, teaching, or some other area — tend to be challenged rather than threatened by multiple possibilities. Instead of retreating to the way things have always been done, they bring freshness and creativity to their work. F. Scott Fitzgerald once astutely described the "test of a first-rate intelligence" as "the ability to hold two opposed ideas in the mind at the same time, and still retain the ability to function." People with such intelligence know how to read situations, shape questions, interpret details, and evaluate competing points of view. Equipped with a healthy respect for facts, they also understand the value of pursuing hunches and exercising their imaginations. Reading literature encourages a suppleness of mind that is helpful in any discipline or work.

Once the requirements for your degree are completed, what ultimately matters are not the courses listed on your transcript but the sensibilities and habits of mind that you bring to your work, friends, family, and, indeed, the rest of your life. A healthy economy changes and grows with the times; people do too if they are prepared for more than simply filling a job description. The range and variety of life that literature affords can help you to interpret your own experiences and the world in which you live.

To discover the insights that literature reveals requires careful reading and sensitivity. One of the purposes of a college introduction to literature class is to cultivate the analytic skills necessary for reading well. Class discussions often help establish a dialogue with a work that perhaps otherwise would not speak to you. Analytic skills can also be developed by writing about what you read. Writing is an effective means of clarifying your responses and ideas because it requires you to account for the author's use of language as well as your own. This book is based on two premises: that reading literature is pleasurable and that reading and understanding a work sensitively by thinking, talking, or writing about it increases the pleasure of the experience of it.

Understanding its basic elements — such as point of view, symbol, theme, tone, irony, and so on — is a prerequisite to an informed appreciation of literature. This kind of understanding allows you to perceive more in a literary work in much the same way that a spectator at a tennis match sees more if he or she understands the rules and conventions of the game. But literature is not simply a spectator sport. The analytic skills that open up literature also have their uses when you watch a television program or film and, more important, when you attempt to sort out the significance of the people, places, and events that constitute your own life. Literature enhances and sharpens your perceptions. What could be more lastingly practical as well as satisfying?

THE CHANGING LITERARY CANON

Perhaps the best reading creates some kind of change in us: we see more clearly; we're alert to nuances; we ask questions that previously didn't occur to us. Henry David Thoreau had that sort of reading in mind when he remarked in *Walden* that the books he valued most were those that caused him to date "a new era in his life from the reading." Readers are sometimes changed by literature, but it is also worth noting that the life of a literary work can also be affected by its readers. Melville's *Moby-Dick,* for example, was not valued as a classic until the 1920s, when critics rescued the novel from the obscurity of being cataloged in many libraries (including Yale's) not under fiction but under cetology, the study of whales. Indeed, many writers contemporary to Melville who were important and popular in the nineteenth century—William Cullen Bryant, Henry Wadsworth Longfellow, and James Russell Lowell, to name a few—are now mostly unread; their names appear more often on elementary schools built early in this century than in anthologies. Clearly, literary reputations and what is valued as great literature change over time and in the eyes of readers.

Such changes have steadily accelerated as the literary *canon*—those works considered by scholars, critics, and teachers to be the most important to read and study—has undergone a significant series of shifts. Writers who previously were overlooked, undervalued, neglected, or studiously ignored have been brought into focus in an effort to create a more diverse literary canon, one that recognizes the contributions of the many cultures that make up American society. Since the 1960s, for example, some critics have reassessed writings by women who had been left out of the standard literary traditions dominated by male writers. Many more female writers are now read alongside the male writers who traditionally populated literary history. Hence, a reader of Mark Twain and Stephen Crane is now just as likely to encounter Kate Chopin in a literary anthology. Until fairly recently Chopin was mostly regarded as a minor local colorist of Louisiana life. In the 1960s, however, the feminist movement helped to establish her present reputation as a significant voice in American literature owing to the feminist concerns so compellingly articulated by her female characters. This kind of enlargement of the canon also resulted from another reform movement of the 1960s. The civil rights movement sensitized literary critics to the political, moral, and aesthetic necessity of rediscovering African American literature, and more recently Asian and Hispanic writers have been making their way into the canon. Moreover, on a broader scale the canon is being revised and enlarged to include the works of writers from parts of the world other than the West, a development that reflects the changing values, concerns, and complexities of recent decades, when literary landscapes have shifted as dramatically as the political boundaries of much of the world.

No semester's reading list—or anthology—can adequately or accurately echo all the new voices competing to be heard as part of the mainstream literary canon, but recent efforts to open up the canon attempt to sensitize readers to the voices of women, minorities, and writers from all over the world. This development has not occurred without its urgent advocates or passionate dissenters. It's no surprise that issues about race, gender, and class often get people off the fence and on their feet (these controversies are discussed further in Chapter 53, "Critical Strategies for Reading"). Although what we regard as literature—whether it's called great, classic, or canonical—continues to generate debate, there is no question that such controversy will continue to reflect readers' values as well as the writers they admire.

FICTION

FICTION

The Elements
of Fiction

1

Reading Fiction

You don't find out you're an artist
because you do something really well.
You find out you're an artist because
when you fail you have something
within you — strength or belief or just
craziness — that picks you back up
again.
— JUNOT DÍAZ

To seek the source, the impulse of a
story is like tearing a flower to pieces for
wantonness.
— KATE CHOPIN

READING FICTION RESPONSIVELY

Reading a literary work responsively can be an intensely demanding activity. Henry David Thoreau — about as intense and demanding a reader and writer as they come — insists that "books must be read as deliberately and reservedly as they were written." Thoreau is right about the necessity for a conscious, sustained involvement with a literary work. Imaginative literature does demand more from us than, say, browsing through *People* magazine in a dentist's waiting room, but Thoreau makes the process sound a little more daunting than it really is. For when we respond to the demands of responsive reading, our efforts are usually rewarded with pleasure as well as understanding. Careful, deliberate reading — the kind that engages a reader's imagination as it calls forth the writer's — is a means of exploration that can take a reader outside whatever circumstance or experience previously defined his or her world. Just as we respond moment by moment to people and situations in our lives, we also respond to literary works as we read them, though we may not be fully aware of how we are affected at each point along the way. The more conscious we are of how and why we respond to works in particular ways, the more likely we are to be imaginatively engaged in our reading.

In a very real sense both the reader and the author create the literary work. How a reader responds to a story, poem, or play will help to determine its meaning. The author arranges the various elements that constitute his or her craft — elements such as plot, character, setting, point of view, symbolism, theme, and style, which you will be examining in subsequent chapters and which are defined in the Glossary of Literary Terms (p. 2123) — but the author cannot completely control the reader's response any more than a person can absolutely predict how a remark or action will be received by a stranger, a friend, or even a family member. Few authors *tell* readers how to respond. Our sympathy, anger, confusion, laughter, sadness, or whatever the feeling might be is left up to us to experience. Writers may have the talent to evoke such feelings, but they don't have the power and authority to enforce them. Because of the range of possible responses produced by imaginative literature, there is no single, correct, definitive response or interpretation. There can be readings that are wrongheaded or foolish, and some readings are better than others — that is, more responsive to a work's details and more persuasive — but that doesn't mean there is only one possible reading of a work (see Chapter 2, "Writing about Fiction").

Experience tells us that different people respond differently to the same work. Consider, for example, how often you've heard Melville's *Moby-Dick* described as one of the greatest American novels. This, however, is how a reviewer in *New Monthly Magazine* described the book when it was published in 1851: it is "a huge dose of hyperbolical slang, maudlin sentimentalism and tragic-comic bubble and squeak." Melville surely did not intend or desire this response; but there it is, and it was not a singular, isolated reaction. This reading — like any reading — was influenced by the values, assumptions, and expectations that the readers brought to the novel from both previous readings and life experiences. The reviewer's refusal to take the book seriously may have caused him to miss the boat from the perspective of many other readers of *Moby-Dick,* but it indicates that even "classics" (perhaps especially those kinds of works) can generate disparate readings.

Consider the following brief story by Kate Chopin, a writer whose fiction (like Melville's) sometimes met with indifference or hostility in her own time. As you read, keep track of your responses to the central character, Mrs. Mallard. Write down your feelings about her in a substantial paragraph when you finish the story. Think, for example, about how you respond to the emotions she expresses concerning news of her husband's death. What do you think of her feelings

Web   Explore contexts for Kate Chopin and approaches to this story at bedfordstmartins.com/meyerlit.

about marriage? Do you think you would react the way she does under similar circumstances?

KATE CHOPIN (1851–1904)

The Story of an Hour   *1894*

Knowing that Mrs. Mallard was afflicted with a heart trouble, great care was taken to break to her as gently as possible the news of her husband's death.

It was her sister Josephine who told her, in broken sentences; veiled hints that revealed in half concealing. Her husband's friend Richards was there, too, near her. It was he who had been in the newspaper office when intelligence of the railroad disaster was received, with Brently Mallard's name leading the list of "killed." He had only taken the time to assure himself of its truth by a second telegram, and had hastened to forestall any less careful, less tender friend in bearing the sad message.

She did not hear the story as many women have heard the same, with a paralyzed inability to accept its significance. She wept at once, with sudden, wild abandonment, in her sister's arms. When the storm of grief had spent itself she went away to her room alone. She would have no one follow her.

There stood, facing the open window, a comfortable, roomy armchair. Into this she sank, pressed down by a physical exhaustion that haunted her body and seemed to reach into her soul.

She could see in the open square before her house the tops of trees that   5 were all aquiver with the new spring life. The delicious breath of rain was in the air. In the street below a peddler was crying his wares. The notes of a distant song which some one was singing reached her faintly, and countless sparrows were twittering in the eaves.

There were patches of blue sky showing here and there through the clouds that had met and piled one above the other in the west facing her window.

She sat with her head thrown back upon the cushion of the chair, quite motionless, except when a sob came up into her throat and shook her, as a child who has cried itself to sleep continues to sob in its dreams.

She was young, with a fair, calm face, whose lines bespoke repression and even a certain strength. But now there was a dull stare in her eyes, whose gaze was fixed away off yonder on one of those patches of blue sky. It was not a glance of reflection, but rather indicated a suspension of intelligent thought.

There was something coming to her and she was waiting for it, fearfully. What was it? She did not know; it was too subtle and elusive to name. But she felt it, creeping out of the sky, reaching toward her through the sounds, the scents, the color that filled the air.

Now her bosom rose and fell tumultuously. She was beginning to recog-   10 nize this thing that was approaching to possess her, and she was striving to beat it back with her will — as powerless as her two white slender hands would have been.

When she abandoned herself a little whispered word escaped her slightly parted lips. She said it over and over under her breath: "free, free, free!" The vacant stare and the look of terror that had followed it went from her eyes.

They stayed keen and bright. Her pulses beat fast, and the coursing blood warmed and relaxed every inch of her body.

She did not stop to ask if it were or were not a monstrous joy that held her. A clear and exalted perception enabled her to dismiss the suggestion as trivial.

She knew that she would weep again when she saw the kind, tender hands folded in death; the face that had never looked save with love upon her, fixed and gray and dead. But she saw beyond that bitter moment a long procession of years to come that would belong to her absolutely. And she opened and spread her arms out to them in welcome.

There would be no one to live for her during those coming years; she would live for herself. There would be no powerful will bending hers in that blind persistence with which men and women believe they have a right to impose a private will upon a fellow-creature. A kind intention or a cruel intention made the act seem no less a crime as she looked upon it in that brief moment of illumination.

And yet she had loved him — sometimes. Often she had not. What did it matter! What could love, the unsolved mystery, count for in face of this possession of self-assertion which she suddenly recognized as the strongest impulse of her being! 15

"Free! Body and soul free!" she kept whispering.

Josephine was kneeling before the closed door with her lips to the keyhole, imploring for admission. "Louise, open the door! I beg; open the door — you will make yourself ill. What are you doing, Louise? For heaven's sake open the door."

"Go away. I am not making myself ill." No; she was drinking in a very elixir of life through that open window.

Her fancy was running riot along those days ahead of her. Spring days, and summer days, and all sorts of days that would be her own. She breathed a quick prayer that life might be long. It was only yesterday she had thought with a shudder that life might be long.

She arose at length and opened the door to her sister's importunities. There was a feverish triumph in her eyes, and she carried herself unwittingly like a goddess of Victory. She clasped her sister's waist, and together they descended the stairs. Richards stood waiting for them at the bottom. 20

Some one was opening the front door with a latchkey. It was Brently Mallard who entered, a little travel-stained, composedly carrying his gripsack and umbrella. He had been far from the scene of accident, and did not even know there had been one. He stood amazed at Josephine's piercing cry; at Richards' quick motion to screen him from the view of his wife.

But Richards was too late.

When the doctors came they said she had died of heart disease — of joy that kills.

A SAMPLE CLOSE READING

An Annotated Section of "The Story of an Hour"

Even as you read a story for the first time, you can highlight passages, circle or underline words, and write responses in the margins. Subsequent readings will yield more insights once you begin to understand how various elements such as plot, characterization, and wording build toward the conclusion and what you perceive to be the story's central ideas. The following annotations for the first eleven paragraphs of "The Story of an Hour" provide a perspective written by someone who had read the work several times. Your own approach might, of course, be quite different—as the sample paper that follows the annotated passage amply demonstrates.

KATE CHOPIN (1851–1904)

The Story of an Hour   1894

Knowing that Mrs. Mallard was afflicted with a heart trouble, great care was taken to break to her as gently as possible the news of her husband's death.

It was her sister Josephine who told her, in broken sentences; veiled hints that revealed in half concealing. Her husband's friend Richards was there, too, near her. It was he who had been in the newspaper office when intelligence of the railroad disaster was received, with Brently Mallard's name leading the list of "killed." He had only taken the time to assure himself of its truth by a second telegram, and had hastened to forestall any less careful, less tender friend in bearing the sad message.

She did not hear the story as many women have heard the same, with a paralyzed inability to accept its significance. She wept at once, with sudden, wild abandonment, in her sister's arms. When the storm of grief had spent itself she went away to her room alone. She would have no one follow her.

There stood, facing the open window, a comfortable, roomy armchair. Into this she sank, pressed down by a physical exhaustion that haunted her body and seemed to reach into her soul.

She could see in the open square before her house the tops of trees that were all aquiver with the new spring life. The delicious breath of rain was in the air. In the street below a peddler was crying his wares. The notes of a distant song which some one was singing reached her faintly, and countless sparrows were twittering in the eaves.

There were patches of blue sky showing here and there through the clouds that had met and piled one above the other in the west facing her window.

She sat with her head thrown back upon the cushion of the chair, quite motionless, except when a sob came up into her throat and shook her, as a child who has cried itself to sleep continues to sob in its dreams.

She was young, with a fair, calm face, whose lines bespoke repression and even a certain strength. But now there was a dull stare in her eyes, whose gaze was fixed away off yonder on

---

5

The title could point to the brevity of the story—only 23 short paragraphs—or to the decisive nature of what happens in a very short period of time. Or both.

Mrs. Mallard's first name (Louise) is not given until paragraph 17, yet her sister Josephine is named immediately. This emphasizes Mrs. Mallard's married identity.

Given the nature of the cause of Mrs. Mallard's death at the story's end, it's worth noting the ambiguous description that she "was afflicted with a heart trouble." Is this one of Chopin's (rather than Josephine's) "veiled hints"?

When Mrs. Mallard weeps with "wild abandonment," the reader is again confronted with an ambiguous phrase: she grieves in an overwhelming manner yet seems to express relief at being abandoned by Brently's death.

These 3 paragraphs create an increasingly "open" atmosphere that leads to the "delicious" outside where there are inviting sounds and "patches of blue sky." There's a definite tension between the inside and outside worlds.

Though still stunned by grief, Mrs. Mallard begins to feel a change come over her owing to her growing awareness of a world outside her room.

What that change is remains "too subtle and elusive to name."

Mrs. Mallard's conflicted struggle is described in passionate, physical terms as if she is "possess[ed]" by a lover she is "powerless" to resist.

Once she has "abandoned" herself (see the "abandonment" in paragraph 3), the reader realizes that her love is to be "free, free, free." Her recognition is evident in the "coursing blood [that] warmed and relaxed every inch of her body."

one of those patches of blue sky. It was not a glance of reflection, but rather indicated a suspension of intelligent thought.

There was something coming to her and she was waiting for it, fearfully. What was it? She did not know; it was too subtle and elusive to name. But she felt it, creeping out of the sky, reaching toward her through the sounds, the scents, the color that filled the air.

Now her bosom rose and fell tumultuously. She was beginning to recognize this thing that was approaching to possess her, and she was striving to beat it back with her will—as powerless as her two white slender hands would have been.

10

When she abandoned herself a little whispered word escaped her slightly parted lips. She said it over and over under her breath: "free, free, free!" The vacant stare and the look of terror that had followed it went from her eyes. They stayed keen and bright. Her pulses beat fast, and the coursing blood warmed and relaxed every inch of her body. . . .

Do you find Mrs. Mallard a sympathetic character? Some readers think that she is callous, selfish, and unnatural—even monstrous—because she ecstatically revels in her newly discovered sense of freedom so soon after learning of her husband's presumed death. Others read her as a victim of her inability to control her own life in a repressive, male-dominated society. Is it possible to hold both views simultaneously, or are they mutually exclusive? Are your views in any way influenced by your being male or female? Does your age affect your perception? What about your social and economic background? Does your nationality, race, or religion in any way shape your attitudes? Do you have particular views about the institution of marriage that inform your assessment of Mrs. Mallard's character? Have other reading experiences—perhaps a familiarity with some of Chopin's other stories—predisposed you one way or another to Mrs. Mallard?

Understanding potential influences might be useful in determining whether a particular response to Mrs. Mallard is based primarily on the story's details and their arrangement or on an overt or a subtle bias that is brought to the story. If you unconsciously project your beliefs and assumptions onto a literary work, you run the risk of distorting it to accommodate your prejudice. Your feelings can be a reliable guide to interpretation, but you should be aware of what those feelings are based on.

Often specific questions about literary works cannot be answered definitively. For example, Chopin does not explain why Mrs. Mallard suffers a heart attack at the end of this story. Is the shock of seeing her "dead" husband simply too much for this woman "afflicted with a heart trouble"? Does she die of what the doctors call a "joy that kills" because she is so glad to see her husband? Is she so profoundly guilty about feeling "free" at her husband's expense that she has a heart attack? Is her death a kind of willed suicide in reaction to her loss of freedom? Your answers to these questions will depend on which details you emphasize in your interpretation of the story and the kinds of perspectives and values you bring to it. If, for example, you read the story from a feminist perspective, you would be likely to pay close attention to Chopin's comments about marriage in paragraph 14. Or if you read the story as an oblique attack on the insensitivity of physicians of the period, you might want to find out whether Chopin wrote elsewhere about doctors (she did) and compare her comments with historic sources. (A number of critical strategies for reading, including feminist and historical approaches, appear in Chapter 53.)

Reading responsively makes you an active participant in the process of creating meaning in a literary work. The experience that you and the author create will most likely not be identical to another reader's encounter with the same work, but then that's true of nearly any experience you'll have, and it is part of the pleasure of reading. Indeed, talking and writing about literature is a way of sharing responses so that they can be enriched and deepened.

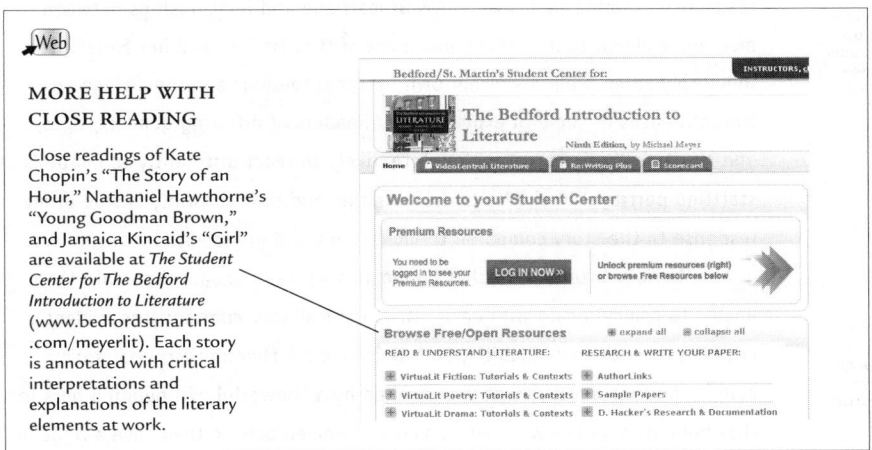

A SAMPLE PAPER

Differences in Responses to Kate Chopin's "The Story of an Hour"

The following paper was written in response to an assignment that called for a three- to four-page discussion of how different readers might interpret Mrs. Mallard's character. The paper is based on the story as well as on the discussion of reader-response criticism (pp. 2060–2062) in Chapter 53, "Critical Strategies for Reading." As that discussion indicates, reader-response criticism is a critical approach that focuses on the reader rather than on the work itself in order to describe how the reader creates meaning from the text.

Wally Villa

Professor Brian

English 210

January 12, 2010

Differences in Responses to

Kate Chopin's "The Story of an Hour"

Kate Chopin's "The Story of an Hour" appears merely to explore a

Thesis providing writer's interpretation of story's purpose

woman's unpredictable reaction to her husband's assumed death and re-

appearance, but actually Chopin offers Mrs. Mallard's bizarre story to reveal

problems that are inherent in the institution of marriage. By offering this

depiction of a marriage that stifles the woman to the point that she

celebrates the death of her kind and loving husband, Chopin challenges her

Introduction setting up other reader responses discussed later in paper

readers to examine their own views of marriage and relationships between

men and women. Each reader's judgment of Mrs. Mallard and her behavior

inevitably stems from his or her own personal feelings about marriage and

the influences of societal expectations. Readers of differing genders, ages,

and marital experiences are, therefore, likely to react differently to Chopin's

startling portrayal of the Mallards' marriage, and that certainly is true of my

response to the story compared to my father's and grandmother's responses.

Marriage often establishes boundaries between people that make them

unable to communicate with each other. The Mallards' marriage was evidently

Analysis of story's portrayal of marriage, with textual evidence

crippled by both their inability to talk to one another and Mrs. Mallard's

conviction that her marriage was defined by a "powerful will bending hers in

that blind persistence with which men and women believe they have a right to

impose a private will upon a fellow-creature" (16). Yet she does not recognize

that it is not just men who impose their will upon women and that the

problems inherent in marriage affect men and women equally. To me, Mrs.

Analysis of character and plot, connecting with story's purpose

Mallard is a somewhat sympathetic character, and I appreciate her longing

to live out the "years to come that would belong to her absolutely" (16).

However, I also believe that she could have tried to improve her own situation

somehow, either by reaching out to her husband or by abandoning the marriage

altogether. Chopin uses Mrs. Mallard's tragedy to illuminate aspects of mar-

riage that are harmful and, in this case, even deadly. Perhaps the Mallards' relationship should be taken as a warning to others: sacrificing one's own happiness in order to satisfy societal expectations can poison one's life and even destroy entire families.

When my father read "The Story of an Hour," his reaction to Mrs. Mallard was more antagonistic than my own. He sees Chopin's story as a timeless "battle of the sexes," serving as further proof that men will never really be able to understand what it is that women want. Mrs. Mallard endures an obviously unsatisfying marriage without ever explaining to her husband that she feels trapped and unfulfilled. Mrs. Mallard dismisses the question of whether or not she is experiencing a "monstrous joy" (16) as trivial, but my father does not think that this is a trivial question. He believes Mrs. Mallard is guilty of a monstrous joy because she selfishly celebrates the death of her husband without ever having allowed him the opportunity to understand her feelings. He believes that, above all, Brently Mallard should be seen as the most victimized character in the story. Mr. Mallard is a good, kind man, with friends who care about him and a marriage that he thinks he can depend on. He "never looked save with love" (16) upon his wife, his only "crime" (16) was his presence in the house, and yet he is the one who is bereaved at the end of the story, for reasons he will never understand. Mrs. Mallard's passion for her newly discovered freedom is perhaps understandable, but according to my father, Mr. Mallard is the character most deserving of sympathy.

Maybe not surprisingly, my grandmother's interpretation of "The Story of an Hour" was radically different from both mine and my father's. My grandmother was married in 1936 and widowed in 1959 and therefore can identify with Chopin's characters, who live at the turn of the century. Her first reaction, aside from her unwavering support for Mrs. Mallard and her predicament, was that this story demonstrates the differences between the ways men and women related to each other a century ago and the way they relate today. Unlike my father, who thinks Mrs. Mallard is too passive, my grandmother believes that Mrs. Mallard doesn't even know that she is feeling repressed until after she is told that Brently is dead. In 1894, divorce was so scandalous and stigmatized that it simply wouldn't have been an option for Mrs. Mallard, and so her only way out of the marriage would have been one

Contrasting summary and analysis of another reader's response

Contrasting summary and analysis of another reader's response

Cultural and historical background providing context for response and story itself

Villa 3

of their deaths. Being relatively young, Mrs. Mallard probably considered herself doomed to a long life in an unhappy marriage. My grandmother also feels that, in spite of all we know of Mrs. Mallard's feelings about her husband and her marriage, she still manages to live up to everyone's expectations of her as a woman both in life and in death. She is a dutiful wife to Brently, as she is expected to be. She weeps "with sudden, wild abandonment" when she hears the news of his death; she locks herself in her room to cope with her new situation, and she has a fatal heart attack upon seeing her husband arrive home. Naturally the male doctors would think that she died of the "joy that kills" (16)—nobody could have guessed that she was unhappy with her life, and she would never have wanted them to know.

Interpretations of "The Story of an Hour" seem to vary according to the gender, age, and experience of the reader. While both male and female readers can certainly sympathize with Mrs. Mallard's plight, female readers—as was evident in our class discussions—seem to relate more easily to her predicament and are quicker to exonerate her of any responsibility for her unhappy situation. Conversely, male readers are more likely to feel compassion for Mr. Mallard, who loses his wife for reasons that will always remain entirely unknown to him. Older readers probably understand more readily the strength of social forces and the difficulty of trying to deny societal expectations concerning gender roles in general and marriage in particular. Younger readers seem to feel that Mrs. Mallard is too passive and that she could have improved her domestic life immeasurably if she had taken the initiative to either improve or end her relationship with her husband. Ultimately, how each individual reader responds to Mrs. Mallard's story reveals his or her own ideas about marriage, society, and how men and women communicate with each other.

Marginal notes:

Analysis supported with textual evidence

Conclusion summarizing reader responses explored in the paper

Villa 4

Work Cited

Chopin, Kate. "The Story of an Hour." *The Bedford Introduction to Literature*. Ed. Michael Meyer. 9th ed. Boston: Bedford/St. Martin's, 2011. 15–16. Print.

Before beginning your own writing assignment on fiction, you should review Chapter 2, "Writing about Fiction," as well as Chapter 54, "Reading and the Writing Process," which provides a step-by-step explanation of how to choose a topic, develop a thesis, and organize various types of writing assignments. If you use outside sources, you should also be familiar with the conventional documentation procedures described in Chapter 55, "The Literary Research Paper."

EXPLORATIONS AND FORMULAS

Each time we pick up a work of fiction, go to the theater, or turn on the television, we have a trace of the same magical expectation that can be heard in the voice of a child who begs, "Tell me a story." Human beings have enjoyed stories ever since they learned to speak. Whatever the motive for creating stories — even if simply to delight or instruct — the basic human impulse to tell and hear stories existed long before the development of written language. Myths about the origins of the world and legends about the heroic exploits of demigods were among the earliest forms of storytelling to develop into oral traditions, which were eventually written down. These narratives are the ancestors of the stories we read on the printed page today. Unlike the early listeners to ancient myths and legends, we read our stories silently, but the pleasure derived from the mysterious power of someone else's artfully arranged words remains largely the same. Every one of us likes a good story.

The stories that appear in anthologies for college students are generally chosen for their high literary quality. Such stories can affect us at the deepest emotional level, reveal new insights into ourselves or the world, and stretch us by exercising our imaginations. They warrant careful reading and close study to appreciate the art that has gone into creating them. The following chapters on plot, character, setting, and the other elements of literature are designed to provide the terms and concepts that can help you understand how a work of fiction achieves its effects and meanings. It is worth acknowledging, however, that many people buy and read fiction that is quite different from the stories usually anthologized in college texts. What about all those paperbacks with exciting, colorful covers near the cash registers in shopping malls and corner drugstores?

These books, known as ***formula fiction,*** are the adventure, western, detective, science fiction, and romance novels that entertain millions of readers annually. What makes them so popular? What do their characters, plots, and themes offer readers that accounts for the tremendous sales of stories with titles like *Caves of Doom, Silent Scream, Colt .45,* and *Forbidden Ecstasy*? Many of the writers included in this book have enjoyed wide popularity and written bestsellers, but there are more readers of formula fiction than there are readers of Ernest Hemingway, William Faulkner, or Joyce Carol Oates, to name only a few. Formula novels do provide entertainment, of course, but that makes them no different from serious stories, if entertainment means pleasure. Any of the stories in this or any other anthology can be read for pleasure.

Formula fiction, though, is usually characterized as escape literature. There are sensible reasons for this description. Adventure stories about soldiers of fortune are eagerly read by men who live pretty average lives doing ordinary jobs. Romance novels about attractive young women falling in love with tall, dark, handsome men are read mostly by women who dream themselves out of their familiar existences. The excitement, violence, and passion that such stories provide are a kind of reprieve from everyday experience.

And yet readers of serious fiction may also use it as a refuge, a liberation from monotony and boredom. Mark Twain's humorous stories have, for example, given countless hours of pleasurable relief to readers who would rather spend time in Twain's light and funny world than in their own. Others might prefer the terror of Edgar Allan Poe's fiction or the painful predicament of two lovers in a Joyce Carol Oates story.

Thus, to get at some of the differences between formula fiction and serious literature, it is necessary to go beyond the motives of the reader to the motives of the writer and the qualities of the work itself.

Unlike serious fiction, the books displayed next to the cash registers (and their short story equivalents on the magazine racks) are written with only one object: to be sold. They are aimed at specific consumer markets that can be counted on to buy them. This does not mean that all serious writers must live in cold garrets writing for audiences who have not yet discovered their work. No one writes to make a career of poverty. It does mean, however, that if a writer's primary purpose is to anticipate readers' generic expectations about when the next torrid love scene, bloody gunfight, or thrilling chase is due, there is little room to be original or to have something significant to say. There is little if any chance to explore seriously a character, idea, or incident if the major focus is not on the integrity of the work itself.

Although the specific elements of formula fiction differ depending on the type of story, some basic ingredients go into all westerns, mysteries, adventures, science fiction, and romances. From the very start, a reader can anticipate a happy ending for the central character, with whom he or she will identify. There may be suspense, but no matter what or how many the obstacles, complications, or near defeats, the hero or heroine succeeds and reaffirms the values and attitudes the reader brings to the story. Virtue triumphs, love conquers all, honesty is the best policy, and hard work guarantees success. Hence, the villains are corralled, the wedding vows are exchanged, the butler confesses, and gold is discovered at the last moment. The visual equivalents of such formula stories are readily available at movie theaters and in television series. Some are better than others, but all are relatively limited by the writer's goal of giving an audience what will sell.

Although formula fiction may not offer many surprises, it provides pleasure to a wide variety of readers. College professors, for example, are just as likely to be charmed by formula stories as anyone else. Readers of serious fiction who revel in exploring more challenging imaginative worlds can also enjoy formulaic stories, which offer little more than an image of the world as a simple place in which our assumptions and desires are confirmed. The familiarity of a given formula is emotionally satisfying because we are secure in our expectations of it. We know at the start of a Sherlock Holmes story that the mystery will be solved by that famous detective's relentless scientific analysis of the clues, but we take pleasure in seeing how Holmes unravels the mystery before us. Similarly, we know that James Bond's wit, grace, charm, courage, and skill will ultimately prevail over the diabolic schemes of eccentric villains, but we volunteer for the mission anyway.

Perhaps that happens for the same reason that we climb aboard a roller coaster: no matter how steep and sharp the curves, we stay on a track that is both exciting and safe. Although excitement, adventure, mystery, and romance are major routes to escape in formula fiction, most of us make that trip only temporarily, for a little relaxation and fun. Momentary relief from our everyday concerns is as healthy and desirable as an occasional daydream or fantasy. Such reading is a form of play because we — like spectators of or participants in a game — experience a formula of excitement, tension, and then release that can fascinate us regardless of how many times the game is played.

Many publishers of formula fiction — such as romance, adventure, or detective stories — issue a set number of new novels each month. Readers can buy them in stores or subscribe to them through the mail. These same publishers send "tip sheets" on request to authors who want to write for a particular series. The details of the formula differ from one series to another, but each tip sheet covers the basic elements that go into a story.

There are many kinds of formulaic romance novels; some include psychological terrors, some use historical settings, and some even incorporate time travel so that the hero or heroine can travel back in time and fall in love, and still others create mystery and suspense. Several publishers have recently released romances that reflect contemporary social concerns and issues; multicultural couples and gay and lesbian relationships as well as more explicit descriptions of sexual activities are now sometimes featured in these books. In general, however, the majority of romance novels are written to appeal to a readership that embraces more traditional societal expectations and values.

The following composite tip sheet summarizes the typical advice offered by publishers of romance novels. These are among the most popular titles published in the United States; it has been estimated that four out of every ten paperbacks sold are romance novels. The categories and the tone of the language in this composite tip sheet are derived from a number of publishers and provide a glimpse of how formula fiction is written and what the readers of romance novels are looking for in their escape literature.

A Composite of a Romance Tip Sheet

Plot

The story focuses on the growing relationship between the heroine and hero. After a number of complications, they discover lasting love and make a permanent commitment to each other in marriage. The plot should move quickly. Background information about the heroine should be kept to a minimum. The hero should appear as early as possible (preferably in the first chapter and no later than the second), so that the hero's and heroine's feelings about each other are in the foreground as they cope with misperceptions that keep them apart until the final pages of the story. The more tension created by their uncertainty about each other's love, the greater the excitement and anticipation for the reader.

Love is the major interest. Do not inject murder, extortion, international intrigue, hijacking, horror, or supernatural elements into the plot. Controversial social issues and politics, if mentioned at all, should never be allowed a significant role. Once the heroine and hero meet, they should clearly be interested in each other, but that interest should be complicated by some kind of misunderstanding. He, for example, might find her too ambitious, an opportunist, cold, or flirtatious; or he might assume that she is attached to someone else. She might think he is haughty, snobbish, power hungry, indifferent, or contemptuous of her. The reader knows what they do not: that eventually these obstacles will be overcome. Interest is sustained by keeping the lovers apart until very near the end so that the reader will stay with the plot to see how they get together.

Heroine

The heroine is a modern American woman between the ages of nineteen and twenty-eight who reflects today's concerns. The story is told in the third person from her point of view. She is attractive and nicely dressed but not glamorous; glitter and sophistication should be reserved for the other woman (the heroine's rival for the hero), whose flashiness will compare unfavorably with the heroine's modesty. When the heroine does dress up, however, her beauty should be stunningly apparent. Her trim figure is appealing but not abundant; a petite healthy appearance is desirable. Both her looks and her clothes should be generously detailed.

Her personality is spirited and independent without being pushy or stubborn because she knows when to give in. Although sensitive, she doesn't cry every time she is confronted with a problem (though she might cry in private moments). A sense of humor is helpful. Because she is on her own, away from parents (usually deceased) or other protective relationships, she is self-reliant as well as vulnerable. The story may begin with her on the verge of an important decision about her life. She is clearly competent but not entirely certain of her own qualities. She does not take her attractiveness for granted or realize how much the hero is drawn to her.

Common careers for the heroine include executive secretary, nurse, teacher, 5 interior designer, assistant manager, department store buyer, travel agent, or struggling photographer (no menial work). She can also be a doctor, lawyer, or other professional. Her job can be described in some detail and made exciting, but it must not dominate her life. Although she is smart, she is not extremely intellectual or defined by her work. Often she meets the hero through work, but her major concerns center on love, marriage, home, and family. White wine is okay, but she never drinks alone — or uses drugs. She may be troubled, frustrated, threatened, and momentarily thwarted in the course of the story, but she never totally gives in to despair or desperation. She has strengths that the hero recognizes and admires.

Hero

The hero should be about ten years older than the heroine and can be foreign or American. He needn't be handsome in a traditional sense, but he must be strongly masculine. Always tall and well built (not brawny or thick) and usually dark, he looks as terrific in a three-piece suit as he does in sports clothes. His clothes reflect good taste and an affluent life-style. Very successful professionally and financially, he is a man in charge of whatever work he's engaged in (financier, doctor, publisher, architect, business executive, airline pilot, artist, etc.). His wealth is manifested in his sophistication and experience.

His past may be slightly mysterious or shrouded by some painful moment (perhaps with a woman) that he doesn't want to discuss. Whatever the circumstance — his wife's death or divorce are common — it was not his fault. Avoid chronic problems such as alcoholism, drug addiction, or sexual dysfunctions. To others he may appear moody, angry, unpredictable, and explosively passionate, but the heroine eventually comes to realize his warm, tender side. He should be attractive not only as a lover but also as a potential husband and father.

Secondary Characters

Because the major interest is in how the heroine will eventually get together with the hero, the other characters are used to advance the action. There are three major types:

(1) *The Other Woman:* Her vices serve to accent the virtues of the heroine; immediately beneath her glamorous sophistication is a deceptive, selfish, mean-spirited, rapacious predator. She may seem to have the hero in her clutches, but she never wins him in the end.

(2) *The Other Man:* He usually falls into two types: (a) the decent sort who is there when the hero isn't around and (b) the selfish sort who schemes rather than loves. Neither is a match for the hero.

(3) *Other Characters:* Like furniture, they fill in the background and are useful for positioning the hero and heroine. These characters are familiar types such as the hero's snobbish aunt, the heroine's troubled younger siblings, the loyal friend, or the office gossip. They should be realistic, but they must not be allowed to obscure the emphasis on the lovers. The hero may have children from a previous marriage, but they should rarely be seen or heard. It's usually simpler and better not to include them.

Setting

The setting is usually contemporary. Romantic, exciting places are best: New York City, London, Paris, Rio, the mountains, the ocean—wherever it is exotic and love's possibilities are the greatest. Marriage may take the heroine and hero to a pretty suburb or small town.

Love Scenes

The hero and heroine may make love before marriage. The choice will depend largely on the heroine's sensibilities and circumstances. She should reflect modern attitudes. If the lovers do engage in premarital sex, it should be made clear that neither is promiscuous, especially the heroine. Even if their relationship is consummated before marriage, their lovemaking should not occur until late in the story. There should be at least several passionate scenes, but complications, misunderstandings, and interruptions should keep the couple from actually making love until they have made a firm commitment to each other. Descriptions

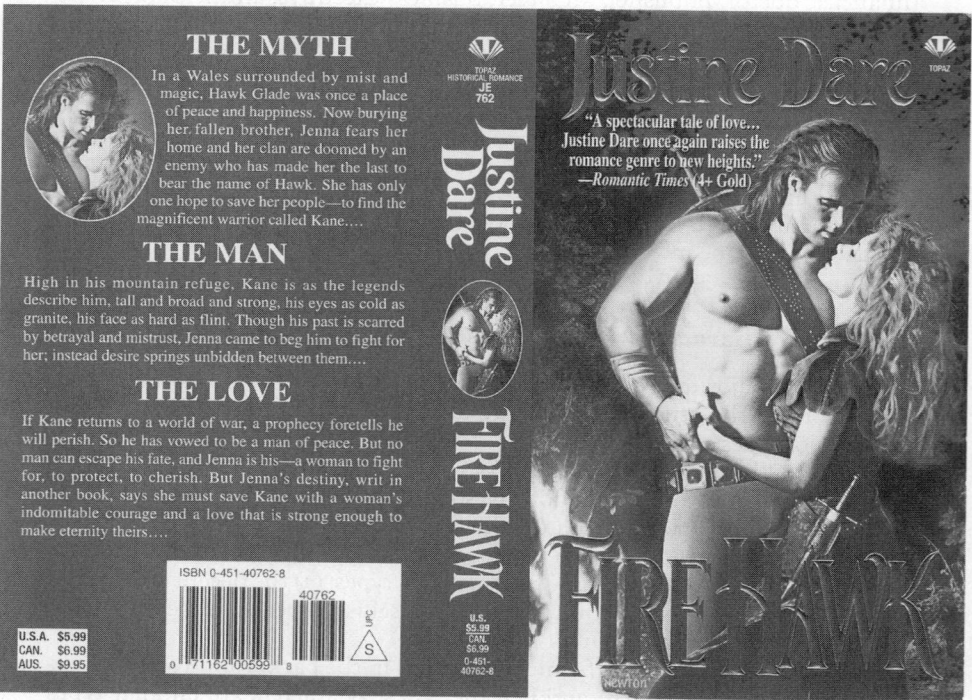

Romance novel. The cover for *FireHawk* (Penguin, 1997) illustrates another convention of romance formula fiction: its packaging demands an image of a man clasping a passionate beauty to his manly chest. As the back-cover copy suggests, this Topaz novel is a historical romance—a subcategory of the romance formula—and so a few of the guidelines on the tip sheet are modified (the setting is medieval Wales rather than contemporary America, for example). But most of the guidelines apply: Kane is strong and so is Jenna's powerful love.
Cover by Richard Newton, from *FireHawk* by Justine Dare, © 1997 Janice Davis Smith.

should appeal to the senses; however, detailed, graphic close-ups are unacceptable. Passion can be presented sensually but not clinically; the lovemaking should be seen through a soft romantic lens. Violence and any out-of-the-way sexual acts should not even be hinted at. No coarse language.

Writing

Avoid extremely complex sentences, very long paragraphs, and lengthy descriptions. Use concise, vivid details to create the heroine's world. Be sure to include full descriptions of the hero's and heroine's physical features and clothes. Allow the reader to experience the romantic mood surrounding the lovers. Show how the heroine feels; do not simply report her feelings. Dialogue should sound like ordinary conversation, and the overall writing should be contemporary English without slang, difficult foreign expressions, strange dialects, racial epithets, or obscenities (*hell, damn,* and a few other mild swears are all right).

Length

55,000 to 65,000 words in ten to twelve chapters. ¹⁵

Considerations for Critical Thinking and Writing

1. **FIRST RESPONSE.** Given the expectations implied by the tip sheet, what generalizations can you make about those likely to write formula fiction? Does the tip sheet change the way you think about romantic fiction or other kinds of formula fiction?

2. Who is the intended audience for this type of romance? Try to describe the audience in detail: How does a romance novel provide escape for these readers?

3. Why is it best that the heroine be "attractive and nicely dressed but not glamorous"? Why do you think publishers advise writers to include detailed descriptions of her clothes? Do you find the heroine appealing? Why or why not?

4. Why should the hero be "about ten years older than the heroine"? If he is divorced, why is it significant that "it was not his fault"?

5. Why do you think the hero and heroine are kept apart by complications until the end of the story? Does the outline of the plot sound familiar to you or remind you of any other stories?

6. Why do you think restrictions are placed on the love scenes?

7. Why are "extremely complex sentences, very long paragraphs, and lengthy descriptions" discouraged?

8. To what extent does the tip sheet describe the strategies used in popular television soap operas? How do you account for the appeal of these shows?

9. Explain how the tip sheet confirms traditional views of male and female roles in society. Does it accommodate any broken traditions?

10. Carefully examine the Topaz Historical Romance cover. How do the cover's images and copy reinforce what readers can expect from a romance novel?

11. Included in the marketing material that accompanies the Topaz Historical Romance is this notation: "Topaz is an Official Sponsor of the Mrs. America Pageant." Why do you suppose the publishers support this contest?

12. Write a tip sheet for another kind of popular formula story, such as a western or a detective story, that you have observed in a novel, television show, or film. How is the plot patterned? How are the characters made familiar? How is the setting related to the story? What are the obligatory scenes? How is the overall style consistent? To get started, you might consider an Agatha Christie novel, an episode from a police series on television, or a James Bond film.

13. Try writing a scene for a formula romance, or read the excerpt from Edgar Rice Burroughs's *Tarzan of the Apes* (p. 75) and try an adventure scene.

A COMPARISON OF TWO STORIES

Each of the following contemporary pieces of fiction is about a woman who experiences deep sorrow. The first, from *A Secret Sorrow* by Karen van der Zee, is an excerpt from a romance by Harlequin Books, a major publisher of formula fiction that has sold well over a billion copies of its romance titles — enough for about 20 percent of the world's population. The second piece, Gail Godwin's "A Sorrowful Woman," is a complete short story that originally appeared in *Esquire;* it is not a formula story. Unlike *A Secret Sorrow,* Godwin's story does not have a standard plot pattern employing familiar character types that appear in a series of separate but similar works.

Read each selection carefully and look for evidence of formulaic writing in the chapters from *A Secret Sorrow.* Pay particular attention to the advice on plotting and characterization offered in the composite tip sheet. As you read Godwin's short story, think about how it is different from van der Zee's excerpt; note also any similarities. The questions that follow the stories should help you consider how the experiences of reading the two are different.

KAREN VAN DER ZEE (B. 1947)

Born and raised in Holland, Karen van der Zee lives in the United States, where she has become a successful romance writer, contributing more than fifteen novels to the popular Harlequin series. This excerpt consists of the final two chapters of *A Secret Sorrow.* This is what has happened so far: the central character, Faye, is recuperating from

By permission of the author.

the psychological effects of a serious car accident in which she received a permanent internal injury. After the accident, she quits her job and breaks her engagement to Greg. She moves into her brother Chuck's house and falls in love with Kai, a visiting Texan and good friend of her brother. At the end of Chapter 10, Kai insists on knowing why she will not marry him and asks, "Who is Doctor Jaworski?"

From **A Secret Sorrow**   *1981*

Chapter Eleven

Faye could feel the blood drain from her face and for one horrifying moment she thought she was going to faint right in Kai's arms. The room tilted and everything swirled around in a wild madman's dance. She clutched at him for support, fighting for control, trying to focus at some point beyond his shoulder. Slowly, everything steadied.

"I . . . I don't know him," she murmured at last. "I. . . ."

He reached in the breast pocket of his shirt, took out a slip of paper, and held it out for her to see. One glance and Faye recognized it as the note from Doctor Martin with Doctor Jaworski's name scrawled on it, thickly underlined.

"How did you get that?" Her voice was a terrified whisper. She was still holding on, afraid she would fall if she let go.

"I found it on the floor in my bedroom. It must have fallen out of your   5 wallet along with everything else on Saturday morning."

Yes — oh God! Her legs were shaking so badly, she knew it was only his arms that kept her from falling.

"Who is Doctor Jaworski, Faye?" His voice was patiently persistent.

"I . . . he. . . ." Her voice broke. "Let me go, please let me go." She felt as if she were suffocating in his embrace and she struggled against him, feebly, but it was no use.

"He's a psychiatrist, isn't he?" His voice was gentle, very gentle, and she looked up at him in stunned surprise.

He knew, oh God, he knew. She closed her eyes, a helpless sense of in-   10 evitability engulfing her.

"You know," she whispered. "How do you know?"

"Simple. Two minutes on the phone to Chicago." He paused. "Doctor Martin — was he one of the doctors who treated you at the hospital?"

"Yes."

"Why did he give you Doctor Jaworski's name? Did he want you to make an appointment with him?"

"Yes." Despondency overtook her. There was no going back now. No es-   15 cape from the truth. No escape from his arms. Resistance faded and she felt numbed and lifeless. It didn't matter any more. Nothing mattered.

"Did you?" Kai repeated.

"Did I what?"

"See him — Doctor Jaworski."

"No."

"Why did Doctor Martin want you to see a psychiatrist?"   20

"I. . . ." Faye swallowed miserably. "It's . . . it's therapy for grieving . . . mourning." She made a helpless gesture with her hand. "When people lose a . . . a wife, or husband for instance, they go through a more or less predictable pattern of emotions. . . ." She gave him a quick glance, then looked away. "Like denial, anger. . . ."

". . . depression, mourning, acceptance," Kai finished for her, and she looked back at him in surprise.

"Yes."

His mouth twisted in a little smile. "I'm not totally ignorant about subjects other than agronomy." There was a momentary pause as he scrutinized her face. "Why did you need that kind of therapy, Faye?"

And then it was back again, the resistance, the revolt against his probing   25 questions. She stiffened in defense—her whole body growing rigid with instinctive rebellion.

"It's none of your business!"

"Oh, yes, it is. We're talking about our life together. Your life and mine."

She strained against him, hands pushing against his chest. "Let me go! Please let me go!" Panic changed into tears. She couldn't take his nearness any more, the feel of his hard body touching hers, the strength of him.

"No, Faye, no. You're going to tell me. Now. I'm not letting you go until you've told me everything. Everything, you hear?"

"I can't!" she sobbed. "I can't!"   30

"Faye," he said slowly, "you'll *have* to. You told me you love me, but you don't want to marry me. You have given me no satisfactory reasons, and I'll be damned if I'm going to accept your lack of explanations."

"You have no right to demand an explanation!"

"Oh, yes, I have. You're part of me, Faye. Part of my life."

"You talk as if you own me!" She was trembling, struggling to get away from him. She couldn't stand there, so close to him with all the pent-up despair inside her, the anger, the fear of what she knew not how to tell him.

His hands were warm and strong on her back, holding her steady. Then,   35 with one hand, he tilted back her head and made her look at him. "You gave me your love—I own that," he said softly. "True loving involves commitment, vulnerability, trust. Don't you trust me, Faye?"

New tears ran silently down her cheeks. "If I told you," she blurted out, "you wouldn't . . . you wouldn't. . . ."

"I wouldn't *what?*"

"You wouldn't want me any more!" The words were wrenched from her in blind, agonizing grief. "You wouldn't *want* me any more!"

He shook his head incredulously. "What makes you think you can make that decision for me? Do you have so little trust in my love for you?"

Faye didn't answer, couldn't answer. Through a mist of tears he was noth-   40 ing but a blur in front of her eyes.

"What is so terrible that you can't tell me?"

She shrank inwardly, as if shriveling away in pain. "Let me go," she whispered. "Please let me go and I'll tell you."

After a moment's hesitation Kai released her. Faye backed away from him, feeling like a terrified animal. She stood with her back against the wall, glad for the support, her whole body shaking. She took a deep breath and wiped her face dry with her hand.

"I'm afraid . . . afraid to marry you."

"Afraid?" He looked perplexed. "Afraid of what? Of me? Of marriage?"   45

Faye closed her eyes, taking another deep breath. "I can't be what you want me to be. We can't have the kind of life you want." She looked at him, standing only a few feet away, anguish tearing through her. "I'm so afraid . . . you'll be disappointed," she whispered.

"Oh God, Faye," he groaned, "I love you." He came toward her and panic surged through her as he held her against the wall, his hands reaching up to catch her face between them.

"Don't," she whispered. "Please, don't touch me." But it was no use. His mouth came down on hers and he kissed her with a hard, desperate passion.

"I love you," he said huskily. "I love you."

Faye wrenched her face free from his hands. "Don't touch me! Please don't   50 touch me!" She was sobbing now, her words barely audible. Her knees gave way and her back slid down along the wall until she crumpled on to the floor, face in her hands.

Kai took a step backward and pulled her up. "Stand up, Faye. For God's sake stand up!" He held her against the wall and she looked at him, seeing every line in his dark face, the intense blue of his eyes, and knew that this was the moment, that there was no more waiting.

And Kai knew it too. His eyes held hers locked in unrelenting demand. "Why should I be disappointed, Faye? *Why?*"

Her heart was thundering in her ears and it seemed as if she couldn't breathe, as if she were going to drown.

"Because . . . because I can't give you children! Because I can't get pregnant! I can't have babies! That's why!" Her voice was an agonized cry, torn from the depths of her misery. She yanked down his arms that held her locked against the wall and moved away from him. And then she saw his face.

It was ashen, gray under his tan. He stared at her as if he had never seen   55 her before.

"Oh my God, Faye. . . ." His voice was low and hoarse. "Why didn't you tell me, why. . . ."

Faye heard no more. She ran out the door, snatching her bag off the chair as she went by. The only thought in her mind was to get away — away from Kai and what was in his eyes.

She reached for Kai's spare set of car keys in her bag, doing it instinctively, knowing she couldn't walk home alone in the dark. How she managed to get the keys in the door lock and in the ignition she never knew. Somehow, she made it home.

The phone rang as Faye opened the front door and she heard Chuck answer it in the kitchen.

"She's just got in," he said into the mouthpiece, smiling at Faye as she   60 came into view. He listened for a moment, nodded. "Okay, fine with me."

Faye turned and walked up the stairs, taking deep breaths to calm her shattered nerves. Kai hadn't wasted any time checking up on her. She didn't care what he was telling Chuck, but she wasn't going to stand there listening to a one-sided conversation. But only a second later Chuck was behind her on the stairs.

"Kai wanted to know whether you'd arrived safely."

"I did, thank you," she said levelly, her voice surprisingly steady.

"I take it you ran out and took off with his car?"

"Did he say that?"   65

"No. He was *worried* about you. He wanted to make sure you went home."
He sounded impatient, and she couldn't blame him. She was making life unbearable for everyone around her. Everybody worried about her. Everybody
loved her. Everything should be right. Only it wasn't.

"Well, I'm home now, and I'm going to bed. Good night."

"Good night, Faye."

Faye lay in bed without any hope of sleep. Mechanically she started to sort
through her thoughts and emotions, preparing mentally for the next confrontation. There would be one, she didn't doubt it for a moment. But she
needed time — time to clear her head, time to look at everything in a reasonable, unemotional way.

It was a temptation to run — get in the car and keep driving, but it would   70
be a stupid thing to do. There was no place for her to go, and Kai would find
her, no matter what. If there was one thing she knew about Kai it was his stubbornness and his persistence. She had to stick it out, right here, get it over
with, deal with it. Only she didn't know how.

She lay listening to the stillness, just a few sounds here and there — the
house creaking, a car somewhere in the distance, a dog barking. She had to
think, but her mind refused to cooperate. She *had* to think, decide what to say
to Kai the next time she saw him, but she couldn't think, she *couldn't think*.

And then, as she heard the door open in the silence, the quiet footsteps
coming up the stairs, she knew it was too late, that time had run out.

Without even knocking he came into her room and walked over to the
bed. She could feel the mattress sag as his weight came down on it. Her heart
was pounding like a sledgehammer, and then his arms came around her and
he drew her against him.

"Faye," he said quietly, "please marry me."

"No," she said thickly. "No." She could feel him stiffen against her and she   75
released herself from his arms and slid off the bed. She switched on the light
and stood near the window, far from the bed, far from Kai. "I don't expect you
to play the gentleman, I don't expect you to throw out a life of dreams just for
the sake of chivalry. You don't have to marry me, Kai." She barely recognized
her own voice. It was like the cool calm sound of a stranger, unemotional, cold.
"You don't have to marry me," she repeated levelly, giving him a steady look.

Her words were underlined by the silence that followed, a silence loaded
with a strange, vibrating energy, a force in itself, filling the room.

Kai rose to his feet, slowly, and the face that looked at her was like that of a
stranger, a dangerous, angry stranger. Never before had she seen him so angry,
so full of hot, fuming fury.

"Shut up," he said in a low, tight voice. "Shut up and stop playing the
martyr!"

The sound of his voice and the words he said shocked Faye into silence. She
stared at him open-mouthed, and then a slow, burning anger arose inside her.

"How dare you! How. . . ."   80

He strode toward her and took her upper arms and shook her. "Shut up
and listen to me! What the hell are you thinking? What the hell did you expect

me to do when you told me? You throw me a bomb and then walk out on me! What did you expect my reaction to be? Was I supposed to stay cool and calm and tell you it didn't matter? Would you have married me then? Well, let me tell you something! It matters! It matters to me! I am not apologizing for my reaction!" He paused, breathing hard. "You know I always wanted children, but what in God's name makes you think you're the only one who has the right to feel bad about it? I have that right too, you hear! I love you, dammit, and I want to marry you, and if we can't have children I have all the right in the world to feel bad about it!"

He stopped talking. He was still breathing hard and he looked at her with stormy blue eyes. Faye felt paralyzed by his tirade and she stared at him, incapable of speech. She couldn't move, she couldn't think.

"Why do you think I want you for my wife?" he continued on a calmer note. "Because you're some kind of baby factory? What kind of man do you think I am? I love *you*, not your procreating ability. So we have a problem. Well, we'll learn to deal with it, one way or another."

There was another silence, and still Faye didn't speak, and she realized she was crying, soundlessly, tears slowly dripping down her cheeks. She was staring at his chest, blindly, not knowing what to think, not thinking at all.

He lifted her chin, gently. "Look at me, Faye."   85

She did, but his face was only a blur.

"Faye, we're in this together—you and I. Don't you see that? It's not just *your* problem, it's *ours*."

"No," she whispered. "No!" She shook her head wildly. "You have a choice, don't you see that? You don't have to marry me. You could marry someone else and have children of your own."

"Oh, God, Faye," he groaned, "you're wrong. Don't you know? Don't you see? I *don't* have a choice. I never did have a choice, or a chance. Not since I met you and fell in love with you. I don't *want* anybody else, don't you understand that? I want you, only you."

She wanted to believe it, give in to him. Never before had she wanted any-   90 thing more desperately than she wanted to give in to him now. But she couldn't, she couldn't. . . . She closed her eyes, briefly, fighting for reason, common sense.

"Kai, I . . . I can't live all my life with your regret and your disappointment. Every time we see some pregnant woman, every time we're with somebody else's children I'll feel I've failed you! I. . . ." Her voice broke and new sobs came unchecked.

He held her very tightly until she calmed down and then he put her from him a little and gave her a dark, compelling look.

"It's not *my* regret, or *my* disappointment," he said with quiet emphasis. "It's *ours*. We're not talking about *you* or *me*. We're talking about *us*. I love you, and you love me, and that's the starting point, that comes first. From then on we're in it together."

Faye moved out of his arms, away from him, but her legs wouldn't carry her and she sank into a chair. She covered her face with her hands and tried desperately to stop the crying, to stop the tears from coming and coming as if they would never end.

"How . . . how can I ever believe it?"   95

"Because I'm asking you to," he said quietly. He knelt in front of her, took her hands away from her wet face. "Look at me, Faye. No other woman can give me what you can—yourself, your love, your warmth, your sense of humor. All the facets of your personality that make up the final you. I've known other women, Faye, but none of them have ever stirred in me any feelings that come close to what I feel for you. You're an original, remember? There's no replacement for an original. There are only copies, and I don't want a copy. To me you're special, and you'll have to believe it, take it on faith. That's what love is all about."

He was holding her hands in his, strong brown hands, and she was looking down on them, fighting with herself, fighting with everything inside her to believe what he was saying, to accept it, to give in to it.

Leaning forward, Kai kissed her gently on the mouth and smiled. "It's all been too much too soon for you, hasn't it? You never really got a chance to get over the shock, and when I fell in love with you it only made things worse." He smiled ruefully and Faye was surprised at his insight.

"Yes," she said. "It all happened too fast."

"Bad timing. If only we could have met later, after you'd sorted it all out in your mind, then it would never have been such a crisis." 100

She looked at him doubtfully. "It wouldn't have changed the facts."

"No, but it might have changed your perspective."

Would it have? she wondered. Could she ever feel confident and secure in her worth as a woman? Or was she at this moment too emotionally bruised to accept that possibility?

"I don't understand," he said, "why I never guessed what was wrong. Now that I know, it all seems so obvious." He looked at her thoughtfully. "Faye," he said gently, "I want you to tell me exactly what happened to you, what Doctor Martin told you."

She stared at him, surprised a little. A thought stirred in the back of her mind. Greg. He had never even asked. The why and the what had not interested him. But Kai, he wanted to know. She swallowed nervously and began the story, slowly, word for word, everything Doctor Martin had said. And he listened, quietly, not interrupting. "So you see," she said at last, "we don't have to hope for any miracles either." 105

"We'll make our own miracles," he said, and smiled. "Come here," he said then, "kiss me."

She did, shyly almost, until he took over and lifted her up and carried her to the bed. He looked down on her, eyes thoughtful. "I won't pretend I understand your feelings about this, the feelings you have about yourself as a woman, but I'll try." He paused for a moment. "Faye," he said then, speaking with slow emphasis, "don't *ever*, not for a single moment, think that you're not good enough for me. You're the best there is, Faye, the very best."

His mouth sought hers and he kissed her with gentle reassurance at first, then with rising ardor. His hands moved over her body, touching her with sensual, intimate caresses.

"You're my woman, Faye, you're mine. . . ."

Her senses reeled. She could never love anyone like she loved him. No one had ever evoked in her this depth of emotion. This was real, this was forever. Kai wanted her as much as ever. No chivalry, this, no game of pretense, she was very sure of that. And when he lifted his face and looked at her, it was all there in his eyes and the wonder of it filled her with joy. 110

"Do you believe me now?" he whispered huskily. "Do you believe I love you and want you and need you?"

She nodded wordlessly, incapable of uttering a sound.

"And do you love me?"

Again she nodded, her eyes in his.

"Okay, then." In one smooth flowing movement he got to his feet. He crossed to the closet, opened it, and took out her suitcases. He put one on the end of the bed and began to pile her clothes in it, taking armfuls out of the closet.

Faye watched incredulously. "What are you doing?" she managed at last.

Kai kept on moving around, opening drawers, taking out her things, filling the suitcase until it could hold no more. "Get dressed. We're going home."

"Home . . . ?"

For a moment he stopped and he looked at her with a deep blue glitter in his eyes. "Yes, *home* — where you belong. With me, in my house, in my bed, in my arms."

"Oh, Kai," she said tremulously, smiling suddenly. "It's midnight!"

His eyes were very dark. "I've waited long enough, I'm not waiting any more. You're coming with me, now. And I'm not letting you out of my sight until we're safely married. I don't want you getting any crazy ideas about running off to save me from myself, or some such notion."

Her throat was dry. "Please, let's not rush into it! Let's think about it first!"

Calmly he zipped up the full suitcase, swung it off the bed, and put it near the door. "I'm not rushing into anything," he said levelly. "I've wanted to marry you for quite a while, remember?"

He crossed to the bed, sat down next to her, and put his arm around her. "Faye, I wish you wouldn't worry so. I'm not going to change my mind. And I haven't shelved my hopes for a family, either." There was a brief silence. "When we're ready to have kids, we'll have them. We'll adopt them. There are orphanages the world over, full of children in need of love and care. We'll do whatever it takes. We'll get them, one way or another."

Faye searched his face, faint hope flickering deep inside her.

"Would you want that?"

"Why not?"

"I don't know, really. I thought you . . . it isn't the same."

"No," he said levelly, "it isn't. Adoption is a different process from pregnancy and birth, but the kids will be ours just the same and we'll love them no less."

"Yes," she said, "yes." And suddenly it seemed as if a light had been turned on inside her, as if suddenly she could see again, a future with Kai, a future with children.

A bronzed hand lifted her face. "Look, Faye, I'll always be sorry. I'll always be sorry not to see you pregnant, not to see you with a big stomach knowing you're carrying my child, but I'll live."

Faye lowered her eyes and tears threatened again. With both his hands he cupped her face.

"Look at me, Faye. I want you to stop thinking of yourself as a machine with a defect. You're not a damaged piece of merchandise, you hear? You're a living, breathing human being, a warm-blooded female, and I love you."

Through a haze of tears she looked at him, giving a weak smile. "I love you too." She put her arms around him and he heaved an unsteady breath.

"Faye," he said huskily, "you're my first and only choice." 135

Chapter Twelve

Kai and Faye had their family, two girls and a boy. They came to them one at a time, from faraway places, with small faces and large dark eyes full of fear. In their faces Faye could read the tragedies of war and death and poverty. They were hungry for love, hungry for nourishment and care. At night they woke in terror, screaming, their memories alive in sleep.

Time passed, and in the low white ranch house under the blue skies of Texas they flourished like the crops in the fields. They grew tall and straight and healthy and the fear in their dark eyes faded. Like their father they wore jeans and boots and large-brimmed hats, and they rode horses and played the guitar. They learned to speak English with a Southern twang.

One day Kai and Faye watched them as they played in the garden, and joy and gratitude overflowed in Faye's heart. Life was good and filled with love.

"They're all ours," she said. Even now after all these years she sometimes still couldn't believe it was really so.

Kai smiled at her. His eyes, still very blue, crinkled at the corners. "Yes, and 140 you're all mine."

"They don't even look like us," she said. "Not even a tiny little bit." No blondes, no redheads.

Taking her in his arms, Kai kissed her. "They're true originals, like their mother. I wouldn't want it any other way."

There was love in his embrace and love in his words and in her heart there was no room now for doubt, no room for sorrow.

Sometimes in the night he would reach for her and she would wake to his touch, his hands on her breast, her stomach, searching. In the warm darkness of their bed she would come to him and they would hold each other close and she knew he had been dreaming.

She knew the dream. She was walking away from him, calling out that she 145 couldn't marry him, the words echoing all around. *"I can't marry you! I can't marry you!"* And Kai was standing there watching her go, terrified, unable to move, his legs frozen to the ground. He wanted to follow her, keep her from leaving, but his legs wouldn't move.

Kai had told her of the dream, of the panic that clutched at him as he watched her walk out of his life. And always he would wake and search for her in the big bed, and she knew of only one way to reassure him. And in the warm afterglow of lovemaking, their bodies close together, she knew that to him she was everything, to him she was the only woman, beautiful, complete, whole.

GAIL GODWIN (B. 1937)

Born in Birmingham, Alabama, Gail Godwin was educated at the University of North
Carolina and the University of Iowa, where
she earned a Ph.D. in English in 1971. She is
a full-time writer who has won grants from
the National Endowment for the Arts, the
Guggenheim Foundation, and the American
Institute for the Arts and Letters. Among
her novels are *Glass People* (1971), *A Mother
and Two Daughters* (1981), *The Finishing School*
(1985), *Evensong* (1999), and *Queen of the Underworld* (2006). Her short stories have been
collected in several volumes including *Dream
Children* (1976) and *Mr. Bedford and the Muses*
(1983).

© Jerry Bauer.

A Sorrowful Woman   *1971*

Once upon a time there was a wife and mother one too many times

One winter evening she looked at them: the husband durable, receptive, gentle;
the child a tender golden three. The sight of them made her so sad and sick she
did not want to see them ever again.

   She told the husband these thoughts. He was attuned to her; he understood such things. He said he understood. What would she like him to do? "If
you could put the boy to bed and read him the story about the monkey who
ate too many bananas, I would be grateful." "Of course," he said. "Why, that's a
pleasure." And he sent her off to bed.

   The next night it happened again. Putting the warm dishes away in the
cupboard, she turned and saw the child's gray eyes approving her movements.
In the next room was the man, his chin sunk in the open collar of his favorite
wool shirt. He was dozing after her good supper. The shirt was the gray of the
child's trusting gaze. She began yelping without tears, retching in between. The
man woke in alarm and carried her in his arms to bed. The boy followed
them up the stairs, saying, "It's all right, Mommy," but this made her scream.
"Mommy is sick," the father said, "go wait for me in your room."

   The husband undressed her, abandoning her only long enough to root beneath the eiderdown for her flannel gown. She stood naked except for her bra,
which hung by one strap down the side of her body; she had not the impetus to
shrug it off. She looked down at the right nipple, shriveled with chill, and
thought, How absurd, a vertical bra. "If only there were instant sleep," she said,
hiccuping, and the husband bundled her into the gown and went out and

came back with a sleeping draught guaranteed swift. She was to drink a little glass of cognac followed by a big glass of dark liquid and afterwards there was just time to say Thank you and could you get him a clean pair of pajamas out of the laundry, it came back today.

The next day was Sunday and the husband brought her breakfast in bed and let her sleep until it grew dark again. He took the child for a walk, and when they returned, red-cheeked and boisterous, the father made supper. She heard them laughing in the kitchen. He brought her up a tray of buttered toast, celery sticks, and black bean soup. "I am the luckiest woman," she said, crying real tears. "Nonsense," he said. "You need a rest from us," and went to prepare the sleeping draught, find the child's pajamas, select the story for the night.

She got up on Monday and moved about the house till noon. The boy, delighted to have her back, pretended he was a vicious tiger and followed her from room to room, growling and scratching. Whenever she came close, he would growl and scratch at her. One of his sharp little claws ripped her flesh, just above the wrist, and together they paused to watch a thin red line materialize on the inside of her pale arm and spill over in little beads. "Go away," she said. She got herself upstairs and locked the door. She called the husband's office and said, "I've locked myself away from him. I'm afraid." The husband told her in his richest voice to lie down, take it easy, and he was already on the phone to call one of the baby-sitters they often employed. Shortly after, she heard the girl let herself in, heard the girl coaxing the frightened child to come and play.

After supper several nights later, she hit the child. She had known she was going to do it when the father would see. "I'm sorry," she said, collapsing on the floor. The weeping child had run to hide. "What has happened to me, I'm not myself anymore." The man picked her tenderly from the floor and looked at her with much concern. "Would it help if we got, you know, a girl in? We could fix the room downstairs. I want you to feel freer," he said, understanding these things. "We have the money for a girl. I want you to think about it."

And now the sleeping draught was a nightly thing, she did not have to ask. He went down to the kitchen to mix it, he set it nightly beside her bed. The little glass and the big one, amber and deep rich brown, the flannel gown and the eiderdown.

The man put out the word and found the perfect girl. She was young, dynamic, and not pretty. "Don't bother with the room, I'll fix it up myself." Laughing, she employed her thousand energies. She painted the room white, fed the child lunch, read edifying books, raced the boy to the mailbox, hung her own watercolors on the fresh-painted walls, made spinach soufflé, cleaned a spot from the mother's coat, made them all laugh, danced in stocking feet to music in the white room after reading the child to sleep. She knitted dresses for herself and played chess with the husband. She washed and set the mother's soft ash-blonde hair and gave her neck rubs, offered to.

The woman now spent her winter afternoons in the big bedroom. She made a fire in the hearth and put on slacks and an old sweater she had loved at school, and sat in the big chair and stared out the window at snow-ridden branches, or went away into long novels about other people moving through other winters.

The girl brought the child in twice a day, once in the later afternoon when he would tell of his day, all of it tumbling out quickly because there was not much time, and before he went to bed. Often now, the man took his wife to dinner. He made a courtship ceremony of it, inviting her beforehand so she could get used to the idea. They dressed and were beautiful together again and went out into the frosty night. Over candlelight he would say, "I think you are better, you know." "Perhaps I am," she would murmur. "You look . . . like a cloistered queen," he said once, his voice breaking curiously.

One afternoon the girl brought the child into the bedroom. "We've been out playing in the park. He found something he wants to give you, a surprise." The little boy approached her, smiling mysteriously. He placed his cupped hands in hers and left a live dry thing that spat brown juice in her palm and leapt away. She screamed and wrung her hands to be rid of the brown juice. "Oh, it was only a grasshopper," said the girl. Nimbly she crept to the edge of the curtain, did a quick knee bend, and reclaimed the creature, led the boy competently from the room.

"The girl upsets me," said the woman to her husband. He sat frowning on the side of the bed he had not entered for so long. "I'm sorry, but there it is." The husband stroked his creased brow and said he was sorry too. He really did not know what they would do without that treasure of a girl. "Why don't you stay here with me in bed," the woman said.

Next morning she fired the girl who cried and said, "I loved the little boy, what will become of him now?" But the mother turned away her face and the girl took down the watercolors from the walls, sheathed the records she had danced to, and went away.

"I don't know what we'll do. It's all my fault, I know. I'm such a burden, I 15 know that."

"Let me think. I'll think of something." (Still understanding these things.)

"I know you will. You always do," she said.

With great care he rearranged his life. He got up hours early, did the shopping, cooked the breakfast, took the boy to nursery school. "We will manage," he said, "until you're better, however long that is." He did his work, collected the boy from the school, came home and made the supper, washed the dishes, got the child to bed. He managed everything. One evening, just as she was on the verge of swallowing her draught, there was a timid knock on her door. The little boy came in wearing his pajamas. "Daddy has fallen asleep on my bed and I can't get in. There's not room."

Very sedately she left her bed and went to the child's room. Things were much changed. Books were rearranged, toys. He'd done some new drawings. She came as a visitor to her son's room, wakened the father and helped him to bed. "Ah, he shouldn't have bothered you," said the man, leaning on his wife. "I've told him not to." He dropped into his own bed and fell asleep with a moan. Meticulously she undressed him. She folded and hung his clothes. She covered his body with the bedclothes. She flicked off the light that shone in his face.

The next day she moved her things into the girl's white room. She put her 20 hairbrush on the dresser; she put a note pad and pen beside the bed. She stocked the little room with cigarettes, books, bread, and cheese. She didn't need much.

At first the husband was dismayed. But he was receptive to her needs. He understood these things. "Perhaps the best thing is for you to follow it through," he said. "I want to be big enough to contain whatever you must do."

All day long she stayed in the white room. She was a young queen, a virgin in a tower; she was the previous inhabitant, the girl with all the energies. She tried these personalities on like costumes, then discarded them. The room had a new view of streets she'd never seen that way before. The sun hit the room in late afternoon and she took to brushing her hair in the sun. One day she decided to write a poem. "Perhaps a sonnet." She took up her pen and pad and began working from words that had lately lain in her mind. She had choices for the sonnet, ABAB or ABBA for a start. She pondered these possibilities until she tottered into a larger choice: she did not have to write a sonnet. Her poem could be six, eight, ten, thirteen lines, it could be any number of lines, and it did not even have to rhyme.

She put down the pen on top of the pad.

In the evenings, very briefly, she saw the two of them. They knocked on her door, a big knock and a little, and she would call Come in, and the husband would smile though he looked a bit tired, yet somehow this tiredness suited him. He would put her sleeping draught on the bedside table and say, "The boy and I have done all right today," and the child would kiss her. One night she tasted for the first time the power of his baby spit.

"I don't think I can see him anymore," she whispered sadly to the man. And the husband turned away, but recovered admirably and said, "Of course, I see." 25

So the husband came alone. "I have explained to the boy," he said. "And we are doing fine. We are managing." He squeezed his wife's pale arm and put the two glasses on her table. After he had gone, she sat looking at the arm.

"I'm afraid it's come to that," she said. "Just push the notes under the door; I'll read them. And don't forget to leave the draught outside."

The man sat for a long time with his head in his hands. Then he rose and went away from her. She heard him in the kitchen where he mixed the draught in batches now to last a week at a time, storing it in a corner of the cupboard. She heard him come back, leave the big glass and the little one outside on the floor.

Outside her window the snow was melting from the branches, there were more people on the streets. She brushed her hair a lot and seldom read anymore. She sat in her window and brushed her hair for hours, and saw a boy fall off his new bicycle again and again, a dog chasing a squirrel, an old woman peek slyly over her shoulder and then extract a parcel from a garbage can.

In the evening she read the notes they slipped under her door. The child 30 could not write, so he drew and sometimes painted his. The notes were painstaking at first; the man and boy offering the final strength of their day to her. But sometimes, when they seemed to have had a bad day, there were only hurried scrawls.

One night, when the husband's note had been extremely short, loving but short, and there had been nothing from the boy, she stole out of her room as she often did to get more supplies, but crept upstairs instead and stood outside their doors, listening to the regular breathing of the man and boy asleep. She hurried back to her room and drank the draught.

She woke earlier now. It was spring, there were birds. She listened for sounds of the man and the boy eating breakfast; she listened for the roar of the motor when they drove away. One beautiful noon, she went out to look at her kitchen in the daylight. Things were changed. He had bought some new dish towels. Had the old ones worn out? The canisters seemed closer to the sink. She got out flour, baking powder, salt, milk (he bought a different brand of butter), and baked a loaf of bread and left it cooling on the table.

The force of the two joyful notes slipped under her door that evening pressed her into the corner of the little room; she had hardly space to breathe. As soon as possible, she drank the draught.

Now the days were too short. She was always busy. She woke with the first bird. Worked till the sun set. No time for hair brushing. Her fingers raced the hours.

Finally, in the nick of time, it was finished one late afternoon. Her veins 35 pumped and her forehead sparkled. She went to the cupboard, took what was hers, closed herself into the little white room and brushed her hair for a while.

The man and boy came home and found: five loaves of warm bread, a roast stuffed turkey, a glazed ham, three pies of different fillings, eight molds of the boy's favorite custard, two weeks' supply of fresh-laundered sheets and shirts and towels, two hand-knitted sweaters (both of the same gray color), a sheath of marvelous watercolor beasts accompanied by mad and fanciful stories nobody could ever make up again, and a tablet full of love sonnets addressed to the man. The house smelled redolently of renewal and spring. The man ran to the little room, could not contain himself to knock, flung back the door.

"Look, Mommy is sleeping," said the boy. "She's tired from doing all our things again." He dawdled in a stream of the last sun for that day and watched his father roll tenderly back her eyelids, lay his ear softly to her breast, test the delicate bones of her wrist. The father put down his face into her fresh-washed hair.

"Can we eat the turkey for supper?" the boy asked.

CONSIDERATIONS FOR CRITICAL THINKING AND WRITING

1. **FIRST RESPONSE.** How did you respond to the excerpt from *A Secret Sorrow* and to "A Sorrowful Woman"? Do you like one more than the other? Is one of the women — Faye or Godwin's unnamed wife — more likable than the other? Why do you think you respond the way you do to the characters and the stories — is your response intellectual, emotional, a result of authorial intent, a mix of these, or something else entirely?

2. Describe what you found appealing in each story. Can you point to passages in both that strike you as especially well written or interesting? Was there anything in either story that did not appeal to you? Why?

3. How do the two women's attitudes toward family life differ? How does that difference constitute the problem in each story?

4. How is the woman's problem in "A Sorrowful Woman" made more complex than Faye's in *A Secret Sorrow*? What is the purpose of the husband and child in Godwin's story?

5. How would you describe the theme — the central point and meaning — in each story?

6. To what extent might "A Sorrowful Woman" be regarded as an unromantic sequel to *A Secret Sorrow*?

7. Can both stories be read a second or third time and still be interesting? Why or why not?

8. Explain how you think a romance formula writer would end "A Sorrowful Woman," or write the ending yourself.

9. Contrast what marriage means in the two stories.

10. Discuss your feelings about the woman in "A Sorrowful Woman." How does she remain a sympathetic character in spite of her refusal to be a traditional wife and mother? (It may take more than one reading of the story to see that Godwin does sympathize with her.)

11. The happy ending of *A Secret Sorrow* may seem like that of a fairy tale, but it is realistically presented because there is nothing strange, mysterious, or fabulous that strains our ability to believe it could happen. In contrast, "A Sorrowful Woman" begins with an epigraph (*"Once upon a time . . ."*) that causes us to expect a fairy-tale ending, but that story is clearly a fairy tale gone wrong. Consider the two stories as fairy tales. How might "A Sorrowful Woman" be read as a dark version of "Sleeping Beauty"?

12. **CRITICAL STRATEGIES.** Read the section on feminist criticism in Chapter 53, "Critical Strategies for Reading." Based on that discussion, what do you think a feminist critic might have to say about these two stories?

Perspectives

KAY MUSSELL (B. 1943)

Are Feminism and Romance Novels Mutually Exclusive?

1997

If feminism and romance are mutually exclusive, a lot of romance writers and readers haven't heard the news yet. In my experience, the only people who think they are mutually exclusive are people who don't know much about romances — or about women, or dare I add about feminism? That last point may be provocative and subject to real debate.

Twenty years ago, when romance novels were getting a lot of attention in the media, I thought that their increased popularity and changing content had something to do with the challenge mounted by feminism to more traditional women. I saw romances back then as a kind of backlash against the more aggressive and controversial aspects of feminism — something that reaffirmed traditional values and made women who hadn't bought into the feminist critique feel validated about their own choices. I also expected romances to fade away as more and more women entered the labor force and became practical feminists if not theoretical or political feminists.

Was I ever wrong! Instead of quietly going the way of the Western (which is much less popular now than it was a few decades ago), romances have become one of the hottest areas of publishing. One reason, of course, is that romances have changed with the times. The newer romances incorporate feminist themes while still reaffirming more traditional notions about love and family. Moreover, many romance writers have openly claimed feminist values and, in the process, rejected easy stereotypes about themselves and their work. For example, see the essays by romance writers collected in Jayne Ann Krentz's *Dangerous Men & Adventurous Women.*

More difficult to illustrate, but I think equally important, is change in feminist thinking itself. Twenty or so years ago, when academic feminists first became interested in the romance genre, there was wider agreement among feminists themselves on what the feminist agenda should be — and conventional romantic relationships, widely assumed to be discriminatory toward women, were not part of it. Thus romances were seen as threatening to female autonomy. But as feminism has matured — and as feminist scholars have come to recognize a broader range of female experience — some scholars have challenged those earlier notions in productive ways.

I don't know how you can read many romances today as anything but feminist. To take just one issue: Heroes and heroines meet each other on a much more equal playing field. Heroes don't always dominate and heroines are frequently right. Heroines have expertise and aren't afraid to show it. Heroes aren't the fount of all wisdom and they actually have things to learn from heroines. This is true of both contemporary and historical romances. I'm not trying to argue that all romances before the 1990s featured unequal relationships or that all romances today are based on equality. That's clearly not the case. But in general heroines today have a lot more independence and authority than their counterparts did in earlier romances. I think that's clear evidence of the influence of feminism on romances and of the ability of romance novels to address contemporary concerns that women share.

From "All About Romance: The Back-Fence for Lovers of Romance Novels"
accessed at *likesbooks.com/mussell.html.*

CONSIDERATIONS FOR CRITICAL THINKING AND WRITING

1. How might the excerpt from *A Secret Sorrow* be read "as a kind of backlash against the more aggressive and controversial aspects of feminism"?

2. Examine some recent romance novel covers and back-cover copy in a bookstore. What evidence is there to support or refute Mussell's claim that "newer romances incorporate feminist themes while still reaffirming more traditional notions about love and family"?

3. Write an essay in which you consider a book, film, or television program that seems to appeal to male fantasies, and explore some of the similarities and differences between male and female tastes in popular fiction.

THOMAS JEFFERSON (1743–1826)

On the Dangers of Reading Fiction   1818

A great obstacle to good education is the inordinate passion prevalent for novels, and the time lost in that reading which should be instructively employed. When this poison infects the mind, it destroys its tone and revolts it against wholesome reading. Reason and fact, plain and unadorned, are rejected. Nothing can engage attention unless dressed in all the figments of fancy, and nothing so bedecked comes amiss. The result is a bloated imagination, sickly judgment, and disgust towards all the real businesses of life. This mass of trash, however, is not without some distinction; some few modeling their narratives, although fictitious, on the incidents of real life, have been able to make them interesting and useful vehicles of a sound morality. . . . For a like reason, too, much poetry should not be indulged. Some is useful for forming style and taste. Pope, Dryden, Thompson, Shakespeare, and of the French, Molière, Racine, the Corneilles, may be read with pleasure and improvement.

Letter to Nathaniel Burwell, March 14, 1818,
in *The Writings of Thomas Jefferson*

CONSIDERATIONS FOR CRITICAL THINKING AND WRITING

1. Jefferson voices several common objections to fiction. What, according to him, are the changes associated with reading fiction? Are these concerns still expressed today? Why or why not? To what extent are Jefferson's arguments similar to twentieth-century objections to watching television?

2. Explain why you agree or disagree that works of fiction should serve as "useful vehicles of a sound morality."

3. How do you think Jefferson would regard Harlequin romances?

ENCOUNTERING FICTION: COMICS AND GRAPHIC STORIES

In the beginning of storytelling was the drawn picture, not the written word. The cave paintings produced thousands of years ago told stories without words, but the development of written language and the invention of printing cast visual storytelling into the shadows until the late nineteenth century when the first comic strips brought words and pictures together in what has become an enormously popular art. From the quirky humor of *Peanuts* characters to the sexy action adventures of Japanese graphic novels, comic strips and graphic stories have become a significant part of the growth of the visual culture that we daily encounter.

Comic strips and graphic stories — told by a series of related drawings containing words that advance the plot — are certainly not to everyone's taste, but their increasing popularity is undeniable. A perusal of the shelf space in your local bookstore devoted to comic books and graphic novels will confirm the growing demand for this kind of storytelling. Like the conventional books that surround them, comic strips and graphic stories vary in quality. The best create seamless relationships between words and images that can be humorous, satirical, disturbing, or provocative. The strips that follow below and throughout the fiction section of *The Bedford Introduction to Literature* by Gene Luen Yang, Edward Gorey, Lynda Barry, Marjane Satrapi, and Matt Groening manage to take on important subjects with seriousness but also with humor. There can be no question that reading a graphic story is not identical to reading a short story, but it is nevertheless a form of reading — and the strips a form of storytelling. What similarities and differences do you find between the narrative elements in the strips and in the short stories you have read?

Gene Luen Yang (b. 1973), *American Born Chinese*

Born in Alameda, California, Gene Luen Yang has been drawing comic books since he was a grammar school student and published his first comics in 1996 under the name Humble comics. He received the prestigious comics Xeric Grant in 1997 for *Gordon Yamamoto and the King of the Geeks,* the story of a not very smart but very likable high-school student. His second graphic novel, *Loyola Chin and the San Peligrin Order,* was followed by *American Born Chinese* (2006), the first book of its kind to be nominated for a National Book Award and the first graphic novel to win the American Library's Printz Award. Yang's latest graphic novel, *The Eternal Smile* (2009), is co-authored with Derek Kirk Kim. Yang currently teaches computer science at a high school in Oakland, California.

In the following excerpt from *American Born Chinese,* Jin Wang is the son of Chinese immigrants who lives in San Francisco's Chinatown before moving to the suburbs. The story focuses on issues associated with immigration and being an outsider trying to establish an authentic identity, topics that Yang handles deftly with humor and compassion in both his writing and visual art. In an interview with the *San Francisco Chronicle,* Yang acknowledges that some of Wang's story is based on his own childhood: "I was Asian and I wore glasses and I was really skinny, and I knew that I was stereotyped as a nerd. So there was part of me that kind of rebelled against that" (October 23, 2006).

EVERY SUNDAY MOTHER USED TO VISIT THE CHINESE HERBALIST JUST AROUND THE CORNER FOR HER ALLERGIES. SHE WOULD ALWAYS TAKE ME ALONG.

SOMETIMES THE APPOINTMENT LASTED FOR WHAT SEEMED LIKE HOURS. I WOULD SIT IN THE FRONT ROOM, LISTENING TO THE HERBALIST'S WIFE CALCULATE BILLS ON HER ABACUS.

CLICK CLACK CLICK

ONE SUNDAY, WHEN BUSINESS WAS ESPECIALLY SLOW AND I WAS ESPECIALLY BORED, THE HERBALIST'S WIFE ASKED,

< SO LITTLE FRIEND, WHAT DO YOU PLAN TO BECOME WHEN YOU GROW UP? >

<...WELL...>

<...I...I WANT TO BE A>

TRANS-FORMER!

..."TRANS- FO- MA?"

< YEAH! > A ROBOT IN DISGUISE! < LIKE THIS ONE! >

< HE CHANGES INTO A TRUCK... >

CLICK
CLICK CLACK

< ...SEE? > MORE THAN MEETS THE EYE!

< IN THE CARTOON, HE'S ALSO GOT A TRAILER THAT MAGICALLY APPEARS WHENEVER HE TRANS-FORMS, BUT ON THE TOY IT'S A SEPARATE PIECE. >

< SO YOU WANT TO BE A...A...> "TRANS-FO-MA," < HUH? >

< YEAH...BUT MA-MA SAYS THAT'S SILLY. LITTLE BOYS DON'T GROW UP TO BE > TRANSFORMERS.

< OH, I WOULDN'T BE SO SURE ABOUT THAT. I'M GOING TO LET YOU IN ON A SECRET, LITTLE FRIEND: >

"Forfeit Your Soul" panel illustrations and text from the book *American Born Chinese*. Text and illustrations by Gene Luen Yang. Copyright 2006 by Gene Lang. Published by First Second Books. Reprinted by arrangement with Henry Holt and Company, LLC.

CONSIDERATIONS AND CONNECTION TO ANOTHER SELECTION

1. Describe how the visual details economically establish the setting.
2. Comment on the use of Yang's sound in the frames. How do they serve to unify the story?
3. Discuss the herbalist's advice. How sound is it?
4. How might the herbalist's "secret" be applied to Gail Godwin's "A Sorrowful Woman" (p. 39)?

2

Writing about
Fiction

Writing permits me to experience life as
any number of strange creations.
— ALICE WALKER

FROM READING TO WRITING

There's no question about it: writing about fiction is a different experience
than reading it. The novelist William Styron amply concedes that writing
to him is not so much about pleasure as it is about work: "Let's face it, writing is hell." Although Styron's lament concerns his own feelings about
writing prose fiction, he no doubt speaks for many other writers, including
essayists. Writing is, of course, work, but it is also a pleasure when it goes
well — when ideas feel solid and the writing is fluid. You can experience
that pleasure as well, if you approach writing as an intellectual and emotional opportunity rather than merely a sentence.

Just as reading fiction requires an imaginative, conscious response, so
does writing about fiction. Composing an essay is not just recording your

interpretive response to a work because the act of writing can change your response as you explore, clarify, and discover relationships you hadn't previously considered or recognized. Most writers discover new ideas and connections as they move through the process of rereading and annotating the text, taking notes, generating ideas, developing a thesis, and organizing an argumentative essay (these matters are detailed in Chapter 54, "Reading and the Writing Process"). To become more conscious of the writing process, first study the following questions specifically aimed at sharpening your response to reading and writing about fiction. Then examine the case study of a student's paper in progress that takes you through writing a first response to reading, brainstorming for a paper topic, writing a first draft, revising, and writing the final paper.

Questions for Responsive Reading and Writing

The following questions can help you consider important elements of fiction that reveal your responses to a story's effects and meanings. The questions are general, so they will not always be relevant to a particular story. Many of them, however, should prove useful for thinking, talking, and writing about a work of fiction. If you are uncertain about the meaning of a term used in a question, consult the Glossary of Literary Terms beginning on page 2123 of this book. You should also find useful the discussion of various critical approaches to literature in Chapter 53, "Critical Strategies for Reading."

PLOT

1. Does the plot conform to a formula? Is it like those of any other stories you have read? Did you find it predictable?

2. What is the source and nature of the conflict for the protagonist? Was your major interest in the story based on what happens next or on some other concern? What does the title reveal now that you've finished the story?

3. Is the story told chronologically? If not, in what order are its events told, and what is the effect of that order on your response to the action?

4. What does the exposition reveal? Are flashbacks used? Did you see any foreshadowings? Where is the climax?

5. Is the conflict resolved at the end? Would you characterize the ending as happy, unhappy, or somewhere in between?

6. Is the plot unified? Is each incident somehow related to some other element in the story?

CHARACTER

7. Do you identify with the protagonist? Who (or what) is the antagonist?

8. Did your response to any characters change as you read? What do you think caused the change? Do any characters change and develop in the course of the story? How?

continued

9. Are round, flat, or stock characters used? Is their behavior motivated and plausible?

10. How does the author reveal characters? Are they directly described or indirectly presented? Are the characters' names used to convey something about them?

11. What is the purpose of the minor characters? Are they individualized, or do they primarily represent ideas or attitudes?

SETTING

12. Is the setting important in shaping your response? If it were changed, would your response to the story's action and meaning be significantly different?

13. Is the setting used symbolically? Are the time, place, and atmosphere related to the theme?

14. Is the setting used as an antagonist?

POINT OF VIEW

15. Who tells the story? Is it a first-person or third-person narrator? Is it a major or minor character or one who does not participate in the action at all? How much does the narrator know? Does the point of view change at all in the course of the story?

16. Is the narrator reliable and objective? Does the narrator appear too innocent, emotional, or self-deluded to be trusted?

17. Does the author directly comment on the action?

18. If it were told from a different point of view, how would your response to the story change? Would anything be lost?

SYMBOLISM

19. Did you notice any symbols in the story? Are they actions, characters, settings, objects, or words?

20. How do the symbols contribute to your understanding of the story?

THEME

21. Did you find a theme? If so, what is it?

22. Is the theme stated directly, or is it developed implicitly through the plot, characters, or some other element?

23. Is the theme a confirmation of your values, or does it challenge them?

STYLE, TONE, AND IRONY

24. Do you think the style is consistent and appropriate throughout the story? Do all the characters use the same kind of language, or did you hear different voices?

25. Would you describe the level of diction as formal or informal? Are the sentences short and simple, long and complex, or some combination?

26. How does the author's use of language contribute to the tone of the story? Did it seem, for example, intense, relaxed, sentimental, nostalgic, humorous, angry, sad, or remote?

27. Do you think the story is worth reading more than once? Does the author's use of language bear close scrutiny so that you feel and experience more with each reading?

CRITICAL STRATEGIES

28. Is there a particular critical approach that seems especially appropriate for this story? (See the discussion of critical strategies for reading beginning on p. 2041.)

29. How might biographical information about the author help you to determine the central concerns of the story?

30. How might historical information about the story provide a useful context for interpretation?

31. What kinds of evidence from the story are you focusing on to support your interpretation? Does your interpretation leave out any important elements that might undercut or qualify your interpretation?

32. To what extent do your own experiences, values, beliefs, and assumptions inform your interpretation?

33. Given that there are a variety of ways to interpret the story, which one seems the most useful to you?

A SAMPLE PAPER IN PROGRESS

The following student paper was written in response to an assignment that asked for a comparison and contrast of the treatment of marriage in the excerpt from Karen van der Zee's novel *A Secret Sorrow* (p. 31) and in Gail Godwin's short story "A Sorrowful Woman" (p. 39). The final draft of the paper is preceded by four distinct phases of composition: (1) an initial response, (2) a brainstorming exercise, (3) a preliminary draft of the paper, and (4) an annotated version of the preliminary draft that shows how the student thought about revising the paper. Maya Leigh's First Response is an informal paper based on questions supplied by the instructor: "How did you respond to each story? Do you like one more than the other? Is one of the women more likable than the other? Why do you think you respond the way you do? Is your response to the characters and the stories primarily intellectual, emotional, a result of authorial intention, a mix of these, or something else entirely?" (Spelling and grammatical errors in Maya's preliminary drafts have been silently corrected so as not to distract from her developing argument.)

A First Response to A Secret Sorrow *and* "A Sorrowful Woman"

Reading the excerpt from the Harlequin I was irritated by the seeming helplessness of Faye; in the first chapter she is constantly on the edge of hysteria and can hardly stand up. I could do without all of the fainting, gasping, and general theatrics. I've read Harlequins before, and I usually skim through that stuff to get to the good romantic parts and the happy ending. What I like about these kinds of romance novels is the happy ending. Even though the ending is kind of clichéd with the white fence and blue skies, there is still something satisfying about having everything work out okay.

The Godwin story, of course, does not have a happy ending. It is a much more powerful story, and it is one that I could read several times, unlike the Harlequin. The Godwin woman bothers me too, because I can't really see what she has to complain about. Her husband is perfectly accommodating and understanding. It seems that if she were unhappy with her life as a wife and mother and wanted to work or do something else, he wouldn't have a problem with it. She seems to throw away her life and hurt her family for nothing.

I enjoyed reading the Godwin story more just because it is well written and more complex, but I liked the ending of the Harlequin more. I think on an emotional level I liked the Harlequin better, and on an intellectual level I liked the Godwin story more. It is more satisfying emotionally to see a romance develop and end happily than it is to see the deterioration of a marriage and the suicide of a depressed woman. I don't really find either character particularly likable; toward the end when the Godwin woman comes out of her room and starts doing things again I begin to feel sympathy for her—I can understand her having a period of depression, but I want her to pull herself out of it, and when she doesn't, I am disappointed. Even though Faye is annoying in the beginning, because everything ends happily I am almost willing to forgive and forget my previous annoyance with her. If the Godwin woman hadn't killed herself and had returned to her family life, I would have liked her better, but because she doesn't I leave the story feeling discouraged.

Brainstorming

By listing these parallel but alternate treatments of marriage in each story, Maya begins to assemble an inventory of relevant topics related to the assignment. What becomes clear to her is that her approach will emphasize the differences in each story's portrayal of marriage.

A Sample Brainstorming List

<u>Marriage</u>

Godwin	*Harlequin*
marriage as end of life — confining, weighty	marriage as end, goal — dreamlike, idyllic
husband — durable, receptive, understanding	husband — understanding, manly
p. 39 sight of family makes her sad and sick	p. 38 watching kids she feels that life is good + filled with love
house in winter — girl paints room white	white house in Texas under blue skies
the power of his baby spit and looking at arm p. 42	in husband's embrace no room for doubt or sorrow p. 38
family makes her sad	family makes her happy
weight pressing on her	weight lifted off her
impersonal — the husband, the child emphasis on roles	Kai, Faye, our children
dead in the end	beautiful, whole, complete in the end
crisis due to fear of always having husband and kid	crisis due to fear of never having husband and kids
feels incomplete and depressed as only wife and mother	feels incomplete and depressed not being wife and mother

---

Revising: First and Second Drafts

Maya's first draft of the paper pursues and develops many of the topics she noted while brainstorming. She explores the differences between each story's treatment of marriage in detail by examining each protagonist's role as wife and mother, her husband's response, the role played by her children, and the ending of each story. The second draft's annotations indicate that Maya has been able to distance herself enough from her first draft to critique its weak moments. In the annotations she recognizes, for example, that she needs a clearer thesis, some stronger transitions between paragraphs, some crisper and more detailed sentences to clarify points, and a more convincing conclusion as well as a more pointed title.

A Sample First Draft: Separate Sorrows

Separate Sorrows

In both the excerpt from *A Secret Sorrow* and "A Sorrowful Woman," by Gail Godwin, the story is centered around ideas of marriage and family. However, marriage and family are presented in very different lights in the two stories. Karen van der Zee presents marriage with children as perfect and somewhat dreamlike; it is what Faye, the heroine of *A Secret Sorrow*, wants, and what is necessary for her happiness. For Godwin's heroine, marriage and family are almost the antithesis of happiness; her home life seems to suffocate her and eventually leads her to commit suicide.

Both of the female protagonists in the two stories experience a crisis of sorts. In *A Secret Sorrow* Faye's crisis comes before marriage. She is distraught and upset because she cannot have children and fears that this will prevent her from marrying the man she loves. Both she and her beloved, Kai, have always wanted a marriage with children, and it is assumed that only under these circumstances will they truly be happy. Faye feels that her inability to have children is a fatal flaw. "Every time we see some pregnant woman, every time we're with somebody else's children I'll feel I've failed you!" (35). In "A Sorrowful Woman," however, the crisis comes after the marriage, when the woman has already procured her husband and child. Faye would be ecstatic in this woman's situation. The protagonist of the Godwin story, however, is not. Her husband and son bring her such sorrow that eventually she is unable to see them at all, and communicates only through notes stuck under her bedroom door. Faye's anxiety and fear is based on the thought of losing her man and never having children. In contrast, Godwin's character has a loving husband and child and is still filled with grief. In a Harlequin such as *A Secret Sorrow*, this is unimaginable; it goes against every formula of romance writing, where books always end with a wedding, and happiness after that is just assumed.

In *A Secret Sorrow*, marriage is portrayed as the end, as the goal of the story. It is what the heroine wants. The author works to let the reader know that only in this way will Faye be fulfilled and happy; it is what the entire story, with all the plot twists and romantic interludes, has been working toward. In "A Sorrowful Woman," marriage is the end, but is not the goal—it is quite literally the end of the woman's life. Though we don't see what her life was like before her emotional crisis, there are hints of it. When she moves into the new room she mentions seeing the streets from a whole new perspective, suggesting the previous monotony of her daily life. In addition, in the final paragraphs of the story when the character bakes pies and bread and washes and folds the laundry, her son says, "she's tired from doing all our things again," (43) giving us an idea of what "our things" were, and what the woman did with her time before becoming ill.

In *A Secret Sorrow* Faye's inability to have children does not end Kai's love for her, and the two go on to get married and adopt children. Faye's married life is described in a very idyllic way—she raises her son and two daughters in a "white ranch house under the blue skies of Texas" (38). In other words, once she is married and has children there is no more anxiety, nothing more to fear. The author leads us to the conclusion that marriage solves all problems and is a source of unending happiness for all. This is a great difference from the Godwin tale, which takes place in the winter and maintains a sense of cold throughout the whole thing. Whenever Godwin describes the family it is not in the light, glowing terms of van der Zee, but always with a sense of weight or guilt or failure about it. The child's trusting gaze makes the protagonist begin "yelping without tears" (39). Any sign of life or love increases her sorrow and makes her want to be rid of it. For example, when the hired girl brings her son to visit her with a grasshopper he's found—something both alive and from the outside world—she gets very upset and forces her husband to fire her. The girl is too much of an infringement on her space, and too much of a reminder of what she can no longer be.

Never is the difference between the two authors' portrayals of marriage more apparent than when both the women are viewing their families. Faye, sitting with her husband and watching her children play, felt that "life was good and filled with love" (38). Godwin's protagonist, on the other hand, says, "The sight of them made her so sad and sick she did not want to see them ever again" (39). When Kai, now her husband, embraces Faye, she feels that, "There was love in his embrace and love in his words and in her heart there was no room now for doubt, no room for sorrow" (38). When Godwin's heroine feels the loving touch of her husband's arm and the kiss of her child she cannot bear it and cuts off all direct contact with them. The situation of her marriage pushes her into a self-imposed imprisonment and lethargy. She feels unbearably sad because she can no longer be who they want and need her to be. She avoids them not because she does not love them, but rather because she loves them so much that it is too painful to see them and feel her failure.

When Faye's fears of losing Kai are assuaged, and she is happily married, it is as though a great weight has been lifted off of her. Godwin's character, on the other hand, feels her marriage as a great weight pressing in on her. The love of her husband and child weighs on her and immobilizes her. When she leaves her room for a day and leaves out freshly baked bread for her husband and son, they express their happiness in the notes they write to her that night, and "the force of the two joyful notes . . . pressed her into the corner of the little room; she hardly had space to breathe" (43). Faye can be a traditional wife and mother, so her family is a source of joy. Godwin's character can no longer do this, and so her family is a representation of her failure, and the guilt presses her further and further into herself, until she can retreat no further and ends her life.

The endings of the two stories are powerful illustrations of the differences between them. In the end of *A Secret Sorrow* the author shows us Faye feeling "beautiful, complete, whole" (38) in her role as wife and mother. Godwin, on the other hand, shows us her heroine dead on her bed. Godwin first gives the reader hope, by showing all that the woman has done, and saying that "the house smelled redolently of renewal and spring" (43). This makes the blow even harder when we then discover, along with the husband and child, the woman's suicide.

Karen van der Zee creates a story full of emotional highs and lows, but one that leads up to—and ends with—marriage. After the marriage all plot twists and traumas come to a halt. Faye is brought to new life by her marriage and children; in it she finds completion of herself and total happiness. Godwin's tale, on the other hand, is full of anguish and emotion, but it all takes place after the marriage. The character she creates is stifled and killed by her marriage. There is no portrayal of unending happiness in her tale, but rather unending woe.

A Sample Second Draft: Separate Sorrows

Maya Leigh
Professor Herlin
English 104
February 11, 2010

*title works for
Godwin—but does
it for van der Zee?*

Separate Sorrows

Karen van der Zee's novel   Gail Godwin's short story

In both the excerpt from *A Secret Sorrow* and "A Sorrowful Woman," ~~by~~
                                                                    plot
~~Gail Godwin~~, the ~~story is~~ centered around ideas of marriage and family.

However, marriage and family are presented in very different lights in the two

stories. Karen van der Zee presents marriage with children as perfect and
            totally fulfilling   protagonist
~~somewhat dream-like~~; it is what Faye, the ~~heroine~~ of *A Secret Sorrow*, wants

and what is necessary for her happiness. For Godwin's ~~heroine,~~ marriage and

*need a clear
thesis here—
is it that SS
endorses
marriage while
SW problem-
atizes it?*

family are almost the antithesis of happiness; her home life seems to suffo-

cate her and eventually leads her to commit suicide.

*does
she? or
is she
con-
sumed
by her
role?*

Both of the female protagonists in the two stories experience a crisis

~~of sorts~~. In *A Secret Sorrow* Faye's crisis comes before marriage. She is dis-

traught and upset because she cannot have children and fears that this will

prevent her from marrying the man she loves. Both she and her beloved, Kai,
                                                  unclear referent
have always wanted a marriage with children, and (it) is assumed that only

under these circumstances will they truly be happy. Faye feels that her inabil-
                            that cuts her off from Kai's love
ity to have children is a fatal flaw. "Every time we see some pregnant woman,

every time we're with somebody else's children I'll feel I've failed you!" (35).

In "A Sorrowful Woman," however, the crisis comes after the marriage, when
                            secured   Unlike who
the woman has already ~~procured~~ her husband and child. Faye would be ec-

static in this woman's situation, ~~T~~he protagonist of ~~the~~ Godwin story ~~how~~-
            Inexplicably,
~~ever,~~ is not. Her husband and son bring her such sorrow that eventually she is
                                        -ing
unable to see them at all, ~~and~~ communicates only through notes stuck under

her bedroom door. Faye's anxiety and fear are based on the thought of losing

her man and never having children. ~~In contrast,~~ Godwin's character has a

Leigh 2

loving husband and child ~~and is still~~ *yet she* filled with grief. ~~In a Harlequin such as A Secret Sorrow,~~ this ~~is~~ unimaginable *it goes against every* formula of *the plot* romance writing; ~~where books~~ always end with a wedding, ~~and happiness after that is just assumed.~~ *with the assumption that the rest is happily ever after.*

(in a Harlequin romance because)
sense of defeat would be
one of the most popular

In *A Secret Sorrow*, marriage is portrayed as ~~the end, as in~~ the goal. ~~It is what the heroine wants. The author~~ *Van der Zee* works to let the reader know that only in this way will Faye be fulfilled and happy; it is what the entire story, with all the plot twists and romantic interludes, ~~has been~~ working toward. In "A Sorrowful Woman," *(marriage is also the end)* but not as in the goal—it is quite literally the end of the woman's life. Though we don't see what her life was like before her emotional crisis, there are hints of it. When she moves into the new room she mentions seeing the streets from a whole new perspective, *need p. ref* suggesting the previous monotony of her daily life. In addition, in the final paragraphs of the story when the character bakes pies and bread and washes and folds the laundry, her son says, "she's tired from doing all our things again" (43), giving us an idea of what "our things" were, and what the woman did with her time before *becoming ill*.

I like this!

is she really ill? or just withdrawing from her life?

In *A Secret Sorrow* Faye's inability to have children does not end Kai's love for her, and the two go on to get married and adopt children. Faye's married life is described in a very idyllic way—she raises her son and two daughters in a "white ranch house under the blue skies of Texas" (38). ~~In other words,~~ once she is married and has children there is no more anxiety, ~~nothing more to fear. The author~~ *because the plot* leads us to the conclusion that marriage solves all problems and is a source of unending happiness ~~for all.~~ This ~~is a~~ great difference from ~~the~~ Godwin's tale, which takes place in the winter and maintains a sense of cold ~~throughout the whole thing.~~ Whenever Godwin describes the family it is ~~not~~ in ~~the light, glowing~~ terms of van der Zee, *that suggest* ~~but~~

need transition

~~always with a sense of~~ weight, or guilt, or failure ~~about it~~. The child's trusting

gaze makes the protagonist begin "yelping without tears" (39). ~~A~~*; and* ~~A~~ny sign of

life or love increases her sorrow and makes her want to be rid of (it.) For *unclear referent*

example, when the hired girl brings her son to visit her with a grasshopper

he's found — something both alive and from the outside world — she gets very

upset and forces her husband to fire ~~her~~ *the girl*. ~~T~~*Apparently,* he girl is too much of an infringe-

ment on her space, and too much of a reminder of what she can no longer be.

Never is the difference between the two authors' portrayals of marriage

more apparent than when both the women are viewing their families. Faye,

sitting with her husband and watching her children play, felt that "life was

good and filled with love" (38). Godwin's protagonist, on the other hand,

says, "The sight of them made her so sad and sick she did not want to see

them ever again" (39). When Kai, now her husband, embraces Faye, she feels

that, "There was love in his embrace and love in his words and in her heart

there was no room now for doubt, no room for sorrow" (38). When Godwin's

heroine feels the loving touch of her husband's arm and the kiss of her child,

she cannot bear it and cuts off all direct contact with them. The situation of

her marriage pushes her into a self-imposed imprisonment and lethargy. She

feels unbearably sad because she can no longer be who they want and need

should I use epigram here? or work into the thesis? her to be. She avoids them not because she does not love them, but rather

because she loves them so much that it is too painful to see them and feel

her failure.

need → transition When Faye's fears of losing Kai are assuaged, and she is happily mar-

ried, it is as though a great weight has been lifted off of her. Godwin's char-

acter, on the other hand, feels her marriage as a great weight pressing in on

her, ~~The love of her husband and child weighs on her and~~ *and* immobiliz~~es~~*ing* her.

When she leaves her room for a day and ~~leaves~~ *puts* out freshly baked bread for

Leigh 4

her husband and son, they express their happiness in the notes they write to

her that night, and "the force of the two joyful notes . . . pressed her into

the corner of the little room; she hardly had space to breathe" (43). Faye can

be a *the* traditional wife and mother, so her family is a source of joy. Godwin's

character can no longer do this, and so her family ~~is a representation of~~ her *'s* *own*

failure, and the guilt presses her further and further into herself/ until she

can retreat no further and ends her life.

The endings of the two stories are powerful illustrations of the

differences between them. In the end of *A Secret Sorrow* the author shows us

Faye feeling "beautiful, complete, whole" (38) in her role as wife and mother.

Godwin, on the other hand, shows us her ~~heroine~~ *protagonist* dead on her bed. Godwin

seems to first gives the reader hope/ by showing all that the woman has done/ and

saying that "the house smelled redolently of renewal and spring" (43). This

makes the blow even harder when we then discover, along with the husband

and child, the woman's ~~suicide~~ *death*.

> *same idyllic surround- ings as VDZ's blue skies?*

Karen van der Zee creates a story full of emotional highs and lows/ but

one that leads up to—and ends with—marriage. After the marriage all plot

twists and traumas come to a halt. Faye is brought to new life by her mar-

riage and children; ~~in it~~ she finds ~~completion of herself~~ *fulfillment* and total happiness.

Godwin's ~~tale, on the other hand,~~ *story, however,* is full of anguish and ~~emotion, but it~~ *confusion (?) that* all

takes place after the marriage. The character she creates is stifled and killed

by her marriage. There is no portrayal of unending happiness in her tale, but

rather unending (woe.) *is this the right word, since she dies?*

> *need some very brief quotes to make conclusion stronger?*

Need to add Works Cited!

Final Paper

The changes noted in Maya's annotations on her second draft are put to good use in the following final draft. By not insisting that Godwin's protagonist actually commits suicide, Maya shifts her attention away from this indeterminable death to the causes and effects of it. This shift leads her to a stronger thesis — that Godwin raises questions about the efficacy of marriage rather than endorsing it as a certain recipe for happiness the way van der Zee does. Maya also incorporates additional revisions, such as transitions (see, for example, the revision between paragraphs 3 and 4), sentence clarity, and a fuller and more persuasive concluding paragraph.

Final Paper: Fulfillment or Failure?
Marriage in A Secret Sorrow *and "A Sorrowful Woman"*

Maya Leigh

Professor Herlin

English 104

February 11, 2010

Fulfillment or Failure?

Marriage in *A Secret Sorrow* and "A Sorrowful Woman"

In both the excerpt from Karen van der Zee's novel *A Secret Sorrow* and in Gail Godwin's short story "A Sorrowful Woman," the plots center around ideas of marriage and family. However, marriage and family are presented in very different lights in the two stories. Karen van der Zee presents marriage with children as perfect and totally fulfilling; it is what Faye, the protagonist of *A Secret Sorrow,* wants and what is necessary for her happiness. For Godwin's unnamed protagonist, marriage and family are almost the antithesis of happiness; her home life seems to suffocate her and eventually leads to her death. *A Secret Sorrow* directly endorses and encourages marriage, whereas "A Sorrowful Woman" indirectly questions and discourages it.

Both of the female protagonists in the two stories experience a crisis. In *A Secret Sorrow* Faye's crisis comes before the marriage. She is distraught and upset because she cannot have children and fears that this will prevent her from marrying the man she loves. Both she and her beloved, Kai, desire marriage with children, and van der Zee suggests that only with these things will they truly be happy. Faye feels that her inability to have children is a fatal flaw that cuts her off from Kai's love. "Every time we see some pregnant woman, every time we're with somebody else's children I'll feel I've failed you!" (35). Faye's anxiety and fear are based on the thought of losing her man and never having children. In "A Sorrowful Woman," however, the crisis comes after the marriage, when the woman has already secured her husband and child. Unlike Faye, who would be ecstatic in this woman's situation, the protagonist of Godwin's story is not. Inexplicably, her husband and son bring

Introduction comparing plots of both stories

Thesis contrasting treatment of marriage in both stories

Discussion of crisis in A Secret Sorrow *with textual evidence*

Discussion of crisis in "A Sorrowful Woman"

her such sorrow that eventually she is unable to see them at all, communi-

Statements
contrasting
crises in the
plots of the
two stories

cating only through notes stuck under her bedroom door. Godwin's character

has a loving husband and child, yet she is still filled with grief. This sense

of defeat would be unimaginable in a Harlequin romance because it goes

against one of the most popular formulas of romance writing: the plot always

ends with a wedding, with the assumption that the rest is happily ever after.

Discussion
contrasting
function of
marriage in
both stories

In *A Secret Sorrow*, marriage is portrayed as the goal. Van der Zee

works to let the reader know that only in this way will Faye be fulfilled and

happy; it is what the entire story, with all the plot twists and romantic inter-

ludes, works toward. Marriage is also the end in "A Sorrowful Woman" but not

as in the goal: it is quite literally the end of the woman's life. Though we

don't see what her life was like before her emotional crisis, there are hints of

it. When she moves into a new bedroom—away from her husband—she

Textual
evidence
supporting
analysis of
"A Sorrowful
Woman"

mentions seeing the streets from a whole new perspective (42), suggesting

the previous monotony of her daily life. In addition, in the final paragraphs

of the story—when the character bakes pies and bread and washes and folds

the laundry—her son says, "She's tired from doing all our things again" (43),

giving us an idea of what "our things" were and what the woman did with

her time before her crisis.

Discussion
contrasting
married life
and family in
both stories,
with textual
evidence

This monotony of marriage is absent in *A Secret Sorrow*. Faye's inability

to have children does not end Kai's love for her, and the two go on to marry

and adopt children. Faye's married life is described in a very idyllic way: she

raises her son and two daughters in a "white ranch house under the blue

skies of Texas" (38). Once she is married and has children, there is no more

anxiety because the plot leads us to the conclusion that marriage solves all

problems and is a source of unending happiness. This greatly differs from

Godwin's tale, which takes place in winter and maintains a sense of cold.

Whenever Godwin describes the family, it is in terms that suggest weight,

guilt, or failure. The child's trusting gaze makes the protagonist begin "yelp-

ing without tears" (39), and any sign of life or love increases her sorrow and

makes her want to be alone. For example, when the hired girl brings her son

to visit her with a grasshopper he's found (41)—something both alive and from the outside world—she gets very upset and forces her husband to fire the girl. Apparently, the girl is too much of an infringement on her space, too much of a reminder of what she can no longer be.

   Never is the difference between the two authors' portrayals of marriage more apparent than when both women are viewing their families. Faye, sitting with her husband and watching her children play, feels that "life was good and filled with love" (38). Godwin's protagonist, on the other hand, says, "The sight of them made her so sad and sick she did not want to see them ever again" (39). When Kai, now her husband, embraces Faye, she feels, "There was love in his embrace and love in his words and in her heart there was no room now for doubt, no room for sorrow" (38). When Godwin's heroine feels the loving touch of her husband's arm and the kiss of her child, she cannot bear it and cuts off all direct contact with them. The situation of her marriage pushes her into a self-imposed imprisonment and lethargy. She feels unbearably sad because she can no longer be who they want and need her to be. She avoids them not because she does not love them but rather because she loves them so much that it is too painful to see them and feel her failure. The epigram to Godwin's story tells us that "Once upon a time there was a wife and a mother one too many times" (39). The addition of "one too many times" to this traditional story opening forces the idea of repetition and monotony: it suggests that it is not that state of being a wife and mother that is inherently bad but rather the fact that that is all Godwin's character is. Day in and day out, too many times over, the woman is just a wife and a mother, and it isn't enough for her.

   In van der Zee's story there could be no such thing as too much motherhood or too much of being a wife. When Faye's fears of losing Kai are assuaged, and she is happily married, it is as though a great weight has been lifted off her. Godwin's character, on the other hand, feels her marriage as a great weight pressing on her and immobilizing her. When she leaves her room for a day and puts out freshly baked bread for her husband and son, they express their happiness in the notes they write to her that night, and "the force of the two joyful notes . . . pressed her into the corner of the little room; she hardly had space to breathe" (43). Faye can be a traditional wife

Analysis contrasting emotions of protagonists in both stories, with textual evidence

Analysis contrasting protagonists' experience of traditional roles, with textual evidence

and mother, so her family is a source of joy. Godwin's character can no longer be the traditional wife and mother, and so her family represents her own failure, and the guilt presses her further and further into herself until she can retreat no further and ends her life.

The endings of the two stories are powerful illustrations of the differences between them. In the end of *A Secret Sorrow* the author shows us Faye feeling "beautiful, complete, whole" (38) in her role as wife and mother. Godwin, on the other hand, shows us her protagonist dead on her bed. Godwin seems to give the reader hope by showing all that the woman has done and saying that "the house smelled redolently of renewal and spring" (43). This makes the blow even harder when we then discover, along with the husband and child, the woman's death. The ambiguous way the death of Godwin's unnamed protagonist is dealt with reinforces the author's negative portrayal of marriage. It isn't explicitly written as a suicide, and Godwin seems to encourage her readers to see it as the inevitable consequence of her marriage.

Van der Zee creates a story full of emotional highs and lows, but one that leads up to and ends with marriage. After the marriage all of the plot twists and traumas come to a halt, replaced with peace and happiness. Faye is brought to new life by her marriage and children; she finds fulfillment of all of her desires in them. Godwin's story, however, is full of postmarital anguish and confusion. The character she creates is stifled and most definitely unfulfilled by her marriage. A burst of creative energy right before her death produces, among other things, "a sheath of marvelous watercolor beasts accompanied by mad and fanciful stories nobody could ever make up again, and a tablet full of love sonnets addressed to the man" (43). It is clear that the woman had talents and desires not met by the routine duties of her marital life. For Faye, the protagonist of *A Secret Sorrow*, marriage is the happily-ever-after ending she has wanted all of her life; for Godwin's protagonist, on the other hand, marriage is just a monotonous and interminable ever after.

Leigh 5

Works Cited

Godwin, Gail. "A Sorrowful Woman." *The Bedford Introduction to Literature*.
    Ed. Michael Meyer. 9th ed. Boston: Bedford/St. Martin's, 2011. 39–43.
    Print.

Van der Zee, Karen. "From *A Secret Sorrow*." *The Bedford Introduction to
    Literature*. Ed. Michael Meyer. 9th ed. Boston: Bedford/St. Martin's,
    2011. 31–38. Print.

3

Plot

I put a group of characters in some sort of predicament, and then watch them try to work themselves free. My job isn't to help them work their way free, or manipulate them to safety — those are jobs which require the noisy jackhammer of plot — but to watch what happens and then write it down.
— STEPHEN KING

Never mistake motion for action.
— ERNEST HEMINGWAY

Created by a writer's imagination, a work of fiction need not be factual or historically accurate. Although actual people, places, and events may be included in fiction, facts are not as important as is the writer's use of them. We can learn much about Russian life in the early part of the nineteenth century from Leo Tolstoy's *War and Peace,* but that historical information is incidental to Tolstoy's exploration of human nature. Tolstoy, like most successful writers, makes us accept as real the world in his novel no matter how foreign it may be to our own reality. One of the ways a writer achieves this acceptance and engagement — and one of

Web Explore the literary element in this chapter at bedfordstmartins.com/meyerlit.

a writer's few obligations — is to interest us in what is happening in the story. We are carried into the writer's fictional world by the plot.

Plot is the author's arrangement of incidents in a story. It is the organizing principle that controls the order of events. This structure is, in a sense, what remains after a writer edits out what is irrelevant to the story being told. We don't need to know, for example, what happens to Rip Van Winkle's faithful dog, Wolf, during his amiable master's twenty-year nap in the Catskill Mountains in order to be enchanted by Washington Irving's story of a henpecked husband. Instead, what is told takes on meaning as it is brought into focus by a skillful writer who selects and orders the events that constitute the story's plot.

Events can be presented in a variety of orders. A chronological arrangement begins with what happens first, then second, and so on, until the last incident is related. That is how "Rip Van Winkle" is told. The events in William Faulkner's "A Rose for Emily," however, are not arranged in chronological order because that would give away the story's surprise ending; instead, Faulkner moves back and forth between the past and present to provide information that leads up to the final startling moment (which won't be given away here either; the story begins on p. 91).

Some stories begin at the end and then lead up to why or how events worked out as they did. If you read the first paragraph of Ralph Ellison's "Battle Royal" (p. 277), you'll find an example of this arrangement that will make it difficult for you to stop reading. Stories can also begin in the middle of things (the Latin term for this common plot strategy is ***in medias res***). In this kind of plot we enter the story on the verge of some important moment. John Updike's "A & P" (p. 733) begins with the narrator, a teenager working at a checkout counter in a supermarket, telling us: "In walks these three girls in nothing but bathing suits." Right away we are brought into the middle of a situation that will ultimately create the conflict in the story.

Another common strategy is the ***flashback,*** a device that informs us about events that happened before the opening scene of a work. Nearly all of Ellison's "Battle Royal" takes the form of a flashback as the narrator recounts how his identity as a black man was shaped by the circumstances that attended a high-school graduation speech he delivered twenty years earlier in a hotel ballroom before a gathering of the town's leading white citizens, most of whom were "quite tipsy." Whatever the plot arrangement, you should be aware of how the writer's conscious ordering of events affects your responses to the action.

EDGAR RICE BURROUGHS (1875–1950)

A great many stories share a standard plot pattern. The following excerpt from Edgar Rice Burroughs's novel *Tarzan of the Apes* provides a conventional plot pattern in which the ***character,*** an imagined person in the story, is confronted with a problem leading to a climactic struggle that is followed by a resolution of the problem. The elements of a conventional plot are easily recognizable to readers familiar with fast-paced, action-packed mysteries, spy thrillers, westerns, or adventure stories. These page-turners are carefully plotted so that the reader is swept up by the action. More serious writers sometimes use similar strategies, but they do so with greater subtlety and for some purpose that goes beyond providing a thrill a minute. The writer of serious fiction is usually less concerned with what happens next to the central character than with why it

Special Collection, Rare Books, Burroughs Memorial Collection, University of Louisville.

happens. In Burroughs's adventure story, however, the emphasis is clearly on action. *Tarzan of the Apes* may add little or nothing to our understanding of life, but it is useful for delineating some important elements of plot. Moreover, it is great fun.

Special Collection, Rare Books, Burroughs Memorial Collection, University of Louisville.

Tarzan first appeared in the October 1912 issue of *The All-Story* magazine, a pulp serial that sold for 15 cents a copy. Instead of publishing the lengthy novel in serial segments, *All-Story* published *Tarzan of the Apes: A Romance of the Jungle* in a single issue that featured a provocative cover and exotic illustrations. The enormous popularity of the *Tarzan* issue led to the publication of the 1914 novel that spawned two dozen books, more than forty movies, hundreds of comic books and radio and television programs, and countless products, from toys to running shoes. Edgar Rice Burroughs became one of the most popular authors of the twentieth century, and Tarzan remains one of the world's best-known characters.

Burroughs's novel, published in 1914 and the first of a series of enormously popular Tarzan books and films, charts the growth to manhood of a child raised in the African jungle by great apes. Tarzan struggles to survive his primitive beginnings and to reconcile what he has learned in the jungle with his equally powerful instincts to be a civilized human being. One of the more exciting moments in Tarzan's development is his final confrontation with his old enemy, Terkoz, a huge tyrannical ape that has kidnapped Jane, a pretty nineteen-year-old from Baltimore, Maryland, who has accompanied her father on an expedition to the jungle.

In the chapter preceding this excerpt, Tarzan falls in love with Jane and writes this pointed, if not eloquent, note to her: "I am Tarzan of the Apes. I want you. I am yours. You are mine." Just as he finishes the note, he hears "the agonized screams of a woman" and rushes to their source to find Esmeralda, Jane's maid, hysterical with fear and grief. She reports that Jane, the fair and gentle embodiment of civilization in the story, has been carried off by a gorilla. Here is the first half of the next chapter, which illustrates how Burroughs plots the sequence of events so that the emphasis is on physical action.

From Tarzan of the Apes   *1914*

From the time Tarzan left the tribe of great anthropoids in which he had been raised, it was torn by continual strife and discord. Terkoz proved a cruel and capricious king, so that, one by one, many of the older and weaker apes, upon whom he was particularly prone to vent his brutish nature, took their families and sought the quiet and safety of the far interior.

But at last those who remained were driven to desperation by the continued truculence of Terkoz, and it so happened that one of them recalled the parting admonition of Tarzan:

"If you have a chief who is cruel, do not do as the other apes do, and attempt, any one of you, to pit yourself against him alone. But, instead, let two or three or four of you attack him together. Then, if you will do this, no chief will dare to be other than he should be, for four of you can kill any chief who may ever be over you."

And the ape who recalled this wise counsel repeated it to several of his fellows, so that when Terkoz returned to the tribe that day he found a warm reception awaiting him.

There were no formalities. As Terkoz reached the group, five huge, hairy   5
beasts sprang upon him.

At heart he was an arrant coward, which is the way with bullies among apes as well as among men; so he did not remain to fight and die, but tore himself away from them as quickly as he could and fled into the sheltering boughs of the forest.

Two more attempts he made to rejoin the tribe, but on each occasion he was set upon and driven away. At last he gave it up, and turned, foaming with rage and hatred, into the jungle.

For several days he wandered aimlessly, nursing his spite and looking for some weak thing on which to vent his pent anger.

It was in this state of mind that the horrible, manlike beast, swinging from tree to tree, came suddenly upon two women in the jungle.

He was right above them when he discovered them. The first intimation Jane Porter had of his presence was when the great hairy body dropped to the earth beside her, and she saw the awful face and the snarling, hideous mouth thrust within a foot of her.

One piercing scream escaped her lips as the brute hand clutched her arm. Then she was dragged toward those awful fangs which yawned at her throat. But ere they touched that fair skin another mood claimed the anthropoid.

The tribe had kept his women. He must find others to replace them. This hairless white ape would be the first of his new household, and so he threw her roughly across his broad, hairy shoulders and leaped back into the trees, bearing Jane away.

Esmeralda's scream of terror had mingled once with that of Jane, and then, as was Esmeralda's manner under stress of emergency which required presence of mind, she swooned.

But Jane did not once lose consciousness. It is true that that awful face, pressing close to hers, and the stench of the foul breath beating upon her nostrils, paralyzed her with terror; but her brain was clear, and she comprehended all that transpired.

With what seemed to her marvelous rapidity the brute bore her through the forest, but still she did not cry out or struggle. The sudden advent of the ape had confused her to such an extent that she thought now that he was bearing her toward the beach.

For this reason she conserved her energies and her voice until she could see that they had approached near enough to the camp to attract the succor she craved.

She could not have known it, but she was being borne farther and farther into the impenetrable jungle.

The scream that had brought Clayton and the two older men stumbling through the undergrowth had led Tarzan of the Apes straight to where Esmeralda lay, but it was not Esmeralda in whom his interest centered, though pausing over her he saw that she was unhurt.

For a moment he scrutinized the ground below and the trees above, until the ape that was in him by virtue of training and environment, combined with the intelligence that was his by right of birth, told his wondrous woodcraft the whole story as plainly as though he had seen the thing happen with his own eyes.

And then he was gone again into the swaying trees, following the high-flung spoor which no other human eye could have detected, much less translated.

At boughs' ends, where the anthropoid swings from one tree to another, there is most to mark the trail, but least to point the direction of the quarry; for there the pressure is downward always, toward the small end of the branch, whether the ape be leaving or entering a tree. Nearer the center of the tree, where the signs of passage are fainter, the direction is plainly marked.

Here, on this branch, a caterpillar has been crushed by the fugitive's great foot, and Tarzan knows instinctively where that same foot would touch in the next stride. Here he looks to find a tiny particle of the demolished larva, oft-times not more than a speck of moisture.

Again, a minute bit of bark has been upturned by the scraping hand, and the direction of the break indicates the direction of the passage. Or some great limb, or the stem of the tree itself has been brushed by the hairy body, and a tiny shred of hair tells him by the direction from which it is wedged beneath the bark that he is on the right trail.

Nor does he need to check his speed to catch these seemingly faint records of the fleeing beast.

To Tarzan they stand out boldly against all the myriad other scars and 25 bruises and signs upon the leafy way. But strongest of all is the scent, for Tarzan is pursuing up the wind, and his trained nostrils are as sensitive as a hound's.

There are those who believe that the lower orders are specially endowed by nature with better olfactory nerves than man, but it is merely a matter of development.

Man's survival does not hinge so greatly upon the perfection of his senses. His power to reason has relieved them of many of their duties, and so they have, to some extent, atrophied, as have the muscles which move the ears and scalp, merely from disuse.

The muscles are there, about the ears and beneath the scalp, and so are the nerves which transmit sensations to the brain, but they are underdeveloped because they are not needed.

Not so with Tarzan of the Apes. From early infancy his survival had depended upon acuteness of eyesight, hearing, smell, touch, and taste far more than upon the more slowly developed organ of reason.

The least developed of all in Tarzan was the sense of taste, for he could eat 30 luscious fruits, or raw flesh, long buried, with almost equal appreciation; but in that he differed but slightly from more civilized epicures.

Almost silently the ape-man sped on in the track of Terkoz and his prey, but the sound of his approach reached the ears of the fleeing beast and spurred it on to greater speed.

Three miles were covered before Tarzan overtook them, and then Terkoz, seeing that further flight was futile, dropped to the ground in a small open glade, that he might turn and fight for his prize or be free to escape unhampered if he saw that the pursuer was more than a match for him.

He still grasped Jane in one great arm as Tarzan bounded like a leopard into the arena which nature had provided for this primeval-like battle.

When Terkoz saw that it was Tarzan who pursued him, he jumped to the conclusion that this was Tarzan's woman, since they were of the same kind — white and hairless — and so he rejoiced at this opportunity for double revenge upon his hated enemy.

To Jane the strange apparition of this godlike man was as wine to sick 35 nerves.

From the description which Clayton and her father and Mr. Philander had given her, she knew that it must be the same wonderful creature who had saved them, and she saw in him only a protector and a friend.

But as Terkoz pushed her roughly aside to meet Tarzan's charge, and she saw the great proportions of the ape and the mighty muscles and the fierce fangs, her heart quailed. How could any vanquish such a mighty antagonist?

Like two charging bulls they came together, and like two wolves sought each other's throat. Against the long canines of the ape was pitted the thin blade of the man's knife.

Jane — her lithe, young form flattened against the trunk of a great tree, her hands tight pressed against her rising and falling bosom, and her eyes wide with mingled horror, fascination, fear, and admiration — watched the primordial ape battle with the primeval man for possession of a woman — for her.

As the great muscles of the man's back and shoulders knotted beneath the 40 tension of his efforts, and the huge biceps and forearm held at bay those mighty tusks, the veil of centuries of civilization and culture were swept from the blurred vision of the Baltimore girl.

When the long knife drank deep a dozen times of Terkoz's heart's blood, and the great carcass rolled lifeless upon the ground, it was a primeval woman who sprang forward with outstretched arms toward the primeval man who had fought for her and won.

And Tarzan?

He did what no red-blooded man needs lessons in doing. He took his woman in his arms and smothered her upturned, panting lips with kisses.

For a moment Jane lay there with half-closed eyes. For a moment — the first in her young life — she knew the meaning of love.

But as suddenly as the veil had been withdrawn it dropped again, and an 45 outraged conscience suffused her face with its scarlet mantle, and a mortified woman thrust Tarzan of the Apes from her and buried her face in her hands.

Tarzan had been surprised when he had found the girl he had learned to love after a vague and abstract manner a willing prisoner in his arms. Now he was surprised that she repulsed him.

He came close to her once more and took hold of her arm. She turned upon him like a tigress, striking his great breast with her tiny hands.

Tarzan could not understand it.

A moment ago, and it had been his intention to hasten Jane back to her people, but that little moment was lost now in the dim and distant past of things which were but can never be again, and with it the good intention had gone to join the impossible.

Since then Tarzan of the Apes had felt a warm, lithe form close pressed to 50 his. Hot, sweet breath against his cheek and mouth had fanned a new flame to life within his breast, and perfect lips had clung to his in burning kisses that had seared a deep brand into his soul — a brand which marked a new Tarzan.

Again he laid his hand upon her arm. Again she repulsed him. And then Tarzan of the Apes did just what his first ancestor would have done.

He took his woman in his arms and carried her into the jungle.

This episode begins with ***exposition,*** the background information the reader needs to make sense of the situation in which the characters are placed. The first eight paragraphs let us know that Terkoz has been overthrown as leader of the ape tribe and that he is roaming the jungle "looking for some weak thing on which to vent his pent anger." This exposition is in the form of a flashback. (Recall that the previous chapter ended with Esmeralda's report of the kidnapping; now we will see what happened.)

Once this information supplies a context for the characters, the plot gains momentum with the ***rising action,*** a complication that intensifies the situation: Terkoz, looking for a victim, discovers the vulnerable Esmeralda and Jane. His first impulse is to kill Jane, but his "mood" changes when he remembers that he has no woman of his own after having been forced to leave the tribe (more exposition). Hence, there is a further complication in the rising action when he decides to carry her off. Just when it seems that the situation could not get any worse, it does. The reader is invited to shudder even more than if Terkoz had made a meal of Jane because she may have to endure the "awful face," "foul breath," and lust of this beast.

At this point we are brought up to the action that ended the preceding chapter. Tarzan races to the rescue by unerringly following the trail from the place where Jane was kidnapped. He relentlessly tracks Terkoz. Unfortunately, Burroughs slows down the pursuit here by including several paragraphs that abstractly consider the evolutionary development of human reliance on reason more than on their senses for survival. This discussion offers a rationale for Tarzan's remarkable ability to track Jane, but it is an interruption in the chase.

When Tarzan finally catches up to Terkoz, the *conflict* of this episode fully emerges. Tarzan must save the woman he loves by defeating his long-standing enemy. For Terkoz seeks to achieve a "double revenge" by killing Tarzan and taking his woman. Terkoz's assumption that Jane is Tarzan's woman is a *foreshadowing*, a suggestion of what is yet to come. In this conflict Tarzan is the *protagonist* or *hero*, the central character who engages our interest and empathy. *Protagonist* is often a more useful term than *hero* or *heroine*, however, because the central character of a story can be despicable as well as heroic. In Edgar Allan Poe's "The Tell-Tale Heart," for example, the central character is a madman and murderer. Terkoz is the *antagonist*, the force that opposes the protagonist.

The battle between Tarzan and Terkoz creates *suspense* because the reader is made anxious about what is going to happen. Burroughs makes certain that the reader will worry about the outcome by having Jane wonder, "How could any vanquish such a mighty antagonist?" If we are caught up in the moment, we watch the battle, as Jane does, with "mingled horror, fascination, fear, and admiration" to see what will happen next. The moment of greatest emotional tension, the *climax*, occurs when Tarzan kills Terkoz. Tarzan's victory is the *resolution* of the conflict, also known as the *dénouement* (a French word meaning the "untying of the knot"). This could have been the conclusion to the episode except that Jane and Tarzan simultaneously discover their "primeval" selves sexually drawn to each other. Burroughs resolves one conflict—the battle with Terkoz—but then immediately creates another—by raising the question of what a respectable professor's daughter from Baltimore is doing in the sweaty arms of a panting, half-naked man.

For a brief moment the cycle of conflict, suspense, and resolution begins again as Jane passionately kisses Tarzan; then her "outraged conscience" causes her to regain her sense of propriety and she pushes him away. Although Tarzan succeeds in the encounter with Terkoz, he is not successful with Jane. However, Burroughs creates suspense for a third time at the very end of the episode, when the "new Tarzan," having been transformed by this sexual awakening, "took his woman in his arms and carried her into the jungle." What will he do next? Despite the novel's implausibility (beginning with the premise that apes could raise a human child) and its heavy use of coincidences (not the least of which is Tarzan's donning a loincloth for the first time only four pages before he meets Jane), the story is difficult to put down. The plot swings us swiftly and smoothly from incident to incident, even if there is an occasional interruption, such as Burroughs's discussion of evolution, in the flow of the action.

Although this pattern of exposition, rising action, conflict, suspense, climax, and resolution provides a useful outline of many plots that emphasize physical action, a greater value of this pattern is that it helps us to see how innovative artists move beyond formula fiction by manipulating and changing the pattern for their own purposes. At the furthest extreme are those modern storytellers who reject traditional plotting techniques in favor of experimental approaches. Instead of including characters who wrestle with conflicts, experimental fiction frequently may concern the writer's own efforts to create a story. Rather than ordering experience, such writers disrupt it by insisting that meanings in fiction are as elusive — or nonexistent — as meanings in life; they are likely to reject both traditional values and traditional forms of writing. Most writers, however, use conflicts in their plots to reveal characters and convey meanings. The nature of those conflicts can help determine how important physical action is to the plot.

The primary conflict that Tarzan experiences in his battle with Terkoz is external. External conflict is popular in adventure stories because the protagonist's physical struggles with a formidable foe or the ever-present dangers of a dense jungle echoing wild screams provide plenty of excitement. External conflicts may place the protagonist in opposition to another individual, nature, or society. Tarzan's battle with societal values begins the moment he instinctively takes Jane in his arms to carry her off into the jungle. He will learn that an individual's conflict with society can be as frustrating as it is complex, which is why so many plots in serious fiction focus on this conflict. It can be seen, to cite only two examples, in a mysterious stranger's alienation from a materialistic culture in Herman Melville's "Bartleby, the Scrivener" (p. 142) and in a young black man's struggle with racism in Ellison's "Battle Royal" (p. 277).

Conflict may also be internal; in such a case some moral or psychological issue must be resolved within the protagonist. Inner conflicts frequently accompany external ones, as in Godwin's "A Sorrowful Woman" (p. 39). Godwin's story is quiet and almost uneventful compared with *Tarzan of the Apes*. The conflict, though puzzling, is more significant in "A Sorrowful Woman" because that story subtly explores some troubling issues that cannot be resolved simply by "huge biceps" or a "lithe, young form." The protagonist struggles with both internal and external forces. We are not told why she withdraws from her considerate husband and beautiful son. There is no exposition to explain why she is hopelessly "sad and sick" of them. There is no readily identifiable antagonist in her way, but there are several possibilities. Her antagonist is some part of herself that cannot find satisfaction in playing the roles of wife and mother, yet her husband and child also seem to bear some of the responsibility, as does the domestic environment that defines her.

Godwin creates questions for the reader rather than suspense. We are compelled to keep asking why the protagonist in her story is so unhappy instead of what is going to happen next. The story ends with her flurry of domestic activity and her death, but we do not feel as if we have come to a resolution. "A Sorrowful Woman" will not let us go because we keep coming back to what causes the protagonist's rejection of her role. Has she gone mad? Are the husband and child not what they seem to be? Is her domestic life stifling rather than nourishing? Does her family destroy rather than support her? Who or what is to blame? No one is able to rescue the sorrowful woman from her conflict, nor does the design of Godwin's plot relieve the reader of the questions the story raises. The meaning of the action is not self-evident as it is in *Tarzan of the Apes*. It must be drawn from a careful reading of the interrelated details and dialogues that constitute this story's action.

Although Burroughs makes enormous demands on Tarzan to survive the perils of the jungle, the author makes few demands on the reader. In part, that's why *Tarzan of the Apes* is so much fun: we sit back while Tarzan does all the work, struggling heroically through all the conflicts Burroughs has planted along his jungle paths. Godwin's story, in contrast, illustrates that there are other kinds of plots, less dependent on action but equally full of conflict. This kind of reading is more demanding, but ultimately more satisfying, because as we confront conflicts in serious fiction we read not only absorbing stories but also ourselves. We are invited not to escape life but to look long and hard at it. Although serious fiction can be as diverting and pleasurable as most standard action-packed plots, serious fiction offers an additional important element: a perspective on experience that reflects rather than deflects life.

The following four stories — Alice Walker's "The Flowers," Joyce Carol Oates's "Three Girls," William Faulkner's "A Rose for Emily," and Andre Dubus's "Killings" — are remarkable for the different kinds of tension produced in each by a subtle use of plot.

ALICE WALKER (B. 1944)

Novelist, poet, and political activist, Alice Walker was born in 1944 to Minnie Tallulah Grant Walker and Willie Lee Walker, sharecroppers in Eatonton, Georgia. A promising student from the beginning, Walker started her collegiate career at Spelman College in Atlanta, but graduated from Sarah Lawrence College in New York in 1965. After teaching history in Mississippi, she won a fellowship from the Radcliffe Institute and went on to teach at Wellesley College, where

Courtesy of Jean Weisinger.

she pioneered one of the first women's studies courses in the country. Walker has published several volumes of poetry, including *Once* (1968), *Revolutionary Petunias and Other Poems* (1973), *Horses Make a Landscape Look More Beautiful* (1984), *Collected Poems* (2005), and a book of essays, *Living by the Word* (1988). Her numerous works of fiction include *In Love and Trouble: Stories of Black Women* (1973), *The Temple of My Familiar* (1989), *The Complete Stories* (1994), *By the Light of My Father's Smile* (1998), *Possessing the Secret of Joy* (1998), *Now Is the Time to Open Your Heart* (2004), and *The Color Purple* (1982), which was made into a major motion picture. The acclaim for her novel *Meridian* (1982) won her a Guggenheim Fellowship and led her to San Francisco, where she still lives. Walker's writing career has been defined largely by political interests that have not waned since the sixties, and she has contributed substantially to the antinuclear and environmental movements, women's rights, and the movement for the protection of indigenous peoples.

The Flowers   1973

It seemed to Myop as she skipped lightly from hen house to pigpen to smoke-house that the days had never been as beautiful as these. The air held a keen-ness that made her nose twitch. The harvesting of the corn and cotton, peanuts and squash, made each day a golden surprise that caused excited little tremors to run up her jaws.

Myop carried a short, knobby stick. She struck out at random at chickens she liked, and worked out the beat of a song on the fence around the pigpen. She felt light and good in the warm sun. She was ten, and nothing existed for her but her song, the stick clutched in her dark brown hand, and the tat-de-ta-ta-ta of accompaniment.

Turning her back on the rusty boards of her family's sharecropper cabin, Myop walked along the fence till it ran into the stream made by the spring. Around the spring, where the family got drinking water, silver ferns and wild-flowers grew. Along the shallow banks pigs rooted. Myop watched the tiny white bubbles disrupt the thin black scale of soil and the water that silently rose and slid away down the stream.

She had explored the woods behind the house many times. Often, in late autumn, her mother took her to gather nuts among the fallen leaves. Today she made her own path, bouncing this way and that way, vaguely keeping an eye out for snakes. She found, in addition to various common but pretty ferns and leaves, an armful of strange blue flowers with velvety ridges and a sweet-suds bush full of the brown, fragrant buds.

By twelve o'clock, her arms laden with sprigs of her findings, she was a mile 5 or more from home. She had often been as far before, but the strangeness of the land made it not as pleasant as her usual haunts. It seemed gloomy in the little cove in which she found herself. The air was damp, the silence close and deep.

Myop began to circle back to the house, back to the peacefulness of the morning. It was then she stepped smack into his eyes. Her heel became lodged in the broken ridge between brow and nose, and she reached down quickly, unafraid, to free herself. It was only when she saw his naked grin that she gave a little yelp of surprise.

He had been a tall man. From feet to neck covered a long space. His head lay beside him. When she pushed back the leaves and layers of earth and debris Myop saw that he'd had large white teeth, all of them cracked or broken, long fingers, and very big bones. All his clothes had rotted away except some threads of blue denim from his overalls. The buckles of the overalls had turned green.

Myop gazed around the spot with interest. Very near where she'd stepped into the head was a wild pink rose. As she picked it to add to her bundle she noticed a raised mound, a ring, around the rose's root. It was the rotted remains of a noose, a bit of shredding plowline, now blending benignly into the soil. Around an overhanging limb of a great spreading oak clung another piece. Frayed, rotted, bleached, and frazzled—barely there—but spinning restlessly in the breeze. Myop laid down her flowers.

And the summer was over.

CONSIDERATIONS FOR CRITICAL THINKING AND WRITING

1. **FIRST RESPONSE.** How do you interpret the final line of the story? What is the effect of the brevity of that sentence?

2. Describe the atmosphere and tone of the first three paragraphs. What emotions do they produce concerning Myop's childhood?

3. How might paragraph 5 be described as an example of foreshadowing?

4. What is the conflict in the story? What is its climax? Is there a resolution to the conflict? Explain.

5. What do you think is the central point of this story?

CONNECTIONS TO OTHER SELECTIONS

1. Discuss the significance of Myop's experience and that of the narrator in Ralph Ellison's "Battle Royal" (p. 277).

2. Write an essay comparing the ending of Walker's story with that of William Faulkner's "A Rose for Emily" (p. 91). What is the effect of the ending on your reading of each story?

JOYCE CAROL OATES (B. 1938)

Raised in upstate New York, Joyce Carol Oates earned degrees at Syracuse University and the University of Wisconsin. Both the range and volume of her writing are extensive. A writer of novels, plays, short stories, poetry, and literary criticism, she has published over eighty books. Oates has described the subject matter of her fiction as "real people in a real society," but her method of expression ranges from the realistic to the

Reprinted by permission of Beth Gwinn.

experimental. Her novels include *them* (1969), *Do with Me What You Will* (1973), *Childwold* (1976), *Bellefleur* (1980), *A Bloodsmoor Romance* (1982), *Marya: A Life* (1986), *You Must Remember This* (1987), *Black Water* (1992), *I'll Take You There* (2003), and *Missing Mom* (2005). Among her collections of short stories are *Marriages and Infidelities* (1972), *Raven's Wing* (1986), *The Assignation* (1988), *Heat* (1991), *Haunted: Tales of the Grotesque* (1994), *Will You Always Love Me? and Other Stories* (1996), *The Collector of Hearts* (1998), *Small Avalanches and Other Stories* (2004), *High Lonesome: New and Selected Stories 1966–2006* (2006), and *Dear Husband* (2009). This story creates some fascinating tension in a famous Manhattan bookstore.

Three Girls

2002

In Strand Used Books on Broadway and Twelfth one snowy March early evening in 1956 when the streetlights on Broadway glimmered with a strange sepia glow, we were two NYU girl-poets drifting through the warehouse of treasures as through an enchanted forest. Just past 6:00 P.M. Above light-riddled Manhattan, opaque night. Snowing, and sidewalks encrusted with ice so there were fewer customers in the Strand than usual at this hour but *there we were*. Among other cranky brooding regulars. In our army-surplus jackets, baggy khaki pants, and zip-up rubber boots. In our matching wool caps (knitted by your restless fingers) pulled down low over our pale-girl foreheads. Enchanted by books. Enchanted by the Strand.

No bookstore of merely "new" books with elegant show window displays drew us like the drafty Strand, bins of books untidy and thumbed through as merchants' sidewalk bins on Fourteenth Street, NEW THIS WEEK, BEST BARGAINS, WORLD CLASSICS, ART BOOKS 50% OFF, REVIEWERS' COPIES, HIGHEST PRICE $1.98, REMAINDERS 25¢–$1.00. Hardcover/paperback. Spotless/battered. Beautiful books/cheaply printed pulp paper. And at the rear and sides in that vast echoing space massive shelves of books books books rising to a ceiling of hammered tin fifteen feet above! Stacked shelves so high they required ladders to negotiate and a monkey nimbleness (like yours) to climb.

We were enchanted with the Strand and with each other in the Strand. Overseen by surly young clerks who were poets like us, or playwrights/actors/artists. In an agony of unspoken young love I watched you. As always on these romantic evenings at the Strand, prowling the aisles sneering at those luckless books, so many of them, unworthy of your attention. Bestsellers, how-tos, arts and crafts, too-simple *histories of*. Women's romances, sentimental love poems. Patriotic books, middlebrow books, books lacking esoteric covers. We were girl-poets passionately enamored of T. S. Eliot but scornful of Robert Frost, whom we'd been made to memorize in high school — slyly we communicated in code phrases from Eliot in the presence of obtuse others in our dining hall and residence. We were admiring of though confused by the poetry of Yeats, we were yet more confused by the lauded worth of Pound, enthusiastically drawn to the bold metaphors of Kafka (that cockroach!) and Dostoevski (sexy murderer Raskolnikov and the Underground Man were our rebel heroes) and

Sartre ("Hell is other people" — we knew this), and had reason to believe that we were their lineage though admittedly we were American middle class, and Caucasian, and female. (Yet we were not "conventional" females. In fact, we shared male contempt for the merely "conventional" female.)

Brooding above a tumble of books that quickened the pulse, almost shyly touching Freud's *Civilization and Its Discontents,* Crane Brinton's *The Age of Reason,* Margaret Mead's *Coming of Age in Samoa,* D. H. Lawrence's *The Rainbow,* Kierkegaard's *Fear and Trembling,* Mann's *Death in Venice* — there suddenly you glided up behind me to touch my wrist (as never you'd done before, had you?) and whispered, "Come here," in a way that thrilled me for its meaning *I have something wonderful/unexpected/startling to show you*. Like poems these discoveries in the Strand were, to us, found poems to be cherished. And eagerly I turned to follow you though disguising my eagerness, "Yes, what?" as if you'd interrupted me, for possibly we'd had a quarrel earlier that day, a flaring up of tense girl-tempers. Yes, you were childish and self-absorbed and given to sulky silences and mercurial moods in the presence of showy superficial people, and I adored and feared you knowing you'd break my heart, my heart that had never before been broken because never before so exposed.

So eagerly yet with my customary guardedness I followed you through 5 a maze of book bins and shelves and stacks to the ceiling ANTHROPOLOGY, ART/ANCIENT, ART/RENAISSANCE, ART/MODERN, ART/ASIAN, ART/WESTERN, TRAVEL, PHILOSOPHY, COOKERY, POETRY/MODERN where the way was treacherously lighted only by bare sixty-watt bulbs, and where customers as cranky as we two stood in the aisles reading books, or sat hunched on footstools glancing up annoyed at our passage, and unquestioning I followed you until at POETRY/MODERN you halted, and pushed me ahead and around a corner, and I stood puzzled staring, not knowing what I was supposed to be seeing until impatiently you poked me in the ribs and pointed, and now I perceived an individual in the aisle pulling down books from shelves, peering at them, clearly absorbed by what she read, a woman nearly my height (I was tall for a girl, in 1956) in a man's navy coat to her ankles and with sleeves past her wrists, a man's beige fedora hat on her head, scrunched low as we wore our knitted caps, and most of her hair hidden by the hat except for a six-inch blond plait at the nape of her neck; and she wore black trousers tucked into what appeared to be salt-stained cowboy boots. Someone we knew? An older, goodlooking student from one of our classes? *A girl-poet like ourselves?* I was about to nudge you in the ribs in bafflement when the blond woman turned, taking down another book from the shelf (e. e. cummings' *Tulips and Chimneys* — always I would remember that title!), and I saw that she was Marilyn Monroe.

Marilyn Monroe. In the Strand. Just like us. And she seemed to be alone. *Marilyn Monroe, alone!*

Wholly absorbed in browsing amid books, oblivious of her surroundings and of us. No one seemed to have recognized her (yet) except you.

Here was the surprise: this woman was/was not Marilyn Monroe. For this woman was an individual wholly absorbed in selecting, leafing through, pausing to read books. You could see that this individual was a *reader*. One of those who *reads*. With concentration, with passion. With her very soul. And it was poetry she was reading, her lips pursed, silently shaping words. Absent-mindedly she wiped her nose on the edge of her hand, so intent was she on what she was reading. For when you truly read poetry, poetry reads *you*.

Still, this woman was—Marilyn Monroe. And despite our common sense, 10
our scorn for the silly clichés of Hollywood romance, still we halfway expected
a Leading Man to join her: Clark Gable, Robert Taylor, Marlon Brando.

Halfway we expected the syrupy surge of movie music, to glide us into the
scene.

But no man joined Marilyn Monroe in her disguise as one of us in the
Strand. No Leading Man, no dark prince.

Like us (we began to see) this Marilyn Monroe required no man.

For what seemed like a long time but was probably no more than half an
hour, Marilyn Monroe browsed in the POETRY/MODERN shelves, as from a distance of approximately ten feet two girl-poets watched covertly, clutching each
other's hands. We were stunned to see that this woman looked very little like
the glamorous "Marilyn Monroe." That figure was a garish blond showgirl, a
Hollywood "sexpot" of no interest to intellectuals (*we* thought, we who knew
nothing of the secret romance between Marilyn Monroe and Arthur Miller);
this figure more resembled us (almost) than she resembled her Hollywood
image. We were dying of curiosity to see whose poetry books Marilyn Monroe
was examining: Elizabeth Bishop, H. D., Robert Lowell, Muriel Rukeyser,
Harry Crosby, Denise Levertov. . . . Five or six of these Marilyn Monroe decided to purchase, then moved on, leather bag slung over her shoulder and
fedora tilted down on her head.

We couldn't resist, we had to follow! Cautious not to whisper together like 15
excited schoolgirls, still less to giggle wildly as we were tempted; you nudged me
in the ribs to sober me, gave me a glare signaling *Don't be rude, don't ruin this for
all of us.* I conceded: I was the more pushy of the two of us, a tall gawky Rima the
Bird Girl with springy carroty-red hair like an exotic bird's crest, while you were
petite and dark haired and attractive with long-lashed Semitic sloe eyes, you the
wily gymnast and I the aggressive basketball player, you the "experimental" poet
and I drawn to "forms," our contrary talents bred in our bones. Which of us
would marry, have babies, disappear into "real" life, and which of us would persevere into her thirties before starting to be published and becoming, in time, a
"real" poet—could anyone have predicted, this snowy March evening in 1956?

Marilyn Monroe drifted through the maze of books and we followed in
her wake as through a maze of dreams, past SPORTS, past MILITARY, past WAR,
past HISTORY/ANCIENT, past the familiar figures of Strand regulars frowning
into books, past surly yawning bearded clerks who took no more heed of the
blond actress than they ever did of us, and so to NATURAL HISTORY where she
paused, and there again for unhurried minutes (the Strand was open until
9:00 P.M.) Marilyn Monroe in her mannish disguise browsed and brooded,
pulling down books, seeking what? at last crouched leafing through an oversized illustrated book (curiosity overcame me! I shoved away your restraining
hand; politely I eased past Marilyn Monroe murmuring "excuse me" without
so much as brushing against her and without being noticed), Charles Darwin's
Origin of Species in a deluxe edition. Darwin! *Origin of Species!* We were poet-
despisers-of-science, or believed we were, or must be, to be true poets in the exalted mode of T. S. Eliot and William Butler Yeats; such a choice, for Marilyn
Monroe, seemed perverse to us. But this book was one Marilyn quickly decided
to purchase, hoisting it into her arms and moving on.

That rakish fedora we'd come to covet, and that single chunky blond
braid. (Afterward we would wonder: Marilyn Monroe's hair in a braid? Never

had we seen Marilyn Monroe with her hair braided in any movie or photo. What did this mean? Did it mean anything? *Had she quit films, and embarked on a new, anonymous life in our midst?*)

Suddenly Marilyn Monroe glanced back at us, frowning as a child might frown (had we spoken aloud? had she heard our thoughts?), and there came into her face a look of puzzlement, not alarm or annoyance but a childlike puzzlement: *Who are you? You two? Are you watching me?* Quickly we looked away. We were engaged in a whispering dispute over a book one of us had fumbled from a shelf, *A History of Botanical Gardens in England*. So we were undetected. We hoped!

But wary now, and sobered. For what if Marilyn Monroe had caught us, and knew that we knew?

She might have abandoned her books and fled the Strand. What a loss for   20 her, and for the books! For us, too.

Oh, we worried at Marilyn Monroe's recklessness! We dreaded her being recognized by a (male) customer or (male) clerk. A girl or woman would have kept her secret (so we thought) but no man could resist staring openly at her, following her, and at last speaking to her. Of course, the blond actress in Strand Used Books wasn't herself, not at all glamorous, or "sexy," or especially blond, in her inconspicuous man's clothing and those salt-stained boots; she might have been anyone, female or male, hardly a Hollywood celebrity, a movie goddess. Yet if you stared, you'd recognize her. If you tried, with any imagination you'd see "Marilyn Monroe." It was like a child's game in which you stare at foliage, grass, clouds in the sky, and suddenly you see a face or a figure, and after that recognition you can't not see the hidden shape, it's staring you in the face. So too with Marilyn Monroe. Once we saw her, it seemed to us she must be seen — and recognized — by anyone who happened to glance at her. If any man saw! We were fearful her privacy would be destroyed. Quickly the blond actress would become surrounded, mobbed. It was risky and reckless of her to have come to Strand Used Books by herself, we thought. Sure, she could shop at Tiffany's, maybe; she could stroll through the lobby of the Plaza, or the Waldorf-Astoria; she'd be safe from fans and unwanted admirers in privileged settings on the Upper East Side, but — here? In the egalitarian Strand, on Broadway and Twelfth?

We were perplexed. Almost, I was annoyed with her. Taking such chances! But you, gripping my wrist, had another, more subtle thought.

"She thinks she's like *us*."

You meant: a human being, anonymous. Female, like us. Amid the ordinary unspectacular customers (predominantly male) of the Strand.

And that was the sadness in it, Marilyn Monroe's wish. To be *like us*. For it   25 was impossible, of course. For anyone could have told Marilyn Monroe, even two young girl-poets, that it was too late for her in history. Already, at age thirty (we could calculate afterward that this was her age) "Marilyn Monroe" had entered history, and there was no escape from it. Her films, her photos. Her face, her figure, her name. To enter history is to be abducted spiritually, with no way back. As if lightning were to strike the building that housed the Strand, as if an actual current of electricity were to touch and transform only one individual in the great cavernous space and that lone individual, by pure chance it might seem, the caprice of fate, would be the young woman with the blond braid and the fedora slanted across her face. Why? Why her, and not another? You could argue that such a destiny is absurd, and undeserved, for one individual among many, and logically you would be correct. And yet: "Marilyn Monroe" has entered history, and you have not. She will endure, though the young woman with the blond braid will die. *And even should she wish to die, "Marilyn Monroe" cannot.*

By this time she—the young woman with the blond braid—was carrying an armload of books. We were hoping she'd almost finished and would be leaving soon, before strangers' rude eyes lighted upon her and exposed her, but no: she surprised us by heading for a section called JUDAICA. In that forbidding aisle, which we'd never before entered, there were books in numerous languages: Hebrew, Yiddish, German, Russian, French. Some of these books looked ancient! Complete sets of the Talmud. Cryptically printed tomes on the cabala. Luckily for us, the titles Marilyn Monroe pulled out were all in English: *Jews of Eastern Europe; The Chosen People: A Complete History of the Jews; Jews of the New World.* Quickly Marilyn Monroe placed her bag and books on the floor, sat on a footstool, and leafed through pages with the frowning intensity of a young girl, as if searching for something urgent, something she knew—knew!—must be there; in this uncomfortable posture she remained for at least fifteen minutes, wetting her fingers to turn pages that stuck together, pages that had not been turned, still less read, for decades. She was frowning, yet smiling too; faint vertical lines appeared between her eyebrows, in the intensity of her concentration; her eyes moved rapidly along lines of print, then returned, and moved more slowly. By this time we were close enough to observe the blond actress's feverish cheeks and slightly parted moist lips that seemed to move silently. *What is she reading in that ancient book, what can possibly mean so much to her? A secret, revealed? A secret, to save her life?*

"Hey you!" a clerk called out in a nasal, insinuating voice.

The three of us looked up, startled.

But the clerk wasn't speaking to us. Not to the blond actress frowning over *The Chosen People,* and not to us who were hovering close by. The clerk had caught someone slipping a book into an overcoat pocket, not an unusual sight at the Strand.

After this mild upset, Marilyn Monroe became uneasy. She turned to look   30 frankly at us, and though we tried clumsily to retreat, her eyes met ours. *She knows!* But after a moment, she simply turned back to her book, stubborn and determined to finish what she was reading, while we continued to hover close by, exposed now, and blushing, yet feeling protective of her. *She has seen us, she knows. She trusts us.* We saw that Marilyn Monroe was beautiful in her anonymity as she had never seemed, to us, to be beautiful as "Marilyn Monroe." All that was makeup, fakery, cartoon sexiness subtle as a kick in the groin. All that was vulgar and infantile. But this young woman was beautiful without makeup, without even lipstick; in her mannish clothes, her hair in a stubby braid. Beautiful: her skin luminous and pale and her eyes a startling clear blue. Almost shyly she glanced back at us, to note that we were still there, and she smiled. *Yes, I see you two. Thank you for not speaking my name.*

Always you and I would remember: that smile of gratitude, and sweetness.

Always you and I would remember: that she trusted us, as perhaps we would not have trusted ourselves.

So many years later, I'm proud of us. We were so young.

Young, headstrong, arrogant, insecure though "brilliant"—or so we'd been led to believe. Not that we thought of ourselves as young: you were nineteen, I was twenty. We were mature for our ages, and we were immature. We were intellectually sophisticated, and emotionally unpredictable. We revered something we called *art*, we were disdainful of something we called *life*. We were overly conscious of ourselves. And yet: how patient, how protective, watching over Marilyn Monroe squatting on a footstool in the JUDAICA stacks as stray customers pushed past muttering "excuse me!" or not even seeming to notice her, or the two of us standing guard. And at last—a relief—Marilyn Monroe shut the unwieldy book, having decided to buy it, and rose from the footstool gathering up her many things. And—this was a temptation!—we held back, not offering to help her carry her things as we so badly wanted to, but only just following at a discreet distance as Marilyn Monroe made her way through the labyrinth of the bookstore to the front counter. (Did she glance back at us? Did she understand you and I were her protectors?) If anyone dared to approach her, we intended to intervene. We would push between Marilyn Monroe and whomever it was. Yet how strange the scene was: none of the other Strand customers, lost in books, took any special notice of her, any more than they took notice of us. Book lovers, especially used-book lovers, are not ones to stare curiously at others, but only at books. At the front of the store—it was a long hike—the cashiers would be more alert, we thought. One of them seemed to be watching Marilyn Monroe approach. Did he know? Could he guess? Was he waiting for her?

Nearing the front counter and the bright fluorescent lights overhead, 35 Marilyn Monroe seemed for the first time to falter. She fumbled to extract out of her shoulder bag a pair of dark glasses and managed to put them on. She turned up the collar of her navy coat. She lowered her hat brim.

Still she was hesitant, and it was then that I stepped forward and said quietly, "Excuse me. Why don't I buy your books for you? That way you won't have to talk to anyone."

The blond actress stared at me through her oversized dark glasses. Her eyes were only just visible behind the lenses. A shy-girl's eyes, startled and grateful.

And so I did. With you helping me. Two girl-poets, side by side, all brisk and businesslike, making Marilyn Monroe's purchases for her: a total of sixteen books!—hardcover and paperback, relatively new books, old battered thumbed-through books—at a cost of $55.85. A staggering sum! Never in my two years of coming into the Strand had I handed over more than a few dollars to the cashier, and this time my hand might have trembled as I pushed twenty-dollar bills at him, half expecting the bristly bearded man to interrogate me: "Where'd you get so much money?" But as usual the cashier hardly gave me a second glance. And Marilyn Monroe, burdened with no books, had already slipped through the turnstile and was awaiting us at the front door.

There, when we handed over her purchases in two sturdy bags, she leaned forward. For a breathless moment we thought she might kiss our cheeks. Instead she pressed into our surprised hands a slender volume she lifted from one of the bags: *Selected Poems of Marianne Moore*. We stammered thanks, but already the blond actress had pulled the fedora down more tightly over her head and had stepped out into the lightly falling snow, headed south on Broadway. We trailed behind her, unable to resist, waiting for her to hail a taxi but she did not. We knew we must not follow her. By this time we were giddy with the strain of the past hour, gripping each other's hands in childlike elation. So happy!

"Oh. Oh God. Marilyn Monroe. She gave us a book. Was any of it real?"   40
It was real: we had *Selected Poems of Marianne Moore* to prove it.

That snowy early evening in March at Strand Used Books. That magical evening of Marilyn Monroe, when I kissed you for the first time.

CONSIDERATIONS FOR CRITICAL THINKING AND WRITING

1. **FIRST RESPONSE.** How do you interpret the story's final sentence? Explain whether you were surprised by it. How does that sentence affect your reading of the rest of the story?

2. Describe the manner in which the narrator tells her story. Which passages are especially effective in revealing her as an undergraduate in love with poetry?

3. Why do you think Marilyn Monroe is so prominent in the story's plot? Why did Oates choose Marilyn Monroe and not, say, Lucille Ball?

4. Comment on Oates's use of suspense. What purpose does it serve?

5. What is the conflict of the story? What is its climax? Is there a resolution to the conflict? Explain.

6. What do you think is the central point of the story?

CONNECTIONS TO OTHER SELECTIONS

1. Discuss the role of Marilyn Monroe in this story and the role of Princip in Fay Weldon's "IND AFF, or Out of Love in Sarajevo" (p. 202). How does each of these historic figures add to the plot of each story?

2. Write an essay comparing the ending of Oates's story with that of David Updike's "Summer" (p. 380). What is the effect of the ending on your reading of each story?

WILLIAM FAULKNER (1897–1962)

Born into an old Mississippi family that had lost its influence and wealth during the Civil War, William Faulkner lived nearly all his life in the South writing about Yoknapatawpha County, an imagined Mississippi county similar to his home in Oxford. Among his novels based on this fictional location are *The Sound and the Fury* (1929), *As I Lay Dying* (1930), *Light in August* (1932), and *Absalom, Absalom!* (1936). Although his writings are regional in their emphasis on local social history, his concerns are broader. In his 1950 acceptance speech for the Nobel Prize for literature, he insisted that the "problems of the human heart in conflict with itself . . . alone can make good writing because only that is worth writing about, worth the agony and the sweat." This commitment is evident in his novels and in *The Collected Stories of William Faulkner* (1950). "A Rose for Emily," about the mysterious life of Emily Grierson, presents a personal conflict rooted in her southern identity. It also contains a grim surprise.

A Rose for Emily   *1931*

I

When Miss Emily Grierson died, our whole town went to her funeral: the men through a sort of respectful affection for a fallen monument, the women mostly out of curiosity to see the inside of her house, which no one save an old manservant — a combined gardener and cook — had seen in at least ten years.

It was a big, squarish frame house that had once been white, decorated with cupolas and spires and scrolled balconies in the heavily lightsome style of the seventies, set on what had once been our most select street. But garages and cotton gins had encroached and obliterated even the august names of that neighborhood; only Miss Emily's house was left, lifting its stubborn and coquettish decay above the cotton wagons and the gasoline pumps — an eyesore among eyesores. And now Miss Emily had gone to join the representatives of those august names where they lay in the cedar-bemused cemetery among the ranked and anonymous graves of Union and Confederate soldiers who fell at the battle of Jefferson.

Alive, Miss Emily had been a tradition, a duty, and a care; a sort of hereditary obligation upon the town, dating from that day in 1894 when Colonel Sartoris, the mayor — he who fathered the edict that no Negro woman should appear on the streets without an apron — remitted her taxes, the dispensation dating from the death of her father on into perpetuity. Not that Miss Emily would have accepted charity. Colonel Sartoris invented an involved tale to the effect that Miss Emily's father had loaned money to the town, which the town, as a matter of business, preferred this way of repaying. Only a man of Colonel Sartoris' generation and thought could have invented it, and only a woman could have believed it.

When the next generation, with its more modern ideas, became mayors and aldermen, this arrangement created some little dissatisfaction. On the first of the year they mailed her a tax notice. February came, and there was no reply. They wrote her a formal letter, asking her to call at the sheriff's office at her convenience. A week later the mayor wrote her himself, offering to call or to send his car for her, and received in reply a note on paper of an archaic shape, in a thin, flowing calligraphy in faded ink, to the effect that she no longer went out at all. The tax notice was also enclosed, without comment.

They called a special meeting of the Board of Aldermen. A deputation 5 waited upon her, knocked at the door through which no visitor had passed since she ceased giving china-painting lessons eight or ten years earlier. They were admitted by the old Negro into a dim hall from which a stairway mounted into still more shadow. It smelled of dust and disuse—a close, dank smell. The Negro led them into the parlor. It was furnished in heavy, leather-covered furniture. When the Negro opened the blinds of one window, they could see that the leather was cracked; and when they sat down, a faint dust rose sluggishly about their thighs, spinning with slow motes in the single sun-ray. On a tarnished gilt easel before the fireplace stood a crayon portrait of Miss Emily's father.

They rose when she entered—a small, fat woman in black, with a thin gold chain descending to her waist and vanishing into her belt, leaning on an ebony cane with a tarnished gold head. Her skeleton was small and spare; perhaps that was why what would have been merely plumpness in another was obesity in her. She looked bloated, like a body long submerged in motionless water, and of that pallid hue. Her eyes, lost in the fatty ridges of her face, looked like two small pieces of coal pressed into a lump of dough as they moved from one face to another while the visitors stated their errand.

She did not ask them to sit. She just stood in the door and listened quietly until the spokesman came to a stumbling halt. Then they could hear the invisible watch ticking at the end of the gold chain.

Her voice was dry and cold. "I have no taxes in Jefferson. Colonel Sartoris explained it to me. Perhaps one of you can gain access to the city records and satisfy yourselves."

"But we have. We are the city authorities, Miss Emily. Didn't you get a notice from the sheriff, signed by him?"

"I received a paper, yes," Miss Emily said. "Perhaps he considers himself 10 the sheriff . . . I have no taxes in Jefferson."

"But there is nothing on the books to show that, you see. We must go by the—"

"See Colonel Sartoris. I have no taxes in Jefferson."

"But, Miss Emily—"

"See Colonel Sartoris." (Colonel Sartoris had been dead almost ten years.) "I have no taxes in Jefferson. Tobe!" The Negro appeared. "Show these gentlemen out."

II

So she vanquished them, horse and foot, just as she had vanquished their fa- 15 thers thirty years before about the smell. That was two years after her father's death and a short time after her sweetheart—the one we believed would marry her—had deserted her. After her father's death she went out very little; after her sweetheart went away, people hardly saw her at all. A few of the ladies had the temerity to call, but were not received, and the only sign of life about the place was the Negro man—a young man then—going in and out with a market basket.

"Just as if a man—any man—could keep a kitchen properly," the ladies said; so they were not surprised when the smell developed. It was another link between the gross, teeming world and the high and mighty Griersons.

A neighbor, a woman, complained to the mayor, Judge Stevens, eighty years old.

"But what will you have me do about it, madam?" he said.

"Why, send her word to stop it," the woman said. "Isn't there a law?"

"I'm sure that won't be necessary," Judge Stevens said. "It's probably just a 20 snake or a rat that nigger of hers killed in the yard. I'll speak to him about it."

The next day he received two more complaints, one from a man who came in diffident deprecation. "We really must do something about it, Judge. I'd be the last one in the world to bother Miss Emily, but we've got to do something." That night the Board of Aldermen met — three graybeards and one younger man, a member of the rising generation.

"It's simple enough," he said. "Send her word to have her place cleaned up. Give her a certain time to do it in, and if she don't . . ."

"Dammit, sir," Judge Stevens said, "will you accuse a lady to her face of smelling bad?"

So the next night, after midnight, four men crossed Miss Emily's lawn and slunk about the house like burglars, sniffing along the base of the brickwork and at the cellar openings while one of them performed a regular sowing motion with his hand out of a sack slung from his shoulder. They broke open the cellar door and sprinkled lime there, and in all the outbuildings. As they recrossed the lawn, a window that had been dark was lighted and Miss Emily sat in it, the light behind her, and her upright torso motionless as that of an idol. They crept quietly across the lawn and into the shadow of the locusts that lined the street. After a week or two the smell went away.

That was when people had begun to feel really sorry for her. People in our 25 town, remembering how old lady Wyatt, her great-aunt, had gone completely crazy at last, believed that the Griersons held themselves a little too high for what they really were. None of the young men were quite good enough for Miss Emily and such. We had long thought of them as a tableau, Miss Emily a slender figure in white in the background, her father a spraddled silhouette in the foreground, his back to her and clutching a horsewhip, the two of them framed by the back-flung front door. So when she got to be thirty and was still single, we were not pleased exactly, but vindicated; even with insanity in the family she wouldn't have turned down all of her chances if they had really materialized.

When her father died, it got about that the house was all that was left to her; and in a way, people were glad. At last they could pity Miss Emily. Being left alone, and a pauper, she had become humanized. Now she too would know the old thrill and the old despair of a penny more or less.

The day after his death all the ladies prepared to call at the house and offer condolence and aid, as is our custom. Miss Emily met them at the door, dressed as usual and with no trace of grief on her face. She told them that her father was not dead. She did that for three days, with the ministers calling on her, and the doctors, trying to persuade her to let them dispose of the body. Just as they were about to resort to law and force, she broke down, and they buried her father quickly.

We did not say she was crazy then. We believed she had to do that. We remembered all the young men her father had driven away, and we knew that with nothing left, she would have to cling to that which had robbed her, as people will.

III

She was sick for a long time. When we saw her again, her hair was cut short, making her look like a girl, with a vague resemblance to those angels in colored church windows — sort of tragic and serene.

The town had just let the contracts for paving the sidewalks, and in the 30
summer after her father's death they began the work. The construction company came with niggers and mules and machinery, and a foreman named
Homer Barron, a Yankee—a big, dark, ready man, with a big voice and eyes
lighter than his face. The little boys would follow in groups to hear him cuss the
niggers, and the niggers singing in time to the rise and fall of picks. Pretty soon
he knew everybody in town. Whenever you heard a lot of laughing anywhere
about the square, Homer Barron would be in the center of the group. Presently
we began to see him and Miss Emily on Sunday afternoons driving in the
yellow-wheeled buggy and the matched team of bays from the livery stable.

At first we were glad that Miss Emily would have an interest, because the
ladies all said, "Of course a Grierson would not think seriously of a Northerner,
a day laborer." But there were still others, older people, who said that even grief
could not cause a real lady to forget *noblesse oblige*°—without calling it *noblesse
oblige.* They just said, "Poor Emily. Her kinsfolk should come to her." She had
some kin in Alabama; but years ago her father had fallen out with them over the
estate of old lady Wyatt, the crazy woman, and there was no communication between the two families. They had not even been represented at the funeral.

And as soon as the old people said, "Poor Emily," the whispering began.
"Do you suppose it's really so?" they said to one another. "Of course it is. What
else could . . ." This behind their hands; rustling of craned silk and satin behind jalousies closed upon the sun of Sunday afternoon as the thin, swift clop-
clop-clop of the matched team passed: "Poor Emily."

She carried her head high enough—even when we believed that she was
fallen. It was as if she demanded more than ever the recognition of her dignity
as the last Grierson; as if it had wanted that touch of earthiness to reaffirm her
imperviousness. Like when she bought the rat poison, the arsenic. That was
over a year after they had begun to say "Poor Emily," and while the two female
cousins were visiting her.

"I want some poison," she said to the druggist. She was over thirty then, still a
slight woman, though thinner than usual, with cold, haughty black eyes in a face
the flesh of which was strained across the temples and about the eye-sockets as you
imagine a lighthouse-keeper's face ought to look. "I want some poison," she said.

"Yes, Miss Emily. What kind? For rats and such? I'd recom—"   35
"I want the best you have. I don't care what kind."
The druggist named several. "They'll kill anything up to an elephant. But
what you want is—"
"Arsenic," Miss Emily said. "Is that a good one?"
"Is . . . arsenic? Yes, ma'am. But what you want—"
"I want arsenic."   40
The druggist looked down at her. She looked back at him, erect, her face
like a strained flag. "Why, of course," the druggist said. "If that's what you
want. But the law requires you to tell what you are going to use it for."
Miss Emily just stared at him, her head tilted back in order to look him eye
for eye, until he looked away and went and got the arsenic and wrapped it up.
The Negro delivery boy brought her the package; the druggist didn't come
back. When she opened the package at home there was written on the box,
under the skull and bones: "For rats."

noblesse oblige: The obligation of people of high social position.

IV

So the next day we all said, "She will kill herself"; and we said it would be the best thing. When she had first begun to be seen with Homer Barron, we had said, "She will marry him." Then we said, "She will persuade him yet," because Homer himself had remarked—he liked men, and it was known that he drank with the younger men in the Elks' Club—that he was not a marrying man. Later we said, "Poor Emily" behind the jalousies as they passed on Sunday afternoon in the glittering buggy, Miss Emily with her head high and Homer Barron with his hat cocked and a cigar in his teeth, reins and whip in a yellow glove.

Then some of the ladies began to say that it was a disgrace to the town and a bad example to the young people. The men did not want to interfere, but at last the ladies forced the Baptist minister—Miss Emily's people were Episcopal—to call upon her. He would never divulge what happened during that interview, but he refused to go back again. The next Sunday they again drove about the streets, and the following day the minister's wife wrote to Miss Emily's relations in Alabama.

So she had blood-kin under her roof again and we sat back to watch developments. At first nothing happened. Then we were sure that they were to be married. We learned that Miss Emily had been to the jeweler's and ordered a man's toilet set in silver, with the letters H. B. on each piece. Two days later we learned that she had bought a complete outfit of men's clothing, including a nightshirt, and we said, "They are married." We were really glad. We were glad because the two female cousins were even more Grierson than Miss Emily had ever been.

So we were not surprised when Homer Barron—the streets had been finished some time since—was gone. We were a little disappointed that there was not a public blowing-off, but we believed that he had gone on to prepare for Miss Emily's coming, or to give her a chance to get rid of the cousins. (By that time it was a cabal, and we were all Miss Emily's allies to help circumvent the cousins.) Sure enough, after another week they departed. And, as we had expected all along, within three days Homer Barron was back in town. A neighbor saw the Negro man admit him at the kitchen door at dusk one evening.

And that was the last we saw of Homer Barron. And of Miss Emily for some time. The Negro man went in and out with the market basket, but the front door remained closed. Now and then we would see her at a window for a moment, as the men did that night when they sprinkled the lime, but for almost six months she did not appear on the streets. Then we knew that this was to be expected too; as if that quality of her father which had thwarted her woman's life so many times had been too virulent and too furious to die.

When we next saw Miss Emily, she had grown fat and her hair was turning gray. During the next few years it grew grayer and grayer until it attained an even pepper-and-salt iron-gray, when it ceased turning. Up to the day of her death at seventy-four it was still that vigorous iron-gray, like the hair of an active man.

From that time on her front door remained closed, save for a period of six or seven years, when she was about forty, during which she gave lessons in china-painting. She fitted up a studio in one of the downstairs rooms, where the daughters and granddaughters of Colonel Sartoris' contemporaries were sent to her with the same regularity and in the same spirit that they were sent to church on Sundays with a twenty-five-cent piece for the collection plate. Meanwhile her taxes had been remitted.

Then the newer generation became the backbone and the spirit of the 50 town, and the painting pupils grew up and fell away and did not send their children to her with boxes of color and tedious brushes and pictures cut from the ladies' magazines. The front door closed upon the last one and remained closed for good. When the town got free postal delivery, Miss Emily alone refused to let them fasten the metal numbers above her door and attach a mailbox to it. She would not listen to them.

Daily, monthly, yearly we watched the Negro grow grayer and more stooped, going in and out with the market basket. Each December we sent her a tax notice, which would be returned by the post office a week later, unclaimed. Now and then we would see her in one of the downstairs windows—she had evidently shut up the top floor of the house—like the carven torso of an idol in a niche, looking or not looking at us, we could never tell which. Thus she passed from generation to generation—dear, inescapable, impervious, tranquil, and perverse.

And so she died. Fell ill in the house filled with dust and shadows, with only a doddering Negro man to wait on her. We did not even know she was sick; we had long since given up trying to get information from the Negro. He talked to no one, probably not even to her, for his voice had grown harsh and rusty, as if from disuse.

She died in one of the downstairs rooms, in a heavy walnut bed with a curtain, her gray head propped on a pillow yellow and moldy with age and lack of sunlight.

V

The Negro met the first of the ladies at the front door and let them in, with their hushed, sibilant voices and their quick, curious glances, and then he disappeared. He walked right through the house and out the back and was not seen again.

The two female cousins came at once. They held the funeral on the second 55 day, with the town coming to look at Miss Emily beneath a mass of bought flowers, with the crayon face of her father musing profoundly above the bier and the ladies sibilant and macabre; and the very old men—some in their brushed Confederate uniforms—on the porch and the lawn, talking of Miss Emily as if she had been a contemporary of theirs, believing that they had danced with her and courted her perhaps, confusing time with its mathematical progression, as the old do, to whom all the past is not a diminishing road but, instead, a huge meadow which no winter ever quite touches, divided from them now by the narrow bottle-neck of the most recent decade of years.

Already we knew that there was one room in that region above stairs which no one had seen in forty years, and which would have to be forced. They waited until Miss Emily was decently in the ground before they opened it.

The violence of breaking down the door seemed to fill this room with pervading dust. A thin, acrid pall as of the tomb seemed to lie everywhere upon this room decked and furnished as for a bridal: upon the valance curtains of faded rose color, upon the rose-shaded lights, upon the dressing table, upon the delicate array of crystal and the man's toilet things backed with tarnished silver, silver so tarnished that the monogram was obscured. Among them lay a collar and tie, as if they had just been removed, which, lifted, left upon the surface a pale crescent in the dust. Upon a chair hung the suit, carefully folded; beneath it the two mute shoes and the discarded socks.

The man himself lay in the bed.

For a long while we just stood there, looking down at the profound and fleshless grin. The body had apparently once lain in the attitude of an embrace, but now the long sleep that outlasts love, that conquers even the grimace of love, had cuckolded him. What was left of him, rotted beneath what was left of the nightshirt, had become inextricable from the bed in which he lay; and upon him and upon the pillow beside him lay that even coating of the patient and biding dust.

Then we noticed that in the second pillow was the indentation of a head.   60 One of us lifted something from it, and leaning forward, that faint and invisible dust dry and acrid in the nostrils, we saw a long strand of iron-gray hair.

Considerations for Critical Thinking and Writing

1. **FIRST RESPONSE.** How might this story be rewritten as a piece of formula fiction? You could write it as a romance, detective, or horror story — whatever strikes your fancy. Does Faulkner's version have elements of formulaic fiction?

2. What is the effect of the final paragraph of the story? How does it contribute to your understanding of Emily? Why is it important that we get this information last rather than at the beginning of the story?

3. What details foreshadow the conclusion of the story? Did you anticipate the ending?

4. Contrast the order of events as they happen in the story with the order in which they are told. How does this plotting create interest and suspense?

5. Faulkner uses a number of gothic elements in this plot: the imposing decrepit house, the decayed corpse, and the mysterious secret horrors connected with Emily's life. How do these elements forward the plot and establish the atmosphere?

6. How does the information provided by the exposition indicate the nature of the conflict in the story? What does Emily's southern heritage contribute to the story?

7. Who or what is the antagonist of the story? Why is it significant that Homer Barron is a construction foreman and a northerner?

8. In what sense does the narrator's telling of the story serve as "A Rose for Emily"? Why do you think the narrator uses *we* rather than *I*?

9. Explain how Emily's reasons for murdering Homer are related to her personal history and to the ways she handled previous conflicts.

10. Discuss how Faulkner's treatment of the North and South contributes to the meaning of the story.

11. Provide an alternative title and explain how the emphasis in your title is reflected in the story.

CONNECTION TO ANOTHER SELECTION

1. Contrast Faulkner's ordering of events with Tim O'Brien's "How to Tell a True War Story" (p. 346). How does each author's arrangement of incidents create different effects on the reader?

2. To what extent do concepts of honor and tradition influence the action in "A Rose for Emily" and "How to Tell a True War Story"?

Perspective

WILLIAM FAULKNER (1897–1962)

On "A Rose for Emily"   1959

Q. What is the meaning of the title "A Rose for Emily"?

A. Oh, it's simply the poor woman had had no life at all. Her father had kept her more or less locked up and then she had a lover who was about to quit her, she had to murder him. It was just "A Rose for Emily" — that's all.

Q. . . . What ever inspired you to write this story?

A. That to me was another sad and tragic manifestation of man's condition in which he dreams and hopes, in which he is in conflict with himself or with his environment or with others. In this case there was the young girl with a young girl's normal aspirations to find love and then a husband and a family, who was brow-beaten and kept down by her father, a selfish man who didn't want her to leave home because he wanted a housekeeper, and it was a natural instinct of — repressed which — you can't repress it — you can mash it down but it comes up somewhere else and very likely in a tragic form, and that was simply another manifestation of man's injustice to man, of the poor tragic human being struggling with its own heart, with others, with its environment, for the simple things which all human beings want. In that case it was a young girl that just wanted to be loved and to love and to have a husband and a family.

Q. And that purely came from your imagination?

A. Well, the story did but the condition is there. It exists. I didn't invent that condition, I didn't invent the fact that young girls dream of someone to love and children and a home, but the story of what her own particular tragedy was was invented, yes. . . .

Q. Sir, it has been argued that "A Rose for Emily" is a criticism of the North, and others have argued saying that it is a criticism of the South. Now, could this story, shall we say, be more properly classified as a criticism of the times?

A. Now that I don't know, because I was simply trying to write about people. The writer uses environment — what he knows — and if there's a symbolism in which the lover represented the North and the woman who murdered him represents the South, I don't say that's not valid and not there, but it was no intention of the writer to say, Now let's see, I'm going to write a piece in which I will use a symbolism for the North and another symbol for the South, that he was simply writing about people, a story which he thought was tragic and true, because it came out of the human heart, the human aspiration, the human — the conflict of conscience with glands, with the Old Adam. It was a conflict not between North and the South so much as between, well you might say, God and Satan.

Q. Sir, just a little more on that thing. You say it's a conflict between God and Satan. Well, I don't quite understand what you mean. Who is — did one represent the —

A. The conflict was in Miss Emily, that she knew that you do not murder people. She had been trained that you do not take a lover. You marry, you don't take a lover. She had broken all the laws of her tradition, her background, and she had finally broken the law of God too, which says you do not take human life. And she knew she was doing wrong, and that's why her own life was wrecked. Instead of murdering one lover, and then to go and take another and when she used him up to murder him, she was expiating her crime.

Q. Was the "Rose for Emily" an idea or a character? Just how did you go about it?

A. That came from a picture of the strand of hair on the pillow. It was a ghost story. Simply a picture of a strand of hair on the pillow in the abandoned house.

From *Faulkner in the University*, edited by
Frederick Gwynn and Joseph Blotner

CONSIDERATIONS FOR CRITICAL THINKING AND WRITING

1. Discuss whether you think Faulkner's explanation of the conflict between "God and Satan" limits or expands the meaning of the story for you.

2. In what sense is "A Rose for Emily" a ghost story?

3. Compare Faulkner's account of how he conceived "A Rose for Emily" with Flannery O'Connor's description of "Good Country People" in the Perspective on page 491. To what extent are their attitudes about symbolism similar?

A SAMPLE CLOSE READING

An Annotated Section of "A Rose for Emily"

Even as you read a story for the first time, you can highlight passages, circle or underline words, and write responses in the margins. Subsequent readings will yield more insights once you begin to understand how various elements such as plot, character, and wording build toward the conclusion and what you perceive to be the story's central ideas. The following annotations for the first six paragraphs of "A Rose for Emily" provide a perspective written by someone who had read the work several times.

WILLIAM FAULKNER (1897–1962)

From *A Rose for Emily*   *1931*

I

The title suggests that the story is an expression of affection and mourning, as well as a tribute, for Emily — despite her bizarre behavior.

The story begins (and ends) with death, and "the fallen monument" signals Emily's special meaning to the narrator and the community.

When Miss Emily Grierson died, our whole town went to her funeral: the men through a sort of respectful affection for a fallen monument, the women mostly out of curiosity to see the inside of her house, which no one save an old man-servant — a combined gardener and cook — had seen in at least ten years.

The importance of the decayed old South setting is emphasized by being detailed even before Emily is described. The Civil War between the North and South is implicitly linked to the garages and gas pumps (the modern) that overtake the old southern neighborhood and hint at a lingering conflict.

It was a big, squarish frame house that had once been white, decorated with cupolas and spires and scrolled balconies in the heavily lightsome style of the seventies, set on what had once been our most select street. But garages and cotton gins had encroached and obliterated even the august names of that neighborhood; only Miss Emily's house was left, lifting its stubborn and coquettish decay above the cotton wagons and the gasoline pumps — an eyesore among eyesores. And now Miss Emily had gone to join the representatives of those august names where they lay in the cedar-bemused cemetery among the ranked and anonymous graves of Union and Confederate soldiers who fell at the battle of Jefferson.

Emily is associated with southern tradition, duty, and privilege that require protection. This helps explain why the townspeople attend her funeral.

Alive, Miss Emily had been a tradition, a duty, and a care; a sort of hereditary obligation upon the town, dating from that day in 1894 when Colonel Sartoris, the mayor — he who fathered the edict that no Negro woman should appear on the streets without an apron — remitted her taxes, the dispensation dating from the death of her father on into perpetuity.

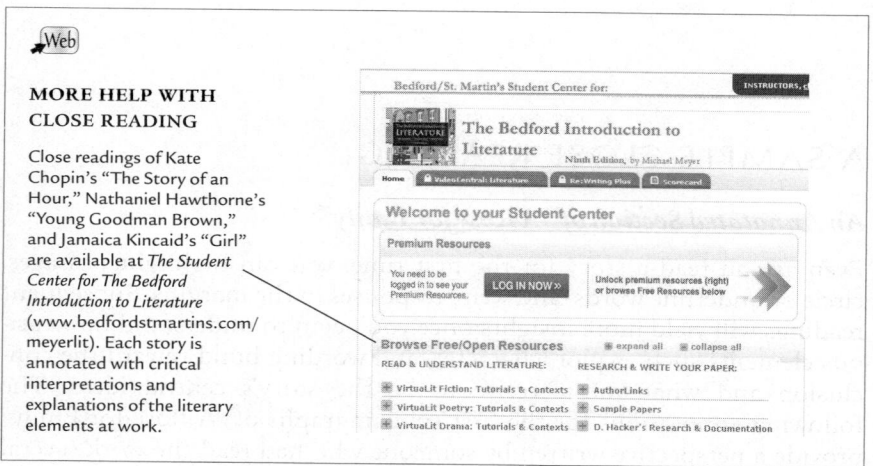

MORE HELP WITH CLOSE READING

Close readings of Kate Chopin's "The Story of an Hour," Nathaniel Hawthorne's "Young Goodman Brown," and Jamaica Kincaid's "Girl" are available at *The Student Center for The Bedford Introduction to Literature* (www.bedfordstmartins.com/meyerlit). Each story is annotated with critical interpretations and explanations of the literary elements at work.

Not that Miss Emily would have accepted charity. Colonel Sartoris invented an involved tale to the effect that Miss Emily's father had loaned money to the town, which the town, as a matter of business, preferred this way of repaying. Only a man of Colonel Sartoris' generation and thought could have invented it, and only a woman could have believed it.

When the next generation, with its more modern ideas, became mayors and aldermen, this arrangement created some little dissatisfaction. On the first of the year they mailed her a tax notice. February came, and there was no reply. They wrote her a formal letter, asking her to call at the sheriff's office at her convenience. A week later the mayor wrote her himself, offering to call or to send his car for her, and received in reply a note on paper of an archaic shape, in a thin, flowing calligraphy in faded ink, to the effect that she no longer went out at all. The tax notice was also enclosed, without comment.

They called a special meeting of the Board of Aldermen. 5 A deputation waited upon her, knocked at the door through which no visitor had passed since she ceased giving china-painting lessons eight or ten years earlier. They were admitted by the old Negro into a dim hall from which a stairway mounted into still more shadow. It smelled of dust and disuse—a close, dank smell. The Negro led them into the parlor. It was furnished in heavy, leather-covered furniture. When the Negro opened the blinds of one window, they could see that the leather was cracked; and when they sat down, a faint dust rose sluggishly about their thighs, spinning with slow motes in the single sun-ray. On a tarnished gilt easel before the fireplace stood a crayon portrait of Miss Emily's father.

> Like Emily, her "archaic," "thin," and "faded" note resists change and "modern ideas." She dismisses any attempts by the town to assess her for taxes or for anything else. She won't even leave the house.

> The description of the "dank" house smelling of "dust and disuse" reinforces Emily's connection with the past and her refusal to let go of it. As the men sit down, "a faint dust rose" around them. The passage of time is alluded to in each of these paragraphs and ultimately emerges as a kind of antagonist.

A SAMPLE STUDENT RESPONSE

Parker 1

Josiah Parker

Professor Altschuler

English 200-A

December 14, 2009

Conflict in the Plot of Faulkner's "A Rose for Emily"

The conflict of William Faulkner's "A Rose for Emily" is the driving force of the story's plot. However, the conflict is not the act of murder, nor is it Miss Emily's bizarre, reclusive lifestyle. The conflict is located instead in

Miss Emily's background, her history. She is portrayed as a hardened, bitter old woman, but we soon realize she herself is a victim. She has been oppressed her entire life by her domineering father, unable to take a suitor and marry, which is what she desires most. This lifelong oppression becomes the central conflict, and is what drives Miss Emily, causing her "to cling to that which had robbed her" (Faulkner, "Rose" 93).

After her father's death, Miss Emily immediately takes a lover, then poisons him when he tries to leave her. Both actions are what Faulkner himself claims "had broken all the laws of her tradition" (Faulkner, "On 'A Rose'" 99). She has been taught her whole life not to take a lover, certainly not to take a life. Her willingness to go against what she has always known to be moral and right creates dramatic tension and advances the story. In this way, the act of murder is nothing more than a portion of the plot, an "incident in the story," rather than the conflict itself (Meyer 73). . . . .

Works Cited

Faulkner, William. "A Rose for Emily." *The Bedford Introduction to Literature*.
    Ed. Michael Meyer. 9th ed. Boston: Bedford/St. Martin's, 2011.
    91–97. Print.

---. "On 'A Rose for Emily.'" *The Bedford Introduction to Literature*. Ed.
    Michael Meyer. 9th ed. Boston: Bedford/St. Martin's, 2011. 98–99.
    Print.

Meyer, Michael, ed. *The Bedford Introduction to Literature*. 9th ed. Boston:
    Bedford/St. Martin's, 2011. 73. Print.

ANDRE DUBUS (1936–1999)

Though a native of Louisiana, where he attended the Christian Brothers School and McNeese State College, Andre Dubus lived much of his life in Massachusetts; many of his stories are set in the Merrimack Valley north of Boston. After college Dubus served as an officer for five years in the Marine Corps. He then took an M.F.A. at the University of Iowa in 1966 and began teaching at Bradford College in Massachusetts. His fiction earned him numerous awards, and he was both a Guggenheim and a MacArthur Fellow. Among his collections of fiction are

© Marion Ettlinger.

Separate Flights (1975); *Adultery and Other Choices* (1977); *Finding a Girl in America* (1980), from which "Killings" is taken; *The Last Worthless Evening* (1986); *Collected Stories* (1988); and *Dancing after Hours* (1996). In 1991 he published *Broken Vessels*, a collection of autobiographical essays. His stories are often tense with violence, anger, tenderness, and guilt; they are populated by characters who struggle to understand and survive their experiences, painful with failure and the weight of imperfect relationships. In "Killings," the basis for a 2001 film titled *In the Bedroom,* Dubus offers a powerful blend of intimate domestic life and shocking violence.

Killings   *1979*

On the August morning when Matt Fowler buried his youngest son, Frank, who had lived for twenty-one years, eight months, and four days, Matt's older son, Steve, turned to him as the family left the grave and walked between their friends, and said: "I should kill him." He was twenty-eight, his brown hair starting to thin in front where he used to have a cowlick. He bit his lower lip, wiped his eyes, then said it again. Ruth's arm, linked with Matt's, tightened; he looked at her. Beneath her eyes there was swelling from the three days she had suffered. At the limousine Matt stopped and looked back at the grave, the casket, and the Congregationalist minister who he thought had probably had a difficult job with the eulogy though he hadn't seemed to, and the old funeral director who was saying something to the six young pallbearers. The grave was on a hill and overlooked the Merrimack, which he could not see from where he stood; he looked at the opposite bank, at the apple orchard with its symmetrically planted trees going up a hill.

Next day Steve drove with his wife back to Baltimore where he managed the branch office of a bank, and Cathleen, the middle child, drove with her husband back to Syracuse. They had left the grandchildren with friends. A month after the funeral Matt played poker at Willis Trottier's because Ruth, who knew this was the second time he had been invited, told him to go, he couldn't sit home with her for the rest of her life, she was all right. After the game Willis went outside to tell everyone good night and, when the others had driven away, he walked with Matt to his car. Willis was a short, silver-haired man who had opened a diner after World War II, his trade then mostly very early breakfast, which he cooked, and then lunch for the men who worked at the leather and shoe factories. He now owned a large restaurant.

"He walks the Goddamn streets," Matt said.

"I know. He was in my place last night, at the bar. With a girl."

"I don't see him. I'm in the store all the time. Ruth sees him. She sees him   5 too much. She was at Sunnyhurst today getting cigarettes and aspirin, and there he was. She can't even go out for cigarettes and aspirin. It's killing her."

"Come back in for a drink."

Matt looked at his watch. Ruth would be asleep. He walked with Willis back into the house, pausing at the steps to look at the starlit sky. It was a cool summer night; he thought vaguely of the Red Sox, did not even know if they were at home tonight; since it happened he had not been able to think about any of the small pleasures he believed he had earned, as he had earned also what was shattered now forever: the quietly harried and quietly pleasurable days of fatherhood. They went inside. Willis's wife, Martha, had gone to bed hours ago, in the rear of the large house which was rigged with burglar and fire alarms. They went downstairs to the game room: the television set suspended from the ceiling, the pool table, the poker table with beer cans, cards, chips, filled ashtrays, and the six chairs where Matt and his friends had sat, the friends picking up the old banter as though he had only been away on vacation; but he could see the affection and courtesy in their eyes. Willis went behind the bar and mixed them each a Scotch and soda; he stayed behind the bar and looked at Matt sitting on the stool.

"How often have you thought about it?" Willis said.

"Every day since he got out. I didn't think about bail. I thought I wouldn't have to worry about him for years. She sees him all the time. It makes her cry."

"He was in my place a long time last night. He'll be back."   10

"Maybe he won't."

"The band. He likes the band."

"What's he doing now?"

"He's tending bar up to Hampton Beach. For a friend. Ever notice even the worst bastard always has friends? He couldn't get work in town. It's just tourists and kids up to Hampton. Nobody knows him. If they do, they don't care. They drink what he mixes."

"Nobody tells me about him."   15

"I hate him, Matt. My boys went to school with him. He was the same then. Know what he'll do? Five at the most. Remember that woman about seven years ago? Shot her husband and dropped him off the bridge in the Merrimack with a hundred-pound sack of cement and said all the way through it that nobody helped her. Know where she is now? She's in Lawrence now, a secretary. And whoever helped her, where the hell is he?"

"I've got a .38 I've had for years, I take it to the store now. I tell Ruth it's for the night deposits. I tell her things have changed: we got junkies here now too. Lots of people without jobs. She knows though."

"What does she know?"

"She knows I started carrying it after the first time she saw him in town. She knows it's in case I see him, and there's some kind of a situation—"

He stopped, looked at Willis, and finished his drink. Willis mixed him another. 20

"What kind of situation?"

"Where he did something to me. Where I could get away with it."

"How does Ruth feel about that?"

"She doesn't know."

"You said she does, she's got it figured out." 25

He thought of her that afternoon: when she went into Sunnyhurst, Strout was waiting at the counter while the clerk bagged the things he had bought; she turned down an aisle and looked at soup cans until he left.

"Ruth would shoot him herself, if she thought she could hit him."

"You got a permit?"

"No."

"I do. You could get a year for that." 30

"Maybe I'll get one. Or maybe I won't. Maybe I'll just stop bringing it to the store."

Richard Strout was twenty-six years old, a high school athlete, football scholarship to the University of Massachusetts where he lasted for almost two semesters before quitting in advance of the final grades that would have forced him not to return. People then said: Dickie can do the work; he just doesn't want to. He came home and did construction work for his father but refused his father's offer to learn the business; his two older brothers had learned it, so that Strout and Sons trucks going about town, and signs on construction sites, now slashed wounds into Matt Fowler's life. Then Richard married a young girl and became a bartender, his salary and tips augmented and perhaps sometimes matched by his father, who also posted his bond. So his friends, his enemies (he had those: fist fights or, more often, boys and then young men who had not fought him when they thought they should have), and those who simply knew him by face and name, had a series of images of him which they recalled when they heard of the killing: the high school running back, the young drunk in bars, the oblivious hard-hatted young man eating lunch at a counter, the bartender who could perhaps be called courteous but not more than that: as he tended bar, his dark eyes and dark, wide-jawed face appeared less sullen, near blank.

One night he beat Frank. Frank was living at home and waiting for September, for graduate school in economics, and working as a lifeguard at Salisbury Beach, where he met Mary Ann Strout, in her first month of separation. She spent most days at the beach with her two sons. Before ten o'clock one night Frank came home; he had driven to the hospital first, and he walked into the living room with stitches over his right eye and both lips bright and swollen.

"I'm all right," he said, when Matt and Ruth stood up, and Matt turned off the television, letting Ruth get to him first: the tall, muscled but slender suntanned boy. Frank tried to smile at them but couldn't because of his lips.

"It was her husband, wasn't it?" Ruth said. 35

"Ex," Frank said. "He dropped in."

Matt gently held Frank's jaw and turned his face to the light, looked at the stitches, the blood under the white of the eye, the bruised flesh.

"Press charges," Matt said.

"No."

"What's to stop him from doing it again? Did you hit him at all? Enough 40
so he won't want to next time?"

"I don't think I touched him."

"So what are you going to do?"

"Take karate," Frank said, and tried again to smile.

"That's not the problem," Ruth said.

"You know you like her," Frank said. 45

"I like a lot of people. What about the boys? Did they see it?"

"They were asleep."

"Did you leave her alone with him?"

"He left first. She was yelling at him. I believe she had a skillet in her
hand."

"Oh for God's sake," Ruth said. 50

Matt had been dealing with that too: at the dinner table on evenings when
Frank wasn't home, was eating with Mary Ann; or, on the other nights—and
Frank was with her every night—he talked with Ruth while they watched television, or lay in bed with the windows open and he smelled the night air and
imagined, with both pride and muted sorrow, Frank in Mary Ann's arms. Ruth
didn't like it because Mary Ann was in the process of divorce, because she had
two children, because she was four years older than Frank, and finally—she
told this in bed, where she had during all of their marriage told him of her
deepest feelings: of love, of passion, of fears about one of the children, of pain
Matt had caused her or she had caused him—she was against it because of
what she had heard: that the marriage had gone bad early, and for most of it
Richard and Mary Ann had both played around.

"That can't be true," Matt said. "Strout wouldn't have stood for it."

"Maybe he loves her."

"He's too hot-tempered. He couldn't have taken that."

But Matt knew Strout had taken it, for he had heard the stories too. He 55
wondered who had told them to Ruth; and he felt vaguely annoyed and
isolated: living with her for thirty-one years and still not knowing what she
talked about with her friends. On these summer nights he did not so much
argue with her as try to comfort her, but finally there was no difference between the two: she had concrete objections, which he tried to overcome. And in
his attempt to do this, he neglected his own objections, which were the same as
hers, so that as he spoke to her he felt as disembodied as he sometimes did in
the store when he helped a man choose a blouse or dress or piece of costume
jewelry for his wife.

"The divorce doesn't mean anything," he said. "She was young and maybe
she liked his looks and then after a while she realized she was living with a bastard. I see it as a positive thing."

"She's not divorced yet."

"It's the same thing. Massachusetts has crazy laws, that's all. Her age is no
problem. What's it matter when she was born? And that other business: even if
it's true, which it probably isn't, it's got nothing to do with Frank, and it's in
the past. And the kids are no problem. She's been married six years; she ought
to have kids. Frank likes them. He plays with them. And he's not going to
marry her anyway, so it's not a problem of money."

"Then what's he doing with her?"

"She probably loves him, Ruth. Girls always have. Why can't we just leave it   60
at that?"

"He got home at six o'clock Tuesday morning."

"I didn't know you knew. I've already talked to him about it."

Which he had: since he believed almost nothing he told Ruth, he went to
Frank with what he believed. The night before, he had followed Frank to the
car after dinner.

"You wouldn't make much of a burglar," he said.

"How's that?"   65

Matt was looking up at him; Frank was six feet tall, an inch and a half
taller than Matt, who had been proud when Frank at seventeen outgrew him;
he had only felt uncomfortable when he had to reprimand or caution him. He
touched Frank's bicep, thought of the young taut passionate body, believed he
could sense the desire, and again he felt the pride and sorrow and envy too, not
knowing whether he was envious of Frank or Mary Ann.

"When you came in yesterday morning, I woke up. One of these mornings
your mother will. And I'm the one who'll have to talk to her. She won't interfere with you. Okay? I know it means —" But he stopped, thinking: I know it
means getting up and leaving that suntanned girl and going sleepy to the car, I
know —

"Okay," Frank said, and touched Matt's shoulder and got into the car.

There had been other talks, but the only long one was their first one: a
night driving to Fenway Park, Matt having ordered the tickets so they could
talk, and knowing when Frank said yes, he would go, that he knew the talk was
coming too. It took them forty minutes to get to Boston, and they talked
about Mary Ann until they joined the city traffic along the Charles River, blue
in the late sun. Frank told him all the things that Matt would later pretend to
believe when he told them to Ruth.

"It seems like a lot for a young guy to take on," Matt finally said.   70

"Sometimes it is. But she's worth it."

"Are you thinking about getting married?"

"We haven't talked about it. She can't for over a year. I've got school."

"I *do* like her," Matt said.

He did. Some evenings, when the long summer sun was still low in the sky,   75
Frank brought her home; they came into the house smelling of suntan lotion
and the sea, and Matt gave them gin and tonics and started the charcoal in the
backyard, and looked at Mary Ann in the lawn chair: long and very light brown
hair (Matt thinking that twenty years ago she would have dyed it blonde), and
the long brown legs he loved to look at; her face was pretty; she had probably
never in her adult life gone unnoticed into a public place. It was in her wide
brown eyes that she looked older than Frank; after a few drinks Matt thought
what he saw in her eyes was something erotic, testament to the rumors about
her; but he knew it wasn't that, or all that: she had, very young, been through a
sort of pain that his children, and he and Ruth, had been spared. In the moments of his recognizing that pain, he wanted to tenderly touch her hair,
wanted with some gesture to give her solace and hope. And he would glance at
Frank, and hope they would love each other, hope Frank would soothe that
pain in her heart, take it from her eyes; and her divorce, her age, and her children did not matter at all. On the first two evenings she did not bring her boys,

and then Ruth asked her to bring them the next time. In bed that night Ruth said, "She hasn't brought them because she's embarrassed. She shouldn't feel embarrassed."

Richard Strout shot Frank in front of the boys. They were sitting on the living room floor watching television, Frank sitting on the couch, and Mary Ann just returning from the kitchen with a tray of sandwiches. Strout came in the front door and shot Frank twice in the chest and once in the face with a 9 mm automatic. Then he looked at the boys and Mary Ann, and went home to wait for the police.

It seemed to Matt that from the time Mary Ann called weeping to tell him until now, a Saturday night in September, sitting in the car with Willis, parked beside Strout's car, waiting for the bar to close, that he had not so much moved through his life as wandered through it, his spirit like a dazed body bumping into furniture and corners. He had always been a fearful father: when his children were young, at the start of each summer he thought of them drowning in a pond or the sea, and he was relieved when he came home in the evenings and they were there; usually that relief was his only acknowledgment of his fear, which he never spoke of, and which he controlled within his heart. As he had when they were very young and all of them in turn, Cathleen too, were drawn to the high oak in the backyard, and had to climb it. Smiling, he watched them, imagining the fall: and he was poised to catch the small body before it hit the earth. Or his legs were poised; his hands were in his pockets or his arms were folded and, for the child looking down, he appeared relaxed and confident while his heart beat with the two words he wanted to call out but did not: *Don't fall.* In winter he was less afraid: he made sure the ice would hold him before they skated, and he brought or sent them to places where they could sled without ending in the street. So he and his children had survived their childhood, and he only worried about them when he knew they were driving a long distance, and then he lost Frank in a way no father expected to lose his son, and he felt that all the fears he had borne while they were growing up, and all the grief he had been afraid of, had backed up like a huge wave and struck him on the beach and swept him out to sea. Each day he felt the same and when he was able to forget how he felt, when he was able to force himself not to feel that way, the eyes of his clerks and customers defeated him. He wished those eyes were oblivious, even cold; he felt he was withering in their tenderness. And beneath his listless wandering, every day in his soul he shot Richard Strout in the face; while Ruth, going about town on errands, kept seeing him. And at nights in bed she would hold Matt and cry, or sometimes she was silent and Matt would touch her tightening arm, her clenched fist.

As his own right fist was now, squeezing the butt of the revolver, the last of the drinkers having left the bar, talking to each other, going to their separate cars which were in the lot in front of the bar, out of Matt's vision. He heard their voices, their cars, and then the ocean again, across the street. The tide was in and sometimes it smacked the sea wall. Through the windshield he looked at the dark red side wall of the bar, and then to his left, past Willis, at Strout's car, and through its windows he could see the now-emptied parking lot, the road, the sea wall. He could smell the sea.

The front door of the bar opened and closed again and Willis looked at Matt then at the corner of the building; when Strout came around it alone Matt got out of the car, giving up the hope he had kept all night (and for the past week) that Strout would come out with friends, and Willis would simply drive away; thinking: *All right then. All right;* and he went around the front of Willis's car, and at Strout's he stopped and aimed over the hood at Strout's blue shirt ten feet away. Willis was aiming too, crouched on Matt's left, his elbow resting on the hood.

"Mr. Fowler," Strout said. He looked at each of them, and at the guns. 80 "Mr. Trottier."

Then Matt, watching the parking lot and the road, walked quickly between the car and the building and stood behind Strout. He took one leather glove from his pocket and put it on his left hand.

"Don't talk. Unlock the front and back and get in."

Strout unlocked the front door, reached in and unlocked the back, then got in, and Matt slid into the back seat, closed the door with his gloved hand, and touched Strout's head once with the muzzle.

"It's cocked. Drive to your house."

When Strout looked over his shoulder to back the car, Matt aimed at his 85 temple and did not look at his eyes.

"Drive slowly," he said. "Don't try to get stopped."

They drove across the empty front lot and onto the road, Willis's headlights shining into the car; then back through town, the sea wall on the left hiding the beach, though far out Matt could see the ocean; he uncocked the revolver; on the right were the places, most with their neon signs off, that did so much business in summer: the lounges and cafés and pizza houses, the street itself empty of traffic, the way he and Willis had known it would be when they decided to take Strout at the bar rather than knock on his door at two o'clock one morning and risk that one insomniac neighbor. Matt had not told Willis he was afraid he could not be alone with Strout for very long, smell his smells, feel the presence of his flesh, hear his voice, and then shoot him. They left the beach town and then were on the high bridge over the channel: to the left the smacking curling white at the breakwater and beyond that the dark sea and the full moon, and down to his right the small fishing boats bobbing at anchor in the cove. When they left the bridge, the sea was blocked by abandoned beach cottages, and Matt's left hand was sweating in the glove. Out here in the dark in the car he believed Ruth knew. Willis had come to his house at eleven and asked if he wanted a nightcap; Matt went to the bedroom for his wallet, put the gloves in one trouser pocket and the .38 in the other and went back to the living room, his hand in his pocket covering the bulge of the cool cylinder pressed against his fingers, the butt against his palm. When Ruth said good night she looked at his face, and he felt she could see in his eyes the gun, and the night he was going to. But he knew he couldn't trust what he saw. Willis's wife had taken her sleeping pill, which gave her eight hours — the reason, Willis had told Matt, he had the alarms installed, for nights when he was late at the restaurant — and when it was all done and Willis got home he would leave ice and a trace of Scotch and soda in two glasses in the game room and tell Martha in the morning that he had left the restaurant early and brought Matt home for a drink.

"He was making it with my wife." Strout's voice was careful, not pleading.

Matt pressed the muzzle against Strout's head, pressed it harder than he wanted to, feeling through the gun Strout's head flinching and moving forward; then he lowered the gun to his lap.

"Don't talk," he said. · 90

Strout did not speak again. They turned west, drove past the Dairy Queen closed until spring, and the two lobster restaurants that faced each other and were crowded all summer and were now also closed, onto the short bridge crossing the tidal stream, and over the engine Matt could hear through his open window the water rushing inland under the bridge; looking to his left he saw its swift moonlit current going back into the marsh which, leaving the bridge, they entered: the salt marsh stretching out on both sides, the grass tall in patches but mostly low and leaning earthward as though windblown, a large dark rock sitting as though it rested on nothing but itself, and shallow pools reflecting the bright moon.

Beyond the marsh they drove through woods, Matt thinking now of the hole he and Willis had dug last Sunday afternoon after telling their wives they were going to Fenway Park. They listened to the game on a transistor radio, but heard none of it as they dug into the soft earth on the knoll they had chosen because elms and maples sheltered it. Already some leaves had fallen. When the hole was deep enough they covered it and the piled earth with dead branches, then cleaned their shoes and pants and went to a restaurant farther up in New Hampshire where they ate sandwiches and drank beer and watched the rest of the game on television. Looking at the back of Strout's head he thought of Frank's grave; he had not been back to it; but he would go before winter, and its second burial of snow.

He thought of Frank sitting on the couch and perhaps talking to the children as they watched television, imagined him feeling young and strong, still warmed from the sun at the beach, and feeling loved, hearing Mary Ann moving about in the kitchen, hearing her walking into the living room; maybe he looked up at her and maybe she said something, looking at him over the tray of sandwiches, smiling at him, saying something the way women do when they offer food as a gift, then the front door opening and this son of a bitch coming in and Frank seeing that he meant the gun in his hand, this son of a bitch and his gun the last person and thing Frank saw on earth.

When they drove into town the streets were nearly empty: a few slow cars, a policeman walking his beat past the darkened fronts of stores. Strout and Matt both glanced at him as they drove by. They were on the main street, and all the stoplights were blinking yellow. Willis and Matt had talked about that too: the lights changed at midnight, so there would be no place Strout had to stop and where he might try to run. Strout turned down the block where he lived and Willis's headlights were no longer with Matt in the back seat. They had planned that too, had decided it was best for just the one car to go to the house, and again Matt had said nothing about his fear of being alone with Strout, especially in his house: a duplex, dark as all the houses on the street were, the street itself lit at the corner of each block. As Strout turned into the driveway Matt thought of the one insomniac neighbor, thought of some man or woman sitting alone in the dark living room, watching the all-night channel from Boston. When Strout stopped the car near the front of the house, Matt said: "Drive it to the back."

He touched Strout's head with the muzzle. 95

"You wouldn't have it cocked, would you? For when I put on the brakes."

Matt cocked it, and said: "It is now."

Strout waited a moment; then he eased the car forward, the engine doing little more than idling, and as they approached the garage he gently braked.

Matt opened the door, then took off the glove and put it in his pocket. He stepped out and shut the door with his hip and said: "All right."

Strout looked at the gun, then got out, and Matt followed him across the grass, and as Strout unlocked the door Matt looked quickly at the row of small backyards on either side, and scattered tall trees, some evergreens, others not, and he thought of the red and yellow leaves on the trees over the hole, saw them falling soon, probably in two weeks, dropping slowly, covering. Strout stepped into the kitchen.

"Turn on the light."   100

Strout reached to the wall switch, and in the light Matt looked at his wide back, the dark blue shirt, the white belt, the red plaid pants.

"Where's your suitcase?"

"My suitcase?"

"Where is it?"

"In the bedroom closet."   105

"That's where we're going then. When we get to a door you stop and turn on the light."

They crossed the kitchen, Matt glancing at the sink and stove and refrigerator: no dishes in the sink or even the dish rack beside it, no grease splashings on the stove, the refrigerator door clean and white. He did not want to look at any more but he looked quickly at all he could see: in the living room magazines and newspapers in a wicker basket, clean ashtrays, a record player, the records shelved next to it, then down the hall where, near the bedroom door, hung a color photograph of Mary Ann and the two boys sitting on a lawn—there was no house in the picture—Mary Ann smiling at the camera or Strout or whoever held the camera, smiling as she had on Matt's lawn this summer while he waited for the charcoal and they all talked and he looked at her brown legs and at Frank touching her arm, her shoulder, her hair; he moved down the hall with her smile in his mind, wondering: was that when they were both playing around and she was smiling like that at him and they were happy, even sometimes, making it worth it? He recalled her eyes, the pain in them, and he was conscious of the circles of love he was touching with the hand that held the revolver so tightly now as Strout stopped at the door at the end of the hall.

"There's no wall switch."

"Where's the light?"

"By the bed."   110

"Let's go."

Matt stayed a pace behind, then Strout leaned over and the room was lighted: the bed, a double one, was neatly made; the ashtray on the bedside table clean, the bureau top dustless, and no photographs; probably so the girl—who *was* she?—would not have to see Mary Ann in the bedroom she believed was theirs. But because Matt was a father and a husband, though never an ex-husband, he knew (and did not want to know) that this bedroom had never been theirs alone. Strout turned around; Matt looked at his lips, his wide jaw, and thought of Frank's doomed and fearful eyes looking up from the couch.

"Where's Mr. Trottier?"

"He's waiting. Pack clothes for warm weather."

"What's going on?"   115

"You're jumping bail."

"Mr. Fowler—"

He pointed the cocked revolver at Strout's face. The barrel trembled but not much, not as much as he had expected. Strout went to the closet and got the suitcase from the floor and opened it on the bed. As he went to the bureau, he said: "He was making it with my wife. I'd go pick up my kids and he'd be there. Sometimes he spent the night. My boys told me."

He did not look at Matt as he spoke. He opened the top drawer and Matt stepped closer so he could see Strout's hands: underwear and socks, the socks rolled, the underwear folded and stacked. He took them back to the bed, arranged them neatly in the suitcase, then from the closet he was taking shirts and trousers and a jacket; he laid them on the bed and Matt followed him to the bathroom and watched from the door while he packed those things a person accumulated and that became part of him so that at times in the store Matt felt he was selling more than clothes.

"I wanted to try to get together with her again." He was bent over the suit-case. "I couldn't even talk to her. He was always with her. I'm going to jail for it; if I ever get out I'll be an old man. Isn't that enough?"   120

"You're not going to jail."

Strout closed the suitcase and faced Matt, looking at the gun. Matt went to his rear, so Strout was between him and the lighted hall; then using his handkerchief he turned off the lamp and said: "Let's go."

They went down the hall, Matt looking again at the photograph, and through the living room and kitchen, Matt turning off the lights and talking, frightened that he was talking, that he was telling this lie he had not planned: "It's the trial. We can't go through that, my wife and me. So you're leaving. We've got you a ticket, and a job. A friend of Mr. Trottier's. Out west. My wife keeps seeing you. We can't have that anymore."

Matt turned out the kitchen light and put the handkerchief in his pocket, and they went down the two brick steps and across the lawn. Strout put the suitcase on the floor of the back seat, then got into the front seat and Matt got in the back and put on his glove and shut the door.

"They'll catch me. They'll check passenger lists."   125

"We didn't use your name."

"They'll figure that out too. You think I wouldn't have done it myself if it was that easy?"

He backed into the street, Matt looking down the gun barrel but not at the profiled face beyond it.

"You were alone," Matt said. "We've got it worked out."

"There's no planes this time of night, Mr. Fowler."   130

"Go back through town. Then north on 125."

They came to the corner and turned, and now Willis's headlights were in the car with Matt.

"Why north, Mr. Fowler?"

"Somebody's going to keep you for a while. They'll take you to the airport." He uncocked the hammer and lowered the revolver to his lap and said wearily: "No more talking."

As they drove back through town, Matt's body sagged, going limp with his   135
spirit and its new and false bond with Strout, the hope his lie had given Strout. He had grown up in this town whose streets had become places of apprehension and pain for Ruth as she drove and walked, doing what she had to do; and for him too, if only in his mind as he worked and chatted six days a week in his store; he wondered now if his lie would have worked, if sending Strout away

would have been enough; but then he knew that just thinking of Strout in Montana or whatever place lay at the end of the lie he had told, thinking of him walking the streets there, loving a girl there (who *was* she?) would be enough to slowly rot the rest of his days. And Ruth's. Again he was certain that she knew, that she was waiting for him.

They were in New Hampshire now, on the narrow highway, passing the shopping center at the state line, and then houses and small stores and sandwich shops. There were few cars on the road. After ten minutes he raised his trembling hand, touched Strout's neck with the gun, and said: "Turn in up here. At the dirt road."

Strout flicked on the indicator and slowed.

"Mr. Fowler?"

"They're waiting here."

Strout turned very slowly, easing his neck away from the gun. In the moon- 140 light the road was light brown, lighter and yellowed where the headlights shone; weeds and a few trees grew on either side of it, and ahead of them were the woods.

"There's nothing back here, Mr. Fowler."

"It's for your car. You don't think we'd leave it at the airport, do you?"

He watched Strout's large, big-knuckled hands tighten on the wheel, saw Frank's face that night: not the stitches and bruised eye and swollen lips, but his own hand gently touching Frank's jaw, turning his wounds to the light. They rounded a bend in the road and were out of sight of the highway: tall trees all around them now, hiding the moon. When they reached the abandoned gravel pit on the left, the bare flat earth and steep pale embankment behind it, and the black crowns of trees at its top, Matt said: "Stop here."

Strout stopped but did not turn off the engine. Matt pressed the gun hard against his neck, and he straightened in the seat and looked in the rearview mirror, Matt's eyes meeting his in the glass for an instant before looking at the hair at the end of the gun barrel.

"Turn it off." 145

Strout did, then held the wheel with two hands, and looked in the mirror.

"I'll do twenty years, Mr. Fowler; at least. I'll be forty-six years old."

"That's nine years younger than I am," Matt said, and got out and took off the glove and kicked the door shut. He aimed at Strout's ear and pulled back the hammer. Willis's headlights were off and Matt heard him walking on the soft thin layer of dust, the hard earth beneath it. Strout opened the door, sat for a moment in the interior light, then stepped out onto the road. Now his face was pleading. Matt did not look at his eyes, but he could see it in the lips.

"Just get the suitcase. They're right up the road."

Willis was beside him now, to his left. Strout looked at both guns. Then he 150 opened the back door, leaned in, and with a jerk brought the suitcase out. He was turning to face them when Matt said: "Just walk up the road. Just ahead."

Strout turned to walk, the suitcase in his right hand, and Matt and Willis followed; as Strout cleared the front of his car he dropped the suitcase and, ducking, took one step that was the beginning of a sprint to his right. The gun kicked in Matt's hand, and the explosion of the shot surrounded him, isolated him in a nimbus of sound that cut him off from all his time, all his history, isolated him standing absolutely still on the dirt road with the gun in his hand, looking down at Richard Strout squirming on his belly, kicking one leg behind him, pushing himself forward, toward the woods. Then Matt went to him and shot him once in the back of the head.

Driving south to Boston, wearing both gloves now, staying in the middle lane and looking often in the rearview mirror at Willis's headlights, he relived the suitcase dropping, the quick dip and turn of Strout's back, and the kick of the gun, the sound of the shot. When he walked to Strout, he still existed within the first shot, still trembled and breathed with it. The second shot and the burial seemed to be happening to someone else, someone he was watching. He and Willis each held an arm and pulled Strout face-down off the road and into the woods, his bouncing sliding belt white under the trees where it was so dark that when they stopped at the top of the knoll, panting and sweating, Matt could not see where Strout's blue shirt ended and the earth began. They pulled off the branches then dragged Strout to the edge of the hole and went behind him and lifted his legs and pushed him in. They stood still for a moment. The woods were quiet save for their breathing, and Matt remembered hearing the movements of birds and small animals after the first shot. Or maybe he had not heard them. Willis went down to the road. Matt could see him clearly out on the tan dirt, could see the glint of Strout's car and, beyond the road, the gravel pit. Willis came back up the knoll with the suitcase. He dropped it in the hole and took off his gloves and they went down to his car for the spades. They worked quietly. Sometimes they paused to listen to the woods. When they were finished Willis turned on his flashlight and they covered the earth with leaves and branches and then went down to the spot in front of the car, and while Matt held the light Willis crouched and sprinkled dust on the blood, backing up till he reached the grass and leaves, then he used leaves until they had worked up to the grave again. They did not stop. They walked around the grave and through the woods, using the light on the ground, looking up through the trees to where they ended at the lake. Neither of them spoke above the sounds of their heavy and clumsy strides through low brush and over fallen branches. Then they reached it: wide and dark, lapping softly at the bank, pine needles smooth under Matt's feet, moonlight on the lake, a small island near its middle, with black, tall evergreens. He took out the gun and threw for the island: taking two steps back on the pine needles, striding with the throw and going to one knee as he followed through, looking up to see the dark shapeless object arcing downward, splashing.

They left Strout's car in Boston, in front of an apartment building on Commonwealth Avenue. When they got back to town Willis drove slowly over the bridge and Matt threw the keys into the Merrimack. The sky was turning light. Willis let him out a block from his house, and walking home he listened for sounds from the houses he passed. They were quiet. A light was on in his living room. He turned it off and undressed in there, and went softly toward the bedroom; in the hall he smelled the smoke, and he stood in the bedroom doorway and looked at the orange of her cigarette in the dark. The curtains were closed. He went to the closet and put his shoes on the floor and felt for a hanger.

"Did you do it?" she said.

He went down the hall to the bathroom and in the dark he washed his hands and face. Then he went to her, lay on his back, and pulled the sheet up to his throat.

"Are you all right?" she said.

"I think so."

Now she touched him, lying on her side, her hand on his belly, his thigh.

"Tell me," she said.

He started from the beginning, in the parking lot at the bar; but soon with   160
his eyes closed and Ruth petting him, he spoke of Strout's house: the order,
the woman presence, the picture on the wall.

"The way she was smiling," he said.

"What about it?"

"I don't know. Did you ever see Strout's girl? When you saw him in town?"

"No."

"I wonder who she was."   165

Then he thought: *not was: is. Sleeping now she is his girl.* He opened his eyes,
then closed them again. There was more light beyond the curtains. With Ruth
now he left Strout's house and told again his lie to Strout, gave him again that
hope that Strout must have for a while believed, else he would have to believe
only the gun pointed at him for the last two hours of his life. And with Ruth he
saw again the dropping suitcase, the darting move to the right: and he told of
the first shot, feeling her hand on him but his heart isolated still, beating on
the road still in that explosion like thunder. He told her the rest, but the words
had no images for him, he did not see himself doing what the words said he
had done; he only saw himself on that road.

"We can't tell the other kids," she said. "It'll hurt them, thinking he got
away. But we mustn't."

"No."

She was holding him, wanting him, and he wished he could make love
with her but he could not. He saw Frank and Mary Ann making love in her
bed, their eyes closed, their bodies brown and smelling of the sea; the other girl
was faceless, bodiless, but he felt her sleeping now; and he saw Frank and
Strout, their faces alive; he saw red and yellow leaves falling on the earth, then
snow: falling and freezing and falling; and holding Ruth, his cheek touching
her breast, he shuddered with a sob that he kept silent in his heart.

CONSIDERATIONS FOR CRITICAL THINKING AND WRITING

1. **FIRST RESPONSE.** How do you feel about Matt's act of revenge? Trace the
   emotions his character produces in you as the plot unfolds.

2. Discuss the significance of the title. Why is "Killings" a more appropriate
   title than "Killers"?

3. What are the effects of Dubus's ordering of events in the story? How
   would the effects be different if the story were told in a chronological
   order?

4. Describe the Fowler family before Frank's murder. How does the murder
   affect Matt?

5. What is learned about Richard from the flashback in paragraphs 32
   through 75? How does this information affect your attitude toward him?

6. What is the effect of the description of Richard shooting Frank in paragraph 76?

7. How well planned is Matt's revenge? Why does he lie to Richard about
   sending him out west?

8. Describe Matt at the end of the story when he tells his wife about the
   killing. How do you think this revenge killing will affect the Fowler
   family?

9. How might "Killings" be considered a love story as well as a murder story?

10. **CRITICAL STRATEGIES.** Read the section on psychological criticism (pp. 2050–52) in Chapter 53, "Critical Strategies for Reading." How do the details of the killing and the disposal of Richard's body reveal Matt's emotions? What is he thinking and feeling as he performs these actions? How did you feel as you read about them?

CONNECTIONS TO OTHER SELECTIONS

1. Compare and contrast Matt's motivation for murder with Emily's in "A Rose for Emily." Which character made you feel more empathy and sympathy for his or her actions? Why?

2. Explore the father-son relationships in "Killings" and William Faulkner's "Barn Burning" (p. 503). Read the section on psychological criticism in Chapter 53, "Critical Strategies for Reading." How do you think a psychological critic would interpret these relationships in each story?

Perspective

A. L. BADER (B. 1902)

Nothing Happens in Modern Short Stories   1945

Any teacher who has ever confronted a class with representative modern short stories will remember the disappointment, the puzzled "so-what" attitude, of certain members of the group. "Nothing happens in some of these stories," "They just end," or "They're not real stories" are frequent criticisms. . . . Sometimes the phrase "Nothing happens" seems to mean that nothing significant happens, but in a great many cases it means that the modern short story is charged with a lack of narrative structure. Readers and critics accustomed to an older type of story are baffled by a newer type. They sense the underlying and unifying design of the one, but they find nothing equivalent to it in the other. Hence they maintain that the modern short story is plotless, static, fragmentary, amorphous — frequently a mere character sketch or vignette, or a mere reporting of a transient moment, or the capturing of a mood or nuance — everything, in fact, except a story.

From "The Structure of the Modern Story" in *College English*

CONSIDERATIONS FOR CRITICAL THINKING AND WRITING

1. What is the basic objection to the "newer type" of short story? How does it differ from the "older type"?

2. Consider any one of the stories from Chapter 18, "An Album of Contemporary Stories" (pp. 631–66), as an example of the newer type. Does anything "happen" in the story? How does it differ from the excerpt from Edgar Rice Burroughs's *Tarzan of the Apes* (p. 75)?

Web Research the authors in this chapter or take quizzes on their works at bedfordstmartins.com/ meyerlit.

3. Read a recent story published in *The New Yorker* or the *Atlantic Monthly* and compare its narrative structure with that of Faulkner's "A Rose for Emily" (p. 91).

ENCOUNTERING FICTION:
COMICS AND GRAPHIC STORIES

EDWARD GOREY (1925–2000), From *The Hapless Child*

Born in Chicago, Edward Gorey read *Dracula, Alice in Wonderland, Frankenstein,* and the works of Victor Hugo by the time he was eight. After one semester at the Art Institute of Chicago (his only formal art training), Gorey was drafted for a three-year stint in the army as a wartime clerk. He went on to study French literature at Harvard, where he roomed with the poet Frank O'Hara, and then worked as illustrator and designer for Doubleday Anchor Books. Since his first book in 1953 *(The Unstrung Harp),* Gorey published nearly one hundred illustrated books and designed sets for theatrical productions. He is best known for *The Gashlycrumb Tinies* (1963), a cautionary alphabet of 26 doomed children ("A is for Amy who fell down the stairs...."). Gorey's works have been described as "macabre, yet delicate; grim but amusing; ghoulish without a drop of blood." Following are excerpts from *The Hapless Child* (1961), a satire of the nineteenth-century gothic novel. In the story, an innocent orphan is unjustly tormented before meeting her tragic demise, ironically under the wheels of a carriage driven by her supposedly dead father. Gorey, who disliked "exhaustive writers" who left nothing for the reader's imagination, preferred to leave his own readers with unanswered questions. He once commented: "[S]ince I leave out most of the connections and very little is pinned down, I feel that I'm doing the minimum damage to other possibilities that might arise in a reader's mind."

THE HAPLESS CHILD

There was once a little girl named Charlotte Sophia.

One day her father, a colonel in the army, was ordered to Africa.

Several months later he was reported killed in a native uprising.

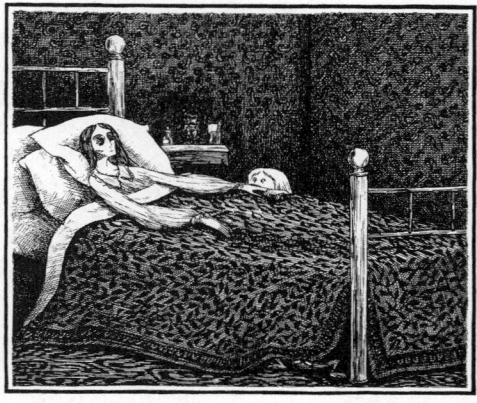

Her mother fell into a decline that proved fatal.

Charlotte Sophia was left in the hands of
the family lawyer.

He at once put her into a boarding-school.

There she was punished by the teachers for things
she hadn't done.

During the day Charlotte Sophia hid as much as possible.

At night she lay awake weeping and weeping.

When she could bear it no longer she fled from the
school at dawn.

CONSIDERATIONS AND CONNECTION TO ANOTHER SELECTION

1. Discuss the use of light and dark in the drawings. How are these shadings related to the plot?
2. Compare the style of the printed letters in Gorey's drawings and in Barry's "Spelling" (p. 183). How is the lettering related to the style and tone of each story?
3. Does this story have a happy ending? Why or why not?
4. Compare the themes in "The Hapless Child" and in "Eleven" by Sandra Cisneros (p. 609).

4

Character

When I find a well-drawn character in fiction or biography, I generally take a warm personal interest in him, for the reason that I have known him before — met him on the river.

— MARK TWAIN

Character is essential to plot. Without characters Burroughs's *Tarzan of the Apes* would be a travelogue through the jungle and Faulkner's "A Rose for Emily" little more than a faded history of a sleepy town in the South. If stories were depopulated, the plots would disappear because characters and plots are interrelated. A dangerous jungle is important only because we care what effect it has on a character. Characters are influenced by events just as events are shaped by characters. Tarzan's physical strength is the result of his growing up in the jungle, and his strength, along with his inherited intelligence, allows him to be master there.

The methods by which a writer creates people in a story so that they seem actually to exist are called *characterization*. Huck Finn never lived, yet those who have read Mark Twain's novel about his adventures along the Mississippi River feel as if they know him. A good writer gives us the illusion that a character is real, but we should also remember that a character is not an actual person but instead has been created by the author. Though we might walk out of a room in which Huck Finn's Pap talks racist nonsense, we would not throw away the book in a similar fit of anger. This illusion of reality is the magic that allows us to move beyond the circumstances of our own lives into a writer's fictional world, where we can encounter everyone from royalty to paupers, murderers, lovers, cheaters, martyrs, artists, destroyers, and, nearly always, some part of ourselves. The life that a writer breathes into a character adds to our own experiences and enlarges our view of the world.

🖱️ Web Explore the literary element in this chapter at bedfordstmartins.com/ meyerlit.

A character is usually but not always a person. In Jack London's *Call of the Wild*, the protagonist is a devoted sled dog; in Herman Melville's *Moby-Dick*, the antagonist is an unfathomable whale. Perhaps the only possible qualification to be placed on character is that whatever it is — whether an animal or even an inanimate object, such as a robot — it must have some recognizable human qualities. The action of the plot interests us primarily because we care about what happens to people and what they do. We may identify with a character's desires and aspirations, or we may be disgusted by his or her viciousness and selfishness. To understand our response to a story, we should be able to recognize the methods of characterization the author uses.

CHARLES DICKENS (1812–1870)

Charles Dickens is well known for creating characters who have stepped off the pages of his fictions into the imaginations and memories of his readers. His characters are successful not because readers might have encountered such people in their own lives, but because his characterizations are vivid and convincing. He manages to make strange and eccentric people appear familiar. The following excerpt from *Hard Times* is the novel's entire first chapter. In it Dickens introduces and characterizes a school principal addressing a classroom full of children.

© National Portrait Gallery, London.

From **Hard Times**   *1854*

"Now, what I want is, Facts. Teach these boys and girls nothing but Facts. Facts alone are wanted in life. Plant nothing else, and root out everything else. You can only form the minds of reasoning animals upon Facts: nothing else will ever be of any service to them. This is the principle on which I bring up my own children, and this is the principle on which I bring up these children. Stick to Facts, sir!"

The scene was a plain, bare, monotonous vault of a schoolroom, and the speaker's square forefinger emphasized his observations by underscoring every sentence with a line on the schoolmaster's sleeve. The emphasis was helped by the speaker's square wall of a forehead, which had his eyebrows for its base, while his eyes found commodious cellarage in two dark caves, overshadowed by the wall. The emphasis was helped by the speaker's mouth, which was wide, thin, and hard set. The emphasis was helped by the speaker's voice, which was inflexible, dry, and dictatorial. The emphasis was helped by the speaker's hair, which bristled on the skirts of his bald head, a plantation of firs to keep the wind from its shining surface, all covered with knobs, like the crust of a plum pie, as if the head had scarcely warehouse-room for the hard facts stored inside. The speaker's obstinate carriage, square coat, square legs, square shoulders — nay, his very neckcloth, trained to take him by the throat with an unaccommodating grasp, like a stubborn fact, as it was — all helped the emphasis.

"In this life, we want nothing but Facts, sir; nothing but Facts!"

The speaker, and the schoolmaster, and the third grown person present, all backed a little, and swept with their eyes the inclined plane of little vessels then and there arranged in order, ready to have imperial gallons of facts poured into them until they were full to the brim.

Dickens withholds his character's name until the beginning of the second chapter; he calls this fact-bound educator Mr. Gradgrind. Authors sometimes put as much time and effort into naming their characters as parents invest in naming their children. Names can be used to indicate qualities that the writer associates with the characters. Mr. Gradgrind is precisely what his name suggests. The "schoolmaster" employed by Gradgrind is Mr. M'Choakumchild. Pronounce this name aloud and you have the essence of this teacher's educational philosophy. In Nathaniel Hawthorne's *The Scarlet Letter,* Chillingworth is cold and relentless in his single-minded quest for revenge. The innocent and youthful protagonist in Herman Melville's *Billy Budd* is nipped in the bud by the evil Claggart, whose name simply sounds unpleasant.

Names are also used in films to suggest a character's nature. One example that is destined to be a classic is the infamous villain Darth Vader, whose name identifies his role as an invader allied with the dark and death. On the heroic side, it makes sense that Marion Morrison decided to change his box-office name to John Wayne in order to play tough, masculine roles because both the first and last of his chosen names are unambiguously male and to the point, while his given name is androgynous. There may also be some significance to the lack of a specific identity. In Godwin's "A Sorrowful Woman" (p. 39) the woman, man, boy, and girl are reduced to a set of domestic functions, and their not being named emphasizes their roles as opposed to their individual identities. Of course, not every name is suggestive of the qualities a character may embody, but it is frequently worth determining what is in a name.

The only way to tell whether a name reveals character is to look at the other information the author supplies about the character. We evaluate fictional characters in much the same way we understand people in our own lives. By piecing together bits of information, we create a context that allows us to interpret their behavior. We can predict, for instance, that an acquaintance who is a chronic complainer is not likely to have anything good to say about a roommate. We interpret words and actions in the light of what we already know about someone, and that is why keeping track of what characters say (and how they say it) along with what they do (and don't do) is important.

Authors reveal characters by other means too. Physical descriptions can indicate important inner qualities; disheveled clothing, a crafty smile, or a blush might communicate as much as or more than what a character says. Characters can also be revealed by the words and actions of others who respond to them. In literature, moreover, we have one great advantage that life cannot offer; a work of fiction can give us access to a person's thoughts. Although in Herman Melville's "Bartleby, the Scrivener" (p. 142) we learn about Bartleby primarily through descriptive details, words, actions, and his relationships with the other characters, Melville allows us to enter the lawyer's consciousness.

Authors have two major methods of presenting characters: ***showing*** and ***telling.*** Characters shown in dramatic situations reveal themselves indirectly by what they say and do. In the first paragraph of the excerpt from *Hard Times,* Dickens shows us some of Gradgrind's utilitarian educational principles by having him speak. We can infer the kind of person he is from his reference to boys and girls as "reasoning animals," but we are not told what to think of him until the second paragraph. It would be impossible to admire Gradgrind after reading the physical description of him and the school that he oversees. The adjectives in the second paragraph make the author's evaluation of Gradgrind's values and personality clear: everything about him is rigidly "square"; his mouth is "thin, and hard set"; his voice is "inflexible, dry, and dictatorial"; and he presides over a "plain, bare, monotonous vault of a schoolroom." Dickens directly lets us know how to feel about Gradgrind, but he does so artistically. Instead of simply being presented with a statement that Gradgrind is destructively practical, we get a detailed and amusing description.

We can contrast Dickens's direct presentation in this paragraph with the indirect showing that Gail Godwin uses in "A Sorrowful Woman." Godwin avoids telling us how we should think about the characters. Their story includes little description and no evaluations or interpretations by the author. To determine the significance of the events, the reader must pay close attention to what the characters say and do. Like Godwin, many twentieth-century authors favor showing over telling because showing allows readers to discover the meanings, which modern authors are often reluctant to impose on an audience for whom fixed meanings and values are not as strong as they once were. However, most writers continue to reveal characters by telling as well as showing when the technique suits their purposes — when, for example, a minor character must be sketched economically or when a long time has elapsed, causing changes in a major character. Telling and showing complement each other.

Characters can be convincing whether they are presented by telling or showing, provided their actions are *__motivated.__* There must be reasons for how they behave and what they say. If adequate motivation is offered, we can understand and find *__plausible__* their actions no matter how bizarre. In "A Rose for Emily" (p. 91), Faulkner makes Emily Grierson's intimacy with a corpse credible by preparing us with information about her father's death along with her inability to leave the past and live in the present. Emily turns out to be **consistent.** Although we are surprised by the ending of the story, the behavior it reveals is compatible with her temperament.

Some kinds of fiction consciously break away from our expectations of traditional realistic stories. Consistency, plausibility, and motivation are not very useful concepts for understanding and evaluating characterizations in modern *absurdist literature,* for instance, in which characters are often alienated from themselves and their environment in an irrational world. In this world there is no possibility for traditional heroic action; instead we find an *__antihero__* who has little control over events. Yossarian from Joseph Heller's *Catch-22* is an example of a protagonist who is thwarted by the absurd terms on which life offers itself to many twentieth-century characters.

In most stories we expect characters to act plausibly and in ways consistent with their personalities, but that does not mean that characters cannot develop and change. A *dynamic* character undergoes some kind of change because of the action of the plot. Huck Finn's view of Jim, the runaway slave in Mark Twain's novel, develops during their experiences on the raft. Huck discovers Jim's humanity and, therefore, cannot betray him because Huck no longer sees his companion as merely the property of a white owner. On the other hand, Huck's friend, Tom Sawyer, is a *__static__* character because he does not change. He remains interested only in high adventure, even at the risk of Jim's life. As static characters often do, Tom serves as a foil to Huck; his frivolous concerns are contrasted with Huck's serious development. A *__foil__* helps to reveal by contrast the distinctive qualities of another character.

The protagonist in a story is usually a dynamic character who experiences some conflict that makes an impact on his or her life. Less commonly, static characters can also be protagonists. Rip Van Winkle wakes up from his twenty-year sleep in Washington Irving's story to discover his family dramatically changed and his country no longer a British colony, but none of these important events has an impact on his character; he continues to be the same shiftless and idle man that he was before he fell asleep. The protagonist in Faulkner's "A Rose for Emily" is also a static character; indeed, she rejects all change. Our understanding of her changes, but she does not. Ordinarily, however, a plot contains one or two dynamic characters with any number of static characters in supporting roles. This is especially true of short stories, in which brevity limits the possibilities of character development.

The extent to which a character is developed is another means by which character can be analyzed. The novelist E. M. Forster coined the terms *flat* and *round* to distinguish degrees of character development. A **flat character** embodies one or two qualities, ideas, or traits that can be readily described in a brief summary. For instance, Mr. M'Choakumchild in Dickens's *Hard Times* stifles students instead of encouraging them to grow. Flat characters tend to be one-dimensional. They are readily accessible because their characteristics are few and simple; they are not created to be psychologically complex.

Some flat characters are immediately recognizable as **stock characters.** These stereotypes are particularly popular in formula fiction, television programs, and action movies. Stock characters are types rather than individuals. The poor but dedicated writer falls in love with a hard-working understudy, who gets nowhere because the corrupt producer favors his boozy, pampered mistress for the leading role. Characters such as these — the loyal servant, the mean stepfather, the henpecked husband, the dumb blonde, the sadistic army officer, the dotty grandmother — are prepackaged; they lack individuality because their authors have, in a sense, not imaginatively created them but simply summoned them from a warehouse of clichés and social prejudices. Stock characters can become fresh if a good writer makes them vivid, interesting, or memorable, but too often a writer's use of these stereotypes is simply weak characterization.

Round characters are more complex than flat or stock characters. Round characters have more depth and require more attention. They may surprise us or puzzle us. Although they are more fully developed, round characters are also more difficult to summarize because we are aware of competing ideas, values, and possibilities in their lives. As a flat character, Huck Finn's alcoholic, bigoted father is clear to us; we know that Pap is the embodiment of racism and irrationality. But Huck is considerably less predictable because he struggles with what Twain calls a "sound heart and a deformed conscience."

In making distinctions between flat and round characters, you must understand that an author's use of a flat character — even as a protagonist — does not necessarily represent an artistic flaw. Moreover, both flat and round characters can be either dynamic or static. Each plot can be made most effective by its own special kind of characterization. Terms such as *round* and *flat* are helpful tools to use to determine what we know about a character, but they are not an infallible measurement of the quality of a story.

The next three stories — May-lee Chai's "Saving Sourdi," Herman Melville's "Bartleby, the Scrivener," and Junot Díaz's "Fiesta, 1980" — offer character studies worthy of close analysis. As you read them, notice the methods of characterization used to bring each to life.

A SAMPLE STUDENT RESPONSE

Crispin Shea

Professor Atwood

English 102

January 20, 2010

Character Development in Dickens's *Hard Times*

In the first chapter of *Hard Times*, by Charles Dickens, the speaker, or focal character, develops slowly and is brought to life through dialogue and description. We understand him as a character not only through what he says, but through how he says it. Learning, to him, means nothing more than absorbing facts; there is no discussion, no debate. Facts are given to the students, "poured into them until they were filled to the brim," and the children must take every word as truth (123). Understanding the speaker's view on learning helps us to understand the man himself, and he quickly becomes a fully developed character: a person hard-nosed and unyielding, with little interest in middle ground.

After the character speaks, Dickens gives us a physical description to reinforce our initial opinion of the speaker. He is described as having a "square wall of a forehead," and eyes that find "commodious cellarage in two dark caves" (123). His mouth is "thin, and hard set" (123). Dickens's description emphasizes the character's rigidity. He portrays the speaker as someone who is callous and difficult. This does not mean, however, that all characters with harsh physical features are unpleasant or villainous (just as attractive characters are not always pleasant). Certainly Dickens could have focused on the speaker's best traits, physical or otherwise, and created a more endearing character. Instead, he focuses on what he wants us to read as the true essence of this particular person, using physical details to "indicate [the character's] important inner qualities" (Meyer 124). . . .

Shea 6

Works Cited

Dickens, Charles. "From *Hard Times*." *The Bedford Introduction to Literature*.
Ed. Michael Meyer. 9th ed. Boston: Bedford/St. Martin's, 2011.
122–23. Print.

Meyer, Michael, ed. *The Bedford Introduction to Literature*. 9th ed. Boston:
Bedford/St. Martin's, 2011. 124. Print.

MAY-LEE CHAI

Courtesy of Jason Doiy.

May-lee Chai, the first of her family to be born in the United States, is a San Francisco author and graduate of Yale University. Chai has worked as a reporter for the Associated Press and taught creative writing at San Francisco State University, the University of Wyoming, and Amherst College. She is the author of *My Lucky Face* (2001), a novel about a woman's marriage in contemporary China; *Glamorous Asians: Short Stories and Essays* (2004); and co-author, with her father, Winberg Chai, of *The Girl from Purple Mountain* (2002), a family memoir about her grandparents' journey from China to America. *Hapa Girl: A Memoir* (2007) describes the bigotry her family encounters in rural South Dakota.

Saving Sourdi 2001

Once, when my older sister, Sourdi, and I were working alone in our family's restaurant, just the two of us and the elderly cook, some men got drunk and I stabbed one of them. I was eleven.

I don't remember where Ma had gone that night. But I remember we were tired and it was late. We were one of the only restaurants that stayed open past nine in those days. The men had been growing louder, until they were our only customers, and, finally, one of them staggered up and put his arm across Sourdi's shoulders. He called her his "China doll," and his friends hooted at this.

Sourdi looked distressed and tried to remove his arm, but he held her tighter. She said, "Please," in her incense-sweet voice, and he smiled and said, "Say it again nice and I might just have to give you a kiss."

That summer we'd just moved to South Dakota. After all the crummy jobs Ma had had to take in Texas, where we'd first come to the U.S., where our sponsors lived, we were so proud to be working in our own restaurant. When we moved to South Dakota, I thought we'd find the real America, the one where we were supposed to be, not the hot sweaty America where we lived packed together in an apartment with bars on the windows on a street where angry boys in cars played loud music and shot guns at each other in the night. The summer we moved to join my uncle's family to run the Silver Palace, I was certain we would at last find the life we deserved.

Now I was panicked. I wanted Ma to be there. Ma would know what to 5 do. She always did. I stood there, chewing my nails, wishing I could make them go away. The men's voices were so loud in my ears, I was drowning in the sound.

I ran into the kitchen. I had this idea to get the cook and the cleaver, but the first thing that caught my eye was this little paring knife on the counter next to a bowl of oranges. I grabbed the knife and ran back out to Sourdi.

"Get away from my sister!" I shouted, waving the paring knife.

The men were silent for about three seconds, then they burst into laughter.

I charged and stabbed the man in the sleeve.

In a movie or a television show this kind of scene always unfolds in slow 10 motion, but everything happened so fast. I stabbed the man, Sourdi jumped free, Ma came rushing in the front door waving her arms. "Omigod! What happen?"

"Jesus Christ!" The man shook his arm as though it were on fire, but the paring knife was stuck in the fabric of his jeans jacket.

I thought Ma would take care of everything now. And I was right, she did, but not the way I had imagined. She started apologizing to the man, and she helped him take off his jacket. She made Sourdi get the first-aid kit from the bathroom, "Quick! Quick!" Ma even tried to put some ointment on his cut, but he just shrugged her off.

I couldn't believe it. I wanted to take the knife back and stab myself. That's how I felt when I heard her say, "No charge, on the house," for their dinner, despite the $50-worth of pitchers they'd had.

Ma grabbed me by the shoulders. "Say you sorry. Say it." I pressed my lips firmly together and hung my head. Then she slapped me.

I didn't start crying until after the men had left. "But, Ma," I said, "he was 15 hurting Sourdi!"

"Then why Sourdi not do something?" Ma twisted my ear. "You not thinking. That your problem. You always not think!"

Afterwards, Sourdi said I was lucky. The knife had only grazed the man's skin. They could have sued us. They could have pressed charges.

"I don't care!" I hissed then. "I shoulda killed him! I shoulda killed that sucker!"

Sourdi's face changed. I'd never seen my sister look like that. Not ever. Especially not at me. I was her favorite. But she looked then the way I felt inside. Like a big bomb was ticking behind her eyes.

We were sitting together in the bathroom. It was late at night, and every- 20
one else was asleep. Sometimes we locked ourselves in the bathroom then, just
the two of us, so we could talk about things like boys at school or who was the
cutest actor on television shows we liked or how we felt when our family
fought, when Uncle and Auntie yelled at each other, or when Ma grew depressed and smoked too much and looked at us as though she wished we'd
never been born.

This night, however, Sourdi looked at me grimly. "Oh, no, Nea. Don't ever
say that. Don't ever talk like that."

I was going to smile and shrug and say something like "I was just kidding," but something inside me couldn't lie tonight. I crossed my arms over
my flat chest, and I stuck out my lower lip, like I'd seen the tough girls at
school do. "Anyone mess like that with me, I'm gonna kill him!"

Sourdi took me by the shoulders then and shook me so hard I thought
she was going to shake my head right off my body. She wouldn't stop even
after I started to cry.

"Stop, stop!" I begged. "I'll be good! I promise, I'll be good!"

Finally, she pushed me away from her and sat on the toilet, with her head 25
in her hands. Although she'd been the one hurting me, she looked as though
she'd been beaten up, the way she sat like that, her shoulders hunched over her
lap, as though she were trying to make herself disappear.

"I was trying to protect you," I said through my tears. "I was trying to save
you. You're so stupid! I should just let that man diss you!"

Sourdi's head shot up and I could see that she had no patience left. Her
eyes were red and her nostrils flared. She stood up and I took a step back
quickly. I thought she was going to grab me and shake me again, but this time
she just put her hand on my arm. "They could take you away. The police, they
could put you in a foster home. All of us."

A chill ran through my whole body, like a live current. We all knew about
foster homes. Rudy Gutierrez in third grade was taken away from his parents
after the teacher noticed some bruises on his back. He'd tried to shoplift some
PayDays from the 7-Eleven and got caught. When his dad got home that weekend, he let him have it. But after the school nurse took a look at him, Rudy was
taken away from his parents and sent to live in a foster home. His parents
couldn't speak English so good and didn't know what was happening until
too late. Anyway, what kind of lawyer could they afford? We heard later from
his cousin in Mrs. Chang's homeroom that Rudy's foster-dad had molested
him. The cousin said Rudy ran away from that home, but he got caught. At any
rate, none of us ever saw him again.

"You want to go to a foster home?" Sourdi asked me.

"No," I whispered. 30

"Then don't be so stupid!"

I started crying again, because I realized Sourdi was right. She kissed me
on the top of my head and hugged me to her. I leaned my head against her soft
breasts that had only recently emerged from her chest and pretended that I was
a good girl and that I would always obey her. What I didn't tell Sourdi was that
I was still a wicked girl. I was glad I'd stabbed that man. I was crying only
because life was so unfair.

We used to say that we'd run away, Sourdi and me. When we were older. After
she graduated. She'd be my legal guardian. We'd go to California to see the

stars. Paris. London. Cambodia even, to light incense for the bones of our father. We'd earn money working in Chinese restaurants in every country we visited. We had enough experience; it had to be worth something.

We'd lie awake all night whispering back and forth. I'd climb into Sourdi's bed, claiming that I couldn't sleep, curling into a ball beside my older sister, the smell of her like salt and garlic and a sweet scent that emanated directly from her skin. Sometimes I'd stroke Sourdi's slick hair, which she plaited into a thick wet braid so that it would be wavy in the morning. I would stay awake all night, pinching the inside of Sourdi's arm, the soft flesh of her thigh, to keep my sister from falling asleep and leaving me alone.

When she first started seeing Duke, I used to think of him as something 35 like a bookmark, just holding a certain space in her life until it was time for her to move on. I never thought of him as a fork in the road, dividing my life with Sourdi from Sourdi's life with men.

In those days, I didn't understand anything.

Ma had hired Duke to wash dishes at the Palace that first summer. At first, we paid him no mind. He was just this funny-looking white kid, hair that stuck up straight from his head when he wasn't wearing his silly baseball cap backwards, skinny as a stalk of bamboo, long legs and long arms that seemed to move in opposition to each other. Chopstick-boy I called him, just to be mean. He took it as a compliment.

I could see why he fell in love with Sourdi. My sister was beautiful. Really beautiful, not like the girls in magazines with their pale, pinched faces, pink and powdery, brittle girls. Sourdi looked like a statue that had been rescued from the sea. She was smooth where I had angles and soft where I was bone. Sourdi's face was round, her nose low and wide, her eyes crescent-shaped like the quarter moon, her hair sleek as seaweed. Her skin was a burnished cinnamon color. Looking at Sourdi, I could pretend I was beautiful, too. She had so much to spare.

At first, Duke and Sourdi only talked behind the Palace, pretending to take a break from the heat of the kitchen. I caught them looking at the stars together.

The first time they kissed, I was there, too. Duke was giving us a ride after 40 school in his pickup. He had the music on loud and the windows were open. It was a hot day for October, and the wind felt like a warm ocean that we could swim in forever. He was going to drop us off at the Palace, but then Duke said he had something to show us, and we circled around the outskirts of town, taking the gravel road that led to the open fields, beyond the highway where the cattle ranches lay. Finally, he pulled off the gravel road and parked.

"You want us to look at cows?" I asked impatiently, crossing my arms.

He laughed at me then and took Sourdi by the hand. We hiked through a ditch to the edge of an empty cornfield long since harvested, the stubble of cornstalks poking up from the black soil, pale and bonelike. The field was laced with a barbed-wire fence to keep the cattle in, though I couldn't see any cows at all. The whole place gave me the creeps.

Duke held the strands of barbed wire apart for Sourdi and me and told us to crawl under the fence.

"Just trust me," he said.

We followed him to a spot in the middle of the field. "It's the center of the 45 world," Duke said. "Look." And he pointed back to where we'd come from, and suddenly I realized the rest of the world had disappeared. The ground had appeared level, but we must have walked into a tiny hollow in the plains, because from where we stood there was only sky and field for as far as our eyes could see. We could no longer see the road or Duke's pickup, our town, or even the green smudge of cottonwoods that grew along the Yankton River or the distant hills of Nebraska. There was nothing overhead, either; the sky was unbroken by clouds, smooth as an empty rice bowl. "It's just us here," Duke said. "We're alone in the whole universe."

All at once, Sourdi began to breathe funny. Her face grew pinched, and she wiped at her eyes with the back of her hand.

"What's wrong?" Duke asked stupidly.

Then Sourdi was running wildly. She took off like an animal startled by a gunshot. She was trying to head back to the road, but she tripped over the cornstalks and fell onto her knees. She started crying for real.

I caught up to her first—I've always been a fast runner. As Duke approached, I put my arms around Sourdi.

"I thought you'd like it," Duke said.   50

"We're city girls," I said, glaring at him. "Why would we like this hick stuff?"

"I'm sorry," Sourdi whispered. "I'm so sorry."

"What are you sorry for? It's his fault!" I pointed out.

Now Duke was kneeling next to Sourdi. He tried to put his arm over her shoulder, too. I was going to push him away, when Sourdi did something very surprising. She put both her arms around his neck and leaned against him, while Duke said soft, dumb-sounding things that I couldn't quite hear. Then they were kissing.

I was so surprised, I stared at them before I forced myself to look away.   55
Then I was the one who felt like running, screaming, for the road.

On the way back to the Palace, Duke and Sourdi didn't talk, but they held hands. The worst part was I was sitting between them.

Ma didn't seem to notice anything for a while, but then with Ma it was always hard to know what she was thinking, what she knew and what she didn't. Sometimes she seemed to go through her days like she was made of stone. Sometimes she erupted like a volcano.

Uncle fired Duke a few weeks later. He said it was because Duke had dropped a tray of dishes. It was during the Saturday lunch rush when Sourdi and I weren't working and couldn't witness what had happened.

"He's a clumsy boy," Ma agreed after work that night, when we all sat around in the back booths and ate our dinner.

Sourdi didn't say anything. She knew Ma knew.   60

She kept seeing Duke, of course. They were both juniors, and there was only one high school in town. Now when I crept into Sourdi's bed at night, when she talked about running away, she meant Duke and her. I was the one who had to pipe up that I was coming with them, too. What we didn't know was that Ma was making plans as well.

Uncle first introduced his friend Mr. Chhay in the winter. I'd had a strange dream the night before. I hadn't remembered it at all until Mr. Chhay walked into the Palace, with his hangdog face and his suit like a salesman's. He sat in a corner booth with Uncle and, while they talked, he shredded a napkin, then took the scraps of paper and rolled them between his thumb and index finger into a hundred tiny red balls. He left them in the ashtray, like a mountain of fish eggs. Seeing them, I remembered my dream.

I was swimming in the ocean. I was just a small child, but I wasn't afraid at all. The sea was liquid turquoise, the sunlight yellow as gold against my skin. Fish were swimming alongside me. I could see through the clear water to the bottom of the sea. The fish were schooling around me and below me, and they brushed against my feet when I kicked the water. Their scales felt like bones scraping my toes. I tried to push them away, but the schools grew more dense, until I was swimming amongst them under the waves.

The fish began to spawn around me and soon the water was cloudy with eggs. I tried to break through the film, but the eggs clung to my skin. The water darkened as we entered a sea of kelp. I pushed against the dark slippery strands like Sourdi's hair. I realized I was pushing against my sister, wrapped in the kelp, suspended just below the surface of the water. Then I woke up.

I thought about that dream seeing that old guy Mr. Chhay with Uncle and 65 I knew they were up to no good. I wanted to warn Sourdi, but she seemed to understand without my having to tell her anything.

Uncle called over to her and introduced her to his friend. But Sourdi wouldn't even look at Mr. Chhay. She kept her eyes lowered, though he tried to smile and talk to her. She whispered so low in reply that no one could understand a word she said. I could tell the man was disappointed when he left. His shoulders seemed barely able to support the weight of his jacket.

Mr. Chhay wrote letters to Uncle, to Ma. He thanked them for their hospitality and enclosed pictures of his business and his house, plus a formal portrait of himself looking ridiculous in another suit, standing in front of some potted plants, his hair combed over the bald spot in the middle of his head.

The next time he came to visit the Palace, he brought gifts. A giant Chinese vase for Ma, Barbie dolls for my younger sisters and cousin, a Christian music cassette tape for me, and a bright red leather purse for Sourdi.

Ma made Sourdi tell him thank you.

And that was all she said to him. 70

But this old guy was persistent. He took us all out to eat at a steakhouse once. He said he wanted to pay back Uncle for some good deed he'd done a long time ago when they both first came to America. I could have told him, Sourdi hated this kind of food. She preferred Mexican, tacos, not this Midwest cowboy stuff. But Ma made us all thank him.

"Thank you, Mr. Chhay," we said dutifully. He'd smiled so all his yellow teeth showed at once. "Oh, please, call me Older Brother," he said.

It was the beginning of the end. I should have fought harder then. I should have stabbed this man, too.

I saw Duke at Sourdi's wedding. She invited him for the ceremony proper, the reception, too, but he didn't show up until the end. I almost didn't see him at all. He was slouching through the parking lot of St. Agnes, wearing his best hightops and the navy-blue suit that his mother had insisted upon buying for graduation. I wasn't used to him looking like a teenage undertaker, but I recognized his loping gait immediately. That afternoon of Sourdi's wedding, he was holding a brown bag awkwardly behind his back, as if trying to conceal the fact that he was drinking as conspicuously as possible.

I was standing inside the bingo hall, before the row of squat windows, my 75
back turned to the festivities, the exploding flash capturing the tipsy toasts,
the in-laws singing off-key to the rented karaoke machine.

Then it really became too much to bear, and I had to escape the terrible
heat, the flickering fluorescent lights. I slipped from the church into the ferocious March wind and gave it my best shot, running across the hard lawn, but
the too-tight heels pinched my toes and the stiff taffeta bodice of the cotton-
candy-pink bridesmaid's dress might as well have been a vise around my rib
cage. I had intended to make it off church property, run to the empty field that
stretched low and dark all the way to the horizon, but I only made it to the end
of the walk near the rectory before vomiting into Sister Kevin's over-tended
tulip patch.

Duke came over and sat on his haunches beside me, while I puked. I let
him hold back my hair, while the wedding cake and wine cooler that I'd tried
poured from my mouth.

Finally, I spat a few times to clear my mouth, then sat back on my rear end.

After a few minutes, I could take a sip from Duke's beer.

We didn't talk. 80

I took out the pack of cigarettes I'd stolen from Ma's purse and lit one. It
took five puffs before I could mask the taste of bile and sugar.

The wind was blowing fiercely from the northwest, whipping my hair
about my face like a widow's veil, throwing dust from the parking lot around
us like wedding rice.

After a long while, Duke stood up and walked back down the sidewalk
lined with yellow daffodils. He walked bow-legged, like all the boys in our town,
farmers' sons, no matter how cool Duke tried to be. I buried my head in my
arms and watched him from under one polyester-covered armpit as he climbed
back into his pickup and pulled away with a screech. As he left the parking lot,
he tossed the brown bag with the empty bottle of Bud out the window. It fell
into the street, where it rolled and rolled until it disappeared into a ditch.

Ma liked Sourdi's husband. He had a steady job, a house. She didn't mind
he was so old and Sourdi just eighteen when they married. In her eyes, eighteen
was a good age to start a family. "I was younger than Sourdi when I get married," Ma liked to say.

When Sourdi sent pictures home for the holidays, Ma ooohed and aaahed 85
as though they were winning lottery tickets. My sister and her old husband in
front of a listing Christmas tree, a pile of presents at their feet. Then, the red-
faced baby sprawled on a pink blanket on the living room carpet, drooling in
its shiny high chair, slumped in its Snugli like a rock around Sourdi's neck.

"Look. Sony," Ma pointed at the big-screen television in the background of
the New Year's pictures. "Sourdi say they got all new washer/dryer, too. Maytag."

When I looked at my sister's pictures, I could see that she looked tired.

Sourdi always said that Ma used to be a very brave woman. She also said that
Ma used to be a beautiful woman who liked to have her hair fixed in salons, who
wore pretty dresses and knew how to dance in all the fashionable styles. I don't
remember this mother. I remember the mother who worked two jobs for us.

I might never have seen Duke again if it were not for Sourdi's strange phone
call one Saturday evening nearly two years after her wedding. I was fourteen
and a half.

At first, I hadn't recognized my older sister's voice. 90

"Who is this?" I demanded, thinking: heavy breathing, prank caller.

"Who d'you think?" Sourdi was crying, a tiny crimped sound that barely crept out of the receiver. Then her voice steadied with anger and grew familiar. "Is Ma there?"

"What's the matter? What happened?"

"Just let me speak to Ma, O.K.?" There was a pause, as Sourdi blew her nose. "Tell her it's important."

I lured Ma from the TV room without alerting my younger sisters. Ma 95 paced back and forth in the kitchen between the refrigerator and the stove, nodding and muttering, "Mmm, mmm, uh-hmm." I could just hear the tinny squeak of Sourdi's panicked voice.

I sat on the floor, hugging my knees, in the doorway to the hall, just out of Ma's line of sight.

Finally, Ma said, in the tone normally reserved for refusing service to the unruly or arguing with a customer who had a complaint, "It's always like this. Every marriage is hard. Sometimes there is nothing you can do —"

Then Ma stopped pacing. "Just minute," she said and she took the phone with her into the bathroom, shutting the door firmly behind her.

When she came out again, twenty-two minutes later, she ignored me completely. She set the phone back on the counter without saying a word.

"So?" I prompted. 100

"I'm tired." Ma rubbed her neck with one hand. "Just let me rest. You girls, it's always something. Don't let your old mother rest."

She yawned extravagantly. She claimed she was too tired to watch any more TV. She had to go to bed, her eyes just wouldn't stay open.

I tried calling Sourdi, but the phone only rang and rang.

The next morning, Sunday, I called first thing, but then *he* picked up, my sister's husband.

"Oh, is this Nea?" he said, so cheerfully it was obvious he was hiding some- 105 thing.

"Yes, I'd like to speak to my sister."

"I'm sorry, Little Sister." I just hated when he called me that. "My wife is out right now. But I'll tell her you called. She'll be sorry she missed you."

It was eight o'clock in the morning, for Chrissake.

"Oh, thank you," I said, sweet as pie. "How's the baby?"

"So well!" Then he launched into a long explanation about his daughter's 110 eating habits, her rather average attempts to crawl, the simple words she was trying to say. For all I knew, Sourdi could have been right there, fixing his breakfast, washing his clothes, cleaning up his messes. I thought of my sister's voice in my ear, the tiny sound like something breaking.

It was all I could do to disguise the disdain in my voice. "Be sure to tell Sourdi to call back. Ma found that recipe she wanted. That special delicious recipe she was looking for. I can't tell you what it is, Ma's secret recipe, but you'll really be surprised."

"Oh, boy," the jerk said. "I didn't know about any secret recipe."

"That's why it's a secret." I hung up. I couldn't breathe. My chest hurt. I could feel my swollen heart pressing against my ribs.

The next afternoon, I tried calling back three more times, but no one answered.

At work that evening, Ma was irritable. She wouldn't look me in the eyes 115
when I tried to get her attention. Some little kid spilled his Coke into a perfectly good plate of House Special Prawns and his parents insisted they be
given a new order—and a new Coke—on the house. There was a minor grease
fire around quarter to nine—the smoke alarms all went off at the same time—
and then the customers started complaining about the cold, too, once we had
opened all the doors and windows to clear the air. Fairly average as far as disasters went, but they put Ma in a sour mood.

Ma was taking a cigarette break out back by the dumpsters, smoke curling
from her nostrils, before I could corner her. She wasn't in the mood to talk, but
after the nicotine fix took hold, she didn't tell me to get back to work, either.

I asked Ma if I could have a smoke. She didn't get angry. She smiled in her
tired way, the edges of her mouth twitching upwards just a little, and said,
"Smoking will kill you." Then she handed me her pack.

"Maybe Sourdi should come back home for a while," I suggested.

"She's a married woman. She has her own family now."

"She's still part of our family." 120

Ma didn't say anything, just tilted her head back and blew smoke at the
stars, so I continued, "Well, don't you think she might be in trouble? She was
crying, you know. It's not like Sourdi." My voice must have slipped a tad, just
enough to sound disrespectful, because Ma jerked upright, took the cigarette
out of her mouth and glared at me.

"What you think? You so smart? You gonna tell me what's what?" Ma
threw her cigarette onto the asphalt. "You not like your sister. Your sister know
how to bear things!"

She stormed back into the kitchen, and Ma ignored me for the rest of the
evening.

I called Sourdi one more time, after Ma and my sisters had gone to bed and I
finally had the kitchen to myself, the moon spilling from the window onto the
floor in a big, blue puddle. I didn't dare turn on the lights.

This time, my sister answered. "Mmm. . . . Hello?" 125

"Sourdi?"

"What time is it?"

"Sssh." My heart beat so loudly, I couldn't hear my own voice. "How are
you doing?"

"Oh, we're fine. The baby, she's doing real good. She's starting to talk—"

"No, no, no. I mean, what happened the other night?" 130

"What?"

Another voice now, low, a man's voice, just beneath the snow on the line.
Then suddenly a shriek.

"Uh-oh. I just woke her up." Sourdi's voice grew fainter as she spoke to
him: "Honey, can you check the baby's diaper?" Then she said to me, "I have to
go. The baby, she's hungry, you know."

"Let him handle it. I have to talk to you a minute, O.K.? Just don't go,
Sourdi. What's going on? What did you say to Ma?"

Sourdi sighed, like a balloon losing its air. "Oh . . . nothing. Look, I really 135
have to go. Talk to you later, Nea." She hung up.

I called back in twenty minutes, surely long enough to change a diaper,
but the phone only rang forlornly, ignored.

I considered taking Ma's car, but then Ma wouldn't be able to get to work and I wasn't sure how long I needed to be gone. Then I thought of Duke.

Even though it was far too late in the night, I called Duke. He was still in town, two years after graduation. I'd heard he was working as a mechanic at the Standard station. I found his number in the phone book.

"It's Nea. Pick up your phone, Duke," I hissed into his machine. "It's an emergency!"

"Nea?!" He was yawning. "My God. What time is it?"   140

"Duke! It's important! It's Sourdi, she's in trouble."

There was a pause while I let him absorb all this.

"You have to drive me to Des Moines. We have to get her."

"What happened?"

"Look, I don't have time to explain. We have to go tonight. It's an emer-   145 gency. A matter of life and death."

"Did you call the police?"

"Don't be stupid. Sourdi would never call the cops. She loves that jerk."

"What?" Duke whispered, "Her husband, he beat her up?"

"Duke, I told you, I can't say anything right now. But you have to help me."

He agreed to meet me at the corner, where there'd be no chance Ma could   150 hear his truck. I'd be waiting.

It was freezing. The wind stung my cheeks, which wasn't a good sign. Could be rain coming, or worse, snow. Even when the roads were clear, it was a good six-hour drive. I didn't want to think how long it would take if we ran into a late-season blizzard.

There was the roar of a souped-up engine and then a spray of gravel. Snoop Doggy Dogg growled over the wind.

"Duke! What took you?"

He put his hand over the door, barring me from climbing up. "You want me to help or not?"

"Don't joke."   155

I pulled myself inside and then made Duke back up rather than run in front of the house. Just in case Ma woke up.

"How come your Ma didn't want to come?"

"She doesn't know."

"Sourdi didn't want to worry her?"

"Mmm." There was no point trying to shout above Snoop Dogg.   160

He was obviously tired. When Duke was tired, he turned his music up even louder than normal. I'd forgotten that. Now the bass underneath the rap was vibrating in my bones. But at least he did as I asked and took off toward the highway.

Soon the squat buildings of town, the used-car lots on the route in from the interstate with their flapping colored flags, and the metal storage units of the Sav-U-Lot passed from view, and there was nothing before us but the black sky and the highway and the patches of snow on the shoulders glowing briefly in the wake of the headlights.

I must have fallen asleep, though I don't remember feeling tired. I was standing on the deck of a boat in an inky ocean, trying to read the stars, but every time I found one constellation, the stars began to blink and fade. I squinted at them, but the stars would not stay in place. Then my head snapped forward as the pickup careened off the shoulder.

The pickup landed in a ditch. Metal glittered in the headlights; the fields on this side of the highway were strung with barbed wire.

We got out by sacrificing our jackets, stuffing them under the back tires 165 until we had enough traction to slide back onto the pavement.

I insisted upon driving. "I got my license," I lied. "And I'm not tired at all."

Duke settled into the passenger seat, his arms folded across his chest, his head tilted back, preparing to go to sleep again.

"D'ya think she'll be happy to see me?" he said out of the blue. "Sourdi sent me a Christmas card with a picture of the baby. Looks just like. . . . But I didn't write back or nothing. She probably thought I was angry. She mad at me, you think?"

"Sourdi's never mad at anybody."

"She must be mad at her husband if she wants you to come get her." 170

"She doesn't know we're coming."

"What!"

"I didn't have time to explain to her."

"You're not running away from home, are you?" Duke's eyes narrowed and his voice grew slow as if he thought he was suddenly being clever.

"Yeah, I'm running away to Des Moines." 175

Once upon a time, in another world, a place almost unimaginable to me sitting in the pickup with Madonna singing "Lucky Star" on the radio, Sourdi had walked across a minefield, carrying me on her back. She was nine and I was four. Because she'd told me, I could see it all clearly, better than if I actually remembered: the startled faces of people who'd tripped a mine, their limbs in new arrangements, the bones peeking through the earth. Sourdi had said it was safest to step on the bodies; that way you knew a mine was no longer there.

This was nothing I would ever tell Duke. It was our own personal story, just for Sourdi and me to share. Nobody's business but ours.

I would walk on bones for my sister, I vowed. I would put my bare feet on rotting flesh. I would save Sourdi.

We found the house in West Des Moines after circling for nearly an hour through the identical streets with their neat lawns and boxy houses and chain link fences. I refused to allow Duke to ask for directions from any of the joggers or the van that sputtered by, delivering the *Register*. He figured people in the neighborhood would know, just ask where the Oriental family lived. I told him to go to hell. Then we didn't talk for a while.

But as soon as we found Locust Street, I recognized the house. I knew it 180 was Sourdi's even though it had been painted a different color since the last set of pictures. The lace undercurtains before the cheerful flowered draperies, the flourishing plants in the windows, next to little trinkets, figurines in glass that caught the light. Every space crammed with something sweet.

The heater in Duke's truck began to make a high-pitched, sick-cat whine as we waited, parked across the street, staring at Sourdi's house.

"So, are we going to just sit here?"

"Shh," I said irritably. "Just wait a minute." Somehow I had imagined that Sourdi would sense our presence, the curtains would stir, and I'd only have to wait a moment for my sister to come running out the front door. But we sat patiently, shivering, staring at Sourdi's house. Nothing moved.

"Her husband's home," I said stupidly. "He hasn't gone to work yet."

"He wouldn't dare try anything. Not with the both of us here. We should just go and knock." 185

"They're probably still asleep."

"Nea, what's the matter with you? What are you afraid of all of a sudden?"

I'd had it with Duke. He just didn't understand anything. I hopped out of the truck and ran through the icy air, my arms wrapped around my body. The sidewalk was slick beneath my sneakers, still damp from the ditch, and I slid onto my knees on the driveway. My right hand broke the fall. A sharp jagged pain shot up to my elbow and stayed there, throbbing. I picked myself up and ran limping to the door and rang.

No one answered for a minute, and then it was him.

"What on earth? Nea!" Sourdi's husband was dressed for work, but he hadn't shaved yet. He looked even older than I remembered, his thinning hair flat across his skull, his bloodshot eyes and swollen lids still heavy from sleep. He might have been handsome once, decades ago, but I saw no evidence of it now. He held the door open and I slipped into the warmth without even removing my shoes first. "How did you get here? Is your mother coming, too?" 190

My eyes started to water, the transition from cold to heat. Slowly the room came into focus. It was a mess. Baby toys on the carpet, shoes in a pile by the door, old newspapers scattered on an end table anchored by a bowl of peanut shells. The TV was blaring somewhere, and a baby was crying.

Sourdi emerged from the kitchen, dressed in a bright pink sweatsuit emblazoned with the head of Minnie Mouse, pink slippers over her feet, the baby on her hip. She had a bruise across her cheekbone and the purple remains of a black eye. Sourdi didn't say anything for a few seconds as she stared at me, blinking, her mouth falling open. "Where's Ma?"

"Home."

"Oh, no." Sourdi's face crumpled. "Is everything all right?"

I couldn't believe how dense my sister had become. We used to be able to communicate without words. "Everything's fine . . . at home. Of course." I tried to give her a look so that she'd understand that I had come to rescue her, but Sourdi stood rigidly in place in the doorway to the kitchen, her mouth twitching, puzzled. 195

"Please, Little Sister, sit down," her husband said. "Let me make you some tea."

Someone banged on the front door, three times. Before I could begin to feel annoyed that Duke couldn't even wait five minutes, that he just had to ruin everything, my sister's husband opened the door again. I didn't bother to turn, instead I watched Sourdi's eyes widen and her wide mouth pucker into an O as she gasped, "Duke!"

"What's goin' on?" Duke said.

Then everyone stared at me with such identical expressions of noncomprehension that I had to laugh. Then I couldn't stop, because I hadn't slept and it was so cold and my nose was running and I didn't have any Kleenex.

"I said, what the hell is going on?" Duke repeated.   200

Sourdi's husband approached Duke. He smiled. "You must be Nea's—"

But by now, Duke had seen Sourdi's bruises. His mouth twisted into a sneer. "You bastard! I oughtta—" He punched Sourdi's husband in the nose. Sourdi screamed, her husband bent over double. Duke drew back his fist again, but Sourdi ran forward and grabbed him. She was punching him on the chest, "Out! Out! You! I'll call the police!" She tried to claw him with her nails, but Duke threw his arms up around his head.

Sourdi's husband stood up. Blood gushed from his nose all over his white shirt and tie.

"Come on!" I said stupidly. "Come on, Sourdi, let's go!"

But it was pretty obvious that she didn't want to leave.   205

The baby began shrieking.

I started crying, too.

After everyone had calmed down, Duke went down the street to the 7-Eleven to get a bag of ice for Mr. Chhay, who kept saying "I'm fine, don't worry," even though his nose had turned a deep scarlet and was starting to swell.

It turned out Sourdi's husband hadn't beaten her up. An economy-size box of baby wipes had fallen off the closet shelf and struck her full in the eye.

While Mr. Chhay went into the bedroom to change his clothes, I sat with   210
Sourdi in the kitchen as she tried to get the squawling baby to eat its breakfast.

"Nea, what's wrong with you?"

"What's wrong with me? Don't you get it? I was trying to help you!"

Sourdi sighed as the baby spat a spoonful of the glop onto the table. "I'm a married woman. I'm not just some girl anymore. I have my own family. You understand that?"

"You were crying." I squinted at my sister. "I heard you."

"I'm gonna have another baby, you know. That's a big step. That's a big   215
thing." She said this as though it explained everything.

"You sound like an old lady. You're only twenty, for Chrissake. You don't have to live like this. Ma is wrong. You can be anything, Sourdi."

Sourdi pinched her nose between two fingers. "Everything's gonna be fine. We just had a little argument, but it's O.K. We had a good talk. He understands now. I'm still gonna go to school. I haven't changed my mind. After the baby gets a little bigger, I mean, both babies. Maybe when they start pre-school."

Just then her husband came back into the kitchen. He had to use the phone to call work. His face looked like a gargoyle's.

Sourdi looked at me then, so disappointed. I knew what she was thinking. She had grown up, and I had merely grown unworthy of her love.

After Duke got back with the ice, he and Sourdi's husband shook hands.   220
Duke kept saying, "Gosh, I'm so sorry," and Mr. Chhay kept repeating, "No problem, don't worry."

Then Sourdi's husband had to go. We followed him to the driveway. My sister kissed him before he climbed into his Buick. He rolled down the window, and she leaned in and kissed him again.

I turned away. I watched Duke standing in the doorway, holding the baby in his arms, cooing at its face. In his tough wannabe clothes, the super-wide jeans and his fancy sneakers and the chain from his wallet to his belt loops, he looked surprisingly young.

Sourdi lent us some blankets and matching his-and-hers Donald and Daisy Duck sweatshirts for the trip back, since our coats were still wet and worthless.

"Don't tell Ma I was here, O.K.?" I begged Sourdi. "We'll be home by afternoon. She'll just think I'm with friends or something. She doesn't have to know, O.K.?"

Sourdi pressed her full lips together into a thin line and nodded in a way 225 that seemed as though she were answering a different question. And I knew that I couldn't trust my sister to take my side anymore.

As we pulled away from Sourdi's house, the first icy snowflakes began to fall across the windshield.

Sourdi stood in the driveway with the baby on her hip. She waved to us as the snow swirled around her like ashes.

She had made her choice, and she hadn't chosen me.

Sourdi told me a story once about a magic serpent, the Naga, with a mouth so large, it could swallow people whole. Our ancestors carved Naga into the stones of Angkor Wat to scare away demons. Sourdi said people used to believe they could come alive in times of great evil and protect the temples. They could eat armies.

I wished I was a Naga. I would have swallowed the whole world in one gulp. 230 But I have no magic powers. None whatsoever.

CONSIDERATIONS FOR CRITICAL THINKING AND WRITING

1. **FIRST RESPONSE.** How does your response to Nea develop over the course of the story? Is she a dynamic or a static character?

2. Explain how Nea and Sourdi serve as character foils to one another.

3. Discuss whether you think Duke is a flat or a round character.

4. What is the effect of the story's being told from Nea's perspective? How might the story be different if it were told from the mother's point of view?

5. Do you think Mr. Chhay is a good or bad husband?

6. How does the information about Nea and Sourdi's trip through the mine-field affect your understanding of Nea's relationship with her sister?

7. Comment on the title. Why wouldn't an alternative like "Nea the Trouble-maker" be appropriate?

CONNECTIONS TO OTHER SELECTIONS

1. Discuss the process of immigrants becoming Americanized in this story and in Chitra Banerjee Divakaruni's "Clothes" (p. 265).

2. Compare the characterization of Nea in "Saving Sourdi" and of Sammy in John Updike's "A & P" (p. 733). In what sense do both characters see themselves as rescuers?

HERMAN MELVILLE (1819–1891)

Hoping to improve his distressed financial situation, Herman Melville left New York and went to sea as a young common sailor. He returned to become an uncommon writer. His experiences at sea became the basis for his early novels: *Typee* (1846), *Omoo* (1847), *Mardi* (1849), *Redburn* (1849), and *White-Jacket* (1850). Ironically, with the publication of his masterpiece, *Moby-Dick* (1851), Melville lost the popular success he had enjoyed with his earlier books because his readers were not ready for its philosophical complexity. Although he wrote more, Melville's works were read less and slipped into obscurity. His final short novel, *Billy Budd,* was not published until the 1920s, when critics rediscovered him. In "Bartleby, the Scrivener," Melville presents a quiet clerk in a law office whose baffling "passive resistance" disrupts the life of his employer, a man who attempts to make sense of Bartleby's refusal to behave reasonably.

Library of Congress, Prints and Photographs Division.

Bartleby, the Scrivener
A Story of Wall Street

1853

I am a rather elderly man. The nature of my avocations, for the last thirty years, has brought me into more than ordinary contact with what would seem an interesting and somewhat singular set of men, of whom, as yet, nothing, that I know of, has ever been written — I mean, the law-copyists, or scriveners. I have known very many of them, professionally and privately, and, if I pleased, could relate diverse histories, at which good-natured gentlemen might smile, and sentimental souls might weep. But I waive the biographies of all other scriveners, for a few passages in the life of Bartleby, who was a scrivener, the strangest I ever saw, or heard of. While, of other law-copyists, I might write the complete life, of Bartleby nothing of that sort can be done. I believe that no materials exist, for a full and satisfactory biography of this man. It is an irreparable loss to literature. Bartleby was one of those beings of whom nothing is ascertainable, except from the original sources, and, in his case, those are very small. What my own astonished eyes saw of Bartleby, *that* is all I know of him, except, indeed, one vague report, which will appear in the sequel.

Ere introducing the scrivener, as he first appeared to me, it is fit I make some mention of myself, my *employés,* my business, my chambers, and general surroundings, because some such description is indispensable to an adequate understanding of the chief character about to be presented. Imprimis:° I am a

Imprimis: In the first place.

man who, from his youth upwards, has been filled with a profound conviction that the easiest way of life is the best. Hence, though I belong to a profession proverbially energetic and nervous, even to turbulence, at times, yet nothing of that sort have I ever suffered to invade my peace. I am one of those unambitious lawyers who never address a jury, or in any way draw down public applause; but, in the cool tranquillity of a snug retreat, do a snug business among rich men's bonds, and mortgages, and title-deeds. All who know me, consider me an eminently *safe* man. The late John Jacob Astor,° a personage little given to poetic enthusiasm, had no hesitation in pronouncing my first grand point to be prudence; my next, method. I do not speak it in vanity, but simply record the fact, that I was not unemployed in my profession by the late John Jacob Astor; a name which, I admit, I love to repeat; for it hath a rounded and orbicular sound to it, and rings like unto bullion. I will freely add, that I was not insensible to the late John Jacob Astor's good opinion.

Some time prior to the period at which this little history begins, my avocations had been largely increased. The good old office, now extinct in the State of New York, of a Master in Chancery, had been conferred upon me. It was not a very arduous office, but very pleasantly remunerative. I seldom lose my temper; much more seldom indulge in dangerous indignation at wrongs and outrages; but I must be permitted to be rash here and declare, that I consider the sudden and violent abrogation of the office of Master in Chancery, by the new Constitution, as a — premature act; inasmuch as I had counted upon a life-lease of the profits, whereas I only received those of a few short years. But this is by the way.

My chambers were up stairs, at No. — Wall Street. At one end, they looked upon the white wall of the interior of a spacious skylight shaft, penetrating the building from top to bottom.

This view might have been considered rather tame than otherwise, defi- 5 cient in what landscape painters call "life." But, if so, the view from the other end of my chambers offered, at least, a contrast, if nothing more. In that direction, my windows commanded an unobstructed view of a lofty brick wall, black by age and everlasting shade; which wall required no spyglass to bring out its lurking beauties, but, for the benefit of all near-sighted spectators, was pushed up to within ten feet of my window-panes. Owing to the great height of the surrounding buildings, and my chambers being on the second floor, the interval between this wall and mine not a little resembled a huge square cistern.

At the period just preceding the advent of Bartleby, I had two persons as copyists in my employment, and a promising lad as an office-boy. First, Turkey; second, Nippers; third, Ginger Nut. These may seem names, the like of which are not usually found in the Directory. In truth, they were nicknames, mutually conferred upon each other by my three clerks, and were deemed expressive of their respective persons or characters. Turkey was a short, pursy Englishman, of about my own age — that is, somewhere not far from sixty. In the morning, one might say, his face was of a fine florid hue, but after twelve o'clock, meridian — his dinner hour — it blazed like a grate full of Christmas coals; and continued blazing — but, as it were, with a gradual wane — till six o'clock, P.M., or thereabouts; after which, I saw no more of the proprietor of

John Jacob Astor (1763-1848): An enormously wealthy American capitalist.

the face, which, gaining its meridian with the sun, seemed to set with it, to rise, culminate, and decline the following day, with the like regularity and undiminished glory. There are many singular coincidences I have known in the course of my life, not the least among which was the fact, that, exactly when Turkey displayed his fullest beams from his red and radiant countenance, just then, too, at that critical moment, began the daily period when I considered his business capacities as seriously disturbed for the remainder of the twenty-four hours. Not that he was absolutely idle, or averse to business then; far from it. The difficulty was, he was apt to be altogether too energetic. There was a strange, inflamed, flurried, flighty recklessness of activity about him. He would be incautious in dipping his pen into his inkstand. All his blots upon my documents were dropped there after twelve o'clock, meridian. Indeed, not only would he be reckless, and sadly given to making blots in the afternoon, but, some days, he went further, and was rather noisy. At such times, too, his face flamed with augmented blazonry, as if cannel coal had been heaped on anthracite. He made an unpleasant racket with his chair; spilled his sand-box; in mending his pens, impatiently split them all to pieces, and threw them on the floor in a sudden passion; stood up, and leaned over his table, boxing his papers about in a most indecorous manner, very sad to behold in an elderly man like him. Nevertheless, as he was in many ways a most valuable person to me, and all the time before twelve o'clock, meridian, was the quickest, steadiest creature, too, accomplishing a great deal of work in a style not easily to be matched — for these reasons, I was willing to overlook his eccentricities, though, indeed, occasionally, I remonstrated with him. I did this very gently, however, because, though the civilest, nay, the blandest and most reverential of men in the morning, yet, in the afternoon, he was disposed, upon provocation, to be slightly rash with his tongue — in fact, insolent. Now, valuing his morning services as I did, and resolved not to lose them — yet, at the same time, made uncomfortable by his inflamed ways after twelve o'clock — and being a man of peace, unwilling by my admonitions to call forth unseemly retorts from him, I took upon me, one Saturday noon (he was always worse on Saturdays) to hint to him, very kindly, that, perhaps, now that he was growing old, it might be well to abridge his labors; in short, he need not come to my chambers after twelve o'clock, but, dinner over, had best go home to his lodgings, and rest himself till tea-time. But no; he insisted upon his afternoon devotions. His countenance became intolerably fervid, as he oratorically assured me — gesticulating with a long ruler at the other end of the room — that if his services in the morning were useful, how indispensable, then, in the afternoon?

"With submission, sir," said Turkey, on this occasion, "I consider myself your right-hand man. In the morning I but marshal and deploy my columns; but in the afternoon I put myself at their head, and gallantly charge the foe, thus" — and he made a violent thrust with the ruler.

"But the blots, Turkey," intimated I.

"True; but, with submission, sir, behold these hairs! I am getting old. Surely, sir, a blot or two of a warm afternoon is not to be severely urged against gray hairs. Old age — even if it blot the page — is honorable. With submission, sir, we *both* are getting old."

This appeal to my fellow-feeling was hardly to be resisted. At all events, I 10 saw that go he would not. So, I made up my mind to let him stay, resolving, nevertheless, to see to it that, during the afternoon, he had to do with my less important papers.

Nippers, the second on my list, was a whiskered, sallow, and, upon the whole, rather piratical-looking young man, of about five-and-twenty. I always deemed him the victim of two evil powers—ambition and indigestion. The ambition was evinced by a certain impatience of the duties of a mere copyist, an unwarrantable usurpation of strictly professional affairs such as the original drawing up of legal documents. The indigestion seemed betokened in an occasional nervous testiness and grinning irritability, causing the teeth to audibly grind together over mistakes committed in copying; unnecessary maledictions, hissed, rather than spoken, in the heat of business; and especially by a continual discontent with the height of the table where he worked. Though of a very ingenious mechanical turn, Nippers could never get this table to suit him. He put chips under it, blocks of various sorts, bits of pasteboard, and at last went so far as to attempt an exquisite adjustment, by final pieces of folded blotting-paper. But no invention would answer. If, for the sake of easing his back, he brought the table-lid at a sharp angle well up towards his chin, and wrote there like a man using the steep roof of a Dutch house for his desk, then he declared that it stopped the circulation in his arms. If now he lowered the table to his waistbands, and stooped over it in writing, then there was a sore aching in his back. In short, the truth of the matter was, Nippers knew not what he wanted. Or, if he wanted anything, it was to be rid of a scrivener's table altogether. Among the manifestations of his diseased ambition was a fondness he had for receiving visits from certain ambiguous-looking fellows in seedy coats, whom he called his clients. Indeed, I was aware that not only was he, at times, considerable of a ward-politician, but he occasionally did a little business at the justices' courts, and was not unknown on the steps of the Tombs.° I have good reason to believe, however, that one individual who called upon him at my chambers, and who, with a grand air, he insisted was his client, was no other than a dun, and the alleged title-deed, a bill. But, with all his failings, and the annoyances he caused me, Nippers, like his compatriot Turkey, was a very useful man to me; wrote a neat, swift hand; and, when he chose, was not deficient in a gentlemanly sort of deportment. Added to this, he always dressed in a gentlemanly sort of way; and so, incidentally, reflected credit upon my chambers. Whereas, with respect to Turkey, I had much ado to keep him from being a reproach to me. His clothes were apt to look oily, and smell of eating-houses. He wore his pantaloons very loose and baggy in summer. His coats were execrable, his hat not to be handled. But while the hat was a thing of indifference to me, inasmuch as his natural civility and deference, as a dependent Englishman, always led him to doff it the moment he entered the room, yet his coat was another matter. Concerning his coats, I reasoned with him; but with no effect. The truth was, I suppose, that a man with so small an income could not afford to sport such a lustrous face and a lustrous coat at one and the same time. As Nippers once observed, Turkey's money went chiefly for red ink. One winter day, I presented Turkey with a highly respectable-looking coat of my own—a padded gray coat, of a most comfortable warmth, and which buttoned straight up from the knee to the neck. I thought Turkey would appreciate the favor, and abate his rashness and

the Tombs: A jail in New York City.

obstreperousness of afternoons. But no; I verily believe that buttoning himself up in so downy and blanket-like a coat had a pernicious effect upon him — upon the same principle that too much oats are bad for horses. In fact, precisely as a rash, restive horse is said to feel his oats, so Turkey felt his coat. It made him insolent. He was a man whom prosperity harmed.

Though, concerning the self-indulgent habits of Turkey, I had my own private surmises, yet, touching Nippers, I was well persuaded that, whatever might be his faults in other respects, he was, at least, a temperate young man. But indeed, nature herself seemed to have been his vintner, and, at his birth, charged him so thoroughly with an irritable, brandy-like disposition, that all subsequent potations were needless. When I consider how, amid the stillness of my chambers, Nippers would sometimes impatiently rise from his seat, and stooping over his table, spread his arms wide apart, seize the whole desk, and move it, and jerk it, with a grim, grinding motion on the floor, as if the table were a perverse voluntary agent, intent on thwarting and vexing him, I plainly perceive that, for Nippers, brandy-and-water were altogether superfluous.

It was fortunate for me that, owing to its peculiar cause — indigestion — the irritability and consequent nervousness of Nippers were mainly observable in the morning, while in the afternoon he was comparatively mild. So that, Turkey's paroxysms only coming on about twelve o'clock, I never had to do with their eccentricities at one time. Their fits relieved each other, like guards. When Nippers' was on, Turkey's was off; and *vice versa*. This was a good natural arrangement, under the circumstances.

Ginger Nut, the third on my list, was a lad, some twelve years old. His father was a carman, ambitious of seeing his son on the bench instead of a cart, before he died. So he sent him to my office, as student at law, errand-boy, cleaner, and sweeper, at the rate of one dollar a week. He had a little desk to himself, but he did not use it much. Upon inspection, the drawer exhibited a great array of the shells of various sorts of nuts. Indeed, to this quick-witted youth, the whole noble science of the law was contained in a nutshell. Not the least among the employments of Ginger Nut, as well as one which he discharged with the most alacrity, was his duty as cake and apple purveyor for Turkey and Nippers. Copying lawpapers being proverbially a dry, husky sort of business, my two scriveners were fain to moisten their mouths very often with Spitzenbergs, to be had at the numerous stalls nigh the Custom House and Post Office. Also, they sent Ginger Nut very frequently for that peculiar cake — small, flat, round, and very spicy — after which he had been named by them. Of a cold morning, when business was but dull, Turkey would gobble up scores of these cakes, as if they were mere wafers — indeed, they sell them at the rate of six or eight for a penny — the scrape of his pen blending with the crunching of the crisp particles in his mouth. Of all the fiery afternoon blunders and flurried rashness of Turkey, was his once moistening a ginger-cake between his lips, and clapping it on to a mortgage, for a seal. I came within an ace of dismissing him then. But he mollified me by making an oriental bow, and saying —

"With submission, sir, it was generous of me to find you in stationery on ₁₅ my own account."

Now my original business — that of a conveyancer and title hunter, and drawer-up of recondite documents of all sorts — was considerably increased by receiving the Master's office. There was now great work for scriveners. Not only must I push the clerks already with me, but I must have additional help.

In answer to my advertisement, a motionless young man one morning stood upon my office threshold, the door being open, for it was summer. I can see that figure now — pallidly neat, pitiably respectable, incurably forlorn! It was Bartleby.

After a few words touching his qualifications, I engaged him, glad to have among my corps of copyists a man of so singularly sedate an aspect, which I thought might operate beneficially upon the flighty temper of Turkey, and the fiery one of Nippers.

I should have stated before that ground-glass folding-doors divided my premises into two parts, one of which was occupied by my scriveners, the other by myself. According to my humor, I threw open these doors, or closed them. I resolved to assign Bartleby a corner by the folding-doors, but on my side of them, so as to have this quiet man within easy call, in case any trifling thing was to be done. I placed his desk close up to a small side-window in that part of the room, a window which originally had afforded a lateral view of certain grimy brickyards and bricks, but which, owing to subsequent erections, commanded at present no view at all, though it gave some light. Within three feet of the panes was a wall, and the light came down from far above, between two lofty buildings, as from a very small opening in a dome. Still further to a satisfactory arrangement, I procured a high green folding screen, which might entirely isolate Bartleby from my sight, though not remove him from my voice. And thus, in a manner, privacy and society were conjoined.

At first, Bartleby did an extraordinary quantity of writing. As if long famishing for something to copy, he seemed to gorge himself on my documents. There was no pause for digestion. He ran a day and night line, copying by sunlight and by candle-light. I should have been quite delighted with his application, had he been cheerfully industrious. But he wrote on silently, palely, mechanically.

It is, of course, an indispensable part of a scrivener's business to verify the accuracy of his copy, word by word. Where there are two or more scriveners in an office, they assist each other in this examination, one reading from the copy, the other holding the original. It is a very dull, wearisome, and lethargic affair. I can readily imagine that, to some sanguine temperaments, it would be altogether intolerable. For example, I cannot credit that the mettlesome poet, Byron, would have contentedly sat down with Bartleby to examine a law document of, say five hundred pages, closely written in a crimpy hand.

Now and then, in the haste of business, it had been my habit to assist in comparing some brief document myself, calling Turkey or Nippers for this purpose. One object I had, in placing Bartleby so handy to me behind the screen, was, to avail myself of his services on such trivial occasions. It was on the third day, I think, of his being with me, and before any necessity had arisen for having his own writing examined, that, being much hurried to complete a small affair I had in hand, I abruptly called to Bartleby. In my haste and natural expectancy of instant compliance, I sat with my head bent over the original on my desk, and my right hand sideways, and somewhat nervously extended with the copy, so that, immediately upon emerging from his retreat, Bartleby might snatch it and proceed to business without the least delay.

In this very attitude did I sit when I called to him, rapidly stating what it was I wanted him to do — namely, to examine a small paper with me. Imagine my surprise, nay, my consternation, when, without moving from his privacy, Bartleby, in a singularly mild, firm voice, replied, "I would prefer not to."

I sat awhile in perfect silence, rallying my stunned faculties. Immediately it occurred to me that my ears had deceived me, or Bartleby had entirely misunderstood my meaning. I repeated my request in the clearest tone I could assume; but in quite as clear a one came the previous reply, "I would prefer not to."

"Prefer not to," echoed I, rising in high excitement, and crossing the room 25 with a stride. "What do you mean? Are you moonstruck? I want you to help me compare this sheet here — take it," and I thrust it towards him.

"I would prefer not to," said he.

I looked at him steadfastly. His face was leanly composed; his gray eye dimly calm. Not a wrinkle of agitation rippled him. Had there been the least uneasiness, anger, impatience, or impertinence in his manner; in other words, had there been anything ordinarily human about him, doubtless I should have violently dismissed him from the premises. But as it was, I should have as soon thought of turning my pale plaster-of-paris bust of Cicero out of doors. I stood gazing at him awhile, as he went on with his own writing, and then reseated myself at my desk. This is very strange, thought I. What had one best do? But my business hurried me. I concluded to forget the matter for the present, reserving it for my future leisure. So, calling Nippers from the other room, the paper was speedily examined.

A few days after this, Bartleby concluded four lengthy documents, being quadruplicates of a week's testimony taken before me in my High Court of Chancery. It became necessary to examine them. It was an important suit, and great accuracy was imperative. Having all things arranged, I called Turkey, Nippers, and Ginger Nut, from the next room, meaning to place the four copies in the hands of my four clerks, while I should read from the original. Accordingly, Turkey, Nippers, and Ginger Nut had taken their seats in a row, each with his document in his hand, when I called to Bartleby to join this interesting group.

"Bartleby! quick, I am waiting."

I heard a slow scrape of his chair legs on the uncarpeted floor, and soon he 30 appeared standing at the entrance of his hermitage.

"What is wanted?" said he, mildly.

"The copies, the copies," said I, hurriedly. "We are going to examine them. There" — and I held towards him the fourth quadruplicate.

"I would prefer not to," he said, and gently disappeared behind the screen.

For a few moments I was turned into a pillar of salt, standing at the head of my seated column of clerks. Recovering myself, I advanced towards the screen, and demanded the reason for such extraordinary conduct.

"*Why* do you refuse?" 35

"I would prefer not to."

With any other man I should have flown outright into a dreadful passion, scorned all further words, and thrust him ignominiously from my presence. But there was something about Bartleby that not only strangely disarmed me, but, in a wonderful manner, touched and disconcerted me. I began to reason with him.

"These are your own copies we are about to examine. It is labor saving to you, because one examination will answer for your four papers. It is common usage. Every copyist is bound to help examine his copy. Is it not so? Will you not speak? Answer!"

"I prefer not to," he replied in a flute-like tone. It seemed to me that, while I had been addressing him, he carefully revolved every statement that I made; fully comprehended the meaning; could not gainsay the irresistible conclusion; but, at the same time, some paramount consideration prevailed with him to reply as he did.

"You are decided, then, not to comply with my request — a request made 40 according to common usage and common sense?"

He briefly gave me to understand, that on that point my judgment was sound. Yes: his decision was irreversible.

It is not seldom the case that, when a man is browbeaten in some unprecedented and violently unreasonable way, he begins to stagger in his own plainest faith. He begins, as it were, vaguely to surmise that, wonderful as it may be, all the justice and all the reason is on the other side. Accordingly, if any disinterested persons are present, he turns to them for some reinforcement for his own faltering mind.

"Turkey," said I, "what do you think of this? Am I not right?"

"With submission, sir," said Turkey, in his blandest tone, "I think that you are."

"Nippers," said I, "what do *you* think of it?" 45

"I think I should kick him out of the office."

(The reader of nice perceptions will have perceived that, it being morning, Turkey's answer is couched in polite and tranquil terms, but Nippers replies in ill-tempered ones. Or, to repeat a previous sentence, Nippers' ugly mood was on duty, and Turkey's off.)

"Ginger Nut," said I, willing to enlist the smallest suffrage in my behalf, "what do *you* think of it?"

"I think, sir, he's a little *luny*," replied Ginger Nut, with a grin.

"You hear what they say," said I, turning towards the screen, "come forth 50 and do your duty."

But he vouchsafed no reply. I pondered a moment in sore perplexity. But once more business hurried me. I determined again to postpone the consideration of this dilemma to my future leisure. With a little trouble we made out to examine the papers without Bartleby, though at every page or two Turkey deferentially dropped his opinion, that this proceeding was quite out of the common; while Nippers, twitching in his chair with a dyspeptic nervousness, ground out, between his set teeth, occasional hissing maledictions against the stubborn oaf behind the screen. And for his (Nippers') part, this was the first and the last time he would do another man's business without pay.

Meanwhile Bartleby sat in his hermitage, oblivious to everything but his own peculiar business there.

Some days passed, the scrivener being employed upon another lengthy work. His late remarkable conduct led me to regard his ways narrowly. I observed that he never went to dinner; indeed, that he never went anywhere. As yet I had never, of my personal knowledge, known him to be outside of my office. He was a perpetual sentry in the corner. At about eleven o'clock though, in the morning, I noticed that Ginger Nut would advance toward the opening in

Bartleby's screen, as if silently beckoned thither by a gesture invisible to me where I sat. The boy would then leave the office, jingling a few pence, and reappear with a handful of ginger-nuts, which he delivered in the hermitage, receiving two of the cakes for his trouble.

He lives, then, on ginger-nuts, thought I; never eats a dinner, properly speaking; he must be a vegetarian, then, but no; he never eats even vegetables, he eats nothing but ginger-nuts. My mind then ran on in reveries concerning the probable effects upon the human constitution of living entirely on ginger-nuts. Ginger-nuts are so called, because they contain ginger as one of their peculiar constituents, and the final flavoring one. Now, what was ginger? A hot, spicy thing. Was Bartleby hot and spicy? Not at all. Ginger, then, had no effect upon Bartleby. Probably he preferred it should have none.

Nothing so aggravates an earnest person as a passive resistance. If the 55 individual so resisted be of a not inhumane temper, and the resisting one perfectly harmless in his passivity, then, in the better moods of the former, he will endeavor charitably to construe to his imagination what proves impossible to be solved by his judgment. Even so, for the most part, I regarded Bartleby and his ways. Poor fellow! thought I, he means no mischief; it is plain he intends no insolence; his aspect sufficiently evinces that his eccentricities are involuntary. He is useful to me. I can get along with him. If I turn him away, the chances are he will fall in with some less indulgent employer, and then he will be rudely treated, and perhaps driven forth miserably to starve. Yes. Here I can cheaply purchase a delicious self-approval. To befriend Bartleby; to humor him in his strange wilfulness, will cost me little or nothing, while I lay up in my soul what will eventually prove a sweet morsel for my conscience. But this mood was not invariable with me. The passiveness of Bartleby sometimes irritated me. I felt strangely goaded on to encounter him in new opposition — to elicit some angry spark from him answerable to my own. But, indeed, I might as well have essayed to strike fire with my knuckles against a bit of Windsor soap. But one afternoon the evil impulse in me mastered me, and the following little scene ensued:

"Bartleby," said I, "when those papers are all copied, I will compare them with you."

"I would prefer not to."

"How? Surely you do not mean to persist in that mulish vagary?"

No answer.

I threw open the folding-doors nearby, and turning upon Turkey and Nip- 60 pers, exclaimed:

"Bartleby a second time says, he won't examine his papers. What do you think of it, Turkey?"

It was afternoon, be it remembered. Turkey sat glowing like a brass boiler; his bald head steaming; his hands reeling among his blotted papers.

"Think of it?" roared Turkey. "I think I'll just step behind his screen, and black his eyes for him!"

So saying, Turkey rose to his feet and threw his arms into a pugilistic position. He was hurrying away to make good his promise, when I detained him, alarmed at the effect of incautiously rousing Turkey's combativeness after dinner.

"Sit down, Turkey," said I, "and hear what Nippers has to say. What do 65 you think of it, Nippers? Would I not be justified in immediately dismissing Bartleby?"

"Excuse me, that is for you to decide, sir. I think his conduct quite unusual, and, indeed, unjust, as regards Turkey and myself. But it may only be a passing whim."

"Ah," exclaimed I, "you have strangely changed your mind, then—you speak very gently of him now."

"All beer," cried Turkey; "gentleness is effects of beer—Nippers and I dined together to-day. You see how gentle *I* am, sir. Shall I go and black his eyes?"

"You refer to Bartleby, I suppose. No, not to-day, Turkey," I replied; "pray, put up your fists."

I closed the doors, and again advanced towards Bartleby. I felt additional 70 incentives tempting me to my fate. I burned to be rebelled against again. I remembered that Bartleby never left the office.

"Bartleby," said I, "Ginger Nut is away; just step around to the Post Office, won't you?" (it was but a three minutes' walk) "and see if there is anything for me."

"I would prefer not to."

"You *will* not?"

"I *prefer* not."

I staggered to my desk, and sat there in a deep study. My blind inveteracy 75 returned. Was there any other thing in which I could procure myself to be ignominiously repulsed by this lean, penniless wight?—my hired clerk? What added thing is there, perfectly reasonable, that he will be sure to refuse to do?

"Bartleby!"

No answer.

"Bartleby," in a louder tone.

No answer.

"Bartleby," I roared. 80

Like a very ghost, agreeably to the laws of magical invocation, at the third summons, he appeared at the entrance of his hermitage.

"Go to the next room, and tell Nippers to come to me."

"I prefer not to," he respectfully and slowly said, and mildly disappeared.

"Very good, Bartleby," said I, in a quiet sort of serenely-severe self-possessed tone, intimating the unalterable purpose of some terrible retribution very close at hand. At the moment I half intended something of the kind. But upon the whole, as it was drawing towards my dinner-hour, I thought it best to put on my hat and walk home for the day, suffering much from perplexity and distress of mind.

Shall I acknowledge it? The conclusion of this whole business was, that it 85 soon became a fixed fact of my chambers, that a pale young scrivener, by the name of Bartleby, had a desk there; that he copied for me at the usual rate of four cents a folio (one hundred words); but he was permanently exempt from examining the work done by him, that duty being transferred to Turkey and Nippers, out of compliment, doubtless, to their superior acuteness; moreover, said Bartleby was never, on any account, to be dispatched on the most trivial errand of any sort; and that even if entreated to take upon him such a matter, it was generally understood that he would "prefer not to"—in other words, that he would refuse point-blank.

As days passed on, I became considerably reconciled to Bartleby. His steadiness, his freedom from all dissipation, his incessant industry (except when he chose to throw himself into a standing revery behind his screen), his great stillness, his unalterableness of demeanor under all circumstances, made him a valuable acquisition. One prime thing was this—*he was always there*—first in the morning, continually through the day, and the last at night. I had a singular confidence in his honesty. I felt my most precious papers perfectly safe in his hands. Sometimes, to be sure, I could not, for the very soul of me, avoid falling into sudden spasmodic passions with him. For it was exceeding difficult to bear in mind all the time those strange peculiarities, privileges, and unheard-of exemptions, forming the tacit stipulations on Bartleby's part under which he remained in my office. Now and then, in the eagerness of dispatching pressing business, I would inadvertently summon Bartleby, in a short, rapid tone, to put his finger, say, on the incipient tie of a bit of red tape with which I was about compressing some papers. Of course, from behind the screen the usual answer, "I prefer not to," was sure to come; and then, how could a human creature, with the common infirmities of our nature, refrain from bitterly exclaiming upon such perverseness—such unreasonableness? However, every added repulse of this sort which I received only tended to lessen the probability of my repeating the inadvertence.

Here it must be said, that, according to the custom of most legal gentlemen occupying chambers in densely populated law buildings, there were several keys to my door. One was kept by a woman residing in the attic, which person weekly scrubbed and daily swept and dusted my apartments. Another was kept by Turkey for convenience sake. The third I sometimes carried in my own pocket. The fourth I knew not who had.

Now, one Sunday morning I happened to go to Trinity Church, to hear a celebrated preacher, and finding myself rather early on the ground I thought I would walk round to my chambers for a while. Luckily I had my key with me; but upon applying it to the lock, I found it resisted by something inserted from the inside. Quite surprised, I called out; when to my consternation a key was turned from within; and thrusting his lean visage at me, and holding the door ajar, the apparition of Bartleby appeared, in his shirt-sleeves, and otherwise in a strangely tattered *deshabille,* saying quietly that he was sorry, but he was deeply engaged just then, and—preferred not admitting me at present. In a brief word or two, he moreover added, that perhaps I had better walk round the block two or three times, and by that time he would probably have concluded his affairs.

Now, the utterly unsurmised appearance of Bartleby, tenanting my law-chambers of a Sunday morning, with his cadaverously gentlemanly *nonchalance,* yet withal firm and self-possessed, had such a strange effect upon me, that incontinently I slunk away from my own door, and did as desired. But not without sundry twinges of impotent rebellion against the mild effrontery of this unaccountable scrivener. Indeed, it was his wonderful mildness chiefly, which not only disarmed me, but unmanned me, as it were. For I consider that one, for the time, is sort of unmanned when he tranquilly permits his hired clerk to dictate to him, and order him away from his own premises. Furthermore, I was full of uneasiness as to what Bartleby could possibly be doing in my office in his shirt-sleeves, and in an otherwise dismantled condition of a Sunday morning. Was anything amiss going on? Nay, that was out of the question. It was not to be thought of for a moment that Bartleby was an immoral person. But what could he be doing there?—copying? Nay again, whatever might be his eccentricities, Bartleby was an eminently decorous person. He would be the last man to sit down to his desk in any state approaching to nudity. Besides, it was Sunday; and there was something about Bartleby that forbade the supposition that he would by any secular occupation violate the proprieties of the day.

Nevertheless, my mind was not pacified; and full of a restless curiosity, at last I returned to the door. Without hindrance I inserted my key, opened it, and entered. Bartleby was not to be seen. I looked round anxiously, peeped behind his screen; but it was very plain that he was gone. Upon more closely examining the place, I surmised that for an indefinite period Bartleby must have ate, dressed, and slept in my office, and that too without plate, mirror, or bed. The cushioned seat of a rickety old sofa in one corner bore the faint impress of a lean, reclining form. Rolled away under his desk, I found a blanket; under the empty grate, a blacking box and brush; on a chair, a tin basin, with soap and a ragged towel; in a newspaper a few crumbs of ginger-nuts and a morsel of cheese. Yes, thought I, it is evident enough that Bartleby has been making his home here, keeping bachelor's hall all by himself. Immediately then the thought came sweeping across me, what miserable friendlessness and loneliness are here revealed! His poverty is great; but his solitude, how horrible! Think of it. Of a Sunday, Wall Street is deserted as Petra;° and every night of every day it is an emptiness. This building, too, which of week-days hums with industry and life, at nightfall echoes with sheer vacancy, and all through Sunday is forlorn. And here Bartleby makes his home; sole spectator of a solitude which he has seen all populous — a sort of innocent and transformed Marius brooding among the ruins of Carthage?°

For the first time in my life a feeling of overpowering stinging melancholy seized me. Before, I had never experienced aught but a not unpleasing sadness. The bond of a common humanity now drew me irresistibly to gloom. A fraternal melancholy! For both I and Bartleby were sons of Adam. I remembered the bright silks and sparkling faces I had seen that day, in gala trim, swan-like sailing down the Mississippi of Broadway; and I contrasted them with the pallid copyist, and thought to myself, Ah, happiness courts the light, so we deem the world is gay; but misery hides aloof, so we deem that misery there is none. These sad fancyings — chimeras, doubtless, of a sick and silly brain — led on to other and more special thoughts, concerning the eccentricities of Bartleby. Presentiments of strange discoveries hovered round me. The scrivener's pale form appeared to me laid out, among uncaring strangers, in its shivering winding-sheet.

Suddenly I was attracted by Bartleby's closed desk, the key in open sight left in the lock.

I mean no mischief, seek the gratification of no heartless curiosity, thought I; besides, the desk is mine, and its contents, too, so I will make bold to look within. Everything was methodically arranged, the papers smoothly placed. The pigeon-holes were deep, and removing the files of documents, I groped into their recesses. Presently I felt something there, and dragged it out. It was an old bandanna handkerchief, heavy and knotted. I opened it, and saw it was a saving's bank.

Petra: An ancient Arabian city whose ruins were discovered in 1812.
Marius . . . of Carthage: Gaius Marius (157–86 B.C.), an exiled Roman general, sought refuge in the African city-state of Carthage, which was destroyed by the Romans in the Third Punic War.

I now recalled all the quiet mysteries which I had noted in the man. I remembered that he never spoke but to answer; that, though at intervals he had considerable time to himself, yet I had never seen him reading — no, not even a newspaper; that for long periods he would stand looking out, at his pale window behind the screen, upon the dead brick wall; I was quite sure he never visited any refectory or eating-house; while his pale face clearly indicated that he never drank beer like Turkey; or tea and coffee even, like other men; that he never went anywhere in particular that I could learn; never went out for a walk, unless, indeed, that was the case at present; that he had declined telling who he was, or whence he came, or whether he had any relatives in the world; that though so thin and pale, he never complained of ill-health. And more than all, I remembered a certain unconscious air of pallid — how shall I call it? — of pallid haughtiness, say, or rather an austere reserve about him, which had positively awed me into my tame compliance with his eccentricities, when I had feared to ask him to do the slightest incidental thing for me, even though I might know, from his long-continued motionlessness, that behind his screen he must be standing in one of those dead-wall reveries of his.

Revolving all these things, and coupling them with the recently discovered 95 fact, that he made my office his constant abiding place and home, and not forgetful of his morbid moodiness; revolving all these things, a prudential feeling began to steal over me. My first emotions had been those of pure melancholy and sincerest pity; but just in proportion as the forlornness of Bartleby grew and grew to my imagination, did that same melancholy merge into fear, that pity into repulsion. So true it is, and so terrible, too, that up to a certain point the thought or sight of misery enlists our best affections; but, in certain special cases, beyond that point it does not. They err who would assert that invariably this is owing to the inherent selfishness of the human heart. It rather proceeds from a certain hopelessness of remedying excessive and organic ill. To a sensitive being, pity is not seldom pain. And when at last it is perceived that such pity cannot lead to effectual succor, common sense bids the soul be rid of it. What I saw that morning persuaded me that the scrivener was the victim of innate and incurable disorder. I might give alms to his body; but his body did not pain him; it was his soul that suffered, and his soul I could not reach.

I did not accomplish the purpose of going to Trinity Church that morning. Somehow, the things I had seen disqualified me for the time from churchgoing. I walked homeward, thinking what I would do with Bartleby. Finally, I resolved upon this — I would put certain calm questions to him the next morning, touching his history, etc., and if he declined to answer them openly and unreservedly (and I supposed he would prefer not), then to give him a twenty dollar bill over and above whatever I might owe him, and tell him his services were no longer required; but that if in any other way I could assist him, I would be happy to do so, especially if he desired to return to his native place, wherever that might be, I would willingly help to defray the expenses. Moreover, if, after reaching home, he found himself at any time in want of aid, a letter from him would be sure of a reply.

The next morning came.

"Bartleby," said I, gently calling to him behind his screen.

No reply.

"Bartleby," said I, in a still gentler tone, "come here; I am not going to ask 100
you to do anything you would prefer not to do—I simply wish to speak to you."

Upon this he noiselessly slid into view.

"Will you tell me, Bartleby, where you were born?"

"I would prefer not to."

"Will you tell me *anything* about yourself?"

"I would prefer not to." 105

"But what reasonable objection can you have to speak to me? I feel friendly
towards you."

He did not look at me while I spoke, but kept his glance fixed upon my
bust of Cicero, which, as I then sat, was directly behind me, some six inches
above my head.

"What is your answer, Bartleby?" said I, after waiting a considerable time
for a reply, during which his countenance remained immovable, only there was
the faintest conceivable tremor of the white attenuated mouth.

"At present I prefer to give no answer," he said, and retired into his hermitage.

It was rather weak in me I confess, but his manner, on this occasion, nettled 110
me. Not only did there seem to lurk in it a certain calm disdain, but his perverseness seemed ungrateful, considering the undeniable good usage and indulgence
he had received from me.

Again I sat ruminating what I should do. Mortified as I was at his behavior, and resolved as I had been to dismiss him when I entered my office, nevertheless I strangely felt something superstitious knocking at my heart, and
forbidding me to carry out my purpose, and denouncing me for a villain if I
dared to breathe one bitter word against this forlornest of mankind. At last, familiarly drawing my chair behind his screen, I sat down and said: "Bartleby,
never mind, then, about revealing your history; but let me entreat you, as a
friend, to comply as far as may be with the usages of this office. Say now, you
will help to examine papers tomorrow or next day: in short, say now, that in a
day or two you will begin to be a little reasonable:—say so, Bartleby."

"At present I would prefer not to be a little reasonable," was his mildly cadaverous reply.

Just then the folding-doors opened, and Nippers approached. He seemed
suffering from an unusually bad night's rest, induced by severer indigestion
than common. He overheard those final words of Bartleby.

"*Prefer not*, eh?" gritted Nippers—"I'd *prefer* him, if I were you, sir," addressing me—"I'd *prefer* him; I'd give him preferences, the stubborn mule!
What is it, sir, pray, that he *prefers* not to do now?"

Bartleby moved not a limb. 115

"Mr. Nippers," said I, "I'd prefer that you would withdraw for the present."

Somehow, of late, I had got into the way of involuntarily using this word
"prefer" upon all sorts of not exactly suitable occasions. And I trembled to
think that my contact with the scrivener had already and seriously affected me
in a mental way. And what further and deeper aberration might it not yet produce? This apprehension had not been without efficacy in determining me to
summary measures.

As Nippers, looking very sour and sulky, was departing, Turkey blandly
and deferentially approached.

"With submission, sir," said he, "yesterday I was thinking about Bartleby here, and I think that if he would but prefer to take a quart of good ale every day, it would do much towards mending him, and enabling him to assist in examining his papers."

"So you have got the word, too," said I, slightly excited.   120

"With submission, what word, sir?" asked Turkey, respectfully crowding himself into the contracted space behind the screen, and by so doing, making me jostle the scrivener. "What word, sir?"

"I would prefer to be left alone here," said Bartleby, as if offended at being mobbed in his privacy.

"*That's* the word, Turkey," said I — "*that's* it."

"Oh, *prefer?* oh yes — queer word. I never use it myself. But, sir, as I was saying, if he would but prefer —"

"Turkey," interrupted I, "you will please withdraw."   125

"Oh certainly, sir, if you prefer that I should."

As he opened the folding-door to retire, Nippers at his desk caught a glimpse of me, and asked whether I would prefer to have a certain paper copied on blue paper or white. He did not in the least roguishly accent the word "prefer." It was plain that it involuntarily rolled from his tongue. I thought to myself, surely I must get rid of a demented man, who already has in some degree turned the tongues, if not the heads of myself and clerks. But I thought it prudent not to break the dismission at once.

The next day I noticed that Bartleby did nothing but stand at his window in his dead-wall revery. Upon asking him why he did not write, he said that he had decided upon doing no more writing.

"Why, how now? what next?" exclaimed I, "do no more writing?"

"No more."   130

"And what is the reason?"

"Do you not see the reason for yourself?" he indifferently replied.

I looked steadfastly at him, and perceived that his eyes looked dull and glazed. Instantly it occurred to me, that his unexampled diligence in copying by his dim window for the first few weeks of his stay with me might have temporarily impaired his vision.

I was touched. I said something in condolence with him. I hinted that of course he did wisely in abstaining from writing for a while; and urged him to embrace that opportunity of taking wholesome exercise in the open air. This, however, he did not do. A few days after this, my other clerks being absent, and being in a great hurry to dispatch certain letters by the mail, I thought that, having nothing else earthly to do, Bartleby would surely be less inflexible than usual, and carry these letters to the Post Office. But he blankly declined. So, much to my inconvenience, I went myself.

Still added days went by. Whether Bartleby's eyes improved or not, I could   135
not say. To all appearance, I thought they did. But when I asked him if they did, he vouchsafed no answer. At all events, he would do no copying. At last, in replying to my urgings, he informed me that he had permanently given up copying.

"What!" exclaimed I; "suppose your eyes should get entirely well — better than ever before — would you not copy then?"

"I have given up copying," he answered, and slid aside.

He remained as ever, a fixture in my chamber. Nay — if that were possible — he became still more of a fixture than before. What was to be done? He would do nothing in the office; why should he stay there? In plain fact, he had now become a millstone to me, not only useless as a necklace, but afflictive to bear. Yet I was sorry for him. I speak less than truth when I say that, on his own account, he occasioned me uneasiness. If he would but have named a single relative or friend, I would instantly have written, and urged their taking the poor fellow away to some convenient retreat. But he seemed alone, absolutely alone in the universe. A bit of wreck in the mid-Atlantic. At length, necessities connected with my business tyrannized over all other considerations. Decently as I could, I told Bartleby that in six days' time he must unconditionally leave the office. I warned him to take measures, in the interval, for procuring some other abode. I offered to assist him in this endeavor, if he himself would but take the first step towards a removal. "And when you finally quit me, Bartleby," added I, "I shall see that you go not away entirely unprovided. Six days from this hour, remember."

At the expiration of that period, I peeped behind the screen, and lo! Bartleby was there.

I buttoned up my coat, balanced myself; advanced slowly towards him, 140 touched his shoulder, and said, "The time has come; you must quit this place; I am sorry for you; here is money; but you must go."

"I would prefer not," he replied, with his back still towards me.

"You *must*."

He remained silent.

Now I had an unbounded confidence in this man's common honesty. He had frequently restored to me sixpences and shillings carelessly dropped upon the floor, for I am apt to be very reckless in such shirt-button affairs. The proceeding, then, which followed will not be deemed extraordinary.

"Bartleby," said I, "I owe you twelve dollars on account; here are thirty-two, 145 the odd twenty are yours — Will you take it?" and I handed the bills towards him.

But he made no motion.

"I will leave them here, then," putting them under a weight on the table. Then taking my hat and cane and going to the door, I tranquilly turned and added — "After you have removed your things from these offices, Bartleby, you will of course lock the door — since every one is now gone for the day but you — and if you please, slip your key underneath the mat, so that I may have it in the morning. I shall not see you again; so good-bye to you. If, hereafter, in your new place of abode, I can be of any service to you, do not fail to advise me by letter. Good-bye, Bartleby, and fare you well."

But he answered not a word; like the last column of some ruined temple, he remained standing mute and solitary in the middle of the otherwise deserted room.

As I walked home in a pensive mood, my vanity got the better of my pity. I could not but highly plume myself on my masterly management in getting rid of Bartleby. Masterly I call it, and such it must appear to any dispassionate thinker. The beauty of my procedure seemed to consist in its perfect quietness. There was no vulgar bullying, no bravado of any sort, no choleric hectoring, and striding to and fro across the apartment, jerking out vehement commands for Bartleby to bundle himself off with his beggarly traps. Nothing of the kind.

Without loudly bidding Bartleby depart—as an inferior genius might have done—I *assumed* the ground that depart he must; and upon that assumption built all I had to say. The more I thought over my procedure, the more I was charmed with it. Nevertheless, next morning, upon awakening, I had my doubts—I had somehow slept off the fumes of vanity. One of the coolest and wisest hours a man has, is just after he awakes in the morning. My procedure seemed as sagacious as ever—but only in theory. How it would prove in practice—there was the rub. It was truly a beautiful thought to have assumed Bartleby's departure; but, after all, that assumption was simply my own, and none of Bartleby's. The great point was, not whether I had assumed that he would quit me, but whether he would prefer to do so. He was more a man of preferences than assumptions.

After breakfast, I walked down town, arguing the probabilities *pro* and *con*. 150 One moment I thought it would prove a miserable failure, and Bartleby would be found all alive at my office as usual; the next moment it seemed certain that I should find his chair empty. And so I kept veering about. At the corner of Broadway and Canal Street, I saw quite an excited group of people standing in earnest conversation.

"I'll take odds he doesn't," said a voice as I passed.

"Doesn't go?—done!" said I, "put up your money."

I was instinctively putting my hand in my pocket to produce my own, when I remembered that this was an election day. The words I had overheard bore no reference to Bartleby, but to the success or non-success of some candidate for the mayoralty. In my intent frame of mind, I had, as it were, imagined that all Broadway shared in my excitement, and were debating the same question with me. I passed on, very thankful that the uproar of the street screened my momentary absent-mindedness.

As I had intended, I was earlier than usual at my office door. I stood listening for a moment. All was still. He must be gone. I tried the knob. The door was locked. Yes, my procedure had worked to a charm; he indeed must be vanished. Yet a certain melancholy mixed with this: I was almost sorry for my brilliant success. I was fumbling under the door mat for the key, which Bartleby was to have left there for me, when accidentally my knee knocked against a panel, producing a summoning sound, and in response a voice came to me from within—"Not yet; I am occupied."

It was Bartleby. 155

I was thunderstruck. For an instant I stood like the man who, pipe in mouth, was killed one cloudless afternoon long ago in Virginia, by summer lightning; at his own warm open window he was killed, and remained leaning out there upon the dreamy afternoon, till some one touched him, when he fell.

"Not gone!" I murmured at last. But again obeying that wondrous ascendancy which the inscrutable scrivener had over me, and from which ascendancy, for all my chafing, I could not completely escape, I slowly went down stairs and out into the street, and while walking round the block, considered what I should next do in this unheard-of perplexity. Turn the man out by an actual thrusting I could not; to drive him away by calling him hard names would not do; calling in the police was an unpleasant idea; and yet, permit him to enjoy his cadaverous triumph over me—this, too, I could not think of. What was to be done? or, if nothing could be done, was there anything further that I could *assume* in the matter? Yes, as before I had prospectively assumed that

Bartleby would depart, so now I might retrospectively assume that departed he was. In the legitimate carrying out of this assumption, I might enter my office in a great hurry, and pretending not to see Bartleby at all, walk straight against him as if he were air. Such a proceeding would in a singular degree have the appearance of a home-thrust. It was hardly possible that Bartleby could withstand such an application of the doctrine of assumption. But upon second thoughts the success of the plan seemed rather dubious. I resolved to argue the matter over with him again.

"Bartleby," said I, entering the office, with a quietly severe expression, "I am seriously displeased. I am pained, Bartleby. I had thought better of you. I had imagined you of such a gentlemanly organization, that in any delicate dilemma a slight hint would suffice—in short, an assumption. But it appears I am deceived. Why," I added, unaffectedly starting, "you have not even touched that money yet," pointing to it, just where I had left it the evening previous.

He answered nothing.

"Will you, or will you not, quit me?" I now demanded in a sudden passion, 160 advancing close to him.

"I would prefer *not* to quit you," he replied, gently emphasizing the *not*.

"What earthly right have you to stay here? Do you pay any rent? Do you pay my taxes? Or is this property yours?"

He answered nothing.

"Are you ready to go on and write now? Are your eyes recovered? Could you copy a small paper for me this morning? or help examine a few lines? or step round to the Post Office? In a word, will you do anything at all, to give a coloring to your refusal to depart the premises?"

He silently retired into his hermitage. 165

I was now in such a state of nervous resentment that I thought it but prudent to check myself at present from further demonstrations. Bartleby and I were alone. I remembered the tragedy of the unfortunate Adams and the still more unfortunate Colt° in the solitary office of the latter; and how poor Colt, being dreadfully incensed by Adams, and imprudently permitting himself to get wildly excited, was at unawares hurried into his fatal act—an act which certainly no man could possibly deplore more than the actor himself. Often it had occurred to me in my ponderings upon the subject that had that altercation taken place in the public street, or at a private residence, it would not have terminated as it did. It was the circumstance of being alone in a solitary office, up stairs, of a building entirely unhallowed by humanizing domestic associations—an uncarpeted office, doubtless, of a dusty, haggard sort of appearance—this it must have been, which greatly helped to enhance the irritable desperation of the hapless Colt.

But when this old Adam of resentment rose in me and tempted me concerning Bartleby, I grappled him and threw him. How? Why, simply by recalling the divine injunction: "A new commandment give I unto you, that ye love one another." Yes, this it was that saved me. Aside from higher considerations, charity often operates as a vastly wise and prudent principle—a great safeguard to its possessor. Men have committed murder for jealousy's sake, and

Adams . . . Colt: Samuel Adams was killed by John C. Colt, brother of the gun maker, during a quarrel in 1842. After a sensational court case, Colt committed suicide just before he was to be hanged.

anger's sake, and hatred's sake, and selfishness' sake, and spiritual pride's sake; but no man, that ever I heard of, ever committed a diabolical murder for sweet charity's sake. Mere self-interest, then, if no better motive can be enlisted, should, especially with high-tempered men, prompt all beings to charity and philanthropy. At any rate, upon the occasion in question, I strove to drown my exasperated feelings towards the scrivener by benevolently construing his conduct. Poor fellow, poor fellow! thought I, he don't mean anything; and besides, he has seen hard times, and ought to be indulged.

I endeavored, also, immediately to occupy myself, and at the same time to comfort my despondency. I tried to fancy, that in the course of the morning, at such time as might prove agreeable to him, Bartleby, of his own free accord, would emerge from his hermitage and take up some decided line of march in the direction of the door. But no. Half-past twelve o'clock came; Turkey began to glow in the face, overturn his inkstand, and become generally obstreperous; Nippers abated down into quietude and courtesy; Ginger Nut munched his noon apple; and Bartleby remained standing at his window in one of his profoundest dead-wall reveries. Will it be credited? Ought I to acknowledge it? That afternoon I left the office without saying one further word to him.

Some days now passed, during which, at leisure intervals I looked a little into "Edwards on the Will," and "Priestley on Necessity."° Under the circumstances, those books induced a salutary feeling. Gradually I slid into the persuasion that these troubles of mine, touching the scrivener, had been all predestined from eternity, and Bartleby was billeted upon me for some mysterious purpose of an all-wise Providence, which it was not for a mere mortal like me to fathom. Yes, Bartleby, stay there behind your screen, thought I; I shall persecute you no more; you are harmless and noiseless as any of these old chairs; in short, I never feel so private as when I know you are here. At last I see it, I feel it; I penetrate to the predestined purpose of my life. I am content. Others may have loftier parts to enact; but my mission in this world, Bartleby, is to furnish you with office-room for such period as you may see fit to remain.

I believe that this wise and blessed frame of mind would have continued with me, had it not been for the unsolicited and uncharitable remarks obtruded upon me by my professional friends who visited the rooms. But thus it often is, that the constant friction of illiberal minds wears out at last the best resolves of the more generous. Though to be sure, when I reflected upon it, it was not strange that people entering my office should be struck by the peculiar aspect of the unaccountable Bartleby, and so be tempted to throw out some sinister observations concerning him. Sometimes an attorney, having business with me, and calling at my office, and finding no one but the scrivener there, would undertake to obtain some sort of precise information from him touching my whereabouts; but without heeding his idle talk, Bartleby would remain standing immovable in the middle of the room. So after contemplating him in that position for a time, the attorney would depart, no wiser than he came.

Also, when a reference was going on, and the room full of lawyers and witnesses, and business driving fast, some deeply-occupied legal gentleman present, seeing Bartleby wholly unemployed, would request him to run round to

170

"*Edwards . . . Necessity*": Jonathan Edwards, in *Freedom of the Will* (1754), and Joseph Priestley, in *Doctrine of Philosophical Necessity* (1777), both argued that human beings do not have free will.

his (the legal gentleman's) office and fetch some papers for him. Thereupon, Bartleby would tranquilly decline, and yet remain idle as before. Then the lawyer would give a great stare, and turn to me. And what could I say? At last I was made aware that all through the circle of my professional acquaintance, a whisper of wonder was running round, having reference to the strange creature I kept at my office. This worried me very much. And as the idea came upon me of his possibly turning out a long-lived man, and keeping occupying my chambers, and denying my authority; and perplexing my visitors; and scandalizing my professional reputation; and casting a general gloom over the premises; keeping soul and body together to the last upon his savings (for doubtless he spent but half a dime a day), and in the end perhaps outlive me, and claim possession of my office by right of his perpetual occupancy: as all these dark anticipations crowded upon me more and more, and my friends continually intruded their relentless remarks upon the apparition in my room; a great change was wrought in me. I resolved to gather all my faculties together, and forever rid me of this intolerable incubus.

Ere revolving any complicated project, however, adapted to this end, I first simply suggested to Bartleby the propriety of his permanent departure. In a calm and serious tone, I commended the idea to his careful and mature consideration. But, having taken three days to meditate upon it, he apprised me, that his original determination remained the same; in short, that he still preferred to abide with me.

What shall I do? I now said to myself, buttoning up my coat to the last button. What shall I do? what ought I to do? what does conscience say I *should* do with this man, or, rather, ghost. Rid myself of him, I must; go, he shall. But how? You will not thrust him, the poor, pale, passive mortal — you will not thrust such a helpless creature out of your door? you will not dishonor yourself by such cruelty? No, I will not, I cannot do that. Rather would I let him live and die here, and then mason up his remains in the wall. What, then, will you do? For all your coaxing, he will not budge. Bribes he leaves under your own paper-weight on your table; in short, it is quite plain that he prefers to cling to you.

Then something severe, something unusual must be done. What! surely you will not have him collared by a constable, and commit his innocent pallor to the common jail? And upon what ground could you procure such a thing to be done? — a vagrant, is he? What! he a vagrant, a wanderer, who refuses to budge? It is because he will *not* be a vagrant, then, that you seek to count him *as* a vagrant. That is too absurd. No visible means of support: there I have him. Wrong again: for indubitably he *does* support himself, and that is the only unanswerable proof that any man can show of his possessing the means so to do. No more, then. Since he will not quit me, I must quit him. I will change my offices; I will move elsewhere, and give him fair notice, that if I find him on my new premises I will then proceed against him as a common trespasser.

Acting accordingly, next day I thus addressed him: "I find these chambers 175 too far from the City Hall; the air is unwholesome. In a word, I propose to remove my offices next week, and shall no longer require your services. I tell you this now, in order that you may seek another place."

He made no reply, and nothing more was said.

On the appointed day I engaged carts and men, proceeded to my chambers, and having but little furniture, everything was removed in a few hours.

Throughout, the scrivener remained standing behind the screen, which I directed to be removed the last thing. It was withdrawn; and, being folded up like a huge folio, left him the motionless occupant of a naked room. I stood in the entry watching him a moment, while something from within me upbraided me.

I re-entered, with my hand in my pocket — and — and my heart in my mouth.

"Good-bye, Bartleby; I am going — good-bye, and God some way bless you; and take that," slipping something in his hand. But it dropped upon the floor, and then — strange to say — I tore myself from him whom I had so longed to be rid of.

Established in my new quarters, for a day or two I kept the door locked, and started at every footfall in the passages. When I returned to my rooms, after any little absence, I would pause at the threshold for an instant, and attentively listen, ere applying my key. But these fears were needless. Bartleby never came nigh me.

I thought all was going well, when a perturbed-looking stranger visited me, inquiring whether I was the person who had recently occupied rooms at No. — Wall Street.

Full of forebodings, I replied that I was.

"Then, sir," said the stranger, who proved a lawyer, "you are responsible for the man you left there. He refuses to do any copying; he refuses to do anything; he says he prefers not to; and he refuses to quit the premises."

"I am very sorry, sir," said I, with assumed tranquillity, but an inward tremor, "but, really, the man you allude to is nothing to me — he is no relation or apprentice of mine, that you should hold me responsible for him."

"In mercy's name, who is he?"

"I certainly cannot inform you. I know nothing about him. Formerly I employed him as a copyist; but he has done nothing for me now for some time past."

"I shall settle him, then — good morning, sir."

Several days passed, and I heard nothing more; and, though I often felt a charitable prompting to call at the place and see poor Bartleby, yet a certain squeamishness, of I know not what, withheld me.

All is over with him, by this time, thought I, at last, when, through another week, no further intelligence reached me. But, coming to my room the day after, I found several persons waiting at my door in a high state of nervous excitement.

"That's the man — here he comes," cried the foremost one, whom I recognized as the lawyer who had previously called upon me alone.

"You must take him away, sir, at once," cried a portly person among them, advancing upon me, and whom I knew to be the landlord of No. — Wall Street. "These gentlemen, my tenants, cannot stand it any longer; Mr. B ——," pointing to the lawyer, "has turned him out of his room, and he now persists in haunting the building generally, sitting upon the banisters of the stairs by day, and sleeping in the entry by night. Everybody is concerned; clients are leaving the offices; some fears are entertained of a mob; something you must do, and that without delay."

Aghast at this torrent, I fell back before it, and would fain have locked myself in my new quarters. In vain I persisted that Bartleby was nothing to me — no more than to any one else. In vain — I was the last person known to have anything to do with him, and they held me to the terrible account. Fearful, then, of being exposed in the papers (as one person present obscurely threatened), I considered the matter, and, at length, said, that if the lawyer would give me a confidential interview with the scrivener, in his (the lawyer's) own room, I would, that afternoon, strive my best to rid them of the nuisance they complained of.

Going up stairs to my old haunt, there was Bartleby silently sitting upon the banister at the landing.

"What are you doing here, Bartleby?" said I.

"Sitting upon the banister," he mildly replied.

I motioned him into the lawyer's room, who then left us.

"Bartleby," said I, "are you aware that you are the cause of great tribulation to me, by persisting in occupying the entry after being dismissed from the office?"

No answer.

"Now one of two things must take place. Either you must do something, or something must be done to you. Now what sort of business would you like to engage in? Would you like to re-engage in copying for some one?"

"No; I would prefer not to make any change."

"Would you like a clerkship in a dry-goods store?"

"There is too much confinement about that. No, I would not like a clerkship; but I am not particular."

"Too much confinement," I cried, "why, you keep yourself confined all the time!"

"I would prefer not to take a clerkship," he rejoined, as if to settle that little item at once.

"How would a bar-tender's business suit you? There is no trying of the eyesight in that."

"I would not like it at all; though, as I said before, I am not particular."

His unwonted wordiness inspired me. I returned to the charge.

"Well, then, would you like to travel through the country collecting bills for the merchants? That would improve your health."

"No, I would prefer to be doing something else."

"How, then, would going as a companion to Europe, to entertain some young gentleman with your conversation—how would that suit you?"

"Not at all. It does not strike me that there is anything definite about that. I like to be stationary. But I am not particular."

"Stationary you shall be, then," I cried, now losing all patience, and, for the first time in all my exasperating connection with him, fairly flying into a passion. "If you do not go away from these premises before night, I shall feel bound—indeed, I *am* bound—to—to quit the premises myself!" I rather absurdly concluded, knowing not with what possible threat to try to frighten his immobility into compliance. Despairing of all further efforts, I was precipitately leaving him, when a final thought occurred to me—one which had not been wholly unindulged before.

"Bartleby," said I, in the kindest tone I could assume under such exciting circumstances, "will you go home with me now—not to my office, but my dwelling—and remain there till we can conclude upon some convenient arrangement for you at our leisure? Come, let us start now, right away."

"No: at present I would prefer not to make any change at all."

I answered nothing; but, effectually dodging every one by the suddenness 215
and rapidity of my flight, rushed from the building, ran up Wall Street towards
Broadway, and, jumping into the first omnibus, was soon removed from pursuit. As soon as tranquillity returned, I distinctly perceived that I had now
done all that I possibly could, both in respect to the demands of the landlord
and his tenants, and with regard to my own desire and sense of duty, to benefit
Bartleby, and shield him from rude persecution. I now strove to be entirely
care-free and quiescent; and my conscience justified me in the attempt;
though, indeed, it was not so successful as I could have wished. So fearful was I
of being again hunted out by the incensed landlord and his exasperated tenants, that, surrendering my business to Nippers, for a few days, I drove about
the upper part of the town and through the suburbs, in my rockaway; crossed
over to Jersey City and Hoboken, and paid fugitive visits to Manhattanville and
Astoria. In fact, I almost lived in my rockaway for the time.

When again I entered my office, lo, a note from the landlord lay upon the
desk. I opened it with trembling hands. It informed me that the writer had
sent to the police, and had Bartleby removed to the Tombs as a vagrant. Moreover, since I knew more about him than any one else, he wished me to appear at
that place, and make a suitable statement of the facts. These tidings had a conflicting effect upon me. At first I was indignant; but, at last, almost approved.
The landlord's energetic, summary disposition, had led him to adopt a procedure which I do not think I would have decided upon myself; and yet, as a last
resort, under such peculiar circumstances, it seemed the only plan.

As I afterwards learned, the poor scrivener, when told that he must be conducted to the Tombs, offered not the slightest obstacle, but, in his pale, unmoving way, silently acquiesced.

Some of the compassionate and curious by-standers joined the party; and
headed by one of the constables arm-in-arm with Bartleby, the silent procession filed its way through all the noise, and heat, and joy of the roaring thor-
oughfares at noon.

The same day I received the note, I went to the Tombs, or, to speak more
properly, the Halls of Justice. Seeking the right officer, I stated the purpose of
my call, and was informed that the individual I described was, indeed, within. I
then assured the functionary that Bartleby was a perfectly honest man, and
greatly to be compassionated, however unaccountably eccentric. I narrated all
I knew, and closed by suggesting the idea of letting him remain in as indulgent
confinement as possible, till something less harsh might be done—though, indeed, I hardly knew what. At all events, if nothing else could be decided upon,
the almshouse must receive him. I then begged to have an interview.

Being under no disgraceful charge, and quite serene and harmless in all 220
his ways, they had permitted him freely to wander about the prison, and, especially, in the inclosed grass-platted yards thereof. And so I found him there,
standing all alone in the quietest of the yards, his face towards a high wall,
while all around, from the narrow slits of the jail windows, I thought I saw
peering out upon him the eyes of murderers and thieves.

"Bartleby!"

"I know you," he said, without looking round—"and I want nothing to say
to you."

"It was not I that brought you here, Bartleby," said I, keenly pained at his
implied suspicion. "And to you, this should not be so vile a place. Nothing

reproachful attaches to you by being here. And see, it is not so sad a place as one might think. Look, there is the sky, and here is the grass."

"I know where I am," he replied, but would say nothing more, and so I left him.

As I entered the corridor again, a broad meat-like man, in an apron, accosted 225
me, and, jerking his thumb over his shoulder, said — "Is that your friend?"

"Yes."

"Does he want to starve? If he does, let him live on the prison fare, that's all."

"Who are you?" asked I, not knowing what to make of such an unofficially speaking person in such a place.

"I am the grub-man. Such gentlemen as have friends here, hire me to provide them with something good to eat."

"Is this so?" said I, turning the turnkey. 230

He said it was.

"Well, then," said I, slipping some silver into the grub-man's hands (for so they called him), "I want you to give particular attention to my friend there; let him have the best dinner you can get. And you must be as polite to him as possible."

"Introduce me, will you?" said the grub-man, looking at me with an expression which seemed to say he was all impatience for an opportunity to give a specimen of his breeding.

Thinking it would prove of benefit to the scrivener, I acquiesced; and, asking the grub-man his name, went up with him to Bartleby.

"Bartleby, this is a friend; you will find him very useful to you." 235

"Your sarvant, sir, your sarvant," said the grub-man, making a low salutation behind his apron. "Hope you find it pleasant here, sir; nice grounds — cool apartments — hope you'll stay with us some time — try to make it agreeable. What will you have for dinner to-day?"

"I prefer not to dine to-day," said Bartleby, turning away. "It would disagree with me; I am unused to dinners." So saying, he slowly moved to the other side of the inclosure, and took up a position fronting the deadwall.

"How's this?" said the grub-man, addressing me with a stare of astonishment. "He's odd, ain't he?"

"I think he is a little deranged," said I, sadly.

"Deranged? deranged is it? Well, now, upon my word, I thought that 240
friend of yourn was a gentleman forger; they are always pale and genteel-like, them forgers. I can't help pity 'em — can't help it, sir. Did you know Monroe Edwards?" he added, touchingly, and paused. Then, laying his hand piteously on my shoulder, sighed, "he died of consumption at Sing-Sing. So you weren't acquainted with Monroe?"

"No, I was never socially acquainted with any forgers. But I cannot stop longer. Look to my friend yonder. You will not lose by it. I will see you again."

Some few days after this, I again obtained admission to the Tombs, and went through the corridors in quest of Bartleby; but without finding him.

"I saw him coming from his cell not long ago," said a turnkey, "may be he's gone to loiter in the yards."

So I went in that direction.

"Are you looking for the silent man?" said another turnkey, passing me. 245
"Yonder he lies — sleeping in the yard there. 'Tis not twenty minutes since I saw him lie down."

The yard was entirely quiet. It was not accessible to the common prisoners. The surrounding walls, of amazing thickness, kept off all sounds behind them. The Egyptian character of the masonry weighed upon me with its gloom. But a soft imprisoned turf grew under foot. The heart of the eternal pyramids, it seemed, wherein, by some strange magic, through the clefts, grass-seed, dropped by birds, had sprung.

Strangely huddled at the base of the wall, his knees drawn up, and lying on his side, his head touching the cold stones, I saw the wasted Bartleby. But nothing stirred. I paused; then went close up to him; stooped over, and saw that his dim eyes were open; otherwise he seemed profoundly sleeping. Something prompted me to touch him. I felt his hand, when a tingling shiver ran up my arm and down my spine to my feet.

The round face of the grub-man peered upon me now. "His dinner is ready. Won't he dine to-day, either? Or does he live without dining?"

"Lives without dining," said I, and closed the eyes.

"Eh! — He's asleep, ain't he?"

"With kings and counselors,"° murmured I. 250

There would seem little need for proceeding further in this history. Imagination will readily supply the meagre recital of poor Bartleby's interment. But, ere parting with the reader, let me say, that if this little narrative has sufficiently interested him, to awaken curiosity as to who Bartleby was, and what manner of life he led prior to the present narrator's making his acquaintance, I can only reply, that in such curiosity I fully share, but am wholly unable to gratify it. Yet here I hardly know whether I should divulge one little item of rumor, which came to my ear a few months after the scrivener's decease. Upon what basis it rested, I could never ascertain; and hence, how true it is I cannot now tell. But, inasmuch as this vague report has not been without a certain suggestive interest to me, however sad, it may prove the same with some others; and so I will briefly mention it. The report was this: that Bartleby had been a subordinate clerk in the Dead Letter Office at Washington, from which he had been suddenly removed by a change in the administration. When I think over this rumor, hardly can I express the emotions which seize me. Dead letters! does it not sound like dead men? Conceive a man by nature and misfortune prone to a pallid hopelessness, can any business seem more fitted to heighten it than that of continually handling these dead letters, and assorting them for the flames? For by the cart-load they are annually burned. Sometimes from out the folded paper the pale clerk takes a ring — the finger it was meant for, perhaps, moulders in the grave; a bank-note sent in swiftest charity — he whom it would relieve, nor eats nor hungers any more; pardon for those who died despairing; hope for those who died unhoping; good tidings for those who died stifled by unrelieved calamities. On errands of life, these letters speed to death.

Ah, Bartleby! Ah, humanity!

"With kings and counselors": From Job 3:13–14: "then had I been at rest, / With kings and counselors of the earth, / which built desolate places for themselves."

Considerations for Critical Thinking and Writing

I. **FIRST RESPONSE.** How does the lawyer's description of himself serve to characterize him? Why is it significant that he is a lawyer? Are his understandings and judgments about Bartleby and himself always sound?

2. Why do you think Turkey, Nippers, and Ginger Nut are introduced to the reader before Bartleby?

3. Describe Bartleby's physical characteristics. How is his physical description a foreshadowing of what happens to him?

4. How does Bartleby's "I would prefer not to" affect the routine of the lawyer and his employees?

5. What is the significance of the subtitle: "A Story of Wall Street"?

6. Who is the protagonist? Whose story is it?

7. Does the lawyer change during the story? Does Bartleby? Who is the antagonist?

8. What motivates Bartleby's behavior? Why do you think Melville withholds the information about the Dead Letter Office until the end of the story? Does this background adequately explain Bartleby?

9. Does Bartleby have any lasting impact on the lawyer?

10. Do you think Melville sympathizes more with Bartleby or with the lawyer?

11. Describe the lawyer's changing attitudes toward Bartleby.

12. Consider how this story could be regarded as a kind of protest with nonnegotiable demands.

13. Discuss the story's humor and how it affects your response to Bartleby.

14. Trace your emotional reaction to Bartleby as he is revealed in the story.

15. **CRITICAL STRATEGIES.** Read the section on biographical criticism (pp. 2048–50) in Chapter 53, "Critical Strategies for Reading," and use the library to learn about Melville's reputation as a writer at the time of his writing "Bartleby." How might this information produce a provocative biographical approach to the story?

CONNECTIONS TO OTHER SELECTIONS

1. Compare Bartleby's withdrawal from life with that of the protagonist in Gail Godwin's "A Sorrowful Woman" (p. 39). Why does each character choose death?

2. How is Melville's use of Bartleby's experience in the Dead Letter Office similar to Nathaniel Hawthorne's use of Brown's forest encounter with the devil in "Young Goodman Brown" (p. 402)? Why is each experience crucial to an understanding of what informs the behavior of these characters?

Perspectives

NATHANIEL HAWTHORNE (1804–1864)

On Herman Melville's Philosophic Stance   *1856*

[Melville] stayed with us from Tuesday till Thursday; and, on the intervening day, we took a pretty long walk together, and sat down in a hollow among the sand hills (sheltering ourselves from the high, cool wind) and smoked a cigar. Melville, as he always does, began to reason of Providence and futurity, and of everything that lies beyond human ken, and informed me that he had "pretty much made up his mind to be annihilated"; but still he does not seem to rest in that anticipation; and, I think, will never rest until he gets hold of a definite belief. It is strange how he persists — and has persisted ever since I knew him, and probably long before — in wandering to-and-fro over these deserts, as dismal and monotonous as the sand hills amid which we were sitting. He can neither believe, nor be comfortable in his unbelief; and he is too honest and courageous not to try to do one or the other. If he were a religious man, he would be one of the most truly religious and reverential; he has a very high and noble nature, and better worth immortality than most of us.

From *The American Notebooks*

CONSIDERATIONS FOR CRITICAL THINKING AND WRITING

1. How does this description of Melville shed light on the central concerns of "Bartleby, the Scrivener"?

2. Which side does Hawthorne seem to be on — "belief" or "unbelief"? Why?

3. Compare Hawthorne's description with Melville's view of Hawthorne (p. 435). What attitudes about life do they share?

4. Write an essay about the issue of "belief" and "unbelief" in "Bartleby, the Scrivener" and Ernest Hemingway's "Soldier's Home" (p. 187).

DAN MCCALL (B. 1940)

On the Lawyer's Character in "Bartleby, the Scrivener"   *1989*

The overwhelming majority of the Bartleby Industry reads the narrator of the story in a way that is not only different from mine but quite incompatible with mine. Every virtue I see in the man, they see as a vice; where I see his strength, they see his weakness; what I see as his genuine responsiveness, they see as his cold self-absorption. Some critics read the story as I do, but we are in a distinct minority. There are several reasons this should be so, and I think I understand at least some of them, but first I should like to present as fairly as I can the majority opinion.

Robert Weisbuch, who has said the Lawyer is Charles Dickens, refers to the Lawyer as "unnatural," "anti-natural," "lifeless," "self-satisfied," "pompous," and "rationalizing." The Lawyer "investigates Bartleby but refuses authentic emotional commitment in so doing," and "Bartleby rightly refuses to credit the Lawyer's false commitment." The Lawyer is guilty of "toadyism" and his final heartbroken outburst, "Ah, Bartleby! Ah, humanity!" is no more than "a someways hollow and unfeeling exclamation."[1] Another critic calls the Lawyer

[1] Robert Weisbuch, "Melville's 'Bartleby' and the Dead Letter of Charles Dickens," *Atlantic Double-Cross: American Literature and British Influence in the Age of Emerson* (Chicago: University of Chicago Press, 1986), pp. 44, 45–47.

a "smug fool" who is "terribly unkind to a very sick man."[2] I had always thought of the Lawyer as a kind of stand-in for us, a figure we could identify with as we struggled to understand Bartleby. On the contrary, the narrator is "deficient in humanity and quite obtuse towards human beings." I must have had it backwards, for "surely this was Melville's intention: to have his reader *not* sympathize with the Lawyer, *not* to identify with him, *not* to put himself in the Lawyer's place" (*his* italics, not mine).[3] Another critic says, "The narrator attains new heights of vague sentimentality rather than a peak of awareness in his climactic and highly revealing sigh: 'Ah, Bartleby! Ah, humanity!'" This reader provides dismissive certainty in answering the question

> Who then is Melville's narrator? He is the sort of man one tends to find in high places: the snug man whose worldly success has convinced him that this is the "best of all possible worlds," and whose virtues cluster around a "prudential" concern for maintaining his own situation. The narrator can never fully understand or truly befriend Bartleby because the narrator is simply too complacent, both philosophically and morally, to sympathize with human dissatisfaction and despair.[4]

Still another reader tells us the Lawyer's commentary "rings with blasphemy" and demonstrates "grotesque manifestations of diseased conscience."[5]

Authority is the enemy here. In the extended quotation just above it is taken for granted that the "sort of man one tends to find in high places" is superficial and selfish. Worldly success is bad for the character. The Lawyer has to be bad, or he wouldn't be in an office on Wall Street. Hershel Parker tells us that "our ultimate opinion" of the Lawyer "is not contempt so much as bleak astonishment at his secure blindness. With a bitterer irony than the narrator is capable of, we murmur something like 'Ah, narrator! Ah, humanity!' In his self-consciously eloquent sequel, after all, the lawyer has merely made his last cheap purchase of a 'delicious self-approval.'" Parker maintains that when "this easy-conscienced" man speaks of kings and counselors, "he is experiencing a comfortable, self-indulgent variety of melancholy"; when he quotes words from the Book of Job he does so "with prideful aptness," and "characteristically perverts them from profound lament to sonorous urbanity."[6]

This last feature of Parker's argument is interesting to me because it reminds me of the first time I read the story, at eighteen. I was overwhelmed by the discovery that Bartleby had died, and I didn't know that "With kings and counselors" was a quotation from the Book of Job. The phrase "With

[2] David Shusterman, "The 'Reader Fallacy' and 'Bartleby, the Scrivener,'" *New England Quarterly* 45 (March 1972): 122–23.

[3] Ibid., p. 121.

[4] Allan Emery, "The Alternatives of Melville's 'Bartleby,'" *Nineteenth-Century Fiction* 31 (1976): 186–87.

[5] William Bysshe Stein, "Bartleby: The Christian Conscience," in *Melville Annual 1965, A Symposium: "Bartleby, the Scrivener,"* ed. Howard P. Vincent (Kent, Ohio: Kent State University Press, 1966), p. 107.

[6] Hershel Parker, "The Sequel in 'Bartleby,'" in *Bartleby the Inscrutable: A Collection of Commentary on Herman Melville's Tale "Bartleby, the Scrivener,"* ed. M. Thomas Inge (Hamden, Conn.: Archon Books, 1979), pp. 159–65, 163–64.

kings and counselors" seemed to me majestic and solemn and final. That "murmured I" put a deep hush around it. But it never occurred to me that the man who said those words was "easy-conscienced" or "self-indulgent" or the sort of man who "characteristically perverts" a "profound lament to sonorous urbanity." The figure of Bartleby seemed so weird and funny and painful, his death at once inevitable and shocking, that I did not see it as an occasion for the man who was telling me about it to make a "last cheap purchase" of "delicious self-approval." I trusted that Lawyer.

Thirty years later, I still do. He seems to me extremely intelligent, whimsical and ironic, generous, self-aware, passionate, and thoroughly competent.

From *The Silence of Bartleby*

CONSIDERATIONS FOR CRITICAL THINKING AND WRITING

1. How does McCall characterize the "majority opinion" on the lawyer's character? What is his opinion of the lawyer?

2. How does McCall's opinion of the lawyer compare with Hawthorne's opinion of Herman Melville in the preceding Perspective?

3. Write an essay explaining whether you find the "majority opinion" or McCall's view of the lawyer more convincing.

JUNOT DÍAZ (B. 1968)

Born in Santo Domingo, Dominican Republic, Junot Díaz moved with his family to the United States when he was seven years old. He grew up in New Jersey and graduated from Rutgers University and then earned an M.F.A. from Cornell University. His short story collection *Drown* (1996) centers on a teenage narrator from the Dominican Republic who makes his way as an impoverished immigrant in New Jersey. "Fiesta, 1980" is drawn from that collection and was featured in *The Best American Short Stories 1997.* Díaz's novel *The Brief Wondrous*

© Scott Lituchy/Star Ledger/CORBIS.

Life of Oscar Wao (2007) was awarded a number of prizes, including the Pulitzer. He teaches creative writing at the Massachusetts Institute of Technology.

Fiesta, 1980 1996

Mami's youngest sister — my Tía° Yrma — finally made it to the United States that year. She and Tío° Miguel got themselves an apartment in the Bronx, off the Grand Concourse, and everybody decided that we should have a party. Actually, my dad decided, but everybody — meaning Mami, Tía Yrma, Tío Miguel, and their neighbors — thought it a dope idea. On the Friday of the party Papi got back from work around six. Right on time. We were all dressed by then, which was a smart move on our part. If Papi had walked in and caught us lounging around in our underwear, man, he would have kicked our asses something serious.

He didn't say nothing to nobody, not even to my moms. He just pushed past her, held up his hand when she tried to talk to him, and jumped into the shower. Rafa gave me the look and I gave it back to him; we both knew Papi had been out with the Puerto Rican woman he was seeing and wanted to wash off the evidence quick.

Mami looked really nice that day. The United States had finally put some meat on her; she was no longer the same flaca° who had arrived here three years before. She had cut her hair short and was wearing tons of cheap-ass jewelry, which on her was kinda attractive. She smelled like herself, which meant she smelled good, like the wind through a tree. She always waited until the last possible minute to put on her perfume because she said it was a waste to spray it on early and then have to spray it on again once you got to the party.

We — meaning me, my brother, my little sister, and Mami — waited for Papi to finish his shower. Mami seemed anxious, in her usual dispassionate way. Her hands adjusted the buckle of her belt over and over again. That morning, when she had gotten us up for school, Mami told us that she wanted to have a good time at the party. I want to dance, she said, but now, with the sun sliding out of the sky like spit off a wall, she seemed ready to just get this over with.

Rafa didn't much want to go to no party either, and me, I never wanted to 5 go anywhere with my family. There was a baseball game in the parking lot outside and we could hear our friends yelling, Hey, and, You suck, to one another. We heard the pop of a ball as it sailed over the cars, the clatter of an aluminum bat dropping to the concrete. Not that me or Rafa loved baseball; we just liked playing with the local kids, thrashing them at anything they were doing. By the sounds of the shouting, we both knew the game was close, either of us could have made a difference. Rafa frowned, and when I frowned back, he put up his fist. Don't you mirror me, he said.

Don't you mirror me, I said.

He punched me — I would have hit him back but right then Papi marched into the living room with his towel around his waist, looking a lot smaller than he did when he was dressed. He had a few strands of hair around his nipples and a surly closed-mouth expression, like maybe he had scalded his tongue or something.

Have they eaten? he asked Mami.

She nodded. I made you something.

You didn't let him eat, did you? 10

Tía/Tío: Aunt/Uncle (all annotations are Spanish translations).
flaca: Thin person.

Dios mio,° she said, letting her arms fall to her side.

Dios mio is right, Papi said.

I was never supposed to eat before our car trips, but earlier, when she had put out our dinner of rice, beans, and sweet platanos, guess who had been the first one to gobble his meal down? You couldn't blame Mami really, she had been busy — cooking, getting ready, dressing my sister Madai. I should have reminded her not to feed me but I hadn't been thinking. Even if I had, I doubt I would have told her.

Papi turned to me. Why did you eat?

Rafa had already inched away from me. I'd once told him I considered him   15
a low-down chickenshit for moving out of the way every time Papi was going to smack me.

Collateral damage, he said. Ever heard of it?

No.

Look it up.

Chickenshit or not, right then I didn't dare glance at him. Papi was old-fashioned; he expected you to attend him, but not stare into his eyes, while you were getting your ass whupped. I studied Papi's bellybutton, which was perfectly round and immaculate. Papi pulled me to my feet by my ear.

If you throw up —   20

I won't, I said, tears in my eyes, more out of reflex than pain.

It's not his fault, Mami said. I fed them before I reminded them about the party.

They've known about this party forever. How did they think we were going to get there? Fly?

He finally let go of my ear and I went back to my seat. Madai was too scared to open her eyes. Being around Papi all her life had turned her into a big-time wuss. Anytime Papi raised his voice her lip would start trembling, like it was some sort of specialized tuning fork. Rafa pretended that he had knuckles to crack, and when I shoved him, he gave me a *Don't start* look. But even that little bit of recognition made me feel better.

I was the one who was always in trouble with my dad. It was like my God-   25
given role to piss him off, to do everything the way he hated. It didn't bother me too much, really. I still wanted him to love me, something that never seemed strange or contradictory until years later, when he was out of our lives.

Before I knew it Papi was dressed and Mami was crossing each one of us, solemnly, like we were heading off to war. We said, in turn, Bendición,° Mami, and she poked us in our five cardinal spots while saying, Que Dios te bendiga.°

This was how we began all our trips, the words that followed me every time I left the house.

None of us said anything else until we were in Papi's Volkswagen van. Brand new, lime green, bought to impress. Oh, we were impressed, considering we couldn't afford no VW van, used or new, but me, each time I got in that VW and Papi went above twenty miles an hour, I vomited. I'd never had trouble with cars before, and that van was like my curse. Mami suspected it was the upholstery. In her mind, American things — appliances, mouthwash,

Dios mio: My God.
Bendición: Blessing, benediction.
Que . . . bendiga: May God bless you.

funny-looking upholstery — all seemed to have an intrinsic badness. Papi was careful about taking me anywhere in the VW, but when he did, like that night, I had to ride up front in Mami's usual seat so I could throw up out a window.

You okay? Mami asked over my shoulder as Papi got us onto the turnpike. She had her hand on the small of my neck. One thing about Mami, even when she was nervous, her palms never sweated.

I'm okay, I said, keeping my eyes straight ahead. I definitely didn't want to 30 trade glances with Papi. He had this one look, furious and sharp, that always left me feeling bruised.

Toma. Mami handed me four mentas.° She had thrown a few out her window at the beginning of our trip, an offering to Eshú;° the rest were for me. Mami considered these candies a cure-all for any disorder.

I took one and sucked it slowly, my tongue knocking it up against my teeth. As always, it helped. We passed Newark Airport without any incident. If Madai had been awake she would have cried because the planes flew so close to the cars.

How's he feeling? Papi asked.

Fine, I said. I glanced back at Rafa and he pretended like he didn't see me. That was the way he was, both at school and at home. When I was in trouble, he didn't know me. Madai was solidly asleep, but even with her face all wrinkled up and drooling she looked cute.

I turned around and concentrated on the candy. Papi even started to joke 35 that we might not have to scrub the van out tonight. He was beginning to loosen up, not checking his watch too much. Maybe he was thinking about that Puerto Rican woman or maybe he was just happy that we were all together. I could never tell. At the toll, he was feeling positive enough to actually get out of the van and search around under the basket for dropped coins. It was something he had once done to amuse Madai, but now it was habit. Cars behind us honked their horns and I slid down in my seat. Rafa didn't care; he just grinned back at the other cars. His actual job was to make sure no cops were coming. Mami shook Madai awake, and as soon as she saw Papi stooping for a couple of quarters she let out this screech of delight that almost took the top of my head off.

That was the end of the good times. Just outside the Washington Bridge, I started feeling woozy. The smell of the upholstery got all up inside my head and I found myself with a mouthful of saliva. Mami's hand tensed on my shoulder and when I caught Papi's eye, he was like, No way. Don't do it.

The first time I got sick in the van Papi was taking me to the library. Rafa was with us and he couldn't believe I threw up. I was famous for my steel-lined stomach. A third-world childhood could give you that. Papi was worried enough that just as quick as Rafa could drop the books off we were on our way home. Mami fixed me one of her honey-and-onion concoctions and that made my stomach feel better. A week later we tried the library again, and on this

---

mentas: Mints.
Eshú: A deity of the roads and protector of travelers.

go-around I couldn't get the window open in time. When Papi got me home, he went and cleaned out the van himself, an expression of asco° on his face. This was a big deal, since Papi almost never cleaned anything himself. He came back inside and found me sitting on the couch; I was feeling like hell.

It's the car, he said to Mami. It's making him sick.

This time the damage was pretty minimal, nothing Papi couldn't wash off the door with a blast of the hose. He was pissed, though; he jammed his finger into my cheek, a nice solid thrust. That was the way he was with his punishments: imaginative. Earlier that year I'd written an essay in school called "My Father the Torturer," but the teacher made me write a new one. She thought I was kidding.

We drove the rest of the way to the Bronx in silence. We only stopped once, 40 so I could brush my teeth. Mami had brought along my toothbrush and a tube of toothpaste and while every car known to man sped by us she stood outside with me so I wouldn't feel alone.

Tío Miguel was about seven feet tall and had his hair combed up and out, into a demi-'fro. He gave me and Rafa big spleen-crushing hugs and then kissed Mami and finally ended up with Madai on his shoulder. The last time I'd seen Tío was at the airport, his first day in the United States. I remembered how he hadn't seemed all that troubled to be in another country.

He looked down at me. Carajo,° Yunior, you look horrible!

He threw up, my brother explained.

I pushed Rafa. Thanks a lot, ass-face.

Hey, he said. Tío asked. 45

Tío clapped a bricklayer's hand on my shoulder. Everybody gets sick sometimes, he said. You should have seen me on the plane over here. Dios mio! He rolled his small Asian-looking eyes for emphasis. I thought we were all going to die.

Everybody could tell he was lying. I smiled like he was making me feel better.

Do you want me to get you a drink? Tío asked. We got beer and rum.

Miguel, Mami said. He's young.

Young? Back in Santo Domingo, he'd be getting laid by now. 50

Mami thinned her lips, which took some doing.

Well, it's true, Tío said.

So, Mami, I said, when do I get to go visit the D.R.?°

That's enough, Yunior.

It's the only pussy you'll ever get, Rafa said to me in English. 55

Not counting your girlfriend, of course.

Rafa smiled. He had to give me that one.

Papi came in from parking the van. He and Miguel gave each other the sort of handshakes that would have turned my fingers into Wonder bread.

Long time, compa'i, Tío said.

Compa'i, ¿como va todo?° 60

---

asco: Disgust.
Carajo: Damn.
D.R.: Dominican Republic.
Compa'i . . . todo: Buddy, how's it going?

Tía came out then, with an apron on and maybe the longest Lee Press-On Nails I've ever seen in my life. There was this one guru guy I'd seen in the *Guinness Book of World Records* who had longer nails, but I tell you, it was close. She gave everybody kisses, told me and Rafa how guapo° we were — Rafa, of course, believed her — told Madai how bella she was, but when she got to Papi, she froze a little, like maybe she'd seen a wasp on the tip of his nose, but then she kissed him all the same. Just a peck really.

Look at that, Rafa whispered to me in English.

Mami told us to join the other kids in the living room. Tío said, Wait a minute, I want to show you the apartment. I was glad Tía said, Hold on, because from what I'd seen so far, the place had been furnished in Contemporary Dominican Tacky. The less I saw, the better. I mean, I liked plastic sofa covers but damn, Tío and Tía had taken it to another level. They had a disco ball hanging in the living room and the type of stucco ceilings that looked like stalactite heaven. The sofas all had golden tassels dangling from their edges.

Tía came out of the kitchen with some people I didn't know and by the time she got done introducing everybody, only Papi and Mami were given the guided tour of the four-room, third-floor apartment. Me and Rafa joined the kids in the living room. Their parents wouldn't be over until late, but the kids had come over anyway. We were hungry, one of the girls explained, a pastelito° in hand. The boy was about three years younger than me but the girl who'd spoken, Leti, was my age. She and another girl were on the sofa together and they were cute as hell.

Leti introduced them: the boy was her brother Wilquins and the other girl   65
was her neighbor Mari. Leti had some serious tetas and I could tell that my brother was going to gun for her. His taste in girls was predictable. He sat down right between Leti and Mari, and by the way they were smiling at him I knew he'd do fine. Neither of the girls gave me more than a cursory one-two, which didn't bother me. Sure, I liked girls, but I was always too terrified to speak to them unless we were arguing or I was calling them stupidos, which was one of my favorite words that year. I turned to Wilquins and asked him what there was to do around here. Mari, who had the lowest voice I'd ever heard, said, He can't speak.

What does that mean?

He's mute.

I looked at Wilquins incredulously. He smiled and nodded, as if he'd won a prize or something.

Does he understand? I asked.

Of course he understands, Rafa said. He's not dumb.   70

I could tell Rafa had said that just to score points with the girls. Both of them nodded. Low-voice Mari said, He's the best student in his grade.

I thought, Not bad for a mute. I sat next to Wilquins. After about two seconds of TV, Wilquins whipped out a bag of dominoes and motioned to me. Did I want to play? Sure. Me and him played Rafa and Leti and we whupped their collective asses twice, which put Rafa in a real bad mood. Leti kept whispering into Rafa's ear, telling him it was okay.

---

guapo: Handsome.
pastelito: Dried fruit-filled pie.

In the kitchen I could hear my parents slipping into their usual modes. Papi's voice was loud and argumentative; you didn't have to be anywhere near him to catch his drift. And Mami, you had to strain your ears to hear her. I went into the kitchen a few times: once so the tíos could show off how much bullshit I'd been able to cram in my head the last few years, another time for a bucket-sized cup of soda. Mami and Tía were frying tostones° and the last of the pastelitos. She appeared happier now, and the way her hands worked on our dinner you would think she had a life somewhere else making rare and precious things. She nudged Tía every now and then, shit they must have been doing all their lives. As soon as Mami saw me, though, she gave me the eye. Don't stay long, that eye said. Don't piss your old man off.

Papi was too busy arguing about Elvis to notice me. Then somebody mentioned Cubans and Papi had plenty to say about them, too.

Maybe I was used to him. His voice — louder than most adults' — didn't   75
bother me none, though the other kids shifted uneasily in their seats. Wilquins got up to raise the volume on the TV, but Rafa said, I wouldn't do that. Muteboy had some balls. He did it anyway and then sat down. Wilquins's pop came into the living room a second later, a bottle of Presidente in hand. That dude must have had Spider-senses or something. Did you raise that? he asked Wilquins, and Wilquins nodded.

Is this your house? Pa Wilquins asked. He looked ready to kick Wilquins's ass but he lowered the volume instead.

See, Rafa said. You nearly got your ass *kicked*.

I met the Puerto Rican woman right after Papi had gotten the van. He was taking me on short trips, trying to cure me of my vomiting. It wasn't really working but I looked forward to our trips, even though at the end of each one I'd be sick. These were the only times me and Papi did anything together. When we were alone he treated me much better, like maybe I was his son or something.

Before each drive Mami always crossed me.

Bendición, Mami, I would say.   80

She would kiss my forehead. Que Dios te bendiga. And then she would give me a handful of mentas because she wanted me to be okay. Mami didn't think these excursions would cure me, but the one time she had brought it up to Papi, he had told her to shut up and what did she know about anything anyway?

Me and Papi didn't talk much. We just drove around our neighborhood. Occasionally he would ask, How is it?

And I would nod, no matter how I felt.

One day I got sick outside of Perth Amboy. Instead of taking me home like he usually did, he went the other way on Industrial Avenue, stopping a few minutes later in front of a light blue house I didn't recognize. It reminded me of the Easter eggs we colored at school, the ones we threw out the bus windows at other cars.

The Puerto Rican woman was there and she helped me clean up. She had   85
dry papery hands and when she rubbed the towel on my chest, she did it hard, like I was a bumper she was waxing. She was very thin and had a cloud of brown hair rising above her narrow face and the sharpest, blackest eyes you've ever seen.

He's cute, she said to Papi. What's your name? she asked me. Are you Rafa?

tostones: Fried plantains.

I shook my head.

Then it's Yunior, right?

I nodded.

You're the smart one, she said, suddenly happy with herself. Maybe you want to see my books?

They weren't hers. I recognized them as ones my father must have left in her house. Papi was a voracious reader, couldn't even go cheating without a paperback in his pocket.

Why don't you go watch TV? Papi suggested. He already had his hand on her ass and didn't care that I was watching. He was looking at her like she was the last piece of chicken on earth.

We got plenty of channels, she said. Use the remote if you want.

The two of them went upstairs and I was too scared of what was happening to poke around. I just sat there, ashamed, expecting something big and fiery to crash down on all our heads. I watched a whole hour of the news before Papi came downstairs and said, Let's go.

About two hours later the women laid out the food and like always nobody but the kids thanked them. It must have been some Dominican tradition or something. There was everything I liked — chicharrónes,° fried chicken, tostones, sancocho,° rice, fried cheese, yucca, avocado, potato salad, a meteor-sized hunk of pernil,° even a tossed salad, which I could do without — but when I joined the other kids around the serving table, Papi said, Oh, no you don't, and took the paper plate out of my hand. His fingers weren't gentle.

What's wrong now? Tía asked, handing me another plate.

He ain't eating, Papi said. Mami pretended to help Rafa with the pernil.

Why can't he eat?

Because I said so.

The adults who didn't know us made like they hadn't heard a thing and Tío just smiled sheepishly and told everybody to go ahead and eat. All the kids — about ten of them now — trooped back into the living room with their plates aheaping, and all the adults ducked into the kitchen and the dining room, where the radio was playing loud-ass bachatas.° I was the only one without a plate. Papi stopped me before I could get away from him. He kept his voice nice and low so nobody else could hear him.

If you eat anything, I'm going to beat you. ¿Entiendes?°

I nodded.

And if your brother gives you any food, I'll beat him, too. Right here in front of everybody. ¿Entiendes?

I nodded again. I wanted to kill him, and he must have sensed it because he gave my head a little shove.

All the kids watched me come in and sit down in front of the TV.

What's wrong with your dad? Leti asked.

He's a dick, I said.

Rafa shook his head. Don't say that shit in front of people.

chicharrónes: Pork rinds.
sancocho: Stew.
pernil: Ham.
bachatas: Wild party music.
¿Entiendes?: Understand?

Easy for you to be nice when you're eating, I said.

Hey, if I was a pukey little baby, I wouldn't get no food either. 110

I almost said something back but I concentrated on the TV. I wasn't going to start it. No fucking way. So I watched Bruce Lee beat Chuck Norris into the floor of the Coliseum and tried to pretend that there was no food anywhere in the house. It was Tía who finally saved me. She came into the living room and said, Since you ain't eating, Yunior, you can at least help me get some ice.

I didn't want to, but she mistook my reluctance for something else.

I already asked your father.

She held my hand while we walked; Tía didn't have any kids but I could tell she wanted them. She was the sort of relative who always remembered your birthday but who you only went to visit because you had to. We didn't get past the first-floor landing before she opened her pocketbook and handed me the first of three pastelitos she had smuggled out of the apartment.

Go ahead, she said. And as soon as you get inside, make sure you brush 115 your teeth.

Thanks a lot, Tía, I said.

Those pastelitos didn't stand a chance.

She sat next to me on the stairs and smoked her cigarette. All the way down on the first floor we could hear the music and the adults and the television. Tía looked a ton like Mami; the two of them were both short and light-skinned. Tía smiled a lot and that was what set them the most apart.

How is it at home, Yunior?

What do you mean? 120

How's it going in the apartment? Are you kids okay?

I knew an interrogation when I heard one, no matter how sugar-coated or oblique it was. I didn't say anything. Don't get me wrong, I loved my tía, but something told me to keep my mouth shut. Maybe it was family loyalty, maybe I just wanted to protect Mami or I was afraid that Papi would find out — it could have been anything really.

Is your mom all right?

I shrugged.

Have there been lots of fights? 125

None, I said. Too many shrugs would have been just as bad as an answer. Papi's at work too much.

Work, Tía said, like it was somebody's name she didn't like.

Me and Rafa, we didn't talk much about the Puerto Rican woman. When we ate dinner at her house, the few times Papi had taken us over there, we still acted like nothing was out of the ordinary. Pass the ketchup, man. No sweat, bro. The affair was like a hole in our living room floor, one we'd gotten so used to circumnavigating that we sometimes forgot it was there.

By midnight all the adults were getting crazy on the dance floor. I was sitting outside Tía's bedroom, where Madai was sleeping, trying not to attract attention. Rafa had me guarding the door; he and Leti were in there, too, with some of the other kids, getting busy no doubt. Wilquins had gone across the hall to bed, so I had only the roaches to mess around with.

Whenever I peered into the main room I saw about twenty moms and dads 130
dancing and drinking beers. Every now and then somebody yelled, Quisqueya!°
And then everybody else would yell and stomp their feet. From what I could see,
my parents seemed to be enjoying themselves.

Mami and Tía spent a lot of time side by side, whispering, and I kept expecting something to come of this, a brawl maybe. I'd never once been out with
my family when it hadn't turned to shit. We were a Doomsday on wheels. We
weren't even theatrical or straight crazy like other families. We fought like
sixth graders, without any real dignity. I guess the whole night I'd been waiting
for a blowup, something between Papi and Mami. This was how I always figured Papi would be exposed, out in public, where everybody would know.

You're a cheater!

But everything was calmer than usual. And Mami didn't look like she was
about to say anything to Papi. The two of them danced every now and then,
but they never lasted more than a song before Mami rejoined Tía in whatever
conversation they were having.

I tried to imagine Mami before Papi. Maybe I was tired, or just sad, thinking about the way my family was. Maybe I already knew how it would all end
up in a few years, Mami without Papi, and that was why I did it. Picturing her
alone wasn't easy. It seemed like Papi had always been with her, even when we
were waiting in Santo Domingo for him to send for us.

The only photograph our family had of Mami as a young woman, before she 135
married Papi, was the one that somebody took of her at an election party, which
I found one day while rummaging for money to go to the arcade. Mami had it
tucked into her immigration papers. In the photo, she's surrounded by laughing
cousins I will never meet who are all shiny from dancing, whose clothes are rumpled and loose. You can tell it's night and hot and that the mosquitoes have been
biting. She sits straight, and even in a crowd she stands out, smiling quietly like
maybe she's the one everybody's celebrating. You can't see her hands but I imagined they're knotting a straw or a bit of thread. This was the woman my father
met a year later on the Malecón, the woman Mami thought she'd always be.

Mami must have caught me studying her because she stopped what she was
doing and gave me a smile, maybe her first one of the night. Suddenly I wanted
to go over and hug her, for no other reason than I loved her, but there were about
eleven fat jiggling bodies between us. So I sat down on the tiled floor and waited.

I must have fallen asleep, because the next thing I knew Rafa was kicking
me and saying, Let's go. He looked like he'd been hitting off those girls; he was
all smiles. I got to my feet in time to kiss Tía and Tío goodbye. Mami was holding the serving dish she had brought with her.

Where's Papi? I asked.

He's downstairs, bringing the van around. Mami leaned down to kiss me.
You were good today, she said. 140

And then Papi burst in and told us to get the hell downstairs before some
pendejo° cop gave him a ticket. More kisses, more handshakes, and then we
were gone.

Quisqueya: A popular name for the Dominican Republic.
pendejo: Dumb ass.

I don't remember being out of sorts after I met the Puerto Rican woman, but I must have been, because Mami only asked me questions when she thought something was wrong in my life. It took her about ten passes but finally she cornered me one afternoon when we were alone in the apartment. Our upstairs neighbors were beating the crap out of their kids, and me and her had been listening to it all afternoon. She put her hand on mine and said, Is everything okay, Yunior? Have you been fighting with your brother?

Me and Rafa had already talked. We'd been in the basement, where our parents couldn't hear us. He told me that yeah, he knew about her.

Papi's taken me there twice now.

Why didn't you tell me? I asked.   145

What the hell was I going to say?

I didn't say anything to Mami either. She watched me, very, very closely. Later I would think, maybe if I had told her, she would have confronted him, would have done something, but who can know these things? I said I'd been having trouble in school, and like that everything was back to normal between us. She put her hand on my shoulder and squeezed, and that was that.

We were on the turnpike, just past Exit 11, when I started feeling it again. I sat up from leaning against Rafa. His fingers smelled and he'd gone to sleep almost as soon as he got into the van. Madai was out, too, but at least she wasn't snoring.

In the darkness, I saw that Papi had a hand on Mami's knee and that the two of them were quiet and still. They weren't slumped back or anything; they were both wide awake, buckled into their seats. I couldn't see either of their faces and no matter how hard I tried I could not imagine their expressions. Every now and then the van was filled with the bright rush of somebody else's headlights. Finally I said, Mami, and they both looked back, already knowing what was happening.

CONSIDERATIONS FOR CRITICAL THINKING AND WRITING

1. **FIRST RESPONSE.** Describe the overall mood of this story. Explain why you think it is mostly sad, humorous, or somewhere in between.

2. Point to five details about Yunior that serve to reveal his character particularly well for you.

3. Characterize Papi. Does his adulterous behavior make him an irrevocably bad father in Yunior's eyes? In yours?

4. How convincing do you find Díaz's description of this immigrant family's life together? Do they behave like a family? Why or why not?

5. How does Rafa serve as a kind of foil to Yunior? What is the purpose of the other minor characters?

6. Why do you think Díaz has Yunior suffer from motion sickness? How is that problem connected to the rest of the plot?

7. What do you think is the story's conflict? Is it resolved?

8. Explain why you think Yunior's school essay title "My Father the Torturer" could or could not be an accurate title for this short story.

CONNECTIONS TO OTHER SELECTIONS

1. Compare the teenage narrator's relationship to authority in "Fiesta, 1980" and in John Updike's "A & P" (p. 733).

2. Discuss how love and hate are at the heart of the father/son relationship in "Fiesta, 1980" and in William Faulkner's "Barn Burning" (p. 503).

ENCOUNTERING FICTION: COMICS AND GRAPHIC STORIES

LYNDA BARRY (B. 1956), *Spelling*

Lynda Barry is the creator of the syndicated comic strip *Ernie Pook's Comeek* and author of more than a dozen illustrated books that she classifies as "autobifictionalography," or part fiction, part autobiography. Barry's characters range from the "life-grooving" Marlys (featured in the following strip, from *Down the Street* [1986]), to herself in *One Hundred Demons* (2002). Her work focuses on childhood and adolescent experience, and among her influences are Dr. Seuss, R. Crumb, Grimm's fairy tales, *Ripley's Believe It or Not!*, cave paintings, and religious art of India. "When I write," said Barry in a 2003 interview, "I don't plan the story first, I don't pencil anything in. . . . I try really hard not to plan anything beyond the movement of the brush and the next word." Barry's first comic strip was published in 1977 in the Evergreen State College student newspaper, where friend and classmate Matt Groening served as co-editor. She lives in a suburb of Chicago with her husband and six parakeets.

"Spelling" by Lynda Barry, © 2000. Used courtesy of Darhansoff, Verrill, Feldman Literary Agents.

CONSIDERATIONS AND CONNECTION TO ANOTHER SELECTION

1. How does Barry's drawing serve to characterize Marlys? Write a paragraph that articulates what the drawing shows about Marlys's character.

2. Why is spelling an especially appropriate and symbolic endeavor in this narrative?

3. Try drawing and writing a fifth frame for "Spelling" that depicts Marlys after her job interview.

4. **CREATIVE RESPONSE.** Reread the brief excerpt from *Hard Times* by Charles Dickens (p. 122) and use it as an inspiration to write a vivid, detailed one-paragraph description of Marlys that captures her character for you.

5

Setting

I love the way a short story can offer a
sharp concentrated insight like a stiletto
thrust. I love the way you can experience
a whole lifetime in a few pages, as you
do in the lines of a poem.
— ANDREA LEE

Setting is the context in which the action of a story occurs. The major elements of setting are time, place, and the social environment that frames the characters. These elements establish the world in which the characters act. In most stories they also serve as more than backgrounds and furnishings. If we are sensitive to the contexts provided by setting, we are better able to understand the behavior of the characters and the significance of their actions. It may be tempting to read quickly through a writer's descriptions and ignore the details of the setting once a geographic location and a historic period are established. But if you read a story so impatiently, the significance of the setting may slip by you. That kind of reading is similar to traveling on interstate highways: a lot of ground gets covered, but very little is seen along the way.

Settings can be used to evoke a mood or atmosphere that will prepare the reader for what is to come. In "Young Goodman Brown" (p. 402), Nathaniel Hawthorne has his pious protagonist leave his wife and village one night to keep an appointment in a New England forest near the site of the seventeenth-century witch trials. This is Hawthorne's description of Brown entering the forest:

> He had taken a dreary road, darkened by all the gloomiest trees of the forest, which barely stood aside to let the narrow path creep through, and closed immediately behind. It was all as lonely as could be; and there is this peculiarity in such a solitude, that the traveler knows not who may be concealed by the innumerable trunks and the thick boughs overhead; so that with lonely footsteps he may yet be passing through an unseen multitude.

The atmosphere established in this descriptive setting is somber and threatening. Careful reading reveals that the forest is not simply the woods; it is a moral wilderness, where anything can happen.

Web Explore the literary element in this chapter at bedfordstmartins.com/meyerlit.

If we ask why a writer chooses to include certain details in a work, then we are likely to make connections that relate the details to some larger purpose, such as the story's meaning. The final scene in Godwin's "A Sorrowful Woman" (p. 39) occurs in the spring, an ironic time for the action to be set because instead of rebirth for the protagonist there is only death. There is usually a reason for placing a story in a particular time or location. Katherine Mansfield has the protagonist in "Miss Brill" (p. 307) discover her loneliness and old age in a French vacation town, a lively atmosphere that serves as a cruel contrast to an elderly (and foreign) lady's painful realization.

Melville's "Bartleby, the Scrivener" (p. 142) takes on meaning as Bartleby's "dead-wall reveries" begin to reflect his shattered vision of life. He is surrounded by walls. A folding screen separates him from others in the office; he is isolated. The office window faces walls; there is no view to relieve the deadening work. Bartleby faces a wall at the prison where he dies; the final wall is death. As the subtitle indicates, this is "A Story of Wall Street." Unless the geographic location or the physical details of a story are used merely as necessary props, they frequently shed light on character and action. All offices have walls, but Melville transforms the walls into an antagonist that represents the limitations Bartleby sees and feels all around him but does not speak of.

Time, location, and the physical features of a setting can all be relevant to the overall purpose of a story. So too is the social environment in which the characters are developed. In Faulkner's "A Rose for Emily" (p. 91) the changes in her southern town serve as a foil for Emily's tenacious hold on a lost past. She is regarded as a "fallen monument," as old-fashioned and peculiar as the "stubborn and coquettish decay" of her house. Neither she nor her house fits into the modern changes that are paving and transforming the town. Without the social context, this story would be mostly an account of a bizarre murder rather than an exploration of the conflicts Faulkner associated with the changing South. Setting enlarges the meaning of Emily's actions.

Some settings have traditional associations that are closely related to the action of a story. Adventure and romance, for example, flourish in the fertile soil of most exotic settings: the film version of Isak Dinesen's novel *Out of Africa* is a lush visual demonstration of how setting can play a significant role in generating the audience's expectations of love and excitement.

Sometimes, writers reverse traditional expectations. When a tranquil garden is the scene for a horrendously bloody murder, we are as much taken by surprise as the victim is. In John Updike's "A & P" (p. 733) there seems to be little possibility for heroic action in so mundane a place as a supermarket, but the setting turns out to be appropriate for the important, unexpected decision the protagonist makes about life. Traditional associations are also disrupted in "A Sorrowful Woman," in which Godwin disassociates home from the safety, security, and comfort usually connected with it by presenting the protagonist's home as a deadly trap. By drawing on traditional associations, a writer can fulfill or disrupt a reader's expectations about a setting in order to complement the elements of the story.

Not every story uses setting as a means of revealing mood, idea, meaning, or characters' actions. Some stories have no particularly significant setting. It is entirely possible to envision a story in which two characters speak to each other about a conflict between them and little or no mention is made of the time or place they inhabit. If, however, a shift in setting would make a serious difference to our understanding of a story, then the setting is probably an important element in the work. Consider how different "Bartleby, the Scrivener" would be if it were set in a relaxed, pleasant, sunny town in the South rather than in the grinding, limiting materialism of Wall Street. Bartleby's withdrawal from life would be less comprehensible and meaningful in such a setting. The setting is integral to that story.

The following three stories — Ernest Hemingway's "Soldier's Home," Andrea Lee's "Anthropology," and Fay Weldon's "IND AFF, or Out of Love in Sarajevo" — include settings that serve to shape their meanings.

ERNEST HEMINGWAY (1899–1961)

In 1918, a year after graduating from high school in Oak Park, Illinois, Ernest Hemingway volunteered as an ambulance driver in World War I. At the Italian front, he was seriously wounded. This experience haunted him and many of the characters in his short stories and novels. *In Our Time* (1925) is a collection of short stories, including "Soldier's Home," that

Courtesy of the Ernest Hemingway Photographic Collection, John Fitzgerald Kennedy Library, Boston.

reflect some of Hemingway's own attempts to readjust to life back home after the war. *The Sun Also Rises* (1926), *A Farewell to Arms* (1929), and *For Whom the Bell Tolls* (1940) are also about war and its impact on people's lives. Hemingway courted violence all his life in war, the bullring, the boxing ring, and big game hunting. When he was sixty-two years old and terminally ill with cancer, he committed suicide by shooting himself with a shotgun. "Soldier's Home" takes place in a small town in Oklahoma; the war, however, is never distant from the protagonist's mind as he struggles to come home again.

Soldier's Home   1925

Krebs went to the war from a Methodist college in Kansas. There is a picture which shows him among his fraternity brothers, all of them wearing exactly the same height and style collar. He enlisted in the Marines in 1917 and did not return to the United States until the second division returned from the Rhine in the summer of 1919.

There is a picture which shows him on the Rhine with two German girls and another corporal. Krebs and the corporal look too big for their uniforms. The German girls are not beautiful. The Rhine does not show in the picture.

By the time Krebs returned to his home town in Oklahoma the greeting of heroes was over. He came back much too late. The men from the town who had been drafted had all been welcomed elaborately on their return. There had been a great deal of hysteria. Now the reaction had set in. People seemed to think it was rather ridiculous for Krebs to be getting back so late, years after the war was over.

At first Krebs, who had been at Belleau Wood, Soissons, the Champagne, St. Mihiel, and in the Argonne° did not want to talk about the war at all. Later he felt the need to talk but no one wanted to hear about it. His town had heard too many atrocity stories to be thrilled by actualities. Krebs found that to be listened to at all he had to lie, and after he had done this twice he, too, had a reaction against the war and against talking about it. A distaste for everything that had happened to him in the war set in because of the lies he had told. All of the times that had been able to make him feel cool and clear inside himself when he thought of them; the times so long back when he had done the one thing, the only thing for a man to do, easily and naturally, when he might have done something else, now lost their cool, valuable quality and then were lost themselves.

His lies were quite unimportant lies and consisted in attributing to himself 5 things other men had seen, done, or heard of, and stating as facts certain apocryphal incidents familiar to all soldiers. Even his lies were not sensational at the pool room. His acquaintances, who had heard detailed accounts of German women found chained to machine guns in the Argonne forest and who could not comprehend, or were barred by their patriotism from interest in, any German machine gunners who were not chained, were not thrilled by his stories.

Belleau Wood ... Argonne: Sites of battles in World War I in which American troops were instrumental in pushing back the Germans.

Krebs acquired the nausea in regard to experience that is the result of untruth or exaggeration, and when he occasionally met another man who had really been a soldier and they talked a few minutes in the dressing room at a dance he fell into the easy pose of the old soldier among other soldiers: that he had been badly, sickeningly frightened all the time. In this way he lost everything.

During this time, it was late summer, he was sleeping late in bed, getting up to walk down town to the library to get a book, eating lunch at home, reading on the front porch until he became bored, and then walking down through the town to spend the hottest hours of the day in the cool dark of the pool room. He loved to play pool.

In the evening he practiced on his clarinet, strolled down town, read, and went to bed. He was still a hero to his two young sisters. His mother would have given him breakfast in bed if he had wanted it. She often came in when he was in bed and asked him to tell her about the war, but her attention always wandered. His father was noncommittal.

Before Krebs went away to the war he had never been allowed to drive the family motor car. His father was in the real estate business and always wanted the car to be at his command when he required it to take clients out into the country to show them a piece of farm property. The car always stood outside the First National Bank building where his father had an office on the second floor. Now, after the war, it was still the same car.

Nothing was changed in the town except that the young girls had grown 10 up. But they lived in such a complicated world of already defined alliances and shifting feuds that Krebs did not feel the energy or the courage to break into it. He liked to look at them, though. There were so many good-looking young girls. Most of them had their hair cut short. When he went away only little girls wore their hair like that or girls that were fast. They all wore sweaters and shirt waists with round Dutch collars. It was a pattern. He liked to look at them from the front porch as they walked on the other side of the street. He liked to watch them walking under the shade of the trees. He liked the round Dutch collars above their sweaters. He liked their silk stockings and flat shoes. He liked their bobbed hair and the way they walked.

When he was in town their appeal to him was not very strong. He did not like them when he saw them in the Greek's ice cream parlor. He did not want them themselves really. They were too complicated. There was something else. Vaguely he wanted a girl but he did not want to have to work to get her. He would have liked to have a girl but he did not want to have to spend a long time getting her. He did not want to get into the intrigue and the politics. He did not want to have to do any courting. He did not want to tell any more lies. It wasn't worth it.

He did not want any consequences. He did not want any consequences ever again. He wanted to live alone without consequences. Besides he did not really need a girl. The army had taught him that. It was all right to pose as though you had to have a girl. Nearly everybody did that. But it wasn't true. You did not need a girl. That was the funny thing. First a fellow boasted how girls mean nothing to him, that he never thought of them, that they could not touch him. Then a fellow boasted that he could not get along without girls, that he had to have them all the time, that he could not go to sleep without them.

That was all a lie. It was all a lie both ways. You did not need a girl unless you thought about them. He learned that in the army. Then sooner or later you always got one. When you were really ripe for a girl you always got one. You did not have to think about it. Sooner or later it would come. He had learned that in the army.

Now he would have liked a girl if she had come to him and not wanted to talk. But here at home it was all too complicated. He knew he could never get through it all again. It was not worth the trouble. That was the thing about French girls and German girls. There was not all this talking. You couldn't talk much and you did not need to talk. It was simple and you were friends. He thought about France and then he began to think about Germany. On the whole he had liked Germany better. He did not want to leave Germany. He did not want to come home. Still, he had come home. He sat on the front porch.

He liked the girls that were walking along the other side of the street. He 15 liked the look of them much better than the French girls or the German girls. But the world they were in was not the world he was in. He would like to have one of them. But it was not worth it. They were such a nice pattern. He liked the pattern. It was exciting. But he would not go through all the talking. He did not want one badly enough. He liked to look at them all, though. It was not worth it. Not now when things were getting good again.

He sat there on the porch reading a book on the war. It was a history and he was reading about all the engagements he had been in. It was the most interesting reading he had ever done. He wished there were more maps. He looked forward with a good feeling to reading all the really good histories when they would come out with good detail maps. Now he was really learning about the war. He had been a good soldier. That made a difference.

One morning after he had been home about a month his mother came into his bedroom and sat on the bed. She smoothed her apron.

"I had a talk with your father last night, Harold," she said, "and he is willing for you to take the car out in the evenings."

"Yeah?" said Krebs, who was not fully awake. "Take the car out? Yeah?"

"Yes. Your father has felt for some time that you should be able to take the 20 car out in the evenings whenever you wished but we only talked it over last night."

"I'll bet you made him," Krebs said.

"No. It was your father's suggestion that we talk the matter over."

"Yeah. I'll bet you made him," Krebs sat up in bed.

"Will you come down to breakfast, Harold?" his mother said.

"As soon as I get my clothes on," Krebs said. 25

His mother went out of the room and he could hear her frying something downstairs while he washed, shaved, and dressed to go down into the dining-room for breakfast. While he was eating breakfast his sister brought in the mail.

"Well, Hare," she said. "You old sleepyhead. What do you ever get up for?"

Krebs looked at her. He liked her. She was his best sister.

"Have you got the paper?" he asked.

She handed him the Kansas City *Star* and he shucked off its brown wrap- 30 per and opened it to the sporting page. He folded the *Star* open and propped it against the water pitcher with his cereal dish to steady it, so he could read while he ate.

"Harold," his mother stood in the kitchen doorway, "Harold, please don't muss up the paper. Your father can't read his *Star* if it's been mussed."

"I won't muss it," Krebs said.

His sister sat down at the table and watched him while he read.

"We're playing indoor over at school this afternoon," she said. "I'm going to pitch."

"Good," said Krebs. "How's the old wing?"   35

"I can pitch better than lots of the boys. I tell them all you taught me. The other girls aren't much good."

"Yeah?" said Krebs.

"I tell them all you're my beau. Aren't you my beau, Hare?"

"You bet."

"Couldn't your brother really be your beau just because he's your brother?"   40

"I don't know."

"Sure you know. Couldn't you be my beau, Hare, if I was old enough and if you wanted to?"

"Sure. You're my girl now."

"Am I really your girl?"

"Sure."   45

"Do you love me?"

"Uh, huh."

"Will you love me always?"

"Sure."

"Will you come over and watch me play indoor?"   50

"Maybe."

"Aw, Hare, you don't love me. If you loved me, you'd want to come over and watch me play indoor."

Krebs's mother came into the dining-room from the kitchen. She carried a plate with two fried eggs and some crisp bacon on it and a plate of buckwheat cakes.

"You run along, Helen," she said. "I want to talk to Harold."

She put the eggs and bacon down in front of him and brought in a jug of   55
maple syrup for the buckwheat cakes. Then she sat down across the table from Krebs.

"I wish you'd put down the paper a minute, Harold," she said.

Krebs took down the paper and folded it.

"Have you decided what you are going to do yet, Harold?" his mother said, taking off her glasses.

"No," said Krebs.

"Don't you think it's about time?" His mother did not say this in a mean   60
way. She seemed worried.

"I hadn't thought about it," Krebs said.

"God has some work for everyone to do," his mother said. "There can be no idle hands in His Kingdom."

"I'm not in His Kingdom," Krebs said.

"We are all of us in His Kingdom."

Krebs felt embarrassed and resentful as always.   65

"I've worried about you so much, Harold," his mother went on. "I know the temptations you must have been exposed to. I know how weak men are. I know what your own dear grandfather, my own father, told us about the Civil War and I have prayed for you. I pray for you all day long, Harold."

Krebs looked at the bacon fat hardening on his plate.

"Your father is worried, too," his mother went on. "He thinks you have lost your ambition, that you haven't got a definite aim in life. Charley Simmons, who is just your age, has a good job and is going to be married. The boys are all settling down; they're all determined to get somewhere; you can see that boys like Charley Simmons are on their way to being really a credit to the community."

Krebs said nothing.

"Don't look that way, Harold," his mother said. "You know we love you 70 and I want to tell you for your own good how matters stand. Your father does not want to hamper your freedom. He thinks you should be allowed to drive the car. If you want to take some of the nice girls out riding with you, we are only too pleased. We want you to enjoy yourself. But you are going to have to settle down to work, Harold. Your father doesn't care what you start in at. All work is honorable as he says. But you've got to make a start at something. He asked me to speak to you this morning and then you can stop in and see him at his office."

"Is that all?" Krebs said.

"Yes. Don't you love your mother, dear boy?"

"No," Krebs said.

His mother looked at him across the table. Her eyes were shiny. She started crying.

"I don't love anybody," Krebs said. 75

It wasn't any good. He couldn't tell her, he couldn't make her see it. It was silly to have said it. He had only hurt her. He went over and took hold of her arm. She was crying with her head in her hands.

"I didn't mean it," he said. "I was just angry at something. I didn't mean I didn't love you."

His mother went on crying. Krebs put his arm on her shoulder.

"Can't you believe me, mother?"

His mother shook her head. 80

"Please, please, mother. Please believe me."

"All right," his mother said chokily. She looked up at him. "I believe you, Harold."

Krebs kissed her hair. She put her face up to him.

"I'm your mother," she said. "I held you next to my heart when you were a tiny baby."

Krebs felt sick and vaguely nauseated. 85

"I know, Mummy," he said. "I'll try and be a good boy for you."

"Would you kneel and pray with me, Harold?" his mother asked.

They knelt down beside the dining-room table and Krebs's mother prayed.

"Now, you pray, Harold," she said.

"I can't," Krebs said. 90

"Try, Harold."

"I can't."

"Do you want me to pray for you?"

"Yes."

So his mother prayed for him and then they stood up and Krebs kissed his 95 mother and went out of the house. He had tried so to keep his life from being complicated. Still, none of it had touched him. He had felt sorry for his mother and she had made him lie. He would go to Kansas City and get a job and she would feel all right about it. There would be one more scene maybe before he got away. He would not go down to his father's office. He would miss that one. He wanted his life to go smoothly. It had just gotten going that way. Well, that was all over now, anyway. He would go over to the schoolyard and watch Helen play indoor baseball.

CONSIDERATIONS FOR CRITICAL THINKING AND WRITING

1. **FIRST RESPONSE.** The title, "Soldier's Home," focuses on the setting. Do you have a clear picture of Krebs's home? Describe it, filling in missing details from your associations of home, Krebs's routine, or anything else you can use.

2. What does the photograph of Krebs, the corporal, and the German girls reveal?

3. Belleau Wood, Soissons, the Champagne, St. Mihiel, and the Argonne were the sites of fierce and bloody fighting. What effect have these battles had on Krebs? Why do you think he won't talk about them to the people at home?

4. Why does Krebs avoid complications and consequences? How has the war changed his attitudes toward work and women? How is his hometown different from Germany and France? What is the conflict in the story?

5. Why do you think Hemingway refers to the protagonist as Krebs rather than Harold? What is the significance of his sister calling him "Hare"?

6. How does Krebs's mother embody the community's values? What does Krebs think of those values?

7. Why can't Krebs pray with his mother?

8. What is the resolution to Krebs's conflict?

9. Comment on the appropriateness of the story's title.

10. Explain how Krebs's war experiences are present throughout the story even though we get no details about them.

11. **CRITICAL STRATEGIES.** Read the section on reader-response criticism (pp. 2060–62) in Chapter 53, "Critical Strategies for Reading," and consider the following: Perhaps, after having been away from home for a time, you have returned to find yourself alienated from your family or friends. Describe your experience. What caused the change? How does this experience affect your understanding of Krebs? Alternately, if alienation hasn't been your experience, how does that difference affect your reading of Krebs?

CONNECTIONS TO OTHER SELECTIONS

1. Contrast the attitudes toward patriotism implicit in this story with those in Tim O'Brien's "How to Tell a True War Story" (p. 346). How do the stories' settings help to account for the differences between them?

2. How might Krebs's rejection of his community's values be related to Sammy's relationship to his supermarket job in John Updike's "A & P" (p. 733)? What details does Updike use to make the setting in "A & P" a comic, though nonetheless serious, version of Krebs's hometown?

3. Explain how the violent details that Tim O'Brien uses to establish the setting in "How to Tell a True War Story" can be considered representative of the kinds of horrors that haunt Krebs after he returns home.

Perspective

ERNEST HEMINGWAY (1899–1961)

On What Every Writer Needs

1954

The most essential gift for a good writer is a built-in, shock-proof, shit detector. This is the writer's radar and all great writers have had it.

From *Writers at Work: The Paris Review Interviews* (Second Series)

CONSIDERATIONS FOR CRITICAL THINKING AND WRITING

1. Hemingway is typically forthright here, but it is tempting to dismiss his point as simply humorous. Take him seriously. What does he insist a good writer must be able to do?

2. How might Krebs in Hemingway's "Soldier's Home" (p. 187) be seen as having a similar kind of "shit detector" and "radar"?

3. Try writing a pithy, quotable statement that makes an observation about reading or writing.

ANDREA LEE (B. 1953)

© Jerry Bauer.

Andrea Lee was born in Philadelphia and earned her bachelor's and master's degrees from Harvard University. While an exchange student in Russia, she began her journalistic career as a staff writer for *The New Yorker*. Her writing has also appeared in *The New York Times Magazine*, *The New York Times Book Review*, *Vogue*, *Time*, and *The Oxford American*. She is the author of the novels *Sarah Phillips* (1984); *Russian Journal* (1981), which was nominated for a National Book Award and won the Jean Stein Award from the National Academy of Arts and Letters; and *Lost Hearts in Italy* (2006). Her short story "Anthropology" appeared in *New Stories from the South: The Year's Best* (2002) and in her collection of short stories, *Interesting Women* (2002).

Anthropology

2002

(My cousin says: Didn't you think about what *they* would think, that they were going to read it, too? Of course Aunt Noah and her friends would read it, if it were about them, the more so because it was in a fancy Northern magazine. They can read. You weren't dealing with a tribe of Mbuti Pygmies.)

It is bad enough and quite a novelty to be scolded by my cousin, who lives in a dusty labyrinth of books in a West Village artists' building and rarely abandons his Olympian bibliotaph's detachment to chide anyone face-to-face. But his chance remark about Pygmies also punishes me in an idiosyncratic way. It makes me remember a girl I knew at Harvard, a girl with the unlikely name of Undine Loving, whom everybody thought was my sister, the way everybody always assumes that young black women with light complexions and middle-class accents are close relations, as if there could be only one possible family of us. Anyway, this Undine — who was, I think, from Chicago and was prettier than I, with a pair of bright hazel eyes in a round, merry face that under cropped hair suggested a boy chorister, and an equally round, high-spirited backside in the tight Levi's she always wore — this Undine was a grad student, the brilliant protégé of a famous anthropologist, and she went off for a year to Zaire to live among Pygmies. They'll think she's a goddess, my boyfriend at the time annoyed me by remarking. After that I was haunted by an irritating vision of Undine: tall, fair, and callipygian among reverent little brown men with peppercorn hair: an African-American Snow White. I lost sight of her after that, but I'm certain that, in the Ituri Forest, Undine was as dedicated a professional who ever took notes — abandoning toothpaste and toilet paper and subjecting herself to the menstrual hut, clear and scientific about her motives. Never even fractionally disturbing the equilibrium of the Lilliputian society she had chosen to observe. Not like me.

Well, of course, I never had a science, never had a plan. (That's obvious, says my cousin.) Two years ago, the summer before I moved to Rome, I went to spend three weeks with my Great-Aunt Noah, in Ball County, North Carolina. It was a freak impulse: a last-minute addressing of my attention to the country I was leaving behind. I hadn't been there since I was a child. I was prompted by a writer's vague instinct that there was a thread to be grasped, a strand, initially finer than spider silk, that might grow firmer and more solid in my hands, might lead to something that for the want of a better term I call *of interest*. I never pretended —

(You wanted to investigate your *roots,* says my cousin flatly.) He extracts a cigarette from a red pack bearing the picture of a clove and the words *Kretek Jakarta* and lights it with the kind of ironic flourish that I imagine he uses to intimidate his students at NYU. The way he says *roots* — that spurious '70s term — is so shaming. It brings back all the jokes we used to make in college about fat black American tourists in polyester dashikis trundling around Senegal in Alex Haley tour buses. Black intellectuals are notorious for their snobbish reverence toward Africa — as if crass human nature didn't exist there, too. And, from his West Village aerie, my cousin regards with the same aggressive piety the patch of coastal North Carolina that, before the diaspora north and west, was home to five generations of our family.

We are sitting at his dining table, which is about the length and width 5 of the Gutenberg Bible, covered with clove ash and Melitta filters and the corrected proofs of his latest article. The article is about the whitewashed "magic houses" of the Niger tribe and how the dense plaster arabesques that ornament their façades, gleaming like cake icing, are echoed faintly across the ocean in the designs of glorious, raucous Bahia. He is very good at what he does, my cousin. And he is the happiest of scholars, a minor celebrity in his field, paid royally by obscure foundations to rove from hemisphere to hemisphere, chasing artistic clues that point to a primeval tropical unity. Kerala, Cameroon, Honduras, the Philippines. Ex-wife, children, a string of over-educated girlfriends left hovering wistfully in the dust behind him. He is always traveling, always alone, always vaguely belonging, always from somewhere else. Once he sent me a postcard from Cochin, signed, "Affectionately yours, The Wandering Negro."

Outside on Twelfth Street, sticky acid-green buds are bursting in a March heat wave. But no weather penetrates this studio, which is as close as a confessional and has two computer screens glowing balefully in the background. As he reprimands me I am observing with fascination that my cousin knows how to smoke like a European. I'm the one who lives in Rome, dammit, and yet it is he who smokes with one hand drifting almost incidentally up to his lips and then flowing bonelessly down to the tabletop. And the half-sweet smell of those ridiculous clove cigarettes has permeated every corner of his apartment, giving it a vague atmosphere of stale festivity as if a wassail bowl were tucked away on his overstuffed bookshelves.

I'd be more impressed by all this exotic intellectualism if I didn't remember him as a boy during the single summer we both spent with Aunt Noah down in Ball County. A sallow bookworm with a towering forehead that now in middle age has achieved a mandarin distinction but was then cartoonish. A greedy solitary boy who stole the crumbling syrupy crust off fruit cobblers and who spent the summer afternoons shut in Aunt Noah's unused living room fussily drawing ironclad ships of the Civil War. The two of us loathed each other, and all that summer we never willingly exchanged a word, except insults as I tore by him with my gang of scabby-kneed girlfriends from down the road.

The memory gives me courage to defend myself. All I did, after all, was write a magazine article.

(An article about quilts and superstitions! A fuzzy folkloristic excursion. You made Aunt Noah and the others look cute and rustic and backward like a mixture of *Amos 'n' Andy* and *The Beverly Hillbillies*. Talk about quilts—you embroidered your information. And you mortally offended them—you called them black.)

But they *are* black.

10

(They don't choose to define themselves that way, and if anybody knows that, you do. We're talking about a group of old people who don't look black and who have always called themselves, if anything, colored. People whose blood has been mixed for so many generations that their lives have been constructed on the idea of being a separate caste. Like in Brazil, or other sensible countries where they accept nuances. Anyway, in ten years Aunt Noah and all those people you visited will be dead. What use was it to upset them by forcing your definitions on them? It's not your place to tell them who they are.)

I nearly burst out laughing at this last phrase, which I haven't heard for a long time. It's not your place to do this, to say that. My cousin used it primly and deliberately as an allusion to the entire structure of family and tradition he thinks I flouted. The phrase is a country heirloom, passed down from women like our grandmother and her sister Eleanora and already sounding archaic on the lips of our mothers in the suburbs of the North. It evokes those towns on the North Carolina–Virginia border, where our families still own land: villages marooned in the tobacco fields, where—as in every other rural community in the world—"place," identity, whether defined by pigmentation, occupation, economic rank, or family name, forms an invisible web that lends structure to daily life. In Ball County everyone knows everyone's place. There, the white-white people, the white-black people like Aunt Noah, and the black-black people all keep to their own niches, even though they may rub shoulders every day and even though they may share the same last names and the same ancestors. Aunt Eleanora became Aunt Noah — Noah as in *know* — because she is a phenomenal chronicler of place and can recite labyrinthine genealogies with the offhand fluency of a bard. When I was little I was convinced that she was called Noah because she had actually been aboard the Ark. And that she had stored in her head — perhaps on tiny pieces of parchment, like the papers in fortune cookies — the name of every child born since the waters receded from Ararat.

I was scared to death when I went down to Ball County after so many years. Am I thinking this or speaking aloud? Something of each. My cousin's face grows less bellicose as he listens. We actually like each other, my cousin and I. Our childhood hostility has been transmogrified into a bond that is nothing like the instinctive understanding that flows between brothers and sisters: It is more a deeply buried iron link of formal respect. When I was still living in Manhattan we rarely saw each other, but we knew we were snobs about the same occult things. That's why I allow him to scold me. That's why I have to try to explain things to him.

I was scared, I continue. The usual last-minute terrors you get when you're about to return to a place where you've been perfectly happy. I was convinced it would be awful: ruin and disillusion, not a blade of grass the way I remembered it. I was afraid above all that I wouldn't be able to sleep. That I would end up lying awake in a suffocating Southern night contemplating a wreath of moths around a lightbulb, and listening to an old woman thumping around in the next bedroom like a revenant in a coffin. I took medication with me. Strong stuff.

(Very practical, says my cousin.)   15

But the minute I got there I knew I wouldn't need it. You know I hate driving, so I took an overnight bus from the Port Authority. There isn't a plane or a train that goes near there. And when I got off the bus in front of Ball County Courthouse at dawn, the air was like milk. Five o'clock in the morning at the end of June and ninety percent humidity. White porches and green leaves swimming in mist. Aunt Noah picked me up and drove me down Route 14 in the Oldsmobile that Uncle Pershing left her. A car as long and slow as Cleopatra's barge. And I just lay back, waking up, and sank into the luxurious realization that you can go home again. From vertical New York, life had turned horizontal as a mattress: tobacco, corn, and soybeans spreading out on either side. And you know the first thing I remembered?

(What?)

What it was like to pee in the cornfields. You know I used to run races through the rows with those girls from down the road, and very often we used to stop and pee, not because we had to, but for the fun of it. I remembered the exact feeling of squatting down in that long corridor of leaves, our feet sinking into the sides of the furrow as we pulled down our Carter's cotton underpants, the heat from the ground blasting up onto our backsides as we pissed lakes into the black dirt.

The last time before my visit that I had seen Aunt Noah was two years earlier at my wedding in Massachusetts. There she elicited great curiosity from my husband's family, a studious clan of New England Brahmins who could not digest the fact that the interracial marriage to which they had agreed with such eager tolerance had allied them with a woman who appeared to be an elderly white Southern housewife. She looked the same as she had at the wedding and very much as she had when we were kids. Eighty-three years old, with smooth, graying hair colored intermittently with Loving Care and styled in a precise 1950s helmet that suited her crisp pastel shirtwaist dresses and flat shoes. The same crumpled pale-skinned face of an aged belle, round and girlish from the front but the profile displaying a blunt leonine nose and calm predator's folds around the mouth — she was born, after all, in the magisterial solar month of July. The same blue-gray eyes, shrewd and humorous, sometimes alight with the intense love of a childless woman for her nieces and nephews but never sentimental, never suffering a fool. And, at odd moments, curiously remote.

Well, you look beautiful, she said, when she saw me get off the bus.   20

And the whole focus of my life seemed to shift around. At the close of my twenties, as I was beginning to feel unbearably adult, crushed by the responsibilities of a recently acquired husband, apartment, and job, here I was offered the brief chance to become a young girl again. Better than being a pampered visiting daughter in my mother's house: a pampered visiting niece.

Driving to her house through the sunrise, she said: I hear you made peace with those in-laws of yours.

Things are okay now, I said, feeling my face get hot. She was referring to a newlywed spat that had overflowed into the two families and brought out all the animosity that had been so dutifully concealed at the wedding.

They used excuses to make trouble between you and your husband. He's a nice boy, so I don't lay blame on your marrying white. But you have to watch out for white folks. No matter how friendly they act at first, you can't trust them.

As always it seemed funny to hear this from the lips of someone who   25 looked like Aunt Noah. Who got teased up North by kids on the street when she walked through black neighborhoods. Until she stopped, as she always did, and told them what was what.

The sky was paling into tropical heat, the mist chased away by the brazen song of a million cicadas. The smell of fertilizer and drying earth flowed through the car windows, and I could feel my pores starting to pump out sweat, as if I'd parachuted into equatorial Africa.

Aunt Noah, I said, just to tweak her, you wouldn't have liked it if I'd married a black-black man.

Oh Lord, honey, no, she said. She put on the blinker and turned off the highway into the gravel driveway. We passed beneath the fringes of the giant willow that shaded the brick ranch house Uncle Pershing built fifty years ago as a palace for his beautiful childless wife. The house designed to rival the houses of rich white people in Ball County. Built and air-conditioned with the rent of dark-skinned tenants who cultivated the acres of tobacco that have belonged to Noah and Pershing's families for two hundred years. They were cousins, Noah and Pershing, and they had married both for love and because marrying cousins was what one did among their people at that time. A nigger is just as bad as white trash, she said, turning off the engine. But honey, there were still plenty of boys you could have chosen from our own kind.

(You stayed two weeks, my cousin says, jealously.)

I was researching folkways, I tell him, keeping a straight face. I was hoping 30 to find a mother lode of West African animism, pithy backwoods expressions, seventeenth-century English thieves' cant, poetic upwellings from the cyclic drama of agriculture, as played out on the Southeastern tidal plain. I wanted to be ravished by the dying tradition of the peasant South, like Jean Toomer.

(My cousin can't resist the reference. *Fecund Southern night, a pregnant Negress,* he declaims, in the orotund voice of a Baptist preacher.)

What I really did during my visit was laze around and let Aunt Noah spoil me. Every morning scrambled eggs, grits, country ham, and hot biscuits with homemade peach preserves. She was up for hours before me, working in her garden. A fructiferous Eden of giant pea vines, prodigious tomato plants, squash blossoms like Victrola horns. She wore a green sun hat that made her look like an elderly infant, blissfully happy. Breakfast over and the house tidy, we would set out on visits where she displayed me in the only way she knew how, as an ornamental young sprig on the family tree. I fell into the gratifying role of the cherished newlywed niece, passed around admiringly like a mail-order collectible doll. Dressing in her frilly pink guest room, I put on charming outfits: long skirts, flowery blouses. I looked like a poster girl for *Southern Living.* Everyone we visited was enchanted. My husband, who telephoned me every night, began to seem very far away: a small white boy's voice sounding for-lornly out of Manhattan.

The people we called on all seemed to be distant relatives of Aunt Noah's and mine, and more than once I nearly fell asleep in a stuffy front room listen-ing to two old voices tracing the spiderweb of connections. I'd decided to write about quilts, and that gave us an excuse to go chasing around Ball County peering at old masterpieces dragged out of mothballs, and new ones stitched out of lurid polyester. Everybody had quilts, and everybody had some variation of the same four family names. Hopper, Osborne, Amiel, Mills. There was Ger-tie Osborne, a little freckled woman with the diction of a Victorian school-mistress who contributed the "Rambling Reader" column to the *Ball County Chronicle.* The tobacco magnate and head deacon P. H. Mills, tall and rich and silent in his white linen suits. Mary Amiel, who lived up the road from Aunt Noah and wrote poetry privately printed in a volume entitled *The Flaming Depths.* Aunt Noah's brother-in-law Hopper Mills, who rode a decrepit Vespa over to check up on her every day at dawn.

I practiced pistol-shooting in the woods and went to the tobacco auction and rode the rope-drawn ferry down at Crenshaw Crossing. And I attended the Mount Moriah Baptist church, where years before I had passed Sunday morn-ings in starched dresses and cotton gloves. The big church stood unchanged under the pines: an air-conditioned Williamsburg copy in brick as vauntingly prosperous as Aunt Noah's ranch house.

After the service, they were all together outside the church, chatting in the 35 pine shade: the fabled White Negroes of Ball County. An enterprising *Ebony* magazine journalist had described them that way once, back in 1955. They were a group who defied conventional logic: Southern landowners of African de-scent who had pale skins and generations of free ancestors. Republicans to a man. People who'd fought to desegregate Greensboro and had marched on

Washington yet still expected their poorer, blacker tenants to address them as Miss Nora or Mr. Fred. Most of them were over seventy: their sons and daughters had escaped years ago to Washington or Atlanta or Los Angeles or New York. To them I was the symbol of all those runaway children, and they loved me to pieces.

(But then you went and called them black. In print, which to people raised on the Bible and the *McGuffey Readers* is as definitive as a set of stone tablets. And you did it not in some academic journal but in a magazine that people buy on newsstands all over the country. To them it was the worst thing they could have read about themselves—)

I didn't—

(Except perhaps being called white.)

I didn't mean—

(It was the most presumptuous thing you could have done. They're old. 40 They've survived, defining themselves in a certain way. We children and grandchildren can call ourselves Afro-American or African-American or black or whatever the week's fashion happens to be.)

You—

(And of course you knew this. We all grew up knowing it. You're a very smart woman, and the question is why you allowed yourself to be so careless. So breezy and destructive. Maybe to make sure you couldn't go back there.)

I say: That's enough. Stop it.

And my cousin, for a minute, does stop. I never noticed before how much he looks like Uncle Pershing. The same mountainous brow and reprobative eyes of a biblical patriarch that look out of framed photographs in Aunt Noah's living room. A memory reawakens of being similarly thundered at, in the course of that childhood summer, when I lied about borrowing Uncle Pershing's pocketknife.

We sit staring at each other across this little cluttered table in Green- 45 wich Village. I am letting him tell me off as I would never allow my brother or my husband—especially my husband. But the buried link between my cousin and me makes the fact that I actually sit and take it inevitable. As I do, it occurs to me that fifty years ago, in the moribund world we are arguing about, it would have been an obvious choice for the two of us to get married. As Ball County cousins always did. And how far we have flown from it all, as if we were genuine emigrants, energetically forgetful of some small, dire old-world country plagued by dictators, drought, locusts, and pogroms. Years ago yet another of our cousins, a dentist in Atlanta, was approached by Aunt Noah about moving his family back to Ball County and taking over her house and land. I remember him grimacing with incredulity about it as we sat over drinks once in an airport bar. Why did the family select him for this honor? he asked, with a strained laugh. The last place anyone would ever want to be, he said.

I don't know what else to do but stumble on with my story.

Aunt Noah was having a good time showing me off. On one of the last days of my visit, she drove me clear across the county to the house where she grew up. I'd never been there, though I knew that was where it had all begun. It was on this land, in the 1740s, before North Carolina statutes about slavery and mixing of races had grown hard and fast, that a Scotch-Irish settler—a debtor or petty thief deported to the pitch-pine wilderness of the penal colony—allowed his handsome half-African, half-Indian bond-servant to marry his only daughter. The handsomeness of the bond-servant is part of the tradition, as is the pregnancy of the daughter. Their descendants took the land and joined the group of farmers and artisans who managed to carve out an independent station between the white planters and the black slaves until after the Civil War. Dissertations and books have been written about them. The name some scholars chose for them has a certain lyricism: Tidewater Free Negroes.

My daddy grew tobacco and was the best blacksmith in the county, Aunt Noah told me. There wasn't a man, black or white, who didn't respect him.

We had turned onto a dirt road that led through fields of tobacco and corn farmed by the two tenant families who divided the old house. It was a nineteenth-century farmhouse, white and green with a rambling porch and fretwork around the eaves. I saw with a pang that the paint was peeling and that the whole structure had achieved the undulating organic shape that signals imminent collapse.

I can't keep it up, and, honey, the tenants just do enough to keep the roof 50
from falling in, she said. Good morning, Hattie, she called out, stopping the car and waving to a woman with cornrowed hair and skin the color of dark plums, who came out of the front door.

Good morning, Miss Nora, said Hattie.

Mama's flower garden was over there, Aunt Noah told me. You never saw such peonies. We had a fish pond and a greenhouse and an icehouse. Didn't have to buy anything except sugar and coffee and flour. And over there was a paddock for trotting horses. You know there was a fair every year where Papa and other of our kind of folks used to race their sulkies. Our own county fair.

She collected the rent, and we drove away. On the road, she stopped and showed me her mother's family graveyard, a mound covered with Amiel and Hopper tombstones rising in the middle of a tobacco field. She told me she paid a boy to clean off the brush.

You know it's hard to see the old place like that, she said. But I don't see any use in holding onto things just for the sake of holding on. You children are all off in the North, marrying your niggers or your white trash—honey, I'm just fooling, you know how I talk—and pretty soon we ugly old folks are going to go. Then there will just be some bones out in the fields and some money in the bank.

That was the night that my husband called from New York with the news 55
we had hoped for: His assignment in Europe was for Rome.

(You really pissed them off, you know, says my cousin, continuing where he left off. You were already in Italy when the article was published, and your mother never told you, but it was quite an item for the rest of the family. There was that neighbor of Aunt Noah's, Dan Mills, who was threatening to sue. They said he was ranting: *I'm not African-American like they printed there! I'm not black!*)

Well, God knows I'm sorry about it now. But really—what could I have called them? The quaint colored folk of the Carolina lowlands? Mulattos and octoroons, like something out of *Mandingo*?

(You could have thought more about it, he says, his voice softening. You could have considered things before plunging into the quilts and the superstitions.)

You know, I tell him, I did talk to Aunt Noah just after the article came out. She said: Oh, honey, some of the folks around here got worked up about what you wrote, but they calmed right down when the TV truck came around and put them on the evening news.

My cousin drums his fingers thoughtfully on the table as I look on with a 60 certain muted glee. I can tell that he isn't familiar with this twist in the story.

(Well — he says.) Rising to brew us another pot of coffee. Public scourging finished; case closed. By degrees he changes the subject to a much-discussed new book on W. E. B. Du Bois in Germany. Have I read about that sojourn in the early 1930s? Du Bois's weirdly prescient musings on American segregation and the National Socialist racial laws?

We talk about this and about his ex-wife and his upcoming trip to Celebes and the recent flood of Nigerian Kok statues on the London art market. Then, irresistibly, we turn again to Ball County. I surprise my cousin by telling him that if I can get back to the States this fall, I may go down there for Thanksgiving. With my husband. Aunt Noah invited us. That's when they kill the pigs, and I want to taste some of that fall barbeque. Why don't you come too? I say.

(Me? I'm not a barbeque fan, he says. Having the grace to flush slightly on the ears. Aren't you afraid that they're going to burn a cross in front of your window? he adds with a smile.)

I'll never write about that place again, I say. Just one thing, though —
(What?) 65
What would you have called them?

He takes his time lighting up another Kretek Jakarta. His eyes, through the foreign smoke, grow as remote as Aunt Noah's, receding in the distance like a highway in a rearview mirror. And I have a moment of false nostalgia. A quick glimpse of an image that never was: a boy racing me down a long corridor of July corn, his big flat feet churning up the dirt where we'd peed to mark our territory like two young dogs, his skinny figure tearing along ahead of me, both of us breaking our necks to get to the vanishing point where the green rows come together and geometry begins. Gone.

His cigarette lit, my cousin shakes his head and gives a short exasperated laugh. (In the end, it doesn't make a damn bit of difference, does it? he says.)

CONSIDERATIONS FOR CRITICAL THINKING AND WRITING

1. **FIRST RESPONSE.** Why is "Anthropology" an appropriate title for this story?

2. How does the narrator's use of language reveal her character?

3. Compare and contrast the narrator with her cousin. Explain why you find them more alike or different from each other.

4. Discuss the differences and similarities between the settings of New York City and Ball County, North Carolina. Why are the settings important elements in the story?

5. Consider the definition of "place" offered in paragraph 12. How might this definition be used to describe accurately both New York City and Ball County?

6. Explain what you think is the essential conflict in the story and whether there is a resolution to it.

CONNECTIONS TO OTHER SELECTIONS

1. Compare the treatment of race in "Anthropology" with Flannery O'Connor's treatment of it in "Revelation" (p. 474).

2. How is the South depicted in "Anthropology" and in William Faulkner's "Barn Burning" (p. 503)? How do these settings contribute to each story's central points?

FAY WELDON (B. 1933)

© Jerry Bauer.

Born in England and raised in New Zealand, Fay Weldon graduated from St. Andrew's University in Scotland. She wrote advertising copy for various companies and was a propaganda writer for the British Foreign Office before turning to fiction. She has written novels, short stories, plays, and radio scripts. In 1971 her script for an episode of *Upstairs, Downstairs* won an award from the Society of Film and Television Arts. She has written more than a score of novels, including *The Fat Woman's Joke* (1967), *Down Among the Women* (1971), *Praxis* (1978), *The Life and Loves of a She-Devil* (1983), *Life Force* (1991), *The Bulgari Connection* (2001), *She May Not Leave* (2005), and *The Stepmother's Diary* (2008), and an equal number of plays and scripts. Her collections of short stories include *Moon over Minneapolis* (1992), *Wicked Women* (American edition, 1997), *A Hard Time to Be a Father* (1998), and *Nothing to Wear and Nowhere to Hide* (2002). Weldon often uses ironic humor to portray carefully drawn female characters coming to terms with the facts of their lives.

IND AFF
or Out of Love in Sarajevo

1988

This is a sad story. It has to be. It rained in Sarajevo, and we had expected fine weather.

The rain filled up Sarajevo's pride, two footprints set into a pavement which mark the spot where the young assassin Princip stood to shoot the Archduke Franz Ferdinand and his wife. (Don't forget his wife: everyone forgets his wife, the archduchess.) That was in the summer of 1914. Sarajevo is a pretty town, Balkan style, mountain-rimmed. A broad, swift, shallow river runs through its center, carrying the mountain snow away, arched by many bridges. The one nearest the two footprints has been named the Princip Bridge. The young man is a hero in these parts. Not only does he bring in the tourists—look, look, the spot, the very spot!—but by his action, as everyone knows, he lit a spark which fired the timber which caused World War I which crumbled the Austro-Hungarian Empire, the crumbling of which made modern Yugoslavia possible. Forty million dead (or was it thirty?) but who cares? So long as he loved his country.

The river, they say, can run so shallow in the summer it's known derisively as "the wet road." Today, from what I could see through the sheets of falling rain, it seemed full enough. Yugoslavian streets are always busy—no one stays home if they can help it (thus can an indecent shortage of housing space create a sociable nation) and it seemed as if by common consent a shield of bobbing umbrellas had been erected two meters high to keep the rain off the streets. It just hadn't worked around Princip's corner.

"Come all this way," said Peter, who was a professor of classical history, "and you can't even see the footprints properly, just two undistinguished puddles." Ah, but I loved him. I shivered for his disappointment. He was supervising my thesis on varying concepts of morality and duty in the early Greek States as evidenced in their poetry and drama. I was dependent upon him for my academic future. He said I had a good mind but not a first-class mind and somehow I didn't take it as an insult. I had a feeling first-class minds weren't all that good in bed.

Sarajevo is in Bosnia, in the center of Yugoslavia, that grouping of unlikely   5 states, that distillation of languages into the phonetic reasonableness of Serbo-Croatian. We'd sheltered from the rain in an ancient mosque in Serbian Belgrade; done the same in a monastery in Croatia; now we spent a wet couple of days in Sarajevo beneath other people's umbrellas. We planned to go on to Montenegro, on the coast, where the fish and the artists come from, to swim and lie in the sun, and recover from the exhaustion caused by the sexual and moral torments of the last year. It couldn't possibly go on raining forever. Could it? Satellite pictures showed black clouds swishing gently all over Europe, over the Balkans, into Asia—practically all the way from Moscow to London, in fact. It wasn't that Peter and myself were being singled out. No. It was raining on his wife, too, back in Cambridge.

Peter was trying to decide, as he had been for the past year, between his wife and myself as his permanent life partner. To this end we had gone away, off the beaten track, for a holiday; if not with his wife's blessing, at least with her knowledge. Were we really, truly suited? We had to be sure, you see, that this was more than just any old professor-student romance; that it was the Real Thing, because the longer the indecision went on the longer Mrs. Piper would be left dangling in uncertainty and distress. They had been married for twenty-four years; they had stopped loving each other a long time ago, of course—but there would be a fearful personal and practical upheaval entailed if he decided to leave permanently and shack up, as he put it, with me. Which I certainly wanted him to do. I loved him. And so far I was winning hands down. It didn't seem much of a contest at all, in fact. I'd been cool and thin and informed on the seat next to him in a Zagreb theater (Mrs. Piper was sweaty and only liked telly); was now eager and anxious for social and political instruction in Sarajevo (Mrs. Piper spat in the face of knowledge, he'd once told me); and planned to be lissome (and I thought topless but I hadn't quite decided: this might be the area where the age difference showed) while I splashed and shrieked like a bathing belle in the shallows of the Montenegrin coast. (Mrs. Piper was a swimming coach: I imagined she smelt permanently of chlorine.)

In fact so far as I could see, it was no contest at all between his wife and myself. But Peter liked to luxuriate in guilt and indecision. And I loved him with an inordinate affection.

Princip's prints are a meter apart, placed as a modern cop on a training shoot-out would place his feet — the left in front at a slight outward angle, the right behind, facing forward. There seemed great energy focused here. Both hands on the gun, run, stop, plant the feet, aim, fire! I could see the footprints well enough, in spite of Peter's complaint. They were clear enough to me.

We went to a restaurant for lunch, since it was too wet to do what we loved to do: that is, buy bread, cheese, sausage, wine, and go off somewhere in our hired car, into the woods or the hills, and picnic and make love. It was a private restaurant — Yugoslavia went over to a mixed capitalist-communist economy years back, so you get either the best or worst of both systems, depending on your mood — that is to say, we knew we would pay more but be given a choice. We chose the wild boar.

"Probably ordinary pork soaked in red cabbage water to darken it," said   10
Peter. He was not in a good mood.

Cucumber salad was served first.

"Everything in this country comes with cucumber salad," complained Peter. I noticed I had become used to his complaining. I supposed that when you had been married a little you simply wouldn't hear it. He was forty-six and I was twenty-five.

"They grow a lot of cucumber," I said.

"If they can grow cucumbers," Peter then asked, "why can't they grow *mange-tout*°?" It seemed a why-can't-they-eat-cake sort of argument to me, but not knowing enough about horticulture not to be outflanked if I debated the point, I moved the subject on to safer ground.

"I suppose Princip's action couldn't really have started World War I," I re-   15
marked. "Otherwise, what a thing to have on your conscience! One little shot and the deaths of thirty million."

"Forty," he corrected me. Though how they reckon these things and get them right I can't imagine. "Of course he didn't start the war. That's just a simple tale to keep the children quiet. It takes more than an assassination to start a war. What happened was that the buildup of political and economic tensions in the Balkans was such that it had to find some release."

"So it was merely the shot that lit the spark that fired the timber that started the war, et cetera?"

"Quite," he said. "World War I would have had to have started sooner or later."

"A bit later or a bit sooner," I said, "might have made the difference of a million or so; if it was you on the battlefield in the mud and the rain you'd notice; exactly when they fired the starting-pistol; exactly when they blew the

---

mange-tout: A sugar pea or bean (French).

final whistle. Is that what they do when a war ends; blow a whistle? So that everyone just comes in from the trenches."

But he wasn't listening. He was parting the flesh of the soft collapsed 20 orangey-red pepper which sat in the middle of his cucumber salad; he was carefully extracting the pips. His nan had once told him they could never be digested, would stick inside and do terrible damage. I loved him for his dexterity and patience with his knife and fork. I'd finished my salad yonks ago, pips and all. I was hungry. I wanted my wild boar.

Peter might be forty-six, but he was six foot two and grizzled and muscled with it, in a dark-eyed, intelligent, broad-jawed kind of way. I adored him. I loved to be seen with him. "Muscular academic, not weedy academic" as my younger sister Clare once said. "Muscular academic is just a generally superior human being: everything works well from the brain to the toes. Weedy academic is when there isn't enough vital energy in the person, and the brain drains all the strength from the other parts." Well, Clare should know. Clare is only twenty-three, but of the superior human variety kind herself, vividly pretty, bright and competent — somewhere behind a heavy curtain of vibrant red hair, which she only parts for effect. She had her first degree at twenty. Now she's married to a Harvard professor of economics seconded to the United Nations. She can even cook. I gave up competing yonks ago. Though she too is capable of self-deception. I would say her husband was definitely of the weedy academic rather than the muscular academic type. And they have to live in Brussels.

The archduke's chauffeur had lost his way, and was parked on the corner trying to recover his nerve when Princip came running out of a café, planted his feet, aimed, and fired. Princip was nineteen — too young to hang. But they sent him to prison for life and, since he had TB to begin with, he only lasted three years. He died in 1918, in an Austrian prison. Or perhaps it was more than TB: perhaps they gave him a hard time, not learning till later, when the Austro-Hungarian Empire collapsed, that he was a hero. Poor Princip, too young to die — like so many other millions. Dying for love of a country.

"I love you," I said to Peter, my living man, progenitor already of three children by his chlorinated, swimming-coach wife.

"How much do you love me?"

"Inordinately! I love you with inordinate affection." It was a joke between 25 us. Ind Aff!

"Inordinate affection is a sin," he'd told me. "According to the Wesleyans. John Wesley° himself worried about it to such a degree he ended up abbreviating it in his diaries, Ind Aff. He maintained that what he felt for young Sophy, the eighteen-year-old in his congregation, was not Ind Aff, which bears the spirit away from God towards the flesh: he insisted that what he felt was a pure and spiritual, if passionate, concern for her soul."

Peter said now, as we waited for our wild boar, and he picked over his pepper, "Your Ind Aff is my wife's sorrow, that's the trouble." He wanted, I knew, one of the long half-wrangles, half soul-sharings that we could keep going for hours, and led to piercing pains in the heart which could only be made better in bed. But our bedroom at the Hotel Europa was small and dark and looked

John Wesley (1703–1791): English religious leader and founder of Methodism.

out into the well of the building—a punishment room if ever there was one. (Reception staff did sometimes take against us.) When Peter had tried to change it in his quasi-Serbo-Croatian, they'd shrugged their Bosnian shoulders and pretended not to understand, so we'd decided to put up with it. I did not fancy pushing hard single beds together—it seemed easier not to have the pain in the heart in the first place. "Look," I said, "this holiday is supposed to be just the two of us, not Mrs. Piper as well. Shall we talk about something else?"

Do not think that the archduke's chauffeur was merely careless, an inefficient chauffeur, when he took the wrong turning. He was, I imagine, in a state of shock, fright, and confusion. There had been two previous attempts on the archduke's life since the cavalcade had entered town. The first was a bomb which got the car in front and killed its driver. The second was a shot fired by none other than young Princip, which had missed. Princip had vanished into the crowd and gone to sit down in a corner café and ordered coffee to calm his nerves. I expect his hand trembled at the best of times—he did have TB. (Not the best choice of assassin, but no doubt those who arrange these things have to make do with what they can get.) The archduke's chauffeur panicked, took the wrong road, realized what he'd done, and stopped to await rescue and instructions just outside the café where Princip sat drinking his coffee.

"What shall we talk about?" asked Peter, in even less of a good mood.

"The collapse of the Austro-Hungarian Empire?" I suggested. "How does 30 an empire collapse? Is there no money to pay the military or the police, so everyone goes home? Or what?" He liked to be asked questions.

"The Hungro-Austrarian Empire," said Peter to me, "didn't so much collapse as fail to exist any more. War destroys social organizations. The same thing happened after World War II. There being no organized bodies left between Moscow and London—and for London read Washington, then as now— it was left to these two to put in their own puppet governments. Yalta, 1944. It's taken the best part of forty-five years for nations of West and East Europe to remember who they are."

"Austro-Hungarian," I said, "not Hungro-Austrarian."

"I didn't say Hungro-Austrarian," he said.

"You did," I said.

"Didn't," he said. "What the hell are they doing about our wild boar? Are 35 they out in the hills shooting it?"

My sister Clare had been surprisingly understanding about Peter. When I worried about him being older, she pooh-poohed it; when I worried about him being married, she said, "Just go for it, sister. If you can unhinge a marriage, it's ripe for unhinging, it would happen sooner or later, it might as well be you. See a catch, go ahead and catch! Go for it!"

Princip saw the archduke's car parked outside, and went for it. Second chances are rare in life: they must be responded to. Except perhaps his second chance was missing in the first place? Should he have taken his cue from fate, and just sat and finished his coffee, and gone home to his mother? But what's a man to do when he loves his country? Fate delivered the archduke into his hands: how could he resist it? A parked car, a uniformed and medaled chest, the persecutor of his country—how could Princip not, believing God to be on his side, but see this as His intervention, push his coffee aside and leap to his feet?

Two waiters stood idly by and watched us waiting for our wild boar. One was young and handsome in a mountainous Bosnian way—flashing eyes, hooked nose, luxuriant black hair, sensuous mouth. He was about my age. He smiled. His teeth were even and white. I smiled back, and instead of the pain in the heart I'd become accustomed to as an erotic sensation, now felt, quite violently, an associated yet different pang which got my lower stomach. The true, the real pain of Ind Aff!

"Fancy him?" asked Peter.

"No," I said. "I just thought if I smiled the wild boar might come quicker." 40

The other waiter was older and gentler: his eyes were soft and kind. I thought he looked at me reproachfully. I could see why. In a world which for once, after centuries of savagery, was finally full of young men, unslaughtered, what was I doing with this man with thinning hair?

"What are you thinking of?" Professor Piper asked me. He liked to be in my head.

"How much I love you," I said automatically, and was finally aware how much I lied. "And about the archduke's assassination," I went on, to cover the kind of tremble in my head as I came to my senses, "and let's not forget his wife, she died too—how can you say World War I would have happened anyway. If Princip hadn't shot the archduke, something else, some undisclosed, unsuspected variable, might have come along and defused the whole political/military situation, and neither World War I nor II ever happened. We'll just never know, will we?"

I had my passport and my travelers' checks with me. (Peter felt it was less confusing if we each paid our own way.) I stood up, and took my raincoat from the peg.

"Where are you going?" he asked, startled. 45

"Home," I said. I kissed the top of his head, where it was balding. It smelt gently of chlorine, which may have come from thinking about his wife so much, but might merely have been that he'd taken a shower that morning. ("The water all over Yugoslavia, though safe to drink, is unusually chlorinated": Guide Book.) As I left to catch a taxi to the airport the younger of the two waiters emerged from the kitchen with two piled plates of roasted wild boar, potatoes duchesse, and stewed peppers. ("Yugoslavian diet is unusually rich in proteins and fats": Guide Book.) I could tell from the glisten of oil that the food was no longer hot, and I was not tempted to stay, hungry though I was. Thus fate — or was it Bosnian willfulness? — confirmed the wisdom of my intent.

And that was how I fell out of love with my professor, in Sarajevo, a city to which I am grateful to this day, though I never got to see very much of it, because of the rain.

It was a silly sad thing to do, in the first place, to confuse mere passing academic ambition with love: to try and outdo my sister Clare. (Professor Piper was spiteful, as it happened, and did his best to have my thesis refused, but I went to appeal, which he never thought I'd dare, and won. I had a first-class mind after all.) A silly sad episode, which I regret. As silly and sad as Princip, poor young man, with his feverish mind, his bright tubercular cheeks, and his inordinate affection for his country, pushing aside his cup of coffee, leaping to his feet, taking his gun in both hands, planting his feet, aiming, and firing — one, two, three shots — and starting World War I. The first one missed, the second got the wife (never forget the wife), and the third got the archduke and a whole generation, and their children, and their children's children, and on and on forever. If he'd just hung on a bit, there in Sarajevo, that June day, he might have come to his senses. People do, sometimes quite quickly.

CONSIDERATIONS FOR CRITICAL THINKING AND WRITING

1. FIRST RESPONSE. Do you agree with Weldon's first line, "This is a sad story"? Explain why or why not.

2. How does the rain establish the mood for the story in the first five paragraphs?

3. Characterize Peter. What details concerning him reveal his personality?

4. Describe the narrator's relationship with Peter. How do you think he regards her? Why is she attracted to him?

5. Why is Sarajevo important for the story's setting? What is the effect of having the story of Princip's assassination of the Archduke Franz Ferdinand and his wife woven through the plot?

6. Describe Mrs. Piper. Though she doesn't appear in the story, she does have an important role. What do you think her role is?

7. What is "Ind Aff"? Why is it an important element of this story?

8. What is the significance of the two waiters (paras. 38–41)? How do they affect the narrator?

9. Why does the narrator decide to go home (para. 46)? Do you think she makes a reasoned or an impulsive decision? Explain why you think so.

10. Discuss the relationship between the personal history and the public history recounted in the story. How are the two interconnected? Explain whether you think it is necessary to be familiar with the assassinations in Sarajevo before reading the story.

11. CRITICAL STRATEGIES. Read the section on cultural criticism (pp. 2055–56) in Chapter 53, "Critical Strategies for Reading." How do you think a cultural critic might describe the nature of the narrator's relationship with her professor given the current attitudes on college campuses concerning teacher-student affairs?

CONNECTIONS TO OTHER SELECTIONS

1. Compare and contrast "IND AFF" and Joyce Carol Oates's "The Lady with the Pet Dog" (p. 237) as love stories. Do you think that the stories end happily, or the way you would want them to end? Are the endings problematic?

2. Explain how Weldon's concept of "Ind Aff" — "inordinate affection" — can be used to make sense of the relationship between Georgiana and Aylmer in Nathaniel Hawthorne's "The Birthmark" (p. 420).

3. How does passion figure in "IND AFF" and in D. H. Lawrence's "The Horse Dealer's Daughter" (p. 701)? Explain how Weldon's and Lawrence's perspectives on passion suggest differing views of love and human relationships.

Perspective

FAY WELDON (B. 1933)

On the Importance of Place in "IND AFF"   1997

I'm the kind of writer who lives mostly in her head, looking inwards not outwards, more sensitive to people than places, unless the place turns out to be some useful metaphor. In Sarajevo, on a book tour, brooding about Ind. Aff., inordinate affection, these days more unkindly known as neurotic dependency, I was taken to see Princip's footsteps in the sidewalk. Fancy fell away. Here was the metaphor taken in physical form — chance and death, so like chance and love. Then later we went up into the hills to eat wild boar and the intellectual Englishmen I was with seemed so pallid and absurd compared to the here-and-now mountain men: people came into perspective inside a landscape. I have a kind of rule of thumb: three preoccupations make a story. I interweaved them, delivered them into paper, and fell back into jet-lagged torpor.

From an interview with Michael Meyer, November 15, 1997

CONSIDERATIONS FOR CRITICAL THINKING AND WRITING

1. Weldon's description of how she began "IND AFF" draws on her personal experience in Sarajevo. How does that experience make its way into the story?

2. Consider Weldon's observation that "here was the metaphor taken in physical form — chance and death, so like chance and love." Do you think her observation works as a summary of the story?

3. Choose any other story in this anthology that can serve as an example of how "people [come] into perspective inside a landscape," and write an essay about it.

A SAMPLE STUDENT RESPONSE

Karita Perez

Professor Hoffs

English 202

November 30, 2009

The Significance of Setting in Weldon's "IND AFF"

In the first line of Fay Weldon's "IND AFF," we are told "This is a sad story" (Weldon 202), and the setting immediately reflects that. The story takes place in Sarajevo, where the skies are dark and the rain never stops. A young woman and her lover (twenty years her senior, and also her university professor) are on holiday visiting the landmark where Archduke Ferdinand was assassinated. The trip is meant to be pleasant, a break from their lives to determine if they are "truly suited" for each other. But just as the rains spoil their trip, their relationship is spoiled by a reality they cannot control. The main character feels guilt and sympathizes with her lover's wife: "it was raining on his wife, too" (203). She begins to see her lover in a new light, and her hopes for something beautiful give way to disappointment.

The setting also creates a mood that shapes the story, what Michael Meyer calls an "atmosphere that will prepare the reader for what is to come" (184). Along with the dismal weather, the descriptions of the landscape represent what the characters are going through. Despite the rains, there is beauty here; the town is "mountain-rimmed," and a "shallow river runs through its center, carrying the mountain snow away, arched by many bridges" (Weldon 202). This majestic scenery can be read as connected to the physical stature of Peter. The main character, despite her doubts, has strong feelings for Peter and is drawn to his height and attractiveness: "he was six foot two and grizzled and muscled with it, in a dark-eyed, intelligent, broad-jawed kind of way. I adored him" (205). . . .

Perez 4

Works Cited

Meyer, Michael, ed. *The Bedford Introduction to Literature*. 9th ed. Boston:

Bedford/St. Martin's, 2011. 184. Print.

Weldon, Fay. "IND AFF, or Out of Love in Sarajevo." *The Bedford Introduction

to Literature*. Ed. Michael Meyer. 9th ed. Boston: Bedford/St. Martin's,

2011. 202–08. Print.

6

Point of View

It is not necessary to portray many characters. The center of gravity should be in two persons: him and her.
— ANTON CHEKHOV

Because one of the pleasures of reading fiction consists of seeing the world through someone else's eyes, it is easy to overlook the eyes that control our view of the plot, characters, and setting. *Point of view* refers to who tells us the story and how it is told. What we know and how we feel about the events in a story are shaped by the author's choice of a point of view. The teller of a story, the *narrator,* inevitably affects our understanding of the characters' actions by filtering what is told through his or her own perspective. The narrator should not be confused with the author who has created the narrative voice because the two are usually distinct (more on this point later).

If the narrative voice is changed, the story will change. Consider, for example, how different "Bartleby, the Scrivener" (p. 142) would be if Melville had chosen to tell the story from Bartleby's point of view instead of the lawyer's. With Bartleby as narrator, much of the mystery concerning his behavior would be lost. The peculiar force of his saying "I would prefer not to" would be lessened amid all the other things he would have to say as narrator. Moreover, the lawyer's reaction — puzzled, upset, outraged, and finally sympathetic to Bartleby — would be lost too. It would be entirely possible, of course, to write a story from Bartleby's point of view, but it would not be the story Melville wrote.

The possible ways of telling a story are many, and more than one point of view can be worked into a single story. However, the various points of view that storytellers draw on can be conveniently grouped into two broad categories: (1) the third-person narrator and (2) the first-person narrator. The third-person narrator uses *he, she,* or *they* to tell the story and does not participate in the action. The first-person narrator uses *I* and is a major or minor partici-pant in the action. A second-person narrator, *you,* is possible but rarely used because of the awkwardness in thrusting the reader into the story, as in "You are minding your own busi-ness on a park bench when a drunk steps out of the bushes and demands your lunch bag."

Let's look now at the most important and most often used variations within first- and third-person narrations.

Web Explore the literary element in this chapter at bedfordstmartins.com/meyerlit.

THIRD-PERSON NARRATOR (Nonparticipant)

1. Omniscient (the narrator takes us inside the character[s])
2. Limited omniscient (the narrator takes us inside one or two characters)
3. Objective (the narrator is outside the character[s])

No type of third-person narrator appears as a character in a story. The *omniscient narrator* is all-knowing. From this point of view, the narrator can move from place to place and pass back and forth through time, slip-ping into and out of characters as no human being possibly could in real life. This narrator can report the characters' thoughts and feelings as well as what they say and do. In the excerpt from *Tarzan of the Apes* (p. 75), Bur-roughs's narrator tells us about events concerning Terkoz in another part of the jungle that long preceded the battle between Terkoz and Tarzan. We also learn Tarzan's and Jane's inner thoughts and emotions during the episode. And Burroughs's narrator describes Terkoz as "an arrant coward" and a bully, thereby evaluating the character for the reader. This kind of in-trusion is called *editorial omniscience.* In contrast, narration that allows characters' actions and thoughts to speak for themselves is known as *neu-tral omniscience.* Most modern writers use neutral omniscience so that readers can reach their own conclusions.

The *limited omniscient narrator* is much more confined than the om-niscient narrator. With limited omniscience the author very often restricts the narrator to the single perspective of either a major or a minor character. Sometimes a narrator can see into more than one character, particularly in a longer work that focuses, for example, on two characters alternately from one chapter to the next. Short stories, however, frequently are restricted by length to a single character's point of view. The way people, places, and events appear to that character is the way they appear to the reader. The reader has access to the thoughts and feelings of the characters revealed by the narrator, but neither the reader nor the character has access to the inner lives of any of the other characters in the story. The events in Katherine Mansfield's "Miss Brill" (p. 307) are viewed entirely through the protagonist's eyes; we see a French vacation town as an elderly woman does. Miss Brill represents the central consciousness of the story. She unifies the story by being present through all the action. We are not told of anything that happens away from the character because the narration is based on her perception of things.

The most intense use of a central consciousness in narration can be seen in the ***stream-of-consciousness technique*** developed by modern writers such as James Joyce, Virginia Woolf, and William Faulkner. This technique takes a reader inside a character's mind to reveal perceptions, thoughts, and feelings on a conscious or unconscious level. A stream of consciousness suggests the flow of thought as well as its content; hence, complete sentences may give way to fragments as the character's mind makes rapid associations free of conventional logic or transitions.

The following passage is from Joyce's *Ulysses,* a novel famous for its extended use of this technique. In this paragraph Joyce takes us inside the mind of a character who is describing a funeral:

> Coffin now. Got here before us, dead as he is. Horse looking round at it with his plume skeowways [askew]. Dull eye: collar tight on his neck, pressing on a bloodvessel or something. Do they know what they cart out of here every day? Must be twenty or thirty funerals every day. Then Mount Jerome for the protestants. Funerals all over the world everywhere every minute. Shovelling them under by the cartload doublequick. Thousands every hour. Too many in the world.

The character's thoughts range from specific observations to speculations about death. Joyce creates the illusion that we are reading the character's thoughts as they occur. The stream-of-consciousness technique provides an intimate perspective on a character's thoughts.

In contrast, the ***objective point of view*** employs a narrator who does not see into the mind of any character. From this detached and impersonal perspective, the narrator reports action and dialogue without telling us directly what the character feels and thinks. We observe the characters in much the same way we would perceive events in a film or play: we supply the meanings; no analysis or interpretation is provided by the narrator. This point of view places a heavy premium on dialogue, actions, and details to reveal character.

In Hemingway's "Soldier's Home" (p. 187), a limited omniscient narration is the predominant point of view. Krebs's thoughts and reaction to being home from the war are made available to the reader by the narrator, who tells us that Krebs "felt embarrassed and resentful" or "sick and vaguely nauseated" by the small-town life he has reentered. Occasionally, however, Hemingway uses an objective point of view when he dramatizes particularly tense moments between Krebs and his mother. In the following excerpt, Hemingway's narrator shows us Krebs's feelings instead of telling us what they are. Krebs's response to his mother's concerns is presented without comment. The external details of the scene reveal his inner feelings.

> "I've worried about you so much, Harold," his mother went on. "I know the temptations you must have been exposed to. I know how weak men are. I know what your own dear grandfather, my own father, told us about the Civil War and I have prayed for you. I pray for you all day long, Harold."
> Krebs looked at the bacon fat hardening on his plate.
> "Your father is worried, too," his mother went on. "He thinks you have lost your ambition, that you haven't got a definite aim in life. Charley Simmons, who is just your age, has a good job and is going to be married. The boys are all settling down; they're all determined to get somewhere; you can see that boys like Charley Simmons are on their way to being really a credit to the community."
> Krebs said nothing.
> "Don't look that way, Harold. . . ."

When Krebs looks at the bacon fat, we can see him cooling and hardening too. Hemingway does not describe the expression on Krebs's face, yet we know it is a look that disturbs his mother as she goes on about what she thinks she knows. Krebs and his mother are clearly tense and upset; the details, action, and dialogue reveal that without the narrator telling the reader how each character feels.

FIRST-PERSON NARRATOR (Participant)

1. Major character
2. Minor character

With a *first-person narrator,* the *I* presents the point of view of only one character's consciousness. The reader is restricted to the perceptions, thoughts, and feelings of that single character. This is Melville's technique with the lawyer in "Bartleby, the Scrivener" (p. 142). Everything learned about the characters, action, and plot comes from the unnamed lawyer. Bartleby remains a mystery because we are limited to what the lawyer knows and reports. The lawyer cannot explain what Bartleby means because he does not entirely know himself. Melville's use of the first person encourages us to identify with the lawyer's confused reaction to Bartleby so that we pay attention not only to the scrivener but to the lawyer's response to him. We are as perplexed as the lawyer and share his effort to make sense of Bartleby.

The lawyer is a major character in Melville's story; indeed, many readers take him to be the protagonist. A first-person narrator can, however, also be a minor character (imagine how different the story would be if it were told by, say, Ginger Nut or by an observer who had little or nothing to do with the action). Faulkner uses an observer in "A Rose for Emily" (p. 91). His *we*, though plural and representative of the town's view of Emily, is nonetheless a first-person narrator.

One of the primary reasons for identifying the point of view in a story is to determine where the author stands in relation to the story. Behind the narrative voice of any story is the author, manipulating events and providing or withholding information. It is a mistake to assume that the narrative voice of a story is the author. The narrator, whether a first-person participant or a third-person nonparticipant, is a creation of the writer. A narrator's perceptions may be accepted, rejected, or modified by an author, depending on how the narrative voice is articulated.

Faulkner seems to have shared the fascination, sympathy, and horror of the narrator in "A Rose for Emily," but Melville must not be so readily identified with the lawyer in "Bartleby, the Scrivener." The lawyer's description of himself as "an eminently *safe* man," convinced "that the easiest way of life is the best," raises the question of how well equipped he is to fathom Bartleby's protest. To make sense of Bartleby, it is also necessary to understand the lawyer's point of view. Until the conclusion of the story, this "*safe* man" is too self-serving, defensive, and obtuse to comprehend the despair embodied in Bartleby and the deadening meaninglessness of Wall Street life.

The lawyer is an **unreliable narrator,** whose interpretation of events is different from the author's. We cannot entirely accept the lawyer's assessment of Bartleby because we see that the lawyer's perceptions are not totally to be trusted. Melville does not expect us, for example, to agree with the lawyer's suggestion that the solution to Bartleby's situation might be to "entertain some young gentleman with your conversation" on a trip to Europe. Given Bartleby's awful silences, this absurd suggestion reveals the lawyer's superficial understanding. The lawyer's perceptions frequently do not coincide with those Melville expects his readers to share. Hence, the lawyer's unreliability preserves Bartleby's mysterious nature while revealing the lawyer's sensibilities. The point of view is artistically appropriate for Melville's purposes because the eyes through which we perceive the plot, characters, and setting are also the subject of the story.

Narrators can be unreliable for a variety of reasons: they might lack self-knowledge, like Melville's lawyer, or they might be innocent and inexperienced, like Ralph Ellison's young narrator in "Battle Royal" (p. 277). Youthful innocence frequently characterizes a **naive narrator** such as Mark

Twain's Huck Finn or Holden Caulfield, J. D. Salinger's twentieth-century version of Huck in *The Catcher in the Rye*. These narrators lack the sophistication to interpret accurately what they see; they are unreliable because the reader must go beyond their understanding of events to comprehend the situations described. Huck and Holden describe their respective social environments, but the reader, with more experience, supplies the critical perspective that each boy lacks. In "Battle Royal" that perspective is supplemented by Ellison's dividing the narration between the young man who experiences events and the mature man who reflects back on those events.

Few generalizations can be made about the advantages or disadvantages of using a specific point of view. What can be said with confidence, however, is that writers choose a point of view to achieve particular effects because point of view determines what we know about the characters and events in a story. We should, therefore, be aware of who is telling the story and whether the narrator sees things clearly and reliably.

The next four works warrant a careful examination of their points of view. In Robert Olen Butler's "Jealous Husband Returns in Form of Parrot," we hear the voice of a parrot—yes, a parrot. In Anton Chekhov's and Joyce Carol Oates's versions of "The Lady with the Pet Dog," we are presented with similar stories told from two different perspectives that make for intriguing comparisons and contrasts. And in Alice Walker's "Roselily" we are presented with a woman's thoughts as she is being married.

ROBERT OLEN BUTLER (B. 1945)

Born in Granite City, Illinois, Robert Olen Butler earned degrees at Northwestern University and the University of Iowa. After a tour of duty in Vietnam and before his success as a writer, he worked for trade publications. He has published ten novels and five collections of short stories. Currently Butler teaches at Florida State University. His first novel, *The Alleys of Eden* (1981), was followed by *Sun Dog* (1982), which was related to his experiences in Vietnam. *A Good Scent from a Strange Mountain* (1992), a collec-

© Elizabeth Dewberry.

tion of short stories that focuses on Vietnamese refugees in the United States, won the Pulitzer Prize. He has also been awarded a Guggenheim Fellowship and a National Endowment for the Arts grant. The following story is from his 1996 collection, *Tabloid Dreams*.

Jealous Husband Returns in Form of Parrot   1995

I never can quite say as much as I know. I look at other parrots and I wonder if it's the same for them, if somebody is trapped in each of them paying some kind of price for living their life in a certain way. For instance, "Hello," I say, and I'm sitting on a perch in a pet store in Houston and what I'm really thinking is Holy shit. It's you. And what's happened is I'm looking at my wife.

"Hello," she says, and she comes over to me and I can't believe how beautiful she is. Those great brown eyes, almost as dark as the center of mine. And her nose — I don't remember her for her nose but its beauty is clear to me now. Her nose is a little too long, but it's redeemed by the faint hook to it.

She scratches the back of my neck.

Her touch makes my tail flare. I feel the stretch and rustle of me back there. I bend my head to her and she whispers, "Pretty bird."

For a moment I think she knows it's me. But she doesn't, of course. I say   5 "Hello" again and I will eventually pick up "pretty bird." I can tell that as soon as she says it, but for now I can only give her another hello. Her fingertips move through my feathers and she seems to know about birds. She knows that to pet a bird you don't smooth his feathers down, you ruffle them.

But of course she did that in my human life, as well. It's all the same for her. Not that I was complaining, even to myself, at that moment in the pet shop when she found me like I presume she was supposed to. She said it again, "Pretty bird," and this brain that works like it does now could feel that tiny little voice of mine ready to shape itself around these sounds. But before I could get them out of my beak there was this guy at my wife's shoulder and all my feathers went slick flat like to make me small enough not to be seen and I backed away. The pupils of my eyes pinned and dilated and pinned again.

He circled around her. A guy that looked like a meat packer, big in the chest and thick with hair, the kind of guy that I always sensed her eyes moving to when I was alive. I had a bare chest and I'd look for little black hairs on the sheets when I'd come home on a day with the whiff of somebody else in the air. She was still in the same goddam rut.

A "hello" wouldn't do and I'd recently learned "good night" but it was the wrong suggestion altogether, so I said nothing and the guy circled her and he was looking at me with a smug little smile and I fluffed up all my feathers, made myself about twice as big, so big he'd see he couldn't mess with me. I waited for him to draw close enough for me to take off the tip of his finger.

But she intervened. Those nut-brown eyes were before me and she said, "I want him."

And that's how I ended up in my own house once again. She bought me a   10 large black wrought-iron cage, very large, convinced by some young guy who clerked in the bird department and who took her aside and made his voice go much too soft when he was doing the selling job. The meat packer didn't like it. I didn't either. I'd missed a lot of chances to take a bite out of this clerk in my stay at the shop and I regretted that suddenly.

But I got my giant cage and I guess I'm happy enough about that. I can pace as much as I want. I can hang upside down. It's full of bird toys. That dangling thing over there with knots and strips of rawhide and a bell at the bottom needs a good thrashing a couple of times a day and I'm the bird to do it. I look at the very dangle of it and the thing is rough, the rawhide and the knotted rope, and I get this restlessness back in my tail, a burning thrashing feeling, and it's like all the times when I was sure there was a man naked with my wife. Then I go to this thing that feels so familiar and I bite and bite and it's very good.

I could have used the thing the last day I went out of this house as a man. I'd found the address of the new guy at my wife's office. He'd been there a month in the shipping department and three times she'd mentioned him. She didn't even have to work with him and three times I heard about him, just dropped into the conversation. "Oh," she'd say when a car commercial came on the television, "that car there is like the one the new man in shipping owns. Just like it." Hey, I'm not stupid. She said another thing about him and then another and right after the third one I locked myself in the bathroom because I couldn't rage about this anymore. I felt like a damn fool whenever I actually said anything about this kind of feeling and she looked at me like she could start hating me real easy and so I was working on saying nothing, even if it meant locking myself up. My goal was to hold my tongue about half the time. That would be a good start.

But this guy from shipping. I found out his name and his address and it was one of her typical Saturday afternoons of vague shopping. So I went to his house, and his car that was just like the commercial was outside. Nobody was around in the neighborhood and there was this big tree in the back of the house going up to a second floor window that was making funny little sounds. I went up. The shade was drawn but not quite all the way. I was holding on to a limb with arms and legs wrapped around it like it was her in those times when I could forget the others for a little while. But the crack in the shade was just out of view and I crawled on along till there was no limb left and I fell on my head. Thinking about that now, my wings flap and I feel myself lift up and it all seems so avoidable. Though I know I'm different now. I'm a bird.

Except I'm not. That's what's confusing. It's like those times when she would tell me she loved me and I actually believed her and maybe it was true and we clung to each other in bed and at times like that I was different. I was the man in her life. I was whole with her. Except even at that moment, holding her sweetly, there was this other creature inside me who knew a lot more about it and couldn't quite put all the evidence together to speak.

My cage sits in the den. My pool table is gone and the cage is sitting in that space and if I come all the way down to one end of my perch I can see through the door and down the back hallway to the master bedroom. When she keeps the bedroom door open I can see the space at the foot of the bed but not the bed itself. That I can sense to the left, just out of sight. I watch the men go in and I hear the sounds but I can't quite see. And they drive me crazy.

I flap my wings and I squawk and I fluff up and I slick down and I throw seed and I attack that dangly toy as if it was the guy's balls, but it does no good. It never did any good in the other life either, the thrashing around I did by myself. In that other life I'd have given anything to be standing in this den with her doing this thing with some other guy just down the hall and all I had to do was walk down there and turn the corner and she couldn't deny it any more.

But now all I can do is try to let it go. I sidestep down to the opposite end of the cage and I look out the big sliding glass doors to the back yard. It's a pretty yard. There are great placid maple trees with good places to roost. There's a blue sky that plucks at the feathers on my chest. There are clouds. Other birds. Fly away. I could just fly away.

I tried once and I learned a lesson. She forgot and left the door to my cage open and I climbed beak and foot, beak and foot, along the bars and curled around to stretch sideways out the door and the vast scene of peace was there at the other end of the room. I flew.

And a pain flared through my head and I fell straight down and the room whirled around and the only good thing was she held me. She put her hands under my wings and lifted me and clutched me to her breast and I wish there hadn't been bees in my head at the time so I could have enjoyed that, but she put me back in the cage and wept awhile. That touched me, her tears. And I looked back to the wall of sky and trees. There was something invisible there between me and that dream of peace. I remembered, eventually, about glass, and I knew I'd been lucky, I knew that for the little fragile-boned skull I was doing all this thinking in, it meant death.

She wept that day but by the night she had another man. A guy with a thick Georgia truck-stop accent and pale white skin and an Adam's apple big as my seed ball. This guy has been around for a few weeks and he makes a whooping sound down the hallway, just out of my sight. At times like that I want to fly against the bars of the cage, but I don't. I have to remember how the world has changed. 20

She's single now, of course. Her husband, the man that I was, is dead to her. She does not understand all that is behind my "hello." I know many words, for a parrot. I am a yellow-nape Amazon, a handsome bird, I think, green with a splash of yellow at the back of my neck. I talk pretty well, but none of my words are adequate. I can't make her understand.

And what would I say if I could? I was jealous in life. I admit it. I would admit it to her. But it was because of my connection to her. I would explain that. When we held each other, I had no past at all, no present but her body, no future but to lie there and not let her go. I was an egg hatched beneath her crouching body, I entered as a chick into her wet sky of a body, and all that I wished was to sit on her shoulder and fluff my feathers and lay my head against her cheek, my neck exposed to her hand. And so the glances that I could see in her troubled me deeply, the movement of her eyes in public to other men, the laughs sent across a room, the tracking of her mind behind her blank eyes, pursuing images of others, her distraction even in our bed, the ghosts that were there of men who'd touched her, perhaps even that very day. I was not part of all those other men who were part of her. I didn't want to connect to all that. It was only her that I would fluff for but these others were there also and I couldn't put them aside. I sensed them inside her and so they were inside me. If I had the words, these are the things I would say.

But half an hour ago there was a moment that thrilled me. A word, a word we all knew in the pet shop, was just the right word after all. This guy with his cowboy belt buckle and rattlesnake boots and his pasty face and his twanging words of love trailed after my wife through the den, past my cage, and I said, "Cracker." He even flipped his head back a little at this in surprise. He'd been called that before to his face, I realized. I said it again, "Cracker." But to him I was a bird and he let it pass. "Cracker," I said. "Hello, cracker." That was even better. They were out of sight through the hall doorway and I hustled along the perch and I caught a glimpse of them before they made the turn to the bed and I said, "Hello, cracker," and he shot me one last glance.

It made me hopeful. I eased away from that end of the cage, moved toward the scene of peace beyond the far wall. The sky is chalky blue today, blue like the brow of the blue-front Amazon who was on the perch next to me for about a week at the store. She was very sweet, but I watched her carefully for a day or two when she first came in. And it wasn't long before she nuzzled up to a cockatoo named Gordo and I knew she'd break my heart. But her color now in the sky is sweet, really. I left all those feelings behind me when my wife showed up. I am a faithful man, for all my suspicions. Too faithful, maybe. I am ready to give too much and maybe that's the problem.

The whooping began down the hall and I focused on a tree out there. A 25 crow flapped down, his mouth open, his throat throbbing, though I could not hear his sound. I was feeling very odd. At least I'd made my point to the guy in the other room. "Pretty bird," I said, referring to myself. She called me "pretty bird" and I believed her and I told myself again, "Pretty bird."

But then something new happened, something very difficult for me. She appeared in the den naked. I have not seen her naked since I fell from the tree and had no wings to fly. She always had a certain tidiness in things. She was naked in the bedroom, clothed in the den. But now she appears from the hallway and I look at her and she is still slim and she is beautiful, I think — at least I clearly remember that as her husband I found her beautiful in this state. Now, though, she seems too naked. Plucked. I find that a sad thing. I am sorry for her and she goes by me and she disappears into the kitchen. I want to pluck some of my own feathers, the feathers from my chest, and give them to her. I love her more in that moment, seeing her terrible nakedness, than I ever have before.

And since I've had success in the last few minutes with words, when she comes back I am moved to speak. "Hello," I say, meaning, You are still connected to me, I still want only you. "Hello," I say again. Please listen to this tiny heart that beats fast at all times for you.

And she does indeed stop and she comes to me and bends to me. "Pretty bird," I say and I am saying, You are beautiful, my wife, and your beauty cries out for protection. "Pretty." I want to cover you with my own nakedness. "Bad bird," I say. If there are others in your life, even in your mind, then there is nothing I can do. "Bad." Your nakedness is touched from inside by the others. "Open," I say. How can we be whole together if you are not empty in the place that I am to fill?

She smiles at this and she opens the door to my cage. "Up," I say, meaning, Is there no place for me in this world where I can be free of this terrible sense of others?

She reaches in now and offers her hand and I climb onto it and I tremble 30 and she says, "Poor baby."

"Poor baby," I say. You have yearned for wholeness too and somehow I failed you. I was not enough. "Bad bird," I say. I'm sorry.

And then the cracker comes around the corner. He wears only his rattlesnake boots. I take one look at his miserable, featherless body and shake my head. We keep our sexual parts hidden, we parrots, and this man is a pitiful sight. "Peanut," I say. I presume that my wife simply has not noticed. But that's foolish, of course. This is, in fact, what she wants. Not me. And she scrapes me off her hand onto the open cage door and she turns her naked back to me and embraces this man and they laugh and stagger in their embrace around the corner.

For a moment I still think I've been eloquent. What I've said only needs repeating for it to have its transforming effect. "Hello," I say. "Hello. Pretty bird. Pretty. Bad bird. Bad. Open. Up. Poor baby. Bad bird." And I am beginning to hear myself as I really sound to her. "Peanut." I can never say what is in my heart to her. Never.

I stand on my cage door now and my wings stir. I look at the corner to the hallway and down at the end the whooping has begun again. I can fly there and think of things to do about all this.

But I do not. I turn instead and I look at the trees moving just beyond the 35
other end of the room. I look at the sky the color of the brow of a blue-front
Amazon. A shadow of birds spanks across the lawn. And I spread my wings. I
will fly now. Even though I know there is something between me and that place
where I can be free of all these feelings, I will fly. I will throw myself there again
and again. Pretty bird. Bad bird. Good night.

CONSIDERATIONS FOR CRITICAL THINKING AND WRITING

1. **FIRST RESPONSE.** Why do you suppose Butler chooses to write the story
   from the point of view of a parrot rather than, say, a dog or a cat?

2. How convincing do you find the story told from the parrot's point of view?

3. How would you characterize the husband before he was transformed into a
   parrot? Has he changed or remained essentially the same?

4. Describe the wife. Explain why you find her sympathetic or not.

5. Comment on the appropriateness of the story's primary setting in a cage.

6. How does Butler manage to extract humor from the painful circumstances
   of the husband's life?

7. What do you think happens at the end of the story? How does that affect
   your interpretation of it?

CONNECTION TO ANOTHER SELECTION

1. Compare the adulterous wife in Butler's story with the one in Joyce Carol
   Oates's "The Lady with the Pet Dog" (p. 237).

ANTON CHEKHOV (1860–1904)

Born in a small town in Russia, Anton
Chekhov gave up the career his medical degree prepared him for in order to devote
himself to writing. His concentration on realistic detail in the hundreds of short stories
he published has had an important influence on fiction writing. Modern drama has
also been strengthened by his plays, among
them these classics: *The Seagull* (1896), *Uncle
Vanya* (1899), *The Three Sisters* (1901), and *The
Cherry Orchard* (1904). Chekhov was a close
observer of people in ordinary situations

© Austrian Archives/CORBIS.

who struggle to live their lives as best they
can. They are not very often completely successful. Chekhov's compassion,
however, makes their failures less significant than their humanity. In "The
Lady with the Pet Dog," love is at the heart of a struggle that begins in
Yalta, a resort town on the Black Sea.

The Lady with the Pet Dog 1899

TRANSLATED BY AVRAHM YARMOLINSKY (1947)

I

A new person, it was said, had appeared on the esplanade: a lady with a pet dog. Dmitry Dmitrich Gurov, who had spent a fortnight at Yalta and had got used to the place, had also begun to take an interest in new arrivals. As he sat in Vernet's confectionery shop, he saw, walking on the esplanade, a fair-haired young woman of medium height, wearing a beret; a white Pomeranian was trotting behind her.

And afterwards he met her in the public garden and in the square several times a day. She walked alone, always wearing the same beret and always with the white dog; no one knew who she was and everyone called her simply "the lady with the pet dog."

"If she is here alone without husband or friends," Gurov reflected, "it wouldn't be a bad thing to make her acquaintance."

He was under forty, but he already had a daughter twelve years old, and two sons at school. They had found a wife for him when he was very young, a student in his second year, and by now she seemed half as old again as he. She was a tall, erect woman with dark eyebrows, stately and dignified and, as she said of herself, intellectual. She read a great deal, used simplified spelling in her letters, called her husband, not Dmitry, but Dimitry, while he privately considered her of limited intelligence, narrow-minded, dowdy, was afraid of her, and did not like to be at home. He had begun being unfaithful to her long ago—had been unfaithful to her often and, probably for that reason, almost always spoke ill of women, and when they were talked of in his presence used to call them "the inferior race."

It seemed to him that he had been sufficiently tutored by bitter experience to call them what he pleased, and yet he could not have lived without "the inferior race" for two days together. In the company of men he was bored and ill at ease, he was chilly and uncommunicative with them; but when he was among women he felt free, and knew what to speak to them about and how to comport himself; and even to be silent with them was no strain on him. In his appearance, in his character, in his whole makeup there was something attractive and elusive that disposed women in his favor and allured them. He knew that, and some force seemed to draw him to them, too.

Oft-repeated and really bitter experience had taught him long ago that with decent people—particularly Moscow people—who are irresolute and slow to move, every affair which at first seems a light and charming adventure inevitably grows into a whole problem of extreme complexity, and in the end a painful situation is created. But at every new meeting with an interesting woman this lesson of experience seemed to slip from his memory, and he was eager for life, and everything seemed so simple and diverting.

One evening while he was dining in the public garden the lady in the beret walked up without haste to take the next table. Her expression, her gait, her dress, and the way she did her hair told him that she belonged to the upper class, that she was married, that she was in Yalta for the first time and alone, and that she was bored there. The stories told of the immorality in Yalta are to a great extent untrue; he despised them, and knew that such stories were made up for the most part by persons who would have been glad to sin themselves if they had had the chance; but when the lady sat down at the next table three paces from him, he recalled these stories of easy conquests, of trips to the mountains, and the tempting thought of a swift, fleeting liaison, a romance with an unknown woman of whose very name he was ignorant suddenly took hold of him.

He beckoned invitingly to the Pomeranian, and when the dog approached him, shook his finger at it. The Pomeranian growled; Gurov threatened it again.

The lady glanced at him and at once dropped her eyes.

"He doesn't bite," she said and blushed.   10

"May I give him a bone?" he asked; and when she nodded he inquired affably, "Have you been in Yalta long?"

"About five days."

"And I am dragging out the second week here."

There was a short silence.

"Time passes quickly, and yet it is so dull here!" she said, not looking   15
at him.

"It's only the fashion to say it's dull here. A provincial will live in Belyov or Zhizdra and not be bored, but when he comes here it's 'Oh, the dullness! Oh, the dust!' One would think he came from Granada."

She laughed. Then both continued eating in silence, like strangers, but after dinner they walked together and there sprang up between them the light banter of people who are free and contented, to whom it does not matter where they go or what they talk about. They walked and talked of the strange light on the sea: the water was a soft, warm, lilac color, and there was a golden band of moonlight upon it. They talked of how sultry it was after a hot day. Gurov told her that he was a native of Moscow, that he had studied languages and literature at the university, but had a post in a bank; that at one time he had trained to become an opera singer but had given it up, that he owned two houses in Moscow. And he learned from her that she had grown up in Petersburg, but had lived in S —— since her marriage two years previously, that she was going to stay in Yalta for about another month, and that her husband, who needed a rest, too, might perhaps come to fetch her. She was not certain whether her husband was a member of a Government Board or served on a Zemstvo Council,° and this amused her. And Gurov learned too that her name was Anna Sergeyevna.

Afterwards in his room at the hotel he thought about her — and was certain that he would meet her the next day. It was bound to happen. Getting into bed he recalled that she had been a schoolgirl only recently, doing lessons like his own daughter; he thought how much timidity and angularity there was still in her laugh and her manner of talking with a stranger. It must have been the first time in her life that she was alone in a setting in which she was followed, looked at, and spoken to for one secret purpose alone, which she could hardly fail to guess. He thought of her slim, delicate throat, her lovely gray eyes.

"There's something pathetic about her, though," he thought, and dropped off.

Zemstvo Council: A district council.

II

A week had passed since they had struck up an acquaintance. It was a holiday. 20
It was close indoors, while in the street the wind whirled the dust about and
blew people's hats off. One was thirsty all day, and Gurov often went into the
restaurant and offered Anna Sergeyevna a soft drink or ice cream. One did not
know what to do with oneself.

In the evening when the wind had abated they went out on the pier to
watch the steamer come in. There were a great many people walking about the
dock; they had come to welcome someone and they were carrying bunches of
flowers. And two peculiarities of a festive Yalta crowd stood out: the elderly
ladies were dressed like young ones and there were many generals.

Owing to the choppy sea, the steamer arrived late, after sunset, and it was
a long time tacking about before it put in at the pier. Anna Sergeyevna peered
at the steamer and the passengers through her lorgnette as though looking for
acquaintances, and whenever she turned to Gurov her eyes were shining. She
talked a great deal and asked questions jerkily, forgetting the next moment
what she had asked; then she lost her lorgnette in the crush.

The festive crowd began to disperse; it was now too dark to see people's
faces; there was no wind any more, but Gurov and Anna Sergeyevna still stood
as though waiting to see someone else come off the steamer. Anna Sergeyevna
was silent now, and sniffed her flowers without looking at Gurov.

"The weather has improved this evening," he said. "Where shall we go
now? Shall we drive somewhere?"

She did not reply.   25

Then he looked at her intently, and suddenly embraced her and kissed her
on the lips, and the moist fragrance of her flowers enveloped him; and at once
he looked round him anxiously, wondering if anyone had seen them.

"Let us go to your place," he said softly. And they walked off together rapidly.

The air in her room was close and there was the smell of the perfume she
had bought at the Japanese shop. Looking at her, Gurov thought: "What encounters life offers!" From the past he preserved the memory of carefree, good-
natured women whom love made gay and who were grateful to him for the
happiness he gave them, however brief it might be; and of women like his wife
who loved without sincerity, with too many words, affectedly, hysterically, with
an expression that it was not love or passion that engaged them but something
more significant; and of two or three others, very beautiful, frigid women,
across whose faces would suddenly flit a rapacious expression—an obstinate
desire to take from life more than it could give, and these were women no
longer young, capricious, unreflecting, domineering, unintelligent, and when
Gurov grew cold to them their beauty aroused his hatred, and the lace on their
lingerie seemed to him to resemble scales.

But here there was the timidity, the angularity of inexperienced youth, a
feeling of awkwardness; and there was a sense of embarrassment, as though
someone had suddenly knocked at the door. Anna Sergeyevna, "the lady with
the pet dog," treated what had happened in a peculiar way, very seriously, as
though it were her fall—so it seemed, and this was odd and inappropriate. Her
features drooped and faded, and her long hair hung down sadly on either side
of her face; she grew pensive and her dejected pose was that of a Magdalene in
a picture by an old master.

"It's not right," she said. "You don't respect me now, you first of all."   30

There was a watermelon on the table. Gurov cut himself a slice and began eating it without haste. They were silent for at least half an hour.

There was something touching about Anna Sergeyevna; she had the purity of a well-bred, naive woman who has seen little of life. The single candle burning on the table barely illumined her face, yet it was clear that she was unhappy.

"Why should I stop respecting you, darling?" asked Gurov. "You don't know what you're saying."

"God forgive me," she said, and her eyes filled with tears. "It's terrible."

"It's as though you were trying to exonerate yourself."   35

"How can I exonerate myself? No. I am a bad, low woman; I despise myself and I have no thought of exonerating myself. It's not my husband but myself I have deceived. And not only just now; I have been deceiving myself for a long time. My husband may be a good, honest man, but he is a flunkey! I don't know what he does, what his work is, but I know he is a flunkey! I was twenty when I married him. I was tormented by curiosity; I wanted something better. 'There must be a different sort of life,' I said to myself. I wanted to live! To live, to live! Curiosity kept eating at me—you don't understand it, but I swear to God I could no longer control myself; something was going on in me: I could not be held back. I told my husband I was ill, and came here. And here I have been walking about as though in a daze, as though I were mad; and now I have become a vulgar, vile woman whom anyone may despise."

Gurov was already bored with her; he was irritated by her naive tone, by her repentance, so unexpected and so out of place; but for the tears in her eyes he might have thought she was joking or play-acting.

"I don't understand, my dear," he said softly. "What do you want?"

She hid her face on his breast and pressed close to him.

"Believe me, believe me, I beg you," she said, "I love honesty and purity,   40 and sin is loathsome to me; I don't know what I'm doing. Simple people say, 'The Evil One has led me astray.' And I may say of myself now that the Evil One has led me astray."

"Quiet, quiet," he murmured.

He looked into her fixed, frightened eyes, kissed her, spoke to her softly and affectionately, and by degrees she calmed down, and her gaiety returned; both began laughing.

Afterwards when they went out there was not a soul on the esplanade. The town with its cypresses looked quite dead, but the sea was still sounding as it broke upon the beach; a single launch was rocking on the waves and on it a lantern was blinking sleepily.

They found a cab and drove to Oreanda.

"I found out your surname in the hall just now: it was written on the   45 board—von Dideritz," said Gurov. "Is your husband German?"

"No; I believe his grandfather was German, but he is Greek Orthodox himself."

At Oreanda they sat on a bench not far from the church, looked down at the sea, and were silent. Yalta was barely visible through the morning mist; white clouds rested motionlessly on the mountaintops. The leaves did not stir on the trees, cicadas twanged, and the monotonous muffled sound of the sea that rose from below spoke of the peace, the eternal sleep awaiting us. So it rumbled below when there was no Yalta, no Oreanda here; so it rumbles now, and it will rumble as indifferently and as hollowly when we are no more. And in this constancy, in this complete indifference to the life and death of each of us, there lies, perhaps, a pledge of our eternal salvation, of the unceasing advance of life upon earth, of unceasing movement towards perfection. Sitting beside a young woman who in the dawn seemed so lovely, Gurov, soothed and spell-bound by these magical surroundings—the sea, the mountains, the clouds, the wide sky—thought how everything is really beautiful in this world when one reflects: everything except what we think or do ourselves when we forget the higher aims of life and our own human dignity.

A man strolled up to them—probably a guard—looked at them and walked away. And this detail, too, seemed so mysterious and beautiful. They saw a steamer arrive from Feodosia, its lights extinguished in the glow of dawn.

"There is dew on the grass," said Anna Sergeyevna, after a silence.

"Yes, it's time to go home."   50

They returned to the city.

Then they met every day at twelve o'clock on the esplanade, lunched and dined together, took walks, admired the sea. She complained that she slept badly, that she had palpitations, asked the same questions, troubled now by jealousy and now by the fear that he did not respect her sufficiently. And often in the square or the public garden, when there was no one near them, he suddenly drew her to him and kissed her passionately. Complete idleness, these kisses in broad daylight exchanged furtively in dread of someone's seeing them, the heat, the smell of the sea, and the continual flitting before his eyes of idle, well-dressed, well-fed people, worked a complete change in him; he kept telling Anna Sergeyevna how beautiful she was, how seductive, was urgently passionate; he would not move a step away from her, while she was often pensive and continually pressed him to confess that he did not respect her, did not love her in the least, and saw in her nothing but a common woman. Almost every evening rather late they drove somewhere out of town, to Oreanda or to the waterfall; and the excursion was always a success, the scenery invariably impressed them as beautiful and magnificent.

They were expecting her husband, but a letter came from him saying that he had eye-trouble, and begging his wife to return home as soon as possible. Anna Sergeyevna made haste to go.

"It's a good thing I am leaving," she said to Gurov. "It's the hand of Fate!"

She took a carriage to the railway station, and he went with her. They were   55 driving the whole day. When she had taken her place in the express, and when the second bell had rung, she said, "Let me look at you once more—let me look at you again. Like this."

She was not crying but was so sad that she seemed ill, and her face was quivering.

"I shall be thinking of you—remembering you," she said. "God bless you; be happy. Don't remember evil against me. We are parting forever—it has to be, for we ought never to have met. Well, God bless you."

The train moved off rapidly, its lights soon vanished, and a minute later there was no sound of it, as though everything had conspired to end as quickly as possible that sweet trance, that madness. Left alone on the platform, and gazing into the dark distance, Gurov listened to the twang of the grasshoppers and the hum of the telegraph wires, feeling as though he had just waked up.

And he reflected, musing, that there had now been another episode or adventure in his life, and it, too, was at an end, and nothing was left of it but a memory. He was moved, sad, and slightly remorseful: this young woman whom he would never meet again had not been happy with him; he had been warm and affectionate with her, but yet in his manner, his tone, and his caresses there had been a shade of light irony, the slightly coarse arrogance of a happy male who was, besides, almost twice her age. She had constantly called him kind, exceptional, high-minded; obviously he had seemed to her different from what he really was, so he had involuntarily deceived her.

Here at the station there was already a scent of autumn in the air; it was a chilly evening.

"It is time for me to go north, too," thought Gurov as he left the platform. 60
"High time!"

III

At home in Moscow the winter routine was already established: the stoves were heated, and in the morning it was still dark when the children were having breakfast and getting ready for school, and the nurse would light the lamp for a short time. There were frosts already. When the first snow falls, on the first day the sleighs are out, it is pleasant to see the white earth, the white roofs; one draws easy, delicious breaths, and the season brings back the days of one's youth. The old limes and birches, white with hoar-frost, have a good-natured look; they are closer to one's heart than cypresses and palms, and near them one no longer wants to think of mountains and the sea.

Gurov, a native of Moscow, arrived there on a fine frosty day, and when he put on his fur coat and warm gloves and took a walk along Petrovka, and when on Saturday night he heard the bells ringing, his recent trip and the places he had visited lost all charm for him. Little by little he became immersed in Moscow life, greedily read three newspapers a day, and declared that he did not read the Moscow papers on principle. He already felt a longing for restaurants, clubs, formal dinners, anniversary celebrations, and it flattered him to entertain distinguished lawyers and actors, and to play cards with a professor at the physicians' club. He could eat a whole portion of meat stewed with pickled cabbage and served in a pan, Moscow style.

A month or so would pass and the image of Anna Sergeyevna, it seemed to him, would become misty in his memory, and only from time to time he would dream of her with her touching smile as he dreamed of others. But more than a month went by, winter came into its own, and everything was still clear in his memory as though he had parted from Anna Sergeyevna only yesterday. And his memories glowed more and more vividly. When in the evening stillness the voices of his children preparing their lessons reached his study, or when he listened to a song or to an organ playing in a restaurant, or when the storm howled in the chimney, suddenly everything would rise up in his memory: what had happened on the pier and the early morning with the mist on the mountains, and the steamer coming from Feodosia, and the kisses. He would pace about his room a long time, remembering and smiling; then his memories passed into reveries, and in his imagination the past would mingle with what was to come. He did not dream of Anna Sergeyevna, but she followed him about everywhere and watched him. When he shut his eyes he saw her before him as though she were there in the flesh; and she seemed to him lovelier, younger, tenderer than she had been, and he imagined himself a finer man than he had been in Yalta. Of evenings she peered out at him from the book-case, from the fireplace, from the corner — he heard her breathing, the caressing rustle of her clothes. In the street he followed the women with his eyes, looking for someone who resembled her.

Already he was tormented by a strong desire to share his memories with someone. But in his home it was impossible to talk of his love, and he had no one to talk to outside; certainly he could not confide in his tenants or in anyone at the bank. And what was there to talk about? He hadn't loved her then, had he? Had there been anything beautiful, poetical, edifying, or simply interesting in his relations with Anna Sergeyevna? And he was forced to talk vaguely of love, of women, and no one guessed what he meant; only his wife would twitch her black eyebrows and say, "The part of a philanderer does not suit you at all, Dimitry."

One evening, coming out of the physicians' club with an official with 65
whom he had been playing cards, he could not resist saying:

"If you only knew what a fascinating woman I became acquainted with at Yalta!"

The official got into his sledge and was driving away, but turned suddenly and shouted: "Dmitry Dmitrich!"

"What is it?"

"You were right this evening: the sturgeon was a bit high."

These words, so commonplace, for some reason moved Gurov to indigna- 70
tion, and struck him as degrading and unclean. What savage manners, what mugs! What stupid nights, what dull, humdrum days! Frenzied gambling, gluttony, drunkenness, continual talk always about the same things! Futile pursuits and conversations always about the same topics take up the better part of one's time, the better part of one's strength, and in the end there is left a life clipped and wingless, an absurd mess, and there is no escaping or getting away from it — just as though one were in a madhouse or a prison.

Gurov, boiling with indignation, did not sleep all night. And he had a headache all the next day. And the following nights too he slept badly; he sat up in bed, thinking, or paced up and down his room. He was fed up with his children, fed up with the bank; he had no desire to go anywhere or to talk of anything.

In December during the holidays he prepared to take a trip and told his wife he was going to Petersburg to do what he could for a young friend — and he set off for S——. What for? He did not know, himself. He wanted to see Anna Sergeyevna and talk with her, to arrange a rendezvous if possible.

He arrived at S—— in the morning, and at the hotel took the best room, in which the floor was covered with gray army cloth, and on the table there was an inkstand, gray with dust and topped by a figure on horseback, its hat in its raised hand and its head broken off. The porter gave him the necessary information: von Dideritz lived in a house of his own on Staro-Goncharnaya Street, not far from the hotel: he was rich and lived well and kept his own horses; everyone in the town knew him. The porter pronounced the name: "Dridiritz."

Without haste Gurov made his way to Staro-Goncharnaya Street and found the house. Directly opposite the house stretched a long gray fence studded with nails.

"A fence like that would make one run away," thought Gurov, looking now 75 at the fence, now at the windows of the house.

He reflected: this was a holiday, and the husband was apt to be at home. And in any case, it would be tactless to go into the house and disturb her. If he were to send her a note, it might fall into her husband's hands, and that might spoil everything. The best thing was to rely on chance. And he kept walking up and down the street and along the fence, waiting for the chance. He saw a beggar go in at the gate and heard the dogs attack him; then an hour later he heard a piano, and the sound came to him faintly and indistinctly. Probably it was Anna Sergeyevna playing. The front door opened suddenly, and an old woman came out, followed by the familiar white Pomeranian. Gurov was on the point of calling to the dog, but his heart began beating violently, and in his excitement he could not remember the Pomeranian's name.

He kept walking up and down, and hated the gray fence more and more, and by now he thought irritably that Anna Sergeyevna had forgotten him, and was perhaps already diverting herself with another man, and that that was very natural in a young woman who from morning till night had to look at that damn fence. He went back to his hotel room and sat on the couch for a long while, not knowing what to do, then he had dinner and a long nap.

"How stupid and annoying all this is!" he thought when he woke and looked at the dark windows: it was already evening. "Here I've had a good sleep for some reason. What am I going to do at night?"

He sat on the bed, which was covered with a cheap gray blanket of the kind seen in hospitals, and he twitted himself in his vexation:

"So there's your lady with the pet dog. There's your adventure. A nice 80 place to cool your heels in."

That morning at the station a playbill in large letters had caught his eye. *The Geisha* was to be given for the first time. He thought of this and drove to the theater.

"It's quite possible that she goes to first nights," he thought.

The theater was full. As in all provincial theaters, there was a haze above the chandelier, the gallery was noisy and restless; in the front row, before the beginning of the performance the local dandies were standing with their hands clasped behind their backs; in the Governor's box the Governor's daughter, wearing a boa, occupied the front seat, while the Governor himself hid modestly behind the portiere and only his hands were visible; the curtain swayed; the orchestra was a long time tuning up. While the audience were coming in and taking their seats, Gurov scanned the faces eagerly.

Anna Sergeyevna, too, came in. She sat down in the third row, and when Gurov looked at her his heart contracted, and he understood clearly that in the whole world there was no human being so near, so precious, and so important to him; she, this little, undistinguished woman, lost in a provincial crowd, with a vulgar lorgnette in her hand, filled his whole life now, was his sorrow and his joy, the only happiness that he now desired for himself, and to the sounds of the bad orchestra, of the miserable local violins, he thought how lovely she was. He thought and dreamed.

A young man with small side-whiskers, very tall and stooped, came in with 85 Anna Sergeyevna and sat down beside her; he nodded his head at every step and seemed to be bowing continually. Probably this was the husband whom at Yalta, in an excess of bitter feeling, she had called a flunkey. And there really was in his lanky figure, his side-whiskers, his small bald patch, something of a flunkey's retiring manner; his smile was mawkish, and in his buttonhole there was an academic badge like a waiter's number.

During the first intermission the husband went out to have a smoke; she remained in her seat. Gurov, who was also sitting in the orchestra, went up to her and said in a shaky voice, with a forced smile:

"Good evening!"

She glanced at him and turned pale, then looked at him again in horror, unable to believe her eyes, and gripped the fan and the lorgnette tightly together in her hands, evidently trying to keep herself from fainting. Both were silent. She was sitting, he was standing, frightened by her distress and not daring to take a seat beside her. The violins and the flute that were being tuned up sang out. He suddenly felt frightened: it seemed as if all the people in the boxes were looking at them. She got up and went hurriedly to the exit; he followed her, and both of them walked blindly along the corridors and up and down stairs, and figures in the uniforms prescribed for magistrates, teachers, and officials of the Department of Crown Lands, all wearing badges, flitted before their eyes, as did also ladies, and fur coats on hangers; they were conscious of drafts and the smell of stale tobacco. And Gurov, whose heart was beating violently, thought:

"Oh, Lord! Why are these people here and this orchestra!"

And at that instant he suddenly recalled how when he had seen Anna Sergeyevna off at the station he had said to himself that all was over between them and that they would never meet again. But how distant the end still was!

On the narrow, gloomy staircase over which it said "To the Amphitheatre," she stopped.

"How you frightened me!" she said, breathing hard, still pale and stunned. "Oh, how you frightened me! I am barely alive. Why did you come? Why?"

"But do understand, Anna, do understand—" he said hurriedly, under his breath. "I implore you, do understand—"

She looked at him with fear, with entreaty, with love; she looked at him intently, to keep his features more distinctly in her memory.

"I suffer so," she went on, not listening to him. "All this time I have been thinking of nothing but you; I live only by the thought of you. And I wanted to forget, to forget; but why, oh, why have you come?"

On the landing above them two high school boys were looking down and smoking, but it was all the same to Gurov; he drew Anna Sergeyevna to him and began kissing her face and her hands.

"What are you doing, what are you doing!" she was saying in horror, pushing him away. "We have lost our senses. Go away today; go away at once— I conjure you by all that is sacred, I implore you—People are coming this way!"

Someone was walking up the stairs.

"You must leave," Anna Sergeyevna went on in a whisper. "Do you hear, Dmitry Dmitrich? I will come and see you in Moscow. I have never been happy; I am unhappy now, and I never, never shall be happy, never! So don't make me suffer still more! I swear I'll come to Moscow. But now let us part. My dear, good, precious one, let us part!"

She pressed his hand and walked rapidly downstairs, turning to look round at him, and from her eyes he could see that she really was unhappy.

Gurov stood for a while, listening, then when all grew quiet, he found his coat and left the theater.

IV

And Anna Sergeyevna began coming to see him in Moscow. Once every two or three months she left S——, telling her husband that she was going to consult a doctor about a woman's ailment from which she was suffering—and her husband did and did not believe her. When she arrived in Moscow she would stop at the Slavyansky Bazar Hotel, and at once send a man in a red cap to Gurov. Gurov came to see her, and no one in Moscow knew of it.

Once he was going to see her in this way on a winter morning (the messenger had come the evening before and not found him in). With him walked his daughter, whom he wanted to take to school: it was on the way. Snow was coming down in big wet flakes.

"It's three degrees above zero,° and yet it's snowing," Gurov was saying to his daughter. "But this temperature prevails only on the surface of the earth; in the upper layers of the atmosphere there is quite a different temperature."

"And why doesn't it thunder in winter, papa?"

He explained that, too. He talked, thinking all the while that he was on his $_{105}$ way to a rendezvous, and no living soul knew of it, and probably no one would ever know. He had two lives: an open one, seen and known by all who needed to know it, full of conventional truth and conventional falsehood, exactly like the lives of his friends and acquaintances; and another life that went on in secret. And through some strange, perhaps accidental, combination of circumstances, everything that was of interest and importance to him, everything that was essential to him, everything about which he felt sincerely and did not deceive himself, everything that constituted the core of his life, was going on concealed from others; while all that was false, the shell in which he hid to cover the truth—his work at the bank, for instance, his discussions at the club, his references to the "inferior race," his appearances at anniversary celebrations with his wife—all that went on in the open. Judging others by himself, he did not believe what he saw, and always fancied that every man led his real, most interesting life under cover of secrecy as under cover of night. The personal life of every individual is based on secrecy, and perhaps it is partly for that reason that civilized man is so nervously anxious that personal privacy should be respected.

Having taken his daughter to school, Gurov went on to the Slavyansky Bazar Hotel. He took off his fur coat in the lobby, went upstairs, and knocked gently at the door. Anna Sergeyevna, wearing his favorite gray dress, exhausted by the journey and by waiting, had been expecting him since the previous evening. She was pale, and looked at him without a smile, and he had hardly entered when she flung herself on his breast. Their kiss was a long, lingering one, as though they had not seen one another for two years.

"Well, darling, how are you getting on there?" he asked. "What news?"

"Wait; I'll tell you in a moment—I can't speak."

---

three degrees above zero: On the Celsius scale; about thirty-eight degrees Fahrenheit.

She could not speak; she was crying. She turned away from him, and pressed her handkerchief to her eyes.

"Let her have her cry; meanwhile I'll sit down," he thought, and he seated 110 himself in an armchair.

Then he rang and ordered tea, and while he was having his tea she remained standing at the window with her back to him. She was crying out of sheer agitation, in the sorrowful consciousness that their life was so sad; that they could only see each other in secret and had to hide from people like thieves! Was it not a broken life?

"Come, stop now, dear!" he said.

It was plain to him that this love of theirs would not be over soon, that the end of it was not in sight. Anna Sergeyevna was growing more and more attached to him. She adored him, and it was unthinkable to tell her that their love was bound to come to an end some day; besides, she would not have believed it!

He went up to her and took her by the shoulders, to fondle her and say something diverting, and at that moment he caught sight of himself in the mirror.

His hair was already beginning to turn gray. And it seemed odd to him 115 that he had grown so much older in the last few years, and lost his looks. The shoulders on which his hands rested were warm and heaving. He felt compassion for this life, still so warm and lovely, but probably already about to begin to fade and wither like his own. Why did she love him so much? He always seemed to women different from what he was, and they loved in him not himself, but the man whom their imagination created and whom they had been eagerly seeking all their lives; and afterwards, when they saw their mistake, they loved him nevertheless. And not one of them had been happy with him. In the past he had met women, come together with them, parted from them, but he had never once loved; it was anything you please, but not love. And only now when his head was gray he had fallen in love, really, truly—for the first time in his life.

Anna Sergeyevna and he loved each other as people do who are very close and intimate, like man and wife, like tender friends; it seemed to them that Fate itself had meant them for one another, and they could not understand why he had a wife and she a husband; and it was as though they were a pair of migratory birds, male and female, caught and forced to live in different cages. They forgave each other what they were ashamed of in their past, they forgave everything in the present, and felt that this love of theirs had altered them both.

Formerly in moments of sadness he had soothed himself with whatever logical arguments came into his head, but now he no longer cared for logic; he felt profound compassion, he wanted to be sincere and tender.

"Give it up now, my darling," he said. "You've had your cry; that's enough. Let us have a talk now, we'll think up something."

Then they spent a long time taking counsel together, they talked of how to avoid the necessity for secrecy, for deception, for living in different cities, and not seeing one another for long stretches of time. How could they free themselves from these intolerable fetters?

"How? How?" he asked, clutching his head. "How?" 120

And it seemed as though in a little while the solution would be found, and then a new and glorious life would begin; and it was clear to both of them that the end was still far off, and that what was to be most complicated and difficult for them was only just beginning.

CONSIDERATIONS FOR CRITICAL THINKING AND WRITING

1. **FIRST RESPONSE.** Consider the following assessment of the story: "No excuses can be made for the lovers' adulterous affair. They behave selfishly and irresponsibly. They are immoral—and so is the story." Explain what you think Chekhov's response to this view would be, given his treatment of the lovers. How does this compare with your own views?

2. Why is it significant that the setting of this story is a resort town? How does the vacation atmosphere affect the action?

3. What does Gurov's view of women reveal about him? Why does he regard them as an "inferior race"?

4. What do we learn about Gurov's wife and Anna's husband? Why do you think Chekhov includes this exposition? How does it affect our view of the lovers?

5. When and why do Gurov's feelings about Anna begin to change? Is he really in love with her?

6. Who or what is the antagonist in this story? What is the nature of the conflict?

7. What is the effect of having Gurov as the central consciousness? How would the story be different if it were told from Anna's perspective?

8. Why do you think Chekhov does not report what ultimately becomes of the lovers? Is there a resolution to the conflict? Is the ending of the story effective?

9. Discuss the validity of Gurov's belief that people lead their real lives in private rather than in public: "The personal life of every individual is based on secrecy, and perhaps it is partly for that reason that civilized man is so nervously anxious that personal privacy should be respected" (para. 105).

10. Describe your response to Gurov in Parts I and II, and discuss how your judgment of him changes in the last two parts of the story.

11. Based on your understanding of the characterizations of Gurov and Anna, consider the final paragraph of the story and summarize what you think will happen to them.

Perspectives

Two Additional Translations of the Final Paragraphs of Anton Chekhov's "The Lady with the Pet Dog"

"A Note on Reading Translations" appears on page 830. Because different translators of the same work make various choices in diction, phrasing, images, and tone as they interpret both the language and the work, they often produce subtly different translations. Compare the following two versions of the final six paragraphs of Chekhov's story with Avrahm Yarmolinsky's 1947 translation, reprinted in this anthology on pages 233–34.

ANTON CHEKHOV (1860–1904)
From "The Lady and the Dog"   *1899*
TRANSLATED BY CONSTANCE GARNETT (1963)

Anna Sergeyevna and he loved each other like people very close and akin, like husband and wife, like tender friends; it seemed to them that fate itself had meant them for one another, and they could not understand why he had a wife and she a husband; and it was as though they were a pair of birds of passage, caught and forced to live in different cages. They forgave each other for what they were ashamed of in their past, they forgave everything in the present, and felt that this love of theirs had changed them both.

In moments of depression in the past he had comforted himself with any arguments that came into his mind, but now he no longer cared for arguments; he felt profound compassion, he wanted to be sincere and tender. . . .

"Don't cry, my darling," he said. "You've had your cry; that's enough. . . . Let us talk now, let us think of some plan."

Then they spent a long while taking counsel together, talked of how to avoid the necessity for secrecy, for deception, for living in different towns and not seeing each other for long at a time. How could they be free from this intolerable bondage?

"How? How?" he asked, clutching his head. "How?"

And it seemed as though in a little while the solution would be found, and then a new and splendid life would begin; and it was clear to both of them that they had still a long, long way to go, and that the most complicated and difficult part of it was only just beginning.

From My Life and Other Stories

ANTON CHEKHOV (1860–1904)
From "A Lady with a Dog"   *1899*
TRANSLATED BY RONALD HINGLEY (1975)

Anne and he loved each other very, very dearly, like man and wife or bosom friends. They felt themselves predestined for each other. That he should have a wife, and she a husband . . . it seemed to make no sense. They were like two migratory birds, a male and a female, caught and put in separate cages. They had forgiven each other the shameful episodes of their past, they forgave each other for the present too, and they felt that their love had transformed them both.

Once, in moments of depression, he had tried to console himself with any argument which came into his head—but now he had no use for arguments. His deepest sympathies were stirred, he only wanted to be sincere and tender.

"Stop, darling," he said. "You've had your cry—that's enough. Now let's talk, let's think of something."

Then they consulted at length about avoiding the need for concealment and deception, for living in different towns, for meeting only at rare intervals. How could they break these intolerable bonds? How, how, how?

He clutched his head and asked the question again and again.

Soon, it seemed, the solution would be found and a wonderful new life would begin. But both could see that they still had a long, long way to travel— and that the most complicated and difficult part was only just beginning.

From The Oxford Chekhov, Vol. IX

Perspective

ANTON CHEKHOV (1860–1904)

On Morality in Fiction   *1890*

You abuse me for objectivity, calling it indifference to good and evil, lack of ideals and ideas, and so on. You would have me, when I describe horse-thieves, say: "Stealing horses is an evil." But that has been known for ages without my saying so. Let the jury judge them; it's my job simply to show what sort of people they are. I write: You are dealing with horse-thieves, so let me tell you that they are not beggars but well-fed people, that they are people of a special cult, and that horse-stealing is not simply theft but a passion. Of course it would be pleasant to combine art with a sermon, but for me personally it is extremely difficult and almost impossible, owing to the conditions of technique. You see, to depict horse-thieves in seven hundred lines I must all the time speak and think in their tone and feel in their spirit, otherwise, if I introduce subjectivity, the image becomes blurred and the story will not be as compact as all short stories ought to be. When I write, I reckon entirely upon the reader to add for himself the subjective elements that are lacking in the story.

From a letter to Aleksey S. Suvorin in Letters on the Short Story,
the Drama, and Other Literary Topics by Anton Chekhov

CONSIDERATIONS FOR CRITICAL THINKING AND WRITING

1. Why does Chekhov reject sermonizing in his fiction?
2. How does his "objectivity" affect your reading of "The Lady with the Pet Dog"?
3. Compare and contrast Chekhov's views with Thomas Jefferson's belief that fiction should offer "sound morality" (p. 46).

Joyce Carol Oates (b. 1938)

A biographical note and photograph of Joyce Carol Oates appear on page 83, before her story "Three Girls."

The Lady with the Pet Dog   *1972*

I

Strangers parted as if to make way for him.

There he stood. He was there in the aisle, a few yards away, watching her.

She leaned forward at once in her seat, her hand jerked up to her face as if to ward off a blow—but then the crowd in the aisle hid him, he was gone. She pressed both hands against her cheeks. He was not here, she had imagined him.

"My God," she whispered.

She was alone. Her husband had gone out to the foyer to make a tele- 5 phone call; it was intermission at the concert, a Thursday evening.

Now she saw him again, clearly. He was standing there. He was staring at her. Her blood rocked in her body, draining out of her head . . . she was going to faint . . . They stared at each other. They gave no sign of recognition. Only when he took a step forward did she shake her head *no—no—keep away*. It was not possible.

When her husband returned, she was staring at the place in the aisle where her lover had been standing. Her husband leaned forward to interrupt that stare.

"What's wrong?" he said. "Are you sick?"

Panic rose in her in long shuddering waves. She tried to get to her feet, panicked at the thought of fainting here, and her husband took hold of her. She stood like an aged woman, clutching the seat before her.

At home he helped her up the stairs and she lay down. Her head was like a 10 large piece of crockery that had to be held still, it was so heavy. She was still panicked. She felt it in the shallows of her face, behind her knees, in the pit of her stomach. It sickened her, it made her think of mucus, of something thick and gray congested inside her, stuck to her, that was herself and yet not her-self—a poison.

She lay with her knees drawn up toward her chest, her eyes hotly open, while her husband spoke to her. She imagined that other man saying, *Why did you run away from me?* Her husband was saying other words. She tried to listen to them. He was going to call the doctor, he said, and she tried to sit up. "No, I'm all right now," she said quickly. The panic was like lead inside her, so thickly congested. How slow love was to drain out of her, how fluid and sticky it was inside her head!

Her husband believed her. No doctor. No threat. Grateful, she drew her husband down to her. They embraced, not comfortably. For years now they had not been comfortable together, in their intimacy and at a distance, and now they struggled gently as if the paces of this dance were too rigorous for them. It was something they might have known once, but had now outgrown. The panic in her thickened at this double betrayal: she drew her husband to her, she caressed him wildly, she shut her eyes to think about that other man.

A crowd of men and women parting, unexpectedly, and there he stood — there he stood — she kept seeing him, and yet her vision blotched at the memory. It had been finished between them, six months before, but he had come out here . . . and she had escaped him, now she was lying in her husband's arms, in his embrace, her face pressed against his. It was a kind of sleep, this love-making. She felt herself falling asleep, her body falling from her. Her eyes shut.

"I love you," her husband said fiercely, angrily.

She shut her eyes and thought of that other man, as if betraying him 15 would give her life a center.

"Did I hurt you? Are you — ?" Her husband whispered.

Always this hot flashing of shame between them, the shame of her husband's near failure, the clumsiness of his love —

"You didn't hurt me," she said.

II

They had said good-by six months before. He drove her from Nantucket, where they had met, to Albany, New York, where she visited her sister. The hours of intimacy in the car had sealed something between them, a vow of silence and impersonality: she recalled the movement of the highways, the passing of other cars, the natural rhythms of the day hypnotizing her toward sleep while he drove. She trusted him, she could sleep in his presence. Yet she could not really fall asleep in spite of her exhaustion, and she kept jerking awake, frightened, to discover that nothing had changed — still the stranger who was driving her to Albany, still the highway, the sky, the antiseptic odor of the rented car, the sense of a rhythm behind the rhythm of the air that might unleash itself at any second. Everywhere on this highway, at this moment, there were men and women driving together, bonded together — what did that mean, to be together? What did it mean to enter into a bond with another person?

No, she did not really trust him; she did not really trust men. He would 20 glance at her with his small cautious smile and she felt a declaration of shame between them.

Shame.

In her head she rehearsed conversations. She said bitterly, "You'll be relieved when we get to Albany. Relieved to get rid of me." They had spent so many days talking, confessing too much, driven to a pitch of childish excitement, laughing together on the beach, breaking into that pose of laughter that seems to eradicate the soul, so many days of this that the silence of the trip was like the silence of a hospital — all these surface noises, these rattles and hums, but an interior silence, a befuddlement. She said to him in her imagination, "One of us should die." Then she leaned over to touch him. She caressed the back of his neck. She said, aloud, "Would you like me to drive for a while?"

They stopped at a picnic area where other cars were stopped — couples, families — and walked together, smiling at their good luck. He put his arm around her shoulders and she sensed how they were in a posture together, a man and a woman forming a posture, a figure, that someone might sketch and show to them. She said slowly, "I don't want to go back. . . ."

Silence. She looked up at him. His face was heavy with her words, as if she had pulled at his skin with her fingers. Children ran nearby and distracted him — yes, he was a father too, his children ran like that, they tugged at his skin with their light, busy fingers.

"Are you so unhappy?" he said.   25

"I'm not unhappy, back there. I'm nothing. There's nothing to me," she said.

They stared at each other. The sensation between them was intense, exhausting. She thought that this man was her savior, that he had come to her at a time in her life when her life demanded completion, an end, a permanent fixing of all that was troubled and shifting and deadly. And yet it was absurd to think this. No person could save another. So she drew back from him and released him.

A few hours later they stopped at a gas station in a small city. She went to the women's rest room, having to ask the attendant for a key, and when she came back her eye jumped nervously onto the rented car — why? did she think he might have driven off without her? — onto the man, her friend, standing in conversation with the young attendant. Her friend was as old as her husband, over forty, with lanky, sloping shoulders, a full body, his hair thick, a dark, burnished brown, a festive color that made her eye twitch a little — and his hands were always moving, always those rapid conversational circles, going nowhere, gestures that were at once a little aggressive and apologetic.

She put her hand on his arm, a claim. He turned to her and smiled and she felt that she loved him, that everything in her life had forced her to this moment and that she had no choice about it.

They sat in the car for two hours, in Albany, in the parking lot of a Howard   30
Johnson's restaurant, talking, trying to figure out their past. There was no future. They concentrated on the past, the several days behind them, lit up with a hot, dazzling August sun, like explosions that already belonged to other people, to strangers. Her face was faintly reflected in the green-tinted curve of the windshield, but she could not have recognized that face. She began to cry; she told herself: *I am not here, this will pass, this is nothing.* Still, she could not stop crying. The muscles of her face were springy, like a child's, unpredictable muscles. He stroked her arms, her shoulders, trying to comfort her. "This is so hard . . . this is impossible . . ." he said. She felt panic for the world outside this car, all that was not herself and this man, and at the same time she understood that she was free of him, as people are free of other people, she would leave him soon, safely, and within a few days he would have fallen into the past, the impersonal past. . . .

"I'm so ashamed of myself!" she said finally.

She returned to her husband and saw that another woman, a shadow-woman, had taken her place — noiseless and convincing, like a dancer performing certain difficult steps. Her husband folded her in his arms and talked to her of his own loneliness, his worries about his business, his health, his mother, kept tranquilized and mute in a nursing home, and her spirit detached itself from her and drifted about the rooms of the large house she lived in with her husband, a shadow-woman delicate and imprecise. There was no boundary to her, no edge. Alone, she took hot baths and sat exhausted in the steaming water, wondering at her perpetual exhaustion. All that winter she noticed the limp, languid weight of her arms, her veins bulging slightly with the pressure of her extreme weariness. *This is fate,* she thought, to be here and not there, to be one person and not another, a certain man's wife and not the wife of another man. The long, slow pain of this certainty rose in her, but it never became clear, it was baffling and imprecise. She could not be serious about it; she kept congratulating herself on her own good luck, to have escaped so easily, to have freed herself. So much love had gone into the first several years of her marriage that there wasn't much left, now, for another man. . . . She was certain of that. But the bath water made her dizzy, all that perpetual heat, and one day in January she drew a razor blade lightly across the inside of her arm, near the elbow, to see what would happen.

Afterward she wrapped a small towel around it, to stop the bleeding. The towel soaked through. She wrapped a bath towel around that and walked through the empty rooms of her home, lightheaded, hardly aware of the stubborn seeping of blood. There was no boundary to her in this house, no precise limit. She could flow out like her own blood and come to no end.

She sat for a while on a blue love seat, her mind empty. Her husband telephoned her when he would be staying late at the plant. He talked to her always about his plans, his problems, his business friends, his future. It was obvious that he had a future. As he spoke she nodded to encourage him, and her heartbeat quickened with the memory of her own, personal shame, the shame of this man's particular, private wife. One evening at dinner he leaned forward and put his head in his arms and fell asleep, like a child. She sat at the table with him for a while, watching him. His hair had gone gray, almost white, at the temples — no one would guess that he was so quick, so careful a man, still fairly young about the eyes. She put her hand on his head, lightly, as if to prove to herself that he was real. He slept, exhausted.

One evening they went to a concert and she looked up to see her lover 35 there, in the crowded aisle, in this city, watching her. He was standing there, with his overcoat on, watching her. She went cold. That morning the telephone had rung while her husband was still home, and she had heard him answer it, heard him hang up — it must have been a wrong number — and when the telephone rang again, at 9:30, she had been afraid to answer it. She had left home to be out of the range of that ringing, but now, in this public place, in this busy auditorium, she found herself staring at that man, unable to make any sign to him, any gesture of recognition. . . .

He would have come to her but she shook her head. *No. Stay away.*

Her husband helped her out of the row of seats, saying, "Excuse us, please. Excuse us," so that strangers got to their feet, quickly, alarmed, to let them pass. Was that woman about to faint? What was wrong?

At home she felt the blood drain slowly back into her head. Her husband embraced her hips, pressing his face against her, in that silence that belonged to the earliest days of their marriage. She thought, *He will drive it out of me.* He made love to her and she was back in the auditorium again, sitting alone, now that the concert was over. The stage was empty; the heavy velvet curtains had not been drawn; the musicians' chairs were empty, everything was silent and expectant; in the aisle her lover stood and smiled at her — Her husband was impatient. He was apart from her, working on her, operating on her; and then, stricken, he whispered, "Did I hurt you?"

The telephone rang the next morning. Dully, sluggishly, she answered it. She recognized his voice at once—that "Anna?" with its lifting of the second syllable, questioning and apologetic and making its claim—"Yes, what do you want?" she said.

"Just to see you. Please—"   40

"I can't."

"Anna, I'm sorry, I didn't mean to upset you—"

"I can't see you."

"Just for a few minutes—I have to talk to you—"

"But why, why now? Why now?" she said.   45

She heard her voice rising, but she could not stop it. He began to talk again, drowning her out. She remembered his rapid conversation. She remembered his gestures, the witty energetic circling of his hands.

"Please don't hang up!" he cried.

"I can't—I don't want to go through it again—"

"I'm not going to hurt you. Just tell me how you are."

"Everything is the same."   50

"Everything is the same with me."

She looked up at the ceiling, shyly. "Your wife? Your children?"

"The same."

"Your son?"

"He's fine—"   55

"I'm so glad to hear that. I—"

"Is it still the same with you, your marriage? Tell me what you feel. What are you thinking?"

"I don't know. . . ."

She remembered his intense, eager words, the movement of his hands, that impatient precise fixing of the air by his hands, the jabbing of his fingers.

"Do you love me?" he said.   60

She could not answer.

"I'll come over to see you," he said.

"No," she said.

What will come next, what will happen?

Flesh hardening on his body, aging. Shrinking. He will grow old, but not   65
soft like her husband. They are two different types: he is nervous, lean, energetic, wise. She will grow thinner, as the tension radiates out from her backbone, wearing down her flesh. Her collarbones will jut out of her skin. Her husband, caressing her in their bed, will discover that she is another woman—she is not there with him—instead she is rising in an elevator in a downtown hotel, carrying a book as a prop, or walking quickly away from that hotel, her head bent and filled with secrets. Love, what to do with it? . . . Useless as moths' wings, as moths' fluttering. . . . She feels the flutterings of silky, crazy wings in her chest.

He flew out to visit her every several weeks, staying at a different hotel each time. He telephoned her, and she drove down to park in an underground garage at the very center of the city.

She lay in his arms while her husband talked to her, miles away, one body fading into another. He will grow old, his body will change, she thought, pressing her cheek against the back of one of these men. If it was her lover, they were in a hotel room: always the propped-up little booklet describing the hotel's many services, with color photographs of its cocktail lounge and dining room and coffee shop. Grow old, leave me, die, go back to your neurotic wife and your sad, ordinary children, she thought, but still her eyes closed gratefully against his skin and she felt how complete their silence was, how they had come to rest in each other.

"Tell me about your life here. The people who love you," he said, as he always did.

One afternoon they lay together for four hours. It was her birthday and she was intoxicated with her good fortune, this prize of the afternoon, this man in her arms! She was a little giddy, she talked too much. She told him about her parents, about her husband. . . . "They were all people I believed in, but it turned out wrong. Now, I believe in you. . . ." He laughed as if shocked by her words. She did not understand. Then she understood. "But I believe truly in you. I can't think of myself without you," she said. . . . He spoke of his wife, her ambitions, her intelligence, her use of the children against him, her use of his younger son's blindness, all of his words gentle and hypnotic and convincing in the late afternoon peace of this hotel room . . . and she felt the terror of laughter, threatening laughter. Their words, like their bodies, were aging.

She dressed quickly in the bathroom, drawing her long hair up around the   70
back of her head, fixing it as always, anxious that everything be the same. Her face was slightly raw, from his face. The rubbing of his skin. Her eyes were too bright, wearily bright. Her hair was blond but not so blond as it had been that summer in the white Nantucket air.

She ran water and splashed it on her face. She blinked at the water. Blind. Drowning. She thought with satisfaction that soon, soon, he would be back home, in that house on Long Island she had never seen, with that woman she had never seen, sitting on the edge of another bed, putting on his shoes. She wanted nothing except to be free of him. Why not be free? *Oh,* she thought suddenly, *I will follow you back and kill you. You and her and the little boy. What is there to stop me?*

She left him. Everyone on the street pitied her, that look of absolute zero.

III

A man and a child, approaching her. The sharp acrid smell of fish. The crashing of waves. Anna pretended not to notice the father with his son — there was something strange about them. That frank, silent intimacy, too gentle, the man's bare feet in the water and the boy a few feet away, leaning away from his father. He was about nine years old and still his father held his hand.

A small yipping dog, a golden dog, bounded near them.

Anna turned shyly back to her reading; she did not want to have to speak   75
to these neighbors. She saw the man's shadow falling over her legs, then over the pages of her book, and she had the idea that he wanted to see what she was reading. The dog nuzzled her; the man called him away.

She watched them walk down the beach. She was relieved that the man had not spoken to her.

She saw them in town later that day, the two of them brown-haired and patient, now wearing sandals, walking with that same look of care. The man's white shorts were soiled and a little baggy. His pullover shirt was a faded green. His face was broad, the cheekbones wide, spaced widely apart, the eyes stark in their sockets, as if they fastened onto objects for no reason, ponderous and edgy. The little boy's face was pale and sharp; his lips were perpetually parted.

Anna realized that the child was blind.

The next morning, early, she caught sight of them again. For some reason she went to the back door of her cottage. She faced the sea breeze eagerly. Her heart hammered. . . . She had been here, in her family's old house, for three days, alone, bitterly satisfied at being alone, and now it was a puzzle to her how her soul strained to fly outward, to meet with another person. She watched the man with his son, his cautious, rather stooped shoulders above the child's small shoulders.

The man was carrying something, it looked like a notebook. He sat on the sand, not far from Anna's spot of the day before, and the dog rushed up to them. The child approached the edge of the ocean, timidly. He moved in short jerky steps, his legs stiff. The dog ran around him. Anna heard the child crying out a word that sounded like "Ty" — it must have been the dog's name — and then the man joined in, his voice heavy and firm.

"Ty —"

Anna tied her hair back with a yellow scarf and went down to the beach.

The man glanced around at her. He smiled. She stared past him at the waves. To talk to him or not to talk — she had the freedom of that choice. For a moment she felt that she had made a mistake, that the child and the dog would not protect her, that behind this man's ordinary, friendly face there was a certain arrogant maleness — then she relented, she smiled shyly.

"A nice house you've got there," the man said.

She nodded her thanks.

The man pushed his sunglasses up on his forehead. Yes, she recognized the eyes of the day before — intelligent and nervous, the sockets pale, untanned.

"Is that your telephone ringing?" he said.

She did not bother to listen. "It's a wrong number," she said.

Her husband calling: she had left home for a few days, to be alone.

But the man, settling himself on the sand, seemed to misinterpret this. He smiled in surprise, one corner of his mouth higher than the other. He said nothing. Anna wondered: *What is he thinking?* The dog was leaping about her, panting against her legs, and she laughed in embarrassment. She bent to pet it, grateful for its busyness. "Don't let him jump up on you," the man said. "He's a nuisance."

The dog was a small golden retriever, a young dog. The blind child, standing now in the water, turned to call the dog to him. His voice was shrill and impatient.

"Our house is the third one down — the white one," the man said.

She turned, startled. "Oh, did you buy it from Dr. Patrick? Did he die?"

"Yes, finally. . . ."

Her eyes wandered nervously over the child and the dog. She felt the nervous beat of her heart out to the very tips of her fingers, the fleshy tips of her fingers: little hearts were there, pulsing. *What is he thinking?* The man had opened his notebook. He had a piece of charcoal and he began to sketch something.

Anna looked down at him. She saw the top of his head, his thick brown hair, the freckles on his shoulders, the quick, deft movement of his hand. Upside down, Anna herself being drawn. She smiled in surprise.

"Let me draw you. Sit down," he said.

She knelt awkwardly a few yards away. He turned the page of the sketch pad. The dog ran to her and she sat, straightening out her skirt beneath her, flinching from the dog's tongue. "Ty!" cried the child. Anna sat, and slowly the pleasure of the moment began to glow in her; her skin flushed with gratitude.

She sat there for nearly an hour. The man did not talk much. Back and forth the dog bounded, shaking itself. The child came to sit near them, in silence. Anna felt that she was drifting into a kind of trance while the man sketched her, half a dozen rapid sketches, the surface of her face given up to him. "Where are you from?" the man asked.

"Ohio. My husband lives in Ohio."

She wore no wedding band.

"Your wife —" Anna began.

"Yes?"

"Is she here?"

"Not right now."

She was silent, ashamed. She had asked an improper question. But the man did not seem to notice. He continued drawing her, bent over the sketch pad. When Anna said she had to go, he showed her the drawings — one after another of her, Anna, recognizably Anna, a woman in her early thirties, her hair smooth and flat across the top of her head, tied behind by a scarf. "Take the one you like best," he said, and she picked one of her with the dog in her lap, sitting very straight, her brows and eyes clearly defined, her lips girlishly pursed, the dog and her dress suggested by a few quick irregular lines.

"Lady with pet dog," the man said.

She spent the rest of that day reading, nearer her cottage. It was not really a cottage — it was a two-story house, large and ungainly and weathered. It was mixed up in her mind with her family, her own childhood, and she glanced up from her book, perplexed, as if waiting for one of her parents or her sister to come up to her. Then she thought of that man, the man with the blind child, the man with the dog, and she could not concentrate on her reading. Someone — probably her father — had marked a passage that must be important, but she kept reading and rereading it: *We try to discover in things, endeared to us on that account, the spiritual glamour which we ourselves have cast upon them; we are disillusioned, and learn that they are in themselves barren and devoid of the charm that they owed, in our minds, to the association of certain ideas. . . .*

She thought again of the man on the beach. She lay the book aside and thought of him: his eyes, his aloneness, his drawings of her.

They began seeing each other after that. He came to her front door in the evening, without the child; he drove her into town for dinner. She was shy and extremely pleased. The darkness of the expensive restaurant released her; she heard herself chatter; she leaned forward and seemed to be offering her face up to him, listening to him. He talked about his work on a Long Island newspaper and she seemed to be listening to him, as she stared at his face, arranging her own face into the expression she had seen in that charcoal drawing. Did he see her like that, then? — girlish and withdrawn and patrician? She felt the weight of his interest in her, a force that fell upon her like a blow. A repeated blow. Of course he was married, he had children — of course she was married, permanently married. This flight from her husband was not important. She had left him before, to be alone, it was not important. Everything in her was slender and delicate and not important.

100

105

110

They walked for hours after dinner, looking at the other strollers, the weekend visitors, the tourists, the couples like themselves. Surely they were mistaken for a couple, a married couple. *This is the hour in which everything is decided,* Anna thought. They had both had several drinks and they talked a great deal. Anna found herself saying too much, stopping and starting giddily. She put her hand to her forehead, feeling faint.

"It's from the sun — you've had too much sun —" he said.

At the door to her cottage, on the front porch, she heard herself asking him if he would like to come in. She allowed him to lead her inside, to close the door. *This is not important,* she thought clearly, *he doesn't mean it, he doesn't love me, nothing will come of it.* She was frightened, yet it seemed to her necessary to give in; she had to leave Nantucket with that act completed, an act of adultery, an accomplishment she would take back to Ohio and to her marriage.

Later, incredibly, she heard herself asking: "Do you . . . do you love me?"

"You're so beautiful!" he said, amazed. 115

She felt this beauty, shy and glowing and centered in her eyes. He stared at her. In this large, drafty house, alone together, they were like accomplices, conspirators. She could not think: how old was she? which year was this? They had done something unforgivable together, and the knowledge of it was tugging at their faces. A cloud seemed to pass over her. She felt herself smiling shrilly.

Afterward, a peculiar raspiness, a dryness of breath. He was silent. She felt a strange, idle fear, a sense of the danger outside this room and this old comfortable bed — a danger that would not recognize her as the lady in that drawing, the lady with the pet dog. There was nothing to say to this man, this stranger. She felt the beauty draining out of her face, her eyes fading.

"I've got to be alone," she told him.

He left, and she understood that she would not see him again. She stood by the window of the room, watching the ocean. A sense of shame overpowered her: it was smeared everywhere on her body, the smell of it, the richness of it. She tried to recall him, and his face was confused in her memory: she would have to shout to him across a jumbled space, she would have to wave her arms wildly. *You love me! You must love me!* But she knew he did not love her, and she did not love him; he was a man who drew everything up into himself, like all men, walking away, free to walk away, free to have his own thoughts, free to envision her body, all the secrets of her body. . . . And she lay down again in the bed, feeling how heavy this body had become, her insides heavy with shame, the very backs of her eyelids coated with shame.

"This is the end of one part of my life," she thought. 120

But in the morning the telephone rang. She answered it. It was her lover: they talked brightly and happily. She could hear the eagerness in his voice, the love in his voice, that same still, sad amazement — she understood how simple life was, there were no problems.

They spent most of their time on the beach, with the child and the dog. He joked and was serious at the same time. He said, once, "You have defined my soul for me," and she laughed to hide her alarm. In a few days it was time for her to leave. He got a sitter for the boy and took the ferry with her to the mainland, then rented a car to drive her up to Albany. She kept thinking: *Now something will happen. It will come to an end.* But most of the drive was silent and hypnotic. She wanted him to joke with her, to say again that she had defined his soul for him, but he drove fast, he was serious, she distrusted the hawkish look of his profile—she did not know him at all. At a gas station she splashed her face with cold water. Alone in the grubby little rest room, shaky and very much alone. In such places are women totally alone with their bodies. The body grows heavier, more evil, in such silence. . . . On the beach everything had been noisy with sunlight and gulls and waves; here, as if run to earth, everything was cramped and silent and dead.

She went outside, squinting. There he was, talking with the station attendant. She could not think as she returned to him whether she wanted to live or not.

She stayed in Albany for a few days, then flew home to her husband. He met her at the airport, near the luggage counter, where her three pieces of pale-brown luggage were brought to him on a conveyer belt, to be claimed by him. He kissed her on the cheek. They shook hands, a little embarrassed. She had come home again.

"How will I live out the rest of my life?" she wondered.   125

In January her lover spied on her: she glanced up and saw him, in a public place, in the DeRoy Symphony Hall. She was paralyzed with fear. She nearly fainted. In this faint she felt her husband's body, loving her, working its love upon her, and she shut her eyes harder to keep out the certainty of his love—sometimes he failed at loving her, sometimes he succeeded, it had nothing to do with her or her pity or her ten years of love for him, it had nothing to do with a woman at all. It was a private act accomplished by a man, a husband, or a lover, in communion with his own soul, his manhood.

Her husband was forty-two years old now, growing slowly into middle age, getting heavier, softer. Her lover was about the same age, narrower in the shoulders, with a full, solid chest, yet lean, nervous. She thought, in her paralysis, of men and how they love freely and eagerly so long as their bodies are capable of love, love for a woman; and then, as love fades in their bodies, it fades from their souls and they become immune and immortal and ready to die.

Her husband was a little rough with her, as if impatient with himself. "I love you," he said fiercely, angrily. And then, ashamed, he said, "Did I hurt you? . . ."

"You didn't hurt me," she said.

Her voice was too shrill for their embrace.   130

While he was in the bathroom she went to her closet and took out that drawing of the summer before. There she was, on the beach at Nantucket, a lady with a pet dog, her eyes large and defined, the dog in her lap hardly more than a few snarls, a few coarse soft lines of charcoal . . . her dress smeared, her arms oddly limp . . . her hands not well drawn at all. . . . She tried to think: did she love the man who had drawn this? did he love her? The fever in her husband's body had touched her and driven her temperature up, and now she stared at the drawing with a kind of lust, fearful of seeing an ugly soul in that woman's face, fearful of seeing the face suddenly through her lover's eyes. She breathed quickly and harshly, staring at the drawing.

And so, the next day, she went to him at his hotel. She wept, pressing against him, demanding of him, "What do you want? Why are you here? Why don't you let me alone?" He told her that he wanted nothing. He expected nothing. He would not cause trouble.

"I want to talk about last August," he said.

"Don't —" she said.

She was hypnotized by his gesturing hands, his nervousness, his obvious   135
agitation. He kept saying, "I understand. I'm making no claims upon you."

They became lovers again.

He called room service for something to drink and they sat side by side on
his bed, looking through a copy of *The New Yorker*, laughing at the cartoons. It
was so peaceful in this room, so complete. They were on a holiday. It was a secret
holiday. Four-thirty in the afternoon, on a Friday, an ordinary Friday: a secret
holiday.

"I won't bother you again," he said.

He flew back to see her again in March, and in late April. He telephoned
her from his hotel — a different hotel each time — and she came down to him at
once. She rose to him in various elevators, she knocked on the doors of various
rooms, she stepped into his embrace, breathless and guilty and already angry
with him, pleading with him. One morning in May, when he telephoned, she
pressed her forehead against the doorframe and could not speak. He kept saying, "What's wrong? Can't you talk? Aren't you alone?" She felt that she was
going insane. Her head would burst. Why, why did he love her, why did he pursue her? Why did he want her to die?

She went to him in the hotel room. A familiar room: had they been here   140
before? "Everything is repeating itself. Everything is stuck," she said. He
framed her face in his hands and said that she looked thinner — was she sick? —
what was wrong? She shook herself free. He, her lover, looked about the same.
There was a small, angry pimple on his neck. He stared at her, eagerly and suspiciously. Did she bring bad news?

"So you love me? You love me?" she asked.

"Why are you so angry?"

"I want to be free of you. The two of us free of each other."

"That isn't true — you don't want that —"

He embraced her. She was wild with that old, familiar passion for him,   145
her body clinging to his, her arms not strong enough to hold him. Ah, what
despair! — what bitter hatred she felt! — she needed this man for her salvation,
he was all she had to live for, and yet she could not believe in him. He embraced
her thighs, her hips, kissing her, pressing his warm face against her, and yet she
could not believe in him, not really. She needed him in order to live, but he was
not worth her love, he was not worth her dying. . . . She promised herself this:
when she got back home, when she was alone, she would draw the razor more
deeply across her arm.

The telephone rang and he answered it: a wrong number.

"Jesus," he said.

They lay together, still. She imagined their posture like this, the two of
them one figure, one substance; and outside this room and this bed there was
a universe of disjointed, separate things, blank things, that had nothing to do
with them. She would not be Anna out there, the lady in the drawing. He
would not be her lover.

"I love you so much . . ." she whispered.

"Please don't cry! We have only a few hours, please. . . ."   150

It was absurd, their clinging together like this. She saw them as a single
figure in a drawing, their arms and legs entwined, their heads pressing mutely

together. Helpless substance, so heavy and warm and doomed. It was absurd that any human being should be so important to another human being. She wanted to laugh: a laugh might free them both.

She could not laugh.

Sometime later he said, as if they had been arguing, "Look. It's you. You're the one who doesn't want to get married. You lie to me—"

"Lie to you?"

"You love me but you won't marry me, because you want something left 155
over—Something not finished—All your life you can attribute your misery to me, to our not being married—you are using me—"

"Stop it! You'll make me hate you!" she cried.

"You can say to yourself that you're miserable because of *me*. We will never be married, you will never be happy, neither one of us will ever be happy—"

"I don't want to hear this!" she said.

She pressed her hands flatly against her face.

She went to the bathroom to get dressed. She washed her face and part of 160
her body, quickly. The fever was in her, in the pit of her belly. She would rush home and strike a razor across the inside of her arm and free that pressure, that fever.

The impatient bulging of the veins: an ordeal over.

The demand of the telephone's ringing: that ordeal over.

The nuisance of getting the car and driving home in all that five o'clock traffic: an ordeal too much for a woman.

The movement of this stranger's body in hers: over, finished.

Now, dressed, a little calmer, they held hands and talked. They had to talk 165
swiftly, to get all their news in: he did not trust the people who worked for him, he had faith in no one, his wife had moved to a textbook publishing company and was doing well, she had inherited a Ben Shahn painting from her father and wanted to "touch it up a little"—she was crazy!—his blind son was at another school, doing fairly well, in fact his children were all doing fairly well in spite of the stupid mistake of their parents' marriage—and what about her? what about her life? She told him in a rush the one thing he wanted to hear: that she lived with her husband lovelessly, the two of them polite strangers, sharing a bed, lying side by side in the night in that bed, bodies out of which souls had fled. There was no longer even any shame between them.

"And what about me? Do you feel shame with me still?" he asked.

She did not answer. She moved away from him and prepared to leave.

Then, a minute later, she happened to catch sight of his reflection in the bureau mirror—he was glancing down at himself, checking himself mechanically, impersonally, preparing also to leave. He too would leave this room: he too was headed somewhere else.

She stared at him. It seemed to her that in this instant he was breaking from her, the image of her lover fell free of her, breaking from her . . . and she realized that he existed in a dimension quite apart from her, a mysterious being. And suddenly, joyfully, she felt a miraculous calm. This man was her husband, truly—they were truly married, here in this room—they had been married haphazardly and accidentally for a long time. In another part of the city she had another husband, a "husband," but she had not betrayed that man, not really. This man, whom she loved above any other person in the world, above even her own self-pitying sorrow and her own life, was her truest lover, her destiny. And she did not hate him, she did not hate herself any longer; she did not wish to die; she was flooded with a strange certainty, a sense of gratitude, of pure selfless energy. It was obvious to her that she had, all along, been behaving correctly; out of instinct.

What triumph, to love like this in any room, anywhere, risking even the craziest of accidents!   170

"Why are you so happy? What's wrong?" he asked, startled. He stared at her. She felt the abrupt concentration in him, the focusing of his vision on her, almost a bitterness in his face, as if he feared her. What, was it beginning all over again? Their love beginning again, in spite of them? "How can you look so happy?" he asked. "We don't have any right to it. Is it because . . . ?"

"Yes," she said.

CONSIDERATIONS FOR CRITICAL THINKING AND WRITING

1. **FIRST RESPONSE.** Which version do you like better—Chekhov's story or Oates's? What's the point of retelling the story?

2. How would this story be different if it were told only in chronological order as it is in Part III? What do Parts I and II contribute to the details and information provided in Part III?

3. Why are Anna and her lover drawn to each other? What do we learn about their spouses that helps explain their attraction? Are there any other explanations?

4. Why is Anna so unhappy after the affair on Nantucket begins? Why does she think of suicide?

5. What is Anna's attitude toward men? Does it change during the story?

6. What details in the story make the narration particularly convincing from a woman's perspective? How might a man tell the story differently?

7. "What triumph, to love like this in any room, anywhere, risking even the craziest of accidents!" Explain this reflection of Anna's (para. 170) and relate it to her character.

8. How does Oates's arrangement of incidents validate Anna's feeling that "everything is repeating itself. Everything is stuck" (para. 140)?

9. Consider whether Anna reaches any kind of resolution to her problems by the end of the story. Is she merely "repeating" herself, or do you think she develops?

10. At the end of paragraph 19, Oates has Anna ask herself the question "What did it mean to enter into a bond with another person?" Write an essay explaining how the story answers that question.

11. **CRITICAL STRATEGIES.** Read the section on new historicist criticism (pp. 2054–55) in Chapter 53, "Critical Strategies for Reading," and consider how the institution of marriage was generally regarded when Chekhov and Oates wrote their respective stories. How do these two different perspectives on marriage compare with your own twenty-first-century point of view? How do you think a new historicist would weight the similarities and differences between these perspectives when comparing these two stories?

CONNECTION TO ANOTHER SELECTION

1. What similarities in setting, plot, and character are there between Oates's version and Chekhov's story? Are there any significant differences?
2. Describe how a familiarity with Chekhov's story affected your reading and expectations of Oates's version. Choose one version of the story and write an essay explaining why you prefer it over the other.

Perspective

MATTHEW C. BRENNAN (B. 1955)

Point of View and Plotting in Chekhov's and Oates's "The Lady with the Pet Dog"   1985

Oates . . . retains Chekhov's third-person point of view. But unlike Chekhov, who focuses on the male lover, Gurov, Oates makes Anna S., the female lover, the center of consciousness. Because Chekhov privileges Gurov, he represents Anna's feelings only when she speaks to Gurov. In fact, when Anna S. expresses her shame to Gurov, Chekhov says, "The solitary candle on the table scarcely lit up her face"; and rather than reveal her inner thoughts he merely tells us, "it was obvious that her heart was heavy." So, by subordinating Anna S. to Gurov, Chekhov gives readers no way to understand the feminine side of a masculine story. In contrast, Oates presents what Chekhov leaves out — the female's experience — and so relegates the male lover (who in her version is nameless) to the limited status Chekhov relegates Anna S.: Oates privileges the point of view of Anna. Furthermore, because Anna S. says she feels "like a madwoman," Oates fragments Chekhov's traditionally chronological plot, which becomes a subtext against which Oates can foreground Anna's confusion, doubt, and struggle to find an identity. . . .

Chekhov develops a conventional, sequential plot. He spreads the five-step plot through the four formal divisions of his story. Part I consists of the exposition, during which Gurov and Anna S. meet at the resort, Yalta. Part II continues the exposition, as the characters become lovers, and it also introduces the rising action as they separate at the train station, Anna S. returning to her home in the town of S——, Gurov to his in Moscow. Then, in Part III, the action continues to rise as Gurov misses Anna and eventually goes to the town of S——. Here, at a concert, the two climactically meet again, and, as Part III ends, Anna S. agrees to come to Moscow. Finally, in Part IV, the action falls as Chekhov describes their affair and dramatizes it in a scene that forms the resolution, through which Gurov realizes, after looking in a mirror, that he is in love for the first time: he and Anna S. really are "as husband and wife" though separated by law.

Oates borrows all these events for her plot, but if Chekhov's is linear, hers is circular. Oates breaks her story into three parts. Part I depicts the climax, immediately giving her version the intensity that the high-strung center of consciousness, Anna, is experiencing. We are with her at the concert hall, where her lover appears and she faints, and then with her back home, where her husband clumsily makes love to her while she thinks of her lover. Part II opens with a flashback to the rising action — when the lover drives Anna to Albany where they separate, just as Chekhov's lovers separate at the train station; next, Part II both repeats the climax (at the concert and in the bedroom) and relates, for the first time, the falling action in which the lovers continue the affair. Part I, then, presents only the climax, and Part II widens the plot to record not just the center, the climax, but also the rising and falling actions that surround it. Part III, however, widens the circular plot still further. Expanding outward from the climactic center, first the plot regresses to embrace the exposition (in which the lovers meet and make love at the resort, in this version Nantucket); then it moves inward again, retracing chronologically the rising action, climax, and falling action; and finally, as Part III concludes, the plot introduces the resolution, rounding out its pattern.

Before the resolution, however, as we witness the falling action (the resumption of the affair) for the second time, Oates stresses the lack of development: Anna says, "'Everything is repeating itself. Everything is stuck.'" By having the plot repeat itself, and so fail to progress toward resolution, Oates conveys Anna's lack of identity: Anna is trapped between two relationships, two "husbands," and hence wavers throughout this version between feeling like "nothing" in her legal husband's house where "there was no boundary to her," "no precise limit," and feeling defined — as "recognizably Anna" — by her illicit lover, her true "husband," who has sketched her portrait, to which she continually refers as if grasping for a rope.

Here, then, with the climax repeated three times and the rising and falling actions twice, the plot finally progresses from this impasse to its resolution. And, appropriately, as the plot finally achieves its completion, so too does Anna, discovering as she symbolically looks into the mirror,

> this man was her husband, truly — they were truly married, here in this room — they had been married haphazardly and accidentally for a long time. In another part of the city she had another husband, a "husband," but she had not betrayed that man, not really. This man, whom she loved above any other person in the world . . . was her truest lover, her destiny.

Oates allows the plot to progress sequentially to the resolution — to integrity — only as Anna's consciousness discovers its true identity, its integration.

From *Notes on Modern American Literature*

CONSIDERATIONS FOR CRITICAL THINKING AND WRITING

1. What does Brennan mean by characterizing Chekhov's story as "masculine" and Oates's as "feminine"? How is each writer's use of point of view related to this question?

2. Brennan describes Chekhov's plot as "linear" and Oates's as "circular." How is this contrast influenced by the writer's use of point of view?

3. Brennan asserts that in Oates's story, "Anna's consciousness discovers its true identity, its integration." Write an essay explaining whether you agree or disagree with this assessment. In your response, consider how Oates's use of point of view affects your reading of Anna's character.

A SAMPLE STUDENT RESPONSE

James Armand

Professor Rosen

English 102

September 8, 2009

Two Versions of the Same Story:

Point of View in Chekhov's and Oates's "The Lady with the Pet Dog"

The narrative point of view in each version of "The Lady with the Pet Dog" provides an in-depth look at how a love affair affects the characters involved. While both versions contain essentially the same plot, the accounts from the point of view of each character are starkly different. Chekhov's version "gives readers no way to understand the feminine side of a masculine story" (Brennan 250), while Oates's version provides just that. Yet each story effectively portrays a main character experiencing conflicting emotions and change.

In Chekhov's story, Gurov initially acts on lust, not love. He views women as "the inferior race" (Chekhov 223) and thinks of Anna as "pathetic" (224). But Anna has a greater effect on him than he anticipates. After their brief affair, he is "tormented by a strong desire to share his memories with someone" (229), and his desire for Anna becomes so strong that he seeks her out at the theater, in spite of the possible consequences. Ultimately, Gurov's views of Anna change, and he experiences love for the first time in his life:

> In the past he had met women, come together with them,
> parted from them, but he had never once loved; it was any-
> thing you please, but not love. And only now when his head
> was gray he had fallen in love, really, truly—for the first time
> in his life. (233)

By shifting to Anna's point of view, Oates provides another layer to the same story. We understand Anna to be more than simply a timid woman enamored with her lover (as she appears in Chekhov's version). Her character is complex. She is pulled between her attraction to her lover and her own morality— "They had done something unforgivable together, the knowledge of it was tugging at their faces. A cloud seemed to pass over her" (Oates 245). Anna has

Armand 2

trouble coming to terms with her infidelity and regrets betraying her husband and family. Yet her love for her lover is too powerful to give up. Having access to Anna's point of view, we gain a deeper understanding of her as a character—something that is not possible in Chekhov's version. . . .

Armand 6

Works Cited

Brennan, Matthew C. "Point of View and Plotting in Chekhov's and Oates's 'The Lady with the Pet Dog.'" *The Bedford Introduction to Literature.* Ed. Michael Meyer. 9th ed. Boston: Bedford/St. Martin's, 2011. 250–51. Print.

Chekhov, Anton. "The Lady with the Pet Dog." *The Bedford Introduction to Literature.* Ed. Michael Meyer. 9th ed. Boston: Bedford/St. Martin's, 2011. 223–34. Print.

Oates, Joyce Carol. "The Lady with the Pet Dog." *The Bedford Introduction to Literature.* Ed. Michael Meyer. 9th ed. Boston: Bedford/St. Martin's, 2011. 237–49. Print.

ALICE WALKER (B. 1944)

A biographical note and photograph of Alice Walker appear on page 81 before her story "The Flowers."

Roselily   *1973*

Dearly Beloved,

She dreams; dragging herself across the world. A small girl in her mother's white robe and veil, knee raised waist high through a bowl of quicksand soup. The man who stands beside her is against this standing on the front porch of her house, being married to the sound of cars whizzing by on highway 61.

we are gathered here

Like cotton to be weighed. Her fingers at the last minute busily removing dry leaves and twigs. Aware it is a superficial sweep. She knows he blames Mississippi for the respectful way the men turn their heads up in the yard, the women stand waiting and knowledgeable, their children held from mischief by teachings from the wrong God. He glares beyond them to the occupants of the cars, white faces glued to promises beyond a country wedding, noses thrust forward like dogs on a track. For him they usurp the wedding.

in the sight of God   5

Yes, open house. That is what country black folks like. She dreams she does not already have three children. A squeeze around the flowers in her hands chokes off three and four and five years of breath. Instantly she is ashamed and frightened in her superstition. She looks for the first time at the preacher, forces humility into her eyes, as if she believes he is, in fact, a man of God. She can imagine God, a small black boy, timidly pulling the preacher's coattail.

to join this man and this woman

She thinks of ropes, chains, handcuffs, his religion. His place of worship. Where she will be required to sit apart with covered head. In Chicago, a word she hears when thinking of smoke, from his description of what a cinder was, which they never had in Panther Burn. She sees hovering over the heads of the clean neighbors in her front yard black specks falling, clinging, from the sky. But in Chicago. Respect, a chance to build. Her children at last from underneath the detrimental wheel. A chance to be on top. What a relief, she thinks. What a vision, a view, from up so high.

in holy matrimony.

Her fourth child she gave away to the child's father who had some money.   10
Certainly a good job. Had gone to Harvard. Was a good man but weak because good language meant so much to him he could not live with Roselily. Could not abide TV in the living room, five beds in three rooms, no Bach except from four to six on Sunday afternoons. No chess at all. She does not forget to worry about her son among his father's people. She wonders if the New England climate will agree with him. If he will ever come down to Mississippi, as his father did, to try to right the country's wrongs. She wonders if he will be stronger than his father. His father cried off and on throughout her pregnancy. Went to skin and bones. Suffered nightmares, retching and falling out of bed. Tried to kill himself. Later told his wife he found the right baby through friends. Vouched for, the sterling qualities that would make up his character.

It is not her nature to blame. Still, she is not entirely thankful. She supposes New England, the North, to be quite different from what she knows. It seems right somehow to her that people who move there to live return home completely changed. She thinks of the air, the smoke, the cinders. Imagines cinders big as hailstones; heavy, weighing on the people. Wonders how this pressure finds its way into the veins, roping the springs of laughter.

If there's anybody here that knows a reason why

But of course they know no reason why beyond what they daily have come to know. She thinks of the man who will be her husband, feels shut away from him because of the stiff severity of his plain black suit. His religion. A lifetime of black and white. Of veils. Covered head. It is as if her children are already gone from her. Not dead, but exalted on a pedestal, a stalk that has no roots. She wonders how to make new roots. It is beyond her. She wonders what one does with memories in a brand-new life. This had seemed easy, until she thought of it. "The reasons why . . . the people who" . . . she thinks, and does not wonder where the thought is from.

these two should not be joined

She thinks of her mother, who is dead. Dead, but still her mother. Joined.   15
This is confusing. Of her father. A gray old man who sold wild mink, rabbit, fox skins to Sears, Roebuck. He stands in the yard, like a man waiting for a train. Her young sisters stand behind her in smooth green dresses, with flowers in their hands and hair. They giggle, she feels, at the absurdity of the wedding. They are ready for something new. She thinks the man beside her should marry one of them. She feels old. Yoked. An arm seems to reach out from behind her and snatch her backward. She thinks of cemeteries and the long sleep of grandparents mingling in the dirt. She believes that she believes in ghosts. In the soil giving back what it takes.

together,

In the city. He sees her in a new way. This she knows, and is grateful. But is it new enough? She cannot always be a bride and virgin, wearing robes and veil. Even now her body itches to be free of satin and voile, organdy and lily of the valley. Memories crash against her. Memories of being bare to the sun. She wonders what it will be like. Not to have to go to a job. Not to work in a sewing plant. Not to worry about learning to sew straight seams in workingmen's overalls, jeans, and dress pants. Her place will be in the home, he has said, repeatedly, promising her rest she had prayed for. But now she wonders. When she is rested, what will she do? They will make babies — she thinks practically about her fine brown body, his strong black one. They will be inevitable. Her hands will be full. Full of what? Babies. She is not comforted.

let him speak

She wishes she had asked him to explain more of what he meant. But she was impatient. Impatient to be done with sewing. With doing everything for three children, alone. Impatient to leave the girls she had known since childhood, their children growing up, their husbands hanging around her, already old, seedy. Nothing about them that she wanted, or needed. The fathers of her children driving by, waving, not waving; reminders of times she would just as soon forget. Impatient to see the South Side, where they would live and build and be respectable and respected and free. Her husband would free her. A romantic hush. Proposal. Promises. A new life! Respectable, reclaimed, renewed. Free! In robe and veil.

or forever hold

She does not even know if she loves him. She loves his sobriety. His refusal to sing just because he knows the tune. She loves his pride. His blackness and his gray car. She loves his understanding of her *condition*. She thinks she loves the effort he will make to redo her into what he truly wants. His love of her makes her completely conscious of how unloved she was before. This is something; though it makes her unbearably sad. Melancholy. She blinks her eyes. Remembers she is finally being married, like other girls. Like other girls, women? Something strains upward behind her eyes. She thinks of the something as a rat trapped, cornered, scurrying to and fro in her head, peering through the windows of her eyes. She wants to live for once. But doesn't know quite what that means. Wonders if she has ever done it. If she ever will. The preacher is odious to her. She wants to strike him out of the way, out of her light, with the back of her hand. It seems to her he has always been standing in front of her, barring her way.

his peace.

The rest she does not hear. She feels a kiss, passionate, rousing, within the general pandemonium. Cars drive up blowing their horns. Firecrackers go off. Dogs come from under the house and begin to yelp and bark. Her husband's hand is like the clasp of an iron gate. People congratulate. Her children press against her. They look with awe and distaste mixed with hope at their new father. He stands curiously apart, in spite of the people crowding about to grasp his free hand. He smiles at them all but his eyes are as if turned inward. He knows they cannot understand that he is not a Christian. He will not explain himself. He feels different, he looks it. The old women thought he was like one of their sons except that he had somehow got away from them. Still a son, not a son. Changed.

She thinks how it will be later in the night in the silvery gray car. How they will spin through the darkness of Mississippi and in the morning be in Chicago, Illinois. She thinks of Lincoln, the president. That is all she knows about the place. She feels ignorant, *wrong*, backward. She presses her worried fingers into his palm. He is standing in front of her. In the crush of well-wishing people, he does not look back.

CONSIDERATIONS FOR CRITICAL THINKING AND WRITING

1. **FIRST RESPONSE.** Describe the story's point of view. How does the point of view affect your understanding of Roselily's character and her circumstances?

2. How does the first paragraph announce the nature of the story's conflict?

3. What do you think Roselily's reflections about her fourth child reveal about her character?

4. What do you learn about Roselily's past? How is that related to her reasons for marrying?

5. Describe the groom. What kind of man is he? What sort of life is Roselily likely to have with him?

6. How are the interspersed lines of the wedding ceremony related to the paragraphs they follow and precede?

7. Why can't the central conflict of this story accurately be described simply as "the bride had cold feet"?

8. **CREATIVE RESPONSE.** Write a paragraph in Walker's style written from the point of view of the groom. You may place it in the story wherever it best fits and serves to reveal something essential about his character.

CONNECTIONS TO OTHER SELECTIONS

1. Discuss the view of marriage in "Roselily" and in Colette's "The Hand" (p. 274).

2. Compare the treatments of the North and the South in "Roselily" and in Faulkner's "A Rose for Emily" (p. 91).

Web Research the authors in this chapter or take quizzes on their works at bedfordstmartins.com/meyerlit.

ENCOUNTERING FICTION: COMICS AND GRAPHIC STORIES

Marjane Satrapi (b. 1969), "The Trip," From *Persepolis*

Marjane Satrapi was born in Rasht, Iran, and grew up in Tehran. The daughter of politically liberal parents but also a princess (her great-grandfather was the last Qadjar emperor of Iran), Satrapi attended Tehran's Lycée Français, and left at age 14 to study illustration in Vienna and Strasbourg. Her graphic memoir, *Persepolis,* excerpted in the following pages, is an account of her experiences as a young girl during the 1979 Iranian Revolution, from the ages of six to fourteen. In her preface she writes: "[T]his old and great civilization has been discussed mostly in connection with fundamentalism, fanaticism, and terrorism. As an Iranian who has lived more than half of my life in Iran, I know that this image is far from the truth. This is why writing *Persepolis* was so important to me." Satrapi's work has been compared to Art Spiegelman's *Maus,* a graphic novel about the Holocaust, a work that greatly influenced her. "When I read him, I thought . . . it's possible to tell a story and make a point this way. It was amazing."

THE TRIP

OH SHIT!

THEY'VE OCCUPIED THE U.S. EMBASSY!!

WHO'S "THEY"?

WHO DO YOU THINK? THE FUNDAMENTALIST STUDENTS HAVE TAKEN THE AMERICANS HOSTAGE!!

REALLY?

THEY CALL IT "A NEST OF SPIES." HA HA! YOU'D THINK IT WAS A JAMES BOND MOVIE.

YOU'RE NOT INTERESTED?

I COULDN'T CARE LESS.

ANYWAY, THE AMERICANS ARE DUMMIES.

MAYBE, BUT NOW NO ONE CAN GO TO THE UNITED STATES.

WHY'S THAT??

THINK ABOUT IT. NO EMBASSY, NO VISA!

SO, MY GREAT DREAM WENT UP IN SMOKE. I WOULDN'T BE ABLE TO GO TO THE UNITED STATES.

KAVEH, THEY CLOSED THE U.S. EMBASSY TODAY. I WON'T BE ABLE TO COME AND SEE YOU...

THE DREAM WASN'T THE USA. IT WAS SEEING MY FRIEND KAVEH, WHO HAD LEFT TO GO LIVE IN THE STATES A YEAR EARLIER.

259

AND THEN SOME DAYS LATER...

THE MINISTRY OF EDUCATION HAS DECREED THAT UNIVERSITIES WILL CLOSE AT THE END OF THE MONTH.

OH NO!

THE EDUCATIONAL SYSTEM AND WHAT IS WRITTEN IN SCHOOL BOOKS, AT ALL LEVELS, ARE DECADENT. EVERYTHING NEEDS TO BE REVISED TO ENSURE THAT OUR CHILDREN ARE NOT LED ASTRAY FROM THE TRUE PATH OF ISLAM.

OF COURSE, OF COURSE!

THAT'S WHY WE'RE CLOSING ALL THE UNIVERSITIES FOR A WHILE. BETTER TO HAVE NO STUDENTS AT ALL THAN TO EDUCATE FUTURE IMPERIALISTS.

THUS, THE UNIVERSITIES WERE CLOSED FOR TWO YEARS.

YOU'LL SEE. SOON THEY'RE ACTUALLY GOING TO FORCE US TO WEAR THE VEIL AND YOU, YOU'LL HAVE TO TRADE YOUR CAR FOR A CAMEL. GOD, WHAT A BACKWARD POLICY!

A CAMEL?

NO MORE UNIVERSITY. AND I WANTED TO STUDY CHEMISTRY. I WANTED TO BE LIKE MARIE CURIE.

I WANTED TO BE AN EDUCATED, LIBERATED WOMAN. AND IF THE PURSUIT OF KNOWLEDGE MEANT GETTING CANCER, SO BE IT.

IT'S I WHO DISCOVERED THE NEWEST RADIOACTIVE ELEMENT.

AND SO ANOTHER DREAM WENT UP IN SMOKE.

MISERY! AT THE AGE THAT MARIE CURIE FIRST WENT TO FRANCE TO STUDY, I'LL PROBABLY HAVE TEN CHILDREN ...

"The Trip" from *Persepolis: The Story of a Childhood*, by Marjane Satrapi, translated by Matthias Ripa and Blake Ferris. © 2003 by L'Association, Paris, France. Used by permission of Pantheon Books, a division of Random House, Inc.

Considerations for Critical Thinking and Writing

1. How does point of view in "The Trip" affect your understanding of the impact of the Islamic Revolution in Iran?

2. What specific cultural and political issues are raised by Satrapi's narrative? How does the strip comment on those issues?

3. How are Islamic fundamentalists portrayed in the strip? Explain whether you think this is a fair depiction.

7

Symbolism

Now mind, I recognize no dichotomy
between art and protest.
— RALPH ELLISON

A **symbol** is a person, object, or event that suggests more than its literal meaning. This basic definition is simple enough, but the use of symbol in literature makes some students slightly nervous because they tend to regard it as a booby trap, a hidden device that can go off during a seemingly harmless class discussion. "I didn't see that when I was reading the story" is a frequently heard comment. This sort of surprise and recognition is both natural and common. Most readers go through a story for the first time getting their bearings, figuring out what is happening to whom and so on. Patterns and significant details often require a second or third reading before they become evident—before a symbol sheds light on a story. Then the details of a work may suddenly fit together, and its meaning may be reinforced, clarified, or enlarged by the symbol. Symbolic meanings are usually embedded in the texture of a story, but they are not "hidden"; instead, they are carefully placed. Reading between the lines (where there is only space) is unnecessary. What is needed is a careful consideration of the elements of the story, a sensitivity to its language, and some common sense.

Common sense is a good place to begin. Symbols appear all around us; anything can be given symbolic significance. Without symbols our lives would be stark and vacant. Awareness of a writer's use of symbols is not all that different from the kinds of perceptions and interpretations that allow us to make sense of our daily lives. We know, for example, that a ring used in a wedding is more than just a piece of jewelry because it suggests the unity and intimacy of a closed circle. The bride's gown may be white because we tend to associate innocence and purity with that color. Or consider the meaning of a small polo pony sewn on a shirt or some other article of clothing. What started as a company trademark has gathered around it a range of meanings suggesting everything from quality and money to preppiness and silliness. The ring, the white gown, and the polo pony trademark are symbolic because each has meanings that go beyond its specific qualities and functions.

Web Explore the literary element in this chapter at bedfordstmartins.com/ meyerlit.

Symbols such as these that are widely recognized by a society or culture are called **conventional symbols.** The Christian cross, the Star of David, a swastika, or a nation's flag all have meanings understood by large groups of people. Certain kinds of experiences also have traditional meanings in Western cultures. Winter, the setting sun, and the color black suggest death, while spring, the rising sun, and the color green evoke images of youth and new beginnings. (It is worth noting, however, that individual cultures sometimes have their own conventions; some Eastern cultures associate white rather than black with death and mourning. And obviously the polo pony trademark would mean nothing to anyone totally unfamiliar with American culture.) These broadly shared symbolic meanings are second nature to us.

Writers use conventional symbols to reinforce meanings. Kate Chopin, for example, emphasizes the spring setting in "The Story of an Hour" (p. 15) as a way of suggesting the renewed sense of life that Mrs. Mallard feels when she thinks herself free from her husband.

A **literary symbol** can include traditional, conventional, or public meanings, but it may also be established internally by the total context of the work in which it appears. In "Soldier's Home" (p. 187), Hemingway does not use Krebs's family home as a conventional symbol of safety, comfort, and refuge from the war. Instead, Krebs's home becomes symbolic of provincial, erroneous presuppositions compounded by blind innocence, sentimentality, and smug middle-class respectability. The symbolic meaning of his home reveals that Krebs no longer shares his family's and town's view of the world. Their notions of love, the value of a respectable job, and a belief in God seem to him petty, complicated, and meaningless. The significance of Krebs's home is determined by the events within the story, which reverse and subvert the traditional associations readers might bring to it. Krebs's interactions with his family and the people in town reveal what home has come to mean to him.

A literary symbol can be a setting, character, action, object, name, or anything else in a work that maintains its literal significance while suggesting other meanings. Symbols cannot be restricted to a single meaning; they are suggestive rather than definitive. Their evocation of multiple meanings allows a writer to say more with less. Symbols are economical devices for evoking complex ideas without having to resort to painstaking explanations that would make a story more like an essay than an experience. The many walls in Melville's "Bartleby, the Scrivener" (p. 142) cannot be reduced to one idea. They have multiple meanings that unify the story. The walls are symbols of the deadening, dehumanizing, restrictive repetitiveness of the office routine, as well as of the confining, materialistic sensibilities of Wall Street. They suggest whatever limits and thwarts human aspirations, including death itself. We don't know precisely what shatters Bartleby's will to live, but the walls in the story, through their symbolic suggestiveness, indicate the nature of the limitations that cause the scrivener to slip into hopelessness and his "dead-wall reveries."

When a character, object, or incident indicates a single, fixed meaning, the writer is using ***allegory*** rather than symbol. Whereas symbols have literal functions as well as multiple meanings, the primary focus in allegory is on the abstract idea called forth by the concrete object. John Bunyan's *Pilgrim's Progress,* published during the seventeenth century, is a classic example of allegory because the characters, action, and setting have no existence beyond their abstract meanings. Bunyan's purpose is to teach his readers the exemplary way to salvation and heaven. The protagonist, named Christian, flees the City of Destruction in search of the Celestial City. Along the way he encounters characters who either help or hinder his spiritual journey. Among them are Mr. Worldly Wiseman, Faithful, Prudence, Piety, and a host of others named after the virtues or vices they display. These characters, places, and actions exist solely to illustrate religious doctrine. Allegory tends to be definitive rather than suggestive. It drives meaning into a corner and keeps it there. Most modern writers prefer the exploratory nature of symbol to the reductive nature of pure allegory.

Stories often include symbols that you may or may not perceive on a first reading. Their subtle use is a sign of a writer's skill in weaving symbols into the fabric of the characters' lives. Symbols may sometimes escape you, but that is probably better than finding symbols where only literal meanings are intended. Allow the text to help you determine whether a symbolic reading is appropriate. Once you are clear about what literally happens, read carefully and notice the placement of details that are emphasized. The pervasive references to time in Faulkner's "A Rose for Emily" (p. 91) and the many kinds of walls that appear throughout "Bartleby, the Scrivener" call attention to themselves and warrant symbolic readings. A symbol, however, need not be repeated to have an important purpose in a story. We don't learn until the very end of "Bartleby, the Scrivener" that Bartleby once worked as a clerk in the Dead Letter Office in Washington, D.C. This information is offered as merely an offhand rumor by the narrator, but its symbolic value is essential for understanding what motivates Bartleby's behavior. Indeed, Bartleby's experiences in the Dead Letter Office suggest enough about the nature of his thwarted hopes and desires to account for Bartleby's rejection of life.

By keeping track of the total context of the story, you should be able to decide whether your reading is reasonable and consistent with the other facts; plenty of lemons in literature yield no symbolic meaning even if they are squeezed. Be sensitive to the meanings that the author associates with people, places, objects, and actions. You may not associate home with provincial innocence as Hemingway does in "Soldier's Home," but a close reading of the story will permit you to see how and why he constructs that symbolic meaning. If you treat stories like people — with tact and care — they ordinarily are accessible and enjoyable.

The next four stories — Chitra Banerjee Divakaruni's "Clothes," Colette's "The Hand," Ralph Ellison's "Battle Royal," and Michael Oppenheimer's "The Paring Knife" — rely on symbols to convey meanings that go far beyond the specific incidents described in their plots.

CHITRA BANERJEE DIVAKARUNI
(B. 1956)

Born in India, Chitra Banerjee Divakaruni left Calcutta when she was nineteen years old to continue her education in the United States, where she worked a variety of odd jobs while earning a master's degree from Wright State University and a Ph.D. from the University of California, Berkeley. She currently teaches in the creative writing department at the University of Houston. Her first collection of short stories, *Arranged Marriage* (which includes "Clothes," reprinted below), was published in 1995; it won several awards including the American Book Award. In addition to a second collection of stories, *The Unknown Errors of Our Lives* (2001), she has published several novels including *Sister of My Heart* (1999), *Vine of Desire* (2002), *The Conch Bearer* (2003), *Queen of Dreams* (2004), and *Shadowland* (2009). Among her three books of poetry, her most recent is *Leaving Yuba City* (1997). Much of her work focuses on Indian immigrant women who find themselves having to balance their lives between their homeland and the United States.

Copyright © by Chitra Banerjee Divakaruni.

Clothes   *1990*

The water of the women's lake laps against my breasts, cool, calming. I can feel it beginning to wash the hot nervousness away from my body. The little waves tickle my armpits, make my sari float up around me, wet and yellow, like a sunflower after rain. I close my eyes and smell the sweet brown odor of the *ritha* pulp my friends Deepali and Radha are working into my hair so it will glisten with little lights this evening. They scrub with more vigor than usual and wash it out more carefully, because today is a special day. It is the day of my bride-viewing.

"Ei, Sumita! Mita! Are you deaf?" Radha says. "This is the third time I've asked you the same question."

"Look at her, already dreaming about her husband, and she hasn't even seen him yet!" Deepali jokes. Then she adds, the envy in her voice only half hidden, "Who cares about friends from a little Indian village when you're about to go live in America?"

I want to deny it, to say that I will always love them and all the things we did together through my growing-up years — visiting the *charak* fair where we always ate too many sweets, raiding the neighbor's guava tree summer afternoons while the grown-ups slept, telling fairy tales while we braided each other's hair in elaborate patterns we'd invented. *And she married the handsome prince who took her to his kingdom beyond the seven seas.* But already the activities of our girlhood seem to be far in my past, the colors leached out of them, like old sepia photographs.

His name is Somesh Sen, the man who is coming to our house with his   5 parents today and who will be my husband "if I'm lucky enough to be chosen," as my aunt says. He is coming all the way from California. Father showed it to me yesterday, on the metal globe that sits on his desk, a chunky pink wedge on the side of a multicolored slab marked *Untd. Sts. of America.* I touched it and felt the excitement leap all the way up my arm like an electric shock. Then it died away, leaving only a beaten-metal coldness against my fingertips.

For the first time it occurred to me that if things worked out the way everyone was hoping, I'd be going halfway around the world to live with a man I hadn't even met. Would I ever see my parents again? *Don't send me so far away,* I wanted to cry, but of course I didn't. It would be ungrateful. Father had worked so hard to find this match for me. Besides, wasn't it every woman's destiny, as Mother was always telling me, to leave the known for the unknown? She had done it, and her mother before her. *A married woman belongs to her husband, her in-laws.* Hot seeds of tears pricked my eyelids at the unfairness of it.

"Mita Moni, little jewel," Father said, calling me by my childhood name. He put out his hand as though he wanted to touch my face, then let it fall to his side. "He's a good man. Comes from a fine family. He will be kind to you." He was silent for a while. Finally he said, "Come, let me show you the special sari I bought in Calcutta for you to wear at the bride-viewing."

"Are you nervous?" Radha asks as she wraps my hair in a soft cotton towel. Her parents are also trying to arrange a marriage for her. So far three families have come to see her, but no one has chosen her because her skin-color is considered too dark. "Isn't it terrible, not knowing what's going to happen?"

I nod because I don't want to disagree, don't want to make her feel bad by saying that sometimes it's worse when you know what's coming, like I do. I knew it as soon as Father unlocked his mahogany *almirah*° and took out the sari.

---

almirah: A large closet.

It was the most expensive sari I had ever seen, and surely the most beau- 10 tiful. Its body was a pale pink, like the dawn sky over the women's lake. The color of transition. Embroidered all over it were tiny stars made out of real gold *zari* thread.

"Here, hold it," said Father.

The sari was unexpectedly heavy in my hands, silk-slippery, a sari to walk carefully in. A sari that could change one's life. I stood there holding it, wanting to weep. I knew that when I wore it, it would hang in perfect pleats to my feet and shimmer in the light of the evening lamps. It would dazzle Somesh and his parents and they would choose me to be his bride.

When the plane takes off, I try to stay calm, to take deep, slow breaths like Father does when he practices yoga. But my hands clench themselves on to the folds of my sari and when I force them open, after the *fasten seat belt* and *no smoking* signs have blinked off, I see they have left damp blotches on the delicate crushed fabric.

We had some arguments about this sari. I wanted a blue one for the journey, because blue is the color of possibility, the color of the sky through which I would be traveling. But Mother said there must be red in it because red is the color of luck for married women. Finally, Father found one to satisfy us both: midnight-blue with a thin red border the same color as the marriage mark I'm wearing on my forehead.

It is hard for me to think of myself as a married woman. I whisper my new 15 name to myself, Mrs. Sumita Sen, but the syllables rustle uneasily in my mouth like a stiff satin that's never been worn.

Somesh had to leave for America just a week after the wedding. He had to get back to the store, he explained to me. He had promised his partner. The store. It seems more real to me than Somesh—perhaps because I know more about it. It was what we had mostly talked about the night after the wedding, the first night we were together alone. It stayed open twenty-four hours, yes, all night, every night, not like the Indian stores which closed at dinnertime and sometimes in the hottest part of the afternoon. That's why his partner needed him back.

The store was called *7-Eleven*. I thought it a strange name, exotic, risky. All the stores I knew were piously named after gods and goddesses—*Ganesh Sweet House, Lakshmi Vastralaya for Fine Saris*—to bring the owners luck.

The store sold all kinds of amazing things—apple juice in cardboard cartons that never leaked; American bread that came in cellophane packages, already cut up; canisters of potato chips, each large grainy flake curved exactly like the next. The large refrigerator with see-through glass doors held beer and wine, which Somesh said were the most popular items.

"That's where the money comes from, especially in the neighborhood where our store is," said Somesh, smiling at the shocked look on my face. (The only places I knew of that sold alcohol were the village toddy shops, "dark, stinking dens of vice," Father called them.) "A lot of Americans drink, you know. It's a part of their culture, not considered immoral, like it is here. And really, there's nothing wrong with it." He touched my lips lightly with his finger. "When you come to California, I'll get you some sweet white wine and you'll see how good it makes you feel. . . ." Now his fingers were stroking my cheeks, my throat, moving downward. I closed my eyes and tried not to jerk away because after all it was my wifely duty.

"It helps if you can think about something else," my friend Madhavi had 20 said when she warned me about what most husbands demanded on the very first night. Two years married, she already had one child and was pregnant with a second one.

I tried to think of the women's lake, the dark cloudy green of the *shapla*° leaves that float on the water, but his lips were hot against my skin, his fingers fumbling with buttons, pulling at the cotton night-sari I wore. I couldn't breathe.

"Bite hard on your tongue," Madhavi had advised. "The pain will keep your mind off what's going on down there."

But when I bit down, it hurt so much that I cried out. I couldn't help it although I was ashamed. Somesh lifted his head. I don't know what he saw on my face, but he stopped right away. "Shhh," he said, although I had made myself silent already. "It's OK, we'll wait until you feel like it." I tried to apologize but he smiled it away and started telling me some more about the store.

And that's how it was the rest of the week until he left. We would lie side by side on the big white bridal pillow I had embroidered with a pair of doves for married harmony, and Somesh would describe how the store's front windows were decorated with a flashing neon Dewar's sign and a lighted Budweiser waterfall *this big*. I would watch his hands moving excitedly through the dim air of the bedroom and think that Father had been right, he was a good man, my husband, a kind, patient man. And so handsome, too, I would add, stealing a quick look at the strong curve of his jaw, feeling luckier than I had any right to be.

The night before he left, Somesh confessed that the store wasn't making 25 much money yet. "I'm not worried, I'm sure it soon will," he added, his fingers pleating the edge of my sari. "But I just don't want to give you the wrong impression, don't want you to be disappointed."

In the half dark I could see he had turned toward me. His face, with two vertical lines between the brows, looked young, apprehensive, in need of protection. I'd never seen that on a man's face before. Something rose in me like a wave.

"It's all right," I said, as though to a child, and pulled his head down to my breast. His hair smelled faintly of the American cigarettes he smoked. "I won't be disappointed. I'll help you." And a sudden happiness filled me.

That night I dreamed I was at the store. Soft American music floated in the background as I moved between shelves stocked high with brightly colored cans and elegant-necked bottles, turning their labels carefully to the front, polishing them until they shone.

Now, sitting inside this metal shell that is hurtling through emptiness, I try to remember other things about my husband: how gentle his hands had been, and his lips, surprisingly soft, like a woman's. How I've longed for them through those drawn-out nights while I waited for my visa to arrive. He will be standing at the customs gate, and when I reach him, he will lower his face to mine. We will kiss in front of everyone, not caring, like Americans, then pull back, look each other in the eye, and smile.

shapla: A water plant.

But suddenly, as I am thinking this, I realize I cannot recall Somesh's face. 30
I try and try until my head hurts, but I can only visualize the black air swirling
outside the plane, too thin for breathing. My own breath grows ragged with
panic as I think of it and my mouth fills with sour fluid the way it does just before I throw up.

I grope for something to hold on to, something beautiful and talismanic
from my old life. And then I remember. Somewhere down under me, low in the
belly of the plane, inside my new brown case which is stacked in the dark with
a hundred others, are my saris. Thick Kanjeepuram silks in solid purples and
golden yellows, the thin hand-woven cottons of the Bengal countryside, green
as a young banana plant, gray as the women's lake on a monsoon morning. Already I can feel my shoulders loosening up, my breath steadying. My wedding
Benarasi, flame-orange, with a wide *palloo*° of gold-embroidered dancing peacocks. Fold upon fold of Dhakais° so fine they can be pulled through a ring.
Into each fold my mother has tucked a small sachet of sandalwood powder to
protect the saris from the unknown insects of America. Little silk sachets,
made from *her* old saris — I can smell their calm fragrance as I watch the American air hostess wheeling the dinner cart toward my seat. It is the smell of my
mother's hands.

I know then that everything will be all right. And when the air hostess
bends her curly golden head to ask me what I would like to eat, I understand
every word in spite of her strange accent and answer her without stumbling
even once over the unfamiliar English phrases.

Late at night I stand in front of our bedroom mirror trying on the clothes
Somesh has bought for me and smuggled in past his parents. I model each one
for him, walking back and forth, clasping my hands behind my head, lips
pouted, left hip thrust out just like the models on TV, while he whispers applause. I'm breathless with suppressed laughter (Father and Mother Sen must
not hear us) and my cheeks are hot with the delicious excitement of conspiracy. We've stuffed a towel at the bottom of the door so no light will shine
through.

I'm wearing a pair of jeans now, marveling at the curves of my hips and
thighs, which have always been hidden under the flowing lines of my saris. I
love the color, the same pale blue as the *nayantara* flowers that grow in my parents' garden. The solid comforting weight. The jeans come with a close-fitting
T-shirt which outlines my breasts.

I scold Somesh to hide my embarrassed pleasure. He shouldn't have been 35
so extravagant. We can't afford it. He just smiles.

The T-shirt is sunrise-orange — the color, I decide, of joy, of my new American life. Across its middle, in large black letters, is written *Great America*. I was
sure the letters referred to the country, but Somesh told me it is the name of
an amusement park, a place where people go to have fun. I think it a wonderful
concept, novel. Above the letters is the picture of a train. Only it's not a train,
Somesh tells me, it's a roller coaster. He tries to explain how it moves, the insane speed, the dizzy ground falling away, then gives up. "I'll take you there,
Mita sweetheart," he says, "as soon as we move into our own place."

palloo: The piece of the sari that goes over the shoulder.
Dhakais: Hand-loomed saris from Bangladesh.

That's our dream (mine more than his, I suspect)—moving out of this two-room apartment where it seems to me if we all breathed in at once, there would be no air left. Where I must cover my head with the edge of my Japan nylon sari (my expensive Indian ones are to be saved for special occasions—trips to the temple, Bengali New Year) and serve tea to the old women that come to visit Mother Sen, where like a good Indian wife I must never address my husband by his name. Where even in our bed we kiss guiltily, uneasily, listening for the giveaway creak of springs. Sometimes I laugh to myself, thinking how ironic it is that after all my fears about America, my life has turned out to be no different from Deepali's or Radha's. But at other times I feel caught in a world where everything is frozen in place, like a scene inside a glass paperweight. It is a world so small that if I were to stretch out my arms, I would touch its cold unyielding edges. I stand inside this glass world, watching helplessly as America rushes by, wanting to scream. Then I'm ashamed. Mita, I tell myself, you're growing westernized. Back home you'd never have felt this way.

We must be patient. I know that. Tactful, loving children. That is the Indian way. "I'm their life," Somesh tells me as we lie beside each other, lazy from lovemaking. He's not boasting, merely stating a fact. "They've always been there when I needed them. I could never abandon them at some old people's home." For a moment I feel rage. You're constantly thinking of them, I want to scream. But what about me? Then I remember my own parents, Mother's hands cool on my sweat-drenched body through nights of fever, Father teaching me to read, his finger moving along the crisp black angles of the alphabet, transforming them magically into things I knew, water, dog, mango tree. I beat back my unreasonable desire and nod agreement.

Somesh has bought me a cream blouse with a long brown skirt. They match beautifully, like the inside and outside of an almond. "For when you begin working," he says. But first he wants me to start college. Get a degree, perhaps in teaching. I picture myself in front of a classroom of girls with blond pigtails and blue uniforms, like a scene out of an English movie I saw long ago in Calcutta. They raise their hands respectfully when I ask a question. "Do you really think I can?" I ask. "Of course," he replies.

I am gratified he has such confidence in me. But I have another plan, a secret that I will divulge to him once we move. What I really want is to work in the store. I want to stand behind the counter in the cream-and-brown skirt set (color of earth, color of seeds) and ring up purchases. The register drawer will glide open. Confident, I will count out green dollars and silver quarters. Gleaming copper pennies. I will dust the jars of gilt-wrapped chocolates on the counter. Will straighten, on the far wall, posters of smiling young men raising their beer mugs to toast scantily clad redheads with huge spiky eyelashes. (I have never visited the store—my in-laws don't consider it proper for a wife—but of course I know exactly what it looks like.) I will charm the customers with my smile, so that they will return again and again just to hear me telling them to have a nice day. [40]

Meanwhile, I will the store to make money for us. Quickly. Because when we move, we'll be paying for two households. But so far it hasn't worked. They're running at a loss, Somesh tells me. They had to let the hired help go. This means most nights Somesh has to take the graveyard shift (that horrible word, like a cold hand up my spine) because his partner refuses to.

"The bastard!" Somesh spat out once. "Just because he put in more money he thinks he can order me around. I'll show him!" I was frightened by the vicious twist of his mouth. Somehow I'd never imagined that he could be angry.

Often Somesh leaves as soon as he has dinner and doesn't get back till after I've made morning tea for Father and Mother Sen. I lie mostly awake those nights, picturing masked intruders crouching in the shadowed back of the store, like I've seen on the police shows that Father Sen sometimes watches. But Somesh insists there's nothing to worry about, they have bars on the windows and a burglar alarm. "And remember," he says, "the extra cash will help us move out that much quicker."

I'm wearing a nightie now, my very first one. It's black and lacy, with a bit of a shine to it, and it glides over my hips to stop outrageously at mid-thigh. My mouth is an O of surprise in the mirror, my legs long and pale and sleek from the hair remover I asked Somesh to buy me last week. The legs of a movie star. Somesh laughs at the look on my face, then says, "You're beautiful." His voice starts a flutter low in my belly.

"Do you really think so?" I ask, mostly because I want to hear him say it 45 again. No one has called me beautiful before. My father would have thought it inappropriate, my mother that it would make me vain.

Somesh draws me close. "Very beautiful," he whispers. "The most beautiful woman in the whole world." His eyes are not joking as they usually are. I want to turn off the light, but "Please," he says, "I want to keep seeing your face." His fingers are taking the pins from my hair, undoing my braids. The escaped strands fall on his face like dark rain. We have already decided where we will hide my new American clothes — the jeans and T-shirt camouflaged on a hanger among Somesh's pants, the skirt set and nightie at the bottom of my suitcase, a sandalwood sachet tucked between them, waiting.

I stand in the middle of our empty bedroom, my hair still wet from the purification bath, my back to the stripped bed I can't bear to look at. I hold in my hands the plain white sari I'm supposed to wear. I must hurry. Any minute now there'll be a knock at the door. They are afraid to leave me alone too long, afraid I might do something to myself.

The sari, a thick voile that will bunch around the waist when worn, is borrowed. White. Widow's color, color of endings. I try to tuck it into the top of the petticoat, but my fingers are numb, disobedient. It spills through them and there are waves and waves of white around my feet. I kick out in sudden rage, but the sari is too soft, it gives too easily. I grab up an edge, clamp down with my teeth and pull, feeling a fierce, bitter satisfaction when I hear it rip.

There's a cut, still stinging, on the side of my right arm, halfway to the elbow. It is from the bangle-breaking ceremony. Old Mrs. Ghosh performed the ritual, since she's a widow, too. She took my hands in hers and brought them down hard on the bedpost, so that the glass bangles I was wearing shattered and multicolored shards flew out in every direction. Some landed on the body that was on the bed, covered with a sheet. I can't call it Somesh. He was gone already. She took an edge of the sheet and rubbed the red marriage mark off my forehead. She was crying. All the women in the room were crying except me. I watched them as though from the far end of a tunnel. Their flared nostrils, their red-veined eyes, the runnels of tears, salt-corrosive, down their cheeks.

It happened last night. He was at the store. "It isn't too bad," he would tell 50 me on the days when he was in a good mood. "Not too many customers. I can put up my feet and watch MTV all night. I can sing along with Michael Jackson as loud as I want." He had a good voice, Somesh. Sometimes he would sing softly at night, lying in bed, holding me. Hindi songs of love, *Mere Sapnon Ki Rani,* queen of my dreams. (He would not sing American songs at home out of respect for his parents, who thought they were decadent.) I would feel his warm breath on my hair as I fell asleep.

Someone came into the store last night. He took all the money, even the little rolls of pennies I had helped Somesh make up. Before he left he emptied the bullets from his gun into my husband's chest.

"Only thing is," Somesh would say about the night shifts, "I really miss you. I sit there and think of you asleep in bed. Do you know that when you sleep you make your hands into fists, like a baby? When we move out, will you come along some nights to keep me company?"

My in-laws are good people, kind. They made sure the body was covered before they let me into the room. When someone asked if my hair should be cut off, as they sometimes do with widows back home, they said no. They said I could stay at the apartment with Mrs. Ghosh if I didn't want to go to the crematorium. They asked Dr. Das to give me something to calm me down when I couldn't stop shivering. They didn't say, even once, as people would surely have in the village, that it was my bad luck that brought death to their son so soon after his marriage.

They will probably go back to India now. There's nothing here for them anymore. They will want me to go with them. You're like our daughter, they will say. Your home is with us, for as long as you want. For the rest of your life. *The rest of my life.* I can't think about that yet. It makes me dizzy. Fragments are flying about my head, multicolored and piercing sharp like bits of bangle glass.

I want you to go to college. Choose a career. I stand in front of a classroom of 55 smiling children who love me in my cream-and-brown American dress. A faceless parade straggles across my eyelids: all those customers at the store that I will never meet. The lace nightie, fragrant with sandalwood, waiting in its blackness inside my suitcase. The savings book where we have $3605.33. *Four thousand and we can move out, maybe next month.* The name of the panty hose I'd asked him to buy me for my birthday: sheer golden-beige. His lips, unexpectedly soft, woman-smooth. Elegant-necked wine bottles swept off shelves, shattering on the floor.

I know Somesh would not have tried to stop the gunman. I can picture his silhouette against the lighted Dewar's sign, hands raised. He is trying to find the right expression to put on his face, calm, reassuring, reasonable. *OK, take the money. No, I won't call the police.* His hands tremble just a little. His eyes darken with disbelief as his fingers touch his chest and come away wet.

I yanked away the cover. I had to see. *Great America, a place where people go to have fun.* My breath roller-coasting through my body, my unlived life gathering itself into a scream. I'd expected blood, a lot of blood, the deep red-black of it crusting his chest. But they must have cleaned him up at the hospital. He was dressed in his silk wedding *kurta.* Against its warm ivory his face appeared remote, stern. The musky aroma of his aftershave lotion that someone must have sprinkled on the body. It didn't quite hide that other smell, thin, sour, metallic. The smell of death. The floor shifted under me, tilting like a wave.

I'm lying on the floor now, on the spilled white sari. I feel sleepy. Or perhaps it is some other feeling I don't have a word for. The sari is seductive-soft, drawing me into its folds.

Sometimes, bathing at the lake, I would move away from my friends, their endless chatter. I'd swim toward the middle of the water with a lazy backstroke, gazing at the sky, its enormous blueness drawing me up until I felt weightless and dizzy. Once in a while there would be a plane, a small silver needle drawn through the clouds, in and out, until it disappeared. Sometimes the thought came to me, as I floated in the middle of the lake with the sun beating down on my closed eyelids, that it would be so easy to let go, to drop into the dim brown world of mud, of water weeds fine as hair.

Once I almost did it. I curled my body inward, tight as a fist, and felt it 60 start to sink. The sun grew pale and shapeless; the water, suddenly cold, licked at the insides of my ears in welcome. But in the end I couldn't.

They are knocking on the door now, calling my name. I push myself off the floor, my body almost too heavy to lift up, as when one climbs out after a long swim. I'm surprised at how vividly it comes to me, this memory I haven't called up in years: the desperate flailing of arms and legs as I fought my way upward; the press of the water on me, heavy as terror; the wild animal trapped inside my chest, clawing at my lungs. The day returning to me as searing air, the way I drew it in, in, in, as though I would never have enough of it.

That's when I know I cannot go back. I don't know yet how I'll manage, here in this new, dangerous land. I only know I must. Because all over India, at this very moment, widows in white saris are bowing their veiled heads, serving tea to in-laws. Doves with cut-off wings.

I am standing in front of the mirror now, gathering up the sari. I tuck in the ripped end so it lies next to my skin, my secret. I make myself think of the store, although it hurts. Inside the refrigerated unit, blue milk cartons neatly lined up by Somesh's hands. The exotic smell of Hills Brothers coffee brewed black and strong, the glisten of sugar-glazed donuts nestled in tissue. The neon Budweiser emblem winking on and off like a risky invitation.

I straighten my shoulders and stand taller, take a deep breath. Air fills me — the same air that traveled through Somesh's lungs a little while ago. The thought is like an unexpected, intimate gift. I tilt my chin, readying myself for the arguments of the coming weeks, the remonstrations. In the mirror a woman holds my gaze, her eyes apprehensive yet steady. She wears a blouse and skirt the color of almonds.

CONSIDERATIONS FOR CRITICAL THINKING AND WRITING

1. **FIRST RESPONSE.** What do you think of the practice of arranging marriages? Sumita initially cries "at the unfairness of it" (para. 6), but how does Divakaruni present Sumita's marriage in the story?

2. Explain how the author weaves into the first section (paras. 1–12) the necessary exposition so that the reader has a rich context in which to understand the plot and characters.

3. How is Somesh characterized? What kind of man, son, and husband is he?

4. Explain how the 7-Eleven is used as a symbol of American life.

5. Gather up all the clothes in the story and explain how they take on symbolic meanings.

6. Consider the use of colors throughout the story—yellow (para. 1), pink (10), blue (14), orange (36), white (48), multicolor (49), cream and brown (40, 55). What significance is associated with each color, and how does each signify an important moment in the plot?

7. Explain why you consider the ending to be happy, unhappy, or indeterminate.

CONNECTIONS TO OTHER SELECTIONS

1. Read Mordecai Marcus on "What Is an Initiation Story?" (p. 288) and consider whether "Clothes" fits his description of that type of plot.

2. Discuss how the settings are related to each story's overall meanings in "Clothes" and in Hemingway's "Soldier's Home" (p. 187).

COLETTE (SIDONIE-GABRIELLE COLETTE / 1873–1954)

Born in Burgundy, France, Sidonie-Gabrielle Colette lived a long and remarkably diverse life. At various points during her career she supported herself as a novelist, music hall performer, and journalist. Her professional life and three marriages helped to shape her keen insights into modern love and women's lives. She is regarded as a significant feminist voice in the twentieth century, and her reputation is firmly fixed by her having been the first woman admitted to the Goncourt Academy and by the continued popularity of her work among readers internationally. Her best-known works include *Mitsou, or, How Girls Grow Wise* (1919), *Chéri* (1920), *Claudine's House* (1922), and *Gigi* (1944). "The Hand" signals a telling moment in the life of a young bride.

The Hand   1924

He had fallen asleep on his young wife's shoulder, and she proudly bore the weight of the man's head, blond, ruddy-complexioned, eyes closed. He had slipped his big arm under the small of her slim, adolescent back, and his strong hand lay on the sheet next to the young woman's right elbow. She smiled to see the man's hand emerging there, all by itself and far away from its owner. Then she let her eyes wander over the half-lit room. A veiled conch shed a light across the bed the color of periwinkle.

"Too happy to sleep," she thought.

Too excited also, and often surprised by her new state. It had been only two weeks since she had begun to live the scandalous life of a newlywed who tastes the joys of living with someone unknown and with whom she is in love. To meet a handsome, blond young man, recently widowed, good at tennis and rowing, to marry him a month later: her conjugal adventure had been little more than a kidnapping. So that whenever she lay awake beside her husband, like tonight, she still kept her eyes closed for a long time, then opened them again in order to savor, with astonishment, the blue of the brand-new curtains, instead of the apricot-pink through which the first light of day filtered into the room where she had slept as a little girl.

A quiver ran through the sleeping body lying next to her, and she tightened her left arm around her husband's neck with the charming authority exercised by weak creatures. He did not wake up.

"His eyelashes are so long," she said to herself.   5

To herself she also praised his mouth, full and likable, his skin the color of pink brick, and even his forehead, neither noble nor broad, but still smooth and unwrinkled.

Her husband's right hand, lying beside her, quivered in turn, and beneath the curve of her back she felt the right arm, on which her whole weight was resting, come to life.

"I'm so heavy . . . I wish I could get up and turn the light off. But he's sleeping so well . . ."

The arm twisted again, feebly, and she arched her back to make herself lighter.

"It's as if I were lying on some animal," she thought.   10

She turned her head a little on the pillow and looked at the hand lying there next to her.

"It's so big! It really is bigger than my whole head."

The light, flowing out from under the edge of a parasol of bluish crystal, spilled up against the hand, and made every contour of the skin apparent, exaggerating the powerful knuckles and the veins engorged by the pressure on the arm. A few red hairs, at the base of the fingers, all curved in the same direction, like ears of wheat in the wind, and the flat nails, whose ridges the nail buffer had not smoothed out, gleamed, coated with pink varnish.

"I'll tell him not to varnish his nails," thought the young wife. "Varnish and pink polish don't go with a hand so . . . a hand that's so . . ."

An electric jolt ran through the hand and spared the young woman from   15
having to find the right adjective. The thumb stiffened itself out, horribly long and spatulate, and pressed tightly against the index finger, so that the hand suddenly took on a vile, apelike appearance.

"Oh!" whispered the young woman, as though faced with something slightly indecent.

The sound of a passing car pierced the silence with a shrillness that seemed luminous. The sleeping man did not wake, but the hand, offended, reared back and tensed up in the shape of a crab and waited, ready for battle. The screeching sound died down and the hand, relaxing gradually, lowered its claws, and became a pliant beast, awkwardly bent, shaken by faint jerks which resembled some sort of agony. The flat, cruel nail of the overlong thumb glistened. A curve in the little finger, which the young woman had never noticed, appeared, and the wallowing hand revealed its fleshy palm like a red belly.

"And I've kissed that hand! . . . How horrible! Haven't I ever looked at it?"

The hand, disturbed by a bad dream, appeared to respond to this startling discovery, this disgust. It regrouped its forces, opened wide, and splayed its tendons, lumps, and red fur like battle dress, then slowly drawing itself in again, grabbed a fistful of the sheet, dug into it with its curved fingers, and squeezed, squeezed with the methodical pleasure of a strangler.

"Oh!" cried the young woman.   20

The hand disappeared and a moment later the big arm, relieved of its burden, became a protective belt, a warm bulwark against all the terrors of night.
But the next morning, when it was time for breakfast in bed — hot chocolate
and toast — she saw the hand again, with its red hair and red skin, and the
ghastly thumb curving out over the handle of a knife.

"Do you want this slice, darling? I'll butter it for you."

She shuddered and felt her skin crawl on the back of her arms and down
her back.

"Oh, no . . . no . . ."

Then she concealed her fear, bravely subdued herself, and, beginning her   25
life of duplicity, of resignation, and of a lowly, delicate diplomacy, she leaned
over and humbly kissed the monstrous hand.

CONSIDERATIONS FOR CRITICAL THINKING AND WRITING

1. **FIRST RESPONSE.** Where is "The Hand" set? How significant is the setting
   of the story?

2. How well did the young woman know her husband before she married
   him? What attracted her to him?

3. How does the wife regard the hand at the very beginning of the story? At
   what point does she begin to change her attitude?

4. Explain how the wife's description of the hand affects your own response
   to it. What prompts her "Oh!" in paragraphs 16 and 20? What do you suppose the wife is thinking at these moments?

5. What powerful feelings does the hand evoke in the wife? How do her descriptions of the hand suggest symbolic readings of it?

6. Describe the conflict in the story. Explain whether there is a resolution to
   this conflict.

7. Do you think the story is more about the husband or about the wife?
   Who is the central character? Explain your choice. Consider also whether
   the characters are static or dynamic.

8. Why do you think the narrator mentions that the husband was "recently
   widowed"?

9. Why do you think the wife kisses her husband's hand in the final paragraph? Write an essay explaining how the kiss symbolizes the nature of
   their relationship.

10. Describe the point of view in the story. Why do you suppose Colette
    doesn't use a first-person perspective that would reveal more intimately
    the wife's perceptions and concerns?

CONNECTIONS TO OTHER SELECTIONS

1. In "The Birthmark" (p. 420) Nathaniel Hawthorne also uses a hand for
   symbolic purposes. Compare the meanings he associates with the hand
   in his story with Colette's. How does each writer invest meanings in a
   central symbol? What are the significant similarities and differences in
   meanings? Write an essay explaining why you find one story more effective than the other.

2. Compare the use of settings in "The Hand" and in John Updike's "A & P" (p. 733). To what extent does each story attach meaning to its setting?

3. How might Gail Godwin's "A Sorrowful Woman" (p. 39) be read as a kind of sequel to "The Hand"?

RALPH ELLISON (1914–1994)

Born in Oklahoma and educated at the Tuskegee Institute in Alabama, where he studied music, Ralph Ellison gained his reputation as a writer on the strength of his only published novel, *Invisible Man* (1952). He also published some scattered short stories and two collections of essays, *Shadow and Act* (1964) and *Going to the Territory* (1986).

Library of Congress, Prints and Photographs Division.

Although his writing was not extensive, it is important because Ellison wrote about race relations in the context of universal human concerns. *Invisible Man* is the story of a young black man who moves from the South to the North and discovers what it means to be black in America. "Battle Royal," published in 1947 as a short story, became the first chapter of *Invisible Man*. It concerns the beginning of the protagonist's long struggle for an adult identity in a world made corrupt by racial prejudice.

Battle Royal   1947

It goes a long way back, some twenty years. All my life I had been looking for something, and everywhere I turned someone tried to tell me what it was. I accepted their answers too, though they were often in contradiction and even self-contradictory. I was naive. I was looking for myself and asking everyone except myself questions which I, and only I, could answer. It took me a long time and much painful boomeranging of my expectations to achieve a realization everyone else appears to have been born with: That I am nobody but myself. But first I had to discover that I am an invisible man!

And yet I am no freak of nature, nor of history. I was in the cards, other things having been equal (or unequal) eighty-five years ago. I am not ashamed of my grandparents for having been slaves. I am only ashamed of myself for having at one time been ashamed. About eighty-five years ago they were told that they were free, united with others of our country in everything pertaining to the common good, and, in everything social, separate like the fingers of the hand. And they believed it. They exulted in it. They stayed in their place, worked hard, and brought up my father to do the same. But my grandfather is the one. He was an odd old guy, my grandfather, and I am told I take after him. It was he who caused the trouble. On his deathbed he called my father to him and said, "Son, after I'm gone I want you to keep up the good fight. I never told you, but our life is a war and I have been a traitor all my born days, a spy in the enemy's country ever since I gave up my gun back in the Reconstruction. Live with your head in the lion's mouth. I want you to overcome 'em with yeses, undermine 'em with grins, agree 'em to death and destruction, let 'em swoller you till they vomit or bust wide open." They thought the old man had gone out of his mind. He had been the meekest of men. The younger children were rushed from the room, the shades drawn and the flame of the lamp turned so low that it sputtered on the wick like the old man's breathing. "Learn it to the young-uns," he whispered fiercely; then he died.

But my folks were more alarmed over his last words than over his dying. It was as though he had not died at all, his words caused so much anxiety. I was warned emphatically to forget what he had said and, indeed, this is the first time it has been mentioned outside the family circle. It had a tremendous effect upon me, however. I could never be sure of what he meant. Grandfather had been a quiet old man who never made any trouble, yet on his deathbed he had called himself a traitor and a spy, and he had spoken of his meekness as a dangerous activity. It became a constant puzzle which lay unanswered in the back of my mind. And whenever things went well for me I remembered my grandfather and felt guilty and uncomfortable. It was as though I was carrying out his advice in spite of myself. And to make it worse, everyone loved me for it. I was praised by the most lily-white men of the town. I was considered an example of desirable conduct — just as my grandfather had been. And what puzzled me was that the old man had defined it as *treachery*. When I was praised for my conduct I felt a guilt that in some way I was doing something that was really against the wishes of the white folks, that if they had understood they would have desired me to act just the opposite, that I should have been sulky and mean, and that that really would have been what they wanted, even though they were fooled and thought they wanted me to act as I did. It made me afraid that some day they would look upon me as a traitor and I would be lost. Still I was more afraid to act any other way because they didn't like that at all. The old man's words were like a curse. On my graduation day I delivered an oration in which I showed that humility was the secret, indeed, the very essence of progress. (Not that I believed this — how could I, remembering my grandfather? — I only believed that it worked.) It was a great success. Everyone praised me and I was invited to give the speech at a gathering of the town's leading white citizens. It was a triumph for our whole community.

It was in the main ballroom of the leading hotel. When I got there I discovered that it was on the occasion of a smoker, and I was told that since I was to be there anyway I might as well take part in the battle royal to be fought by some of my schoolmates as part of the entertainment. The battle royal came first.

All of the town's big shots were there in their tuxedoes, wolfing down the 5 buffet foods, drinking beer and whiskey and smoking black cigars. It was a large room with a high ceiling. Chairs were arranged in neat rows around three sides of a portable boxing ring. The fourth side was clear, revealing a gleaming space of polished floor. I had some misgivings over the battle royal, by the way. Not from a distaste for fighting, but because I didn't care too much for the other fellows who were to take part. They were tough guys who seemed to have no grandfather's curse worrying their minds. No one could mistake their toughness. And besides, I suspected that fighting a battle royal might detract from the dignity of my speech. In those pre-invisible days I visualized myself as a potential Booker T. Washington. But the other fellows didn't care too much for me either, and there were nine of them. I felt superior to them in my way, and I didn't like the manner in which we were all crowded together into the servants' elevator. Nor did they like my being there. In fact, as the warmly lighted floors flashed past the elevator we had words over the fact that I, by taking part in the fight, had knocked one of their friends out of a night's work.

We were led out of the elevator through a rococo hall into an anteroom and told to get into our fighting togs. Each of us was issued a pair of boxing gloves and ushered out into the big mirrored hall, which we entered looking cautiously about us and whispering, lest we might accidentally be heard above the noise of the room. It was foggy with cigar smoke. And already the whiskey was taking effect. I was shocked to see some of the most important men of the town quite tipsy. They were all there—bankers, lawyers, judges, doctors, fire chiefs, teachers, merchants. Even one of the more fashionable pastors. Something we could not see was going on up front. A clarinet was vibrating sensuously and the men were standing up and moving eagerly forward. We were a small tight group, clustered together, our bare upper bodies touching and shining with anticipatory sweat; while up front the big shots were becoming increasingly excited over something we still could not see. Suddenly I heard the school superintendent, who had told me to come, yell, "Bring up the shines, gentlemen! Bring up the little shines!"

We were rushed up to the front of the ballroom, where it smelled even more strongly of tobacco and whiskey. Then we were pushed into place. I almost wet my pants. A sea of faces, some hostile, some amused, ringed around us, and in the center, facing us, stood a magnificent blonde—stark naked. There was dead silence. I felt a blast of cold air chill me. I tried to back away, but they were behind me and around me. Some of the boys stood with lowered heads, trembling. I felt a wave of irrational guilt and fear. My teeth chattered, my skin turned to goose flesh, my knees knocked. Yet I was strongly attracted and looked in spite of myself. Had the price of looking been blindness, I would have looked. The hair was yellow like that of a circus kewpie doll, the face heavily powdered and rouged, as though to form an abstract mask, the eyes hollow and smeared a cool blue, the color of a baboon's butt. I felt a desire to spit upon her as my eyes brushed slowly over her body. Her breasts were firm and round as the domes of East Indian temples, and I stood so close as to see the fine skin texture and beads of pearly perspiration glistening like dew around the pink and erected buds of her nipples. I wanted at one and the same time to run from the room, to sink through the floor, or go to her and cover her from my eyes and the eyes of the others with my body; to feel the soft thighs, to caress her and destroy her, to love her and murder her, to hide from her, and yet to stroke where below the small American flag tattooed upon her belly her thighs formed a capital V. I had a notion that of all in the room she saw only me with her impersonal eyes.

And then she began to dance, a slow sensuous movement; the smoke of a hundred cigars clinging to her like the thinnest of veils. She seemed like a fair bird-girl girdled in veils calling to me from the angry surface of some gray and threatening sea. I was transported. Then I became aware of the clarinet playing and the big shots yelling at us. Some threatened us if we looked and others if we did not. On my right I saw one boy faint. And now a man grabbed a silver pitcher from a table and stepped close as he dashed ice water upon him and stood him up and forced two of us to support him as his head hung and moans issued from his thick bluish lips. Another boy began to plead to go home. He was the largest of the group, wearing dark red fighting trunks much too small to conceal the erection which projected from him as though in answer to the insinuating low-registered moaning of the clarinet. He tried to hide himself with his boxing gloves.

And all the while the blonde continued dancing, smiling faintly at the big shots who watched her with fascination, and faintly smiling at our fear. I noticed a certain merchant who followed her hungrily, his lips loose and drooling. He was a large man who wore diamond studs in a shirtfront which swelled with the ample paunch underneath, and each time the blonde swayed her undulating hips he ran his hand through the thin hair of his bald head and, with his arms upheld, his posture clumsy like that of an intoxicated panda, wound his belly in a slow and obscene grind. This creature was completely hypnotized. The music had quickened. As the dancer flung herself about with a detached expression on her face, the men began reaching out to touch her. I could see their beefy fingers sink into the soft flesh. Some of the others tried to stop them as she began to move around the floor in graceful circles, as they gave chase, slipping and sliding over the polished floor. It was mad. Chairs went crashing, drinks were spilt, as they ran laughing and howling after her. They caught her just as she reached a door, raised her from the floor, and tossed her as college boys are tossed at a hazing, and above her red, fixed-smiling lips I saw the terror and disgust in her eyes, almost like my own terror and that which I saw in some of the other boys. As I watched, they tossed her twice and her soft breasts seemed to flatten against the air and her legs flung wildly as she spun. Some of the more sober ones helped her to escape. And I started off the floor, heading for the anteroom with the rest of the boys.

Some were still crying in hysteria. But as we tried to leave we were stopped and ordered to get into the ring. There was nothing to do but what we were told. All ten of us climbed under the ropes and allowed ourselves to be blindfolded with broad bands of white cloth. One of the men seemed to feel a bit sympathetic and tried to cheer us up as we stood with our backs against the ropes. Some of us tried to grin. "See that boy over there?" one of the men said. "I want you to run across at the bell and give it to him right in the belly. If you don't get him, I'm going to get you. I don't like his looks." Each of us was told the same. The blindfolds were put on. Yet even then I had been going over my speech. In my mind each word was as bright as flame. I felt the cloth pressed into place, and frowned so that it would be loosened when I relaxed.

But now I felt a sudden fit of blind terror. I was unused to darkness. It was as though I had suddenly found myself in a dark room filled with poisonous cottonmouths. I could hear the bleary voices yelling insistently for the battle royal to begin.

"Get going in there!"

10

"Let me at that big nigger!"

I strained to pick up the school superintendent's voice, as though to squeeze some security out of that slightly more familiar sound.

"Let me at those black sonsabitches!" someone yelled.   15

"No, Jackson, no!" another voice yelled. "Here, somebody, help me hold Jack."

"I want to get at that ginger-colored nigger. Tear him limb from limb," the first voice yelled.

I stood against the ropes trembling. For in those days I was what they called ginger-colored, and he sounded as though he might crunch me between his teeth like a crisp ginger cookie.

Quite a struggle was going on. Chairs were being kicked about and I could hear voices grunting as with a terrific effort. I wanted to see, to see more desperately than ever before. But the blindfold was tight as a thick skin-puckering scab and when I raised my gloved hands to push the layers of white aside a voice yelled, "Oh, no you don't, black bastard! Leave that alone!"

"Ring the bell before Jackson kills him a coon!" someone boomed in the   20 sudden silence. And I heard the bell clang and the sound of the feet scuffling forward.

A glove smacked against my head. I pivoted, striking out stiffly as someone went past, and felt the jar ripple along the length of my arm to my shoulder. Then it seemed as though all nine of the boys had turned upon me at once. Blows pounded me from all sides while I struck out as best I could. So many blows landed upon me that I wondered if I were not the only blindfolded fighter in the ring, or if the man called Jackson hadn't succeeded in getting me after all.

Blindfolded, I could no longer control my motions. I had no dignity. I stumbled about like a baby or a drunken man. The smoke had become thicker and with each new blow it seemed to sear and further restrict my lungs. My saliva became like hot bitter glue. A glove connected with my head, filling my mouth with warm blood. It was everywhere. I could not tell if the moisture I felt upon my body was sweat or blood. A blow landed hard against the nape of my neck. I felt myself going over, my head hitting the floor. Streaks of blue light filled the black world behind the blindfold. I lay prone, pretending that I was knocked out, but felt myself seized by hands and yanked to my feet. "Get going, black boy! Mix it up!" My arms were like lead, my head smarting from blows. I managed to feel my way to the ropes and held on, trying to catch my breath. A glove landed in my mid-section and I went over again, feeling as though the smoke had become a knife jabbed into my guts. Pushed this way and that by the legs milling around me, I finally pulled erect and discovered that I could see the black, sweat-washed forms weaving in the smoky-blue atmosphere like drunken dancers weaving to the rapid drumlike thuds of blows.

Everyone fought hysterically. It was complete anarchy. Everybody fought everybody else. No group fought together for long. Two, three, four, fought one, then turned to fight each other, were themselves attacked. Blows landed below the belt and in the kidney, with the gloves open as well as closed, and with my eye partly opened now there was not so much terror. I moved carefully, avoiding blows, although not too many to attract attention, fighting from group to group. The boys groped about like blind, cautious crabs crouching to protect their mid-sections, their heads pulled in short against their shoulders, their arms stretched nervously before them, with their fists testing the smoke-filled air like the knobbed feelers of hypersensitive snails. In one corner I glimpsed a boy violently punching the air and heard him scream in pain as he smashed his hand against a ring post. For a second I saw him bent over holding his hand, then going down as a blow caught his unprotected head. I played one group against the other, slipping in and throwing a punch then stepping out of range while pushing the others into the melee to take the blows blindly aimed at me. The smoke was agonizing and there were no rounds, no bells at three minute intervals to relieve our exhaustion. The room spun round me, a swirl of lights, smoke, sweating bodies surrounded by tense white faces. I bled from both nose and mouth, the blood spattering upon my chest.

The men kept yelling, "Slug him, black boy! Knock his guts out!"

"Uppercut him! Kill him! Kill that big boy!"   25

Taking a fake fall, I saw a boy going down heavily beside me as though we were felled by a single blow, saw a sneaker-clad foot shoot into his groin as the two who had knocked him down stumbled upon him. I rolled out of range, feeling a twinge of nausea.

The harder we fought the more threatening the men became. And yet, I had begun to worry about my speech again. How would it go? Would they recognize my ability? What would they give me?

I was fighting automatically when suddenly I noticed that one after another of the boys was leaving the ring. I was surprised, filled with panic, as though I had been left alone with an unknown danger. Then I understood. The boys had arranged it among themselves. It was the custom for the two men left in the ring to slug it out for the winner's prize. I discovered this too late. When the bell sounded two men in tuxedoes leaped into the ring and removed the blindfold. I found myself facing Tatlock, the biggest of the gang. I felt sick at my stomach. Hardly had the bell stopped ringing in my ears than it clanged again and I saw him moving swiftly toward me. Thinking of nothing else to do I hit him smash on the nose. He kept coming, bringing the rank sharp violence of stale sweat. His face was a black blank of a face, only his eyes alive—with hate of me and aglow with a feverish terror from what had happened to us all. I became anxious. I wanted to deliver my speech and he came at me as though he meant to beat it out of me. I smashed him again and again, taking his blows as they came. Then on a sudden impulse I struck him lightly and as we clinched, I whispered, "Fake like I knocked you out, you can have the prize."

"I'll break your behind," he whispered hoarsely.

"For *them?*"   30

"For *me,* sonofabitch!"

They were yelling for us to break it up and Tatlock spun me half around with a blow, and as a joggled camera sweeps in a reeling scene, I saw the howling red faces crouching tense beneath the cloud of blue-gray smoke. For a moment the world wavered, unraveled, flowed, then my head cleared and Tatlock bounced before me. That fluttering shadow before my eyes was his jabbing left hand. Then falling forward, my head against his damp shoulder, I whispered,

"I'll make it five dollars more."

"Go to hell!"

But his muscles relaxed a trifle beneath my pressure and I breathed, 35 "Seven?"

"Give it to your ma," he said, ripping me beneath the heart.

And while I still held him I butted him and moved away. I felt myself bombarded with punches. I fought back with hopeless desperation. I wanted to deliver my speech more than anything else in the world, because I felt that only these men could judge truly my ability, and now this stupid clown was ruining my chances. I began fighting carefully now, moving in to punch him and out again with my greater speed. A lucky blow to his chin and I had him going too — until I heard a loud voice yell, "I got my money on the big boy."

Hearing this, I almost dropped my guard. I was confused: Should I try to win against the voice out there? Would not this go against my speech, and was not this a moment for humility, for nonresistance? A blow to my head as I danced about sent my right eye popping like a jack-in-the-box and settled my dilemma. The room went red as I fell. It was a dream fall, my body languid and fastidious as to where to land, until the floor became impatient and smashed up to meet me. A moment later I came to. An hypnotic voice said FIVE emphatically. And I lay there, hazily watching a dark red spot of my own blood shaping itself into a butterfly, glistening and soaking into the soiled gray world of the canvas.

When the voice drawled TEN I was lifted up and dragged to a chair. I sat dazed. My eye pained and swelled with each throb of my pounding heart and I wondered if now I would be allowed to speak. I was wringing wet, my mouth still bleeding. We were grouped along the wall now. The other boys ignored me as they congratulated Tatlock and speculated as to how much they would be paid. One boy whimpered over his smashed hand. Looking up front, I saw attendants in white jackets rolling the portable ring away and placing a small square rug in the vacant space surrounded by chairs. Perhaps, I thought, I will stand on the rug to deliver my speech.

Then the M.C. called to us, "Come on up here boys and get your money." 40 We ran forward to where the men laughed and talked in their chairs, waiting. Everyone seemed friendly now.

"There it is on the rug," the man said. I saw the rug covered with coins of all dimensions and a few crumpled bills. But what excited me, scattered here and there, were the gold pieces.

"Boys, it's all yours," the man said. "You get all you grab."

"That's right, Sambo," a blond man said, winking at me confidentially.

I trembled with excitement, forgetting my pain. I would get the gold and the bills, I thought. I would use both hands. I would throw my body against the boys nearest me to block them from the gold.

"Get down around the rug now," the man commanded, "and don't anyone 45 touch it until I give the signal."

"This ought to be good," I heard.

As told, we got around the square rug on our knees. Slowly the man raised his freckled hand as we followed it upward with our eyes.

I heard, "These niggers look like they're about to pray!"

Then, "Ready," the man said. "Go!"

I lunged for a yellow coin lying on the blue design of the carpet, touching 50 it and sending a surprised shriek to join those rising around me. I tried frantically to remove my hand but could not let go. A hot, violent force tore through my body, shaking me like a wet rat. The rug was electrified. The hair bristled up on my head as I shook myself free. My muscles jumped, my nerves jangled, writhed. But I saw that this was not stopping the other boys. Laughing in fear and embarrassment, some were holding back and scooping up the coins knocked off by the painful contortions of the others. The men roared above us as we struggled.

"Pick it up, goddamnit, pick it up!" someone called like a bass-voiced parrot. "Go on, get it!"

I crawled rapidly around the floor, picking up the coins, trying to avoid the coppers and to get greenbacks and the gold. Ignoring the shock by laughing, as I brushed the coins off quickly, I discovered that I could contain the electricity — a contradiction, but it works. Then the men began to push us onto the rug. Laughing embarrassedly, we struggled out of their hands and kept after the coins. We were all wet and slippery and hard to hold. Suddenly I saw a boy lifted into the air, glistening with sweat like a circus seal, and dropped, his wet back landing flush upon the charged rug, heard him yell and saw him literally dance upon his back, his elbows beating a frenzied tattoo upon the floor, his muscles twitching like the flesh of a horse stung by many flies. When he finally rolled off, his face was gray and no one stopped him when he ran from the floor amid booming laughter.

"Get the money," the M.C. called. "That's good hard American cash!"

And we snatched and grabbed, snatched and grabbed. I was careful not to come too close to the rug now, and when I felt the hot whiskey breath descend upon me like a cloud of foul air I reached out and grabbed the leg of a chair. It was occupied and I held on desperately.

"Leggo, nigger! Leggo!"

The huge face wavered down to mine as he tried to push me free. But my body was slippery and he was too drunk. It was Mr. Colcord, who owned a chain of movie houses and "entertainment palaces." Each time he grabbed me I slipped out of his hands. It became a real struggle. I feared the rug more than I did the drunk, so I held on, surprising myself for a moment by trying to topple *him* upon the rug. It was such an enormous idea that I found myself actually carrying it out. I tried not to be obvious, yet when I grabbed his leg, trying to tumble him out of the chair, he raised up roaring with laughter, and, looking at me with soberness dead in the eye, kicked me viciously in the chest. The chair leg flew out of my hand and I felt myself going and rolled. It was as though I had rolled through a bed of hot coals. It seemed a whole century would pass before I would roll free, a century in which I was seared through the deepest levels of my body to the fearful breath within me and the breath seared and heated to the point of explosion. It'll all be over in a flash, I thought as I rolled clear. It'll all be over in a flash.

But not yet, the men on the other side were waiting, red faces swollen as though from apoplexy as they bent forward in their chairs. Seeing their fingers coming toward me I rolled away as a fumbled football rolls off the receiver's fingertips, back into the coals. That time I luckily sent the rug sliding out of place and heard the coins ringing against the floor and the boys scuffling to pick them up and the M.C. calling, "All right, boys, that's all. Go get dressed and get your money."

I was limp as a dish rag. My back felt as though it had been beaten with wires.

55

When we had dressed the M.C. came in and gave us each five dollars, except Tatlock, who got ten for being last in the ring. Then he told us to leave. I was not to get a chance to deliver my speech, I thought. I was going out into the dim alley in despair when I was stopped and told to go back. I returned to the ballroom, where the men were pushing back their chairs and gathering in groups to talk.

The M.C. knocked on a table for quiet. "Gentlemen," he said, "we almost   60 forgot an important part of the program. A most serious part, gentlemen. This boy was brought here to deliver a speech which he made at his graduation yesterday . . ."

"Bravo!"

"I'm told that he is the smartest boy we've got out there in Greenwood. I'm told that he knows more big words than a pocket-sized dictionary."

Much applause and laughter.

"So now, gentlemen, I want you to give him your attention."

There was still laughter as I faced them, my mouth dry, my eye throbbing.   65 I began slowly, but evidently my throat was tense, because they began shouting, "Louder! Louder!"

"We of the younger generation extol the wisdom of that great leader and educator," I shouted, "who first spoke these flaming words of wisdom: 'A ship lost at sea for many days suddenly sighted a friendly vessel. From the mast of the unfortunate vessel was seen a signal: "Water, water; we die of thirst!" The answer from the friendly vessel came back: "Cast down your bucket where you are." The captain of the distressed vessel, at last heeding the injunction, cast down his bucket, and it came up full of fresh sparkling water from the mouth of the Amazon River.' And like him I say, and in his words, 'To those of my race who depend upon bettering their condition in a foreign land, or who underestimate the importance of cultivating friendly relations with the Southern white man, who is his next-door neighbor, I would say: "Cast down your bucket where you are" — cast it down in making friends in every manly way of the people of all races by whom we are surrounded . . .'"

I spoke automatically and with such fervor that I did not realize that the men were still talking and laughing until my dry mouth, filling up with blood from the cut, almost strangled me. I coughed, wanting to stop and go to one of the tall brass, sand-filled spittoons to relieve myself, but a few of the men, especially the superintendent, were listening and I was afraid. So I gulped it down, blood, saliva, and all, and continued. (What powers of endurance I had during those days! What enthusiasm! What a belief in the rightness of things!) I spoke even louder in spite of the pain. But still they talked and still they laughed, as though deaf with cotton in dirty ears. So I spoke with greater emotional emphasis. I closed my ears and swallowed blood until I was nauseated. The speech seemed a hundred times as long as before, but I could not leave out a single word. All had to be said, each memorized nuance considered, rendered. Nor was that all. Whenever I uttered a word of three or more syllables a group of voices would yell for me to repeat it. I used the phrase "social responsibility" and they yelled:

"What's that word you say, boy?"

"Social responsibility," I said.

"What?"   70

"Social . . ."

"Louder."

". . . responsibility."

"More!"

"Respon—"

"Repeat!"

"—sibility."

The room filled with the uproar of laughter until, no doubt, distracted by having to gulp down my blood, I made a mistake and yelled a phrase I had often seen denounced in newspaper editorials, heard debated in private.

"Social . . ."

"What?" they yelled.

". . . equality—"

The laughter hung smokelike in the sudden stillness. I opened my eyes, puzzled. Sounds of displeasure filled the room. The M.C. rushed forward. They shouted hostile phrases at me. But I did not understand.

A small dry mustached man in the front row blared out, "Say that slowly, son!"

"What, sir?"

"What you just said!"

"Social responsibility, sir," I said.

"You weren't being smart, were you, boy?" he said, not unkindly.

"No, sir!"

"You sure that about 'equality' was a mistake?"

"Oh, yes, sir," I said. "I was swallowing blood."

"Well, you had better speak more slowly so we can understand. We mean to do right by you, but you've got to know your place at all times. All right, now, go on with your speech."

I was afraid. I wanted to leave but I wanted also to speak and I was afraid they'd snatch me down.

"Thank you, sir," I said, beginning where I had left off, and having them ignore me as before.

Yet when I finished there was a thunderous applause. I was surprised to see the superintendent come forth with a package wrapped in white tissue paper, and, gesturing for quiet, address the men.

"Gentlemen, you see that I did not overpraise this boy. He makes a good speech and some day he'll lead his people in the proper paths. And I don't have to tell you that that is important in these days and times. This is a good, smart boy, and so to encourage him in the right direction, in the name of the Board of Education I wish to present him a prize in the form of this . . ."

He paused, removing the tissue paper and revealing a gleaming calfskin brief case.

". . . in the form of this first-class article from Shad Whitmore's shop."

"Boy," he said, addressing me, "take this prize and keep it well. Consider it a badge of office. Prize it. Keep developing as you are and some day it will be filled with important papers that will help shape the destiny of your people."

I was so moved that I could hardly express my thanks. A rope of bloody saliva forming a shape like an undiscovered continent drooled upon the leather and I wiped it quickly away. I felt an importance that I had never dreamed.

"Open it and see what's inside," I was told.

My fingers a-tremble, I complied, smelling the fresh leather and finding an official-looking document inside. It was a scholarship to the state college for Negroes. My eyes filled with tears and I ran awkwardly off the floor.

I was overjoyed; I did not even mind when I discovered that the gold pieces I had scrambled for were brass pocket tokens advertising a certain make of automobile.

When I reached home everyone was excited. Next day the neighbors came to congratulate me. I even felt safe from grandfather, whose deathbed curse usually spoiled my triumphs. I stood beneath his photograph with my brief case in hand and smiled triumphantly into his stolid black peasant's face. It was a face that fascinated me. The eyes seemed to follow everywhere I went.

That night I dreamed I was at a circus with him and that he refused to laugh at the clowns no matter what they did. Then later he told me to open my brief case and read what was inside and I did, finding an official envelope stamped with the state seal; and inside the envelope I found another and another, endlessly, and I thought I would fall of weariness. "Them's years," he said. "Now open that one." And I did and in it I found an engraved document containing a short message in letters of gold. "Read it," my grandfather said. "Out loud!"

"To Whom It May Concern," I intoned. "Keep This Nigger-Boy Running." 105 I awoke with the old man's laughter ringing in my ears.

(It was a dream I was to remember and dream again for many years after. But at that time I had no insight into its meaning. First I had to attend college.)

Considerations for Critical Thinking and Writing

1. **FIRST RESPONSE.** Discuss how the protagonist's expectations are similar to what has come to be known as the American dream — the assumption that ambition, hard work, perseverance, intelligence, and virtue always lead to success. Do you believe in the American dream?

2. How does the first paragraph of the story sum up the conflict that the narrator confronts? In what sense is he "invisible"?

3. Why do his grandfather's last words cause so much anxiety in the family? What does his grandfather mean when he says, "I want you to overcome 'em with yeses, undermine 'em with grins, agree 'em to death" (para. 2)?

4. What is the symbolic significance of the naked blonde? What details reveal that she represents more than a sexual tease in the story?

5. How does the battle in the boxing ring and the scramble for money afterward suggest the kind of control whites have over blacks in the story?

6. Why is it significant that the town is named Greenwood and that the briefcase award comes from Shad Whitmore's shop? Can you find any other details that serve to reinforce the meaning of the story?

7. What is the narrator's perspective as an educated adult telling the story, in contrast to his assumptions and beliefs as a recent high school graduate? How is this contrast especially evident in the speech before the "leading white citizens" of the town?

8. How can the dream at the end of the story be related to the major incidents that precede it?

9. Given the grandfather's advice, explain how "meekness" can be a "dangerous activity" and a weapon against oppression.

10. Imagine the story as told from a third-person point of view. How would this change the story? Do you think the story would be more or less effective told from a third-person point of view? Explain your answer.

11. CRITICAL STRATEGIES. Read the section on mythological criticism (pp. 2058–60) in Chapter 53, "Critical Strategies for Reading," and "What Is an Initiation Story?" by Mordecai Marcus (following). Discuss "Battle Royal" as an archetypal initiation story.

CONNECTIONS TO OTHER SELECTIONS

1. Compare and contrast Ellison's view of the South with William Faulkner's in "A Rose for Emily" (p. 91).

2. Compare and contrast this story with M. Carl Holman's poem "Mr. Z" (p. 1254).

Perspective

MORDECAI MARCUS (B. 1925)

What Is an Initiation Story?

1960

An initiation story may be said to show its young protagonist experiencing a significant change of knowledge about the world or himself, or a change of character, or of both, and this change must point or lead him toward an adult world. It may or may not contain some form of ritual, but it should give some evidence that the change is at least likely to have permanent effects.

Initiation stories obviously center on a variety of experiences and the initiations vary in effect. It will be useful, therefore, to divide initiations into types according to their power and effect. First, some initiations lead only to the threshold of maturity and understanding but do not definitely cross it. Such stories emphasize the shocking effect of experience, and their protagonists tend to be distinctly young. Second, some initiations take their protagonists across a threshold of maturity and understanding but leave them enmeshed in a struggle for certainty. These initiations sometimes involve self-discovery. Third, the most decisive initiations carry their protagonists firmly into maturity and understanding, or at least show them decisively embarked toward maturity. These initiations usually center on self-discovery. For convenience, I will call these types tentative, uncompleted, and decisive initiations.

From "What Is an Initiation Story?" in *The Journal of Aesthetics and Art Criticism*

CONSIDERATIONS FOR CRITICAL THINKING AND WRITING

1. For a work to be classified as an initiation story, why should it "give some evidence that the change [in the protagonist] is at least likely to have permanent effects"?

2. Marcus divides initiations into three broad types: tentative, uncompleted, and decisive. Explain how you would categorize the initiation in Ellison's "Battle Royal."

A SAMPLE CLOSE READING

An Annotated Section of "Battle Royal"

Even as you read a story for the first time, you can highlight passages, circle or underline words, and write responses in the margins. Subsequent readings will yield more insights once you begin to understand how various elements such as plot, character, and wording build toward the conclusion and what you perceive to be the story's central ideas. The following annotations for paragraphs 3–6 of "Battle Royal" provide a perspective written by someone who had read the work several times.

RALPH ELLISON (1914–1994)

Battle Royal   1947

. . . On my graduation day I delivered an oration in which I showed that humility was the secret, indeed, the very essence of progress. (Not that I believed this—how could I, remembering my grandfather?—I only believed that it worked.) It was a great success. Everyone praised me and I was invited to give the speech at a gathering of the town's leading white citizens. It was a triumph for our whole community.

It was in the main ballroom of the leading hotel. When I got there I discovered that it was on the occasion of a smoker, and I was told that since I was to be there anyway I might as well take part in the battle royal to be fought by some of my schoolmates as part of the entertainment. The battle royal came first.

All of the town's big shots were there in their tuxedoes, wolfing down the buffet foods, drinking beer and whiskey and smoking black cigars. It was a large room with a high ceiling. Chairs were arranged in neat rows around three sides of a portable boxing ring. The fourth side was clear, revealing a gleaming space of polished floor. I had some misgivings over the battle royal, by the way. Not from a distaste for fighting, but because I didn't care too much for the other fellows who were to take part. They were tough guys who seemed to have no grandfather's curse worrying their minds. No one could

> On his "graduation day," the narrator is about to be initiated into a world of racial degradations that will make him an "invisible man."

> The narrator's "humility" is a pragmatic strategy to achieve success in a white world and connects him to his grandfather's subversive advice "to overcome 'em with yeses."

> The "leading" whites in the "leading" hotel represent the respectable pillars of the community, but they are only leading the blacks to a battle with each other rather than to some kind of recognition and "triumph."

> The town's leaders are described as "wolfing" down their food, an appropriate image for their predatory relationship to the boys.

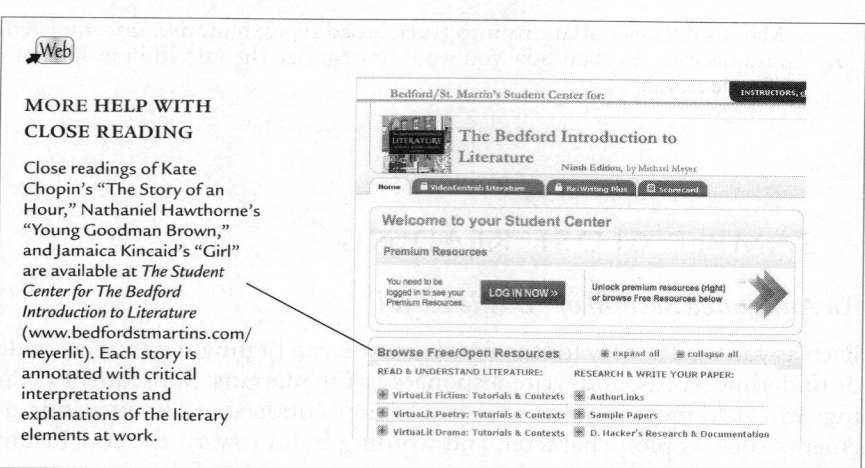

**MORE HELP WITH
CLOSE READING**

Close readings of Kate Chopin's "The Story of an Hour," Nathaniel Hawthorne's "Young Goodman Brown," and Jamaica Kincaid's "Girl" are available at *The Student Center for The Bedford Introduction to Literature* (www.bedfordstmartins.com/meyerlit). Each story is annotated with critical interpretations and explanations of the literary elements at work.

The narrator's "dignity" exists in his own mind but not in the minds of the whites or his fellow fighters.

The advice that the narrator quotes from Washington, a symbol of racial accommodation, in his speech (para. 66) is undercut by the battle royal to come.

mistake their toughness. And besides, I suspected that fighting a battle royal might detract from the dignity of my speech. In those pre-invisible days I visualized myself as a potential Booker T. Washington. But the other fellows didn't care too much for me either, and there were nine of them. I felt superior to them in my way, and I didn't like the manner in which we were all crowded together into the servants' elevator. Nor did they like my being there. In fact, as the warmly lighted floors flashed past the elevator we had words over the fact that I, by taking part in the fight, had knocked one of their friends out of a night's work.

We were led out of the elevator through a rococo hall into an anteroom and told to get into our fighting togs. Each of us was issued a pair of boxing gloves and ushered out into the big mirrored hall, which we entered looking cautiously about us and whispering, lest we might accidentally be heard above the noise of the room. It was foggy with cigar smoke. And already the whiskey was taking effect. I was shocked to see some of the most important men of the town quite tipsy. They were all there — bankers, lawyers, judges, doctors, fire chiefs, teachers, merchants. Even one of the more fashionable pastors. Something we could not see was going on up front. A clarinet was vibrating sensuously and the men were standing up and moving eagerly forward. We were a small tight group, clustered together, our bare upper bodies touching and shining with anticipatory sweat; while up front the big shots were becoming increasingly excited over something we still could not see. Suddenly I heard the school superintendent, who had told me to come, yell, "Bring up the shines, gentlemen! Bring up the little shines!"

The narrator's innocence is demonstrated by his shocked response to seeing "the most important men of the town," including a pastor, at the smoker.

The school superintendent not only participates but appears to be in charge of the smoker. His yelling "Bring up the shines" is filled with unintended irony.

A SAMPLE STUDENT RESPONSE

Katz 1

Lila Katz

Professor West

English 200

February 2, 2010

Symbolism in Ellison's "Battle Royal"

In Ralph Ellison's story "Battle Royal," a young African American man, proud of his achievements, is asked to read his high school graduation speech to the "town's big shots" (278). The event, which the narrator initially looks forward to as "a triumph for our whole community" (278), turns out to be a spectacle of ridicule and abuse. He and other young black men are degraded and forced to fight gladiator-style—all for the amusement of drunken white men. This experience, as horrible as it is, allows the main character to better understand the world and the place he is expected to occupy in it. The story can be considered a coming-of-age or initiation story, in which the main character experiences change. Ellison's character is taken "across a threshold of maturity and understanding" yet is still "enmeshed in a struggle for certainty" (Marcus 288). And through the story's powerful symbolism, the reader can better understand that struggle.

The battle itself can be read as a representation of the society in which the narrator lives—in which nothing makes sense, in which whites hold the power, and in which blacks must struggle against racism and violence. In this battle, part of the narrator's initiation into society, the young black men are stripped of power, blindfolded, and turned against each other. The lead-up to the battle, the dance of the naked white woman branded with an American flag tattoo, is symbolic, too. Read as a representation of America, she is what the young black men cannot have. In the aftermath of the battle, when it is time for the men to finally be paid, they are forced to crawl on the floor and grapple not for money but for worthless tokens. Ellison offers these symbols to define the inequalities of race and class that the African Americans endure in the story. . . .

Katz 4

Works Cited

Ellison, Ralph. "Battle Royal." *The Bedford Introduction to Literature.* Ed.
      Michael Meyer. 9th ed. Boston: Bedford/St. Martin's, 2011. 277–87. Print.

Marcus, Mordecai. "What Is an Initiation Story?" *The Bedford Introduction to*
      Literature. Ed. Michael Meyer. 9th ed. Boston: Bedford/St. Martin's,
      2011. 288. Print.

MICHAEL OPPENHEIMER (B. 1943)

Born in Berkeley, California, Michael Oppenheimer grew up on a cattle ranch
in the Rocky Mountains of southwest Colorado. He graduated from Antioch
College and earned a master of arts in English and art at Lone Mountain
College/University of San Francisco. Oppenheimer has published short stories
and worked as a reporter, teacher, and publisher of a press; he currently lives in
Bellingham, Washington, where he creates kinetic environmental art.

The Paring Knife   1982

I found a knife under the refrigerator while the woman I love and I were cleaning our house. It was a small paring knife that we lost many years before and
had since forgotten about. I showed the knife to the woman I love and she said,
"Oh. Where did you find it?" After I told her, she put the knife on the table and
then went into the next room and continued to clean. While I cleaned the
kitchen floor, I remembered something that happened four years before that
explained how the knife had gotten under the refrigerator.

We had eaten a large dinner and had drunk many glasses of wine. We
turned all the lights out, took our clothing off, and went to bed. We thought
we would make love, but something happened and we had an argument while
making love. We had never experienced such a thing. We both became extremely angry. I said some very hurtful things to the woman I love. She kicked
at me in bed and I got out and went into the kitchen. I fumbled for a chair and
sat down. I wanted to rest my arms on the table and then rest my head in my
arms, but I felt the dirty dishes on the table and they were in the way. I became
incensed. I swept everything that was on the table onto the floor. The noise
was tremendous, but then the room was very quiet and I suddenly felt sad. I
thought I had destroyed everything. I began to cry. The woman I love came

into the kitchen and asked if I was all right. I said, "Yes." She turned the light on and we looked at the kitchen floor. Nothing much was broken, but the floor was very messy. We both laughed and then went back to bed and made love. The next morning we cleaned up the mess, but obviously overlooked the knife.

I was about to ask the woman I love if she remembered that incident when she came in from the next room and without saying a word, picked up the knife from the table and slid it back under the refrigerator.

CONSIDERATIONS FOR CRITICAL THINKING AND WRITING

1. **FIRST RESPONSE.** Why do you think the woman slides the knife back under the refrigerator at the end of the story?
2. Consider whether the knife is used as a conventional symbol or as a literary symbol in the story.
3. Discuss the significance of the title.
4. How does the flashback in the second paragraph provide the necessary exposition to create the elements of a complex plot?
5. **CREATIVE RESPONSE.** Rewrite the second paragraph without revising the first and third paragraphs so that the woman's motivation for sliding the knife under the refrigerator must be read in a very different way than you read it now.

CONNECTIONS TO OTHER SELECTIONS

1. Compare the narrator's emotions at the end of this story and in Colette's "The Hand" (p. 274).
2. Explain how symbolism is central to understanding the resolution of the conflicts in "The Paring Knife" and in Raymond Carver's "Popular Mechanics" (p. 334).

8

Theme

To produce a mighty book, you must choose a mighty theme.
— HERMAN MELVILLE,
from *Moby-Dick*, 1851

Theme is the central idea or meaning of a story. It provides a unifying point around which the plot, characters, setting, point of view, symbols, and other elements of a story are organized. In some works the theme is explicitly stated. Nathaniel Hawthorne's "Wakefield," for example, begins with the author telling the reader that the point of his story is "done up neatly, and condensed into the final sentence." Most modern writers, however, present their themes implicitly (as Hawthorne does in the majority of his stories), so determining the underlying meaning of a work often requires more effort than it does from the reader of "Wakefield." One reason for the difficulty is that the theme is fused into the elements of the story, and these must be carefully examined in relation to one another as well as to the work as a whole. But then that's the value of determining the theme, for it requires a close analysis of all the elements of a work. Such a close reading often results in sharper insights into this overlooked character or that seemingly unrelated incident. Accounting for the details and seeing how they fit together result in greater understanding of the story. Such familiarity creates pleasure in much the same way that a musical piece heard more than once becomes a rich experience rather than simply a repetitive one.

Themes are not always easy to express, but some principles can aid you in articulating the central meaning of a work. First distinguish between the theme of a story and its subject. They are not equivalents. Many stories share identical subjects, such as fate, death, innocence, youth, loneliness, racial prejudice, and disillusionment. Yet each story usually makes its own statement about the subject and expresses some view of life. Hemingway's "Soldier's Home" (p. 187) and Faulkner's "Barn Burning" (p. 503) both describe young men who are unhappy at home and decide that they must leave, but the meaning of each story is quite different. A thematic generalization about "Soldier's Home" could be something like this: "The brutal experience of war can alienate a person from those — even family and friends — who are innocent of war's reality." The theme of Faulkner's story could be stated this way: "No matter how much one might love one's father, there comes a time when family loyalties must be left behind in order to be true to one's self."

Web Explore the literary element in this chapter at bedfordstmartins.com/meyerlit.

These two statements of theme do not definitively sum up each story — there is no single, absolute way of expressing a work's theme — but they do describe a central idea in each. Furthermore, the emphasis in each of these themes could be modified or expanded because interpretations of interesting, complex works are always subject to revision. People have different responses to life, and so it is hardly surprising that responses to literature are not identical. When theme is considered, the possibilities for meaning are usually expanded and not reduced to categories such as "right" or "wrong."

Although readers may differ in their interpretations of a story, that does not mean that *any* interpretation is valid. If we were to assert that the soldier's dissatisfactions in Hemingway's story could be readily eliminated by his settling down to marriage and a decent job (his mother's solution), we would have missed Hemingway's purposes in writing the story; we would have failed to see how Krebs's war experiences have caused him to reexamine the assumptions and beliefs that previously nurtured him but now seem unreal to him. We would have to ignore much in the story in order to arrive at such a reading. To be valid, the statement of the theme should be responsive to the details of the story. It must be based on evidence within the story rather than solely on experiences, attitudes, or values the reader brings to the work — such as personally knowing a war veteran who successfully adjusted to civilian life after getting a good job and marrying. Familiarity with the subject matter of a story can certainly be an aid to interpretation, but it should not get in the way of seeing the author's perspective.

Sometimes readers too hastily conclude that a story's theme always consists of a moral, some kind of lesson that is dramatized by the various elements of the work. There are stories that do this—Hawthorne's "Wakefield," for example. Here are the final sentences in his story about a middle-aged man who drops out of life for twenty years:

> He has left us much food for thought, a portion of which shall lend its wisdom to a moral, and be shaped into a figure. Amid the seeming confusion of our mysterious world, individuals are so nicely adjusted to a system, and systems to one another and to a whole, that, by stepping aside for a moment, a man exposes himself to a fearful risk of losing his place forever. Like Wakefield, he may become, as it were, the Outcast of the Universe.

Most stories, however, do not include such direct caveats about the conduct of life. A tendency to look for a lesson in a story can produce a reductive and inaccurate formulation of its theme. Consider the damage done to Colette's "The Hand" (p. 274) if its theme is described as this: "Adolescents are too young to cope with the responsibilities of marriage." Colette's focus in this story is on the young woman's response to her husband's powerful sexuality and dominance rather than on her inability to be a good wife.

In fact, a good many stories go beyond traditional moral values to explore human behavior instead of condemning or endorsing it. Chekhov's treatment of the adulterous affair between Gurov and Anna in "The Lady with the Pet Dog" (p. 223) portrays a love that is valuable and true despite the conventional moral codes it violates. That is not to say that the reader must agree with Chekhov's attitude that such love has a validity of its own. We are obligated to see that Chekhov is sympathetic to the lovers but not necessarily obligated to approve of their actions. All that is required is our willingness to explore with the author the issues set before us. The themes we encounter in literature may challenge as well as reassure us.

Determining the theme of a story can be a difficult task because all the story's elements may contribute to its central idea. Indeed, you may discover that finding the theme is more challenging than coming to grips with the author's values as they are revealed in the story. There is no precise formula that can take you to the center of a story's meaning and help you to articulate it. However, several strategies are practical and useful once you have read the story. Apply these pointers during a second or third reading:

1. Pay attention to the title of the story. It often provides a lead to a major symbol (Faulkner's "Barn Burning," p. 503) or to the subject around which the theme develops (Godwin's "A Sorrowful Woman," p. 39).
2. Look for details in the story that have potential for symbolic meanings. Careful consideration of names, places, objects, minor characters, and incidents can lead you to the central meaning—for example, think of the stripper in Ellison's "Battle Royal" (p. 277). Be especially attentive to elements you did not understand on the first reading.
3. Decide whether the protagonist changes or develops some important insight as a result of the action. Carefully examine any generalizations the protagonist or narrator makes about the events in the story.

4. When you formulate the theme of the story in your own words, write it down in one or two complete sentences that make some point about the subject matter. Revenge may be the subject of a story, but its theme should make a statement about revenge: "Instead of providing satisfaction, revenge defeats the best in one's self" is one possibility.

5. Be certain that your expression of the theme is a generalized statement rather than a specific description of particular people, places, and incidents in the story. Contrast the preceding statement of a theme on revenge with this too-specific one: "In Nathaniel Hawthorne's *The Scarlet Letter,* Roger Chillingworth loses his humanity owing to his single-minded attempts to punish Arthur Dimmesdale for fathering a child with Chillingworth's wife, Hester." Hawthorne's theme is not restricted to a single fictional character named Chillingworth but to anyone whose life is ruined by revenge. Be certain that your statement of theme does not focus on only part of the story. The theme just cited for *The Scarlet Letter,* for example, relegates Hester to the status of a minor character. What it says about Chillingworth is true, but the statement is incomplete as a generalization about the novel.

6. Be wary of using clichés as a way of stating theme. They tend to short-circuit ideas instead of generating them. It may be tempting to resort to something like "Love conquers all" as a statement of the theme of Chekhov's "The Lady with the Pet Dog"; however, even the slightest second thought reveals how much more ambiguous the ending of that story is.

7. Be aware that some stories emphasize theme less than others. Stories that have as their major purpose adventure, humor, mystery, or terror may have little or no theme. In Edgar Allan Poe's "The Pit and the Pendulum," for example, the protagonist is not used to condemn torture; instead, he becomes a sensitive gauge to measure the pain and horror he endures at the hands of his captors.

What is most valuable about articulating the theme of a work is the process by which the theme is determined. Ultimately, the theme is expressed by the story itself and is inseparable from the experience of reading the story. Tim O'Brien's explanation of "How to Tell a True War Story" (p. 346) is probably true of most kinds of stories: "In a true war story, if there's a moral [or theme] at all, it's like the thread that makes the cloth. You can't tease it out. You can't extract the meaning without unraveling the deeper meaning." Describing the theme should not be a way to consume a story, to be done with it. It is a means of clarifying our thinking about what we've read and probably felt intuitively.

Stephen Crane's "The Bride Comes to Yellow Sky," Katherine Mansfield's "Miss Brill," Dagoberto Gilb's "Love in L.A.," and Daly Walker's "I Am the Grass" are four stories whose respective themes emerge from the authors' skillful use of plot, character, setting, and symbol.

STEPHEN CRANE (1871–1900)

Born in Newark, New Jersey, Stephen Crane attended Lafayette College and Syracuse University and then worked as a free-lance journalist in New York City. He wrote newspaper pieces, short stories, poems, and novels for his entire, brief adult life. His first book, *Maggie: A Girl of the Streets* (1893), is a story about New York slum life and prostitution. His most famous novel, *The Red Badge of Courage* (1895), gives readers a vivid, convincing re-creation of Civil War battles, even though Crane had never been to war. However, Crane was personally familiar with the American West, where he

© Bettmann/CORBIS.

traveled as a reporter. "The Bride Comes to Yellow Sky" includes some of the ingredients of a typical popular western—a confrontation between a marshal and a drunk who shoots up the town—but the story's theme is less predictable and more serious than the plot seems to suggest.

The Bride Comes to Yellow Sky　　　　　　　　　　*1898*

I

The great Pullman was whirling onward with such dignity of motion that a glance from the window seemed simply to prove that the plains of Texas were pouring eastward. Vast flats of green grass, dull-hued spaces of mesquit and cactus, little groups of frame houses, woods of light and tender trees, all were sweeping into the east, sweeping over the horizon, a precipice.

A newly married pair had boarded this coach at San Antonio. The man's face was reddened from many days in the wind and sun, and a direct result of his new black clothes was that his brick-colored hands were constantly performing in a most conscious fashion. From time to time he looked down respectfully at his attire. He sat with a hand on each knee, like a man waiting in a barber's shop. The glances he devoted to other passengers were furtive and shy.

The bride was not pretty, nor was she very young. She wore a dress of blue cashmere, with small reservations of velvet here and there, and with steel buttons abounding. She continually twisted her head to regard her puff sleeves, very stiff, straight, and high. They embarrassed her. It was quite apparent that she had cooked, and that she expected to cook, dutifully. The blushes caused by the careless scrutiny of some passengers as she had entered the car were strange to see upon this plain, under-class countenance, which was drawn in placid, almost emotionless lines.

They were evidently very happy. "Ever been in a parlor-car before?" he asked, smiling with delight.

"No," she answered; "I never was. It's fine, ain't it?"

5

"Great! And then after a while we'll go forward to the diner, and get a big lay-out. Finest meal in the world. Charge a dollar."

"Oh, do they?" cried the bride. "Charge a dollar? Why, that's too much — for us — ain't it, Jack?"

"Not this trip, anyhow," he answered bravely. "We're going to go the whole thing."

Later he explained to her about the trains. "You see, it's a thousand miles from one end of Texas to the other; and this train runs right across it, and never stops but four times." He had the pride of an owner. He pointed out to her the dazzling fittings of the coach; and in truth her eyes opened wider as she contemplated the sea-green figured velvet, the shining brass, silver, and glass, the wood that gleamed as darkly brilliant as the surface of a pool of oil. At one end a bronze figure sturdily held a support for a separated chamber, and at convenient places on the ceiling were frescoes in olive and silver.

To the minds of the pair, their surroundings reflected the glory of their   10 marriage that morning in San Antonio; this was the environment of their new estate; and the man's face in particular beamed with an elation that made him appear ridiculous to the negro porter. This individual at times surveyed them from afar with an amused and superior grin. On other occasions he bullied them with skill in ways that did not make it exactly plain to them that they were being bullied. He subtly used all the manners of the most unconquerable kind of snobbery. He oppressed them; but of this oppression they had small knowledge, and they speedily forgot that infrequently a number of travelers covered them with stares of derisive enjoyment. Historically there was supposed to be something infinitely humorous in their situation.

"We are due in Yellow Sky at 3:42," he said, looking tenderly into her eyes.

"Oh, are we?" she said, as if she had not been aware of it. To evince surprise at her husband's statement was part of her wifely amiability. She took from a pocket a little silver watch; and as she held it before her, and stared at it with a frown of attention, the new husband's face shone.

"I bought it in San Anton' from a friend of mine," he told her gleefully.

"It's seventeen minutes past twelve," she said, looking up at him with a kind of shy and clumsy coquetry. A passenger, noting this play, grew excessively sardonic, and winked at himself in one of the numerous mirrors.

At last they went to the dining-car. Two rows of negro waiters, in glowing   15 white suits, surveyed their entrance with the interest, and also the equanimity, of men who had been forewarned. The pair fell to the lot of a waiter who happened to feel pleasure in steering them through their meal. He viewed them with the manner of a fatherly pilot, his countenance radiant with benevolence. The patronage, entwined with the ordinary deference, was not plain to them. And yet, as they returned to their coach, they showed in their faces a sense of escape.

To the left, miles down a long purple slope, was a little ribbon of mist where moved the keening Rio Grande. The train was approaching it at an angle, and the apex was Yellow Sky. Presently it was apparent that, as the distance from Yellow Sky grew shorter, the husband became commensurately restless. His brick-red hands were more insistent in their prominence. Occasionally he was even rather absent-minded and far-away when the bride leaned forward and addressed him.

As a matter of truth, Jack Potter was beginning to find the shadow of a deed weigh upon him like a leaden slab. He, the town marshal of Yellow Sky, a man known, liked, and feared in his corner, a prominent person, had gone to

San Antonio to meet a girl he believed he loved, and there, after the usual prayers, had actually induced her to marry him, without consulting Yellow Sky for any part of the transaction. He was now bringing his bride before an innocent and unsuspecting community.

Of course people in Yellow Sky married as it pleased them in accordance with a general custom; but such was Potter's thought of his duty to his friends, or of their idea of his duty, or of an unspoken form which does not control men in these matters, that he felt he was heinous. He had committed an extraordinary crime. Face to face with this girl in San Antonio, and spurred by his sharp impulse, he had gone headlong over all the social hedges. At San Antonio he was like a man hidden in the dark. A knife to sever any friendly duty, any form, was easy to his hand in that remote city. But the hour of Yellow Sky — the hour of daylight — was approaching.

He knew full well that his marriage was an important thing to his town. It could only be exceeded by the burning of the new hotel. His friends could not forgive him. Frequently he had reflected on the advisability of telling them by telegraph, but a new cowardice had been upon him. He feared to do it. And now the train was hurrying him toward a scene of amazement, glee, and reproach. He glanced out of the window at the line of haze swinging slowly in toward the train.

Yellow Sky had a kind of brass band, which played painfully, to the delight 20 of the populace. He laughed without heart as he thought of it. If the citizens could dream of his prospective arrival with his bride, they would parade the band at the station and escort them, amid cheers and laughing congratulations, to his adobe home.

He resolved that he would use all the devices of speed and plainscraft in making the journey from the station to his house. Once within that safe citadel, he could issue some sort of vocal bulletin, and then not go among the citizens until they had time to wear off a little of their enthusiasm.

The bride looked anxiously at him. "What's worrying you, Jack?"

He laughed again. "I'm not worrying, girl; I'm only thinking of Yellow Sky."

She flushed in comprehension.

A sense of mutual guilt invaded their minds and developed a finer ten- 25 derness. They looked at each other with eyes softly aglow. But Potter often laughed the same nervous laugh; the flush upon the bride's face seemed quite permanent.

The traitor to the feelings of Yellow Sky narrowly watched the speeding landscape. "We're nearly there," he said.

Presently the porter came and announced the proximity of Potter's home. He held a brush in his hand, and, with all his airy superiority gone, he brushed Potter's new clothes as the latter slowly turned this way and that way. Potter fumbled out a coin and gave it to the porter, as he had seen others do. It was a heavy and muscle-bound business, as that of a man shoeing his first horse.

The porter took their bag, and as the train began to slow they moved forward to the hooded platform of the car. Presently the two engines and their long string of coaches rushed into the station of Yellow Sky.

"They have to take water here," said Potter, from a constricted throat and in mournful cadence, as one announcing death. Before the train stopped his eye had swept the length of the platform, and he was glad and astonished to see there was none upon it but the station-agent, who, with a slightly hurried and anxious air, was walking toward the water-tanks. When the train had halted, the porter alighted first, and placed in position a little temporary step.

"Come on, girl," said Potter, hoarsely. As he helped her down they each 30 laughed on a false note. He took the bag from the negro, and bade his wife cling to his arm. As they slunk rapidly away, his hang-dog glance perceived that they were unloading the two trunks, and also that the station-agent, far ahead near the baggage-car, had turned and was running toward him, making gestures. He laughed, and groaned as he laughed, when he noted the first effect of his marital bliss upon Yellow Sky. He gripped his wife's arm firmly to his side, and they fled. Behind them the porter stood, chuckling fatuously.

II

The California express on the Southern Railway was due at Yellow Sky in twenty-one minutes. There were six men at the bar of the Weary Gentleman saloon. One was a drummer° who talked a great deal and rapidly; three were Texans who did not care to talk at that time; and two were Mexican sheep-herders, who did not talk as a general practice in the Weary Gentleman saloon. The bar-keeper's dog lay on the board walk that crossed in front of the door. His head was on his paws, and he glanced drowsily here and there with the constant vigilance of a dog that is kicked on occasion. Across the sandy street were some vivid green grass-plots, so wonderful in appearance, amid the sands that burned near them in a blazing sun, that they caused a doubt in the mind. They exactly resembled the grass mats used to represent lawns on the stage. At the cooler end of the railway station, a man without a coat sat in a tilted chair and smoked his pipe. The fresh-cut bank of the Rio Grande circled near the town, and there could be seen beyond it a great plum-colored plain of mesquit.

Save for the busy drummer and his companions in the saloon, Yellow Sky was dozing. The new-comer leaned gracefully upon the bar, and recited many tales with the confidence of a bard who has come upon a new field.

" — and at the moment that the old man fell downstairs with the bureau in his arms, the old woman was coming up with two scuttles of coal, and of course — "

The drummer's tale was interrupted by a young man who suddenly appeared in the open door. He cried: "Scratchy Wilson's drunk, and has turned loose with both hands." The two Mexicans at once set down their glasses and faded out of the rear entrance of the saloon.

The drummer, innocent and jocular, answered: "All right, old man. S'pose 35 he has? Come in and have a drink, anyhow."

But the information had made such an obvious cleft in every skull in the room that the drummer was obliged to see its importance. All had become instantly solemn. "Say," said he, mystified, "what is this?" His three companions made the introductory gesture of eloquent speech; but the young man at the door forestalled them.

"It means, my friend," he answered, as he came into the saloon, "that for the next two hours this town won't be a health resort."

The barkeeper went to the door, and locked and barred it; reaching out of the window, he pulled in heavy wooden shutters, and barred them. Immediately

---

drummer: Traveling salesman.

a solemn, chapel-like gloom was upon the place. The drummer was looking from one to another.

"But, say," he cried, "what is this, anyhow? You don't mean there is going to be a gun-fight?"

"Don't know whether there'll be a fight or not," answered one man, 40 grimly; "but there'll be some shootin'—some good shootin'."

The young man who had warned them waved his hand. "Oh, there'll be a fight fast enough, if any one wants it. Anybody can get a fight out there in the street. There's a fight just waiting."

The drummer seemed to be swayed between the interest of a foreigner and a perception of personal danger.

"What did you say his name was?" he asked.

"Scratchy Wilson," they answered in chorus.

"And will he kill anybody? What are you going to do? Does this happen 45 often? Does he rampage around like this once a week or so? Can he break in that door?"

"No; he can't break down that door," replied the barkeeper. "He's tried it three times. But when he comes you'd better lay down on the floor, stranger. He's dead sure to shoot at it, and a bullet may come through."

Thereafter the drummer kept a strict eye upon the door. The time had not yet called for him to hug the floor, but, as a minor precaution, he sidled near the wall. "Will he kill anybody?" he said again.

The men laughed low and scornfully at the question.

"He's out to shoot, and he's out for trouble. Don't see any good in experimentin' with him."

"But what do you do in a case like this? What do you do?" 50

A man responded: "Why, he and Jack Potter—"

"But," in chorus the other men interrupted, "Jack Potter's in San Anton'."

"Well, who is he? What's he got to do with it?"

"Oh, he's the town marshal. He goes out and fights Scratchy when he gets on one of these tears."

"Wow!" said the drummer, mopping his brow. "Nice job he's got." 55

The voices had toned away to mere whisperings. The drummer wished to ask further questions, which were born of an increasing anxiety and bewilderment; but when he attempted them, the men merely looked at him in irritation and motioned him to remain silent. A tense waiting hush was upon them. In the deep shadows of the room their eyes shone as they listened for sounds from the street. One man made three gestures at the barkeeper; and the latter, moving like a ghost, handed him a glass and a bottle. The man poured a full glass of whisky, and set down the bottle noiselessly. He gulped the whisky in a swallow, and turned again toward the door in immovable silence. The drummer saw that the barkeeper, without a sound, had taken a Winchester from beneath the bar. Later he saw this individual beckoning to him, so he tiptoed across the room.

"You better come with me back of the bar."

"No thanks," said the drummer, perspiring; "I'd rather be where I can make a break for the back door."

Whereupon the man of bottles made a kindly but peremptory gesture. The drummer obeyed it, and, finding himself seated on a box with his head below the level of the bar, balm was laid upon his soul at sight of various zinc and copper fittings that bore a resemblance to armor-plate. The barkeeper took a seat comfortably upon an adjacent box.

"You see," he whispered, "this here Scratchy Wilson is a wonder with a 60 gun — a perfect wonder; and when he goes on the war-trail, we hunt our holes — naturally. He's about the last one of the old gang that used to hang out along the river here. He's a terror when he's drunk. When he's sober he's all right — kind of simple — wouldn't hurt a fly — nicest fellow in town. But when he's drunk — whoo!"

There were periods of stillness. "I wish Jack Potter was back from San Anton'," said the barkeeper. "He shot Wilson up once — in the leg — and he would sail in and pull out the kinks in this thing."

Presently they heard from a distance the sound of a shot, followed by three wild yowls. It instantly removed a bond from the men in the darkened saloon. There was a shuffling of feet. They looked at each other. "Here he comes," they said.

III

A man in a maroon-colored flannel shirt, which had been purchased for purposes of decoration, and made principally by some Jewish women on the East Side of New York, rounded a corner and walked into the middle of the main street of Yellow Sky. In either hand the man held a long, heavy, blue-black revolver. Often he yelled, and these cries rang through a semblance of a deserted village, shrilly flying over the roofs in a volume that seemed to have no relation to the ordinary vocal strength of a man. It was as if the surrounding stillness formed the arch of a tomb over him. These cries of ferocious challenge rang against walls of silence. And his boots had red tops with gilded imprints, of the kind beloved in winter by little sledding boys on the hillsides of New England.

The man's face flamed in a rage begot of whisky. His eyes, rolling, and yet keen for ambush, hunted the still doorways and windows. He walked with the creeping movement of the midnight cat. As it occurred to him, he roared menacing information. The long revolvers in his hands were as easy as straws; they were removed with an electric swiftness. The little fingers of each hand played sometimes in a musician's way. Plain from the low collar of the shirt, the cords of his neck straightened and sank, straightened and sank, as passion moved him. The only sounds were his terrible invitations. The calm adobes preserved their demeanor at the passing of this small thing in the middle of the street.

There was no offer of fight — no offer of fight. The man called to the sky. 65 There were no attractions. He bellowed and fumed and swayed his revolvers here and everywhere.

The dog of the barkeeper of the Weary Gentleman saloon had not appreciated the advance of events. He yet lay dozing in front of his master's door. At sight of the dog, the man paused and raised his revolver humorously. At sight of the man, the dog sprang up and walked diagonally away, with a sullen head, and growling. The man yelled, and the dog broke into a gallop. As it was about to enter the alley, there was a loud noise, a whistling, and something spat the ground directly before it. The dog screamed, and, wheeling in terror, galloped headlong in a new direction. Again there was a noise, a whistling, and sand was kicked viciously before it. Fear-stricken, the dog turned and flurried like an animal in a pen. The man stood laughing, his weapons at his hips.

Ultimately the man was attracted by the closed door of the Weary Gentleman saloon. He went to it and, hammering with a revolver, demanded drink.

The door remaining imperturbable, he picked a bit of paper from the walk, and nailed it to the framework with a knife. He then turned his back contemptuously upon this popular resort and, walking to the opposite side of the street and spinning there on his heel quickly and lithely, fired at the bit of paper. He missed it by a half inch. He swore at himself, and went away. Later he comfortably fusilladed the windows of his most intimate friend. The man was playing with this town; it was a toy for him.

But still there was no offer of fight. The name of Jack Potter, his ancient antagonist, entered his mind, and he concluded that it would be a glad thing if he should go to Potter's house, and by bombardment induce him to come out and fight. He moved in the direction of his desire, chanting Apache scalp-music.

When he arrived at it, Potter's house presented the same still front as had 70
the other adobes. Taking up a strategic position, the man howled a challenge. But this house regarded him as might a great stone god. It gave no sign. After a decent wait, the man howled further challenges, mingling with them wonderful epithets.

Presently there came the spectacle of a man churning himself into deepest rage over the immobility of a house. He fumed at it as the winter wind attacks a prairie cabin in the North. To the distance there should have gone the sound of a tumult like the fighting of two hundred Mexicans. As necessity bade him, he paused for breath or to reload his revolvers.

IV

Potter and his bride walked sheepishly and with speed. Sometimes they laughed together shamefacedly and low.

"Next corner, dear," he said finally.

They put forth the efforts of a pair walking bowed against a strong wind. Potter was about to raise a finger to point the first appearance of the new home when, as they circled the corner, they came face to face with a man in a maroon-colored shirt, who was feverishly pushing cartridges into a large revolver. Upon the instant the man dropped his revolver to the ground and, like lightning, whipped another from its holster. The second weapon was aimed at the bridegroom's chest.

There was a silence. Potter's mouth seemed to be merely a grave for his 75
tongue. He exhibited an instinct to at once loosen his arm from the woman's grip, and he dropped the bag to the sand. As for the bride, her face had gone as yellow as old cloth. She was a slave to hideous rites, gazing at the apparitional snake.

The two men faced each other at a distance of three paces. He of the revolver smiled with a new and quiet ferocity.

"Tried to sneak up on me," he said. "Tried to sneak up on me!" His eyes grew more baleful. As Potter made a slight movement, the man thrust his revolver venomously forward. "No, don't you do it, Jack Potter. Don't you move a finger toward a gun just yet. Don't you move an eyelash. The time has come for me to settle with you and I'm goin' to do it my own way, and loaf along with no interferin'. So if you don't want a gun bent on you, just mind what I tell you."

Potter looked at his enemy. "I ain't got a gun on me, Scratchy," he said. "Honest, I ain't." He was stiffening and steadying, but yet somewhere at the back of his mind a vision of the Pullman floated: the sea-green figured velvet, the shining brass, silver, and glass, the wood that gleamed as darkly brilliant as the surface of a pool of oil — all the glory of marriage, the environment of the new estate. "You know I fight when it comes to fighting, Scratchy Wilson; but I ain't got a gun on me. You'll have to do all the shootin' yourself."

His enemy's face went livid. He stepped forward, and lashed his weapon to and fro before Potter's chest. "Don't you tell me you ain't got no gun on you, you whelp. Don't tell me no lie like that. There ain't a man in Texas ever seen you without no gun. Don't take me for no kid." His eyes blazed with light, and his throat worked like a pump.

"I ain't takin' you for no kid," answered Potter. His heels had not moved 80 an inch backward. "I'm takin' you for a damn fool. I tell you I ain't got a gun, and I ain't. If you're goin' to shoot me up, you better begin now; you'll never get a chance like this again."

So much enforced reasoning had told on Wilson's rage; he was calmer. "If you ain't got a gun, why ain't you got a gun?" he sneered. "Been to Sunday-school?"

"I ain't got a gun because I've just come from San Anton' with my wife. I'm married," said Potter. "And if I'd thought there was going to be any galoots like you prowling around when I brought my wife home, I'd had a gun, and don't you forget it."

"Married!" said Scratchy, not at all comprehending.

"Yes, married. I'm married," said Potter, distinctly.

"Married?" said Scratchy. Seemingly for the first time, he saw the droop- 85 ing, drowning woman at the other man's side. "No!" he said. He was like a creature allowed a glimpse of another world. He moved a pace backward, and his arm, with the revolver, dropped to his side. "Is this the lady?" he asked.

"Yes; this is the lady," answered Potter.

There was another period of silence.

"Well," said Wilson at last, slowly, "I s'pose it's all off now."

"It's all off if you say so, Scratchy. You know I didn't make the trouble." Potter lifted his valise.

"Well, I 'low it's off, Jack," said Wilson. He was looking at the ground. 90 "Married!" He was not a student of chivalry; it was merely that in the presence of this foreign condition he was a simple child of the earlier plains. He picked up his starboard revolver, and, placing both weapons in their holsters, he went away. His feet made funnel-shaped tracks in the heavy sand.

CONSIDERATIONS FOR CRITICAL THINKING AND WRITING

1. **FIRST RESPONSE.** Think of a western you've read or seen: any of Larry Mc-Murtry's books would work, such as *Lonesome Dove* or *Evening Star.* Compare and contrast the setting, characters, action, and theme in Crane's story with your western.

2. What is the nature of the conflict Marshal Potter feels on the train in Part I? Why does he feel that he committed a "crime" in bringing home a bride to Yellow Sky?

3. What is the function of the "drummer," the traveling salesman, in Part II?

4. How do Mrs. Potter and Scratchy Wilson serve as foils for each other? What does each represent in the story?

5. What is the significance of the setting?

6. How does Crane create suspense about what will happen when Marshal Potter meets Scratchy Wilson? Is suspense the major point of the story?

7. Is Scratchy Wilson too drunk, comical, and ineffective to be a sympathetic character? What is the meaning of his conceding that "I s'pose it's all off now" at the end of Part IV? Is he a dynamic or a static character?

8. What details seem to support the story's theme? Consider, for example, the descriptions of the bride's clothes and Scratchy Wilson's shirt and boots.

9. Explain why the heroes in western stories are rarely married and why Crane's use of marriage is central to his theme.

10. **CRITICAL STRATEGIES.** Read the section on gender strategies (pp. 2056–58) in Chapter 53, "Critical Strategies for Reading." Explore the heterosexual and potentially homosexual issues that a gender critic might discover in the story.

CONNECTIONS TO OTHER SELECTIONS

1. Although Scratchy Wilson and the title character in Katherine Mansfield's "Miss Brill" (below) are radically different kinds of people, they share a painful recognition at the end of their stories. What does each of them learn? Discuss whether you think what each of them learns is of equal importance in changing his or her life.

2. Write an essay comparing Crane's use of suspense with William Faulkner's in "A Rose for Emily" (p. 91).

KATHERINE MANSFIELD (1888–1923)

Born in New Zealand, Katherine Mansfield moved to London when she was a young woman and began writing short stories. Her first collection, *In a German Pension,* appeared in 1911. Subsequent publications, which include *Bliss and Other Stories* (1920) and *The Garden Party* (1922), secured her reputation as an important writer. The full range of her short stories is available in *The Collected Short Stories of Katherine Mansfield* (1945). Mansfield tends to focus her stories on intelligent, sensitive protagonists who undergo subtle but important changes in their lives. In "Miss Brill," an aging Englishwoman

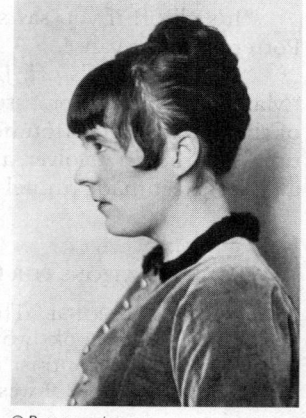
© Bettmann/CORBIS.

spends the afternoon in a park located in an unnamed French vacation town watching the activities of the people around her. Through those observations, Mansfield characterizes Miss Brill and permits us to see her experience a moment that changes her view of the world as well as of herself.

Miss Brill   1922

Although it was so brilliantly fine — the blue sky powdered with gold and great spots of light like white wine splashed over the Jardins Publiques — Miss Brill was glad that she had decided on her fur. The air was motionless, but when you opened your mouth there was just a faint chill, like a chill from a glass of iced water before you sip, and now and again a leaf came drifting — from nowhere, from the sky. Miss Brill put up her hand and touched her fur. Dear little thing! It was nice to feel it again. She had taken it out of its box that afternoon, shaken out the moth-powder, given it a good brush, and rubbed the life back into the dim little eyes. "What has been happening to me?" said the sad little eyes. Oh, how sweet it was to see them snap at her again from the red eiderdown! . . . But the nose, which was of some black composition, wasn't at all firm. It must have had a knock, somehow. Never mind — a little dab of black sealing-wax when the time came — when it was absolutely necessary. . . . Little rogue! Yes, she really felt like that about it. Little rogue biting its tail just by her left ear. She could have taken it off and laid it on her lap and stroked it. She felt a tingling in her hands and arms, but that came from walking, she supposed. And when she breathed, something light and sad — no, not sad, exactly — something gentle seemed to move in her bosom.

There were a number of people out this afternoon, far more than last Sunday. And the band sounded louder and gayer. That was because the Season had begun. For although the band played all the year round on Sundays, out of season it was never the same. It was like someone playing with only the family to listen; it didn't care how it played if there weren't any strangers present. Wasn't the conductor wearing a new coat, too? She was sure it was new. He scraped with his foot and flapped his arms like a rooster about to crow, and the bandsmen sitting in the green rotunda blew out their cheeks and glared at the music. Now there came a little "flutey" bit — very pretty! — a little chain of bright drops. She was sure it would be repeated. It was; she lifted her head and smiled.

Only two people shared her "special" seat: a fine old man in a velvet coat, his hands clasped over a huge carved walking-stick, and a big old woman, sitting upright, with a roll of knitting on her embroidered apron. They did not speak. This was disappointing, for Miss Brill always looked forward to the conversation. She had become really quite expert, she thought, at listening as though she didn't listen, at sitting in other people's lives just for a minute while they talked around her.

She glanced, sideways, at the old couple. Perhaps they would go soon. Last Sunday, too, hadn't been as interesting as usual. An Englishman and his wife, he wearing a dreadful Panama hat and she button boots. And she'd gone on the whole time about how she ought to wear spectacles; she knew she needed them; but that it was no good getting any; they'd be sure to break and they'd never keep on. And he'd been so patient. He'd suggested everything — gold rims, the kind that curved round your ears, little pads inside the bridge. No, nothing would please her. "They'll always be sliding down my nose!" Miss Brill had wanted to shake her.

The old people sat on the bench, still as statues. Never mind, there was always the crowd to watch. To and fro, in front of the flower-beds and the band rotunda, the couples and groups paraded, stopped to talk, to greet, to buy a handful of flowers from the old beggar who had his tray fixed to the railings. Little children ran among them, swooping and laughing; little boys with big white silk bows under their chins, little girls, little French dolls, dressed up in velvet and lace. And sometimes a tiny staggerer came suddenly rocking into the open from under the trees, stopped, stared, as suddenly sat down "flop," until its small high-stepping mother, like a young hen, rushed scolding to its rescue. Other people sat on the benches and green chairs, but they were nearly always the same, Sunday after Sunday, and — Miss Brill had often noticed — there was something funny about nearly all of them. They were odd, silent, nearly all old, and from the way they stared they looked as though they'd just come from dark little rooms or even — even cupboards!

Behind the rotunda the slender trees with yellow leaves down drooping, and through them just a line of sea, and beyond the blue sky with gold-veined clouds.

Tum-tum-tum tiddle-um! tiddle-um! tum tiddley-um tum ta! blew the band.

Two young girls in red came by and two young soldiers in blue met them, and they laughed and paired and went off arm-in-arm. Two peasant women with funny straw hats passed, gravely, leading beautiful smoke-colored donkeys. A cold, pale nun hurried by. A beautiful woman came along and dropped her bunch of violets, and a little boy ran after to hand them to her, and she took them and threw them away as if they'd been poisoned. Dear me! Miss Brill didn't know whether to admire that or not! And now an ermine toque and a gentleman in grey met just in front of her. He was tall, stiff, dignified, and she was wearing the ermine toque she'd bought when her hair was yellow. Now everything, her hair, her face, even her eyes, was the same color as the shabby ermine, and her hand, in its cleaned glove, lifted to dab her lips, was a tiny yellowish paw. Oh, she was so pleased to see him — delighted! She rather thought they were going to meet that afternoon. She described where she'd been — everywhere, here, there, along by the sea. The day was so charming — didn't he agree? And wouldn't he, perhaps? . . . But he shook his head, lighted a cigarette, slowly breathed a great deep puff into her face, and, even while she was still talking and laughing, flicked the match away and walked on. The ermine toque was alone; she smiled more brightly than ever. But even the band seemed to know what she was feeling and played more softly, played tenderly, and the drum beat, "The Brute! The Brute!" over and over. What would she do? What was going to happen now? But as Miss Brill wondered, the ermine toque turned, raised her hand as though she'd seen some one else, much nicer, just over there, and pattered away. And the band changed again and played more quickly, more gaily than ever, and the old couple on Miss Brill's seat got up and marched away, and such a funny old man with long whiskers hobbled along in time to the music and was nearly knocked over by four girls walking abreast.

Oh, how fascinating it was! How she enjoyed it! How she loved sitting here, watching it all! It was like a play. It was exactly like a play. Who could believe the sky at the back wasn't painted? But it wasn't till a little brown dog trotted on solemn and then slowly trotted off, like a little "theatre" dog, a little dog that had been drugged, that Miss Brill discovered what it was that made it so exciting. They were all on the stage. They weren't only the audience, not only looking on; they were acting. Even she had a part and came every Sunday. No doubt somebody would have noticed if she hadn't been there; she was part of the performance after all. How strange she'd never thought of it like that before! And yet it explained why she made such a point of starting from home at just the same time each week — so as not to be late for the performance — and it also explained why she had quite a queer, shy feeling at telling her English pupils how she spent her Sunday afternoons. No wonder! Miss Brill nearly laughed out loud. She was on the stage. She thought of the old invalid gentleman to whom she read the newspaper four afternoons a week while he slept in the garden. She had got quite used to the frail head on the cotton pillow, the hollowed eyes, the open mouth, and the high pinched nose. If he'd been dead she mightn't have noticed for weeks; she wouldn't have minded. But suddenly he knew he was having the paper read to him by an actress! "An actress!" The old head lifted; two points of light quivered in the old eyes. "An actress — are ye?" And Miss Brill smoothed the newspaper as though it were the manuscript of her part and said gently: "Yes, I have been an actress for a long time."

The band had been having a rest. Now they started again. And what they 10 played was warm, sunny, yet there was just a faint chill — a something, what was it? — not sadness — no, not sadness — a something that made you want to sing. The tune lifted, lifted, the light shone; and it seemed to Miss Brill that in another moment all of them, all the whole company, would begin singing. The young ones, the laughing ones who were moving together, they would begin, and the men's voices, very resolute and brave, would join them. And then she too, she too, and the others on the benches — they would come in with a kind of accompaniment — something low, that scarcely rose or fell, something so beautiful — moving. . . . And Miss Brill's eyes filled with tears and she looked smiling at all the other members of the company. Yes, we understand, we understand, she thought — though what they understood she didn't know.

Just at that moment a boy and a girl came and sat down where the old couple had been. They were beautifully dressed; they were in love. The hero and heroine, of course, just arrived from his father's yacht. And still soundlessly singing, still with that trembling smile, Miss Brill prepared to listen.

"No, not now," said the girl. "Not here, I can't."

"But why? Because of that stupid old thing at the end there?" asked the boy. "Why does she come here at all — who wants her? Why doesn't she keep her silly old mug at home?"

"It's her fu-fur which is so funny," giggled the girl. "It's exactly like a fried whiting."

"Ah, be off with you!" said the boy in an angry whisper. Then: "Tell me, ma 15 petite chère ——"

"No, not here," said the girl. "Not *yet.*"

On her way home she usually bought a slice of honey-cake at the baker's. It was her Sunday treat. Sometimes there was an almond in her slice, sometimes not. It made a great difference. If there was an almond it was like carrying home a tiny present — a surprise — something that might very well not have been there.

She hurried on the almond Sundays and struck the match for the kettle in quite a dashing way.

But today she passed the baker's by, climbed the stairs, went into the little dark room — her room like a cupboard — and sat down on the red eiderdown. She sat there for a long time. The box that the fur came out of was on the bed. She unclasped the necklet quickly; quickly, without looking, laid it inside. But when she put the lid on she thought she heard something crying.

CONSIDERATIONS FOR CRITICAL THINKING AND WRITING

1. **FIRST RESPONSE.** There is almost no physical description of Miss Brill in the story. What do you think she looks like? Develop a detailed description that would be consistent with her behavior.

2. How does the calculated omission of Miss Brill's first name contribute to her characterization?

3. What details make Miss Brill more than a stock characterization of a frail old lady?

4. What do Miss Brill's observations about the people she encounters reveal about her?

5. What is the conflict in the story? Who or what is the antagonist?

6. Locate the climax of the story. How is it resolved?

7. What is the purpose of the fur piece? What is the source of the crying in the final sentence of the story?

8. Is Miss Brill a static or a dynamic character?

9. Describe Miss Brill's sense of herself at the end of the story.

10. Discuss the function of the minor characters mentioned in the story. Analyze how Mansfield used them to reveal Miss Brill's character.

CONNECTIONS TO OTHER SELECTIONS

1. Compare Miss Brill's recognition with that of the narrator in Fay Weldon's "IND AFF, or Out of Love in Sarajevo" (p. 202).

2. Write an essay comparing the themes in "Miss Brill" and James Joyce's "Eveline" (p. 536).

DAGOBERTO GILB (B. 1950)

Born in Los Angeles, Dagoberto Gilb was a journeyman carpenter who considered both Los Angeles and El Paso to be home. He is a professor of creative writing at Texas State University in San Marcos. Among his literary prizes are the James D. Phelan Award in literature, the Whiting Award, and a Guggenheim Foundation fellowship. He has also won a National Endowment for the Arts Creative Writing Fellowship. Gilb's

© Bret Brookshire.

fiction has been published in a variety of journals including *The Threepenny Review, ZYZZYVA,* and *American Short Fiction.* His stories — collected in *The Magic of Blood* (1993), from which "Love in L.A." is taken, and *Woodcuts of Women* (2001) — often reflect his experiences as a worker moving between Los Angeles and El Paso. In 1994 he published his first novel, *The Last Known Residence of Mickey Acuña,* and in 2003 he published a collection of essays, *Gritos.* He has also edited *Hecho en Tejas: An Anthology of Texas Mexican Literature* (2006).

Love in L.A.   1993

Jake slouched in a clot of near motionless traffic, in the peculiar gray of concrete, smog, and early morning beneath the overpass of the Hollywood Freeway on Alvarado Street. He didn't really mind because he knew how much worse it could be trying to make a left onto the onramp. He certainly didn't do that every day of his life, and he'd assure anyone who'd ask that he never would either. A steady occupation had its advantages and he couldn't deny thinking about that too. He needed an FM radio in something better than this '58 Buick he drove. It would have crushed velvet interior with electric controls for the L.A. summer, a nice warm heater and defroster for the winter drives at the beach, a cruise control for those longer trips, mellow speakers front and rear of course, windows that hum closed, snuffing out that nasty exterior noise of freeways. The fact was that he'd probably have to change his whole style. Exotic colognes, plush, dark nightclubs, maitais and daiquiris, necklaced ladies in satin gowns, misty and sexy like in a tequila ad. Jake could imagine lots of possibilities when he let himself, but none that ended up with him pressed onto a stalled freeway.

Jake was thinking about this freedom of his so much that when he glimpsed its green light he just went ahead and stared bye bye to the steadily employed. When he turned his head the same direction his windshield faced, it was maybe one second too late. He pounced the brake pedal and steered the front wheels away from the tiny brakelights but the smack was unavoidable. Just one second sooner and it would only have been close. One second more and he'd be crawling up the Toyota's trunk. As it was, it seemed like only a harmless smack, much less solid than the one against his back bumper.

Jake considered driving past the Toyota but was afraid the traffic ahead would make it too difficult. As he pulled up against the curb a few carlengths ahead, it occurred to him that the traffic might have helped him get away too. He slammed the car door twice to make sure it was closed fully and to give himself another second more, then toured front and rear of his Buick for damage on or near the bumpers. Not an impressionable scratch even in the chrome. He perked up. Though the car's beauty was secondary to its ability to start and move, the body and paint were clean except for a few minor dings. This stood out as one of his few clearcut accomplishments over the years.

Before he spoke to the driver of the Toyota, whose looks he could see might present him with an added complication, he signaled to the driver of the car that hit him, still in his car and stopped behind the Toyota, and waved his hands and shook his head to let the man know there was no problem as far as he was concerned. The driver waved back and started his engine.

"It didn't even scratch my paint," Jake told her in that way of his. "So how you doin? Any damage to the car? I'm kinda hoping so, just so it takes a little more time and we can talk some. Or else you can give me your phone number now and I won't have to lay my regular b.s. on you to get it later."

He took her smile as a good sign and relaxed. He inhaled her scent like it was clean air and straightened out his less than new but not unhip clothes.

"You've got Florida plates. You look like you must be Cuban."

"My parents are from Venezuela."

"My name's Jake." He held out his hand.

"Mariana."

They shook hands like she'd never done it before in her life.

"I really am sorry about hitting you like that." He sounded genuine. He fondled the wide dimple near the cracked taillight. "It's amazing how easy it is to put a dent in these new cars. They're so soft they might replace waterbeds soon." Jake was confused about how to proceed with this. So much seemed so unlikely, but there was always possibility. "So maybe we should go out to breakfast somewhere and talk it over."

"I don't eat breakfast."

"Some coffee then."

"Thanks, but I really can't."

"You're not married, are you? Not that that would matter that much to me. I'm an openminded kinda guy."

She was smiling. "I have to get to work."

"That sounds boring."

"I better get your driver's license," she said.

Jake nodded, disappointed. "One little problem," he said. "I didn't bring it. I just forgot it this morning. I'm a musician," he exaggerated greatly, "and, well, I dunno, I left my wallet in the pants I was wearing last night. If you have some paper and a pen I'll give you my address and all that."

He followed her to the glove compartment side of her car.

"What if we don't report it to the insurance companies? I'll just get it fixed for you."

"I don't think my dad would let me do that."

"Your dad? It's not your car?"

"He bought it for me. And I live at home."

"Right." She was slipping away from him. He went back around to the back of her new Toyota and looked over the damage again. There was the trunk lid, the bumper, a rear panel, a taillight.

"You do have insurance?" she asked, suspicious, as she came around the back of the car.

"Oh yeah," he lied.

"I guess you better write the name of that down too."

He made up a last name and address and wrote down the name of an insurance company an old girlfriend once belonged to. He considered giving a real phone number but went against that idea and made one up.

"I act too," he lied to enhance the effect more. "Been in a couple of movies."

She smiled like a fan.

"So how about your phone number?" He was rebounding maturely.

She gave it to him.

"Mariana, you are beautiful," he said in his most sincere voice.   35

"Call me," she said timidly.

Jake beamed. "We'll see you, Mariana," he said holding out his hand. Her hand felt so warm and soft he felt like he'd been kissed.

Back in his car he took a moment or two to feel both proud and sad about his performance. Then he watched the rear view mirror as Mariana pulled up behind him. She was writing down the license plate numbers on his Buick, ones that he'd taken off a junk because the ones that belonged to his had expired so long ago. He turned the ignition key and revved the big engine and clicked into drive. His sense of freedom swelled as he drove into the now moving street traffic, though he couldn't stop the thought about that FM stereo radio and crushed velvet interior and the new car smell that would even make it better.

CONSIDERATIONS FOR CRITICAL THINKING AND WRITING

1. **FIRST RESPONSE.** Is "Love in L.A." a love story? Try to argue that it is. (If the story ended with paragraph 37, how would your interpretation of the story be affected?)

2. What is the effect of setting the story's action in a Los Angeles traffic jam on the Hollywood Freeway?

3. Characterize Jake. What do his thoughts in the first two paragraphs reveal about him? About how old do you think he is?

4. There is little physical description of Jake in the story, but given what you learn about him, how would you describe his physical features and the way he dresses?

5. What causes Jake to smack into the back of Mariana's car? What is revealed about his character by the manner in which he has the accident?

6. Describe how Jake responds to Mariana when he introduces himself to her, especially in paragraph 12. What does his behavior reveal about his character?

7. How does Mariana respond to Jake? Explain whether you think she is a round or flat character.

8. Explain how their respective cars serve to characterize Jake and Mariana.

9. What does the final paragraph reveal about each character?

10. In a sentence or two write down what you think the story's theme is. How does the title contribute to that theme?

CONNECTION TO ANOTHER SELECTION

1. Compare and contrast the themes in "Love in L.A." and Fay Weldon's "IND AFF, or Out of Love in Sarajevo" (p. 202).

A SAMPLE STUDENT RESPONSE

Randall Patterson

Professor Kahane

English 102

September 28, 2009

The Theme of Deception in Gilb's "Love in L.A."

Jake, the main character of Dagoberto Gilb's "Love in L.A.," sits in traffic and dreams of a better life. There are things he desires: a better car with an FM radio, heater and defroster, cruise control, "mellow speakers," and "windows that hum closed" (311). However, Jake is unwilling to earn these things. Instead, he is irresponsible; he lies and cheats to get (or try to get) what he wants. And while Jake appears to get away with his irresponsible behavior, there are consequences.

Deception is a clear theme throughout the story. Jake pities the people in traffic who have to "make a left onto the onramp" to get to their jobs, and vows "he certainly didn't do that every day of his life, and . . . he never would" (Gilb 311). So he instead shirks his responsibility. After getting in an accident with Mariana, we learn that he has no car insurance, no driver's license, and that his plates are stolen. Jake will not be held responsible for the accident, but he is ultimately trapped in a world of dishonesty, a world he will never find fulfilling. He spends all his time dreaming of something better: "he couldn't stop the thought about that FM stereo radio and crushed velvet interior and the new car smell that would even make it better" (313). It seems that although Jake does not change dramatically in this story, he does become more self-aware. He feels "both proud and sad about his performance" (313) and perhaps is beginning to realize he will never find happiness as long as he continues his pattern of deception. . . .

Work Cited

Gilb, Dagoberto. "Love in L.A." *The Bedford Introduction to Literature*. Ed. Michael Meyer. 9th ed. Boston: Bedford/St. Martin's, 2011. 311–13. Print.

DALY WALKER (B. 1940)

Born in Winchester, Indiana, Daly Walker was an undergraduate at Ohio Wesleyan University, and his education culminated in his medical and surgical training at Indiana University and the University of Wisconsin. Though he has not yet published a book, his fiction has appeared in *The Atlantic* (where he published "I Am the Grass") and in other periodicals such as *The Sewanee Review* and *The Sycamore Review*. With a surgical practice in Florida, Daly serves as a reminder that writing fiction is not always a full-time endeavor for everyone and that powerful

Courtesy of the author.

stories can be produced by writers who are not necessarily self-described professionals. He began writing fiction only after he was forty years old, long after he had served in the Vietnam War in 1967–68 and well into his career as a physician. "I Am the Grass" evokes the pain and terrible suffering that exist in any war, while simultaneously creating a convincing portrait of a veteran who tries to make some personal sense out of it.

I Am the Grass — 2000

Because I love my wife and daughter, and because I want them to believe I am a good man, I have never talked to them about my year as a grunt with the 25th infantry in Vietnam. I cannot tell my thirteen-year-old that once, drunk on Ba Muoi Ba beer, I took a girl her age into a thatched-roof hooch in Tay Ninh City and did her on a bamboo mat. I cannot tell my wife, who paints watercolors of songbirds, that on a search-and-destroy mission I emptied my M-60 machine gun into two beautiful white egrets that were wading in the muddy water of a paddy. I cannot tell them how I sang "Happy Trails" as I shoved two wounded Viet Cong out the door of a medevac chopper hovering twenty feet above the tarmac of a battalion aid station. I cannot tell them how I lay in a ditch and used my M-60 to gun down a skinny, black-haired farmer I thought was a VC, nearly blowing his head off. I cannot tell them how I completed the decapitation with a machete, and then stuck his head on a pole on top of a mountain called Nui Ba Den. All these things fester in me like the tiny fragment of shrapnel embedded in my skull, haunt me like the corpse of the slim dark man I killed. I cannot talk about these things that I wish I could forget but know that I never will.

Twenty years have passed since the summer of 1968, when I flew home from the war and my "freedom bird" landed in the night at Travis Air Force Base, near San Francisco. I knew that in the city, soldiers in uniform were taunted in the streets by flower children. So I slipped quietly into a restroom and changed from my dress khakis into jeans and a flannel shirt. Nobody was there to say "Welcome home, soldier." It was as if I were an exile in my own country. I felt deceived and confused, and most of all angry, but I wasn't sure at whom to direct my anger or where to go or what to do, so I held everything inside and went about forming a life day by day.

After I was discharged from the Army, I went home to Chicago and hung around there for a couple of years, haunted by memories and nameless faces. Devoid of hope or expectations, smoking dope and dreaming dreams of torment, I drifted from one meaningless endeavor to the next. I studied drawing at the art academy, cut grass with the grounds crew at Soldier Field, parked cars at the Four Seasons. Nothing seemed to matter; nothing changed what I was. I was still fire and smoke, a loaded gun, a dead survivor, a little girl on a bamboo mat, a headless corpse. I was still in the killing zone.

Gradually I grew weary of my hollowness, ran out of pity for my own self-pity. I wanted to take my life and shake it by the hair. I decided to use the GI Bill and give college a try.

I enrolled at the University of Wisconsin at Madison, the headquarters of 5 the Weathermen and the SDS. I lived in a run-down rooming house on Mifflen Street, among all the long-haired war protesters and scruffy peaceniks. During the day I went to classes and worked as an orderly at a Catholic hospital, but at night, after work, I went back to my room to study alone. Through the window of my room I could see mobs of students marching through the streets, chanting "Ho, Ho, Ho Chi Minh" and "Bring home the war." What did they know about war? I watched them, and I wanted to kick their hippie asses.

It was in caring for the patients at the hospital that I seemed to find what I had been searching for. While bathing or feeding a patient I felt simply good. It was better than my best trips with Mary Jane. I decided to apply to medical school, and I was accepted.

One night when I was a senior med student, a couple of radical war protesters blew up the Army Mathematics Research Center on campus. The explosion shook my bed in the hospital call room like the rocket that blasted me out of sleep the night of the Tet Offensive. I have never been a brave man, and I lay there in the dark with my heart pounding, thinking I was back in Firebase Zulu the night we were overrun. A nurse called me to the emergency room to help resuscitate a theoretical physicist who had been pulled from under the rubble. His chest was crushed and both his lungs were collapsed. He didn't need resuscitation. He needed a body bag. The war I was trying to escape had followed me home.

Now I practice plastic surgery in Lake Forest, a North Shore Chicago suburb of stone walls, German cars, and private clubs. On my arm is a scar from the laser surgery that removed a tattoo I woke up with one morning in a Bangkok whorehouse. The tattoo was a cartoon in blue and red ink of a baby in diapers, wearing an Army helmet and a parachute with the inscription "Airborne." I feel that I am two people at once, two people fighting within myself. One is a family man and a physician who lives a comfortable external life. The other is a war criminal with an atrophied soul. Nothing I do can revive it.

Even as a surgeon I have a split personality. I sculpt women's bodies with breast augmentations, tummy tucks, face-lifts, and liposuction. I like the money, but I'm bored with these patients and their vanity, their urgent need for surgical enhancement. I am also a reconstructive plastic surgeon who loves Z-plastying a scar from a dog bite on a little girl's cheek or skin grafting a burn on the neck of a small boy who fell against a space heater. I love reconstructing a lobster-claw deformity of the hand so that a child can hold a spoon and fork. I'm no Albert Schweitzer, but every summer I spend a couple of weeks in Haiti or Kenya or Guatemala with Operation Smile, repairing cleft palates and lips. Removing the bandages and seeing the results of my skill sends a chill up my neck, makes me feel like something of a decent man, a healer.

Today, in late September, I am sitting in a window seat in a Thai Airways 10
jet on its way from Bangkok to Ho Chi Minh City. I am headed to the Khanh Hoa Hospital, in Nha Trang, for two weeks of my own little Operation Smile, repairing the cleft palates and lips of children on whose land I once wreaked havoc, whose parents and grandparents I murdered and whom, somewhere deep inside me, I still hold in contempt.

I stare out the airplane window at tufts of white clouds that look like bursts of artillery flak, and I break into a sweat, remembering the descent of the airliner that flew me, a machine gunner, an Airborne Ranger, an eighteen-year-old pissed-off, pot-smoking warrior, cannon fodder, to Vietnam. The pilot lurched into a steep, spiraling dive to minimize the plane's exposure time to ground fire. I pitched forward in my seat, the belt cutting into my belly, my heart pounding. Until that moment I had felt immortal, but then fear came to me in an image of my own death by a bullet to the brain, and I realized how little I mattered, how quickly and simply and anonymously the end could come. I believed that I would never return home to my room with the old oak dresser and corner desk that my mother dusted and polished with lemon oil. Tears filled my eyes.

With the plane in a long, gentle glide, I gaze out the window and search for remnants of the war. I see a green patchwork of paddies and fields of grass, dirt roads whose iron-red dust choked me, whose mud caked my jungle boots. A sampan floats down a river. Smoke curls lazily from a thatched-roof shack. An ox pulls a cart. The land seems asleep, and the war only a dream. I drop back in the seat and close my eyes. Stirring in my chest is the feeling that a dangerous demon is setting itself free inside me.

I spend the night in Saigon at the Bong Song Hotel, a mildewing walk-up not far from the Museum of American War Crimes. The toilet doesn't flush. The ceiling fan croaks so loudly that I turn it off. Oily tropical heat drenches the room, and I can hear rats skittering across the floor. I feel as I once did trying to grab a little shut-eye before going out on ambush patrol. I can't sleep. My mind is filled with the image of myself dragging the lifeless body of a kid named Dugan by the ankles through mud.

In the orange light of dawn I board an old minivan that will take me north to the hospital in Nha Trang. The tottering vehicle weaves through streets teeming with bicycles, three-wheeled cyclos, motorbikes, an occasional car. People gawk at me as if I were a zoo animal of a breed they have never seen before. The driver is Tran, a spindly man with wispy Ho Chi Minh chin whiskers. He has been assigned to be my guide and interpreter, but he is really the People's Committee watchdog. When I was here before, I would have called him a gook or a slope, a dink motherfucker, and those are the words that come to me now when I look at Tran. I picture his head on a pole.

We cross the Saigon River on Highway One, Vietnam's aorta, the artery con- 15
necting Hanoi with Saigon. The French called Highway One *"la rue sans joie."* We

called it "the street to sorrow." During the war I often traveled this road in convoys of tanks and half-tracks whose treads pulverized the pavement. I was always high on Buddha grass. Armed to the teeth. Frightened and mean. I was so young. I didn't know what I was doing here. A few miles out of Saigon, Tran slows and points to a vast empty plain overgrown with olive-drab grass and scrub brush.

"This Long Binh," he says.

"Stop," I say.

He pulls off the road and parks by a pile of rusty wire and scrap metal. I climb out of the van and stand, looking at acres of elephant grass blasted by the tropical sun. I think of Long Binh when it was an enormous military base, a sandbag city of tents, barbed wire, and bunkers. We called it LBJ, for "Long Binh Jail." It was where I spent my first night "in country," sweat-soaked on a sagging cot, listening to the distant chunk of artillery, fear clawing at my chest. Now all I see is emptiness. Nothing to verify my past, nothing to commune with. How hot it is. How quiet.

Since Nam, I have spent a lot of nights with bottles of wine, reading the poetry of war — Homer and Kipling, Sandburg and Komunyakaa. Through the haze of my thoughts, words by Sandburg are moving. The words are about grass and war and soldiers in Austerlitz and Gettysburg and Waterloo, but they are about this place, too. *Shove them under and let me work — I am the grass; I cover all.* I gaze out at Long Binh's grass. It ripples in hot wind like folds of silk.

I climb back into the van, and we jostle on through paddies and rubber plantations, green groves of bamboo and banana trees. I have the strange feeling that my life has shrunk, that just around the bend an ambush will be waiting. I lean forward in my seat and ask Tran if he remembers Long Binh when the American soldiers were here.

"Vietnam believe it better not to remind of the past." He speaks looking straight ahead through aviator sunglasses. "We live in present with eye on future." The words sound rote, as if he is quoting from a propaganda paper. "Vietnam want to be thought of as country, not war, not just problem in other country's past."

On a berm old women in conical hats spread rice and palm fronds to dry in the sun. Charcoal fumes waft from cooking fires. White-shirted children with red kerchiefs tied around their necks march to school. Two men, brown and bent like cashew nuts, face each other over a big teak log and pull a cross-cut saw back and forth slowly, rhythmically. For a brief moment the smell of gunpowder comes back to me, and I see little Asian men running headlong through tall grass, firing weapons and screaming. I see GIs running through smoke with green canvas stretchers.

The arrangements for my mission in the coastal city of Nha Trang were made through Dr. Lieh Viet Dinh, the director of Khanh Hoa Hospital. The morning after my arrival, Dinh sends word to my hotel that he wants to meet me for a welcoming meal at a restaurant on the South China Sea. I have been told that Dinh was once in the North Vietnamese army and now is a high official in the province's Communist Party. What does he want? For me to say I'm sorry?

I hire a cyclo driver to pedal me to the restaurant. Mopeds with their exhaust tinting the air blue and bicycles piled high with cordwood tangle the streets. The Sunday-afternoon sun is so bright it hurts my eyes. But there is a cool ocean breeze and the scent of bougainvillaea in the air. Under flame trees with brilliant-orange blossoms barbers trim hair and clean wax from ears. Street vendors hawk flowers and loaves of French bread. Everywhere I look, I see Vietnamese getting on with their lives. I marvel at their serenity. They are no different from the people that I was taught to distrust, that I once machine-gunned. This street is no different from streets that I once helped to fill with rubble and bodies. A man on a Honda raises his index finger and calls, "Hey, Joe. U.S. number one." But I look away from him.

The restaurant is a rickety tile-roofed pagoda perched on stilts over a 25 beach of sand the color of crème brûlée. Below, in a natural aquarium, sand sharks and tropical fish dart among the rocks. In the distance a soft vapor hangs over mountain islands in the bay. The restaurant is empty except for a gnarly little man sitting alone at a table with the sun splashing off turquoise water behind him. He is a militant figure with penetrating black eyes and hollow, acne-scarred cheeks that give him a look of toughness, a look that says, You could never defeat me no matter how many bombs you dropped. I know he is Dinh. The contempt that boiled inside me during the war bubbles up. I can feel it in my chest.

He calls to me to join him. I settle into a wooden chair across from him and extend my hand for him to shake, but he ignores it and offers a stiff little bow of his head. Nervousness dries up the saliva in my mouth. A waitress in a blue *ao dai* brings us bottles of Ba Muoi Ba beer. With her lustrous black hair and slim, silk-sheathed figure, she is beautiful and exotic like a tropical bird. The shy young girl with a dimple in her cheek that I took on the bamboo mat in Tay Ninh would be about her age now. I wonder what became of her.

In English that I have to listen to closely to understand, Dinh talks for a while about the Khanh Hoa Hospital, the only hospital for the one million people of his province. He tells me that my visit has been advertised on television, and that thirty children with cleft lips to be repaired will be there. His jaw tight, his voice intimidating, he tells me that the hospital has trouble getting medicine and equipment because of the American embargo. I pick up my bottle of beer and press it to my lips and tilt it. The liquid is warm, with the slight formaldehyde taste that I remember from the war. I look at Dinh's slanty black eyes and stained teeth, thinking how easy it would be to kill him. I've been taught to do it with a gun or a knife or my hands. It would come back to me quickly, like sitting down at a piano and playing a song that you mastered a long time ago but haven't played in years. Suddenly the thought of operating on little children in all this heat and dirt, with archaic equipment, jolts me back into the present. I ask him who will give the anesthesia.

"My doctors," he says. "Vietnamese doctors as good as any in the world."

The waitress brings a plate of lightly fried rice paper, bowls of rice and noodles, and a platter of sea bass smothered in peppers, onions, and peanuts. She gives me chopsticks and Dinh a metal spoon. When we begin to eat, I see Dinh's hands for the first time. I am startled. Now I know why he didn't shake with me. His thumbs are missing. I watch him spoon rice onto his plate, clutching the utensil in his thumbless hand. He has learned a pinch grip between his second and third digits, like children I have operated on who were born with floating thumbs or congenital absence of the first metacarpal bone. Using his fingers as if they were tongs, he wraps some fish in a sheet of the rice paper and dips it in nuoc cham sauce. The sauce smells rancid, and a sourness rises up my esophagus.

"I hear you in Vietnam during war," Dinh says between bites of fish and rice. 30
"Yes," I say. I can't take my eyes off his hands.
"Where?" he asks.
"South of here, along the Cambodian border near Tay Ninh."
"You see Nui Ba Den," he says. "How you call it? The black virgin mountain. This fish good. Dip your fish in nuoc cham."
I picture that black-haired man's head skewered on a bamboo pole. 35
"Yeah, I've seen Nui Ba Den," I say, feeling as if he must somehow know what I did on top of the mountain.
"Were you Army surgeon?"
"No. That was before I went to medical school. I was with the infantry." I take a gulp of beer. "That was a long time ago."
"Not so long ago," Dinh says. His lips curl into a smile that is filled with crooked yellow teeth. "Americans always think time longer than it is. Americans very impatient. Vietnamese very patient. We believe life is circle. Everything comes and goes. Why grasp and cling? Always things will come around again if you give them time. Patience is why we win victory."
In the filthy little village across the bay I can see tin-roofed shacks, teem- 40
ing streets, the haze of smoke from cooking fires — the thick stew of peasant life.
"How about you?" I ask. "Were you a doctor during the war?"
He wipes his mouth with his shirt-sleeve and says, "In war against French colonialists, I was Vietminh infantry man. Fifteen years old."
He raises a maimed hand and, with a wave motion to demonstrate high altitude, tells how he twice climbed the mountains of Laos and Cambodia on the Ho Chi Minh Trail — once to fight the French and once to fight the Americans and their Vietnamese puppets. He was wounded at Dien Bien Phu. I wonder if that was when he lost his thumbs. I'm fascinated by his thumblessness. The ability to oppose a thumb and a finger is what sets us apart from lemurs and baboons.
"We have little to fight with," Dinh says. "After we shoot our guns, we pick up empty cartridges to use again. We eat nothing but tapioca roots and half a can of rice a day. For seven years I fight hungry."
I listen to him tell of his wars, and it takes me back to mine. Cold-sweat 45
nights peering out of a muddy bunker through concertina wire at tracers and shadows. Waiting. Listening. Grim patrols through elephant grass and jungle greased with moonlight. I can hear screams, see faces of the dead. What is memory and what is a dream? When it comes to the war, nothing seems true. It seems impossible that something that tragic, that unspeakable, was once a part of my life. Suddenly I'm overwhelmed with emotion. I wonder if Dinh ever feels like crying. In the shallows below the restaurant a sea turtle snaps at silver fish trapped in a net.
"How about in the war against America?" I ask. "Were you a doctor then?"
"I was surgeon in the war against you and your South Vietnamese puppets."
"Where did you serve?" I ask. "Were you in a hospital?"
"My hospital the forest. My operating table the soil of the jungle." He holds up both hands and rotates them for me to see. "I have thumbs then. I clever surgeon. I operate on everything from head to toes." He looks up at the ceiling as if an airplane were circling overhead. "Your B-fifty-twos drop big bombs. They make earth shake. They scare hell out of me."

Dinh flashes a smile that makes me uncomfortable. He takes a drink of beer.   50
"Were you wounded?" I ask.

"You mean my hands?"

"Yeah. What happened?"

He rests them on the table, displaying them as he talks. He tells me that he was captured in the central highlands, not by Americans but by South Vietnamese Special Forces in their purple berets. When they learned he was a doctor, they chose him for torture. They tied him to a stake under merciless sun and every day pulled out one of his fingernails with a pair of pliers. At night they locked him up in a tiger cage. He speaks softly. On the eleventh day they cut off his thumbs. Then they cooked them in a soup and told him to drink it. He hadn't eaten for two weeks, so he did.

"How did you survive?" I ask. "Why didn't you go crazy?"   55

"I pretended to be somewhere else. Somewhere at a time after our victory. I always knew we would win."

Dinh looks at my hands.

"You lucky," he says. "You have thumbs to do surgery. I can't even eat with chopsticks." He raises his hands, flexing his fingers. He glares at me with eyes as hard and black as gun bores. "This should happen to no one."

We finish our meal in silence. Under the afternoon sun the restaurant is stifling, and I feel queasy. I can get down only a little rice. But Dinh eats hungrily, shoveling in the food with his spoon as if to make up for all those years of rice and tapioca roots. When his plate is clean, he rinses his hands in a bowl of hot lime water with tea leaves floating on the surface.

He looks up at me and says, "To take the smell of fish from your skin."   60

In the morning I walk from my hotel through steamy air, on streets boiling with people, to the hospital. Around the entryway dozens of crippled peasants and ragged children with skin sores squat on the powdery earth. Everything is dusty. I understand why Vietnamese peasants call themselves "the dust of life." A boy with weight-lifter arms calls to me in English from a bicycle that he pedals with his hands. He wants me to fix his paralyzed legs.

Khanh Hoa's pale-yellow façade gives me an impression of cleanliness and light, but inside, the wards are dim and grungy, with no glass or screens in the windows to keep out flies and mosquitoes. Often two patients occupy a single narrow bed, with family members sleeping on the floor nearby to assist with the feeding and bathing, the emptying of bedpans. A tiny, toothless woman with skin like teakwood waves a bamboo fan over a wasted man on a mattress without sheets. She gazes at me with longing. Everywhere I go, someone with sorrowful eyes looks at me as if I were Jesus.

During my first week I don't have any more conversations with Dinh, but I see him every morning when he comes in his white lab coat to the surgery suite to watch me operate. At the door he slips off his sandals and pads barefoot into the room, where he stands at the head of the table, his black eyes peering at the children whose lips are like hook-ripped fish mouths. He rarely speaks, and when he does, it is usually to address the Vietnamese doctors and nurses in a tone that suggests sarcasm.

It is impossible to know what his silence toward me means, but I become immersed in my work, and I don't worry about him. Once the operation starts, my concentration is complete, my only concern the child's face, framed in blue towels and bathed in bright light. I have always been gifted at drawing and carving, and with a scalpel in my hand I feel like an artist, forming something beautiful out of chaos. I love mapping out flaps of skin around a child's mouth and then rotating them over the cleft to create a nice Cupid's bow of lip with a clean vermilion border. My sutures are like the brushstrokes of a portrait. Dinh must envy the collaboration of my brain and fingers.

Between cases I rest in the doctors' lounge at a wooden table. I drink a pot 65 of pale-tan tea, eat litchi fruit, and look out into the hospital courtyard that serves as the waiting room. I often see Dinh with his hands hidden in the pockets of his lab coat, squatting in the dust, talking with the parents of the cleft-lipped children who are undergoing surgery. His face, glistening under the hot sun, looks as if it has been oiled. His chronic scowl has become a comforting smile.

At the end of my first week I call my wife and daughter to tell them that all is going well. When I report that I have repaired eighteen cleft lips without a complication, my wife seems proud of me. I am getting to like the nurses and doctors in the operating room. My feelings of guilt and ambivalence are being replaced by a sense of good will and atonement, as if Vietnam and I were two bad people who had unexpectedly done something nice for each other. But on Sunday, Dinh sends word for me to meet him in his "cabinet," as he calls his private office. I worry that I have done something wrong.

The room is the size of an armoire and sparsely furnished. A single bookcase contains the medical texts of the hospital's meager library. On the wall is a little green lizard and a yellowed photograph of Ho Chi Minh. From a cassette player on a homemade wooden table comes the music of a symphony orchestra playing Vivaldi's *The Four Seasons*. The hospital sewer system is backed up, and the air smells brackish. My stomach churns. I sit in a straight-backed chair across a metal desk from Dinh. My office in Lake Forest, with its Oriental carpet and polished cherry furniture, seems infinitely far away.

"Vivaldi," I say to break the silence.

Dinh looks up from a journal article in which he is underlining with a wooden pencil. His face, shadowed by years of hardship, is expressionless. He wears a white shirt and a clip-on red rayon tie. He has a small Band-Aid on his chin where, I assume, he nicked himself shaving. I imagine him handling a razor, buttoning a shirt, tying a tie or shoestrings. Without a thumb's ability to pinch and oppose, even simple tasks must be difficult for him.

"Do you enjoy Vivaldi?" he asks. 70

"*The Four Seasons* is one of my favorites. When did you develop a taste for Western music?"

"When I was in medical school in Hanoi, French doctors play music in surgery room. Music only good thing about Frenchmen. Music good healing medicine. I play music to calm my patients."

He clicks off the tape and hands me the article he has been reading. It is a reprint from a French journal of hand surgery. I leaf through its pages, scanning illustrations that depict an operation in which a toe is transferred to the hand to replace a missing thumb.

"Can you make thumb?" Dinh asks.

I sit for a moment, remembering my last toe transplant, performed a couple of years ago. It was on a young farm boy who had lost his thumb in a corn picker.

"Yes," I say. "I've done this operation. Not often, but I've done it."

"I want you do this to me," Dinh says.

"Here? Now? You want me to make you a thumb?"

"Yes. I want you make me new thumb."

It is as if, fighting a losing battle, I suddenly see the enemy waving a white flag. For a moment I look at his narrow, bony hands with the red ridges of scar tissue where thumbs once protruded.

"It's a very hard operation," I say. "Quite delicate. A microvascular procedure. Even under perfect conditions it often doesn't work."

"I watch you operate." Dinh lowers his eyes and his voice. "You very careful surgeon. I know you can do."

"Let me see your hand."

He extends his right hand toward me. I rise and move around the desk. I take his hand in mine and turn it slowly, studying skin tone and temperature. His radial pulse bounds against my fingers. His nail beds are pink with good capillary circulation. The skin of the palm is creased and thickly callused.

"Thumb reconstruction must be carefully planned," I say. "You don't just jump into it. There are several techniques to consider."

In my mind I review them: using a skin flap and a bone graft from the pelvis; pollicization, in which the index finger is rotated to oppose the third finger; and my favorite technique, which uses a tube graft of abdominal skin — but it has to be staged over several weeks.

"The new thumb must be free of pain," I say, carefully palpating the bones of his hand, searching for the missing thumb's metacarpal. I find it intact. "It has to have sensation so it can recognize objects. It has to be long enough to touch the tip of opposing digits. It must be flexible."

"You don't have to teach me," Dinh says gruffly. "I know about this. I read everything in literature. Toe transplant best for me."

"I'm not so sure about that."

"Toe transplant best."

"Maybe so, but you're the patient this time. I'm the doctor. Let me decide."

I bend over and lift his dusty foot into my lap. I slip off his tire-tread sandal. His foot is the size of my daughter's, the toenails poorly cared for. My fingers find strong dorsalis pedis and posterior tibial pulses at the ankle. I would prefer to transplant the second toe, but his is very small; I decide the big toe would make a better thumb.

"What you find?" he asks anxiously.

"You have good circulation and a metacarpal bone."

"So what you think? Toe transplant?"

I look up at Dinh's face. It is pale yellow, contrasting with the density of shadowed books and wall behind him. His haughty eyes have softened into a look of hope and longing.

"I agree," I say. "A toe transplant would be best for you."

"You must do it, then," he says.

"Maybe you could come to the States and have it done."

"I no rich American. No can get visa."

"There's a good chance the graft won't take. I don't have an operating microscope or some of the instruments I use."

He flexes and unflexes the four fingers on his right hand and smiles.

"Do it here tomorrow. I want to hold chopsticks again. I tired of eating like a Frenchman."

"Look," I say, "you don't realize how many things could go wrong." 105

"It work. I know it work."

I think how the fortunes of the Vietnamese always seem to be in the hands of others.

"Okay," I say. "I'll do it. A local anesthetic would be safest. Would that be all right?"

"Pain no matter. You do it."

"You're on. But don't be surprised if it doesn't work." 110

That night I lie awake under the mosquito net on my bed, reviewing the technique of toe transplantation, suturing in my mind tendons and tiny digital nerves, minute veins and arteries. Tropical heat drenches me. The bark of dogs comes in from the street. When I finally fall asleep, I dream again of the man whose head I severed and stuck on the end of a pole. We meet in the Cao Dia temple in Tay Ninh, a vast, gaudy cathedral with a vaulted ceiling, pillars wound with gilded dragons and pink serpents, and a giant eye over the altar. He stands naked in front of me, holding his head with its sheen of black hair in the crook of his elbow.

The surgery suite is high ceilinged, with dirty windows and yellow tile walls, like the restroom in an old train station. The air is drowsy with the odor of ether that leaks from U.S. Army surplus anesthesia machines. Outside the operating room I attach magnifying loupes to a pair of glasses. I focus the lenses on the lines of my fingertips and begin scrubbing my hands in cold water at an old porcelain sink. Through the door I see Dinh sedated and strapped to the operating table. Bathed in fierce white light, with his arms extended on boards at right angles to his body, he looks as if he has been crucified. I have sent an orderly to his office for his cassette player, and *The Four Seasons* plays softly at the head of the table.

For a moment I rinse my hands, designing in my mind skin incisions and tendon transfers. In the past, to decrease operating time and diminish my fatigue, I used a second surgical team to prepare the recipient site in the hand while I removed the donor tissue from the foot, but here I am alone.

With water dripping from my elbows, I step into the room. Suddenly I feel a surge of force, a sense of power that has been mine in no other place but surgery, except when my finger was on the trigger of an M-60.

The instruments I have brought with me lie on trays and tables. My 115 weapons are tenotomy scissors and mosquito hemostats, atraumatic forceps and spring-loaded needle holders. A scrub technician, who worked as an interpreter in a MASH unit during the war, hands me a towel. Two masked nurses prep Dinh's foot and hand with a soap solution. The surgery team's spirits are high. Listening to them talk is like hearing finches chirp.

Gowned and gloved, I sit on a stool beside Dinh's right hand. I adjust the light and begin the numbing with an injection of Xylocaine. The prick of the needle rouses him in his narcotized slumber, and he groans.

"Everyone ready? Let's go. Knife."

The nurse pops the handle of the scalpel into my palm. A stillness settles over me and passes into my hand.

Dissecting out the filamentous vessels and nerves that once brought blood and sensation to Dinh's thumb is tedious and takes more than an hour. While I work, a nurse sits at Dinh's head, murmuring to him and wiping his forehead with a wet cloth. I wonder what Dinh is thinking. Is he remembering the men who cut off his thumbs? Is he dreaming of what he might do if he met them again? When all the digital nerves and vessels and tendons are isolated and tagged with black-silk sutures, I cover the hand with a sterile towel. Before I move to Dinh's foot to harvest his spare part, I step to the head of the table.

"It's going well," I say. "You all right?"   120

"Don't worry about Dinh," he replies. "Worry about operation."

I make a circular incision around the base of the phalanx, taking care to preserve skin in the web space so that the defect can be closed without a skin graft. When the toe is finally transected, with its trailing tentacles of tendons, nerves, and vessels, it looks like a baby squid. I wrap it in saline-soaked gauze and carry it to the hand. I'm tired and sweating. My back hurts. My eyes ache. I feel as if I were on a long forced march.

First I join the bones, using wires to fuse the toe's bone to the hand's metacarpal in a position of flexion and pronation, to provide Dinh with a good pinch. Next I unite the tendons with strong nylon sutures — extensor hallucis longus to extensor pollicis longus, flexor hallucis longus to flexor pollicis longus.

Fighting off fatigue, I begin the most critical and tedious part of the procedure — the anastomosis of filamentous nerves and vessels. It is like sewing strands of hair together. Under the magnification of the lenses the delicate instruments seem big and blunt; the slightest tremor of my fingers appears to be an awkward jerk. Blood oozes into the wound and obscures my vision. A few drops seem like a crimson flood.

"Suck. Will someone please suck."   125

I take a stitch in the digital artery, and Dinh's hand rises from the drapes. I push it down, pinning it to the table.

"Goddamn it," I say. "Hold still, Dinh."

"*Dau*," Dinh moans in pain. "*Dau. Dau.*"

"He feel it," the nurse says.

"More Xylocaine," I say. His hand jerks again. "Hurry up, Goddamn it.   130 Xylocaine."

After four hours Dinh has a new thumb, pinned in place by Kirschner wires through the bones and a neat ring of black-nylon skin sutures. Exhausted, I sit for a moment cradling his hand in mine and staring at my work. The graft is cool and cadaveric, as pale as plaster, but it twitches slightly with his pulse. I haven't prayed in years, and doubt that it does any good, but I silently ask the Lord to give the transplant life. The nurse hands me a sterile dressing, and I wrap Dinh's fingers in loose layers of fluffy gauze followed by a light cast of plaster of paris. I strip off my gloves and step to the head of the table. I look down at Dinh's face, resting my hand on his shoulder. His pitted cheeks puff with each breath, and his half-closed eyelids flutter.

"All done, Dinh," I say.

"How does it look?" he asks groggily.

"Like a thumb."

Dinh believes that our lives move in circles, repeating themselves endlessly like 135
the four seasons, like the cycle of his country's rice crop. Planting. Weeding
and waiting. Harvesting. Fallowness. Planting again. If things don't work out,
so what? Another chance will come around, the way winter always gives in to
spring. But I believe that my life is somehow outside these circles, that I am on
a straight march toward something final, and on that journey to the end of
existence, the journey itself is all there is. When I fail along the way, when
something I need eludes me because of a mistake I have made, the mistake itself
becomes a defeat, and I am left with only loss, with emptiness, uncertainty,
and regret.

Because that is my nature, the fate of Dinh's transplanted toe takes on a
monumental importance. I lie awake at night in unbearable heat, sweating and
worrying about infection and thrombosis. Each morning, before I start my
surgery schedule, I visit Dinh in his stark hospital room, with its metal cot
and the clay pot that serves as a bedside commode. Peering up at me from his
pillow through circular Uncle Ho wire-rims, he seems calm and confident,
talking of all the things that will be easier for him to do with his new thumb —
holding a pen when he writes haiku, picking hibiscus blooms for his wife's
table, playing his bamboo flute, and, of course, eating with chopsticks. He says
he may even do a little minor surgery. The thought of him trying to operate
makes me cringe.

One day I show him a few snapshots of my daughter. He leafs through the
pictures and nods politely. Then he talks about all the children I operated on
who can now smile and suck their bottles. The children, tender and pliant, are
what is important, he tells me, not old people like him, who have become dry
and rigid and whose lives are behind them.

When I examine him, I am relieved to find that he is free of fever. His pain
is minimal. The dressing smells clean, and a little blood stains the cast, which
is a good sign. The graft has to be taking. I begin to look forward to removing
the dressing and seeing a nice new pink thumb. It will be a kind of miracle.

The day before I am to leave Vietnam is the day of atonement, the time of
truth, the moment to unwrap Dinh's hand and see if his thumb is viable. It is
also the end of the rice harvest, and the farmers are burning off the fields to
the west of the city. As I walk to the hospital, I can see a gray haze of smoke
hanging over a horizon curtained with flames. It is a scorched-earth image,
reminiscent of napalm and war.

In the surgery clinic I meet Dinh, sitting in a wheelchair with his ban- 140
daged hand in a sling and a confident smile on his face. Hoa, a petite nurse
with a pretty smile and pearl earrings, places his hand on a white towel. A hush
hangs over the room. My heart gallops. I cut the cast with heavy scissors and
begin carefully unwinding the dressing. The gauze is stuck with dried blood,
so I moisten it with saline and let it soak for a few minutes while I re-dress his
foot. I am pleased to find the donor-site incision clean and healing well, but
when I peel the last layer of gauze from his hand, I smell the faint odor of
necrosis. Dinh's new thumb is the cold clay color of mildewed meat. I feel his
eyes on me. I want to leave now, get on an airplane and fly home, let someone

else amputate the dead thumb, let someone else clean up my mess. I glance up at his face. He is staring at the dead toe. God damn this dirty little Job of a country. Nothing turns out right here. I look out the window. The monsoon season is only a few days away, and already it is raining. Big drops kick up dust like rifle fire.

"It doesn't look good," I say. "Maybe I should re-dress it and give it a little more time."

"Gangrene," he says. "It dead. Take it off."

In the operating room everyone works in silence. On the table Dinh looks small and fragile, exhausted, as if he had just climbed one of those mountains on the Ho Chi Minh Trail. I pull the Kirschner wires from his hand with a hemostat and snip the nylon sutures. It is a bloodless operation. The necrotic transplant falls off onto blue drapes, stiff and cold, no longer a thumb or a toe. Looking at it, I can scarcely believe my childish hope that it would survive. I pick it up with sterile forceps and drop it into a stainless-steel pan. I think of Dinh's torturers in their purple berets chopping off his thumbs with a big knife. I see him drinking soup made with his own flesh and bone.

The day of my departure Dinh sends a driver in an old Toyota to take me to the airport. I am disappointed that he isn't riding with me, but something tells me he will be waiting for me in the terminal. I want to apologize to him because the transplant didn't work, and then have him laugh and say no problem, that in his next life he will have thumbs.

I check my bags at the ticket counter and hurry to the lounge, hoping that Dinh will be waiting there in a rattan chair with his bandaged foot propped up while he drinks a cup of green tea. Over the door to the sunny room a sign announces, NHA TRANG A GOOD PLACE FOR RESORT. With my heart hammering high in my chest, I step inside. No Dinh. The lounge is empty and silent except for the groan of a ceiling fan that churns warm, viscous air.

I move heavily between tables and out glass doors onto the tarmac. Silence surrounds me. The sun. The quiet blue sky. I stand for a while, gazing at tall brown grass and prickly pears that sprout through cracks in the airstrip. Concrete revetments built during the war to shelter American F-4 fighter jets from rocket attacks are empty and crumbling, like mausoleums of an earlier civilization. Beside the runway rests the rusty carcass of a US C141 Starlifter. I watch an old F-4, now a Vietnamese fighter jet with rocket launchers riveted to its wings, practice a touchdown. The plane bounces on the concrete, its tires screeching like the cry of some fierce predator. The gray gunship rises into sparkling blue sky. My eyes follow its flight until it disappears into the glare of the sun.

Soon an Air Vietnam passenger plane lands on the runway and taxies to the tarmac, where it shimmies to a stop. It is an old Russian turboprop with a dented skin and chipped blue-and-white paint. I have heard that Air Vietnam's planes are in poor repair because the airline has trouble getting parts, and that Japanese businessmen refuse to use it.

I mount the steps into the aircraft. Inside the fuselage, heat and the oily odor of fuel squeeze the breath out of me. Only two other travelers are on board, a mamasan in a conical hat and the baby she carries in a broad sling around her waist. She stands in the aisle, swaying back and forth to rock the infant. I choose a window seat with tattered upholstery. Soon the engines on the wings cough and sputter to life. I try to buckle my seat belt, but the clasp doesn't work. I shake my head and smile. In Vietnam danger has always been ubiquitous, life tenuous. For some reason I welcome the risky ride. It makes me feel a part of the land.

CONSIDERATIONS FOR CRITICAL THINKING AND WRITING

1. **FIRST RESPONSE.** Discuss whether you think this story is primarily about war or peace.

2. Comment on the purpose and effect of the first paragraph. How does it draw you into the narrator's conflicted sense of himself?

3. How might the Vietnam setting be described as an antagonist in the story?

4. Choose a paragraph in which Walker uses details particularly well to create a mood, set a scene, or unify the plot, and discuss how that effect is achieved through his carefully chosen language.

5. Does Dinh function as a character foil to the narrator, or is their relationship to one another more complex? Explain your response by considering Dinh's "thumblessness" and the narrator's efforts to surgically repair him.

6. Trace the narrator's reaction to Vietnam and its people from the beginning to the end of the story. Explain why you think his attitudes remain constant or change.

7. Can you find the story's theme (or themes) stated directly in a specific paragraph, or is it developed implicitly through the plot, characters, symbols, or some other element?

8. The title derives from an eleven-line poem by Carl Sandburg titled "Grass" (1918) that the narrator quotes in the context of revisiting Long Binh (para. 19). Read the entire poem (it's available online or in the library) and comment on how it is related to the theme(s) in Walker's story.

9. Discuss the thematic connections between the narrator's description of his first flight into Vietnam (paras. 10–12) and his last flight out (paras. 144–48). How do these two scenes frame his story?

10. **CREATIVE RESPONSE.** Rewrite the final section (paras. 144–48) from Dinh's point of view. How does this shift in perspective change the theme for you?

CONNECTIONS TO OTHER SELECTIONS

1. Walker has cited Tim O'Brien as an influence on his writing. Compare O'Brien's treatment of the Vietnam War in "How to Tell a True War Story" (p. 346) with Walker's and his narrator's observation, "When it comes to the war, nothing seems true" (para. 45).

2. Compare the response of Walker's protagonist to being "haunted by memories" of war (para. 3) to that of Ernest Hemingway's Krebs in "Soldier's Home" (p. 187). How do they resolve the conflicts produced by their haunting memories?

9

Style, Tone, and Irony

I like it when there is some feeling of threat or sense of menace in short stories. I think a little menace is fine to have in a story.
— RAYMOND CARVER

STYLE

Style is a concept that everyone understands on some level because in its broadest sense it refers to the particular way in which anything is made or done. Style is everywhere around us. The world is saturated with styles in cars, clothing, buildings, teaching, dancing, music, politics — in anything that reflects a distinctive manner of expression or design. Consider, for example, how a tune sung by the Beatles differs from the same tune performed by a string orchestra. There's no mistaking the two styles.

Authors also have different characteristic styles. *Style* refers to the distinctive manner in which a writer arranges words to achieve particular effects. That arrangement includes individual word choices and matters such as the length of sentences, their structure and tone, and the use of irony.

Diction refers to a writer's choice of words. Because different words evoke different associations in a reader's mind, the writer's choice of words is crucial in controlling a reader's response. The diction must be appropriate for the characters and the situations in which the author places them. Consider how inappropriate it would have been if Melville had had Bartleby respond to the lawyer's requests with "Hell no!" instead of "I would prefer not to." The word *prefer* and the tentativeness of *would* help reinforce the scrivener's mildness, his dignity, and even his seeming reasonableness — all of which frustrate the lawyer's efforts to get rid of him. Bartleby, despite his passivity, seems to be in control of the situation. If he were to shout "Hell no!" he would appear angry, aggressive, desperate, and too informal, none of which would fit with his solemn, conscious decision to die. Melville makes the lawyer the desperate party by carefully choosing Bartleby's words.

> Web Explore the literary elements in this chapter at bedfordstmartins.com/meyerlit.

Sentence structure is another element of a writer's style. Hemingway's terse, economical sentences are frequently noted and readily perceived. Here are the concluding sentences of Hemingway's "Soldier's Home" (p. 187), in which Krebs decides to leave home:

> He had tried so to keep his life from being complicated. Still, none of it had touched him. He had felt sorry for his mother and she had made him lie. He would go to Kansas City and get a job and she would feel all right about it. There would be one more scene maybe before he got away. He would not go down to his father's office. He would miss that one. He wanted his life to go smoothly. It had just gotten going that way. Well, that was all over now, anyway. He would go over to the schoolyard and watch Helen play indoor baseball.

Hemingway expresses Krebs's thought the way Krebs thinks. The style avoids any "complicated" sentence structures. Seven of the eleven sentences begin with the word *He.* There are no abstractions or qualifications. We feel as if we are listening not only to *what* Krebs thinks but to *how* he thinks. The style reflects his firm determination to make, one step at a time, a clean, unobstructed break from his family and the entangling complications they would impose on him.

Contrast this straightforward style with Vladimir Nabokov's description of a woman in his short story "The Vane Sisters." The sophisticated narrator teaches French literature at a women's college and is as observant as he is icily critical of the woman he describes in this passage:

> Her fingernails were gaudily painted, but badly bitten and not clean. Her lovers were a silent young photographer with a sudden laugh and two older men, brothers, who owned a small printing establishment across the street. I wondered at their tastes whenever I glimpsed, with a secret shudder, the higgledy-piggledy striation of black hairs that showed all along her pale shins through the nylon of her stockings with the scientific distinctness of a preparation flattened under glass; or when I felt, at her every movement, the dullish,

stalish, not particularly conspicuous but all-pervading and depressing emanation that her seldom bathed flesh spread from under weary perfumes and creams.

This portrait — etched with a razor blade — is restrained but devastating. The woman's fingernails are "gaudily painted." She has no taste in men either. One of her lovers is "silent" except for a "sudden laugh," a telling detail that suggests a strikingly odd personality. Her other lovers, the two brothers (!), run a "small" business. We are invited to "shudder" along with the narrator as he vividly describes the "striation of black hairs" on her legs; we see the woman as if she were displayed under a microscope, an appropriate perspective given the narrator's close inspection. His scrutiny is relentless, and its object smells as awful as it looks (notice the difference in the language between this blunt description and the narrator's elegant distaste). He finds the woman "depressing" because the weight of her unpleasantness oppresses him.

The narrator reveals nearly as much about himself as about the woman, but Nabokov leaves the reader with the task of assessing the narrator's fastidious reactions. The formal style of this description is appropriately that of an educated, highly critical, close observer of life who knows how to convey the "dullish, stalish" essence of this woman. But, you might ask, what about the curious informality of "higgledy-piggledy"? Does that fit the formal professorial voice? Given Nabokov's well-known fascination with wit and, more important, the narrator's obvious relish for verbally slicing this woman into a slide specimen, the term is revealed as appropriately chosen once the reader sees the subtle, if brutal, pun on *piggledy*.

Hemingway's and Nabokov's uses of language are very different, yet each style successfully fuses what is said with how it is said. We could write summaries of both passages, but our summaries, owing to their styles, would not have the same effect as the originals. And that makes all the difference.

TONE

Style reveals **tone,** the author's implicit attitude toward the people, places, and events in a story. When we speak, tone is conveyed by our voice inflections, our wink of an eye, or some other gesture. A professor who says "You're going to fail the next exam" may be indicating concern, frustration, sympathy, alarm, humor, or indifference, depending on the tone of voice. In a literary work that spoken voice is unavailable; instead we must rely on the context in which a statement appears to interpret it correctly.

In Chopin's "The Story of an Hour" (p. 15), for example, we can determine that the author sympathizes with Mrs. Mallard despite the fact that her grief over her husband's assumed death is mixed with joy. Though

Mrs. Mallard thinks she's lost her husband, she experiences relief because she feels liberated from an oppressive male-dominated life. That's why she collapses when she sees her husband alive at the end of the story. Chopin makes clear by the tone of the final line ("When the doctors came they said she had died of heart disease — of joy that kills") that the men misinterpret both her grief and joy, for in the larger context of Mrs. Mallard's emotions we see, unlike the doctors, that her death may well have been caused not by a shock of joy but by an overwhelming recognition of her lost freedom.

If we are sensitive to tone, we can get behind a character and see him or her from the author's perspective. In Melville's "Bartleby, the Scrivener" (p. 142) everything is told from the lawyer's point of view, but the tone of his remarks often separates him from the author's values and attitudes. When the lawyer characterizes himself at the beginning of the story, his use of language effectively allows us to see Melville disapproving of what the lawyer takes pride in:

> The late John Jacob Astor, a personage little given to poetic enthusiasm, had no hesitation in pronouncing my first grand point to be prudence; my next, method. I do not speak it in vanity.

But, of course, he is vain and a name-dropper as well. He likes the "rounded and orbicular sound" of Astor's name because it "rings like unto bullion." Tone, here, helps to characterize the lawyer. Melville doesn't tell us that the lawyer is status conscious and materialistic; instead, we discover that through the tone. This stylistic technique is frequently an important element for interpreting a story. An insensitivity to tone can lead a reader astray in determining the theme of a work. Regardless of who is speaking in a story, it is wise to listen for the author's voice too.

IRONY

One of the enduring themes in literature is that things are not always what they seem to be. What we see — or think we see — is not always what we get. The unexpected complexity that often surprises us in life — what Herman Melville in *Moby-Dick* called the "universal thump" — is fertile ground for writers of imaginative literature. They cultivate that ground through the use of *irony,* a device that reveals a reality different from what appears to be true.

Verbal irony consists of a person saying one thing but meaning the opposite. If a student driver smashes into a parked car and the angry instructor turns to say "You sure did well today," the statement is an example of verbal irony. What is meant is not what is said. Verbal irony that is calculated to hurt someone by false praise is commonly known as **sarcasm.** In literature, however, verbal irony is usually not openly aggressive; instead, it is more subtle and restrained though no less intense.

In Godwin's "A Sorrowful Woman" (p. 39), a woman retreats from her family because she cannot live in the traditional role that her husband and son expect of her. When the husband tries to be sympathetic about her withdrawal from family life, the narrator tells us three times that "he understood such things" and that in "understanding these things" he tried to be patient by "[s]till understanding these things." The narrator's repetition of these phrases constitutes verbal irony because they call attention to the fact that the husband doesn't understand his wife at all. His "understanding" is really only a form of condescension that represents part of her problem rather than a solution.

Situational irony exists when there is an incongruity between what is expected to happen and what actually happens. For instance, at the climactic showdown between Marshal Potter and Scratchy Wilson in Crane's "The Bride Comes to Yellow Sky" (p. 298), there are no gunshots, only talk — and what subdues Wilson is not Potter's strength and heroism but the fact that the marshal is now married. To take one more example, the protagonist in Godwin's "A Sorrowful Woman" seems, by traditional societal standards, to have all that a wife and mother could desire in a family, but, given her needs, that turns out not to be enough to sustain even her life, let alone her happiness. In each of these instances the ironic situation creates a distinction between appearances and realities and brings the reader closer to the central meaning of the story.

Another form of irony occurs when an author allows the reader to know more about a situation than a character knows. *Dramatic irony* creates a discrepancy between what a character believes or says and what the reader understands to be true. In Flannery O'Connor's "Revelation" (p. 474) the insecure Mrs. Turpin, as a member of "the home-and-land owner" class, believes herself to be superior to "niggers," "white-trash," and mere "home owners." She takes pride in her position in the community and in what she perceives to be her privileged position in relation to God. The reader, however, knows that her remarks underscore her failings rather than any superiority. Dramatic irony can be an effective way for an author to have a character unwittingly reveal himself or herself.

As you read Raymond Carver's "Popular Mechanics," Susan Minot's "Lust," Tim O'Brien's "How to Tell a True War Story," and Z. Z. Packer's "Brownies," pay attention to the authors' artful use of style, tone, and irony to convey meanings.

RAYMOND CARVER (1938–1988)

Born in 1938 in Clatskanie, Oregon, to working-class parents, Carver grew up in Yakima, Washington, was educated at Humboldt State College in California, and did graduate work at the University of Iowa. He married at age nineteen and during his college years worked at a series of low-paying jobs to help support his family. These difficult years eventually ended in divorce. He taught at a number of universities, among them the University of California, Berkeley; the University of Iowa; the University of Texas, El Paso; and Syracuse University. Carver's collections of stories include *Will You Please Be Quiet, Please?* (1976); *What We Talk about When We Talk about Love* (1981), from which "Popular Mechanics" is taken; *Cathedral* (1984); and *Where I'm Calling From: New and Selected Stories* (1988). Though extremely brief, "Popular Mechanics" describes a stark domestic situation with a startling conclusion.

© Marion Ettlinger.

Popular Mechanics   *1981*

Early that day the weather turned and the snow was melting into dirty water. Streaks of it ran down from the little shoulder-high window that faced the backyard. Cars slushed by on the street outside, where it was getting dark. But it was getting dark on the inside too.

He was in the bedroom pushing clothes into a suitcase when she came to the door.

I'm glad you're leaving! I'm glad you're leaving! she said. Do you hear?

He kept on putting his things into the suitcase.

Son of a bitch! I'm so glad you're leaving! She began to cry. You can't even 5
look me in the face, can you?

Then she noticed the baby's picture on the bed and picked it up.

He looked at her and she wiped her eyes and stared at him before turning and going back to the living room.

Bring that back, he said.

Just get your things and get out, she said.

He did not answer. He fastened the suitcase, put on his coat, looked 10
around the bedroom before turning off the light. Then he went out to the living room.

She stood in the doorway of the little kitchen, holding the baby.

I want the baby, he said.

Are you crazy?

No, but I want the baby. I'll get someone to come by for his things.

You're not touching this baby, she said.   15

The baby had begun to cry and she uncovered the blanket from around his head.

Oh, oh, she said, looking at the baby.

He moved toward her.

For God's sake! she said. She took a step back into the kitchen.

I want the baby. 20
Get out of here!

She turned and tried to hold the baby over in a corner behind the stove.

But he came up. He reached across the stove and tightened his hands on the baby.

Let go of him, he said.

Get away, get away! she cried. 25

The baby was red-faced and screaming. In the scuffle they knocked down a flowerpot that hung behind the stove.

He crowded her into the wall then, trying to break her grip. He held on to the baby and pushed with all his weight.

Let go of him, he said.

Don't, she said. You're hurting the baby, she said.

I'm not hurting the baby, he said. 30

The kitchen window gave no light. In the near-dark he worked on her fisted fingers with one hand and with the other hand he gripped the screaming baby up under an arm near the shoulder.

She felt her fingers being forced open. She felt the baby going from her.

No! she screamed just as her hands came loose.

She would have it, this baby. She grabbed for the baby's other arm. She caught the baby around the wrist and leaned back.

But he would not let go. He felt the baby slipping out of his hands and he 35 pulled back very hard.

In this manner, the issue was decided.

CONSIDERATIONS FOR CRITICAL THINKING AND WRITING

1. **FIRST RESPONSE.** Discuss the story's final lines. What is the "issue" that is "decided"?

2. Though there is little description of the setting in this story, how do the few details that are provided help to establish the tone?

3. How do small actions take on larger significance in the story? Consider the woman picking up the baby's picture and the knocked-down flowerpot.

4. Why is this couple splitting up? Do we know? Does it matter? Explain your response.

5. Discuss the title of the story. The original title was "Mine." Which do you think is more effective?

6. What is the conflict? How is it resolved?

7. Read I Kings 3 in the Bible for the story of Solomon. How might "Popular Mechanics" be read as a retelling of this story? What significant differences do you find in the endings of each?

8. Explain how Carver uses irony to convey theme.

CONNECTIONS TO OTHER SELECTIONS

1. Compare Carver's style with Ernest Hemingway's in "Soldier's Home" (p. 187).

2. How is the ending of "Popular Mechanics" similar to the ending of Nathaniel Hawthorne's "The Birthmark" (p. 420)?

Perspective

JOHN BARTH (B. 1930)

On Minimalist Fiction   *1987*

Minimalism (of one sort or another) is the principle (one of the principles, anyhow) underlying (what I and many another interested observer consider to be perhaps) the most impressive phenomenon on the current (North American, especially the United States) literary scene (the gringo equivalent of *el boom* in the Latin American novel): I mean the new flowering of the (North) American short story (in particular the kind of terse, oblique, realistic or hyperrealistic, slightly plotted, extrospective, cool-surfaced fiction associated in the last five or ten years with such excellent writers as Frederick Barthelme, Ann Beattie, Raymond Carver, Bobbie Ann Mason, James Robison, Mary Robison, and Tobias Wolff, and both praised and damned under such labels as "K-Mart realism," "hick chic," "Diet-Pepsi minimalism," and "post-Vietnam, post-literary, postmodernist blue-collar neo-early-Hemingwayism"). . . .

The genre of the short story, as Poe distinguished it from the traditional tale in his 1842 review of Hawthorne's first collection of stories, is an early manifesto of modern narrative minimalism: "In the whole composition there should be no word written, of which the tendency . . . is not to the pre-established design. . . . Undue length is . . . to be avoided." Poe's codification informs such later nineteenth-century masters of terseness, selectivity, and implicitness (as opposed to leisurely once-upon-a-timelessness, luxuriant abundance, explicit and extended analysis) as Guy de Maupassant and Anton Chekhov. Show, don't tell, said Henry James in effect and at length in his prefaces to the 1908 New York edition of his novels. And don't tell a word more than you absolutely need to, added young Ernest Hemingway, who thus described his "new theory" in the early 1920's: "You could omit anything if you knew that you omitted, and the omitted part would strengthen the story and make people feel something more than they understood. . . ."

Old or new, fiction can be minimalist in any or all of several ways. There are minimalisms of unit, form, and scale: short words, short sentences and paragraphs, [and] super-short stories. . . . There are minimalisms of style: a stripped-down vocabulary; a stripped-down syntax that avoids periodic sentences, serial predications, and complex subordinating constructions; a stripped-down rhetoric that may eschew figurative language altogether; a stripped-down, non-emotive tone. And there are minimalisms of material: minimal characters, minimal exposition ("all that David Copperfield kind of crap," says J. D. Salinger's *Catcher in the Rye*), minimal *mises en scène*, minimal action, minimal plot.

From *Weber Studies*

CONSIDERATIONS FOR CRITICAL THINKING AND WRITING

1. To what extent do Ernest Hemingway's "Soldier's Home" (p. 187) and Raymond Carver's "Popular Mechanics" fulfill Barth's description of minimalist fiction? How does each story suggest that less is more?

2. Write an essay explaining why one of the short stories by Nathaniel Hawthorne, William Faulkner, or Flannery O'Connor in this anthology is not a minimalist story.

A SAMPLE STUDENT RESPONSE

Hansen 1

Skyler Hansen

Professor Ríos

English 200

November 16, 2009

The Minimalist Style of Carver's "Popular Mechanics"

Raymond Carver provides little information in the story "Popular Mechanics." We are not given a complete background of the characters or vivid descriptions of setting. Even the dialogue is limited, and we are thrown into a scene already in progress. However, even though Carver does not tell us "a word more than [he] absolutely need[s] to" (Barth 336), all the necessary elements of a story are right there in front of us. Despite the minimalist style, we understand the characters and their motives by reading closely.

The plot of the story is simple: in the wake of a bitter fight, a man packs his suitcase and is about to leave the mother of his child. Many seemingly important details are missing. We're not certain whether the couple is married or what they are arguing about. We don't even know their names. However, all the story's complexities are there. The main conflict emerges when the man decides that he wants the baby. And while we might initially assume this has always been his intention, we realize that's not the case. He first plans to take a picture of the baby, and when the woman won't let him, he suddenly decides to raise the stakes:

> He did not answer. He fastened the suitcase, put on his
> coat, looked around the bedroom before turning off the light.
> Then he went out to the living room.
>
> She stood in the doorway of the little kitchen, holding the
> baby.
>
> I want the baby, he said. (334)

Here, we are practically able to watch the man's thought process. He feels so much anger toward the woman that he wants to hurt her before he leaves. As he packs, he searches for something he can take from her, and finally decides on the baby. His motive has little (perhaps nothing) to do with the child. He seeks only to devastate the child's mother.

Though the story appears to be open-ended, the resolution is clear. The two struggle for the baby, forcefully, violently, unwilling to give in to the other:

> She caught the baby around the wrist and leaned back.
>
> But he would not let go. He felt the baby slipping out of
> his hands and he pulled back very hard.
>
> In this manner, the issue was decided. (335)

While we do not know the extent of the damage, or what will become of these people, we do know that the baby suffers most as a result of the altercation, a theme Carver makes clear. . . .

Works Cited

Barth, John. "On Minimalist Fiction." *The Bedford Introduction to
   Literature.* Ed. Michael Meyer. 9th ed. Boston: Bedford/St. Martin's,
   2011. 336. Print.

Carver, Raymond. "Popular Mechanics." *The Bedford Introduction to Literature.*
   Ed. Michael Meyer. 9th ed. Boston: Bedford/St. Martin's, 2011.
   334–35. Print.

SUSAN MINOT (B. 1956)

Born and raised in Massachusetts, Susan Minot earned a B.A. at Brown University and an M.F.A. at Columbia University. Before devoting herself full-time to writing, Minot worked as an assistant editor at *Grand Street* magazine. Her stories have appeared in *The Atlantic, Harper's, The New Yorker, Mademoiselle,* and *Paris Review.* Her short stories have been collected in *Lust and Other Stories* (1989), and she has published four novels — *Monkeys* (1986), *Folly* (1992), *Evening* (1998), and *Rapture* (2002), as well as one volume of poetry, *Poems 4 A.M.* (2002).

Courtesy of Dinah Minot Hubley.

Lust   *1984*

Leo was from a long time ago, the first one I ever saw nude. In the spring before the Hellmans filled their pool, we'd go down there in the deep end, with baby oil, and like that. I met him the first month away at boarding school. He had a halo from the campus light behind him. I flipped.

Roger was fast. In his illegal car, we drove to the reservoir, the radio blaring, talking fast, fast, fast. He was always going for my zipper. He got kicked out sophomore year.

By the time the band got around to playing "Wild Horses," I had tasted Bruce's tongue. We were clicking in the shadows on the other side of the amplifier, out of Mrs. Donovan's line of vision. It tasted like salt, with my neck bent back, because we had been dancing so hard before.

Tim's line: "I'd like to see you in a bathing suit." I knew it was his line when he said the exact same thing to Annie Hines.

You'd go on walks to get off campus. It was raining like hell, my sweater as 5
sopped as a wet sheep. Tim pinned me to a tree, the woods light brown and dark brown, a white house half hidden with the lights already on. The water was as loud as a crowd hissing. He made certain comments about my forehead, about my cheeks.

We started off sitting at one end of the couch and then our feet were squished against the armrest and then he went over to turn off the TV and came back after he had taken off his shirt and then we slid onto the floor and he got up again to close the door, then came back to me, a body waiting on the rug.

You'd try to wipe off the table or to do the dishes and Willie would untuck your shirt and get his hands up under in front, standing behind you, making puffy noises in your ear.

He likes it when I wash my hair. He covers his face with it and if I start to say something, he goes, "Shush."

For a long time, I had Philip on the brain. The less they noticed you, the more you got them on the brain.

My parents had no idea. Parents never really know what's going on, espe- 10
cially when you're away at school most of the time. If she met them, my mother might say, "Oliver seems nice" or "I like that one" without much of an opinion. If she didn't like them, "He's a funny fellow, isn't he?" or "Johnny's perfectly nice but a drink of water." My father was too shy to talk to them at all unless they played sports and he'd ask them about that.

The sand was almost cold underneath because the sun was long gone. Eben piled a mound over my feet, patting around my ankles, the ghostly surf rumbling behind him in the dark. He was the first person I ever knew who died, later that summer, in a car crash. I thought about it for a long time.

"Come here," he says on the porch.
I go over to the hammock and he takes my wrist with two fingers.
"What?"
He kisses my palm then directs my hand to his fly. 15

Songs went with whichever boy it was. "Sugar Magnolia" was Tim, with the line "Rolling in the rushes / down by the riverside." With "Darkness Darkness," I'd picture Philip with his long hair. Hearing "Under My Thumb" there'd be the smell of Jamie's suede jacket.

We hid in the listening rooms during study hall. With a record cover over the door's window, the teacher on duty couldn't look in. I came out flushed and heady and back at the dorm was surprised how red my lips were in the mirror.

One weekend at Simon's brother's, we stayed inside all day with the shades down, in bed, then went out to Store 24 to get some ice cream. He stood at the magazine rack and read through *MAD* while I got butterscotch sauce, craving something sweet.

I could do some things well. Some things I was good at, like math or painting or even sports, but the second a boy put his arm around me, I forgot about wanting to do anything else, which felt like a relief at first until it became like sinking into a muck.

It was different for a girl. 20

When we were little, the brothers next door tied up our ankles. They held the door of the goat house and wouldn't let us out till we showed them our underpants. Then they'd forget about being after us and when we played whiffle ball, I'd be just as good as they were.

Then it got to be different. Just because you have on a short skirt, they yell from the cars, slowing down for a while, and if you don't look, they screech off and call you a bitch.

"What's the matter with me?" they say, point-blank.

Or else, "Why won't you go out with me? I'm not asking you to get married," about to get mad.

Or it'd be, trying to be reasonable, in a regular voice, "Listen, I just want to   25 have a good time."

So I'd go because I couldn't think of something to say back that wouldn't be obvious, and if you go out with them, you sort of have to do something.

I sat between Mack and Eddie in the front seat of the pickup. They were having a fight about something. I've a feeling about me.

Certain nights you'd feel a certain surrender, maybe if you'd had wine. The surrender would be forgetting yourself and you'd put your nose to his neck and feel like a squirrel, safe, at rest, in a restful dream. But then you'd start to slip from that and the dark would come in and there'd be a cave. You make out the dim shape of the windows and feel yourself become a cave, filled absolutely with air, or with a sadness that wouldn't stop.

Teenage years. You know just what you're doing and don't see the things that start to get in the way.

Lots of boys, but never two at the same time. One was plenty to keep you   30 in a state. You'd start to see a boy and something would rush over you like a fast storm cloud and you couldn't possibly think of anyone else. Boys took it differently. Their eyes perked up at any little number that walked by. You'd act like you weren't noticing.

The joke was that the school doctor gave out the pill like aspirin. He didn't ask you anything. I was fifteen. We had a picture of him in assembly, holding up an IUD shaped like a T. Most girls were on the pill, if anything, because they couldn't handle a diaphragm. I kept the dial in my top drawer like my mother and thought of her each time I tipped out the yellow tablets in the morning before chapel.

If they were too shy, I'd be more so. Andrew was nervous. We stayed up with his family album, sharing a pack of Old Golds. Before it got light, we turned on the TV. A man was explaining how to plant seedlings. His mouth jerked to the side in a tic. Andrew thought it was a riot and kept imitating him. I laughed to be polite. When we finally dozed off, he dared to put his arm around me, but that was it.

You wait till they come to you. With half fright, half swagger, they stand one step down. They dare to touch the button on your coat then lose their nerve and quickly drop their hand so you—you'd do anything for them. You touch their cheek.

The girls sit around in the common room and talk about boys, smoking their heads off.

"What are you complaining about?" says Jill to me when we talk about 35 problems.

"Yeah," says Giddy. "You always have a boyfriend."

I look at them and think, As if.

I thought the worst thing anyone could call you was a cock-teaser. So, if you flirted, you had to be prepared to go through with it. Sleeping with someone was perfectly normal once you had done it. You didn't really worry about it. But there were other problems. The problems had to do with something else entirely.

Mack was during the hottest summer ever recorded. We were renting a house on an island with all sorts of other people. No one slept during the heat wave, walking around the house with nothing on which we were used to because of the nude beach. In the living room, Eddie lay on top of a coffee table to cool off. Mack and I, with the bedroom door open for air, sweated and sweated all night.

"I can't take this," he said at three A.M. "I'm going for a swim." He and 40 some guys down the hall went to the beach. The heat put me on edge. I sat on a cracked chest by the open window and smoked and smoked till I felt even worse, waiting for something—I guess for him to get back.

One was on a camping trip in Colorado. We zipped our sleeping bags together, the coyotes' hysterical chatter far away. Other couples murmured in other tents. Paul was up before sunrise, starting a fire for breakfast. He wasn't much of a talker in the daytime. At night, his hand leafed about in the hair at my neck.

There'd be times when you overdid it. You'd get carried away. All the next day, you'd be in a total fog, delirious, absent-minded, crossing the street and nearly getting run over.

The more girls a boy has, the better. He has a bright look, having reaped fruits, blooming. He stalks around, sure-shouldered, and you have the feeling he's got more in him, a fatter heart, more stories to tell. For a girl, with each boy it's as though a petal gets plucked each time.

Then you start to get tired. You begin to feel diluted, like watered-down stew.

Oliver came skiing with us. We lolled by the fire after everyone had gone to 45 bed. Each creak you'd think was someone coming downstairs. The silver loop bracelet he gave me had been a present from his girlfriend before.

On vacations, we went skiing, or you'd go south if someone invited you. Some people had apartments in New York that their families hardly ever used. Or summer houses, or older sisters. We always managed to find someplace to go.

We made the plan at coffee hour. Simon snuck out and met me at Main Gate after lights-out. We crept to the chapel and spent the night in the balcony. He tasted like onions from a submarine sandwich.

The boys are one of two ways: either they can't sit still or they don't move. In front of the TV, they won't budge. On weekends they play touch football while we sit on the sidelines, picking blades of grass to chew on, and watch. We're always watching them run around. We shiver in the stands, knocking our boots together to keep our toes warm, and they whizz across the ice, chopping their sticks around the puck. When they're in the rink, they refuse to look at you, only eyeing each other beneath low helmets. You cheer for them but they don't look up, even if it's a face-off when nothing's happening, even if they're doing drills before any game has started at all.

Dancing under the pink tent, he bent down and whispered in my ear. We slipped away to the lawn on the other side of the hedge. Much later, as he was leaving the buffet with two plates of eggs and sausage, I saw the grass stains on the knees of his white pants.

Tim's was shaped like a banana, with a graceful curve to it. They're all different. Willie's like a bunch of walnuts when nothing was happening, another's as thin as a thin hot dog. But it's like faces; you're never really surprised. 50

Still, you're not sure what to expect.

I look into his face and he looks back. I look into his eyes and they look back at mine. Then they look down at my mouth so I look at his mouth, then back to his eyes then, backing up, at his whole face. I think, Who? Who are you? His head tilts to one side.
I say, "Who are you?"
"What do you mean?"
"Nothing." 55
I look at his eyes again, deeper. Can't tell who he is, what he thinks.
"What?" he says. I look at his mouth.
"I'm just wondering," I say and go wandering across his face. Study the chin line. It's shaped like a persimmon.
"Who are you? What are you thinking?"
He says, "What the hell are you talking about?" 60

Then they get mad after, when you say enough is enough. After, when it's easier to explain that you don't want to. You wouldn't dream of saying that maybe you weren't really ready to in the first place.

Gentle Eddie. We waded into the sea, the waves round and plowing in, buffalo-headed, slapping our thighs. I put my arms around his freckled shoulders and he held me up, buoyed by the water, and rocked me like a sea shell.

I had no idea whose party it was, the apartment jam-packed, stepping over people in the hallway. The room with the music was practically empty, the bare floor, me in red shoes. This fellow slides onto one knee and takes me around the waist and we rock to jazzy tunes, with my toes pointing heavenward, and waltz and spin and dip to "Smoke Gets in Your Eyes" or "I'll Love You Just for Now." He puts his head to my chest, runs a sweeping hand down my inside thigh and we go loose-limbed and sultry and as smooth as silk and I stamp my red heels and he takes me into a swoon. I never saw him again after that but I thought, I could have loved that one.

You wonder how long you can keep it up. You begin to feel as if you're showing through, like a bathroom window that only lets in grey light, the kind you can't see out of.

They keep coming around. Johnny drives up at Easter vacation from Balti-   65
more and I let him in the kitchen with everyone sound asleep. He has friends waiting in the car.

"What are you, crazy? It's pouring out there," I say.

"It's okay," he says. "They understand."

So he gets some long kisses from me, against the refrigerator, before he goes because I hate those girls who push away a boy's face as if she were made out of Ivory soap, as if she's that much greater than he is.

The note on my cubby told me to see the headmaster. I had no idea for what. He had received complaints about my amorous displays on the town green. It was Willie that spring. The headmaster told me he didn't care what I did but that Casey Academy had a reputation to uphold in the town. He lowered his glasses on his nose. "We've got twenty acres of woods on this campus," he said. "If you want to smooch with your boyfriend, there are twenty acres for you to do it out of the public eye. You read me?"

Everybody'd get weekend permissions for different places, then we'd all go   70
to someone's house whose parents were away. Usually there'd be more boys than girls. We raided the liquor closet and smoked pot at the kitchen table and you'd never know who would end up where, or with whom. There were always disasters. Ceci got bombed and cracked her head open on the banister and needed stitches. Then there was the time Wendel Blair walked through the picture window at the Lowes' and got slashed to ribbons.

He scared me. In bed, I didn't dare look at him. I lay back with my eyes closed, luxuriating because he knew all sorts of expert angles, his hands never fumbling, going over my whole body, pressing the hair up and off the back of my head, giving an extra hip shove, as if to say *There*. I parted my eyes slightly, keeping the screen of my lashes low because it was too much to look at him, his mouth loose and pink and parted, his eyes looking through my forehead, or kneeling up, looking through my throat. I was ashamed but couldn't look him in the eye.

You wonder about things feeling a little off-kilter. You begin to feel like a piece of pounded veal.

At boarding school, everyone gets depressed. We go in and see the housemother, Mrs. Gunther. She got married when she was eighteen. Mr. Gunther was her high school sweetheart, the only boyfriend she ever had.

"And you knew you wanted to marry him right off?" we ask her.

She smiles and says, "Yes."   75

"They always want something from you," says Jill, complaining about her boyfriend.

"Yeah," says Giddy. "You always feel like you have to deliver something."

"You do," says Mrs. Gunther. "Babies."

After sex, you curl up like a shrimp, something deep inside you ruined, slammed in a place that sickens at slamming, and slowly you fill up with an overwhelming sadness, an elusive gaping worry. You don't try to explain it, filled with the knowledge that it's nothing after all, everything filling up finally and absolutely with death. After the briskness of loving, loving stops. And you roll over with death stretched out alongside you like a feather boa, or a snake, light as air, and you . . . you don't even ask for anything or try to say something to him because it's obviously your own damn fault. You haven't been able to — to what? To open your heart. You open your legs but can't, or don't dare anymore, to open your heart.

It starts this way: 80

You stare into their eyes. They flash like all the stars are out. They look at you seriously, their eyes at a low burn and their hands no matter what starting off shy and with such a gentle touch that the only thing you can do is take that tenderness and let yourself be swept away. When, with one attentive finger they tuck the hair behind your ear, you —

You do everything they want.

Then comes after. After when they don't look at you. They scratch their balls, stare at the ceiling. Or if they do turn, their gaze is altogether changed. They are surprised. They turn casually to look at you, distracted, and get a mild distracted surprise. You're gone. Their blank look tells you that the girl they were fucking is not there anymore. You seem to have disappeared.

CONSIDERATIONS FOR CRITICAL THINKING AND WRITING

1. **FIRST RESPONSE.** What do you think of the narrator? Why? Do you agree with the definition the story offers for *lust*?

2. Do you think that the narrator's depiction of male and female responses to sex are accurate? Explain why or why not.

3. How effective is the narrator's description of teenage sex? What do you think she means when she says "You know just what you're doing and don't see the things that start to get in the way" (para. 29)?

4. What is the story's conflict? Explain whether you think the conflict is resolved.

5. Discuss the story's tone. Is it what you expected from the title?

6. What do you think is the theme of "Lust"? Does its style carry its theme?

7. What is the primary setting for the story? What does it reveal about the nature of the narrator's economic and social class?

8. In a *Publisher's Weekly* interview (November 6, 1992), Minot observed, "There's more fictional material in unhappiness and disappointment and frustration than there is in happiness. Who was it said, 'Happiness is like a blank page'?" What do you think of this observation?

CONNECTIONS TO OTHER SELECTIONS

1. Compare the treatments of youthful sexuality in "Lust" and David Updike's "Summer" (p. 380). Do you prefer one story to the other? Why?

2. Write an essay explaining the sort of advice the narrator of Fay Weldon's "IND AFF, or Out of Love in Sarajevo" (p. 202) might give to the narrator of "Lust." You might try writing this in the form of a letter.

TIM O'BRIEN (B. 1946)

Born in Austin, Minnesota, Tim O'Brien was educated at Macalester College and Harvard University. He was drafted to serve in the Vietnam War and received a Purple Heart. His work is heavily influenced by his service in the war. His first book, *If I Die in a Combat Zone, Box Me Up and Ship Me Home* (1973), is a blend of fiction and actual experiences during his tour of duty. *Going after Cacciato,* judged by many critics to be the best work of American fiction about the Vietnam War, won the National Book Award in 1978. He has also published five other novels, *North-*

© Marion Ettlinger.

ern Lights (1974), *The Nuclear Age* (1985), *In the Lake of the Woods* (1994), *Tomcat in Love* (1998), and *July, July* (2002). "How to Tell a True War Story" is from a collection of interrelated stories titled *The Things They Carried* (1990). Originally published in *Esquire,* this story is at once grotesque and beautiful in its attempt to be true to experience.

How to Tell a True War Story   1987

This is true.

I had a buddy in Vietnam. His name was Bob Kiley, but everybody called him Rat.

A friend of his gets killed, so about a week later Rat sits down and writes a letter to the guy's sister. Rat tells her what a great brother she had, how strack° the guy was, a number one pal and comrade. A real soldier's soldier, Rat says. Then he tells a few stories to make the point, how her brother would always volunteer for stuff nobody else would volunteer for in a million years, danger-ous stuff, like doing recon° or going out on these really badass night patrols.

---

strack: A strict military appearance.
doing recon: Reconnaissance, or exploratory survey of enemy territory.

Stainless steel balls, Rat tells her. The guy was a little crazy, for sure, but crazy in a good way, a real daredevil, because he liked the challenge of it, he liked testing himself, just man against gook. A great, great guy, Rat says.

Anyway, it's a terrific letter, very personal and touching. Rat almost bawls writing it. He gets all teary telling about the good times they had together, how her brother made the war seem almost fun, always raising hell and lighting up villes° and bringing smoke to bear every which way. A great sense of humor, too. Like the time at this river when he went fishing with a whole damn crate of hand grenades. Probably the funniest thing in world history, Rat says, all that gore, about twenty zillion dead gook fish. Her brother, he had the right attitude. He knew how to have a good time. On Halloween, this real hot spooky night, the dude paints up his body all different colors and puts on this weird mask and goes out on ambush almost stark naked, just boots and balls and an M-16. A tremendous human being, Rat says. Pretty nutso sometimes, but you could trust him with your life.

And then the letter gets very sad and serious. Rat pours his heart out. He   5
says he loved the guy. He says the guy was his best friend in the world. They were like soul mates, he says, like twins or something, they had a whole lot in common. He tells the guy's sister he'll look her up when the war's over.

So what happens?

Rat mails the letter. He waits two months. The dumb cooze never writes back.

A true war story is never moral. It does not instruct, nor encourage virtue, nor suggest models of proper human behavior, nor restrain men from doing the things they have always done. If a story seems moral, do not believe it. If at the end of a war story you feel uplifted, or if you feel that some small bit of rectitude has been salvaged from the larger waste, then you have been made the victim of a very old and terrible lie. There is no rectitude whatsoever. There is no virtue. As a first rule of thumb, therefore, you can tell a true war story by its absolute and uncompromising allegiance to obscenity and evil. Listen to Rat Kiley. *Cooze,* he says. He does not say *bitch.* He certainly does not say *woman,* or *girl.* He says *cooze.* Then he spits and stares. He's nineteen years old — it's too much for him — so he looks at you with those big gentle killer eyes and says *cooze,* because his friend is dead, and because it's so incredibly sad and true: she never wrote back.

You can tell a true war story if it embarrasses you. If you don't care for obscenity, you don't care for the truth; if you don't care for the truth, watch how you vote. Send guys to war, they come home talking dirty.

Listen to Rat: "Jesus Christ, man, I write this beautiful fucking letter, I   10
slave over it, and what happens? The dumb cooze never writes back."

The dead guy's name was Curt Lemon. What happened was, we crossed a muddy river and marched west into the mountains, and on the third day we took a break along a trail junction in deep jungle. Right away, Lemon and Rat Kiley started goofing off. They didn't understand about the spookiness. They were kids; they just didn't know. A nature hike, they thought, not even a war, so they went off into the shade of some giant trees — quadruple canopy, no

---

villes: Villages.

sunlight at all — and they were giggling and calling each other motherfucker and playing a silly game they'd invented. The game involved smoke grenades, which were harmless unless you did stupid things, and what they did was pull out the pin and stand a few feet apart and play catch under the shade of those huge trees. Whoever chickened out was a motherfucker. And if nobody chickened out, the grenade would make a light popping sound and they'd be covered with smoke and they'd laugh and dance around and then do it again.

It's all exactly true.

It happened nearly twenty years ago, but I still remember that trail junction and the giant trees and a soft dripping sound somewhere beyond the trees. I remember the smell of moss. Up in the canopy there were tiny white blossoms, but no sunlight at all, and I remember the shadows spreading out under the trees where Lemon and Rat Kiley were playing catch with smoke grenades. Mitchell Sanders sat flipping his yo-yo. Norman Bowker and Kiowa and Dave Jensen were dozing, or half-dozing, and all around us were those ragged green mountains.

Except for the laughter things were quiet.

At one point, I remember, Mitchell Sanders turned and looked at me, not 15 quite nodding, then after a while he rolled up his yo-yo and moved away.

It's hard to tell what happened next.

They were just goofing. There was a noise, I suppose, which must've been the detonator, so I glanced behind me and watched Lemon step from the shade into bright sunlight. His face was suddenly brown and shining. A handsome kid, really. Sharp gray eyes, lean and narrow-waisted, and when he died it was almost beautiful, the way the sunlight came around him and lifted him up and sucked him high into a tree full of moss and vines and white blossoms.

In any war story, but especially a true one, it's difficult to separate what happened from what seemed to happen. What seems to happen becomes its own happening and has to be told that way. The angles of vision are skewed. When a booby trap explodes, you close your eyes and duck and float outside yourself. When a guy dies, like Lemon, you look away and then look back for a moment and then look away again. The pictures get jumbled; you tend to miss a lot. And then afterward, when you go to tell about it, there is always that surreal seemingness, which makes the story seem untrue, but which in fact represents the hard and exact truth as it seemed.

In many cases a true war story cannot be believed. If you believe it, be skeptical. It's a question of credibility. Often the crazy stuff is true and the normal stuff isn't because the normal stuff is necessary to make you believe the truly incredible craziness.

In other cases you can't even tell a true war story. Sometimes it's just 20 beyond telling.

I heard this one, for example, from Mitchell Sanders. It was near dusk and we were sitting at my foxhole along a wide, muddy river north of Quang Ngai. I remember how peaceful the twilight was. A deep pinkish red spilled out on the river, which moved without sound, and in the morning we would cross the river and march west into the mountains. The occasion was right for a good story.

"God's truth," Mitchell Sanders said. "A six-man patrol goes up into the mountains on a basic listening-post operation. The idea's to spend a week up there, just lie low and listen for enemy movement. They've got a radio along, so if they hear anything suspicious — anything — they're supposed to call in artillery or gunships, whatever it takes. Otherwise they keep strict field discipline. Absolute silence. They just listen."

He glanced at me to make sure I had the scenario. He was playing with his yo-yo, making it dance with short, tight little strokes of the wrist.

His face was blank in the dusk.

"We're talking hardass LP.° These six guys, they don't say boo for a solid   25
week. They don't got tongues. *All* ears."

"Right," I said.

"Understand me?"

"Invisible."

Sanders nodded.

"Affirm," he said. "Invisible. So what happens is, these guys get themselves   30
deep in the bush, all camouflaged up, and they lie down and wait and that's all they do, nothing else, they lie there for seven straight days and just listen. And man, I'll tell you — it's spooky. This is mountains. You don't *know* spooky till you been there. Jungle, sort of, except it's way up in the clouds and there's always this fog — like rain, except it's not raining — everything's all wet and swirly and tangled up and you can't see jack, you can't find your own pecker to piss with. Like you don't even have a body. Serious spooky. You just go with the vapors — the fog sort of takes you in. . . . And the sounds, man. The sounds carry forever. You hear shit nobody should *ever* hear."

Sanders was quiet for a second, just working the yo-yo, then he smiled at me. "So, after a couple days the guys start hearing this real soft, kind of wacked-out music. Weird echoes and stuff. Like a radio or something, but it's not a radio, it's this strange gook music that comes right out of the rocks. Faraway, sort of, but right up close, too. They try to ignore it. But it's a listening post, right? So they listen. And every night they keep hearing this crazyass gook concert. All kinds of chimes and xylophones. I mean, this is wilderness — no way, it can't be real — but there it *is,* like the mountains are tuned in to Radio Fucking Hanoi. Naturally they get nervous. One guy sticks Juicy Fruit in his ears. Another guy almost flips. Thing is, though, they can't report music. They can't get on the horn and call back to base and say, 'Hey, listen, we need some firepower, we got to blow away this weirdo gook rock band.' They can't do that. It wouldn't go down. So they lie there in the fog and keep their mouths shut. And what makes it extra bad, see, is the poor dudes can't horse around like normal. Can't joke it away. Can't even talk to each other except maybe in whispers, all hush-hush, and that just revs up the willies. All they do is listen."

Again there was some silence as Mitchell Sanders looked out on the river. The dark was coming on hard now, and off to the west I could see the mountains rising in silhouette, all the mysteries and unknowns.

"This next part," Sanders said quietly, "you won't believe."

"Probably not," I said.

"You won't. And you know why?"   35

LP: Listening post.

"Why?"

He gave me a tired smile. "Because it happened. Because every word is absolutely dead-on true."

Sanders made a little sound in his throat, like a sigh, as if to say he didn't care if I believed it or not. But he did care. He wanted me to believe, I could tell. He seemed sad, in a way.

"These six guys, they're pretty fried out by now, and one night they start hearing voices. Like at a cocktail party. That's what it sounds like, this big swank gook cocktail party somewhere out there in the fog. Music and chitchat and stuff. It's crazy, I know, but they hear the champagne corks. They hear the actual martini glasses. Real hoity-toity, all very civilized, except this isn't civilization. This is Nam.

"Anyway, the guys try to be cool. They just lie there and groove, but after a   40
while they start hearing—you won't believe this—they hear chamber music. They hear violins and shit. They hear this terrific mama-san soprano. Then after a while they hear gook opera and a glee club and the Haiphong Boys Choir and a barbershop quartet and all kinds of weird chanting and Buddha-Buddha stuff. The whole time, in the background, there's still that cocktail party going on. All these different voices. Not human voices, though. Because it's the mountains. Follow me? The rock—it's *talking*. And the fog, too, and the grass and the goddamn mongooses. Everything talks. The trees talk politics, the monkeys talk religion. The whole country. Vietnam, the place talks.

"The guys can't cope. They lose it. They get on the radio and report enemy movement—a whole army, they say—and they order up the firepower. They get arty° and gunships. They call in air strikes. And I'll tell you, they fuckin' crash that cocktail party. All night long, they just smoke those mountains. They make jungle juice. They blow away trees and glee clubs and whatever else there is to blow away. Scorch time. They walk napalm up and down the ridges. They bring in the Cobras and F-4s, they use Willie Peter and HE° and incendiaries. It's all fire. They make those mountains burn.

"Around dawn things finally get quiet. Like you never even *heard* quiet before. One of those real thick, real misty days—just clouds and fog, they're off in this special zone—and the mountains are absolutely dead-flat silent. Like Brigadoon°— pure vapor, you know? Everything's all sucked up inside the fog. Not a single sound, except they still *hear* it.

"So they pack up and start humping. They head down the mountain, back to base camp, and when they get there they don't say diddly. They don't talk. Not a word, like they're deaf and dumb. Later on this fat bird colonel comes up and asks what the hell happened out there. What'd they hear? Why all the ordnance? The man's ragged out, he gets down tight on their case. I mean, they spent six trillion dollars on firepower, and this fatass colonel wants answers, he wants to know what the fuckin' story is.

"But the guys don't say zip. They just look at him for a while, sort of funny-like, sort of amazed, and the whole war is right there in that stare. It says everything you can't ever say. It says, man, you got *wax* in your ears. It says,

---

arty: Artillery.
Willie Peter and HE: White phosphorus, an incendiary substance, and high explosives.
Brigadoon: A fictional village in Scotland that only appears once every one hundred years; subject of a popular American musical (1947).

poor bastard, you'll never know—wrong frequency—you don't *even* want to hear this. Then they salute the fucker and walk away, because certain stories you don't ever tell."

You can tell a true war story by the way it never seems to end. Not then, not 45
ever. Not when Mitchell Sanders stood up and moved off into the dark.

It all happened.

Even now I remember that yo-yo. In a way, I suppose, you had to be there, you had to hear it, but I could tell how desperately Sanders wanted me to believe him, his frustration at not quite getting the details right, not quite pinning down the final and definitive truth.

And I remember sitting at my foxhole that night, watching the shadows of Quang Ngai, thinking about the coming day and how we would cross the river and march west into the mountains, all the ways I might die, all the things I did not understand.

Late in the night Mitchell Sanders touched my shoulder.

"Just came to me," he whispered. "The moral, I mean. Nobody listens. 50
Nobody hears nothing. Like that fatass colonel. The politicians, all the civilian types, what they need is to go out on LP. The vapors, man. Trees and rocks— you got to *listen* to your enemy."

And then again, in the morning, Sanders came up to me. The platoon was preparing to move out, checking weapons, going through all the little rituals that preceded a day's march. Already the lead squad had crossed the river and was filing off toward the west.

"I got a confession to make," Sanders said. "Last night, man, I had to make up a few things."

"I know that."

"The glee club. There wasn't any glee club."

"Right." 55

"No opera."

"Forget it, I understand."

"Yeah, but listen, it's still true. Those six guys, they heard wicked sound out there. They heard sound you just plain won't believe."

Sanders pulled on his rucksack, closed his eyes for a moment, then almost smiled at me.

I knew what was coming but I beat him to it. 60

"All right," I said, "what's the moral?"

"Forget it."

"No, go ahead."

For a long while he was quiet, looking away, and the silence kept stretching out until it was almost embarrassing. Then he shrugged and gave me a stare that lasted all day.

"Hear that quiet, man?" he said. "There's your moral." 65

In a true war story, if there's a moral at all, it's like the thread that makes the cloth. You can't tease it out. You can't extract the meaning without unraveling the deeper meaning. And in the end, really, there's nothing much to say about a true war story, except maybe "Oh."

True war stories do not generalize. They do not indulge in abstraction or analysis.

For example: War is hell. As a moral declaration the old truism seems perfectly true, and yet because it abstracts, because it generalizes, I can't believe it with my stomach. Nothing turns inside.

It comes down to gut instinct. A true war story, if truly told, makes the stomach believe.

This one does it for me. I've told it before — many times, many versions — but   70
here's what actually happened.

We crossed the river and marched west into the mountains. On the third day, Curt Lemon stepped on a booby-trapped 105 round. He was playing catch with Rat Kiley, laughing, and then he was dead. The trees were thick; it took nearly an hour to cut an LZ for the dustoff.°

Later, higher in the mountains, we came across a baby VC° water buffalo. What it was doing there I don't know — no farms or paddies — but we chased it down and got a rope around it and led it along to a deserted village where we set for the night. After supper Rat Kiley went over and stroked its nose.

He opened up a can of C rations, pork and beans, but the baby buffalo wasn't interested.

Rat shrugged.

He stepped back and shot it through the right front knee. The animal did   75
not make a sound. It went down hard, then got up again, and Rat took careful aim and shot off an ear. He shot it in the hindquarters and in the little hump at its back. He shot it twice in the flanks. It wasn't to kill; it was just to hurt. He put the rifle muzzle up against the mouth and shot the mouth away. Nobody said much. The whole platoon stood there watching, feeling all kinds of things, but there wasn't a great deal of pity for the baby water buffalo. Lemon was dead. Rat Kiley had lost his best friend in the world. Later in the week he would write a long personal letter to the guy's sister, who would not write back, but for now it was a question of pain. He shot off the tail. He shot away chunks of meat below the ribs. All around us there was the smell of smoke and filth, and deep greenery, and the evening was humid and very hot. Rat went to automatic. He shot randomly, almost casually, quick little spurts in the belly and butt. Then he reloaded, squatted down, and shot it in the left front knee. Again the animal fell hard and tried to get up, but this time it couldn't quite make it. It wobbled and went down sideways. Rat shot it in the nose. He bent forward and whispered something, as if talking to a pet, then he shot it in the throat. All the while the baby buffalo was silent, or almost silent, just a light bubbling sound where the nose had been. It lay very still. Nothing moved except the eyes, which were enormous, the pupils shiny black and dumb.

Rat Kiley was crying. He tried to say something, but then cradled his rifle and went off by himself.

The rest of us stood in a ragged circle around the baby buffalo. For a time no one spoke. We had witnessed something essential, something brand-new and profound, a piece of the world so startling there was not yet a name for it.

Somebody kicked the baby buffalo.

It was still alive, though just barely, just in the eyes.

LZ for the dustoff: Landing zone for a helicopter evacuation of a casualty.
VC: Vietcong (North Vietnamese).

"Amazing," Dave Jensen said. "My whole life, I never seen anything like it." 80

"Never?"

"Not hardly. Not once."

Kiowa and Mitchell Sanders picked up the baby buffalo. They hauled it across the open square, hoisted it up, and dumped it in the village well.

Afterward, we sat waiting for Rat to get himself together.

"Amazing," Dave Jensen kept saying. 85

"For sure."

"A new wrinkle. I never seen it before."

Mitchell Sanders took out his yo-yo.

"Well, that's Nam," he said. "Garden of Evil. Over here, man, every sin's real fresh and original."

How do you generalize? 90

War is hell, but that's not the half of it, because war is also mystery and terror and adventure and courage and discovery and holiness and pity and despair and longing and love. War is nasty; war is fun. War is thrilling; war is drudgery. War makes you a man; war makes you dead.

The truths are contradictory. It can be argued, for instance, that war is grotesque. But in truth war is also beauty. For all its horror, you can't help but gape at the awful majesty of combat. You stare out at tracer rounds unwinding through the dark like brilliant red ribbons. You crouch in ambush as a cool, impassive moon rises over the nighttime paddies. You admire the fluid symmetries of troops on the move, the harmonies of sound and shape and proportion, the great sheets of metal-fire streaming down from a gunship, the illumination rounds, the white phosphorous, the purply black glow of napalm, the rocket's red glare. It's not pretty, exactly. It's astonishing. It fills the eye. It commands you. You hate it, yes, but your eyes do not. Like a killer forest fire, like cancer under a microscope, any battle or bombing raid or artillery barrage has the aesthetic purity of absolute moral indifference—a powerful, implacable beauty—and a true war story will tell the truth about this, though the truth is ugly.

To generalize about war is like generalizing about peace. Almost everything is true. Almost nothing is true. At its core, perhaps, war is just another name for death, and yet any soldier will tell you, if he tells the truth, that proximity to death brings with it a corresponding proximity to life. After a fire fight, there is always the immense pleasure of aliveness. The trees are alive. The grass, the soil—everything. All around you things are purely living, and you among them, and the aliveness makes you tremble. You feel an intense, out-of-the-skin awareness of your living self—your truest self, the human being you want to be and then become by the force of wanting it. In the midst of evil you want to be a good man. You want decency. You want justice and courtesy and human concord, things you never knew you wanted. There is a kind of largeness to it; a kind of godliness. Though it's odd, you're never more alive than when you're almost dead. You recognize what's valuable. Freshly, as if for the first time, you love what's best in yourself and in the world, all that might be lost. At the hour of dusk you sit at your foxhole and look out on a wide river turning pinkish red, and at the mountains beyond, and although in the morning you must cross the river and go into the mountains and do terrible things and maybe die, even so, you find yourself studying the fine colors on the river, you feel wonder and awe at the setting of the sun, and you are filled with a hard, aching love for how the world could be and always should be, but now is not.

Mitchell Sanders was right. For the common soldier, at least, war has the feel — the spiritual texture — of a great ghostly fog, thick and permanent. There is no clarity. Everything swirls. The old rules are no longer binding, the old truths no longer true. Right spills over into wrong. Order blends into chaos, love into hate, ugliness into beauty, law into anarchy, civility into savagery. The vapors suck you in. You can't tell where you are, or why you're there, and the only certainty is absolute ambiguity.

In war you lose your sense of the definite, hence your sense of truth itself, 95 and therefore it's safe to say that in a true war story nothing much is ever very true.

Often in a true war story there is not even a point, or else the point doesn't hit you until twenty years later, in your sleep, and you wake up and shake your wife and start telling the story to her, except when you get to the end you've forgotten the point again. And then for a long time you lie there watching the story happen in your head. You listen to your wife's breathing. The war's over. You close your eyes. You smile and think, Christ, what's the *point?*

This one wakes me up.

In the mountains that day, I watched Lemon turn sideways. He laughed and said something to Rat Kiley. Then he took a peculiar half step, moving from shade into bright sunlight, and the booby-trapped 105 round blew him into a tree. The parts were just hanging there, so Norman Bowker and I were ordered to shinny up and peel him off. I remember the white bone of an arm. I remember pieces of skin and something wet and yellow that must've been the intestines. The gore was horrible, and stays with me, but what wakes me up twenty years later is Norman Bowker singing "Lemon Tree" as we threw down the parts.

You can tell a true war story by the questions you ask. Somebody tells a story, let's say, and afterward you ask, "Is it true?" and if the answer matters, you've got your answer.

For example, we've all heard this one. Four guys go down a trail. A grenade 100 sails out. One guy jumps on it and takes the blast and saves his three buddies.

Is it true?

The answer matters.

You'd feel cheated if it never happened. Without the grounding reality, it's just a trite bit of puffery, pure Hollywood, untrue in the way all such stories are untrue. Yet even if it did happen — and maybe it did, anything's possible — even then you know it can't be true, because a true war story does not depend upon that kind of truth. Happeningness is irrelevant. A thing may happen and be a total lie; another thing may not happen and be truer than the truth. For example: four guys go down a trail. A grenade sails out. One guy jumps on it and takes the blast, but it's a killer grenade and everybody dies anyway. Before they die, though, one of the dead guys says, "The fuck you do *that* for?" and the jumper says, "Story of my life, man," and the other guy starts to smile but he's dead.

That's a true story that never happened.

Twenty years later, I can still see the sunlight on Lemon's face. I can see him 105
turning, looking back at Rat Kiley, then he laughed and took that curious half
step from shade into sunlight, his face suddenly brown and shining, and when his
foot touched down, in that instant, he must've thought it was the sunlight that
was killing him. It was not the sunlight. It was a rigged 105 round. But if I could
ever get the story right, how the sun seemed to gather around him and pick him
up and lift him into a tree, if I could somehow recreate the fatal whiteness of that
light, the quick glare, the obvious cause and effect, then you would believe the last
thing Lemon believed, which for him must've been the final truth.

Now and then, when I tell this story, someone will come up to me afterward
and say she liked it. It's always a woman. Usually it's an older woman of kindly
temperament and humane politics. She'll explain that as a rule she hates war
stories, she can't understand why people want to wallow in blood and gore.
But this one she liked. Sometimes, even, there are little tears. What I should do,
she'll say, is put it all behind me. Find new stories to tell.

I won't say it but I'll think it.

I'll picture Rat Kiley's face, his grief, and I'll think, *You dumb cooze.*

Because she wasn't listening.

It wasn't a war story. It was a love story. It was a ghost story. 110

But you can't say that. All you can do is tell it one more time, patiently,
adding and subtracting, making up a few things to get at the real truth. No
Mitchell Sanders, you tell her. No Lemon, no Rat Kiley. And it didn't happen
in the mountains, it happened in this little village on the Batangan Peninsula,
and it was raining like crazy, and one night a guy named Stink Harris woke up
screaming with a leech on his tongue. You can tell a true war story if you just
keep on telling it.

In the end, of course, a true war story is never about war. It's about the
special way that dawn spreads out on a river when you know you must cross
the river and march into the mountains and do things you are afraid to do. It's
about love and memory. It's about sorrow. It's about sisters who never write
back and people who never listen.

CONSIDERATIONS FOR CRITICAL THINKING AND WRITING

1. **FIRST RESPONSE.** What implicit problem is created about the story by its
   first line, "This is true"? How is the notion of "truth" problematized
   throughout the story and subjected to irony?

2. Why is Rat Kiley so upset over Curt Lemon's sister not writing back?

3. How are you affected by the descriptions of Curt Lemon being blown up
   in paragraphs 17, 98, and 105?

4. Analyze the story told about the six-man patrol in paragraphs 19–65. How
   is this story relevant to the rest of the plot?

5. What emotions did you feel as you read about the shooting of the water
   buffalo? How does paragraph 75 achieve these effects?

6. Explain what you think O'Brien means when he writes "After a fire fight,
   there is always the immense pleasure of aliveness" (para. 93).

7. Trace the narrator's comments about what constitutes a true war story. What
   do you think these competing and contradictory ideas finally add up to?

8. Characterize the narrator. Why must he repeatedly "keep on telling" his war story?

9. Consider O'Brien's use of profanity and violence in this story. Do you think they are essential or merely sensational?

10. **CRITICAL STRATEGIES.** Read the discussion concerning historical criticism (pp. 2052–56) in Chapter 53, "Critical Strategies for Reading," and research American protests and reactions to the war in Vietnam. How are these responses relevant to O'Brien's story, particularly paragraphs 1–10 and 106–11?

CONNECTIONS TO OTHER SELECTIONS

1. Imagine Krebs from Ernest Hemingway's "Soldier's Home" (p. 187) writing a letter home recommending "How to Tell a True War Story" to his parents. Write that letter from Krebs's point of view.

2. How does the treatment of violence in O'Brien's story compare with that in Andre Dubus's "Killings" (p. 103)? Write an essay that points to specific descriptions and explains the function of the violence in each story.

Z. Z. PACKER (B. 1973)

Born in 1973 in Chicago, Packer received a B.A. from Yale University in 1994, an M.A. from Johns Hopkins University in 1995, and an M.F.A. from the University of Iowa in 1999. She was also a Stegner Fellow at Stanford University and has received many other prestigious awards such as the Rona Jaffe Writers Foundation Grant in 1997, the Ms. Giles Whiting Award in 1999, the Bellingham Review Award for the short story "Brownies" (1999), and a Guggenheim Fellowship in 2005. Her work has appeared in *Seventeen*, *Harper's*, *The Best American Short Stories* (2000), and *Ploughshares*. Her short story "Drink-

© Marion Ettlinger.

ing Coffee Elsewhere" was published in *The New Yorker*'s summer 2000 Debut Fiction issue and is also the title story for a collection she published in 2003. Packer now lives in San Francisco, where she is working on a novel.

Brownies   1999

By our second day at Camp Crescendo, the girls in my Brownie troop had decided to kick the asses of each and every girl in Brownie Troop 909. Troop 909 was doomed from the first day of camp; they were white girls, their complexions a blend of ice cream: strawberry, vanilla. They turtled out from their bus in pairs, their rolled-up sleeping bags chromatized with Disney characters: Sleeping Beauty, Snow White, Mickey Mouse; or the generic ones cheap parents bought: washed-out rainbows, unicorns, curly-eyelashed frogs. Some clutched Igloo coolers and still others held on to stuffed toys like pacifiers, looking all around them like tourists determined to be dazzled.

Our troop was wending its way past their bus, past the ranger station, past the colorful trail guide drawn like a treasure map, locked behind glass.

"Man, did you smell them?" Arnetta said, giving the girls a slow once-over, "They smell like Chihuahuas. *Wet* Chihuahuas." Their troop was still at the entrance, and though we had passed them by yards, Arnetta raised her nose in the air and grimaced.

Arnetta said this from the very rear of the line, far away from Mrs. Margolin, who always strung our troop behind her like a brood of obedient ducklings. Mrs. Margolin even looked like a mother duck — she had hair cropped close to a small ball of a head, almost no neck, and huge, miraculous breasts. She wore enormous belts that looked like the kind that weightlifters wear, except hers would be cheap metallic gold or rabbit fur covered with gigantic fake sunflowers, and often these belts would become nature lessons in and of themselves. "See," Mrs. Margolin once said to us, pointing to her belt, "this one's made entirely from the feathers of baby pigeons."

The belt layered with feathers was uncanny enough, but I was more disturbed by the realization that I had never actually *seen* a baby pigeon. I searched weeks for one, in vain — scampering after pigeons whenever I was downtown with my father.

But nature lessons were not Mrs. Margolin's top priority. She saw the position of troop leader as an evangelical post. Back at the A.M.E. church where our Brownie meetings were held, Mrs. Margolin was especially fond of imparting religious aphorisms by means of acrostics — "Satan" was the "Serpent Always Tempting and Noisome"; she'd refer to the "Bible" as "Basic Instructions Before Leaving Earth." Whenever she quizzed us on these, expecting to hear the acrostics parroted back to her, only Arnetta's correct replies soared over our vague mumblings. "Jesus?" Mrs. Margolin might ask expectantly, and Arnetta alone would dutifully answer, "Jehovah's Example, Saving Us Sinners."

Arnetta always made a point of listening to Mrs. Margolin's religious talk and giving her what she wanted to hear. Because of this, Arnetta could have blared through a megaphone that the white girls of Troop 909 were "wet Chihuahuas" without so much as a blink from Mrs. Margolin. Once, Arnetta killed the troop goldfish by feeding it a french fry covered in ketchup, and when Mrs. Margolin demanded that she explain what had happened, claimed the goldfish had been eyeing her meal for *hours,* then the fish — giving in to temptation — had leapt up and snatched a whole golden fry from her fingertips.

"*Serious* Chihuahua," Octavia added, and though neither Arnetta nor Octavia could *spell* "Chihuahua," had ever *seen* a Chihuahua, trisyllabic words had gained a sort of exoticism within our fourth-grade set at Woodrow Wilson Elementary. Arnetta and Octavia would flip through the dictionary, determined to work the vulgar-sounding ones like "Djibouti" and "asinine" into conversation.

"*Caucasian* Chihuahuas," Arnetta said.

That did it. The girls in my troop turned elastic: Drema and Elise doubled up on one another like inextricably entwined kites; Octavia slapped her belly;

Janice jumped straight up in the air, then did it again, as if to slam-dunk her own head. They could not stop laughing. No one had laughed so hard since a boy named Martez had stuck a pencil in the electric socket and spent the whole day with a strange grin on his face.

"Girls, girls," said our parent helper, Mrs. Hedy. Mrs. Hedy was Octavia's mother, and she wagged her index finger perfunctorily, like a windshield wiper. "Stop it, now. Be good." She said this loud enough to be heard, but lazily, bereft of any feeling or indication that she meant to be obeyed, as though she could say these words again at the exact same pitch if a button somewhere on her were pressed.

But the rest of the girls didn't stop; they only laughed louder. It was the word "Caucasian" that got them all going. One day at school, about a month before the Brownie camping trip, Arnetta turned to a boy wearing impossibly high-ankled floodwater jeans and said, "What are you? *Caucasian?*" The word took off from there, and soon everything was Caucasian. If you ate too fast you ate like a Caucasian, if you ate too slow you ate like a Caucasian. The biggest feat anyone at Woodrow Wilson could do was to jump off the swing in midair, at the highest point in its arc, and if you fell (as I had, more than once) instead of landing on your feet, knees bent Olympic gymnast–style, Arnetta and Octavia were prepared to comment. They'd look at each other with the silence of passengers who'd narrowly escaped an accident, then nod their heads, whispering with solemn horror, "*Caucasian.*"

Even the only white kid in our school, Dennis, got in on the Caucasian act. That time when Martez stuck a pencil in the socket, Dennis had pointed and yelled, "That was *so* Caucasian!"

When you lived in the south suburbs of Atlanta, it was easy to forget about whites. Whites were like those baby pigeons: real and existing, but rarely seen or thought about. Everyone had been to Rich's to go clothes shopping, everyone had seen white girls and their mothers coo-cooing over dresses; everyone had gone to the downtown library and seen white businessmen swish by importantly, wrists flexed in front of them to check the time as though they would change from Clark Kent into Superman at any second. But those images were as fleeting as cards shuffled in a deck, whereas the ten white girls behind us — *invaders,* Arnetta would later call them — were instantly real and memorable, with their long, shampoo-commercial hair, straight as spaghetti from the box. This alone was reason for envy and hatred. The only black girl most of us had ever seen with hair that long was Octavia, whose hair hung past her butt like a Hawaiian hula dancer's. The sight of Octavia's mane prompted other girls to listen to her reverentially, as though whatever she had to say would somehow activate their own follicles. For example, when, on the first day of camp, Octavia made as if to speak, and everyone fell silent. "Nobody," Octavia said, "calls us niggers."

At the end of that first day, when half of our troop made their way back to 15 the cabin after tag-team restroom visits, Arnetta said she'd heard one of the Troop 909 girls call Daphne a nigger. The other half of the girls and I were helping Mrs. Margolin clean up the pots and pans from the campfire ravioli dinner. When we made our way to the restrooms to wash up and brush our teeth, we met up with Arnetta midway.

"Man, I completely heard the girl," Arnetta reported. "Right, Daphne?"

Daphne hardly ever spoke, but when she did, her voice was petite and tinkly, the voice one might expect from a shiny new earring. She'd written a poem once, for Langston Hughes Day, a poem brimming with all the teacher-winning ingredients — trees and oceans, sunsets and moons — but what cinched the poem for the grown-ups, snatching the win from Octavia's musical ode to Grandmaster Flash and the Furious Five, were Daphne's last lines:

> You are my father, the veteran
> When you cry in the dark
> It rains and rains and rains in my heart

She'd always worn clean, though faded, jumpers and dresses when Chic jeans were the fashion, but when she went up to the dais to receive her prize journal, pages trimmed in gold, she wore a new dress with a velveteen bodice and a taffeta skirt as wide as an umbrella. All the kids clapped, though none of them understood the poem. I'd read encyclopedias the way others read comics, and I didn't get it. But those last lines pricked me, they were so eerie, and as my father and I ate cereal, I'd whisper over my Froot Loops, like a mantra, *"You are my father, the veteran. You are my father, the veteran, the veteran, the veteran,"* until my father, who acted in plays as Caliban and Othello and was not a veteran, marched me up to my teacher one morning and said, "Can you tell me what's wrong with this kid?"

I thought Daphne and I might become friends, but I think she grew spooked by me whispering those lines to her, begging her to tell me what they meant, and I soon understood that two quiet people like us were better off quiet alone.

"Daphne? Didn't you hear them call you a nigger?" Arnetta asked, giving   20 Daphne a nudge.

The sun was setting behind the trees, and their leafy tops formed a canopy of black lace for the flame of the sun to pass through. Daphne shrugged her shoulders at first, then slowly nodded her head when Arnetta gave her a hard look.

Twenty minutes later, when my restroom group returned to the cabin, Arnetta was still talking about Troop 909. My restroom group had passed by some of the 909 girls. For the most part, they deferred to us, waving us into the restrooms, letting us go even though they'd gotten there first.

We'd seen them, but from afar, never within their orbit enough to see whether their faces were the way all white girls appeared on TV — ponytailed and full of energy, bubbling over with love and money. All I could see was that some of them rapidly fanned their faces with their hands, though the heat of the day had long passed. A few seemed to be lolling their heads in slow circles, half purposefully, as if exercising the muscles of their necks, half ecstatically, like Stevie Wonder.

"We can't let them get away with that," Arnetta said, dropping her voice to a laryngitic whisper. "We can't let them get away with calling us niggers. I say we teach them a lesson." She sat down cross-legged on a sleeping bag, an embittered Buddha, eyes glimmering acrylic-black. "We can't go telling Mrs. Margolin, either. Mrs. Margolin'll say something about doing unto others and the path of righteousness and all. Forget that shit." She let her eyes flutter irreverently till they half closed, as though ignoring an insult not worth returning. We could all hear Mrs. Margolin outside, gathering the last of the metal campware.

Nobody said anything for a while. Usually people were quiet after Arnetta   25
spoke. Her tone had an upholstered confidence that was somehow both regal
and vulgar at once. It demanded a few moments of silence in its wake, like the
ringing of a church bell or the playing of taps. Sometimes Octavia would ditto
or dissent to whatever Arnetta had said, and this was the signal that others
could speak. But this time Octavia just swirled a long cord of hair into pretzel
shapes.

   "*Well?*" Arnetta said. She looked as if she had discerned the hidden severity of the situation and was waiting for the rest of us to catch up. Everyone
looked from Arnetta to Daphne. It was, after all, Daphne who had supposedly
been called the name, but Daphne sat on the bare cabin floor, flipping through
the pages of the Girl Scout handbook, eyebrows arched in mock wonder, as if
the handbook were a catalogue full of bright and startling foreign costumes.
Janice broke the silence. She clapped her hands to broach her idea of a plan.

   "They gone be sleeping," she whispered conspiratorially, "then we gone
sneak into they cabin, then we'll put daddy longlegs in they sleeping bags. Then
they'll wake up. Then we gone beat 'em up till they're as flat as frying pans!" She
jammed her fist into the palm of her hand, then made a sizzling sound.

   Janice's country accent was laughable, her looks homely, her jumpy acro-
batics embarrassing to behold. Arnetta and Octavia volleyed amused, arrogant
smiles whenever Janice opened her mouth, but Janice never caught the hint,
spoke whenever she wanted, fluttered around Arnetta and Octavia futilely offering her opinions to their departing backs. Whenever Arnetta and Octavia
shooed her away, Janice loitered until the two would finally sigh and ask,
"What *is* it, Miss Caucausoid? What do you *want?*"

   "Shut up, Janice," Octavia said, letting a fingered loop of hair fall to her
waist as though just the sound of Janice's voice had ruined the fun of her hair
twisting.

   Janice obeyed, her mouth hung open in a loose grin, unflappable, unhurt.   30

   "All right," Arnetta said, standing up. "We're going to have a secret meeting and talk about what we're going to do."

   Everyone gravely nodded her head. The word "secret" had a built-in importance, the modifier form of the word carried more clout than the noun. A
secret meant nothing; it was like gossip: just a bit of unpleasant knowledge
about someone who happened to be someone other than yourself. A secret
meeting, or a secret *club* was entirely different.

   That was when Arnetta turned to me as though she knew that doing so
was both a compliment and a charity.

   "Snot, you're not going to be a bitch and tell Mrs. Margolin, are you?"

   I had been called "Snot" ever since first grade, when I'd sneezed in class   35
and two long ropes of mucus had splattered a nearby girl.

   "Hey," I said. "Maybe you didn't hear them right — I mean — "

   "Are you gonna tell on us or not?" was all Arnetta wanted to know, and by the
time the question was asked, the rest of our Brownie troop looked at me as though
they'd already decided their course of action, me being the only impediment.

Camp Crescendo used to double as a high-school-band and field hockey camp
until an arcing field hockey ball landed on the clasp of a girl's metal barrette,
knifing a skull nerve and paralyzing the right side of her body. The camp
closed down for a few years and the girl's teammates built a memorial, filling

the spot on which the girl fell with hockey balls, on which they had painted — all in nail polish — get-well tidings, flowers, and hearts. The balls were still stacked there, like a shrine of ostrich eggs embedded in the ground.

On the second day of camp, Troop 909 was dancing around the mound of hockey balls, their limbs jangling awkwardly, their cries like the constant summer squeal of an amusement park. There was a stream that bordered the field hockey lawn, and the girls from my troop settled next to it, scarfing down the last of lunch: sandwiches made from salami and slices of tomato that had gotten waterlogged from the melting ice in the cooler. From the stream bank, Arnetta eyed the Troop 909 girls, scrutinizing their movements to glean inspiration for battle.

"Man," Arnetta said, "we could bumrush them right now if that damn 40 lady would *leave.*"

The 909 troop leader was a white woman with the severe pageboy hairdo of an ancient Egyptian. She lay on a picnic blanket, sphinx-like, eating a banana, sometimes holding it out in front of her like a microphone. Beside her sat a girl slowly flapping one hand like a bird with a broken wing. Occasionally, the leader would call out the names of girls who'd attempted leapfrogs and flips, or of girls who yelled too loudly or strayed far from the circle.

"I'm just glad Big Fat Mama's not following us here," Octavia said. "At least we don't have to worry about her." Mrs. Margolin, Octavia assured us, was having her Afternoon Devotional, shrouded in mosquito netting, in a clearing she'd found. Mrs. Hedy was cleaning mud from her espadrilles in the cabin.

"I handled them." Arnetta sucked on her teeth and proudly grinned. "I told her we was going to gather leaves."

"Gather leaves," Octavia said, nodding respectfully. "That's a good one. Especially since they're so mad-crazy about this camping thing." She looked from ground to sky, sky to ground. Her hair hung down her back in two braids like a squaw's. "I mean, I really don't know why it's even called *camping* — all we ever do with Nature is find some twigs and say something like, 'Wow, this fell from a tree.'" She then studied her sandwich. With two disdainful fingers, she picked out a slice of dripping tomato, the sections congealed with red slime. She pitched it into the stream embrowned with dead leaves and the murky effigies of other dead things, but in the opaque water, a group of small silver-brown fish appeared. They surrounded the tomato and nibbled.

"Look!" Janice cried. "Fishes! Fishes!" As she scrambled to the edge of the 45 stream to watch, a covey of insects threw up tantrums from the wheatgrass and nettle, a throng of tiny electric machines, all going at once. Octavia sneaked up behind Janice as if to push her in. Daphne and I exchanged terrified looks. It seemed as though only we knew that Octavia was close enough — and bold enough — to actually push Janice into the stream. Janice turned around quickly, but Octavia was already staring serenely into the still water as though she was gathering some sort of courage from it. "What's so funny?" Janice said, eyeing them all suspiciously.

Elise began humming the tune to "Karma Chameleon," all the girls joining in, their hums light and facile. Janice also began to hum, against everyone else, the high-octane opening chords of "Beat It."

"I love me some Michael Jackson," Janice said when she'd finished humming, smacking her lips as though Michael Jackson were a favorite meal. "I *will* marry Michael Jackson."

Before anyone had a chance to impress upon Janice the impossibility of this, Arnetta suddenly rose, made a sun visor of her hand, and watched Troop 909 leave the field hockey lawn.

"Dammit!" she said. "We've got to get them *alone.*"

"They won't ever be alone," I said. All the rest of the girls looked at me, for 50
I usually kept quiet. If I spoke even a word, I could count on someone calling me Snot. Everyone seemed to think that we could beat up these girls; no one entertained the thought that they might fight *back.* "The only time they'll be unsupervised is in the bathroom."

"Oh shut up, Snot," Octavia said.

But Arnetta slowly nodded her head. "The bathroom," she said. "The bathroom," she said, again and again. "The bathroom! The bathroom!"

According to Octavia's watch, it took us five minutes to hike to the restrooms, which were midway between our cabin and Troop 909's. Inside, the mirrors above the sinks returned only the vaguest of reflections, as though someone had taken a scouring pad to their surfaces to obscure the shine. Pine needles, leaves, and dirty, flattened wads of chewing gum covered the floor like a mosaic. Webs of hair matted the drain in the middle of the floor. Above the sinks and below the mirrors, stacks of folded white paper towels lay on a long metal counter. Shaggy white balls of paper towels sat on the sinktops in a line like corsages on display. A thread of floss snaked from a wad of tissues dotted with the faint red-pink of blood. One of those white girls, I thought, had just lost a tooth.

Though the restroom looked almost the same as it had the night before, it somehow seemed stranger now. We hadn't noticed the wooden rafters coming together in great V's. We were, it seemed, inside a whale, viewing the ribs of the roof of its mouth.

"Wow. It's a mess," Elise said. 55

"You can say that again."

Arnetta leaned against the doorjamb of a restroom stall. "This is where they'll be again," she said. Just seeing the place, just having a plan seemed to satisfy her. "We'll go in and talk to them. You know, 'How you doing? How long'll you be here?' That sort of thing. Then Octavia and I are gonna tell them what happens when they call any one of us a nigger."

"I'm going to say something, too," Janice said.

Arnetta considered this. "Sure," she said. "Of course. Whatever you want."

Janice pointed her finger like a gun at Octavia and rehearsed the line she'd 60
thought up, "'We're gonna teach you a *lesson*!' That's what I'm going to say." She narrowed her eyes like a TV mobster. "'We're gonna teach you little girls a lesson!'"

With the back of her hand, Octavia brushed Janice's finger away. "You couldn't teach me to shit in a toilet."

"But," I said, "what if they say, 'We didn't say that? We didn't call anyone an N-I-G-G-E-R.'"

"Snot," Arnetta said, and then sighed. "Don't think. Just fight. If you even know how."

Everyone laughed except Daphne. Arnetta gently laid her hand on Daphne's shoulder. "Daphne. You don't have to fight. We're doing this for you."

Daphne walked to the counter, took a clean paper towel, and carefully un- 65
folded it like a map. With it, she began to pick up the trash all around. Everyone watched.

"C'mon," Arnetta said to everyone. "Let's beat it." We all ambled toward the doorway, where the sunshine made one large white rectangle of light. We were immediately blinded, and we shielded our eyes with our hands and our forearms.

"Daphne?" Arnetta asked. "Are you coming?"

We all looked back at the bending girl, the thin of her back hunched like the back of a custodian sweeping a stage, caught in limelight. Stray strands of her hair were lit near-transparent, thin fiber-optic threads. She did not nod yes to the question, nor did she shake her head no. She abided, bent. Then she began again, picking up leaves, wads of paper, the cotton fluff innards from a torn stuffed toy. She did it so methodically, so exquisitely, so humbly, she must have been trained. I thought of those dresses she wore, faded and old, yet so pressed and clean. I then saw the poverty in them; I then could imagine her mother, cleaning the houses of others, returning home, weary.

"I guess she's not coming."

We left her and headed back to our cabin, over pine needles and leaves, 70 taking the path full of shade.

"What about our secret meeting?" Elise asked.

Arnetta enunciated her words in a way that defied contradiction: "We just had it."

It was nearing our bedtime, but the sun had not yet set.

"Hey, your mama's coming," Arnetta said to Octavia when she saw Mrs. Hedy walk toward the cabin, sniffling. When Octavia's mother wasn't giving bored, parochial orders, she sniffled continuously, mourning an imminent divorce from her husband. She might begin a sentence, "I don't know what Robert will do when Octavia and I are gone. Who'll buy him cigarettes?" and Octavia would hotly whisper, *"Mama,"* in a way that meant: Please don't talk about our problems in front of everyone. Please shut up.

But when Mrs. Hedy began talking about her husband, thinking about 75 her husband, seeing clouds shaped like the head of her husband, she couldn't be quiet, and no one could dislodge her from the comfort of her own woe. Only one thing could perk her up — Brownie songs. If the girls were quiet, and Mrs. Hedy was in her dopey, sorrowful mood, she would say, "Y'all know I like those songs, girls. Why don't you sing one?" Everyone would groan, except me and Daphne. I, for one, liked some of the songs.

"C'mon, everybody," Octavia said drearily. "She likes the Brownie song best."

We sang, loud enough to reach Mrs. Hedy:

"I've got something in my pocket;
It belongs across my face.
And I keep it very close at hand
    in a most convenient place.
I'm sure you couldn't guess it
If you guessed a long, long while.
So I'll take it out and put it on —
It's a great big Brownie smile!"

The Brownie song was supposed to be sung cheerfully, as though we were elves in a workshop, singing as we merrily cobbled shoes, but everyone except me hated the song so much that they sang it like a maudlin record, played on the most sluggish of rpms.

"That was good," Mrs. Hedy said, closing the cabin door behind her. "Wasn't that nice, Linda?"

"Praise God," Mrs. Margolin answered without raising her head from the 80
chore of counting out Popsicle sticks for the next day's craft session.

"Sing another one," Mrs. Hedy said. She said it with a sort of joyful aggression, like a drunk I'd once seen who'd refused to leave a Korean grocery.

"God, Mama, get over it," Octavia whispered in a voice meant only for Arnetta, but Mrs. Hedy heard it and started to leave the cabin.

"Don't go," Arnetta said. She ran after Mrs. Hedy and held her by the arm. "We haven't finished singing." She nudged us with a single look. "Let's sing the 'Friends Song.' For Mrs. Hedy."

Although I liked some of the songs, I hated this one:

> Make new friends
> But keep the o-old,
> One is silver
> And the other gold.

If most of the girls in the troop could be any type of metal, they'd be 85
bunched-up wads of tinfoil, maybe, or rusty iron nails you had to get tetanus shots for.

"No, no, no," Mrs. Margolin said before anyone could start in on the "Friends Song." "An uplifting song. Something to lift her up and take her mind off all these earthly burdens."

Arnetta and Octavia rolled their eyes. Everyone knew what song Mrs. Margolin was talking about, and no one, no one, wanted to sing it.

"Please, no," a voice called out. "Not 'The Doughnut Song.'"

"Please not 'The Doughnut Song,'" Octavia pleaded.

"I'll brush my teeth two times if I don't have to sing 'The Doughnut—'" 90

"Sing!" Mrs. Margolin demanded.

We sang:

> "Life without Jesus is like a do-ough-nut!
> Like a do-ooough-nut!
> Like a do-ooough-nut!
> Life without Jesus is like a do-ough-nut!
> There's a hole in the middle of my soul!"

There were other verses, involving other pastries, but we stopped after the first one and cast glances toward Mrs. Margolin to see if we could gain a reprieve. Mrs. Margolin's eyes fluttered blissfully. She was half asleep.

"Awww," Mrs. Hedy said, as though giant Mrs. Margolin were a cute baby, "Mrs. Margolin's had a long day."

"Yes indeed," Mrs. Margolin answered. "If you don't mind, I might just go 95
to the lodge where the beds are. I haven't been the same since the operation."

I had not heard of this operation, or when it had occurred, since Mrs. Margolin had never missed the once-a-week Brownie meetings, but I could see from Daphne's face that she was concerned, and I could see that the other girls had decided that Mrs. Margolin's operation must have happened long ago in some remote time unconnected to our own. Nevertheless, they put on sad faces. We had all been taught that adulthood was full of sorrow and pain, taxes and bills, dreaded work and dealings with whites, sickness, and death. I tried to do what the others did. I tried to look silent.

"Go right ahead, Linda," Mrs. Hedy said. "I'll watch the girls." Mrs. Hedy seemed to forget about divorce for a moment; she looked at us with dewy eyes, as if we were mysterious, furry creatures. Meanwhile, Mrs. Margolin walked through the maze of sleeping bags until she found her own. She gathered a neat stack of clothes and pajamas slowly, as though doing so was almost painful. She took her toothbrush, her toothpaste, her pillow. "All right!" Mrs. Margolin said, addressing us all from the threshold of the cabin. "Be in bed by nine." She said it with a twinkle in her voice, letting us know she was allowing us to be naughty and stay up till nine-fifteen.

"C'mon everybody," Arnetta said after Mrs. Margolin left. "Time for us to wash up."

Everyone watched Mrs. Hedy closely, wondering whether she would insist on coming with us since it was night, making a fight with Troop 909 nearly impossible. Troop 909 would soon be in the bathroom, washing their faces, brushing their teeth—completely unsuspecting of our ambush.

"We won't be long," Arnetta said. "We're old enough to go to the restrooms   100 by ourselves."

Ms. Hedy pursed her lips at this dilemma. "Well, I guess you Brownies are almost Girl Scouts, right?"

"Right!"

"Just one more badge," Drema said.

"And about," Octavia droned, "a million more cookies to sell." Octavia looked at all of us, *Now's our chance,* her face seemed to say, but our chance to do *what,* I didn't exactly know.

Finally, Mrs. Hedy walked to the doorway where Octavia stood dutifully   105 waiting to say goodbye but looking bored doing it. Mrs. Hedy held Octavia's chin. "You'll be good?"

"Yes, Mama."

"And remember to pray for me and your father? If I'm asleep when you get back?"

"Yes, Mama."

When the other girls had finished getting their toothbrushes and washcloths and flashlights for the group restroom trip, I was drawing pictures of tiny birds with too many feathers. Daphne was sitting on her sleeping bag, reading.

"You're not going to come?" Octavia asked.   110

Daphne shook her head.

"I'm gonna stay, too," I said. "I'll go to the restroom when Daphne and Mrs. Hedy go."

Arnetta leaned down toward me and whispered so that Mrs. Hedy, who'd taken over Mrs. Margolin's task of counting Popsicle sticks, couldn't hear. "No, Snot. If we get in trouble, you're going to get in trouble with the rest of us."

We made our way through the darkness by flashlight. The tree branches that had shaded us just hours earlier, along the same path, now looked like arms sprouting menacing hands. The stars sprinkled the sky like spilled salt. They seemed fastened to the darkness, high up and holy, their places fixed and definite as we stirred beneath them.

Some, like me, were quiet because we were afraid of the dark; others were   115 talking like crazy for the same reason.

"Wow!" Drema said, looking up. "Why are all the stars out here? I never see stars back on Oneida Street."

"It's a camping trip, that's why," Octavia said. "You're supposed to see stars on camping trips."

Janice said, "This place smells like my mother's air freshener."

"These woods are *pine*," Elise said. "Your mother probably uses *pine* air freshener."

Janice mouthed an exaggerated "Oh," nodding her head as though she just then understood one of the world's great secrets. 120

No one talked about fighting. Everyone was afraid enough just walking through the infinite deep of the woods. Even though I didn't fight to fight, was afraid of fighting, I felt I was part of the rest of the troop; like I was defending something. We trudged against the slight incline of the path, Arnetta leading the way.

"You know," I said, "their leader will be there. Or they won't even be there. It's dark already. Last night the sun was still in the sky. I'm sure they're already finished."

Arnetta acted as if she hadn't heard me. I followed her gaze with my flashlight, and that's when I saw the squares of light in the darkness. The bathroom was just ahead.

But the girls were there. We could hear them before we could see them.

"Octavia and I will go in first so they'll think there's just two of us, then wait till I say, 'We're gonna teach you a lesson,'" Arnetta said. "Then, bust in. That'll surprise them." 125

"That's what I was supposed to say," Janice said.

Arnetta went inside, Octavia next to her. Janice followed, and the rest of us waited outside.

They were in there for what seemed like whole minutes, but something was wrong. Arnetta hadn't given the signal yet. I was with the girls outside when I heard one of the Troop 909 girls say, "NO. That did NOT happen!"

That was to be expected, that they'd deny the whole thing. What I hadn't expected was *the voice* in which the denial was said. The girl sounded as though her tongue were caught in her mouth. "That's a BAD word!" the girl continued. "We don't say BAD words!"

"Let's go in," Elise said. 130

"No," Drema said, "I don't want to. What if we get beat up?"

"Snot?" Elise turned to me, her flashlight blinding. It was the first time anyone had asked my opinion, though I knew they were just asking because they were afraid.

"I say we go inside, just to see what's going on."

"But Arnetta didn't give us the signal," Drema said. "She's supposed to say, 'We're gonna teach you a lesson,' and I didn't hear her say it."

"C'mon," I said. "Let's just go in." 135

We went inside. There we found the white girls — about five girls huddled up next to one big girl. I instantly knew she was the owner of the voice we'd heard. Arnetta and Octavia inched toward us as soon as we entered.

"Where's Janice?" Elise asked, then we heard a flush. "Oh."

"I think," Octavia said, whispering to Elise, "they're retarded."

"We ARE NOT retarded!" the big girl said, though it was obvious that she was. That they all were. The girls around her began to whimper.

"They're just pretending," Arnetta said, trying to convince herself. "I know 140 they are."

Octavia turned to Arnetta. "Arnetta. Let's just leave."

Janice came out of a stall, happy and relieved, then she suddenly remembered her line, pointed to the big girl, and said, "We're gonna teach you a lesson."

"Shut up, Janice," Octavia said, but her heart was not in it. Arnetta's face was set in a lost, deep scowl. Octavia turned to the big girl and said loudly, slowly, as if they were all deaf, "We're going to leave. It was nice meeting you, O.K.? You don't have to tell anyone that we were here. O.K.?"

"Why not?" said the big girl, like a taunt. When she spoke, her lips did not meet, her mouth did not close. Her tongue grazed the roof of her mouth, like a little pink fish. "You'll get in trouble. I know. *I* know."

Arnetta got back her old cunning. "If you said anything, then you'd be a 145 tattletale."

The girl looked sad for a moment, then perked up quickly. A flash of genius crossed her face. "I *like* tattletale."

"It's all right, girls. It's gonna be all right!" the 909 troop leader said. All of Troop 909 burst into tears. It was as though someone had instructed them all to cry at once. The troop leader had girls under her arm, and all the rest of the girls crowded about her. It reminded me of a hog I'd seen on a field trip, where all the little hogs gathered about the mother at feeding time, latching onto her teats. The 909 troop leader had come into the bathroom, shortly after the big girl had threatened to tell. Then the ranger came, then, once the ranger had radioed the station, Mrs. Margolin arrived with Daphne in tow.

The ranger had left the restroom area, but everyone else was huddled just outside, swatting mosquitoes.

"Oh. They *will* apologize," Mrs. Margolin said to the 909 troop leader, but she said this so angrily, I knew she was speaking more to us than to the other troop leader. "When their parents find out, every one a them will be on punishment."

"It's all right, it's all right," the 909 troop leader reassured Mrs. Margolin. 150 Her voice lilted in the same way it had when addressing the girls. She smiled the whole time she talked. She was like one of those TV-cooking-show women who talk and dice onions and smile all at the same time.

"See. It could have happened. I'm not calling your girls fibbers or anything." She shook her head ferociously from side to side, her Egyptian-style pageboy flapping against her cheeks like heavy drapes. "It *could* have happened. See. Our girls are *not* retarded. They are *delayed* learners." She said this in a syrupy instructional voice, as though our troop might be delayed learners as well. "We're from the Decatur Children's Academy. Many of them just have special needs."

"Now we won't be able to walk to the bathroom by ourselves!" the big girl said.

"Yes you will," the troop leader said, "but maybe we'll wait till we get back to Decatur —"

"I don't want to wait!" the girl said. "I want my Independence badge!"

The girls in my troop were entirely speechless. Arnetta looked stoic, as   155
though she were soon to be tortured but was determined not to appear
weak. Mrs. Margolin pursed her lips solemnly and said, "Bless them, Lord.
Bless them."

In contrast, the Troop 909 leader was full of words and energy. "Some of
our girls are echolalic—" She smiled and happily presented one of the girls
hanging onto her, but the girl widened her eyes in horror, and violently withdrew herself from the center of attention, sensing she was being sacrificed for
the village sins. "Echolalic," the troop leader continued. "That means they will
say whatever they hear, like an echo—that's where the word comes from. It
comes from 'echo.'" She ducked her head apologetically, "I mean, not all of
them have the most *progressive* of parents, so if they heard a bad word, they
might have repeated it. But I guarantee it would not have been *intentional*."

Arnetta spoke. "I saw her say the word. I heard her." She pointed to a
small girl, smaller than any of us, wearing an oversized T-shirt that read: "Eat
Bertha's Mussels."

The troop leader shook her head and smiled, "That's impossible. She
doesn't speak. She can, but she doesn't."

Arnetta furrowed her brow. "No. It wasn't her. That's right. It was *her*."

The girl Arnetta pointed to grinned as though she'd been paid a compli-   160
ment. She was the only one from either troop actually wearing a full uniform:
the mocha-colored A-line shift, the orange ascot, the sash covered with badges,
though all the same one—the Try-It patch. She took a few steps toward Arnetta and made a grand sweeping gesture toward the sash. "See," she said, full
of self-importance, "I'm a Brownie." I had a hard time imagining this girl calling anyone a "nigger"; the girl looked perpetually delighted, as though she
would have cuddled up with a grizzly if someone had let her.

On the fourth morning, we boarded the bus to go home.

The previous day had been spent building miniature churches from Popsicle sticks. We hardly left the cabin. Mrs. Margolin and Mrs. Hedy guarded us
so closely, almost no one talked for the entire day.

Even on the day of departure from Camp Crescendo, all was serious and
silent. The bus ride began quietly enough. Arnetta had to sit beside Mrs. Margolin; Octavia had to sit beside her mother. I sat beside Daphne, who gave me
her prize journal without a word of explanation.

"You don't want it?"

She shook her head no. It was empty.   165

Then Mrs. Hedy began to weep. "Octavia," Mrs. Hedy said to her daughter
without looking at her, "I'm going to sit with Mrs. Margolin. All right?"

Arnetta exchanged seats with Mrs. Hedy. With the two women up front,
Elise felt it safe to speak. "Hey," she said, then she set her face into a placid, vacant
stare, trying to imitate that of a Troop 909 girl. Emboldened, Arnetta made a
gesture of mock pride toward an imaginary sash, the way the girl in full uniform
had done. Then they all made a game of it, trying to do the most exaggerated
imitations of the Troop 909 girls, all without speaking, all without laughing
loud enough to catch the women's attention.

Daphne looked down at her shoes, white with sneaker polish. I opened the
journal she'd given me. I looked out the window, trying to decide what to

write, searching for lines, but nothing could compare with what Daphne had written, *"My father, the veteran,"* my favorite line of all time. It replayed itself in my head, and I gave up trying to write.

By then, it seemed that the rest of the troop had given up making fun of the girls in Troop 909. They were now quietly gossiping about who had passed notes to whom in school. For a moment the gossiping fell off, and all I heard was the hum of the bus as we sped down the road and the muffled sounds of Mrs. Hedy and Mrs. Margolin talking about serious things.

"You know," Octavia whispered, "why did *we* have to be stuck at a camp 170 with retarded girls? You know?"

"*You* know why," Arnetta answered. She narrowed her eyes like a cat. "My mama and I were in the mall in Buckhead, and this white lady just kept looking at us. I mean, like we were foreign or something. Like we were from China."

"What did the woman say?" Elise asked.

"Nothing," Arnetta said. "She didn't say nothing."

A few girls quietly nodded their heads.

"There was this time," I said, "when my father and I were in the mall and—" 175
"Oh shut up, Snot," Octavia said.

I stared at Octavia, then rolled my eyes from her to the window. As I watched the trees blur, I wanted nothing more than to be through with it all: the bus ride, the troop, school—all of it. But we were going home. I'd see the same girls in school the next day. We were on a bus, and there was nowhere else to go.

"Go on, Laurel," Daphne said to me. It seemed like the first time she'd spoken the whole trip, and she'd said my name. I turned to her and smiled weakly so as not to cry, hoping she'd remember when I'd tried to be her friend, thinking maybe that her gift of the journal was an invitation of friendship. But she didn't smile back. All she said was, "What happened?"

I studied the girls, waiting for Octavia to tell me to shut up again before I even had a chance to utter another word, but everyone was amazed that Daphne had spoken. The bus was silent. I gathered my voice. "Well," I said. "My father and I were in this mall, but *I* was the one doing the staring." I stopped and glanced from face to face. I continued. "There were these white people dressed like Puritans or something, but they weren't Puritans. They were Mennonites. They're these people who, if you ask them to do a favor, like paint your porch or something, they have to do it. It's in their rules."

"That sucks," someone said. 180

"C'mon," Arnetta said. "You're lying."

"I am not."

"How do you know that's not just some story someone made up?" Elise asked, her head cocked full of daring. "I mean, who's gonna do whatever you ask?"

"It's not made up. I know because when I was looking at them, my father said, 'See those people? If you ask them to do something, they'll do it. Anything you want.'"

No one would call anyone's father a liar—then they'd have to fight the per- 185 son. But Drema parsed her words carefully. "How does your *father* know that's not just some story? Huh?"

"Because," I said, "he went up to the man and asked him would he paint our porch, and the man said yes. It's their religion."

"Man, I'm glad I'm a Baptist," Elise said, shaking her head in sympathy for the Mennonites.

"So did the guy do it?" Drema asked, scooting closer to hear if the story got juicy.

"Yeah," I said. "His whole family was with him. My dad drove them to our house. They all painted our porch. The woman and girl were in bonnets and long, long skirts with buttons up to their necks. The guy wore this weird hat and these huge suspenders."

"Why," Arnetta asked archly, as though she didn't believe a word, "would someone pick a *porch*? If they'll do anything, why not make them paint the whole *house*? Why not ask for a hundred bucks?"   190

I thought about it, and then remembered the words my father had said about them painting our porch, though I had never seemed to think about his words after he'd said them.

"He said," I began, only then understanding the words as they uncoiled from my mouth, "it was the only time he'd have a white man on his knees doing something for a black man for free."

I now understood what he meant, and why he did it, though I didn't like it. When you've been made to feel bad for so long, you jump at the chance to do it to others. I remembered the Mennonites bending the way Daphne had bent when she was cleaning the restroom. I remembered the dark blue of their bonnets, the black of their shoes. They painted the porch as though scrubbing a floor. I was already trembling before Daphne asked quietly, "Did he thank them?"

I looked out the window. I could not tell which were the thoughts and which were the trees. "No," I said, and suddenly knew there was something mean in the world that I could not stop.

Arnetta laughed. "If I asked them to take off their long skirts and bonnets   195 and put on some jeans, would they do it?"

And Daphne's voice, quiet, steady: "Maybe they would. Just to be nice."

CONSIDERATIONS FOR CRITICAL THINKING AND WRITING

1. **FIRST RESPONSE.** What kinds of expectations are set up by the title "Brownies"? Explain how the story meets those expectations and goes beyond them.

2. What does the style of the story's first paragraph tell you about the narrator's voice and personality?

3. Describe Arnetta and Laurel in terms of their attitudes toward life. How does Packer make you feel about each of them? How does the author achieve those effects?

4. Why do you suppose we are not given the narrator's first name until paragraph 178? What is the effect of not learning her name until almost the end of the story?

5. Discuss the ironies that accompany the use of the words *Caucasian* and *nigger* in the story.

6. How does Packer foreshadow the fact that the Troop 909 girls have mental retardation?

7. Explain how the father's interaction with the Mennonites is related to the Brownies' experience at camp.

8. What do you think this story says about racism? What makes this theme so complicated in "Brownies"?

CONNECTIONS TO OTHER SELECTIONS

1. How is revenge important to the plot of "Brownies" and of Edgar Allan Poe's "The Cask of Amontillado" (p. 727)?

2. Discuss how racial issues are treated in "Brownies" and Ralph Ellison's "Battle Royal" (p. 277).

Web Research the authors in this chapter or take quizzes on their works at bedfordstmartins.com/ meyerlit.

RICK MOODY (B. 1961)

© David Katzenstein/CORBIS.

Born in New York City, Rick Moody grew up in Connecticut and earned his undergraduate degree at Brown University and his M.F.A. at Columbia University. His first of four novels, *Garden State* (1992), won the Pushcart Editor's Choice Award. *The Ice Storm* (1994) was made into a popular film directed by Ang Lee in 1997 and was followed by two more novels: *Purple America* (1996) and *The Diviners* (2005). Moody has also published three collections of short stories and novellas: *The Ring of Brightest Angels Along Heaven* (1995); *Demonology* (2001), which collects "Boys"; and *Right Livelihoods* (2007). "Boys" was included in *The Best American Short Stories 2001*, in which Moody describes how this experimental story began. He had heard a fellow writer, Max Steele, use the phrase "Then the boys entered the house" at a reading and found himself "preoccupied" with what is "perhaps the most essential gesture in a boy's life." He then "started playing around with the sentence."

Boys   2000

Boys enter the house, boys enter the house. Boys, and with them the ideas of boys (ideas leaden, reductive, inflexible), enter the house. Boys, two of them, wound into hospital packaging, boys with infant-pattern baldness, slung in the arms of parents, boys dreaming of breasts, enter the house. Twin boys, kettles on the boil, boys in hideous vinyl knapsacks that young couples from Edison, N.J., wear on their shirt fronts, knapsacks coated with baby saliva and staphylococcus and milk vomit, enter the house. Two boys, one striking the other with a rubberized hot dog, enter the house. Two boys, one of them striking the other with a willow switch about the head and shoulders, the other crying, enter the house. Boys enter the house speaking nonsense. Boys enter the house calling for mother. On a Sunday, in May, a day one might nearly describe as perfect, an ice cream truck comes slowly down the lane, chimes inducing salivation, and children run after it, not long after which boys dig a hole in the back yard and bury their younger sister's dolls two feet down, so that she will never find these dolls and these dolls will rot in hell, after which boys enter the house. Boys, trailing after their father like he is the Second Goddamned Coming of Christ Goddamned Almighty, enter the house, repair to the basement to watch baseball. Boys enter the house, site of devastation, and repair immediately to the kitchen, where they mix lighter fluid, vanilla pudding, drain-opening lye, balsamic vinegar, blue food coloring, calamine lotion, cottage cheese, ants, a plastic lizard one of them received in his Christmas stocking, tacks, leftover mashed potatoes, Spam, frozen lima beans, and chocolate syrup in a medium-sized saucepan and heat over a low flame until thick, afterward transferring the contents of this saucepan into a Pyrex lasagna dish, baking the Pyrex lasagna dish in the oven for nineteen minutes before attempting to persuade their sister that she should eat the mixture; later they smash three family heirlooms (the last, a glass egg, intentionally) in a two-and-a-half-hour stretch, whereupon they are sent to their bedroom until freed, in each case thirteen minutes after. Boys enter the house, starchy in pressed shirts and flannel pants that itch so bad, fresh from Sunday school instruction, blond and brown locks (respectively) plastered down but even so with a number of cowlicks protruding at odd angles, disconsolate and humbled, uncertain if boyish things — such as shooting at the neighbor's dog with a pump-action BB gun and gagging the fat boy up the street with a bandanna and showing their shriveled boy-penises to their younger sister — are exempted from the commandment to *Love the Lord thy God with all thy heart and with all thy soul and with all thy mind, and thy neighbor as thyself.* Boys enter the house in baseball gear (only one of the boys can hit): in their spikes, in mismatched tube socks that smell like Stilton cheese. Boys enter the house in soccer gear. Boys enter the house carrying skates. Boys enter the house with lacrosse sticks, and soon after, tossing a lacrosse ball lightly in the living room, they destroy a lamp. One boy enters the house sporting basketball clothes, the other wearing jeans and a sweatshirt. One boy enters the house bleeding profusely and is taken out to get stitches, the other watches. Boys enter the house at the end of term carrying report cards, sneak around the house like spies of foreign nationality, looking for a place to hide the report cards for the time being (under a toaster? in a medicine cabinet?). One boy with a black eye enters the house, one boy without. Boys with acne enter the house and squeeze and prod large skin blemishes in front of their sister. Boys with acne-treatment products hidden about their persons enter the house. Boys, standing just up the street, sneak cigarettes behind a willow in the Elys' yard, wave smoke away from their natural fibers, hack terribly, experience nausea, then enter the house. Boys call each other *Retard, Homo, Geek,* and, later, *Neckless Thug, Theater Fag,* and enter the house exchanging further epithets. Boys enter house with nose-hair clippers, chase sister around house threatening to depilate her eyebrows. She cries. Boys attempt to induce girls to whom they would not have spoken only six or eight months prior to enter the house with them. Boys enter the house with girls efflorescent and homely and attempt to induce girls to sneak into their bedroom, as they still share a single bedroom; girls refuse.

Boys enter the house, go to separate bedrooms. Boys, with their father (an arm around each of them), enter the house, but of the monologue preceding and succeeding this entrance, not a syllable is preserved. Boys enter the house having masturbated in a variety of locales. Boys enter the house having masturbated in train-station bathrooms, in forests, in beach houses, in football bleachers at night under the stars, in cars (under a blanket), in the shower, backstage, on a plane, the boys masturbate constantly, identically, three times a day in some cases, desire like a madness upon them, at the mere sound of certain words, words that sound like other words, *interrogative* reminding them of *intercourse, beast* reminding them of *breast, sects* reminding them of *sex,* and so forth, the boys are not very smart yet, and as they enter the house they feel, as always, immense shame at the scale of this self-abusive cogitation, seeing a classmate, seeing a billboard, seeing a fire hydrant, seeing things that should not induce thoughts of masturbation (their sister, e.g.) and then thinking of masturbation anyway. Boys enter the house, go to their rooms, remove sexually explicit magazines from hidden stashes, put on loud music, feel despair. Boys enter the house worried; they argue. The boys are ugly, they are failures, they will never be loved, they enter the house. Boys enter the house and kiss their mother, who feels differently now they have outgrown her. Boys enter the house, kiss their mother, she explains the seriousness of their sister's difficulty, her diagnosis. Boys enter the house, having attempted to locate the spot in their yard where the dolls were buried, eight or nine years prior, without success; they go to their sister's room, sit by her bed. Boys enter the house and tell their completely bald sister jokes about baldness. Boys hold either hand of their sister, laying aside differences, having trudged grimly into the house. Boys skip school, enter house, hold vigil. Boys enter the house after their parents have both gone off to work, sit with their sister and with their sister's nurse. Boys enter the house carrying cases of beer. Boys enter the house, very worried now, didn't know more worry was possible. Boys enter the house carrying controlled substances, neither having told the other that he is carrying a controlled substance, though an intoxicated posture seems appropriate under the circumstances. Boys enter the house weeping and hear weeping around them. Boys enter the house embarrassed, silent, anguished, keening, afflicted, angry, woeful, grief-stricken. Boys enter the house on vacation, each clasps the hand of the other with genuine warmth, the one wearing dark colors and having shaved a portion of his head, the other having grown his hair out longish and wearing, uncharacteristically, a tie-dyed shirt. Boys enter the house on vacation and argue bitterly about politics (other subjects are no longer discussed), one boy supporting the Maoist insurgency in a certain Southeast Asian country, one believing that to change the system you need to work inside it; one boy threatens to beat the living shit out of the other, refuses crème brûlée, though it is created by his mother in order to keep the peace. One boy writes home and thereby enters the house only through a mail slot: he argues that the other boy is crypto-fascist, believing that the market can seek its own level on questions of ethics and morals; boys enter the house on vacation and announce future professions; boys enter the house on vacation and change their minds about professions; boys enter the house on vacation, and one boy brings home a sweetheart but throws a tantrum when it is suggested that the sweetheart will have to retire on the folding bed in the basement; the other boy, having no sweetheart, is distant and withdrawn, preferring to talk late into the night about family members gone from this world. Boys enter the house several weeks apart. Boys enter the house on days of heavy rain. Boys enter the house, in different calendar years, and upon entering, the boys seem to do nothing but compose manifestos, for the benefit of parents; they follow their mother around the place, having fashioned these manifestos in celebration of brand-new independence: *Mom, I like to lie in bed late into the morning watching game shows,* or, *I'm never going to date anyone but artists from now on, mad girls, dreamers, practicers of black magic,* or, *A man should eat bologna, sliced meats are important,* or, *An American should bowl at least once a year,* but these manifestos apply only for brief spells, after which they are reversed or discarded. Boys don't enter the house at all, except as ghostly afterimages of younger selves, fleeting images of sneakers dashing up a staircase; soggy towels on the floor of the bathroom; blue jeans coiled like asps in the basin of the washing machine; boys as an absence of boys, blissful at first, you put a thing down on a spot, put this book down, come back later, it's still there; you buy a box of cookies, eat three, later three are missing. Nevertheless, when boys next enter the house, which they ultimately must do, it's a relief, even if it's only in preparation for weddings of acquaintances from boyhood, one boy has a beard, neatly trimmed, the other has rakish sideburns, one boy wears a hat, the other boy thinks hats are ridiculous, one boy wears khakis pleated at the waist, the other wears denim, but each changes into his suit (one suit fits well, one is a little tight), as though suits are the liminary marker of adulthood. Boys enter the house after the wedding and they are slapping each other on the back and yelling at anyone who will listen, *It's a party!* One boy enters the house, carried by friends, having been arrested (after the wedding) for driving while intoxicated, complexion ashen; the other boy tries to keep his mouth shut: the car is on its side in a ditch, the car has the top half of a tree broken over its bonnet, the car has struck another car, which has in turn struck a third, *Everyone will have seen.* One boy misses his brother horribly, misses the past, misses a time worth being nostalgic over, a time that never existed, back when they set their sister's playhouse on fire; the other boy avoids all mention of that time; each of them is once the boy who enters the house alone, missing the other, each is devoted and each callous, and each plays his part on the telephone, over the course of months. Boys enter the house with fishing gear, according to prearranged date and time, arguing about whether to use lures or live bait, in order to meet their father for the fishing adventure, after which boys enter the house again, almost immediately, with live bait, having settled the question; boys boast of having caught fish in the past, though no fish has ever been caught: *Remember when the blues were biting?* Boys enter the house carrying their father, slumped. Happens so fast. Boys rush into the house leading EMTs to the couch in the living room where the body lies, boys enter the house, boys enter the house, boys enter the house. Boys hold open the threshold, awesome threshold that has welcomed them when they haven't even been able to welcome themselves, that threshold which welcomed them when they had to be taken in, here is its tarnished knocker, here is its euphonious bell, here's where the boys had to sand the door down because it never would hang right in the frame, here are the scuff marks from when boys were on the wrong side of the door demanding, here's where there were once milk bottles for the milkman, here's where the newspaper always landed, here's the mail slot, here's the light on the front step, illuminated, here's where the boys are standing, as that beloved man is carried out. Boys, no longer boys, exit.

CONSIDERATIONS FOR CRITICAL THINKING AND WRITING

1. **FIRST RESPONSE.** Write a paragraph that describes in detail the style of this story. In what ways is it conventional as well as unconventional?

2. What is the story's basic plot? What actually happens? Does it have any kind of pattern to it?

3. Who are the major characters? Is there an antagonist who produces a conflict? Explain why or why not.

4. How well do you think Moody captures boys' lives?

5. How is the plot related to the story's style?

6. What do you think is the significance of the final sentence?

CONNECTIONS TO OTHER SELECTIONS

1. Discuss how time is conveyed stylistically in this narrative and in Mark Halliday's "Young Man on Sixth Avenue" (p. 615).

2. Compare the literary styles and their effects in this story and in David Foster Wallace's "Incarnations of Burned Children" (p. 617).

ENCOUNTERING FICTION: COMICS AND GRAPHIC STORIES

Matt Groening (B. 1954), *Life in Hell*

A native of Portland, Oregon, cartoon artist Matt Groening moved to Los Angeles in 1977 to become a writer for television. There he began recording his observations of life in the comic strip *Life in Hell*, a strip that he began as "an ongoing series of self-help cartoons." First published in 1980 in the *Los Angeles Reader*, *Life in Hell* was quickly syndicated and has been collected in many volumes beginning with *Love Is Hell* (1984). In his preface to *The Big Book of Hell*, from which the following cartoon is reprinted, Groening writes: "All my life I've been torn between frivolity and despair, between the desire to amuse and the desire to annoy, between dread-filled insomnia and a sense of my own goofiness. Just like you, I worry about love and sex and work and suffering and injustice and death, but I also dig drawing bulgy-eyed rabbits with tragic overbites." Groening is best known as the creator of *The Simpsons*, an animated sit-com satirizing family, life, and culture in America. He describes its central character, Bart Simpson, as "a more entertaining version of myself."

From *The Big Book of Hell* © 1990 by Matt Groening. All rights reserved. Reprinted by permission of Pantheon Books, a division of Random House, Inc., NY. Courtesy of Acme Features Syndicate.

CONSIDERATIONS AND CONNECTION TO ANOTHER SELECTION

1. What do you think of the father's explanation of death? What does he think about his own ideas?

2. What is the story's tone? How do the images and the words set the tone?

3. Does this strip rely more heavily on the drawings or on the words for its meanings? Explain your answer.

4. Discuss the perspective on death in Groening's strip and in Tim O'Brien's "How to Tell a True War Story" (p. 346).

10

Combining the
Elements of Fiction:
A Writing Process

A skillful artist has constructed a tale.
He has not fashioned his thoughts to
accommodate his incidents, but having
deliberately conceived a certain single
effect to be wrought, he then invents
such incidents . . . as may best serve him
in establishing the preconceived effect.
There should be no word written of
which the tendency, direct or indirect, is
not to the one pre-established design.

— EDGAR ALLAN POE, Review of
Hawthorne's *Twice-Told Tales*

THE ELEMENTS TOGETHER

The elements of fiction that you have examined in Chapters 1–9 provide
terms and concepts that enable you to think, talk, and write about fiction
in a variety of ways. As those chapters have indicated, there are many
means available to you for determining a story's effects and meanings. By
considering elements of fiction such as characterization, conflict, setting,
point of view, symbolism, style, and theme, you can better articulate your
understanding of a particular work. A careful reading of the work's elements allows you to see how the parts contribute to the whole.

    The parts or elements of a story work together rather than in isolation to
create a particular kind of experience, emotion, or insight for a reader. The
symbolic significance of the free and easy Mississippi River setting of *The
Adventures of Huckleberry Finn,* for example, cannot be excavated from Huck's
first-person point of view. Nor can the "smothery" ways of the corrupt towns

along the river be understood without the pious frauds, hypocrites, cowards, and other sordid characters that populate them. Add the plot that has Jim on the run from slavery and the unconscious ironic tone that Mark Twain invests in Huck — all constitute interrelated elements that add up to serious themes commenting on nineteenth-century society. Understanding the ways in which these elements work together produces a richer and more satisfying reading of a plot that might otherwise be read simply as a children's story.

MAPPING THE STORY

Writing about a story requires your creation of a clear path that a reader can take in order to follow your experience and understanding of the work. The path offers perspectives and directions that are informed by what caught your attention along the way. Your paper points out what you thought worth revisiting and taking the reader to see. Whatever the thesis of the paper, your role as a guide remains the same as you move from one element of the story to the next, offering an overall impression about the story. And as you already know, the best tours are always guided by informed and interesting voices.

This chapter presents an example of how one student, Janice Reardon, arrived at a thesis, combining her understanding of several elements of fiction for an assigned topic on David Updike's short story "Summer." After reviewing the elements of fiction covered in Chapters 1–9, Janice read the story several times, paying careful attention to plot, character, setting, point of view, symbolism, and so on. She then developed her ideas by brainstorming, drafting, and using the Questions for Writing (listed after the story) to develop her thesis into a statement that makes a definite claim about a specific idea and provides a clear sense of direction for the paper to come. As you read "Summer," think about what you might want to say about the relationship — or lack thereof — between Homer and Sandra. Pay attention to how the various elements of fiction work together to establish or reinforce that relationship.

DAVID UPDIKE (B. 1957)

Born in Ipswich, Massachusetts, David Updike is the son of author John Updike. David received his B.A. in art history at Harvard and his M.A. from Teachers College, Columbia University. His acclaimed children's books include *An Autumn Tale* (1988), *A Spring Story* (1989), *Seven Times Eight* (1990), *The Sounds of Summer* (1993), and *A Helpful Alphabet of* © Jerry Bauer.

Friendly Objects (1998), which he co-authored with his father. "Summer," a poignant tale for adults, is part of *Out on the Marsh: Stories* (1988), a collection of his short fiction; his short stories have also appeared in *The New Yorker.* Updike resides in Cambridge, Massachusetts.

Summer   *1985*

It was the first week in August, the time when summer briefly pauses, shifting between its beginning and its end: the light had not yet begun to change, the leaves were still full and green on the trees, the nights were still warm. From the woods and fields came the hiss of crickets; the line of distant mountains was still dulled by the edge of summer haze, the echo of fireworks was replaced by the rumble of thunder and the hollow premonition of school, too far off to imagine though dimly, dully felt. His senses were consumed by the joy of their own fulfillment: the satisfying swat of a tennis ball, the dappled damp and light of the dirt road after rain, the alternating sensations of sand, mossy stone, and pine needles under bare feet. His days were spent in the adolescent pursuit of childhood pleasures: tennis, a haphazard round of golf, a variant of baseball adapted to the local geography: two pine trees as foul poles, a broomstick as the bat, the apex of the small, secluded house the dividing line between home runs and outs. On rainy days they swatted bottle tops across the living room floor, and at night vented budding cerebral energy with games of chess thoughtfully played over glasses of iced tea. After dinner they would paddle the canoe to the middle of the lake, and drift beneath the vast, blue-black dome of sky, looking at the stars and speaking softly in tones which, with the waning summer, became increasingly philosophical: the sky's blue vastness, the distance and magnitude of stars, an endless succession of numbers, gave way to a rising sensation of infinity, eternity, an imagined universe with no bounds. But the sound of the paddle hitting against the side of the canoe, the faint shadow of surrounding mountains, the cry of a nocturnal bird brought them back to the happy, cloistered finity of their world, and they paddled slowly home and went to bed.

Homer woke to the slant and shadow of a summer morning, dressed in their shared cabin, and went into the house where Mrs. Thyme sat alone, looking out across the flat blue stillness of the lake. She poured him a cup of coffee and they quietly talked, and it was then that his happiness seemed most tangible. In this summer month with the Thymes, freed from the complications of his own family, he had released himself to them and, as interim member — friend, brother, surrogate son — he lived in a blessed realm between two worlds.

From the cool darkness of the porch, smelling faintly of moldy books and kerosene and the tobacco of burning pipes, he sat looking through the screen to the lake, shimmering beneath the heat of a summer afternoon: a dog lay sleeping in the sun, a bird hopped along a swaying branch, sunlight came in through the trees and collapsed on the sandy soil beside a patch of moss, or mimicked the shade and cadence of stones as they stepped to the edge of a lake where small waves lapped a damp rock and washed onto a sandy shore. An inverted boat lay decaying under a tree, a drooping American flag hung from its gnarled pole, a haphazard dock started out across the cove toward distant islands through which the white triangle of a sail silently moved.

The yellowed pages of the book from which he occasionally read swam before him: ". . . Holmes clapped the hat upon his head. It came right over the forehead and settled on the bridge of his nose. 'It is a question of cubic capacity' said he . . ." Homer looked up. The texture of the smooth, unbroken air was cleanly divided by the sound of a slamming door, echoing up into the woods around him. Through the screen he watched Fred's sister Sandra as she came ambling down the path, stepping lightly between the stones in her bare feet. She held a towel in one hand, a book in the other, and wore a pair of pale blue shorts — faded relics of another era. At the end of the dock she stopped, raised her hands above her head, stretching, and then sat down. She rolled over onto her stomach and, using the book as a pillow, fell asleep.

Homer was amused by the fact, that although she did this every day, she   5 didn't get any tanner. When she first came in her face was faintly flushed, and there was a pinkish line around the snowy band where her bathing suit strap had been, but the back of her legs remained an endearing, pale white, the color of eggshells, and her back acquired only the softest, brownish blur. Sometimes she kept her shoes on, other times a shirt, or sweater, or just collapsed onto the seat of the boat, her pale eyelids turned upward toward the pale sun; and as silently as she arrived, she would leave, walking back through the stones with the same, casual sway of indifference. He would watch her, hear the distant door slam, the shower running in the far corner of the house. Other times he would just look up and she would be gone.

On the tennis court she was strangely indifferent to his heroics. When the crucial moment arrived — Homer serving in the final game of the final set — the match would pause while she left, walking across the court, stopping to call the dog, swaying out through the gate. Homer watched her as she went down the path, and, impetus suddenly lost, he double faulted, stroked a routine backhand over the back fence, and the match was over.

When he arrived back at the house she asked him who won, but didn't seem to hear his answer. "I wish I could go sailing," she said, looking distractedly out over the lake.

At night, when he went out to the cottage where he and Fred slept, he could see her through the window as she lay on her bed, reading, her arm folded beneath her head like a leaf. Her nightgown, pulled and buttoned to her chin, pierced him with a regret that had no source or resolution, and its imagined texture floated in the air above him as he lay in bed at night, suspended in the surrounding darkness, the scent of pine, the hypnotic cadence of his best friend's breathing.

Was it that he had known her all his life, and as such had grown up in the shadow of her subtle beauty? Was it the condensed world of the lake, the silent reverence of surrounding woods, mountains, which heightened his sense of her and brought the warm glow of her presence into soft, amorous focus? She had the hair of a baby, the freckles of a child, and the sway of motherhood. Like his love, her beauty rose up in the world which spawned and nurtured it, and found in the family the medium in which it thrived, and in Homer distilled to a pure distant longing for something he had never had.

One day they climbed a mountain, and as the components of family and   10
friends strung out along the path on their laborious upward hike, he found
himself tromping along through the woods with her with nobody else in sight.
Now and then they would stop by a stream, or sit on a stump, or stone, and he
would speak to her, and then they would set off again, he following her. But in
the end this day exhausted him, following her pale legs and tripping sneakers
over the ruts and stones and a thousand roots, all the while trying to suppress
a wordless, inarticulate passion, and the last mile or so he left her, sprinting
down the path in a reckless, solitary release, howling into the woods around
him. He was lying on the grass, staring up into the patterns of drifting clouds
when she came ambling down. "Wher'd you go? I thought I'd lost you," she
said, and sat heavily down in the seat of the car. On the ride home, his elbow
hopelessly held in the warm crook of her arm, he resolved to release his love,
give it up, on the grounds that it was too disruptive to his otherwise placid life.
But in the days to follow he discovered that his resolution had done little to
change her, and her life went on its oblivious, happy course without him.

His friendship with Fred, meanwhile, continued on its course of athletic
and boyhood fulfillment. Alcohol seeped into their diet, and an occasional cigarette, and at night they would drive into town, buy two enormous cans of
Australian beer and sit at a small cove by the lake, talking. One night on the
ride home Fred accelerated over a small bridge, and as the family station
wagon left the ground their heads floated up to the ceiling, touched, and then
came crashing down as the car landed and Fred wrestled the car back onto
course. Other times they would take the motorboat out onto the lake and
make sudden racing turns around buoys, sending a plume of water into the air
and everything in the boat crashing to one side. But always with these adventures Homer felt a pang of absence, and was always relieved when they headed
back toward the familiar cove, and home.

As August ran its merciless succession of beautiful days, Sandra drifted in
and out of his presence in rising oscillations of sorrow and desire. She worked
at a bowling alley on the other side of the lake, and in the evening Homer and
Fred would drive the boat over, bowl a couple of strings, and wait for her to get
off work. Homer sat at the counter and watched her serve up sloshing cups of
coffee, secretly loathing the leering gazes of whiskered truck drivers, and loving her oblivious, vacant stare in answer, hip cocked, hand on counter, gazing
up into the neon air above their heads. When she was finished, they would pile
into the boat and skim through darkness the four or five miles home, and it
was then, bundled beneath sweaters and blankets, the white hem of her wait-
ressing dress showing through the darkness, their hair swept in the wind and
their voices swallowed by the engine's slow, steady growl, that he felt most
powerless to her attraction. As the boat rounded corners he would close his
eyes and release himself to gravity, his body's warmth swaying into hers, guis-
ing his attraction in the thin veil of centrifugal force. Now and then he would
lean into the floating strands of her hair and speak into her fragrance, watching her smile swell in the pale half-light of the moon, the umber glow of the
boat's rear light, her laughter spilling backward over the swirling "V" of wake.

Into the humid days of August a sudden rain fell, leaving the sky a hard, unbroken
blue and the nights clear and cool. In the morning when he woke, leaving Fred a

heap of sighing covers in his bed, he stepped out into the first rays of sunlight that came through the branches of the trees and sensed, in the cool vapor that rose from damp pine needles, the piercing cry of a blue jay, that something had changed. That night as they ate dinner—hamburgers and squash and corn-on-the-cob—everyone wore sweaters, and as the sun set behind the undulating line of distant mountains—burnt, like a filament of summer into his blinking eyes—it was with an autumnal tint, a reddish glow. Several days later the tree at the end of the point bloomed with a sprig of russet leaves, one or two of which occasionally fell, and their lives became filled with an unspoken urgency. Life of summer went on in the silent knowledge that, with the slow, inexorable seepage of an hourglass, it was turning into fall. Another mountain was climbed, annual tennis matches were arranged and played. Homer and Fred became unofficial champions of the lake by trouncing the elder Dewitt boys, unbeaten in several years. "Youth, youth," glum Billy Dewitt kept saying over iced tea afterward, in jest, though Homer could tell he was hiding some greater sense of loss.

And the moment, the conjunction of circumstance that, through the steady exertion of will, minor adjustments of time and place, he had often tried to induce, never happened. She received his veiled attentions with a kind of amused curiosity, as if smiling back on innocence. One night they had been the last ones up, and there was a fleeting, shuddering moment before he stepped through the woods to his cabin and she went to her bed that he recognized, in a distant sort of way, as the moment of truth. But to touch her, or kiss her, seemed suddenly incongruous, absurd, contrary to something he could not put his finger on. He looked down at the floor and softly said goodnight. The screen door shut quietly behind him and he went out into the darkness and made his way through the unseen sticks and stones, and it was only then, tripping drunkenly on a fallen branch, that he realized he had never been able to imagine the moment he distantly longed for.

The Preacher gave a familiar sermon about another summer having run 15 its course, the harvest of friendship reaped, and a concluding prayer that, "God willing, we will all meet again in June." That afternoon Homer and Fred went sailing, and as they swept past a neighboring cove Homer saw in its sullen shadows a girl sitting alone in a canoe, and in an eternal, melancholy signal of parting, she waved to them as they passed. And there was something in the way that she raised her arm which, when added to the distant impression of her fullness, beauty, youth, filled him with longing as their boat moved inexorably past, slapping the waves, and she disappeared behind a crop of trees.

The night before they were to leave they were all sitting in the living room after dinner—Mrs. Thyme sewing, Fred folded up with the morning paper, Homer reading on the other end of the couch where Sandra was lying—when the dog leapt up and things shifted in such a way that Sandra's bare foot was lightly touching Homer's back. Mrs. Thyme came over with a roll of newspaper, hit the dog on the head and he leapt off. But to Homer's surprise Sandra's foot remained, and he felt, in the faint sensation of exerted pressure, the passive emanation of its warmth, a distant signal of acquiescence. And as the family scene continued as before it was with the accompanying drama of Homer's hand, shielded from the family by a haphazard wall of pillows, migrating over the couch to where, in a moment of breathless abandon, settled softly on the cool hollow of her arch. She laughed at something her mother had said, her toe twitched, but her foot remained. It was only then, in the presence of the family, that he realized she was his accomplice, and that, though this was as far as it would ever go, his love had been returned.

CONSIDERATIONS FOR CRITICAL THINKING AND WRITING

1. **FIRST RESPONSE.** How do you respond to this love story? Would the story be more satisfying if Homer and Sandra openly acknowledged their feelings for each other and kissed at the end? Why or why not?

2. What details in the first paragraph evoke particular feelings about August? What sort of mood is created by these details?

3. How is Homer's attraction to Sandra made evident in paragraphs 5 through 9?

4. Why do you think August is described as a "merciless succession of beautiful days" (para. 12)?

5. Analyze the images in paragraph 13 that evoke the impending autumn. What does Billy Dewitt's lament about "youth, youth" add to this description?

6. Discuss the transition between paragraphs 14 and 15. How is the mood effectively changed between the night and the next day?

7. What effect does Homer's friendship with Fred and his relationship with the Thyme family have on your understanding of his reticent attraction to Sandra?

8. What, if any, significance can you attach to the names of Homer, Sandra, Thyme, and the Dewitt boys?

9. How successful do you think Updike is in evoking youthful feeling about summer in this story? Explain why you responded positively or negatively to this evocation of summer.

CONNECTIONS TO OTHER SELECTIONS

1. Compare David Updike's treatment of summer as the setting of his story with John Updike's use of summer as the setting in "A & P" (p. 733).

2. Discuss "Summer" and Dagoberto Gilb's "Love in L.A." (p. 311) as love stories. Explain why you might prefer one over the other.

As you read "Summer," what potential paper topics occurred to you? Annotating the text and brainstorming are both good ways to identify moments in a text that you will feel moved to write about if your instructor does not assign a paper topic to you. Even after you come up with a topic — say, the relationship between Homer and Sandra — you still need to turn it into a thesis. The following questions should prove useful in choosing a topic that you can develop into a thesis, the central idea of your paper. As you become increasingly engaged in your topic, you're likely to discover and perhaps change your ideas, so at the beginning stages it's best to regard your thesis as tentative. This will allow you to remain open to unexpected insights along the way.

DEVELOPING A TOPIC INTO A REVISED THESIS

1. If the topic is assigned, have you specifically addressed the prescribed subject matter?

2. If you choose your own topic, have you used your annotations, notes, and first response writing to help you find a suitable topic?

3. Is the topic too broad or too narrow? Is the topic focused enough to be feasible and manageable for the assigned length of the paper?

4. Is the topic too difficult or specialized for you to write about successfully? If you need information and expertise that goes well beyond the scope of the assignment, would it be better to choose another topic?

5. Is the topic too simple or obvious to allow you to develop a strong thesis?

6. Once you have focused your topic, what do you think you want to say about it? What is the central idea — the tentative thesis — of the paper?

7. Have you asked questions about the topic to help generate a thesis?

8. Have you tried brainstorming or freewriting as a means of producing ideas that would lead to a thesis?

9. Have you tried writing a rough outline or simply jotting down ideas to see if your tentative thesis can be supported or qualified and made firmer?

10. Is your thesis statement precise or vague? What is the central argument that your thesis makes?

11. Does the thesis help provide an organizing principle — a sense of direction — for the paper?

12. Does the thesis statement consist of one or more complete declarative sentences (not framed as a question) written in clear language that express a complete idea?

13. Is the thesis supported by specific references to the text you are discussing? Have you used brief quotations to illustrate important points and provide evidence for the argument?

14. Is everything included in the paper in some way related to the thesis? Should any sentences or paragraphs be deleted because they are irrelevant to the central point?

15. Does the thesis appear in the introductory paragraph? If not, is there a particular reason for including it later in the paper?

16. If during the course of writing the paper you shifted direction or changed your mind about its central point, have you revised (or completely revamped) your thesis to reflect that change?

17. Have you developed a thesis that genuinely interests you? Are you interested enough in the thesis to write a paper that will also engage your reader?

A SAMPLE BRAINSTORMING LIST

After Janice has read the story twice carefully, she is ready to start working on turning the assigned topic into a defined thesis. Her instructor asked the class to answer the first question in the Considerations for Critical Thinking and Writing: *Would the story be more satisfying if Homer and Sandra openly acknowledged their feelings for each other and kissed at the end?* Janice uses the technique of brainstorming to come up with a more specific approach to the topic, thinking carefully about elements of the story like plot, setting, action, character, symbolism, tone, and theme.

> — *plot with subtle drama — why?*
>
> — *"blessed realm between two worlds" — adolescence, the school years, real home life (Homer with another family), state of desire before culmination*
>
> — *action: regular, familiar, relatively uneventful, savoring state of vague desire*
>
> — *setting: tranquil, idyllic, familiar, warm, unabrasive "happy, cloistered finity of their world" — unthreatening, known; things happen as they're expected to; navigable, happy, image of summer*
>
> — *character: Homer is shy but sensitive; Sandra seems a little more in control; both are on the threshold of adulthood*
>
> — *symbolism: "blessed realm between two worlds" — adolescent summer life on the lake vs. school and the adult world, summer month with Thymes vs. real home life*
>
> — *tone: easy, light tone, vague but pleasant romantic longing*
>
> — *theme: love acknowledged but kept as part of summer life*

A SAMPLE FIRST THESIS

Reviewing her brainstorming list, Janice sees a connection between the plot and the setting that helps her to address the question and to draft a thesis.

> David Updike's short story "Summer" is a love story with little drama or complication. This lack of action in the plot is mirrored by Updike's rendering of the setting and general atmosphere, which are evoked by the description of the picturesque cabin on a lake, the season of summer, and the symbolic "season" of adolescence. The fact that there is no great culmination to Homer's attraction to Sandra is not a failure of the characters or of the fiction's drama. Instead, this nearly actionless plot captures and reflects the sense of adolescence and summer as a state of protected happiness.

A SAMPLE REVISED THESIS

After this initial attempt at a thesis, Janice asks herself several of the Questions for Writing on page 385 and writes out her responses, realizing along the way how she needs to revise her thesis.

Is the topic (that the action reflects the setting to create a sense of "happy, cloistered finity") too simple? I could discuss whether the story succeeds in creating this sense. It does — through description of setting and of Homer's thoughts.

Is the thesis statement precise? Not quite; I think I need to say in the thesis what would be appealing about "between two worlds." Updike describes it in positive tones, but suggests with the word "cloistered" that there's something they're closing themselves away from, implies there's a world outside. Why is the cloistered state happy and blessed? (I should also comment on the religious terminology, but maybe not in the thesis statement, since it's not the most important descriptive technique in the story.)

Does my thesis offer a direction for the paper, an organizing principle? I think that if I add onto the last sentence something about why the "realm between two worlds" is blessed, I'd be able to organize the paper as a discussion moving between action and setting to argue that the lack of action isn't a failure but a kind of fulfillment or contentment.

Is the thesis supported by specific references to the text you are discussing? Instead of saying "protected happiness" I should use one of the quotes I've been mentioning: "the happy, cloistered finity of their world" (para. 1) and "a blessed realm between two worlds" (para. 2).

David Updike's short story "Summer" involves little action or complication, but this lack of action in the plot is made meaningful by the rendering of the idyllic setting. Combined, these create a particular sense of summer, the symbolic "season" of adolescence, and of adolescent love. The fact that there is no great culmination to Homer's attraction to Sandra is not a failure of the characters or of the plot. Instead, the light tone of this nearly actionless plot captures and reflects the theme — a sense of adolescence and summer as a "blessed realm between two worlds" (para. 2), in which the characters are relatively free of the constraints of more complex adult relationships but may enjoy something of adult consciousness of feeling.

Compare the two thesis statements. Does the revised version seem more effective to you? Why or why not? Can you think of ways of further improving the revised version? Do you think the thesis would be more effective if more or fewer elements were included in it?

Before you begin writing your own paper, review the Questions for Responsive Reading and Writing (pp. 53–55) in Chapter 2, "Writing about Fiction." These questions will help you to focus and sharpen your critical thinking and writing. You'll also find help in Chapter 54, "Reading and the Writing Process," which offers a systematic overview of choosing a topic, developing a thesis, and organizing various types of assignments. If you use outside sources for the paper, be sure to acknowledge them adequately by using the conventional documentation procedures detailed in Chapter 55, "The Literary Research Paper."

A SAMPLE STUDENT RESPONSE

Janice Reardon

Professor Halovanic

English 102

January 21, 2010

Plot and Setting in David Updike's "Summer"

David Updike's short story "Summer" is a love story with little drama or complication, but the lack of action in the plot is made meaningful by the rendering of the idyllic setting, as well as through metaphor and subtle detail. Combined, these elements create a particular sense of summer, the symbolic "season" of adolescence, and of adolescent love. The fact that there is no great culmination to Homer's attraction to Sandra is not a failure of Updike's characters or plot. Instead, the light tone of this nearly actionless plot reflects a specific period of adolescence, a moment between one stage of life and the next. During this time, the characters experience—perhaps for the first time—adult emotions, yet they are still free of the constraints of more complex adult relationships.

From the start, the story establishes a theme of transition through setting. The story takes place in early August "when summer briefly pauses, shifting between its beginning and its end" (380). The days are still long and warm, yet change looms. The sound of fireworks is replaced by distant thunder. Thoughts of the approaching school year become stronger. This setting (both the physical setting as well as the time of year) is a metaphor for the characters, who are also dealing with change. The characters are caught in this same "pause" of summer, experiencing changes in their lives, anticipating other changes to come.

Also like the setting, the characters are at a midpoint, poised between where they have been and where they are going. Both Homer and Sandra are maturing. Homer suddenly has an interest in Sandra, though he has known her all his life. He sees her as having "the hair of a baby, the freckles of a child, and the sway of motherhood" (381). This description suggests the dichotomy of adolescence, a time when a person is caught "between two worlds" (380), between youth and adulthood. Though they recognize the changes they are going through, the characters still cling to their childhood. Homer spends his days playing games: tennis, golf, baseball. Sandra wears shorts faded by time—"faded relics of another era" (381)—a token of her past, perhaps one she is unwilling to give up just yet. These characters are pulled between what they have been all their lives and what lies ahead. They are no longer children and not quite adults, but the emotions they experience are no less real or significant.

    The story has few active scenes, and Updike focuses on internal monologue and detail; it is this inaction that drives the plot. Homer does little to express his love for Sandra. He spends his days watching her intently as she lies in the sun, but he loathes the truck drivers' "leering gazes" (382) in the bowling alley diner where Sandra works. He deals with his newfound love for Sandra by focusing on and analyzing detail, much like the reader of the story. He cannot tell Sandra how he feels, even when the moment warrants it. When they are the last two awake and share a subtle, intimate moment, the thought of kissing her seems "absurd," and Homer can only look at the floor and say goodnight (383). At times, Homer even tries to use his inaction to get what he wants. When the pain of Sandra's seeming indifference becomes too much, he decides to give up his love for her, only to find that she continues on her "oblivious, happy course without him" (382). But it is Homer's inaction that helps us to understand what he is going through; in many ways his inaction creates more drama than action would.

    While Homer does little to act on his love for Sandra, he does *react*. His desire for Sandra causes him to go to extremes. During their hike, when Homer is overcome by his "inarticulate passion" for Sandra, he runs from her at full speed, "howling into the woods" (382). At other times, he and Fred behave recklessly, speeding their car over bridges, racing their motor-boat between buoys. They get in the habit of having a beer and a cigarette each night. These impulsive actions are a "solitary release" for Homer, a way for him to expend some of the anguish he's experiencing (382). This is not uncommon in life or in fiction. Sammy in John Updike's "A & P" reacts similarly to a difficult situation. After seeing two teenage girls

Reardon 3

humiliated by his boss, Sammy decides to take a stand. He quits his job, despite the possibility of upsetting his parents:

> "Sammy, you don't want to do this to your Mom and Dad,"
> he tells me. It's true, I don't. But it seems to me that
> once you begin a gesture it's fatal not to go through
> with it. (737)

Here, Sammy, like Homer, acts without considering the consequences, a behavior common to adolescents.

Keeping with the themes of time and transition, the story ends when the summer ends. The nights grow cold; the preacher speaks of "another summer having run its course" (D. Updike 383). It is only then that Homer and Sandra share a simple, tender moment, a touch, and Homer's love for Sandra is finally—albeit subtly—requited. And with this small dramatic peak, the characters enter a new phase of adulthood. The two will no longer live "between two worlds." They will move on to the next stage of their lives, taking with them memories: memories of this period of their lives, of summer, and of each other.

Reardon 4

Works Cited

Updike, David. "Summer." *The Bedford Introduction to Literature*. Ed. Michael
    Meyer. 9th ed. Boston: Bedford/St. Martin's, 2011. 380–84. Print.
Updike, John. "A & P." *The Bedford Introduction to Literature*. Ed. Michael
    Meyer. 9th ed. Boston: Bedford/St. Martin's, 2011. 733–38. Print.

Approaches
to Fiction

11

A Study of
Nathaniel Hawthorne

[My] book, if you would see anything
in it, requires to be read in the clear,
brown, twilight atmosphere in which it
was written; if opened in the sunshine,
it is apt to look exceedingly like a
volume of blank pages.

— HAWTHORNE, Preface to
Twice-Told Tales (1851)

The three short stories by Nathaniel Hawthorne included in this chapter
provide an opportunity to study a major fiction writer in depth. Getting
to know an author's work is similar to developing a friendship with someone: the more encounters, the more intimate the relationship becomes. Familiarity with a writer's concerns
and methods in one story can help to illuminate another story. As we become accustomed to someone's
voice — a friend's or a writer's — we become attuned to
nuances in tone and meaning. The nuances in Haw-
thorne's fiction warrant close analysis. Although the stories included are
not wholly representative of his work, they suggest some of the techniques
and concerns that characterize it. The three stories provide a useful context

Web Explore
contexts for Nathaniel
Hawthorne and ap-
proaches to "Young
Goodman Brown" at
bedfordstmartins
.com/meyerlit.

Nath⁺ Hathorne

"The Old Manse." The Hawthornes spent some of their happiest years (from the summer of 1842 to 1846) at the Old Manse, a house built by the family of Ralph Waldo Emerson (c. 1770). The garden held a special attraction for Hawthorne, as he describes in *Mosses from an Old Manse:* "I used to visit and revisit it a dozen times a day, and stand in deep contemplation over my vegetable progeny with a love that nobody could share or conceive of who had never taken part in the process of creation. It was one of the most bewitching sights in the world, to observe a hill of beans thrusting aside the soil, or a row of early peas just peeping forth sufficiently to trace a line of delicate green. . . ." © Lee Snider.

"The Witch of the Woodlands"
(above). Because Hawthorne's
family tree included a judge who
participated in the Salem witchcraft trials (1692–93), witchcraft
was an important theme in Hawthorne's writing. This illustration
from an eighteenth-century book
on witchcraft features "a grave
and dark-clad company" such
as Goodman Brown describes
(see "Young Goodman Brown,"
p. 402). Witches were thought
to commune in the forest and
associate with evil creatures or
strange animals known as
"familiars."
By permission of the Peabody Essex
Museum.

Nathaniel Hawthorne (right).
Age 36, in an 1840 portrait by
Charles Osgood.
By permission of the Peabody Essex
Museum.

for reading individual stories. Moreover, the works invite comparisons and contrasts in their styles and themes. Following the three stories are some brief commentaries by and about Hawthorne that establish additional contexts for understanding his fiction.

A BRIEF BIOGRAPHY AND INTRODUCTION

Nathaniel Hawthorne (1804–1864) once described himself as "the obscurest man of letters in America." During the early years of his career, this self-assessment was mostly accurate, but the publication of *The Scarlet Letter* in 1850 marked the beginning of Hawthorne's reputation as a major American writer. His novels and short stories have entertained and challenged generations of readers; they have wide appeal because they can be read on many levels. Hawthorne skillfully creates an atmosphere of complexity and ambiguity that makes it difficult to reduce his stories to a simple view of life. The moral and psychological issues that he examines through the conflicts his characters experience are often intricate and mysterious. Readers are frequently made to feel that in exploring Hawthorne's characters they are also encountering some part of themselves.

Hawthorne achieved success as a writer only after a steady and intense struggle. His personal history was hardly conducive to producing a professional writer. Born in Salem, Massachusetts, Hawthorne came from a Puritan family of declining fortunes that prided itself on an energetic pursuit of practical matters such as law and commerce. He never knew his father, a sea captain who died in Dutch Guiana when Hawthorne was only four years old, but he did have a strong imaginative sense of an early ancestor, who as a Puritan judge persecuted Quakers, and of a later ancestor, who was a judge during the Salem witchcraft trials. His forebears seemed to haunt Hawthorne, so that in some ways he felt more involved in the past than in the present.

In "The Custom-House," the introduction to *The Scarlet Letter,* Hawthorne considers himself in relation to his severe Puritan ancestors:

> No aim, that I have ever cherished, would they recognize as laudable; no success of mine . . . would they deem otherwise than worthless, if not positively disgraceful. "What is he?" murmurs one gray shadow of my forefathers to the other. "A writer of story-books! What kind of a business in life, — what mode of glorifying God, or being serviceable to mankind in his day and generation, — may that be? Why, the degenerate fellow might as well have been a fiddler!" Such are the compliments bandied between my great-grandsires and myself, across the gulf of time! And yet, let them scorn me as they will, strong traits of their nature have intertwined with mine.

Hawthorne's sense of what his forebears might think of his work caused him to worry that the utilitarian world was more real and important than his imaginative creations. This issue became a recurring theme in his work.

Despite the Puritan strain in Hawthorne's sensibilities and his own deep suspicion that a literary vocation was not serious or productive work, Hawthorne was determined to become a writer. He found encouragement at Bowdoin College in Maine and graduated in 1825 with a class that included the poet Henry Wadsworth Longfellow and Franklin Pierce, who would be elected president of the United States in the early 1850s. After graduation Hawthorne returned to his mother's house in Salem, where for the next twelve years he read New England history as well as writers such as John Milton, William Shakespeare, and John Bunyan. During this time he lived a relatively withdrawn life devoted to developing his literary art. Hawthorne wrote and revised stories as he sought a style that would express his creative energies. Many of these early efforts were destroyed when they did not meet his high standards. His first novel, *Fanshawe,* was published anonymously in 1828; it concerns a solitary young man who fails to realize his potential and dies young. Hawthorne very nearly succeeded in reclaiming and destroying all the published copies of this work. It was not attributed to the author until after his death; not even his wife was aware that he had written it. The stories eventually published as *Twice-Told Tales* (1837) represent work that was carefully revised and survived Hawthorne's critical judgments.

Writing did not provide an adequate income, so like nearly all nineteenth-century American writers, Hawthorne had to take on other employment. He worked in the Boston Custom House from 1839 through 1840 to save money to marry Sophia Peabody, but he lost that politically appointed job when administrations changed. In 1841 he lived at Brook Farm, a utopian community founded by idealists who hoped to combine manual labor with art and philosophy. Finding that monotonous physical labor left little time for thinking and writing, Hawthorne departed after seven months. The experience failed to improve his financial situation, but it did eventually serve as the basis for a novel, *The Blithedale Romance* (1852).

Married in the summer of 1842, Hawthorne and his wife moved to the Old Manse in Concord, Massachusetts, where their neighbors included Ralph Waldo Emerson, Henry David Thoreau, Amos Bronson Alcott, and other writers and thinkers who contributed to the lively literary environment of that small town. Although Hawthorne was on friendly terms with these men, his skepticism concerning human nature prevented him from sharing either their optimism or their faith in radical reform of individuals or society. Hawthorne's view of life was chastened by a sense of what he called in "Wakefield" the "iron tissue of necessity." His sensibilities were more akin to Herman Melville's. When Melville and Hawthorne met while Hawthorne was living in the Berkshires of western Massachusetts, they responded to each other intensely. Melville admired the "power of blackness" he discovered in Hawthorne's writings and dedicated *Moby-Dick* to him.

During the several years he lived in the Old Manse, Hawthorne published a second collection of *Twice-Told Tales* (1842) and additional stories in

Mosses from an Old Manse (1846). To keep afloat financially, he worked in the Salem Custom House from 1846 until 1849, when he again lost his job through a change in administrations. This time, however, he discovered that by leaving the oppressive materialism of the Custom House he found more energy to write: "So little adapted is the atmosphere of a Custom House to the delicate harvest of fancy and sensibility, that, had I remained there through ten Presidencies yet to come, I doubt whether the tale of 'The Scarlet Letter' would ever have been brought before the public. My imagination was a tarnished mirror [there.]" Free of the Custom House, Hawthorne was at the height of his creativity and productivity during the early 1850s. In addition to *The Scarlet Letter* and *The Blithedale Romance,* he wrote *The House of the Seven Gables* (1851); *The Snow-Image, and Other Twice-Told Tales* (1852); a campaign biography of his Bowdoin classmate, *The Life of Franklin Pierce* (1852); and two collections of stories for children, *A Wonder Book* (1852) and *Tanglewood Tales* (1853).

Hawthorne's financial situation improved during the final decade of his life. In 1853 his friend President Pierce appointed him to the U.S. consulship in Liverpool, where he remained for the next four years. Following a tour of Europe from 1858 to 1860, Hawthorne and his family returned to Concord, and he published *The Marble Faun* (1860), his final completed work of fiction. He died while traveling through New Hampshire with former President Pierce.

Hawthorne's stories are much more complex than the melodramatic but usually optimistic fiction published in many magazines contemporary to him. Instead of cheerfully confirming public values and attitudes, his work tends to be dark and brooding. Modern readers remain responsive to Hawthorne's work—despite the fact that his nineteenth-century style takes some getting used to—because his psychological themes are as fascinating as they are disturbing. The range of his themes is not broad, but their treatment is remarkable for its insights.

Hawthorne wrote about individuals who suffer from inner conflicts caused by sin, pride, untested innocence, hidden guilt, perverse secrecy, cold intellectuality, and isolation. His characters are often consumed by their own passions, whether those passions are motivated by an obsession with goodness or evil. He looks inside his characters and reveals to us that portion of their hearts, minds, and souls that they keep from the world and even from themselves. This emphasis accounts for the private, interior, and sometimes gloomy atmosphere in Hawthorne's works. His stories rarely end on a happy note because the questions his characters raise are almost never completely answered. Rather than positing solutions to the problems and issues his characters encounter, Hawthorne leaves us with ambiguities suggesting that experience cannot always be fully understood and controlled. Beneath the surface appearances in his stories lurk ironies and shifting meanings that point to many complex truths instead of a single simple moral.

The following three Hawthorne stories provide an opportunity to study this writer in some depth. These stories are not intended to be entirely representative of the 120 or so that Hawthorne wrote, but they do offer some sense of the range of his techniques and themes. Hawthorne's fictional world of mysterious incidents and sometimes bizarre characters increases in meaning the more his stories are read in the context of one another.

Chronology

1804	Born on July 4 in Salem, Massachusetts.
1808	Hawthorne's father, a sea captain, dies in Surinam, Dutch Guiana, leaving the family dependent on relatives.
1821–25	Attends Bowdoin College in Maine. Franklin Pierce (later to become president) and Henry Wadsworth Longfellow are classmates. Graduates eighteenth in a class of thirty-eight.
1828	Publishes *Fanshawe: A Tale* anonymously at his own expense.
1830–37	Publishes numerous stories in periodicals anonymously or pseudonymously, collected in *Twice-Told Tales*.
1838	Becomes engaged to Sophia Peabody.
1839–40	Works in Boston Custom House.
1841	From April to November, lives at the utopian Brook Farm Community.
1842–45	Marries (eventually has three children) and lives at the Old Manse in Concord, Massachusetts, where he meets Ralph Waldo Emerson and Henry David Thoreau.
1846	Publishes his second collection of stories, *Mosses from an Old Manse*.
1846–49	Works as a surveyor in the Salem Custom House.
1850	Publishes *The Scarlet Letter;* becomes a friend of Herman Melville.
1851	Publishes *The House of the Seven Gables; The Snow-Image, and Other Twice-Told Tales;* and *True Stories from History and Biography*.
1852	Publishes *The Blithedale Romance; A Wonder Book for Girls and Boys;* and *The Life of Franklin Pierce*, a campaign biography.
1853–57	Serves as United States Consul at Liverpool on appointment by President Pierce.
1857–59	Lives in Rome and Florence.
1860	Publishes *The Marble Faun;* returns to Concord.
1863	Publishes *Our Old Home: A Series of English Sketches*.
1864	Dies on May 19 at Plymouth, New Hampshire.

Young Goodman Brown 1835

Young Goodman Brown came forth at sunset into the street at Salem village; but put his head back, after crossing the threshold, to exchange a parting kiss with his young wife. And Faith, as the wife was aptly named, thrust her own pretty head into the street, letting the wind play with the pink ribbons of her cap while she called to Goodman Brown.

"Dearest heart," whispered she, softly and rather sadly, when her lips were close to his ear, "prithee put off your journey until sunrise and sleep in your own bed tonight. A lone woman is troubled with such dreams and such thoughts that she's afeared of herself sometimes. Pray tarry with me this night, dear husband, of all nights in the year."

"My love and my Faith," replied young Goodman Brown, "of all nights in the year, this one night must I tarry away from thee. My journey, as thou callest it, forth and back again, must needs be done 'twixt now and sunrise. What, my sweet, pretty wife, dost thou doubt me already, and we but three months married?"

"Then God bless you!" said Faith, with the pink ribbons; "and may you find all well when you come back."

"Amen!" cried Goodman Brown. "Say thy prayers, dear Faith, and go to 5 bed at dusk, and no harm will come to thee."

So they parted; and the young man pursued his way until, being about to turn the corner by the meeting-house, he looked back and saw the head of Faith still peeping after him with a melancholy air, in spite of her pink ribbons.

"Poor little Faith!" thought he, for his heart smote him. "What a wretch am I to leave her on such an errand! She talks of dreams, too. Methought as she spoke there was trouble in her face, as if a dream had warned her what work is to be done tonight. But no, no; 't would kill her to think it. Well, she's a blessed angel on earth; and after this one night I'll cling to her skirts and follow her to heaven."

With this excellent resolve for the future, Goodman Brown felt himself justified in making more haste on his present evil purpose. He had taken a dreary road, darkened by all the gloomiest trees of the forest, which barely stood aside to let the narrow path creep through, and closed immediately behind. It was all as lonely as could be; and there is this peculiarity in such a solitude, that the traveler knows not who may be concealed by the innumerable trunks and the thick boughs overhead; so that with lonely footsteps he may yet be passing through an unseen multitude.

"There may be a devilish Indian behind every tree," said Goodman Brown to himself; and he glanced fearfully behind him as he added, "What if the devil himself should be at my very elbow!"

His head being turned back, he passed a crook of the road, and, looking 10 forward again, beheld the figure of a man, in grave and decent attire, seated at the foot of an old tree. He arose at Goodman Brown's approach and walked onward side by side with him.

"You are late, Goodman Brown," said he. "The clock of the Old South was striking as I came through Boston, and that is full fifteen minutes agone."

"Faith kept me back a while," replied the young man, with a tremor in his voice, caused by the sudden appearance of his companion, though not wholly unexpected.

It was now deep dusk in the forest, and deepest in that part of it where these two were journeying. As nearly as could be discerned, the second traveler was about fifty years old, apparently in the same rank of life as Goodman Brown, and bearing a considerable resemblance to him, though perhaps more in expression than features. Still they might have been taken for father and son. And yet, though the elder person was as simply clad as the younger, and as simple in manner too, he had an indescribable air of one who knew the world, and who would not have felt abashed at the governor's dinner table or in King William's court, were it possible that his affairs should call him thither. But the only thing about him that could be fixed upon as remarkable was his staff, which bore the likeness of a great black snake, so curiously wrought that it might almost be seen to twist and wriggle itself like a living serpent. This, of course, must have been an ocular deception, assisted by the uncertain light.

"Come, Goodman Brown," cried his fellow-traveler, "this is a dull pace for the beginning of a journey. Take my staff, if you are so soon weary."

"Friend," said the other, exchanging his slow pace for a full stop, "having 15 kept covenant by meeting thee here, it is my purpose now to return whence I came. I have scruples touching the matter thou wot'st° of."

"Sayest thou so?" replied he of the serpent, smiling apart. "Let us walk on, nevertheless, reasoning as we go; and if I convince thee not thou shalt turn back. We are but a little way in the forest yet."

"Too far! too far!" exclaimed the goodman, unconsciously resuming his walk. "My father never went into the woods on such an errand, nor his father before him. We have been a race of honest men and good Christians since the days of the martyrs; and shall I be the first of the name of Brown that ever took this path and kept"—

"Such company, thou wouldst say," observed the elder person, interpreting his pause. "Well said, Goodman Brown! I have been as well acquainted with your family as with ever a one among the Puritans; and that's no trifle to say. I helped your grandfather, the constable, when he lashed the Quaker woman so smartly through the streets of Salem; and it was I that brought your father a pitch-pine knot, kindled at my own hearth, to set fire to an Indian village, in King Philip's war.° They were my good friends, both; and many a pleasant walk have we had along this path, and returned merrily after midnight. I would fain be friends with you for their sake."

"If it be as thou sayest," replied Goodman Brown, "I marvel they never spoke of these matters; or, verily, I marvel not, seeing that the least rumor of the sort would have driven them from New England. We are a people of prayer, and good works to boot, and abide no such wickedness."

"Wickedness or not," said the traveler with the twisted staff, "I have a very 20 general acquaintance here in New England. The deacons of many a church have drunk the communion wine with me; the selectmen of divers towns make me their chairman; and a majority of the Great and General Court are

---

wot'st: Know.
King Philip's war (1675–76): War between the colonists and an alliance of Indian tribes led by Metacan (also known as Metacomet), leader of the Wampanoags, who was called King Philip by the colonists.

firm supporters of my interest. The governor and I, too — But these are state secrets."

"Can this be so?" cried Goodman Brown, with a stare of amazement at his undisturbed companion. "Howbeit, I have nothing to do with the governor and council; they have their own ways, and are no rule for a simple husband-man like me. But, were I to go on with thee, how should I meet the eye of that good old man, our minister, at Salem village? Oh, his voice would make me tremble both Sabbath day and lecture day."

Thus far the elder traveler had listened with due gravity; but now burst into a fit of irrepressible mirth, shaking himself so violently that his snakelike staff actually seemed to wriggle in sympathy.

"Ha! ha! ha!" shouted he again and again; then composing himself, "Well, go on, Goodman Brown, go on; but, prithee, don't kill me with laughing."

"Well, then, to end the matter at once," said Goodman Brown, consider-ably nettled, "there is my wife, Faith. It would break her dear little heart; and I'd rather break my own."

"Nay, if that be the case," answered the other, "e'en go thy ways, Goodman Brown. I would not for twenty old women like the one hobbling before us that Faith should come to any harm." | 25

As he spoke he pointed his staff at a female figure on the path, in whom Goodman Brown recognized a very pious and exemplary dame, who had taught him his catechism in youth, and was still his moral and spiritual adviser, jointly with the minister and Deacon Gookin.

"A marvel, truly that Goody Cloyse should be so far in the wilderness at nightfall," said he. "But with your leave, friend, I shall take a cut through the woods until we have left this Christian woman behind. Being a stranger to you, she might ask whom I was consorting with and whither I was going."

"Be it so," said his fellow-traveler. "Betake you to the woods, and let me keep the path."

Accordingly the young man turned aside, but took care to watch his com-panion, who advanced softly along the road until he had come within a staff's length of the old dame. She, meanwhile, was making the best of her way, with singular speed for so aged a woman, and mumbling some indistinct words — a prayer, doubtless — as she went. The traveler put forth his staff and touched her withered neck with what seemed the serpent's tail.

"The devil!" screamed the pious old lady. | 30

"Then Goody Cloyse knows her old friend?" observed the traveler, con-fronting her and leaning on his writhing stick.

"Ah, forsooth, and is it your worship indeed?" cried the good dame. "Yea, truly is it, and in the very image of my old gossip, Goodman Brown, the grand-father of the silly fellow that now is. But — would your worship believe it? — my broomstick hath strangely disappeared, stolen, as I suspect, by that unhanged witch, Goody Cory, and that, too, when I was all anointed with the juice of smallage, and cinquefoil, and wolfsbane" —

"Mingled with fine wheat and the fat of a newborn babe," said the shape of old Goodman Brown.

"Ah, your worship knows the recipe," cried the old lady, cackling aloud. "So, as I was saying, being all ready for the meeting, and no horse to ride on, I made up my mind to foot it; for they tell me there is a nice young man to be taken into communion tonight. But now your good worship will lend me your arm, and we shall be there in a twinkling."

"That can hardly be," answered her friend. "I may not spare you my arm, 35 Goody Cloyse; but here is my staff, if you will."

So saying, he threw it down at her feet, where, perhaps, it assumed life, being one of the rods which its owner had formerly lent to the Egyptian magi. Of this fact, however, Goodman Brown could not take cognizance. He had cast up his eyes in astonishment, and, looking down again, beheld neither Goody Cloyse nor the serpentine staff, but his fellow-traveler alone, who waited for him as calmly as if nothing had happened.

"That old woman taught me my catechism," said the young man; and there was a world of meaning in this simple comment.

They continued to walk onward, while the elder traveler exhorted his companion to make good speed and persevere in the path, discoursing so aptly that his arguments seemed rather to spring up in the bosom of his auditor than to be suggested by himself. As they went, he plucked a branch of maple to serve for a walking stick, and began to strip it of the twigs and little boughs, which were wet with evening dew. The moment his fingers touched them they became strangely withered and dried up as with a week's sunshine. Thus the pair proceeded, at a good free pace, until suddenly, in a gloomy hollow of the road, Goodman Brown sat himself down on the stump of a tree and refused to go any farther.

"Friend," he said, stubbornly, "my mind is made up. Not another step will I budge on this errand. What if a wretched old woman do choose to go to the devil when I thought she was going to heaven: is that any reason why I should quit my dear Faith and go after her?"

"You will think better of this by and by," said his acquaintance, compos- 40 edly. "Sit here and rest yourself a while; and when you feel like moving again, there is my staff to help you along."

Without more words, he threw his companion the maple stick, and was as speedily out of sight as if he had vanished into the deepening gloom. The young man sat a few moments by the roadside, applauding himself greatly, and thinking with how clear a conscience he should meet the minister in his morning walk, nor shrink from the eye of good old Deacon Gookin. And what calm sleep would be his that very night, which was to have been spent so wickedly, but so purely and sweetly now, in the arms of Faith! Amidst these pleasant and praiseworthy meditations, Goodman Brown heard the tramp of horses along the road, and deemed it advisable to conceal himself within the verge of the forest, conscious of the guilty purpose that had brought him thither, though now so happily turned from it.

On came the hoof tramps and the voices of the riders, two grave old voices, conversing soberly as they drew near. These mingled sounds appeared to pass along the road, within a few yards of the young man's hiding-place; but, owing doubtless to the depth of the gloom at that particular spot, neither the travelers nor their steeds were visible. Though their figures brushed the small boughs by the wayside, it could not be seen that they intercepted, even for a moment, the faint gleam from the strip of bright sky athwart which they must have passed. Goodman Brown alternately crouched and stood on tiptoe, pulling aside the branches and thrusting forth his head as far as he durst without discerning so much as a shadow. It vexed him the more, because he could have sworn, were such a thing possible, that he recognized the voices of the minister and Deacon Gookin, jogging along quietly, as they were wont to do, when bound to some ordination or ecclesiastical council. While yet within hearing, one of the riders stopped to pluck a switch.

"Of the two, reverend sir," said the voice like the deacon's, "I had rather miss an ordination dinner than tonight's meeting. They tell me that some of our community are to be here from Falmouth and beyond, and others from Connecticut and Rhode Island, besides several of the Indian powwows, who, after their fashion, know almost as much deviltry as the best of us. Moreover, there is a goodly young woman to be taken into communion."

"Mighty well, Deacon Gookin!" replied the solemn old tones of the minister. "Spur up, or we shall be late. Nothing can be done, you know, until I get on the ground."

The hoofs clattered again; and the voices, talking so strangely in the empty air, passed on through the forest, where no church had ever been gathered or solitary Christian prayed. Whither, then, could these holy men be journeying so deep into the heathen wilderness? Young Goodman Brown caught hold of a tree for support, being ready to sink down on the ground, faint and overburdened with the heavy sickness of his heart. He looked up to the sky, doubting whether there really was a heaven above him. Yet there was the blue arch, and the stars brightening in it. 45

"With heaven above and Faith below, I will yet stand firm against the devil!" cried Goodman Brown.

While he still gazed upward into the deep arch of the firmament and had lifted his hands to pray, a cloud, though no wind was stirring, hurried across the zenith and hid the brightening stars. The blue sky was still visible, except directly overhead, where this black mass of cloud was sweeping swiftly northward. Aloft in the air, as if from the depths of the cloud, came a confused and doubtful sound of voices. Once the listener fancied that he could distinguish the accents of townspeople of his own, men and women, both pious and ungodly, many of whom he had met at the communion table, and had seen others rioting at the tavern. The next moment, so indistinct were the sounds, he doubted whether he had heard aught but the murmur of the old forest, whispering without a wind. Then came a stronger swell of those familiar tones, heard daily in the sunshine at Salem village, but never until now from a cloud of night. There was one voice, of a young woman, uttering lamentations, yet with an uncertain sorrow, and entreating for some favor, which, perhaps, it would grieve her to obtain; and all the unseen multitude, both saints and sinners, seemed to encourage her onward.

"Faith!" shouted Goodman Brown, in a voice of agony and desperation; and the echoes of the forest mocked him, crying, "Faith! Faith!" as if bewildered wretches were seeking her all through the wilderness.

The cry of grief, rage, and terror was yet piercing the night, when the unhappy husband held his breath for a response. There was a scream, drowned immediately in a louder murmur of voices, fading into far-off laughter, as the dark cloud swept away, leaving the clear and silent sky above Goodman Brown. But something fluttered lightly down through the air and caught on the branch of a tree. The young man seized it, and beheld a pink ribbon.

"My Faith is gone!" cried he after one stupefied moment. "There is no good on earth; and sin is but a name. Come, devil; for to thee is this world given." 50

And, maddened with despair, so that he laughed loud and long, did Goodman Brown grasp his staff and set forth again, at such a rate that he seemed to fly along the forest path rather than to walk or run. The road grew wilder and drearier and more faintly traced, and vanished at length, leaving him in the heart of the dark wilderness, still rushing onward with the instinct that guides mortal man to evil. The whole forest was peopled with frightful sounds — the creaking of the trees, the howling of wild beasts, and the yell of Indians; while sometimes the wind tolled like a distant church bell, and sometimes gave a broad roar around the traveler, as if all Nature were laughing him to scorn. But he was himself the chief horror of the scene, and shrank not from its other horrors.

"Ha! ha! ha!" roared Goodman Brown when the wind laughed at him. "Let us hear which will laugh loudest. Think not to frighten me with your deviltry. Come witch, come wizard, come Indian powwow, come devil himself, and here comes Goodman Brown. You may as well fear him as he fear you."

In truth, all through the haunted forest there could be nothing more frightful than the figure of Goodman Brown. On he flew among the black pines, brandishing his staff with frenzied gestures, now giving vent to an inspiration of horrid blasphemy, and now shouting forth such laughter as set all the echoes of the forest laughing like demons around him. The fiend in his own shape is less hideous than when he rages in the breast of man. Thus sped the demoniac on his course, until, quivering among the trees, he saw a red light before him, as when the felled trunks and branches of a clearing have been set on fire, and throw up their lurid blaze against the sky, at the hour of midnight. He paused, in a lull of the tempest that had driven him onward, and heard the swell of what seemed a hymn, rolling solemnly from a distance with the weight of many voices. He knew the tune; it was a familiar one in the choir of the village meeting-house. The verse died heavily away, and was lengthened by a chorus, not of human voices, but of all the sounds of the benighted wilderness pealing in awful harmony together. Goodman Brown cried out, and his cry was lost to his own ear by its unison with the cry of the desert.

In the interval of silence he stole forward until the light glared full upon his eyes. At one extremity of an open space, hemmed in by the dark wall of the forest, arose a rock, bearing some rude, natural resemblance either to an altar or a pulpit, and surrounded by four blazing pines, their tops aflame, their stems untouched, like candles at an evening meeting. The mass of foliage that had overgrown the summit of the rock was all on fire, blazing high into the night and fitfully illuminating the whole field. Each pendent twig and leafy festoon was in a blaze. As the red light arose and fell, a numerous congregation alternately shone forth, then disappeared in shadow, and again grew, as it were, out of the darkness, peopling the heart of the solitary woods at once.

"A grave and dark-clad company," quoth Goodman Brown.   55

In truth they were such. Among them, quivering to and fro between gloom and splendor, appeared faces that would be seen next day at the council board of the province, and others which, Sabbath after Sabbath, looked devoutly heavenward, and benignantly over the crowded pews, from the holiest pulpits in the land. Some affirm that the lady of the governor was there. At least there were high dames well known to her, and wives of honored husbands, and widows, a great multitude, and ancient maidens, all of excellent repute, and fair young girls, who trembled lest their mothers should espy them. Either the sudden gleams of light flashing over the obscure field bedazzled Goodman Brown, or he recognized a score of the church members of Salem village famous for their especial sanctity. Good old Deacon Gookin had arrived, and waited at the skirts of that venerable saint, his revered pastor. But, irreverently consorting with these grave, reputable, and pious people, these elders of the church, these chaste dames and dewy virgins, there were men of dissolute lives and women of spotted fame, wretches given over to all mean and filthy vice, and suspected even of horrid crimes. It was strange to see that the good shrank not from the wicked, nor were the sinners abashed by the saints. Scattered also among their pale-faced enemies were the Indian priests, or powwows, who had often scared their native forest with more hideous incantations than any known to English witchcraft.

"But where is Faith?" thought Goodman Brown; and, as hope came into his heart, he trembled.

Another verse of the hymn arose, a slow and mournful strain, such as the pious love, but joined to words which expressed all that our nature can conceive of sin, and darkly hinted at far more. Unfathomable to mere mortals is the lore of fiends. Verse after verse was sung; and still the chorus of the desert swelled between like the deepest tone of a mighty organ; and with the final peal of that dreadful anthem there came a sound, as if the roaring wind, the rushing streams, the howling beasts, and every other voice of the unconcerted wilderness were mingling and according with the voice of guilty man in homage to the prince of all. The four blazing pines threw up a loftier flame, and obscurely discovered shapes and visages of horror on the smoke wreaths above the impious assembly. At the same moment the fire on the rock shot redly forth and formed a glowing arch above its base, where now appeared a figure. With reverence be it spoken, the figure bore no slight similitude, both in garb and manner, to some grave divine of the New England churches.

"Bring forth the converts!" cried a voice that echoed through the field and rolled into the forest.

At the word, Goodman Brown stepped forth from the shadow of the trees 60 and approached the congregation, with whom he felt a loathful brotherhood by the sympathy of all that was wicked in his heart. He could have well-nigh sworn that the shape of his own dead father beckoned him to advance, looking downward from a smoke wreath, while a woman, with dim features of despair, threw out her hand to warn him back. Was it his mother? But he had no power to retreat one step, nor to resist, even in thought, when the minister and good old Deacon Gookin seized his arms and led him to the blazing rock. Thither came also the slender form of a veiled female, led between Goody Cloyse, that pious teacher of the catechism, and Martha Carrier, who had received the devil's promise to be queen of hell. A rampant hag was she. And there stood the proselytes beneath the canopy of fire.

"Welcome, my children," said the dark figure, "to the communion of your race. Ye have found thus young your nature and your destiny. My children, look behind you!"

They turned; and flashing forth, as it were, in a sheet of flame, the fiend worshipers were seen; the smile of welcome gleamed darkly on every visage.

"There," resumed the sable form, "are all whom ye have reverenced from youth. Ye deemed them holier than yourselves and shrank from your own sin, contrasting it with their lives of righteousness and prayerful aspirations heavenward. Yet here are they all in my worshiping assembly. This night it shall be granted you to know their secret deeds: how hoary-bearded elders of the church have whispered wanton words to the young maids of their households;

how many a woman, eager for widows' weeds, has given her husband a drink at bedtime and let him sleep his last sleep in her bosom; how beardless youths have made haste to inherit their fathers' wealth; and how fair damsels—blush not, sweet ones—have dug little graves in the garden, and bidden me, the sole guest, to an infant's funeral. By the sympathy of your human hearts for sin ye shall scent out all the places—whether in church, bedchamber, street, field, or forest—where crime has been committed, and shall exult to behold the whole earth one stain of guilt, one mighty blood spot. Far more than this. It shall be yours to penetrate, in every bosom, the deep mystery of sin, the fountain of all wicked arts, and which inexhaustibly supplies more evil impulses than human power—than my power at its utmost—can make manifest in deeds. And now, my children, look upon each other."

They did so; and, by the blaze of the hell-kindled torches, the wretched man beheld his Faith, and the wife her husband, trembling before that unhallowed altar.

"Lo, there ye stand, my children," said the figure, in a deep and solemn   65
tone, almost sad with its despairing awfulness, as if his once angelic nature could yet mourn for our miserable race. "Depending upon one another's hearts, ye had still hoped that virtue were not all a dream. Now are ye undeceived. Evil is the nature of mankind. Evil must be your only happiness. Welcome again, my children, to the communion of your race."

"Welcome," repeated the fiend worshipers; in one cry of despair and triumph.

And there they stood, the only pair, as it seemed, who were yet hesitating on the verge of wickedness in this dark world. A basin was hollowed, naturally, in the rock. Did it contain water, reddened by the lurid light? or was it blood? or, perchance, a liquid flame? Herein did the shape of evil dip his hand and prepare to lay the mark of baptism upon their foreheads, that they might be partakers of the mystery of sin, more conscious of the secret guilt of others, both in deed and thought, than they could now be of their own. The husband cast one look at his pale wife, and Faith at him. What polluted wretches would the next glance show them to each other, shuddering alike at what they disclosed and what they saw!

"Faith! Faith!" cried the husband, "look up to heaven, and resist the wicked one."

Whether Faith obeyed he knew not. Hardly had he spoken when he found himself amid calm night and solitude, listening to a roar of the wind which died heavily away through the forest. He staggered against the rock, and felt it chill and damp; while a hanging twig, that had been all on fire, besprinkled his cheek with the coldest dew.

The next morning young Goodman Brown came slowly into the street of   70
Salem village, staring around him like a bewildered man. The good old minister was taking a walk along the graveyard to get an appetite for breakfast and meditate his sermon, and bestowed a blessing, as he passed, on Goodman Brown. He shrank from the venerable saint as if to avoid an anathema. Old Deacon Gookin was at domestic worship, and the holy words of his prayer were heard through the open window. "What God doth the wizard pray to?" quoth Goodman Brown. Goody Cloyse, that excellent old Christian, stood in the early sunshine at her own lattice, catechizing a little girl who had brought her a pint of morning's milk. Goodman Brown snatched away the child as from

the grasp of the fiend himself. Turning the corner by the meeting-house, he spied the head of Faith, with the pink ribbons, gazing anxiously forth, and bursting into such joy at sight of him that she skipped along the street and almost kissed her husband before the whole village. But Goodman Brown looked sternly and sadly into her face, and passed on without a greeting.

Had Goodman Brown fallen asleep in the forest and only dreamed a wild dream of a witch-meeting?

Be it so if you will; but, alas! it was a dream of evil omen for young Goodman Brown. A stern, a sad, a darkly meditative, a distrustful, if not a desperate man did he become from the night of that fearful dream. On the Sabbath day, when the congregation were singing a holy psalm, he could not listen because an anthem of sin rushed loudly upon his ear and drowned all the blessed strain. When the minister spoke from the pulpit with power and fervid eloquence, and, with his hand on the open Bible, of the sacred truths of our religion, and of saintlike lives and triumphant deaths, and of future bliss or misery unutterable, then did Goodman Brown turn pale, dreading lest the roof should thunder down upon the gray blasphemer and his hearers. Often, awaking suddenly at midnight, he shrank from the bosom of Faith; and at morning or eventide, when the family knelt down at prayer, he scowled and muttered to himself, and gazed sternly at his wife, and turned away. And when he had lived long, and was borne to his grave a hoary corpse, followed by Faith, an aged woman, and children and grandchildren, a goodly procession, besides neighbors not a few, they carved no hopeful verse upon his tombstone, for his dying hour was gloom.

CONSIDERATIONS FOR CRITICAL THINKING AND WRITING

1. **FIRST RESPONSE.** Try to summarize "Young Goodman Brown" with a tidy moral. Is it possible? What makes this story complex?

2. What is the significance of Goodman Brown's name?

3. What is the symbolic value of the forest in this story? How are the descriptions of the forest contrasted with those of Salem village?

4. Characterize Goodman Brown at the beginning of the story. Why does he go into the forest? What does he mean when he says "Faith kept me back a while" (para. 12)?

5. What function do Faith's ribbons have in the story?

6. What foreshadows Goodman Brown's meeting with his "fellow-traveler" (para. 14)? Who is he? How do we know that Brown is keeping an appointment with a supernatural being?

7. The narrator describes the fellow-traveler's staff wriggling like a snake but then says, "This, of course, must have been an ocular deception, assisted by the uncertain light" (para. 13). What is the effect of this and other instances of ambiguity in the story?

8. What does Goodman Brown discover in the forest? What does he come to think of his ancestors, the church and state, Goody Cloyse, and even his wife?

9. Is Salem populated by hypocrites who cover hideous crimes with a veneer of piety and respectability? Do Faith and the other characters Brown sees when he returns from the forest appear corrupt to you?

10. Near the end of the story the narrator asks, "Had Goodman Brown fallen asleep in the forest and only dreamed a wild dream of a witch-meeting?" (para. 71). Was it a dream, or did the meeting actually happen? How does the answer to this question affect your reading of the story? Write an essay giving an answer to the narrator's question.

11. How is Goodman Brown changed by his experience in the forest? Does the narrator endorse Brown's unwillingness to trust anyone?

12. Consider the story as a criticism of the village's hypocrisy.

13. **CRITICAL STRATEGIES.** Read the section on psychological criticism (pp. 2050–52) in Chapter 53, "Critical Strategies for Reading," and discuss this story as an inward, psychological journey in which Goodman Brown discovers the power of blackness in himself but refuses to acknowledge that dimension of his personality.

CONNECTIONS TO OTHER SELECTIONS

1. Compare and contrast Goodman Brown's reasons for withdrawal with those of Melville's Bartleby (p. 142). Do you find yourself more sympathetic with one character than the other? Explain.

2. To what extent is Hawthorne's use of dreams crucial in this story and in "The Birthmark" (p. 420)? Explain how Hawthorne uses dreams as a means to complicate our view of his characters.

3. What does Goodman Brown's pursuit of sin have in common with Aylmer's quest for perfection in "The Birthmark"? How do these pursuits reveal the characters' personalities and shed light on the theme of each story?

The Minister's Black Veil   *1836*
A Parable°

The sexton stood in the porch of Milford meeting-house, pulling lustily at the bell-rope. The old people of the village came stooping along the street. Children, with bright faces, tript merrily beside their parents, or mimicked a graver gait, in the conscious dignity of their Sunday clothes. Spruce bachelors looked sidelong at the pretty maidens, and fancied that the Sabbath sunshine made them prettier than on weekdays. When the throng had mostly streamed into the porch, the sexton began to toll the bell, keeping his eye on the Reverend Mr. Hooper's door. The first glimpse of the clergyman's figure was the signal for the bell to cease its summons.

"But what has good Parson Hooper got upon his face?" cried the sexton in astonishment.

All within hearing immediately turned about, and beheld the semblance of Mr. Hooper, pacing slowly his meditative way towards the meeting-house.

Another clergyman in New England, Mr. Joseph Moody, of York, Maine, who died about eighty years since, made himself remarkable by the same eccentricity that is here related of the Reverend Mr. Hooper. In his case, however, the symbol had a different import. In early life he had accidentally killed a beloved friend; and from that day till the hour of his own death, he hid his face from men. [Hawthorne's note.]

With one accord they started, expressing more wonder than if some strange minister were coming to dust the cushions of Mr. Hooper's pulpit.

"Are you sure it is our parson?" inquired Goodman Gray of the sexton.

"Of a certainty it is good Mr. Hooper," replied the sexton. "He was to have 5 exchanged pulpits with Parson Shute of Westbury; but Parson Shute sent to excuse himself yesterday, being to preach a funeral sermon."

The cause of so much amazement may appear sufficiently slight. Mr. Hooper, a gentlemanly person of about thirty, though still a bachelor, was dressed with due clerical neatness, as if a careful wife had starched his band, and brushed the weekly dust from his Sunday's garb. There was but one thing remarkable in his appearance. Swathed about his forehead, and hanging down over his face, so low as to be shaken by his breath, Mr. Hooper had on a black veil. On a nearer view, it seemed to consist of two folds of crape, which entirely concealed his features, except the mouth and chin, but probably did not intercept his sight, farther than to give a darkened aspect to all living and inanimate things. With this gloomy shade before him, good Mr. Hooper walked onward, at a slow and quiet pace, stooping somewhat and looking on the ground, as is customary with abstracted men, yet nodding kindly to those of his parishioners who still waited on the meeting-house steps. But so wonder-struck were they, that his greeting hardly met with a return.

"I can't really feel as if good Mr. Hooper's face was behind that piece of crape," said the sexton.

"I don't like it," muttered an old woman, as she hobbled into the meeting-house. "He has changed himself into something awful, only by hiding his face."

"Our parson has gone mad!" cried Goodman Gray, following him across the threshold.

A rumor of some unaccountable phenomenon had preceded Mr. Hooper 10 into the meeting-house, and set all the congregation astir. Few could refrain from twisting their heads towards the door; many stood upright, and turned directly about; while several little boys clambered upon the seats, and came down again with a terrible racket. There was a general bustle, a rustling of the women's gowns and shuffling of the men's feet, greatly at variance with that hushed repose which should attend the entrance of the minister. But Mr. Hooper appeared not to notice the perturbation of his people. He entered with an almost noiseless step, bent his head mildly to the pews on each side, and bowed as he passed his oldest parishioner, a white-haired great-grandsire, who occupied an arm-chair in the center of the aisle. It was strange to observe, how slowly this venerable man became conscious of something singular in the appearance of his pastor. He seemed not fully to partake of the prevailing wonder, till Mr. Hooper had ascended the stairs, and showed himself in the pulpit, face to face with his congregation, except for the black veil. That mysterious emblem was never once withdrawn. It shook with his measured breath as he gave out the psalm; it threw its obscurity between him and the holy page, as he read the Scriptures; and while he prayed, the veil lay heavily on his uplifted countenance. Did he seek to hide it from the dread Being whom he was addressing?

Such was the effect of this simple piece of crape, that more than one woman of delicate nerves was forced to leave the meeting-house. Yet perhaps the pale-faced congregation was almost as fearful a sight to the minister, as his black veil to them.

Mr. Hooper had the reputation of a good preacher, but not an energetic one: he strove to win his people heavenward, by mild persuasive influences, rather than to drive them thither, by the thunders of the Word. The sermon which he now delivered, was marked by the same characteristics of style and manner, as the general series of his pulpit oratory. But there was something, either in the sentiment of the discourse itself, or in the imagination of the auditors, which made it greatly the most powerful effort that they had ever heard from their pastor's lips. It was tinged, rather more darkly than usual, with the gentle gloom of Mr. Hooper's temperament. The subject had reference to secret sin, and those sad mysteries which we hide from our nearest and dearest, and would fain conceal from our own consciousness, even forgetting that the Omniscient can detect them. A subtle power was breathed into his words. Each member of the congregation, the most innocent girl, and the man of hardened breast, felt as if the preacher had crept upon them, behind his awful veil, and discovered their hoarded iniquity of deed or thought. Many spread their clasped hands on their bosoms. There was nothing terrible in what Mr. Hooper said; at least, no violence; and yet, with every tremor of his melancholy voice, the hearers quaked. An unsought pathos came hand in hand with awe. So sensible were the audience of some unwonted attribute in their minister, that they longed for a breath of wind to blow aside the veil, almost believing that a stranger's visage would be discovered, though the form, gesture, and voice were those of Mr. Hooper.

At the close of the services, the people hurried out with indecorous confusion, eager to communicate their pent-up amazement, and conscious of lighter spirits, the moment they lost sight of the black veil. Some gathered in little circles, huddled closely together, with their mouths all whispering in the center; some went homeward alone, wrapt in silent meditation; some talked loudly, and profaned the Sabbath-day with ostentatious laughter. A few shook their sagacious heads, intimating that they could penetrate the mystery; while one or two affirmed that there was no mystery at all, but only that Mr. Hooper's eyes were so weakened by the midnight lamp, as to require a shade. After a brief interval, forth came good Mr. Hooper also, in the rear of his flock. Turning his veiled face from one group to another, he paid due reverence to the hoary heads, saluted the middle-aged with kind dignity, as their friend and spiritual guide, greeted the young with mingled authority and love, and laid his hands on the little children's heads to bless them. Such was always his custom on the Sabbath-day. Strange and bewildered looks repaid him for his courtesy. None, as on former occasions, aspired to the honor of walking by their pastor's side. Old Squire Saunders, doubtless by an accidental lapse of memory, neglected to invite Mr. Hooper to his table, where the good clergyman had been wont to bless the food, almost every Sunday since his settlement. He returned, therefore, to the parsonage, and, at the moment of closing the door, was observed to look back upon the people, all of whom had their eyes fixed upon the minister. A sad smile gleamed faintly from beneath the black veil, and flickered about his mouth, glimmering as he disappeared.

"How strange," said a lady, "that a simple black veil, such as any woman might wear on her bonnet, should become such a terrible thing on Mr. Hooper's face!"

"Something must surely be amiss with Mr. Hooper's intellects," observed 15 her husband, the physician of the village. "But the strangest part of the affair is the effect of this vagary, even on a sober-minded man like myself. The black veil, though it covers only our pastor's face, throws its influence over his whole person, and makes him ghost-like from head to foot. Do you not feel it so?"

"Truly do I," replied the lady; "and I would not be alone with him for the world. I wonder he is not afraid to be alone with himself!"

"Men sometimes are so," said her husband.

That afternoon service was attended with similar circumstances. At its conclusion, the bell tolled for the funeral of a young lady. The relatives and friends were assembled in the house, and the more distant acquaintances stood about the door, speaking of the good qualities of the deceased, when their talk was interrupted by the appearance of Mr. Hooper, still covered with his black veil. It was now an appropriate emblem. The clergyman stepped into the room where the corpse was laid, and bent over the coffin, to take a last farewell of his deceased parishioner. As he stooped, the veil hung straight down from his forehead, so that, if her eye-lids had not been closed for ever, the dead maiden might have seen his face. Could Mr. Hooper be fearful of her glance, that he so hastily caught back the black veil? A person, who watched the interview between the dead and living, scrupled not to affirm, that, at the instant when the clergyman's features were disclosed, the corpse had slightly shuddered, rustling the shroud and muslin cap, though the countenance retained the composure of death. A superstitious old woman was the only witness of this prodigy. From the coffin, Mr. Hooper passed into the chamber of the mourners, and thence to the head of the staircase, to make the funeral prayer. It was a tender and heart-dissolving prayer, full of sorrow, yet so imbued with celestial hopes, that the music of a heavenly harp, swept by the fingers of the dead, seemed faintly to be heard among the saddest accents of the minister. The people trembled, though they but darkly understood him, when he prayed that they, and himself, and all of mortal race, might be ready, as he trusted this young maiden had been, for the dreadful hour that should snatch the veil from their faces. The bearers went heavily forth, and the mourners followed, saddening all the street, with the dead before them, and Mr. Hooper in his black veil behind.

"Why do you look back?" said one in the procession to his partner.

"I had a fancy," replied she, "that the minister and the maiden's spirit were 20 walking hand in hand."

"And so had I, at the same moment," said the other.

That night, the handsomest couple in Milford village were to be joined in wedlock. Though reckoned a melancholy man, Mr. Hooper had a placid cheerfulness for such occasions, which often excited a sympathetic smile, where livelier merriment would have been thrown away. There was no quality of his disposition which made him more beloved than this. The company at the wedding awaited his arrival with impatience, trusting that the strange awe, which had gathered over him throughout the day, would now be dispelled. But such was not the result. When Mr. Hooper came, the first thing that their eyes rested on was the same horrible black veil, which had added deeper gloom to the funeral, and could portend nothing but evil to the wedding. Such was its immediate effect on the guests, that a cloud seemed to have rolled duskily from beneath the black crape, and dimmed the light of the candles. The bridal pair stood up before the minister. But the bride's cold fingers quivered in the tremulous hand of the bridegroom, and her death-like paleness caused a whisper, that the maiden who had been buried a few hours before, was come from her grave to be married. If ever another wedding were so dismal, it was that famous one, where they tolled the wedding-knell. After performing the ceremony, Mr. Hooper raised a glass of wine to his lips, wishing happiness to the new-married couple, in a strain of mild pleasantry that ought to have brightened the features of the guests, like a cheerful gleam from the hearth. At that instant, catching a glimpse of his figure in the looking-glass, the black veil involved his own spirit in the horror with which it overwhelmed all others. His frame shuddered — his lips grew white — he spilt the untasted wine upon the carpet — and rushed forth into the darkness. For the Earth, too, had on her Black Veil.

The next day, the whole village of Milford talked of little else than Parson Hooper's black veil. That, and the mystery concealed behind it, supplied a topic for discussion between acquaintances meeting in the street, and good women gossiping at their open windows. It was the first item of news that the tavernkeeper told to his guests. The children babbled of it on their way to school. One imitative little imp covered his face with an old black handkerchief, thereby so affrighting his playmates, that the panic seized himself, and he well nigh lost his wits by his own waggery.

It was remarkable, that, of all the busy-bodies and impertinent people in the parish, not one ventured to put the plain question to Mr. Hooper, wherefore he did this thing. Hitherto, whenever there appeared the slightest call for such interference, he had never lacked advisers, nor shown himself averse to be guided by their judgment. If he erred at all, it was by so painful a degree of self-distrust, that even the mildest censure would lead him to consider an indifferent action as a crime. Yet, though so well acquainted with this amiable weakness, no individual among his parishioners chose to make the black veil a subject of friendly remonstrance. There was a feeling of dread, neither plainly confessed nor carefully concealed, which caused each to shift the responsibility upon another, till at length it was found expedient to send a deputation of the church, in order to deal with Mr. Hooper about the mystery, before it should grow into a scandal. Never did an embassy so ill discharge its duties. The minister received them with friendly courtesy, but became silent, after they were seated, leaving to his visitors the whole burthen of introducing their important business. The topic, it might be supposed, was obvious enough. There was the black veil, swathed round Mr. Hooper's forehead, and concealing every feature above his placid mouth, on which, at times, they could perceive the glimmering of a melancholy smile. But that piece of crape, to their imagination, seemed to hang down before his heart, the symbol of a fearful secret between him and them. Were the veil but cast aside, they might speak freely of it, but not till then. Thus they sat a considerable time, speechless, confused, and shrinking uneasily from Mr. Hooper's eye, which they felt to be fixed upon them with an invisible glance. Finally, the deputies returned abashed to their constituents, pronouncing the matter too weighty to be handled, except by a council of the churches, if, indeed, it might not require a general synod.

But there was one person in the village, unappalled by the awe with which 25 the black veil had impressed all beside herself. When the deputies returned without an explanation, or even venturing to demand one, she, with the calm energy of her character, determined to chase away the strange cloud that appeared to be settling round Mr. Hooper, every moment more darkly than before. As his plighted wife, it should be her privilege to know what the black veil concealed. At the minister's first visit, therefore, she entered upon the subject, with a direct simplicity, which made the task easier both for him and her. After he had seated himself, she fixed her eyes steadfastly upon the veil, but could discern nothing of the dreadful gloom that had so overawed the multitude: it was but a double fold of crape, hanging down from his forehead to his mouth, and slightly stirring with his breath.

"No," said she aloud, and smiling, "there is nothing terrible in this piece of crape, except that it hides a face which I am always glad to look upon. Come, good sir, let the sun shine from behind the cloud. First lay aside your black veil: then tell me why you put it on."

Mr. Hooper's smile glimmered faintly.

"There is an hour to come," said he, "when all of us shall cast aside our veils. Take it not amiss, beloved friend, if I wear this piece of crape till then."

"Your words are a mystery too," returned the young lady. "Take away the veil for them, at least."

"Elizabeth, I will," said he, "so far as my vow may suffer me. Know, then, 30 this veil is a type and a symbol, and I am bound to wear it ever, both in light and darkness, in solitude and before the gaze of multitudes, and as with strangers, so with my familiar friends. No mortal eye will see it withdrawn. This dismal shade must separate me from the world: even you, Elizabeth, can never come behind it!"

"What grievous affliction hath befallen you," she earnestly inquired, "that you should thus darken your eyes for ever?"

"If it be a sign of mourning," replied Mr. Hooper, "I, perhaps, like most other mortals, have sorrows dark enough to be typified by a black veil."

"But what if the world will not believe that it is the type of an innocent sorrow?" urged Elizabeth. "Beloved and respected as you are, there may be whispers, that you hide your face under the consciousness of secret sin. For the sake of your holy office, do away this scandal!"

The color rose into her cheeks, as she intimated the nature of the rumors that were already abroad in the village. But Mr. Hooper's mildness did not forsake him. He even smiled again — that same sad smile, which always appeared like a faint glimmering of light, proceeding from the obscurity beneath the veil.

"If I hide my face for sorrow, there is cause enough," he merely replied; 35 "and if I cover it for secret sin, what mortal might not do the same?"

And with this gentle, but unconquerable obstinacy, did he resist all her entreaties. At length Elizabeth sat silent. For a few moments she appeared lost in thought, considering, probably, what new methods might be tried, to withdraw her lover from so dark a fantasy, which, if it had no other meaning, was perhaps a symptom of mental disease. Though of a firmer character than his own, the tears rolled down her cheeks. But, in an instant, as it were, a new feeling took the place of sorrow: her eyes were fixed insensibly on the black veil, when, like a sudden twilight in the air, its terrors fell around her. She arose, and stood trembling before him.

"And do you feel it then at last?" said he mournfully.

She made no reply, but covered her eyes with her hand, and turned to leave the room. He rushed forward and caught her arm.

"Have patience with me, Elizabeth!" cried he passionately. "Do not desert me, though this veil must be between us here on earth. Be mine, and hereafter there shall be no veil over my face, no darkness between our souls! It is but a mortal veil — it is not for eternity! Oh! you know not how lonely I am, and how frightened to be alone behind my black veil. Do not leave me in this miserable obscurity for ever!"

"Lift the veil but once, and look me in the face," said she.   40

"Never! It cannot be!" replied Mr. Hooper.

"Then, farewell!" said Elizabeth.

She withdrew her arm from his grasp, and slowly departed, pausing at the door, to give one long, shuddering gaze, that seemed almost to penetrate the mystery of the black veil. But, even amid his grief, Mr. Hooper smiled to think that only a material emblem had separated him from happiness, though the horrors which it shadowed forth, must be drawn darkly between the fondest of lovers.

From that time no attempts were made to remove Mr. Hooper's black veil, or, by a direct appeal, to discover the secret which it was supposed to hide. By persons who claimed a superiority to popular prejudice, it was reckoned merely an eccentric whim, such as often mingles with the sober actions of men otherwise rational, and tinges them all with its own semblance of insanity. But with the multitude, good Mr. Hooper was irreparably a bugbear. He could not walk the streets with any peace of mind, so conscious was he that the gentle and timid would turn aside to avoid him, and that others would make it a point of hardihood to throw themselves in his way. The impertinence of the latter class compelled him to give up his customary walk, at sunset, to the burial ground, for when he leaned pensively over the gate, there would always be faces behind the grave-stones, peeping at his black veil. A fable went the rounds that the stare of the dead people drove him thence. It grieved him, to the very depth of his kind heart, to observe how the children fled from his approach, breaking up their merriest sports, while his melancholy figure was yet afar off. Their instinctive dread caused him to feel, more strongly than aught else, that a preternatural horror was interwoven with the threads of the black crape. In truth, his own antipathy to the veil was known to be so great, that he never willingly passed before a mirror, nor stooped to drink at a still fountain, lest, in its peaceful bosom, he should be affrighted by himself. This was what gave plausibility to the whispers, that Mr. Hooper's conscience tortured him for some great crime, too horrible to be entirely concealed, or otherwise than so obscurely intimated. Thus, from beneath the black veil, there rolled a cloud into the sunshine, an ambiguity of sin or sorrow, which enveloped the poor minister, so that love or sympathy could never reach him. It was said, that ghost and fiend consorted with him there. With self-shudderings and outward terrors, he walked continually in its shadow, groping darkly within his own soul, or gazing through a medium that saddened the whole world. Even the lawless wind, it was believed, respected his dreadful secret, and never blew aside the veil. But still good Mr. Hooper sadly smiled, at the pale visages of the worldly throng as he passed by.

Among all its bad influences, the black veil had the one desirable effect, of   45
making its wearer a very efficient clergyman. By the aid of his mysterious emblem — for there was no other apparent cause — he became a man of awful power, over souls that were in agony for sin. His converts always regarded him

with a dread peculiar to themselves, affirming, though but figuratively, that, before he brought them to celestial light, they had been with him behind the black veil. Its gloom, indeed, enabled him to sympathize with all dark affections. Dying sinners cried aloud for Mr. Hooper, and would not yield their breath till he appeared; though ever, as he stooped to whisper consolation, they shuddered at the veiled face so near their own. Such were the terrors of the black veil, even when Death had bared his visage! Strangers came long distances to attend service at his church, with the mere idle purpose of gazing at his figure, because it was forbidden them to behold his face. But many were made to quake ere they departed! Once, during Governor Belcher's administration, Mr. Hooper was appointed to preach the election sermon. Covered with his black veil, he stood before the chief magistrate, the council, and the representatives, and wrought so deep an impression, that the legislative measures of that year were characterized by all the gloom and piety of our earliest ancestral sway.

In this manner Mr. Hooper spent a long life, irreproachable in outward act, yet shrouded in dismal suspicions; kind and loving, though unloved, and dimly feared; a man apart from men, shunned in their health and joy, but ever summoned to their aid in mortal anguish. As years wore on, shedding their snows above his sable veil, he acquired a name throughout the New-England churches, and they called him Father Hooper. Nearly all his parishioners, who were of mature age when he was settled, had been borne away by many a funeral: he had one congregation in the church, and a more crowded one in the churchyard; and having wrought so late into the evening, and done his work so well, it was now good Father Hooper's turn to rest.

Several persons were visible by the shaded candlelight, in the death-chamber of the old clergyman. Natural connections he had none. But there was the decorously grave, though unmoved physician, seeking only to mitigate the last pangs of the patient whom he could not save. There were the deacons, and other eminently pious members of his church. There, also, was the Reverend Mr. Clark, of Westbury, a young and zealous divine, who had ridden in haste to pray by the bedside of the expiring minister. There was the nurse, no hired handmaiden of death, but one whose calm affection had endured thus long, in secrecy, in solitude, amid the chill of age, and would not perish, even at the dying hour. Who, but Elizabeth! And there lay the hoary head of good Father Hooper upon the death-pillow, with the black veil still swathed about his brow and reaching down over his face, so that each more difficult gasp of his faint breath caused it to stir. All through life that piece of crape had hung between him and the world: it had separated him from cheerful brotherhood and woman's love, and kept him in that saddest of all prisons, his own heart; and still it lay upon his face, as if to deepen the gloom of his darksome chamber, and shade him from the sunshine of eternity.

For some time previous, his mind had been confused, wavering doubtfully between the past and the present, and hovering forward, as it were, at intervals, into the indistinctness of the world to come. There had been feverish turns, which tossed him from side to side, and wore away what little strength he had. But in his most convulsive struggles, and in the wildest vagaries of his intellect, when no other thought retained its sober influence, he still showed an awful solicitude lest the black veil should slip aside. Even if his bewildered soul could have forgotten, there was a faithful woman at his pillow, who, with averted

eyes, would have covered that aged face, which she had last beheld in the come-
liness of manhood. At length the death-stricken old man lay quietly in the torpor of mental and bodily exhaustion, with an imperceptible pulse, and breath
that grew fainter and fainter, except when a long, deep, and irregular inspiration seemed to prelude the flight of his spirit.

The minister of Westbury approached the bedside.

"Venerable Father Hooper," said he, "the moment of your release is at   50
hand. Are you ready for the lifting of the veil, that shuts in time from eternity?"

Father Hooper at first replied merely by a feeble motion of his head; then,
apprehensive, perhaps, that his meaning might be doubtful, he exerted himself to speak.

"Yea," said he, in faint accents, "my soul hath a patient weariness until
that veil be lifted."

"And is it fitting," resumed the Reverend Mr. Clark, "that a man so given
to prayer, of such a blameless example, holy in deed and thought, so far as
mortal judgment may pronounce; is it fitting that a father in the church
should leave a shadow on his memory, that may seem to blacken a life so pure?
I pray you, my venerable brother, let not this thing be! Suffer us to be glad-
dened by your triumphant aspect, as you go to your reward. Before the veil of
eternity be lifted, let me cast aside this black veil from your face!"

And thus speaking, the Reverend Mr. Clark bent forward to reveal the
mystery of so many years. But, exerting a sudden energy, that made all the
beholders stand aghast, Father Hooper snatched both his hands from beneath
the bedclothes, and pressed them strongly on the black veil, resolute to struggle,
if the minister of Westbury would contend with a dying man.

"Never!" cried the veiled clergyman. "On earth, never!"   55

"Dark old man!" exclaimed the affrighted minister, "with what horrible
crime upon your soul are you now passing to the judgment?"

Father Hooper's breath heaved; it rattled in his throat; but, with a mighty
effort, grasping forward with his hands, he caught hold of life, and held it back
till he should speak. He even raised himself in bed; and there he sat, shivering
with the arms of death around him, while the black veil hung down, awful, at
that last moment, in the gathered terrors of a life-time. And yet the faint, sad
smile, so often there, now seemed to glimmer from its obscurity, and linger on
Father Hooper's lips.

"Why do you tremble at me alone?" cried he, turning his veiled face round
the circle of pale spectators. "Tremble also at each other! Have men avoided
me, and women shown no pity, and children screamed and fled, only for my
black veil? What, but the mystery which it obscurely typifies, has made this
piece of crape so awful? When the friend shows his inmost heart to his friend;
the lover to his best-beloved; when man does not vainly shrink from the eye of
his Creator, loathsomely treasuring up the secret of his sin; then deem me a
monster, for the symbol beneath which I have lived, and die! I look around me,
and, lo! on every visage a Black Veil!"

While his auditors shrank from one another, in mutual affright, Father
Hooper fell back upon his pillow, a veiled corpse, with a faint smile lingering
on the lips. Still veiled, they laid him in his coffin, and a veiled corpse they bore
him to the grave. The grass of many years has sprung up and withered on that
grave, the burial-stone is moss-grown, and good Mr. Hooper's face is dust; but
awful is still the thought, that it moldered beneath the Black Veil!

CONSIDERATIONS FOR CRITICAL THINKING AND WRITING

1. **FIRST RESPONSE.** Why do you think Hooper wears the veil? Explain whether you think Hooper is right or wrong to wear it.

2. Describe the veil Hooper wears. How does it affect his vision?

3. Characterize the townspeople. How does the community react to the veil?

4. What is Hooper's explanation for why he wears the veil? Is he more or less effective as a minister because he wears it?

5. What is the one feature of Hooper's face that we see? What does that feature reveal about him?

6. Describe what happens at the funeral and wedding ceremonies at which Hooper officiates. How are the incidents at these events organized around the veil?

7. Why does Elizabeth think "it should be her privilege to know what the black veil concealed" (para. 25)? Why doesn't Hooper remove it at her request?

8. How does Elizabeth react to Hooper's refusal to take off the veil? Why is her response especially significant?

9. How do others in town explain why Hooper wears the veil? Do these explanations seem adequate to you? Why or why not?

10. Why is Hooper buried with the veil? Of what significance is it that grass "withered" on his grave (para. 59)?

11. Describe the story's point of view. How would a first-person narrative change the story dramatically?

CONNECTIONS TO OTHER SELECTIONS

1. How might this story be regarded as a sequel to "Young Goodman Brown"? How are the themes similar?

2. Explain how Faith in "Young Goodman Brown," Georgiana in "The Birthmark" (below), and Elizabeth in "The Minister's Black Veil" are used to reveal some truth about the central male characters in each story. Describe the similarities that you see among these women characters.

3. Compare Hawthorne's use of symbol in "The Minister's Black Veil" and "The Birthmark." Write an essay explaining which symbol you think works more effectively to evoke the theme of its story.

The Birthmark   1843

In the latter part of the last century there lived a man of science, an eminent proficient in every branch of natural philosophy, who not long before our story opens had made experience of a spiritual affinity more attractive than any chemical one. He had left his laboratory to the care of an assistant, cleared his fine countenance from the furnace smoke, washed the stain of acids from his fingers, and persuaded a beautiful woman to become his wife. In those days when the comparatively recent discovery of electricity and other kindred mysteries of Nature seemed to open paths into the region of miracle, it was not unusual for the love of science to rival the love of woman in its depth and absorbing energy. The higher intellect, the imagination, the spirit, and even the heart might all find their congenial aliment in pursuits which, as some of their ardent votaries believed, would ascend from one step of powerful intelligence to another, until the philosopher should lay his hand on the secret of creative force and perhaps make new worlds for himself. We know not whether Aylmer possessed this degree of faith in man's ultimate control over Nature. He had devoted himself, however, too unreservedly to scientific studies ever to be weaned from them by any second passion. His love for his young wife might prove the stronger of the two; but it could only be by intertwining itself with his love of science, and uniting the strength of the latter to his own.

Such a union accordingly took place, and was attended with truly remarkable consequences and a deeply impressive moral. One day, very soon after their marriage, Aylmer sat gazing at his wife with a trouble in his countenance that grew stronger until he spoke.

"Georgiana," said he, "has it never occurred to you that the mark upon your cheek might be removed?"

"No, indeed," said she, smiling; but perceiving the seriousness of his manner, she blushed deeply. "To tell you the truth it has been so often called a charm that I was simple enough to imagine it might be so."

"Ah, upon another face perhaps it might," replied her husband; "but never 5 on yours. No, dearest Georgiana, you came so nearly perfect from the hand of Nature that this slightest possible defect, which we hesitate whether to term a defect or a beauty, shocks me, as being the visible mark of earthly imperfection."

"Shocks you, my husband!" cried Georgiana, deeply hurt; at first reddening with momentary anger, but then bursting into tears. "Then why did you take me from my mother's side? You cannot love what shocks you!"

To explain this conversation it must be mentioned that in the center of Georgiana's left cheek there was a singular mark, deeply interwoven, as it were, with the texture and substance of her face. In the usual state of her complexion — a healthy though delicate bloom — the mark wore a tint of deeper crimson, which imperfectly defined its shape amid the surrounding rosiness. When she blushed it gradually became more indistinct, and finally vanished amid the triumphant rush of blood that bathed the whole cheek with its brilliant glow. But if any shifting motion caused her to turn pale, there was the mark again, a crimson stain upon the snow, in what Aylmer sometimes deemed an almost fearful distinctness. Its shape bore not a little similarity to the human hand, though of the smallest pygmy size. Georgiana's lovers were wont to say that some fairy at her birth hour had laid her tiny hand upon the infant's cheek, and left this impress there in token of the magic endowments that were to give her such sway over all hearts. Many a desperate swain would have risked life for the privilege of pressing his lips to the mysterious hand. It must not be concealed, however, that the impression wrought by this fairy sign manual varied exceedingly, according to the difference of temperament in the beholders. Some fastidious persons — but they were exclusively of her own sex — affirmed that the bloody hand, as they chose to call it, quite destroyed the effect of Georgiana's beauty, and rendered her countenance even hideous. But it would be as reasonable to say that one of those small blue stains which sometimes occur in the purest statuary marble would convert the Eve of Powers to a monster.

Masculine observers, if the birthmark did not heighten their admiration, contented themselves with wishing it away, that the world might possess one living specimen of ideal loveliness without the semblance of a flaw. After his marriage, — for he thought little or nothing of the matter before, — Aylmer discovered that this was the case with himself.

Had she been less beautiful, — if Envy's self could have found aught else to sneer at, — he might have felt his affection heightened by the prettiness of this mimic hand, now vaguely portrayed, now lost, now stealing forth again and glimmering to and fro with every pulse of emotion that throbbed within her heart; but seeing her otherwise so perfect, he found this one defect grow more and more intolerable with every moment of their united lives. It was the fatal flaw of humanity which Nature, in one shape or another, stamps ineffaceably on all her productions, either to imply that they are temporary and finite, or that their perfection must be wrought by toil and pain. The crimson hand expressed the ineludible gripe° in which mortality clutches the highest and purest of earthly mold, degrading them into kindred with the lowest, and even with the very brutes, like whom their visible frames return to dust. In this manner, selecting it as the symbol of his wife's liability to sin, sorrow, decay, and death, Aylmer's somber imagination was not long in rendering the birthmark a frightful object, causing him more trouble and horror than ever Georgiana's beauty, whether of soul or sense, had given him delight.

At all the seasons which should have been their happiest, he invariably and without intending it, nay, in spite of a purpose to the contrary, reverted to this one disastrous topic. Trifling as it at first appeared, it so connected itself with innumerable trains of thought and modes of feeling that it became the central point of all. With the morning twilight Aylmer opened his eyes upon his wife's face and recognized the symbol of imperfection; and when they sat together at the evening hearth his eyes wandered stealthily to her cheek, and beheld, flickering with the blaze of the wood fire, the spectral hand that wrote mortality where he would fain have worshiped. Georgiana soon learned to shudder at his gaze. It needed but a glance with the peculiar expression that his face often wore to change the roses of her cheek into a deathlike paleness, amid which the crimson hand was brought strongly out, like a bas-relief of ruby on the whitest marble.

Late one night when the lights were growing dim, so as hardly to betray the stain on the poor wife's cheek, she herself, for the first time, voluntarily took up the subject.

"Do you remember, my dear Aylmer," said she, with a feeble attempt at a smile, "have you any recollection of a dream last night about this odious hand?"

"None! none whatever!" replied Aylmer, starting; but then he added, in a dry, cold tone, affected for the sake of concealing the real depth of his emotion, "I might well dream of it; for before I fell asleep it had taken a pretty firm hold of my fancy."

"And you did dream of it?" continued Georgiana hastily, for she dreaded lest a gush of tears should interrupt what she had to say. "A terrible dream! I wonder that you can forget it. Is it possible to forget this one expression? — 'It is in her heart now; we must have it out!' Reflect, my husband; for by all means I would have you recall that dream."

gripe: Grip.

The mind is in a sad state when Sleep, the all-involving, cannot confine her specters within the dim region of her sway, but suffers them to break forth, affrighting this actual life with secrets that perchance belong to a deeper one. Aylmer now remembered his dream. He had fancied himself with his servant Aminadab, attempting an operation for the removal of the birthmark; but the deeper went the knife, the deeper sank the hand, until at length its tiny grasp appeared to have caught hold of Georgiana's heart; whence, however, her husband was inexorably resolved to cut or wrench it away.

When the dream had shaped itself perfectly in his memory, Aylmer sat in his wife's presence with a guilty feeling. Truth often finds its way to the mind close muffled in robes of sleep, and then speaks with uncompromising directness of matters in regard to which we practice an unconscious self-deception during our waking moments. Until now he had not been aware of the tyrannizing influence acquired by one idea over his mind, and of the lengths which he might find in his heart to go for the sake of giving himself peace.

"Aylmer," resumed Georgiana solemnly, "I know not what may be the cost to both of us to rid me of this fatal birthmark. Perhaps its removal may cause cureless deformity; or it may be the stain goes as deep as life itself. Again: do we know that there is a possibility, on any terms, of unclasping the firm grip of this little hand which was laid upon me before I came into the world?"

"Dearest Georgiana, I have spent much thought upon the subject," hastily interrupted Aylmer. "I am convinced of the perfect practicability of its removal."

"If there be the remotest possibility of it," continued Georgiana, "let the attempt be made at whatever risk. Danger is nothing to me; for life, while this hateful mark makes me the object of your horror and disgust, — life is a burden which I would fling down with joy. Either remove this dreadful hand, or take my wretched life! You have deep science. All the world bears witness of it. You have achieved great wonders. Cannot you remove this little, little mark, which I cover with the tips of two small fingers? Is this beyond your power, for the sake of your own peace, and to save your poor wife from madness?"

"Noblest, dearest, tenderest wife," cried Aylmer rapturously, "doubt not my power. I have already given this matter the deepest thought — thought which might almost have enlightened me to create a being less perfect than yourself. Georgiana, you have led me deeper than ever into the heart of science. I feel myself fully competent to render this dear cheek as faultless as its fellow; and then, most beloved, what will be my triumph when I shall have corrected what Nature left imperfect in her fairest work! Even Pygmalion, when his sculptured woman assumed life, felt not greater ecstasy than mine will be."

"It is resolved, then," said Georgiana, faintly smiling. "And, Aylmer, spare me not, though you should find the birthmark take refuge in my heart at last."

Her husband tenderly kissed her cheek — her right cheek — not that which bore the impress of the crimson hand.

The next day Aylmer apprised his wife of a plan that he had formed whereby he might have opportunity for the intense thought and constant watchfulness which the proposed operation would require; while Georgiana, likewise, would enjoy the perfect repose essential to its success. They were to seclude themselves in the extensive apartments occupied by Aylmer as a laboratory, and where, during his toilsome youth, he had made discoveries in the elemental powers of Nature that had roused the admiration of all the learned societies in Europe. Seated calmly in this laboratory, the pale philosopher had investigated the secrets of the highest cloud region and of the profoundest mines; he had satisfied himself of the causes that kindled and kept alive the fires of the volcano; and had explained the mystery of fountains, and how it is that they gush forth, some so bright and pure, and others with such rich medicinal virtues, from the dark bosom of the earth. Here, too, at an earlier period, he had studied the wonders of the human frame, and attempted to fathom the very process by which Nature assimilates all her precious influences from earth and air, and from the spiritual world, to create and foster man, her masterpiece. The latter pursuit, however, Aylmer had long laid aside in unwilling recognition of the truth — against which all seekers sooner or later stumble — that our great creative Mother, while she amuses us with apparently working in the broadest sunshine, is yet severely careful to keep her own secrets, and, in spite of her pretended openness, shows us nothing but results. She permits us, indeed, to mar, but seldom to mend, and, like a jealous patentee, on no account to make. Now, however, Aylmer resumed these half-forgotten investigations, — not, of course, with such hopes or wishes as first suggested them, but because they involved much physiological truth and lay in the path of his proposed scheme for the treatment of Georgiana.

As he led her over the threshold of the laboratory, Georgiana was cold and tremulous. Aylmer looked cheerfully into her face, with intent to reassure her, but was so startled with the intense glow of the birthmark upon the whiteness of her cheek that he could not restrain a strong convulsive shudder. His wife fainted.

"Aminadab! Aminadab!" shouted Aylmer, stamping violently on the floor.

Forthwith there issued from an inner apartment a man of low stature, but bulky frame, with shaggy hair hanging about his visage, which was grimed with the vapors of the furnace. This personage had been Aylmer's underworker during his whole scientific career, and was admirably fitted for that office by his great mechanical readiness, and the skill with which, while incapable of comprehending a single principle, he executed all the details of his master's experiments. With his vast strength, his shaggy hair, his smoky aspect, and the indescribable earthiness that encrusted him, he seemed to represent man's physical nature; while Aylmer's slender figure, and pale, intellectual face, were no less apt a type of the spiritual element. 25

"Throw open the door of the boudoir, Aminadab," said Aylmer, "and burn a pastille."

"Yes, master," answered Aminadab, looking intently at the lifeless form of Georgiana; and then he muttered to himself, "If she were my wife, I'd never part with that birthmark."

When Georgiana recovered consciousness she found herself breathing an atmosphere of penetrating fragrance, the gentle potency of which had recalled her from her deathlike faintness. The scene around her looked like enchantment. Aylmer had converted those smoky, dingy, somber rooms, where he had spent his brightest years in recondite pursuits, into a series of beautiful apartments not unfit to be the secluded abode of a lovely woman. The walls were hung with gorgeous curtains, which imparted the combination of grandeur and grace that no other species of adornment can achieve; and as they fell from the ceiling to the floor, their rich and ponderous folds, concealing all angles and straight lines, appeared to shut in the scene from infinite space. For aught Georgiana knew, it might be a pavilion among the clouds. And Aylmer, excluding the sunshine, which would have interfered with his chemical processes, had supplied its place with perfumed lamps, emitting flames of various hue, but all uniting in a soft, empurpled radiance. He now knelt by his wife's side, watching her earnestly, but without alarm; for he was confident in his science, and felt that he could draw a magic circle round her within which no evil might intrude.

"Where am I? Ah, I remember," said Georgiana faintly; and she placed her hand over her cheek to hide the terrible mark from her husband's eyes.

"Fear not, dearest!" exclaimed he. "Do not shrink from me! Believe me, 30 Georgiana, I even rejoice in this single imperfection, since it will be such a rapture to remove it."

"Oh, spare me!" sadly replied his wife. "Pray do not look at it again. I never can forget that convulsive shudder."

In order to soothe Georgiana, and, as it were, to release her mind from the burden of actual things, Aylmer now put in practice some of the light and playful secrets which science had taught him among its profounder lore. Airy figures, absolutely bodiless ideas, and forms of unsubstantial beauty came and danced before her, imprinting their momentary footsteps on beams of light. Though she had some indistinct idea of the method of these optical phenomena, still the illusion was almost perfect enough to warrant the belief that her husband possessed sway over the spiritual world. Then again, when she felt a wish to look forth from her seclusion, immediately, as if her thoughts were answered, the procession of external existence flitted across a screen. The scenery and the figures of actual life were perfectly represented, but with that bewitching, yet indescribable difference which always makes a picture, an image, or a shadow so much more attractive than the original. When wearied of this, Aylmer bade her cast her eyes upon a vessel containing a quantity of earth. She did so, with little interest at first; but was soon startled to perceive the germ of a plant shooting upward from the soil. Then came the slender stalk; the leaves gradually unfolded themselves; and amid them was a perfect and lovely flower.

"It is magical!" cried Georgiana. "I dare not touch it."

"Nay, pluck it," answered Aylmer: "pluck it, and inhale its brief perfume while you may. The flower will wither in a few moments and leave nothing save its brown seed vessels; but thence may be perpetuated a race as ephemeral as itself."

But Georgiana had no sooner touched the flower than the whole plant 35 suffered a blight, its leaves turning coal-black as if by the agency of fire.

"There was too powerful a stimulus," said Aylmer thoughtfully.

To make up for this abortive experiment, he proposed to take her portrait by a scientific process of his own invention. It was to be effected by rays of light striking upon a polished plate of metal. Georgiana assented; but, on looking at the result, was affrighted to find the features of the portrait blurred and indefinable; while the minute figure of a hand appeared where the cheek should have been. Aylmer snatched the metallic plate and threw it into a jar of corrosive acid.

Soon, however, he forgot these mortifying failures. In the intervals of study and chemical experiment he came to her flushed and exhausted, but seemed invigorated by her presence, and spoke in glowing language of the resources of his art. He gave a history of the long dynasty of the alchemists, who spent so many ages in quest of the universal solvent by which the golden principle might be elicited from all things vile and base. Aylmer appeared to believe that, by the plainest scientific logic, it was altogether within the limits of possibility to discover this long-sought medium; "but," he added, "a philosopher who should go deep enough to acquire the power would attain too lofty a wisdom to stoop to the exercise of it." Not less singular were his opinions in regard to the elixir vitae. He more than intimated that it was at his option to concoct a liquid that should prolong life for years, perhaps interminably; but that it would produce a discord in Nature which all the world, and chiefly the quaffer of the immortal nostrum, would find cause to curse.

"Aylmer, are you in earnest?" asked Georgiana, looking at him with amazement and fear. "It is terrible to possess such power, or even to dream of possessing it."

"Oh, do not tremble, my love," said her husband. "I would not wrong   40 either you or myself by working such inharmonious effects upon our lives; but I would have you consider how trifling, in comparison, is the skill requisite to remove this little hand."

At the mention of the birthmark, Georgiana, as usual, shrank as if a redhot iron had touched her cheek.

Again Aylmer applied himself to his labors. She could hear his voice in the distant furnace-room giving directions to Aminadab, whose harsh, uncouth, misshapen tones were audible in response, more like the grunt or growl of a brute than human speech. After hours of absence, Aylmer reappeared and proposed that she should now examine his cabinet of chemical products and natural treasures of the earth. Among the former he showed her a small vial, in which, he remarked, was contained a gentle yet most powerful fragrance, capable of impregnating all the breezes that blow across a kingdom. They were of inestimable value, the contents of that little vial; and, as he said so, he threw some of the perfume into the air and filled the room with piercing and invigorating delight.

"And what is this?" asked Georgiana, pointing to a small crystal globe containing a gold-colored liquid. "It is so beautiful to the eye that I could imagine it the elixir of life."

"In one sense it is," replied Aylmer; "or rather, the elixir of immortality. It is the most precious poison that ever was concocted in this world. By its aid I could apportion the lifetime of any mortal at whom you might point your finger. The strength of the dose would determine whether he were to linger out years, or drop dead in the midst of a breath. No king on his guarded throne could keep his life if I, in my private station, should deem that the welfare of millions justified me in depriving him of it."

"Why do you keep such a terrific drug?" inquired Georgiana in horror.   45

"Do not mistrust me, dearest," said her husband, smiling; "its virtuous potency is yet greater than its harmful one. But see! here is a powerful cosmetic. With a few drops of this in a vase of water, freckles may be washed away as easily as the hands are cleansed. A stronger infusion would take the blood out of the cheek, and leave the rosiest beauty a pale ghost."

"Is it with this lotion that you intend to bathe my cheek?" asked Georgiana, anxiously.

"Oh, no," hastily replied her husband; "this is merely superficial. Your case demands a remedy that shall go deeper."

In his interviews with Georgiana, Aylmer generally made minute inquiries as to her sensations and whether the confinement of the rooms and the temperature of the atmosphere agreed with her. These questions had such a particular drift that Georgiana began to conjecture that she was already subjected to certain physical influences, either breathed in with the fragrant air or taken with her food. She fancied likewise, but it might be altogether fancy, that there was a stirring up of her system — a strange, indefinite sensation creeping through her veins, and tingling, half painfully, half pleasurably, at her heart. Still, whenever she dared to look into the mirror, there she beheld herself pale as a white rose and with the crimson birthmark stamped upon her cheek. Not even Aylmer now hated it so much as she.

To dispel the tedium of the hours which her husband found it necessary 50 to devote to the processes of combination and analysis, Georgiana turned over the volumes of his scientific library. In many dark old tomes she met with chapters full of romance and poetry. They were the works of the philosophers of the middle ages, such as Albertus Magnus, Cornelius Agrippa, Paracelsus, and the famous friar who created the prophetic Brazen Head. All these antique naturalists stood in advance of their centuries, yet were imbued with some of their credulity, and therefore were believed, and perhaps imagined themselves to have acquired from the investigation of Nature a power above Nature, and from physics a sway over the spiritual world. Hardly less curious and imaginative were the early volumes of the Transactions of the Royal Society, in which the members, knowing little of the limits of natural possibility, were continually recording wonders or proposing methods whereby wonders might be wrought.

But to Georgiana the most engrossing volume was a large folio from her husband's own hand, in which he had recorded every experiment of his scientific career, its original aim, the methods adopted for its development, and its final success or failure, with the circumstances to which either event was attributable. The book, in truth, was both the history and emblem of his ardent, ambitious, imaginative, yet practical and laborious life. He handled physical details as if there were nothing beyond them; yet spiritualized them all, and redeemed himself from materialism by his strong and eager aspiration towards the infinite. In his grasp the veriest clod of earth assumed a soul. Georgiana, as she read, reverenced Aylmer and loved him more profoundly than ever, but with a less entire dependence on his judgment than heretofore. Much as he had accomplished, she could not but observe that his most splendid successes were almost invariably failures, if compared with the ideal at which he aimed. His brightest diamonds were the merest pebbles, and felt to be so by himself, in comparison with the inestimable gems which lay hidden beyond his reach. The volume, rich with achievements that had won renown for its author, was yet as melancholy a record as ever mortal hand had penned. It was the sad confession and continual exemplification of the shortcomings of the composite man, the spirit burdened with clay and working in matter, and of the despair that assails the higher nature at finding itself so miserably thwarted by the earthly part. Perhaps every man of genius in whatever sphere might recognize the image of his own experience in Aylmer's journal.

So deeply did these reflections affect Georgiana that she laid her face upon the open volume and burst into tears. In this situation she was found by her husband.

"It is dangerous to read in a sorcerer's books," said he with a smile, though his countenance was uneasy and displeased. "Georgiana, there are pages in that volume which I can scarcely glance over and keep my senses. Take heed lest it prove as detrimental to you."

"It has made me worship you more than ever," said she.

"Ah, wait for this one success," rejoined he, "then worship me if you will. I shall deem myself hardly unworthy of it. But come, I have sought you for the luxury of your voice. Sing to me, dearest." 55

So she poured out the liquid music of her voice to quench the thirst of his spirit. He then took his leave with a boyish exuberance of gaiety, assuring her that her seclusion would endure but a little longer, and that the result was already certain. Scarcely had he departed when Georgiana felt irresistibly impelled to follow him. She had forgotten to inform Aylmer of a symptom which for two or three hours past had begun to excite her attention. It was a sensation in the fatal birthmark, not painful, but which induced a restlessness throughout her system. Hastening after her husband, she intruded for the first time into the laboratory.

The first thing that struck her eye was the furnace, that hot and feverish worker, with the intense glow of its fire, which by the quantities of soot clustered above it seemed to have been burning for ages. There was a distilling apparatus in full operation. Around the room were retorts, tubes, cylinders, crucibles, and other apparatus of chemical research. An electrical machine stood ready for immediate use. The atmosphere felt oppressively close, and was tainted with gaseous odors which had been tormented forth by the processes of science. The severe and homely simplicity of the apartment, with its naked walls and brick pavement, looked strange, accustomed as Georgiana had become to the fantastic elegance of her boudoir. But what chiefly, indeed almost solely, drew her attention, was the aspect of Aylmer himself.

He was pale as death, anxious and absorbed, and hung over the furnace as if it depended upon his utmost watchfulness whether the liquid which it was distilling should be the draught of immortal happiness or misery. How different from the sanguine and joyous mien that he had assumed for Georgiana's encouragement!

"Carefully now, Aminadab; carefully, thou human machine; carefully, thou man of clay!" muttered Aylmer, more to himself than his assistant. "Now, if there be a thought too much or too little, it is all over."

"Ho! ho!" mumbled Aminadab. "Look, master! look!" 60

Aylmer raised his eyes hastily, and at first reddened, then grew paler than ever, on beholding Georgiana. He rushed towards her and seized her arm with a gripe that left the print of his fingers upon it.

"Why do you come hither? Have you no trust in your husband?" cried he impetuously. "Would you throw the blight of that fatal birthmark over my labors? It is not well done. Go, prying woman, go!"

"Nay, Aylmer," said Georgiana with the firmness of which she possessed no stinted endowment, "it is not you that have a right to complain. You mistrust your wife; you have concealed the anxiety with which you watch the development of this experiment. Think not so unworthily of me, my husband. Tell me all the risk we run, and fear not that I shall shrink; for my share in it is far less than your own."

"No, no, Georgiana!" said Aylmer impatiently; "it must not be."

"I submit," replied she calmly. "And, Aylmer, I shall quaff whatever 65 draught you bring me; but it will be on the same principle that would induce me to take a dose of poison if offered by your hand."

"My noble wife," said Aylmer, deeply moved, "I knew not the height and depth of your nature until now. Nothing shall be concealed. Know, then, that this crimson hand, superficial as it seems, has clutched its grasp into your being with a strength of which I had no previous conception. I have already administered agents powerful enough to do aught except to change your entire physical system. Only one thing remains to be tried. If that fails us we are ruined."

"Why did you hesitate to tell me this?" asked she.

"Because, Georgiana," said Aylmer in a low voice, "there is danger."

"Danger? There is but one danger — that this horrible stigma shall be left upon my cheek!" cried Georgiana. "Remove it, remove it, whatever be the cost, or we shall both go mad!"

"Heaven knows your words are too true," said Aylmer sadly. "And now, 70 dearest, return to your boudoir. In a little while all will be tested."

He conducted her back and took leave of her with a solemn tenderness which spoke far more than his words how much was now at stake. After his departure Georgiana became rapt in musings. She considered the character of Aylmer, and did it completer justice than at any previous moment. Her heart exulted, while it trembled, at his honorable love — so pure and lofty that it would accept nothing less than perfection nor miserably make itself contented with an earthlier nature than he had dreamed of. She felt how much more precious was such a sentiment than that meaner kind which would have borne with the imperfection for her sake, and have been guilty of treason to holy love by degrading its perfect idea to the level of the actual; and with her whole spirit she prayed that, for a single moment, she might satisfy his highest and deepest conception. Longer than one moment she well knew it could not be; for his spirit was ever on the march, ever ascending, and each instant required something that was beyond the scope of the instant before.

The sound of her husband's footsteps aroused her. He bore a crystal goblet containing a liquor colorless as water, but bright enough to be the draught of immortality. Aylmer was pale; but it seemed rather the consequence of a highly wrought state of mind and tension of spirit than of fear or doubt.

"The concoction of the draught has been perfect," said he, in answer to Georgiana's look. "Unless all my science have deceived me, it cannot fail."

"Save on your account, my dearest Aylmer," observed his wife, "I might wish to put off this birthmark of mortality by relinquishing mortality itself in preference to any other mode. Life is but a sad possession to those who have attained precisely the degree of moral advancement at which I stand. Were I weaker and blinder it might be happiness. Were I stronger, it might be endured hopefully. But, being what I find myself, methinks I am of all mortals the most fit to die."

"You are fit for heaven without tasting death!" replied her husband. "But 75 why do we speak of dying? The draught cannot fail. Behold its effect upon this plant."

On the window seat there stood a geranium diseased with yellow blotches, which had overspread all its leaves. Aylmer poured a small quantity of the liquid upon the soil in which it grew. In a little time, when the roots of the plant had taken up the moisture, the unsightly blotches began to be extinguished in a living verdure.

"There needed no proof," said Georgiana quietly. "Give me the goblet. I joyfully stake all upon your word."

"Drink, then, thou lofty creature!" exclaimed Aylmer, with fervid admiration. "There is no taint of imperfection on thy spirit. Thy sensible frame, too, shall soon be all perfect."

She quaffed the liquid and returned the goblet to his hand.

"It is grateful," said she, with a placid smile. "Methinks it is like water 80 from a heavenly fountain; for it contains I know not what of unobtrusive fragrance and deliciousness. It allays a feverish thirst that had parched me for many days. Now, dearest, let me sleep. My earthly senses are closing over my spirit like the leaves around the heart of a rose at sunset."

She spoke the last words with a gentle reluctance, as if it required almost more energy than she could command to pronounce the faint and lingering syllables. Scarcely had they loitered through her lips ere she was lost in slumber. Aylmer sat by her side, watching her aspect with the emotions proper to a man the whole value of whose existence was involved in the process now to be tested. Mingled with this mood, however, was the philosophic investigation characteristic of the man of science. Not the minutest symptom escaped him. A heightened flush of the cheek, a slight irregularity of breath, a quiver of the eyelid, a hardly perceptible tremor through the frame, — such were the details which, as the moments passed, he wrote down in his folio volume. Intense thought had set its stamp upon every previous page of that volume, but the thoughts of years were all concentrated upon the last.

While thus employed, he failed not to gaze often at the fatal hand, and not without a shudder. Yet once, by a strange and unaccountable impulse, he pressed it with his lips. His spirit recoiled, however, in the very act; and Georgiana, out of the midst of her deep sleep, moved uneasily and murmured as if in remonstrance. Again Aylmer resumed his watch. Nor was it without avail. The crimson hand, which at first had been strongly visible upon the marble paleness of Georgiana's cheek, now grew more faintly outlined. She remained not less pale than ever; but the birthmark, with every breath that came and went, lost somewhat of its former distinctness. Its presence had been awful; its departure was more awful still. Watch the stain of the rainbow fading out of the sky, and you will know how that mysterious symbol passed away.

"By Heaven! it is well-nigh gone!" said Aylmer to himself, in almost irrepressible ecstasy. "I can scarcely trace it now. Success! success! And now it is like the faintest rose color. The lightest flush of blood across her cheek would overcome it. But she is so pale!"

He drew aside the window curtain and suffered the light of natural day to fall into the room and rest upon her cheek. At the same time he heard a gross, hoarse chuckle, which he had long known as his servant Aminadab's expression of delight.

"Ah, clod! ah, earthly mass!" cried Aylmer, laughing in a sort of frenzy, 85 "you have served me well! Matter and spirit—earth and heaven—have both done their part in this! Laugh, thing of the senses! You have earned the right to laugh."

These exclamations broke Georgiana's sleep. She slowly unclosed her eyes and gazed into the mirror which her husband had arranged for that purpose. A faint smile flitted over her lips when she recognized how barely perceptible was now that crimson hand which had once blazed forth with such disastrous brilliancy as to scare away all their happiness. But then her eyes sought Aylmer's face with a trouble and anxiety that he could by no means account for.

"My poor Aylmer!" murmured she.

"Poor? Nay, richest, happiest, most favored!" exclaimed he. "My peerless bride, it is successful! You are perfect!"

"My poor Aylmer," she repeated, with a more than human tenderness, "you have aimed loftily; you have done nobly. Do not repent that with so high and pure a feeling, you have rejected the best the earth could offer. Aylmer, dearest Aylmer, I am dying!"

Alas! it was too true! The fatal hand had grappled with the mystery of life, 90 and was the bond by which an angelic spirit kept itself in union with a mortal frame. As the last crimson tint of the birthmark — that sole token of human imperfection — faded from her cheek, the parting breath of the now perfect woman passed into the atmosphere, and her soul, lingering a moment near her husband, took its heavenward flight. Then a hoarse, chuckling laugh was heard again! Thus ever does the gross fatality of earth exult in its invariable triumph over the immortal essence which, in this dim sphere of half development, demands the completeness of a higher state. Yet, had Aylmer reached a profounder wisdom, he need not thus have flung away the happiness which would have woven his mortal life of the selfsame texture with the celestial. The momentary circumstance was too strong for him; he failed to look beyond the shadowy scope of time, and, living once for all in eternity, to find the perfect future in the present.

CONSIDERATIONS FOR CRITICAL THINKING AND WRITING

1. **FIRST RESPONSE.** Consider this story as an early version of our contemporary obsession with physical perfection. What significant similarities — and differences — do you find?

2. Is Aylmer evil? Is he simply a stock version of a mad scientist? In what sense might he be regarded as an idealist?

3. What does the birthmark symbolize? How does Aylmer's view of it differ from the other perspectives provided in the story? What is the significance of its handlike shape?

4. Does Aylmer love Georgiana? Why does she allow him to risk her life to remove the birthmark?

5. In what sense can Aylmer be characterized as guilty of the sin of pride?

6. How is Aminadab a foil for Aylmer?

7. What is the significance of the descriptions of Aylmer's laboratory?

8. What do Aylmer's other experiments reveal about the nature of his work? How do they constitute foreshadowings of what will happen to Georgiana?

9. What is the theme of the story? What point is made about what it means to be a human being?

10. Despite the risks to Georgiana, Aylmer conducts his experiments in the hope and expectation of achieving a higher good. He devotes his life to science, and yet he is an egotist. Explain.

11. Discuss the extent to which Georgiana is responsible for her own death.

CONNECTIONS TO OTHER SELECTIONS

1. Compare Aylmer's unwillingness to accept things as they are with Goodman Brown's refusal to be a part of a community he regards as fallen.

2. What similarities do you see in Aylmer's growing feelings about the "crimson hand" on Georgiana's cheek and the young wife's feelings about her husband's hand in Colette's "The Hand" (p. 274)? How do Aylmer and the young wife cope with these feelings? How do you account for the differences between them?

Perspectives on Hawthorne

NATHANIEL HAWTHORNE
On Solitude   1837

Dear Sir,

Not to burthen you with my correspondence, I have delayed a rejoinder to your very kind and cordial letter, until now. It gratifies me to find that you have occasionally felt an interest in my situation. . . . You would have been nearer the truth if you had pictured me as dwelling in an owl's nest; for mine is about as dismal; and, like the owl I seldom venture abroad till after dark. By some witchcraft or other — for I really cannot assign any reasonable why and wherefore — I have been carried apart from the main current of life, and find it impossible to get back again. Since we last met . . . I have secluded myself from society; and yet I never meant any such thing, nor dreamed what sort of life I was going to lead. I have made a captive of myself and put me into a dungeon, and now I cannot find the key to let myself out — and if the door were open, I should be almost afraid to come out. You tell me that you have met with troubles and changes. I know not what they may have been; but I can assure you that trouble is the next best thing to enjoyment, and that there is no fate in this world so horrible as to have no share in either its joys or sorrows. For the last ten years, I have not lived, but only dreamed about living. It may be true that there have been some unsubstantial pleasures here in the shade, which I should have missed in the sunshine, but you cannot conceive how utterly devoid of satisfaction all my retrospects are. I have laid up no treasure of pleasant remembrances, against old age; but there is some comfort in thinking that my future years can hardly fail to be more varied, and therefore more tolerable, than the past.

You give me more credit than I deserve, in supposing that I have led a studious life. I have, indeed, turned over a good many books, but in so desultory a way that it cannot be called study, nor has it left me the fruits of study. As to my literary efforts, I do not think much of them — neither is it worthwhile to be ashamed of them. They would have been better, I trust, if written under more favorable circumstances. I have had no external excitement — no consciousness that the public would like what I wrote, nor much hope nor a very passionate desire that they should do so. Nevertheless, having nothing else to be ambitious of, I have felt considerably interested in literature; and if my writings had made any decided impression, I should probably have been stimulated to greater exertions; but there has been no warmth of approbation, so that I have always written with benumbed fingers. I have another great difficulty, in the lack of materials; for I have seen so little of the world, that I have nothing but thin air to concoct my stories of, and it is not easy to give a lifelike semblance to such shadowy stuff. Sometimes, through a peep-hole, I have caught a glimpse of the real world; and the two or three articles, in which I have portrayed such glimpses, please me better than the others. I have now, or shall soon have, one sharp spur to exertion, which I lacked at an earlier period; for I see little prospect but that I must scribble for a living. But this troubles me much less than you would suppose. I can turn my pen to all sorts of drudgery, such as children's books, etc., and by and by, I shall get some editorship that will answer my purpose. Frank Pierce, who was with us at college, offered me his influence to obtain an office in the Exploring Expedition; but I believe that he was mistaken in supposing that a vacancy existed. If such a post were attainable, I should certainly accept it; for, though fixed so long to one spot, I have always had a desire to run around the world.

The copy of my Tales was sent to Mr. Owen's, the bookseller's in Cambridge. I am glad to find that you had read and liked some of the stories. To be sure, you could not well help flattering me a little; but I value your praise too highly not to have faith in its sincerity. When I last heard from the publisher — which was not very recently — the book was doing pretty well. Six or seven hundred copies had been sold. I suppose, however, these awful times have now stopped the sale.

I intend in a week or two to come out of my owl's nest, and not return to it till late in the summer — employing the interval in making a tour somewhere in New England. You, who have the dust of distant countries on your "sandal-shoon," cannot imagine how much enjoyment I shall have in this little excursion. Whenever I get abroad, I feel just as young as I did, ten years ago. What a letter I am inflicting on you! I trust you will answer it.

Yours sincerely,
Nath. Hawthorne.

From a letter to Henry Wadsworth Longfellow, June 4, 1837

CONSIDERATIONS FOR CRITICAL THINKING AND WRITING

1. How does Hawthorne regard his solitude? How does he feel it has affected his life and writing?

2. Hawthorne explains to Longfellow, one of his Bowdoin classmates, that "there is no fate in this world so horrible as to have no share in either its joys or sorrows" (para. 1). Explain how this idea is worked into "Young Goodman Brown" (p. 402).

3. Does Hawthorne indicate any positive results for having lived in his "owl's nest" (para. 1)? Consider how "The Minister's Black Veil" (p. 411) and this letter shed light on each other.

NATHANIEL HAWTHORNE
On the Power of the Writer's Imagination   *1850*

. . . Moonlight, in a familiar room, falling so white upon the carpet, and showing all its figures so distinctly—making every object so minutely visible, yet so
unlike a morning or noontide visibility—is a medium the most suitable for a
romance-writer° to get acquainted with his illusive guests. There is the little
domestic scenery of the well-known apartment; the chairs, with each its separate individuality; the center-table, sustaining a work-basket, a volume or two,
and an extinguished lamp; the sofa; the book-case; the picture on the wall—all
these details, so completely seen, are so spiritualized by the unusual light, that
they seem to lose their actual substance, and become things of intellect. Nothing is too small or too trifling to undergo this change, and acquire dignity
thereby. A child's shoe; the doll, seated in her little wicker carriage; the hobbyhorse—whatever, in a word, has been used or played with, during the day, is
now invested with a quality of strangeness and remoteness, though still almost
as vividly present as by daylight. Thus, therefore, the floor of our familiar room
has become a neutral territory, somewhere between the real world and fairy-
land, where the Actual and the Imaginary may meet, and each imbue itself
with the nature of the other. Ghosts might enter here, without affrighting us.
It would be too much in keeping with the scene to excite surprise, were we to
look about us and discover a form, beloved, but gone hence, now sitting quietly in a streak of this magic moonshine, with an aspect that would make us
doubt whether it had returned from afar, or had never once stirred from our
fireside.

The somewhat dim coal-fire has an essential influence in producing the
effect which I would describe. It throws its unobtrusive tinge throughout the
room, with a faint ruddiness upon the walls and ceiling, and a reflected
gleam from the polish of the furniture. This warmer light mingles itself with
the cold spirituality of the moonbeams, and communicates, as it were, a heart
and sensibilities of human tenderness to the forms which fancy summons up.
It converts them from snow-images into men and women. Glancing at the
looking-glass, we behold—deep within its haunted verge—the smouldering
glow of the half-extinguished anthracite, the white moonbeams on the floor,
and a repetition of all the gleam and shadow of the picture, with one remove
farther from the actual, and nearer to the imaginative. Then, at such an hour,
and with this scene before him, if a man, sitting all alone, cannot dream
strange things, and make them look like truth, he need never try to write
romances.

From *The Scarlet Letter*

---

romance-writer: Hawthorne distinguished romance writing from novel writing. In the preface to *The House of the Seven Gables* he writes:

> The latter form of composition is presumed to aim at a very minute fidelity, not merely to
> the possible, but to the probable and ordinary course of man's experience. The former—
> while, as a work of art, it must rigidly subject itself to laws, and while it sins unpardon-
> ably so far as it may swerve aside from the truth of the human heart—has fairly a right to
> present that truth under circumstances, to a great extent, of the writer's own choosing or
> creation.

CONSIDERATIONS FOR CRITICAL THINKING AND WRITING

1. Explain how Hawthorne uses light as a means of invoking the transforming powers of the imagination.

2. How do Hawthorne's stories fulfill his definition of romance writing? Why can't they be regarded as realistic?

3. Choose one story and discuss it as an attempt to evoke "the truth of the human heart."

NATHANIEL HAWTHORNE

On His Short Stories   *1851*

[These stories] have the pale tint of flowers that blossomed in too retired a shade — the coolness of a meditative habit, which diffuses itself through the feeling and observation of every sketch. Instead of passion there is sentiment; and, even in what purport to be pictures of actual life, we have allegory, not always warmly dressed in its habiliments of flesh and blood as to be taken into the reader's mind without a shiver. Whether from lack of power, or an unconquerable reserve, the Author's touches have often an effect of tameness; the merriest man can hardly contrive to laugh at his broadest humor; the tenderest woman, one would suppose, will hardly shed warm tears at his deepest pathos. The book, if you would see anything in it, requires to be read in the clear brown, twilight atmosphere in which it was written; if opened in the sunshine, it is apt to look exceedingly like a volume of blank pages.

> From the preface to the 1851 edition of *Twice-Told Tales*

CONSIDERATIONS FOR CRITICAL THINKING AND WRITING

1. How does Hawthorne characterize his stories? Does his assessment accurately describe the stories you've read?

2. Why is a "twilight atmosphere" more conducive to an appreciation of Hawthorne's art than "sunshine"?

3. Write a one-page description of Hawthorne's stories in which you generalize about his characteristic approach to one of these elements: plot, character, setting, symbol, theme, tone.

HERMAN MELVILLE (1819–1891)

On Nathaniel Hawthorne's Tragic Vision   *1851*

There is a certain tragic phase of humanity which, in our opinion, was never more powerfully embodied than by Hawthorne. We mean the tragicalness of human thought in its own unbiased, native, and profounder workings. We think that in no recorded mind has the intense feeling of the visable truth ever entered more deeply than into this man's. By visable truth, we mean the apprehension of the absolute condition of present things as they strike the eye of the man who fears them not, though they do their worst to him — the man who, like Russia or the British Empire, declares himself a sovereign nature (in himself) amid the powers of heaven, hell, and earth. He may perish; but so long as he exists he insists upon treating with all Powers upon an equal basis. If any of those other Powers choose to withhold certain secrets, let them; that does not impair my sovereignty in myself; that does not make me tributary. And perhaps, after all, there is *no* secret. We incline to think that the Problem of the Universe is like the Freemason's° mighty secret, so terrible to all children. It turns out, at last, to consist in a triangle, a mallet, and an apron — nothing more! . . . There is the grand truth about Nathaniel Hawthorne. He says NO! in thunder; but the Devil himself cannot make him say *yes*. For all men who say *yes*, lie; and all men who say *no* — why, they are in the happy condition of judicious, unincumbered travelers in Europe; they cross the frontiers into Eternity with nothing but a carpetbag — that is to say, the Ego. Whereas those *yes*-gentry, they travel with heaps of baggage, and, damn them! they will never get through the Custom House. What's the reason, Mr. Hawthorne, that in the last stages of metaphysics a fellow always falls to *swearing* so? I could rip an hour.

From a letter to Hawthorne, April 16(?), 1851

Freemason: A member of the secret fraternity of Freemasonry.

CONSIDERATIONS FOR CRITICAL THINKING AND WRITING

1. What qualities in Hawthorne does Melville admire?
2. Explain how these qualities are embodied in one of the Hawthorne stories.
3. How might Melville's lawyer in "Bartleby, the Scrivener" (p. 142) be characterized as one of "those *yes*-gentry"?

GAYLORD BREWER (B. 1965)

The Joys of Secret Sin   2006

— after Hawthorne

"For the Earth, too, had on her Black Veil"?
Can you blame her? The better to avoid
the humbug of these two soldiers of melancholy —
that young, good man who soils the world
with his dark dream; a sweat-lipped preacher   5
smugly trembling behind twin folds of crape.

The Earth doesn't appreciate her name
sullied — always, winds howling and bestial
cries. Wife and fiancée fare no better —
poor plump Faith, her pink ribbons disavowed;   10
long-suffering Elizabeth, left old by cryptic

evasions. Who in the village doesn't
recognize the human face or needs reminding?

Black veil on every visage? Dying hour of gloom?
That's the rectitude that compels them all —   15
deacon, farmer, child, maiden, hag —
toward your welcoming smile, avuncular wink,
kindly dip of black staff, so curiously
entwined it seems almost to writhe. There,
just ahead: the forest's mossy, crooked path,   20
a canopy of flames, a guiltless hearth of stone.

CONSIDERATIONS FOR CRITICAL THINKING AND WRITING

1. Write a paraphrase of this poem. How does it provide a reading of "Young
   Goodman Brown" and "The Minister's Black Veil"?
2. **CREATIVE RESPONSE.** Using Brewer's poem as a source of inspiration (but not
   necessarily its style and form), try writing a poem based on your reading of
   "The Birthmark."

Two Complementary Critical Readings

JUDITH FETTERLEY (B. 1938)

A Feminist Reading of "The Birthmark"   *1978*

It is testimony at once to Hawthorne's ambivalence, his seeking to cover with
one hand what he uncovers with the other; and to the pervasive sexism of our
culture that most readers would describe "The Birthmark" as a story of failure
rather than as the success story it really is — the demonstration of how to murder your wife and get away with it. It is, of course, possible to read "The Birthmark" as a story of misguided idealism, a tale of the unhappy consequences
of man's nevertheless worthy passion for perfecting and transcending nature;
and this is the reading usually given it. This reading, however, ignores the
significance of the form idealism takes in the story. It is not irrelevant that
"The Birthmark" is about a man's desire to perfect his wife, nor is it accidental
that the consequence of this idealism is the wife's death. In fact, "The Birthmark" provides a brilliant analysis of the sexual politics of idealization and a
brilliant exposure of the mechanisms whereby hatred can be disguised as love,
neurosis can be disguised as science, murder can be disguised as idealization,
and success can be disguised as failure. Thus, Hawthorne's insistence in his
story on the metaphor of disguise serves as both warning and clue to a feminist reading. . . .

One cannot imagine this story in reverse — that is, a woman's discovering an
obsessive need to perfect her husband and deciding to perform experiments
on him — nor can one imagine the story being about a man's conceiving such
an obsession for another man. It is woman, and specifically woman as wife,
who elicits the obsession with imperfection and the compulsion to achieve

perfection, just as it is man, and specifically man as husband, who is thus obsessed and compelled. In addition, it is clear from the summary that the imagined perfection is purely physical. Aylmer is not concerned with the quality of Georgiana's character or with the state of her soul, for he considers her "fit for heaven without tasting death." Rather, he is absorbed in her physical appearance, and perfection for him is equivalent to physical beauty. Georgiana is an exemplum of woman as beautiful object, reduced to and defined by her body. . . . "The Birthmark" demonstrates the fact that the idealization of women has its source in a profound hostility toward women and that it is at once a disguise for this hostility and the fullest expression of it. . . .

. . . Unable to accept himself for what he is, Aylmer constructs a mythology of science and adopts the character of a scientist to disguise his true nature and to hide his real motives, from himself as well as others. As a consequence, he acquires a way of acting out these motives without in fact having to be aware of them. One might describe "The Birthmark" as an exposé of science because it demonstrates the ease with which science can be invoked to conceal highly subjective motives. "The Birthmark" is an exposure of the realities that underlie the scientist's posture of objectivity and rationality and the claims of science to operate in an amoral and value-free world. Pale Aylmer, the intellectual scientist, is a mask for the brutish, earthy, soot-smeared Aminadab, just as the mythology of scientific research and objectivity finally masks murder, disguising Georgiana's death as just one more experiment that failed. . . .

The implicit feminism in "The Birthmark" is considerable. On one level the story is a study of sexual politics, of the powerlessness of women and of the psychology which results from that powerlessness. Hawthorne dramatizes the fact that woman's identity is a product of men's responses to her: "It must not be concealed, however, that the impression wrought by this fairy sign manual varied exceedingly, according to the difference of temperament in the beholders." To those who love Georgiana, her birthmark is evidence of her beauty; to those who envy or hate her, it is an object of disgust. It is Aylmer's repugnance for the birthmark that makes Georgiana blanch, thus causing the mark to emerge as a sharply defined blemish against the whiteness of her cheek. Clearly, the birthmark takes on its character from the eye of the beholder. And just as clearly Georgiana's attitude toward her birthmark varies in response to different observers and definers. Her self-image derives from internalizing the attitudes toward her of the man or men around her. Since what surrounds Georgiana is an obsessional attraction expressed as a total revulsion, the result is not surprising: continual self-consciousness that leads to a pervasive sense of shame and a self-hatred that terminates in an utter readiness to be killed. "The Birthmark" demonstrates the consequences to women of being trapped in the laboratory of man's mind, the object of unrelenting scrutiny, examination, and experimentation.

From The Resisting Reader: A Feminist Approach to American Fiction

CONSIDERATIONS FOR CRITICAL THINKING AND WRITING

1. In what sense does Fetterley regard "The Birthmark" as a "success story" (para. 1)? How does her feminist perspective inform this view?

2. Why do you think Fetterley argues that it is impossible to imagine reversing the male-female roles in this story?

3. How does Fetterley make a case for reading the story as an "exposé of science" (para. 3)? Explain why science is described as an essentially male activity.

4. Although Fetterley does not include "The Minister's Black Veil" (p. 411) in her discussion, might it not be argued that it too harbors an "implicit feminism" (para. 4)? Write an analysis of the Reverend Mr. Hooper from a feminist perspective.

JAMES QUINN (B. 1937) AND ROSS BALDESSARINI (B. 1937)
A Psychological Reading of "The Birthmark" 1981

Hawthorne's art in the creation of character in many ways anticipates modern psychoanalytic psychology. As a literary psychologist, he excels at revealing unconscious sources of obsessed behavior. In "The Birthmark," Aylmer, a scientist whose ambition may be to control nature, provides an exceptionally good example of an obsessive character. He is obsessed with imperfection in human nature and is unable to achieve a mature human relationship. . . .

. . . What has happened to make Aylmer feel this way? What indeed ails him? The question is a natural one, but useless. Hawthorne does not supply an answer and by this omission seems to suggest that insights into human behavior are likely to be subjective, imperfect, unsatisfying. What is important is not the cause of obsessive thought or compulsive behavior but the effects.

The dramatic situation here is that Aylmer, by marrying Georgiana, is forced to deal with a conflict between his earlier, somewhat distant view of her as an intellectualized feminine ideal and her present tangible reality. Clearly one meaning of the red hand is a mark of her accessibility to touch, that is, of her sexuality. It also includes conflict between personal idealization and reality — a classical and ubiquitous obsessional neurotic conflict. While Aylmer's struggle is virtually universal, his fixation on Georgiana's blemish approaches a symptom that is considered characteristic of obsessive-compulsive neurosis in modern-day psychopathological terms.[1] The function of such neurotic symptoms in the psychic economy is to inhibit intolerable anxiety by focusing on an isolated and somewhat concrete representation so as to avoid a larger emotional conflict.

[1] Most of the characteristics of the illness can be found in the official definition of obsessive-compulsive disorder stated in the third edition of the American Psychiatric Association's (1980) *Diagnostic and Statistical Manual of Mental Disorders* (DSM-III):

> The essential features are recurrent obsessions and/or compulsions. Obsessions are defined as recurrent, persistent ideas, thoughts, images, or impulses which are ego-alien; that is, they are not experienced as voluntarily produced, but rather as ideas that invade the field of consciousness. Attempts are made to ignore or suppress them. Compulsions are behaviors which are not experienced as the outcome of the individual's own volition, but are accompanied by both a sense of subjective compulsion and a desire to resist (at least initially). (p. 234)

The psychoanalytic theorist Fenichel has written, "Many compulsive neu-rotics have to worry very much about small and apparently insignificant things. In analysis, these small things turn out to be substitutes for important ones."[2] And further: "Compulsive neurotics try to use external objects for the solution or relief of their inner conflicts" (p. 293). As "the compulsive neurotic tends . . . to extend the range of his symptoms . . ." (p. 294), so Aylmer's reac-tion to the birthmark grew "more and more intolerable with every moment of their . . . lives," presumably as a result of Georgiana's unavoidable presence. What at first seemed a trifling matter "so connected itself with innumerable trains of thought and modes of feeling that it became the *central point of all*" [stress added]. Like Parson Hooper [in "The Minister's Black Veil"], Aylmer is another Hawthornian victim of morbid forces, largely internal, beyond his control. Surely Aylmer's aversion owes its intensity and its obsessive character precisely to the fact that it is not accessible to conscious examination.[3] . . .

He draws distinct lines between good and bad as does . . . Young Goodman Brown, who must see Faith, indeed all women, as Madonna or whore and who therefore remains immature and uncommitted. Aylmer, too, is like an adoles-cent, unable to find a point of equilibrium between two poles of thought, not realizing that "to be is to be imperfect, that the price of human existence is imperfection."[4]

An ironic aspect of such obsessed and morbid behavior so often seen in Hawthorne's works is that the more one struggles to attain perfection or to retain an unreasonable fixed idea, the more one is caught up in dealing with its opposite — imperfection and destruction. . . .

Up to this point we have been concerned with Hawthorne's presentation of Aylmer as one more neurotic and troubled obsessional soul. More important, however, is Aylmer's dramatically exaggerated representation of a more general struggle to adjust the ideal and the real. Likewise the birthmark can be viewed on more than one level. It is a mark of Georgiana's accessibility to touch, of her sexuality. It is suggestive of the scarlet letter — another public sign of secret and lustful sin, of "putting hands upon" in a sexual sense, of being touched, tainted, having sexuality and womanly characteristics. And, within the Judeo-Christian tradition . . . it seems to Hawthorne to symbolize the fallen and sin-ful nature of man. In an even wider application, it symbolizes the mortality of all mankind.

We miss the point, however, if we connect the birthmark solely with neu-rotic conflicts of atypical individuals or even with the hold death has on every-one, for the mark is also connected with sexuality and new life, indeed with

---

[2] Otto Fenichel, *The Psychoanalytic Theory of Neurosis* (New York, 1945), p. 290.

[3] In Freudian theory, certain ideas heavily charged or invested with affect or emotion con-stantly press toward conscious recognition or awareness, and certain impulses toward overt satisfaction or fulfillment. What we note in this tale is something close to "isolation of affect" or suppression and limitation or restriction of a highly charged emotion. The feeling and its source seem to be a form of anxiety, fear of being harmed through intimacy — metaphorically a problem in the category of castration anxiety or fear of being found want-ing (already castrated). The idea that the birthmark is a castration symbol has already been suggested by Simon Lesser, *Fiction and the Unconscious*, p. 88.

[4] Terence Martin, *Nathaniel Hawthorne* (New Haven, 1965), p. 70.

aspiration to beauty and achievement and with the joy and energy for living. The importance of Hawthorne's psychological symbol is not the susceptibility of man to sin and death, but the special manner in which the marked woman suffers her fate: it is Aylmer who kills her. When the inward life concentrates narcissistically on self, demonic violence flares up in the lust to control and possess another person. Yet the first to be destroyed is Aylmer himself, who steps out of the procession of life, suffering from an incapacity to accept and integrate human emotions.

From *University of Hartford Studies in Literature:*
A Journal of Interdisciplinary Criticism

CONSIDERATIONS FOR CRITICAL THINKING AND WRITING

1. According to Quinn and Baldessarini, why isn't it fruitful to inquire into the causes of Aylmer's obsession? Explain why you agree or disagree with their assessment.

2. How might Aylmer, Parson Hooper, and Goodman Brown all be regarded as exhibiting obsessive behavior?

3. Write an essay that discusses how and why this psychoanalytic reading leads to a focus on Aylmer while Judith Fetterley's feminist reading leads to an emphasis on Georgiana. For a discussion of psychological and feminist readings see Chapter 53, "Critical Strategies for Reading."

4. Explain what you think a psychological reading of Georgiana would make of her character.

SUGGESTED TOPICS FOR LONGER PAPERS

1. Consider the setting of each of the Hawthorne stories in this chapter. Why are they significant? How are they related to the stories' respective themes? In your essay, determine which story relies most heavily on setting to convey its meanings.

2. Read the Perspective concerning Hawthorne and solitude (p. 432) and do some biographical research on Hawthorne's attitudes toward solitude and human isolation. How do details about his life shed light on the solitary or isolated characters in the three stories you have read in this chapter?

Web   Research Nathaniel Hawthorne or take quizzes on his works at bedfordstmartins.com/meyerlit.

12

A Study of Flannery O'Connor

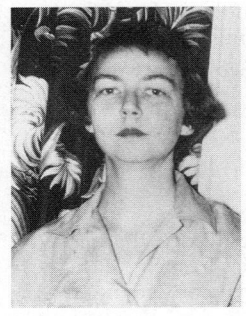

In most English classes the short story has become a kind of literary specimen to be dissected. Every time a story of mine appears in a Freshman anthology, I have a vision of it, with its little organs laid open, like a frog in a bottle.
— FLANNERY O'CONNOR

I am always having it pointed out to me that life in Georgia is not at all the way I picture it, that escaped criminals do not roam the roads exterminating families, nor Bible salesmen prowl about looking for girls with wooden legs.
— FLANNERY O'CONNOR

When Flannery O'Connor (1925–1964) died of lupus before her fortieth birthday, her work was cruelly cut short. Nevertheless, she had completed two novels, *Wise Blood* (1952) and *The Violent Bear It Away* (1960), as well as thirty-one short stories. Despite her brief life and relatively modest output, her work is regarded as among the most distinguished American fiction of the mid-twentieth century. Her two collections of short stories, *A Good Man Is Hard to Find* (1955) and *Everything That Rises Must Converge* (1965), were included in *The Complete Stories of Flannery O'Connor* (1971), which won the National Book Award. The stories included in this chapter offer a glimpse into the work of this important twentieth-century writer.

Cheers,
Flannery

A BRIEF BIOGRAPHY AND INTRODUCTION

O'Connor's fiction grapples with living a spiritual life in a secular world. Although this major concern is worked into each of her stories, she takes a broad approach to spiritual issues by providing moral, social, and psychological contexts that offer a wealth of insights and passion that her readers have found both startling and absorbing. Her stories are challenging because her characters, who initially seem radically different from people we know, turn out to be, by the end of each story, somehow familiar—somehow connected to us.

O'Connor inhabited simultaneously two radically different worlds. The world she created in her stories is populated with bratty children, malcontents, incompetents, pious frauds, bewildered intellectuals, deformed cynics, rednecks, hucksters, racists, perverts, and murderers who experience dramatically intense moments that surprise and shock readers. Her personal life, however, was largely uneventful. She humorously acknowledged its quiet nature in 1958 when she claimed that "there won't be any biographies of me because, for only one reason, lives spent between the house and the chicken yard do not make exciting copy."

A broad outline of O'Connor's life may not offer very much "exciting copy," but it does provide clues about why she wrote such powerful fiction. The only child of Catholic parents, O'Connor was born in Savannah, Georgia, where she attended a parochial grammar school and high school. When she was thirteen, her father became ill with disseminated lupus, a rare, incurable blood disease, and had to abandon his real-estate business. The family moved to Milledgeville in central Georgia, where her mother's family had lived for generations. Because there were no Catholic schools in Milledgeville, O'Connor attended a public high school. In 1942, the year after her father died of lupus, O'Connor graduated from high school and enrolled in Georgia State College for Women. There she wrote for the literary magazine until receiving her diploma in 1945. Her stories earned her a fellowship to the Writers' Workshop at the University of Iowa, and for two years she learned to write steadily and seriously. She sold her first story to *Accent* in 1946 and earned her master of fine arts degree in 1947. She wrote stories about life in the rural South, and this subject matter, along with her devout Catholic perspective, became central to her fiction.

With her formal education behind her, O'Connor was ready to begin her professional career at the age of twenty-two. Equipped with determination ("No one can convince me that I shouldn't rewrite as much as I do") and offered the opportunity to be around other practicing writers, she moved to New York, where she worked on her first novel, *Wise Blood*. In 1950, however, she was diagnosed as having lupus, and, returning to Georgia for treatment, she took up permanent residence on her mother's farm in Milledgeville. There she lived a severely restricted but productive life, writing stories and raising peacocks.

With the exception of O'Connor's early years in Iowa and New York and some short lecture trips to other states, she traveled little. Although

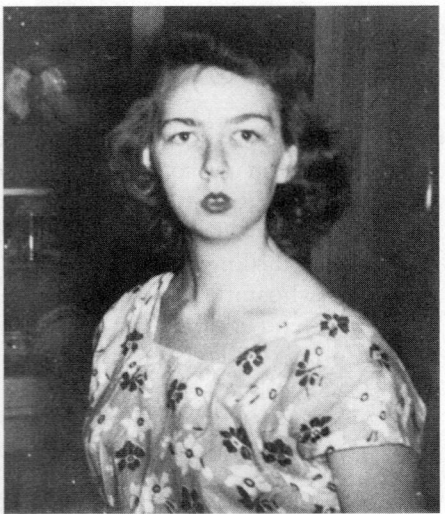

Flannery O'Connor (above left) at age 12 and (above right) in her teens (age 16 or 17). O'Connor, whose youth was marked by the declining health and death of her father, once wrote, "[A]nybody who has survived childhood has enough information about life to last him the rest of the days."

Courtesy of Ina Dillard Russell Library Special Collections, Georgia College and State University.

Flannery O'Connor and a Self-Portrait. The author poses in front of an accurate, if rather fierce self-portrait with one of her beloved ring-necked pheasants. As a child, O'Connor enjoyed raising birds, a passion that was sparked when one of her chickens, "a buff Cochin Bantam [that] had the distinction of being able to walk either forward or backward" was reported on in the press. "I had to have more and more chickens. . . . I wanted one with three legs or three wings but nothing in that line turned up. . . . My quest, whatever it was for, ended with peacocks," she wrote.

Reprinted by permission of Bettmann/CORBIS.

The *Corinthian* Staff (above). Flannery O'Connor (seated, center) as editor of the *Corinthian*, the literary magazine at Georgia State College for Women (now Georgia College and State University). O'Connor attended the college from 1942 through 1945, and earned a B.A. in social science.

"Targets." As a student, O'Connor created humorous cartoons that lampooned aspects of campus life (many of which satirized the presence of the Navy at the school) that were published in the *Corinthian,* in the school newspaper, *The Colonnade,* and in the yearbook. In the cartoon shown here, O'Connor targets the WAVES (Women Accepted for Military Service), a group that marched about the campus in lockstep and represented to her a rigid conformity against which she rebelled.

she made a pilgrimage to Lourdes (apparently more for her mother's sake than for her own) and then to Rome for an audience with the pope, her life was centered in the South. Like those of William Faulkner and many other southern writers, O'Connor's stories evoke the rhythms of rural southern speech and manners in insulated settings where widely diverse characters mingle. Also like Faulkner, she created works whose meanings go beyond their settings. She did not want her fiction to be seen in the context of narrowly defined regionalism: she complained that "in almost every hamlet you'll find at least one old lady writing epics in Negro dialect and probably two or three old gentlemen who have impossible historical novels on the way." Refusing to be caricatured, she knew that "the woods are full of regional writers, and it is the great horror of every serious Southern writer that he will become one of them." O'Connor's stories are rooted in rural southern culture, but in a larger sense they are set within the psychological and spiritual landscapes of the human soul. This interior setting universalizes local materials in much the same way that Nathaniel Hawthorne's New England stories do. Indeed, O'Connor once described herself as "one of his descendants": "I feel more of a kinship with him than any other American."

O'Connor's deep spiritual convictions coincide with the traditional emphasis on religion in the South, where, she said, there is still the belief "that man has fallen and that he is only perfectible by God's grace, not by his own unaided efforts." Although O'Connor's Catholicism differs from the prevailing Protestant fundamentalism of the South, the religious ethos so pervasive even in rural southern areas provided fertile ground for the spiritual crises her characters experience. In a posthumous collection of her articles, essays, and reviews aptly titled *Mystery and Manners* (1969), she summarized her basic religious convictions:

> I am no disbeliever in spiritual purpose and no vague believer. I see from the standpoint of Christian orthodoxy. This means that for me the meaning of life is centered in our Redemption by Christ and what I see in the world I see in its relation to that. I don't think that this is a position that can be taken halfway or one that is particularly easy in these times to make transparent in fiction.

O'Connor realized that she was writing against the grain of the readers who discovered her stories in the *Partisan Review, Sewanee Review, Mademoiselle,* or *Harper's Bazaar.* Many readers thought that Christian dogma would make her writing doctrinaire, but she insisted that the perspective of Christianity allowed her to interpret the details of life and guaranteed her "respect for [life's] mystery." O'Connor's stories contain no prepackaged prescriptions for living, no catechisms that lay out all the answers. Instead, her characters struggle with spiritual questions in bizarre, incongruous situations. Their lives are grotesque — even comic — precisely because they do not understand their own spiritual natures. Their actions are extreme and abnormal. O'Connor explains the reasons for this in *Mystery and Manners;* she says she sought to expose the "distortions" of "modern life" that appear "normal" to her audience. Hence, she used "violent means" to convey her vision to a

Flannery O'Connor and Pet Peacock at Andalusia Farm. Following her graduation from Georgia State Women's College, O'Connor attended the University of Iowa, where she received her M.F.A. in 1947. She left Iowa for the Yaddo Foundation's artist colony in Saratoga Springs, New York, in 1948 and later lived in New York City and Connecticut. In 1950, as she was working on her first novel (*Wise Blood*), O'Connor began to experience symptoms of lupus, and returned to Milledgeville, Georgia, in 1951. Instead of moving back to her home in town, she and her mother moved to Andalusia, the family farm (shown here) where she lived until her death in 1964. At Andalusia farm, O'Connor wrote in the mornings until noon; the rest of the day she spent minding her birds and entertaining friends. Andalusia, arguably, provided an inspiration for and landscape for her fiction — it was here that O'Connor completed *Wise Blood* and wrote *A Good Man Is Hard to Find* (1955), *The Violent Bear It Away* (1960), and *Everything That Rises Must Converge* (published posthumously, in 1965).

"hostile audience." "When you can assume that your audience holds the same beliefs you do, you can relax a little and use more normal means of talking to it." But when the audience holds different values, "you have to make your vision apparent by shock—to the hard of hearing you shout, and for the almost-blind you draw large and startling figures." O'Connor's characters lose or find their soul-saving grace in painful, chaotic circumstances that bear little or no resemblance to the slow but sure progress to the Celestial City of repentant pilgrims in traditional religious stories.

Because her characters are powerful creations who live convincing, even if ugly, lives, O'Connor's religious beliefs never supersede her storytelling. One need not be either Christian or Catholic to appreciate her concerns about human failure and degradation and her artistic ability to render fictional lives that are alternately absurdly comic and tragic. The ironies that abound in her work leave plenty of room for readers of all persuasions. O'Connor's work is narrow in the sense that her concerns are emphatically spiritual, but her compassion and her belief in human possibilities — even among the most unlikely characters — afford her fictions a capacity for wonder that is exhilarating. Her precise, deft use of language always reveals more than it seems to tell.

Like Hawthorne's fiction, O'Connor's stories present complex experiences that cannot be tidily summarized; it takes the entire story to suggest the meanings. Read the following three stories for the pleasure of entering the remarkable world O'Connor creates. You're in for some surprises.

Chronology

1925	Born on March 25 in Savannah, Georgia.
1938	Moves with family to Milledgeville, Georgia; enters the public Peabody High School.
1941	Father dies of lupus.
1942	Graduates from Peabody High School; enters Georgia State College for Women (now Georgia College and State University).
1943–45	Writes stories and poems for college literary magazine; graduates from Georgia State with an undergraduate degree in English.
1945–47	Enters writing program at the University of Iowa and earns a master of fine arts degree in creative writing.
1948–49	Attends Yaddo artists' colony near Saratoga Springs, New York, for several months; lives in New York and Connecticut.
1950	After an illness, returns to Milledgeville and is diagnosed as suffering from lupus, an incurable disease. Lives on her family's dairy farm the rest of her life.
1952	*Wise Blood* receives mixed reviews and upsets some Milledgeville residents.
1955	*A Good Man Is Hard to Find and Other Stories* receives critical praise; the Guggenheim foundation rejects her fellowship application for a second time.
1956	A degenerating hip forces her to use crutches; the first telephone is installed on the farm.
1957	Lectures at several universities; dislikes a television version of the short story "The Life You Save May Be Your Own"; receives a grant from the National Institute of Arts and Letters.
1958	Visits Lourdes and Rome.
1960	Publishes *The Violent Bear It Away*.
1962–63	Receives honorary doctorate from Saint Mary's women's college of the University of Notre Dame; speaks at a number of colleges in the South about her writing.
1964	Dies on August 3, 1964.
1965	*Everything That Rises Must Converge* published posthumously.

A Good Man Is Hard to Find   1953

The grandmother didn't want to go to Florida. She wanted to visit some of her connections in east Tennessee and she was seizing at every chance to change Bailey's mind. Bailey was the son she lived with, her only boy. He was sitting on the edge of his chair at the table, bent over the orange sports section of the *Journal.* "Now look here, Bailey," she said, "see here, read this," and she stood with one hand on her thin hip and the other rattling the newspaper at his bald head. "Here this fellow that calls himself The Misfit is aloose from the Federal Pen and headed toward Florida and you read here what it says he did to these people. Just you read it. I wouldn't take my children in any direction with a criminal like that aloose in it. I couldn't answer to my conscience if I did."

Bailey didn't look up from his reading so she wheeled around then and faced the children's mother, a young woman in slacks, whose face was as broad and innocent as a cabbage and was tied around with a green headkerchief that had two points on the top like a rabbit's ears. She was sitting on the sofa, feeding the baby his apricots out of a jar. "The children have been to Florida before," the old lady said. "You all ought to take them somewhere else for a change so they would see different parts of the world and be broad. They never have been to east Tennessee."

The children's mother didn't seem to hear her but the eight-year-old boy, John Wesley, a stocky child with glasses, said, "If you don't want to go to Florida, why dontcha stay at home?" He and the little girl, June Star, were reading the funny papers on the floor.

"She wouldn't stay at home to be queen for a day," June Star said without raising her yellow head.

"Yes and what would you do if this fellow, The Misfit, caught you?" the 5
grandmother asked.

"I'd smack his face," John Wesley said.

"She wouldn't stay at home for a million bucks," June Star said. "Afraid she'd miss something. She has to go everywhere we go."

"All right, Miss," the grandmother said. "Just remember that the next time you want me to curl your hair."

June Star said her hair was naturally curly.

The next morning the grandmother was the first one in the car, ready to 10
go. She had her big black valise that looked like the head of a hippopotamus in one corner, and underneath it she was hiding a basket with Pitty Sing, the cat, in it. She didn't intend for the cat to be left alone in the house for three days because he would miss her too much and she was afraid he might brush against one of the gas burners and accidentally asphyxiate himself. Her son, Bailey, didn't like to arrive at a motel with a cat.

She sat in the middle of the back seat with John Wesley and June Star on either side of her. Bailey and the children's mother and the baby sat in front and they left Atlanta at eight forty-five with the mileage on the car at 55890. The grandmother wrote this down because she thought it would be interesting to say how many miles they had been when they got back. It took them twenty minutes to reach the outskirts of the city.

The old lady settled herself comfortably, removing her white cotton gloves and putting them up with her purse on the shelf in front of the back window. The children's mother still had on slacks and still had her head tied up in a green kerchief, but the grandmother had on a navy blue straw sailor hat with a bunch of white violets on the brim and a navy blue dress with a small white dot in the print. Her collars and cuffs were white organdy trimmed with lace and at her neckline she had pinned a purple spray of cloth violets containing a sachet. In case of an accident, anyone seeing her dead on the highway would know at once that she was a lady.

She said she thought it was going to be a good day for driving, neither too hot nor too cold, and she cautioned Bailey that the speed limit was fifty-five miles an hour and that the patrolmen hid themselves behind billboards and small clumps of trees and sped out after you before you had a chance to slow down. She pointed out interesting details of the scenery: Stone Mountain; the blue granite that in some places came up to both sides of the highway; the brilliant red clay banks slightly streaked with purple; and the various crops that made rows of green lace-work on the ground. The trees were full of silver-white sunlight and the meanest of them sparkled. The children were reading comic magazines and their mother had gone back to sleep.

"Let's go through Georgia fast so we won't have to look at it much," John Wesley said.

"If I were a little boy," said the grandmother, "I wouldn't talk about my 15 native state that way. Tennessee has the mountains and Georgia has the hills."

"Tennessee is just a hillbilly dumping ground," John Wesley said, "and Georgia is a lousy state too."

"You said it," June Star said.

"In my time," said the grandmother, folding her thin veined fingers, "children were more respectful of their native states and their parents and everything else. People did right then. Oh look at the cute little pickaninny!" she said and pointed to a Negro child standing in the door of a shack. "Wouldn't that make a picture, now?" she asked and they all turned and looked at the little Negro out of the back window. He waved.

"He didn't have any britches on," June Star said.

"He probably didn't have any," the grandmother explained. "Little niggers 20 in the country don't have things like we do. If I could paint, I'd paint that picture," she said.

The children exchanged comic books.

The grandmother offered to hold the baby and the children's mother passed him over the front seat to her. She set him on her knee and bounced him and told him about the things they were passing. She rolled her eyes and screwed up her mouth and stuck her leathery thin face into his smooth bland one. Occasionally he gave her a faraway smile. They passed a large cotton field with five or six graves fenced in the middle of it, like a small island. "Look at the graveyard!" the grandmother said, pointing it out. "That was the old family burying ground. That belonged to the plantation."

"Where's the plantation?" John Wesley asked.

"Gone With the Wind," said the grandmother. "Ha. Ha."

When the children finished all the comic books they had brought, they 25 opened the lunch and ate it. The grandmother ate a peanut butter sandwich and an olive and would not let the children throw the box and the paper napkins out the window. When there was nothing else to do they played a game by choosing a cloud and making the other two guess what shape it suggested. John Wesley took one the shape of a cow and June Star guessed a cow and John

Wesley said, no, an automobile, and June Star said he didn't play fair, and they began to slap each other over the grandmother.

The grandmother said she would tell them a story if they would keep quiet. When she told a story, she rolled her eyes and waved her head and was very dramatic. She said once when she was a maiden lady she had been courted by a Mr. Edgar Atkins Teagarden from Jasper, Georgia. She said he was a very good-looking man and a gentleman and that he brought her a watermelon every Saturday afternoon with his initials cut in it, E.A.T. Well, one Saturday, she said, Mr. Teagarden brought the watermelon and there was nobody at home and he left it on the front porch and returned in his buggy to Jasper, but she never got the watermelon, she said, because a nigger boy ate it when he saw the initials, E.A.T.! This story tickled John Wesley's funny bone and he giggled and giggled but June Star didn't think it was any good. She said she wouldn't marry a man that just brought her a watermelon on Saturday. The grandmother said she would have done well to marry Mr. Teagarden because he was a gentleman and had bought Coca-Cola stock when it first came out and that he had died only a few years ago, a very wealthy man.

They stopped at The Tower for barbecued sandwiches. The Tower was a part stucco and part wood filling station and dance hall set in a clearing outside of Timothy. A fat man named Red Sammy Butts ran it and there were signs stuck here and there on the building and for miles up and down the highway saying, TRY RED SAMMY'S FAMOUS BARBECUE. NONE LIKE FAMOUS RED SAMMY'S! RED SAM! THE FAT BOY WITH THE HAPPY LAUGH. A VETERAN! RED SAMMY'S YOUR MAN!

Red Sammy was lying on the bare ground outside The Tower with his head under a truck while a gray monkey about a foot high, chained to a small chinaberry tree, chattered nearby. The monkey sprang back into the tree and got on the highest limb as soon as he saw the children jump out of the car and run toward him.

Inside, The Tower was a long dark room with a counter at one end and tables at the other and dancing space in the middle. They all sat down at a board table next to the nickelodeon and Red Sam's wife, a tall burnt-brown woman with hair and eyes lighter than her skin, came and took their order. The children's mother put a dime in the machine and played "The Tennessee Waltz," and the grandmother said that tune always made her want to dance. She asked Bailey if he would like to dance but he only glared at her. He didn't have a naturally sunny disposition like she did and trips made him nervous. The grandmother's brown eyes were very bright. She swayed her head from side to side and pretended she was dancing in her chair. June Star said play something she could tap to so the children's mother put in another dime and played a fast number and June Star stepped out onto the dance floor and did her tap routine.

"Ain't she cute?" Red Sam's wife said, leaning over the counter. "Would you like to come be my little girl?"

"No I certainly wouldn't," June Star said. "I wouldn't live in a broken-down place like this for a million bucks!" and she ran back to the table.

"Ain't she cute?" the woman repeated, stretching her mouth politely.

"Aren't you ashamed?" hissed the grandmother.

Red Sam came in and told his wife to quit lounging on the counter and hurry up with these people's order. His khaki trousers reached just to his hip bones and his stomach hung over them like a sack of meal swaying under his shirt. He came over and sat down at a table nearby and let out a combination sigh and yodel. "You can't win," he said. "You can't win," and he wiped his sweating red face off with a gray handkerchief. "These days you don't know who to trust," he said. "Ain't that the truth?"

"People are certainly not nice like they used to be," said the grandmother.   35

"Two fellers come in here last week," Red Sammy said, "driving a Chrysler. It was a old beat-up car but it was a good one and these boys looked all right to me. Said they worked at the mill and you know I let them fellers charge the gas they bought? Now why did I do that?"

"Because you're a good man!" the grandmother said at once.

"Yes'm, I suppose so," Red Sam said as if he were struck with this answer.

His wife brought the orders, carrying the five plates all at once without a tray, two in each hand and one balanced on her arm. "It isn't a soul in this green world of God's that you can trust," she said. "And I don't count nobody out of that, not nobody," she repeated, looking at Red Sammy.

"Did you read about that criminal, The Misfit, that's escaped?" asked the   40
grandmother.

"I wouldn't be a bit surprised if he didn't attack this place right here," said the woman. "If he hears about it being here, I wouldn't be none surprised to see him. If he hears it's two cent in the cash register, I wouldn't be a tall surprised if he. . . ."

"That'll do," Red Sam said. "Go bring these people their Co'-Colas," and the woman went off to get the rest of the order.

"A good man is hard to find," Red Sammy said. "Everything is getting terrible. I remember the day you could go off and leave your screen door unlatched. Not no more."

He and the grandmother discussed better times. The old lady said that in her opinion Europe was entirely to blame for the way things were now. She said the way Europe acted you would think we were made of money and Red Sam said it was no use talking about it, she was exactly right. The children ran outside into the white sunlight and looked at the monkey in the lacy chinaberry tree. He was busy catching fleas on himself and biting each one carefully between his teeth as if it were a delicacy.

They drove off again into the hot afternoon. The grandmother took cat   45
naps and woke up every few minutes with her own snoring. Outside of Toombsboro she woke up and recalled an old plantation that she had visited in this neighborhood once when she was a young lady. She said the house had six white columns across the front and that there was an avenue of oaks leading up to it and two little wooden trellis arbors on either side in front where you sat down with your suitor after a stroll in the garden. She recalled exactly which road to turn off to get to it. She knew that Bailey would not be willing to lose any time looking at an old house, but the more she talked about it, the more she wanted to see it once again and find out if the little twin arbors were still standing. "There was a secret panel in this house," she said craftily, not telling the truth but wishing that she were, "and the story went that all the family silver was hidden in it when Sherman° came through but it was never found. . . ."

Sherman: William Tecumseh Sherman (1820–1891), Union Army commander who led infamous marches through the South during the Civil War.

"Hey!" John Wesley said. "Let's go see it! We'll find it! We'll poke all the woodwork and find it! Who lives there? Where do you turn off at? Hey Pop, can't we turn off there?"

"We never have seen a house with a secret panel!" June Star shrieked. "Let's go to the house with the secret panel! Hey Pop, can't we go see the house with the secret panel!"

"It's not far from here, I know," the grandmother said. "It won't take over twenty minutes."

Bailey was looking straight ahead. His jaw was as rigid as a horseshoe. "No," he said.

The children began to yell and scream that they wanted to see the house 50 with the secret panel. John Wesley kicked the back of the front seat and June Star hung over her mother's shoulder and whined desperately into her ear that they never had any fun even on their vacation, that they could never do what THEY wanted to do. The baby began to scream and John Wesley kicked the back of the seat so hard that his father could feel the blows in his kidney.

"All right!" he shouted and drew the car to a stop at the side of the road. "Will you all shut up? Will you all just shut up for one second? If you don't shut up, we won't go anywhere."

"It would be very educational for them," the grandmother murmured.

"All right," Bailey said, "but get this: this is the only time we're going to stop for anything like this. This is the one and only time."

"The dirt road that you have to turn down is about a mile back," the grandmother directed. "I marked it when we passed."

"A dirt road," Bailey groaned.   55

After they had turned around and were headed toward the dirt road, the grandmother recalled other points about the house, the beautiful glass over the front doorway and the candle-lamp in the hall. John Wesley said that the secret panel was probably in the fireplace.

"You can't go inside this house," Bailey said. "You don't know who lives there."

"While you all talk to the people in front, I'll run around behind and get in a window," John Wesley suggested.

"We'll all stay in the car," his mother said.

They turned onto the dirt road and the car raced roughly along in a swirl 60 of pink dust. The grandmother recalled the times when there were no paved roads and thirty miles was a day's journey. The dirt road was hilly and there were sudden washes in it and sharp curves on dangerous embankments. All at once they would be on a hill, looking down over the blue tops of trees for miles around, then the next minute, they would be in a red depression with the dust-coated trees looking down on them.

"This place had better turn up in a minute," Bailey said, "or I'm going to turn around."

The road looked as if no one had traveled on it for months.

"It's not much farther," the grandmother said and just as she said it, a horrible thought came to her. The thought was so embarrassing that she turned red in the face and her eyes dilated and her feet jumped up, upsetting her valise in the corner. The instant the valise moved, the newspaper top she had over the basket under it rose with a snarl and Pitty Sing, the cat, sprang onto Bailey's shoulder.

The children were thrown to the floor and their mother, clutching the baby, was thrown out the door onto the ground; the old lady was thrown into the front seat. The car turned over once and landed right-side-up in a gulch off the side of the road. Bailey remained in the driver's seat with the cat — gray-striped with a broad white face and an orange nose — clinging to his neck like a caterpillar.

As soon as the children saw they could move their arms and legs, they 65 scrambled out of the car, shouting, "We've had an ACCIDENT!" The grandmother was curled up under the dashboard, hoping she was injured so that Bailey's wrath would not come down on her all at once. The horrible thought she had before the accident was that the house she had remembered so vividly was not in Georgia but in Tennessee.

Bailey removed the cat from his neck with both hands and flung it out the window against the side of a pine tree. Then he got out of the car and started looking for the children's mother. She was sitting against the side of the red gutted ditch, holding the screaming baby, but she only had a cut down her face and a broken shoulder. "We've had an ACCIDENT!" the children screamed in a frenzy of delight.

"But nobody's killed," June Star said with disappointment as the grandmother limped out of the car, her hat still pinned to her head but the broken front brim standing up at a jaunty angle and the violet spray hanging off the side. They all sat down in the ditch, except the children, to recover from the shock. They were all shaking.

"Maybe a car will come along," said the children's mother hoarsely.

"I believe I have injured an organ," said the grandmother, pressing her side, but no one answered her. Bailey's teeth were clattering. He had on a yellow sport shirt with bright blue parrots designed in it and his face was as yellow as the shirt. The grandmother decided that she would not mention that the house was in Tennessee.

The road was about ten feet above and they could see only the tops of the 70 trees on the other side of it. Behind the ditch they were sitting in there were more woods, tall and dark and deep. In a few minutes they saw a car some distance away on top of a hill, coming slowly as if the occupants were watching them. The grandmother stood up and waved both arms dramatically to attract their attention. The car continued to come on slowly, disappeared around a bend and appeared again, moving even slower, on top of the hill they had gone over. It was a big black battered hearse-like automobile. There were three men in it.

It came to a stop just over them and for some minutes, the driver looked down with a steady expressionless gaze to where they were sitting, and didn't speak. Then he turned his head and muttered something to the other two and they got out. One was a fat boy in black trousers and a red sweat shirt with a silver stallion embossed on the front of it. He moved around on the right side of them and stood staring, his mouth partly open in a kind of loose grin. The other had on khaki pants and a blue striped coat and a gray hat pulled down very low, hiding most of his face. He came around slowly on the left side. Neither spoke.

The driver got out of the car and stood by the side of it, looking down at them. He was an older man than the other two. His hair was just beginning to gray and he wore silver-rimmed spectacles that gave him a scholarly look. He had a long creased face and didn't have on any shirt or undershirt. He had on blue jeans that were too tight for him and was holding a black hat and a gun. The two boys also had guns.

"We've had an ACCIDENT!" the children screamed.

The grandmother had the peculiar feeling that the bespectacled man was someone she knew. His face was as familiar to her as if she had known him all her life but she could not recall who he was. He moved away from the car and began to come down the embankment, placing his feet carefully so that he wouldn't slip. He had on tan and white shoes and no socks, and his ankles were red and thin. "Good afternoon," he said. "I see you all had you a little spill."

"We turned over twice!" said the grandmother. 75

"Oncet," he corrected. "We seen it happen. Try their car and see will it run, Hiram," he said quietly to the boy with the gray hat.

"What you got that gun for?" John Wesley asked. "Whatcha gonna do with that gun?"

"Lady," the man said to the children's mother, "would you mind calling them children to sit down by you? Children make me nervous. I want all you all to sit down right together there where you're at."

"What are you telling US what to do for?" June Star asked.

Behind them the line of woods gaped like a dark open mouth. "Come 80 here," said their mother.

"Look here now," Bailey said suddenly, "we're in a predicament! We're in. . . ."

The grandmother shrieked. She scrambled to her feet and stood staring. "You're The Misfit!" she said. "I recognized you at once!"

"Yes'm," the man said, smiling slightly as if he were pleased in spite of himself to be known, "but it would have been better for all of you, lady, if you hadn't of reckernized me."

Bailey turned his head sharply and said something to his mother that shocked even the children. The old lady began to cry and The Misfit reddened.

"Lady," he said, "don't you get upset. Sometimes a man says things he 85 don't mean. I don't reckon he meant to talk to you thataway."

"You wouldn't shoot a lady, would you?" the grandmother said and removed a clean handkerchief from her cuff and began to slap at her eyes with it.

The Misfit pointed the toe of his shoe into the ground and made a little hole and then covered it up again. "I would hate to have to," he said.

"Listen," the grandmother almost screamed, "I know you're a good man. You don't look a bit like you have common blood. I know you must come from nice people!"

"Yes mam," he said, "finest people in the world." When he smiled he showed a row of strong white teeth. "God never made a finer woman than my mother and my daddy's heart was pure gold," he said. The boy with the red sweat shirt had come around behind them and was standing with his gun at his hip. The Misfit squatted down on the ground. "Watch them children, Bobby Lee," he said. "You know they make me nervous." He looked at the six of them huddled together in front of him and he seemed to be embarrassed as if he couldn't think of anything to say. "Ain't a cloud in the sky," he remarked, looking up at it. "Don't see no sun but don't see no cloud neither."

"Yes, it's a beautiful day," said the grandmother. "Listen," she said, "you 90 shouldn't call yourself The Misfit because I know you're a good man at heart. I can just look at you and tell."

"Hush!" Bailey yelled. "Hush! Everybody shut up and let me handle this!" He was squatting in the position of a runner about to sprint forward but he didn't move.

"I pre-chate that, lady," The Misfit said and drew a little circle in the ground with the butt of his gun.

"It'll take a half a hour to fix this here car," Hiram called, looking over the raised hood of it.

"Well, first you and Bobby Lee get him and that little boy to step over yonder with you," The Misfit said, pointing to Bailey and John Wesley. "The boys want to ast you something," he said to Bailey. "Would you mind stepping back in them woods there with them?"

"Listen," Bailey began, "we're in a terrible predicament! Nobody realizes 95 what this is," and his voice cracked. His eyes were as blue and intense as the parrots in his shirt and he remained perfectly still.

The grandmother reached up to adjust her hat brim as if she were going to the woods with him but it came off in her hand. She stood staring at it and after a second she let it fall to the ground. Hiram pulled Bailey up by the arm as if he were assisting an old man. John Wesley caught hold of his father's hand and Bobby Lee followed. They went off toward the woods and just as they reached the dark edge, Bailey turned and supporting himself against a gray naked pine trunk, he shouted, "I'll be back in a minute, Mamma, wait on me!"

"Come back this instant!" his mother shrilled but they all disappeared into the woods.

"Bailey Boy!" the grandmother called in a tragic voice but she found she was looking at The Misfit squatting on the ground in front of her. "I just know you're a good man," she said desperately. "You're not a bit common!"

"Nome, I ain't a good man," The Misfit said after a second as if he had considered her statement carefully, "but I ain't the worst in the world neither. My daddy said I was a different breed of dog from my brothers and sisters. 'You know,' Daddy said, 'it's some that can live their whole life out without asking about it and it's others has to know why it is, and this boy is one of the latters. He's going to be into everything!'" He put on his black hat and looked up suddenly and then away deep into the woods as if he were embarrassed again. "I'm sorry I don't have on a shirt before you ladies," he said, hunching his shoulders slightly. "We buried our clothes that we had on when we escaped and we're just making do until we can get better. We borrowed these from some folks we met," he explained.

"That's perfectly all right," the grandmother said. "Maybe Bailey has an 100 extra shirt in his suitcase."

"I'll look and see terrectly," The Misfit said.

"Where are they taking him?" the children's mother screamed.

"Daddy was a card himself," The Misfit said. "You couldn't put anything over on him. He never got in trouble with the Authorities though. Just had the knack of handling them."

"You could be honest too if you'd only try," said the grandmother. "Think how wonderful it would be to settle down and live a comfortable life and not have to think about somebody chasing you all the time."

The Misfit kept scratching in the ground with the butt of his gun as if he 105 were thinking about it. "Yes'm, somebody is always after you," he murmured.

The grandmother noticed how thin his shoulder blades were just behind his hat because she was standing up looking down on him. "Do you ever pray?" she asked.

He shook his head. All she saw was the black hat wiggle between his shoulder blades. "Nome," he said.

There was a pistol shot from the woods, followed closely by another. Then silence. The old lady's head jerked around. She could hear the wind move through the tree tops like a long satisfied insuck of breath. "Bailey Boy!" she called.

"I was a gospel singer for a while," The Misfit said. "I been most everything. Been in the arm service, both land and sea, at home and abroad, been twict married, been an undertaker, been with the railroads, plowed Mother Earth, been in a tornado, seen a man burnt alive oncet," and he looked up at the children's mother and the little girl who were sitting close together, their faces white and their eyes glassy; "I even seen a woman flogged," he said.

"Pray, pray," the grandmother began, "pray, pray. . . ."   110

"I never was a bad boy that I remember of," The Misfit said in an almost dreamy voice, "but somewheres along the line I done something wrong and got sent to the penitentiary. I was buried alive," and he looked up and held her attention to him by a steady stare.

"That's when you should have started to pray," she said. "What did you do to get sent to the penitentiary that first time?"

"Turn to the right, it was a wall," The Misfit said, looking up again at the cloudless sky. "Turn to the left, it was a wall. Look up it was a ceiling, look down it was a floor. I forget what I done, lady. I set there and set there, trying to remember what it was I done and I ain't recalled it to this day. Oncet in a while, I would think it was coming to me, but it never come."

"Maybe they put you in by mistake," the old lady said vaguely.

"Nome," he said. "It wasn't no mistake. They had the papers on me."   115

"You must have stolen something," she said.

The Misfit sneered slightly. "Nobody had nothing I wanted," he said. "It was a head-doctor at the penitentiary said what I had done was kill my daddy but I known that for a lie. My daddy died in nineteen ought nineteen of the epidemic flu and I never had a thing to do with it. He was buried in the Mount Hopewell Baptist churchyard and you can see for yourself."

"If you would pray," the old lady said, "Jesus would help you."

"That's right," The Misfit said.

"Well then, why don't you pray?" she asked trembling with delight suddenly. 120

"I don't want no hep," he said. "I'm doing all right by myself."

Bobby Lee and Hiram came ambling back from the woods. Bobby Lee was dragging a yellow shirt with bright blue parrots in it.

"Throw me that shirt, Bobby Lee," The Misfit said. The shirt came flying at him and landed on his shoulder and he put it on. The grandmother couldn't name what the shirt reminded her of. "No, lady," The Misfit said while he was buttoning it up, "I found out the crime don't matter. You can do one thing or you can do another, kill a man or take a tire off his car, because sooner or later you're going to forget what it was you done and just be punished for it."

The children's mother had begun to make heaving noises as if she couldn't get her breath. "Lady," he asked, "would you and that little girl like to step off yonder with Bobby Lee and Hiram and join your husband?"

"Yes, thank you," the mother said faintly. Her left arm dangled helplessly 125 and she was holding the baby, who had gone to sleep, in the other. "Hep that lady up, Hiram," The Misfit said as she struggled to climb out of the ditch, "and Bobby Lee, you hold onto that little girl's hand."

"I don't want to hold hands with him," June Star said. "He reminds me of a pig."

The fat boy blushed and laughed and caught her by the arm and pulled her off into the woods after Hiram and her mother.

Alone with The Misfit, the grandmother found that she had lost her voice. There was not a cloud in the sky nor any sun. There was nothing around her but woods. She wanted to tell him that he must pray. She opened and closed her mouth several times before anything came out. Finally she found herself saying, "Jesus, Jesus," meaning Jesus will help you, but the way she was saying it, it sounded as if she might be cursing.

"Yes'm," The Misfit said as if he agreed. "Jesus thown everything off balance. It was the same case with Him as with me except He hadn't committed any crime and they could prove I had committed one because they had the papers on me. Of course," he said, "they never shown me my papers. That's why I sign myself now. I said long ago, you get your signature and sign everything you do and keep a copy of it. Then you'll know what you done and you can hold up the crime to the punishment and see do they match and in the end you'll have something to prove you ain't been treated right. I call myself The Misfit," he said, "because I can't make what all I done wrong fit what all I gone through in punishment."

There was a piercing scream from the woods, followed closely by a pistol 130 report. "Does it seem right to you, lady, that one is punished a heap and another ain't punished at all?"

"Jesus!" the old lady cried. "You've got good blood! I know you wouldn't shoot a lady! I know you come from nice people! Pray! Jesus, you ought not to shoot a lady. I'll give you all the money I've got!"

"Lady," The Misfit said, looking beyond her far into the woods, "there never was a body that give the undertaker a tip."

There were two more pistol reports and the grandmother raised her head like a parched old turkey hen crying for water and called, "Bailey Boy, Bailey Boy!" as if her heart would break.

"Jesus was the only One that ever raised the dead," The Misfit continued, "and He shouldn't have done it. He thown everything off balance. If He did what He said, then it's nothing for you to do but thow away everything and follow Him, and if He didn't, then it's nothing for you to do but enjoy the few minutes you got left the best way you can—by killing somebody or burning down his house or doing some other meanness to him. No pleasure but meanness," he said and his voice had become almost a snarl.

"Maybe He didn't raise the dead," the old lady mumbled, not knowing 135 what she was saying and feeling so dizzy that she sank down in the ditch with her legs twisted under her.

"I wasn't there so I can't say He didn't," The Misfit said. "I wisht I had of been there," he said, hitting the ground with his fist. "It ain't right I wasn't there because if I had of been there I would of known. Listen lady," he said in a high voice, "if I had of been there I would of known and I wouldn't be like I am now." His voice seemed about to crack and the grandmother's head cleared for an instant. She saw the man's face twisted close to her own as if he were going to cry and she murmured, "Why you're one of my babies. You're one of my own children!" She reached out and touched him on the shoulder. The Misfit sprang back as if a snake had bitten him and shot her three times through the chest. Then he put his gun down on the ground and took off his glasses and began to clean them.

Hiram and Bobby Lee returned from the woods and stood over the ditch, looking down at the grandmother who half sat and half lay in a puddle of blood with her legs crossed under her like a child's and her face smiling up at the cloudless sky.

Without his glasses, The Misfit's eyes were red-rimmed and pale and defenseless-looking. "Take her off and thow her where you thown the others," he said, picking up the cat that was rubbing itself against his leg.

"She was a talker, wasn't she?" Bobby Lee said, sliding down the ditch with a yodel.

"She would of been a good woman," The Misfit said, "if it had been some-   140 body there to shoot her every minute of her life."

"Some fun!" Bobby Lee said.

"Shut up, Bobby Lee," The Misfit said. "It's no real pleasure in life."

Considerations for Critical Thinking and Writing

1. **FIRST RESPONSE.** How does O'Connor portray the family? What is comic about them? What qualities about them are we meant to take seriously? Are you shocked by what happens to them? Does your attitude toward them remain constant during the course of the story?

2. How do the grandmother's concerns about the trip to Florida foreshadow events in the story?

3. Describe the grandmother. How does O'Connor make her the central character?

4. What is Red Sammy's purpose in the story? Relate his view of life to the story's conflicts.

5. Characterize The Misfit. What makes him so? Can he be written off as simply insane? How does the grandmother respond to him?

6. Why does The Misfit say that "Jesus thown everything off balance" (para. 129)? What does religion have to do with the brutal action of this story?

7. What does The Misfit mean at the end when he says about the grandmother, "She would of been a good woman . . . if it had been somebody there to shoot her every minute of her life"?

8. Describe the story's tone. Is it consistent? What is the effect of O'Connor's use of tone?

9. How is coincidence used to advance the plot? How do coincidences lead to ironies in the story?

10. Explain how the title points to the story's theme.

Connections to Other Selections

1. What makes "A Good Man Is Hard to Find" so difficult to interpret in contrast, say, to Hawthorne's "The Birthmark" (p. 420)?

2. How does this family compare with the Snopeses in Faulkner's "Barn Burning" (p. 503)? Which family are you more sympathetic to?

3. Consider the criminal behavior of The Misfit and Abner Snopes. What motivates each character? Explain the significant similarities and differences between them.

Good Country People   1955

Besides the neutral expression that she wore when she was alone, Mrs. Freeman had two others, forward and reverse, that she used for all her human dealings. Her forward expression was steady and driving like the advance of a heavy truck. Her eyes never swerved to left or right but turned as the story turned as if they followed a yellow line down the center of it. She seldom used the other expression because it was not often necessary for her to retract a statement, but when she did, her face came to a complete stop, there was an almost imperceptible movement of her black eyes, during which they seemed to be receding, and then the observer would see that Mrs. Freeman, though she might stand there as real as several grain sacks thrown on top of each other, was no longer there in spirit. As for getting anything across to her when this was the case, Mrs. Hopewell had given it up. She might talk her head off. Mrs. Freeman could never be brought to admit herself wrong on any point. She would stand there and if she could be brought to say anything, it was something like, "Well, I wouldn't of said it was and I wouldn't of said it wasn't," or letting her gaze range over the top kitchen shelf where there was an assortment of dusty bottles, she might remark, "I see you ain't ate many of them figs you put up last summer."

They carried on their most important business in the kitchen at breakfast. Every morning Mrs. Hopewell got up at seven o'clock and lit her gas heater and Joy's. Joy was her daughter, a large blonde girl who had an artificial leg. Mrs. Hopewell thought of her as a child though she was thirty-two years old and highly educated. Joy would get up while her mother was eating and lumber into the bathroom and slam the door, and before long, Mrs. Freeman would arrive at the back door. Joy would hear her mother call, "Come on in," and then they would talk for a while in low voices that were indistinguishable in the bathroom. By the time Joy came in, they had usually finished the weather report and were on one or the other of Mrs. Freeman's daughters, Glynese or Carramae, Joy called them Glycerin and Caramel. Glynese, a redhead, was eighteen and had many admirers; Carramae, a blonde, was only fifteen but already married and pregnant. She could not keep anything in her stomach. Every morning Mrs. Freeman told Mrs. Hopewell how many times she had vomited since the last report.

Mrs. Hopewell liked to tell people that Glynese and Carramae were two of the finest girls she knew and that Mrs. Freeman was a *lady* and that she was never ashamed to take her anywhere or introduce her to anybody they might meet. Then she would tell how she had happened to hire the Freemans in the first place and how they were a godsend to her and how she had had them four years. The reason for her keeping them so long was that they were not trash.

They were good country people. She had telephoned the man whose name they had given as a reference and he had told her that Mr. Freeman was a good farmer but that his wife was the nosiest woman ever to walk the earth. "She's got to be into everything," the man said. "If she don't get there before the dust settles, you can bet she's dead, that's all. She'll want to know all your business. I can stand him real good," he had said, "but me nor my wife neither could have stood that woman one more minute on this place." That had put Mrs. Hopewell off for a few days.

She had hired them in the end because there were no other applicants but she had made up her mind beforehand exactly how she would handle the woman. Since she was the type who had to be into everything, then, Mrs. Hopewell decided, she would not only let her be into everything, she would *see to it* that she was into everything — she would give her the responsibility of everything, she would put her in charge. Mrs. Hopewell had no bad qualities of her own but she was able to use other people's in such a constructive way that she never felt the lack. She had hired the Freemans and she had kept them four years.

Nothing is perfect. This was one of Mrs. Hopewell's favorite sayings. 5 Another was: that is life! And still another, the most important, was: well, other people have their opinions too. She would make these statements, usually at the table, in a tone of gentle insistence as if no one held them but her, and the large hulking Joy, whose constant outrage had obliterated every expression from her face, would stare just a little to the side of her, her eyes icy blue, with the look of someone who has achieved blindness by an act of will and means to keep it.

When Mrs. Hopewell said to Mrs. Freeman that life was like that, Mrs. Freeman would say, "I always said so myself." Nothing had been arrived at by anyone that had not first been arrived at by her. She was quicker than Mr. Freeman. When Mrs. Hopewell said to her after they had been on the place a while, "You know, you're the wheel behind the wheel," and winked, Mrs. Freeman had said, "I know it. I've always been quick. It's some that are quicker than others."

"Everybody is different," Mrs. Hopewell said.

"Yes, most people is," Mrs. Freeman said.

"It takes all kinds to make the world."

"I always said it did myself." 10

The girl was used to this kind of dialogue for breakfast and more of it for dinner; sometimes they had it for supper too. When they had no guest they ate in the kitchen because that was easier. Mrs. Freeman always managed to arrive at some point during the meal and to watch them finish it. She would stand in the doorway if it were summer but in the winter she would stand with one elbow on top of the refrigerator and look down on them, or she would stand by the gas heater, lifting the back of her skirt slightly. Occasionally she would stand against the wall and roll her head from side to side. At no time was she in any hurry to leave. All this was very trying on Mrs. Hopewell but she was a woman of great patience. She realized that nothing is perfect and that in the Freemans she had good country people and that if, in this day and age, you get good country people, you had better hang onto them.

She had had plenty of experience with trash. Before the Freemans she had averaged one tenant family a year. The wives of these farmers were not the kind you would want to be around you for very long. Mrs. Hopewell, who had divorced her husband long ago, needed someone to walk over the fields with her; and when Joy had to be impressed for these services, her remarks were usually so ugly and her face so glum that Mrs. Hopewell would say, "If you can't come pleasantly, I don't want you at all," to which the girl, standing square and rigid-shouldered with her neck thrust slightly forward, would reply, "If you want me, here I am—LIKE I AM."

Mrs. Hopewell excused this attitude because of the leg (which had been shot off in a hunting accident when Joy was ten). It was hard for Mrs. Hopewell to realize that her child was thirty-two now and that for more than twenty years she had had only one leg. She thought of her still as a child because it tore her heart to think instead of the poor stout girl in her thirties who had never danced a step or had any *normal* good times. Her name was really Joy but as soon as she was twenty-one and away from home, she had had it legally changed. Mrs. Hopewell was certain that she had thought and thought until she had hit upon the ugliest name in any language. Then she had gone and had the beautiful name, Joy, changed without telling her mother until after she had done it. Her legal name was Hulga.

When Mrs. Hopewell thought the name, Hulga, she thought of the broad blank hull of a battleship. She would not use it. She continued to call her Joy to which the girl responded but in a purely mechanical way.

Hulga had learned to tolerate Mrs. Freeman who saved her from taking 15 walks with her mother. Even Glynese and Carramae were useful when they occupied attention that might otherwise have been directed at her. At first she had thought she could not stand Mrs. Freeman for she had found that it was not possible to be rude to her. Mrs. Freeman would take on strange resentments and for days together she would be sullen but the source of her displeasure was always obscure; a direct attack, a positive leer, blatant ugliness to her face—these never touched her. And without warning one day, she began calling her Hulga.

She did not call her that in front of Mrs. Hopewell who would have been incensed but when she and the girl happened to be out of the house together, she would say something and add the name Hulga to the end of it, and the big spectacled Joy-Hulga would scowl and redden as if her privacy had been intruded upon. She considered the name her personal affair. She had arrived at it first purely on the basis of its ugly sound and then the full genius of its fitness had struck her. She had a vision of the name working like the ugly sweating Vulcan° who stayed in the furnace and to whom, presumably, the goddess had to come when called. She saw it as the name of her highest creative act. One of her major triumphs was that her mother had not been able to turn her dust into Joy, but the greater one was that she had been able to turn it herself into Hulga. However, Mrs. Freeman's relish for using the name only irritated her. It was as if Mrs. Freeman's beady steel-pointed eyes had penetrated far enough behind her face to reach some secret fact. Something about her seemed to fascinate Mrs. Freeman and then one day Hulga realized that it was the artificial leg. Mrs. Freeman had a special fondness for the details of secret infections, hidden deformities, assaults upon children. Of diseases, she preferred the lingering or incurable. Hulga had heard Mrs. Hopewell give her the details

Vulcan: Roman god of fire.

of the hunting accident, how the leg had been literally blasted off, how she had never lost consciousness. Mrs. Freeman could listen to it any time as if it had happened an hour ago.

When Hulga stumped into the kitchen in the morning (she could walk without making the awful noise but she made it — Mrs. Hopewell was certain — because it was ugly-sounding), she glanced at them and did not speak. Mrs. Hopewell would be in her red kimono with her hair tied around her head in rags. She would be sitting at the table, finishing her breakfast and Mrs. Freeman would be hanging by her elbow outward from the refrigerator, looking down at the table. Hulga always put her eggs on the stove to boil and then stood over them with her arms folded, and Mrs. Hopewell would look at her — a kind of indirect gaze divided between her and Mrs. Freeman — and would think that if she would only keep herself up a little, she wouldn't be so bad looking. There was nothing wrong with her face that a pleasant expression wouldn't help. Mrs. Hopewell said that people who looked on the bright side of things would be beautiful even if they were not.

Whenever she looked at Joy this way, she could not help but feel that it would have been better if the child had not taken the Ph.D. It had certainly not brought her out any and now that she had it, there was no more excuse for her to go to school again. Mrs. Hopewell thought it was nice for girls to go to school to have a good time but Joy had "gone through." Anyhow, she would not have been strong enough to go again. The doctors had told Mrs. Hopewell that with the best of care, Joy might see forty-five. She had a weak heart. Joy had made it plain that if it had not been for this condition, she would be far from these red hills and good country people. She would be in a university lecturing to people who knew what she was talking about. And Mrs. Hopewell could very well picture her there, looking like a scarecrow and lecturing to more of the same. Here she went about all day in a six-year-old skirt and a yellow sweat shirt with a faded cowboy on a horse embossed on it. She thought this was funny; Mrs. Hopewell thought it was idiotic and showed simply that she was still a child. She was brilliant but she didn't have a grain of sense. It seemed to Mrs. Hopewell that every year she grew less like other people and more like herself — bloated, rude, and squint-eyed. And she said such strange things! To her own mother she had said — without warning, without excuse, standing up in the middle of a meal with her face purple and her mouth half full — "Woman! do you ever look inside? Do you ever look inside and see what you are *not*? God!" she had cried sinking down again and staring at her plate, "Malebranche° was right: we are not our own light. We are not our own light!" Mrs. Hopewell had no idea to this day what brought that on. She had only made the remark, hoping Joy would take it in, that a smile never hurt anyone.

The girl had taken the Ph.D. in philosophy and this left Mrs. Hopewell at a complete loss. You could say, "My daughter is a nurse," or "My daughter is a schoolteacher," or even, "My daughter is a chemical engineer." You could not say, "My daughter is a philosopher." That was something that had ended with the Greeks and Romans. All day Joy sat on her neck in a deep chair, reading. Sometimes she went for walks but she didn't like dogs or cats or birds or flowers or nature or nice young men. She looked at nice young men as if she could smell their stupidity.

Malebranche: Nicolas Malebranche (1638–1715), a French philosopher.

One day Mrs. Hopewell had picked up one of the books the girl had just 20 put down and opening it at random, she read, "Science, on the other hand, has to assert its soberness and seriousness afresh and declare that it is concerned solely with what-is. Nothing—how can it be for science anything but a horror and a phantasm? If science is right, then one thing stands firm: science wishes to know nothing of nothing. Such is after all the strictly scientific approach to Nothing. We know it by wishing to know nothing of Nothing." These words had been underlined with a blue pencil and they worked on Mrs. Hopewell like some evil incantation in gibberish. She shut the book quickly and went out of the room as if she were having a chill.

This morning when the girl came in, Mrs. Freeman was on Carramae. "She thrown up four times after supper," she said, "and was up twict in the night after three o'clock. Yesterday she didn't do nothing but ramble in the bureau drawer. All she did. Stand up there and see what she could run up on."

"She's got to eat," Mrs. Hopewell muttered, sipping her coffee, while she watched Joy's back at the stove. She was wondering what the child had said to the Bible salesman. She could not imagine what kind of a conversation she could possibly have had with him.

He was a tall gaunt hatless youth who had called yesterday to sell them a Bible. He had appeared at the door, carrying a large black suitcase that weighted him so heavily on one side that he had to brace himself against the door facing. He seemed on the point of collapse but he said in a cheerful voice, "Good morning, Mrs. Cedars!" and set the suitcase down on the mat. He was not a bad-looking young man though he had on a bright blue suit and yellow socks that were not pulled up far enough. He had prominent face bones and a streak of sticky-looking brown hair falling across his forehead.

"I'm Mrs. Hopewell," she said.

"Oh!" he said, pretending to look puzzled but with his eyes sparkling, "I 25 saw it said 'The Cedars' on the mailbox so I thought you was Mrs. Cedars!" and he burst out in a pleasant laugh. He picked up the satchel and under cover of a pant, he fell forward into her hall. It was rather as if the suitcase had moved first, jerking him after it. "Mrs. Hopewell!" he said and grabbed her hand. "I hope you are well!" and he laughed again and then all at once his face sobered completely. He paused and gave her a straight earnest look and said, "Lady, I've come to speak of serious things."

"Well, come in," she muttered, none too pleased because her dinner was almost ready. He came into the parlor and sat down on the edge of a straight chair and put the suitcase between his feet and glanced around the room as if he were sizing her up by it. Her silver gleamed on the two sideboards; she decided he had never been in a room as elegant as this.

"Mrs. Hopewell," he began, using her name in a way that sounded almost intimate, "I know you believe in Chrustian service."

"Well yes," she murmured.

"I know," he said and paused, looking very wise with his head cocked on one side, "that you're a good woman. Friends have told me."

Mrs. Hopewell never liked to be taken for a fool. "What are you selling?" 30 she asked.

"Bibles," the young man said and his eye raced around the room before he added, "I see you have no family Bible in your parlor, I see that is the one lack you got!"

Mrs. Hopewell could not say, "My daughter is an atheist and won't let me keep the Bible in the parlor." She said, stiffening slightly, "I keep my Bible by my bedside." This was not the truth. It was in the attic somewhere.

"Lady," he said, "the word of God ought to be in the parlor."

"Well, I think that's a matter of taste," she began. "I think . . ."

"Lady," he said, "for a Chrustian, the word of God ought to be in every room in the house besides in his heart. I know you're a Chrustian because I can see it in every line of your face." 35

She stood up and said, "Well, young man, I don't want to buy a Bible and I smell my dinner burning."

He didn't get up. He began to twist his hands and looking down at them, he said softly, "Well lady, I'll tell you the truth — not many people want to buy one nowadays and besides, I know I'm real simple. I don't know how to say a thing but to say it. I'm just a country boy." He glanced up into her unfriendly face. "People like you don't like to fool with country people like me!"

"Why!" she cried, "good country people are the salt of the earth! Besides, we all have different ways of doing, it takes all kinds to make the world go 'round. That's life!"

"You said a mouthful," he said.

"Why, I think there aren't enough good people in the world!" she said, stirred. "I think that's what's wrong with it!" 40

His face had brightened. "I didn't introduce myself," he said. "I'm Manley Pointer from out in the country around Willohobie, not even from a place, just from near a place."

"You wait a minute," she said. "I have to see about my dinner." She went out to the kitchen and found Joy standing near the door where she had been listening.

"Get rid of the salt of the earth," she said, "and let's eat."

Mrs. Hopewell gave her a pained look and turned the heat down under the vegetables. "*I* can't be rude to anybody," she murmured and went back into the parlor.

He had opened the suitcase and was sitting with a Bible on each knee. 45

"You might as well put those up," she told him. "I don't want one."

"I appreciate your honesty," he said. "You don't see any more real honest people unless you go way out in the country."

"I know," she said, "real genuine folks!" Through the crack in the door she heard a groan.

"I guess a lot of boys come telling you they're working their way through college," he said, "but I'm not going to tell you that. Somehow," he said, "I don't want to go to college. I want to devote my life to Chrustian service. See," he said, lowering his voice, "I got this heart condition. I may not live long. When you know it's something wrong with you and you may not live long, well then, lady . . ." He paused, with his mouth open, and stared at her.

He and Joy had the same condition! She knew that her eyes were filling with tears but she collected herself quickly and murmured, "Won't you stay for dinner? We'd love to have you!" and was sorry the instant she heard herself say it. 50

"Yes mam," he said in an abashed voice, "I would sher love to do that!"

Joy had given him one look on being introduced to him and then throughout the meal had not glanced at him again. He had addressed several remarks

to her, which she had pretended not to hear. Mrs. Hopewell could not understand deliberate rudeness, although she lived with it, and she felt she had
always to overflow with hospitality to make up for Joy's lack of courtesy. She
urged him to talk about himself and he did. He said he was the seventh child
of twelve and that his father had been crushed under a tree when he himself
was eight years old. He had been crushed very badly, in fact, almost cut in two
and was practically not recognizable. His mother had got along the best she
could by hard working and she had always seen that her children went to Sunday School and that they read the Bible every evening. He was now nineteen
years old and he had been selling Bibles for four months. In that time he had
sold seventy-seven Bibles and had the promise of two more sales. He wanted to
become a missionary because he thought that was the way you could do most
for people. "He who losest his life shall find it," he said simply and he was so
sincere, so genuine and earnest that Mrs. Hopewell would not for the world
have smiled. He prevented his peas from sliding onto the table by blocking
them with a piece of bread which he later cleaned his plate with. She could see
Joy observing sidewise how he handled his knife and fork and she saw too that
every few minutes, the boy would dart a keen appraising glance at the girl as if
he were trying to attract her attention.

After dinner Joy cleared the dishes off the table and disappeared and Mrs.
Hopewell was left to talk with him. He told her again about his childhood and
his father's accident and about various things that had happened to him.
Every five minutes or so she would stifle a yawn. He sat for two hours until
finally she told him she must go because she had an appointment in town. He
packed his Bibles and thanked her and prepared to leave, but in the doorway
he stopped and wrung her hand and said that not on any of his trips had he
met a lady as nice as her and he asked if he could come again. She had said she
would always be happy to see him.

Joy had been standing in the road, apparently looking at something in the
distance, when he came down the steps toward her, bent to the side with his
heavy valise. He stopped where she was standing and confronted her directly.
Mrs. Hopewell could not hear what he said but she trembled to think what Joy
would say to him. She could see that after a minute Joy said something and
that then the boy began to speak again, making an excited gesture with his free
hand. After a minute Joy said something else at which the boy began to speak
once more. Then to her amazement, Mrs. Hopewell saw the two of them walk
off together, toward the gate. Joy had walked all the way to the gate with him
and Mrs. Hopewell could not imagine what they had said to each other, and
she had not yet dared to ask.

Mrs. Freeman was insisting upon her attention. She had moved from the 55
refrigerator to the heater so that Mrs. Hopewell had to turn and face her in
order to seem to be listening. "Glynese gone out with Harvey Hill again last
night," she said. "She had this sty."

"Hill," Mrs. Hopewell said absently, "is the one who works in the garage?"

"Nome, he's the one that goes to chiropractor school," Mrs. Freeman said.
"She had this sty. Been had it two days. So she says when he brought her in the
other night he says, 'Lemme get rid of that sty for you,' and she says, 'How?'
and he says, 'You just lay yourself down acrost the seat of that car and I'll show
you.' So she done it and he popped her neck. Kept on a-popping it several

times until she made him quit. This morning," Mrs. Freeman said, "she ain't got no sty. She ain't got no traces of a sty."

"I never heard of that before," Mrs. Hopewell said.

"He ast her to marry him before the Ordinary,"° Mrs. Freeman went on, "and she told him she wasn't going to be married in no *office.*"

"Well, Glynese is a fine girl," Mrs. Hopewell said. "Glynese and Carramae   60 are both fine girls."

"Carramae said when her and Lyman was married Lyman said it sure felt sacred to him. She said he said he wouldn't take five hundred dollars for being married by a preacher."

"How much would he take?" the girl asked from the stove.

"He said he wouldn't take five hundred dollars," Mrs. Freeman repeated.

"Well we all have work to do," Mrs. Hopewell said.

"Lyman said it just felt more sacred to him," Mrs. Freeman said. "The doc-   65 tor wants Carramae to eat prunes. Says instead of medicine. Says them cramps is coming from pressure. You know where I think it is?"

"She'll be better in a few weeks," Mrs. Hopewell said.

"In the tube," Mrs. Freeman said. "Else she wouldn't be as sick as she is."

Hulga had cracked her two eggs into a saucer and was bringing them to the table along with a cup of coffee that she had filled too full. She sat down carefully and began to eat, meaning to keep Mrs. Freeman there by questions if for any reason she showed an inclination to leave. She could perceive her mother's eye on her. The first round-about question would be about the Bible salesman and she did not wish to bring it on. "How did he pop her neck?" she asked.

Mrs. Freeman went into a description of how he had popped her neck. She said he owned a '55 Mercury but that Glynese said she would rather marry a man with only a '36 Plymouth who would be married by a preacher. The girl asked what if he had a '32 Plymouth and Mrs. Freeman said what Glynese had said was a '36 Plymouth.

Mrs. Hopewell said there were not many girls with Glynese's common   70 sense. She said what she admired in those girls was their common sense. She said that reminded her that they had had a nice visitor yesterday, a young man selling Bibles. "Lord," she said, "he bored me to death but he was so sincere and genuine I couldn't be rude to him. He was just good country people, you know," she said, "—just the salt of the earth."

"I seen him walk up," Mrs. Freeman said, "and then later—I seen him walk off," and Hulga could feel the slight shift in her voice, the slight insinuation, that he had not walked off alone, had he? Her face remained expressionless but the color rose into her neck and she seemed to swallow it down with the next spoonful of egg. Mrs. Freeman was looking at her as if they had a secret together.

"Well, it takes all kinds of people to make the world go 'round," Mrs. Hopewell said. "It's very good we aren't all alike."

"Some people are more alike than others," Mrs. Freeman said.

Hulga got up and stumped, with about twice the noise that was necessary, into her room and locked the door. She was to meet the Bible salesman at ten o'clock at the gate. She had thought about it half the night. She had started

Ordinary: Justice of the peace.

thinking of it as a great joke and then she had begun to see profound implications in it. She had lain in bed imagining dialogues for them that were insane on the surface but that reached below to depths that no Bible salesman would be aware of. Their conversation yesterday had been of this kind.

He had stopped in front of her and had simply stood there. His face was 75
bony and sweaty and bright, with a little pointed nose in the center of it, and his look was different from what it had been at the dinner table. He was gazing at her with open curiosity, with fascination, like a child watching a new fantastic animal at the zoo, and he was breathing as if he had run a great distance to reach her. His gaze seemed somehow familiar but she could not think where she had been regarded with it before. For almost a minute he didn't say anything. Then on what seemed an insuck of breath, he whispered, "You ever ate a chicken that was two days old?"

The girl looked at him stonily. He might have just put this question up for consideration at the meeting of a philosophical association. "Yes," she presently replied as if she had considered it from all angles.

"It must have been mighty small!" he said triumphantly and shook all over with little nervous giggles, getting very red in the face, and subsiding finally into his gaze of complete admiration, while the girl's expression remained exactly the same.

"How old are you?" he asked softly.

She waited some time before she answered. Then in a flat voice she said, "Seventeen."

His smiles came in succession like waves breaking on the surface of a little 80
lake. "I see you got a wooden leg," he said. "I think you're brave. I think you're real sweet."

The girl stood blank and solid and silent.

"Walk to the gate with me," he said. "You're a brave sweet little thing and I liked you the minute I seen you walk in the door."

Hulga began to move forward.

"What's your name?" he asked, smiling down on the top of her head.

"Hulga," she said. 85

"Hulga," he murmured, "Hulga. Hulga. I never heard of anybody name Hulga before. You're shy, aren't you, Hulga?" he asked.

She nodded, watching his large red hand on the handle of the giant valise.

"I like girls that wear glasses," he said. "I think a lot. I'm not like these people that a serious thought don't ever enter their heads. It's because I may die."

"I may die too," she said suddenly and looked up at him. His eyes were very small and brown, glittering feverishly.

"Listen," he said, "don't you think some people was meant to meet on 90
account of what all they got in common and all? Like they both think serious thoughts and all?" He shifted the valise to his other hand so that the hand nearest her was free. He caught hold of her elbow and shook it a little. "I don't work on Saturday," he said. "I like to walk in the woods and see what Mother Nature is wearing. O'er the hills and far away. Pic-nics and things. Couldn't we go on a pic-nic tomorrow? Say yes, Hulga," he said and gave her a dying look as if he felt his insides about to drop out of him. He had even seemed to sway slightly toward her.

During the night she had imagined that she seduced him. She imagined that the two of them walked on the place until they came to the storage barn beyond the two back fields and there, she imagined, that things came to such a pass that she very easily seduced him and that then, of course, she had to reckon with his remorse. True genius can get an idea across even to an inferior mind. She imagined that she took his remorse in hand and changed it into a deeper understanding of life. She took all his shame away and turned it into something useful.

She set off for the gate at exactly ten o'clock, escaping without drawing Mrs. Hopewell's attention. She didn't take anything to eat, forgetting that food is usually taken on a picnic. She wore a pair of slacks and a dirty white shirt, and as an afterthought, she had put some Vapex° on the collar of it since she did not own any perfume. When she reached the gate no one was there.

She looked up and down the empty highway and had the furious feeling that she had been tricked, that he had only meant to make her walk to the gate after the idea of him. Then suddenly he stood up, very tall, from behind a bush on the opposite embankment. Smiling, he lifted his hat which was new and wide-brimmed. He had not worn it yesterday and she wondered if he had bought it for the occasion. It was toast-colored with a red and white band around it and was slightly too large for him. He stepped from behind the bush still carrying the black valise. He had on the same suit and the same yellow socks sucked down in his shoes from walking. He crossed the highway and said, "I knew you'd come!"

The girl wondered acidly how he had known this. She pointed to the valise and asked, "Why did you bring your Bibles?"

He took her elbow, smiling down on her as if he could not stop. "You can 95 never tell when you'll need the word of God, Hulga," he said. She had a moment in which she doubted that this was actually happening and then they began to climb the embankment. They went down into the pasture toward the woods. The boy walked lightly by her side, bouncing on his toes. The valise did not seem to be heavy today; he even swung it. They crossed half the pasture without saying anything and then, putting his hand easily on the small of her back, he asked softly, "Where does your wooden leg join on?"

She turned an ugly red and glared at him and for an instant the boy looked abashed. "I didn't mean you no harm," he said. "I only meant you're so brave and all. I guess God takes care of you."

"No," she said, looking forward and walking fast, "I don't even believe in God."

At this he stopped and whistled. "No!" he exclaimed as if he were too astonished to say anything else.

She walked on and in a second he was bouncing at her side, fanning with his hat. "That's very unusual for a girl," he remarked, watching her out of the corner of his eye. When they reached the edge of the wood, he put his hand on her back again and drew her against him without a word and kissed her heavily.

The kiss, which had more pressure than feeling behind it, produced that 100 extra surge of adrenaline in the girl that enables one to carry a packed trunk out of a burning house, but in her, the power went at once to the brain. Even before he released her, her mind, clear and detached and ironic anyway, was regarding him from a great distance, with amusement but with pity. She had

Vapex: Trade name for a nasal spray.

never been kissed before and she was pleased to discover that it was an unexceptional experience and all a matter of the mind's control. Some people might enjoy drain water if they were told it was vodka. When the boy, looking expectant but uncertain, pushed her gently away, she turned and walked on, saying nothing as if such business, for her, were common enough.

He came along panting at her side, trying to help her when he saw a root that she might trip over. He caught and held back the long swaying blades of thorn vine until she had passed beyond them. She led the way and he came breathing heavily behind her. Then they came out on a sunlit hillside, sloping softly into another one a little smaller. Beyond, they could see the rusted top of the old barn where the extra hay was stored.

The hill was sprinkled with small pink weeds. "Then you ain't saved?" he asked suddenly, stopping.

The girl smiled. It was the first time she had smiled at him at all. "In my economy," she said, "I'm saved and you are damned but I told you I didn't believe in God."

Nothing seemed to destroy the boy's look of admiration. He gazed at her now as if the fantastic animal at the zoo had put its paw through the bars and given him a loving poke. She thought he looked as if he wanted to kiss her again and she walked on before he had the chance.

"Ain't there somewheres we can sit down sometime?" he murmured, his 105 voice softening toward the end of the sentence.

"In that barn," she said.

They made for it rapidly as if it might slide away like a train. It was a large two-story barn, cool and dark inside. The boy pointed up the ladder that led into the loft and said, "It's too bad we can't go up there."

"Why can't we?" she asked.

"Yer leg," he said reverently.

The girl gave him a contemptuous look and putting both hands on the 110 ladder, she climbed it while he stood below, apparently awestruck. She pulled herself expertly through the opening and then looked down at him and said, "Well, come on if you're coming," and he began to climb the ladder, awkwardly bringing the suitcase with him.

"We won't need the Bible," she observed.

"You never can tell," he said, panting. After he had got into the loft, he was a few seconds catching his breath. She had sat down in a pile of straw. A wide sheath of sunlight, filled with dust particles, slanted over her. She lay back against a bale, her face turned away, looking out the front opening of the barn where hay was thrown from a wagon into the loft. The two pink-speckled hillsides lay back against a dark ridge of woods. The sky was cloudless and cold blue. The boy dropped down by her side and put one arm under her and the other over her and began methodically kissing her face, making little noises like a fish. He did not remove his hat but it was pushed far enough back not to interfere. When her glasses got in his way, he took them off of her and slipped them into his pocket.

The girl at first did not return any of the kisses but presently she began to and after she had put several on his cheek, she reached his lips and remained there, kissing him again and again as if she were trying to draw all the breath out of him. His breath was clear and sweet like a child's and the kisses were sticky like a child's. He mumbled about loving her and about knowing when he first seen her that he loved her, but the mumbling was like the sleepy fretting of a child being put to sleep by his mother. Her mind, throughout this, never stopped or lost itself for a second to her feelings. "You ain't said you loved me none," he whispered finally, pulling back from her. "You got to say that."

She looked away from him off into the hollow sky and then down at a black ridge and then down farther into what appeared to be two green swelling lakes. She didn't realize he had taken her glasses but this landscape could not seem exceptional to her for she seldom paid any close attention to her surroundings.

"You got to say it," he repeated. "You got to say you love me."   115

She was always careful how she committed herself. "In a sense," she began, "if you use the word loosely, you might say that. But it's not a word I use. I don't have illusions. I'm one of those people who see *through* to nothing."

The boy was frowning. "You got to say it. I said it and you got to say it," he said.

The girl looked at him almost tenderly. "You poor baby," she murmured. "It's just as well you don't understand," and she pulled him by the neck, face-down, against her. "We are all damned," she said, "but some of us have taken off our blindfolds and see that there's nothing to see. It's a kind of salvation."

The boy's astonished eyes looked blankly through the ends of her hair. "Okay," he almost whined, "but do you love me or don'tcher?"

"Yes," she said and added, "in a sense. But I must tell you something. There   120 mustn't be anything dishonest between us." She lifted his head and looked him in the eye. "I am thirty years old," she said. "I have a number of degrees."

The boy's look was irritated but dogged. "I don't care," he said. "I don't care a thing about what all you done. I just want to know if you love me or don'tcher?" and he caught her to him and wildly planted her face with kisses until she said, "Yes, yes."

"Okay then," he said, letting her go. "Prove it."

She smiled, looking dreamily out on the shifty landscape. She had seduced him without even making up her mind to try. "How?" she asked, feeling that he should be delayed a little.

He leaned over and put his lips to her ear. "Show me where your wooden leg joins on," he whispered.

The girl uttered a sharp little cry and her face instantly drained of color.   125 The obscenity of the suggestion was not what shocked her. As a child she had sometimes been subject to feelings of shame but education had removed the last traces of that as a good surgeon scrapes for cancer; she would no more have felt it over what he was asking than she would have believed in his Bible. But she was as sensitive about the artificial leg as a peacock about his tail. No one ever touched it but her. She took care of it as someone else would his soul, in private and almost with her own eyes turned away. "No," she said.

"I known it," he muttered, sitting up. "You're just playing me for a sucker."

"Oh no no!" she cried. "It joins on at the knee. Only at the knee. Why do you want to see it?"

The boy gave her a long penetrating look. "Because," he said, "it's what makes you different. You ain't like anybody else."

She sat staring at him. There was nothing about her face or her round freezing-blue eyes to indicate that this had moved her; but she felt as if her heart had stopped and left her mind to pump her blood. She decided that for the first time in her life she was face to face with real innocence. This boy, with an instinct that came from beyond wisdom, had touched the truth about her. When after a minute, she said in a hoarse high voice, "All right," it was like surrendering to him completely. It was like losing her own life and finding it again, miraculously, in his.

Very gently he began to roll the slack leg up. The artificial limb, in a white   130 sock and brown flat shoe, was bound in a heavy material like canvas and ended in an ugly jointure where it was attached to the stump. The boy's face and his voice were entirely reverent as he uncovered it and said, "Now show me how to take it off and on."

She took it off for him and put it back on again and then he took it off himself, handling it as tenderly as if it were a real one. "See!" he said with a delighted child's face. "Now I can do it myself!"

"Put it back on," she said. She was thinking that she would run away with him and that every night he would take the leg off and every morning put it back on again. "Put it back on," she said.

"Not yet," he murmured, setting it on its foot out of her reach. "Leave it off for a while. You got me instead."

She gave a little cry of alarm but he pushed her down and began to kiss her again. Without the leg she felt entirely dependent on him. Her brain seemed to have stopped thinking altogether and to be about some other function that it was not very good at. Different expressions raced back and forth over her face. Every now and then the boy, his eyes like two steel spikes, would glance behind him where the leg stood. Finally she pushed him off and said, "Put it back on me now."

"Wait," he said. He leaned the other way and pulled the valise toward him   135 and opened it. It had a pale blue spotted lining and there were only two Bibles in it. He took one of these out and opened the cover of it. It was hollow and contained a pocket flask of whiskey, a pack of cards, and a small blue box with printing on it. He laid these out in front of her one at a time in an evenly-spaced row, like one presenting offerings at the shrine of a goddess. He put the blue box in her hand. THIS PRODUCT TO BE USED ONLY FOR THE PREVENTION OF DISEASE, she read, and dropped it. The boy was unscrewing the top of the flask. He stopped and pointed, with a smile, to the deck of cards. It was not an ordinary deck but one with an obscene picture on the back of each card. "Take a swig," he said, offering her the bottle first. He held it in front of her, but like one mesmerized, she did not move.

Her voice when she spoke had an almost pleading sound. "Aren't you," she murmured, "aren't you just good country people?"

The boy cocked his head. He looked as if he were just beginning to understand that she might be trying to insult him. "Yeah," he said, curling his lip slightly, "but it ain't held me back none. I'm as good as you any day in the week."

"Give me my leg," she said.

He pushed it farther away with his foot. "Come on now, let's begin to have us a good time," he said coaxingly. "We ain't got to know one another good yet."

"Give me my leg!" she screamed and tried to lunge for it but he pushed her   140 down easily.

"What's the matter with you all of a sudden?" he asked, frowning as he screwed the top on the flask and put it quickly back inside the Bible. "You just a while ago said you didn't believe in nothing. I thought you was some girl!"

Her face was almost purple. "You're a Christian!" she hissed. "You're a fine Christian! You're just like them all—say one thing and do another. You're a perfect Christian, you're . . ."

The boy's mouth was set angrily. "I hope you don't think," he said in a lofty indignant tone, "that I believe in that crap! I may sell Bibles but I know which end is up and I wasn't born yesterday and I know where I'm going!"

"Give me my leg!" she screeched. He jumped up so quickly that she barely saw him sweep the cards and the blue box into the Bible and throw the Bible into his valise. She saw him grab the leg and then she saw it for an instant slanted forlornly across the inside of the suitcase with a Bible at either side of its opposite ends. He slammed the lid shut and snatched up the valise and swung it down the hole and then stepped through himself.

When all of him had passed but his head, he turned and regarded her with 145 a look that no longer had any admiration in it. "I've gotten a lot of interesting things," he said. "One time I got a woman's glass eye this way. And you needn't to think you'll catch me because Pointer ain't really my name. I use a different name at every house I call at and don't stay nowhere long. And I'll tell you another thing, Hulga," he said, using the name as if he didn't think much of it, "you ain't so smart. I been believing in nothing ever since I was born!" and then the toast-colored hat disappeared down the hole and the girl was left, sitting on the straw in the dusty sunlight. When she turned her churning face toward the opening, she saw his blue figure struggling successfully over the green speckled lake.

Mrs. Hopewell and Mrs. Freeman, who were in the back pasture, digging up onions, saw him emerge a little later from the woods and head across the meadow toward the highway. "Why, that looks like that nice dull young man that tried to sell me a Bible yesterday," Mrs. Hopewell said, squinting. "He must have been selling them to the Negroes back in there. He was so simple," she said, "but I guess the world would be better off if we were all that simple."

Mrs. Freeman's gaze drove forward and just touched him before he disappeared under the hill. Then she returned her attention to the evil-smelling onion shoot she was lifting from the ground. "Some can't be that simple," she said. "I know I never could."

CONSIDERATIONS FOR CRITICAL THINKING AND WRITING

1. **FIRST RESPONSE.** What do you think of Hulga's conviction that intelligence and education are incompatible with religious faith?

2. Why is it significant that Mrs. Hopewell's daughter has two names? How do the other characters' names serve to characterize them?

3. Why do you think Mrs. Freeman and Mrs. Hopewell are introduced before Hulga? What do they contribute to Hulga's story?

4. Identify the conflict in this story. How is it resolved?

5. Hulga and the Bible salesman play a series of jokes on each other. How are these deceptions related to the theme?

6. What is the effect of O'Connor's use of the phrase "good country people" throughout the story? Why is it an appropriate title?

7. The Bible salesman's final words to Hulga are "You ain't so smart. I been believing in nothing ever since I was born!" What religious values are expressed in the story?

8. After the Bible salesman leaves Hulga at the end of the story, O'Connor adds two more paragraphs concerning Mrs. Hopewell and Mrs. Freeman. What is the purpose of these final paragraphs?

9. Hulga's perspective on life is ironic, but she is also the subject of O'Connor's irony. Explain how O'Connor uses irony to reveal Hulga's character.

10. This story would be different if told from Hulga's point of view. Describe how the use of a limited omniscient narrator contributes to the story's effects.

CONNECTIONS TO OTHER SELECTIONS

1. How do Mrs. Hopewell's assumptions about life compare with those of Krebs's mother in Hemingway's "Soldier's Home" (p. 187)? Explain how the conflict in each story is related to what the mothers come to represent in the eyes of the central characters.

2. Discuss the treatment of faith in this story and in Hawthorne's "Young Goodman Brown" (p. 402).

Revelation   1964

The doctor's waiting room, which was very small, was almost full when the Turpins entered and Mrs. Turpin, who was very large, made it look even smaller by her presence. She stood looming at the head of the magazine table set in the center of it, a living demonstration that the room was inadequate and ridiculous. Her little bright black eyes took in all the patients as she sized up the seating situation. There was one vacant chair and a place on the sofa occupied by a blond child in a dirty blue romper who should have been told to move over and make room for the lady. He was five or six, but Mrs. Turpin saw at once that no one was going to tell him to move over. He was slumped down in the seat, his arms idle at his sides and his eyes idle in his head; his nose ran unchecked.

Mrs. Turpin put a firm hand on Claud's shoulder and said in a voice that included anyone who wanted to listen, "Claud, you sit in that chair there," and gave him a push down into the vacant one. Claud was florid and bald and sturdy, somewhat shorter than Mrs. Turpin, but he sat down as if he were accustomed to doing what she told him to.

Mrs. Turpin remained standing. The only man in the room besides Claud was a lean stringy old fellow with a rusty hand spread out on each knee, whose eyes were closed as if he were asleep or dead or pretending to be so as not to get up and offer her his seat. Her gaze settled agreeably on a well-dressed gray-haired lady whose eyes met hers and whose expression said: if that child belonged to me, he would have some manners and move over—there's plenty of room there for you and him too.

Claud looked up with a sigh and made as if to rise.

"Sit down," Mrs. Turpin said. "You know you're not supposed to stand on   5
that leg. He has an ulcer on his leg," she explained.

Claud lifted his foot onto the magazine table and rolled his trouser leg up to reveal a purple swelling on a plump marble-white calf.

"My!" the pleasant lady said. "How did you do that?"

"A cow kicked him," Mrs. Turpin said.

"Goodness!" said the lady.

Claud rolled his trouser leg down.   10

"Maybe the little boy would move over," the lady suggested, but the child did not stir.

"Somebody will be leaving in a minute," Mrs. Turpin said. She could not understand why a doctor—with as much money as they made charging five dollars a day to just stick their head in the hospital door and look at you— couldn't afford a decent-sized waiting room. This one was hardly bigger than a garage. The table was cluttered with limp-looking magazines and at one end of it there was a big green glass ash tray full of cigarette butts and cotton wads with little blood spots on them. If she had had anything to do with the running of the place, that would have been emptied every so often. There were no chairs against the wall at the head of the room. It had a rectangular-shaped panel in it that permitted a view of the office where the nurse came and went and the secretary listened to the radio. A plastic fern in a gold pot sat in the opening and trailed its fronds down almost to the floor. The radio was softly playing gospel music.

Just then the inner door opened and a nurse with the highest stack of yellow hair Mrs. Turpin had ever seen put her face in the crack and called for the next patient. The woman sitting beside Claud grasped the two arms of her chair and hoisted herself up; she pulled her dress free from her legs and lumbered through the door where the nurse had disappeared.

Mrs. Turpin eased into the vacant chair, which held her tight as a corset. "I wish I could reduce," she said, and rolled her eyes and gave a comic sigh.

"Oh, *you* aren't fat," the stylish lady said.   15

"Ooooo I am too," Mrs. Turpin said. "Claud he eats all he wants to and never weighs over one hundred and seventy-five pounds, but me I just look at something good to eat and I gain some weight," and her stomach and shoulders shook with laughter. "You can eat all you want to, can't you, Claud?" she asked, turning to him.

Claud only grinned.

"Well, as long as you have such a good disposition," the stylish lady said, "I don't think it makes a bit of difference what size you are. You just can't beat a good disposition."

Next to her was a fat girl of eighteen or nineteen, scowling into a thick blue book which Mrs. Turpin saw was entitled *Human Development*. The girl raised her head and directed her scowl at Mrs. Turpin as if she did not like her looks. She appeared annoyed that anyone should speak while she tried to read. The poor girl's face was blue with acne and Mrs. Turpin thought how pitiful it was to have a face like that at that age. She gave the girl a friendly smile but the girl only scowled the harder. Mrs. Turpin herself was fat but she had always had good skin, and though she was forty-seven years old, there was not a wrinkle in her face except around her eyes from laughing too much.

Next to the ugly girl was the child, still in exactly the same position, and   20 next to him was a thin leathery old woman in a cotton print dress. She and Claud had three sacks of chicken feed in their pump house that was in the same print. She had seen from the first that the child belonged with the old woman. She could tell by the way they sat—kind of vacant and white-trashy, as if they would sit there until Doomsday if nobody called and told them to get up. And at right angles but next to the well-dressed pleasant lady was a lank-faced woman who was certainly the child's mother. She had on a yellow sweat shirt and wine-colored slacks, both gritty-looking, and the rims of her lips were stained with snuff. Her dirty yellow hair was tied behind with a little piece of red paper ribbon. Worse than niggers any day, Mrs. Turpin thought.

The gospel hymn playing was, "When I looked up and He looked down," and Mrs. Turpin, who knew it, supplied the last line mentally, "And wona these days I know I'll we-eara crown."

Without appearing to, Mrs. Turpin always noticed people's feet. The well-dressed lady had on red and gray suede shoes to match her dress. Mrs. Turpin had on her good black patent leather pumps. The ugly girl had on Girl Scout shoes and heavy socks. The old woman had on tennis shoes and the white-trashy mother had on what appeared to be bedroom slippers, black straw with gold braid threaded through them — exactly what you would have expected her to have on.

Sometimes at night when she couldn't go to sleep, Mrs. Turpin would occupy herself with the question of who she would have chosen to be if she couldn't have been herself. If Jesus had said to her before he made her, "There's only two places available for you. You can either be a nigger or white-trash," what would she have said? "Please, Jesus, please," she would have said, "just let me wait until there's another place available," and he would have said, "No, you have to go right now and I have only those two places so make up your mind." She would have wiggled and squirmed and begged and pleaded but it would have been no use and finally she would have said, "All right, make me a nigger then — but that don't mean a trashy one." And he would have made her a neat clean respectable Negro woman, herself but black.

Next to the child's mother was a red-headed youngish woman, reading one of the magazines and working a piece of chewing gum, hell for leather, as Claud would say. Mrs. Turpin could not see the woman's feet. She was not white-trash, just common. Sometimes Mrs. Turpin occupied herself at night naming the classes of people. On the bottom of the heap were most colored people, not the kind she would have been if she had been one, but most of them; then next to them — not above, just away from — were the white-trash; then above them were the homeowners, and above them the home-and-land owners, to which she and Claud belonged. Above she and Claud were people with a lot of money and much bigger houses and much more land. But here the complexity of it would begin to bear in on her, for some of the people with a lot of money were common and ought to be below she and Claud and some of the people who had good blood had lost their money and had to rent and then there were colored people who owned their homes and land as well. There was a colored dentist in town who had two red Lincolns and a swimming pool and a farm with registered white-face cattle on it. Usually by the time she had fallen asleep all the classes of people were moiling and roiling around in her head, and she would dream they were all crammed in together in a box car, being ridden off to be put in a gas oven.

"That's a beautiful clock," she said and nodded to her right. It was a big wall clock, the face encased in a brass sunburst.

"Yes, it's very pretty," the stylish lady said agreeably. "And right on the dot too," she added, glancing at her watch.

The ugly girl beside her cast an eye upward at the clock, smirked, then looked directly at Mrs. Turpin and smirked again. Then she returned her eyes to her book. She was obviously the lady's daughter because, although they didn't look anything alike as to disposition, they both had the same shape of face and the same blue eyes. On the lady they sparkled pleasantly but in the girl's seared face they appeared alternately to smolder and to blaze.

What if Jesus had said, "All right, you can be white-trash or a nigger or ugly"!

Mrs. Turpin felt an awful pity for the girl, though she thought it was one thing to be ugly and another to act ugly.

The woman with the snuff-stained lips turned around in her chair and 30 looked up at the clock. Then she turned back and appeared to look a little to the side of Mrs. Turpin. There was a cast in one of her eyes. "You want to know wher you can get you one of themther clocks?" she asked in a loud voice.

"No, I already have a nice clock," Mrs. Turpin said. Once somebody like her got a leg in the conversation, she would be all over it.

"You can get you one with green stamps," the woman said. "That's most likely wher he got hisn. Save you up enough, you can get you most anythang. I got me some joo'ry."

Ought to have got you a wash rag and some soap, Mrs. Turpin thought.

"I get contour sheets with mine," the pleasant lady said.

The daughter slammed her book shut. She looked straight in front of her, 35 directly through Mrs. Turpin and on through the yellow curtain and the plate glass window which made the wall behind her. The girl's eyes seemed lit all of a sudden with a peculiar light, an unnatural light like night road signs give. Mrs. Turpin turned her head to see if there was anything going on outside that she should see, but she could not see anything. Figures passing cast only a pale shadow through the curtain. There was no reason the girl should single her out for her ugly looks.

"Miss Finley," the nurse said, cracking the door. The gum-chewing woman got up and passed in front of her and Claud and went into the office. She had on red high-heeled shoes.

Directly across the table, the ugly girl's eyes were fixed on Mrs. Turpin as if she had some very special reason for disliking her.

"This is wonderful weather, isn't it?" the girl's mother said.

"It's good weather for cotton if you can get the niggers to pick it," Mrs. Turpin said, "but niggers don't want to pick cotton any more. You can't get the white folks to pick it and now you can't get the niggers—because they got to be right up there with the white folks."

"They gonna *try* anyways," the white-trash woman said, leaning forward. 40

"Do you have one of the cotton-picking machines?" the pleasant lady asked.

"No," Mrs. Turpin said, "they leave half the cotton in the field. We don't have much cotton anyway. If you want to make it farming now, you have to have a little of everything. We got a couple of acres of cotton and a few hogs and chickens and just enough white-face that Claud can look after them himself."

"One thang I don't want," the white-trash woman said, wiping her mouth with the back of her hand. "Hogs. Nasty stinking things, a-gruntin and a-rootin all over the place."

Mrs. Turpin gave her the merest edge of her attention. "Our hogs are not dirty and they don't stink," she said. "They're cleaner than some children I've seen. Their feet never touch the ground. We have a pig parlor—that's where you raise them on concrete," she explained to the pleasant lady, "and Claud scoots them down with the hose every afternoon and washes off the floor." Cleaner by far than that child right there, she thought. Poor nasty little thing. He had not moved except to put the thumb of his dirty hand into his mouth.

The woman turned her face away from Mrs. Turpin. "I know I wouldn't 45 scoot down no hog with no hose," she said to the wall.

You wouldn't have no hog to scoot down, Mrs. Turpin said to herself.

"A-gruntin and a-rootin and a-groanin," the woman muttered.

"We got a little of everything," Mrs. Turpin said to the pleasant lady. "It's no use in having more than you can handle yourself with help like it is. We found enough niggers to pick our cotton this year but Claud he has to go after them and take them home again in the evening. They can't walk that half a mile. No they can't. I tell you," she said and laughed merrily, "I sure am tired of buttering up niggers, but you got to love em if you want em to work for you. When they come in the morning, I run out and I say, 'Hi yawl this morning?' and when Claud drives them off to the field I just wave to beat the band and they just wave back." And she waved her hand rapidly to illustrate.

"Like you read out of the same book," the lady said, showing she understood perfectly.

"Child, yes," Mrs. Turpin said. "And when they come in from the field, 50 I run out with a bucket of icewater. That's the way it's going to be from now on," she said. "You may as well face it."

"One thang I know," the white-trash woman said. "Two thangs I ain't going to do: love no niggers or scoot down no hog with no hose." And she let out a bark of contempt.

The look that Mrs. Turpin and the pleasant lady exchanged indicated they both understood that you had to *have* certain things before you could *know* certain things. But every time Mrs. Turpin exchanged a look with the lady, she was aware that the ugly girl's peculiar eyes were still on her, and she had trouble bringing her attention back to the conversation.

"When you got something," she said, "you got to look after it." And when you ain't got a thing but breath and britches, she added to herself, you can afford to come to town every morning and just sit on the Court House coping and spit.

A grotesque revolving shadow passed across the curtain behind her and was thrown palely on the opposite wall. Then a bicycle clattered down against the outside of the building. The door opened and a colored boy glided in with a tray from the drugstore. It had two large red and white paper cups on it with tops on them. He was a tall, very black boy in discolored white pants and a green nylon shirt. He was chewing gum slowly, as if to music. He set the tray down in the office opening next to the fern and stuck his head through to look for the secretary. She was not in there. He rested his arms on the ledge and waited, his narrow bottom stuck out, swaying to the left and right. He raised a hand over his head and scratched the base of his skull.

"You see that button there, boy?" Mrs. Turpin said. "You can punch that 55 and she'll come. She's probably in the back somewhere."

"Is that right?" the boy said agreeably, as if he had never seen the button before. He leaned to the right and put his finger on it. "She sometime out," he said and twisted around to face his audience, his elbows behind him on the counter. The nurse appeared and he twisted back again. She handed him a dollar and he rooted in his pocket and made the change and counted it out to her. She gave him fifteen cents for a tip and he went out with the empty tray. The heavy door swung to slowly and closed at length with the sound of suction. For a moment no one spoke.

"They ought to send all them niggers back to Africa," the white-trash woman said. "That's wher they come from in the first place."

"Oh, I couldn't do without my good colored friends," the pleasant lady said.

"There's a heap of things worse than a nigger," Mrs. Turpin agreed. "It's all kinds of them just like it's all kinds of us."

"Yes, and it takes all kinds to make the world go round," the lady said in 60 her musical voice.

As she said it, the raw-complexioned girl snapped her teeth together. Her lower lip turned downwards and inside out, revealing the pale pink inside of her mouth. After a second it rolled back up. It was the ugliest face Mrs. Turpin had ever seen anyone make and for a moment she was certain that the girl had made it at her. She was looking at her as if she had known and disliked her all her life—all of Mrs. Turpin's life, it seemed too, not just all the girl's life. Why, girl, I don't even know you, Mrs. Turpin said silently.

She forced her attention back to the discussion. "It wouldn't be practical to send them back to Africa," she said. "They wouldn't want to go. They got it too good here."

"Wouldn't be what they wanted—if I had anythang to do with it," the woman said.

"It wouldn't be a way in the world you could get all the niggers back over there," Mrs. Turpin said. "They'd be hiding out and lying down and turning sick on you and wailing and hollering and raring and pitching. It wouldn't be a way in the world to get them over there."

"They got over here," the trashy woman said. "Get back like they got over." 65

"It wasn't so many of them then," Mrs. Turpin explained.

The woman looked at Mrs. Turpin as if here was an idiot indeed but Mrs. Turpin was not bothered by the look, considering where it came from.

"Nooo," she said, "they're going to stay here where they can go to New York and marry white folks and improve their color. That's what they all want to do, every one of them, improve their color."

"You know what comes of that, don't you?" Claud asked.

"No, Claud, what?" Mrs. Turpin said. 70

Claud's eyes twinkled. "White-faced niggers," he said with never a smile.

Everybody in the office laughed except the white-trash and the ugly girl. The girl gripped the book in her lap with white fingers. The trashy woman looked around her from face to face as if she thought they were all idiots. The old woman in the feed sack dress continued to gaze expressionless across the floor at the high-top shoes of the man opposite her, the one who had been pretending to be asleep when the Turpins came in. He was laughing heartily, his hands still spread out on his knees. The child had fallen to the side and was lying now almost face down in the old woman's lap.

While they recovered from their laughter, the nasal chorus on the radio kept the room from silence.

"You go to blank blank
And I'll go to mine

But we'll all blank along
To-geth-ther,
And all along the blank
We'll hep each other out
Smile-ling in any kind of
Weath-ther!"

Mrs. Turpin didn't catch every word but she caught enough to agree with the spirit of the song and it turned her thoughts sober. To help anybody out that needed it was her philosophy of life. She never spared herself when she found somebody in need, whether they were white or black, trash or decent. And of all she had to be thankful for, she was most thankful that this was so. If Jesus had said, "You can be high society and have all the money you want and be thin and svelte-like, but you can't be a good woman with it," she would have had to say, "Well don't make me that then. Make me a good woman and it don't matter what else, how fat or how ugly or how poor!" Her heart rose. He had not made her a nigger or white-trash or ugly! He had made her herself and given her a little of everything. Jesus, thank you! she said. Thank you thank you thank you! Whenever she counted her blessings she felt as buoyant as if she weighed one hundred and twenty-five pounds instead of one hundred and eighty.

"What's wrong with your little boy?" the pleasant lady asked the white- 75 trashy woman.

"He has a ulcer," the woman said proudly. "He ain't give me a minute's peace since he was born. Him and her are just alike," she said, nodding at the old woman, who was running her leathery fingers through the child's pale hair. "Look like I can't get nothing down them two but Co' Cola and candy."

That's all you try to get down em, Mrs. Turpin said to herself. Too lazy to light the fire. There was nothing you could tell her about people like them that she didn't know already. And it was not just that they didn't have anything. Because if you gave them everything, in two weeks it would all be broken or filthy or they would have chopped it up for lightwood. She knew all this from her own experience. Help them you must, but help them you couldn't.

All at once the ugly girl turned her lips inside out again. Her eyes fixed like two drills on Mrs. Turpin. This time there was no mistaking that there was something urgent behind them.

Girl, Mrs. Turpin exclaimed silently, I haven't done a thing to you! The girl might be confusing her with somebody else. There was no need to sit by and let herself be intimidated. "You must be in college," she said boldly, looking directly at the girl. "I see you reading a book there."

The girl continued to stare and pointedly did not answer. 80

Her mother blushed at this rudeness. "The lady asked you a question, Mary Grace," she said under her breath.

"I have ears," Mary Grace said.

The poor mother blushed again. "Mary Grace goes to Wellesley College," she explained. She twisted one of the buttons on her dress. "In Massachusetts," she added with a grimace. "And in the summer she just keeps right on studying. Just reads all the time, a real book worm. She's done real well at Wellesley; she's taking English and Math and History and Psychology and Social Studies," she rattled on, "and I think it's too much. I think she ought to get out and have fun."

The girl looked as if she would like to hurl them all through the plate glass window.

"Way up north," Mrs. Turpin murmured and thought, well, it hasn't done much for her manners. 85

"I'd almost rather to have him sick," the white-trash woman said, wrenching the attention back to herself. "He's so mean when he ain't. Look like some children just take natural to meanness. It's some gets bad when they get sick but he was the opposite. Took sick and turned good. He don't give me no trouble now. It's me waitin to see the doctor," she said.

If I was going to send anybody back to Africa, Mrs. Turpin thought, it would be your kind, woman. "Yes, indeed," she said aloud, but looking up at the ceiling, "it's a heap of things worse than a nigger." And dirtier than a hog, she added to herself.

"I think people with bad dispositions are more to be pitied than anyone on earth," the pleasant lady said in a voice that was decidedly thin.

"I thank the Lord he has blessed me with a good one," Mrs. Turpin said. "The day has never dawned that I couldn't find something to laugh at."

"Not since she married me anyways," Claud said with a comical straight face. 90

Everybody laughed except the girl and the white-trash.

Mrs. Turpin's stomach shook. "He's such a caution," she said, "that I can't help but laugh at him."

The girl made a loud ugly noise through her teeth.

Her mother's mouth grew thin and tight. "I think the worst thing in the world," she said, "is an ungrateful person. To have everything and not appreciate it. I know a girl," she said, "who has parents who would give her anything, a little brother who loves her dearly, who is getting a good education, who wears the best clothes, but who can never say a kind word to anyone, who never smiles, who just criticizes and complains all day long."

"Is she too old to paddle?" Claud asked. 95

The girl's face was almost purple.

"Yes," the lady said, "I'm afraid there's nothing to do but leave her to her folly. Some day she'll wake up and it'll be too late."

"It never hurt anyone to smile," Mrs. Turpin said. "It just makes you feel better all over."

"Of course," the lady said sadly, "but there are just some people you can't tell anything to. They can't take criticism."

"If it's one thing I am," Mrs. Turpin said with feeling, "it's grateful. When I think who all I could have been besides myself and what all I got, a little of everything, and a good disposition besides, I just feel like shouting, 'Thank you, Jesus, for making everything the way it is!' It could have been different!" For one thing, somebody else could have got Claud. At the thought of this, she was flooded with gratitude and a terrible pang of joy ran through her. "Oh thank you, Jesus, Jesus, thank you!" she cried aloud. 100

The book struck her directly over her left eye. It struck almost at the same instant that she realized the girl was about to hurl it. Before she could utter a sound, the raw face came crashing across the table toward her, howling. The girl's fingers sank like clamps into the soft flesh of her neck. She heard the mother cry out and Claud shout, "Whoa!" There was an instant when she was certain that she was about to be in an earthquake.

All at once her vision narrowed and she saw everything as if it were happening in a small room far away, or as if she were looking at it through the wrong end of a telescope. Claud's face crumpled and fell out of sight. The nurse ran in, then out, then in again. Then the gangling figure of the doctor rushed out of the inner door. Magazines flew this way and that as the table turned over. The girl fell with a thud and Mrs. Turpin's vision suddenly reversed itself and she saw everything large instead of small. The eyes of the white-trashy woman were staring hugely at the floor. There the girl, held down on one side by the nurse and on the other by her mother, was wrenching and turning in their grasp. The doctor was kneeling astride her, trying to hold her arm down. He managed after a second to sink a long needle into it.

Mrs. Turpin felt entirely hollow except for her heart which swung from side to side as if it were agitated in a great empty drum of flesh.

"Somebody that's not busy call for the ambulance," the doctor said in the off-hand voice young doctors adopt for terrible occasions.

Mrs. Turpin could not have moved a finger. The old man who had been sit- 105 ting next to her skipped nimbly into the office and made the call, for the secretary still seemed to be gone.

"Claud!" Mrs. Turpin called.

He was not in his chair. She knew she must jump up and find him but she felt like some one trying to catch a train in a dream, when everything moves in slow motion and the faster you try to run the slower you go.

"Here I am," a suffocated voice, very unlike Claud's, said.

He was doubled up in the corner on the floor, pale as paper, holding his leg. She wanted to get up and go to him but she could not move. Instead, her gaze was drawn slowly downward to the churning face on the floor, which she could see over the doctor's shoulder.

The girl's eyes stopped rolling and focused on her. They seemed a much 110 lighter blue than before, as if a door that had been tightly closed behind them was now open to admit light and air.

Mrs. Turpin's head cleared and her power of motion returned. She leaned forward until she was looking directly into the fierce brilliant eyes. There was no doubt in her mind that the girl did know her, knew her in some intense and personal way, beyond time and place and condition. "What you got to say to me?" she asked hoarsely and held her breath, waiting, as for a revelation.

The girl raised her head. Her gaze locked with Mrs. Turpin's. "Go back to hell where you came from, you old wart hog," she whispered. Her voice was low but clear. Her eyes burned for a moment as if she saw with pleasure that her message had struck its target.

Mrs. Turpin sank back in her chair.

After a moment the girl's eyes closed and she turned her head wearily to the side.

The doctor rose and handed the nurse the empty syringe. He leaned over 115 and put both hands for a moment on the mother's shoulders, which were shaking. She was sitting on the floor, her lips pressed together, holding Mary Grace's hand in her lap. The girl's fingers were gripped like a baby's around her thumb. "Go on to the hospital," he said. "I'll call and make the arrangements."

"Now let's see that neck," he said in a jovial voice to Mrs. Turpin. He began to inspect her neck with his first two fingers. Two little moon-shaped lines like pink fish bones were indented over her windpipe. There was the beginning of an angry red swelling above her eye. His fingers passed over this also.

"Lea' me be," she said thickly and shook him off. "See about Claud. She kicked him."

"I'll see about him in a minute," he said and felt her pulse. He was a thin gray-haired man, given to pleasantries. "Go home and have yourself a vacation the rest of the day," he said and patted her on the shoulder.

Quit your pattin me, Mrs. Turpin growled to herself.

"And put an ice pack over that eye," he said. Then he went and squatted   120
down beside Claud and looked at his leg. After a moment he pulled him up and Claud limped after him into the office.

Until the ambulance came, the only sounds in the room were the tremulous moans of the girl's mother, who continued to sit on the floor. The white-trash woman did not take her eyes off the girl. Mrs. Turpin looked straight ahead at nothing. Presently the ambulance drew up, a long dark shadow, behind the curtain. The attendants came in and set the stretcher down beside the girl and lifted her expertly onto it and carried her out. The nurse helped the mother gather up her things. The shadow of the ambulance moved silently away and the nurse came back in the office.

"That ther girl is going to be a lunatic, ain't she?" the white-trash woman asked the nurse, but the nurse kept on to the back and never answered her.

"Yes, she's going to be a lunatic," the white-trash woman said to the rest of them.

"Po' critter," the old woman murmured. The child's face was still in her lap. His eyes looked idly out over her knees. He had not moved during the disturbance except to draw one leg up under him.

"I thank Gawd," the white-trash woman said fervently, "I ain't a lunatic."   125

Claud came limping out and the Turpins went home.

As their pick-up truck turned into their own dirt road and made the crest of the hill, Mrs. Turpin gripped the window ledge and looked out suspiciously. The land sloped gracefully down through a field dotted with lavender weeds and at the start of the rise their small yellow frame house, with its little flower beds spread out around it like a fancy apron, sat primly in its accustomed place between two giant hickory trees. She would not have been startled to see a burnt wound between two blackened chimneys.

Neither of them felt like eating so they put on their house clothes and lowered the shade in the bedroom and lay down, Claud with his leg on a pillow and herself with a damp washcloth over her eye. The instant she was flat on her back, the image of a razor-backed hog with warts on its face and horns coming out behind its ears snorted into her head. She moaned, a low quiet moan.

"I am not," she said tearfully, "a wart hog. From hell." But the denial had no force. The girl's eyes and her words, even the tone of her voice, low but clear, directed only to her, brooked no repudiation. She had been singled out for the message, though there was trash in the room to whom it might justly have been applied. The full force of this fact struck her only now. There was a woman there who was neglecting her own child but she had been overlooked. The message had been given to Ruby Turpin, a respectable, hard-working, church-going woman. The tears dried. Her eyes began to burn instead with wrath.

She rose on her elbow and the washcloth fell into her hand. Claud was   130
lying on his back, snoring. She wanted to tell him what the girl had said. At the

same time, she did not wish to put the image of herself as a wart hog from hell into his mind.

"Hey, Claud," she muttered and pushed his shoulder.

Claud opened one pale baby blue eye.

She looked into it warily. He did not think about anything. He just went his way.

"Wha, whasit?" he said and closed the eye again.

"Nothing," she said. "Does your leg pain you?"

"Hurts like hell," Claud said.   135

"It'll quit terreckly," she said and lay back down. In a moment Claud was snoring again. For the rest of the afternoon they lay there. Claud slept. She scowled at the ceiling. Occasionally she raised her fist and made a small stabbing motion over her chest as if she was defending her innocence to invisible guests who were like the comforters of Job, reasonable-seeming but wrong.

About five-thirty Claud stirred. "Got to go after those niggers," he sighed, not moving.

She was looking straight up as if there were unintelligible handwriting on the ceiling. The protuberance over her eye had turned a greenish-blue. "Listen here," she said.

"What?"   140

"Kiss me."

Claud leaned over and kissed her loudly on the mouth. He pinched her side and their hands interlocked. Her expression of ferocious concentration did not change. Claud got up, groaning and growling, and limped off. She continued to study the ceiling.

She did not get up until she heard the pick-up truck coming back with the Negroes. Then she rose and thrust her feet in her brown oxfords, which she did not bother to lace, and stumped out onto the back porch and got her red plastic bucket. She emptied a tray of ice cubes into it and filled it half full of water and went out into the back yard. Every afternoon after Claud brought the hands in, one of the boys helped him put out hay and the rest waited in the back of the truck until he was ready to take them home. The truck was parked in the shade under one of the hickory trees.

"Hi yawl this evening?" Mrs. Turpin asked grimly, appearing with the bucket and the dipper. There were three women and a boy in the truck.

"Us doin nicely," the oldest woman said. "Hi you doin?" and her gaze   145
struck immediately on the dark lump on Mrs. Turpin's forehead. "You done fell down, ain't you?" she asked in a solicitous voice. The old woman was dark and almost toothless. She had on an old felt hat of Claud's set back on her head. The other two women were younger and lighter and they both had new bright green sunhats. One of them had hers on her head; the other had taken hers off and the boy was grinning beneath it.

Mrs. Turpin set the bucket down on the floor of the truck. "Yawl hep yourselves," she said. She looked around to make sure Claud had gone. "No, I didn't fall down," she said, folding her arms. "It was something worse than that."

"Ain't nothing bad happen to you!" the old woman said. She said it as if they all knew that Mrs. Turpin was protected in some special way by Divine Providence. "You just had you a little fall."

"We were in town at the doctor's office for where the cow kicked Mr. Turpin," Mrs. Turpin said in a flat tone that indicated they could leave off their foolishness. "And there was this girl there. A big fat girl with her face all broke out. I could look at that girl and tell she was peculiar but I couldn't tell how. And me and her mama was just talking and going along and all of a sudden WHAM! She throws this big book she was reading at me and . . ."

"Naw!" the old woman cried out.

"And then she jumps over the table and commences to choke me." 150

"Naw!" they all exclaimed, "naw!"

"Hi come she do that?" the old woman asked. "What ail her?"

Mrs. Turpin only glared in front of her.

"Somethin ail her," the old woman said.

"They carried her off in an ambulance," Mrs. Turpin continued, "but 155 before she went she was rolling on the floor and they were trying to hold her down to give her a shot and she said something to me." She paused. "You know what she said to me?"

"What she say?" they asked.

"She said," Mrs. Turpin began, and stopped, her face very dark and heavy. The sun was getting whiter and whiter, blanching the sky overhead so that the leaves of the hickory tree were black in the face of it. She could not bring forth the words. "Something real ugly," she muttered.

"She sho shouldn't said nothin ugly to you," the old woman said. "You so sweet. You the sweetest lady I know."

"She pretty too," the one with the hat on said.

"And stout," the other one said. "I never knowed no sweeter white lady." 160

"That's the truth befo' Jesus," the old woman said. "Amen! You des as sweet and pretty as you can be."

Mrs. Turpin knew exactly how much Negro flattery was worth and it added to her rage. "She said," she began again and finished this time with a fierce rush of breath, "that I was an old wart hog from hell."

There was an astounded silence.

"Where she at?" the youngest woman cried in a piercing voice.

"Lemme see her. I'll kill her!" 165

"I'll kill her with you!" the other one cried.

"She b'long in the sylum," the old woman said emphatically. "You the sweetest white lady I know."

"She pretty too," the other two said. "Stout as she can be and sweet. Jesus satisfied with her!"

"Deed he is," the woman declared.

Idiots! Mrs. Turpin growled to herself. You could never say anything intel- 170 ligent to a nigger. You could talk at them but not with them. "Yawl ain't drunk your water," she said shortly. "Leave the bucket in the truck when you're finished with it. I got more to do than just stand around and pass the time of day," and she moved off and into the house.

She stood for a moment in the middle of the kitchen. The dark protuberance over her eye looked like a miniature tornado cloud which might any moment sweep across the horizon of her brow. Her lower lip protruded dangerously. She squared her massive shoulders. Then she marched into the front of the house and out the side door and started down the road to the pig parlor. She had the look of a woman going single-handed, weaponless, into battle.

The sun was deep yellow now like a harvest moon and was riding westward very fast over the far tree line as if it meant to reach the hogs before she did.

The road was rutted and she kicked several good-sized stones out of her path as she strode along. The pig parlor was on a little knoll at the end of a lane that ran off from the side of the barn. It was a square of concrete as large as a small room, with a board fence about four feet high around it. The concrete floor sloped slightly so that the hog wash could drain off into a trench where it was carried to the field for fertilizer. Claud was standing on the outside, on the edge of the concrete, hanging onto the top board, hosing down the floor inside. The hose was connected to the faucet of a water trough nearby.

Mrs. Turpin climbed up beside him and glowered down at the hogs inside. There were seven long-snouted bristly shoats in it—tan with liver-colored spots—and an old sow a few weeks off from farrowing. She was lying on her side grunting. The shoats were running about shaking themselves like idiot children, their little slit pig eyes searching the floor for anything left. She had read that pigs were the most intelligent animal. She doubted it. They were supposed to be smarter than dogs. There had even been a pig astronaut. He had performed his assignment perfectly but died of a heart attack afterwards because they left him in his electric suit, sitting upright throughout his examination when naturally a hog should be on all fours.

A-gruntin and a-rootin and a-groanin.

"Gimme that hose," she said, yanking it away from Claud. "Go on and carry them niggers home and then get off that leg." 175

"You look like you might have swallowed a mad dog," Claud observed, but he got down and limped off. He paid no attention to her humors.

Until he was out of earshot, Mrs. Turpin stood on the side of the pen, holding the hose and pointing the stream of water at the hind quarters of any shoat that looked as if it might try to lie down. When he had had time to get over the hill, she turned her head slightly and her wrathful eyes scanned the path. He was nowhere in sight. She turned back again and seemed to gather herself up. Her shoulders rose and she drew in her breath.

"What do you send me a message like that for?" she said in a low fierce voice, barely above a whisper but with the force of a shout in its concentrated fury. "How am I a hog and me both? How am I saved and from hell too?" Her free fist was knotted and with the other she gripped the hose, blindly pointing the stream of water in and out of the eye of the old sow whose outraged squeal she did not hear.

The pig parlor commanded a view of the back pasture where their twenty beef cows were gathered around the hay-bales Claud and the boy had put out. The freshly cut pasture sloped down to the highway. Across it was their cotton field and beyond that a dark green dusty wood which they owned as well. The sun was behind the wood, very red, looking over the paling of the trees like a farmer inspecting his own hogs.

"Why me?" she rumbled. "It's no trash around here, black or white, that I 180 haven't given to. And break my back to the bone every day working. And do for the church."

She appeared to be the right size woman to command the arena before her. "How am I a hog?" she demanded. "Exactly how am I like them?" and she jabbed the stream of water at the shoats. "There was plenty of trash there. It didn't have to be me.

"If you like trash better, go get yourself some trash then," she railed. "You could have made me trash. Or a nigger. If trash is what you wanted why didn't you make me trash?" She shook her fist with the hose in it and a watery snake appeared momentarily in the air. "I could quit working and take it easy and be filthy," she growled. "Lounge about the sidewalks all day drinking root beer. Dip snuff and spit in every puddle and have it all over my face. I could be nasty.

"Or you could have made me a nigger. It's too late for me to be a nigger," she said with deep sarcasm, "but I could act like one. Lay down in the middle of the road and stop traffic. Roll on the ground."

In the deepening light everything was taking on a mysterious hue. The pasture was growing a peculiar glassy green and the streak of highway had turned lavender. She braced herself for a final assault and this time her voice rolled out over the pasture. "Go on," she yelled, "call me a hog! Call me a hog again. From hell. Call me a wart hog from hell. Put that bottom rail on top. There'll still be a top and bottom!"

A garbled echo returned to her.   185

A final surge of fury shook her and she roared, "Who do you think you are?"

The color of everything, field and crimson sky, burned for a moment with a transparent intensity. The question carried over the pasture and across the highway and the cotton field and returned to her clearly like an answer from beyond the wood.

She opened her mouth but no sound came out of it.

A tiny truck, Claud's, appeared on the highway, heading rapidly out of sight. Its gears scraped thinly. It looked like a child's toy. At any moment a bigger truck might smash into it and scatter Claud's and the niggers' brains all over the road.

Mrs. Turpin stood there, her gaze fixed on the highway, all her muscles   190
rigid, until in five or six minutes the truck reappeared, returning. She waited until it had had time to turn into their own road. Then like a monumental statue coming to life, she bent her head slowly and gazed, as if through the very heart of mystery, down into the pig parlor at the hogs. They had settled all in one corner around the old sow who was grunting softly. A red glow suffused them. They appeared to pant with a secret life.

Until the sun slipped finally behind the tree line, Mrs. Turpin remained there with her gaze bent to them as if she were absorbing some abysmal life-giving knowledge. At last she lifted her head. There was only a purple streak in the sky, cutting through a field of crimson and leading, like an extension of the highway, into the descending dusk. She raised her hands from the side of the pen in a gesture hieratic and profound. A visionary light settled in her eyes. She saw the streak as a vast swinging bridge extending upward from the earth through a field of living fire. Upon it a vast horde of souls were rumbling toward heaven. There were whole companies of white-trash, clean for the first time in their lives, and bands of black niggers in white robes, and battalions of freaks and lunatics shouting and clapping and leaping like frogs. And bringing up the end of the procession was a tribe of people whom she recognized at once as those who, like herself and Claud, had always had a little of everything and the God-given wit to use it right. She leaned forward to observe them closer. They were marching behind the others with great dignity, accountable as they had always been for good order and common sense and respectable behavior. They alone were on key. Yet she could see by their shocked and altered faces that even their virtues were being burned away. She lowered her hands and gripped the rail of the hog pen, her eyes small but fixed unblinkingly on what lay ahead. In a moment the vision faded but she remained where she was, immobile.

At length she got down and turned off the faucet and made her slow way on the darkening path to the house. In the woods around her the invisible cricket choruses had struck up, but what she heard were the voices of the souls climbing upward into the starry field and shouting hallelujah.

CONSIDERATIONS FOR CRITICAL THINKING AND WRITING

1. **FIRST RESPONSE.** Does your attitude toward Mrs. Turpin change or remain the same during the story? Do you *like* her more at some points than at others? Explain why.

2. Why is it appropriate that the two major settings for the action in this story are a doctor's waiting room and a "pig parlor"?

3. How does Mrs. Turpin's treatment of her husband help to characterize her?

4. Mrs. Turpin notices people's shoes. What does this and her thoughts about "classes of people" (para. 24) reveal about her? How does she see herself in relation to other people?

5. Why does Mary Grace attack Mrs. Turpin?

6. Why is it significant that the book Mary Grace reads is *Human Development*? What is the significance of her name?

7. What does the background music played on the radio contribute to the story?

8. To whom does Mrs. Turpin address this anguished question: "What do you send me a message [Mary Grace's whispered words telling her "Go back to hell where you came from, you old wart hog"] like that for?" (para. 178). Why is Mrs. Turpin so angry and bewildered?

9. What is the "abysmal life-giving knowledge" that Mrs. Turpin discovers in the next to the last paragraph? Why is it "abysmal"? How is it "life-giving"?

10. Given the serious theme, consider whether the story's humor is appropriate.

11. When Mrs. Turpin returns home bruised, a hired African American woman tells her that nothing really "bad" happened: "You just had you a little fall" (para. 147). Pay particular attention to the suggestive language of this sentence, and discuss its significance in relation to the rest of the story.

12. **CRITICAL STRATEGIES.** Choose a critical approach from Chapter 53, "Critical Strategies for Reading," that you think is particularly useful for explaining the themes of this story.

CONNECTIONS TO OTHER SELECTIONS

1. Compare and contrast Mary Grace with Hulga of "Good Country People."

2. Explain how "Revelation" could be used as a title for any of the O'Connor stories you have read.

3. Discuss Mrs. Turpin's prideful hypocrisy in connection with the racial attitudes expressed by the white men at the "smoker" in Ellison's "Battle Royal" (p. 277). How do pride and personal illusions inform these characters' racial attitudes?

4. Explore the nature of the "revelation" in O'Connor's story and in John Updike's "A & P" (p. 733).

Perspectives on O'Connor

FLANNERY O'CONNOR

On Faith 1955

I write the way I do because (not though) I am a Catholic. This is a fact and nothing covers it like the bald statement. However, I am a Catholic peculiarly possessed of the modern consciousness, the thing Jung° describes as unhistorical, solitary, and guilty. To possess this within the Church is to bear a burden, the necessary burden for the conscious Catholic. It's to feel the contemporary situation at the ultimate level. I think that the Church is the only thing that is going to make the terrible world we are coming to endurable; the only thing that makes the Church endurable is that it is somehow the body of Christ and that on this we are fed. It seems to be a fact that you suffer as much from the Church as for it but if you believe in the divinity of Christ, you have to cherish the world at the same time that you struggle to endure it. This may explain the lack of bitterness in the stories.

From a letter to "A," July 20, 1955, in *The Habit of Being*

Jung: Carl Jung (1875–1961), a Swiss psychiatrist.

CONSIDERATIONS FOR CRITICAL THINKING AND WRITING

1. Consider how O'Connor's fiction expresses her belief that "you have to cherish the world at the same time that you struggle to endure it."
2. Do you agree that "bitterness" is absent from O'Connor's stories? Explain why or why not.

FLANNERY O'CONNOR

On the Materials of Fiction 1969

The beginning of human knowledge is through the senses, and the fiction writer begins where human perception begins. He appeals through the senses, and you cannot appeal to the senses with abstractions. It is a good deal easier for most people to state an abstract idea than to describe and thus re-create some object that they actually see. But the world of the fiction writer is full of matter, and this is what the beginning fiction writers are very loath to create. They are concerned primarily with unfleshed ideas and emotions. They are apt to be reformers and to want to write because they are possessed not by a story but by the bare bones of some abstract notion. They are conscious of problems, not of people, of questions and issues, not of the texture of existence, of case histories and of everything that has a sociological smack, instead of with all those concrete details of life that make actual the mystery of our position on earth. . . .

One of the most common and saddest spectacles is that of a person of really fine sensibility and acute psychological perception trying to write fiction by using these [abstract] qualities alone. This type of writer will put down one intensely emotional or keenly perceptive sentence after the other, and the result will be complete dullness. The fact is that the materials of the fiction writer are the humblest. Fiction is about everything human and we are made out of dust, and if you scorn getting yourself dusty, then you shouldn't try to write fiction. It's not a grand enough job for you.

From "The Nature and Aim of Fiction" in *Mystery and Manners*

CONSIDERATIONS FOR CRITICAL THINKING AND WRITING

1. Explain O'Connor's idea that "the materials of the fiction writer are the humblest" (para. 2) by reference to the materials and details of her stories.

2. Choose a substantial paragraph from an O'Connor story and describe how it "appeals through the senses" (para. 1).

3. Write an essay in which you agree or disagree with the following statement: Hawthorne's fiction is a good example of the kinds of mistakes that O'Connor attributes to a beginning fiction writer.

FLANNERY O'CONNOR

On the Use of Exaggeration and Distortion   1969

When I write a novel in which the central action is a baptism, I am very well aware that for a majority of my readers, baptism is a meaningless rite, and so in my novel I have to see that this baptism carries enough awe and mystery to jar the reader into some kind of emotional recognition of its significance. To this end I have to bend the whole novel — its language, its structure, its action. I have to make the reader feel, in his bones if nowhere else, that something is going on here that counts. Distortion in this case is an instrument; exaggeration has a purpose, and the whole structure of the story or novel has been made what it is because of belief. This is not the kind of distortion that destroys; it is the kind that reveals, or should reveal.

From "Novelist and Believer" in *Mystery and Manners*

CONSIDERATIONS FOR CRITICAL THINKING AND WRITING

1. It has been observed that in many of O'Connor's works the central action takes the form of some kind of "baptism" that initiates, tests, or purifies a character. Select a story that illustrates this generalization, and explain how the conflict results in a kind of baptism.

2. O'Connor says that exaggeration and distortion reveal something in her stories. What is the effect of such exaggeration and distortion? Typically,

what is revealed by it? Focus your comments on a single story to illustrate your points.

3. Do you think that O'Connor's stories have anything to offer a reader who has no religious faith? Explain why or why not.

FLANNERY O'CONNOR

On Theme and Symbol   1969

When you can state the theme of a story, when you can separate it from the story itself, then you can be sure the story is not a very good one. The meaning of a story has to be embodied in it, has to be made concrete in it. A story is a way to say something that can't be said any other way, and it takes every word in the story to say what the meaning is. You tell a story because a statement would be inadequate. When anybody asks what a story is about, the only proper thing is to tell him to read the story. The meaning of fiction is not abstract meaning but experienced meaning, and the purpose of making statements about the meaning of a story is only to help you to experience that meaning more fully.

The peculiar problem of the short-story writer is how to make the action he describes reveal as much of the mystery of existence as possible. He has only a short space to do it in and he can't do it by statement. He has to do it by showing, not by saying, and by showing the concrete — so that his problem is really how to make the concrete work double time for him.

In good fiction, certain of the details will tend to accumulate meaning from the action of the story itself, and when this happens they become symbolic in the way they work. I once wrote a story called "Good Country People," in which a lady Ph.D. has her wooden leg stolen by a Bible salesman whom she has tried to seduce. Now I'll admit that, paraphrased in this way, the situation is simply a low joke. The average reader is pleased to observe anybody's wooden leg being stolen. But without ceasing to appeal to him and without making any statements of high intention, this story does manage to operate at another level of experience, by letting the wooden leg accumulate meaning. Early in the story, we're presented with the fact that the Ph.D. is spiritually as well as physically crippled. She believes in nothing but her own belief in nothing, and we perceive that there is a wooden part of her soul that corresponds to her wooden leg. Now of course this is never stated. The fiction writer states as little as possible. The reader makes this connection from things he is shown. He may not even know that he makes the connection, but the connection is there nevertheless and it has its effect on him. As the story goes on, the wooden leg continues to accumulate meaning. The reader learns how the girl feels about her leg, how her mother feels about it, and how the country woman on the place feels about it; and finally, by the time the Bible salesman comes along, the leg has accumulated so much meaning that it is, as the saying goes, loaded. And when the Bible salesman steals it, the reader realizes that he has taken away part of the girl's personality and has revealed her deeper affliction to her for the first time.

If you want to say that the wooden leg is a symbol, you can say that. But it is a wooden leg first, and as a wooden leg it is absolutely necessary to the story. It has its place on the literal level of the story, but it operates in depth as well as on the surface. It increases the story in every direction, and this is essentially the way a story escapes being short.

Now a little might be said about the way in which this happens. I wouldn't want you to think that in that story I sat down and said, "I am now going to write a story about a Ph.D. with a wooden leg, using the wooden leg as a symbol for another kind of affliction." I doubt myself if many writers know what they are going to do when they start out. When I started writing that story, I didn't know there was going to be a Ph.D. with a wooden leg in it. I merely found myself one morning writing a description of two women that I knew something about, and before I realized it, I had equipped one of them with a daughter with a wooden leg. As the story progressed, I brought in the Bible salesman, but I had no idea what I was going to do with him. I didn't know he was going to steal that wooden leg until ten or twelve lines before he did it, but when I found out that this was what was going to happen, I realized that it was inevitable. This is a story that produces a shock for the reader, and I think one reason for this is that it produced a shock for the writer.

Now despite the fact that this story came about in this seemingly mindless fashion, it is a story that almost no rewriting was done on. It is a story that was under control throughout the writing of it, and it might be asked how this kind of control comes about, since it is not entirely conscious.

From "Writing Short Stories" in *Mystery and Manners*

CONSIDERATIONS FOR CRITICAL THINKING AND WRITING

1. Why is a "statement" (para. 1) inadequate to convey the meaning of a story?
2. O'Connor describes how the wooden leg "continues to accumulate meaning" (para. 3) in "Good Country People" (p. 460). Choose another story by O'Connor and explain how something specific and concrete is invested with symbolic meaning.

JOSEPHINE HENDIN (B. 1946)
On O'Connor's Refusal to "Do Pretty" 1970

There is, in the memory of one Milledgeville matron, the image of O'Connor at nineteen or twenty who, when invited to a wedding shower for an old family friend, remained standing, her back pressed against the wall, scowling at the group of women who had sat down to lunch. Neither the devil nor her mother could make her say yes to this fiercely gracious female society, but Flannery O'Connor could not say no even in a whisper. She could not refuse the invitation but she would not accept it either. She did not exactly "fuss" but neither did she "do pretty."

From *The World of Flannery O'Connor*

CONSIDERATIONS FOR CRITICAL THINKING AND WRITING

1. How is O'Connor's personality revealed in this anecdote about her ambivalent response to society? Allow the description to be suggestive for you, and flesh out a brief portrait of her.

2. Consider how this personality makes itself apparent in any one of O'Connor's stories you have read. How does the anecdote help to characterize the narrator's voice in the story?

3. To what extent do you think biographical details such as this — assuming the Milledgeville matron's memory to be accurate — can shed light on a writer's works?

CLAIRE KATZ (B. 1935)
The Function of Violence in O'Connor's Fiction   *1974*

From the moment the reader enters O'Connor's backwoods, he is poised on the edge of a pervasive violence. Characters barely contain their rage; images reflect a hostile nature; and even the Christ to whom the characters are ultimately driven is a threatening figure . . . full of the apocalyptic wrath of the Old Testament.

O'Connor's conscious purpose is evident enough . . . : to reveal the need for grace in a world grotesque without a transcendent context. "I have found that my subject in fiction is the action of grace in territory largely held by the devil," she wrote [in *Mystery and Manners*], and she was not vague about what the devil is: "an evil intelligence determined on its own supremacy." It would seem that for O'Connor, given the fact of original Sin, any intelligence determined on its own supremacy was intrinsically evil. For in each work, it is the impulse toward secular autonomy, the smug confidence that human nature is perfectible by its own efforts, that she sets out to destroy, through an act of violence so intense that the character is rendered helpless, a passive victim of a superior power. Again and again she creates a fiction in which a character attempts to live autonomously, to define himself and his values, only to be jarred back to what she calls "reality" — the recognition of helplessness in the face of contingency, and the need for absolute submission to the power of Christ.

From "Flannery O'Connor's Rage of Vision"
in *American Literature*

CONSIDERATIONS FOR CRITICAL THINKING AND WRITING

1. Choose an O'Connor story, and explain how grace — the divine influence from God that redeems a person — is used in it to transform a character.

2. Which O'Connor characters can be accurately described as having an "evil intelligence determined on its own supremacy" (para. 2)? Choose one character, and write an essay explaining how this description is central to the conflict of the story.

3. Compare an O'Connor story with one of Hawthorne's "in which a character attempts to live autonomously, to define himself and his values, only to be jarred back to . . . 'reality'—the recognition of helplessness in the face of contingency . . ." (para. 2).

EDWARD KESSLER (B. 1927)
On O'Connor's Use of History   1986

In company with other Southern writers . . . who aspire to embrace a lost tradition and look on history as a repository of value, Flannery O'Connor seems a curious anomaly. She wrote of herself: "I am a Catholic peculiarly possessed of the modern consciousness . . . unhistorical, solitary, and guilty." Likewise her characters comprise a gallery of misfits isolated in a present and sentenced to a lifetime of exile from the human community. In O'Connor's fiction, the past neither justifies nor even explains what is happening. If she believed, for example, in the importance of the past accident that maimed Joy in "Good Country People," she could have demonstrated how the event predetermined her present rejection of both human and external nature; but Joy's past is parenthetical: "Mrs. Hopewell excused this attitude because of the leg (which had been shot off in a hunting accident when Joy was ten)." Believing that humankind is fundamentally flawed, O'Connor spends very little time constructing a past for her characters. The cure is neither behind us nor before us but within us; therefore, the past—even historical time itself—supplies only a limited base for self-discovery.

From *Flannery O'Connor and the Language of Apocalypse*

CONSIDERATIONS FOR CRITICAL THINKING AND WRITING

1. Consider how O'Connor uses history in any one of her stories in this anthology and compare that "unhistorical" vision with Hawthorne's in "Young Goodman Brown" (p. 402) or "The Minister's Black Veil" (p. 411).

2. Write an essay in which you discuss Kessler's assertion that for O'Connor the "past is parenthetical," in contrast to most southern writers, who "embrace a lost tradition and look on history as a repository of value." For your point of comparison choose either William Faulkner's "A Rose for Emily" (p. 91) or "Barn Burning" (p. 503).

Time Magazine, on *A Good Man Is Hard to Find*   1962

Highly unladylike . . . a brutal irony, a slam-bang humor, and a style of writing as balefully direct as a death sentence.

From a *Time* magazine blurb quoted on the cover of the second American edition of *A Good Man Is Hard to Find*

1. How accurate do you think this blurb is in characterizing the three O'Connor stories in this chapter?

2. **CREATIVE RESPONSE.** Write your own blurb for the three stories and be prepared to justify your pithy description.

Two Complementary Critical Readings

A. R. COULTHARD (B. 1940)
On the Visionary Ending of "Revelation"　　　*1983*

The second part of the story does not keep pace with its rollicking opening, but its psychological realism gives Mrs. Turpin's ultimate redemption a hard-edged credibility. When the protagonist returns home, her first impulse is, quite naturally, to resist the message of grace brought by the girl: "'I am not,' she said tearfully, 'a wart hog. From hell.' But the denial had no force." Unable to reject the charge, Mrs. Turpin turns to resentment: "The message had been given to Ruby Turpin, a respectable, hard-working, church-going woman. The tears dried. Her eyes began to burn instead with wrath." Next she attempts to exorcise the girl's demonic words by confessing them to her black fieldhands:

> "She said," she began again and finished this time with a fierce rush of breath, "that I was an old wart hog from hell."
> There was an astounded silence.
> "Where she at?" the youngest woman cried in a piercing voice.
> "Lemme see her. I'll kill her!"
> "I'll kill her with you!" the other one cried.
> "She b'long in the sylum," the old woman said emphatically. "You the sweetest white lady I know."
> "She pretty too," the other two said. "Stout as she can be and sweet. Jesus satisfied with her!"
> "Deed he is," the woman declared.
> Idiots! Mrs. Turpin growled to herself.

This little scene is both funny and thematically significant. Mrs. Turpin's refusal to accept the phony image of herself as a good woman offered by the blacks is a step toward facing the truth.

Mrs. Turpin's next step is literal. She climbs the hill to the hogpen, apparently considering it the appropriate place to reason out the meaning of being called a wart hog from hell. Once there, Ruby gets right down to business: "What do you send me a message like that for?" she demands. "How am I a hog and me both?" Then she yells, "Go on, call me a hog! Call me a hog again. From hell. Call me a wart hog from hell." She ends her harangue by hilariously roaring at God, "Who do you think you are?" In this scene, Ruby begins to grow into a sympathetic, even lovable, character. As O'Connor said, "You got to be a very big woman to shout at the Lord across a hogpen." You also got to believe.

God answers Mrs. Turpin by sending her an epiphany which is so unobtrusively presented that at first it seems to be only description: "A tiny truck, Claud's, appeared on the highway, heading rapidly out of sight. Its gears scraped thinly. It looked like a child's toy. At any moment a bigger truck might smash into it and scatter Claud's and the niggers' brains all over the road." The answer to Ruby's question is that God is omnipotent and that Ruby, like all mortals, is an insignificant, vulnerable creature whose life can end at any moment. Her response to this new knowledge is immediate: "Then like a monumental statue coming to life, she bent her head slowly and gazed, as if through the very heart of mystery, down into the pig parlor at the hogs."

The story originally ended at this point, but O'Connor decided that "something else was needed." Fortunately, what she added is not a concluding mini-sermon but a supernatural vision which is perfectly in keeping with the seriocomic tone of the story:

> A visionary light settled in her eyes . . . a vast horde of souls were rumbling toward heaven. There were whole companies of white-trash, clean for the first time in their lives, and bands of black niggers in white robes, and battalions of freaks and lunatics shouting and clapping and leaping like frogs. And bringing up the end of the procession was a tribe of people whom she recognized at once as those . . . like herself and Claud. . . . They were marching behind the others with great dignity. . . . They alone were on key. Yet she could see by their shocked and altered faces that even their virtues were being burned away.

This vision demolishes Ruby's earlier neat ranking of people, and its concluding sentence, which could have quotation marks around "virtues," completes her education by telling her that no one deserves grace and that we receive it only because of God's mysterious mercy. The epiphany takes, and the story ends with Ruby, "her eyes small but fixed unblinkingly on what lay ahead," prepared to face a humbler and more demanding life.

Though at least one reader whom O'Connor respected found "Revelation" pessimistic and considered the protagonist evil, O'Connor's main worry was that the story would "be taken to be one designed to make fun of Ruby," probably because her weaknesses are so vividly shown. But the great achievement of the protagonist's characterization is that Ruby Turpin retains her humanity to the end and does not, upon receiving grace, turn into an inspirational symbol. At the same time, O'Connor has made her conversion believable by dramatizing it in action and dialogue consistent with both Mrs. Turpin's humorous traits and her serious role in the story. "Revelation" is not only a delightful comedy but a profound dramatization of redemption as well.

From American Literature

CONSIDERATIONS FOR CRITICAL THINKING AND WRITING

1. According to Coulthard, how does O'Connor avoid turning the end of the story into a "mini-sermon" (para. 4)?

2. How would your response to the story be different if it ended as O'Connor first intended it to — without the concluding paragraph? How would you regard Mrs. Turpin if this paragraph did not appear in the story?

3. Write an essay in response to this judgment of "Revelation": "Religion and comedy don't mix; therefore, the comic tone of 'Revelation' is inappropriate to the concluding religious epiphany."

MARSHALL BRUCE GENTRY (B. 1953)
On the Revised Ending of "Revelation"   *1986*

The precise significance of Mrs. Turpin's vision of hordes on a fiery bridge is not altogether a matter of critical agreement. And O'Connor's letters show her to have been inconsistent in her opinion of "Revelation" while she was writing it. It was the ending of the story that most troubled her, and the sequence of versions shows O'Connor trying to make clear that Ruby is not entirely corrupt. In a letter dated 25 December 1963, O'Connor mentioned that a friend who had read a draft of "Revelation" had called Mrs. Turpin "evil" and had suggested that O'Connor omit the final vision, which the friend considered to be a confirmation of Mrs. Turpin's evilness. O'Connor's reaction was, "I am not going to leave it out. I am going to deepen it so that there'll be no mistaking Ruby is not just an evil Glad Annie." As she finished revising the story, O'Connor made the final vision less obviously of Mrs. Turpin's making. One late draft, for example, contains the statement that the Turpins, "marching behind the others" toward heaven "with great dignity," were "driving them, in fact, ahead of themselves, still responsible as they had always been for good order and common sense and respectable behavior." In the published text, the Turpins are still at the end of the procession, but there is no mention of them "driving" the others on, and they are "accountable" rather than "still responsible." Another significant difference between the draft and the published text is the addition in the final version of the fact that Mrs. Turpin sees that her "virtues" are "being burned away." In both these revisions there is less emphasis on Mrs. Turpin's smug perspective, more emphasis on what shocks her.

The final version makes the vision more clearly redemptive, and one apparent implication of the revisions is that Mrs. Turpin's revelation is supernatural in origin. This implication is misleading, however; there is still much in Mrs. Turpin's vision to suggest that she produces it, and the primary effect of O'Connor's revisions is to make Mrs. Turpin's unconscious more clearly responsible for her vision of entry into a heavenly community. This view may seem peculiar when one considers Mrs. Turpin's bigotry and banality, but one's impression of that bigotry and banality is the result of the narrator's emphasis in describing Mrs. Turpin. The narrator emphasizes the ridiculous aspects of Mrs. Turpin rather than making fully apparent the tracks she has laid to carry herself to the oven in which individuality is renounced and the ideal of heavenly community achieved.

From *Flannery O'Connor's Religion of the Grotesque*

CONSIDERATIONS FOR CRITICAL THINKING AND WRITING

1. What reservations, according to Gentry, did O'Connor have about the story's ending? For what purpose did O'Connor revise the manuscript?

2. How does Gentry's reading of the ending compare with Coulthard's? Which reading do you find closer to your own? Why?

3. Write an essay that considers Gentry's final charge that Mrs. Turpin appears "ridiculous" at the end of the story in contrast to Coulthard's assessment that she "retains her humanity."

[Web] Research Flannery O'Connor or take quizzes on her works at bedfordstmartins.com/meyerlit.

SUGGESTED TOPICS FOR LONGER PAPERS

1. Discuss O'Connor's use of humor in the stories you've read in this chapter. As the basis of your discussion consider at least one humorous moment or scene in each story and characterize the tone of her humor. What generalizations can you make about the tone of the humor in her stories? How does O'Connor use humor to affect the reader's understanding of her themes?

2. O'Connor's fiction is often populated with peculiar characters who seem to demand psychological interpretation. O'Connor, however, made clear in a March 28, 1961, letter that "I am not interested in abnormal psychology." Research psychological readings of one of the stories in this chapter and argue for or against reading her characters from a psychological point of view. You may need to do your own psychological analysis of a character or two to argue for or against its relevance to the story.

13

A CRITICAL CASE STUDY

William Faulkner's "Barn Burning"

The writer's only responsibility is to his art. . . . He has a dream. It anguishes him so much he must get rid of it. He has no peace until then.
— WILLIAM FAULKNER

It is the writer's privilege to help man endure by lifting his heart.
— WILLIAM FAULKNER

This chapter offers several critical approaches to a well-known short story by William Faulkner. Though there are many possible critical approaches to any given work (see Chapter 53, "Critical Strategies for Reading," for a discussion of a variety of methods), and there are numerous studies of Faulkner from formalist, biographical, historical, mythological, psychological, sociological, and other perspectives, it is worth noting that each reading of a work or writer is predicated on accepting certain assumptions about literature and life. Those assumptions or premises may be complementary or mutually exclusive, and they may appeal to you or appall you. What is interesting, however, is how various approaches reveal the text (as well as its readers and critics) by calling attention to certain elements or leaving others out. The following critical excerpts suggest only a portion of the range of

William Faulkner

possibilities, but even a small representation of approaches can help you to raise new questions, develop insights, recognize problems, and suggest additional ways of reading the text.

WILLIAM FAULKNER (1897–1962)

A biographical note for William Faulkner appears on page 90, before his story "A Rose for Emily." In "Barn Burning" Faulkner portrays a young boy's love and revulsion for his father, a frightening man who lives by a "ferocious conviction in the rightness of his own actions."

William Faulkner, Author Photo for *Sanctuary*, 1931. William Faulkner (1897–1962) was born in New Albany, Mississippi, the first of four sons born to Murry and Maud Butler Falkner (as their name was then spelled). He was named after his deceased great-grandfather, William Clark Falkner—family patriarch, lawyer, politician, planter, businessman, railroad financier, and best-selling writer (*The White Rose of Memphis*)—who was known as the "Old Colonel." When Faulkner was five, his family moved forty miles west to the town of Oxford in Lafayette County. Following the move, Murry's father abruptly sold the railroad founded by the "Old Colonel," and Murry was forced to take a series of jobs in Oxford to support his family. Oxford and its surrounding county—its landscape, history, and inhabitants—became a rich source for William Faulkner's writing and the inspiration for his fictional Yoknapatawpha County. "Beginning with *Sartoris* [1929, his third novel]," Faulkner wrote, "I discovered that my own little postage stamp of native soil was worth writing about, and that I would never live long enough to exhaust it." (Top, p. 501) Shown here is Relbue Price's Oxford Hardware Store, the business that Murry Falkner became affiliated with following the decline of his once-successful livery stable business. (Bottom, p. 501) Across the street from the hardware store was Goodwin and Brown's Commissary, a general store that Faulkner would have visited as a boy.

Courtesy of the Colfield Collection, Southern Media Archive, University of Mississippi. Special Collections.

The Oxford Hardware Store, Oxford, Mississippi.

Goodwin and Brown's Commissary, Oxford, Mississippi.

Rowan Oak. In 1930, Faulkner purchased a large, dilapidated plantation house in Oxford known as "The Bailey Place." The house predated the Civil War and was set on thirty-two acres (known as "Bailey's Woods") where Faulkner had played as a boy. He renamed the house "Rowan Oak," and from 1930 on, he did most of his writing here. Despite the financial strain that Rowan Oak presented, the house and land also represented for Faulkner the reclaiming of the genteel life of "The Colonel": Faulkner would never inherit a plantation, so he bought one. Courtesy of the Library of Congress.

William Faulkner (May 6, 1955). The author in the spot where he did most of his writing— his living room at Rowan Oak—bent over a glass-topped table with a pen.
© Bettmann/CORBIS.

Barn Burning

The store in which the Justice of the Peace's court was sitting smelled of cheese. The boy, crouched on his nail keg at the back of the crowded room, knew he smelled cheese, and more: from where he sat he could see the ranked shelves close-packed with the solid, squat, dynamic shapes of tin cans whose labels his stomach read, not from the lettering which meant nothing to his mind but from the scarlet devils and the silver curve of fish — this, the cheese which he knew he smelled and the hermetic meat which his intestines believed he smelled coming in intermittent gusts momentary and brief between the other constant one, the smell and sense just a little of fear because mostly of despair and grief, the old fierce pull of blood. He could not see the table where the Justice sat and before which his father and his father's enemy (*our enemy* he thought in that despair; *ourn! mine and hisn both! He's my father!*) stood, but he could hear them, the two of them that is, because his father had said no word yet:

"But what proof have you, Mr. Harris?"

"I told you. The hog got into my corn. I caught it up and sent it back to him. He had no fence that would hold it. I told him so, warned him. The next time I put the hog in my pen. When he came to get it I gave him enough wire to patch up his pen. The next time I put the hog up and kept it. I rode down to his house and saw the wire I gave him still rolled on to the spool in his yard. I told him he could have the hog when he paid me a dollar pound fee. That evening a nigger came with the dollar and got the hog. He was a strange nigger. He said, 'He say to tell you wood and hay kin burn.' I said, 'What?' 'That whut he say to tell you,' the nigger said. 'Wood and hay kin burn.' That night my barn burned. I got the stock out but I lost the barn."

"Where is the nigger? Have you got him?"

"He was a strange nigger, I tell you. I don't know what became of him." 5

"But that's not proof. Don't you see that's not proof?"

"Get that boy up here. He knows." For a moment the boy thought too that the man meant his older brother until Harris said, "Not him. The little one. The boy," and, crouching, small for his age, small and wiry like his father, in patched and faded jeans even too small for him, with straight, uncombed, brown hair and eyes gray and wild as storm scud, he saw the men between himself and the table part and become a lane of grim faces, at the end of which he saw the Justice, a shabby, collarless, graying man in spectacles, beckoning him. He felt no floor under his bare feet; he seemed to walk beneath the palpable weight of the grim turning faces. His father, stiff in his black Sunday coat donned not for the trial but for the moving, did not even look at him. *He aims for me to lie,* he thought, again with that frantic grief and despair. *And I will have to do hit.*

"What's your name, boy?" the Justice said.

"Colonel Sartoris Snopes," the boy whispered.

"Hey?" the Justice said. "Talk louder. Colonel Sartoris? I reckon anybody 10 named for Colonel Sartoris in this country can't help but tell the truth, can they?" The boy said nothing. *Enemy! Enemy!* he thought; for a moment he could not even see, could not see that the Justice's face was kindly nor discern that his voice was troubled when he spoke to the man named Harris: "Do you want me to question this boy?" But he could hear, and during those subsequent long seconds while there was absolutely no sound in the crowded little room save that of quiet and intent breathing it was as if he had swung outward at the end of a grape vine, over a ravine, and at the top of the swing had been caught in a prolonged instant of mesmerized gravity, weightless in time.

"No!" Harris said violently, explosively. "Damnation! Send him out of here!" Now time, the fluid world, rushed beneath him again, the voices coming to him again through the smell of cheese and sealed meat, the fear and despair and the old grief of blood:

"This case is closed. I can't find against you, Snopes, but I can give you advice. Leave this country and don't come back to it."

His father spoke for the first time, his voice cold and harsh, level, without emphasis: "I aim to. I don't figure to stay in a country among people who . . ." he said something unprintable and vile, addressed to no one.

"That'll do," the Justice said. "Take your wagon and get out of this country before dark. Case dismissed."

His father turned, and he followed the stiff black coat, the wiry figure   15
walking a little stiffly from where a Confederate provost's man's musket ball had taken him in the heel on a stolen horse thirty years ago, followed the two backs now, since his older brother had appeared from somewhere in the crowd, no taller than the father but thicker, chewing tobacco steadily, between the two lines of grim-faced men and out of the store and across the worn gallery and down the sagging steps and among the dogs and half-grown boys in the mild May dust, where as he passed a voice hissed:

"Barn burner!"

Again he could not see, whirling; there was a face in a red haze, moonlike, bigger than the full moon, the owner of it half again his size, he leaping in the red haze toward the face, feeling no blow, feeling no shock when his head struck the earth, scrabbling up and leaping again, feeling no blow this time either and tasting no blood, scrabbling up to see the other boy in full flight and himself already leaping into pursuit as his father's hand jerked him back, the harsh, cold voice speaking above him: "Go get in the wagon."

It stood in a grove of locusts and mulberries across the road. His two hulking sisters in their Sunday dresses and his mother and her sister in calico and sunbonnets were already in it, sitting on or among the sorry residue of the dozen and more movings which even the boy could remember — the battered stove, the broken beds and chairs, the clock inlaid with mother-of-pearl, which would not run, stopped at some fourteen minutes past two o'clock of a dead and forgotten day and time, which had been his mother's dowry. She was crying, though when she saw him she drew her sleeve across her face and began to descend from the wagon. "Get back," the father said.

"He's hurt. I got to get some water and wash his . . ."

"Get back in the wagon," his father said. He got in too, over the tail-gate.   20
His father mounted to the seat where the older brother already sat and struck the gaunt mules two savage blows with the peeled willow, but without heat. It was not even sadistic; it was exactly that same quality which in later years would cause his descendants to over-run the engine before putting a motor car in motion, striking and reining back in the same movement. The wagon went on, the store with its quiet crowd of grimly watching men dropped behind; a curve in the road hid it. *Forever* he thought. *Maybe he's done satisfied now, now that he has* . . . stopping himself, not to say it aloud even to himself. His mother's hand touched his shoulder.

"Does hit hurt?" she said.

"Naw," he said. "Hit don't hurt. Lemme be."

"Can't you wipe some of the blood off before hit dries?"

"I'll wash to-night," he said. "Lemme be, I tell you."

The wagon went on. He did not know where they were going. None of them ever did or ever asked, because it was always somewhere, always a house of sorts waiting for them a day or two days or even three days away. Likely his father had already arranged to make a crop on another farm before he . . . Again he had to stop himself. He (the father) always did. There was something about his wolflike independence and even courage when the advantage was at least neutral which impressed strangers, as if they got from his latent ravening ferocity not so much a sense of dependability as a feeling that his ferocious conviction in the rightness of his own actions would be of advantage to all whose interest lay with his.

That night they camped, in a grove of oaks and beeches where a spring ran. The nights were still cool and they had a fire against it, of a rail lifted from a nearby fence and cut into lengths — a small fire, neat, niggard almost, a shrewd fire; such fires were his father's habit and custom always, even in freezing weather. Older, the boy might have remarked this and wondered why not a big one; why should not a man who had not only seen the waste and extravagance of war, but who had in his blood an inherent voracious prodigality with material not his own, have burned everything in sight? Then he might have gone a step farther and thought that that was the reason: that niggard blaze was the living fruit of nights passed during those four years in the woods hiding from all men, blue or gray, with his strings of horses (captured horses, he called them). And older still, he might have divined the true reason: that the element of fire spoke to some deep mainspring of his father's being, as the element of steel or of powder spoke to other men, as the one weapon for the preservation of integrity, else breath were not worth the breathing, and hence to be regarded with respect and used with discretion.

But he did not think this now and he had seen those same niggard blazes all his life. He merely ate his supper beside it and was already half asleep over his iron plate when his father called him, and once more he followed the stiff back, the stiff and ruthless limp, up the slope and on to the starlit road where, turning, he could see his father against the stars but without face or depth — a shape black, flat, and bloodless as though cut from tin in the iron folds of the frockcoat which had not been made for him, the voice harsh like tin and without heat like tin:

"You were fixing to tell them. You would have told him."

He didn't answer. His father struck him with the flat of his hand on the side of the head, hard but without heat, exactly as he had struck the two mules at the store, exactly as he would strike either of them with any stick in order to kill a horse fly, his voice still without heat or anger. "You're getting to be a man. You got to learn. You got to learn to stick to your own blood or you ain't going to have any blood to stick to you. Do you think either of them, any man there this morning, would? Don't you know all they wanted was a chance to get at me because they knew I had them beat? Eh?" Later, twenty years later, he was to tell himself, "If I had said they wanted only truth, justice, he would have hit me again." But now he said nothing. He was not crying. He just stood there. "Answer me," his father said.

"Yes," he whispered. His father turned.

"Get on to bed. We'll be there tomorrow."

Tomorrow they were there. In the early afternoon the wagon stopped before a paintless two-room house identical almost with the dozen others it had stopped before even in the boy's ten years, and again, as on the other dozen occasions, his mother and aunt got down and began to unload the wagon, although his two sisters and his father and brother had not moved.

"Likely hit ain't fitten for hawgs," one of the sisters said.

"Nevertheless, fit it will and you'll hog it and like it," his father said. "Get out of them chairs and help your Ma unload."

The two sisters got down, big, bovine, in a flutter of cheap ribbons; one of them drew from the jumbled wagon bed a battered lantern, the other a worn broom. His father handed the reins to the older son and began to climb stiffly over the wheel. "When they get unloaded, take the team to the barn and feed them." Then he said, and at first the boy thought he was still speaking to his brother: "Come with me."

"Me?" he said.

"Yes," his father said. "You."

"Abner," his mother said. His father paused and looked back — the harsh level stare beneath the shaggy, graying, irascible brows.

"I reckon I'll have a word with the man that aims to begin tomorrow owning me body and soul for the next eight months."

They went back up the road. A week ago — or before last night, that is — he would have asked where they were going, but not now. His father had struck him before last night but never before had he paused afterward to explain why; it was as if the blow and the following calm, outrageous voice still rang, repercussed, divulging nothing to him save the terrible handicap of being young, the light weight of his few years, just heavy enough to prevent his soaring free of the world as it seemed to be ordered but not heavy enough to keep him footed solid in it, to resist it and try to change the course of events.

Presently he could see the grove of oaks and cedars and the other flowering trees and shrubs where the house would be, though not the house yet. They walked beside a fence massed with honeysuckle and Cherokee roses and came to a gate swinging open between two brick pillars, and now, beyond a sweep of drive, he saw the house for the first time and at that instant he forgot his father and the terror and despair both, and even when he remembered his father again (who had not stopped) the terror and despair did not return. Because, for all the twelve movings, they had sojourned until now in a poor country, a land of small farms and fields and houses, and he had never seen a house like this before. *Hit's big as a courthouse* he thought quietly, with a surge of peace and joy whose reason he could not have thought into words, being too young for that: *They are safe from him. People whose lives are a part of this peace and dignity are beyond his touch, he no more to them than a buzzing wasp: capable of stinging for a little moment but that's all; the spell of this peace and dignity rendering even the barns and stable and cribs which belong to it impervious to the puny flames he might contrive . . .* this, the peace and joy, ebbing for an instant as he looked again at the stiff black back, the stiff and implacable limp of the figure which was not dwarfed by the house, for the reason that it had never looked big anywhere and which now, against the serene columned backdrop, had more than ever that impervious quality of something cut ruthlessly from tin, depthless, as though, sidewise to the sun, it would cast no shadow. Watching him, the boy remarked the absolutely undeviating course which his father held and saw the stiff foot come squarely down in a pile of fresh droppings where a horse had stood in the drive and which his father could have avoided by a simple change of stride. But it ebbed only for a moment, though he could not have thought this into words either, walking on in the spell of the house, which he could even want but without envy, without sorrow, certainly never with that ravening and jealous rage which unknown to him walked in the ironlike black coat before him: *Maybe he will feel it too. Maybe it will even change him now from what maybe he couldn't help but be.*

They crossed the portico. Now he could hear his father's stiff foot as it came down on the boards with clocklike finality, a sound out of all proportion to the displacement of the body it bore and which was not dwarfed either by the white door before it, as though it had attained to a sort of vicious and ravening minimum not to be dwarfed by anything — the flat, wide, black hat, the formal coat of broadcloth which had once been black but which had now that friction-glazed greenish cast of the bodies of old house flies, the lifted sleeve which was too large, the lifted hand like a curled claw. The door opened so promptly that the boy knew the Negro must have been watching them all the time, an old man with neat grizzled hair, in a linen jacket, who stood barring the door with his body, saying, "Wipe yo foots, white man, fo you come in here. Major ain't home nohow."

"Get out of my way, nigger," his father said, without heat too, flinging the door back and the Negro also and entering, his hat still on his head. And now the boy saw the prints of the stiff foot on the doorjamb and saw them appear on the pale rug behind the machinelike deliberation of the foot which seemed to bear (or transmit) twice the weight which the body compassed. The Negro was shouting "Miss Lula! Miss Lula!" somewhere behind them, then the boy, deluged as though by a warm wave by a suave turn of the carpeted stair and a pendant glitter of chandeliers and a mute gleam of gold frames, heard the swift feet and saw her too, a lady — perhaps he had never seen her like before either — in a gray, smooth gown with lace at the throat and an apron tied at the waist and the sleeves turned back, wiping cake or biscuit dough from her hands with a towel as she came up the hall, looking not at his father at all but at the tracks on the blond rug with an expression of incredulous amazement.

"I tried," the Negro cried. "I tole him to . . ."

"Will you please go away?" she said in a shaking voice. "Major de Spain is not at home. Will you please go away?" 45

His father had not spoken again. He did not speak again. He did not even look at her. He just stood stiff in the center of the rug, in his hat, the shaggy iron-gray brows twitching slightly above the pebble-colored eyes as he appeared to examine the house with brief deliberation. Then with the same deliberation he turned; the boy watched him pivot on the good leg and saw the stiff foot drag round the arc of the turning, leaving a final long and fading smear. His father never looked at it, he never once looked down at the rug. The Negro held the door. It closed behind them, upon the hysteric and indistinguishable woman-wail. His father stopped at the top of the steps and scraped his boot clean on the edge of it. At the gate he stopped again. He stood for a moment, planted stiffly on the stiff foot, looking back at the house. "Pretty and white, ain't it?" he said. "That's sweat. Nigger sweat. Maybe it ain't white enough yet to suit him. Maybe he wants to mix some white sweat with it."

Two hours later the boy was chopping wood behind the house within which his mother and aunt and the two sisters (the mother and aunt, not the two girls, he knew that; even at this distance and muffled by walls the flat loud voices of the two girls emanated an incorrigible idle inertia) were setting up the stove to prepare a meal; when he heard the hooves and saw the linen-clad man on a fine sorrel mare, whom he recognized even before he saw the rolled rug in front of the Negro youth following on a fat bay carriage horse — a suffused, angry face vanishing, still at full gallop, beyond the corner of the house where his father and brother were sitting in the two tilted chairs; and a moment later, almost before he could have put the axe down, he heard the hooves again and watched the sorrel mare go back out of the yard, already galloping again. Then his father began to shout one of the sisters' names, who presently emerged backward from the kitchen door dragging the rolled rug along the ground by one end while the other sister walked behind it.

"If you ain't going to tote, go on and set up the wash pot," the first said.

"You, Sarty!" the second shouted. "Set up the wash pot!" His father appeared at the door, framed against that shabbiness, as he had been against that other bland perfection, impervious to either, the mother's anxious face at his shoulder.

"Go on," the father said. "Pick it up." The two sisters stopped, broad, lethargic; stooping, they presented an incredible expanse of pale cloth and a flutter of tawdry ribbons.   50

"If I thought enough of a rug to have to git hit all the way from France I wouldn't keep hit where folks coming in would have to tromp on hit," the first said. They raised the rug.

"Abner," the mother said. "Let me do it."

"You go back and git dinner," his father said. "I'll tend to this."

From the woodpile through the rest of the afternoon the boy watched them, the rug spread flat in the dust beside the bubbling wash pot, the two sisters stooping over it with that profound and lethargic reluctance, while the father stood over them in turn, implacable and grim, driving them though never raising his voice again. He could smell the harsh homemade lye they were using; he saw his mother come to the door once and look toward them with an expression not anxious now but very like despair; he saw his father turn, and he fell to with the axe and saw from the corner of his eye his father raise from the ground a flattish fragment of field stone and examine it and return to the pot, and this time his mother actually spoke: "Abner. Abner. Please don't. Please, Abner."

Then he was done too. It was dusk; the whippoorwills had already begun.   55 He could smell coffee from the room where they would presently eat the cold food remaining from the midafternoon meal, though when he entered the house he realized they were having coffee again probably because there was a fire on the hearth, before which the rug now lay spread over the backs of the two chairs. The tracks of his father's foot were gone. Where they had been were now long, water-cloudy scoriations resembling the sporadic course of a lilliputian mowing machine.

It still hung there while they ate the cold food and then went to bed, scattered without order or claim up and down the two rooms, his mother in one bed, where his father would later lie, the older brother in the other, himself, the aunt, and the two sisters on pallets on the floor. But his father was not in bed yet. The last thing the boy remembered was the depthless, harsh silhouette of the hat and coat bending over the rug and it seemed to him that he had not even closed his eyes when the silhouette was standing over him, the fire almost dead behind it, the stiff foot prodding him awake. "Catch up the mule," his father said.

When he returned with the mule his father was standing in the black door, the rolled rug over his shoulder. "Ain't you going to ride?" he said.

"No. Give me your foot."

He bent his knee into his father's hand, the wiry, surprising power flowed smoothly, rising, he rising with it, on to the mule's bare back (they had owned a saddle once; the boy could remember it though not when or where) and with the same effortlessness his father swung the rug up in front of him. Now in the starlight they retraced the afternoon's path, up the dusty road rife with honeysuckle, through the gate and up the black tunnel of the drive to the lightless house, where he sat on the mule and felt the rough warp of the rug drag across his thighs and vanish.

"Don't you want me to help?" he whispered. His father did not answer and now he heard again that stiff foot striking the hollow portico with that wooden and clocklike deliberation, that outrageous overstatement of the weight it carried. The rug, hunched, not flung (the boy could tell that even in the darkness) from his father's shoulder struck the angle of wall and floor with a sound unbelievably loud, thunderous, then the foot again, unhurried and enormous; a light came on in the house and the boy sat, tense, breathing steadily and quietly and just a little fast, though the foot itself did not increase its beat at all, descending the steps now; now the boy could see him.

"Don't you want to ride now?" he whispered. "We kin both ride now," the light within the house altering now, flaring up and sinking. *He's coming down the stairs now,* he thought. He had already ridden the mule up beside the horse block; presently his father was up behind him and he doubled the reins over and slashed the mule across the neck, but before the animal could begin to trot the hard, thin arm came around him, the hard, knotted hand jerking the mule back to a walk.

In the first red rays of the sun they were in the lot, putting plow gear on the mules. This time the sorrel mare was in the lot before he heard it at all, the rider collarless and even bareheaded, trembling, speaking in a shaking voice as the woman in the house had done, his father merely looking up once before stooping again to the hame he was buckling, so that the man on the mare spoke to his stooping back:

"You must realize you have ruined that rug. Wasn't there anybody here, any of your women . . ." he ceased, shaking, the boy watching him, the older brother leaning now in the stable door, chewing, blinking slowly and steadily at nothing apparently. "It cost a hundred dollars. But you never had a hundred dollars. You never will. So I'm going to charge you twenty bushels of corn against your crop. I'll add it in your contract and when you come to the commissary you can sign it. That won't keep Mrs. de Spain quiet but maybe it will teach you to wipe your feet before you enter her house again."

Then he was gone. The boy looked at his father, who still had not spoken or even looked up again, who was now adjusting the logger-head in the hame.

"Pap," he said. His father looked at him — the inscrutable face, the shaggy brows beneath which the gray eyes glinted coldly. Suddenly the boy went toward him, fast, stopping as suddenly. "You done the best you could!" he cried.

60

65

"If he wanted hit done different why didn't he wait and tell you how? He won't git no twenty bushels! He won't git none! We'll gether hit and hide hit! I kin watch . . ."

"Did you put the cutter back in that straight stock like I told you?"

"No, sir," he said.

"Then go do it."

That was Wednesday. During the rest of that week he worked steadily, at what was within his scope and some which was beyond it, with an industry that did not need to be driven nor even commanded twice; he had this from his mother, with the difference that some at least of what he did he liked to do, such as splitting wood with the half-size axe which his mother and aunt had earned, or saved money somehow, to present him with at Christmas. In company with the two older women (and on one afternoon, even one of the sisters), he built pens for the shoat and the cow which were part of his father's contract with the landlord, and one afternoon, his father being absent, gone somewhere on one of the mules, he went to the field.

They were running a middle buster now, his brother holding the plow 70 straight while he handled the reins, and walking beside the straining mule, the rich black soil shearing cool and damp against his bare ankles, he thought *Maybe this is the end of it. Maybe even that twenty bushels that seems hard to have to pay for just a rug will be a cheap price for him to stop forever and always from being what he used to be;* thinking, dreaming now, so that his brother had to speak sharply to him to mind the mule: *Maybe he even won't collect the twenty bushels. Maybe it will all add up and balance and vanish—corn, rug, fire; the terror and grief, the being pulled two ways like between two teams of horses—gone, done with for ever and ever.*

Then it was Saturday; he looked up from beneath the mule he was harnessing and saw his father in the black coat and hat. "Not that," his father said. "The wagon gear." And then, two hours later, sitting in the wagon bed behind his father and brother on the seat, the wagon accomplished a final curve, and he saw the weathered paintless store with its tattered tobacco- and patent-medicine posters and the tethered wagons and saddle animals below the gallery. He mounted the gnawed steps behind his father and brother, and there again was the lane of quiet, watching faces for the three of them to walk through. He saw the man in spectacles sitting at the plank table and he did not need to be told this was a Justice of the Peace; he sent one glare of fierce, exultant, partisan defiance at the man in collar and cravat now, whom he had seen but twice before in his life, and that on a galloping horse, who now wore on his face an expression not of rage but of amazed unbelief which the boy could not have known was at the incredible circumstance of being sued by one of his own tenants, and came and stood against his father and cried at the Justice: "He ain't done it! He ain't burnt . . ."

"Go back to the wagon," his father said.

"Burnt?" the Justice said. "Do I understand this rug was burned too?"

"Does anybody here claim it was?" his father said. "Go back to the wagon." But he did not, he merely retreated to the rear of the room, crowded as that other had been, but not to sit down this time, instead, to stand pressing among the motionless bodies, listening to the voices:

"And you claim twenty bushels of corn is too high for the damage you did 75 to the rug?"

"He brought the rug to me and said he wanted the tracks washed out of it. I washed the tracks out and took the rug back to him."

"But you didn't carry the rug back to him in the same condition it was in before you made the tracks on it."

His father did not answer, and now for perhaps half a minute there was no sound at all save that of breathing, the faint, steady suspiration of complete and intent listening.

"You decline to answer that, Mr. Snopes?" Again his father did not answer. "I'm going to find against you, Mr. Snopes. I'm going to find that you were responsible for the injury to Major de Spain's rug and hold you liable for it. But twenty bushels of corn seems a little high for a man in your circumstances to have to pay. Major de Spain claims it cost a hundred dollars. October corn will be worth about fifty cents. I figure that if Major de Spain can stand a ninety-five dollar loss on something he paid cash for, you can stand a five-dollar loss you haven't earned yet. I hold you in damages to Major de Spain to the amount of ten bushels of corn over and above your contract with him, to be paid to him out of your crop at gathering time. Court adjourned."

It had taken no time hardly, the morning was but half begun. He thought they would return home and perhaps back to the field, since they were late, far behind all other farmers. But instead his father passed on behind the wagon, merely indicating with his hand for the older brother to follow with it, and crossed the road toward the blacksmith shop opposite, pressing on after his father, overtaking him, speaking, whispering up at the harsh, calm face beneath the weathered hat: "He won't git no ten bushels neither. He won't git one. We'll . . ." until his father glanced for an instant down at him, the face absolutely calm, the grizzled eyebrows tangled above the cold eyes, the voice almost pleasant, almost gentle:

"You think so? Well, we'll wait till October anyway."

The matter of the wagon — the setting of a spoke or two and the tightening of the tires — did not take long either, the business of the tires accomplished by driving the wagon into the spring branch behind the shop and letting it stand there, the mules nuzzling into the water from time to time, and the boy on the seat with the idle reins, looking up the slope and through the sooty tunnel of the shed where the slow hammer rang and where his father sat on an upended cypress bolt, easily, either talking or listening, still sitting there when the boy brought the dripping wagon up out of the branch and halted it before the door.

"Take them on to the shade and hitch," his father said. He did so and returned. His father and the smith and a third man squatting on his heels inside the door were talking, about crops and animals; the boy, squatting too in the ammoniac dust and hoof-parings and scales of rust, heard his father tell a long and unhurried story out of the time before the birth of the older brother even when he had been a professional horsetrader. And then his father came up beside him where he stood before a tattered last year's circus poster on the other side of the store, gazing rapt and quiet at the scarlet horses, the incredible poisings and convolutions of tulle and tights and the painted leers of comedians, and said, "It's time to eat."

But not at home. Squatting beside his brother against the front wall, he watched his father emerge from the store and produce from a paper sack a

80

segment of cheese and divide it carefully and deliberately into three with his pocket knife and produce crackers from the same sack. They all three squatted on the gallery and ate, slowly, without talking; then in the store again, they drank from a tin dipper tepid water smelling of the cedar bucket and of living beech trees. And still they did not go home. It was a horse lot this time, a tall rail fence upon and along which men stood and sat and out of which one by one horses were led, to be walked and trotted and then cantered back and forth along the road while the slow swapping and buying went on and the sun began to slant westward, they — the three of them — watching and listening, the older brother with his muddy eyes and his steady, inevitable tobacco, the father commenting now and then on certain of the animals, to no one in particular.

It was after sundown when they reached home. They ate supper by lamp- 85
light, then, sitting on the doorstep, the boy watched the night fully accomplish, listening to the whippoorwills and the frogs, when he heard his mother's voice: "Abner! No! No! Oh, God. Oh, God. Abner!" and he rose, whirled, and saw the altered light through the door where a candle stub now burned in a bottle neck on the table and his father, still in the hat and coat, at once formal and burlesque as though dressed carefully for some shabby and ceremonial violence, emptying the reservoir of the lamp back into the five-gallon kerosene can from which it had been filled, while the mother tugged at his arm until he shifted the lamp to the other hand and flung her back, not savagely or viciously, just hard, into the wall, her hands flung out against the wall for balance, her mouth open and in her face the same quality of hopeless despair as had been in her voice. Then his father saw him standing in the door.

"Go to the barn and get that can of oil we were oiling the wagon with," he said. The boy did not move. Then he could speak.

"What . . ." he cried. "What are you . . ."

"Go get that oil," his father said. "Go."

Then he was moving, running, outside the house, toward the stable: this the old habit, the old blood which he had not been permitted to choose for himself, which had been bequeathed him willy nilly and which had run for so long (and who knew where, battening on what of outrage and savagery and lust) before it came to him. *I could keep on,* he thought. *I could run on and on and never look back, never need to see his face again. Only I can't. I can't,* the rusted can in his hand now, the liquid sploshing in it as he ran back to the house and into it, into the sound of his mother's weeping in the next room, and handed the can to his father.

"Ain't you going to even send a nigger?" he cried. "At least you sent a nig- 90
ger before!"

This time his father didn't strike him. The hand came even faster than the blow had, the same hand which had set the can on the table with almost excruciating care flashing from the can toward him too quick for him to follow it, gripping him by the back of his shirt and on to tiptoe before he had seen it quit the can, the face stooping at him in breathless and frozen ferocity, the cold, dead voice speaking over him to the older brother who leaned against the table, chewing with that steady, curious, sidewise motion of cows:

"Empty the can into the big one and go on. I'll catch up with you."

"Better tie him up to the bedpost," the brother said.

"Do like I told you," the father said. Then the boy was moving, his bunched shirt and the hard, bony hand between his shoulder-blades, his toes just touching the floor, across the room and into the other one, past the sisters sitting with spread heavy thighs in the two chairs over the cold hearth, and to where his mother and aunt sat side by side on the bed, the aunt's arms about his mother's shoulders.

"Hold him," the father said. The aunt made a startled movement. "Not 95 you," the father said. "Lennie. Take hold of him. I want to see you do it." His mother took him by the wrist. "You'll hold him better than that. If he gets loose don't you know what he is going to do? He will go up yonder." He jerked his head toward the road. "Maybe I'd better tie him."

"I'll hold him," his mother whispered.

"See you do then." Then his father was gone, the stiff foot heavy and measured upon the boards, ceasing at last.

Then he began to struggle. His mother caught him in both arms, he jerking and wrenching at them. He would be stronger in the end, he knew that. But he had no time to wait for it. "Lemme go!" he cried. "I don't want to have to hit you!"

"Let him go!" the aunt said. "If he don't go, before God, I am going up there myself!"

"Don't you see I can't?" his mother cried. "Sarty! Sarty! No! No! Help me, 100 Lizzie!"

Then he was free. His aunt grasped at him but it was too late. He whirled, running, his mother stumbled forward on to her knees behind him, crying to the nearer sister. "Catch him, Net! Catch him!" But that was too late too, the sister (the sisters were twins, born at the same time, yet either of them now gave the impression of being, encompassing as much living meat and volume and weight as any other two of the family) not yet having begun to rise from the chair, her head, face, alone merely turned, presenting to him in the flying instant an astonishing expanse of young female features untroubled by any surprise even, wearing only an expression of bovine interest. Then he was out of the room, out of the house, in the mild dust of the starlit road and the heavy rifeness of honeysuckle, the pale ribbon unspooling with terrific slowness under his running feet, reaching the gate at last and turning in, running, his heart and lungs drumming, on up the drive toward the lighted house, the lighted door. He did not knock, he burst in, sobbing for breath, incapable for the moment of speech; he saw the astonished face of the Negro in the linen jacket without knowing when the Negro had appeared.

"De Spain!" he cried, panted. "Where's . . ." then he saw the white man too emerging from a white door down the hall. "Barn!" he cried. "Barn!"

"What?" the white man said. "Barn?"

"Yes!" the boy cried. "Barn!"

"Catch him!" the white man shouted. 105

But it was too late this time too. The Negro grasped his shirt, but the entire sleeve, rotten with washing, carried away, and he was out that door too and in the drive again, and had actually never ceased to run even while he was screaming into the white man's face.

Behind him the white man was shouting, "My horse! Fetch my horse!" and he thought for an instant of cutting across the park and climbing the fence into the road, but he did not know the park nor how high the vine-massed fence might be and he dared not risk it. So he ran on down the drive, blood and breath roaring; presently he was in the road again though he could not see it. He could not hear either: the galloping mare was almost upon him before he heard her, and even then he held his course, as if the very urgency of his wild grief and need must in a moment more find him wings, waiting until the ultimate instant to hurl himself aside and into the weed-choked roadside ditch as the horse thundered past and on, for an instant in furious silhouette against the stars, the tranquil early summer night sky which, even before the shape of the horse and rider vanished, strained abruptly and violently upward: a long, swirling roar incredible and soundless, blotting the stars, and he springing up and into the road again, running again, knowing it was too late yet still running even after he heard the shot and, an instant later, two shots, pausing now without knowing he had ceased to run, crying "Pap! Pap!," running again before he knew he had begun to run, stumbling, tripping over something and scrabbling up again without ceasing to run, looking backward over his shoulder at the glare as he got up, running on among the invisible trees, panting, sobbing, "Father! Father!"

At midnight he was sitting on the crest of a hill. He did not know it was midnight and he did not know how far he had come. But there was no glare behind him now and he sat now, his back toward what he had called home for four days anyhow, his face toward the dark woods which he would enter when breath was strong again, small, shaking steadily in the chill darkness, hugging himself into the remainder of his thin, rotten shirt, the grief and despair now no longer terror and fear but just grief and despair. *Father. My father,* he thought. "He was brave!" he cried suddenly, aloud but not loud, no more than a whisper: "He was! He was in the war! He was in Colonel Sartoris' cav'ry!" not knowing that his father had gone to that war a private in the fine old European sense, wearing no uniform, admitting the authority of and giving fidelity to no man or army or flag, going to war as Malbrouck° himself did: for booty—it meant nothing and less than nothing to him if it were enemy booty or his own.

The slow constellations wheeled on. It would be dawn and then sun-up after a while and he would be hungry. But that would be tomorrow and now he was only cold, and walking would cure that. His breathing was easier now and he decided to get up and go on, and then he found that he had been asleep because he knew it was almost dawn, the night almost over. He could tell that from the whippoorwills. They were everywhere now among the dark trees below him, constant and inflectioned and ceaseless, so that, as the instant for giving over to the day birds drew nearer and nearer, there was no interval at all between them. He got up. He was a little stiff, but walking would cure that too as it would the cold, and soon there would be the sun. He went on down the hill, toward the dark woods within which the liquid silver voices of the birds called unceasing—the rapid and urgent beating of the urgent and quiring heart of the late spring night. He did not look back.

Malbrouck: John Churchill, duke of Marlborough (1650–1722), English military commander who led the armies of England and Holland in the War of Spanish Succession.

CONSIDERATIONS FOR CRITICAL THINKING AND WRITING

1. **FIRST RESPONSE.** Who is "Barn Burning" about? Explain your choice.
2. Is Sarty a dynamic or a static character? Why? Which term best describes his father? Why?

3. Who is the central character in this story? Explain your choice.

4. How are Sarty's emotions revealed in the story's opening paragraphs? What seems to be the function of the italicized passages there and elsewhere?

5. What do we learn from the story's exposition that helps us understand Abner's character? How does his behavior reveal his character? What do other people say about him?

6. How does Faulkner's physical description of Abner further our understanding of his personality?

7. Explain how the justice of the peace, Mr. Harris, and Major de Spain serve as foils to Abner. Discuss whether you think they are round or flat characters.

8. Who are the story's stock characters? What is their purpose?

9. Explain how the description of Major de Spain's house helps to frame the main conflicts that Sarty experiences in his efforts to remain loyal to his father.

10. Write an essay describing Sarty's attitudes toward his father as they develop and change throughout the story.

11. What do you think happens to Sarty's father and brother at the end of the story? How does your response to this question affect your reading of the last paragraph?

12. How does the language of the final paragraph suggest a kind of resolution to the conflicts Sarty has experienced?

CONNECTIONS TO OTHER SELECTIONS

1. Compare and contrast Faulkner's characterizations of Abner Snopes in this story and Miss Emily in "A Rose for Emily" (p. 91). How does the author generate sympathy for each character even though both are guilty of terrible crimes? Which character do you find more sympathetic? Explain why.

2. How does Abner Snopes's motivation for revenge compare with Matt Fowler's in Andre Dubus's "Killings" (p. 103)? How do the victims of each character's revenge differ and thereby help to shape the meanings of each story?

3. Read the section on mythological criticism in Chapter 53, "Critical Strategies for Reading." How do you think a mythological critic would make sense of Sarty Snopes and Matt Fowler?

Perspectives on Faulkner

JANE HILES (B. 1951)

Hiles uses a biographical approach (see pp. 2048–50 in Chapter 53, "Critical Strategies for Reading") to determine Faulkner's intentions in his characterization of how Sarty responds to the conflicts he feels about his father.

Blood Ties in "Barn Burning" 1985

"'You're getting to be a man. . . . You got to learn to stick to your own blood or you ain't going to have any blood to stick to you'": Abner Snopes's admonition to his son, Colonel Sartoris (or "Sarty"), introduces a central issue in Faulkner's "Barn Burning" — the kinship bond, which the story's narrator calls the "old fierce pull of blood." The interpretive crux of the work is a conflict between determinism, represented by the blood tie that binds Sarty to his clan, and free will, dramatized by the boy's ultimate repudiation of family ties and his decampment. Dissonances between the structure and the imagery of the work develop and amplify Sarty's conflict: viewed in the light of the narrator's deterministic assumptions, the story's denouement is a red herring which only appears to resolve the complexities created by evocative language. Sarty's seeming interruption of the antisocial pattern established by his father is actually a continuation of it, and the ostensible resolution of his moral dilemma actually no resolution at all. . . .

In an interview in Japan sixteen years after the publication of "Barn Burning," Faulkner delivered an appraisal of the phenomenon of clannishness that bears considerable relevance to Abner Snopes's defensive posture in "Barn Burning":

> Yes, we are country people and we have never had too much in material possessions because 60 or 70 years ago we were invaded and we were conquered. So we have been thrown back on our selves not only for entertainment but certain [sic] amount of defense. We have to be clannish just like the people in the Scottish highlands, each springing to defend his own blood whether it be right or wrong. Just a matter of custom and habit, we have to do it; interrelated that way, and usually there is hereditary head [sic] of the whole lot, as usually, the oldest son of the oldest son and each looked upon as chief of his own particular clan. That is the tone they live by. But I am sure it is because only a comparatively short time ago we were invaded by our own people — speaking in our own language which is always a pretty savage sort of warfare.

In Faulkner's estimation, the old pull of blood transcends considerations of caste, class, and occupation:

> . . . [I]t is regional. It is through what we call the "South." It doesn't matter what the people do. They can be land people, farmers, and industrialists, but there still exists the feeling of blood, of clan, blood for blood. It is pretty general through all the classes.[1]

Faulkner's explanation of the phenomenon of Southern clannishness touches upon a number of the issues that arise in "Barn Burning." In each case, alienation from the politically and economically dominant group leads to dependence upon an alternative source of security. Just as beleaguered Southerners, Faulkner suggests, have had to look to themselves for "defense" since the South was defeated, so Ab Snopes must turn to his kin for defense not only from Union troops but also from the landed Southern aristocrat who, in what Ab perceives as a failure of paternalism, "aims to begin . . . owning

---

[1] James B. Meriwether and Michael Millgate, eds., *Lion in the Garden* (New York: Random House, 1968), p. 191.

[him] body and soul." The clan's identifying characteristic, then, is its orientation to survival. Perhaps most interestingly, the comments made in the interview impinge upon the central issue of the morality of Sarty's choice. Faulkner's recognition here of a private code of honor suggests that Sarty's conduct is somewhat more questionable than is generally recognized, and his articulation in the interview of a necessity for clannishness suggests at least a modicum of sympathy for the "custom and habit" of "each springing to defend his own blood whether it be right or wrong."

From *Mississippi Quarterly: The Journal of Southern Culture*

CONSIDERATIONS FOR CRITICAL THINKING AND WRITING

1. To what extent does Faulkner's description of clannishness in the South affect your understanding of whether Sarty resolves his dilemma at the end of the story?

2. Do you agree with Hiles that "Sarty's conduct is somewhat more questionable than is generally recognized" (para. 4)?

BENJAMIN DeMOTT   (1924–2005)

DeMott pays close attention to matters of culture, race, class, and power that affect Abner Snopes, and from those perspectives Abner is seen as more than simply malevolent.

Abner Snopes as a Victim of Class   *1988*

We know that Ab Snopes is harsh to his wife, his sons, and his daughters, and that he is particularly cruel to his stock. We know that his hatred of the planters with whom he enters into sharecropping agreements repeatedly issues in acts of wanton destruction. We know that he's ridden with suspicion of his own closest kin, expecting them to betray him. And we know that — worse than any of this — he often behaves with fearful coldness to those who try desperately to communicate the loving respect they feel for him.

Given such a combination of racism, destructiveness, and blank insensitivity, it's tempting to imagine Ab as a figure in whom ignorance and brutality obliterate every sympathetic impulse, every normative response to peace, dignity, or beauty. Major de Spain seems to reach something close to that conclusion after the rug-laundering episode ("Wasn't there anybody here, any of your women . . ."). And although Ab's son is intensely loyal to his father and indignant at the injustice of the Major's twenty-bushel "charge" for the destruction of the rug, Sarty clearly has a conviction that "peace and dignity" are somehow *"beyond his [father's] touch, he no more to them than a buzzing wasp."* Is there anything to be made of Ab Snopes except a person whose raging malevolence has badly stunted if not crippled his humanity?

Denying the force of the malevolence is impossible—but tracing it solely to ignorance and insensitivity falsifies Ab's nature. Uneducated, probably illiterate, schooled in none of the revolutionary traditions which, in urban settings, were shaping popular protests against "economic injustice" when this story was written in the late 1930s, Ab nevertheless has managed, through the exercise of his own primitive intelligence, to make sense of his world, to arrive at a vision of the relations between labor, money, and the beautiful. It's a vision that's miles away from transforming itself into a broadly historical account of capital accumulation. Ab Snopes can't frame a theory to himself about, say, proletarian enslavement; he has no language in which to imagine a class solidarity leading to political action aimed at securing justice and truth. Indeed, he would explode at the notion that considerations of truth and justice have any pertinence either to the interests of the authorities opposing him or to his own interests in defying them. ("Later, twenty years later, [Sarty] was to tell himself, 'If I had said they wanted only truth, justice, he would have hit me again.'") For Ab Snopes the only principle lending significance to his war with the de Spains of this world is that of blood loyalty—determination to beat your personal enemy if you can and keep faith, at all costs, with your clan.

Yet despite all this, Ab does see that part of the power of the beautiful and the orderly to command our respect depends upon our refusal to remind ourselves that they have been brought into existence by other people's labor—by effort that often in history has been slave labor and has seldom been fairly recompensed. Sarty Snopes, grown up, presumably arrives finally at an understanding both that his father's situation was one of economic oppression and that the oppressors, when sitting in a court of law, are capable of attempting to reach beyond selfishness to a decent distribution of justice. But his father had, at the time, no grip on any of this.

Yet Ab is not a fool, and brutality and insensitivity are not the only features of character that we can make out in him. What we need also to summon is the terrible frustration of an undeveloped mind—aware of the weight of an immense unfairness, aware of the habit of the weak perpetually to behave as though the elegance, grace, beauty, and order found often in the neighborhoods of the rich somehow were traceable exclusively to the superior nature of the rich—and yet unable to move forward from either awareness to anything approaching rational protest. His rage cannot become a force leading toward any positive principle; it has no way to express itself except in viciousness to those closest at hand. It can't begin to make a serious bid for admiration, because whatever inclination we might have to admire it is instantly crossed by repugnance at the cruelty inherent in it.

But it remains true that, together with the ignorance and brutality in Ab Snopes, there is a ferocious, primitive undeceivedness in his reading of the terms of the relationship between rich and poor, lucky and unlucky, advantaged and disadvantaged. Ab Snopes has seen a portion of the truth of the world that many on his level, and most who are luckier, never see. We can damn him for allowing that truth to wreck his humanity, but when we fully bring him to life as a character, it's impossible not to include with our indictment a sense of pity.

From *Close Imagining: An Introduction to Literature*

CONSIDERATIONS FOR CRITICAL THINKING AND WRITING

1. DeMott acknowledges Abner's ignorance and brutality, but he also presents him as a man who suffers injustices. What are those injustices? Discuss whether you think they warrant a more balanced assessment of Abner's character.

2. Why doesn't Abner protest his "oppression" (para. 4)? Given DeMott's perspective on him, how might Abner — in another story — have been the hero rather than a terrible source of conflict?

3. To what extent can DeMott's approach to Abner's circumstances be described as a Marxist perspective? (For a discussion of Marxist criticism see pp. 2053–54.)

GAYLE EDWARD WILSON (B. 1931)

The following analysis combines psychology and myth as a means of understanding the conflicts in "Barn Burning." The "Apollonian man" alluded to in the discussion (para. 1) refers to the myth of Apollo and implies a person who values order, community, balance, and self-knowledge to establish true relations between the individual and his world.

Conflict in "Barn Burning" 1990

Ruth Benedict's descriptions of two major patterns of culture provide an advantageous starting point for a discussion of the way in which Faulkner develops the content of "Barn Burning." The Paranoid way of life, she comments, has "no political organization. In a strict sense it has no legality."[1] As a consequence of the Paranoid man's adherence to this life-style, he is "lawless," and is feared as a warrior who will hesitate "at no treachery" (p. 121). In such a culture, "every man's hand is against every other man," and as a result each man relies upon blood ties to form social alliances and to sanction his actions (pp. 122–23). The Apollonian man, on the other hand, "keeps to the middle of the road, stays within the known map," and strives to fulfill his civic role in terms of the expectations of the community at large (p. 70). Men in such a society, although the blood tie is relatively important as a bond, turn to the community and its collected wisdom, as it is embodied in the law, for the approval of their actions and for their security. Thus the sanction for a man's "acts comes from the formal structure, not the individual" (p. 99) — from the community, not the blood kin. In "Barn Burning" Faulkner develops the ideas contained in these descriptions of dissimilar life-styles in a way which creates the central tension in the story and keeps it constantly before the reader. The reader is thus made aware of the pervasiveness of Sarty's *"terror and the grief, the being pulled two ways like between two teams of horses."*

[1] *Patterns of Culture* (New York, 1959), p. 122.

The tension is made evident by the presence of effects which follow from actions taken in accord with the dominant characteristic of each life-style. Abner's "wolflike independence . . . his latent ravening ferocity . . . [and] conviction in the rightness of his own actions," which have frequently manifested themselves in acts of destruction against the property of an established community, clearly mark him as a follower of the Paranoid way. As such, his actions inevitably, and repeatedly, alienate him from each settled society into which he moves. His disregard for a "formal structure" of any kind is indicated by such a minor detail as that which occurs when Abner fuels his fire with "a rail lifted from a nearby fence and cut into lengths," an act which is symbolic of his rejection of any societally imposed limits. It is by burning barns, however, that Abner's Paranoid life-style and its consequences are most forcefully dramatized. At Abner's trial for barn burning, Sarty sees the men "between himself and the table part and become a lane of grim faces." Abner and Sarty then walk between the "two lines of grim-faced men" and they leave a "quiet crowd of grimly watching men." This separation of the Snopes family from the larger society as a consequence of acts motivated by Abner's "ravening ferocity" is underscored by the Justice's command to Abner: "Take your wagon and get out of this country before dark." The Snopes's wagon, containing "the sorry residue of the dozen and more movings," becomes, therefore, a symbol of the transient and nomadic way of life which the Snopes family is forced to adopt because of Abner's adherence to the Paranoid way. The de Spain tenant house and the manner in which the Snopes family lives in it are also effects of a life-style which is not concerned with permanence or order or boundaries or limits. The house is a "paintless two-room" structure "identical almost with the dozen others" in which the family has lived as a result of its nomadic existence, and the members of the family are found "scattered without order or claim up and down the two rooms."

On the other hand, the Harris and de Spain barns represent productivity and fertility, permanence and continuity, because they house the equipment, stock, and seed by which a society produces the goods to sustain and perpetuate itself. A barn and its contents are the effects of a society which is built upon the willingness of men to subordinate their unfettered desires to a communal consensus in order to develop a permanent community. The importance of a barn to the Apollonian way is illustrated by Sarty's thoughts when he sees the effect brought about by what a barn symbolizes. When he comes upon the de Spain house for the first time, he feels that "*the spell*" of "*peace and dignity*" cast by the magnificent house will render "*even the barns and stable and cribs which belong to it impervious to the puny flames he* [Abner] *might contrive.*" The sight of this apotheosis of the Apollonian way has a profound effect on Sarty: he "at that instant . . . forgot his father. . . ." It is most revealing that Sartoris should compare this house which symbolizes the "*peace and dignity*" of the Apollonian way with another kind of building which, because of what it represents, embodies the very essence of an ordered society: "*Hit's big as a courthouse* he thought quietly, with a surge of peace and joy."

Essentially, it is the concept of law, as symbolized by the de Spain house, that gives Sarty his sense of "peace and joy," for it is the law that provides man with the peace necessary to develop the "formal structure" of a communal, stable society. Without law, as Hobbes tells us, "there is no place for Industry; because the fruit thereof is uncertain: and consequently no Culture of the

Earth; . . . no commodius Building; . . . no Society; and which is worst of all, continuall feare, and danger of violent death; And the life of man, solitary, poore, nasty, brutish, and short."[2] At its best, the law is moderate, even, and impartial. It protects as well as punishes; it is an elaborately worked out system designed to join men together in a common purpose, to insure the presumption of innocence until guilt is proved, and to make the punishment commensurate with the crime. In "Barn Burning" the primacy of the law in an Apollonian society is made quite evident. It is represented in a minor way by the contract in which Snopes engages with de Spain to work for eight months in return for a share of the crop. It is developed in a major way in the two trials which take place. In the first trial, the law protects Abner from unwarranted conclusions. Concerning the charge that Abner burned Harris's barn, the Justice asks Harris, "But what proof have you, Mr. Harris?" Harris tells of the Negro who appeared and gave him the cryptic message, "'wood and hay kin burn,'" to which the Justice replies, "But that's not proof. Don't you see that's not proof?" In the second trial, de Spain's unreasonable assessment of twenty bushels of corn in payment for the rug Abner ruined is not allowed. Abner is fined ten bushels, not twenty, as de Spain had wanted. For the men in "Barn Burning," . . . then, the law and its equitable application to all men is the *sine qua non* of the Apollonian way. . . . It is this belief in the law and its extensions of "justice" and "civilization" which guides and controls the behavior of the Apollonian man. This is the same realization that young Sarty is only able to articulate "twenty years" after Abner strikes him for not being willing to lie in his defense at the trial. "'If I had said they only wanted truth, justice, he would have hit me again.'"

From *Mississippi Quarterly*

[2] Chapter XIII, "*Of the NATURAL CONDITION of Mankind, as concerning their Felicity, and Misery,*" *Leviathan* . . . (1651) in *Seventeenth-Century Verse and Prose,* ed. Helen White, Ruth Wallerstein, and Ricardo Quintana (New York, 1967), I, 223.

CONSIDERATIONS FOR CRITICAL THINKING AND WRITING

1. What distinctions are drawn between the "Paranoid man" and the "Apollonian man" (para. 1)? How do these two different types serve to frame the conflicts in "Barn Burning"?

2. How is Snopes's wagon an appropriate symbol of the "Paranoid way" (para. 1), and how are the Harris and de Spain barns fitting symbols of the "Apollonian way" (para. 3)?

3. In an essay explain why you think Sarty chooses one way of life over the other at the end of the story.

4. Compare Wilson's description of the story's conflicts with Hiles's and DeMott's.

JAMES FERGUSON (B. 1928)

Ferguson's formalist approach (see pp. 2046–48 in Chapter 53, "Critical Strategies for Reading") relates Faulkner's use of point of view to his thematic concerns in the story.

Narrative Strategy in "Barn Burning"   1991

The point of view is largely limited to the consciousness of Sarty Snopes, but in spite of his sensitivity and his intuitive sense of right and wrong, the little boy is far too young to understand his father and the complexities of the moral choice he must make. To enhance the pathos of his situation and the drama of Sarty's initiation into life, Faulkner felt the need for the occasional intrusion of an authorial voice giving the reader insights far beyond the capabilities of the youthful protagonist. A passage, for example, about the fires Abner Snopes builds affords us a sense of the rationale for the man's actions, of his strangely perverse integrity, which could not be supplied to us by the consciousness of his son:

> The nights were still cool and they had a fire against it, of a rail lifted from a nearby fence and cut into lengths — a small fire, neat, niggard almost, a shrewd fire; such fires were his father's habit and custom always, even in freezing weather. Older, the boy might have remarked this and wondered why not a big one; why should not a man who had not only seen the waste and extravagance of war, but who had in his blood an inherent voracious prodigality with material not his own, have burned everything in sight? Then he might have gone a step farther and thought that that was the reason: that niggard blaze was the living fruit of nights passed during those four years in the woods hiding from all men, blue or gray, with his strings of horses (captured horses, he called them). And older still, he might have divined the true reason: that the element of fire spoke to some deep mainspring of his father's being, as the element of steel or of powder spoke to other men, as the one weapon for the preservation of integrity, else breath were not worth the breathing, and hence to be regarded with respect and used with discretion.

Again, near the end of the story, after Sarty has betrayed his father, there is another brief shift away from the consciousness of the protagonist:

> "He was brave!" he cried suddenly, aloud but not loud, no more than a whisper: "He was! He was in the war! He was in Colonel Sartoris' cav'ry!" not knowing that his father had gone to that war a private in the fine old European sense, wearing no uniform, admitting the authority of and giving fidelity to no man or army or flag, going to war as Malbrouck himself did: for booty — it meant nothing and less than nothing to him if it were enemy booty or his own.

"Barn Burning" is incomparably richer than it would have been without such additions not only because they supply us with ironies otherwise unavailable to us but also because these manipulations of point of view dramatize *on the level of technique* the thematic matter of the story. The tensions between the awareness of the boy and the information supplied us by the authorial voice undergird and emphasize the conflicts between youth and age, innocence and sophistication, intuition and abstraction, decency and corruption, all of which lie at the core of the work.

From *Faulkner's Short Fiction*

CONSIDERATIONS FOR CRITICAL THINKING AND WRITING

1. In the first passage quoted by Ferguson how does the narrator's analysis of Abner Snopes become progressively sophisticated in explaining his reasons for building a small fire?

2. What other examples of shifts away from the consciousness of Sarty to a more informed point of view can you find in the story? Choose what you judge to be a significant example and write an essay about how Faulkner's use of point of view contributes to the story's themes.

Questions for Writing

INCORPORATING THE CRITICS

The following questions can help you to incorporate materials from critical essays into your own writing about a literary work. You may initially feel intimidated by the prospect of responding to the arguments of professional critics in your own paper. However, the process will not defeat you if you have clearly formulated your own response to the literary work and are able to distinguish it from the critics' perspectives. Reading the critics can help you to develop your own thesis — perhaps, to cite just two examples, by using them as supporting evidence or by arguing with them in order to clarify or qualify their points about the literary work. As you write and discover how to advance your thesis, you'll find yourself participating in a dialogue with the critics. This sort of conversation will help you to improve your thinking and hone your argument.

Keep in mind that the work of professional critics is a means of enriching your understanding of a literary work rather than a substitution for your own analysis and interpretation of that work. Quoting, paraphrasing, or summarizing a critic's perspective does not relieve you of the obligation of choosing a topic, organizing information, developing a thesis, and arguing your point of view by citing sufficient evidence from the text you are examining. These matters are discussed in further detail in Chapter 54, "Reading and the Writing Process." You should also be familiar with the methods for documenting sources that are explained in Chapter 55, "The Literary Research Paper"; this chapter also contains important information about how to avoid plagiarism.

No doubt you won't find all literary criticism equally useful: some critics' arguments won't address your own areas of concern; some will be too difficult for you to get a handle on; and some will seem wrongheaded. However, much of the criticism you read will serve to make a literary work more accessible and interesting to you, and disagreeing with others' arguments will often help you to develop your own ideas about a work. When you use the work of critics in your own writing, you should consider the following questions. Responding to these

continued

questions will help you to ensure that you have a clear understanding of what a critic is arguing about a work, to what extent you agree with that argument, and how you plan to incorporate and respond to the critic's reading in your own paper. The more questions you can ask yourself in response to this list or as a result of your own reading, the more you'll be able to think critically about how you are approaching both the critics and the literary work under consideration.

1. Have you read the literary work carefully and taken notes of your own impressions before reading any critical perspectives so that your initial insights are not lost to the arguments made by the critics? Have you articulated your own responses to the work in a journal entry prior to reading the critics?

2. Are you sufficiently familiar with the literary work that you can determine the accuracy, fairness, and thoroughness of the critic's use of evidence from the work?

3. Have you read the critic's piece carefully? Try summarizing the critic's argument in a brief paragraph. Do you understand the nature and purpose of the critic's argument? Which passages are especially helpful to you? Which seem unclear? Why?

4. Is the critic's reading of the literary work similar to or different from your own reading? Why do you agree or disagree? What generational, historical, cultural, or biographical considerations might help to account for any differences between the critic's responses and your own?

5. How has your reading of the critic influenced your understanding of the literary work? Do issues that previously seemed unimportant now seem significant? What are these issues, and how does a consideration of them affect your reading of the work?

6. Are you too quickly revising or even discarding your own reading because the critic's perspective seems so polished and persuasive? Are you making use of your reading notes and the responses in your journal entries?

7. How would you classify the critic's approach? Through what kind of lens does the critic view the literary work? Is the critical approach formalist, biographical, psychological, sociological, mythological, reader-response, deconstructionist, or some combination of these or possibly other strategies? (For a discussion of these approaches, see Chapter 53, "Critical Strategies for Reading.")

8. What biases, if any, can you detect in the critic's approach? How might, for example, a southern critic's reading of "Barn Burning" differ from a northern critic's?

9. Can you determine how other critics have responded to the critic's work? Is the critic's work cited and taken seriously in other critics' books and articles? Is the work dated by having been superseded by subsequent studies?

10. Are any passages or topics that you deem important left out by the critic? Do these omissions qualify or refute the critic's argument?

11. What judgments does the critic seem to make about the work? Is the work regarded, for example, as significant, unified, representative, trivial, inept, or irresponsible? Do you agree with these judgments? If not, can you develop and support a thesis about your difference of opinion?

12. What important disagreements do critics reveal in their approaches to the work? Do you find one perspective more convincing than another? Why? Is there a way of resolving their conflicting views that could serve as a thesis for your paper?

13. Can you extend or qualify the critic's argument to matters in the literary text that are not covered by the critic's perspective? Will this allow you to develop your own topic while acknowledging the critic's useful insights?

14. Have you quoted, paraphrased, or summarized the critic accurately and fairly? Have you avoided misrepresenting the critic's arguments in any way?

15. Are the critic's words, ideas, opinions, and insights adequately acknowledged and documented in the correct format? Do you understand the difference between common knowledge and plagiarism? Have you avoided quoting excessively? Are the quotations smoothly integrated into your own text?

16. Are you certain that your incorporation of the critic's work is for the purpose of developing your paper's thesis rather than for name-dropping or padding your paper? How can you explain to yourself why the critic's work is useful for your argument?

A SAMPLE STUDENT PAPER

The Fires of Class Conflict in "Barn Burning" (excerpt)

The following excerpt consists of the first few paragraphs of a paper in which the student develops a thesis based on her reading of critical perspectives by Benjamin DeMott (p. 517) and Gayle Edward Wilson (p. 519). Sonia Metzger uses the two critics' different approaches to "Barn Burning" to develop a thesis that goes beyond either critic's perspective. The rest of her paper (not included) argues her thesis that a recognition of the class conflicts suppressed by Faulkner in the story makes Abner Snopes's violent response to the economic power inherent in Major de Spain's Apollonian values appear to be justifiable, rather than merely the desperate activity of a Paranoid man. Abner has good reason to fear Apollonian values because de Spain's world is carefully constructed to exclude him while simultaneously exploiting him.

Metzger 1

Sonia Metzger

Professor Wolf

English 109

April 15, 2010

The Fires of Class Conflict in

"Barn Burning"

The central conflict in William Faulkner's "Barn Burning" concerns a young boy named Sarty Snopes who must choose between loyalty to his father and his family and loyalty to society and humanity. A first reading of the story probably leaves most readers with the sense that the boy must turn away from his father's vicious sensibilities if he is to grow into a responsible adult. Sarty faces tremendous pressure from his father to lie in court so that his father will not be convicted of barn burning. He knows his father wants him "to stick to your own blood or you ain't going to have any blood to stick to you" (505).

Thesis identifying conflict of story, supported with textual evidence

Unlike the selfish, mean, vengeful father who despises the wealth and gentility of the southern aristocracy and is relentless in his contempt for the upper-class world of Major de Spain, Sarty is a gentle, vulnerable character who engages our sympathy. He is divided between wanting his father's love and loving the "peace and dignity" (506) that de Spain's house evokes within him. Gayle Edward Wilson, one of the critics I've read, mostly agrees with this view of the story's conflict, but Benjamin DeMott goes beyond the focus on Sarty's conflicted conscience to examine another, more subtle dimension of the story—the reasons for Abner Snopes's ferocious rejection of the world he wants to burn down.

Writer's analysis of central character and conflict

Identification of two critics' views of conflict

Our understanding of Abner and his son is, according to Wilson, deepened by employing two concepts from Ruth Benedict's *Patterns of Culture* that she calls the "Paranoid man" and the "Apollonian man" (519). Abner is a version of the Paranoid man. His culture consists of a lawless, clannish, fierce world in which his nomadic, lonely existence is characterized by violence, hatred, force, and destruction. Except for blood ties, he rejects forms of any kind: the stability created by the Apollonian man (Major de Spain) through law and order in a community is his enemy. He will not be bound by any societal regulations; instead, he destroys any sense of community

Analysis of critics' views, set in contrast to each other

through his barn burning and his erratic antisocial behavior. For Wilson, Sarty must turn away from the Paranoid man to the Apollonian man if he is to pledge his loyalty to justice and civilization (521). This conflict is also recognized by Benjamin DeMott, who acknowledges Abner's harshness, cruelty, destructiveness, paranoia, and coldness but who also raises an important question that shifts some of our focus from Sarty onto Abner: "Is there anything to be made of Ab Snopes except a person whose raging malevolence has badly stunted if not crippled his humanity?" (517).

By considering when "Barn Burning" was written—during the depression of the late 1930s—DeMott suggests a kind of defense for understanding and even sympathizing with Abner by pointing to issues of class and power embedded in the capitalistic culture and the nearly slave-labor conditions endured by Abner. This version of Abner is not merely brutish but also suffering from "the terrible frustration of an undeveloped mind—aware of the weight of an immense unfairness . . . and yet unable to move forward . . . to anything approaching rational protest" (518). DeMott suggests that Abner warrants our pity rather than total repudiation and that he, however imperfectly, does feel (even if he doesn't comprehend) the pain produced by the miserable gap between the rich and the poor. With this gap in mind, I want to go further than DeMott goes and argue, using Wilson's categories, that Faulkner's portrayal of Apollonian values avoids confronting the economic oppression that Abner experiences but that neither he nor Sarty can articulate. Abner may fit much of the description associated with the Paranoid man, but there are important social reasons for his rightfully fearing the economic power of the Apollonian man.

Writer's response to critics' views

Works Cited

DeMott, Benjamin. "Abner Snopes as a Victim of Class." *The Bedford Introduction to Literature*. Ed. Michael Meyer. 9th ed. Boston: Bedford/St. Martin's, 2011. 517–518. Print.

(Continued on page 528.)

Faulkner, William. "Barn Burning." *The Bedford Introduction to Literature.* Ed. Michael Meyer. 9th ed. Boston: Bedford/St. Martin's, 2011. 503–514. Print.

Wilson, Gayle Edward. "Conflict in 'Barn Burning.'" *The Bedford Introduction to Literature.* Ed. Michael Meyer. 9th ed. Boston: Bedford/St. Martin's, 2011. 519–521. Print.

Suggested Topics for Longer Papers

1. Write a character analysis of Abner Snopes. Does he change or develop through the course of the story? Do you identify with him in any way? Think about whether you might characterize his behavior as criminal, insane, or heroic.

2. A great many articles and portions of books have been written about "Barn Burning." Scan these sources to get an overview of the kinds of critical approaches that have been applied to the story, and write a selective survey of how criticism about "Barn Burning" has evolved over the past three or four decades. Which approaches seem the most useful and revealing to you?

Web Research William Faulkner or take quizzes on his works at bedfordstmartins.com/meyerlit.

14

A CULTURAL CASE STUDY
James Joyce's "Eveline"

Ireland is the old sow that eats her farrow.
— JAMES JOYCE

I've put in [my writing] so many enigmas and puzzles that it will keep the professors busy for centuries arguing over what I meant.
— JAMES JOYCE

Close reading is an essential and important means of appreciating the literary art of a text. This formalist approach to literature explores the subtle, complex relationships between how a work is constructed using elements such as plot, characterization, point of view, diction, metaphor, symbol, irony, and other literary techniques to create a coherent structure that contributes to a work's meaning. (For a more detailed discussion of formalistic approaches to literary works, see Chapter 53, "Critical Strategies for Reading.") The formalist focuses on the text itself rather than the historical, political, economic, and other contexts of a text. A formalist reading of *The Scarlet Letter,* for example, is more likely to examine how the book is structured around a series of scenes in which the main characters appear on or near the town scaffold than to analyze how the text portrays the social and religious values of Nathaniel Hawthorne or of seventeenth-century Puritan New Englanders. Although recent literary criticism has continued to demonstrate the importance of close readings to discover how a text creates its effects on a reader, scholars also have made a sustained effort to place literary texts in their historical and cultural contexts.

Cultural critics, like literary historians, place literary works in the contexts of their times, but they do not restrict themselves to major historical moments or figures. Instead of focusing on, perhaps, Hawthorne's friendship with Herman Melville, a cultural critic might examine the relationship between Hawthorne's writing and popular contemporary domestic novels that are now obscure. Cultural critics might even examine the classic comic book version of *The Scarlet Letter* or one of its many film versions to gain insight into how our culture has reinterpreted Hawthorne's writing. The materials used by cultural critics are taken from both "high culture" and popular culture. A cultural critic's approach to James Joyce's work might include discussions of Dublin's saloons, political pamphlets, and Catholic sexual mores as well as connections to Ezra Pound or T. S. Eliot.

The documents that follow Joyce's "Eveline" in this chapter offer a glimpse of how cultural criticism can be used to provide a rich and revealing historical context for a literary work. They include two early twentieth-century photographs of Dublin, a portion of a temperance tract, a letter from an Irish woman who emigrated to Australia, and a plot synopsis of the opera *The Bohemian Girl:* all these documents figure in one way or another in "Eveline." These documents are suggestive rather than exhaustive, but they do evoke some of the culture contemporary to Joyce that informs the world he creates in "Eveline" and thereby allow readers to gain a broader and deeper understanding of the story itself.

A BRIEF BIOGRAPHY AND INTRODUCTION

James Joyce (1882–1941) was born in Dublin, Ireland, during a time of political upheaval. The country had endured nearly a century of economic depression and terrible famine and continued to suffer under what many Irish regarded as British oppression. Irish nationalism and independence movements attempted to counter British economic exploitation and cultural arrogance. Joyce, influenced by a climate in which ecclesiastical privilege and governmental authority were at once powerful and suspect, believed the Irish were also unable to free themselves from the Catholic church's compromises and their own political ineptitude. Change was in the air, but Ireland was slow to be moved by the reform currents already rippling through the Continent.

Modernism, as it was developing on the Continent, challenged traditional attitudes about God, humanity, and society. Scientific and industrial advances created not only material progress but also tremendous social upheaval, which sometimes produced a sense of discontinuity, fragmentation, alienation, and despair. Firm certainties gave way to anxious doubts, and the past was considered more as something to be overcome than as something to revere. Heroic action seemed remote and theatrical to a writer like Joyce, who rejected the use of remarkable historic events in his fiction and instead focused on the everyday lives of ordinary people trying to make sense of themselves.

Joyce himself came from a declining middle-class family of more than a dozen children, eventually reduced to poverty by his father's drinking. Nevertheless, Joyce received a fine classical education at Jesuit schools, including University College, Dublin. His strict early education was strongly traditional in its Catholicism, but when he entered University College, he rejected both his religion and his national heritage. By the time he took his undergraduate degree in 1902, he was more comfortable casting himself as an alienated writer than as a typical citizen of Dublin, who he thought lived a life of mediocrity, sentimentality, and self-deception. While at college he studied modern languages and taught himself Norwegian so he could read the plays of Henrik Ibsen in their original language (see p. 1709 for Ibsen's *A Doll House*). Joyce responded deeply to Ibsen's dramatizations of troubled individuals who repudiate public morality and social values in their efforts to create lives of integrity amid stifling families, institutions, and cultures.

After graduation Joyce left Dublin for Paris to study medicine, but that career soon ended when he dropped out of the single course for which he had registered. Instead, he wrote poetry, which was eventually published in 1907 as *Chamber Music*. In 1903 he returned to Dublin to be with his mother, then dying of cancer. The next summer he met Nora Barnacle, while she was working in a Dublin boardinghouse. After leaving Dublin with Nora in 1905 to return to the Continent, he visited his native city only a few times (the final visit was in 1912), and he lived the rest of his life in Europe. From 1920 until shortly before his death, Joyce settled in Paris, where he enjoyed the stimulation of living amid writers and artists. He lived with Nora his entire life, having two children and eventually marrying her in 1931.

Joyce earned a living by teaching at a Berlitz language school, tutoring, and working in a bank, but mostly he gathered impressions of the world around him — whether in Trieste, Zurich, Rome, or Paris — that he would incorporate into his literary work. His writings, however, were always about life in Ireland rather than the European cities in which he lived. Fortunately, Joyce's talents attracted several patrons who subsidized his income and helped him to publish.

Dubliners, Joyce's first major publication in fiction, was a collection of stories that he published in 1914 and that included "Eveline." Two years later Joyce published *A Portrait of the Artist as a Young Man,* a novel. Joyce

THE IRISH HOMESTEAD

The Organ of Irish Agricultural and Industrial Development

By Post 1½d.

SEPTEMBER 10, 1904.   THE IRISH HOMESTEAD.   761

to observe, and that the principles which underlie the science of modern agriculture can be instilled into their minds." The question is: How far is it practicable and desirable to introduce into our own colony methods which have proved successful in other lands, and which have done so much to improve the position of the farmers, financially, socially, and intellectually?

OUR WEEKLY STORY.

EVELINE.
By STEPHEN DÆDALUS.

She sat at the window watching the evening invade the avenue. Her head was leaned against the window-curtain, and in her nostrils was the odour of dusty cretonne. She was tired. Few people passed. The man out of the last house passed on his way home; she heard his footsteps clacking along the concrete pavement, and afterwards crunching on the cinder path before the new red houses. One time there used to be a field there, in which they used to play in the evening with other people's children. Then a man from Belfast bought the field and built houses in it—not like their little brown houses, but bright brick houses, with shining roofs. The children of the avenue used to play together in that field—the Devines, the Waters, the Dunns, little Keogh the cripple, and her brothers and sisters. Ernest, however, never played; he was too grown-up. Her father used often to hunt them in out of the field with his blackthorn stick, but usually little Keogh used to keep "nix," and call out when he saw her father coming. Still they seemed to have been rather happy then. Her father was not so bad then, and besides her mother was alive. That was a long time ago; she and her brothers and sisters were all grown up; her mother was dead; Tizzie Dunn was dead, too, and the Waters had gone back to England. Everything changes; now she was going to go away, to leave her home.

Home! She looked round the room, passing in review all its familiar objects. How many times she had dusted it, once a week at least. It was the "best" room, but it seemed to secrete dust everywhere. She had known the room for ten years—more—twelve years, and knew everything in it. Now she was going away. And yet during all those years she had never found out the name of the Australian priest whose yellowing photograph hung on the wall, just above the broken harmonium. He had been a friend of her father's—a school friend. When he showed the photograph to a friend, her father used to pass it with a casual word, "In Australia now—Melbourne."

She had consented to go away—to leave her home. Was it wise—was it honourable? She tried to weigh each side of the question in her mind. In her home at least she had shelter and food; she had those whom she had known all her life about her. She had to work of course both in the house and at business. What would they think of her in the Stores when they discovered she had gone away? Think her a fool, perhaps, and fill up her place by advertisement. Miss Gavan would probably be glad. She, too, would not be sorry to be out of Miss Gavan's clutches. Miss Gavan had an "edge" on her, and used her superior position mercilessly, particularly whenever there were people listening. It was—"Miss Hill, will you please attend to these ladies?" "A little bit smarter, Miss Hill, if you please." She would not cry many tears at leaving the Stores. In her new home in a distant, unknown country, surely she would be free from such indignities! She would then be a married woman—she, Eveline. She would be treated with respect. She would not be treated as her mother had been treated. Even now—at her age, she was over nineteen—she sometimes felt herself in danger of her father's violence. Latterly he had begun to threaten her, saying what he would do were it not for her dead mother's sake. And now she had nobody to protect her. Ernest was dead, and Harry, who was in the church-decorating business, was nearly always down somewhere in the country. Besides, the invariable squabble for money on Saturday nights had begun to weary her unspeakably. She always gave her entire wages—seven shillings—and Harry always sent up what he could, but the trouble was to get any money from her father. He said she used to squander the money, that she had no head, that he wasn't going to give her his hard-earned money to throw about the streets, and much more, for he was usually fairly bad on Saturday night. In the end he would give her the money, and ask her had she any intention of buying Sunday's dinner. Then she had to rush out as quickly as she could and do her marketing, holding her black leather purse tightly in her hand as she elbowed her way through the crowds, and returning home late under her load of provisions. She had had hard work to keep the house together, and to see that the two young children who had been left to her charge went to school regularly and got their meals regularly. It was hard work—a hard life—but now that she was about to leave it she did not find it a wholly undesirable life.

She was about to explore another life with Frank. Frank was very kind, manly, open-hearted. She was to go away with him by the night boat to be his wife, and to live with him in Buenos Ayres, where he had a home waiting for her. How well she remembered the first time she had seen him (he was lodging in a house on the main road where she used to visit). A few weeks ago it seemed. He was standing at the gate, his peaked cap pushed back on his head, and his hair tumbled forward over a face of bronze. Then they had come to know each other. He used to meet her outside the Stores every evening, and see her home. He took her to see the "Bohemian Girl," and she felt elated as she sat in an unaccustomed part of the theatre with him. He was very fond of music, and sang a little. People knew that they were courting, and when Frank sang about the lass that loves a sailor she always felt pleasantly confused. He used to call her "Poppens" out of fun. First it had been an excitement for her to have a young man, and then she had begun to like him. He had tales of distant countries. He had started as a deck boy at a pound a month on a ship of the Allan line going out to Canada. He told her the names of the ships he had been on, and the names of the different services. He had sailed through the Straits of Magellan, and he told her stories of the terrible Patagonians. He had fallen on his feet in Buenos Ayres, he said, and had come over to the old country just for a holiday. Of course, her father had found out the affair, and had forbidden her to have anything to do with him. "I know these sailor fellows," her father said. Frank and her father were at sharp words and after that she had to meet her lover secretly.

The evening deepened in the avenue. The white of two letters lying in her lap grew indistinct. One was to Harry; the other was to her father. Ernest had been her favourite, but she liked Harry, too. Her father was not so bad she noticed; he would miss her. Sometimes he could be very nice. Not long before, when she had been laid up for a day, he had read her out a ghost-story, and made toast for her at the fire. Another day, when her mother had been alive, they had all gone for a picnic to the Hill of Howth. She remembered her father putting on her mother's bonnet to make the children laugh.

Her time was running out, but she continued to sit by the window, leaning her head against the window-curtain, inhaling the odour of dusty cretonne. Down far in the avenue she could hear a street organ playing. She knew the air. Strange that it should come that very night to remind her of the promise to her mother, her promise to keep the home together as long as she could. She remembered the last night of her mother's illness; she was again in the close dark room at the other side of the hall, and outside she heard a melancholy air of Italy. The organ-player had been ordered to go away and given sixpence. She remembered her father strutting back into the sick room, saying:—"Damned Italians! coming over here!" As she mused the pitiful vision of her mother's life laid its spell on the very quick of her being—that life of commonplace sacrifices closing in final craziness. She trembled as she heard again her mother's voice saying constantly with foolish insistence: "Derevaun Seraun! Derevaun Seraun!"

She stood up in a sudden impulse of terror. Escape! She must escape! Frank would save her. He would give her life, perhaps love, too. But she wanted to live. Why should she be unhappy? She had a right to happiness. Frank would take her in his arms, fold her in his arms. He would save her.

She stood among the swaying crowd in the station at the North Wall. He held her hand, and she knew that he was speaking to her, saying something about the passage over again. The station was full of soldiers with brown baggages. Through the wide doors of the sheds she caught a glimpse of the black mass of the boat lying in beside the quay wall, with illumined portholes. She answered nothing. She felt her cheek pale and cold, and, out of a maze of distress, she prayed to God to direct her, to show her what was her duty. The boat blew a long, mournful whistle into the mist. If she went, to-morrow she would be on the sea with Frank, steaming towards Buenos Ayres. Their passage had been booked. Could she still draw back, after all he had done for her? Her distress awoke a nausea in her body, and she kept moving her lips in silent fervent prayer.

A bell clanged upon her heart. She felt him seize her hand:

"Come!"

All the seas of the world tumbled about her heart. He was drawing her into them: he would drown her. She gripped with both hands at the iron railing.

"Come!"

No! No! No! It was impossible. Her hands clutched the iron in frenzy. Amid the seas she sent a cry of anguish!

"Eveline! Evvy!"

He rushed beyond the barrier and called to her to follow. He was shouted at to go on, but he still called to her. She set her white face to him, passive, like a helpless animal. Her eyes gave him no sign of love, or farewell, or recognition.

First Publication of "Eveline." In 1904, the editor of the farmer's magazine *The Irish Homestead* asked James Joyce to write some "simple" stories about Irish life. The magazine published "The Sisters," "Eveline," and "After the Race," before deciding that Joyce's work was not suitable for *Homestead* readers. After some initial trouble with his publisher over the risk of libel, Joyce in 1914 published the stories in *Dubliners,* a book that he called "a moral history" of his country. "I call the series *Dubliners,*" he writes, "to betray the soul of that hemiplegia or paralysis which many consider a city." Though Joyce never lived in Dublin again after he eloped with Nora Barnacle in 1905, Dublin is the setting of almost all of his work. Shown here is a facsimile of the first publication of "Eveline," on September 10, 1904. Joyce signed the story "Stephen Daedalus," his early pen name and the name of the protagonist in *A Portrait of the Artist as a Young Man* (1915) who later reappears in *Ulysses* (1922). **Joyce is shown here at age twenty-two,** the year his stories appeared in *The Irish Homestead.*

James Joyce with Nora and Friends (top). James Joyce, Nora Barnacle (left), and their friends the Sullivans, seated at a piano in Paris. Joyce grew up in a musical family and was said to have a beautiful tenor voice. He loved music and frequently incorporated it in his writing — his works contain thousands of musical references and allusions.
Courtesy of the Poetry/Rare Books Collection, UB Libraries, State University of New York at Buffalo.

James Joyce in Paris (right). James Joyce and Sylvia Beach, proprietor of the Parisian bookstore Shakespeare & Company, during the "roaring twenties." In 1920 Joyce and his family relocated to Paris, and in 1922, Beach published the first edition of *Ulysses*.
© Bettmann/CORBIS.

strongly identified with the protagonist, who, like Joyce, rejected custom and tradition. If the price of independence from deadening sensibilities, crass materialism, and a circumscribed life was alienation, then so be it. Joyce believed that if the artist was to see clearly and report what he saw freshly, it was necessary to stand outside the commonplace responses to experience derived from family, church, or country. His next novel, *Ulysses* (1922), is regarded by many readers as Joyce's masterpiece. This remarkably innovative novel is an account of one day in the life of an Irish Jew named Leopold Bloom, who, despite his rather ordinary life in Dublin, represents a microcosm of all human experience. Joyce's stream-of-consciousness technique revealed the characters' thoughts as they experienced them (see p. 214 for a discussion of this technique). These uninhibited thoughts were censored in the United States until 1933, when a judge ruled in a celebrated court case that the book was not obscene. Though *Ulysses* is Joyce's most famous book, *Finnegans Wake* (1939) is his most challenging. Even more unconventional and experimental than *Ulysses,* it endlessly plays with language within a fluid dream world in which the characters' experiences evolve into continuously expanding meanings produced through complex allusions and elaborate puns in multiple languages. The novel's plot defies summation, but its language warrants exploration, which is perhaps best begun by hearing a recording of Joyce reading aloud from the book. His stylistic innovations in *Ulysses* and *Finnegans Wake* had as great an influence on literature as the automobile and the radio did on people's daily lives, when people started covering more ground and hearing more voices than ever before.

Dubliners is Joyce's quarrel with his native city, and his homage to it. Written between 1904 and 1907, it is the most accessible of Joyce's works. It consists of a series of fifteen stories about characters who struggle with oppressive morality, plodding routines, somber shadows, self-conscious decency, restless desires, and frail gestures toward freedom. These stories contain no conventional high drama or action-filled episodes; instead, they are made up of small, quiet moments that turn out to be important in their characters' lives. Most of the characters are on the brink of discovering something, such as loss, shame, failure, or death. Typically, the protagonist suddenly experiences a deep realization about himself or herself, a truth that is grasped in an ordinary rather than melodramatic moment. Joyce called such a moment — when a character is overcome by a flash of recognition — an **epiphany** and defined it as a "sudden spiritual manifestation, whether in the vulgarity of speech or gesture or in a memorable phase of the mind itself." Even the most commonplace experience might yield a spontaneous insight into the essential nature of a person or situation. Joyce's characters may live ordinary lives cluttered with mundane details, but their lives have significance. Indeed, they seem to stumble onto significance when they least expect it.

Joyce weaves his characters' dreams and longings into the texture of Dublin life, a social fabric that appears to limit his characters' options. He once explained to his publisher that his intention in *Dubliners* "was to write a chapter of the moral history of my country," and he focused on Dublin because that city seemed to him "the center of paralysis." The major causes of his characters' paralysis are transmitted by their family life, Catholicism, economic situations, and vulnerability to political forces. His characters have lives consisting largely of self-denial and drab duties, but they also have an irrepressible desire for something more — as in "Eveline," which focuses on a dutiful daughter's efforts to run away with her lover.

Chronology

1882	Born on February 2 in Dublin, Ireland.
1888–98	Studies at Jesuit schools in preparation for university.
1898–1902	Attends University College, Dublin, another Jesuit school, and graduates with a degree in modern languages.
1902	Studies medicine in Paris but soon abandons it for writing.
1903	Returns to be at his mother's deathbed in Dublin.
1904	Meets Nora Barnacle, with whom he will have two children and live his entire life.
1905	Moves to the Continent to teach at the Berlitz school in Trieste and write.
1907	After working in a bank for a year in Rome, he returns to Trieste; publishes *Chamber Music,* a volume of poems.
1912	Makes his final visit to Ireland.
1914	Publishes *Dubliners* after eight years of censorship battles.
1916	Publishes *A Portrait of the Artist as a Young Man.*
1917	Has the first of a series of debilitating eye operations.
1918	Publishes *Exiles,* a play.
1920	Settles in Paris with his family.
1922	Publishes *Ulysses* amid controversy concerning its alleged obscenity.
1927	Publishes *Pomes Penyeach.*
1931	Marries Nora Barnacle.
1934	Publishes *Collected Poems.*
1939	Publishes *Finnegans Wake.*
1940	After the German occupation of Paris, the Joyces move to Zurich.
1941	Dies of a perforated ulcer on January 13 at Zurich.

Eveline 1914

She sat at the window watching the evening invade the avenue. Her head was leaned against the window curtains and in her nostrils was the odor of dusty cretonne. She was tired.

Few people passed. The man out of the last house passed on his way home; she heard his footsteps clacking along the concrete pavement and afterwards crunching on the cinder path before the new red houses. One time there used to be a field there in which they used to play every evening with other people's children. Then a man from Belfast bought the field and built houses in it—not like their little brown houses but bright brick houses with shining roofs. The children of the avenue used to play together in that field—the Devines, the Waters, the Dunns, little Keogh the cripple, she and her brothers and sisters. Ernest, however, never played: he was too grown up. Her father used often to hunt them in out of the field with his blackthorn stick; but usually little Keogh used to keep *nix* and call out when he saw her father coming. Still they seemed to have been rather happy then. Her father was not so bad then; and besides, her mother was alive. That was a long time ago; she and her brothers and sisters were all grown up; her mother was dead. Tizzie Dunn was dead, too, and the Waters had gone back to England. Everything changes. Now she was going to go away like the others, to leave her home.

Home! She looked round the room, reviewing all its familiar objects which she had dusted once a week for so many years, wondering where on earth all the dust came from. Perhaps she would never see again those familiar objects from which she had never dreamed of being divided. And yet during all those years she had never found out the name of the priest whose yellowing photograph hung on the wall above the broken harmonium beside the colored print of the promises made to Blessed Margaret Mary Alacoque. He had been a school friend of her father. Whenever he showed the photograph to a visitor her father used to pass it with a casual word:

—He is in Melbourne now.

She had consented to go away, to leave her home. Was that wise? She tried 5 to weigh each side of the question. In her home anyway she had shelter and food; she had those whom she had known all her life about her. Of course she had to work hard both in the house and at business. What would they say of her in the Stores when they found out that she had run away with a fellow? Say she was a fool, perhaps; and her place would be filled up by advertisement. Miss Gavan would be glad. She had always had an edge on her, especially whenever there were people listening.

—Miss Hill, don't you see these ladies are waiting?

—Look lively, Miss Hill, please.

She would not cry many tears at leaving the Stores.

But in her new home, in a distant unknown country, it would not be like that. Then she would be married—she, Eveline. People would treat her with respect then. She would not be treated as her mother had been. Even now, though she was over nineteen, she sometimes felt herself in danger of her father's violence. She knew it was that that had given her the palpitations. When they were growing up he had never gone for her, like he used to go for

Harry and Ernest, because she was a girl; but latterly he had begun to threaten her and say what he would do to her only for her dead mother's sake. And now she had nobody to protect her. Ernest was dead and Harry, who was in the church decorating business, was nearly always down somewhere in the country. Besides, the invariable squabble for money on Saturday nights had begun to weary her unspeakably. She always gave her entire wages — seven shillings — and Harry always sent up what he could but the trouble was to get any money from her father. He said she used to squander the money, that she had no head, that he wasn't going to give her his hard-earned money to throw about the streets, and much more, for he was usually fairly bad of a Saturday night. In the end he would give her the money and ask her had she any intention of buying Sunday's dinner. Then she had to rush out as quickly as she could and do her marketing, holding her black leather purse tightly in her hand as she elbowed her way through the crowds and returning home late under her load of provisions. She had hard work to keep the house together and to see that the two young children who had been left to her charge went to school regularly and got their meals regularly. It was hard work — a hard life — but now that she was about to leave it she did not find it a wholly undesirable life.

She was about to explore another life with Frank. Frank was very kind,   10
manly, open-hearted. She was to go away with him by the night-boat to be his wife and to live with him in Buenos Aires where he had a home waiting for her. How well she remembered the first time she had seen him; he was lodging in a house on the main road where she used to visit. It seemed a few weeks ago. He was standing at the gate, his peaked cap pushed back on his head and his hair tumbled forward over a face of bronze. Then they had come to know each other. He used to meet her outside the Stores every evening and see her home. He took her to see *The Bohemian Girl* and she felt elated as she sat in an unaccustomed part of the theater with him. He was awfully fond of music and sang a little. People knew that they were courting and, when he sang about the lass that loves a sailor, she always felt pleasantly confused. He used to call her Poppens out of fun. First of all it had been an excitement for her to have a fellow and then she had begun to like him. He had tales of distant countries. He had started as a deck boy at a pound a month on a ship of the Allan Line going out to Canada. He told her the names of the ships he had been on and the names of the different services. He had sailed through the Straits of Magellan and he told her stories of the terrible Patagonians. He had fallen on his feet in Buenos Aires, he said, and had come over to the old country just for a holiday. Of course, her father had found out the affair and had forbidden her to have anything to say to him.

— I know these sailor chaps, he said.

One day he had quarreled with Frank and after that she had to meet her lover secretly.

The evening deepened in the avenue. The white of two letters in her lap grew indistinct. One was to Harry; the other was to her father. Ernest had been her favorite but she liked Harry too. Her father was becoming old lately, she noticed; he would miss her. Sometimes he could be very nice. Not long before, when she had been laid up for a day, he had read her out a ghost story and made toast for her at the fire. Another day, when their mother was alive, they had all gone for a picnic to the Hill of Howth. She remembered her father putting on her mother's bonnet to make the children laugh.

Her time was running out but she continued to sit by the window, leaning her head against the window curtain, inhaling the odor of dusty cretonne. Down far in the avenue she could hear a street organ playing. She knew the air. Strange that it should come that very night to remind her of the promise to her mother, her promise to keep the home together as long as she could. She remembered the last night of her mother's illness; she was again in the close dark room at the other side of the hall and outside she heard a melancholy air of Italy. The organ-player had been ordered to go away and given sixpence. She remembered her father strutting back into the sickroom saying:

—Damned Italians! coming over here!   15

As she mused the pitiful vision of her mother's life laid its spell on the very quick of her being—that life of commonplace sacrifices closing in final craziness. She trembled as she heard again her mother's voice saying constantly with foolish insistence:

—Derevaun Seraun! Derevaun Seraun!°

She stood up in a sudden impulse of terror. Escape! She must escape! Frank would save her. He would give her life, perhaps love, too. But she wanted to live. Why should she be unhappy? She had a right to happiness. Frank would take her in his arms, fold her in his arms. He would save her.

She stood among the swaying crowd in the station at the North Wall. He held her hand and she knew that he was speaking to her, saying something about the passage over and over again. The station was full of soldiers with brown baggages. Through the wide doors of the sheds she caught a glimpse of the black mass of the boat, lying in beside the quay wall, with illumined portholes. She answered nothing. She felt her cheek pale and cold and, out of a maze of distress, she prayed to God to direct her, to show her what was her duty. The boat blew a long mournful whistle into the mist. If she went, tomorrow she would be on the sea with Frank, steaming toward Buenos Aires. Their passage had been booked. Could she still draw back after all he had done for her? Her distress awoke a nausea in her body and she kept moving her lips in silent fervent prayer.

A bell clanged upon her heart. She felt him seize her hand: 20
—Come!

All the seas of the world tumbled about her heart. He was drawing her into them: he would drown her. She gripped with both hands at the iron railing.
—Come!

No! No! No! It was impossible. Her hands clutched the iron in frenzy. Amid the seas she sent a cry of anguish!

—Eveline! Evvy!   25

He rushed beyond the barrier and called to her to follow. He was shouted at to go on but he still called to her. She set her white face to him, passive, like a helpless animal. Her eyes gave him no sign of love or farewell or recognition.

Derevaun Seraun!: "The end of pleasure is pain!" (Gaelic).

CONSIDERATIONS FOR CRITICAL THINKING AND WRITING

1. **FIRST RESPONSE.** Explain why you agree or disagree with Eveline's decision.

2. Describe the character of Eveline. What do you think she looks like? Though there are no physical details about her in the story, write a one-page description of her as you think she would appear at the beginning of the story looking out the window.

3. Describe the physical setting of Eveline's home. How does she feel about living at home?

4. What sort of relationship does Eveline have with her father? Describe the range of her feelings toward him.

5. How is Frank characterized? Why does Eveline's father forbid them to see each other?

6. Why does thinking of her mother make Eveline want to "escape"?

7. Before she meets him at the dock, how does Eveline expect Frank to change her life?

8. Why doesn't she go with Frank to Buenos Aires?

9. What associations do you have about Buenos Aires? What symbolic value does this Argentine city have in the story?

10. Read carefully the water imagery in the final paragraphs of the story. How does this imagery help to suggest Eveline's reasons for not leaving with Frank?

CONNECTIONS TO OTHER SELECTIONS

1. How does Eveline's response to her life at home compare with that of the narrator in D. H. Lawrence's "The Horse Dealer's Daughter" (p. 701)? Write an essay that explores the similarities and differences in their efforts to escape to something better.

2. Write an essay about the meaning of "home" to the protagonists in "Eveline" and Ernest Hemingway's "Soldier's Home" (p. 187).

DOCUMENTS

CONSIDERATIONS FOR CRITICAL THINKING AND WRITING

1. Describe what this photograph tells you. What does it tell you about life in Dublin? Explain whether you think this photograph confirms or challenges the view of Dublin presented by Joyce in "Eveline."

2. Write an essay describing the mood evoked by this photograph, and compare it with the tone associated with urban life in "Eveline."

OOLE ST.DUBLIN.7880.W.L.

Poole Street in Dublin. The street in this photograph, taken during the period 1880–1914, gives a sense of the "little brown house" that Eveline calls home.
Courtesy of the National Library of Ireland.

THE ALLIANCE TEMPERANCE ALMANACK
On the Resources of Ireland   *1910*

The Alliance Temperance Almanack was published in London. The following excerpt describes the cost of Ireland's drinking habits in economic terms.

Much of the public attention is at this time drawn to the wants of the labouring poor of Ireland, and the great decay of her trade and manufactures. It may therefore be worth while to lay before our countrymen some calculations of the quantity of produce and employment which might arise from the whole population of that country agreeing to apply the vast sum, which, as stated below, is spent annually on whiskey in Ireland, to the encouragement of home manufactures, and the employment of the people. These advantages would follow in the most simple and natural course from the purchase of those articles of prime necessity, or of substantial comfort, the desire for which arises in the mind of every poor man whose habits do not lead him to prefer whiskey to domestic happiness. The Linen Manufacture, which *was* the staple trade of that island, the woollen trade, and the other more useful and indispensable occupations in a civilized community, are chiefly referred to; and the observer will be struck with the immense loss which that country sustains from the propensity to the use of Distilled Spirits.

"It appears from parliamentary returns, that the average quantity of Whiskey which paid excise duty in Ireland for each of the years 1826, 1827, 1828, and 1829, was Ten millions of Gallons. To this, if there be added one-sixth for reduction of strength by retailers, and also about Two Millions, Five Hundred Thousand Gallons made, but which did not pay duty, we shall have a total of upwards of *Fourteen Millions of Gallons, costing, at nine shillings per gallon, by retail, Six Millions Three Hundred Thousand Pounds sterling;* and being equal to a yearly consumption of more than Two Gallons for every man, woman, and child of our population."

•   •   •

The above remarks, though intended exclusively for Ireland, apply with great force to the United Kingdom generally. The ardent spirits, at full proof, on which duty was paid for home consumption in the year ending January 6, 1830, amounted to *twenty-seven millions five hundred and thirteen thousand two hundred and sixty gallons,* imperial measure. To this if we add, at a very low estimate as above, one-sixth, for the reduction of strength by retailers, without computing either the adulterations notoriously made, the spirits smuggled from the continent, or the still greater quantity produced by illicit distillation in Scotland and Ireland, we find that we have expended in one year for ardent spirits, *eighteen millions nine hundred and eleven thousand six hundred and fifty-eight pounds, ten shillings.*

Table I. Shewing that the sum of Six Millions Three Hundred Thousand Pounds, which the People of Ireland pay annually for Whiskey, if expended as follows, would provide

1. The population of Ireland, (computed at eight millions) with 2½ yards of linen each, amounting to 20,000,000 yards, at 1s. 3d. per yard	£1,250,000
2. Ten thousand men in each county in Ireland with 3½ yards of Corduroy each, amounting to 1,120,000 yards, at 1s. per yard	56,000
3. Four thousand men in each county with 3 yards of Kersey each, amounting to 384,000 yards, at 2s. 4d. per yard	44,800
4. Ten thousand men in each county with 2½ yards of Broad Cloth, amounting to 720,000 yards, at 4s. per yard	144,000
5. Four thousand men in each county with one hat each, amounting to 128,000 hats, at 5s. per hat	32,000
6. Three millions of women and children with 1¼ yard of Check, amounting to 3,750,000 yards, at 10d. per yard.	156,250
7. One million of women and children with 6 yards of stuff each, amounting to 6,000,000 yards, at 8d. per yard	200,000
8. Three millions of women and children with 6 yards of printed calico, each, amounting to 18,000,000 yards, at 8d. per yard	600,000
9. Three hundred and twenty thousand women with 2¼ yards of grey cloaking, amounting to 720,000 yards, at 2s. 8d. per yard	96,000
10. Four millions of men, women, and children, with 2½ yards of Flannel each, amounting to 10,000,000 yards, at 1s. per yard	500,000
11. Four millions of men, women, and children, with one pair of shoes each, at 5s. per pair	1,000,000
12. Four millions of men, women and children, with one pair of stockings each, at 1s. 3d. per pair	250,000
13. Ten thousand families in each county with one pair of blankets each, amounting to 320,000 pair, at 10s. per pair	160,000
14. Four hundred tons of oatmeal for each county, amounting to 12,800 tons, at £15 per ton	192,000
15. Three hundred tons of wheat meal for each county, amounting to 9,600 tons, at £18 per ton	172,800
16. Two thousand pigs for each county, amounting to 64,000 pigs at £2 per pig	128,000
17. Two thousand sheep for each county, amounting to 64,000 sheep, at £1 5s. per sheep	80,000
18. Five hundred cows for each county, amounting to 16,000 cows, at £10 per cow	160,000
19. And pay one thousand labourers in each county, (reclaiming land, &c.) amounting to 32,000 labourers, at 6s. per week each, or £15 12s. per year	499,200
20. And support 1,000 aged and infirm in each county, amounting to 32,000 at 6d. per day, or £9 per year each	288,000
21. And build fifty school-houses in each county, amounting to 1,600 at £100 each	160,000
22. And pay fifty school-masters at £50, and fifty school-mistresses at £30 per year, in each county, amounting to 3,200 teachers, at an average salary of £40 each	128,000
23. Leaving for other charitable purposes	2,950
Total	£6,300,000

Let us now see what might be done by a proper application of the money, which the most moderate habitual tippler spends on whiskey in the course of a year.

One glass of whiskey per day, commonly called by drinking men *"their morning,"* costs (at three half-pence per glass) Two pounds Five Shillings and Seven-pence Half-penny, yearly! which sum, if laid by, would provide the following clothing, viz.: —

	£	s	d
Three yards of Kersey for great coat, at 2s. 4d. per yard	£0	7	0
Two yards and a quarter of Broad Cloth for coat and waistcoat, at 5s. 4d. per yard	0	12	0
Three yards and a half of Corduroy for Trowsers, at 1s. per yard	0	3	6
Two Neck Handkerchiefs	0	1	7½
One Hat	0	5	0
One Pair of Shoes	0	7	0
Two Pair of Stockings	0	8	0
Two Shirts	0	8	6
	£2	5	7½

Six million three hundred thousand sovereigns in gold would extend in a line from the town of Roscommon to the Circular Road of Dublin, being a distance of 66¾ Irish miles, or 85 English miles, and would require 49 horses and carts to draw them, at one ton weight each draft.

The same sum, if laid down in shillings, would extend in a line of 1442 Irish miles, or 1835 English miles, and would require 669 horses and carts to draw them, at one ton weight each draft.

The same sum, if laid down in penny pieces, would extend in a line of 25,000 miles, equal to the computed distance round the globe!

The three last year's expenditure on whiskey, say £18,900,000, would afford nine guineas for each family (four persons), in Ireland, allowing the population as already stated, at eight millions of souls!

Note. — The cost of ardent spirits in the United Kingdom which exceeds *eighteen millions nine hundred and eleven thousand pounds sterling, yearly,* would, on the calculations given, afford employment to *four hundred and twenty-eight thousand seven hundred and fifty men;* circulating among them nearly *six million pounds sterling* in wages only.

Our magistrates have already publicly declared that this enormous expenditure of £18,911,658 10s. is not to be regarded as merely useless, but horribly injurious; and their testimony is amply supported by the voice of *ninety five thousand offenders* committed within the past year to the prisons of England and Wales only. On high authority it is asserted that four-fifths of the crimes, three-fourths of the beggary, and one-half of all the madness of our countrymen arise from drinking. Have we nothing to learn from America, where, by the associated efforts of the sober and intelligent for the purpose of discouraging the use of ardent spirits, their consumption is already diminished one-third throughout the whole Union?

From *The Alliance Temperance Almanack* for 1910

CONSIDERATIONS FOR CRITICAL THINKING AND WRITING

1. Describe the tone of this analysis of Ireland's consumption of alcohol. Why is it significant that this temperance publication originates from England?

2. What sort of economic argument is made here? Explain why you do or do not find it convincing.

3. How does this document speak to the conditions of Eveline Hill's life? Pay particular attention to paragraph 9 of the story.

BRIDGET BURKE

A Letter Home from an Irish Emigrant   1882

The excerpt below comes from a letter written by Bridget Burke, who, at the age of twenty-one, emigrated from Galway, Ireland, to Brisbane, Australia. Though her spelling is rough, her affection for her brother John is clear.

Dear John

I am 40 Miles from My uncle. I feal Quare without a Home to goe to when on My sunday out. I often wish to Have you out Heare. I ame verry strange out Here. I cannot make free with any body. I often Have a Walk with Patt [her brother] & Has a long yarn of Home. He is verry Kind became a steady fellow since He Left Home & also I could not expect My father to be a bit better than My Uncle. His wife & children is all right it is a nice place to go but it is to [too] far away but My brother is near me & comes to see me 2 or 3 times a week. We often Have some fun talking of the Old times at Home.

Dear John you wanted to know How do I Like the Country or what sort of people are heare. John that Queston I cannot answer. There is all sortes black & white misted & married together & Living in pretty Cotages Just the same as the white people. Thire is English Irish French German Italian black Chineease and not forgetin the Juse [Jews]. There are verry rich fancy John white girls marrid to a black man & Irish girls to [too] & to Yellow Chinaman with their Hair platted down there[?] black back. Sow [so] you see that girls dont care what the do in this Country. The would do anny think [anything] before the worke & a great Lot of them does worse[?] than that same. & this is a fine Country for a Young person that can take care of himselfe.

Now John I must ask you for all my Aunts & Uncles Cousins friends & Neighbours sweet Harts & all also did Cannopy die yet. Now John I must Conclude Hoping that You will send me as Long a Letter as I have send you & Lett me know all about Home. Dirrect Your Letter as[?] Patt told you for me, I Have more[?] to say but remaning yours fond sister for ever

BDB

From David Fitzpatrick, *Oceans of Consolation: Personal Accounts of Irish Migration to Australia,* Cornell University Press (1994)

CONSIDERATIONS FOR CRITICAL THINKING AND WRITING

1. How does Bridget feel about living in Australia? How does she feel about Ireland?

2. How is Australia's social structure different from Ireland's?

3. How does this letter help to fill in Eveline's feelings about leaving Ireland for Buenos Aires?

4. Research life in Buenos Aires during the first fifteen years of the twentieth century. What would it have been like to live there then? How would it be different from Ireland?

A Plot Synopsis of The Bohemian Girl   *1843*

The following synopsis recounts the story of The Bohemian Girl, *a well-loved opera by Michael William Balfe that played in the principal capitals of Europe, North America, and South America. It gives a sense of the romantic narrative Eveline and Frank would have seen at the opera.*

The action of this drama commences at the chateau of Count Arnheim, in Austria. The peasantry and retainers of the Count are making preparations for the chase, when Thaddeus, a Polish exile and fugitive from the Austrian troops, arrives in search of shelter and concealment. Here he encounters a band of Gipsies, headed by one Devilshoof, who, learning from Thaddeus that he is pursued by soldiers, gives him a disguise, conceals him, and puts the pursuing troops on the wrong track. Just at this time, shouts of distress are heard, and Florestein appears surrounded by huntsmen. The Count's child and her attendant have been attacked by an infuriated stag in the forest, and are probably destroyed. Hearing this, Thaddeus seizes a rifle, and hastens to their relief, and by a well-aimed shot kills the animal, and saves them from destruction. The Count now returns in time to hear of the peril of his darling child, and to see Thaddeus bearing her wounded form in his arms. Overjoyed to find her still alive, the Count overwhelms Thaddeus with grateful thanks, and invites him to join in the festivities about to take place. Thaddeus at first declines, but being warmly entreated to remain, at length consents to do so. They seat themselves at table, and the Count proposes as a toast, "Health and long life to the Emperor!" All except Thaddeus do honor to the toast, and his silence being observed, the Count challenges him to empty his goblet as the rest have done. Thaddeus, to the surprise of all, dashes the wine to the earth; this, of course, produces a burst of indignation. The assembled guests are infuriated by such an indignity to their monarch, and threaten the life of Thaddeus. At this moment Devilshoof returns, and at once takes sides with Thaddeus. The Count orders Devilshoof to be secured. The attendants seize and carry him into the castle. Thaddeus departs, and festivities are resumed. During the *fête*, Devilshoof escapes, taking with him the Count's infant daughter, Arline; and his flight being almost immediately discovered, the greatest excitement prevails. Peasants, huntsmen, and attendants hasten in search of the daring fugitive, and he is seen bearing the child across a dangerous precipice; he escapes, and the unhappy father sinks in despair as the First Act ends.

by Michael William Balfe

The Bohemian Girl. Carefully chosen fragments of opera and popular music are woven into stories in *Dubliners,* providing texture and advancing the dramatic action. In "Eveline" Frank takes Eveline to a performance of an operetta by Michael William Balfe: "He took her to see *The Bohemian Girl* and she felt elated as she sat in an unaccustomed part of the theater with him. . . . He had tales of distant countries." Shown here is the original poster advertising the operetta (1843). The white castle in the upper left corner of the image reflects Eveline's yearning for "another life."
© Mucha Trust.

Twelve years are supposed to elapse, and we are transported to the city of Presburg, in the suburbs of which the Gipsies are encamped with the Queen of their tribe in whose tent dwells the Count's daughter, Arline, now a fine young woman. Florestein, a foppish *attaché* to the Court, is met by Devilshoof and his companions, who relieve him of his jewelry, among which is a medallion, which Devilshoof carries off. Thaddeus, who has joined the tribe, is now enamored of

Arline, and he tells her that it was he who saved her life in infancy, but he still carefully conceals from her the secret of her birth. Arline confesses her love for Thaddeus, and they are betrothed according to the custom of the Gipsy tribe.

A grand fair is in progress in the plaza of the city, and hither, of course, come all the Gipsies, who add to the gayety and life of the scene by their peculiar dances, songs, etc. Florestein appears, and is quite fascinated by the beauty of Arline. While trying to engage her attention, he perceives his medallion hanging on her neck and claims it, charging her with having stolen it. This leads to great excitement: the guard is called, Arline is arrested, and the crowd dispersed by the soldiery. The supposed culprit is brought before Count Arnheim; Florestein presses the charge, and circumstances strengthen the appearance of guilt against Arline, when the Count perceives the mark left by the wound inflicted by the deer on Arline's arm. He asks its origin. She repeats the story as related to her by Thaddeus. The Count recognizes his long-lost child, and the Act ends with an effective *tableau*.

In the Third Act we find Arline restored to her rank and the home of her father; but the change in her prospects does not diminish her love for Thaddeus. He, daring all dangers for an interview, seeks and finds her here. He comes to bid her farewell, and prays that she will, even when surrounded by other admirers, give a thought to him who saved her life, and who loves her. She promises fidelity, and declares herself his and his only. Here we find that the Gipsy Queen, who also loves Thaddeus, has been plotting to take him from Arline. By her device the medallion was discovered in the possession of Arline. Even now she is conspiring to separate the lovers, but her plots fail. Thaddeus relates his history to Count Arnheim, who, in gratitude to the preserver of his child, bestows her upon him. Desire for vengeance now fills the heart of the Gipsy Queen; she induces one of her tribe to fire at Thaddeus as he is embracing Arline, but by a timely movement of Devilshoof the bullet reaches her own heart.

From *The Bohemian Girl,* edited by Richard Aldrich (1902)

CONSIDERATIONS FOR CRITICAL THINKING AND WRITING

1. Describe the action of this opera. How does its plot compare with Eveline's life?

2. Why do you suppose Joyce has Frank take Eveline to this particular opera?

3. One of the songs of *The Bohemian Girl* is titled "Tis Sad to Leave Our Fatherland" and contains these verses: "Without / friends, and without a home, my country too! yes, I'm exiled from thee; what / fate, what fate awaits me here, now! Pity, Heav'n! oh calm my despair!" How do these lines shed light on Eveline's situation?

SUGGESTED TOPICS FOR LONGER PAPERS

1. Write an essay that discusses the theme(s) of this story. Is the theme presented directly, or is it offered implicitly through other elements of the story? Explain whether the theme reinforces your own values or challenges them.

2. Research biographical resources to describe in detail Joyce's attitudes toward Dublin, and explain how they are reflected in "Eveline."

Web Research James Joyce or take quizzes on his work at bedfordstmartins.com/ meyerlit.

15

A THEMATIC CASE STUDY
The Literature of the South

The Southern writer is forced from all sides to make his gaze extend beyond the surface, beyond mere problems, until it touches that realm which is the concern of prophets and poets.
— FLANNERY O'CONNOR

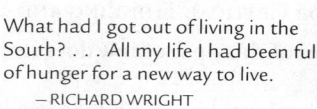

What had I got out of living in the South? . . . All my life I had been full of hunger for a new way to live.
— RICHARD WRIGHT

This chapter provides a variety of materials that are thematically related to the American South. Theme — the central or dominant idea in a literary work — provides a unifying point around which literary elements such as plot, character, setting, and point of view are organized. For a detailed discussion of theme and some strategies for determining theme, see Chapter 8.

The documents that follow are offered as a means of supplementing and contextualizing the short stories by southern writers or about southern life reprinted in this anthology. (A list of twelve such stories appears below.) Taken together, they compose a small anthology that furnishes an opportunity to read intensely fiction that is thematically related to the South. The stories range from the nineteenth to the twenty-first centuries, and the authors include Mark Twain, William Faulkner, Flannery O'Connor, Ralph Ellison, and Alice Walker.

Readers of southern literature have found the region and its literary production fascinating owing to its complexity, variety, and resonance. As O'Connor explains it in *Mystery and Manners,* "We in the South live in a society that is rich in contradiction, rich in irony, rich in contrast, and particularly rich in speech." The South, owing to the issues associated with the Civil War, is a curious study: it is at once peculiarly American and distinct from the rest of the country. Secession was not only a political act but also a state of mind. The materials in this chapter amply explore topics related to southern identities and shed light on the southern short stories in this anthology. The documents range from attempts to define southern culture by such cultural critics as W. J. Cash and Irving Howe to observations about southern writing by such writers as O'Connor and Margaret Walker. In addition, photographs, paintings, and other works of art provide visual representations of southern life. These materials provide a ready context for grasping southern themes in fiction and offer a deeper pleasure and understanding of the short stories.

Related short stories

Ralph Ellison, "Battle Royal," p. 277

William Faulkner, "A Rose for Emily," p. 91

William Faulkner, "Barn Burning," p. 503

Andrea Lee, "Anthropology," p. 193

Flannery O'Connor, "A Good Man Is Hard to Find," p. 449

Flannery O'Connor, "Good Country People," p. 460   (30 rock)?

Flannery O'Connor, "Revelation," p. 474

Katherine Anne Porter, "The Witness," p. 732

Lee Smith, "The Happy Memories Club," p. 588

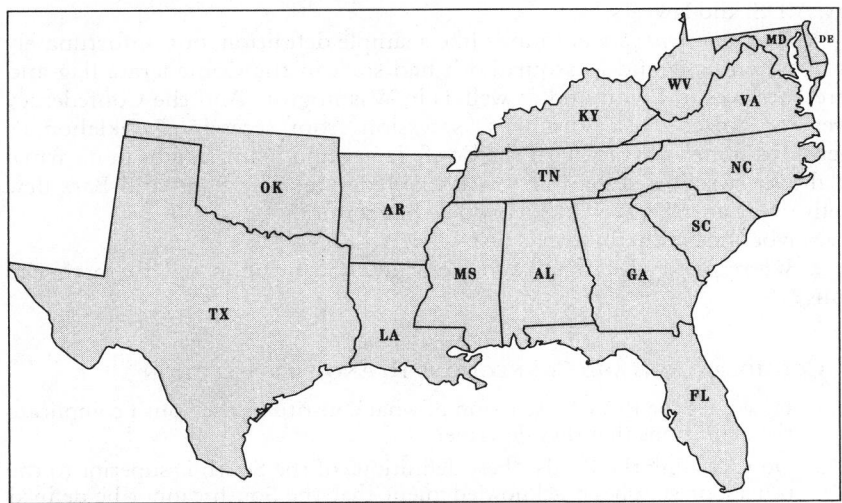

U.S. Bureau of the Census, "The South."
Courtesy of U.S. Census Bureau/The National Archives.

Mark Twain, "The Story of the Good Little Boy," p. 604
Alice Walker, "The Flowers," p. 82
Alice Walker, "Roselily," p. 253

JOHN SHELTON REED AND DALE VOLBERG REED
Definitions of the South   1996

In 1787 Charles Pinckney said, "When I say Southern, I mean Maryland, and the states to the southward of her." But it's not that simple now, if it ever was. Here are three of the most common definitions, and what's wrong with them.

1. *Below the Mason-Dixon Line* once meant south of the Pennsylvania-Maryland boundary, surveyed in the 1760s by two Englishmen, Charles Mason and Jeremiah Dixon. The line gained significance in the nineteenth century when all of the states north of it had abolished slavery. "Below the Mason-Dixon Line" came to mean "in the South," and it has kept that meaning in innumerable popular and country songs as well as in common speech. But the only recent definition of the South that uses the real Mason-Dixon line as a boundary is —

2. *The Bureau of the Census definition.* The Census Bureau's South includes West Virginia, Maryland, Delaware, and the District of Columbia, as well as Oklahoma and twelve less questionable states. (But it doesn't simply include all of the 1860 slave states and territories: Missouri's not in it.) Few other definitions of the South are that inclusive. These days most stop at the Potomac, and even the southern suburbs of Washington are known in some circles as "occupied Virginia." Generally speaking, the "Census South" is more urban, richer, and better educated than the actual South. It also has more armed robbery, AIDS, and lawyers.

3. *The Confederate States* sounds like a simple definition, but unfortunately it's not. Kentucky and Missouri both had stars in the Confederate flag and representatives in Richmond as well as in Washington. And the Confederacy never recognized West Virginia's "secession from secession." Oklahoma's Cherokees signed a treaty with the Confederacy and many fought in its army: Oklahoma wasn't a state, but was it Confederate? The Stars and Bars flew briefly over Santa Fe, New Mexico: does that count?

Maybe the best definition is just —

4. *Where people think they're in the South.* You want to tell them they're wrong?

CONSIDERATIONS AND CONNECTIONS TO ANOTHER SELECTION

1. How does the Reeds' discussion of what constitutes the South complicate the definitions that they describe?

2. Do you think the Reeds' "best definition" of the South is superior to the others, or simply an acknowledgment that the South cannot be defined satisfactorily in geographic terms? Explain your answer.

3. How does your own definition of the South compare with the Reeds'?
4. What do you think the authors would think of the definition of the South that, in effect, emerges from Andrea Lee's "Anthropology" (p. 193)?

W. J. CASH (1900–1941)
The Old and the New South   1941

What the Old South of the legend in its classical form was like is more or less familiar to everyone. It was a sort of stage piece out of the eighteenth century, wherein gesturing gentlemen move soft-spokenly against a background of rose gardens and dueling grounds, through always gallant deeds, and lovely ladies, in farthingales, never for a moment lost that exquisite remoteness which has been the dream of all men and the possession of none. Its social pattern was manorial, its civilization that of the Cavalier, its ruling class an aristocracy coextensive with the planter group — men often entitled to quarter the royal arms of St. George and St. Andrew on their shields, and in every case descended from the old gentlefolk who for many centuries had made up the ruling classes of Europe.

They dwelt in large and stately mansions, preferably white and with columns and Grecian entablature. Their estates were feudal baronies, their slaves quite too numerous ever to be counted, and their social life a thing of Old World splendor and delicacy. What had really happened here, indeed, was that the gentlemanly idea, driven from England by Cromwell,° had taken refuge in the South and fashioned for itself a world to its heart's desire: a world singularly polished and mellow and poised, wholly dominated by ideals of honor and chivalry and *noblesse*° — all those sentiments and values and habits of action which used to be, especially in Walter Scott,° invariably assigned to the gentleman born and the Cavalier.

Beneath these was a vague race lumped together indiscriminately as the poor whites — very often, in fact, as the "white-trash." These people belonged in the main to a physically inferior type, having sprung from the most part from the convict servants, redemptioners, and debtors of old Virginia and Georgia, with a sprinkling of the most unsuccessful sort of European peasants and farm laborers and the dregs of the European town slums. And so, of course, the gulf between them and the master classes was impassable, and their ideas and feelings did not enter into the make-up of the prevailing Southern civilization.

But in the legend of the New South, the Old South is supposed to have been destroyed by the Civil War and the thirty years that followed it, to have been swept both socially and mentally into the limbo of things that were and are not, to give place to a society which has been rapidly and increasingly

Cromwell: Oliver Cromwell, politician and military leader (1599–1658) in the English Civil War; parliamentary forces defeated the royalists (known as Cavaliers).
noblesse: Nobility.
Walter Scott: Scottish novelist (1771–1832).

Metro-Goldwyn-Mayer's *Gone with the Wind* (1939). Vivien Leigh stars as the heroine Scarlett O'Hara in the epic motion picture based on Margaret Mitchell's best-selling 1936 novel of the Old South, the story of a southern belle seeking love and refuge during the tumultuous years of the Civil War and Reconstruction, who ultimately returns to her family's beloved plantation. Though hugely popular, the book and film were criticized by audiences of their time for glorifying slavery and stereotyping African Americans. How does this image reflect W. J. Cash's description of the "Old South"?
© John Springer Collection/CORBIS.

industrialized and modernized both in body and in mind — which now, indeed, save for a few quaint survivals and gentle sentimentalities and a few shocking and inexplicable brutalities such as lynching, is almost as industrialized and modernized in its outlook as the North. Such an idea is obviously inconsistent with the general assumption of the South's great difference, but paradox is the essence of popular thinking, and millions — even in the South itself — placidly believe in both notions.

These legends, however, bear little relation to reality. There was an Old South, to be sure, but it was another thing than this. And there is a New South. Industrialization and commercialization have greatly modified the land, including its ideology. . . . Nevertheless, the extent of the change and of the break between the Old South that was and the South of our time has been vastly exaggerated. The South, one might say, is a tree with many age rings, with its limbs and trunk bent and twisted by all the winds of the years, but with its tap root in the Old South. Or, better still, it is like one of those churches one sees in England. The façade and towers, the windows and clerestory, all the exterior and superstructure are late Gothic of one sort or another, but look

"The Old Plantation Home." This lithograph, created in 1872 by the popular firm of Currier and Ives, presents a romanticized, postwar view of life on the plantation. In this mythic image, slaves are portrayed as happy children and the plantation as a benevolent, familial institution. How does this image relate to Cash's arguments about the "Old" and "New" South?

Reprinted Courtesy of the Library of Congress.

into its nave, its aisles, and its choir and you find the old mighty Norman arches of the twelfth century. And if you look into its crypt, you may even find stones cut by Saxon, brick made by Roman hands.

The mind of the section, that is, is continuous with the past. And its primary form is determined not nearly so much by industry as by the purely agricultural conditions of that past. So far from being modernized, in many ways it has actually always marched away, as to this day it continues to do, from the present toward the past.

CONSIDERATIONS AND CONNECTIONS TO OTHER SELECTIONS

1. What is the paradox that Cash observes in popular descriptions of how the Old South evolved into the New South? How does he resolve that paradox?

2. Explain how the class distinctions between southern gentility and "white trash" described by Cash are at the center of the conflict in Faulkner's "Barn Burning" (p. 503).

3. What do you think Cash means when he writes that the mind of the South "is continuous with the past"? How is this idea presented in Katherine Anne Porter's "The Witness" (p. 732)?

4. How does the still from *Gone with the Wind* evoke "the Old South of the legend" as described by Cash? How is that myth further extended in the Currier and Ives print *"The Old Plantation Home"*?

IRVING HOWE (1920–1993)

The Southern Myth   *1951*

Until very recently, regional consciousness has remained stronger in the South than in any other part of the United States. This "historical lag" is the source of whatever is most distinctive in Southern thought and feeling. After its defeat in the Civil War, the South could not participate fully and freely in the "normal" development of American society—that is, industrialism and large-scale capitalism arrived there later and with far less force than in the North or West. By the Reconstruction period New England regional consciousness was in decline and by the turn of the century the same was probably true for the Midwest; but the South, because it was a pariah region or because its recalcitrance in defeat forced the rest of the nation to treat it as such, felt its sectional identity most acutely during the very decades when the United States was becoming a self-conscious nation. While the other regions meekly submitted to dissolution, the South worked desperately to keep itself intact. Through an exercise of the will, it insisted that the regional memory be the main shaper of its life.

Perhaps because it had so little else to give its people, the South nurtured in them a generous and often obsessive sense of the past. The rest of the country might be committed to commercial expansion or addicted to the notion of progressive optimism, but the South, even if it cared to, was unable to accept these dominant American values; it had been left behind, it was living on the margin of history—a position that often provides the sharpest perspective on history. During the decades that followed the defeat of the South, its writers could maintain a relation to American life comparable, in miniature, to the relation in the nineteenth century between Russian writers and European life. For while nineteenth-century Russia was the most backward country on the continent, its writers managed to use that backwardness as a vantage-point from which to observe West-European life and thereby to arrive at a profound and withering criticism of bourgeois morality. Precisely because Russia was trailing the capitalist West, the Russian writers could examine the bourgeois code without hesitation or illusion. It was this crucial advantage of distance, this perspective from the social rear, that was the major dispensation the South could offer its writers.

And it gave them something else: a compact and inescapable subject. The Southern writer did not have to cast about for his materials, he hardly enjoyed a spontaneous choice in his use of them, for they welled within him like a dream recurrent since childhood. Faulkner has given a vivid if somewhat romantic description of this subject in *Intruder in the Dust*:

> . . . For every Southern boy fourteen years old, not once but whenever he wants it, there is the instance when it's still not two o'clock on that July afternoon in 1863, the brigades are in position behind the rail fence, the guns are laid and ready in the woods and the furled flags are already loosened to break out and Pickett himself with his long oiled ringlets and his hat in one hand probably and his sword in the other looking up the hill waiting for Longstreet to give the word and it's all in the balance, it hasn't happened yet, it hasn't even begun. . . .

But of course it has happened, it must begin. The basic Southern subject is the defeat of the homeland, though its presentation can vary from the magnolia romancing of *The White Rose of Memphis* to the despairing estimate of

The Battle of Gettysburg, 1863, by John Richards. The largest and most decisive battle of the Civil War took place on July 1 through July 3, 1863, in Gettysburg, Pennsylvania. Here the Union army turned back the last major invasion of the North by General Robert E. Lee's Army of Northern Virginia. Losses were heavy on both sides — more than 51,000 soldiers were killed in a mere three days, making Gettysburg the war's bloodiest battle. It is this battle that Faulkner refers to in *Intruder in the Dust.* (See page 554.)
© Bettman/CORBIS.

social loss in *The Sound and the Fury.* Nor does it matter, for the moment, whether one defines the Southern subject, in Allen Tate's words, as "the destruction by war and the later degradation by carpetbaggers and scalawags, and a consequent lack of moral force and imagination in the cynical material-ism of the New South," or as the defeat of a reactionary slaveowning class fol-lowed by its partial recapture of power through humiliating alliances with Northern capital and a new scrofulous commercial class of local origin. Regardless of which interpretation one accepts, the important point is that this subject, like a thick cloud of memory, has been insistently and implacably *there.* The Southern writer could romanticize it, reject it, enlarge it into an image of the general human situation; he could not escape it. And precisely this ubiquity of subject matter provided him with some very considerable advantages. Not so long before the Civil War, Hawthorne had remarked that "No author can conceive of the difficulty of writing a romance about a country where there is no shadow, no antiquity, no picturesque and gloomy wrong, not anything but a commonplace prosperity." But now the War and Reconstruction gave the Southern writers all that Hawthorne had found lacking: all but antiq-uity. And there were ruins to take the place of that.

CONSIDERATIONS AND CONNECTIONS TO OTHER SELECTIONS

1. In what sense, according to Howe, was the South "left behind" the rest of the country, and how did that affect the region's perceptions of itself?

2. Explain how the South's memory of the Civil War is woven into the plot of William Faulkner's "A Rose for Emily" (p. 91). How is this memory related to the story's theme?

3. Choose any of the stories about the South listed on pages 549–50 and explain how "regional memory" is central to its setting and theme.

4. How does the painting *The Battle of Gettysburg* (p. 555) serve as an illustration of Howe's point about the South's relationship to its own past?

FLANNERY O'CONNOR (1925–1964)

The Regional Writer   1963

The present state of the South is one wherein nothing can be taken for granted, one in which our identity is obscured and in doubt. In the past, the things that have seemed to many to make us ourselves have been very obvious things, but now no amount of nostalgia can make us believe they will characterize us much longer. Prophets have already been heard to say that in twenty years there'll be no such thing as Southern literature. It will be ironical indeed if the Southern writer has discovered he can live in the South and the Southern audience has become aware of its literature just in time to discover that being Southern is relatively meaningless, and that soon there is going to be precious little difference in the end-product whether you are a writer from Georgia or a writer from Hollywood, California.

It's in these terms that the Georgia part of being a Georgia writer has some positive significance.

It is not a matter of so-called local color, it is not a matter of losing our peculiar quaintness. Southern identity is not really connected with mocking-birds and beaten biscuits and white columns any more than it is with hookworm and bare feet and muddy clay roads. Nor is it necessarily shown forth in the antics of our politicians, for the development of power obeys strange laws of its own. An identity is not to be found on the surface; it is not accessible to the poll-taker; it is not something that *can* become a cliché. It is not made from the mean average or the typical, but from the hidden and often the most extreme. It is not made from what passes, but from those qualities that endure, regardless of what passes, because they are related to truth. It lies very deep. In its entirety, it is known only to God, but of those who look for it, none gets so close as the artist.

The best American fiction has always been regional. The ascendancy passed roughly from New England to the Midwest to the South; it has passed to and stayed longest wherever there has been a shared past, a sense of alikeness, and the possibility of reading a small history in a universal light. In these things the South still has a degree of advantage. It is a slight degree and getting slighter, but it is a degree of kind as well as of intensity, and it is enough to feed great literature if our people — whether they be newcomers or have roots here — are enough aware of it to foster its growth in themselves.

Trinity — Elvis, Jesus, and Robert E. Lee (1994).   The Southern painter Clyde Broadway (b. 1944) offers a humorous commentary on southern culture, bringing together the popular (Elvis), the sacred (Jesus), and the heroic (Lee), in a work that mimics religious votive painting. Flannery O'Connor once wrote: "the South . . . is most certainly Christ-haunted. The Southerner, who isn't convinced of it, is very much afraid that he may have been formed in the image and likeness of God. Ghosts can be very fierce and instructive. They cast strange shadows, particularly in our literature." Do other figures "haunt" southern literature?
Gift of the Roger H. Ogden Collection, Ogden Museum of Southern Arts, University of New Orleans. © 1994, Clyde Broadway.

CONSIDERATIONS AND CONNECTIONS TO OTHER SELECTIONS

1. Why do you think O'Connor insists that "the best American fiction has always been regional"? Explain why you agree or disagree.

2. O'Connor asserts that southern identity is "not made from the mean average or the typical, but from the hidden and often the most extreme." How is this idea manifested in O'Connor's "A Good Man Is Hard to Find" (p. 449), "Good Country People" (p. 460), or "Revelation" (p. 474)?

3. To what extent is a southern regional identity present in Andrea Lee's "Anthropology" (p. 193)? Discuss whether you think Lee's story illustrates O'Connor's concern that being southern will become "relatively meaningless."

4. Consider the satiric painting *Trinity—Elvis, Jesus, and Robert E. Lee* (above) as a possible example of how, according to O'Connor, southern identity is formed. Explain why you think she would or would not regard this painting as an accurate evocation of southern spirituality.

"Bus Station, Colored Waiting Room, Memphis, Tennessee" (ca. 1960s). At age fourteen, Memphis native Ernest C. Withers (1922–2007) began taking pictures documenting the African American experience of the South. This image documents the Jim Crow institutional segregation that would eventually be dismantled by the civil rights movement. Legal segregation in the United States was especially widespread in the South from the 1870s through the 1950s and 1960s. Margaret Walker writes that segregation "separated and polarized" society. Further, it "ostracized the artistic accomplishments of Black people and ignored their literature." © Ernest C. Withers Estate, courtesy Panopticon Gallery, Boston, MA.

Margaret Walker (1915–1998)

The Southern Writer and Race   *1971*

The southern writer, like all American writers, but perhaps with more intensity, deals largely with race. He or she cannot escape the ever present factor of race and the problems of race as they have grown out of the southern society and affected all of America. The treatment first of the Black man, or the Negro, in southern fiction has been not only the problem of character delineation but also the moral problem of race. The subject of race has been romanticized, and realistically portrayed, and the characters have ranged from wooden stereotypes — flat, mindless, and caricatured as buffoons — to deft and skillful portrayal of both realistic and humanistic proportions. The subject of race has become theme and conflict and character development in southern literature.

   Perhaps the single most glaring fault Black Americans find with southern literature by white writers is in the psychology and philosophy, which of necessity in most instances is racist. This has to be understood in terms of the society, the values emphasized in American education, the nature of slavery and

Elizabeth Eckford. On September 4, 1957, following the Supreme Court's decision to deseg-regate U.S. schools (*Brown v. Board of Education*), fifteen-year-old Elizabeth Eckford attempted to enter Little Rock Central High School. Eckford was pursued by an angry mob that kicked and spat at her, and a wall of National Guardsmen, ordered in by the governor of Arkansas, blocked her entry.

Courtesy of the Library of Congress.

"Sanitation Workers' Strike, Memphis, Tennessee" (1968). Powerful images of the civil rights struggle, such as this famous photograph by Ernest C. Withers, appeared in national newspapers in the 1950s and 1960s and helped mobilize the movement across the country.

© Ernest C. Withers Estate, courtesy Panopticon Gallery, Boston, MA.

segregation, which not only have kept the races apart, separated and polarized in two segregated societies but have ostracized the artistic accomplishments of Black people and ignored their literature. The earliest writers, Black and white, were fighting a racial battle, the white writers were writing apologies for slavery and the Black writers were protesting against the inhumanity of the slave system. With the substitution of segregation, the white child was educated to regard race as more important than humanity and the Black child was educated to imitate a white world as superior to his and thus taught to hate himself. The battle and the conflict can be seen in the literature.

CONSIDERATIONS AND CONNECTIONS TO OTHER SELECTIONS

1. Why does Walker argue that the southern writer "cannot escape the ever present factor of race"?

2. Consider Faulkner's characterization of Tobe in "A Rose for Emily" (p. 91). Using Walker's terms, explain why you think Tobe is a wooden stereotype or a realistic portrayal of a black man.

3. Walker observes that under segregation "the Black child was educated to imitate a white world as superior to his and thus taught to hate himself." How is this dramatized in Ellison's "Battle Royal" (p. 277)?

4. Discuss the relationship between the racial tensions portrayed in the photographs by Ernest C. Withers (pp. 558, 559) and in Ellison's "Battle Royal."

RICHARD WRIGHT (1908–1960)

The Ethics of Living Jim Crow   1937

My first lesson in how to live as a Negro came when I was quite small. We were living in Arkansas. Our house stood behind the railroad tracks. Its skimpy yard was paved with black cinders. Nothing green ever grew in that yard. The only touch of green we could see was far away, beyond the tracks, over where the white folks lived. But cinders were good enough for me and I never missed the green growing things. And anyhow cinders were fine weapons. You could always have a nice hot war with huge black cinders. All you had to do was crouch behind the brick pillars of a house with your hands full of gritty ammunition. And the first woolly black head you saw pop out from behind another row of pillars was your target. You tried your very best to knock it off. It was great fun.

I never fully realized the appalling disadvantages of a cinder environment till one day the gang to which I belonged found itself engaged in a war with the white boys who lived beyond the tracks. As usual we laid down our cinder barrage, thinking that this would wipe the white boys out. But they replied with a steady bombardment of broken bottles. We doubled our cinder barrage, but they hid behind trees, hedges, and the sloping embankments of their lawns. Having no such fortifications, we retreated to the brick pillars of our homes. During the retreat a broken milk bottle caught me behind the ear, opening a deep gash which bled profusely. The sight of blood pouring over my face completely demoralized our ranks. My fellow-combatants left me standing paralyzed

Watching the Good Trains Go By (1964). Romare Bearden (1911–1988) was born in Charlotte, North Carolina, but in 1914 his family joined the Great Migration of southern blacks, moving to the Harlem section of New York City to seek greater opportunities. Bearden, who visited Charlotte throughout his childhood, said he created art in order to "possess the meaning of his southern childhood and northern upbringing." This collage presents his memories of Charlotte, a center of community activities and a major hub for southern railroads, surrounded by cotton fields and farms. For Bearden, the train, just one of the many images at work in this collage, symbolized black migration after slavery, provided jobs, and clocked time. Like the Beardens, author Richard Wright left the South looking for a better life. Born in Mississippi (1908), the son of an illiterate sharecropper, Wright moved to Chicago, New York, and later, to Paris. He is best known for his groundbreaking novel *Native Son* (1940), which portrayed the dehumanization of blacks in a racist society, and *Black Boy* (1945), an autobiography of his childhood in the South.

© Romare Bearden, *Watching the Good Trains Go By*, 1964.

in the center of the yard, and scurried for their homes. A kind neighbor saw me and rushed me to a doctor, who took three stitches in my neck.

I sat brooding on my front steps, nursing my wound and waiting for my mother to come from work. I felt that a grave injustice had been done me. It was all right to throw cinders. The greatest harm a cinder could do was leave a bruise. But broken bottles were dangerous; they left you cut, bleeding, and helpless.

When night fell, my mother came from the white folks' kitchen. I raced down the street to meet her. I could just feel in my bones that she would understand. I knew she would tell me exactly what to do next time. I grabbed her hand and babbled out the whole story. She examined my wound, then slapped me.

"How come yuh didn't hide?" she asked me. "How come yuh awways fightin'?"

I was outraged, and bawled. Between sobs I told her that I didn't have any trees or hedges to hide behind. There wasn't a thing I could have used as a trench. And you couldn't throw very far when you were hiding behind the brick pillars of a house. She grabbed a barrel stave, dragged me home, stripped me naked, and beat me till I had a fever of one hundred and two. She would smack my rump with the stave, and, while the skin was still smarting, impart to me gems of Jim Crow wisdom. I was never to throw cinders any more. I was never to fight any more wars. I was never, never, under any conditions, to fight *white* folks again. And they were absolutely right in clouting me with the broken milk bottle. Didn't I know she was working hard every day in the hot kitchens of the white folks to make money to take care of me? When was I ever going to learn to be a good boy? She couldn't be bothered with my fights. She finished by telling me that I ought to be thankful to God as long as I lived that they didn't kill me.

All that night I was delirious and could not sleep. Each time I closed my eyes I saw monstrous white faces suspended from the ceiling, leering at me.

From that time on, the charm of my cinder yard was gone. The green trees, the trimmed hedges, the cropped lawns grew very meaningful, became a symbol. Even today when I think of white folks, the hard, sharp outlines of white houses surrounded by trees, lawns, and hedges are present somewhere in the background of my mind. Through the years they grew into an overreaching symbol of fear.

It was a long time before I came in close contact with white folks again. . . .

CONSIDERATIONS AND CONNECTIONS TO OTHER SELECTIONS

1. What "lesson in how to live as a Negro" did Wright learn?
2. Compare and contrast the "cinder environment" that Wright describes with the environment of the "white boys who lived beyond the tracks." How does Wright's attitude toward both environments change by the end of the essay?
3. How does Wright's experience as a child in the South connect with Margaret Walker's observations about segregation and the differences between the education of blacks and whites? (See "The Southern Writer and Race," p. 558.)

DONALD R. NOBLE (B. 1941)

The Future of Southern Writing   *1985*

[O]ne can assume that [in the future] race will still be a major subject for Southern literature. . . . The stories of gross cruelty, lynching, and brutality will be fewer and give way to more subtle examinations of race relations in an integrated society. Southerners will continue to be a church-going people, but the role of fundamentalist religion will be diminished in the literature ahead as the influence of the church in the community diminishes. The sense of community itself, long understood as an identifying mark of Southern writing, will also be weaker. Strangers are moving in, and now probably not everyone residing in a small town was born there.

Along with this diminution in sense of community, the South seems to be joining the nation in other attitudes as well. There is more non-teleological thinking, for example, less sense of a master plan. The South will not soon be a nest of nihilists or existentialists, but concerns will move from communal to personal; and chaos and disorder that have been depicted in much Southern literature, as in Shakespearean drama, as a rending of the social fabric, a wound to the body politic, will now be seen in personal and domestic terms, not communal ones. Southerners feel increasingly isolated, alienated from their society, albeit less so than New Yorkers or Los Angelenos, perhaps, and this sense of isolation from kin and neighbors will be a theme of future writing.

As a smaller number of Southerners remain on the land, this central relationship will play a smaller part in Southern writing. The characters of the writing of the future will earn their livings not just as farmers or sheriffs or the owners of small businesses, but as professional people, executives with large corporations, as real estate and life insurance salesmen, and the literature will be set more often in offices, factories, suburbs, and country clubs and less in the fields or woods. The characters of future Southern literature will be a more diverse group. Many will have been sent by their corporations; some will have come from Germany or Japan, perhaps, but they will be making their homes in the South. Because many of them will not have Southern accents, and because radio and television are having their effects on regional speech, there will be less dialect in Southern literature. Phonetic spelling and orthographic humor are already nearly dead and will expire. There will still be Southern speech, of course, but it will be rendered more subtly, through the pronunciations of a few chosen words, through expressions and idioms, through the cadence and lilt of particular regions and groups, such as the way a sorority girl's voice rises at the end of each phrase, making it into a question and an appeal for agreement and approval.

A good portion of the Southern literature of the past has been written by women. Before 1930 or so, much of it was sentimental, popular, and secondrate, but after 1930 Welty, O'Connor, and others have stood in the first rank. But in the future an even higher percentage will be by women, and more importantly, it will be more and more about the question of being female. We can surely look for more frank and even angry writing from Southern women who see themselves as having been denied access in the past to educational opportunities, jobs, full freedom, by having been assigned narrow roles or by having been put up on a pedestal too high to jump off.

Without question, a larger share of the literature will be written by blacks. As educational opportunities for blacks continue to improve there will be more writers; as the economic situation for blacks improves there will be more readers. White readers will, of course, buy and learn from black writings, but the creation of a larger market of black readers is bound to help the black writers. There is every sign this is already underway. There are also indications that this black writing will be different in kind. Rather than focusing on the relations between the races, it will be more frank. It will be about family life, status, love, pain, prejudice, *within* the black community, a community that is still a mystery to most whites, in and out of the South.

CONSIDERATIONS AND CONNECTIONS TO OTHER SELECTIONS

1. How does Noble's characterization of the South differ from W. J. Cash's assessment (p. 551)? According to Noble, what has caused the greatest changes in the South?

2. How does Andrea Lee's "Anthropology" (p. 193) illustrate some of the major developments in the South referred to by Noble?

3. Compare any two stories listed on pages 549–50 and discuss the way in which regional speech is rendered. Which rendition of southern dialogue do you prefer? Explain why.

LEE SMITH (B. 1944)
On Southern Change and Permanence   2001

The South was two-thirds rural in the 1930s. Now it is over two-thirds urban. One half of all Southerners were farmworkers in the thirties; now that figure is at 2 percent. And out of those farmworkers in the thirties, one half were tenant farmers. Now we have no tenant farmers, but migrant workers instead.

As the largest metro areas continue to attract people and jobs, the viability of rural life comes increasingly into question. One half of all the new jobs in this country are being created in the South, with nine out of ten of them in Texas, Florida, and a dozen metropolitan areas. . . .

Our Southern birth rate, which used to be famously *above* the national average, is now below it. This means that immigration is defining the South's population. Ten years from now, Texas will have a 57 percent nonwhite population. Florida will have a 54 percent nonwhite population. Some of the "big nine" states that now contain half the U.S. population will be eclipsed by the "New South": Georgia, North Carolina, and Virginia. Among African Americans, there was a great migration out of the South in the twenties, the thirties, and on into the fifties. But in the 1970s more blacks started moving *to* the South — in many instances, back to the South — than leaving it. That trend has now accelerated. . . .

Some things never change. Some Southern food will never go out of style, no matter how much it may get *nouveau*ed. And large parts of the South still look a lot like they used to — the Appalachian coal country where I'm from, for instance, and the old Cotton Belt. As a whole, we Southerners are still religious, and we are still violent. We'll bring you a casserole, but we'll kill you, too. Southern women, both black and white, have always been more likely than Northern women to work outside the home, despite the image projected by such country lyrics as "Get your biscuits in the oven and your buns in the bed, this women's liberation is a-going to your head." It was not because we were so liberated; it's because we were so poor. This, too, is changing: now our per capita income is at 92 percent of the national average.

With all these changes, what should I tell my student, one of my very favorite students, who burst into tears after we attended a reading together at which Elizabeth Spencer read her fine short story entitled "Cousins." "I'll *never* be a Southern writer!" my student wailed. "I don't even *know* my cousins!" Raised in a military household, relocated many times, she had absolutely no sense of place, no sense of past, no sense of family. How did she spend her childhood? I asked. In the mall in Fayetteville, North Carolina, she tearfully confessed, sneaking cigarettes and drinking Cokes.

I told her she was lucky.

But she was also right. For a writer cannot pick her material any more than she can pick her parents; her material is given to her by the circumstances of her birth, by how she first hears language. And if she happens to be Southern, these given factors may already be trite, even before she sits down at her computer to begin. Her neurasthenic, fragile Aunt Lena is already trite, her mean, scary cousin Bobby Lee is already trite, her columned, shuttered house in Natchez is already trite. Far better to start out from the mall in Fayetteville, illicit cigarette in hand, with no cousins to hold her back, and venture forth fearlessly into the New South. . . .

[Storytelling] is the main thing that has not changed about the South, in my opinion — that will never change. We Southerners love a story, and will tell you *anything*. Narrative is as necessary to us as air. We use the story to transmit information as well as to wile away the time. In periods of stress and change, the story becomes even more important. In the telling of it we discover or affirm who we are, why we exist, what we should do. The story brings order and delight. Its form is inherently pleasing, and deeply satisfying to us. Because it has a beginning, middle, and end, it gives a recognizable shape to the muddle and chaos of our lives.

Considerations and Connections to Other Selections

1. According to Smith, what kind of story do statistics tell about the South?

2. How will Smith's student necessarily differ, as a southern writer, from her predecessors? To what extent can she be a true southern writer?

3. Compare Smith's ideas about the changing nature of the South with Donald R. Noble's views. Do you think they essentially agree or disagree in their assessment of the South? Explain.

4. Choose a Faulkner or O'Connor story from the list on pages 549–50 and discuss whether that story could have been set in the South if it had been written during the past five years.

16

A THEMATIC CASE STUDY
Humor and Satire

[W]hat so many of our beard-tugging critics and the long-suffering students . . . seem to have lost sight of is that stories are meant as entertainment.
—T. CORAGHESSAN BOYLE

Let's get serious: although some austere readers may assume that humor and satire require a rationale or apology, a reading life without laughter would be grimly monochromed and dull. We laugh in color, not just in black and white, because humor is often used as a play of light that allows us to perceive shades of meaning that might otherwise be invisible. Wit, irony, exaggeration, understatement, caricature, parody, and any number of other methods through which a writer opens our eyes to the complexities of human experience illuminate what high seriousness sometimes demands is no laughing matter. Flannery O'Connor's fiction, for example, is heavily freighted with pain, perversity, and tragic attempts at religious salvation, but a responsive reader will also find that her stories include startling humor, despite the presence of murder, a stolen artificial leg, and some lunatic characters (see her three stories in Chapter 12, "A Study of Flannery O'Connor"). Even Herman Melville's weird protagonist in "Bartleby, the Scrivener" (p. 142), who engages in a suicidal withdrawal from life, is invested with a comic dimension. To test this idea, try reading the very brief story that begins this chapter, E. Annie Proulx's "55 Miles to the Gas Pump."

566

Of course people don't always agree about what's amusing, owing to their personal sensibilities and experiences. "That's not funny" is a sentiment that commonly measures the difference in varying responses. Humor can open people's eyes, but it can also cause people to shut them if they feel offended by it. A passionate animal-rights advocate might find T. Coraghessan Boyle's satiric ironies in "Carnal Knowledge" (p. 569) viciously biting, while another reader might believe that the topic of a family pet's death wholly removes any possibilities for humor in Ron Hansen's "My Kid's Dog" (p. 584). Other readers, however, might find one or both of these stories hilarious — and revealing.

As Mark Twain makes surprisingly clear in "The Story of the Good Little Boy" (p. 604), even Sunday school can be unexpectedly funny, because humor often asserts that nothing is sacred. It wears social restraints lightly and refuses to sit still, preferring that others grapple with discomfort. Perhaps Lee Smith's feisty, wheelchair-bound elderly protagonist in "The Happy Memories Club" (p. 588) best expresses the subversive nature of humor. Labeled "inappropriate" (a term demanding compliance that has always crippled humor) by the staff of the retirement home where she resides, this colorful character forthrightly announces at the beginning of the story that "I've always done exactly what I was supposed to do — now I intend to do what I want." Like the stories in this chapter, she's disruptive and she's funny, but she's also serious.

E. ANNIE PROULX (B. 1935)

© Jerry Bauer.

Edna Annie Proulx was born in 1935 and did not finish her first book until 1988. She received a B.A. from the University of Vermont in 1969 and a master's degree from Sir George Williams University, both in history, and later became a freelance writer of articles for magazines in the United States. She published short stories occasionally until she had enough to make her first collection, *Heart Songs and Other Stories* (1988), which she followed with the novel *Postcards* in 1992. Her breakthrough novel was *The Shipping News* (1993), which won both the Pulitzer Prize and the National Book Award, and she has since produced two novels, *Accordion Crimes* (1996) and *The Old Ace in the Hole* (2003), and three books of short stories, *Close Range: Wyoming Stories* (1999), *Bad Dirt: Wyoming Stories 2* (2004), and *Fine Just the Way It Is: Wyoming Stories 3* (2008). Setting her works in places as distant as Newfoundland and Wyoming, Proulx conveys her dark, comic stories by creating a strong sense of place, using her talent for keen detail and for reproducing the peculiarities of local speech. *The Shipping News* and the short story "Brokeback Mountain" from *Close Range* were made into popular films.

55 Miles to the Gas Pump   1999

Rancher Croom in handmade boots and filthy hat, that walleyed cattleman, stray hairs like curling fiddle string ends, that warm-handed, quick-foot dancer on splintery boards or down the cellar stairs to a rack of bottles of his own strange beer, yeasty, cloudy, bursting out in garlands of foam, Rancher Croom at night galloping drunk over the dark plain, turning off at a place he knows to arrive at a canyon brink where he dismounts and looks down on tumbled rock, waits, then steps out, parting the air with his last roar, sleeves surging up windmill arms, jeans riding over boot tops, but before he hits he rises again to the top of the cliff like a cork in a bucket of milk.

Mrs. Croom on the roof with a saw cutting a hole into the attic where she has not been for twelve years thanks to old Croom's padlocks and warnings, whets to her desire, and the sweat flies as she exchanges the saw for a chisel and hammer until a ragged slab of peak is free and she can see inside: just as she thought: the corpses of Mr. Croom's paramours — she recognizes them from their photographs in the paper: MISSING WOMAN — some desiccated as jerky and much the same color, some moldy from lying beneath roof leaks, and all of them used hard, covered with tarry handprints, the marks of boot heels, some bright blue with the remnants of paint used on the shutters years ago, one wrapped in newspaper nipple to knee.

When you live a long way out you make your own fun.

CONSIDERATIONS FOR CRITICAL THINKING AND WRITING

1. **FIRST RESPONSE.** Do you think this story is humorous? Why or why not?
2. What kinds of assumptions about rural and urban life are made in the story? To what extent does Proulx challenge or endorse conventional views of rural and urban values?
3. Consider whether Mr. and Mrs. Croom are round, flat, or stock characters.
4. Is there a resolution to the conflict(s) in the plot?
5. How important is the setting?
6. Write a sentence that expresses your reading of the theme.
7. Describe the style and tone of each paragraph. How do they contribute to the theme?
8. **CREATIVE RESPONSE.** Substitute Proulx's title and final paragraph with your own. How do these changes affect your interpretation of the entire work?

CONNECTIONS TO OTHER SELECTIONS

1. Despite their brevity, how do "55 Miles to the Gas Pump" and Raymond Carver's "Popular Mechanics" (p. 334) manage to create compelling fictional worlds?

2. Compare Proulx's humorous treatment of the West to Stephen Crane's in "The Bride Comes to Yellow Sky" (p. 298).

3. Consider the use of irony in Proulx's story and in Mark Twain's "The Story of the Good Little Boy" (p. 604). Explain why you find the endings of the stories similar or different in tone.

T. Coraghessan Boyle (b. 1948)

Photograph of T. C. Boyle. By permission of the author.

Born in Peekskill, New York, T. Coraghessan Boyle earned a doctorate at the University of Iowa and has taught at the University of Southern California. Among his literary awards is a National Endowment for the Arts Creative Writing Fellowship and the PEN/Faulkner Award for fiction. His fiction has appeared in a variety of periodicals including the *North American Review, The New Yorker, Harper's, The Atlantic,* and *Playboy.* His novels include *Water Music* (1981), *Budding Projects* (1984), *World's End* (1987), *East Is East* (1990), *The Road to Wellville* (1993), *Drop City* (2003), *Talk Talk* (2006), and *The Woman* (2009). His short stories are collected in *Descent of Man* (1979); *Greasy Lake and Other Stories* (1985); *If the River Was Whiskey* (1989); *Without a Hero and Other Stories* (1994), from which "Carnal Knowledge" is reprinted; *T. C. Boyle Stories: The Collected Stories of T. Coraghessan Boyle* (1998); *After the Plague and Other Stories* (2001); and *Tooth and Claw* (2005).

Carnal Knowledge   1994

I'd never really thought much about meat. It was there in the supermarket in a plastic wrapper; it came between slices of bread with mayo and mustard and a dill pickle on the side; it sputtered and smoked on the grill till somebody flipped it over, and then it appeared on the plate, between the baked potato and the julienne carrots, neatly cross-hatched and floating in a puddle of red juice. Beef, mutton, pork, venison, dripping burgers, and greasy ribs — it was all the same to me, food, the body's fuel, something to savor a moment on the tongue before the digestive system went to work on it. Which is not to say I was totally unconscious of the deeper implications. Every once in a while I'd eat at home, a quartered chicken, a package of Shake 'n Bake, Stove Top stuffing, and frozen peas, and as I hacked away at the stippled yellow skin and pink flesh of the sanitized bird I'd wonder at the darkish bits of organ clinging to the ribs — what was that, liver? kidney? — but in the end it didn't make me any less fond of Kentucky Fried or Chicken McNuggets. I saw those ads in the magazines, too, the ones that showed the veal calves penned up in their own waste, their limbs atrophied and their veins so pumped full of antibiotics they couldn't control their bowels, but when I took a date to Anna Maria's, I could never resist the veal scallopini.

And then I met Alena Jorgensen.

It was a year ago, two weeks before Thanksgiving—I remember the date because it was my birthday, my thirtieth, and I'd called in sick and gone to the beach to warm my face, read a book, and feel a little sorry for myself. The Santa Anas were blowing and it was clear all the way to Catalina, but there was an edge to the air, a scent of winter hanging over Utah, and as far as I could see in either direction I had the beach pretty much to myself. I found a sheltered spot in a tumble of boulders, spread a blanket, and settled down to attack the pastrami on rye I'd brought along for nourishment. Then I turned to my book—a comfortingly apocalyptic tract about the demise of the planet—and let the sun warm me as I read about the denuding of the rain forest, the poisoning of the atmosphere, and the swift silent eradication of species. Gulls coasted by overhead. I saw the distant glint of jetliners.

I must have dozed, my head thrown back, the book spread open in my lap, because the next thing I remember, a strange dog was hovering over me and the sun had dipped behind the rocks. The dog was big, wild-haired, with one staring blue eye, and it just looked at me, ears slightly cocked, as if it expected a Milk-Bone or something. I was startled—not that I don't like dogs, but here was this woolly thing poking its snout in my face—and I guess that I must have made some sort of defensive gesture, because the dog staggered back a step and froze. Even in the confusion of the moment I could see that there was something wrong with this dog, an unsteadiness, a gimp, a wobble to its legs. I felt a mixture of pity and revulsion—had it been hit by a car, was that it?— when all at once I became aware of a wetness on the breast of my windbreaker, and an unmistakable odor rose to my nostrils: I'd been pissed on.

Pissed on. As I lay there unsuspecting, enjoying the sun, the beach, the solitude, this stupid beast had lifted its leg and used me as a pissoir—and now it was poised there on the edge of the blanket as if it expected a reward. A sudden rage seized me. I came up off the blanket with a curse, and it was only then that a dim apprehension seemed to seep into the dog's other eye, the brown one, and it lurched back and fell on its face, just out of reach. And then it lurched and fell again, bobbing and weaving across the sand like a seal out of water. I was on my feet now, murderous, glad to see that the thing was hobbled—it would simplify the task of running it down and beating it to death.

"Alf!" a voice called, and as the dog floundered in the sand, I turned and saw Alena Jorgensen poised on the boulder behind me. I don't want to make too much of the moment, don't want to mythologize it or clutter the scene with allusions to Aphrodite rising from the waves or accepting the golden apple from Paris, but she was a pretty impressive sight. Bare-legged, fluid, as tall and uncompromising as her Nordic ancestors, and dressed in a Gore-Tex bikini and hooded sweatshirt unzipped to the waist, she blew me away, in any event. Piss-spattered and stupefied, I could only gape up at her.

"You bad boy," she said, scolding, "you get out of there." She glanced from the dog to me and back again. "Oh, you bad boy, what have you done?" she demanded, and I was ready to admit to anything, but it was the dog she was addressing, and the dog flopped over in the sand as if it had been shot. Alena skipped lightly down from the rock, and in the next moment, before I could protest, she was rubbing at the stain on my windbreaker with the wadded-up hem of her sweatshirt.

I tried to stop her — "It's all right," I said, "it's nothing," as if dogs routinely pissed on my wardrobe — but she wouldn't hear of it.

"No," she said, rubbing, her hair flying in my face, the naked skin of her thigh pressing unconsciously to my own, "no, this is terrible, I'm so embarrassed — Alf, you bad boy — I'll clean it for you, I will, it's the least — oh, look at that, it's stained right through to your T-shirt —"

I could smell her, the mousse she used in her hair, a lilac soap or perfume, 10 the salt-sweet odor of her sweat — she'd been jogging, that was it. I murmured something about taking it to the cleaner's myself.

She stopped rubbing and straightened up. She was my height, maybe even a fraction taller, and her eyes were ever so slightly mismatched, like the dog's: a deep earnest blue in the right iris, shading to sea-green and turquoise in the left. We were so close we might have been dancing. "Tell you what," she said, and her face lit with a smile, "since you're so nice about the whole thing, and most people wouldn't be, even if they knew what poor Alf has been through, why don't you let me wash it for you — and the T-shirt too?"

I was a little disconcerted at this point — I was the one who'd been pissed on, after all — but my anger was gone. I felt weightless, adrift, like a piece of fluff floating on the breeze. "Listen," I said, and for the moment I couldn't look her in the eye, "I don't want to put you to any trouble . . ."

"I'm ten minutes up the beach, and I've got a washer and dryer. Come on, it's no trouble at all. Or do you have plans? I mean, I could just pay for the cleaner's if you want . . ."

I was between relationships — the person I'd been seeing off and on for the past year wouldn't even return my calls — and my plans consisted of taking a solitary late-afternoon movie as a birthday treat, then heading over to my mother's for dinner and the cake with the candles. My Aunt Irene would be there, and so would my grandmother. They would exclaim over how big I was and how handsome and then they would begin to contrast my present self with my previous, more diminutive incarnations, and finally work themselves up to a spate of reminiscence that would continue unabated till my mother drove them home. And then, if I was lucky, I'd go out to a singles bar and make the acquaintance of a divorced computer programmer in her mid-thirties with three kids and bad breath.

I shrugged. "Plans? No, not really. I mean, nothing in particular." 15

Alena was housesitting a one-room bungalow that rose stumplike from the sand, no more than fifty feet from the tide line. There were trees in the yard behind it and the place was sandwiched between glass fortresses with crenellated decks, whipping flags, and great hulking concrete pylons. Sitting on the couch inside, you could feel the dull reverberation of each wave hitting the shore, a slow steady pulse that forever defined the place for me. Alena gave me a faded UC Davis sweatshirt that nearly fit, sprayed a stain remover on my T-shirt and windbreaker, and in a single fluid motion flipped down the lid of the washer and extracted two beers from the refrigerator beside it.

There was an awkward moment as she settled into the chair opposite me and we concentrated on our beers. I didn't know what to say. I was disoriented, giddy, still struggling to grasp what had happened. Fifteen minutes earlier I'd been dozing on the beach, alone on my birthday and feeling sorry for myself, and now I was ensconced in a cozy beach house, in the presence of Alena Jorgensen and her naked spill of leg, drinking a beer. "So what do you do?" she said, setting her beer down on the coffee table.

I was grateful for the question, too grateful maybe. I described to her at length how dull my job was, nearly ten years with the same agency, writing ad copy, my brain gone numb with disuse. I was somewhere in the middle of a blow-by-blow account of our current campaign for a Ghanian vodka distilled from calabash husks when she said, "I know what you mean," and told me she'd dropped out of veterinary school herself. "After I saw what they did to the animals. I mean, can you see neutering a dog just for our convenience, just because it's easier for us if they don't have a sex life?" Her voice grew hot. "It's the same old story, species fascism at its worst."

Alf was lying at my feet, grunting softly and looking up mournfully out of his staring blue eye, as blameless a creature as ever lived. I made a small noise of agreement and then focused on Alf. "And your dog," I said, "he's arthritic? Or is it hip dysplasia or what?" I was pleased with myself for the question — aside from "tapeworm," "hip dysplasia" was the only veterinary term I could dredge up from the memory bank, and I could see that Alf's problems ran deeper than worms.

Alena looked angry suddenly. "Don't I wish," she said. She paused to draw   20 a bitter breath. "There's nothing wrong with Alf that wasn't inflicted on him. They tortured him, maimed him, mutilated him."

"Tortured him?" I echoed, feeling the indignation rise in me — this beautiful girl, this innocent beast. "Who?"

Alena leaned forward and there was real hate in her eyes. She mentioned a prominent shoe company — spat out the name, actually. It was an ordinary name, a familiar one, and it hung in the air between us, suddenly sinister. Alf had been part of an experiment to market booties for dogs — suede, cordovan, patent leather, the works. The dogs were made to pace a treadmill in their booties, to assess wear; Alf was part of the control group.

"Control group?" I could feel the hackles rising on the back of my neck.

"They used eighty-grit sandpaper on the treads, to accelerate the process." Alena shot a glance out the window to where the surf pounded the shore; she bit her lip. "Alf was one of the dogs without booties."

I was stunned. I wanted to get up and comfort her, but I might as well have   25 been grafted to the chair. "I don't believe it," I said. "How could anybody —"

"Believe it," she said. She studied me a moment, then set down her beer and crossed the room to dig through a cardboard box in the corner. If I was moved by the emotion she'd called up, I was moved even more by the sight of her bending over the box in her Gore-Tex bikini; I clung to the edge of the chair as if it were a plunging roller coaster. A moment later she dropped a dozen file folders in my lap. The uppermost bore the name of the shoe company, and it was crammed with news clippings, several pages of a diary relating to plant operations and workers' shifts at the Grand Rapids facility, and a floor plan of the laboratories. The folders beneath it were inscribed with the names of cosmetics firms, biomedical research centers, furriers, tanners, meatpackers. Alena perched on the edge of the coffee table and watched as I shuffled through them.

"You know the Draize test?"

I gave her a blank look.

"They inject chemicals into rabbits' eyes to see how much it'll take before they go blind. The rabbits are in cages, thousands of them, and they take a needle and jab it into their eyes — and you know why, you know in the name of what great humanitarian cause this is going on, even as we speak?"

I didn't know. The surf pounded at my feet. I glanced at Alf and then back 30 into her angry eyes.

"Mascara, that's what. Mascara. They torture countless thousands of rabbits so women can look like sluts."

I thought the characterization a bit harsh, but when I studied her pale lashes and tight lipstickless mouth, I saw that she meant it. At any rate, the notion set her off, and she launched into a two-hour lecture, gesturing with her flawless hands, quoting figures, digging through her files for the odd photo of legless mice or morphine-addicted gerbils. She told me how she'd rescued Alf herself, raiding the laboratory with six other members of the Animal Liberation Front, the militant group in honor of which Alf had been named. At first, she'd been content to write letters and carry placards, but now, with the lives of so many animals at stake, she'd turned to more direct action: harassment, vandalism, sabotage. She described how she'd spiked trees with Earth-First!ers in Oregon, cut miles of barbed-wire fence on cattle ranches in Nevada, destroyed records in biomedical research labs up and down the coast and insinuated herself between the hunters and the bighorn sheep in the mountains of Arizona. I could only nod and exclaim, smile ruefully and whistle in a low "holy cow!" sort of way. Finally, she paused to level her unsettling eyes on me. "You know what Isaac Bashevis Singer said?"

We were on our third beer. The sun was gone. I didn't have a clue.

Alena leaned forward. "'Every day is Auschwitz for the animals.'"

I looked down into the amber aperture of my beer bottle and nodded my 35 head sadly. The dryer had stopped an hour and a half ago. I wondered if she'd go out to dinner with me, and what she could eat if she did. "Uh, I was wondering," I said, "if . . . if you might want to go out for something to eat —"

Alf chose that moment to heave himself up from the floor and urinate on the wall behind me. My dinner proposal hung in the balance as Alena shot up off the edge of the table to scold him and then gently usher him out the door. "Poor Alf," she sighed, turning back to me with a shrug. "But listen, I'm sorry if I talked your head off — I didn't mean to, but it's rare to find somebody on your own wavelength."

She smiled. *On your own wavelength:* the words illuminated me, excited me, sent up a tremor I could feel all the way down in the deepest nodes of my reproductive tract. "So how about dinner?" I persisted. Restaurants were running through my head — would it have to be veggie? Could there be even a whiff of grilled flesh on the air? Curdled goat's milk and tabbouleh, tofu, lentil soup, sprouts: *Every day is Auschwitz for the animals.* "No place with meat, of course."

She just looked at me.

"I mean, I don't eat meat myself," I lied, "or actually, not anymore" — since the pastrami sandwich, that is — "but I don't really know any place that . . ." I trailed off lamely.

"I'm a Vegan," she said. 40

After two hours of blind bunnies, butchered calves and mutilated pups, I couldn't resist the joke. "I'm from Venus myself."

She laughed, but I could see she didn't find it all that funny. Vegans didn't eat meat or fish, she explained, or milk or cheese or eggs, and they didn't wear wool or leather — or fur, of course.

"Of course," I said. We were both standing there, hovering over the coffee table. I was beginning to feel a little foolish.

"Why don't we just eat here," she said.

The deep throb of the ocean seemed to settle in my bones as we lay there in bed   45 that night, Alena and I, and I learned all about the fluency of her limbs and the sweetness of her vegetable tongue. Alf sprawled on the floor beneath us, wheezing and groaning in his sleep, and I blessed him for his incontinence and his doggy stupidity. Something was happening to me — I could feel it in the way the boards shifted under me, feel it with each beat of the surf — and I was ready to go along with it. In the morning, I called in sick again.

Alena was watching me from bed as I dialed the office and described how the flu had migrated from my head to my gut and beyond, and there was a look in her eye that told me I would spend the rest of the day right there beside her, peeling grapes and dropping them one by one between her parted and expectant lips. I was wrong. Half an hour later, after a breakfast of brewer's yeast and what appeared to be some sort of bark marinated in yogurt, I found myself marching up and down the sidewalk in front of a fur emporium in Beverly Hills, waving a placard that read HOW DOES IT FEEL TO WEAR A CORPSE? in letters that dripped like blood.

It was a shock. I'd seen protest marches on TV, antiwar rallies and civil rights demonstrations and all that, but I'd never warmed my heels on the pavement or chanted slogans or felt the naked stick in my hand. There were maybe forty of us in all, mostly women, and we waved our placards at passing cars and blocked traffic on the sidewalk. One woman had smeared her face and hands with cold cream steeped in red dye, and Alena had found a ratty mink stole somewhere — the kind that features whole animals sewed together, snout to tail, their miniature limbs dangling — and she'd taken a can of crimson spray paint to their muzzles so that they looked freshly killed. She brandished this grisly banner on a stick high above her head, whooping like a savage and chanting, "Fur is death, fur is death," over and over again till it became a mantra for the crowd. The day was unseasonably warm, the Jaguars glinted in the sun and the palms nodded in the breeze, and no one, but for a single tight-lipped salesman glowering from behind the store's immaculate windows, paid the slightest bit of attention to us.

I marched out there on the street, feeling exposed and conspicuous, but marching nonetheless — for Alena's sake and for the sake of the foxes and martens and all the rest, and for my own sake too: with each step I took I could feel my consciousness expanding like a balloon, the breath of saintliness seeping steadily into me. Up to this point I'd worn suede and leather like anybody else, ankle boots and Air Jordans, a bombardier jacket I'd had since high school. If I'd drawn the line with fur, it was only because I'd never had any use for it. If I lived in the Yukon — and sometimes, drowsing through a meeting at work, I found myself fantasizing about it — I would have worn fur, no compunction, no second thoughts.

But not anymore. Now I was the protestor, a placard waver, now I was fighting for the right of every last weasel and lynx to grow old and die gracefully, now I was Alena Jorgensen's lover and a force to be reckoned with. Of course, my feet hurt and I was running sweat and praying that no one from work would drive by and see me there on the sidewalk with my crazy cohorts and denunciatory sign.

We marched for hours, back and forth, till I thought we'd wear a groove in 50 the pavement. We chanted and jeered and nobody so much as looked at us twice. We could have been Hare Krishnas, bums, antiabortionists, or lepers, what did it matter? To the rest of the world, to the uninitiated masses to whose sorry number I'd belonged just twenty-four hours earlier, we were invisible. I was hungry, tired, discouraged. Alena was ignoring me. Even the woman in red-face was slowing down, her chant a hoarse whisper that was sucked up and obliterated in the roar of traffic. And then, as the afternoon faded toward rush hour, a wizened silvery old woman who might have been an aging star or a star's mother or even the first dimly remembered wife of a studio exec got out of a long white car at the curb and strode fearlessly toward us. Despite the heat—it must have been eighty degrees at this point—she was wearing an ankle-length silver fox coat, a bristling shouldery wafting mass of peltry that must have decimated every burrow on the tundra. It was the moment we'd been waiting for.

A cry went up, shrill and ululating, and we converged on the lone old woman like a Cheyenne war party scouring the plains. The man beside me went down on all fours and howled like a dog. Alena slashed the air with her limp mink, and the blood sang in my ears. "Murderer!" I screamed, getting into it. "Torturer! Nazi!" The strings in my neck were tight. I didn't know what I was saying. The crowd gibbered. The placards danced. I was so close to the old woman I could smell her—her perfume, a whiff of mothballs from the coat—and it intoxicated me, maddened me, and I stepped in front of her to block her path with all the seething militant bulk of my one hundred eighty-five pounds of sinew and muscle.

I never saw the chauffeur. Alena told me afterward that he was a former kickboxing champion who'd been banned from the sport for excessive brutality. The first blow seemed to drop down from above, a shell lobbed from deep within enemy territory; the others came at me like a windmill churning in a storm. Someone screamed. I remember focusing on the flawless rigid pleats of the chauffeur's trousers, and then things got a bit hazy.

I woke to the dull thump of the surf slamming at the shore and the touch of Alena's lips on my own. I felt as if I'd been broken on the wheel, dismantled, and put back together again. "Lie still," she said, and her tongue moved against my swollen cheek. Stricken, I could only drag my head across the pillow and gaze into the depths of her parti-colored eyes. "You're one of us now," she whispered.

Next morning I didn't even bother to call in sick.

By the end of the week I'd recovered enough to crave meat, for which I felt 55 deeply ashamed, and to wear out a pair of vinyl huaraches on the picket line. Together, and with various coalitions of antivivisectionists, militant Vegans, and cat lovers, Alena and I tramped a hundred miles of sidewalk, spray-painted inflammatory slogans across the windows of supermarkets and burger stands, denounced tanners, furriers, poulterers, and sausage makers, and somehow found time to break up a cockfight in Pacoima. It was exhilarating, heady, dangerous. If I'd been disconnected in the past, I was plugged in now. I felt righteous — for the first time in my life I had a cause — and I had Alena, Alena above all. She fascinated me, fixated me, made me feel like a tomcat leaping in and out of second-story windows, oblivious to the free-fall and the picket fence below. There was her beauty, of course, a triumph of evolution and the happy interchange of genes going all the way back to the cavemen, but it was more than that — it was her commitment to animals, to the righting of wrongs, to morality that made her irresistible. Was it love? The term is something I've always had difficulty with, but I suppose it was. Sure it was. Love, pure and simple. I had it, it had me.

"You know what?" Alena said one night as she stood over the miniature stove, searing tofu in oil and garlic. We'd spent the afternoon demonstrating out front of a tortilla factory that used rendered animal fat as a congealing agent, after which we'd been chased three blocks by an overweight assistant manager at Von's who objected to Alena's spray-painting MEAT IS DEATH over the specials in the front window. I was giddy with the adolescent joy of it. I sank into the couch with a beer and watched Alf limp across the floor to fling himself down and lick at a suspicious spot on the floor. The surf boomed like thunder.

"What?" I said.

"Thanksgiving's coming."

I let it ride a moment, wondering if I should invite Alena to my mother's for the big basted bird stuffed with canned oysters and buttered bread crumbs, and then realized it probably wouldn't be such a great idea. I said nothing.

She glanced over her shoulder. "The animals don't have a whole lot to be   60
thankful for, that's for sure. It's just an excuse for the meat industry to butcher a couple million turkeys, is all it is." She paused; hot safflower oil popped in the pan. "I think it's time for a little road trip," she said. "Can we take your car?"

"Sure, but where are we going?"

She gave me her Gioconda smile. "To liberate some turkeys."

In the morning I called my boss to tell him I had pancreatic cancer and wouldn't be in for a while, then we threw some things in the car, helped Alf scrabble into the back seat, and headed up Route 5 for the San Joaquin Valley. We drove for three hours through a fog so dense the windows might as well have been packed with cotton. Alena was secretive, but I could see she was excited. I knew only that we were on our way to rendezvous with a certain "Rolfe," a longtime friend of hers and a big name in the world of ecotage and animal rights, after which we would commit some desperate and illegal act, for which the turkeys would be eternally grateful.

There was a truck stalled in front of the sign for our exit at Calpurnia Springs, and I had to brake hard and jerk the wheel around twice to keep the tires on the pavement. Alena came up out of her seat and Alf slammed into the armrest like a sack of meal, but we made it. A few minutes later we were gliding through the ghostly vacancy of the town itself, lights drifting past in a nimbus of fog, glowing pink, yellow, and white, and then there was only the blacktop road and the pale void that engulfed it. We'd gone ten miles or so when Alena instructed me to slow down and began to study the right-hand shoulder with a keen, unwavering eye.

The earth breathed in and out. I squinted hard into the soft drifting glow   65
of the headlights. "There, there!" she cried and I swung the wheel to the right,
and suddenly we were lurching along a pitted dirt road that rose up from the
blacktop like a goat path worn into the side of a mountain. Five minutes later
Alf sat up in the back seat and began to whine, and then a crude unpainted
shack began to detach itself from the vagueness around us.

   Rolfe met us on the porch. He was tall and leathery, in his fifties, I guessed,
with a shock of hair and rutted features that brought Samuel Beckett to mind.
He was wearing gumboots and jeans and a faded lumberjack shirt that looked
as if it had been washed a hundred times. Alf took a quick pee against the side
of the house, then fumbled up the steps to roll over and fawn at his feet.

   "Rolfe!" Alena called, and there was too much animation in her voice, too
much familiarity, for my taste. She took the steps in a bound and threw herself
in his arms. I watched them kiss, and it wasn't a fatherly-daughterly sort of
kiss, not at all. It was a kiss with some meaning behind it, and I didn't like it.
Rolfe, I thought: What kind of name is that?

   "Rolfe," Alena gasped, still a little breathless from bouncing up the steps
like a cheerleader, "I'd like you to meet Jim."

   That was my signal. I ascended the porch steps and held out my hand.
Rolfe gave me a look out of the hooded depths of his eyes and then took my
hand in a hard calloused grip, the grip of the wood splitter, the fence mender,
the liberator of hothouse turkeys and laboratory mice. "A pleasure," he said,
and his voice rasped like sandpaper.

   There was a fire going inside, and Alena and I sat before it and warmed our   70
hands while Alf whined and sniffed and Rolfe served Red Zinger tea in Japanese cups the size of thimbles. Alena hadn't stopped chattering since we
stepped through the door, and Rolfe came right back at her in his woodsy rasp,
the two of them exchanging names and news and gossip as if they were talking
in code. I studied the reproductions of teal and widgeon that hung from the
peeling walls, noted the case of Heinz vegetarian beans in the corner and the
half-gallon of Jack Daniel's on the mantel. Finally, after the third cup of tea,
Alena settled back in her chair — a huge old Salvation Army sort of thing with a
soiled antimacassar — and said, "So what's the plan?"

   Rolfe gave me another look, a quick predatory darting of the eyes, as if he
weren't sure I could be trusted, and then turned back to Alena. "Hedda
Gabler's Range-Fed Turkey Ranch," he said. "And no, I don't find the name
cute, not at all." He looked at me now, a long steady assay. "They grind up the
heads for cat food, and the neck, the organs, and the rest, that they wrap up in
paper and stuff back in the body cavity like it was a war atrocity or something.
Whatever did a turkey go and do to us to deserve a fate like that?"

   The question was rhetorical, even if it seemed to have been aimed at me,
and I made no response other than to compose my face in a look that wedded
grief, outrage, and resolve. I was thinking of all the turkeys I'd sent to their
doom, of the plucked wishbones, the pope's noses,° and the crisp browned
skin I used to relish as a kid. It brought a lump to my throat, and something
more: I realized I was hungry.

   "Ben Franklin wanted to make them our national symbol," Alena chimed
in, "did you know that? But the meat eaters won out."

---

pope's noses: Slang for the fleshy tail sections of turkeys and other poultry.

"Fifty thousand birds," Rolfe said, glancing at Alena and bringing his incendiary gaze back to rest on me. "I have information they're going to start slaughtering them tomorrow, for the fresh-not-frozen market."

"Yuppie poultry," Alena's voice was drenched in disgust.   75

For a moment, no one spoke. I became aware of the crackling of the fire. The fog pressed at the windows. It was getting dark.

"You can see the place from the highway," Rolfe said finally, "but the only access is through Calpurnia Springs. It's about twenty miles — twenty-two point three, to be exact."

Alena's eyes were bright. She was gazing on Rolfe as if he'd just dropped down from heaven. I felt something heave in my stomach.

"We strike tonight."

Rolfe insisted that we take my car — "Everybody around here knows my   80 pickup, and I can't take any chances on a little operation like this" — but we did mask the plates, front and back, with an inch-thick smear of mud. We blackened our faces like commandos and collected our tools from the shed out back — tin snips, a crowbar, and two five-gallon cans of gasoline. "Gasoline?" I said, trying the heft of the can. Rolfe gave me a craggy look. "To create a diversion," he said. Alf, for obvious reasons, stayed behind in the shack.

If the fog had been thick in daylight, it was impenetrable now, the sky collapsed upon the earth. It took hold of the headlights and threw them back at me till my eyes began to water from the effort of keeping the car on the road. But for the ruts and bumps we might have been floating in space. Alena sat up front between Rolfe and me, curiously silent. Rolfe didn't have much to say either, save for the occasional grunted command: "Hang a right here"; "Hard left"; "Easy, easy." I thought about meat and jail and the heroic proportions to which I was about to swell in Alena's eyes and what I intended to do to her when we finally got to bed. It was 2:00 A.M. by the dashboard clock.

"Okay," Rolfe said, and his voice came at me so suddenly it startled me, "pull over here — and kill the lights."

We stepped out into the hush of night and eased the doors shut behind us. I couldn't see a thing, but I could hear the not-so-distant hiss of traffic on the highway, and another sound, too, muffled and indistinct, the gentle unconscious suspiration of thousands upon thousands of my fellow creatures. And I could smell them, a seething rancid odor of feces and feathers and naked scaly feet that crawled down my throat and burned my nostrils. "Whew," I said in a whisper, "I can smell them."

Rolfe and Alena were vague presences at my side. Rolfe flipped open the trunk and in the next moment I felt the heft of a crowbar and a pair of tin snips in my hand. "Listen, you, Jim," Rolfe whispered, taking me by the wrist in his iron grip and leading me half-a-dozen steps forward. "Feel this?"

I felt a grid of wire, which he promptly cut: *snip, snip, snip.*   85

"This is their enclosure — they're out there in the day, scratching around in the dirt. You get lost, you follow this wire. Now, you're going to take a section out of this side, Alena's got the west side and I've got the south. Once that's done I signal with the flashlight and we bust open the doors to the turkey houses — they're these big low white buildings, you'll see them when you get close — and flush the birds out. Don't worry about me or Alena. Just worry about getting as many birds out as you can."

I was worried. Worried about everything, from some half-crazed farmer with a shotgun or AK-47 or whatever they carried these days, to losing Alena in the fog, to the turkeys themselves: How big were they? Were they violent? They had claws and beaks, didn't they? And how were they going to feel about me bursting into their bedroom in the middle of the night?

"And when the gas cans go up, you hightail it back to the car, got it?"

I could hear the turkeys tossing in their sleep. A truck shifted gears out on the highway. "I think so," I whispered.

"And one more thing — be sure to leave the keys in the ignition." 90

This gave me pause. "But —"

"The getaway." Alena was so close I could feel her breath on my ear. "I mean, we don't want to be fumbling around for the keys when all hell is breaking loose out there, do we?"

I eased open the door and reinserted the keys in the ignition, even though the automatic buzzer warned me against it. "Okay," I murmured, but they were already gone, soaked up in the shadows and the mist. At this point my heart was hammering so loudly I could barely hear the rustling of the turkeys — this is crazy, I told myself, it's hurtful and wrong, not to mention illegal. Spray-painting slogans was one thing, but this was something else altogether. I thought of the turkey farmer asleep in his bed, an entrepreneur working to make America strong, a man with a wife and kids and a mortgage . . . but then I thought of all those innocent turkeys consigned to death, and finally I thought of Alena, long-legged and loving, and the way she came to me out of the darkness of the bathroom and the boom of the surf. I took the tin snips to the wire.

I must have been at it half an hour, forty-five minutes, gradually working my way toward the big white sheds that had begun to emerge from the gloom up ahead, when I saw Rolfe's flashlight blinking off to my left. This was my signal to head to the nearest shed, snap off the padlock with my crowbar, fling open the doors, and herd a bunch of cranky suspicious gobblers out into the night. It was now or never. I looked twice round me and then broke for the near shed in an awkward crouching gait. The turkeys must have sensed that something was up — from behind the long white windowless wall there arose a watchful gabbling, a soughing of feathers that fanned up like a breeze in the treetops. *Hold on, you toms and hens,* I thought, *freedom is at hand.* A jerk of the wrist, and the padlock fell to the ground. Blood pounded in my ears, I took hold of the sliding door and jerked it open with a great dull booming reverberation — and suddenly, there they were, turkeys, thousands upon thousands of them, cloaked in white feathers under a string of dim yellow bulbs. The light glinted in their reptilian eyes. Somewhere a dog began to bark.

I steeled myself and sprang through the door with a shout, whirling the 95 crowbar over my head, "All right!" I boomed, and the echo gave it back to me a hundred times over, "this is it! Turkeys, on your feet!" Nothing. No response. But for the whisper of rustling feathers and the alertly cocked heads, they might have been sculptures, throw pillows, they might as well have been dead and butchered and served up with yams and onions and all the trimmings. The barking of the dog went up a notch. I thought I heard voices.

The turkeys crouched on the concrete floor, wave upon wave of them, stupid and immovable; they perched in the rafters, on shelves and platforms, huddled in wooden stalls. Desperate, I rushed into the front rank of them, swinging my crowbar, stamping my feet, and howling like the wishbone plucker I once was. That did it. There was a shriek from the nearest bird and the others took it up till an unholy racket filled the place, and now they were moving, tumbling down from their perches, flapping their wings in a storm of dried excrement and pecked-over grain, pouring across the concrete floor till it vanished beneath them. Encouraged, I screamed again — "Yeeee-ha-ha-ha-ha!" — and beat at the aluminum walls with the crowbar as the turkeys shot through the doorway and out into the night.

It was then that the black mouth of the doorway erupted with light and the *ka-boom!* of the gas cans sent a tremor through the earth. *Run!* a voice screamed in my head, and the adrenaline kicked in and all of a sudden I was scrambling for the door in a hurricane of turkeys. They were everywhere, flapping their wings, gobbling and screeching, loosing their bowels in panic. Something hit the back of my legs and all at once I was down amongst them, on the floor, in the dirt and feathers and wet turkey shit. I was a roadbed, a turkey expressway. Their claws dug at my back, my shoulders, the crown of my head. Panicked now, choking on feathers and dust and worse, I fought to my feet as the big screeching birds launched themselves round me, and staggered out into the barnyard. "There! Who's that there?" a voice roared, and I was off and running.

What can I say? I vaulted turkeys, kicked them aside like so many foot-balls, slashed and tore at them as they sailed through the air. I ran till my lungs felt as if they were burning right through my chest, disoriented, bewildered, terrified of the shotgun blast I was sure would cut me down at any moment. Behind me the fire raged and lit the fog till it glowed blood-red and hellish. But where was the fence? And where the car?

I got control of my feet then and stood stock-still in a flurry of turkeys, squinting into the wall of fog. Was that it? Was that the car over there? At that moment I heard an engine start up somewhere behind me — a familiar engine with a familiar coughing gurgle in the throat of the carburetor — and then the lights blinked on briefly three hundred yards away. I heard the engine race and listened, helpless, as the car roared off in the opposite direction. I stood there a moment longer, forlorn and forsaken, and then I ran blindly off into the night, putting the fire and the shouts and the barking and the incessant mindless squawking of the turkeys as far behind me as I could.

When dawn finally broke, it was only just perceptibly, so thick was the fog. I'd 100 made my way to a blacktop road — which road and where it led I didn't know — and sat crouched and shivering in a clump of weed just off the shoulder. Alena wouldn't desert me, I was sure of that — she loved me, as I loved her; needed me, as I needed her — and I was sure she'd be cruising along the back roads looking for me. My pride was wounded, of course, and if I never laid eyes on Rolfe again I felt I wouldn't be missing much, but at least I hadn't been drilled full of shot, savaged by farm dogs, or pecked to death by irate turkeys. I was sore all over, my shin throbbed where I'd slammed into something substantial while vaulting through the night, there were feathers in my hair, and my face and arms were a mosaic of cuts and scratches and long trailing fissures of dirt. I'd been sitting there for what seemed like hours, cursing Rolfe, developing suspicions about Alena and unflattering theories about environmentalists in general, when finally I heard the familiar slurp and roar of my Chevy Citation cutting through the mist ahead of me.

Rolfe was driving, his face impassive. I flung myself into the road like a tattered beggar, waving my arms over my head and giving vent to my joy, and he very nearly ran me down. Alena was out of the car before it stopped, wrapping me up in her arms, and then she was bundling me into the rear seat with Alf and we were on our way back to the hideaway. "What happened?" she cried, as if she couldn't have guessed. "Where were you? We waited as long as we could."

I was feeling sulky, betrayed, feeling as if I was owed a whole lot more than a perfunctory hug and a string of insipid questions. Still, as I told my tale I began to warm to it—they'd got away in the car with the heater going, and I'd stayed behind to fight the turkeys, the farmers, and the elements, too, and if that wasn't heroic, I'd like to know what was. I looked into Alena's admiring eyes and pictured Rolfe's shack, a nip or two from the bottle of Jack Daniel's, maybe a peanut-butter-and-tofu sandwich, and then the bed, with Alena in it. Rolfe said nothing.

Back at Rolfe's, I took a shower and scrubbed the turkey droppings from my pores, then helped myself to the bourbon. It was ten in the morning and the house was dark—if the world had ever been without fog, there was no sign of it here. When Rolfe stepped out on the porch to fetch an armload of firewood, I pulled Alena down into my lap. "Hey," she murmured, "I thought you were an invalid."

She was wearing a pair of too-tight jeans and an oversize sweater with nothing underneath it. I slipped my hand inside the sweater and found something to hold on to. "Invalid?" I said, nuzzling at her sleeve. "Hell, I'm a turkey liberator, an ecoguerrilla, a friend of the animals and the environment, too."

She laughed, but she pushed herself up and crossed the room to stare out   105
the occluded window. "Listen, Jim," she said, "what we did last night was great, really great, but it's just the beginning." Alf looked up at her expectantly. I heard Rolfe fumbling around on the porch, the thump of wood on wood. She turned around to face me now. "What I mean is, Rolfe wants me to go up to Wyoming for a little bit, just outside of Yellowstone—"

Me? Rolfe wants me? There was no invitation in that, no plurality, no acknowledgment of all we'd done and meant to each other. "For what?" I said. "What do you mean?"

"There's this grizzly—a pair of them, actually—and they've been raiding places outside the park. One of them made off with the mayor's Doberman the other night and the people are up in arms. We—I mean Rolfe and me and some other people from the old Bolt Weevils in Minnesota?—we're going to go up there and make sure the Park Service—or the local yahoos—don't eliminate them. The bears, I mean."

My tone was corrosive. "You and Rolfe?"

"There's nothing between us, if that's what you're thinking. This has to do with animals, that's all."

"Like us?"   110

She shook her head slowly. "Not like us, no. We're the plague on this planet, don't you know that?"

Suddenly I was angry. Seething. Here I'd crouched in the bushes all night, covered in turkey crap, and now I was part of a plague. I was on my feet. "No, I don't know that."

She gave me a look that let me know it didn't matter, that she was already gone, that her agenda, at least for the moment, didn't include me and there was no use arguing about it. "Look," she said, her voice dropping as Rolfe slammed back through the door with a load of wood, "I'll see you in L.A. in a month or so, okay?" She gave me an apologetic smile. "Water the plants for me?"

An hour later I was on the road again. I'd helped Rolfe stack the wood beside the fireplace, allowed Alena to brush my lips with a good-bye kiss, and then stood there on the porch while Rolfe locked up, lifted Alf into the bed of his pickup, and rumbled down the rutted dirt road with Alena at his side. I watched till their brake lights dissolved in the drifting gray mist, then fired up the Citation and lurched down the road behind them. *A month or so:* I felt hollow inside. I pictured her with Rolfe, eating yogurt and wheat germ, stopping at motels, wrestling grizzlies, and spiking trees. The hollowness opened up, cored me out till I felt as if I'd been plucked and gutted and served up on a platter myself.

I found my way back through Calpurnia Springs without incident—there were no roadblocks, no flashing lights and grim-looking troopers searching trunks and back seats for a tallish thirty-year-old ecoterrorist with turkey tracks down his back—but after I turned onto the highway for Los Angeles, I had a shock. Ten miles up the road my nightmare materialized out of the gloom: red lights everywhere, signal flares and police cars lined up on the shoulder. I was on the very edge of panicking, a beat away from cutting across the median and giving them a run for it, when I saw the truck jackknifed up ahead. I slowed to forty, thirty, and then hit the brakes again. In a moment I was stalled in a line of cars and there was something all over the road, ghostly and white in the fog. At first I thought it must have been flung from the truck, rolls of toilet paper or crates of soap powder ruptured on the pavement. It was neither. As I inched closer, the tires creeping now, the pulse of the lights in my face, I saw that the road was coated in feathers, turkey feathers. A storm of them. A blizzard. And more: there was flesh there too, slick and greasy, a red pulp ground into the surface of the road, thrown up like slush from the tires of the car ahead of me, ground beneath the massive wheels of the truck. Turkeys. Turkeys everywhere.

The car crept forward. I flicked on the windshield wipers, hit the washer button, and for a moment a scrim of diluted blood obscured the windows and the hollowness opened up inside of me till I thought it would suck me inside out. Behind me, someone was leaning on his horn. A trooper loomed up out of the gloom, waving me on with the dead yellow eye of his flashlight. I thought of Alena and felt sick. All there was between us had come to this, expectations gone sour, a smear on the road. I wanted to get out and shoot myself, turn myself in, close my eyes, and wake up in jail, in a hair shirt, in a straitjacket, anything. It went on. Time passed. Nothing moved. And then, miraculously, a vision began to emerge from behind the smeared glass and the gray belly of the fog, lights glowing golden in the waste. I saw the sign, Gas / Food / Lodging, and my hand was on the blinker.

It took me a moment, picturing the place, the generic tile, the false cheer of the lights, the odor of charred flesh hanging heavy on the air, Big Mac, three-piece dark meat, carne asada, cheeseburger. The engine coughed. The lights glowed. I didn't think of Alena then, didn't think of Rolfe or grizzlies or the doomed bleating flocks and herds, or of the blind bunnies and cancerous mice — I thought only of the cavern opening inside me and how to fill it. "Meat," and I spoke the word aloud, talking to calm myself as if I'd awakened from a bad dream, "it's only meat."

CONSIDERATIONS FOR CRITICAL THINKING AND WRITING

1. **FIRST RESPONSE.** How do your own views of vegetarianism and animal rights' groups influence your response to this story?

2. Comment on how Boyle achieves humorous effects through his first-person narrator in the story's first paragraph.

3. Describe the tone of the first-person narrator. How does he regard the world — the people, situations, and events — he encounters? Why is it especially appropriate that he has a job writing copy for an advertising agency?

4. How does Boyle's style reveal the narrator's character? Select several paragraphs to illustrate your points.

5. How does the narrator use irony? Select three instances of his use of irony, and discuss their effects and what they reveal about him.

6. How does Boyle create a genuinely comic character with Alf? What is the narrator's relationship with Alf?

7. Characterize Alena. Why is the narrator both attracted to her and puzzled by her?

8. How do you think the story would differ if it were told from Alena's point of view?

9. What is your response to Alena's descriptions of commercial experiments on animals? How does the narrator respond to them?

10. What is the narrator's view of the protests he engages in with Alena? Discuss specific passages to support your answer.

11. How does paragraph 93 explain the narrator's willingness to go along with the raid on the turkey farm?

12. Describe the narrator's response to Rolfe. How does Boyle make Rolfe into a comic figure?

13. What is the major conflict in the story? How is it resolved in the story's final paragraphs?

14. How do the story's last words, "it's only meat," shed light on the significance of the title? What does a dictionary tell you about possible readings of the title?

15. **CRITICAL STRATEGIES.** Read the discussion on new historicist criticism (pp. 2054–55) in Chapter 53, "Critical Strategies for Reading," and describe how a new historicist might use "Carnal Knowledge" to describe aspects of American life in the early 1990s.

CONNECTIONS TO OTHER SELECTIONS

1. What do Alena and Nathaniel Hawthorne's Goodman Brown (p. 402) have in common as reformers? Are there also significant differences?

2. Write an essay comparing Boyle's humorous treatment of animal rights issues with Ron Hansen's humorous approach to his son's dog's death in "My Kid's Dog," which follows.

RON HANSEN (B. 1947)

Born in Omaha, Nebraska, Ron Hansen holds a B.A. from Creighton University, an M.F.A. from the University of Iowa, and an M.A. in spirituality from Santa Clara University. He has received numerous fellowships and awards, including the Award in Literature from the American Academy and Institute of Arts and Letters. Hansen has taught writing and literature at Stanford, the University of Michigan, Cornell, and the University of Iowa, and is currently the Gerard Manley Hopkins, S.J., Professor in the Arts and Humanities at Santa Clara University. He is the author of seven novels — *Desperadoes: A Novel* (1979), *The Assassination of Jesse James by the Coward Robert Ford* (1983), *Mariette in Ecstasy* (1992), *Atticus* (1996), *Hitler's Niece* (1999), *Isn't It Romantic?* (2003), and *Exiles* (2008) — a collection of short fiction, *Nebraska: Stories* (1989), and a children's book, *The Shadowmaker* (1987). Hansen's works tend to smudge generic lines, partaking freely of popular modes such as the murder mystery and the western, and to emphasize spiritual conflicts within his characters.

My Kid's Dog   2003

My kid's dog died.
　Sparky.
　I hated that dog.
　The feeling was mutual.
　We got off on the wrong foot. Whining in his pen those first nights. My 5
squirt gun in his face and him blinking from the water. And then the holes in
the yard. The so-called accidents in the house. His nose snuffling into my
Brooks Brothers trousers. Him slurping my fine Pilsner beer or sneaking bites
of my Dagwood sandwich when I fell asleep on the sofa. Also his inability to
fetch, to take a joke, to find the humor in sudden air horns. To be dandled,
roughhoused, or teased. And then the growling, the skulking, the snapping at
my ankles, the hiding from me under the house, and literally thousands of abject refusals to obey. Like, *Who the hell are you?*
　You'd have thought he was a cat. When pushed to the brink I shouted, "I'll
cut your face off and show it to you," and the small-brained mammal just
stared at me.
　But with the kids or my wife little Foo-Foo was a changeling, conning them
with the tail, the prance, the peppiness, the soft chocolate eyes, the sloppy
expressions of love, the easy tricks that if I performed I'd get no credit for.
　Oh, we understood each other all right. I was on to him.
　And then, at age ten, and none too soon, he kicked the bucket. You'd think
that would be it. End of story. But no, he had to get even.
　Those who have tears, prepare to shed them.   10
　I was futzing with the hinges on the front-yard gate on a Saturday afternoon, my tattersall shirtsleeves rolled up and mind off in Oklahoma, when I
noticed Fido in the California shade, snoozing, but for once a little wistful too,

and far more serene than he usually was in my offensive presence. I tried to surprise him with my standard patriarchal shout, but it was no go, so I walked over and prodded the little guy with my wingtip. Nothing doing. And not so much as a flutter in his oddly abstracted face. Surely this was the big sleep, I thought.

She who must be obeyed was at the mall, provisioning, so I was safe from objection or inquiry on that account. I then made an inventory of my progeny: Buzz in the collegiate East, in the realm of heart-attack tuitions, Zack in the netherworld of the surf shop, Suzy, my last kid, on her bike and somewhere with her cousin. Were I to bury Rover with due haste and dispatch I could forestall the waterworks, even convince them that he'd signed up with the circus, run afoul of Cruella De Vil° — anything but died.

I got a green tarpaulin from the garage and laid it out on the front lawn where I hesitated before using my shoe to roll Spot into his funeral shroud, then dragged him back into the victory garden where summer's dying zucchini plants were in riot. With trusty spade I dug his burial place, heaped earth atop him, tamped it down with satisfying *whumps.*

I was feeling good about myself, heroic, as if, miraculously, compassion and charity had invaded not only my bones but my sinewy muscle tissues. I fixed myself a tall glass of gin and tonic and watched the first quarter of the USC football game.

And then pangs of conscience assailed me. Hadn't my investigation of said demise of Precious been rather cursory? Wouldn't I, myself, closely cross-examine a suspect whose emotions were clouded, whose nefarious wishes were well established, whose veterinary skills were without credential? The innocence of my childhood had been spoiled with the tales of Edgar Allan Poe, so it was not difficult to conjure images of Scruffy clawing through tarpaulin and earth as he fought for one last gasp of air, air that others could more profitably use.

I marched out to the garden with aforementioned spade and with great lumbar strain exhumed our darling lapdog. Considering the circumstances, he seemed none the worse for wear, but I did detect a marked disinclination to respirate, which I took as a sign either of his inveterate stubbornness or of his having reached the Stygian shore. The latter seemed more likely. I heard in my fuddled head a line from *The Wild Bunch* when a critically injured gunman begs his outlaw gang to "finish it." And in the healing spirit of Hippocrates I lifted high the shovel and whanged it down on Harvey's head.

To my relief, not a whimper issued from him. I was confident he was defunct.

With care I shrouded and buried him again, committing earth to earth and dust to dust and so on, and with spritelike step conveyed myself to the kitchen where I made another gin and tonic and, in semiprone position, settled into the game's third quarter, the fabled Trojan running attack grinding out, it would seem, another win.

I was shocked awake by the impertinence of a ringing telephone, which I, with due caution, answered. It was my wife's friend Vicki inquiring about the pooch, for it was her assertion that Snip had fancied a taste of her son's upper calf and without invitation or permission to do so had partaken of same

15

Cruella De Vil: A fictional character popularized in Disney films who kidnapped puppies.

within the last twenty-four hours. Even while I was wondering what toxicity lurked in the child's leg and to what extent the poison was culpably responsible for our adored pet's actionable extinction, a loss we would feel for our lifetimes, Vicki insisted that I have the dog checked out by a vet to ascertain if he had rabies.

Cause of death: rabies? It seemed unlikely. Notwithstanding his surliness, 20 there'd been no Cujoesque frothing or lunging at car windows; but my familiarity with torts has made me both careful and rather unctuous in confrontation with a plaintiff, and so I assured the complainant that I would accede to her request.

Off to the back yard again, my pace that of a woebegone trudge, and with my implement of agriculture I displaced the slack and loosened earth. This was getting old. With an accusatory tone I said, "You're doing this on purpose, aren't you," and I took his silence as a plea of nolo contendere.°

My plan, of course, was to employ the Oldsmobile 88 to transport my burden to the canine's autopsy at Dr. Romo's office just a half mile away. However, upon settling into its plush front seat, it came to my attention that Zack — he who is but a sojourner on this earth — had not thought to replenish the fuel he'd used up on his trip to the Hollywood Bowl last night. The vehicle was not in a condition of plenitude. Would not ferry us farther than a block.

With Buster lying in the altogether on the driveway, not yet unsightly but no calendar page, I went into the house and found an old leather suitcase in the attic, then stuffed the mutt into the larger flapped compartment before hefting him on his final journey to those veterinary rooms he always shivered in.

I am, as I may have implied, a man of depth, perspicacity, and nearly Olympian strength, but I found myself hauling my heavy and lifeless cargo to Dr. Romo's with a pronounced lack of vigor and resolve. The September afternoon was hot, the Pasadena streets were vacant, the entire world seemed to have found entertainment and surcease in ways that I had not. I was, in a word, in a sweaty snit, and after many panting and pain-filled stops, my spine in Quasimodo configuration and my right arm gradually inching longer than my left, it was all I could do not to heave the suitcase containing Wonderdog into a haulaway behind the Chinese restaurant.

But during our joint ordeal I had developed a grudging affection for our 25 pet; he who'd been so quick to defend my kith and kin against the noise of passing trucks, who took loud notice of the squirrels outside, who held fast in the foyer, hackles raised, fearlessly barking, whenever company arrived at the front door. With him I seemed calm, masterful, and uneccentric, the Superior Man that the *I Ching* talks so much about. Without him, I thought, I would be otherwise.

I put down the suitcase to shake the ache from my fingers and subtract affliction from my back, and it was then that my final indignity came. An angel of mercy spied my plight, braked his ancient Cadillac, and got out, his facial piercings and tattoos and shoot-the-marbles eyes belying the kindness and decency of his heart as he asked, "Can I help you with that suitcase?"

"I can handle it."

"Are you sure?"

---

nolo contendere: Latin for "I do not wish to contend."

"I'm just two blocks away."

"What the heck's in it?" he asked.   30

And for some reason I said, "A family heirloom."

"Wow!" he said. "Why don't you put it in my trunk and I'll help you with it? I got nothin' better to do."

Well, I did not just fall off the turnip truck. I would have been, in other circumstances, suspicious. But I was all too aware of the weight and worthlessness of my cumbrance, and so I granted his specified offer, hoisting the deceased into the Seville and slamming down the trunk lid. And, in evidence of our fallen state, my Samaritan immediately took off without me, jeering and peeling rubber and speeding west toward Los Angeles.

I could only lift my hand in a languid wave. *So long, old sport.*

Our world being the location of penance and recrimination, it was only   35 right that my last kid should pedal up to me on her bike just then and ask, "Daddy, what are you doing here?"

Waving to a guy, I thought, *who's about to become an undertaker.*

And then I confessed. Sparky's sudden death, the burial, not the exhumation and execution attempt, but the imputation of rabies and my arduous efforts to acquit his reputation with a pilgrimage to the vet's.

Suzy took it in with sangfroid for a little while, but then the lip quivered and tears spilled from her gorgeous eyes, and as I held her close she begged me to get her another dog just like Sparky. And that was Sparky's final revenge, for I said, "Okay, honey. Another dog, just like him."

CONSIDERATIONS FOR CRITICAL THINKING AND WRITING

1. **FIRST RESPONSE.** What's so funny about a family's dog dying? How does Hansen transform this unpromising subject matter into humorous material?

2. Is there anything likable about the narrator despite the way he treats Sparky and his wife and children? Explain why or why not.

3. How does the narrator's use of language help to characterize him? Choose a paragraph in which his language seems representative of his personality, and analyze the way in which his diction and phrasing reveals his character.

4. Point to specific moments in the story when Hansen further complicates the plot and delays resolving the story's conflicts.

5. Trace the names that the narrator calls the dog throughout the story. Do they suggest anything about how he really feels about him?

6. In what sense is this story a revenge plot?

7. Discuss the tone of the final paragraph. Is it consistent with the rest of the story? Why or why not?

CONNECTIONS TO OTHER SELECTIONS

1. Compare the opening lines of this story with the openings of several others in this anthology. Discuss how their respective writers immediately engage their readers' interest.

2. Compare the tone of this revenge story with that of Edgar Allan Poe's "The Cask of Amontillado" (p. 727).

LEE SMITH (B. 1944)

Born in the Appalachian coal-mining town of Grundy, Virginia, Lee Smith was educated at Hollins College, where she and fellow-student Annie Dillard (the essayist and novelist) taught themselves to be go-go dancers for a female rock band named the Virginia Woolfs—a calling that quickly gave way to fiction writing as well as eventually teaching at North Carolina State University. During her senior year, Smith began writing a novel that was published as her first book, *The Last Day the Dog Bushes Bloomed* (1968). Since then she has published three collections of short stories—*Cakewalk* (1981), *Me and My Baby View the Eclipse* (1990), and *News of the Spirit* (1997)—along with more than ten novels, including *Fancy Street* (1973), *Black Mountain Breakdown* (1981), *Fair and Tender Ladies* (1988), *Devil's Dream* (1996), *The Last Girls* (2003), and *On Agate Hill* (2006). Her literary prizes include two O. Henry Awards, the Southern Critics Circle Award, and the Robert Penn Warren Prize for fiction. "Narrative," writes Smith, "is as necessary to me as breathing air. I write for the reason I've always done so: simply to survive." In "The Happy Memories Club" Smith creates a narrator who also insists on telling a story.

Bryan Regan Photography, Raleigh, NC.

The Happy Memories Club   1995

I may be old, but I'm not dead.

Perhaps you are surprised to hear this. You may be surprised to learn that people like me are still capable of original ideas, intelligent insights, and intense feelings. Passionate love affairs, for example, are not uncommon here. Pacemakers cannot regulate the wild, unbridled yearnings of the heart. You do not wish to know this, I imagine. This knowledge is probably upsetting to you, as it is upsetting to my sons, who do not want to hear, for instance, about my relationship with Dr. Solomon Marx, the historian. "Please, Mom," my son Alex said, rolling his eyes. "Come on, Mama," my son Johnny said. "Can't you maintain a little dignity here?" *Dignity,* said Johnny, who runs a chain of miniature-golf courses! "I have had enough dignity to last me for the rest of my life, thank you," I told Johnny.

I've always done exactly what I was supposed to do—now I intend to do what I want.

"Besides, Dr. Solomon Marx is the joy of my life," I told them. This remained true even when my second surgery was less than successful, obliging me to take to this chair. It remained true until Solomon's most recent stroke, five weeks ago, which has paralyzed him below the waist and caused his thoughts to become disordered, so that he cannot always remember things, or the words for things. A survivor himself, Solomon is an expert on the Holocaust. He has numbers tattooed on his arm. He used to travel the world, speaking about the Holocaust. Now he can't remember what to call it.

"Well, I think it's a blessing," said one of the nurses — that young Miss 5 Rogers. "The Holocaust was just awful."

"It is not a blessing, you ignorant bitch," I told her. "It is the end; our memories are all we've got." I put myself in reverse and sped off before she could reply. I could feel her staring at me as I motored down the hall. I am sure she wrote something in her ever-present notebook. "Inappropriate" and "unmanageable" are among the words they use, unpleasant and inaccurate adjectives all.

The words Solomon can't recall are always nouns.

"My dear," he said to me one day recently, when they had wheeled him out into the Residence Center lobby, "what did you say your name was?" He knew it, of course, deep in his heart's core, as well as he knew his own.

"Alice Scully," I said.

"Ah. Alice Scully," he said. "And what is it that we used to do together, 10 Alice Scully, which brought me such intense — oh, so big —" His eyes were like bright little beads in his pinched face. "It was of the greatest, ah —"

"Sex," I told him. "You loved it."

He grinned at me. "Oh, yes," he said. "Sex. It was sex, indeed."

"Mrs. Scully!" his nurse snapped.

Now I have devised a little game to help Solomon remember nouns. It works like this. Whenever they bring him out, I go over to him and clasp my hands together as if I were hiding something in them. "If you can guess what I've got here," I say, "I'll give you a kiss."

He squints in concentration, fishing for nouns. If he gets one, I give him 15 a kiss.

Some days are better than others.

This is true for us all, of course. We can't be expected to remember everything we know.

In my life I was a teacher, and a good one. I taught English in the days when it was English, not "language arts." I taught for forty years at the Sandy Point School, in Sandy Point, Virginia, where I lived with my husband, Harold Scully, and raised four sons, three of them Harold's. Harold owned and ran the Trent Riverside Pharmacy until the day he dropped dead in his drugstore counting out antibiotics for a Methodist preacher. His mouth and his eyes were wide open, as if whatever he found on the other side surprised him mightily. I was sorry to see this, since Harold was not a man who liked surprises.

I must say I gave him none. I was a good wife to Harold, though I was at first dismayed to learn that this role entailed taking care of his parents from the day of our marriage until their deaths. They both lived long lives, and his mother went blind at the end. But we lived in their house, the largest house in Sandy Point, right on the old tidal river, and their wealth enabled us to send our own sons off to the finest schools and even, in Robert's case, to medical school.

Harold's parents never got over Harold's failure to get into medical school 20 himself. In fact, he barely made it through pharmacy school. As far as I know, however, he was a good pharmacist, never poisoning anybody or mixing up prescriptions. He loved to look at the orderly rows of bottles on his shelves. He loved labeling. Often he dispensed medical advice to his customers: which cough medicine worked best, what to put on a boil. People trusted him. Harold got a great deal of pleasure from his job and from his standing in the community.

I taught school at first because I was trained to do it and because I wanted to. I was never one to plan a menu or clip a recipe out of a magazine. I left all that to Harold's mother and to the family housekeeper, Lucille.

Anyway, I loved teaching. I loved to diagram sentences on the board, precisely separating the subject from the predicate with a vertical line, the linking verb from the predicate adjective with a slanted line, and so forth. The children used to try to stump me by making up long sentences they thought I couldn't diagram, sentences so complex that my final diagram on the board looked like a blueprint for a cathedral, with flying buttresses everywhere, all the lines connecting.

I loved geography, as well — tracing roads, tracing rivers. I loved to trace the route of the pony express, of the Underground Railroad, of De Soto's search for gold. I told them the story of that bumbling fool Zebulon Pike, who set out in 1805 to find the source of the Mississippi River and ended up a year later at the glorious peak they named for him, Pike's Peak, which my sister, Rose, and I visited in 1926 on our cross-country odyssey with my brother John and his wife. In the photograph taken at Pike's Peak, I am seated astride a donkey, wearing a polka-dot dress and a floppy hat, while the western sky goes on and on endlessly behind me.

I taught my students these things: the first flight in a power-driven airplane was made by Wilbur and Orville Wright at Kitty Hawk, North Carolina, on December 17, 1903; Wisconsin is the "Badger State"; the Dutch bought Manhattan Island from the Indians for twenty-four dollars in 1626; you can't sink in the Great Salt Lake. Now these facts ricochet in my head like pinballs, and I do not intend, thank you very much, to enter the Health Center for "better care."

I never tired of telling my students the story of the Mississippi River — how a 25 scarlet oak leaf falling into Lake Itasca, in Minnesota, travels first north and then east through a wild, lonely landscape of lakes and rapids as if it were heading for Lake Superior, over the Falls of St. Anthony, down through Minneapolis and St. Paul, past bluffs and prairies and islands, to be joined by the Missouri River just above St. Louis, and then by the Ohio, where the water grows more than a mile wide — you can't see across it. My scarlet leaf meanders with eccentric loops and horseshoe curves down, down, down the great continent, through the delta, to New Orleans and beyond, past the great fertile mud plain shaped like a giant goose's foot, and into the Gulf of Mexico.

"And what happens to the leaf *then*, Mrs. Scully?" some student would never fail to ask.

"Ah," I would say, "then our little leaf becomes a part of the universe" — leaving them to ponder *that*!

I was known as a hard teacher but a fair one, and many of my students came back in later years to tell me how much they had learned.

Here at Marshwood, a "total" retirement community, they want us to become children again, forgoing intelligence. This is why I was so pleased when the announcement went up on the bulletin board about a month ago:

WRITING GROUP TO MEET

WEDNESDAY, 3:00 P.M.

Ah, I thought, that promising infinitive "to meet." For, like many former 30 English teachers, I had thought that someday I might like "to write."

At the appointed day and hour I motored over to the library (a euphemism since the room contains mostly well-worn paperbacks by Jacqueline Susann and Louis L'Amour). I was dismayed to find Martha Louise Clapton already in charge. The idea had been hers, I learned; I should have known. She's the type who tries to run everything. Martha Louise Clapton has never liked me, having had her eye on Solomon, to no avail, for years before my arrival. She inclined her frizzy blue head ever so slightly to acknowledge my entrance.

"As I was just saying, Alice, several of us have discovered in mealtime conversation that in fact we've been writing for years, in our journals and letters and whatnot, and so I said to myself, 'Martha Louise, why not form a writing group?' and *voilà*."

"*Voilà*," I said, edging into the circle.

So it began.

Besides Martha Louise and myself, the writing group included Joy Richter, a 35 minister's widow with a preference for poetry; Miss Elena Grier, who taught Shakespeare for years and years at a girls' preparatory school in Nashville, Tennessee; Frances Mason, whose husband lay in a coma over at the Health Center (another euphemism — you never leave the Health Center); Shirley Lassiter, who had buried three husbands and still thought of herself as a belle; and Sam Hofstetter, a retired lawyer, deaf as a post. We agreed to meet again in the library one week later. Each of us should bring some writing to share with the others.

"What's that?" Sam Hofstetter said. We wrote the time and place down on a little piece of paper and gave it to him. He folded the paper carefully, placing it in his pocket. "Could you make copies of the writing, please?" he asked. He inclined his silver head and tapped his ear significantly. We all agreed. Of course we agreed — we outnumber the men four to one, poor old things. In a place like this they get more attention than you would believe.

Then Joy Richter said that she probably couldn't afford to make copies. She said she was on a limited budget.

I said I felt sure we could use the Xerox machine in the manager's office, especially since we needed it for the writing group.

"Oh, I don't know." Frances Mason started wringing her hands. "They might not let us."

"I'll take care of it," Martha Louise said majestically. "Thank you, Alice, for 40 your suggestion. Thank you, everyone, for joining the group."

I had wondered if I might suffer initially from writer's block, but nothing of that sort occurred. In fact I was flooded by memories — overwhelmed, engulfed, as I sat in my chair by the picture window, writing on my lap board. I was not even aware of the world outside, my head was so full of the people and places of the past, rising up in my mind as they were then, in all the fullness of life, and myself as I was then, that headstrong girl longing to leave her home in east Virginia and walk in the world at large.

I wrote and wrote. I wrote for three days. I wrote until I felt satisfied, and then I stopped. I felt better than I had in years, full of new life and freedom (a paradox, since I am more and more confined to this chair).

During that week Solomon guessed "candy," "ring," and "Anacin." He was getting better. I was not. I ignored certain symptoms in order to attend the Wednesday meeting of the writing group.

Martha Louise led off. Her blue eyes looked huge, like lakes, behind her glasses. "They just don't make families like they used to," she began, and continued with an account of growing up on a farm in Ohio, how her parents struggled to make ends meet, how the children strung popcorn and cut out paper ornaments to trim the tree when they had no money for Christmas, how they pulled taffy and laid it out on a marble slab, and how each older child had a little one to take care of. "We were poor but we were happy," Martha Louise concluded. "It was an ideal childhood."

"Oh, Martha Louise," Frances Mason said tremulously, "that was just 45 beautiful."

Everyone agreed.

Too many adjectives, I thought, but I held my tongue.

Next Joy Richter read a poem about seeing God in everything: "the stuff of day" was a phrase I rather liked. Joy Richter apparently saw God in a shiny red apple, in a dewy rose, in her husband's kind blue eyes, in photographs of her grandchildren. The poem was pretty good, but it would have been better if she hadn't tried so hard to rhyme it.

Miss Elena then presented a sonnet comparing life to a merry-go-round. The final couplet went

> Lost children, though you're old, remember well
> The joy and music of life's carousel.

This was not bad, and I said so. Frances Mason read a reminiscence about 50 her husband's return from the Second World War, which featured the young Frances "hovering upon the future" in a porch swing as she "listened for the tread of his beloved boot." The military theme was continued by Sam Hofstetter, who read (loudly) an account of Army life titled "Somewhere in France." Shirley Lassiter was the only one whose story was not about herself. Instead it was fiction evidently modeled on a romance novel, for it involved a voluptuous debutante who had to choose between two men. Both of them were rich, and both of them loved her, but one had a fatal disease, and for some reason this young woman didn't know which one.

"Why not?" boomed the literal Sam.

"It's a mystery, silly," Shirley Lassiter said. "That's the plot." Shirley Lassiter had a way of resting her jeweled hands on her enormous bosom as if it were a shelf. "I don't want to give the plot away," she said. Clearly, she did not have a brain in her head.

Then came my turn.

I began to read the story of my childhood. I had grown up in the tiny coastal town of Waterville, Maryland. I was the fourth child in a family of five, with three older brothers and a baby sister. My father, who was in the oyster business, killed himself when I was six and Rose was only three. He went out into the Chesapeake Bay in an old rowboat, chopped a hole in the bottom of it with an ax, and then shot himself in the head with a revolver. He meant to finish the job. He did not sink as planned, however, because a fisherman witnessed the act, and hauled his body to shore.

This left Mama with five children to raise and no means of support. She was forced to turn our home into a boardinghouse, keeping mostly teachers from Goucher College and salesmen passing through, although two old widows, Mrs. Flora Lewis and Mrs. Virginia Prince, stayed with us for years. Miss Flora, as we called her, had to have a cup of warm milk every night at bedtime; I will never forget it. It could be neither too hot nor too cold. I was the one who took it up to her, stepping so carefully up the dark back stair.

Nor will I forget young Miss Day from Richmond, a teacher, who played the piano beautifully. She used to play "Clair de Lune" and "Für Elise" on the old upright in the parlor. I would already have been sent to bed, and so I'd lie there trembling in the dark, seized by feelings I couldn't name, as the notes floated up to me and Rose in our little room, in our white iron bed wrought with roses and figures of nymphs. Miss Day was jilted some years later, we heard, her virtue lost and her reputation ruined.

Every Sunday, Mama presided over the big tureen at breakfast, when we'd have boiled fish and crisp little johnnycakes. To this day I have never tasted anything as good as those johnnycakes. Mama's face was flushed, and her hair escaped its bun to curl in damp tendrils as she dished up the breakfast plates. I thought she was beautiful. I'm sure she could have married again had she chosen to do so, but her heart was full of bitterness at the way her life had turned out, and she never forgave our father, or looked at another man.

Daddy had been a charmer, by all accounts. He carried a silver-handled cane and allowed me to play with his gold pocket watch when I was especially good. He took me to harness races, where we cheered for a horse he owned, a big roan named Joe Cord. On these excursions I wore a white dress and stockings and patent-leather shoes. And how Daddy could sing! He had a lovely baritone voice. I remember him on bended knee singing "Daisy, Daisy, give me your answer, do" to Mama, who pretended to be embarrassed but was not. I remember his bouncing Rose up and down on his lap and singing, "This is the way the lady rides."

After his death the boys went off to sea as soon as they could, and I was obliged to work in the kitchen and take care of Rose. Kitchen work in a boardinghouse is never finished. This is why I have never liked to cook since, though I know how to do it, I can assure you.

We had a summer kitchen outside, so that it wouldn't heat up the whole house when we were cooking or canning. It had a kerosene stove. I remember one time when we were putting up blackberry jam, and one of those jars simply blew up. We had blackberry jam all over the place. Glass cut the Negro girl, Ocie, who was helping out, and I was surprised to see that her blood was as red as mine.

As time went on, Mama grew sadder and withdrew from us, sometimes barely speaking for days on end. My great joy was Rose, a lively child with golden curls and skin so fair you could see the blue veins beneath it. I slept with Rose every night and played with her every day. Since Mama was indisposed, we could do whatever we wanted, and we had the run of the town, just like boys. We'd go clamming in the bay with an inner tube floating out behind us, tied to my waist by a rope. We'd feel the clams with our feet and rake them up, flipping them into a net attached to the inner tube. Once, we went on a sailing trip with a cousin of ours, Bud Ned Black, up the Chickahominy River for a load of brick. But the wind failed and we got stuck there. We just *sat* on that river, for what seemed like days and days. Rose fussed and fumed while Cap'n Bud Ned drank whiskey and chewed tobacco and did not appear to mind the situation, so long as his supplies held out. But Rose was impatient — always, always so impatient.

"Alice," she said dramatically, as we sat staring out at the shining water, the green trees at its edge, the wheeling gulls, "I will *die* if we don't move. I will die here," Rose said, though Bud Ned and I laughed at her.

But Rose meant it. As she grew older, she had to go here, go there, do this, do that, have this, have that — she hated being poor and living in the boarding-house, and could not wait to grow up and go away.

We both developed a serious taste for distance when our brother John and his wife took us motoring across the country. I was sixteen. I loved that trip, from the first stage of planning our route on the map to finally viewing the great mountains, which sprang straight up from the desert like apparitions. Of course, we had never seen such mountains; they took my breath away. I remember how Rose flung her arms out wide to the world as we stood in the cold wind on Pike's Peak. I believe we could have gone on driving and driving forever. But we had to return, and I had to resume my duties, letting go the girl John had hired so that Mama would permit my absence. John was our sweetest brother, but they are all dead now, all my brothers, and Rose, too.

I have outlived everyone.

Only yesterday Rose and I were little girls, playing a game we loved so well, a game that strikes me now as terribly dangerous. This memory is more vivid than any other in my life.

It is late night, summertime. Rose and I have sneaked out of the boarding-house, down the tiny back stair past the gently sighing widows' rooms; past Mama's room, door open, moonlight ghostly on the mosquito netting draped from the canopy over her bed; past the snoring salesmen's rooms, stepping tip-toe across the wide-plank kitchen floor, wincing at each squeak; and out the kitchen door into moonlight so bright that it leaves shadows. Darting from tree to tree, we cross the yard and attain the sidewalk, moving rapidly past the big sleeping houses with their shutters yawning open to the cool night air, down the sidewalk to the edge of town where the sidewalk ends and the road goes on forever through miles and miles of peanut fields and other towns and other fields, toward Baltimore.

Rose and I lie down flat in the middle of the road, which still retains the heat of the day, and let it warm us head to toe as we dream aloud of what the future holds. At different times Rose planned to be an aviator, a doctor, and a film actress living in California, with an orange tree in her yard. Even her most domestic dreams were grand. "I'll have a big house and lots of servants and a husband who loves me *so much,*" Rose would say, "and a yellow convertible touring car, and six children, and we will be rich and they will never have to work, and I will put a silk scarf on my head and we will all go out riding on Sunday."

Even then I said I would be a teacher, because I was always good in school, but I would be a missionary teacher, enlightening natives in some far-off corner

65

of the world. Even as I said it, though, I believe I knew it would not come to pass, for I was bound to stay at home, as Rose was bound to go.

But we'd lie there looking up at the sky, and dream our dreams, and wait 70 for the thrill of an oncoming vehicle, which we could hear coming a long time away, and could feel throughout the length of our bodies as it neared us. We would roll off the pavement and in the peanut field just as the car approached, our hearts pounding. Sometimes we nearly dozed on that warm road — and once we were almost killed by a potato truck.

Gradually, as Mama retreated to her room, I took over the running of the boardinghouse, and Mama's care as well. At eighteen Rose ran away with a fast-talking furniture salesman who had been boarding with us. They settled finally in Ohio, and had three children, and her life was not glamorous in the least, though better than some, and we wrote to each other every week until her death, of ovarian cancer, at thirty-nine.

This was as far as I'd gotten.

I quit reading aloud and looked around the room. Joy Richter was ashen, Miss Elena Grier was mumbling to herself, and Shirley Lassiter was breathing heavily and fluttering her fingers at her throat. Sam Hofstetter stared fixedly at me with the oddest expression on his face, and Frances Mason wept openly, shaking with sobs.

"Alice! Now just look at what you've done!" Martha Louise said to me severely. "Meeting adjourned!"

I had to miss the third meeting of the writing group, because Dr. Culbertson 75 sent me to the Health Center for treatment and further tests (euphemisms both). Dr. Culbertson then went so far as to consult with my son Robert, also a doctor, about what to do with me next. Dr. Culbertson believed that I ought to move to the Health Center, for "better care." Of course I called Robert immediately and gave him a piece of my mind.

That was yesterday.

I know they are discussing me by telephone — Robert, Alex, Johnny, and Carl. Lines are buzzing up and down the East Coast.

I came here when I had to, because I did not want any of their wives to get stuck with me, as I had gotten stuck with Harold's mother and father. Now I expect some common decency and respect. At times like this I wish for daughters, who often, I feel, have more compassion and understanding than sons.

Even Carl, the child of my heart, says I had "better listen to the doctor."

Instead I have been listening to this voice too long silent inside me, the 80 voice of myself, as I write page after page propped up in bed in the Health Center.

Today is Wednesday. I have skipped certain of my afternoon medications. At 2:15 I buzz for Sheila, my favorite, a tall young nurse's aide with the grace of a gazelle. "Sheila," I say, "I need for you to help me dress, dear, and then roll my chair over here, if you will. My own chair, I mean. I have to go to a meeting."

Sheila looks at my chart and then back at me, her eyes wide. "It doesn't say . . ." she begins.

"Dr. Culbertson said it would be perfectly all right," I assure her. I pull a $20.00 bill from my purse, which I keep right beside me in bed, and hand it to her. "I know it's a lot of trouble, but it's very important," I say. "I think I'll just slip on the red sweater and the black wraparound skirt — that's so easy to get on. "They're both in the drawer, dear."

"Okay, honey," Sheila says, and she gets me dressed and sets me in my chair. I put on lipstick and have Sheila fluff up my hair in the back where it's gotten so flat from lying in bed. Sheila hands me my purse and my notebook, and then I'm off, waving to the girls at the nurses' station as I purr past them. They wave back. I feel fine now. I take the elevator down to the first floor and then motor through the lobby, speaking to acquaintances. I pass the gift shop, the newspaper stand, and all the waiting rooms.

It's chilly outside. I head up the walkway past the par three golf course, where I spy Parker Howard, ludicrous in those bright-green pants they sell to old men, putting on the third hole. "Hi, Parker!" I cry.

"Hello, Alice," he calls. "Nice to see you out!" He sinks the putt.

I enter the Multipurpose Building and head for the library, where the writers' group is already in progress. Driving over from the Health Center took longer than I'd expected.

Miss Elena is reading, but she stops and looks up when I come in, her mouth a perfect O. Everybody looks at Martha Louise.

"Why, Alice," Martha Louise says. She clears her throat. "We didn't expect that you would be joining us today. We heard that you were in the Health Center."

"I was," I say. "But I'm out now."

"Evidently," Martha Louise says.

I ride up to the circular table, set my brake, get out my notebook, and ask Miss Elena for a copy of whatever she's reading. Wordless, she slides one over. But she still does not resume. They're all looking at me.

"What is it?" I ask.

"Well, Alice, last week, when you were absent, we laid out some ground rules for this writing group." Martha Louise gains composure as she goes along. "We are all in agreement here, Alice, that if this is to be a pleasant and meaningful club for all of us, we need to restrict our subject matter to what everyone enjoys."

"So?" I don't get it.

"We've also adopted an official name for the group." Now Martha Louise is as cheerful as a robin.

"It's the Happy Memories Club," she announces, and they all nod.

I am beginning to get it.

"You mean to tell me —" I start.

"I mean to tell you that if you wish to be a part of this group, Alice Scully, you will have to calm yourself down, and keep your subject matter in check. We don't come here to be upset," Martha Louise says serenely.

They are all watching me closely now, Sam Hofstetter in particular. I think they expect an outburst.

But I won't give them the satisfaction.

"Fine," I say. This is a lie. "That sounds just fine to me. Good idea!" I smile at everybody.

There is a perceptible relaxation then, an audible settling back into chairs, as Miss Elena resumes her reading. It's a travelogue named "Shakespeare and His Haunts," about a tour she made to England several years ago. But I find myself unable to listen. I simply can't hear Elena, or Joy, who reads next, or even Sam.

"Well, is that it for today? Anybody else?" Martha Louise raps her knuckles   105
against the table. "I brought something," I say, "but I don't have copies."

I look at Sam, who shrugs and smiles and says I should go ahead anyway.
Everybody else looks at Martha Louise.

"Well, go on, then," she directs tartly, and I begin.

After Rose's disappearance, my mother took to her bed and turned her
face to the wall, leaving me in charge of everything. Oh, how I worked! I
worked like a dog, long hours, a cruelly unnatural life for a spirited young
woman. Yet I persevered. People in the town, including our minister, complimented me; I was discussed and admired. Our boardinghouse stayed full,
and somehow I managed, with Ocie's help, to get the meals on the table. I
smiled and chattered at mealtime. Yet inside I was starving, starving for love
and life.

Thus it was not surprising, I suppose, that I should fall for the first man
who showed any interest in me. He was a schoolteacher who had been educated at the university, in Charlottesville, a thin, dreamy young man from one
of the finest families in Virginia. His grandfather had been the governor. He
used to sit out by the sound every evening after supper, reading, and one day I
joined him there. It was a lovely June evening; the sound was full of sailboats,
and the sky above us was as round and blue as a bowl.

"I was reading a poem about a girl with beautiful yellow hair," he said,   110
"and then I look up and what do I see? A real girl with beautiful yellow
hair."

For some reason I started to cry, not even caring what my other boarders
thought as they sat up on the porch looking out over this landscape in which
we figured.

"Come here," he said, and he took my hand and led me behind the old
rose-covered boathouse, where he pulled me to him and kissed me curiously,
as if it were an experiment.

His name was Carl Redding Armistead III. He had the reedy look of a poet,
but all the assurance of the privileged class. I was older than he, but he was
more experienced. He was well educated, and had been to Europe several times.

"You pretty thing," he said, and kissed me again. The scent of the roses
was everywhere.

I went that night to his room, and before the summer was out, we had lain   115
together in nearly every room of the boardinghouse. We were crazy for each
other by then, and I didn't care what might happen, or who knew. On Saturday
evenings I'd leave a cold supper for the rest, and Carl and I would take the skiff
and row out to Sand Island, where the wild ponies were, and take off all our
clothes and make love. Sometimes my back would be red and bleeding from
the rough black sand and the broken shells on the beach.

"Just a minute! Just a minute here!" Martha Louise is pounding on the
table, and Frances Mason is crying, as usual. Sam Hofstetter is staring at me in
a manner that indicates that he has heard every word I've said.

"Well, I think that's terrific!" Shirley Lassiter giggles and bats her painted
blue eyelids at us all.

Of course this romance did not last. Nothing that intense can be sustained,
though the loss of such intensity can scarcely be borne. Quite simply, Carl and I
foundered upon the prospect of the future. He had to go on to the world that
awaited him; I could not leave Mama. Our final parting was bitter—we were

spent, exhausted by the force of what had passed between us. He did not even look back as he sped away in his little red sports car, nor did I cry.

Nor did I ever tell him about the existence of Carl, my son, whom I bore defiantly out of wedlock nine months later, telling no one who the father was. Oh, those were hard, black days! I was ostracized by the very people who had formerly praised me, and ogled by the men in my boardinghouse, who now considered me a fallen woman. I wore myself to a frazzle taking care of Mama and the baby at the same time.

One night, I remember, I was so tired that I felt that I would actually die,   120 yet little Carl would not stop crying. Nothing would quiet him—not rocking, not the breast, not walking the room. He had an oddly unpleasant cry, like a cat mewing. I remember looking out my window at the quiet town where everyone slept—everyone on this earth, I felt, except me. I held Carl out at arm's length and looked hard at him in the streetlight, at his red, twisted little face. I had an awful urge to throw him out the window—

"That's enough!" several of them say at once. Martha Louise is standing.

But it is Miss Elena who speaks. "I cannot believe," she say severely, "that out of your entire life, Alice Scully, this is all you can find to write about. What of your long marriage to Mr. Scully? Your seven grandchildren? Those of us who have not been blessed with grandchildren would give—"

Of course I loved Harold Scully. Of course I love my grandchildren. I love Solomon, too. I love them all. Miss Elena is like my sons, too terrified to admit to herself how many people we can love, how various we are. She does not want to hear it any more than they do, any more than you do. You all want us to *never change, never change.*

I did not throw my baby out the window after all, and my mother finally died, and I sold the boardinghouse then and was able, at last, to go to school.

Out of the corner of my eye I see Dr. Culbertson appear at the library door,   125 accompanied by a man I do not know. Martha Louise says, "I simply cannot believe that a former *English teacher*—"

This strikes me as very funny. My mind is filled with enormous sentences as I back up my chair and then start forward, out the other door and down the hall and outside into the sweet spring day, where the sunshine falls on my face as it did in those days on the beach, my whole body hot and aching and sticky with sweat and salt and blood, the wild ponies paying us no mind as they ate the tall grass that grew at the edge of the dunes. Sometimes the ponies came so close that we could reach out and touch them. Their coats were shaggy and rough and full of burrs, I remember.

Oh, I remember everything as I cruise forward on the sidewalk that neatly separates the rock garden from the golf course. I turn right at the corner, instead of left toward the Health Center. "Fore!" Parker Howard shouts, waving at me. *A former English teacher,* Martha Louise said. These sidewalks are like diagrams, parallel lines and dividers: oh, I could diagram anything. The semicolon, I used to say, is like a little scale; it must have items of equal rank, I'd warn them. Do not use a semicolon between a clause and a phrase, or a main clause and a subordinate clause. Do not write *I loved Carl Redding Armistead; a rich man's son.* Do not write *If I had really loved Carl Armistead; I would have left with him despite all obstacles.* Do not write *I still feel his touch; which has thrilled me throughout my life.*

I turn at the top of the hill and motor along the sidewalk toward the Residence Center, hoping to see Solomon. The sun is in my eyes. Do not carelessly link two sentences with a comma. Do not write *I want to see Solomon again, he has meant so much to me.* To correct this problem, subordinate one of the parts. *I want to see Solomon, because he has meant so much to me.* Because he has meant. So much. To me. Fragments. Fragments all. I push the button to open the door into the Residence Center, and sure enough, they've brought him out. They've dressed him in his Madras plaid shirt and wheeled him in front of the television, which he hates. I cruise right over.

"Solomon," I say, but at first he doesn't respond when he looks at me. I come even closer. "Solomon!" I say sharply, bumping his wheelchair. He notices me then, and a little light comes into his eyes.

I cup my hands. "Solomon," I say, "I'll give you a kiss if you can guess what   130
I've got in my hands."

He looks at me for a while longer.

"Now, Mrs. Scully," his nurse starts.

"Come on," I say. "What have I got in here?"

"An elephant," Solomon finally says.

"Close enough!" I cry, and lean right over to kiss his sweet old cheek, being   135
unable to reach his mouth.

"Mrs. Scully," his nurse starts again, but I'm gone, I'm history, I'm out the front door and around the parking circle and up the long entrance drive to the highway. It all connects. Everything connects. The sun is bright, the dogwoods are blooming, the state flower of Virginia is the dogwood, I can still see the sun on the Chickahominy River and my own little sons as they sail their own little boats in a tidal pool by the Chesapeake Bay, they were all blond boys once, though their hair would darken later, Annapolis is the capital of Maryland, the first historic words ever transmitted by telegraph came to Maryland: "What hath God wrought?" The sun is still shining. It glares off the snow on Pike's Peak, it gleams through the milky blue glass of the old apothecary jar in the window of Harold Scully's shop, it warms the asphalt on that road where Rose and I lie waiting, waiting, waiting.

CONSIDERATIONS FOR CRITICAL THINKING AND WRITING

1. **FIRST RESPONSE.** Smith has observed about the humor in her writing that "I tend to see life fairly tragically. If you do that, you've got two choices: you can either go in the closet and sit in the dark or you can make jokes. . . ." How accurately do you think this describes her writing strategy in "The Happy Memories Club"?

2. How effective do you think Smith's descriptions of life in Marshwood are in evoking life in an old-age home? What is the significance of the setting?

3. Characterize Alice as a young and old woman. Explain whether or not her character seems to be consistent.

4. Why is Alice's point of view crucial to the story? Imagine it written in the third person. How would that change your reading of it?

5. What does Alice's story-within-the-story add to your understanding of her character?

6. How does the plot of Alice's written story about herself relate to the larger plot that frames it? Are there significant parallels or contrasts between them?

7. What is the purpose of the minor characters in Marshwood? How are they connected to the conflict in the plot? Consider especially their response to Alice's reading about her early life.

8. Consider the symbolic value of Alice's discussion of punctuation in paragraphs 127–28. How is it related to the theme?

9. "It all connects. Everything connects." Discuss the potential meaning of these lines in the story's final paragraph.

10. Consider the tone of the title. How do you interpret its meaning?

CONNECTIONS TO OTHER SELECTIONS

1. Discuss the treatment of old age in Smith's story and in Peter Meinke's "The Cranes" (p. 621). Explain why each is so convincing.

2. Consider Alice's assertion that "our memories are all we've got" (para. 6) in relation to Kelly Cherry's poem "Alzheimer's" (p. 1008). How does the poem implicitly comment on Solomon Marx's condition in Smith's story?

JOYCE CAROL OATES (B. 1938)

A biographical note and photograph of Joyce Carol Oates appear on page 83, before her story "Three Girls."

Hi Howya Doin   2007

Good-looking husky guy six-foot-four in late twenties or early thirties, Caucasian male, as the initial police report will note, he's solid-built as a fire hydrant, carries himself like an athlete, or an ex-athlete just perceptibly thickening at the waist, otherwise in terrific condition like a bronze figure in motion, sinewy arms pumping as he runs, long muscled legs, chiseled-muscled calves, he's hurtling along the moist woodchip path at the western edge of the university arboretum at approximately six P.M., Thursday evening, and there comes, from the other direction, a woman jogger on the path, female in her late thirties, flushed face, downturned eyes, dark hair threaded with gray like cobwebs, an awkward runner, fleshy lips parted, holds her arms stiff at her sides, in a shrunken pullover shirt with a faded tiger cat on its front, not-large but sizable breasts shaking as she runs, mimicked in the slight shaking of her cheeks, and her hips in carrot-colored sweatpants, this is Madeline Hersey frowning at the woodchip path before her, Madeline's exasperating habit of staring at the ground when she runs, oblivious of the arboretum, though at this time in May it's dazzling with white dogwood, pink dogwood, vivid yellow forsythia, Madeline is a lab technician at Squibb, lost in a labyrinth of her own tangled thoughts (career, lover, lover's "learning disabled" child), startled out of her reverie by the loud aggressive-friendly greeting *Hi! Howya doin!* flung out at her like a playful slap on the buttocks as the tall husky jogger passes Madeline with the most fleeting of glances, big-toothed bemused smile, and Madeline loses her stride, in a faltering voice *Fine — thank you —* but the other jogger is past, unhearing and now on the gravel path behind the university hospital, now on the grassy towpath beside the old canal, in the greenly lushness of University Dells Park where, in the late afternoon, into dusk joggers are running singly and in couples, in groups of three or more, track-team runners from the local high school, college students, white-haired older runners both male and female, to these the husky jogger in skin-tight mustard-yellow T-shirt, short navy-blue shorts showing his chiseled thigh muscles, size-twelve Nikes calls out *Hi Howya doin* in a big bland booming voice, *Hi Howya doin* and a flash of big horsy teeth, long pumping legs, pumping arms, it's his practice to come up close behind a solitary jogger, a woman maybe, a girl, or an older man, so many "older" men (forties, fifties, sixties, and beyond) in the university community, sometimes a younger guy who's sweated through his clothes, beginning to breathe through his mouth, size-twelve Nikes striking the earth like mallets, *Hi! Howya doin!* jolting Kyle Lindeman out of dreamy-sexy thoughts, jolting Michelle Rossley out of snarled anxious thoughts, there's Diane Hendricks who'd been an athlete in high school now twenty pounds overweight, divorced, no kid, replaying in her head a quarrel she'd had with a woman friend, goddamn she's angry! goddamn she's not going to call Ginny back, this time! trying to calm her rush of thoughts like churning roiling water, trying to measure her breaths Zen-fashion, inhale, exhale, inhale and out of nowhere into this reverie a tall husky hurtling figure bears down upon her, toward her, veering into her line of vision, instinctively Diane bears to the right to give him plenty of room to pass her, hopes this is no one she knows from work, no one who knows her, trying not to look up at him, tall guy, husky, must weigh two-twenty, works out, has got to be an athlete, or ex-athlete, a pang of sexual excitement courses through her, or is it sexual dread even as *Hi! Howya doin!* rings out loud and bemused like an elbow in Diane's left breast as the stranger pounds past her, in his wake an odor of male sweat, acrid-briny male sweat and an impression of big glistening teeth bared in a brainless grin or is it a mock-grin, death's-head grin? — thrown off stride, self-conscious and stumbling, Diane manages to stammer *Fine — I'm fine* as if the stranger brushing past her is interested in her, or in her well-being, in the slightest, what a fool Diane is! — yet another day, moist-bright morning in the university dells along the path beside the seed-stippled lagoon where amorous-combative male mallard ducks are pursuing female ducks with much squawking, flapping of wings, and splashing water, there comes the tall husky jogger, Caucasian male six-foot-four, two-twenty pounds, no ID as the initial police report will note, on this occasion the jogger is wearing a skin-tight black Judas Priest T-shirt, very short white-nylon shorts revealing every surge, ripple, sheen of chiseled thigh muscles, emerging out of a shadowy pathway at the edge of the birch woods to approach Dr. Rausch of the university's geology department, older man, just slightly vain of being "fit," dark-tinted aviator glasses riding the bridge of his perspiring nose, Dr. Rausch panting as he runs, not running so fast as he'd like, rivulets of sweat like melting grease down his back, sides, sweating through his shirt, in baggy khaki shorts to the knee, Dr. Rausch grinding his jaws in thought (departmental budget cuts! his youngest daughter's wrecked marriage! his wife's biopsy next morning at seven A.M., he will drive her to the medical center and wait for her, return her home and yet somehow get to the tenure committee meeting he's chairing at eleven A.M.) when *Hi! Howya doin!* jolts Dr. Rausch as if the husky jogger in the black Judas Priest T-shirt has extended a playful size-twelve foot into Dr. Rausch's path to trip him, suddenly he's thrown off-stride, poor old guy, hasn't always been sixty-four years old, sunken-chested, skinny white legs sprouting individual hairs like wires, hard little pot belly straining at the unbelted waistline of the khaki shorts, Dr. Rausch looks up squinting, is this someone he knows? should know? who knows *him*? across the vertiginous span of thirty years in the geology department Dr. Rausch has had so many students, but before he can see who this is, or make a panting effort to reply in the quick-casual way of youthful joggers, the husky jogger has passed by Dr. Rausch without a second glance, legs like pistons of muscle, shimmering sweat-film like a halo about his body, fair-brown, russet-brown hair in curls like wood shavings lifting halo-like from his large uplifted head, big toothy smile, large broad nose made for deep breathing, enormous dark nostrils that look as if thumbs have been shoved into them, soon again this shimmering male figure appears on the far side of the dells, another afternoon on the Institute grounds, hard-pounding feet, muscled arms pumping, on this day a navy blue T-shirt faded from numerous launderings, another time the very short navy-blue shorts, as he runs he exudes a yeasty body odor, sighting a solitary male jogger ahead he quickens his pace to overtake him, guy in his early twenties, university student, no athlete, about five-eight, skinny guy, running with some effort, breathing through his mouth, and in his head a swirl of numerals, symbols, equations, quantum optics, quantum noise, into this reverie *Hi! Howya doin* is like a firecracker tossed by a prankish kid, snappishly the younger jogger replies *I'm okay* as his face flushes, how like high school, junior high kids pushing him around, in that instant he's remembering, almost now limping, lost the stride, now life seems pointless, you know it's pointless, you live, you die, look how his grandfather died, what's the point, there is none, as next day, next week, late Friday afternoon of the final week in May along the canal towpath past Linden Road where there are fewer joggers looming up suddenly in your line of vision, approaching you, a tall husky male jogger running in the center of the path, instinctively you bear to the right, instinctively you turn your gaze downward, no eye contact on the towpath, you've been lost in thought, coils of thought like electric currents burning-hot, scalding-hot, the very pain, anguish, futility of your thoughts, for what is your soul but your thoughts, upright flame cupped between your hands silently pleading *Don't speak to me, respect my privacy please* even as the oncoming jogger continues to approach, in the center of the path, inexorably, unstoppably, curly hairs on his arms shimmering with a bronze-roseate glow, big teeth bared in a smile *Hi! Howya doing!* loud and bland and booming mock-friendly, and out of the pocket of your nylon jacket you fumble to remove the snub-nosed, twenty-two-caliber Smith & Wesson revolver you'd stolen from your stepfather's lodge in Jackson Hole, Wyoming, three years before, hateful of the old drunk asshole you'd waited for him to ask if you'd taken it, were you the one to take his gun that's unlicensed, and your stepfather never asked, and you never told, and you lift the toy-like gun in a hand trembling with excitement, with trepidation, with anticipation, aim at the face looming at you like a balloon-face up close and fire and the bullet leaps like magic from the toy-weapon with unexpected force and short-range accuracy and enters the face at the forehead directly above the big-nostriled nose, in an instant the husky jogger in the mustard-yellow T-shirt drops to his knees on the path, already the mustard-yellow T-shirt is splashed with blood, on his belly now and brawny arms outspread, face flattened against the path fallen silent and limp as a cloth puppet when the puppeteer has lost interest and dropped the puppet, he's dead, *That's how I'm doin.*

CONSIDERATIONS FOR CRITICAL THINKING AND WRITING

1. **FIRST RESPONSE.** How is the style of this story particularly suited to jogging?
2. What is the effect of the narrator mentioning the "initial police report" in the second line?
3. Explain how the male jogger is a character foil to Madeline Hersey. How do the other joggers' responses to him further define his character?
4. How might this story be regarded as a kind of sociology of jogging? Consider whether or not it seems like an accurate rendition of it to you.
5. How does Oates subtly convey the passage of time in the narrative?
6. The inevitable question: Is this story funny? Why or why not?

CONNECTIONS TO OTHER SELECTIONS

1. Compare the tone of the humor in this revenge story with that in Ron Hansen's "My Kid's Dog" (p. 584).
2. Comment on the ways in which style is related to content in "Hi Howya Doin" and in Rick Moody's "Boys" (p. 371).

MARK TWAIN (1835–1910)

Mark Twain is the pen name of Samuel Clemens, born in Missouri in 1835. Twain spent most of his childhood in Hannibal, Missouri, on the Mississippi River, and after the death of his father when he was eleven, he worked at a series of jobs to help support his family. A newspaper job prepared him to wander east working for papers and exploring St. Louis, New York, and Philadelphia. Later he trained as a steamboat pilot on the Mississippi and piloted boats professionally until the onset of the Civil War.

© Bettmann/CORBIS.

Clemens had used a couple of different pseudonyms for minor publications before this point, but in 1863 he signed a travel narrative "Mark Twain," from a boating term that means "two fathoms deep," and the name for the great American humorist was created. Twain gained fame in 1865 with his story "The Celebrated Jumping

Frog of Calaveras County," which appeared in New York–based *The Saturday Press*. He then became a traveling correspondent, writing pieces on his travels to Europe and the Middle East, and returned to the United States in 1870, when he married and moved to Connecticut. Twain produced *Roughing It* (1872) and *The Gilded Age* (1873) while he toured the country lecturing, and in 1876 published *The Adventures of Tom Sawyer*, an instant hit. His subsequent publications include *A Tramp Abroad* (1880), *The Prince and the Pauper* (1881), and the masterpiece *The Adventures of Huckleberry Finn* (1884). Often traveling and lecturing, Twain wrote several more books, including story collections, *The Tragedy of Pudd'nhead Wilson* (1894), and *Tom Sawyer, Detective* (1896), before he died in Italy in 1910. His work is noted for the combination of rough humor and vernacular language it often uses to convey keen social insights. In "The Story of the Good Little Boy" Twain offers his version of a Sunday-school lesson.

The Story of the Good Little Boy   *1870*

Once there was a good little boy by the name of Jacob Blivens. He always obeyed his parents, no matter how absurd and unreasonable their demands were; and he always learned his book, and never was late at Sabbath-school. He would not play hookey, even when his sober judgment told him it was the most profitable thing he could do. None of the other boys could ever make that boy out, he acted so strangely. He wouldn't lie, no matter how convenient it was. He just said it was wrong to lie, and that was sufficient for him. And he was so honest that he was simply ridiculous. The curious ways that that Jacob had, surpassed everything. He wouldn't play marbles on Sunday, he wouldn't rob birds' nests, he wouldn't give hot pennies to organ-grinders' monkeys; he didn't seem to take any interest in any kind of rational amusement. So the other boys used to try to reason it out and come to an understanding of him, but they couldn't arrive at any satisfactory conclusion. As I said before, they could only figure out a sort of vague idea that he was "afflicted," and so they took him under their protection, and never allowed any harm to come to him.

   This good little boy read all the Sunday-school books; they were his greatest delight. This was the whole secret of it. He believed in the good little boys they put in the Sunday-school books; he had every confidence in them. He longed to come across one of them alive once; but he never did. They all died before his time, maybe. Whenever he read about a particularly good one he turned over quickly to the end to see what became of him, because he wanted to travel thousands of miles and gaze on him; but it wasn't any use; that good little boy always died in the last chapter, and there was a picture of the funeral, with all his relations and the Sunday-school children standing around the grave in pantaloons that were too short, and bonnets that were too large, and everybody crying into handkerchiefs that had as much as a yard and a half of stuff in them. He was always headed off in this way. He never could see one of those good little boys on account of his always dying in the last chapter.

Jacob had a noble ambition to be put in a Sunday-school book. He wanted to be put in, with pictures representing him gloriously declining to lie to his mother, and her weeping for joy about it; and pictures representing him standing on the doorstep giving a penny to a poor beggar-woman with six children, and telling her to spend it freely, but not to be extravagant, because extravagance is a sin; and pictures of him magnanimously refusing to tell on the bad boy who always lay in wait for him around the corner as he came from school, and welted him over the head with a lath, and then chased him home, saying, "Hi! hi!" as he proceeded. That was the ambition of young Jacob Blivens. He wished to be put in a Sunday-school book. It made him feel a little uncomfortable sometimes when he reflected that the good little boys always died. He loved to live, you know, and this was the most unpleasant feature about being a Sunday-school-book boy. He knew it was not healthy to be good. He knew it was more fatal than consumption to be so supernaturally good as the boys in the books were; he knew that none of them had ever been able to stand it long, and it pained him to think that if they put him in a book he wouldn't ever see it, or even if they did get the book out before he died it wouldn't be popular without any picture of his funeral in the back part of it. It couldn't be much of a Sunday-school book that couldn't tell about the advice he gave to the community when he was dying. So at last, of course, he had to make up his mind to do the best he could under the circumstances—to live right, and, hang on as long as he could, and have his dying speech all ready when his time came.

But somehow nothing ever went right with this good little boy; nothing ever turned out with him the way it turned out with the good little boys in the books. They always had a good time, and the bad boys had the broken legs; but in his case there was a screw loose somewhere, and it all happened just the other way. When he found Jim Blake stealing apples, and went under the tree to read to him about the bad little boy who fell out of a neighbor's apple tree and broke his arm, Jim fell out of the tree, too, but he fell on *him* and broke *his* arm, and Jim wasn't hurt at all. Jacob couldn't understand that. There wasn't anything in the books like it.

And once, when some bad boys pushed a blind man over in the mud, and   5 Jacob ran to help him up and receive his blessing, the blind man did not give him any blessing at all, but whacked him over the head with his stick and said he would like to catch him shoving *him* again, and then pretending to help him up. This was not in accordance with any of the books. Jacob looked them all over to see.

One thing that Jacob wanted to do was to find a lame dog that hadn't any place to stay, and was hungry and persecuted, and bring him home and pet him and have that dog's imperishable gratitude. And at last he found one and was happy; and he brought him home and fed him, but when he was going to pet him the dog flew at him and tore all the clothes off him except those that were in front, and made a spectacle of him that was astonishing. He examined authorities, but he could not understand the matter. It was of the same breed of dogs that was in the books, but it acted very differently. Whatever this boy did he got into trouble. The very things the boys in the books got rewarded for turned out to be about the most unprofitable things he could invest in.

Once, when he was on his way to Sunday-school, he saw some bad boys starting off pleasuring in a sailboat. He was filled with consternation, because he knew from his reading that boys who went sailing on Sunday invariably got drowned. So he ran out on a raft to warn them, but a log turned with him and slid him into the river. A man got him out pretty soon, and the doctor pumped the water out of him, and gave him a fresh start with his bellows, but he caught cold and lay sick abed nine weeks. But the most unaccountable thing about it was that the bad boys in the boat had a good time all day, and then reached home alive and well in the most surprising manner. Jacob Blivens said there was nothing like these things in the books. He was perfectly dumbfounded.

When he got well he was a little discouraged, but he resolved to keep on trying anyhow. He knew that so far his experiences wouldn't do to go in a book, but he hadn't yet reached the allotted term of life for good little boys, and he hoped to be able to make a record yet if he could hold on till his time was fully up. If everything else failed he had his dying speech to fall back on.

He examined his authorities, and found that it was now time for him to go to sea as a cabin-boy. He called on a ship-captain and made his application, and when the captain asked for his recommendations he proudly drew out a tract and pointed to the word, "To Jacob Blivens, from his affectionate teacher." But the captain was a coarse, vulgar man, and he said, "Oh, that be blowed! *that* wasn't any proof that he knew how to wash dishes or handle a slush-bucket, and he guessed he didn't want him." This was altogether the most extraordinary thing that ever happened to Jacob in all his life. A compliment from a teacher, on a tract, had never failed to move the tenderest emotions of ship-captains, and open the way to all offices of honor and profit in their gift — it never had in any book that ever *he* had read. He could hardly believe his senses.

This boy always had a hard time of it. Nothing ever came out according to the authorities with him. At last, one day, when he was around hunting up bad little boys to admonish, he found a lot of them in the old iron-foundry fixing up a little joke on fourteen or fifteen dogs, which they had tied together in long procession, and were going to ornament with empty nitroglycerin cans made fast to their tails. Jacob's heart was touched. He sat down on one of those cans (for he never minded grease when duty was before him), and he took hold of the foremost dog by the collar, and turned his reproving eye upon wicked Tom Jones. But just at that moment Alderman McWelter, full of wrath, stepped in. All the bad boys ran away, but Jacob Blivens rose in conscious innocence and began one of those stately little Sunday-school-book speeches which always commence with "Oh, sir!" in dead opposition to the fact that no boy, good or bad, ever starts a remark with "Oh, sir." But the alderman never waited to hear the rest. He took Jacob Blivens by the ear and turned him around, and hit him a whack in the rear with the flat of his hand; and in an instant that good little boy shot out through the roof and soared away toward the sun, with the fragments of those fifteen dogs stringing after him like the tail of a kite. And there wasn't a sign of that alderman or that old iron-foundry left on the face of the earth; and, as for young Jacob Blivens, he never got a chance to make his last dying speech after all his trouble fixing it up, unless he made it to the birds; because, although the bulk of him came down all right in a tree-top in an adjoining county, the rest of him was apportioned around among four townships, and so they had to hold five inquests on him to find out whether he was dead or not, and how it occurred. You never saw a boy scattered so.[1]

10

---

[1] This glycerin catastrophe is borrowed from a floating newspaper item, whose author's name I would give if I knew it. M.T.

Thus perished the good little boy who did the best he could, but didn't come out according to the books. Every boy who ever did as he did prospered except him. His case is truly remarkable. It will probably never be accounted for.

CONSIDERATIONS FOR CRITICAL THINKING AND WRITING

1. FIRST RESPONSE. This story is about the death of a child. What's so funny about that?

2. What is the story's central irony?

3. Which sentences are particularly effective in imitating the style of Sunday-school books? Which sentences are clearly Twain's style? What is the effect of having both styles side by side?

4. How does the story's irony reveal Twain's attitude toward Jacob? Find specific passages to support your points.

5. What sort of lesson does Twain's version of Sunday-school instruction teach?

6. Is there a serious point to the humor here? What is the theme of the story?

7. It might be tempting to sum up this story with something like "Nice guys finish last." Discuss the adequacy of this as a statement of theme.

8. Characterize the tone of voice that tells the story. Is it indignant, amused, cynical, bitter, disinterested, or what?

CONNECTIONS TO OTHER SELECTIONS

1. Compare Jacob's fate with that of the central character in Ralph Ellison's "Battle Royal" (p. 277).

2. Write an essay explaining the extent to which this story and Stephen Crane's "The Bride Comes to Yellow Sky" (p. 298) are dependent on a reader's familiarity with the formulaic qualities of Sunday-school stories or traditional westerns.

17

A THEMATIC CASE STUDY
Remarkably Short-Short Stories

The beauty of literature is you allow
readers to see things through other
people's eyes.
—SANDRA CISNEROS

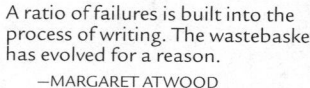

A ratio of failures is built into the
process of writing. The wastebasket
has evolved for a reason.
—MARGARET ATWOOD

All of the nine very short stories in this chapter are fewer than three pages in
length and can be read in less than five minutes. These numbers do not measure what the stories achieve as works of literature, however. Their remarkably focused form gives you an intense opportunity to read fiction carefully
and deliberately in order to enhance your understanding and pleasure.

Short-short stories have developed into a genre of their own in recent
years; they are known variously as *sudden, flash, fast, quick, micro,* or *mini fiction.* A number of anthologies have now compiled stories that are only a
few pages long. Authors enjoy the challenge of writing in such an intense
and disciplined form, while readers appreciate the express journeys into
writers' imaginations that are skillfully mapped and allow readers to travel
at their own pace. These brief works do not sacrifice complexity, depth,

seriousness, or subtlety. You'll find in these stories some characters who will make you laugh, wince, feel wistful, and experience the full weight of human loss and tragedy. Moreover, while the plots are not long, they are intriguing because they engage the characters in conflicts that are crucial to them and will likely matter to you. Give it five minutes. You'll see.

SANDRA CISNEROS (B. 1954)

Born to a Mexican father and a Mexican American mother, Sandra Cisneros grew up in Chicago along with her six brothers. She earned a B.A. in English at Loyola University of Chicago and an M.F.A. in creative writing at the University of Iowa. She has taught creative writing at a number of universities and currently is writer-in-residence at Our Lady of the Lake University in San Antonio. Her poetry and fiction have won her a number of awards including two National Endowment for the Arts fellowships and a MacArthur fellowship. Her fiction includes two novels, *House on Mango Street* (1984) and

© Gene Blevins/CORBIS.

Caramelo (2002), and a collection of short stories, *Woman Hollering Creek and Other Stories* (1991), from which "Eleven" is taken.

Eleven   *1983*

What they don't understand about birthdays and what they never tell you is that when you're eleven, you're also ten, and nine, and eight, and seven, and six, and five, and four, and three, and two, and one. And when you wake up on your eleventh birthday you expect to feel eleven, but you don't. You open your eyes and everything's just like yesterday, only it's today. And you don't feel eleven at all. You feel like you're still ten. And you are—underneath the year that makes you eleven.

Like some days you might say something stupid, and that's the part of you that's still ten. Or maybe some days you might need to sit on your mama's lap because you're scared, and that's the part of you that's five. And maybe one day when you're all grown up maybe you will need to cry like if you're three, and that's okay. That's what I tell Mama when she's sad and needs to cry. Maybe she's feeling three.

Because the way you grow old is kind of like an onion or like the rings inside a tree trunk or like my little wooden dolls that fit one inside the other, each year inside the next one. That's how being eleven years old is.

You don't feel eleven. Not right away. It takes a few days, weeks even, sometimes even months before you say Eleven when they ask you. And you don't feel smart eleven, not until you're almost twelve. That's the way it is.

Only today I wish I didn't have only eleven years rattling inside me like   5
pennies in a tin Band-Aid box. Today I wish I was one hundred and two instead of eleven because if I was one hundred and two I'd have known what to say when Mrs. Price put the red sweater on my desk. I would've known how to tell her it wasn't mine instead of just sitting there with that look on my face and nothing coming out of my mouth.

"Whose is this?" Mrs. Price says, and she holds the red sweater up in the air for all the class to see. "Whose? It's been sitting in the coatroom for a month."

"Not mine," says everybody. "Not me."

"It has to belong to somebody," Mrs. Price keeps saying, but nobody can remember. It's an ugly sweater with red plastic buttons and a collar and sleeves all stretched out like you could use them for a jump rope. It's maybe a thousand years old and even if it belonged to me I wouldn't say so.

Maybe because I'm skinny, maybe because she doesn't like me, that stupid Sylvia Saldivar says, "I think it belongs to Rachel." An ugly sweater like that, all raggedy and old, but Mrs. Price believes her; Mrs. Price takes the sweater and puts it right on my desk, but when I open my mouth nothing comes out.

"That's not, I don't, you're not . . . Not mine," I finally say in a little voice   10
that was maybe me when I was four.

"Of course it's yours," Mrs. Price says. "I remember you wearing it once." Because she's older and the teacher, she's right and I'm not.

Not mine, not mine, not mine, but Mrs. Price is already turning to page thirty-two and math problem number four. I don't know why but all of a sudden I'm feeling sick inside, like the part of me that's three wants to come out of my eyes, only I squeeze them shut tight and bite down on my teeth real hard and try to remember today I am eleven, eleven.

Mama is making a cake for me tonight, and when Papa comes home everybody will sing Happy birthday, happy birthday to you.

But when the sick feeling goes away and I open my eyes, the red sweater's still sitting there like a big red mountain. I move the red sweater to the corner of my desk with my ruler. I move my pencil and books and eraser as far from it as possible. I even move my chair a little to the right. Not mine, not mine, not mine.

In my head I'm thinking how long till lunchtime, how long till I can take   15
the red sweater and throw it over the schoolyard fence, or leave it hanging on a parking meter, or bunch it up into a little ball and toss it in the alley. Except when math period ends Mrs. Price says loud and in front of everybody, "Now, Rachel, that's enough," because she sees I've shoved the red sweater to the tippy-tip corner of my desk and it's hanging all over the edge like a waterfall, but I don't care.

"Rachel," Mrs. Price says. She says it like she's getting mad. "You put that sweater on right now and no more nonsense."

"But it's not —"

"Now!" Mrs. Price says.

This is when I wish I wasn't eleven, because all the years inside of me — ten, nine, eight, seven, six, five, four, three, two, and one — are pushing at the back of my eyes when I put one arm through one sleeve of the sweater that smells like cottage cheese, and then the other arm through the other and stand there with my arms apart like if the sweater hurts me and it does, all itchy and full of germs that aren't even mine.

That's when everything I've been holding in since this morning, since 20 when Mrs. Price put the sweater on my desk, finally lets go, and all of a sudden I'm crying in front of everybody. I wish I was invisible but I'm not. I'm eleven and it's my birthday today and I'm crying like I'm three in front of everybody. I put my head down on the desk and bury my face in my stupid clown-sweater arms. My face all hot and spit coming out of my mouth because I can't stop the little animal noises from coming out of me, until there aren't any more tears left in my eyes, and it's just my body shaking like when you have the hiccups, and my whole head hurts like when you drink milk too fast.

But the worst part is right before the bell rings for lunch. That stupid Phyllis Lopez, who is even dumber than Sylvia Saldivar, says she remembers the red sweater is hers! I take it off right away and give it to her, only Mrs. Price pretends like everything's okay.

Today I'm eleven. There's a cake Mama's making for tonight, and when Papa comes home from work we'll eat it. There'll be candles and presents and everybody will sing Happy birthday, happy birthday to you, Rachel, only it's too late.

I'm eleven today. I'm eleven, ten, nine, eight, seven, six, five, four, three, two, and one, but I wish I was one hundred and two. I wish I was anything but eleven, because I want today to be far away already, far away like a runaway balloon, like a tiny *o* in the sky, so tiny-tiny you have to close your eyes to see it.

CONSIDERATIONS FOR CRITICAL THINKING AND WRITING

1. **FIRST RESPONSE.** Although this story certainly focuses on what it means to be eleven years old, in what sense might it also be considered a meditation on the meaning of birthdays in general?

2. How does Rachel's use of language — particularly her images and metaphors — seem appropriate for an eleven-year-old girl?

3. Discuss the importance of the repetition of numbers throughout the story as a way of describing Rachel's emotions.

4. Comment on the thematic significance of Rachel's observation concerning Mrs. Price: "Because she's older and the teacher, she's right and I'm not" (para. 11).

CONNECTIONS TO OTHER SELECTIONS

1. Discuss the teacher's impact on the student in this story and in Judy Page Heitzman's poem "The Schoolroom on the Second Floor of the Knitting Mill" (p. 878).

2. Compare the experience of the young girl in this story with that of the girl in Alice Walker's "The Flowers" (p. 82). How does each work achieve powerful effects in only two pages?

RON CARLSON (B. 1947)

Born in Logan, Utah, Ron Carlson is emeritus professor of English at Arizona State University. He has published his fiction widely in magazines such as *The New Yorker, Esquire,* and *Harper's.* To date he has published four novels, the most recent being *Five Skies* (2007), and four collections of short stories, the last *A Kind of Flying* (2003). On his own work Carlson has commented: "I think all stories, long and short, require astonishing attention. . . . Attention is the ruler of craft."

Max   *1986*

Max is a crotch dog. He has powerful instinct and insistent snout, and he can ruin a cocktail party faster than running out of ice. This urge of his runs deeper than any training can reach. He can sit, heel, fetch; he'll even fetch a thrown snowball from a snowfield, bringing a fragment of it back to you delicately in his mouth. And then he'll poke your crotch, and be warned: it is no gentle nuzzling.

So when our friend Maxwell came by for a drink to introduce us to his new girlfriend, our dog Max paddled up to him and jabbed him a sharp one, a stroke so clean and fast it could have been a boxing glove on a spring. Maxwell, our friend, lost his breath and sat on the couch suddenly and heavily, unable to say anything beyond a hoarse whisper of "*Scotch.* Just *scotch.* No ice."

Cody put Max out on the back porch, of course, where he has spent a good measure of this long winter, and Maxwell took a long nourishing sip on his scotch and began recovering. He's not athletic at all, but I admired the way he had folded, crumpling just like a ballplayer taking an inside pitch in the nuts. It wasn't enough to change my whole opinion of him, but it helped me talk to him civilly for five minutes while Cody calmed the dog. I think I had seen a sly crocodile smile on Max's face after he'd struck, pride in a job well done, possibly, and then again, possibly a deeper satisfaction. He had heard Cody and me talk about Maxwell before, and Max is a smart dog.

Maxwell, his color returning, was now explaining that his new girlfriend, Laurie, would be along in a minute; she had been detained at aerobics class. Life at the museum was hectic and lovely, he was explaining. It was frustrating for him to be working with folk so ignorant of what made a good show, of counterpoint, of even the crudest elements of art. Let alone business, the business of curating, the business of public responsibility, the business in general. I was hoping to get him on his arch tirade about how the average intelligence in his department couldn't make a picture by connecting the dots, a routine which Cody could dial up like a phone number. But I wasn't going to get it tonight; he was already on business, his favorite topic.

The truth is that Maxwell is a simple crook. He uses his office to travel like 5 a pasha; he damages borrowed work, sees to the insurance, and then buys some of it for himself; he only mounts three shows a year; and he only goes in four days a week.

Cody came in for one of her favorite parts, Maxwell's catalogue (including stores and prices) of the clothing and jewelry he was wearing tonight. Cody always asked about the clerks, and so his glorious monologue was sprinkled with diatribes about the help. Old Maxwell.

When his girlfriend, Laurie, finally did arrive, breathless and airy at the same time, Maxwell had all three rings on the coffee table and he was showing Cody his new watch. Laurie tossed her head three times taking off her coat; we were in for a record evening.

Maxwell would show her off for a while, making disparaging remarks about exercise *of any kind,* and she would admire his rings, ranking them like tokens on the table, going into complex and aesthetic reasons for her choices. I would fill her full of the white wine that all of Maxwell's girlfriends drink, and then when she asked where the powder room was, I would rise with her and go into the kitchen, wait, count to twenty-five while selecting another Buckhorn out of the fridge, and let Max in.

CONSIDERATIONS FOR CRITICAL THINKING AND WRITING

1. **FIRST RESPONSE.** Why do you think the story is titled "Max" rather than "Maxwell"?

2. What details are especially effective in characterizing Maxwell and his girlfriend?

3. How does the narrator serve as an implicit foil to Maxwell?

4. **CREATIVE RESPONSE.** Write an additional final paragraph that describes what happens when Max is let back into the house, a paragraph that is worthy of the humor in the rest of the story.

5. Why do you think Carlson didn't write that paragraph?

CONNECTIONS TO OTHER SELECTIONS

1. Compare "Max" and Ron Hansen's "My Kid's Dog" (p. 584) as revenge stories.

2. Discuss the point of view and tone of the narration in "Max" and T. Coraghessan Boyle's "Carnal Knowledge" (p. 569).

JAYNE ANNE PHILLIPS (B. 1952)

Born in Buckhannon, West Virginia, Jayne Anne Phillips earned a B.A. from West Virginia University and within five years published three collections of short stories. The third of those collections, *Black Tickets* (1979), from which "Cheers" is taken, created a national reputation for her work. She has published four novels, most recently *Lark and Termite* (2009). Her work has been awarded a Guggenheim and two National Endowment for the Arts fellowships. She directs the creative writing M.F.A. program at Rutgers Newark, the State University of New Jersey.

Cheers   *1979*

The sewing woman lived across the tracks, down past Arey's Feed Store. Row of skinny houses on a mud alley. Her rooms smelled of salted grease and old newspaper. Behind the ironing board she was thin, scooping up papers that shuffled open in her hands. Her eyebrows were arched sharp and painted on.

She made cheerleading suits for ten-year-olds. Threading the machine, she clicked her red nails on the needle and pulled my shirt over my head. In the other room the kids watched *Queen for a Day*. She bent over me. I saw each eyelash painted black and hard and separate. Honey, she said. Turn around this way. And on the wall there was a postcard of orange trees in Florida. A man in a straw hat reached up with his hand all curled. Beautiful Bounty said the card in wavy red letters.

I got part of it made up, she said, fitting the red vest. You girls are bout the same size as mine. All you girls are bout the same. She pursed her red lips and pinched the cloth together. Tell me somethin Honey. How'd I manage all these kids an no man. On television there was loud applause for the queen, whose roses were sharp and real. Her machine buzzed like an animal beside the round clock. She frowned as she pressed the button with her foot, then furled the red cloth out and pulled me to her. Her pointed white face was smudged around the eyes. I watched the pale strand of scalp in her hair. There, she said.

When I left she tucked the money in her sweater. She had pins between her teeth and lipstick gone grainy in the cracks of her mouth. I had a red swing skirt and a bumpy *A* on my chest. Lord, she said. You do look pretty.

CONSIDERATIONS FOR CRITICAL THINKING AND WRITING

1. **FIRST RESPONSE.** How did you respond to "Cheers" on a first reading? What sorts of ironies emerge from this story on a second or third reading?

2. What can you say about the setting that is relevant to the story's tone?

3. Comment on the sewing woman's makeup. What purpose do you think it has thematically in the story?

4. Discuss the significance of the title.

CONNECTIONS TO OTHER SELECTIONS

1. Contrast the significance of the nature experience that the ten-year-old has in "Cheers" with that of the experience of Rachel in Sandra Cisneros's "Eleven" (p. 609).

2. Discuss the use of irony in "Cheers" and Mark Twain's "The Story of the Good Little Boy" (p. 604).

MARK HALLIDAY (B. 1949)

Born in Ann Arbor, Michigan, Mark Halliday earned a B.A. and an M.A. from Brown University and a Ph.D. from Brandeis University. A teacher at Ohio University, his short stories and poems have appeared in a variety of periodicals, including *The Massachusetts Review, Michigan Quarterly Review, Chicago Review,* and *The New Republic.* Among his four collections of poetry, *Little Star* was selected by the National Poetry Series for publication in 1987. He has also written a critical study on poet Wallace Stevens titled *Stevens and the Interpersonal* (1991).

Young Man on Sixth Avenue   *1995*

He was a young man in the big city. He was a young man in the biggest, the most overwhelming city—and he was not overwhelmed. For see, he strode across Fifth Avenue just before the light changed, and his head was up in the sharp New York wind and he was thriving upon the rock of Manhattan, in 1938. His legs were long and his legs were strong; there was no question about his legs; they were unmistakable in their length and strength; they were as bold and dependable as any American machine, moving him across Fifth just in time, his brown shoes attaining the sidewalk without any faltering, his gait unaware of the notion that legs might ever want to rest. Forty-ninth Street! He walked swiftly through the haste and blare, through the chilly exclamation points of taxis and trucks and people. He was a man! In America, '38, New York, two o'clock in the afternoon, sunlight chopping down between buildings, Forty-ninth Street. And his hair was so dark, almost black, and it had a natural wave in it recognized as a handsome feature by everyone, recognized universally, along with his dark blue eyes and strong jaw. Women saw him, they all had to see him, all the young women had to perceive him reaching the corner of Forty-ninth and Sixth, and they had to know he was a candidate. He knew they knew. He knew they knew he would *get* some of them, and he moved visibly tall with the tall potential of the not-finite twentieth-century getting that would be his inheritance; and young women who glanced at him on Sixth Avenue knew that he knew. They felt that they or their sisters would have to take him into account, and they touched their scarves a little nervously.

He was twenty-five years old, and this day in 1938 was the present. It was so obviously and totally the present, so unabashed and even garish with its presentness, beamingly right there right now like Rita Hayworth,° all Sixth Avenue was in fact at two o'clock a thumping bright Rita Hayworth and the young man strode south irresistibly. If there was only one thing he knew, crossing Forty-eighth, it was that this day was the present, out of which uncounted glories could and must blossom—when?—in 1938, or in 1939, soon, or in the big brazen decade ahead, in 1940, soon; so he walked with fistfuls of futures that could happen in all his pockets.

And his wavy hair was so dark, almost black. And he knew the right restaurant for red roast beef, not too expensive. And in his head were some sharp ideas about Dreiser, and Thomas Wolfe, and John O'Hara.

On Forty-seventh between two buildings (buildings taller even than him) there was an unexpected zone of deep shade. He paused for half a second, and he shivered for some reason. Briskly then, briskly he moved ahead.

Rita Hayworth (1918–87):   A Hollywood movie star.

In the restaurant on Seventh Avenue he met his friend John for a witty late lunch. Everything was — the whole lunch was good. It was right. And what they said was both hilarious and notably well-informed. And then soon he was taking the stairs two at a time up to an office on Sixth for his interview. The powerful lady seemed to like his sincerity and the clarity of his eyes — a hard combination to beat — and the even more powerful man in charge sized him up and saw the same things, and he got the job.

That job lasted three years, then came the War, then another job, then Judy, and the two kids, and a better job in Baltimore, and those years — those years. And those years. "Those years" — and the kids went to college with new typewriters. In the blue chair, with his work on his lapboard, after a pleasant dinner of macaroni and sausage and salad, he dozed off. Then he was sixty. Sixty? Then he rode back and forth on trains, Judy became ill, doctors offered opinions, comas were deceptive, Judy died. But the traffic on Coleytown Road next morning still moved casually too fast. And in a minute he was seventy-five and the phone rang with news that witty John of the great late lunches was dead. The house pulsed with silence.

Something undone? What? The thing that would have saved — what? Waking in the dark — maybe something unwritten, that would have made people say "*Yes* that's why you matter so much." Ideas about Wolfe. Dreiser. Or some lost point about John O'Hara.

Women see past him on the street in this pseudo-present and he feels they are so stupid and walks fierce for a minute but then his shoulders settle closer to his skeleton with the truth about these women: not especially stupid; only young. In this pseudo-present he blinks at a glimpse of that young man on Sixth Avenue, young man as if still out there in the exclamation of Sixth Avenue — that young man ready to stride across — but a taxi makes him step back to the curb, he'll have to wait a few more seconds, he can wait.

CONSIDERATIONS FOR CRITICAL THINKING AND WRITING

1. **FIRST RESPONSE.** Do you identify with the young man as he is described in the first paragraph? Is he appealing to you? Why or why not?

2. Why do you think this story opens in 1938? Why is the Manhattan setting important?

3. The American novelists Theodore Dreiser, Thomas Wolfe, and John O'Hara are mentioned in paragraphs 3 and 7. Of what significance are these novelists in this story? You may have to look up these writers in an encyclopedic entry or a dictionary of American literary biographies to answer this question.

4. What is the conflict in the story?

5. Locate the climax in the story. Is there a resolution to the conflict? Explain.

CONNECTIONS TO OTHER SELECTIONS

1. Discuss the significance of the Manhattan setting in "Young Man on Sixth Avenue" and in Xu Xi's "Famine" (p. 657).

2. Write an essay comparing the ending of Halliday's story with that of Raymond Carver's "Popular Mechanics" (p. 334). What is the effect of the ending on your reading of each story?

DAVID FOSTER WALLACE   (1962–2008)

Born in Ithaca, New York, David Foster Wallace grew up in Illinois and graduated with a B.A. from Amherst College and an M.F.A. from the University of Arizona. He taught in the English department at Illinois State University and then became a professor of English at Pomona College. His essays and fiction appeared in magazines ranging from *The New Yorker* to *The Paris Review.* These, along with his two novels — *The Broom of the System* (1987) and *Infinite Jest* (1996) — and three short story collections — *Girl with Curious Hair* (1989), *Brief Interviews with Hideous Men* (1999), and *Oblivion* (2004) — earned

© Gary Hannabarger/CORBIS.

him a meteoric literary reputation as an innovative writer. "Incarnations of Burned Children" was originally published in *Esquire.*

Incarnations of Burned Children   *2000*

The daddy was around the side of the house hanging a door for the tenant when he heard the child's screams and the Mommy's voice gone high between them. He could move fast, and the back porch gave onto the kitchen, and before the screen door had banged shut behind him the Daddy had taken the scene in whole, the overturned pot on the floortile before the stove and the burner's blue jet and the floor's pool of water still steaming as its many arms extended, the toddler in his baggy diaper standing rigid with steam coming off his hair and his chest and shoulders scarlet and his eyes rolled up and mouth open very wide and seeming somehow separate from the sounds that issued, the Mommy down on one knee with the dishrag dabbing pointlessly at him and matching the screams with cries of her own, hysterical so she was almost frozen. Her one knee and the bare little soft feet were still in the steaming pool and the Daddy's first act was to take the child under the arms and lift him away from it and take him to the sink, where he threw out plates and struck the tap to let cold well water run over the boy's feet while with his cupped hand he gathered and poured or flung cold water over his head and shoulders and chest, wanting first to see the steam stop coming off him, the Mommy over his shoulder invoking God until he sent her for towels and gauze if they had it, the Daddy moving quickly and well and his man's mind empty of everything but purpose, not yet aware of how smoothly he moved or that he'd ceased to hear the high screams because to hear them would freeze him and make impossible what had to be done to help his child, whose screams were regular as breath and went on so long they'd become already a thing in the kitchen, something else to move quickly around. The tenant side's door outside hung half off its top hinge and moved slightly in the wind, and a bird in the oak across the driveway appeared to observe the door with a cocked head as the cries still came from inside. The worst scalds seemed to be the right arm and shoulder, the chest and stomach's red was fading to pink under the cold water and his feet's soft soles weren't blistered that the Daddy could see, but the toddler still made little fists and screamed except now merely on reflex from fear, the Daddy would know he thought possible later, small face distended and thready veins standing out at the temples and the Daddy kept saying he was here he was here, adrenaline ebbing and an anger at the Mommy for allowing this thing to happen just starting to gather in wisps at his mind's extreme rear still hours from expression. When the Mommy returned he wasn't sure whether to wrap the child in a towel or not but he wet the towel down and did, swaddled him tight and lifted his baby out of the sink and set him on the kitchen table's edge to soothe him while the Mommy tried to check the feet's soles with one hand waving around in the area of her mouth and uttering objectless words while the Daddy bent in and was face to face with the child on the table's checked edge repeating the fact that he was here and trying to calm the toddler's cries but still the child breathlessly screamed, a high pure shining sound that could stop his heart and his bitty lips and gums now tinged with the light blue of a low flame the Daddy thought, screaming as if almost still under the tilted pot in pain. A minute, two like this that seemed much longer, with the Mommy at the Daddy's side talking sing-song at the child's face and the lark on the limb with its head to the side and the hinge going white in a line from the weight of the canted door until the first wisp of steam came lazy from under the wrapped towel's hem and the parents' eyes met and widened — the diaper, which when they opened the towel and leaned their little boy back on the checkered cloth and unfastened the softened tabs and tried to remove it resisted slightly with new high cries and was hot, their baby's diaper burned their hand and they saw where the real water'd fallen and pooled and been burning their baby all this time while he screamed for them to help him and they hadn't, hadn't thought and when they got it off and saw the state of what was there the Mommy said their God's first name and grabbed the table to keep her feet while the father turned away and threw a haymaker at the air of the kitchen and cursed both himself and the world for not the last time while his child might now have been sleeping if not for the rate of his breathing and the tiny stricken motions of his hands in the air above where he lay, hands the size of a grown man's thumb that had clutched the Daddy's thumb in the crib while he'd watched the Daddy's mouth move in song, his head cocked and seeming to see way past him into something his eyes made the Daddy lonesome for in a sideways way. If you've never wept and want to, have a child. Break your heart inside and something will a child is the twangy song the Daddy hears again as if the radio's lady was almost there with him looking down at what they've done, though hours later what the Daddy won't most forgive is how badly he wanted a cigarette right then as they diapered the child as best they could in gauze and two crossed handtowels and the Daddy lifted him like a newborn with his skull in one palm and ran him out to the hot truck and burned custom rubber all the way to town and the clinic's ER with the tenant's door hanging open like that all day until the hinge gave but by then it was too late, when it wouldn't stop and they couldn't make it the child had learned to leave himself and watch the whole rest unfold from a point overhead, and whatever was lost never thenceforth mattered, and the child's body expanded and walked about and drew pay and lived its life untenanted, a thing among things, its self's soul so much vapor aloft, falling as rain and then rising, the sun up and down like a yoyo.

CONSIDERATIONS FOR CRITICAL THINKING AND WRITING

1. **FIRST RESPONSE.** Describe the emotions this narration produces in you. What elements in the story are most effective in creating them for you?

2. How do you interpret the ending of this story? What do you think happens at the very end?

3. At one point the narrator steps in front of the action and addresses the reader: "If you've never wept and want to, have a child." Explain whether that sentence adequately sums up the theme of the story for you.

4. What do you make of the title?

CONNECTIONS TO OTHER SELECTIONS

1. Describe the unconventional style of Wallace's story and Joyce Carol Oates's "Hi Howya Doin" (p. 600). How is the style related to content in each story?

2. Compare the relationship between the husband and wife in "Incarnations of Burned Children" and in "Popular Mechanics" by Raymond Carver (p. 334).

LYDIA DAVIS (B. 1947)

Born in Northampton, Massachusetts, Lydia Davis graduated from Barnard College in 1970, after which she began work as a translator of French literature. Her success as a translator can be measured in part by the French government's awarding her the Chevalier of the Order of Arts. She has won high praise particularly for her translations of Marcel Proust. As a fiction writer, Davis has appeared in numerous literary periodicals while publishing one novel, *End of the Story* (1995), and four collections of short stories: *Break It Down* (1986); *Almost No Memory* (1997); *Samuel Johnson Is Indignant* (2001), the collection from which "Letter to a Funeral Parlor" is reprinted; and *Varieties of Disturbances: Stories* (2007). Among the prestigious literary prizes that Davis has been awarded are fellowships from the MacArthur and Guggenheim foundations, a Lannan Literary Award, and a Whiting Writer's Award. She has taught at several schools, including Bard College and the University at Albany.

© Jerry Bauer.

Davis is well known for her brief, compact, sharp, and often humorous fictions that survey contemporary life. "In such a form," she observes, "each word has to be right."

Letter to a Funeral Parlor   *2001*

Dear Sir,

I am writing to you to object to the word "cremains," which was used by your representative when he met with my mother and me two days after my father's death.

We had no objection to your representative, personally, who was respectful and friendly and dealt with us in a sensitive way. He did not try to sell us an expensive urn, for instance.

What startled and disturbed us was the word "cremains." You in the business must have invented this word and you are used to it. We the public do not hear it very often. We don't lose a close friend or a family member very many times in our life, and years pass in between, if we are lucky. Even less often do we have to discuss what is to be done with a family member or close friend after their death.

We noticed that before the death of my father you and your representative used the words "loved one" to refer to him. That was comfortable for us, even if the ways in which we loved him were complicated.

Then we were sitting there in our chairs in the living room trying not to 5 weep in front of your representative, who was opposite us on the sofa, and we were very tired first from sitting up with my father, and then from worrying about whether he was comfortable as he was dying, and then from worrying about where he might be now that he was dead, and your representative referred to him as "the cremains."

At first we did not even know what he meant. Then, when we realized, we were frankly upset. "Cremains" sounds like something invented as a milk substitute in coffee, like Cremora, or Coffee-Mate. Or it sounds like some kind of chipped beef dish.

As one who works with words for a living, I must say that any invented word, like "Porta Potti" or "pooper-scooper," has a cheerful or even jovial ring to it that I don't think you really intended when you invented the word "cremains." In fact, my father himself, who was a professor of English and is now being called "the cremains," would have pointed out to you the alliteration in "Porta Potti" and the rhyme in "pooper-scooper." Then he would have told you that "cremains" falls into the same category as "brunch" and is known as a portmanteau word.

There is nothing wrong with inventing words, especially in a business. But a grieving family is not prepared for this one. We are not even used to our loved one being gone. You could very well continue to employ the term "ashes." We are used to it from the Bible, and are even comforted by it. We would not misunderstand. We would know that these ashes are not like the ashes in a fireplace.

Yours sincerely.

CONSIDERATIONS FOR CRITICAL THINKING AND WRITING

1. **FIRST RESPONSE.** Why does it make sense that the author of this story is also a professional translator? What does that fact suggest about her sensitivity to diction and tone?

2. Describe the movement of the story's plot. What elements of a typical plot (see the glossary entry for *plot*) can you find in the story?

3. Which paragraphs seem particularly humorous to you? Explain why the story does or doesn't make a serious point.

4. To what extent do you think these eight paragraphs constitute a short story?

CONNECTIONS TO OTHER SELECTIONS

1. Compare the style, tone, and irony of Davis's story with Annie Proulx's "55 Miles to the Gas Pump" (p. 568).

2. Discuss the attitudes expressed about language usage in "Letter to a Funeral Parlor" and in Barbara Hamby's poem "Ode to American English" (p. 817).

PETER MEINKE (B. 1932)

Born in Brooklyn, New York, Peter Meinke was educated at Hamilton College (B.A., 1955), the University of Michigan (M.A., 1961), and the University of Minnesota (Ph.D., 1965). He has taught literature and creative writing at a number of schools, including Hamline University, Eckerd College, and Old Dominion University. Among his many poetry books are *Nightwatch on the Chesapeake* (1987), *Scars* (1996), and *The Contracted World* (2006), which are notable for their powerful use of detail from everyday life as well as simple — and serious — humor. They have earned him two National Endowment for the Arts fellowships. Though Meinke is primarily a poet, he has also published two collections of short stories: *Piano Tuner* (1986), which won the Flannery O'Connor Award, and *Unheard Music* (2007). In a 1990 interview in *Clockwatch Review,* Meinke discussed the similarities he sees between short stories and poetry: "I think that certainly poetry and short stories are more alike than short stories and novels, because that's the main decision — leaving out the boffo endings, leaving out conversations that are extraneous. There's a big empty spot around poems and short stories, certainly. That's the thing they have very strongly in common." "The Cranes" is a fine example of the kind of literary economy that Meinke believes poetry and short stories often share.

The Cranes   *1987*

"Oh!" she said, "what are those, the huge white ones?" Along the marshy shore two tall and stately birds, staring motionless toward the Gulf, towered above the bobbing egrets and scurrying plovers.

"Well, I can't believe it," he said. "I've been coming here for years and never saw one."

"But what are they? Don't make me guess or anything; it makes me feel dumb." They leaned forward in the car, and the shower curtain spread over the front seat crackled and hissed.

"They've got to be whooping cranes, nothing else so big." One of the birds turned gracefully, as if to acknowledge the old Dodge parked alone in the tall grasses. "See the black legs and black wingtips? Big! Why don't I have my binoculars?" He looked at his wife and smiled.

"Well," he continued after a while, "I've seen enough birds. But whooping cranes, they're rare. Not many left." 5

"They're lovely. They make the little birds look like clowns."

"I could use a few clowns," he said. "A few laughs never hurt anybody."

"Are you all right?" She put a hand on his thin arm. "I feel I'm responsible. Maybe this is the wrong thing."

"God, no!" His voice changed. "No way. I can't smoke, can't drink martinis, no coffee, no candy. I not only can't leap buildings in a single bound, I can hardly get up the goddamn stairs."

She was smiling. "Do you remember the time you drank nine martinis and 10 asked that young priest to step outside and see whose side God was on?"

"What a jerk I was! How have you put up with me all this time?"

"Oh no! I was proud of you. You were so funny, and that priest was a snot."

"Now you tell me." The cranes were moving slowly over a small hillock, wings opening and closing like bellows. "It's all right. It's enough," he said again. "How old am I anyway, 130?"

"Really," she said, "it's me. Ever since the accident it's been one thing after another. I'm just a lot of trouble to everybody."

"Let's talk about something else," he said. "Do you want to listen to the 15 radio? How about turning on that preacher station so we can throw up?"

"No," she said, "I just want to watch the birds. And listen to you."

"You must be pretty tired of that."

She turned her head from the window and looked into his eyes. "I never got tired of listening to you. Never."

"Well, that's good," he said. "It's just that when my mouth opens, your eyes tend to close."

"They do not!" she said, and began to laugh, but the laugh turned into a 20 cough and he had to pat her on the back until she stopped. They leaned back in silence and looked toward the Gulf stretching out beyond the horizon. In the distance, the water looked like metal, still and hard.

"I wish they'd court," he said. "I wish we could see them court, the cranes. They put on a show. He bows like Nijinksy and jumps straight up in the air."

"What does she do?"

"She lies down and he lands on top of her."

"No," she said, "I'm serious."

"Well, I forget. I've never seen it. But I do remember that they mate for life 25 and live a long time. They're probably older than we are. Their feathers are falling out and their kids never write."

She was quiet again. He turned in his seat, picked up an object wrapped in a plaid towel, and placed it between them in the front. "Here's looking at *you*, kid," he said.

"Do they really mate for life? I'm glad — they're so beautiful."

"Yep. Audubon said that's why they're almost extinct: a failure of imagination."

"I don't believe that," she said. "I think there'll always be whooping cranes."

"Why not?" he said.   30

"I wish the children were more settled. I keep thinking it's my fault."

"You think everything's your fault. Nicaragua. Ozone depletion. Nothing is your fault. They'll be fine, and anyway, they're not children anymore. Kids are different today, that's all. You were terrific." He paused. "You were terrific in ways I couldn't tell the kids about."

"I should hope not." She laughed and began coughing again, but held his hand when he reached over. When the cough subsided they sat quietly, looking down at their hands as if they were objects in a museum. "I used to have pretty hands," she said.

"I remember."

"Do you? Really?"   35

"I remember everything," he said.

"You always forgot everything."

"Well, now I remember."

"Did you bring something for your ears?"

"No, I can hardly hear anything, anyway." But he turned his head at a sud- 40
den squabble among the smaller birds. The cranes were stepping delicately away from the commotion.

"I'm tired," she said.

"Yes." He leaned over and kissed her, barely touching her lips. "Tell me," he said, "did I really drink nine martinis?"

But she had already closed her eyes and only smiled. Outside, the wind ruffled the bleached-out grasses, and the birds in the white glare seemed almost transparent. The hull of the car gleamed beetle-like — dull and somehow sinister in its metallic isolation.

Suddenly, the two cranes plunged upward, their great wings beating the air and their long slender necks pointed like arrows toward the sun.

CONSIDERATIONS FOR CRITICAL THINKING AND WRITING

1. **FIRST RESPONSE.** What happens at the end of "The Cranes"? What do you think this story is about?

2. Does the couple's behavior seem motivated and plausible to you? Explain why or why not.

3. Point to incidences of suspenseful foreshadowing and discuss how they affect your understanding of the plot. Were you aware of the foreshadowing elements on a first reading or only after subsequent readings?

4. How might the cranes be read as both conventional and literary symbols in this story?

CONNECTIONS TO OTHER SELECTIONS

1. Consider how symbols convey the central meanings of "The Cranes" and of either Kate Chopin's "The Story of an Hour" (p. 15) or Gail Godwin's "A Sorrowful Woman" (p. 39).

2. How do you think this couple would respond to the funeral parlor representative's use of the word "cremains" in Lydia Davis's "Letter to a Funeral Parlor" (p. 620)?

MARGARET ATWOOD (B. 1939)

© Kathy deWitt/Alamy.

Born in Ottawa, Ontario, Margaret Atwood was educated at the University of Toronto and Harvard University. She has been writing fiction and poetry since she was a child; along the way she has done odd jobs and been a screenwriter and a teacher. Among her collections of short stories are *Dancing Girls* (1977), *Bluebeard's Egg* (1983), *Wilderness Tips* (1991), and *Moral Disorder* (2006). Her highly successful novels include *Surfacing* (1972), *The Handmaid's Tale* (1986), *Cat's Eye* (1989), *The Robber Bride* (1993), *Alias Grace* (1995), *The Blind Assassin* (2000), *Oryx and Crake* (2003), and *Year of the Flood* (2009). She has also written twelve books of poetry. Atwood has enhanced the appreciation of Canadian literature through her editing of *The New Oxford Book of Canadian Verse in English* (1982) and *The Oxford Book of Canadian Short Stories in English* (1986). Her own work closely examines the weight of the complex human relationships that complicate her characters' lives. In "Happy Endings," taken from her collection of short works, *Good Bones and Simple Murders* (1994), Atwood has fun with some of the conventional expectations placed on contemporary writers.

Happy Endings   1983

John and Mary meet.
What happens next?
If you want a happy ending, try A.

A. John and Mary fall in love and get married. They both have worthwhile and remunerative jobs which they find stimulating and challenging. They buy a charming house. Real estate values go up. Eventually, when they can afford live-in help, they have two children, to whom they are devoted. The children turn out well. John and Mary have a stimulating and challenging sex life and worthwhile friends. They go on fun vacations together. They retire. They both have hobbies which they find stimulating and challenging. Eventually they die. This is the end of the story.

B. Mary falls in love with John but John doesn't fall in love with Mary. He merely uses her body for selfish pleasure and ego gratification of a tepid kind. He comes to her apartment twice a week and she cooks him dinner, you'll notice that he doesn't even consider her worth the price of a dinner out, and after he's eaten the dinner he fucks her and after that he falls asleep, while she does the dishes so he won't think she's untidy, having all those dirty dishes lying around, and puts on fresh lipstick so she'll look good when he wakes up, but when he wakes up he doesn't even notice, he puts on his socks and his shorts and his pants and his shirt and his tie and his shoes, the reverse order from the one in which he took them off. He doesn't take off Mary's clothes, she takes them off herself, she acts as if she's dying for it every time, not because she likes sex exactly, she doesn't, but she wants John to think she does because if they do it often enough surely he'll get used to her, he'll come to depend on her and they will get married, but John goes out the door with hardly so much as a good-night and three days later he turns up at six o'clock and they do the whole thing over again.

Mary gets run-down. Crying is bad for your face, everyone knows that and so does Mary but she can't stop. People at work notice. Her friends tell her John is a rat, a pig, a dog, he isn't good enough for her, but she can't believe it. Inside John, she thinks, is another John, who is much nicer. This other John will emerge like a butterfly from a cocoon, a Jack from a box, a pit from a prune, if the first John is only squeezed enough.

One evening John complains about the food. He has never complained about the food before. Mary is hurt.

Her friends tell her they've seen him in a restaurant with another 5 woman, whose name is Madge. It's not even Madge that finally gets to Mary: it's the restaurant. John has never taken Mary to a restaurant. Mary collects all the sleeping pills and aspirins she can find, and takes them and a half a bottle of sherry. You can see what kind of a woman she is by the fact that it's not even whiskey. She leaves a note for John. She hopes he'll discover her and get her to the hospital in time and repent and then they can get married, but this fails to happen and she dies.

John marries Madge and everything continues as in A.

C. John, who is an older man, falls in love with Mary, and Mary, who is only twenty-two, feels sorry for him because he's worried about his hair falling out. She sleeps with him even though she's not in love with him. She met him at work. She's in love with someone called James, who is twenty-two also and not yet ready to settle down.

John on the contrary settled down long ago: this is what is bothering him. John has a steady, respectable job and is getting ahead in his field, but Mary isn't impressed by him, she's impressed by James, who has a motorcycle and a fabulous record collection. But James is often away on his motorcycle, being free. Freedom isn't the same for girls, so in the meantime Mary spends Thursday evenings with John. Thursdays are the only days John can get away.

John is married to a woman called Madge and they have two children, a charming house which they bought just before the real estate values went up, and hobbies which they find stimulating and challenging, when they have the time. John tells Mary how important she is to him, but of course he can't leave his wife because a commitment is a commitment. He goes on about this more than is necessary and Mary finds it boring, but older men can keep it up longer so on the whole she has a fairly good time.

One day James breezes in on his motorcycle with some top-grade California hybrid and James and Mary get higher than you'd believe possible and they climb into bed. Everything becomes very underwater, but along comes John, who has a key to Mary's apartment. He finds them stoned and entwined. He's hardly in any position to be jealous, considering Madge, but nevertheless he's overcome with despair. Finally he's middle-aged, in two years he'll be bald as an egg and he can't stand it. He purchases a handgun, saying he needs it for target practice — this is the thin part of the plot, but it can be dealt with later — and shoots the two of them and himself. 10

Madge, after a suitable period of mourning, marries an understanding man called Fred and everything continues as in A, but under different names.

D. Fred and Madge have no problems. They get along exceptionally well and are good at working out any little difficulties that may arise. But their charming house is by the seashore and one day a giant tidal wave approaches. Real estate values go down. The rest of the story is about what caused the tidal wave and how they escape from it. They do, though thousands drown, but Fred and Madge are virtuous and lucky. Finally on high ground they clasp each other, wet and dripping and grateful, and continue as in A.

E. Yes, but Fred has a bad heart. The rest of the story is about how kind and understanding they both are until Fred dies. Then Madge devotes herself to charity work until the end of A. If you like, it can be "Madge," "cancer," "guilty and confused," and "bird watching."

F. If you think this is all too bourgeois, make John a revolutionary and Mary a counterespionage agent and see how far that gets you. Remember, this is Canada. You'll still end up with A, though in between you may get a lustful brawling saga of passionate involvement, a chronicle of our times, sort of.

You'll have to face it, the endings are the same however you slice it. Don't be deluded by any other endings, they're all fake, either deliberately fake, with malicious intent to deceive, or just motivated by excessive optimism if not by downright sentimentality. 15

The only authentic ending is the one provided here:
John and Mary die. John and Mary die. John and Mary die.

So much for endings. Beginnings are always more fun. True connoisseurs, however, are known to favor the stretch in between, since it's the hardest to do anything with.

That's about all that can be said for plots, which anyway are just one thing after another, a what and a what and a what.

Now try How and Why. 20

CONSIDERATIONS FOR CRITICAL THINKING AND WRITING

1. **FIRST RESPONSE.** Why do you suppose that happy endings are widely popular with so many readers? How do you think about them?
2. Which of the endings from A through F do you find most compelling? Why?
3. What does Atwood satirize in this story?
4. What do you think is the theme of "Happy Endings"?

CONNECTIONS TO OTHER SELECTIONS

1. **FIRST RESPONSE.** Try rewriting the end of Sandra Cisneros's "Eleven" (p. 609) or David Foster Wallace's "Incarnations of Burned Children" (p. 617) by supplying a happy ending. Then discuss whether your ending seems convincing to you.
2. Compare the treatment of fiction writing in "Happy Endings" and Tim O'Brien's "How to Tell a True War Story" (p. 346).

TERRY L. TILTON

The following story by Terry L. Tilton appeared as a contest winner in *The World's Shortest Stories,* edited by Steve Moss. The book is described on the cover as follows: "Murder. Love. Horror. Suspense. All this and much more in the most amazing short stories ever written — each one just fifty-five words long!" And indeed they are all limited to fifty-five words — every one drawn from stories submitted in a contest with the winners selected for publication. If Terry L. Tilton has published more than these fifty-five words, they are not readily available, but here's a story that provided a positive answer to a question that the editor raised in his introduction: "Does such a stingy word count allow for a really satisfying read?" That's a good question. See what you think.

That Settles That   *1998*

Tom was a handsome, fun-loving young man, albeit a bit drunk when he got into the argument with Sam, his roommate of just two months.

"You can't. You can *not* write a short story in just 55 words, you idiot!"

Sam shot him dead on the spot

"Oh, yes you can," Sam said, smiling.

CONSIDERATIONS FOR CRITICAL THINKING AND WRITING

1. **FIRST RESPONSE.** How satisfying a read is this as a short story?
2. Specifically, what elements of fiction can you identify in these fifty-five words?
3. **CREATIVE RESPONSE.** Write your own short story using precisely fifty-five words.

A Collection
of Stories

18

An Album of
Contemporary Stories

Writers lie. So do tape recorders and
video cameras. So does memory. As a
fiction writer this doesn't bother me
at all. I only have to be true to my
imagination, to the characters I create
and the events that I cause. In fiction,
the writer is God, without quarreling
apostles, without competing deities
and without any foot-dragging villagers.
— AMY BLOOM

The sixteen short stories in this collection represent a broad variety of styles and themes. They are written by men and women from a number of countries whose lives collectively span the nineteenth and twentieth centuries. The four stories in Chapter 18, "An Album of Contemporary Stories"—each written within the past ten years—offer a sustained opportunity to explore the fiction being produced today. The four stories in Chapter 19, "An Album of World Literature," by writers from Botswana, Egypt, Colombia, and China, introduce themes and styles from traditions that might differ quite a bit from your own. Inevitably, you will find some of the following stories more appealing than others, but every one of them is worth a careful reading, the kind of reading rewarded by pleasure and understanding.

AMY BLOOM (B. 1953)

Born and raised in the suburbs of New York
City, Amy Bloom "started writing unexpectedly." Bloom reports that before she began
writing she had "picked peanuts, scooped
felafel, waitressed up and down the East
Coast, tended bar, written catalogue copy,
and worked as a psychotherapist, for both
the worried well and the very ill." Her first
book, a collection of short stories, *Come to Me*
(1993), was nominated for the National Book
Award. It was followed by *Love Invents Us*
(1998), *A Blind Man Can See How Much I Love
You* (2000), *Normal* (2002), and *Away* (2007).
Currently teaching creative writing at Yale
University, Bloom lives in Connecticut and contributes to *The New Yorker,*
The Atlantic, and a variety of other magazines here and abroad.

© Marion Ettlinger.

By-and-by   2004

Every death is violent.
    The iris, the rainbow of the eye, closes down. The pupil spreads out like
black water. It seems natural, if you are there, to push the lid down, to ease the
pleated shade over the ball, to the lower lashes. The light is out, close the door.

Mrs. Warburg called me at midnight. I heard the click of her lighter and the
tiny crackle of burning tobacco. Her ring bumped against the receiver.
    "Are you comfortable, darling?"
    I was pretty comfortable. I was lying on her daughter's bed, with my feet   5
on Anne's yellow comforter, wearing Anne's bathrobe.
    "Do you feel like talking tonight?"
    Mrs. Warburg was the only person I felt like talking to. My boyfriend was
away. My mother was away. My father was dead. I worked in a felafel joint on
Charles Street where only my boss spoke English.
    I heard Mrs. Warburg swallow. "You have a drink, too. This'll be our little
party."
    Mrs. Warburg and I had an interstate, telephonic rum-and-Coke party
twice a week the summer Anne was missing. Mrs. Warburg told me about their
problems with the house; they had some roof mold and a crack in the foundation, and Mr. Warburg was not handy.
    "Roof mold," she said. "When you get married, you move into a nice pre-   10
war six in the city and let some other girl worry about roof mold. You go out
dancing."
    I know people say — but it's not true — you see it in movies cascades of hair
tumbling out of the coffin, long, curved nails growing over the clasped hands.

It's not true. When you're dead, you're dead and although some cells take longer to die than others, after a few hours everything is gone. The brain cells die fast, and blood pools in the soft, pressed places: the scapula, the lower back, the calves. If the body is not covered up, it produces a particular smell called cadaverine, and flies pick up the scent from a mile away. First, just one fly, then the rest. They lay fly eggs and ants come, drawn to the eggs, and sometimes wasps, and always maggots. Beetles and moths, the household kind that eat your sweaters, finish the body; they undress the flesh from the bone. They are the clean-up crew.

Mrs. Warburg and I only talked about Anne in passing and only about Anne in the past. Anne's tenth birthday had a Hawaiian theme. They made a hotdog luau in the backyard and served raspberry punch; they played pin-the-lei-on-the-donkey and had grass skirts for all the girls. "Anne might have been a little old for that, even then. She was a sophisticate from birth," Mrs. Warburg said. I was not a sophisticate from birth. I was an idiot from birth, and that is why when the police first came to look for Anne, I said a lot of things that sounded like lies.

Mrs. Warburg loved to entertain; she said Anne was her mother's daughter. We did like to have parties, and Mrs. Warburg made me tell her what kind of hors d'oeuvres we had. She was glad we served pigs-in-blankets because that's what she served when she was just starting out, although she'd actually made hers. And did one of us actually make the marinara sauce, at least, and was Anne actually eating pork sausage and she knew it must be me who made pineapple-upside-down cake, because that was not in her daughter's repertoire, and she hoped we used wine glasses but she had the strong suspicion we poured wine out of the box into paper cups, which was true. I told her Anne had spray-painted some of our third-hand furniture bright gold and when we lit the candles and turned out the lights, our apartment looked extremely glamorous.

"Oh, we love glamorous," Mrs. Warburg said.

In the Adirondacks, the Glens Falls trail and the old mining roads sometimes overlap. Miles of trail, around Speculator and Johnsburg are as smooth and neatly edged as garden paths. These are the old Fish Hill Mining Company roads and they will take you firmly and smoothly from the center of Hamilton County to the center of the woods and up the mountainside. Eugene Trask took Anne and her boyfriend, Teddy Ross, when they were loading up Teddy's van in the Glens Falls parking lot. He stabbed Teddy twice in the chest with his hunting knife, and tied him to a tree and stabbed him again, and left him and his backpack right there, next to the wooden sign about No Drinking, No Hunting. He took Anne with him, in Teddy's car. They found Teddy's body three days later and his parents buried him two days after that, back in Virginia.

Eugene Trask killed another boy just a few days before he killed Teddy. Some kids from Schenectady were celebrating their high school graduation with an overnight camping trip, and when Eugene Trask came upon them, he tied them all to different trees, far enough apart so they couldn't see each other, and then he killed the boy who'd made him mad. While he was stabbing him, the same way he stabbed Teddy, two sharp holes in his heart and then a slash across his chest, for emphasis, for something, the other kids slipped out of their ropes and ran. By the time they came back with people from town, Eugene

Trask had circled around the woods and was running through streams where the dogs could not catch his scent.

The heart is really two hearts and four parts: the right and the left, and the up and the down. The left heart pumps the blood through the body. Even when there is nothing more for it to do, even when you have already lost ten ounces of blood, which is all an average-sized person needs to lose to bring on heart failure, the left heart keeps pumping, bringing old news to nowhere. The right heart sits still as a cave, a thin scrim of blood barely covering its floor. The less air you have, the faster the whole heart beats. Still less and the bronchioles, hollow, spongy flutes of the lungs, whistle and squeeze dry until they lie flat and hard, like plates on the table, and when there is no more air and no more blood to bring help from the furthest reaches of the body, the lungs crack and chip like old china.

Mrs. Warburg and I both went to psychics.

She said, "A psychic in East Cleveland. What's *that* tell you?" which is why I kept talking to her even after Mr. Warburg said he didn't think it was helping. Mrs. Warburg's psychic lived in a run-down split-level ranch house with lime-green shag carpeting. Her psychic wore a white smock and white shoes like a nurse and she got Mrs. Warburg confused with her three o'clock, who was coming for a reading on her pancreatic cancer. Mrs. Warburg's psychic didn't know where Anne was.

My psychic was on West Cedar Street, in a tiny apartment two blocks away   20 from us on Beacon Hill. My boss's wife had lost a diamond earring and the psychic found it, she said. He looked like a graduate student. He was barefoot. He saw me looking down and flexed his feet.

"Helps me concentrate," he said.

We sat down at a dinette table and he held my hands between his. He inhaled and closed his eyes. I couldn't remember if I had the twenty dollars with me or not.

"Don't worry about it," he said.

We sat for three minutes, and I watched the hands on the grandfather clock behind him. My aunt had the same clock, with the flowers carved in cherrywood climbing up the maple box.

"It's very dark," he said. "I'm sorry. It's very dark where she is."   25

I found the money and he pushed it back at me, and not just out of kindness, I didn't think.

I told Mrs. Warburg my psychic didn't know anything either.

The police came on Saturday and again on Monday, but not the same ones. On Monday it was detectives from New York, and they didn't treat me like the worried roommate. They reminded me that I told the Boston police I'd last seen Anne at two o'clock on Thursday, before she went to Teddy's. They said someone else had told them Anne came back to our apartment at four o'clock, to get her sleeping bag. I said yes, I remembered, I was napping and she woke me up, because it was really my sleeping bag, I lent it to her for the trip. Yes, I did see her at four, not just at two.

Were you upset she was going on this trip with Ted? they said.

Teddy, I said. Why would I be upset?   30

They looked around our apartment, where I had to walk through her little bedroom to use the bathroom and she had to walk through my little bedroom to get to the front door, as if it was obvious why I'd be upset.

Maybe you didn't like him, they said.

I like him, I said.

Maybe he was cutting into your time with Annie.

Anne, I said, and they looked at each other as if it was very significant that I had corrected them.

Anne, they said. So maybe Teddy got in the way of your friendship with Anne?

I rolled my eyes. No, I said, we double-dated sometimes, it was cool.

They looked at their notes.

You have a boyfriend? they said. We'd like to talk to him too.

Sure, I said, he's in Maine with his family, but you can talk to him.

They shrugged a little. Maine, with his parents, was not a promising lead.

They pressed me a little more about my latent lesbian feelings for Anne and my unexpressed and unrequited love for Teddy, and I said that I thought maybe I had forgotten to tell the Boston police that I had worked double shifts every day last week and that I didn't own a car. They smiled and shrugged again.

If you think of anything, they said.

It's very dark where she is, is what I thought.

The police talked to me and they talked to Rose Trask, Eugene's sister, too. She said Eugene was a worthless piece of shit. She said he owed her money and if they found him she'd like it back, please. She hid Eugene's hunting knife at the bottom of her root cellar, under the onions, and she hid Eugene in her big, old-fashioned chimney until they left. Later, they made her go up in the helicopter to help them find him, and they made her call out his name over their loud-speaker ("Eugene, I love you. Eugene, it will be okay."). While they circled the park, which is three times the size of Yellowstone, she told the police that Eugene had worked on their uncle's farm from the time he was seven, because he was big for his age, and that he knew his way around the woods because their father threw him out of the house naked, in the middle of the night, whenever he wet his bed, which he did all his life.

Mrs. Warburg said she had wanted to be a dancer and she made Anne take jazz and tap and modern all through school but what Anne really loved was talking. Debate Club, Rhetoric, Student Court, Model U.N., anything that gave you plenty of opportunity for arguing and persuading, she liked. I said I knew that because I had had to live with Anne for four years and she argued and persuaded me out of cheap shoes and generic toilet paper and my mother's winter coat. She bought us matching kimonos in Chinatown. I told Mrs. Warburg that it was entirely due to Anne that I was able to walk through the world like a normal person.

Mrs. Warburg said, "Let me get another drink."

I lay back on Anne's bed and sipped my beer. Mrs. Warburg and I had agreed that since I didn't always remember to get rum for our parties, I could make do with beer. Anne actually liked beer, Mrs. Warburg said. Mr. Warburg liked Scotch. Mrs. Warburg went right down the middle, she felt, with the rum-and-Coke.

"Should we have gone to Teddy's funeral?" she said.

I didn't think so. Mrs. Warburg had never met Teddy, and I certainly didn't 50 want to go. I didn't want to sit with his family, or sit far behind them, hoping that since Teddy was dead, Anne was alive, or that if Anne had to be dead, she'd be lying in a white casket, with bushels of white carnations around her, and Teddy would be lying someplace dark and terrible and unseen.

"I think Anne might have escaped," Mrs. Warburg said. "I really do. I think she might have gotten out of those awful mountains and she might have found a rowboat or something, she's wonderful on water, you should see her on Lake Erie but it could be because of the trauma she doesn't—"

Mr. Warburg got on the line.

"It's three o'clock in the morning," he said. "Mrs. Warburg needs to sleep. So do you, I'm sure."

Eugene Trask and Anne traveled for four days. He said, at his trial, that she was a wonderful conversationalist. He said that talking to her was a pleasure and that they had had some very lively discussions, which he felt she had enjoyed. At the end of the fourth day, he unbuckled his belt so he could rape her again, in a quiet pine grove near Lake Pleasant, and while he was distracted with his shirttail and zipper, she made a grab for his hunting knife. He hit her on the head with the butt of his rifle, and when she got up, he hit her again. Then he stabbed her twice, just like Teddy, two to the heart. He didn't want to shoot her, he said. He put her bleeding body in the back of an orange Buick he'd stolen in Speculator, and he drove to an abandoned mine. He threw her down the thirty-foot shaft, dumped the Buick in Mineville, and walked through the woods to his sister's place. They had hamburgers and mashed potatoes and sat on Rose's back step and watched a pair of red-tailed hawks circling the spruce. Rose washed out his shirt and pants and ironed them dry, and he left early the next morning, with two meatloaf sandwiches in his jacket pocket. They caught Eugene Trask when one of his stolen cars broke down. They shot him in the leg. He said he didn't remember anything since he'd skipped his last arraignment two months ago. He said he was subject to fits of amnesia. He had fancy criminal lawyers who took his case because the hunt for Eugene Trask had turned out to be the biggest manhunt in the tristate area since the Lindbergh baby. There were reporters everywhere, Mrs. Warburg said. Mr. Feldman and Mr. Barone told Eugene that if he lied to them they would not be able to defend him adequately, so he drew them maps of where they could find Anne's body, and also two other girls who had been missing for six months. Mr. Feldman and Mr. Barone felt that they could not reveal this information to the police or to the Warburgs or to the other families because it would violate Eugene's confidentiality. After the trial, after Eugene was transferred to Fishkill Correctional Facility, two kids were playing in an old mine near Speculator, looking for garnets and gold and arrowheads, and they found Anne's body.

The dead body makes its own way. It stiffens and then it relaxes and then it 55 softens. The flesh turns to a black thick cream. If I had put my arms around her to carry her up the gravel path and home, if I had reached out to steady her, my hand would have slid through her skin like a spoon through custard, and she would have fallen away from me, held in only by her clothes. If I had hidden in the timbered walls of the mine, waiting until Eugene Trask heard the reassuring one-two thump of the almost emptied body on the mine car tracks, I might have seen her as I see her now. Her eyes open and blue, her cheeks pink underneath the streaks of clay and dust, and she is breathing, her chest is rising and falling, too fast and too shallow, like a bird in distress, but rising and falling.

We are all in the cave. Mrs. Warburg went back to her life, without me, after Anne's funeral that winter (did those children find her covered with the first November snow?), and Mr. Warburg resurfaced eight years later, remarried to a woman who became friends with my aunt Rita in Beachwood. Aunt Rita said the new Mrs. Warburg was lovely. She said the first Mrs. Warburg had made herself into a complete invalid, round-the-clock help, but even so she died alone, Rita said, in their old house. She didn't know from what. Eugene was shot and killed trying to escape from Fishkill. Two bullets to the heart, one to the lungs. Mrs. Warburg sent me the clipping. Rose Trask married and had two children, Cheryl and Eugene. Rose and Cheryl and little Eugene drowned in 1986, boating on Lake Champlain. Mrs. Warburg sent me the clipping. My young father, still slim and handsome and a good dancer, collapsed on our roof trying to straighten our ancient TV antennae and Eugene Trask pulled his feet out from under him, over the gutters and thirty feet down. Don't let the sun catch you crying, my father used to say. Maybe your nervous system doesn't get the message to swallow the morning toast and you are strangled and thrown to the kitchen floor by Eugene Trask while your wife and children watch. Maybe a cluster of secret tumors bloom from skull to spine, opening their petals so you can be beaten unconscious by Eugene Trask on the way to work. Everyone dies of heart failure, Eugene Trask said at his trial.

I don't miss the dead less, I miss them more. I miss the tall pines around Lake Pleasant, I miss the brown-and-gray cobblestones on West Cedar Street, I miss the red-tailed hawks that fly so often in pairs. I miss the cheap red wine in a box and I miss the rum-and-Coke. I miss Anne's wet gold hair drying as we sat on the fire escape. I miss the hotdog luau and driving to dance lessons after breakfast at Bruegger's Bagels. I miss the cold mornings on the farm, when the handle of the bucket bit into my small hands and my feet slid over the frozen dew. I miss the hot grease spattering around the felafel balls and the urgent clicking of Hebrew. I miss the new green leaves, shaking in the June rain. I miss standing on my father's shiny shoes as we danced to the Tennessee Waltz and my mother made me a paper fan so I could flirt like a Southern belle, tapping my nose with the fan. I miss every piece of my dead. Every piece is stacked high like cordwood within me, and my heart, both sides, and all four parts, is their reliquary.

CONNECTIONS TO OTHER SELECTIONS

1. Compare the way Bloom creates tension and suspense in her story with Andre Dubus's strategies in "Killings" (p. 103).

2. Discuss how the themes of "By-and-by" and Jhumpa Lahiri's "Hell-Heaven" (p. 638) are stories about grief.

JHUMPA LAHIRI (b. 1967)

Born in London and raised in Rhode Island, Jhumpa Lahiri is the daughter of Bengali parents. She graduated from Barnard College with a B.A. in English and went on to earn four degrees from Boston University — master's degrees in English, creative writing, and comparative studies in literature and the arts, and a Ph.D. in Renaissance studies. In 1998 Lahiri published three stories in *The New Yorker*, and the following year published her first book, the short story collection *Interpreter of Maladies* (1999), which won her the 2000 Pulitzer Prize for fiction. Her second collection, *Unaccustomed Earth*,

Marc Royce/CORBIS.

appeared in 2008. She has also published a novel, *The Namesake* (2003). She currently resides in New York City. Lahiri locates her stories between the cultures of the United States and India, using lavish description of setting and the elaboration of cultural tradition to illuminate her characters' inner worlds.

Hell–Heaven   2008

Pranab Chakraborty wasn't technically my father's younger brother. He was a fellow Bengali from Calcutta who had washed up on the barren shores of my parents' social life in the early seventies, when they lived in a rented apartment in Central Square and could number their acquaintances on one hand. But I had no real uncles in America, and so I was taught to call him Pranab Kaku. Accordingly, he called my father Shyamal Da, always addressing him in the polite form, and he called my mother Boudi, which is how Bengalis are supposed to address an older brother's wife, instead of using her first name, Aparna. After Pranab Kaku was befriended by my parents, he confessed that on the day we met him he had followed my mother and me for the better part of an afternoon around the streets of Cambridge, where she and I tended to roam after I got out of school. He had trailed behind us along Massachusetts Avenue and in and out of the Harvard Coop, where my mother liked to look at discounted housewares. He wandered with us into Harvard Yard, where my mother often sat on the grass on pleasant days and watched the stream of students and professors filing busily along the paths, until, finally, as we were climbing the steps to Widener Library so that I could use the bathroom, he tapped my mother on the shoulder and inquired, in English, if she might be a Bengali. The answer to his question was clear, given that my mother was wearing the red and white bangles unique to Bengali married women, and a common Tangail sari, and had a thick stem of vermilion powder in the center parting of her hair, and the full round face and large dark eyes that are so typical of Bengali women. He noticed the two or three safety pins she wore fastened to the thin gold bangles that were behind the red and white ones, which she would use to replace a missing hook on a blouse or to draw a string through a petticoat at a moment's notice, a practice he associated strictly with his mother and sisters and aunts in Calcutta. Moreover, Pranab Kaku had overheard my mother speaking to me in Bengali, telling me that I couldn't buy an issue of *Archie* at the Coop. But back then, he also confessed, he was so new to America that he took nothing for granted and doubted even the obvious.

My parents and I had lived in Central Square for three years prior to that day; before that, we lived in Berlin, where I was born and where my father had finished his training in microbiology before accepting a position as a researcher at Mass General, and before Berlin my mother and father had lived in India, where they were strangers to each other, and where their marriage had been arranged. Central Square is the first place I can recall living, and in my memories of our apartment, in a dark brown shingled house on Ashburton Place, Pranab Kaku is always there. According to the story he liked to recall often, my mother invited him to accompany us back to our apartment that very afternoon and prepared tea for the two of them; then, after learning that he had not had a proper Bengali meal in more than three months, she served him the leftover curried mackerel and rice that we had eaten for dinner the night before. He remained into the evening for a second dinner after my father got home, and after that he showed up for dinner almost every night, occupying the fourth chair at our square Formica kitchen table and becoming a part of our family in practice as well as in name.

He was from a wealthy family in Calcutta and had never had to do so much as pour himself a glass of water before moving to America, to study engineering at MIT. Life as a graduate student in Boston was a cruel shock, and in his first month he lost nearly twenty pounds. He had arrived in January, in the middle of a snowstorm, and at the end of a week he had packed his bags and gone to Logan, prepared to abandon the opportunity he'd worked toward all his life, only to change his mind at the last minute. He was living on Trowbridge Street in the home of a divorced woman with two young children who were always screaming and crying. He rented a room in the attic and was permitted to use the kitchen only at specified times of the day and instructed always to wipe down the stove with Windex and a sponge. My parents agreed that it was a terrible situation, and if they'd had a bedroom to spare they would have offered it to him. Instead, they welcomed him to our meals and opened up our apartment to him at any time, and soon it was there he went between classes and on his days off, always leaving behind some vestige of himself: a nearly finished pack of cigarettes, a newspaper, a piece of mail he had not bothered to open, a sweater he had taken off and forgotten in the course of his stay.

I remember vividly the sound of his exuberant laughter and the sight of his lanky body slouched or sprawled on the dull, mismatched furniture that had come with our apartment. He had a striking face, with a high forehead and a thick mustache, and overgrown, untamed hair that my mother said made him look like the American hippies who were everywhere in those days. His long legs jiggled rapidly up and down wherever he sat, and his elegant hands trembled when he held a cigarette between his fingers, tapping the ashes into a teacup that my mother began to set aside for this exclusive purpose. Though he was a scientist by training, there was nothing rigid or predictable or orderly about him. He always seemed to be starving, walking through the door and announcing that he hadn't had lunch, and then he would eat ravenously, reaching behind my mother to steal cutlets as she was frying them, before she had a chance to set them properly on a plate with red onion salad. In private, my parents remarked that he was a brilliant student, a star at Jadavpur who had come to MIT with an impressive assistantship, but Pranab Kaku was cavalier about his classes, skipping them with frequency. "These Americans are learning equations I knew at Usha's age," he would complain. He was stunned that my second-grade teacher didn't assign any homework and that at the age of seven I hadn't yet been taught square roots or the concept of pi.

He appeared without warning, never phoning beforehand but simply 5 knocking on the door the way people did in Calcutta and calling out "Boudi!" as he waited for my mother to let him in. Before we met him, I would return from school and find my mother with her purse in her lap and her trench coat on, desperate to escape the apartment where she had spent the day alone. But now I would find her in the kitchen, rolling out dough for luchis, which she normally made only on Sundays for my father and me, or putting up new curtains she'd bought at Woolworth's. I did not know, back then, that Pranab Kaku's visits were what my mother looked forward to all day, that she changed into a new sari and combed her hair in anticipation of his arrival, and that she planned, days in advance, the snacks she would serve him with such nonchalance. That she lived for the moment she heard him call out "Boudi!" from the porch and that she was in a foul humor on the days he didn't materialize.

It must have pleased her that I looked forward to his visits as well. He showed me card tricks and an optical illusion in which he appeared to be severing his own thumb with enormous struggle and strength and taught me to memorize multiplication tables well before I had to learn them in school. His hobby was photography. He owned an expensive camera that required thought before you pressed the shutter, and I quickly became his favorite subject, round-faced, missing teeth, my thick bangs in need of a trim. They are still the pictures of myself I like best, for they convey that confidence of youth I no longer possess, especially in front of a camera. I remember having to run back and forth in Harvard Yard as he stood with the camera, trying to capture me in motion, or posing on the steps of university buildings and on the street and against the trunks of trees. There is only one photograph in which my mother appears; she is holding me as I sit straddling her lap, her head tilted toward me, her hands pressed to my ears as if to prevent me from hearing something. In that picture, Pranab Kaku's shadow, his two arms raised at angles to hold the camera to his face, hovers in the corner of the frame, his darkened, featureless shape superimposed on one side of my mother's body. It was always the three of us. I was always there when he visited. It would have been inappropriate for my mother to receive him in the apartment alone; this was something that went without saying.

They had in common all the things she and my father did not: a love of music, film, leftist politics, poetry. They were from the same neighborhood in North Calcutta, their family homes within walking distance, the facades familiar to them once the exact locations were described. They knew the same shops, the same bus and tram routes, the same holes-in-the-wall for the best jelabis and moghlai parathas. My father, on the other hand, came from a suburb twenty miles outside Calcutta, an area that my mother considered the wilderness, and even in her bleakest hours of homesickness she was grateful that my father had at least spared her a life in the stern house of her in-laws, where she would have had to keep her head covered with the end of her sari at all times and use an outhouse that was nothing but a raised platform with a hole, and where, in the rooms, there was not a single painting hanging on the walls. Within a few weeks, Pranab Kaku had brought his reel-to-reel over to our apartment, and he played for my mother medley after medley of songs from the Hindi films of their youth. They were cheerful songs of courtship, which transformed the quiet life in our apartment and transported my mother back to the world she'd left behind in order to marry my father. She and Pranab Kaku would try to recall which scene in which movie the songs were from, who the actors were and what they were wearing. My mother would describe Raj Kapoor and Nargis singing under umbrellas in the rain, or Dev Anand strumming a guitar on the beach in Goa. She and Pranab Kaku would argue passionately about these matters, raising their voices in playful combat, confronting each other in a way she and my father never did.

Because he played the part of a younger brother, she felt free to call him Pranab, whereas she never called my father by his first name. My father was thirty-seven then, nine years older than my mother. Pranab Kaku was twenty-five. My father was a lover of silence and solitude. He had married my mother to placate his parents; they were willing to accept his desertion as long as he had a wife. He was wedded to his work, his research, and he existed in a shell that neither my mother nor I could penetrate. Conversation was a chore for him; it required an effort he preferred to expend at the lab. He disliked excess in anything, voiced no cravings or needs apart from the frugal elements of his daily routine: cereal and tea in the mornings, a cup of tea after he got home, and two different vegetable dishes every night with dinner. He did not eat with the reckless appetite of Pranab Kaku. My father had a survivor's mentality. From time to time, he liked to remark, in mixed company and often with no relevant provocation, that starving Russians under Stalin had resorted to eating the glue off the back of their wallpaper. One might think that he would have felt slightly jealous, or at the very least suspicious, about the regularity of Pranab Kaku's visits and the effect they had on my mother's behavior and mood. But my guess is that my father was grateful to Pranab Kaku for the companionship he provided, freed from the sense of responsibility he must have felt for forcing her to leave India, and relieved, perhaps, to see her happy for a change.

In the summer, Pranab Kaku bought a navy-blue Volkswagen Beetle and began to take my mother and me for drives through Boston and Cambridge, and soon outside the city, flying down the highway. He would take us to India Tea and Spices in Watertown, and one time he drove us all the way to New Hampshire to look at the mountains. As the weather grew hotter, we started going, once or twice a week, to Walden Pond. My mother always prepared a picnic of hard-boiled eggs and cucumber sandwiches and talked fondly about the winter picnics of her youth, grand expeditions with fifty of her relatives, all taking the train into the West Bengal countryside. Pranab Kaku listened to these stories with interest, absorbing the vanishing details of her past. He did not turn a deaf ear to her nostalgia, like my father, or listen uncomprehending, like me. At Walden Pond, Pranab Kaku would coax my mother through the woods, and lead her down the steep slope to the water's edge. She would unpack the picnic things and sit and watch us as we swam. His chest was matted with thick dark hair, all the way to his waist. He was an odd sight, with his pole-thin legs and a small, flaccid belly, like an otherwise svelte woman who has had a baby and not bothered to tone her abdomen. "You're making me fat, Boudi," he would complain after gorging himself on my mother's cooking. He swam noisily, clumsily, his head always above the water; he didn't know how to blow bubbles or hold his breath, as I had learned in swimming class. Wherever we went, any stranger would have naturally assumed that Pranab Kaku was my father, that my mother was his wife.

It is clear to me now that my mother was in love with him. He wooed her as   10 no other man had, with the innocent affection of a brother-in-law. In my mind, he was just a family member, a cross between an uncle and a much older brother, for in certain respects my parents sheltered and cared for him in much the same way they cared for me. He was respectful of my father, always seeking his advice about making a life in the West, about setting up a bank account and getting a job, and deferring to his opinions about Kissinger and Watergate. Occasionally, my mother would tease him about women, asking about female Indian students at MIT or showing him pictures of her younger cousins in India. "What do you think of her?" she would ask. "Isn't she pretty?" She knew that she could never have Pranab Kaku for herself, and I suppose it was her attempt to keep him in the family. But, most important, in the beginning he was totally dependent on her, needing her for those months in a way my father never did in the whole history of their marriage. He brought to my mother the first and, I suspect, the only pure happiness she ever felt. I don't think even my birth made her as happy. I was evidence of her marriage to my father, an assumed consequence of the life she had been raised to lead. But Pranab Kaku was different. He was the one totally unanticipated pleasure in her life.

In the fall of 1974, Pranab Kaku met a student at Radcliffe named Deborah, an American, and she began to accompany him to our house. I called Deborah by her first name, as my parents did, but Pranab Kaku taught her to call my father Shyamal Da and my mother Boudi, something with which Deborah gladly complied. Before they came to dinner for the first time, I asked my mother, as she was straightening up the living room, if I ought to address her as Deborah Kakima, turning her into an aunt as I had turned Pranab into an uncle. "What's the point?" my mother said, looking back at me sharply. "In a few weeks, the fun will be over and she'll leave him." And yet Deborah remained by his side, attending the weekend parties that Pranab Kaku and my parents were becoming more involved with, gatherings that were exclusively Bengali with the exception of her. Deborah was very tall, taller than both my parents and nearly as tall as Pranab Kaku. She wore her long brass-colored hair center-parted, as my mother did, but it was gathered into a low ponytail instead of a braid, or it spilled messily over her shoulders and down her back in a way that my mother considered indecent. She wore small silver spectacles and not a trace of makeup, and she studied philosophy. I found her utterly beautiful, but according to my mother she had spots on her face, and her hips were too small.

For a while, Pranab Kaku still showed up once a week for dinner on his own, mostly asking my mother what she thought of Deborah. He sought her approval, telling her that Deborah was the daughter of professors at Boston College, that her father published poetry, and that both her parents had PhDs. When he wasn't around, my mother complained about Deborah's visits, about having to make the food less spicy, even though Deborah said she liked spicy food, and feeling embarrassed to put a fried fish head in the dal. Pranab Kaku taught Deborah to say *khub bhalo* and *aacha* and to pick up certain foods with her fingers instead of with a fork. Sometimes they ended up feeding each other, allowing their fingers to linger in each other's mouth, causing my parents to look down at their plates and wait for the moment to pass. At larger gatherings, they kissed and held hands in front of everyone, and when they were out of earshot my mother would talk to the other Bengali women. "He used to be so different. I don't understand how a person can change so suddenly. It's just hell–heaven, the difference," she would say, always using the English words for her self-concocted, backward metaphor.

The more my mother began to resent Deborah's visits, the more I began to anticipate them. I fell in love with Deborah, the way young girls often fall in love with women who are not their mothers. I loved her serene gray eyes, the ponchos and denim wrap skirts and sandals she wore, her straight hair that she let me manipulate into all sorts of silly styles. I longed for her casual appearance; my mother insisted whenever there was a gathering that I wear one of my ankle-length, faintly Victorian dresses, which she referred to as maxis, and have party hair, which meant taking a strand from either side of my head and joining them with a barrette at the back. At parties, Deborah would, eventually, politely slip away, much to the relief of the Bengali women with whom she was expected to carry on a conversation, and she would play with me. I was older than all my parents' friends' children, but with Deborah I had a companion. She knew all about the books I read, about Pippi Longstocking and Anne of Green Gables. She gave me the sorts of gifts my parents had neither the money nor the inspiration to buy: a large book of Grimm's *Fairy Tales* with watercolor illustrations on thick, silken pages, wooden puppets with hair fashioned from yarn. She told me about her family, three older sisters and two brothers, the youngest of whom was closer to my age than to hers. Once, after visiting her parents, she brought back three Nancy Drews, her name written in a girlish hand at the top of the first page, and an old toy she'd had, a small paper theater set with interchangeable backdrops, the exterior of a castle and a ballroom and an open field. Deborah and I spoke freely in English, a language in which, by that age, I expressed myself more easily than Bengali, which I was required to speak at home. Sometimes she asked me how to say this or that in Bengali; once, she asked me what *asobbho* meant. I hesitated, then told her it was what my mother called me if I had done something extremely naughty, and Deborah's face clouded. I felt protective of her, aware that she was unwanted, that she was resented, aware of the nasty things people said.

Outings in the Volkswagen now involved the four of us, Deborah in the front, her hand over Pranab Kaku's while it rested on the gearshift, my mother and I in the back. Soon, my mother began coming up with reasons to excuse herself, headaches and incipient colds, and so I became part of a new triangle. To my surprise, my mother allowed me to go with them, to the Museum of Fine Arts and the Public Garden and the Aquarium. She was waiting for the affair to end, for Deborah to break Pranab Kaku's heart and for him to return to us, scarred and penitent. I saw no sign of their relationship foundering. Their open affection for each other, their easily expressed happiness, was a new and romantic thing to me. Having me in the backseat allowed Pranab Kaku and Deborah to practice for the future, to try on the idea of a family of their own. Countless photographs were taken of me and Deborah, of me sitting on

Deborah's lap, holding her hand, kissing her on the cheek. We exchanged what I believed were secret smiles, and in those moments I felt that she understood me better than anyone else in the world. Anyone would have said that Deborah would make an excellent mother one day. But my mother refused to acknowledge such a thing. I did not know at the time that my mother allowed me to go off with Pranab Kaku and Deborah because she was pregnant for the fifth time since my birth and was so sick and exhausted and fearful of losing another baby that she slept most of the day. After ten weeks, she miscarried once again and was advised by her doctor to stop trying.

By summer, there was a diamond on Deborah's left hand, something my mother had never been given. Because his own family lived so far away, Pranab Kaku came to the house alone one day, to ask for my parents' blessing before giving her the ring. He showed us the box, opening it and taking out the diamond nestled inside. "I want to see how it looks on someone," he said, urging my mother to try it on, but she refused. I was the one who stuck out my hand, feeling the weight of the ring suspended at the base of my finger. Then he asked for a second thing: he wanted my parents to write to his parents, saying that they had met Deborah and that they thought highly of her. He was nervous, naturally, about telling his family that he intended to marry an American girl. He had told his parents all about us, and at one point my parents had received a letter from them, expressing appreciation for taking such good care of their son and for giving him a proper home in America. "It needn't be long," Pranab Kaku said. "Just a few lines. They'll accept it more easily if it comes from you." My father thought neither ill nor well of Deborah, never commenting or criticizing as my mother did, but he assured Pranab Kaku that a letter of endorsement would be on its way to Calcutta by the end of the week. My mother nodded her assent, but the following day I saw the teacup Pranab Kaku had used all this time as an ashtray in the kitchen garbage can, in pieces, and three Band-Aids taped to my mother's hand.

Pranab Kaku's parents were horrified by the thought of their only son marrying an American woman, and a few weeks later our telephone rang in the middle of the night: it was Mr. Chakraborty telling my father that they could not possibly bless such a marriage, that it was out of the question, that if Pranab Kaku dared to marry Deborah he would no longer acknowledge him as a son. Then his wife got on the phone, asking to speak to my mother and attacked her as if they were intimate, blaming my mother for allowing the affair to develop. She said that they had already chosen a wife for him in Calcutta, that he'd left for America with the understanding that he'd go back after he had finished his studies and marry this girl. They had bought the neighboring flat in their building for Pranab and his betrothed, and it was sitting empty, waiting for his return. "We thought we could trust you, and yet you have betrayed us so deeply," his mother said, taking out her anger on a stranger in a way she could not with her son. "Is this what happens to people in America?" For Pranab Kaku's sake, my mother defended the engagement, telling his mother that Deborah was a polite girl from a decent family. Pranab Kaku's parents pleaded with mine to talk him out of it, but my father refused, deciding that it was not their place to get embroiled. "We are not his parents," he told my mother. "We can tell him they don't approve but nothing more." And so my parents told Pranab Kaku nothing about how his parents had berated them and blamed them, and threatened to disown Pranab Kaku, only that

15

they had refused to give him their blessing. In the face of this refusal, Pranab Kaku shrugged. "I don't care. Not everyone can be as open-minded as you," he told my parents. "Your blessing is blessing enough."

After the engagement, Pranab Kaku and Deborah began drifting out of our lives. They moved in together, to an apartment in Boston, in the South End, a part of the city my parents considered unsafe. We moved as well, to a house in Natick. Though my parents had bought the house, they occupied it as if they were still tenants, touching up scuff marks with leftover paint and reluctant to put holes in the walls, and every afternoon when the sun shone through the living-room window my mother closed the blinds so that our new furniture would not fade. A few weeks before the wedding, my parents invited Pranab Kaku to the house alone, and my mother prepared a special meal to mark the end of his bachelorhood. It would be the only Bengali aspect of the wedding; the rest of it would be strictly American, with a cake and a minister and Deborah in a long white dress and veil. There is a photograph of the dinner, taken by my father, the only picture, to my knowledge, in which my mother and Pranab Kaku appear together. The picture is slightly blurry; I remember Pranab Kaku explaining to my father how to work the camera, and so he is captured looking up from the kitchen table and the elaborate array of food my mother had prepared in his honor, his mouth open, his long arm outstretched and his finger pointing, instructing my father how to read the light meter or some such thing. My mother stands beside him, one hand placed on top of his head in a gesture of blessing, the first and last time she was to touch him in her life. "She will leave him," my mother told her friends afterward. "He is throwing his life away."

The wedding was at a church in Ipswich, with a reception at a country club. It was going to be a small ceremony, which my parents took to mean one or two hundred people as opposed to three or four hundred. My mother was shocked that fewer than thirty people had been invited, and she was more perplexed than honored that, of all the Bengalis Pranab Kaku knew by then, we were the only ones on the list. At the wedding we sat, like the other guests, first on the hard wooden pews of the church and then at a long table that had been set up for lunch. Though we were the closest thing Pranab Kaku had to a family that day, we were not included in the group photographs that were taken on the grounds of the country club, with Deborah's parents and grandparents and her many siblings, and neither my mother nor my father got up to make a toast. My mother did not appreciate the fact that Deborah had made sure that my parents, who did not eat beef, were given fish instead of filet mignon like everyone else. She kept speaking in Bengali, complaining about the formality of the proceedings, and the fact that Pranab Kaku, wearing a tuxedo, barely said a word to us because he was too busy leaning over the shoulders of his new American in-laws as he circled the table. As usual, my father said nothing in response to my mother's commentary, quietly and methodically working through his meal, his fork and knife occasionally squeaking against the surface of the china, because he was accustomed to eating with his hands. He cleared his plate and then my mother's, for she had pronounced the food inedible, and then he announced that he had overeaten and had a stomachache. The only time my mother forced a smile was when Deborah appeared behind her chair, kissing her on the cheek and asking if we were enjoying ourselves.

When the dancing started, my parents remained at the table, drinking tea, and after two or three songs they decided that it was time for us to go home, my mother shooting me looks to that effect across the room, where I was dancing in a circle with Pranab Kaku and Deborah and the other children at the wedding. I wanted to stay, and when, reluctantly, I walked over to where my parents sat, Deborah followed me. "Boudi, let Usha stay. She's having such a good time," she said to my mother. "Lots of people will be heading back your way, someone can drop her off in a little while." But my mother said no, I had had plenty of fun already and forced me to put on my coat over my long puff-sleeved dress. As we drove home from the wedding I told my mother, for the first but not the last time in my life, that I hated her.

The following year, we received a birth announcement from the Chakrabortys, a picture of twin girls, which my mother did not paste into an album or display on the refrigerator door. The girls were named Srabani and Sabitri, but were called Bonny and Sara. Apart from a thank-you card for our wedding gift, it was their only communication; we were not invited to the new house in Marblehead, bought after Pranab Kaku got a high-paying job at Stone & Webster. For a while, my parents and their friends continued to invite the Chakrabortys to gatherings, but because they never came, or left after staying only an hour, the invitations stopped. Their absences were attributed, by my parents and their circle, to Deborah, and it was universally agreed that she had stripped Pranab Kaku not only of his origins but of his independence. She was the enemy, he was her prey, and their example was invoked as a warning, and as vindication, that mixed marriages were a doomed enterprise. Occasionally, they surprised everyone, appearing at a pujo for a few hours with their two identical little girls who barely looked Bengali and spoke only English and were being raised so differently from me and most of the other children. They were not taken to Calcutta every summer, they did not have parents who were clinging to another way of life and exhorting their children to do the same. Because of Deborah, they were exempt from all that, and for this reason I envied them. "Usha, look at you, all grown up and so pretty," Deborah would say whenever she saw me, rekindling, if only for a minute, our bond of years before. She had cut off her beautiful long hair by then, and had a bob. "I bet you'll be old enough to babysit soon," she would say. "I'll call you — the girls would love that." But she never did.

I began to grow out of my girlhood, entering middle school and developing crushes on the American boys in my class. The crushes amounted to nothing; in spite of Deborah's compliments, I was always overlooked at that age. But my mother must have picked up on something, for she forbade me to attend the dances that were held the last Friday of every month in the school cafeteria, and it was an unspoken law that I was not allowed to date. "Don't think you'll get away with marrying an American, the way Pranab Kaku did," she would say from time to time. I was thirteen, the thought of marriage irrelevant to my life. Still, her words upset me, and I felt her grip on me tighten. She would fly into a rage when I told her I wanted to start wearing a bra, or if I wanted to go to Harvard Square with a friend. In the middle of our arguments, she often conjured Deborah as her antithesis, the sort of woman she refused to be. "If she were your mother, she would let you do whatever you wanted, because she wouldn't care. Is that what you want, Usha, a mother who doesn't care?" When I began menstruating, the summer before I started ninth grade, my mother gave me a speech, telling me that I was to let no boy touch me, and then she asked if I knew how a woman became pregnant. I told her what I had been taught in science, about the sperm fertilizing the egg, and then she asked if I knew how, exactly, that happened. I saw the terror in her eyes and so, though I knew that aspect of procreation as well, I lied, and told her it hadn't been explained to us.

I began keeping other secrets from her, evading her with the aid of my friends. I told her I was sleeping over at a friend's when really I went to parties, drinking beer and allowing boys to kiss me and fondle my breasts and press their erections against my hip as we lay groping on a sofa or the backseat of a car. I began to pity my mother; the older I got, the more I saw what a desolate life she led. She had never worked, and during the day she watched soap operas to pass the time. Her only job, every day, was to clean and cook for my father and me. We rarely went to restaurants, my father always pointing out, even in cheap ones, how expensive they were compared with eating at home. When my mother complained to him about how much she hated life in the suburbs and how lonely she felt, he said nothing to placate her. "If you are so unhappy, go back to Calcutta," he would offer, making it clear that their separation would not affect him one way or the other. I began to take my cues from my father in dealing with her, isolating her doubly. When she screamed at me for talking too long on the telephone, or for staying too long in my room, I learned to scream back, telling her that she was pathetic, that she knew nothing about me, and it was clear to us both that I had stopped needing her, definitively and abruptly, just as Pranab Kaku had.

Then, the year before I went off to college, my parents and I were invited to the Chakrabortys' home for Thanksgiving. We were not the only guests from my parents' old Cambridge crowd; it turned out that Pranab Kaku and Deborah wanted to have a sort of reunion of all the people they had been friendly with back then. Normally, my parents did not celebrate Thanksgiving; the ritual of a large sit-down dinner and the foods that one was supposed to eat was lost on them. They treated it as if it were Memorial Day or Veterans Day — just another holiday in the American year. But we drove out to Marblehead, to an impressive stone-faced house with a semicircular gravel driveway clogged with cars. The house was a short walk from the ocean; on our way, we had driven by the harbor overlooking the cold, glittering Atlantic, and when we stepped out of the car we were greeted by the sound of gulls and waves. Most of the living-room furniture had been moved to the basement and extra tables joined to the main one to form a giant U. They were covered with tablecloths, set with white plates and silverware, and had centerpieces of gourds. I was struck by the toys and dolls that were everywhere, dogs that shed long yellow hairs on everything, all the photographs of Bonny and Sara and Deborah decorating the walls, still more plastering the refrigerator door. Food was being prepared when we arrived, something my mother always frowned upon, the kitchen a chaos of people and smells and enormous dirtied bowls.

Deborah's family, whom we remembered dimly from the wedding, was there, her parents and her brothers and sisters and their husbands and wives and boyfriends and babies. Her sisters were in their thirties, but, like Deborah, they could have been mistaken for college students, wearing jeans and clogs and fisherman sweaters, and her brother Matty, with whom I had danced in a circle at the wedding, was now a freshman at Amherst, with wide-set green eyes and wispy brown hair and a complexion that reddened easily. As soon as I saw Deborah's siblings, joking with one another as they chopped and stirred things in the kitchen, I was furious with my mother for making a scene before we left the house and forcing me to wear a shalwar kameez. I knew they assumed, from my clothing, that I had more in common with the other Bengalis than with them. But Deborah insisted on including me, setting me to work peeling apples with Matty, and out of my parents' sight I was given beer to drink. When the meal was ready, we were told where to sit, in an alternating boy-girl formation that made the Bengalis uncomfortable. Bottles of wine were lined up on the table. Two turkeys were brought out, one stuffed with sausage and one without. My mouth watered at the food, but I knew that afterward, on our way home, my mother would complain that it was all tasteless and bland. "Impossible," my mother said, shaking her hand over the top of her glass when someone tried to pour her a little wine.

　　Deborah's father, Gene, got up to say grace, and asked everyone at the　25 table to join hands. He bowed his head and closed his eyes. "Dear Lord, we thank you today for the food we are about to receive," he began. My parents were seated next to each other, and I was stunned to see that they complied, that my father's brown fingers lightly clasped my mother's pale ones. I noticed Matty seated on the other side of the room and saw him glancing at me as his father spoke. After the chorus of Amens, Gene raised his glass and said, "Forgive me, but I never thought I'd have the opportunity to say this: Here's to Thanksgiving with the Indians." Only a few people laughed at the joke.

　　Then Pranab Kaku stood up and thanked everyone for coming. He was relaxed from alcohol, his once wiry body beginning to thicken. He started to talk sentimentally about his early days in Cambridge, and then suddenly he recounted the story of meeting me and my mother for the first time, telling the guests about how he had followed us that afternoon. The people who did not know us laughed, amused by the description of the encounter, and by Pranab Kaku's desperation. He walked around the room to where my mother was sitting and draped a lanky arm around her shoulder, forcing her, for a brief moment, to stand up. "This woman," he declared, pulling her close to his side, "this woman hosted my first real Thanksgiving in America. It might have been an afternoon in May, but that first meal at Boudi's table was Thanksgiving to me. If it weren't for that meal, I would have gone back to Calcutta." My mother looked away, embarrassed. She was thirty-eight, already going gray, and she looked closer to my father's age than to Pranab Kaku's; regardless of his waistline, he retained his handsome, carefree looks. Pranab Kaku went back to his place at the head of the table, next to Deborah, and concluded, "And if that had been the case I'd have never met you, my darling," and he kissed her on the mouth in front of everyone, to much applause, as if it were their wedding day all over again.

　　After the turkey, smaller forks were distributed and orders were taken for three different kinds of pie, written on small pads by Deborah's sisters, as if they were waitresses. After dessert, the dogs needed to go out, and Pranab Kaku volunteered to take them. "How about a walk on the beach?" he suggested, and Deborah's side of the family agreed that that was an excellent idea. None of the Bengalis wanted to go, preferring to sit with their tea and cluster together, at last, at one end of the room, speaking freely after the forced chitchat with the Americans during the meal. Matty came over and sat in the chair beside me that was now empty, encouraging me to join the walk. When I hesitated, pointing to my inappropriate clothes and shoes but also aware of my mother's silent fury at the sight of us together, he said, "I'm sure Deb can lend you something." So I went upstairs, where Deborah gave me a pair of her jeans and a thick sweater and some sneakers, so that I looked like her and her sisters.

She sat on the edge of her bed, watching me change, as if we were girlfriends, and she asked if I had a boyfriend. When I told her no, she said, "Matty thinks you're cute."

"He told you?"

"No, but I can tell."   30

As I walked back downstairs, emboldened by this information, in the jeans I'd had to roll up and in which I felt finally like myself, I noticed my mother lift her eyes from her teacup and stare at me, but she said nothing, and off I went, with Pranab Kaku and his dogs and his in-laws, along a road and then down some steep wooden steps to the water. Deborah and one of her sisters stayed behind, to begin the cleanup and see to the needs of those who remained. Initially, we all walked together, in a single row across the sand, but then I noticed Matty hanging back, and so the two of us trailed behind, the distance between us and the others increasing. We began flirting, talking of things I no longer remember, and eventually we wandered into a rocky inlet and Matty fished a joint out of his pocket. We turned our backs to the wind and smoked it, our cold fingers touching in the process, our lips pressed to the same damp section of the rolling paper. At first I didn't feel any effect, but then, listening to him talk about the band he was in, I was aware that his voice sounded miles away, and that I had the urge to laugh, even though what he was saying was not terribly funny. It felt as if we were apart from the group for hours, but when we wandered back to the sand we could still see them, walking out onto a promontory to watch the sun set.

It was dark by the time we all headed back to the house, and I dreaded seeing my parents while I was still high. But when we got there Deborah told me that my parents, feeling tired, had left, agreeing to let someone drive me home later. A fire had been lit and I was told to relax and have more pie as the leftovers were put away and the living room slowly put back in order. Of course, it was Matty who drove me home, and sitting in my parents' driveway I kissed him, at once thrilled and terrified that my mother might walk onto the lawn in her nightgown and discover us. I gave Matty my phone number, and for a few weeks I thought of him constantly, and hoped foolishly that he would call.

In the end, my mother was right, and fourteen years after that Thanksgiving, after twenty-three years of marriage, Pranab Kaku and Deborah got divorced. It was he who had strayed, falling in love with a married Bengali woman, destroying two families in the process. The other woman was someone my parents knew, though not very well. Deborah was in her forties by then, Bonny and Sara away at college. In her shock and grief, it was my mother whom Deborah turned to, calling and weeping into the phone. Somehow, through all the years, she had continued to regard us as quasi in-laws, sending flowers when my grandparents died and giving me a compact edition of the *O.E.D.*° as a college-graduation present. "You knew him so well. How could he do something like this?" Deborah

---

O.E.D.: Oxford English Dictionary.

asked my mother. And then, "Did you know anything about it?" My mother answered truthfully that she did not. Their hearts had been broken by the same man, only my mother's had long ago mended, and in an odd way, as my parents approached their old age, she and my father had grown fond of each other, out of habit if nothing else. I believe my absence from the house, once I left for college, had something to do with this, because over the years, when I visited, I noticed a warmth between my parents that had not been there before, a quiet teasing, a solidarity, a concern when one of them fell ill. My mother and I had also made peace; she had accepted the fact that I was not only her daughter but a child of America as well. Slowly, she accepted that I dated one American man, and then another, and then yet another, that I slept with them, and even that I lived with one though we were not married. She welcomed my boyfriends into our home and when things didn't work out she told me I would find someone better. After years of being idle, she decided, when she turned fifty, to get a degree in library science at a nearby university.

On the phone, Deborah admitted something that surprised my mother: that all these years she had felt hopelessly shut out of a part of Pranab Kaku's life. "I was so horribly jealous of you back then, for knowing him, understanding him in a way I never could. He turned his back on his family, on all of you, really, but I still felt threatened. I could never get over that." She told my mother that she had tried, for years, to get Pranab Kaku to reconcile with his parents, and that she had also encouraged him to maintain ties with other Bengalis, but he had resisted. It had been Deborah's idea to invite us to their Thanksgiving; ironically, the other woman had been there, too. "I hope you don't blame me for taking him away from your lives, Boudi. I always worried that you did."

My mother assured Deborah that she blamed her for nothing. She con- 35 fessed nothing to Deborah about her own jealousy of decades before, only that she was sorry for what had happened, that it was a sad and terrible thing for their family. She did not tell Deborah that a few weeks after Pranab Kaku's wedding, while I was at a Girl Scout meeting and my father was at work, she had gone through the house, gathering up all the safety pins that lurked in drawers and tins, and adding them to the few fastened to her bracelets. When she'd found enough, she pinned them to her sari one by one, attaching the front piece to the layer of material underneath, so that no one would be able to pull the garment off her body. Then she took a can of lighter fluid and a box of kitchen matches and stepped outside, into our chilly backyard, which was full of leaves needing to be raked. Over her sari she was wearing a knee-length lilac trench coat, and to any neighbor she must have looked as though she'd simply stepped out for some fresh air. She opened up the coat and removed the tip from the can of lighter fluid and doused herself, then buttoned and belted the coat. She walked over to the garbage barrel behind our house and disposed of the fluid, then returned to the middle of the yard with the box of matches in her coat pocket. For nearly an hour she stood there, looking at our house, trying to work up the courage to strike a match. It was not I who saved her, or my father, but our next-door neighbor, Mrs. Holcomb, with whom my mother had never been particularly friendly. She came out to rake the leaves in her yard, calling out to my mother and remarking how beautiful the sunset was. "I see you've been admiring it for a while now," she said. My mother agreed, and then she went back into the house. By the time my father and I came home in the early evening, she was in the kitchen boiling rice for our dinner, as if it were any other day.

My mother told Deborah none of this. It was to me that she confessed, after my own heart was broken by a man I'd hoped to marry.

CONNECTIONS TO OTHER SELECTIONS

1. Compare the social and cultural conflicts in "Hell–Heaven" with those in Chitra Banerjee Divakaruni's "Clothes" (p. 265).
2. Discuss "Hell–Heaven" and Amy Bloom's "By-and-by" (p. 632) as stories about grief.

JOHN UPDIKE (1932–2009)

© Jerry Bauer.

John Updike grew up in the small town of Shillington, Pennsylvania, and on a family farm nearby. Academic success in school earned him a scholarship to Harvard, where he studied English and graduated in 1954. He soon sold his first story and poem to *The New Yorker.* Also an artist, Updike studied drawing in Oxford, England, and returned to take a position on the staff at *The New Yorker.* His first book, a collection of poems titled *The Carpentered Hen and Other Tame Creatures,* appeared in 1958, and the following year he published a book of stories and a novel, *The Poorhouse Fair,* which received the Rosenthal Foundation Award in 1960. Updike produced his second novel, *Rabbit, Run,* in the same year. The prolific Updike lived in Massachusetts the rest of his life and continued to publish essays, poems, a novel, or a book of stories nearly every year since 1959, including *The Centaur* (1963), winner of the National Book Award; *Rabbit Is Rich* (1981) and *Rabbit at Rest* (1990), both Pulitzer Prize winners; and *The Witches of Eastwick* (1984), which was made into a major motion picture (Warner Bros., 1987). His last novel was *Terrorist* (2006), and his last short story collection was *My Father's Tears and Other Stories* (2009). Updike's fiction is noted for its exemplary use of storytelling conventions, its unique prose style, and its engaging picture of middle-class American life.

Outage   *2008*

The weatherpersons on television, always eager for ratings-boosting disasters, had predicted a fierce autumn storm for New England, with driving rain and high winds. Brad Morris, who worked at home while his wife, Jane, managed a boutique on Boston's Newbury Street, glanced out his windows now and then at the swaying trees — oaks still tenacious of their rusty leaves, maples letting go in gusts of gold and red — but was unimpressed by the hyped news event. Rain came down heavily a half hour at a time, then pulled back into a silvery sky of fast-moving, fuzzy-bottomed clouds. The worst seemed to be over, when, in midafternoon, his computer died under his eyes. The financial figures he had been painstakingly assembling swooned as a group, sucked into the dead blank screen like glittering water pulled down a drain. Around him, the house seemed to sigh, as all its lights and little engines, its computerized timers and indicators, simultaneously shut down. The sound of wind and rain lashing the trees outside infiltrated the silence. A beam creaked. A loose shutter banged. The drip from a plugged gutter tapped heavily, like a bully nagging for attention, on the wooden cover of a cellar-window well.

The lines bringing the Morrises' house electricity and telephone service and cable television came up, on three poles, through two acres of woods. Brad stepped outside in the storm's lull, in the strangely luminous air, to see if he could spot any branches fallen on his lines. He saw none, and no window lights in the nearest house, barely visible through the woods whose leaves in summer hid it entirely. The tops of the tallest trees were heaving in a wind he barely felt; a spatter of thick cold drops sent him back into the house, where drifts of shadow were sifting into the corners and the furnace ticked in the basement as its metal cooled. Without electricity, there was nothing to do.

He opened the refrigerator and was surprised by its failure to greet him with a welcoming inner light. The fireplace in the den emitted a sour scent of damp wood ash. Wind whistled in crevices he had not known existed, under the eaves and at the edges of the storm windows. He felt impotent, and amused by his impotence, in this emergency. He remembered some letters he had planned to mail at the post office in his suburb's little downtown, and a check he had intended to deposit at the bank. So he did have something to do: he collected these pieces of paper, and put on a tan water-resistant zippered jacket and a Red Sox cap. The burglar alarm by the front door was peeping and blinking, softly, as if to itself. Brad punched the reset button; the device fell silent, and he went out the door.

It seemed odd that his car started as usual. Wet leaves were plastered over the driveway and the narrow macadam roads of this development; the neighborhood had been built all at once, twenty years ago, on the land of an unprofitable farm. He drove cautiously, especially around the duck pond, beside a vanished barn, where, in a snowstorm ten years ago, a teen-ager had slid through a rail fence and sunk his parents' Mercedes up to its hubcaps. The downtown — two churches, a drugstore, a Dunkin' Donuts, a pizza shop, a mostly Italian restaurant, two beauty parlors, a dress shop, a bridal shop, a few more stores that came and went in the same chronically vacated premises, an insurance agent and a lawyer on the floor above a realty office, a dentist, a bank branch, and a post office — was without electricity but busier than usual, the sidewalk full of pedestrians in this gleaming gray lull.

Brad was startled by the sight of two young women embracing, before they 5 began to converse, as if renewing a long-neglected acquaintance. People stood talking, discussing their fate in small groups. Shopwindows usually bright were dark, and it occurred to him that, of course, people had been flushed onto the sidewalk by the outage. The health-food store, its crammed shelves of bagged nuts and bottled vitamins and refrigerated tofu sandwiches, and the fruit store, its rival in healthy nutrition across the street, were both caves of forbidding darkness behind their display windows.

But it did not occur to him that the bank, usually so receptive to his deposits, would have a taped notice on its glass doors declaring the location of the nearest other branch, and that, although he could see the tellers chatting on the padded bench where applicants for mortgages and perpetrators of overdrafts customarily languished, he could no more gain access to his money than he could have laid hands on the fish in an aquarium. The bank manager, an excitable tall woman in a severe suit, was actually patrolling the sidewalk; she told Brad breathlessly, "I'm so sorry, Mr. Morris. Our A.T.M., alarms, everything is down. I was just checking to see if the hardware store had any power."

"Myra, I think we're all in the same boat," Brad reassured her; yet he understood her incredulity. He himself did not expect that the post office, though open to box users and seekers of the inside mail slots, would be also closed to transactions; everything had been computerized by a United States Postal Service zealous to modernize, and now not a single letter could be weighed or a single stamp sold, even had there been light enough to see. The afternoon was darkening. In danger of completing no errands at all, he tested the door of the health-food store. The latch released, and he heard a giggle in the shadows. "Are you open?" he called.

"To you, sure," answered the voice of the young proprietress, curly-haired, perpetually tan Olivia. Brad groped toward the back, where a single squat perfumed candle illuminated bins of little plastic bags; they shimmered with blobby reflections. He brought to the counter a bag of what he hoped were roasted but unsalted cashews. "The register's out. All contributions accepted," Olivia joked, and made change out of her own purse for what he, holding it close to his eyes, verified was a five-dollar bill.

The transaction had felt flirtatious to him, and the atmosphere of the downtown, beneath its drooping festoon of useless cables, seemed festive. Automobiles paraded past with burning headlights. The ominous thickening in the air stirred the pedestrians to take shelter again. There was a brimming, an overflow of good nature, and a transparency: something occluding had been removed, baring neglected possibilities. Hurrying back into the shelter of his car, Brad laughed with irrational pleasure.

Fresh drops speckled his windshield as he turned in to his neighborhood, through a break in the stone wall that had once marked the bounds of the farm. "Private Way," a painted sign said sternly. A woman in white — a shiny vinyl raincoat and silly-looking white running shoes — was walking in the middle of the narrow road. With fluttering gestures she motioned him to stop. He recognized a newish neighbor, a wispy blonde who had moved a few years ago, with her husband and two growing boys, into a house invisible from the Morrises'. They met only a few times a year, at cocktail parties or zoning-appeals-board hearings. She looked like a ghost, beckoning him. He braked, and lowered the car window. "Oh, Brad," she said, with breathy relief. "It's you. What's happening?" she asked. "All my electricity went out, even the telephones."

"Mine, too," he said, to reassure her. "Everybody's. A tree must have fallen on a power line somewhere, in this wind. It happens, Lynne." He was pleased to have fished her name up from his memory: Lynne Willard.

She came close enough to his open window for him to see that she was actually trembling, her lips groping like those of a child near tears. Her eyes stared above his car roof as if scanning the treetops for rescue. She brought her focus down to his face and shakily explained, "Willy's away. In Chicago, all week. I'm up there all alone, now the boys are both off to boarding school. I didn't know what I should do, so I put on sneakers and set off walking."

Brad remembered those boys as sly and noisy, waiting in blazers for the day-school bus at the end of the road, just outside the tumbled-down field-stone wall. If they were now old enough for boarding school, then this woman was not as young as she seemed. Her face, narrowed by a knotted head scarf, was white, except for the tip of her nose, which was pink like a rabbit's. Her eyelids also were pink; they looked rubbed, and her eyes watered. "I like your hat," she said, to fill the lengthening silence. "Are you a fan?"

"No more than normal."

"They won the World Series."   15

"That is true. Get in the car, Lynne," he said, his powers of reassurance deepening. "I'll drive you home. There's nothing downtown. Nobody knows how long the outage will be. Even the bank and post office didn't know. The only thing open was the health-food store."

"I was taking a walk," she said, as if this hadn't been quite established. "I can keep going."

"Don't you notice? The rain is starting up again. The skies are about to let loose."

Blinking, pressing her lips together to suppress their tremor—the lower had a trick of twitching sideways—she walked around in front of his head-lights. He leaned across the seat to tug at the door handle and push open the passenger door for her, as if she couldn't do it for herself. Sliding in, with a slither of white vinyl, she confessed, "There was a beeping in the house I had to get away from. Willy's not even in Boston, where I could call him."

"I think that's your burglar alarm," Brad told her. "Or some other alarm that   20 doesn't like losing current. I'll come inside, if I may, and look at the problem."

She had brought a pleasant smell with her into the car, a smell from his childhood, like cough drops or licorice. "You may," she said, settling back on his leather car seat. "I got so afraid," she went on, with a wry twist to her mouth, as if to laugh at herself, or in memory of a long-ago self.

He had never been to the Willards' place. Their driveway was fringed with more elaborate plantings—gnarly little azaleas, bare of leaf, and euonymus still blaring forth that surreal autumnal magenta—than the Morrises', and their parking area was covered in larger, whiter stones than the brown half-inch pebbles that Brad's wife had insisted on despite their tendency (which he had pointed out) to scatter into the lawn during winter snowplowing. But the basic house, a good-sized clapboarded neo-Colonial twenty years old, with a gratuitous swath of brick façade, looked much like his. Lynne hadn't locked the front door, just walked out in her panic. Trailing behind her, Brad was surprised by the lithe swiftness with which she climbed the steps of the flagstone porch and let herself back in, holding the storm door for him as she opened the other.

Inside, the beeping was distinct and insistent, but not the urgent, ever-louder bleating of alarm mode. He turned the wrong way at first; the floor plan of this house was different from his, with the family room on the left instead of the right, and the kitchen beyond it, not beside it. The furnishings, though, looked much the same — the modern taste of twenty years ago, boxy and stuffed, bare wood and monochrome wool, coffee tables of thick glass on cruciform legs of stainless steel, all mixed with Orientals and family antiques. These possessions looked slightly smarter and less tired than those in his home; but then Brad tended to glamorize what other people had.

"Over here," Lynne said, "next to the closet" — the very front-hall closet in which she was hanging up her vinyl coat. The snug knit gray dress she wore beneath it looked to him as if she had come from a ladies' luncheon that noon. Using her toes, she pried off her sneakers without bothering to unlace them — perhaps to avoid bending over beneath his eyes — and tossed them onto the closet floor.

"Yes," he said, moving to the panel. "It's just like mine." He lifted his hand 25 to touch it, then thought to ask, "May I?"

"Help yourself," she said. Her voice, in her own house, had become almost slangy, shedding its quaver. "Be my guest."

He pushed the little rectangular button labelled Reset. The beeping sharply stopped. Coming close up behind him, she marvelled. "That's all it takes?"

"Apparently," he said. "That tells it the current shutoff wasn't a home invasion. Not that I'm much of a hand with technology."

She giggled in obscure delight. What he had smelled in the car, he realized, had had alcohol in it, mixed with licorice from long ago. "Willy's such a prick," she told Brad. "He knows all this stuff but never shares it. Tell me," she said, "as a man. Do you think he really has to spend all this time in Chicago?"

Brad said cautiously, "Business can be very demanding. At a certain level 30 men — and women in business, too, of course — have to look each other in the eye. I used to be on planes all the time and have meetings and so on myself, but I found working at home was more efficient. With all this electronic communication everywhere, there's really no need to get out all that much. But then I don't know Will — Mr. Willard's business." His words, nervously excessive, seemed to have an echo in the unfamiliar house — or, rather, felt absorbed by its partial strangeness, the sounds falling into the many little differences between this house and his own. The rain, as he had foretold, had returned, whispering and drumming outside, and bringing inside a deeper shade of darkness. The wind whipped bursts of wet pellets across the windows.

"Me neither. Could I offer you a drink?" this woman asked, nervous herself. She added with another giggle, "Since you've *gotten* out." She gestured toward her becalmed kitchen. "I can't offer you coffee."

"What have *you* been drinking?" Brad asked her.

Her eyes widened, as if to compensate for the lack of light. "How did you know it was anything? Some girlfriends and I finished off lunch with anisette."

"In the car," he answered her, "you smelled sweet," and moved closer, as if to verify.

Her kisses did not taste of licorice. There in the family room, where the great 35 plasma TV screen stared blankly and the morning *Globe* lay, still in its plastic wrapper, where it had been tossed onto the sofa unread, Lynne kissed dryly, tentatively, as if testing her lipstick. Then her lips warmed to the fit; her face pushed up at his and her fidgety hands went around his back, to its small and the nape of his neck, and Brad dizzily wondered if he wasn't too far, too suddenly, out on a limb. But no, he reassured himself, this was human and harmless, this sheltered contact while the rain thrashed outside and the light inside the rooms dimmed by imperceptible notches. His impulse was to keep smoothing her hair, where it had been tangled and pressed flat beneath her head scarf. His hands trembled, as her lips had. Their faces grew hot; their caresses through their clothes began to feel clumsy. "We should go upstairs," she said huskily. "Anybody going by could look inside."

"Who would go by in this weather?" he asked.

"He gets a lot of FedExes," she said. Climbing the stairs ahead of him — carpeted in pale green, where his and Jane's were maroon — Lynne continued the unidentified pronoun. "He calls me every day, often around now. I guess it leaves his nights free." Brad, slightly winded at the head of the stairs, from having held his breath while admiring her haunches as they moved in the snug knit dress, asked, "Did you mean it, that your phone doesn't work, either?"

"Yeah, some penny-pinching system he got installed, so it's all the same wires. I don't understand it exactly. In our new car, I can't do the radio stations. They give you too many options now."

"Exactly," he agreed.

The rooms upstairs had a different layout from those in his house, and   40
the one she led him into was barer and smaller than the master bedroom would have been. Photographs on the bureau showed her boys, at various stages, and older people, though still young, in fifties clothes, perhaps her parents, or Willy's. The color in various framed vacation snapshots had bleached out, shifting register. On the wall a paper poster showed a woman draped only in a tiger skin stretched out on a Lamborghini. Lynne stood a moment by the window. "Look," she said. "You can see your house, now that the leaves are down." It took Brad some seconds to make it out — a pale shadow, the tint of smoke, through the intervening trees.

"You have good eyes," he told her. He did not want to feel that this neighbor was much younger than he, but an age difference was declared in how calmly and quickly she shed her clothes, as if it were no big deal. Oh, but it *was* a big deal, she was so lovely, all bony and downy and pale and fat in the right places, drifting back and forth in the shadowy room to put her folded clothes on chairs, simple straight-backed boys' chairs. When he had seen her in the center of the road he had thought for an instant she was a ghost, and there was a ghostly detached quality in the way she moved, her lips crimped in that twist of self-criticism he had noticed in the car, when she had slid in beside him.

She came to him to help him undress, something Jane never did. This servile act, her small face frowning as she worked at his shirt buttons, excited him so that he ceased to feel nervous, out on a limb — ceased to listen to the rain and wind. The storm of blood inside him drowned them out. The tip of her tongue crept out between her lips in her concentration. The front fringe of her hair, which the scarf had left uncovered, showed a few gleaming droplets and smelled of rain, another scent from boyhood. "God," he said. "I love this." He had kept himself, with an effort, from saying "you."

"It's not over," she promised, in the light voice of a woman talking to a girlfriend. "There's more, Brad."

The electricity came on. All over the upstairs, wallpaper patterns and wood moldings popped into clarity. Downstairs, in the kitchen, the dishwasher surged into its next phase. By the front door, the burglar alarm resumed its beeping, at a shriller pitch. The furnace in the basement, at a pitch below that of the wind, ignited and began, with a roar steadier than the wind, to reintroduce warmth into the cooling house. Amplified, eager voices downstairs proclaimed that Lynne had been watching television news an hour ago, before she panicked. Her face, so close to his that their breaths mingled, jumped back, like a cut to the commercial. "Oh, dear," she said, her rubbed-looking eyes coming back into focus.

"To the rescue," he said. He began to redo his buttons.   45

"You don't have to go." But she, too, in her nakedness, was embarrassed; her cheeks blazed as if with a rash.

"I think I do. He," he said, "might call. Even she might, if the outage has made the news in Boston. You'll be fine now. Listen. Lynne. The alarm has stopped beeping. It's saying, 'All is well. All is normal.' It's saying, 'Get that man out of my house.' "

"No," she weakly protested.

"It's saying, 'I'm in charge now.' " Brad turned his eyes from her nakedness, his wispy blonde's. "It's saying," he told her, " 'This is how it is. This is reality.' "

CONNECTIONS TO OTHER SELECTIONS

1. Discuss Updike's use of symbols in "Outage" and in his story "A & P" (p. 733).

2. Compare the endings of "Outage" and Fay Weldon's "IND AFF, or Out of Love in Sarajevo" (p. 202).

XU XI (B. 1954)

Raised in Hong Kong and a resident there until her mid-twenties, Xu Xi graduated from the M.F.A. Program for Poets and Writers at the University of Massachusetts and teaches at Vermont College. She has published three novels — *Chinese Walls* (1994), *Hong Kong Rose* (1997), and *The Unwalled City* (2001) — and three collections of stories and essays — *Daughters of Hui* (1996), *History's Fiction* (2001), and *Overleaf Hong Kong* (2004). "Famine" was chosen for the *O. Henry Prize Stories 2006.*

© AFP/Getty.

Famine   2004

I escape. I board Northwest 18 to New York, via Tokyo. The engine starts, there is no going back. Yesterday, I taught the last English class and left my job of thirty-two years. Five weeks earlier, A-Ma died of heartbreak, within days of my father's sudden death. He was ninety-five, she ninety. Unlike

A-Ba, who saw the world by crewing on tankers, neither my mother nor I ever left Hong Kong.

Their deaths rid me of responsibility at last, and I could forfeit my pension and that dreary existence. I am fifty-one and an only child, unmarried.

I never expected my parents to take so long to die.

This meal is *luxurious,* better than anything I imagined.

My colleagues who fly every summer complain of the indignities of travel. 5 Cardboard food, cramped seats, long lines, and these days, too much security nonsense, they say. They fly Cathay, our "national" carrier. This makes me laugh. We have never been a nation; "national" isn't our adjective. *Semantics,* they say, dismissive, just as they dismiss what I say of debt, that it is not an inevitable state, or that children exist to be taught, not spoilt. My colleagues live in overpriced, new, mortgaged flats and indulge 1 to 2.5 children. Most of my students are uneducable.

Back, though, to this in-flight meal. Smoked salmon and cold shrimp, endive salad, strawberries and melon to clean the palate. Then, steak with mushrooms, potatoes *au gratin,* a choice between a shiraz or cabernet sauvignon. Three cheeses, white chocolate mousse, coffee, and port or a liqueur or brandy. Foods from the pages of a novel, perhaps.

My parents ate sparingly, long after we were no longer impoverished, and disdained "unhealthy" Western diets. A-Ba often said that the only thing he really discovered from travel was that the world was hungry, and that there would never be enough food for everyone. It was why, he said, he did not miss the travel when he retired.

I have no complaints of my travels so far.

My complaining colleagues do not fly business. This seat is an *island* of a bed, surrounded by air. I did not mean to fly in dignity, but having never traveled in summer, or at all, I didn't plan months ahead, long before flights filled up. I simply rang the airlines and booked Northwest, the first one that had a seat, only in business class.

Friends and former students, who do fly business when their companies 10 foot the bill, were horrified. *You* paid *full fare? No one does!* I have money, I replied, why shouldn't I? *But you've given up your "rice bowl." Think of the future.*

I hate rice, always have, even though I never left a single grain, because under my father's watchful glare, A-Ma inspected my bowl. Every meal, even after her eyes dimmed.

The Plaza Suite is nine hundred square feet, over three times the size of home. I had wanted the Vanderbilt or Ambassador and would have settled for the Louis XV, but they were all booked, by those more important than I, no doubt. Anyway, this will have to do. "Nothing unimportant" happens here at the Plaza is what their website literature claims.

The porter arrives, and wheels my bags in on a trolley.

My father bought our tiny flat in a village in Shatin with his disability settlement. When he was forty-five and I one, a falling crane crushed his left leg and groin, thus ending his sailing and procreating career. Shatin isn't very rural anymore, but our home has denied progress its due. We didn't get a phone till I was in my thirties.

I tip the porter five dollars and begin unpacking the leather luggage set. 15 There is too much space for my things.

Right about now, you're probably wondering, along with my colleagues, former students, and friends, *What on earth does she think she's doing?* It was what my parents shouted when I was twelve and went on my first hunger strike.

My parents were illiterate, both refugees from China's rural poverty. A-Ma fried tofu at Shatin market. Once A-Ba recovered from his accident, he worked there also as a cleaner, cursing his fate. They expected me to support them as soon as possible, which should have been after six years of primary school, the only compulsory education required by law in the sixties.

As you see, I clearly had no choice but to strike, since my exam results proved I was smart enough for secondary school. My father beat me, threatened to starve me. *How dare I,* when others were genuinely hungry, unlike me, the only child of a tofu seller who always ate. *Did I want him and A-Ma to die of hunger just to send me to school? How dare I risk their longevity and old age?*

But I was unpacking a Spanish leather suitcase when the past, that country bumpkin's territory, so rudely interrupted.

Veronica, whom I met years ago at university while taking a literature 20 course, foisted this luggage on me. She runs her family's garment enterprise, and is married to a banker. Between them and their three children, they own four flats, three cars, and at least a dozen sets of luggage. Veronica invites me out to dinner (she always pays) whenever she wants to complain about her family. Lately, we've dined often.

"Kids," she groaned over our rice porridge, two days before my trip. "My daughter won't use her brand-new Loewe set because, she says, that's *passé*. All her friends at Stanford sling these canvas bags with one fat strap. Canvas, imagine. Not even leather."

"Ergonomics," I told her, annoyed at this bland and inexpensive meal. "It's all about weight and balance." And cost, I knew, because the young overspend to conform, just as Veronica eats rice porridge because she's overweight and no longer complains that I'm thin.

She continued. "You're welcome to take the set if you like."

"Don't worry yourself. I can use an old school bag."

"But that's barely a cabin bag! Surely not enough to travel with." 25

In the end, I let her nag me into taking this set, which is more bag than clothing.

Veronica sounded worried when I left her that evening. "Are you *sure* you'll be okay?"

And would she worry, I wonder, if she could see me now, here, in this suite, this enormous space where one night's bill would have taken my parents years, no, *decades,* to earn and even for me, four years' pay, at least when I first started teaching in my rural enclave (though you're thinking, of course, quite correctly, *Well, what about inflation,* the thing economists cite to dismiss these longings of an English teacher who has spent her life instructing those who care not a whit for our "official language," the one they never speak, at least not if they can choose, especially not now when there is, increasingly, a choice).

My unpacking is done; the past need not intrude. I draw a bath, as one does in English literature, to wash away the heat and grime of both cities in summer. *Why New York?* Veronica asked, at the end of our last evening together. Because,

I told her, it will be like nothing I've ever known. For the first time since we've known each other, Veronica actually seemed to envy *me*, although perhaps it was my imagination.

The phone rings, and it's "Guest Relations" wishing to welcome me and offer   30
hospitality. The hotel must wonder, since I grace no social register. I ask for a table at Lutèce tonight. Afterwards, I tip the concierge ten dollars for successfully making the reservation. As you can see, I am no longer an ignorant bumpkin, even though I never left the schools in the New Territories, our urban countryside now that no one farms anymore. Besides, Hong Kong magazines detail lives of the rich and richer so I've read of the famous restaurant and know about the greasy palms of New Yorkers.

I order tea and scones from Room Service. It will hold me till dinner at eight.

The first time I ever tasted tea and scones was at the home of my private student. To supplement income when I enrolled in Teacher Training, I tutored Form V students who needed to pass the School Certificate English exam. This was the compromise I agreed to with my parents before they would allow me to qualify as a teacher. Oh yes, there was a second hunger strike two years prior, before they would let me continue into Form IV. That time, I promised to keep working in the markets after school with A-Ma, which I did.

Actually, my learning English at all was a stroke of luck, since I was *hardly* at a "name school" of the elite. An American priest taught at my secondary school, so I heard a native speaker. He wasn't a very good teacher, but he paid attention to me because I was the only student who liked the subject. A little attention goes a long way.

Tea and scones! I am *supposed* to be eating, not dwelling on the ancient past. The opulence of the tray Room Service brings far surpasses what that pretentious woman served, mother of the hopeless boy, my first private student of many, who only passed his English exam because he cheated (he paid a friend to sit the exam for him), not that I'd ever tell since he's now a wealthy international businessman of some repute who can hire staff to communicate in English with the rest of the world, since he still cannot, at least not with any credibility. That scone ("from Cherikoff," she bragged) was cold and dry, hard as a rock.

Hot scones, oozing with butter. To ooze. I like the lasciviousness of that   35
word, with its excess of vowels, the way an excess of wealth allows people to waste kindness on me, as my former student still does, every lunar new year, by sending me a *laisee* packet with a generous check which I deposit in my parents' bank account, the way I surrender all my earnings, as any filial and responsible unmarried child should, or so they said.

I eat two scones oozing with butter and savor tea enriched by cream and sugar, here at this "greatest hotel in the world," to vanquish, once and for all, my parents' fear of death and opulence.

Eight does not come soon enough. In the taxi on the way to Lutèce, I ponder the question of pork.

When we were poor but not impoverished, A-Ma once dared to make pork for dinner. It was meant to be a treat, to give me a taste of meat, because I complained that tofu was bland. A-Ba became a vegetarian after his accident and prohibited meat at home; eunuchs are angry people. She dared because he was not eating with us that night, a rare event in our family (I think some sailors he used to know invited him out).

I shat a tapeworm the next morning — almost ten inches long — and she never cooked pork again.

I have since tasted properly cooked pork, naturally, since it's unavoidable in 40 Chinese cuisine. In my twenties, I dined out with friends, despite my parents' objections. But friends marry and scatter; the truth is that there is no one but family in the end, so over time, I submitted to their way of being and seldom took meals away from home, meals my mother cooked virtually till the day she died.

I am distracted. The real question, of course, is whether or not I should order pork tonight.

I did not expect this trip to be fraught with pork!

At Lutèce, I have the distinct impression that the two couples at the next table are talking about me. Perhaps they pity me. People often pitied me my life. *Starved of affection,* they whispered, although why they felt the need to whisper what everyone could hear I failed to understand. All I desired was greater gastronomic variety, but my parents couldn't bear the idea of my eating without them. I ate our plain diet and endured their perpetual skimping because they did eventually learn to leave me alone. That much filial propriety was reasonable payment. I just didn't expect them to *stop* complaining, to fear for what little fortune they had, because somewhere someone was less fortunate than they. That fear made them cling hard to life, forcing me to suffer their fortitude, their good health, and their longevity.

I should walk over to those overdressed people and tell them how things are, about famine, I mean, the way I tried to tell my students, the way my parents dinned it into me as long as they were alive.

Famine has no menu! The waiter waits as I take too long to study the 45 menu. He does not seem patient, making him an oxymoron in his profession. My students would no more learn the oxymoron than they would learn about famine. *Daughter, did you lecture your charges today about famine?* A-Ba would ask every night before dinner. *Yes,* I learned to lie, giving him the answer he needed. This waiter could take a lesson in patience from me.

Finally, I look up at this man who twitches, and do not order pork. *Very good,* he says, as if I should be graded for my literacy in menus. He returns shortly with a bottle of the most expensive red available, and now I *know* the people at the next table are staring. The minute he leaves, the taller of the two men from that table comes over.

"Excuse me, but I believe we met in March? At the U.S. Consulate cocktail in Hong Kong? You're Kwai-sin Ho, aren't you?" He extends his hand. "Peter Martin."

Insulted, it's my turn to stare at this total stranger. I look *nothing* like that simpering socialite who designs wildly fashionable hats that are all the rage in Asia. Hats! We don't have the weather for hats, especially not those things, which are good for neither warmth nor shelter from the sun.

Besides, what use are hats for the hungry?

I do not accept his hand. "I'm her twin sister," I lie. "Kwai-sin and I are 50 estranged."

He looks like he's about to protest, but retreats. After that, they don't stare, although I am sure they discuss me now that I've contributed new gossip for those who are nurtured by the crumbs of the rich and famous. But at least I can eat in peace.

It's my outfit, probably. Kwai-sin Ho is famous for her *cheongsams,* which is all she ever wears, the way I do. It was my idea. When we were girls together in school, I said the only thing I'd ever wear when I grew up was the *cheongsam,* the shapely dress with side slits and a neck-strangling collar. She grimaced and said they weren't fashionable, that only spinster schoolteachers and prostitutes wore them, which, back in the sixties, wasn't exactly true, but Kwai-sin was never too bright or imaginative.

That was long ago, before she became Kwai-sin in the *cheongsam* once these turned fashionable again, long before her father died and her mother became the mistress of a prominent businessman who whisked them into the stratosphere high above mine. For a little while, she remained my friend, but then we grew up, she married one of the shipping Hos, and became the socialite who refused, albeit politely, to recognize me the one time we bumped into each other at some function in Hong Kong.

So now, vengeance is mine. I will not entertain the people who fawn over her and possess no powers of recognition.

Food is getting sidelined by memory. This is unacceptable. I cannot allow all 55 these intrusions. I must get back to the food, which is, after all, the point of famine.

This is due to a lack of diligence, as A-Ma would say, this lazy meandering from what's important, this succumbing to sloth. My mother was terrified of sloth, almost as much as she was terrified of my father.

She used to tell me an old legend about sloth.

There once was a man so lazy he wouldn't even lift food to his mouth. When he was young, his mother fed him, but as his mother aged, she couldn't. So he marries a woman who will feed him as his mother did. For a time, life is bliss.

Then one day, his wife must return to her village to visit her dying mother. "How will I eat?" he exclaims in fright. The wife conjures this plan. She bakes a gigantic cookie and hangs it on a string around his neck. All the lazy man must do is bend forward and eat. "Wonderful!" he says, and off she goes, promising to return.

On the first day, the man nibbles the edge of the cookie. Each day, he nib- 60 bles further. By the fourth day, he's eaten so far down there's no more cookie unless he turns it, which his wife expected he would since he could do this with his mouth.

However, the man's so lazy he lies down instead and waits for his wife's return. As the days pass, his stomach growls and begins to eat itself. Yet the man still won't turn the cookie. By the time his wife comes home, the lazy man has starved to death.

Memory causes such unaccountable digressions! There I was in Lutèce, noticing that people pitied me. Pity made my father livid, which he took out on A-Ma and me. Anger was his one escape from timidity. He wanted no sympathy for either his dead limb or useless genitals.

Perhaps people find me odd rather than pitiful. I will describe my appearance and let you judge. I am thin but not emaciated and have strong teeth. This latter feature is most unusual for a Hong Kong person of my generation. Many years ago, a dentist courted me. He taught me well about oral hygiene, trained as he had been at an American university. Unfortunately, he was slightly rotund, which offended A-Ba. I think A-Ma wouldn't have minded the marriage, but she always sided with my father, who believed it wise to marry one's own physical type (illiteracy did not prevent him from developing philosophies, as you've already witnessed). I was then in my mid-thirties. After the dentist, there were no other men and as a result, I never left home, which is our custom for unmarried women and men, a loathsome custom but difficult to overthrow. We all must pick our battles, and my acquiring English, which my parents naturally knew not a word, was a sufficiently drastic defiance to last a lifetime, or at least till they expired.

This dinner at Lutèce has come and gone, and you haven't tasted a thing. It's what happens when we converse overmuch and do not concentrate on the food. At home, we ate in the silence of A-Ba's rage.

What a shame, but never mind, I promise to share the bounty next time. 65 This meal must have been good because the bill is in the thousands. I pay by traveler's checks because, not believing in debt, I own no credit cards.

Last night's dinner weighs badly, despite my excellent digestion, so I take a long walk late in the afternoon and end up in Chelsea. New York streets are dirtier than I imagined. Although I did not really expect pavements of gold, in my deepest fantasies, there did reign a glitter and sheen.

No one talks to me here.

The air is fetid with the day's leftover heat and odors. Under a humid, darkening sky, I almost trip over a body on the corner of Twenty-fourth and Seventh. It cannot be a corpse! Surely cadavers aren't left to rot in the streets.

A-Ma used to tell of a childhood occurrence in her village. An itinerant had stolen food from the local pig trough. The villagers caught him, beat him senseless, cut off his tongue and arms, and left him to bleed to death behind the rubbish heap. In the morning, my mother was at play, and while running, tripped over the body. She fell into a blood pool beside him. The corpse's eyes were open.

He surely didn't mean to steal, she always said in the telling, her eyes burning 70 from the memory. *Try to forget,* my father would say. My parents specialized in memory. They both remained lucid and clearheaded till they died.

But this body moves. It's a man awakening from sleep. He mumbles something. Startled, I move away. He is still speaking. I think he's saying he's hungry.

I escape. A taxi whisks me back to my hotel, where my table is reserved at the restaurant.

The ceiling at the Oak Room is roughly four times the height of an average basketball player. The ambience is not as seductive as promised by the Plaza's literature. The problem with reading the wrong kind of literature is that you are bound to be disappointed.

This is a man's restaurant, with a menu of many steaks. Hemingway and Fitzgerald used to eat here. Few of my students have heard of these two, and none of them will have read a single book by either author.

As an English teacher, especially one who was not employed at a "name 75 school" of the elite, I became increasingly marginal. Colleagues and friends converse in Cantonese, the only official language out of our three that people live as well as speak. The last time any student read an entire novel was well over twenty years ago. English literature is not on anyone's exam roster anymore; to desire it in a Chinese colony is as irresponsible as it was of me to master it in our former British one.

Teaching English is little else than a linguistic requirement. Once, it was my passion and flight away from home. Now it is merely my entrée to this former men's club.

But I must order dinner and stop thinking about literature.

The entrées make my head spin, so I turn to the desserts. There is no gooseberry tart! Ever since *David Copperfield,* I have wanted to taste a gooseberry tart (or perhaps it was another book, I don't remember). I tell the boy with the water jug this.

He says. "The magician, madam?"

"The orphan," I reply.   80

He stands, openmouthed, without pouring water. What is this imbecility of the young? They neither serve nor wait.

The waiter appears. "Can I help with the menu?"

"Why?" I snap. "It isn't heavy."

But what upsets me is the memory of my mother's story, which I'd long forgotten until this afternoon, just as I hoped to forget about the teaching of English literature, about the uselessness of the life I prepared so hard for.

The waiter hovers. "Are you feeling okay?"   85

I look up at the sound of his voice and realize my hands are shaking. Calming myself, I say, "*Au jus.* The prime rib, please, and escargots to start," and on and on I go, ordering in the manner of a man who retreats to a segregated club, who indulges in oblivion because he can, who shuts out the stirrings of the groin and the heart.

I wake to a ringing phone. Housekeeping wants to know if they may clean. It's already past noon. This must be jet lag. I tell Housekeeping, Later.

It's so *comfortable* here that I believe it is possible to forget.

I order brunch from Room Service. Five-star hotels in Hong Kong serve brunch buffets on weekends. The first time I went to one, Veronica paid. We were both students at university. She wasn't wealthy, but her parents gave her spending money, whereas my entire salary (I was already a working teacher by then) belonged to my parents. The array of food made my mouth water. *Pace yourself,* Veronica said. *It's all you can eat.* I wanted to try everything, but gluttony frightened me.

Meanwhile, A-Ba's voice. *After four or more days without food, your stomach* 90 *begins to eat itself,* and his laugh, dry and caustic.

But I was choosing brunch.

Mimosa. Smoked salmon. Omelet with Swiss cheese and chives. And salad, the expensive kind that's imported back home, crisp Romaine in a Caesar. Room Service asks what I'd like for dessert, so I say chocolate ice-cream sundae. Perhaps I'm more of a bumpkin than I care to admit. My colleagues, former students, and friends would consider my choices boring, unsophisticated, lacking in culinary imagination. They're right, I suppose, since everything I've eaten since coming to New York I could just as easily have obtained back home. They can't understand, though. It's not *what* but *how much.* How opulent. The opulence is what counts to stop the cannibalism of internal organs.

Will that be all?

I am tempted to say, Bring me an endless buffet, whatever your chef concocts, whatever your tongues desire.

How long till my money runs out, my finite account, ending this sweet exile? 95

Guest Relations knocks, insistent. I have not let anyone in for three days. I open the door wide to show the manager that everything is fine, that their room is not wrecked, that I am not crazy even if I'm not on the social register. If you read the news, as I do, you know it's necessary to allay fears. So I do, because I do not wish to give the wrong impression. I am not a diva or an excessively famous person who trashes hotel rooms because she can.

I say, politely, that I've been a little unwell, nothing serious, and to please have Housekeeping stop in now. The "please" is significant; it shows I am not odd, that I am, in fact, cognizant of civilized language in English. The manager withdraws, relieved.

For dinner tonight, I decide on two dozen oysters, lobster, and filet mignon. I select a champagne and the wines, one white and one red. Then, it occurs to me that since this is a suite, I can order enough food for a party, so I tell Room Service that there will be a dozen guests for dinner, possibly more. *Very good,* he says, and asks how many extra bottles of champagne and wine, to which I reply, As many as needed.

My students will be my guests. They more or less were visitors during those years I tried to teach. You mustn't think I was always disillusioned, though I seem so now. To prove it to you I'll invite all my colleagues, the few friends I have, like Veronica, the dentist who courted me and his wife and two children, even Kwai-sin and my parents. I bear no grudges; I am not bitter towards them. What I'm uncertain of is whether or not they will come to my supper.

This room, this endless meal, can save me. I feel it. I am vanquishing my 100 fear of death and opulence.

There was a time we did not care about opulence and we dared to speak of death. You spoke of famine because everyone knew the stories from China were true. Now, even in this country, people more or less know. You could educate students about starvation in China or Africa or India because they knew it to be true, because they saw the hunger around them, among the beggars in our streets, and for some, even in their own homes. There was a time it was better *not* to have space, or things to put in that space, and to dream of having instead, because no one had much, except royalty and movie stars and they were *meant* to be fantasy— untouchable, unreal—somewhere in a dream of manna and celluloid.

But you can't speak of famine anymore. Anorexia's fashionable and desirably profitable on runways, so students simply *can't see the hunger.* My colleagues and friends also can't, and refuse to speak of it, changing the subject to what they prefer to see. Even our journalists can't seem to see, preferring the reality they fashion rather than the reality that is. I get angry, but then, when I'm calm, I am simply baffled. Perhaps my parents, and friends and colleagues and memory, are right, that I *am* too stubborn, perhaps even too slothful because instead of *seeing* reality, I've hidden in my parents' home, in my life as a teacher, even though the years were dreary and long, when what I truly wanted, what I desired, was to embrace the opulence, forsake the hunger, but was too lazy to turn the cookie instead.

I mustn't be angry at them, by which I mean all the "thems" I know and don't know, the big impersonal "they." Like a good English teacher I tell my students, you *must* define the "they." Students are students and continue to make the same mistakes, and all I can do is remind them that "they" are you and to please, please, try to remember because language is a root of life.

Most of the people can't be wrong all the time. Besides, whose fault is it if the dream came true? Postdream is like postmodern; no one understands it, but everyone condones its existence.

Furthermore, what you can't, or won't see, *doesn't* exist.   105

Comfort, like food, exists, *surrounds* me here.

Not wishing to let anger get the better of me, I eat. Like the Romans, I disgorge and continue. It takes hours to eat three lobsters and three steaks, plus consume five glasses of champagne and six of wine, yet still the food is not enough.

The guests arrive and more keep coming. Who would have thought all these people would show up, all these people I thought I left behind. Where do they come from? My students, colleagues, the dentist and his family, a horde of strangers. Even Kwai-sin and her silly hats, and do you know something, we *do* look a little alike, so Peter Martin wasn't completely wrong. I changed my language to change my life, but still the past throngs, bringing all these people and their Cantonese chatter. The food is not enough, the food is never enough.

Room Service obliges round the clock.

Veronica arrives and I feel a great relief, because the truth is, I no longer   110
cared for her anymore when all we ate was rice porridge. It was mean-spirited, I was ungrateful, forgetting that once she fed me my first buffet, teasing my appetite. *Come out, travel,* she urged over the years. It's not her fault I stayed at home, afraid to abandon my responsibility, traveling only in my mind.

Finally, my parents arrive. My father sits down first to the feast. His leg is whole, and sperm gushes out from between his legs. *It's not so bad here,* he says, and gestures for my mother to join him. This is good. A-Ma will eat if A-Ba does, they're like that, those two. My friends don't understand, not even Veronica. She repeats now what she often has said, that my parents are "controlling." Perhaps, I say, but that's unimportant. I'm only interested in not being responsible anymore.

The noise in the room is deafening. We can barely hear each other above the din. Cantonese is a noisy language, unlike Mandarin or English, but it is alive. This suite that was too empty is stuffed with people, all needing to be fed.

I gaze at the platters of food, piled in this space with largesse. What does it matter if there *are* too many mouths to feed? A phone call is all it takes to get more food, and more. I am fifty-one and have waited too long to eat. They're right, they're all right. If I give in, if I let go, I will vanquish my fears. *This* is bliss, truly.

A-Ma smiles at the vast quantities of food. This pleases me because she so rarely smiles. She says, *Not like lazy cookie man, hah?*

Feeling benevolent, I smile at my parents. *No, not like him,* I say. *Now, eat.*   115

CONNECTIONS TO OTHER SELECTIONS

1. Compare the cultural ambitions of the narrator in "Famine" with those of the man in Mark Halliday's "Young Man on Sixth Avenue" (p. 615).

2. Discuss the narrator's symbolic relationship to food in "Famine" and in Junot Díaz's "Fiesta, 1980" (p. 171).

19

An Album of
World Literature

Literature is where I go to explore the
highest and lowest places in human
society and in the human spirit, where I
hope to find not absolute truth but the
truth of the tale, of the imagination and
of the heart.
— SALMAN RUSHDIE

© Jerry Bauer.

BESSIE HEAD (BOTSWANA / 1937–1986)

Born in Pietermaritzburg, South Africa, Bessie Head was the daughter of
a black father and a white mother. After growing up in a foster home and
orphanage, she taught grammar school and wrote fiction for a local paper.
In her twenties she moved to a farm commune in Botswana to avoid the
apartheid of her homeland. Her first novel, *When Rain
Clouds Gather,* was published in 1969. Her collection of
stories, *The Collector of Treasures and Other Botswana Village Tales* (1977), was followed by two other novels,
Serowe: Village of the Rain Wind (1981) and *A Bewitched
Crossroad* (1984). Head's familiarity with oppression and the daily difficulties endured by its victims produced in her work a heightened sensitivity to

Web Research
the authors in this
chapter or take quizzes
on their works at
bedfordstmartins.com/
meyerlit.

the necessity for human decency. In "The Prisoner Who Wore Glasses," oppression and decency turn out to be complex matters.

The Prisoner Who Wore Glasses

1974

Scarcely a breath of wind disturbed the stillness of the day and the long rows of cabbages were bright green in the sunlight. Large white clouds drifted slowly across the deep blue sky. Now and then they obscured the sun and caused a chill on the backs of the prisoners who had to work all day long in the cabbage field. This trick the clouds were playing with the sun eventually caused one of the prisoners who wore glasses to stop work, straighten up, and peer shortsightedly at them. He was a thin little fellow with a hollowed-out chest and comic knobbly knees. He also had a lot of fanciful ideas because he smiled at the clouds.

"Perhaps they want me to send a message to the children," he thought, tenderly, noting that the clouds were drifting in the direction of his home some hundred miles away. But before he could frame the message, the warder in charge of his work span° shouted: "Hey, what you tink you're doing, Brille?"

The prisoner swung round, blinking rapidly, yet at the same time sizing up the enemy. He was a new warder, named Jacobus Stephanus Hannetjie. His eyes were the color of the sky but they were frightening. A simple, primitive, brutal soul gazed out of them. The prisoner bent down quickly and a message was quietly passed down the line: "We're in for trouble this time, comrades."

"Why?" rippled back up the line.

"Because he's not human," the reply rippled down and yet only the 5 crunching of the spades as they turned over the earth disturbed the stillness.

This particular work span was known as Span One. It was composed of ten men and they were all political prisoners. They were grouped together for convenience as it was one of the prison regulations that no black warder should be in charge of a political prisoner lest this prisoner convert him to his views. It never seemed to occur to the authorities that this very reasoning was the strength of Span One and a clue to the strange terror they aroused in the warders. As political prisoners they were unlike the other prisoners in the sense that they felt no guilt nor were they outcasts of society. All guilty men instinctively cower, which was why it was the kind of prison where men got knocked out cold with a blow at the back of the head from an iron bar. Up until the arrival of Warder Hannetjie, no warder had dared beat any member of Span One and no warder had lasted more than a week with them. The battle was entirely psychological. Span One was assertive and it was beyond the scope of white warders to handle assertive black men. Thus, Span One had got out of control. They were the best thieves and liars in the camp. They lived all day on raw cabbages. They chatted and smoked tobacco. And since they moved, thought, and acted as one, they had perfected every technique of group concealment.

span: Squad.

Trouble began that very day between Span One and Warder Hannetjie. It was because of the shortsightedness of Brille. That was the nickname he was given in prison and is the Afrikaans word for someone who wears glasses. Brille could never judge the approach of the prison gates and on several previous occasions he had munched on cabbages and dropped them almost at the feet of the warder and all previous warders had overlooked this. Not so Warder Hannetjie.

"Who dropped that cabbage?" he thundered.

Brille stepped out of line.

"I did," he said meekly.   10

"Alright," said Hannetjie. "The whole Span goes three meals off."

"But I told you I did it," Brille protested.

The blood rushed to Warder Hannetjie's face.

"Look 'ere," he said. "I don't take orders from a kaffir.° I don't know what kind of kaffir you tink you are. Why don't you say Baas? I'm your Baas. Why don't you say Baas, hey?"

Brille blinked his eyes rapidly but by contrast his voice was strangely calm.   15

"I'm twenty years older than you," he said. It was the first thing that came to mind but the comrades seemed to think it a huge joke. A titter swept up the line. The next thing Warder Hannetjie whipped out a knobkerrie° and gave Brille several blows about the head. What surprised his comrades was the speed with which Brille had removed his glasses or else they would have been smashed to pieces on the ground.

That evening in the cell Brille was very apologetic.

"I'm sorry, comrades," he said. "I've put you into a hell of a mess."

"Never mind, brother," they said. "What happens to one of us, happens to all."

"I'll try to make up for it, comrades," he said. "I'll steal something so that   20 you don't go hungry."

Privately, Brille was very philosophical about his head wounds. It was the first time an act of violence had been perpetrated against him but he had long been a witness of extreme, almost unbelievable human brutality. He had twelve children and his mind traveled back that evening through the sixteen years of bedlam in which he had lived. It had all happened in a small drab little three-bedroomed house in a small drab little street in the Eastern Cape and the children kept coming year after year because neither he nor Martha ever managed the contraceptives the right way and a teacher's salary never allowed moving to a bigger house and he was always taking exams to improve his salary only to have it all eaten up by hungry mouths. Everything was pretty horrible, especially the way the children fought. They'd get hold of each other's heads and give them a good bashing against the wall. Martha gave up somewhere along the line so they worked out a thing between them. The bashings, biting, and blood were to operate in full swing until he came home. He was to be the bogey-man and when it worked he never failed to have a sense of godhead at the way in which his presence could change savages into fairly reasonable human beings.

---

kaffir: A black South African; often used as a disparaging term.
knobkerrie: A club.

Yet somehow it was this chaos and mismanagement at the center of his life that drove him into politics. It was really an ordered beautiful world with just a few basic slogans to learn along with the rights of mankind. At one stage, before things became very bad, there were conferences to attend, all very far away from home.

"Let's face it," he thought ruefully. "I'm only learning right now what it means to be a politician. All this while I've been running away from Martha and the kids."

And the pain in his head brought a hard lump to his throat. That was what the children did to each other daily and Martha wasn't managing and if Warder Hannetjie had not interrupted him that morning he would have sent the following message: "Be good comrades, my children. Cooperate, then life will run smoothly."

The next day Warder Hannetjie caught this old man of twelve children stealing grapes from the farm shed. They were an enormous quantity of grapes in a ten-gallon tin and for this misdeed the old man spent a week in the isolation cell. In fact, Span One as a whole was in constant trouble. Warder Hannetjie seemed to have eyes at the back of his head. He uncovered the trick about the cabbages, how they were split in two with the spade and immediately covered with earth and then unearthed again and eaten with split-second timing. He found out how tobacco smoke was beaten into the ground and he found out how conversations were whispered down the wind. 25

For about two weeks Span One lived in acute misery. The cabbages, tobacco, and conversations had been the pivot of jail life to them. Then one evening they noticed that their good old comrade who wore the glasses was looking rather pleased with himself. He pulled out a four-ounce packet of tobacco by way of explanation and the comrades fell upon it with great greed. Brille merely smiled. After all, he was the father of many children. But when the last shred had disappeared, it occurred to the comrades that they ought to be puzzled. Someone said: "I say, brother. We're watched like hawks these days. Where did you get the tobacco?"

"Hannetjie gave it to me," said Brille.

There was a long silence. Into it dropped a quiet bombshell.

"I saw Hannetjie in the shed today," and the failing eyesight blinked rapidly. "I caught him in the act of stealing five bags of fertilizer and he bribed me to keep my mouth shut."

There was another long silence. 30

"Prison is an evil life," Brille continued, apparently discussing some irrelevant matter. "It makes a man contemplate all kinds of evil deeds."

He held out his hand and closed it.

"You know, comrades," he said. "I've got Hannetjie. I'll betray him tomorrow."

Everyone began talking at once.

"Forget it, brother. You'll get shot."

Brille laughed. 35

"I won't," he said. "That is what I mean about evil. I am a father of children and I saw today that Hannetjie is just a child and stupidly truthful. I'm going to punish him severely because we need a good warder."

The following day, with Brille as witness, Hannetjie confessed to the theft of the fertilizer and was fined a large sum of money. From then on Span One did very much as they pleased while Warder Hannetjie stood by and said nothing. But it was Brille who carried this to extremes. One day, at the close of work Warder Hannetjie said: "Brille, pick up my jacket and carry it back to the camp."

"But nothing in the regulations say I'm your servant, Hannetjie," Brille replied coolly.

"I've told you not to call me Hannetjie. You must say, 'Baas,'" but Warder 40 Hannetjie's voice lacked conviction. In turn, Brille squinted up at him.

"I'll tell you something about this Baas business, Hannetjie," he said. "One of these days we are going to run the country. You are going to clean my car. Now I have a fifteen-year-old son and I'd die of shame if you had to tell him that I ever called you Baas."

Warder Hannetjie went red in the face and picked up his coat.

On another occasion Brille was seen to be walking about the prison yard, openly smoking tobacco. On being taken before the prison commander he claimed to have received the tobacco from Warder Hannetjie. All throughout the tirade from his chief, Warder Hannetjie failed to defend himself but his nerve broke completely. He called Brille to one side.

"Brille," he said. "This thing between you and me must end. You may not know it but I have a wife and children and you're driving me to suicide."

"Why don't you like your own medicine, Hannetjie?" Brille asked quietly.   45

"I can give you anything you want," Warder Hannetjie said in desperation.

"It's not only me but the whole of Span One," said Brille, cunningly. "The whole of Span One wants something from you."

Warder Hannetjie brightened with relief.

"I tink I can manage if it's tobacco you want," he said.

Brille looked at him, for the first time struck with pity, and guilt.   50

He wondered if he had carried the whole business too far. The man was really a child.

"It's not tobacco we want, but you," he said. "We want you on our side. We want a good warder because without a good warder we won't be able to manage the long stretch ahead."

Warder Hannetjie interpreted this request in his own fashion and his interpretation of what was good and human often left the prisoners of Span One speechless with surprise. He had a way of slipping off his revolver and picking up a spade and digging alongside Span One. He had a way of producing unheard-of luxuries like boiled eggs from his farm nearby and things like cigarettes, and Span One responded nobly and got the reputation of being the best work span in the camp. And it wasn't only take from their side. They were awfully good at stealing certain commodities like fertilizer which were needed on the farm of Warder Hannetjie.

CONNECTIONS TO OTHER SELECTIONS

1. Discuss how the issue of race relations is presented in "The Prisoner Who Wore Glasses" and Ralph Ellison's "Battle Royal" (p. 277). Compare Brille's strategy of dealing with racial issues with the strategy suggested by the last words from the grandfather in "Battle Royal" (para. 2).

2. Compare Brille's character with Abner Snopes's in William Faulkner's "Barn Burning" (p. 503). How does each character cope with oppression?

NAGUIB MAHFOUZ

(EGYPT / 1911–2006)

© Thomas Hartwell/CORBIS.

Born in Cairo, Egypt, Naguib Mahfouz graduated from Cairo University in 1934 and spent most of his life writing while working as a government employee in the Ministry of Islamic Affairs until his retirement in 1971. He continued to write fiction and published nearly forty novels along with fourteen collections of short stories. His reputation in the Arab world is secure, and he has been celebrated internationally since 1988, when he was awarded the Nobel Prize in literature. Among his most popular novels translated into English are *Miramar* (1978), *Children of Gebelawi* (1981), and *Sugar Street: The Cairo Trilogy* (1992). "The Answer Is No" is reprinted from *The Time and the Place and Other Stories* (1991).

The Answer Is No   *1991*

TRANSLATED BY DENYS JOHNSON-DAVIES

The important piece of news that the new headmaster had arrived spread through the school. She heard of it in the women teachers' common room as she was casting a final glance at the day's lessons. There was no getting away from joining the other teachers in congratulating him, and from shaking him by the hand too. A shudder passed through her body, but it was unavoidable.

"They speak highly of his ability," said a colleague of hers. "And they talk too of his strictness."

It had always been a possibility that might occur, and now it had. Her pretty face paled, and a staring look came to her wide black eyes.

When the time came, the teachers went in single file, decorously attired, to his open room. He stood behind his desk as he received the men and women. He was of medium height, with a tendency to portliness, and had a spherical face, hooked nose, and bulging eyes; the first thing that could be seen of him was a thick, puffed-up mustache, arched like a foam-laden wave. She advanced with her eyes fixed on his chest. Avoiding his gaze, she stretched out her hand. What was she to say? Just what the others had said? However, she kept silent, uttered not a word. What, she wondered, did his eyes express? His rough hand shook hers, and he said in a gruff voice, "Thanks." She turned elegantly and moved off.

She forgot her worries through her daily tasks, though she did not look in good shape. Several of the girls remarked, "Miss is in a bad mood." When she returned to her home at the beginning of the Pyramids Road, she changed her clothes and sat down to eat with her mother. "Everything all right?" inquired her mother, looking her in the face.

"Badran, Badran Badawi," she said briefly. "Do you remember him? He's been appointed our headmaster."

"Really!"

Then, after a moment of silence, she said, "It's of no importance at all — it's an old and long-forgotten story."

After eating, she took herself off to her study to rest for a while before correcting some exercise books. She had forgotten him completely. No, not completely. How could he be forgotten completely? When he had first come to give her a private lesson in mathematics, she was fourteen years of age. In fact not quite fourteen. He had been twenty-five years older, the same age as her father. She had said to her mother, "His appearance is a mess, but he explains things well." And her mother had said, "We're not concerned with what he looks like; what's important is how he explains things."

He was an amusing person, and she got on well with him and benefited   10 from his knowledge. How, then, had it happened? In her innocence she had not noticed any change in his behavior to put her on her guard. Then one day he had been left on his own with her, her father having gone to her aunt's clinic. She had not the slightest doubts about a man she regarded as a second father. How, then, had it happened? Without love or desire on her part the thing had happened. She had asked in terror about what had occurred, and he had told her, "Don't be frightened or sad. Keep it to yourself and I'll come and propose to you the day you come of age."

And he had kept his promise and had come to ask for her hand. By then she had attained a degree of maturity that gave her an understanding of the dimensions of their tragic position. She had found that she had no love or respect for him and that he was as far as he could be from her dreams and from the ideas she had formed of what constituted an ideal and moral person. But what was to be done? Her father had passed away two years ago, and her mother had been taken aback by the forwardness of the man. However, she had said to her, "I know your attachment to your personal independence, so I leave the decision to you."

She had been conscious of the critical position she was in. She had either to accept or to close the door forever. It was the sort of situation that could force her into something she detested. She was the rich, beautiful girl, a byword in Abbasiyya for her nobility of character, and now here she was struggling helplessly in a well-sprung trap, while he looked down at her with rapacious eyes. Just as she had hated his strength, so too did she hate her own weakness. To have abused her innocence was one thing, but for him to have the upper hand now that she was fully in possession of her faculties was something else. He had said, "So here I am, making good my promise because I love you." He had also said, "I know of your love of teaching, and you will complete your studies at the College of Science."

She had felt such anger as she had never felt before. She had rejected coercion in the same way as she rejected ugliness. It had meant little to her to sacrifice marriage. She had welcomed being on her own, for solitude accompanied by self-respect was not loneliness. She had also guessed he was after her money. She had told her mother quite straightforwardly, "No," to which her mother had replied, "I am astonished you did not make this decision from the first moment."

The man had blocked her way outside and said, "How can you refuse? Don't you realize the outcome?" And she had replied with an asperity he had not expected, "For me any outcome is preferable to being married to you."

After finishing her studies, she had wanted something to do to fill her 15 spare time, so she had worked as a teacher. Chances to marry had come time after time, but she had turned her back on them all.

"Does no one please you?" her mother asked her.

"I know what I'm doing," she had said gently.

"But time is going by."

"Let it go as it pleases, I am content."

Day by day she becomes older. She avoids love, fears it. With all her strength 20 she hopes that life will pass calmly, peacefully, rather than happily. She goes on persuading herself that happiness is not confined to love and motherhood. Never has she regretted her firm decision. Who knows what the morrow holds? But she was certainly unhappy that he should again make his appearance in her life, that she would be making of the past a living and painful present.

Then, the first time he was alone with her in his room, he asked her, "How are you?"

She answered coldly, "I'm fine."

He hesitated slightly before inquiring, "Have you not . . . I mean, did you get married?"

In the tone of someone intent on cutting short a conversation, she said, "I told you, I'm fine."

CONNECTIONS TO OTHER SELECTIONS

1. Discuss the similarities and differences between the older men in "The Answer Is No" and Fay Weldon's "IND AFF, or Out of Love in Sarajevo" (p. 202).

2. In an essay compare the protagonists' decisions not to marry in "The Answer Is No" and James Joyce's "Eveline" (p. 536).

GABRIEL GARCÍA MÁRQUEZ
(COLOMBIA / B. 1927)

Fiction writer, essayist, journalist, and writer of scripts for screen and stage, Gabriel García Márquez is one of the most widely read and discussed authors in the history of Latin American literature. Born in Aracataca, Colombia, García Márquez spent his first eight years listening to his grandmother weave matter-of-fact stories in which the living and the dead coexisted without distinction, a style that profoundly influenced the magic realism of his work years later. In 1936,

© Bettmann/CORBIS.

García Márquez moved to Sucre and lived with his parents for four years before going on to secondary school in Zipaquira, and then to study law at the Universidad Nacional in the capital city of Bogotá. The young García Márquez's talents were recognized early. At the age of nineteen, he published his first story, "The Third Resignation," in the newspaper *El Espectador,* and it appeared with an introductory note hailing him as the "new genius of Colombian letters." This recognition allowed García Márquez to abandon his university course and pursue a career in journalism that took him to Rome in 1954 as the European correspondent for *El Espectador.* The following year, he published a short story collection, *Leafstorm and Other Stories,* and later wrote the novel *In Evil Hour* (1962) while working for the Cuban news agency La Prensa in Colombia, Havana, and New York City. Later the author moved to Mexico City, where a gust of inspiration led him to risk financial ruin and write for a year in seclusion. The result was the 1967 publication of his masterpiece, *One Hundred Years of Solitude,* which brought him international fame and the ability to use his journalism in the service of left-wing causes worldwide. His other publications include *The Autumn of the Patriarch* (1975), *Chronicle of a Death Foretold* (1982), *Love in the Time of Cholera* (1985), *The General in His Labyrinth* (1990), and *Strange Pilgrims* (1993). García Márquez was awarded the Nobel Prize for Literature in 1982.

One of These Days   1962

Monday dawned warm and rainless. Aurelio Escovar, a dentist without a degree, and a very early riser, opened his office at six. He took some false teeth, still mounted in their plaster mold, out of the glass case and put on the table a fistful of instruments which he arranged in size order, as if they were on display. He wore a collarless striped shirt, closed at the neck with a golden stud, and pants held up by suspenders. He was erect and skinny, with a look that rarely corresponded to the situation, the way deaf people have of looking.

When he had things arranged on the table, he pulled the drill toward the dental chair and sat down to polish the false teeth. He seemed not to be thinking about what he was doing, but worked steadily, pumping the drill with his feet, even when he didn't need it.

After eight he stopped for a while to look at the sky through the window, and he saw two pensive buzzards who were drying themselves in the sun on the ridgepole of the house next door. He went on working with the idea that before lunch it would rain again. The shrill voice of his eleven-year-old son interrupted his concentration.

"Papa."

"What?"   5

"The Mayor wants to know if you'll pull his tooth."

"Tell him I'm not here."

He was polishing a gold tooth. He held it at arm's length, and examined it with his eyes half closed. His son shouted again from the little waiting room.

"He says you are, too, because he can hear you."

The dentist kept examining the tooth. Only when he had put it on the 10
table with the finished work did he say:

"So much the better."

He operated the drill again. He took several pieces of a bridge out of a cardboard box where he kept the things he still had to do and began to polish the gold.

"Papa."

"What?"

He still hadn't changed his expression. 15

"He says if you don't take out his tooth, he'll shoot you."

Without hurrying, with an extremely tranquil movement, he stopped pedaling the drill, pushed it away from the chair, and pulled the lower drawer of the table all the way out. There was a revolver. "O.K.," he said. "Tell him to come and shoot me."

He rolled the chair over opposite the door, his hand resting on the edge of the drawer. The Mayor appeared at the door. He had shaved the left side of his face, but the other side, swollen and in pain, had a five-day-old beard. The dentist saw many nights of desperation in his dull eyes. He closed the drawer with his fingertips and said softly:

"Sit down."

"Good morning," said the Mayor.

"Morning," said the dentist. 20

While the instruments were boiling, the Mayor leaned his skull on the headrest of the chair and felt better. His breath was icy. It was a poor office: an old wooden chair, the pedal drill, a glass case with ceramic bottles. Opposite the chair was a window with a shoulder-high cloth curtain. When he felt the dentist approach, the Mayor braced his heels and opened his mouth.

Aurelio Escovar turned his head toward the light. After inspecting the infected tooth, he closed the Mayor's jaw with a cautious pressure of his fingers.

"It has to be without anesthesia," he said.

"Why?"

"Because you have an abscess." 25

The Mayor looked him in the eye. "All right," he said, and tried to smile. The dentist did not return the smile. He brought the basin of sterilized instruments to the worktable and took them out of the water with a pair of cold tweezers, still without hurrying. Then he pushed the spittoon with the tip of his shoe, and went to wash his hands in the washbasin. He did all this without looking at the Mayor. But the Mayor didn't take his eyes off him.

It was a lower wisdom tooth. The dentist spread his feet and grasped the tooth with the hot forceps. The Mayor seized the arms of the chair, braced his feet with all his strength, and felt an icy void in his kidneys, but didn't make a sound. The dentist moved only his wrist. Without rancor, rather with a bitter tenderness, he said:

"Now you'll pay for our twenty dead men."

The Mayor felt the crunch of bones in his jaw, and his eyes filled with tears. 30
But he didn't breathe until he felt the tooth come out. Then he saw it through his tears. It seemed so foreign to his pain that he failed to understand his torture of the five previous nights.

Bent over the spittoon, sweating, panting, he unbuttoned his tunic and reached for the handkerchief in his pants pocket. The dentist gave him a clean cloth.

"Dry your tears," he said.

The Mayor did. He was trembling. While the dentist washed his hands, he saw the crumbling ceiling and a dusty spider web with spider's eggs and dead insects. The dentist returned, drying his hands. "Go to bed," he said, "and gargle with salt water." The Mayor stood up, said goodbye with a casual military salute, and walked toward the door, stretching his legs, without buttoning up his tunic.

"Send the bill," he said.

"To you or the town?"   35

The Mayor didn't look at him. He closed the door and said through the screen: "It's the same damn thing."

CONNECTIONS TO OTHER SELECTIONS

1. Discuss the power relationships in "One of These Days" and in Bessie Head's "The Prisoner Who Wore Glasses" (p. 668). How are the powerless empowered in each story?

2. Compare and contrast the treatment of revenge in "One of These Days" and Edgar Allan Poe's "The Cask of Amontillado" (p. 727).

TATYANA TOLSTAYA (RUSSIA / B. 1951)

Born in Leningrad, Tatyana Tolstaya graduated from Leningrad University in 1974 and now lives in New Jersey. Though she is the great-grandniece of Leo Tolstoy, Tolstaya's enthusiastic reception in Russia is firmly based on her remarkable talents rather than on her ancestry. Her stories often appear in Russian literary journals, but she is not a prolific writer. Her collection of short stories, *On the Golden Porch,* immediately sold out when it was first published in Moscow in 1987, and the English translation established her as an important voice when it was published in the United States in 1989. *Sleepwalker in a Fog* was published in English translation in 1991, followed by a novel, *The Slynx* (2007), and a collection of stories, *White Walls* (2007). Instead of focusing on social and political issues, Tolstaya's sensuous style explores the inner lives of her characters, who are defined by their perceptions and emotions rather than by national borders. Her writing is characterized by the kind of metaphoric intensity found more typically in poetry than in prose.

See the Other Side   *2007*

TRANSLATED, FROM THE RUSSIAN, BY JAMEY GAMBRELL

A hot day in May in Ravenna, the small Italian city where Dante is buried. Once upon a time — right at the start of the fifth century A.D. — the Emperor Honorius transferred the capital of the Western Roman Empire to this city. There was a port here then, but the sea has since receded, and in its place are swamps, roses, dust, and vineyards. Ravenna is famous for its mosaics; hordes of tourists

move from one church to another, craning their necks to glimpse the dim lustre
of tiny multicolored smalti high up under dusky vaults. It is possible to make
out something in those vaults, but not very much. The glossy postcards,
though terribly bright, flat, and cheap-looking, will give you a better view.

I'm suffocating and hot. I'm depressed. My father died, and I loved him so
much! Once, long, long ago, almost forty years back, he passed through
Ravenna and sent me a postcard of one of these famous mosaics. On the back —
in pencil, for some reason; he must have been in a hurry — he wrote, "Sweetheart! I have never seen anything so sublime (see the other side) in my life!
Makes you want to cry! Oh, if only you were here! Your Father!"

Each sentence ends with a silly exclamation point — he was young, he was
cheerful, maybe he'd had a glass of wine. I can see him with his felt hat cocked in
the manner of the late fifties, a cigarette between his white teeth — which were still
his own then — beads of sweat on his forehead. Tall, slim, handsome: his eyes shine
happily behind the glass circles of his spectacles. . . . The postcard — which he
dropped in a mailbox, lightheartedly entrusting it to two unreliable postal services,
the Italian and the Russian — depicts Heaven: the Lord sits amid a blindingly green
paradise of eternal spring, white sheep grazing all around. Those two unreliable
postal services had bent the corners of the postcard, but it didn't matter — the
message was received and everything could be seen.

If Heaven exists, then my father is there now. Where else would he be? The
only thing is, he died — he died and he doesn't write me postcards with exclamation points anymore; he no longer sends tidings from all parts of the globe:
I'm here, I love you. Do you love me? Do you share my pleasure and joy? Do you see the
beauty that I see? Greetings! Here's a postcard! Here's a cheap, glossy photograph — I was
here! It's wonderful! Oh, if only you could be here, too!

He travelled all over the world, and he liked the world. Now, as much as I   5
can, I follow in his footsteps. I go to the same towns and try to see them through
his eyes, try to imagine him young, turning that corner, climbing those steps,
leaning on the railing of the embankment with a cigarette between his teeth.

This time I'm in Ravenna, a stuffy, exhausting place, like all tourist destina-
tions where crowds fill narrow streets. It's a dead, hollow, hot town, with no place
to sit down. The tomb of Dante, exiled from his native Florence. The tomb of
Theodorich. The mausoleum of Galla Placidia, sister of Flavius Honorius, the
very man who made Ravenna the capital of the Western Empire. Fifteen centuries
passed. Everything changed. Dust gathered; the mosaics crumbled. What was
once important is now unimportant; what once excited has vanished in the sands.
The sea itself has receded, and where merry green waves once splashed there are
wastelands, vineyards, silence. Forty years — a whole lifetime — ago, my father
strolled and laughed here; his myopic eyes squinted; he sat at a sidewalk table,
drank red wine, and tore off bites of pizza with his own, strong teeth. The dark-
blue night fell. And on a postcard balanced on the edge of the table, in pencil, he
scribbled a few hurried words to me, scattering exclamation points and expressing his delight and his love for the world.

The overcast sky is stifling. It's hot, but the sun can't be seen. Dust is
everywhere. Land that was once at the bottom of the sea now lies around the
town in wide, fertile fields; where crabs once crawled, donkeys pick their way;
in place of seaweed, roses grow. Everything has gone to seed. Along the once
splendid streets of the capital of the Western world, disappointed American
tourists in pink sweatshirts wander, unhappy that the travel agency has tricked

them yet again: everything in Europe is so dinky, so small, so old! Fifteen centuries. Dante's grave. The tomb of Galla Placidia. My father's grave. Some sort of naïve green paradise on a crumpled postcard.

What was it that so amazed him here? I find the right church, I look up — yes, there's something green there, high up under the vault. White sheep on a green meadow. The usual dim light. The discordant hum of tourists below. Their fingers point. They look for explanations in their guidebooks: such-and-such a century, such-and-such a style. Everything is the same everywhere, always. You can hardly see.

In every Italian church there's a box on the wall for donations; and, for those who are interested, these boxes often provide an additional service. If you put in three hundred lira — twenty-five cents — for a brief moment spotlights are turned on near the ceiling, bathing the stones of the mosaic in fresh white light. The colors brighten. You can see details. The crowd gets excited; its hum grows louder. Only twenty-five cents. You've already come so far; you've paid for the plane ticket, for the train, the hotel, the pizza, the cold drinks, the coffee. How can you now begrudge a few extra cents? But many do. They're annoyed; they weren't forewarned. They want to see Heaven for free. They wait around for some other generous, impatient person to deposit a coin in the slot of that swindling Italian apparatus — all Italians are swindlers, isn't that right? Then the spotlights flare, and for a moment, too short for the human eye to adjust, paradise is greener, the sheep more innocent, the Lord — kinder. . . . And then the lights go off, and the din of the tourists turns from a momentary grumble of protest to a greedy growl to whispered disappointment. Once again, everything is immersed in gloom.

I wander from church to church along with the crowd. I listen to its muffled, multilingual murmur, like the rush of the sea; a slow human whirlpool spins me around, and tired, empty faces flash by — as empty as my own; eyeglasses glint; the pages of guidebooks rustle. I squeeze through the narrow doors of churches, push past my neighbors, trying, like everyone else, to get a better view, trying not to become irritated. After all, I think, if Heaven does exist it's likely that I'll enter it with just such a flock of sheep, of people — old, not all that smart, a bit greedy. Because if Heaven isn't for people like us, then who is it for, I'd like to know? Are there really so many others — special people, people who are noticeably better than us ordinary, statistically average souls? No, there aren't, so in all likelihood I will have to plod across those green meadows with a herd of American tourists, disgruntled that everything is so ancient and small. And, if that is the case, then Heaven must be awful and boring — which, by definition, seems wrong. Everything in Heaven should be utterly sublime.

"I have never seen anything so sublime (see the other side) in my life!" my father wrote. See the other side. An ordinary paradise. What did he see that I don't see?

I squeeze into a small building, of which the early-twentieth-century Russian traveller Pavel Muratov wrote in his famous book "Images of Italy":

> The blue of the ceiling of the mausoleum of Galla Placidia is unusually dark and deep — almost inscrutably so. Depending on the light penetrating through the small windows, it will shimmer, in a wonderful and unexpectedly marvellous manner, with a greenish, lilac, or crimson hue. It is against this background that the famous depiction of the youthful Good Shepherd, sitting among snow-white sheep, is placed. The half-circles near the windows are decorated with a large ornamental motif of deer drinking from a spring. Garlands of

10

fruit and leaves wind along the lower arches. On viewing their magnificence one cannot help but think that never has mankind arrived at a more satisfactory solution to the problem of decorating a church wall. Owing to the small size of the mausoleum chapel, the mosaics do not create the impression of vain, cold pomp. The air surrounding the sarcophagus, shining with the blue fire of the mosaics, which once contained the embalmed body of the Empress, is a worthy dream of an ardently religious imagination. Was this not what the artists of stained glass in the Gothic cathedrals strove to achieve, only in a different way?

Marvellous words! But, having pushed my way into the chapel, I can't see anything. Perhaps Muratov's guide illuminated the church with a torch, but now it's simply dark in here, and whatever scant light makes its way through the windows is blocked by tourists' backs. The crowd stands dense and stubborn, elbow to elbow. We need to put some coins into the light box, but no one is in a hurry; everyone is waiting for someone else to do it. I'm in no hurry, either. "I've put coins in many times," my internal voice says. "Let someone else do it this time." A minute passes in the stuffy dark. Another minute. Each of us thinks, I won't give in. The darkness presses on our heads. It smells like mice, mold, and something else, too, something very old—as though time itself had an odor. Then the human smells come through: aging flesh, perfume, breath mints, sweat, tobacco. This is how it will be right after death: there will be the sound of others breathing and sniffling in the dark; heat, anticipation, a subtle hostility toward one's fellow-travellers; a polite decision not to show this hostility; egotism, stubbornness, hope, doubt. The waiting room for Heaven—where else is there to go? "I have never seen anything so sublime (see the other side) in my life! Makes you want to cry!" my father wrote from paradise.

Finally, the familiar click resounds—someone has taken the plunge. The lights come on. For a brief moment, the briefest moment—the eye doesn't have time to take it all in, the eye casts about—the dull, hot darkness overhead becomes a starry sky, a dark-blue cupola with huge, shimmering stars that seem startlingly close. "Ahhhhh!" comes the sound from below, and then the light goes out, and again there's darkness, darker even than before. And again the click, and the fantastic, multicolored stars, like spinning Ferris wheels, and that very same "air . . . shining with the blue fire"—a momentary vision—and again gloom. And again the clatter of a falling coin, followed by the click—the glorious vision, don't go, stay with us!—and again the blow of darkness. The sinners stand as though enchanted, their faces lifted. A path has opened in the darkness, a promise has been made, evidence has been presented: all will be saved, no explanations necessary—the magical dark-blue abyss, raised above us by nameless artists, speaks for itself, sings in a wordless language. The blue flows down toward the garlands of fruit and leaves. . . . Everything disappears, but again and again the lights flash on, the fête is endless, and any minute now the angels will begin to sing. Let there be light!

I squeeze carefully through the crowd. I want to see the insatiable being 15 who has mounted these fireworks, who has rolled back the walls of the sepulchre with light.

He sits in a wheelchair, his face lowered. There's a box of coins in his lap. His hand gropes for one and sticks it into the slot, and, while the blue is tinted with lilac and crimson fire, a female guide hurriedly whispers in his ear words that I can't make out, and that, even if I could, I wouldn't understand: I don't know this language.

The man is blind. He has the reserved and patient expression of all blind people; his eyelids are closed, his head bowed, his ear bent toward his companion. What is she to him — daughter, wife, or simply someone hired to accompany him on his travels? He listens to her whisper and occasionally nods his head: yes, yes. He wants to hear more; he puts in coin after coin. He throws coins into the darkness, and from the darkness sounds a voice that tells him, as much as it is possible, about the great comfort of beauty.

He listens his fill, nods, and smiles, then the woman deftly wheels his chair through the crowd and out of the mausoleum. People look at them; he doesn't care, and she's probably used to it. The chair bounces along the cobblestones of the square, affording the blind man a little additional suffering. A light rain drips from the clouds but soon stops.

"See the other side." But there's nothing on the other side. On the other side there's only darkness, heat, silence, irritation, doubt, dejection. On the other side there's the depiction, worn with age, of something that was important long, long ago, but not to me. "Makes you want to cry!" Father wrote, forty years ago, of the beauty that struck him then (and perhaps of something greater as well). I want to cry, because he no longer exists, I don't know where he has gone, and all that's left of him is a mountain of papers and this postcard of a green Heaven, which I move from volume to volume like a bookmark.

But maybe that is not the way things are; maybe everything was calculated   20
long ago, a plan laid out that has only now taken effect? An anonymous Byzantine master, inspired by faith, imagined the beauty of the Lord's garden. He expressed it in his language as well as he could; perhaps he was even frustrated that he didn't have the skill to do more. Centuries passed. My father arrived in Ravenna, lifted his head, saw the vision of Eden, bought a cheap little picture of the picture, and sent it to me with love fortified by exclamation points — everyone chooses his own language. And, if he hadn't sent it, I wouldn't have come here. I wouldn't have come to this dark chapel. I wouldn't have encountered the blind man. I wouldn't have seen how, with a wave of his hand, the blue light of Heaven's threshold could flare on the other side of darkness.

Because we are just as blind — no, a thousand times blinder than that old man in the wheelchair. We hear whispers but we plug our ears; we are shown but we turn away. We have no faith: we're afraid to believe, because we're afraid that we'll be deceived. We are certain that we're in the tomb. We are certain that there's nothing in the dark. There can't be anything in the dark.

The blind man and his guide move away down the narrow streets of the small, dead town. The woman pushes the chair and says something, bending down toward the blind man's ear, and no doubt she falters, chooses her words, words that I would never choose. He laughs at something, and she straightens his collar. She adds coins to the box in his lap, then goes into a taverna and brings out a slice of pizza. He eats gratefully, messily, his hands touching the invisible, marvellous food in the darkness.

CONNECTIONS TO OTHER SELECTIONS

1. How is faith a significant thematic issue in "See the Other Side" and in Flannery O'Connor's "Revelation" (p. 474).

2. Compare the light in the church in Tolstaya's story to that in Emily Dickinson's poem "There's a certain Slant of light" (p. 2085).

20

Stories for Further Reading

The ability of writers to imagine what is not the self, to familiarize the strange and mystify the familiar, is the test of their power.
— TONI MORRISON

AP/Wide World Photos.

JOSEPH CONRAD (1857–1924)

Born Jozef Teodore Konrad Nalecz Korze-
niowski in Poland (then occupied by Russia), Joseph Conrad went to sea at an early age
and joined the French and English merchant
services traveling to Africa, South America,
India, Australia, and other exotic places. During his early twenties, he learned English
aboard British vessels but did not begin writing fiction until his mid-thirties. He published his first novel, *Almayer's Folly,* in 1895
and left the sea to marry an Englishwoman

Mary Evans Picture Library/The Image Works.

and settle in London, where he established himself as a major novelist, writing thirteen novels and nearly thirty short stories. *Typhoon* (1902), *An Outcast of the Island* (1896), *Lord Jim* (1900), and *Victory* (1915) are among the novels that reflect his experiences at sea and the remarkable locations he passed through. His most famous novel, *Heart of Darkness* (1902), explores the tensions between European life and the horrors of inner darkness that Conrad found in Africa and in his characters. European traders in the Congo instituted a ruthless colonialism that Conrad exposes in the novel and also in his short story "An Outpost of Progress" written four years earlier. Filled with political, racial, religious, and philosophical complexities that are compounded by irony, "An Outpost of Progress" calls into question the deeply held assumptions of civilization.

An Outpost of Progress 1897

I

There were two white men in charge of the trading station. Kayerts, the chief, was short and fat; Carlier, the assistant, was tall, with a large head and a very broad trunk perched upon a long pair of thin legs. The third man on the staff was a Sierra Leone nigger, who maintained that his name was Henry Price. However, for some reason or other, the natives down the river had given him the name of Makola, and it stuck to him through all his wanderings about the country. He spoke English and French with a warbling accent, wrote a beautiful hand, understood bookkeeping, and cherished in his innermost heart the worship of evil spirits. His wife was a negress from Loanda, very large and very noisy. Three children rolled about in sunshine before the door of his low, shed-like dwelling. Makola, taciturn and impenetrable, despised the two white men. He had charge of a small clay storehouse with a dried-grass roof, and pretended to keep a correct account of beads, cotton cloth, red kerchiefs, brass wire, and other trade goods it contained. Besides the storehouse and Makola's hut, there was only one large building in the cleared ground of the station. It was built neatly of reeds, with a verandah on all the four sides. There were three rooms in it. The one in the middle was the living-room, and had two rough tables and a few stools in it. The other two were the bedrooms for the white men. Each had a bedstead and a mosquito net for all furniture. The plank floor was littered with the belongings of the white men; open half-empty boxes, torn wearing apparel, old boots; all the things dirty, and all the things broken, that accumulate mysteriously round untidy men. There was also another dwelling-place some distance away from the buildings. In it, under a tall cross much out of the perpendicular, slept the man who had seen the beginning of all this; who had planned and had watched the construction of this outpost of progress. He had been, at home, an unsuccessful painter who, weary of pursuing fame on an empty stomach, had gone out there through high protections. He had been the first chief of that station. Makola had watched the energetic artist die of fever in the just finished house with his

usual kind of "I told you so" indifference. Then, for a time, he dwelt alone with
his family, his account books, and the Evil Spirit that rules the lands under the
equator. He got on very well with his god. Perhaps he had propitiated him by a
promise of more white men to play with, by and by. At any rate the director of
the Great Trading Company, coming up in a steamer that resembled an enormous sardine box with a flat-roofed shed erected on it, found the station in
good order, and Makola as usual quietly diligent. The director had the cross
put up over the first agent's grave, and appointed Kayerts to the post. Carlier
was told off as second in charge. The director was a man ruthless and efficient,
who at times, but very imperceptibly, indulged in grim humour. He made a
speech to Kayerts and Carlier, pointing out to them the promising aspect of
their station. The nearest trading-post was about three hundred miles away. It
was an exceptional opportunity for them to distinguish themselves and to
earn percentages on the trade. This appointment was a favour done to begin-
ners. Kayerts was moved almost to tears by his director's kindness. He would,
he said, by doing his best, try to justify the flattering confidence, &c., &c. Kayerts had been in the Administration of the Telegraphs, and knew how to
express himself correctly. Carlier, an ex-non-commissioned officer of cavalry
in an army guaranteed from harm by several European Powers, was less
impressed. If there were commissions to get, so much the better; and, trailing a
sulky glance over the river, the forests, the impenetrable bush that seemed to
cut off the station from the rest of the world, he muttered between his teeth,
"We shall see, very soon."

Next day, some bales of cotton goods and a few cases of provisions having been thrown on shore, the sardine-box steamer went off, not to return
for another six months. On the deck the director touched his cap to the two
agents, who stood on the bank waving their hats, and turning to an old servant of the Company on his passage to headquarters, said, "Look at those
two imbeciles. They must be mad at home to send me such specimens. I told
those fellows to plant a vegetable garden, build new storehouses and fences,
and construct a landing-stage. I bet nothing will be done! They won't know
how to begin. I always thought the station on this river useless, and they just
fit the station!"

"They will form themselves there," said the old stager with a quiet smile.

"At any rate, I am rid of them for six months," retorted the director.

The two men watched the steamer round the bend, then, ascending arm   5
in arm the slope of the bank, returned to the station. They had been in this
vast and dark country only a very short time, and as yet always in the midst of
other white men, under the eye and guidance of their superiors. And now, dull
as they were to the subtle influences of surroundings, they felt themselves very
much alone, when suddenly left unassisted to face the wilderness; a wilderness
rendered more strange, more incomprehensible by the mysterious glimpses of
the vigorous life it contained. They were two perfectly insignificant and incapable individuals, whose existence is only rendered possible through the high
organization of civilized crowds. Few men realize that their life, the very
essence of their character, their capabilities and their audacities, are only the
expression of their belief in the safety of their surroundings. The courage, the
composure, the confidence; the emotions and principles; every great and every
insignificant thought belongs not to the individual but to the crowd: to the
crowd that believes blindly in the irresistible force of its institutions and of its

morals, in the power of its police and of its opinion. But the contact with pure unmitigated savagery, with primitive nature and primitive man, brings sudden and profound trouble into the heart. To the sentiment of being alone of one's kind, to the clear perception of the loneliness of one's thoughts, of one's sensations — to the negation of the habitual, which is safe, there is added the affirmation of the unusual, which is dangerous; a suggestion of things vague, uncontrollable, and repulsive, whose discomposing intrusion excites the imagination and tries the civilized nerves of the foolish and the wise alike.

Kayerts and Carlier walked arm in arm, drawing close to one another as children do in the dark; and they had the same, not altogether unpleasant, sense of danger which one half suspects to be imaginary. They chatted persistently in familiar tones. "Our station is prettily situated," said one. The other assented with enthusiasm, enlarging volubly on the beauties of the situation. Then they passed near the grave. "Poor devil!" said Kayerts. "He died of fever, didn't he?" muttered Carlier, stopping short. "Why," retorted Kayerts, with indignation, "I've been told that the fellow exposed himself recklessly to the sun. The climate here, everybody says, is not at all worse than at home, as long as you keep out of the sun. Do you hear that, Carlier? I am chief here, and my orders are that you should not expose yourself to the sun!" He assumed his superiority jocularly, but his meaning was serious. The idea that he would, perhaps, have to bury Carlier and remain alone, gave him an inward shiver. He felt suddenly that this Carlier was more precious to him here, in the centre of Africa, than a brother could be anywhere else. Carlier, entering into the spirit of the thing, made a military salute and answered in a brisk tone, "Your orders shall be attended to, chief!" Then he burst out laughing, slapped Kayerts on the back and shouted, "We shall let life run easily here! Just sit still and gather in the ivory those savages will bring. This country has its good points, after all!" They both laughed loudly while Carlier thought: That poor Kayerts; he is so fat and unhealthy. It would be awful if I had to bury him here. He is a man I respect. . . . Before they reached the verandah of their house they called one another "my dear fellow."

The first day they were very active, pottering about with hammers and nails and red calico, to put up curtains, make their house habitable and pretty; resolved to settle down comfortably to their new life. For them an impossible task. To grapple effectually with even purely material problems requires more serenity of mind and more lofty courage than people generally imagine. No two beings could have been more unfitted for such a struggle. Society, not from any tenderness, but because of its strange needs, had taken care of those two men, forbidding them all independent thought, all initiative, all departure from routine; and forbidding it under pain of death. They could only live on condition of being machines. And now, released from the fostering care of men with pens behind the ears, or of men with gold lace on the sleeves, they were like those lifelong prisoners who, liberated after many years, do not know what use to make of their freedom. They did not know what use to make of their faculties, being both, through want of practice, incapable of independent thought.

At the end of two months Kayerts often would say, "If it was not for my Melie, you wouldn't catch me here." Melie was his daughter. He had thrown up his post in the Administration of the Telegraphs, though he had been for seventeen years perfectly happy there, to earn a dowry for his girl. His wife was dead, and the child was being brought up by his sisters. He regretted the streets, the pavements, the cafés, his friends of many years; all the things he used to see, day after day; all the thoughts suggested by familiar things — the thoughts effortless, monotonous, and soothing of a Government clerk; he regretted all the gossip, the small enmities, the mild venom, and the little jokes of Government offices. "If I had had a decent brother-in-law," Carlier would remark, "a fellow with a heart, I would not be here." He had left the army and had made himself so obnoxious to his family by his laziness and impudence, that an exasperated brother-in-law had made superhuman efforts to procure him an appointment in the Company as a second-class agent. Having not a penny in the world he was compelled to accept this means of livelihood as soon as it became quite clear to him that there was nothing more to squeeze out of his relations. He, like Kayerts, regretted his old life. He regretted the clink of sabre and spurs on a fine afternoon, the barrack-room witticisms, the girls of garrison towns; but, besides, he had also a sense of grievance. He was evidently a much ill-used man. This made him moody, at times. But the two men got on well together in the fellowship of their stupidity and laziness. Together they did nothing, absolutely nothing, and enjoyed the sense of the idleness for which they were paid. And in time they came to feel something resembling affection for one another.

They lived like blind men in a large room, aware only of what came in contact with them (and of that only imperfectly), but unable to see the general aspect of things. The river, the forest, all the great land throbbing with life, were like a great emptiness. Even the brilliant sunshine disclosed nothing intelligible. Things appeared and disappeared before their eyes in an unconnected and aimless kind of way. The river seemed to come from nowhere and flow nowhither. It flowed through a void. Out of that void, at times, came canoes, and men with spears in their hands would suddenly crowd the yard of the station. They were naked, glossy black, ornamented with snowy shells and glistening brass wire, perfect of limb. They made an uncouth babbling noise when they spoke, moved in a stately manner, and sent quick, wild glances out of their startled, never-resting eyes. Those warriors would squat in long rows, four or more deep, before the verandah, while their chiefs bargained for hours with Makola over an elephant tusk. Kayerts sat on his chair and looked down on the proceedings, understanding nothing. He stared at them with his round blue eyes, called out to Carlier, "Here, look! look at that fellow there — and that other one, to the left. Did you ever see such a face? Oh, the funny brute!"

Carlier, smoking native tobacco in a short wooden pipe, would swagger up 10 twirling his moustaches, and surveying the warriors with haughty indulgence, would say —

"Fine animals. Brought any bone? Yes? It's not any too soon. Look at the muscles of that fellow — third from the end. I wouldn't care to get a punch on the nose from him. Fine arms, but legs no good below the knee. Couldn't make cavalry men of them." And after glancing down complacently at his own shanks, he always concluded: "Pah! Don't they stink! You, Makola! Take that herd over to the fetish" (the storehouse was in every station called the fetish, perhaps because of the spirit of civilization it contained) "and give them up some of the rubbish you keep there. I'd rather see it full of bone than full of rags."

Kayerts approved.

"Yes, yes! Go and finish that palaver over there, Mr. Makola. I will come round when you are ready, to weigh the tusk. We must be careful." Then turning to his companion: "This is the tribe that lives down the river; they are rather aromatic. I remember, they had been once before here. D'ye hear that row? What a fellow has got to put up with in this dog of a country! My head is split."

Such profitable visits were rare. For days the two pioneers of trade and progress would look on their empty courtyard in the vibrating brilliance of vertical sunshine. Below the high bank, the silent river flowed on glittering and steady. On the sands in the middle of the stream, hippos and alligators sunned themselves side by side. And stretching away in all directions, surrounding the insignificant cleared spot of the trading post, immense forests, hiding fateful complications of fantastic life, lay in the eloquent silence of mute greatness. The two men understood nothing, cared for nothing but for the passage of days that separated them from the steamer's return. Their predecessor had left some torn books. They took up these wrecks of novels, and, as they had never read anything of the kind before, they were surprised and amused. Then during long days there were interminable and silly discussions about plots and personages. In the centre of Africa they made acquaintance of Richelieu and of d'Artagnan, of Hawk's Eye and of Father Goriot, and of many other people. All these imaginary personages became subjects for gossip as if they had been living friends. They discounted their virtues, suspected their motives, decried their successes; were scandalized at their duplicity or were doubtful about their courage. The accounts of crimes filled them with indignation, while tender or pathetic passages moved them deeply. Carlier cleared his throat and said in a soldierly voice, "What nonsense!" Kayerts, his round eyes suffused with tears, his fat cheeks quivering, rubbed his bald head, and declared, "This is a splendid book. I had no idea there were such clever fellows in the world." They also found some old copies of a home paper. That print discussed what it was pleased to call "Our Colonial Expansion" in high-flown language. It spoke much of the rights and duties of civilization, of the sacredness of the civilizing work, and extolled the merits of those who went about bringing light, and faith and commerce to the dark places of the earth. Carlier and Kayerts read, wondered, and began to think better of themselves. Carlier said one evening, waving his hand about, "In a hundred years, there will be perhaps a town here. Quays, and warehouses, and barracks, and — and — billiard-rooms. Civilization, my boy, and virtue — and all. And then, chaps will read that two good fellows, Kayerts and Carlier, were the first civilized men to live in this very spot!" Kayerts nodded, "Yes, it is a consolation to think of that." They seemed to forget their dead predecessor; but, early one day, Carlier went out and replanted the cross firmly. "It used to make me squint whenever I walked that way," he explained to Kayerts over the morning coffee. "It made me squint, leaning over so much. So I just planted it upright. And solid, I promise you! I suspended myself with both hands to the crosspiece. Not a move. Oh, I did that properly."

At times Gobila came to see them. Gobila was the chief of the neighbouring villages. He was a gray-headed savage, thin and black, with a white cloth round his loins and a mangy panther skin hanging over his back. He came up with long strides of his skeleton legs, swinging a staff as tall as himself, and, entering the common room of the station, would squat on his heels to the left of the door. There he sat, watching Kayerts, and now and then making a   15 speech which the other did not understand. Kayerts, without interrupting his occupation, would from time to time say in a friendly manner: "How goes it, you old image?" and they would smile at one another. The two whites had a liking for that old and incomprehensible creature, and called him Father Gobila. Gobila's manner was paternal, and he seemed really to love all white men. They all appeared to him very young, indistinguishably alike (except for stature), and he knew that they were all brothers, and also immortal. The death of the artist, who was the first white man whom he knew intimately, did not disturb this belief, because he was firmly convinced that the white stranger had pretended to die and got himself buried for some mysterious purpose of his own, into which it was useless to inquire. Perhaps it was his way of going home to his own country? At any rate, these were his brothers, and he transferred his absurd affection to them. They returned it in a way. Carlier slapped him on the back, and recklessly struck off matches for his amusement. Kayerts was always ready to let him have a sniff at the ammonia bottle. In short, they behaved just like that other white creature that had hidden itself in a hole in the ground. Gobila considered them attentively. Perhaps they were the same being with the other — or one of them was. He couldn't decide — clear up that mystery; but he remained always very friendly. In consequence of that friendship the women of Gobila's village walked in single file through the reedy grass, bringing every morning to the station, fowls, and sweet potatoes, and palm wine, and sometimes a goat. The Company never provisions the stations fully, and the agents required those local supplies to live. They had them through the goodwill of Gobila, and lived well. Now and then one of them had a bout of fever, and the other nursed him with gentle devotion. They did not think much of it. It left them weaker, and their appearance changed for the worse. Carlier was hollow-eyed and irritable. Kayerts showed a drawn, flabby face above the rotundity of his stomach, which gave him a weird aspect. But being constantly together, they did not notice the change that took place gradually in their appearance, and also in their dispositions.

Five months passed in that way.

Then, one morning, as Kayerts and Carlier, lounging in their chairs under the verandah, talked about the approaching visit of the steamer, a knot of armed men came out of the forest and advanced towards the station. They were strangers to that part of the country. They were tall, slight, draped classically from neck to heel in blue fringed cloths, and carried percussion muskets over their bare right shoulders. Makola showed signs of excitement, and ran out of the storehouse (where he spent all his days) to meet these visitors. They came into the courtyard and looked about them with steady, scornful glances. Their leader, a powerful and determined-looking Negro with bloodshot eyes, stood in front of the verandah and made a long speech. He gesticulated much, and ceased very suddenly.

There was something in his intonation, in the sounds of the long sentences he used, that startled the two whites. It was like a reminiscence of something not exactly familiar, and yet resembling the speech of civilized men. It sounded like one of those impossible languages which sometimes we hear in our dreams.

"What lingo is that?" said the amazed Carlier. "In the first moment I fancied the fellow was going to speak French. Anyway, it is a different kind of gibberish to what we ever heard."

"Yes," replied Kayerts. "Hey, Makola, what does he say? Where do they 20 come from? Who are they?"

But Makola, who seemed to be standing on hot bricks, answered hurriedly, "I don't know. They come from very far. Perhaps Mrs. Price will understand. They are perhaps bad men."

The leader, after waiting for a while, said something sharply to Makola, who shook his head. Then the man, after looking round, noticed Makola's hut and walked over there. The next moment Mrs. Makola was heard speaking with great volubility. The other strangers — they were six in all — strolled about with an air of ease, put their heads through the door of the store-room, congregated round the grave, pointed understandingly at the cross, and generally made themselves at home.

"I don't like those chaps — and, I say, Kayerts, they must be from the coast; they've got firearms," observed the sagacious Carlier.

Kayerts also did not like those chaps. They both, for the first time, became aware that they lived in conditions where the unusual may be dangerous, and that there was no power on earth outside of themselves to stand between them and the unusual. They became uneasy, went in and loaded their revolvers. Kayerts said, "We must order Makola to tell them to go away before dark."

The strangers left in the afternoon, after eating a meal prepared for them 25 by Mrs. Makola. The immense woman was excited, and talked much with the visitors. She rattled away shrilly, pointing here and there at the forests and at the river. Makola sat apart and watched. At times he got up and whispered to his wife. He accompanied the strangers across the ravine at the back of the station-ground, and returned slowly looking very thoughtful. When questioned by the white men he was very strange, seemed not to understand, seemed to have forgotten French — seemed to have forgotten how to speak altogether. Kayerts and Carlier agreed that the nigger had had too much palm wine.

There was some talk about keeping a watch in turn, but in the evening everything seemed so quiet and peaceful that they retired as usual. All night they were disturbed by a lot of drumming in the villages. A deep, rapid roll near by would be followed by another far off — then all ceased. Soon short appeals would rattle out here and there, then all mingle together, increase, become vigorous and sustained, would spread out over the forest, roll through the night, unbroken and ceaseless, near and far, as if the whole land had been one immense drum booming out steadily an appeal to heaven. And through the deep and tremendous noise sudden yells that resembled snatches of songs from a madhouse darted shrill and high in discordant jets of sound which seemed to rush far above the earth and drive all peace from under the stars.

Carlier and Kayerts slept badly. They both thought they had heard shots fired during the night — but they could not agree as to the direction. In the morning Makola was gone somewhere. He returned about noon with one of yesterday's strangers, and eluded all Kayerts' attempts to close with him: had become deaf apparently. Kayerts wondered. Carlier, who had been fishing off the bank, came back and remarked while he showed his catch, "The niggers seem to be in a deuce of a stir; I wonder what's up. I saw about fifteen canoes cross the river during the two hours I was there fishing." Kayerts, worried, said, "Isn't this Makola very queer to-day?" Carlier advised, "Keep all our men together in case of some trouble."

II

There were ten station men who had been left by the Director. Those fellows, having engaged themselves to the Company for six months (without having any idea of a month in particular and only a very faint notion of time in general), had been serving the cause of progress for upwards of two years. Belonging to a tribe from a very distant part of the land of darkness and sorrow, they did not run away, naturally supposing that as wandering strangers they would be killed by the inhabitants of the country; in which they were right. They lived in straw huts on the slope of a ravine overgrown with reedy grass, just behind the station buildings. They were not happy, regretting the festive incantations, the sorceries, the human sacrifices of their own land; where they also had parents, brothers, sisters, admired chiefs, respected magicians, loved friends, and other ties supposed generally to be human. Besides, the rice rations served out by the Company did not agree with them, being a food unknown to their land, and to which they could not get used. Consequently they were unhealthy and miserable. Had they been of any other tribe they would have made up their minds to die—for nothing is easier to certain savages than suicide—and so have escaped from the puzzling difficulties of existence. But belonging, as they did, to a warlike tribe with filed teeth, they had more grit, and went on stupidly living through disease and sorrow. They did very little work, and had lost their splendid physique. Carlier and Kays doctored them assiduously without being able to bring them back into condition again. They were mustered every morning and told off to different tasks—grass-cutting, fence-building, tree-felling, &c., &c., which no power on earth could induce them to execute efficiently. The two whites had practically very little control over them.

In the afternoon Makola came over to the big house and found Kayerts watching three heavy columns of smoke rising above the forests. "What is that?" asked Kayerts. "Some villages burn," answered Makola, who seemed to have regained his wits. Then he said abruptly: "We have got very little ivory; bad six months' trading. Do you like get a little more ivory?"

"Yes," said Kayerts, eagerly. He thought of percentages which were low. 30

"Those men who came yesterday are traders from Loanda who have got more ivory than they can carry home. Shall I buy? I know their camp."

"Certainly," said Kayerts. "What are those traders?"

"Bad fellows," said Makola, indifferently. "They fight with people, and catch women and children. They are bad men, and got guns. There is a great disturbance in the country. Do you want ivory?"

"Yes," said Kayerts. Makola said nothing for a while. Then: "Those workmen of ours are no good at all," he muttered, looking round. "Station in very bad order, sir. Director will growl. Better get a fine lot of ivory, then he say nothing."

"I can't help it; the men won't work," said Kayerts. "When will you get that 35 ivory?"

"Very soon," said Makola. "Perhaps to-night. You leave it to me, and keep indoors, sir. I think you had better give some palm wine to our men to make a dance this evening. Enjoy themselves. Work better tomorrow. There's plenty palm wine—gone a little sour."

Kayerts said "yes," and Makola, with his own hands carried big calabashes to the door of his hut. They stood there till the evening, and Mrs. Makola looked into every one. The men got them at sunset. When Kayerts and Carlier retired, a big bonfire was flaring before the men's huts. They could hear their shouts and drumming. Some men from Gobila's village had joined the station hands, and the entertainment was a great success.

In the middle of the night, Carlier waking suddenly, heard a man shout loudly; then a shot was fired. Only one. Carlier ran out and met Kayerts on the verandah. They were both startled. As they went across the yard to call Makola, they saw shadows moving in the night. One of them cried, "Don't shoot! It's me, Price." Then Makola appeared close to them. "Go back, go back, please," he urged, "you spoil all." "There are strange men about," said Carlier. "Never mind; I know," said Makola. Then he whispered, "All right. Bring ivory. Say nothing! I know my business." The two white men reluctantly went back to the house, but did not sleep. They heard footsteps, whispers, some groans. It seemed as if a lot of men came in, dumped heavy things on the ground, squabbled a long time, then went away. They lay on their hard beds and thought: "This Makola is invaluable." In the morning Carlier came out, very sleepy, and pulled at the cord of the big bell. The station hands mustered every morning to the sound of the bell. That morning nobody came. Kayerts turned out also, yawning. Across the yard they saw Makola come out of his hut, a tin basin of soapy water in his hand. Makola, a civilized nigger, was very neat in his person. He threw the soapsuds skillfully over a wretched little yellow cur he had, then turning his face to the agent's house, he shouted from the distance, "All the men gone last night!"

They heard him plainly, but in their surprise they both yelled out together: "What?" Then they stared at one another. "We are in a proper fix now," growled Carlier. "It's incredible!" muttered Kayerts. "I will go to the huts and see," said Carlier, striding off. Makola coming up found Kayerts standing alone.

"I can hardly believe it," said Kayerts, tearfully. "We took care of them as if 40 they had been our children."

"They went with the coast people," said Makola after a moment of hesitation.

"What do I care with whom they went — the ungrateful brutes!" exclaimed the other. Then with sudden suspicion, and looking hard at Makola, he added: "What do you know about it?"

Makola moved his shoulders, looking down on the ground. "What do I know? I think only. Will you come and look at the ivory I've got there? It is a fine lot. You never saw such."

He moved towards the store. Kayerts followed him mechanically, thinking about the incredible desertion of the men. On the ground before the door of the fetish lay six splendid tusks.

"What did you give for it?" asked Kayerts, after surveying the lot with 45 satisfaction.

"No regular trade," said Makola. "They brought the ivory and gave it to me. I told them to take what they most wanted in the station. It is a beautiful lot. No station can show such tusks. Those traders wanted carriers badly, and our men were no good here. No trade, no entry in books; all correct."

Kayerts nearly burst with indignation. "Why!" he shouted, "I believe you have sold our men for these tusks!" Makola stood impassive and silent. "I — I — will — I," stuttered Kayerts. "You fiend!" he yelled out.

"I did the best for you and the Company," said Makola imperturbably. "Why you shout so much? Look at this tusk."

"I dismiss you! I will report you—I won't look at the tusk. I forbid you to touch them. I order you to throw them into the river. You—you!"

"You very red, Mr. Kayerts. If you are so irritable in the sun, you will get 50 fever and die—like the first chief!" pronounced Makola impressively.

They stood still, contemplating one another with intense eyes, as if they had been looking with effort across immense distances. Kayerts shivered. Makola had meant no more than he said, but his words seemed to Kayerts full of ominous menace! He turned sharply and went away to the house. Makola retired into the bosom of his family; and the tusks, left lying before the store, looked very large and valuable in the sunshine.

Carlier came back on the verandah. "They're all gone, hey?" asked Kayerts from the far end of the common room in a muffled voice. "You did not find anybody?"

"Oh, yes," said Carlier, "I found one of Gobila's people lying dead before the hut—shot through the body. We heard that shot last night."

Kayerts came out quickly. He found his companion staring grimly over the yard at the tusks, away by the store. They both sat in silence for a while. Then Kayerts related his conversation with Makola. Carlier said nothing. At the midday meal they ate very little. They hardly exchanged a word that day. A great silence seemed to lie heavily over the station and press on their lips. Makola did not open the store; he spent the day playing with his children. He lay full-length on a mat outside his door, and the youngsters sat on his chest and clambered all over him. It was a touching picture. Mrs. Makola was busy cooking all day as usual. The white men made a somewhat better meal in the evening. Afterwards, Carlier smoking his pipe strolled over to the store; he stood for a long time over the tusks, touched one or two with his foot, even tried to lift the largest one by its small end. He came back to his chief, who had not stirred from the verandah, threw himself in the chair and said—

"I can see it! They were pounced upon while they slept heavily after drink- 55 ing all that palm wine you've allowed Makola to give them. A put-up job! See? The worst is, some of Gobila's people were there, and got carried off too, no doubt. The least drunk woke up, and got shot for his sobriety. This is a funny country. What will you do now?"

"We can't touch it, of course," said Kayerts.

"Of course not," assented Carlier.

"Slavery is an awful thing," stammered out Kayerts in an unsteady voice.

"Frightful—the sufferings," grunted Carlier with conviction.

They believed their words. Everybody shows a respectful deference to cer- 60 tain sounds that he and his fellows can make. But about feelings people really know nothing. We talk with indignation or enthusiasm; we talk about oppression, cruelty, crime, devotion, self-sacrifice, virtue, and we know nothing real beyond the words. Nobody knows what suffering or sacrifice mean—except, perhaps the victims of the mysterious purpose of these illusions.

Next morning they saw Makola very busy setting up in the yard the big scales used for weighing ivory. By and by Carlier said: "What's that filthy scoundrel up to?" and lounged out into the yard. Kayerts followed. They stood watching. Makola took no notice. When the balance was swung true, he tried to lift a tusk into the scale. It was too heavy. He looked up helplessly without a word, and for a minute they stood round that balance as mute and still as three statues. Suddenly Carlier said: "Catch hold of the other end, Makola—you beast!" and together they swung the tusk up. Kayerts trembled in every limb. He muttered, "I say! O! I say!" and putting his hand in his pocket found there a dirty bit of paper and the stump of a pencil. He turned his back on the others, as if about to do something tricky, and noted stealthily the weights which Carlier shouted out to him with unnecessary loudness. When all was over Makola whispered to himself: "The sun's very strong here for the tusks." Carlier said to Kayerts in a careless tone: "I say, chief, I might just as well give him a lift with this lot into the store."

As they were going back to the house Kayerts observed with a sigh: "It had to be done." And Carlier said: "It's deplorable, but, the men being Company's men the ivory is Company's ivory. We must look after it." "I will report to the Director, of course," said Kayerts. "Of course; let him decide," approved Carlier.

At midday they made a hearty meal. Kayerts sighed from time to time. Whenever they mentioned Makola's name they always added to it an opprobrious epithet. It eased their conscience. Makola gave himself a half-holiday, and bathed his children in the river. No one from Gobila's villages came near the station that day. No one came the next day, and the next, nor for a whole week. Gobila's people might have been dead and buried for any sign of life they gave. But they were only mourning for those they had lost by the witchcraft of white men, who had brought wicked people into their country. The wicked people were gone, but fear remained. Fear always remains. A man may destroy everything within himself, love and hate and belief, and even doubt; but as long as he clings to life he cannot destroy fear: the fear, subtle, indestructible, and terrible, that pervades his being; that tinges his thoughts; that lurks in his heart; that watches on his lips the struggle of his last breath. In his fear, the mild old Gobila offered extra human sacrifices to all the Evil Spirits that had taken possession of his white friends. His heart was heavy. Some warriors spoke about burning and killing, but the cautious old savage dissuaded them. Who could foresee the woe those mysterious creatures, if irritated, might bring? They should be left alone. Perhaps in time they would disappear into the earth as the first one had disappeared. His people must keep away from them, and hope for the best.

Kayerts and Carlier did not disappear, but remained above on this earth, that, somehow, they fancied had become bigger and very empty. It was not the absolute and dumb solitude of the post that impressed them so much as an inarticulate feeling that something from within them was gone, something that worked for their safety, and had kept the wilderness from interfering with their hearts. The images of home; the memory of people like them, of men that thought and felt as they used to think and feel, receded into distances made indistinct by the glare of unclouded sunshine. And out of the great silence of the surrounding wilderness, its very hopelessness and savagery seemed to approach them nearer, to draw them gently, to look upon them, to envelop them with a solicitude irresistible, familiar, and disgusting.

Days lengthened into weeks, then into months. Gobila's people drummed 65 and yelled to every new moon, as of yore, but kept away from the station. Makola and Carlier tried once in a canoe to open communications, but were received with a shower of arrows, and had to fly back to the station for dear life. That attempt set the country up and down the river into an uproar that could be very distinctly heard for days. The steamer was late. At first they spoke of delay jauntily, then anxiously, then gloomily. The matter was becoming serious. Stores were running short. Carlier cast his lines off the bank, but the river was low, and the fish kept out in the stream. They dared not stroll far away from the station to shoot. Moreover, there was no game in the impenetrable forest. Once Carlier shot a hippo in the river. They had no boat to secure it, and it sank. When it floated up it drifted away, and Gobila's people secured the carcass. It was the occasion for a national holiday, but Carlier had a fit of rage over it and talked about the necessity of exterminating all the niggers before the country could be made habitable. Kayerts mooned about silently; spent hours looking at the portrait of his Melie. It represented a little girl with long bleached tresses and a rather sour face. His legs were much swollen, and he could hardly walk. Carlier, undermined by fever, could not swagger any more, but kept tottering about, still with a devil-may-care air, as became a man who remembered his crack regiment. He had become hoarse, sarcastic, and inclined to say unpleasant things. He called it "being frank with you." They had long ago reckoned their percentages on trade, including in them that last deal of "this infamous Makola." They had also concluded not to say anything about it. Kayerts hesitated at first — was afraid of the Director.

"He has seen worse things done on the quiet," maintained Carlier, with a hoarse laugh. "Trust him! He won't thank you if you blab. He is no better than you or me. Who will talk if we hold our tongues? There is nobody here."

That was the root of the trouble! There was nobody there; and being left there alone with their weakness, they became daily more like a pair of accomplices than like a couple of devoted friends. They had heard nothing from home for eight months. Every evening they said, "To-morrow we shall see the steamer." But one of the Company's steamers had been wrecked, and the Director was busy with the other, relieving very distant and important stations on the main river. He thought that the useless station, and the useless men, could wait. Meantime Kayerts and Carlier lived on rice boiled without salt, and cursed the Company, all Africa, and the day they were born. One must have lived on such diet to discover what ghastly trouble the necessity of swallowing one's food may become. There was literally nothing else in the station but rice and coffee; they drank the coffee without sugar. The last fifteen lumps Kayerts had solemnly locked away in his box, together with a half-bottle of cognac, "in case of sickness," he explained. Carlier approved. "When one is sick," he said, "any little extra like that is cheering."

They waited. Rank grass began to sprout over the courtyard. The bell never rang now. Days passed, silent, exasperating, and slow. When the two men spoke, they snarled; and their silences were bitter, as if tinged by the bitterness of their thoughts.

One day after a lunch of boiled rice, Carlier put down his cup untasted, and said: "Hang it all! Let's have a decent cup of coffee for once. Bring out that sugar, Kayerts!"

"For the sick," muttered Kayerts, without looking up.   70

"For the sick," mocked Carlier. "Bosh! . . . Well! I am sick."

"You are no more sick than I am, and I go without," said Kayerts in a peaceful tone.

"Come! out with that sugar, you stingy old slave-dealer."

Kayerts looked up quickly. Carlier was smiling with marked insolence. And suddenly it seemed to Kayerts that he had never seen that man before.

Who was he? He knew nothing about him. What was he capable of? There was a surprising flash of violent emotion within him, as if in the presence of something undreamt-of, dangerous, and final. But he managed to pronounce with composure—

"That joke is in very bad taste. Don't repeat it."   75

"Joke!" said Carlier, hitching himself forward on his seat. "I am hungry—I am sick—don't joke! I hate hypocrites. You are a hypocrite. You are a slave-dealer. I am a slave-dealer. There's nothing but slave-dealers in this cursed country. I mean to have sugar in my coffee to-day, anyhow!"

"I forbid you to speak to me in that way," said Kayerts with a fair show of resolution.

"You!—What?" shouted Carlier, jumping up.

Kayerts stood up also. "I am your chief," he began, trying to master the shakiness of his voice.

"What?" yelled the other. "Who's chief? There's no chief here. There's noth-   80 ing here: there's nothing but you and I. Fetch the sugar—you pot-bellied ass."

"Hold your tongue. Go out of this room," screamed Kayerts. "I dismiss you—you scoundrel!"

Carlier swung a stool. All at once he looked dangerously in earnest. "You flabby, good-for-nothing civilian—take that!" he howled.

Kayerts dropped under the table, and the stool struck the grass inner wall of the room. Then, as Carlier was trying to upset the table, Kayerts in desperation made a blind rush, head low, like a cornered pig would do, and overturning his friend, bolted along the verandah, and into his room. He locked the door, snatched his revolver, and stood panting. In less than a minute Carlier was kicking at the door furiously, howling, "If you don't bring out that sugar, I will shoot you at sight, like a dog. Now then—one—two—three. You won't? I will show you who's the master."

Kayerts thought the door would fall in, and scrambled through the square hole that served for a window in his room. There was then the whole breadth of the house between them. But the other was apparently not strong enough to break in the door, and Kayerts heard him running round. Then he also began to run laboriously on his swollen legs. He ran as quickly as he could, grasping the revolver, and unable yet to understand what was happening to him. He saw in succession Makola's house, the store, the river, the ravine, and the low bushes; and he saw all those things again as he ran for the second time round the house. Then again they flashed past him. That morning he could not have walked a yard without a groan.

And now he ran. He ran fast enough to keep out of sight of the other man.   85

Then as, weak and desperate, he thought, "Before I finish the next round I shall die," he heard the other man stumble heavily, then stop. He stopped also. He had the back and Carlier the front of the house, as before. He heard him drop into a chair cursing, and suddenly his own legs gave way, and he slid down into a sitting posture with his back to the wall. His mouth was as dry as a cinder, and his face was wet with perspiration—and tears. What was it all about? He thought it must be a horrible illusion; he thought he was dreaming; he thought he was going mad! After a while he collected his senses. What did they quarrel about? That sugar! How absurd! He would give it to him—didn't want it himself. And he began scrambling to his feet with a sudden feeling of security. But before he had fairly stood upright, a common-sense reflection occurred to him and drove him back into despair. He thought: "If I give way now to that brute of a soldier, he will begin this horror again tomorrow—and the day after—every day—raise other pretensions, trample on me, torture me, make me his slave—and I will be lost! Lost! The steamer may not come for days—may never come." He shook so that he had to sit down on the floor again. He shivered forlornly. He felt he could not, would not move any more. He was completely distracted by the sudden perception that the position was without issue—that death and life had in a moment become equally difficult and terrible.

All at once he heard the other push his chair back; and he leaped to his feet with extreme facility. He listened and got confused. Must run again! Right or left? He heard footsteps. He darted to the left, grasping his revolver, and at the very same instant, as it seemed to him, they came into violent collision. Both shouted surprise. A loud explosion took place between them; a roar of red fire, thick smoke; and Kayerts, deafened and blinded, rushed back thinking: "I am hit—it's all over." He expected the other to come round—to gloat over his agony. He caught hold of an upright of the roof—"All over!" Then he heard a crashing fall on the other side of the house, as if somebody had tumbled headlong over a chair—then silence. Nothing more happened. He did not die. Only his shoulder felt as if it had been badly wrenched, and he had lost his revolver. He was disarmed and helpless! He waited for his fate. The other man made no sound. It was a stratagem. He was stalking him now! Along what side? Perhaps he was taking aim this very minute!

After a few moments of an agony frightful and absurd, he decided to go and meet his doom. He was prepared for every surrender. He turned the corner, steadying himself with one hand on the wall; made a few paces, and nearly swooned. He had seen on the floor, protruding past the other corner, a pair of turned-up feet. A pair of white naked feet in red slippers. He felt deadly sick, and stood for a time in profound darkness. Then Makola appeared before him, saying quietly: "Come along, Mr. Kayerts. He is dead." He burst into tears of gratitude; a loud, sobbing fit of crying. After a time he found himself sitting in a chair and looking at Carlier, who lay stretched on his back. Makola was kneeling over the body.

"Is this your revolver?" asked Makola, getting up.

"Yes," said Kayerts; then he added very quickly, "He ran after me to shoot 90
me—you saw!"

"Yes, I saw," said Makola. "There is only one revolver; where's his?"

"Don't know," whispered Kayerts in a voice that had become suddenly very faint.

"I will go and look for it," said the other, gently. He made the round along the verandah, while Kayerts sat still and looked at the corpse. Makola came back empty-handed, stood in deep thought, then stepped quietly into the dead man's room, and came out directly with a revolver, which he held up before Kayerts. Kayerts shut his eyes. Everything was going round. He found life more terrible and difficult than death. He had shot an unarmed man.

After meditating for a while, Makola said softly, pointing at the dead man who lay there with his right eye blown out—

"He died of fever." Kayerts looked at him with a stony stare. "Yes," repeated 95
Makola, thoughtfully, stepping over the corpse, "I think he died of fever. Bury him to-morrow."

And he went away slowly to his expectant wife, leaving the two white men alone on the verandah.

Night came, and Kayerts sat unmoving on his chair. He sat quiet as if he had taken a dose of opium. The violence of the emotions he had passed through produced a feeling of exhausted serenity. He had plumbed in one short afternoon the depths of horror and despair, and now found repose in the conviction that life had no more secrets for him: neither had death! He sat by the corpse thinking; thinking very actively, thinking very new thoughts. He seemed to have broken loose from himself altogether. His old thoughts, convictions, likes and dislikes, things he respected and things he abhorred, appeared in their true light at last! Appeared contemptible and childish, false and ridiculous. He revelled in his new wisdom while he sat by the man he had killed. He argued with himself about all things under heaven with that kind of wrong-headed lucidity which may be observed in some lunatics. Incidentally he reflected that the fellow dead there had been a noxious beast anyway; that men died every day in thousands; perhaps in hundreds of thousands — who could tell? — and that in the number, that one death could not possibly make any difference; couldn't have any importance, at least to a thinking creature. He, Kayerts, was a thinking creature. He had been all his life, till that moment, a believer in a lot of nonsense like the rest of mankind — who are fools; but now he thought! He knew! He was at peace; he was familiar with the highest wisdom! Then he tried to imagine himself dead, and Carlier sitting in his chair watching him; and his attempt met with such unexpected success, that in a very few moments he became not at all sure who was dead and who was alive. This extraordinary achievement of his fancy startled him, however, and by a clever and timely effort of mind he saved himself just in time from becoming Carlier. His heart thumped, and he felt hot all over at the thought of that danger. Carlier! What a beastly thing! To compose his now disturbed nerves — and no wonder! — he tried to whistle a little. Then, suddenly, he fell asleep, or thought he had slept; but at any rate there was a fog, and somebody had whistled in the fog.

He stood up. The day had come, and a heavy mist had descended upon the land: the mist penetrating, enveloping, and silent; the morning mist of tropical lands; the mist that clings and kills; the mist white and deadly, immaculate and poisonous. He stood up, saw the body, and threw his arms above his head with a cry like that of a man who, waking from a trance, finds himself immured forever in a tomb. *"Help! . . . My God!"*

A shriek inhuman, vibrating and sudden, pierced like a sharp dart the white shroud of that land of sorrow. Three short, impatient screeches followed, and then, for a time, the fog-wreaths rolled on, undisturbed, through a formidable silence. Then many more shrieks, rapid and piercing, like the yells of some exasperated and ruthless creature, rent the air. Progress was calling to Kayerts from the river. Progress and civilization and all the virtues. Society was calling to its accomplished child to come, to be taken care of, to be instructed, to be judged, to be condemned; it called him to return to that rubbish heap from which he had wandered away, so that justice could be done.

Kayerts heard and understood. He stumbled out of the verandah, leaving the other man quite alone for the first time since they had been thrown there together. He groped his way through the fog, calling in his ignorance upon the 100 invisible heaven to undo its work. Makola flitted by in the mist, shouting as he ran —

"Steamer! Steamer! They can't see. They whistle for the station. I go ring the bell. Go down to the landing, sir. I ring."

He disappeared. Kayerts stood still. He looked upwards; the fog rolled low over his head. He looked round like a man who has lost his way; and he saw a dark smudge, a cross-shaped stain, upon the shifting purity of the mist. As he began to stumble towards it, the station bell rang in a tumultuous peal its answer to the impatient clamour of the steamer.

The Managing Director of the Great Civilizing Company (since we know that civilization follows trade) landed first, and incontinently lost sight of the steamer. The fog down by the river was exceedingly dense; above, at the station, the bell rang unceasing and brazen.

The Director shouted loudly to the steamer:

"There is nobody down to meet us; there may be something wrong, 105 though they are ringing. You had better come, too!"

And he began to toil up the steep bank. The captain and the engine-driver of the boat followed behind. As they scrambled up the fog thinned, and they could see their Director a good way ahead. Suddenly they saw him start forward, calling to them over his shoulder: — "Run! Run to the house! I've found one of them. Run, look for the other!"

He had found one of them! And even he, the man of varied and startling experience, was somewhat discomposed by the manner of this finding. He stood and fumbled in his pockets (for a knife) while he faced Kayerts, who was hanging by a leather strap from the cross. He had evidently climbed the grave, which was high and narrow, and after tying the end of the strap to the arm, had swung himself off. His toes were only a couple of inches above the ground; his arms hung stiffly down; he seemed to be standing rigidly at attention, but with one purple cheek playfully posed on the shoulder. And, irreverently, he was putting out a swollen tongue at his Managing Director.

JAMAICA KINCAID (B. 1949)

Jamaica Kincaid was born Elaine Potter Richardson on the Caribbean island of Antigua. She moved to New York in 1965 to work as an au pair, studied photography at both the New School for Social Research and Franconia College, and changed her name to Jamaica Kincaid in 1973 with her first publication, "When I Was 17," a series of interviews. Over the next few years, she wrote for *The New Yorker* magazine, first as a freelancer

By permission of Trix Rosen.

and then as a staff writer. In 1978, Kincaid wrote her first piece of fiction, "Girl," published in *The New Yorker* and included in her debut short story collection, *At the Bottom of the River* (1983), which won an award from the Academy and Institute of Arts and Letters and was nominated for the PEN/Faulkner Award. Her other work includes *Annie John* (1985), *Lucy* (1990), *Autobiography of My Mother* (1994), and three nonfiction books, *A Small Place* (1988), *My Brother* (1997), and *Mr. Potter* (2002). Whether autobiographical fiction or nonfiction, her work usually focuses on the perils of postcolonial society, paralleled by an examination of rifts in mother-daughter relationships.

Web Explore contexts for Jamaica Kincaid and approaches to "Girl" at bedfordstmartins.com/ meyerlit.

Girl   1978

Wash the white clothes on Monday and put them on the stone heap; wash the color clothes on Tuesday and put them on the clothesline to dry; don't walk barehead in the hot sun; cook pumpkin fritters in very hot sweet oil; soak your little cloths right after you take them off; when buying cotton to make yourself a nice blouse, be sure that it doesn't have gum on it, because that way it won't hold up well after a wash; soak salt fish overnight before you cook it; is it true that you sing benna° in Sunday school?; always eat your food in such a way that it won't turn someone else's stomach; on Sundays try to walk like a lady and not like the slut you are so bent on becoming; don't sing benna in Sunday school; you mustn't speak to wharf-rat boys, not even to give directions; don't eat fruits on the street — flies will follow you; *but I don't sing benna on Sundays at all and never in Sunday school;* this is how to sew on a button; this is how to make a buttonhole for the button you have just sewed on; this is how to hem a dress when you see the hem coming down and so to prevent yourself from looking like the slut I know you are so bent on becoming; this is how you iron your father's khaki shirt so that it doesn't have a crease; this is how you iron your father's khaki pants so that they don't have a crease; this is how you grow okra — far from the house, because okra tree harbors red ants; when you are growing dasheen,° make sure it gets plenty of water or else it makes your throat itch when you are eating it; this is how you sweep a corner; this is how you sweep a whole house; this is how you sweep a yard; this is how you smile to someone you don't like too much; this is how you smile to someone you don't like at all; this is how you smile to someone you like completely; this is how you set a table for tea; this is how you set a table for dinner; this is how you set a table for dinner with an important guest; this is how you set a table for lunch; this is how you set a table for breakfast; this is how to behave in the presence of men who don't know you very well, and this way they won't recognize immediately the slut I have warned you against becoming; be sure to wash every day, even if it is with your own spit; don't squat down to play marbles — you are not a boy, you know; don't pick people's flowers — you might catch

benna: Calypso music.
dasheen: The edible rootstock of taro, a tropical plant.

something; don't throw stones at blackbirds, because it might not be a black-bird at all; this is how to make a bread pudding; this is how to make doukona;° this is how to make pepper pot;° this is how to make a good medicine for a cold; this is how to make a good medicine to throw away a child before it even becomes a child; this is how to catch a fish; this is how to throw back a fish you don't like, and that way something bad won't fall on you; this is how to bully a man; this is how a man bullies you; this is how to love a man, and if this doesn't work there are other ways, and if they don't work don't feel too bad about giving up; this is how to spit up in the air if you feel like it, and this is how to move quick so that it doesn't fall on you; this is how to make ends meet; always squeeze bread to make sure it's fresh; *but what if the baker won't let me feel the bread?;* you mean to say that after all you are really going to be the kind of woman who the baker won't let near the bread?

doukona: A spicy plantain pudding.
pepper pot: A stew.

D. H. LAWRENCE (1885–1930)

David Herbert Lawrence was born near Nottingham, England, in 1885. As a teenager, he worked as a factory clerk but became ill and, during his recuperation, became drawn to writing and teaching. He received a teaching certificate from University College, Nottingham, in 1908, having already published his first story. Lawrence achieved literary success early, publishing poems in the prestigious *English Review,* whose editor helped him to publish his first novel, *The White Peacock* (1911), which he followed with *The Trespasser* (1912) and *Sons and Lovers* (1913). In the meantime, he

© Hulton-Deutsch Collection/CORBIS.

eloped with Freida Weekly, the German wife of a professor in Nottingham, and they were married in 1914. After World War I, Lawrence and his wife left England and never again resided there. The couple lived in Italy and traveled and lived in Ceylon, Australia, the United States, and Mexico. Lawrence published several novels and books of nonfiction along the way, including *The Rainbow* (1915), *Women in Love* (1920), *Lost Girl* (1920), *Aaron's Rod* (1922), *The Plumed Serpent* (1926), *Movements in European History* (1921), *Studies in Classic American Literature* (1923), and two books on psychoanalysis. Lawrence had already transgressed norms of decency with *The Rainbow,* considered obscene in England, and his next work, *Lady Chatterley's Lover,* was published privately in 1928 because of its explicit sexual descriptions. Also the author of plays, poems, and such famous short stories as "The Odour of Chrysanthemums" and "Daughters of the Vicar," Lawrence innovated in ways that go far beyond his challenge to standards of obscenity. His works characteristically probe the nature of unconscious experience and promote a new receptiveness to sexuality, intuition, and emotion. In 1930, Lawrence died of tuberculosis in the south of France.

The Horse Dealer's Daughter   1922

"Well, Mabel, and what are you going to do with yourself?" asked Joe, with foolish flippancy. He felt quite safe himself. Without listening for an answer, he turned aside, worked a grain of tobacco to the tip of his tongue, and spat it out. He did not care about anything, since he felt safe himself.

The three brothers and the sister sat round the desolate breakfast-table, attempting some sort of desultory consultation. The morning's post had given the final tap to the family fortunes, and all was over. The dreary dining-room itself, with its heavy mahogany furniture, looked as if it were waiting to be done away with.

But the consultation amounted to nothing. There was a strange air of ineffectuality about the three men, as they sprawled at table, smoking and reflecting vaguely on their own condition. The girl was alone, a rather short, sullen-looking young woman of twenty-seven. She did not share the same life as her brothers. She would have been good-looking, save for the impressive fixity of her face, "bull-dog," as her brothers called it.

There was a confused tramping of horses' feet outside. The three men all sprawled round in their chairs to watch. Beyond the dark holly bushes that separated the strip of lawn from the high-road, they could see a cavalcade of shire horses swinging out of their own yard, being taken for exercise. This was the last time. These were the last horses that would go through their hands. The young men watched with critical, callous looks. They were all frightened at the collapse of their lives, and the sense of disaster in which they were involved left them no inner freedom.

Yet they were three fine, well-set fellows enough. Joe, the eldest, was a man 5 of thirty-three, broad and handsome in a hot, flushed way. His face was red, he twisted his black mustache over a thick finger, his eyes were shallow and restless. He had a sensual way of uncovering his teeth when he laughed, and his bearing was stupid. Now he watched the horses with a glazed look of helplessness in his eyes, a certain stupor of downfall.

The great draft-horses swung past. They were tied head to tail, four of them, and they heaved along to where a lane branched off from the high-road, planting their great hoofs floutingly in the fine black mud, swinging their great rounded haunches sumptuously, and trotting a few sudden steps as they were led into the lane, round the corner. Every movement showed a massive, slumbrous strength, and a stupidity which held them in subjection. The groom at the head looked back, jerking the leading rope. And the cavalcade moved out of sight up the lane, the tail of the last horse, bobbed up tight and stiff, held out taut from the swinging great haunches as they rocked behind the hedges in a motionlike sleep.

Joe watched with glazed hopeless eyes. The horses were almost like his own body to him. He felt he was done for now. Luckily he was engaged to a woman as old as himself, and therefore her father, who was steward of a neigh-boring estate, would provide him with a job. He would marry and go into har-ness. His life was over, he would be a subject animal now.

He turned uneasily aside, the retreating steps of the horses echoing in his ears. Then, with foolish restlessness, he reached for the scraps of bacon-rind from the plates, and making a faint whistling sound, flung them to the terrier that lay against the fender. He watched the dog swallow them, and waited till the creature looked into his eyes. Then a faint grin came on his face, and in a high, foolish voice he said:

"You won't get much more bacon, shall you, you little b ———?"

The dog faintly and dismally wagged its tail, then lowered its haunches,   10 circled round, and lay down again.

There was another helpless silence at the table. Joe sprawled uneasily in his seat, not willing to go till the family conclave was dissolved. Fred Henry, the second brother, was erect, clean-limbed, alert. He had watched the passing of the horses with more *sang-froid*.° If he was an animal, like Joe, he was an animal which controls, not one which is controlled. He was master of any horse, and he carried himself with a well-tempered air of mastery. But he was not master of the situations of life. He pushed his coarse brown mustache upwards, off his lip, and glanced irritably at his sister, who sat impassive and inscrutable.

"You'll go and stop with Lucy for a bit, shan't you?" he asked. The girl did not answer.

"I don't see what else you can do," persisted Fred Henry.

"Go as a skivvy,"° Joe interpolated laconically.

The girl did not move a muscle.   15

"If I was her, I should go in for training for a nurse," said Malcolm, the youngest of them all. He was the baby of the family, a young man of twenty-two, with a fresh, jaunty *museau*.°

But Mabel did not take any notice of him. They had talked at her and round her for so many years, that she hardly heard them at all.

The marble clock on the mantelpiece softly chimed the half-hour, the dog rose uneasily from the hearth-rug and looked at the party at the breakfast-table. But still they sat on in ineffectual conclave.

"Oh, all right," said Joe suddenly, apropos of nothing. "I'll get a move on."

He pushed back his chair, straddled his knees with a downward jerk, to get   20 them free, in horsey fashion, and went to the fire. Still he did not go out of the room; he was curious to know what the others would do or say. He began to charge his pipe, looking down at the dog and saying in a high, affected voice:

"Going wi' me? Going wi' me are ter? Tha'rt goin' further than tha counts on just now, dost hear?"

The dog faintly wagged its tail, the man stuck out his jaw and covered his pipe with his hands, and puffed intently, losing himself in the tobacco, look-ing down all the while at the dog with an absent brown eye. The dog looked up at him in mournful distrust. Joe stood with his knees stuck out, in real horsey fashion.

sang-froid: Coolness, composure.
skivvy: Domestic worker.
museau: Slang for *face*.

"Have you had a letter from Lucy?" Fred Henry asked of his sister.

"Last week," came the neutral reply.

"And what does she say?"   25

There was no answer.

"Does she *ask* you to go and stop there?" persisted Fred Henry.

"She says I can if I like."

"Well, then, you'd better. Tell her you'll come on Monday."

This was received in silence.   30

"That's what you'll do then, is it?" said Fred Henry, in some exasperation.

But she made no answer. There was a silence of futility and irritation in the room. Malcolm grinned fatuously.

"You'll have to make up your mind between now and next Wednesday," said Joe loudly, "or else find yourself lodgings on the curbstone."

The face of the young woman darkened, but she sat on immutable.

"Here's Jack Fergusson!" exclaimed Malcolm, who was looking aimlessly 35 out of the window.

"Where?" exclaimed Joe loudly.

"Just gone past."

"Coming in?"

Malcolm craned his neck to see the gate.

"Yes," he said.   40

There was a silence. Mabel sat on like one condemned, at the head of the table. Then a whistle was heard from the kitchen. The dog got up and barked sharply. Joe opened the door and shouted:

"Come on."

After a moment a young man entered. He was muffled up in overcoat and a purple woolen scarf, and his tweed cap, which he did not remove, was pulled down on his head. He was of medium height, his face was rather long and pale, his eyes looked tired.

"Hello, Jack! Well, Jack!" exclaimed Malcolm and Joe. Fred Henry merely said: "Jack."

"What's doing?" asked the newcomer, evidently addressing Fred Henry.   45

"Same. We've got to be out by Wednesday. Got a cold?"

"I have — got it bad, too."

"Why don't you stop in?"

"*Me* stop in? When I can't stand on my legs, perhaps I shall have a chance," the young man spoke huskily. He had a slight Scotch accent.

"It's a knock-out, isn't it," said Joe, boisterously, "if a doctor goes round 50 croaking with a cold. Looks bad for the patients, doesn't it?"

The young doctor looked at him slowly.

"Anything the matter with *you,* then?" he asked sarcastically.

"Not as I know of. Damn your eyes, hope not. Why?"

"I thought you were very concerned about the patients, wondered if you might be one yourself."

"Damn it, no, I've never been patient to no flaming doctor, and hope I 55 never shall be," returned Joe.

At this point Mabel rose from the table, and they all seemed to become aware of her existence. She began putting the dishes together. The young doctor looked at her, but did not address her. He had not greeted her. She went out of the room with the tray, her face impassive and unchanged.

"When are you off then, all of you?" asked the doctor.

"I'm catching the eleven-forty," replied Malcolm. "Are you goin' down wi' th' trap,° Joe?"

"Yes, I've told you I'm going down wi' th' trap, haven't I?"

"We'd better be getting her in then. So long, Jack, if I don't see you before I 60 go," said Malcolm, shaking hands.

He went out, followed by Joe, who seemed to have his tail between his legs.

"Well, this is the devil's own," exclaimed the doctor, when he was left alone with Fred Henry. "Going before Wednesday, are you?"

"That's the orders," replied the other.

"Where, to Northampton?"

"That's it." 65

"The devil!" exclaimed Fergusson, with quiet chagrin.

And there was silence between the two.

"All settled up, are you?" asked Fergusson.

"About."

There was another pause. 70

"Well, I shall miss yer, Freddy, boy," said the young doctor.

"And I shall miss thee, Jack," returned the other.

"Miss you like hell," mused the doctor.

Fred Henry turned aside. There was nothing to say. Mabel came in again, to finish clearing the table.

"What are *you* going to do, then, Miss Pervin?" asked Fergusson. "Going to 75 your sister's, are you?"

Mabel looked at him with her steady, dangerous eyes, that always made him uncomfortable, unsettling his superficial ease.

"No," she said.

"Well, what in the name of fortune *are* you going to do? Say what you mean to do," cried Fred Henry, with futile intensity.

But she only averted her head, and continued her work. She folded the white table-cloth, and put on the chenille cloth.

"The sulkiest bitch that ever trod!" muttered her brother. 80

But she finished her task with perfectly impassive face, the young doctor watching her interestedly all the while. Then she went out.

Fred Henry stared after her, clenching his lips, his blue eyes fixing in sharp antagonism, as he made a grimace of sour exasperation.

"You could bray her into bits, and that's all you'd get out of her," he said, in a small, narrowed tone.

The doctor smiled faintly.

"What's she *going* to do, then?" he asked. 85

"Strike me if *I* know!" returned the other.

There was a pause. Then the doctor stirred.

"I'll be seeing you tonight, shall I?" he said to his friend.

"Ay—where's it to be? Are we going over to Jessdale?"

"I don't know. I've got such a cold on me. I'll come round to the 'Moon 90 and Stars,' anyway."

"Let Lizzie and May miss their night for once, eh?"

"That's it—if I feel as I do now."

---

trap: A light two-wheeled carriage.

"All's one ——"

The two young men went through the passage and down to the back door together. The house was large, but it was servantless now, and desolate. At the back was a small bricked houseyard and beyond that a big square, graveled fine and red, and having stables on two sides. Sloping, dank, winter-dark fields stretched away on the open sides.

But the stables were empty. Joseph Pervin, the father of the family, had 95 been a man of no education, who had become a fairly large horse dealer. The stables had been full of horses, there was a great turmoil and come-and-go of horses and of dealers and grooms. Then the kitchen was full of servants. But of late things had declined. The old man had married a second time, to retrieve his fortunes. Now he was dead and everything was gone to the dogs, there was nothing but debt and threatening.

For months, Mabel had been servantless in the big house, keeping the home together in penury for her ineffectual brothers. She had kept house for ten years. But previously it was with unstinted means. Then, however brutal and coarse everything was, the sense of money had kept her proud, confident. The men might be foul-mouthed, the women in the kitchen might have bad reputations, her brothers might have illegitimate children. But so long as there was money, the girl felt herself established, and brutally proud, reserved.

No company came to the house, save dealers and coarse men. Mabel had no associates of her own sex, after her sister went away. But she did not mind. She went regularly to church, she attended to her father. And she lived in the memory of her mother, who had died when she was fourteen, and whom she had loved. She had loved her father, too, in a different way, depending upon him, and feeling secure in him, until at the age of fifty-four he married again. And then she had set hard against him. Now he had died and left them all hopelessly in debt.

She had suffered badly during the period of poverty. Nothing, however, could shake the curious, sullen, animal pride that dominated each member of the family. Now, for Mabel, the end had come. Still she would not cast about her. She would follow her own way just the same. She would always hold the keys of her own situation. Mindless and persistent, she endured from day to day. Why should she think? Why should she answer anybody? It was enough that this was the end, and there was no way out. She need not pass any more darkly along the main street of the small town, avoiding every eye. She need not demean herself any more, going into the shops and buying the cheapest food. This was at an end. She thought of nobody, not even of herself. Mindless and persistent, she seemed in a sort of ecstasy to be coming nearer to her fulfillment, her own glorification, approaching her dead mother, who was glorified.

In the afternoon she took a little bag, with shears and sponge and a small scrubbing-brush, and went out. It was a gray, wintry day, with saddened, dark green fields and an atmosphere blackened by the smoke of foundries not far off. She went quickly, darkly along the causeway, heeding nobody, through the town to the churchyard.

There she always felt secure, as if no one could see her, although as a mat- 100 ter of fact she was exposed to the stare of everyone who passed along under the churchyard wall. Nevertheless, once under the shadow of the great looming church, among the graves, she felt immune from the world, reserved within the thick churchyard wall as in another country.

Carefully she clipped the grass from the grave, and arranged the pinky white, small chrysanthemums in the tin cross. When this was done, she took an empty jar from a neighboring grave, brought water, and carefully, most scrupulously sponged the marble headstone and the coping-stone.

It gave her sincere satisfaction to do this. She felt in immediate contact with the world of her mother. She took minute pains, went through the park in a state bordering on pure happiness, as if in performing this task she came into a subtle, intimate connection with her mother. For the life she followed here in the world was far less real than the world of death she inherited from her mother.

The doctor's house was just by the church. Fergusson, being a mere hired assistant, was slave to the countryside. As he hurried now to attend to the out-patients in the surgery, glancing across the graveyard with his quick eye, he saw the girl at her task at the grave. She seemed so intent and remote, it was like looking into another world. Some mystical element was touched in him. He slowed down as he walked, watching her as if spellbound.

She lifted her eyes, feeling him looking. Their eyes met. And each looked again at once, each feeling, in some way, found out by the other. He lifted his cap and passed on down the road. There remained distinct in his consciousness, like a vision, the memory of her face, lifted from the tombstone in the churchyard, and looking at him with slow, large, portentous eyes. It *was* portentous, her face. It seemed to mesmerize him. There was a heavy power in her eyes which laid hold of his whole being, as if he had drunk some powerful drug. He had been feeling weak and done before. Now the life came back into him, he felt delivered from his own fretted, daily self.

He finished his duties at the surgery as quickly as might be, hastily filling up the bottles of the waiting people with cheap drugs. Then, in perpetual haste, he set off again to visit several cases in another part of his round, before teatime. At all times he preferred to walk if he could, but particularly when he was not well. He fancied the motion restored him.

The afternoon was falling. It was gray, deadened, and wintry, with a slow, moist, heavy coldness sinking in and deadening all the faculties. But why should he think or notice? He hastily climbed the hill and turned across the dark green fields, following the black cinder-track. In the distance, across a shallow dip in the country, the small town was clustered like smoldering ash, a tower, a spire, a heap of low, raw, extinct houses. And on the nearest fringe of the town, sloping into the dip, was Oldmeadow, the Pervins' house. He could see the stables and the outbuildings distinctly, as they lay towards him on the slope. Well, he would not go there many more times! Another resource would be lost to him, another place gone: the only company he cared for in the alien, ugly little town he was losing. Nothing but work, drudgery, constant hastening from dwelling to dwelling among the colliers and the iron-workers. It wore him out, but at the same time he had a craving for it. It was a stimulant to him to be in the homes of the working people, moving, as it were, through the innermost body of their life. His nerves were excited and gratified. He could come so near, into the very lives of the rough, inarticulate, powerful emotional men and women: He grumbled, he said he hated the hellish hole. But as a matter of fact it excited him, the contact with the rough, strongly-feeling people was a stimulant applied direct to his nerves.

Below Oldmeadow, in the green, shallow, soddened hollow of fields, lay a square, deep pond. Roving across the landscape, the doctor's quick eye detected a figure in black passing through the gate of the field, down towards the pond. He looked again. It would be Mabel Pervin. His mind suddenly became alive and attentive.

Why was she going down there? He pulled up on the path on the slope above, and stood staring. He could just make sure of the small black figure moving in the hollow of the failing day. He seemed to see her in the midst of such obscurity, that he was like a clairvoyant, seeing rather with the mind's eye than with ordinary sight. Yet he could see her positively enough, whilst he kept his eye attentive. He felt, if he looked away from her, in the thick, ugly falling dusk, he would lose her altogether.

He followed her minutely as she moved, direct and intent, like something transmitted rather than stirring in voluntary activity, straight down from the field towards the pond. There she stood on the bank for a moment. She never raised her head. Then she waded slowly into the water.

He stood motionless as the small black figure walked slowly and deliber- 110 ately towards the center of the pond, very slowly, gradually moving deeper into the motionless water, and still moving forward as the water got up to her breast. Then he could see her no more in the dusk of the dead afternoon.

"There!" he exclaimed. "Would you believe it?"

And he hastened straight down, running over the wet, soddened fields, pushing through the hedges, down into the depression of callous wintry obscurity. It took him several minutes to come to the pond. He stood on the bank, breathing heavily. He could see nothing. His eyes seemed to penetrate the dead water. Yes, perhaps that was the dark shadow of her black clothing beneath the surface of the water.

He slowly ventured into the pond. The bottom was deep, soft clay, he sank in, and the water clasped dead cold round his legs. As he stirred he could smell the cold, rotten clay that fouled up into the water. It was objectionable in his lungs. Still, repelled and yet not heeding, he moved deeper into the pond. The cold water rose over his thighs, over his loins, upon his abdomen. The lower part of his body was all sunk in the hideous cold element. And the bottom was so deeply soft and uncertain, he was afraid of pitching with his mouth underneath. He could not swim, and was afraid.

He crouched a little, spreading his hands under the water and moving them round, trying to feel for her. The dead cold pond swayed upon his chest. He moved again, a little deeper, and again, with his hands underneath, he felt all around under the water. And he touched her clothing. But it evaded his fingers. He made a desperate effort to grasp it.

And so doing he lost his balance and went under, horribly, suffocating in 115 the foul earthy water, struggling madly for a few moments. At last, after what seemed an eternity, he got his footing, rose again into the air, and looked around. He gasped, and knew he was in the world. Then he looked at the water. She had risen near him. He grasped her clothing, and drawing her nearer, turned to make his way to land again.

He went very slowly, carefully, absorbed in the slow progress. He rose higher, climbing out of the pond. The water was now only about his legs; he was thankful, full of relief to be out of the clutches of the pond. He lifted her and staggered on to the bank, out of the horror of wet, gray clay.

He laid her down on the bank. She was quite unconscious and running with water. He made the water come from her mouth, he worked to restore her. He did not have to work very long before he could feel the breathing begin again in her; she was breathing naturally. He worked a little longer. He could feel her live beneath his hands; she was coming back. He wiped her face, wrapped her in his overcoat, looked round into the dim, dark gray world, then lifted her and staggered down the bank and across the fields.

It seemed an unthinkably long way, and his burden so heavy he felt he would never get to the house. But at last he was in the stable-yard, and then in the house-yard. He opened the door and went into the house. In the kitchen he laid her down on the hearth-rug and called. The house was empty. But the fire was burning in the grate.

Then again he kneeled to attend to her. She was breathing regularly, her eyes were wide open and as if conscious, but there seemed something missing in her look. She was conscious in herself, but unconscious of her surroundings.

He ran upstairs, took blankets from a bed, and put them before the fire to   120
warm. Then he removed her saturated, earthy-smelling clothing, rubbed her dry with a towel, and wrapped her naked in the blankets. Then he went into the dining-room, to look for spirits. There was a little whiskey. He drank a gulp himself, and put some into her mouth.

The effect was instantaneous. She looked full into his face, as if she had been seeing him for some time, and yet had only just become conscious of him.

"Dr. Fergusson?" she said.

"What?" he answered.

He was divesting himself of his coat, intending to find some dry clothing upstairs. He could not bear the smell of the dead, clayey water, and he was mortally afraid for his own health.

"What did I do?" she asked.   125

"Walked into the pond," he replied. He had begun to shudder like one sick, and could hardly attend to her. Her eyes remained full on him, he seemed to be going dark in his mind, looking back at her helplessly. The shuddering became quieter in him, his life came back to him, dark and unknowing, but strong again.

"Was I out of my mind?" she asked, while her eyes were fixed on him all the time.

"Maybe, for the moment," he replied. He felt quiet, because his strength had come back. The strange fretful strain had left him.

"Am I out of my mind now?" she asked.

"Are you?" he reflected a moment. "No," he answered truthfully, "I don't   130
see that you are." He turned his face aside. He was afraid now, because he felt dazed, and felt dimly that her power was stronger than his, in this issue. And she continued to look at him fixedly all the time. "Can you tell me where I shall find some dry things to put on?" he asked.

"Did you dive into the pond for me?" she asked.

"No," he answered. "I walked in. But I went in overhead as well."

There was silence for a moment. He hesitated. He very much wanted to go upstairs to get into dry clothing. But there was another desire in him. And she seemed to hold him. His will seemed to have gone to sleep, and left him, standing there slack before her. But he felt warm inside himself. He did not shudder at all, though his clothes were sodden on him.

"Why did you?" she asked.

"Because I didn't want you to do such a foolish thing," he said.   135

"It wasn't foolish," she said, still gazing at him as she lay on the floor, with a sofa cushion under her head. "It was the right thing to do. *I* knew best, then."

"I'll go and shift these wet things," he said. But still he had not the power to move out of her presence, until she sent him. It was as if she had the life of his body in her hands, and he could not extricate himself. Or perhaps he did not want to.

Suddenly she sat up. Then she became aware of her own immediate condition. She felt the blankets about her, she knew her own limbs. For a moment it seemed as if her reason were going. She looked round, with wild eyes, as if seeking something. He stood still with fear. She saw her clothing lying scattered.

"Who undressed me?" she asked, her eyes resting full and inevitable on his face.

"I did," he replied, "to bring you round."   140

For some moments she sat and gazed at him, awfully, her lips parted.

"Do you love me, then?" she asked.

He only stood and stared at her, fascinated. His soul seemed to melt.

She shuffled forward on her knees, and put her arms round him, round his legs, as he stood there, pressing her breasts against his knees and thighs, clutching him with strange, convulsive certainty, pressing his thighs against her, drawing him to her face, her throat, as she looked up at him with flaring, humble eyes of transfiguration, triumphant in first possession.

"You love me," she murmured, in strange transport, yearning and tri-   145 umphant and confident. "You love me. I know you love me, I know."

And she was passionately kissing his knees, through the wet clothing, passionately and indiscriminately kissing his knees, his legs, as if unaware of everything.

He looked down at the tangled wet hair, the wild, bare, animal shoulders. He was amazed, bewildered, and afraid. He had never thought of loving her. He had never wanted to love her. When he rescued her and restored her, he was a doctor, and she was a patient. He had had no single personal thought of her. Nay, this introduction of the personal element was very distasteful to him, a violation of his professional honor. It was horrible to have her there embracing his knees. It was horrible. He revolted from it, violently. And yet — and yet — he had not the power to break away.

She looked at him again, with the same supplication of powerful love, and that same transcendent, frightening light of triumph. In view of the delicate flame which seemed to come from her face like a light, he was powerless. And yet he had never intended to love her. He had never intended. And something stubborn in him could not give way.

"You love me," she repeated, in a murmur of deep, rhapsodic assurance. "You love me."

Her hands were drawing him, drawing him down to her. He was afraid,   150 even a little horrified. For he had, really, no intention of loving her. Yet her hands were drawing him towards her. He put out his hand quickly to steady himself, and grasped her bare shoulder. A flame seemed to burn the hand that grasped her soft shoulder. He had no intention of loving her: his whole will was against his yielding. It was horrible. And yet wonderful was the touch of her shoulders, beautiful the shining of her face. Was she perhaps mad? He had a horror of yielding to her. Yet something in him ached also.

He had been staring away at the door, away from her. But his hand remained on her shoulder. She had gone suddenly very still. He looked down at her. Her eyes were now wide with fear, with doubt, the light was dying from her face, a shadow of terrible grayness was returning. He could not bear the touch of her eyes' question upon him, and the look of death behind the question.

With an inward groan he gave way, and let his heart yield towards her. A sudden gentle smile came on his face. And her eyes, which never left his face, slowly, slowly filled with tears. He watched the strange water rise in her eyes, like some slow fountain coming up. And his heart seemed to burn and melt away in his breast.

He could not bear to look at her any more. He dropped on his knees and caught her head with his arms and pressed her face against his throat. She was very still. His heart, which seemed to have broken, was burning with a kind of agony in his breast. And he felt her slow, hot tears wetting his throat. But he could not move.

He felt the hot tears wet his neck and the hollows of his neck, and he remained motionless, suspended through one of man's eternities. Only now it had become indispensable to him to have her face pressed close to him; he could never let her go again. He could never let her head go away from the close clutch of his arm. He wanted to remain like that for ever, with his heart hurting him in a pain that was also life to him. Without knowing, he was looking down on her damp, soft brown hair.

Then, as it were suddenly, he smelt the horrid stagnant smell of that water. 155 And at the same moment she drew away from him and looked at him. Her eyes were wistful and unfathomable. He was afraid of them, and he fell to kissing her, not knowing what he was doing. He wanted her eyes not to have that terrible, wistful, unfathomable look.

When she turned her face to him again, a faint delicate flush was glowing, and there was again dawning that terrible shining of joy in her eyes, which really terrified him, and yet which he now wanted to see, because he feared the look of doubt still more.

"You love me?" she said, rather faltering.

"Yes." The word cost him a painful effort. Not because it wasn't true. But because it was too newly true, the *saying* seemed to tear open again his newly-torn heart. And he hardly wanted it to be true, even now.

She lifted her face to him, and he bent forward and kissed her on the mouth, gently, with the one kiss that is an eternal pledge. And as he kissed her his heart strained again in his breast. He never intended to love her. But now it was over. He had crossed over the gulf to her, and all that he had left behind had shriveled and become void.

After the kiss, her eyes again slowly filled with tears. She sat still, away 160 from him, with her face drooped aside, and her hands folded in her lap. The tears fell very slowly. There was complete silence. He too sat there motionless and silent on the hearth-rug. The strange pain of his heart that was broken seemed to consume him. That he should love her? That this was love! That he should be ripped open in this way! Him, a doctor! How they would all jeer if they knew! It was agony to him to think they might know.

In the curious naked pain of the thought he looked again to her. She was still sitting there drooped into a muse. He saw a tear fall, and his heart flared hot. He saw for the first time that one of her shoulders was quite uncovered, one arm bare, he could see one of her small breasts; dimly, because it had become almost dark in the room.

"Why are you crying?" he asked, in an altered voice.

She looked up at him, and behind her tears the consciousness of her situation for the first time brought a dark look of shame to her eyes.

"I'm not crying, really," she said, watching him, half frightened.

He reached his hand, and softly closed it on her bare arm.   165

"I love you! I love you!" he said in a soft, low vibrating voice, unlike himself.

She shrank, and dropped her head. The soft, penetrating grip of his hand on her arm distressed her. She looked up at him.

"I want to go," she said. "I want to go and get you some dry things."

"Why?" he said. "I'm all right."

"But I want to go," she said. "And I want you to change your things."   170

He released her arm, and she wrapped herself in the blanket, looking at him rather frightened. And still she did not rise.

"Kiss me," she said wistfully.

He kissed her, but briefly, half in anger.

Then, after a second, she rose nervously, all mixed up in the blanket. He watched her in her confusion as she tried to extricate herself and wrap herself up so that she could walk. He watched her relentlessly, as she knew. And as she went, the blanket trailing, and as he saw a glimpse of her feet and her white leg, he tried to remember her as she was when he had wrapped her in the blanket. But then he didn't want to remember, because she had been nothing to him then, and his nature revolted from remembering her as she was when she was nothing to him.

A tumbling, muffled noise from within the dark house startled him. Then   175
he heard her voice: "There are clothes." He rose and went to the foot of the stairs, and gathered up the garments she had thrown down. Then he came back to the fire, to rub himself down and dress. He grinned at his own appearance when he had finished.

The fire was sinking, so he put on coal. The house was now quite dark, save for the light of a street-lamp that shone in faintly from beyond the holly trees. He lit the gas with matches he found on the mantelpiece. Then he emptied the pockets of his own clothes, and threw all his wet things in a heap into the scullery. After which he gathered up her sodden clothes, gently, and put them in a separate heap on the copper-top in the scullery.

It was six o'clock on the clock. His own watch had stopped. He ought to go back to the surgery. He waited, and still she did not come down. So he went to the foot of the stairs and called:

"I shall have to go."

Almost immediately he heard her coming down. She had on her best dress of black voile, and her hair was tidy, but still damp. She looked at him — and in spite of herself, smiled.

"I don't like you in those clothes," she said.   180

"Do I look a sight?" he answered.

They were shy of one another.

"I'll make you some tea," she said.

"No, I must go."

"Must you?" And she looked at him again with the wide, strained, doubt-   185
ful eyes. And again, from the pain of his breast, he knew how he loved her. He went and bent to kiss her, gently, passionately, with his heart's painful kiss.

"And my hair smells so horrible," she murmured in distraction. "And I'm so awful, I'm so awful! Oh, no, I'm too awful." And she broke into bitter, heart-broken sobbing. "You can't want to love me, I'm horrible."

"Don't be silly, don't be silly," he said, trying to comfort her, kissing her, holding her in his arms. "I want you, I want to marry you, we're going to be married, quickly, quickly — tomorrow if I can."

But she only sobbed terribly, and cried:

"I feel awful. I feel awful. I feel I'm horrible to you."

"No, I want you, I want you," was all he answered, blindly, with that ter-   190
rible intonation which frightened her almost more than her horror lest he should *not* want her.

JACK LONDON (1876–1916)

Hulton Archive/Getty Images.

Born in San Francisco, Jack London was raised in Oakland, California. Though he never completed a degree at the University of California, Berkeley, his informal education ranged widely throughout the world from oyster pirating in San Francisco Bay to seal hunting in Japan and Siberia. By the time he was twenty-one, he was in Alaska attempting to strike it rich in the Klondike Gold Rush. These early experiences provided rich materials for the start of his writing career so that within six years he did, indeed, find gold in *The Call of the Wild* (1903), which became an international best-seller. Among his later works were *White Fang* (1906), *The Sea-Wolf* (1904), and *The Iron Heel* (1908). During his lifetime, London was enormously prolific and arguably the most popular American writer in the world. He demonstrated in both his career and his plots how to survive.

To Build a Fire   *1908*

Day had broken cold and grey, exceedingly cold and grey, when the man turned aside from the main Yukon trail and climbed the high earth-bank, where a dim and little-travelled trail led eastward through the fat spruce timberland. It was a steep bank, and he paused for breath at the top, excusing the act to himself by looking at his watch. It was nine o'clock. There was no sun nor hint of sun, though there was not a cloud in the sky. It was a clear day, and yet there seemed an intangible pall over the face of things, a subtle gloom that made the day dark, and that was due to the absence of sun. This fact did not worry the man. He was used to the lack of sun. It had been days since he had seen the sun, and he knew that a few more days must pass before that cheerful orb, due south, would just peep above the skyline and dip immediately from view.

The man flung a look back along the way he had come. The Yukon lay a mile wide and hidden under three feet of ice. On top of this ice were as many feet of snow. It was all pure white, rolling in gentle undulations where the ice jams of the freeze-up had formed. North and south, as far as his eye could see, it was unbroken white, save for a dark hairline that curved and twisted from around the spruce-covered island to the south, and that curved and twisted away into the north, where it disappeared behind another spruce-covered island. This dark hairline was the trail — the main trail — that led south five hundred miles to the Chilcoot Pass, Dyea, and salt water; and that led north seventy miles to Dawson, and still on to the north a thousand miles to Nulato, and finally to St. Michael, on Bering Sea, a thousand miles and half a thousand more.

But all this — the mysterious, far-reaching hairline trail, the absence of sun from the sky, the tremendous cold, and the strangeness and weirdness of it all — made no impression on the man. It was not because he was long used to it. He was a newcomer in the land, a *chechaquo*, and this was his first winter. The trouble with him was that he was without imagination. He was quick and alert in the things of life, but only in the things, and not in the significances. Fifty degrees below zero meant eighty-odd degrees of frost. Such fact impressed him as being cold and uncomfortable, and that was all. It did not lead him to meditate upon his frailty as a creature of temperature, and upon man's frailty in general, able only to live within certain narrow limits of heat and cold; and from there on it did not lead him to the conjectural field of immortality and man's place in the universe. Fifty degrees below zero stood for a bite of frost that hurt and that must be guarded against by the use of mittens, ear flaps, warm moccasins, and thick socks. Fifty degrees below zero. That there should be anything more to it than that was a thought that never entered his head.

As he turned to go on, he spat speculatively. There was a sharp explosive crackle that startled him. He spat again. And again, in the air, before it could fall to the snow, the spittle crackled. He knew that at fifty below spittle crackled on the snow, but this spittle had crackled in the air. Undoubtedly it was colder than fifty below — how much colder he did not know. But the temperature did not matter. He was bound for the old claim on the left fork of Henderson Creek, where the boys were already. They had come over across the divide from the Indian Creek country, while he had come the roundabout way to take a look at the possibilities of getting out logs in the spring from the islands in the Yukon. He would be in to camp by six o'clock; a bit after dark, it was true, but the boys would be there, a fire would be going, and a hot supper would be ready. As for lunch, he pressed his hand against the protruding bundle under his jacket. It was also under his shirt, wrapped up in a handkerchief and lying against the naked skin. It was the only way to keep the biscuits from freezing. He smiled agreeably to himself as he thought of those biscuits, each cut open and sopped in bacon grease, and each enclosing a generous slice of fried bacon.

He plunged in among the big spruce trees. The trail was faint. A foot of 5 snow had fallen since the last sled had passed over, and he was glad he was without a sled, travelling light. In fact, he carried nothing but the lunch wrapped in the handkerchief. He was surprised, however, at the cold. It certainly was cold, he concluded, as he rubbed his numb nose and cheekbones with his mittened hand. He was a warm-whiskered man, but the hair on his face did not protect the high cheekbones and the eager nose that thrust itself aggressively into the frosty air.

At the man's heels trotted a dog, a big native husky, the proper wolf-dog, grey-coated and without any visible or temperamental difference from its brother, the wild wolf. The animal was depressed by the tremendous cold. It knew that it was no time for travelling. Its instinct told it a truer tale than was told to the man by the man's judgment. In reality, it was not merely colder than fifty below zero; it was colder than sixty below, than seventy below. It was seventy-five below zero. Since the freezing point is thirty-two above zero, it meant that one hundred and seven degrees of frost obtained. The dog did not know anything about thermometers. Possibly in its brain there was no sharp consciousness of a condition of very cold such as was in the man's brain. But the brute had its instinct. It experienced a vague but menacing apprehension that subdued it and made it slink along at the man's heels, and that made it question eagerly every unwonted movement of the man as if expecting him to go into camp or to seek shelter somewhere and build a fire. The dog had learned fire, and it wanted fire, or else to burrow under the snow and cuddle its warmth away from the air.

The frozen moisture of its breathing had settled on its fur in a fine powder of frost, and especially were its jowls, muzzle, and eyelashes whitened by its crystalled breath. The man's red beard and moustache were likewise frosted, but more solidly, the deposit taking the form of ice and increasing with every warm, moist breath he exhaled. Also, the man was chewing tobacco, and the muzzle of ice held his lips so rigidly that he was unable to clear his chin when he expelled the juice. The result was that a crystal beard of the colour and solidity of amber was increasing its length on his chin. If he fell down it would shatter itself, like glass, into brittle fragments. But he did not mind the appendage. It was the penalty all tobacco chewers paid in that country, and he had been out before in two cold snaps. They had not been so cold as this, he knew, but by the spirit thermometer at Sixty Mile he knew they had been registered at fifty below and at fifty-five.

He held on through the level stretch of woods for several miles, crossed a wide flat of nigger heads, and dropped down a bank to the frozen bed of a small stream. This was Henderson Creek, and he knew he was ten miles from the forks. He looked at his watch. It was ten o'clock. He was making four miles an hour, and he calculated that he would arrive at the forks at half-past twelve. He decided to celebrate that event by eating his lunch there.

The dog dropped in again at his heels, with a tail drooping discouragement, as the man swung along the creek bed. The furrow of the old sled trail was plainly visible, but a dozen inches of snow covered up the marks of the last runners. In a month no man had come up or down that silent creek. The man held steadily on. He was not much given to thinking, and just then particularly he had nothing to think about save that he would eat lunch at the forks and that at six o'clock he would be in camp with the boys. There was nobody to talk to; and, had there been, speech would have been impossible because of the ice muzzle on his mouth. So he continued monotonously to chew tobacco and to increase the length of his amber beard.

Once in a while the thought reiterated itself that it was very cold and that he had never experienced such cold. As he walked along he rubbed his cheekbones and nose with the back of his mittened hand. He did this automatically, now and 10 again changing hands. But, rub as he would, the instant he stopped his cheek-bones went numb, and the following instant the end of his nose went numb. He was sure to frost his cheeks; he knew that, and experienced a pang of regret that he had not devised a nose strap of the sort Bud wore in cold snaps. Such a strap passed across the cheeks, as well, and saved them. But it didn't matter much, after all. What were frosted cheeks? A bit painful, that was all; they were never serious.

Empty as the man's mind was of thoughts, he was keenly observant, and he noticed the changes in the creeks, the curves and bends and timber jams, and always he sharply noted where he placed his feet. Once, coming round a bend, he shied abruptly, like a startled horse, curved away from the place where he had been walking, and retreated several paces back along the trail. The creek he knew was frozen clear to the bottom—no creek could contain water in that arctic winter—but he knew also that there were springs that bubbled out from the hillsides and ran along under the snow and on top of the ice of the creek. He knew that the coldest snaps never froze these springs, and he knew likewise their danger. They were traps. They hid pools of water under the snow that might be three inches deep, or three feet. Sometimes a skin of ice half an inch thick covered them, and in turn was covered by snow. Sometimes there were alternate layers of water and ice skin, so that when one broke through he kept on breaking through for a while, sometimes wetting himself to the waist.

That was why he had shied in such a panic. He had felt the give under his feet and heard the crackle of a snow-hidden ice skin. And to get his feet wet in such a temperature meant trouble and danger. At the very least it meant delay, for he would be forced to stop and build a fire, and under its protection to bare his feet while he dried his socks and moccasins. He stood and studied the creek bed and its banks, and decided that the flow of water came from the right. He reflected awhile, rubbing his nose and cheeks, then skirted to the left, stepping gingerly and testing the footing for each step. Once clear of the danger, he took a fresh chew of tobacco and swung along at his four-mile gait.

In the course of the next two hours he came upon several similar traps. Usually the snow above the hidden pools had a sunken, candied appearance that advertised the danger. Once again, however, he had a close call; and once, suspecting danger, he compelled the dog to go on in front. The dog did not want to go. It hung back until the man shoved it forward, and then it went quickly across the white, unbroken surface. Suddenly it broke through, floundered to one side, and got away to firmer footing. It had wet its forefeet and legs, and almost immediately the water that clung to it turned to ice. It made quick efforts to lick the ice off its legs, then dropped down in the snow and began to bite out the ice that had formed between the toes. This was a matter of instinct. To permit the ice to remain would mean sore feet. It did not know this. It merely obeyed the mysterious prompting that arose from the deep crypts of its being. But the man knew, having achieved a judgment on the subject, and he removed the mitten from his right hand and helped to tear out the ice particles. He did not expose his fingers more than a minute, and was astonished at the swift numbness that smote them. It certainly was cold. He pulled on the mitten hastily, and beat the hand savagely across his chest.

At twelve o'clock the day was at its brightest. Yet the sun was too far south on its winter journey to clear the horizon. The bulge of the earth intervened between it and Henderson Creek, where the man walked under a clear sky at noon and cast no shadow. At half-past twelve, to the minute, he arrived at the forks of the creek. He was pleased at the speed he had made. If he kept it up, he would certainly be with the boys by six. He unbuttoned his jacket and shirt and drew forth his lunch. The action consumed no more than a quarter of a minute, yet in that brief moment the numbness laid hold of the exposed fingers. He did not put the mitten on, but, instead, struck the fingers a dozen sharp smashes against his leg. Then he sat down on a snow-covered log to eat. The sting that followed upon the striking of his fingers against his leg ceased so quickly that he was startled. He had had no chance to take a bite of biscuit. He struck the fingers repeatedly and returned them to the mitten, baring the other hand for the purpose of eating. He tried to take a mouthful, but the ice muzzle prevented. He had forgotten to build a fire and thaw out. He chuckled at his foolishness, and as he chuckled he noted the numbness creeping into the exposed fingers. Also, he noted that the stinging which had first come to his toes when he sat down was already passing away. He wondered whether the toes were warm or numb. He moved them inside the moccasins and decided that they were numb.

He pulled the mitten on hurriedly and stood up. He was a bit frightened. 15 He stamped up and down until the stinging returned into the feet. It certainly was cold, was his thought. That man from Sulphur Creek had spoken the truth when telling how cold it sometimes got in the country. And he had laughed at him at the time! That showed one must not be too sure of things. There was no mistake about it, it *was* cold. He strode up and down, stamping his feet and threshing his arms, until reassured by the returning warmth. Then he got out matches and proceeded to make a fire. From the undergrowth, where high water of the previous spring had lodged a supply of seasoned twigs, he got his firewood. Working carefully from a small beginning, he soon had a roaring fire, over which he thawed the ice from his face and in the protection of which he ate his biscuits. For the moment the cold of space was outwitted. The dog took satisfaction in the fire, stretching out close enough for warmth and far enough away to escape being singed.

When the man had finished, he filled his pipe and took his comfortable time over a smoke. Then he pulled on his mittens, settled the ear-flaps of his cap firmly about his ears, and took the creek trail up the left fork. The dog was disappointed and yearned back towards the fire. This man did not know cold. Possibly all the generations of his ancestry had been ignorant of cold, of real cold, of cold one hundred and seven degrees below freezing point. But the dog knew; all its ancestry knew, and it had inherited the knowledge. And it knew that it was not good to walk abroad in such fearful cold. It was the time to lie snug in a hole in the snow and wait for a curtain of cloud to be drawn across the face of outer space whence this cold came. On the other hand, there was no keen intimacy between the dog and the man. The one was the toil slave of the other, and the only caresses it had ever received were the caresses of the whip lash and of harsh and menacing throat sounds that threatened the whip lash. So the dog made no effort to communicate its apprehension to the man. It was not concerned in the welfare of the man; it was for its own sake that it yearned back towards the fire. But the man whistled, and spoke to it with the sound of whip lashes, and the dog swung in at the man's heels and followed after.

The man took a chew of tobacco and proceeded to start a new amber beard. Also, his moist breath quickly powdered with white his moustache, eyebrows, and lashes. There did not seem to be so many springs on the left fork of the Henderson, and for half an hour the man saw no signs of any. And then it happened. At a place where there were no signs, where the soft, unbroken snow seemed to advertise solidity beneath, the man broke through. It was not deep. He wet himself half-way to the knees before he floundered out to the firm crust.

He was angry, and cursed his luck aloud. He had hoped to get into camp with the boys at six o'clock, and this would delay him an hour, for he would have to build a fire and dry out his footgear. This was imperative at that low temperature — he knew that much; and he turned aside to the bank, which he climbed. On top, tangled in the underbrush about the trunks of several small spruce trees, was a high-water deposit of dry firewood — sticks and twigs, principally, but also larger portions of seasoned branches and fine, dry, last year's grasses. He threw down several large pieces on top of the snow. This served for a foundation and prevented the young flame from drowning itself in the snow it otherwise would melt. The flame he got by touching a match to a small shred of birch bark that he took from his pocket. This burned even more readily than paper. Placing it on the foundation, he fed the young flame with wisps of dry grass and with the tiniest dry twigs.

He worked slowly and carefully, keenly aware of his danger. Gradually, as the flame grew stronger, he increased the size of the twigs with which he fed it. He squatted in the snow pulling the twigs out from their entanglement in the brush and feeding directly to the flame. He knew there must be no failure. When it is seventy-five below zero, a man must not fail in his first attempt to build a fire — that is, if his feet are wet. If his feet are dry, and he fails, he can run along the trail for half a mile and restore his circulation. But the circulation of wet and freezing feet cannot be restored by running when it is seventy-five below. No matter how fast he runs, the wet feet will freeze the harder.

All this the man knew. The old-timer on Sulphur Creek had told him   20 about it the previous fall, and now he was appreciating the advice. Already all sensation had gone out of his feet. To build the fire he had been forced to remove his mittens, and the fingers had quickly gone numb. His pace of four miles an hour had kept his heart pumping blood to the surface of his body and to all the extremities. But the instant he stopped, the action of the pump eased down. The cold of space smote the unprotected tip of the planet, and he, being on that unprotected tip, received the full force of the blow. The blood of his body recoiled before it. The blood was alive, like the dog, and like the dog it wanted to hide away and cover itself up from the fearful cold. So long as he walked four miles an hour, he pumped that blood, willy-nilly, to the surface; but now it ebbed away and sank down into the recesses of his body. The extremities were the first to feel its absence. His wet feet froze the faster, and his exposed fingers numbed the faster, though they had not yet begun to freeze. Nose and cheeks were already freezing, while the skin of all his body chilled as it lost its blood.

But he was safe. Toes and nose and cheeks would be only touched by the frost, for the fire was beginning to burn with strength. He was feeding it with twigs the size of his finger. In another minute he would be able to feed it with branches the size of his wrist, and then he could remove his wet footgear, and, while it dried, he could keep his naked feet warm by the fire, rubbing them at first, of course, with snow. The fire was a success. He was safe. He remembered the advice of the old-timer on Sulphur Creek, and smiled. The old-timer had been very serious in laying down the law that no man must travel alone in the Klondike after fifty below. Well, here he was; he had had the accident; he was alone; and he had saved himself. Those old-timers were rather womanish, some of them, he thought. All a man had to do was to keep his head, and he was all right. Any man who was a man could travel alone. But it was surprising, the rapidity with which his cheeks and nose were freezing. And he had not thought his fingers could go lifeless in so short a time. Lifeless they were, for he could scarcely make them move together to grip a twig, and they seemed remote from his body and from him. When he touched a twig, he had to look and see whether or not he had hold of it. The wires were pretty well down between him and his finger ends.

All of which counted for little. There was the fire, snapping and crackling and promising life with every dancing flame. He started to untie his moccasins. They were coated with ice; the thick German socks were like sheaths of iron halfway to the knees; and the moccasin strings were like rods of steel all twisted and knotted as by some conflagration. For a moment he tugged with his numb fingers, then, realizing the folly of it, he drew his sheath knife.

But before he could cut the strings, it happened. It was his own fault, or, rather, his mistake. He should not have built the fire under the spruce tree. He should have built it in the open. But it had been easier to pull the twigs from the brush and drop them directly on the fire. Now the tree under which he had done this carried a weight of snow on its boughs. No wind had blown for weeks, and each bough was fully freighted. Each time he had pulled a twig he had communicated a slight agitation to the tree — an imperceptible agitation, so far as he was concerned, but an agitation sufficient to bring about the disaster. High up in the tree one bough capsized its load of snow. This fell on the boughs beneath, capsizing them. This process continued, spreading out and involving the whole tree. It grew like an avalanche, and it descended without warning upon the man and the fire, and the fire was blotted out! Where it had burned was a mantle of fresh and disordered snow.

The man was shocked. It was as though he had just heard his own sentence of death. For a moment he sat and stared at the spot where the fire had been. Then he grew very calm. Perhaps the old-timer on Sulphur Creek was right. If he had only had a trail mate he would have been in no danger now. The trail mate could have built the fire. Well, it was up to him to build the fire over again, and this second time there must be no failure. Even if he succeeded, he would most likely lose some toes. His feet must be badly frozen by now, and there would be some time before the second fire was ready.

Such were his thoughts, but he did not sit and think them. He was busy all 25 the time they were passing through his mind. He had made a new foundation for a fire, this time in the open, where no treacherous tree could blot it out. Next he gathered dry grasses and tiny twigs from the high-water flotsam. He could not bring his fingers together to pull them out, but he was able to gather them by the handful. In this way he got many rotten twigs and bits of green moss that were undesirable, but it was the best he could do. He worked methodically, even collecting an armful of the larger branches to be used later when the fire gathered strength. And all the while the dog sat and watched him, a certain yearning wistfulness in its eyes, it looked upon him as the fire provider, and the fire was slow in coming.

When all was ready, the man reached in his pocket for a second piece of birch bark. He knew the bark was there, and, though he could not feel it with his fingers, he could hear its crisp rustling as he fumbled for it. Try as he would, he could not clutch hold of it. And all the time, in his consciousness, was the knowledge that each instant his feet were freezing. This thought tended to put him in a panic, but he fought against it and kept calm. He pulled on his mittens with his teeth, and threshed his arms back and forth, beating his hands with all his might against his sides. He did this sitting down, and he stood up to do it; and all the while the dog sat in the snow, its wolf brush of a tail curled around warmly over its forefeet, its sharp wolf ears pricked forward intently as it watched the man. And the man, as he beat and threshed with his arms and hands, felt a great surge of envy as he regarded the creature that was warm and secure in its natural covering.

After a time he was aware of the first faraway signals of sensation in his beaten fingers. The faint tingling grew stronger till it evolved into a stinging ache that was excruciating, but which the man hailed with satisfaction. He stripped the mitten from his right hand and fetched forth the birch bark. The exposed fingers were quickly going numb again. Next he brought out his bunch of sulphur matches. But the tremendous cold had already driven the life out of his fingers. In his effort to separate one match from the others, the whole bunch fell in the snow. He tried to pick it out of the snow, but failed. The dead fingers could neither touch nor clutch. He was very careful. He drove the thought of his freezing feet, and nose, and cheeks, out of his mind, devoting his whole soul to the matches. He watched, using the sense of vision in place of that of touch, and when he saw his fingers on each side the bunch, he closed them — that is, he willed to close them, for the wires were down, and the fingers did not obey. He pulled the mitten on the right hand, and beat it fiercely against the knee. Then with both mittened hands, he scooped the bunch of matches, along with much snow, into his lap. Yet he was no better off.

After some manipulation he managed to get the bunch between the heels of his mittened hands. In this fashion he carried it to his mouth. The ice crackled and snapped when by a violent effort he opened his mouth. He drew the lower jaw in, curled the upper lip out of the way, and scraped the bunch with his upper teeth in order to separate a match. He succeeded in getting one, which he dropped on his lap. He was no better off. He could not pick it up. Then he devised a way. He picked it up in his teeth and scratched it on his leg. Twenty times he scratched before he succeeded in lighting it. As it flamed he held it with his teeth to the birch bark. But the burning brimstone went up his nostrils and into his lungs, causing him to cough spasmodically. The match fell into the snow and went out.

The old-timer on Sulphur Creek was right, he thought in the moment of controlled despair that ensued: after fifty below, a man should travel with a partner. He beat his hands, but failed in exciting any sensation. Suddenly he bared both hands, removing the mittens with his teeth. He caught the whole bunch between the heels of his hands. His arm muscles not being frozen enabled him to press the hand heels tightly against the matches. Then he scratched the bunch along his leg. It flared into flame, seventy sulphur matches at once! There was no wind to blow them out. He kept his head to one side to escape the strangling fumes, and held the blazing bunch to the birch bark. As he so held it, he became aware of sensation in his hand. His flesh was burning. He could smell it. Deep down below the surface he could feel it.

The sensation developed into pain that grew acute. And still he endured it, holding the flame of the matches clumsily to the bark that would not light readily because his own burning hands were in the way, absorbing most of the flame.

At last, when he could endure no more, he jerked his hands apart. The blazing matches fell sizzling into the snow, but the birch bark was alight. He began laying dry grasses and the tiniest twigs on the flame. He could not pick and choose, for he had to lift the fuel between the heels of his hands. Small pieces of rotten wood and green moss clung to the twigs, and he bit them off as well as he could with his teeth. He cherished the flame carefully and awkwardly. It meant life, and it must not perish. The withdrawal of blood from the surface of his body now made him begin to shiver, and he grew more awkward. A large piece of green moss fell squarely on the little fire. He tried to poke it out with his fingers, but his shivering frame made him poke too far, and he disrupted the nucleus of the little fire, the burning grasses and tiny twigs separating and scattering. He tried to poke them together again, but in spite of the tenseness of the effort, his shivering got away with him, and the twigs were hopelessly scattered. Each twig gushed a puff of smoke and went out. The fire provider had failed. As he looked apathetically about him, his eyes chanced on the dog, sitting across the ruins of the fire from him, in the snow, making restless, hunching movements, slightly lifting one forefoot and then the other, shifting its weight back and forth on them with wistful eagerness.

The sight of the dog put a wild idea into his head. He remembered the tale of the man, caught in a blizzard, who killed a steer and crawled inside the carcass, and so was saved. He would kill the dog and bury his hands in the warm body until the numbness went out of them. Then he could build another fire. He spoke to the dog, calling it to him; but in his voice was a strange note of fear that frightened the animal, who had never known the man to speak in such a way before. Something was the matter, and its suspicious nature sensed danger — it knew not what danger but somewhere, somehow, in its brain arose an apprehension of the man. It flattened its ears down at the sound of the man's voice, and its restless, hunching movements and the liftings and shiftings of its forefeet became more pronounced; but it would not come to the man. He got on his hands and knees and crawled towards the dog. This unusual posture again excited suspicion, and the animal sidled mincingly away.

The man sat up in the snow for a moment and struggled for calmness. Then he pulled on his mittens, by means of his teeth, and got upon his feet. He glanced down at first in order to assure himself that he was really standing up, for the absence of sensation in his feet left him unrelated to the earth. His erect position in itself started to drive the webs of suspicion from the dog's mind; and when he spoke peremptorily, with the sound of whip lashes in his voice, the dog rendered its customary allegiance and came to him. As it came within reaching distance, the man lost his control. His arms flashed out to the dog, and he experienced genuine surprise when he discovered that his hands could not clutch, that there was neither bend nor feeling in the fingers. He had forgotten for the moment that they were frozen and that they were freezing more and more. All this happened quickly, and before the animal could get away, he encircled its body with his arms. He sat down in the snow, and in this fashion held the dog, while it snarled and whined and struggled.

But it was all he could do, hold its body encircled in his arms and sit there. He realized he could not kill the dog. There was no way to do it. With his help-less hands he could neither draw nor hold his sheath knife nor throttle the animal. He released it, and it plunged wildly away, with tail between its legs, and still snarling. It halted forty feet away and surveyed him curiously, with ears pricked forward.

The man looked down at his hands in order to locate them, and found them hanging on the ends of his arms. It struck him as curious that one should have to use his eyes in order to find out where his hands were. He began thresh-ing his arms back and forth, beating the mittened hands against his sides. He did this for five minutes, violently, and his heart pumped enough blood up to the surface to put a stop to his shivering. But no sensation was aroused in the hands. He had an impression that they hung like weights on the ends of his arms, but when he tried to run the impression down, he could not find it.

A certain fear of death, dull and oppressive, came to him. This fear quickly 35 became poignant as he realized that it was no longer a mere matter of freezing his fingers and toes, or of losing his hands and feet, but that it was a matter of life and death with the chances against him. This threw him into a panic, and he turned and ran up the creek bed along the old, dim trail. The dog joined in behind him and kept up with him. He ran blindly, without intention, in fear such as he had never known in his life. Slowly, as he ploughed and floundered through the snow, he began to see things again — the banks of the creek, the old timber jams, the leafless aspens, and the sky. The running made him feel better. He did not shiver. Maybe, if he ran on, his feet would thaw out; and, anyway, if he ran far enough, he would reach camp and the boys. Without doubt he would lose some fingers and toes and some of his face; but the boys would take care of him, and save the rest of him when he got there. And at the same time there was another thought in his mind that said he would never get to the camp and the boys; that it was too many miles away, that the freezing had too great a start on him, and that he would soon be stiff and dead. This thought he kept in the background and refused to consider. Sometimes it pushed itself forward and demanded to be heard, but he thrust it back and strove to think of other things.

It struck him as curious that he could run at all on feet so frozen that he could not feel them when they struck the earth and took the weight of his body. He seemed to himself to skim along above the surface, and to have no connection with the earth. Somewhere he had once seen a winged Mercury, and he wondered if Mercury felt as he felt when skimming over the earth.

His theory of running until he reached camp and the boys had one flaw in it: he lacked the endurance. Several times he stumbled, and finally he tottered, crumpled up, and fell. When he tried to rise, he failed. He must sit and rest, he decided, and next time he would merely walk and keep on going. As he sat and regained his breath, he noted that he was feeling quite warm and comfortable. He was not shivering, and it even seemed that a warm glow had come to his chest and trunk. And yet, when he touched his nose or cheeks, there was no sensation. Running would not thaw them out. Nor would it thaw out his hands and feet. Then the thought came to him that the frozen portions of his body must be extending. He tried to keep this thought down, to forget it, to think of something else; he was aware of the panicky feeling that it caused, and he was afraid of the panic. But the thought asserted itself, and persisted, until it produced a vision of his body totally frozen. This was too much, and he made another wild run along the trail. Once he slowed down to a walk, but the thought of the freezing extending itself made him run again.

And all the time the dog ran with him, at his heels. When he fell down a second time, it curled its tail over its forefeet and sat in front of him, facing him, curiously eager and intent. The warmth and security of the animal angered him, and he cursed it till it flattened down its ears appeasingly. This time the shivering came more quickly upon the man. He was losing in his battle with the frost. It was creeping into his body from all sides. The thought of it drove him on, but he ran no more than a hundred feet, when he staggered and pitched headlong. It was his last panic. When he had recovered his breath and control, he sat up and entertained in his mind the conception of meeting death with dignity. However, the conception did not come to him in such terms. His idea of it was that he had been making a fool of himself, running around like a chicken with its head cut off — such was the simile that occurred to him. Well, he was bound to freeze anyway, and he might as well take it decently. With this new-found peace of mind came the first glimmerings of drowsiness. A good idea, he thought, to sleep off to death. It was like taking an anaesthetic. Freezing was not so bad as people thought. There were lots worse ways to die.

He pictured the boys finding his body next day. Suddenly he found himself with them, coming along the trail looking for himself. And, still with them, he came around a turn in the trail and found himself lying in the snow. He did not belong with himself any more, for even then he was out of himself, standing with the boys and looking at himself in the snow. It certainly was cold, was his thought. When he got back to the States he could tell the folks what real cold was. He drifted on from this to a vision of the old-timer on Sulphur Creek. He could see him quite clearly, warm and comfortable, and smoking a pipe.

"You were right, old hoss; you were right," the man mumbled to the old-timer of Sulphur Creek. 40

Then the man drowsed off into what seemed to him the most comfortable and satisfying sleep he had ever known. The dog sat facing him and waiting. The brief day drew to a close in a long, slow twilight. There were no signs of a fire to be made, and, besides, never in the dog's experience had it known a man to sit like that in the snow and make no fire. As the twilight drew on, its eager yearning for the fire mastered it, and with a great lifting and shifting of forefeet, it whined softly, then flattened its ears down in anticipation of being chidden by the man. But the man remained silent. Later the dog whined loudly. And still later it crept close to the man and caught the scent of death. This made the animal bristle and back away. A little longer it delayed, howling under the stars that leaped and danced and shone brightly in the cold sky. Then it turned and trotted up the trail in the direction of the camp it knew, where were the other food providers and fire providers.

Katherine Mansfield (1888–1923)

A biographical note and photograph of Katherine Mansfield appear on page 306 before her story "Miss Brill."

The Fly   *1923*

"Y'are very snug in here," piped old Mr. Woodifield, and he peered out of the great, green-leather arm-chair by his friend the boss's desk as a baby peers out of its pram. His talk was over; it was time for him to be off. But he did not want to go. Since he had retired, since his . . . stroke, the wife and the girls kept him boxed up in the house every day of the week except Tuesday. On Tuesday he was dressed and brushed and allowed to cut back to the City for the day. Though what he did there the wife and girls couldn't imagine. Made a nuisance of himself to his friends, they supposed. . . . Well, perhaps so. All the same, we cling to our last pleasures as the tree clings to its last leaves. So there sat old Woodifield, smoking a cigar and staring almost greedily at the boss, who rolled in his office chair, stout, rosy, five years older than he, and still going strong, still at the helm. It did one good to see him.

Wistfully, admiringly, the old voice added, "It's snug in here, upon my word!"

"Yes, it's comfortable enough," agreed the boss, and he flipped the *Financial Times* with a paper-knife. As a matter of fact he was proud of his room; he liked to have it admired, especially by old Woodifield. It gave him a feeling of deep, solid satisfaction to be planted there in the midst of it in full view of that frail old figure in the muffler.

"I've had it done up lately," he explained, as he had explained for the past — how many? — weeks. "New carpet," and he pointed to the bright red carpet with a pattern of large white rings. "New furniture," and he nodded towards the massive bookcase and the table with legs like twisted treacle. "Electric heating!" He waved almost exultantly towards the five transparent, pearly sausages glowing so softly in the tilted copper pan.

But he did not draw old Woodifield's attention to the photograph over the 5 table of a grave-looking boy in uniform standing in one of those spectral photographers' parks with photographers' storm-clouds behind him. It was not new. It had been there for over six years.

"There was something I wanted to tell you," said old Woodifield, and his eyes grew dim remembering. "Now what was it? I had it in my mind when I started out this morning." His hands began to tremble, and patches of red showed above his beard.

Poor old chap, he's on his last pins, thought the boss. And, feeling kindly, he winked at the old man, and said jokingly, "I tell you what. I've got a little drop of something here that'll do you good before you go out into the cold again. It's beautiful stuff. It wouldn't hurt a child." He took a key off his watch-chain, unlocked a cupboard below his desk, and drew forth a dark, squat bottle. "That's the medicine," said he. "And the man from whom I got it told me on the strict Q.T. it came from the cellars at Windsor Castle."

Old Woodifield's mouth fell open at the sight. He couldn't have looked more surprised if the boss had produced a rabbit.

"It's whisky, ain't it?" he piped feebly.

The boss turned the bottle and lovingly showed him the label. Whisky it was. 10

"D'you know," said he, peering up at the boss wonderingly, "they won't let me touch it at home." And he looked as though he was going to cry.

"Ah, that's where we know a bit more than the ladies," cried the boss, swooping across for two tumblers that stood on the table with the water-bottle, and pouring a generous finger into each. "Drink it down. It'll do you good. And don't put any water with it. It's sacrilege to tamper with stuff like this. Ah!" He tossed off his, pulled out his handkerchief, hastily wiped his moustaches, and cocked an eye at old Woodifield, who was rolling his in his chaps.

The old man swallowed, was silent a moment, and then said faintly, "It's nutty!"

But it warmed him; it crept into his chill old brain — he remembered.

"That was it," he said, heaving himself out of his chair. "I thought you'd   15 like to know. The girls were in Belgium last week having a look at poor Reggie's grave, and they happened to come across your boy's. They're quite near each other, it seems."

Old Woodifield paused, but the boss made no reply. Only a quiver in his eyelids showed that he heard.

"The girls were delighted with the way the place is kept," piped the old voice. "Beautifully looked after. Couldn't be better if they were at home. You've not been across, have yer?"

"No, no!" For various reasons the boss had not been across.

"There's miles of it," quavered old Woodifield, "and it's all as neat as a garden. Flowers growing on all the graves. Nice broad paths." It was plain from his voice how much he liked a nice broad path.

The pause came again. Then the old man brightened wonderfully.   20

"D'you know what the hotel made the girls pay for a pot of jam?" he piped. "Ten francs! Robbery, I call it. It was a little pot, so Gertrude says, no bigger than a half-crown. And she hadn't taken more than a spoonful when they charged her ten francs. Gertrude brought the pot away with her to teach 'em a lesson. Quite right, too; it's trading on our feelings. They think because we're over there having a look round we're ready to pay anything. That's what it is." And he turned towards the door.

"Quite right, quite right!" cried the boss, though what was quite right he hadn't the least idea. He came round by his desk, followed the shuffling footsteps to the door, and saw the old fellow out. Woodifield was gone.

For a long moment the boss stayed, staring at nothing, while the grey-haired office messenger, watching him, dodged in and out of his cubby-hole like a dog that expects to be taken for a run. Then: "I'll see nobody for half an hour, Macey," said the boss. "Understand? Nobody at all."

"Very good, sir."

The door shut, the firm heavy steps recrossed the bright carpet, the fat   25 body plumped down in the spring chair, and leaning forward, the boss covered his face with his hands. He wanted, he intended, he had arranged to weep. . . .

It had been a terrible shock to him when old Woodifield sprang that remark upon him about the boy's grave. It was exactly as though the earth had opened and he had seen the boy lying there with Woodifield's girls staring down at him. For it was strange. Although over six years had passed away, the boss never thought of the boy except as lying unchanged, unblemished in his uniform, asleep for ever. "My son!" groaned the boss. But no tears came yet. In the past, in the first few months and even years after the boy's death, he had only to say those words to be overcome by such grief that nothing short of a violent fit of weeping could relieve him. Time, he had declared then, he had told everybody, could make no difference. Other men perhaps might recover, might live their loss down, but not he. How was it possible? His boy was an only son. Ever since his birth the boss had worked at building up this business for him;

it had no other meaning if it was not for the boy. Life itself had come to have no other meaning. How on earth could he have slaved, denied himself, kept going all those years without the promise for ever before him of the boy's stepping into his shoes and carrying on where he left off?

And that promise had been so near being fulfilled. The boy had been in the office learning the ropes for a year before the war. Every morning they had started off together; they had come back by the same train. And what congratulations he had received as the boy's father! No wonder; he had taken to it marvellously. As to his popularity with the staff, every man jack of them down to old Macey couldn't make enough of the boy. And he wasn't in the least spoilt. No, he was just his bright natural self, with the right word for everybody, with that boyish look and his habit of saying, "Simply splendid!"

But all that was over and done with as though it never had been. The day had come when Macey had handed him the telegram that brought the whole place crashing about his head. "Deeply regret to inform you . . ." And he had left the office a broken man, with his life in ruins.

Six years ago, six years. . . . How quickly time passed! It might have happened yesterday. The boss took his hands from his face; he was puzzled. Something seemed to be wrong with him. He wasn't feeling as he wanted to feel. He decided to get up and have a look at the boy's photograph. But it wasn't a favourite photograph of his; the expression was unnatural. It was cold, even stern-looking. The boy had never looked like that.

At that moment the boss noticed that a fly had fallen into his broad inkpot, 30 and was trying feebly but desperately to clamber out again. Help! help! said those struggling legs. But the sides of the inkpot were wet and slippery; it fell back again and began to swim. The boss took up a pen, picked the fly out of the ink, and shook it on to a piece of blotting-paper. For a fraction of a second it lay still on the dark patch that oozed round it. Then the front legs waved, took hold, and, pulling its small, sodden body up, it began the immense task of cleaning the ink from its wings. Over and under, over and under, went a leg along a wing as the stone goes over and under the scythe. Then there was a pause, while the fly, seeming to stand on the tips of its toes, tried to expand first one wing and then the other. It succeeded at last, and, sitting down, it began, like a minute cat, to clean its face. Now one could imagine that the little front legs rubbed against each other lightly, joyfully. The horrible danger was over; it had escaped; it was ready for life again.

But just then the boss had an idea. He plunged his pen back into the ink, leaned his thick wrist on the blotting-paper, and as the fly tried its wings down came a great heavy blot. What would it make of that? What indeed! The little beggar seemed absolutely cowed, stunned, and afraid to move because of what would happen next. But then, as if painfully, it dragged itself forward. The front legs waved, caught hold, and, more slowly this time, the task began from the beginning.

He's a plucky little devil, thought the boss, and he felt a real admiration for the fly's courage. That was the way to tackle things; that was the right spirit. Never say die; it was only a question of. . . . But the fly had again finished its laborious task, and the boss had just time to refill his pen, to shake fair and square on the new-cleaned body yet another dark drop. What about it this time? A painful moment of suspense followed. But behold, the front legs were again waving; the boss felt a rush of relief. He leaned over the fly and said to it tenderly, "You artful little b . . ." And he actually had the brilliant notion of breathing on it to help the drying process. All the same, there was something timid and weak about its efforts now, and the boss decided that this time should be the last, as he dipped the pen deep into the inkpot.

It was. The last blot fell on the soaked blotting-paper, and the draggled fly lay in it and did not stir. The back legs were stuck to the body; the front legs were not to be seen.

"Come on," said the boss. "Look sharp!" And he stirred it with his pen — in vain. Nothing happened or was likely to happen. The fly was dead.

The boss lifted the corpse on the end of the paper-knife and flung it into 35 the waste-paper basket. But such a grinding feeling of wretchedness seized him that he felt positively frightened. He started forward and pressed the bell for Macey.

"Bring me some fresh blotting-paper," he said sternly, "and look sharp about it." And while the old dog padded away he fell to wondering what it was he had been thinking about before. What was it? It was . . . He took out his handkerchief and passed it inside his collar. For the life of him he could not remember.

EDGAR ALLAN POE (1809–1849)

Edgar Allan Poe grew up in the home of John Allan, in Richmond, Virginia, after his mother died in 1811, and he was educated in Scotland and England for five years before completing his classical education in Richmond. After a short stint at the University of Virginia, Poe went to Boston, where he began publishing his poetry. His foster father sent him to West Point Military Academy, but Poe was expelled and moved on to New York, where he published a book of poems inspired by the Romantic movement. Mov-

Courtesy of the Library of Congress.

ing among editorial jobs in Baltimore, Richmond, and New York, Poe married his thirteen-year-old cousin Virginia Clemm. Early in his story-writing career, Poe published his only novel-length piece, *The Narrative of Arthur Gordon Pym* (1838), and the following year, he began to work in the genre of the supernatural and horrible, with the stories "William Wilson" and "The Fall of the House of Usher." He gained publicity with the detective story "The Murders in the Rue Morgue," became nationally famous with the publication of his poem "The Raven" in 1845, and died four years later in Baltimore after a drinking binge. Poe theorized that the short story writer should plan every word toward the achievement of a certain effect, and that stories should be read in a single sitting. Morbidity and dreamlike flights of fancy, for which Poe is often recognized, do not detract from his lucid crafting of suspense and his erudite control of language and symbol.

The Cask of Amontillado   *1846*

The thousand injuries of Fortunato I had borne as I best could; but when he ventured upon insult, I vowed revenge. You, who so well know the nature of my soul, will not suppose, however, that I gave utterance to a threat. *At length* I would be avenged; this was a point definitely settled—but the very definitiveness with which it was resolved precluded the idea of risk. I must not only punish, but punish with impunity. A wrong is unredressed when retribution overtakes its redresser. It is equally unredressed when the avenger fails to make himself felt as such to him who has done the wrong.

It must be understood, that neither by word nor deed had I given Fortunato cause to doubt my good-will. I continued, as was my wont, to smile in his face, and he did not perceive that my smile *now* was at the thought of his immolation.

He had a weak point—this Fortunato—although in other regards he was a man to be respected and even feared. He prided himself on his connoisseurship in wine. Few Italians have the true virtuoso spirit. For the most part their enthusiasm is adopted to suit the time and opportunity—to practise imposture upon the British and Austrian *millionnaires*. In painting and gemmary Fortunato, like his countrymen, was a quack—but in the matter of old wines he was sincere. In this respect I did not differ from him materially: I was skilful in the Italian vintages myself, and bought largely whenever I could.

It was about dusk, one evening during the supreme madness of the carnival season, that I encountered my friend. He accosted me with excessive warmth, for he had been drinking much. The man wore motley. He had on a tight-fitting parti-striped dress, and his head was surmounted by the conical cap and bells. I was so pleased to see him, that I thought I should never have done wringing his hand.

I said to him: "My dear Fortunato, you are luckily met. How remarkably 5 well you are looking to-day! But I have received a pipe° of what passes for Amontillado, and I have my doubts."

"How?" said he. "Amontillado? A pipe? Impossible! And in the middle of the carnival!"

"I have my doubts," I replied; "and I was silly enough to pay the full Amontillado price without consulting you in the matter. You were not to be found, and I was fearful of losing a bargain."

"Amontillado!"

"I have my doubts."

"Amontillado!"   10

"And I must satisfy them."

"Amontillado!"

"As you are engaged, I am on my way to Luchesi. If any one has a critical turn, it is he. He will tell me ——"

"Luchesi cannot tell Amontillado from Sherry."

"And yet some fools will have it that his taste is a match for your own."   15

"Come, let us go."

"Whither?"

"To your vaults."

---

pipe: A large keg.

"My friend, no; I will not impose upon your good nature. I perceive you have an engagement. Luchesi ——"

"I have no engagement; — come." 20

"My friend, no. It is not the engagement, but the severe cold with which I perceive you are afflicted. The vaults are insufferably damp. They are encrusted with nitre."

"Let us go, nevertheless. The cold is merely nothing. Amontillado! You have been imposed upon. And as for Luchesi, he cannot distinguish Sherry from Amontillado."

Thus speaking, Fortunato possessed himself of my arm. Putting on a mask of black silk, and drawing a *roquelaire°* closely about my person, I suffered him to hurry me to my palazzo.

There were no attendants at home; they had absconded to make merry in honor of the time. I had told them that I should not return until the morning, and had given them explicit orders not to stir from the house. These orders were sufficient, I well knew, to insure their immediate disappearance, one and all, as soon as my back was turned.

I took from their sconces two flambeaux, and giving one to Fortunato, 25 bowed him through several suites of rooms to the archway that led into the vaults. I passed down a long and winding staircase, requesting him to be cautious as he followed. We came at length to the foot of the descent, and stood together on the damp ground of the catacombs of the Montresors.

The gait of my friend was unsteady, and the bells upon his cap jingled as he strode.

"The pipe?" said he.

"It is farther on," said I; "but observe the white web-work which gleams from these cavern walls."

He turned toward me, and looked into my eyes with two filmy orbs that distilled the rheum of intoxication.

"Nitre?" he asked, at length.

"Nitre," I replied. "How long have you had that cough?" 30

"Ugh! ugh! ugh! — ugh! ugh! ugh! — ugh! ugh! ugh! — ugh! ugh! ugh! — ugh! ugh! ugh!"

My poor friend found it impossible to reply for many minutes.

"It is nothing," he said, at last.

"Come," I said, with decision, "we will go back; your health is precious. 35 You are rich, respected, admired, beloved; you are happy, as once I was. You are a man to be missed. For me it is no matter. We will go back; you will be ill, and I cannot be responsible. Besides, there is Luchesi ——"

"Enough," he said; "the cough is a mere nothing; it will not kill me. I shall not die of a cough."

"True — true," I replied; "and, indeed, I had no intention of alarming you unnecessarily; but you should use all proper caution. A draught of this Medoc will defend us from the damps."

Here I knocked off the neck of a bottle which I drew from a long row of its fellows that lay upon the mould.

"Drink," I said, presenting him the wine.

---

roquelaire: A short cloak.

He raised it to his lips with a leer. He paused and nodded to me familiarly, 40
while his bells jingled.

"I drink," he said, "to the buried that repose around us."

"And I to your long life."

He again took my arm, and we proceeded.

"These vaults," he said, "are extensive."

"The Montresors," I replied, "were a great and numerous family." 45

"I forget your arms."

"A huge human foot d'or,° in a field azure; the foot crushes a serpent rampant whose fangs are imbedded in the heel."

"And the motto?"

"Nemo me impune lacessit."°

"Good!" he said. 50

The wine sparkled in his eyes and the bells jingled. My own fancy grew warm with the Medoc. We had passed through walls of piled bones, with casks and puncheons intermingling into the inmost recesses of the catacombs. I paused again, and this time I made bold to seize Fortunato by an arm above the elbow.

"The nitre!" I said; "see, it increases. It hangs like moss upon the vaults. We are below the river's bed. The drops of moisture trickle among the bones. Come, we will go back ere it is too late. Your cough ——"

"It is nothing," he said; "let us go on. But first, another draught of the Medoc."

I broke and reached him a flagon of De Grâve. He emptied it at a breath. His eyes flashed with a fierce light. He laughed and threw the bottle upward with a gesticulation I did not understand.

I looked at him in surprise. He repeated the movement — a grotesque one. 55

"You do not comprehend?" he said.

"Not I," I replied.

"Then you are not of the brotherhood."

"How?"

"You are not of the masons." 60

"Yes, yes," I said; "yes, yes."

"You? Impossible! A mason?"

"A mason," I replied.

"A sign," he said.

"It is this," I answered, producing a trowel from beneath the folds of my 65
roquelaire.

"You jest," he exclaimed, recoiling a few paces. "But let us proceed to the Amontillado."

"Be it so," I said, replacing the tool beneath the cloak, and again offering him my arm. He leaned upon it heavily. We continued our route in search of the Amontillado. We passed through a range of low arches, descended, passed on, and descending again, arrived at a deep crypt, in which the foulness of the air caused our flambeaux rather to glow than flame.

At the most remote end of the crypt there appeared another less spacious. Its walls had been lined with human remains, piled to the vault overhead, in the

---

d'or: Of gold.
Nemo . . . lacessit (Latin): No one wounds me with impunity.

fashion of the great catacombs of Paris. Three sides of this interior crypt were still ornamented in this manner. From the fourth the bones had been thrown down, and lay promiscuously upon the earth, forming at one point a mound of some size. Within the wall thus exposed by the displacing of the bones, we perceived a still interior recess, in depth about four feet, in width three, in height six or seven. It seemed to have been constructed for no especial use within itself, but formed merely the interval between two of the colossal supports of the roof of the catacombs, and was backed by one of their circumscribing walls of solid granite.

It was in vain that Fortunato, uplifting his dull torch, endeavored to pry into the depth of the recess. Its termination the feeble light did not enable us to see.

"Proceed," I said; "herein is the Amontillado. As for Luchesi —— " 70

"He is an ignoramus," interrupted my friend, as he stepped unsteadily forward, while I followed immediately at his heels. In an instant he had reached the extremity of the niche, and finding his progress arrested by the rock, stood stupidly bewildered. A moment more and I had fettered him to the granite. In its surface were two iron staples, distant from each other about two feet, horizontally. From one of these depended a short chain, from the other a padlock. Throwing the links about his waist, it was but the work of a few seconds to secure it. He was too much astounded to resist. Withdrawing the key I stepped back from the recess.

"Pass your hand," I said, "over the wall; you cannot help feeling the nitre. Indeed it is *very* damp. Once more let me *implore* you to return. No? Then I must positively leave you. But I must first render you all the little attentions in my power."

"The Amontillado!" ejaculated my friend, not yet recovered from his astonishment.

"True," I replied; "the Amontillado."

As I said these words I busied myself among the pile of bones of which I 75 have before spoken. Throwing them aside, I soon uncovered a quantity of building stone and mortar. With these materials and with the aid of my trowel, I began vigorously to wall up the entrance of the niche.

I had scarcely laid the first tier of the masonry when I discovered that the intoxication of Fortunato had in a great measure worn off. The earliest indication I had of this was a low moaning cry from the depth of the recess. It was *not* the cry of a drunken man. There was then a long and obstinate silence. I laid the second tier, and the third, and the fourth; and then I heard the furious vibrations of the chain. The noise lasted for several minutes, during which, that I might hearken to it with the more satisfaction, I ceased my labors and sat down upon the bones. When at last the clanking subsided, I resumed the trowel, and finished without interruption the fifth, the sixth, and the seventh tier. The wall was now nearly upon a level with my breast. I again paused, and holding the flambeaux over the masonwork, threw a few feeble rays upon the figure within.

A succession of loud and shrill screams, bursting suddenly from the throat of the chained form, seemed to thrust me violently back. For a brief moment I hesitated — I trembled. Unsheathing my rapier, I began to grope with it about the recess; but the thought of an instant reassured me. I placed my hand upon the solid fabric of the catacombs, and felt satisfied. I reapproached the wall. I replied to the yells of him who clamored. I reechoed — I aided — I surpassed them in volume and in strength. I did this, and the clamorer grew still.

It was now midnight, and my task was drawing to a close. I had completed the eighth, the ninth, and the tenth tier. I had finished a portion of the last and the eleventh; there remained but a single stone to be fitted and plastered in. I struggled with its weight; I placed it partially in its destined position. But now there came from out the niche a low laugh that erected the hairs upon my head. It was succeeded by a sad voice, which I had difficulty in recognizing as that of the noble Fortunato. The voice said —

"Ha! ha! ha! — he! he! — a very good joke indeed — an excellent jest. We will have many a rich laugh about it at the palazzo — he! he! he! — over our wine — he! he! he!"

"The Amontillado!" I said. 80

"He! he! he! — he! he! he! — yes, the Amontillado. But is it not getting late? Will not they be awaiting us at the palazzo, the Lady Fortunato and the rest? Let us be gone."

"Yes," I said, "let us be gone."

"For the love of God, Montresor!"

"Yes," I said, "for the love of God!"

But to these words I hearkened in vain for a reply. I grew impatient. I called 85 aloud:

"Fortunato!"

No answer. I called again:

"Fortunato!"

No answer still, I thrust a torch through the remaining aperture and let it fall within. There came forth in return only a jingling of the bells. My heart grew sick — on account of the dampness of the catacombs. I hastened to make an end of my labor. I forced the last stone into its position; I plastered it up. Against the new masonry I re-erected the old rampart of bones. For the half of a century no mortal has disturbed them. *In pace requiescat!*°

In pace requiescat! (Latin): In peace may he rest!

KATHERINE ANNE PORTER (1890–1980)

Born in Indian Creek, Texas, Katherine Anne Porter was raised by her grandmother and married her first of four husbands at the age of sixteen. At various points in her life she made a living as a journalist and teacher as well as a stage and film performer. Her extensive travels, multiple husbands, and many acknowledged lovers provided much of the material about human relations that makes its way into her fiction. Her collections of stories include *Flowering Judas* (1930), *The Leaning Tower* (1944), and *Collected Stories* (1965), which was awarded both

Papers of Katherine Anne Porter, Special Collections, University of Maryland Libraries.

the Pulitzer Prize and the National Book Award. Her novels include *Pale Horse, Pale Rider: Three Short Novels* (1939) and *Ship of Fools* (1962). "The Witness," one of her many stories about the South, evokes reflections on the old order of slavery.

The Witness   1935

Uncle Jimbilly was so old and had spent so many years bowed over things, putting them together and taking them apart, making them over and making them do, he was bent almost double. His hands were closed and stiff from gripping objects tightly, while he worked at them, and they could not open altogether even if a child took the thick black fingers and tried to turn them back. He hobbled on a stick; his purplish skull showed through patches in his wool, which had turned greenish gray and looked as if the moths had got at it.

He mended harness and put half soles on the other Negroes' shoes, he built fences and chicken coops and barn doors; he stretched wires and put in new window panes and fixed sagging hinges and patched up roofs; he repaired carriage tops and cranky plows. Also he had a gift for carving miniature tombstones out of blocks of wood; give him almost any kind of piece of wood and he could turn out a tombstone, shaped very like the real ones, with carving, and a name and date on it if they were needed. They were often needed, for some small beast or bird was always dying and having to be buried with proper ceremonies: the cart draped as a hearse, a shoe-box coffin with a pall over it, a profuse floral outlay, and, of course, a tombstone. As he worked, turning the long blade of his bowie knife deftly in circles to cut a flower, whittling and smoothing the back and sides, stopping now and then to hold it at arm's length and examine it with one eye closed, Uncle Jimbilly would talk in a low, broken, abstracted murmur, as if to himself; but he was really saying something he meant one to hear. Sometimes it would be an incomprehensible ghost story; listen ever so carefully, at the end it was impossible to decide whether Uncle Jimbilly himself had seen the ghost, whether it was a real ghost at all, or only another man dressed like one; and he dwelt much on the horrors of slave times.

"Dey used to take 'em out and tie 'em down and whup 'em," he muttered, "wid gret big leather strops inch thick long as yo' ahm, wid round holes bored in 'em so's evey time dey hit 'em de hide and de meat done come off dey bones in little round chunks. And wen dey had whupped 'em wid de strop till dey backs was all raw and bloody, dey spread dry cawnshucks on dey backs and set 'em afire and pahched 'em, and den dey poured vinega all ovah 'em . . . Yassuh. And den, the ve'y nex day dey'd got to git back to work in the fiels or dey'd do the same thing right ovah agin. Yassah. Dat was it. If dey didn't git back to work dey got it all right ovah agin."

The children—three of them: a serious, prissy older girl of ten, a thoughtful sad looking boy of eight, and a quick flighty little girl of six—sat disposed around Uncle Jimbilly and listened with faint tinglings of embarrassment. They knew, of course, that once upon a time Negroes had been slaves; but they had all been freed long ago and were now only servants. It was hard to realize that Uncle Jimbilly had been born in slavery, as the Negroes were always saying. The children thought that Uncle Jimbilly had got over his slavery very well. Since they had known him, he had never done a single thing that anyone told him to do. He did his work just as he pleased and when he pleased. If you wanted a tombstone, you had to be very careful about the way you asked for it. Nothing could have been more impersonal and faraway than his tone and manner of talking about slavery, but they wriggled a little and felt guilty. Paul would have changed the subject, but Miranda, the little quick one, wanted to know the worst. "Did they act like that to you, Uncle Jimbilly?" she asked.

"No, *mam*," said Uncle Jimbilly. "Now whut name you want on dis one? 5 Dey nevah did. Dey done 'em dat way in the rice swamps. I always worked right here close to the house or in town with Miss Sophia. Down in the swamps . . ."

"Didn't they ever die, Uncle Jimbilly?" asked Paul.

"Cose dey died," said Uncle Jimbilly, "cose dey died—dey died," he went on, pursing his mouth gloomily, "by de thousands and tens upon thousands."

"Can you carve 'Safe in Heaven' on that, Uncle Jimbilly?" asked Maria in her pleasant, mincing voice.

"To put over a tame jackrabbit, Missy?" asked Uncle Jimbilly indignantly. He was very religious. "A heathen like dat? No, *mam*. In de swamps dey used to stake 'em out all day and all night, and all day and all night and all day wid dey hans and feet tied so dey couldn't scretch and let de muskeeters eat 'em alive. De muskeeters 'ud bite 'em tell dey was all swole up like a balloon all over, and you could heah 'em howlin and prayin all ovah the swamp. Yassuh. Dat was it. And nary a drop of watah noh a moufful of braid . . . Yassuh, dat's it. Lawd, dey done it. Hosanna! Now take dis yere tombstone and don' bother me no more . . . or I'll . . ."

Uncle Jimbilly was apt to be suddenly annoyed and you never knew why. He 10 was easily put out about things, but his threats were always so exorbitant that not even the most credulous child could be terrified by them. He was always going to do something quite horrible to somebody and then he was going to dispose of the remains in a revolting manner. He was going to skin somebody alive and nail the hide on the barn door, or he was just getting ready to cut off somebody's ears with a hatchet and pin them on Bongo, the crop-eared brindle dog. He was often all prepared in his mind to pull somebody's teeth and make a set of false teeth for Ole Man Ronk . . . Ole Man Ronk was a tramp who had been living all summer in the little cabin behind the smokehouse. He got his rations along with the Negroes and sat all day mumbling his naked gums. He had skimpy black whiskers which appeared to be set in wax, and angry red eyelids. He took morphine, it was said; but what morphine might be, or how he took it, or why, no one seemed to know . . . Nothing could have been more unpleasant than the notion that one's teeth might be given to Ole Man Ronk.

The reason why Uncle Jimbilly never did any of these things he threatened was, he said, because he never could get round to them. He always had so much other work on hand he never seemed to get caught up on it. But some day, somebody was going to get a mighty big surprise, and meanwhile everybody had better look out.

JOHN UPDIKE (1932–2009)

A biographical note and photograph of John Updike appear on page 651 before his story "Outage."

A & P   *1961*

In walks these three girls in nothing but bathing suits. I'm in the third checkout slot, with my back to the door, so I don't see them until they're over by the bread. The one that caught my eye first was the one in the plaid green two-piece.

She was a chunky kid, with a good tan and a sweet broad soft-looking can with those two crescents of white just under it, where the sun never seems to hit, at the top of the backs of her legs. I stood there with my hand on a box of HiHo crackers trying to remember if I rang it up or not. I ring it up again and the customer starts giving me hell. She's one of these cash-register-watchers, a witch about fifty with rouge on her cheekbones and no eyebrows, and I know it made her day to trip me up. She'd been watching cash registers for fifty years and probably never seen a mistake before.

By the time I got her feathers smoothed and her goodies into a bag — she gives me a little snort in passing, if she'd been born at the right time they would have burned her over in Salem — by the time I get her on her way the girls had circled around the bread and were coming back, without a pushcart, back my way along the counters, in the aisle between the checkouts and the Special bins. They didn't even have shoes on. There was this chunky one, with the two-piece — it was bright green and the seams on the bra were still sharp and her belly was still pretty pale so I guessed she just got it (the suit) — there was this one, with one of those chubby berry-faces, the lips all bunched together under her nose, this one, and a tall one, with black hair that hadn't quite frizzed right, and one of these sunburns right across under the eyes, and a chin that was too long — you know, the kind of girl other girls think is very "striking" and "attractive" but never quite makes it, as they very well know, which is why they like her so much — and then the third one, that wasn't quite so tall. She was the queen. She kind of led them, the other two peeking around and making their shoulders round. She didn't look around, not this queen, she just walked straight on slowly, on these long white prima-donna legs. She came down a little hard on her heels, as if she didn't walk in her bare feet that much, putting down her heels and then letting the weight move along to her toes as if she was testing the floor with every step, putting a little deliberate extra action into it. You never know for sure how girls' minds work (do you really think it's a mind in there or just a little buzz like a bee in a glass jar?) but you got the idea she had talked the other two into coming in here with her, and now she was showing them how to do it, walk slow and hold yourself straight.

She had on a kind of dirty-pink — beige maybe, I don't know — bathing suit with a little nubble all over it and, what got me, the straps were down. They were off her shoulders looped loose around the cool tops of her arms, and I guess as a result the suit had slipped a little on her, so all around the top of the cloth there was this shining rim. If it hadn't been there you wouldn't have known there could have been anything whiter than those shoulders. With the straps pushed off, there was nothing between the top of the suit and the top of her head except just *her,* this clean bare plane of the top of her chest down from the shoulder bones like a dented sheet of metal tilted in the light. I mean, it was more than pretty.

She had sort of oaky hair that the sun and salt had bleached, done up in a bun that was unraveling, and a kind of prim face. Walking into the A & P with your straps down, I suppose it's the only kind of face you *can* have. She held her head so high her neck, coming up out of those white shoulders, looked kind of stretched, but I didn't mind. The longer her neck was, the more of her there was.

She must have felt in the corner of her eye me and over my shoulder Stoke- sie in the second slot watching, but she didn't tip. Not this queen. She kept her eyes moving across the racks, and stopped, and turned so slow it made my stomach rub the inside of my apron, and buzzed to the other two, who kind of huddled against her for relief, and then they all three of them went up the cat-and-dogfood-breakfast-cereal-macaroni-rice-raisins-seasonings-spreads-spaghetti-soft-drinks-crackers-and-cookies aisle. From the third slot I look straight up this aisle to the meat counter, and I watched them all the way. The fat one with the tan sort of fumbled with the cookies, but on second thought she put the package back. The sheep pushing their carts down the aisle — the girls were walking against the usual traffic (not that we have one-way signs or anything) — were pretty hilarious. You could see them, when Queenie's white shoulders dawned on them, kind of jerk, or hop, or hiccup, but their eyes snapped back to their own baskets and on they pushed. I bet you could set off dynamite in an A & P and the people would by and large keep reaching and checking oatmeal off their lists and muttering "Let me see, there was a third thing, began with A, asparagus, no, ah, yes, applesauce!" or whatever it is they do mutter. But there was no doubt, this jiggled them. A few houseslaves in pin curlers even looked around after pushing their carts past to make sure what they had seen was correct.

You know, it's one thing to have a girl in a bathing suit down on the beach, where what with the glare nobody can look at each other much anyway, and another thing in the cool of the A & P, under the fluorescent lights, against all those stacked packages, with her feet paddling along naked over our checkerboard green-and-cream rubber-tile floor.

"Oh Daddy," Stokesie said beside me. "I feel so faint."

"Darling," I said. "Hold me tight." Stokesie's married, with two babies chalked up on his fuselage already, but as far as I can tell that's the only difference. He's twenty-two, and I was nineteen this April.

"Is it done?" he asks, the responsible married man finding his voice. I forgot to say he thinks he's going to be manager some sunny day, maybe in 1990 when it's called the Great Alexandrov and Petrooshki Tea Company or something.

What he meant was, our town is five miles from a beach, with a big summer colony out on the Point, but we're right in the middle of town, and the women generally put on a shirt or shorts or something before they get out of the car into the street. And anyway these are usually women with six children and varicose veins mapping their legs and nobody, including them, could care less. As I say, we're right in the middle of town, and if you stand at our front doors you can see two banks and the Congregational church and the newspaper store and three real-estate offices and about twenty-seven old freeloaders tearing up Central Street because the sewer broke again. It's not as if we're on the Cape, we're north of Boston and there's people in this town haven't seen the ocean for twenty years.

The girls had reached the meat counter and were asking McMahon something. He pointed, they pointed, and they shuffled out of sight behind a pyramid of Diet Delight peaches. All that was left for us to see was old McMahon patting his mouth and looking after them sizing up their joints. Poor kids, I began to feel sorry for them, they couldn't help it.

Now here comes the sad part of the story, at least my family says it's sad, but I don't think it's so sad myself. The store's pretty empty, it being Thursday afternoon, so there was nothing much to do except lean on the register and wait for the girls to show up again. The whole store was like a pinball machine and I didn't know which tunnel they'd come out of. After a while they come around out of the far aisle, around the light bulbs, records at discount of the Caribbean Six or Tony Martin Sings or some such gunk you wonder they waste the wax on, sixpacks of candy bars, and plastic toys done up in cellophane that fall apart when a kid looks at them anyway. Around they come, Queenie still leading the way, and holding a little gray jar in her hands. Slots Three through Seven are unmanned and I could see her wondering between Stokes and me, but Stokesie with his usual luck draws an old party in baggy gray pants who stumbles up with four giant cans of pineapple juice (what do these bums *do* with all that pineapple juice? I've often asked myself). So the girls come to me. Queenie puts down the jar and I take it into my fingers icy cold. Kingfish Fancy Herring Snacks in Pure Sour Cream: 49¢. Now her hands are empty, not a ring or a bracelet, bare as God made them, and I wonder where the money's coming from. Still with that prim look she lifts a folded dollar bill out of the hollow at the center of her nubbled pink top. The jar went heavy in my hand. Really, I thought that was so cute.

Then everybody's luck begins to run out. Lengel comes in from haggling with a truck full of cabbages on the lot and is about to scuttle into that door marked MANAGER behind which he hides all day when the girls touch his eye. Lengel's pretty dreary, teaches Sunday school and the rest, but he doesn't miss that much. He comes over and says, "Girls, this isn't the beach."

Queenie blushes, though maybe it's just a brush of sunburn I was noticing for the first time, now that she was so close. "My mother asked me to pick up a jar of herring snacks." Her voice kind of startled me, the way voices do when you see the people first, coming out so flat and dumb yet kind of tony, too, the way it ticked over "pick up" and "snacks." All of a sudden I slid right down her voice into the living room. Her father and the other men were standing around in ice-cream coats and bow ties and the women were in sandals picking up herring snacks on toothpicks off a big glass plate and they were all holding drinks the color of water with olives and sprigs of mint in them. When my parents have somebody over they get lemonade and if it's a real racy affair Schlitz in tall glasses with "They'll Do It Every Time" cartoons stenciled on.

"That's all right," Lengel said. "But this isn't the beach." His repeating this struck me as funny, as if it had just occurred to him, and he had been thinking all these years the A & P was a great big dune and he was the head lifeguard. He didn't like my smiling — as I say he doesn't miss much — but he concentrates on giving the girls that sad Sunday-school-superintendent stare.

Queenie's blush is no sunburn now, and the plump one in plaid, that I liked better from the back — a really sweet can — pipes up, "We weren't doing any shopping. We just came in for the one thing."

"That makes no difference," Lengel tells her, and I could see from the way his eyes went that he hadn't noticed she was wearing a two-piece before. "We want you decently dressed when you come in here."

"We *are* decent," Queenie says suddenly, her lower lip pushing, getting sore now that she remembers her place, a place from which the crowd that runs the A & P must look pretty crummy. Fancy Herring Snacks flashed in her very blue eyes.

"Girls, I don't want to argue with you. After this come in here with your shoulders covered. It's our policy." He turns his back. That's policy for you. Policy is what the kingpins want. What the others want is juvenile delinquency.

All this while, the customers had been showing up with their carts but, 20 you know, sheep, seeing a scene, they had all bunched up on Stokesie, who shook open a paper bag as gently as peeling a peach, not wanting to miss a word. I could feel in the silence everybody getting nervous, most of all Lengel, who asks me, "Sammy, have you rung up their purchase?"

I thought and said "No" but it wasn't about that I was thinking. I go through the punches, 4, 9, GROC. TOT — it's more complicated than you think, and after you do it often enough, it begins to make a little song, that you hear words to, in my case "Hello *(bing)* there, you *(gung)* hap-py *pee*-pul *(splat)!*" — the *splat* being the drawer flying out. I uncrease the bill, tenderly as you may imagine, it just having come from between the two smoothest scoops of vanilla I had ever known were there, and pass a half and a penny into her narrow pink palm, and nestle the herrings in a bag and twist its neck and hand it over, all the time thinking.

The girls, and who'd blame them, are in a hurry to get out, so I say "I quit" to Lengel quick enough for them to hear, hoping they'll stop and watch me, their unsuspected hero. They keep right on going, into the electric eye; the door flies open and they flicker across the lot to their car, Queenie and Plaid and Big Tall Goony-Goony (not that as raw material she was so bad), leaving me with Lengel and a kink in his eyebrow.

"Did you say something, Sammy?"

"I said I quit."

"I thought you did."   25

"You didn't have to embarrass them."

"It was they who were embarrassing us."

I started to say something that came out "Fiddle-de-doo." It's a saying of my grandmother's, and I know she would have been pleased.

"I don't think you know what you're saying," Lengel said.

"I know you don't," I said. "But I do." I pull the bow at the back of my 30 apron and start shrugging it off my shoulders. A couple customers that had been heading for my slot begin to knock against each other, like scared pigs in a chute.

Lengel sighs and begins to look very patient and old and gray. He's been a friend of my parents for years. "Sammy, you don't want to do this to your Mom and Dad," he tells me. It's true, I don't. But it seems to me that once you begin a gesture it's fatal not to go through with it. I fold the apron, "Sammy" stitched in red on the pocket, and put it on the counter, and drop the bow tie on top of it. The bow tie is theirs, if you've ever wondered. "You'll feel this for the rest of your life," Lengel says, and I know that's true, too, but remembering how he made the pretty girl blush makes me so scrunchy inside I punch the No Sale tab and the machine whirs "pee-pul" and the drawer splats out. One advantage to this scene taking place in summer, I can follow this up with a clean exit, there's no fumbling around getting your coat and galoshes, I just saunter into the electric eye in my white shirt that my mother ironed the night before, and the door heaves itself open, and outside the sunshine is skating around on the asphalt.

I look around for my girls, but they're gone, of course. There wasn't anybody but some young married screaming with her children about some candy they didn't get by the door of a powder-blue Falcon station wagon. Looking back in the big windows, over the bags of peat moss and aluminum lawn furniture stacked on the pavement, I could see Lengel in my place in the slot, checking the sheep through. His face was dark gray and his back stiff, as if he'd just had an injection of iron, and my stomach kind of fell as I felt how hard the world was going to be to me hereafter.

POETRY

POETRY

The Elements
of Poetry

21

Reading Poetry

Ink runs from the corners of my mouth.
There is no happiness like mine.
I have been eating poetry.
— MARK STRAND

© Lilo Raymond.

READING POETRY RESPONSIVELY

Perhaps the best way to begin reading poetry responsively is not to allow
yourself to be intimidated by it. Come to it, initially at least, the way you
might listen to a song on the radio. You probably listen to a song several
times before you hear it all, before you have a sense of how it works, where
it's going, and how it gets there. You don't worry about analyzing a song
when you listen to it, even though after repeated experiences with it you
know and anticipate a favorite part and know, on some level, why it works
for you. Give yourself a chance to respond to poetry. The hardest work has
already been done by the poet, so all you need to do at the start is listen for
the pleasure produced by the poet's arrangement of words.

Try reading the following poem aloud. Read it aloud before you read it
silently. You may stumble once or twice, but you'll make sense of it if you
pay attention to its punctuation and don't stop at the end of every line
where there is no punctuation. The title gives you an initial sense of what
the poem is about.

MARGE PIERCY (B. 1936)

The Secretary Chant

1973

My hips are a desk.
From my ears hang
chains of paper clips.
Rubber bands form my hair.
My breasts are wells of mimeograph ink.   5
My feet bear casters.
Buzz. Click.
My head is a badly organized file.
My head is a switchboard
where crossed lines crackle.   10
Press my fingers
and in my eyes appear
credit and debit.
Zing. Tinkle.
My navel is a reject button.   15
From my mouth issue canceled reams.
Swollen, heavy, rectangular
I am about to be delivered
of a baby
Xerox machine.   20
File me under W
because I wonce
was
a woman.

What is your response to this secretary's chant? The point is simple
enough — she feels dehumanized by her office functions — but the pleasures are manifold. Piercy makes the speaker's voice sound mechanical by
using short bursts of sound and by having her make repetitive, flat, matter-
of-fact statements ("My breasts . . . My feet . . . My head . . . My navel").
"The Secretary Chant" makes a serious statement about how such women
are reduced to functionaries. The point is made, however, with humor, as
we are asked to visualize the misappropriation of the secretary's body — her
identity — as it is transformed into little more than a piece of office equipment, which seems to be breaking down in the final lines, when we learn
that she "wonce / was / a woman." Is there the slightest hint of something
subversive in this misspelling of "once"? Maybe so, but the humor is clear
enough, particularly if you try to make a drawing of what this dehumanized secretary has become.

The next poem creates a different kind of mood. Think about the title,
"Those Winter Sundays," before you begin reading the poem. What associations do you have with winter Sundays? What emotions does the phrase
evoke in you?

ROBERT HAYDEN (1913–1980)

Those Winter Sundays   1962

Sundays too my father got up early
and put his clothes on in the blueblack cold,
then with cracked hands that ached
from labor in the weekday weather made
banked fires blaze. No one ever thanked him.   5

I'd wake and hear the cold splintering, breaking.
When the rooms were warm, he'd call,
and slowly I would rise and dress,
fearing the chronic angers of that house,

Speaking indifferently to him,   10
who had driven out the cold
and polished my good shoes as well.
What did I know, what did I know
of love's austere and lonely offices?

Does the poem match the feelings you have about winter Sundays? Either way, your response can be useful in reading the poem. For most of us, Sundays are days at home; they might be cozy and pleasant experiences or they might be dull and depressing. Whatever they are, Sundays are more evocative than, say, Tuesdays. Hayden uses that response to call forth a sense of missed opportunity in the poem. The person who reflects on those winter Sundays didn't know until much later how much he had to thank his father for "love's austere and lonely offices." This is a poem about a cold past and a present reverence for his father—elements brought together by the phrase "Winter Sundays." *His* father? You may have noticed that the poem doesn't use a masculine pronoun; hence the voice could be a woman's. Does the gender of the voice make any difference to your reading? Would it make any difference about which details are included or what language is used?

What is most important about your initial readings of a poem is that you ask questions. If you read responsively, you'll find yourself asking all kinds of questions about the words, descriptions, sounds, and structure of a poem. The specifics of those questions will be generated by the particular poem. We don't, for example, ask how humor is achieved in "Those Winter Sundays" because there is none, but it is worth asking what kind of tone is established by the description of "the chronic angers of that house." The remaining chapters in this part of the book will help you to formulate and answer questions about a variety of specific elements in poetry, such as speaker, image, metaphor, symbol, rhyme, and rhythm. For the moment, however, read the following poem several times and note your response at different points in the poem. Then write down a half-dozen or so questions about what produces your response to the poem. To answer questions, it's best to know first what the questions are, and that's what the rest of this chapter is about.

JOHN UPDIKE (1932–2009)

Dog's Death 1969

She must have been kicked unseen or brushed by a car.
Too young to know much, she was beginning to learn
To use the newspapers spread on the kitchen floor
And to win, wetting there, the words, "Good dog! Good dog!"

We thought her shy malaise was a shot reaction. 5
The autopsy disclosed a rupture in her liver.
As we teased her with play, blood was filling her skin
And her heart was learning to lie down forever.

Monday morning, as the children were noisily fed
And sent to school, she crawled beneath the youngest's bed. 10
We found her twisted and limp but still alive.
In the car to the vet's, on my lap, she tried

To bite my hand and died. I stroked her warm fur
And my wife called in a voice imperious with tears.
Though surrounded by love that would have upheld her, 15
Nevertheless she sank and, stiffening, disappeared.

Back home, we found that in the night her frame,
Drawing near to dissolution, had endured the shame
Of diarrhoea and had dragged across the floor
To a newspaper carelessly left there. *Good dog.* 20

Here's a simple question to get started with your own questions: What would the poem's effect have been if Updike had titled it "Good Dog" instead of "Dog's Death"?

THE PLEASURE OF WORDS

The impulse to create and appreciate poetry is as basic to human experience as language itself. Although no one can point to the precise origins of poetry, it is one of the most ancient of the arts, because it has existed ever since human beings discovered pleasure in language. The tribal ceremonies of peoples without written languages suggest that the earliest primitive cultures incorporated rhythmic patterns of words into their rituals. These chants, very likely accompanied by the music of a simple beat and the dance of a measured step, expressed what people regarded as significant and memorable in their lives. They echoed the concerns of the chanters and the listeners by chronicling acts of bravery, fearsome foes, natural disasters, mysterious events, births, deaths, and whatever else brought people pain or pleasure, bewilderment or revelation. Later cultures, such as the ancient Greeks, made poetry an integral part of religion.

Thus, from its very beginnings, poetry has been associated with what has mattered most to people. These concerns — whether natural or supernatural — can, of course, be expressed without vivid images, rhythmic patterns, and pleasing sounds, but human beings have always sensed a magic in words that goes beyond rational, logical understanding. Poetry is not simply a method of communication; it is a unique experience in itself.

What is special about poetry? What makes it valuable? Why should we read it? How is reading it different from reading prose? To begin with, poetry pervades our world in a variety of forms, ranging from advertising jingles to song lyrics. These may seem to be a long way from the chants heard around a primitive campfire, but they serve some of the same purposes. Like poems printed in a magazine or book, primitive chants, catchy jingles, and popular songs attempt to stir the imagination through the carefully measured use of words.

Although reading poetry usually makes more demands than does the kind of reading we use to skim a magazine or newspaper, the appreciation of poetry comes naturally enough to anyone who enjoys playing with words. Play is an important element of poetry. Consider, for example, how the following words appeal to the children who gleefully chant them in playgrounds:

> I scream, you scream
> We all scream
> For ice cream.

These lines are an exuberant evocation of the joy of ice cream. Indeed, chanting the words turns out to be as pleasurable as eating ice cream. In poetry, the expression of the idea is as important as the idea expressed.

But is "I scream . . ." poetry? Some poets and literary critics would say that it certainly is one kind of poem because the children who chant it experience some of the pleasures of poetry in its measured beat and repeated sounds. However, other poets and critics would define poetry more narrowly and insist, for a variety of reasons, that this isn't true poetry but merely **doggerel,** a term used for lines whose subject matter is trite and whose rhythm and sounds are monotonously heavy-handed.

Although probably no one would argue that "I scream . . ." is a great poem, it does contain some poetic elements that appeal, at the very least, to children. Does that make it poetry? The answer depends on one's definition, but poetry has a way of breaking loose from definitions. Because there are nearly as many definitions of poetry as there are poets, Edwin Arlington Robinson's succinct observations are useful: "poetry has two outstanding characteristics. One is that it is undefinable. The other is that it is eventually unmistakable."

This comment places more emphasis on how a poem affects a reader than on how a poem is defined. By characterizing poetry as "undefinable," Robinson acknowledges that it can include many different purposes, subjects, emotions, styles, and forms. What effect does the following poem have on you?

WILLIAM HATHAWAY (B. 1944)

Oh, Oh
1982

My girl and I amble a country lane,
moo cows chomping daisies, our own
sweet saliva green with grass stems.
"Look, look," she says at the crossing,
"the choo-choo's light is on." And sure
enough, right smack dab in the middle
of maple dappled summer sunlight
is the lit headlight—so funny.
An arm waves to us from the black window.
We wave gaily to the arm. "When I hear
trains at night I dream of being president,"
I say dreamily. "And me first lady," she
says loyally. So when the last boxcars,
named after wonderful, faraway places,
and the caboose chuckle by we look   15
eagerly to the road ahead. And there,
poised and growling, are fifty Hell's Angels.

© William Hathaway.

A SAMPLE CLOSE READING

An Annotated Version of "Oh, Oh"

After you've read a poem two or three times, a deeper, closer reading—line by line, word by word, syllable by syllable—will help you discover even more about the poem. Ask yourself: What happens (or does not happen) in the poem? What are the poem's central ideas? How do the poem's words, images, and sounds, for example, contribute to its meaning? What is the poem's overall tone? How is the poem put together?

You can flesh out your close reading by writing your responses in the margins of the page. The following interpretive notes offer but one way to read Hathaway's poem.

The title offers an interjection expressing strong emotion and foreboding.

WILLIAM HATHAWAY (B. 1944)
Oh, Oh

1982

The informal language conjures up an idyllic picture of a walk in the country, where the sights, sounds, and tastes are full of pleasure.

The carefully orchestrated *d*s, *m*s, *p*s, and *s*s of lines 6–8 create sounds that are meant to be savored.

Filled with confidence and hope, the couple imagines a successful future together in exotic locations. Even the train is happy for them as it "chuckle[s]" in approval of their dreams.

The visual effect of the many *o*s in lines 1–5 (and 15) suggests an innocent, wide-eyed openness to experience while the repetitive *oo* sounds echo a kind of reassuring, satisfied cooing.

"Right smack dab in the middle" of the poem, the "black window" hints that all is not well.

Not until the very last line does "the road ahead" yield a terrifying surprise. The strategically "poised" final line derails the leisurely movement of the couple and brings their happy story to a dead stop. The emotional reversal parked in the last few words awaits the reader as much as it does the couple. The sight and sound of the motorcycle gang signal that what seemed like heaven is, in reality, hell: Oh, oh.

My girl and I amble a country lane,
moo cows chomping daisies, our own
sweet saliva green with grass stems.
"Look, look," she says at the crossing,
"the choo-choo's light is on." And sure   5
enough, right smack dab in the middle
of maple dappled summer sunlight
is the lit headlight — so funny.
An arm waves to us from the black window.
We wave gaily to the arm. "When I hear   10
trains at night I dream of being president,"
I say dreamily. "And me first lady," she
says loyally. So when the last boxcars,
named after wonderful, faraway places,
and the caboose chuckle by we look   15
eagerly to the road ahead. And there,
poised and growling, are fifty Hell's Angels.

MORE HELP WITH CLOSE READING

Close readings of Andrew Marvell's "To His Coy Mistress," Elizabeth Bishop's "The Fish," and Theodore Roethke's "My Papa's Waltz" are available at *The Student Center for The Bedford Introduction to Literature* (www.bedfordstmartins.com/meyerlit). As you explore each poem, highlighted sections are annotated with critical interpretations and explanations of literary elements at work.

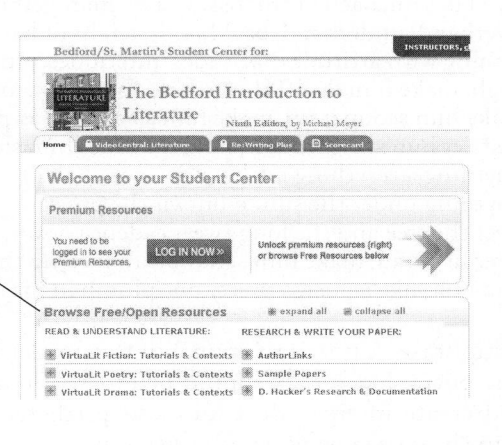

Hathaway's poem serves as a convenient reminder that poetry can be full of surprises. Full of confidence, this couple, like the reader, is unprepared for the shock to come. When we see those "fifty Hell's Angels," we are confronted with something like a bucket of cold water in the face.

But even though our expectations are abruptly and powerfully reversed, we are finally invited to view the entire episode from a safe distance — the distance provided by the delightful humor in this poem. After all, how seriously can we take a poem that is titled "Oh, Oh"? The poet has his way with us, but we are brought in on the joke, too. The terror takes on comic proportions as the innocent couple is confronted by no fewer than *fifty* Hell's Angels. This is the kind of raucous overkill that informs a short animated film produced some years ago titled *Bambi Meets Godzilla:* you might not have seen it, but you know how it ends. The poem's good humor comes through when we realize how pathetically inadequate the response of "Oh, Oh" is to the circumstances.

As you can see, reading a description of what happens in a poem is not the same as experiencing a poem. The exuberance of "I scream . . ." and the surprise of Hathaway's "Oh, Oh" are in the hearing or reading rather than in the retelling. A *paraphrase* is a prose restatement of the central ideas of a poem in your own language. Consider the difference between the following poem and the paraphrase that follows it. What is missing from the paraphrase?

ROBERT FRANCIS (1901–1987)

Catch   1950

Two boys uncoached are tossing a poem together,
Overhand, underhand, backhand, sleight of hand, every hand,
Teasing with attitudes, latitudes, interludes, altitudes,
High, make him fly off the ground for it, low, make him stoop,
Make him scoop it up, make him as-almost-as-possible miss it,   5
Fast, let him sting from it, now, now fool him slowly,
Anything, everything tricky, risky, nonchalant,
Anything under the sun to outwit the prosy,
Over the tree and the long sweet cadence down,
Over his head, make him scramble to pick up the meaning,   10
And now, like a posy, a pretty one plump in his hands.

Paraphrase: A poet's relationship to a reader is similar to a game of catch. The poem, like a ball, should be pitched in a variety of ways to challenge and create interest. Boredom and predictability must be avoided if the game is to be engaging and satisfying.

. . .

A paraphrase can help us achieve a clearer understanding of a poem, but, unlike a poem, it misses all of the sport and fun. It is the poem that "outwit[s] the prosy" because the poem serves as an example of what it suggests poetry should be. Moreover, the two players — the poet and the reader — are "uncoached." They know how the game is played, but their expectations do not preclude spontaneity and creativity or their ability to surprise and be surprised. The solid pleasure of the workout — of reading poetry — is the satisfaction derived from exercising your imagination and intellect.

That pleasure is worth emphasizing. Poetry uses language to move and delight even when it includes a cast of fifty Hell's Angels. The pleasure is in having the poem work its spell on us. For that to happen, it is best to relax and enjoy poetry rather than worry about definitions of it. Pay attention to what the poet throws you. We read poems for emotional and intellectual discovery — to feel and to experience something about the world and ourselves. The ideas in poetry — what can be paraphrased in prose — are important, but the real value of a poem consists in the words that work their magic by allowing us to feel, see, and be more than we were before. Perhaps the best way to approach a poem is similar to what Francis's "Catch" implies: expect to be surprised, stay on your toes, and concentrate on the delivery.

A SAMPLE STUDENT ANALYSIS

Tossing Metaphors Together in "Catch"

The following sample paper on Robert Francis's "Catch" was written in response to an assignment that asked students to discuss the use of metaphor in the poem. Notice that Chris Leggett's paper is clearly focused and well organized. His discussion of the use of metaphor in the poem stays on track from beginning to end without any detours concerning unrelated topics (for a definition of **metaphor,** see pp. 2134–35). His title draws on the central metaphor of the poem, and he organizes the paper around four key words used in the poem: "attitudes, latitudes, interludes, altitudes." These constitute the heart of the paper's four substantive paragraphs, and they are effectively framed by introductory and concluding paragraphs. Moreover, the transitions between paragraphs clearly indicate that the author was not merely tossing a paper together.

Chris Leggett

Professor Lyles

English 203-1

November 9, 2009

Tossing Metaphors Together in "Catch"

Exploration of the meaning of the word *catch*.

The word "catch" is an attention getter. It usually means something is about to be hurled at someone and that he or she is expected to catch it. "Catch" can also signal a challenge to another player if the toss is purposefully difficult. Robert Francis, in his poem "Catch," uses the extended metaphor of two boys playing catch to explore the considerations a poet makes when

Thesis statement identifying purpose of poem's metaphors.

"tossing a poem together" (line 1). Line 3 of "Catch" enumerates these considerations metaphorically as "attitudes, latitudes, interludes, [and] altitudes." While regular prose is typically straightforward and easily understood, poetry usually takes great effort to understand and appreciate. To exemplify this,

Reference to specific language in poem, around which the paper is organized.

Francis presents the reader not with a normal game of catch with the ball flying back and forth in a repetitive and predictable fashion, but with a physically challenging game in which one must concentrate, scramble, and exert oneself to catch the ball, as one must stretch the intellect to truly grasp a poem.

Introductory analysis of the poem's purpose.

The first consideration mentioned by Francis is attitude. Attitude, when applied to the game of catch, indicates the ball's pitch in flight—upward, downward, or straight. It could also describe the players' attitudes toward each other or toward the game in general. Below this literal level lies *attitude*'s

Analysis of the meaning of *attitude* in the poem.

meaning in relation to poetry. Attitude in this case represents a poem's tone. A poet may "teas[e] with attitude" (3) by experimenting with different tones to achieve the desired mood. The underlying tone of "Catch" is a playful one, set

Discussion of how the attitude metaphor contributes to poem's tone.

and reinforced by the use of a game. This playfulness is further reinforced by such words and phrases as "teasing" (3), "outwit" (8), and "fool him" (6).

Considered also in the metaphorical game of catch is latitude, which, when applied to the game, suggests the range the object may be thrown—

Analysis of the meaning of *latitude* in the poem.

how high, how low, or how far. Poetic latitude, along similar lines, concerns a poem's breadth, or the scope of topic. Taken one level further, latitude suggests freedom from normal restraints or limitations, indicating the ability to

Leggett 2

go outside the norm to find originality of expression. The entire game of catch described in Francis's poem reaches outside the normal expectations of something being merely tossed back and forth in a predictable manner. The ball is thrown in almost every conceivable fashion, "overhand, underhand . . . every hand" (2). Other terms describing the throws—such as "tricky," "risky," "fast," "slowly," and "Anything under the sun"(6-8)—express endless latitude for avoiding predictability in Francis's game of catch and metaphorically in writing poetry.

> Discussion of how the latitude metaphor contributes to the poem's scope and message.

During a game of catch the ball may be thrown at different intervals, establishing a steady rhythm or a broken, irregular one. Other intervening features, such as the field being played on or the weather, could also affect the game. These features of the game are alluded to in the poem by the use of the word "interludes." "Interlude" in the poetic sense represents the poem's form, which can similarly establish or diminish rhythm or enhance meaning. Lines 6 and 9, respectively, show a broken and a flowing rhythm. Line 6 begins rapidly as a hard toss that stings the catcher's hand is described. The rhythm of the line is immediately slowed, however, by the word "now" followed by a comma, followed by the rest of the line. In contrast, line 9 flows smoothly as the reader visualizes the ball flying over the tree and sailing downward. The words chosen for this line function perfectly. The phrase "the long sweet cadence down" establishes a sweet rhythm that reads smoothly and rolls off the tongue easily. The choice of diction not only affects the poem's rhythmic flow but also establishes through connotative language the various levels at which the poem can be understood, represented in "Catch" as altitude.

> Analysis of the meaning of *interlude* in the poem.

> Discussion of how the interlude metaphor contributes to the poem's form and rhythm.

While "altitudes" when referring to the game of catch means how high an object is thrown, in poetry it could refer to the level of diction, lofty or down-to-earth, formal or informal. It suggests also the levels at which a poem can be comprehended, the literal as well as the interpretive. In Francis's game of catch, the ball is thrown high to make the player reach, low to "make him stoop" (4), or "over his head [to] make him scramble" (10), implying that the player should have to exert himself to catch it. So too, then, should the reader of poetry put great effort into understanding the full meaning of a poem. Francis exemplifies

> Analysis of the meaning of *altitudes* in the poem.

Discussion of how the altitude metaphor contributes to the poem's literal and symbolic meanings, with references to specific language.

this consideration in writing poetry by giving "Catch" not only an enjoyable literal meaning concerning the game of catch, but also a rich metaphorical meaning—reflecting the process of writing poetry. Francis uses several phrases and words with multiple meanings. The phrase "tossing a poem to-gether" (1) can be understood as tossing something back and forth or the process of constructing a poem. While "prosy" (8) suggests prose itself, it also means the mundane or the ordinary. In the poem's final line the word "posy" of course represents a flower, while it is also a variant of the word "poesy," meaning poetry, or the practice of composing poetry.

Conclusion summarizing ideas explored in paper.

Francis effectively describes several considerations to be taken in writing poetry in order to "outwit the prosy" (8). His use of the extended metaphor in "Catch" shows that a poem must be unique, able to be comprehended on multiple levels, and a challenge to the reader. The various rhythms in the lines of "Catch" exemplify the ideas they express. While achieving an enjoyable poem on the literal level, Francis has also achieved a rich metaphorical meaning. The poem offers a good workout both physically and intellectually.

Work Cited

Francis, Robert. "Catch." *The Bedford Introduction to Literature*. Ed. Michael Meyer. 9th ed. Boston: Bedford/St. Martin's, 2011. 750. Print.

Before beginning your own writing assignment on poetry, you should review Chapter 22, "Writing about Poetry: From Inquiry to Final Paper," and Chapter 54, "Reading and the Writing Process," which provides a step-by-step overview of how to choose a topic, develop a thesis, and organize various types of writing assignments. If you are using outside sources in your paper, you should make sure that you are familiar with the conventional documentation procedures described in Chapter 55, "The Literary Research Paper."

Poets often remind us that beauty can be found in unexpected places. What is it that Elizabeth Bishop finds so beautiful about the "battered" fish she describes in the following poem?

Web Explore contexts for Elizabeth Bishop and approaches to this poem at bedfordstmartins.com/meyerlit.

ELIZABETH BISHOP (1911–1979)
The Fish   1946

I caught a tremendous fish
and held him beside the boat
half out of water, with my hook
fast in a corner of his mouth.
He didn't fight.   5
He hadn't fought at all.
He hung a grunting weight,
battered and venerable
and homely. Here and there
his brown skin hung in strips   10
like ancient wall-paper,
and its pattern of darker brown
was like wall-paper:
shapes like full-blown roses
stained and lost through age.   15
He was speckled with barnacles,
fine rosettes of lime,
and infested
with tiny white sea-lice,
and underneath two or three   20
rags of green weed hung down.
While his gills were breathing in
the terrible oxygen
— the frightening gills,
fresh and crisp with blood,   25
that can cut so badly—
I thought of the coarse white flesh
packed in like feathers,
the big bones and the little bones,
the dramatic reds and blacks   30
of his shiny entrails,
and the pink swim-bladder
like a big peony.
I looked into his eyes
which were far larger than mine   35
but shallower, and yellowed,
the irises backed and packed
with tarnished tinfoil
seen through the lenses
of old scratched isinglass.   40
They shifted a little, but not
to return my stare.
— It was more like the tipping
of an object toward the light.
I admired his sullen face,   45
the mechanism of his jaw,
and then I saw

that from his lower lip
— if you could call it a lip —
grim, wet, and weapon-like,   50
hung five old pieces of fish-line,
or four and a wire leader
with the swivel still attached,
with all their five big hooks
grown firmly in his mouth.   55
A green line, frayed at the end
where he broke it, two heavier lines,
and a fine black thread
still crimped from the strain and snap
when it broke and he got away.   60
Like medals with their ribbons
frayed and wavering,
a five-haired beard of wisdom
trailing from his aching jaw.
I stared and stared   65
and victory filled up
the little rented boat,
from the pool of bilge
where oil had spread a rainbow
around the rusted engine   70
to the bailer rusted orange,
the sun-cracked thwarts,
the oarlocks on their strings,
the gunnels — until everything
was rainbow, rainbow, rainbow!   75
And I let the fish go.

CONSIDERATIONS FOR CRITICAL THINKING AND WRITING

1. **FIRST RESPONSE.** Which lines in this poem provide especially vivid details of the fish? What makes these descriptions effective?

2. How is the fish characterized? Is it simply a weak victim because it "didn't fight" (line 5)?

3. Comment on lines 65–76. In what sense has "victory filled up" the boat (66), given that the speaker finally lets the fish go?

The speaker in Bishop's "The Fish" ends on a triumphantly joyful note. The ***speaker*** is the voice used by the author in the poem; like the narrator in a work of fiction, the speaker is often a created identity rather than the author's actual self. The two should not automatically be equated. Contrast the attitude toward life of the speaker in "The Fish" with that of the speaker in the following poem.

PHILIP LARKIN (1922–1985)
A Study of Reading Habits   *1964*

When getting my nose in a book
Cured most things short of school,
It was worth ruining my eyes
To know I could still keep cool,
And deal out the old right hook   5
To dirty dogs twice my size.

Later, with inch-thick specs,
Evil was just my lark:
Me and my cloak and fangs
Had ripping times in the dark.   10
The women I clubbed with sex!
I broke them up like meringues.

Don't read much now: the dude
Who lets the girl down before
The hero arrives, the chap   15
Who's yellow and keeps the store,
Seem far too familiar. Get stewed:
Books are a load of crap.

     What the speaker sees and describes in "The Fish" is close if not identical to Bishop's own vision and voice. The joyful response to the fish is clearly shared by the speaker and the poet, between whom there is little or no distance. In "A Study of Reading Habits," however, Larkin distances himself from a speaker whose sensibilities he does not wholly share. The poet — and many readers — might identify with the reading habits described by the speaker in the first twelve lines, but Larkin uses the last six lines to criticize the speaker's attitude toward life as well as reading. The speaker recalls in lines 1–6 how as a schoolboy he identified with the hero, whose virtuous strength always triumphed over "dirty dogs," and in lines 7–12 he recounts how his schoolboy fantasies were transformed by adolescence into a fascination with violence and sex. This description of early reading habits is pleasantly amusing, because many readers of popular fiction will probably recall having moved through similar stages, but at the end of the poem the speaker provides more information about himself than he intends to.

     As an adult the speaker has lost interest in reading because it is no longer an escape from his own disappointed life. Instead of identifying with heroes or villains, he finds himself identifying with minor characters who are irresponsible and cowardly. Reading is now a reminder of his failures, so he turns to alcohol. His solution, to "Get stewed" because "Books are a load of crap," is obviously self-destructive. The speaker is ultimately exposed by Larkin as someone who never grew beyond fantasies. Getting drunk is consistent with the speaker's immature reading habits. Unlike the speaker, the poet understands that life is often distorted by escapist fantasies, whether through a steady diet of popular fiction or through alcohol. The speaker in this poem, then, is not Larkin but a created identity whose voice is filled with disillusionment and delusion.

The problem with Larkin's speaker is that he misreads books as well as his own life. Reading means nothing to him unless it serves as an escape from himself. It is not surprising that Larkin has him read fiction rather than poetry because poetry places an especially heavy emphasis on language. Fiction, indeed any kind of writing, including essays and drama, relies on carefully chosen and arranged words, but poetry does so to an even greater extent. Notice, for example, how Larkin's deft use of trite expressions and slang characterizes the speaker so that his language reveals nearly as much about his dreary life as what he says. Larkin's speaker would have no use for poetry.

What is "unmistakable" in poetry (to use Robinson's term again) is its intense, concentrated use of language — its emphasis on individual words to convey meanings, experiences, emotions, and effects. Poets never simply process words; they savor them. Words in poems frequently create their own tastes, textures, scents, sounds, and shapes. They often seem more sensuous than ordinary language, and readers usually sense that a word has been hefted before making its way into a poem. Although poems are crafted differently from the ways a painting, sculpture, or musical composition is created, in each form of art the creator delights in the medium. Poetry is carefully orchestrated so that the words work together as elements in a structure to sustain close, repeated readings. The words are chosen to interact with one another to create the maximum desired effect, whether the purpose is to capture a mood or feeling, create a vivid experience, express a point of view, narrate a story, or portray a character.

Here is a poem that looks quite different from most *verse,* a term used for lines composed in a measured rhythmical pattern, which are often, but not necessarily, rhymed.

ROBERT MORGAN (B. 1944)

Mountain Graveyard   1979

for the author of "Slow Owls"

Spore Prose

stone	notes
slate	tales
sacred	cedars
heart	earth
asleep	please
hated	death

Though unconventional in its appearance, this is unmistakably poetry because of its concentrated use of language. The poem demonstrates how serious play with words can lead to some remarkable discoveries. At first glance "Mountain Graveyard" may seem intimidating. What, after all, does this list of words add up to? How is it in any sense a poetic use of language? But if the words are examined closely, it is not difficult to see how they work. The wordplay here is literally in the form of a game. Morgan uses a series of **anagrams** (words made from the letters of other words, such as *read* and *dare*) to evoke feelings about death. "Mountain Graveyard" is one of several poems that Morgan has called "Spore Prose" (another anagram) because he finds in individual words the seeds of poetry. He wrote the poem in honor of the fiftieth birthday of another poet, Jonathan Williams, the author of "Slow Owls," whose title is also an anagram.

The title, "Mountain Graveyard," indicates the poem's setting, which is also the context in which the individual words in the poem interact to provide a larger meaning. Morgan's discovery of the words on the stones of a graveyard is more than just clever. The observations he makes among the silent graves go beyond the curious pleasure a reader experiences in finding that the words *sacred cedars,* referring to evergreens common in cemeteries, consist of the same letters. The surprise and delight of realizing the connection between *heart* and *earth* are tempered by the more sober recognition that everyone's story ultimately ends in the ground. The hope that the dead are merely asleep is expressed with a plea that is answered grimly by a hatred of death's finality.

Little is told in this poem. There is no way of knowing who is buried or who is looking at the graves, but the emotions of sadness, hope, and pain are unmistakable — and are conveyed in fewer than half the words of this sentence. Morgan takes words that initially appear to be a dead, prosaic list and energizes their meanings through imaginative juxtapositions.

The following poem also involves a startling discovery about words. With the peculiar title "l(a," the poem cannot be read aloud, so there is no sound, but is there sense, a **theme** — a central idea or meaning — in the poem?

E. E. CUMMINGS (1894–1962)

l(a   *1958*

l(a

le

af

fa

ll

© Bettmann/CORBIS.

s)
one
l

iness

CONSIDERATIONS FOR CRITICAL THINKING AND WRITING

1. **FIRST RESPONSE.** Discuss the connection between what appears inside and outside the parentheses in this poem.

2. What does Cummings draw attention to by breaking up the words? How do this strategy and the poem's overall shape contribute to its theme?

3. Which seems more important in this poem — what is expressed or the way it is expressed?

Although "Mountain Graveyard" and "l(a" do not resemble the kind of verse that readers might recognize immediately as poetry on a page, both are actually a very common type of poem, called the *lyric,* usually a brief poem that expresses the personal emotions and thoughts of a single speaker. Lyrics are often written in the first person, but sometimes — as in "Mountain Graveyard" and "l(a" — no speaker is specified. Lyrics present a subjective mood, emotion, or idea. Very often they are about love or death, but almost any subject or experience that evokes some intense emotional response can be found in lyrics. In addition to brevity and emotional intensity, lyrics are also frequently characterized by their musical qualities. The word *lyric* derives from the Greek word *lyre,* meaning a musical instrument that originally accompanied the singing of a lyric. Lyric poems can be organized in a variety of ways, such as the sonnet, elegy, and ode (see Chapter 29), but it is enough to point out here that lyrics are an extremely popular kind of poetry with writers and readers.

The following anonymous lyric was found in a sixteenth-century manuscript.

ANONYMOUS

Western Wind

c. 1500

Western wind, when wilt thou blow,
The small rain down can rain?
Christ, if my love were in my arms,
And I in my bed again!

This speaker's intense longing for his lover is characteristic of lyric poetry. He impatiently addresses the western wind that brings spring to England and could make it possible for him to be reunited with the woman he loves. We do not know the details of these lovers' lives because this poem focuses on the speaker's emotion. We do not learn why the lovers are apart or if they will be together again. We don't even know if the speaker is a man. But those issues are not really important. The poem gives us a feeling rather than a story.

   A poem that tells a story is called a ***narrative poem.*** Narrative poetry may be short or very long. An ***epic,*** for example, is a long narrative poem on a serious subject chronicling heroic deeds and important events. Among the most famous epics are Homer's *Iliad* and *Odyssey,* the Old English *Beowulf,* Dante's *Divine Comedy,* and John Milton's *Paradise Lost.* More typically, however, narrative poems are considerably shorter, as is the case with the following poem, which tells the story of a child's memory of her father.

REGINA BARRECA (B. 1957)

Nighttime Fires   *1986*

When I was five in Louisville
we drove to see nighttime fires. Piled seven of us,
all pajamas and running noses, into the Olds,
drove fast toward smoke. It was after my father
lost his job, so not getting up in the morning
gave him time: awake past midnight, he
      read old newspapers
with no news, tried crosswords until he split
      the pencil
between his teeth, mad. When he heard
the wolf whine of the siren, he woke my mother,
and she pushed and shoved   10
us all into waking. Once roused we longed for burnt wood
and a smell of flames high into the pines. My old man liked
driving to rich neighborhoods best, swearing in a good mood
as he followed fire engines that snaked like dragons
and split the silent streets. It was festival, carnival.   15

If there were a Cadillac or any car
in a curved driveway, my father smiled a smile
from a secret, brittle heart.
His face lit up in the heat given off by destruction
like something was being made, or was being set right.   20
I bent my head back to see where sparks
ate up the sky. My father who never held us
would take my hand and point to falling cinders that
covered the ground like snow, or, excited, show us
the swollen collapse of a staircase. My mother   25
watched my father, not the house. She was happy
only when we were ready to go, when it was finally over
and nothing else could burn.
Driving home, she would sleep in the front seat
as we huddled behind. I could see his quiet face in the   30
rearview mirror, eyes like hallways filled with smoke.

Courtesy of Robert Benson, © 2004.

This narrative poem could have been a short story if the poet had wanted to say more about the "brittle heart" of this unemployed man whose daughter so vividly remembers the desperate pleasure he took in watching fire consume other people's property. Indeed, a reading of William Faulkner's famous short story "Barn Burning" (p. 503) suggests how such a character can be further developed and how his child responds to him. The similarities between Faulkner's angry character and the poem's father, whose "eyes [are] like hallways filled with smoke," are coincidental, but the characters' sense of "something . . . being set right" by flames is worth comparing. Although we do not know everything about this man and his family, we have a much firmer sense of their story than we do of the story of the couple in "Western Wind."

Although narrative poetry is still written, short stories and novels have largely replaced the long narrative poem. Lyric poems tend to be the predominant type of poetry today. Regardless of whether a poem is a narrative or a lyric, however, the strategies for reading it are somewhat different from those for reading prose. Try these suggestions for approaching poetry.

Suggestions for Approaching Poetry

1. Assume that it will be necessary to read a poem more than once. Give yourself a chance to become familiar with what the poem has to offer. Like a piece of music, a poem becomes more pleasurable with each encounter.

2. Pay attention to the title; it will often provide a helpful context for the poem and serve as an introduction to it. Larkin's "A Study of Reading Habits" is precisely what its title describes.

3. As you read the poem for the first time, avoid becoming entangled in words or lines that you don't understand. Instead, give yourself a chance to take in the entire poem before attempting to resolve problems encountered along the way.

4. On a second reading, identify any words or passages that you don't understand. Look up words you don't know; these might include names, places, historical and mythical references, or anything else that is unfamiliar to you.

5. Read the poem aloud (or perhaps have a friend read it to you). You'll probably discover that some puzzling passages suddenly fall into place when you hear them. You'll find that nothing helps, though, if the poem is read in an artificial, exaggerated manner. Read in as natural a voice as possible, with slight pauses at line breaks. Silent reading is preferable to imposing a te-tumpty-te-tum reading on a good poem.

6. Read the punctuation. Poems use punctuation marks — in addition to the space on the page — as signals for readers. Be especially careful not to assume that the end of a line marks the end of a sentence, unless it is concluded by punctuation. Consider, for example, the opening lines of Hathaway's "Oh, Oh":

> My girl and I amble a country lane,
> moo cows chomping daisies, our own
> sweet saliva green with grass stems.

Line 2 makes little or no sense if a reader stops after "own." Keeping track of the subjects and verbs will help you find your way among the sentences.

7. Paraphrase the poem to determine whether you understand what happens in it. As you work through each line of the poem, a paraphrase will help you to see which words or passages need further attention.

8. Try to get a sense of who is speaking and what the setting or situation is. Don't assume that the speaker is the author; often it is a created character.

9. Assume that each element in the poem has a purpose. Try to explain how the elements of the poem work together.

10. Be generous. Be willing to entertain perspectives, values, experiences, and subjects that you might not agree with or approve of. Even if baseball bores you, you should be able to comprehend its imaginative use in Francis's "Catch."

11. Try developing a coherent approach to the poem that helps you to shape a discussion of the text. See Chapter 53, "Critical Strategies for Reading," to review formalist, biographical, historical, psychological, feminist, and other possible critical approaches.

12. Don't expect to produce a definitive reading. Many poems do not resolve all of the ideas, issues, or tensions in them, and so it is not always possible to drive their meaning into an absolute corner. Your reading will explore rather than define the poem. Poems are not trophies to be stuffed and mounted. They're usually more elusive. And don't be afraid that a close reading will damage the poem. Poems aren't hurt when we analyze them; instead, they come alive as we experience them and put into words what we discover through them.

A list of more specific questions using the literary terms and concepts discussed in the following chapters begins on page 791. That list, like the suggestions just made, raises issues and questions that can help you to read just about any poem closely. These strategies should be a useful means for getting inside poems to understand how they work. Furthermore, because reading poetry inevitably increases sensitivity to language, you're likely to find yourself a better reader of words in any form — whether in a novel, a newspaper editorial, an advertisement, a political speech, or a conversation — after having studied poetry. In short, many of the reading skills that make poetry accessible also open up the world you inhabit.

You'll probably find some poems amusing or sad, some fierce or tender, and some fascinating or dull. You may find, too, some poems that will get inside you. Their kinds of insights — the poet's and yours — are what Emily Dickinson had in mind when she defined poetry this way: "If I read a book and it makes my whole body so cold no fire can ever warm me, I know that it is poetry. If I feel physically as if the top of my head were taken off, I know that it is poetry." Dickinson's response may be more intense than most — poetry was, after all, at the center of her life — but you, too, might find yourself moved by poems in unexpected ways. In any case, as Edwin Arlington Robinson knew, poetry is, to an alert and sensitive reader, "eventually unmistakable."

BILLY COLLINS (B. 1941)

Introduction to Poetry   *1988*

I ask them to take a poem
and hold it up to the light
like a color slide

or press an ear against its hive.

I say drop a mouse into a poem   5
and watch him probe his way out,

or walk inside the poem's room
and feel the walls for a light switch.

I want them to water-ski
across the surface of a poem   10
waving at the author's name on the shore.

But all they want to do
is tie the poem to a chair with rope
and torture a confession out of it.

They begin beating it with a hose   15
to find out what it really means.

CONSIDERATIONS FOR CRITICAL THINKING AND WRITING

1. **FIRST RESPONSE.** In what sense does this poem offer suggestions for approaching poetry? What kinds of advice does the speaker provide in lines 1–11?

2. How does the mood of the poem change beginning in line 12? What do you make of the shift from "them" to "they"?

3. Paraphrase the poem. How is your paraphrase different from what is included in the poem?

ENCOUNTERING POETRY:
IMAGES OF POETRY
IN POPULAR CULTURE

Although poets may find it painful to acknowledge, poetry is not nearly as popular as prose among contemporary readers. A quick prowl through almost any bookstore reveals many more shelves devoted to novels or biographies, for example, than the meager space allotted to poetry. Moreover, few poems are made into films (although there have been some exceptions, such as Alfred, Lord Tennyson's "The Charge of the Light Brigade" [p. 965]), and few collections of poetry have earned their authors extraordinary wealth or celebrity status.

Despite these facts, however, there is plenty of poetry being produced that saturates our culture and suggests just how essential it is to our lives. When in 2001 Billy Collins was named the poet laureate of the United States, he shrewdly observed that "we should notice that there is no *prose* laureate." What Collins implicitly acknowledges here is the importance of poetry. He acknowledges the idea that poetry is central to any literature because it is the art closest to language itself; its emphasis on getting each word just right speaks to us and for us. The audience for poetry may be relatively modest in comparison to the readership of prose, but there is nothing shy about poetry's presence in contemporary life. Indeed, a particularly observant person might find it difficult to reach the end of a day without encountering poetry in some shape or form.

You may, for instance, read yet again that magnetic poem composed on your refrigerator door as you reach for your breakfast juice, or perhaps you'll be surprised by some poetic lines while riding the bus or subway, where you might encounter a Poetry in Motion poster, featuring the work of a local poet or well-known author such as Dorothy Parker. What the poems have in common is the celebration of language as a means of surprising, delighting, provoking, or inspiring their readers. There's no obligation and no quiz. The poems are for the taking: all for pleasure.

The following portfolio of images—including provocative posters, a humorous cartoon, poetry-related art in public spaces, and vibrant photographs from the poetry slam scene—illustrate the significance of poetry in our culture. These images recognize the importance not only of such canonical authors as Carl Sandburg and T. S. Eliot but also of aspiring poets— spoken word performers or Magnetic Poetry authors, for example—whose works reflect the growth of poetry as a popular form of expression.

Perhaps the largest, most recent explosion of poetry can be found on the Internet. As Poetry Portal (poetry-portal.com) indicates, the number of poetry sites is staggering; these include sites that provide poems, audio readings, e-zines, reviews, criticism, festivals, slams, conferences, workshops, and even collaborative poetry writing in real time. This growth in poetry on the Internet is significant because it reflects an energy and vitality about the poetic activity in our daily lives. Poetry may not be rich and famous, but it is certainly alive and well. Consider, for example, the following images of poetry that can be found in contemporary life. What do they suggest to you about the nature of poetry and its audience?

DOROTHY PARKER, *Unfortunate Coincidence*

Begun in New York City in 1992, the Poetry in Motion program has spread from coast to coast on buses and subways. Offering works ranging from ancient Chinese poetry to contemporary poetry, Poetry in Motion posters give riders more to read than their own reflections in the window. In this example, Dorothy Parker, a poet known for her sharp wit, becomes a presence on a New York subway car.

This poster was part of the New York City Poetry in Motion® program, which is a registered trademark of MTA/New York City Transit and the Poetry Society of America. "Unfortunate Coincidence," copyright 1926, renewed © 1954 by Dorothy Parker, from *The Portable Dorothy Parker* by Dorothy Parker, edited by Marion Meade. Used by permission of Viking Penguin, a division of Penguin Group (USA) Inc.

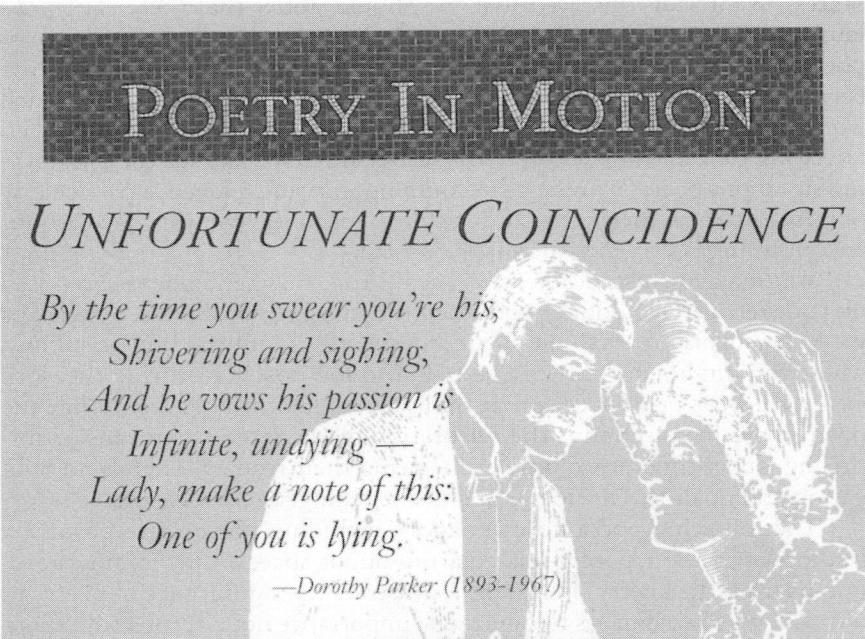

CONSIDERATIONS FOR CRITICAL THINKING AND WRITING

1. How does the unromantic nature of this poem seem especially appropriate for New York City subway riders?
2. What kinds of poetry do you find on billboards or public transportation in your own environment? If there is none, what poem would you choose to post on a bus or train in your area?

CARL SANDBURG, *Window*

This mural, painted on a station wall of the Chicago El, features the poem "Window," from a collection of poems by Carl Sandburg titled *Chicago*. This work transforms the evening commute into an encounter with a vivid image.

CONSIDERATIONS FOR CRITICAL THINKING AND WRITING

1. Discuss the effectiveness of the images in these two lines.

2. **CREATIVE RESPONSE.** Try writing two lines of vivid imagery that capture the movement seen from a quickly moving automobile during daylight.

This *New Yorker* cartoon by Roz Chast (b. 1954) updates lines from T. S. Eliot's "The Love Song of J. Alfred Prufrock" (page 1216, lines 120–24) with the kind of language used in the popular J. Crew clothing catalog. Though published in 1917, Eliot's poem clearly remains fashionable.

CONSIDERATIONS FOR CRITICAL THINKING AND WRITING

1. Read "The Love Song of J. Alfred Prufrock" (p. 1216) and compare the speaker's personality to the kind of image associated with the typical J. Crew customer. How does this comparison serve to explain the humor in the cartoon?

2. Explain why you think the J. Crew company would be flattered or annoyed to have its image treated this way in a cartoon.

TIM TAYLOR, *I shake the delicate apparatus*

Magnetic Poetry™ kits are available in a number of languages, including Yiddish, Norwegian, and sign language, along with a variety of thematic versions such as those dedicated to cats, love, art, rock and roll, college, and Shakespeare. This poem by Tim Taylor (b. 1957) graces his Manhattan apartment refrigerator and is but one example of the creative expression that poetry magnets inspire in kitchens around the world.

Reprinted by permission of Tim Taylor (poem) and Pelle Cass (image).

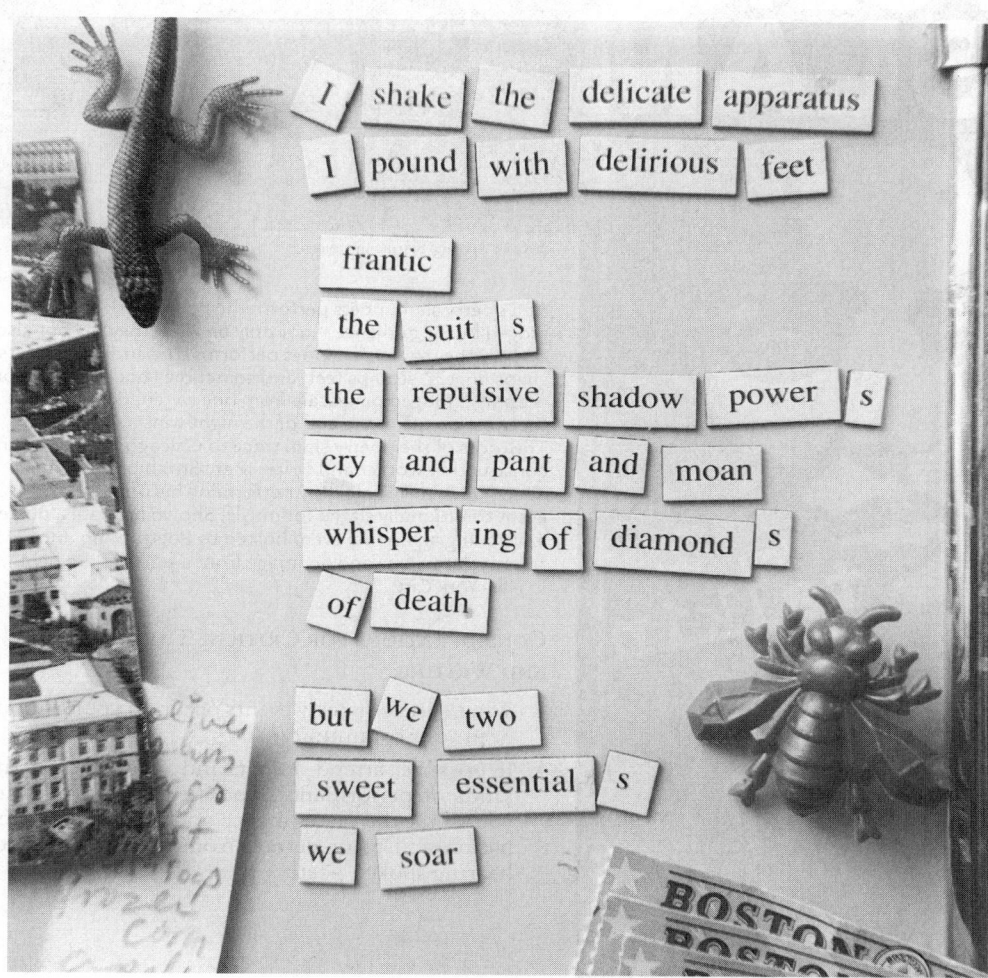

CONSIDERATIONS FOR CRITICAL THINKING AND WRITING

1. Write a paragraph that describes what you think is the essential meaning of this poem.
2. How do you explain the enormous popularity of Magnetic Poetry?

© Kevin Fleming/Bettmann/CORBIS.

At a poetry slam, poets perform their own work and are judged by the audience—not only on what they say but also on how they say it. As a poet performs, the audience cheers, snaps fingers, stomps feet, and sometimes boos the poet off the stage. Judged on a scale from one to ten, the poet with the most points at the end of the night wins a cash prize. The roots of the poetry slam trace to Chicago in 1984, when construction worker and writer Marc Smith broke format at an "open mike" night by performing his poetry at an event traditionally slated for music. Shown here are a poster advertising an annual event hosted by Poetry Slam, Inc. (poetryslam.com) and an image from a poetry slam held in New York City.

CONSIDERATIONS FOR CRITICAL THINKING AND WRITING

1. What sorts of poetry events occur on your campus or in your community?

2. If possible, attend a slam and comment on the kinds of performances you see. Explain whether you think the performance and audience participation add to or detract from the experience of hearing spoken poetry.

Reprinted by permission of Eric Dunn (designer/copy-writer) and Mike Wigton (copywriter).

Poetry-portal.com

Poetry Portal (poetry-portal.com), offering access to databases of poems and a cornucopia of online resources about poetry, is an excellent site to begin an exploration of poetry on the Internet.

Reprinted by permission of poetry-portal.com and Colin John Holcombe.

CONSIDERATIONS FOR CRITICAL THINKING AND WRITING

1. Log on to the home page of poetry-portal.com and explore some of the online sites listed there. Describe three sites that you found particularly interesting. Any surprises?

2. In what sense does the Poetry Portal demonstrate that poetry is, indeed, a "community"?

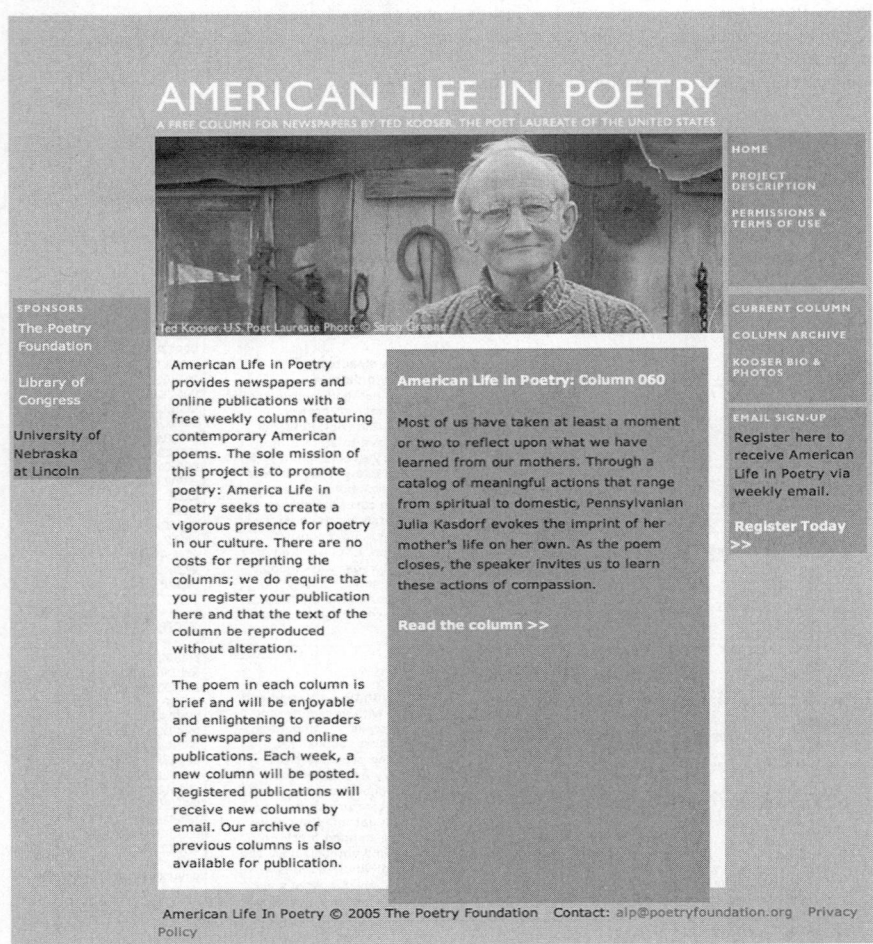

American Life in Poetry (americanlifeinpoetry.org) is a weekly newspaper column featuring a contemporary poem and brief introduction. Initiated by Ted Kooser, a poet laureate of the United States, and supported by the Poetry Foundation in partnership with the Library of Congress, this popular source is distributed free to newspapers and online publications. The site provides countless readers with a wide variety of high-quality, accessible poems. The reprint from the Detroit *Metro Times* (*next page*), featuring a poem by David Allan Evans, offers an engaging example of the weekly column.

© The Poetry Foundation.

David Allan Evans, *Neighbors*

April 6-12, 2005

metrotimes

detroit's weekly alternative   www.metrotimes.com • free

ART BAR

POETRY FOR THE PEOPLE: New Pulitzer-winner Ted Kooser, America's 13th poet laureate, gets us. He's no suit sitting in an office consulting ancient texts. For 35 years, he worked in the insurance business. "I wrote each morning ... and I often took my fresh drafts of poems and showed them to my secretary. ... If she didn't understand them, I went home and worked to make them more clear."

Kooser received funding as poet laureate and founded "American Life In Poetry," a free weekly newspaper column. *Metro Times* readers love to be talked to straight up, so we've signed up. Here's our and Kooser's premiere. If we don't have room in print, find it faithfully on our Web site. Kooser is excited *MT* signed on – "This is wonderful news! ... REALLY a start!"

Reprinted from Train Windows, *Ohio University Press, 1976, by permission of the author, whose most recent book is* The Bull Rider's Advice: New and Selected Poems. *This weekly column is supported by The Poetry Foundation, The Library of Congress, and the department of English at the University of Nebraska, Lincoln.*

AMERICAN LIFE IN POETRY

by Ted Kooser, U.S. poet laureate

We all know that the manner in which people behave toward one another can tell us a lot about their private lives. In this amusing poem by David Allan Evans, poet laureate of South Dakota, we learn something about a marriage by being shown a couple as they take on an ordinary household task.

Neighbors

They live alone
together,

she with her wide hind
and bird face,
he with his hung belly
and crewcut.

They never talk
but keep busy.

Today they are
washing windows
(each window together)
she on the inside,
he on the outside.
He squirts Windex
at her face,
she squirts Windex
at his face.

Now they are waving
to each other
with rags,

not smiling.

Courtesy of the Detroit *Metro Times*, the Poetry Foundation, and David Allan Evans.

CONSIDERATIONS FOR CRITICAL THINKING AND WRITING

1. Put together a cluster of images that reflect your encounters with poetry. Where do you find poetry? How is it used? What do these images suggest to you about the state of poetry in contemporary culture?

2. Surely not all manifestations of poetry in popular culture represent good poetry. Does bad poetry undercut good poetry? Does it cheapen its value? At this point in your study of poetry — the beginning — how do you define a good poem or a bad poem?

3. What is your favorite poem? Where did you first encounter it? Why is it important to you? Alternatively, if you can't come up with a favorite poem, why can't you?

POETRY IN POPULAR FORMS

Before you try out these strategies for reading on a few more poems, it is worth acknowledging that the verse that enjoys the widest readership appears not in collections, magazines, or even anthologies for students, but in greeting cards. A significant amount of the personal daily mail delivered in the United States consists of greeting cards. That represents millions of lines of verse going by us on the street and in planes over our heads. These verses share some similarities with the poetry included in this anthology, but there are also important differences that indicate the need for reading serious poetry closely rather than casually.

The popularity of greeting cards is easy to explain: just as many of us have neither the time nor the talent to make gifts for birthdays, weddings, anniversaries, graduations, Valentine's Day, Mother's Day, and other holidays, we are unlikely to write personal messages when cards conveniently say them for us. Although impersonal, cards are efficient and convey an important message no matter what the occasion for them: I care. These greetings are rarely serious poetry; they are not written to be. Nevertheless, they demonstrate the impulse in our culture to generate and receive poetry.

In a handbook for greeting-card freelancers, a writer and past editor of such verse began with this advice:

> Once you determine what you want to say — and in this regard it is best to stick to one basic idea — you must choose your words to do several things at the same time:
>
> 1. Your idea must be expressed as a complete idea; it must have a beginning, a middle, and an end.
>
> 2. There must be coherence in your verse. Every line must be linked logically and smoothly with its neighbors.
>
> 3. Your expressions . . . must be conversational. High-flown language rarely comes off successfully in greeting-card writing.
>
> 4. You must write with emphasis — and something else: enthusiasm. It's necessary to create interest in that all-important first line. From that point on, writing your verse is a matter of developing your idea and bringing it to a peak of emphasis in the last line. Occasionally you will find that you have shot your wad too early in the verse, and whatever you say after that point sounds like an afterthought.
>
> 5. You must do all of the above and at the same time make everything come out right in the meter-and-rhyme department.[1]

This advice is followed by a list of approximately fifty of the most frequently used rhyme sounds accompanied by rhyming words, such as *love, of, above* for the sound *uv*. The point of these prescriptions is that the verse

---

[1] Chris Fitzgerald, "Conventional Verse: The Sentimental Favorite," *The Greeting Card Writer's Handbook,* ed. H. Joseph Chadwick (Cincinnati: Writer's Digest, 1975), 13, 17.

must be written so that it is immediately accessible — consumable — by both the buyer and the recipient. Writers of these cards are expected to avoid any complexity.

Compare the following greeting-card verse with the poem that comes after it. "Magic of Love," by Helen Farries, has been a longtime favorite in a major greeting-card company's "wedding line"; with different endings it has been used also in valentines and friendship cards.

HELEN FARRIES

Magic of Love   *date unknown*

There's a wonderful gift that can give you a lift,
It's a blessing from heaven above!
It can comfort and bless, it can bring happiness —
It's the wonderful MAGIC OF LOVE!

Like a star in the night, it can keep your faith bright,   5
Like the sun, it can warm your hearts, too —
It's a gift you can give every day that you live,
And when given, it comes back to you!

When love lights the way, there is joy in the day
And all troubles are lighter to bear,   10
Love is gentle and kind, and through love you will find
There's an answer to your every prayer!

May it never depart from your two loving hearts,
May you treasure this gift from above —
You will find if you do, all your dreams will come true,   15
In the wonderful MAGIC OF LOVE!

JOHN FREDERICK NIMS (1913–1999)

Love Poem   *1947*

My clumsiest dear, whose hands shipwreck vases,
At whose quick touch all glasses chip and ring,
Whose palms are bulls in china, burs in linen,
And have no cunning with any soft thing

Except all ill-at-ease fidgeting people: 5
The refugee uncertain at the door
You make at home; deftly you steady
The drunk clambering on his undulant floor.

Unpredictable dear, the taxi drivers' terror,
Shrinking from far headlights pale as a dime   10
Yet leaping before red apoplectic streetcars —
Misfit in any space. And never on time.

A wrench in clocks and the solar system. Only
With words and people and love you move at ease.
In traffic of wit expertly maneuver   15
And keep us, all devotion, at your knees.

Forgetting your coffee spreading on our flannel,
Your lipstick grinning on our coat,
So gaily in love's unbreakable heaven
Our souls on glory of spilt bourbon float.   20

Be with me, darling, early and late. Smash glasses—
I will study wry music for your sake.
For should your hands drop white and empty
All the toys of the world would break.

CONSIDERATIONS FOR CRITICAL THINKING AND WRITING

1. **FIRST RESPONSE.** Read these two works aloud. How are they different? How
   the same?
2. To what extent does the advice to would-be greeting-card writers apply to
   each work?
3. Compare the two speakers. Which do you find more appealing? Why?
4. How does Nims's description of love differ from Farries's?

In contrast to poetry, which transfigures and expresses an emotion or
experience through an original use of language, the verse in "Magic of
Love" relies on *clichés* — ideas or expressions that have become tired and
trite from overuse, such as describing love as "a blessing from heaven
above." Clichés anesthetize readers instead of alerting them to the possibility of fresh perceptions. They are used to draw out *stock responses* —
predictable, conventional reactions to language, characters, symbols, or
situations; God, heaven, the flag, motherhood, hearts, puppies, and peace
are some often-used objects of stock responses. Advertisers manufacture
careers from this sort of business.

Clichés and stock responses are two of the major ingredients of sentimentality in literature. **Sentimentality** exploits the reader by inducing responses that exceed what the situation warrants. This pejorative term
should not be confused with *sentiment,* which is synonymous with *emotion*
or *feeling.* Sentimentality cons readers into falling for the mass murderer
who is devoted to stray cats, and it requires that we not think twice about
what we're feeling because those tears shed for the little old lady, the rage
aimed at the vicious enemy soldier, and the longing for the simple virtues
of poverty might disappear under the slightest scrutiny. The experience of
sentimentality is not unlike biting into a swirl of cotton candy; it's momentarily sweet but wholly insubstantial.

Clichés, stock responses, and sentimentality are generally the hallmarks
of weak writing. Poetry — the kind that is unmistakable — achieves freshness, vitality, and genuine emotion that sharpen our perceptions of life.

Although the most widely read verse is found in greeting cards, the most widely *heard* poetry appears in song lyrics. Not all songs are poetic, but a good many share the same effects and qualities as poems. Consider these lyrics by Bruce Springsteen.

BRUCE SPRINGSTEEN (B. 1949)

You're Missing   2002

Shirts in the closet, shoes in the hall
Mama's in the kitchen, baby and all
Everything is everything
Everything is everything
But you're missing   5

Coffee cups on the counter, jackets on the chair
Papers on the doorstep, you're not there
Everything is everything
Everything is everything
But you're missing   10

Pictures on the nightstand, TV's on in the den
Your house is waiting, your house is waiting
For you to walk in, for you to walk in
But you're missing, you're missing
You're missing when I shut out the lights   15
You're missing when I close my eyes
You're missing when I see the sun rise
You're missing

Children are asking if it's alright
Will you be in our arms tonight?   20

Morning is morning, the evening falls I have
Too much room in my bed, too many phone calls
How's everything, everything?
Everything, everything
You're missing, you're missing   25

God's drifting in heaven, devil's in the mailbox
I got dust on my shoes, nothing but teardrops

CONSIDERATIONS FOR CRITICAL THINKING AND WRITING

1. **FIRST RESPONSE.** How do the descriptions of home and the phrases that are repeated evoke a particular kind of mood in this song?

2. Explain whether you think this song can be accurately called a narrative poem. How would you describe its theme?

3. How does your experience of reading "You're Missing" compare with listening to Springsteen singing the song (available on *The Rising*)?

S. Pearl Sharp (b. 1942)

It's the Law: A Rap Poem   *1991*

You can learn about the state of the U.S.A.
By the laws we have on the books today.
The rules we break are the laws we make
The things that we fear, we legislate.

We got laws designed to keep folks in line   5
Laws for what happens when you lose your mind
Laws against stealing, laws against feeling,
The laws we have are a definite sign
That our vision of love is going blind.
(They probably got a law against this rhyme.)   10
Unh-hunh . . . . .

We got laws for cool cats & laws for dirty dogs
Laws about where you can park your hog
Laws against your mama and your papa, too
Even got a law to make the laws come true.   15
It's against the law to hurt an ol' lady,
It's against the law to steal a little baby,
The laws we make are what we do to each other
There is no law to make brother love brother
Hmmm   20

Now this respect thang is hard for some folks to do
They don't respect themselves so they can't respect you
This is the word we should get around —
These are the rules: we gonna run 'em on down.
Listen up!:   25

It ain't enough to be cute,
It ain't enough to be tough
You gotta walk tall
You gotta strut your stuff

You gotta learn to read, you gotta learn to write.   30
Get the tools you need to win this fight
Get your common sense down off the shelf
Start in the mirror . . . . Respect your Self!

When you respect yourself you keep your body clean
You walk tall, walk gentle, don't have to be mean   35
You keep your mind well fed, you keep a clear head
And you think 'bout who you let in your bed —
Unh-hunh . . . . . .

When you respect yourself you come to understand
That your body is a temple for a natural plan,   40
It's against that plan to use drugs or dope —
Use your heart and your mind when you need to cope . . .
It's the law!

We got laws that got started in '86
And laws made back when the Indians got kicked   45
If we want these laws to go out of favor
Then we've got to change our behavior

Change what!? you say, well let's take a look
How did the laws get on the books? Yeah.
I said it up front but let's get tougher   50
The laws we make are what we do to each other

If you never shoot at me then I don't need
A law to keep you from shooting at me, do you see?
There's a universal law that's tried and true
Says Don't do to me—   55
What you don't want done to you
Unh-hunh!
Don't do to me—
What you don't want done to you
It's the law!   60

CONSIDERATIONS FOR CRITICAL THINKING AND WRITING

1. **FIRST RESPONSE.** According to this rap poem, what do laws reveal "about the state of the U.S.A." (line 1)?

2. How are the "laws" different from the "rules" prescribed in the middle stanzas of the poem?

3. What is the theme of this rap poem?

Perspective

ROBERT FRANCIS (1901–1987)

On "Hard" Poetry   *1965*

When Robert Frost said he liked poems hard he could scarcely have meant he liked them difficult. If he had meant difficult he would have said he didn't like them easy. What he said was that he didn't like them soft.

Poems can be soft in several ways. They can be soft in form (invertebrate). They can be soft in thought and feeling (sentimental). They can be soft with excess verbiage. Frost used to advise [writers] to squeeze the water out of a poem. He liked poems dry. What is dry tends to be hard, and what is hard is always dry, except perhaps on the outside.

Yet though hardness here does not mean difficulty, some difficulty naturally goes with hardness. A hard poem may not be hard to read but is hard to write. Not too hard, preferably. Not so hard to write that there is no flow in the writer. But hard enough for the growing poem to meet with some healthy resistance. Frost often found this healthy resistance in a tight rhyme scheme and strict meter. There are other ways of getting good resistance, of course.

And in the reader too, a hard poem will bring some difficulty. Preferably not too much. Not enough difficulty to completely baffle him. Ideally a hard poem should not be too hard to make sense of, but hard to exhaust its meaning and its beauty.

"What I care about is the hardness of the poems. I don't like them soft, I want them to be little pebbles, but placed where they won't dislodge easily. And I'd like them to be little pebbles of precious stone — precious, or semi-precious" ([Robert Frost] interview with John Ciardi, *Saturday Review,* March 21, 1959).

Here is hard prose talking about hard poetry. Frost was never shrewder or more illuminating. Here, as well as in anything else he ever said, is his flavor.

What contemporary of his can you imagine saying this or anything like it?

In 1843 Emerson jotted in his journal: "Hard clouds and hard expressions, and hard manners, I love."

From *The Satirical Rogue on Poetry*

CONSIDERATIONS FOR CRITICAL THINKING AND WRITING

1. What is the distinction between "hard" and "soft" poetry?
2. Explain whether you would characterize Bruce Springsteen's "You're Missing" (p. 777) as hard or soft.
3. **CREATIVE RESPONSE.** Given Francis's brief essay and his poem "Catch" (p. 750), write a review of Helen Farries's "Magic of Love" (p. 775) as you think Francis would.

POEMS FOR FURTHER STUDY

PETER PEREIRA (B. 1959)

Anagrammer   *2003*

If you believe in the magic of language,
then *Elvis* really *Lives*
and *Princess Diana* foretold *I end as car spin.*

If you believe the letters themselves
contain a power within them,   5
then you understand
what makes *outside tedious,*
how *desperation* becomes *a rope ends it.*

The circular logic that allows *senator* to become *treason,*
and *treason* to become *atoners.*   10

That *eleven plus two* is *twelve plus one,*
and an *admirer* is also *married.*

That if you could just re-arrange things the right way
you'd find your true life,

the right path, the answer to your questions: 15
you'd understand how *the Titanic*
turns into *that ice tin,*
and *debit card* becomes *bad credit.*

How *listen* is the same as *silent,*
and not one letter separates *stained* from *sainted.*   20

CONSIDERATIONS FOR CRITICAL THINKING AND WRITING

1. **FIRST RESPONSE.** How is "the magic of language" (line 1) created in the poem?
2. Explain what you think is the poem's theme.
3. **CREATIVE RESPONSE.** Try savoring the letters in your own first and/or last name by writing some anagrams for them.

CONNECTION TO ANOTHER SELECTION

1. Compare Pereira's use of anagrams in this poem with Robert Morgan's in "Mountain Graveyard" (p. 758). How does each poem employ anagrams to achieve its effects?

MARY OLIVER (B. 1935)

The Poet with His Face in His Hands   *2005*

You want to cry aloud for your
mistakes. But to tell the truth the world
doesn't need any more of that sound.

So if you're going to do it and can't
stop yourself, if your pretty mouth can't   5
hold it in, at least go by yourself across

the forty fields and the forty dark inclines
of rocks and water to the place where
the falls are flinging out their white sheets

like crazy, and there is a cave behind all that   10
jubilation and water fun and you can
stand there, under it, and roar all you

want and nothing will be disturbed; you can
drip with despair all afternoon and still,
on a green branch, its wings just lightly touched   15

by the passing foil of the water, the thrush,
puffing out its spotted breast, will sing
of the perfect, stone-hard beauty of everything.

CONSIDERATIONS FOR CRITICAL THINKING AND WRITING

1. **FIRST RESPONSE.** Describe the kind of poet the speaker characterizes. What is the speaker's attitude toward that sort of poet?

2. Explain which single phrase used by the speaker to describe the poet most reveals for you the speaker's attitude toward the poet.

3. How is nature contrasted with the poet?

CONNECTION TO ANOTHER SELECTION

1. Compare the thematic use of nature in Oliver's poem and in Elizabeth Bishop's "The Fish" (p. 755).

LISA PARKER (B. 1972)

Snapping Beans   1998

For Fay Whitt

I snapped beans into the silver bowl
that sat on the splintering slats
of the porchswing between my grandma and me.
I was home for the weekend,
from school, from the North,   5
Grandma hummed "What A Friend We Have In Jesus"
as the sun rose, pushing its pink spikes
through the slant of cornstalks,
through the fly-eyed mesh of the screen.
We didn't speak until the sun overcame   10
the feathered tips of the cornfield
and Grandma stopped humming. I could feel
the soft gray of her stare
against the side of my face
when she asked, *How's school a-goin'?*   15
I wanted to tell her about my classes,
the revelations by book and lecture,
as real as any shout of faith
and potent as a swig of strychnine.
She reached the leather of her hand   20
over the bowl and cupped
my quivering chin; the slick smooth of her palm
held my face the way she held tomatoes
under the spigot, careful not to drop them,
and I wanted to tell her   25
about the nights I cried into the familiar
heartsick panels of the quilt she made me,
wishing myself home on the evening star.
I wanted to tell her
the evening star was a planet,   30
that my friends wore noserings and wrote poetry
about sex, about alcoholism, about Buddha.
I wanted to tell her how my stomach burned
acidic holes at the thought of speaking in class,

speaking in an accent, speaking out of turn,   35
how I was tearing, splitting myself apart
with the slow-simmering guilt of being happy
despite it all.
I said, *School's fine.*
We snapped beans into the silver bowl between us   40
and when a hickory leaf, still summer green,
skidded onto the porchfront,
Grandma said,
It's funny how things blow loose like that.

CONSIDERATIONS FOR CRITICAL THINKING AND WRITING

1. **FIRST RESPONSE.** Describe the speaker's feelings about starting a life at college. How do those feelings compare with your own experiences?

2. How does the grandmother's world differ from the speaker's at school? What details especially reveal those differences?

3. Given that the poem is about how "school['s] a-goin'" (line 15), why do you think the title is "Snapping Beans"?

4. Discuss the significance of the grandmother's response to the hickory leaf in line 44. How do you read the last line?

CONNECTION TO ANOTHER SELECTION

1. Discuss the treatment of the grandmothers in this poem and in "Behind Grandma's House" by Gary Soto (p. 914).

ALBERTO RÍOS (B. 1952)

Seniors   *1985*

William cut a hole in his Levi's pocket
so he could flop himself out in class
behind the girls so the other guys
could see and shit what guts we all said.
All Konga wanted to do over and over   5
was the rubber band trick, but he showed
everyone how, so nobody wanted to see
anymore and one day he cried, just cried
until his parents took him away forever.
Maya had a Hotpoint refrigerator standing   10
in his living room, just for his family to show
anybody who came that they could afford it.

Me, I got a French kiss, finally, in the catholic
darkness, my tongue's farthest half vacationing
loudly in another mouth like a man in Bermudas,   15

Courtesy of Alberto Ríos.

and my body jumped against a flagstone wall,
I could feel it through her thin, almost
nonexistent body: I had, at that moment, that moment,
a hot girl on a summer night, the best of all
the things we tried to do. Well, she   20
let me kiss her, anyway, all over.

Or it was just a flagstone wall
with a flaw in the stone, an understanding cavity
for burning young men with smooth dreams —
the true circumstance is gone, the true   25
circumstances about us all then
are gone. But when I kissed her, all water,
she would close her eyes, and they into somewhere
would disappear. Whether she was there
or not, I remember her, clearly, and she moves   30
around the room, sometimes, until I sleep.

I have lain on the desert in watch
low in the back of a pick-up truck
for nothing in particular, for stars, for
the things behind stars, and nothing comes   35
more than the moment: always now, here in a truck,
the moment again to dream of making love and sweat,
this time to a woman, or even to all of them
in some allowable way, to those boys, then,
who couldn't cry, to the girls before they were   40
women, to friends, me on my back, the sky over me
pressing its simple weight into her body
on me, into the bodies of them all, on me.

Considerations for Critical Thinking and Writing

1. **FIRST RESPONSE.** Comment on the use of slang in the poem. Does it surprise you? How does it characterize the speaker?

2. How does the language of the final stanza differ from that of the first stanza? To what purpose?

3. Write an essay that discusses the speaker's attitudes toward sex and life. How are they related?

Connection to Another Selection

1. Think about "Seniors" as a kind of love poem and compare the speaker's voice here with the one in T. S. Eliot's "The Love Song of J. Alfred Prufrock" (p. 1216). How are these two voices used to evoke different cultures? Of what value is love in these cultures?

ALFRED, LORD TENNYSON (1809–1892)

Crossing the Bar   *1889*

Sunset and evening star,
   And one clear call for me!
And may there be no moaning of the bar,°   *sandbar*
   When I put out to sea,

But such a tide as moving seems asleep,   5
   Too full for sound and foam,
When that which drew from out the boundless deep
   Turns again home.

Twilight and evening bell,
   And after that the dark!   10
And may there be no sadness of farewell,
   When I embark;

For tho' from out our bourne of Time and Place
   The flood may bear me far,
I hope to see my Pilot face to face   15
   When I have crost the bar.

CONSIDERATIONS FOR CRITICAL THINKING AND WRITING

1. **FIRST RESPONSE.** How does Tennyson make clear that this poem is about more than a sea journey?
2. Why do you think Tennyson directed to his publishers to place "Crossing the Bar" as the last poem in all collections of his poetry?
3. Discuss the purpose of the punctuation (or its absence) at the end of each line.

CONNECTION TO ANOTHER SELECTION

1. Compare the speaker's mood in "Crossing the Bar" with that in Dylan Thomas's "Do Not Go Gentle into That Good Night" (p. 981).

LI HO (791–817)

A Beautiful Girl Combs Her Hair   *date unknown*

TRANSLATED BY DAVID YOUNG

Awake at dawn
she's dreaming
by cool silk curtains

fragrance of spilling hair
half sandalwood, half aloes   5

windlass creaking at the well
singing jade

the lotus blossom wakes, refreshed

her mirror
two phoenixes   10
a pool of autumn light

standing on the ivory bed
loosening her hair
watching the mirror

one long coil, aromatic silk   15
a cloud down to the floor

drop the jade comb — no sound

delicate fingers
pushing the coils into place
color of raven feathers   20

shining blue-black stuff
the jewelled comb will hardly hold it

spring wind makes me restless
her slovenly beauty upsets me

eighteen and her hair's so thick   25
she wears herself out fixing it!

she's finished now
the whole arrangement in place

in a cloud-patterned skirt
she walks with even steps   30
a wild goose on the sand

turns away without a word
where is she off to?

down the steps to break a spray of
        cherry blossoms   35

CONSIDERATIONS FOR CRITICAL THINKING AND WRITING

1. **FIRST RESPONSE.** Try to paraphrase the poem. What is lost by rewording?

2. How does the speaker use sensuous language to create a vivid picture of the girl?

3. What are the speaker's feelings toward the girl? Do they remain the same throughout the poem?

CONNECTIONS TO OTHER SELECTIONS

1. Compare the description of hair in this poem with that in Cathy Song's "The White Porch" (p. 861). What significant similarities do you find?

2. Write an essay that explores the differing portraits in this poem and in Sylvia Plath's "Mirror" (p. 879). Which portrait is more interesting to you? Explain why.

BILLY COLLINS (B. 1941)

Marginalia   *1998*

Sometimes the notes are ferocious,
skirmishes against the author
raging along the borders of every page
in tiny black script.
If I could just get my hands on you,   5
Kierkegaard,° or Conor Cruise O'Brien,°
they seem to say,
I would bolt the door and beat some logic into your head.

Other comments are more offhand, dismissive —
"Nonsense." "Please!" "HA!!" —   10
that kind of thing.
I remember once looking up from my reading,
my thumb as a bookmark,
trying to imagine what the person must look like
who wrote "Don't be a ninny"   15
alongside a paragraph in *The Life of Emily Dickinson.*

Students are more modest
needing to leave only their splayed footprints
along the shore of the page.

One scrawls "Metaphor" next to a stanza of Eliot's.°   20
Another notes the presence of "Irony"
fifty times outside the paragraphs of *A Modest Proposal.*°

Or they are fans who cheer from the empty bleachers,
hands cupped around their mouths.
"Absolutely," they shout   25
to Duns Scotus° and James Baldwin.°
"Yes." "Bull's-eye." "My man!"
Check marks, asterisks, and exclamation points
rain down along the sidelines.

And if you have managed to graduate from college   30
without ever having written "Man vs. Nature"
in a margin, perhaps now
is the time to take one step forward.

We have all seized the white perimeter as our own
and reached for a pen if only to show   35
we did not just laze in an armchair turning pages;
we pressed a thought into the wayside,
planted an impression along the verge.

6 *Kierkegaard:* Søren Aaby Kierkegaard (1813–1855), Danish philosopher and theologian; *Conor Cruise O'Brien* (1917–2008): Irish historian, critic, and statesman.   20 *Eliot's:* Thomas Stearns Eliot (1888–1965), American-born English poet and critic (see p. 1213).   22 *A Modest Proposal:* An essay by English satirist Jonathan Swift (1667–1745).   26 *Duns Scotus* (1265?–1308): Scottish theologian; *James Baldwin* (1924–1987): African American essayist and novelist.

Even Irish monks in their cold scriptoria°
jotted along the borders of the Gospels   40
brief asides about the pains of copying,
a bird singing near their window,
or the sunlight that illuminated their page —
anonymous men catching a ride into the future
on a vessel more lasting than themselves.   45

And you have not read Joshua Reynolds,°
they say, until you have read him
enwreathed with Blake's° furious scribbling.

Yet the one I think of most often,
the one that dangles from me like a locket,   50
was written in the copy of *Catcher in the Rye*°
I borrowed from the local library
one slow, hot summer.
I was just beginning high school then,
reading books on a davenport in my parents' living room,   55
and I cannot tell you
how vastly my loneliness was deepened,
how poignant and amplified the world before me seemed,
when I found on one page

a few greasy looking smears   60
and next to them, written in soft pencil —
by a beautiful girl, I could tell,
whom I would never meet —
"Pardon the egg salad stains, but I'm in love."

39 *scriptoria:* Rooms in a monastery used for writing and copying.   46 *Joshua Reynolds*
(1723–1792): English portrait artist who entertained many of the important writers of his
time.   48 *Blake's:* William Blake (1757–1827), English mystic and poet.   51 *Catcher in the
Rye:* A novel (1951) about adolescence by American author J. D. Salinger (b. 1919).

CONSIDERATIONS FOR CRITICAL THINKING AND WRITING

1. **FIRST RESPONSE.** How does your own experience of finding notations written in the margins of books compare with the speaker's?

2. How does Collins use humor to characterize the speaker?

3. Given the poem's final sixteen lines, consider how the title might go beyond simply announcing the subject matter of the poem.

CONNECTIONS TO OTHER SELECTIONS

1. Discuss the speakers' responses to reading in this poem and in Philip
   Larkin's "A Study of Reading Habits" (p. 757). How is reading used as a
   measure of each speaker's character?

2. Describe the speakers' attitudes toward books in this poem and in Anne
   Bradstreet's "The Author to Her Book" (p. 868).

CHRISTIAN BÖK (B. 1966)

Vowels   *2001*

loveless vessels

we vow
solo love

we see
love solve loss

else we see
love sow woe

selves we woo
we lose

losses we levee
we owe

we sell
loose vows

so we love
less well

so low
so level

wolves evolve

© Christian Yde Frostholm.   10

15

CONSIDERATIONS FOR CRITICAL THINKING AND WRITING

1. **FIRST RESPONSE.** What do you think Bök is up to in this poem? How is the title related to the lines that follow it?

2. Paraphrase the narrative that the poem tells.

3. **CREATIVE RESPONSE.** Using Bök's strategy and style, choose a single word and try writing your own poem in the same manner.

22

Writing about Poetry:
From Inquiry to Final Paper

Poems reveal secrets when they are analyzed. The poet's pleasure in finding ingenious ways to enclose her secrets should be matched by the reader's pleasure in unlocking and revealing secrets.

— DIANE WAKOSKI

© Robert Turney.

FROM READING TO WRITING

Writing about poetry can be a rigorous means of testing the validity of your own reading of a poem. Anyone who has been asked to write several pages about a fourteen-line poem knows how intellectually challenging this exercise is, because it means paying close attention to language. Such scrutiny of words, however, sensitizes you not only to the poet's use of language but also to your own use of language. At first you may feel intimidated by having to compose a paper that is longer than the poem you're writing about, but a careful reading will reveal that there's plenty to write about what the poem says and how it says it. Keep in mind that your job is not to produce a definitive reading of the poem—even Carl Sandburg once confessed that "I've written some poetry I don't understand myself." It is enough to develop an interesting thesis and to present it clearly and persuasively.

An interesting thesis will come to you if you read and reread, take notes, annotate the text, and generate ideas (for a discussion of this process, see Chapter 54, "Reading and the Writing Process"). Although it requires energy to read closely and to write convincingly about the charged language found in poetry, there is nothing mysterious about such reading and writing. This chapter provides a set of questions designed to sharpen your reading and writing about poetry. Following these questions is a sample paper that offers a clear and well-developed thesis concerning Elizabeth Bishop's "Manners."

Questions for Responsive Reading and Writing

The following questions can help you respond to important elements that reveal a poem's effects and meanings. The questions are general, so not all of them will necessarily be relevant to a particular poem. Many, however, should prove useful for thinking, talking, and writing about each poem in this collection. If you are uncertain about the meaning of a term used in a question, consult the Glossary of Literary Terms beginning on page 2123.

Before addressing these questions, read the poem you are studying in its entirety. Don't worry about interpretation on a first reading; allow yourself the pleasure of enjoying whatever makes itself apparent to you. Then on subsequent readings, use the questions to understand and appreciate how the poem works.

1. Who is the speaker? Is it possible to determine the speaker's age, sex, sensibilities, level of awareness, and values?

2. Is the speaker addressing anyone in particular?

3. How do you respond to the speaker? Favorably? Negatively? What is the situation? Are there any special circumstances that inform what the speaker says?

4. Is there a specific setting of time and place?

5. Does reading the poem aloud help you to understand it?

6. Does a paraphrase reveal the basic purpose of the poem?

7. What does the title emphasize?

8. Is the theme presented directly or indirectly?

9. Do any allusions enrich the poem's meaning?

10. How does the diction reveal meaning? Are any words repeated? Do any carry evocative connotative meanings? Are there any puns or other forms of verbal wit?

11. Are figures of speech used? How does the figurative language contribute to the poem's vividness and meaning?

(continued)

12. Do any objects, persons, places, events, or actions have allegorical or symbolic meanings? What other details in the poem support your interpretation?

13. Is irony used? Are there any examples of situational irony, verbal irony, or dramatic irony? Is understatement or paradox used?

14. What is the tone of the poem? Is the tone consistent?

15. Does the poem use onomatopoeia, assonance, consonance, or alliteration? How do these sounds affect you?

16. What sounds are repeated? If there are rhymes, what is their effect? Do they seem forced or natural? Is there a rhyme scheme? Do the rhymes contribute to the poem's meaning?

17. Do the lines have a regular meter? What is the predominant meter? Are there significant variations? Does the rhythm seem appropriate for the poem's tone?

18. Does the poem's form—its overall structure—follow an established pattern? Do you think the form is a suitable vehicle for the poem's meaning and effects?

19. Is the language of the poem intense and concentrated? Do you think it warrants more than one or two close readings?

20. Did you enjoy the poem? What, specifically, pleased or displeased you about what was expressed and how it was expressed?

21. Is there a particular critical approach that seems especially appropriate for this poem? (See Chapter 53, "Critical Strategies for Reading.")

22. How might biographical information about the author help to determine the poem's central concerns?

23. How might historical information about the poem provide a useful context for interpretation?

24. To what extent do your own experiences, values, beliefs, and assumptions inform your interpretation?

25. What kinds of evidence from the poem are you focusing on to support your interpretation? Does your interpretation leave out any important elements that might undercut or qualify your interpretation?

26. Given that there are a variety of ways to interpret the poem, which one seems the most useful to you?

ELIZABETH BISHOP (1911–1979)

Manners

1965

for a Child of 1918

My grandfather said to me
as we sat on the wagon seat,
"Be sure to remember to always
speak to everyone you meet."

Web Explore contexts for Elizabeth Bishop and approaches to this poem at bedfordstmartins.com/ meyerlit.

We met a stranger on foot.
My grandfather's whip tapped his hat.
"Good day, sir. Good day. A fine day."
And I said it and bowed where I sat.

Then we overtook a boy we knew
with his big pet crow on his shoulder.
"Always offer everyone a ride;
don't forget that when you get older,"

© Bettmann/CORBIS.

my grandfather said. So Willy
climbed up with us, but the crow
gave a "Caw!" and flew off. I was worried.
How would he know where to go?

But he flew a little way at a time
from fence post to fence post, ahead;
and when Willy whistled he answered.
"A fine bird," my grandfather said,   20

"and he's well brought up. See, he answers
nicely when he's spoken to.
Man or beast, that's good manners.
Be sure that you both always do."

When automobiles went by,   25
the dust hid the people's faces,
but we shouted "Good day! Good day!
Fine day!" at the top of our voices.

When we came to Hustler Hill,
he said that the mare was tired,   30
so we all got down and walked,
as our good manners required.

A SAMPLE CLOSE READING

An Annotated Version of "Manners"

The following annotations represent insights about the relationship of
various elements at work in the poem gleaned only after several close
readings. Don't expect to be able to produce these kinds of interpretive
notes on a first reading because such perceptions will not be apparent
until you've read the poem and then gone back to the beginning to discover how each word, line, and stanza contributes to the overall effect.
Writing your responses in the margins of the page can be a useful means
of recording your impressions as well as discovering new insights as you
read the text closely.

Elizabeth Bishop (1911–1979)

Manners   1965

for a Child of 1918

Title refers to what is socially correct, polite and/or decent behavior.

WWI ended in 1918 and denotes a shift in values and manners that often follows rapid social changes brought about by war.

Wagon seat suggests a simpler past—as does simple language and informal diction of the child speaker.

My grandfather said to me
as we sat on the wagon seat,
"Be sure to remember to always
speak to everyone you meet."

We met a stranger on foot.   5
My grandfather's whip tapped his hat.
"Good day, sir. Good day. A fine day."
And I said it and bowed where I sat.

Grandfather seems kind, but he also carries a whip that reinforces his authoritative voice.

Idea that values "always" transcend time is emphasized by the grandfather's urging: "don't forget."

Then we overtook a boy we knew
with his big pet crow on his shoulder.   10
"Always offer everyone a ride;
don't forget that when you get older,"

"My grandfather," repeated four times in first five stanzas, reflects the child's affection and a sense of belonging in his world. The crow, however, worries the child and indicates an uncertain future.

my grandfather said. So Willy
climbed up with us, but the crow
gave a "Caw!" and flew off. I was worried.   15
How would he know where to go?

But he flew a little way at a time
from fence post to fence post, ahead;
and when Willy whistled he answered.
"A fine bird," my grandfather said,   20

Predictable quatrains and *abcb* rhyme scheme throughout the poem take the worry out of where they—and the crow—are headed.

Third time the grandfather says "always." This and the inverted syntax of line 24 call attention, again, to idea that good manners are forever important.

"and he's well brought up. See, he answers
nicely when he's spoken to.
Man or beast, that's good manners.
Be sure that you both always do."

When automobiles went by,   25
the dust hid the people's faces,

The modern symbolic automobile races by raising dust that obscures everyone's vision and forces them to shout. Rhymes in lines 26 and 28 are off (unlike all the other rhymes) just enough to suggest the dissonant future that will supersede the calm wagon ride.

but we shouted "Good day! Good day!

Fine day!" at the top of our voices.

> The horse, like the simple past it symbolizes, is weakened by the hustle of modern life, but even so, "our" good manners prevail, internalized from the grandfather's values.

When we came to Hustler Hill,

he said that the mare was tired,   30

so we all got down and walked,

as our good manners required.

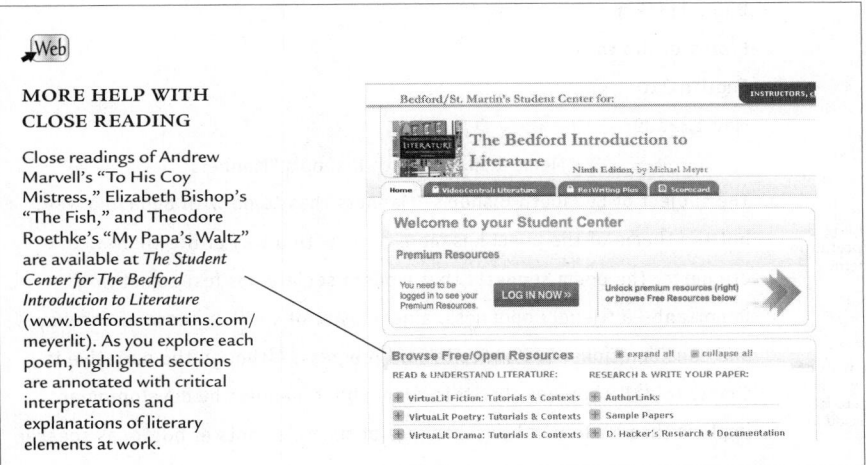

**MORE HELP WITH
CLOSE READING**

Close readings of Andrew Marvell's "To His Coy Mistress," Elizabeth Bishop's "The Fish," and Theodore Roethke's "My Papa's Waltz" are available at *The Student Center for The Bedford Introduction to Literature* (www.bedfordstmartins.com/meyerlit). As you explore each poem, highlighted sections are annotated with critical interpretations and explanations of literary elements at work.

A SAMPLE STUDENT ANALYSIS

Memory in Elizabeth Bishop's "Manners"

The following sample paper on Elizabeth Bishop's "Manners" was written in response to an assignment that called for a 750-word discussion of the ways in which at least five of the following elements work to develop and reinforce the poem's themes:

diction and tone	irony	form
images	sound and rhyme	speaker
figures of speech	rhythm and meter	setting and situation
symbols		

In her paper, Debra Epstein discusses the ways in which a number of these elements contribute to what she sees as a central theme of "Manners": the loss of a way of life that Bishop associates with the end of World War I. Not all of the elements of poetry are covered equally in Epstein's paper because some, such as the speaker and setting, are more important to her argument than others. Notice how rather than merely listing each of the elements, Epstein mentions them in her discussion as she needs to in order to develop the thesis that she clearly and succinctly expresses in her opening paragraph.

Web Research the poets in this chapter at bedfordstmartins.com/meyerlit.

Epstein 1

Debra Epstein

Professor Brown

English 210

May 1, 2009

Memory in Elizabeth Bishop's "Manners"

Thesis providing interpretation of poem.

The subject of Elizabeth Bishop's "Manners" has to do with behaving well, but the theme of the poem has more to do with a way of life than with etiquette. The poem suggests that modern society has lost something important—a friendly openness, a generosity of spirit, a sense of decency and consideration—in its race toward progress. Although the narrative is simply told, Bishop enriches this poem about manners by developing an implicit theme through her subtle use of such elements of poetry as speaker, setting, rhyme, meter, symbol, and images.

Statement of elements in poem to be discussed in paper.

Summary of poem's narrative and introduction to discussion of elements.

The dedication suggests that the speaker is "a Child of 1918" who accompanies his or her grandfather on a wagon ride and who is urged to practice good manners by greeting people, offering everyone a ride, and speaking when spoken to by anyone. During the ride they say hello to a stranger, give a ride to a boy with a pet crow, shout greetings to a passing automobile, and get down from the wagon when they reach a hill because the horse is tired. They walk because "good manners required" (line 32) such consideration, even for a horse. This summary indicates what goes on in the poem but not its significance. That requires a closer look at some of the poem's elements.

Analysis of speaker in poem.

Given the speaker's simple language (there are no metaphors or similes and only a few words out of thirty-two lines are longer than two syllables), it seems likely that he or she is a fairly young child, rather than an adult reminiscing. (It is interesting to note that Bishop herself, though not identical with the speaker, would have been seven in 1918.) Because the speaker is a young child who uses simple diction, Bishop has to show us the ride's significance indirectly rather than having the speaker explicitly state it.

The setting for the speaker's narrative is important because 1918 was the year World War I ended, and it marked the beginning of a new era of technology that was the result of rapid industrialization during the war. Horses and wagons would soon be put out to pasture. The grandfather's manners emphasize a time gone by; the child must be told to "remember" what the grandfather says because he or she will take that advice into a new and very different world.

Analysis of poem's setting.

The grandfather's world of the horse and wagon is uncomplicated, and this is reflected in both the simple quatrains that move predictably along in an *abcb* rhyme scheme and the frequent anapestic meter (ăs wĕ săt ŏn thĕ wăgŏn [2]) that pulls the lines rapidly and lightly. The one moment Bishop breaks the set rhyme scheme is in the seventh stanza when the automobile (the single four-syllable word in the poem) rushes by in a cloud of dust so that people cannot see or hear each other. The only off rhymes in the poem—"faces" (26) and "voices" (28)—are also in this stanza, which suggests that the automobile and the people in it are somehow off or out of sync with what goes on in the other stanzas. The automobile is a symbol of a way of life in which people—their faces hidden—and manners take a back seat to speed and noise. The people in the car don't wave, don't offer a ride, and don't speak when spoken to.

Analysis of rhyme scheme and meter.

Analysis of symbols.

Maybe the image of the crow's noisy cawing and flying from post to post is a foreshadowing that should prepare readers for the automobile. The speaker feels "worried" about the crow's apparent directionlessness: "How would he know where to go?" (16). However, neither the child nor the grandfather (nor the reader on a first reading) clearly sees the two worlds that Bishop contrasts in the final stanza.

Analysis of images.

"Hustler Hill" is the perfect name for what finally tires out the mare. There is no hurry for the grandfather and child, but there is for those people

Conclusion supporting thesis on poem's theme.

Epstein 3

in the car and the postwar hustle and bustle they represent. The fast-paced future overtakes the tired symbol of the past in the poem. The pace slows as the wagon passengers get down to walk, but the reader recognizes that the grandfather's way has been lost to a world in which good manners are not required.

Epstein 4

Work Cited

Bishop, Elizabeth. "Manners." *The Bedford Introduction to Literature.* Ed. Michael Meyer. 9th ed. Boston: Bedford/St. Martin's, 2011. 792–93. Print.

23

Word Choice, Word Order, and Tone

By permission of The Granger Collection, New York.

I still feel that a poet has a duty to words, and that words can do wonderful things. And it's too bad to just let them lie there without doing anything with and for them.

— GWENDOLYN BROOKS

WORD CHOICE

Diction

Like all good writers, poets are keenly aware of ***diction,*** their choice of words. Poets, however, choose words especially carefully because the words in poems call attention to themselves. Characters, actions, settings, and symbols may appear in a poem, but in the foreground, before all else, is the poem's language. Also, poems are usually briefer than other forms of writing. A few inappropriate words in a 200-page novel (which would have about 100,000 words) create fewer problems than they would in a 100-word poem. Functioning in a compressed atmosphere, the words in a poem must convey meanings gracefully and economically. Readers therefore have to be alert to the ways in which those meanings are released.

Web Explore the poetic elements in this chapter at bedfordstmartins.com/meyerlit.

Although poetic language is often more intensely charged than ordinary speech, the words used in poetry are not necessarily different from everyday speech. Inexperienced readers may sometimes assume that language must be high-flown and out of date to be included in a poem: instead of reading about a boy "enjoying a swim," they expect to read about a boy "disporting with pliant arm o'er a glassy wave." During the eighteenth century this kind of **poetic diction** — the use of elevated language rather than ordinary language — was highly valued in English poetry, but since the nineteenth century poets have generally overridden the distinctions that were once made between words used in everyday speech and those used in poetry. Today all levels of diction can be found in poetry.

A poet, like any writer, has several levels of diction from which to choose; they range from formal to middle to informal. **Formal diction** consists of a dignified, impersonal, and elevated use of language. Notice, for example, the formality of Thomas Hardy's description of the sunken luxury liner *Titanic* in this stanza from "The Convergence of the Twain" (the entire poem appears on p. 818):

> In a solitude of the sea
> Deep from human vanity,
> And the Pride of Life that planned her, stilly couches she.

There is nothing casual or relaxed about these lines. Hardy's use of "stilly," meaning "quietly" or "calmly," is purely literary; the word rarely, if ever, turns up in everyday English.

The language used in Sharon Olds's "Last Night" (p. 816) represents a less formal level of diction; the speaker uses a **middle diction** spoken by most educated people. Consider how Olds's speaker struggles the next day to comprehend her passion:

> Love? It was more like dragonflies
> in the sun, 100 degrees at noon,
> the ends of their abdomens stuck together, I
> close my eyes when I remember.

The words used to describe this encounter are common enough, yet it is precisely Olds's use of language that evokes the extraordinary nature of this couple's connection.

Informal diction is evident in Philip Larkin's "A Study of Reading Habits" (p. 757). The speaker's account of his early reading is presented **colloquially,** in a conversational manner that in this instance includes slang expressions not used by the culture at large:

> When getting my nose in a book
> Cured most things short of school,
> It was worth ruining my eyes
> To know I could still keep cool,
> And deal out the old right hook
> To dirty dogs twice my size.

This level of diction is clearly not that of Hardy's or Olds's speakers.

Poets may also draw on another form of informal diction, called *dialect.* Dialects are spoken by definable groups of people from a particular geographic region, economic group, or social class. New England dialects are often heard in Robert Frost's poems, for example. Gwendolyn Brooks uses a black dialect in "We Real Cool" (p. 827) to characterize a group of pool players. Another form of diction related to particular groups is *jargon,* a category of language defined by a trade or profession. Sociologists, photographers, carpenters, baseball players, and dentists, for example, all use words that are specific to their fields. Sally Croft offers an appetizing dish of cookbook jargon in "Home-Baked Bread" (p. 857).

Many levels of diction are available to poets. The variety of diction to be found in poetry is enormous, and that is how it should be. No language is foreign to poetry because it is possible to imagine any human voice as the speaker of a poem. When we say a poem is formal, informal, or somewhere in between, we are making a descriptive statement rather than an evaluative one. What matters in a poem is not only which words are used but how they are used.

Denotations and Connotations

One important way that the meaning of a word is communicated in a poem is through sound: snakes *hiss,* saws *buzz.* This and other matters related to sound are discussed in Chapter 27. Individual words also convey meanings through denotations and connotations. *Denotations* are the literal, dictionary meanings of a word. For example, *bird* denotes a feathered animal with wings (other denotations for the same word include a shuttlecock, an airplane, or an odd person), but in addition to its denotative meanings, *bird* also carries *connotations*—associations and implications that go beyond a word's literal meanings. Connotations derive from how the word has been used and the associations people make with it. Therefore, the connotations of *bird* might include fragility, vulnerability, altitude, the sky, or freedom, depending on the context in which the word is used. Consider also how different the connotations are for the following types of birds: hawk, dove, penguin, pigeon, chicken, peacock, duck, crow, turkey, gull, owl, goose, coot, and vulture. These words have long been used to refer to types of people as well as birds. They are rich in connotative meanings.

Connotations derive their resonance from a person's experiences with a word. Those experiences may not always be the same, especially when the people having them are in different times and places. *Theater,* for instance, was once associated with depravity, disease, and sin, whereas today the word usually evokes some sense of high culture and perhaps visions of elegant opulence. In several ethnic communities in the United States many people would find *squid* appetizing, but elsewhere the word is likely to produce negative connotations. Readers must recognize, then, that words written in other times and places may have unexpected connotations. Annotations usually help in these matters, which is why it makes sense to pay attention to them when they are available.

Ordinarily, though, the language of poetry is accessible, even when the circumstances of the reader and the poet are different. Although connotative language may be used subtly, it mostly draws on associations experienced by many people. Poets rely on widely shared associations rather than the idiosyncratic response that an individual might have to a word. Someone who has received a severe burn from a fireplace accident may associate the word *hearth* with intense pain instead of home and family life, but that reader must not allow a personal experience to undermine the response the poet intends to evoke. Connotative meanings are usually public meanings.

Perhaps this can be seen most clearly in advertising, where language is also used primarily to convey moods and feelings rather than information. For instance, three decades of increasing interest in nutrition and general fitness have created a collective consciousness that advertisers have capitalized on successfully. Knowing that we want to be slender or lean or slim (not *spare* or *scrawny* and certainly not *gaunt*), advertisers have created a new word to describe beers, wines, sodas, cheeses, canned fruits, and other products that tend to overload what used to be called sweatclothes and sneakers. The word is *lite*. The assumed denotative meaning of *lite* is "low in calories," but as close readers of ingredient labels know, some *lites* are heavier than regularly prepared products. There can be no doubt about the connotative meaning of *lite*, however. Whatever is *lite* cannot hurt you; less is more. Even the word is lighter than *light;* there is no unnecessary droopy *g* or plump *h*. *Lite* is a brilliantly manufactured use of connotation.

Connotative meanings are valuable because they allow poets to be economical and suggestive simultaneously. In this way emotions and attitudes are carefully woven into the texture of the poem's language. Read the following poem and pay close attention to the connotative meanings of its words.

RANDALL JARRELL (1914–1965)

The Death of the Ball Turret Gunner   1945

From my mother's sleep I fell into the State
And I hunched in its belly till my wet fur froze.
Six miles from earth, loosed from its dream of life,
I woke to black flack and the nightmare fighters.
When I died they washed me out of the turret with a hose.

The title of this poem establishes the setting and the speaker's situation. Like the setting of a short story, the setting of a poem is important when the time and place influence what happens. "The Death of the Ball Turret Gunner" is set in the midst of a war and, more specifically, in a ball turret—a Plexiglas sphere housing machine guns on the underside of a bomber. The speaker's situation obviously places him in extreme danger; indeed, his fate is announced in the title.

Although the poem is written in the first-person singular, its speaker is clearly not the poet. Jarrell uses a ***persona,*** a speaker created by the poet. In this poem the persona is a disembodied voice that makes the gunner's story all the more powerful. What is his story? A paraphrase might read something like this:

> After I was born, I grew up to find myself at war, cramped into the turret of a bomber's belly some 31,000 feet above the ground. Below me were exploding shells from antiaircraft guns and attacking fighter planes. I was killed, but the bomber returned to base, where my remains were cleaned out of the turret so the next man could take my place.

This paraphrase is accurate, but its language is much less suggestive than the poem's. The first line of the poem has the speaker emerge from his "mother's sleep," the anesthetized sleep of her giving birth. The phrase also suggests the comfort, warmth, and security he knew as a child. This safety was left behind when he "fell," a verb that evokes the danger and involuntary movement associated with his subsequent "State" (*fell* also echoes, perhaps, the fall from innocence to experience related in the Bible).

Several dictionary definitions appear for the noun *state;* it can denote a territorial unit, the power and authority of a government, a person's social status, or a person's emotional or physical condition. The context provided by the rest of the poem makes clear that "State" has several denotative meanings here: because it is capitalized, it certainly refers to the violent world of a government at war, but it also refers to the gunner's vulnerable status as well as his physical and emotional condition. By having "State" carry more than one meaning, Jarrell has created an intentional ambiguity. ***Ambiguity*** allows for two or more simultaneous interpretations of a word, a phrase, an action, or a situation, all of which can be supported by the context of a work. Through his ambiguous use of "State," Jarrell connects the horrors of war not just to bombers and gunners but to the governments that control them.

Related to this ambiguity is the connotative meaning of "State" in the poem. The context demands that the word be read with a negative charge. The word is not used with patriotic pride but to suggest an anonymous, impersonal "State" that kills rather than nurtures the life in its "belly." The state's "belly" is a bomber, and the gunner is "hunched" like a fetus in the cramped turret, where, in contrast to the warmth of his mother's womb, everything is frozen, even the "wet fur" of his flight jacket (newborn infants have wet fur too). The gunner is not just 31,000 feet from the ground but "Six miles from earth." *Six miles* has roughly the same denotative meaning as 31,000 feet, but Jarrell knew that the connotative meaning of *six miles* makes the speaker's position seem even more remote and frightening.

When the gunner is born into the violent world of war, he finds himself waking up to a "nightmare" that is all too real. The poem's final line is grimly understated, but it hits the reader with the force of an exploding shell: what the State-bomber-turret gives birth to is a gruesome death that is merely one of an endless series. It may be tempting to reduce the theme of this poem to the idea that "war is hell," but Jarrell's target is more specific. He implicates the "State," which routinely executes such violence, and he does so without preaching or hysterical denunciations. Instead, his use of language conveys his theme subtly and powerfully.

WORD ORDER

Meanings in poems are conveyed not only by denotations and connotations but also by the poet's arrangement of words into phrases, clauses, and sentences to achieve particular effects. The ordering of words into meaningful verbal patterns is called *syntax.* A poet can manipulate the syntax of a line to place emphasis on a word; this is especially apparent when a poet varies normal word order. In Emily Dickinson's "A narrow Fellow in the Grass" (p. 2), for example, the speaker says about the snake that "His notice sudden is." Ordinarily, that would be expressed as "his notice is sudden." By placing the verb *is* unexpectedly at the end of the line, Dickinson creates the sense of surprise we feel when we suddenly come upon a snake. Dickinson's inversion of the standard word order also makes the final sound of the line a hissing *is.*

TONE

Tone is the writer's attitude toward the subject, the mood created by all of the elements in the poem. Writing, like speech, can be characterized as serious or light, sad or happy, private or public, angry or affectionate, bitter or nostalgic, or by any other attitudes and feelings that human beings experience. In Jarrell's "The Death of the Ball Turret Gunner," the tone is clearly serious; the voice in the poem even sounds dead. Listen again to the persona's final words: "When I died they washed me out of the turret with a hose." The brutal, restrained matter-of-factness of this line is effective because the reader is called on to supply the appropriate anger and despair — a strategy that makes those emotions all the more convincing.

Consider how tone is used to convey meaning in the next poem, inspired by the poet's contemplation of mortality.

JUDITH ORTIZ COFER (B. 1952)

Common Ground 1987

Blood tells the story of your life
in heartbeats as you live it;
bones speak in the language
of death, and flesh thins
with age when up 5
through your pores rises
the stuff of your origin.

    These days,
when I look into the mirror I see
my grandmother's stern lips 10
speaking in parentheses at the corners
of my mouth of pain and deprivation
I have never known. I recognize
my father's brows arching in disdain
over the objects of my vanity, my mother's 15
nervous hands smoothing lines
just appearing on my skin,
like arrows pointing downward
to our common ground.

CONSIDERATIONS FOR CRITICAL THINKING AND WRITING

1. **FIRST RESPONSE.** How do you interpret the title? How did your idea of its meaning change as you read the poem?
2. What is the relationship between the first and second stanzas?
3. How does this poem make you feel? What is its tone? How do the diction and imagery create the tone?

COLETTE INEZ (B. 1931)

Back When All Was Continuous Chuckles 2004

after a line by Anselm Hollo °

Doris and I were helpless on the Beeline Bus
laughing at what was it? "What did the moron
who killed his mother and father eat
at the orphan's picnic?" "Crow?" Har-har.

Anselm Hollo: Finnish poet (b. 1934) who teaches creative writing in the United States.

The bus was grinding towards Hempstead,   5
past the cemetery whose stones Doris
and I found hilarious. Freaky ghouls and skeletons.
"What did the dead man say to the ghost?"

"I like the movie better than the book."
Even "I don't get it" was funny.   10
The war was on, rationing, sirens.
Silly billies, we poked each other's arms

with balled fists, held hands and howled
at crabby ladies in funny hats, dusty feathers,
fake fruit. Doris' mom wore this headgear   15
before she got the big C which no one said out loud.

In a shadowy room her skin seemed gray
as moon dust on Smith Street, as Doris' house
where we tiptoed down the hall.
Sometimes we heard moans from the back room   20

and I helped wring out cloths while Doris
brought water in a glass held to her mother's lips.
But soon we were flipping through joke books
and writhing on the floor, war news shut off

back when we pretended all was continuous chuckles,   25
and we rode the bus past Greenfield's rise
where stones, trumpeting angels,
would bear names we later came to recognize.

CONSIDERATIONS FOR CRITICAL THINKING AND WRITING

1. **FIRST RESPONSE.** Compare the difference between the title and its slightly revised version as it appears in line 25. How does that difference reveal the theme?

2. At what point does the tone of the poem shift from chuckles to something else?

3. What is the effect of the rhymes in lines 26 and 28? How do the rhymes serve to reinforce the poem's theme?

CONNECTION TO ANOTHER SELECTION

1. Discuss the tone of this poem and that of Gwendolyn Brooks's "We Real Cool" (p. 827).

The next work is a ***dramatic monologue,*** a type of poem in which a character — the speaker — addresses a silent audience in such a way as to reveal unintentionally some aspect of his or her temperament or personality. What tone is created by Machan's use of a persona?

KATHARYN HOWD MACHAN (B. 1952)

Hazel Tells LaVerne   *1976*

last night
im cleanin out my
howard johnsons ladies room
when all of a sudden
up pops this frog   5
musta come from the sewer
swimmin aroun an tryin ta
climb up the sida the bowl
so i goes ta flushm down
but sohelpmegod he starts talkin   10
bout a golden ball
an how i can be a princess
me a princess
well my mouth drops
all the way to the floor   15
an he says
kiss me just kiss me
once on the nose
well i screams
ya little green pervert   20
an i hitsm with my mop
an has ta flush
the toilet down three times
me
a princess   25

CONSIDERATIONS FOR CRITICAL THINKING AND WRITING

1. **FIRST RESPONSE.** What do you imagine the situation and setting are for this poem? Do you like this revision of the fairy tale "The Frog Prince"?

2. What creates the poem's humor? How does Hazel's use of language reveal her personality? Is her treatment of the frog consistent with her character?

3. Although it has no punctuation, this poem is easy to follow. How does the arrangement of the lines organize Hazel's speech for clarity and emphasis?

4. What is the theme? Is it conveyed through denotative or connotative language?

5. **CREATIVE RESPONSE.** Write what you think might be LaVerne's reply to Hazel. First, write LaVerne's response as a series of ordinary sentences, and then try editing and organizing them into poetic lines.

CONNECTION TO ANOTHER SELECTION

1. Although Robert Browning's "My Last Duchess" (p. 910) is a more complex poem than Machan's, both use dramatic monologues to reveal character. How are the strategies in each poem similar?

A SAMPLE STUDENT RESPONSE

Alex Georges

Professor Myerov

English 200

October 2, 2009

Tone in Katharyn Howd Machan's "Hazel Tells LaVerne"

"Tone," Michael Meyer writes, "is the writer's attitude toward the subject, the mood created by all of the elements of the poem" (804) and is used to convey meaning and character. In her dramatic monologue, "Hazel Tells LaVerne," the poet Katharyn Howd Machan reveals through the persona of Hazel—a funny, tough-talking, no-nonsense cleaning lady—a satirical revision of "The Frog Prince" fairy tale. Hazel's attitude toward the possibility of a fairy-tale romance is evident in her response to the frog prince. She has no use for him or his offers "bout a golden ball / an how i can be a princess" (lines 11-12). If Hazel is viewed by the reader as a princess, it is clear from her words and tone that she is far from a traditional one.

Machan's word choice and humorous tone also reveal much about Hazel's personality and circumstances. Through the use of slang, alternate spellings, and the omission of punctuation, we learn a great deal about the character:

> well i screams
>
> ya little green pervert
>
> an i hitsm with my mop
>
> an has ta flush
>
> the toilet down three times
>
> me
>
> a princess (19-25)

Listening to her speak, the reader understands that Hazel, a cleaner at Howard Johnson's, does not have an extensive education. She speaks in the colloquial, running words into one another and using phrases like "ya little green pervert" (20) and "i screams" (19). The lack of complete sentences,

capital letters, and punctuation adds to her informal tone. Hazel's speech defines her social status, brings out details of her personality, and gives the reader
her view of herself. She is accustomed to the thankless daily grind of work and
will not allow herself even a moment's fantasy of becoming a princess. It is a
notion that she has to flush away—literally, has "ta flush . . . down three
times." She tells LaVerne that the very idea of such fantasy is absurd to her, as
she states in the final lines: "me / a princess" (24-25).

Works Cited

Machan, Katharyn Howd. "Hazel Tells LaVerne." *The Bedford Introduction to
Literature*. Ed. Michael Meyer. 9th ed. Boston: Bedford/St. Martin's,
2011. 807. Print.

Meyer, Michael, ed. *The Bedford Introduction to Literature*. 9th ed. Boston:
Bedford/St. Martin's, 2011. 804. Print.

MARTÍN ESPADA (B. 1957)
Latin Night at the Pawnshop   *1987*

Chelsea, Massachusetts
Christmas, 1987

The apparition of a salsa band
gleaming in the Liberty Loan
pawnshop window:

Golden trumpet,
silver trombone,   5
congas, maracas, tambourine,

all with price tags dangling
like the city morgue ticket
on a dead man's toe.

CONSIDERATIONS FOR CRITICAL THINKING AND WRITING

1. **FIRST RESPONSE.** What is "Latin" about this night at the pawnshop?
2. What kind of tone is created by the poet's word choice and by the poem's rhythm?
3. Does it matter that this apparition occurs on Christmas night? Why or why not?
4. What do you think is the central point of this poem?

How do the speaker's attitude and tone change during the course of this next poem?

PAUL LAURENCE DUNBAR (1872–1906)
To a Captious Critic   1903

Dear critic, who my lightness so deplores,
Would I might study to be prince of bores,
Right wisely would I rule that dull estate —
But, sir, I may not; till you abdicate.

CONSIDERATIONS FOR CRITICAL THINKING AND WRITING

1. **FIRST RESPONSE.** How do Dunbar's vocabulary and syntax signal the level of diction used in the poem?
2. Describe the speaker's tone. How does it characterize the speaker as well as the critic?
3. **CREATIVE RESPONSE.** Using "To a Captious Critic" as a model, try writing a four-line witty reply to someone in your own life — perhaps a roommate, coach, teacher, waiter, dentist, or anyone else who provokes a strong response in you.

DICTION AND TONE IN FOUR LOVE POEMS

The first three of these love poems share the same basic situation and theme: a male speaker addresses a female (in the first poem it is a type of female) urging that love should not be delayed because time is short. This theme is as familiar in poetry as it is in life. In Latin this tradition is known as *carpe diem,* "seize the day." Notice how the poets' diction helps create a distinctive tone in each poem, even though the subject matter and central ideas are similar (although not identical) in all three.

ROBERT HERRICK (1591–1674)

To the Virgins, to Make Much of Time   1648

Gather ye rose-buds while ye may,
   Old Time is still a-flying;
And this same flower that smiles today,
   Tomorrow will be dying.

The glorious lamp of heaven, the sun,
   The higher he's a-getting,
The sooner will his race be run,
   And nearer he's to setting.

That age is best which is the first,
   When youth and blood are warmer;
But being spent, the worse, and worst
   Times still succeed the former.

Then be not coy, but use your time,
   And while ye may, go marry;
For having lost but once your prime,   15
   You may for ever tarry.

Courtesy of the National Portrait Gallery, London.

CONSIDERATIONS FOR CRITICAL THINKING AND WRITING

1. **FIRST RESPONSE.** Would there be any change in meaning if the title of this poem were "To Young Women, to Make Much of Time"? Do you think the poem can apply to young men, too?

2. What do the virgins have in common with the flowers (lines 1–4) and the course of the day (5–8)?

3. How does the speaker develop his argument? What will happen to the virgins if they don't "marry"? Paraphrase the poem.

4. What is the tone of the speaker's advice?

The next poem was also written in the seventeenth century, but it includes some words that have changed in usage and meaning over the past three hundred years. The title of Andrew Marvell's "To His Coy Mistress" requires some explanation. "Mistress" does not refer to a married man's illicit lover but to a woman who is loved and courted — a sweetheart. Marvell uses "coy" to describe a woman who is reserved and shy rather than coquettish or flirtatious. Often such shifts in meanings over time are explained in the notes that accompany reprintings of poems. You should keep in mind, however, that it is helpful to have a reasonably thick dictionary available when you are reading poetry. The most thorough is the *Oxford English Dictionary (OED)*, which provides histories of words. The *OED* is a multivolume leviathan, but there are other useful unabridged dictionaries and desk dictionaries.

Web Explore contexts for Andrew Marvell and approaches to this poem at bedfordstmartins.com/meyerlit.

Knowing its original meaning can also enrich your understanding of why a contemporary poet chooses a particular word. Elizabeth Bishop begins "The Fish" (p. 755) this way: "I caught a tremendous fish." We know immediately in this context that "tremendous" means very large. In addition, given that the speaker clearly admires the fish in the lines that follow, we might even understand "tremendous" in the colloquial sense of wonderful and extraordinary. But a dictionary gives us some further relevant insights. Because, by the end of the poem, we see the speaker thoroughly moved as a result of the encounter with the fish ("everything / was rainbow, rainbow, rainbow!"), the dictionary's additional information about the history of *tremendous* shows why it is the perfect adjective to introduce the fish. The word comes from the Latin *tremere* (to tremble) and therefore once meant "such as to make one tremble." That is precisely how the speaker is at the end of the poem: deeply affected and trembling. Knowing the origin of *tremendous* gives us the full heft of the poet's word choice.

Although some of the language in "To His Coy Mistress" requires annotations for the modern reader, this poem continues to serve as a powerful reminder that time is a formidable foe, even for lovers.

Andrew Marvell (1621–1678)

To His Coy Mistress   *1681*

Courtesy of the National Portrait Gallery, London.

Had we but world enough, and time,
This coyness, lady, were no crime.
We would sit down, and think which way
To walk, and pass our long love's day.
Thou by the Indian Ganges'° side   5
Shouldst rubies find; I by the tide
Of Humber° would complain.° I would   *write love songs*
Love you ten years before the Flood,
And you should, if you please, refuse
Till the conversion of the Jews.   10
My vegetable love should grow°
Vaster than empires, and more slow;
An hundred years should go to praise
Thine eyes and on thy forehead gaze,
Two hundred to adore each breast,   15
But thirty thousand to the rest:

---

5 *Ganges:* A river in India sacred to the Hindus.   7 *Humber:* A river that flows through Marvell's native town, Hull.   11 *My vegetable love . . . grow:* A slow, unconscious growth.

An age at least to every part,
And the last age should show your heart.
For, lady, you deserve this state,
Nor would I love at lower rate.   20
    But at my back I always hear
Time's wingèd chariot hurrying near;
And yonder all before us lie
Deserts of vast eternity.
Thy beauty shall no more be found,   25
Nor in thy marble vault shall sound
My echoing song; then worms shall try
That long preserved virginity,
And your quaint honor turn to dust,
And into ashes all my lust.   30
The grave's a fine and private place,
But none, I think, do there embrace.
    Now, therefore, while the youthful hue
Sits on thy skin like morning dew,
And while thy willing soul transpires°   *breathes forth*   35
At every pore with instant fires,
Now let us sport us while we may,
And now, like amorous birds of prey,
Rather at once our time devour
Than languish in his slow-chapped° power.   *slow-jawed*   40
Let us roll all our strength and all
Our sweetness up into one ball,
And tear our pleasures with rough strife
Thorough° the iron gates of life.   *through*
Thus, though we cannot make our sun   45
Stand still, yet we will make him run.

CONSIDERATIONS FOR CRITICAL THINKING AND WRITING

1. **FIRST RESPONSE.** Do you think this *carpe diem* poem is hopelessly dated, or does it speak to our contemporary concerns?

2. This poem is divided into a three-part argument. Briefly summarize each section: if (lines 1–20), but (21–32), therefore (33–46).

3. What is the speaker's tone in lines 1–20? How much time would he spend adoring his mistress? Is he sincere? How does he expect his mistress to respond to these lines?

4. How does the speaker's tone change beginning with line 21? What is his view of time in lines 21–32? What does this description do to the lush and leisurely sense of time in lines 1–20? How do you think his mistress would react to lines 21–32?

5. In the final lines of Herrick's "To the Virgins, to Make Much of Time" (p. 811), the speaker urges the virgins to "go marry." What does Marvell's speaker urge in lines 33–46? How is the pace of these lines (notice the verbs) different from that of the first twenty lines of the poem?

6. This poem is sometimes read as a vigorous but simple celebration of flesh. Is there more to the theme than that?

The third in this series of *carpe diem* poems is a twenty-first-century work. The language of Ann Lauinger's "Marvell Noir" is more immediately accessible than that of Marvell's "To His Coy Mistress"; an ordinary dictionary will quickly identify any words unfamiliar to a reader. But the title might require a dictionary of biography for the reference to Marvell, as well as a dictionary of allusions to provide a succinct description that explains the reference to film noir. An ***allusion*** is a brief cultural reference to a person, a place, a thing, an event, or an idea in history or literature. Allusive words, like connotative words, are both suggestive and economical; poets use allusions to conjure up biblical authority, scenes from Shakespeare's plays, historic figures, wars, great love stories, and anything else that might serve to deepen and enrich their own work. The title of "Marvell Noir" makes two allusions that an ordinary dictionary may not explain, because it alludes to Marvell's most famous poem, "To His Coy Mistress," and to dark crime films (*noir* is "black" in French) of the 1940s that were often filmed in black and white featuring tough-talking, cynical heroes such as Humphrey Bogart and hardened, cold women like Joan Crawford. Lauinger assumes that her reader will understand the allusions.

Allusions imply reading and cultural experiences shared by the poet and reader. Literate audiences once had more in common than they do today because more people had similar economic, social, and educational backgrounds. But a judicious use of specialized dictionaries, encyclopedias, and other reference tools can help you decipher allusions that grow out of this body of experience. As you read more, you'll be able to make connections based on your own experiences with literature. In a sense, allusions make available what other human beings have deemed worth remembering, and that is certainly an economical way of supplementing and enhancing your own experience.

Lauinger's version of the *carpe diem* theme follows. What strikes you as particularly modern about it?

ANN LAUINGER

Marvell Noir

2005

Sweetheart, if we had the time,
A week in bed would be no crime.
I'd light your Camels, pour your Jack;
You'd do shiatsu on my back.
When you got up to scramble eggs,   5
I'd write a sonnet to your legs,

And you could watch my stubble grow.
Yes, gorgeous, we'd take it slow.
I'd hear the whole sad tale again:
A roadhouse band; you can't trust men;   10
He set you up; you had to eat,
And bitter with the bittersweet
Was what they dished you; Ginger lied;
You weren't there when Sanchez died;
You didn't know the pearls were fake . . .   15
Aw, can it, sport! Make no mistake,
You're in it, doll, up to your eyeballs!
Tears? Please! You'll dilute our highballs,
And make that angel face a mess
For the nice Lieutenant. I confess   20
I'm nuts for you — but take the rap?
You must think I'm some other sap!
And, precious, I kind of wish I was.
Well, when they spring you, give a buzz;
Guess I'll get back to Archie's wife,   25
And you'll get twenty-five to life.
You'll have time then, more than enough,
To reminisce about the stuff
That dreams are made of, and the men
You suckered. Sadly, in the pen   30
Your kind of talent goes to waste.
But Irish bars are more my taste
Than iron ones: stripes ain't my style.
You're going down; I promise I'll
Come visit every other year.   35
Now kiss me, sweet — the squad car's here.

CONSIDERATIONS FOR CRITICAL THINKING AND WRITING

1. **FIRST RESPONSE.** How does Lauinger's poem evoke Marvell's *carpe diem* poem (p. 812) and the tough-guy tone of a "noir" narrative, a crime story or thriller that is especially dark?

2. Discuss the ways in which time is a central presence in the poem.

3. Explain the allusion to dreams in lines 28–29.

CONNECTION TO ANOTHER SELECTION

1. Compare the speaker's voice in this poem with that of the speaker in "To His Coy Mistress" (p. 812). What significant similarities and differences do you find?

This fourth love poem is a twentieth-century work in which the speaker's voice is a woman's. How does it sound different from the way the men speak in the previous three poems?

SHARON OLDS (B. 1942)

Last Night   *1996*

The next day, I am almost afraid.
Love? It was more like dragonflies
in the sun, 100 degrees at noon,
the ends of their abdomens stuck together, I
close my eyes when I remember. I hardly   5
knew myself, like something twisting and
twisting out of a chrysalis,
enormous, without language, all
head, all shut eyes, and the humming
like madness, the way they writhe away,   10
and do not leave, back, back,
away, back. Did I know you? No kiss,
no tenderness — more like killing, death-grip
holding to life, genitals
like violent hands clasped tight   15
barely moving, more like being closed
in a great jaw and eaten, and the screaming
I groan to remember it, and when we started
to die, then I refuse to remember,
the way a drunkard forgets. After,   20
you held my hands extremely hard as my
body moved in shudders like the ferry when its
axle is loosed past engagement, you kept me
sealed exactly against you, our hairlines
wet as the arc of a gateway after   25
a cloudburst, you secured me in your arms till I slept —
that was love, and we woke in the morning
clasped, fragrant, buoyant, that was
the morning after love.

CONSIDERATIONS FOR CRITICAL THINKING AND WRITING

1. **FIRST RESPONSE.** How is your response to this poem affected by the fact that the speaker is female? Explain why this is or isn't a *carpe diem* poem.

2. Comment on the descriptive passages of "Last Night." Which images seem especially vivid to you? How do they contribute to the poem's meaning?

3. Explain how the poem's tone changes from beginning to end.

CONNECTIONS TO OTHER SELECTIONS

1. How does the speaker's description of intimacy compare with Herrick's and Marvell's?

2. Compare the speaker's voice in Olds's poem with the voice you imagine for the coy mistress in Marvell's poem.

3. **CRITICAL STRATEGIES.** Read the section on formalist criticism (pp. 2046–48) in Chapter 53, "Critical Strategies for Reading," and compare the themes in Olds's poem and Philip Larkin's "A Study of Reading Habits" (p. 757) the way you think a feminist critic might analyze them.

POEMS FOR FURTHER STUDY

BARBARA HAMBY (B. 1929)

Ode to American English   2004

I was sitting in Paris one day missing English, American, really,
    with its pill-popping Hungarian goulash of everything
from Anglo-Saxon to Zulu, because British English
    is not the same, if the paperback dictionary I bought
at Brentano's on the Avenue de l'Opéra is any indication,   5
    too cultured by half. Oh, the English know their delphiniums,
but what about doowop, donuts, Dick Tracy, Tricky Dick?
    With their elegant Oxfordian accents, how could they
understand my yearning for the hotrod, hotdog, hot flash
    vocabulary of the U.S. of A., the fragmented fandango   10
of Dagwood's everyday flattening of Mr. Beasley on the sidewalk,
    fetuses floating on billboards, drive-by monster
hip-hop stereos shaking the windows of my dining room
    like a 7.5 earthquake, Ebonics, Spanglish, "you know"
used as a comma and period, the inability of 90% of the population   15
    to get the past perfect. *I have went, I have saw,*
I have tooken Jesus into my heart, the battle cry of the Bible Belt,
    but no one uses the King James anymore, only plain-speak
versions, in which Jesus, raising Lazarus from the dead, says,
    "Dude, wake up," and the L-man bolts up like a B-movie   20
mummy. "Whoa, I was toasted." Yes, ma'am, I miss the mongrel
    plenitude of American English, its fall-guy, rat-terrier,
dog-pound neologisms, the bomb of it all, the rushing River Jordan
    backwoods mutability of it, the low-rider, boom-box cruise of it,
from New Joisey to Ha-wah-ya with its sly dog, malasada-scarfing   25
    beach blanket lingo to the ubiquitous Valley Girl's
like-like stuttering, shopaholic rant. I miss its quotidian beauty,
    its querulous back-biting righteous indignation, its preening
rotgut flag-waving cowardice. *Suffering Succotash*, sputters
    Sylvester the Cat; *sine die,°* say the pork-bellied legislators   30
of the swamps and plains. I miss all those guys, their Tweety-bird
    resilience, their Doris Day optimism, the candid unguent
of utter unhappiness on every channel, the midnight televangelist
    euphoric stew, the junk mail-voice mail vernacular.

---

30 *sine die:* Latin for "without a day"; indefinitely.

On every *boulevard* and *rue* I miss the Tarzan cry of Johnny   35
  Weismueller, Johnny Cash, Johnny B. Goode,
and all the smart-talking, gum-snapping hard-girl dialogue,
  finger-popping x-rated street talk, sports babble,
Cheetoes, Cheerios, chili-dog diatribes. Yeah, I miss 'em all,
  sitting here on my sidewalk throne sipping champagne,   40
verses lined up like hearses, metaphors juking, nouns zipping
  in my head like Corvettes on dexedrine, French verbs
slitting my throat, yearning for James Dean to jump my curb.

CONSIDERATIONS FOR CRITICAL THINKING AND WRITING

1. **FIRST RESPONSE.** Consult the Glossary of Literary Terms (p. 2123) for the definition of *ode*. How does this poem constitute an ode to American English?

2. Explain how the diction of this poem is vital to its meaning. What is it about American English that causes the speaker to admire it so much?

3. What kind of characterization of American life is presented by the varieties of English cataloged in the poem?

CONNECTIONS TO OTHER SELECTIONS

1. Discuss the strategic use of American phrasing in this poem and in Florence Cassen Mayers's "All-American Sestina" (p. 984), and compare the tone of each poem.

2. Write an essay comparing the themes of Hamby's poem and Lydia Huntley Sigourney's "Indian Names" (p. 1346). Compare how the diction of each poem controls its tone.

THOMAS HARDY (1840–1928)

The Convergence of the Twain   1912

Lines on the Loss of the "Titanic"°

I

In a solitude of the sea
Deep from human vanity,
And the Pride of Life that planned her, stilly couches she.

II

Steel chambers, late the pyres
Of her salamandrine fires,°   5
Cold currents thrid,° and turn to rhythmic tidal lyres.   *thread*

"Titanic": A luxurious ocean liner, reputed to be unsinkable, which sank after hitting an iceberg on its maiden voyage in 1912. Only a third of the 2,200 passengers survived. 5 *salamandrine fires:* Salamanders were, according to legend, able to survive fire; hence the ship's fires burned even though under water.

III

Over the mirrors meant
To glass the opulent
The sea-worm crawls — grotesque, slimed, dumb, indifferent.

IV

Jewels in joy designed   10
To ravish the sensuous mind
Lie lightless, all their sparkles bleared and black and blind.

V

Dim moon-eyed fishes near
Gaze at the gilded gear
And query: "What does this vaingloriousness down here?"   15

VI

Well: while was fashioning
This creature of cleaving wing,
The Immanent Will that stirs and urges everything

VII

Prepared a sinister mate
For her — so gaily great —   20
A Shape of Ice, for the time far and dissociate.

VIII

And as the smart ship grew
In stature, grace, and hue,
In shadowy silent distance grew the Iceberg too.

IX

Alien they seemed to be: 25
No mortal eye could see
The intimate welding of their later history,

X

Or sign that they were bent
By paths coincident
On being anon twin halves of one august event,   30

XI

Till the Spinner of the Years
Said "Now!" And each one hears,
And consummation comes, and jars two hemispheres.

CONSIDERATIONS FOR CRITICAL THINKING AND WRITING

1. **FIRST RESPONSE.** Describe a contemporary disaster comparable to the sinking of the *Titanic*. How was your response to it similar to or different from the speaker's response to the fate of the *Titanic*?

2. How do the words used to describe the ship in this poem reveal the speaker's attitude toward the *Titanic*?

3. The diction of the poem suggests that the *Titanic* and the iceberg participate in something like an arranged marriage. What specific words imply this?

4. Who or what causes the disaster? Does the speaker assign responsibility?

DAVID R. SLAVITT (B. 1935)

Titanic   1983

Who does not love the *Titanic*?
If they sold passage tomorrow for that same crossing,
who would not buy?

To go down . . . We all go down, mostly
alone. But with crowds of people, friends, servants,   5
well fed, with music, with lights! Ah!

And the world, shocked, mourns, as it ought to do
and almost never does. There will be the books and movies
to remind our grandchildren who we were
and how we died, and give them a good cry.   10

Not so bad, after all. The cold
water is anesthetic and very quick.
The cries on all sides must be a comfort.

We all go: only a few, first-class.

CONSIDERATIONS FOR CRITICAL THINKING AND WRITING

1. **FIRST RESPONSE.** What, according to the speaker in this poem, is so compelling about the *Titanic*? Do you agree?

2. Discuss the speaker's tone. Is "Titanic" merely a sarcastic poem?

3. What is the effect of the poem's final line? What emotions does it elicit?

CONNECTION TO ANOTHER SELECTION

1. How does "Titanic" differ in its attitude toward opulence from "The Convergence of the Twain" (p. 818)?

2. Which poem, "Titanic" or "The Convergence of the Twain," is more emotionally satisfying to you? Explain why.

3. Compare the speakers' tones in "Titanic" and "The Convergence of the Twain."

4. **CRITICAL STRATEGIES.** Read the section on Marxist criticism (pp. 2053–54) in Chapter 53, "Critical Strategies for Reading," and analyze the attitudes toward opulence that are manifested in the two poems.

PETER MEINKE (B. 1932)

(Untitled)

1991

this is a poem to my son Peter
whom I have hurt a thousand times
whose large and vulnerable eyes
have glazed in pain at my ragings
thin wrists and fingers hung   5
boneless in despair, pale freckled back
bent in defeat, pillow soaked
by my failure to understand.
I have scarred through weakness
and impatience your frail confidence forever   10
because when I needed to strike
you were there to be hurt and because
I thought you knew
you were beautiful and fair
your bright eyes and hair   15
but now I see that no one knows that
about himself, but must be told
and retold until it takes hold
because I think anything can be killed
after a while, especially beauty   20
so I write this for life, for love, for
you, my oldest son Peter, age 10,
going on 11.

CONSIDERATIONS FOR CRITICAL THINKING AND WRITING

1. **FIRST RESPONSE.** How would you characterize the speaker? The son is described physically but not the father. What sort of physical description do you think would reveal the father?

2. Why do you think the poem ends with "going on 11"? Would it have made any difference to the tone or meaning if the poem ended at line 22?

3. **CREATIVE RESPONSE.** Provide at least two titles for this untitled work and explain your rationale for each.

Joanne Diaz (b. 1972)

On My Father's Loss of Hearing   2006

I'd like to see more poems treat the deaf
as being abled differently, not lost
or missing something, weakened, deficient.
                    —from a listserv for the deaf

Abled differently — so vague compared
with deaf, obtuse but true to history,
from deave: to deafen, stun, amaze with noise.
Perhaps that's what we've done — amazed
          him with
our sorrows and complaints, the stupid jabs,
the loneliness of boredom in the house,

Courtesy of Jason Reblando.

our wants so foreign to his own. What else
is there but loss? He's lost the humor of
sarcastic jokes, the snarky dialogue
of British films eludes him, phone calls   10
cast him adrift in that cochlear maze
that thrums and bristles even now, when
it doesn't have to: an unnecessary kind
of elegance, the vestige of a sense

no longer obligated to transmit   15
the crack of thawing ice that fills the yard's
wide dip in winter, or the scrape of his
dull rake in spring, its prongs' vibration thrilled
by grass and peat moss. Imagine his desires
released like saffron pistils in the wind;   20
mark their trace against the cords of wood

he spent the summer splitting. See his quiet
flicker like a film, a Super-8
projected on the wall, and all of us
there, laughing on the porch without a sound.   25
No noisome cruelty, no baffled rage,
no aging children sullen in their lack.
Love hurts much less in this serenity.

Considerations for Critical Thinking and Writing

1. **First response.** Why does the speaker prefer the word *deaf* to the phrase "abled differently" as a means of describing her father? Which description do you prefer? Why?

2. Explain how sound and silence move through the poem from beginning to end.

3. Choose a single word from each stanza that strikes you as particularly effective, and explain why you think Diaz chose it over other possibilities.

4. What do you make of the poem's final line? How does it relate to the tone of the rest of the poem?

CONNECTION TO ANOTHER SELECTION

1. Discuss the relationship between love and pain in "On My Father's Loss of Hearing" and in the Meinke poem that precedes it.

MARY OLIVER (B. 1935)

Oxygen

2005

Everything needs it: bone, muscles, and even,
while it calls the earth its home, the soul.
So the merciful, noisy machine

stands in our house working away in its
lung-like voice. I hear it as I kneel   5
before the fire, stirring with a

stick of iron, letting the logs
lie more loosely. You, in the upstairs room,
are in your usual position, leaning on your

right shoulder which aches   10
all day. You are breathing
patiently; it is a

beautiful sound. It is
your life, which is so close
to my own that I would not know   15

where to drop the knife of
separation. And what does this have to do
with love, except

everything? Now the fire rises
and offers a dozen, singing, deep-red   20
roses of flame. Then it settles

to quietude, or maybe gratitude, as it feeds
as we all do, as we must, upon the invisible gift:
our purest, sweet necessity: the air.

CONSIDERATIONS FOR CRITICAL THINKING AND WRITING

1. FIRST RESPONSE. Though this is a poem about someone who is seriously ill, its tone isn't sad. Why not?
2. What is the connection between the loved one's breathing and the fire? How does the speaker's choice of words to describe each connect them?
3. In what sense might this celebration of oxygen be considered a love poem?

CATHY SONG (B. 1955)

The Youngest Daughter 1983

The sky has been dark
for many years.
My skin has become as damp
and pale as rice paper
and feels the way 5
mother's used to before the drying sun
parched it out there in the fields.

    Lately, when I touch myself,
my hands react as if
I had just touched something 10
hot enough to burn.
My skin, aspirin-colored,
tingles with migraine. Mother
has been massaging the left side of my face
especially in the evenings 15
when it flares up.

This morning
her breathing was graveled,
her voice gruff with affection
when I took her into the bath. 20
She was in good humor,
making jokes about her great breasts,
floating in the milky water
like two walruses,
flaccid and whiskered around the nipples. 25
I scrubbed them with a sour taste
in my mouth, thinking:
six children and an old man
have sucked from these brown nipples.

I was almost tender 30
when I came to the blue bruises
that freckle her body,
places where she has been injecting insulin
for thirty years, ever since
I can remember. I soaped her slowly, 35
she sighed deeply, her eyes closed.

In the afternoons
when she has rested,
she prepares our ritual of tea and rice,
garnished with a shred of gingered fish, 40
a slice of pickled turnip
a token for my white body.
We eat in the familiar silence.
She knows I am not to be trusted,

even now planning my escape.   45
As I toast to her health
with the tea she has poured,
a thousand cranes curtain the window,
fly up in a sudden breeze.

CONSIDERATIONS FOR CRITICAL THINKING AND WRITING

1. **FIRST RESPONSE.** Though the speaker is the youngest daughter in the family, how old do you think she is based on the description of her in the poem? What, specifically, makes you think so?

2. How would you characterize the relationship between mother and daughter? How are lines 44–45 ("She knows I am not to be trusted, / even now planning my escape") particularly revealing of the nature of the relationship?

3. Interpret the final four lines of the poem. Why do you think it ends with this image?

JOHN KEATS (1795–1821)

Ode on a Grecian Urn   *1819*

I

Thou still unravished bride of quietness,
    Thou foster-child of silence and slow time,
Sylvan° historian, who canst thus express
    A flowery tale more sweetly than our rhyme:
What leaf-fringed legend haunts about thy shape   5
    Of deities or mortals, or of both,
        In Tempe or the dales of Arcady?°
What men or gods are these? What maidens loath?
    What mad pursuit? What struggle to escape?
        What pipes and timbrels? What wild ecstasy?   10

II

Heard melodies are sweet, but those unheard
    Are sweeter; therefore, ye soft pipes, play on;
Not to the sensual ear, but, more endeared,
    Pipe to the spirit ditties of no tone:
Fair youth, beneath the trees, thou canst not leave   15
    Thy song, nor ever can those trees be bare;
        Bold Lover, never, never canst thou kiss,
Though winning near the goal — yet, do not grieve;
    She cannot fade, though thou hast not thy bliss,
        For ever wilt thou love, and she be fair!   20

---

3 *Sylvan:* Rustic. The urn is decorated with a forest scene.   7 *Tempe, Arcady:* Beautiful rural valleys in Greece.

III

Ah, happy, happy boughs! that cannot shed
   Your leaves, nor ever bid the Spring adieu;
And, happy melodist, unwearièd,
   For ever piping songs for ever new;
More happy love! more happy, happy love!   25
   For ever warm and still to be enjoyed,
      For ever panting, and for ever young;
All breathing human passion far above,
   That leaves a heart high-sorrowful and cloyed,
      A burning forehead, and a parching tongue.   30

IV

Who are these coming to the sacrifice?
   To what green altar, O mysterious priest,
Lead'st thou that heifer lowing at the skies,
   And all her silken flanks with garlands drest?
What little town by river or sea shore,   35
   Or mountain-built with peaceful citadel,
      Is emptied of this folk, this pious morn?
And, little town, thy streets for evermore
   Will silent be; and not a soul to tell
      Why thou art desolate, can e'er return.   40

V

O Attic° shape! Fair attitude! with brede°
   Of marble men and maidens overwrought,
With forest branches and the trodden weed;
   Thou, silent form, dost tease us out of thought
As doth eternity: Cold Pastoral!   45
   When old age shall this generation waste,
      Thou shalt remain, in midst of other woe
Than ours, a friend to man, to whom thou say'st,
   Beauty is truth, truth beauty — that is all
      Ye know on earth, and all ye need to know.   50

41 *Attic:* Possessing classic Athenian simplicity; *brede:* Design.

CONSIDERATIONS FOR CRITICAL THINKING AND WRITING

1. **FIRST RESPONSE.** What does the speaker's diction reveal about his attitude toward the urn in this ode? Does his view develop or change?

2. How is the happiness in stanza 3 related to the assertion in lines 11–12 that "Heard melodies are sweet, but those unheard / Are sweeter"?

3. What is the difference between the world depicted on the urn and the speaker's world?

4. What do lines 49 and 50 suggest about the relation of art to life? Why is the urn described as a "Cold Pastoral" (line 45)?

5. Which world does the speaker seem to prefer, the urn's or his own?

6. Describe the overall tone of the poem.

CONNECTIONS TO OTHER SELECTIONS

1. Write an essay comparing the view of time in this ode with that in Marvell's "To His Coy Mistress" (p. 812). Pay particular attention to the connotative language in each poem.

2. Compare the tone and attitude toward life in this ode with those in John Keats's "To Autumn" (p. 858).

GWENDOLYN BROOKS (1917–2000)

We Real Cool   1960

The Pool Players.
Seven at the Golden Shovel.

We real cool. We
Left school. We

Lurk late. We
Strike straight. We

Sing sin. We
Thin gin. We

Jazz June. We
Die soon.

CONSIDERATIONS FOR CRITICAL THINKING AND WRITING

1. **FIRST RESPONSE.** How does the speech of the pool players in this poem help to characterize them? What is the effect of the pronouns coming at the ends of the lines? How would the poem sound if the pronouns came at the beginnings of lines?

2. What is the author's attitude toward the players? Is there a change in tone in the last line?

3. How is the pool hall's name related to the rest of the poem and its theme?

JOAN MURRAY (B. 1945)

We Old Dudes   2006

We old dudes. We
White shoes. We

Golf ball. We
Eat mall. We

Soak teeth. We
Palm Beach; We

Vote red. We
Soon dead.

CONSIDERATIONS FOR CRITICAL THINKING AND WRITING

1. **FIRST RESPONSE.** Consider the poem's humor. To what extent does it make a serious point?
2. What does the reference to Palm Beach tell you about these "old dudes"?
3. **CREATIVE RESPONSE.** Write a poem similar in style that characterizes your life as a student.

CONNECTION TO ANOTHER SELECTION

1. Compare the themes of "We Old Dudes" and Brooks's "We Real Cool." How do the two poems speak to each other?

ALICE JONES (B. 1949)

The Larynx   *1993*

Under the epiglottic flap
the long-ringed tube sinks
its shaft down to the bronchial
    fork, divides from two
to four then infinite branches,   5
each ending finally in a clump
    of transparent sacs knit
with small vessels into a mesh
that sponge-like soaks up breath
    and gives it off with a push   10
from the diaphragm's muscular wall,
forces wind out of the lungs'
wide tree, up through this organ's
    single pipe, through the puzzle
box of gristle, where resonant   15
    plates of cartilage fold
    into shield, horns, bows,
    bound by odd half-spirals
of muscles that modulate air
as it rises through this empty place   20
    at our core, where lip-like
folds stretch across the vestibule,
small and tough, they flutter,
    bend like birds' wings finding
    just the right angle to stay   25
airborne; here the cords arch
in the hollow of this ancient instrument,
    curve and vibrate to make a song.

CONSIDERATIONS FOR CRITICAL THINKING AND WRITING

1. **FIRST RESPONSE.** What is the effect of having this poem written as one long sentence? How does the length of the sentence contribute to the poem's meaning?

2. Make a list of words and phrases from the poem that strike you as scientific, and compare those with a list of words that seem poetic. How do they compete or complement each other in terms of how they affect your reading?

3. Comment on the final three lines. How would your interpretation of this poem change if it ended before the semicolon in line 26?

CONNECTION TO ANOTHER SELECTION

1. Compare the diction and the ending in "The Larynx" with those of "The Foot" (p. 955), another poem by Jones.

LOUIS SIMPSON (B. 1923)

In the Suburbs   *1963*

There's no way out.
You were born to waste your life.
You were born to this middleclass life

As others before you
Were born to walk in procession
To the temple, singing.

CONSIDERATIONS FOR CRITICAL THINKING AND WRITING

1. **FIRST RESPONSE.** Is the title of this poem especially significant? What images does it conjure up for you?

2. What does the repetition in lines 2–3 suggest?

3. Discuss the possible connotative meanings of lines 5 and 6. Who are the "others before you"?

CONNECTION TO ANOTHER SELECTION

1. Write an essay on suburban life based on this poem and John Ciardi's "Suburban" (p. 1247).

HERBERT LOMAS (B. 1924)

The Fly's Poem about Emily°   *2008*

Beelzebub° sent me.
I ate their meat.
I was the fly on
the dead poet's feet.

The Fly's Poem about Emily: See Emily Dickinson's poem "I heard a Fly buzz — when I died —"
(p. 1065).   1 *Beelzebub:* An ancient name for a devil or demon; also called "Lord of the Flies."

I've a good tube   5
for the scents of food.
I love life
and find death good.

My little head
is as black as my tube,   10
but when she died
I buzzed and survived.

Later I ate her.
My buzz is no bell,
but I'm remembered on earth   15
as well as in hell,

and I was eating her sweat
when God received her.

CONSIDERATIONS FOR CRITICAL THINKING AND WRITING

1. **FIRST RESPONSE.** Explain why you think it is essential (or not) to read Dickinson's poem in order to appreciate this poem.
2. Characterize the fly by the tone of its language. What kinds of emotions does the language produce in you?
3. Consider whether there is any humor in the poem. Or is it all grim?

CONNECTION TO ANOTHER SELECTION

1. How does this poem, read alongside Emily Dickinson's "I heard a Fly buzz—when I died—" (p. 1065), create a kind of dialogue about the nature of death?

A NOTE ON READING TRANSLATIONS

Sometimes translation can inadvertently be a comic business. Consider, for example, the discovery made by John Steinbeck's wife, Elaine, when in a Yokohama bookstore she asked for a copy of her husband's famous novel *The Grapes of Wrath* and learned that it had been translated into Japanese as *Angry Raisins*. Close but no cigar (perhaps translated as: Nearby, yet no smoke). As amusing as that *Angry Raisins* title is, it teaches an important lesson about the significance of a poet's or a translator's choices when crafting a poem: a powerful piece moves us through diction and tone, both built word by careful word. Translations are frequently regarded as merely vehicular, a way to arrive at the original work. It is, of course, the original work—its spirit, style, and meaning—that most readers expect to find in a translation. Even so, it is important to understand that a translation is *by nature* different from the original—and that despite that difference, a fine translation can be an important part of the journey and become part of the literary landscape itself.

Reading a translation of a poem is not the same as reading the original, but neither is watching two different performances of *Hamlet*. The translator provides a reading of the poem in much the same way that a director shapes the play. Each interprets the text from a unique perspective.

Basically, there are two distinct approaches to translation: literal translations and adaptations. A literal translation sets out to create a word-for-word equivalent that is absolutely faithful to the original. As simple and direct as this method may sound, literal translations are nearly impossible over extended passages because of the structural differences between languages. Moreover, the meaning of a single word in one language may not exist in another language, or it may require a phrase, clause, or entire sentence to capture its implications. Adaptations of works offer broader, more open-ended approaches to translation. Unlike a literal translation, an adaptation moves beyond denotative meanings in an attempt to capture the spirit of a work so that its idioms, dialects, slang, and other conventions are re-created in the language of the translation.

The question we ask of an adaptation should not be "Is this exactly how the original reads?" Instead, we ask, "Is this an insightful, graceful rendering worth reading?" To translate poetry it is not enough to know the language of the original; it is also necessary that the translator be a poet. A translated poem is more than a collation of decisions based on dictionaries and grammars; it must also be poetry. However undefinable poetry may be, it is unmistakable in its intense use of language. Poems are not merely translated; they are savored.

Three Translations of a Poem by Sappho

Sappho, born about 630 B.C. and a native of the Greek island of Lesbos, is the author of a hymn to Aphrodite, the goddess of love and beauty in Greek myth. The three translations that follow suggest how widely translations can differ from one another. The first, by Henry T. Wharton, is intended to be a literal prose translation of the original Greek.

SAPPHO (CA. 630 B.C.–CA. 570 B.C.)

Immortal Aphrodite of the broidered throne   *date unknown*

TRANSLATED BY HENRY T. WHARTON (1885)

Immortal Aphrodite of the broidered throne, daughter of Zeus, weaver of wiles, I pray thee break not my spirit with anguish and distress, O Queen. But come hither, if ever before thou

© Bettmann/CORBIS.

didst hear my voice afar, and listen, and leaving thy father's golden house camest with chariot yoked, and fair fleet sparrows drew thee, flapping fast their wings around the dark earth, from heaven through mid sky. Quickly arrived they; and thou, blessed one, smiling with immortal countenance, didst ask What now is befallen me, and Why now I call, and What I in my mad heart most desire to see. "What Beauty now wouldst thou draw to love thee? Who wrongs thee, Sappho? For even if she flies she shall soon follow, and if she rejects gifts shall yet give, and if she loves not shall soon love, however loth." Come, I pray thee, now too, and release me from cruel cares; and all that my heart desires to accomplish, accomplish thou, and be thyself my ally.

Beautiful-throned, immortal Aphrodite

TRANSLATED BY THOMAS WENTWORTH HIGGINSON (1871)

Beautiful-throned, immortal Aphrodite,
Daughter of Zeus, beguiler, I implore thee,
Weigh me not down with weariness and anguish
    O Thou most holy!

Come to me now, if ever thou in kindness   5
Hearkenedst my words, — and often hast thou hearkened —
Heeding, and coming from the mansions golden
    Of thy great Father,

Yoking thy chariot, borne by the most lovely
Consecrated birds, with dusky-tinted pinions,   10
Waving swift wings from utmost heights of heaven
    Through the mid-ether;

Swiftly they vanished, leaving thee, O goddess,
Smiling, with face immortal in its beauty,
Asking why I grieved, and why in utter longing   15
    I had dared call thee;

Asking what I sought, thus hopeless in desiring,
Wildered in brain, and spreading nets of passion —
Alas, for whom? and saidst thou, "Who has harmed thee?
    "O my poor Sappho!   20

"Though now he flies, ere long he shall pursue thee;
"Fearing thy gifts, he too in turn shall bring them;
"Loveless to-day, to-morrow he shall woo thee,
    "Though thou shouldst spurn him."

Thus seek me now, O holy Aphrodite!   25
Save me from anguish; give me all I ask for,
Gifts at thy hand; and thine shall be the glory,
    Sacred protector!

Prayer to my lady of Paphos

TRANSLATED BY MARY BARNARD (1958)

Dapple-throned Aphrodite,
eternal daughter of God,
snare-knitter! Don't, I beg you,

cow my heart with grief! Come,
as once when you heard my far-   5
off cry and, listening, stepped

from your father's house to your
gold car, to yoke the pair whose
beautiful thick-feathered wings

oaring down mid-air from heaven   10
carried you to light swiftly
on dark earth; then, blissful one,

smiling your immortal smile
you asked, What ailed me now that
made me call you again? What   15

was it that my distracted
heart most wanted? "Whom has
Persuasion to bring round now

"to your love? Who, Sappho, is
unfair to you? For, let her   20
run, she will soon run after;

"if she won't accept gifts, she
will one day give them; and if
she won't love you — she soon will

"love, although unwillingly . . ."   25
If ever — come now! Relieve
this intolerable pain!

What my heart most hopes will
happen, make happen; you your-
self join forces on my side!   30

CONSIDERATIONS FOR CRITICAL THINKING AND WRITING

1. **FIRST RESPONSE.** Try rewriting Wharton's prose version in contemporary language. How does your prose version differ in tone from Wharton's?

2. Explain which translation seems closest to Wharton's prose version.

3. Discuss the images and metaphors in Higginson's and Barnard's versions. Which version is more appealing to you? Explain why.

4. Explain which version seems to you to be the most contemporary in its use of language.

Two Translations of a Poem by Pablo Neruda

The following poem by the Chilean Nobel Prize–winner Pablo Neruda is in its original Spanish. By using a substantial Spanish/English dictionary, you might be able to translate it into English even if you are unfamiliar with Spanish. Following the poem are two translations that offer some subtle and intriguing differences in their approaches to the poem.

© Luis Poirot.

PABLO NERUDA (1904–1973)

Verbo   *1968*

Voy a arrugar esta palabra,
voy a torcerla,
sí,
es demasiado lisa,
es como si un gran perro o un gran río   5
le hubíera repasado lengua o agua
durante muchos años.

Quiero que en la palabra
se vea la aspereza,
la sal ferruginosa,   10
la fuerza desdentada
de la tierra,
la sangre
de los que hablaron y de los que no hablaron.

Quiero ver la sed   15
adentro de las sílabas:
quiero tocar el fuego
en el sonido:
quiero sentir la oscuridad
del grito. Quiero   20
palabras ásperas
como piedras vírgenes.

Word

TRANSLATED BY BEN BELITT (1974)

I'm going to crumple this word,
to twist it,
yes,
it's too slick
like a big dog or a river   5
had been lapping it down with its tongue, or water
had worn it away with the years.

I want gravel
to show in the word,
the ferruginous salt,   10
the gap-toothed power
of the soil.
There must be a blood-letting
for talker and non-talker alike.

I want to see thirst   15
in the syllables,
touch fire
in the sound;
feel through the dark
for the scream. Let   20
my words be acrid
as virginal stone.

Word

TRANSLATED BY KRISTIN LINKLATER (1992)

I'm going to crumple this word,
I'm going to twist it,
yes,
it's too smooth,
it's as though a big dog or a big river   5
had been licking it over and over with tongue or water
for many years.

I want the word
to reveal the roughness,
the ferruginous salt,   10
the toothless strength
of the earth,
the blood
of those who talked and of those who did not talk.

I want to see the thirst   15
inside the syllables,

I want to touch the fire
in the sound:
I want to feel the darkness
of the scream. I want   20
rough words,
like virgin rocks.

CONSIDERATIONS FOR CRITICAL THINKING AND WRITING

1. **FIRST RESPONSE.** Discuss whether or not the two translations convey the same essential themes.

2. What are the major differences that you see in diction, syntax, and tone between the translations?

3. Which translation do you think is the most effective? Explain why you prefer one translation over another.

Web Research the poets in this chapter at bedfordstmartins.com/meyerlit.

24

Images

© Daniel J. Harper.

Between my finger and my thumb
The squat pen rests.
I'll dig with it.
— SEAMUS HEANEY

POETRY'S APPEAL TO THE SENSES

A poet, to borrow a phrase from Henry James, is one on whom nothing is lost. Poets take in the world and give us impressions of what they experience through images. An *image* is language that addresses the senses. The most common images in poetry are visual; they provide verbal pictures of the poets' encounters — real or imagined — with the world. But poets also create images that appeal to our other senses. Li Ho arouses several senses in "A Beautiful Girl Combs Her Hair" (p. 785):

Awake at dawn
she's dreaming
by cool silk curtains

fragrance of spilling hair
half sandalwood, half aloes

windlass creaking at the well
singing jade

5

837

These vivid images deftly blend textures, fragrances, and sounds that tease out the sensuousness of the moment. Images give us the physical world to experience in our imaginations. Some poems, like the following one, are written to do just that; they make no comment about what they describe.

Web Explore the poetic element in this chapter at bedfordstmartins.com/meyerlit.

WILLIAM CARLOS WILLIAMS (1883–1963)

Poem

1934

As the cat
climbed over
the top of

the jamcloset
first the right   5
forefoot

carefully
then the hind
stepped down

into the pit of   10
the empty
flowerpot

This poem defies paraphrase because it is all an image of agile movement. No statement is made about the movement; the title, "Poem" — really no title — signals Williams's refusal to comment on the movements. To impose a meaning on the poem, we'd probably have to knock over the flowerpot.

We experience the image in Williams's "Poem" more clearly because of how the sentence is organized into lines and groups of lines, or stanzas. Consider how differently the sentence is read if it is arranged as prose:

> As the cat climbed over the top of the jamcloset, first the right forefoot carefully then the hind stepped down into the pit of the empty flowerpot.

The poem's line and stanza division transforms what is essentially an awkward prose sentence into a rhythmic verbal picture. Especially when the poem is read aloud, this line and stanza division allows us to feel the image we see. Even the lack of a period at the end suggests that the cat is only pausing.

Images frequently do more than offer only sensory impressions, however. They also convey emotions and moods, as in the following poem.

JEANNETTE BARNES   (B. 1956)

Battle-Piece   1999

Confederate monument, Ocean Pond, Olustee, Florida, 1864

Picknickers sojourn here an hour,
get their fill, get gone.
Seldom, they quickstep as far downhill
as this bivouac; they miss sting, snap,

grit in clenched teeth, carbine, cartridge,   5
cap, *hurrah boys.* Cannon-cracks
the peal, the clap of doom.

Into the billows, white, filthy,
choked by smoke, Clem, Eustace, Willy —
it would be useless to name names or call them all.   10

Anyway, that's done already. Every fall
sons of sons and reverent veterans' wives
lay wreaths, a prize of plastic daisies,

everlasting. Nobody calls this lazy.
It's August, and it's late, it's afternoon,   15
heat-mist glistens on slick granite, sun

fingers through sleek pines, their edges cropped
like the clipped elegant grass. It is a shock
to see a caisson blown

to flinders; a horse shrieks,   20
the mortar-shell zooms, spiral-
ripping tender belly. Oh, yes, here

are raked paths, cindered, sweet trees
and cool water. That whimper
you do not hear now was the doves,   25
spooning. Evening calls you all, eager

as spruce-gum-chewing, apple-filching boys
to pull one long last gulp of switchel
as if, now, somebody's sons had almost done

haying. Keen to victual, nearly home, feature the sharp   30
surprise when, smooth as oiled stone
stroking the clean edge of a scythe, these boys achieved
each his marble pillow, astonished by the sky.

CONSIDERATIONS FOR CRITICAL THINKING AND WRITING

1. **FIRST RESPONSE.** Contrast the images used to describe the present moment
   at the battle site with the images used to describe the actual battle.

2. Describe the speaker's tone. What do the images reveal about the speaker's
   emotions?

3. Analyze the diction and images of the final stanza. What makes it so powerful?

What mood is established in this next poem's view of Civil War troops moving across a river?

WALT WHITMAN (1819–1892)

Cavalry Crossing a Ford

1865

A line in long array where they wind betwixt green islands,
They take a serpentine course, their arms flash in the sun — hark to the
    musical clank,
Behold the silvery river, in it the splashing horses loitering stop to drink,
Behold the brown-faced men, each group, each person, a picture, the
    negligent rest on the saddles,
Some emerge on the opposite bank, others are just entering the ford — while,
Scarlet and blue and snowy white,
The guidon flags flutter gaily in the wind.

CONSIDERATIONS FOR CRITICAL THINKING AND WRITING

1. FIRST RESPONSE. Do the colors and sounds establish the mood of this poem? What *is* the mood?
2. How would the poem's mood have been changed if Whitman had used "look" or "see" instead of "behold" (lines 3–4)?
3. Where is the speaker as he observes this troop movement?
4. Does "serpentine" in line 2 have an evil connotation in this poem? Explain your answer.

Whitman seems to capture momentarily all of the troop's actions, and through carefully chosen, suggestive details — really very few — he succeeds in making "each group, each person, a picture." Specific details, even when few are provided, give us the impression that we see the entire picture; it is as if those are the details we would remember if we had viewed the scene ourselves. Notice, too, that the movement of the "line in long array" is emphasized by the continuous winding syntax of the poem's lengthy lines.

Movement is also central to the next poem, in which action and motion are created through carefully chosen verbs.

DAVID SOLWAY (B. 1941)

Windsurfing

1993

It rides upon the wrinkled hide
of water, like the upturned hull
of a small canoe or kayak
waiting to be righted — yet its law

is opposite to that of boats,   5
it floats upon its breastbone and
brings whatever spine there is to light.
A thin shaft is slotted into place.
Then a puffed right-angle of wind
pushes it forward, out into the bay,   10
where suddenly it glitters into speed,
tilts, knifes up, and for the moment's
nothing but a slim projectile
of cambered fiberglass,
peeling the crests.   15

        The man's
clamped to the mast, taut as a guywire.
Part of the sleek apparatus
he controls, immaculate nerve
of balance, plunge and curvet,   20
he clinches all component movements
into single motion.
It bucks, stalls, shudders, yaws, and dips
its hissing sides beneath the surface
that sustains it, tensing   25
into muscle that nude ellipse
of lunging appetite and power.

And now the mechanism's wholly
dolphin, springing toward its prey
of spume and beaded sunlight,   30
tossing spray, and hits the vertex
of the wide, salt glare of distance,
and reverses.

        Back it comes through
a screen of particles,   35
scalloped out of water, shimmer
and reflection, the wind snapping
and lashing it homeward,
shearing the curve of the wave,
breaking the spell of the caught breath   40
and articulate play of sinew, to enter
the haven of the breakwater
and settle in a rush of silence.

Now the crossing drifts
in the husk of its wake   45
and nothing's the same again
as, gliding elegantly on a film of water,
the man guides
his brash, obedient legend
into shore.   50

CONSIDERATIONS FOR CRITICAL THINKING AND WRITING

1. **FIRST RESPONSE.** Draw a circle around the verbs that seem especially effective in conveying a strong sense of motion, and explain why they are effective.

2. How is the man made to seem to be one with his board and sail?

3. How does the rhythm of the poem change beginning with line 45?

CONNECTIONS TO OTHER SELECTIONS

1. Consider the effects of the images in "Windsurfing" and Li Ho's "A Beautiful Girl Combs Her Hair" (p. 785). In an essay, explain how these images elicit the emotional responses they do.

2. Compare the descriptions in "Windsurfing" and Elizabeth Bishop's "The Fish" (p. 755). How does each poet appeal to your senses to describe windsurfing and fishing?

"Windsurfing" is awash with images of speed, fluidity, and power. Even the calming aftermath of the breakwater is described as a "rush of silence," adding to the sense of motion that is detailed and expanded throughout the poem.

Poets choose details the way they choose the words to present those details: only telling ones will do. Consider the images Theodore Roethke uses in "Root Cellar."

THEODORE ROETHKE (1908–1963)

Root Cellar 1948

Nothing would sleep in that cellar, dank as a ditch,
Bulbs broke out of boxes hunting for chinks in the dark,
Shoots dangled and drooped,
Lolling obscenely from mildewed crates,
Hung down long yellow evil necks, like tropical snakes.   5
And what a congress of stinks!
Roots ripe as old bait,
Pulpy stems, rank, silo-rich,
Leaf-mold, manure, lime, piled against slippery planks.
Nothing would give up life: 10
Even the dirt kept breathing a small breath.

CONSIDERATIONS FOR CRITICAL THINKING AND WRITING

1. **FIRST RESPONSE.** Explain why you think this is a positive or negative rendition of a root cellar.

2. What senses are engaged by the images in this poem? Is the poem simply a series of sensations, or do the detailed images make some kind of point about the root cellar?

3. What controls the choice of details in the poem? Why isn't there, for example, a rusty shovel leaning against a dirt wall or a worn gardener's glove atop one of the crates?

4. Look up *congress* in a dictionary for its denotative meanings. Explain why "congress of stinks" (line 6) is especially appropriate given the nature of the rest of the poem's imagery.

5. What single line in the poem suggests a theme?

6. **CREATIVE RESPONSE.** Try writing a poem of ten lines or so that consists of a series of evocative images that creates a strong impression about something you know well.

The tone of the images and mood of the speaker are consistent in Roethke's "Root Cellar." In Matthew Arnold's "Dover Beach," however, they shift as the theme is developed.

MATTHEW ARNOLD (1822–1888)

Dover Beach
1867

The sea is calm tonight.
The tide is full, the moon lies fair
Upon the straits;—on the French coast the light
Gleams and is gone; the cliffs of England stand,
Glimmering and vast, out in the tranquil bay.   5
Come to the window, sweet is the night-air!
Only, from the long line of spray
Where the sea meets the moon-blanched land,
Listen! you hear the grating roar
Of pebbles which the waves draw back, and fling,   10
At their return, up the high strand,
Begin, and cease, and then again begin,
With tremulous cadence slow, and bring
The eternal note of sadness in.

Sophocles long ago   15
Heard it on the Aegean, and it brought
Into his mind the turbid ebb and flow
Of human misery;° we
Find also in the sound a thought,
Hearing it by this distant northern sea.   20

The Sea of Faith
Was once, too, at the full, and round earth's shore

15–18 *Sophocles . . . misery:* In *Antigone* (lines 656–77), Sophocles likens the disasters that beset the house of Oedipus to a "mounting tide."

Lay like the folds of a bright girdle furled.
But now I only hear
Its melancholy, long, withdrawing roar,   25
Retreating, to the breath
Of the night-wind, down the vast edges drear
And naked shingles° of the world.   *pebble beaches*

Ah, love, let us be true
To one another! for the world, which seems   30
To lie before us like a land of dreams,
So various, so beautiful, so new,
Hath really neither joy, nor love, nor light,
Nor certitude, nor peace, nor help for pain;
And we are here as on a darkling plain   35
Swept with confused alarms of struggle and flight,
Where ignorant armies clash by night.

CONSIDERATIONS FOR CRITICAL THINKING AND WRITING

1. **FIRST RESPONSE.** Discuss what you consider to be this poem's central point. How do the speaker's descriptions of the ocean work toward making that point?

2. Contrast the images in lines 4–8 and 9–13. How do they reveal the speaker's mood? To whom is he speaking?

3. What is the cause of the "sadness" in line 14? What is the speaker's response to the ebbing "Sea of Faith"? Is there anything to replace his sense of loss?

4. What details of the beach seem related to the ideas in the poem? How is the sea used differently in lines 1–14 and 21–28?

5. Describe the differences in tone between lines 1–8 and 35–37. What has caused the change?

6. **CRITICAL STRATEGIES.** Read the section on mythological strategies (pp. 2058–60) in Chapter 53, "Critical Strategies for Reading," and discuss how you think a mythological critic might make use of the allusion to Sophocles in this poem.

CONNECTIONS TO OTHER SELECTIONS

1. Explain how the images in Wilfred Owen's "Dulce et Decorum Est" (p. 852) develop further the ideas and sentiments suggested by Arnold's final line concerning "ignorant armies clash[ing] by night."

2. Contrast the theme of Arnold's poem with Alfred, Lord Tennyson's "The Charge of the Light Brigade" (p. 965). How does Arnold's poem create a very different mood from that of Tennyson's poem?

Consider the poetic appetite for images displayed in the celebration of chile peppers in the following passionate poem.

Jimmy Santiago Baca (b. 1952)

Green Chile   *1989*

I prefer red chile over my eggs
and potatoes for breakfast.
Red chile *ristras*° decorate my door,   *a braided string of peppers*
dry on my roof, and hang from eaves.
They lend open-air vegetable stands   5
historical grandeur, and gently swing
with an air of festive welcome.
I can hear them talking in the wind,
haggard, yellowing, crisp, rasping
tongues of old men, licking the breeze.   10

       But grandmother loves green chile.
When I visit her,
she holds the green chile pepper
in her wrinkled hands.
Ah, voluptuous, masculine,   15
an air of authority and youth simmers
from its swan-neck stem, tapering to a flowery
collar, fermenting resinous spice.
A well-dressed gentleman at the door
my grandmother takes sensuously in her hand,   20
rubbing its firm glossed sides,
caressing the oily rubbery serpent,
with mouth-watering fulfillment,
fondling its curves with gentle fingers.
Its bearing magnificent and taut   25
as flanks of a tiger in mid-leap,
she thrusts her blade into
and cuts it open, with lust
on her hot mouth, sweating over the stove,
bandanna round her forehead,   30
mysterious passion on her face
and she serves me green chile con carne
between soft warm leaves of corn tortillas,
with beans and rice — her sacrifice
to her little prince.   35
I slurp from my plate
with last bit of tortilla, my mouth burns
and I hiss and drink a tall glass of cold water.

All over New Mexico, sunburned men and women
drive rickety trucks stuffed with gunny-sacks   40
of green chile, from Belen, Veguita, Willard, Estancia,
San Antonio y Socorro, from fields
to roadside stands, you see them roasting green chile
in screen-sided homemade barrels, and for a dollar a bag,
we relive this old, beautiful ritual again and again.   45

CONSIDERATIONS FOR CRITICAL THINKING AND WRITING

1. **FIRST RESPONSE.** What's the difference between red and green chiles in this poem? Find the different images the speaker uses to distinguish between the two.

2. What kinds of images are used to describe the grandmother's preparation of green chile? What is the effect of those images?

3. **CREATIVE RESPONSE.** Try writing a description — in poetry or prose — that uses vivid images to evoke a powerful response (either positive or negative) to a particular food.

POEMS FOR FURTHER STUDY

AMY LOWELL (1874–1925)

The Pond   *1919*

Cold, wet leaves
Floating on moss-colored water,
And the croaking of frogs —
Cracked bell-notes in the twilight.

CONSIDERATIONS FOR CRITICAL THINKING AND WRITING

1. **FIRST RESPONSE.** This poem is not a complete sentence. What is missing? Does it matter in terms of understanding what is described by the images?

2. What senses are stimulated by the images? Which sense seems to be the most dominant in the poem? Why?

3. **CREATIVE RESPONSE.** Is the title of the poem necessary to convey its meaning? Choose an appropriate alternate title and explain how it subtly suggests something different from "The Pond."

H. D. (HILDA DOOLITTLE/1886–1961)

Heat   *1916*

O wind, rend open the heat,
cut apart the heat,
rend it to tatters.

Fruit cannot drop
through this thick air —
fruit cannot fall into heat   5
that presses up and blunts
the points of pears
and rounds the grapes.

Cut the heat —   10
plough through it,
turning it on either side
of your path.

CONSIDERATIONS FOR CRITICAL THINKING AND WRITING

1. **FIRST RESPONSE.** Is this poem more about heat or fruit? Explain your answer.
2. What physical properties are associated with heat in this poem?
3. Explain the effect of the description of fruit in lines 4–9.
4. Why is the image of the cutting plow especially effective in lines 10–13?

LINDA PASTAN (B. 1932)

Pass/Fail   *1975*

Examination dreams are reported to persist even into old age . . .
                         —Time *magazine*

You will never graduate
from this dream
of blue books.
No matter how
you succeed awake,   5
asleep there is a test
waiting to be failed.
The dream beckons
with two dull pencils,
but you haven't even   10
taken the course;
when you reach for a book —
it closes its door
in your face; when
you conjugate a verb —   15
it is in the wrong
language.
Now the pillow becomes
a blank page. Turn it
to the cool side;   20
you will still smother
in all of the feathers
that have to be learned
by heart.

CONSIDERATIONS FOR CRITICAL THINKING AND WRITING

1. **FIRST RESPONSE.** How well do the images in this poem capture for you the anxieties about taking exams?

2. Instead of a first-person point of view, Pastan uses the second person. Does her strategy make any difference to your reading of "Pass/Fail"?

3. **CREATIVE RESPONSE.** Write a poem in Pastan's style that expresses your experience taking examinations.

CONNECTION TO ANOTHER SELECTION

1. Discuss the significance of being graded in this poem and in Pastan's "Marks" (p. 883).

RUTH FAINLIGHT (B. 1931)

Crocuses   2006

Pale, bare, tender stems rising
from the muddy winter-faded grass,

shivering petals the almost luminous
blue and mauve of bruises on the naked

bodies of men, women, children
herded into a forest clearing

before the shouted order, crack of gunfire,
final screams and prayers and moans.

CONSIDERATIONS FOR CRITICAL THINKING AND WRITING

1. **FIRST RESPONSE.** Comment on Fainlight's choice of title. What effect does it have on your reading of the poem?

2. Trace your response to each image in the poem and describe the poem's tone as it moves from line to line.

3. **CREATIVE RESPONSE.** Try writing an eight-line poem in the style of Fainlight's based on images that gradually but radically shift in tone.

MARY ROBINSON (1758–1800)

London's Summer Morning   1806

Who has not wak'd to list° the busy sounds   listen to
Of summer's morning, in the sultry smoke
Of noisy London? On the pavement hot
The sooty chimney-boy, with dingy face
And tatter'd covering, shrilly bawls his trade,   5
Rousing the sleepy housemaid. At the door
The milk-pail rattles, and the tinkling bell
Proclaims the dustman's office; while the street

Is lost in clouds impervious. Now begins
The din of hackney-coaches, waggons, carts;   10
While tinmen's shops, and noisy trunk-makers,
Knife-grinders, coopers, squeaking cork-cutters,
Fruit-barrows, and the hunger-giving cries
Of vegetable venders, fill the air.
Now ev'ry shop displays its varied trade,   15
And the fresh-sprinkled pavement cools the feet
Of early walkers. At the private door
The ruddy housemaid twirls the busy mop,
Annoying the smart 'prentice, or neat girl,
Tripping with band-box° lightly. Now the sun   *hat box*   20
Darts burning splendour on the glitt'ring pane,
Save where the canvas awning throws a shade
On the gay merchandize. Now, spruce and trim,
In shops (where beauty smiles with industry),
Sits the smart damsel; while the passenger   25
Peeps thro' the window, watching ev'ry charm.
Now pastry dainties catch the eye minute
Of humming insects, while the limy snare
Waits to enthral them. Now the lamp-lighter
Mounts the tall ladder, nimbly vent'rous,   30
To trim the half-fill'd lamp; while at his feet
The pot-boy° yells discordant! All along   *drink server*
The sultry pavement, the old-clothes-man cries
In tones monotonous, and side-long views
The area for his traffic: now the bag   35
Is slily open'd, and the half-worn suit
(Sometimes the pilfer'd treasure of the base
Domestic spoiler), for one half its worth,
Sinks in the green abyss. The porter now
Bears his huge load along the burning way;   40
And the poor poet wakes from busy dreams,
To paint the summer morning.

CONSIDERATIONS FOR CRITICAL THINKING AND WRITING

1. **FIRST RESPONSE.** How effective is this picture of a London summer morning? Which images do you find particularly effective?

2. How does the end of the poem bring us full circle to its beginning? What effect does this structure have on your understanding of the poem?

3. **CREATIVE RESPONSE.** Try writing about the start of your own day—in the dormitory, at home, the start of a class—using a series of images that provide a vivid sense of what happens and how you experience it.

CONNECTION TO ANOTHER SELECTION

1. How does Robinson's description of London differ from William Blake's "London," the next poem? What would you say is the essential difference in purpose between the two poems?

WILLIAM BLAKE (1757–1827)

London 1794

I wander through each chartered° street,   *defined by law*
Near where the chartered Thames does flow,
And mark in every face I meet
Marks of weakness, marks of woe.

In every cry of every man, 5
In every Infant's cry of fear,
In every voice, in every ban,
The mind-forged manacles I hear.

How the Chimney-sweeper's cry
Every black'ning Church appalls; 10
And the hapless Soldier's sigh
Runs in blood down Palace walls.

But most through midnight streets I hear
How the youthful Harlot's curse
Blasts the new-born Infant's tear, 15
And blights with plagues the Marriage hearse.

CONSIDERATIONS FOR CRITICAL THINKING AND WRITING

1. **FIRST RESPONSE.** What feelings do the visual images in this poem suggest to you?

2. What is the predominant sound heard in the poem?

3. What is the meaning of line 8? What is the cause of the problems that the speaker sees and hears in London? Does the speaker suggest additional causes?

4. The image in lines 11 and 12 cannot be read literally. Comment on its effectiveness.

5. How does Blake's use of denotative and connotative language enrich this poem's meaning?

6. An earlier version of Blake's last stanza appeared this way:

   > But most the midnight harlot's curse
   > From every dismal street I hear,
   > Weaves around the marriage hearse
   > And blasts the new-born infant's tear.

   Examine carefully the differences between the two versions. How do Blake's revisions affect his picture of London life? Which version do you think is more effective? Why?

A SAMPLE STUDENT RESPONSE

Anna Tamara

Professor Burton

English 211

September 30, 2009

Imagery in William Blake's "London" and Mary Robinson's

"London's Summer Morning"

Both William Blake and Mary Robinson use strong imagery to examine and bring to life the city of London, yet each writer paints a very different picture. The images in both poems "[address] the senses," as Meyer writes (837). But while Blake's images depict a city weighed down by oppression and poverty, Robinson's images are lighter, happier, and, arguably, idealized. Both poems use powerful imagery in very different ways to establish theme.

In Blake's poem, oppression and social discontent are defined by the speaker, who sees "weakness" and "woe" (line 4) in the faces he meets; he hears cries of men and children and "mind-forged manacles" (8). And, through imagery, the poem makes a political statement:

> How the Chimney-sweeper's cry
>
> Every black'ning Church appalls;
>
> And the hapless Soldier's sigh
>
> Runs in blood down Palace walls. (9-12)

These images indicate the speaker's dark view of the religious and governmental institutions that he believes cause the city's suffering. The "black'ning Church" and bloody "Palace walls" can be seen to represent misused power and corruption, while the "manacles" are the rules and physical and psychological burdens that lead to societal ills. In Blake's view of London, children are sold into servitude (as chimney sweeps) and soldiers pay in blood.

Robinson's poem, on the other hand, offers the reader a pleasant view of a sunny London morning through a different series of images. The reader hears "the tinkling bell" (7) and sees a bright moment in which "the sun / Darts burning splendour on the glitt'ring pane" (20-21). Even the chimney-boy is shown in a rosy glow. Though he is described as having a "dingy face / and

Tamara 2

tatter'd covering," he wakes the "sleepy" house servant when he "shrilly bawls his trade" (4-6). In contrast to the chimney-sweep of Blake's "London," Robinson's boy is painted as a charming character who announces the morning amid a backdrop of happy workers. Also unlike Blake's London, Robinson's is a city of contentment in which a "ruddy housemaid twirls the busy mop" (18) . . .

Tamara 4

Works Cited

Blake, William. "London." *The Bedford Introduction to Literature*. Ed. Michael
    Meyer. 9th ed. Boston: Bedford/St. Martin's, 2011. 850. Print.

Meyer, Michael, ed. *The Bedford Introduction to Literature*. 9th ed. Boston:
    Bedford/St. Martin's, 2011. 837. Print.

Robinson, Mary. "London's Summer Morning." *The Bedford Introduction to
    Literature*. Ed. Michael Meyer. 9th ed. Boston: Bedford/St. Martin's,
    2011. 848–49. Print.

WILFRED OWEN (1893–1918)

Dulce et Decorum Est   *1920*

Bent double, like old beggars under sacks,
Knock-kneed, coughing like hags, we cursed through
        sludge,
Till on the haunting flares we turned our backs,
And towards our distant rest began to trudge.

Men marched asleep. Many had lost their boots,   5
But limped on, blood-shod. All went lame, all blind;
Drunk with fatigue; deaf even to the hoots
Of gas-shells dropping softly behind.

Gas! GAS! Quick, boys! — An ecstasy of fumbling,
Fitting the clumsy helmets just in time,   10
But someone still was yelling out and stumbling

And flound'ring like a man in fire or lime. —
Dim through the misty panes and thick green light,
As under a green sea, I saw him drowning.

In all my dreams before my helpless sight   15
He plunges at me, guttering, choking, drowning.

If in some smothering dreams, you too could pace
Behind the wagon that we flung him in,
And watch the white eyes writhing in his face,
His hanging face, like a devil's sick of sin,   20
If you could hear, at every jolt, the blood
Come gargling from the froth-corrupted lungs
Bitter as the cud
Obscene as cancer,
Of vile, incurable sores on innocent tongues, —   25
My friend, you would not tell with such high zest
To children ardent for some desperate glory,
The old lie: *Dulce et decorum est*
Pro patria mori.

CONSIDERATIONS FOR CRITICAL THINKING AND WRITING

1. **FIRST RESPONSE.** The Latin quotation in lines 28 and 29 is from Horace: "It is sweet and fitting to die for one's country." Owen served as a British soldier during World War I and was killed. Is this poem unpatriotic? What is its purpose?

2. Which images in the poem are most vivid? To which senses do they speak?

3. Describe the speaker's tone. What is his relationship to his audience?

4. How are the images of the soldiers in this poem different from the images that typically appear in recruiting posters?

MARVIN BELL (B. 1937)

The Uniform   *1994*

Of the sleeves, I remember their weight, like wet wool,
on my arms, and the empty ends which hung past my hands.
Of the body of the shirt, I remember the large buttons
and larger buttonholes, which made a rack of wheels
down my chest and could not be quickly unbuttoned.   5
Of the collar, I remember its thickness without starch,
by which it lay against my clavicle without moving.
Of my trousers, the same — heavy, bulky, slow to give
for a leg, a crowded feeling, a molasses to walk in.
Of my boots, I remember the brittle soles, of a material   10
that had not been made love to by any natural substance,
and the laces: ropes to make prisoners of my feet.
Of the helmet, I remember the webbed, inner liner,

a brittle plastic underwear on which wobbled
the crushing steel pot then strapped at the chin.   15
Of the mortar, I remember the mortar plate,
heavy enough to kill by weight, which I carried by rope.
Of the machine gun, I remember the way it fit
behind my head and across my shoulder blades
as I carried it, or, to be precise, as it rode me.   20
Of tactics, I remember the likelihood of shooting
the wrong man, the weight of the rifle bolt, the difficulty
of loading while prone, the shock of noise.
For earplugs, some used cigarette filters or toilet paper.
I don't hear well now, for a man of my age,   25
and the doctor says my ears were damaged and asks
if I was in the Army, and of course I was but then
a wounded eardrum wasn't much in the scheme.

CONSIDERATIONS FOR CRITICAL THINKING AND WRITING

1. **FIRST RESPONSE.** What overall impression do the speaker's images convey about his uniform?

2. Write a description of the speaker's uniform using adjectives that are not in the poem.

3. Which lines seem especially revealing to you of the speaker's attitude toward his time in the army?

CONNECTION TO ANOTHER SELECTION

1. Compare the vision of war expressed in "Uniform" with that in Wilfred Owen's "Dulce et Decorum Est" (p. 852).

PATRICIA SMITH (B. 1955)

What It's Like to Be a Black Girl (for Those of You Who Aren't)   *1991*

First of all, it's being 9 years old and
feeling like you're not finished, like your
edges are wild, like there's something,
everything, wrong. it's dropping food coloring
in your eyes to make them blue and suffering   5
their burn in silence. it's popping a bleached
white mophead over the kinks of your hair and
primping in front of the mirrors that deny your
reflection. it's finding a space between your
legs, a disturbance at your chest, and not knowing   10
what to do with the whistles. it's jumping
double dutch until your legs pop, it's sweat
and vaseline and bullets, it's growing tall and
wearing a lot of white, it's smelling blood in

your breakfast, it's learning to say fuck with   15
grace but learning to fuck without it, it's
flame and fists and life according to motown,
it's finally having a man reach out for you
then caving in
around his fingers.   20

CONSIDERATIONS FOR CRITICAL THINKING AND WRITING

1. **FIRST RESPONSE.** Describe the speaker's tone. What images in particular contribute to it? How do you account for the selected tone?

2. How does the speaker characterize her life? On which elements of it does she focus?

3. Discuss the poem's final image. What sort of emotions does it elicit in you?

RAINER MARIA RILKE (1875–1926)

The Panther   *1927*

TRANSLATED BY STEPHEN MITCHELL

His vision, from the constantly passing bars,
has grown so weary that it cannot hold
anything else. It seems to him there are
a thousand bars; and behind the bars, no world.

As he paces in cramped circles, over and over,   5
the movement of his powerful soft strides
is like a ritual dance around a center
in which a mighty will stands paralyzed.

Only at times, the curtain of the pupils
lifts, quietly — . An image enters in,   10
rushes down through the tensed, arrested muscles,
plunges into the heart and is gone.

CONSIDERATIONS FOR CRITICAL THINKING AND WRITING

1. **FIRST RESPONSE.** Why do you think Rilke chooses a panther rather than, say, a lion as the subject of the poem's images?

2. What kind of "image enters in" the heart of the panther in the final stanza?

3. How are images of confinement achieved in the poem? Why doesn't Rilke describe the final image in lines 10–12?

CONNECTION TO ANOTHER SELECTION

1. Write an essay explaining how a sense of movement is achieved by the images and rhythms in this poem and in Emily Dickinson's "A Bird came down the Walk —" (p. 920).

JANE KENYON (1947–1995)

The Blue Bowl

1990

Like primitives we buried the cat
with his bowl. Bare-handed
we scraped sand and gravel
back into the hole.

They fell with a hiss   5

and thud on his side,
on his long red fur, the white feathers
between his toes, and his
long, not to say aquiline, nose.

We stood and brushed each other off.   10
There are sorrows keener than these.

Silent the rest of the day, we worked,
ate, stared, and slept. It stormed
all night; now it clears, and a robin
burbles from a dripping bush   15
like the neighbor who means well
but always says the wrong thing.

CONSIDERATIONS FOR CRITICAL THINKING AND WRITING

1. **FIRST RESPONSE.** How do the descriptions of the cat—for example, "the white feathers / between his toes"—affect your reading of the poem?

2. Why do you think Kenyon titles the poem "The Blue Bowl" rather than, perhaps, "The Cat's Bowl"?

3. What is the effect of being reminded that "There are sorrows keener than these"?

4. Why is the robin's song "the wrong thing"?

CONNECTION TO ANOTHER SELECTION

1. Write an essay comparing the death of this cat with the death of the dog in John Updike's "Dog's Death" (p. 746). Which poem draws a more powerful response from you? Explain why.

DONNA MASINI (B. 1954)

Slowly

2004

I watched a snake once, swallow a rabbit.
Fourth grade, the reptile zoo
the rabbit stiff, nose in, bits of litter stuck to its fur,

its head clenched in the wide
jaws of the snake, the snake   5
sucking it down its long throat.

All throat that snake—I couldn't tell
where the throat ended, the body
began. I remember the glass

case, the way that snake   10
took its time (all the girls, groaning, shrieking
but weren't we amazed, fascinated,

saying we couldn't look, but looking, weren't we
held there, weren't we
imagining—what were we imagining?).   15

Mrs. Peterson urged us to *move on girls,*
but we couldn't move. It was like
watching a fern unfurl, a minute

hand move across a clock. I didn't know why
the snake didn't choke, the rabbit never   20
moved, how the jaws kept opening

wider, sucking it down, just so
I am taking this in, slowly,
taking it into my body:

this grief. How slow   25
the body is to realize.
You are never coming back.

Considerations for Critical Thinking and Writing

1. **First Response.** What, ultimately, is this poem about?
2. Comment on the effectiveness of the short, quick images in the first stanza in establishing the setting and plot.
3. Explain how time is depicted through the poem's images.

Connection to Another Selection

1. Compare the treatment of grief in "Slowly" and in Jane Kenyon's "The Blue Bowl" (p. 856).

Sally Croft (b. 1935)
Home-Baked Bread   *1981*

Nothing gives a household a greater sense of stability and common comfort than the aroma of cooling bread. Begin, if you like, with a loaf of whole wheat, which requires neither sifting nor kneading, and go on from there to more cunning triumphs.
                                               —The Joy of Cooking

What is it she is not saying?
Cunning triumphs. It rings
of insinuation. Step into my kitchen,

I have prepared a cunning triumph
for you. Spices and herbs
sealed in this porcelain jar,   5

a treasure of my great-aunt
who sat up past midnight
in her Massachusetts bedroom
when the moon was dark. Come,   10
rest your feet. I'll make
you tea with honey and slices

of warm bread spread with peach butter.
I picked the fruit this morning
still fresh with dew. The fragrance   15
is seductive? I hoped you would say that.
See how the heat rises
when the bread opens. Come,

we'll eat together, the small flakes
have scarcely any flavor. What cunning   20
triumphs we can discover in my upstairs room
where peach trees breathe their sweetness
beside the open window and
sun lies like honey on the floor.

CONSIDERATIONS FOR CRITICAL THINKING AND WRITING

1. **FIRST RESPONSE.** Why does the speaker in this poem seize on the phrase
   "cunning triumphs" from the *Joy of Cooking* excerpt?

2. Distinguish between the voice we hear in lines 1–3 and the second voice in
   lines 3–24. Who is the "you" in the poem?

3. Why is the word "insinuation" an especially appropriate choice in line 3?

4. How do the images in lines 20–24 bring together all of the senses evoked in
   the preceding lines?

5. **CREATIVE RESPONSE.** Write a paragraph — or stanza — that describes the sensuous (and perhaps sensual) qualities of a food you enjoy.

JOHN KEATS (1795–1821)

To Autumn   *1819*

I

Season of mists and mellow fruitfulness,
    Close bosom-friend of the maturing sun;
Conspiring with him how to load and bless
    With fruit the vines that round the thatch-eves run;
To bend with apples the mossed cottage-trees,   5
    And fill all fruit with ripeness to the core;
        To swell the gourd, and plump the hazel shells
    With a sweet kernel; to set budding more,

And still more, later flowers for the bees,
Until they think warm days will never cease,   10
    For summer has o'er-brimmed their clammy cells.

II

Who hath not seen thee oft amid thy store?
    Sometimes whoever seeks abroad may find
Thee sitting careless on a granary floor,
    Thy hair soft-lifted by the winnowing wind;   15
Or on a half-reaped furrow sound asleep,
    Drowsed with the fume of poppies, while thy hook°   *scythe*
      Spares the next swath and all its twinèd flowers:
And sometimes like a gleaner thou dost keep
    Steady thy laden head across a brook;   20
    Or by a cider-press, with patient look,
      Thou watchest the last oozings hours by hours.

III

Where are the songs of spring? Ay, where are they?
    Think not of them, thou hast thy music too —
While barred clouds bloom the soft-dying day,   25
    And touch the stubble-plains with rosy hue;
Then in a wailful choir the small gnats mourn
    Among the river swallows,° borne aloft   *willows*
      Or sinking as the light wind lives or dies;
And full-grown lambs loud bleat from hilly bourn;°   *territory*   30
    Hedge-crickets sing; and now with treble soft
    The redbreast whistles from a garden-croft,
      And gathering swallows twitter in the skies.

CONSIDERATIONS FOR CRITICAL THINKING AND WRITING

1. **FIRST RESPONSE.** How is autumn made to seem like a person in each stanza of this ode?

2. Which senses are most emphasized in each stanza?

3. How is the progression of time expressed in the ode?

4. How does the imagery convey tone? Which words have especially strong connotative values?

5. What is the speaker's view of death?

CONNECTIONS TO OTHER SELECTIONS

1. Compare this poem's tone and perspective on death with those of Robert Frost's "After Apple-Picking" (p. 1106).

2. Write an essay comparing the significance of this poem's images of "mellow fruitfulness" (line 1) with that of the images of ripeness in Theodore Roethke's "Root Cellar" (p. 842). Explain how the images in each poem lead to very different feelings about the same phenomenon.

C. K. WILLIAMS (B. 1936)

Shock

1999

Furiously a crane
in the scrap yard out of whose grasp
a car it meant to pick up slipped,
lifts and lets fall, lifts and lets fall
the steel ton of its clenched pincers
onto the shuddering carcass
which spurts fragments of anguished glass
until it's sufficiently crushed
to be hauled up and flung onto
the heap from which one imagines
it'll move on to the shredding
or melting down that awaits it.

© Christopher Felver/CORBIS.

Also somewhere a crow
with less evident emotion
punches its beak through the dead   15
breast of a dove or albino
sparrow until it arrives at
a coil of gut it can extract,
then undo with a dexterous twist
an oily stretch just the right length   20
to be devoured, the only
suggestion of violation
the carrion jerked to one side
in involuntary dismay.

Splayed on the soiled pavement   25
the dove or sparrow; dismembered
in the tangled remnants of itself
the wreck, the crane slamming once more
for good measure into the all
but dematerialized hulk,   30
then luxuriously swaying
away, as, gorged, glutted, the crow
with savage care unfurls the full,
luminous glitter of its wings,
so we can preen, too, for so much   35
so well accomplished, so well seen.

CONSIDERATIONS FOR CRITICAL THINKING AND WRITING

1. **FIRST RESPONSE.** What do you think is the significance of the poem's title?
2. What connections can you make between the images in stanzas 1 and 2?
3. Explain how the third stanza develops a theme from the images provided
   in the first two stanzas.

Ezra Pound (1885–1972)

In a Station of the Metro°   1913

The apparition of these faces in the crowd;
Petals on a wet, black bough.

Metro: Underground railroad in Paris.

Considerations for Critical Thinking and Writing

1. **First Response.** Why is the title essential for this poem?
2. What kind of mood does the image in the second line convey?
3. Why is "apparition" (line 1) a better word choice than, say, "appearance" or "sight"?
4. **Creative Response.** Write a two-line vivid image for a poem titled "At a Desk in the Library."

Cathy Song (b. 1955)

The White Porch   1983

I wrap the blue towel
after washing,
around the damp
weight of hair, bulky
as a sleeping cat,   5
and sit out on the porch.
Still dripping water,
it'll be dry by supper,
by the time the dust
settles off your shoes,   10
though it's only five
past noon. Think
of the luxury: how to use
the afternoon like the stretch
of lawn spread before me.   15
There's the laundry,
sun-warm clothes at twilight,
and the mountain of beans
in my lap. Each one,
I'll break and snap   20
thoughtfully in half.

But there is this slow arousal.
The small buttons
of my cotton blouse
are pulling away from my body.   25
I feel the strain of threads,
the swollen magnolias

heavy as a flock of birds
in the tree. Already,
the orange sponge cake   30
is rising in the oven.
I know you'll say it makes
your mouth dry
and I'll watch you
drench your slice of it   35
in canned peaches
and lick the plate clean.

So much hair, my mother
used to say, grabbing
the thick braided rope   40
in her hands while we washed
the breakfast dishes, discussing
dresses and pastries.
My mind often elsewhere
as we did the morning chores together.   45
Sometimes, a few strands
would catch in her gold ring.
I worked hard then,
anticipating the hour
when I would let the rope down   50
at night, strips of sheets,
knotted and tied,
while she slept in tight blankets.
My hair, freshly washed
like a measure of wealth,   55
like a bridal veil.
Crouching in the grass,
you would wait for the signal,
for the movement of curtains
before releasing yourself   60
from the shadow of moths.
Cloth, hair and hands,
smuggling you in.

CONSIDERATIONS FOR CRITICAL THINKING AND WRITING

1. **FIRST RESPONSE.** How is hair made erotic in this poem? Discuss the images
   that you deem especially effective.
2. Who is the "you" to whom the speaker refers in each stanza?
3. What role does the mother play in this poem about desire?
4. Why do you think the poem is titled "The White Porch"?

CONNECTIONS TO OTHER SELECTIONS

1. Compare the images used to describe the speaker's "slow arousal" (line 22)
   in this poem with Sally Croft's images in "Home-Baked Bread" (p. 857).
   What similarities do you see? What makes each description so effective?

2. Write an essay comparing the images of sensuality in this poem with those in Li Ho's "A Beautiful Girl Combs Her Hair" (p. 785). Which poem seems more erotic to you? Why?

Perspective

T. E. Hulme (1883–1917)
On the Differences between Poetry and Prose   *1924*

In prose as in algebra concrete things are embodied in signs or counters which are moved about according to rules, without being visualized at all in the process. There are in prose certain type situations and arrangements of words, which move as automatically into certain other arrangements as do functions in algebra. One only changes the *X*'s and the *Y*'s back into physical things at the end of the process. Poetry, in one aspect at any rate, may be considered as an effort to avoid this characteristic of prose. It is not a counter language, but a visual concrete one. It is a compromise for a language of intuition which would hand over sensations bodily. It always endeavors to arrest you, and to make you continuously see a physical thing, to prevent you gliding through an abstract process. It chooses fresh epithets and fresh metaphors, not so much because they are new, and we are tired of the old, but because the old cease to convey a physical thing and become abstract counters. A poet says a ship "coursed the seas" to get a physical image, instead of the counter word "sailed." Visual meanings can only be transferred by the new bowl of metaphor; prose is an old pot that lets them leak out. Images in verse are not mere decoration, but the very essence of an intuitive language. Verse is a pedestrian taking you over the ground, prose — a train which delivers you at a destination.

From "Romanticism and Classicism," in *Speculations,*
edited by Herbert Read

CONSIDERATIONS FOR CRITICAL THINKING AND WRITING

1. What distinctions does Hulme make between poetry and prose? Which seems to be the most important difference?

2. Write an essay that discusses Hulme's claim that poetry "is a compromise for a language of intuition which would hand over sensations bodily."

Web Research the poets in this chapter at bedfordstmartins.com/ meyerlit.

25

Figures of Speech

© Bettmann/CORBIS.

Like a piece of ice on a hot stove the
poem must ride on its own melting.
— ROBERT FROST

Figures of speech are broadly defined as a way of saying one thing in terms of something else. An overeager funeral director might, for example, be described as a vulture. Although figures of speech are indirect, they are designed to clarify, not obscure, our understanding of what they describe. Poets frequently use them because, as Emily Dickinson said, the poet's work is to "tell all the Truth but tell it slant" to capture the reader's interest and imagination. But figures of speech are not limited to poetry. Hearing them, reading them, or using them is as natural as using language itself.

Suppose that in the middle of a class discussion concerning the economic causes of World War II your history instructor introduces a series of statistics by saying, "Let's get down to brass tacks." Would anyone be likely to expect a display of brass tacks for students to examine? Of course not. To interpret the statement literally would be to wholly misunderstand the instructor's point that the time has come for a close look at the economic circumstances leading to the war. A literal response transforms the statement into the sort of hilariously bizarre material often found in a sketch by Woody Allen.

The class does not look for brass tacks because, in a nutshell, they understand that the instructor is speaking figuratively. They would understand, too, that in the preceding sentence "in a nutshell" refers to brevity and conciseness rather than to the covering of a kernel of a nut. Figurative language makes its way into our everyday speech and writing as well as into literature because it is a means of achieving color, vividness, and intensity.

Consider the difference, for example, between these two statements:

Literal: The diner strongly expressed anger at the waiter.
Figurative: The diner leaped from his table and roared at the waiter.

The second statement is more vivid because it creates a picture of ferocious anger by likening the diner to some kind of wild animal, such as a lion or tiger. By comparison, "strongly expressed anger" is neither especially strong nor especially expressive; it is flat. Not all figurative language avoids this kind of flatness, however. Figures of speech such as "getting down to brass tacks" and "in a nutshell" are clichés because they lack originality and freshness. Still, they suggest how these devices are commonly used to give language some color, even if that color is sometimes a bit faded.

There is nothing weak about William Shakespeare's use of figurative language in the following passage from *Macbeth*. Macbeth has just learned that his wife is dead, and he laments her loss as well as the course of his own life.

WILLIAM SHAKESPEARE (1564–1616)

From Macbeth *(Act V, Scene v)*   *1605–1606*

Tomorrow, and tomorrow, and tomorrow
Creeps in this petty pace from day to day
To the last syllable of recorded time;
And all our yesterdays have lighted fools
The way to dusty death. Out, out, brief candle!   5
Life's but a walking shadow, a poor player,
That struts and frets his hour upon the stage,
And then is heard no more. It is a tale
Told by an idiot, full of sound and fury,
Signifying nothing.   10

This passage might be summarized as "life has no meaning," but such a brief paraphrase does not take into account the figurative language that reveals the depth of Macbeth's despair and his view of the absolute meaninglessness of life. By comparing life to a "brief candle," Macbeth emphasizes the darkness and death that surround human beings. The light of life is too brief and unpredictable to be of any comfort. Indeed, life for Macbeth is a "walking shadow," futilely playing a role that is more farcical than dramatic, because life is, ultimately, a desperate story filled with pain and devoid of significance. What the figurative language provides, then, is the emotional force of Macbeth's assertion; his comparisons are disturbing because they are so apt.

The remainder of this chapter discusses some of the most important figures of speech used in poetry. A familiarity with them will help you to understand how poetry achieves its effects.

SIMILE AND METAPHOR

The two most common figures of speech are simile and metaphor. Both compare things that are ordinarily considered unlike each other. A *simile* makes an explicit comparison between two things by using words such as *like, as, than, appears,* or *seems:* "A sip of Mrs. Cook's coffee is like a punch in the stomach." The force of the simile is created by the differences between the two things compared. There would be no simile if the comparison were stated this way: "Mrs. Cook's coffee is as strong as the cafeteria's coffee." This is a literal comparison because Mrs. Cook's coffee is compared with something like it, another kind of coffee. Consider how simile is used in this poem.

Web Explore the poetic elements in this chapter at bedfordstmartins.com/ meyerlit.

MARGARET ATWOOD (B. 1939)

you fit into me 1971

you fit into me
like a hook into an eye

a fish hook
an open eye

© Sophie Bassouls/CORBIS SYGMA.

If you blinked on a second reading, you got the point of this poem because you recognized that the simile "like a hook into an eye" gives way to a play on words in the final two lines. There the hook and eye, no longer a pleasant domestic image of a clothing fastener or door latch that fits closely together, become a literal, sharp fishhook and a human eye. The wordplay qualifies the simile and drastically alters the tone of this poem by creating a strong and unpleasant surprise.

A *metaphor,* like a simile, makes a comparison between two unlike things, but it does so implicitly, without words such as *like* or *as:* "Mrs. Cook's coffee is a punch in the stomach." Metaphor asserts the identity of dissimilar things. Macbeth tells us that life *is* a "brief candle," life *is* "a walking shadow," life *is* "a poor player," life *is* "a tale / Told by an idiot." Metaphor transforms people, places, objects, and ideas into whatever the poet imagines them to be, and if metaphors are effective, the reader's experience, understanding, and appreciation of what is described are enhanced. Metaphors are frequently more demanding than similes because they are not signaled by particular words. They are both subtle and powerful.

Here is a poem about presentiment, a foreboding that something terrible is about to happen.

EMILY DICKINSON (1830–1886)

Presentiment — is that long Shadow — on the lawn —

ca. 1863

Presentiment — is that long Shadow — on the lawn —
Indicative that Suns go down —

The notice to the startled Grass
That Darkness — is about to pass —

The metaphors in this poem define the abstraction "Presentiment." The sense of foreboding that Dickinson expresses is identified with a particular moment — the moment when darkness is just about to envelop an otherwise tranquil, ordinary scene. The speaker projects that fear onto the "startled Grass" so that it seems any life must be frightened by the approaching "Shadow" and "Darkness" — two richly connotative words associated with death. The metaphors obliquely tell us ("tell it slant" was Dickinson's motto, remember) that presentiment is related to a fear of death, and, more important, the metaphors convey the feelings that attend that idea.

Some metaphors are more subtle than others because their comparison of terms is less explicit. Notice the difference between the following two metaphors, both of which describe a shaggy derelict refusing to leave the warmth of a hotel lobby: "He was a mule standing his ground" is a quite explicit comparison. The man is a mule; X is Y. But this metaphor is much more covert: "He brayed his refusal to leave." This second version is an ***implied metaphor*** because it does not explicitly identify the man with a mule. Instead it hints at or alludes to the mule. Braying is associated with mules and is especially appropriate in this context because of the mule's reputation for stubbornness. Implied metaphors can slip by readers, but they offer the alert reader the energy and resonance of carefully chosen, highly concentrated language.

Some poets write extended comparisons in which part or all of the poem consists of a series of related metaphors or similes. Extended metaphors are more common than extended similes. In "Catch" (p. 750), Robert Francis creates an *extended metaphor* that compares poetry to a game of catch. The entire poem is organized around this comparison. Because these comparisons are at work throughout the entire poem, they are called *controlling metaphors.* Extended comparisons can serve as a poem's organizing principle; they are also a reminder that in good poems metaphor and simile are not merely decorative but inseparable from what is expressed.

Notice the controlling metaphor in this poem, published posthumously by a woman whose contemporaries identified her more as a wife and mother than as a poet. Bradstreet's first volume of poetry, *The Tenth Muse,* was published by her brother-in-law in 1650 without her prior knowledge.

ANNE BRADSTREET (CA. 1612–1672)

The Author to Her Book

1678

Thou ill-formed offspring of my feeble brain,
Who after birth did'st by my side remain,
Till snatched from thence by friends, less wise than true,
Who thee abroad exposed to public view;
Made thee in rags, halting, to the press to trudge,   5
Where errors were not lessened, all may judge.
At thy return my blushing was not small,
My rambling brat (in print) should mother call;
I cast thee by as one unfit for light,
Thy visage was so irksome in my sight;   10
Yet being mine own, at length affection would
Thy blemishes amend, if so I could:
I washed thy face, but more defects I saw,
And rubbing off a spot, still made a flaw.
I stretched thy joints to make thee even feet,   15
Yet still thou run'st more hobbling than is meet;
In better dress to trim thee was my mind,
But nought save homespun cloth in the house I find.
In this array, 'mongst vulgars may'st thou roam;
In critics' hands beware thou dost not come;   20
And take thy way where yet thou are not known.
If for thy Father asked, say thou had'st none;
And for thy Mother, she alas is poor,
Which caused her thus to send thee out of door.

The extended metaphor likening her book to a child came naturally to Bradstreet and allowed her to regard her work both critically and affectionately. Her conception of the book as her child creates just the right tone of amusement, self-deprecation, and concern.

The controlling metaphor in the following poem is identified by the title.

JAY ROGOFF (B. 1954)

Death's Theater

2006

It's not all tragedy; he's not averse
to melodrama if everyone gets shot,
or musical comedy if the plot
is big and earthy, with a crop of chorus
girls good enough to eat. He loves a farce,   5
that nervous frenzy, those doors slamming shut
in your face. He's Mr. Opening Night,
top hat and cape, arriving in a hearse,
knocking them dead, each show a limited run:
one performance, curtain up, curtain down.   10
He'll undertake conning supporting roles,
rebuild the sets, rewrite your lines. He peddles
tickets, and pens reviews in which you shine.
He sends flowers. He coughs through your big scene.

CONSIDERATIONS FOR CRITICAL THINKING AND WRITING

1. **FIRST RESPONSE.** How is the somber topic of this poem lightened in tone by Rogoff's use of the controlling metaphor?
2. Which words or phrases seem especially carefully chosen to evoke Death's presence throughout the poem?
3. Consider the possible meanings of the title and their relevance to the poem's themes.

OTHER FIGURES

Perhaps the humblest figure of speech — if not one of the most familiar — is the pun. A *pun* is a play on words that relies on a word having more than one meaning or sounding like another word. For example, "A fad is in one era and out the other" is the sort of pun that produces obligatory groans. But most of us find pleasant and interesting surprises in puns. Here's one that has a slight edge to its humor.

EDMUND CONTI (B. 1929)

Pragmatist   *1985*

Apocalypse soon
Coming our way
Ground zero at noon
Halve a nice day.

Grimly practical under the circumstances, the pragmatist divides the familiar cheerful cliché by half. As simple as this poem is, its tone is mixed because it makes us laugh and wince at the same time.

Puns can be used to achieve serious effects as well as humorous ones. Although we may have learned to underrate puns as figures of speech, it is a mistake to underestimate their power and the frequency with which they appear in poetry. A close examination, for example, of Henry Reed's "Naming of Parts" (p. 907), Robert Frost's "Design" (p. 1116), or almost any lengthy passage from a Shakespeare play will confirm the value of puns.

Synecdoche is a figure of speech in which part of something is used to signify the whole: a neighbor is a "wagging tongue" (a gossip); a criminal is placed "behind bars" (in prison). Less typically, synecdoche refers to the whole used to signify the part: "Germany invaded Poland"; "Princeton won the fencing match." Clearly, certain individuals participated in these activities, not all of Germany or Princeton. Another related figure of speech is *metonymy,* in which something closely associated with a subject is substituted for it: "She preferred the silver screen [motion pictures] to reading." "At precisely ten o'clock the paper shufflers [office workers] stopped for coffee."

Synecdoche and metonymy may overlap and are therefore sometimes difficult to distinguish. Consider this description of a disapproving minister entering a noisy tavern: "As those pursed lips came through the swinging door, the atmosphere was suddenly soured." The pursed lips signal the presence of the minister and are therefore a synecdoche, but they additionally suggest an inhibiting sense of sin and guilt that makes the bar patrons feel uncomfortable. Hence the pursed lips are also a metonymy, as they are in this context so closely connected with religion. Although the distinction between synecdoche and metonymy can be useful, a figure of speech is usually labeled a metonymy when it overlaps categories.

Knowing the precise term for a figure of speech is, finally, less important than responding to its use in a poem. Consider how metonymy and synecdoche convey the tone and meaning of the following poem.

DYLAN THOMAS (1914–1953)
The Hand That Signed the Paper   1936

The hand that signed the paper felled a city;
Five sovereign fingers taxed the breath,
Doubled the globe of dead and halved a
      country;
These five kings did a king to death.

The mighty hand leads to a sloping shoulder,
The finger joints are cramped with chalk;
A goose's quill has put an end to murder
That put an end to talk.

The hand that signed the treaty bred a fever,
And famine grew, and locusts came;
Great is the hand that holds dominion over
Man by a scribbled name.

The five kings count the dead but do not soften
The crusted wound nor stroke the brow;
A hand rules pity as a hand rules heaven;
Hands have no tears to flow.

© Hulton-Deutsch Collection/CORBIS.

10

15

The "hand" in this poem is a synecdoche for a powerful ruler because it is a part of someone used to signify the entire person. The "goose's quill" is a metonymy that also refers to the power associated with the ruler's hand. By using these figures of speech, Thomas depersonalizes and ultimately dehumanizes the ruler. The final synecdoche tells us that "Hands have no tears to flow." It makes us see the political power behind the hand as remote and inhuman. How is the meaning of the poem enlarged when the speaker says, "A hand rules pity as a hand rules heaven"?

One of the ways writers energize the abstractions, ideas, objects, and animals that constitute their created worlds is through ***personification,*** the attribution of human characteristics to nonhuman things: temptation pursues the innocent; trees scream in the raging wind; mice conspire in the cupboard. We are not explicitly told that these things are people; instead, we are invited to see that they behave like people. Perhaps it is human vanity that makes personification a frequently used figure of speech. Whatever the reason, personification, a form of metaphor that connects the nonhuman with the human, makes the world understandable in human terms. Consider this concise example from William Blake's *The Marriage of Heaven and Hell,* a long poem that takes delight in attacking conventional morality: "Prudence is a rich ugly old maid courted by Incapacity." By personifying prudence, Blake transforms what is usually considered a virtue into a comic figure hardly worth emulating.

Often related to personification is another rhetorical figure called **apostrophe,** an address either to someone who is absent and therefore cannot hear the speaker or to something nonhuman that cannot comprehend. Apostrophe provides an opportunity for the speaker of a poem to think aloud, and often the thoughts expressed are in a formal tone. John Keats, for example, begins "Ode on a Grecian Urn" (p. 825) this way: "Thou still unravished bride of quietness." Apostrophe is frequently accompanied by intense emotion that is signaled by phrasing such as "O Life." In the right hands — such as Keats's — apostrophe can provide an intense and immediate voice in a poem, but when it is overdone or extravagant it can be ludicrous. Modern poets are more wary of apostrophe than their predecessors because apostrophizing strikes many self-conscious twenty-first-century sensibilities as too theatrical. Thus modern poets tend to avoid exaggerated situations in favor of less charged though equally meditative moments, as in this next poem, with its amusing, half-serious cosmic twist.

JANICE TOWNLEY MOORE (B. 1939)

To a Wasp   1984

You must have chortled
finding that tiny hole
in the kitchen screen. Right
into my cheese cake batter
you dived,   5
no chance to swim ashore,
no saving spoon,
the mixer whirring
your legs, wings, stinger,
churning you into such   10
delicious death.
Never mind the bright April day.
Did you not see
rising out of cumulus clouds
That fist aimed at both of us?   15

Moore's apostrophe "To a Wasp" is based on the simplest of domestic circumstances; there is almost nothing theatrical or exaggerated in the poem's tone until "That fist" in the last line, when exaggeration takes center stage. As a figure of speech, exaggeration is known as **overstatement** or **hyperbole** and adds emphasis without intending to be literally true: "The teenage boy ate everything in the house." Notice how the speaker of Andrew Marvell's "To His Coy Mistress" (p. 812) exaggerates his devotion in the following overstatement:

An hundred years should go to praise
Thine eyes and on thy forehead gaze,
Two hundred to adore each breast,
But thirty thousand to the rest:

That comes to 30,500 years. What is expressed here is heightened emotion, not deception.

The speaker also uses the opposite figure of speech, **understatement,** which says less than is intended. In the next section he sums up why he cannot take 30,500 years to express his love:

The grave's a fine and private place,
But none, I think, do there embrace.

The speaker is correct, of course, but by deliberately understating— saying "I think" when he is actually certain—he makes his point, that death will overtake their love, all the more emphatic. Another powerful example of understatement appears in the final line of Randall Jarrell's "The Death of the Ball Turret Gunner" (p. 802), when the disembodied voice of the machine-gunner describes his death in a bomber: "When I died they washed me out of the turret with a hose."

Paradox is a statement that initially appears to be self-contradictory but that, on closer inspection, turns out to make sense: "The pen is mightier than the sword." In a fencing match, anyone would prefer the sword, but if the goal is to win the hearts and minds of people, the art of persuasion can be more compelling than swordplay. To resolve the paradox, it is necessary to discover the sense that underlies the statement. If we see that "pen" and "sword" are used as metonymies for writing and violence, then the paradox rings true. **Oxymoron** is a condensed form of paradox in which two contradictory words are used together. Combinations such as "sweet sorrow," "silent scream," "sad joy," and "cold fire" indicate the kinds of startling effects that oxymorons can produce. Paradox is useful in poetry because it arrests a reader's attention by its seemingly stubborn refusal to make sense, and once a reader has penetrated the paradox, it is difficult to resist a perception so well earned. Good paradoxes are knotty pleasures. Here is a simple but effective one.

J. PATRICK LEWIS (B. 1942)
The Unkindest Cut   *1993*

Knives can harm you, heaven forbid;
Axes may disarm you, kid;
Guillotines are painful, but
There's nothing like a paper cut!

We all know how bloody paper cuts can be, but this quatrain is also a humorous version of "the pen is mightier than the sword." The wounds escalate to the paper cut, which paradoxically is more damaging than even the broad blade of a guillotine. "The unkindest cut" of all (an allusion to Shakespeare's *Julius Caesar*, III.ii.188) is produced by chilling words on a page rather than cold steel, but it is more painfully fatal nonetheless.

The following poems are rich in figurative language. As you read and study them, notice how their figures of speech vivify situations, clarify ideas, intensify emotions, and engage your imagination. Although the terms for the various figures discussed in this chapter are useful for labeling the particular devices used in poetry, they should not be allowed to get in the way of your response to a poem. Don't worry about rounding up examples of figurative language. First relax and let the figures work their effects on you. Use the terms as a means of taking you further into poetry, and they will serve your reading well.

POEMS FOR FURTHER STUDY

GARY SNYDER (B. 1930)

How Poetry Comes to Me 1992

It comes blundering over the
Boulders at night, it stays
Frightened outside the
Range of my campfire
I go to meet it at the
Edge of the light

CONSIDERATIONS FOR CRITICAL THINKING AND WRITING

1. **FIRST RESPONSE.** How does personification in this poem depict the creative process?

2. Why do you suppose Snyder makes each successive line shorter?

3. **CREATIVE RESPONSE.** How would eliminating the title change your understanding of the poem? Substitute another title that causes you to reinterpret it.

A SAMPLE STUDENT RESPONSE

Jennifer Jackson

Professor Kahane

English 215

October 16, 2009

Metaphor in Gary Snyder's "How Poetry Comes to Me"

"A metaphor," Michael Meyer writes, "makes a comparison between two unlike things . . . implicitly, without words such as *like* or *as*" (866). In his poem "How Poetry Comes to Me," Gary Snyder uses metaphor to compare poetic inspiration and creativity with a kind of wild creature.

In this work, poetry itself is both an ungraceful beast and a timid animal. It is something big and unwieldy, that "comes blundering over the / Boulders at night" (lines 1-2). The word "blunder" suggests that poetic inspiration moves clumsily, blindly—not knowing where it will go next—and somewhat dangerously. Yet it is hesitant and "stays / Frightened outside the / Range of [the] campfire" (2-4). According to Snyder's poem, the creature poetry comes only part way to meet the poet; the poet has to go to meet it on its terms, "at the / Edge of the light" (5-6). The metaphor of the poem as wild animal tells the reader that poetic inspiration is elusive and unpredictable. It must be sought out carefully or it will run back over the boulders, by the way it came. . . .

Works Cited

Meyer, Michael, ed. *The Bedford Introduction to Literature*. 9th ed. Boston: Bedford/St. Martin's, 2011. 866. Print.

Snyder, Gary. "How Poetry Comes to Me." *The Bedford Introduction to Literature*. Ed. Michael Meyer. 9th ed. Boston: Bedford/St. Martin's, 2011. 874. Print.

Margaret Atwood (b. 1939)

February 1995

Winter. Time to eat fat
and watch hockey. In the pewter mornings, the cat,
a black fur sausage with yellow
Houdini eyes, jumps up on the bed and tries
to get onto my head. It's his 5
way of telling whether or not I'm dead.
If I'm not, he wants to be scratched; if I am
he'll think of something. He settles
on my chest, breathing his breath
of burped-up meat and musty sofas, 10
purring like a washboard. Some other tomcat,
not yet a capon, has been spraying our front door,
declaring war. It's all about sex and territory,
which are what will finish us off
in the long run. Some cat owners around here 15
should snip a few testicles. If we wise
hominids were sensible, we'd do that too,
or eat our young, like sharks.
But it's love that does us in. Over and over
again, *He shoots, he scores!* and famine 20
crouches in the bedsheets, ambushing the pulsing
eiderdown, and the windchill factor hits
thirty below, and pollution pours
out of our chimneys to keep us warm.
February, month of despair, 25
with a skewered heart in the centre.
I think dire thoughts, and lust for French fries
with a splash of vinegar.
Cat, enough of your greedy whining
and your small pink bumhole. 30
Off my face! You're the life principle,
more or less, so get going
on a little optimism around here.
Get rid of death. Celebrate increase. Make it be spring.

Considerations for Critical Thinking and Writing

1. **First response.** How do your own associations with February compare
   with the speaker's?
2. Explain how the poem is organized around an extended metaphor that
   defines winter as a "Time to eat fat / and watch hockey" (lines 1–2).
3. Explain the paradox in "it's love that does us in" (line 19).
4. What theme(s) do you find in the poem? How is the cat central to them?

WILLIAM CARLOS WILLIAMS (1883–1963)

To Waken an Old Lady

1921

Old age is
a flight of small
cheeping birds
skimming
bare trees   5
above a snow glaze.
Gaining and failing
they are buffeted
by a dark wind —
But what?   10
On harsh weedstalks
the flock has rested,
the snow
is covered with broken
seedhusks   15
and the wind tempered
by a shrill
piping of plenty.

CONSIDERATIONS FOR CRITICAL THINKING AND WRITING

1. **FIRST RESPONSE.** Consider the images and figures of speech in this poem and explain why you think it is a positive or negative assessment of old age.

2. How does the title relate to the rest of the poem?

CONNECTION TO ANOTHER SELECTION

1. Discuss the shift in tone in "To Waken an Old Lady" and in Colette Inez's "Back When All Was Continuous Chuckles" (p. 805).

ERNEST SLYMAN (B. 1946)

Lightning Bugs

1988

In my backyard,
They burn peepholes in the night
And take snapshots of my house.

CONSIDERATIONS FOR CRITICAL THINKING AND WRITING

1. **FIRST RESPONSE.** Explain why the title is essential to this poem.

2. What makes the description of the lightning bugs effective? How do the second and third lines complement each other?

3. **CREATIVE RESPONSE.** As Slyman has done, take a simple, common fact of nature and make it vivid by using a figure of speech to describe it.

PETER MEINKE (B. 1932)

Unnatural Light

After the break-in
we hung spotlights on the garage outside
Light-sensitive they flare on at dusk
fade out at dawn night-blooming suns
on crime watch   5

Through the dense dark
light pulses under oak and laurel
pulling the stems of periwinkle and begonia
the crimson bougainvillea on the trellis
the calamondin with its bitter fruit   10
When the wind blows in their shadows
slide like burglars along the wall
beyond our barred windows
around the shaky birdhouse
spilling crumbs   15

And the white azaleas confused
by so much light confess their startling secrets
three months early   The others farther out
huddle in natural darkness playing it safe
keeping mum   20

CONSIDERATIONS FOR CRITICAL THINKING AND WRITING

1. **FIRST RESPONSE.** Why do you suppose Meinke substitutes spacing for punctuation in this poem?
2. Describe the controlling metaphor. In which lines does it appear?
3. Discuss whether the tone of this poem is light or dark.

CONNECTION TO ANOTHER SELECTION

1. Compare "Unnatural Light" and Emily Dickinson's "Presentiment — is that long Shadow — on the lawn — " (p. 867) as meditations on being "Light-sensitive," as Meinke puts it.

JUDY PAGE HEITZMAN (B. 1952)

The Schoolroom on the Second Floor of the Knitting Mill

While most of us copied letters out of books,
Mrs. Lawrence carved and cleaned her nails.
Now the red and buff cardinals at my back-room window
make me miss her, her room, her hallway,
even the chimney outside   5
that broke up the sky.

In my memory it is afternoon.
Sun streams in through the door
next to the fire escape where we are lined up
getting our coats on to go out to the playground,   10
the tether ball, its towering height, the swings.
She tells me to make sure the line
does not move up over the threshold.
That would be dangerous.
So I stand guard at the door.   15
Somehow it happens
the way things seem to happen when we're not really looking,
or we are looking, just not the right way.
Kids crush up like cattle, pushing me over the line.

Judy is not a good leader is all Mrs. Lawrence says.   20
She says it quietly. Still, everybody hears.
Her arms hang down like sausages.
I hear her every time I fail.

CONSIDERATIONS FOR CRITICAL THINKING AND WRITING

1. **FIRST RESPONSE.** Does your impression of Mrs. Lawrence change from the beginning to the end of the poem? How so?

2. How can line 2 be read as an implied metaphor?

3. Discuss the use of similes in the poem. How do they contribute to the poem's meaning?

SYLVIA PLATH (1932–1963)

Mirror   *1963*

I am silver and exact. I have no
     preconceptions.
Whatever I see I swallow immediately
Just as it is, unmisted by love or dislike.
I am not cruel, only truthful —
The eye of a little god, four-cornered.
Most of the time I meditate on the
     opposite wall.
It is pink, with speckles. I have looked
     at it so long
I think it is a part of my heart. But it flickers.
Faces and darkness separate us over and over.

© Bettmann/CORBIS.

Now I am a lake. A woman bends over me,   10
Searching my reaches for what she really is.
Then she turns to those liars, the candles or the moon.
I see her back, and reflect it faithfully.
She rewards me with tears and an agitation of hands.
I am important to her. She comes and goes.   15

Each morning it is her face that replaces the darkness.
In me she has drowned a young girl, and in me an old woman
Rises toward her day after day, like a terrible fish.

CONSIDERATIONS FOR CRITICAL THINKING AND WRITING

1. **FIRST RESPONSE.** What is the effect of the personification in this poem? How would our view of the aging woman be different if she, rather than the mirror, told her story?

2. What is the mythical allusion in "Now I am a lake" (line 10)?

3. In what sense can "candles or the moon" be regarded as "liars" (line 12)? Explain this metaphor.

4. Discuss the effectiveness of the simile in the poem's final line.

WILLIAM WORDSWORTH (1770–1850)

London, 1802

1802

Milton!° thou should'st be living at this hour:
England hath need of thee: she is a fen
Of stagnant waters: altar, sword, and pen,
Fireside, the heroic wealth of hall and bower,
Have forfeited their ancient English dower   5
Of inward happiness. We are selfish men;
Oh! raise us up, return to us again;
And give us manners, virtue, freedom, power.
Thy soul was like a star, and dwelt apart:
Thou hadst a voice whose sound was like the sea: 10
Pure as the naked heavens, majestic, free,
So didst thou travel on life's common way,
In cheerful godliness; and yet thy heart
The lowliest duties on herself did lay.

1 *Milton:* John Milton (1608–1674), poet, famous especially for his religious epic *Paradise Lost* and his defense of political freedom.

CONSIDERATIONS FOR CRITICAL THINKING AND WRITING

1. **FIRST RESPONSE.** Describe the poem's tone. Is it nostalgic, angry, or something else?

2. Explain the metonymies in lines 3–6 of this poem. What is the speaker's assessment of England?

3. How would the effect of the poem be different if it were in the form of an address to Wordsworth's contemporaries rather than an apostrophe to Milton? What qualities does Wordsworth attribute to Milton by the use of figurative language?

4. **CRITICAL STRATEGIES.** Read the section on literary history criticism (pp. 2052–53) in Chapter 53, "Critical Strategies for Reading," and use the library to find out about the state of London in 1802. How does the poem reflect or refute the social values of its time?

JIM STEVENS (B. 1922)

Schizophrenia

1992

It was the house that suffered most.

It had begun with slamming doors, angry feet scuffing the carpets,
dishes slammed onto the table,
greasy stains spreading on the cloth.

Certain doors were locked at night,　　　　　　　　　　　　　　　5
feet stood for hours outside them,
dishes were left unwashed, the cloth
disappeared under a hardened crust.

The house came to miss the shouting voices,
the threats, the half-apologies, noisy　　　　　　　　　　　　10
reconciliations, the sobbing that followed.

Then lines were drawn, borders established,
some rooms declared their loyalties,
keeping to themselves, keeping out the other.
The house divided against itself.　　　　　　　　　　　　　　15

Seeing cracking paint, broken windows,
the front door banging in the wind,
the roof tiles flying off, one by one,
the neighbors said it was a madhouse.

It was the house that suffered most.　　　　　　　　　　　　20

CONSIDERATIONS FOR CRITICAL THINKING AND WRITING

1. **FIRST RESPONSE.** What is the effect of personifying the house in this poem?
2. How are the people who live in the house characterized? What does their behavior reveal about them? How does the house respond to them?
3. Comment on the title. If the title were missing, what, if anything, would be missing from the poem? Explain your answer.

WALT WHITMAN (1819–1892)

A Noiseless Patient Spider

1868

A noiseless patient spider,
I mark'd where on a little promontory it stood isolated,
Mark'd how to explore the vacant vast surrounding,
It launch'd forth filament, filament, filament, out of itself,
Ever unreeling them, ever tirelessly speeding them.　　　　　　5

And you O my soul where you stand,
Surrounded, detached, in measureless oceans of space,

Ceaselessly musing, venturing, throwing, seeking
　　the spheres to connect them,
Till the bridge you will need be form'd, till the ductile anchor hold,
Till the gossamer thread you fling catch somewhere, O my soul.　　　　10

CONSIDERATIONS FOR CRITICAL THINKING AND WRITING

1. **FIRST RESPONSE.** Spiders are not usually regarded as pleasant creatures. Why does the speaker in this poem liken his soul to one? What similarities are there in the poem between spider and soul? Are there any significant differences?

2. How do the images of space relate to the connections made between the speaker's soul and the spider?

JOHN DONNE (1572–1631)

A Valediction: Forbidding Mourning　　　　*1611*

As virtuous men pass mildly away,
　　And whisper to their souls to go,
While some of their sad friends do say,
　　The breath goes now, and some say, no:

So let us melt, and make no noise,　　　　　　　　　　　　　　　　5
　　No tear-floods, nor sigh-tempests move;
'Twere profanation of our joys
　　To tell the laity our love.

Moving of th' earth° brings harms and fears,　　　　　　　　*earthquakes*
　　Men reckon what it did and meant,　　　　　　　　　　　　10
But trepidation of the spheres,°
　　Though greater far, is innocent.

Dull sublunary° lovers' love
　　(Whose soul is sense) cannot admit
Absence, because it doth remove　　　　　　　　　　　　　　15
　　Those things which elemented° it.　　　　　　　　　　　　*composed*

But we by a love so much refined,
　　That ourselves know not what it is,
Inter-assured of the mind,
　　Care less, eyes, lips, and hands to miss.　　　　　　　　20

Our two souls therefore, which are one,
　　Though I must go, endure not yet
A breach, but an expansion,
　　Like gold to airy thinness beat.

11 *trepidation of the spheres:* According to Ptolemaic astronomy, the planets sometimes moved violently, like earthquakes, but these movements were not felt by people on earth.
13 *sublunary:* Under the moon; hence, mortal and subject to change.

If they be two, they are two so   25
　　As stiff twin compasses are two;
Thy soul the fixed foot, makes no show
　　To move, but doth, if th' other do.

And though it in the center sit,
　　Yet when the other far doth roam,   30
It leans, and hearkens after it,
　　And grows erect, as that comes home.

Such wilt thou be to me, who must
　　Like th' other foot, obliquely run;
Thy firmness makes my circle just,°   35
　　And makes me end, where I begun.

35 *circle just:* The circle is a traditional symbol of perfection.

CONSIDERATIONS FOR CRITICAL THINKING AND WRITING

1. **FIRST RESPONSE.** A valediction is a farewell. Donne wrote this poem for his wife before leaving on a trip to France. What kind of "mourning" is the speaker forbidding?

2. Explain how the simile in lines 1–4 is related to the couple in lines 5–8. Who is described as dying?

3. How does the speaker contrast the couple's love to "sublunary lovers' love" (line 13)?

4. Explain the similes in lines 24 and 25–36.

LINDA PASTAN (B. 1932)

Marks   *1978*

My husband gives me an A
for last night's supper,
an incomplete for my ironing,
a B plus in bed.
My son says I am average,   5
an average mother, but if
I put my mind to it
I could improve.
My daughter believes
in Pass/Fail and tells me   10
I pass. Wait 'til they learn
I'm dropping out.

CONSIDERATIONS FOR CRITICAL THINKING AND WRITING

1. **FIRST RESPONSE.** Explain the appropriateness of the controlling metaphor in this poem. How does it reveal the woman's relationship to her family?

2. Discuss the meaning of the title.

3. How does the last line serve as both the climax of the woman's story and the poem's controlling metaphor?

Kay Ryan (b. 1945)

Hailstorm   *2005*

Like a storm
of hornets, the
little white planets
layer and relayer
as they whip around
in their high orbits,
getting more and
more dense before
they crash against
our crust. A maelstrom
of ferocious little
fists and punches,
so hard to believe
once it's past.

© Christopher Felver/CORBIS.

Considerations for Critical Thinking and Writing

1. **FIRST RESPONSE.** Describe the progression in violence from the simile to the metaphor as the hailstorm develops.
2. Why is "maelstrom" just the right word in line 10?
3. **CREATIVE RESPONSE.** Try writing a poem in a similar style using one or two striking similes or metaphors to describe a thunderstorm, snowstorm, or windstorm.

Ronald Wallace (b. 1945)

Building an Outhouse   *1991*

Is not unlike building a poem: the pure
mathematics of shape; the music of hammer
and tenpenny nail, of floor joist, stud wall,
and sill; the cut wood's sweet smell.

If the Skil saw rear up in your unpracticed hand,   5
cussing, hawking its chaw of dust,
and you're lost in the pounding particulars
of fly rafters, siding, hypotenuse, and load,
until nothing seems level or true
but the scorn of the tape's clucked tongue,   10

let the nub of your plainspoken pencil prevail
and it's up! Functional. Tight as a sonnet.
It will last forever (or at least for awhile)
though the critics come sit on it, and sit on it.

CONSIDERATIONS FOR CRITICAL THINKING AND WRITING

1. **FIRST RESPONSE.** Explain how the poem's diction contributes to the extended simile. Why is the language of building especially appropriate here?

2. What is the effect of the repetition and sounds in the final line? How does that affect the poem's tone?

3. Consult the Glossary of Literary Terms (p. 2123) for the definition of a sonnet. To what extent does "Building an Outhouse" conform to a sonnet's structure?

ELAINE MAGARRELL (B. 1928)

The Joy of Cooking 1988

I have prepared my sister's tongue,
scrubbed and skinned it,
trimmed the roots, small bones, and gristle.
Carved through the hump it slices thin and neat.
Best with horseradish   5
and economical — it probably will grow back.
Next time perhaps a creole sauce
or mold of aspic?

I will have my brother's heart,
which is firm and rather dry,   10
slow cooked. It resembles muscle
more than organ meat
and needs an apple-onion stuffing
to make it interesting at all.
Although beef heart serves six   15
my brother's heart barely feeds two.
I could also have it braised
and served in sour sauce.

CONSIDERATIONS FOR CRITICAL THINKING AND WRITING

1. **FIRST RESPONSE.** Describe the poem's tone. Do you find it amusing, bitter, or something else?

2. How are the tongue and heart used to characterize the sister and brother in this poem?

3. How is the speaker's personality revealed in the poem's language?

CONNECTION TO ANOTHER SELECTION

1. Write an essay that explains how cooking becomes a way of talking about something else in this poem and in Sally Croft's "Home-Baked Bread" (p. 857).

Ruth Fainlight (b. 1931)

The Clarinettist   *2002*

Pale round arms raising her clarinet
at the exact angle, she sways, then halts,
poised for the music

like a horse that gathers itself up before the leap
with the awkward, perfect, only   5
possible movement

an alto in a quattrocento chorus, blond head
lifted from the score, open-mouthed
for hallelujah

a cherub on a ceiling cornice leaning out   10
from heaped-up clouds of opalescent pink,
translucent blue

a swimmer breasting frothy surf like ripping through
lace curtains, a dancer centred as a spinning top,
an August moon   15

alone, in front of the orchestra, the conductor's
other, and unacknowledged opposite,
she starts the tune.

Considerations for Critical Thinking and Writing

1. **FIRST RESPONSE.** This poem is structured as one long sentence. How does
   this structure create a kind of suspense as the clarinettist is "poised for the
   music" (line 3)?

2. How do the similes and metaphors capture the moment that the clarinettist "starts the tune" (line 18)? What sort of description of her emerges from
   them?

3. **CREATIVE RESPONSE.** Create a similar three-line stanza that adds to
   Fainlight's description and maintains the poem's tone.

Perspective

John R. Searle (b. 1932)

Figuring Out Metaphors   *1979*

If you hear somebody say, "Sally is a block of ice," or, "Sam is a pig," you are
likely to assume that the speaker does not mean what he says literally, but that
he is speaking metaphorically. Furthermore, you are not likely to have very
much trouble figuring out what he means. If he says, "Sally is a prime number between 17 and 23," or "Bill is a barn door," you might still assume he is

speaking metaphorically, but it is much harder to figure out what he means. The existence of such utterances—utterances in which the speaker means metaphorically something different from what the sentence means literally—poses a series of questions for any theory of language and communication: What is metaphor, and how does it differ from both literal and other forms of figurative utterances? Why do we use expressions metaphorically instead of saying exactly and literally what we mean? How do metaphorical utterances work, that is, how is it possible for speakers to communicate to hearers when speaking metaphorically inasmuch as they do not say what they mean? And why do some metaphors work and others do not?

From *Expression and Meaning*

CONSIDERATIONS FOR CRITICAL THINKING AND WRITING

1. Searle poses a series of important questions. Write an essay that explores one of these questions, basing your discussion on the poems in this chapter.

2. **CREATIVE RESPONSE.** Try writing a brief poem that provides a context for the line "Sally is a prime number between 17 and 23" or the line "Bill is a barn door." Your task is to create a context so that either one of these metaphoric statements is as readily understandable as "Sally is a block of ice" or "Sam is a pig." Share your poem with your classmates and explain how the line generated the poem you built around it.

Web Research the poets in this chapter at bedfordstmartins.com/ meyerlit.

26

Symbol, Allegory, and Irony

© Barbara Savage Cheresh.

Poetry is serious business; literature
is the apparatus through which the
world tries to keep intact its important
ideas and feelings.
— MARY OLIVER

SYMBOL

A *symbol* is something that represents something else. An object, a person,
a place, an event, or an action can suggest more than its literal meaning.
A handshake between two world leaders might be simply a greeting, but if
it is done ceremoniously before cameras, it could be a symbolic gesture signifying unity, issues resolved, and joint policies that will be followed. We live
surrounded by symbols. When a $100,000 Mercedes-
Benz comes roaring by in the fast lane, we get a quick
glimpse of not only an expensive car but an entire
lifestyle that suggests opulence, broad lawns, executive
offices, and power. One of the reasons some buyers are
willing to spend roughly the cost of five Chevrolets for a single Mercedes-
Benz is that they are aware of the car's symbolic value. A symbol is a vehicle

Web Explore
the poetic elements
in this chapter at
bedfordstmartins.com/
meyerlit.

for two things at once: it functions as itself, and it implies meanings beyond itself.

The meanings suggested by a symbol are determined by the context in which they appear. The Mercedes could symbolize very different things depending on where it was parked. Would an American political candidate be likely to appear in a Detroit blue-collar neighborhood with such a car? Probably not. Although a candidate might be able to afford the car, it would be an inappropriate symbol for someone seeking votes from all of the people. As a symbol, the German-built Mercedes would backfire if voters perceived it as representing an entity partially responsible for layoffs of automobile workers or, worse, as a sign of decadence and corruption. Similarly, a huge portrait of Mao Tse-tung conveys different meanings to residents of Beijing than it would to farmers in Prairie Center, Illinois. Because symbols depend on contexts for their meaning, literary artists provide those contexts so that the reader has enough information to determine the probable range of meanings suggested by a symbol.

In the following poem, the speaker describes walking at night. How is the night used symbolically?

ROBERT FROST (1874–1963)

Acquainted with the Night   1928

I have been one acquainted with the night.
I have walked out in rain — and back in rain.
I have outwalked the furthest city light.

I have looked down the saddest city lane.
I have passed by the watchman on his beat   5
And dropped my eyes, unwilling to explain.

I have stood still and stopped the sound of feet
When far away an interrupted cry
Came over houses from another street,

But not to call me back or say good-by;   10
And further still at an unearthly height
One luminary clock against the sky

Proclaimed the time was neither wrong nor right.
I have been one acquainted with the night.

In approaching this or any poem, you should read for literal meanings first and then allow the elements of the poem to invite you to symbolic readings, if they are appropriate. Here the somber tone suggests that the lines have symbolic meaning, too. The flat matter-of-factness created by the repetition of "I have" (lines 1–5, 7, 14) understates the symbolic subject matter of the poem, which is, finally, more about the "night" located in the speaker's mind or soul than it is about walking away from a city and back again. The speaker is "acquainted with the night." The importance of this phrase is emphasized by Frost's title and by the fact that he begins and ends the poem with it. Poets frequently use this kind of repetition to alert readers to details that carry more than literal meanings.

The speaker in this poem has personal knowledge of the night but does not indicate specifically what the night means. To arrive at the potential meanings of the night in this context, it is necessary to look closely at its connotations, along with the images provided in the poem. The connotative meanings of night suggest, for example, darkness, death, and grief. By drawing on these connotations, Frost uses a ***conventional symbol*** — something that is recognized by many people to represent certain ideas. Roses conventionally symbolize love or beauty; laurels, fame; spring, growth; the moon, romance. Poets often use conventional symbols to convey tone and meaning.

Frost uses the night as a conventional symbol, but he also develops it into a ***literary*** or ***contextual symbol*** that goes beyond traditional, public meanings. A literary symbol cannot be summarized in a word or two. It tends to be as elusive as experience itself. The night cannot be reduced to or equated with darkness or death or grief, but it evokes those associations and more. Frost took what perhaps initially appears to be an overworked, conventional symbol and prevented it from becoming a cliché by deepening and extending its meaning.

The images in "Acquainted with the Night" lead to the poem's symbolic meaning. Unwilling, and perhaps unable, to explain explicitly to the watchman (and to the reader) what the night means, the speaker nevertheless conveys feelings about it. The brief images of darkness, rain, sad city lanes, the necessity for guards, the eerie sound of a distressing cry coming over rooftops, and the "luminary clock against the sky" proclaiming "the time was neither wrong nor right" all help to create a sense of anxiety in this tight-lipped speaker. Although we cannot know what unnamed personal experiences have acquainted the speaker with the night, the images suggest that whatever the night means, it is somehow associated with insomnia, loneliness, isolation, coldness, darkness, death, fear, and a sense of alienation from humanity and even time. Daylight — ordinary daytime thoughts and life itself — seems remote and unavailable in this poem. The night is literally the period from sunset to sunrise, but, more important, it is an internal state of being felt by the speaker and revealed through the images.

Frost used symbols rather than an expository essay that would explain the conditions that cause these feelings because most readers can provide their own list of sorrows and terrors that evoke similar emotions. Through symbol, the speaker's experience is compressed and simultaneously expanded by the personal darkness that each reader brings to the poem. The suggestive nature of symbols makes them valuable for poets and evocative for readers.

ALLEGORY

Unlike expansive, suggestive symbols, **allegory** is a narration or description usually restricted to a single meaning because its events, actions, characters, settings, and objects represent specific abstractions or ideas. Although the elements in an allegory may be interesting in themselves, the emphasis tends to be on what they ultimately mean. Characters may be given names such as Hope, Pride, Youth, and Charity; they have few, if any, personal qualities beyond their abstract meanings. These personifications are a form of extended metaphor, but their meanings are severely restricted. They are not symbols because, for instance, the meaning of a character named Charity is precisely that virtue.

There is little or no room for broad speculation and exploration in allegories. If Frost had written "Acquainted with the Night" as an allegory, he might have named his speaker Loneliness and had him leave the City of Despair to walk the Streets of Emptiness, where Crime, Poverty, Fear, and other characters would define the nature of city life. The literal elements in an allegory tend to be de-emphasized in favor of the message. Symbols, however, function both literally and symbolically, so that "Acquainted with the Night" is about both a walk and a sense that something is terribly wrong.

Allegory especially lends itself to **didactic poetry,** which is designed to teach an ethical, moral, or religious lesson. Many stories, poems, and plays are concerned with values, but didactic literature is specifically created to convey a message. "Acquainted with the Night" does not impart advice or offer guidance. If the poem argued that city life is self-destructive or sinful, it would be didactic; instead, it is a lyric poem that expresses the emotions and thoughts of a single speaker.

Although allegory is often enlisted in didactic causes because it can so readily communicate abstract ideas through physical representations, not all allegories teach a lesson. Here is a poem describing a haunted palace while also establishing a consistent pattern that reveals another meaning.

EDGAR ALLAN POE (1809–1849)
The Haunted Palace   *1839*

I

In the greenest of our valleys,
   By good angels tenanted,
Once a fair and stately palace —
   Radiant palace — reared its head.

In the monarch Thought's dominion —   5
    It stood there!
Never seraph spread a pinion
    Over fabric half so fair.

II

Banners yellow, glorious, golden,
    On its roof did float and flow;   10
(This — all this — was in the olden
    Time long ago)
And every gentle air that dallied,
    In that sweet day,
Along the ramparts plumed and pallid,   15
    A wingèd odor went away.

III

Wanderers in that happy valley
    Through two luminous windows saw
Spirits moving musically
    To a lute's well-tunèd law,   20
Round about a throne, where sitting
    (Porphyrogene!)°   *born to purple, royal*
In state his glory well befitting,
    The ruler of the realm was seen.

IV

And all with pearl and ruby glowing   25
    Was the fair palace door,
Through which came flowing, flowing, flowing
    And sparkling evermore,
A troop of Echoes whose sweet duty
    Was but to sing,   30
In voices of surpassing beauty,
    The wit and wisdom of their king.

V

But evil things, in robes of sorrow,
    Assailed the monarch's high estate;
(Ah, let us mourn, for never morrow   35
    Shall dawn upon him, desolate!)
And, round about his home, the glory
    That blushed and bloomed
Is but a dim-remembered story
    Of the old time entombed.   40

VI

And travelers now within that valley,
   Through the red-litten windows see
Vast forms that move fantastically
   To a discordant melody;
While, like a rapid ghastly river,   45
   Through the pale door,
A hideous throng rush out forever,
   And laugh — but smile no more.

     On one level this poem describes how a once happy palace is desolated by "evil things" (line 33). If the reader pays close attention to the diction, however, an allegorical meaning becomes apparent on a second reading. A systematic pattern develops in the choice of words used to describe the palace, so that it comes to stand for a human mind. The palace, banners, windows, door, echoes, and throng are equated with a person's head, hair, eyes, mouth, voice, and laughter. That mind, once harmoniously ordered, is overthrown by evil, haunting thoughts that lead to the mad laughter in the poem's final lines. Once the general pattern is seen, the rest of the details fall neatly into place to strengthen the parallels between the surface description of a palace and the allegorical representation of a disordered mind.

     Modern writers generally prefer symbol over allegory because they tend to be more interested in opening up the potential meanings of an experience instead of transforming it into a closed pattern of meaning. Perhaps the major difference is that while allegory may delight a reader's imagination, symbol challenges and enriches it.

IRONY

Another important resource writers use to take readers beyond literal meanings is *irony,* a technique that reveals a discrepancy between what appears to be and what is actually true. Here is a classic example in which appearances give way to the underlying reality.

EDWIN ARLINGTON ROBINSON (1869–1935)

Richard Cory   1897

Whenever Richard Cory went down town,
We people on the pavement looked at him:
He was a gentleman from sole to crown,
Clean favored, and imperially slim.

And he was always quietly arrayed,   5
And he was always human when he talked;
But still he fluttered pulses when he said,
"Good-morning," and he glittered when he walked.

And he was rich — yes, richer than a king —
And admirably schooled in every grace: 10
In fine, we thought that he was everything
To make us wish that we were in his place.

So on we worked, and waited for the light,
And went without the meat, and cursed the bread;
And Richard Cory, one calm summer night,   15
Went home and put a bullet through his head.

Richard Cory seems to have it all. Those less fortunate, the "people on the pavement," regard him as well-bred, handsome, tasteful, and richly endowed with both money and grace. Until the final line of the poem, the reader, like the speaker, is charmed by Cory's good fortune, so quietly expressed in his decent, easy manner. That final, shocking line, however, shatters the appearances of Cory's life and reveals him to have been a desperately unhappy man. While everyone else assumes that Cory represented "everything" to which they aspire, the reality is that he could escape his miserable life only as a suicide. This discrepancy between what appears to be true and what actually exists is known as *situational irony:* what happens is entirely different from what is expected. We are not told why Cory shoots himself; instead, the irony in the poem shocks us into the recognition that appearances do not always reflect realities.

Words are also sometimes intended to be taken at other than face value. *Verbal irony* is saying something different from what is meant. If after reading "Richard Cory," you said, "That rich gentleman sure was happy," your statement would be ironic. Your tone of voice would indicate that just the opposite was meant; hence verbal irony is usually easy to detect in spoken language. In literature, however, a reader can sometimes take literally what a writer intends ironically. The remedy for this kind of misreading is to pay close attention to the poem's context. There is no formula that can detect verbal irony, but contradictory actions and statements as well as the use of understatement and overstatement can often be signals that verbal irony is present.

A SAMPLE STUDENT RESPONSE

Cipriano Diaz

Professor Young

English 200

September 16, 2009

Irony in Edwin Arlington Robinson's "Richard Cory"

In Edwin Arlington Robinson's poem "Richard Cory," appearances are not reality. The character Richard Cory, viewed by the townspeople as "richer than a king" (line 9) and "a gentleman from sole to crown" (3), is someone who inspires envy. The poem's speaker says, "we thought that he was every-thing / To make us wish that we were in his place" (11-12). However, the final shocking line of the poem creates a situational irony that emphasizes the difference between what seems—and what really is.

In lines 1 through 14, the speaker sets up a shining, princely image of Cory, associating him with such regal words as "imperially" (4), "crown" (3), and "king" (9). Cory is viewed by the townspeople from the "pavement" as if he is on a pedestal (2); far below him, those who must work and "[go] without meat" stand in stark contrast (14). Further, not only is Cory a gentle-man, he is so good-looking that he "flutter[s] the pulses" (7) of those around him when he speaks. He's a rich man who "glitter[s] when he walk[s]" (8). He is also a decent man who is "always human when he talk[s]" (6). However, this noble image of Cory is unexpectedly shattered "one calm summer night" in the final couplet (15). What the speaker and townspeople believed Cory to be and aspired to imitate was merely an illusion. The irony is that what Cory seemed to be—a happy, satisfied man—is exactly what he was not. . . .

Work Cited

Robinson, Edwin Arlington. "Richard Cory." *The Bedford Introduction to Literature*. Ed. Michael Meyer. 9th ed. Boston: Bedford/St. Martin's, 2011. 893. Print.

Consider how verbal irony is used in this poem.

KENNETH FEARING (1902–1961)

AD

1938

Wanted: Men;
Millions of men are *wanted at once* in a big new field;
New, tremendous, thrilling, great.
If you've ever been a figure in the chamber of horrors,
If you've ever escaped from a psychiatric ward,   5
If you thrill at the thought of throwing poison into wells, have heavenly
    visions of people, by the thousands, dying in flames—

You are the very man we want
We mean business and our business is *you*
Wanted: A race of brand-new men.   10

Apply: Middle Europe;
No skill needed;
No ambition required; no brains wanted and no character allowed;

Take a permanent job in the coming profession
Wages: *Death.*   15

This poem was written as Nazi troops stormed across Europe at the start of World War II. The advertisement suggests on the surface that killing is just an ordinary job, but the speaker indicates through understatement that there is nothing ordinary about the "business" of this "*coming profession.*" Fearing uses verbal irony to indicate how casually and mindlessly people are prepared to accept the horrors of war.

"AD" is a *satire,* an example of the literary art of ridiculing a folly or vice in an effort to expose or correct it. The object of satire is usually some human frailty; people, institutions, ideas, and things are all fair game for satirists. Fearing satirizes the insanity of a world mobilizing itself for war: his irony reveals the speaker's knowledge that there is nothing "*New, tremendous, thrilling,* [or] *great*" about going off to kill and be killed. The implication of the poem is that no one should respond to advertisements for war. The poem serves as a satiric corrective to those who would troop off armed with unrealistic expectations: wage war, and the wages consist of death.

Dramatic irony is used when a writer allows a reader to know more about a situation than a character does. This creates a discrepancy between what a character says or thinks and what the reader knows to be true. Dramatic irony is often used to reveal character. In the following poem the speaker delivers a public address that ironically tells us more about him than it does about the patriotic holiday he is commemorating.

E. E. CUMMINGS (1894–1962)

next to of course god america i   1926

"next to of course god america i
love you land of the pilgrims' and so forth oh
say can you see by the dawn's early my
country 'tis of centuries come and go
and are no more what of it we should worry   5
in every language even deafanddumb
thy sons acclaim your glorious name by gorry
by jingo by gee by gosh by gum
why talk of beauty what could be more beaut-
iful than these heroic happy dead   10
who rushed like lions to the roaring slaughter
they did not stop to think they died instead
then shall the voice of liberty be mute?"

He spoke. And drank rapidly a glass of water

This verbal debauch of chauvinistic clichés (notice the run-on phrases
and lines) reveals that the speaker's relationship to God and country is not,
as he claims, one of love. His public address suggests a hearty mindlessness
that leads to "roaring slaughter" rather than to reverence or patriotism.
Cummings allows the reader to see through the speaker's words to their
dangerous emptiness. What the speaker means and what Cummings
means are entirely different. Like Fearing's "AD," this poem is a satire that
invites the reader's laughter and contempt in order to deflate the benighted attitudes expressed in it.

When a writer uses God, destiny, or fate to dash the hopes and expectations of a character or humankind in general, it is called **cosmic irony.**
In "The Convergence of the Twain" (p. 818), for example, Thomas Hardy
describes how "The Immanent Will" brought together the *Titanic* and a
deadly iceberg. Technology and pride are no match for "the Spinner of the
Years." Here's a painfully terse version of cosmic irony.

STEPHEN CRANE (1871–1900)

A Man Said to the Universe   1899

A man said to the universe:
"Sir, I exist!"
"However," replied the universe,
"The fact has not created in me
A sense of obligation."

Unlike in "The Convergence of the Twain," there is the slightest bit of humor in Crane's poem, but the joke is on us.

Irony is an important technique that allows a writer to distinguish between appearances and realities. In situational irony a discrepancy exists between what we expect to happen and what actually happens; in verbal irony a discrepancy exists between what is said and what is meant; in dramatic irony a discrepancy exists between what a character believes and what the reader knows to be true; and in cosmic irony a discrepancy exists between what a character aspires to and what universal forces provide. With each form of irony, we are invited to move beyond surface appearances and sentimental assumptions to see the complexity of experience. Irony is often used in literature to reveal a writer's perspective on matters that previously seemed settled.

POEMS FOR FURTHER STUDY

Bob Hicok (b. 1960)

Making it in poetry   2004

The young teller
at the credit union
asked why so many
small checks
from universities?   5
Because I write
poems I said. Why
haven't I heard
of you? Because
I write poems   10
I said.

Considerations for Critical Thinking and Writing

1. **First Response.** Explain how the speaker's verbal irony is central to the poem's humor.

2. What sort of portrait of the poet-speaker emerges from this very brief poem?

Connection to Another Selection

1. Compare the lives of the poets in Hicok's poem and in Richard Wakefield's "In a Poetry Workshop" (p. 1350).

JANE KENYON (1947–1995)

Surprise

1996

He suggests pancakes at the local diner,
followed by a walk in search of mayflowers,
while friends convene at the house
bearing casseroles and a cake, their cars
pulled close along the sandy shoulders
of the road, where tender ferns unfurl
in the ditches, and this year's budding leaves
push last year's spectral leaves from the tips
of the twigs of the ash trees. The gathering
itself is not what astounds her, but the casual   10
accomplishment with which he has lied.

Courtesy of Donald Hall.

CONSIDERATIONS FOR CRITICAL THINKING AND WRITING

1. **FIRST RESPONSE.** Does it matter that this poem is set in the spring?
2. Consider the connotative meaning of "ash trees" in line 9. Why are they particularly appropriate?
3. Why do you suppose Kenyon uses "astounds" rather than "surprises" in line 10? Use a dictionary to help you determine the possible reasons for this choice.
4. Discuss the irony in the poem.

CONNECTION TO ANOTHER SELECTION

1. Write an essay on the nature of the surprises in Kenyon's poem and in Hathaway's "Oh, Oh" (p. 748). Include in your discussion a comparison of the tone and irony in each poem.

MARTÍN ESPADA (B. 1957)

Bully

1990

Boston, Massachusetts, 1987

In the school auditorium
the Theodore Roosevelt statue
is nostalgic
for the Spanish-American War,
each fist lonely for a saber   5
or the reins of anguish-eyed horses,
or a podium to clatter with speeches
glorying in the malaria of conquest.

But now the Roosevelt school
is pronounced *Hernández.*   10
Puerto Rico has invaded Roosevelt
with its army of Spanish-singing children

in the hallways,
brown children devouring
the stockpiles of the cafeteria,   15
children painting *Taíno* ancestors°
that leap naked across murals.

Roosevelt is surrounded
by all the faces
he ever shoved in eugenic spite   20
and cursed as mongrels, skin of one race,
hair and cheekbones of another.

Once Marines tramped
from the newsreel of his imagination;
now children plot to spray graffiti   25
in parrot-brilliant colors
across the Victorian mustache
and monocle.

16 Taíno *ancestors:* The most culturally developed Indian tribe in the Caribbean when
Columbus arrived in Hispaniola in 1492.

CONSIDERATIONS FOR CRITICAL THINKING AND WRITING

1. **FIRST RESPONSE.** Describe the speaker's sense of the past as well as the present. In what sense do two very different cultures collide in this poem?

2. What do you think is the poem's central theme? How do the images and
   symbols work together to contribute to the theme?

3. **CRITICAL STRATEGIES.** Read the section on new historicist and cultural criticism (pp. 2054–56) in Chapter 53, "Critical Strategies for Reading," and
   then do some research on Theodore Roosevelt's role in the Spanish-American
   War and on what was happening in the Boston public school system in the
   late 1980s. How does this information affect your reading of the poem?

KEVIN PIERCE (B. 1958)

Proof of Origin   2005

*NEWSWIRE — A U.S. judge ordered a Georgia school district to remove from textbooks
stickers challenging the theory of evolution.*

Though close to their hearts is the version that starts
With Adam and Eve and no clothes,
What enables their grip as the stickers they strip
Is Darwinian thumbs that oppose°.

CONSIDERATIONS FOR CRITICAL THINKING AND WRITING

1. **FIRST RESPONSE.** How do the rhymes contribute to the humorous tone?
2. Discuss the levels of irony in the poem.
3. How do you read the title? Can it be explained in more than one way?

CARL SANDBURG (1878–1967)

Buttons

1905

I have been watching the war map slammed up for advertising in front
    of the newspaper office.
Buttons — red and yellow buttons — blue and black buttons — are shoved
    back and forth across the map.

A laughing young man, sunny with freckles,
Climbs a ladder, yells a joke to somebody in the crowd,
And then fixes a yellow button one inch west
And follows the yellow button with a black button one inch west.

(Ten thousand men and boys twist on their bodies in a red soak along a
    river edge,
Gasping of wounds, calling for water, some rattling death in their
    throats.)
Who would guess what it cost to move two buttons one inch on the war
    map here in front of the newspaper office where the freckle-faced
    young man is laughing to us?

CONSIDERATIONS FOR CRITICAL THINKING AND WRITING

1. **FIRST RESPONSE.** Why is the date of this poem significant?
2. Discuss the symbolic meaning of the buttons and whether you think the symbolism is too spelled out or not.
3. What purpose does the "laughing young man, sunny with freckles" (line 3) serve in the poem?

CONNECTION TO ANOTHER SELECTION

1. Discuss the symbolic treatment of war in this poem, Kenneth Fearing's "AD" (p. 896), and Henry Reed's "Naming of Parts" (p. 907).

WALLACE STEVENS (1879–1955)

Anecdote of the Jar

1923

I placed a jar in Tennessee,
And round it was, upon a hill.
It made the slovenly wilderness
Surround that hill.

The wilderness rose up to it,   5
And sprawled around, no longer wild.
The jar was round upon the ground
And tall and of a port in air.

It took dominion everywhere.
The jar was gray and bare.   10
It did not give of bird or bush,
Like nothing else in Tennessee.

CONSIDERATIONS FOR CRITICAL THINKING AND WRITING

1. **FIRST RESPONSE.** How is the jar different from its surroundings? What effect does the jar's placement have upon the "slovenly wilderness" (line 3)?

2. What do you make of all the "round" sounds in lines 2, 4, 6, and 7? How do they echo the relationship between the jar and the wilderness?

3. In what sense might this poem be regarded as an anecdote about the power and limitations of art and nature?

CONNECTION TO ANOTHER SELECTION

1. Compare the thematic function of the jar in Stevens's poem with that of the urn in John Keats's "Ode on a Grecian Urn" (p. 825). What important similarities and differences do you see in the meanings of each? Discuss why you think Stevens and Keats have similar or different ideas about art.

MAY SWENSON (1919–1989)

All That Time 1991

© Oscar White/CORBIS.

I saw two trees embracing.
One leaned on the other
as if to throw her down.
But she was the upright one.
Since their twin youth, maybe she
had been pulling him toward her
all that time,

and finally almost uprooted him.
He was the thin, dry, insecure one,
the most wind-warped, you could see.
And where their tops tangled
it looked like he was crying
on her shoulder.
On the other hand, maybe he

had been trying to weaken her,   15
break her, or at least
make her bend
over backwards for him
just a little bit.
And all that time   20
she was standing up to him

the best she could.
She was the most stubborn,
the straightest one, that's a fact.
But he had been willing   25
to change himself —
even if it was for the worse —
all that time.

At the top they looked like one
tree, where they were embracing.   30
It was plain they'd be
always together.

Too late now to part.
When the wind blew, you could hear
them rubbing on each other.   35

CONSIDERATIONS FOR CRITICAL THINKING AND WRITING

1. **FIRST RESPONSE.** Paraphrase the allegory in the poem.
2. Explain why you think the narrative does or doesn't have a happy ending.
3. Discuss the title's significance. How might the theme of the poem shift for you if the title were instead "Too late now to part" (line 33)?

WILLIAM STAFFORD (1914–1993)

Traveling through the Dark   1962

Traveling through the dark I found a deer
dead on the edge of the Wilson River road.
It is usually best to roll them into the canyon:
that road is narrow; to swerve might make more dead.

By glow of the tail-light I stumbled back of the car   5
and stood by the heap, a doe, a recent killing;
she had stiffened already, almost cold.
I dragged her off; she was large in the belly.

My fingers touching her side brought me the reason —
her side was warm; her fawn lay there waiting,   10
alive, still, never to be born.
Beside that mountain road I hesitated.

The car aimed ahead its lowered parking lights;
under the hood purred the steady engine.
I stood in the glare of the warm exhaust turning red;   15
around our group I could hear the wilderness listen.

I thought hard for us all — my only swerving —
then pushed her over the edge into the river.

CONSIDERATIONS FOR CRITICAL THINKING AND WRITING

1. **FIRST RESPONSE.** Notice the description of the car in this poem: the "glow of the tail-light" (line 5), the "lowered parking lights" (13), and how the engine "purred" (14). How do these and other details suggest symbolic meanings for the car and the "recent killing" (line 6)?

2. Discuss the speaker's tone. Does the speaker seem, for example, tough, callous, kind, sentimental, confused, or confident?

3. What is the effect of the last stanza's having only two lines rather than the established four lines of the previous stanzas?

4. Discuss the appropriateness of this poem's title. In what sense has the speaker "thought hard for us all" (line 17) ? What are those thoughts?

5. Is this a didactic poem?

JULIO MARZÁN (B. 1946)

Ethnic Poetry   *1994*

The ethnic poet said: "The earth is maybe
a huge maraca / and the sun a trombone /
and life / is to move your ass / to slow beats."
The ethnic audience roasted a suckling pig.

The ethnic poet said: "Oh thank Goddy, Goddy /   5
I be me, my toenails curled downward /
deep, deep, deep into Mama earth."
The ethnic audience shook strands of sea shells.

The ethnic poet said: "The sun was created black /
so we should imagine light / and also dream /   10
a walrus emerging from the broken ice."
The ethnic audience beat on sealskin drums.

The ethnic poet said: "Reproductive organs /
Eagles nesting California redwoods /
Shut up and listen to my ancestors."   15
The ethnic audience ate fried bread and honey.

The ethnic poet said: "Something there is that
doesn't love a wall / That sends
the frozen-ground-swell under it."
The ethnic audience deeply understood humanity.   20

CONSIDERATIONS FOR CRITICAL THINKING AND WRITING

1. **FIRST RESPONSE.** What is the implicit definition of ethnic poetry in this poem?

2. The final stanza quotes lines from Robert Frost's "Mending Wall" (p. 1100). Read the entire poem. Why do you think Marzán chooses these lines and this particular poem as one kind of ethnic poetry?

3. What is the poem's central irony? Pay particular attention to the final line. What is being satirized here?

4. **CRITICAL STRATEGIES.** Read the section on the literary canon (pp. 2044–46) in Chapter 53, "Critical Strategies for Reading," and discuss how the formation of the literary canon is related to the theme of "Ethnic Poetry."

CONNECTION TO ANOTHER SELECTION

1. Write an essay that discusses the speakers' ideas about what poetry should be in "Ethnic Poetry" and in Langston Hughes's "Formula" (p. 1142).

MARK HALLIDAY (B. 1949)

Graded Paper

1991

On the whole this is quite successful work:
your main argument about the poet's ambivalence —
how he loves the very things he attacks —
is mostly persuasive and always engaging.

At the same time,   5
             there are spots
where your thinking becomes, for me,
alarmingly opaque, and your syntax seems to jump
backwards through unnecessary hoops,
as on p. 2 where you speak of "precognitive awareness   10
not yet disestablished by the shell that encrusts
each thing that a person actually says"
or at the top of p. 5 where your discussion of
"subverbal undertow miming the subversion of self-belief
woven counter to desire's outreach"   15
leaves me groping for firmer footholds.
(I'd have said it differently,
or rather, said something else.)
And when you say that women "could not fulfill themselves" (p. 6)
"in that era" (only forty years ago, after all!)   20
are you so sure that the situation is so different today?
Also, how does Whitman bluff his way into
your penultimate paragraph? He is the *last* poet
I would have quoted in this context!
What plausible way of behaving   25
does the passage you quote represent? Don't you think
literature should ultimately reveal possibilities for *action*?

Please notice how I've repaired your use of semicolons.

And yet, despite what may seem my cranky response,
I do admire the freshness of   30
your thinking and your style; there is
a vitality here; your sentences thrust themselves forward
with a confidence as impressive as it is cheeky. . . .
You are not
        me, finally,   35
and though this is an awkward problem, involving
the inescapable fact that you are so young, so young
it is also a delightful provocation.

A−

CONSIDERATIONS FOR CRITICAL THINKING AND WRITING

1. **FIRST RESPONSE.** How do you characterize the grader of this paper based on the comments about the paper?

2. Is the speaker a man or a woman? What makes you think so? Does the gender of the speaker affect your reading of the poem? How?

3. Explain whether or not you think the teacher's comments on the paper are consistent with the grade awarded it. How do you account for the grade?

CONNECTION TO ANOTHER SELECTION

1. Compare the ways in which Halliday reveals the speaker's character in this poem with the strategies used by Robert Browning in "My Last Duchess" (p. 910).

CHARLES SIMIC (B. 1938)

The Storm   2008

I'm going over to see what those weeds
By the stone wall are worried about.
Perhaps, they don't care for the way
The shadows creep across the lawn
In the silence of the afternoon.   5

The sky keeps being blue,
Though we hear no birds,
See no butterflies among the flowers
Or ants running over our feet.

Trees, you bend your branches ever so slightly   10
In deference to something
About to make its entrance
Of which we know nothing,
Spellbound as we are by the deepening quiet,
The light just beginning to dim.   15

CONSIDERATIONS FOR CRITICAL THINKING AND WRITING

1. **FIRST RESPONSE.** How does the diction of this poem invite more than just a literal reading about a storm?

2. How does Simic manipulate sound in the poem to help create its tone?

3. Describe how the images in each stanza advance the sense of the storm's progression.

CONNECTION TO ANOTHER SELECTION

1. Write a comparative analysis of the themes of "The Storm" and Emily Dickinson's "Presentiment — is that long Shadow — on the lawn —" (p. 867).

JAMES MERRILL (1926–1995)

Casual Wear

1984

Your average tourist: Fifty. 2.3
Times married. Dressed, this year, in Ferdi Plinthbower
Originals. Odds 1 to 9
Against her strolling past the Embassy

Today at noon. Your average terrorist: 5
Twenty-five. Celibate. No use for trends,
At least in clothing. Mark, though, where it ends.
People have come forth made of colored mist

Unsmiling on one hundred million screens
To tell of his prompt phone call to the station,   10
"Claiming responsibility" — devastation
Signed with a flourish, like the dead wife's jeans.

CONSIDERATIONS FOR CRITICAL THINKING AND WRITING

1. **FIRST RESPONSE.** What is the effect of the statistics in this poem?
2. Describe the speaker's tone. Is it appropriate for the subject matter? Explain why or why not.
3. Comment on the ironies that emerge from the final two lines. How are the tourist and terrorist linked by the speaker's description? Explain why you think the speaker sympathizes more with the tourist or the terrorist — or with neither.

CONNECTION TO ANOTHER SELECTION

1. Compare the satire in this poem with that in Peter Meinke's "The ABC of Aerobics" (p. 1022). What is satirized in each poem? Which satire do you think is more pointed?

HENRY REED (1914–1986)

Naming of Parts

Today we have naming of parts. Yesterday,
We had daily cleaning. And tomorrow morning,
We shall have what to do after firing. But today,
Today we have naming of parts. Japonica
Glistens like coral in all of the neighboring gardens,   5
          And today we have naming of parts.

This is the lower sling swivel. And this
Is the upper sling swivel, whose use you will see,
When you are given your slings. And this is the piling swivel,
Which in your case you have not got. The branches   10

Hold in the gardens their silent, eloquent gestures,
        Which in our case we have not got.

This is the safety-catch, which is always released
With an easy flick of the thumb. And please do not let me
See anyone using his finger. You can do it quite easy   15
If you have any strength in your thumb. The blossoms
Are fragile and motionless, never letting anyone see
        Any of them using their finger.

And this you can see is the bolt. The purpose of this
Is to open the breech, as you see. We can slide it   20
Rapidly backwards and forwards: we call this
Easing the spring. And rapidly backwards and forwards
The early bees are assaulting and fumbling the flowers:
        They call it easing the Spring.

They call it easing the Spring: it is perfectly easy   25
If you have any strength in your thumb: like the bolt,
And the breech, and the cocking-piece, and the point of balance,
Which in our case we have not got; and the almond-blossom
Silent in all of the gardens and the bees going backwards and forwards,
        For today we have naming of parts.   30

CONSIDERATIONS FOR CRITICAL THINKING AND WRITING

1. **FIRST RESPONSE.** Characterize the two speakers in this poem. Identify the
    lines spoken by each. How do their respective lines differ in tone?

2. What is the effect of the last line of each stanza?

3. How do ambiguities and puns contribute to the poem's meaning?

4. What symbolic contrast is made between the rifle instruction and the gar-
    dens? How is this contrast ironic?

RACHEL HADAS (B. 1948)

The Compact   *2003*

The short steep ride in the red bus uphill
from the Girls' School to the Boys' School left
time to whip our compacts out and powder
cheeks, noses. What for? For the boys? Well, yes,
we might have answered if we had been asked.   5
No one asked. Good thing. We didn't know.
Those uphill rides were forty years ago.

If every gesture halves a hidden whole,
if every moment twins a hidden half,
then my thumb clicking that pink plastic catch   10
(sweet whiff of powder; flash of a tiny mirror)
opens not only the compact but also

the first half of a parenthesis
stretching its arms out, longing to be closed.

CONSIDERATIONS FOR CRITICAL THINKING AND WRITING

1. **FIRST RESPONSE.** Discuss the denotative meanings of the "compact" as well as its potential symbolic meanings.
2. Why is it appropriate that the bus is red (rather than a yellow school bus) and that the trip is an uphill ride?
3. How do the final lines create an effective ending for the poem?

BRUCE WEIGL (B. 1949)

Snowy Egret   1985

My neighbor's boy has lifted his father's shotgun and stolen
down to the backwaters of the Elizabeth
and in the moon he's blasted a snowy egret
from the shallows it stalked for small fish.

Midnight. My wife wakes me. He's in the backyard   5
with a shovel, so I go down half drunk with pills
that let me sleep to see what I can see and if it's safe.
The boy doesn't hear me come across the dewy grass.
He says through tears he has to bury it.
He says his father will kill him   10
and he digs until the hole is deep enough and gathers
the egret carefully into his arms
as if not to harm the blood-splattered wings
gleaming in the flashlight beam.

His man's muscled shoulders   15
shake with the weight of what he can't set right no matter what,
but one last time he tries to stay a child, sobbing,
Please don't tell.
He says he only meant to flush it from the shadows,
he only meant to watch it fly   20
but the shot spread too far
ripping into the white wings
spanned awkwardly for a moment
until it glided into brackish death.

I want to grab his shoulders,   25
shake the lies loose from his lips, but he hurts enough;
he burns with shame for what he's done,
with fear for his hard father's
fists I've seen crash down on him for so much less.
I don't know what to do but hold him.   30
If I let go he'll fly to pieces before me.

What a time we share, that can make a good boy steal away,
wiping out from the blue face of the pond
what he hadn't even known he loved, blasting
such beauty into nothing.   35

CONSIDERATIONS FOR CRITICAL THINKING AND WRITING

1. **FIRST RESPONSE.** Describe the boy's relationship with his father. Why is that important in the speaker's account of the boy's actions?

2. Describe how Weigl's use of both the past and present affects your reading of the narrative.

3. Read line 19, "He says he only meant to flush it from the shadows," symbolically. What significance does it take on as the narrative develops?

ROBERT BROWNING (1812–1889)

My Last Duchess   *1842*

Courtesy of the National Portrait Gallery, London.

Ferrara°

That's my last Duchess painted on the wall,
Looking as if she were alive. I call
That piece a wonder, now: Frà Pandolf's°
          hands
Worked busily a day, and there she stands.
Will't please you sit and look at her? I said
"Frà Pandolf" by design, for never read
Strangers like you that pictured countenance,
The depth and passion of its earnest glance,
But to myself they turned (since none puts by
The curtain I have drawn for you, but I)   10
And seemed as they would ask me, if they durst,
How such a glance came there; so, not the first
Are you to turn and ask thus. Sir, 'twas not
Her husband's presence only, called that spot
Of joy into the Duchess' cheek: perhaps   15
Frà Pandolf chanced to say "Her mantle laps
Over my lady's wrist too much," or "Paint
Must never hope to reproduce the faint
Half-flush that dies along her throat": such stuff
Was courtesy, she thought, and cause enough   20
For calling up that spot of joy. She had

Ferrara: In the sixteenth century, the duke of this Italian city arranged to marry a second time after the mysterious death of his very young first wife.   3 *Frà Pandolf:* A fictitious artist.

A heart — how shall I say? — too soon made glad,
Too easily impressed; she liked whate'er
She looked on, and her looks went everywhere.
Sir, 'twas all one! My favor at her breast,   25
The dropping of the daylight in the West,
The bough of cherries some officious fool
Broke in the orchard for her, the white mule
She rode with round the terrace — all and each
Would draw from her alike the approving speech,   30
Or blush, at least. She thanked men, — good! but thanked
Somehow — I know not how — as if she ranked
My gift of a nine-hundred-years-old name
With anybody's gift. Who'd stoop to blame
This sort of trifling? Even had you skill   35
In speech — which I have not — to make your will
Quite clear to such an one, and say, "Just this
Or that in you disgusts me; here you miss,
Or there exceed the mark" — and if she let
Herself be lessoned so, nor plainly set   40
Her wits to yours, forsooth, and made excuse,
— E'en then would be some stooping; and I choose
Never to stoop. Oh sir, she smiled, no doubt,
Whene'er I passed her; but who passed without
Much the same smile? This grew; I gave commands;   45
Then all smiles stopped together. There she stands
As if alive. Will't please you rise? We'll meet
The company below, then. I repeat,
The Count your master's known munificence
Is ample warrant that no just pretense   50
Of mine for dowry will be disallowed;
Though his fair daughter's self, as I avowed
At starting, is my object. Nay, we'll go
Together down, sir. Notice Neptune, though,
Taming a sea-horse, thought a rarity,   55
Which Claus of Innsbruck° cast in bronze for me!

56 *Claus of Innsbruck:* Also a fictitious artist.

CONSIDERATIONS FOR CRITICAL THINKING AND WRITING

1. **FIRST RESPONSE.** What do you think happened to the duchess?
2. To whom is the duke addressing his remarks about the duchess in this poem? What is ironic about the situation?
3. Why was the duke unhappy with his first wife? What does this reveal about him? What does the poem's title suggest about his attitude toward women in general?
4. What seems to be the visitor's response (lines 53–54) to the duke's account of his first wife?

CONNECTION TO ANOTHER SELECTION

1. Write an essay describing the ways in which the speakers of "My Last Duchess" and Katharyn Howd Machan's "Hazel Tells LaVerne" (p. 807) inadvertently reveal themselves.

WILLIAM BLAKE (1757–1827)

The Chimney Sweeper   *1789*

When my mother died I was very young,
And my father sold me while yet my tongue
Could scarcely cry " 'weep! 'weep! 'weep! 'weep!"
So your chimneys I sweep, and in soot I sleep.

There's little Tom Dacre, who cried when his head,   5
That curled like a lamb's back, was shaved: so I said
"Hush, Tom! never mind it, for when your head's bare
You know that the soot cannot spoil your white hair."

And so he was quiet, and that very night,
As Tom was a-sleeping, he had such a sight!   10
That thousands of sweepers, Dick, Joe, Ned, and Jack,
Were all of them locked up in coffins of black.

And by came an Angel who had a bright key,
And he opened the coffins and set them all free;
Then down a green plain leaping, laughing, they run,   15
And wash in a river, and shine in the sun.

Then naked and white, all their bags left behind,
They rise upon clouds and sport in the wind;
And the Angel told Tom, if he'd be a good boy,
He'd have God for his father, and never want joy.   20

And so Tom awoke; and we rose in the dark,
And got with our bags and our brushes to work.
Though the morning was cold, Tom was happy and warm;
So if all do their duty they need not fear harm.

CONSIDERATIONS FOR CRITICAL THINKING AND WRITING

1. **FIRST RESPONSE.** Discuss the validity of this statement: " 'The Chimney Sweeper' is a sentimental poem about a shameful eighteenth-century social problem; such a treatment of child abuse cannot be taken seriously."

2. Characterize the speaker in this poem and describe his tone. Is his tone the same as the poet's? Consider especially lines 7, 8, and 24.

3. What is the symbolic value of the dream in lines 11 to 20?

4. Why is irony central to the meaning of this poem?

WALT WHITMAN (1819–1892)

From *Song of Myself*   *1881*

6

A child said *What is the grass?* fetching it to me with full hands;
How could I answer the child? I do not know what it is any more than he.

I guess it must be the flag of my disposition, out of hopeful green stuff
    woven.

Or I guess it is the handkerchief of the Lord,
A scented gift and remembrancer designedly dropt,   5
Bearing the owner's name someway in the corners, that we may see and
    remark, and say *Whose?*

Or I guess the grass is itself a child, the produced babe of the vegetation.

Or I guess it is a uniform hieroglyphic,
And it means, Sprouting alike in broad zones and narrow zones,
Growing among black folks as among white,   10
Kanuck, Tuckahoe, Congressman, Cuff,° I give them the same, I receive
    them the same.

And now it seems to me the beautiful uncut hair of graves.

Tenderly will I use you curling grass,
It may be you transpire from the breasts of young men,
It may be if I had known them I would have loved them,   15
It may be you are from old people, or from offspring taken soon out of
    their mothers' laps,
And here you are the mothers' laps.

This grass is very dark to be from the white heads of old mothers,
Darker than the colorless beards of old men,
Dark to come from under the faint red roofs of mouths.   20

O I perceive after all so many uttering tongues,
And I perceive they do not come from the roofs of mouths for nothing.

I wish I could translate the hints about the dead young men and women,
And the hints about old men and mothers, and the offspring taken soon
    out of their laps.

What do you think has become of the young and old men?   25
And what do you think has become of the women and children?

They are alive and well somewhere,
The smallest sprout shows there is really no death,
And if ever there was it led forward life, and does not wait at the end to
    arrest it,
And ceas'd the moment life appear'd.   30

All goes onward and outward . . . and nothing collapses,
And to die is different from what any one supposed, and luckier.

11 *Kanuck . . . Cuff:* Kanuck, a French Canadian; Tuckahoe, a Virginian; Cuff, an African American.

CONSIDERATIONS FOR CRITICAL THINKING AND WRITING

1. **FIRST RESPONSE.** What does the grass mean to the speaker? Describe the various symbolic possibilities offered in lines 1–11. What seems to be the most important symbolic meaning?

2. Describe the tone of lines 12–26. Explain why these lines are or aren't representative of the poem's entire tone.

3. How does the final line compare with your own view of death?

CONNECTION TO ANOTHER SELECTION

1. Compare attitudes toward death in Whitman's poem and in Emily Dickinson's "I heard a Fly buzz—when I died—" (p. 1065).

GARY SOTO (B. 1952)

Behind Grandma's House   *1985*

Courtesy of Gary Soto.

At ten I wanted fame. I had a comb
And two Coke bottles, a tube of Bryl-creem.
I borrowed a dog, one with
Mismatched eyes and a happy tongue,
And wanted to prove I was tough
In the alley, kicking over trash cans,
A dull chime of tuna cans falling.
I hurled light bulbs like grenades
And men teachers held their heads,
Fingers of blood lengthening
On the ground. I flicked rocks at cats,
Their goofy faces spurred with foxtails.
I kicked fences. I shooed pigeons.
I broke a branch from a flowering peach
And frightened ants with a stream of spit.   15
I said "*Chale*," "In your face," and "No way
Daddy-O" to an imaginary priest
Until grandma came into the alley,
Her apron flapping in a breeze,
Her hair mussed, and said, "Let me help you,"   20
And punched me between the eyes.

CONSIDERATIONS FOR CRITICAL THINKING AND WRITING

1. **FIRST RESPONSE.** What is the central irony of this poem?

2. How does the speaker characterize himself at ten?

3. Though the "grandma" appears only briefly, she seems, in a sense, fully characterized. How would you describe her? Why do you think she says, "Let me help you"?

CONNECTION TO ANOTHER SELECTION

1. Write an essay comparing the themes of "Behind Grandma's House" and Bruce Weigl's "Snowy Egret" (p. 909).

Perspective

EZRA POUND (1885–1972)

On Symbols 1912

I believe that the proper and perfect symbol is the natural object, that if a man uses "symbols" he must so use them that their symbolic function does not obtrude; so that *a* sense, and the poetic quality of the passage, is not lost to those who do not understand the symbol as such, to whom, for instance, a hawk is a hawk.

From "Prolegomena," *Poetry Review,* February 1912

CONSIDERATIONS FOR CRITICAL THINKING AND WRITING

1. Discuss whether you agree with Pound that the "perfect symbol" is a "natural object" that does not insist on being read as a symbol.
2. Write an essay in which you discuss Bruce Weigl's "Snowy Egret" (p. 909) as an example of the "perfect symbol" Pound proposes.

Web Research the poets in this chapter at bedfordstmartins.com/ meyerlit.

27

Sounds

Bettmann/CORBIS.

In a poem the words should be as
pleasing to the ear as the meaning is
to the mind.
— MARIANNE MOORE

LISTENING TO POETRY

Poems yearn to be read aloud. Much of their energy, charm, and beauty
come to life only when they are heard. Poets choose and arrange words for
their sounds as well as for their meanings. Most poetry is best read with
your lips, teeth, and tongue because they serve to articulate the effects that sound may have in a poem. When   Web Explore
a voice is breathed into a good poem, there is pleasure   the poetic elements
in the reading, the saying, and the hearing.   in this chapter at
                                                           bedfordstmartins.com/
  The earliest poetry — before writing and painting —   meyerlit.
was chanted or sung. The rhythmic quality of such oral performances
served two purposes: it helped the chanting bard remember the lines and it
entertained audiences with patterned sounds of language, which were
sometimes accompanied by musical instruments. Poetry has always been
closely related to music. Indeed, as the word suggests, lyric poetry evolved

from songs. "Western Wind" (p. 760), an anonymous Middle English lyric, survived as song long before it was written down. Had Robert Frost lived in a nonliterate society, he probably would have sung some version—a very different version to be sure—of "Acquainted with the Night" (p. 889) instead of writing it down. Even though Frost creates a speaking rather than a singing voice, the speaker's anxious tone is distinctly heard in any careful reading of the poem.

Like lyrics, early narrative poems were originally part of an anonymous oral folk tradition. A *ballad* such as "Bonny Barbara Allan" (p. 1315) told a story that was sung from one generation to the next until it was finally transcribed. Since the eighteenth century, this narrative form has sometimes been imitated by poets who write *literary ballads.* John Keats's "La Belle Dame sans Merci" (p. 1335) is, for example, a more complex and sophisticated nineteenth-century reflection of the original ballad traditions that developed in the fifteenth century and earlier. In considering poetry as sound, we should not forget that poetry traces its beginnings to song.

These next lines exemplify poetry's continuing relation to song. What poetic elements can you find in this ballad, which was adapted by Paul Simon and Art Garfunkel and became a popular antiwar song in the 1960s?

ANONYMOUS

Scarborough Fair   *date unknown*

Where are you going? To Scarborough Fair?
Parsley, sage, rosemary, and thyme,
Remember me to a bonny lass there,
For once she was a true lover of mine.

Tell her to make me a cambric shirt,   5
Parsley, sage, rosemary, and thyme,
Without any needle or thread work'd in it,
And she shall be a true lover of mine.

Tell her to wash it in yonder well,
Parsley, sage, rosemary, and thyme,   10
Where water ne'er sprung nor a drop of rain fell,
And she shall be a true lover of mine.

Tell her to plough me an acre of land,
Parsley, sage, rosemary, and thyme,
Between the sea and the salt sea strand,   15
And she shall be a true lover of mine.

Tell her to plough it with one ram's horn,
Parsley, sage, rosemary, and thyme,
And sow it all over with one peppercorn,
And she shall be a true lover of mine.   20

Tell her to reap it with a sickle of leather,
Parsley, sage, rosemary, and thyme,
And tie it all up with a tom tit's feather,
And she shall be a true lover of mine.

Tell her to gather it all in a sack,   25
Parsley, sage, rosemary, and thyme,
And carry it home on a butterfly's back,
And then she shall be a true lover of mine.

CONSIDERATIONS FOR CRITICAL THINKING AND WRITING

1. **FIRST RESPONSE.** What do you associate with "Parsley, sage, rosemary, and thyme"? What images does this poem evoke? How so?

2. What kinds of demands does the speaker make on his former lover? What do these demands have in common?

3. What is the tone of this ballad?

4. Choose a contemporary song that you especially like and examine the lyrics. Write an essay explaining whether or not you consider the lyrics poetic.

Of course, reading "Scarborough Fair" is not the same as hearing it. Like the lyrics of a song, many poems must be heard — or at least read with listening eyes — before they can be fully understood and enjoyed. The sounds of words are a universal source of music for human beings. This has been so from ancient tribes to bards to the two-year-old child in a bakery gleefully chanting "Cuppitycake, cuppitycake!"

Listen to the sound of this poem as you read it aloud. How do the words provide, in a sense, their own musical accompaniment?

JOHN UPDIKE (1932–2009)

Player Piano   *1958*

My stick fingers click with a snicker
And, chuckling, they knuckle the keys;
Light-footed, my steel feelers flicker
And pluck from these keys melodies.

My paper can caper; abandon   5
Is broadcast by dint of my din,
And no man or band has a hand in
The tones I turn on from within.

At times I'm a jumble of rumbles,
At others I'm light like the moon,   10
But never my numb plunker fumbles,
Misstrums me, or tries a new tune.

The speaker in this poem is a piano that can play automatically by means of a mechanism that depresses keys in response to signals on a perforated roll. Notice how the speaker's voice approximates the sounds of a piano. In each stanza a predominant sound emerges from the carefully chosen words. How is the sound of each stanza tuned to its sense?

Like Updike's "Player Piano," this next poem is also primarily about sounds.

May Swenson (1919–1989)

A Nosty Fright
1984

The roldengod and the soneyhuckle,
the sack eyed blusan and the wistle theed
are all tangled with the oison pivy,
the fallen nine peedles and the wumbleteed.

A mipchunk caught in a wobceb tried   5
to hip and skide in a dandy sune
but a stobler put up a EEP KOFF sign.
Then the unfucky lellow met a phytoon

and was sept out to swea. He difted for drays
till a hassgropper flying happened to spot   10
the boolish feast all debraggled and wet,
covered with snears and tot.

Loonmight shone through the winey poods
where rushmooms grew among risted twoots.
Back blats flew betreen the twees   15
and orned howls hounded their soots.

A kumkpin stood with tooked creeth
on the sindow will of a house
where a icked wold itch lived all alone
except for her stoombrick, a mitten and a kouse.   20

"Here we part," said hassgropper.
"Pere we hart," said mipchunk, too.
They purried away on opposite haths,
both scared of some "Bat!" or "Scoo!"

October was ending on a nosty fright   25
with scroans and greeches and chanking clains,
with oblins and gelfs, coaths and urses,
skinning grulls and stoodblains.

Will it ever be morning, Nofember virst,
skue bly and the sappy hun, our friend?   30
With light breaves of wall by the fayside?
I sope ho, so that this oem can pend.

At just the right moments Swenson transposes letters to create amusing sound effects and wild wordplays. Although there is a story lurking in "A Nosty Fright," any serious attempt to interpret its meaning is confronted with "a EEP KOFF sign." Instead, we are invited to enjoy the delicious sounds the poet has cooked up.

Few poems revel in sound so completely. More typically, the sounds of a poem contribute to its meaning rather than become its meaning. Consider how sound is used in the next poem.

EMILY DICKINSON   (1830–1886)

A Bird came down the Walk—   c. 1862

A Bird came down the Walk —
He did not know I saw —
He bit an Angleworm in halves
And ate the fellow, raw,

And then he drank a Dew   5
From a convenient Grass —
And then hopped sidewise to the Wall
To let a Beetle pass —

He glanced with rapid eyes
That hurried all around —   10
They looked like frightened Beads, I thought —
He stirred his Velvet Head

Like one in danger, Cautious,
I offered him a Crumb
And he unrolled his feathers   15
And rowed him softer home —

Than Oars divide the Ocean,
Too silver for a seam —
Or Butterflies, off Banks of Noon
Leap, plashless as they swim.   20

This description of a bird offers a close look at how differently a bird moves when it hops on the ground than when it flies in the air. On the ground the bird moves quickly, awkwardly, and irregularly as it plucks up a worm, washes it down with dew, and then hops aside to avoid a passing beetle. The speaker recounts the bird's rapid, abrupt actions from a somewhat superior, amused perspective. By describing the bird in human terms (as if, for example, it chose to eat the worm "raw"), the speaker is almost condescending. But when the attempt to offer a crumb fails and the frightened bird flies off, the speaker is left looking up instead of down at the bird.

With that shift in perspective the tone shifts from amusement to awe in response to the bird's graceful flight. The jerky movements of lines 1 to 13 give way to the smooth motion of lines 15 to 20. The pace of the first three stanzas is fast and discontinuous. We tend to pause at the end of each line, and this reinforces a sense of disconnected movements. In contrast, the final six lines are to be read as a single sentence in one flowing movement, lubricated by various sounds.

Read again the description of the bird flying away. Several *o*-sounds contribute to the image of the serene, expansive, confident flight, just as the *s*-sounds serve as smooth transitions from one line to the next. Notice how these sounds are grouped in the following vertical columns:

unrolled	softer	too	his	Ocean	Banks
rowed	Oars	Noon	feathers	silver	plashless
home	Or		softer	seam	as
Ocean	off		Oars	Butterflies	swim

This blending of sounds (notice how "Leap, plashless" brings together the *p*- and *l*-sounds without a ripple) helps convey the bird's smooth grace in the air. Like a feathered oar, the bird moves seamlessly in its element.

The repetition of sounds in poetry is similar to the function of the tones and melodies that are repeated, with variations, in music. Just as the patterned sounds in music unify a work, so do the words in poems, which have been carefully chosen for the combinations of sounds they create. These sounds are produced in a number of ways.

The most direct way in which the sound of a word suggests its meaning is through **onomatopoeia,** which is the use of a word that resembles the sound it denotes: *quack, buzz, rattle, bang, squeak, bowwow, burp, choo-choo, ding-a-ling, sizzle.* The sound and sense of these words are closely related, but such words represent a very small percentage of the words available to us. Poets usually employ more subtle means for echoing meanings.

Onomatopoeia can consist of more than just single words. In its broadest meaning the term refers to lines or passages in which sounds help to convey meanings, as in these lines from Updike's "Player Piano":

> My stick fingers click with a snicker
> And, chuckling, they knuckle the keys.

The sharp, crisp sounds of these two lines approximate the sounds of a piano; the syllables seem to "click" against one another. Contrast Updike's rendition with the following lines:

> My long fingers play with abandon
> And, laughing, they cover the keys.

The original version is more interesting and alive because the sounds of the words are pleasurable and reinforce the meaning through a careful blending of consonants and vowels.

Alliteration is the repetition of the same consonant sounds at the beginnings of nearby words: "*descending dewd*rops," "*luscious lemons.*" Sometimes the term is also used to describe the consonant sounds within words: "tre*spa*sser's re*p*roach," "*wedded lady.*" Alliteration is based on sound rather than spelling. "*Keen*" and "*car*" alliterate, but "*car*" does not alliterate with "*cite.*" Rarely is heavy-handed alliteration effective. Used too self-consciously, it can be distracting instead of strengthening meaning or emphasizing a relation between words. Consider the relentless *h*'s in this line: "Horrendous horrors haunted Helen's happiness." Those *h*'s certainly suggest that Helen is being pursued, but they have a more comic than serious effect because they are overdone.

Assonance is the repetition of the same vowel sound in nearby words: "as*lee*p under a tr*ee*," "t*i*me and t*i*de," "h*au*nt" and "*aw*esome," "*ea*ch evening." Both alliteration and assonance help to establish relations among words in a line or a series of lines. Whether the effect is *euphony* (lines that are musically pleasant to the ear and smooth, like the final lines of Dickinson's "A Bird came down the Walk—") or *cacophony* (lines that are discordant and difficult to pronounce, like the claim that "never my numb plunker fumbles" in Updike's "Player Piano"), the sounds of words in poetry can be as significant as the words' denotative or connotative meanings.

A SAMPLE STUDENT RESPONSE

Lee 1

Ryan Lee

Professor McDonough

English 211

December 1, 2009

Sound in Emily Dickinson's "A Bird came down the Walk—"

In her poem "A Bird came down the Walk—" Emily Dickinson uses the sound and rhythm of each line to reflect the motion of a bird walking awkwardly—and then flying gracefully. Particularly when read aloud, the staccato phrases and stilted breaks in lines 1 through 14 create a sense of the bird's movement on land, quick and off-balanced, which helps bring the scene to life.

The first three stanzas are structured to make the bird's movement consistent. The bird hops around, eating worms while keeping guard for any threats. Vulnerable on the ground, the bird is intensely aware of danger:

> He glanced with rapid eyes
>
> That hurried all around—
>
> They looked like frightened Beads, I thought—
>
> He stirred his Velvet Head (9-12)

In addition to choosing words that portray the bird as cautious—it "glanced with rapid eyes" (9) that resemble "frightened Beads" (11)—Dickinson chooses to end each line abruptly. This abrupt halting of sound allows the reader to experience the bird's fear more immediately, and the effect is similar to the missing of a beat or a breath.

These halting lines stand in contrast to the smoothness of the last six lines, during which the bird takes flight. The sounds in these lines are pleasingly soft, and rich in the "s" sound. The bird

> unrolled his feathers
>
> And rowed him softer home—
>
>
> Than Oars
>
> divide the Ocean,
>
> Too silver for a seam— (15-18). . . .

Work Cited

Dickinson, Emily. "A Bird came down the Walk—." *The Bedford Introduction to Literature*. Ed. Michael Meyer. 9th ed. Boston: Bedford/St. Martin's, 2011. 920. Print.

This next poem provides a feast of sounds. Read the poem aloud and try to determine the effects of its sounds.

GALWAY KINNELL (B. 1927)

Blackberry Eating   1980

Photo by Charlie Nye.

I love to go out in late September
among the fat, overripe, icy, black
        blackberries
to eat blackberries for breakfast,
the stalks very prickly, a penalty
they earn for knowing the black art
of blackberry-making; and as I stand among
        them
lifting the stalks to my mouth, the ripest
        berries
fall almost unbidden to my tongue,
as words sometimes do, certain peculiar words
like *strengths* or *squinched*,   10
many-lettered, one-syllabled lumps,
which I squeeze, squinch open, and splurge well
in the silent, startled, icy, black language
of blackberry-eating in late September.

CONSIDERATIONS FOR CRITICAL THINKING AND WRITING

1. **FIRST RESPONSE.** What types of sounds does Kinnell use throughout this poem? What categories can you place them in? What is the effect of these sounds?

2. How do lines 4–6 fit into the poem? What does this prickly image add to the poem?

3. Explain what you think the poem's theme is.

4. Write an essay that considers the speaker's love of blackberry eating along with the speaker's appetite for words. How are the two blended in the poem?

RHYME

Like alliteration and assonance, **rhyme** is a way of creating sound patterns. Rhyme, broadly defined, consists of two or more words or phrases that repeat the same sounds: *happy* and *snappy*. Rhyme words often have similar spellings, but that is not a requirement of rhyme; what matters is that the words sound alike: *vain* rhymes with *reign* as well as *rain*. Moreover, words may look alike but not rhyme at all. In **eye rhyme** the spellings are similar, but the pronunciations are not, as with *bough* and *cough,* or *brow* and *blow.*

Not all poems use rhyme. Many great poems have no rhymes, and many weak verses use rhyme as a substitute for poetry. These are especially apparent in commercial messages and greeting-card lines. At its worst, rhyme is merely a distracting decoration that can lead to dullness and predictability. But used skillfully, rhyme creates lines that are memorable and musical.

Here is a poem using rhyme that you might remember the next time you are in a restaurant.

RICHARD ARMOUR (1906–1989)

Going to Extremes   1954

Shake and shake
   The catsup bottle
None'll come —
   And then a lot'll.

The experience recounted in Armour's poem is common enough, but the rhyme's humor is special. The final line clicks the poem shut — an effect that is often achieved by the use of rhyme. That click provides a sense of a satisfying and fulfilled form. Rhymes have a number of uses: They can emphasize words, direct a reader's attention to relations between words, and provide an overall structure for a poem.

Rhyme is used in the following poem to imitate the sound of cascading water.

ROBERT SOUTHEY (1774–1843)

From "The Cataract of Lodore"   1820

   "How does the water

  Come down at Lodore?"
. . . .
From its sources which well
  In the tarn on the fell;
    From its fountains   5
    In the mountains,
  Its rills and its gills;
Through moss and through brake,
    It runs and it creeps
    For awhile, till it sleeps   10
    In its own little lake.
  And thence at departing,
  Awakening and starting,
  It runs through the reeds
    And away it proceeds,   15

Through meadow and glade,
    In sun and in shade,
And through the wood-shelter,
        Among crags in its flurry,
            Helter-skelter,
            Hurry-scurry.
Here it comes sparkling,
And there it lies darkling;
Now smoking and frothing
    Its tumult and wrath in,
        Till in this rapid race
            On which it is bent,
            It reaches the place
            Of its steep descent.

        The cataract strong
        Then plunges along,
    Striking and raging
    As if a war waging
Its caverns and rocks among:
        Rising and leaping,
        Sinking and creeping,
        Swelling and sweeping,
    Showering and springing,
        Flying and flinging,
        Writhing and ringing,
Eddying and whisking,
Spouting and frisking,
Turning and twisting,
        Around and around
        With endless rebound!
    Smiting and fighting,
        A sight to delight in;
    Confounding, astounding,
Dizzying and deafening the ear with its sound.
· ·
Dividing and gliding and sliding,
And falling and brawling and spawling,
And driving and riving and striving,
And sprinkling and twinkling and wrinkling,
And sounding and bounding and rounding,
And bubbling and troubling and doubling,
And grumbling and rumbling and tumbling,
And clattering and battering and shattering;
Retreating and beating and meeting and sheeting,
Delaying and straying and playing and spraying,
Advancing and prancing and glancing and dancing,
Recoiling, turmoiling and toiling and boiling,
And gleaming and streaming and steaming and beaming,
And rushing and flushing and brushing and gushing,
And flapping and rapping and clapping and slapping,

20

25

30

35

40

45

50

55

60

And curling and whirling and purling and twirling,   65
And thumping and plumping and bumping and jumping,
And dashing and flashing and splashing and clashing;
And so never ending, but always descending,
Sounds and motions forever and ever are blending,
All at once and all o'er, with a mighty uproar;   70
And this way the water comes down at Lodore.

    This deluge of rhymes consists of "Sounds and motions forever and ever . . . blending" (line 69). The pace quickens as the water creeps from its mountain source and then descends in rushing cataracts. As the speed of the water increases, so do the number of rhymes, until they run in fours: "dashing and flashing and splashing and clashing" (line 67). Most rhymes meander through poems instead of flooding them; nevertheless, Southey's use of rhyme suggests how sounds can flow with meanings. "The Cataract of Lodore" has been criticized, however, for overusing onomatopoeia. Some readers find the poem silly; others regard it as a brilliant example of sound effects. What do you think?

    A variety of types of rhyme is available to poets. The most common form, **_end rhyme,_** comes at the ends of lines (lines 14–17).

> It runs through the reeds
>   And away it proceeds,
> Through meadow and glade,
>   In sun and in shade.

Internal rhyme places at least one of the rhymed words within the line, as in "Dividing and gliding and sliding" (line 50) or, more subtly, in the fourth and final words of "In mist or cloud, on mast or shroud."

    The rhyming of single-syllable words such as *glade* and *shade* is known as **_masculine rhyme,_** as we see in these lines from A. E. Housman:

> Loveliest of trees, the cherry now
> Is hung with bloom along the bough.

Rhymes using words of more than one syllable are also called masculine when the same sound occurs in a final stressed syllable, as in *defend, contend; betray, away.* A **_feminine rhyme_** consists of a rhymed stressed syllable followed by one or more rhymed unstressed syllables, as in *butter, clutter; gratitude, attitude; quivering, shivering.* This rhyme is evident in John Millington Synge's verse:

> Lord confound this surly sister,
> Blight her brow and blotch and blister.

    All of the examples so far have been **_exact rhymes_** because they share the same stressed vowel sounds as well as any sounds that follow the vowel. In **_near rhyme_** (also called **_off rhyme, slant rhyme,_** and **_approximate rhyme_**), the sounds are almost but not exactly alike. There are several kinds of near rhyme. One of the most common is ***consonance,*** an identical consonant sound preceded by a different vowel sound: *home, same; worth, breath; trophy, daffy*. Near rhyme can also be achieved by using different vowel sounds with identical consonant sounds: *sound, sand; kind, conned; fellow, fallow*. The dissonance of *blade* and *blood* in the following lines from Wilfred Owen helps to reinforce their grim tone:

> Let the boy try along this bayonet-blade
> How cold steel is, and keen with hunger of blood.

Near rhymes greatly broaden the possibility for musical effects in English, a language that, compared with Spanish or Italian, contains few exact rhymes. Do not assume, however, that a near rhyme represents a failed attempt at exact rhyme. Near rhymes allow a musical subtlety and variety and can avoid the sometimes overpowering jingling effects that exact rhymes may create.

These basic terms hardly exhaust the ways in which the sounds in poems can be labeled and discussed, but the terms can help you to describe how poets manipulate sounds for effect. Read "God's Grandeur" (p. 929) aloud and try to determine how the sounds of the lines contribute to their sense.

Perspective

DAVID LENSON (B. 1945)

On the Contemporary Use of Rhyme 1988

One impediment to a respectable return to rhyme is the popular survival of "functional" verse: greeting cards, pedagogical and mnemonic devices ("Thirty days hath September"), nursery rhymes, advertising jingles, and of course song lyrics. Pentameters, irregular rhymes, and free verse aren't much use in songwriting, where the meter has to be governed by the time signature of the music.

Far from universities, there has been a revival of rhymed couplets in rap music, in which, to the accompaniment of synthesizers, vocalists deliver lengthy first-person narratives in tetrameter. While most writing teachers would dismiss such lyrics as doggerel, the aim of the songs is really not so far from that of Alexander Pope: to use rhyme to sharpen social insight, in the hope that the world may be reordered.

From *The Chronicle of Higher Education*, February 24, 1988

CONSIDERATIONS FOR CRITICAL THINKING AND WRITING

1. Read some contemporary song lyrics from a wide range of groups or vocalists. Is Lenson correct in his assessment that irregular rhyme is not much use in songwriting?

2. Examine the rhymed couplets of some rap music. Discuss whether they are used "to sharpen social insight." What is the effect of using rhymes in rap music?

3. What is your own response to rhymed poetry? Do you like yours with or without? What do you think informs your preference?

SOUND AND MEANING

GERARD MANLEY HOPKINS (1844–1889)

God's Grandeur   *1877*

The world is charged with the grandeur of God.
  It will flame out, like shining from shook foil;°   *shaken gold foil*
  It gathers to a greatness, like the ooze of oil
Crushed.° Why do men then now not reck his rod?°
Generations have trod, have trod, have trod;   5
  And all is seared with trade; bleared, smeared with toil;
  And wears man's smudge and shares man's smell: the soil
Is bare now, nor can foot feel, being shod.

And for all this, nature is never spent;
  There lives the dearest freshness deep down things;
And though the last lights off the black West went   10
  Oh, morning, at the brown brink eastward, springs —
Because the Holy Ghost over the bent
  World broods with warm breast and with ah! bright wings.

4 *Crushed:* Olives crushed in their oil; *reck his rod:* Obey God.

    The subject of this poem is announced in the title and the first line: "The world is charged with the grandeur of God." The poem is a celebration of the power and greatness of God's presence in the world, but the speaker is also perplexed and dismayed by people who refuse to recognize God's authority and grandeur as they are manifested in the creation. Instead of glorifying God, "men" have degraded the earth through meaningless toil and cut themselves off from the spiritual renewal inherent in the beauty of nature. The relentless demands of commerce and industry have blinded people to the earth's natural and spiritual resources. Despite this abuse and insensitivity to God's grandeur, however, "nature is never spent"; the morning light that "springs" in the east redeems the "black West" of the night and is a sign that the spirit of the Holy Ghost is ever present in the world. This summary of the poem sketches some of the thematic significance of the lines, but it does not do justice to how they are organized around the use of sound. Hopkins's poem, unlike Southey's "The Cataract of Lodore," uses sounds in a subtle and complex way.

    In the opening line Hopkins uses alliteration — a device apparent in almost every line of the poem — to connect "Go*d*" to the "wor*ld*," which is "charged" with his "grandeur." These consonants unify the line as well. The alliteration in lines 2 and 3 suggests a harmony in the creation: the *f*'s in "*f*lame" and "*f*oil," the *sh*'s in "*sh*ining" and "*sh*ook," the *g*'s in "*g*athers" and "*g*reatness," and the visual (not alliterative) similarities of "*ooze* of *oil*" emphasize a world that is held together by God's will.

That harmony is abruptly interrupted by the speaker's angry question in line 4: "Why do men then now not reck his rod?" The question is as painful to the speaker as it is difficult to pronounce. The arrangement of the alliteration ("*now*," "*not*"; "*reck*," "*rod*"), the assonance ("*not*," "*rod*"; "*men*," "*then*," "*reck*"), and the internal rhyme ("*men*," "*then*") contribute to the difficulty in saying the line—a difficulty associated with human behavior. That behavior is introduced in line 5 by the repetition of "have trod" to emphasize the repeated mistakes—sins—committed by human beings. The tone is dirgelike because humanity persists in its mistaken path rather than progressing. The speaker's horror at humanity is evident in the cacophonous sounds of lines 6 to 8. Here the alliteration of "*sm*eared," "*sm*udge," and "*sm*ell" along with the internal rhymes of "*seared*," "*bleared*," and "*smeared*" echo the disgust with which the speaker views humanity's "toil" with the "soil," an end rhyme that calls attention to our mistaken equation of nature with production rather than with spirituality.

In contrast to this cacophony, the final six lines build toward the joyful recognition of the new possibilities that accompany the rising sun. This recognition leads to the euphonic description of the "Holy Gh*o*st *o*ver" (notice the reassuring consistency of the assonance) the world. Traditionally represented as a dove, the Holy Ghost brings love and peace to the "*w*orld," and "*b*roods *w*ith *w*arm *b*reast and *w*ith ah! *b*right *w*ings." The effect of this alliteration is mellifluous: the sound bespeaks the harmony that prevails at the end of the poem resulting from the speaker's recognition that "nature is never spent" because God loves and protects the world.

The sounds of "God's Grandeur" enhance the poem's theme; more can be said about its sounds, but it is enough to point out here that for this poem the sound strongly echoes the theme in nearly every line. Here are some more poems in which sound plays a significant role.

POEMS FOR FURTHER STUDY

THOMAS LUX (B. 1946)

Onomatopoeia

1994

The word sounds like the thing.
The sound of the word next to
the sound of another word
sounds like the thing feels
or you desire it to feel. You want   5

this alive
from its insides
and the mind, the denotative, the dictionary
means naught: what you want
to be known must be known   10
cellularly, belly-wise,
or on the tongue: *cerulean blue,*
for example, or *punch drunk.*
Those who live elsewhere
than their bodies don't buy it, don't like it,   15
this in-the-body; the science
and the math tests on it
are yet inconclusive.
There's always this little humming
beneath the surface   20
of the painting, the dance, the play
(the good ones) that tells your heart
that it — the painting, the dance, the play — tells
a truth: *dewlap, dewlap,*
it's dawn's time, it says — the sound   25
provides the thing its lungs, mouth,
and blood-beat. The sound, the noise of the sound, is
the thing — the deaf can hear it,
the blind see it, this tuning fork
beneath the breastbone, sweetly   30
accompanying its song.

CONSIDERATIONS FOR CRITICAL THINKING AND WRITING

1. **FIRST RESPONSE.** Compare Lux's poetic definition of *onomatopoeia* with the textbook definition on page 921. What does Lux's treatment of *onomatopoeia* add to the standard definition?

2. Which lines contain images that particularly emphasize the physical sensation that sounds evoke for those who live "in-the-body" (line 16)?

3. **CREATIVE RESPONSE.** Write a sentence — or a short poem — that consists almost exclusively of onomatopoetic words.

CONNECTION TO ANOTHER SELECTION

1. Choose a poem from this chapter and write an essay that explains how its "sound, the noise of the sound, is / the thing" (lines 27–28).

MOLLY PEACOCK (B. 1947)

Of Night   2008

A city mouse darts from the paws of night.
A body drops from the jaws of night.
A woman denies the laws of night,
awake and trapped in the *was* of night.

A young man turns in the gauze of night,   5
unraveling the cause of night:
that days extend their claws at night
to reenact old wars at night,
though dreams can heal old sores at night
and spring begins its thaw at night,   10
while worry bones are gnawed at night.
He sips her through a straw at night.
Verbs whisper in the clause of night.
A finger to her lips
                   the pause of night.

CONSIDERATIONS FOR CRITICAL THINKING AND WRITING

1. **FIRST RESPONSE.** Describe the overall tone created by the images through line 8. Discuss the relationship between those images and the ones in the final six lines in terms of what you think the poem's theme might be.

2. What is the effect of the line-end repetitions? Comment also on Peacock's use of internal near rhymes.

3. Why do you think Peacock chose to space line 14 the way she did?

LEWIS CARROLL (CHARLES LUTWIDGE DODGSON/1832–1898)

Jabberwocky   *1871*

'Twas brillig, and the slithy toves
     Did gyre and gimble in the wabe:
All mimsy were the borogoves,
     And the mome raths outgrabe.

"Beware the Jabberwock, my son!   5
     The jaws that bite, the claws that catch!
Beware the Jubjub bird, and shun
     The frumious Bandersnatch!"

He took his vorpal sword in hand;
     Long time the manxome foe he sought —   10
So rested he by the Tumtum tree,
     And stood awhile in thought.

And, as in uffish thought he stood,
     The Jabberwock, with eyes of flame,
Came whiffling through the tulgey wood,   15
     And burbled as it came!

One, two! One, two! And through and through
     The vorpal blade went snicker-snack!
He left it dead, and with its head
     He went galumphing back.   20

"And hast thou slain the Jabberwock?
     Come to my arms, my beamish boy!

O frabjous day! Callooh, Callay!"
   He chortled in his joy.

'Twas brillig, and the slithy toves   25
   Did gyre and gimble in the wabe:
All mimsy were the borogoves,
   And the mome raths outgrabe.

CONSIDERATIONS FOR CRITICAL THINKING AND WRITING

1. **FIRST RESPONSE.** What happens in this poem? Does it have any meaning?

2. Not all of the words used in this poem appear in dictionaries. In *Through the Looking Glass,* Humpty Dumpty explains to Alice that "'slithy' means 'lithe and slimy.' 'Lithe' is the same as 'active.' You see it's like a portmanteau — there are two meanings packed up into one word." Are there any other portmanteau words in the poem?

3. Which words in the poem sound especially meaningful, even if they are devoid of any denotative meanings?

CONNECTION TO ANOTHER SELECTION

1. Compare Carroll's strategies for creating sound and meaning with those used by Swenson in "A Nosty Fright" (p. 919).

HARRYETTE MULLEN (B. 1953)

Blah-Blah   *2002*

Ack-ack, aye-aye.
Baa baa, Baba, Bambam, Bebe, Berber, Bibi, blah-blah, Bobo,
    bonbon,
booboo, Bora Bora, Boutros Boutros, bye-bye.
Caca, cancan, Cece, cha-cha, chichi, choo-choo, chop chop,
    chow chow, Coco, cocoa,
come come, cuckoo.   5
Dada, Dee Dee, Didi, dindin, dodo, doodoo, dumdum,
    Duran Duran.
Fifi, fifty-fifty, foofoo, froufrou.
Gaga, Gigi, glug-glug, go-go, goody-goody, googoo, grisgris.
Haha, harhar, hear hear, heehee, hey hey, hip-hip, hoho,
    Hsing-Hsing, hubba-hubba, humhum.
is is, It'sIts.   10
JarJar, Jo Jo, juju.
Kiki, knock knock, Koko, Kumkum.
Lala, Lili, Ling-Ling looky-looky, Lulu.
Mahi mahi, mama, Mau Mau, Mei-Mei, Mimi, Momo, murmur,
    my my.
Na Na, No-no, now now.   15
Oh-oh, oink oink.

Pago Pago, Palau Palau, papa, pawpaw, peepee, Phen Fen,
    pooh-pooh, poopoo, pupu, putt-putt.
Rah-rah, ReRe.
Shih-Shih, Sing Sing, Sirhan Sirhan, Sen Sen, Sisi, so-so.
Tata, taki-taki, talky-talky, Tam Tam, Tartar, teetee, Tintin,   20
Tingi Tingi, tom-tom, toot toot, tsetse, tsk tsk, tutu,
    tumtum, tut tut.
Van Van, veve, vroom-vroom.
Wahwah, Walla Walla, weewee, win-win.
Yadda yadda Yari Yari, yaya, ylang ylang, yo-yo, yuk-yuk,
    yum-yum.
Zizi, ZsaZsa, Zouzou, Zuzu.   25

CONSIDERATIONS FOR CRITICAL THINKING AND WRITING

1. **FIRST RESPONSE.** The title probably makes sense to you, but does the rest of the poem? Why or why not?

2. Read the poem aloud, and describe the poem's sound effects.

3. **CREATIVE RESPONSE.** Write ten lines of your own alliterative string of words and read it aloud to hear what it sounds like.

CONNECTION TO ANOTHER SELECTION

1. Compare Mullen's strategies for emphasizing sound in her poem with those of May Swenson in "A Nosty Fright" (p. 919) and Lewis Carroll in "Jabberwocky" (p. 932).

WILLIAM HEYEN (B. 1940)

The Trains   1984

Signed by Franz Paul Stangl, Commandant,
there is in Berlin a document,
an order of transmittal from Treblinka:

248 freight cars of clothing,
400,000 gold watches,
25 freight cars of women's hair.   5

Some clothing was kept, some pulped for paper.
The finest watches were never melted down.
All the women's hair was used for mattresses, or dolls.

Would these words like to use some of that same paper?   10
One of those watches may pulse in your own wrist.
Does someone you know collect dolls, or sleep on human hair?

He is dead at last, Commandant Stangl of Treblinka,
but the camp's three syllables still sound like freight cars
straining around a curve, Treblinka,   15

Treblinka. Clothing, time in gold watches,
women's hair for mattresses and dolls' heads.
Treblinka. The trains from Treblinka.

CONSIDERATIONS FOR CRITICAL THINKING AND WRITING

1. **FIRST RESPONSE.** How does the sound of the word *Treblinka* inform your understanding of the poem?

2. Why does the place name of Treblinka continue to resonate over time? To learn more about Treblinka, search the Web, perhaps starting at ushm.org, the site of the United States Holocaust Memorial Museum.

3. Why do you suppose Heyen uses the word *in* instead of *on* in line 11?

4. Why is sound so important for establishing the tone of this poem? In what sense do "the camp's three syllables still sound like freight cars" (line 14)?

5. **CRITICAL STRATEGIES.** Read the section on reader-response strategies (pp. 2060–62) in Chapter 53, "Critical Strategies for Reading." How does this poem make you feel? Why?

JOHN DONNE (1572–1631)

Song   *1633*

Go and catch a falling star,
   Get with child a mandrake root,°
Tell me where all past years are,
   Or who cleft the Devil's foot,
Teach me to hear mermaids singing,   5
   Or to keep off envy's stinging,
        And find
        What wind
Serves to advance an honest mind.

If thou be'st borne to strange sights,   10
   Things invisible to see,
Ride ten thousand days and nights,
   Till age snow white hairs on thee,
Thou, when thou return'st, wilt tell me
   All strange wonders that befell thee,   15
        And swear
        Nowhere
Lives a woman true, and fair.

If thou findst one, let me know,
   Such a pilgrimage were sweet —   20
Yet do not, I would not go,
   Though at next door we might meet;

---

2 *mandrake root:* This V-shaped root resembles the lower half of the human body.

Though she were true, when you met her,
  And last, till you write your letter,
       Yet she 25
       Will be
False, ere I come, to two or three.

CONSIDERATIONS FOR CRITICAL THINKING AND WRITING

1. **FIRST RESPONSE.** What is the speaker's tone in this poem? What is his view of a woman's love? What does the speaker's use of hyperbole reveal about his emotional state?

2. Do you think Donne wants the speaker's argument to be taken seriously? Is there any humor in the poem?

3. Most of these lines end with masculine rhymes. What other kinds of rhymes are used for end rhymes?

ALEXANDER POPE (1688–1774)

From An Essay on Criticism 1711

But most by numbers° judge a poet's song;   *versification*
And smooth or rough, with them, is right or wrong;
In the bright muse though thousand charms conspire,
Her voice is all these tuneful fools admire;
Who haunt Parnassus° but to please their ear, 5
Not mend their minds; as some to church repair,
Not for the doctrine, but the music there.
These equal syllables alone require,
Though oft the ear the open vowels tire;
While expletives° their feeble aid do join; 10
And ten low words oft creep in one dull line;
While they ring round the same unvaried chimes,
With sure returns of still expected rhymes;
Where'er you find "the cooling western breeze,"
In the next line, it "whispers through the trees": 15
If crystal streams "with pleasing murmurs creep,"
The reader's threatened (not in vain) with "sleep":
Then, at the last and only couplet fraught
With some unmeaning thing they call a thought,
A needless Alexandrine° ends the song, 20
That, like a wounded snake, drags its slow length along.
Leave such to tune their own dull rhymes, and know
What's roundly smooth, or languishingly slow;
And praise the easy vigor of a line,

5 *Parnassus:* A Greek mountain sacred to the Muses.   10 *expletives:* Unnecessary words used to fill a line, as the *do* in this line.   20 *Alexandrine:* A twelve-syllable line, as line 21.

Where Denham's strength, and Waller's° sweetness join.   25
True ease in writing comes from art, not chance,
As those move easiest who have learned to dance.
'Tis not enough no harshness gives offense,
The sound must seem an echo to the sense:
Soft is the strain when Zephyr° gently blows,   *the west wind*   30
And the smooth stream in smoother numbers flows;
But when loud surges lash the sounding shore,
The hoarse, rough verse should like the torrent roar:
When Ajax° strives some rock's vast weight to throw,
The line too labors, and the words move slow;   35
Not so, when swift Camilla° scours the plain,
Flies o'er th' unbending corn, and skims along the main.

25 *Denham's . . . Waller's:* Sir John Denham (1615–1669) and Edmund Waller (1606–1687) were
poets who used heroic couplets.   34 *Ajax:* A Greek warrior famous for his strength in the
Trojan War.   36 *Camilla:* A goddess famous for her delicate speed.

CONSIDERATIONS FOR CRITICAL THINKING AND WRITING

1. **FIRST RESPONSE.** In these lines Pope describes some faults he finds in
   poems and illustrates those faults within the lines that describe them. How
   do the sounds in lines 4, 9, 10, 11, and 21 illustrate what they describe?

2. What is the objection to the "expected rhymes" in lines 12–17? How do they
   differ from Pope's end rhymes?

3. Some lines discuss how to write successful poetry. How do lines 23, 24,
   32–33, 35, 36, and 37 illustrate what they describe?

4. Do you agree that in a good poem "The sound must seem an echo to
   the sense" (line 29)?

HAKI R. MADHUBUTI (B. 1942)

The B Network   *1998*

brothers bop & pop and be-bop in cities locked up
and chained insane by crack and other acts
of desperation computerized in pentagon cellars producing
boppin brothers boastin of being better, best & beautiful.

if the boppin brothers are beautiful where are the sisters   5
who seek brotherman with a drugless head unbossed or beaten
by the bodacious West?

in a time of big wind being blown by boastful brothers,
will other brothers beat back backwardness to better & best
without braggart bosses beatin butts,   10
takin names and diggin graves?

beatin badness into bad may be urban but is it beautiful & serious?
or is it betrayal in an era of prepared easy death hangin on
corners trappin young brothers before they know the
difference between big death and big life?   15

brothers bop & pop and be-bop in cities locked up
and chained insane by crack and other acts
of desperation computerized in pentagon cellars producing
boppin brothers boastin of being better, best, beautiful
and definitely not *Black*.   20

the critical best is that
brothers better be the best if they are to avoid backwardness
brothers better be the best if they are to conquer beautiful bigness
Comprehend that bad is only *bad* if it's big, Black and better
than boastful braggarts belittling our best and brightest   25
with bosses seeking inches when miles are better.

brothers need to bop to being Black & bright & above board
the black train of beautiful wisdom that is bending this bind
toward a new & knowledgeable beginning that is
bountiful & bountiful & beautiful   30
While be-boppin to be
better than the test,
brotherman.

better yet write the exam.

CONSIDERATIONS FOR CRITICAL THINKING AND WRITING

1. **FIRST RESPONSE.** Read this poem aloud. How is that a different experience from reading it silently?

2. Why has the poet included all those words beginning with *b*? How do you explain the title?

3. What is the speaker's assessment of the status of African Americans in the United States? What sort of advice, if any, is offered to them?

4. Comment on the possible interpretations of the final line.

CONNECTION TO ANOTHER SELECTION

1. Compare the style and themes of "The B Network" with those of Langston Hughes's "Dream Boogie" (p. 1147).

ANDREW HUDGINS (B. 1951)

The Cow   2006

I love the red cow
with all of my heart.
She's gentle when pulling
my cherry-red cart.

We take her rich milk   5
and swallow it down.

With nothing, it's white,
with chocolate brown.

When she grows too feeble
to give us fresh cream,   10
we'll slit her red throat,
hang her from a beam,

and pull out her insides
to throw to the dogs,
just as we do   15
when we slaughter the hogs.

We've now owned six cows
that I can remember.
We drain them and gut them,
skin and dismember,   20

package and label them,
and stock up the freezer.
We all love beefsteak—
from baby to geezer!

Tossed on the grill,   25
the bloody steaks sputter.
As a last, grateful tribute,
so humble we stutter,

we offer up thanks
with a reverent mutter—   30
then slather her chops
with her own creamy butter.

CONSIDERATIONS FOR CRITICAL THINKING AND WRITING

1. **FIRST RESPONSE.** Describe the tone of each stanza. How do the rhymes serve
   to establish the tone?
2. Characterize the speaker. How do you reconcile what is said in the first
   stanza with the description in the final stanza?
3. This poem appeared in the July/August 2006 humor issue of *Poetry*. How
   does that context affect your reading of it?
4. **CREATIVE RESPONSE.** Bring something to the table yourself: add a four-line
   stanza in Hudgins's style that rhymes and concludes the meal.

PAUL HUMPHREY (B. 1915)

Blow   *1983*

Her skirt was lofted by the gale;
When I, with gesture deft,
Essayed to stay her frisky sail
She luffed, and laughed, and left.

CONSIDERATIONS FOR CRITICAL THINKING AND WRITING

1. **FIRST RESPONSE.** How do alliteration and assonance contribute to the euphonic effects in this poem?

2. What is the poem's controlling metaphor? Why is it especially appropriate?

3. Explain the ambiguity of the title.

ROBERT FRANCIS (1901–1987)

The Pitcher   1953

His art is eccentricity, his aim
How not to hit the mark he seems to aim at,

His passion how to avoid the obvious,
His technique how to vary the avoidance.

The others throw to be comprehended. He   5
Throws to be a moment misunderstood.

Yet not too much. Not errant, arrant, wild,
But every seeming aberration willed.

Not to, yet still, still to communicate
Making the batter understand too late.   10

CONSIDERATIONS FOR CRITICAL THINKING AND WRITING

1. **FIRST RESPONSE.** Explain how each pair of lines in this poem works together to describe the pitcher's art.

2. Consider how the poem itself works the way a good pitcher does. Which lines illustrate what they describe?

3. Comment on the effects of the poem's rhymes. How are the final two lines different in their rhyme from the previous lines? How does sound echo sense in lines 9–10?

4. Write an essay that examines "The Pitcher" as an extended metaphor for talking about poetry. How well does the poem characterize strategies for writing poetry as well as pitching?

5. Write an essay that develops an extended comparison between writing or reading poetry and playing or watching another sport.

CONNECTION TO ANOTHER SELECTION

1. Write an essay comparing "The Pitcher" with another work by Francis, "Catch" (p. 750). One poem defines poetry implicitly, the other defines it explicitly. Which poem do you prefer? Why?

HELEN CHASIN (B. 1938)

The Word Plum   *1968*

The word *plum* is delicious

pout and push, luxury of
self-love, and savoring murmur
full in the mouth and falling
like fruit   5

taut skin
pierced, bitten, provoked into
juice, and tart flesh

question
and reply, lip and tongue   10
of pleasure.

CONSIDERATIONS FOR CRITICAL THINKING AND WRITING

1. **FIRST RESPONSE.** What is the effect of the repetitions of the alliteration and assonance throughout the poem? How does it contribute to the poem's meaning?

2. Which sounds in the poem are like the sounds one makes while eating a
   plum?

3. Discuss the title. Explain whether you think this poem is more about the
   word *plum* or about the plum itself. Can the two be separated in the poem?

CONNECTION TO ANOTHER SELECTION

1. How is Galway Kinnell's "Blackberry Eating" (p. 924) similar in technique
   to Chasin's poem? Try writing such a poem yourself: choose a food to
   describe that allows you to evoke its sensuousness in sounds.

RICHARD WAKEFIELD (B. 1952)

The Bell Rope   *2005*

In Sunday school the boy who learned a psalm
by heart would get to sound the steeple bell
and send its tolling through the sabbath calm
to call the saved and not-so-saved as well.
For lack of practice all the lines are lost—   5
something about how angels' hands would bear
me up to God—but on one Pentecost
they won me passage up the steeple stair.
I leapt and grabbed the rope up high to ride
it down, I touched the floor, the rope went slack,   10
the bell was silent. Then, beatified,

I rose, uplifted as the rope pulled back.
I leapt and fell again; again it took
me up, but still the bell withheld its word —
until at last the church foundation shook   15
in bass approval, felt as much as heard,
and after I let go the bell tolled long
and loud as if repaying me for each
unanswered pull with heaven-rending song
a year of Sunday school could never teach   20
and that these forty years can not obscure.
Some nights when sleep won't come I think of how
just once there came an answer, clear and sure.
If I could find that rope I'd grasp it now.

CONSIDERATIONS FOR CRITICAL THINKING AND WRITING

1. **FIRST RESPONSE.** Describe the rhyme scheme and then read the poem aloud. How does Wakefield manage to avoid making this heavily rhymed poem sound clichéd or sing-songy?

2. Comment on the appropriateness of Wakefield's choice of diction and how it relates to the poem's images.

3. Explain how sound becomes, in a sense, the theme of the poem.

CONNECTION TO ANOTHER SELECTION

1. Compare the images and themes of "The Bell Rope" with those in Robert Frost's "Birches" (p. 1107).

JOHN KEATS (1795–1821)

Ode to a Nightingale   *1819*

I

My heart aches, and a drowsy numbness pains
    My sense, as though of hemlock° I had drunk,   *a poison*
Or emptied some dull opiate to the drains
    One minute past, and Lethe-wards° had sunk:
'Tis not through envy of thy happy lot,   5
    But being too happy in thine happiness —
        That thou, light-wingèd Dryad° of the trees,   *wood nymph*
            In some melodious plot
Of beechen green, and shadows numberless,
    Singest of summer in full-throated ease.   10

---

4 *Lethe-wards:* Toward Lethe, the river of forgetfulness in the Hades of Greek mythology.

II

O, for a draught of vintage! that hath been
  Cooled a long age in the deep-delved earth,
Tasting of Flora° and the country green,   *goddess of flowers*
  Dance, and Provençal song,° and sunburnt mirth!
O for a beaker full of the warm South,   15
  Full of the true, the blushful Hippocrene,°
    With beaded bubbles winking at the brim,
      And purple-stainèd mouth;
That I might drink, and leave the world unseen,
    And with thee fade away into the forest dim.   20

III

Fade far away, dissolve, and quite forget
  What thou among the leaves hast never known,
The weariness, the fever, and the fret
  Here, where men sit and hear each other groan;
Where palsy shakes a few, sad, last gray hairs,   25
  Where youth grows pale, and specter-thin, and dies,
    Where but to think is to be full of sorrow
      And leaden-eyed despairs,
  Where Beauty cannot keep her lustrous eyes;
    Or new Love pine at them beyond tomorrow.   30

IV

Away! away! for I will fly to thee,
  Not charioted by Bacchus and his pards,°
But on the viewless wings of Poesy,
  Though the dull brain perplexes and retards:
Already with thee! tender is the night,   35
  And haply the Queen-Moon is on her throne,
    Clustered around by all her starry Fays;
      But here there is no light,
Save what from heaven is with the breezes blown
    Through verdurous glooms and winding mossy ways.   40

V

I cannot see what flowers are at my feet,
  Nor what soft incense hangs upon the boughs,
But, in embalmèd° darkness, guess each sweet   *perfumed*
  Wherewith the seasonable month endows

---

14 *Provençal song:* The medieval troubadours of Provence, France, were known for their singing.   16 *Hippocrene:* The fountain of the Muses in Greek mythology.   32 *Bacchus and his pards:* The Greek god of wine traveled in a chariot drawn by leopards.

The grass, the thicket, and the fruit-tree wild; 45
   What hawthorn, and the pastoral eglantine;
     Fast fading violets covered up in leaves;
      And mid-May's eldest child,
  The coming musk-rose, full of dewy wine,
     The murmurous haunt of flies on summer eves. 50

VI

Darkling° I listen; and for many a time   *in the dark*
   I have been half in love with easeful Death,
Called him soft names in many a musèd rhyme,
   To take into the air my quiet breath;
Now more than ever seems it rich to die, 55
   To cease upon the midnight with no pain,
     While thou art pouring forth thy soul abroad
      In such an ecstasy!
  Still wouldst thou sing, and I have ears in vain —
     To thy high requiem become a sod. 60

VII

Thou wast not born for death, immortal Bird!
   No hungry generations tread thee down;
The voice I hear this passing night was heard
   In ancient days by emperor and clown:
Perhaps the selfsame song that found a path 65
  Through the sad heart of Ruth,° when, sick for home,
     She stood in tears amid the alien corn:
      The same that oft-times hath
  Charmed magic casements, opening on the foam
     Of perilous seas, in faery lands forlorn. 70

VIII

Forlorn! the very word is like a bell
   To toll me back from thee to my sole self!
Adieu! the fancy cannot cheat so well
   As she is famed to do, deceiving elf.
Adieu! adieu! thy plaintive anthem fades 75
  Past the near meadows, over the still stream,
     Up the hill side; and now 'tis buried deep
      In the next valley-glades:
  Was it a vision, or a waking dream?
     Fled is that music: — Do I wake or sleep? 80

66 *Ruth:* A young widow in the Bible (see the book of Ruth).

CONSIDERATIONS FOR CRITICAL THINKING AND WRITING

1. **FIRST RESPONSE.** Why does the speaker in this ode want to leave his world for the nightingale's? What might the nightingale symbolize?

2. How does the speaker attempt to escape his world? Is he successful?

3. What changes the speaker's view of death at the end of stanza VI?

4. What does the allusion to Ruth (line 66) contribute to the ode's meaning?

5. In which lines is the imagery especially sensuous? How does this effect add to the conflict presented?

6. What calls the speaker back to himself at the end of stanza VII and the beginning of stanza VIII?

7. Choose a stanza and explain how sound is related to its meaning.

8. How regular is the stanza form of this ode?

HOWARD NEMEROV (B. 1920)

Because You Asked about the Line between Prose and Poetry   1980

Sparrows were feeding in a freezing drizzle
That while you watched turned into pieces of snow
Riding a gradient invisible
From silver aslant to random, white, and slow.

There came a moment that you couldn't tell.
And then they clearly flew instead of fell.

CONSIDERATIONS FOR CRITICAL THINKING AND WRITING

1. **FIRST RESPONSE.** Describe the distinction that this poem makes between prose and poetry. How does the poem itself become an example of that distinction?

2. Identify the kinds of rhymes Nemerov employs. How do the rhymes in the first and second stanzas differ from each other?

3. Comment on the poem's punctuation. How is it related to theme?

28

Patterns of Rhythm

I would define, in brief, the Poetry of
words as the Rhythmical Creation of
Beauty. Its sole arbiter is Taste.
— EDGAR ALLAN POE[1]

The rhythms of everyday life surround us in regularly recurring movements and sounds. As you read these words, your heart pulsates while
somewhere else a clock ticks, a cradle rocks, a drum beats, a dancer sways, a
foghorn blasts, a wave recedes, or a child skips. We may tend to overlook
rhythm because it is so tightly woven into the fabric of
our experience, but it is there nonetheless, one of the
conditions of life. Rhythm is also one of the conditions
of speech because the voice alternately rises and falls as
words are stressed or unstressed and as the pace quick-
ens or slackens. In poetry *rhythm* refers to the recurrence of stressed and
unstressed sounds. Depending on how the sounds are arranged, this can
result in a pace that is fast or slow, choppy or smooth.

Web Explore
the poetic element
in this chapter at
bedfordstmartins.com/
meyerlit.

[1] Photograph by W. S. Hartshorn. 1848. Prints and Photographs Division, Library of Congress.

SOME PRINCIPLES OF METER

Poets use rhythm to create pleasurable sound patterns and to reinforce meanings. "Rhythm," Edith Sitwell once observed, "might be described as, to the world of sound, what light is to the world of sight. It shapes and gives new meaning." Prose can use rhythm effectively too, but prose that does so tends to be an exception. The following exceptional lines are from a speech by Winston Churchill to the House of Commons after Allied forces lost a great battle to German forces at Dunkirk during World War II:

> We shall not flag or fail. We shall go on to the end. We shall fight in France, we shall fight on the seas and oceans, we shall fight with growing confidence and growing strength in the air, we shall defend our island, whatever the cost may be, we shall fight on the beaches, we shall fight on the landing grounds, we shall fight in the fields and in the streets, we shall fight in the hills; we shall never surrender.

The stressed repetition of "we shall" bespeaks the resolute singleness of purpose that Churchill had to convey to the British people if they were to win the war. Repetition is also one of the devices used in poetry to create rhythmic effects. In the following excerpt from "Song of the Open Road," Walt Whitman urges the pleasures of limitless freedom on his reader:

> Allons!° the road is before us!   *Let's go!*
> It is safe — I have tried it — my own feet have tried it well — be not detain'd!
> Let the paper remain on the desk unwritten, and the book on the
>   shelf unopen'd!
> Let the tools remain in the workshop! Let the money remain unearn'd!
> Let the school stand! mind not the cry of the teacher!   5
> Let the preacher preach in his pulpit! Let the lawyer plead in the
>   court, and the judge expound the law.
>
> Camerado,° I give you my hand!   *friend*
> I give you my love more precious than money,
> I give you myself before preaching or law;
> Will you give me yourself? will you come travel with me?   10
> Shall we stick by each other as long as we live?

These rhythmic lines quickly move away from conventional values to the open road of shared experiences. Their recurring sounds are created not by rhyme or alliteration and assonance (see Chapter 27) but by the repetition of words and phrases.

Although the repetition of words and phrases can be an effective means of creating rhythm in poetry, the more typical method consists of patterns of accented or unaccented syllables. Words contain syllables that are either stressed or unstressed. A **stress** (or **accent**) places more emphasis on one syllable than on another. We say "*syl*lable" not "syl*la*ble," "*em*phasis" not "em*pha*sis." We routinely stress syllables when we speak: "*Is* she con*tent* with the *con*tents of the *yel*low *pack*age?" To distinguish between two people we might say "Is *she* con*tent*...?" In this way stress can be used to emphasize a particular word in a sentence. Poets often arrange words so that the desired meaning is suggested by the rhythm; hence emphasis is controlled by the poet rather than left entirely to the reader.

When a rhythmic pattern of stresses recurs in a poem, the result is **meter.** Taken together, all the metrical elements in a poem make up what is called the poem's **prosody.** *Scansion* consists of measuring the stresses in a line to determine its metrical pattern. Several methods can be used to mark lines. One widely used system uses ′ for a stressed syllable and ˘ for an unstressed syllable. In a sense, the stress mark represents the equivalent of tapping one's foot to a beat:

> Hickory, dickory, dock,
> The mouse ran up the clock.
> The clock struck one,
> And down he run,
> Hickory, dickory, dock.

In the first two lines and the final line of this familiar nursery rhyme we hear three stressed syllables. In lines 3 and 4, where the meter changes for variety, we hear just two stressed syllables. The combination of stresses provides the pleasure of the rhythm we hear.

To hear the rhythms of "Hickory, dickory, dock" does not require a formal study of meter. Nevertheless, an awareness of the basic kinds of meter that appear in English poetry can enhance your understanding of how a poem achieves its effects. Understanding the sound effects of a poem and having a vocabulary with which to discuss those effects can intensify your pleasure in poetry. Although the study of meter can be extremely technical, the terms used to describe the basic meters of English poetry are relatively easy to comprehend.

The **foot** is the metrical unit by which a line of poetry is measured. A foot usually consists of one stressed and one or two unstressed syllables. A vertical line is used to separate the feet: "The clock | struck one" consists of two feet. A foot of poetry can be arranged in a variety of patterns; here are five of the chief ones:

Foot	Pattern	Example
iamb	˘ ′	away
trochee	′ ˘	Lovely
anapest	˘ ˘ ′	understand
dactyl	′ ˘ ˘	desperate
spondee	′ ′	dead set

The most common lines in English poetry contain meters based on iambic feet. However, even lines that are predominantly iambic will often include variations to create particular effects. Other important patterns include trochaic, anapestic, and dactylic feet. The spondee is not a sustained meter but occurs for variety or emphasis.

Iambic
What kĕpt | hĭs eyĕs | frŏm gĭv | ĭng bắck | thĕ gáze
Trochaic
Hĕ wăs | loúdĕr | thăn thĕ | préachĕr
Anapestic
Ĭ ăm callĕd | tŏ thĕ frónt | ŏf thĕ roóm
Dactylic
Sĭng ĭt áll | mérrĭlў

These meters have different rhythms and can create different effects. Iambic and anapestic are known as **rising meters** because they move from unstressed to stressed sounds, while trochaic and dactylic are known as **falling meters.** Anapests and dactyls tend to move more lightly and rapidly than iambs or trochees. Although no single kind of meter can be considered always better than another for a given subject, it is possible to determine whether the meter of a specific poem is appropriate for its subject. A serious poem about a tragic death would most likely not be well served by lilting rhythms. Keep in mind, too, that though one or another of these four basic meters might constitute the predominant rhythm of a poem, variations can occur within lines to change the pace or call attention to a particular word.

A **line** is measured by the number of feet it contains. Here, for example, is an iambic line with three feet: "If shĕ | shŏuld wríte | ă nóte." These are the names for line lengths:

monometer: one foot	pentameter: five feet
dimeter: two feet	hexameter: six feet
trimeter: three feet	heptameter: seven feet
tetrameter: four feet	octameter: eight feet

By combining the name of a line length with the name of a foot, we can describe the metrical qualities of a line concisely. Consider, for example, the pattern of feet and length of this line:

I didn't want the boy to hit the dog.

The iambic rhythm of this line falls into five feet; hence it is called **iambic pentameter.** Iambic is the most common pattern in English poetry because its rhythm appears so naturally in English speech and writing. Unrhymed iambic pentameter is called **blank verse;** Shakespeare's plays are built on such lines.

Less common than the iamb, trochee, anapest, or dactyl is the **spondee,** a two-syllable foot in which both syllables are stressed (´ ´). Note the effect of the spondaic foot at the beginning of this line:

Dead sét | ăgaínst | thĕ plán | hĕ wént | ăwáy.

Spondees can slow a rhythm and provide variety and emphasis, particularly in iambic and trochaic lines. A line that ends with a stressed syllable is said to have a ***masculine ending,*** whereas a line that ends with an extra unstressed syllable is said to have a ***feminine ending.*** Consider, for example, these two lines from Timothy Steele's "Waiting for the Storm" (the entire poem appears on p. 952):

feminine: Thĕ sánd | ăt my féet | grŏw cóld | er,
masculine: Thĕ dámp | aír chíll | ănd spréad.

The effects of English meters are easily seen in the following lines by Samuel Taylor Coleridge, in which the rhythm of each line illustrates the meter described in it:

Trochee trips from long to short;
From long to long in solemn sort
Slow Spondee stalks; strong foot yet ill able
Ever to come up with Dactylic trisyllable.
Iambics march from short to long —
With a leap and a bound the swift Anapests throng.

The speed of a line is also affected by the number of pauses in it. A pause within a line is called a ***caesura*** and is indicated by a double vertical line (‖). A caesura can occur anywhere within a line and need not be indicated by punctuation:

Camerado, ‖ I give you my hand!
I give you my love ‖ more precious than money.

A slight pause occurs within each of these lines and at its end. Both kinds of pauses contribute to the lines' rhythm.

When a line has a pause at its end, it is called an ***end-stopped line.*** Such pauses reflect normal speech patterns and are often marked by punctuation. A line that ends without a pause and continues into the next line for its meaning is called a ***run-on line.*** Running over from one line to another is also called ***enjambment.*** The first and eighth lines of the following poem are run-on lines; the rest are end-stopped.

WILLIAM WORDSWORTH (1770–1850)

My Heart Leaps Up   *1807*

My heart leaps up when I behold
  A rainbow in the sky:
So was it when my life began;
So is it now I am a man;

So be it when I shall grow old,
   Or let me die!
The child is father of the Man;
And I could wish my days to be
Bound each to each by natural piety.

Run-on lines have a different rhythm from end-stopped lines. Lines 3 and 4 and lines 8 and 9 are iambic, but the effect of their two rhythms is very different when we read these lines aloud. The enjambment of lines 8 and 9 reinforces their meaning; just as the "days" are bound together, so are the lines.

The rhythm of a poem can be affected by several devices: the kind and number of stresses within lines, the length of lines, and the kinds of pauses that appear within lines or at their ends. In addition, as we saw in Chapter 27, the sound of a poem is affected by alliteration, assonance, rhyme, and consonance. These sounds help to create rhythms by controlling our pronunciations, as in the following lines by Alexander Pope (the entire poem appears on p. 936):

Soft is the strain when Zephyr gently blows,
And the smooth stream in smoother numbers flows;
But when loud surges lash the sounding shore,
The hoarse, rough verse should like the torrent roar.

These lines are effective because their rhythm and sound work with their meaning.

Suggestions for Scanning a Poem

These suggestions should help you in talking about a poem's meter.

1. After reading the poem through, read it aloud and mark the stressed syllables in each line. Then mark the unstressed syllables.

2. From your markings, identify what kind of foot is dominant (iambic, trochaic, dactylic, or anapestic) and divide the lines into feet, keeping in mind that the vertical line marking a foot may come in the middle of a word as well as at its beginning or end.

3. Determine the number of feet in each line. Remember that there may be variations; some lines may be shorter or longer than the predominant meter. What is important is the overall pattern. Do not assume that variations represent the poet's inability to fulfill the overall pattern. Notice the effects of variations and whether they emphasize words and phrases or disrupt your expectation for some other purpose.

4. Listen for pauses within lines and mark the caesuras; many times there will be no punctuation to indicate them.

5. Recognize that scansion does not always yield a definitive measurement of a line. Even experienced readers may differ over the scansion of a given line. What is important is not a precise description of the line but an awareness of how a poem's rhythms contribute to its effects.

The following poem demonstrates how you can use an understanding of meter and rhythm to gain a greater appreciation for what a poem is saying.

TIMOTHY STEELE (B. 1948)
Waiting for the Storm 1986

Breeze sent | a wrink | ling dark | ness
Across | the bay. || I knelt
Beneath | an up | turned boat,
And, mo | ment by mo | ment, felt

The sand | at my feet | grow cold | er,
The damp | air chill | and spread.
Then the | first rain | drops sound | ed
On the hull | above | my head.

The predominant meter of this poem is iambic trimeter, but there is plenty of variation as the storm rapidly approaches and finally begins to pelt the sheltered speaker. The emphatic spondee ("Breeze sent") pushes the darkness quickly across the bay while the caesura at the end of the sentence in line 2 creates a pause that sets up a feeling of suspense and expectation that is measured in the ticking rhythm of line 4, a run-on line that brings us into the chilly sand and air of the second stanza. Perhaps the most impressive sound effect used in the poem appears in the second syllable of "sounded" in line 7. That "ed" precedes the sound of the poem's final word, "head," just as if it were the first drop of rain hitting the hull above the speaker. The visual, tactile, and auditory images make "Waiting for the Storm" an intense sensory experience.

A SAMPLE STUDENT RESPONSE

Marco Pacini

Professor Fierstein

English 201

November 2, 2009

The Rhythm of Anticipation in Timothy Steele's "Waiting for the Storm"

In his poem "Waiting for the Storm," Timothy Steele uses run-on lines, or enjambment, to create a feeling of anticipation. Every line ends unfinished or is a continuation of the previous line, so we must read on to gain completion. This open-ended rhythm mirrors the waiting experienced by the speaker of the poem.

Nearly every line of the poem leaves the reader in suspense:

> I knelt
> Beneath an upturned boat,
> And moment by moment, felt
>
> The sand at my feet grow colder,
> The damp air chill and spread. (2-6)

Action is interrupted at every line break. We have to wait to find out where the speaker knelt and what was felt, since information is given in small increments. So, like the speaker, we must take in the details of the storm little by little, "moment by moment" (4). Even when the first drops of rain hit the hull, the poem ends before we can see or feel the storm's full force, and we are left waiting, in a continuous state of anticipation. . . .

Work Cited

Steele, Timothy. "Waiting for the Storm." *The Bedford Introduction to Literature*. Ed. Michael Meyer. 9th ed. Boston: Bedford/St. Martin's, 2011. 952. Print.

This next poem also reinforces meanings through its use of meter and rhythm.

WILLIAM BUTLER YEATS (1865–1939)

That the Night Come

1912

She lived | in storm | and strife,
Her soul | had such | desire
For what | proud death | may bring
That it | could not | endure
The com | mon good | of life,   5
But lived | as 'twere | a king
That packed | his mar | riage day
With ban | neret | and pen | non,
Trumpet | and ket | tledrum,
And the | outrag | eous can | non,   10
To bun | dle time | away
That the | night come.

Scansion reveals that the predominant meter here is iambic trimeter: Each line contains three stressed and unstressed syllables that form a regular, predictable rhythm through line 7. That rhythm is disrupted, however, when the speaker compares the woman's longing for what death brings to a king's eager anticipation of his wedding night. The king packs the day with noisy fanfares and celebrations to fill up time and distract himself. Unable to accept "The common good of life," the woman fills her days with "storm and strife." In a determined effort "To bundle time away," she, like the king, impatiently awaits the night.

Lines 8–10 break the regular pattern established in the first seven lines. The extra unstressed syllable in lines 8 and 10 along with the trochaic feet in lines 9 ("trumpet") and 10 ("And the") interrupt the basic iambic trimeter and parallel the woman's and the king's frenetic activity. These lines thus echo the inability of the woman and king to "endure" regular or normal time. The last line is the most irregular in the poem. The final two accented syllables sound like the deep resonant beats of a kettledrum or a cannon firing. The words "night come" dramatically remind us that what the woman anticipates is not a lover but the mysterious finality of death. The meter serves, then, in both its regularity and variations to reinforce the poem's meaning and tone.

The following poems are especially rich in their rhythms and sounds. As you read and study them, notice how patterns of rhythm and the sounds of words reinforce meanings and contribute to the poems' effects. And, perhaps most important, read the poems aloud so that you can hear them.

POEMS FOR FURTHER STUDY

ALFRED, LORD TENNYSON (1809–1892)

Break, Break, Break   *1842*

Break, break, break,
   On thy cold gray stones, O Sea!
And I would that my tongue could utter
   The thoughts that arise in me.

O, well for the fisherman's boy,   5
   That he shouts with his sister at play!
O, well for the sailor lad,
   That he sings in his boat on the bay!

And the stately ships go on
   To their haven under the hill;   10
But O for the touch of a vanished hand,
   And the sound of a voice that is still!

Break, break, break
   At the foot of thy crags, O Sea!
But the tender grace of a day that is dead   15
   Will never come back to me.

CONSIDERATIONS FOR CRITICAL THINKING AND WRITING

1. **FIRST RESPONSE.** Paraphrase the poem and describe its tone.
2. How do lines 1 and 13 differ from the predominant meter of the rest of the lines? How do these lines control the poem's tone?
3. What is the effect of the repetition? What does "break" refer to in addition to the waves?

ALICE JONES (B. 1949)

The Foot   *1993*

Our improbable support, erected
on the osseous architecture
of the calcaneus, talus, cuboid,
navicular, cuneiforms, metatarsals,
phalanges, a plethora of hinges,   5

all strung together by gliding
tendons, covered by the pearly
plantar fascia, then fat-padded
to form the sole, humble surface
of our contact with earth.   10

Here the body's broadest tendon
anchors the heel's fleshy base,

the finely wrinkled skin stretches
forward across the capillaried arch,
to the ball, a balance point.   15

A wide web of flexor tendons
and branched veins maps the dorsum,
fades into the stub-laden bone
splay, the stuffed sausage sacks
of toes, each with a tuft   20

of proximal hairs to introduce
the distal nail, whose useless
curve remembers an ancestor,
the vanished creature's wild
and necessary claw.   25

CONSIDERATIONS FOR CRITICAL THINKING AND WRITING

1. **FIRST RESPONSE.** What is the effect of the diction? What sort of tone is established by the use of anatomical terms? How do the terms affect the rhythm?

2. Jones has described the form of "The Foot" as "five stubby stanzas." Explain why the lines of this poem may or may not warrant this description of the stanzas.

3. **CRITICAL STRATEGIES.** Read the section on formalist strategies (pp. 2046–48) in Chapter 53, "Critical Strategies for Reading." Describe the effect of the final stanza. How would your reading be affected if the poem ended after the comma in the middle of line 22?

A. E. HOUSMAN (1859–1936)

When I was one-and-twenty   1896

When I was one-and-twenty
  I heard a wise man say,
"Give crowns and pounds and guineas
  But not your heart away;
Give pearls away and rubies   5
  But keep your fancy free."
But I was one-and-twenty,
  No use to talk to me.

When I was one-and-twenty
  I heard him say again,   10
"The heart out of the bosom
  Was never given in vain;
'Tis paid with sighs a plenty
  And sold for endless rue."
And I am two-and-twenty,   15
  And oh, 'tis true, 'tis true.

CONSIDERATIONS FOR CRITICAL THINKING AND WRITING

1. **FIRST RESPONSE.** How does the basic metrical pattern affect your understanding of the speaker?

2. How do lines 1–8 parallel lines 9–16 in their use of rhyme and metaphor? Are there any significant differences between the stanzas?

3. What do you think has happened to change the speaker's attitude toward love?

4. Explain why you agree or disagree with the advice given by the "wise man."

5. What is the effect of the repetition in line 16?

RITA DOVE (B. 1952)

Fox Trot Fridays   *2001*

Thank the stars there's a day
each week to tuck in

the grief, lift your pearls, and
stride brush stride

quick-quick with a   5
heel-ball-toe. Smooth

as Nat King Cole's
slow satin smile,

easy as taking
one day at a time: 10

one man and
one woman,

rib to rib,
with no heartbreak in sight —

just the sweep of Paradise   15
and the space of a song

to count all the wonders in it.

CONSIDERATIONS FOR CRITICAL THINKING AND WRITING

1. **FIRST RESPONSE.** Explain how the rhythm of the lines is aptly partnered with the fox trot.

2. Do some background research so that you can discuss why Dove chooses Nat King Cole as the right kind of singer for this poem.

3. The fox trot is more than a dance step for Dove. What is its appeal in this poem?

RACHEL HADAS (B. 1948)

The Red Hat

1995

It started before Christmas. Now our son
officially walks to school alone.
Semi-alone, it's accurate to say:
I or his father track him on the way.
He walks up on the east side of West End,   5
we on the west side. Glances can extend
(and do) across the street; not eye contact.
Already ties are feeling and not fact.
Straus Park is where these parallel paths part;
he goes alone from there. The watcher's heart   10
stretches, elastic in its love and fear,
toward him as we see him disappear,
striding briskly. Where two weeks ago,
holding a hand, he'd dawdle, dreamy, slow,
he now is hustled forward by the pull   15
of something far more powerful than school.

The mornings we turn back to are no more
than forty minutes longer than before,
but they feel vastly different — flimsy, strange,
wavering in the eddies of this change,   20
empty, unanchored, perilously light
since the red hat vanished from our sight.

CONSIDERATIONS FOR CRITICAL THINKING AND WRITING

1. FIRST RESPONSE. What emotions do the parents experience throughout the
   poem? How do you think the boy feels? Does the metrical pattern affect
   your understanding of the parents or the boy?

2. What prevents the rhymed couplets in this poem from sounding sing-
   songy? What is the predominant meter?

3. What is it that "pull[s]" the boy along in lines 15–16?

4. Why do you think Hadas titled the poem "The Red Hat" rather than, for
   example, "Paths Part" (line 9)?

5. CRITICAL STRATEGIES. Read the section on psychological strategies (pp.
   2050–52) in Chapter 53, "Critical Strategies for Reading." How does the
   speaker reveal her personal psychology in this poem?

ROBERT HERRICK (1591–1674)

Delight in Disorder

1648

A sweet disorder in the dress
Kindles in clothes a wantonness.
A lawn° about the shoulders thrown   *linen scarf*
Into a fine distraction;

An erring lace, which here and there   5
Enthralls the crimson stomacher,
A cuff neglectful, and thereby
Ribbons to flow confusedly;
A winning wave, deserving note,
In the tempestuous petticoat;   10
A careless shoestring, in whose tie
I see a wild civility;
Do more bewitch me than when art
Is too precise in every part.

CONSIDERATIONS FOR CRITICAL THINKING AND WRITING

1. **FIRST RESPONSE.** Why does the speaker in this poem value "disorder" so highly? How do the poem's organization and rhythmic order relate to its theme? Are they "precise in every part" (line 14)?

2. Which words in the poem indicate disorder? Which words indicate the speaker's response to that disorder? What are the connotative meanings of each set of words? Why are they appropriate? What do they suggest about the woman and the speaker?

3. Write a short essay in which you agree or disagree with the speaker's views on dress.

BEN JONSON (1573–1637)

Still to Be Neat   *1609*

Still° to be neat, still to be dressed,   *continually*
As you were going to a feast;
Still to be powdered, still perfumed;
Lady, it is to be presumed,
Though art's hid causes are not found,   5
All is not sweet, all is not sound.

Give me a look, give me a face
That makes simplicity a grace;
Robes loosely flowing, hair as free;
Such sweet neglect more taketh me   10
Then all th' adulteries of art.
They strike mine eyes, but not my heart.

CONSIDERATIONS FOR CRITICAL THINKING AND WRITING

1. **FIRST RESPONSE.** What are the speaker's reservations about the lady in the first stanza? What do you think "sweet" means in line 6?

2. What does the speaker want from the lady in the second stanza? How has the meaning of "sweet" shifted from line 6 to line 10? What other words in the poem are especially charged with connotative meanings?

3. How do the rhythms of Jonson's lines help to reinforce meanings? Pay particular attention to lines 6 and 12.

1. Write an essay comparing the themes of "Still to Be Neat" and Herrick's preceding poem, "Delight in Disorder." How do the speakers make similar points but from different perspectives?

2. How does the rhythm of "Still to Be Neat" compare with that of "Delight in Disorder"? Which do you find more effective? Explain why.

SONIA SANCHEZ (B. 1934)

Summer Words of
a Sistuh Addict   1969

© Christopher Felver/CORBIS.

the first day i shot dope
was on a sunday.
              i had just come
home from church
              got mad at my motha
cuz she got mad at me. u dig?
              went out. shot up
behind a feelen against her.
              it felt good.   10
gooder than dooing it. yeah.
              it was nice.
i did it. uh huh. i did it.   uh. huh.
i want to do it again. it felt so gooooood.
              and as the sistuh
              sits in her silent/   15
              remembered/high
              someone leans for
              ward gently asks her:
                  sistuh.
                  did u   20
                  finally
              learn how to hold yo/mother?
and the music of the day
              drifts in the room
to mingle with the sistuh's young tears.   25
      and we all sing.

1. **FIRST RESPONSE.** Comment on the effect of the spelling and grammar in the poem.

2. Describe the difference in the rhythm and tone in lines 1 to 13 in contrast with those in lines 14 to 26. How do you account for the difference?

3. In what sense does the "sistuh's" speech consist of those "Summer Words" referred to in the title?

WILLIAM BLAKE (1757–1827)

The Lamb

1789

Courtesy of the National Portrait Gallery, London.

> Little Lamb, who made thee?
> Dost thou know who made thee?
> Gave thee life, and bid thee feed
> By the stream and o'er the mead;
> Gave thee clothing of delight,
> Softest clothing, wooly, bright;
> Gave thee such a tender voice,
> Making all the vales rejoice?
>> Little Lamb, who made thee?
>> Dost thou know who made thee?
>
>> Little Lamb, I'll tell thee,
>> Little Lamb, I'll tell thee:
> He is callèd by thy name,
> For he calls himself a Lamb.
> He is meek, and he is mild;   15
> He became a little child.
> I a child, and thou a lamb,
> We are callèd by his name.
>> Little Lamb, God bless thee!
>> Little Lamb, God bless thee!   20

CONSIDERATIONS FOR CRITICAL THINKING AND WRITING

1. **FIRST RESPONSE.** This poem is from Blake's *Songs of Innocence.* Describe its tone. How do the meter, rhyme, and repetition help to characterize the speaker's voice?

2. Why is it significant that the animal addressed by the speaker is a lamb? What symbolic value would be lost if the animal were, for example, a doe?

3. How does the second stanza answer the question raised in the first? What is the speaker's view of the creation?

WILLIAM BLAKE (1757–1827)

The Tyger

1794

Tyger! Tyger! burning bright
In the forests of the night,
What immortal hand or eye
Could frame thy fearful symmetry?

In what distant deeps or skies   5
Burnt the fire of thine eyes?
On what wings dare he aspire?
What the hand dare seize the fire?

And what shoulder, and what art,
Could twist the sinews of thy heart?   10
And when thy heart began to beat,
What dread hand? and what dread feet?

What the hammer? what the chain?
In what furnace was thy brain?
What the anvil? what dread grasp   15
Dare its deadly terrors clasp?

When the stars threw down their spears,
And watered heaven with their tears,
Did he smile his work to see?
Did he who made the Lamb make thee?   20

Tyger! Tyger! burning bright
In the forests of the night,
What immortal hand or eye
Dare frame thy fearful symmetry?

Considerations for Critical Thinking and Writing

1. **FIRST RESPONSE.** This poem from Blake's *Songs of Experience* is often paired with "The Lamb." Describe the poem's tone. Is the speaker's voice the same here as in "The Lamb"? Which words are repeated, and how do they contribute to the tone?

2. What is revealed about the nature of the tiger by the words used to describe its creation? What do you think the tiger symbolizes?

3. Unlike in "The Lamb," more than one question is raised in "The Tyger." What are these questions? Are they answered?

4. Compare the rhythms in "The Lamb" and "The Tyger." Each basically uses a seven-syllable line, but the effects are very different. Why?

5. Using these two poems as the basis of your discussion, describe what distinguishes innocence from experience.

Carl Sandburg (1878–1967)

Chicago   *1916*

Hog Butcher for the World,
Tool Maker, Stacker of Wheat,
Player with Railroads and the Nation's Freight Handler;
Stormy, husky, brawling,
City of the Big Shoulders: 5

They tell me you are wicked and I believe them, for I have seen your painted
        women under the gas lamps luring the farm boys.
And they tell me you are crooked and I answer: Yes, it is true I have seen the
        gunman kill and go free to kill again.

And they tell me you are brutal and my reply is: On the faces of women and
　　children I have seen the marks of wanton hunger.
And having answered so I turn once more to those who sneer at this my city,
　　and I give them back the sneer and say to them:
Come and show me another city with lifted head singing so proud to be alive
　　and coarse and strong and cunning.　　　　　　　　　　　　　　　　　　10
Flinging magnetic curses amid the toil of piling job on job, here is a tall bold
　　slugger set vivid against the little soft cities;
Fierce as a dog with tongue lapping for action, cunning as a savage pitted
　　against the wilderness,
　Bareheaded,
　Shoveling,
　Wrecking,　　　　　　　　　　　　　　　　　　　　　　　　　　　　15
　Planning,
　Building, breaking, rebuilding,
Under the smoke, dust all over his mouth, laughing with white teeth,
Under the terrible burden of destiny laughing as a young man laughs,
Laughing even as an ignorant fighter laughs who has never lost a battle,　　20
Bragging and laughing that under his wrist is the pulse, and under his ribs
　　the heart of the people,
　Laughing!
Laughing the stormy, husky, brawling laughter of Youth, half-naked,
　　sweating, proud to be Hog Butcher, Tool Maker, Stacker of Wheat,
　　Player with Railroads and Freight Handler to the Nation.

CONSIDERATIONS FOR CRITICAL THINKING AND WRITING

1. **FIRST RESPONSE.** Sandburg's personification of Chicago creates a strong
   identity for the city. Explain why you find the city attractive or not.

2. How do the length and rhythm of lines 1 to 5 compare with those of the
   final lines?

3. **CREATIVE RESPONSE.** Using "Chicago" as a model for style, try writing a
   tribute or condemnation about a place that you know well. Make an effort
   to use vivid images and stylistic techniques that capture its rhythms.

CONNECTION TO ANOTHER SELECTION

1. Compare "Chicago" with William Blake's "London" (p. 850) in style and theme.

MARK DOTY (B. 1953)

Tunnel Music　　　　　　　　　　　　　　　　　　　　　　　　　*1995*

Times Square, the shuttle's quick chrome
flies open and the whole car floods with
— what is it? Infernal industry, the tunnels
under Manhattan broken into hell at last?

Guttural churr and whistle and grind　　　　　　　　　　　　　　　5
of the engines that spin the poles?

Enormous racket, ungodly. What it is
is percussion: nine black guys

with nine lovely and previously unimagined
constructions of metal ripped and mauled,   10
welded and oiled: scoured chemical drums,
torched rims, unnamable disks of chrome.

Artifacts of wreck? The end of industry?
A century's failures reworked, bent,
hammered out, struck till their shimmying   15
tumbles and ricochets from tile walls:

anything dinged, busted or dumped
can be beaten till it sings.
A kind of ghostly joy in it, though
this music's almost unrecognizable,   20

so utterly of the coming world it is.

CONSIDERATIONS FOR CRITICAL THINKING AND WRITING

1. **FIRST RESPONSE.** How do these lines capture the rhythms and sounds of
   both the subway and the metal drums?

2. Why do you suppose Doty chooses Times Square as his stop rather than,
   say, Penn Station or 125th Street?

3. Discuss the significance of the last line. To what extent would you read the
   poem differently if it ended at line 20?

CONNECTION TO ANOTHER SELECTION

1. Compare the themes in Doty's poem with those in Carl Sandburg's
   "Chicago."

MARK TURPIN (B. 1953)

Sledgehammer's Song   *2003*

The way you hold the haft,
The way it climbs a curve,
A manswung curve,
The way it undoes what was done.
The way a stake sinks,   5
Cement splits or a stud
Spins off its nails.

The way shoulders shrug.
The way the breezes waft
And wake and tease a cheek,   10
The way it undoes what was done.
The way a cabinet cracks

And rakes and bares
The nail-scarred wall beneath.

The way a stance is spread,   15
The way the steel head pings
And thrums and thuds,
The way it undoes what was done.
The way a bathtub breaks:
Pieces barrowed, porcelain   20
Left in a bin.

The way sight is stark.
The way the weight wills the arms,
The back and heart,
The way it undoes what was done.   25
The way the weight is weighed,
Stalling the swing,
The sorrow mid-arc.

CONSIDERATIONS FOR CRITICAL THINKING AND WRITING

1. **FIRST RESPONSE.** Explain how the meter of these lines gets into the swing of a sledgehammer's work.

2. Why is the repetition at the beginning of many lines particularly appropriate for this poem?

3. Is this hammer work depicted as simply mindlessly destructive or as something else? Explain your response with reference to the poem's diction and images.

ALFRED, LORD TENNYSON (1809–1892)
The Charge of the Light Brigade   *1855*

1

Half a league, half a league,
   Half a league onward,
All in the valley of Death
   Rode the six hundred.
"Forward, the Light Brigade!   5
Charge for the guns!" he said:
Into the valley of Death
   Rode the six hundred.

2

"Forward, the Light Brigade!"
Was there a man dismayed?   10

Not though the soldier knew
   Some one had blundered:
Their's not to make reply,
Their's not to reason why,
Their's but to do and die: 15
Into the valley of Death
   Rode the six hundred.

3

Cannon to right of them,
Cannon to left of them,
Cannon in front of them   20
   Volleyed and thundered;
Stormed at with shot and shell,
Boldly they rode and well,
Into the jaws of Death,
Into the mouth of Hell   25
   Rode the six hundred.

4

Flashed all their sabers bare,
Flashed as they turned in air
Sabring the gunners there,
Charging an army, while   30
   All the world wondered:
Plunged in the battery-smoke
Right through the line they broke;
Cossack and Russian
Reeled from the saber-stroke   35
   Shattered and sundered.
Then they rode back, but not
   Not the six hundred.

5

Cannon to right of them,
Cannon to left of them,
Cannon behind them   40
   Volleyed and thundered;
Stormed at with shot and shell,
While horse and hero fell,
They that had fought so well
Came through the jaws of Death,
Back from the mouth of Hell,   45
All that was left of them,
   Left of six hundred.

6

When can their glory fade?   50
O the wild charge they made!
    All the world wondered.
Honor the charge they made!
Honor the Light Brigade,
    Noble six hundred!   55

CONSIDERATIONS FOR CRITICAL THINKING AND WRITING

1. **FIRST RESPONSE.** How do the meter and rhyme contribute to the meaning of this poem's lines?

2. What is the speaker's attitude toward war?

3. Describe the tone, paying particular attention to stanza 2.

CONNECTION TO ANOTHER SELECTION

1. Compare the theme of "The Charge of the Light Brigade" with that of Wilfred Owen's "Dulce et Decorum Est" (p. 852).

THEODORE ROETHKE (1908–1963)

My Papa's Waltz   *1948*

[Web] Explore
contexts for Theodore
Roethke and approaches
to this poem at
bedfordstmartins.com/
meyerlit.

The whiskey on your breath
Could make a small boy dizzy;
But I hung on like death:
Such waltzing was not easy.

We romped until the pans   5
Slid from the kitchen shelf;
My mother's countenance
Could not unfrown itself.

The hand that held my wrist
Was battered on one knuckle;   10
At every step you missed
My right ear scraped a buckle.

You beat time on my head
With a palm caked hard by dirt,
Then waltzed me off to bed   15
Still clinging to your shirt.

CONSIDERATIONS FOR CRITICAL THINKING AND WRITING

1. **FIRST RESPONSE.** What details characterize the father in this poem? How does the speaker's choice of words reveal his feeling about his father? Is the remembering speaker still a boy?

2. Characterize the rhythm of the poem. Does it move "like death" (line 3), or is it more like a waltz? Is the rhythm regular throughout the poem? What is its effect?

3. Comment on the appropriateness of the title. Why do you suppose Roethke didn't use "My Father's Waltz"?

THYLIAS MOSS (B. 1954)

Tornados

1991

Truth is, I envy them
not because they dance; I out jitterbug them
as I'm shuttled through and through legs
strong as looms, weaving time. They
do black more justice than I, frenzy   5
of conductor of philharmonic and electricity, hair
on end, result of the charge when horns and strings release
the pent up Beethoven and Mozart. Ions played

instead of notes. The movement
is not wrath, not hormone swarm because   10
I saw my first forming above the church a surrogate
steeple. The morning of my first baptism and
salvation already tangible, funnel for the spirit
coming into me without losing a drop, my black
guardian angel come to rescue me before all the words   15

get out, *I looked over Jordan and what did I see coming for*
to carry me home. Regardez, it all comes back, even the first
grade French, when the tornado stirs up the past, bewitched spoon
lost in its own spin, like a roulette wheel that won't
be steered, like the world. They drove me underground,   20
tornado watches and warnings, atomic bomb drills. Adult
storms so I had to leave the room. Truth is

the tornado is a perfect nappy curl, tightly wound,
spinning wildly when I try to tamper with its nature, shunning
the hot comb and pressing oil even though if absolutely straight   25
I'd have the longest hair in the world. Bouffant tornadic
crown taking the royal path on a trip to town, stroll down
Tornado Alley where it intersects Memory Lane. Smoky spirit-
clouds, shadows searching for what cast them.

CONSIDERATIONS FOR CRITICAL THINKING AND WRITING

1. **FIRST RESPONSE.** What connections does the speaker make between herself and the tornado? Explain why you think they are primarily positive or negative.

2. Describe the poem's rhythm. Do you find any moments where the lines' rhythm reflects their meaning?

3. Could the title of this poem just as effectively have been "Bouffant Tornadic Crown" (lines 26–27)? Explain why or why not.

FLOYD SKLOOT (B. 1947)

Winter Solstice　2005

I wake in darkness and fog to the hoofbeat of deer
racing across the hill's frosted crest from east to west.
As in a dream, within the rise and fall of wind I hear
the rise and fall of the deer pack's breath
as it becomes the beat of my heart within my chest.　5
I am fitted so close to my wife's body her breath
seems to be my breath as we curl together, awake
but not awake, her back rising against my rising chest
in the lingering pre-dawn dark.
Now, in the space between our breath, silence comes to rest.　10

CONSIDERATIONS FOR CRITICAL THINKING AND WRITING

1. **FIRST RESPONSE.** What emotions do these images produce in you?
2. Explain how the meter and rhyme contribute to the poem's tone.
3. Comment on the significance of the title. How is it related to the images in the poem?

Perspective

LOUISE BOGAN (1897–1970)

On Formal Poetry　1953

What is formal poetry? It is poetry written in form. And what is *form*? The elements of form, so far as poetry is concerned, are meter and rhyme. Are these elements merely mold and ornaments that have been impressed upon poetry from without? Are they indeed restrictions which bind and fetter language and the thought and emotion behind, under, within language in a repressive way? Are they arbitrary rules which have lost all validity since they have been broken to good purpose by "experimental poets," ancient and modern? Does the breaking up of form, or its total elimination, always result in an increase of power and of effect; and is any return to form a sort of relinquishment of freedom, or retreat to old fogeyism?

From *A Poet's Alphabet*

CONSIDERATIONS FOR CRITICAL THINKING AND WRITING

1. Choose one of the questions Bogan raises and write an essay in response to it using two or three poems from this chapter to illustrate your answer.
2. **CREATIVE RESPONSE.** Try writing a poem in meter and rhyme. Does the experience make your writing feel limited or not?

Web Research the poets in this chapter at bedfordstmartins.com/ meyerlit.

29

Poetic Forms

© Tom Jorgensen/ The University of Iowa.

A short poem need not be small.
— MARVIN BELL

Poems come in a variety of shapes. Although the best poems always have their own unique qualities, many of them also conform to traditional patterns. Frequently the **form** of a poem — its overall structure or shape — follows an already established design. A poem that can be categorized by the patterns of its lines, meter, rhymes, and stanzas is considered a **fixed form** because it follows a prescribed model such as a sonnet. However, poems written in a fixed form do not always fit models precisely; writers sometimes work variations on traditional forms to create innovative effects.

Not all poets are content with variations on traditional forms. Some prefer to create their own structures and shapes. Poems that do not conform to established patterns of meter, rhyme, and stanza are called **free verse** or **open form** poetry. (See Chapter 30 for further discussion of open forms.) This kind of poetry creates its own ordering principles through the careful arrangement of words and phrases in line lengths that embody rhythms appropriate to the meaning. Modern and contemporary poets in particular have learned to use the blank space on the page as a significant functional element (for a striking example, see Cummings's "in Just-," p. 1000). Good poetry of this kind is structured in ways that can be as demanding, interesting, and satisfying as fixed forms. Open and fixed forms represent different poetic styles, but they are identical in the sense that both use language in concentrated ways to convey meanings, experiences, emotions, and effects.

SOME COMMON POETIC FORMS

A familiarity with some of the most frequently used fixed forms of poetry is useful because it allows for a better understanding of how a poem works. Classifying patterns allows us to talk about the effects of established rhythm and rhyme and to recognize how significant variations from them affect the pace and meaning of the lines. An awareness of form also allows us to anticipate how a poem is likely to proceed. As we shall see, a sonnet creates a different set of expectations in a reader from those of, say, a limerick. A reader isn't likely to find in limericks the kind of serious themes that often make their way into sonnets. The discussion that follows identifies some of the important poetic forms frequently encountered in English poetry.

The shape of a fixed-form poem is often determined by the way in which the lines are organized into stanzas. A *stanza* consists of a grouping of lines, set off by a space, that usually has a set pattern of meter and rhyme. This pattern is ordinarily repeated in other stanzas throughout the poem. What is usual is not obligatory, however; some poems may use a different pattern for each stanza, somewhat like paragraphs in prose.

Traditionally, though, stanzas do share a common **rhyme scheme,** the pattern of end rhymes. We can map out rhyme schemes by noting patterns of rhyme with lowercase letters: the first rhyme sound is designated *a,* the second becomes *b,* the third *c,* and so on. Using this system, we can describe the rhyme scheme in the following poem this way: *aabb, ccdd, eeff.*

A. E. HOUSMAN (1859–1936)

Loveliest of trees, the cherry now   *1896*

Loveliest of trees, the cherry now	*a*
Is hung with bloom along the bough,	*a*
And stands about the woodland ride	*b*
Wearing white for Eastertide.	*b*
Now, of my threescore years and ten,	*c*
Twenty will not come again,	*c*
And take from seventy springs a score,	*d*
It only leaves me fifty more.	*d*
And since to look at things in bloom	*e*
Fifty springs are little room,	*e*

5

10

About the woodlands I will go   *f*
To see the cherry hung with snow.   *f*

CONSIDERATIONS FOR CRITICAL THINKING AND WRITING

1. **FIRST RESPONSE.** What is the speaker's attitude in this poem toward time and life?

2. Why is spring an appropriate season for the setting rather than, say, winter?

3. Paraphrase each stanza. How do the images in each reinforce the poem's themes?

4. Lines 1 and 12 are not intended to rhyme, but they are close. What is the effect of the near rhyme of "now" and "snow"? How does the rhyme enhance the theme?

Poets often create their own stanzaic patterns; hence there is an infinite number of kinds of stanzas. One way of talking about stanzaic forms is to describe a given stanza by how many lines it contains.

A *couplet* consists of two lines that usually rhyme and have the same meter; couplets are frequently not separated from each other by space on the page. A *heroic couplet* consists of rhymed iambic pentameter. Here is an example from Alexander Pope's "Essay on Criticism":

One science only will one genius fit;   *a*
So vast is art, so narrow human wit: *a*
Not only bounded to peculiar arts,   *b*
But oft in those confined to single parts.   *b*

A *tercet* is a three-line stanza. When all three lines rhyme, they are called a *triplet.* Two triplets make up this captivating poem.

ROBERT HERRICK (1591–1674)

Upon Julia's Clothes   *1648*

Whenas in silks my Julia goes,   *a*
Then, then, methinks, how sweetly flows   *a*
That liquefaction of her clothes.   *a*

Next, when I cast mine eyes, and see   *b*
That brave vibration, each way free,   *b*
O, how that glittering taketh me!   *b*

CONSIDERATIONS FOR CRITICAL THINKING AND WRITING

1. **FIRST RESPONSE.** What purpose does alliteration serve in this poem?

2. Comment on the effect of the meter. How is it related to the speaker's description of Julia's clothes?

3. Look up the word *brave* in the *Oxford English Dictionary*. Which of its meanings is appropriate to describe Julia's movement? Some readers interpret lines 4–6 to mean that Julia has no clothes on. What do you think?

CONNECTION TO ANOTHER SELECTION

1. Compare the tone of this poem with that of Paul Humphrey's "Blow" (p. 939). Are the situations and speakers similar? Is there any difference in tone between these two poems?

Terza rima consists of an interlocking three-line rhyme scheme: *aba, bcb, cdc, ded,* and so on. Dante's *Divine Comedy* uses this pattern, as does Robert Frost's "Acquainted with the Night" (p. 889) and Percy Bysshe Shelley's "Ode to the West Wind" (p. 993).

A *quatrain,* or four-line stanza, is the most common stanzaic form in the English language and can have various meters and rhyme schemes (if any). The most common rhyme schemes are *aabb, abba, aaba,* and *abcb.* This last pattern is especially characteristic of the popular **ballad stanza,** which consists of alternating eight- and six-syllable lines. Samuel Taylor Coleridge adopted this pattern in "The Rime of the Ancient Mariner"; here is one representative stanza:

> All in a hot and copper sky
> The bloody Sun, at noon,
> Right up above the mast did stand,
> No bigger than the Moon.

There are a number of longer stanzaic forms, and the list of types of stanzas could be extended considerably, but knowing these three most basic patterns should prove helpful to you in talking about the form of a great many poems. In addition to stanzaic forms, there are fixed forms that characterize entire poems. Lyric poems can be, for example, sonnets, villanelles, sestinas, or epigrams.

Sonnet

The **sonnet** has been a popular literary form in English since the sixteenth century, when it was adopted from the Italian *sonnetto,* meaning "little song." A sonnet consists of fourteen lines, usually written in iambic pentameter. Because the sonnet has been such a favorite form, writers have experimented with many variations on its essential structure. Nevertheless, there are two basic types of sonnets: the Italian and the English.

The **Italian sonnet** (also known as the **Petrarchan sonnet,** from the fourteenth-century Italian poet Petrarch) divides into two parts. The first eight lines (the **octave**) typically rhyme *abbaabba.* The final six lines (the **sestet**) may vary; common patterns are *cdecde, cdcdcd,* and *cdccdc.* Very often the octave presents a situation, an attitude, or a problem that the sestet comments upon or resolves, as in John Keats's "On First Looking into Chapman's Homer."

JOHN KEATS (1795–1821)

On First Looking into Chapman's Homer°   *1816*

Much have I traveled in the realms of gold,
   And many goodly states and kingdoms
      seen;
   Round many western islands have I been
Which bards in fealty to Apollo° hold.
Oft of one wide expanse had I been told
   That deep-browed Homer ruled as his
      demesne;

Courtesy of the National Portrait Gallery, London.

   Yet did I never breathe its pure serene°   *atmosphere*
Till I heard Chapman speak out loud and bold:
Then felt I like some watcher of the skies
   When a new planet swims into his ken;   10
Or like stout Cortez° when with eagle eyes
   He stared at the Pacific — and all his men
Looked at each other with a wild surmise —
   Silent, upon a peak in Darien.

Chapman's Homer: Before reading George Chapman's (ca. 1560–1634) poetic Elizabethan translations of Homer's *Iliad* and *Odyssey,* Keats had known only stilted and pedestrian eighteenth-century translations. 4 *Apollo:* Greek god of poetry. 11 *Cortez:* Vasco Núñez de Balboa, not Hernando Cortés, was the first European to sight the Pacific from Darien, a peak in Panama.

CONSIDERATIONS FOR CRITICAL THINKING AND WRITING

1. **FIRST RESPONSE.** How do the images shift from the octave to the sestet? How does the tone change? Does the meaning change as well?

2. What is the controlling metaphor of this poem?

3. What is it that the speaker discovers?

4. How does the rhythm of the lines change between the octave and the sestet? How does that change reflect the tones of both the octave and the sestet?

5. Does Keats's mistake concerning Cortés and Balboa affect your reading of the poem? Explain why or why not.

The Italian sonnet pattern is also used in the next sonnet, but notice that the thematic break between octave and sestet comes within line 9 rather than between lines 8 and 9. This unconventional break helps to reinforce the speaker's impatience with the conventional attitudes he describes.

WILLIAM WORDSWORTH (1770–1850)

The World Is Too Much with Us   *1807*

The world is too much with us; late and soon,
Getting and spending, we lay waste our powers;
Little we see in Nature that is ours;
We have given our hearts away, a sordid boon!
This Sea that bares her bosom to the moon;   5
The winds that will be howling at all hours,
And are up-gathered now like sleeping flowers;
For this, for everything, we are out of tune;
It moves us not. — Great God! I'd rather be
A Pagan suckled in a creed outworn;   10
So might I, standing on this pleasant lea,
Have glimpses that would make me less forlorn;
Have sight of Proteus rising from the sea;
Or hear old Triton blow his wreathèd horn.

CONSIDERATIONS FOR CRITICAL THINKING AND WRITING

1. **FIRST RESPONSE.** What is the speaker's complaint in this sonnet? How do the conditions described affect him?
2. Look up "Proteus" and "Triton." What do these mythological allusions contribute to the sonnet's tone?
3. What is the effect of the personification of the sea and wind in the octave?

CONNECTION TO ANOTHER SELECTION

1. Compare the theme of this sonnet with that of Gerard Manley Hopkins's "God's Grandeur" (p. 929).

The **English sonnet,** more commonly known as the **Shakespearean sonnet,** is organized into three quatrains and a couplet, which typically rhyme *abab cdcd efef gg.* This rhyme scheme is more suited to English poetry because English has fewer rhyming words than Italian. English sonnets, because of their four-part organization, also have more flexibility about where thematic breaks can occur. Frequently, however, the most pronounced break or turn comes with the concluding couplet.

In the following Shakespearean sonnet, the three quatrains compare the speaker's loved one to a summer's day and explain why the loved one is even more lovely. The couplet bestows eternal beauty and love upon both the loved one and the sonnet.

WILLIAM SHAKESPEARE (1564–1616)
Shall I compare thee to a summer's day?   1609

Shall I compare thee to a summer's day?
Thou art more lovely and more temperate:
Rough winds do shake the darling buds of May,
And summer's lease hath all too short a date.
Sometime too hot the eye of heaven shines,   5
And often is his gold complexion dimmed;
And every fair from fair sometime declines,
By chance, or nature's changing course, untrimmed.
But thy eternal summer shall not fade,
Nor lose possession of that fair thou ow'st°   *possess*   10
Nor shall death brag thou wand'rest in his shade,
When in eternal lines to time thou grow'st.
      So long as men can breathe or eyes can see,
      So long lives this, and this gives life to thee.

CONSIDERATIONS FOR CRITICAL THINKING AND WRITING

1. **FIRST RESPONSE.** Describe the shift in tone and subject matter that begins in line 9.
2. Why is the speaker's loved one more lovely than a summer's day? What qualities does he admire in the loved one?
3. What does the couplet say about the relation between art and love?
4. Which syllables are stressed in the final line? How do these syllables relate to the line's meaning?

Sonnets have been the vehicles for all kinds of subjects, including love, death, politics, and cosmic questions. Although most sonnets tend to treat their subjects seriously, this fixed form does not mean a fixed expression; humor is also possible in it. Compare this next Shakespearean sonnet with "Shall I compare thee to a summer's day?" They are, finally, both love poems, but their tones are markedly different.

WILLIAM SHAKESPEARE (1564–1616)
My mistress' eyes are nothing like the sun   1609

My mistress' eyes are nothing like the sun;
Coral is far more red than her lips' red;
If snow be white, why then her breasts are dun;
If hairs be wires, black wires grow on her head.
I have seen roses damasked red and white,   5
But no such roses see I in her cheeks;
And in some perfumes is there more delight
Than in the breath that from my mistress reeks.

I love to hear her speak, yet well I know
That music hath a far more pleasing sound;   10
I grant I never saw a goddess go:
My mistress, when she walks, treads on the ground.
     And yet, by heaven, I think my love as rare
     As any she,° belied with false compare.   *lady*

CONSIDERATIONS FOR CRITICAL THINKING AND WRITING

1. **FIRST RESPONSE.** What does "mistress" mean in this sonnet? Write a description of this particular mistress based on the images used in the sonnet.

2. What sort of person is the speaker? Does he truly love the woman he describes?

3. In what sense are this sonnet and "Shall I compare thee to a summer's day?" about poetry as well as love?

EDNA ST. VINCENT MILLAY (1892–1950)

I will put Chaos into fourteen lines   1954

© CORBIS.

I will put Chaos into fourteen lines
And keep him there; and let him thence escape
If he be lucky; let him twist, and ape
Flood, fire, and demon — his adroit designs
Will strain to nothing in the strict confines
Of this sweet Order, where, in pious rape,
I hold his essence and amorphous shape,
Till he with Order mingles and combines.
Past are the hours, the years, of our duress,
His arrogance, our awful servitude: 10
I have him. He is nothing more nor less
Than something simple not yet understood;
I shall not even force him to confess;
Or answer. I will only make him good.

CONSIDERATIONS FOR CRITICAL THINKING AND WRITING

1. **FIRST RESPONSE.** Does the poem contain "Chaos"? If so, how? If not, why not?

2. What properties of a sonnet does this poem possess?

3. What do you think is meant by the phrase "pious rape" in line 6?

4. What is the effect of the personification in the poem?

CONNECTION TO ANOTHER SELECTION

1. Compare the theme of this poem with that of Robert Frost's "Design" (p. 1116).

A SAMPLE STUDENT RESPONSE

Alexia Sykes

Professor Jones

English 211

December 1, 2009

The Fixed Form in Edna St. Vincent Millay's

"I will put Chaos into fourteen lines"

In her poem "I will put Chaos into fourteen lines," Edna St. Vincent Millay does exactly what her title promises. Though the poem is of a fixed form, using patterns in meter, rhyme, line, and stanza, a sense of chaos is created through a complex structure, only to be calmed in the last six lines by a simpler rhyme scheme.

The first octave of the poem is structured *abbaabba,* a structure commonly found in sonnets. Although this is a fixed structure, the rhyme scheme is so complex that a chaotic tone is established:

> Flood, Fire, and demon—his adroit designs
> Will strain to nothing in the strict confines
> Of this sweet Order, where, in pious rape,
> I hold his essence and amorphous shape,
> Till he with Order mingles and combines. (lines 4-8)

Rhyming couplets are fired at the reader and the seemingly haphazard pattern gives the impression that there is little or no structure at all, particularly on a first reading. It is difficult to determine the framework of the poem, and the absence of a decipherable structure creates in the reader a feeling of randomness, the same disorder mentioned by the speaker. It is not until the end of the poem that relief is provided. The final six lines contain a much simpler, more repetitive structure: *cdcdcd.* This rhyme scheme provides stability and consistency. The pattern is simple and predictable; order is restored. Chaos has been tamed and made "good" (14) by the poem's form. . . .

Sykes 3

Work Cited

Millay, Edna St. Vincent. "I will put Chaos into fourteen lines." *The Bedford*
    Introduction to Literature. Ed. Michael Meyer. 9th ed. Boston: Bedford/St.
    Martin's, 2011. 977. Print.

MOLLY PEACOCK (B. 1947)

Desire   *1984*

It doesn't speak and it isn't schooled,
like a small foetal animal with wettened fur.
It is the blind instinct for life unruled,
visceral frankincense and animal myrrh.
It is what babies bring to kings,   5
an eyes-shut, ears-shut medicine of the heart
that smells and touches endings and beginnings
without the details of time's experienced *part-*
fit-into-part-fit-into-part. Like a paw,
it is blunt; like a pet who knows you   10
and nudges your knee with its snout — but more raw
and blinder and younger and more divine, too,
than the tamed wild — it's the drive for what is real,
deeper than the brain's detail: the drive to feel.

CONSIDERATIONS FOR CRITICAL THINKING AND WRITING

1. **FIRST RESPONSE.** Taken together, what do all of the metaphors that appear
   in this poem reveal about the speaker's conception of desire?

2. What is the "it" being described in lines 3–5? How do the allusions to the
   three wise men relate to the other metaphors used to define desire?

3. How is this English sonnet structured? What is the effect of its irregular
   meter?

CONNECTION TO ANOTHER SELECTION

1. Compare the treatment of desire in this poem with that of Sharon Olds's
   "Last Night" (p. 816). In an essay, identify the theme of each poem and compare their conceptions of desire. How alike are these two poems?

MARK JARMAN (B. 1952)

Unholy Sonnet

1993

After the praying, after the hymn-singing,
After the sermon's trenchant commentary
On the world's ills, which make ours secondary,
After communion, after the hand-wringing,
And after peace descends upon us, bringing   5
Our eyes up to regard the sanctuary
And how the light swords through it, and how, scary
In their sheer numbers, motes of dust ride, clinging —
There is, as doctors say about some pain,
Discomfort knowing that despite your prayers,   10
Your listening and rejoicing, your small part
In this communal stab at coming clean,
There is one stubborn remnant of your cares
Intact. There is still murder in your heart.

CONSIDERATIONS FOR CRITICAL THINKING AND WRITING

1. **FIRST RESPONSE.** Describe the rhyme scheme and structure of this sonnet. Explain why it is an English or Italian sonnet.

2. What are the effects of the use of "after" in lines 1, 2, 4, and 5 and "there" in lines 9, 13, and 14?

3. In what sense might this poem be summed up as a "communal stab" (line 12)? Discuss the accuracy of this assessment.

4. **CREATIVE RESPONSE.** Try writing a reply to the theme of Jarman's poem using the same sonnet form that he uses.

CONNECTION TO ANOTHER SELECTION

1. Jarman has said that his "Unholy Sonnets" (there are about twenty of them) are modeled after John Donne's *Holy Sonnets* but that he does not share the same Christian assumptions about faith and mercy that inform Donne's sonnets. Instead, Jarman says, he "work[s] against any assumption or shared expression of faith, to write a devotional poetry against the grain." Keeping this statement in mind, write an essay comparing and contrasting the tone and theme of Jarman's sonnet with those of John Donne's "Death Be Not Proud" (p. 1030).

X. J. KENNEDY (B. 1929)

"The Purpose of Time Is to Prevent Everything from Happening at Once"

2002

Suppose your life a folded telescope
Durationless, collapsed in just a flash
As from your mother's womb you, bawling, drop
Into a nursing home. Suppose you crash

Your car, your marriage — toddler laying waste   5
A field of daisies, schoolkid, zit-faced teen
With lover zipping up your pants in haste
Hearing your parents' tread downstairs — all one.

Einstein was right. That would be too intense.
You need a chance to preen, to give a dull   10
Recital before an indifferent audience
Equally slow in jeering you and clapping.
Time takes its time unraveling. But, still,
You'll wonder when your life ends: Huh? What happened?

CONSIDERATIONS FOR CRITICAL THINKING AND WRITING

1. **FIRST RESPONSE.** Comment on how the images in the octave manage to sum up a human life.
2. How serious a reflection on the passage of time is this poem?
3. What kind of sonnet is it? Why might a fixed form be a more appropriate ordering principle for the theme of this poem than an open form?

Villanelle

The **villanelle** is a fixed form consisting of nineteen lines of any length divided into six stanzas: five tercets and a concluding quatrain. The first and third lines of the initial tercet rhyme; these rhymes are repeated in each subsequent tercet (*aba*) and in the final two lines of the quatrain (*abaa*). Moreover, line 1 appears in its entirety as lines 6, 12, and 18, while line 3 appears as lines 9, 15, and 19. This form may seem to risk monotony, but in competent hands a villanelle can create haunting echoes, as in Dylan Thomas's "Do Not Go Gentle into That Good Night."

DYLAN THOMAS (1914–1953)

Do Not Go Gentle into That Good Night   *1952*

Do not go gentle into that good night,
Old age should burn and rave at close of day;
Rage, rage against the dying of the light.

Though wise men at their end know dark is right,
Because their words had forked no lightning they   5
Do not go gentle into that good night.

Good men, the last wave by, crying how bright
Their frail deeds might have danced in a green bay,
Rage, rage against the dying of the light.

Wild men who caught and sang the sun in flight,   10
And learn, too late, they grieved it on its way,
Do not go gentle into that good night.

Grave men, near death, who see with blinding sight
Blind eyes could blaze like meteors and be gay,
Rage, rage against the dying of the light.   15

And you, my father, there on the sad height,
Curse, bless, me now with your fierce tears, I pray.
Do not go gentle into that good night.
Rage, rage against the dying of the light.

CONSIDERATIONS FOR CRITICAL THINKING AND WRITING

1. **FIRST RESPONSE.** How does Thomas vary the meanings of the poem's two
   refrains: "Do not go gentle into that good night" and "Rage, rage against
   the dying of the light"?

2. Thomas's father was close to death when this poem was written. How does
   the tone contribute to the poem's theme?

3. How is "good" used in line 1?

4. Characterize the men who are "wise" (line 4), "Good" (7), "Wild" (10), and
   "Grave" (13).

5. What do figures of speech contribute to this poem?

6. Discuss this villanelle's sound effects.

WENDY COPE (B. 1945)

Lonely Hearts   *1986*

Can someone make my simple wish come true?
Male biker seeks female for touring fun.
Do you live in North London? Is it you?

Gay vegetarian whose friends are few,
I'm into music, Shakespeare and the sun.   5
Can someone make my simple wish come true?

Executive in search of something new —
Perhaps bisexual woman, arty, young.
Do you live in North London? Is it you?

Successful, straight and solvent? I am too —   10
Attractive Jewish lady with a son.
Can someone make my simple wish come true?

I'm Libran, inexperienced and blue —
Need slim non-smoker, under twenty-one.
Do you live in North London? Is it you?   15

Please write (with photo) to Box 152
Who knows where it may lead once we've begun?
Can someone make my simple wish come true?
Do you live in North London? Is it you?

CONSIDERATIONS FOR CRITICAL THINKING AND WRITING

1. **FIRST RESPONSE.** Why does the repetitive form of the villanelle seem particularly appropriate for the subject matter of "Lonely Hearts"?

2. How closely does "Lonely Hearts" conform to the conventional form of the villanelle? Are there any significant variations that produce interesting effects?

3. How are the several speakers' voices in the poem unified by tone?

Sestina

Although the **sestina** usually does not rhyme, it is perhaps an even more demanding fixed form than the villanelle. A sestina consists of thirty-nine lines of any length divided into six six-line stanzas and a three-line concluding stanza called an **envoy.** The difficulty lies in repeating the six words at the ends of the first stanza's lines at the ends of the lines in the other five six-line stanzas as well. Those words must also appear in the final three lines, where they often resonate important themes. The sestina originated in the Middle Ages, but contemporary poets continue to find it a fascinating and challenging form.

ALGERNON CHARLES SWINBURNE (1837–1909)

Sestina   1872

I saw my soul at rest upon a day
As a bird sleeping in the nest of night,
Among soft leaves that give the starlight way
To touch its wings but not its eyes with light;
So that it knew as one in visions may,   5
And knew not as men waking, of delight.

This was the measure of my soul's delight;
It had no power of joy to fly by day,
Nor part in the large lordship of the light;
But in a secret moon-beholden way   10
Had all its will of dreams and pleasant night,
And all the love and life that sleepers may.

But such life's triumph as men waking may
It might not have to feed its faint delight
Between the stars by night and sun by day,   15
Shut up with green leaves and a little light;
Because its way was as a lost star's way,
A world's not wholly known of day or night.

All loves and dreams and sounds and gleams of night
Made it all music that such minstrels may,   20
And all they had they gave it of delight;
But in the full face of the fire of day
What place shall be for any starry light,
What part of heaven in all the wide sun's way?

Yet the soul woke not, sleeping by the way,   25
Watched as a nursling of the large-eyed night,
And sought no strength nor knowledge of the day,
Nor closer touch conclusive of delight,
Nor mightier joy nor truer than dreamers may,
Nor more of song than they, nor more of light.   30

For who sleeps once and sees the secret light
Whereby sleep shows the soul a fairer way
Between the rise and rest of day and night,
Shall care no more to fare as all men may,
But be his place of pain or of delight,   35
There shall he dwell, beholding night as day.

Song, have thy day and take thy fill of light
Before the night be fallen across thy way;
Sing while he may, man hath no long delight.

CONSIDERATIONS FOR CRITICAL THINKING AND WRITING

1. **FIRST RESPONSE.** How are the six end words — "day," "night," "way," "light," "may," and "delight" — central to the sestina's meaning?

2. Number the end words of the first stanza 1, 2, 3, 4, 5, and 6, and then use those numbers for the corresponding end words in the remaining five stanzas to see how the pattern of the line-end words is worked out in this sestina. Also locate the six end words in the envoy.

3. Underline the images that seem especially vivid to you. What effects do they create? What is the tone of the sestina?

4. **CRITICAL STRATEGIES.** Read the section on psychological strategies (pp. 2050–52) in Chapter 53, "Critical Strategies for Reading." Write a brief essay explaining why you think a poet might derive pleasure from writing in a fixed form such as a villanelle or sestina. Can you think of similar activities outside the field of writing in which discipline and restraint give pleasure? How might this reflect an author's personal psychology?

FLORENCE CASSEN MAYERS (B. 1940)

All-American Sestina   *1996*

One nation, indivisible
two-car garage
three strikes you're out
four-minute mile

five-cent cigar   5
six-string guitar

six-pack Bud
one-day sale
five-year warranty
two-way street   10
fourscore and seven years ago
three cheers

three-star restaurant
sixty-
four-dollar question   15
one-night stand
two-pound lobster
five-star general

five-course meal
three sheets to the wind   20
two bits
six-shooter
one-armed bandit
four-poster

four-wheel drive   25
five-and-dime
hole in one
three-alarm fire
sweet sixteen
two-wheeler   30

two-tone Chevy
four rms, hi flr, w/vu
six-footer
high five
three-ring circus   35
one-room schoolhouse

two thumbs up, five-karat diamond
Fourth of July, three-piece suit
six feet under, one-horse town

CONSIDERATIONS FOR CRITICAL THINKING AND WRITING

1. **FIRST RESPONSE.** Discuss the significance of the title; what is "All-American" about this sestina?

2. How is the structure of this poem different from that of a conventional sestina? (What structural requirement does Mayers add for this sestina?)

3. Do you think important themes are raised by this poem, as is traditional for a sestina? If so, what are they? If not, what is being played with by using this convention?

CONNECTION TO ANOTHER SELECTION

1. Describe and compare the strategy used to create meaning in "All-American Sestina" with that used by E. E. Cummings in "next to of course god america i" (p. 897).

Epigram

An *epigram* is a brief, pointed, and witty poem. Although most rhyme and often are written in couplets, epigrams take no prescribed form. Instead, they are typically polished bits of compressed irony, satire, or paradox. Here is an epigram that defines itself.

SAMUEL TAYLOR COLERIDGE (1772–1834)
What Is an Epigram?

1802

What is an epigram? A dwarfish whole;
Its body brevity, and wit its soul.

These additional examples by A. R. Ammons, David McCord, and Paul Laurence Dunbar satisfy Coleridge's definition.

A. R. AMMONS (B. 1926)
Coward

1975

Bravery runs in my family.

DAVID McCORD (1897–1997)
Epitaph on a Waiter

By and by
God caught his eye.

PAUL LAURENCE DUNBAR (1872–1906)
Theology

1896

There is a heaven, for ever, day by day,
The upward longing of my soul doth tell
    me so.
There is a hell, I'm quite as sure; for pray,
If there were not, where would my
        neighbors go?

Courtesy of the Ohio Historical Society.

CONSIDERATIONS FOR CRITICAL THINKING AND WRITING

1. **FIRST RESPONSE.** In what sense is each of these epigrams, as Coleridge puts it, a "dwarfish whole"?

2. Explain which of these epigrams, in addition to being witty, makes a serious point.

3. **CREATIVE RESPONSE.** Try writing a few epigrams that say something memorable about whatever you choose to focus on.

Limerick

The *limerick* is always light and humorous. Its usual form consists of five predominantly anapestic lines rhyming *aabba;* lines 1, 2, and 5 contain three feet, while lines 3 and 4 contain two. Limericks have delighted everyone from schoolchildren to sophisticated adults, and they range in subject matter from the simply innocent and silly to the satiric or obscene. The sexual humor helps to explain why so many limericks are written anonymously. Here is one that is anonymous but more concerned with physics than physiology.

ANONYMOUS

There was a young lady named Bright

There was a young lady named Bright,
Who traveled much faster than light,
    She started one day
    In a relative way,
And returned on the previous night.

This next one is a particularly clever definition of a limerick.

LAURENCE PERRINE (1915–1995)

The limerick's never averse   *1982*

The limerick's never averse
To expressing itself in a terse
    Economical style,
    And yet, all the while,
The limerick's *always* a verse.

CONSIDERATIONS FOR CRITICAL THINKING AND WRITING

1. **FIRST RESPONSE.** How does this limerick differ from others you know? How is it similar?

2. Scan Perrine's limerick. How do the lines measure up to the traditional fixed metrical pattern?

3. **CREATIVE RESPONSE.** Try writing a limerick. Use the following basic pattern.

```
 ˘ ˘ ´   ˘ ˘ ´   ˘ ˘ ´
 ˘ ˘ ´      ˘ ˘ ´      ˘ ˘ ´
           ˘ ˘ ´      ˘ ˘ ´
           ˘ ˘ ´      ˘ ˘ ´
 ˘ ˘ ´      ˘ ˘ ´      ˘ ˘ ´
```

You might begin with a friend's name or the name of your school or town. Your instructor is, of course, fair game, too, provided your tact matches your wit.

The next selection is a real tongue twister.

KEITH CASTO

She Don't Bop

1987

A nervous young woman named Trudy
Was at odds with a horn player, Rudy.
His horn so annoyed her
The neighbors would loiter
To watch Rudy toot Trudy fruity.

Haiku

Another brief fixed poetic form, borrowed from the Japanese, is the **haiku.** A haiku is usually described as consisting of seventeen syllables organized into three unrhymed lines of five, seven, and five syllables. Owing to language difference, however, English translations of haiku are often only approximated, because a Japanese haiku exists in time (Japanese syllables have duration). The number of syllables in our sense is not as significant as the duration in Japanese. These poems typically present an intense emotion or vivid image of nature, which, in the Japanese, are also designed to lead to a spiritual insight.

MATSUO BASHŌ (1644–1694)

Under cherry trees

date unknown

Under cherry trees
Soup, the salad, fish and all . . .
Seasoned with petals.

CAROLYN KIZER (B. 1925)

After Bashō   *1984*

Tentatively, you
slip onstage this evening,
pallid, famous moon.

SONIA SANCHEZ (B. 1935)

c'mon man hold me   *1998*

c'mon man hold me
touch me before time love me
from behind your eyes.

CONSIDERATIONS FOR CRITICAL THINKING AND WRITING

1. **FIRST RESPONSE.** What different emotions do these three haiku evoke?
2. What differences and similarities are there between the effects of a haiku and those of an epigram?
3. **CREATIVE RESPONSE.** Compose a haiku. Try to make it as allusive and suggestive as possible.

Elegy

An elegy in classical Greek and Roman literature was written in alternating hexameter and pentameter lines. Since the seventeenth century, however, the term *elegy* has been used to describe a lyric poem written to commemorate someone who is dead. The word is also used to refer to a serious meditative poem produced to express the speaker's melancholy thoughts. Elegies no longer conform to a fixed pattern of lines and stanzas, but their characteristic subject is related to death and their tone is mournfully contemplative.

THEODORE ROETHKE (1908–1963)

Elegy for Jane   *1953*
My Student, Thrown by a Horse

I remember the neckcurls, limp and damp as tendrils;
And her quick look, a sidelong pickerel smile;
And how, once startled into talk, the light syllables leaped for her,
And she balanced in the delight of her thought,

A wren, happy, tail into the wind,   5
Her song trembling the twigs and small branches.
The shade sang with her;
The leaves, their whispers turned to kissing;
And the mold sang in the bleached valleys under the rose.

Oh, when she was sad, she cast herself down into such a pure depth,   10
Even a father could not find her:
Scraping her cheek against straw;
Stirring the clearest water.

My sparrow, you are not here,
Waiting like a fern, making a spiny shadow.   15
The sides of wet stones cannot console me,
Nor the moss, wound with the last light.

If only I could nudge you from this sleep,
My maimed darling, my skittery pigeon.
Over this damp grave I speak the words of my love: 20
I, with no rights in this matter,
Neither father nor lover.

CONSIDERATIONS FOR CRITICAL THINKING AND WRITING

1. **FIRST RESPONSE.** Does this elegy use any kind of formal pattern for its structure? What holds it together?

2. List the images that compare Jane to nature. How is she depicted by these images?

3. Describe the shift in tone that begins in line 14. How do the speaker's feelings change in lines 14–22?

4. What is the significance of Jane's having been the speaker's student? How does that affect your reading of lines 21–22?

CONNECTION TO ANOTHER SELECTION

1. Compare "Elegy for Jane" with A. E. Housman's "To an Athlete Dying Young" (p. 1331). How does each poem avoid sentimentality in its description of a young person who had died?

ANDREW HUDGINS (B. 1951)

Elegy for My Father, Who Is Not Dead   1991

One day I'll lift the telephone
and be told my father's dead. He's ready.
In the sureness of his faith, he talks
about the world beyond this world
as though his reservations have   5

been made. I think he wants to go,
a little bit — a new desire
to travel building up, an itch
to see fresh worlds. Or older ones.
He thinks that when I follow him   10
he'll wrap me in his arms and laugh,
the way he did when I arrived
on earth. I do not think he's right.
He's ready. I am not. I can't
just say good-bye as cheerfully   15
as if he were embarking on a trip
to make my later trip go well.
I see myself on deck, convinced
his ship's gone down, while he's convinced
I'll see him standing on the dock   20
and waving, shouting, Welcome back.

CONSIDERATIONS FOR CRITICAL THINKING AND WRITING

1. **FIRST RESPONSE.** Why does this speaker elegize his father if the father "is not dead"?

2. How does the speaker's view of immortality differ from his father's?

3. Explain why you think this is an optimistic or a pessimistic poem — or explain why these two categories fail to describe the poem.

4. In what sense can this poem be regarded as an elegy?

CONNECTION TO ANOTHER SELECTION

1. Write an essay comparing attitudes toward death in this poem and in Dylan Thomas's "Do Not Go Gentle into That Good Night" (p. 981). Both speakers invoke their fathers, nearer to death than they are; what impact does this invocation have?

BRENDAN GALVIN (B. 1938)

An Evel Knievel° Elegy   *2008*

We have all felt our parachutes
malfunctioning at a job interview
or cocktail party, with bystanders
reading the freefall on our faces,
and some of us have imagined   5

Evel Knievel (1938–2007): American motorcycle stunt performer whose daredevil jumps over lines of vehicles, canyons, and rivers were nationally televised in the 1960s and 70s.

how it must have felt for you
above the Snake River Canyon
or the fountains outside Caesar's
Palace, though a mental bungee
reversed our flops before we were   10
converted to sacks of poker chips and spent
a month or more in a coma. You were
our star-spangled Icarus,° Evel,
while we dressed off the rack
for working lives among the common   15
asps and vipers, never jumping
the rattlers in what you and
the networks considered a sport.
Stunts, Evel. We loved their heights
and distances from our gray quotidian   20
so much we bought the kids three
hundred million dollars' worth
of your wheels and getups. You were
our airborne Elvis, and rode
your rocket-powered bike through fire.   25
Which we admired, though some,
annealing or annulled, knew that
they stand in fire all their lives,
and turned away, and didn't applaud,
and would not suffer the loss   30
of your departure.

Icarus: In Greek mythology, a character who fell to the earth and died after refusing to heed his father's advice about not flying too close to the sun on manufactured wings of wax and feathers that melted from the heat.

CONSIDERATIONS FOR CRITICAL THINKING AND WRITING

1. **FIRST RESPONSE.** To what extent is this poem a meditation upon popular culture as well as an elegy for Evel Knievel?

2. Discuss Galvin's use of metaphor to characterize Knievel. Choose three metaphors that seem especially vivid to you and explain why.

3. Discuss the thematic significance of lines 26 to 31. How would you read the poem differently if it ended in the middle of line 26?

Ode

An **ode** is characterized by a serious topic and formal tone, but no pre-scribed formal pattern describes all odes. In some odes the pattern of each stanza is repeated throughout, while in others each stanza introduces a new pattern. Odes are lengthy lyrics that often include lofty emotions conveyed by a dignified style. Typical topics include truth, art, freedom, justice, and the meaning of life. Frequently such lyrics tend to be more public than private, and their speakers often use apostrophe.

PERCY BYSSHE SHELLEY (1792–1822)

Ode to the West Wind   *1820*

I

O wild West Wind, thou breath of Autumn's being,
Thou, from whose unseen presence the leaves dead
Are driven, like ghosts from an enchanter fleeing,

Yellow, and black, and pale, and hectic red,
Pestilence-stricken multitudes: O thou,   5
Who chariotest to their dark wintry bed

The wingèd seeds, where they lie cold and low,
Each like a corpse within its grave, until
Thine azure sister of the Spring shall blow

Her clarion o'er the dreaming earth, and fill   10
(Driving sweet buds like flocks to feed in air)
With living hues and odors plain and hill:

Wild Spirit, which art moving everywhere;
Destroyer and preserver; hear, oh, hear!

II

Thou on whose stream, mid the steep sky's commotion,   15
Loose clouds like earth's decaying leaves are shed,
Shook from the tangled boughs of Heaven and Ocean,

Angels° of rain and lightning: there are spread   *messengers*
On the blue surface of thine airy surge,
Like the bright hair uplifted from the head   20

Of some fierce Maenad,° even from the dim verge
Of the horizon to the zenith's height,
The locks of the approaching storm. Thou dirge

Of the dying year, to which this closing night
Will be the dome of a vast sepulcher,   25
Vaulted with all thy congregated might

Of vapors, from whose solid atmosphere
Black rain, and fire, and hail will burst: oh, hear!

III

Thou who didst waken from his summer dreams
The blue Mediterranean, where he lay,   30
Lulled by the coil of his crystálline streams,

---

21 *Maenad:* In Greek mythology, a frenzied worshipper of Dionysus, god of wine and fertility.

Beside a pumice isle in Baiae's bay,°
And saw in sleep old palaces and towers
Quivering within the wave's intenser day,

All overgrown with azure moss and flowers   35
So sweet, the sense faints picturing them! Thou
For whose path the Atlantic's level powers

Cleave themselves into chasms, while far below
The sea-blooms and the oozy woods which wear
The sapless foliage of the ocean, know   40

Thy voice, and suddenly grow gray with fear,
And tremble and despoil themselves: oh, hear!

IV

If I were a dead leaf thou mightest bear;
If I were a swift cloud to fly with thee;
A wave to pant beneath thy power, and share   45

The impulse of thy strength, only less free
Than thou, O uncontrollable! If even
I were as in my boyhood, and could be

The comrade by thy wanderings over Heaven,
As then, when to outstrip thy skyey speed   50
Scarce seemed a vision; I would ne'er have striven

As thus with thee in prayer in my sore need.
Oh, lift me as a wave, a leaf, a cloud!
I fall upon the thorns of life! I bleed!

A heavy weight of hours has chained and bowed   55
One too like thee: tameless, and swift, and proud.

V

Make me thy lyre,° even as the forest is:
What if my leaves are falling like its own!
The tumult of thy mighty harmonies

Will take from both a deep, autumnal tone,   60
Sweet though in sadness. Be thou, Spirit fierce,
My spirit! Be thou me, impetuous one!

Drive my dead thoughts over the universe
Like withered leaves to quicken a new birth!
And, by the incantation of this verse,   65

---

32 *Baiae's bay:* A bay in the Mediterranean Sea.   57 *Make me thy lyre:* Sound is produced
on an Aeolian lyre, or wind harp, by wind blowing across its strings.

Scatter, as from an unextinguished hearth
Ashes and sparks, my words among mankind!
Be through my lips to unawakened earth

The trumpet of a prophecy! O Wind,
If Winter comes, can Spring be far behind?   70

CONSIDERATIONS FOR CRITICAL THINKING AND WRITING

1. **FIRST RESPONSE.** Write a summary of each of this ode's five sections.
2. What is the speaker's situation? What is his "sore need" (line 52)? What does the speaker ask of the wind in lines 57–70?
3. What does the wind signify in this ode? How is it used symbolically?
4. Determine the meter and rhyme of the first five stanzas. How do these elements contribute to the ode's movement? Is this pattern continued in the other four sections?

BARON WORMSER (B. 1948)

Labor   2008

I spent a couple of years during my undestined
Twenties on a north woods acreage
That grew, as the locals poetically phrased it,
"Stones and rocks." I loved it.

No real insulation in the old farmhouse,   5
Which meant ten cords of hardwood,
Which meant a muscled mantra of cutting,
Yarding, splitting, stacking and burning.

I was the maul coming down *kerchunk*
On the round of maple; I was the hellacious   10
Screeching saw; I was the fire.
I was fiber and grew imperceptibly.

I lost interest in everything except for trees.
Career, ambition and politics bored me.
I loved putting on my steel-toe, lace-up   15
Work boots in the morning. I loved the feel

Of my feet on grass slick with dew or frost
Or ice-skimmed mud or crisp snow crust.
I loved the moment after I felled a tree
When it was still again and I felt the awe   20

Of what I had done and awe for the tree that had
Stretched toward the sky for silent decades.
On Saturday night the regulars who had worked
In the woods forever mocked me as I limped into

The bar out on the state highway. "Workin' hard   25
There, sonny, or more like hardly workin'?"
I cradled my bottle between stiff raw hands,
Felt a pinching tension in the small of my back,

Inhaled ripe sweat, damp flannel,
Cheap whiskey then nodded — a happy fool.   30
They grinned back. Through their proper
Scorn I could feel it. They loved it too.

for Hayden Carruth

CONSIDERATIONS FOR CRITICAL THINKING AND WRITING

1. **FIRST RESPONSE.** To what extent does the poem conform to the definitions of an ode?

2. What is it about tree cutting that so enthralls the speaker?

3. Do you think this poem is sentimental? Why or why not?

4. **CREATIVE RESPONSE.** Write an ode concerning an activity that you know well and can express strong feelings about, using vivid images and metaphors.

CONNECTION TO ANOTHER SELECTION

1. Compare the themes in "Labor" and in Mark Turpin's "Sledgehammer's Song" (p. 964).

Parody

A ***parody*** is a humorous imitation of another, usually serious, work. It can take any fixed or open form because parodists imitate the tone, language, and shape of the original. While a parody may be teasingly close to a work's style, it typically deflates the subject matter to make the original seem absurd. Parody can be used as a kind of literary criticism to expose the defects in a work, but it is also very often an affectionate acknowledgment that a well-known work has become both institutionalized in our culture and fair game for some fun. Read Robert Frost's "The Road Not Taken" (p. 1095) and then study this parody.

BLANCHE FARLEY (B. 1937)

The Lover Not Taken   1984

Committed to one, she wanted both
And, mulling it over, long she stood,
Alone on the road, loath
To leave, wanting to hide in the undergrowth.
This new guy, smooth as a yellow wood   5

Really turned her on. She liked his hair,
His smile. But the other, Jack, had a claim
On her already and she had to admit, he did wear
Well. In fact, to be perfectly fair,
He understood her. His long, lithe frame   10

Beside hers in the evening tenderly lay.
Still, if this blond guy dropped by someday,
Couldn't way just lead on to way?
No. For if way led on and Jack
Found out, she doubted if he would ever come back.   15

Oh, she turned with a sigh.
Somewhere ages and ages hence,
She might be telling this. "And I —"
She would say, "stood faithfully by."
But by then who would know the difference?   20

With that in mind, she took the fast way home,
The road by the pond, and phoned the blond.

CONSIDERATIONS FOR CRITICAL THINKING AND WRITING

1. **FIRST RESPONSE.** To what degree does this poem duplicate Frost's style? How does it differ?

2. Does this parody seem successful to you? Explain what you think makes a successful parody.

3. **CREATIVE RESPONSE.** Choose a poet whose work you know reasonably well or would like to know better and determine what is characteristic about his or her style. Then choose a poem to parody. It's probably best to attempt a short poem or a section of a long work. If you have difficulty selecting an author, you might consider Herrick, Blake, Keats, Dickinson, Whitman, Hughes, or Frost, as a number of their works are included in this book.

Picture Poem

By arranging lines into particular shapes, poets can sometimes organize typography into *picture poems* of what they describe. Words have been arranged into all kinds of shapes, from apples to light bulbs. Notice how the shape of this next poem (on the following page) embodies its meaning.

MICHAEL McFEE (B. 1954)

In Medias Res° 1985

His waist
like the plot
thickens, wedding
pants now breathtaking,
belt no longer the cinch   5
it once was, belly's cambium
expanding to match each birthday,
his body a wad of anonymous tissue
swung in the same centrifuge of years
that separates a house from its foundation,   10
undermining sidewalks grim with joggers
and loose-filled graves and families
and stars collapsing on themselves,
no preservation society capable
of plugging entropy's dike,   15
under his zipper's sneer
a belly hibernation-
soft, ready for
the kill.

In Medias Res: A Latin term for a story that begins "in the middle of things."

CONSIDERATIONS FOR CRITICAL THINKING AND WRITING

1. **FIRST RESPONSE.** Explain how the title is related to this poem's shape and meaning.

2. Identify the puns. How do they work in the poem?

3. What is "cambium" (line 6)? Why is the phrase "belly's cambium" especially appropriate?

4. What is the tone of this poem? Is it consistent throughout?

Perspective

ELAINE MITCHELL (B. 1924)

Form 1994

Is it a corset
or primal wave?
Don't try to force it.

Even endorse it
to shape and deceive.   5
Ouch, too tight a corset.

Take it off. No remorse. It
's an ace up your sleeve.
No need to force it.

Can you make a horse knit?   10
Who would believe?
Consider. Of course, it

might be a resource. Wit,
your grateful slave.
Form. Sometimes you force it,   15

sometimes divorce it
to make it behave.
So don't try to force it.
Respect a good corset.

CONSIDERATIONS FOR CRITICAL THINKING AND WRITING

1. **FIRST RESPONSE.** What is the speaker's attitude toward form?

2. Explain why you think the form of this poem does or does not conform to the speaker's advice.

3. Why is the metaphor of a corset an especially apt image for this poem?

Web Research the poets in this chapter at bedfordstmartins.com/meyerlit.

30

Open Form

By permission of David Geier and New Directions.

I believe every space and comma is a living part of the poem and has its function, just as every muscle and pore of the body has its function. And the way the lines are broken is a functioning part essential to the poem's life.
— DENISE LEVERTOV

Many poems, especially those written in the past century, are composed of lines that cannot be scanned for a fixed or predominant meter. Moreover, very often these poems do not rhyme. Known as *free verse* (from the French, *vers libre*), such lines can derive their rhythmic qualities from the repetition of words, phrases, or grammatical structures; the arrangement of words on the printed page; or some other means. In recent years the term *open form* has been used in place of *free verse* to avoid the erroneous suggestion that this kind of poetry lacks all discipline and shape.

Although the following two poems do not use measurable meters, they do have rhythm.

E. E. CUMMINGS (1894–1962)
in Just-

1923

in Just-
spring   when the world is mud-
luscious the little
lame balloonman

whistles   far   and wee   5

and eddieandbill come
running from marbles and
piracies and it's
spring

when the world is puddle-wonderful   10

the queer
old balloonman whistles
far   and   wee
and bettyandisbel come dancing

from hop-scotch and jump-rope and   15

it's
spring
and

    the

        goat-footed   20

balloonMan   whistles
far
and
wee

CONSIDERATIONS FOR CRITICAL THINKING AND WRITING

1. **FIRST RESPONSE.** What is the effect of this poem's arrangement of words and use of space on the page? How would the effect differ if the text were written out in prose?

2. What is the effect of Cummings's combining the names "eddieandbill" (line 6) and "bettyandisbel" (line 14)?

3. The allusion in line 20 refers to Pan, a Greek god associated with nature. How does this allusion add to the meaning of the poem?

WALT WHITMAN (1819–1892)

From "I Sing the Body Electric"   *1855*

O my body! I dare not desert the likes of you in other men and women,
    nor the likes of the parts of you,
I believe the likes of you are to stand or fall with the likes of the soul, (and
    that they are the soul,)
I believe the likes of you shall stand or fall with my poems, and that they
    are my poems.
Man's, woman's, child's, youth's, wife's, husband's, mother's, father's,
    young man's, young woman's poems.

Head, neck, hair, ears, drop and tympan of the
    ears.
Eyes, eye-fringes, iris of the eye, eyebrows, and
    the waking or sleeping of the lids,
Mouth, tongue, lips, teeth, roof of the mouth,
    jaws, and the jaw-hinges,
Nose, nostrils of the nose, and the partition,
Cheeks, temples, forehead, chin, throat, back
    of the neck, neck-slue,
Strong shoulders, manly beard, scapula, hind-
    shoulders, and the ample
    side-round of the chest,
Upper-arm, armpit, elbow-socket, lower-arm,
    arm-sinews, arm-bones,
Wrist and wrist-joints, hand, palm, knuckles,
    thumb, forefinger, finger-joints, finger-
    nails,

Courtesy of the Bayley-Whitman Collection
of Ohio Wesleyan University of Delaware,
Ohio.

Broad breast-front, curling hair of the breast,
    breast-bone, breast-side,
Ribs, belly, backbone, joints of the backbone,
Hips, hip-sockets, hip-strength, inward and outward round, man-balls,
    man-root,   15
Strong set of thighs, well carrying the trunk above,
Leg-fibers, knee, knee-pan, upper-leg, under-leg,
Ankles, instep, foot-ball, toes, toe-joints, the heel;
All attitudes, all the shapeliness, all the belongings of my or your body or
    of any one's body, male or female,
The lung-sponges, the stomach-sac, the bowels sweet and clean,   20
The brain in its folds inside the skull-frame,
Sympathies, heart-valves, palate-valves, sexuality, maternity,
Womanhood, and all that is a woman, and the man that comes from
    woman,
The womb, the teats, nipples, breast-milk, tears, laughter, weeping, love-
    looks, love-perturbations and risings,
The voice, articulation, language, whispering, shouting aloud,   25
Food, drink, pulse, digestion, sweat, sleep, walking, swimming,
Poise on the hips, leaping, reclining, embracing, arm-curving and
    tightening,
The continual changes of the flex of the mouth, and around the eyes,
The skin, the sunburnt shade, freckles, hair,
The curious sympathy one feels when feeling with the hand the naked
    meat of the body,   30
The circling rivers the breath, and breathing it in and out,
The beauty of the waist, and thence of the hips, and thence downward
    toward the knees,
The thin red jellies within you or within me, the bones and the marrow
    in the bones,
The exquisite realization of health;
O I say these are not the parts and poems of the body only, but of the soul, 35
O I say now these are the soul!

1. **FIRST RESPONSE.** What informs this speaker's attitude toward the human body?

2. Read the poem aloud. Is it simply a tedious enumeration of body parts, or do the lines achieve some kind of rhythmic cadence?

Perspective

WALT WHITMAN (1819–1892)

On Rhyme and Meter   1855

The poetic quality is not marshaled in rhyme or uniformity or abstract addresses to things nor in melancholy complaints or good precepts, but is the life of these and much else and is in the soul. The profit of rhyme is that it drops seeds of a sweeter and more luxuriant rhyme, and of uniformity that it conveys itself into its own roots in the ground out of sight. The rhyme and uniformity of perfect poems show the free growth of metrical laws and bud from them as unerringly and loosely as lilacs or roses on a bush, and take shapes as compact as the shapes of chestnuts and oranges and melons and pears, and shed the perfume impalpable to form. The fluency and ornaments of the finest poems or music or orations or recitations are not independent but dependent. All beauty comes from beautiful blood and a beautiful brain. If the greatnesses are in conjunction in a man or woman it is enough . . . the fact will prevail through the universe . . . but the gaggery and gilt of a million years will not prevail. Who troubles himself about his ornaments or fluency is lost.

From the preface to the 1855 edition of Leaves of Grass

Considerations for Critical Thinking and Writing

1. According to Whitman, what determines the shape of a poem?

2. Why does Whitman prefer open forms over fixed forms such as the sonnet?

3. Is Whitman's poetry devoid of any structure or shape? Choose one of his poems (listed in the index) to illustrate your answer.

A SAMPLE STUDENT RESPONSE

Avery Bloom

Professor Rios

English 212

October 7, 2009

The Power of Walt Whitman's Open Form Poem

"I Sing the Body Electric"

Walt Whitman's "I Sing the Body Electric" is an ode to the human body. The poem is open form, without rhymes or consistent meter, and instead relies almost entirely on the use of language and the structure of lists to affect the reader. The result is a thorough inventory of parts of the body that illustrates the beauty of the human form and its intimate connection to the soul.

At times, Whitman lists the parts of the body with almost complete objectivity, making it difficult to understand the poem's purpose. The poem initially appears to do little more than recite the names of body parts: "Head, neck, hair, ears, drop and tympan of the ears" (line 5); "Mouth, tongue, lips, teeth, roof of the mouth, jaws, and the jaw-hinges" (7). There are no end rhymes, but the exhaustive and detailed list of body parts—from the brain to "the thin red jellies . . . , the bones and the marrow in the bones" (33)— offers language that has a certain rhythm. The language and rhythm of the list creates a visual image full of energy and momentum that builds, emphasizing the body's functions and movements. As Michael Meyer writes, open form poems "rely on an intense use of language to establish rhythms and relations between meaning and form. [They] use the arrangement of words and phrases . . . to create unique forms" (page 1005). No doubt Whitman chose the open form for this work—relying on his "intense use of language" and the rhythm of the list—because it allowed a basic structure that held together but did not restrain, and a full freedom and range of motion to create a poem that is alive with movement and electricity. . . .

Bloom 4

Works Cited

Meyer, Michael, ed. *The Bedford Introduction to Literature.* 9th ed. Boston:
    Bedford/St. Martin's, 2011. 1005. Print.

Whitman, Walt. "From 'I Sing the Body Electric.'" *The Bedford Introduction to
    literature.* Ed. Michael Meyer. 9th ed. Boston: Bedford/St. Martin's,
    2011. 1001–02. Print.

Open form poetry is sometimes regarded as formless because it is un-like the strict fixed forms of a sonnet, villanelle, or sestina. But even though open form poems may not employ traditional meters and rhymes, they still rely on an intense use of language to establish rhythms and relations between meaning and form. Open form poems use the arrangement of words and phrases on the printed page, pauses, line lengths, and other means to create unique forms that express their particular meaning and tone.

Cummings's "in Just-" and the excerpt from Whitman's "I Sing the Body Electric" demonstrate how the white space on a page and rhythmic cadences can be aligned with meaning, but there is one kind of open form poetry that doesn't even look like poetry on a page. A ***prose poem*** is printed as prose and represents, perhaps, the most clear opposite of fixed forms. Here is a brief example.

ROBERT HASS (B. 1941)

A Story about the Body   *1989*

The young composer, working that summer at an artists' colony, had watched her for a week. She was Japanese, a painter, almost sixty, and he thought he was in love with her. He loved her work, and her work was like the way she moved her body, used her hands, looked at him directly when she made amused and considered answers to his questions. One night, walking back from a concert, they came to her door and she turned to him and said, "I think you would like to have me. I would like that too, but I must tell you that I have had a double mastectomy," and when he didn't understand, "I've lost both my breasts." The radiance that he had carried around in his belly and chest cavity — like music — withered very quickly, and he made himself look at her when he said, "I'm sorry. I don't think I could." He walked back to his own cabin through the pines, and in the morning he found a small blue bowl on the porch outside his door. It looked to be full of rose petals, but he found when he picked it up that the rose petals were on top; the rest of the bowl — she must have swept them from the corners of her studio — was full of dead bees.

CONSIDERATIONS FOR CRITICAL THINKING AND WRITING

1. **FIRST RESPONSE.** Why this title? What other potential titles can you come up with that evoke your reading of the poem?
2. What impression about the "young composer" do you derive from the poem?
3. Why are bees very appropriate in the final line rather than, for example, moths?

CONNECTIONS TO OTHER SELECTIONS

1. Discuss the treatments of love in this poem and in John Frederick Nims's "Love Poem" (p. 775).
2. Read T. E. Hulme's "On the Differences between Poetry and Prose" (p. 863) and write an essay on what you think Hulme would have to say about "A Story about the Body."

RICHARD HAGUE (B. 1947)

Directions for Resisting the SAT   *1996*

Do not believe in October or May
or in any Saturday morning with pencils.
Do not observe the rules of gravity,
commas, history.
Lie about numbers.   5
Blame your successes,
every one of them,
on rotten luck.
Resign all clubs and committees.
Go down with the ship — any ship.   10
Speak nothing like English.
Desire to live whole,
like an oyster or snail,
and follow no directions.
Listen to no one.   15

Make your marks on everything.

CONSIDERATIONS FOR CRITICAL THINKING AND WRITING

1. **FIRST RESPONSE.** What is the speaker's subversive message? What do you think of the advice offered?

2. What kinds of assumptions do you suppose Hague makes about readers' attitudes toward the SAT? To what extent do you share those attitudes?

3. Discuss Hague's use of spacing and line breaks. What is the effect of the space between lines 15 and 16?

CONNECTION TO ANOTHER SELECTION

1. Compare the treatment of tests in this poem and in Linda Pastan's "Pass / Fail" (p. 847).

Much of the poetry published today is written in open form; however, many poets continue to take pleasure in the requirements imposed by fixed forms. Some write both fixed form and open form poetry. Each kind offers rewards to careful readers as well. Here are several more open form poems that establish their own unique patterns.

GALWAY KINNELL (B. 1927)

After Making Love We Hear Footsteps   *1980*

For I can snore like a bullhorn
or play loud music
or sit up talking with any reasonably sober Irishman
and Fergus will only sink deeper
into his dreamless sleep, which goes by all in one flash,   5
but let there be that heavy breathing
or a stifled come-cry anywhere in the house
and he will wrench himself awake
and make for it on the run — as now, we lie together,
after making love, quiet, touching along the length of our bodies,   10
familiar touch of the long-married,
and he appears — in his baseball pajamas, it happens,
the neck opening so small
he has to screw them on, which one day may make him wonder
about the mental capacity of baseball players —   15
and says, "Are you loving and snuggling? May I join?"
He flops down between us and hugs us and snuggles himself to sleep,
his face gleaming with satisfaction at being this very child.

In the half darkness we look at each other
and smile   20
and touch arms across his little, startlingly muscled body —
this one whom habit of memory propels to the ground of his making,
sleeper only the mortal sounds can sing awake,
this blessing love gives again into our arms.

CONSIDERATIONS FOR CRITICAL THINKING AND WRITING

1. **FIRST RESPONSE.** Explore Kinnell's line endings. Why does he break the lines where he does?

2. How does the speaker's language reveal his character?

3. Describe the shift in tone between lines 18 and 19 with the shift in focus from child to adults. How does the use of space here emphasize this shift?

4. Do you think this poem is sentimental? Explain why or why not.

CONNECTION TO ANOTHER SELECTION

1. Discuss how this poem helps to bring into focus the sense of loss Robert Frost evokes in "Home Burial" (p. 1102).

KELLY CHERRY (B. 1940)

Alzheimer's   1990

He stands at the door, a crazy old man
Back from the hospital, his mind rattling
Like the suitcase, swinging from his hand,
That contains shaving cream, a piggy bank,
A book he sometimes pretends to read,   5
His clothes. On the brick wall beside him
Roses and columbine slug it out for space, claw the mortar.
The sun is shining, as it does late in the afternoon
In England, after rain.
Sun hardens the house, reifies it,   10
Strikes the iron grillwork like a smithy
And sparks fly off, burning in the bushes —
The rosebushes —
While the white wood trim defines solidity in space.
This is his house. He remembers it as his,   15
Remembers the walkway he built between the front room
And the garage, the rhododendron he planted in back,
The car he used to drive. He remembers himself,
A younger man, in a tweed hat, a man who loved
Music. There is no time for that now. No time for music,   20
The peculiar screeching of strings, the luxurious
Fiddling with emotion.
Other things have become more urgent.
Other matters are now of greater import, have more
Consequence, must be attended to. The first   25
Thing he must do, now that he is home, is decide who
This woman is, this old, white-haired woman
Standing here in the doorway,
Welcoming him in.

Considerations for Critical Thinking and Writing

1. **FIRST RESPONSE.** Why is it impossible to dismiss the character in this poem as merely "a crazy old man" (line 1)?

2. Discuss the effect of the line breaks in lines 1–6 of the poem's first complete sentence. How do the line breaks contribute to the meaning of these lines?

3. What do the images in lines 6–20 indicate about the nature of the man's memory?

4. Why is the final image of the "white-haired woman" especially effective? How does the final line serve as the poem's emotional climax?

WILLIAM CARLOS WILLIAMS (1883–1963)

The Red Wheelbarrow   *1923*

so much depends
upon

a red wheel
barrow

glazed with rain
water

beside the white
chickens.

Considerations for Critical Thinking and Writing

1. **FIRST RESPONSE.** What "depends upon" the things mentioned in the poem? What is the effect of these images? Do they have a particular meaning?

2. Do these lines have any kind of rhythm?

3. How does this poem resemble a haiku? How is it different?

NATASHA TRETHEWEY (B. 1966)

On Captivity   *2007*

Being all Stripped as Naked as We were Born, and endeavoring to hide our Nakedness,
these Cannaballs took [our] Books, and tearing out the Leaves would give each of us a
Leaf to cover us . . .

                                            — Jonathan Dickinson, 1699

At the hands now
        of their captors, those
                they've named *savages,*
        do they say the word itself
savagely — hissing   5

that first letter,
            the serpent's image,
                        releasing
            thought into speech?
For them now,   10

everything is flesh
            as if their thoughts, made
                        suddenly corporeal,
            reveal even more
their nakedness —   15

the shame of it:
            their bodies rendered
                        plain as the natives' —
            homely and pale,
their ordinary sex,   20

the secret illicit hairs
            that do not (cannot)
                        cover enough.
            This is how they are brought,
naked as newborns,   25

to knowledge. Adam and Eve
            in the New World,
                        they have only the Bible
            to cover them. Think of it:
a woman holding before her   30

the torn leaves of *Genesis,*
            and a man covering himself
                        with the Good Book's
            frontispiece — his own name
inscribed on the page.   35

CONSIDERATIONS FOR CRITICAL THINKING AND WRITING

1. **FIRST RESPONSE.** Trethewey has written about the sources of her epigraph:
    "Because the conquerors made use of the written word to claim land
    [in North America] inhabited by native people, I found the detail of settlers
    forced to cover themselves with torn pages from books a compelling irony"
    (*The Best American Poetry 2008,* p. 182). How does this comment contribute to
    the central irony in the poem?

2. Discuss Trethewey's use of alliteration in lines 1 to 9.

3. In what sense are the captors "brought, / naked as newborns, / to knowledge"
    (lines 24–26)?

GARY GILDNER (B. 1938)

First Practice   1984

After the doctor checked to see
we weren't ruptured,
the man with the short cigar took us
under the grade school,
where we went in case of attack   5
or storm, and said
he was Clifford Hill, he was
a man who believed dogs
ate dogs, he had once killed
for his country, and if   10
there were any girls present
for them to leave now.
                        No one
left. OK, he said, he said I take
that to mean you are hungry   15
men who hate to lose as much
as I do. OK. Then
he made two lines of us
facing each other,
and across the way, he said,   20
is the man you hate most
in the world,
and if we are to win
that title I want to see how.
But I don't want to see   25
any marks when you're dressed,
he said. He said, *Now*.

CONSIDERATIONS FOR CRITICAL THINKING AND WRITING

1. **FIRST RESPONSE.** Do you recognize this coach? How does he compare with sports coaches you have known?

2. Comment on the significance of Clifford Hill's name.

3. Locate examples of irony in the poem and explain how they contribute to the theme.

4. Discuss the effect of line spacing in line 13.

CONNECTION TO ANOTHER SELECTION

1. Write an essay comparing the coach in this poem and the teacher in Judy Page Heitzman's "The Schoolroom on the Second Floor of the Knitting Mill" (p. 878).

MARILYN NELSON WANIEK (B. 1946)
Emily Dickinson's Defunct 1978

She used to
pack poems
in her hip pocket.
Under all the
gray old lady 5
clothes she was
dressed for action.
She had hair,
imagine,
in certain places, and 10
believe me
she smelled human
on a hot summer day.
Stalking snakes
or counting 15
the thousand motes
in sunlight
she walked just
like an Indian.
She was New England's 20
favorite daughter,
she could pray
like the devil.
She was a
two-fisted woman, 25
this babe.
All the flies
just stood around
and buzzed
when she died. 30

CONSIDERATIONS FOR CRITICAL THINKING AND WRITING

1. FIRST RESPONSE. How does the speaker characterize Dickinson? Explain why this characterization is different from the popular view of Dickinson.

2. How does the diction of the poem serve to characterize the speaker?

3. Discuss the function of the poem's title.

CONNECTIONS TO OTHER SELECTIONS

1. Waniek alludes to at least two other poems in "Emily Dickinson's Defunct." The title refers to E. E. Cummings's "Buffalo Bill 's" (p. 1323), and the final lines (27–30) refer to Dickinson's "I heard a Fly buzz — when I died —" (p. 1065). Read those poems and write an essay discussing how they affect your reading of Waniek's poem.

JEFFREY HARRISON   (B. 1957)

The Names of Things   *2006*

Just after breakfast and still
waking up, I take the path cut
through the meadow, my mind caught
in some rudimentary stage,
the stems of timothy bending   5
inward with the weight of a single
drop of condensed fog clinging
to each of their fuzzy heads
that brush wetly against my jeans.
Out on a rise, the lupines stand   10
like a choir singing their purples,
pinks and whites to the buttercups
spread thickly through the grasses—
and to the sparser daisies, orange
hawkweed, pink and white clover,   15
purple vetch, butter-and-eggs.
It's a pleasure to name things
as long as one doesn't get
hung up about it. A pleasure, too,
to pick up the dirt road and listen   20
to my sneakers soaked with dew
scrunching on the damp pinkish sand—
that must be feldspar, an element
of granite, I remember from
fifth grade. I don't know what   25
this black salamander with yellow spots
is called—I want to say yellow-
spotted salamander, as if names
innocently sprang from things
themselves. Purple columbines   30
nod in a ditch, escapees
from someone's garden. It isn't
until I'm on my way back
that they remind me of the school
shootings in Colorado,   35
the association clinging to the spurs
of their delicate, complex blooms.
And I remember the hawk
in hawkweed, and that it's also
called devil's paintbrush, and how   40
lupines are named after wolves . . .
how like second thoughts the darker
world encroaches even on these
fields protected as a sanctuary,
something ulterior always   45

creeping in like seeds carried
in the excrement of these buoyant
goldfinches, whose yellow bodies
are as bright as joy itself,
but whose species name in Latin   50
means "sorrowful."

CONSIDERATIONS FOR CRITICAL THINKING AND WRITING

1. **FIRST RESPONSE.** "It's a pleasure to name things / as long as one doesn't get /
   hung up about it" (lines 17–19). Do you think these lines adequately sum up
   the theme of this poem?

2. Locate and describe the shift in tone as this meditation on names progresses.

3. Discuss the effect of the images and their meanings in lines 42 to 51.

CONNECTION TO ANOTHER SELECTION

1. Compare the themes in this poem and in Robert Frost's "Nothing Gold
   Can Stay" (p. 1113).

JULIO MARZÁN (B. 1946)

The Translator at the Reception for Latin American Writers   *1997*

Air-conditioned introductions,
then breezy Spanish conversation
fan his curiosity to know
what country I come from.
"Puerto Rico and the Bronx."   5

Spectacled downward eyes
translate disappointment
like a poison mushroom
puffed in his thoughts as if,
after investing a sizable   10
intellectual budget, transporting
a huge cast and camera crew
to film on location
Mayan pyramid grandeur,
indigenes whose ancient gods   15
and comet-tail plumage
inspire a glorious epic
of revolution across a continent,
he received a lurid script
for a social documentary   20
rife with dreary streets

and pathetic human interest,
meager in the profits of high culture.

Understandably he turns,
catches up with the hostess,   25
praising the uncommon quality
of her offerings of cheese.

CONSIDERATIONS FOR CRITICAL THINKING AND WRITING

1. **FIRST RESPONSE.** What is the speaker's attitude toward the person he meets
   at the reception? What lines in particular lead you to that conclusion?

2. Why is that person so disappointed about the answer, "Puerto Rico and the
   Bronx" (line 5)?

3. Explain lines 6 to 23. How do they reveal both the speaker and the person
   encountered at the reception?

4. Why is the setting of this poem significant?

TODD BOSS (B. 1968)

Advance   2008

With a squeal, the already
otherworldly broadcast
stuttered,
            scattered,
                        leaving   5
only a tattered hiss.
                        At first
my father's fingers
                        fussed
the dial of our radio,   10
                        signals
fritzed as a flintless lighter,

then he leaned in closer,
intent on
            teasing   15
                        the news
we needed
            out of that box.
I never saw him touch more
slightly anything or anyone,   20
all his
            fingertips navigating
in and out of
                        nonsense for
the lifeline of our lives,   25

before
      swiping it off.
           Now
no more news was ours but
the storm's dark musings   30
on the matter.

          Even last
fall's fruit, jarred in the root
cellar just around the corner,
sucked   35
        its cupped lids
                tighter.

CONSIDERATIONS FOR CRITICAL THINKING AND WRITING

1. **FIRST RESPONSE.** Explain which words evoke the sounds of tuning the radio, and how.

2. Describe the ways in which Boss creates tension and suspense in the poem.

3. Type out the poem as a prose paragraph. How is the experience of reading the paragraph different from that of reading the poem? What do the line breaks of the poem contribute to your reading experience?

ROBERT MORGAN (B. 1944)

Overalls
1990

Even the biggest man will look
babylike in overalls, bib
up to his neck holding the trousers
high on his belly, with no chafing
at the waist, no bulging over   5
the belt. But it's the pockets on
the chest that are most interesting,
buttons and snaps like medals, badges,
flaps open with careless ease, thin
sheath for the pencil, little pockets   10
and pouches and the main zipper
compartment like a wallet over
the heart and the slit where the watch
goes, an eye where the chain is caught.
Every bit of surface is taken   15
up with patches, denim mesas
and envelopes, a many-level
cloth topography. And below,
the loops for hammers and pliers
like holsters for going armed   20
and armored yet free-handed
into the field another day
for labor's playful war with time.

CONSIDERATIONS FOR CRITICAL THINKING AND WRITING

1. **FIRST RESPONSE.** How does the poem's last line announce its theme?

2. Why is it that the "pockets on / the chest . . . are most interesting" (lines 6–7) to the speaker?

3. Describe the way images of childhood and adulthood, along with work and war, are interwoven in Morgan's treatment of overalls.

LOUISE GLÜCK (B. 1943)

March   *2008*

Photo © Sigrid Estrada.

The light stays longer in the sky,
    but it's a cold light,
it brings no relief from winter.

My neighbor stares out the window,
talking to her dog. He's sniffing the garden,
trying to reach a decision about the
    dead flowers.

It's a little early for all this.
Everything's still very bare—
nevertheless, something's different today
    from yesterday.

We can see the mountain: the peak's glittering where the ice
    catches the light.
But on the sides the snow's melted, exposing bare rock.   10

My neighbor's calling the dog, making
    her unconvincing doglike sounds.
The dog's polite; he raises his head when she calls,
but he doesn't move. So she goes on calling,
her failed bark slowly deteriorating into a human voice.

All her life she dreamed of living by the sea   15
but fate didn't put her there.
It laughed at her dreams;
it locked her up in the hills, where no one escapes.

The sun beats down on the earth, the earth flourishes.
And every winter, it's as though the rock underneath the earth rises   20
higher and higher and the earth becomes rock, cold and rejecting.

She says hope killed her parents, it killed her grandparents.
It rose up each spring with the wheat
and died between the heat of summer and the raw cold.
In the end, they told her to live near the sea,   25
as though that would make a difference.

By late spring she'll be garrulous, but now she's down to two words,
never and *only,* to express this sense that life's cheated her.

Never the cries of the gulls, only, in summer, the crickets, cicadas.
Only the smell of the field, when all she wanted   30
was the smell of the sea, of disappearance.

The sky above the fields has turned a sort of grayish pink
as the sun sinks. The clouds are silk yarn, magenta and crimson.

And everywhere the earth is rustling, not lying still.
And the dog senses this stirring; his ears twitch.   35

He walks back and forth, vaguely remembering
from other years this elation. The season of discoveries
is beginning. Always the same discoveries, but to the dog
intoxicating and new, not duplicitous.

I tell my neighbor we'll be like this   40
when we lose our memories. I ask her if she's ever seen the sea
and she says, once, in a movie.
It was a sad story, nothing worked out at all.

The lovers part. The sea hammers the shore, the mark each wave leaves
wiped out by the wave that follows.   45
Never accumulation, never one wave trying to build on another,
never the promise of shelter —

The sea doesn't change as the earth changes;
it doesn't lie.
You ask the sea, what can you promise me   50
and it speaks the truth; it says *erasure*.

Finally the dog goes in.
We watch the crescent moon,
very faint at first, then clearer and clearer
as the night grows dark.   55
Soon it will be the sky of early spring, stretching
      above the stubborn ferns and violets.

Nothing can be forced to live.
The earth is like a drug now, like a voice from far away,
a lover or master. In the end, you do what the voice tells you.
It says forget, you forget.   60
It says begin again, you begin again.

CONSIDERATIONS FOR CRITICAL THINKING AND WRITING

1. **FIRST RESPONSE.** Consider whether or not this is "a sad story, [in which] nothing worked out at all" (line 43).

2. What distinctions between living inland and by the sea does the speaker make through the use of imagery?

3. Comment on the significance of the personification in lines 48 to 51.

4. Discuss the meaning and tone of the final stanza.

CONNECTION TO ANOTHER SELECTION

1. Compare Glück's seasonal description in "March" with Margaret Atwood's in "February" (p. 876). Which poem do you find more evocative in capturing the particular qualities of the month? Why?

LINDA PASTAN (B. 1932)

To a Daughter Leaving Home   *1988*

When I taught you
at eight to ride
a bicycle, loping along
beside you
as you wobbled away   5
on two round wheels,
my own mouth rounding
in surprise when you pulled
ahead down the curved
path of the park,   10
I kept waiting
for the thud
of your crash as I
sprinted to catch up,
while you grew   15
smaller, more breakable
with distance,
pumping, pumping
for your life, screaming
with laughter,   20
the hair flapping
behind you like a
handkerchief waving
goodbye.

CONSIDERATIONS FOR CRITICAL THINKING AND WRITING

1. **FIRST RESPONSE.** Comment on the appropriateness of the extended metaphor as a means of creating the theme for this poem. What other extended metaphors do you think would work just as well to convey the same theme?

2. Replace Pastan's title with your own so that the poem's tone is slightly shifted but the theme is still consistent with the body of the poem.

3. **CREATIVE RESPONSE.** Write an open form poem using an extended metaphor for some aspect of your life at school.

CONNECTION TO ANOTHER SELECTION

1. Compare the themes in Pastan's poem and in Rachel Hadas's "The Red Hat" (p. 958).

ANONYMOUS

The Frog

What a wonderful bird the frog are!
When he stand he sit almost;
When he hop he fly almost.
He ain't got no sense hardly;
He ain't got no tail hardly either.
When he sit, he sit on what he ain't got almost.

CONSIDERATIONS FOR CRITICAL THINKING AND WRITING

1. **FIRST RESPONSE.** How is the poem a description of the speaker as well as of a frog?
2. Though this poem is ungrammatical, it does have a patterned structure. How does the pattern of sentences create a formal structure?

TATO LAVIERA (B. 1951)

AmeRícan

1985

we gave birth to a new generation,
AmeRícan, broader than lost gold
never touched, hidden inside the
puerto rican mountains.

we gave birth to a new generation,   5
AmeRícan, it includes everything
imaginable you-name-it-we-got-it
society.

we gave birth to a new generation,
AmeRícan salutes all folklores,   10
european, indian, black, spanish,
and anything else compatible:

AmeRícan,   singing to composer pedro flores'° palm
             trees high up in the universal sky!

AmeRícan,   sweet soft spanish danzas gypsies   15
             moving lyrics la *española*° cascabelling   *Spanish*
             presence always singing at our side!

AmeRícan,   beating jíbaro° modern troubadours
             crying guitars romantic continental
             bolero love songs!   20

AmeRícan,   across forth and across back
             back across and forth back

13 *pedro flores:* Puerto Rican composer of popular romantic songs.   18 *jíbaro:* A particular style of music played by Puerto Rican mountain farmers.

forth across and back and forth
our trips are walking bridges!

it all dissolved into itself, the attempt   25
was truly made, the attempt was truly
absorbed, digested, we spit out
the poison, we spit out the malice,
we stand, affirmative in action,
to reproduce a broader answer to the   30
marginality that gobbled us up abruptly!

AmeRícan,   walking plena-rhythms° in new york,
strutting beautifully alert, alive,
many turning eyes wondering,
admiring!   35

AmeRícan,   defining myself my own way any way many
ways Am e Rícan, with the big R and the
accent on the í!

AmeRícan,   like the soul gliding talk of gospel
boogie music!   40

AmeRícan,   speaking new words in spanglish tenements,
fast tongue moving street corner *"que
corta"*° talk being invented at the insistence   *that cuts*
of a smile!

AmeRícan,   abounding inside so many ethnic english   45
people, and out of humanity, we blend
and mix all that is good!

AmeRícan,   integrating in new york and defining our
own *destino,*° our own way of life,   *destiny*

AmeRícan,   defining the new america, humane america,   50
admired america, loved america, harmonious
america, the world in peace, our energies
collectively invested to find other civili-
zations, to touch God, further and further,
to dwell in the spirit of divinity!   55

AmeRícan,   yes, for now, for i love this, my second
land, and i dream to take the accent from
the altercation, and be proud to call
myself american, in the u.s. sense of the
word, AmeRícan, America!   60

32 *plena-rhythms:* African–Puerto Rican folklore, music, and dance.

CONSIDERATIONS FOR CRITICAL THINKING AND WRITING

1. **FIRST RESPONSE.** How does the arrangement of lines communicate a sense of energy and vitality?
2. How does the speaker portray Puerto Ricans living in the United States?
3. How does the poet describe the United States?

CONNECTION TO ANOTHER SELECTION

1. In an essay compare the themes, styles, and tones of "AmeRícan" and Barbara Hamby's "Ode to American English" (p. 817).

PETER MEINKE (B. 1932)

The ABC of Aerobics 1983

Air seeps through alleys and our diaphragms
balloon blackly with this mix of
carbon monoxide and the thousand corrosives a city
doles out free to its constituents;
everyone's jogging through Edgemont Park,   5
frightened by death and fatty tissue,
gasping at the maximal heart rate,
hoping to outlive all the others streaming
in the lanes like lemmings lurching toward their last
jump. I join in despair   10
knowing my arteries jammed with
lint and tobacco, lard and bourbon — my
medical history a noxious marsh:
newts and moles slink through the sodden veins,
owls hoot in the lungs' dark branches;   15
probably I shall keel off the john like
queer Uncle George and lie on the bathroom floor
raging about Shirley Clark, my true love in
seventh grade, God bless her wherever she lives
tied to that turkey who hugely   20
undervalues the beauty of her tiny earlobes, one
view of which (either one: they are both perfect)
would add years to my life and I could skip these
x-rays, turn in my insurance card, and trade
yoga and treadmills and jogging and zen and   25
zucchini for drinking and dreaming of her, breathing hard.

CONSIDERATIONS FOR CRITICAL THINKING AND WRITING

1. FIRST RESPONSE. How does the title help to establish a pattern throughout the poem? How does the pattern contribute to the poem's meaning?

2. How does the speaker feel about exercise? How do his descriptions of his physical condition serve to characterize him?

3. A primer is a book that teaches children to read or introduces them, in an elementary way, to the basics of a subject. The title "The ABC of Aerobics" indicates that this poem is meant to be a primer. What is it trying to teach us? Is its final lesson serious or ironic?

4. Discuss Meinke's use of humor. Is it effective?

CONNECTIONS TO OTHER SELECTIONS

1. Write an essay comparing the humor in Meinke's poem and in Andrew Hudgins's "The Cow" (p. 938)
2. Compare the voice in this poem with that in Galway Kinnell's "After Making Love We Hear Footsteps" (p. 1007). Which do you find more appealing? Why?

CHRISTINA GEROGIANNIS (B. 1981)

Headland   *2007*

1

There is no sadness
but held in the bedroom of the
rented house from two years ago.

I should say no
definite sadness.   5

2

On the dresser:
a small sample of jasper.
Late summer, the house smelled of bleach.

In every corner we tried
to clean it of the day.   10

3

The telephone rang in the living day.
After that, the prepared slideshow, the
walking in and walking out.

The photos on corkboard.
The ordeal over.   15

4

The quilt stained white in places
from mopping bleach onto the ceiling
and not moving the quilt.

I could smell bleach underneath and
thought of the acres around the house.   20

5

Here, in the driveway,
is Celeste in her workout clothes.
This is ending everything.

Quarries, unfamiliar, not
just unfamiliar —   25

6

Home is over for us.
Here, in the kitchen,
we learn of a new death.

Celeste is polite and leaves. Acres surround
the house, protection from nothing, really.   30

7

In the living world I collected rocks
and minerals, and was interested in
telescopes, meridians. Hills, quarries —

the land at home, whatever it was.
At this hour, clean. Later, start again.   35

QUESTIONS FOR CRITICAL THINKING AND WRITING

1. **FIRST RESPONSE.** What is lost in "Headland"? How does "no definite sadness" characterize feelings about a place that has been lost?

2. What does Gerogiannis achieve by describing emotions, places, and objects
   in ambiguous terms? Are there parallel details to "no definite sadness" that
   characterize the absences referred to in the poem?

3. Is "Headland" a place, a geological formation, or a mental territory? How
   does this affect your sense of the title?

CONNECTION TO ANOTHER SELECTION

1. Why are the speaker's sensory perceptions jumbled in this poem? Discuss
   "Headland" in terms Emily Dickinson identifies in "The Bustle in a House"
   (p. 1069).

SANDRA M. GILBERT (B. 1936)

Chairlift   *2005*

What does it allegorize, such unseemly
haste at the beginning
and the end —

the swift attendants gripping, heaving
each of us   5
into a steady place,

and then the long slow silent
journey over
and up the mountain, swaying

in sunshine or buffeted   10
by churning
winds, the sea beyond, with its tiny

sails and lonesome
cloudscapes, and all along,
under the bob of the shadow   15

that hangs below every chair,
a real live human
world of vines and gardens

boiling and blooming and getting
sparser as the humming   20
cables clamber

higher, steeper, until
soon there are only empty
meadows, knots of forest, channels

of frigid   25
granite or ice,
though just before someone suddenly

drags you off
at the summit,
just before the circling seats   30

descend for another
round, you notice
lying in the last deep

weedy cutbank,
all by itself,   35
one mateless leather clog. . . .

Considerations for Critical Thinking and Writing

1. **First response.** Explain why you consider the chairlift to function as an allegory or as a symbol in the poem.

2. How does the end punctuation of the first and last stanzas contribute to the tone of the poem?

3. **Critical strategies.** Read the section on mythological strategies (pp. 2058–60) in Chapter 53, "Critical Strategies for Reading." How might this poem be read as a literary archetype?

MARY STEWART HAMMOND (B. 1953)

The Big Fish Story   2006

Late fall and not a soul around for miles.
Just me and my man. And those scallopers
trolling a few hundred feet offshore I'm pointing to
saying *no, non, nein, nyet, nej,*
in every language including body English,   5
to his idea that we take off all our clothes
smack in the middle of the lawn
in broad daylight and go swimming!
This is the line he throws me: "But, sweetheart,
the young have given up scalloping. Those   10
are all old men out there. Their eyesight
is terrible." Which explains why
I'm naked in the water off the coast
of Massachusetts on the fourteenth of October
and loving it, the water still summer warm,   15
feeling like silk, like the feel of his flesh
drawing over my skin when we're landed
on a bed, so I swim off out of his reach
lolling and rolling, diving and surfacing,
floating on my back for his still good eyes.   20
I know what he has in mind and what
I have in mind is to play him for a while
for that line I swallowed, delay the moment
I'll do a slow crawl over to him,
wrap my legs around his waist, and   25
reel him in — just the fish he was after.

CONSIDERATIONS FOR CRITICAL THINKING AND WRITING

1. **FIRST RESPONSE.** How does the speaker's language serve to characterize her?
2. How does Hammond make this narrative both playful and erotic?

Found Poem

This next selection is a ***found poem,*** unintentional verse discovered in a
nonpoetic context, such as a conversation, news story, or an advertisement.
Found poems are playful reminders that the words in poems are very often
the language we use every day. Whether such found language should be regarded as a poem is an issue left for you to consider.

DONALD JUSTICE (1925–2004)
Order in the Streets   1969

(*From instructions printed on a child's toy, Christmas 1968, as reported in the* New York Times)

1. 2. 3.
Switch on.

Jeep rushes
to the scene
of riot   5

Jeep goes
in all directions
by mystery action.

Jeep stops periodically
to turn hood over   10

machine gun appears
with realistic
shooting noise.

After putting down riot,
jeep goes   15
back to the headquarters.

CONSIDERATIONS FOR CRITICAL THINKING AND WRITING

1. **FIRST RESPONSE.** What is the effect of arranging these instructions in discrete lines? How are the language and meaning enhanced by this arrangement?

2. **CREATIVE RESPONSE.** Look for phrases or sentences in ads, textbooks, labels, or directions — in anything that might inadvertently contain provocative material that would be revealed by arranging the words in verse lines. You may even discover some patterns of rhyme and rhythm. After arranging the lines, explain why you organized them as you did.

Web Research the poets in this chapter at bedfordstmartins.com/meyerlit.

31

Combining the Elements of Poetry: A Writing Process

© Bettmann/CORBIS.

In poetry you have a form looking for a subject and a subject looking for a form. When they come together successfully you have a poem.
—W. H. AUDEN

THE ELEMENTS TOGETHER

The elements of poetry that you have studied in the first ten chapters of this section offer a vocabulary and a series of perspectives that open up avenues of inquiry into a poem. As you have learned, there are many potential routes that you can take. By asking questions about the speaker, diction, figurative language, sounds, rhythm, tone, or theme, you clarify your understanding while simultaneously sensitizing yourself to elements and issues especially relevant to the poem under consideration. This process of careful, informed reading allows you to see how the various elements of the poem reinforce its meanings.

A poem's elements do not exist in isolation, however. They work together to create a complete experience for the reader. Knowing how the elements combine helps you to understand the poem's structure and to appreciate it as a whole. Robert Herrick's "Delight in Disorder" (p. 958), for example, is more easily understood (and the humor of the poem is better appreciated) when meter and rhyme are considered together with the poem's meaning. Musing about how he is more charmed by a naturally disheveled appearance than by those that seem contrived, the speaker lists several attributes of dishevelment and concludes that they

> Do more bewitch me than when art
> Is too precise in every part.

Noticing how the couplet's precise and sing-songy rhythm combines with the solid, obvious, and final rhyme of *art* / *part* helps in understanding what the speaker means by "too precise," as the lines are a little too precise themselves. Noticing this, you may even want to chart how rhythm and rhyme work together throughout the early (more disheveled) lines of the poem. Finding a pattern in the ways the elements work together throughout the poem will help you understand how the poem works.

MAPPING THE POEM

When you write about a poem, you are, in some ways, providing a guide for a place that might otherwise seem unfamiliar and remote. Put simply, writing enables you to chart a work so that you can comfortably move around in it to discuss or write about what interests you. Your paper represents a record and a map of your intellectual journey through the poem, pointing out the things worth noting and your impressions about them. Your role as writer is to offer insights into the challenges, pleasures, and discoveries that the poem harbors. These insights are a kind of sightseeing, as you navigate the various elements of the poem to make some overall point about it.

This chapter shows you how one student, Rose Bostwick, moves through the stages of writing about how a poem's elements combine for a final effect. Included here are Rose's annotated version of the poem, her first response, her informal outline, and the final draft of an explication of John Donne's "Death Be Not Proud." A detailed explanation of what is implicit in a poem, an ***explication*** requires a line-by-line examination of the poem. (For more on explication, see page 2084 in Chapter 54, "Reading and the Writing Process.") After reviewing the elements of poetry covered in the preceding chapters, Rose read the poem (which follows) several times, paying careful attention to diction, figurative language, irony, symbol, rhythm, sound, and so on. Her final paper is more concerned with the overall effect of the combination of elements than with a line-by-line breakdown, and her annotated version of the poem details her attention to that task. As you read and reread "Death Be Not Proud," keep notes on how *you* think the elements of this poem work together and to what overall effect.

JOHN DONNE (1572–1631)

John Donne, now regarded as a major poet of the early seventeenth century, wrote love poems at the beginning of his career but shifted to religious themes after converting from Catholicism to Anglicanism in the early 1590s. Although trained in law, he was also ordained a priest and became dean of St. Paul's Cathedral in London in 1621. The following poem, from "Holy Sonnets," reflects both his religious faith and his ability to create elegant arguments in verse.

Courtesy of the National Portrait Gallery, London.

Death Be Not Proud   1611

Death be not proud, though some have callèd thee
Mighty and dreadful, for thou art not so;
For those whom thou think'st thou dost overthrow
Die not, poor Death, nor yet canst thou kill me.
From rest and sleep, which but thy pictures° be,   *images* 5
Much pleasure; then from thee much more must flow,
And soonest our best men with thee do go,
Rest of their bones, and soul's delivery.°   *deliverance*
Thou art slave to Fate, Chance, kings, and desperate men,
And dost with Poison, War, and Sickness dwell;   10
And poppy or charms can make us sleep as well,
And better than thy stroke; why swell'st° thou then?   *swell with pride*
One short sleep past, we wake eternally
And death shall be no more; Death, thou shalt die.

CONSIDERATIONS FOR CRITICAL THINKING AND WRITING

1. FIRST RESPONSE. Why doesn't the speaker fear death? Explain why you find the argument convincing or not.

2. How does the speaker compare death with rest and sleep in lines 5 to 8? What is the point of this comparison?

3. Discuss the poem's rhythm by examining the breaks and end-stopped lines. How does the poem's rhythm contribute to its meaning?

4. What are the signs that this poem is structured as a sonnet?

ASKING QUESTIONS ABOUT THE ELEMENTS

After reading a poem, use the Questions for Responsive Reading and Writing (pp. 791–92) to help you think, talk, and write about any poem. Before you do, though, be sure that you have read the poem several times without worrying actively about interpretation. With poetry, as with all literature, it's important to allow yourself the pleasure of enjoying whatever makes itself apparent to you. On subsequent readings, use the questions to understand and appreciate how the poem works; remember to keep in mind that not all questions will necessarily be relevant to a particular poem. A good starting point is to ask yourself what elements are exemplified in the parts of the poem that especially interest you. Then ask the Questions for Responsive Reading and Writing that relate to those elements. Finally, as you begin to get a sense of what elements are important to the poem and how those elements fit together, it often helps to put your impressions on paper.

A SAMPLE CLOSE READING

An Annotated Version of "Death Be Not Proud"

As she read the poem closely several times, Rose annotated it with impressions and ideas that would lead to insights on which her analysis would be built. Her close examination of the poem's elements allowed her to understand how its parts contribute to its overall effect; her annotations provide a useful map of her thinking.

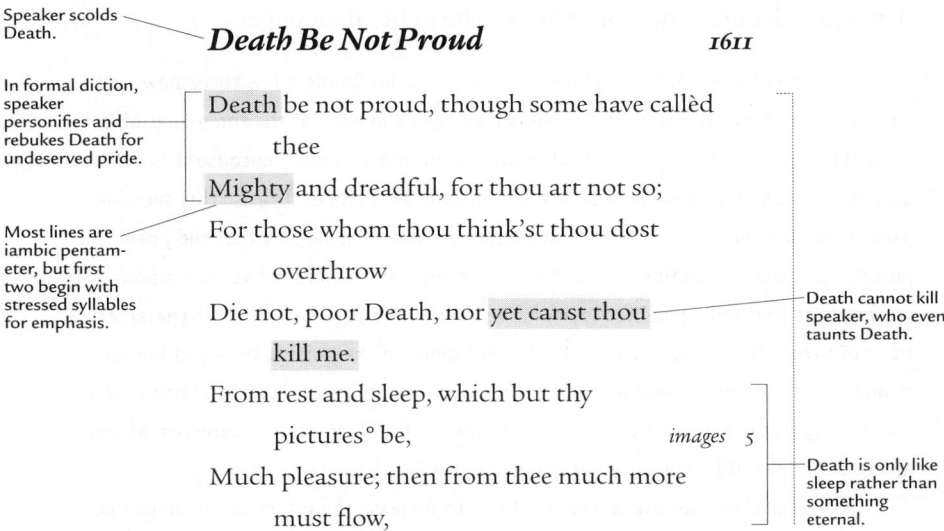

Speaker scolds Death.

Death Be Not Proud   1611

In formal diction, speaker personifies and rebukes Death for undeserved pride.

Death be not proud, though some have callèd
    thee
Mighty and dreadful, for thou art not so;
For those whom thou think'st thou dost
    overthrow
Die not, poor Death, nor yet canst thou
    kill me.
From rest and sleep, which but thy
    pictures° be,   *images* 5
Much pleasure; then from thee much more
    must flow,

Most lines are iambic pentameter, but first two begin with stressed syllables for emphasis.

Death cannot kill speaker, who even taunts Death.

Death is only like sleep rather than something eternal.

And soonest our best men with thee do go,

Rest of their bones, and soul's

delivery.°   *deliverance*

Thou art slave to Fate, Chance, kings, and

desperate men,

And dost with Poison, War, and Sickness

dwell;   10

And poppy or charms can make us sleep

as well,

And better than thy stroke; why

swell'st° thou then?   *swell with pride*

One short sleep past, we wake eternally

And death shall be no more; Death, thou

shalt die.

> Each quatrain (4-line stanza) develops the argument that Death is ultimately weak and cannot be justly proud or rightly feared, building toward the conclusion of final two lines.

> Rather than a power, Death is a slave to other forces.

> Argument in the couplet climaxes with allusion to humanity's resurrection and death of Death itself. In addition to Christianity, does sonnet form finally control Death too?

A SAMPLE FIRST RESPONSE

After Rose carefully read "Death Be Not Proud" and had a sense of how the elements work, she took the first step toward a formal explication by writing informally about the relevant elements and addressing the question *Why doesn't the speaker fear death? Explain why you find the argument convincing or not.* Note that at this point, she was not as concerned with textual evidence and detail as she would need to be in her final paper.

I've read the poem "Death Be Not Proud" by John Donne a few times now, and I have a sense of how it works. The poem is a sonnet, and each of the three quatrains presents a piece of the argument that Death should not be proud, because it is not really all-powerful, and may even be a source of pleasure. As a reader, I resist this seeming paradox at first, but I know it must be a trick, a riddle of some sort that the poem will proceed to untangle. I think one of the reasons the poem comes off as such a powerful statement is that Donne at first seems to be playful and paradoxical in his characterizations of Death. He's almost teasing Death. But beneath the teasing tone you feel the strong foundation of the real reason Death should not be proud—Donne's faith in the immortality of the soul. The poem begins to feel more solemn as it progresses, as the hints at the idea of immortality become more clearly articulated.

Donne utilizes two literary conventions to increase the effect of this poem: he uses the convention of personifying death, so that he can address it directly, and he uses the metaphor of death as a kind of sleep. These two things determine the tone and the progression from playful to solemn in the poem.

The last clause of the poem (line 14) plays with the paradoxical-seeming character of what he's been declaring. Ironically, it seems the only thing susceptible to death is death itself. Or, when death becomes powerless is when it only has power over itself.

ORGANIZING YOUR THOUGHTS

Showing in a paper how different elements of a particular poem work together is often quite challenging. While you may have a clear intuitive sense of what elements are important to the poem and how they complement one another, it is important to organize your thoughts in such a way as to make the relationships clear to your audience. The simplest way is to go line by line, but that can quickly become rote for writer and reader. Because you will want to organize your paper in the way that best serves your thesis, it may help to write an informal outline that charts how you think the argument moves. You may find, for example, that the argument is not persuasive if you start with the final lines and go back to the beginning of the poem or passage. However you decide to organize your argument, keep in mind that a single idea, or thesis, will have to run throughout the entire paper.

A SAMPLE INFORMAL OUTLINE

In her informal outline (following), Rose discovers that her argument works best if she begins at the beginning. Note that, though her later paper concerns itself with how several elements of poetry contribute to the poem's theme and message, her informal outline concerns itself much more with what that message is and how it develops as the poem progresses. She will fill in the details later.

Thesis: From the very first word, addressing "Death" directly, Donne uses the literary conventions of personifying death and comparing it to sleep to begin an argument that Death should not be proud of its might or dreadfulness. But these two elements of his argument come to be seen as the superficial points when the true reason for death's powerlessness becomes clear. The Christian belief in the immortality of the soul is the reason for death's powerlessness and likeness to sleep.

Body of essay: Show how argument proceeds by quatrains from playful address to Death, and statement that Death is much like sleep, its "picture," to statement that Death is "slave" to other forces (and so should not be proud of being the mightiest), to the couplet, which articulates clearly the idea of immortality and gives the final paradox, "Death, thou shalt die."

<u>Conclusion</u>: *Donne's faith in the immortality of the soul enables him to "prove" in this argument that Death is truly like its metaphorical representation, sleep. Faith allows him to derive a source for this conventional trope, and it allows him to state his truth in paradoxes. He relies on the conventional idea that death is an end, and a conqueror, and the only all-powerful force, to make the paradoxes that lend his argument the force of mystery — the mystery of faith.*

THE ELEMENTS AND THEME

As you create an informal outline, your understanding of the poem will grow, change, and finally, solidify. You will develop a much clearer sense of what the poem's elements combine to create, and you will have chosen a scheme for organizing your argument. The next step before drafting is to determine the paper's thesis, which will not only keep your paper focused but will also help you center your thoughts. For papers that discuss how the elements of poetry come together, the thesis is a single and concise statement of what the elements combine to create — the idea around which all the elements revolve. In the earlier discussion of Robert Herrick's "Delight in Disorder," for example, the two elements, rhythm and rhyme, work together to create the speaker's self-directed irony. To state this as a thesis, we might say that by making his own rhythm and rhyme "too precise," Herrick's speaker is making fun of himself while complimenting a certain type of woman. (You may ask yourself if he's doing a little flirting.)

Once you understand how all of the elements of the poem fit together and have articulated your understanding in the thesis statement, the next step is to flesh out your argument. By including quotations from the poem to illustrate the points you will be making, you will better explain exactly how each element relates to the others and, more specifically, to your thesis, and you will have created a finished paper that helps readers navigate the poem's geography.

A SAMPLE EXPLICATION

The Use of Conventional Metaphors for Death in John Donne's "Death Be Not Proud"

In Rose's final draft, she focuses on the use of metaphor in "Death Be Not Proud." Her essay provides a coherent reading that relates each line of the poem to the speaker's intense awareness of death. Although the essay discusses each stanza in order, the introductory paragraph provides a brief overview explaining how the poem's metaphor and arguments contribute to its total meaning. In addition, Rose does not hesitate to discuss a line out of sequence when it can be usefully connected to another phrase. She also works quotations into her sentences to support her points. When she adds something to a quotation to clarify it, she encloses her words in brackets so that they will not be mistaken for the poet's, and she uses a slash to indicate line divisions: "soonest . . . with thee do go, / [for] Rest of their bones, and soul's delivery." Finally, Rose is sure to cite the line numbers for any direct quotations from the poem. As you read through her final draft, remember that the word *explication* comes from the Latin *explicare,* "to unfold." How successful do you think Rose is at unfolding this poem to reveal how its elements — here ranging from metaphor, structure, meter, personification, paradox, and irony to theme — contribute to its meaning?

Bostwick 1

Rose Bostwick

English 101

Professor Hart

February 24, 2009

The Use of Conventional Metaphors for Death

in John Donne's "Death Be Not Proud"

In the sonnet that begins "Death be not proud . . ." John Donne argues that death is not "mighty and dreadful" but is more like its metaphorical representation, sleep. Death, Donne puts forth, is even a source of pleasure and rest. The poet builds this argument on two foundations. One is made up of the metaphors and literary conventions for death: death is compared with sleep and is often personified so that it can be addressed directly. The poem is an address to death that at first seems paradoxical and somewhat playful, but which then rises in all the emotion of faith as it reveals the second foundation of the argument—the Christian belief in the immortality of the soul. Seen against the backdrop of this belief, death loses its powerful threat and is seen as only a metaphorical sleep, or rest.

> Thesis providing interpretation of the poem's use of metaphor and how it contributes to the poem's central argument.

<table>
<tr><td>

Discussion of how form and meter contribute to the poem's central argument.

</td><td>

The poem is an ironic argument that proceeds according to the structure of the sonnet form. Each quatrain contains a new development or aspect of the argument, and the final couplet serves as a conclusion. The metrical scheme is mainly iambic pentameter, but in several places in the poem, the stress pattern is altered for emphasis. For example, the first foot of the poem is inverted, so that "Death," the first word, receives the stress. This announces to us right away that Death is being personified and addressed. This inversion also serves to begin the poem energetically and forcefully. The second line behaves in the same way. The first syllable of "Mighty" receives the stress, emphasizing the meaning of the word and its assumed relation to Death.

</td></tr>
</table>

Discussion of how personification contributes to the poem's central argument.

This first quatrain offers the first paradox and sets up the argument that death has been conventionally personified with the wrong attributes, might and dreadfulness. The poet tells death not to be proud, "though some have called thee / Mighty and dreadful," because, he says, death is "not so" (lines 1–2). Donne will turn this conventional characterization of death on its head with the paradox of the third and fourth lines: he says the people overthrown by death (as if by a conqueror) "Die not, poor death, nor yet canst thou kill me." These lines establish the paradox of death not being able to cause death.

Discussion of how metaphor of sleep and idea of immortality support the poem's central argument.

The next quatrain will not begin to answer the question of why this paradox is so, but will posit another slight paradox—the idea of death as pleasurable. In lines 5–8, Donne uses the literary convention of describing death as a metaphorical sleep, or rest, to construct the argument that death must give pleasure: "From rest and sleep, which but thy pictures be, / Much pleasure; then from thee much more must flow" (5–6). At this point, the argument seems almost playful, but is carefully hinting at the solemnity of the deeper foundation of the belief in immortality. The metaphor of sleep for death includes the idea of waking; one doesn't sleep forever. The next two lines put forth the idea that death is pleasurable enough to be desired by "our best men" who "soonest . . . with thee do go, / [for] Rest of their bones, and soul's delivery" (7–8). This last line comes closer to announcing the true reason for death's powerlessness and pleasure: it is the way to the "soul's delivery" from the body and life on earth, and implicitly, into another, better realm.

Bostwick 3

A new reason for death's powerlessness arises in the next four lines. The poet says to death:

> Thou art slave to Fate, Chance, kings, and desperate men,
>
> And dost with Poison, War, and Sickness dwell;
>
> And poppy or charms can make us sleep as well,
>
> And better than thy stroke; why swell'st thou then? (9–12)

Donne argues here that there are forces more powerful than death that actually control it. Fate and chance determine when death occurs, and to whom it comes. Kings, with the powers of law and war, can summon death and throw it on whom they wish. And desperate men, murderers or suicides, can also summon death with the strength of their emotions. In lines 11 and 12, Donne again uses the metaphor of death as a kind of sleep, but says that drugs or "charms" give one a better sleep than death. And he asks playfully why death should be so proud, after all these illustrations of its weakness have been given: "why swell'st thou then?" (12).

Finally, with the last couplet, Donne reveals the true, deeper reason behind his argument that death should not be proud of its power. These lines also offer an explanation of the metaphor for death of sleep, or rest: "One short sleep past, we wake eternally / And death shall be no more; Death, thou shalt die" (13–14). After death, the soul lives on, according to Christian theology and belief. In the Christian heaven, where the soul is immortal, death will no longer exist, and so this last paradox, "Death, thou shalt die," becomes true. Again in this line, a significant inversion of metrical stress occurs. "Death," in the second clause, receives the stress, recalling the first line, emphasizing that it is an address and giving the clause a forceful sense of finality. His belief in the immortality of the soul enables Donne to "prove" in this argument that death is in actuality like its metaphorical representation, sleep. His faith allows him to derive a source for this conventional metaphor and to "disprove" the metaphor of death as an all-powerful conqueror. His Christian beliefs also allow him to state his truth in paradoxes, the mysteries that are justified by the mystery of faith.

Margin notes:

Discussion of how language and tone contribute to the poem's central argument.

Discussion of function of religious faith in the poem and how word order and meter create emphasis.

Conclusion supporting thesis in context of poet's beliefs.

Bostwick 4

Work Cited

Donne, John. "Death Be Not Proud." *The Bedford Introduction to Literature.* Ed. Michael Meyer. 9th ed. Boston: Bedford/St. Martin's, 2011. 1030. Print.

Before you begin writing your own paper on poetry, review the Suggestions for Approaching Poetry (pp. 762–63) and Chapter 22, "Writing about Poetry: From Inquiry to Final Paper," particularly the Questions for Responsive Reading and Writing (pp. 791–92). These suggestions and questions will help you to focus and sharpen your critical thinking and writing. You'll also find help in Chapter 54, "Reading and the Writing Process," which offers a systematic overview of choosing a topic, developing a thesis, and organizing various types of assignments. If you use outside sources for the paper, be sure to acknowledge them adequately by using the conventional documentation procedures detailed in Chapter 55, "The Literary Research Paper."

Web Research John Donne at bedfordstmartins.com/meyerlit.

Approaches
to Poetry

32

A Study of Emily Dickinson

My business is circumference.
— EMILY DICKINSON

In this chapter you'll find a variety of poems by Emily Dickinson so that you can study her work in some depth. While this collection is not wholly representative of her work, it does offer enough poems to suggest some of the techniques and concerns that characterize her writings. The poems speak not only to readers but also to one another. That's natural enough: the more familiar you are with a writer's work, the easier it is to perceive and enjoy the strategies and themes the poet uses. If you are asked to write about a number of poems by the same author, you may find useful the Questions for Writing about an Author in Depth (pp. 1082–83) and the sample paper on Dickinson's attitudes toward religious faith in four of her poems (pp. 1085–88).

Emily E. Dickinson.

This daguerreotype of Emily Dickinson, taken shortly after her sixteenth birthday, and the silhouette (*opposite page*), created when she was fourteen years old, are the only authenticated mechanically produced images of the poet.

A BRIEF BIOGRAPHY

Emily Dickinson (1830–1886) grew up in a prominent and prosperous household in Amherst, Massachusetts. Along with her younger sister, Lavinia, and older brother, Austin, she experienced a quiet and reserved family life headed by her father, Edward Dickinson. In a letter to Austin at law school, she once described the atmosphere in her father's house as

(*Below*) This recently discovered print of a mid-1850s daguerreotype, acquired by the scholar Philip F. Gura in 2000, may represent the poet in her twenties.
By permission of the Collection of Philip and Leslie Gura.

(*Right*) The silhouette shows Dickinson at age fourteen.
Amherst College Archives and Special Collections. Used by permission of the Trustees of Amherst College.

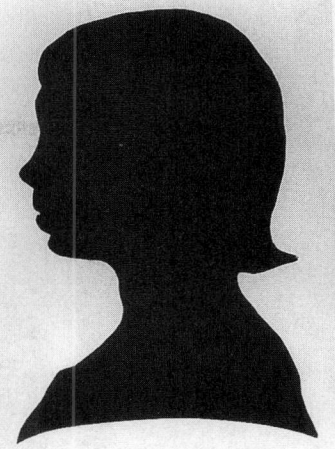

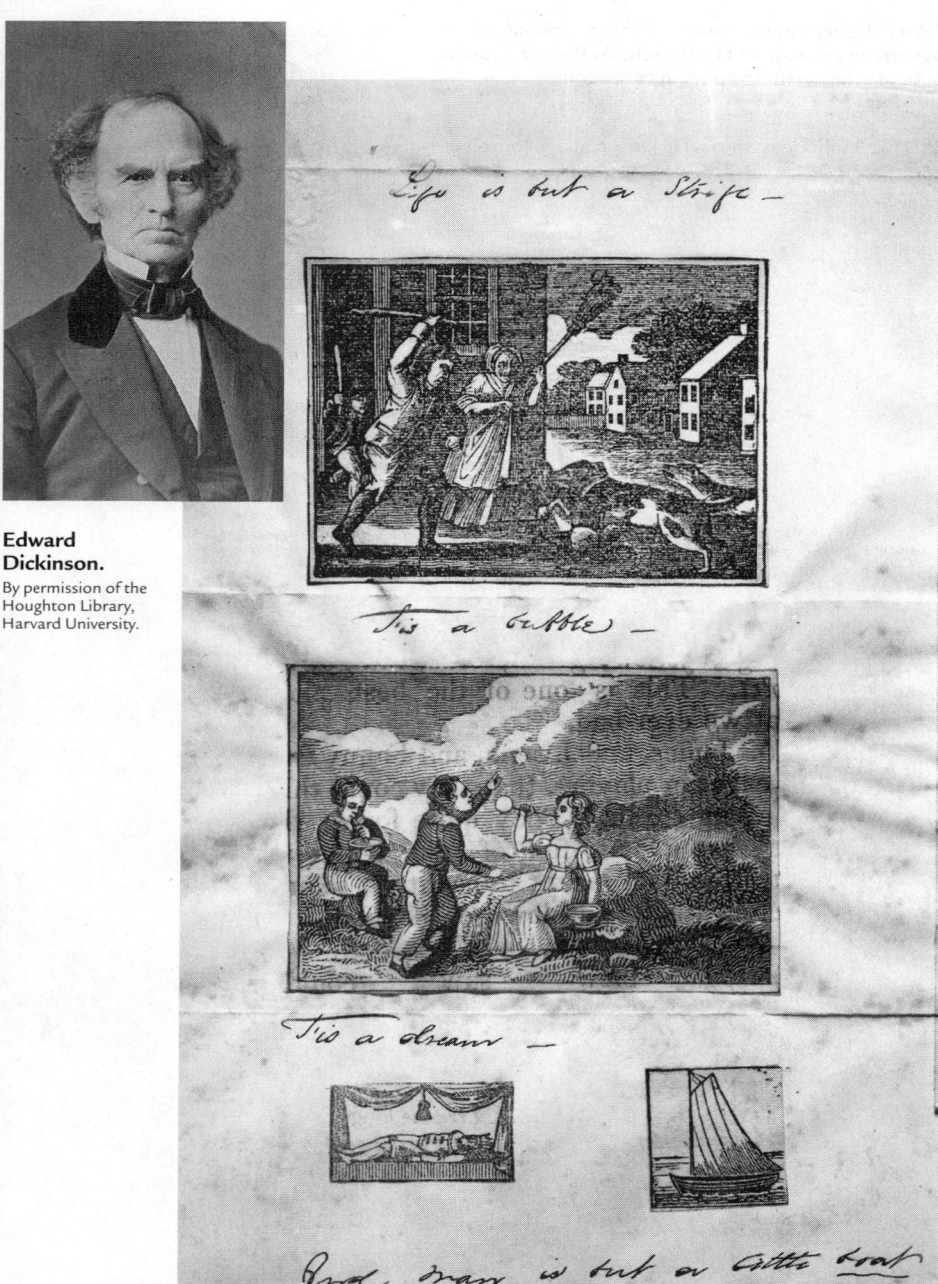

Edward Dickinson.

Letter from Emily Dickinson to cousin William Cowper Dickinson.

Susan Gilbert Dickinson.
Courtesy of the Todd-Bingham Picture
Collection, Manuscripts and Archives,
Yale University Library. © The President
and Fellows of Yale University.

Letter from Emily Dickinson to Susan Gilbert Dickinson.
By permission of the Houghton Library, Harvard University MS Am 1118.5 (B114). © The President and Fellows of Harvard
College.

(*Opposite page*) Shown here are the poet's father, Edward Dickinson, a prominent public
figure in Amherst, and a page from a letter sent to her cousin William Cowper Dickinson.
Emily Dickinson sometimes included in her correspondence images cut from books and
magazines. This illustrated letter reads, "Life is but a Strife — / T'is a bubble — / T'is a dream — /
And man is but a little *boat* / Which paddles down the stream —"

(*This page*) Following a party held next door at the home of Dickinson's brother, Austin, and
sister-in-law Susan (*top*), the poet was reprimanded by her father for staying out too late. The
next day, Dickinson wrote a playful note to Susan that included a cartoon poking fun at her
father. The note reads, "My 'position'" and features an image of a young person pursued by
a dragonlike creature, cut from the Dickinsons' copy of the *New England Primer*, a book of
moral lessons. The note concludes: "P.S. — Lest you misapprehend, the unfortunate insect
upon the *left* is Myself, while the Reptile upon the *right*, is my more immediate friends, and
connections [*sic*]."

"pretty much all sobriety." Her mother, Emily Norcross Dickinson, was not as powerful a presence in her life; she seems not to have been as emotionally accessible as Dickinson would have liked. Her daughter is said to have characterized her as not the sort of mother "to whom you hurry when you are troubled." Both parents raised Dickinson to be a cultured Christian woman who would one day be responsible for a family of her own. Her father attempted to protect her from reading books that might "joggle" her mind, particularly her religious faith, but Dickinson's individualistic instincts and irreverent sensibilities created conflicts that did not allow her to fall into step with the conventional piety, domesticity, and social duty prescribed by her father and the orthodox Congregationalism of Amherst.

The Dickinsons were well known in Massachusetts. Her father was a lawyer and served as the treasurer of Amherst College (a position Austin eventually took up as well), and her grandfather was one of the college's founders. Although nineteenth-century politics, economics, and social issues do not appear in the foreground of her poetry, Dickinson lived in a family environment that was steeped in them: her father was an active town official and served in the General Court of Massachusetts, the state senate, and the U.S. House of Representatives.

Dickinson, however, withdrew not only from her father's public world but also from almost all social life in Amherst. She refused to see most people, and aside from a single year at South Hadley Female Seminary (now Mount Holyoke College), one excursion to Philadelphia and Washington, and several brief trips to Boston to see a doctor about eye problems, she lived all her life in her father's house. She dressed only in white and developed a reputation as a reclusive eccentric. Dickinson selected her own society carefully and frugally. Like her poetry, her relationship to the world was intensely reticent. Indeed, during the last twenty years of her life she rarely left the house.

Though Dickinson never married, she had significant relationships with several men who were friends, confidants, and mentors. She also enjoyed an intimate relationship with her friend Susan Huntington Gilbert, who became her sister-in-law by marrying Austin. Susan and her husband lived next door and were extremely close with Dickinson. Biographers have attempted to find in a number of her relationships the source for the passion of some of her love poems and letters. Several possibilities have been put forward as the person she addressed in three letters as "Dear Master": Benjamin Newton, a clerk in her father's office who talked about books with her; Samuel Bowles, editor of the *Springfield Republican* and friend of the family; the Reverend Charles Wadsworth, a Presbyterian preacher with a reputation for powerful sermons; and an old friend and widower, Judge Otis P. Lord. Despite these speculations, no biographer has been able to identify definitively the object of Dickinson's love. What matters, of course, is not with whom she was in love — if, in fact, there was any single person — but that she wrote about such passions so intensely and convincingly in her poetry.

Choosing to live life internally within the confines of her home, Dickinson brought her life into sharp focus, for she also chose to live within the limitless expanses of her imagination — a choice she was keenly aware of and which she described in one of her poems this way: "I dwell in Possibility—" (p. 1062). Her small circle of domestic life did not impinge on her creative sensibilities. Like Henry David Thoreau, she simplified her life so that doing without was a means of being within. In a sense she redefined the meaning of deprivation because being denied something — whether faith, love, literary recognition, or some other desire — provided a sharper, more intense understanding than she would have experienced had she achieved what she wanted: "'Heaven,'" she wrote, "is what I cannot reach!" This poem (p. 1056) — along with many others, such as "Water, is taught by thirst" (p. 1053) and "Success is counted sweetest / By those who ne'er succeed" (p. 1052) — suggests just how persistently she saw deprivation as a way of sensitizing herself to the value of what she was missing. For Dickinson, hopeful expectation was always more satisfying than achieving a golden moment. Perhaps that's one reason she was so attracted to John Keats's poetry (see, for example, his "Ode on a Grecian Urn," p. 825).

Dickinson enjoyed reading Keats as well as Emily and Charlotte Brontë; Robert and Elizabeth Barrett Browning; Alfred, Lord Tennyson; and George Eliot. Even so, these writers had little or no effect on the style of her writing. In her own work she was original and innovative, but she did draw on her knowledge of the Bible, classical myths, and Shakespeare for allusions and references in her poetry. She also used contemporary popular church hymns, transforming their standard rhythms into free-form hymn meters. Among American writers she appreciated Ralph Waldo Emerson and Thoreau, but she apparently felt Walt Whitman was better left unread. She once mentioned to Thomas Wentworth Higginson, a leading critic with whom she corresponded about her poetry, that as for Whitman "I never read his Book — but was told that he was disgraceful" (for the kind of Whitman poetry she had been warned against, see his "I Sing the Body Electric," p. 1001). Nathaniel Hawthorne, however, intrigued her with his faith in the imagination and his dark themes: "Hawthorne appals — entices," a remark that might be used to describe her own themes and techniques.

AN INTRODUCTION TO HER WORK

Today, Dickinson is regarded as one of America's greatest poets, but when she died at the age of fifty-six after devoting most of her life to writing poetry, her nearly two thousand poems — only a dozen of which were published, anonymously, during her lifetime — were unknown except to a small number of friends and relatives. Dickinson was not recognized as a major poet until the twentieth century, when modern readers ranked her as a major new voice whose literary innovations were unmatched by any other nineteenth-century poet in the United States.

Dickinson neither completed many poems nor prepared them for publication. She wrote her drafts on scraps of paper, grocery lists, and the backs of recipes and used envelopes. Early editors of her poems took the liberty of making them more accessible to nineteenth-century readers when several volumes of selected poems were published in the 1890s. The poems were made to appear like traditional nineteenth-century verse by assigning them titles, rearranging their syntax, normalizing their grammar, and regularizing their capitalizations. Instead of dashes, editors used standard punctuation; instead of the highly elliptical telegraphic lines so characteristic of her poems, editors added articles, conjunctions, and prepositions to make them more readable and in line with conventional expectations. In addition, the poems were made more predictable by organizing them into categories such as friendship, nature, love, and death. Not until 1955, when Thomas Johnson published Dickinson's complete works in a form that attempted to be true to her manuscript versions, did readers have the opportunity to see the full range of her style and themes.

Like that of Robert Frost, Dickinson's popular reputation has sometimes relegated her to the role of a New England regionalist who writes quaint uplifting verses that touch the heart. In 1971 that image was mailed first class all over the country by the U.S. Postal Service. In addition to issuing a commemorative stamp featuring a portrait of Dickinson, the Postal Service affixed the stamp to a first-day-of-issue envelope that included an engraved rose and one of her poems. Here's the poem chosen from among the nearly two thousand she wrote:

If I can stop one Heart from breaking   *c. 1864*

If I can stop one Heart from breaking
I shall not live in vain
If I can ease one Life the Aching
or cool one Pain

Or help one fainting Robin
Unto his Nest again
I shall not live in Vain.

This is typical not only of many nineteenth-century popular poems but also of the kind of verse that can be found in contemporary greeting cards. The speaker tells us what we imagine we should think about and makes the point simply with a sentimental image of a "fainting Robin." To point out that robins don't faint or that altruism isn't necessarily the only rule of conduct by which one should live one's life is to make trouble for this poem. Moreover, its use of language is unexceptional; the metaphors used, like that robin, are a bit weary. If this poem were characteristic of Dickinson's poetry, the U.S. Postal Service probably would not have been urged to issue a stamp in her honor, nor would you be reading her poems in this anthology or many others. Here's a poem by Dickinson that is more typical of her writing:

If I shouldn't be alive   *c. 1860*

If I shouldn't be alive
When the Robins come,
Give the one in Red Cravat,
A Memorial crumb.

If I couldn't thank you,
Being fast asleep,
You will know I'm trying
With my Granite lip!

This poem is more representative of Dickinson's sensibilities and techniques. Although the first stanza sets up a rather mild concern that the speaker might not survive the winter (a not uncommon fear for those who fell prey to pneumonia, for example, during Dickinson's time), the concern can't be taken too seriously—a gentle humor lightens the poem when we realize that all robins have red cravats and are therefore the speaker's favorite. Furthermore, the euphemism that describes the speaker "Being fast asleep" in line 6 makes death seem not so threatening after all. But the sentimental expectations of the first six lines—lines that could have been written by any number of popular nineteenth-century writers—are dashed by the penultimate word of the last line. *Granite* is the perfect word here because it forces us to reread the poem and to recognize that it's not about feeding robins or offering a cosmetic treatment of death; rather, it's a bone-chilling description of a corpse's lip that evokes the cold, hard texture and grayish color of tombstones. These lips will never say "thank you" or anything else.

Instead of the predictable rhymes and sentiments of "If I can stop one Heart from breaking," this poem is unnervingly precise in its use of language and tidily points out how much emphasis Dickinson places on an individual word. Her use of near rhyme with "asleep" and "lip" brilliantly mocks a euphemistic approach to death by its jarring dissonance. This is a better poem, not because it's grim or about death, but because it demonstrates Dickinson's skillful use of language to produce a shocking irony.

Dickinson found irony, ambiguity, and paradox lurking in the simplest and commonest experiences. The materials and subject matter of her poetry are quite conventional. Her poems are filled with robins, bees, winter light, household items, and domestic duties. These materials represent the range of what she experienced in and around her father's house. She used them because they constituted so much of her life and, more important, because she found meanings latent in them. Though her world was simple, it was also complex in its beauties and its terrors. Her lyric poems capture impressions of particular moments, scenes, or moods, and she characteristically focuses on topics such as nature, love, immortality, death, faith, doubt, pain, and the self.

Though her materials were conventional, her treatment of them was innovative because she was willing to break whatever poetic conventions stood in the way of the intensity of her thought and images. Her conciseness, brevity, and wit are tightly packed. Typically she offers her observations via one or two images that reveal her thought in a powerful manner. She once characterized her literary art by writing, "My business is circumference." Her method is to reveal the inadequacy of declarative statements by evoking qualifications and questions with images that complicate firm assertions and affirmations. In one of her poems she describes her strategies this way: "Tell all the Truth but tell it slant—/ Success in Circuit lies" (p. 1070). This might well stand as a working definition of Dickinson's aesthetics and is embodied in the following poem:

The Thought beneath so slight a film —   *c. 1860*

The Thought beneath so slight a film —
Is more distinctly seen —
As laces just reveal the surge —
Or Mists — the Apennine°   *Italian mountain range*

Paradoxically, "Thought" is more clearly understood precisely because a slight "film"—in this case language—covers it. Language, like lace, enhances what it covers and reveals it all the more—just as a mountain range is more engaging to the imagination if it is covered in mists rather than starkly presenting itself. Poetry for Dickinson intensifies, clarifies, and organizes experience.

Dickinson's poetry is challenging because it is radical and original in its rejection of most traditional nineteenth-century themes and techniques. Her poems require active engagement from the reader because she seems to leave out so much with her elliptical style and remarkable contracting metaphors. But these apparent gaps are filled with meaning if we are sensitive to her use of devices such as personification, allusion, symbolism, and startling syntax and grammar. Because her use of dashes is sometimes puzzling, it helps to read her poems aloud to hear how carefully the words are arranged. What might initially seem intimidating on a silent page can surprise the reader with meaning when heard. It's also worth keeping in mind that Dickinson was not always consistent in her views and that they can change from poem to poem, depending on how she felt at a given moment. For example, her definition of religious belief in " 'Faith' is a fine invention" (p. 1084) reflects an ironically detached wariness in contrast to the faith embraced in "I never saw a Moor—" (p. 1085). Dickinson was less interested in absolute answers to questions than she was in examining and exploring their "circumference."

Because Dickinson's poems are all relatively brief (none is longer than fifty lines), they invite browsing and sampling, but perhaps a useful way into their highly metaphoric and witty world is this "how to" poem that reads almost like a recipe:

To make a prairie it takes a clover and one bee   *date unknown*

To make a prairie it takes a clover and one bee,
One clover, and a bee,
And revery.
The revery alone will do,
If bees are few.

This quiet but infinite claim for a writer's imagination brings together the range of ingredients in Dickinson's world of domestic and ordinary natural details. Not surprisingly, she deletes rather than adds to the recipe, because the one essential ingredient is the writer's creative imagination. *Bon appétit.*

Chronology

1830	Born December 10 in Amherst, Massachusetts.
1840	Starts her first year at Amherst Academy.
1847–48	Graduates from Amherst Academy and attends South Hadley Female Seminary (now Mount Holyoke College).
1855	Visits Philadelphia and Washington, D.C.
1857	Ralph Waldo Emerson lectures in Amherst.
1862	Starts corresponding with Thomas Wentworth Higginson, asking for advice about her poems.
1864	Visits Boston for eye treatments.
1870	Higginson visits her in Amherst.
1873	Higginson visits her for a second and final time.
1874	Her father dies in Boston.
1875	Her mother suffers from paralysis.
1882	Her mother dies.

1886	Dies on May 15 in Amherst, Massachusetts.
1890	First edition of her poetry, edited by Mabel Loomis Todd and Thomas Wentworth Higginson, is published.
1955	Thomas H. Johnson publishes *The Poems of Emily Dickinson* in three volumes, thereby making available her poetry known to that date.

Success is counted sweetest

c. 1859

Success is counted sweetest
By those who ne'er succeed.
To comprehend a nectar
Requires sorest need.

Not one of all the purple Host   5
Who took the Flag today
Can tell the definition
So clear of Victory

As he defeated — dying —
On whose forbidden ear   10
The distant strains of triumph
Burst agonized and clear!

CONSIDERATIONS FOR CRITICAL THINKING AND WRITING

1. **FIRST RESPONSE.** How is "success" defined in this poem? To what extent does that definition agree with your own understanding of the word?
2. What do you think is meant by the use of "comprehend" in line 3? How can a nectar be comprehended?
3. Why do the defeated understand victory better than the victorious?
4. Discuss the effect of the poem's final line.

CONNECTION TO ANOTHER SELECTION

1. In an essay compare the themes of this poem with those of John Keats's "Ode on a Grecian Urn" (p. 825).

Some things that fly there be —

c. 1859

Some things that fly there be —
Birds — Hours — the Bumblebee —
Of these no Elegy.

Some things that stay there be —
Grief — Hills — Eternity —
Nor this behooveth me.

There are that resting, rise.
Can I expound the skies?
How still the Riddle lies!

CONSIDERATIONS FOR CRITICAL THINKING AND WRITING

1. **FIRST RESPONSE.** Given the question the speaker raises in line 8, what do you suppose is the nature of the "Riddle" (line 9) in this poem?

2. What distinction is made between the "things that fly" in the first stanza and the "things that stay" in the second stanza?

3. Discuss the connotative value of the diction in line 7. How might this suggest some possible themes for the poem?

Water, is taught by thirst   *c. 1859*

Water, is taught by thirst.
Land — by the Oceans passed.
Transport — by throe —
Peace — by its battles told —
Love, by Memorial Mold —
Birds, by the Snow.

CONSIDERATIONS FOR CRITICAL THINKING AND WRITING

1. **FIRST RESPONSE.** Which image in the poem do you find most powerful? Explain why.

2. How is the paradox of each line of the poem resolved? How is the first word of each line "taught" by the phrase that follows it?

3. **CREATIVE RESPONSE.** Try your hand at writing similar lines in which something is "taught."

CONNECTIONS TO OTHER SELECTIONS

1. What does this poem have in common with "Success is counted sweetest" (p. 1052)? Which poem do you think is more effective? Explain why.

2. How is the crucial point of this poem related to "I like a look of Agony" (p. 1058)?

Safe in their Alabaster Chambers —   *1859 version*

Safe in their Alabaster Chambers —
Untouched by Morning
And untouched by Noon —
Sleep the meek members of the Resurrection —
Rafter of satin,   5
And Roof of stone.

Light laughs the breeze
In her Castle above them —
Babbles the Bee in a stolid Ear,
Pipe the Sweet Birds in ignorant cadence —   10
Ah, what sagacity perished here!

Safe in their Alabaster Chambers —   *1861 version*

Safe in their Alabaster Chambers —
Untouched by Morning —
And untouched by Noon —
Lie the meek members of the Resurrection —
Rafter of Satin — and Roof of Stone!   5

Grand go the Years — in the Crescent — above them —
Worlds scoop their arcs —
And Firmaments — row —
Diadems — drop — and Doges° — surrender —
Soundless as dots — on a Disc of Snow —   10

9 *Doges:* Chief magistrates of Venice from the twelfth to the sixteenth centuries.

CONSIDERATIONS FOR CRITICAL THINKING AND WRITING

1. **FIRST RESPONSE.** Dickinson permitted the 1859 version of this poem, entitled "The Sleeping," to be printed in the *Springfield Republican.* The second version she sent privately to Thomas Wentworth Higginson. Why do you suppose she would agree to publish the first but not the second version?

2. Are there any significant changes in the first stanzas of the two versions? If you answered yes, explain the significance of the changes.

3. Describe the different kinds of images used in the two second stanzas. How do those images affect the tones and meanings of those stanzas?

4. Discuss why you prefer one version of the poem to the other.

CONNECTIONS TO OTHER SELECTIONS

1. Compare the theme in the 1861 version with the theme of Robert Frost's "Design" (p. 1116).

2. In an essay discuss the attitude toward death in the 1859 version and in "Apparently with no surprise" (p. 1085).

Portraits are to daily faces   *c. 1860*

Portraits are to daily faces
As an Evening West,
To a fine, pedantic sunshine —
In a satin Vest!

CONSIDERATIONS FOR CRITICAL THINKING AND WRITING

1. **FIRST RESPONSE.** Dickinson once described her literary art this way: "My business is circumference." Does this poem fit her characterization of her poetry?

2. How is the basic strategy of this poem similar to the following statement: "Doorknob is to door as button is to sweater"?

3. Identify the four metonymies in the poem. Pay close attention to their connotative meanings.

4. If you don't know the meaning of "pedantic" (line 3), look it up in a dictionary. How does its meaning affect your reading of "fine" (line 3)?

CONNECTIONS TO OTHER SELECTIONS

1. Compare Dickinson's view of poetry in this poem with Robert Francis's perspective in "Catch" (p. 750). What important similarities and differences do you find?

2. Write an essay describing Robert Frost's strategy in "Mending Wall" (p. 1100) or "Birches" (p. 1107) as the "business of circumference."

3. How is the theme of this poem related to the central idea in "The Thought beneath so slight a film —" (p. 1050)?

4. Compare the use of the word "fine" here with its use in "'Faith' is a fine invention" (p. 1084).

Some keep the Sabbath going to Church —   *c. 1860*

Some keep the Sabbath going to Church —
I keep it, staying at Home —
With a Bobolink for a Chorister —
And an Orchard, for a Dome —

Some keep the Sabbath in Surplice°   *holy robes*   5
I just wear my Wings —
And instead of tolling the Bell, for Church,
Our little Sexton — sings.

God preaches, a noted Clergyman —
And the sermon is never long,   10
So instead of getting to Heaven, at last —
I'm going, all along.

CONSIDERATIONS FOR CRITICAL THINKING AND WRITING

1. **FIRST RESPONSE.** What is the effect of referring to "Some" people (line 1)?

2. Characterize the speaker's tone.

3. How does the speaker distinguish himself or herself from those who go to church?

4. How might "Surplice" (line 5) be read as a pun?

5. According to the speaker, how should the Sabbath be observed?

CONNECTION TO ANOTHER SELECTION

1. Write an essay that discusses nature in this poem and in Walt Whitman's "When I Heard the Learn'd Astronomer" (p. 1351).

"Heaven" — is what I cannot reach!

c. 1861

"Heaven" — is what I cannot reach!
The Apple on the Tree —
Provided it do hopeless — hang —
That — "Heaven" is — to Me!

The Color, on the Cruising Cloud —   5
The interdicted Land —
Behind the Hill — the House behind —
There — Paradise — is found!

Her teasing Purples — Afternoons —
The credulous — decoy —   10
Enamored — of the Conjuror —
That spurned us — Yesterday!

CONSIDERATIONS FOR CRITICAL THINKING AND WRITING

1. **FIRST RESPONSE.** How does the speaker define heaven? How does that definition compare with conventional views of heaven?
2. Look up the myth of Tantalus and explain the allusion in line 3.
3. Given the speaker's definition of heaven, how do you think he or she would describe hell?

CONNECTIONS TO OTHER SELECTIONS

1. Write an essay that discusses desire in this poem and in "Water, is taught by thirst" (p. 1053).
2. Discuss the speakers' attitudes toward pleasure in this poem and in Sharon Olds's "Last Night" (p. 816).

"Hope" is the thing with feathers —

c. 1861

"Hope" is the thing with feathers —
That perches in the soul —
And sings the tune without the words —
And never stops — at all —

And sweetest — in the Gale — is heard —   5
And sore must be the storm —
That could abash the little Bird
That kept so many warm —

I've heard it in the chillest land —
And on the strangest Sea —   10
Yet, never, in Extremity,
It asked a crumb — of Me.

CONSIDERATIONS FOR CRITICAL THINKING AND WRITING

1. **FIRST RESPONSE.** Why do you think the speaker defines hope in terms of a
   bird? Why is this metaphor more appropriate than, say, a dog?

2. Discuss the effects of the rhymes in each stanza.

3. What is the central point of the poem?

CONNECTIONS TO OTHER SELECTIONS

1. Compare the tone of this definition of hope with that of "'Faith' is a fine
   invention" (p. 1084). How is "Extremity" (line 11) handled differently than
   the "Emergency" (4) in the latter poem?

2. Compare the strategies used to define hope in this poem and heaven in the
   preceding poem, "'Heaven' — is what I cannot reach!" Which poem, in your
   opinion, creates a more successful definition? In an essay explain why.

The Robin's my Criterion for Tune —   *c. 1861*

The Robin's my Criterion for Tune —
Because I grow — where Robins do —
But, were I Cuckoo born —
I'd swear by him —
The ode familiar — rules the Noon —   5
The Buttercup's, my Whim for Bloom —
Because, we're Orchard sprung —
But, were I Britain born,
I'd Daisies spurn —
None but the Nut — October fit —   10
Because, through dropping it,
The Seasons flit — I'm taught —
Without the Snow's Tableau
Winter, were lie — to me —
Because I see — New Englandly —   15
The Queen, discerns like me —
Provincially —

CONSIDERATIONS FOR CRITICAL THINKING AND WRITING

1. **FIRST RESPONSE.** What does this poem suggest about the importance Dickinson invests in the sense of place in her poetry?

2. How does the dictionary define *provincial*? How does the speaker define
   provincial in the poem?

3. Choose another Dickinson poem from the collection in this anthology and
   explain how the poet sees "New Englandly" (line 15) in it.

I like a look of Agony

c. 1861

I like a look of Agony,
Because I know it's true —
Men do not sham Convulsion,
Nor simulate, a Throe —

The Eyes glaze once — and that is Death —
Impossible to feign
The Beads upon the Forehead
By homely Anguish strung.

CONSIDERATIONS FOR CRITICAL THINKING AND WRITING

1. **FIRST RESPONSE.** Why does the speaker "like a look of Agony"? How do you respond to her appreciation of "Convulsion" (line 3)?

2. Discuss the image of "The Eyes glaze once —" (line 5). Why is that a particularly effective metaphor for death?

3. Characterize the speaker. One critic described the voice in this poem as "almost a hysterical shriek." Explain why you agree or disagree.

CONNECTION TO ANOTHER SELECTION

1. Write an essay on Dickinson's attitudes toward pain and deprivation, using this poem and " 'Heaven' — is what I cannot reach!" (p. 1056).

Wild Nights — Wild Nights!

c. 1861

Wild Nights — Wild Nights!
Were I with thee
Wild Nights should be
Our luxury!

Futile — the Winds —
To a Heart in port —   5
Done with the Compass —
Done with the Chart!

Rowing in Eden —
Ah, the Sea!
Might I but moor — Tonight —   10
In Thee!

CONSIDERATIONS FOR CRITICAL THINKING AND WRITING

1. **FIRST RESPONSE.** Thomas Wentworth Higginson, Dickinson's mentor, once said he was afraid that some "malignant" readers might "read into [a poem like this] more than that virgin recluse ever dreamed of putting there." What do you think?

2. Look up the meaning of *luxury* in a dictionary. Why does this word work especially well here?

3. Given the imagery of the final stanza, do you think the speaker is a man or a woman? Explain why.

4. **CRITICAL STRATEGIES.** Read the section on psychological strategies (pp. 2050–52) in Chapter 53, "Critical Strategies for Reading." What do you think this poem reveals about the author's personal psychology?

CONNECTION TO ANOTHER SELECTION

1. Write an essay that compares the voice, figures of speech, and theme of this poem with those of Margaret Atwood's "you fit into me" (p. 866).

What Soft — Cherubic Creatures —   *1862*

What Soft — Cherubic Creatures —
These Gentlewomen are —
One would as soon assault a Plush —
Or violate a Star —

Such Dimity° Convictions —   *sheer cotton fabric* 5
A Horror so refined
Of freckled Human Nature —
Of Deity — ashamed —

It's such a common — Glory —
A Fisherman's — Degree —   10
Redemption — Brittle Lady —
Be so — ashamed of Thee —

CONSIDERATIONS FOR CRITICAL THINKING AND WRITING

1. **FIRST RESPONSE.** Characterize the "Gentlewomen" in this poem.

2. How do the sounds produced in the first line help to reinforce meaning?

3. What are "Dimity Convictions" (line 5), and what do they make "Of freckled Human Nature" (line 7)?

4. Discuss the irony in the final stanza.

CONNECTION TO ANOTHER SELECTION

1. How are the "Gentlewomen" in this poem similar to the "Gentlemen" in "'Faith' is a fine invention" (p. 1084)?

The Soul selects her own Society —   *c. 1862*

The Soul selects her own Society —
Then — shuts the Door —
To her divine Majority —
Present no more —

Manuscript page for "What Soft—Cherubic Creatures—" (p. 1059), taken from one of Dickinson's forty fascicles—small booklets hand-sewn with white string that contained her poetry as well as other miscellaneous writings. These fascicles are important for Dickinson scholars, as this manuscript page makes clear: her style to some extent resists translation into the conventions of print.

Unmoved — she notes the Chariots — pausing —   5
At her low Gate —
Unmoved — an Emperor be kneeling
Upon her Mat —

I've known her — from an ample nation —
Choose One —   10
Then — close the Valves of her attention —
Like Stone —

CONSIDERATIONS FOR CRITICAL THINKING AND WRITING

1. FIRST RESPONSE. Characterize the speaker. Is she self-reliant and self-sufficient? cold? angry?

2. Why do you suppose the "Soul" in this poem is female? Would it make any difference if it were male?

3. Discuss the effect of the images in the final two lines. Pay particular attention to the meanings of "Valves" in line 11.

Much Madness is divinest Sense —   *c. 1862*

Much Madness is divinest Sense —
To a discerning Eye —
Much Sense — the starkest Madness —
'Tis the Majority
In this, as All, prevail —
Assent — and you are sane —
Demur — you're straightway dangerous —
And handled with a Chain —

CONSIDERATIONS FOR CRITICAL THINKING AND WRITING

1. FIRST RESPONSE. Thomas Wentworth Higginson's wife once referred to Dickinson as the "partially cracked poetess of Amherst." Assuming that Dickinson had some idea of how she was regarded by "the Majority" (line 4), how might this poem be seen as an insight into her life?

2. Discuss the conflict between the individual and society in this poem. Which images are used to describe each? How do these images affect your attitudes about them?

3. Comment on the effectiveness of the poem's final line.

CONNECTION TO ANOTHER SELECTION

1. Discuss the theme of self-reliance in this poem and in the preceding poem, "The Soul selects her own Society —."

I dwell in Possibility —

c. 1862

I dwell in Possibility —
A fairer House than Prose —
More numerous of Windows —
Superior — for Doors —

Of Chambers as the Cedars —   5
Impregnable of Eye —
And for an Everlasting Roof
The Gambrels° of the Sky —   *angled roofs*

Of Visitors — the fairest —
For Occupation — This —   10
The spreading wide my narrow Hands
To gather Paradise —

CONSIDERATIONS FOR CRITICAL THINKING AND WRITING

1. **FIRST RESPONSE.** What distinction is made between poetry and prose in this poem? Explain why you agree or disagree with the speaker's distinctions.

2. What is the poem's central metaphor in the second and third stanzas?

3. How does the use of metaphor in this poem become a means for the speaker to envision and create a world beyond the circumstances of his or her actual life?

CONNECTIONS TO OTHER SELECTIONS

1. Compare what this poem says about poetry and prose with T. E. Hulme's comments in "On the Differences between Poetry and Prose" (p. 863).

2. How can the speaker's sense of expansiveness in this poem be reconciled with the speaker's insistence on contraction in "The Soul selects her own Society —" (p. 1059)? Are these poems contradictory? Explain why or why not.

They dropped like Flakes —

1862

They dropped like Flakes —
They dropped like Stars —
Like Petals from a Rose —
When suddenly across the June
A wind with fingers — goes —

They perished in the Seamless Grass —
No eye could find the place —
But God can summon every face
On his Repealless — List.

CONSIDERATIONS FOR CRITICAL THINKING AND WRITING

1. **FIRST RESPONSE.** How are the similes in the first three lines related to one another?
2. What do you think is happening in lines 4–5?
3. Explain why you find the final two lines either alarming or comforting.

CONNECTION TO ANOTHER SELECTION

1. Compare the tone and themes of this poem with those in "Apparently with no surprise" (p. 1085).

After great pain, a formal feeling comes —   *c. 1862*

After great pain, a formal feeling comes —
The Nerves sit ceremonious, like Tombs —
The stiff Heart questions was it He, that bore,
And Yesterday, or Centuries before?

The Feet, mechanical, go round —   5
Of Ground, or Air, or Ought —
A Wooden way
Regardless grown,
A Quartz contentment, like a stone —

This is the Hour of Lead —   10
Remembered, if outlived,
As Freezing persons, recollect the Snow —
First — Chill — then Stupor — then the letting go —

CONSIDERATIONS FOR CRITICAL THINKING AND WRITING

1. **FIRST RESPONSE.** What do you think has caused the speaker's pain?
2. How does the rhythm of the lines create a slow, somber pace?
3. Discuss why "the Hour of Lead" (line 10) could serve as a useful title for this poem.

CONNECTIONS TO OTHER SELECTIONS

1. How might this poem be read as a kind of sequel to "The Bustle in a House" (p. 1069)?
2. Write an essay that discusses this poem in relation to Robert Frost's "Home Burial" (p. 1102).

Pain — has an Element of Blank —   *c. 1862*

Pain — has an Element of Blank —
It cannot recollect
When it begun — or if there were
A time when it was not —

It has no Future — but itself —
Its Infinite contain
Its Past — enlightened to perceive
New Periods — of Pain.

CONSIDERATIONS FOR CRITICAL THINKING AND WRITING

1. **FIRST RESPONSE.** What does the speaker say is the relationship between pain and time?

2. Explain why you think this poem refers primarily to physical or emotional pain — or both.

3. Comment on Dickinson's choice of "enlightened" in line 7. Why do you suppose she didn't choose a word like *fated* or *doomed*?

CONNECTION TO ANOTHER SELECTION

1. Consider the significance of pain in this poem and in Dickinson's "I like a look of Agony" (p. 1058).

The Morning after Wo —   *c. 1862*

The Morning after Wo —
'Tis frequently the Way —
Surpasses all that rose before —
For utter Jubilee —

As Nature did not care —   5
And piled her Blossoms on —
And further to parade a Joy
Her Victim stared upon —

The Birds declaim their Tunes —
Pronouncing every word   10
Like Hammers — Did they know they fell
Like Litanies of Lead —

On here and there — a creature —
They'd modify the Glee
To fit some Crucifixel Clef —   15
Some Key of Calvary —

CONSIDERATIONS FOR CRITICAL THINKING AND WRITING

1. **FIRST RESPONSE.** How does the diction of this poem serve to identify the nature of the "Wo" in line 1?

2. Paraphrase the disjuncture the speaker describes between what the "Victim" (line 8) experiences and how "Nature" (5) responds to "wo."

3. Examine carefully Dickinson's use of sound and rhythm and explain how that affects tone.

CONNECTION TO ANOTHER SELECTION

1. Compare the themes of "The Morning after Wo —" and "The Bustle in a House" (p. 1069).

I heard a Fly buzz — when I died —   *c. 1862*

I heard a Fly buzz — when I died —
The Stillness in the Room
Was like the Stillness in the Air —
Between the Heaves of Storm —

The Eyes around — had wrung them dry —   5
And Breaths were gathering firm
For that last Onset — when the King
Be witnessed — in the Room —

I willed my Keepsakes — Signed away
What portion of me be   10
Assignable — and then it was
There interposed a Fly —

With Blue — uncertain stumbling Buzz —
Between the light — and me —
And then the Windows failed — and then   15
I could not see to see —

CONSIDERATIONS FOR CRITICAL THINKING AND WRITING

1. **FIRST RESPONSE.** What was expected to happen "when the King" was "witnessed" (lines 7–8)? What happened instead?

2. Why do you think Dickinson chooses a fly rather than perhaps a bee or gnat?

3. What is the effect of the last line? Why not end the poem with "I could not see" instead of the additional "to see"?

4. Discuss the sounds in the poem. Are there any instances of onomatopoeia?

CONNECTIONS TO OTHER SELECTIONS

1. Contrast the symbolic significance of the fly with that of the spider in Walt Whitman's "A Noiseless Patient Spider" (p. 881).

2. Consider the meaning of "light" (line 14) in this poem and in "There's a certain Slant of light" (p. 2085).

3. Compare the themes in Dickinson's poem and in Herbert Lomas's "The Fly's Poem about Emily" (p. 829).

One need not be a Chamber — to be Haunted —   *c. 1863*

One need not be a Chamber — to be Haunted —
One need not be a House —
The Brain has Corridors — surpassing
Material Place —

Far safer, of a Midnight Meeting   5
External Ghost
Than its interior Confronting —
That Cooler Host.

Far safer, through an Abbey gallop,
The Stones a'chase —   10
Than Unarmed, one's a'self encounter —
In lonesome Place —

Ourself behind ourself, concealed —
Should startle most —
Assassin hid in our Apartment   15
Be Horror's least.

The Body — borrows a Revolver —
He bolts the Door —
O'erlooking a superior spectre —
Or More —   20

CONSIDERATIONS FOR CRITICAL THINKING AND WRITING

1. **FIRST RESPONSE.** Paraphrase the poem. Which stanza is most difficult to paraphrase? Why?

2. What is the poem's controlling metaphor? Explain why you think it is effective or not.

3. What is the "superior spectre" in line 19?

CONNECTIONS TO OTHER SELECTIONS

1. Compare and contrast this poem with Edgar Allan Poe's "The Haunted Palace" (p. 891) and Jim Stevens's "Schizophrenia" (p. 881). In an essay explain which poem you find the most frightening.

Because I could not stop for Death —   *c. 1863*

Because I could not stop for Death —
He kindly stopped for me —
The Carriage held but just Ourselves —
And Immortality.

We slowly drove — He knew no haste   5
And I had put away
My labor and my leisure too,
For His Civility —

We passed the School, where Children strove
At Recess — in the Ring —   10
We passed the Fields of Gazing Grain —
We passed the Setting Sun —

Or rather — He passed Us —
The Dews drew quivering and chill —
For only Gossamer, my Gown —   15
My Tippet° — only Tulle —   *shawl*

We paused before a House that seemed
A Swelling of the Ground —
The Roof was scarcely visible —
The Cornice — in the Ground —   20

Since then — 'tis Centuries — and yet
Feels shorter than the Day
I first surmised the Horses' Heads
Were toward Eternity —

CONSIDERATIONS FOR CRITICAL THINKING AND WRITING

1. **FIRST RESPONSE.** Why couldn't the speaker "stop for Death"?
2. How is death personified in this poem? How does the speaker respond to him? Why are they accompanied by Immortality?
3. What is the significance of the things they "passed" in the third stanza?
4. What is the "House" in lines 17–20?
5. Discuss the rhythm of the lines. How, for example, is the rhythm of line 14 related to its meaning?

CONNECTIONS TO OTHER SELECTIONS

1. Compare the tone of this poem with that of Dickinson's "Apparently with no surprise" (p. 1085).
2. Write an essay comparing Dickinson's view of death in this poem and in "If I shouldn't be alive" (p. 1049). Which poem is more powerful for you? Explain why.

I felt a Cleaving in my Mind —   *c. 1864*

I felt a Cleaving in my Mind —
As if my Brain had split —
I tried to match it — Seam by Seam —
But could not make them fit.

The thought behind, I strove to join
Unto the thought before —
But Sequence ravelled out of Sound
Like Balls — upon a Floor.

CONSIDERATIONS FOR CRITICAL THINKING AND WRITING

1. **FIRST RESPONSE.** What is going on in the speaker's mind?

2. What is the poem's controlling metaphor? Describe the simile in lines 7 and 8. How does it clarify the first stanza?

3. Discuss the rhymes. How do they reinforce meaning?

CONNECTION TO ANOTHER SELECTION

1. Compare the power of the speaker's mind described here with the power of imagination described in "To make a prairie it takes a clover and one bee" (p. 1051).

A Light exists in Spring

c. 1864

A Light exists in Spring
Not present on the Year
At any other period —
When March is scarcely here

A Color stands abroad   5
On Solitary Fields
That Science cannot overtake
But Human Nature feels.

It waits upon the Lawn,
It shows the furthest Tree   10
Upon the furthest Slope you know
It almost speaks to you.

Then as Horizons step
Or Noons report away
Without the Formula of sound   15
It passes and we stay —

A quality of loss
Affecting our Content
As Trade had suddenly encroached
Upon a Sacrament.   20

CONSIDERATIONS FOR CRITICAL THINKING AND WRITING

1. **FIRST RESPONSE.** Based on Dickinson's description, how would you characterize the nature of the light on a New England March day? How is that light different from that of a summer's day?

2. What kinds of feelings are evoked in the speaker by the light?

3. How are "Science" and "Trade" (lines 7, 19) depicted in contrast to what "Human Nature feels" (8)?

CONNECTION TO ANOTHER SELECTION

1. Compare Dickinson's thematic use of light in this poem and in "There's a certain Slant of light" (p. 2085).

Oh Sumptuous moment   *c. 1868*

Oh Sumptuous moment
Slower go
That I may gloat on thee —
'Twill never be the same to starve
Now I abundance see —

Which was to famish, then or now —
The difference of Day
Ask him unto the Gallows led —
With morning in the sky

CONSIDERATIONS FOR CRITICAL THINKING AND WRITING

1. FIRST RESPONSE. How do the sounds of the first stanza contribute to its meaning?

2. What kind of experience do you imagine the speaker is describing?

3. How do the final three lines shed light on the meaning of lines 1 to 6?

CONNECTIONS TO OTHER SELECTIONS

1. Compare and contrast the themes of this poem, "Water, is taught by thirst" (p. 1053), and "'Heaven' — is what I cannot reach!" (p. 1056).

The Bustle in a House   *c. 1866*

The Bustle in a House
The Morning after Death
Is solemnest of industries
Enacted upon Earth —

The Sweeping up the Heart
And putting Love away
We shall not want to use again
Until Eternity.

CONSIDERATIONS FOR CRITICAL THINKING AND WRITING

1. FIRST RESPONSE. What is the relationship between love and death in this poem?

2. Why do you think mourning (notice the pun in line 2) is described as industry?

3. Discuss the tone of the poem's ending. Consider whether you think it is hopeful, sad, resigned, or some other mood.

CONNECTIONS TO OTHER SELECTIONS

1. Compare this poem with "After great pain, a formal feeling comes—" (p. 1063). Which poem is, for you, a more powerful treatment of mourning?
2. How does this poem qualify "I like a look of Agony" (p. 1058)? Does it contradict the latter poem? Explain why or why not.

Tell all the Truth but tell it slant—

c. 1868

Tell all the Truth but tell it slant—
Success in Circuit lies
Too bright for our infirm Delight
The Truth's superb surprise

As Lightning to the Children eased
With explanation kind
The Truth must dazzle gradually
Or every man be blind—

CONSIDERATIONS FOR CRITICAL THINKING AND WRITING

1. FIRST RESPONSE. What do you think the first line means? Why should truth be told "slant" and circuitously?
2. How does the second stanza explain the first?
3. How is this poem an example of its own theme?

CONNECTIONS TO OTHER SELECTIONS

1. How does the first stanza of "I know that He exists" (p. 1084) suggest an idea similar to this poem's? Why do you think the last eight lines of the former aren't similar in theme to this poem?
2. Write an essay on Dickinson's attitudes about the purpose and strategies of poetry by considering this poem as well as "The Thought beneath so slight a film—" (p. 1050) and "Portraits are to daily faces" (p. 1054).

There is no Frigate like a Book

c. 1873

There is no Frigate like a Book
To take us Lands away
Nor any Coursers like a Page
Of prancing Poetry—

This Traverse may the poorest take
Without oppress of Toll —
How frugal is the Chariot
That bears the Human soul.

CONSIDERATIONS FOR CRITICAL THINKING AND WRITING

1. **FIRST RESPONSE.** Which lines present reading as a mode of transportation? Why do you think that is an effective controlling metaphor in a poem about the value of books?

2. How does the poem's rhythm suggest a kind of "prancing Poetry" (line 4)?

CONNECTION TO ANOTHER SELECTION

1. Compare the use of extended metaphor in this poem with that in "I dwell in Possibility—" (p. 1062). How consistent is the use of extended metaphor in each poem, and what is the effect?

Fame is the one that does not stay —   *c. 1879*

Fame is the one that does not stay —
Its occupant must die
Or out of sight of estimate
Ascend incessantly —
Or be that most insolvent thing
A Lightning in the Germ —
Electrical the embryo
But we demand the Flame

CONSIDERATIONS FOR CRITICAL THINKING AND WRITING

1. **FIRST RESPONSE.** How is "fame" defined in this poem? Does the definition seem to correspond with what you know of Dickinson's relationship to fame?

2. Check a dictionary for definitions of "Germ" (line 6). How is Dickinson using the word?

3. Discuss the possible meanings of the final two lines.

CONNECTION TO ANOTHER SELECTION

1. To what extent might Dickinson's "Success is counted sweetest" (p. 1052) serve as a commentary on this poem?

Perspectives on Emily Dickinson

EMILY DICKINSON

A Description of Herself   1862

Mr Higginson,

Your kindness claimed earlier gratitude — but I was ill — and write today, from my pillow.

Thank you for the surgery — it was not so painful as I supposed. I bring you others° — as you ask — though they might not differ —

While my thought is undressed — I can make the distinction, but when I put them in the Gown — they look alike, and numb.

You asked how old I was? I made no verse — but one or two° — until this winter — Sir —

I had a terror — since September — I could tell to none — and so I sing, as the Boy does by the Burying Ground — because I am afraid — You inquire my Books — For Poets — I have Keats — and Mr and Mrs Browning. For Prose — Mr Ruskin — Sir Thomas Browne — and the Revelations. I went to school — but in your manner of the phrase — had no education. When a little Girl, I had a friend, who taught me Immortality — but venturing too near, himself — he never returned — Soon after, my Tutor, died — and for several years, my Lexicon — was my only companion — Then I found one more — but he was not contented I be his scholar — so he left the Land.

You ask of my Companions Hills — Sir — and the Sundown — and a Dog — large as myself, that my Father bought me — They are better than Beings — because they know — but do not tell — and the noise in the Pool, at Noon — excels my Piano. I have a Brother and Sister — My Mother does not care for thought — and Father, too busy with his Briefs — to notice what we do — He buys me many Books — but begs me not to read them — because he fears they joggle the Mind. They are religious — except me — and address an Eclipse, every morning — whom they call their "Father." But I fear my story fatigues you — I would like to learn — Could you tell me how to grow — or is it unconveyed — like Melody — or Witchcraft?

From a letter to Thomas Wentworth Higginson, April 25, 1862

others: Dickinson had sent poems to Higginson for his opinions and enclosed more with this letter.   *one or two:* Actually she had written almost 300 poems.

CONSIDERATIONS FOR CRITICAL THINKING AND WRITING

1. What impression does this letter give you of Dickinson?
2. What kinds of thoughts are there in the foreground of her thinking?
3. To what extent is the style of her letter writing like that of her poetry?

THOMAS WENTWORTH HIGGINSON (1823–1911)

On Meeting Dickinson for the First Time   *1870*

A large county lawyer's house, brown brick, with great trees & a garden — I sent up my card. A parlor dark & cool & stiffish, a few books & engravings & an open piano. . . .

A step like a pattering child's in entry & in glided a little plain woman with two smooth bands of reddish hair & a face a little like Belle Dove's; not plainer — with no good feature — in a very plain & exquisitely clean white pique & a blue net worsted shawl. She came to me with two day lilies which she put in a sort of childlike way into my hand & said "These are my introduction" in a soft frightened breathless childlike voice — & added under her breath Forgive me if I am frightened; I never see strangers & hardly know what I say — but she talked soon & thenceforward continuously — & deferentially — sometimes stopping to ask me to talk instead of her — but readily recommencing . . . thoroughly ingenuous & simple . . . & saying many things which you would have thought foolish & I wise — & some things you wd. hv. liked. I add a few over the page. . . .

"Women talk; men are silent; that is why I dread women."

"My father only reads on Sunday — he reads *lonely* & *rigorous* books."

"If I read a book [and] it makes my whole body so cold no fire ever can warm me I know *that* is poetry. If I feel physically as if the top of my head were taken off, I know *that* is poetry. These are the only ways I know it. Is there any other way."

"How do most people live without any thoughts. There are many people in the world (you must have noticed them in the street) How do they live. How do they get strength to put on their clothes in the morning"

"When I lost the use of my Eyes it was a comfort to think there were so few real *books* that I could easily find some one to read me all of them"

"Truth is such a *rare* thing it is delightful to tell it."

"I find ecstasy in living — the mere sense of living is joy enough"

I asked if she never felt want of employment, never going off the place & never seeing any visitor "I never thought of conceiving that I could ever have the slightest approach to such a want in all future time" (& added) "I feel that I have not expressed myself strongly enough."

From a letter to his wife, August 16, 1870

CONSIDERATIONS FOR CRITICAL THINKING AND WRITING

1. How old is Dickinson when Higginson meets her? Does this description seem commensurate with her age? Explain why or why not.

2. Choose one of the quotations from Dickinson that Higginson includes and write an essay about what it reveals about her.

Mabel Loomis Todd (1856–1932)

The Character *of Amherst*   *1881*

I must tell you about the *character* of Amherst. It is a lady whom the people call the *Myth*. She is a sister of Mr. Dickinson, & seems to be the climax of all the family oddity. She has not been outside of her own house in fifteen years, except once to see a new church, when she crept out at night, & viewed it by moonlight. No one who calls upon her mother & sister ever see her, but she allows little children once in a great while, & one at a time, to come in, when she gives them cake or candy, or some nicety, for she is very fond of little ones. But more often she lets down the sweetmeat by a string, out of a window, to them. She dresses wholly in white, & her mind is said to be perfectly wonderful. She writes finely, but no one *ever* sees her. Her sister, who was at Mrs. Dickinson's party, invited me to come & sing to her mother sometime. . . . People tell me the *myth* will hear every note — she will be near, but unseen. . . . Isn't that like a book? So interesting.

From a letter to her parents, November 6, 1881

Considerations for Critical Thinking and Writing

1. Todd, who in the 1890s would edit Dickinson's poems and letters, had known her for only two months when she wrote this letter. How does Todd characterize Dickinson?

2. Does this description seem positive or negative to you? Explain your answer.

3. A few of Dickinson's poems, such as "Much Madness is divinest Sense —" (p. 1061), suggest that she was aware of this perception of her. Refer to her poems in discussing Dickinson's response to this perception.

Richard Wilbur (b. 1921)

On Dickinson's Sense of Privation   *1960*

What did Emily Dickinson do, as a poet, with her sense of privation? One thing she quite often did was to pose as the laureate and attorney of the empty-handed, and question God about the economy of His creation. Why, she asked, is a fatherly God so sparing of His presence? Why is there never a sign that prayers are heard? Why does Nature tell us no comforting news of its Maker? Why do some receive a whole loaf, while others must starve on a crumb? Where is the benevolence in shipwreck and earthquake? By asking such questions as these, she turned complaint into critique, and used her own sufferings as experiential evidence about the nature of the deity. The God who emerges from these poems is a God who does not answer, an unrevealed God whom one cannot confidently approach through Nature or through doctrine.

But there was another way in which Emily Dickinson dealt with her sentiment of lack — another emotional strategy which was both more frequent and more fruitful. I refer to her repeated assertion of the paradox that privation is more plentiful than plenty; that to renounce is to possess the more; that "The

Banquet of abstemiousness / Defaces that of wine." We all know how the poet illustrated this ascetic paradox in her behavior—how in her latter years she chose to live in relative retirement, keeping the world, even in its dearest aspects, at a physical remove. She would write her friends, telling them how she missed them, then flee upstairs when they came to see her; afterward, she might send a note of apology, offering the odd explanation that "We shun because we prize." Any reader of Dickinson biographies can furnish other examples, dramatic or homely, of this prizing and shunning, this yearning and renouncing: in my own mind's eye is a picture of Emily Dickinson watching a gay circus caravan from the distance of her chamber window.

> From "Sumptuous Destitution" in *Emily Dickinson: Three Views,*
> by Richard Wilbur, Louise Bogan, and Archibald MacLeish

CONSIDERATIONS FOR CRITICAL THINKING AND WRITING

1. Which poems by Dickinson reprinted in this anthology suggest that she was "the laureate and attorney of the empty-handed"?
2. Which poems suggest that "privation is more plentiful than plenty"?
3. Of these two types of poems, which do you prefer? Write an essay that explains your preference.

SANDRA M. GILBERT (B. 1936) AND
SUSAN GUBAR (B. 1944)

On Dickinson's White Dress   1979

Today a dress that the Amherst Historical Society assures us is *the* white dress Dickinson wore—or at least one of her "Uniforms of Snow"—hangs in a drycleaner's plastic bag in the closet of the Dickinson homestead. Perfectly preserved, beautifully flounced and tucked, it is larger than most readers would have expected this self-consciously small poet's dress to be, and thus reminds visiting scholars of the enduring enigma of Dickinson's central metaphor, even while it draws gasps from more practical visitors, who reflect with awe upon the difficulties of maintaining such a costume. But what exactly did the literal and figurative whiteness of this costume represent? What rewards did it offer that would cause an intelligent woman to overlook those practical difficulties? Comparing Dickinson's obsession with whiteness to [Herman] Melville's, William R. Sherwood suggests that "it reflected in her case the Christian mystery and not a Christian enigma . . . a decision to announce . . . the assumption of a worldly death that paradoxically involved regeneration." This, he adds, her gown—"a typically slant demonstration of truth"—should have revealed "to anyone with the wit to catch on."[1]

We might reasonably wonder, however, if Dickinson herself consciously intended her wardrobe to convey any one message. The range of associations

[1] *Circumference and Circumstance: Stages in the Mind and Art of Emily Dickinson* (New York: Columbia UP, 1968) 152, 231.

her white poems imply suggests, on the contrary, that for her, as for Melville, white is the ultimate symbol of enigma, paradox, and irony, "not so much a color as the visible absence of color, and at the same time the concrete of all colors." Melville's question [in *Moby-Dick*] might, therefore, also be hers: "is it for these reasons that there is such a dumb blankness, full of meaning, in a wide landscape of snows—a colorless, all-color of atheism from which we shrink?" And his concluding speculation might be hers too, his remark "that the mystical cosmetic which produces every one of [Nature's] hues, the great principle of light, for ever remains white or colorless in itself, and if operating without medium upon matter, would touch all objects . . . with its own blank tinge." For white, in Dickinson's poetry, frequently represents both the energy (the white heat) of Romantic creativity, and the loneliness (the polar cold) of the renunciation or tribulation Romantic creativity may demand, both the white radiance of eternity—or Revelation—and the white terror of a shroud.

From *The Madwoman in the Attic: The Woman Writer*
and the Nineteenth-Century Literary Imagination

CONSIDERATIONS FOR CRITICAL THINKING AND WRITING

1. What meanings do Gilbert and Gubar attribute to Dickinson's white dress?
2. Discuss the meaning of the implicit whiteness in "Safe in their Alabaster Chambers—" (pp. 1053–54) and "After great pain, a formal feeling comes—" (p. 1063). To what extent do these poems incorporate the meanings of whiteness that Gilbert and Gubar suggest?
3. What other reasons can you think of that might account for Dickinson's wearing only white?

CYNTHIA GRIFFIN WOLFF (B. 1935)
On the Many Voices in Dickinson's Poetry   1986

There were many "Voices." This fact has sometimes puzzled Dickinson's readers. One poem may be delivered in a child's Voice; another in the Voice of a young woman scrutinizing nature and the society in which she makes her place. Sometimes the Voice is that of a woman self-confidently addressing her lover in a language of passion and sexual desire. At still other times, the Voice of the verse seems so precariously balanced at the edge of hysteria that even its calmest observations grate like the shriek of dementia. There is the Voice of the housewife and the Voice that has recourse to the occasionally agonizing, occasionally regal language of the conversion experience of latter-day New England Puritanism. In some poems the Voice is distinctive principally because it speaks in the aftermath of wounding and can comprehend extremities of pain. Moreover, these Voices are not always entirely distinct from one another: the child's Voice that opens a poem may yield to the Voice of a young woman speaking the idiom of ardent love; in a different poem, the speaker may fall into a mood of almost religious contemplation in an attempt to analyze or define such abstract entities as loneliness or madness or eternity; the diction of the housewife may be conflated with the sovereign language of the New Jerusalem, and taken together, they may render some aspect of the word-smith's labor. No manageable set of discrete categories suffices to capture the diversity of discourse, and any attempt to simplify Dickinson's methods does violence to the verse.

Yet there is a paradox here. This is, by no stretch of the imagination, a body of poetry that might be construed as a series of lyrics spoken by many different people. Disparate as these many Voices are, somehow they all appear to issue from the same "self." . . . It is the enigmatic "Emily Dickinson" readers suppose themselves to have found in this poetry, even in the extreme case when Dickinson's supposed speaker is male. One explanation for this sense of intrinsic unity in the midst of diversity is the persistence with which Dickinson addresses the same set of problems, using a remarkably durable repertoire of linguistic modes. Evocations of injury and wounding—threats to the coherence of the self—appear in the earliest poems and continue until the end; ways of rendering face-to-face encounters change, but this preoccupation with "interview" is sustained by metaphors of "confrontation" that weave throughout. The summoning of one or another Voice in a given poem, then, is not an unself-conscious emotive reflection of Emily Dickinson's mood at the moment of creation. Rather, each different Voice is a calculated tactic, an attempt to touch her readers and engage them intimately with the poetry. Each Voice had its unique advantages; each its limitations. A poet self-conscious in her craft, she calculated this element as carefully as every other.

From *Emily Dickinson*

CONSIDERATIONS FOR CRITICAL THINKING AND WRITING

1. From the poems in this anthology, try adding to the list of voices Wolff cites.
2. Despite the many voices in Dickinson's poetry, why, according to Wolff, is there still a "sense of intrinsic unity" in her poetry?
3. Choose a Dickinson poem and describe how the choice of voice is a "calculated tactic."

PAULA BENNETT (B. 1936)
On "I heard a Fly buzz—when I died—"   *1990*

Dickinson's rage against death, a rage that led her at times to hate both life and death, might have been alleviated, had she been able to gather hard evidence about an afterlife. But, of course, she could not. "The *Bareheaded life*—under the grass—," she wrote to Samuel Bowles in c. 1860, "worries one like a Wasp." If death was the gate to a better life in "the childhood of the kingdom of Heaven," as the sentimentalists—and Christ—claimed, then, perhaps, there was compensation and healing for life's woes. . . . But how do we know? What can we know? In "I heard a Fly buzz—when I died," Dickinson concludes that we do not know much. . . .

Like many people in her period, Dickinson was fascinated by death-bed scenes. How, she asked various correspondents, did this or that person die? In particular, she wanted to know if their deaths revealed any information about the nature of the afterlife. In this poem, however, she imagines her own death-bed scene, and the answer she provides is grim, as grim (and, at the same time, as ironically mocking) as anything she ever wrote.

In the narrowing focus of death, the fly's insignificant buzz, magnified tenfold by the stillness in the room, is all that the speaker hears. This kind of distortion in scale is common. It is one of the "illusions" of perception. But here it is horrifying because it defeats every expectation we have. Death is supposed to be an experience of awe. It is the moment when the soul, departing the body, is taken up by God. Hence the watchers at the bedside wait for the moment when the "King" (whether God or death) "be witnessed" in the room. And hence the speaker assigns away everything but that which she expects God (her soul) or death (her body) to take.

What arrives instead, however, is neither God nor death but a fly, "[w]ith Blue — uncertain — stumbling Buzz," a fly, that is, no more secure, no more sure, than we are. Dickinson had associated flies with death once before in the exquisite lament, "How many times these low feet / staggered." In this poem, they buzz "on the / chamber window," and speckle it with dirt, reminding us that the housewife, who once protected us from such intrusions, will protect us no longer. Their presence is threatening but only in a minor way, "dull" like themselves. They are a background noise we do not have to deal with yet.

In "I heard a Fly buzz," on the other hand, there is only one fly and its buzz is not only foregrounded. Before the poem is over, the buzz takes up the entire field of perception, coming between the speaker and the "light" (of day, of life, of knowledge). It is then that the "Windows" (the eyes that are the windows of the soul as well as, metonymically, the light that passes through the panes of glass) "fail" and the speaker is left in darkness — in death, in ignorance. She cannot "see" to "see" (understand).

Given that the only sure thing we know about "life after death" is that flies — in their adult form and more particularly, as maggots — devour us, the poem is at the very least a grim joke. In projecting her death-bed scene, Dickinson confronts her ignorance and gives back the only answer human knowledge can with any certainty give. While we may hope for an afterlife, no one, not even the dying, can prove it exists.

From *Emily Dickinson: Woman Poet*

CONSIDERATIONS FOR CRITICAL THINKING AND WRITING

1. According to Bennett, what is the symbolic value of the fly?
2. Does Bennett leave out any significant elements of the poem in her analysis? Explain why you think she did or did not.
3. Choose a Dickinson poem and write a detailed analysis that attempts to account for all of its major elements.

MARTHA NELL SMITH (B. 1953)

On "Because I could not stop for Death—" *1993*

That this poem begins and ends with humanity's ultimate dream of self-importance — Immortality and Eternity — could well be the joke central to its meaning, for Dickinson carefully surrounds the fantasy of living ever after with the dirty facts of life — dusty carriage rides, schoolyards, and farmers' fields. Many may contend that, like the Puritans and metaphysicals before her, Dickinson pulls the sublime down to the ridiculous but unavoidable facts of existence, thus imbues life on earth with its real import. On the other hand, Dickinson may have argued otherwise. Very late in her life, she wrote, "When Jesus tells us about his Father, we distrust him. When he shows us his Home, we turn away, but when he confides to us that he is 'acquainted with Grief,' we listen, for that is also an Acquaintance of our own." Instead of sharing their faith, Dickinson may be showing the community around her, most of whom were singing "When we all get to Heaven what a day of rejoicing that will be," how selfishly selective is their belief in a system that bolsters egocentrism by assuring believers not only that their individual identities will survive death, but also that they are one of the exclusive club of the saved. Waiting for the return of Eden or Paradise, which "is always eligible" and which she "never believed . . . to be a superhuman site," those believers may simply find themselves gathering dust. Surrounded by the faithful, Dickinson struggled with trust and doubt in Christian promises herself, but whether she believed in salvation or even in immortality is endlessly debatable. Readers can select poems and letters and construct compelling arguments to prove that she did or did not. But for every declaration evincing belief, there is one like that to Elizabeth Holland:

> The Fiction of "Santa Claus" always reminds me of the reply to my early question of "Who made the Bible" — "Holy Men moved by the Holy Ghost," and though I have now ceased my investigations, the Solution is insufficient —

What "Because I could not stop for Death —" will not allow is any hard and fast conclusion to be drawn about the matter. Once again . . . by mixing tropes and tones Dickinson underscores the importance of refusing any single-minded response to a subject and implicitly attests to the power in continually opening possibilities by repeatedly posing questions.

From *Comic Power in Emily Dickinson,* by Suzanne Juhasz,
Cristanne Miller, and Martha Nell Smith

CONSIDERATIONS FOR CRITICAL THINKING AND WRITING

1. In what sense, according to Smith, could a joke be central to the meaning of "Because I could not stop for Death —"?

2. Compare the potential joke in this poem and in "I know that He exists" (p. 1084). How is your reading of each poem influenced by considering them together?

3. Read the sample paper on "Religious Faith in Four Poems by Emily Dickinson" (pp. 1085–88) and write an analysis of "Because I could not stop for Death —" that supports or refutes the paper's thesis.

RONALD WALLACE (B. 1945)

Miss Goff   1994

When Zack Pulanski brought the plastic vomit
and slid it slickly to the vinyl floor
and raised his hand, and her tired eyes fell on it
with horror, the heartless classroom lost in laughter
as the custodian slyly tossed his saw dust on it   5
and pushed it, grinning, through the door,
she reached into her ancient corner closet
and found some Emily Dickinson mimeos there

which she passed out. And then, herself
passed out on the cold circumference of her desk.   10
And everybody went their merry ways
but me, who, chancing on one unexpected phrase
after another, sat transfixed until dusk.
Me and Miss Goff, the top of our heads taken off.

CONSIDERATIONS FOR CRITICAL THINKING AND WRITING

1. How does the joke played on Miss Goff in the first stanza give way to something more serious in the second stanza? Explain the shift in tone.

2. Characterize Miss Goff. How does the poem's diction reveal some of her
   personality?

3. Dickinson once described her own poetry by writing that "my business is
   circumference," and she made an attempt to define poetry with this comment: "If I read a book [and] it makes my whole body so cold no fire ever
   can warm me, I know *that* is poetry. If I feel physically as if the top of my
   head were taken off, I know *that* is poetry." How are these statements relevant to your understanding of Wallace's poem?

4. Discuss the use of irony in "Miss Goff."

Two Complementary Critical Readings

CHARLES R. ANDERSON (1902–1999)

Eroticism in "Wild Nights — Wild Nights!"   1960

The frank eroticism of this poem might puzzle the biographer of a spinster,
but the critic can only be concerned with its effectiveness as a poem. Unless
one insists on taking the "I" to mean Emily Dickinson, there is not even any reversal of the lovers' roles (which has been charged, curiously enough, as a fault
in this poem). The opening declaration — "Wild Nights should be / Our luxury!" — sets the key of her song, for *luxuria* included the meaning of lust as well
as lavishness of sensuous enjoyment, as she was Latinist enough to know. This
is echoed at the end in "Eden," her recurring image, in letters and poems, for

the paradise of earthly love. The theme here is that of sexual passion which is lawless, outside the rule of "Chart" and "Compass." But it lives by a law of its own, the law of Eden, which protects it from mundane wind and wave.

This is what gives the magic to her climactic vision, "Rowing in Eden," sheltered luxuriously in those paradisiac waters while the wild storms of this world break about them. Such love was only possible before the Fall. Since then the bower of bliss is frugal of her leases, limiting each occupant to "an instant" she says in another poem, for "Adam taught her Thrift / Bankrupt once through his excesses." In the present poem she limits her yearning to the mortal term, just "Tonight." But this echoes the surge of ecstasy that initiated her song and gives the reiterated "Wild Nights!" a double reference, to the passionate experience in Eden as well as to the tumult of the world shut out by it. So she avoids the chief pitfall of the love lyric, the tendency to exploit emotion for its own sake. Instead she generates out of the conflicting aspects of love, its ecstasy and its brevity, the symbol that contains the poem's meaning.

From *Emily Dickinson's Poetry: Stairway of Surprise*

CONSIDERATIONS FOR CRITICAL THINKING AND WRITING

1. According to Anderson, what is the theme of "Wild Nights — Wild Nights!"?

2. How does Anderson discuss the poem's "frank eroticism"? How detailed is his discussion?

3. If there is a "reversal of the lovers' roles" in this poem, do you think it represents, as some critics have charged, "a fault in this poem"? Explain why or why not.

4. Compare Anderson's treatment of this poem with David S. Reynolds's reading that follows. Discuss which one you find more useful and explain why.

DAVID S. REYNOLDS (B. 1949)
Popular Literature and "Wild Nights — Wild Nights!"   1988

It is not known whether Dickinson had read any of the erotic literature of the day or if she knew of the stereotype of the sensual woman. Given her fascination with sensational journalism and with popular literature in general, it is hard to believe she would not have had at least some exposure to erotic literature. At any rate, her treatment of the daring theme of woman's sexual fantasy in this deservedly famous poem bears comparison with erotic themes as they appeared in popular sensational writings. The first stanza of the poem provides an uplifting or purification of sexual fantasy not distant from the effect of [Walt] Whitman's cleansing rhetoric, which, as we have seen, was consciously designed to counteract the prurience of the popular "love plot." Dickinson's repeated phrase "Wild Nights" is a simple but dazzling metaphor that communicates wild passion — even lust — but simultaneously lifts sexual desire out of the scabrous by fusing it with the natural image of the night. The second verse introduces a second nature image, the turbulent sea and the contrasting quiet port, which at once universalizes the passion and purifies it further by distancing it through a more abstract metaphor. Also, the second verse makes clear that this is not a poem of sexual consummation but rather of pure fantasy and sexual impossibility. Unlike popular erotic literature, the poem portrays neither a consummated seduction nor the heartless deception that it involves. There is instead a pure, fervent fantasy whose frustration is figured forth in the contrasting images of the ocean (the longed-for-but-never-achieved consummation) and the port (the reality of the poet's isolation). The third verse begins with an image, "Rowing in Eden," that further uplifts sexual passion by yoking it with a religious archetype. Here as elsewhere, Dickinson capitalizes nicely on the new religious style, which made possible such fusions of the divine and the earthly. The persona's concluding wish to "moor" in the sea expresses the sustained intense sexual longing and the simultaneous frustration of that longing. In the course of the poem, Dickinson has communicated great erotic passion, and yet, by effectively projecting this passion through unusual nature and religious images, has rid it of even the tiniest residue of sensationalism.

From *Beneath the American Renaissance: The Subversive Imagination in the Age of Emerson and Melville*

CONSIDERATIONS FOR CRITICAL THINKING AND WRITING

1. According to Reynolds, how do Dickinson's images provide a "cleansing" effect in the poem?

2. Explain whether you agree that the poem portrays a "pure, fervent fantasy" or something else.

3. Does Reynolds's reading of the poem compete with Anderson's or complement it? Explain your answer.

4. Given the types of critical strategies described in Chapter 53, how would you characterize Anderson's and Reynolds's approaches?

Questions for Writing about an Author in Depth

As you read multiple works by the same author, you're likely to be struck by the similarities and differences in those selections. You'll begin to recognize situations, events, characters, issues, perspectives, styles, and strategies — even recurring words or phrases — that provide a kind of signature, making the poems in some way identifiable with that particular writer.

The following questions can help you to respond to multiple works by the same author. They should help you to listen to how a writer's works can speak to one another and to you. Additional useful questions can be found in other chapters of this book. See Chapter 22, "Writing about Poetry: From Inquiry to Final Paper," and Arguing about Literature (p. 2073) in Chapter 54, "Reading and the Writing Process."

1. What topics reappear in the writer's work? What seem to be the major concerns of the author?

2. Does the author have a definable worldview that can be discerned from work to work? Is, for example, the writer liberal, conservative, apolitical, or religious?

3. What social values come through in the author's work? Does he or she seem to identify with a particular group or social class?

4. Is there a consistent voice or point of view from work to work? Is it a persona or the author's actual self?

5. How much of the author's own life experiences and historical moment make their way into the works?

6. Does the author experiment with style from work to work, or are the works mostly consistent with one another?

7. Can the author's work be identified with a literary tradition, such as *carpe diem* poetry, that aligns his or her work with that of other writers?

8. What is distinctive about the author's writing? Is the language innovative? Are the themes challenging? Are the voices conventional? Is the tone characteristic?

9. Could you identify another work by the same author without a name being attached to it? What are the distinctive features that allow you to do so?

10. Do any of the writer's works seem *not* to be by that writer? Why?

11. What other writers are most like this author in style and content? Why?

12. Has the writer's work evolved over time? Are there significant changes or developments? Are there new ideas and styles, or do the works remain largely the same?

13. How would you characterize the author's writing habits? Is it possible to anticipate what goes on in different works, or are you surprised by their content or style?

14. Can difficult or ambiguous passages in a work be resolved by referring to a similar passage in another work?

15. What does the writer say about his or her own work? Do you trust the teller or the tale? Which do you think is more reliable?

A SAMPLE IN-DEPTH STUDY

The following paper was written for an assignment that called for an analysis (about 750 words) on any topic that could be traced in three or four poems by Dickinson. The student, Michael Weitz, chose "'Faith' is a fine invention," "I know that He exists," "I never saw a Moor—," and "Apparently with no surprise."

Previous knowledge of a writer's work can set up useful expectations in a reader. In the case of the four Dickinson poems included in this section, religion emerges as a central topic linked to a number of issues, including faith, immortality, skepticism, and the nature of God. The student selected these poems because he noticed Dickinson's intense interest in religious faith owing to the many poems that explore a variety of religious attitudes in her work. He chose these four because they were closely related, but he might have found equally useful clusters of poems about love, nature, domestic life, or writing. What especially intrigued him was some of the information he read about Dickinson's sternly religious father and the orthodox nature of the religious values of her hometown of Amherst, Massachusetts. Because this paper was not a research paper, he did not pursue these issues beyond the level of the general remarks provided in an introduction to her poetry (though he might have). He did, however, use this biographical and historical information as a means of framing his search for poems that were related to one another. In doing so he discovered consistent concerns along with contradictory themes that became the basis of his paper.

"Faith" is a fine invention

c. *1860*

"Faith" is a fine invention
When Gentlemen can *see* —
But *Microscopes* are prudent
In an Emergency.

I know that He exists

c. *1862*

I know that He exists.
Somewhere — in Silence —
He has hid his rare life
From our gross eyes.

'Tis an instant's play.   5
'Tis a fond Ambush —
Just to make Bliss
Earn her own surprise!

But — should the play
Prove piercing earnest —   10
Should the glee-glaze —
In Death's — stiff — stare —

Would not the fun
Look too expensive!
Would not the jest —   15
Have crawled too far!

I never saw a Moor —

c. 1865

I never saw a Moor —
I never saw the Sea —
Yet know I how the Heather looks
And what a Billow be.

I never spoke with God
Nor visited in Heaven —
Yet certain am I of the spot
As if the Checks were given —

Apparently with no surprise

c. 1884

Apparently with no surprise
To any happy Flower
The Frost beheads it at its play —
In accidental power —
The blond Assassin passes on —
The Sun proceeds unmoved
To measure off another Day
For an Approving God.

A SAMPLE STUDENT PAPER

Religious Faith in Four Poems by Emily Dickinson

Weitz 1

Michael Weitz
Professor Pearl
English 270
May 5, 2009

Religious Faith in Four Poems by Emily Dickinson

Throughout much of her poetry, Emily Dickinson wrestles with complex
notions of God, faith, and religious devotion. She adheres to no consistent
view of religion; rather, her poetry reveals a vision of God and faith that is
constantly evolving. Dickinson's gods range from the strict and powerful Old

Introduction
providing
overview
of faith in
Dickinson's
work.

Testament father to a loving spiritual guide to an irrational and ridiculous imaginary figure. Through these varying images of God, Dickinson portrays contrasting images of the meaning and validity of religious faith. Her work reveals competing attitudes toward religious devotion as conventional religious piety struggles with a more cynical perception of God and religious worship.

Dickinson's "I never saw a Moor—" reveals a vision of traditional religious sensibilities. Although the speaker readily admits that "I never spoke with God / Nor visited in Heaven" (lines 5-6), her devout faith in a supreme being does not waver. The poem appears to be a straightforward profession of true faith stemming from the argument that the proof of God's existence is the universe's existence. Dickinson's imagery therefore evolves from the natural to the supernatural, first establishing her convictions that moors and seas exist, in spite of her lack of personal contact with either. This leads to the foundation of her religious faith, again based not on physical experience but on intellectual convictions. The speaker professes that she believes in the existence of Heaven even without conclusive evidence: "Yet certain am I of the spot / As if the Checks were given—" (7-8). But the appearance of such idealistic views of God and faith in "I never saw a Moor—" are transformed in Dickinson's other poems into a much more skeptical vision of the validity of religious piety.

While faith is portrayed as an authentic and deeply important quality in "I never saw a Moor—," Dickinson's "'Faith' is a fine invention" portrays faith as much less essential. Faith is defined in the poem as "a fine invention" (1), suggesting that it is created by man for man and therefore is not a crucial aspect of the natural universe. Thus the strong idealistic faith of "I never saw a Moor—" becomes discredited in the face of scientific rationalism. The speaker compares religious faith with actual microscopes, both of which are meant to enhance one's vision in some way. But "Faith" is useful only "When Gentlemen can *see*—" already (2); "In an Emergency," when one ostensibly cannot see, "*Microscopes* are prudent" (4, 3). Dickinson pits religion against science, suggesting that science, with its tangible evidence and rational attitude, is a more reliable lens through which to view the world. Faith is irreverently reduced to a mere "invention" and one that is ultimately less useful than microscopes or other scientific instruments.

Marginal annotations:

Thesis analyzing poet's attitudes toward God and religion.

Analysis of religious piety in "I never saw a Moor—" supported with textual evidence.

Contrast between attitudes in "Moor" and other poems.

Analysis of scientific rationalism in "'Faith' is a fine invention" supported with textual evidence.

Weitz 3

Rational, scientific observations are not the only contributing factor to the portrayal of religious skepticism in Dickinson's poems; nature itself is seen to be incompatible in some ways with conventional religious ideology. In "Apparently with no surprise," the speaker recognizes the inexorable cycle of natural life and death as a morning frost kills a flower. But the tension in this poem stems not from the "happy Flower" (2) struck down by the frost's "accidental power" (4) but from the apparent indifference of the "Approving God" (8) who condones this seemingly cruel and unnecessary death. God is seen as remote and uncompromising, and it is this perceived distance between the speaker and God that reveals the increasing absurdity of traditional religious faith. The speaker understands that praying to God or believing in religion cannot change the course of nature, and as a result feels so helplessly distanced from God that religious faith becomes virtually meaningless.

Dickinson's religious skepticism becomes even more explicit in "I know that He exists," in which the speaker attempts to understand the connection between seeing God and facing death. In this poem Dickinson characterizes God as a remote and mysterious figure; the speaker mockingly asserts, "I know that He exists" (1), even though "He has hid his rare life / From our gross eyes" (3-4). The skepticism toward religious faith revealed in this poem stems from the speaker's recognition of the paradoxical quest that people undertake to know and to see God. A successful attempt to see God, to win the game of hide-and-seek that He apparently is orchestrating, results inevitably in death. With this recognition the speaker comes to view religion as an absurd and reckless game in which the prize may be "Bliss" (7) but more likely is "Death's—stiff—stare—" (12). For, to see God and to meet one's death as a result certainly suggests that the game of trying to see God (the so-called "fun" of line 13) is much "too expensive" and that religion itself is a "jest" that, like the serpent in Genesis, has "crawled too far" (14–16).

Ultimately, the vision of religious faith that Dickinson describes in her poems is one of suspicion and cynicism. She cannot reconcile the physical world to the spiritual existence that Christian doctrine teaches, and as a result the traditional perception of God becomes ludicrous. "I never saw a Moor—" does attempt to sustain a conventional vision of religious devotion, but Dickinson's poems overall are far more likely to suggest that God is elusive, indifferent, and

Analysis of God and nature in "Apparently with no surprise" supported with textual evidence.

Analysis of characterization of God in "I know that He exists" supported with textual evidence.

Conclusion
providing
well-
supported
final analysis
of poet's
views on God
and faith.

often cruel, thus undermining the traditional vision of God as a loving father worthy of devout worship. Thus, not only religious faith but also those who are religiously faithful become targets for Dickinson's irreverent criticism of conventional belief.

Works Cited

Dickinson, Emily. "Apparently with no surprise." *The Bedford Introduction to Literature*. Ed. Michael Meyer. 9th ed. Boston. Bedford/St. Martin's, 2011. 1085. Print.

---. "'Faith' is a fine invention."*The Bedford Introduction to Literature*. Ed. Michael Meyer. 9th ed. Boston. Bedford/St. Martin's, 2011. 1084. Print.

---. "I know that He exists." *The Bedford Introduction to Literature*. Ed. Michael Meyer. 9th ed. Boston. Bedford/St. Martin's, 2011. 1084. Print.

---. "I never saw a Moor—." *The Bedford Introduction to Literature*. Ed. Michael Meyer. 9th ed. Boston. Bedford/St. Martin's, 2011. 1085. Print.

SUGGESTED TOPICS FOR LONGER PAPERS

1. Irony is abundant in Dickinson's poetry. Choose five poems from this chapter that strike you as especially ironic and discuss her use of irony in each. Taken individually and collectively, what do these poems suggest to you about the poet's sensibilities and her ways of looking at the world?

2. Readers have sometimes noted that Dickinson's poetry does not reflect very much of the social, political, economic, religious, and historical events of her lifetime. Using the poems in this chapter as the basis of your discussion, what can you say about the contexts in which Dickinson wrote? What kind of world do you think she inhabited, and how did she respond to it?

Web Research
Emily Dickinson at
bedfordstmartins.com/
meyerlit.

33

A Study of Robert Frost

A poem . . . begins as a lump in the throat, a sense of wrong, a home-sickness, a love-sickness. . . . It finds the thought and the thought finds the words.

— ROBERT FROST

Every poem is doubtlessly affected by the personal history of its composer, but Robert Frost's poems are especially known for their reflection of New England life. Although the poems included in this chapter evoke the landscapes of Frost's life and work, the depth and range of those landscapes are far more complicated than his popular reputation typically acknowledges. He was an enormously private man and a much more subtle poet than many of his readers have expected him to be. His poems warrant careful, close readings. As you explore his poetry, you may find useful the Questions

Robert Frost

for Writing about an Author in Depth (p. 1082) as a means of stimulating your thinking about his life and work.

A BRIEF BIOGRAPHY

Few poets have enjoyed the popular success that Robert Frost (1874–1963) achieved during his lifetime, and no twentieth-century American poet has had his or her work as widely read and honored. Frost is as much associated with New England as the stone walls that help define its landscape; his reputation, however, transcends regional boundaries. Although he was named poet laureate of Vermont only two years before his death, he was for many years the nation's unofficial poet laureate. Frost collected honors the way some people pick up burrs on country walks. Among his awards were four Pulitzer Prizes, the Bollingen Prize, a Congressional Medal, and dozens of honorary degrees. Perhaps his most moving appearance was his

Robert Frost at age eighteen (1892), the year he graduated from high school. "Education," Frost once said, "is the ability to listen to almost anything without losing your temper or your self-confidence."

Courtesy of Rauner Special Collections Library, Dartmouth College.

Robert Frost at age forty-seven (1921) at Stone Cottage in Shaftsbury, Vermont. Frost wrote, "I would have written of me on my stone: / I had a lover's quarrel with the world." Courtesy of Rauner Special Collections Library, Dartmouth College.

Robert Frost at his writing desk in Franconia, New Hampshire, 1915. "I have never started a poem whose end I knew," Frost said, "writing a poem is discovering."

recitation of "The Gift Outright" for millions of Americans at the inauguration of John F. Kennedy in 1961.

Frost's recognition as a poet is especially remarkable because his career as a writer did not attract any significant attention until he was nearly forty years old. He taught himself to write while he labored at odd jobs, taught school, or farmed.

Frost's early identity seems very remote from the New England soil. Although his parents were descended from generations of New Englanders, he was born in San Francisco and was named Robert Lee Frost after the Confederate general. After his father died in 1885, his mother moved the family back to Massachusetts to live with relatives. Frost graduated from high school sharing valedictorian honors with the classmate who would become his wife three years later. Between high school and marriage, he attended Dartmouth College for a few months and then taught. His teaching prompted him to enroll at Harvard in 1897, but after less than two years he withdrew without a degree (though Harvard would eventually award him an honorary doctorate in 1937, four years after Dartmouth conferred its honorary degree on him). For the next decade, Frost read and wrote poems when he was not chicken farming or teaching. In 1912, he sold his farm and moved his family to England, where he hoped to find the audience that his poetry did not have in America.

Three years in England made it possible for Frost to return home as a poet. His first two volumes of poetry, *A Boy's Will* (1913) and *North of Boston* (1914), were published in England. During the next twenty years, honors and awards were conferred on collections such as *Mountain Interval* (1916), *New Hampshire* (1923), *West-Running Brook* (1928), and *A Further Range* (1936). These are the volumes on which most of Frost's popular and critical reputation rests. Later collections include *A Witness Tree* (1942), *A Masque of Reason* (1945), *Steeple Bush* (1947), *A Masque of Mercy* (1947), *Complete Poems* (1949), and *In the Clearing* (1962). In addition to publishing his works, Frost endeared himself to audiences throughout the country by presenting his poetry almost as conversations. He also taught at a number of schools, including Amherst College, the University of Michigan, Harvard University, Dartmouth College, and Middlebury College.

Frost's countless poetry readings generated wide audiences eager to claim him as their poet. The image he cultivated resembled closely what the public likes to think a poet should be. Frost was seen as a lovable, wise old man; his simple wisdom and cracker-barrel sayings appeared comforting and homey. From this Yankee rustic, audiences learned that "There's a lot yet that isn't understood" or "We love the things we love for what they are" or "Good fences make good neighbors."

In a sense, Frost packaged himself for public consumption. "I am . . . my own salesman," he said. When asked direct questions about the meanings of his poems, he often winked or scratched his head to give the impression that the customer was always right. To be sure, there is a simplicity in Frost's language, but that simplicity does not fully reflect the depth of the man, the complexity of his themes, or the richness of his art.

The folksy optimist behind the public lectern did not reveal his private troubles to his audiences, although he did address those problems at his writing desk. Frost suffered from professional jealousies, anger, and depression. His family life was especially painful. Three of his four children died: a son at the age of four, a daughter in her late twenties from tuberculosis, and another son by suicide. His marriage was filled with tension. Although Frost's work is landscaped with sunlight, snow, birches, birds, blueberries, and squirrels, it is important to recognize that he was also intimately "acquainted with the night," a phrase that serves as the haunting title of one of his poems (see p. 889).

As a corrective to Frost's popular reputation, one critic, Lionel Trilling, described the world Frost creates in his poems as a "terrifying universe," characterized by loneliness, anguish, frustration, doubts, disappointment, and despair. To point this out is not to annihilate the pleasantness and even good-natured cheerfulness that can be enjoyed in Frost's poetry, but it is to say that Frost is not so one-dimensional as he is sometimes assumed to be. Frost's poetry requires readers who are alert and willing to penetrate the simplicity of its language to see the elusive and ambiguous meanings that lie below the surface.

AN INTRODUCTION TO HIS WORK

Frost's treatment of nature helps to explain the various levels of meaning in his poetry. The familiar natural world his poems evoke is sharply detailed. We hear icy branches clicking against themselves, we see the snow-white trunks of birches, we feel the smarting pain of a twig lashing across a face. The aspects of the natural world Frost describes are designated to give pleasure, but they are also frequently calculated to provoke thought. His use of nature tends to be symbolic. Complex meanings are derived from simple facts, such as a spider killing a moth or the difference between fire and ice (see "Design," p. 1116, and "Fire and Ice," p. 1112). Although Frost's strategy is to talk about particular events and individual experiences, his poems evoke universal issues.

Frost's poetry has strong regional roots and is "versed in country things," but it flourishes in any receptive imagination because, in the final analysis, it is concerned with human beings. Frost's New England landscapes are the occasion rather than the ultimate focus of his poems. Like the rural voices he creates in his poems, Frost typically approaches his themes indirectly. He explained the reason for this in a talk titled "Education by Poetry":

> Poetry provides the one permissible way of saying one thing and meaning another. People say, "Why don't you say what you mean?" We never do that, do we, being all of us too much poets. We like to talk in parables and in hints and in indirections — whether from diffidence or some other instinct.

The result is that the settings, characters, and situations that make up the subject matter of Frost's poems are vehicles for his perceptions about life.

In "Stopping by Woods on a Snowy Evening" (p. 1112), for example, Frost uses the kind of familiar New England details that constitute his poetry for more than descriptive purposes. He shapes them into a meditation on the tension we sometimes feel between life's responsibilities and the "lovely, dark, and deep" attraction that death offers. When the speaker's horse "gives his harness bells a shake," we are reminded that we are confronting a universal theme as well as a quiet moment of natural beauty.

Among the major concerns that appear in Frost's poetry are the fragility of life, the consequences of rejecting or accepting the conditions of one's life, the passion of inconsolable grief, the difficulty of sustaining intimacy, the fear of loneliness and isolation, the inevitability of change, the tensions between the individual and society, and the place of tradition and custom.

Whatever theme is encountered in a poem by Frost, a reader is likely to agree with him that "the initial delight is in the surprise of remembering something I didn't know." To achieve that fresh sense of discovery, Frost allowed himself to follow his instincts; his poetry

> inclines to the impulse, it assumes direction with the first line laid down, it runs a course of lucky events, and ends in a clarification of life — not necessarily a great clarification, such as sects and cults are founded on, but in a momentary stay against confusion.

This description from "On the Figure a Poem Makes" (see p. 1118 for the complete essay), Frost's brief introduction to *Complete Poems,* may sound as if his poetry is formless and merely "lucky," but his poems tend to be more conventional than experimental: "The artist in me," as he put the matter in one of his poems, "cries out for design."

From Frost's perspective, "free verse is like playing tennis with the net down." He exercised his own freedom in meeting the challenges of rhyme and meter. His use of fixed forms such as couplets, tercets, quatrains, blank verse, and sonnets was not slavish because he enjoyed working them into the natural English speech patterns — especially the rhythms, idioms, and tones of speakers living north of Boston — that give voice to his themes. Frost often liked to use "Stopping by Woods on a Snowy Evening" as an example of his graceful way of making conventions appear natural and inevitable. He explored "the old ways to be new."

Frost's eye for strong, telling details was matched by his ear for natural speech rhythms. His flexible use of what he called "iambic and loose iambic" enabled him to create moving lyric poems that reveal the personal thoughts of a speaker and dramatic poems that convincingly characterize people caught in intense emotional situations. The language in his poems appears to be little more than a transcription of casual and even rambling speech, but it is in actuality Frost's poetic creation, carefully crafted to reveal the joys and sorrows that are woven into people's daily lives. What is missing from Frost's poems is artificiality, not art. Consider this poem.

The Road Not Taken   *1916*

Two roads diverged in a yellow wood,
And sorry I could not travel both
And be one traveler, long I stood
And looked down one as far as I could
To where it bent in the undergrowth;   5

Then took the other, as just as fair,
And having perhaps the better claim,
Because it was grassy and wanted wear;
Though as for that the passing there
Had worn them really about the same,   10

And both that morning equally lay
In leaves no step had trodden black.
Oh, I kept the first for another day!
Yet knowing how way leads on to way,
I doubted if I should ever come back.   15

I shall be telling this with a sigh
Somewhere ages and ages hence:
Two roads diverged in a wood, and I—
I took the one less traveled by,
And that has made all the difference.   20

This poem intrigues readers because it is at once so simple and so deeply resonant. Recalling a walk in the woods, the speaker describes how he came to a fork in the road, which forced him to choose one path over another. Though "sorry" that he "could not travel both," he made a choice after carefully weighing his two options. This, essentially, is what happens in the poem; there is no other action. However, the incident is charged with symbolic significance by the speaker's reflections on the necessity and consequences of his decision.

The final stanza indicates that the choice concerns more than simply walking down a road, for the speaker says that choosing the "less traveled" path has affected his entire life—that "that has made all the difference." Frost draws on a familiar enough metaphor when he compares life to a journey, but he is also calling attention to a less commonly noted problem: despite our expectations, aspirations, appetites, hopes, and desires, we can't have it all. Making one choice precludes another. It is impossible to determine what particular decision the speaker refers to: perhaps he had to choose a college, a career, a spouse; perhaps he was confronted with mutually exclusive ideas, beliefs, or values. There is no way to know because Frost wisely creates a symbolic choice and implicitly invites us to supply our own circumstances.

The speaker's reflections about his choice are as central to an understanding of the poem as the choice itself; indeed, they may be more central. He describes the road taken as "having perhaps the better claim, / Because it was grassy and wanted wear"; he prefers the "less traveled" path. This seems to be an expression of individualism, which would account for "the difference" his choice made in his life. But Frost complicates matters by having the speaker also acknowledge that there was no significant difference between the two roads; one was "just as fair" as the other; each was "worn . . . really about the same"; and "both that morning equally lay / In leaves no step had trodden black."

The speaker imagines that in the future, "ages and ages hence," he will recount his choice with "a sigh" that will satisfactorily explain the course of his life, but Frost seems to be having a little fun here by showing us how the speaker will embellish his past decision to make it appear more dramatic. What we hear is someone trying to convince himself that the choice he made significantly changed his life. When he recalls what happened in the "yellow wood," a color that gives a glow to that irretrievable moment when his life seemed to be on verge of a momentous change, he appears more concerned with the path he did not choose than with the one he took. Frost shrewdly titles the poem to suggest the speaker's sense of loss at not being able to "travel both" roads. When the speaker's reflections about his choice are examined, the poem reveals his nostalgia instead of affirming his decision to travel a self-reliant path in life.

The rhymed stanzas of "The Road Not Taken" follow a pattern established in the first five lines (*abaab*). This rhyme scheme reflects, perhaps, the speaker's efforts to shape his life into a pleasing and coherent form. The natural speech rhythms Frost uses allow him to integrate the rhymes unobtrusively, but there is a slight shift in lines 19 and 20, when the speaker asserts self-consciously that the "less traveled" road—which we already know to be basically the same as the other road—"made all the difference." Unlike all of the other rhymes in the poem, "difference" does not rhyme precisely with "hence." The emphasis that must be placed on "differ*ence*" to make it rhyme perfectly with "hence" may suggest that the speaker is trying just a little too hard to pattern his life on his earlier choice in the woods.

Perhaps the best way to begin reading Frost's poetry is to accept the invitation he placed at the beginning of many volumes of his poems. "The Pasture" means what it says, of course; it is about taking care of some farm chores, but it is also a means of "saying one thing in terms of another."

The Pasture   *1913*

I'm going out to clean the pasture spring;
I'll only stop to rake the leaves away
(And wait to watch the water clear, I may):
I shan't be gone long.—You come too.

I'm going out to fetch the little calf
That's standing by the mother. It's so young
It totters when she licks it with her tongue.
I sha'n't be gone long.—You come too.

"The Pasture" is a simple but irresistible songlike invitation to the pleasure of looking at the world through the eyes of a poet.

Chronology

1874	Born on March 26 in San Francisco.
1885	Father dies and family moves to Lawrence, Massachusetts.
1892	Graduates from Lawrence High School.
1893–94	Studies at Dartmouth College.
1895	Marries his high school sweetheart, Elinor White.
1897–99	Studies at Harvard College.

1900	Moves to a farm in West Derry, New Hampshire.
1912	Moves to England, where he farms and writes.
1913	*A Boy's Will* is published in London.
1914	*North of Boston* is published in London.
1915	Moves to a farm near Franconia, New Hampshire.
1916	Elected to National Institute of Letters.
1917–20	Teaches at Amherst College.
1919	Moves to South Shaftsbury, Vermont.
1921–23	Teaches at the University of Michigan.
1923	*Selected Poems* and *New Hampshire* are published; the latter is awarded a Pulitzer Prize.
1928	*West-Running Brook* is published.
1930	*Collected Poems* is published.
1936	*A Further Range* is published; teaches at Harvard.
1938	Wife dies.
1939–42	Teaches at Harvard.
1942	*A Witness Tree,* which is awarded a Pulitzer Prize, is published.
1943–49	Teaches at Dartmouth.
1945	*A Masque of Reason* is published.
1947	*Steeple Bush* and *A Masque of Mercy* are published.
1949	*Complete Poems* (enlarged) is published.
1961	Reads "The Gift Outright" at President John F. Kennedy's inauguration.
1963	Dies on January 29 in Boston.

Mowing   *1913*

There was never a sound beside the wood but one,
And that was my long scythe whispering to the ground.
What was it it whispered? I knew not well myself;
Perhaps it was something about the heat of the sun,
Something, perhaps, about the lack of sound —   5
And that was why it whispered and did not speak.
It was no dream of the gift of idle hours,
Or easy gold at the hand of fay or elf:
Anything more than the truth would have seemed too weak
To the earnest love that laid the swale in rows,   10
Not without feeble-pointed spikes of flowers
(Pale orchises), and scared a bright green snake.

The fact is the sweetest dream that labour knows.
My long scythe whispered and left the hay to make.

CONSIDERATIONS FOR CRITICAL THINKING AND WRITING

1. **FIRST RESPONSE.** Describe the tone of "Mowing." How does reading the poem aloud affect your understanding of it?
2. Discuss the image of the scythe. Do you think it has any symbolic value? Explain why or why not.
3. Paraphrase the poem. What do you think its theme is?
4. Describe the type of sonnet Frost uses in "Mowing."

My November Guest   *1913*

My Sorrow, when she's here with me,
   Thinks these dark days of autumn rain
Are beautiful as days can be;
She loves the bare, the withered tree;
   She walks the sodden pasture lane.   5

Her pleasure will not let me stay.
   She talks and I am fain to list:
She's glad the birds are gone away,
She's glad her simple worsted grey
   Is silver now with clinging mist.   10

The desolate, deserted trees,
   The faded earth, the heavy sky,
The beauties she so truly sees,
She thinks I have no eye for these,
   And vexes me for reason why.   15

Not yesterday I learned to know
   The love of bare November days
Before the coming of the snow,
But it were vain to tell her so,
   And they are better for her praise.   20

CONSIDERATIONS FOR CRITICAL THINKING AND WRITING

1. **FIRST RESPONSE.** How is "Sorrow" personified? What sort of relationship does the speaker have with her?
2. What kind of tone do the poem's images create?
3. What do you think is this poem's theme?

CONNECTION TO ANOTHER SELECTION

1. Compare Frost's treatment of November with Margaret Atwood's evocation of "February" (p. 876). Explain why you prefer one poem over the other.

Storm Fear

1913

When the wind works against us in the dark,
And pelts with snow
The lower chamber window on the east,
And whispers with a sort of stifled bark,
The beast,   5
"Come out! Come out!" —
It costs no inward struggle not to go,
Ah, no!
I count our strength,
Two and a child,   10
Those of us not asleep subdued to mark
How the cold creeps as the fire dies at length, —
How drifts are piled,
Dooryard and road ungraded,
Till even the comforting barn grows far away,   15
And my heart owns a doubt
Whether 'tis in us to arise with day
And save ourselves unaided.

CONSIDERATIONS FOR CRITICAL THINKING AND WRITING

1. **FIRST RESPONSE.** What is the "inward struggle" (line 7) in this poem?

2. How is winter depicted by the speaker? What emotions does winter produce in the speaker?

3. Describe the rhyme scheme and its effects on your reading the poem aloud.

CONNECTION TO ANOTHER SELECTION

1. Compare the perspectives on nature in "Storm Fear" and in Emily Dickinson's "Presentiment — is that long Shadow — on the lawn — " (p. 867). How are they both poems about fear?

Mending Wall

1914

Something there is that doesn't love a wall,
That sends the frozen-ground-swell under it,
And spills the upper boulders in the sun;
And makes gaps even two can pass abreast.
The work of hunters is another thing: 5
I have come after them and made repair
Where they have left not one stone on a stone,
But they would have the rabbit out of hiding,
To please the yelping dogs. The gaps I mean,
No one has seen them made or heard them made,   10

But at spring mending-time we find them there.
I let my neighbor know beyond the hill;
And on a day we meet to walk the line
And set the wall between us once again.
We keep the wall between us as we go.   15
To each the boulders that have fallen to each.
And some are loaves and some so nearly balls
We have to use a spell to make them balance:
"Stay where you are until our backs are turned!"
We wear our fingers rough with handling them.   20
Oh, just another kind of outdoor game,
One on a side. It comes to little more:
There where it is we do not need the wall:
He is all pine and I am apple orchard.
My apple trees will never get across   25
And eat the cones under his pines, I tell him.
He only says, "Good fences make good neighbors."
Spring is the mischief in me, and I wonder
If I could put a notion in his head:
"*Why* do they make good neighbors? Isn't it   30
Where there are cows? But here there are no cows.
Before I built a wall I'd ask to know
What I was walling in or walling out,
And to whom I was like to give offense.
Something there is that doesn't love a wall,   35
That wants it down." I could say "Elves" to him,
But it's not elves exactly, and I'd rather
He said it for himself. I see him there
Bringing a stone grasped firmly by the top
In each hand, like an old-stone savage armed.   40
He moves in darkness as it seems to me,
Not of woods only and the shade of trees.
He will not go behind his father's saying,
And he likes having thought of it so well
He says again, "Good fences make good neighbors."   45

CONSIDERATIONS FOR CRITICAL THINKING AND WRITING

1. **FIRST RESPONSE.** What might the "Something" be that "doesn't love a wall" (line 1)? Why does the speaker remind his neighbor each spring that the wall needs to be repaired? Is it ironic that the *speaker* initiates the mending? Is there anything good about the wall?

2. How do the speaker and his neighbor differ in sensibilities? What is suggested about the neighbor in lines 41 and 42?

3. The neighbor likes the saying "Good fences make good neighbors" so well that he repeats it (lines 27, 45). Does the speaker also say something twice? What else suggests that the speaker's attitude toward the wall is not necessarily Frost's?

4. Although the speaker's language is colloquial, what is poetic about the sounds and rhythms he uses?

5. This poem was first published in 1914; Frost read it to an audience when he visited Russia in 1962. What do these facts suggest about the symbolic value of "Mending Wall"?

CONNECTIONS TO OTHER SELECTIONS

1. How do you think the neighbor in this poem would respond to Dickinson's idea of imagination in "To make a prairie it takes a clover and one bee" (p. 1051)?

2. What similarities and differences does the neighbor have with the people Frost describes in "Neither Out Far nor In Deep" (p. 1114)?

Home Burial   1914

He saw her from the bottom of the stairs
Before she saw him. She was starting down,
Looking back over her shoulder at some fear.
She took a doubtful step and then undid it
To raise herself and look again. He spoke   5
Advancing toward her: "What is it you see
From up there always — for I want to know."
She turned and sank upon her skirts at that,
And her face changed from terrified to dull.
He said to gain time: "What is it you see,"   10
Mounting until she cowered under him.
"I will find out now — you must tell me, dear."
She, in her place, refused him any help
With the least stiffening of her neck and silence.
She let him look, sure that he wouldn't see,   15
Blind creature; and awhile he didn't see.
But at last he murmured, "Oh," and again, "Oh."

"What is it — what?" she said.

                                 "Just that I see."

"You don't," she challenged. "Tell what it is."   20

"The wonder is I didn't see at once.
I never noticed it from here before.
I must be wonted° to it — that's the reason.   *accustomed*
The little graveyard where my people are!
So small the window frames the whole of it.   25
Not so much larger than a bedroom, is it?
There are three stones of slate and one of marble,
Broad-shouldered little slabs there in the sunlight
On the sidehill. We haven't to mind *those*.

But I understand: it is not the stones,   30
But the child's mound —"

                "Don't, don't, don't, don't," she cried.

She withdrew, shrinking from beneath his arm
That rested on the banister, and slid downstairs;
And turned on him with such a daunting look,   35
He said twice over before he knew himself:
"Can't a man speak of his own child he's lost?"

"Not you! — Oh, where's my hat? Oh, I don't need it!
I must get out of here. I must get air.
I don't know rightly whether any man can."   40

"Amy! Don't go to someone else this time.
Listen to me. I won't come down the stairs."
He sat and fixed his chin between his fists.
"There's something I should like to ask you, dear."

"You don't know how to ask it."   45

                "Help me, then."
Her fingers moved the latch for all reply.

"My words are nearly always an offense.
I don't know how to speak of anything
So as to please you. But I might be taught,   50
I should suppose. I can't say I see how.
A man must partly give up being a man
With women-folk. We could have some arrangement
By which I'd bind myself to keep hands off
Anything special you're a-mind to name.   55
Though I don't like such things 'twixt those that love.
Two that don't love can't live together without them.
But two that do can't live together with them."
She moved the latch a little. "Don't — don't go.
Don't carry it to someone else this time.   60
Tell me about it if it's something human.
Let me into your grief. I'm not so much
Unlike other folks as your standing there
Apart would make me out. Give me my chance.
I do think, though, you overdo it a little.   65
What was it brought you up to think it the thing
To take your mother-loss of a first child
So inconsolably — in the face of love.
You'd think his memory might be satisfied —"

"There you go sneering now!"   70

                "I'm not, I'm not!

You make me angry. I'll come down to you.
God, what a woman! And it's come to this,
A man can't speak of his own child that's dead."

"You can't because you don't know how to speak.   75
If you had any feelings, you that dug
With your own hand — how could you? — his little grave;
I saw you from that very window there,
Making the gravel leap and leap in air,
Leap up, like that, like that, and land so lightly   80
And roll back down the mound beside the hole.
I thought, Who is that man? I didn't know you.
And I crept down the stairs and up the stairs
To look again, and still your spade kept lifting.
Then you came in. I heard your rumbling voice   85
Out in the kitchen, and I don't know why,
But I went near to see with my own eyes.
You could sit there with the stains on your shoes
Of the fresh earth from your own baby's grave
And talk about your everyday concerns.   90
You had stood the spade up against the wall
Outside there in the entry, for I saw it."

"I shall laugh the worst laugh I ever laughed.
I'm cursed. God, if I don't believe I'm cursed."

"I can repeat the very words you were saying.   95
'Three foggy mornings and one rainy day
Will rot the best birch fence a man can build.'
Think of it, talk like that at such a time!
What had how long it takes a birch to rot
To do with what was in the darkened parlor   100
You *couldn't* care! The nearest friends can go
With anyone to death, comes so far short
They might as well not try to go at all.
No, from the time when one is sick to death,
One is alone, and he dies more alone.   105
Friends make pretense of following to the grave.
But before one is in it, their minds are turned
And making the best of their way back to life
And living people, and things they understand.
But the world's evil. I won't have grief so   110
If I can change it. Oh, I won't, I won't!"

"There, you have said it all and you feel better.
You won't go now. You're crying. Close the door.
The heart's gone out of it: why keep it up.
Amy! There's someone coming down the road!"   115

"*You* — oh, you think the talk is all. I must go —
Somewhere out of this house. How can I make you —"

"If — you — do!" She was opening the door wider.
"Where do you mean to go? First tell me that.
I'll follow and bring you back by force. I *will!* —"   120

Considerations for Critical Thinking and Writing

1. **FIRST RESPONSE.** This poem tells a story of a relationship. Is the husband insensitive and indifferent to his wife's grief? Characterize the wife. Has Frost invited us to sympathize with one character more than with the other?

2. How has the burial of the child within sight of the stairway window affected the relationship of the couple in this poem? Is the child's grave a symptom or a cause of the conflict between them?

3. What is the effect of splitting the iambic pentameter pattern in lines 18 and 19, 31 and 32, 45 and 46, and 70 and 71?

4. Is the conflict resolved at the conclusion of the poem? Do you think the husband and wife will overcome their differences?

The Wood-Pile   1914

Out walking in the frozen swamp one gray day,
I paused and said, "I will turn back from here.
No, I will go on farther — and we shall see."
The hard snow held me, save where now and then
One foot went through. The view was all in lines   5
Straight up and down of tall slim trees
Too much alike to mark or name a place by
So as to say for certain I was here
Or somewhere else: I was just far from home.
A small bird flew before me. He was careful   10
To put a tree between us when he lighted,
And say no word to tell me who he was
Who was so foolish as to think what *he* thought.
He thought that I was after him for a feather —
The white one in his tail; like one who takes   15
Everything said as personal to himself.
One flight out sideways would have undeceived him.
And then there was a pile of wood for which
I forgot him and let his little fear
Carry him off the way I might have gone,   20
Without so much as wishing him good-night.
He went behind it to make his last stand.
It was a cord of maple, cut and split
And piled — and measured, four by four by eight.
And not another like it could I see.   25
No runner tracks in this year's snow looped near it.
And it was older sure than this year's cutting,
Or even last year's or the year's before.
The wood was gray and the bark warping off it
And the pile somewhat sunken. Clematis   30
Had wound strings round and round it like a bundle.
What held it though on one side was a tree
Still growing, and on one a stake and prop,

These latter about to fall. I thought that only
Someone who lived in turning to fresh tasks   35
Could so forget his handiwork on which
He spent himself, the labor of his ax,
And leave it there far from a useful fireplace
To warm the frozen swamp as best it could
With the slow smokeless burning of decay.   40

CONSIDERATIONS FOR CRITICAL THINKING AND WRITING

1. **FIRST RESPONSE.** What symbolic value can you find in the speaker's account of his discovery of the woodpile?

2. Write a paraphrase of the poem.

3. How does the "small bird" (line 10) figure in the poem? Why do you think it's there? How is it related to the woodpile?

4. Characterize the speaker's tone. How does the rhythm of the poem's lines help to create the tone?

CONNECTIONS TO OTHER SELECTIONS

1. Write an essay comparing the speaker in this poem to the speaker in "Stopping by Woods on a Snowy Evening" (p. 1112). How, in each poem, do simple activities reveal something important about the speaker?

2. Discuss the speakers' sense of time in "The Wood-Pile" and in "Nothing Gold Can Stay" (p. 1113).

After Apple-Picking   *1914*

My long two-pointed ladder's sticking through a tree
Toward heaven still,
And there's a barrel that I didn't fill
Beside it, and there may be two or three
Apples I didn't pick upon some bough.   5
But I am done with apple-picking now.
Essence of winter sleep is on the night,
The scent of apples: I am drowsing off.
I cannot rub the strangeness from my sight
I got from looking through a pane of glass   10
I skimmed this morning from the drinking trough
And held against the world of hoary grass.
It melted, and I let it fall and break.
But I was well
Upon my way to sleep before it fell,   15
And I could tell
What form my dreaming was about to take.
Magnified apples appear and disappear,
Stem end and blossom end,
And every fleck of russet showing clear.   20
My instep arch not only keeps the ache,

It keeps the pressure of a ladder-round.
I feel the ladder sway as the boughs bend.
And I keep hearing from the cellar bin
The rumbling sound 25
Of load on load of apples coming in.
For I have had too much
Of apple-picking: I am overtired
Of the great harvest I myself desired.
There were ten thousand thousand fruit to touch, 30
Cherish in hand, lift down, and not let fall.
For all
That struck the earth,
No matter if not bruised or spiked with stubble,
Went surely to the cider-apple heap 35
As of no worth.
One can see what will trouble
This sleep of mine, whatever sleep it is.
Were he not gone,
The woodchuck could say whether it's like his 40
Long sleep, as I describe its coming on,
Or just some human sleep.

Considerations for Critical Thinking and Writing

1. **FIRST RESPONSE.** How does this poem illustrate Frost's view that "Poetry provides the one permissible way of saying one thing and meaning another"? When do you first sense that the detailed description of apple picking is being used that way?

2. What comes after apple picking? What does the speaker worry about in the dream beginning in line 18?

3. Why do you suppose Frost uses apples rather than, say, pears or squash?

Birches   1916

When I see birches bend to left and right
Across the lines of straighter darker trees,
I like to think some boy's been swinging them.
But swinging doesn't bend them down to stay
As ice-storms do. Often you must have seen them 5
Loaded with ice a sunny winter morning
After a rain. They click upon themselves
As the breeze rises, and turn many-colored
As the stir cracks and crazes their enamel.
Soon the sun's warmth makes them shed crystal shells 10
Shattering and avalanching on the snow-crust —
Such heaps of broken glass to sweep away
You'd think the inner dome of heaven had fallen.
They are dragged to the withered bracken by the load,

And they seem not to break; though once they are bowed 15
So low for long, they never right themselves:
You may see their trunks arching in the woods
Years afterwards, trailing their leaves on the ground
Like girls on hands and knees that throw their hair
Before them over their heads to dry in the sun. 20
But I was going to say when Truth broke in
With all her matter-of-fact about the ice-storm,
I should prefer to have some boy bend them
As he went out and in to fetch the cows —
Some boy too far from town to learn baseball, 25
Whose only play was what he found himself,
Summer or winter, and could play alone.
One by one he subdued his father's trees
By riding them down over and over again
Until he took the stiffness out of them, 30
And not one but hung limp, not one was left
For him to conquer. He learned all there was
To learn about not launching out too soon
And so not carrying the tree away
Clear to the ground. He always kept his poise 35
To the top branches, climbing carefully
With the same pains you use to fill a cup
Up to the brim, and even above the brim.
Then he flung outward, feet first, with a swish,
Kicking his way down through the air to the ground. 40
So was I once myself a swinger of birches.
And so I dream of going back to be.
It's when I'm weary of considerations,
And life is too much like a pathless wood
Where your face burns and tickles with the cobwebs 45
Broken across it, and one eye is weeping
From a twig's having lashed across it open.
I'd like to get away from earth awhile
And then come back to it and begin over.
May no fate willfully misunderstand me 50
And half grant what I wish and snatch me away
Not to return. Earth's the right place for love:
I don't know where it's likely to go better.
I'd like to go by climbing a birch tree,
And climb black branches up a snow-white trunk, 55
Toward heaven, till the tree could bear no more,
But dipped its top and set me down again.
That would be good both going and coming back.
One could do worse than be a swinger of birches.

CONSIDERATIONS FOR CRITICAL THINKING AND WRITING

1. **FIRST RESPONSE.** What do you think the swinging of birches symbolizes?

2. Why does the speaker in this poem prefer the birches to have been bent by boys instead of ice storms?

3. How is "earth" (line 52) described in the poem? Why does the speaker choose it over "heaven" (line 56)?

4. How might the effect of this poem be changed if it were written in heroic couplets instead of blank verse?

5. **CRITICAL STRATEGIES.** Read the section on reader-response strategies (pp. 2060–62) in Chapter 53, "Critical Strategies for Reading." Trace your response to this poem over three successive careful readings. How does your understanding of the poem change or develop?

An Old Man's Winter Night   1916

All out-of-doors looked darkly in at him
Through the thin frost, almost in separate stars,
That gathers on the pane in empty rooms.
What kept his eyes from giving back the gaze
Was the lamp tilted near them in his hand.   5
What kept him from remembering what it was
That brought him to that creaking room was age.
He stood with barrels round him — at a loss.
And having scared the cellar under him
In clomping here, he scared it once again   10
In clomping off — and scared the outer night,
Which has its sounds, familiar, like the roar
Of trees and crack of branches, common things,
But nothing so like beating on a box.
A light he was to no one but himself   15
Where now he sat, concerned with he knew what,
A quiet light, and then not even that.
He consigned to the moon, such as she was,
So late-arising, to the broken moon
As better than the sun in any case   20
For such a charge, his snow upon the roof,
His icicles along the wall to keep;
And slept. The log that shifted with a jolt
Once in the stove, disturbed him and he shifted,
And eased his heavy breathing, but still slept.   25
One aged man — one man — can't keep a house,
A farm, a countryside, or if he can,
It's thus he does it of a winter night.

CONSIDERATIONS FOR CRITICAL THINKING AND WRITING

1. **FIRST RESPONSE.** Describe the tone of this poem. Which images are especially effective in evoking the old man, the winter, and night?

2. What emotions do you feel for the old man? Is this a sentimental poem?

3. Comment on the sounds described in the poem. What effects do they create?

CONNECTIONS TO OTHER SELECTIONS

1. Compare the speaker in "The Road Not Taken" (p. 1095) with the old man in this poem. Are they essentially similar or different? Explain your response in an essay.
2. Discuss images of winter and night in "An Old Man's Winter Night" and "Stopping by Woods on a Snowy Evening" (p. 1112).

"Out, Out —"°

1916

The buzz-saw snarled and rattled in the yard
And made dust and dropped stove-length sticks of wood,
Sweet-scented stuff when the breeze drew across it.
And from there those that lifted eyes could count
Five mountain ranges one behind the other   5
Under the sunset far into Vermont.
And the saw snarled and rattled, snarled and rattled,
As it ran light, or had to bear a load.
And nothing happened: day was all but done.
Call it a day, I wish they might have said   10
To please the boy by giving him the half hour
That a boy counts so much when saved from work.
His sister stood beside them in her apron
To tell them "Supper." At the word, the saw,
As if to prove saws knew what supper meant,   15
Leaped out at the boy's hand, or seemed to leap —
He must have given the hand. However it was,
Neither refused the meeting. But the hand!
The boy's first outcry was a rueful laugh,
As he swung toward them holding up the hand   20
Half in appeal, but half as if to keep
The life from spilling. Then the boy saw all —
Since he was old enough to know, big boy
Doing a man's work, though a child at heart —
He saw all spoiled. "Don't let him cut my hand off —   25
The doctor, when he comes. Don't let him, sister!"
So. But the hand was gone already.
The doctor put him in the dark of ether.
He lay and puffed his lips out with his breath.
And then — the watcher at his pulse took fright.   30
No one believed. They listened at his heart.
Little — less — nothing! — and that ended it.
No more to build on there. And they, since they
Were not the one dead, turned to their affairs.

"Out, Out —": From Act V, Scene v, of Shakespeare's *Macbeth.*

CONSIDERATIONS FOR CRITICAL THINKING AND WRITING

1. **FIRST RESPONSE.** This narrative poem is about the accidental death of a Vermont boy. What is the purpose of the story? Some readers have argued that the final lines reveal the speaker's callousness and indifference. What do you think?

2. How does Frost's allusion to *Macbeth* contribute to the meaning of this poem? Does the speaker seem to agree with the view of life expressed in Macbeth's lines?

3. **CRITICAL STRATEGIES.** Read the section on Marxist criticism (pp. 2053–54) in Chapter 53, "Critical Strategies for Reading." How do you think a Marxist critic would interpret the family and events described in this poem?

CONNECTIONS TO OTHER SELECTIONS

1. What are the similarities and differences in theme between this poem and Frost's "Nothing Gold Can Stay" (p. 1113)?

2. Write an essay comparing how grief is handled by the boy's family in this poem and by the couple in "Home Burial" (p. 1102).

3. Compare the tone and theme of "'Out, Out—'" with those of Stephen Crane's "A Man Said to the Universe" (p. 897).

The Oven Bird   *1916*

There is a singer everyone has heard,
Loud, a mid-summer and a mid-wood bird,
Who makes the solid tree trunks sound again.
He says that leaves are old and that for flowers
Mid-summer is to spring as one to ten.   5
He says the early petal-fall is past
When pear and cherry bloom went down in showers
On sunny days a moment overcast;
And comes that other fall we name the fall.
He says the highway dust is over all.   10
The bird would cease and be as other birds
But that he knows in singing not to sing.
The question that he frames in all but words
Is what to make of a diminished thing.

CONSIDERATIONS FOR CRITICAL THINKING AND WRITING

1. **FIRST RESPONSE.** What kind of sonnet is this poem? What is the relationship between the octave and the sestet?

2. The ovenbird is a warbler that makes its domed nest on the ground. What kinds of observations does the speaker have it make about spring, summer, and fall?

3. The final two lines invite symbolic readings. What do you make of them?

4. **CRITICAL STRATEGIES.** Read the section on critical thinking (pp. 2041–44) in Chapter 53, "Critical Strategies for Reading," and then research critical commentary on this poem. Write an essay describing the range of interpretations that you find. Which interpretation do you think is the most convincing? Why?

Fire and Ice   1923

Some say the world will end in fire,
Some say in ice.
From what I've tasted of desire
I hold with those who favor fire.
But if it had to perish twice,
I think I know enough of hate
To say that for destruction ice
Is also great
And would suffice.

CONSIDERATIONS FOR CRITICAL THINKING AND WRITING

1. **FIRST RESPONSE.** What characteristics of human behavior does the speaker associate with fire and ice?

2. What theories about the end of the world are alluded to in lines 1 and 2?

3. How does the speaker's use of understatement and rhyme affect the tone of this poem?

Stopping by Woods on a Snowy Evening   1923

Whose woods these are I think I know.
His house is in the village, though;
He will not see me stopping here
To watch his woods fill up with snow.

My little horse must think it queer   5
To stop without a farmhouse near
Between the woods and frozen lake
The darkest evening of the year.

He gives his harness bells a shake
To ask if there is some mistake.   10
The only other sound's the sweep
Of easy wind and downy flake.

The woods are lovely, dark and deep,
But I have promises to keep,
And miles to go before I sleep,   15
And miles to go before I sleep.

1. **FIRST RESPONSE.** What is the significance of the setting in this poem? How is tone conveyed by the images?

2. What does the speaker find appealing about the woods? What is the purpose of the horse in the poem?

3. Although the last two lines are identical, they are not read at the same speed. Why the difference? What is achieved by the repetition?

4. What is the poem's rhyme scheme? What is the effect of the rhyme in the final stanza?

CONNECTION TO ANOTHER SELECTION

1. What do you think Frost might have to say about "A Parodic Interpretation of 'Stopping by Woods on a Snowy Evening'" by Herbert R. Coursen Jr. (p. 1121)?

Nothing Gold Can Stay   *1923*

Nature's first green is gold,
Her hardest hue to hold.
Her early leaf's a flower;
But only so an hour.
The leaf subsides to leaf.
So Eden sank to grief,
So dawn goes down to day.
Nothing gold can stay.

CONSIDERATIONS FOR CRITICAL THINKING AND WRITING

1. **FIRST RESPONSE.** What is meant by "gold" in the poem? Why can't it "stay"?

2. What do the leaf, humanity, and a day have in common?

CONNECTION TO ANOTHER SELECTION

1. Write an essay comparing the tone and theme of "Nothing Gold Can Stay" with those of Robert Herrick's "To the Virgins, to Make Much of Time" (p. 811).

Unharvested   *1936*

A scent of ripeness from over a wall.
And come to leave the routine road
And look for what had made me stall,
There sure enough was an apple tree
That had eased itself of its summer load,   5
And of all but its trivial foliage free,
Now breathed as light as a lady's fan.

For there there had been an apple fall
As complete as the apple had given man.
The ground was one circle of solid red.   10

May something go always unharvested!
May much stay out of our stated plan,
Apples or something forgotten and left,
So smelling their sweetness would be no theft.

CONSIDERATIONS FOR CRITICAL THINKING AND WRITING

1. **FIRST RESPONSE.** Why does the speaker like the idea of some things going unharvested?

2. Explain why this poem is about more than just apples. What lines especially invite deeper readings?

3. What kind of sonnet is this poem? Discuss the effects created by Frost's use of meter and rhyme.

4. **CRITICAL STRATEGIES.** Read the section on mythological criticism (pp. 2058–60) in Chapter 53, "Critical Strategies for Reading." How do you think a mythological critic would interpret "Unharvested"?

CONNECTION TO ANOTHER SELECTION

1. Compare the themes in this poem and in "After Apple-Picking" (p. 1106).

Neither Out Far nor In Deep   1936

The people along the sand
All turn and look one way.
They turn their back on the land.
They look at the sea all day.

As long as it takes to pass   5
A ship keeps raising its hull;
The wetter ground like glass
Reflects a standing gull.

The land may vary more;
But wherever the truth may be —   10
The water comes ashore,
And the people look at the sea.

They cannot look out far.
They cannot look in deep.
But when was that ever a bar   15
To any watch they keep?

Neither Out Far nor In Deep

The people along the sand
All turn and look one way.
They turn their backs on the land;
They look at the sea all day.

As long as it takes to pass
A ship keeps raising its hull.
The wetter ground like glass
Reflects a standing gull.

The land may vary more,
But wherever the truth may be—
The water comes ashore
And the people look at the sea.

They cannot look out far;
They cannot look in deep;
But when was that ever a bar
To any watch they keep.

Robert Frost

With the permission of The Yale Review.

Manuscript page for Robert Frost's "Neither Out Far nor In Deep" (p. 1114), which was first published in *The Yale Review* in 1934 and later, with a few punctuation changes, in *A Further Range* in 1936.

CONSIDERATIONS FOR CRITICAL THINKING AND WRITING

1. **FIRST RESPONSE.** Frost built this poem around a simple observation that raises some questions. Why do people at the beach almost always face the ocean? What feelings and thoughts are evoked by looking at the ocean?

2. Notice how the verb *look* takes on added meaning as the poem progresses. What are the people looking for?

3. How does the final stanza extend the poem's significance?

4. Does the speaker identify with the people described, or does he ironically distance himself from them?

Design   1936

I found a dimpled spider, fat and white,
On a white heal-all,° holding up a moth
Like a white piece of rigid satin cloth —
Assorted characters of death and blight
Mixed ready to begin the morning right,   5
Like the ingredients of a witches' broth —
A snow-drop spider, a flower like a froth,
And dead wings carried like a paper kite.

What had the flower to do with being white,
The wayside blue and innocent heal-all?   10
What brought the kindred spider to that height,
Then steered the white moth thither in the night?
What but design of darkness to appall? —
If design govern in a thing so small.

2 *heal-all:* A common flower, usually blue, once used for medicinal purposes.

CONSIDERATIONS FOR CRITICAL THINKING AND WRITING

1. **FIRST RESPONSE.** What kinds of speculations are raised in the poem's final two lines? Consider the meaning of the title. Is there more than one way to read it?

2. How does the division of the octave and sestet in this sonnet serve to organize the speaker's thoughts and feelings? What is the predominant rhyme? How does that rhyme relate to the poem's meaning?

3. Which words seem especially rich in connotative meanings? Explain how they function in the sonnet.

CONNECTIONS TO OTHER SELECTIONS

1. Compare the ironic tone of "Design" with the tone of William Hathaway's "Oh, Oh" (p. 748). What would you have to change in Hathaway's poem to make it more like Frost's?

2. In an essay discuss Frost's view of God in this poem and Dickinson's perspective in "I know that He exists" (p. 1084).

3. Compare "Design" with "In White," Frost's early version of it (following).

Perspectives on Robert Frost

ROBERT FROST

"In White": An Early Version of "Design"   1912

A dented spider like a snow drop white
On a white Heal-all, holding up a moth
Like a white piece of lifeless satin cloth —
Saw ever curious eye so strange a sight? —
Portent in little, assorted death and blight   5
Like the ingredients of a witches' broth? —
The beady spider, the flower like a froth,
And the moth carried like a paper kite.

What had that flower to do with being white,
The blue prunella every child's delight.   10
What brought the kindred spider to that height?
(Make we no thesis of the miller's° plight.)   *miller moth*
What but design of darkness and of night?
Design, design! Do I use the word aright?

CONSIDERATIONS FOR CRITICAL THINKING AND WRITING

1. Read "In White" and "Design" (p. 1116) aloud. Which version sounds better to you? Why?

2. Compare these versions line for line, paying particular attention to word choice. List the differences and try to explain why you think Frost revised the lines.

3. How does the change in titles reflect a shift in emphasis in the poem?

ROBERT FROST

On the Living Part of a Poem   1914

The living part of a poem is the intonation entangled somehow in the syntax, idiom, and meaning of a sentence. It is only there for those who have heard it previously in conversation. . . . It is the most volatile and at the same time important part of poetry. It goes and the language becomes dead language, the poetry dead poetry. With it go the accents, the stresses, the delays that are not the property of vowels and syllables but that are shifted at will with the sense. Vowels have length there is no denying. But the accent of sense supersedes all other accent, overrides it and sweeps it away. I will find you the word *come* variously used in various passages, a whole, half, third, fourth, fifth, and sixth note. It is as long as the sense makes it. When men no longer know the intonations on which we string our words they will fall back on what I may call the absolute length of our syllables, which is the length we would give them in passages that meant nothing. . . . I say you can't read a single good sentence with the salt in it unless you have previously heard it spoken. Neither can you with the help of all the characters and diacritical marks pronounce a single word unless you have previously heard it actually pronounced. Words exist in the mouth not books.

From a letter to Sidney Cox in *A Swinger of Birches: A Portrait of Robert Frost*

CONSIDERATIONS FOR CRITICAL THINKING AND WRITING

1. Why does Frost place so much emphasis on hearing poetry spoken?

2. Choose a passage from "Home Burial" (p. 1102) or "After Apple-Picking" (p. 1106) and read it aloud. How does Frost's description of his emphasis on intonation help explain the effects he achieves in the passage you have selected?

3. Do you think it is true that all poetry must be heard? Do "words exist in the mouth not books"?

AMY LOWELL (1874–1925)

On Frost's Realistic Technique 1915

I have said that Mr. Frost's work is almost photographic. The qualification was unnecessary, it is photographic. The pictures, the characters, are reproduced directly from life, they are burnt into his mind as though it were a sensitive plate. He gives out what has been put in unchanged by any personal mental process. His imagination is bounded by what he has seen, he is confined within the limits of his experience (or at least what might have been his experience) and bent all one way like the windblown trees of New England hillsides.

From a review of *North of Boston*, *The New Republic*, February 20, 1915

CONSIDERATIONS FOR CRITICAL THINKING AND WRITING

1. Consider the "photographic" qualities of Frost's poetry by discussing particular passages that strike you as having been "reproduced directly from life."

2. Write an essay that supports or refutes Lowell's assertion that "He gives out what has been put in unchanged by any personal mental process."

ROBERT FROST

On the Figure a Poem Makes 1939

Abstraction is an old story with the philosophers, but it has been like a new toy in the hands of the artists of our day. Why can't we have any one quality of poetry we choose by itself? We can have in thought. Then it will go hard if we can't in practice. Our lives for it.

Granted no one but a humanist much cares how sound a poem is if it is only *a* sound. The sound is the gold in the ore. Then we will have the sound out alone and dispense with the inessential. We do till we make the discovery that the object in writing poetry is to make all poems sound as different as possible from each other, and the resources for that of vowels, consonants, punctuation, syntax, words, sentences, meter are not enough. We need the help of context — meaning — subject matter. That is the greatest help towards variety. All that can be done with words is soon told. So also with meters — particularly in our language where there are virtually but two, strict iambic and loose iambic. The ancients with many were still poor if they depended on meters for all tune. It is painful to watch our sprung-rhythmists straining at the point of omitting one short from a foot for relief from monotony. The possibilities for tune from the dramatic tones of meaning struck across the rigidity of a limited meter are endless. And we are back in poetry as merely one more art of having something to say, sound or unsound. Probably better if sound, because deeper and from wider experience.

Then there is this wildness whereof it is spoken. Granted again that it has an equal claim with sound to being a poem's better half. If it is a wild tune, it is a poem. Our problem then is, as modern abstractionists, to have the wildness pure; to be wild with nothing to be wild about. We bring up as aberrationists, giving way to undirected associations and kicking ourselves from one chance suggestion to another in all directions as of a hot afternoon in the life of a grasshopper. Theme alone can steady us down. Just as the first mystery was how a poem could have a tune in such a straightness as meter, so the second mystery is how a poem can have wildness and at the same time a subject that shall be fulfilled.

It should be of the pleasure of a poem itself to tell how it can. The figure a poem makes. It begins in delight and ends in wisdom. The figure is the same as for love. No one can really hold that the ecstasy should be static and stand still in one place. It begins in delight, it inclines to the impulse, it assumes direction with the first line laid down, it runs a course of lucky events, and ends in a clarification of life — not necessarily a great clarification, such as sects and cults are founded on, but in a momentary stay against confusion. It has denouement. It has an outcome that though unforeseen was predestined from the first image of the original mood — and indeed from the very mood. It is but a trick poem and no poem at all if the best of it was thought of first and saved for the last. It finds its own name as it goes and discovers the best waiting for it in some final phrase at once wise and sad — the happy-sad blend of the drinking song.

No tears in the writer, no tears in the reader. No surprise for the writer, no surprise for the reader. For me the initial delight is in the surprise of remembering something I didn't know I knew. I am in a place, in a situation, as if I had materialized from cloud or risen out of the ground. There is a glad recognition of the long lost and the rest follows. Step by step the wonder of unexpected supply keeps going. The impressions most useful to my purpose seem always those I was unaware of and so made no note of at the time when taken, and the conclusion is come to that like giants we are always hurling experience ahead of us to pave the future with against the day when we may want to strike a line of purpose across it for somewhere. The line will have the more charm for not being mechanically straight. We enjoy the straight crookedness of a good walking stick. Modern instruments of precision are being used to make things crooked as if by eye and hand in the old days.

I tell how there may be a better wildness of logic than of inconsequence. But the logic is backward, in retrospect, after the act. It must be more felt than seen ahead like prophecy. It must be a revelation, or a series of revelations, as much for the poet as for the reader. For it to be that there must have been the greatest freedom of the material to move about in it and to establish relations in it regardless of time and space, previous relation, and everything but affinity. We prate of freedom. We call our schools free because we are not free to stay away from them till we are sixteen years of age. I have given up my democratic prejudices and now willingly set the lower classes free to be completely taken care of by the upper classes. Political freedom is nothing to me. I bestow it right and left. All I would keep for myself is the freedom of my material — the condition of body and mind now and then to summons aptly from the vast chaos of all I have lived through.

Scholars and artists thrown together are often annoyed at the puzzle of where they differ. Both work for knowledge; but I suspect they differ most importantly in the way their knowledge is come by. Scholars get theirs with conscientious thoroughness along projected lines of logic; poets theirs cavalierly and as it happens in and out of books. They stick to nothing deliberately, but let what will stick to them like burrs where they walk in the fields. No acquirement is on assignment, or even self-assignment. Knowledge of the second kind is much more available in the wild free ways of wit and art. A school boy may be defined as one who can tell you what he knows in the order in which he learned it. The artist must value himself as he snatches a thing from some previous order in time and space into a new order with not so much as a ligature clinging to it of the old place where it was organic.

More than once I should have lost my soul to radicalism if it had been the originality it was mistaken for by its young converts. Originality and initiative are what I ask for my country. For myself the originality need be no more than the freshness of a poem run in the way I have described: from delight to wisdom. The figure is the same as for love. Like a piece of ice on a hot stove the poem must ride on its own melting. A poem may be worked over once it is in being, but may not be worried into being. Its most precious quality will remain its having run itself and carried away the poet with it. Read it a hundred times: it will forever keep its freshness as a metal keeps its fragrance. It can never lose its sense of a meaning that once unfolded by surprise as it went.

From *Complete Poems of Robert Frost*

CONSIDERATIONS FOR CRITICAL THINKING AND WRITING

1. Frost places a high premium on sound in his poetry because it "is the gold in the ore." Choose one of Frost's poems in this book and explain the effects of its sounds and how they contribute to its meaning.

2. Discuss Frost's explanation of how his poems are written. In what sense is the process both spontaneous and "predestined"?

3. What do you think Frost means when he says he's given up his "democratic prejudices"? Why is "political freedom" nothing to him?

4. Write an essay that examines in more detail the ways scholars and artists "come by" knowledge.

5. Explain what you think Frost means when he writes, "Like a piece of ice on a hot stove the poem must ride on its own melting."

ROBERT FROST

On the Way to Read a Poem   1951

The way to read a poem in prose or verse is in the light of all the other poems ever written. We may begin anywhere. We *duff* into our first. We read that imperfectly (thoroughness with it would be fatal), but the better to read the second. We read the second the better to read the third, the third the better to read the fourth, the fourth better to read the fifth, the fifth the better to read the first again, or the second if it so happens. For poems are not meant to be read in course any more than they are to be made a study of. I once made a resolve never to put any book to any use it wasn't intended for by its author. Improvement will not be a progression but a widening circulation. Our instinct is to settle down like a revolving dog and make ourselves at home among the poems, completely at our ease as to how they should be taken. The same people will be apt to take poems right as know how to take a hint when there is one and not to take a hint when none is intended. Theirs is the ultimate refinement.

From "Poetry and School," *Atlantic Monthly,* June 1951

CONSIDERATIONS FOR CRITICAL THINKING AND WRITING

1. Given your own experience, how good is Frost's advice about reading in general and his poems in particular?

2. In what sense is a good reader like a "revolving dog" and a person who knows "how to take a hint"?

3. Frost elsewhere in this piece writes, "One of the dangers of college to anyone who wants to stay a human reader (that is to say a humanist) is that he will become a specialist and lose his sensitive fear of landing on the lovely too hard. (With beak and talon.)" Write an essay in response to this concern. Do you agree with Frost's distinction between a "human reader" and a "specialist"?

HERBERT R. COURSEN JR. (B. 1932)

A Parodic Interpretation of "Stopping by Woods on a Snowy Evening"   1962

Much ink has spilled on many pages in exegesis of this little poem. Actually, critical jottings have only obscured what has lain beneath critical noses all these years. To say that the poem means merely that a man stops one night to observe a snowfall, or that the poem contrasts the mundane desire for creature comfort with the sweep of aesthetic appreciation, or that it renders worldly responsibilities paramount, or that it reveals the speaker's latent death-wish is to miss the point rather badly. Lacking has been that mind simple enough to see what is *really* there. . . .

The "darkest evening of the year" in New England is December 21st, a date near that on which the western world celebrates Christmas. It may be that December 21st *is* the date of the poem, or (and with poets this seems more likely) that this is the closest the poet can come to Christmas without giving it all away. Who has "promises to keep" at or near this date, and who must traverse much territory to fulfill these promises? Yes, and who but St. Nick would know the location of *each* home? Only he would know who had "just settled down for a long winter's nap" (the poem's third line — "He will not see me stopping here" — is clearly a veiled allusion) and would not be out inspecting his acreage this night. The unusual phrase "fill up with snow," in the poem's fourth line, is a transfer of Santa's occupational preoccupation to the countryside; he is mulling the filling of countless stockings hung above countless fireplaces by countless careful children. "Harness bells," of course, allude to "Sleighing Song," a popular Christmas tune of the time the poem was written in which the refrain "Jingle Bells! Jingle Bells!" appears; thus again are we put on the Christmas track. The "little horse," like the date, is another attempt at poetic obfuscation. Although the "rein-reindeer" ambiguity has been eliminated from the poem's final version,[1] probably because too obvious, we may speculate that the animal is really a reindeer disguised as a horse by the poet's desire for obscurity, a desire which we must concede has been fulfilled up to now.

The animal is clearly concerned, like the faithful Rudolph — another possible allusion (post facto, hence unconscious) — lest his master fail to complete his mission. Seeing no farmhouse in the second quatrain, but pulling a load of presents, no wonder the little beast wonders! It takes him a full two quatrains to rouse his driver to remember all the empty stockings which hang ahead. And Santa does so reluctantly at that, poor soul, as he ponders the myriad farmhouses and villages which spread between him and his own "winter's nap." The modern St. Nick, lonely and overworked, tosses no "Happy Christmas to all and to all a good night!" into the precipitation. He merely shrugs his shoulders and resignedly plods away.

From "The Ghost of Christmas Past: 'Stopping by Woods
on a Snowy Evening,' " *College English,* December 1962

[1] The original draft contained the following line: "That bid me give the reins a shake" (Stageberg-Anderson, *Poetry as Experience* [New York, 1952], p. 457). [Coursen's note.]

CONSIDERATIONS FOR CRITICAL THINKING AND WRITING

1. Is this critical spoof at all credible? Does the interpretation hold any water? Is the evidence reasonable? Why or why not? Which of the poem's details are accounted for and which are ignored?

2. Choose a Frost poem and try writing a parodic interpretation of it.

3. What criteria do you use to distinguish between a sensible interpretation of a poem and an absurd one?

PETER D. POLAND

On "Neither Out Far nor In Deep"   1994

Robert Frost's cryptic little lyric "Neither Out Far nor In Deep" remains as elusive as "the truth" that is so relentlessly pursued in the poem itself. The poem is very much "about" this search for truth, and scholars, for the most part, persistently maintain that such effort is both necessary and noble, adding slowly but inexorably to the storehouse of human knowledge. Suggestive though such an interpretation might be, it distorts Frost's intentions — as a close examination of the curious image of "a standing gull," located strategically at the very heart of this enigmatic work (lines 7–8, its literal and thematic center), will reveal.

As "the people" stare vacantly seaward in search of "the truth," mesmerized by the mysterious, limitless sea, they closely resemble standing (as opposed to flying) gulls. Never directly stated, this comparison, so crucial to the poem's meaning, is clearly implied, and it works very much to the people's disadvantage. For the gull is doing what comes naturally, staring into the teeming sea that is its source of life (that is, of food), and it is merely resting from its life-sustaining labors. "The people," implies Frost, in literally and symbolically turning their backs on their domain, the land, to stare incessantly seaward, are unnatural. Their efforts are life-denying in the extreme.

Frost underscores the life-denying nature of their mindless staring by introducing not a flock of standing gulls, but a single gull only — surprising in that standing gulls (or, more accurately, terns, which typically station themselves en masse by the water's edge) are rarely found alone. The solitary gull points up just what "the people" are doing and how isolating and dehumanizing such activity is. So absorbed are they in their quest for "truth" that they have become oblivious of all else but their own solipsistic pursuit. They have cut themselves off from the land world and all that it represents (struggles and suffering, commitments, obligations, responsibilities) and from one another as well. They have become isolates, like the solitary gull that they resemble. Furthermore, Frost emphasizes not the bird itself but only its reflected image in the glassy surface of the shore; it is the reflected image that is the object of our concern, for it bears significantly on "the people" themselves. In an ironic version of Plato's Parable of the Cave, these relentless pursuers of truth have willfully turned their backs on the only "reality" they can ever know — the land world and all that it represents — and in so doing have been reduced to insubstantial images, shadowy reflections of true human beings engaged in genuinely fruitful human endeavor. Nameless, faceless, mindless, they have become pale copies of the real thing.

All of this adds up to one inescapable conclusion: "The people" are indeed "gulls" — that is, "dupes." In their search for ultimate reality they have been tricked, cheated, conned. It is all a fraud, insists Frost (for all that they do see is the occasional passing ship mentioned in lines 5 and 6), and he clearly holds their vain efforts in contempt. As the final stanzas make dramatically clear, they are wasting away their lives in a meaningless quest, for whatever it is and wherever it might be, "the truth" is surely not here. In short, they can look "Neither Out Far nor In Deep." So why bother?

The poem cries out for comparison with Frost's most famous work, his personal favorite, "Stopping by Woods on a Snowy Evening," wherein the seductive woods — "lovely, dark and deep" — recall the mysterious sea of "Neither Out Far nor In Deep." But the narrator of "Stopping by Woods" realizes how dangerously alluring the woods are. He realizes that he has "promises to keep," that he cannot "sleep" in the face of his societal obligations, and so he shortly turns homeward. "The people" of the present poem, however, continue to "look at the sea all day," seduced by its deep, dark, mysterious depths. Turning their backs on the land world, their world, they have violated their promises; they are asleep to their human responsibilities, as their comparison to the reflected image of a solitary gull suggests. For "gulls" they surely are.

From *The Explicator* 52.2 (Winter 1994)

Considerations for Critical Thinking and Writing

1. Do you agree with Poland's interpretation of this poem or do you agree with the other readers he mentions who argue that the people on the shore are engaged in a "necessary and noble" pursuit of the truth?

2. How does Poland use "Stopping by Woods on a Snowy Evening" (p. 1112) to further his argument?

3. Explain whether or not you think Poland's reading of "Neither Out Far nor In Deep" is consistent with your understanding of Frost's attitudes toward human aspiration in "Birches" (p. 1107).

Derek Walcott (b. 1930)

The Road Taken   1996

Robert Frost: the icon of Yankee values, the smell of wood smoke, the sparkle of dew, the reality of farmhouse dung, the jocular honesty of an uncle.

Why is the favorite figure of American patriotism not paternal but avuncular? Because uncles are wiser than fathers. They have humor, they keep their distance, they are bachelors, they can't be fooled by rhetoric. Frost loved playing the uncle, relishing the dry enchantment of his own voice, the homely gravel in the throat, the keep-your-distance pseudo-rusticity that suspected every stranger, meaning every reader. The voice is like its weather. It tells you to stay away until you are invited. Its first lines, in the epigraph to Frost's 1949 *Complete Poems,* are not so much invitations as warnings.

> I'm going out to clean the pasture spring;
> I'll only stop to rake the leaves away
> (And wait to watch the water clear, I may):
> I sha'n't be gone long. — You come too.

From the very epigraph, then, the surly ambiguities slide in. Why "I may"? Not for the rhyme, the desperation of doggerel, but because of this truth: that it would take too long to watch the agitated clouded water settle, that is, for as long as patience allows the poet to proceed to the next line. (Note that the parentheses function as a kind of container, or bank, or vessel, of the churned spring.) The refrain, "You come too." An invitation? An order? And how sincere is either? That is the point of Frost's tone, the authoritative but ambiguous distance of a master ironist.

Frost is an autocratic poet rather than a democratic poet. His invitations are close-lipped, wry, quiet; neither the voice nor the metrical line has the open-armed municipal mural expansion of the other democratic poet, Whitman. The people in Frost's dramas occupy a tight and taciturn locale. They are not part of Whitman's parade of blacksmiths, wheelwrights made communal by work. Besieged and threatened, their virtues are as cautious and measured as the scansion by which they are portrayed.

From Joseph Brodsky, Seamus Heaney, and Derek Walcott,
Homage to Robert Frost

CONSIDERATIONS FOR CRITICAL THINKING AND WRITING

1. Why does Walcott characterize Frost as more of an uncle than a father? Explain why you agree or disagree.
2. Choose one of Frost's poems in this anthology and use it to demonstrate that he is a "master ironist."
3. Write an essay that fleshes out Walcott's observation that the people in Frost's poems are "Besieged and threatened, their virtues . . . as cautious and measured as the scansion by which they are portrayed."

Two Complementary Critical Readings

RICHARD POIRIER (B. 1925)

On Emotional Suffocation in "Home Burial"   1977

Frost's poetry recurrently dramatizes the discovery that the sharing of a "home" can produce imaginations of uncontrollable threat inside or outside. "Home" can become the source of those fears from which it is supposed to protect us; it can become the habitation of that death whose anguish it is supposed to ameliorate. And this brings us to one of Frost's greatest poetic dramatizations of the theme, "Home Burial." [T]he pressure is shared by a husband and wife, but . . . the role of the husband is ambiguous. Though he does his best to comprehend the wife's difficulties, he is only partly able to do so. The very title of the poem means something about the couple as well as about the dead child buried in back of the house. It is as if "home" were a burial plot for all of them.

The opening lines of Frost's dramatic narratives are usually wonderfully deft in suggesting the metaphoric nature of "home," the human opportunities or imperatives which certain details represent for a husband or a wife. . . . [I]n "Home Burial," the couple are trapped inside the house, which is described as a kind of prison, or perhaps more aptly, a mental hospital. Even the wife's glance out the window can suggest to the husband the desperation she feels within the confines of what has always been his family's "home"; it looks directly on the family graveyard which now holds the body of their recently dead child: [lines 1–30 of "Home Burial" are quoted here].

The remarkable achievement here is that the husband and wife have become so nearly inarticulate in their animosities that the feelings have been transferred to a vision of household arrangements and to their own bodily movements. They and the house conspire together to create an aura of suffocation. . . . Frost's special genius is in the placement of words. The first line poses the husband as a kind of spy; the opening of the second line suggests a habituated wariness on her part, but from that point to line 5 we are shifted back to his glimpse of her as she moves obsessively again, as yet unaware of being watched, to the window. Suggestions of alienation, secretiveness, male intimidation ("advancing toward her") within a situation of mutual distrust, a miasmic fear inside as well as outside the house — we are made to sense this before anyone speaks. Initially the fault seems to lie mostly with the husband. But as soon as she catches him watching her, and as soon as he begins to talk, it is the grim mutuality of their dilemma and the shared responsibilities for it that sustain the dramatic intelligence and power of the poem.

From *Robert Frost: The Work of Knowing*

CONSIDERATIONS FOR CRITICAL THINKING AND WRITING

1. According to Poirier, how can the couple's home be regarded as a kind of "mental hospital"? Compare Poirier's view with Kearns's description in the following perspective on the house as a "marital asylum."

2. Explain why you agree or disagree that the husband's behavior is a form of "male intimidation."

3. Write an essay that discusses the "grim mutuality" of the couple's "dilemma."

KATHERINE KEARNS (B. 1949)

On the Symbolic Setting of "Home Burial"   1987

"Home Burial" may be used to clarify Frost's intimate relationships between sex, death, and madness. The physical iconography is familiar — a stairwell, a window, a doorway, and a grave — elements which Frost reiterates throughout his poetry. The marriage in "Home Burial" has been destroyed by the death of a first and only son. The wife is in the process of leaving the house, crossing the threshold from marital asylum into freedom. The house is suffocating her. Her window view of the graveyard is not enough and is, in fact, a maddening reminder that she could not enter the earth with her son. With its transparent barrier, the window is a mockery of a widened vision throughout Frost's poetry and seems to incite escape rather than quelling it; in "Home Burial" the woman can "see" through the window and into the grave in a way her husband cannot, and the fear is driving her down the steps toward the door—"She was starting down—/ Looking back over her shoulder at some fear"—even before she sees her husband. He threatens to follow his wife and bring her back by force, as if he is the cause of her leaving, but his gesture will be futile because it is based on the mistaken assumption that she is escaping him. Pathetically, he is merely an obstacle toward which she reacts at first dully and then with angry impatience. He is an inanimate part of the embattled household, her real impetus for movement comes from the grave.

The house itself, reduced symbolically and literally to a womblike passageway between the bedroom and the threshold, is a correlative for the sexual tension generated by the man's insistence on his marital rights. He offers to "give up being a man" by binding himself "to keep hands off," but their marriage is already sexually damaged and empty. The man and woman move in an intricate dance, she coming downward and then retracing a step, he "Mounting until she cower[s] under him," she "shrinking from beneath his arm" to slide downstairs. Randall Jarrell examines the image of the woman sinking into "a modest, compact, feminine bundle" upon her skirts;[1] it might be further observed that this childlike posture is also very much a gesture of sexual denial, body bent, knees drawn up protectively against the breasts, all encompassed by voluminous skirts. The two are in profound imbalance, and Frost makes the wife's speech and movements the poetic equivalent of stumbling and resistance; her lines are frequently eleven syllables, and often are punctuated by spondees whose forceful but awkward slowness embodies the woman's vacillations "from terrified to dull," and from frozen and silent immobility to anger. Her egress from the house will be symbolic verification of her husband's impotence, and if she leaves it and does not come back, the house will rot as the best birch fence will rot. Unfilled, without a woman with child, it will fall into itself, an image that recurs throughout Frost's poetry. Thus the child's grave predicts the dissolution of household, . . . almost a literal "home burial."

From "'The Place Is the Asylum': Women and Nature in Robert Frost's Poetry," *American Literature,* May 1987

[1] "Robert Frost's 'Home Burial,'" in *The Moment of Poetry,* ed. Don Cameron Allen (Baltimore: Johns Hopkins UP, 1962), p. 104.

CONSIDERATIONS FOR CRITICAL THINKING AND WRITING

1. How does Kearns's discussion of the stairwell, window, doorway, and grave shed light on your reading of "Home Burial"?

2. Discuss whether Kearns sympathizes more with the wife or the husband. Which character do you feel more sympathetic toward? Do you think Frost sides with one or the other? Explain your response.

3. Write an essay in which you agree or disagree with Kearns's assessment that "the wife is in the process of . . . crossing the threshold from marital asylum into freedom."

SUGGESTED TOPICS FOR LONGER PAPERS

1. Research Frost's popular reputation and compare that with recent biographical accounts of his personal life. How does knowledge of his personal life affect your reading of his poetry?

2. Frost has been described as a cheerful poet of New England who creates pleasant images of the region as well as a poet who creates a troubling, frightening world bordered by anxiety, anguish, doubts, and darkness. How do the poems in this chapter support both of these readings of Frost's poetry?

Web Research
Robert Frost at
bedfordstmartins.com/
meyerlit.

34

A Study of Langston Hughes

I believe that poetry should be direct, comprehensible, and the epitome of simplicity.
— LANGSTON HUGHES

The poetry of Langston Hughes represents a significant chapter in twentieth-century American literature. The poetry included here both chronicles and evokes African American life during the middle decades of the last century. Moreover, it celebrates the culture and heritage of what is called the "Harlem Renaissance" of the 1920s, which has continued to be a vital tradition and presence in American life. As you introduce yourself to Hughes's innovative techniques and the cultural life embedded in his poetry, keep in mind the Questions for Writing about an Author in Depth (p. 1082), which can serve as a guide in your explorations.

Langston Hughes

(*Left*) The publication of *The Weary Blues* in 1926 established Hughes as an important figure in the Harlem Renaissance, a cultural movement characterized by an explosion of black literature, theater, music, painting, and political and racial consciousness that began after the First World War. A stamp commemorating the centennial of Hughes's birth (2002) is but one illustration of his lasting impact on American poetry and culture.

(*Below*) Langston Hughes claimed that Walt Whitman, Carl Sandburg, and Paul Laurence Dunbar were his greatest influences as a poet. However, the experience of black America from the 1920s through the 1960s, the life and language of Harlem, and a love of jazz and the blues clearly shaped the narrative and lyrical experimentation of his poetry. This image of a couple dancing in a Harlem night club is a snapshot of the life that influenced Hughes's work.

© Bettmann/CORBIS.

In this 1932 image taken by African American photographer James VanDerZee, a Harlem couple in raccoon coats poses with a Cadillac on West 127th Street. VanDerZee once commented, "I tried to pose each person in such a way as to tell a story." His work offered America a dazzling view of black middle-class life in the 1920s and 1930s.
© Donna M. VanDerZee.

A BRIEF BIOGRAPHY

Even as a child, Langston Hughes (1902–1967) was wrapped in an important African American legacy. He was raised by his maternal grandmother, who was the widow of Lewis Sheridan Leary, one of the band of men who participated in John Brown's raid on the federal arsenal at Harpers Ferry in 1859. The raid was a desperate attempt to ignite an insurrection that would ultimately liberate slaves in the South. It was a failure. Leary was killed, but the shawl he wore, which was returned to his wife bloodstained and riddled with bullet holes, was proudly worn by Hughes's grandmother fifty years after the raid, and she used it to cover her grandson at night when he was a young boy.

Throughout his long career as a professional writer, Hughes remained true to the African American heritage he celebrated in his writings, which were frankly "racial in theme and treatment, derived from the life I know." In an influential essay published in *The Nation,* "The Negro Artist and the

The famous Lafayette Theatre, located near 132nd street on 7th Avenue, known during the Harlem Renaissance as the "Boulevard of Dreams," was one of New York's first theaters to desegregate (c. 1912). The theater (now a church) seated 2,000 people and, beginning in 1916, employed its own Lafayette Players, who performed popular and classical plays for almost exclusively black audiences. Known as the "House Beautiful" to many of its patrons, the Lafayette also showcased the blues singer Bessie Smith, the jazz composer Duke Ellington, and other prominent African American performers. Shown here is the vibrant opening night of Shakespeare's *Macbeth*, staged by Orson Welles, featuring leading actors Canada Lee and Rose McLendon, with a musical score by James P. Johnson (1936).
The Granger Collection, New York.

Racial Mountain" (1926), he insisted on the need for black artists to draw on their heritage rather than "to run away spiritually from . . . race":

> We younger Negro artists who create now intend to express our individual dark-skinned selves without fear or shame. If white people are pleased, we are glad. If they are not, it doesn't matter. We know we are beautiful. And ugly too. The tom-tom cries and the tom-tom laughs. If colored people are pleased we are glad. If they are not, their displeasure doesn't matter either. We build our temples for tomorrow, strong as we know how, and we stand on top of the mountain, free within ourselves.

That freedom was hard won for Hughes. His father, James Nathaniel Hughes, could not accommodate the racial prejudice and economic frustration that were the result of James's black and white racial ancestry. James abandoned his wife, Carrie Langston Hughes, only one year after their son was born in Joplin, Missouri, and went to find work in Mexico,

Langston Hughes testifying before the Senate Investigations Subcommittee — Senator Joseph McCarthy's subcommittee on subversive activities — on March 27, 1953. Hughes testified: "From my point [of view] it doesn't matter what the form of government is if the rights of the minorities and the poor people are respected, and if they have a chance to advance equally."
© Bettmann/CORBIS.

where he hoped the color of his skin would be less of an issue than in the United States. During the periods when Hughes's mother shuttled from city to city in the Midwest looking for work, she sent her son to live with his grandmother.

Hughes's spotty relationship with his father—a connection he developed in his late teens and maintained only sporadically thereafter—consisted mostly of arguments about his becoming a writer rather than an engineer and businessman as his father wished. Hughes's father could not appreciate or even tolerate his son's ambition to write about the black experience, and Hughes (whose given name was also James but who refused to be identified by it) could not abide his father's contempt for blacks. Consequently, his determination, as he put it in "The Negro Artist," "to express our individual dark-skinned selves without fear or shame" was not only a profound response to African American culture but also an intensely personal commitment that made a relationship with his own father impossible. Though Hughes had been abandoned by his father, he nevertheless felt an early and deep connection to his ancestors, as he reveals in the following poem, written while crossing the Mississippi River by train as he traveled to visit his father in Mexico, just a month after his high school graduation.

The Negro Speaks of Rivers   1921

I've known rivers:
I've known rivers ancient as the world and older than the
    flow of human blood in human veins.

My soul has grown deep like the rivers.

I bathed in the Euphrates when dawns were young.   5
I built my hut near the Congo and it lulled me to sleep.
I looked upon the Nile and raised the pyramids above it.
I heard the singing of the Mississippi when Abe Lincoln
    went down to New Orleans, and I've seen its muddy
    bosom turn all golden in the sunset.   10

I've known rivers:
Ancient, dusky rivers.

My soul has grown deep like the rivers.

This poem appeared in *The Crisis,* the official publication of the National Association for the Advancement of Colored People, which eventually published more of Hughes's poems than any other magazine or journal. This famous poem's simple and direct free verse makes clear that Africa's "dusky rivers" run concurrently with the poet's soul as he draws spiritual strength as well as individual identity from the collective experience of his ancestors. The themes of racial pride and personal dignity work their way through some forty books that Hughes wrote, edited, or compiled during his forty-five years of writing.

AN INTRODUCTION TO HIS WORK

Hughes's works include volumes of poetry, novels, short stories, essays, plays, opera librettos, histories, documentaries, autobiographies, biographies, anthologies, children's books, and translations, as well as radio and television scripts. This impressive body of work makes him an important literary artist and a leading African American voice of the twentieth century. First and foremost, he considered himself a poet. He set out to be a poet who could address himself to the concerns of his people in poems that could be read with no formal training or extensive literary background. He wanted his poetry to be "direct, comprehensible, and the epitome of simplicity."

Hughes's poetry echoes the voices of ordinary African Americans and the rhythms of their music. He drew on an oral tradition of working-class folk poetry that embraced black vernacular language at a time when some middle-class blacks of the 1920s felt that the use of the vernacular was an embarrassing handicap and an impediment to social progress. Hughes's response to such concerns was unequivocal; at his readings, some of which were accompanied by jazz musicians or singers, his innovative voice found an appreciative audience. As Hughes very well knew, much of the pleasure associated with his poetry comes from reading it aloud; his many recorded readings give testimony to that pleasure.

The blues can be heard moving through Hughes's poetry as well as in the works of many of his contemporaries associated with the Harlem Renaissance, a movement of African American writers, painters, sculptors, actors, and musicians who were active in New York City's Harlem of the 1920s. Hughes's introduction to the "laughter and pain, hunger and heartache" of blues music began the year he spent at Columbia University. He dropped out after only two semesters because he preferred the night life and culture of Harlem to academic life. The sweet, sad blues songs captured for Hughes the intense pain and yearning that he saw around him and that he incorporated into his poems. He also reveled in the jazz music of Harlem and discovered in its open forms and improvisations an energy and freedom that significantly influenced the style of his poetry.

Hughes's life, like the jazz music that influenced his work, was characterized by improvisation and openness. After leaving Columbia, he worked a series of odd jobs and then traveled as a merchant seaman to Africa and Europe from 1923 to 1924. He jumped ship to work for several months in the kitchen of a Paris nightclub. As he broadened his experience through travel, he continued to write poetry. After his return to the United States in 1925 he published poems in two black magazines, *The Crisis* and *Opportunity,* and met the critic Carl Van Vechten, who sent his poems to the publisher Alfred A. Knopf. He also—as a busboy in a Washington, D.C., hotel—met the poet Vachel Lindsay, who was instrumental in advancing Hughes's reputation as a poet. In 1926 Hughes published his first volume of poems,

The Weary Blues, and enrolled in Lincoln University in Pennsylvania, his education funded by a generous patron. His second volume of verse, *Fine Clothes to the Jew,* appeared in 1927, and by the time he graduated from Lincoln in 1929 he was reading his poems publicly on a book tour of the South. Hughes ended the decade as more than a promising poet; as Countee Cullen pronounced in a mixed review of *The Weary Blues* (mixed because Cullen believed that African American poets should embrace universal themes rather than racial themes), Hughes had "arrived."

Hughes wrote more prose than poetry during the 1930s, publishing his first novel, *Not without Laughter* (1930), and a collection of stories, *The Ways of White Folks* (1934). In addition to writing a variety of magazine articles, he also worked on a number of plays and screenplays. Many of his poems from this period reflect proletarian issues. During this decade Hughes's travels took him to all points of the compass — Cuba, Haiti, the Soviet Union, China, Japan, Mexico, France, and Spain — but his general intellectual movement was decidedly toward the left. Hughes was attracted to the American Communist Party, owing to its insistence on equality for all working-class people regardless of race. Like many other Americans of the thirties, he turned his attention away from the exotic twenties and focused on the economic and political issues attending the Great Depression that challenged the freedom and dignity of common humanity.

During World War II, Hughes helped the war effort by writing jingles and catchy verses to sell war bonds and to bolster morale. His protest poems of the thirties were largely replaced by poems that returned to earlier themes centered on the everyday lives of African Americans. In 1942 Hughes described his new collection of poems, *Shakespeare in Harlem,* as "light verse. Afro-American in the blues mood . . . to be read aloud, crooned, shouted, recited, and sung. Some with gestures, some not — as you like." Soon after this collection appeared, the character of Jesse B. Simple emerged from Hughes's 1943 newspaper column for the Chicago *Defender.* Hughes developed this popular urban African American character in five humorous books published over a fifteen-year period: *Simple Speaks His Mind* (1950), *Simple Takes a Wife* (1953), *Simple Stakes a Claim* (1957), *The Best of Simple* (1961), and *Simple's Uncle Sam* (1965). Two more poetry collections appeared in the forties: *Fields of Wonder* (1947) and *One-Way Ticket* (1949).

In the 1950s and 1960s Hughes's poetry again revealed the strong influence of black music, especially in the rhythms of *Montage of a Dream Deferred* (1951) and *Ask Your Mama: 12 Moods for Jazz* (1961). From the poem "Harlem" (p. 1148) in *Montage of a Dream Deferred,* Lorraine Hansberry derived the title of her 1959 play *A Raisin in the Sun.* This is only a small measure of Hughes's influence on his fellow African American writers, but it is suggestive nonetheless. For some in the 1950s, however, Hughes and his influence occasioned suspicion. He was watched closely by the FBI and the Special Committee on Un-American Activities of the House of Representatives because of his alleged communist activities in the 1930s. Hughes denied that he was ever a member of the Communist party, but he and others, including Albert Einstein and Paul Robeson, were characterized as "dupes and fellow travelers" by *Life* magazine in 1949. Hughes was subpoenaed to appear before Senator Joseph McCarthy's subcommittee on subversive activities in 1953 and listed by the FBI as a security risk until 1959. His anger and indignation over these attacks from the right can be seen in his poem "Un-American Investigators," published posthumously in *The Panther and the Lash* (1967).

Despite the tremendous amount that Hughes published, including two autobiographies, *The Big Sea* (1940) and *I Wonder as I Wander* (1956), he remains somewhat elusive. He never married or had friends who can lay claim to truly knowing him beyond what he wanted them to know (even though several biographies have been published). And yet Hughes is well known — not for his personal life but for his treatment of the possibilities of African American experiences and identities. Like Walt Whitman, one of his favorite writers, Hughes created a persona that spoke for more than himself. Consider Hughes's voice in the following poem.

I, Too   1925

I, too, sing America.

I am the darker brother.
They send me to eat in the kitchen
When company comes,
But I laugh,   5
And eat well,
And grow strong.

Tomorrow,
I'll be at the table
When company comes.   10
Nobody'll dare
Say to me,
"Eat in the kitchen,"
Then.

Besides,   15
They'll see how beautiful I am
And be ashamed —

I, too, am America.

The "darker brother" who celebrates America is certain of a better future when he will no longer be shunted aside by "company." The poem is characteristic of Hughes's faith in the racial consciousness of African Americans, a consciousness that reflects their integrity and beauty while simultaneously demanding respect and acceptance from others: "Nobody'll dare / Say to me, / 'Eat in the kitchen,' / Then."

Hughes's poetry reveals his hearty appetite for all humanity, his insistence on justice for all, and his faith in the transcendent possibilities of joy and hope that make room for everyone at America's table.

Chronology

1902	Born on February 1, in Joplin, Missouri.
1903–14	Lives primarily with his grandmother in Lawrence, Kansas.
1920	Graduates from high school in Cleveland.
1921–22	Attends Columbia University for one year but then drops out to work odd jobs and discover Harlem.
1923–24	Travels to Africa and Europe while working on a merchant ship.
1926	Publishes his first collection of poems, *The Weary Blues,* and enters Lincoln University in Pennsylvania.
1929	Graduates from Lincoln University.
1930	Publishes his first novel, *Not without Laughter.*
1932	Travels to the Soviet Union.
1934	Publishes his first collection of short stories, *The Ways of White Folks.*
1935	His play *Mulatto* is produced on Broadway.
1937	Covers the Spanish Civil War for the Baltimore *Afro-American.*
1938–39	Founds African American theaters in Harlem and Los Angeles.
1940	Publishes his first autobiography, *The Big Sea.*
1943	Creates the character of Simple in columns for the Chicago *Defender.*
1947	Is poet-in-residence at Atlanta University.
1949	Teaches at University of Chicago's Laboratory School.
1950	Publishes his first volume of Simple sketches, *Simple Speaks His Mind.*
1951	Publishes a translation of Federico García Lorca's *Gypsy Ballads.*
1953	Is subpoenaed to appear before Senator Joseph McCarthy's subcommittee on subversive activities in Washington, D.C.
1954–55	Publishes a number of books for young readers, including *The First Book of Jazz* and *Famous American Negroes.*
1956	Publishes his second autobiography, *I Wonder as I Wander.*
1958	Publishes *The Langston Hughes Reader.*
1960	Publishes *An African Treasury: Articles, Essays, Stories, Poems by Black Africans.*
1961	Is inducted into the National Institute of Arts and Letters.
1962	Publishes *Fight for Freedom: The Story of the NAACP.*

1963	Publishes *Five Plays by Langston Hughes.*
1964	Publishes *New Negro Poets: U.S.A.*
1965	Defends Martin Luther King Jr. from attacks by militant blacks.
1966	Is appointed by President Lyndon B. Johnson to lead the American delegation to the First World Festival of Negro Arts in Dakar.
1967	Dies on May 22 in New York City; his last volume of poems, *The Panther and the Lash,* is published posthumously.
1994	*The Collected Poems of Langston Hughes,* edited by Arnold Rampersad and David Roessel, is published.

Negro   1922

I am a Negro:
   Black as the night is black,
   Black like the depths of my Africa.

I've been a slave:
   Caesar told me to keep his door-steps clean.   5
   I brushed the boots of Washington.

I've been a worker:
   Under my hand the pyramids arose.
   I made mortar for the Woolworth Building.

I've been a singer: 10
   All the way from Africa to Georgia
   I carried my sorrow songs.
   I made ragtime.

I've been a victim:
   The Belgians cut off my hands in the Congo.   15
   They lynch me still in Mississippi.

I am a Negro:
   Black as the night is black,
   Black like the depths of my Africa.

CONSIDERATIONS FOR CRITICAL THINKING AND WRITING

1. **FIRST RESPONSE.** What sort of identity does the speaker claim for the "Negro"? What is the effect of the litany of roles?

2. What is the effect of the repetition of the first and last stanzas?

3. What kind of history of black people does the speaker describe?

CONNECTIONS TO OTHER SELECTIONS

1. How does Hughes's use of night and blackness in "Negro" help to explain their meaning in the poem "Dream Variations" (p. 1141)?

2. Write an essay comparing the treatment of oppression in "Negro" with that in William Blake's "The Chimney Sweeper" (p. 912).

Danse Africaine   *1922*

The low beating of the tom-toms,
The slow beating of the tom-toms,
    Low . . . slow
    Slow . . . low —
    Stirs your blood.   5
        Dance!
A night-veiled girl
    Whirls softly into a
    Circle of light.
    Whirls softly . . . slowly,   10
Like a wisp of smoke around the fire —
    And the tom-toms beat,
    And the tom-toms beat,
And the low beating of the tom-toms
    Stirs your blood.   15

CONSIDERATIONS FOR CRITICAL THINKING AND WRITING

1. **FIRST RESPONSE.** How do the sounds of this poem build its meaning? (What *is* its meaning?)

2. What effect do the repeated rhythms have? You may need to read the poem aloud to answer.

CONNECTION TO ANOTHER SELECTION

1. **CREATIVE RESPONSE.** Try rewriting this poem based on the prescription for poetry in Hughes's "Formula" (p. 1142).

Jazzonia   *1923*

Oh, silver tree!
Oh, shining rivers of the soul!

In a Harlem cabaret
Six long-headed jazzers play.
A dancing girl whose eyes are bold   5
Lifts high a dress of silken gold.

Oh, singing tree!
Oh, shining rivers of the soul!

Were Eve's eyes
In the first garden   10

Just a bit too bold?
Was Cleopatra gorgeous
In a gown of gold?

Oh, shining tree!
Oh, silver rivers of the soul!   15

In a whirling cabaret
Six long-headed jazzers play.

CONSIDERATIONS FOR CRITICAL THINKING AND WRITING

1. **FIRST RESPONSE.** Does "Jazzonia" capture what you imagine a Harlem cabaret to have been like? Discuss the importance of the setting.

2. What is the effect of the variations in lines 1–2, 7–8, and 14–15?

3. What do the allusions to Eve and Cleopatra add to the poem's meaning? Are the questions raised about them answered?

CONNECTION TO ANOTHER SELECTION

1. Compare in an essay the rhythms of "Jazzonia" and "Danse Africaine" (p. 1140).

Dream Variations   1924

To fling my arms wide
In some place of the sun,
To whirl and to dance
Till the white day is done.
Then rest at cool evening   5
Beneath a tall tree
While night comes on gently,
    Dark like me —
That is my dream!

To fling my arms wide   10
In the face of the sun,
Dance! Whirl! Whirl!
Till the quick day is done.
Rest at pale evening . . .
A tall, slim tree . . .   15
Night coming tenderly
    Black like me.

CONSIDERATIONS FOR CRITICAL THINKING AND WRITING

1. **FIRST RESPONSE.** What distinctions are made in the poem between night and day? Which is the dream?

2. Describe the speaker's "Dream." How might the dream be understood metaphorically?

3. How do the rhythms of the lines contribute to the poem's effects?

CONNECTIONS TO OTHER SELECTIONS

1. In an essay compare and contrast the meanings of darkness and the night in this poem and in William Stafford's "Traveling through the Dark" (p. 903).
2. Discuss the significance of the dream in this poem and in "Dream Boogie" (p. 1147).

Cross   *1925*

My old man's a white old man
And my old mother's black.
If ever I cursed my white old man
I take my curses back.

If ever I cursed my black old mother   5
And wished she were in hell,
I'm sorry for that evil wish
And now I wish her well.

My old man died in a fine big house.
My ma died in a shack.   10
I wonder where I'm gonna die,
Being neither white nor black?

CONSIDERATIONS FOR CRITICAL THINKING AND WRITING

1. **FIRST RESPONSE.** What do you think has caused the speaker to retract his or her hard feelings about his or her parents?
2. Discuss the possible meaning of the title.
3. Why do you think the speaker regrets having "cursed" his or her father and mother? Is it possible to determine if the speaker is male or female? Why or why not?
4. What informs the speaker's attitude toward life?

CONNECTION TO ANOTHER SELECTION

1. Read the perspective by Robert Francis, "On 'Hard' Poetry" (p. 779), and write an essay explaining why you would characterize "Cross" as "hard" or "soft" poetry.

Formula   *1926*

Poetry should treat
    Of lofty things
Soaring thoughts
    And birds with wings.

The Muse of Poetry   5
    Should not know

That roses
    In manure grow.

The Muse of Poetry
    Should not care   10
That earthly pain
    Is everywhere.

Poetry!
    Treats of lofty things:
Soaring thoughts   15
    And birds with wings.

CONSIDERATIONS FOR CRITICAL THINKING AND WRITING

1. **FIRST RESPONSE.** What makes this poem a parody? What assumptions about poetry are being made fun of?

2. How does "Formula" fit the prescriptions offered in the advice to greeting-card freelancers (p. 774)?

CONNECTIONS TO OTHER SELECTIONS

1. Choose any two poems by Hughes in this collection and explain why they do not fit the "Formula."

2. Write an essay that explains how Helen Farries's "Magic of Love" (p. 775) conforms to the ideas about poetry presented in "Formula."

Esthete in Harlem   1926

Strange,
That in this nigger place
I should meet life face to face;
When, for years, I had been seeking
Life in places gentler-speaking,
Until I came to this vile street
And found Life stepping on my feet!

CONSIDERATIONS FOR CRITICAL THINKING AND WRITING

1. **FIRST RESPONSE.** Why might an esthete find Harlem strange? What changes the speaker's mind?

2. Discuss the effect of the enjambment in lines 6–7.

Lenox Avenue: Midnight   1926

The rhythm of life
Is a jazz rhythm,
Honey.
The gods are laughing at us.

The broken heart of love, 5
The weary, weary heart of pain, —
    Overtones,
    Undertones,
To the rumble of street cars,
To the swish of rain. 10

Lenox Avenue,
Honey.
Midnight,
And the gods are laughing at us.

CONSIDERATIONS FOR CRITICAL THINKING AND WRITING

1. **FIRST RESPONSE.** What, in your own experience, is the equivalent of what Lenox Avenue is for the speaker?
2. For so brief a poem there are many sounds in these fourteen lines. What are they? How do they reinforce the poem's meanings?
3. What do you think is the poem's theme?

CONNECTIONS TO OTHER SELECTIONS

1. In an essay compare the theme of this poem with that of Emily Dickinson's "I know that He exists" (p. 1084).
2. Compare and contrast the speaker's tone in this poem with that of the speaker in Thomas Hardy's "Hap" (p. 1326).

Song for a Dark Girl 1927

Way Down South in Dixie
    (Break the heart of me)
They hung my black young lover
    To a cross roads tree.

Way Down South in Dixie 5
    (Bruised body high in air)
I asked the white Lord Jesus
    What was the use of prayer.

Way down South in Dixie
    (Break the heart of me) 10
Love is a naked shadow
    On a gnarled and naked tree.

CONSIDERATIONS FOR CRITICAL THINKING AND WRITING

1. **FIRST RESPONSE.** What allusion is made in the first line of each stanza? How is that allusion ironic?

2. What *is* "the use of prayer" (line 8) in this poem? Is the question answered? What, in particular, leads you to your conclusion?

3. Discuss the relationship between love and hatred in the poem.

CONNECTION TO ANOTHER SELECTION

1. Compare the speakers' sensibilities in this poem and in Emily Dickinson's "If I can stop one Heart from breaking" (p. 1048). What kinds of cultural assumptions are implicit in each speaker's voice?

Red Silk Stockings   1927

Put on yo' red silk stockings,
Black gal.
Go out an' let de white boys
Look at yo' legs.

Ain't nothin' to do for you, nohow,   5
Round this town, —
You's too pretty.

Put on yo' red silk stockings, gal,
An' tomorrow's chile'll
Be a high yaller.   10

Go out an' let de white boys
Look at yo' legs.

CONSIDERATIONS FOR CRITICAL THINKING AND WRITING

1. **FIRST RESPONSE.** Who do you think is speaking? Describe his or her tone.

2. Discuss the racial dimensions of this poem.

3. Write a response from the girl — does she put on the red silk stockings? Explain why you imagine her reacting in a certain way.

CONNECTION TO ANOTHER SELECTION

1. Write an essay that compares relations between whites and blacks in this poem and in "Song for a Dark Girl" (p. 1144).

Rent-Party° Shout: For a Lady Dancer   1930

Whip it to a jelly!
Too bad Jim!
Mamie's got ma man —
An' I can't find him.

Rent-Party: In Harlem during the 1920s, parties were given that charged admission to raise money for rent.

Shake that thing! O!   5
Shake it slow!
That man I love is
Mean an' low.
Pistol an' razor!
Razor an' gun!   10
If I sees ma man he'd
Better run—
For I'll shoot him in de shoulder,
Else I'll cut him down,
Cause I knows I can find him   15
When he's in de ground—
Then can't no other women
Have him layin' round.
So play it, Mr. Nappy!
Yo' music's fine!   20
I'm gonna kill that
Man o' mine!

CONSIDERATIONS FOR CRITICAL THINKING AND WRITING

1. **FIRST RESPONSE.** Describe the type of music you think might be played at this party today.
2. In what sense is this poem a kind of "Shout"?
3. How is the speaker's personality characterized by her use of language?
4. How does Hughes's use of short lines affect your reading of the poem?

50-50   1942

I'm all alone in this world, she said,
Ain't got nobody to share my bed,
Ain't got nobody to hold my hand—
The truth of the matter's
I ain't got no man.   5

Big Boy opened his mouth and said,
Trouble with you is
You ain't got no head!
If you had a head and used your mind
You could have *me* with you   10
All the time.

She answered, Babe, what must I do?

He said, Share your bed—
And your money, too.

CONSIDERATIONS FOR CRITICAL THINKING AND WRITING

1. **FIRST RESPONSE.** What do you think is the speaker's attitude toward Big Boy? What's yours?

2. Discuss the significance of the title.

3. **CREATIVE RESPONSE.** Write an additional stanza giving the woman's reply to Big Boy.

125th Street°   *1950*

Face like a chocolate bar
full of nuts and sweet.

Face like a jack-o'-lantern,
candle inside.

Face like a slice of melon,
grin that wide.

125th Street: The main street in Harlem.

CONSIDERATIONS FOR CRITICAL THINKING AND WRITING

1. **FIRST RESPONSE.** How do these three similes create a vivid picture of 125th Street?

2. How does this poem confirm the poet Marvin Bell's observation that "a short poem need not be small"?

Dream Boogie   *1951*

Good morning, daddy!
Ain't you heard
The boogie-woogie rumble
Of a dream deferred?
Listen closely: 5
You'll hear their feet
Beating out and beating out a —

   You think
   It's a happy beat?

Listen to it closely: 10
Ain't you heard
something underneath
like a —

What did I say?

Sure,   15
I'm happy!
Take it away!

Hey, pop!
Re-bop!
Mop!   20

Y-e-a-h!

CONSIDERATIONS FOR CRITICAL THINKING AND WRITING

1. **FIRST RESPONSE.** Answer the question, *"You think / It's a happy beat?"* (lines 8–9).
2. Discuss the poem's musical qualities. Which lines are most musical?
3. Describe the competing tones in the poem. Which do you think is predominant?

CONNECTIONS TO OTHER SELECTIONS

1. In an essay compare and contrast the thematic tensions in this poem and in "Harlem" (below).
2. How are the "dreams" different in "Dream Boogie" and "Dream Variations" (p. 1141)?

Harlem   1951

What happens to a dream deferred?

    Does it dry up
like a raisin in the sun?
Or fester like a sore —
And then run?
Does it stink like rotten meat?   5
Or crust and sugar over —
like a syrupy sweet?

Maybe it just sags
like a heavy load.   10

Or does it explode?

CONSIDERATIONS FOR CRITICAL THINKING AND WRITING

1. **FIRST RESPONSE.** Could the question asked in this poem be raised by any individual or group whose dreams and aspirations are thwarted? Why or why not?
2. In some editions of Hughes's poetry the title of this poem is "Dream Deferred." How would this change affect your reading of the poem's symbolic significance?

3. How might the final line be completed as a simile? What is the effect of the speaker not completing the simile? Why is this an especially useful strategy?

CONNECTION TO ANOTHER SELECTION

1. Write an essay on the themes of "Harlem" and James Merrill's "Casual Wear" (p. 907).

Motto   1951

I play it cool
And dig all jive
That's the reason
I stay alive.

My motto,
As I lived and learn,
   is:
Dig And Be Dug
In Return.

CONSIDERATIONS FOR CRITICAL THINKING AND WRITING

1. **FIRST RESPONSE.** Write a paraphrase of the poem. How useful do you think this principle is to live by?
2. Discuss Hughes's use of line spacing in the second stanza.

CONNECTION TO ANOTHER SELECTION

1. Compare the themes of "Motto" and Gwendolyn Brooks's "We Real Cool" (p. 827).

Old Walt   1954

Old Walt Whitman
Went finding and seeking,
Finding less than sought
Seeking more than found,
Every detail minding   5
Of the seeking or the finding.

Pleasured equally
In seeking as in finding,
Each detail minding,
Old Walt went seeking   10
And finding.

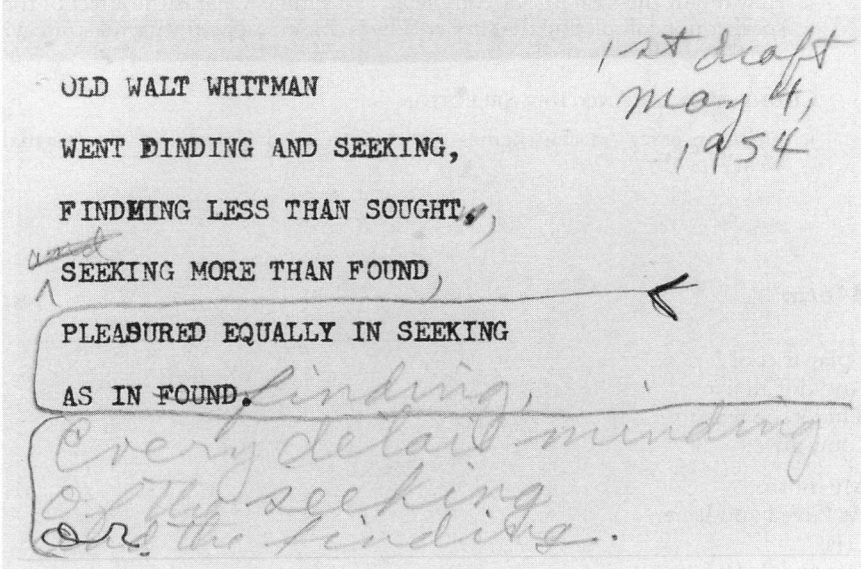

Manuscript page for "Old Walt" (1954) showing an earlier stage of the poem with Hughes's revisions.

Reprinted by permission of Harold Ober Associates, Incorporated.

CONSIDERATIONS FOR CRITICAL THINKING AND WRITING

1. **FIRST RESPONSE.** Read any poem by Whitman in this book. Do you agree with the speaker's take on Whitman's poetry?

2. Write an explication of "Old Walt." (For a discussion of how to explicate a poem, see the sample explication on p. 1034.)

3. What is the effect of the poem's repeated sounds?

4. To what extent do you think lines 3 and 4 could be used to describe Hughes's poetry as well as Whitman's?

High to Low   1949

God knows
We have our troubles, too—
One trouble is you:
you talk too loud,
cuss too loud,   5
look too black,
don't get anywhere,
and sometimes it seems
you don't even care.
The way you send your kids to school   10

stockings down,
(not Ethical Culture)
the way you shout out loud in church,
(not St. Phillips)
and the way you lounge on doorsteps   15
just as if you were down South,
(not at 409)
the way you clown —
the way, in other words,
you let me down —   20
me, trying to uphold the race
and you —
well, you can see,
we have our problems,
too, with you.   25

CONSIDERATIONS FOR CRITICAL THINKING AND WRITING

1. **FIRST RESPONSE.** Characterize the speaker. How does the speaker characterize the "you" in the poem?
2. Do you think Hughes empathizes with the speaker or with those being spoken to? Which one do you find more appealing? Why?
3. To what extent are racial matters complicated by class issues in the poem?

CONNECTION TO ANOTHER SELECTION

1. Compare the speaker in "High to Low" with the central character in M. Carl Holman's "Mr. Z" (p. 1254) in terms of their racial attitudes.

Perspectives on Langston Hughes

LANGSTON HUGHES

On Harlem Rent Parties   1940

Then [in the late twenties and early thirties] it was that house-rent parties began to flourish — and not always to raise the rent either. But, as often as not, to have a get-together of one's own, where you could do the black-bottom with no stranger behind you trying to do it, too. Non-theatrical, non-intellectual Harlem was an unwilling victim of its own vogue. It didn't like to be stared at by white folks. But perhaps the downtowners never knew this — for the cabaret owners, the entertainers, and the speakeasy proprietors treated them fine — as long as they paid.

   The Saturday night rent parties that I attended were often more amusing than any night club, in small apartments where God knows who lived — because the guests seldom did — but where the piano would often be augmented by a guitar, or an odd cornet, or somebody with a pair of drums walking in off the

---

We got yellow girls, we've got black and tan
Will you have a good time? - YEAH MAN !

𝔄 𝔖𝔬𝔠𝔦𝔞𝔩 𝔚𝔥𝔦𝔰𝔱 𝔓𝔞𝔯𝔱𝔶

—GIVEN BY—

MARY WINSTON

147 West 145th Street   Apt. 5

SATURDAY EVE., MARCH 19th, 1932

GOOD MUSIC   **REFRESHMENTS**

---

street. And where awful bootleg whiskey and good fried fish or steaming chitterling were sold at very low prices. And the dancing and singing and impromptu entertaining went on until dawn came in at the windows.

These parties, often termed whist parties or dances, were usually announced by brightly colored cards stuck in the grille of apartment house elevators. Some of the cards were highly entertaining in themselves.

Almost every Saturday night when I was in Harlem I went to a house-rent party. I wrote lots of poems about house-rent parties, and ate there at many a fried fish and pig's foot—with liquid refreshments on the side. I met ladies' maids and truck drivers, laundry workers and shoe shine boys, seamstresses and porters. I can still hear their laughter in my ears, hear the soft slow music, and feel the floor shaking as the dancers danced.

From "When the Negro Was in Vogue," in *The Big Sea*

CONSIDERATIONS FOR CRITICAL THINKING AND WRITING

1. What, according to Hughes, was the appeal of the rent parties in contrast to the nightclubs?
2. Describe the tone in which Hughes recounts his memory of these parties.

JAMES A. EMANUEL (B. 1921)

Hughes's Attitudes toward Religion   1973

Religion, because of its historical importance during and after slavery, is an undeniably useful theme in the work of any major black writer. In a writer whose special province for almost forty-five years was more recent black experience, the theme is doubly vital. Hughes's personal religious orientation is pertinent.

Asked about it by the Reverend Dana F. Kennedy of the "Viewpoint" radio and television show (on December 10, 1960), the poet responded:

> I grew up in a not very religious family, but I had a foster aunt who saw that I went to church and Sunday school . . . and I was very much moved, always, by the, shall I say, the rhythms of the Negro church . . . of the spirituals, . . . of those wonderful old-time sermons. . . . There's great beauty in the mysticism of much religious writing, and great help there — but I also think that we live in a world . . . of solid earth and vegetables and a need for jobs and a need for housing. . . .

Two years earlier, the poet had told John Kirkwood of British Columbia's *Vancouver Sun* (December 3, 1958): "I'm not anti-Christian. I'm not against anyone's religion. Religion is one of the innate needs of mankind. What I am against is the misuse of religion. But I won't ridicule it. . . . Whatever part of God is in anybody is not to be played with, and everybody has got a part of God in them."

These typical public protestations by Hughes boil down to his insistence that religion is naturally sacred and beautiful, and that its needed sustenance must not be exploited.

> From "Christ in Alabama: Religion in the Poetry of Langston Hughes,"
> in *Modern Black Poets,* edited by Donald B. Gibson

CONSIDERATIONS FOR CRITICAL THINKING AND WRITING

1. Why do you think Emanuel asserts that, owing to slavery, religion "is an undeniably useful theme in the work of any major black writer"?
2. How does Hughes's concern for the "solid earth and vegetables and a need for jobs and a need for housing" qualify his attitudes toward religion?

KAREN JACKSON FORD

Hughes's Aesthetics of Simplicity   1992

The repression of the great bulk of Hughes's poems is the result of chronic critical scorn for their simplicity. Throughout his long career, but especially after his first two volumes of poetry (readers were at ficxrst willing to assume that a youthful poet might grow to be more complex), his books received their harshest reviews for a variety of "flaws" that all originate in an aesthetics of simplicity. From his first book, *The Weary Blues* (1926), to his last one, *The Panther and the Lash* (1967), the reviews invoke a litany of faults: the poems are superficial, infantile, silly, small, unpoetic, common, jejune, iterative, and, of course, simple.[1] Even his admirers reluctantly conclude that Hughes's poetics failed. Saunders Redding flatly opposes simplicity and artfulness. "While Hughes's rejection of his own growth shows an admirable loyalty to his self-commitment as the poet of the 'simple, Negro commonfolk' . . . it does a

---

[1] Reviews in which these epithets appear are collected in Edward J. Mullen, *Critical Essays on Langston Hughes* (Boston: G. K. Hall, 1986). [Ford's note.]

disservice to his art."[2] James Baldwin, who recognizes the potential of simplicity as an artistic principle, faults the poems for "tak[ing] refuge . . . in a fake simplicity in order to avoid the very difficult simplicity of the experience."[3]

Despite a lifetime of critical disappointments, then, Hughes remained loyal to the aesthetic program he had outlined in 1926 in his decisive poetic treatise, "The Negro Artist and the Racial Mountain." There he had predicted that the common people would "give to this world its truly great Negro artist, the one who is not afraid to be himself," a poet who would explore the "great field of unused [folk] material ready for his art" and recognize that this source would provide "sufficient matter to furnish a black artist with a lifetime of creative work."[4] This is clearly a portrait of the poet Hughes would become, and he maintained his fidelity to this ideal at great cost to his literary reputation.

From "Do Right to Write Right: Langston Hughes's Aesthetics of Simplicity,"
Twentieth Century Literature 38.4 (1992)

[2] Redding's comments appear in Mullen 74. [Ford's note.]
[3] Baldwin's comments appear in Mullen 85. [Ford's note.]
[4] *The Nation* 122 (1926): 692. [Ford's note.]

CONSIDERATIONS FOR CRITICAL THINKING AND WRITING

1. What was Hughes's rationale for the value of simplicity in his poetry?
2. Explain whether or not you think there is any justification for regarding Hughes's poetry as "superficial" and too "simple."

DAVID CHINITZ (B. 1962)

The Romanticization of Africa in the 1920s   *1997*

In Europe black culture was an exotic import; in America it was domestic and increasingly mass-produced. If postwar [World War I] disillusionment judged the majority culture mannered, neurotic, and repressive, Americans had an easily accessible alternative. The need for such an Other produced a discourse in which black Americans figured as barely civilized exiles from the jungle, with — so the clichés ran — tom-toms beating in their blood and dark laughter in their souls. The African American became a model of "natural" human behavior to contrast with the falsified, constrained and impotent modes of the "civilized."

Far from being immune to the lure of this discourse, for the better part of the 1920s Hughes asserted an open pride in the supposed primitive qualities of his race, the atavistic legacy of the African motherland. Unlike most of those who romanticized Africa, Hughes had at least some firsthand experience of the continent; yet he processed what he saw there in images conditioned by European primitivism, rendering "[the land] wild and lovely, the people dark and beautiful, the palm trees tall, the sun bright, and the rivers deep."[1] His short story "Luani of the Jungle," in attempting to glorify aboriginal African vigor as against European anemia, shows how predictable and unextraordinary even

[1] *The Big Sea.* 1940. N.Y.: Thunder's Mouth, 1986, 11. [Chinitz's note.]

Hughes's primitivism could be. To discover in the descendants of idealized Africans the same qualities of innate health, spontaneity, and naturalness requires no great leap; one has only to identify the African American as a displaced primitive, as Hughes does repeatedly in his first book, *The Weary Blues:*

> They drove me out of the forest.
> They took me away from the jungles.
> I lost my trees.
> I lost my silver moons.
>
> Now they've caged me
> In the circus of civilization.[2]

Hughes depicts black atavism vividly and often gracefully, yet in a way that is entirely consistent with the popular iconography of the time. His African Americans retain "among the skyscrapers" the primal fears and instincts of their ancestors "among the palms in Africa."[3] The scion of Africa is still more than half primitive: "All the tom-toms of the jungles beat in my blood, / And all the wild hot moons of the jungles shine in my soul."[4]

From "Rejuvenation through Joy: Langston Hughes, Primitivism and Jazz,"
in *American Literary History,* Spring 1997

[2] *The Weary Blues.* N.Y.: Knopf, 1926, 100. [Chinitz's note.]
[3] Ibid. 101.
[4] Ibid. 102.

CONSIDERATIONS FOR CRITICAL THINKING AND WRITING

1. According to Chinitz, why did Europeans and Americans romanticize African culture?

2. Consider the poems published by Hughes in the 1920s reprinted in this anthology. Explain whether you find any "primitivism" in these poems.

3. Later in this essay, Chinitz points out that Hughes eventually rejected the "reductive mischaracterizations of black culture, the commercialism, the sham sociology, and the downright silliness of the primitivist fad." Choose and discuss a poem from this anthology that you think reflects Hughes's later views of primitivism.

Two Complementary Critical Readings

ARNOLD RAMPERSAD (B. 1941)

On the Persona in "The Negro Speaks of Rivers"   1985

Here, the persona moves steadily from dimly starred personal memory ("I've known rivers") toward a rendezvous with modern history (Lincoln going down the Mississippi and seeing the horror of slavery that, according to legend, would make him one day free the slaves). The death wish, benign but suffusing, of its images of rivers older than human blood, of souls grown as deep as these rivers, gives way steadily to an altering, ennobling vision whose final effect gleams in the evocation of the Mississippi's "muddy bosom" turning at last "all golden in the sunset." Personal anguish has been alchemized by the poet into a gracious meditation on his race, whose despised ("muddy") culture and history, irradiated by the poet's vision, changes within the poem from mud into gold. This is a classic example of the essential process of creativity in Hughes.

The poem came to him, according to Hughes (accurately, it seems clear) about ten months after his Mexican illness, when he was riding a train from Cleveland to Mexico to rejoin his father. The time was sundown, the place the Mississippi outside St. Louis. "All day on the train I had been thinking of my father," he would write in *The Big Sea*. "Now it was just sunset and we crossed the Mississippi, slowly, over a long bridge. I looked out of the window of the Pullman at the great muddy river flowing down toward the heart of the South, and I began to think what that river, the old Mississippi, had meant to Negroes in the past — how to be sold down the river was the worst fate that could overtake a slave in bondage. Then I remembered reading how Abraham Lincoln had made a trip down the Mississippi on a raft, and how he had seen slavery at its worst, and had decided within himself that it should be removed from American life. Then I began to think of other rivers in our past — the Congo, and the Niger, and the Nile in Africa — and the thought came to me: 'I've known rivers,' and I put it down on the back of an envelope I had in my pocket, and within the space of ten or fifteen minutes, as the train gathered speed in the dusk, I had written this poem."

From "The Origins of Poetry in Langston Hughes,"
Southern Review 21.3 (1985)

CONSIDERATIONS FOR CRITICAL THINKING AND WRITING

1. How does the biographical information that Rampersad provides affect your reading of "The Negro Speaks of Rivers" (p. 1134)?

2. Describe how the poem's images support Rampersad's assertion that Hughes's personal experience is "alchemized" into a reflection on the history of his race.

ADRIAN OKTENBERG (B. 1947)

Memory in "The Negro Speaks of Rivers" 1987

"The Negro Speaks of Rivers" . . . is only the beginning of a long chain of poems by Hughes which confront, distill, extend, and transform the historical experience of black people into an art both limpid and programmatic. . . . The "I" of the poem is not that of "a" Negro but "the" Negro, suggesting the whole of the people and their history. Most of the consonants — *d*'s, *n*'s, *l*'s, *s*'s — are soft, and of the vowels, long *o*'s reoccur, contributing by sound the effect of an ancient voice. The tone of the repeated declarative sentences is muted, lulling. Every element of the poem combines to suggest that when the Negro speaks of rivers it is with the accumulated wisdom of a sage. The function of a sage is to impart the sometimes secret but long accumulated history of a people to its younger members so that they might make the lessons of the past active in the future. This impartation occurs in the central stanza of the poem:

I bathed in the Euphrates when dawns were young.
I built my hut near the Congo and it lulled me to sleep.
I looked upon the Nile and raised the pyramids above it.
I heard the singing of the Mississippi when Abe Lincoln
     went down to New Orleans, and I've seen its muddy
     bosom turn all golden in the sunset.

Moving by suggestion, by naming particular rivers and particular activities per-formed nearby, the poem implicates the whole history of African and American slavery without ever articulating the word. "I bathed in the Euphrates" and "I built my hut near the Congo" are the normal activities of natural man per-formed in his natural habitat. That may be an unnecessarily anthropological way of putting it, but the lines are the equivalent of the speaker having said, "I made my life undisturbed in the place where I lived." The shift—and the lesson—occurs in the next two lines. Raising the pyramids above the Nile was the act of slaves, and if ever "Abe Lincoln went down to New Orleans," it would have been in the context of American slavery and the Civil War. Implicit in the history of a people who had first been free and then enslaved is the vision of freedom regained, and therein lies the program. The final line of the poem, "My soul has grown deep like the rivers," suggests wisdom in the word *deep*. The wisdom imparted by the poem, beyond the memory of the suffering of slavery, includes a more deeply embedded memory of freedom. This is perhaps the more powerful memory, or the more sustaining one, and even if deferred, will reemerge in one form or another.

From "From the Bottom Up: Three Radicals of the Thirties" in
A Gift of Tongues: Critical Challenges in Contemporary American Poetry,
edited by Marie Harris and Kathleen Aguero

CONSIDERATIONS FOR CRITICAL THINKING AND WRITING

1. Oktenberg characterizes the speaker of the poem as having "the accumu-lated wisdom of a sage." Does the knowledge that Hughes was only nineteen years old when he wrote this poem affect your response to Oktenberg's characterization? Explain why or why not.

2. Discuss whether you think Oktenberg's reading competes with or comple-ments Rampersad's interpretation.

SUGGESTED TOPICS FOR LONGER PAPERS

1. Discuss Hughes's use of rhyme, meter, and sounds in five poems of your choice. How do these elements contribute to the poems' meanings?

2. Taken together, how do Hughes's poems provide a critique of relations between blacks and whites in America?

35
A Study of Billy Collins: The Author Reflects on Five Poems

More interesting to me than what a poem means is how it travels. In the classroom, I like to substitute for the question, "What is the meaning of the poem?" other questions: "How does this poem go?" or "How does this poem travel through itself in search of its own ending?"

—BILLY COLLINS

© Juliet van Otteren.

Billy Collins selected the five poems presented in this chapter and provided commentaries for each so that readers of this anthology might gain a sense of how he, a former poet laureate and teacher, writes and thinks about poetry. In his perspectives on the poems, Collins explores a variety of literary elements ranging from the poems' origins, allusions, images, metaphors, symbols, and tone to his strategies for maintaining his integrity and sensitivity to both language and the reader. Be advised, however, that these discussions do not constitute CliffsNotes to the poems; Collins does not interpret a single one of them for us. Instead of "beating it with a hose / to find out what it really means," as he writes in his poem "Introduction to Poetry" (p. 764), he "hold[s] it up to the light" so that we can see more clearly how each poem works. He explains that the purpose of his discussions is to have students "see how a poem gets written from the opening lines, through the shifts and maneuvers of the body to whatever closure the poem manages to achieve . . . to make the process of writing a poem less mysterious without taking away the mystery that is at the heart of every good poem."

Along with Collins's illuminating and friendly tutorial, the chapter also provides some additional contexts, such as photos from the poet's personal collection; screen shots that offer a look at his unique—and dynamic—Web presence, including a collection of short animated films set to his work; a collection of draft manuscript pages; and an interview with Michael Meyer.

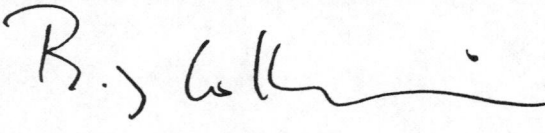

A BRIEF BIOGRAPHY AND AN INTRODUCTION TO HIS WORK

Born in New York City in 1941, Billy Collins grew up in Queens, the only child of a nurse and an electrician. His father had hoped that he might go to the Harvard Business School, but following his own lights, he earned a Ph.D. at the University of California, Riverside, in Romantic poetry, and

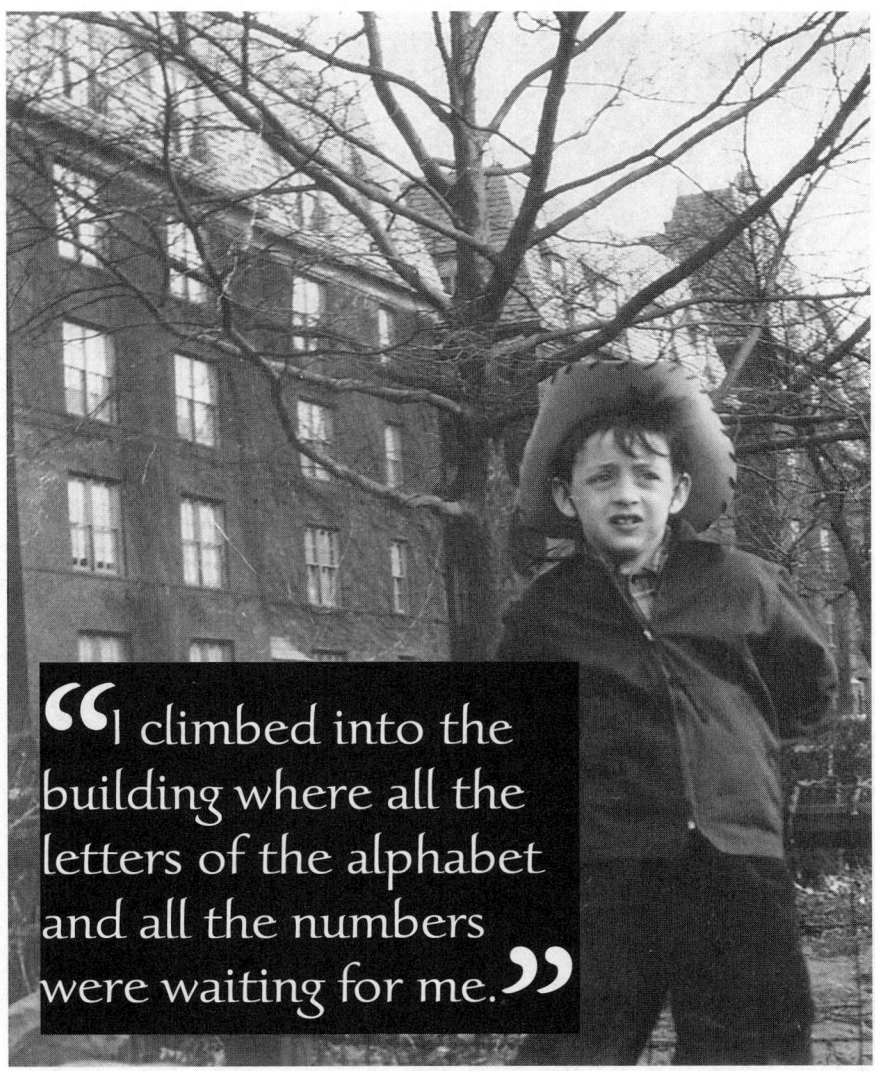

"I climbed into the building where all the letters of the alphabet and all the numbers were waiting for me."

Billy Collins on his first day as a student at St. Joan of Arc School, Jackson Heights, N.Y., 1948.
© Courtesy of Billy Collins.

then began a career in the English department at Lehman College, City University of New York, where he taught writing and literature for more than thirty years. He has also tutored writers at the National University of Ireland at Galway, Sarah Lawrence University, Arizona State University, Columbia University, and Rollins College. Along the way, he wrote poems that eventually earned him a reputation among many people as the most popular living poet in America.

Billy Collins on his first day at Holy Cross College, 1959.
© Courtesy of Billy Collins.

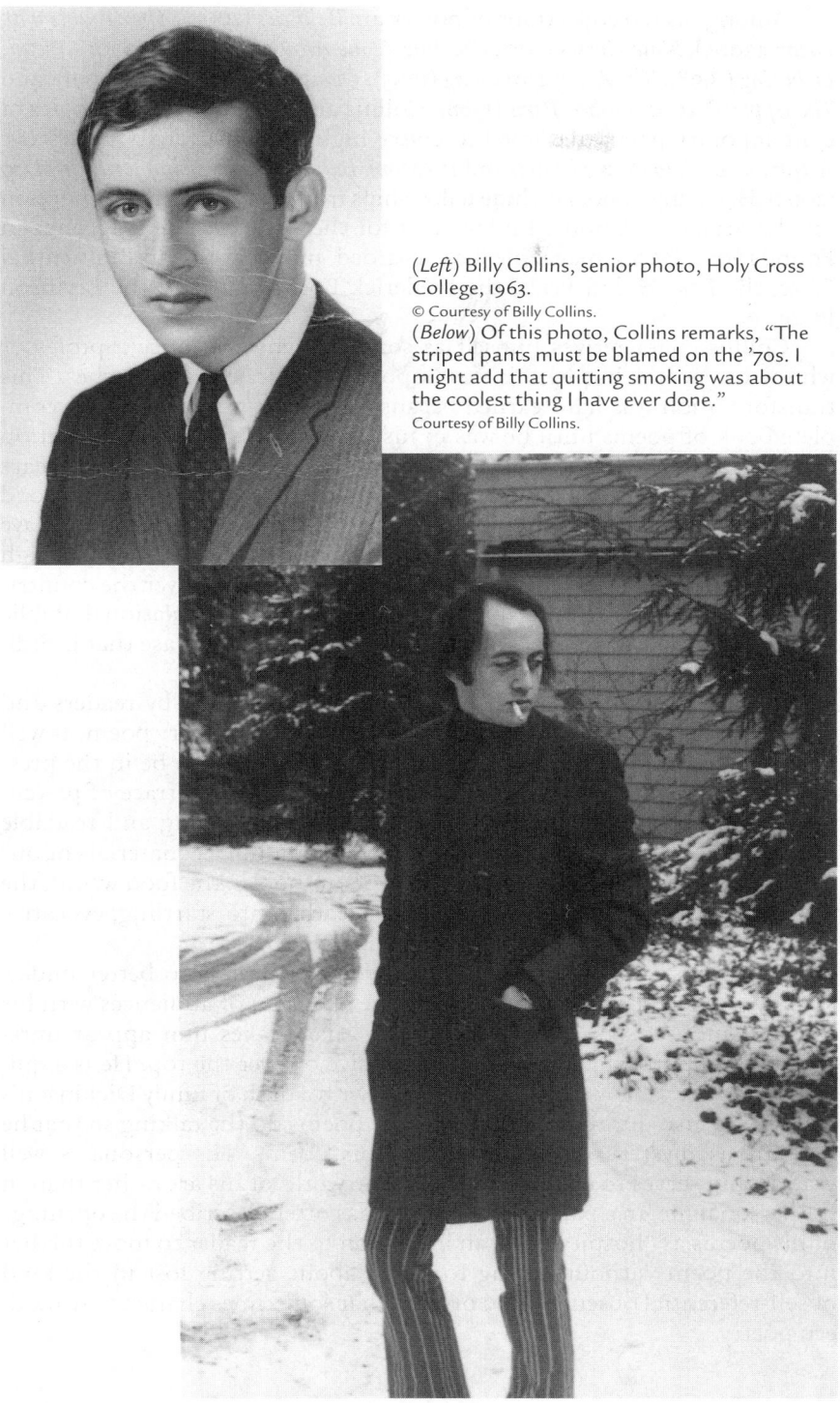

(*Left*) Billy Collins, senior photo, Holy Cross College, 1963.
© Courtesy of Billy Collins.
(*Below*) Of this photo, Collins remarks, "The striped pants must be blamed on the '70s. I might add that quitting smoking was about the coolest thing I have ever done."
Courtesy of Billy Collins.

Among his ten collections of poetry are *Ballistics* (2008), *The Trouble with Poetry* (2005), *Nine Horses* (2002), *Sailing Alone Around the Room* (2001), *Picnic, Lightning* (1998), *The Art of Drowning* (1995), *Questions About Angels* (1991), and *The Apple That Astonished Paris* (1988). Collins also edited two anthologies of contemporary poetry designed to entice high school students: *Poetry 180: A Turning Back to Poetry* (2003) and *180 More: Extraordinary Poems for Every Day* (2005). His many honors include fellowships from the New York Foundation for the Arts, the National Endowment for the Arts, and the Guggenheim Foundation. *Poetry* magazine has awarded him the Oscar Blumenthal Prize, the Bess Hokin Prize, the Frederick Bock Prize, and the Levinson Prize.

Collins characterizes himself as someone who was once a professor who wrote poems but who is now a poet who occasionally teaches. This transformation was hard earned because he didn't publish his first complete book of poems until he was in his early forties, with no expectation that twenty years later he would be named United States Poet Laureate (a gift of hope to writers everywhere). Just as writing poetry has been good for Billy Collins, he has been good for poetry. Both their reputations have risen simultaneously owing to his appeal to audiences that pack high school auditoriums, college halls, and public theaters all over the country. His many popular readings—including broadcasts on National Public Radio—have helped to make him a best-selling poet, a phrase that is ordinarily an oxymoron in America.

Unlike many poetry readings, Collins's are attended by readers and fans who come to whoop, holler, and cheer after nearly every poem, as well as to laugh out loud. His audiences are clearly relieved to be in the presence of a poet who speaks to them (not down) without a trace of pretension, superiority, or presumption. His work is welcoming and readable because he weaves observations about the commonplace materials of our lives—the notes we write in the margins of our books, the food we eat, the way we speak, even the way we think of death—into startling, evocative insights that open our eyes wider than they were before.

To understand Collins's attraction to audiences is to better understand his appeal on the page. He wins the affection of audiences with his warmth and genial charm, an affability that makes him appear unreserved and approachable but never intrusive or over the top. He is a quieter, suburban version of Walt Whitman—with a dash of Emily Dickinson's reserve. He gives just enough and lets the poems do the talking so that he remains as mysteriously appealing as his poems. His persona is well crafted and serves to engage readers in the world of his art rather than in his personal life. In a parallel manner, he has often described the openings of his poems as "hospitable"—an invitation to the reader to move further into the poem without having to worry about getting lost in the kind of self-referential obscurity and opacity that sometimes characterize modern poetry.

(*Above*) The poet with his dog, Luke. Scarsdale, N.Y., 1970s.
Courtesy of Billy Collins.
(*Left*) Billy Collins, in his office at Lehman College, 1984.
Courtesy of Billy Collins.

Perhaps not surprisingly, some critics and fellow poets have objected that Collins's poems may sometimes bear up to little more than the pleasures of one reading. Collins, however, believes immediate pleasure can be a primary motivation for reading poetry, and he argues that a poem using simple language should not be considered simpleminded. In his work the ordinary, the everyday, and the familiar often become curious, unusual, and surprising the more closely the poems are read. In interviews, he has compared a first reading of his poems to a reading of the large *E* at the top of an eye chart in an optometrist's office. What starts out clear and unambiguous gradually becomes more complicated and demanding as we squint to make our way to the end. That big *E*—it might be read as "enter"—welcomes us in and gives us the confidence to enjoy the experience, but it doesn't mean that there aren't challenges ahead. The casual, "easy" read frequently becomes a thought-provoking compound of humor, irony, and unconventional wisdom. Humor is such an essential part of Collins's work that in 2004 he was the first recipient of the Poetry Foundation's Mark Twain Award for Humor in Poetry. Given this remarkable trifecta of humor, popularity, and book sales, it is hardly to be unexpected that Collins gives some of his colleagues—as Mark Twain might have put it—the "fantods," but his audiences and readers eagerly anticipate whatever poetic pleasures he will offer them next. In any case, Whitman made the point more than 150 years ago in his preface to *Leaves of Grass*: "The proof of a poet is that his country absorbs him as affectionately as he has absorbed it."

Chronology

1941	Born on March 22 in New York City.
1941–59	Raised in Queens, New York.
1963	Graduates from Holy Cross College with a B.A.
1965	Graduates from the University of California, Riverside, with an M.A.
1968	Begins teaching literature at Lehman College of the City University of New York.
1971	Receives Ph.D. from University of California, Riverside.
1978	*Pokerface* (Kenmore Press).
1980	*Video Poems* (Applezaba Press).
1988	*The Apple That Astonished Paris* (University of Arkansas Press).

The poems "Nostalgia" (p. 1169) and "Questions About Angels" (p. 1172) are from *Questions About Angels*, published in 1991 by the University of Pittsburgh Press.

1991	*Questions About Angels,* which wins the National Poetry Series award (William Morrow & Co.).
1995	*The Art of Drowning* (University of Pittsburgh Press).
1997	Releases a CD of thirty-three poems, *The Best Cigarette.*
1998	*Picnic, Lightning* (University of Pittsburgh Press).
2000	*Taking Off Emily Dickinson's Clothes* (Picador UK).
2000	Appointed Distinguished Professor at Lehman College.
2001	*Sailing Alone Around the Room* (Random House).
2001–03	Appointed United States poet laureate for two terms.
2002	*Nine Horses* (Random House).
2003	*Poetry 180: A Turning Back to Poetry* (Random House).
2004	First Recipient of the Poetry Foundation's Mark Twain Award for Humor in Poetry.
2004–06	Appointed New York State poet laureate.
2005	*The Trouble with Poetry and Other Poems* (Random House).
2006	*She Was Just Seventeen* (Modern Haiku Press).
2008	*Ballistics* (Random House).
2008–09	Appointed the Irving Bacheller Chair at Rollins College.

The Art of Drowning

Billy Collins

U.S. POET LAUREATE

The poem "Osso Buco" (p. 1167) is from *The Art of Drowning,* published in 1995 by the University of Pittsburgh Press.

The cover art of *The Art of Drowning,* by Billy Collins, © 1995, is reprinted by permission of the University of Pittsburgh Press.

Billy Collins
Nine Horses
Poems

THE TROUBLE WITH POETRY
AND OTHER POEMS
BILLY COLLINS

The poem "Litany" (p. 1174) is from *Nine Horses,* published in 2002 by Random House. The poem "Building with Its Face Blown Off" (p. 1176) is from *The Trouble with Poetry,* published in 2005 by Random House.

"Book cover," copyright © 2002, from *Nine Horses* by Billy Collins. Used by permission of Random House, Inc.

"Book cover," copyright © 2005, from *The Trouble with Poetry* by Billy Collins. Used by permission of Random House, Inc.

BILLY COLLINS

"How Do Poems Travel?" 2008

Asking a poet to examine his or her own work is a bit like trying to get a puppy interested in looking in a mirror. Parakeets take an interest in their own reflections but not puppies, who are too busy smelling everything and tumbling over themselves to have time for self-regard. Maybe the difficulty is that most imaginative poems issue largely from the intuitive right side of the brain, whereas literary criticism draws on the brain's more rational, analytic left side. So, writing about your own writing involves getting up, moving from one room of the brain to another, and taking all the furniture with you. When asked about the source of his work, one contemporary poet remarked that if he knew where his poems came from, he would go there and never come back. What he was implying is that much of what goes on in the creative moment takes place on a stealthy level beneath the writer's conscious awareness. If creative work did not offer access to this somewhat mysterious, less than rational region, we would all be writing annual reports or law briefs, not stories, plays, and poems.

Just because you don't know what you are doing doesn't mean you are not doing it; so let me say what I do know about the writing process. While writing a poem, I am also listening to it. As the poem gets underway, I am pushing it forward — after all, I am the one holding the pencil — but I am also ready to be pulled in the direction that the poem seems to want to go. I am willfully writing the poem, but I am also submitting to the poem's will. Emerson once compared writing poetry to ice-skating. I think he meant that both the skater on a frozen pond and the poet on the page might end up going places they didn't intend to go. And Mario Andretti, the Grand Prix driver, once remarked that "If you think everything is under control, you're just not driving fast enough."

Total control over any artistic material eliminates the possibility of surprise. I would not bother to start a poem if I already knew how it was going to end. I try to "maintain the benefits of my ignorance," as another poet put it, letting the poem work toward an understanding of itself (and of me) as I go along. In a student essay, the idea is to stick to the topic. In much imaginative poetry, the pleasure lies in finding a way to escape the initial topic, to transcend the subject and ride the poem into strange, unforeseen areas. As poet John Ashbery put it: "In the process of writing, all sorts of unexpected things happen that shift the poet away from his plan; these accidents are really what we mean whenever we talk about Poetry." Readers of poetry see only the finished product set confidently on the page; but the process of writing a poem involves uncertainty, ambiguity, improvisation, and surprise.

I think of poetry as the original travel literature in that a poem can take me to an imaginative place where I have never been. A good poem often progresses by a series of associative leaps, including sudden shifts in time and space, all of which results in a kind of mental journey. I never know the ending of the poem when I set out, but I am aware that I am moving the poem toward some destination, and when I find the ending, I recognize it right away. More interesting to me than what a poem means is how it travels. In the classroom, I

like to substitute for the question, "What is the meaning of the poem?" other
questions: "How does this poem go?" or "How does this poem travel through
itself in search of its own ending?" Maybe a few of my poems that follow will
serve as illustrations, and I hope what I have said so far will help you articulate
how poems go and how they find their endings.

BILLY COLLINS

Osso Buco°   1995

I love the sound of the bone against the plate
and the fortress-like look of it
lying before me in a moat of risotto,
the meat soft as the leg of an angel
who has lived a purely airborne existence.   5
And best of all, the secret marrow,
the invaded privacy of the animal
prized out with a knife and swallowed down
with cold, exhilarating wine.

I am swaying now in the hour after dinner,   10
a citizen tilted back on his chair,
a creature with a full stomach—
something you don't hear much about in poetry,
that sanctuary of hunger and deprivation.
You know: the driving rain, the boots by the door,   15
small birds searching for berries in winter.

But tonight, the lion of contentment
has placed a warm, heavy paw on my chest,
and I can only close my eyes and listen
to the drums of woe throbbing in the distance   20
and the sound of my wife's laughter
on the telephone in the next room,
the woman who cooked the savory osso buco,
who pointed to show the butcher the ones she wanted.
She who talks to her faraway friend   25
while I linger here at the table
with a hot, companionable cup of tea,
feeling like one of the friendly natives,
a reliable guide, maybe even the chief's favorite son.

Somewhere, a man is crawling up a rocky hillside   30
on bleeding knees and palms, an Irish penitent
carrying the stone of the world in his stomach;
and elsewhere people of all nations stare
at one another across a long, empty table.

Osso Buco: An Italian veal dish; translated as "hole [*buco*] bone [*osso*]."

But here, the candles give off their warm glow,   35
the same light that Shakespeare and Izaak Walton wrote by,
the light that lit and shadowed the faces of history.
Only now it plays on the blue plates,
the crumpled napkins, the crossed knife and fork.

In a while, one of us will go up to bed   40
and the other one will follow.
Then we will slip below the surface of the night
into miles of water, drifting down and down
to the dark, soundless bottom
until the weight of dreams pulls us lower still,   45
below the shale and layered rock,
beneath the strata of hunger and pleasure,
into the broken bones of the earth itself,
into the marrow of the only place we know.

BILLY COLLINS

On Writing "Osso Buco"   *2008*

The critic Terry Eagleton pointed out that "writing is just language which can
function perfectly well in the physical absence of its author." In other words,
the author does not have to accompany his or her writing into the world to act
as its interpreter or chaperone. One way for a poem to achieve that kind of
independence is to exhibit a certain degree of clarity, at least in the opening
lines. The ideal progression of a poem is from the clear to the mysterious. A
poem that begins simply can engage the reader by establishing a common
ground and then lead the reader into more challenging, less familiar territory.
Robert Frost's poems are admirable models of this process of deepening. Of
course, if the initial engagement is not made early, it's hard to see how the participation of a reader can be counted on.

   "Osso Buco" opens with a gourmand's appreciation of a favorite dish, one
commonly served up in Italian restaurants. The one thing I knew at the outset
was that the poem was going to be a meditation on the subject of contentment.
Misery, despondency, melancholy, and just plain human wretchedness are more
likely to be the moods of poetry. Indeed, happiness in serious literature is often
mistaken for a kind of cowlike stupidity. I thought I would address that imbalance by taking on the challenge of writing about the pleasures of a full stomach. Even the gloomiest of philosophers admits that there are occasional
interruptions in the despondency that is the human lot; so why not pay those
moments some poetic attention?

   To me, the image of "the lion of contentment" suggested a larger set of
metaphors connected to African exploration that might add glue to the poem.
A metaphor can be deployed in one line of a poem and then dropped, but other
times the poem develops an interest in its own language and a metaphor can be
extended and explored. The result can bind together a number of disparate
thoughts by giving them a common vocabulary. Thus, in this extended metaphor

that begins with "the lion of contentment," "drums of woe" are heard "throbbing in the distance," and later the speaker feels like "one of the friendly natives" or "even the chief's favorite son."

In the fourth stanza, the camera pulls back from the domestic scene of the poem and its mood of contentment to survey examples of human suffering taking place elsewhere. The man with bleeding knees is a reference to the religious pilgrims who annually climb Croagh Patrick, a rocky mountain in the west of Ireland. The image of the "long, empty table" is meant to express the condition of world hunger and famine. But the poem offers those images only in contrast to its insistent theme: satisfaction. Back in the kitchen, there is the candle-lit scene of pleasures recently taken. The mention of Shakespeare and Izaak Walton, who wrote *The Compleat Angler,* a whimsical book on the pleasures of fly-fishing, adds some historic perspective and shows the speaker to be a person of some refinement, an appreciator of literature, history, and, of course, food.

The poem so far has made two noticeable maneuvers, shifting to a global then a historical perspective, but in the final stanza the poem takes its biggest turn when it hits upon the resolving metaphor of geology. The couple retires to bed — another pleasure — descends into sleep, then deeper into dreams, then deeper still through the layers of the earth and into its very center, a "marrow" which harkens back to the bone marrow of the eaten calf. Thus the poem travels from the domestic setting of a kitchen to the plains of Africa, a mountain in Ireland, then back to the kitchen before boring into the core of the earth itself — a fairly extensive journey for a poem of only fifty lines, but not untypical of the kind of ground a lyric poem can quickly cover.

BILLY COLLINS

Nostalgia   *1991*

Remember the 1340s? We were doing a dance called
    the Catapult.
You always wore brown, the color craze of the decade,
and I was draped in one of those capes that were popular,
the ones with unicorns and pomegranates in needlework.
Everyone would pause for beer and onions in the afternoon,   5
and at night we would play a game called "Find the Cow."
Everything was hand-lettered then, not like today.

Where has the summer of 1572 gone? Brocade and sonnet
marathons were the rage. We used to dress up in the flags
of rival baronies and conquer one another in cold rooms
    of stone.   10
Out on the dance floor we were all doing the Struggle
while your sister practiced the Daphne all alone in her room.
We borrowed the jargon of farriers for our slang.
These days language seems transparent, a badly broken code.

The 1790s will never come again. Childhood was big.   15
People would take walks to the very tops of hills
and write down what they saw in their journals without
          speaking.
Our collars were high and our hats were extremely soft.
We would surprise each other with alphabets made of twigs.
It was a wonderful time to be alive, or even dead.   20

I am very fond of the period between 1815 and 1821.
Europe trembled while we sat still for our portraits.
And I would love to return to 1901 if only for a moment,
time enough to wind up a music box and do a
          few dance steps,
or shoot me back to 1922 or 1941, or at least let me   25
recapture the serenity of last month when we picked
berries and glided through afternoons in a canoe.

Even this morning would be an improvement over
          the present.
I was in the garden then, surrounded by the hum of bees
and the Latin names of flowers, watching the early light   30
flash off the slanted windows of the greenhouse
and silver the limbs on the rows of dark hemlocks.

As usual, I was thinking about the moments of the past,
letting my memory rush over them like water
rushing over the stones on the bottom of a stream.   35
I was even thinking a little about the future, that place
where people are doing a dance we cannot imagine,
a dance whose name we can only guess.

Billy Collins

On Writing "Nostalgia"   2008

"Nostalgia" offers me the opportunity to say something about poetic form. Broadly speaking, *form* can mean any feature of a poem that keeps it together and gives it unity. Form is the nails and glue that hold the emotions and thoughts of a poem in place. Naturally, poets are in the business of self-expression, but paradoxically they are always looking for limits. Form can be inherited — the sonnet is an enduring example — or the poet may make up his own rules as he goes along. He might even decide at some point to break the very rules he just imposed upon himself. In either case, formal rules give the poet an enclosed space in which to work, and they keep the poem from descending into chaos or tantrum. As poet Stephen Dunn put it, "form is the pressure that an artist puts on his material in order to see what it will bear."

    The Irish poet W. B. Yeats felt that "all that is personal will rot unless it is packed in ice and salt." For a formalist poet like Yeats, "ice and salt," which were common food preservatives of his day, probably meant rhyme and meter. After Walt Whitman showed in *Leaves of Grass* (1855) that poems could be written without those two traditional supporting pillars, poets still had many other formal devices at their disposal. Just because poets could now write poems without a design of rhyme words at the ends of lines or a regular meter such as iambic pentameter did not mean they had abandoned form. Some of these alternative formal strategies would include line length, stanza choice, repetition, rhetorical development (beginning–middle–end), and thematic recurrence as well as patterns of sound and imagery. Focusing on form allows us to see that poetry can combine a high level of imaginative freedom with the imposition of boundaries and rules of procedure. For the reader, the coexistence of these two contrary elements — liberty and restriction — may be said to create a pleasurable tension found to a higher degree in poetry than in any other literary genre.

An apparent formal element in "Nostalgia," besides its use of stanza breaks, is the chronological sequence it obediently follows. After the absurd opening question (to which the only answer is no), the poem moves forward from the Middle Ages (the 1340s would place us smack in the middle of the Black Death) to the Renaissance, to the beginnings of English Romanticism, that being 1798, when the first edition of *Lyrical Ballads,* a poetic collaboration between Wordsworth and Coleridge, was published. The poem then continues to travel forward in time, but now more whimsically with dates that seem plucked out of the air — 1901, 1922, 1941 — before arriving rather abruptly at "last month" and then "this morning." If nothing else, the poem demonstrates poetry's freedom from normal time constraints as it manages to travel more than 600 years from the Middle Ages to the present in only twenty-eight lines.

When the poem does arrive at the present, the speaker morphs from a kind of thousand-year-old man into an actual person, a sympathetic fellow who likes to garden and who appreciates the sounds and sights of the natural world. The imaginary historical journey of the poem ends amid the bees and flowers of the speaker's garden, where he continues to dwell nostalgically on the past until his attention turns to the future, really the only place left for him to go. Having relinquished his power as an eyewitness to centuries of human civilization, the speaker trails off in a dreamy speculation about the unknowable dance crazes of the future.

The poem takes a lot of imaginative liberties in the oddness of its premise and its free-ranging images, yet, formally speaking, it is held together by a strict chronological line drawn from the distant historical past right through the present moment and into the future.

I don't recall how a lot of my poems got started, but I do remember that this poem arose out of a kind of annoyance. Just as a grain of sand can irritate an oyster into producing a pearl by coating it with a smooth surface, so a poem may be irked into being. What was bugging me in this case was the popular twentieth-century habit of breaking the past into decades ("the fifties," "the sixties," and so forth), constructs which amounted to little more than a collage of stereotypes. What a gross simplification of this mysterious, invisible thing we call the past, I thought. Even worse, each decade was so sentimentalized as to make one feel that its passing was cause for feelings of melancholy and regret. "Nostalgia," then, is a poem with a motive, that is, to satirize that kind of enforced nostalgia.

BILLY COLLINS

Questions About Angels   1991

Of all the questions you might want to ask
about angels, the only one you ever hear
is how many can dance on the head of a pin.

No curiosity about how they pass the eternal time
besides circling the Throne chanting in Latin   5
or delivering a crust of bread to a hermit on earth
or guiding a boy and girl across a rickety wooden bridge.

Do they fly through God's body and come out singing?
Do they swing like children from the hinges
of the spirit world saying their names backwards and
        forwards?
Do they sit alone in little gardens changing colors?   10

What about their sleeping habits, the fabric of their robes,
their diet of unfiltered divine light?
What goes on inside their luminous heads? Is there a wall
these tall presences can look over and see hell?   15

If an angel fell off a cloud, would he leave a hole
in a river and would the hole float along endlessly
filled with the silent letters of every angelic word?

If an angel delivered the mail, would he arrive
in a blinding rush of wings or would he just assume   20
the appearance of the regular mailman and
whistle up the driveway reading the postcards?

No, the medieval theologians control the court.
The only question you ever hear is about
the little dance floor on the head of a pin   25
where halos are meant to converge and drift invisibly.

It is designed to make us think in millions,
billions, to make us run out of numbers and collapse
into infinity, but perhaps the answer is simply one:
one female angel dancing alone in her stocking feet,   30
a small jazz combo working in the background.

She sways like a branch in the wind, her beautiful
eyes closed, and the tall thin bassist leans over
to glance at his watch because she has been dancing
forever, and now it is very late, even for musicians.   35

BILLY COLLINS
On Writing "Questions About Angels"   *2008*

I find that it doesn't take much to get a poem going. A poem can start casually with something trivial and then develop significance along the way. The first inkling may act as a keyhole that allows the poet to look into an imaginary room. When I started to write "Questions About Angels," I really had nothing on my mind except that odd, speculative question: How many angels can dance on the head of a pin? Seemingly unanswerable, the question originated as an attempt to mock certain medieval philosophers (notably Thomas Aquinas) who sought to solve arcane theological mysteries through the sheer application of reason. I had first heard the question when I was studying theology at a Jesuit college, but well before that, the phrase had made its way into the mainstream of modern parlance. It was typical of me to want to begin a poem with something everyone knows and then proceed from there. The poem found a direction to go in when it occurred to me to open up the discussion to include other questions. At that point, it was "Game on."

My investigation really begins in the second stanza, which draws on traditional images of angels in religious art, either worshipping God or paying helpful visits to earth, assisting the poor and protecting the innocent. Then the questions become more fanciful — off-the-wall, really: "Do they fly through God's body and come out singing?" No doubt you could come up with questions of your own about angel behavior; clearly, that has become the poem's game — an open inquiry into the spirit life of these creatures.

After the poem's most bizarre question, which involves a hole that a fallen angel has left in a river, the interrogation descends into the everyday with the image of an angel delivering mail, not gloriously "in a blinding rush of wings" but just like "the regular mailman." After a reminder of the monopoly "the medieval theologians" seem to have on questions about angels, the poem makes a sudden turn (one I did not see coming) by offering a simple, irreducible answer to that unanswerable question. On the little word "but" (line 29), the poem drops down abruptly from "billions" to "one," and the scene shrinks from heaven to a jazz club located in eternity.

In the process of composing a poem, the poet is mentally juggling many concerns, one of the most dominant and persistent being how the poem is going to find a place to end, a point where the journey of the poem was meant to stop, a point where the poet does not want to say any more, and the reader has heard just enough. In this case, the moment she appeared — rather miraculously, as I remember — I knew that this beautiful angel "dancing alone in her stocking feet" was how the poem would close. She was the hidden destination the poem was moving toward all along without my knowing it. I had only to add the detail of the bored bassist and the odd observation that even musicians playing in eternity cannot be expected to stay awake forever.

BILLY COLLINS

Litany   **2002**

> *You are the bread and the knife,*
> *The crystal goblet and the wine.*
>   *— Jacques Crickillon*

You are the bread and the knife,
the crystal goblet and the wine.
You are the dew on the morning grass,
and the burning wheel of the sun.
You are the white apron of the baker,   5
and the marsh birds suddenly in flight.

However, you are not the wind in the orchard,
the plums on the counter,
or the house of cards.
And you are certainly not the pine-scented air.   10
There is no way you are the pine-scented air.

It is possible that you are the fish under the bridge,
maybe even the pigeon on the general's head,
but you are not even close
to being the field of cornflowers at dusk.   15

And a quick look in the mirror will show
that you are neither the boots in the corner
nor the boat asleep in its boathouse.

It might interest you to know,
speaking of the plentiful imagery of the world,   20
that I am the sound of rain on the roof.

I also happen to be the shooting star,
the evening paper blowing down an alley,
and the basket of chestnuts on the kitchen table.

I am also the moon in the trees   25
and the blind woman's teacup.
But don't worry, I am not the bread and the knife.
You are still the bread and the knife.
You will always be the bread and the knife,
not to mention the crystal goblet and — somehow —   30
      the wine.

BILLY COLLINS

On Writing "Litany" 2008

As the epigraph to this poem indicates, "Litany" was written in reaction to another poem, a love poem I came across in a literary magazine by a poet I had not heard of. What struck me about his poem was its reliance on a strategy that had its heyday in the love sonnets of the Elizabethan age, namely, the convention of flattering the beloved by comparing her to various aspects of nature. Typically, her eyes were like twin suns, her lips red as coral or rubies, her skin pure as milk, and her breath as sweet as flowers or perfume. Such exaggerations were part of the overall tendency to idealize women who were featured in the courtly love poetry of the time, each of whom was as unattainable as she was beautiful and as cruel as she was fair. It took Shakespeare to point out the ridiculousness of these hyperboles, questioning in one of his sonnets the very legitimacy of comparisons ("Shall I compare thee to a summer's day?" [p. 976]), then drenching the whole process with the cold water of realism ("My mistress' eyes are nothing like the sun" [p. 976]). You might think that would have put an end to the practice, but the habit of appealing to women's vanity through comparisons persists even in the poetry of today. That poem in the magazine prompted me to respond.

Starting with the same first two lines, "Litany" seeks to rewrite the earlier poem by offering a corrective. It aims to point out the latent silliness in such comparisons and perhaps the potential absurdity at the heart of metaphor itself. The poem even wants us to think about the kind of romantic relationships that would permit such discourse.

The poem opens by adding some new metaphors (morning dew, baker's apron, marsh birds) to the pile, but in the second stanza, the poem reverses direction by trading in flattery for a mock-serious investigation of what this woman might be and what she is not. Instead of appealing to her sense of her own beauty, the speaker is perfectly willing to insult her by bringing up her metaphoric shortcomings. By the time he informs her that "There is no way you are the pine-scented air" and "you are not even close / to being the field of corn-flowers at dusk," we know that this is a different kind of love poem altogether.

The second big turn comes in the fifth stanza when the speaker unexpectedly begins comparing himself to such things as "the sound of rain on the roof." Notice that the earlier comparisons were not all positive. The "pigeon on the general's head" should remind us of an equestrian statue in a park, and we all know what pigeons like to do to statues. But the speaker is not the least bit ashamed to flatter himself with a string of appealing images including a "shooting star," a "basket of chestnuts," and "the moon in the trees." Turning attention away from the "you" of the poem to the speaker is part of the poem's impertinence — the attentive lover turns into an egomaniac — but it echoes a strategy used by Shakespeare himself. Several of his sonnets begin by being about the beloved but end by being about the poet, specifically about his power to bestow immortality on the beloved through his art. Thus, what begins as a love poem ends as a self-love poem.

The last thing to notice is that "Litany" has a circular structure: it ends by swinging back to its beginning, to the imagery of the epigraph. True to the cheekiness of the speaker, his last words are devoted to tossing the woman a bit of false reassurance that she is still and will always be "the bread and the knife." For whatever that's worth.

BILLY COLLINS

Building with Its Face Blown Off   *2005*

How suddenly the private
is revealed in a bombed-out city,
how the blue and white striped wallpaper

of a second story bedroom is now
exposed to the lightly falling snow   5
as if the room had answered the explosion

wearing only its striped pajamas.
Some neighbors and soldiers
poke around in the rubble below

and stare up at the hanging staircase,   10
the portrait of a grandfather,
a door dangling from a single hinge.

And the bathroom looks almost embarrassed
by its uncovered ochre walls,
the twisted mess of its plumbing,   15

the sink sinking to its knees,
the ripped shower curtain,
the torn goldfish trailing bubbles.

It's like a dollhouse view
as if a child on its knees could reach in   20
and pick up the bureau, straighten a picture.

Or it might be a room on a stage
in a play with no characters,
no dialogue or audience,

no beginning, middle and end—   25
just the broken furniture in the street,
a shoe among the cinder blocks,

a light snow still falling
on a distant steeple, and people
crossing a bridge that still stands.   30

And beyond that—crows in a tree,
the statue of a leader on a horse,
and clouds that look like smoke,

and even farther on, in another country
on a blanket under a shade tree,   35
a man pouring wine into two glasses

and a woman sliding out
the wooden pegs of a wicker hamper
filled with bread, cheese, and several kinds of olives.

Perspective

On "Building with Its Face Blown Off": Michael Meyer Interviews Billy Collins   2009

Meyer: The subject matter of your poetry is well known for being typically about the patterns and rhythms of everyday life, along with its delights, humor, ironies, and inevitable pain. "Building with Its Face Blown Off," however, explicitly concerns war and is implicitly political. What prompted this minority report in your writing?

Collins: It's true that I usually steer away from big historical subjects in my poems. I don't want to assume a level of authority beyond what a reader might trust, nor do I want to appear ridiculous by taking a firm stand against some moral horror that any other humane person would naturally oppose. A few years back, I consciously avoided joining the movement called "Poets against the War" because I thought it was as self-obviating as "Generals for the War." A direct approach to subjects as enormous as war or slavery or genocide carries the risk that the poet will be smothered under the weight of the topic. Plus, readers are already morally wired to respond in a certain way to such things. As a writer, you want to *create* an emotion, not merely activate one that already exists in the reader. And who wants to preach to the choir? I have come across few readers of poetry who are all for war; and, besides, poets have enough work to do without trying to convert the lost. William Butler Yeats put it best in his "On Being Asked for a War Poem":

> I think it better that in times like these
> A poet's mouth be silent, for in truth
> We have no gift to set a statesman right;
> He has had enough of meddling who can please
> A young girl in the indolence of her youth,
> Or an old man upon a winter's night.

Before poetry can be political, it must be personal.

That's my dim view of poems that do little more than declare that the poet, walking the moral high road, is opposed to ethically reprehensible acts. But the world does press in on us, and I was stopped in my tracks one morning when I saw in a newspaper still another photograph of a bombed-out building, which echoed all the similar images I had seen for too many decades in too many conflicts around the world in Dresden, Sarajevo, or Baghdad, wherever shells happen to fall. That photograph revealed one personal aspect of the war: the apartment of a family blown wide open for all to see. "Building with Its Face Blown Off" was my response.

Meyer: The images in the poem have a photojournalistic quality, but they are snapped through the lens of personification rather than a camera. Isn't a picture better than a thousand words?

Collins: I wanted to avoid the moralistic antiwar rhetoric that the underlying subject invites, so I stuck to the visual. A photojournalist once observed that to capture the horrors of war, you don't have to go to the front lines and photograph actual armed conflict: just take a picture of a child's shoe lying on a road. That picture would be worth many words, but as a poet I must add, maybe not quite a thousand. In this poem, I wanted to downplay the horrible violence of the destruction by treating the event as a mere social embarrassment, an invasion of domestic privacy. As Chekhov put it, if you want to get the reader emotionally involved, write cold. For the same reason, I deployed nonviolent metaphors such as the dollhouse and the theater, where the fourth wall is absent. The poem finds a way to end by withdrawing from the scene like a camera pulling back to reveal a larger world. Finally, we are looking down as from a blimp on another country, one where the absence of war provides the tranquility that allows a man and a woman to have a picnic.

A reader once complimented me for ending this poem with olives, the olive branch being a traditional symbol of peace. Another reader heard an echo of Ernest Hemingway's short story "In Another Country," which concerns World War I. Just between you and me, neither of these references had ever occurred to me; but I am always glad to take credit for such happy accidents even if it is similar to drawing a target around a bullet hole. No writer can—or should want to—have absolute control over the reactions of his readers.

Meyer: In your essay on writing "Nostalgia," you point out that "formal rules give the poet an enclosed space in which to work, and they keep the poem from descending into chaos or tantrum" (p. 1170). How does form in "Building with Its Face Blown Off" prevent its emotions and thoughts from being reduced to a prose bumper sticker such as "War is hell"?

Collins: I hope what keeps this poem from getting carried away with its traumatic subject is its concentration on the photograph so that the poem maintains a visual, even cinematic, focus throughout. You could think of the poem as a one-minute movie—a short subject about a big topic. Another sign of apparent form here is the division of the poem into three-line stanzas, or tercets, which slow down the reader's progress through the poem. Just as readers should pause slightly at the end of every poetic line (even an unpunctuated one—the equivalent of half a comma), they should also observe a little pause between stanzas. Poetry is famous for condensing large amounts of mental and emotional material into small packages, and it also encourages us to slow down from the speed at which we usually absorb information. The stanzas give the poem a look of regularity, and some of them make visible the grammatical structure of the poem's sentences. Regular stanzas suggest that the poem comes in sections, and they remind us that poetry is a spatial arrangement of words on the page. Think of such stanzas as stones in a stream; the reader steps from one to the next to get to other side.

Meyer: In a classroom discussion of the final two stanzas, one of my students read the couple's picnic scene as "offering an image of hope and peace in contrast to the reckless destruction that precedes it," while another student countered that the scene appeared to be a depiction of "smug indifference and apathy to suffering." Care to comment?

Billy Collins Action Poetry Web site.
In a 2003 interview with the American Booksellers Association, Billy Collins explained that his goal as United States poet laureate was for poetry "to pop up in unexpected places, like the daily announcement in high schools and on airplanes." At the Web site for the Billy Collins Action Poetry film project (www.bcactionpoet.org), you can view artful new interpretations of the poet's work and hear them read aloud by Collins himself, in what makes for an imaginative and elegant combination of poetry and technology.
Produced by the J. Walter Thompson ad agency and the Sundance Channel.

Collins: I find it fascinating that such contrary views of the poem's ending could exist. Probably the most vexing question in poetry studies concerns interpretation. One thing to keep in mind is that readers of poetry, students especially, are much more preoccupied with "meaning" than poets are. While I am writing, I am not thinking about the poem's meaning; I am only trying to write a good poem, which involves securing the form of the poem and getting the poem to hold together so as to stay true to itself. Thinking about what my poem means would only distract me from the real work of poetry. Neurologically speaking, I am trying to inhabit the intuitive side of the brain, not the analytical side where critical thought and "study questions" come from. "Meaning," if I think of it at all, usually comes as an afterthought.

But the question remains: How do poets react to interpretations of their work? Generally speaking, once a poem is completed and then published, it is out of the writer's hands. I'm disposed to welcome interpretations that I did not consciously intend — that doesn't mean my unconscious didn't play a role — as long as those readings do not twist the poem out of shape. In "Building with Its Face Blown Off," I added the picnicking couple simply as a sharp contrast to the scene of destruction in the war-torn city. The man and woman are free to enjoy the luxury of each other's company, the countryside, wine, cheese, and even a choice of olives. Are they a sign of hope? Well, yes, insofar as they show us that the whole world is not at war. Smugness? Not so much to my mind, even though that strikes me as a sensible reaction. But if a reader claimed that the couple represented Adam and Eve, or more absurdly, Antony and Cleopatra, or Donny and Marie Osmond, then I would question the person's common sense or sanity. I might even ring for Security. Mainly, the couple is there simply to show us what is no longer available to the inhabitants of the beleaguered city and to give me a place to end the poem.

The Library of Congress   Poem # [   ] GO

POETRY 180

Poetry 180
a poem a day for american high schools

list of all 180 poems
poetry and literature center

RSS Feeds

Welcome to Poetry 180. Poetry can and should be an important part of our daily lives. Poems can inspire and make us think about what it means to be a member of the human race. By just spending a few minutes reading a poem each day, new worlds can be revealed.

Poetry 180 is designed to make it easy for students to hear or read a poem on each of the 180 days of the school year. I have selected the poems you will find here with high school students in mind. They are intended to be listened to, and I suggest that all members of the school community be included as readers. A great time for the readings would be following the end of daily announcements over the public address system.

Listening to poetry can encourage students and other learners to become members of the circle of readers for whom poetry is a vital source of pleasure. I hope Poetry 180 becomes an important and enriching part of the school day.

Billy Collins
Former Poet Laureate of the United States

more about this program | how to read a poem out loud | read our legal notices

Billy Collins writes: "Poetry can and should be an important part of our daily lives. Poems can inspire and make us think about what it means to be a member of the human race. By just spending a few minutes reading a poem each day, new worlds can be revealed." As United States poet laureate, Collins instituted an ongoing student program through the Library of Congress, called "Poetry 180: A Poem a Day for American High Schools." He chose 180 poems for the project — one for each day of the public school year — and offered some advice on reading poems aloud. (See loc.gov/poetry/180, where the poems can be read online.)
Library of Congress.

1st

Dec 14
08   faucets

Splash ?

The Bath

Nothing much to ~~really~~ tell really —
the soap resting in its soap dish,
hot water blasting from the spigot
hills of bubbles rising,
~~my ankles cro~~
only ankles crossed

and the mirror going blind ~~into~~ with steam
But there is
¶ ~~and~~ A the wish to apologize .
to RWB Lewis for letting his
              American Adam
slip from my wet hands into the water

¶ the book I propped up to dry
tub-side, like a diving bird
drying ~~its~~ its wings on the shore of
                a ~~volcanic~~ isle.
                prehistoric, //

A draft of the unpublished poem "The Bath" from an entry in one of Collins's notebooks, dated December 14, 2008.
Courtesy of Billy Collins.

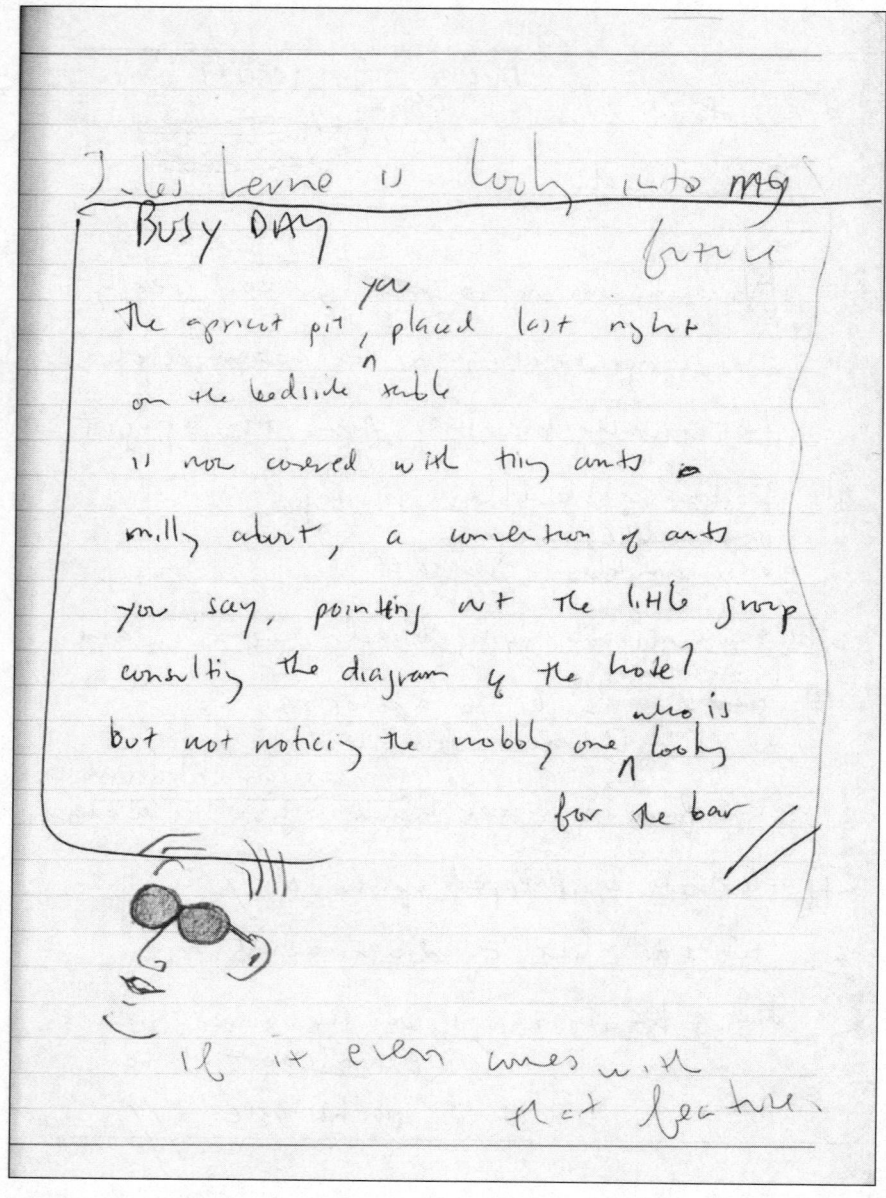

A draft of the unpublished poem "Busy Day" from an undated page of Collins's notebooks.
Courtesy of Billy Collins.

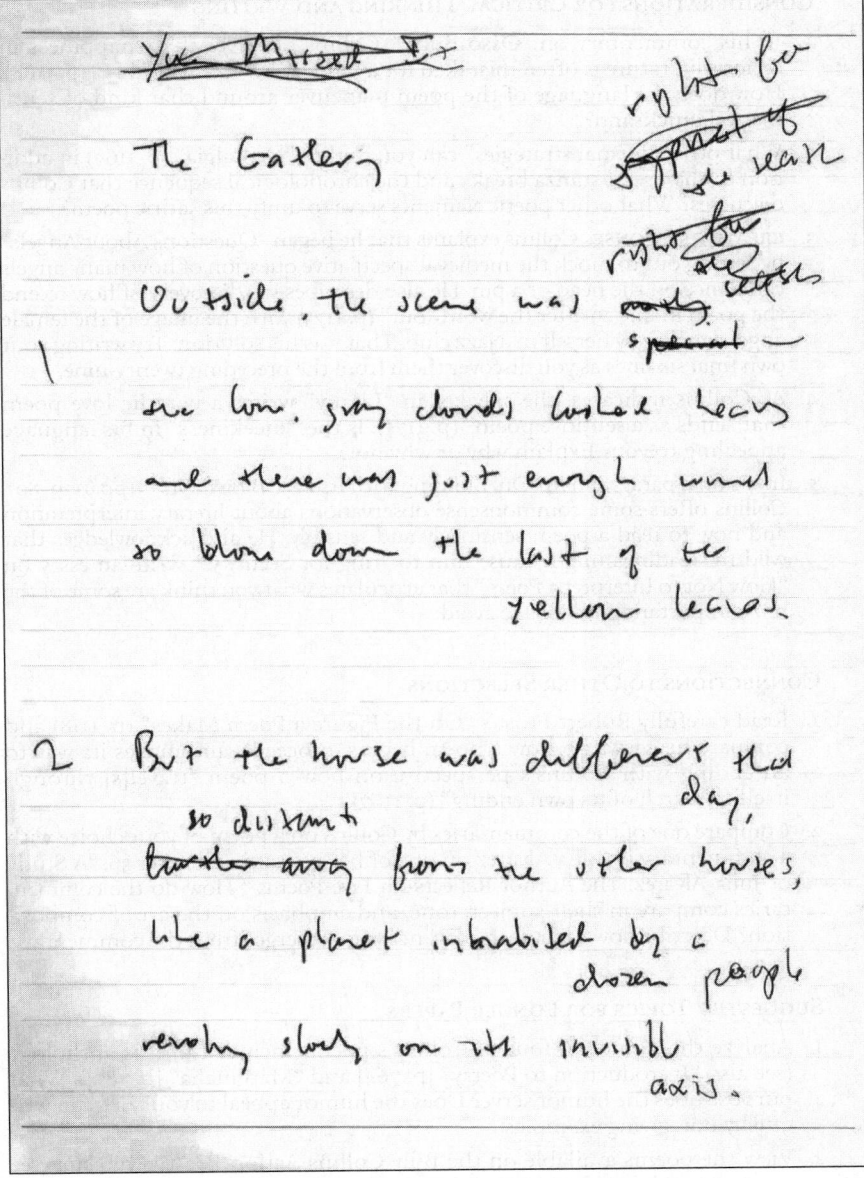

A draft page of "The Gathering" (working title) from an undated page in Collins's notebooks. Published in 2006 in *The New York Times* as "For Your Digestion; The Gathering." Courtesy of Billy Collins.

CONSIDERATIONS FOR CRITICAL THINKING AND WRITING

1. In his commentary on "Osso Buco," Collins observes that "happiness in serious literature is often mistaken for a kind of cowlike stupidity" (p. 1168). How does the language of the poem maneuver around that kind of sentimental quicksand?

2. What other "formal strategies" can you find in "Nostalgia" (p. 1169) in addition to the use of stanza breaks and the chronological sequence that Collins discusses? What other poetic elements serve to unify this satiric poem?

3. CREATIVE RESPONSE. Collins explains that he began "Questions About Angels" by setting out to mock the medieval speculative question of how many angels can dance on the head of a pin. He also describes his discovery of how to end the poem in line 29 after the word "but" (p. 1173) with the image of the female angel dancing by herself in a jazz club. That was his solution. Try writing your own final six lines as you discover them from the preceding twenty-nine.

4. As Collins indicates, the speaker in "Litany" writes a parodic love poem that "ends as a self-love poem" (p. 1175). Is the "cheekiness" in his language appealing to you? Explain why or why not.

5. In his final paragraph in "On 'Building with Its Face Blown Off' " (pp. 1179–80), Collins offers some commonsense observations about literary interpretation and how to read a poem sensitively and sensibly. He also acknowledges that wild misreadings might cause him to "ring for Security." Write an essay on "How Not to Interpret a Poem" that articulates what you think are some of the most important problems to avoid.

CONNECTIONS TO OTHER SELECTIONS

1. Read carefully Robert Frost's "On the Figure a Poem Makes" (p. 1118) and compare his views on how a poem begins, proceeds, and makes its way to an ending with Collins's perspective on how a poem "travel[s] through itself in search of its own ending" (p. 1167).

2. Compare one of the commentaries by Collins on a poem of your choice with a commentary by Julia Alvarez on one of her poems in Chapter 36, "A Study of Julia Alvarez: The Author Reflects on Five Poems." How do the commentaries compare in their subject, tone, and emphasis on the art of composition? Describe how each poet's distinct voice emerges from the commentary.

SUGGESTED TOPICS FOR LONGER PAPERS

1. Analyze the humor in four of Collins's poems included in this anthology (see also "Introduction to Poetry" [p. 764] and "Marginalia" [p. 787]). What purpose does the humor serve? Does the humor appeal to you? Explain why or why not, giving examples.

2. View the poems available on the Billy Collins Action Poetry Web site (see page 1179 and www.bcactionpoet.org), where you can find visual interpretations of individual poems and hear Collins read the poems aloud. Choose three of the poems and write an analysis of how the visual and auditory representations affect your response to the poems' language. Explain why you think this approach enhances or diminishes — or is simply different from — reading the poem on a page.

36

A Study of Julia Alvarez:
The Author Reflects
on Five Poems

© Daniel Cima.

When I'm asked what made me into a writer, I point to the watershed experience of coming to this country. Not understanding the language, I had to pay close attention to each word — great training for a writer.

— JULIA ALVAREZ

This chapter offers five poems, chosen by Julia Alvarez for this anthology, with commentaries written by the poet herself. Alvarez's insights on each work, in addition to accompanying images and documents, provide a variety of contexts — personal, cultural, and historical — for understanding and appreciating her poems.

In her introductions to each of the poems, Alvarez shares her reasons for writing, what was on her mind when she wrote each work, what she thinks now looking back at them, as well as a bird's-eye view into her writing process (see especially the drafts of the poem in progress on pp. 1204–06). She also evokes the voices of those who have inspired her — muses that range from women talking and cooking in a kitchen to a character in *The Arabian Nights* to the poets Walt Whitman, Langston Hughes, and others. Alvarez writes, "A poem can be a resting place for the soul . . . a world teeming with discoveries and luminous little *ah-ha!* moments, a 'place for the genuine,' as Marianne Moore calls it." Read on and find out, for example, who her real "First Muse" was, and what, according to Alvarez, a famous American poet and the Chiquita Banana have in common.

In addition to Alvarez's inviting and richly detailed introductions, the chapter also presents a number of visual contexts, such as a photo of a 1963 civil rights demonstration in Queens, New York; the poet's passport photo taken at age ten, just before she moved back to the United States; a collection of draft manuscript pages; and an image of one of Alvarez's poems set in a bronze plaque in a sidewalk — part of "Library Way" in New York City. Further, a critical essay — which complements Alvarez's own perspectives throughout the chapter — by Kelli Lyon Johnson (p. 1211) allows readers to consider Alvarez's work in a critical framework. (For a discussion on reading a work alongside critical theory, see Chapter 53, "Critical Strategies for Reading," p. 2041.)

A BRIEF BIOGRAPHY

Although Julia Alvarez was born (1950) in New York City, she lived in the Dominican Republic until she was ten years old. She returned to New York after her father, a physician, was connected to a plot to overthrow the dictatorship of Rafael Trujillo, and the family had to flee. Growing up in Queens was radically different from the Latino Caribbean world she experienced during her early childhood. A new culture and new language sensitized Alvarez to her surroundings and her use of language so that emigration from the Dominican Republic to Queens was the beginning of her movement toward becoming a writer. Alvarez quotes the Polish poet Czeslaw Milosz's assertion that "Language is the only homeland" to explain her own sense that what she really settled into was not so much the United States as the English language.

Her fascination with English continued into high school and took shape in college as she became a serious writer — first at Connecticut College from 1967 to 1969 and then at Middlebury College, where she earned her B.A. in 1971. At Syracuse University she was awarded the American Academy of Poetry Prize and, in 1975, earned an M.A. in creative writing.

Since then Alvarez has served as a writer-in-residence for the Kentucky Arts Commission, the Delaware Arts Council, and the Arts Council of Fayetteville, North Carolina. She has taught at California State College (Fresno), College of Sequoias, Phillips Andover Academy, the University of

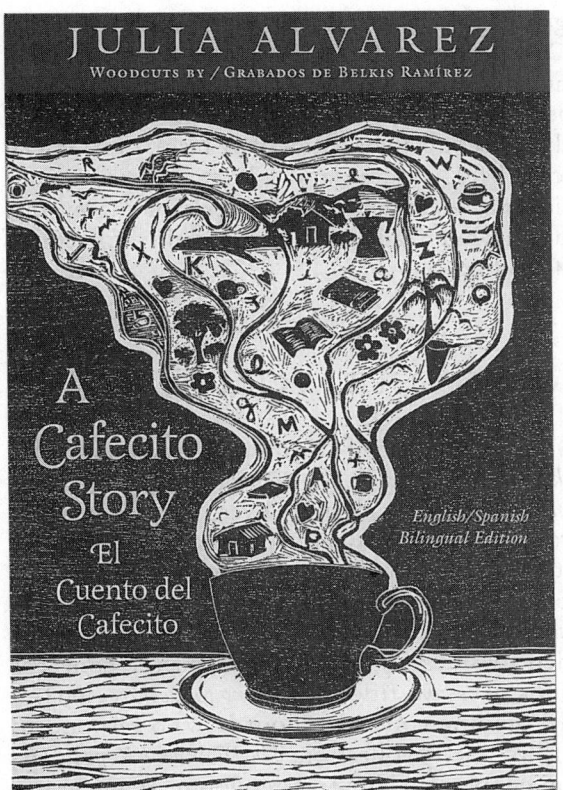

(*Left*) *A Cafecito Story* (2001), which Alvarez describes as a modern "eco-parable" or "green fable" and love story, was inspired by the author's work with local coffee growers in the Dominican Republic.

Reprinted from A Cafecito Story, copyright Julia Alvarez 2001, 2002 with the permission of Chelsea Green Publishing.

(*Below*) Julia Alvarez with students from Middlebury College at her coffee farm, Alta Gracia, in the Dominican Republic.

Photograph courtesy of Fundación Finca Alta Gracia.

Vermont, George Washington University, the University of Illinois, and, since 1988, at Middlebury College, where she has been a professor of literature and creative writing and is currently a part-time writer-in-residence. Alvarez divides her time between Vermont and the Dominican Republic where she and her husband have set up an organic coffee farm, Alta Gracia, that supports a literacy school for children and adults. *A Cafecito Story* (2001), which Alvarez considers a "green fable" or "eco-parable," grew out of their experiences promoting fair trade and sustainability for coffee farmers in the Dominican Republic.

AN INTRODUCTION TO HER WORK

Alvarez's poetry has been widely published in journals and magazines ranging from the *New Yorker* to *Mirabella* to the *Kenyon Review*. Her first book of poems, *Homecoming* (1984; a new expanded verison, *Homecoming: New and Collected Poems*, was published in 1996 by Plume/Penguin), uses simple — yet incisive — language to explore issues related to love, domestic life, and work. Her second book of poetry, *The Other Side/El Otro Lado* (1995), is a collection of meditations on her childhood memories of immigrant life that shaped her adult identity and sensibilities. Some of these concerns are also manifested in her book of essays, titled *Something to Declare* (1998), a collection that describes her abiding concerns about how to respond to competing cultures. In her third poetry collection, *The Woman I Kept to Myself* (2004), Alvarez reflects on her personal life and development as a writer from the vantage point of her mid-fifties in seventy-five poems, each consisting of three ten-line stanzas.

In addition to writing a number of books for children and young adults, Alvarez has also published six novels. The first, *How the García Girls Lost Their Accents* (1991), is a collection of fifteen separate but interrelated stories that cover thirty years of the lives of the García sisters from the late 1950s to the late 1980s. Drawing on her own experiences, Alvarez describes the sisters fleeing the Dominican Republic and growing up Latina in the United States. *In the Time of the Butterflies* (1994) is a fictional account of a true story concerning four sisters who opposed Trujillo's dictatorship. Three of the sisters were murdered in 1960 by the government, and the surviving fourth sister recounts the events of their personal and political lives that led to her sisters' deaths. Shaped by the history of Dominican freedom and tyranny, the novel also explores the sisters' relationships to each other and their country.

In ¡*Yo!* (1997), Alvarez focuses on Yolanda, one of the García sisters from her first novel, who is now a writer. Written in the different voices of Yo's friends and family members, this fractured narrative constructs a complete picture of a woman who uses her relationships as fodder for fiction, a woman who is self-centered, aggravating, and finally lovable — who is deeply embedded in American culture while remaining aware of her Dominican roots. ¡*Yo!*, which means "I" in English, is a meditation on points of view and narrative.

In the Name of Salomé (2000) is a fictional account of Salomé Ureña, who was born in the 1850s and considered to be "the Emily Dickinson of the Dominican Republic," and her daughter's efforts late in life to reconcile her relationship to her mother's reputation and her own response to Castro's revolution in Cuba. Alvarez published her sixth and most recent novel, *Saving the World*, in 2006, a story that also links two women's lives, one from the past and one from the present, around personal and political issues concerning humanitarian efforts to end smallpox in the nineteenth century and the global AIDS epidemic in the twenty-first century.

Chronology

1950	Born on March 27 in New York City.
1950–60	Raised in the Dominican Republic.
1960	Alvarez family flees the Dominican Republic for New York City after her father joins efforts to overthrow the dictatorship of Rafael Trujillo.
1961	Rafael Trujillo is assassinated.
1967–69	Attends Connecticut College.
1971	Graduates from Middlebury College with a B.A.
1975	Graduates from Syracuse University with an M.A.
1979–80	Attends Bread Loaf School of English.
1979–81	Instructor at Phillips Andover Academy.
1981–83	Visiting assistant professor at University of Vermont.
1984	Publishes *Homecoming*, a volume of poems, and *The Housekeeping Book*, a handmade book of a series of "housekeeping poems," illustrated by Carol MacDonald and Rene Schall.
1984–85	Visiting writer-in-residence at George Washington University.
1985–88	Assistant professor of English at University of Illinois.
1987–88	Awarded a National Endowment for the Arts Fellowship.
1988–98	Professor of English at Middlebury College.
1988–Present	Writer-in-residence at Middlebury College.
1991	Publishes *How the García Girls Lost Their Accents*, a novel.
1994	Publishes *In the Time of the Butterflies*, a novel.
1995	Publishes *The Other Side/El Otro Lado*, a volume of poems.
1996	Publishes *Homecoming: New and Collected Poems*, a reissue of *Homecoming* (1984) with new work included.
1997	Publishes *¡Yo!*, a novel.
1998	Publishes *Something to Declare*, a collection of essays, and *Seven Trees*, a handmade volume of poems.
2000	Publishes *In the Name of Salomé*, a novel, and *The Secret Footprints*, a picture book for children.

2001	Publishes *A Cafecito Story,* a novel or "eco-parable," and *How Tía Lola Came to ~~Visit~~ Stay,* a novel for young adults.
2002	Publishes *The Woman I Kept to Myself,* a volume of poems, and *Before We Were Free,* a novel for young adults.
2004	Publishes *A Gift of Gracias: The Legend of Altagracia,* a picture book for children, and *Finding Miracles,* a novel for young adults.
2006	Publishes *Saving the World,* a novel.
2007	Publishes *Once Upon a Quinceañera: Coming of Age in the USA,* a memoir and cultural study of ceremonies for Latina girls when they turn fifteen.
2009	Publishes *Return to Sender,* a children's novel.

In "Queens, 1963" Alvarez remembers the neighborhood she lived in when she was a thirteen-year-old and how "Everyone seemed more American / than we, newly arrived." The tensions that arose when new immigrants and ethnic groups moved onto the block were mirrored in many American neighborhoods in 1963. Indeed, the entire nation was made keenly aware of such issues as integration when demonstrations were organized across the South and a massive march on Washington in support of civil rights for African Americans drew hundreds of thousands of demonstrators who listened to Martin Luther King Jr. deliver his electrifying "I have a dream" speech. But the issues were hardly resolved, as evidenced by 1963's two best-selling books: *Happiness Is a Warm Puppy* and *Security Is a Thumb and a Blanket,* by Charles M. Schulz of *Peanuts* cartoon fame. The popularity of these books is, perhaps, understandable given the tensions that moved across the country and which seemed to culminate on November 22, 1963, when President Kennedy was assassinated in Dallas, Texas. These events are not mentioned in "Queens, 1963," but they are certainly part of the context that helps us to understand Alvarez's particular neighborhood. In the following introductory essay, Alvarez reflects on the cultural moment of 1963 and her reasons for writing the poem.

Julia Alvarez

On Writing "Queens, 1963"   2006

I remember when we finally bought our very own house after three years of living in rentals. Back then, Queens, New York, was not the multicultural, multilingual place it is today. But the process was beginning. Our neighborhood was sprinkled with ethnicities, some who had been here longer than others. The Germans down the block—now we would call them German Americans—had been Americans for a couple of generations as had our Jewish neighbors, and most definitely, the Midwesterners across the street. Meanwhile, the Greek family next door were newcomers as were we, our accents still heavy, our cooking

Julia Alvarez, age ten, in her 1960 passport photo.
Courtesy of Julia Alvarez.

smells commingling across our backyard fences during mealtimes: their Greek lamb with rosemary, our Dominican habichuelas with sofrito.°

It seemed a peaceable enough kingdom until a black family moved in across the street. What a ruckus got started! Of course, it was the early 1960s: the civil rights movement was just getting under way in this country. Suddenly, our neighborhood was faced with discrimination, but coming from the very same people who themselves had felt discrimination from other, more mainstream Americans. It was my first lesson in hypocrisy and in realizing that America was still an experiment in process. The words on the Statue of Liberty

habichuelas with sofrito: Kidney beans prepared with a sautéed mixture of spices, herbs, garlic, onion, pepper, and tomato.

(see "Sometimes the Words Are So Close," p. 1203) were only a promise, not yet a practice in the deep South or in Queens, New York.

In writing this poem I wanted to suggest the many ethnic families in the neighborhood. Of course, I couldn't use their real names and risk being sued. (Though, come to think of it, I've never heard of a poem being sued, have you?) Plus, there is the matter of failing memory. (This was forty-two years ago!) So I chose names that suggested other languages, other places, and also — always the poet's ear at work — names that fit in with the rhythm and cadence of the lines.

JULIA ALVAREZ

Queens, 1963

1992

Everyone seemed more American
than we, newly arrived,
foreign dirt still on our soles.
By year's end, a sprinkler waving
like a flag on our mowed lawn,   5
we were blended into the block,
owned our own mock Tudor house.
Then the house across the street
sold to a black family.
Cop cars patrolled our block   10
from the Castellucci's at one end
to the Balakian's on the other.
We heard rumors of bomb threats,
a burning cross on their lawn.
(It turned out to be a sprinkler.)   15
Still the neighborhood buzzed.
The barber's family, Haralambides,
our left-side neighbors, didn't want trouble.
They'd come a long way to be free!
Mr. Scott, the retired plumber,   20
and his plump midwestern wife,
considered moving back home
where white and black got along
by staying where they belonged.
They had cultivated our street   25
like the garden she'd given up
on account of her ailing back,
bad knees, poor eyes, arthritic hands.
She went through her litany daily.
Politely, my mother listened —   30
¡Ay, Mrs. Scott, qué pena!°
— her Dominican good manners
still running on automatic.
The Jewish counselor next door,

31 *qué pena:* What a shame!

had a practice in her house;   35
clients hurried up her walk
ashamed to be seen needing.
(I watched from my upstairs window,
gloomy with adolescence,
and guessed how they too must have   40
hypocritical old-world parents.)
Mrs. Bernstein said it was time
the neighborhood opened up.
As the first Jew on the block,
she remembered the snubbing she got   45
a few years back from Mrs. Scott.
But real estate worried her,
our houses' plummeting value.
She shook her head as she might
at a client's grim disclosures.   50
Too bad the world works this way.
The German girl playing the piano
down the street abruptly stopped
in the middle of a note.
I completed the tune in my head   55
as I watched *their* front door open.
A dark man in a suit
with a girl about my age
walked quickly into a car.
My hand lifted but fell   60
before I made a welcoming gesture.
On her face I had seen a look
from the days before we had melted
into the United States of America.
It was hardness mixed with hurt.   65
It was knowing she never could be
the right kind of American.
A police car followed their car.
Down the street, curtains fell back.
Mrs. Scott swept her walk   70
as if it had just been dirtied.
Then the German piano commenced
downward scales as if tracking
the plummeting real estate.
One by one I imagined the houses   75
sinking into their lawns,
the grass grown wild and tall
in the past tense of this continent
before the first foreigners owned
any of this free country.   80

CONSIDERATIONS FOR CRITICAL THINKING AND WRITING

1. **FIRST RESPONSE.** What nationalities are the people in this neighborhood in
   the New York City borough of Queens? Are they neighborly to each other?

2. In line 3, why do you suppose Alvarez writes "foreign dirt still on our soles" rather than "foreign soil still on our shoes"? What does Alvarez's word choice suggest about her feelings for her native country?

3. Characterize the speaker. How old is she? How does she feel about having come from the Dominican Republic? About living in the United States?

4. Do you think this poem is optimistic or pessimistic about racial relations in the United States? Explain your answer by referring to specific details in the poem.

CONNECTIONS TO OTHER SELECTIONS

1. Compare the use of irony in "Queens, 1963" with that in John Ciardi's "Suburban" (p. 1247). How does irony contribute to each poem?

2. Discuss the problems immigrants encounter in this poem and in Chitra Banerjee Divakaruni's "Indian Movie, New Jersey" (Crossing Boundaries insert, p. I).

3. Write an essay comparing and contrasting the tone and theme in "Queens, 1963" and in Tato Laviera's "AmeRícan" (p. 1020).

Queens Civil Rights Demonstration   *1963*

In this photograph police remove a Congress of Racial Equality (CORE) demonstrator from a Queens construction site. Demonstrators blocked the delivery entrance to the site because they wanted more African Americans and Puerto Ricans hired in the building-trade industry.
Reprinted by permission of AP/Wide World Photos.

CONSIDERATIONS FOR CRITICAL THINKING AND WRITING

1. Discuss the role played by the police in this photograph and in "Queens, 1963." What attitudes toward the police do the photograph and the poem display?
2. How do you think the Scotts and Mrs. Bernstein would have responded to this photograph in 1963?
3. Compare the tensions in "Queens, 1963" to those depicted in this photo. How do the speaker's private reflections relate to this public protest?

Perspective

MARNY REQUA (B. 1971)

From an Interview with Julia Alvarez   1997

M.R. What was it like when you came to the United States?

J.A. When we got to Queens, it was really a shock to go from a totally Latino, *familia* Caribbean world into this very cold and kind of forbidding one in which we didn't speak the language. I didn't grow up with a tradition of writing or reading books at all. People were always telling stories but it wasn't a tradition of literary . . . reading a book or doing something solitary like that. Coming to this country I discovered books, I discovered that it was a way to enter into a portable homeland that you could carry around in your head. You didn't have to suffer what was going on around you. I found in books a place to go. I became interested in language because I was learning a language intentionally at the age of ten. I was wondering, "Why is it that word and not another?" which any writer has to do with their language. I always say I came to English late but to the profession early. By high school I was pretty set: that's what I want to do, be a writer.

M.R. Did you have culture shock returning to the Dominican Republic as you were growing up?

J.A. The culture here had an effect on me — at the time this country was coming undone with protests and flower children and drugs. Here I was back in the Dominican Republic and I wouldn't keep my mouth shut. I had my own ideas and I had my own politics, and it, I just didn't gel anymore with the family. I didn't quite feel I ever belonged in this North American culture and I always had this nostalgia that when I went back I'd belong, and then I found out I didn't belong there either.

M.R. Was it a source of inspiration to have a foot in both cultures?

J.A. I only came to that later. [Then], it was a burden because I felt torn. I wanted to be part of one culture and then part of the other. It was a time when the model for the immigrant was that you came and you became an American and you cut off your ties and that was that. My parents had that frame of mind, because they were so afraid, and they were "Learn your English" and "Become one of them," and that left out so much. Now I see the richness. Part of what I want to do with my work is that complexity, that richness. I don't want it to be simplistic and either/or.

From "The Politics of Fiction," *Frontera* magazine 5 (1997)

CONSIDERATIONS FOR CRITICAL THINKING AND WRITING

1. What do you think Alvarez means when she describes books as "a portable homeland that you could carry around in your head"?
2. Why is it difficult for Alvarez to feel that she belongs in either the Dominican or the North American culture?
3. Alvarez says that in the 1960s "the model for the immigrant was that you came and you became an American and you cut off your ties and that was that." Do you think this model has changed in the United States since then? Explain your response.
4. How might this interview alter your understanding of "Queens, 1963"? What light is shed, for example, on the speaker's feeling that her family "blended into the block" in line 6?

JULIA ALVAREZ

On Writing "Housekeeping Cages" and Her Housekeeping Poems   *1998*

I can still remember the first time I heard my own voice on paper. It happened a few years after I graduated from a creative writing master's program. I had earned a short-term residency at Yaddo, the writer's colony, where I was assigned a studio in the big mansion — the tower room at the top of the stairs. The rules were clear: we artists and writers were to stick to our studios during the day and come out at night for supper and socializing. Nothing was to come between us and our work.

I sat up in my tower room, waiting for inspiration. All around me I could hear the typewriters going. Before me lay a blank sheet of paper, ready for the important work I had come there to write. That was the problem, you see. I was trying to do IMPORTANT work and so I couldn't hear myself think. I was trying to pitch my voice to "Turning and turning in the widening gyre," or, "Of man's first disobedience, and the fruit of that forbidden tree, " or, "Sing in me, Muse, and through me tell the story." I was tuning my voice to these men's voices because I thought that was the way I had to sound if I wanted to be a writer. After all, the writers I read and admired sounded like that.

But the voice I heard when I listened to myself think was the voice of a woman, sitting in her kitchen, gossiping with a friend over a cup of coffee. It was the voice of Gladys singing her sad boleros, Belkis putting color on my face with tales of her escapades, Tití naming the orchids, Ada telling me love stories as we made the beds. I had, however, never seen voices like these in print. So, I didn't know poems could be written in those voices, *my* voice.

So there I was at Yaddo, trying to write something important and coming up with nothing. And then, hallelujah — I heard the vacuum going up and down the hall. I opened the door and introduced myself to the friendly, sweating woman, wielding her vacuum cleaner. She invited me down to the kitchen so we wouldn't disturb the other guests. There I met the cook, and as we all sat, drinking coffee, I paged through her old cookbook, *knead, poach, stew, whip, score, julienne, whisk, sauté, sift.* Hmm. I began hearing a music in these words. I jotted down the names of implements:

> Cup, spoon, ladle, pot, kettle,
> grater and peeler,
> colander, corer,
> waffle iron, small funnel.

"You working on a poem there?" the cook asked me.
I shook my head.

A little later, I went upstairs and wrote down in my journal this beautiful vocabulary of my girlhood. As I wrote, I tapped my foot on the floor to the rhythm of the words. I could see Mami and the aunts with the cook in the kitchen bending their heads over a pot of habichuelas, arguing about what flavor was missing — what could it be they had missed putting in it? And then, the thought of Mami recalled Gladys, the maid who loved to sing, and that thought led me through the house, the mahogany furniture that needed dusting, the beds that needed making, the big bin of laundry that needed washing.

That day, I began working on a poem about dusting. Then another followed on sewing; then came a sweeping poem, an ironing poem. Later, I would collect these into a series I called "the housekeeping poems," poems using the metaphors, details, language of my first apprenticeship as a young girl. Even later, having found my woman's voice, I would gain confidence to explore my voice as a Latina and to write stories and poems using the metaphors, details, rhythms of that first world I had left behind in Spanish.

But it began, first, by discovering my woman's voice at Yaddo where I had found it as a child. Twenty years after learning to sing with Gladys, I was reminded of the lessons I had learned in childhood: that my voice would not be found up in a tower, in those upper reaches or important places, but down in the kitchen among the women who first taught me about service, about passion, about singing as if my life depended on it.

From *Something to Declare*

Julia Alvarez
Housekeeping Cages   *1994*

Sometimes people ask me why I wrote a series of poems about housekeeping if I'm a feminist. Don't I want women to be liberated from the oppressive roles they were condemned to live? I don't see housekeeping that way. They were the crafts we women had, sewing, embroidering, cooking, spinning, sweeping, even the lowly dusting. And like Dylan Thomas said, we sang in our chains like the sea. Isn't it already thinking from the point of view of the oppressor to say to ourselves, what we did was nothing?

You use what you have, you learn to work the structure to create what you need. I don't feel that writing in traditional forms is giving up power, going over to the enemy. The word belongs to no one, the houses built of words belong to no one. We have to take them back from those who think they own them.

Sometimes I get in a mood. I tell myself I am taken over. I am writing under somebody else's thumb and tongue. See, English was not my first language. It was, in fact, a colonizing language to my Spanish Caribbean. But then Spanish was also a colonizer's language; after all, Spain colonized Quisqueya. There's no getting free. We are always writing in a form imposed on us. But then, I'm Scheherazade in the Sultan's room. I use structures to survive and triumph! To say what's important to me as a woman and as a Latina.

I think of form as territory that has been colonized, but that you can free. See, I feel subversive in formal verse. A voice is going to inhabit that form that was barred from entering it before! That's what I tried in the "33" poems, to use my woman's voice in a sonnet as I would use it sitting in the kitchen with a close friend, talking womanstuff. In school, I was always trying to inhabit those forms as the male writers had. To pitch my voice to "Of man's first disobedience, and the fruit. . . ." If it didn't hit the key of "Sing in me, Muse, and through me tell the story," how could it be important poetry? The only kind.

While I was in graduate school some of the women in the program started a Women's Writing Collective in Syracuse. We were musing each other into unknown writing territory. One woman advised me to listen to my own voice, deep inside, and put that down on paper. But what I heard when I listened were voices that said things like "Don't put so much salt on the lettuce, you'll wilt the salad!" I'd never heard that in a poem. So how could it be poetry? Then, with the "33" sonnet sequence, I said, I'm going to go in there and I'm going to sound like myself. I took on the whole kaboodle. I was going into form, sonnets no less. Wow.

What I wanted from the sonnet was the tradition that it offered as well as the structure. The sonnet tradition was one in which women were caged in golden cages of beloved, in perfumed gas chambers of stereotype. I wanted to go in that heavily mined and male labyrinth with the string of my own voice. I wanted to explore it and explode it too. I call my sonnets free verse sonnets. They have ten syllables per line, and the lines are in a loose iambic pentameter. But they are heavily enjambed and the rhymes are often slant-rhymes, and the rhyme scheme is peculiar to each sonnet. One friend read them and said, "I didn't know they were sonnets. They sounded like you talking!"

By learning to work the sonnet structure and yet remaining true to my own voice, I made myself at home in that form. When I was done with it, it was a totally different form from the one I learned in school. I have used other traditional forms. In my poem about sweeping, since you sweep with the broom and you dance — it's a coupling — I used rhyming couplets. I wrote a poem of advice mothers give to their daughters in a villanelle, because it's such a nagging form. But mostly the sonnet is the form I've worked with. It's the classic form in which we women were trapped, love objects, and I was trapped inside that voice and paradigm, and I wanted to work my way out of it.

My idea of traditional forms is that as women much of our heritage is trapped in them. But the cage can turn into a house if you housekeep it the right way. You housekeep it by working the words just so.

From *A Formal Feeling Comes: Poems in Form by Contemporary Women,*
edited by Annie Finch

CONSIDERATIONS FOR CRITICAL THINKING AND WRITING

1. How does Alvarez connect housekeeping to "writing in traditional forms"?

2. Compare "Sometimes the Words Are So Close" (Sonnet 42, p. 1203) to Alvarez's description in her essay of how she writes sonnets. How closely does the poem's form follow her description?

3. Why does Alvarez consider "Dusting" (p. 1200) and "Ironing Their Clothes" (p. 1201) to be feminist poems? How can the poems be read as feminist in their sensibility?

JULIA ALVAREZ

On Writing "Dusting"   2006

Finally, I took the leap and began to write poems in my own voice and the voices of the women in my past, who inevitably were talking about their work, housekeeping. I had to trust that those voices, while not conventionally important, still had something to say. At school, I had been taught the formal canon of literature: epic poems with catalogues of ships, poems about wars and the rumors of wars. Why not write a poem in the voice of a mother cataloguing the fabrics, with names as beautiful as those of ships ("gabardine, organdy, wool, madras" from "Naming the Fabrics") or a poem about sweeping while watching a news report about the Vietnam War on TV ("How I Learned to Sweep")? Each time I delved into one of the housekeeping "arts," I discovered deeper, richer materials and metaphors than I had anticipated. This is wonderful news for a writer. As Robert Frost once said about rhymes in a poem, "No surprise for the writer, no surprise for the reader." The things we discover while writing what we write tingle with that special energy and delight of not just writing a poem, but enlarging our understanding.

Dusting is the lowliest of the housekeeping arts. Any little girl with a rag can dust. But rather than dust, the little girl in my poem is writing her name on the furniture, something her mother keeps correcting. What a perfect metaphor for the changing roles of women which I've experienced in my own life: the mother believing that a woman's place is in the home, not in the public sphere; the girl from a younger generation wanting to make a name for herself.

And in writing "Dusting," I also discovered a metaphor about writing. A complicated balancing act: like the mother, the artist has to disappear in her work; it's the poem that counts, not the name or celebrity of the writer. But the artist also needs the little girl's pluck and ambition to even imagine a public voice for herself. Otherwise, she'd be swallowed up in self-doubt, silenced by her mother's old-world way of viewing a woman's role.

Julia Alvarez

Dusting   1981

Each morning I wrote my name
on the dusty cabinet, then crossed
the dining table in script, scrawled
in capitals on the backs of chairs,
practicing signatures like scales   5
while Mother followed, squirting
linseed from a burping can
into a crumpled-up flannel.

She erased my fingerprints
from the bookshelf and rocker,   10
polished mirrors on the desk
scribbled with my alphabets.
My name was swallowed in the towel
with which she jeweled the table tops.
The grain surfaced in the oak   15
and the pine grew luminous.
But I refused with every mark
to be like her, anonymous.

CONSIDERATIONS FOR CRITICAL THINKING AND WRITING

1. **FIRST RESPONSE.** Describe the central conflict between the speaker and the mother.

2. Explain why the image of dusting is a particularly appropriate metaphor for evoking the central conflict.

3. Discuss the effect of the rhymes in lines 15–18.

4. Consider the tone of each stanza. Explain why you see them as identical or not.

CONNECTION TO ANOTHER SELECTION

1. Discuss the mother-daughter relationships in "Dusting" and in Cathy Song's "The Youngest Daughter" (p. 824).

Julia Alvarez

On Writing "Ironing Their Clothes"   2006

Maybe because ironing is my favorite of all the housekeeping chores, this is my favorite of the housekeeping poems. In the apprenticeship of household arts, ironing is for the advanced apprentice. After all, think about it, you're wielding an instrument that could cause some damage: you could burn yourself, you could burn the clothes. I was not allowed to iron clothes until I was older and could be trusted to iron all different kinds of fabrics ("gabardine, organdy, wool, madras") just right.

Again, think of how ironing someone's clothes can be a metaphor for all kinds of things. You have this power to take out the wrinkles and worries from someone's outer skin! You can touch and caress and love someone and not be told that you are making a nuisance of yourself!

In writing this poem I wanted the language to mirror the process. I wanted the lines to suggest all the fussy complications of trying to get your iron into hard corners and places ("I stroked the yoke, / the breast pocket, collar and cuffs, / until the rumpled heap relaxed . . .") and then the smooth sailing of a line that sails over the line break into the next line ("into the shape / of my father's broad chest . . ."). I wanted to get the hiss of the iron in those last four lines. I revised and revised this poem, especially the verbs, most especially the verbs that have to do the actual work of the iron. When I finally got that last line with its double rhymes ("express / excess"; "love / cloth"), I felt as if I'd done a whole laundry basket worth of ironing just right.

Julia Alvarez

Ironing Their Clothes   1981

With a hot glide up, then down, his shirts,
I ironed out my father's back, cramped
and worried with work. I stroked the yoke,
the breast pocket, collar and cuffs,
until the rumpled heap relaxed into the shape   5
of my father's broad chest, the shoulders shrugged off
the world, the collapsed arms spread for a hug.
And if there'd been a face above the buttondown neck,
I would have pressed the forehead out, I would
have made a boy again out of that tired man!   10

If I clung to her skirt as she sorted the wash
or put out a line, my mother frowned,
a crease down each side of her mouth.
This is no time for love! But here
I could linger over her wrinkled bedjacket,   15
kiss at the damp puckers of her wrists
with the hot tip. Here I caressed
collars, scallops, ties, pleats which made
her outfits test of the patience of my passion.
Here I could lay my dreaming iron on her lap.   20

The smell of baked cotton rose from the board
and blew with a breeze out the window
to the family wardrobe drying on the clothesline,
all needing a touch of my iron. Here I could tickle
the underarms of my big sister's petticoat   25

or secretly pat the backside of her pajamas.
For she too would have warned me not to muss
her fresh blouses, starched jumpers, and smocks,
all that my careful hand had ironed out,
forced to express my excess love on cloth.   30

CONSIDERATIONS FOR CRITICAL THINKING AND WRITING

1. **FIRST RESPONSE.** Explain how the speaker expresses her love for her family in the extended metaphor of ironing.

2. How are ironing and the poem itself expressions of the speaker's "excess love" (line 30)? In what sense is her love excessive?

3. Explain how the speaker's relationship to her father differs from how she relates to her mother.

CONNECTION TO ANOTHER SELECTION

1. **CREATIVE RESPONSE.** Compare the descriptions of mothers in this poem and in Alvarez's "Dusting" (p. 1200). Write a one-paragraph character sketch that uses vivid details and metaphoric language to describe them.

JULIA ALVAREZ

On Writing "Sometimes the Words Are So Close"   2006
From the "33" Sonnet Sequence

I really believe that being a reader turns you into a writer. You connect with the voice in a poem at a deeper and more intimate level than you do with practically anyone in your everyday life. Seems like the years fall away, differences fall away, and when George Herbert asks in his poem, "The Flower,"

Who would have thought my shrivel'd heart
Could have recover'd greennesse?

You want to stroke the page and answer him, "I did, George." Instead you write a poem that responds to the feelings in his poem; you recover greenness for him and for yourself.

With the "33" sonnet sequence, I wanted the voice of the speaker to sound like a real woman speaking. A voice at once intimate and also somehow universal, essential. This sonnet #42 ["Sometimes the Words Are So Close"] is the last one in the sequence, a kind of final "testimony" about what writing is all about.

I mentioned that when you love something you read, you want to respond to it. You want to say it again, in fresh new language. Robert Frost speaks to this impulse in the poet when he says, "Don't borrow, steal!" Well, I borrowed / stole two favorite passages. One of them is from the poem on the Statue of

Liberty, which was written by Emma Lazarus (1849–1887), titled "The New Colossus" [p. 1336]. These lines will sound familiar to you, I'm sure:

> "Give me your tired, your poor,
> Your huddled masses yearning to breathe free,
> The wretched refuse of your teeming shore.
> Send these, the homeless, tempest-tost to me,
> I lift my lamp beside the golden door!"

I think of these lines, not just as an invitation to the land of the brave and home of the free, but an invitation to poetry! A poem can be a resting place for the soul yearning to breathe free, a form that won't tolerate the misuses and abuses of language, a world teeming with discoveries and luminous little *ah-ha!* moments, a "place for the genuine," as Marianne Moore calls it in her poem, "On Poetry." William Carlos Williams said that we can't get the news from poems, practical information, hard facts, but "men die daily for lack of what is found there."

I not only agreed with this idea, but I wanted to say so in my own words, and so I echoed those lines from the Statue of Liberty in my sonnet:

> Those of you lost and yearning to be free,
> who hear these words, take heart from me.

Another favorite line comes from Walt Whitman's book-length "Leaves of Grass": "Who touches this [book] touches a man." As a young, lonely immigrant girl reading Whitman, those words made me feel so accompanied, so connected. And so I borrowed / stole that line and made it my own at the end of this poem.

JULIA ALVAREZ

Sometimes the Words Are So Close   1982
From the "33" Sonnet Sequence

Sometimes the words are so close I am
more who I am when I'm down on paper
than anywhere else as if my life were
practicing for the real me I become
unbuttoned from the anecdotal and   5
unnecessary and undressed down
to the figure of the poem, line by line,
the real text a child could understand.
Why do I get confused living it through?
Those of you lost and yearning to be free,   10
who hear these words, take heart from me.
I once was in as many drafts as you.
But briefly, essentially, here I am.
Who touches this poem touches a woman.

Drafts of "Sometimes the Words Are So Close": A Poet's Writing Process

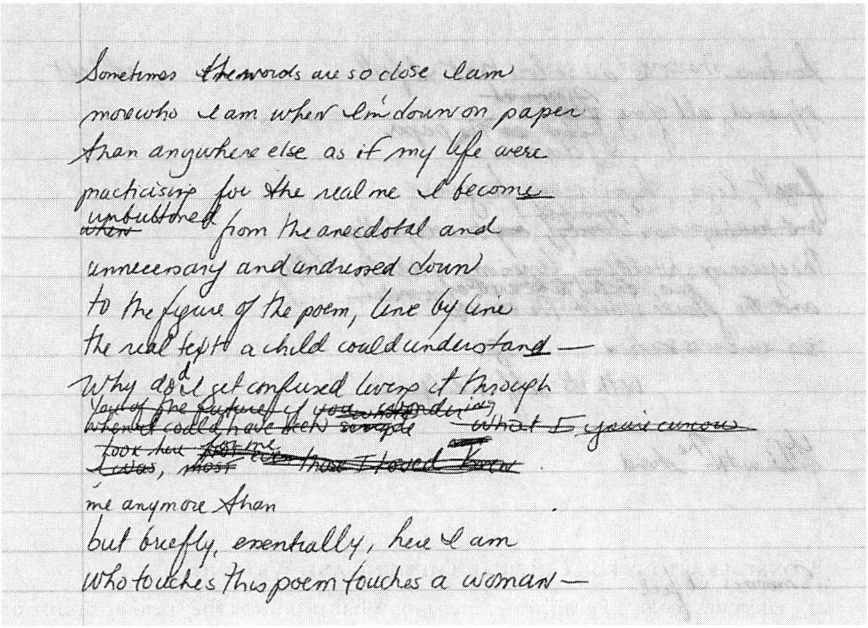

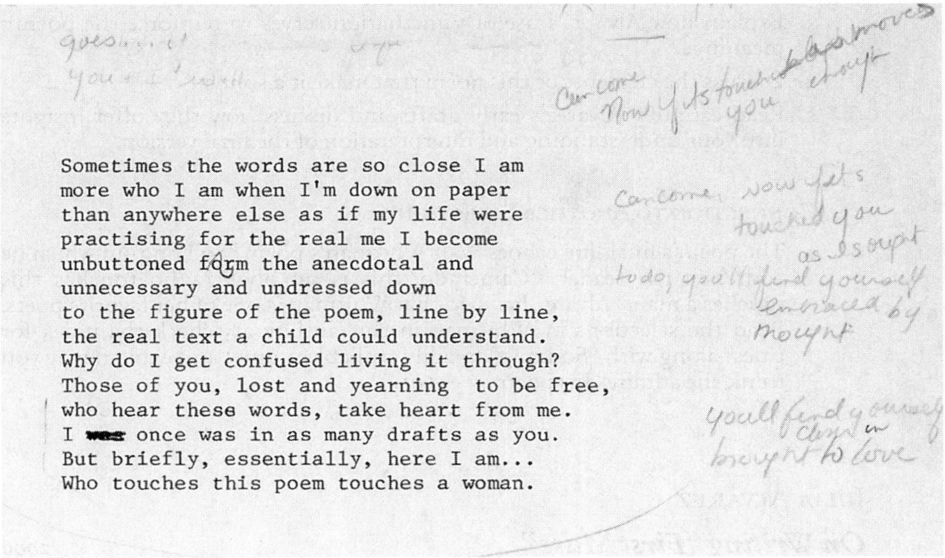

[handwritten draft]

Sometimes the words are so close I am
more who I am when I'm down on paper
than anywhere else as if my life were
practising for the real me I become
~~when~~ unbuttoned from the anecdotal and
unnecessary and undressed down
to the figure of the poem, line by line
the real text a child could understand —
Why do I get confused living it through
~~You of the future of you wondering~~
~~when I could have been scrupel~~ ~~what I, you're curious~~
~~took here fretting~~ ~~those I loved love~~
me anymore than
but briefly, essentially, here I am
Who touches this poem touches a woman —

[typed draft]

```
Sometimes the words are so close I am
more who I am when I'm down on paper
than anywhere else as if my life were
practising for the real me I become
unbuttoned form the anecdotal and
unnecessary and undressed down
to the figure of the poem, line by line,
the real text a child could understand.
Why do I get confused living it through?
Those of you, lost and yearning  to be free,
who hear these words, take heart from me.
I was once was in as many drafts as you.
But briefly, essentially, here I am...
Who touches this poem touches a woman.
```

[handwritten notes, right margin]

goes...

you

Can come
Now if its touched last moves
you chough

Can come now lets
touched you
as I sought
to do, you'll find yourself
embraced by
thought

you'll find yourself
brought to love

> Sometimes the words are so close I am
> more who I am when I'm down on paper
> than anywhere else as if my life were
> practising for the real me I become
> unbuttoned from the anecdotal and
> unnecessary and undressed down
> to the figure of the poem, line by line,
> the real text a child could understand.
> Why do I get confused living it through?
> Those of you, lost and yearning to be free,
> who hear these words, take heart from me.
> I once was in as many drafts as you.
> But briefly, essentially, here I am...
> Who touches this poem touches a woman.

pretentious

CONSIDERATIONS FOR CRITICAL THINKING AND WRITING

1. **FIRST RESPONSE.** Paraphrase lines 1–9. What produces the speaker's sense of frustration?

2. How do lines 10–14 resolve the question raised in line 9?

3. Explain how Alvarez's use of punctuation serves to reinforce the poem's meanings.

4. Discuss the elements of this poem that make it a sonnet.

5. Read carefully Alvarez's early drafts and discuss how they offer insights into your understanding and interpretation of the final version.

CONNECTION TO ANOTHER SELECTION

1. The poem's final line echoes Walt Whitman's poem "So Long" in which he addresses the reader: "Camerado, this is no book,/Who touches this touches a man." Alvarez has said that Whitman is one of her favorite poets. Read the selections by Whitman in this anthology (check the index for titles) along with "So Long" (readily available online) and explain why you think she admires his poetry.

JULIA ALVAREZ

On Writing "First Muse" 2006

I have to come clean about calling this poem, "First Muse."

I had another first muse in Spanish. Her name was Scheherazade and I read about her in a book my aunt gave me called *The Arabian Nights*. Scheherazade saves her life by telling the murderous sultan incredible tales night after night for 1001 nights. Listening to her stories, the sultan is transformed. He no

Those of you, lost and yearning to be free,
who hear these words, take heart from me.
I once was in as many drafts as you.
But briefly, essentially, here I am. . . .
Who touches this poem touches a woman.

-Julia Alvarez
(1950-), "33"

An excerpt from Alvarez's poem "Sometimes the Words Are So Close" is set by sculptor Gregg LeFevre in a bronze plaque on 41st Street in New York City, and is part of the "Library Way" — a display sponsored by the Grand Central Partnership of sidewalk plaques leading to the landmark New York Public Library's Humanities and Social Sciences Library on Fifth Avenue that feature literary quotations from forty-four artists and writers including Lucille Clifton, John Milton, and Pablo Picasso.

Courtesy of the Grand Central Partnership, New York, and Gregg LeFevre.

longer wants to kill all the women in his kingdom. In fact, he falls in love with Scheherazade. This young lady saves her own life, the lives of all the women in her kingdom, and by changing him, she also saves the sultan's soul just by telling stories. Right then, I knew what I wanted to be when I grew up. You bet. A storyteller.

Of course, back then, I was growing up in the Dominican Republic, living in a cruel and dangerous dictatorship myself. My own father was a member of an underground freedom movement to depose this dictator. Like Scheherazade, my life and the life of many Dominicans was in danger. But stories like the ones in *The Arabian Nights* helped me dream that the world was a more exciting and mysterious place than I could even imagine. That I was free to travel on the magic carpet of Scheherazade's tales even if the dictatorship did not allow me to drive one town over without inspection and permission.

When I came into English and became a reader, I had new dreams. I wanted to be an American writer. But as I mentioned earlier, the United States of the early '60s was still a long way off from the multicultural "revolution" of the late '80s and '90s. All the writers we read in my English class were Anglo Americans, and many of them were male. Still, the words they put down on paper invited everyone to partake of them. The authors were talking directly to me, asking me questions ("Who would have thought my shrivel'd heart . . . ?"), inviting me to be intimate with their words ("Who touches this [book] touches a man"). That's what I loved about reading: the great egalitarian democracy between the covers of books. The table set for all. The portable homeland. I wanted to be a part of that world. I often say that when I left the Dominican Republic in 1960, I landed, not in the United States, but in the English language, and that's where I put down deep roots by becoming a writer.

But the world beyond the covers of books did not mirror this great democracy. As you read in "Queens, 1963," the reality was disappointing. There were gated communities within this great free country. Places where immigrants and blacks need not apply. One of them was the guarded canon of literature. I still recall the famous writer who made the pronouncement that one could not write in English unless it was one's mother tongue. I was filled with self-doubt, and since I didn't have any examples in what we were reading in school that this pronouncement was wrong, I thought he was right.

Back then, Latino stories were the province of sociology, not literature. As for popular media, the only "Hispanics" on TV were Ricky Ricardo, with his laughable accent, and Chiquita Banana, selling fruit for the United Fruit Company. But as I said about writing in form, you find yourself caught in a structure or negative paradigm and you turn it on its head. You use it to get free. I listened to Chiquita singing, "I'm Chiquita Banana and I've come to say," and I began to get her message: *I'm a Latina woman, and I am claiming it openly, and what's more I've got something to say.* I felt the same rush of hope when I read Langston Hughes's "I, Too" [This poem appears on p. 1137]. In that poem, Mr. Hughes promised himself that "Tomorrow, / I'll be at the table" of American literature. And there he was in my English textbook. He had made good on his promise to himself, to me!

The civil rights struggle didn't just happen on buses and in places of business or on picket lines in Birmingham, Alabama, or Queens, New York. It also happened on paper. Chiquita Banana and Langston Hughes were right. There is a place for all our voices in the great inclusive world of literature. I feel honored and privileged to be part of that great liberating movement of words on paper, springing us all free with their magic and power, connecting us with ourselves and with each other.

JULIA ALVAREZ

First Muse   1999

When I heard the famous poet pronounce
"One can only write poems in the tongue
in which one first said *Mother,*" I was stunned.
Lately arrived in English, I slipped down

into my seat and fought back tears, thinking 5
of all those notebooks filled with bogus poems
I'd have to burn, thinking maybe there was
a little loophole, maybe just maybe
Mami had sung me lullabies she'd learned
from wives stationed at the embassy, 10

thinking maybe she'd left the radio on
beside my crib tuned to the BBC
or Voice of America, maybe her friend
from boarding school had sent a talking doll
who spoke in English? Maybe I could be 15
the one exception to this writing rule?
For months I suffered from bad writer's-block,
which I envisioned, not as a blank page,
but as a literary border guard
turning me back to Spanish on each line. 20

I gave up writing, watched lots of TV,
and you know how it happens that advice
comes from unlikely quarters? *She* came on,
sassy, olive-skinned, hula-hooping her hips,
a basket of bananas on her head, 25
her lilting accent so full of feeling
it seemed the way the heart would speak English
if it could speak. I touched the screen and sang
my own heart out with my new muse, *I am*
Chiquita Banana and I'm here to say . . . 30

CONSIDERATIONS FOR CRITICAL THINKING AND WRITING

1. **FIRST RESPONSE.** What do you think the "famous poet" had in mind by insisting that "'One can only write poems in the tongue / in which one first said *Mother*'" (lines 2–3)? Explain why you agree or disagree with this statement.

2. How does the speaker preserve the serious nature of her bilingualism while simultaneously treating the topic humorously?

3. How and why does Chiquita Banana serve as the speaker's "new muse"?

CONNECTIONS TO OTHER SELECTIONS

1. Discuss the speakers' passion for language as it is revealed in "First Muse," "Sometimes the Words Are So Close" (p. 1203), and "Dusting" (p. 1200).

2. Compare the themes concerning writing and ethnicity in "First Muse" and in Julio Marzán's "Ethnic Poetry" (p. 904).

3. Consider the speakers' reactions in "First Muse" and in Judy Page Heitzman's "The Schoolroom on the Second Floor of the Knitting Mill" (p. 878) to the authoritative voice each hears. What effects do these powerful voices have on the speakers' lives?

A songbook featuring an image of the Chiquita Banana character referenced in Alvarez's "First Muse."

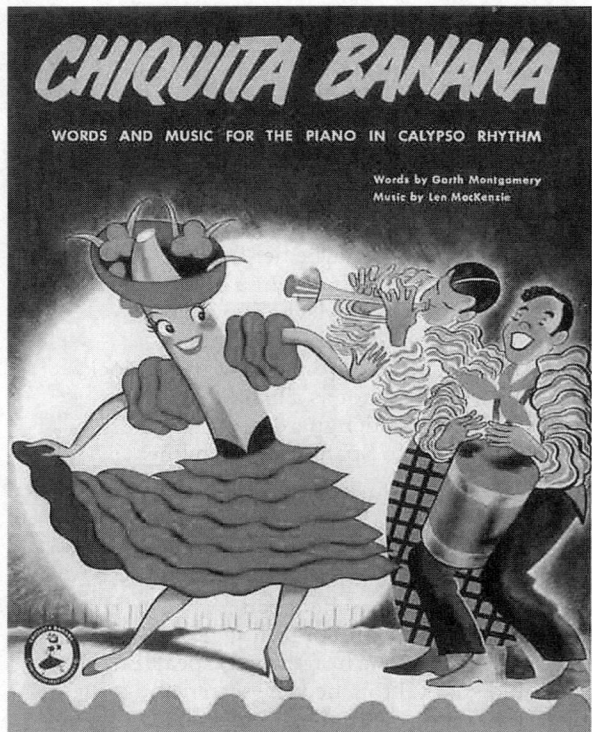

Web For more images of this character, go to bedfordstmartins.com/meyerlit.

CONSIDERATIONS FOR CRITICAL THINKING AND WRITING

1. How does this cover for the sheet music of Chiquita Banana's song illustrate the character's "sassy" tone (line 24) alluded to in the final stanza of "First Muse"?

2. In "First Muse," Alvarez humorously contemplates that if her mother had "left the radio on / beside my crib tuned to the BBC / or Voice of America," she might have learned English as an infant (lines 11–13). How does a careful analysis of the sheet music illustration suggest the difference between Chiquita's voice and that of the BBC or Voice of America?

3. The Chiquita Brands International corporation maintains a Web site (www.chiquita.com) that provides a history of its advertisements from the 1940s to the present, including recordings of the Chiquita song. How do you think the images of "Miss Chiquita" and her song served as a "new muse" for Alvarez when she was starting out as a writer?

Perspective

Kelli Lyon Johnson (b. 1969)
Mapping an Identity   *2005*

Alvarez poses the problem of how we are to understand and represent identity within the multiple migrations that characterize an increasingly global society. By "mapping a country that's not on the map," Alvarez, a Dominican immigrant forced into exile in the United States, is undertaking a journey that places her at the forefront of contemporary American letters.

The question of identity and agency is particularly acute for women, postcolonial peoples, and others upon whom an identity has traditionally been imposed. Given Alvarez's success, both commercial and artistic, a variety of groups have claimed her as a member of their communities: as woman, ethnic, exile, diaspora, Caribbean, Dominican, Latina, and American. In the keynote address at a conference for Caribbean Studies, Doña Aída Cartagena Portalatín, "the grand woman of letters in the Dominican Republic" (*Something*[1] 171) gently chides Alvarez for writing in English. "Come back to your country, to your language," she tells Alvarez. "You are a Dominican" (171). By conflating linguistic, national, and cultural identity, Portalatín underscores the importance of these factors for constructing a literary tradition that includes displaced writers like Alvarez, who quite consciously has not adopted for writing the language of her country of origin.

In response to such comments, Alvarez has asserted her own self-definition as both (and neither) Dominican and American by writing "a new place on the map" (*Something* 173). Placing herself among a multiethnic group of postcolonial authors who write in English — "Michael Ondaatje in Toronto, Maxine Hong Kingston in San Francisco, Seamus Heaney in Boston, Bharati Mukherjee in Berkeley, Marjorie Agosín in Wellesley, Edwidge Danticat in Brooklyn" (173) — Alvarez, like these authors, has altered contemporary American literature by stretching the literary cartography of the Americas. These authors have brought, through their writings, their own countries of origin into a body of work in which the word *American* expands across continents and seas and begins to recapture its original connotation.

Alvarez has also claimed membership among a *comunidad* of U.S. Latina writers — Sandra Cisneros, Ana Castillo, Judith Ortiz Cofer, Lorna Dee Cervantes, Cherríe Moraga, Helena María Viramontes, and Denise Chávez — despite her fears that "the cage of definition" will enclose her writing "with its 'Latino subject matter,' 'Latino style,' 'Latino concerns'" (169). Like these authors, Alvarez seeks to write women into a postcolonial tradition of literature that has historically excluded women, particularly in writings of exile. To counter imposed definitions and historical silences, Alvarez has found that "the best way to define myself is through stories and poems" (169). The space that Alvarez maps is thus a narrative space: the site of her emerging cartography of identity and exile.

From *Julia Alvarez: Writing a New Place on the Map*

---

[1] *Something to Declare*, Alvarez's collection of essays published in 1998.

CONSIDERATIONS FOR CRITICAL THINKING AND WRITING

1. Based on your reading of the poems in this chapter, which community identity — "woman, ethnic, exile, diaspora, Caribbean, Dominican, Latina, and American" — best describes Alvarez for you?

2. In what sense does Alvarez's poetry expand "the literary cartography of the Americas"?

3. Consider "First Muse" as Alvarez's response to Portalatín's suggestion that she should write in Spanish rather than English and "[c]ome back to your country, to your language."

37

A CRITICAL CASE STUDY
T. S. Eliot's "The Love Song of J. Alfred Prufrock"

Genuine poetry can communicate
before it is understood.
—T. S. ELIOT

This chapter provides several critical approaches to a challenging but highly rewarding poem by T. S. Eliot. After studying this poem, you're likely to find yourself quoting bits of its striking imagery. At the very least, you'll recognize the lines when you hear other people fold them into their own conversations. This poem has elicited numerous critical approaches because it raises so many issues relating to history, biography, imagery, symbolism, irony, myth, and other matters. The following critical excerpts offer a small

T. S. Eliot

T. S. Eliot began writing poetry as a student. He is shown here in 1906 at age eighteen, during his first year at Harvard. In 1910, Eliot continued his studies abroad at the Sorbonne in Paris and at age twenty-three completed his first draft of "The Love Song of J. Alfred Prufrock" during the summer of 1911. Later in his life Eliot said, "Immature poets imitate; mature poets steal."

Reprinted by permission of the Houghton Library, Harvard University.

and partial sample of the possible formalist, biographical, historical, mythological, psychological, sociological, and other perspectives that have attempted to shed light on the poem (see Chapter 53, "Critical Strategies for Reading," for a discussion of a variety of critical methods). They should help you to enjoy the poem more by raising questions, providing insights, and inviting you further into the text.

A BRIEF BIOGRAPHY

Born into a prominent New England family that had moved to St. Louis, Missouri, Thomas Stearns Eliot (1888–1965) was a major figure in English literature between the two world wars. He studied literature and philosophy at Harvard and on the Continent, subsequently choosing to live in England for most of his life and becoming a citizen of that country in 1927. Many writers have been powerfully influenced by his allusive and challenging poetry, particularly his treatment of postwar life in *The Waste Land* (1922)

This portrait of T. S. Eliot is by the Modernist painter and writer Wyndham Lewis. The modernist movement of art and literature, dating from the late nineteenth to the mid-twentieth centuries, represented a rejection of tradition, a radical departure from Victorian sentimentality, and a move toward more experimental forms of expression. Modernist writers included T. S. Eliot, James Joyce, and Virginia Woolf. One of the themes explored by modernist authors like Eliot is alienation. He once said, "[Poetry] may make us from time to time a little more aware of the deeper unnamed feelings which form the substratum of our being, to which we rarely penetrate; for our lives are mostly a constant evasion of ourselves."

T. S. Eliot (November 10, 1959), in a pose that suggests the Prufrock persona, holding a book containing some of his earlier work during a press conference at the University of Chicago. © Bettmann/CORBIS.

and his exploration of religious questions in *The Four Quartets* (1943). In addition, he wrote plays, including *Murder in the Cathedral* (1935) and *The Cocktail Party* (1950). He was awarded the Nobel Prize for Literature in 1948. In "The Love Song of J. Alfred Prufrock" Eliot presents a comic but serious figure who expresses through a series of fragmented images the futility, boredom, and meaninglessness associated with much of modern life.

T. S. ELIOT (1888–1965)
The Love Song of J. Alfred Prufrock 1917

S'io credesse che mia risposta fosse
A persona che mai tornasse al mondo,
Questa fiamma staria senza più scosse.
Ma perciocchè giammai di questo fondo

Non tornò vivo alcun, s'i'odo il vero,
Senza tema d'infamia ti rispondo.°

    Let us go then, you and I,
When the evening is spread out against the sky
Like a patient etherized upon a table;
Let us go, through certain half-deserted streets,
The muttering retreats   5
Of restless nights in one-night cheap hotels
And sawdust restaurants with oyster-shells:
Streets that follow like a tedious argument
Of insidious intent
To lead you to an overwhelming question . . .   10

Oh, do not ask, "What is it?"
Let us go and make our visit.

In the room the women come and go
Talking of Michelangelo.

    The yellow fog that rubs its back upon the window panes,   15
The yellow smoke that rubs its muzzle on the window panes
Licked its tongue into the corners of the evening,
Lingered upon the pools that stand in drains,
Let fall upon its back the soot that falls from chimneys,
Slipped by the terrace, made a sudden leap,   20
And seeing that it was a soft October night,
Curled once about the house, and fell asleep.

    And indeed there will be time°
For the yellow smoke that slides along the street,
Rubbing its back upon the window panes;   25
There will be time, there will be time
To prepare a face to meet the faces that you meet;
There will be time to murder and create,
And time for all the works and days° of hands
That lift and drop a question on your plate: 30
Time for you and time for me,
And time yet for a hundred indecisions,
And for a hundred visions and revisions,
Before the taking of a toast and tea.

Epigraph: *S'io credesse . . . rispondo:* Dante's *Inferno,* 27:58–63. In the Eighth Chasm of the Inferno, Dante and Virgil meet Guido da Montefeltro, one of the False Counselors, who is punished by being enveloped in an eternal flame. When Dante asks Guido to tell his life story, the spirit replies: "If I thought that my answer were to one who might ever return to the world, this flame would shake no more; but since from this depth none ever returned alive, if what I hear is true, I answer you without fear of infamy."

23 *there will be time:* An allusion to Ecclesiastes 3:1–8: "To everything there is a season, and a time to every purpose under heaven. . . ."

29 *works and days:* Hesiod's eighth-century B.C. poem *Works and Days* gives practical advice on how to conduct one's life in accordance with the seasons.

In the room the women come and go   35
Talking of Michelangelo.

    And indeed there will be time
To wonder, "Do I dare?" and, "Do I dare?" —
Time to turn back and descend the stair,
With a bald spot in the middle of my hair —   40
(They will say: "How his hair is growing thin!")
My morning coat, my collar mounting firmly to the chin,
My necktie rich and modest, but asserted by a simple pin —
(They will say: "But how his arms and legs are thin!")
Do I dare   45
Disturb the universe?
In a minute there is time
For decisions and revisions which a minute will reverse.

    For I have known them all already, known them all:
Have known the evenings, mornings, afternoons,   50
I have measured out my life with coffee spoons;
I know the voices dying with a dying fall
Beneath the music from a farther room.
    So how should I presume?

    And I have known the eyes already, known them all —   55
The eyes that fix you in a formulated phrase.
And when I am formulated, sprawling on a pin,
When I am pinned and wriggling on the wall,
Then how should I begin
To spit out all the butt-ends of my days and ways?   60
    And how should I presume?

    And I have known the arms already, known them all —
Arms that are braceleted and white and bare
(But in the lamplight, downed with light brown hair!)
    Is it perfume from a dress   65
    That makes me so digress?
Arms that lie along a table, or wrap about a shawl.
    And should I then presume?
    And how should I begin?

    Shall I say, I have gone at dusk through narrow streets,   70
And watched the smoke that rises from the pipes
Of lonely men in shirtsleeves, leaning out of windows? . . .

I should have been a pair of ragged claws
Scuttling across the floors of silent seas.

    And the afternoon, the evening, sleeps so peacefully!   75
Smoothed by long fingers,
Asleep . . . tired . . . or it malingers,
Stretched on the floor, here beside you and me.
Should I, after tea and cakes and ices,
Have the strength to force the moment to its crisis?   80
But though I have wept and fasted, wept and prayed,

Though I have seen my head (grown slightly bald) brought in upon a platter,°
I am no prophet — and here's no great matter;
I have seen the moment of my greatness flicker,
And I have seen the eternal Footman hold my coat, and snicker,   85
    And in short, I was afraid.

    And would it have been worth it, after all,
After the cups, the marmalade, the tea,
Among the porcelain, among some talk of you and me,
Would it have been worth while   90
To have bitten off the matter with a smile,
To have squeezed the universe into a ball°
To roll it toward some overwhelming question,
To say: "I am Lazarus,° come from the dead,
Come back to tell you all, I shall tell you all" —   95
If one, settling a pillow by her head,
    Should say: "That is not what I meant at all;
        That is not it, at all."

    And would it have been worth it, after all,
Would it have been worth while,   100
After the sunsets and the dooryards and the sprinkled streets,
After the novels, after the teacups, after the skirts that trail along the floor —
And this, and so much more? —
It is impossible to say just what I mean!
But as if a magic lantern threw the nerves in patterns on a screen: 105
Would it have been worth while
If one, settling a pillow or throwing off a shawl,
And turning toward the window, should say:
    "That is not it at all,
    That is not what I meant, at all."   110

No! I am not Prince Hamlet, nor was meant to be;
Am an attendant lord,° one that will do
To swell a progress,° start a scene or two,   *state procession*
Advise the prince: withal, an easy tool,
Deferential, glad to be of use,   115
Politic, cautious, and meticulous;
Full of high sentence, but a bit obtuse;
At times, indeed, almost ridiculous —
Almost, at times, the Fool.

I grow old . . . I grow old . . .   120
I shall wear the bottoms of my trousers rolled.

82 *head . . . upon a platter:* At Salome's request, Herod had John the Baptist decapitated and
had the severed head delivered to her on a platter (see Matt. 14:1–12 and Mark 6:17–29).

92 *squeezed the universe into a ball:* See Andrew Marvell's "To His Coy Mistress" (p. 812), lines
41–42: "Let us roll all our strength and all / Our sweetness up into one ball."

94 *Lazarus:* The brother of Mary and Martha who was raised from the dead by Jesus (John
11:1–44). In Luke 16:19–31, a rich man asks that another Lazarus return from the dead to warn
the living about their treatment of the poor.

112 *attendant lord:* Like Polonius in Shakespeare's *Hamlet.*

Shall I part my hair behind? Do I dare to eat a peach?
I shall wear white flannel trousers, and walk upon the beach.
I have heard the mermaids singing, each to each.

I do not think that they will sing to me.   125

I have seen them riding seaward on the waves,
Combing the white hair of the waves blown back
When the wind blows the water white and black.

We have lingered in the chambers of the sea
By seagirls wreathed with seaweed red and brown,   130
Till human voices wake us, and we drown.

CONSIDERATIONS FOR CRITICAL THINKING AND WRITING

1. **FIRST RESPONSE.** What does J. Alfred Prufrock's name connote? How would you characterize him?

2. What do you think is the purpose of the epigraph from Dante's *Inferno*?

3. What is it that Prufrock wants to do? How does he behave? What does he think of himself? Which parts of the poem answer these questions?

4. Who is the "you" of line 1 and the "we" in the final lines?

5. Discuss the poem's imagery. How does the imagery reveal Prufrock's character? Which images seem especially striking to you?

CONNECTIONS TO OTHER SELECTIONS

1. Write an essay comparing Prufrock's sense of himself as an individual with that of Walt Whitman's speaker in "One's-Self I Sing" (p. 1351).

2. Discuss in an essay the tone of "The Love Song of J. Alfred Prufrock" and Robert Frost's "Acquainted with the Night" (p. 889).

Perspectives on T. S. Eliot

ELISABETH SCHNEIDER (1897–1984)

Schneider uses a biographical approach to the poem to suggest that part of what went into the characterization of Prufrock were some of Eliot's own sensibilities.

Hints of Eliot in Prufrock   1952

Perhaps never again did Eliot find an epigraph quite so happily suited to his use as the passage from the *Inferno* which sets the underlying serious tone for *Prufrock* and conveys more than one level of its meaning: "S'io credesse che mia risposta . . . ," lines in which Guido da Montefeltro consents to tell his story to Dante only because he believes that none ever returns to the world of the living from his depth. One in Hell can bear to expose his shame only to another of the damned; Prufrock speaks to, will be understood only by, other Prufrocks (the "you and I" of the opening, perhaps), and, I imagine the epigraph also hints, Eliot himself is speaking to those who know this kind of hell. The poem, I need hardly say, is not in a literal sense autobiographical: for one thing, though it is clear that Prufrock will never marry, the poem was published in the year of Eliot's own first marriage. Nevertheless, friends who knew the young Eliot almost all describe him, retrospectively but convincingly, in Prufrockian terms; and Eliot himself once said of dramatic monologue in general that what we normally hear in it "is the voice of the poet, who has put on the costume and make-up either of some historical character, or of one out of fiction." . . . I suppose it to be one of the many indirect clues to his own poetry planted with evident deliberation throughout his prose. "What every poet starts from," he also once said, "is his own emotions," and, writing of Dante, he asserted that the *Vita nuova* "could only have been written around a personal experience," a statement that, under the circumstances, must be equally applicable to Prufrock; Prufrock was Eliot, though Eliot was much more than Prufrock. We miss the whole tone of the poem, however, if we read it as social satire only. Eliot was not either the dedicated apostle in theory, or the great exemplar in practice, of complete "depersonalization" in poetry that one influential early essay of his for a time led readers to suppose.

From "Prufrock and After: The Theme of Change," *PMLA*, October 1952

Considerations for Critical Thinking and Writing

1. Though Schneider concedes that the poem is not literally autobiographical, she does assert that "Prufrock was Eliot." How does she argue this point? Explain why you find her argument convincing or unconvincing.

2. Find information in the library or online about Eliot's early career when he was writing this poem. To what extent does the poem reveal his circumstances and concerns at that point in his life?

Barbara Everett

Everett's discussion of tone is used to make a distinction between Eliot and his characterization of Prufrock.

The Problem of Tone in Prufrock   1974

Eliot's poetry presents a peculiar problem as far as tone is concerned. *Tone* really means the way the attitude of a speaker is manifested by the inflections of his speaking voice. Many critics have already recognized that for a mixture of reasons it is difficult, sometimes almost impossible, to ascertain Eliot's tone in this way. It is not that the poetry lacks "voice," for in fact Eliot has an extraordinarily recognizable poetic voice, often imitated and justifying his own comment in the . . . *Paris Review* that "in a poem you're writing for your own voice, which is very important. You're thinking in terms of your own voice." It is this authoritative, idiosyncratic, and exact voice that holds our complete attention in poem after poem, however uninterested we are in what opinions it may seem or happen to be expressing. But Eliot too seems uninterested in what opinions it may happen to be expressing, for he invariably dissociates himself from his poems before they are even finished — before they are hardly begun — by balancing a derisory name or title against an "I," by reminding us that there is always going to be a moment at which detachment will take place or has taken place, a retrospective angle from which, far in the future, critical judgment alters the scene, and the speaking voice of the past has fallen silent. "I have known them all already, known them all." Thus whatever started to take place in the beginning of a poem by Eliot cannot truly be said to be Eliot's opinion because at some extremely early stage he began that process of dissociation to be loosely called "dramatization," a process reflected in the peculiar distances of the tone, as though everything spoken was in inverted commas.

From "In Search of Prufrock," Critical Quarterly, Summer 1974

CONSIDERATIONS FOR CRITICAL THINKING AND WRITING

1. According to Everett, why is it difficult to describe Eliot's tone in his poetry?

2. How does Eliot's tone make it difficult to make an autobiographical connection between Prufrock and Eliot?

3. How does Everett's reading of the relationship between Prufrock and Eliot differ from Schneider's in the preceding Perspective?

MICHAEL L. BAUMANN   (B. 1926)

Baumann takes a close look at the poem's images in his formalist efforts to make a point about Prufrock's character.

The "Overwhelming Question" for Prufrock   *1981*

Most critics . . . have seen the overwhelming question related to sex. . . . They have implicitly assumed — and given their readers to understand — that Prufrock's is the male's basic question: Can I?

    The poet and critic Delmore Schwartz once said that "J. Alfred Prufrock is unable to make love to women of his own class and kind because of shyness, self-consciousness, and fear of rejection."[1] This is undoubtedly true, but

---

[1] "T. S. Eliot as the International Hero," *Partisan Review,* 12 (1945), 202; rpt. in *T. S. Eliot: A Selected Critique,* ed. Leonard Unger (New York: Rinehart & Company, Inc., 1948), 46.

Prufrock's inability to *feel* love has something to do with his inability to *make* love, too. . . . A simple desire, lust, is more than honest Prufrock can cope with as he mounts the stairs.

But Prufrock is coping with another, less simple desire as well. . . . If birth, copulation, and death is all there is, then, once we are born, once we have copulated, only death remains (for the male of the species, at least). Prufrock, having "known them all already, known them all," having "known the evenings, mornings, afternoons," having "measured out" his life "with coffee spoons," desires death. The "overwhelming question" that assails him would no longer be the romantic rhetorical "Is life worth living?" (to which the answer is obviously No), but the more immediate shocker: "Should one commit suicide?" which is to say: "Should I?" . . .

. . . The poem makes clear that Prufrock wants more than the "entire destruction of consciousness as we understand it," a notion Prufrock expresses by wishing he were "a pair of ragged claws, / Scuttling across the floors of silent seas." Prufrock wants death itself, physical death, and the poem, I believe, is explicit about this desire.

Not only does Prufrock seem to be tired of time — "time yet for a hundred indecisions" — a tiredness that goes far beyond the acedia Prufrock is generally credited with feeling, if only because "there will be time to murder and create," time, in other words (in one sense at least) to copulate, but Prufrock is also tired of his own endless vanities, from feeling he must "prepare a face to meet the faces that you meet," to having to summon up those ironies with which to contemplate his own thin arms and legs, and, indeed, to asking if, in the rather tedious enterprise of preparing for copulation, the moment is worth "forcing to its crisis." No wonder Prufrock compares himself to John the Baptist and, in conjuring up this first concrete image of his own death, sees his head brought in upon a platter. That would be the easy way out. He had, after all, "wept and fasted, wept and prayed," but he realizes he is no prophet — and no Salome will burst into passion, will ignite for him. When the eternal Footman, Death, who holds his coat, snickers, he does so because Prufrock has let "the moment" of his "greatness" flicker, because Prufrock was unable to comply with the one imperative greatness would have thrust upon him: to kill himself. Prufrock explains: "I was afraid." Yet the achievement of his vision at the end of the poem, his being able to linger "in the chambers of the sea / By seagirls wreathed with seaweed red and brown," is an act of the imagination that only physical death can complete, unless Prufrock wants human voices to wake him, and drown him. His romantic vision demands the voluntary act: suicide. It is to be expected that he will fail in this too, as he has failed in everything else.

From "Let Us Ask 'What Is It,'" *Arizona Quarterly,* Spring 1981

CONSIDERATIONS FOR CRITICAL THINKING AND WRITING

1. Describe the evidence used by Baumann to argue that Prufrock contemplates suicide.
2. Explain in an essay why you do or do not find Baumann's argument convincing.

3. Later in his essay Baumann connects Prufrock's insistence that "No, I am not Prince Hamlet" with Hamlet's "To be or not to be" speech. How do you think this reference might be used to support Baumann's argument in this excerpt?

FREDERIK L. RUSCH (B. 1938)

Rusch makes use of the insights developed by Erich Fromm, a social psychologist who believed "psychic forces [are] a process of constant interaction between man's needs and the social and historical reality in which he participates."

Society and Character in
"The Love Song of J. Alfred Prufrock"   *1984*

In looking at fiction, drama, and poetry from the Frommian point of view, the critic understands literature to be social portrayal as well as character portrayal or personal statement. Society and character are inextricably joined. The Frommian approach opens up the study of literary work, giving a social context to its characters, which suggests why those characters behave as they do. The Frommian approach recognizes human beings for what they are — basically gregarious individuals who are interdependent upon each other, in need of each other, and thus, to a certain degree, products of their social environments, although those environments may be inimical to their mental well-being. That is, as stated earlier, the individual's needs and drives have a social component and are not purely biological. The Frommian approach to literature assumes that a writer is — at least by implication — analyzing society and its setting as well as character. . . .

In T. S. Eliot's "The Love Song of J. Alfred Prufrock," Prufrock is talking to himself, expressing a fantasy or daydream. In his monologue, Prufrock, as noted by Grover Smith, "is addressing, as if looking into a mirror, his whole public personality."[1] Throughout the poem, Prufrock is extremely self-conscious, believing that the people in his imaginary drawing room will examine him as a specimen insect, "sprawling on a pin, / . . . pinned and wriggling on the wall. . . ." Of course, self-consciousness — being conscious of one's self — is not necessarily neurotic. Indeed, it is part of being a human being. It is only when self-consciousness, which has always led man to feel a separation from nature, becomes obsessive that we have a problem. Prufrock is certainly obsessed with his self-consciousness, convinced that everyone notices his balding head, his clothes (his prudent frocks), his thin arms and legs.

[1] Grover Smith, *T. S. Eliot's Poetry and Plays: A Study in Sources and Meaning* (Chicago: U of Chicago P, 1962), 16.

On one level, however, Prufrock is merely expressing the pain that all human beings must feel. Although his problem is extreme, he is quite representative of the human race:

> Self-awareness, reason, and imagination have disrupted the "harmony" that characterizes animal existence. Their emergence has made man into an anomaly, the freak of the universe. He is part of nature, subject to her physical laws and unable to change them, yet he transcends nature. He is set apart while being a part; he is homeless, yet chained to the home he shares with all creatures. . . . Being aware of himself, he realizes his powerlessness and the limitations of his existence. He is never free from the dichotomy of his existence: he cannot rid himself of his mind, even if he would want to; he cannot rid himself of his body as long as he is alive — and his body makes him want to be alive.[2]

This is the predicament of the human being. His self-awareness has made him feel separate from nature. This causes pain and sorrow. What, then, is the solution to the predicament? Fromm believed that mankind filled the void of alienation from nature with the creation of a culture, a society: "Man's existential, and hence unavoidable disequilibrium can be relatively stable when he has found, with the support of his culture, a more or less adequate way of coping with his existential problems" (*Destructiveness* 225). But, unfortunately for Prufrock, his culture and society do not allow him to overcome his existential predicament. The fact is, he is bored by his modern, urban society.

In image after image, Prufrock's mind projects boredom:

> For I have known them all already, known them all:
> Have known the evenings, mornings, afternoons,
> I have measured out my life with coffee spoons. . . .
> . . . .
>
> And I have known the eyes already, known them all —
> . . . .
>
> Then how should I begin
> To spit out all the butt-ends of my days and ways?
> . . . .
>
> And I have known the arms already, known them all — . . . .

Prufrock is completely unstimulated by his social environment, to the point of near death. The evening in which he proposes to himself to make a social visit is "etherized upon a table." The fog, as a cat, falls asleep; it is "tired . . . or it malingers, / Stretched on the floor. . . ."

Prufrock, living in a city of "half-deserted streets, / . . . one-night cheap hotels / And sawdust restaurants with oyster-shells," gets no comfort, no nurturing from his environment. He is, in the words of Erich Fromm, a "modern mass man . . . isolated and lonely" (*Destructiveness* 107). He lives in a destructive environment. Instead of providing communion with fellow human beings, it alienates him through boredom. Such boredom leads to "a state of chronic depression" that can cause the pathology of "insufficient inner productivity"

---

[2] Erich Fromm, *The Anatomy of Human Destructiveness* (New York: Holt, Rinehart & Winston, 1973), 225.

in the individual (*Destructiveness* 243). Such a lack of productivity is voiced by Prufrock when he confesses that he is neither Hamlet nor John the Baptist.

An interesting tension in "The Love Song of J. Alfred Prufrock" is caused by the reader's knowledge that Prufrock understands his own predicament quite well. Although he calls himself a fool, he has wisdom about himself and his predicament. This, however, only reinforces his depression and frustration. In his daydream, he is able to reveal truths about himself that, while they lead to self-understanding, apparently cannot alleviate his problems in his waking life. The poem suggests no positive movement out of the predicament. Prufrock is like a patient cited by Fromm, who under hypnosis envisioned "a black barren place with many masks," and when asked what the vision meant said "that everything was dull, dull, dull; that the masks represent the different roles he takes to fool people into thinking he is feeling well" (*Destructiveness* 246). Likewise, Prufrock understands that "There will be time, there will be time / To prepare a face to meet the faces that you meet. . . ." But despite his understanding of the nature of his existence, he cannot attain a more productive life.

It was Fromm's belief that with boredom "the decisive conditions are to be found in the overall environmental situation. . . . It is highly probable that even cases of severe depression-boredom would be less frequent and less intense . . . in a society where a mood of hope and love of life predominated. But in recent decades the opposite is increasingly the case, and thus a fertile soil for the development of individual depressive states is provided" (*Destructiveness* 251). There is no "mood of hope and love of life" in Prufrock's society. Prufrock is a lonely man, as lonely as "the lonely men in shirt-sleeves, leaning out of windows" of his fantasy. His only solution is to return to the animal state that his race was in before evolving into human beings.

Animals are one with nature, not alienated from their environments. They *are* nature, unselfconscious. Prufrock would return to a preconscious existence in the extreme: "I should have been a pair of ragged claws / Scuttling across the floors of silent seas." Claws *without a head* surely would not be alienated, bored, or depressed. They would seek and would need no psychological nurturing from their environment. And in the end Prufrock's fantasy of becoming claws is definitely more positive for him than his life as a human being. He completes his monologue with depressing irony, to say the least: it is with human voices waking us, bringing us back to human society, that we drown.

> From "Approaching Literature through the Social Psychology of
> Erich Fromm" in *Psychological Perspectives on Literature:
> Freudian Dissidents and Non-Freudians,* edited by Joseph Natoli

CONSIDERATIONS FOR CRITICAL THINKING AND WRITING

1. According to Rusch, why is Fromm's approach useful for understanding Prufrock's character as well as his social context?

2. In what ways is Prufrock "representative of the human race" (para. 3)? Is he like any other characters you have read about in this anthology? Explain your response.

3. In an essay consider how Rusch's analysis of Prufrock might be used to support Baumann's argument that Prufrock's "overwhelming question" is whether or not he should kill himself (p. 1223).

ROBERT SWARD (B. 1933)

Sward, a poet, provides a detailed explication, framed by his own personal experiences during the Korean War.

A Personal Analysis of "The Love Song of J. Alfred Prufrock"   1996

In 1952, sailing to Korea as a U.S. Navy librarian for Landing Ship Tank 914, I read T. S. Eliot's "The Love Song of J. Alfred Prufrock." Ill-educated, a product of Chicago's public-school system, I was nineteen-years-old and, awakened by Whitman, Eliot, and Williams, had just begun writing poetry. I was also reading all the books I could get my hands on.

    Eliot had won the Nobel Prize in 1948 and, curious, I was trying to make sense of poems like "Prufrock" and "The Waste Land."

    "What do you know about T. S. Eliot?" I asked a young officer who'd been to college and studied English literature. I knew from earlier conversations that we shared an interest in what he called "modern poetry." A yeoman third class, two weeks at sea and bored, I longed for someone to talk to. "T. S. Eliot was born in St. Louis, Missouri, but he lives now in England and is studying to become an Englishman," the officer said, tapping tobacco into his pipe. "The 'T. S.' stands for 'tough shit.' You read Eliot's 'Love Song of J. Alfred Prufrock,' what one English prof called 'the first poem of the modern movement,' and if you don't understand it, 'tough shit.' All I can say is that's some love song."

    An anthology of poetry open before us, we were sitting in the ship's all-metal, eight by eight-foot library eating bologna sandwiches and drinking coffee. Fortunately, the captain kept out of sight and life on the slow-moving (eight to ten knots), flat-bottomed amphibious ship was unhurried and anything but formal.

    "Then why does Eliot bother calling it a love song?" I asked, as the ship rolled and the coffee sloshed onto a steel table. The tight metal room smelled like a cross between a diesel engine and a New York deli.

    "Eliot's being ironic, sailor. 'Prufrock' is the love song of a sexually repressed and horny man who has no one but himself to sing to." Drawing on his pipe, the officer scratched his head. "Like you and I, Mr. Prufrock is a lonely man on his way to a war zone. We're sailing to Korea and we know the truth, don't we? We may never make it back. Prufrock marches like a brave soldier to a British drawing room that, he tells us, may be the death of him. He's a mock heroic figure who sings of mermaids and peaches and drowning."

    Pointing to lines 129–31, the officer read aloud:

> We have lingered in the chambers of the sea
> By seagirls wreathed with seaweed red and brown,
> Till human voices wake us and we drown.

    "Prufrock is also singing because he's a poet. Prufrock *is* T. S. Eliot and, the truth is, Eliot is so much like Prufrock that he has to distance himself from his creation. That's why he gives the man that pompous name. Did you know

'Tough Shit,' as a young man, sometimes signed himself 'T. Stearns Eliot'? You have to see the humor — the irony — in 'Prufrock' to understand the poem."

"I read it, I hear it in my head, but I still don't get it," I confessed. "What is 'Prufrock' about?"

"'Birth, death and copulation, that's all there is.' That's what Eliot himself says. Of course the poem also touches on aging, social status, and fashion."

"Aging and fashion?" I asked.

The officer threw back his head and recited:

(They will say: "How his hair is growing thin!")
My morning coat, my collar mounting firmly to the chin,
My necktie rich and modest, but asserted by a simple pin.

He paused, then went on:

I grow old . . . I grow old . . .
I shall wear the bottoms of my trousers rolled.

"At the time the poem was written it was fashionable for young men to roll their trousers. In lines 120–21, Thomas Stearns Prufrock is laughing at himself for being middle-aged and vain.

"Anyway, 'The Love Song of J. Alfred Prufrock' is an interior monologue," said the officer, finishing his bologna sandwich and washing it down with dark rum. Wiping mustard from his mouth, he continued. "The whole thing takes place in J. Alfred Prufrock's head. That's clear, isn't it?"

I had read [Robert] Browning's "My Last Duchess" and understood about interior monologues.

"Listen, sailor: Prufrock thinks about drawing rooms, but he never actually sets foot in one. Am I right?"

"Yeah," I said after rereading the first ten lines. "I think so."

"The poem is about what goes through Prufrock's mind on his way to some upper-class drawing room. It's a foggy evening in October, and what Mr. Prufrock really needs is a drink. He's a tightass Victorian, a lonely teetotaling intellectual. Anyone else would forget the toast and marmalade and step into a pub and ask for a pint of beer."

Setting down his pipe, the naval officer opened the flask and refilled our coffee mugs.

"Every time I think I know what 'Prufrock' means it turns out to mean something else," I said. "Eliot uses too many symbols. Why doesn't he just say what he means?"

"The city — 'the lonely men in shirt-sleeves' and the 'one-night cheap hotels' — are masculine," said the officer. "That's what cities are like, aren't they: ugly and oppressive. What's symbolic — or should I say, what's obscure — about that?"

"Nothing," I said. "That's the easy part — Prufrock walking along like that."

"Okay," said the officer. "And in contrast to city streets, you've got the oppressive drawing room that, in Prufrock's mind, is feminine — 'Arms that are braceleted and white and bare' and 'the marmalade, the tea, / Among the porcelain, among some talk of you and me.'" Using a pencil, the officer underlined those images in the paperback anthology.

"You ever been to a tea party, Sward?"

"No, sir, I haven't. Not like Prufrock's."

"Well," said the officer, "I have and I have a theory about that 'overwhelming question' Prufrock wants to ask in line 10 — and again in line 93. Twice in the poem we hear about an 'overwhelming question.' What do you think he's getting at with that 'overwhelming question,' sailor?"

"Prufrock wants to ask the women what they're doing with their lives, but he's afraid they'll laugh at him," I said.

"Guess again, Sward," he said leaning back in his chair, stretching his arms.

"What's your theory, sir?"

"Sex," said the officer. "On the one hand, it's true, he wants to fit in and play the game because, after all, he's privileged. He belongs in the drawing room with the clever Englishwomen. At the same time he fantasizes. If he could, I think he'd like to shock them. Prufrock longs to put down his dainty porcelain teacup and shout, 'I am Lazarus, come from the dead, / Come back to tell you all, I shall tell you all.'"

"Why doesn't he do it?" I asked.

"Because Prufrock is convinced no matter what he says he won't reach them. He feels the English gentlewomen he's dealing with are unreachable. He believes his situation is as hopeless as theirs. He's dead and they're dead, too. That's why the poem begins with an image of sickness, 'a patient etherized upon a table,' and ends with people drowning. Prufrock is tough shit, man."

"You said you think there's a connection between Eliot the poet and J. Alfred Prufrock," I said.

"Of course there's a connection. Tommy Eliot from St. Louis, Missouri," said the officer. "Try as he will, he doesn't fit in. His English friends call him 'The American' and laugh. Tom Eliot the outsider with his rolled umbrella. T. S. Eliot is a self-conscious, make-believe Englishman and you have to understand that to understand 'Prufrock.'

"The poem is dark and funny at the same time. It's filled with humor and Prufrock is capable of laughing at himself. Just read those lines, 'Is it perfume from a dress / That makes me so digress?'"

"You were talking about Prufrock being sexually attracted to the women. How could that be if he is, as you say, 'dead.'" I asked.

"By 'dead' I mean desolate, inwardly barren, godforsaken. Inwardly, spiritually, Prufrock is a desolate creature. He's a moral man, he's a civilized man, but he's also hollow. But there's hope for him. In spite of himself, Prufrock is drawn to women.

"Look at line 64. He's attracted and repelled. Prufrock attends these teas, notices the women's arms 'downed with light brown hair!' and it scares the hell out of him because what he longs to do is to get them onto a drawing-room floor or a beach somewhere and bury his face in that same wonderfully tantalizing 'light brown hair.' What do you think of that, sailor?"

"I think you're right, sir."

"Then tell me this, Mr. Sward: Why doesn't he ask the overwhelming question? Hell, man, maybe it's not sexual. Maybe I'm wrong. Maybe what he wants to do is to ask some question like what you yourself suggested: 'What's the point in going on living when, in some sense, we're all already dead?'"

"I think he doesn't ask the question because he's so repressed, sir. He longs for physical contact, like you say, but he also wants another kind of intimacy, and he's afraid to ask for it and it's making him crazy."

"That's right, sailor. He's afraid. Eliot wrote the poem in 1911 when women were beginning to break free."

"Break free of what?" I asked.

"Of the prim and proper Victorian ideal. Suffragettes, feminists they called themselves. At the time Eliot wrote 'Prufrock,' women in England and America were catching on to the fact that they were disfranchised and had begun fighting for the right to vote, among other things, and for liberation, equality with men.

"Of course Prufrock is more prim and proper than the bored, overcivilized women in the poem. And it's ironic, isn't it, that he doesn't understand that the women are one step ahead of him. What you have in Prufrock is a man who tries to reconcile the image of real women with 'light brown hair' on their arms with some ideal, women who are a cross between the goddess Juno and a sweet Victorian maiden."

"Prufrock seems to know pretty well what he's feeling," I said. "He's not a liar and he's not a coward. To be honest, sir, I identify with Prufrock. He may try on one mask or another, but he ends up removing the mask and exposing himself."

"Now, about interior monologues: to understand 'Prufrock' you have to understand that most poems have one or more speakers and an audience, implied or otherwise. Let's go back to line 1. Who is this 'you and I' Eliot writes about?"

"Prufrock is talking to both his inner self and the reader," I said.

"How do you interpret the first ten lines?" the officer asked, pointing with his pencil.

"'Let us go then, you and I,' he's saying, let us stroll, somnolent and numb as a sedated patient, through these seedy 'half-deserted streets, / The muttering retreats / Of restless nights in one-night cheap hotels.'"

"That's it, sailor. And while one might argue that Prufrock 'wakes' at the end of the poem, he is for the most part a ghostly inhabitant of a world that is, for him, a sort of hell. He is like the speaker in the Italian epigraph from Dante's *Inferno,* who says, essentially, 'Like you, reader, I'm in purgatory and there is no way out. Nobody ever escapes from this pit and, for that reason, I can speak the truth without fear of ill fame.'

"Despairing and sick of heart, Prufrock is a prisoner. Trapped in himself and trapped in society, he attends another and another in an endless series of effete, decorous teas.

In the room the women come and go
Talking of Michelangelo.

"Do you get it now? Do you see what I mean when I say 'tough shit'?" said the officer.

"Yeah, I'm beginning to," I said.

"T. S. Eliot's 'Prufrock' has become so much a part of the English language that people who have never read the poem are familiar with phrases like 'I have measured out my life with coffee spoons' and 'I grow old . . . I grow old . . . / I shall wear the bottoms of my trousers rolled' and 'Do I dare to eat a peach?' and 'In the room the women come and go.'

"Do you get it now? Eliot's irregularly rhymed, 131-line interior monologue has become part of the monologue all of us carry on in our heads. We are all of us, whether we know it or not, love-hungry, sex-crazed soldiers and sailors, brave, bored and lonely. At some level in our hearts, we are all J. Alfred Prufrock, every one of us, and we are all sailing into a war zone from which, as the last line of the poem implies, we may never return."

From "T. S. Eliot's 'Love Song of J. Alfred Prufrock'" in *Touchstones: American Poets on a Favorite Poem,* edited by Robert Pack and Jay Parini

CONSIDERATIONS FOR CRITICAL THINKING AND WRITING

1. How satisfactory is this reading of the poem? Are any significant portions of the poem left out of this reading?

2. Compare the tone of this critical approach to any other in this chapter. Explain why you prefer one over another.

3. Using Sward's personal approach, write an analysis of a poem of your choice in this anthology.

SUGGESTED TOPICS FOR LONGER PAPERS

1. "The Love Song of J. Alfred Prufrock" has proved to be popular among generations of college students who are fond of quoting bits of the poem. What do you think accounts for that popularity among your own generation? Alternatively, why doesn't this poem speak to your concerns or those of your generation?

2. Of the five critical perspectives on the poem provided in this chapter, which did you find to be the most satisfying reading? Explain your response by describing how your choice opened up the poem more than the other four perspectives.

38

A THEMATIC CASE STUDY
Love and Longing

National Portrait Gallery,
London.

For a man to become a poet . . .
he must be in love or miserable.

— GEORGE GORDON, LORD BYRON

Behind all of the elements that make up a poem, and even behind its cultural contexts and critical reception, lies its theme. Its idea and the point around which the entire poem revolves, the theme is ultimately what we respond to — or fail to respond to. All of the other elements, in fact, are typically there to contribute to the theme, whether or not that theme is explicitly stated. Reading thematically means extending what you have learned about the analysis of individual elements at work in the poem to make connections between the text and the world we inhabit.

This chapter, organized into a case study on love poems, focuses on a single theme as it reappears throughout various parts of poetic history. These poems have much to say about human experience — experience that is contradictory, confusing, complicated, and fascinating. You'll find diverse perspectives from different historical, cultural, generational, or political moments. You'll also discover writers who aim to entertain, to describe, to convince, and to complain. After reading these poems in the context of one another, you're

Web Research the
poets in this chapter at
bedfordstmartins.com/
meyerlit.

likely to come away with a richer understanding of how the themes of love play out in your own life.

Poems about love have probably enchanted and intrigued their hearers since people began making poetry. Like poetry itself, love is, after all, about intensity, acute impressions, and powerful responsibilities. The emotional dimensions of love do not lend themselves to analytic expository essays. Although such writing can be satisfying intellectually, it is most inadequate for evoking and capturing the thick excitement and swooning reveries that love engenders. The poems in this section include spiritual as well as physical explorations of love that range over five centuries. As you'll see, poetic responses to love by men and women can be quite similar as well as different from one another, just as poems from different periods can reflect a variety of values and attitudes toward love. It is indeed an engaging theme — but as you read, don't forget to pay attention to the formal elements of each of these selections and how they work together to create the poem's particular points about love. Also, remember to read not only for the presence of love; many other themes can be found in these works, and many other connections can be made to the literature elsewhere in this anthology.

The oldest love poem in this case study, Christopher Marlowe's "The Passionate Shepherd to His Love," opens with the line, "Come live with me and be my love." This famous pastoral lyric set a tone for love poetry that has been replicated since its publication. Before concluding with "Then live with me and be my love," Marlowe embraces the kinds of generous pleasure that readers have traditionally and happily received for centuries. The feelings, if not the particular images, are likely to be quite familiar to you.

CHRISTOPHER MARLOWE (1564–1593)

The Passionate Shepherd to His Love   1599?

Come live with me and be my love,
And we will all the pleasure prove
That valleys, groves, hills, and fields,
Woods, or steepy mountain yields.

And we will sit upon the rocks,   5
Seeing the shepherds feed their flocks,
By shallow rivers to whose falls
Melodious birds sing madrigals.

And I will make thee beds of roses
And a thousand fragrant posies,   10
A cap of flowers, and a kirtle°   *dress or skirt*
Embroidered all with leaves of myrtle;

A gown made of the finest wool
Which from our pretty lambs we pull;
Fair lined slippers for the cold,   15
With buckles of the purest gold;

A belt of straw and ivy buds,
With coral clasps and amber studs:
And if these pleasures may thee move,
Come live with me, and be my love.   20

The shepherd swains shall dance and sing
For thy delight each May morning:
If these delights thy mind may move,
Then live with me and be my love.

CONSIDERATIONS FOR CRITICAL THINKING AND WRITING

1. **FIRST RESPONSE.** How persuasive do you find the shepherd's arguments to
   his potential lover?

2. What do you think might be the equivalent of the shepherd's arguments in
   the twenty-first century? What kinds of appeals and images of love would
   be made by a contemporary lover?

3. Try writing a response to the shepherd from the female's point of view
   using Marlowe's rhythms, rhyme scheme, and quatrains.

CONNECTION TO ANOTHER SELECTION

1. Read Sir Walter Raleigh's "The Nymph's Reply to the Shepherd" (p. 1339).
   How does the nymph's response compare with your imagined reply?

While Marlowe's shepherd focuses his energies on convincing his potential love to join him (in the delights associated with love), the speaker in
the following sonnet by William Shakespeare demonstrates his love for poetry as well and focuses on the beauty of the object of the poem. In doing
so, he introduces a theme that has become a perennial challenge to love —
the corrosive, destructive nature of what Shakespeare shockingly calls
"sluttish time." His resolution of this issue is intriguing: see if you agree
with it.

WILLIAM SHAKESPEARE (1564–1616)
Not marble, nor the gilded monuments   1609

Not marble, nor the gilded monuments
Of princes, shall outlive this powerful rhyme;
But you shall shine more bright in these conténts
Than unswept stone, besmeared with sluttish time.
When wasteful war shall statues overturn,   5

And broils root out the work of masonry,
Nor Mars his° swords nor war's quick fire shall burn   *possessive of Mars*
The living record of your memory.
'Gainst death and all-oblivious enmity
Shall you pace forth; your praise shall still find room   10
Even in the eyes of all posterity
That wear this world out to the ending doom.
   So, till the judgment that yourself arise,
   You live in this, and dwell in lovers' eyes.

CONSIDERATIONS FOR CRITICAL THINKING AND WRITING

1. **FIRST RESPONSE.** What do you think is the central point of this poem? Explain whether you agree or disagree with its theme.
2. How does "sluttish time" (line 4) represent the poem's major conflict?
3. Consider whether this poem is more about the poet's loved one or the poet's love of his own poetry.

CONNECTIONS TO OTHER SELECTIONS

1. Compare the theme of this poem with that of Andrew Marvell's "To His Coy Mistress" (p. 812), paying particular attention to the speaker's beliefs about how time affects love.
2. Discuss whether you find this love poem more or less appealing than Marlowe's "The Passionate Shepherd to His Love." As you make this comparison, explain what the criteria for an appealing love poem should be.

As Shakespeare's speaker presents a love that will withstand the destruction of time, Anne Bradstreet's "To My Dear and Loving Husband" evokes a marital love that confirms a connection that transcends space and matter as well as time. Although Bradstreet wrote more than three centuries ago, such devotion remains undated for many (but, of course, not all) readers of love poetry. She begins, naturally enough, with the pleasure and paradox of how two people can be one.

ANNE BRADSTREET (c. 1612–1672)

To My Dear and Loving Husband   *1678*

If ever two were one, then surely we.
If ever man were loved by wife, then thee;
If ever wife was happy in a man,
Compare with me, ye women, if you can.
I prize thy love more than whole mines of gold   5
Or all the riches that the East doth hold.

My love is such that rivers cannot quench,
Nor ought but love from thee, give recompense.
Thy love is such I can no way repay,
The heavens reward thee manifold, I pray.   10
Then while we live, in love let's so persevere
That when we live no more, we may live ever.

CONSIDERATIONS FOR CRITICAL THINKING AND WRITING

1. **FIRST RESPONSE.** Describe the poem's tone. Is it what you'd expect from a seventeenth-century Puritan? Why or why not?

2. Explain whether Bradstreet's devotion is directed more toward her husband here on earth or toward the eternal rewards of heaven.

3. What is the paradox of the final line? How is it resolved?

CONNECTION TO ANOTHER SELECTION

1. How does the theme of this poem compare with that of Bradstreet's "Before the Birth of One of Her Children" (p. 1317)? Explain why you find the poems consistent or contradictory.

The remaining poems in this case study are modern and contemporary pieces that both maintain and revise the perspectives on love provided by Marlowe, Shakespeare, and Bradstreet. As you read them, consider what each adds to your understanding of the others and of love in general.

ELIZABETH BARRETT BROWNING (1806–1861)

How Do I Love Thee?
Let Me Count the Ways   *1850*

How do I love thee? Let me count the ways.
I love thee to the depth and breadth and height
My soul can reach, when feeling out of sight
For the ends of being and ideal grace.
I love thee to the level of every day's   5
Most quiet need, by sun and candle-light.
I love thee freely, as men strive for right.
I love thee purely, as they turn from praise.
I love thee with the passion put to use
In my old griefs, and with my childhood's faith.   10
I love thee with a love I seemed to lose
With my lost saints. I love thee with the breath,
Smiles, tears, of all my life; and, if God choose,
I shall but love thee better after death.

CONSIDERATIONS FOR CRITICAL THINKING AND WRITING

1. **FIRST RESPONSE.** This poem has remained extraordinarily popular for more than 150 years. Why do you think it has been so often included in collections of love poems? What is its appeal? Does it speak to a contemporary reader? To you?

2. Comment on the effect of the diction. What kind of tone does it create?

3. Would you characterize this poem as having a religious theme — or is love a substitute for religion?

CONNECTION TO ANOTHER SELECTION

1. Compare and contrast the images, tone, and theme of this poem with those of Christina Rossetti's "Promises Like Pie-Crust" (p. 1343). Explain why you find one poem more promising than the other.

EDNA ST. VINCENT MILLAY (1892–1950)

Recuerdo° 1922

We were very tired, we were very merry —
We had gone back and forth all night on the
    ferry.
It was bare and bright, and smelled like a
    stable —
But we looked into a fire, we leaned across a
    table,
We lay on a hill-top underneath the moon;   5
And the whistles kept blowing, and the dawn
    came soon.

We were very tired, we were very merry —
We had gone back and forth all night on the ferry;
And you ate an apple, and I ate a pear,
From a dozen of each we had bought somewhere;   10
And the sky went wan, and the wind came cold,
And the sun rose dripping, a bucketful of gold.

We were very tired, we were very merry,
We had gone back and forth all night on the ferry.
We hailed, "Good morrow, mother!" to a shawl-covered head,   15
And bought a morning paper, which neither of us read;
And she wept, "God bless you!" for the apples and pears,
And we gave her all our money but our subway fares.

Recuerdo: I remember (Spanish).

CONSIDERATIONS FOR CRITICAL THINKING AND WRITING

1. **FIRST RESPONSE.** This poem was a very popular representation of New York City bohemian life in Greenwich Village during the 1920s. What do you think made "Recuerdo" so appealing then?

2. How does the repetition in the first two lines of each stanza connect sound to sense through the rhythm of the lines?

3. Explain how love and generosity are evoked in the poem.

CONNECTION TO ANOTHER SELECTION

1. Discuss how the couple in this poem essentially follows the advice provided in the next selection, E. E. Cummings's "since feeling is first."

E. E. CUMMINGS (1894–1962)

since feeling is first   1926

since feeling is first
who pays any attention
to the syntax of things
will never wholly kiss you;

wholly to be a fool   5
while Spring is in the world

my blood approves,
and kisses are a better fate
than wisdom
lady i swear by all flowers. Don't cry   10
—the best gesture of my brain is less than
your eyelids' flutter which says

we are for each other:then
laugh,leaning back in my arms
for life's not a paragraph   15

And death i think is no parenthesis

CONSIDERATIONS FOR CRITICAL THINKING AND WRITING

1. **FIRST RESPONSE.** What is the speaker's initial premise? Why is it crucial to his argument? What is his argument?

2. Does this poem fit into the *carpe diem* tradition? How?

3. How are nature and society presented as being in conflict? Why is this relevant to the speaker's argument?

4. List and describe the grammatical metaphors in the poem. How do they further the speaker's argument?

CONNECTIONS TO OTHER SELECTIONS

1. Contrast the theme of this poem with that of Marlowe's "The Passionate Shepherd to His Love" (p. 1233). How do you account for the differences, in both style and content, between the two love poems?

2. Discuss attitudes toward "feeling" in this poem and in Molly Peacock's "Desire" (p. 979).

Mark Doty (b. 1953)

The Embrace   1998

© Kenneth Chen.

You weren't well or really ill yet
    either;
just a little tired, your handsomeness
tinged by grief or anticipation,
    which brought
to your face a thoughtful, deepening
    grace.

I didn't for a moment doubt you
    were dead.   5
I knew that to be true still, even in
    the dream.
You'd been out — at work maybe? —
having a good day, almost energetic.

We seemed to be moving from some old house
where we'd lived, boxes everywhere, things   10
in disarray: that was the *story* of my dream,
but even asleep I was shocked out of narrative

by your face, the physical fact of your face:
inches from mine, smooth-shaven, loving, alert.
Why so difficult, remembering the actual look   15
of you? Without a photograph, without strain?

So when I saw your unguarded, reliable face,
your unmistakable gaze opening all the warmth
and clarity of you — warm brown tea — we held
each other for the time the dream allowed.   20

Bless you. You came back, so I could see you
once more, plainly, so I could rest against you
without thinking this happiness lessened anything,
without thinking you were alive again.

Considerations for Critical Thinking and Writing

1. **First response.** In what sense can "The Embrace" be read as a love poem? Explain why it does or doesn't fit your definition of a love poem.

2. Describe the tone of each of the stanzas and trace your emotional response to them as you move through the poem. What is your emotional reaction to the entire poem?

3. Describe the relation between death and love in the poem. How is that relation central to the theme?

JOAN MURRAY (B. 1945)
Play-by-Play   *1997*

Yaddo°

Would it surprise the young men
playing softball on the hill to hear the women
on the terrace admiring their bodies:
the slim waist of the pitcher, the strength
of the runner's legs, the torso of the catcher   5
rising off his knees to toss the ball back to the mound?
Would it embarrass them
to hear two women, sitting together after dinner,
praising even their futile motions:
the flex of a batter's hips   10
before his missed swing, the wide-spread stride
of a man picked off his base, the intensity
on the new man's face
as he waits on deck and fans the air?

Would it annoy them, the way some women   15
take offense when men caress them with their eyes?
And why should it surprise me that these women,
well past sixty, haven't put aside desire
but sit at ease and in pleasure,
watching the young men move above the rose garden   20
where the marble Naiads
pose and yawn in their fountain?
Who better than these women, with their sweaters
draped across their shoulders, their perspectives
honed from years of lovers, to recognize   25
the beauty that would otherwise
go unnoticed on this hill?
And will it compromise their pleasure
if I sit down at their table to listen
to the play-by-play and see it through their eyes?   30

Would it distract the young men if they realized
that three women laughing softly on the terrace
above closed books and half-filled wineglasses
are moving beside them on the field?
Would they want to know how they've been   35
held to the light till some motion or expression
showed the unsuspected loveliness
in a common shape or face?
Wouldn't they have liked to see how they looked
down there, as they stood for a moment at the plate,   40

Yaddo: An artist's colony in Saratoga Springs, New York.

bathed in the light of perfect expectation,
before their shadows lengthened, before they
walked together up the darkened hill,
so beautiful they would not have
recognized themselves?   45

CONSIDERATIONS FOR CRITICAL THINKING AND WRITING

1. **FIRST RESPONSE.** How would you answer the series of nine questions posed by the speaker?
2. What do you think the young men would have to say to the older women gazing at them?
3. Explain how the "marble Naiads" (line 21) help to set the tone.
4. Discuss the significance of the title.

CONNECTION TO ANOTHER SELECTION

1. Write an essay on the nature of desire in this poem and in Molly Peacock's "Desire" (p. 979).

BILLIE BOLTON (B. 1950)

Memorandum   2004

TO: My Boyfriend from Hell
FR: Me
RE: Shit I Never Want to Hear Another Word About as Long as I Live

1. Your Addled Thoughts. Anything about your ongoing interest in Lucy Liu's legs, Shania Twain's bellybutton, or Reese Witherspoon's whatever; your must-see TV dramas, your fantasy baseball addiction, or your addictions period. Anything about going anywhere with you at any time including, but not limited to: Sam's Club, Big Lots, Waffle House,

Photograph courtesy of Ashley G. Stollar.

church fish fries, local snake round-ups or Amvet turkey shoots, unless you promise to be the turkey.

2. Your Wireless Connection. Anything about your stage-four cell phone habit; the dames who have your cell phone number and why; who's on your speed-dial list or who left a voice mail message; anything about cell phone rebates, late fees, roaming charges, contracts or dropping your cell phone in the john by accident, even if you flush it and walk away.

3. Your Adolescent Only Child. Anything about his bed-wetting or fire-setting habits; his gang affiliation, court dates or swastika tattoo; anything about his tantrums, seizures or deep psychological need for video games and fruit roll-ups; anything about his pathological grudge against mankind or his particular beef against me.

4. Your Significant Others (female). Anything about the redneck redhead you banged in high school, the long-haired potheads you balled in your hippie days, the white trash airhead you married or the blue-haired battle-ax who pats you on the rump and pays for your dinner. Anything about your devotion to your long-suffering mother, your loopy sisters, or even the Blessed Virgin.

CONSIDERATIONS FOR CRITICAL THINKING AND WRITING

1. FIRST RESPONSE. What makes this a poem rather than simply a memo?
2. How does the speaker's diction and choice of details reveal her own personality?
3. CREATIVE RESPONSE. Using Bolton's style, tone, and form as inspiration, write a reply from the boyfriend's point of view.

CONNECTION TO ANOTHER SELECTION

1. Compare the use of descriptive detail to create tone in "Memorandum" and in Michelle Boisseau's "Self-Pity's Closet" (p. 1287)

MICHAEL RYAN (B. 1946)

Bunny   2004

In the scarred desk behind me
in history class,
she lulled her nyloned knee
against my ass,

its message pressing home   5
as dully we went
from the interminable Fall of Rome
to the Council of Trent

and through the even duller
steel town afternoons,   10
locked in a collar
of dim green rooms,

old nuns, and ever new
bewilderment
1962.   15
Like the hood ornament

on some chopped down hot rod
of the apocalypse,
above the blackboard stood
the crucifix   20

flanked on either slope
of its tiny Calvary
by color headshots of the Pope
and John F. Kennedy—

an arrangement meant to convey   25
not thievery being done
but God's work every day
by The Two Johns

drawing us like dynamos
through them to heaven   30
while we shook in our rows
as if on toboggans.

So what if we had known
what JFK was doing
in Laos and Vietnam,   35
and who he was screwing

(including the teenage mistress
of the head of the Mafia,
delivered to the White House
like a midnight pizza)?   40

The greater world to me,
present and past,
was the space between Bunny's knee
and my ass,

and I needed it collapsed   45
as soon as class began.
So what that I thought she had
the brains of a pecan,

mascara so black and thick
she must have smeared it on   50
with a popsicle stick,
and a nickname incredibly dumb?

Each day when she had helped me
annihilate an hour,
and we were going away,   55
I'd stare at her,

and she'd stare back and wink
I know you live off it:
one flashlight blink
at the bottom of a pit.   60

CONSIDERATIONS FOR CRITICAL THINKING AND WRITING

1. **FIRST RESPONSE.** How does the speaker's diction reveal his sensibilities?
   How would you describe him?

2. How does the speaker characterize his Catholic school? Are the images he uses to describe it nostalgic and sentimental? Explain why or why not.

3. What do you think are his feelings for Bunny?

CONNECTIONS TO OTHER SELECTIONS

1. Discuss the treatment of time in this poem and in Shakespeare's "Not marble, nor the gilded monuments" (p. 1234).

2. Compare the speaker's tribute to Bunny with the speaker's devotion in Browning's "How Do I Love Thee? Let Me Count the Ways" (p. 1236). Which poem do you find more moving and convincing? Why?

SUGGESTED TOPICS FOR LONGER PAPERS

1. Choose one of the love poems in this chapter and compare its themes with the lyrics of a contemporary love song in terms of poetic elements such as diction, tone, images, figures of speech, sounds, and rhythms.

2. Select any two poems from this chapter that were published before 1900 and compare them in style and theme with two poems published after 1900. Which set of poems, the early or the later, comes closest to representing your own sensibilities concerning love? Explain why.

39

A THEMATIC CASE STUDY
Humor and Satire

I think like a poet, and behave like a poet. Occasionally I need to sit in the corner for bad behavior.
— GARY SOTO

© Gary Soto.

There is nothing wrong with a poetry that is entertaining and easy to understand.
— CHARLES BUKOWSKI

© Beinecke Library, Yale University.

Poetry can be a hoot. There are plenty of poets that leave you smiling, grinning, chuckling, and laughing out loud because they use language that is witty, surprising, teasing, or satirical. Occasionally, their subject matter is simply wacky. There's a poem in this chapter, for example, titled "Commercial Leech Farming Today" (p. 1258), that deftly squeezes humor out of bloodsucking leeches grown for treating surgical patients. Although the material might not sound promising, Thomas Lux's treatment shapes this unlikely topic into a memorable satiric theme.

Sadly, however, poetry is too often burdened with a reputation for only being formal and serious, and readers sometimes show their deference by feeling intimidated and humbled in its earnest, weighty presence. After all, poetry frequently concerns itself with matters of great consequence: its themes contemplate subjects such as God and immortality, love and death, war and peace, injustice and outrage, racism and societal ills, deprivation and disease, alienation and angst, totalitarianism and terrorism, as well as a host of other tragic grievances and agonies that humanity might suffer. For readers of *The Onion,* a widely distributed satirical newspaper also available online, this prevailing grim reputation is humorously framed in a bogus story about National Poetry Month, celebrated each April to increase an awareness of the value of poetry in American life. The brief article (April 27, 2005) quotes a speaker at a fund-raising meeting of the "American Poetry Prevention Society" who cautions that "we must stop this scourge before more lives are exposed to poetry." He warns that "young people, particularly morose high-school and college students, are very susceptible to this terrible affliction." *The Onion*'s satire peels away the erroneous assumption that sorrow and tears are the only appropriate responses to a poetry "infection."

Poetry — at least in its clichéd popular form — is nearly always morosely dressed in black and rarely smiles. This severe image of somber profundity unfortunately tailors our expectations so that we assume that serious poetry cannot be playful and even downright funny or, putting the issue another way, that humorous poetry cannot be thoughtful and significant. The poems in this chapter demonstrate that serious poems can be funny and that comic poems can be thoughtful. Their humor, sometimes subtle, occasionally even savage, will serve to remind you that laughter engenders thought as well as pleasure.

FLEUR ADCOCK (B. 1934)

The Video

When Laura was born, Ceri watched.
They all gathered around Mum's bed —
Dad and the midwife and Mum's sister
and Ceri. "Move over a bit," Dad said —
he was trying to focus the camcorder   5
on Mum's legs and the baby's head.

After she had a little sister,
and Mum had gone back to being thin,
and was twice as busy, Ceri played
the video again and again.   10
She watched Laura come out, and then,
in reverse, she made her go back in.

CONSIDERATIONS FOR CRITICAL THINKING AND WRITING

1. **FIRST RESPONSE.** How does the humor in the final line produce the theme?

2. Discuss the appropriateness of Adcock's choice of "watched" in lines 1 and 11. What does the word suggest about Ceri?

3. How does the rhyme scheme affect your reading of the poem?

JOHN CIARDI (1916–1986)

Suburban   *1978*

Yesterday Mrs. Friar phoned. "Mr. Ciardi,
   how do you do?" she said. "I am sorry to say
this isn't exactly a social call. The fact is
   your dog has just deposited — forgive me —
a large repulsive object in my petunias."   5

I thought to ask, "Have you checked the rectal grooving
   for a positive I.D.?" My dog, as it happened,
was in Vermont with my son, who had gone fishing —
   if that's what one does with a girl, two cases of beer,
and a borrowed camper. I guessed I'd get no trout.   10

But why lose out on organic gold for a wise crack?
   "Yes, Mrs. Friar," I said, "I understand."
"Most kind of you," she said. "Not at all," I said.
   I went with a spade. She pointed, looking away.
"I always have loved dogs," she said, "but really!"   15

I scooped it up and bowed. "The animal of it.
   I hope this hasn't upset you, Mrs. Friar."
"Not really," she said, "but really!" I bore the turd
   across the line to my own petunias
and buried it till the glorious resurrection   20

when even these suburbs shall give up their dead.

CONSIDERATIONS FOR CRITICAL THINKING AND WRITING

1. **FIRST RESPONSE.** How does the speaker transform Mrs. Friar into a symbolic figure of the suburbs?
2. Why do you suppose Ciardi focuses on this particular incident to make a comment on the suburbs? What is the speaker's attitude toward suburban life?
3. **CREATIVE RESPONSE.** Write a one-paragraph physical description of Mrs. Friar that captures her character.

CONNECTION TO ANOTHER SELECTION

1. Compare the speakers' voices in "Suburban" and in John Updike's "Dog's Death" (p. 746).

DAISY FRIED (B. 1967)

Wit's End   *2000*

My father says, "Face it, you live
   in a civilization of mirrors and sinks,"
      invading my real room, the bathroom.

I pull down an eyelid till I see the pained
    pink meniscus underneath. I "O"
        my mouth, poke the mascara wand   5

at my eyelashes, not missing
    by much. It's makeup's premonition
        of sex in the house he can't stand.

The bathroom's littered with eyeliners,
    tweezers, kisslipped tissues. I shed snarls   10
        of hair in the shower like saffron threads,

red kelp. In the mirror I paint myself a clownface
    copied from *Sassy, Seventeen, Glamour.* He
        stands in the doorway, loving   15

the used-to-be lovable 12-year-old
    formerly his. We look in the mirror:
        blush welts, orange, riding low

on my cheeks, pink lipstick leaking
    from my lip corners. Glitter-white
        chevrons for eyelids; Cover Girl fails   20

again to cover my nose-zits. Reflected, behind me,
    tangles of the unwashed bras I don't need
        trail from shower rod, shampoo rack,

hot-cold dial, soapdish, stopcock.   25
    He hates it: me mooning, me sighing,
        me incessantly hairbrushing, singing stupid

love songs. "I'll buy back the gunk!" he says.
    He'll pay twice what I spent if only I'll stop.
        I stand by the tub in the bathroom,   30

my real room. I prop up a leg, I pull up
    my skirt, start shaving thigh-stubble. I shove
        the door shut between us with my ass.

Considerations for Critical Thinking and Writing

1. **FIRST RESPONSE.** What images and figures of speech make Fried's description of this father-daughter relationship convincing?

2. In what sense is the bathroom for the speaker "my real room" (lines 3 and 31)?

3. How does the title sum up the poem's familial conflict?

4. Explain why you think Fried treats the speaker mostly satirically or sympathetically.

Connections to Other Selections

1. Compare the tone and theme of "Wit's End" with those of Li Ho's "A Beautiful Girl Combs Her Hair" (p. 785).

2. How might the daughter in "Wit's End" be considered a youthful version of the speaker in Sylvia Plath's "Mirror" (p. 879)?

RONALD WALLACE (B. 1945)

In a Rut   2002

She dogs me while
I try to take a catnap.
Of course, I'm playing possum but
I can feel her watching me,
eagle-eyed, like a hawk.   5
She snakes over to my side
of the bed, and continues to
badger me. I may be a rat, but
I won't let her get my goat.
I refuse to make an   10
ass of myself, no matter
how mulish I feel.
I'm trying to make a
bee-line for sleep, but
You're a turkey! she says, and   15
I'm thinking she's no
spring chicken. She *is* a busy beaver,
though, always trying to ferret
things out. She's a bit batty,
in fact, a bit cuckoo, but   20
What's your beef, now? I say.
*Get your head out
of the sand,* she replies. *What
are you—a man, or a mouse?*
That's a lot of bull, I think;   25
she can be a real bear.
Don't horse around, now, she says.
You know you can't weasel out of it!
She's having a whale of a time,
thinking she's got me skunked, thinking   30
that she's out-foxed me.
But I know she's just crying wolf,
and I won't be cowed. Feeling
my oats now, I merely look sheepish;
I give her the hang-dog look;   35
I give her the lion's share.
I give her something to crow about.
Oh, lovey-dove, I intone.
We're all odd ducks, strange
birds; this won't be my swan-   40
song, after all. She's in hog-

heaven now, ready to pig-out.
Oh, my stallion, she says, *Oh,*
my lambkin! You are
a real animal, you know!   45

CONSIDERATIONS FOR CRITICAL THINKING AND WRITING

1. **FIRST RESPONSE.** Explain whether or not Wallace's orchestration of over-used phrases redeems them from being simply clichés.

2. How does the title contribute to your understanding of the poem's plot?

3. **CREATIVE RESPONSE.** Choose a set of familiar related expressions from sports, school, politics, religion, or whatever comes naturally to you, and write your own version of a poem that imitates Wallace's playful use of clichés.

CONNECTION TO ANOTHER SELECTION

1. Compare Wallace's organizing strategy in this poem and E. E. Cummings's technique in "next to of course god america i" (p. 897).

HOWARD NEMEROV (1920–1991)

Walking the Dog   *1980*

Two universes mosey down the street
Connected by love and a leash and nothing else.
Mostly I look at lamplight through the leaves
While he mooches along with tail up and snout down,
Getting a secret knowledge through the nose   5
Almost entirely hidden from my sight.

We stand while he's enraptured by a bush
Till I can't stand our standing any more
And haul him off; for our relationship
Is patience balancing to this side tug   10
And that side drag; a pair of symbionts
Contented not to think each other's thoughts.

What else we have in common's what he taught,
Our interest in shit. We know its every state
From steaming fresh through stink to nature's way   15
Of sluicing it downstreet dissolved in rain
Or drying it to dust that blows away.
We move along the street inspecting it.

His sense of it is keener far than mine,
And only when he finds the place precise   20
He signifies by sniffing urgently
And circles thrice about, and squats, and shits.
Whereon we both with dignity walk home
And just to show who's master I write the poem.

CONSIDERATIONS FOR CRITICAL THINKING AND WRITING

1. **FIRST RESPONSE.** How does the form of this poem give it dignity despite its topic? Explain why you experience the poem as amusing or repugnant.

2. How might you read the poem differently if the last line were deleted?

3. Compare the tone of stanzas 1 and 2 with that of 3 and 4. Discuss whether or not the two sets of stanzas are consistent and compatible.

4. Who do you think is finally the master? Explain why.

CONNECTIONS TO OTHER SELECTIONS

1. Discuss the speakers' attitudes toward dogs in "Walking the Dog" and in John Ciardi's "Suburban" (p. 1247). How does humor inform those attitudes?

2. Consider the subject matter of this poem and Ronald Wallace's "Building an Outhouse" (p. 884). Some readers might argue that the subject matter is tasteless and not suitable for poetic treatment. What do you think?

LINDA PASTAN (B. 1932)

Jump Cabling   *1984*

When our cars	touched,
When you lifted the hood	of mine
To see the intimate workings	underneath,
When we were bound	together
By a pulse of pure	energy,
When my car like the	princess
In the tale woke with a	start,

I thought why not ride the rest of the way together?

CONSIDERATIONS FOR CRITICAL THINKING AND WRITING

1. **FIRST RESPONSE.** How is the word spacing in the poem related to its meaning?

2. Discuss the diction. How does it enhance the theme?

3. **CREATIVE RESPONSE.** Using Pastan's word spacing as a jumping-off point, write an alternate version of "Jump Cabling" in which the car does not start.

CONNECTION TO ANOTHER SELECTION

1. Compare the style and theme of this poem with that of Pastan's "Marks" (p. 883).

PETER SCHMITT (B. 1958)

Friends with Numbers 1995

If you make friends with numbers,
you don't need any other friends.
  —Shakuntala Devi, math genius

They are not hard to get to know:
6 and 9 keep changing their minds,
8 cuts the most graceful figure
but sleeps for an eternity,
and 7, lucky 7, takes   5
an arrow to his heart always.
5, halfway to somewhere, only
wants to patch his unicycle
tire, and 4, who'd like to stand for
something solid, has never had   10
two feet on the ground, yet flutters
gamely in the breeze like a flag.
3, for all his literary
accomplishments and pretensions
to immortality, is still   15
(I can tell you) not half the man
8 is asleep or awake. 1,
little 1. I know him better
than all the others, these numbers
who are all my friends. Only 2,   20
that strange smallest prime, can I count
as just a passing acquaintance.
Divisible by only 1
and herself, she seems on the verge,
yet, of always coming apart.   25
And though she eludes me, swanlike,
though I'd love to know her better,
still I am fine, there are others,
many, I have friends in numbers.

CONSIDERATIONS FOR CRITICAL THINKING AND WRITING

1. **FIRST RESPONSE.** How does the personification of numbers create characters in the poem?

2. Explain how the speaker's use of language helps to characterize him.

3. Discuss the various ways in which the single digits are transformed into individual visual images.

CONNECTION TO ANOTHER SELECTION

1. Discuss the originality—the fresh and unusual approach to their respective subject matter—in Schmitt's poem and in Christian Bök's "Vowels" (p. 789). What makes these poems so interesting?

MARTÍN ESPADA (B. 1957)

The Community College Revises Its Curriculum in Response to Changing Demographics

2000

SPA 100 Conversational Spanish
2 credits

The course
is especially concerned
with giving police
the ability
to express themselves
tersely
in matters of interest
to them

CONSIDERATIONS FOR CRITICAL THINKING AND WRITING

1. FIRST RESPONSE. What sort of political comment do you think Espada makes in this poem?
2. Would this be a poem without the title? Explain your answer.
3. CREATIVE RESPONSE. Choose a course description from your school's catalog and organize the catalog copy into poetic lines. Provide your poem with a title that offers a provocative commentary about it.

CONNECTION TO ANOTHER SELECTION

1. Compare the themes in Espada's poem and in Donald Justice's "Order in the Streets" (p. 1027).

DENISE DUHAMEL (B. 1961)

Language Police Report

2006

After Diane Ravitch's The Language Police

The busybody (banned as sexist, demeaning to older women) who lives next door called my daughter a tomboy (banned as sexist) when she climbed the jungle (banned; replaced with "rain forest") gym. Then she had the nerve to call her an egghead and a bookworm (both banned as offensive; replaced with "intellectual") because she read fairy (banned because suggests homosexuality; replace with "elf") tales.

I'm tired of the Language Police turning a deaf ear (banned as handicapism) to my complaints. I'm no Pollyanna (banned as sexist) and will not accept any lame (banned as offensive; replace with "walks with a cane") excuses at this time.

If Alanis Morissette can play God (banned) in *Dogma* (banned as ethnocentric; replace with "Doctrine" or "Belief"), why can't my daughter play stickball (banned as regional or ethnic bias) on boy's night out (banned as sexist)? Why can't she build a snowman (banned, replace with "snow person") without that fanatic (banned as ethnocentric; replace with "believer," "follower," or "adherent") next door telling her she's going to hell (banned; replaced with "heck" or "darn")?

Do you really think this is what the Founding Fathers (banned as sexist; replace with "the Founders" or "the Framers") had in mind? That we can't even enjoy our Devil (banned)-ed ham sandwiches in peace? I say put a stop to this cult (banned as ethnocentric) of PC old wives' tales (banned as sexist; replace with "folk wisdom") and extremist (banned as ethnocentric; replace with "believer," "follower," or "adherent") conservative duffers (banned as demeaning to older men).

As an heiress (banned as sexist; replace with "heir") to the first amendment, I feel that only a heretic (use with caution when comparing religions) would try to stop American vernacular from flourishing in all its inspirational (banned as patronizing when referring to a person with disabilities) splendor.

CONSIDERATIONS FOR CRITICAL THINKING AND WRITING

1. **FIRST RESPONSE.** Duhamel has explained that she was inspired to write this prose poem after reading a list of words banned as "politically incorrect" in Diane Ravitch's study of editorial censorship, *The Language Police: How Pressure Groups Restrict What Students Learn.* She found this abuse of language both "horrifying and hilarious" (*The Best of American Poetry 2007*, p. 132). What do you think?

2. What is the speaker's basic argument against the "Language Police"?

3. **CREATIVE RESPONSE.** Write a stanza of your own that adds to the list.

CONNECTION TO ANOTHER SELECTION

1. Compare the attitudes expressed toward language in this poem and in Barbara Hamby's "Ode to American English" (p. 817).

M. CARL HOLMAN (1919–1988)

Mr. Z   *1967*

Taught early that his mother's skin was the sign of error,
He dressed and spoke the perfect part of honor;
Won scholarships, attended the best schools,
Disclaimed kinship with jazz and spirituals;
Chose prudent, raceless views for each situation,   5
Or when he could not cleanly skirt dissension,
Faced up to the dilemma, firmly seized
Whatever ground was Anglo-Saxonized.

In diet, too, his practice was exemplary:
Of pork in its profane forms he was wary;   10

Expert in vintage wines, sauces and salads,
His palate shrank from cornbread, yams and collards.

He was as careful whom he chose to kiss:
His bride had somewhere lost her Jewishness,
But kept her blue eyes; an Episcopalian   15
Prelate proclaimed them matched chameleon.
Choosing the right addresses, here, abroad,
They shunned those places where they might be barred;
Even less anxious to be asked to dine
Where hosts catered to kosher accent or exotic skin.   20

And so he climbed, unclogged by ethnic weights,
An airborne plant, flourishing without roots.
Not one false note was struck — until he died:
His subtly grieving widow could have flayed
The obit writers, ringing crude changes on a clumsy phrase: 25
"One of the most distinguished members of his race."

CONSIDERATIONS FOR CRITICAL THINKING AND WRITING

1. **FIRST RESPONSE.** What is the central irony of Mr. Z's life? What do you think of him?
2. Explain whether you find Holman's satiric portrait to be fair or unfair.
3. Discuss the poem's rhythms and rhymes. How do they contribute to the tone?
4. What does Mr. Z's name suggest about his identity?

CONNECTION TO ANOTHER SELECTION

1. Discuss the preference for "Anglo-Saxonized" (line 8) appearances in "Mr. Z" and in Janice Mirikitani's "Recipe" (Crossing Boundaries insert, p. L).

GARY SOTO (B. 1952)

Mexicans Begin Jogging   *1995*

At the factory I worked
In the fleck of rubber, under the press
Of an oven yellow with flame,
Until the border patrol opened
Their vans and my boss waved for us to run.   5
"Over the fence, Soto," he shouted,
And I shouted that I was American.
"No time for lies," he said, and pressed
A dollar in my palm, hurrying me
Through the back door.   10

Since I was on his time, I ran
And became the wag to a short tail of Mexicans —

Ran past the amazed crowds that lined
The street and blurred like photographs, in rain.
I ran from that industrial road to the soft   15
Houses where people paled at the turn of an autumn sky.
What could I do but yell *vivas*
To baseball, milkshakes, and those sociologists
Who would clock me
As I jog into the next century   20
On the power of a great, silly grin.

CONSIDERATIONS FOR CRITICAL THINKING AND WRITING

1. **FIRST RESPONSE.** What ironies are present in this poem?
2. Soto was born and raised in Fresno, California. How does this fact affect your reading of the first stanza?
3. In what different ways does the speaker become "the wag" (line 12) in this poem? (You may want to look up the word to consider all possible meanings.)
4. Explain lines 17–21. What serious point is being made in these humorous lines?

CONNECTION TO ANOTHER SELECTION

1. Compare the speakers' ironic attitudes toward exercise in this poem and in Peter Meinke's "The ABC of Aerobics" (p. 1022).

BOB HICOK (B. 1960)

Spam leaves an aftertaste   2002

What does the Internet know that it sends me
unbidden the offer of a larger penis?
I'm flattered by the energy devoted
to the architecture of my body.
Brain waves noodling on girth, length, curvature   5
possibly, pictures drawn on napkins
of the device, teeth for holding, cylinder —
pneumatic, hydraulic — for stretching
who I am into who I shall be. But of all
messages to drop from the digital ether,   10
hope lives in the communiqué that I can find
out anything about anyone. So I've asked:
who am I, why am I here, if a train
leaving Chicago is subsidized
by the feds, is the romance of travel   15

dead? I'd like the skinny on where I'll be
when I die, to have a map, a seismic map
of past and future emotions, to be told
how to keep the violence I do to myself
from becoming the grenades I pitch   20
at others. The likes of Snoop.com
never get back to me, though I need
to know most of all if any of this helps.
How we can scatter our prayers so wide,
if we've become more human or less   25
in being able to share the specific
in a random way, or was it better
to ask the stars for peace or rain,
to trust the litany of our need
to the air's imperceptible embrace? Just   30
this morning I got a message
asking is anyone out there. I replied
no, I am not, are you not there too,
needing me, and if not, come over, I have
a small penis but aspirations   35
for bigger things, faith among them,
and by that I mean you and I
face to face, mouths
making the sounds once known
as conversation.   40

CONSIDERATIONS FOR CRITICAL THINKING AND WRITING

1. **FIRST RESPONSE.** Comment on the humor Hicok uses to satirize how our lives have been affected by the Internet.

2. What is the serious theme that the speaker's humor leads the reader to contemplate? How does this theme complicate the poem's tone?

3. How do your own experiences with spam compare with the speaker's?

CONNECTIONS TO OTHER SELECTIONS

1. How might Hicok's poem be considered a latter-day version of T. S. Eliot's "The Love Song of J. Alfred Prufrock" (p. 1216)?

2. Discuss the perspective on American contemporary life implicit in "Spam leaves an aftertaste" with respect to the view offered in Tony Hoagland's "America" (p. 1291).

THOMAS LUX (B. 1946)

Commercial Leech Farming Today

1997

—for Robert Sacherman

Although it never rivaled wheat, soybean,
cattle and so on farming
there was a living
in leeches
and after a period of decline   5
there is again
a living to be made
from this endeavor: they're used to reduce
the blood in tissues
after plastic surgery — eyelifts, tucks,   10
wrinkle erad, or in certain
microsurgeries — reattaching a finger, penis.
I love the capitalist
spirit. As in most businesses
the technology has improved: instead   15
of driving an elderly horse
into a leech pond, letting him die
by exsanguination,
and hauling him out
to pick the bloated blossoms   20
from his hide, it's now done at Biopharm
(the showcase operation in Swansea,
Wales) — temp control, tanks, aerator
pumps, several species,
each for a specific job. Once, 19th century,   25
they were applied to the temple
as a treatment for mental
illness. Today we know
their exact chemistry: hirudin,
a blood thinner in their saliva,   30
also an anesthesia
and dilators for the wound area.
Don't you love
the image: the Dr. lays a leech along
the tiny stitches of an eyelift.   35
Where they go after their work is done
I don't know
but I've heard no complaints
from Animal Rights
so perhaps they're retired   40
to a lake or adopted
as pets, maybe the best looking
kept to breed. I don't know. I like the story,
I like the going backwards

to ignorance   45
to come forward to vanity. I like
the small role they can play
in beauty
or the reattachment of a part,
I like the story because it's true.   50

CONSIDERATIONS FOR CRITICAL THINKING AND WRITING

1. **FIRST RESPONSE.** Why does the speaker "like the story" (line 43) about leech farming so much? What does it symbolize to him or her?
2. How does Lux characterize the nature of contemporary life?
3. Explain how the humor in this poem moves beyond the simply bizarre to the satirical.

CONNECTION TO ANOTHER SELECTION

1. Discuss the perspectives on human vanity offered in Lux's poem and in Alice Jones's "The Foot" (p. 955).

LEE UPTON (B. 1953)

Dyserotica   *2007*

There is utopia
and there is dystopia.
There is erotica

and there is . . .
what you've written.   5
Somehow —

as if what two
at a minimum
people might do

or could do   10
in another lifetime —
if suddenly shipwrecked, for instance,

or if it was the end of the world
and they alone were left to procreate —
as if your words must be   15

the antidote to desire,
the corrective trip to the morgue,
the inoculation we haven't been waiting for . . .

although even your dyserotica
becomes erotic for some of us: 20
what else are death bed

confessions for?
Forgive me for not being impressed
by your image of spiders

crawling the mouth of Aphrodite.   25
I know you don't love me,
but why do you have to brag about it?

CONSIDERATIONS FOR CRITICAL THINKING AND WRITING

1. **FIRST RESPONSE.** How is "dyserotica" (line 19) defined in this poem? Why is it so painful to the speaker?
2. Are you — in contrast to the speaker — impressed with the image in lines 24–25? Why or why not?
3. Discuss the tone of the final line.

CONNECTION TO ANOTHER SELECTION

1. Compare the theme and tone of "Dyserotica" with those of Billie Bolton's "Memorandum" (p. 1241).

X. J. KENNEDY (B. 1929)

On a Young Man's Remaining an Undergraduate for Twelve Years   2006

Sweet scent of pot, the mellow smell of beer,
    Frat-house debates on sex, on God's existence
Lasting all night, vacations thrice a year,
    Pliant coeds who put up no resistance

Are all life is. Who'd give a damn for earning,   5
    Who'd struggle by degrees to lofty places
When he can loll, adrift in endless learning,
    In a warm sea of academic stasis?

He's famous now: the everlasting kid.
    After conducting an investigation,   10
Two deans resigned, to do just what he did.
    They couldn't fault his ratiocination.

CONSIDERATIONS FOR CRITICAL THINKING AND WRITING

1. **FIRST RESPONSE.** Comment on the description of undergraduate life in the first stanza and the effect of the enjambment in lines 4 and 5.
2. Discuss the sound effects in stanza three. How are they related to sense?
3. Why is "ratiocination" (line 12) just the right word in this context?

40

A THEMATIC CASE STUDY
Milestones

I like to think of all good poetry as
providing more oxygen into the
atmosphere; it just makes it easier to
breathe.
— KAY RYAN

Christopher Felver/CORBIS.

The thematic center of this chapter focuses on milestones in people's lives. The various literary elements that contribute to the idea or point of each poem are there to enhance moments that seem particularly striking, moving, or memorable. Not surprisingly, this type of moment is the frequent purview of the lyric, a poem that typically expresses the subjective mood, emotion, or idea of a single speaker. Taken together, the poems in this chapter represent a variety of poetic responses ranging from sly observations on young love to painful reflections on birth and death. These poems won't necessarily reflect the complicated and pivotal moments in your own life, but they might make you more sensitive to them and perhaps encourage you to think more deeply about what they mean to you.

Most of these poems have been published within the past ten years, and so their contemporary nature should allow you to make vivid and accessible connections to the world you inhabit and the language you speak and read. Your own experience will provide the necessary annotations. As you read, think about how each of the poems captures a moment charged with some kind of recollection, experience, emotion, energy, insight, or meaning that is somehow transformative.

Steeped in expectation and desire, the young couple in Allen Braden's "Sweethearts" seem like ideal pictures from a high school yearbook—almost.

ALLEN BRADEN (B. 1968)

Sweethearts

2000

One Friday late at night they grope their way
through the pale statuary and fallen leaves

for a hollow to lie in where they fit perfectly
the way their perfect bodies fit one another.

It seems quite natural that he is the star   5
this season and she the head cheerleader.

Once or twice she recalls something else
unforgettable she wants to say but does not.

They touch as if to say, *Don't ever forget this,*
are young enough to wring love from elegy   10

with the vertigo of their longing, the rush
of uncovering and pushing flesh against flesh.

One tiny act is all it takes to bury themselves
in some small excuse for somewhere else,

anywhere but right here where his ambitions   15
will be planed down on the graveyard shift

and hers will be spent waiting on tables
with trays of coffee, hot cakes and syrup.

CONSIDERATIONS FOR CRITICAL THINKING AND WRITING

1. **FIRST RESPONSE.** How is the stanzaic form of this poem especially appropriate for its subject matter?

2. How do you think the speaker regards the romantic relationship of this couple? What does his choice of words and images reveal?

3. In what sense can this Friday night be seen as a milestone in this couple's life together?

CONNECTION TO ANOTHER SELECTION

1. Discuss the treatment of love in "Sweethearts" and in Billie Bolton's "Memorandum" (p. 1241).

The remaining poems in this chapter depict a variety of milestones in people's lives. You'll notice that the moments don't necessarily have to be big and dramatic to be important and moving. No car chases; no explosions.

BARON WORMSER (B. 1948)

Shoplifting   *1997*

The store dick lays a hand on your shoulder
Three steps from the exit. He asks what's
In your pockets but it's more like a statement
Than a question. Two candy bars and a roll of film.

Your stomach melts and your heart starts to beat   5
Like when you used to race on the playground.
He tells you to sit down on the bench by the doors.
Usually there are some old people sitting there

Gabbling about bargains but no one's around
This late in the evening. You expect the manager   10
To show up and give you a lecture about kids
Nowadays but he doesn't

And when the cop appears he doesn't say
Anything special beyond you'll have to go to court.
When he gives you the paper he's almost smiling   15
Or he's not there at all, he's not seeing you.

Thoughts, thoughts . . . your head's raw dough
One moment, light as a balloon the next.
They're always playing a song in the background
In these stores that you can't quite identify.   20

Your foot's tapping to the vacant beat
And after the cop leaves and you
Can leave you don't for some minutes.
You don't even own a camera.

CONSIDERATIONS FOR CRITICAL THINKING AND WRITING

1. **FIRST RESPONSE.** What is the effect of the speaker's addressing the reader in the second person ("you")?
2. Identify the figurative language in the poem. Why do you think there is so little of it?
3. How convincing to you is this portrait of a young shoplifter being caught in the act?

CONNECTION TO ANOTHER SELECTION

1. Consider how Michelle Boisseau's "Self-Pity's Closet" (p. 1287) offers a potential commentary on Wormser's shoplifter.

JAN BEATTY (B. 1952)

My Father Teaches Me to Dream 1996

You want to know what work is?
I'll tell you what work is:
Work is work.
You get up. You get on the bus.
You don't look from side to side. 5
You keep your eyes straight ahead.
That way nobody bothers you—see?
You get off the bus. You work all day.
You get back on the bus at night. Same thing.
You go to sleep. You get up. 10
You do the same thing again.
Nothing more. Nothing less.
There's no handouts in this life.
All this other stuff you're looking for—
it ain't there. 15
Work is work.

CONSIDERATIONS FOR CRITICAL THINKING AND WRITING

1. **FIRST RESPONSE.** How likely is it that the son or daughter of this father actually asked for a definition of work? What do you imagine prompted the start of this explanation?

2. Discuss the effect of the use of repeated words and phrases. How are they related to the father's message?

3. Consider what the title reveals about the "you" of the poem.

CONNECTION TO ANOTHER SELECTION

1. Compare this father's vision of work with the perspective of the young man in Baron Wormser's "Labor" (p. 995). How might the difference between the two be explained?

MARILYN NELSON (B. 1946)

How I Discovered Poetry 1997

It was like soul-kissing, the way the words
filled my mouth as Mrs. Purdy read from her desk.
All the other kids zoned an hour ahead to 3:15,
but Mrs. Purdy and I wandered lonely as clouds borne
by a breeze off Mount Parnassus. She must have seen 5
the darkest eyes in the room brim: The next day
she gave me a poem she'd chosen especially for me
to read to the all except for me white class.
She smiled when she told me to read it, smiled harder,
said oh yes I could. She smiled harder and harder 10

until I stood and opened my mouth to banjo playing
darkies, pickaninnies, disses and dats. When I finished
my classmates stared at the floor. We walked silent
to the buses, awed by the power of words.

CONSIDERATIONS FOR CRITICAL THINKING AND WRITING

1. **FIRST RESPONSE.** Trace your response to Miss Purdy from the beginning to
   the end of the poem.
2. What do the allusions to William Wordsworth's poem "I Wandered Lonely
   as a Cloud" (see p. 1353) and Mount Parnassus (look it up) in lines 4 and 5
   suggest to you about the speaker?
3. How do you interpret the tone of the final two lines?

CONNECTION TO ANOTHER SELECTION

1. How does Nelson's description of discovering poetry compare with Ronald
   Wallace's in "Miss Goff" (p. 1080)?

CHARLES SIMIC (B. 1938)

In the Library   *2008*

for Octavio

There's a book called
"A Dictionary of Angels."
No one has opened it in fifty years,
I know, because when I did,
The covers creaked, the pages   5
Crumbled. There I discovered

The angels were once as plentiful
As species of flies.
The sky at dusk
Used to be thick with them.   10
You had to wave both arms
Just to keep them away.

Now the sun is shining
Through the tall windows.
The library is a quiet place.   15
Angels and gods huddled
In dark unopened books.
The great secret lies
On some shelf Miss Jones
Passes every day on her rounds.   20

She's very tall, so she keeps
Her head tipped as if listening.
The books are whispering.
I hear nothing, but she does.

CONSIDERATIONS FOR CRITICAL THINKING AND WRITING

1. **FIRST RESPONSE.** What does the speaker discover about the library and Miss Jones that makes this a striking experience?

2. Why do you think Simic chooses a book of angels as the source of this discovery? And why does he mention the flies?

3. **CREATIVE RESPONSE.** What sort of poem do you think might be written with the title "In the Computer"?

CONNECTION TO ANOTHER SELECTION

1. Compare the book lovers from "In the Library" and Billy Collins's "Marginalia" (p. 787).

TREVOR WEST KNAPP (B. 1958)

Touch

2001

We speak of the pain of childbirth, referring,
of course, to the mother, but what is pain
to the mother, the one through whose body
the course unwinds? She understands already
what kind of world she must return to,   5
how it daily hones its many edges
against human skin, unlike the child whose
untried limbs inch toward it, pressing now
so firmly against her he feels for the first time
the pinch of bone against bone and is seared   10
by the friction. Isn't he the one
on whom the real burden falls, the one
to whom resilience means nothing yet? His
tender skin like a small measure of cloth
unfolding before the blade under which   15
he will, for a lifetime, bruise
and heal: Crush of the long descent, grip
of the steadying hands, brush of breath
against cheek, even the constant barrage
of the microscopic, the tiny plink-plink   20
of the dust motes knocking against him
before custom makes him numb to it. No wonder
the startled mouth cries out,
each pore suddenly hungry
in the withering, nourishing light.   25

CONSIDERATIONS FOR CRITICAL THINKING AND WRITING

1. **FIRST RESPONSE.** What kind of passage does the speaker envision birth to be for an infant?

2. Discuss the effectiveness of the imagery in evoking pain.

3. Is this a grim view of birth? Overly sensitive? Empathetic? Tender? What do you think?

CONNECTION TO ANOTHER SELECTION

1. Consider whether or not this poem on childbirth and Anne Bradstreet's "Before the Birth of One of Her Children" (p. 1317) have anything to say to each other. What kind of dialogue emerges by placing them side by side?

SANDRA M. GILBERT (B. 1936)

How We Didn't Tell Her   2008

that the housekeeper said that
the gardener said that
someone named

Jean or Jeannie or Jenny
who was his friend or maybe   5
his boss had said that

today that just
today he was hit by a car
& he was killed he died

at once in the prime   10
of his handsome youth he
who was her youngest her

onetime baby ice-cream
cone with dimpled arms
& scrumptious tummy he   15

who gardened & prayed
for purity on earth
but we said let's wait let's

wait to tell her till we're
sure & we called the gardener   20
the housekeeeper the irrigation lady

the police the coroner
the highway patrol the neighbors
we called everyone but her

until at last the gardener   25
said no no how could the housekeeper
get it so wrong it wasn't

him it was someone else who was
hit by a car and killed
today & we rejoiced & were   30

glad we hadn't told her because
his handsome flesh his pulsing
prime returned to us as a gift

more precious than before
& as for the other one, the other   35
mother's son who really died

today we let him go we
didn't give him
another thought.

CONSIDERATIONS FOR CRITICAL THINKING AND WRITING

1. **FIRST RESPONSE.** Read the poem aloud. How does the lack of punctuation (except for the final period) contribute to your reading and understanding of what happens in the narrative?

2. Comment on the rhythm of the lines and its relationship to their meaning.

3. How would the tone and theme of this poem shift if it ended at line 34?

CONNECTION TO ANOTHER SELECTION

1. Compare the ending of this poem and of Robert Frost's " 'Out, Out—' " (p. 1110) in terms of their attitudes toward mortality.

ANNE CARSON (B. 1950)

Father's Old Blue Cardigan   2000

Now it hangs on the back of the kitchen chair
where I always sit, as it did
on the back of the kitchen chair where he always sat.

I put it on whenever I come in,
as he did, stamping   5
the snow from his boots.

I put it on and sit in the dark.
He would not have done this.
Coldness comes paring down from the moonbone in the sky.

His laws were a secret.   10
But I remember the moment at which I knew
he was going mad inside his laws.

He was standing at the turn of the driveway when I arrived.
He had on the blue cardigan with the buttons done up all the way to the top.
Not only because it was a hot July afternoon   15

but the look on his face—
as a small child who has been dressed by some aunt early in the morning
for a long trip

on cold trains and windy platforms
will sit very straight at the edge of his seat   20
while the shadows like long fingers

over the haystacks that sweep past
keep shocking him
because he is riding backwards.

CONSIDERATIONS FOR CRITICAL THINKING AND WRITING

1. **FIRST RESPONSE.** What does the speaker realize in the moment when the father's face reveals that a profound change has come over him?

2. Describe the effect of the simile in lines 17–24. What kinds of emotions does it evoke?

3. Why do you suppose Carson titled the poem "Father's Old Blue Cardigan" rather than, for example, "The Look on His Face"?

CONNECTION TO ANOTHER SELECTION

1. Compare the ways in which the speakers in this poem and in Rachel Loden's "Locked Ward: Newtown, Connecticut" (p. 1292) cope with madness in a parent.

BARBARA CROOKER (B. 1945)

On the Edge of Adolescence, My Middle Daughter Learns to Play the Saxophone   *2000*

For Rebecca

Her hair, that halo of red gold curls,
has thickened, coarsened,
lost its baby fineness,
and the sweet smell of childhood
that clung to her clothes   5
has just about vanished.
Now she's getting moody,
moaning about her hair,
clothes that aren't the right brands,
boys that tease.   10
She clicks over the saxophone keys
with gritty fingernails polished in pink pearl,
grass stains on the knees
of her sister's old designer jeans.
She's gone from sounding like the smoke detector   15
through Old MacDonald and Jingle Bells.
Soon she'll master these keys,
turn notes into liquid gold,
wail that reedy brass.
Soon, she'll be a woman.   20
She's gonna learn to play the blues.

CONSIDERATIONS FOR CRITICAL THINKING AND WRITING

1. **FIRST RESPONSE.** Do you think the title is too long or just right? Explain why.
2. Why do these observations about the daughter's pending transformation seem more like a mother's than a father's?
3. The last line couldn't be better. Why?

CONNECTION TO ANOTHER SELECTION

1. Discuss Daisy Fried's "Wit's End" (p. 1247) as a kind of sequel to the story of the young girl in this poem.

LUISA LOPEZ (B. 1957)

Junior Year Abroad 2002

We were amateurs, that winter in Paris.

The summer before we agreed:
he would come over to keep me company at Christmas.
But the shelf life of my promise expired
before the date on his airline ticket.   5
So we ended up together under a French muslin sky.

Together alone.

Certainly I was alone, inside dark hair, inside foreign blankets,
against white sheets swirling like a cocoon,
covering my bare skin,   10
keeping me apart.
The invited man snored beside me not knowing
I didn't love him anymore.

At first I tried,
perky as a circus pony waiting at the airport gate   15
to be again as I once had been.
But even during the first night
betrayal, the snake under the evergreen,
threw me into nightmares
of floods and dying birds.   20

You see, a new boy just last month
had raised my shy hand to his warm mouth
and kissed the inside of my palm.
I thought "this is impossible,
too close to Christmas, too soon, too dangerous."   25

In Paris I concede:
deceiving my old lover, the one now stirring in his sleep
is even more dangerous.
See him opening his eyes, looking at my face,
dropping his eyes to my breasts and smiling   30
as if he were seeing two old friends? Dangerous.

When I move away and hold the sheet against
myself he,
sensing what this means,
refuses, adamant yet polite,   35
to traffic in the currency of my rejection.

He made a journey. I offered a welcome.
Why should he give me up?

CONSIDERATIONS FOR CRITICAL THINKING AND WRITING

1. **FIRST RESPONSE.** This poem is about strength and dominance as much as it is about love and attraction. Discuss the ways in which the two characters are vying for control.

2. Why is the setting important? How might the sense of the poem be different if this were happening during a typical school year as opposed to "Junior Year Abroad"?

3. Do you think the speaker has the right to reject her old boyfriend under these circumstances? Does the old boyfriend have the right to expect a "welcome" (line 37) since he was invited to visit?

4. The speaker is wrapped in sheets that are like a "cocoon" (line 9). What does this suggest about the changes she is experiencing during this encounter?

CONNECTION TO ANOTHER SELECTION

1. Compare this 2002 poem about young love with A. E. Housman's poem "When I was one-and-twenty" (p. 956), published in 1896. How much has the situation changed in a hundred years?

YUSEF KOMUNYAKAA (B. 1947)

Slam, Dunk, & Hook   *1992*

Fast breaks. Lay ups. With Mercury's
Insignia on our sneakers,
We outmaneuvered the footwork
Of bad angels. Nothing but a hot
Swish of strings like silk   5
Ten feet out. In the roundhouse
Labyrinth our bodies
Created, we could almost
Last forever, poised in midair
Like storybook sea monsters.   10
A high note hung there
A long second. Off
The rim. We'd corkscrew
Up & dunk balls that exploded
The skullcap of hope & good   15
Intention. Bug-eyed, lanky,
All hands & feet . . . sprung rhythm.

We were metaphysical when girls
Cheered on the sidelines.
Tangled up in a falling,   20
Muscles were a bright motor
Double-flashing to the metal hoop
Nailed to our oak.
When Sonny Boy's mama died
He played nonstop all day, so hard   25
Our backboard splintered.
Glistening with sweat, we jibed
& rolled the ball off our
Fingertips. Trouble
Was there slapping a blackjack   30
Against an open palm.
Dribble, drive to the inside, feint,
& glide like a sparrow hawk.
Layups. Fast breaks.
We had moves we didn't know   35
We had. Our bodies spun

On swivels of bone & faith,
Through a lyric slipknot
Of joy, & we knew we were
Beautiful & dangerous.   40

CONSIDERATIONS FOR CRITICAL THINKING AND WRITING

1. **FIRST RESPONSE.** Why and how is basketball more than just a game to these players? What kind of symbolic significance does it hold for them?

2. Explain how the rhythm of the lines follows the rhythm of the game.

3. Why do you think the nostalgic speaker characterizes the players as not only "beautiful" but "dangerous" (line 40)?

CONNECTION TO ANOTHER SELECTION

1. Contrast the team experience described in this poem with that in Gary Gildner's "First Practice" (p. 1011).

SUGGESTED TOPICS FOR LONGER PAPERS

1. Choose one of the writers represented in this chapter and read more poems in his or her collections. Write an analysis of five poems that you think make an interesting and coherent thematic grouping that reveals important elements of the poet's style and characteristic content.

2. Put together a portfolio of several popular songs about the same "milestone" topic (romance, school, work, road tripping, or whatever interests you) and analyze them in terms of their style, themes, or historical context.

41

A THEMATIC CASE STUDY
The Natural World

Writing is my salvation. If I didn't write, what would I do?
—MAXINE KUMIN

© Bettmann/CORBIS.

This chapter is a collection of poems thematically related to the natural environment we inhabit. Though poets may have a popular (and mistaken) reputation for being somewhat ethereal in their concerns, they still breathe the same air as the rest of us. Not surprisingly, because poets instinctively draw inspiration from nature, they are often as delighted to praise its vivid joys as they are compelled to warn us when it is abused. Having neither the technical knowledge of scientists nor the political means of legislators to defend the environment, poets nevertheless lend a voice to remind us of its pleasures, importance, and urgent fragility. The celebration of nature has always, of course, been a major poetic genre, but only fairly recently has poetry treated nature as a cause célèbre.

The poems in this chapter provide some contemporary reflections on our relationship to nature. Though they are not representative of all of the kinds of environmental poetry being written today, these twelve poems do offer a range of voices and issues that can serve as prompts for seeing and responding to your own natural environment through poetic language. You'll find among them detailed and vivid observations of nature, as well as meditations on climate change, the sustainability of the wild, and, indeed, the future of the planet. Some of the voices are quietly thoughtful, while others are ironic or funny, and a couple will even holler at you.

The first poem, "Birdsong Interpreted" by Tom Disch, may not seem like an especially inviting welcome, but it helps to explain why you're invited in the first place.

TOM DISCH (1940–2008)

Birdsong Interpreted   2007

Scuse me? Scuse M? This is *my* territory.
Didja hear what I said? I said, Go away!
No trespassing! Vamoose! Amscray!
Everything was hunky-dory
Till *you* disturbed the eco-balance.   5
I homestead here and you're Jack Palance
Terrorizing godly folk.
Leave! or I will have a stroke.
I will! I kid you not. I'll sing
My heart out, pop a valve, expire: 10
This nest will be my funeral pyre.
I'm warning you: if songs could sting,
If trills could kill, my dear sweet thing,
You wouldn't linger longer here.
Jug jug, pu-whee! — now, disappear!   15

CONSIDERATIONS FOR CRITICAL THINKING AND WRITING

1. **FIRST RESPONSE.** Jack Palance (1919–2006) was famous for his film roles as a menacing villain dressed in black, especially in westerns, who disrupted peaceful towns. What does he symbolize in this poem?

2. How does the speaker's diction and speech pattern characterize the bird?

3. What serious point breaks through the poem's humor?

CONNECTION TO ANOTHER SELECTION

1. Compare the speaker's tone in "Birdsong Interpreted" and that in Herbert Lomas's "The Fly's Poem about Emily" (p. 829).

The rest of the poems in this chapter explore the natural world inhabited with human beings. What is never absent, however, is the human perception that creates the poems.

JANE HIRSHFIELD (B. 1953)

Happiness 1994

I think it was from the animals
that St. Francis learned
it is possible to cast yourself
on the earth's good mercy and live.
From the wolf who cast off   5
the deep fierceness of her first heart
and crept into the circle of sunlight
in full wariness and wolf-hunger,
and was fed, and lived; from the birds
who came fearless to him until he   10
had no choice but return that courage.
Even the least amoeba touched on all sides
by the opulent Other, even the baleened
plankton fully immersed in their fate —
for what else might happiness be   15
than to be porous, opened, rinsed through
by the beings and things?
Nor could he forget those other companions,
the shifting, ethereal, shapeless:
Hopelessness, Desperateness, Loneliness,   20
even the fire-tongued Anger —
for they too waited with the patient Lion,
the glossy Rooster, the drowsy Mule, to step
out of the trees' protection and come in.

CONSIDERATIONS FOR CRITICAL THINKING AND WRITING

1. **FIRST RESPONSE.** Look up some of the legends associated with St. Francis as the patron saint of animals and the environment. How do they inform the speaker's description of happiness?

2. Discuss the way nature is envisioned in the poem.

3. How is happiness defined by the speaker? To what extent does this definition match your own perspective?

CONNECTION TO ANOTHER SELECTION

1. Contrast the view of nature presented in "Happiness" with that in Emily Dickinson's "Apparently with no surprise" (p. 1085) and Robert Frost's "Design" (p. 1116).

Leslie Marmon Silko (b. 1948)

Love Poem   1970

© Christopher Felver/CORBIS.

Rain smell comes with the wind
               out of the southwest.

Smell of sand dunes
          tall grass glistening
               in the rain.
Warm raindrops that fall easy
            (this woman)

The summer is born.
Smell of her breathing new life
            small gray toads on
   damp sand.

(this woman)
          whispering to dark wide leaves
          white moon blossoms dripping
                 tracks in the   15
   sand.

Rain smell
      I am full of hunger
      deep and longing to touch
wet tall grass, green and strong beneath.   20

This woman loved a man
and she breathed to him
           her damp earth song.

I am haunted by this story
I remember it in cottonwood leaves   25
            their fragrance in
   the shade.

I remember it in the wide blue sky
when the rain smell comes with the wind.

Considerations for Critical Thinking and Writing

1. **First response.** How are the erotic and a sensitivity to the environment joined in the language of this poem's images?

2. Discuss the effects of Silko's use of line spacing on your reading.

3. Explain why this poem is both sensuous and sensual.

Connection to Another Selection

1. Compare how nature is used to express longing in "Love Poem" and in Molly Peacock's "Desire" (p. 979).

MARGARET ATWOOD (B. 1939)

A Holiday   *1984*

My child in the smoke of the fire
playing at barbarism,
the burst meat dripping down her
chin, soot smearing
her cheek and her hair infested with twigs,   5
under a huge midsummer-leafed tree
in the rain, the shelter
of poles and canvas down
the road if needed:

This could be where we   10
end up, learning the minimal
with maybe no tree, no rain,
no shelter, no roast carcasses
of animals to renew us

at a time when language   15
will shrink to the word *hunger*
and the word *none*.

Mist lifts from the warm lake
hit by the cold drizzle:
too much dust in the stratosphere   20
this year, they say. Unseasonal.

Here comes the ice,
here comes something,
we can all feel it
like a breath, a footstep,   25
here comes nothing
with its calm eye of fire.

What we're having right
now is a cookout,
sausages on peeled sticks.   30
The blades of grass are still with us.
My daughter forages,
grace plumps the dusty berries,
two or three hot and squashed in her fist.

So far we do it.   35
for fun. So far is
where we've gone
and no farther.

CONSIDERATIONS FOR CRITICAL THINKING AND WRITING

1. **FIRST RESPONSE.** How does Atwood create suspense in this poem?
2. How does the imagery reveal the speaker's thoughts about society's relationship to nature?
3. Consider the potential ironies present in the title.

CONNECTION TO ANOTHER SELECTION

1. Discuss the treatment of air in "A Holiday" and in Mary Oliver's "Oxygen" (p. 823).

MAXINE KUMIN (B. 1925)
Though He Tarry   2007

© Bettmann/CORBIS.

I believe with perfect faith in
the coming of the Messiah
and though he tarry I will
wait daily for his coming
said Maimonides° in 1190
or so and 44 percent
of people polled in the USA
in 2007 are also waiting
for him to show up in person—
though of course he won't <u>be</u> a person.

Do we want to save our planet,
the only one we know of,
so the faithful 44 percent
can be in a state of high alert
in case he arrives in person   15
though of course he won't <u>be</u> a person?

According to Stephen Jay Gould
        science and religion are
        non-overlapping magisteria°
        See each elbowing the other   20
        to shove over on the bed
        they're condemned to share?
        See how they despise, shrink back
        from accidental touching?
It's no surprise that   25
60 percent of scientists
say they are nonbelievers.

But whether you're churchy or not
what about the planet?
Damn all of you with dumpsters.   30

---

5 *Maimonides* (c. 1135?–1204): A famous medieval Jewish philosopher.
19 *non-overlapping magisteria*: Stephen Jay Gould (1941–2002), an American evolutionary biologist and historian of science, published an article titled "Nonoverlapping Magisteria" in *Natural History* (March 1997) in which he described religion and science as two "magisteria" or domains of inquiry that neither overlap nor conflict with one another: "No such conflict should exist because each subject has a legitimate magisterium, or domain of teaching authority—and these do not overlap."

Damn all who do not compost.
Damn all who tie their dogs out
on bare ground, without water.
Damn all who debeak chickens
and all who eat them, damn   35
CEOs with bonuses,
corporate jets, trophy wives.

Damn venal human nature
lurching our way to a sorry
and probably fiery finale. . . .   40
If only he'd strap his angel wings on
in the ether and get his licensed
and guaranteed ass down here —
though of course he won't <u>be</u> a person —
if only he wouldn't tarry.   45

CONSIDERATIONS FOR CRITICAL THINKING AND WRITING

1. **FIRST RESPONSE.** Explain why you think this poem is more about the existence of God or the existence of the planet.

2. Describe the speaker's tone and whether or not you think it is appropriate for the poem's subject matter.

3. Comment on the significance of the title.

CONNECTION TO ANOTHER SELECTION

1. Compare the themes in this poem and in Gerard Manley Hopkins's "God's Grandeur" (p. 929).

GAIL WHITE (B. 1945)

Dead Armadillos   2000

The smart armadillo stays
on the side of the road
where it was born. The dumb ones
get a sudden urge to check the pickings
across the asphalt, and nine   5
times out of ten, collide
with a ton of moving metal.
They're on my daily route — soft shells
of land crustacea, small blind knights
in armor. No one cares.   10
There is no Save the Armadillo
Society. The Sierra Club and Greenpeace
take no interest. There are too
damned many armadillos, and beauty,
like money, is worth more when it's scarce.   15

Give us time. Let enough of them
try to cross the road.
When we're down to the last half dozen,
we'll see them with the eyes of God.

CONSIDERATIONS FOR CRITICAL THINKING AND WRITING

1. **FIRST RESPONSE.** Why do you think White chooses armadillos rather than, say, foxes to make her point?

2. What keeps this poem from becoming preachy?

3. How does the poem's language reveal the speaker's character?

CONNECTION TO ANOTHER SELECTION

1. Discuss the similarities in theme in "Dead Armadillos" and Margaret Atwood's "A Holiday" (p. 1277).

DAVE LUCAS (B. 1980)

November   2007

October's brief, bright gush is over.
Leaf-lisp and fetch, their cold-tea smell
raked to the curb in copper- and shale-
stained piles, or the struck-match-sweet of sulfur

becoming smoke. The overcast
sky the same slight ambergris.
Hung across it, aghast surprise
of so many clotted, orphaned nests.

CONSIDERATIONS FOR CRITICAL THINKING AND WRITING

1. **FIRST RESPONSE.** What overall impression does this poem convey about the month of November? How does it serve as a dramatic contrast to October?

2. Carefully examine the diction in each line to determine how the poem's images achieve their effects.

3. **CREATIVE RESPONSE.** Choose two consecutive months that offer striking climatic environmental changes in the region where you live and write a two-stanza poem that includes vivid diction and images.

CONNECTION TO ANOTHER SELECTION

1. Consider the tone and theme of "November" and of Robert Frost's "Nothing Gold Can Stay" (p. 1113).

Walt McDonald (b. 1934)

Coming Across It   *1988*

Cans rattle in the alley, a cat
prowling, or a man down on his luck
and starving. Neon on buildings

above us blinks like those eyes
in the dark, too slow for a cat,   5
lower than a man, like fangs,

yellow gold. Crowds shove us toward
something that crouches, this blind
alley like a cave. Someone shouts

Otter, and suddenly a sharp nose   10
wedges into focus, pelt shining,
webbed mammal feet begging for room.

Like a tribe, we huddle here
in the city and call *Here, otter,*
otter, asking how far to the river,   15

the police, the safest zoo. We call it
cute, call it ugly, maybe diseased
or lonely, amazed to find something wild

in the city. We wait for someone
with a gun or net to rescue it.   20
We talk to strangers like brothers,

puzzling what should be done
with dark alleys, with garbage,
with vermin that run free at night.

We keep our eyes on it, keep calling   25
softly to calm it. But if we had
clubs, we'd kill it.

Considerations for Critical Thinking and Writing

1. **First response.** How is suspense created and sustained in the poem?

2. How do these city people respond to "something wild / in the city" (lines 18–19)?

3. How is the otter described? What is the effect of repeatedly referring to the animal as "it"?

Connection to Another Selection

1. Discuss how the unexpected encounter between civilization and nature produces anxiety in "Coming Across It" and in Alden Nowlan's "The Bull Moose" (following).

ALDEN NOWLAN (1933–1983)

The Bull Moose

1962

Down from the purple mist of trees on the mountain,
lurching through forests of white spruce and cedar,
stumbling through tamarack swamps,
came the bull moose
to be stopped at last by a pole-fenced pasture.   5

Too tired to turn or, perhaps, aware
there was no place left to go, he stood with the cattle.
They, scenting the musk of death, seeing his great head
like the ritual mask of a blood god, moved to the other end
of the field, and waited.   10

The neighbors heard of it, and by afternoon
cars lined the road. The children teased him
with alder switches and he gazed at them
like an old, tolerant collie. The women asked
if he could have escaped from a Fair.   15

The oldest man in the parish remembered seeing
a gelded moose yoked with an ox for plowing.
The young men snickered and tried to pour beer
down his throat, while their girl friends took their pictures.

The bull moose let them stroke his tick-ravaged flanks,   20
let them pry open his jaws with bottles, let a giggling girl
plant a little purple cap
of thistles on his head.

When the wardens came, everyone agreed it was a shame
to shoot anything so shaggy and cuddlesome.   25
He looked like the kind of pet
women put to bed with their sons.

So they held their fire. But just as the sun dropped in the river
the bull moose gathered his strength
like a scaffolded king, straightened and lifted his horns   30
so that even the wardens backed away as they raised their rifles.
When he roared, people ran to their cars. All the young men
leaned on their automobile horns as he toppled.

CONSIDERATIONS FOR CRITICAL THINKING AND WRITING

1. **FIRST RESPONSE.** How does the speaker present the moose and the towns-people? How are the moose and townspeople contrasted? Discuss specific lines to support your response.

2. Explain how the symbols in this poem point to a conflict between humanity and nature. What do you think the speaker's attitude toward this conflict is?

3. **CRITICAL STRATEGIES.** Read the section on mythological criticism (pp. 2058–60) in Chapter 53, "Critical Strategies for Reading," and write an essay on "The Bull Moose" that approaches the poem from a mythological perspective.

CONNECTION TO ANOTHER SELECTION

1. In an essay compare and contrast how the animals portrayed in "The Bull Moose" and in Stafford's "Traveling through the Dark" (p. 903) are used as symbols.

ROBERT B. SHAW (B. 1947)

Wild Turkeys   2006

Out of the woods and into the side yard
they come in a slow march, a band of three,
dowdy, diaconal in somber plumes
that so englobe their awkward, ambling bodies
it is hard to believe their pipestem legs   5
truly support them as they promenade.
Their raw red necks and bare heads — slaty blue —
go with the legs, austere, deliberate, wiry,
seconding every step with a prim nod,
while now and then pausing to stoop and nip   10
whatever seeds or beetles their bead-eyes
have got a bead on. When they reach the foot
of the hill they advance gamely, helping themselves
with little hops and only a faint stirring
of wings, going up with uncanny lightness,   15
almost as though inflated (which in a sense
they are, given the air caught up inside
their fusty basketry of quills and pinions).
Whether on forage or reconnaissance,
they know where they are going with no hustle;   20
they are as much unwavering as wild.
Soon they pace out of sight, three emissaries
of shadow taking time to appraise sunshine
on a warm day two weeks before Thanksgiving,
intent as Pilgrims turning out for a hanging.   25

CONSIDERATIONS FOR CRITICAL THINKING AND WRITING

1. **FIRST RESPONSE.** These wild turkeys ultimately promenade through quite a lot of history. How does the appearance of Thanksgiving and the Pilgrims in the last two lines add to their "slow march" (line 2)?

2. Comment on the character of the turkeys that arises from Shaw's description of them.

3. Discuss the tone of the last line. What thoughts and feelings does it leave you contemplating?

CONNECTION TO ANOTHER SELECTION

1. Compare the elements of style used to characterize the birds in "Wild Turkeys" and in Tom Disch's "Birdsong Interpreted" (p. 1274). How do the poetic styles match the birds' characters?

PAUL ZIMMER (B. 1934)

What I Know about Owls   1996

They can break the night like glass.
They can hear a tick turn over in
The fur of a mouse thirty acres away.
Their eyes contain a tincture of magic
So potent they see cells dividing in   5
The hearts of their terrified victims.
You cannot hear their dismaying who,
You cannot speak their awesome name
Without ice clattering in your arteries.

But in daytime owls rest in blindness,   10
Their liquids no longer boiling.
There is a legend that if you are
Careful and foolishly ambitious,
You can gently stroke for luck and life
The delicate feathers on their foreheads,   15
Risking always that later on some
Quiet night when you least expect it,
The owl remembering your transgression,
Will slice into your lamplight like a razor,
Bring you down splayed from your easy chair,   20
Your ribcage pierced, organs raked
From their nests, and your head slowly
Rolling down its bloody pipe into
The fierce acids of its stomach.

CONSIDERATIONS FOR CRITICAL THINKING AND WRITING

1. **FIRST RESPONSE.** What does the speaker find both admirable and fearsome about owls?

2. As gruesome as this poem is, consider whether or not it qualifies as a celebration and appreciation of owls.

3. On a larger scale, what does this poem suggest about humanity's relationship to nature?

CONNECTION TO ANOTHER SELECTION

1. Write an essay comparing the views of nature offered in Zimmer's poem and in Andrew Hudgins's "The Cow" (p. 938).

SUGGESTED TOPICS FOR LONGER PAPERS

1. Write an analysis of Gail White's "Dead Armadillos" (p. 1279), Walt McDonald's "Coming Across It" (p. 1281), and Alden Nowlan's "The Bull Moose" (p. 1282) as commentaries on our civilization's problematic relationship to the wild. How does each poem add to and extend a consideration of the issue?

2. Use the Internet to find the lyrics of popular songs written within the past five years about environmental issues. Choose three and write a comparative analysis of their style and themes.

A THEMATIC CASE STUDY
Crossing Boundaries

As immigrants we have this enormous
raw material. . . . We draw from a dual
culture, with two sets of worldviews
and paradigms juxtaposing each other.
— CHITRA BANERJEE DIVAKARUNI

This chapter brings together six poems and a variety of images that center
upon the theme of crossing borders. The borders referred to in these poems
mark not only geographic or political divisions but also the uncertain and
indeterminate borders associated with culture, class, race, ethnicity, and gender. Even if we have never left our home state or country, we have all moved
back and forth across such defining lines as we negotiate the margins and
edges of our personal identities within the particular worlds we inhabit. Any
first-year college student, for example, knows that college life and demanding course work represent a significant border crossing: increased academic
challenges, responsibility, and autonomy likely reflect an entirely new culture
for the student. By Thanksgiving vacation, students know (as do their parents and friends) that they've crossed an invisible border that causes a slight
shift in their identity because they've done some growing and maturing.

A

The poems and visuals in this chapter explore a wide range of border crossings. Phillis Wheatley was kidnapped and forced across borders in 1761 when she was brought to America as a slave. Her poem "On Being Brought from Africa to America" offers a fascinating argument against racism. Wheatley's perspective is deepened by a diagram of a ship and an advertisement for an auction that vividly illustrate how slaves were transported and marketed. Racial tensions are internalized in Pat Mora's "Legal Alien" and Jacalyn López García's "I Just Wanted to Be Me," which describe the dilemma of being raised as a Mexican American. Sandra M. Gilbert examines the pain caused by ethnic stereotyping in "Mafioso," which is complemented by a revealing photograph of Italian immigrant children as they are processed at Ellis Island. The anxieties felt by new immigrants and their yearnings for the life they left behind are the subject of Chitra Banerjee Divakaruni's "Indian Movie, New Jersey," which is paired with an optimistic cover of a Bollywood film soundtrack. The prejudice that causes some of the anxiety in that poem is also evident in Janice Mirikitani's "Recipe," a satire commenting on the impact of Western beauty ideals on Japanese girls and women. The relevance of that problem is brought home in the accompanying photograph by Chiaki Tsukumo of a child holding one of Japan's most popular dolls. Finally, Thomas Lynch's "Liberty" provides an amusing but pointed look at an Irish American who finds suburban life to be a lamentable state compared to the life of his ancestors in Ireland. The photograph of a crowded, working-class Boston suburb that follows the poem tidily captures Lynch's themes.

A list of additional thematically related poems is located at the end of this chapter.

■ **Transcendence and Borders.** Born in West Africa, Phillis Wheatley was kidnapped and brought to America in 1761 and sold to John and Susannah Wheatley of Boston. She was taught to read and write and was then freed at about the age of thirteen. Her remarkable intelligence and talents led Susannah to help her publish *Poems on Various Subjects, Religious and Moral* in 1773. The influence of religion on her poetry is clearly evident in "On Being Brought from Africa to America." Wheatley's response to having been a slave in America is complicated by her acceptance of the religion, language, and even the literary style of the white culture that she found there. The harsh nature of slavery is apparent, however, in the diagram of a slave ship and a slave-auction advertisement. Do these documents qualify Wheatley's description of her origins and the new world into which she was brought as a slave?

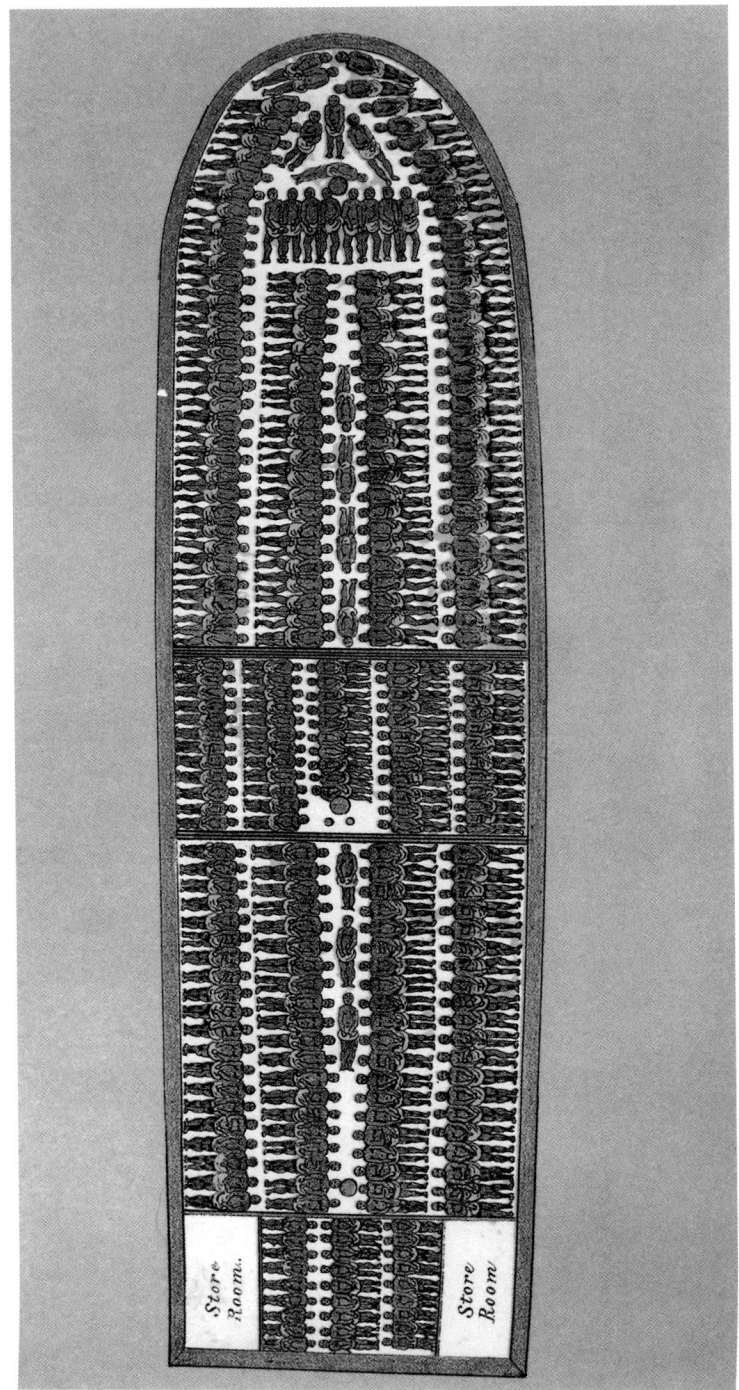

Diagram of an Eighteenth-Century Slave Ship. Often tightly packed and confined in spaces smaller than graves, slaves were subjected to inadequate ventilation and extremely unsanitary conditions. Many died of suffocation or disease during the 3,700-mile voyage from Africa to America.

PHILLIS WHEATLEY (1753?–1784)

On Being Brought from Africa to America

1773

'Twas mercy brought me from my pagan land,
Taught my benighted soul to understand
That there's a God — that there's a Saviour too;
Once I redemption neither sought nor knew.
Some view our sable race with scornful eye —
"Their color is a diabolic dye."
Remember, Christians, Negroes black as Cain°
May be refined, and join the angelic train.

7 *Cain:* In the Bible, Cain murdered Abel and was therefore "marked" by God. That mark has been interpreted by some readers as the origin of dark-skinned people (see Genesis 4:1–15).

CONSIDERATIONS FOR CRITICAL THINKING AND WRITING

1. How does the speaker argue against the pervasive racist views concerning Africans in the eighteenth century?

2. Do you find the argument convincing? Explain whether your own refutation of racism would be argued on similar or other grounds.

3. What arguments are put forth on the slave-auction poster? What attitudes are revealed by its author's choice of words?

Negroes for Sale.

A Cargo of very fine stout Men and Women, in good order and fit for immediate service, just imported from the Windward Coast of Africa, in the Ship Two Brothers.— Conditions are one half Cash or Produce, the other half payable the first of January next, giving Bond and Security if required.

The Sale to be opened at 10 o'Clock each Day, in Mr. Bourdeaux's Yard, at No, 48, on the Bay.

May 19, 1784.   JOHN MITCHELL.

Thirty Seasoned Negroes

To be Sold for Credit, at Private Sale.

AMONGST which is a Carpenter, none of whom are known to be dishonest.

Also, to be sold for Cash, a regular bred young Negroe Man-Cook, born in this Country, who served several Years under an exceeding good French Cook abroad, and his Wife a middle aged Washer-Woman, (both very honest) and their two Children. Likewise, a young Man a Carpenter.

For Terms apply to the Printer.

1784 Slave-Auction Advertisement. In preparation for sale at auction, slaves were fed and washed by the ship's crew. Tar or palm oil was used to disguise sores or wounds caused by poor conditions on board.
© CORBIS.

4. Consider Wheatley's poem alongside the slave-ship diagram and the advertisement for a slave auction. How do you account for the speaker's attitude toward slavery and redemption in relation to the historical realities of slavery?

CONNECTION TO ANOTHER SELECTION

1. Compare the tone and theme of Wheatley's poem with those of Langston Hughes's "I, Too" (p. 1137).

■ **Identity and Borders.** In "Legal Alien" Pat Mora explores the difficulties of living in two different cultures simultaneously. The poem's speaker, both Mexican and American, worries that each cultural identity displaces the other, leaving the speaker standing alone between both worlds. Similarly, Jacalyn López García, a multimedia artist who combines computer art, video, and music CD-ROMs to create complex images, explores the dilemmas that she encountered while being raised as a Mexican American. How do the poem and the image evoke the tensions produced by trying to assimilate into a new culture while trying to hold on to the cultural values brought from one's native country?

PAT MORA (B. 1942)

Legal Alien   *1985*

Bi-lingual, Bi-cultural,
able to slip from "How's life?"
to *"Me'stan volviendo loca,"*°
able to sit in a paneled office
drafting memos in smooth English,   5
able to order in fluent Spanish
at a Mexican restaurant,
American but hyphenated,
viewed by Anglos as perhaps exotic,
perhaps inferior, definitely different,   10
viewed by Mexicans as alien,
(their eyes say, "You may speak
Spanish but you're not like me")
an American to Mexicans
a Mexican to Americans   15
a handy token
sliding back and forth
between the fringes of both worlds

3 *Me'stan . . . loca:* They are driving me crazy.

I NEVER

MY MOTHER'S STORY

"I raised my children speaking English only because I did not want them to have an accent."

WANTED

"I thought it would be easier for them."

TO BE

"After all, I spoke English, having attended an American school in Casas Grandes, Mexico."

"WHITE"

"But I never had the privileges of being "white".

"I Just Wanted to Be Me" (1997), by Jacalyn López García. In her multimedia exhibit *Glass Houses*, García explores family history and issues of identity. "As we crossed the Mexican border, the border patrol would ask me my citizenship. I would reply, 'American' because my parents taught me to say that. But in California, people would ask me 'What are you?'... I would proudly reply 'Mexican.' It wasn't until I became a teenager that I claimed I was 'Mexican-American.'" Once, a white neighbor reported to authorities that García's mother was undocumented. "I was only seven years old when my mother was deported, my brother was six. The Christmas tree stayed up until Mom returned home in April of the following year." Reprinted by permission of Jacalyn López García.

by smiling
by masking the discomfort   20
of being pre-judged
Bi-laterally.

CONSIDERATIONS FOR CRITICAL THINKING AND WRITING

1. **FIRST RESPONSE.** What is the nature of the discomfort the speaker experiences as an "American but hyphenated" (line 8)? Explain whether you think the advantages outweigh the disadvantages.

2. What qualities do you think make someone an American? How does your description compare with your classmates' views? How do you account for the differences or similarities?

3. Discuss the appropriateness of the poem's title. How does it encapsulate the speaker's emotional as well as official status?

4. How do poet Pat Mora and artist Jacalyn López García incorporate multiple voices into their work? Why do you think they do so?

CONNECTION TO ANOTHER SELECTION

1. Compare and contrast the speakers' responses to "sliding back and forth / between the fringes of both worlds" (lines 17–18) in Mora's "Legal Alien" and in Julia Alvarez's "Queens, 1963" (p. 1192).

■ **Immigration and Borders.** Ethnic stereotypes are the legacy Sandra M. Gilbert examines in "Mafioso." Her poem raises important questions about the way in which popular culture shapes our assumptions about and perceptions of ethnic groups. How much of what we regard as quintessentially Italian American is generated by films like *The Godfather* or television programs like *The Sopranos*? How did most immigrants actually work to become Americans once they arrived on the country's shores? A glimpse of the nature of that struggle is suggested by the 1911 photograph of three boys undergoing an examination at Ellis Island. Do you think the photograph supports or qualifies Gilbert's assessment of the difficulties immigrants faced upon their arrival in America?

SANDRA M. GILBERT (B. 1936)

Mafioso   *1979*

Frank Costello eating spaghetti in a cell at San Quentin,
Lucky Luciano mixing up a mess of bullets and
calling for parmesan cheese,
Al Capone baking a sawed-off shotgun into a
huge lasagna —   5
                        are you my uncles, my
only uncles?

            O Mafiosi,
bad uncles of the barren
cliffs of Sicily — was it only you   10
that they transported in barrels
like pure olive oil
across the Atlantic?

                Was *it* only you
who got out at Ellis Island with   15
black scarves on your heads and cheap cigars
and no English and a dozen children?

No carts were waiting, gallant with paint,
no little donkeys plumed like the dreams of peacocks.
Only the evil eyes of a thousand buildings   20
stared across at the echoing debarkation center,
making it seem so much smaller than a piazza,

only a half dozen Puritan millionaires stood on the wharf,
in the wind colder than the impossible snows of the Abruzzi,
ready with country clubs and dynamos   25

to grind the organs out of you.

"Baggage Examined Here" (1911). Between 1880 and 1920, nearly four million Italian immigrants came to the United States, most arriving in New York City and settling in cities along the East Coast. While first- and second-class steamship passengers were quickly inspected on board and allowed to disembark in Manhattan, third-class passengers, such as the boys in this photo, were taken to Ellis Island, where they were subjected to a series of medical examinations and interviews. Inspectors marked the immigrants' clothing with chalk, indicating the need for further examination: *Sc* for scalp disease, *G* for goiter, *H* for hernia, *L* for lameness, or *S* for senility.

© Bettmann/CORBIS.

CONSIDERATIONS FOR CRITICAL THINKING AND WRITING

1. FIRST RESPONSE. In what sense are the gangsters Frank Costello, Lucky Luciano, and Al Capone in the first stanza to be understood as "bad uncles" (line 9)? How does the speaker feel about the "uncles"?

2. Explain how nearly all of the images in the poem are associated with Italian life. Does the poem reinforce stereotypes about Italians or invoke images about them for some other purpose? If so, what other purpose?

3. What sort of people are the "Puritan millionaires" (line 23)? What is their relationship to the "bad uncles"?

4. Consider the photograph. Why was it taken? What does this image convey about attitudes toward working-class immigrants processed at Ellis Island? How do the words "Baggage Examined Here" function in the image? How do these words connect with the last line of Gilbert's poem ("to grind the organs out of you")? What comments are the photograph and poem making about the experience?

CONNECTIONS TO OTHER SELECTIONS

1. Discuss the ways in which ethnicity is used to create meaning in "Mafioso" and in Jimmy Santiago Baca's "Green Chile" (p. 845).

2. How do the attitudes conveyed in "Mafioso" and the photograph "Baggage Examined Here" compare with the sentiments expressed in Emma Lazarus's "The New Colossus" (p. 1336), the poem inscribed at the base of the Statue of Liberty?

■ **Expectations and Borders.** The immigrants' dream of America is deeply present in Chitra Banerjee Divakaruni's "Indian Movie, New Jersey." The hopeful expectation that immigrants bring with them takes on a nostalgic and melancholy tone as the speaker contrasts America as imagined to the country that is experienced. The Indian movie offers yet another dream that suggests a powerful yearning for a different kind of life than the one found in New Jersey. Is the movie version of India any more or less real than the speaker's picture of America? Is this poem more about disillusionment or delusion?

CHITRA BANERJEE DIVAKARUNI (B. 1956)

Indian Movie, New Jersey

1990

Not like the white filmstars, all rib
and gaunt cheekbone, the Indian sex-goddess
smiles plumply from behind a flowery
branch. Below her brief red skirt, her thighs
are satisfying-solid, redeeming   5
as tree trunks. She swings her hips
and the men-viewers whistle. The lover-hero
dances in to a song, his lip-sync

a little off, but no matter, we
know the words already and sing along.   10
It is safe here, the day
golden and cool so no one sweats,
roses on every bush and the Dal Lake
clean again.
        The sex-goddess switches   15
to thickened English to emphasize
a joke. We laugh and clap. Here
we need not be embarrassed by words
dropping like lead pellets into foreign ears.
The flickering movie-light   20
wipes from our faces years of America, sons
who want mohawks and refuse to run
the family store, daughters who date
on the sly.
        When at the end the hero   25
dies for his friend who also
loves the sex-goddess and now can marry her,
we weep, understanding. Even the men
clear their throats to say, "What *qurbani*!°   *sacrifice*
What *dosti*!"° After, we mill around   *friendship* 30
unwilling to leave, exchange greetings
and good news: a new gold chain, a trip
to India. We do not speak
of motel raids, canceled permits, stones
thrown through glass windows, daughters and sons   35
raped by Dotbusters.°
        In this dim foyer
we can pull around us the faint, comforting smell
of incense and *pakoras,*° can arrange   *fried appetizers*
our children's marriages with hometown boys and girls,
open a franchise, win a million   40
in the mail. We can retire
in India, a yellow two-storied house
with wrought-iron gates, our own
Ambassador car. Or at least   45
move to a rich white suburb, Summerfield
or Fort Lee, with neighbors that will
talk to us. Here while the film-songs still echo
in the corridors and restrooms, we can trust
in movie truths: sacrifice, success, love and luck,   50
the America that was supposed to be.

36 *Dotbusters:* New Jersey gangs that attack Indians.

CONSIDERATIONS FOR CRITICAL THINKING AND WRITING

I. **FIRST RESPONSE.** Why does the speaker feel comfortable at the movies? How is the world inside the theater different from life outside in New Jersey?

Rawal Films, *Ladki Pasand Hai* (*I Like This Girl*) (1971). India's massive Hindi-language film industry, known as Bollywood (a play on the word Hollywood, with the *B* representing Bombay), produces twice as many films as Hollywood each year, with a huge international audience. Bollywood films are churned out so quickly that sometimes scripts are handwritten and actors on set shoot scenes for multiple films. Traditionally, these colorful extravaganzas, chock-full of singing, dancing, and multiple costume changes, stick to a "boy meets girl" formula — a hero and heroine fall in love and then struggle for family approval. This image is from the soundtrack to a 1971 film with a typical Bollywood plot.
Reprinted by permission of HMV/Odeon. Courtesy of Niall Richardson.

2. Explain the differences portrayed by the speaker between life in India and life in New Jersey. What connotative values are associated with each location in the poem? Discuss the irony in the final two lines.

3. How do the ideas and values of the Bollywood poster contrast with the realities conveyed in the last part of the poem?

CONNECTION TO ANOTHER SELECTION

1. Explain how the speaker's idea of "the America that was supposed to be" (line 51) compares with the nation described in Florence Cassen Mayers's "All-American Sestina" (p. 984).

■ **Beauty and Borders.** Janice Mirikitani, a third-generation Japanese American, reflects upon dominant cultural standards of beauty in "Recipe." Women who do not meet such standards — especially women of color — can be faced with complicated decisions about how they want to appear, decisions that go far more than skin deep. Chiaki Tsukumo's 2003 photograph of a young Tokyo girl holding a popular Western-style doll demonstrates how powerful Western concepts of beauty are, even among non-Western people. Why are "Round Eyes" so desirable? What kind of price is paid for such a desire?

JANICE MIRIKITANI (B. 1942)

Recipe

1987

Round Eyes

Ingredients: scissors, Scotch magic transparent tape,
eyeliner — water based, black.
Optional: false eyelashes.

Cleanse face thoroughly.   5

For best results, powder entire face, including eyelids.
    (lighter shades suited to total effect desired)

With scissors, cut magic tape $^1/_{16}"$ wide, $^3/_4" - ^1/_2"$ long —
depending on length of eyelid.

Stick firmly onto mid–upper eyelid area   10
    (looking down into handmirror facilitates finding
    adequate surface)

If using false eyelashes, affix first on lid, folding any
excess lid over the base of eyelash with glue.

Paint black eyeliner on tape and entire lid.   15

Do not cry.

CONSIDERATIONS FOR CRITICAL THINKING AND WRITING

1. **FIRST RESPONSE.** Discuss your response to the poem's final line.
2. Why does Mirikitani write the poem in recipe form? What is the effect of the very specific details of this recipe?
3. Why is "false eyelashes" (line 4) a particularly resonant phrase in the context of this poem?
4. Consider and note the Licca doll's hair, eyes, and costume in the photograph by Chiaki Tsukumo. How do you account for the success of the Licca doll? What do you make of the toymaker's claim that the doll makes "girls' dreams and wishes come true"? What dreams and wishes do you think the toymaker is selling? How do the ideals that the toymaker (Takara) associates with the Licca doll compare with those associated with Barbie?
5. How does the paragraph connect with Mirikitani's satirical poem?

"Girl with Licca Doll," by Chiaki Tsukumo (2003). According to the Japanese toymaker Takara, "Licca-chan was developed to make girls' dreams and wishes come true" and "to nurture kindness, gentleness, and love in children." A fan's personal Web site notes that Licca-chan "hates arithmetic, but she's good at language, music, and art." Her favorite books are *Anne of Green Gables* and *A Little Princess*, and she loves eating ice cream and window-shopping. First introduced in 1967, the doll has since sold nearly fifty million units and become, according to the toymaker, a national character that has inspired a Licca-chan generation of women consumers.
Reprinted by permission of the Associated Press.

CONNECTION TO ANOTHER SELECTION

1. How might the voice in Michelle Boisseau's "Self-Pity's Closet" (p. 1287) be read as a version of the speaker in "Recipe"?

■ **Freedom and Borders.**   Thomas Lynch's "Liberty" is an amusing protest against conformity, the kind of middling placidity often associated with suburban life in America. The blustery Irish speaker in this poem laments the lost world his ancestors inhabited in Ireland and longs for the "form[s] of freedom" that they once enjoyed. Though the speaker may cause us to smile, his complaint is serious nonetheless. The potential validity of his assessment of suburban life is presented visually in the accompanying photograph of Somerville, Massachusetts, a suburb of Boston. How might Lynch's speaker be considered a resident of one of those houses? Does the arrangement of the streets and houses help to explain the attitudes expressed in the poem? What are your own views about the suburbs?

THOMAS LYNCH (B. 1948)

Liberty

1998

Some nights I go out and piss on the front lawn
as a form of freedom — liberty from
porcelain and plumbing and the Great Beyond
beyond the toilet and the sewage works.
Here is the statement I am trying to make: 5
to say I am from a fierce bloodline of men
who made their water in the old way, under stars
that overarched the North Atlantic where
the River Shannon empties into sea.
The ex-wife used to say, "Why can't you pee   10
in concert with the most of humankind
who do their business tidily indoors?"
It was gentility or envy, I suppose,
because I could do it anywhere, and do
whenever I begin to feel encumbered.   15
Still, there is nothing, here in the suburbs,
as dense as the darkness in West Clare
nor any equivalent to the nightlong wind
that rattles in the hedgerow of whitethorn there
on the east side of the cottage yard in Moveen.   20
It was market day in Kilrush, years ago:
my great-great-grandfather bargained with tinkers
who claimed it was whitethorn that Christ's crown was made from.
So he gave them two and six and brought them home —
mere saplings then — as a gift for the missus,   25
who planted them between the house and garden.
For years now, men have slipped out the back door
during wakes or wedding feasts or nights of song
to pay their homage to the holy trees
and, looking up into that vast firmament,   30
consider liberty in that last townland where
they have no crowns, no crappers and no ex-wives.

CONSIDERATIONS FOR CRITICAL THINKING AND WRITING

1. **FIRST RESPONSE.** Does "gentility or envy" (line 13) get in the way of your enjoyment and appreciation of this poem? Explain why or why not.

2. Characterize the speaker and explain why you find him engaging or not. What sort of "liberty" does he insist upon?

3. Consider Alex MacLean's aerial photograph of Somerville, Massachusetts. What strikes you about this landscape? What is the thinking behind this example of city planning? How does such a plan affect personal freedoms, and how might it inspire rebellion such as that of the speaker in Lynch's poem?

"Somerville, Massachusetts," by Alex MacLean (1993). Between 1870 and 1915, new streetcar lines in the Boston suburb of Somerville spurred major population growth in the area. Many of the newcomers were immigrants, including Irish workers attracted by plentiful jobs at the brickyards and in the slaughtering and meatpacking industry. The two-family houses in this photograph were built around 1910 to house the new population. By World War II, these neighborhoods swelled to a population density said to be greater than that of Calcutta.
Reprinted by permission of Alex S. MacLean/Landslides.

CONNECTION TO ANOTHER SELECTION

1. Discuss Lynch's treatment of suburban life and compare it with that of John Ciardi in "Suburban" (p. 1247). What similarities are there in the themes and metaphoric strategies of these two poems?

SUGGESTED TOPICS FOR LONGER PAPERS

1. Write an essay that develops a common theme or thread that you find in all six poems presented in this chapter. You may explore similarities or differences concerning any aspect of the border crossings they examine.

2. Choose one of the poems listed on the next page and research at least three images that complement, extend, or qualify the poem. Select rich images that allow you to write an essay explaining how they are thematically connected to the idea of crossing boundaries in the poem.

Selections related to this chapter

An Anthology
of Poems

42

An Album of
Contemporary Poems

Now the role of poetry is not simply to
hold understanding in place but to help
create and hold a realm of experience.
Poetry has become a kind of tool for
knowing the world in a particular way.
        —JANE HIRSHFIELD

© Jerry Bauer.

MICHELLE BOISSEAU (B. 1955)

Born in Cincinnati, Michelle Boisseau earned a B.A. and M.A. from Ohio
University and a Ph.D. from the University of Houston. She teaches literature and writing courses at the University of Missouri,
Kansas City. She has received a National Endowment
for the Arts fellowship and prizes from the Poetry Society of America. Her poetry collections include *No Pri-
vate Life* (1990); *Understory* (1996), winner of the Morse Prize; and *Trembling
Air* (2003).

Web Research the
poets in this chapter at
bedfordstmartins.com/
meyerlit.

Self-Pity's Closet   *2003*

Depression, loneliness, anger, shame, envy,
appetite without hunger, unquenchable
thirst, secret open wounds, long parades
of punishments, resentment honed and glinting

in the sun, the wind driving a few leaves,   5
an empty bird call, the grass bent down, far off
a dog barking and barking, the skin sticky,
the crotch itchy, the tongue stinking, the eyes,
words thrust from the mouth like bottles off a bridge,
tangy molasses of disgust, dank memory   10
of backs, of eyebrows raised and cool expressions
after your vast and painful declarations,
subtle humiliations creeping up
like the smell of wet upholstery, dial tone
in the brain, the conviction that your friends   15
never really loved you, the certitude
you deserved no better, never have, stains
in the carpet, the faucet drilling the sink,
the nights raining spears of stars, the days bland
and blank as newspapers eaten slowly   20
in the bathtub, the clock, the piano,
heavy impatient books, slippery pens,
the radio, a bug bouncing against
the window: go away, make it all go away.

CONNECTIONS TO OTHER SELECTIONS

1. Compare the pain experienced by the speaker in this poem with the
   speaker's pain in T. S. Eliot's "The Love Song of J. Alfred Prufrock" (p. 1216).
   How do the images in each poem reveal the speaker's state of mind?

2. Discuss the themes you find in this poem and in Edgar Allan Poe's "The
   Haunted Palace" (p. 891). Explain whether or not you think the differences
   between these two poems are greater than their similarities.

EAMON GRENNAN (B. 1941)

Born in Dublin, Ireland, Eamon Grennan has lived most of his life in the
United States since the early 1960s, though he is a frequent visitor to his
homeland. After completing his education at University College, Dublin,
and Harvard University, he began teaching at Vassar College, where he is a
professor of English. His poetry has won him a number of honors and
awards, including fellowships from the National Endowment for the Arts,
the National Endowment for the Humanities, and the John Guggenheim
Foundation. His most recent collections of poems include *Selected and New
Poems* (2000), *Still Life with Waterfall* (2002), *Renvyle, Winter* (2003), *The Quick
of It* (2005), and *Matter of Fact: Poems* (2008).

Herringbone   2007

By a dark green altar of moss
the ruffled herringbone twirl
of water: on its downstream
escalator two mallards snatch
a ride at the speed of water,   5
then take to air in a flurry of
flashes (brown, white, royal blue)
where the current crack-foams
over stone. Brisk thinkers
on the wing, they manage a   10
brusque trajectory to clear
the bridge, its one eye shining,
shivery with watershadow.

Time to weigh the few things
learned: the loud clean sound   15
the titmouse makes in April;
hearty whicker-whinny
of the flicker; the eight-note
plaintive song that says
somewhere inside the naked   20
network of hedges a white-
throated sparrow is uttering
something, letting silence settle,
then again saying it, finding it
right and sufficient   25
                    Isn't that
a lovely bit of herringbone tweed,
my mother would say, savoring
the word so you could see
and feel it. Likewise these simple   30
singers laying claim to space
make me feel the sturdy substance
of the air I walk through, the
life they make — as my mother
always did — a daily habit of.   35

Connections to Other Selections

1. Describe how sound is central to the effects and meanings of this poem
   and of Galway Kinnell's "Blackberry Eating" (p. 924).
2. Compare the themes of "Herringbone" and Mary Oliver's "The Poet with
   His Face in His Hands" (p. 781).

MARY STEWART HAMMOND (B. 1953)

Raised in Virginia and Maryland, Mary Stewart Hammond now lives in New York City, where she teaches master poetry classes for the New York Writer's Workshop. Her first book, *Out of Canaan* (1991), won the Great Lakes Colleges' Best First Collection of Poetry prize. Her poems have appeared in a variety of magazines and journals, such as *American Poetry Review, Atlantic Monthly,* the *New Yorker, Paris Review, Yale Review,* and *Shenandoah.* She has been awarded fellowships at the MacDowell Colony and Yaddo.

High Ground   2008

My husband and I sit in cones of electric light
reading in down-filled, chintz-covered armchairs
in our pretty little parlor in our pretty second home.
The tinnitus of crickets and the hiss of the sprinkler system
seep through screened doors and windows.   5
Thousands of miles away people are drowning.

In droves. For days. They stuff rags under their doors.
They perch on rooftops screaming, to us, to high heaven, to
anyone, for help. The water is rising. They dog-paddle
into our parlor exhausted. They are in despair. The wind   10
is roaring. They are the size of pixels. They can't be heard.
Bach's Brandenburg Concerto #6 fills the room.

Last night my husband dreamed we were standing in water.
The water was rising. It was clear. It was potable.
But it was rising. It was reaching our mouths.   15
We interpret his dream as empathy. But that's just a dream.
We, of course, can swim. Join us. Two hundred feet away
the sea kisses and kisses our shore.

CONNECTIONS TO OTHER SELECTIONS

1. Compare the narrative strategy of this poem with that in "Building with Its Face Blown Off" by Billy Collins (p. 1176).
2. Discuss the speakers' responses to witnessing human suffering on television in "High Ground" and in James Merrill's "Casual Wear" (p. 907).

TONY HOAGLAND (B. 1953)

Born in Fort Bragg, North Carolina, Tony Hoagland has published collections of poetry that include *Sweet Rain* (1993), awarded the Brittingham Prize in Poetry; *Donkey Gospel* (1998), awarded the James Laughlin Award of the Academy of American Poets; *What Narcissism Means to Me* (2003); and *Hard*

Rain (2005). He has received writing grants from the Guggenheim Foundation, the National Endowment for the Arts, and the Academy of Arts and Letters. He teaches in the graduate program at the University of Houston.

America   *2003*

Then one of the students with blue hair and a tongue stud
Says that America is for him a maximum-security prison

Whose walls are made of RadioShacks and Burger Kings, and MTV episodes
Where you can't tell the show from the commercials,

And as I consider how to express how full of shit I think he is,   5
He says that even when he's driving to the mall in his Isuzu

Trooper with a gang of his friends, letting rap music pour over them
Like a boiling Jacuzzi full of ballpeen hammers, even then he feels

Buried alive, captured and suffocated in the folds
Of the thick satin quilt of America   10

And I wonder if this is a legitimate category of pain,
Or whether he is just spin doctoring a better grade,

And then I remember that when I stabbed my father in the dream last night,
It was not blood but money

That gushed out of him, bright green hundred-dollar bills   15
Spilling from his wounds, and — this is the weird part —,

He gasped, "Thank god — those Ben Franklins were
Clogging up my heart —

And so I perish happily,
Freed from that which kept me from my liberty" —   20

Which is when I knew it was a dream, since my dad
Would never speak in rhymed couplets,

And I look at the student with his acne and cell phone and phony ghetto
      clothes
And I think, "I am asleep in America too,

And I don't know how to wake myself either,"   25
And I remember what Marx said near the end of his life:

"I was listening to the cries of the past,
When I should have been listening to the cries of the future."

But how could he have imagined 100 channels of 24-hour cable
Or what kind of nightmare it might be   30

When each day you watch rivers of bright merchandise run past you
And you are floating in your pleasure boat upon this river

Even while others are drowning underneath you
And you see their faces twisting in the surface of the waters

And yet it seems to be your own hand 35
Which turns the volume higher?

Connections to Other Selections

1. Discuss the treatment of self-pity in "America" and in Michelle Boisseau's "Self-Pity's Closet" (p. 1287).

2. Explain how "America" and Barbara Hamby's "Ode to American English" (p. 817) offer contrasting visions of American life and culture.

Rachel Loden (b. 1948)

Born in Washington, D.C., Rachel Loden grew up in New York, Connecticut, and California. Her first book, *Hotel Imperium* (1999), won the Contemporary Poetry Series Competition and was named one of the ten best poetry books of the year by the *San Francisco Chronicle*, which called it "quirky and beguiling." Loden has also published four chapbooks, including *The Last Campaign* (1998) and *The Richard Nixon Snow Globe* (2005). Her second full-length book, *Dick of the Dead*, was published by Ashahta Press in 2009. Her work appears in numerous anthologies, among them two editions of *The Best American Poetry* (1995 and 2005). Awards include a Pushcart Prize, a fellowship in poetry from the California Arts Council, and a grant from the Fund for Poetry.

© Jussi Ketonen.

Locked Ward: Newtown, Connecticut 2005

Your tight-lipped jailer beckons
and I trail her like a moon.

The padding of her strange white shoes,
the doors she unlocks one by one —

then you are there on the edge of a cot 5
like a whipped child, with your eyes down.

There are no sharp objects in here,
only the malignant shapes

that dance out
when the strappings are undone.   10

I have brought you what you wanted
from home. A robe, a sweater—

an irony, as though what you wanted
could be mine to give so

easily. Oh I   15
would wrap you up and carry you away

to some all-powerful physician
or at least some place

they'd let you rave in peace.
Silence of the years, the sins against   20

the white page. Carried always out to sea
by the foul winds off the laundry,

the stains that cannot be removed
by any washing of the hands.

The years are mute. And yet   25
there is no end to the lament

of daughters, no end
to the sharp objects in the heart.

CONNECTIONS TO OTHER SELECTIONS

1. Discuss the parent-daughter relationship as it is revealed by the images in Loden's poem and in Cathy Song's "The Youngest Daughter" (p. 824).
2. Compare the themes in Loden's poem and in Emily Dickinson's "One need not be a Chamber—to be Haunted—" (p. 1066).

SUSAN MINOT (B. 1956)

Born and raised in Massachusetts, Susan Minot earned a B.A. at Brown University and an M.F.A. at Columbia University. Before devoting herself full-time to writing, Minot worked as an assistant editor at *Grand Street* magazine. Her stories have appeared in the *Atlantic Monthly, Harper's,* the *New Yorker, Mademoiselle,* and *Paris Review.* Her short stories have been collected in *Lust and Other Stories* (1989), and she has published four novels—*Monkeys* (1986), *Folly* (1992), *Evening* (1998), and *Rapture* (2002), as well as one volume of poetry: *Poems 4 A.M.* (2002).

Courtesy of Dinah Minot Hubley.

My Husband's Back   2005

Sunday evening.
Breakdown hour. Weeping into
a pot of burnt rice. Sun dimmed
like a light bulb gone out
behind a gray lawn of snow.   5
The baby flushed with the flu
asleep on a pillow.
The fire won't catch.
The wet wood's caked
with ice. Sitting   10
on the couch my spine
collides with all its bones
and I watch my husband
peer past the glass grate
and blow.   15
His back in a snug plaid shirt
gray and white
leaning into the woodstove
is firm and compact
like a young man's back.   20

And the giant world which swirls
in my head
stopping most thought
suddenly ceases
to spin. It sits   25
right there, the back I love,
animal and gamine, leaning
on one arm.
I could crawl on it forever
the one point in the world   30
turns out
I have travelled everywhere
to get to.

CONNECTIONS TO OTHER SELECTIONS

1. Compare Minot's "My Husband's Back" and Anne Bradstreet's "To My
   Dear and Loving Husband" (p. 1235) as love poems.
2. Discuss the speakers' tones and treatment of domestic life in Minot's poem
   and in Galway Kinnell's "After Making Love We Hear Footsteps" (p. 1007).

ROBERT MORGAN (B. 1944)

Robert Morgan is a poet and novelist who has been widely praised as the
poet laureate of Appalachia. Morgan was born and raised in North Carolina
in a small, isolated valley in the Blue Ridge Mountains. He earned his B.A.

from the University of North Carolina at Chapel Hill and his M.A. from the University of North Carolina at Greensboro. He has published six books of fiction since 1969, including *The Hinterlands* (1994), *The Truest Pleasure* (1995), and *Brave Enemies* (2008). He has been widely published in such magazines as *Atlantic Monthly, New Republic, Poetry, Southern Review, Yale Review, Carolina Quarterly,* and *New England Review*. He has also published ten volumes of poetry, his latest titled *The Strange Attractor* (2004). In 1971 he began teaching at Cornell University, where, since 1992, he has been Kappa Alpha Professor of English. He has won several awards, including four National Endowment for the Arts fellowships and a Guggenheim Fellowship, and his poetry has appeared in *New Stories from the South* and *Prize Stories: The O. Henry Awards*. His novel *Gap Creek* (1999) was selected for Oprah's Book Club, and *Boone, A Biography* (2007) was awarded the Thomas Wolfe Prize.

Fever Wit

2000

If a child or young adult lay
near crisis with a temperature,
bedclothes hot as from an iron,
face swollen bright as a blown coal,
neighbors and kin would gather round,   5
sitting near the bedside, leaning
close, awaiting words uttered from
delirium, the scattered phrase
and mutter from hot throat and brain.
Every mumble seemed a message   10
to interpret, each groan and wince,
jerk and whisper, a report in
testimony from other tongues,
as though the sick child glowing with
infection could see beyond in   15
fever intoxication, become
a filament for lighting their
ordinary lives with lightning glimpse
burned through the secret boundary,
the ill one privileged to say   20
across and not distort or resist
the wisdom of sickness, the vision
from pain-fire's further peaks, before
the dreaded sweat, the chill descent.

CONNECTIONS TO OTHER SELECTIONS

1. Compare the theme of this poem with that of Emily Dickinson's "Tell all the Truth but tell it slant —" (p. 1070).
2. Discuss the "neighbors and kin" (line 5) of this poem and "The people along the sand" in Robert Frost's "Neither Out Far nor In Deep" (p. 1114).

ALBERTO RÍOS (B. 1952)

Born in Nogales, Arizona, Alberto Ríos grew up on the border between Mexico and Arizona, which is the subject of his memoir *Capriotoda* (1999). He earned a bachelor's degree and an M.F.A. from the University of Arizona. He has published several short story collections and a number of poetry collections, including *Whispering to Fool the Wind* (1982), *The Lime Orchard Woman* (1988), *Teodoro Luna's Two Kisses* (1990), *The Smallest Muscle in the Human Body* (2002), and *The Theater of Night* (2006). Among his many awards are the Arizona Governor's Arts Award and fellowships from the Guggenheim Foundation and the National Endowment for the Arts. He teaches at Arizona State University.

The Gathering Evening   2002

Shadows are the patient apprentices of everything.
They follow what might be followed,

Sit with what will not move.
They take notes all day long —

We don't pay attention, we don't see   5
The dark writing of the pencil, the black notebook.

Sometimes, if you are watching carefully,
A shadow will move. You will turn to see

What has made it move, but nothing.
The shadows transcribe all night.   10

Transcription is their sleep.
We mistake night as a setting of the sun:

Night is all of them comparing notes,
So many gathering that their crowd

Makes the darkness everything.   15
Patient, patient, quiet and still.

One day they will have learned it all.
One day they will step out, in front,

And we will follow them, be their shadows,
And work for our turn —   20

The centuries it takes
To learn what waiting has to teach.

CONNECTIONS TO OTHER SELECTIONS

1. Compare the treatment of shadows in this poem and in Emily Dickinson's "Presentiment — is that long Shadow — on the lawn —" (p. 867).
2. Discuss the significance of the night in this poem and in Robert Frost's "Acquainted with the Night" (p. 889).

CATHY SONG (B. 1955)

Of Chinese and Korean descent, Cathy Song was born in Honolulu, Hawaii. After receiving her B.A. from Wellesley College, she pursued an M.A. in creative writing at Boston University. The recipient of a number of grants and awards, including the Shelley Memorial Award from the Poetry Society of America and the Hawaii Award for Literature, she has taught creative writing at various universities. Her work frequently focuses on the world of family and ancestry. Among her collections of poetry are *Picture Bride* (1983), *Frameless Windows, Squares of Light* (1988), *School Figures* (1994), *The Land of Bliss* (2001), and *Cloud Moving Hands* (2007).

A Poet in the House   *2001*

© School Figures.

Emily's job was to think.
She was the only one of us
who had that to do.
    — *Lavinia Dickinson*

Seemingly small her work,
minute to the point of invisibility —
she vanished daily into paper, famished,
hungry for her next encounter —
but she opened with a string of humble
words necessity,
necessary as the humble work
of bringing well to water, roast to knife,
    cake to frost,
the coarse, loud, grunting labor of the rest of us
who complained not at all   10
for the noises she heard
we deemed divine, if
claustrophobic and esoteric —
and contented ourselves to the apparent,
the menial, set our heads   15
to the task of daily maintenance,
the simple order at the kitchen table,
while she struggled with a different thing —
the pressure seized upon her mind —
we could ourselves not bear such strain   20
and, in gratitude, heaved the bucket,
squeezed the rag, breathed the sweet,
homely odor of soap.
Lifting dirt from the floor
I swear   25
we could hear her thinking.

CONNECTIONS TO OTHER SELECTIONS

1. Compare Song's assessment of the life of a poet with the view expressed in Howard Nemerov's "Walking the Dog" (p. 1250).

2. Discuss the perspective on Dickinson in this poem and in Ronald Wallace's "Miss Goff" (p. 1080).

C. K. WILLIAMS (B. 1936)

Born in Newark, New Jersey, and educated at Bucknell University and the University of Pennsylvania, C. K. Williams has worked as a therapist, an editor, and a writer and has taught creative writing at a number of schools, including Boston, Columbia, Drexel, George Mason, and Princeton Universities. His collections of poetry include *A Dream of Mind* (1992); *Repair* (1999), awarded the Pulitzer Prize; *The Singing* (2003), awarded the National Book Award; and *Collected Poems* (2006). Among his other awards are a Guggenheim Fellowship, the National Book Critics Circle Award, *The Paris Review*'s Connor Prize, and the Ruth Lilly Poetry Prize.

The United States
2007

The rusting, decomposing hulk of the United States
is moored across Columbus Boulevard from Ikea,
rearing weirdly over the old municipal pier
on the mostly derelict docks in Philadelphia.

I'd forgotten how immense it is: I can't imagine   5
which of the hundreds of portholes looked in
on the four-man cabin five flights down
I shared that first time I ran away to France.

We were told we were the fastest thing afloat,
and we surely were; even from the tiny deck   10
where passengers from tourist were allowed
our wake boiled ever vaster out behind.

That such a monster could be lifted by mere waves
and in the storm that hit us halfway across
tossed left and right until we vomited   15
seemed a violation of some natural law.

At Le Havre we were out of scale with everything;
when a swarm of tiny tugs nudged like piglets
at the teat the towering mass of us in place,
all the continent of Europe looked small.   20

Now, behind its ravelling chain-link fence,
the ship's a somnolent carcass, cables lashed

like lilliputian leashes to its prow, its pocking,
once pure paint discoloring to blood.

Upstream, the shells of long-abandoned factories   25
crouch for miles beneath the interstate;
the other way the bridge named after Whitman
hums with traffic toward the suburbs past his grave;

and "America's mighty flagship" waits here,
to be auctioned, I suppose, stripped of anything   30
it might still have of worth, and towed away
and torched to pieces on a beach in Bangladesh.

CONNECTIONS TO OTHER SELECTIONS

1. Discuss Williams's symbolic use of the ship in "The United States" compared with Thomas Hardy's in "The Convergence of the Twain" (p. 818) and David R. Slavitt's in "Titanic" (p. 820).

2. Compare the images and attitudes expressed toward the United States in this poem and in Tony Hoagland's "America" (p. 1291).

43

An Album of
World Literature

My poetry has passed through the same
stages of my life; from a solitary childhood and an adolescence cornered in
distant, isolated countries, I set out to
make myself a part of the great human
multitude.

— PABLO NERUDA

© Luis Poirot.

ANNA AKHMATOVA (RUSSIA / 1889–1966)

Born in Russia, Anna Akhmatova was a poet and translator who was
regarded as a major modern poet. Although she was expelled from the
Union of Soviet Writers during Stalin's rule, she was reclaimed by her
country in the 1960s. Her poetry is characterized by its
clarity, precision, and simplicity. Her work is translated
in *Complete Poems of Anna Akhmatova* (1990).

(Web) Research the
poets in this chapter at
bedfordstmartins.com/
meyerlit.

Lot's Wife   1922

TRANSLATED BY RICHARD WILBUR

The just man followed then his angel guide
Where he strode on the black highway, hulking and bright;
But a wild grief in his wife's bosom cried,
Look back, it is not too late for a last sight

Of the red towers of your native Sodom, the square   5
Where once you sang, the gardens you shall mourn,
And the tall house with empty windows where
You loved your husband and your babes were born.

She turned, and looking on the bitter view
Her eyes were welded shut by mortal pain;   10
Into transparent salt her body grew,
And her quick feet were rooted in the plain.

Who would waste tears upon her? Is she not
The least of our losses, this unhappy wife?
Yet in my heart she will not be forgot   15
Who, for a single glance, gave up her life.

CONNECTIONS TO OTHER SELECTIONS

1. Discuss the use of biblical allusions in "Lot's Wife" and in William Butler Yeats's "The Second Coming" (p. 1356). How is an understanding of the allusions crucial to interpreting each poem?
2. Consider the "unhappy wife" (line 14) in this poem and in Linda Pastan's "Marks" (p. 883). Discuss how you regard the wife in each poem.

CLARIBEL ALEGRÍA   (EL SALVADOR / B. 1924)

Born in Estelí, Nicaragua, Claribel Alegría moved with her family to El Salvador within a year of her birth. A 1948 graduate of George Washington University, she considers herself a Salvadoran, and much of her writing reflects the political upheaval of recent Latin American history. In 1978 she was awarded the Casa de las Americas Prize for her book *I Survive*. A bilingual edition of her major works, *Flowers from the Volcano,* was published in 1982. Recent translated collections of her poetry include *Sorrow* (1999) and *Casting Off* (2003).

I Am Mirror   *1978*

TRANSLATED BY ELECTA ARENAL AND MARSHA GABRIELA DREYER

Water sparkles
on my skin
and I don't feel it
water streams
down my back   5
I don't feel it
I rub myself with a towel
I pinch myself in the arm

I don't feel
frightened I look at myself in the mirror   10
she also pricks herself
I begin to get dressed
stumbling
from the corners
shouts like lightning bolts   15
tortured eyes
scurrying rats
and teeth shoot forth
although I feel nothing
I wander through the streets: 20
children with dirty faces
ask me for charity
child prostitutes
who are not yet fifteen
the streets are paved with pain   25
tanks that approach
raised bayonets
bodies that fall
weeping
finally I feel my arm   30
I am no longer a phantom
I hurt
therefore I exist
I return to watch the scene:
children who run   35
bleeding
women with panic
in their faces
this time it hurts me less
I pinch myself again   40
and already I feel nothing
I simply reflect
what happens at my side
the tanks
are not tanks   45
nor are the shouts
shouts
I am a blank mirror
that nothing penetrates
my surface   50
is hard
is brilliant
is polished
I became a mirror
and I am fleshless   55
scarcely preserving
a vague memory
of pain.

1. Compare the ways in which Alegría uses mirror images to reflect life in El Salvador with Sylvia Plath's concerns in "Mirror" (p. 879).

2. Write an essay comparing the speaker's voice in this poem with that in William Blake's "London" (p. 850). How do the speakers evoke emotional responses to what they describe?

YEHUDA AMICHAI (ISRAEL / 1924–2000)

Considered a leading Hebrew poet, Yehuda Amichai was born in Germany in 1924 and later moved with his family to Jerusalem. Amichai fought with the Jewish Brigade of the British Army during World War II and in the War of Independence. After the war, he attended Hebrew University. His first volume of poetry, *Achshav Uve-Yamin HaAharim* (*Now and in Other Days*), appeared in 1955 and immediately attracted the interest of the poetry-reading public. Widely read and admired outside his country, his works have been translated into thirty-three languages. His *Collected Poems* appeared in 1963; he was also the author of two novels and a book of short stories. *The Selected Poems of Yehuda Amichai* was published in 1996.

Jerusalem, 1985   *1985*

TRANSLATED BY CHANA BLOCH

Scribbled wishes stuck between the stones
of the Wailing Wall:
bits of crumpled, wadded paper.

And across the way, stuck in an old iron gate
half-hidden by jasmine:
"Couldn't make it,
I hope you'll understand."

CONNECTION TO ANOTHER SELECTION

1. Consider the use of irony in this poem and in Emily Dickinson's "I know that He exists" (p. 1084).

FAZIL HÜSNÜ DAĞLARCA (TURKEY / 1914–2008)

Born in Istanbul, Turkey, Fazil Hüsnü Dağlarca was one of Turkey's most important and prolific poets of the twentieth century. He began publishing poetry as a young military officer and continued throughout his career as a journal editor and book publisher. In 1968 he received the International Poetry Forum's Turkish Award. Over the course of his career he published more than fifty books for adults and children. The translator of this poem, Talât Sait Halman, translated some of Dağlarca's poetry in *Selected Poems* (1969).

Dead   1984

TRANSLATED FROM THE TURKISH BY TALÂT SAIT HALMAN

Whichever neighborhood has no clergyman
I shall die there.
Let no one see how beautiful
Are all the things I have, my feet, my hair.

In the name of the dead, free and immaculate,   5
A fish in unknown seas,
Am I not a Muslim, heaven knows,
Yet no crowds for me, please.

Don't let them make me wear a shroud,
In sky safeguard my darkness from misery,   10
Don't shake me as I go from shoulder to shoulder,
For all my parts are fancy free.

No prayer can turn my remoteness
From the other worlds into a reality.
Don't let them wash my body, don't: 15
I am madly in love with the warmth inside me.

CONNECTIONS TO OTHER SELECTIONS

1 Discuss the speaker's attitude toward religion in "Dead" and in the excerpt from Walt Whitman's "Song of Myself" (p. 913).

2. Compare the treatment of death in this poem and in Emily Dickinson's "I heard a Fly buzz—when I died—" (p. 1065).

MAHMOUD DARWISH (PALESTINE / B. 1942)

Born in Al Birweh, a village near Galilee in what is now Israel, Mahmoud Darwish has devoted his life and writing to his Palestinian homeland, from which he has been exiled. His commitment to independence for Palestine is evident in his work for the Palestine Liberation Organization and in his publication of more than twenty books of poetry that include *Sand and Other Poems* (1986), *Adam of Two Edens* (2000), and *The Raven's Ink* (2001). In 2001 he was awarded the Lannan Prize for Cultural Freedom. Darwish remains a major literary voice for the Palestinians.

Identity Card   1980

TRANSLATED FROM THE ARABIC BY DENYS JOHNSON-DAVIES

Put it on record.
   I am an Arab
And the number of my card is fifty thousand
I have eight children
And the ninth is due after summer.   5
What's there to be angry about?

Put it on record.
   I am an Arab
Working with comrades of toil in a quarry.
I have eight children   10
For them I wrest the loaf of bread,
The clothes and exercise books
From the rocks
And beg for no alms at your door,
   Lower not myself at your doorstep.   15
   What's there to be angry about?

Put it on record.
   I am an Arab.
I am a name without a title,
Patient in a country where everything   20
Lives in a whirlpool of anger.
   My roots
   Took hold before the birth of time
   Before the burgeoning of the ages,
   Before cypress and olive trees,   25
   Before the proliferation of weeds.

My father is from the family of the plough
   Not from highborn nobles.
And my grandfather was a peasant
   Without line or genealogy.   30
My house is a watchman's hut
   Made of sticks and reeds.
Does my status satisfy you?
   I am a name without a surname.

Put it on record.   35
   I am an Arab.
Color of hair: jet black.
Color of eyes: brown.
My distinguishing features:
   On my head the *'iqal* cords over a *keffiyeh*   40
   Scratching him who touches it.
My address:
   I'm from a village, remote, forgotten,
   Its streets without name
   And all its men in the fields and quarry.   45

What's there to be angry about?

Put it on record.
  I am an Arab.
You stole my forefathers' vineyards
  And land I used to till,
  I and all my children,
  And you left us and all my grandchildren
  Nothing but these rocks.
  Will your government be taking them too
  As is being said?   55

So!
  Put it on record at the top of page one:
  I don't hate people,
  I trespass on no one's property.
And yet, if I were to become hungry   60
  I shall eat the flesh of my usurper.
  Beware, beware of my hunger
  And of my anger!

50 appears at line "And land I used to till,"

CONNECTIONS TO OTHER SELECTIONS

1. Discuss the relation between anger and political history in "Identity Card" and in Langston Hughes's "Harlem" (p. 1148).

2. Consider "Identity Card" and Pablo Neruda's "The United Fruit Co." (p. 1309) as two personal responses to political events. In what sense do the two poems speak to each other?

MARNE L. KILATES (PHILIPPINES / B. 1952)

Marne L. Kilates is a Filipino translator and poet. He has published three collections of poems: *Children of the Snarl and Other Poems* (1987), *Poems en Route* (1998), both of which won the Manila Critic Circle's National Book Award, and *Mostly in Monsoon Weather* (2006).

Python in the Mall   *1998*

A serpent-like creature has taken residence
in the dark recesses of a new shopping mall.
Supposedly the offspring of the mall tycoon
himself, the creature feeds, by preference,
on nubile virgins.
              —Tabloid story

She hatched in the dank
Basements of our gullibility,
Warmed in the gasp of our telling,

Curling in the tongues
Of housewives and clerks. 5

We gave her a body half-serpent,
Half-voluptuary, and a taste
For maidens and movie stars
Who began to vanish mysteriously
Behind the curtains of boutique 10
Fitting rooms and water closets,
Never to be seen again,
Or only to be found in the parking
Cellars, wandering dazed
Into the headlights of shoppers' cars. 15

How she fed on our thirst
For wonders, fattened on our fear
Of vacant places. Slowly
We embellished the patterns
On her scales and admired 20
The sinuous grace of her spine.

Avidly we filled our multifarious
Hungers at her belly, and lapped
The marvelous tales of her forked
Tongue. And as the gleaming temples 25
Of her worship rose in the midst
Of our squalor, how we trembled
At the seduction of her voice,
O what adoring victims we became.

CONNECTIONS TO OTHER SELECTIONS

1. Discuss the treatment of materialism in "Python in the Mall" and in Tony Hoagland's "America" (p. 1291).
2. Compare the themes in this poem and in William Wordsworth's "The World Is Too Much with Us" (p. 975).

TASLIMA NASRIN (BANGLADESH / B. 1962)

Born in Mymensingh, East Pakistan (now Bangladesh), Taslima Nasrin earned her medical degree in 1984. In addition to working as a physician in Dacca hospitals, she has made a career as a prolific writer of fiction, poetry, and nonfiction, focusing particularly on women's oppression. Her widely translated writing has been condemned by conservative mullahs and religious fundamentalists, who have demanded that her books be banned and that she be executed. Since the early 1990s she has lived in the United States, Calcutta, and Europe, where the European Parliament awarded her the Sakharov Prize in Freedom of Thought in 1994. Her collections of poetry include *The Game in Reverse* (1995).

At the Back of Progress...   *1995*

TRANSLATED FROM THE BENGALI BY CAROLYNE WRIGHT AND MOHAMMAD NURUL HUDA

The fellow who sits in the air-conditioned office
is the one who in his youth raped
          a dozen or so young girls
and at the cocktail party, he's secretly stricken with lust
fastening his eyes on the belly button of some lovely.   5
In the five-star hotels, this fellow frequently
        tries out his different tastes
        in sex acts with a variety of women.
This fellow goes home and beats his wife
        over a handkerchief   10
        or a shirt collar.
This fellow sits in his office and talks with people
        puffing on a cigarette
        and shuffling through his files.

        Ringing the bell he calls his employee   15
          shouts at him
        orders the bearer to bring tea
        and drinks.
    This fellow gives out character references for people.

The employee who's speaking in such a low voice   20
that no one knows or would ever suspect
how much he could raise his voice at home,
        how foul his language could be
        how vile his behavior.
Gathering with his buddies, he buys some movie tickets   25
and kicking back on the porch outside, indulges
        in loud harangues on politics, art and literature.
Someone is committing suicide   his mother
        or his grandmother
        or his great-grandmother.   30
Returning home he beats his wife
        over a bar of soap or
        the baby's pneumonia.

The bearer who brings the tea
who keeps the lighter in his pocket   35
and who gets a couple of *tākā* as a tip:
he's divorced his first wife for her sterility,
his second wife for giving birth to a daughter,
he's divorced his third wife for not bringing dowry.
Returning home, this fellow beats his fourth wife   40
over a couple of green chiles or a handful of cooked rice.

Connections to Other Selections

1. Discuss the status of women in Nasrin's poem and in Marge Piercy's "The Secretary Chant" (p. 744).
2. Compare the treatment of men in Nasrin's poem and in Daisy Fried's "Wit's End" (p. 1247). How do the cultural differences depicted in the poems result in divergent tones?

Pablo Neruda (Chile / 1904–1973)

Born in Chile, Pablo Neruda insisted all of his life on the connection between poetry and politics. He was an activist and a Chilean diplomat in a number of countries during the 1920s and 1930s and remained politically active until his death. Neruda was regarded as a great and influential poet (he was awarded the Nobel Prize in 1971) whose poetry ranged from specific political issues to the yearnings of romantic love. Among his many works are *Twenty Love Poems and a Song of Despair* (1924), *Residence on Earth* (three series, 1925–45), *Spain in the Heart* (1937), *The Captain's Verses* (1952), and *Memorial of Isla Negra* (1964).

The United Fruit Co.   *1950*

TRANSLATED BY ROBERT BLY

When the trumpet sounded, it was
all prepared on the earth,
and Jehovah parceled out the earth
to Coca-Cola, Inc., Anaconda,
Ford Motors, and other entities: 5
The Fruit Company, Inc.
reserved for itself the most succulent,
the central coast of my own land,
the delicate waist of America.
It rechristened its territories   10
as the "Banana Republics"
and over the sleeping dead,
over the restless heroes
who brought about the greatness,
the liberty and the flags,   15
it established the comic opera:
abolished the independencies,
presented crowns of Caesar,
unsheathed envy, attracted
the dictatorship of the flies,   20
Trujillo flies, Tacho flies,
Carias flies, Martinez flies,
Ubico flies, damp flies

of modest blood and marmalade,
drunken flies who zoom   25
over the ordinary graves,
circus flies, wise flies
well trained in tyranny.

Among the bloodthirsty flies
the Fruit Company lands its ships,   30
taking off the coffee and the fruit;
the treasure of our submerged
territories flows as though
on plates into the ships.

Meanwhile Indians are falling   35
into the sugared chasms
of the harbors, wrapped
for burial in the mist of the dawn:
a body rolls, a thing
that has no name, a fallen cipher,   40
a cluster of dead fruit
thrown down on the dump.

CONNECTIONS TO OTHER SELECTIONS

1. Discuss the political perspective in this poem and in Julio Marzán's "The
   Translator at the Reception for Latin American Writers" (p. 1014). What
   significant similarities are there between the two poems?
2. Contrast the treatment of fruit in this poem and in Galway Kinnell's
   "Blackberry Eating" (p. 924).

OCTAVIO PAZ (MEXICO / 1914–1998)

Born in Mexico City, Octavio Paz studied at the National Autonomous
University and in 1943 helped found one of Mexico's most important literary reviews, the *Prodigal Son*. He served in the Mexican diplomatic corps in
Paris, New Delhi, and New York. Much of Paz's poetry reflects Hispanic
traditions and European modernism as well as Buddhism. In 1990 he
received the Nobel Prize for Literature. Paz's major works include *Sun Stone*
(1958), *The Violent Season* (1958), *Salamander* (1962), *Blanco* (1966), *Eastern
Rampart* (1968), *Renga* (1971), and *Collected Poems, 1957–1987* (1987).

The Street   1963

A long silent street.
I walk in blackness and I stumble and fall
and rise, and I walk blind, my feet
stepping on silent stones and dry leaves.

Someone behind me also stepping on stones, leaves: 5
if I slow down, he slows;
if I run, he runs. I turn: nobody.
Everything dark and doorless.
Turning and turning among these corners
which lead forever to the street   10
where nobody waits for, nobody follows me,
where I pursue a man who stumbles
and rises and says when he sees me: nobody.

CONNECTIONS TO OTHER SELECTIONS

1. How does the speaker's anxiety in this poem compare with that in Robert Frost's "Acquainted with the Night" (p. 889)?
2. Write an essay comparing the tone of this poem and that of Langston Hughes's "Lenox Avenue: Midnight" (p. 1143).

YOUSIF AL-SA'IGH (IRAQ / B. 1932)

Born in Mousil, Yousif al-Sa'igh was educated at the University of Baghdad and is a teacher and writer of poetry, fiction, and nonfiction. His work has appeared in more than fourteen books. *Poems,* his collected poetry translated into English, was published in 1992. "An Iraqi Evening" offers a poignant glimpse of his country's home front during a war.

An Iraqi Evening   *1992*

TRANSLATED BY SAADI A SIMAWE, RALPH SAVARESE, AND CHUCK MILLER

Clips from the battlefield
in an Iraqi evening:
a peaceable home
two boys
preparing their homework   5
a little girl
absentmindedly drawing on scrap paper
funny pictures.
— breaking news coming shortly.
The entire house becomes ears   10
ten Iraqi eyes glued to the screen in frightened silence.
Smells mingle:
the smell of war
and the smell of just baked bread.
The mother raises her eyes to a photo on the wall   15

whispering
— May God protect you
and she begins preparing supper
quietly
and in her mind
clips float past of the battlefield   20
carefully selected for hope.

  [18 Feburary 1986]°

[18 February 1986]: The Iran-Iraq war was fought from 1980 to 1988 and claimed an estimated 150,000 Iraqis.

CONNECTIONS TO OTHER SELECTIONS

1. Compare the attitudes expressed toward war in "An Iraqi Evening" and in Alfred, Lord Tennyson's "The Charge of the Light Brigade" (p. 965).

2. Discuss how the images in "An Iraqi Evening" and in Dylan Thomas's "The Hand That Signed the Paper" (p. 871) create the respective tone for each poem.

SHU TING (CHINA / B. 1952)

Born in the Fujian Province of China, Shu Ting (whose real name is Gong Peiyu) was forced in 1969 to live in the countryside for three years because her father was accused of being hostile to the Cultural Revolution. There she began to read Western literature and write. On her return to the city of Xiamen in 1972, she worked in factories and continued writing poetry that made her one of China's most popular poets and a member of the Chinese Writers' Association. She has been a correspondent for the *Beijing Review* and continues to write poetry that has been translated into ten languages. Two of her poetry collections have been translated into English: *Selected Poems* (1994) and *The Mist of My Heart* (1995).

O Motherland, Dear Motherland   1979

TRANSLATED BY FANG DAI, DENNIS DING, AND EDWARD MORIN

I am the old broken waterwheel beside your river
That has composed a centuries-old song of weariness;
I'm the smoke-smudged miner's lamp on your forehead
That lights your snail-like crawl through the cave of history.
I'm the withered rice-ear, the washed-out roadbed,   5
The barge mired in a silt shoal
As the tow rope cuts

Deeply into your shoulder
— O Motherland.

I am poverty,   10
I'm sorrow,
I'm the bitterly painful hope
Of your generations.
I am the flowers strewn from Apsara's° flowing sleeves
That after thousands of years still have not reached earth   15
— O Motherland.

I am your untarnished ideal
Just broken away from the cobweb of myths;
I'm a bud of the ancient lotus blanketed under your snow,
I'm your smiling dimple wet with tears;   20
Your newly drawn lime-white starting line.
I'm the scarlet dawn emerging with long shimmering rays
— O Motherland.

I am numbered among your billions,
The sum of your nine million square kilometers.   25
You with the scar-blemished breast
Have nurtured me,
Me the confused, the ponderer, the seething,
So that from my body of flesh and blood
You might eke out   30
Your prosperity, your glory, and your freedom
— O Motherland,
My dear Motherland.

14 *Apsara's:* Flying Apsaras, or spirits, played music for the Buddhas.

CONNECTIONS TO OTHER SELECTIONS

1. Compare the speaker's tone in this poem and in Mahmoud Darwish's "Identity Card" (p. 1305).
2. Discuss the view of China in this poem and the perspective on the United States in Florence Cassen Mayers's "All-American Sestina" (p. 984).

TOMAS TRANSTRÖMER (SWEDEN / B. 1931)

Born in Stockholm, Tomas Transtromer has had his work translated more than any other contemporary Scandinavian poet. He has worked as a psychologist with juvenile offenders and people with disabilities. His poetry collections include *Night Vision* (1971), *Windows and Stones: Selected Poems* (1972), *Truth Barriers* (1978), *Selected Poems* (1981), and *New Selected Poems* (1997). Among his awards are the Petrarch Prize (1981) and a lifetime subsidy from the government of Sweden.

April and Silence

1991

TRANSLATED BY ROBIN FULTON

Spring lies desolate.
The velvet-dark ditch
crawls by my side
without reflections.

The only thing that shines   5
is yellow flowers.

I am carried in my shadow
like a violin
in its black box.

The only thing I want to say   10
glitters out of reach
like the silver
in a pawnbroker's.

CONNECTIONS TO OTHER SELECTIONS

1. Discuss the description of spring in this poem and in William Carlos
   Williams's "Spring and All" (p. 1352).

2. In an essay explain how the dictions used in this poem and in Martín
   Espada's "Latin Night at the Pawnshop" (p. 809) contribute to the poems'
   meanings and tone.

44

A Collection
of Poems

© Imogen Cunningham Trust.

If there were no poetry on any day in the
world, poetry would be invented that
day. For there would be an intolerable
hunger.
— MURIEL RUKEYSER

ANONYMOUS (TRADITIONAL SCOTTISH BALLAD)

Bonny Barbara Allan

date unknown

It was in and about the Martinmas° time,
    When the green leaves were afalling,
That Sir John Graeme, in the West Country,
    Fell in love with Barbara Allan.

He sent his men down through the town,   5
    To the place where she was dwelling:
"Oh haste and come to my master dear,
    Gin° ye be Barbara Allan."   *if*

Web Research the
poets in this chapter at
bedfordstmartins.com/
meyerlit.

---

1 *Martinmas:* St. Martin's Day, November 11.

O hooly,° hooly rose she up,   *slowly*
    To the place where he was lying,   10
And when she drew the curtain by:
    "Young man, I think you're dying."

"O it's I'm sick, and very, very sick,
    And 'tis a' for Barbara Allan." —
"O the better for me ye's never be,   15
    Tho your heart's blood were aspilling."

"O dinna ye mind,° young man," she said,   *don't you remember*
    "When ye was in the tavern adrinking,
That ye made the health° gae round and round,   *toasts*
    And slighted Barbara Allan?"   20

He turned his face unto the wall,
    And death was with him dealing:
"Adieu, adieu, my dear friends all,
    And be kind to Barbara Allan."

And slowly, slowly raise her up,   25
    And slowly, slowly left him,
And sighing said she could not stay,
    Since death of life had reft him.

She had not gane a mile but twa,
    When she heard the dead-bell ringing,   30
And every jow° that the dead-bell geid,   *stroke*
    It cried, "Woe to Barbara Allan!"

"O mother, mother, make my bed!
    O make it saft and narrow!
Since my love died for me today,   35
    I'll die for him tomorrow."

WILLIAM BLAKE (1757–1827)

The Garden of Love   *1794*

I went to the Garden of Love,
And saw what I never had seen:
A Chapel was built in the midst,
Where I used to play on the green.

And the gates of this Chapel were shut,   5
And "Thou shalt not" writ over the door;
So I turned to the Garden of Love
That so many sweet flowers bore;

And I saw it was filled with graves,
And tomb-stones where flowers should be;   10
And Priests in black gowns were walking their rounds,
And binding with briars my joys and desires.

WILLIAM BLAKE (1757–1827)

Infant Sorrow

1794

My mother groand! my father wept.
Into the dangerous world I leapt:
Helpless naked piping loud:
Like a fiend hid in a cloud.

Struggling in my father's hands:
Striving against my swadling bands
Bound and weary I thought best
To sulk upon my mother's breast.

ANNE BRADSTREET (CA. 1612–1672)

Before the Birth of One of Her Children

1678

All things within this fading world hath end,
Adversity doth still our joys attend;
No ties so strong, no friends so dear and sweet,
But with death's parting blow is sure to meet.
The sentence past is most irrevocable,   5
A common thing, yet oh, inevitable.
How soon, my Dear, death may my steps attend,
How soon't may be thy lot to lose thy friend,
We both are ignorant, yet love bids me
These farewell lines to recommend to thee,   10
That when that knot's untied that made us one,
I may seem thine, who in effect am none.
And if I see not half my days that's due,
What nature would, God grant to yours and you;
The many faults that well you know I have   15
Let be interred in my oblivious grave;
If any worth or virtue were in me,
Let that live freshly in thy memory
And when thou feel'st no grief, as I no harms,
Yet love thy dead, who long lay in thine arms,   20
And when thy loss shall be repaid with gains
Look to my little babes, my dear remains.
And if thou love thyself, or loved'st me,
These O protect from stepdame's° injury.   *stepmother's*
And if chance to thine eyes shall bring this verse,   25
With some sad sighs honor my absent hearse;
And kiss this paper for thy love's dear sake,
Who with salt tears this last farewell did take.

ELIZABETH BARRETT BROWNING (1806–1861)

When our two souls stand up erect and strong   1850

When our two souls stand up erect and strong,
Face to face, silent, drawing nigh and nigher,
Until the lengthening wings break into fire
At either curvèd point — what bitter wrong
Can the earth do to us, that we should not long   5
Be here contented? Think. In mounting higher,
The angels would press on us and aspire
To drop some golden orb of perfect song
Into our deep, dear silence. Let us stay
Rather on earth, Belovèd, — where the unfit   10
Contrarious moods of men recoil away
And isolate pure spirits, and permit
A place to stand and love in for a day,
With darkness and the death-hour rounding it.

ROBERT BROWNING (1812–1889)

Meeting at Night   1845

The gray sea and the long black land;
And the yellow half-moon large and low;
And the startled little waves that leap
In firey ringlets from their sleep,
As I gain the cove with pushing prow,   5
And quench its speed i' the slushy sand.

Then a mile of warm sea-scented beach;
Three fields to cross till a farm appears;
A tap at the pane, the quick sharp scratch
And blue spurt of a lighted match,   10
And a voice less loud, through its joys and fears,
Than the two hearts beating each to each!

ROBERT BROWNING (1812–1889)

Parting at Morning   1845

Round the cape of a sudden came the sea,
And the sun looked over the mountain's rim:
And straight was a path of gold for him,
And the need of a world of men for me.

ROBERT BURNS (1759–1796)

A Red, Red Rose   *1799*

O my luve's like a red, red rose
That's newly sprung in June;
O my luve's like the melodie
That's sweetly played in tune.

As fair art thou, my bonny lass,   5
So deep in luve am I;
And I will luve thee still my dear,
Till a' the seas gang° dry —   *go*

Till a' the seas gang dry, my dear,
And the rocks melt wi' the sun: 10
O I will luve thee still, my dear,
While the sands o' life shall run.

And fare thee weel, my only luve,
And fare thee weel awhile!
And I will come again, my luve,   15
Though it were a thousand mile.

GEORGE GORDON, LORD BYRON (1788–1824)

She Walks in Beauty   *1814*

From Hebrew Melodies

I

She walks in Beauty, like the night
    Of cloudless climes and starry skies;
And all that's best of dark and bright
    Meet in her aspect and her eyes:
Thus mellowed to that tender light   5
    Which Heaven to gaudy day denies.

II

One shade the more, one ray the less,
    Had half impaired the nameless grace
Which waves in every raven tress,
    Or softly lightens o'er her face;   10
Where thoughts serenely sweet express,
    How pure, how dear their dwelling-place.

III

And on that cheek, and o'er that brow,
    So soft, so calm, yet eloquent,
The smiles that win, the tints that glow,   15
    But tell of days in goodness spent,
A mind at peace with all below,
    A heart whose love is innocent!

LUCILLE CLIFTON (B. 1936)

this morning (for the girls of eastern high school)   *1987*

© Christopher Felver.

this morning
this morning
        i met myself

coming in

a bright
jungle girl
shining
quick as a snake
a tall
tree girl a
me girl   10

        i met myself
this morning
coming in

and all day   15
i have been
a black bell
ringing
i survive

       survive   20

survive

SAMUEL TAYLOR COLERIDGE (1772–1834)

Kubla Khan: or, a Vision in a Dream°   *1798*

In Xanadu did Kubla Khan°
  A stately pleasure-dome decree:
Where Alph, the sacred river, ran
Through caverns measureless to man
   Down to a sunless sea.   5

So twice five miles of fertile ground
With walls and towers were girdled round:
And here were gardens bright with sinuous rills
Where blossomed many an incense-bearing tree;
And there were forests ancient as the hills,   10
Enfolding sunny spots of greenery.

But oh! that deep romantic chasm which slanted
Down the green hill athwart a cedarn cover!°
A savage place! as holy and enchanted
As e'er beneath a waning moon was haunted   15
By woman wailing for her demon-lover!
And from this chasm, with ceaseless turmoil seething,
As if this earth in fast thick pants were breathing,
A mighty fountain momently was forced,
Amid whose swift half-intermitted burst   20
Huge fragments vaulted like rebounding hail,
Of chaffy grain beneath the thresher's flail:
And 'mid these dancing rocks at once and ever
It flung up momently the sacred river.
Five miles meandering with a mazy motion   25
Through wood and dale the sacred river ran,
Then reached the caverns measureless to man,
And sank in tumult to a lifeless ocean:
And 'mid this tumult Kubla heard from far
Ancestral voices prophesying war!   30
   The shadow of the dome of pleasure
    Floated midway on the waves;
   Where was heard the mingled measure
    From the fountain and the caves.
It was a miracle of rare device,   35
A sunny pleasure-dome with caves of ice!

Vision in a Dream: This poem came to Coleridge in an opium-induced dream, but he was interrupted by a visitor while writing it down. He was later unable to remember the rest of the poem.

1 *Kubla Khan:* The historical Kublai Khan (1216–1294, grandson of Genghis Khan) was the founder of the Mongol dynasty in China.

13 *athwart . . . cover:* Spanning a grove of cedar trees.

A damsel with a dulcimer
In a vision once I saw:
It was an Abyssinian maid,
And on her dulcimer she played,   40
Singing of Mount Abora.
Could I revive within me
Her symphony and song,
To such a deep delight 'twould win me,
That with music loud and long,   45
I would build that dome in air,
That sunny dome! those caves of ice!
And all who heard should see them there,
And all should cry, Beware! Beware!
His flashing eyes, his floating hair!   50
Weave a circle round him thrice,
And close your eyes with holy dread,
For he on honey-dew hath fed,
And drunk the milk of Paradise.

WYN COOPER (B. 1957)

Puritan Impulse   1999

I talk the least
of what I covet
most, seldom look
at what I wish to see,
turn my nose away   5
from what smells best,
refuse to listen
to my favorite opera,
La Traviata,
even when it's sung   10
in town for free.
The Van Gogh show
can't make me walk
the block to view it,
no chef can intuit   15
what I might want,
and handing me jars
of caviar while
popping Veuve Cliquot
is not what I call love.   20

The rain last night
froze on the birches,
and today they bend
almost to breaking.
The sun makes every   25

branch distinct, too bright
to look at for long.
And that's excuse
enough for me
to look back down   30
to the road
I walk on, ice
on the pavement
so clear it's blue.

E. E. CUMMINGS (1894–1962)

Buffalo Bill 's°   *1923*

Buffalo Bill 's
defunct
       who used to
       ride a watersmooth-silver
              stallion   5
and break onetwothreefourfive pigeonsjustlikethat
                    Jesus

he was a handsome man
              and what i want to know is
how do you like your blueeyed boy   10
Mister Death

Buffalo Bill: William Frederick Cody (1846–1917) was an American frontier scout and Indian killer turned international circus showman with his Wild West show, which employed Sitting Bull and Annie Oakley.

JOHN DONNE (1572–1631)

The Apparition   *c. 1600*

When by thy scorn, O murderess, I am dead,
    And that thou thinkst thee free
From all solicitation from me,
Then shall my ghost come to thy bed,
And thee, feigned vestal, in worse arms shall see;   5
Then thy sick taper° will begin to wink,   *candle*
And he, whose thou art then, being tired before,
Will, if thou stir, or pinch to wake him, think
    Thou call'st for more,
And in false sleep will from thee shrink.   10
And then, poor aspen wretch, neglected, thou,

Bathed in a cold quicksilver sweat, wilt lie
　　A verier° ghost than I.　　　　　　　　　　　　　　　　*truer*
What I will say, I will not tell thee now,
Lest that preserve thee; and since my love is spent,　　15
I had rather thou shouldst painfully repent,
Than by my threatenings rest still innocent.

JOHN DONNE (1572–1631)

Batter My Heart　　　　　　　　　　　　　　　　　　　*1610*

Batter my heart, three-personed God; for You
As yet but knock, breathe, shine, and seek to mend;
That I may rise and stand, o'erthrow me, and bend
Your force, to break, blow, burn, and make me new.
I, like an usurped town, to another due,　　　　　　　　5
Labor to admit You, but Oh, to no end!
Reason, Your viceroy in me, me should defend,
But is captived, and proves weak or untrue.
Yet dearly I love You, and would be loved fain.
But am betrothed unto Your enemy:　　　　　　　　　　10
Divorce me, untie, or break that knot again,
Take me to You, imprison me, for I,
Except You enthrall me, never shall be free,
Nor ever chaste, except You ravish me.

JOHN DONNE (1572–1631)

The Flea　　　　　　　　　　　　　　　　　　　　　　*1633*

Mark but this flea, and mark in this°
How little that which thou deny'st me is;
It sucked me first, and now sucks thee,
And in this flea our two bloods mingled be;
Thou know'st that this cannot be said　　　　　　　　　5
A sin, nor shame, nor loss of maidenhead,
　　　Yet this enjoys before it woo,
　　　And pampered swells with one blood made of two,
　　　And this, alas, is more than we would do.°

Oh stay, three lives in one flea spare,　　　　　　　　　10
Where we almost, yea more than, married are.
This flea is you and I, and this
Our marriage bed, and marriage temple is;

---

1 *mark in this:* Take note of the moral lesson in this object.　　9 *more than we would do:* That
is, if we do not join our blood in conceiving a child.

Though parents grudge, and you, we're met
And cloistered in these living walls of jet.   15
    Though use° make you apt to kill me,   *habit*
    Let not to that, self-murder added be,
    And sacrilege, three sins in killing three.

Cruel and sudden, hast thou since
Purpled thy nail in blood of innocence?   20
Wherein could this flea guilty be,
Except in that drop which it sucked from thee?
Yet thou triumph'st, and say'st that thou
Find'st not thyself, nor me, the weaker now;
    'Tis true; then learn how false, fears be;   25
    Just so much honor, when thou yield'st to me,
    Will waste, as this flea's death took life from thee.

GEORGE ELIOT (MARY ANN EVANS / 1819–1880)

In a London Drawingroom   *1865*

The sky is cloudy, yellowed by the smoke.
For view there are the houses opposite,
Cutting the sky with one long line of wall
Like solid fog: far as the eye can stretch
Monotony of surface and of form   5
Without a break to hang a guess upon.
No bird can make a shadow as it flies,
For all its shadow, as in ways o'erhung
By thickest canvas, where the golden rays
Are clothed in hemp. No figure lingering   10
Pauses to feed the hunger of the eye
Or rest a little on the lap of life.
All hurry on and look upon the ground
Or glance unmarking at the passersby.
The wheels are hurrying, too, cabs, carriages   15
All closed, in multiplied identity.
The world seems one huge prison-house and court
Where men are punished at the slightest cost,
With lowest rate of color, warmth, and joy.

KATIE FORD (B. 1975)

Ark   *2008*

We love the stories of flood and the few
told to prepare in advance by their god.
In that story, the saved are
always us, meaning:
whoever holds the book.

CHARLOTTE PERKINS GILMAN (1860–1935)

Queer People   *1899*

The people people work with best
    Are often very queer
The people people own by birth
    Quite shock your first idea;
The people people choose for friends
    Your common sense appall,
But the people people marry
    Are the queerest folks of all.

THOMAS HARDY (1840–1928)

Hap   *1866*

If but some vengeful god would call to me
From up the sky, and laugh: "Thou suffering thing,
Know that thy sorrow is my ecstasy,
That thy love's loss is my hate's profiting!"

Then would I bear it, clench myself, and die,   5
Steeled by the sense of ire unmerited;
Half-eased in that a Powerfuller than I
Had willed and meted me the tears I shed.

But not so. How arrives it joy lies slain,
And why unblooms the best hope ever sown?   10
— Crass Casualty obstructs the sun and rain,
And dicing Time for gladness casts a moan. . . .
These purblind Doomsters had as readily strown
Blisses about my pilgrimage as pain.

THOMAS HARDY (1840–1928)

In Time of "The Breaking of Nations"°   *1915*

1

Only a man harrowing clods
    In a slow silent walk
With an old horse that stumbles and nods
    Half asleep as they stalk.

2

Only thin smoke without flame   5
    From the heaps of couch-grass;

The Breaking of Nations: See Jeremiah 51:20: "Thou art my battle axe and weapons of war: for with thee will I break in pieces the nations, and with thee will I destroy kingdoms."

Yet this will go onward the same
    Though Dynasties pass.

3

Yonder a maid and her wight°   *man*
    Come whispering by: 10
War's annals will cloud into night
    Ere their story die.

FRANCES E. W. HARPER (1825–1911)

Learning to Read   *1872*

Very soon the Yankee teachers
    Came down and set up school;
But oh! how the Rebs did hate it, —
    It was agin' their rule

Our masters always tried to hide   5
    Book learning from our eyes;
Knowledge did'nt agree with slavery —
    'Twould make us all too wise.

But some of us would try to steal
    A little from the book,
And put the words together,   10
    And learn by hook or crook.

I remember Uncle Caldwell,
    Who took pot-liquor fat
And greased the pages of his book,   15
    And hid it in his hat.

And had his master ever seen
    The leaves upon his head,
He'd have thought them greasy papers,
    But nothing to be read.   20

And there was Mr. Turner's Ben
    Who heard the children spell,
And picked the words right up by heart,
    And learned to read 'em well.

Well the Northern folks kept sending   25
    The Yankee teachers down
And they stood right up and helped us,
    Though Rebs did sneer and frown,

And, I longed to read my Bible,
    For precious words it said;   30
But when I begun to learn it,
    Folks just shook their heads,

And said there is no use trying,
    Oh! Chloe, you're too late;
But as I was rising sixty,
    I had no time to wait.   35

So I got a pair of glasses,
    And straight to work I went,
And never stopped till I could read
    The hymns and Testament.   40

Then I got a little cabin —
    A place to call my own —
And I felt as independent
    As the queen upon her throne.

GEORGE HERBERT (1593–1633)

The Collar   *1633*

I struck the board° and cried, "No more;   *table*
        I will abroad!
What? shall I ever sigh and pine?
My lines and life are free, free as the road,
    Loose as the wind, as large as store.°   5
        Shall I be still in suit?°   *serving another*
    Have I no harvest but a thorn
    To let me blood, and not restore
What I have lost with cordial° fruit?   *restorative*
        Sure there was wine   10
    Before my sighs did dry it; there was corn
        Before my tears did drown it.
    Is the year only lost to me?
        Have I no bays° to crown it,   *triumphal wreaths*
No flowers, no garlands gay? All blasted?   15
        All wasted?
    Not so, my heart; but there is fruit,
        And thou hast hands.
    Recover all thy sigh-blown age
On double pleasures: leave thy cold dispute   20
Of what is fit, and not. Forsake thy cage,
        Thy rope of sands,
Which petty thoughts have made, and made to thee
    Good cable, to enforce and draw,
        And be thy law,   25
    While thou didst wink and wouldst not see.
        Away! take heed;
        I will abroad.

5 *store:* A storehouse or warehouse.

Call in thy death's-head° there; tie up thy fears.
　　　　　He that forbears　　　　　　　　　　　　　　30
　　　　To suit and serve his need,
　　　　Deserves his load."
But as I raved and grew more fierce and wild
　　　　At every word,
Methought I heard one calling, *Child!*　　　　　　　35
　　　　And I replied, *My Lord.*

29 *death's-head:* A skull, reminder of mortality.

Gerard Manley Hopkins (1844–1889)

Hurrahing in Harvest　　　　　　　　　　　*1877*

Summer ends now; now, barbarous in beauty, the stooks° arise　*sheaves*
　　Around; up above, what wind-walks! what lovely behaviour
　　Of silk-sack clouds! has wilder, wilful-wavier
Meal-drift moulded ever and melted across skies?

I walk, I lift up, I lift up heart, eyes,　　　　　　　　　　5
　　Down all that glory in the heavens to glean our Saviour;
　　And, éyes, heárt, what looks, what lips yet gave you a
Rapturous love's greeting of realer, of rounder replies?

And the azurous hung hills are his world-wielding shoulder
　　Majestic — as a stallion stalwart, very-violet-sweet! —　　10
These things, these things were here and but the beholder
　　Wanting; which two when they once meet,
The heart rears wings bold and bolder
　　And hurls for him, O half hurls earth for him off under his feet.

Gerard Manley Hopkins (1844–1889)

Pied Beauty　　　　　　　　　　　　　　*1877*

Glory be to God for dappled things —
　　For skies of couple-color as a brinded cow;
　　　　For rose-moles all in stipple upon trout that swim;
Fresh-firecoal chestnut-falls;° finches' wings;　　*fallen chestnut*
　　Landscape plotted and pieced — fold, fallow, and plow;　　5
　　　　And all trades, their gear and tackle and trim.

All things counter, original, spare, strange;
　　Whatever is fickle, freckled (who knows how?)
　　　　With swift, slow; sweet, sour; adazzle, dim;
He fathers-forth whose beauty is past change:　　　　　　10
　　　　Praise him.

GERARD MANLEY HOPKINS (1844–1889)

The Windhover°

1877

To Christ Our Lord

I caught this morning morning's minion,° king-   favorite
    dom of daylight's dauphin, dapple-dawn-drawn Falcon,
    in his riding
Of the rolling level underneath him steady air, and striding
High there, how he rung upon the rein of a wimpling wing
In his ecstasy! then off, off forth on swing,   5
    As a skate's heel sweeps smooth on a bow-bend: the hurl and gliding
    Rebuffed the big wind. My heart in hiding
Stirred for a bird, — the achieve of, the mastery of the thing!

Brute beauty and valour and act, oh, air, pride, plume, here
    Buckle!° AND the fire that breaks from thee then, a billion   10
Times told lovelier, more dangerous, O my chevalier!

    No wonder of it: shéer plód makes plough down sillion°   furrow
Shine, and blue-bleak embers, ah my dear,
    Fall, gall themselves, and gash gold-vermilion.

The Windhover: "A name for the kestrel [a kind of small hawk], from its habit of hovering or hanging with its head to the wind" [*OED*].   10 *Buckle:* To join, to equip for battle, to crumple.

A. E. HOUSMAN (1859–1936)

Is my team ploughing

1896

"Is my team ploughing,
    That I was used to drive
And hear the harness jingle
    When I was man alive?"

Ay, the horses trample,   5
    The harness jingles now;
No change though you lie under
    The land you used to plough.

"Is football playing
    Along the river shore,   10
With lads to chase the leather,
    Now I stand up no more?"

Ay, the ball is flying,
    The lads play heart and soul;
The goal stands up, the keeper   15
    Stands up to keep the goal.

"Is my girl happy,
    That I thought hard to leave,
And has she tired of weeping
    As she lies down at eve?"   20

Ay, she lies down lightly,
    She lies not down to weep:
Your girl is well contented.
    Be still, my lad, and sleep.

"Is my friend hearty,   25
    Now I am thin and pine,
And has he found to sleep in
    A better bed than mine?"

Yes, lad, I lie easy,
    I lie as lads would choose;   30
I cheer a dead man's sweetheart,
    Never ask me whose.

A. E. HOUSMAN (1859–1936)

To an Athlete Dying Young   *1896*

The time you won your town the race
We chaired° you through the marketplace;
Man and boy stood cheering by,
And home we brought you shoulder-high.

Today, the road all runners come,   5
Shoulder-high we bring you home,
And set you at your threshold down,
Townsman of a stiller town.

Smart lad, to slip betimes away
From fields where glory does not stay,   10
And early though the laurel° grows
It withers quicker than the rose.

Eyes the shady night has shut
Cannot see the record cut,
And silence sounds no worse than cheers   15
After earth has stopped the ears:

Now you will not swell the rout
Of lads that wore their honors out,
Runners whom renown outran
And the name died before the man.   20

2 *chaired:* Carried on the shoulders in triumphal parade.   11 *laurel:* Flowering shrub
traditionally used to fashion wreaths of honor.

To set, before its echoes fade,
The fleet foot on the sill of shade,
And hold to the low lintel up
The still-defended challenge-cup.

And round that early-laureled head   25
Will flock to gaze the strengthless dead,
And find unwithered on its curls
The garland briefer than a girl's.

JULIA WARD HOWE (1819–1910)

Battle-Hymn of the Republic   1862

Mine eyes have seen the glory of the coming of the Lord:
He is trampling out the vintage where the grapes of wrath are stored;
He hath loosed the fateful lightning of his terrible swift sword:
      His truth is marching on.

I have seen Him in the watch-fires of a hundred circling camps;   5
They have builded Him an altar in the evening dews and damps;
I can read His righteous sentence by the dim and flaring lamps.
      His day is marching on.

I have read a fiery gospel, writ in burnished rows of steel:
"As ye deal with my contemners, so with you my grace shall deal;   10
Let the Hero, born of woman, crush the serpent with his heel,
      Since God is marching on."

He has sounded forth the trumpet that shall never call retreat;
He is sifting out the hearts of men before his judgment-seat:
Oh! be swift, my soul, to answer Him! be jubilant, my feet!   15
      Our God is marching on.

In the beauty of the lilies Christ was born across the sea,
With a glory in his bosom that transfigures you and me:
As he died to make men holy, let us die to make men free,
   While God is marching on.   20

ANDREW HUDGINS (B. 1951)

The Cadillac in the Attic   2003

After the tenant moved out, died, disappeared —
the stories vary — the landlord
walked downstairs, bemused, and told his wife,
"There's a Cadillac in the attic,"

and there was. An old one, sure, and one   5
with sloppy paint, bald tires,

and orange rust chewing at the rocker panels,
but still and all, a Cadillac in the attic.

He'd battled transmission, chassis, engine block,
even the huge bench seats,   10
up the folding stairs, heaved them through the trapdoor,
and rebuilt a Cadillac in the attic.

Why'd he do it? we asked. But we know why.
For the reasons we would do it: for the looks
of astonishment he'd never see but could imagine.   15
For the joke. A Cadillac in the attic!

And for the meaning, though we aren't sure what it means.
And of course he did it for pleasure,
the pleasure on his lips of all those short vowels
and three hard clicks: the Cadillac in the attic.   20

BEN JONSON (1573–1637)

On My First Son   *1603*

Farewell, thou child of my right hand,° and joy.
My sin was too much hope of thee, loved boy;
Seven years thou wert lent to me, and I thee pay,
Exacted by thy fate, on the just day.°   *his birthday*
Oh, could I lose all father° now. For why   *fatherhood*   5
Will man lament the state he should envỳ? —
To have so soon 'scaped world's and flesh's rage,
And, if no other misery, yet age.
Rest in soft peace, and asked, say, "Here doth lie
Ben Jonson his best piece of poetry,"   10
For whose sake henceforth all his vows be such
As what he loves may never like too much.

1 *child of my right hand:* This phrase translates the Hebrew name "Benjamin," Jonson's son.

BEN JONSON (1573–1637)

To Celia   *1616*

Drink to me only with thine eyes,
    And I will pledge with mine;
Or leave a kiss but in the cup,
    And I'll not ask for wine.
The thirst that from the soul doth rise   5
    Doth ask a drink divine;
But might I of Jove's nectar sup,
    I would not change for thine.

I sent thee late a rosy wreath,
 Not so much honoring thee   10
As giving it a hope that there
 It could not withered be.
But thou thereon didst only breathe,
 And sent'st it back to me;
Since when it grows, and smells, I swear,   15
 Not of itself but thee.

JOHN KEATS (1795–1821)

To one who has been long in city pent   *1816*

To one who has been long in city pent,
 'Tis very sweet to look into the fair
 And open face of heaven, — to breathe a prayer
Full in the smile of the blue firmament.
Who is more happy, when, with heart's content,   5
 Fatigued he sinks into some pleasant lair
 Of wavy grass, and reads a debonair
And gentle tale of love and languishment?

Returning home at evening, with an ear
 Catching the notes of Philomel,° — an eye   *A nightingale*   10
Watching the sailing cloudlet's bright career,
 He mourns that day so soon has glided by:
E'en like the passage of an angel's tear
 That falls through the clear ether silently.

JOHN KEATS (1795–1821)

When I have fears that I may cease to be   *1818*

When I have fears that I may cease to be
 Before my pen has gleaned my teeming brain,
Before high-piled books, in charactery,°   *print*
 Hold like rich garners the full ripened grain;
When I behold, upon the night's starred face,   5
 Huge cloudy symbols of a high romance,
And think that I may never live to trace
 Their shadows, with the magic hand of chance;
And when I feel, fair creature of an hour,
 That I shall never look upon thee more,   10
Never have relish in the faery° power   *magic*
 Of unreflecting love; — then on the shore
Of the wide world I stand alone, and think
Till love and fame to nothingness do sink.

JOHN KEATS (1795–1821)

La Belle Dame sans Merci°

1819

O what can ail thee, knight-at-arms,
    Alone and palely loitering?
The sedge has withered from the lake,
    And no birds sing.

O what can ail thee, knight-at-arms,   5
    So haggard and so woe-begone?
The squirrel's granary is full,
    And the harvest's done.

I see a lily on thy brow,
    With anguish moist and fever dew,   10
And on thy cheeks a fading rose
    Fast withereth too.

I met a lady in the meads,
    Full beautiful — a faery's child,
Her hair was long, her foot was light,   15
    And her eyes were wild.

I made a garland for her head,
    And bracelets too, and fragrant zone;°   *belt*
She looked at me as she did love,
    And made sweet moan.   20

I set her on my pacing steed,
    And nothing else saw all day long,
For sidelong would she bend, and sing
    A faery's song.

She found me roots of relish sweet,   25
    And honey wild, and manna dew,
And sure in language strange she said,
    "I love thee true."

She took me to her elfin grot,
    And there she wept, and sighed full sore,   30
And there I shut her wild wild eyes
    With kisses four.

And there she lullèd me asleep,
    And there I dreamed — Ah! woe betide!
The latest° dream I ever dreamed   *last* 35
    On the cold hill side.

I saw pale kings and princes too,
    Pale warriors, death-pale were they all;
They cried — "La Belle Dame sans Merci
    Hath thee in thrall!"   40

La Belle Dame sans Merci: This title is borrowed from a medieval poem and means "The Beautiful Lady without Mercy."

I saw their starved lips in the gloom,
    With horrid warning gapèd wide,
And I awoke and found me here,
    On the cold hill's side.

And this is why I sojourn here,   45
    Alone and palely loitering,
Though the sedge has withered from the lake,
    And no birds sing.

JOHN KEATS (1795–1821)

Written in Disgust of Vulgar Superstition   *1816*

The church bells toll a melancholy round,
    Calling the people to some other prayers,
    Some other gloominess, more dreadful cares,
More hearkening to the sermon's horrid sound.
Surely the mind of man is closely bound   5
    In some black spell; seeing that each one tears
    Himself from fireside joys, and Lydian° airs,
And converse high of those with glory crown'd.
Still, still they toll, and I should feel a damp, —
    A chill as from a tomb, did I not know   10
That they are dying like an outburnt lamp;
    That 'tis their sighing, wailing ere they go
    Into oblivion; — that fresh flowers will grow,
And many glories of immortal stamp.

7 *Lydian:* Soft, sweet music.

EMMA LAZARUS (1849–1887)

The New Colossus   *1883*

Not like the brazen giant of Greek fame,
With conquering limbs astride from land to land;
Here at our sea-washed, sunset gates shall stand
A mighty woman with a torch, whose flame
Is the imprisoned lightning, and her name   5
Mother of Exiles. From her beacon-hand
Glows world-wide welcome; her mild eyes command
The air-bridged harbor that twin cities frame.
"Keep, ancient lands, your storied pomp!" cries she
With silent lips. "Give me your tired, your poor,   10
Your huddled masses yearning to breathe free,
The wretched refuse of your teeming shore.
Send these, the homeless, tempest-tost to me,
I lift my lamp beside the golden door!"

PHILLIS LEVIN (B. 1954)

May Day   *2008*

I've decided to waste my life again,
Like I used to: get drunk on
The light in the leaves, find a wall
Against which something can happen,

Whatever may have happened   5
Long ago — let a bullet hole echoing
The will of an executioner, a crevice
In which a love note was hidden,

Be a cell where a struggling tendril
Utters a few spare syllables at dawn.   10
I've decided to waste my life
In a new way, to forget whoever

Touched a hair on my head, because
It doesn't matter what came to pass,
Only that it passed, because we repeat   15
Ourselves, we repeat ourselves.

I've decided to walk a long way
Out of the way, to allow something
Dreaded to waken for no good reason,
Let it go without saying,   20

Let it go as it will to the place
It will go without saying: a wall
Against which a body was pressed
For no good reason, other than this.

HENRY WADSWORTH LONGFELLOW (1807–1882)

Snow-Flakes   *1863*

Out of the bosom of the Air,
    Out of the cloud-folds of her garments shaken,
Over the woodlands brown and bare
    Over the harvest-fields forsaken,
        Silent, and soft, and slow   5
        Descends the snow.

Even as our cloudy fancies take
    Suddenly shape in some divine expression,
Even as the troubled heart doth make
In the white countenance confession,   10
    The troubled sky reveals
    The grief it feels.

This is the poem of the air,
    Slowly in silent syllables recorded;
This is the secret of despair,   15
    Long in its cloudy bosom hoarded,
        Now whispered and revealed
        To wood and field.

EDNA ST. VINCENT MILLAY (1892–1950)

First Fig   *1918*

My candle burns at both ends;
    It will not last the night;
But ah, my foes, and oh, my friends —
    It gives a lovely light!

JOHN MILTON (1608–1674)

On the Late Massacre in Piedmont°   *1655*

Avenge, O Lord, thy slaughtered saints, whose bones
        Lie scattered on the Alpine mountains cold;
        Even them who kept thy truth so pure of old,
When all our fathers worshiped stocks and stones,°
Forget not: in thy book record their groans   5
        Who were thy sheep, and in their ancient fold
        Slain by the bloody Piedmontese, that rolled
Mother with infant down the rocks.° Their moans
The vales redoubled to the hills, and they
        To heaven. Their martyred blood and ashes sow   10
O'er all the Italian fields, where still doth sway
        The triple Tyrant;° that from these may grow
        A hundredfold, who, having learnt thy way,
        Early may fly the Babylonian woe.°

On the Late Massacre . . . : Milton's protest against the treatment of the Waldenses, members
of a Puritan sect living in the Piedmont region of northwest Italy, was not limited to this
sonnet. It is thought that he wrote Oliver Cromwell's appeals to the duke of Savoy and to
others to end the persecution.

4 *When . . . stones:* In Milton's Protestant view, English Catholics had worshiped their stone
and wooden statues in the twelfth century, when the Waldensian sect was formed.

5–8 *in thy book . . . rocks:* On Easter Day, 1655, 1,700 members of the Waldensian sect were
massacred in Piedmont by the duke of Savoy's forces.

12 *triple Tyrant:* The Pope, with his three-crowned tiara, has authority on earth and in
Heaven and Hell.

14 *Babylonian woe:* The destruction of Babylon, symbol of vice and corruption, at the end of
the world (see Rev. 17-18). Protestants interpreted the "Whore of Babylon" as the Roman
Catholic Church.

JOHN MILTON (1608–1674)

When I consider how my light is spent   *c. 1655*

When I consider how my light is spent,°
      Ere half my days in this dark world and wide,
      And that one talent° which is death to hide
Lodged with me useless, though my soul more bent
To serve therewith my Maker, and present   5
      My true account, lest He returning chide;
      "Doth God exact day-labor, light denied?"
I fondly° ask. But Patience, to prevent   *foolishly*
That murmur, soon replies, "God doth not need
      Either man's work or His own gifts. Who best   10
      Bear His mild yoke, they serve Him best. His state
Is kingly: thousands at His bidding speed,
      And post o'er land and ocean without rest;
      They also serve who only stand and wait."

1 *how my light is spent:* Milton had been totally blind since 1651.   3 *that one talent:* Refers to Jesus's parable of the talents (units of money), in which a servant entrusted with a talent buries it rather than invests it and is punished on his master's return (Matt. 25:14–30).

SIR WALTER RALEIGH (1554–1618)

The Nymph's Reply to the Shepherd   *1600*

If all the world and love were young,
And truth in every shepherd's tongue,
These pretty pleasures might me move
To live with thee and be thy love.

Time drives the flocks from field to fold,   5
When rivers rage and rocks grow cold,
And Philomel° becometh dumb;   *nightingale*
The rest complains of cares to come.

The flowers do fade, and wanton fields
To wayward winter reckoning yields;   10
A honey tongue, a heart of gall,
Is fancy's spring, but sorrow's fall.

Thy gowns, thy shoes, thy beds of roses,
Thy cap, thy kirtle, and thy posies
Soon break, soon wither, soon forgotten—   15
In folly ripe, in reason rotten.

Thy belt of straw and ivy buds,
Thy coral clasps and amber studs,

All these in me no means can move
To come to thee and be thy love.   20

But could youth last and love still breed,
Had joys no date° nor age no need,   *end*
Then these delights my mind might move
To live with thee and be thy love.

ALBERTO RÍOS (B. 1952)

Northern Desert Towns in the Turn
of the Old Century   *2005*

1

In town, in Cucurpe and Rayón,
In those small places and on those dirt streets

My grandmother walked with her sisters.
They were girls then, and could remember themselves laughing.

In those days there was a rabies for great civilization,   5
For suits, for Paris, for starch, for good grades, for musical societies.

People went to Saturday dances. Women wore their hair up.
Men walked with canes, fancy for walking but as much to hit the dogs

Biting at their capes—which the dogs thought
With all that black flailing in the summer wind   10

Was something attacking their masters,
The dogs having no understanding of civilized refinement,

Content themselves to walk on all fours
Unclothed, barking at will, and urinating in the neighbors' yards.

2

The invisible wall between the town and the desert,   15
It was the dare of the town drawn as a line in the sand,

A dare against Nature and the sun, a dare against everything
The townspeople knew and imagined in the distance,

A dare as strong in its intent as the great barricades of history
All those stories, all those walls and wire and water,   20

All those protections trying to raise themselves
Against the enemy, against the distant *out-there*.

But in a later century people would come to this place anyway
In shorts, sandals, and half-sleeved shirts.

The townspeople and the visitors would watch and nod,   25
Looking at each other. After all this time

The desert people marveled at the *out-there*
When it came in as it should from the sun.

3

The towns in the northern desert
Had taken care of themselves.   30

In the middle of the desert they bloomed
And a song came up

From them, sometimes, in the evening.
Smoke rose at dinnertime, and early light.

Rain and harvesting the corn   35
All meant something to the town.

When the electricity came, and the new lights,
The cars and the tourists,

Everything was different. Rayón and Cucurpe,
Magdalena and Imuris, all the other small towns,   40

They became old, like my grandmother and her sisters.
Together they waited to see what would come next.

CHRISTINA GEORGINA ROSSETTI
(1830–1894)

Some Ladies Dress in Muslin Full and White   *c. 1848*

Some ladies dress in muslin full and
        white,
Some gentlemen in cloth succinct and black;
Some patronise a dog-cart, some a hack,
        Some think a painted clarence only
            right.
        Youth is not always such a pleasing
            sight:
Witness a man with tassels on his back;
Or woman in a great-coat like a sack,
        Towering above her sex with horrid height.
If all the world were water fit to drown,
        There are some whom you would not teach to swim,   10

Rather enjoying if you saw them sink:
    Certain old ladies dressed in girlish pink,
With roses and geraniums on their gown.
        Go to the basin, poke them o'er the rim —

CHRISTINA GEORGINA ROSSETTI (1830–1894)

In Progress   *1862*

Ten years ago it seemed impossible
    That she should ever grow so calm as this,
    With self-remembrance in her warmest kiss
And dim dried eyes like an exhausted well.
Slow-speaking when she has some fact to tell,   5
    Silent with long-unbroken silences,
    Centred in self yet not unpleased to please,
Gravely monotonous like a passing bell.

Mindful of drudging daily common things,
    Patient at pastime, patient at her work,   10
Wearied perhaps but strenuous certainly.
Sometimes I fancy we may one day see
    Her head shoot forth seven stars from where they lurk
And her eyes lightnings and her shoulders wings.

CHRISTINA GEORGINA ROSSETTI (1830–1894)

The World   *1862*

By day she wooes me, soft, exceeding fair:
But all night as the moon so changeth she;
Loathsome and foul with hideous leprosy
    And subtle serpents gliding in her hair.
    By day she wooes me to the outer air,   5
Ripe fruits, sweet flowers, and full satiety:
But thro' the night, a beast she grins at me,
    A very monster void of love and prayer.
By day she stands a lie: by night she stands
    In all the naked horror of the truth   10
With pushing horns and clawed and clutching hands.
    Is this a friend indeed; that I should sell
My soul to her, give her my life and youth,
Till my feet, cloven too, take hold on hell?

Christina Georgina Rossetti (1830–1894)

Promises Like Pie-Crust°

Promise me no promises,
    So will I not promise you;
Keep we both our liberties,
    Never false and never true:
Let us hold the die uncast,   5
    Free to come as free to go;
For I cannot know your past,
    And of mine what can you know?

You, so warm, may once have been
    Warmer towards another one;   10
I, so cold, may once have seen
    Sunlight, once have felt the sun:
Who shall show us if it was
    Thus indeed in time of old?
Fades the image from the glass   15
    And the fortune is not told.

If you promised, you might grieve
    For lost liberty again;
If I promised, I believe
    I should fret to break the chain: 20
Let us be the friends we were,
    Nothing more but nothing less;
Many thrive on frugal fare
    Who would perish of excess.

Pie-Crust: An old English proverb: "Promises are like pie-crust, made to be broken."

Siegfried Sassoon (1886–1967)

"They"

The Bishop tells us: "When the boys come back
They will not be the same; for they'll have fought
In a just cause: they lead the last attack
On Anti-Christ; their comrades' blood has bought
New right to breed an honourable race,   5
They have challenged Death and dared him face to face."

"We're none of us the same!" the boys reply.
"For George lost both his legs; and Bill's stone blind;
Poor Jim's shot through the lungs and like to die;
And Bert's gone syphilitic: you'll not find   10
A chap who's served that hasn't found *some* change."
And the Bishop said: "The ways of God are strange!"

WILLIAM SHAKESPEARE (1564–1616)

That time of year thou mayst in me behold   1609

That time of year thou mayst in me behold
When yellow leaves, or none, or few, do hang
Upon those boughs which shake against the cold,
Bare ruined choirs, where late the sweet birds sang.
In me thou see'st the twilight of such day   5
As after sunset fadeth in the west;
Which by and by black night doth take away,
Death's second self,° that seals up all in rest.   *sleep*
In me thou see'st the glowing of such fire,
That on the ashes of his youth doth lie,   10
As the deathbed whereon it must expire,
Consumed with that which it was nourished by.
    This thou perceiv'st, which makes thy love more strong,
    To love that well which thou must leave ere long.

WILLIAM SHAKESPEARE (1564–1616)

When forty winters shall besiege thy brow   1609

When forty winters shall besiege thy brow
And dig deep trenches in thy beauty's field,
Thy youth's proud livery, so gazed on now,
Will be a tattered weed,° of small worth held.   *garment*
Then being asked where all thy beauty lies,   5
Where all the treasure of thy lusty days,
To say within thine own deep-sunken eyes
Were an all-eating shame and thriftless praise.
How much more praise deserved thy beauty's use
If thou couldst answer, "This fair child of mine   10
Shall sum my count and make my old excuse,"
Proving his beauty by succession thine.
    This were to be new made when thou art old,
    And see thy blood warm when thou feel'st it cold.

WILLIAM SHAKESPEARE (1564–1616)

When, in disgrace with Fortune and men's eyes   1609

When, in disgrace with Fortune and men's eyes,
I all alone beweep my outcast state,
And trouble deaf heaven with my bootless cries,
And look upon myself and curse my fate,

Wishing me like to one more rich in hope,   5
Featured like him, like him with friends possessed,
Desiring this man's art, and that man's scope,
With what I most enjoy contented least,
Yet in these thoughts myself almost despising,
Haply I think on thee, and then my state,   10
Like to the lark at break of day arising
From sullen earth, sings hymns at heaven's gate;
    For thy sweet love remembered such wealth brings
    That then I scorn to change my state with kings.

PERCY BYSSHE SHELLEY (1792–1822)

Ozymandias°   *1818*

I met a traveler from an antique land
Who said: Two vast and trunkless legs of stone
Stand in the desert. . . . Near them, on the sand,
Half sunk, a shattered visage lies, whose frown,
And wrinkled lip, and sneer of cold command,   5
Tell that its sculptor well those passions read
Which yet survive, stamped on these lifeless things,
The hand that mocked them, and the heart that fed:
And on the pedestal these words appear:
"My name is Ozymandias, King of Kings: 10
Look on my works, ye Mighty, and despair!"
Nothing beside remains. Round the decay
Of that colossal wreck, boundless and bare
The lone and level sands stretch far away.

Ozymandias: Greek name for Ramses II, pharaoh of Egypt for sixty-seven years during the thirteenth century B.C. His colossal statue lies prostrate in the sands of Luxor. Napoleon's soldiers measured it (56 feet long, ear 3½ feet long, weight 1,000 tons). Its inscription, according to the Greek historian Diodorus Siculus, was "I am Ozymandias, King of Kings; if anyone wishes to know what I am and where I lie, let him surpass me in some of my exploits."

SIR PHILIP SIDNEY (1554–1586)

Loving in Truth, and Fain in Verse
My Love to Show   *1591*

Loving in truth, and fain in verse my love to show,
That she, dear she, might take some pleasure of my pain,
Pleasure might cause her read, reading might make her know,
Knowledge might pity win, and pity grace obtain,
I sought fit words to paint the blackest face of woe,   5

Studying inventions fine, her wits to entertain,
Oft turning others' leaves, to see if thence would flow
Some fresh and fruitful showers upon my sunburnt brain.
But words came halting forth, wanting Invention's stay;
Invention, Nature's child, fled step-dame° Study's blows;   *stepmother* 10
And others' feet still seemed but strangers in my way.
Thus great with child to speak, and helpless in my throes,
Biting my truant pen, beating myself for spite:
"Fool," said my Muse to me, "look in thy heart and write."

LYDIA HUNTLEY SIGOURNEY (1791–1865)

Indian Names   *1834*

*"How can the red men be forgotten, while so many of
our states and territories, bays, lakes and rivers, are
indelibly stamped by names of their giving?"*

Ye say they all have passed away,
    That noble race and brave,
That their light canoes have vanished
    From off the crested wave;
That 'mid the forests where they roamed   5
    There rings no hunter shout,
But their name is on your waters,
    Ye may not wash it out.

'Tis where Ontario's billow
    Like Ocean's surge is curled,   10
Where strong Niagara's thunders wake
    The echo of the world.
Where red Missouri bringeth
    Rich tribute from the west,
And Rappahannock sweetly sleeps   15
    On green Virginia's breast.

Ye say their cone-like cabins,
    That clustered o'er the vale,
Have fled away like withered leaves
    Before the autumn gale,   20
But their memory liveth on your hills,
    Their baptism on your shore,
Your everlasting rivers speak
    Their dialect of yore.

Old Massachusetts wears it,   25
    Within her lordly crown,
And broad Ohio bears it,
    Amid his young renown;

Connecticut hath wreathed it
    Where her quiet foliage waves,   30
And bold Kentucky breathed it hoarse
    Through all her ancient caves.

Wachuset hides its lingering voice
    Within his rocky heart,
And Alleghany graves its tone   35
    Throughout his lofty chart;
Monadnock on his forehead hoar
    Doth seal the sacred trust,
Your mountains build their monument,
    Though ye destroy their dust.   40

Ye call these red-browed brethren
    The insects of an hour,
Crushed like the noteless worm amid
    The regions of their power;
Ye drive them from their father's lands,   45
    Ye break of faith the seal,
But can ye from the court of Heaven
    Exclude their last appeal?

Ye see their unresisting tribes,
    With toilsome step and slow,   50
On through the trackless desert pass,
    A caravan of woe;
Think ye the Eternal's ear is deaf?
    His sleepless vision dim?
Think ye the *soul's blood* may not cry   55
    From that far land to him?

ALFRED, LORD TENNYSON (1809–1892)

Ulysses°

1833

    It little profits that an idle king,
By this still hearth, among these barren crags,
Matched with an agèd wife,° I mete and dole   *Penelope*
Unequal laws unto a savage race,
That hoard, and sleep, and feed, and know not me.   5
    I cannot rest from travel; I will drink
Life to the lees. All times I have enjoyed
Greatly, have suffered greatly, both with those
That loved me, and alone; on shore, and when

Ulysses: Ulysses, the hero of Homer's epic poem the *Odyssey*, is presented by Dante in *The Inferno*, XXVI, as restless after his return to Ithaca and eager for new adventures.

Through scudding drifts the rainy Hyades°   10
Vexed the dim sea. I am become a name;
For always roaming with a hungry heart
Much have I seen and known — cities of men
And manners, climates, councils, governments,
Myself not least, but honored of them all —   15
And drunk delight of battle with my peers,
Far on the ringing plains of windy Troy.
I am a part of all that I have met;
Yet all experience is an arch wherethrough
Gleams that untraveled world, whose margin fades   20
For ever and for ever when I move.
How dull it is to pause, to make an end,
To rust unburnished, not to shine in use!
As though to breathe were life. Life piled on life
Were all too little, and of one to me   25
Little remains; but every hour is saved
From that eternal silence, something more,
A bringer of new things; and vile it were
For some three suns to store and hoard myself,
And this gray spirit yearning in desire   30
To follow knowledge like a sinking star,
Beyond the utmost bound of human thought.

    This is my son, mine own Telemachus,
To whom I leave the scepter and the isle —
Well-loved of me, discerning to fulfill   35
This labor, by slow prudence to make mild
A rugged people, and through soft degrees
Subdue them to the useful and the good.
Most blameless is he, centered in the sphere
Of common duties, decent not to fail   40
In offices of tenderness, and pay
Meet adoration to my household gods,
When I am gone. He works his work, I mine.

    There lies the port; the vessel puffs her sail:
There gloom the dark, broad seas. My mariners,   45
Souls that have toiled, and wrought, and thought with me —
That ever with a frolic welcome took
The thunder and the sunshine, and opposed
Free hearts, free foreheads — you and I are old;
Old age hath yet his honor and his toil.   50
Death closes all; but something ere the end,
Some work of noble note, may yet be done,
Not unbecoming men that strove with Gods.
The lights begin to twinkle from the rocks;

10 *Hyades:* Five stars in the constellation Taurus, supposed by the ancients to predict rain when they rose with the sun.

The long day wanes; the slow moon climbs; the deep   55
Moans round with many voices. Come, my friends.
'Tis not too late to seek a newer world.
Push off, and sitting well in order smite
The sounding furrows; for my purpose holds
To sail beyond the sunset, and the baths   60
Of all the western stars, until I die.
It may be that the gulfs will wash us down;
It may be we shall touch the Happy Isles,°
And see the great Achilles,° whom we knew.
Though much is taken, much abides; and though   65
We are not now that strength which in old days
Moved earth and heaven, that which we are, we are:
One equal temper of heroic hearts,
Made weak by time and fate, but strong in will
To strive, to seek, to find, and not to yield.   70

63 *Happy Isles:* Elysium, the home after death of heroes and others favored by the gods. It was thought by the ancients to lie beyond the sunset in the uncharted Atlantic.   64 *Achilles:* The hero of Homer's *Iliad.*

ALFRED, LORD TENNYSON (1809–1892)

Tears, Idle Tears   1847

Tears, idle tears, I know not what they mean,
Tears from the depth of some divine despair
Rise in the heart, and gather to the eyes,
In looking on the happy Autumn-fields,
And thinking of the days that are no more.   5

Fresh as the first beam glittering on a sail,
That brings our friends up from the underworld,
Sad as the last which reddens over one
That sinks with all we love below the verge;
So sad, so fresh, the days that are no more.   10

Ah, sad and strange as in dark summer dawns
The earliest pipe of half-awaken'd birds
To dying ears, when unto dying eyes
The casement° slowly grows a glimmering square;   *window*
So sad, so strange, the days that are no more.   15

Dear as remember'd kisses after death,
And sweet as those by hopeless fancy feign'd
On lips that are for others; deep as love,
Deep as first love, and wild with all regret;
O Death in Life, the days that are no more.   20

RICHARD WAKEFIELD (B. 1952)

In a Poetry Workshop

1999

Let us begin with the basics of modern verse.
Meter, of course, is forbidden, and lines must be,
like life, broken arbitrarily
lest anyone mistake us for budding Wordsworths
(don't be alarmed if you've never heard of him). 5
Rhyme is allowed, but only in moderation
and preferably very slant. Alliteration
and assonance must only be used at whim
so the reader doesn't think we're playing God
by sneaking in a pattern of sounds and echoes. 10
As for subjects, the modern poet knows
that modern readers prefer the decidedly odd,
so flowers, except for weeds, are out, and love,
except the very weed-like, is also out.
So thistles and incest are fine to write about 15
but roses and happy marriage get the shove
into the editor's outbox with hardly a glance.
Now note that language matters, so "I" must be
in lower case, thus "i," to show that we
don't put on airs despite our government grants. 20
This also shows we've read our Marx and know
the self is a bourgeois fiction. We understand
the common speech, and so the ampersand,
pronounced "uhn," replaces "and," although
judicious use of allusions to classical thought 25
will keep the great unwashed from getting our drift,
while those outside of Plato's cave will lift
a knowing eyebrow, declaring our work "well-wrought."
And speaking of work, this is not a "class":
We modern poets roll up our sleeves and write 30
our verse in "workshops," no place for sissies, we fight
to find "a voice," and only the fittest pass.
I've summarized these rules in a convenient list,
it's wallet-sized, laminated, so keep
it handy, use it, recite it in your sleep. 35
First poems are due tomorrow. You're dismissed.

WALT WHITMAN (1819–1892)

I Heard You Solemn-Sweet Pipes of the Organ

1861

I heard you solemn-sweet pipes of the organ as last Sunday
morn I pass'd the church,
Winds of autumn, as I walk'd the woods at dusk I heard your
long-stretch'd sighs up above so mournful,

I heard the perfect Italian tenor singing at the opera, I heard
    the soprano in the midst of the quartet singing;
Heart of my love! you too I heard murmuring low through
    one of the wrists around my head,
Heard the pulse of you when all was still ringing little bells
    last night under my ear.

WALT WHITMAN (1819–1892)
When I Heard the Learn'd Astronomer   *1865*

When I heard the learn'd astronomer,
When the proofs, the figures, were ranged in columns before me,
When I was shown the charts and diagrams, to add, divide, and measure them,
When I sitting heard the astronomer where he lectured with much applause
    in the lecture-room,
How soon unaccountable I became tired and sick,
Till rising and gliding out I wandered off by myself,
In the mystical moist night-air, and from time to time,
Looked up in perfect silence at the stars.

WALT WHITMAN (1819–1892)
One's-Self I Sing   *1867*

One's-Self I sing, a simple separate person,
Yet utter the word Democratic, the word En-Masse.

Of physiology from top to toe I sing,
Not physiognomy alone nor brain alone is worthy for the Muse, I say the
    Form complete is worthier far,
The Female equally with the Male I sing.

Of Life immense in passion, pulse, and power,
Cheerful, for freest action formed under the laws divine,
The Modern Man I sing.

MILLER WILLIAMS (B. 1930)
Thinking about Bill, Dead of AIDS   *1989*

We did not know the first thing about
how blood surrenders to even the smallest threat
when old allergies turn inside out,

the body rescinding all its normal orders
to all defenders of flesh, betraying the head,   5
pulling its guards back from all its borders.

Thinking of friends afraid to shake your hand,
we think of your hand shaking, your mouth set,
your eyes drained of any reprimand.

Loving, we kissed you, partly to persuade   10
both you and us, seeing what eyes had said,
that we were loving and we were not afraid.

If we had had more, we would have given more.
As it was we stood next to your bed,
stopping, though, to set our smiles at the door.   15

Not because we were less sure at the last.
Only because, not knowing anything yet,
we didn't know what look would hurt you least.

WILLIAM CARLOS WILLIAMS (1883–1963)

Spring and All   *1923*

By the road to the contagious hospital
under the surge of the blue
mottled clouds driven from the
northeast — a cold wind. Beyond, the
waste of broad, muddy fields   5
brown with dried weeds, standing and fallen

patches of standing water
and scattering of tall trees

All along the road the reddish
purplish, forked, upstanding, twiggy   10
stuff of bushes and small trees
with dead, brown leaves under them
leafless vines —

Lifeless in appearance, sluggish
dazed spring approaches —   15

They enter the new world naked,
cold, uncertain of all
save that they enter. All about them
the cold, familiar wind —

Now the grass, tomorrow   20
the stiff curl of wildcarrot leaf
One by one objects are defined —
It quickens: clarity, outline of leaf

But now the stark dignity of
entrance — Still, the profound change   25
has come upon them: rooted, they
grip down and begin to awaken

WILLIAM CARLOS WILLIAMS (1883–1963)

This Is Just to Say   *1934*

I have eaten
the plums
that were in
the icebox

and which   5
you were probably
saving
for breakfast

Forgive me
they were delicious   10
so sweet
and so cold

WILLIAM WORDSWORTH (1770–1850)

A Slumber Did My Spirit Seal   *1800*

A slumber did my spirit seal;
  I had no human fears —
She seemed a thing that could not feel
  The touch of earthly years.

No motion has she now, no force;
  She neither hears nor sees;
Rolled round in earth's diurnal course.
  With rocks, and stones, and trees.

By permission of Dove Cottage, the
Wordsworth Trust.

WILLIAM WORDSWORTH (1770–1850)

I Wandered Lonely as a Cloud   *1807*

I wandered lonely as a cloud
That floats on high o'er vales and hills,
When all at once I saw a crowd,
A host, of golden daffodils,
Beside the lake, beneath the trees,   5
Fluttering and dancing in the breeze.

Continuous as the stars that shine
And twinkle on the milky way,
They stretched in never-ending line
Along the margin of a bay;   10

Ten thousand saw I at a glance,
Tossing their heads in sprightly dance.

The waves beside them danced, but they
Outdid the sparkling waves in glee;
A poet could not but be gay,   15
In such a jocund company;
I gazed — and gazed — but little thought
What wealth the show to me had brought:

For oft, when on my couch I lie
In vacant or in pensive mood,   20
They flash upon that inward eye
Which is the bliss of solitude;
And then my heart with pleasure fills,
And dances with the daffodils.

WILLIAM WORDSWORTH (1770–1850)

It Is a Beauteous Evening, Calm and Free   1807

It is a beauteous evening, calm and free,
The holy time is quiet as a Nun
Breathless with adoration; the broad sun
Is sinking down in its tranquillity;
The gentleness of heaven broods o'er the Sea: 5
Listen! the mighty Being is awake,
And doth with his eternal motion make
A sound like thunder — everlastingly.
Dear Child! dear Girl! that walkest with me here,
If thou appear untouched by solemn thought,   10
Thy nature is not therefore less divine:
Thou liest in Abraham's bosom all the year;
And worshipp'st at the Temple's inner shrine,
God being with thee when we know it not.

WILLIAM WORDSWORTH (1770–1850)

The Solitary Reaper°   1807

Behold her, single in the field,
Yon solitary Highland lass!
Reaping and singing by herself;
Stop here, or gently pass!
Alone she cuts and binds the grain,   5
And sings a melancholy strain;
O listen! for the vale profound
Is overflowing with the sound.

No nightingale did ever chaunt
More welcome notes to weary bands   10
Of travelers in some shady haunt
Among Arabian sands.
A voice so thrilling ne'er was heard
In springtime from the cuckoo-bird,
Breaking the silence of the seas   15
Among the farthest Hebrides.

Will no one tell me what she sings? —
Perhaps the plaintive numbers flow
For old, unhappy, far-off things,
And battles long ago.   20
Or is it some more humble lay,
Familiar matter of today?
Some natural sorrow, loss, or pain,
That has been, and may be again?

Whate'er the theme, the maiden sang   25
As if her song could have no ending;
I saw her singing at her work,
And o'er the sickle bending —
I listened, motionless and still;
And, as I mounted up the hill,   30
The music in my heart I bore
Long after it was heard no more.

The Solitary Reaper: Dorothy Wordsworth (William's sister) wrote that the poem was suggested by this sentence in Thomas Wilkinson's *Tour of Scotland:* "Passed a female who was reaping alone; she sung in Erse, as she bended over her sickle; the sweetest human voice I ever heard; her strains were tenderly melancholy, and felt delicious, long after they were heard no more."

WILLIAM WORDSWORTH (1770–1850)

Mutability   1822

From low to high doth dissolution climb,
And sink from high to low, along a scale
Of awful° notes, whose concord shall not fail;   *awe-filled*
A musical but melancholy chime,
Which they can hear who meddle not with crime,   5
Nor avarice, nor over-anxious care.
Truth fails not; but her outward forms that bear
The longest date do melt like frosty rime,
That in the morning whitened hill and plain
And is no more; drop like the tower sublime   10
Of yesterday, which royally did wear
His crown of weeds, but could not even sustain
Some casual shout that broke the silent air,
Or the unimaginable touch of Time.

WILLIAM BUTLER YEATS (1865–1939)

The Second Coming°   *1921*

Turning and turning in the widening gyre°
The falcon cannot hear the falconer;
Things fall apart; the center cannot hold;
Mere anarchy is loosed upon the world,
The blood-dimmed tide is loosed, and
     everywhere
The ceremony of innocence is drowned;
The best lack all conviction, while the worst
Are full of passionate intensity.

Surely some revelation is at hand;
Surely the Second Coming is at hand.   10
The Second Coming! Hardly are those words out
When a vast image out of *Spiritus Mundi*°   *Soul of the world*
Troubles my sight: somewhere in sands of the desert
A shape with lion body and the head of a man,
A gaze blank and pitiless as the sun,   15
Is moving its slow thighs, while all about it
Reel shadows of the indignant desert birds.
The darkness drops again; but now I know
That twenty centuries of stony sleep
Were vexed to nightmare by a rocking cradle,   20
And what rough beast, its hour come round at last,
Slouches towards Bethlehem to be born?

© Hulton-Deutsch Collection/CORBIS.

The Second Coming: According to Matthew 24:29–44, Christ will return to earth after a time of tribulation to reward the righteous and establish the millennium of heaven on earth. Yeats saw his troubled time as the end of the Christian era and feared the portents of the new cycle.

1 *gyre:* Widening spiral of a falcon's flight, used by Yeats to describe the cycling of history.

WILLIAM BUTLER YEATS (1865–1939)

Leda and the Swan°   *1924*

A sudden blow: the great wings beating still
Above the staggering girl, her thighs caressed
By the dark webs, her nape caught in his bill,
He holds her helpless breast upon his breast.

How can those terrified vague fingers push   5
The feathered glory from her loosening thighs?

Leda and the Swan: In Greek myth, Zeus in the form of a swan seduced Leda and fathered Helen of Troy (whose abduction started the Trojan War) and Clytemnestra, Agamemnon's wife and murderer. Yeats thought of Zeus's appearance to Leda as a type of annunciation, like the angel appearing to Mary.

And how can body, laid in that white rush,
But feel the strange heart beating where it lies?

A shudder in the loins engenders there
The broken wall, the burning roof and tower   10
And Agamemnon dead.
                  Being so caught up,
So mastered by the brute blood of the air,
Did she put on his knowledge with his power
Before the indifferent beak could let her drop?   15

WILLIAM BUTLER YEATS (1865–1939)
Sailing to Byzantium°   *1927*

I

That is no country for old men.° The young
In one another's arms, birds in the trees
— Those dying generations — at their song,
The salmon-falls, the mackerel-crowded seas
Fish, flesh, or fowl, commend all summer long   5
Whatever is begotten, born and dies.
Caught in that sensual music all neglect
Monuments of unaging intellect.

II

An aged man is but a paltry thing,
A tattered coat upon a stick, unless   10
Soul clap its hands and sing, and louder sing
For every tatter in its mortal dress,
Nor is there singing school but studying
Monuments of its own magnificence;
And therefore I have sailed the seas and come   15
To the holy city of Byzantium.

III

O sages standing in God's holy fire
As in the gold mosaic of a wall,

Byzantium: Old name for the modern city of Istanbul, capital of the Eastern Roman Empire, ancient artistic and intellectual center. Yeats uses Byzantium as a symbol for "artificial" (and therefore, deathless) art and beauty, as opposed to the beauty of the natural world, which is bound to time and death.

1 *That . . . men:* Ireland, part of the time-bound world.

Come from the holy fire, perne in a gyre,°
And be the singing-masters of my soul.   20
Consume my heart away; sick with desire
And fastened to a dying animal
It knows not what it is; and gather me
Into the artifice of eternity.

IV

Once out of nature I shall never take   25
My bodily form from any natural thing,
But such a form as Grecian goldsmiths make
Of hammered gold and gold enameling
To keep a drowsy Emperor awake;°
Or set upon a golden bough° to sing   30
To lords and ladies of Byzantium
Of what is past, or passing, or to come.

19 *perne in a gyre:* Bobbin making a spiral pattern.   27–29 *such . . . awake:* "I have read
somewhere that in the Emperor's palace at Byzantium was a tree made of gold and silver,
and artificial birds that sang." [Yeats's note.]   30 *golden bough:* In Greek legend, Aeneas had
to pluck a golden bough from a tree in order to descend into Hades. As soon as the bough
was plucked, another grew in its place.

WILLIAM BUTLER YEATS (1865–1939)

Crazy Jane Talks with the Bishop   *1933*

I met the Bishop on the road
And much said he and I.
"Those breasts are flat and fallen now,
Those veins must soon be dry;
Live in a heavenly mansion,   5
Not in some foul sty."

"Fair and foul are near of kin,
And fair needs foul," I cried.
"My friends are gone, but that's a truth
Nor grave nor bed denied,   10
Learned in bodily lowliness
And in the heart's pride.

"A woman can be proud and stiff
When on love intent;
But Love has pitched his mansion in   15
The place of excrement;
For nothing can be sole or whole
That has not been rent."

DRAMA

The Study
of Drama

45

Reading Drama

I regard the theater as serious business, one that makes or should make man more human, which is to say, less alone.
— ARTHUR MILLER

I think theatre is a spiritual experience. There is an exchange of light and energy between an audience and the actors. It can be life altering.
— JOSEFINA LOPEZ

READING DRAMA RESPONSIVELY

The publication of a short story, novel, or poem represents for most writers the final step in a long creative process that might have begun with an idea, issue, emotion, or question that demanded expression. *Playwrights* — writers who make plays — may begin a work in the same way as other writers, but rarely are they satisfied with only its publication because most dramatic literature — what we call *plays* — is written to be performed by actors on a stage before an audience. Playwrights typically create a play keeping in mind not only readers but also actors, producers, directors, costumers, designers, technicians, and a theater full of other support staff who have a hand in presenting the play to a live audience.

Drama is literature equipped with arms, legs, tears, laughs, whispers, shouts, and gestures that are alive and immediate. Indeed, the word *drama* derives from the Greek word *dran,* meaning "to do" or "to perform." The text of many plays — the *script* — may come to life fully only when the written words are transformed into a performance. Although there are plays that do not invite production, they are relatively few. Such plays, written to be read rather than performed, are called *closet dramas.* In this kind of work (primarily associated with nineteenth-century English literature), literary art outweighs all other considerations. The majority of playwrights, however, view the written word as the beginning of a larger creation and hope that a producer will deem their scripts worthy of production.

Given that most playwrights intend their works to be performed, it might be argued that reading a play is a poor substitute for seeing it acted on a stage — perhaps something like reading a recipe without having access to the ingredients and a kitchen. This analogy is tempting, but it overlooks the literary dimensions of a script; the words we hear on a stage were written first. Read from a page, these words can feed an imagination in ways that a recipe cannot satisfy a hungry cook. We can fill in a play's missing faces, voices, actions, and settings in much the same way that we imagine these elements in a short story or novel. Like any play director, we are free to include as many ingredients as we have an appetite for.

This imaginative collaboration with the playwright creates a mental world that can be nearly as real and vivid as a live performance. Sometimes readers find that they prefer their own reading of a play to a director's interpretation. Shakespeare's Hamlet, for instance, has been presented as a whining son, but you may read him as a strong prince. Rich plays often accommodate a wide range of imaginative responses to their texts. Reading, then, is an excellent way to appreciate and evaluate a production of a play. Moreover, reading is valuable in its own right because it allows us to enter the playwright's created world even when a theatrical production is unavailable.

Reading a play, however, requires more creative imagining than sitting in an audience watching actors on a stage presenting lines and actions before you. As a reader you become the play's director; you construct an interpretation based on the playwright's use of language, development of character, arrangement of incidents, description of settings, and directions for staging. Keeping track of the playwright's handling of these elements will help you to organize your response to the play. You may experience suspense, fear, horror, sympathy, or humor, but whatever experience a play evokes, ask yourself why you respond to it as you do. You may discover that your assessment of Hamlet's character is different from someone else's, but whether you find him heroic, indecisive, neurotic, or a complex of competing qualities, you'll be better equipped to articulate your interpretation of him if you pay attention to your responses and ask yourself questions as you read. Consider, for example, how his reactions might be similar to or different from your own. How does his language reveal his character? Does his behavior seem justified? How would you play the role yourself? What actor do you think might best play the Hamlet that you have created in your imagination? Why would he or she (women have also played Hamlet onstage) fill the role best?

These kinds of questions (see Questions for Responsive Reading and Writing, p. 1408) can help you to think and talk about your responses to a play. Happily, such questions needn't — and often can't — be fully answered as you read the play. Frequently you must experience the entire play before you can determine how its elements work together. That's why reading a play can be such a satisfying experience. You wouldn't think of asking a live actor onstage to repeat her lines because you didn't quite comprehend their significance, but you can certainly reread a page in a book. Rereading allows you to replay language, characters, and incidents carefully and thoroughly to your own satisfaction.

Trifles

In the following play, Susan Glaspell skillfully draws on many dramatic elements and creates an intense story that is as effective on the page as it is in the theater. Glaspell wrote *Trifles* in 1916 for the Provincetown Players on Cape Cod, in Massachusetts. Their performance of the work helped her develop a reputation as a writer sensitive to feminist issues. The year after *Trifles* was produced, Glaspell transformed the play into a short story titled "A Jury of Her Peers." (A passage from the story appears on p. 1378 for comparison.)

Provided courtesy of the Lear Center for Special Collections & Archives, Connecticut College.

Glaspell's life in the Midwest provided her with the setting for *Trifles*. Born and raised in Davenport, Iowa, she graduated from Drake University in 1899 and then worked for a short time as a reporter on the *Des Moines News*, until her short stories were accepted in magazines such as *Harper's* and *Ladies' Home Journal*. Glaspell moved to the Northeast when she was in her early thirties to continue writing fiction and drama. She published some twenty plays, novels, and more than forty short stories. *Alison's House*, based on Emily Dickinson's life, earned her a Pulitzer Prize for drama in 1931. *Trifles* and "A Jury of Her Peers" remain, however, Glaspell's best-known works.

Glaspell wrote *Trifles* to complete a bill that was to feature several one-act plays by Eugene O'Neill. In *The Road to the Temple* (1926) she recalls how the play came to her as she sat in the theater looking at a bare stage. First, "the stage became a kitchen. . . . Then the door at the back opened, and people all bundled up came in — two or three men. I wasn't sure which, but sure enough about the two women, who hung back, reluctant to enter that kitchen. When I was a newspaper reporter out in Iowa, I was sent down-state to do a murder trial, and I never forgot going to the kitchen of a woman who had been locked up in town."

Trifles is about a murder committed in a midwestern farmhouse, but the play goes beyond the kinds of questions raised by most whodunit stories. The murder is the occasion instead of the focus. The play's major concerns are the moral, social, and psychological aspects of the assumptions and perceptions of the men and women who search for the murderer's motive. Glaspell is finally more interested in the meaning of Mrs. Wright's life than in the details of Mr. Wright's death.

As you read the play, keep track of your responses to the characters and note in the margin the moments when Glaspell reveals how men and women respond differently to the evidence before them. What do those moments suggest about the kinds of assumptions these men and women make about themselves and each other? How do their assumptions compare with your own?

[Web] Explore contexts for Susan Glaspell and approaches to this play at bedfordstmartins.com/meyerlit.

Susan Glaspell (1882–1948)

Trifles

1916

CHARACTERS

George Henderson, county attorney
Henry Peters, sheriff
Lewis Hale, a neighboring farmer
Mrs. Peters
Mrs. Hale

SCENE: The kitchen in the now abandoned farmhouse of John Wright, a gloomy kitchen, and left without having been put in order — unwashed pans under the sink, a loaf of bread outside the breadbox, a dish towel on the table — other signs of in-completed work. At the rear the outer door opens and the Sheriff comes in followed by the County Attorney and Hale. The Sheriff and Hale are men in middle life, the County Attorney is a young man; all are much bundled up and go at once to the stove. They are followed by the two women — the Sheriff's wife first; she is a slight wiry woman, a thin nervous face. Mrs. Hale is larger and would ordinarily be called more comfortable looking, but she is disturbed now and looks fearfully about as she enters. The women have come in slowly, and stand close together near the door.

County Attorney (rubbing his hands): This feels good. Come up to the fire, ladies.

Mrs. Peters (after taking a step forward): I'm not — cold.

Sheriff (unbuttoning his overcoat and stepping away from the stove as if to mark the beginning of official business): Now, Mr. Hale, before we move things about, you explain to Mr. Henderson just what you saw when you came here yesterday morning.

County Attorney: By the way, has anything been moved? Are things just as you left them yesterday?

Sheriff (looking about): It's just about the same. When it dropped below zero last night I thought I'd better send Frank out this morning to make a fire for us — no use getting pneumonia with a big case on, but I told him not to touch anything except the stove — and you know Frank.

County Attorney: Somebody should have been left here yesterday.

Sheriff: Oh — yesterday. When I had to send Frank to Morris Center for that man who went crazy — I want you to know I had my hands full yesterday. I knew you could get back from Omaha by today and as long as I went over everything here myself —

County Attorney: Well, Mr. Hale, tell just what happened when you came here yesterday morning.

Hale: Harry and I had started to town with a load of potatoes. We came along the road from my place and as I got here I said, "I'm going to see if I can't get John Wright to go in with me on a party telephone." I spoke to Wright about it once before and he put me off, saying folks talked too much anyway, and all he asked was peace and quiet — I guess you know about how much he talked himself; but I thought maybe if I went to the house and talked about it before his wife, though I said to Harry that I didn't know as what his wife wanted made much difference to John —

County Attorney: Let's talk about that later, Mr. Hale. I do want to talk about that, but tell now just what happened when you got to the house.

Hale: I didn't hear or see anything; I knocked at the door, and still it was all quiet inside. I knew they must be up, it was past eight o'clock. So I knocked again, and I thought I heard somebody say, "Come in." I wasn't sure, I'm not sure yet, but I opened the door — this door *(indicating the door by which the two women are still standing)* and there in that rocker — *(pointing to it)* sat Mrs. Wright. *(They all look at the rocker.)*

County Attorney: What — was she doing?

Hale: She was rockin' back and forth. She had her apron in her hand and was kind of — pleating it.

County Attorney: And how did she — look?

Hale: Well, she looked queer.

County Attorney: How do you mean — queer?

Hale: Well, as if she didn't know what she was going to do next. And kind of done up.

County Attorney: How did she seem to feel about your coming?

Hale: Why, I don't think she minded — one way or other. She didn't pay much attention. I said, "How do, Mrs. Wright, it's cold, ain't it?" And she said, "Is it?" — and went on kind of pleating at her apron. Well, I was surprised; she didn't ask me to come up to the stove, or to set down, but just sat there, not even looking at me, so I said, "I want to see John." And then she — laughed. I guess you would call it a laugh. I thought of Harry and the team outside, so I said a little sharp: "Can't I see John?" "No," she says, kind o' dull like. "Ain't he home?" says I. "Yes," says she, "he's home." "Then why can't I see him?" I asked her, out of patience. "'Cause he's dead," says she. *"Dead?"* says I. She just nodded her head, not getting a bit excited, but rockin' back and forth. "Why—where is he?" says I, not knowing what to say. She just pointed upstairs—like that *(himself pointing to the room above)*. I started for the stairs, with the idea of going up there. I walked from there to here—then I says, "Why, what did he die of?" "He died of a rope round his neck," says she, and just went on pleatin' at her apron. Well, I went out and called Harry. I thought I might—need help. We went upstairs and there he was lyin'—

County Attorney: I think I'd rather have you go into that upstairs, where you can point it all out. Just go on now with the rest of the story.

Hale: Well, my first thought was to get that rope off. It looked . . . *(stops; his face twitches)* . . . but Harry, he went up to him, and he said, "No, he's dead all right, and we'd better not touch anything." So we went back downstairs. She was still sitting that same way. "Has anybody been notified?" I asked. "No," says she, unconcerned. "Who did this, Mrs. Wright?" said Harry. He said it businesslike—and she stopped pleatin' of her apron. "I don't know," she says. "You don't *know*?" says Harry. "No," says she. "Weren't you sleepin' in the bed with him?" says Harry. "Yes," says she, "but I was on the inside." "Somebody slipped a rope round his neck and strangled him and you didn't wake up?" says Harry. "I didn't wake up," she said after him. We must 'a' looked as if we didn't see how that could be, for after a minute she said, "I sleep sound." Harry was going to ask her more questions but I said maybe we ought to let her tell her story first to the coroner, or the sheriff, so Harry went fast as he could to Rivers' place, where there's a telephone.

County Attorney: And what did Mrs. Wright do when she knew that you had gone for the coroner?

Hale: She moved from the rocker to that chair over there *(pointing to a small chair in the corner)* and just sat there with her hands held together and looking down. I got a feeling that I ought to make some conversation, so I said I had come in to see if John wanted to put in a telephone, and at that she started to laugh, and then she stopped and looked at me—scared. *(The County Attorney, who has had his notebook out, makes a note.)* I dunno, maybe it wasn't scared. I wouldn't like to say it was. Soon Harry got back, and then Dr. Lloyd came and you, Mr. Peters, and so I guess that's all I know that you don't.

County Attorney (looking around): I guess we'll go upstairs first—and then out to the barn and around there. *(To the Sheriff.)* You're convinced that there was nothing important here—nothing that would point to any motive?

Sheriff: Nothing here but kitchen things. *(The County Attorney, after again looking around the kitchen, opens the door of a cupboard closet. He gets up on a chair and looks on a shelf. Pulls his hand away, sticky.)*

County Attorney: Here's a nice mess. *(The women draw nearer.)*

Mrs. Peters (to the other woman): Oh, her fruit; it did freeze. *(To the Lawyer.)* She worried about that when it turned so cold. She said the fire'd go out and her jars would break.

Sheriff (rises): Well, can you beat the woman! Held for murder and worryin' about her preserves.

County Attorney: I guess before we're through she may have something more serious than preserves to worry about.

Hale: Well, women are used to worrying over trifles. *(The two women move a little closer together.)*

County Attorney (with the gallantry of a young politician): And yet, for all their worries, what would we do without the ladies? *(The women do not unbend. He goes to the sink, takes a dipperful of water from the pail, and pouring it into a basin, washes his hands. Starts to wipe them on the roller towel, turns it for a cleaner place.)* Dirty towels! *(Kicks his foot against the pans under the sink.)* Not much of a housekeeper, would you say, ladies?

Mrs. Hale (stiffly): There's a great deal of work to be done on a farm.

County Attorney: To be sure. And yet *(with a little bow to her)* I know there are some Dickson county farmhouses which do not have such roller towels. *(He gives it a pull to expose its full length again.)*

Mrs. Hale: Those towels get dirty awful quick. Men's hands aren't always as clean as they might be.

County Attorney: Ah, loyal to your sex, I see. But you and Mrs. Wright were neighbors. I suppose you were friends, too.

Mrs. Hale (shaking her head): I've not seen much of her of late years. I've not been in this house — it's more than a year.

County Attorney: And why was that? You didn't like her?

Mrs. Hale: I liked her all well enough. Farmers' wives have their hands full, Mr. Henderson. And then —

County Attorney: Yes — ?

Mrs. Hale (looking about): It never seemed a very cheerful place.

County Attorney: No — it's not cheerful. I shouldn't say she had the homemaking instinct.

Mrs. Hale: Well, I don't know as Wright had, either.

County Attorney: You mean that they didn't get on very well?

Mrs. Hale: No, I don't mean anything. But I don't think a place'd be any cheerfuller for John Wright's being in it.

County Attorney: I'd like to talk more of that a little later. I want to get the lay of things upstairs now. *(He goes to the left where three steps lead to a stair door.)*

Sheriff: I suppose anything Mrs. Peters does'll be all right. She was to take in some clothes for her, you know, and a few little things. We left in such a hurry yesterday.

County Attorney: Yes, but I would like to see what you take, Mrs. Peters, and keep an eye out for anything that might be of use to us.

Mrs. Peters: Yes, Mr. Henderson. *(The women listen to the men's steps on the stairs, then look about the kitchen.)*

Mrs. Hale: I'd hate to have men coming into my kitchen, snooping around and criticizing. *(She arranges the pans under sink which the lawyer had shoved out of place.)*

Mrs. Peters: Of course it's no more than their duty.

Mrs. Hale: Duty's all right, but I guess that deputy sheriff that came out to make the fire might have got a little of this on. *(Gives the roller towel a pull.)* Wish I'd thought of that sooner. Seems mean to talk about her for not having things slicked up when she had to come away in such a hurry.

Mrs. Peters (who has gone to a small table in the left rear corner of the room, and lifted one end of a towel that covers a pan): She had bread set. *(Stands still.)*

Mrs. Hale (eyes fixed on a loaf of bread beside the breadbox, which is on a low shelf at the other side of the room. Moves slowly toward it.): She was going to put this in there. *(Picks up loaf, then abruptly drops it. In a manner of returning to familiar things.)* It's a shame about her fruit. I wonder if it's all gone. *(Gets up on the chair and looks.)* I think there's some here that's all right, Mrs. Peters. Yes — here; *(holding it toward the window)* this is cherries, too. *(Looking again.)* I declare I believe that's the only one. *(Gets down, bottle in her hand. Goes to the sink and wipes it off on the outside.)* She'll feel awful bad after all her hard work in the hot weather. I remember the afternoon I put up my cherries last summer. *(She puts the bottle on the big kitchen table, center of the room. With a sigh, is about to sit down in the rocking-chair. Before she is seated realizes what chair it is; with a slow look at it, steps back. The chair which she has touched rocks back and forth.)*

Mrs. Peters: Well, I must get those things from the front room closet. *(She goes to the door at the right, but after looking into the other room, steps back.)* You coming with me, Mrs. Hale? You could help me carry them. *(They go in the other room; reappear, Mrs. Peters carrying a dress and skirt, Mrs. Hale following with a pair of shoes.)* My, it's cold in there. *(She puts the clothes on the big table, and hurries to the stove.)*

Mrs. Hale (examining the skirt): Wright was close. I think maybe that's why she kept so much to herself. She didn't even belong to the Ladies' Aid. I suppose she felt she couldn't do her part, and then you don't enjoy things when you feel shabby. I heard she used to wear pretty clothes and be lively, when she was Minnie Foster, one of the town girls singing in the choir. But that — oh, that was thirty years ago. This all you want to take in?

Mrs. Peters: She said she wanted an apron. Funny thing to want, for there isn't much to get you dirty in jail, goodness knows. But I suppose just to make her feel more natural. She said they was in the top drawer in this cupboard. Yes, here. And then her little shawl that always hung behind the door. *(Opens stair door and looks.)* Yes, here it is. *(Quickly shuts door leading upstairs.)*

Mrs. Hale (abruptly moving toward her): Mrs. Peters?

Mrs. Peters: Yes, Mrs. Hale?

Mrs. Hale: Do you think she did it?

Mrs. Peters (in a frightened voice): Oh, I don't know.

Mrs. Hale: Well, I don't think she did. Asking for an apron and her little shawl. Worrying about her fruit.

Mrs. Peters (starts to speak, glances up, where footsteps are heard in the room above. In a low voice): Mr. Peters says it looks bad for her. Mr. Henderson is awful sarcastic in a speech and he'll make fun of her sayin' she didn't wake up.

Mrs. Hale: Well, I guess John Wright didn't wake when they was slipping that rope under his neck.

Mrs. Peters: No, it's strange. It must have been done awful crafty and still. They say it was such a — funny way to kill a man, rigging it all up like that.

Mrs. Hale: That's just what Mr. Hale said. There was a gun in the house. He says that's what he can't understand.

Mrs. Peters: Mr. Henderson said coming out that what was needed for the case was a motive; something to show anger, or — sudden feeling.

Mrs. Hale (who is standing by the table): Well, I don't see any signs of anger around here. *(She puts her hand on the dish towel which lies on the table, stands looking down at table, one-half of which is clean, the other half messy.)* It's wiped to here. *(Makes a move as if to finish work, then turns and looks at loaf of bread outside the breadbox. Drops towel. In that voice of coming back to familiar things.)* Wonder how they are finding things upstairs. I hope she had it a little more red-up up there. You know, it seems kind of *sneaking.* Locking her up in town and then coming out here and trying to get her own house to turn against her!

Mrs. Peters: But, Mrs. Hale, the law is the law.

Mrs. Hale: I s'pose 'tis. *(Unbuttoning her coat.)* Better loosen up your things, Mrs. Peters. You won't feel them when you go out. *(Mrs. Peters takes off her fur tippet, goes to hang it on hook at back of room, stands looking at the under part of the small corner table.)*

Mrs. Peters: She was piecing a quilt. *(She brings the large sewing basket and they look at the bright pieces.)*

Mrs. Hale: It's a log cabin pattern. Pretty, isn't it? I wonder if she was goin' to quilt it or just knot it? *(Footsteps have been heard coming down the stairs. The Sheriff enters followed by Hale and the County Attorney.)*

Sheriff: They wonder if she was going to quilt it or just knot it! *(The men laugh, the women look abashed.)*

County Attorney (rubbing his hands over the stove): Frank's fire didn't do much up there, did it? Well, let's go out to the barn and get that cleared up. *(The men go outside.)*

Mrs. Hale (resentfully): I don't know as there's anything so strange, our takin' up our time with little things while we're waiting for them to get the evidence. *(She sits down at the big table smoothing out a block with decision.)* I don't see as it's anything to laugh about.

Mrs. Peters (apologetically): Of course they've got awful important things on their minds. *(Pulls up a chair and joins Mrs. Hale at the table.)*

Mrs. Hale (examining another block): Mrs. Peters, look at this one. Here, this is the one she was working on, and look at the sewing! All the rest of it has been so nice and even. And look at this! It's all over the place! Why, it looks as if she didn't know what she was about! *(After she has said this they look at each other, then start to glance back at the door. After an instant Mrs. Hale has pulled at a knot and ripped the sewing.)*

Mrs. Peters: Oh, what are you doing, Mrs. Hale?

Mrs. Hale (mildly): Just pulling out a stitch or two that's not sewed very good. *(Threading a needle.)* Bad sewing always made me fidgety.

Mrs. Peters (nervously): I don't think we ought to touch things.

Mrs. Hale: I'll just finish up this end. *(Suddenly stopping and leaning forward.)* Mrs. Peters?

Mrs. Peters: Yes, Mrs. Hale?

Mrs. Hale: What do you suppose she was so nervous about?

Mrs. Peters: Oh—I don't know. I don't know as she was nervous. I sometimes sew awful queer when I'm just tired. *(Mrs. Hale starts to say something, looks at Mrs. Peters, then goes on sewing.)* Well, I must get these things wrapped up. They may be through sooner than we think. *(Putting apron and other things together.)* I wonder where I can find a piece of paper, and string. *(Rises.)*

Mrs. Hale: In that cupboard, maybe.

Mrs. Peters (looking in cupboard): Why, here's a bird-cage. *(Holds it up.)* Did she have a bird, Mrs. Hale?

Mrs. Hale: Why, I don't know whether she did or not—I've not been here for so long. There was a man around last year selling canaries cheap, but I don't know as she took one; maybe she did. She used to sing real pretty herself.

Mrs. Peters (glancing around): Seems funny to think of a bird here. But she must have had one, or why would she have a cage? I wonder what happened to it?

Mrs. Hale: I s'pose maybe the cat got it.

Mrs. Peters: No, she didn't have a cat. She's got that feeling some people have about cats—being afraid of them. My cat got in her room and she was real upset and asked me to take it out.

Mrs. Hale: My sister Bessie was like that. Queer, ain't it?

Mrs. Peters (examining the cage): Why, look at this door. It's broke. One hinge is pulled apart.

Mrs. Hale (looking too): Looks as if someone must have been rough with it.

Mrs. Peters: Why, yes. *(She brings the cage forward and puts it on the table.)*

Mrs. Hale: I wish if they're going to find any evidence they'd be about it. I don't like this place.

Mrs. Peters: But I'm awful glad you came with me, Mrs. Hale. It would be lonesome for me sitting here alone.

Mrs. Hale: It would, wouldn't it? *(Dropping her sewing.)* But I tell you what I do wish, Mrs. Peters. I wish I had come over sometimes when *she* was here. I— *(looking around the room)*—wish I had.

Mrs. Peters: But of course you were awful busy, Mrs. Hale—your house and your children.

Mrs. Hale: I could've come. I stayed away because it weren't cheerful—and that's why I ought to have come. I—I've never liked this place. Maybe because it's down in a hollow and you don't see the road. I dunno what it is, but it's a lonesome place and always was. I wish I had come over to see Minnie Foster sometimes. I can see now—*(Shakes her head.)*

Mrs. Peters: Well, you mustn't reproach yourself, Mrs. Hale. Somehow we just don't see how it is with other folks until—something turns up.

Mrs. Hale: Not having children makes less work—but it makes a quiet house, and Wright out to work all day, and no company when he did come in. Did you know John Wright, Mrs. Peters?

Mrs. Peters: Not to know him; I've seen him in town. They say he was a good man.

Mrs. Hale: Yes—good; he didn't drink, and kept his word as well as most, I guess, and paid his debts. But he was a hard man, Mrs. Peters. Just to pass the time of day with him—*(Shivers.)* Like a raw wind that gets to the bone. *(Pauses, her eye falling on the cage.)* I should think she would 'a' wanted a bird. But what do you suppose went with it?

Mrs. Peters: I don't know, unless it got sick and died. *(She reaches over and swings the broken door, swings it again, both women watch it.)*

Mrs. Hale: You weren't raised round here, were you? *(Mrs. Peters shakes her head.)* You didn't know—her?

Mrs. Peters: Not till they brought her yesterday.

Mrs. Hale: She—come to think of it, she was kind of like a bird herself—real sweet and pretty, but kind of timid and—fluttery. How—she—did—change. *(Silence: then as if struck by a happy thought and relieved to get back to everyday things.)* Tell you what, Mrs. Peters, why don't you take the quilt in with you? It might take up her mind.

Mrs. Peters: Why, I think that's a real nice idea, Mrs. Hale. There couldn't possibly be any objection to it could there? Now, just what would I take? I wonder if her patches are in here — and her things. *(They look in the sewing basket.)*

Mrs. Hale: Here's some red. I expect this has got sewing things in it. *(Brings out a fancy box.)* What a pretty box. Looks like something somebody would give you. Maybe her scissors are in here. *(Opens box. Suddenly puts her hand to her nose.)* Why — *(Mrs. Peters bends nearer, then turns her face away.)* There's something wrapped up in this piece of silk.

Mrs. Peters: Why, this isn't her scissors.

Mrs. Hale *(lifting the silk):* Oh, Mrs. Peters — it's — *(Mrs. Peters bends closer.)*

Mrs. Peters: It's the bird.

Mrs. Hale *(jumping up):* But, Mrs. Peters — look at it! Its neck! Look at its neck! It's all — other side *to.*

Mrs. Peters: Somebody — wrung — its — neck. *(Their eyes meet. A look of growing comprehension, of horror. Steps are heard outside. Mrs. Hale slips box under quilt pieces, and sinks into her chair. Enter Sheriff and County Attorney. Mrs. Peters rises.)*

County Attorney *(as one turning from serious things to little pleasantries):* Well, ladies, have you decided whether she was going to quilt it or knot it?

Mrs. Peters: We think she was going to — knot it.

County Attorney: Well, that's interesting, I'm sure. *(Seeing the bird-cage.)* Has the bird flown?

Mrs. Hale *(putting more quilt pieces over the box):* We think the — cat got it.

County Attorney *(preoccupied):* Is there a cat? *(Mrs. Hale glances in a quick covert way at Mrs. Peters.)*

Mrs. Peters: Well, not *now.* They're superstitious, you know. They leave.

County Attorney *(to Sheriff Peters, continuing an interrupted conversation):* No sign at all of anyone having come from the outside. Their own rope. Now let's go up again and go over it piece by piece. *(They start upstairs.)* It would have to have been someone who knew just the — *(Mrs. Peters sits down. The two women sit there not looking at one another, but as if peering into something and at the same time holding back. When they talk now it is in the manner of feeling their way over strange ground, as if afraid of what they are saying, but as if they cannot help saying it.)*

Mrs. Hale: She liked the bird. She was going to bury it in that pretty box.

Mrs. Peters *(in a whisper):* When I was a girl — my kitten — there was a boy took a hatchet, and before my eyes — and before I could get there — *(Covers her face an instant.)* If they hadn't held me back I would have — *(catches herself, looks upstairs where steps are heard, falters weakly)* — hurt him.

Mrs. Hale *(with a slow look around her):* I wonder how it would seem never to have had any children around. *(Pause.)* No, Wright wouldn't like the bird — a thing that sang. She used to sing. He killed that, too.

Mrs. Peters *(moving uneasily):* We don't know who killed the bird.

Mrs. Hale: I knew John Wright.

Mrs. Peters: It was an awful thing was done in this house that night, Mrs. Hale. Killing a man while he slept, slipping a rope around his neck that choked the life out of him.

Mrs. Hale: His neck. Choked the life out of him. *(Her hand goes out and rests on the bird-cage.)*

Mrs. Peters (with rising voice): We don't know who killed him. We don't *know.*

Mrs. Hale (her own feeling not interrupted): If there'd been years and years of nothing, then a bird to sing to you, it would be awful — still, after the bird was still.

Mrs. Peters (something within her speaking): I know what stillness is. When we homesteaded in Dakota, and my first baby died — after he was two years old, and me with no other then —

Mrs. Hale (moving): How soon do you suppose they'll be through looking for the evidence?

Mrs. Peters: I know what stillness is. *(Pulling herself back.)* The law has got to punish crime, Mrs. Hale.

Mrs. Hale (not as if answering that): I wish you'd seen Minnie Foster when she wore a white dress with blue ribbons and stood up there in the choir and sang. *(A look around the room.)* Oh, I *wish* I'd come over here once in a while! That was a crime! That was a crime! Who's going to punish that?

Mrs. Peters (looking upstairs): We mustn't — take on.

Mrs. Hale: I might have known she needed help! I know how things can be — for women. I tell you, it's queer, Mrs. Peters. We live close together and we live far apart. We all go through the same things — it's all just a different kind of the same thing. *(Brushes her eyes, noticing the bottle of fruit, reaches out for it.)* If I was you I wouldn't tell her her fruit was gone. Tell her it *ain't.* Tell her it's all right. Take this in to prove it to her. She — she may never know whether it was broke or not.

Mrs. Peters (takes the bottle, looks about for something to wrap it in; takes petticoat from the clothes brought from the other room, very nervously begins winding this around the bottle. In a false voice): My, it's a good thing the men couldn't hear us. Wouldn't they just laugh! Getting all stirred up over a little thing like a — dead canary. As if that could have anything to do with — with — wouldn't they *laugh! (The men are heard coming down stairs.)*

Mrs. Hale (under her breath): Maybe they would — maybe they wouldn't.

County Attorney: No, Peters, it's all perfectly clear except a reason for doing it. But you know juries when it comes to women. If there was some definite thing. Something to show — something to make a story about — a thing that would connect up with this strange way of doing it — *(The women's eyes meet for an instant. Enter Hale from outer door.)*

Hale: Well, I've got the team around. Pretty cold out there.

County Attorney: I'm going to stay here a while by myself. *(To the Sheriff.)* You can send Frank out for me, can't you? I want to go over everything. I'm not satisfied that we can't do better.

Sheriff: Do you want to see what Mrs. Peters is going to take in? *(The Lawyer goes to the table, picks up the apron, laughs.)*

County Attorney: Oh, I guess they're not very dangerous things the ladies have picked out. *(Moves a few things about, disturbing the quilt pieces which cover the box. Steps back.)* No, Mrs. Peters doesn't need supervising. For that matter a sheriff's wife is married to the law. Ever think of it that way, Mrs. Peters?

Mrs. Peters: Not — just that way.

Sheriff (chuckling): Married to the law. *(Moves toward the other room.)* I just want you
     to come in here a minute, George. We ought to take a look at these windows.
County Attorney (scoffingly): Oh, windows!
Sheriff: We'll be right out, Mr. Hale. *(Hale goes outside. The Sheriff follows the
     County Attorney into the other room. Then Mrs. Hale rises, hands tight together,
     looking intensely at Mrs. Peters, whose eyes make a slow turn, finally meeting Mrs.
     Hale's. A moment Mrs. Hale holds her, then her own eyes point the way to where the
     box is concealed. Suddenly Mrs. Peters throws back quilt pieces and tries to put the
     box in the bag she is wearing. It is too big. She opens box, starts to take bird out, can-
     not touch it, goes to pieces, stands there helpless. Sound of a knob turning in the other
     room. Mrs. Hale snatches the box and puts it in the pocket of her big coat. Enter
     County Attorney and Sheriff.)*
County Attorney (facetiously): Well, Henry, at least we found out that she was
     not going to quilt it. She was going to — what is it you call it, ladies?
Mrs. Hale (her hand against her pocket): We call it — knot it, Mr. Henderson.

     Curtain

Considerations for Critical Thinking and Writing

1. **FIRST RESPONSE.** Describe the setting of this play. What kind of atmo-
    sphere is established by the details in the opening scene? Does the atmo-
    sphere change through the course of the play?

2. Where are Mrs. Hale and Mrs. Peters while Mr. Hale explains to the county
    attorney how the murder was discovered? How does their location suggest
    the relationship between the men and the women in the play?

3. What kind of person was Minnie Foster before she married? How do you
    think her marriage affected her?

4. Characterize John Wright. Why did his wife kill him?

5. Why do the men fail to see the clues that Mrs. Hale and Mrs. Peters dis-
    cover?

6. What is the significance of the birdcage and the dead bird? Why do Mrs.
    Hale and Mrs. Peters respond so strongly to them? How do you respond?

7. Why don't Mrs. Hale and Mrs. Peters reveal the evidence they have uncov-
    ered? What would you have done?

8. How do the men's conversations and actions reveal their attitudes toward
    women?

9. Why do you think Glaspell allows us only to hear about Mr. and Mrs.
    Wright? What is the effect of their never appearing on stage?

10. Does your impression of Mrs. Wright change during the course of the
    play? If so, what changes it?

11. What is the significance of the play's last line, spoken by Mrs. Hale: "We
    call it — knot it, Mr. Henderson"? Explain what you think the tone of Mrs.
    Hale's voice is when she says this line. What is she feeling? What are you
    feeling?

12. Explain the significance of the play's title. Do you think *Trifles* or "A Jury of
    Her Peers," Glaspell's title for the short story version of the play, is more
    appropriate? Can you think of other titles that capture the play's central
    concerns?

13. If possible, find a copy of "A Jury of Her Peers" in the library (reprinted in *The Best Short Stories of 1917*, ed. E. J. O'Brien [Boston: Small, Maynard, 1918], pp. 256–82), and write an essay that explores the differences between the play and the short story. (An alternative is to work with the excerpt on p. 1378.)

14. **CRITICAL STRATEGIES.** Read the section on formalist criticism (pp. 2046–48) in Chapter 53, "Critical Strategies for Reading." Several times the characters say things that they don't mean, and this creates a discrepancy between what appears to be and what is actually true. Point to instances of irony in the play and explain how they contribute to its effects and meanings. (For discussions of irony elsewhere in this book, see the Index of Terms.)

CONNECTIONS TO OTHER SELECTIONS

1. Compare and contrast how Glaspell provides background information in *Trifles* with how Sophocles does so in *Oedipus the King* (p. 1422).

2. Write an essay comparing the views of marriage in *Trifles* and in Kate Chopin's short story "The Story of an Hour" (p. 15). What similarities do you find in the themes of these two works? Are there any significant differences between the works?

3. In an essay compare Mrs. Wright's motivation for committing murder with that of Matt Fowler, the central character from Andre Dubus's short story "Killings" (p. 103). To what extent do you think they are responsible for and guilty of these crimes?

A SAMPLE CLOSE READING

An Annotated Section of Trifles

As you read a play for the first time, highlight lines, circle or underline words, and record your responses in the margins. These responses will allow you to retrieve initial reactions and questions that in subsequent readings you can pursue and resolve. Just as the play is likely to have layered meanings, so too will your own readings as you gradually piece together a variety of elements such as exposition, plot, and character that will lead you toward their thematic significance. The following annotations for an excerpt from *Trifles* offer an interpretation that was produced by several readings of the play. Of course, your annotations could be quite different, depending upon your own approach to the play.

The following excerpt appears about two pages into this nine-page play and is preceded by a significant amount of exposition that establishes the bleak midwestern farm setting and some details about Mrs. Wright, who is the prime suspect in the murder of her husband. Prior to this dialogue, only the male characters speak as they try to discover a motive for the crime.

County Attorney *(looking around):* I guess we'll go upstairs first—and then out to the barn and around there. *(To the Sheriff.)* You're convinced that there was nothing important here—nothing that would point to any motive?

Sheriff: Nothing here but kitchen things. *(The County Attorney, after again looking around the kitchen, opens the door of a cupboard closet. He gets up on a chair and looks on a shelf. Pulls his hand away, sticky.)*

County Attorney: Here's a nice mess. *(The women draw nearer.)*

Mrs. Peters *(to the other woman):* Oh, her fruit; it did freeze. *(To the Lawyer.)* She worried about that when it turned so cold. She said the fire'd go out and her jars would break.

Sheriff *(rises):* Well, can you beat the woman! Held for murder and worryin' about her preserves.

County Attorney: I guess before we're through she may have something more serious than preserves to worry about.

Hale: Well, women are used to worrying over trifles. *(The two women move a little closer together.)*

County Attorney *(with the gallantry of a young politician):* And yet, for all their worries, what would we do without the ladies? *(The women do not unbend. He goes to the sink, takes a dipperful of water from the pail, and pouring it into a basin, washes his hands. Starts to wipe them on the roller towel, turns it for a cleaner place.)* Dirty towels! *(Kicks his foot against the pans under the sink.)* Not much of a housekeeper, would you say, ladies?

Mrs. Hale *(stiffly):* There's a great deal of work to be done on a farm.

County Attorney: To be sure. And yet *(with a little bow to her)* I know there are some Dickson county farmhouses which do not have such roller towels. *(He gives it a pull to expose its full length again.)*

Mrs. Hale: Those towels get dirty awful quick. Men's hands aren't always as clean as they might be.

County Attorney: Ah, loyal to your sex, I see. But you and Mrs. Wright were neighbors. I suppose you were friends, too.

Mrs. Hale *(shaking her head):* I've not seen much of her of late years. I've not been in this house—it's more than a year.

County Attorney: And why was that? You didn't like her?

Mrs. Hale: I liked her all well enough. Farmers' wives have their hands full, Mr. Henderson. And then—

County Attorney: Yes—?

Mrs. Hale *(looking about):* It never seemed a very cheerful place.

The Sheriff unknowingly announces a major conflict in the play that echoes the title: from a male point of view, there is nothing of any importance to be found in the kitchen—or in women's domestic lives. Mr. Hale confirms this by pronouncing such matters "trifles."

The County Attorney weighs in with his assessment of this "sticky" situation by calling it a "mess" from which he pulls away.

As the Attorney pulls away, the women move closer together (sides are slowly being drawn), and Mrs. Peters says more than she realizes when she observes, "Oh, her fruit; it did freeze." This anticipates our understanding of the cold, fruitless life that drove Mrs. Wright to murder.

The Sheriff's exasperation about women worrying about "preserves" will ironically help preserve the secret of Mrs. Wright—a woman who was beaten down by her husband but who cannot be beaten by these male authorities.

The Attorney has an eye for dirty towels but not for the real "dirt" embedded in the Wrights' domestic life.

The female characters are identified as "Mrs.," which emphasizes their roles as wives, while the men are autonomous and identified by their professions.

Mrs. Hale's comment begins a process of mitigating Mrs. Wright's murder of her husband. He—husbands, men—must share some of the guilt, too.

In contrast to men (a nice irony), farmers' wives' hands are full of responsibilities for which they receive little credit owing to the males' assumption that they fill their lives with trifles.

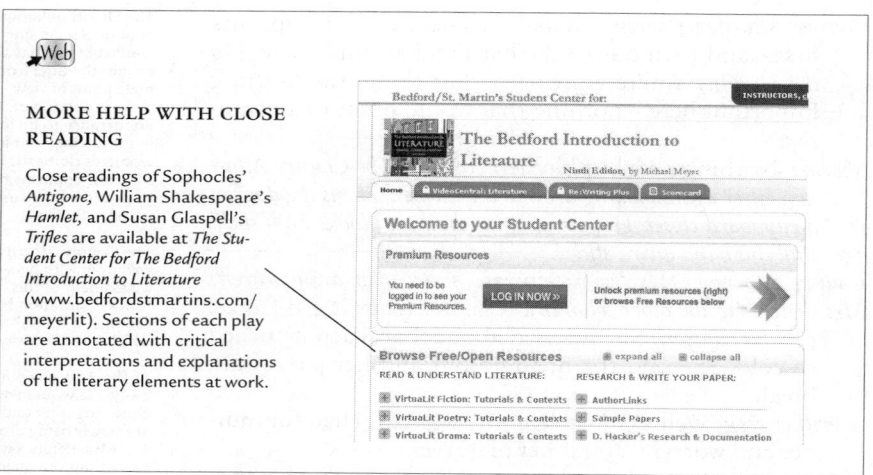

MORE HELP WITH CLOSE READING

Close readings of Sophocles' *Antigone*, William Shakespeare's *Hamlet*, and Susan Glaspell's *Trifles* are available at *The Student Center for The Bedford Introduction to Literature* (www.bedfordstmartins.com/meyerlit). Sections of each play are annotated with critical interpretations and explanations of the literary elements at work.

Perspective

Susan Glaspell (1882–1948)

From the Short Story Version of Trifles   1917

When Martha Hale opened the storm-door and got a cut of the north wind, she ran back for her big woolen scarf. As she hurriedly wound that round her head her eye made a scandalized sweep of her kitchen. It was no ordinary thing that called her away—it was probably farther from ordinary than anything that had ever happened in Dickson County. But what her eye took in was that her kitchen was in no shape for leaving: her bread all ready for mixing, half the flour sifted and half unsifted.

She hated to see things half done; but she had been at that when the team from town stopped to get Mr. Hale, and then the sheriff came running in to say his wife wished Mrs. Hale would come too—adding, with a grin, that he guessed she was getting scarey and wanted another woman along. So she had dropped everything right where it was.

"Martha!" now came her husband's impatient voice. "Don't keep folks waiting out here in the cold."

She again opened the storm-door, and this time joined the three men and the one woman waiting for her in the big two-seated buggy.

After she had the robes tucked around her she took another look at the woman who sat beside her on the back seat. She had met Mrs. Peters the year before at the county fair, and the thing she remembered about her was that she didn't seem like a sheriff's wife. She was small and thin and didn't have a strong voice. Mrs. Gorman, sheriff's wife before Gorman went out and Peters came in, had a voice that somehow seemed to be backing up the law with every word. But if Mrs. Peters didn't look like a sheriff's wife, Peters made it up in looking like a sheriff. He was to a dot the kind of man who could get himself elected sheriff—a heavy man with a big voice, who was particularly genial with the law-abiding, as if to make it plain that he knew the difference between criminals and noncriminals. And right there it came into Mrs. Hale's mind, with a stab, that this man who was so pleasant and lively with all of them was going to the Wrights' now as a sheriff.

"The country's not very pleasant this time of year," Mrs. Peters at last ventured, as if she felt they ought to be talking as well as the men.

Mrs. Hale scarcely finished her reply, for they had gone up a little hill and could see the Wright place now, and seeing it did not make her feel like talking. It looked very lonesome this cold March morning. It had always been a lonesome-looking place. It was down in a hollow, and the poplar trees around it were lonesome-looking trees. The men were looking at it and talking about what had happened. The county attorney was bending to one side of the buggy, and kept looking steadily at the place as they drew up to it.

"I'm glad you came with me," Mrs. Peters said nervously, as the two women were about to follow the men in through the kitchen door.

Even after she had her foot on the door-step, her hand on the knob, Martha Hale had a moment of feeling she could not cross that threshold. And the reason it seemed she couldn't cross it now was simply because she hadn't crossed it before. Time and time again it had been in her mind, "I ought to go over and see Minnie Foster"—she still thought of her as Minnie Foster, though for twenty years she had been Mrs. Wright. And then there was always something to do and Minnie Foster would go from her mind. But *now* she could come.

The men went over to the stove. The women stood close together by the door. Young Henderson, the county attorney, turned around and said, "Come up to the fire, ladies."

Mrs. Peters took a step forward, then stopped. "I'm not—cold," she said.

And so the two women stood by the door, at first not even so much as looking around the kitchen.

The men talked for a minute about what a good thing it was the sheriff had sent his deputy out that morning to make a fire for them, and then Sheriff Peters stepped back from the stove, unbuttoned his outer coat, and leaned his hands on the kitchen table in a way that seemed to mark the beginning of official business. "Now, Mr. Hale," he said in a sort of semiofficial voice, "before we move things about, you tell Mr. Henderson just what it was you saw when you came here yesterday morning."

The county attorney was looking around the kitchen.

"By the way," he said, "has anything been moved?" He turned to the sheriff. "Are things just as you left them yesterday?"

Peters looked from cupboard to sink; from that to a small worn rocker a little to one side of the kitchen table.

"It's just the same."

"Somebody should have been left here yesterday," said the county attorney.

"Oh—yesterday," returned the sheriff, with a little gesture as of yesterday having been more than he could bear to think of. "When I had to send Frank to Morris Center for that man who went crazy—let me tell you, I had my hands full *yesterday*. I knew you could get back from Omaha by to-day, George, and as long as I went over everything here myself—"

"Well, Mr. Hale," said the county attorney, in a way of letting what was past and gone go, "tell just what happened when you came here yesterday morning."

Mrs. Hale, still leaning against the door, had that sinking feeling of the mother whose child is about to speak a piece. Lewis often wandered along and got things mixed up in a story. She hoped he would tell this straight and plain, and not say unnecessary things that would just make things harder for Minnie Foster. He didn't begin at once, and she noticed that he looked queer — as if standing in that kitchen and having to tell what he had seen there yesterday morning made him almost sick.

"Yes, Mr. Hale?" the county attorney reminded.

"Harry and I had started to town with a load of potatoes," Mrs. Hale's husband began.

Harry was Mrs. Hale's oldest boy. He wasn't with them now, for the very good reason that those potatoes never got to town yesterday and he was taking them this morning, so he hadn't been home when the sheriff stopped to say he wanted Mr. Hale to come over to the Wright place and tell the county attorney his story there, where he could point it all out. With all Mrs. Hale's other emotions came the fear that maybe Harry wasn't dressed warm enough — they hadn't any of them realized how that north wind did bite.

"We come along this road," Hale was going on, with a motion of his hand to the road over which they had just come, "and as we got in sight of the house I says to Harry, 'I'm goin' to see if I can't get John Wright to take a telephone.' You see," he explained to Henderson, "unless I can get somebody to go in with me they won't come out this branch road except for a price *I* can't pay. I'd spoke to Wright about it once before; but he put me off, saying folks talked too much anyway, and all he asked was peace and quiet — guess you know about how much he talked himself. But I thought maybe if I went to the house and talked about it before his wife, and said all the women-folks liked the telephones, and that in this lonesome stretch of road it would be a good thing — well, I said to Harry that that was what I was going to say — though I said at the same time that I didn't know as what his wife wanted made much difference to John —"

Now, there he was! — saying things he didn't need to say. Mrs. Hale tried to catch her husband's eye, but fortunately the county attorney interrupted with:

"Let's talk about that a little later, Mr. Hale. I do want to talk about that, but I'm anxious now to get along to just what happened when you got here."

From "A Jury of Her Peers"

CONSIDERATIONS FOR CRITICAL THINKING AND WRITING

1. In this opening scene from the story, how is the setting established differently from the way it is in the play (p. 1366)?

2. What kind of information is provided in the opening paragraphs of the story that is missing from the play's initial scene? What is emphasized early in the story but not in the play?

3. Which version brings us into more intimate contact with the characters? How is that achieved?

4. Does the short story's title, "A Jury of Her Peers," suggest any shift in emphasis from the play's title, *Trifles*?

5. Explain why you prefer one version over the other.

ELEMENTS OF DRAMA

Trifles is a **one-act play;** in other words, the entire play takes place in a single location and unfolds as one continuous action. As in a short story, the characters in a one-act play are presented economically, and the action is sharply focused. In contrast, full-length plays can include many characters as well as different settings in place and time. The main divisions of a full-length play are typically **acts;** their ends are indicated by lowering a curtain or turning up the houselights. Playwrights frequently employ acts to accommodate changes in time, setting, characters on stage, or mood. In many full-length plays, such as Shakespeare's *Hamlet,* acts are further divided into **scenes;** according to tradition a scene changes when the location of the action changes or when a new character enters. Acts and scenes are **conventions** that are understood and accepted by audiences because they have come, through usage and time, to be recognized as familiar techniques. The major convention of a one-act play is that it typically consists of only a single scene; nevertheless, one-act plays contain many of the elements of drama that characterize their full-length counterparts.

[Web] Explore the literary elements in this chapter at bedfordstmartins.com/meyerlit.

One-act plays create their effects through compression. They especially lend themselves to modestly budgeted productions with limited stage facilities, such as those put on by little theater groups. However, the potential of a one-act play to move audiences and readers is not related to its length. As *Trifles* shows, one-acts represent a powerful form of dramatic literature.

The single location that composes the **setting** for *Trifles* is described at the very beginning of the play; it establishes an atmosphere that will later influence our judgment of Mrs. Wright. The "gloomy" kitchen is disordered, bare, and sparsely equipped with a stove, sink, rocker, cupboard, two tables, some chairs, three doors, and a window. These details are just enough to allow us to imagine the stark, uninviting place where Mrs. Wright spent most of her time. Moreover, "signs of incompleted work," coupled with the presence of the sheriff and county attorney, create an immediate tension by suggesting that something is terribly wrong. Before a single word is spoken, **suspense** is created as the characters enter. This suspenseful situation causes an anxious uncertainty about what will happen next.

The setting is further developed through the use of **exposition,** a device that provides the necessary background information about the characters and their circumstances. For example, we immediately learn through **dialogue** — the verbal exchanges between characters — that Mr. Henderson, the county attorney, is just back from Omaha. This establishes the setting as somewhere in the Midwest, where winters can be brutally cold and barren. We also find out that John Wright has been murdered and that his wife has been arrested for the crime.

Even more important, Glaspell deftly characterizes the Wrights through exposition alone. Mr. Hale's conversation with Mr. Henderson explains how Mr. Wright's body was discovered, but it also reveals that Wright was a noncommunicative man, who refused to share a "party telephone" and who did not consider "what his wife wanted." Later Mrs. Hale adds to this characterization when she tells Mrs. Peters that though Mr. Wright was an honest, good man who paid his bills and did not drink, he was a "hard man" and "Like a raw wind that gets to the bone." Mr. Hale's description of Mrs. Wright sitting in the kitchen dazed and disoriented gives us a picture of a shattered, exhausted woman. But it is Mrs. Hale who again offers further insights when she describes how Minnie Foster, a sweet, pretty, timid young woman who sang in the choir, was changed by her marriage to Mr. Wright and by her childless, isolated life on the farm.

This information about Mr. and Mrs. Wright is worked into the dialogue throughout the play in order to suggest the nature of the ***conflict*** or struggle between them, a motive, and, ultimately, a justification for the murder. In the hands of a skillful playwright, exposition is not merely a mechanical device; it can provide important information while simultaneously developing characterizations and moving the action forward.

The action is shaped by the ***plot,*** the author's arrangement of incidents in the play that gives the story a particular focus and emphasis. Plot involves more than simply what happens; it involves how and why things happen. Glaspell begins with a discussion of the murder. Why? She could have begun with the murder itself: the distraught Mrs. Wright looping the rope around her husband's neck. The moment would be dramatic and horribly vivid. We neither see the body nor hear very much about it. When Mr. Hale describes finding Mr. Wright's body, Glaspell has the county attorney cut him off by saying, "I think I'd rather have you go into that upstairs, where you can point it all out. Just go on now with the rest of the story." It is precisely the "rest of the story" that interests Glaspell. Her arrangement of incidents prevents us from sympathizing with Mr. Wright. We are, finally, invited to see Mrs. Wright instead of her husband as the victim.

Mr. Henderson's efforts to discover a motive for the murder appear initially to be the play's focus, but the real conflicts are explored in what seems to be a ***subplot,*** a secondary action that reinforces or contrasts with the main plot. The discussions between Mrs. Hale and Mrs. Peters and the tensions between the men and the women turn out to be the main plot because they address the issues that Glaspell chooses to explore. Those issues are not about murder but about marriage and how men and women relate to each other.

The ***protagonist*** of *Trifles,* the central character with whom we tend to identify, is Mrs. Hale. The ***antagonist,*** the character who is in some kind of opposition to the central character, is the county attorney, Mr. Henderson. These two characters embody the major conflicts presented in the play because each speaks for a different set of characters who represent disparate values. Mrs. Hale and Mr. Henderson are developed less individually than as representative types.

Mrs. Hale articulates a sensitivity to Mrs. Wright's miserable life as well as an awareness of how women are repressed in general by men; she also helps Mrs. Peters to arrive at a similar understanding. When Mrs. Hale defends Mrs. Wright's soiled towels from Mr. Henderson's criticism, Glaspell has her say more than the county attorney is capable of hearing. The *stage directions,* the playwright's instructions about how the actors are to move and behave, indicate that Mrs. Hale responds "stiffly" to Mr. Henderson's disparagements: "Men's hands aren't always as clean as they might be." Mrs. Hale eventually comes to see that the men are, in a sense, complicit because it was insensitivity like theirs that drove Mrs. Wright to murder.

Mr. Henderson, on the other hand, represents the law in a patriarchal, conventional society that blithely places a minimal value on the concerns of women. In his attempt to gather evidence against Mrs. Wright, he implicitly defends men's severe dominance over women. He also patronizes Mrs. Hale and Mrs. Peters. Like Sheriff Peters and Mr. Hale, he regards the women's world as nothing more than "kitchen things" and "trifles." Glaspell, however, patterns the plot so that the women see more about Mrs. Wright's motives than the men do and shows that the women have a deeper understanding of justice.

Many plays are plotted in what has come to be called a *pyramidal pattern,* because the plot is divided into three essential parts. Such plays begin with a *rising action,* in which complication creates conflict for the protagonist. The resulting tension builds to the second major division, known as the *climax,* when the action reaches a final *crisis,* a turning point that has a powerful effect on the protagonist. The third part consists of *falling action;* here the tensions are diminished in the *resolution* of the plot's conflicts and complications (the resolution is also referred to as the *conclusion* or *dénouement,* a French word meaning "unknotting"). These divisions may occur at different times. There are many variations to this pattern. The terms are helpful for identifying various moments and movements within a given plot, but they are less useful if seen as a means of reducing dramatic art to a formula.

Because *Trifles* is a one-act play, this pyramidal pattern is less elaborately worked out than it might be in a full-length play, but the basic elements of the pattern can still be discerned. The complication consists mostly of Mrs. Hale's refusal to assign moral or legal guilt to Mrs. Wright's murder of her husband. Mrs. Hale is able to discover the motive in the domestic details that are beneath the men's consideration. The men fail to see the significance of the fruit jars, messy kitchen, and badly sewn quilt.

At first Mrs. Peters seems to voice the attitudes associated with the men. Unlike Mrs. Hale, who is "more comfortable looking," Mrs. Peters is "a slight wiry woman" with "a thin nervous face" who sounds like her husband, the sheriff, when she insists, "the law is the law." She also defends the men's patronizing attitudes, because "they've got awful important things on their minds." But Mrs. Peters is a *foil* — a character whose behavior and values contrast with the protagonist's—only up to a point. When the most telling clue is discovered, Mrs. Peters suddenly understands, along with Mrs. Hale, the motive for the killing. Mrs. Wright's caged life was no longer tolerable to her after her husband had killed the bird (which was the one bright spot in her life and which represents her early life as the young Minnie Foster). This revelation brings about the climax, when the two women must decide whether to tell the men what they have discovered. Both women empathize with Mrs. Wright as they confront this crisis, and their sense of common experience leads them to withhold the evidence.

This resolution ends the play's immediate conflicts and complications. Presumably, without a motive the county attorney will have difficulty prosecuting Mrs. Wright—at least to the fullest extent of the law. However, the larger issues related to the ***theme,*** the central idea or meaning of the play, are left unresolved. The men have both missed the clues and failed to perceive the suffering that acquits Mrs. Wright in the minds of the two women. The play ends with Mrs. Hale's ironic answer to Mr. Henderson's question about quilting. When she says "knot it," she gives him part of the evidence he needs to connect Mrs. Wright's quilting with the knot used to strangle her husband. Mrs. Hale knows—and we know—that Mr. Henderson will miss the clue she offers because he is blinded by his own self-importance and assumptions.

Though brief, *Trifles* is a masterful representation of dramatic elements working together to keep both audiences and readers absorbed in its characters and situations.

Naked Lunch

Born in Lancaster, Pennsylvania, Michael Hollinger earned a B.A. in music at Oberlin Conservatory and a master of arts degree in theater from Villanova University, where he now teaches theater. His comedies and dramas have been widely produced in the United States and abroad. Among his plays are *An Empty Plate in the Café Du Grand Boeuf* (1994), *Red Herring* (1996), *Hot Air* (1997), *Tiny Island* (1998), *Eureka* (1999), and *Opus* (2006). He has also written three short films and co-authored *Philadelphia Diary* with Bruce Graham and Sonia Sanchez for PBS. His writing awards include the Roger L. Stevens Award from the Kennedy Center's Fund for Outstanding New American Plays, the Barrymore Award for Outstanding New Play, and the Otto Haas Award for Emerging Theatre Artist. Hollinger's extensive music background strongly influences

Courtesy of the Arden Theatre Company.

his work as a playwright. He has said about his own work, "Plays are music to me; characters are instruments, scenes are movements; tempo, rhythm and dynamics are critical; and melody and counterpoint are always set in relief by rests—beats, pauses, the spaces between." *Naked Lunch* (2003) is one of a group of sixteen plays written by various playwrights for *Trepidation Nation: A Phobic Anthology,* which was produced at the 2002–2003 Humana Festival by the Actor Theatre of Louisville.

MICHAEL HOLLINGER   (B. 1962)

Naked Lunch   2003

Lights up on Vernon and Lucy sitting at a small dining-room table, eating. There's a small vase with too many flowers in it, or a large vase with too few. A bottle of wine has been opened. Vernon regales Lucy as he vigorously devours a steak. Lucy discreetly nibbles on her corn-on-the-cob.

Vernon: Larry thinks the whole show's a fake. He says the guy's just an actor and all the crocs are trained. I said, you can't train a crocodile! It's not like some poodle you can teach to ride a bike. It's got this reptile brain, a million years old. All it knows, or wants to know, is whether or not you're juicy. Anyway, this one show the guy's sneaking up on a mother protecting her nest. And she's huge—I mean, this thing could swallow a Buick. And the guy's really playing it up: *(Australian accent.)* "Amazing—look at the size of those teeth!" But just—

(He stops, looking at Lucy. Pause. She looks up from her corn.)

Lucy: What.
Vernon: What's the matter?
Lucy: I'm listening.
Vernon: You're not eating your steak.
Lucy: Oh. No.
Vernon: How come?
Lucy: I'll just eat the corn.

(She returns to nibbling.)

Vernon: What's wrong with the steak?
Lucy: Nothing.
Vernon: Then eat it. It's good.
Lucy: I'd . . . rather not.
Vernon: Why not?

(Pause.)

Lucy: I'm vegetarian.

(Beat.)

Vernon: What?
Lucy: I don't eat meat anymore.
Vernon: Since when?

Lucy: Since we, you know. Broke up.

> (*Pause.*)

Vernon: Just like that?

Lucy: Well —

Vernon: You break up with me and boom next day you start eating tofu?

Lucy: I'd been thinking about it for a while.

Vernon: First I ever heard of it.

Lucy: Well, I'd been thinking. (*Pause. Lucy picks up her corn again, guiding him back to the story:*) So anyway, the guy's sneaking up on the mother . . .

Vernon: Was it because of me?

Lucy: No . . .

Vernon: Something I said, or did . . .

Lucy: It's nothing like that.

Vernon: You were always fond of cataloguing the careless things I said and did . . .

Lucy: I just did some soul-searching, that's all.

> (*Beat.*)

Vernon: Soul-searching.

Lucy: About a lot of things.

Vernon: And your soul said to you "no more meat."

Lucy: You make it sound silly when you say it like that.

Vernon: Then what, what did your soul tell you?

> (*Beat. Lucy exhales heavily and sets down her corn.*)

Lucy: I decided I didn't want to eat anything with a face.

> (*Beat.*)

Vernon: A *face?*

> (*He gets up, stands behind her and looks at her plate.*)

Lucy: Vern . . .

Vernon: I don't see any face . . .

Lucy: This doesn't have to be a big deal . . .

Vernon: I don't see a face. Do you see a face?

> (*He lifts the plate toward her face.*)

Lucy: There's other reasons.

Vernon: No face.

> (*He sets the plate down again.*)

Lucy: I've been reading things.

Vernon: What things?

Lucy: You know, health reports . . .

Vernon: You can't believe that stuff.

Lucy: What do you mean?

Vernon: You can't! One day they say bran's good for you — "Want to live forever? Eat more bran." — the next day they find out bran can kill you.

Lucy: Whatever.

Vernon: Too much bran boom you're dead.

Lucy: There are diseases you can get from meat.

Vernon: Like what?

Lucy: Well, listeria . . .

Vernon: That's chicken. Chicken and turkey.

Lucy: Or Mad Cow.

Vernon: *Mad Cow?* Did you — That's not even — that's *English,* they have that in England. This isn't English meat, this is from, I don't know, Kansas, or . . . *Wyoming.*

Lucy: Even so, —

Vernon: No. Now you're making stuff up.

Lucy: I'm not; I saw an article —

Vernon: You're just being paranoid, this whole . . . You know what this is? Do you?

Lucy: What.

Vernon: Carnophobia.

Lucy: "Carnophobia"?

Vernon: It's a word, look it up.

Lucy: It's not like I'm scared of meat . . .

Vernon: How do you think this makes me feel?

Lucy: Look, let's just drop it.

Vernon: Huh?

Lucy: We were doing so well . . .

Vernon: I invite you over, cook a nice steak, set out flowers, napkins, the whole nine yards . . .

Lucy: I appreciate the napkins.

Vernon: . . . figure I'll open a bottle of wine, apologize . . . maybe we'll get naked, be like old times.

Lucy: So let's start over.

Vernon: Then you get *carnophobic* on me.

Lucy: Can we?

Vernon: Throw it in my face.

Lucy: Please?

Vernon: Start *cataloguing* what's wrong with everything . . .

Lucy: I never meant this to be a big deal. *(Beat. She puts her hand on his. He looks at her.)* I really didn't.

> *(Long pause.)*

Vernon: Then eat it.

> *(Beat.)*

Lucy: Vern . . . *(He picks up her fork, jams it into her steak, and cuts off a bite with his knife.)* Why do you always have to —

> *(He extends the piece of meat toward Lucy's mouth.)*

Vernon: Eat the meat.

Lucy: I don't want to.

Vernon: *Eat the meat.*

Lucy: Vernon . . .

Vernon: I SAID EAT THE MEAT! *(They are locked in a struggle, he menacing, she terrified. Long pause. Finally, Lucy opens her mouth and takes the bite into it. Pause.)* Chew. *(She chews for fifteen or twenty seconds.)* Swallow. *(She swallows. Cheerfully, without malice:)* Good, isn't it. *(Lucy nods obediently.)* Nice and juicy. (*He stabs his fork into his own steak, cuts off a bite and lifts it.*) See, nothing to be afraid of.

(*He pops it into his mouth and begins cutting another. After a moment, Lucy goes back to her corn. They eat in absolute silence. Lights fade.*)

"Naked Lunch — *a frozen moment when everyone sees what is on the end of every fork.*" — William S. Burroughs

CONSIDERATIONS FOR CRITICAL THINKING AND WRITING

1. **FIRST RESPONSE.** Do you identify more with Vernon or Lucy? Which character seems more sympathetic to you? Explain why.

2. What do you think is the significance of the set directions calling for "a small vase with too many flowers in it, or a large vase with too few"?

3. Why won't Lucy eat meat?

4. Why is it so important to Vernon that Lucy eat the steak?

5. Which character would you describe as the antagonist? What do you think is the play's central conflict?

6. Discuss the tone of the final moments of the play when Vernon cuts the steak for Lucy. Is the central conflict resolved? Why or why not?

7. How would you describe the play's theme?

8. Discuss the significance of the title. How is it related to your understanding of the play's theme?

9. In the biographical head note to the play, Hollinger describes how his plays share some of the same qualities as music. Reread his explanation of this comparison and discuss how the literary elements of *Naked Lunch* are similar to music.

CONNECTIONS TO OTHER SELECTIONS

1. Compare the theme of *Naked Lunch* with that of Susan Glaspell's *Trifles* (p. 1366).

2. Discuss the symbolic significance of the steak dinner in *Naked Lunch* and the birdcage and the dead bird in *Trifles*.

Mistaken Identity

Born in Massachusetts and raised in Virginia, Sharon E. Cooper has been writing plays since she was in high school. She was associated with the Kennedy Center Playwriting Intensive Program and lives in New York, where she is a member of the Milk Can Theatre Company, a collective of playwrights and directors who

Julie Fei-Fan Balzer.

provide readings, workshops, and productions for their plays. Among her short plays produced at Milk Can were *The Match* (2006), *Running* (2007), *P.O.V.* (2007), *In the Meantime* (2008), and *A Visit to the Bronx* (2008). *Mistaken Identity,* which premiered at the Open Space Center in Reisterstown, Maryland, in 2003, starts the way a good many shaky blind dates begin but then takes an interesting turn.

SHARON E. COOPER (B. 1975)

Mistaken Identity

2004
(2008 Revised)

CHARACTERS

Kali Patel, 29. Single lesbian Hindu of Indian heritage; social worker who works as much as possible; lives in Leicester, England.
Steve Dodd, 32. Single straight guy, desperate to marry, raised Baptist but attends church only on Christmas and Easter; studying abroad for his final year as an undergraduate.

SETTING: The Castle, a pub in Kirby Muxlowe in Leicester, England.

TIME: The present.

> *(Lights up on Steve and Kali in a busy pub on their first date. They are in the middle of dinner.)*

Steve: You must get tired of fish and chips all the time. Why do y'all call them "chips"? When they're french fries, I mean. And you ever notice when people swear, they say, "Excuse my French." Not me. Nope. I have nothing against the French.

Kali: Right, well, I'm not French, Steve, now am I?

Steve: I just didn't want you to think I was prejudiced against the French or *anyone else.* . . . They're like your neighbors, the French. And your neighbors are like my neighbors. And like a good neighbor, State Farm is there. Have you heard that commercial?

Kali: What? No. Steve—

Steve: It's for insurance. Y'all must not play it here. (*Pause.*) So I know that you all do the "arranged marriage thing." Rashid and I had a long talk about it. Of course, Rashid and I wanted you to approve, too, Kali.

Kali: How twenty-first century of you and my brother. Steve . . .

Kali: I'm gay. / *Steve:* Will you marry me?

Kali: Come again? / *Steve:* What?

Kali: How could you ask me to . . . / *Steve:* Well, I can't believe this.

Kali: Bloody hell, stop talking while I'm talking . . . / *Steve:* This is very strange.

Kali: So—what?

Steve: This new information is, well, new, and changes things, I guess.

Kali: You guess? What the hell is wrong with you? I'm sorry, Steve, you just happened to show up at the end of a very long line of a lot of very bad dates. You know, movies where the bloke negotiates holding your hand while you're just trying to eat popcorn; running across De Montfort University in the pouring rain; dropping a bowling ball on the bloke's pizza.

Steve: You had me until the bowling ball. Kali, this doesn't make sense. I invite you out on a lovely date. We eat fish and chips—when I would rather be eating a burger or lasagna—

Kali: Steve, I'm sorry.

Steve: I figured we would have a nice long traditional wedding with the colorful tents. All of my family would be there. We're more of the Christmas/Easter Christians, so we'd do your religion and I would wear—

Kali: (*Overlapping.*) You don't know anything about my people. What are you—

Steve: (*Overlapping.*) Ooohhh, yes, I do. I saw *Monsoon Wedding.* And the director's cut! And I saw *Slumdog Millionaire* like three times. Three times. Unbelievable!

Kali: Yes, this makes loads of sense at the end of the day. I am a lesbian who has to date every Hindu bloke in England until her brother gets so desperate that he sets her up with a cowboy—

Steve: I take offense to that.

Kali: (*Overlapping.*) But I should feel sorry for *you* because *you* watched *two,* count them, *two* movies about Indian people in your entire life and ordered fish when there are hamburgers on the menu! Forgive *me* for being so insensitive.

Steve: I ordered fish because I wanted you to like me. And I'm sure I've seen other Asian movies. Like all those fighting movies. You know, the ones where women are jumping through the air—

Kali: Aaahhh! Do you see how all of this is a moot point now?

Steve: I'm confused. Let's review.

Kali: Please, no, bloody hell, let's not review. Let's get the waiter. Haven't you had enough?

(*She gets up. He follows.*)

Steve: (*Overlapping.*) Why is your brother setting up his *lesbian* sister—

Kali: (*Overlapping.*) Will you please keep your voice down?

Steve: (*Overlapping.*)—up on dates for marriage and tricking well-meaning men—specifically me—into proposing to her? I'm here to finish my business degree, but I wasn't born yesterday. So I took a few years off and changed careers a few times, was a fireman—

Kali: (*Overlapping.*) What does that have to do with anything?

Steve: And I'm thirty-two years old, but that doesn't mean—

Kali: Mate, are you going to keep on and on?

Steve: Why did your brother put me through this? This isn't one of those new reality shows: "Little Brothers Set Up Their Lesbian Sisters." Is there a camera under the table? (*He looks.*) Let's talk about this. (*He sits back down.*) I'm a good listener. Go ahead. (*Pause.*) I'm listening. (*Pause.*) You have to say something if you want this to continue with what we call in America, a conversation.

Kali: Are you done?

Steve: Go ahead.

(*She sits.*)

Kali: I guess I was hoping you wouldn't tell Rashid.

Steve: He doesn't know?

Kali: You are finishing your bachelor's degree, is that right?

Steve: If you're so "bloody" smart, I'm wondering why you would tell me, a man that is friends with your brother and sits next to him twice a week in eight A.M. classes—why would you tell *me* you're a lesbian and *not* your brother?

Kali: Maybe for the same reason you would ask a woman you've never met before to marry you.

Steve: Your brother made it sound like it would be easy. I've been looking for that.

Kali: (*Overlapping.*) Look, you seem very nice, you do.

Steve: I am very nice.

Kali: And at the end of the day, I hope you find someone you like.

Steve: I like how you say "at the end of the day" and I like how you say "bloke" and "mate." It's so endearing. And you're beautiful and small and your hair falls on your back so.

Kali: Steve, being a lesbian is not negotiable. And don't start with how sexy it would be to be with me or to watch me and another woman—

Steve: (*Overlapping.*) Kali, I didn't say any of that.

Kali: You didn't have to. Up until a few minutes ago, you thought I was a quiet, subservient Asian toy for sale from her brother. Steve, go get a doll. She can travel with you to America whenever you want. In the meantime, I'll continue to be a loud, abrasive (*Whispering.*) lesbian while my brother sets me up with every bloke on the street—and they don't even have to be Hindu anymore! Do you have any idea what that's like? (*Pause.*) How would you know?

Steve: You're right. I wouldn't.

Kali: Steve, why did you want to be with me? I mean, before.

Steve: I figured that we would have visited my family in the winter when it's so cold here. I would have been willing to stay here when I'm done with school and we would get a nice little place by the—

Kali: Steve, we hadn't even shared dessert yet.

Steve: Don't blame me for all of this. Five minutes ago, we were on a date.

Kali: We're just two people in a pub.

Steve: Kali, do you remember the last time someone—man, woman, I don't care—had their hand down the small of your back or leaned into you like it didn't matter where you ended and they began?

Kali: Yes, I do remember that. And that was strangely poetic.

Steve: You don't have to sound so surprised. Anyway, I remember that feeling. Three years ago, at a Fourth of July celebration—you know, that's the holiday—

Kali: Yes, Steve, I know the holiday.

Steve: She was the only woman I ever really loved. I knew it was ending. Could taste it. I just held her as the fireworks went off and the dust got in our skin. Figured I would hold on, hoping that would keep me for a while. You know how they say babies will die if they're left alone too long. Always wondered if it's true for bigger people, too. Like how long would we last?

... She left with her Pilates mat and Snoopy slippers a few days later. I bet it hasn't been three years for you.

Kali: No, it hasn't. But you wouldn't want to hear about that.

Steve: Why not?

Kali: Come on, Steve, I'm not here for your fantasies —

Steve: This thing where you assume you know what I'm thinking — it's gettin' old.

Kali: I'm . . . sorry. I do have a woman in my life, Michele — She's a teacher for people that are deaf. We've been together for eleven months. The longest we were away from each other was this one time for three weeks. She was at a retreat where they weren't allowed to talk — you know, total immersion. So she would call and I would say, "Is it beautiful there, love?" and she would hit a couple of buttons. Sometimes she would leave me messages: "beep, beep, beep beep beep beep." It didn't matter that she didn't say anything . . . But I can't take her home for Diwali.

Steve: What's that?

Kali: It's a festival of lights where —

Steve: You mean like Hanukkah.

Kali: No, like Diwali. It's a New Year's celebration where we remember ancestors, family, and friends. And reflect back and look to the future.

Steve: It sounds nice. You know, my mother has been asking me for grandchildren since I turned twenty-seven. Every year at Christmas, it's the same: "I can't wait to hang another stocking for my grandchildren, if I ever get to have them."

Kali: Now, imagine that same conversation, well, not about Christmas, and what if you could never give that to them — could never bring someone home for any holiday for the rest of your life?

Steve: Then why don't you just tell them the truth?

Kali: I can't say, Mum, Daddy, Rashid, I've chosen women over men — it's not a hamburger over fish. You just don't know how they'll react. I'd run the risk of not being allowed to see my nieces. I'm so exhausted from hiding, I can barely breathe.

Steve: So stop hiding.

Kali: Have you been listening to what I've been saying?

Steve: Have you?

Kali: Are you going to tell my brother?

Steve: Do you want me to?

Kali: I don't know.

Steve: I've never thought about that thing that you said.

Kali: Which thing would that be?

Steve: The one where maybe you can't see your nieces 'cause you're gay. That must suck.

Kali: Yes, well, thanks for trying to make me feel better.

Steve: Listen, you get to decide what you tell your family and when. As far as I'm concerned, I'll tell Rashid tomorrow that we're getting married. Or I can tell him you're a lesbian, and if he doesn't let you be with his kids anymore, I'll punch him in the face. That was me kidding.

Kali: You're funny. *(Pause.)* Maybe I told you because somewhere deep down, I do want him to know. But I don't know if I can take the risk.

Steve: You don't have to rush.

Kali: I just wish it could be more simple. Like, why can't what I want be part of the whole picket-fence thing? That's pretty ridiculous, huh?

Steve: We're all looking for that. My grandparents met before World War II, dated for seven days in a row, and my grandfather asked my grandmother to go with him to Louisiana, where he'd be stationed. She said, "Is that a proposal?" And he said, "Of course it is." And they've been together ever since. And I just want that, too. Huh—asking you to marry me on a first date! You must think I'm pretty desperate, huh?

Kali: Not any more than the rest of us . . . Oh, hell, do you want to have some dessert?

Steve: Oh, hell, sure. You know, we're going to share dessert.

Kali: Hey, mate, no one said anything about sharing.

Steve: I would go home with you for Diwali. I mean, as friends. If you ever wanted one around. You're a nice girl, Kali. I mean woman, mate, bloke. I mean—

Kali: Sssshhhh. Let's just get some dessert.

(Lights fade as they motion for the waiter. Blackout.)

CONSIDERATIONS FOR CRITICAL THINKING AND WRITING

1. **FIRST RESPONSE.** Did you find this play humorous and enjoyable? Why or why not?
2. How does Cooper establish Steve's character in his first few speeches? At what point is his character made more complex?
3. How important is the brother's role in the plot?
4. What serious issues—and conflicts—emerge from the humor of this play?
5. Is there a climax? Are the conflicts resolved?
6. Discuss the potential meanings of the title.

CONNECTIONS TO ANOTHER SELECTION

1. Compare Steve's character with that of Vernon's in Michael Hollinger's *Naked Lunch* (p. 1385). What is the essential difference between them? Are there any significant similarities?
2. **CREATIVE RESPONSE.** Write the dessert scene that ends *Mistaken Identity* so that it matches the tone of *Naked Lunch*.

DRAMA IN POPULAR FORMS

Audiences for live performances of plays have been thinned by high ticket prices but perhaps even more significantly by the impact of motion pictures and television. Motion pictures, the original threat to live theater, have in turn been superseded by television (along with videocassettes and DVDs), now the most popular form of entertainment in America. Television audiences are measured in the millions. Probably more people have seen a single weekly episode of a top-rated prime-time program such as *ER* in one evening than have viewed a live performance of *Hamlet* in nearly four hundred years.

Though most of us are seated more often before a television than before live actors, our limited experience with the theater presents relatively few obstacles to appreciation because many of the basic elements of drama are similar whether the performance is on a screen or on a stage. Television has undoubtedly seduced audiences that otherwise might have been attracted to the theater, but television obviously satisfies some aspects of our desire for drama and can be seen as a potential introduction to live theater rather than as its irresistible rival.

Significant differences do, of course, exist between television and theater productions. Most obviously, television's special camera effects can capture phenomena such as earthquakes, raging fires, car chases, and space travel that cannot be realistically rendered on a live stage. The presentation of characters and the plotting of action are also handled differently owing to both the possibilities and limitations of television and the theater. Television's multiple camera angles and close-ups provide a degree of intimacy that cannot be duplicated by actors on stage, yet this intimacy does not achieve the immediacy that live actors create. On commercial television the plot must accommodate itself to breaks in the action so that advertisements can be aired at regular intervals. Beyond these and many other differences, however, there are enough important similarities that the experience of watching television shows can enhance our understanding of a theater production.

Seinfeld

Seinfeld, which aired on NBC, was first produced during the summer of 1989. Although the series ended in the spring of 1998, it remains popular in syndicated reruns. No one expected the half-hour situation comedy that evolved from the pilot to draw some twenty-seven million viewers per week who avidly watched Jerry Seinfeld playing himself as a standup comic. Nominated for numerous Emmys, the show became one of the most popular programs of the 1990s. Although *Seinfeld* portrays a relatively narrow band of contemporary urban life — four thirtysomething characters living in New York City's Upper West Side — its quirky humor and engaging characters have attracted vast numbers of devoted fans who have conferred on it a kind of cult status. If you haven't watched an episode on television, noticed the T-shirts and posters, or read *Seinlanguage* (a best-selling collection of Seinfeld's monologues), you can catch up on the Internet, where fans discuss the popularity and merits of the show.

The setting for *Seinfeld* is determined by its subject matter, which is everyday life in Manhattan. Most of the action alternates between two principal locations: Jerry's modest one-bedroom apartment on West 81st Street and the characters' favorite restaurant in the neighborhood. Viewers are often surprised to learn that the show was filmed on a soundstage before a live audience in Studio City, California, because the sights, sounds, and seemingly unmistakable texture of Manhattan appear in background shots so that the city functions almost as a major character in many episodes. If you ever find yourself on the corner of Broadway and 112th Street, you'll recognize the facade of Jerry's favorite restaurant; but don't bother to look for the building that matches the exterior shot of his apartment building because it is in Los Angeles, as are the scenes in which the characters actually appear on the street. The care with which the sets are created suggests how important the illusion of the New York City environment is to the show.

As the central character, Jerry begins and ends each episode with a standup comedy act delivered before a club audience. These monologues (played down in later episodes) are connected to the events in the episodes and demonstrate with humor and insight that ordinary experience — such as standing in line at a supermarket or getting something caught in your teeth — can be a source of genuine humor. For Jerry, life is filled with daily annoyances that he copes with by making sharp humorous observations. Here's a brief instance from "The Pitch" (not reprinted in the excerpt on p. 1396) in which Jerry is in the middle of a conversation with friends when he is interrupted by a phone call.

> *Jerry (into phone):* Hello?
> *Man (v[oice] o[ver]):* Hi, would you be interested in switching over to T.M.I. long distance service?
> *Jerry:* Oh gee, I can't talk right now, why don't you give me your home number and I'll call you later?
> *Man (v[oice] o[ver]):* Uh, well I'm sorry, we're not allowed to do that.
> *Jerry:* Oh, I guess you don't want people calling you at home.
> *Man (v[oice] o[ver]):* No.
> *Jerry:* Well now you know how I feel.
> *Hangs up.*

This combination of polite self-assertion and humor is Jerry's first line of defense in his ongoing skirmishes with the irritations of daily life. Unthreatening in his Nikes and neatly pressed jeans, Jerry nonetheless knows how to give it back when he is annoyed. Seinfeld has described his fictional character as a "nice, New York Jewish boy," but his character's bemused and pointed observations reveal a tough-mindedness that is often wittily on target.

Jerry's life and apartment are continually invaded by his three closest friends: George, Kramer, and Elaine. His refrigerator is the rallying point from which they feed each other lines over cardboard takeout cartons and containers of juice. Jerry's success as a standup comic is their cue to enjoy his groceries as well as his company, but they know their intrusions are welcome because the refrigerator is always restocked.

Jerry's closest friend is George Costanza (played by Jason Alexander), a frequently unemployed, balding, pudgy schlemiel. Any straightforward description of his behavior and sensibilities makes him sound starkly unappealing: he is hypochondriacal, usually upset and depressed, inept with women, embarrassingly stingy, and persistently demanding while simultaneously displaying a vain and cocky nature. As intolerable as he can be, he is nonetheless endearing. The pleasure of his character is in observing how he talks his way into trouble and then attempts to talk his way out of it to Jerry's amazement and amusement.

Across the hall from Jerry's apartment lives Kramer (played by Michael Richards), who is strategically located so as to be the mooch in Jerry's life. Known only as Kramer (until an episode later than "The Pitch" revealed his first name to be Cosmo), his slapstick twitching, tripping, and falling serve as a visual contrast to all the talking that goes on. His bizarre schemes and eccentric behavior have their physical counterpart in his vertical hair and his outrageous thrift-shop shirts from the 1960s.

Elaine Benes (played by Julia Louis-Dreyfus), on the other hand, is a sharp-tongued, smart, sexy woman who can hold her own and is very definitely a female member of this boys' club. As Jerry's ex-girlfriend, she provides some interesting romantic tension while serving as a sounding board for the relationship issues that George and Jerry obsess about. Employed at a book company at the time of the episode reprinted here, she, like George and Kramer, is also in the business of publishing her daily problems in Jerry's apartment.

The plots of most *Seinfeld* episodes are generated by the comical situations that Jerry and his friends encounter during the course of their daily lives. Minor irritations develop into huge conflicts that are offbeat, irreverent, or even absurd. The characters have plenty of time to create conflicts in their lives over such everyday situations as dealing with parents, finding an apartment, getting a date, riding the subway, ordering a meal, and losing a car in a mall parking garage. The show's screwball plots involve freewheeling misadventures that are played out in unremarkable but hilarious conversations.

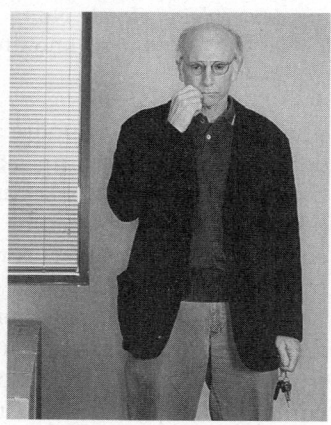

© Dan Winters.

The following scenes from *Seinfeld* are from a script titled "The Pitch" that concerns Jerry's and George's efforts to develop a television show for NBC. The script is loosely based on events that actually occurred when Jerry Seinfeld and his real-life friend Larry David (the author of "The Pitch") sat down to discuss ideas for the pilot NBC produced in 1989. As brief as these scenes are, they contain some of the dramatic elements found in a play.

Larry David (b. 1947)

Seinfeld   *1992*

"The Pitch"
[The following excerpted scenes do not appear one after the other in the original script but are interspersed through several subplots involving Kramer and Elaine.]

ACT ONE

Scene A: *Int[erior] comedy club bar—night*

> *Jerry and George are talking. Suits enter, Stu and Jay.*

Stu: Excuse me, Jerry? I'm Stu Chermak. I'm with NBC.
Jerry: Hi.
Stu: Could we speak for a few moments?
Jerry: Sure, sure.
Jay: Hi, Jay Crespi.
Jerry: Hello.
George: C-R-E-S-P-I?
Jay: That's right.
George: I'm unbelievable at spelling last names. Give me a last name.
Jay: Mm, I'm not —
Jerry: George.
George (backing off): Huh? All right, fine.
Stu: First of all, that was a terrific show.
Jerry: Oh thank you very much.
Stu: And basically, I just wanted to let you know that we've been discussing you at some of our meetings and we'd be very interested in doing something.
Jerry: Really? Wow.
Stu: So, if you have an idea for like a TV show for yourself, well, we'd just love to talk about it.
Jerry: I'd be very interested in something like that.
Stu: Well, here, why don't you give us a call and maybe we can develop a series.

> *They start to exit.*

Jerry: Okay. Great. Thanks.
Stu: It was very nice meeting you.
Jerry: Thank you.
Jay: Nice meeting you.
Jerry: Nice meeting you.

> *George returns.*

George: What was that all about?
Jerry: They said they were interested in me.
George: For what?
Jerry: You know, a TV show.
George: Your own show?
Jerry: Yeah, I guess so.
George: They want you to do a TV show?
Jerry: Well, they want me to come up with an idea. I mean, I don't have any ideas.
George: Come on, how hard is that? Look at all the junk that's on TV. You want an idea? Here's an idea. You coach a gymnastics team in high school. And you're married. And your son's not interested in gymnastics and you're pushing him into gymnastics.
Jerry: Why should I care if my son's into gymnastics?
George: Because you're a gymnastics teacher. It's only natural.
Jerry: But gymnastics is not for everybody.

George: I know, but he's your son.

Jerry: So what?

George: All right, forget that idea, it's not for you. . . . Okay, okay, I got it, I got it. You run an antique store.

Jerry: Yeah and . . . ?

George: And people come in the store and you get involved in their lives.

Jerry: What person who runs an antique store gets involved in people's lives?

George: Why not?

Jerry: So someone comes in to buy an old lamp and all of a sudden I'm getting them out of a jam? I could see if I was a pharmacist because a pharmacist knows what's wrong with everybody that comes in.

George: I know, but antiques are very popular right now.

Jerry: No they're not, they used to be.

George: Oh yeah, like you know.

Jerry: Oh like you do.

Cut to:

ACT ONE

SCENE B: *Int[erior] Jerry's apartment — day*

Jerry and Kramer.

Kramer: . . . And you're the manager of the circus.

Jerry: A circus?

Kramer: Come on, this is a great idea. Look at the characters. You've got all these freaks on the show. A woman with a moustache? I mean, who wouldn't tune in to see a woman with a moustache? You've got the tallest man in the world; the guy who's just a head.

Jerry: I don't think so.

Kramer: Look Jerry, the show isn't about the circus, it's about watching freaks.

Jerry: I don't think the network will go for it.

Kramer: Why not?

Jerry: Look, I'm not pitching a show about freaks.

Kramer: Oh come on Jerry, you're wrong. People they want to watch freaks. This is a "can't miss."

ACT ONE

SCENE C: *Int[erior] coffee shop — lunchtime — day*

Jerry and George enter.

George: So, what's happening with the TV show? You come up with anything?

Jerry: No, nothing.

George: Why don't they have salsa on the table?

Jerry: What do you need salsa for?

George: Salsa is now the number one condiment in America.

Jerry: You know why? Because people like to say "salsa." "Excuse me, do you have salsa?" "We need more salsa." "Where is the salsa? No salsa?"

George: You know it must be impossible for a Spanish person to order seltzer and not get salsa. *(Angry.)* "I wanted seltzer, not salsa."

Jerry: "Don't you know the difference between seltzer and salsa? You have the seltzer after the salsa!"

George: See, this should be the show. This is the show.

Jerry: What?

George: This. Just talking.

Jerry (dismissing): Yeah, right.

George: I'm really serious. I think that's a good idea.

Jerry: Just talking? What's the show about?

George: It's about nothing.

Jerry: No story?

George: No, forget the story.

Jerry: You've got to have a story.

George: Who says you gotta have a story? Remember when we were waiting for that table in that Chinese restaurant that time? That could be a TV show.

Jerry: And who is on the show? Who are the characters?

George: I could be a character.

Jerry: You?

George: You could base a character on me.

Jerry: So on the show there's a character named George Costanza?

George: Yeah. There's something wrong with that? I'm a character. People are always saying to me, "You know you're quite a character."

Jerry: And who else is on the show?

George: Elaine could be a character. Kramer.

Jerry: Now he's a character. . . . So, everyone I know is a character on the show.

George: Right.

Jerry: And it's about nothing?

George: Absolutely nothing.

Jerry: So you're saying, I go in to NBC and tell them I got this idea for a show about nothing.

George: *We* go into NBC.

Jerry: We? Since when are you a writer?

George: Writer. We're talking about a sit-com.

Jerry: You want to go with me to NBC?

George: Yeah, I think we really got something here.

Jerry: What do we got?

George: An idea.

Jerry: What idea?

George: An idea for the show.

Jerry: I still don't know what the idea is.

George: It's about nothing.

Jerry: Right.

George: Everybody's doing something, we'll do nothing.

Jerry: So we go into NBC, we tell them we've got an idea for a show about nothing.

George: Exactly.

Jerry: They say, "What's your show about?" I say, "Nothing."
George: There you go.

> *A beat.*

Jerry: I think you may have something there.

> *Cut to:*

ACT ONE

SCENE D: *Int[erior] Jerry's apartment—day*

> *Jerry and Kramer.*

Jerry: So it would be about my real life. And one of the characters would be based on you.
Kramer (thinks): No. I don't think so.
Jerry: What do you mean you don't think so?
Kramer: I don't like it.
Jerry: I don't understand. What don't you like about it?
Kramer: I don't like the idea of a character based on me.
Jerry: Why not?
Kramer: Doesn't sit well.
Jerry: You're my neighbor. There's got to be a character based on you.
Kramer: That's your problem, buddy.
Jerry: I don't understand what the big deal is.
Kramer: Hey I'll tell you what, you can do it on one condition.
Jerry: Whatever you want.
Kramer: I get to play Kramer.
Jerry: You can't play Kramer.
Kramer: I am Kramer.
Jerry: But you can't act.

ACT ONE

SCENE G: *Int[erior] NBC reception area—day*

> *Jerry and George.*

Jerry (to himself): Salsa, seltzer. Hey excuse me, you got any salsa? No not seltzer, salsa. *(George doesn't react.)* What's the matter?
George (nervous): Nothing.
Jerry: You sure? You look a little pale.
George: No, I'm fine. I'm good. I'm fine. I'm very good.
Jerry: What are you, nervous?
George: No, not nervous. I'm good, very good. *(A beat, then: explodes.)* I can't do this! Can't do this!
Jerry: What?

George: I can't do this! I can't do it. I have tried. I'm here. It's impossible.

Jerry: This was your idea.

George: What idea? I just said something. I didn't know you'd listen to me.

Jerry: Don't worry about it. They're just TV executives.

George: They're men with jobs, Jerry! They wear suits and ties. They're married, they have secretaries.

Jerry: I told you not to come.

George: I need some water. I gotta get some water.

Jerry: They'll give us water inside.

George: Really? That's pretty good. . . .

> *Receptionist enters.*

Receptionist: They're ready for you.

George: Okay, okay, look, you do all the talking, okay?

Jerry: Relax. Who are they?

George: Yeah, they're not better than me.

Jerry: Course not.

George: Who are they?

Jerry: They're nobody.

George: What about me?

Jerry: What about you?

George: Why them? Why not me?

Jerry: Why not you?

George: I'm as good as them.

Jerry: Better.

George: You really think so?

Jerry: No.

> *Door opens, Jerry and George P.O.V., the four execs stand up.*
>
> *Fade out.*

ACT TWO

SCENE G: *Int[erior] NBC president's office — day*

> *The mood is jovial. Stu Chermak is there — along with Susan Ross, Jay Crespi, and Russell Dalrymple, the head of the network.*

Stu (to Jerry): The bit, the bit I really liked was where the parakeet flew into the mirror. Now that's funny.

George: The parakeet in the mirror. That is a good one, Stu.

Jerry: Yeah, it's one of my favorites.

Russell: What about you George, have you written anything we might know?

George: Well, possibly. I wrote an off-Broadway show, "La Cocina." . . . Actually it was off-off-Broadway. It was a comedy about a Mexican chef.

Jerry: Oh it was very funny. There was one great scene with the chef — what was his name?

George: Pepe.

Jerry: Oh Pepe, yeah Pepe. And, uh, he was making tamales.

Susan: Oh, he actually cooked on the stage?

George: No, no, he mimed it. That's what was so funny about it.

Russell: So what have you two come up with?

Jerry: Well we've thought about this in a variety of ways. But the basic idea is I will play myself.

George (interrupting, to Jerry): May I?

Jerry: Go ahead.

George: I think I can sum up the show for you with one word. NOTHING.

Russell: Nothing?

George: Nothing.

Russell: What does that mean?

George: The show is about nothing.

Jerry (to George): Well, it's not about nothing.

George (to Jerry): No, it's about nothing.

Jerry: Well, maybe in philosophy. But even nothing is something.

> *Jerry and George glare at each other. Receptionist sticks her head in.*

Receptionist: Mr. Dalrymple, your niece is on the phone.

Russell: I'll call back.

George: D-A-L-R-I-M-P-E-L.

Russell: Not even close.

George: Is it with a "y"?

Russell: No.

Susan: What's the premise?

Jerry: . . . Well, as I was saying, I would play myself. And as a comedian, living in New York, and I have a friend and a neighbor and an ex-girlfriend, which is all true.

George: Yeah, but nothing happens on the show. You see, it's just like life. You know, you eat, you go shopping, you read. You eat, you read, you go shopping.

Russell: You read? You read on the show?

Jerry: Well I don't know about the reading. We didn't discuss the reading.

Russell: All right, tell me, tell me about the stories. What kind of stories?

George: Oh no, no stories.

Russell: No stories? So what is it?

George: What'd you do today?

Russell: I got up and came to work.

George: There's a show. That's a show.

Russell (confused): How is that a show?

Jerry: Well, uh, maybe something happens on the way to work.

George: No, no, no. Nothing happens.

Jerry: Well, something happens.

Russell: Well why am I watching it?

George: Because it's on TV.

Russell: Not yet.

George: Okay, uh, look, if you want to just keep on doing the same old thing, then maybe this idea is not for you. I for one will not compromise my artistic integrity. And I'll tell you something else. This is the show and we're not going to change it. *(To Jerry.)* Right?

Jerry: How about this? I manage a circus . . .

CONSIDERATIONS FOR CRITICAL THINKING AND WRITING

1. **FIRST RESPONSE.** What does George mean when he says the proposed show should be about "nothing"? Why is George's idea both a comic and a serious proposal?

2. How does the stage direction "Suits enter" serve to characterize Stu and Jay? Write a description of how you think they would look.

3. What is revealed about George's character when he spells Crespi's and Dalrymple's names?

4. Discuss Kramer's assertion that people "want to watch freaks." Do you think this line could be used to sum up accurately audience responses to *Seinfeld*?

5. Choose a scene, and explain how humor is worked into it. What other emotions are evoked in the scene?

6. View an episode of *Seinfeld*. How does reading a script compare with watching the show? Which do you prefer? Why?

7. **CRITICAL STRATEGIES.** Read the section on reader-response criticism (pp. 2060–62) in Chapter 53, "Critical Strategies for Reading," and discuss why you like or dislike "The Pitch" and *Seinfeld* in general. Try to account for your personal response to the script and the show.

CONNECTION TO ANOTHER SELECTION

1. In an essay explain whether or not you think David Ives's play *Moby-Dude, Or: The Three-Minute Whale* (p. 1801) fills George's prescription that a story should be about "nothing."

Like those of many plays, the settings for these scenes are not detailed. Jerry's apartment and the coffee shop are, to cite only two examples, not described at all. We are told only that it is lunchtime in the coffee shop. Even without a set designer's version of these scenes, we readily create a mental picture of these places that provides a background for the characters. In the coffee shop scene we can assume that Jerry and George are having lunch, but we must supply the food, the plates and cutlery, the tables and chairs, and the other customers. For the television show sets were used that replicated the details of a Manhattan coffee shop, right down to the menus and cash register. If the scene were presented on a stage, a set designer might use minimal sets and props to suggest the specific location. The director of such a production would rely on the viewers' imagination to create the details of the setting.

As brief as they are, these scenes include some exposition to provide the necessary background about the characters and their circumstances. We learn through dialogue, for example, that George is not a writer and that he doesn't think it takes very much talent to write a sit-com even though he's unemployed. These bits of information help to characterize George and allow an audience to place his attitudes and comments in a larger context that will be useful for understanding how other characters read them. Rather than dramatizing background information, the scriptwriter arranges incidents to create a particular focus and effect while working in the necessary exposition through dialogue.

The plot in these scenes shapes the conflicts to emphasize humor. As in any good play, incidents are carefully arranged to achieve a particular effect. In the first scene we learn that NBC executives are interested in having Jerry do his own television show. We also learn, through his habit of spelling people's last names when he meets them, that George is a potential embarrassment. The dialogue between Jerry and George quickly establishes the conflict. The NBC executives would like to produce a TV show with Jerry provided that he can come up with an idea for the series; Jerry, however, has no ideas (here's the complication of the pyramidal plot pattern discussed in Elements of Drama, p. 1381). This complication sets up a conflict for Jerry because George assumes that he can help Jerry develop an idea for the show, which, after all, shouldn't be any more difficult than spelling a stranger's name. As George says, "How hard is that? Look at all the junk that's on TV."

All of a sudden everyone is an expert on scriptwriting. George's off-the-wall suggestions that the premise for the show be Jerry's running an antique shop or teaching gymnastics are complemented by Kramer's idea that Jerry be "the manager of the circus" because "people they want to watch freaks." As unhelpful as Kramer's suggestion is, there is some truth here as well as humor, given his own freakish behavior. However, it is George who comes through with the most intriguing suggestion. As a result of the exuberantly funny riff he and Jerry do on "the difference between seltzer and salsa," George suddenly realizes that the show should be "about nothing" — that it should consist of nothing more than Jerry talking and hanging out with his friends George, Elaine, and Kramer. Jerry's initial skepticism gives way as he seriously considers George's proposal and is intrigued enough to bring George with him to the NBC offices to make the pitch. His decision to bring George to the meeting can only, of course, complicate matters further.

Before the meeting with the NBC executives, George is stricken with one of his crises of confidence when he compares himself to the "men with jobs" who are married and have secretaries. Characteristically, George's temporary lack of confidence shifts to an equally ill-timed arrogance once the meeting begins. He usurps Jerry's role and makes the pitch himself: "Nothing happens on the show. You see, it's just like life. You know, you eat, you go shopping, you read. You eat, you read, you go shopping." The climax occurs when George refuses even to consider any of the reservations the executives have about "nothing" happening on the show. George's insistence that he not compromise his "artistic integrity" creates a crisis for Jerry, a turning point that makes him realize that George's ridiculous arrogance might cost him his opportunity to have a TV show. Jerry's final lines to the executives — "How about this? I manage a circus . . ." — work two ways: he resignedly acknowledges that something — not "nothing" — has just happened and that George is, indeed, something of a freak.

The falling action and resolution typical of a pyramidal plot are not present in "The Pitch" because the main plot is not resolved until a later episode. "The Pitch" also contains several subplots not included in the scenes excerpted in this book. Like the main plot, these subplots involving Elaine, Kramer, and a few minor characters are not resolved until later episodes. Self-contained series episodes are increasingly rare on television, as programmers attempt to hook viewers week after week by creating suspense once associated with serialized stories that appeared weekly or monthly in magazines.

The theme of "The Pitch" is especially interesting because it self-reflexively comments on the basic premise of *Seinfeld* scripts: they are all essentially about "nothing" in that they focus on the seemingly trivial details of the four main characters' lives. The unspoken irony of this theme is that such details are in fact significant because it is just such small, everyday activities that constitute most people's lives.

Perspective

GEOFFREY O'BRIEN (B. 1948)

On Seinfeld *as Sitcom Moneymaker*   *1997*

If *Seinfeld* is indeed, in the words of *Entertainment Weekly,* "the defining sitcom of our age" (one wonders how many such ages, each defined by its own sitcom, have already elapsed), the question remains what exactly it defines. Deliberate satire is alien to the spirit of the enterprise. *Seinfeld* has perfected a form in which anything can be invoked — masturbation, Jon Voight, death, kasha, deafness, faked orgasms, Salman Rushdie, Pez dispensers — without assuming the burden of saying anything about it (thereby avoiding the "social message" trap of programs like Norman Lear's *All in the Family* or *Maude*).

The show does not comment on anything except, famously, itself, in the series of episodes where Jerry and George create a pilot for a sitcom "about nothing," a sitcom identical to the one we are watching. This ploy — which ultimately necessitates a whole set of look-alikes to impersonate the cast of the show-within-a-show *Jerry* — ties in with the recursive, alternate-universe mode of such comedies as *The Purple Rose of Cairo* and *Groundhog Day,* while holding back just this side of the paranormal. If conspiracy theories surface from time to time, it is purely for amusement value, as in the episode where a spitting incident at the ballpark becomes the occasion for an elaborate parody — complete with Zapruder-like home movie° — of the Single Bullet Theory (figuring in this context as the ultimate joke on the idea of explanation).

The result is a vastly entertaining mosaic of observed bits and traits and frames. Imagine some future researcher trying to annotate any one of these episodes, like a Shakespearean scholar dutifully noting that "tapsters were proverbially poor at arithmetic." It would not merely be a matter of explaining jokes and cultural references and curt showbiz locutions — "He does fifteen minutes on Ovaltine" or "They cancelled Rick James" — but of explicating

Zapruder-like home movie: A reference to the Dallas bystander who captured John F. Kennedy's assassination on film.

(always assuming that they were detected in the first place) each shrug and curtailed expostulation and deftly averted glance.

Where it might once have been asked if *Seinfeld* was a commentary on society, the question now should probably be whether society has not been reconfigured as a milieu for commenting on *Seinfeld.* If the craziness enacted on the show is nothing more than the usual business of comedy, the craziness that swirls around it in the outside world is of a less hilarious order. Comedy and money have always been around, but not always in such intimate linkage, and certainly not on so grandiose a scale. In the fifteenth century, the fate of Tudor commerce was not perceived to hinge on the traveling English players who wowed foreign audiences as far afield as Denmark.

The information-age money culture for which *Seinfeld* is only another, fatter, bargaining chip clearly lost its sense of humor a long time ago, a fact that becomes ever more apparent as we move into an economy where sit-coms replace iron and steel as principal products and where fun is not merely big business but seemingly the only business. The once-endearing razzmatazz of showbiz hype warps into a perceptible desperation that registers all too plainly how much is at stake for the merchandisers. One becomes uncomfortably aware of them looming behind the audience, running electronic analyses of the giggles, and nervously watching for the dreaded moment when the laughter begins to dry up. It all begins to seem too much like work even for the audience, who may well begin to wonder why they should be expected to care about precisely how much their amusement is worth to the ticket-sellers.

As for the actual creators of the fun, I would imagine that—allowing for difference of scale and pressure—they go about their work pretty much the same way regardless of the going price for a good laugh. Some years ago, in a dusty corner of Languedoc,° I watched a dented circus truck pull up unannounced along the roadside. The family of performers who clambered out proceeded to set up a makeshift stage, which in a few hours time was ready for their show: a display of tumbling and magic that could have been presented without significant difference in the fifteenth century. After two hours of sublime entertainment, they passed the hat around and drove away toward the next bend in the road. It is strange to think of the fate of empires, even entertainment empires, hinging on such things.

From the *New York Review of Books,* August 14, 1997

Languedoc: A region in southern France.

CONSIDERATIONS FOR CRITICAL THINKING AND WRITING

1. In what sense might *Seinfeld* be described as "the defining sitcom of our age"? Do you think this is an accurate description of the show? Why or why not?

2. Explain why you agree or disagree with O'Brien's assertion that *Seinfeld* "does not comment on anything except, famously, itself."

3. Comment on O'Brien's idea that "comedy and money have always been around, but not always in such intimate linkage." How does *Seinfeld* fit into an "information-age money culture"?

46

Writing about Drama

When you create drama, you look for
the best conflict.
— JANE ANDERSON

FROM READING TO WRITING

Because dramatic literature is written to be performed, writing about reading a play may seem twice removed from what playwrights intend the experience of drama to be: a live audience responding to live actors. Although
reading a play creates distance between yourself and a performance of it,
reading a play can actually bring you closer to understanding that what
supports a stage production of any play is the literary dimension of a
script. Writing about that script — examining carefully how the language
of the stage directions, setting, exposition, dialogue, plot, and other dramatic elements serve to produce effects and meanings — can enhance an
imaginative re-creation of a performance. In a sense, writing about a play
gauges your own interpretative response as an audience member — the difference, of course, is that instead of applauding, you are typing.

"There's the rub," as Hamlet might say, because you're working with
the precision of your fingertips rather than with the hearty response of

your palms. Composing an essay about drama records more than your response to a play; writing also helps you explore, clarify, and discover dimensions of the play you may not have perceived by simply watching a performance of it. Writing is work, of course, but it's the kind of work that brings you closer to your own imagination as well as to the play. That process is more accessible if you read carefully, take notes, and annotate the text to generate ideas (for a discussion of this process see Chapter 54, "Reading and the Writing Process"). This chapter offers a set of questions to help you read and write about drama and includes a sample paper that argues for a feminist reading of Susan Glaspell's *Trifles*.

Questions for Responsive Reading and Writing

The questions in this chapter can help you consider important elements that reveal a play's effects and meanings. These questions are general and will not, therefore, always be relevant to a particular play. Many of them, however, should prove to be useful for thinking, talking, and writing about drama. If you are uncertain about the meaning of a term used in a question, consult the Glossary of Literary Terms beginning on page 2123.

1. Did you enjoy the play? What, specifically, pleased or displeased you about what was expressed and how it was expressed?

2. What is the significance of the play's title? How does it suggest the author's overall emphasis?

3. What information do the stage directions provide about the characters, action, and setting? Are these directions primarily descriptive, or are they also interpretive?

4. How is the exposition presented? What does it reveal? How does the playwright's choice *not* to dramatize certain events on stage help to determine what the focus of the play is?

5. In what ways is the setting important? Would the play be altered significantly if the setting were changed?

6. Are foreshadowings used to suggest what is to come? Are flashbacks used to dramatize what has already happened?

7. What is the major conflict the protagonist faces? What complications constitute the rising action? Where is the climax? Is the conflict resolved?

8. Are one or more subplots used to qualify or complicate the main plot? Is the plot unified so that each incident somehow has a function that relates it to some other element in the play?

9. Does the author purposely avoid a pyramidal plot structure of rising action, climax, and falling action? Is the plot experimental? Is the plot logically and chronologically organized, or is it fantastical or absurd? What effects are produced by the plot? How does it reflect the author's view of life?

10. Who is the protagonist? Who (or what) is the antagonist?

11. By what means does the playwright reveal character? What do the characters' names, physical qualities, actions, and words convey about them? What do the characters reveal about each other?

12. What is the purpose of the minor characters? Are they individualized, or do they primarily represent ideas or attitudes? Are any character foils used?

13. Do the characters all use the same kind of language, or is their speech differentiated? Is it formal or informal? How do the characters' diction and manner of speaking serve to characterize them?

14. Does your response to the characters change in the course of the play? What causes the change?

15. Are words and images repeated in the play so that they take on special meanings? Which speeches seem particularly important? Why?

16. How does the playwright's use of language contribute to the tone of the play? Is the dialogue, for example, predominantly light, humorous, relaxed, sentimental, sad, angry, intense, or violent?

17. Are any symbols used in the play? Which actions, characters, settings, objects, or words convey more than their literal meanings?

18. Are any unfamiliar theatrical conventions used that present problems in understanding the play? How does knowing more about the nature of the theater from which the play originated help to resolve these problems?

19. Is the theme stated directly, or is it developed implicitly through the plot, characters, or some other element? Does the theme confirm or challenge most people's values?

20. How does the play reflect the values of the society in which it is set and in which it was written?

21. How does the play reflect or challenge your own values?

22. Is there a recording, film, or videocassette of the play available in your library or media center? How does this version compare with your own reading?

23. How would you produce the play on a stage? Consider scenery, costumes, casting, and characterizations. What would you emphasize most in your production?

24. Is there a particular critical approach that seems especially appropriate for this play? (See Chapter 53, "Critical Strategies for Reading," which begins on p. 2041.)

25. How might biographical information about the author help the reader to grasp the central concerns of the play?

26. How might historical information about the play provide a useful context for interpretation?

27. To what extent do your own experiences, values, beliefs, and assumptions inform your interpretation?

28. What kinds of evidence from the play are you focusing on to support your interpretation? Does your interpretation leave out any important elements that might undercut or qualify your interpretation?

29. Given that there are a variety of ways to interpret the play, which one seems the most useful to you?

A SAMPLE STUDENT PAPER

The Feminist Evidence in Trifles

The following paper was written in response to an assignment that required an analysis — about 750 words — of an assigned play. Chris Duffy's paper argues that although *Trifles* was written over ninety years ago, it should be seen as a feminist play because its treatment of the tensions between men and women deliberately reveals the oppressiveness that women have had to cope with in their everyday lives. The paper discusses a number of the play's elements, but the discussion is unified through its focus on how the women characters are bound together by a set of common concerns. Notice that page numbers are provided to document quoted passages.

Chris Duffy

Professor Barrina-Barrou

English 109-2

March 6, 2009

The Feminist Evidence in *Trifles*

Despite its early publication date, Susan Glaspell's *Trifles* (1916) can

General thesis statement

be regarded as a work of feminist literature. The play depicts the life of a woman who has been suppressed, oppressed, and subjugated by a patronizing, patriarchal husband. Mrs. Wright is eventually driven to kill her "hard" (1372) husband who has stifled every last twitch of her identity. *Trifles* dramatizes the hypocrisy and ingrained discrimination of male-dominated society while simultaneously speaking to the dangers for women who succumb to such hierarchies. Because Mrs. Wright follows the role

More specific thesis offering analysis, with supporting evidence

mapped by her husband and is directed by society's patriarchal expectations, her identity is lost somewhere along the way. However, Mrs. Hale and Mrs. Peters quietly insist on preserving their own identities by protecting Mrs. Wright from the men who seek to convict her of murder.

Analysis of Mrs. Wright through perspectives of female characters

Mrs. Wright is described as someone who used to have a flair for life. Her neighbor, Mrs. Hale, comments that the last time Mrs. Wright appeared happy and vivacious was before she was married or, more important, when

Duffy 2

she was Minnie Foster and not Mrs. Wright. Mrs. Hale laments, "I heard she used to wear pretty clothes and be lively, when she was Minnie Foster, one of the town girls singing in the choir" (1370). But after thirty years of marriage, Mrs. Wright is now worried about her canned preserves freezing and being without an apron while she is in jail. This subservient image was so accepted in society that Mrs. Peters, the sheriff's wife, speculates that Mrs. Wright must want her apron in order to "feel more natural" (1370). Any other roles would be considered uncharacteristic.

This wifely role is predicated on the supposition that women have no ability to make complicated decisions, to think critically, or to rely on themselves. As the title suggests, the men in this story think of homemaking as much less important than a husband's breadwinning role. Mr. Hale remarks, "Well, women are used to worrying over trifles" (1369), and Sheriff Peters assumes the insignificance of "kitchen things" (1368). Hence, women are forced into a domestic, secondary role, like it or not, and are not even respected for that. Mr. Hale, Sheriff Peters, and the county attorney all dismiss the dialogue between Mrs. Peters and Mrs. Hale as feminine chitchat. Further, the county attorney allows the women to leave the Wrights' house unsupervised because he sees Mrs. Peters as merely an extension of her husband.

Even so, the domestic system the men have set up for their wives and their disregard for them after the rules and boundaries have been laid down prove to be the men's downfall. The evidence that Mrs. Wright killed her husband is woven into Mrs. Hale's and Mrs. Peters's conversations about Mrs. Wright's sewing and her pet bird. The knots in her quilt match those in the rope used to strangle Mr. Wright, and the bird, the last symbol of Mrs. Wright's vitality to be taken by her husband, is found dead. Unable to play the role of subservient wife anymore, Mrs. Wright is foreign to herself and therefore lives a lie. As Mrs. Hale proclaims, "Why, it looks as if she didn't know what she was about!" (1371).

Mrs. Hale, however, does ultimately understand what Mrs. Wright is about. She comprehends the desperation, loneliness, and pain that Mrs. Wright experienced, and she instinctively knows that the roles Mrs. Wright

Margin notes:

Analysis of role of women through perspectives of male characters

Discussion of Mrs. Hale's identification with Mrs. Wright

played—even that of murderer—are scripted by the male-dominated circumstances of her life. As Mrs. Hale shrewdly and covertly observes in the context of a discussion about housecleaning with the county attorney: "Men's hands aren't always as clean as they might be" (1369). In fact, even Mrs. Hale feels some guilt for not having made an effort to visit Mrs. Wright over the years to help relieve the monotony of Mrs. Wright's life with her husband:

> I might have known she needed help! I know how things can
> be—for women. I tell you, it's queer, Mrs. Peters. We live close
> together and we live far apart. We all go through the same
> things—it's all just a different kind of the same thing. (1374)

Mrs. Hale cannot help identifying with her neighbor.

In contrast, Mrs. Peters is initially reluctant to support Mrs. Wright. Not only is she married to the sheriff, but, as the county attorney puts it, "a sheriff's wife is married to the law" (1374) as well. She reminds Mrs. Hale that "the law has got to punish crime" (1374), even if it means revealing the existence of the dead bird and exposing the motive that could convict Mrs. Wright of murdering her husband. But finally Mrs. Peters also becomes complicit in keeping information from her husband and other men. She too—owing to the loss of her first child—understands what loss means and what Mrs. Hale means when she says that women "all go through the same things" (1374).

The women in *Trifles* cannot, as the play reveals, be trifled with. Although Glaspell wrote the play over ninety years ago, it continues to be relevant to contemporary relationships between men and women. Its essentially feminist perspective provides a convincing case for the necessity of women to move beyond destructive stereotypes and oppressive assumptions in order to be true to their own significant—not trifling—experiences.

[margin note:] Discussion of Mrs. Peters's identification with Mrs. Wright

[margin note:] Conclusion summarizing analysis

(Student paper continues after the Plays in Performance insert.)

Oedipus the King (top): At center stage is Jocasta (Ching Valdes-Aran) in a scene from the 1993 production of *Oedipus the King* (p. 1422) at Philadelphia's Wilma Theater, directed by Blanka Zizka and Jiri Zizka. © T. Charles Erikson.

Antigone (bottom): Martha Henry as Antigone (p. 1465) in a scene from the 1971 production at the Repertory Theatre of Lincoln Center. © Martha Swope.

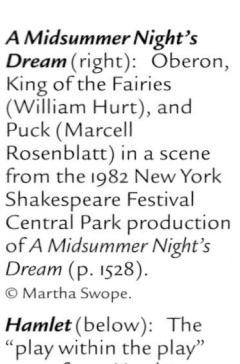

A Midsummer Night's Dream (right): Oberon, King of the Fairies (William Hurt), and Puck (Marcell Rosenblatt) in a scene from the 1982 New York Shakespeare Festival Central Park production of *A Midsummer Night's Dream* (p. 1528).
© Martha Swope.

Hamlet (below): The "play within the play" scene from *Hamlet* (p. 1585).
N. R. Farbman, *Life Magazine,* © Time Inc.

A Doll House: Owen Teale and Janet McTeer in a scene from the 1997 Bill Kenwright London production of *A Doll House* (p. 1709) performed at New York's Belasco Theater — winner of the 1997 Tony Award for Best Revival of a Play. © Joan Marcus.

Real Women Have Curves: America Ferrera and Ingrid Oliu in a 2002 HBO adaptation — winner of the Dramatic Audience Award at that year's Sundance Film Festival — of *Real Women Have Curves* (p. 1831). Everett Collection.

Doubt (above): Cherry Jones as Sister Aloysius and Brian F. O'Byrne as Father Flynn in the 2004 world premiere of *Doubt* (p. 1938) at the Manhattan Theatre Club.

© Sara Krulwich/The New York Times/ Redux.

Rodeo (right): Margo Martindale in *Rodeo* (p. 1804), during the Sixth Annual Humana Festival of New American Plays, at the Actors Theatre of Louisville, Kentucky, in 1982.

Richard C. Trigg, photographer. Courtesy of the Actors Theatre of Louisville.

Fences (left): Mary Alice and James Earl Jones in the Yale Repertory Theatre's 1985 production of *Fences* (p. 1988).
The Image Works.

Trying to Find Chinatown (below): Richard Thompson as Benjamin and Zar Acayan as Ronnie in *Trying to Find Chinatown* (p. 1825), during the 20th Annual Humana Festival of New American Plays, at the Actor's Theatre of Louisville, Kentucky, in 1996.
Courtesy of the Actors Theatre of Louisville.

Death of a Salesman (above): Willy (Lee J. Cobb) with sons Hap (Cameron Mitchell) and Biff (Arthur Kennedy) in *Death of a Salesman* (p. 1869). W. Eugene Smith, *Life Magazine*, © 1949 Time Inc.

No Child . . . (right): Playwright and actor Nilaja Sun performs a scene from her solo show, *No Child . . .* (p. 1969), in a 2008 Berkeley Repertory Theatre production. Carol Rosegg.

Playwriting 101: A scene from the 2003 Kaleidoscope Theatre Company production (New York) of Rich Orloff's *Playwriting 101* (p. 1814).

Larissa Kiel, Daniel Kaufman, and William Green in The Kaleidoscope Theatre Company production of *Playwriting 101: The Rooftop Lesson.* (Photo by Rick Tormone.)

Wanda's Visit: Julie Sweeney, Jim Penson, Jeff Brown, and Colleen Pearson rehearse a scene from *Wanda's Visit* (p. 1785), E. M. Pearson Theater at Concordia University — St. Paul, 1997. Brad Stauffer Photography.

Duffy 4

Work Cited

Glaspell, Susan. "Trifles." *The Bedford Introduction to Literature*. Ed. Michael

Meyer. 9th ed. Boston: Bedford/St. Martin's, 2011. 1366–75. Print.

47

A Study of Sophocles

I depict men as they ought to be . . .
— SOPHOCLES

Not all things are to be discovered;
many are better concealed.
— SOPHOCLES

Sophocles lived a long, productive life (496?–406 B.C.) in Athens. During his life Athens became a dominant political and cultural power after the Persian Wars, but before he died, Sophocles witnessed the decline of Athens as a result of the Peloponnesian Wars and the city's subsequent surrender to Sparta. He saw Athenian culture reach remarkable heights as well as collapse under enormous pressures.

Sophocles embodied much of the best of Athenian culture; he enjoyed success as a statesman, general, treasurer, priest, and, of course, prize-winning dramatist. Although surviving fragments indicate that he wrote over 120 plays, only a handful remain intact. Those that survive consist of the three plays he wrote about Oedipus and his children — *Oedipus the King, Oedipus at Colonus,* and *Antigone* — and four additional tragedies: *Philoctetes, Ajax, Maidens of Trachis,* and *Electra.*

His plays won numerous prizes at festival competitions because of his careful, subtle plotting and the sense of inevitability with which their action is charged. Moreover, his development of character is richly complex. Instead of relying on the extreme situations and exaggerated actions

Web Explore contexts for Sophocles at bedfordstmartins.com/ meyerlit.

that earlier tragedians used, Sophocles created powerfully motivated characters who even today fascinate audiences with their psychological depth.

In addition to crafting sophisticated tragedies for the Greek theater, Sophocles introduced several important innovations to the stage. Most important, he broke the tradition of using only two actors; adding a third resulted in more complicated relationships and intricate dialogue among characters. As individual actors took center stage more often, Sophocles reduced the role of the chorus (discussed on p. 1417). This shift placed even more emphasis on the actors, although the chorus remained important as a means of commenting on the action and establishing its tone. Sophocles was

Map of Ancient Greece. During Sophocles' time, the city-state of Athens (center, left) was the leading cultural and intellectual center of Greece — until the Peloponnesian Wars (431 –404 B.C.) and Athens' defeat in 404 B.C. by the city-state of Sparta (below Athens, to the left).

also the first dramatist to write plays with specific actors in mind, a development that many later playwrights, including Shakespeare, exploited usefully. But without question Sophocles' greatest contribution to drama was *Oedipus the King*, which, it has been argued, is the most influential drama ever written.

Chronology

c. 496 B.C.   Born at Colonus.

480   Athenian victory over the Persians at Salamis. (Sophocles participates as a musician in the victory celebration.)

468   Sophocles' first triumph (over Aeschylus) in the drama competition at the Festival of Dionysus.

443–42   Serves as one of the treasurers of the league against Persia.

c. 441   Writes *Antigone*.

431   The Peloponnesian War begins. This conflict among the Greek states (including Athens and Sparta) lasts nearly thirty years.

c. 430   Writes *Oedipus the King*.

413   Athenian force defeated in Sicily. Sophocles is chosen as one of the leaders to deal with the Sicilian crisis.

406   Sophocles dies.

404   Athens capitulates to Sparta.

401   *Oedipus at Colonus* produced posthumously.

THEATRICAL CONVENTIONS OF GREEK DRAMA

More than twenty-four hundred years have passed since 430 B.C., when Sophocles' *Oedipus the King* was probably first produced on a Greek stage. We inhabit a vastly different planet than Sophocles' audience did, yet concerns about what it means to be human in a world that frequently runs counter to our desires and aspirations have remained relatively constant. The ancient Greeks continue to speak to us. But inexperienced readers or viewers may have some initial difficulty understanding the theatrical conventions used in classical Greek tragedies such as *Oedipus the King* and *Antigone*. If Sophocles were alive today, he would very likely need some sort of assistance with the conventions of an Arthur Miller play or a television production of *Seinfeld*.

Classical Greek drama developed from religious festivals that paid homage to Dionysus, the god of wine and fertility. Most of the details of these festivals have been lost, but we do know that they included dancing and singing that celebrated legends about Dionysus. From these choral songs developed stories of both Dionysus and mortal culture-heroes. These heroes became the subject of playwrights whose works were produced in contests at the festivals. The Dionysian festivals lasted more than five hundred years, but relatively few of their plays have survived. Among the works of the three great writers of tragedy, only seven plays each by Sophocles and Aeschylus (525?–456 B.C.) and nineteen plays by Euripides (480?–406 B.C.) survive.

Plays were such important events in Greek society that they were partially funded by the state. The Greeks associated drama with religious and community values as well as entertainment. In a sense, their plays celebrate their civilization; in approving the plays, audiences applauded their own culture. The enormous popularity of the plays is indicated by the size of surviving amphitheaters. Although information about these theaters is sketchy, we do know that most of them had a common form. They were built into hillsides with rising rows of seats accommodating more than fourteen thousand people. These seats partially encircled an *orchestra* or "dancing place," where the *chorus* of a dozen or so men chanted lines and danced.

Tradition credits the Greek poet Thespis with adding an actor who was separate from the choral singing and dancing of early performances. A second actor was subsequently included by Aeschylus and a third, as noted earlier, by Sophocles. These additions made possible the conflicts and complicated relationships that evolved into the dramatic art we know today. The two or three male actors who played all the roles appeared behind the orchestra in front of the *skene,* a stage building that served as dressing rooms. As Greek theater evolved, a wall of the skene came to be painted to suggest a palace or some other setting, and the roof was employed to indicate, for instance, a mountain location. Sometimes gods were lowered from the roof by mechanical devices to set matters right among the mortals below. This method of rescuing characters from complications beyond their abilities to resolve was known in Latin as *deus ex machina* ("god from the machine"), a term now used to describe any improbable means by which an author provides a too-easy resolution for a story.

Inevitably, the conventions of the Greek theaters affected how plays were presented. Few if any scene changes occurred because the amphitheater stage was set primarily for one location. If an important event happened somewhere else, it was reported by a minor character, such as a messenger. The chorus also provided necessary background information. In *Oedipus the King* and *Antigone,* the choruses, acting as townspeople, also assess the characters' strengths and weaknesses, praising them for their virtues, chiding them for their rashness, and giving them advice. The reactions of the chorus provide a connection between the actors and audience

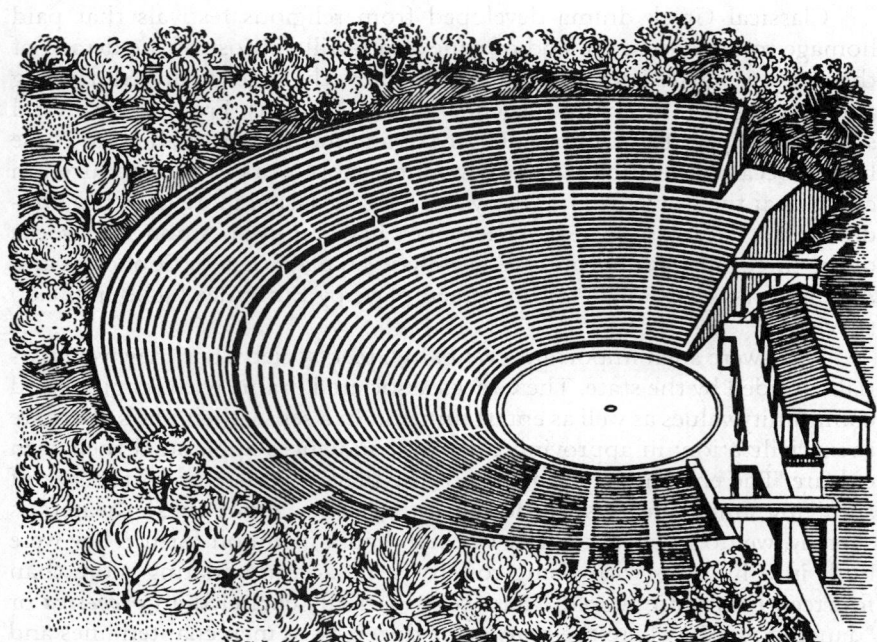

Classical Greek Theater. Based on scholarly sources, this drawing represents the features typical of a classical theater. (Drawing by Gerda Becker. From Kenneth Macgowan and William Melnitz, *The Living Stage,* © 1990 by Prentice Hall / A Division of Simon & Schuster.)

because the chorus is at once a participant in and an observer of the action. In addition, the chorus helps structure the action by indicating changes in scene or mood. Thus the chorus could be used in a variety of ways to shape the audience's response to the play's action and characters.

Actors in classical Greek amphitheaters faced considerable challenges. An intimate relationship with the audience was impossible because many spectators would have been too far away to see a facial expression or subtle gesture. Indeed, some in the audience would have had difficulty even hearing the voices of individual actors. To compensate for these disadvantages, actors wore large masks that extravagantly expressed the major characters' emotions or identified the roles of minor characters. The masks also allowed the two or three actors in a performance to play all the characters without confusing the audience. Each mask was fitted so that the mouthpiece amplified the actor's voice. The actors were further equipped with padded costumes and elevated shoes (***cothurni*** or ***buskins***) that made them appear larger than life.

As a result of these adaptive conventions, Greek plays tend to emphasize words — formal, impassioned speeches — more than physical action. We are invited to ponder actions and events rather than to see all of them enacted. Although the stark simplicity of Greek theater does not offer an audience realistic detail, the classical tragedies that have survived present characters in dramatic situations that transcend theatrical conventions. Tragedy, it seems, has always been compelling for human beings, regardless of the theatrical forms it has taken.

A Greek tragedy is typically divided into five parts: prologue, parodos, episodia, stasimon, and exodus. In some translations these terms appear as headings, but in more recent translations, as those by Robert Fagles included here, the headings do not appear. Still, understanding these terms provides a sense of the overall rhythm of a Greek play. The opening speech or dialogue is known as the ***prologue*** and usually gives the exposition necessary to follow the subsequent action. In the ***parodos*** the chorus makes its first entrance and gives its perspective on what the audience has learned in the prologue. Several ***episodia,*** or episodes, follow, in which characters engage in dialogue that frequently consists of heated debates dramatizing the play's conflicts. Following each episode is a choral ode or ***stasimon,*** in which the chorus responds to and interprets the preceding dialogue. The ***exodus,*** or last scene, follows the final episode and stasimon; in it the resolution occurs and the characters leave the stage.

The effect of alternating dialogues and choral odes has sometimes been likened to that of opera. Greek tragedies were written in verse, and the stasima were chanted or sung as the chorus moved rhythmically, so the plays have a strong musical element that is not always apparent on the printed page. If we remember their musical qualities, we are less likely to forget that no matter how terrifying or horrific the conflicts they describe, these plays are stately, measured, and dignified works that reflect a classical Greek sense of order and proportion.

TRAGEDY

Newspapers are filled with daily reports of tragedies: a child is struck and crippled by a car; an airplane plunges into a suburban neighborhood; a volcano erupts and kills thousands. These unexpected instances of suffering are commonly and accurately described as tragic, but they are not tragedies in the literary sense of the term. A literary ***tragedy*** presents courageous individuals who confront powerful forces within or outside themselves with a dignity that reveals the breadth and depth of the human spirit in the face of failure, defeat, and even death.

Aristotle (384–322 B.C.), in his *Poetics,* defined *tragedy* on the basis of the plays contemporary to him. His definition has generated countless variations, qualifications, and interpretations, but we still derive our literary understanding of this term from Aristotle.

The protagonist of a Greek tragedy is someone regarded as extraordinary rather than typical: a great man or woman brought from happiness to agony. The character's stature is important because it makes his or her fall

all the more terrifying. The protagonist also carries mythic significance for the audience. Oedipus and Antigone, for example, are not only human beings but legendary figures from a distant, revered past. Although the gods do not appear onstage in either *Oedipus the King* or *Antigone,* their power is ever present as the characters invoke their help or attempt to defy them. In addition, Greek tragedy tends to be public rather than private. The fate of the community — the state — is often linked with that of the protagonist, as when Thebes suffers a plague as a result of Oedipus's mistaken actions.

The protagonists of classical Greek tragedies (and of those of Shakespeare) are often rulers of noble birth who represent the monarchical values of their periods, but in modern tragedies the protagonists are more likely to reflect democratic values that make it possible for anyone to be a suitable subject. What is finally important is not so much the protagonist's social stature as a greatness of character that steadfastly confronts suffering, whether it comes from supernatural, social, or psychological forces. Although Greek tragic heroes were aristocrats, the nobility of their characters was more significant than their inherited titles and privileges.

The protagonist's eminence and determination to complete some task or goal make him or her admirable in Greek tragedy, but that does not free the protagonist from what Aristotle described as "some error or frailty" that brings about his or her misfortune. The term Aristotle used for this weakness is *hamartia.* This word has frequently been interpreted to mean that the protagonist's fall is the result of an internal *tragic flaw,* such as an excess of pride, ambition, passion, or some other character trait that leads directly to disaster.

Sometimes, however, misfortunes are not the result of a character flaw but of misunderstood events that overtake and thwart the protagonist's best intentions. Thus, virtue can lead to tragedy too. *Hamartia* has also been interpreted to mean "wrong act" — a mistake based not on a personal failure but on circumstances outside the protagonist's personality and control. Many readers find that a combination of these two interpretations sheds the most light on the causes of the tragic protagonist's fall. Both internal and external forces can lead to downfall because the protagonist's personality may determine crucial judgments that result in mistaken actions.

However the idea of tragic flaw is understood, it is best not to use it as a means of reducing the qualities of a complex character to an adjective or two that labels Oedipus as guilty of "overweening pride" (the Greek term for which is *hubris* or *hybris*) or Antigone as "fated." The protagonists of tragedies require more careful characterization than a simplistic label can provide.

Whatever the causes of the tragic protagonist's downfall, he or she accepts responsibility for it. Hence, even in his or her encounter with failure (and possibly death) the tragic protagonist displays greatness of character.

Perhaps it is the witnessing of this greatness, which seems both to accept and to transcend human limitations, that makes audiences feel relief rather than hopelessness at the end of a tragedy. Aristotle described this response as a ***catharsis,*** or purgation of the emotions of "pity and fear." We are faced with the protagonist's misfortune, which often seems out of proportion to his or her actions, and so we are likely to feel compassionate pity. Simultaneously, we may experience fear because the failure of the protagonist, who is so great in stature and power, is a frightening reminder of our own vulnerabilities. Ultimately, however, both these negative emotions are purged because the tragic protagonist's suffering is an affirmation of human values — even if they are not always triumphant — rather than a despairing denial of them.

Nevertheless, tragedies are disturbing. Instead of coming away with the reassurance of a happy ending, we must take solace in the insight produced by the hero's suffering. And just as our expectations are changed, so are the protagonist's. Aristotle described the moment in the plot when this change occurs as a ***reversal*** (*peripeteia*), the point when the hero's fortunes turn in an unexpected direction. He more specifically defined this term as meaning an action performed by a character that has the opposite of its intended effect. An example cited by Aristotle is the messenger's attempts to relieve Oedipus's anxieties about his relationship to his father and mother. Instead, the messenger reveals previously unknown information that eventually results in a ***recognition*** (*anagnorisis*); Oedipus discovers the terrible truth that he has killed his father and married his mother.

Tragedy is typically filled with ironies because there are so many moments in the plot when what seems to be turns out to be radically different from what actually is. Because of this, a particular form of irony called ***dramatic irony*** is also known as ***tragic irony.*** In dramatic irony, the meaning of a character's words or actions is understood by the audience but not by the character. Audiences of Greek tragedy shared with the playwrights a knowledge of the stories on which many tragic plots were based. Consequently, they frequently were aware of what was going to happen before the characters were. When Oedipus declares that he will seek out the person responsible for the plague that ravishes his city, the audience already knows that the person Oedipus pursues is himself.

Oedipus the King

A familiarity with the Oedipus legend allows modern readers to appreciate the series of ironies that unfolds in Sophocles' *Oedipus the King*. In the opening scene, Oedipus appears with a "telltale limp." As an infant, he had been abandoned by his parents, Laius and Jocasta, the king and queen of Thebes, because a prophecy warned that their son would kill his father and marry his mother. They instructed a servant to leave him on a mountain to die. The infant's feet were pierced and pinned together, but he was not left on the mountain; instead the servant, out of pity, gave him to a shepherd, who in turn presented him to the king and queen of Corinth. They named him Oedipus (for "swollen foot") and raised him as their own son.

On reaching manhood, Oedipus learned from an oracle that he would kill his father and marry his mother; to avoid this horrendous fate, he left Corinth forever. In his travels, Oedipus found his way blocked by a chariot at a crossroads; in a fit of anger, he killed the servants and their passenger. That passenger, unknown to Oedipus, was his real father. In Thebes, Oedipus successfully answered the riddle of the Sphinx, a winged lion with a woman's head. The reward for defeating this dreaded monster was both the crown and the dead king's wife. Oedipus and Jocasta had four children and prospered. But when the play begins, Oedipus's rule is troubled by a plague that threatens to destroy Thebes, and he is determined to find the cause of the plague in order to save the city again.

Oedipus the King is widely recognized as the greatest of the surviving Greek tragedies. Numerous translations are available (Robert Fagles's recent highly regarded translations of *Oedipus the King* and *Antigone,* the choice here, are especially accessible to modern readers. For an excerpt from another version of *Oedipus the King,* see Perspectives on Sophocles, p. 1506). The play has absorbed readers for centuries because Oedipus's character — his intelligence, confidence, rashness, and suffering — represents powers and limitations that are both exhilarating and chastening. Although no reader or viewer is likely to identify with Oedipus's extreme circumstances, anyone can appreciate his heroic efforts to find the truth about himself. In that sense, he is one of us — at our best.

SOPHOCLES (496?–406 B.C.)

Oedipus the King   *c. 430 B.C.*

TRANSLATED BY ROBERT FAGLES

CHARACTERS

Oedipus, king of Thebes
A Priest of Zeus
Creon, brother of Jocasta
A Chorus of Theban citizens and their *Leader*
Tiresias, a blind prophet
Jocasta, the queen, wife of Oedipus
A Messenger from Corinth
A Shepherd

See Plays in Performance insert.

A Messenger from inside the palace
Antigone, Ismene, daughters of Oedipus and Jocasta
Guards and attendants
Priests of Thebes

TIME AND SCENE: The royal house of Thebes. Double doors dominate the facade;
a stone altar stands at the center of the stage.

Many years have passed since Oedipus solved the riddle of the Sphinx and
ascended the throne of Thebes, and now a plague has struck the city. A procession
of priests enters; suppliants, broken and despondent, they carry branches wound
in wool and lay them on the altar.

The doors open. Guards assemble. Oedipus comes forward, majestic but for a
telltale limp, and slowly views the condition of his people.

Oedipus: Oh my children, the new blood of ancient Thebes,
     why are you here? Huddling at my altar,
     praying before me, your branches wound in wool.°
     Our city reeks with the smoke of burning incense,
     rings with cries for the Healer and wailing for the dead.   5
     I thought it wrong, my children, to hear the truth
     from others, messengers. Here I am myself—
     you all know me, the world knows my fame:
     I am Oedipus.

          Helping a Priest to his feet.

               Speak up, old man. Your years,
     your dignity—you should speak for the others.   10
     Why here and kneeling, what preys upon you so?
     Some sudden fear? some strong desire?
     You can trust me; I am ready to help,
     I'll do anything. I would be blind to misery
     not to pity my people kneeling at my feet.   15
Priest: Oh Oedipus, king of the land, our greatest power!
     You see us before you, men of all ages
     clinging to your altars. Here are boys,
     still too weak to fly from the nest,
     and here the old, bowed down with the years,   20
     the holy ones—a priest of Zeus° myself—and here
     the picked, unmarried men, the young hope of Thebes.
     And all the rest, your great family gathers now,
     branches wreathed, massing in the squares,
     kneeling before the two temples of queen Athena°   25
     or the river-shrine where the embers glow and die
     and Apollo sees the future in the ashes.
                              Our city—

---

3 *wool:* Wool was used in offerings to Apollo, god of poetry, the sun, prophecy, and healing.
21 *Zeus:* The highest Olympian deity and father of Apollo.   25 *Athena:* Goddess of wisdom and protector of Greek cities.

look around you, see with your own eyes —
our ship pitches wildly, cannot lift her head
from the depths, the red waves of death . . .   30
Thebes is dying. A blight on the fresh crops
and the rich pastures, cattle sicken and die,
and the women die in labor, children stillborn,
and the plague, the fiery god of fever hurls down
on the city, his lightning slashing through us —   35
raging plague in all its vengeance, devastating
the house of Cadmus!° And Black Death luxuriates
in the raw, wailing miseries of Thebes.

Now we pray to you. You cannot equal the gods,
your children know that, bending at your altar.   40
But we do rate you first of men,
both in the common crises of our lives
and face-to-face encounters with the gods.
You freed us from the Sphinx; you came to Thebes
and cut us loose from the bloody tribute we had paid   45
that harsh, brutal singer. We taught you nothing,
no skill, no extra knowledge, still you triumphed.
A god was with you, so they say, and we believe it —
you lifted up our lives.
                          So now again,
Oedipus, king, we bend to you, your power —   50
we implore you, all of us on our knees:
find us strength, rescue! Perhaps you've heard
the voice of a god or something from other men,
Oedipus . . . what do you know?
The man of experience — you see it every day —   55
his plans will work in a crisis, his first of all.
Act now — we beg you, best of men, raise up our city!
Act, defend yourself, your former glory!
Your country calls you savior now
for your zeal, your action years ago.   60
Never let us remember of your reign:
you helped us stand, only to fall once more.
Oh raise up our city, set us on our feet.
The omens were good that day you brought us joy —
be the same man today!   65
Rule our land, you know you have the power,
but rule a land of the living, not a wasteland.
Ship and towered city are nothing, stripped of men
alive within it, living all as one.

Oedipus: My children,
I pity you. I see — how could I fail to see   70
what longings bring you here? Well I know
you are sick to death, all of you,

---

37 *Cadmus:* The legendary founder of Thebes.

but sick as you are, not one is sick as I.
Your pain strikes each of you alone, each
in the confines of himself, no other. But my spirit   75
grieves for the city, for myself and all of you.
I wasn't asleep, dreaming. You haven't wakened me—
I've wept through the nights, you must know that,
groping, laboring over many paths of thought.
After a painful search I found one cure: 80
I acted at once. I sent Creon,
my wife's own brother, to Delphi°—
Apollo the Prophet's oracle—to learn
what I might do or say to save our city.

Today's the day. When I count the days gone by   85
it torments me . . . what is he doing?
Strange, he's late, he's gone too long.
But once he returns, then, then I'll be a traitor
if I do not do all the god makes clear.
Priest: Timely words. The men over there   90
are signaling—Creon's just arriving.
Oedipus:

Sighting Creon, then turning to the altar.

                                        Lord Apollo,
let him come with a lucky word of rescue,
shining like his eyes!
Priest: Welcome news, I think—he's crowned, look,
and the laurel wreath is bright with berries.   95
Oedipus: We'll soon see. He's close enough to hear—

Enter Creon from the side; his face is shaded with a wreath.

Creon, prince, my kinsman, what do you bring us?
What message from the god?
Creon: Good news.
I tell you even the hardest things to bear,
if they should turn out well, all would be well.   100
Oedipus: Of course, but what were the god's *words*? There's no hope
and nothing to fear in what you've said so far.
Creon: If you want my report in the presence of these . . .

Pointing to the priests while drawing Oedipus toward the palace.

I'm ready now, or we might go inside.
Oedipus: Speak out,
speak to us all. I grieve for these, my people,   105
far more than I fear for my own life.
Creon: Very well,
I will tell you what I heard from the god.
Apollo commands us—he was quite clear—
"Drive the corruption from the land,

82 *Delphi:* The shrine where the oracle of Apollo held forth.

> don't harbor it any longer, past all cure,   110
> don't nurse it in your soil — root it out!"

Oedipus: How can we cleanse ourselves — what rites?
> What's the source of the trouble?

Creon: Banish the man, or pay back blood with blood.
> Murder sets the plague-storm on the city.

Oedipus: Whose murder?   115
> Whose fate does Apollo bring to light?

Creon: Our leader,
> my lord, was once a man named Laius,
> before you came and put us straight on course.

Oedipus: I know —
> or so I've heard. I never saw the man myself.

Creon: Well, he was killed, and Apollo commands us now —   120
> he could not be more clear,
> "Pay the killers back — whoever is responsible."

Oedipus: Where on earth are they? Where to find it now,
> the trail of the ancient guilt so hard to trace?

Creon: "Here in Thebes," he said.   125
> Whatever is sought for can be caught, you know,
> whatever is neglected slips away.

Oedipus: But where,
> in the palace, the fields or foreign soil,
> where did Laius meet his bloody death?

Creon: He went to consult an oracle, he said,   130
> and he set out and never came home again.

Oedipus: No messenger, no fellow-traveler saw what happened?
> Someone to cross-examine?

Creon: No,
> they were all killed but one. He escaped,
> terrified, he could tell us nothing clearly,   135
> nothing of what he saw — just one thing.

Oedipus: What's that?
> One thing could hold the key to it all,
> a small beginning gives us grounds for hope.

Creon: He said thieves attacked them — a whole band,
> not single-handed, cut King Laius down.

Oedipus: A thief,   140
> so daring, wild, he'd kill a king? Impossible,
> unless conspirators paid him off in Thebes.

Creon: We suspected as much. But with Laius dead
> no leader appeared to help us in our troubles.

Oedipus: Trouble? Your *king* was murdered — royal blood!   145
> What stopped you from tracking down the killer
> then and there?

Creon: The singing, riddling Sphinx.
> She . . . persuaded us to let the mystery go
> and concentrate on what lay at our feet.

Oedipus: No,
> I'll start again — I'll bring it all to light myself!   150

Apollo is right, and so are you, Creon,
to turn our attention back to the murdered man.
Now you have *me* to fight for you, you'll see:
I am the land's avenger by all rights
and Apollo's champion too.   155
But not to assist some distant kinsman, no,
for my own sake I'll rid us of this corruption.
Whoever killed the king may decide to kill me too,
with the same violent hand — by avenging Laius
I defend myself.

To the priests.

                Quickly, my children.   160
Up from the steps, take up your branches now.

To the guards.

One of you summon the city here before us,
tell them I'll do everything. God help us,
we will see our triumph — or our fall.

Oedipus and Creon enter the palace, followed by the guards.

Priest: Rise, my sons. The kindness we came for   165
Oedipus volunteers himself.
Apollo has sent his word, his oracle —
Come down, Apollo, save us, stop the plague.

The priests rise, remove their branches, and exit to the side. Enter a Chorus, the citizens of Thebes, who have not heard the news that Creon brings. They march around the altar, chanting.

Chorus: Zeus!
Great welcome voice of Zeus, what do you bring?
What word from the gold vaults of Delphi   170
comes to brilliant Thebes? I'm racked with terror —
                      terror shakes my heart
and I cry your wild cries, Apollo, Healer of Delos°
I worship you in dread . . . what now, what is your price?
some new sacrifice? some ancient rite from the past   175
come round again each spring? —
                what will you bring to birth?
Tell me, child of golden Hope
      warm voice that never dies!

You are the first I call, daughter of Zeus   180
deathless Athena — I call your sister Artemis,°
heart of the market place enthroned in glory,
                  guardian of our earth —
I call Apollo astride the thunderheads of heaven —
O triple shield against death, shine before me now!   185

173 *Delos:* Apollo was born on this sacred island.   181 *Artemis:* Apollo's sister, goddess of hunting, the moon, and chastity.

If ever, once in the past, you stopped some ruin
launched against our walls
        you hurled the flame of pain
far, far from Thebes — you gods
    come now, come down once more!

                   No, no   190
the miseries numberless, grief on grief, no end —
too much to bear, we are all dying
O my people . . .
     Thebes like a great army dying
and there is no sword of thought to save us, no   195
and the fruits of our famous earth, they will not ripen
no and the women cannot scream their pangs to birth —
screams for the Healer, children dead in the womb
       and life on life goes down
                you can watch them go   200
    like seabirds winging west, outracing the day's fire
down the horizon, irresistibly
       streaking on to the shores of Evening
                       Death
so many deaths, numberless deaths on deaths, no end —
Thebes is dying, look, her children   205
stripped of pity . . .
     generations strewn on the ground
unburied, unwept, the dead spreading death
and the young wives and gray-haired mothers with them
cling to the altars, trailing in from all over the city —   210
Thebes, city of death, one long cortege
      and the suffering rises
            wails for mercy rise
     and the wild hymn for the Healer blazes out
clashing with our sobs our cries of mourning —   215
     O golden daughter of god, send rescue
     radiant as the kindness in your eyes!
Drive him back! — the fever, the god of death
             that raging god of war
not armored in bronze, not shielded now, he burns me,   220
battle cries in the onslaught burning on —
O rout him from our borders!
Sail him, blast him out to the Sea-queen's chamber
          the black Atlantic gulfs
     or the northern harbor, death to all   225
where the Thracian surf comes crashing.
Now what the night spares he comes by day and kills —
the god of death.

       O lord of the stormcloud,
you who twirl the lightning, Zeus, Father,

thunder Death to nothing!   230

Apollo, lord of the light, I beg you —
            whip your longbow's golden cord
showering arrows on our enemies — shafts of power
champions strong before us rushing on!

Artemis, Huntress,   235
torches flaring over the eastern ridges —
                ride Death down in pain!

God of the headdress gleaming gold, I cry to you —
your name and ours are one, Dionysus° —
            come with your face aflame with wine   240
                        your raving women's cries°
            your army on the march! Come with the lightning
come with torches blazing, eyes ablaze with glory!
Burn that god of death that all gods hate!

*Oedipus enters from the palace to address the Chorus, as if addressing the entire
city of Thebes.*

Oedipus: You pray to the gods? Let me grant your prayers.   245
        Come, listen to me — do what the plague demands:
        you'll find relief and lift your head from the depths.

        I will speak out now as a stranger to the story,
        a stranger to the crime. If I'd been present then,
        there would have been no mystery, no long hunt   250
        without a clue in hand. So now, counted
        a native Theban years after the murder,
        to all of Thebes I make this proclamation:
        if any one of you knows who murdered Laius,
        the son of Labdacus, I order him to reveal   255
        the whole truth to me. Nothing to fear,
        even if he must denounce himself,
        let him speak up
        and so escape the brunt of the charge —
        he will suffer no unbearable punishment,   260
        nothing worse than exile, totally unharmed.

        Oedipus pauses, waiting for a reply.

                                Next,
        if anyone knows the murderer is a stranger,
        a man from alien soil, come, speak up.
        I will give him a handsome reward, and lay up
        gratitude in my heart for him besides.   265

---

239 *Dionysus:* God of fertility and wine.   241 *your . . . cries:* Dionysus was attended by
female celebrants.

Silence again, no reply.

But if you keep silent, if anyone panicking,
trying to shield himself or friend or kin,
rejects my offer, then hear what I will do.
I order you, every citizen of the state
where I hold throne and power: banish this man —   270
whoever he may be — never shelter him, never
speak a word to him, never make him partner
to your prayers, your victims burned to the gods.
Never let the holy water touch his hands.
Drive him out, each of you, from every home.   275
He is the plague, the heart of our corruption,
as Apollo's oracle has revealed to me
just now. So I honor my obligations:
I fight for the god and for the murdered man.

Now my curse on the murderer. Whoever he is,   280
a lone man unknown in his crime
or one among many, let that man drag out
his life in agony, step by painful step —
I curse myself as well . . . if by any chance
he proves to be an intimate of our house,   285
here at my hearth, with my full knowledge,
may the curse I just called down on him strike me!

These are your orders: perform them to the last.
I command you, for my sake, for Apollo's, for this country
blasted root and branch by the angry heavens.   290
Even if god had never urged you on to act,
how could you leave the crime uncleansed so long?
A man so noble — your king, brought down in blood —
you should have searched. But I am the king now,
I hold the throne that he held then, possess his bed   295
and a wife who shares our seed . . . why, our seed
might be the same, children born of the same mother
might have created blood-bonds between us
if his hope of offspring hadn't met disaster —
but fate swooped at his head and cut him short.   300
So I will fight for him as if he were my father,
stop at nothing, search the world
to lay my hands on the man who shed his blood,
the son of Labdacus descended of Polydorus,
Cadmus of old and Agenor, founder of the line: 305
their power and mine are one.
                              Oh dear gods,
my curse on those who disobey these orders!
Let no crops grow out of the earth for them —
shrivel their women, kill their sons,
burn them to nothing in this plague   310

that hits us now, or something even worse.
But you, loyal men of Thebes who approve my actions,
may our champion, Justice, may all the gods
be with us, fight beside us to the end!

Leader: In the grip of your curse, my king, I swear   315
I'm not the murderer, cannot point him out.
As for the search, Apollo pressed it on us —
he should name the killer.

Oedipus: Quite right,
but to force the gods to act against their will —
no man has the power.

Leader: Then if I might mention   320
the next best thing . . .

Oedipus: The third best too —
don't hold back, say it.

Leader: I still believe . . .
Lord Tiresias sees with the eyes of Lord Apollo.
Anyone searching for the truth, my king,
might learn it from the prophet, clear as day.   325

Oedipus: I've not been slow with that. On Creon's cue
I sent the escorts, twice, within the hour.
I'm surprised he isn't here.

Leader: We need him —
without him we have nothing but old, useless rumors.

Oedipus: Which rumors? I'll search out every word.   330

Leader: Laius was killed, they say, by certain travelers.

Oedipus: I know — but no one can find the murderer.

Leader: If the man has a trace of fear in him
he won't stay silent long,
not with your curses ringing in his ears.   335

Oedipus: He didn't flinch at murder,
he'll never flinch at words.

*Enter Tiresias, the blind prophet, led by a boy with escorts in attendance. He
remains at a distance.*

Leader: Here is the one who will convict him, look,
they bring him on at last, the seer, the man of god.
The truth lives inside him, him alone.

Oedipus: O Tiresias,   340
master of all the mysteries of our life,
all you teach and all you dare not tell,
signs in the heavens, signs that walk the earth!
Blind as you are, you can feel all the more
what sickness haunts our city. You, my lord,   345
are the one shield, the one savior we can find.

We asked Apollo — perhaps the messengers
haven't told you — he sent his answer back:
"Relief from the plague can only come one way.
Uncover the murderers of Laius,   350

put them to death or drive them into exile."
So I beg you, grudge us nothing now, no voice,
no message plucked from the birds, the embers
or the other mantic ways within your grasp.
Rescue yourself, your city, rescue me —   355
rescue everything infected by the dead.
We are in your hands. For a man to help others
with all his gifts and native strength:
that is the noblest work.

Tiresias: How terrible — to see the truth
when the truth is only pain to him who sees!   360
I knew it well, but I put it from my mind,
else I never would have come.

Oedipus: What's this? Why so grim, so dire?

Tiresias: Just send me home. You bear your burdens,
I'll bear mine. It's better that way,   365
please believe me.

Oedipus: Strange response — unlawful,
unfriendly too to the state that bred and raised you;
you're withholding the word of god.

Tiresias: I fail to see
that your own words are so well-timed.
I'd rather not have the same thing said of me . . .   370

Oedipus: For the love of god, don't turn away,
not if you know something. We beg you,
all of us on our knees.

Tiresias: None of you knows —
and I will never reveal my dreadful secrets,
not to say your own.   375

Oedipus: What? You know and you won't tell?
You're bent on betraying us, destroying Thebes?

Tiresias: I'd rather not cause pain for you or me.
So why this . . . useless interrogation?
You'll get nothing from me.

Oedipus: Nothing! You,   380
you scum of the earth, you'd enrage a heart of stone!
You won't talk? Nothing moves you?
Out with it, once and for all!

Tiresias: You criticize my temper . . . unaware
of the one *you* live with, you revile me.   385

Oedipus: Who could restrain his anger hearing you?
What outrage — you spurn the city!

Tiresias: What will come will come.
Even if I shroud it all in silence.

Oedipus: What will come? You're bound to *tell* me that. 390

Tiresias: I'll say no more. Do as you like, build your anger
to whatever pitch you please, rage your worst —

Oedipus: Oh I'll let loose, I have such fury in me —
now I see it all. You helped hatch the plot,
you did the work, yes, short of killing him   395

with your own hands — and given eyes I'd say
you did the killing single-handed!
Tiresias: Is that so!
I charge you, then, submit to that decree
you just laid down: from this day onward
speak to no one, not these citizens, not myself.   400
You are the curse, the corruption of the land!
Oedipus: You, shameless —
aren't you appalled to start up such a story?
You think you can get away with this?
Tiresias: I have already.
The truth with all its power lives inside me.   405
Oedipus: Who primed you for this? Not your prophet's trade.
Tiresias: You did, you forced me, twisted it out of me.
Oedipus: What? Say it again — I'll understand it better.
Tiresias: Didn't you understand, just now?
Or are you tempting me to talk?   410
Oedipus: No, I can't say I grasped your meaning.
Out with it, again!
Tiresias: I say you are the murderer you hunt.
Oedipus: That obscenity, twice — by god, you'll pay.
Tiresias: Shall I say more, so you can really rage?   415
Oedipus: Much as you want. Your words are nothing — futile.
Tiresias: You cannot imagine . . . I tell you,
you and your loved ones live together in infamy,
you cannot see how far you've gone in guilt.
Oedipus: You think you can keep this up and never suffer?   420
Tiresias: Indeed, if the truth has any power.
Oedipus: It does
but not for you, old man. You've lost your power,
stone-blind, stone-deaf — senses, eyes blind as stone!
Tiresias: I pity you, flinging at me the very insults
each man here will fling at you so soon.
Oedipus: Blind,   425
lost in the night, endless night that nursed you!
You can't hurt me or anyone else who sees the light —
you can never touch me.
Tiresias: True, it is not your fate
to fall at my hands. Apollo is quite enough,
and he will take some pains to work this out.   430
Oedipus: Creon! Is this conspiracy his or yours?
Tiresias: Creon is not your downfall, no, you are your own.
Oedipus: O power —
wealth and empire, skill outstripping skill
in the heady rivalries of life,
what envy lurks inside you! Just for this,   435
the crown the city gave me — I never sought it,
they laid it in my hands — for this alone, Creon,
the soul of trust, my loyal friend from the start
steals against me . . . so hungry to overthrow me

he sets this wizard on me, this scheming quack,   440
this fortune-teller peddling lies, eyes peeled
for his own profit — seer blind in his craft!

Come here, you pious fraud. Tell me,
when did you ever prove yourself a prophet?
When the Sphinx, that chanting Fury kept her deathwatch here,   445
why silent then, not a word to set our people free?
There was a riddle, not for some passer-by to solve —
it cried out for a prophet. Where were you?
Did you rise to the crisis? Not a word,
you and your birds, your gods — nothing.   450
No, but I came by, Oedipus the ignorant,
I stopped the Sphinx! With no help from the birds,
the flight of my own intelligence hit the mark.

And this is the man you'd try to overthrow?
You think you'll stand by Creon when he's king?
You and the great mastermind —   455
you'll pay in tears, I promise you, for this,
this witch-hunt. If you didn't look so senile
the lash would teach you what your scheming means!
Leader: I'd suggest his words were spoken in anger,   460
Oedipus . . . yours too, and it isn't what we need.
The best solution to the oracle, the riddle
posed by god — we should look for that.
Tiresias: You are the king no doubt, but in one respect,
at least, I am your equal: the right to reply.   465
I claim that privilege too.
I am not your slave. I serve Apollo.
I don't need Creon to speak for me in public.
                                                      So,
you mock my blindness? Let me tell you this.
You with your precious eyes,   470
you're blind to the corruption of your life,
to the house you live in, those you live with —
who *are* your parents? Do you know? All unknowing
you are the scourge of your own flesh and blood,
the dead below the earth and the living here above,   475
and the double lash of your mother and your father's curse
will whip you from this land one day, their footfall
treading you down in terror, darkness shrouding
your eyes that now can see the light!
                                         Soon, soon
you'll scream aloud — what haven won't reverberate?   480
What rock of Cithaeron° won't scream back in echo?
That day you learn the truth about your marriage,
the wedding-march that sang you into your halls,
the lusty voyage home to the fatal harbor!

481 *Cithaeron:* The mountains where Oedipus was abandoned as an infant.

And a load of other horrors you'd never dream   485
will level you with yourself and all your children.

There. Now smear us with insults — Creon, myself
and every word I've said. No man will ever
be rooted from the earth as brutally as you.
Oedipus: Enough! Such filth from him? Insufferable —   490
what, still alive? Get out —
faster, back where you came from — vanish!
Tiresias: I'd never have come if you hadn't called me here.
Oedipus: If I thought you'd blurt out such absurdities,
you'd have died waiting before I'd had you summoned.   495
Tiresias: Absurd, am I? To you, not to your parents:
the ones who bore you found me sane enough.
Oedipus: Parents — who? Wait . . . who is my father?
Tiresias: This day will bring your birth and your destruction.
Oedipus: Riddles — all you can say are riddles, murk and darkness.   500
Tiresias: Ah, but aren't you the best man alive at solving riddles?
Oedipus: Mock me for that, go on, and you'll reveal my greatness.
Tiresias: Your great good fortune, true, it was your ruin.
Oedipus: Not if I saved the city — what do I care?
Tiresias: Well then, I'll be going.

> *To his attendant.*

                                      Take me home, boy.   505
Oedipus: Yes, take him away. You're a nuisance here.
Out of the way, the irritation's gone.

> *Turning his back on Tiresias, moving toward the palace.*

Tiresias: I will go,
once I have said what I came here to say.
I'll never shrink from the anger in your eyes —
you can't destroy me. Listen to me closely: 510
the man you've sought so long, proclaiming,
cursing up and down, the murderer of Laius —
he is here. A stranger,
you may think, who lives among you,
he soon will be revealed a native Theban   515
but he will take no joy in the revelation.
Blind who now has eyes, beggar who now is rich,
he will grope his way toward a foreign soil,
a stick tapping before him step by step.

> *Oedipus enters the palace.*

Revealed at last, brother and father both   520
to the children he embraces, to his mother
son and husband both — he sowed the loins
his father sowed, he spilled his father's blood!

Go in and reflect on that, solve that.
And if you find I've lied   525

from this day onward call the prophet blind.

Tiresias and the boy exit to the side.

Chorus: Who —
   who is the man the voice of god denounces
   resounding out of the rocky gorge of Delphi?
      The horror too dark to tell,
   whose ruthless bloody hands have done the work?   530
   His time has come to fly
      to outrace the stallions of the storm
         his feet a streak of speed —
   Cased in armor, Apollo son of the Father
   lunges on him, lightning-bolts afire!   535
   And the grim unerring Furies°
      closing for the kill.

             Look,
   the word of god has just come blazing
   flashing off Parnassus'° snowy heights!
      That man who left no trace —   540
   after him, hunt him down with all our strength!
   Now under bristling timber
      up through rocks and caves he stalks
         like the wild mountain bull —
   cut off from men, each step an agony, frenzied, racing blind   545
   but he cannot outrace the dread voices of Delphi
   ringing out of the heart of Earth,
      the dark wings beating around him shrieking doom
         the doom that never dies, the terror —

   The skilled prophet scans the birds and shatters me with terror!   550
   I can't accept him, can't deny him, don't know what to say,
   I'm lost, and the wings of dark foreboding beating —
   I cannot see what's come, what's still to come . . .
   and what could breed a blood feud between
      Laius' house and the son of Polybus?°
   I know of nothing, not in the past and not now,   555
   no charge to bring against our king, no cause
   to attack his fame that rings throughout Thebes —
      not without proof — not for the ghost of Laius,
      not to avenge a murder gone without a trace.   560

   Zeus and Apollo know, they know, the great masters
      of all the dark and depth of human life.
   But whether a mere man can know the truth,
   whether a seer can fathom more than I —
   there is no test, no certain proof   565
      though matching skill for skill
   a man can outstrip a rival. No, not till I see

---

536 *Furies:* Three spirits who avenged evildoers.   539 *Parnassus:* A mountain in Greece associated with Apollo.   555 *Polybus:* The King of Corinth, who is thought to be Oedipus's father.

these charges proved will I side with his accusers.
We saw him then, when the she-hawk° swept against him,
saw with our own eyes his skill, his brilliant triumph — 570
  there was the test — he was the joy of Thebes!
  Never will I convict my king, never in my heart.

Enter Creon from the side.

Creon: My fellow-citizens, I hear King Oedipus
  levels terrible charges at me. I had to come.
  I resent it deeply. If, in the present crisis, 575
  he thinks he suffers any abuse from me,
  anything I've done or said that offers him
  the slightest injury, why, I've no desire
  to linger out this life, my reputation a shambles.
  The damage I'd face from such an accusation 580
  is nothing simple. No, there's nothing worse:
  branded a traitor in the city, a traitor
  to all of you and my good friends.
Leader: True,
  but a slur might have been forced out of him,
  by anger perhaps, not any firm conviction. 585
Creon: The charge was made in public, wasn't it?
  I put the prophet up to spreading lies?
Leader: Such things were said . . .
  I don't know with what intent, if any.
Creon: Was his glance steady, his mind right 590
  when the charge was brought against me?
Leader: I really couldn't say. I never look
  to judge the ones in power.

The doors open. Oedipus enters.

                      Wait,
  here's Oedipus now.
Oedipus: You — here? You have the gall
  to show your face before the palace gates? 595
  You, plotting to kill me, kill the king —
  I see it all, the marauding thief himself
  scheming to steal my crown and power!
                              Tell me,
  in god's name, what did you take me for,
  coward or fool, when you spun out your plot? 600
  Your treachery — you think I'd never detect it
  creeping against me in the dark? Or sensing it,
  not defend myself? Aren't you the fool,
  you and your high adventure. Lacking numbers,
  powerful friends, out for the big game of empire — 605
  you need riches, armies to bring that quarry down!
Creon: Are you quite finished? It's your turn to listen
  for just as long as you've . . . instructed me.
  Hear me out, then judge me on the facts.

569 *she-hawk:* The Sphinx.

Oedipus: You've a wicked way with words, Creon,   610
    but I'll be slow to learn — from you.
    I find you a menace, a great burden to me.
Creon: Just one thing, hear me out in this.
Oedipus: Just one thing,
    don't tell me you're not the enemy, the traitor.
Creon: Look, if you think crude, mindless stubbornness   615
    such a gift, you've lost your sense of balance.
Oedipus: If you think you can abuse a kinsman,
    then escape the penalty, you're insane.
Creon: Fair enough, I grant you. But this injury
    you say I've done you, what is it?   620
Oedipus: Did you induce me, yes or no,
    to send for that sanctimonious prophet?
Creon: I did. And I'd do the same again.
Oedipus: All right then, tell me, how long is it now
    since Laius . . .
Creon: Laius — what did *he* do?
Oedipus: Vanished,   625
    swept from sight, murdered in his tracks.
Creon: The count of the years would run you far back . . .
Oedipus: And that far back, was the prophet at his trade?
Creon: Skilled as he is today, and just as honored.
Oedipus: Did he ever refer to me then, at that time?
Creon: No,   630
    never, at least, when I was in his presence.
Oedipus: But you did investigate the murder, didn't you?
Creon: We did our best, of course, discovered nothing.
Oedipus: But the great seer never accused me then — why not?
Creon: I don't know. And when I don't, *I* keep quiet.   635
Oedipus: You do know this, you'd tell it too —
    if you had a shred of decency.
Creon: What?
    If I know, I won't hold back.
Oedipus: Simply this:
    if the two of you had never put heads together,
    we'd never have heard about *my* killing Laius.   640
Creon: If that's what he says . . . well, you know best.
    But now I have a right to learn from you
    as you just learned from me.
Oedipus: Learn your fill,
    you never will convict me of the murder.
Creon: Tell me, you're married to my sister, aren't you?   645
Oedipus: A genuine discovery — there's no denying that.
Creon: And you rule the land with her, with equal power?
Oedipus: She receives from me whatever she desires.
Creon: And I am the third, all of us are equals?
Oedipus: Yes, and it's there you show your stripes —   650
    you betray a kinsman.
Creon: Not at all.
    Not if you see things calmly, rationally,

as I do. Look at it this way first:
who in his right mind would rather rule
and live in anxiety than sleep in peace?   655
Particularly if he enjoys the same authority.
Not I, I'm not the man to yearn for kingship,
not with a king's power in my hands. Who would?
No one with any sense of self-control.
Now, as it is, you offer me all I need,   660
not a fear in the world. But if I wore the crown . . .
there'd be many painful duties to perform,
hardly to my taste.
                    How could kingship
please me more than influence, power
without a qualm? I'm not that deluded yet,   665
to reach for anything but privilege outright,
profit free and clear.
Now all men sing my praises, all salute me,
now all who request your favors curry mine.
I'm their best hope: success rests in me.   670
Why give up that, I ask you, and borrow trouble?
A man of sense, someone who sees things clearly
would never resort to treason.
No, I've no lust for conspiracy in me,
nor could I ever suffer one who does.   675

Do you want proof? Go to Delphi yourself,
examine the oracle and see if I've reported
the message word-for-word. This too:
if you detect that I and the clairvoyant
have plotted anything in common, arrest me,   680
execute me. Not on the strength of one vote,
two in this case, mine as well as yours.
But don't convict me on sheer unverified surmise.

How wrong it is to take the good for bad,
purely at random, or take the bad for good.   685
But reject a friend, a kinsman? I would as soon
tear out the life within us, priceless life itself.
You'll learn this well, without fail, in time.
Time alone can bring the just man to light;
the criminal you can spot in one short day.
Leader: Good advice,   690
    my lord, for anyone who wants to avoid disaster.
    Those who jump to conclusions may be wrong.
Oedipus: When my enemy moves against me quickly,
    plots in secret, I move quickly too, I must,
    I plot and pay him back. Relax my guard a moment,   695
    waiting his next move — he wins his objective,
    I lose mine.
Creon: What do you want?
    You want me banished?

Oedipus: No, I want you dead.
Creon: Just to show how ugly a grudge can . . .
Oedipus: So,
    still stubborn? you don't think I'm serious?   700
Creon: I think you're insane.
Oedipus: Quite sane — in my behalf.
Creon: Not just as much in mine?
Oedipus: You — my mortal enemy?
Creon: What if you're wholly wrong?
Oedipus: No matter — I must rule.
Creon: Not if you rule unjustly.
Oedipus: Hear him, Thebes, my city!
Creon: My city too, not yours alone!   705
Leader: Please, my lords.

    Enter Jocasta from the palace.

                    Look, Jocasta's coming,
        and just in time too. With her help
        you must put this fighting of yours to rest.
Jocasta: Have you no sense? Poor misguided men,
    such shouting — why this public outburst?   710
    Aren't you ashamed, with the land so sick,
    to stir up private quarrels?

    To Oedipus.

    Into the palace now. And Creon, you go home.
    Why make such a furor over nothing?
Creon: My sister, it's dreadful . . . Oedipus, your husband,   715
    he's bent on a choice of punishments for me,
    banishment from the fatherland or death.
Oedipus: Precisely. I caught him in the act, Jocasta,
    plotting, about to stab me in the back.
Creon: Never — curse me, let me die and be damned   720
    if I've done you any wrong you charge me with.
Jocasta: Oh god, believe it, Oedipus,
    honor the solemn oath he swears to heaven.
    Do it for me, for the sake of all your people.

    The Chorus begins to chant.

Chorus: Believe it, be sensible   725
    give way, my king, I beg you!
Oedipus: What do you want from me, concessions?
Chorus: Respect him — he's been no fool in the past
    and now he's strong with the oath he swears to god.
Oedipus: You know what you're asking?
Chorus: I do.
Oedipus: Then out with it!   730
Chorus: The man's your friend, your kin, he's under oath —
    don't cast him out, disgraced
    branded with guilt on the strength of hearsay only.

Oedipus: Know full well, if that's what you want
    you want me dead or banished from the land.
Chorus: Never—   735
    no, by the blazing Sun, first god of the heavens!
      Stripped of the gods, stripped of loved ones,
    let me die by inches if that ever crossed my mind.
    But the heart inside me sickens, dies as the land dies
    and now on top of the old griefs you pile this,   740
    your fury—both of you!
Oedipus: Then let him go,
    even if it does lead to my ruin, my death
    or my disgrace, driven from Thebes for life.
    It's you, not him I pity—your words move me.
    He, wherever he goes, my hate goes with him.   745
Creon: Look at you, sullen in yielding, brutal in your rage—
    you'll go too far. It's perfect justice:
    natures like yours are hardest on themselves.
Oedipus: Then leave me alone—get out!
Creon: I'm going.
    You're wrong, so wrong. These men know I'm right.   750

    Exit to the side. The Chorus turns to Jocasta.

Chorus: Why do you hesitate, my lady
      why not help him in?
Jocasta: Tell me what's happened first.
Chorus: Loose, ignorant talk started dark suspicions
    and a sense of injustice cut deeply too.   755
Jocasta: On both sides?
Chorus: Oh yes.
Jocasta: What did they say?
Chorus: Enough, please, enough! The land's so racked already
    or so it seems to me . . .
    End the trouble here, just where they left it.
Oedipus: You see what comes of your good intentions now?   760
    And all because you tried to blunt my anger.
Chorus: My king,
    I've said it once, I'll say it time and again—
      I'd be insane, you know it,
    senseless, ever to turn my back on you.
    You who set our beloved land—storm-tossed, shattered—   765
    straight on course. Now again, good helmsman,
    steer us through the storm!

    The Chorus draws away, leaving Oedipus and Jocasta side by side.

Jocasta: For the love of god,
    Oedipus, tell me too, what is it?
    Why this rage? You're so unbending.
Oedipus: I will tell you. I respect you, Jocasta,   770
    much more than these . . .

    Glancing at the Chorus.

Creon's to blame, Creon schemes against me.
Jocasta: Tell me clearly, how did the quarrel start?
Oedipus: He says *I* murdered Laius — I am guilty.
Jocasta: How does he know? Some secret knowledge   775
    or simple hearsay?
Oedipus: Oh, he sent his prophet in
    to do his dirty work. You know Creon,
    Creon keeps his own lips clean.
Jocasta: A prophet?
    Well then, free yourself of every charge!
    Listen to me and learn some peace of mind: 780
    no skill in the world,
    nothing human can penetrate the future.
    Here is proof, quick and to the point.
    An oracle came to Laius one fine day
    (I won't say from Apollo himself   785
    but his underlings, his priests) and it said
    that doom would strike him down at the hands of a son,
    our son, to be born of our own flesh and blood. But Laius,
    so the report goes at least, was killed by strangers,
    thieves, at a place where three roads meet . . . my son —   790
    he wasn't three days old and the boy's father
    fastened his ankles, had a henchman fling him away
    on a barren, trackless mountain.
                              There, you see?
    Apollo brought neither thing to pass. My baby
    no more murdered his father than Laius suffered —   795
    his wildest fear — death at his own son's hands.
    That's how the seers and their revelations
    mapped out the future. Brush them from your mind.
    Whatever the god needs and seeks
    he'll bring to light himself, with ease.
Oedipus: Strange,   800
    hearing you just now . . . my mind wandered,
    my thoughts racing back and forth.
Jocasta: What do you mean? Why so anxious, startled?
Oedipus: I thought I heard you say that Laius
    was cut down at a place where three roads meet.   805
Jocasta: That was the story. It hasn't died out yet.
Oedipus: Where did this thing happen? Be precise.
Jocasta: A place called Phocis, where two branching roads,
    one from Daulia, one from Delphi,
    come together — a crossroads.   810
Oedipus: When? How long ago?
Jocasta: The heralds no sooner reported Laius dead
    than you appeared and they hailed you king of Thebes.
Oedipus: My god, my god — what have you planned to do to me?
Jocasta: What, Oedipus? What haunts you so?
Oedipus: Not yet.   815
    Laius — how did he look? Describe him.

Had he reached his prime?
Jocasta: He was swarthy,
    and the gray had just begun to streak his temples,
    and his build . . . wasn't far from yours.
Oedipus: Oh no no,
    I think I've just called down a dreadful curse   820
    upon myself—I simply didn't know!
Jocasta: What are you saying? I shudder to look at you.
Oedipus: I have a terrible fear the blind seer can see.
    I'll know in a moment. One thing more—
Jocasta: Anything,
    afraid as I am—ask, I'll answer, all I can.   825
Oedipus: Did he go with a light or heavy escort,
    several men-at-arms, like a lord, a king?
Jocasta: There were five in the party, a herald among them,
    and a single wagon carrying Laius.
Oedipus: Ai—
    now I can see it all, clear as day.   830
    Who told you all this at the time, Jocasta?
Jocasta: A servant who reached home, the lone survivor.
Oedipus: So, could he still be in the palace—even now?
Jocasta: No indeed. Soon as he returned from the scene
    and saw you on the throne with Laius dead and gone,   835
    he knelt and clutched my hand, pleading with me
    to send him into the hinterlands, to pasture,
    far as possible, out of sight of Thebes.
    I sent him away. Slave though he was,
    he'd earned that favor—and much more.   840
Oedipus: Can we bring him back, quickly?
Jocasta: Easily. Why do you want him so?
Oedipus: I'm afraid,
    Jocasta, I have said too much already.
    That man—I've got to see him.
Jocasta: Then he'll come.
    But even I have a right, I'd like to think,   845
    to know what's torturing you, my lord.
Oedipus: And so you shall—I can hold nothing back from you,
    now I've reached this pitch of dark foreboding.
    Who means more to me than you? Tell me,
    whom would I turn toward but you   850
    as I go through all this?

    My father was Polybus, king of Corinth.
    My mother, a Dorian, Merope. And I was held
    the prince of the realm among the people there,
    till something struck me out of nowhere,   855
    something strange . . . worth remarking perhaps,
    hardly worth the anxiety I gave it.
    Some man at a banquet who had drunk too much
    shouted out—he was far gone, mind you—

that I am not my father's son. Fighting words! 860
I barely restrained myself that day
but early the next I went to mother and father,
questioned them closely, and they were enraged
at the accusation and the fool who let it fly.
So as for my parents I was satisfied, 865
but still this thing kept gnawing at me,
the slander spread — I had to make my move.

                          And so,
unknown to mother and father I set out for Delphi,
and the god Apollo spurned me, sent me away
denied the facts I came for, 870
but first he flashed before my eyes a future
great with pain, terror, disaster — I can hear him cry,
"You are fated to couple with your mother, you will bring
a breed of children into the light no man can bear to see —
you will kill your father, the one who gave you life!" 875
I heard all that and ran. I abandoned Corinth,
from that day on I gauged its landfall only
by the stars, running, always running
toward some place where I would never see
the shame of all those oracles come true. 880
And as I fled I reached that very spot
where the great king, you say, met his death.
Now, Jocasta, I will tell you all.
Making my way toward this triple crossroad
I began to see a herald, then a brace of colts 885
drawing a wagon, and mounted on the bench . . . a man,
just as you've described him, coming face-to-face,
and the one in the lead and the old man himself
were about to thrust me off the road — brute force —
and the one shouldering me aside, the driver, 890
I strike him in anger! — and the old man, watching me
coming up along his wheels — he brings down
his prod, two prongs straight at my head!
I paid him back with interest!
Short work, by god — with one blow of the staff 895
in this right hand I knock him out of his high seat,
roll him out of the wagon, sprawling headlong —
I killed them all — every mother's son!

Oh, but if there is any blood-tie
between Laius and this stranger . . . 900
what man alive more miserable than I?
More hated by the gods? *I* am the man
no alien, no citizen welcomes to his house,
law forbids it — not a word to me in public,
driven out of every hearth and home. 905
And all these curses I — no one but I
brought down these piling curses on myself!

And you, his wife, I've touched your body with these,
the hands that killed your husband cover you with blood.

Wasn't I born for torment? Look me in the eyes!   910
I am abomination — heart and soul!
I must be exiled, and even in exile
never see my parents, never set foot
on native earth again. Else I'm doomed
to couple with my mother and cut my father down . . .   915
Polybus who reared me, gave me life.
                                    But why, why?
Wouldn't a man of judgment say — and wouldn't he be right —
some savage power has brought this down upon my head?

Oh no, not that, you pure and awesome gods,
never let me see that day! Let me slip   920
from the world of men, vanish without a trace
before I see myself stained with such corruption,
stained to the heart.
Leader: My lord, you fill our hearts with fear.
But at least until you question the witness,   925
do take hope.
Oedipus: Exactly. He is my last hope —
I'm waiting for the shepherd. He is crucial.
Jocasta: And once he appears, what then? Why so urgent?
Oedipus: I'll tell you. If it turns out that his story
matches yours, I've escaped the worst.   930
Jocasta: What did I say? What struck you so?
Oedipus: You said *thieves* —
he told you a whole band of them murdered Laius.
So, if he still holds to the same number,
I cannot be the killer. One can't equal many.
But if he refers to one man, one alone,   935
clearly the scales come down on me:
I am guilty.
Jocasta: Impossible. Trust me,
I told you precisely what he said,
and he can't retract it now;
the whole city heard it, not just I.   940
And even if he should vary his first report
by one man more or less, still, my lord,
he could never make the murder of Laius
truly fit the prophecy. Apollo was explicit:
my son was doomed to kill my husband . . . my son,   945
poor defenseless thing, he never had a chance
to kill his father. They destroyed him first.

So much for prophecy. It's neither here nor there.
From this day on, I wouldn't look right or left.
Oedipus: True, true. Still, that shepherd,   950

someone fetch him — now!
Jocasta: I'll send at once. But do let's go inside.
    I'd never displease you, least of all in this.

Oedipus and Jocasta enter the palace.

Chorus: Destiny guide me always
    Destiny find me filled with reverence   955
        pure in word and deed.
    Great laws tower above us, reared on high
    born for the brilliant vault of heaven —
        Olympian sky their only father,
    nothing mortal, no man gave them birth,   960
    their memory deathless, never lost in sleep:
    within them lives a mighty god, the god does not grow old.

    Pride breeds the tyrant
    violent pride, gorging, crammed to bursting
        with all that is overripe and rich with ruin —   965
    clawing up to the heights, headlong pride
    crashes down the abyss — sheer doom!
        No footing helps, all foothold lost and gone,
    But the healthy strife that makes the city strong —
    I pray that god will never end that wrestling: 970
    god, my champion, I will never let you go.

    But if any man comes striding, high and mighty
        in all he says and does,
    no fear of justice, no reverence
    for the temples of the gods —   975
        let a rough doom tear him down,
    repay his pride, breakneck, ruinous pride!
    If he cannot reap his profits fairly
        cannot restrain himself from outrage —
    mad, laying hands on the holy things untouchable!   980

        Can such a man, so desperate, still boast
        he can save his life from the flashing bolts of god?
        If all such violence goes with honor now
        why join the sacred dance?

    Never again will I go reverent to Delphi,   985
        the inviolate heart of Earth
    or Apollo's ancient oracle at Abae
    or Olympia of the fires —
        unless these prophecies all come true
    for all mankind to point toward in wonder.   990
    King of kings, if you deserve your titles
        Zeus, remember, never forget!
    You and your deathless, everlasting reign.

        They are dying, the old oracles sent to Laius,
        now our masters strike them off the rolls.   995

Nowhere Apollo's golden glory now —
the gods, the gods go down.

Enter Jocasta from the palace, carrying a suppliant's branch wound in wool.

Jocasta: Lords of the realm, it occurred to me,
just now, to visit the temples of the gods,
so I have my branch in hand and incense too. 1000
Oedipus is beside himself. Racked with anguish,
no longer a man of sense, he won't admit
the latest prophecies are hollow as the old —
he's at the mercy of every passing voice
if the voice tells of terror. 1005
I urge him gently, nothing seems to help,
so I turn to you, Apollo, you are nearest.

*Placing her branch on the altar, while an old herdsman enters from the side,
not the one just summoned by the king but an unexpected messenger from
Corinth.*

I come with prayers and offerings . . . I beg you,
cleanse us, set us free of defilement!
Look at us, passengers in the grip of fear, 1010
watching the pilot of the vessel go to pieces.

Messenger:

Approaching Jocasta and the Chorus.

Strangers, please, I wonder if you could lead us
to the palace of the king . . . I think it's Oedipus.
Better, the man himself — you know where he is?

Leader: This is his palace, stranger. He's inside. 1015
But here is his queen, his wife and mother
of his children.

Messenger: Blessings on you, noble queen,
queen of Oedipus crowned with all your family —
blessings on you always!

Jocasta: And the same to you, stranger, you deserve it . . . 1020
such a greeting. But what have you come for?
Have you brought us news?

Messenger: Wonderful news —
for the house, my lady, for your husband too.

Jocasta: Really, what? Who sent you?

Messenger: Corinth.
I'll give you the message in a moment. 1025
You'll be glad of it — how could you help it? —
though it costs a little sorrow in the bargain.

Jocasta: What can it be, with such a double edge?

Messenger: The people there, they want to make your Oedipus
king of Corinth, so they're saying now. 1030

Jocasta: Why? Isn't old Polybus still in power?

Messenger: No more. Death has got him in the tomb.

Jocasta: What are you saying? Polybus, dead? — dead?

Messenger: If not,
if I'm not telling the truth, strike me dead too.

Jocasta:

> *To a servant.*

> Quickly, go to your master, tell him this! 1035

> You prophecies of the gods, where are you now?
> This is the man that Oedipus feared for years,
> he fled him, not to kill him — and now he's dead,
> quite by chance, a normal, natural death,
> not murdered by his son.

Oedipus:

> *Emerging from the palace.*

> Dearest,
> what now? Why call me from the palace? 1040

Jocasta:

> *Bringing the Messenger closer.*

> Listen to *him*, see for yourself what all
> those awful prophecies of god have come to.

Oedipus: And who is he? What can he have for me?

Jocasta: He's from Corinth, he's come to tell you 1045
> your father is no more — Polybus — he's dead!

Oedipus:

> *Wheeling on the Messenger.*

> What? Let me have it from your lips.

Messenger: Well,
> if that's what you want first, then here it is:
> make no mistake, Polybus is dead and gone.

Oedipus: How — murder? sickness? — what? what killed him? 1050

Messenger: A light tip of the scales can put old bones to rest.

Oedipus: Sickness then — poor man, it wore him down.

Messenger: That,
> and the long count of years he'd measured out.

Oedipus: So!
> Jocasta, why, why look to the Prophet's hearth,
> the fires of the future? Why scan the birds 1055
> that scream above our heads? They winged me on
> to the murder of my father, did they? That was my doom?
> Well look, he's dead and buried, hidden under the earth,
> and here I am in Thebes, I never put hand to sword —
> unless some longing for me wasted him away, 1060
> then in a sense you'd say I caused his death.
> But now, all those prophecies I feared — Polybus
> packs them off to sleep with him in hell!
> They're nothing, worthless.

Jocasta: There.
> Didn't I tell you from the start? 1065

Oedipus: So you did. I was lost in fear.

Jocasta: No more, sweep it from your mind forever.

Oedipus: But my mother's bed, surely I must fear—
Jocasta: Fear?
    What should a man fear? It's all chance,
    chance rules our lives. Not a man on earth   1070
    can see a day ahead, groping through the dark.
    Better to live at random, best we can.
    And as for this marriage with your mother—
    have no fear. Many a man before you,
    in his dreams, has shared his mother's bed.   1075
    Take such things for shadows, nothing at all—
    Live, Oedipus,
    as if there's no tomorrow!
Oedipus: Brave words,
    and you'd persuade me if mother weren't alive.
    But mother lives, so for all your reassurances   1080
    I live in fear, I must.
Jocasta: But your father's death,
    that, at least, is a great blessing, joy to the eyes!
Oedipus: Great, I know . . . but I fear *her*—she's still alive.
Messenger: Wait, who is this woman, makes you so afraid?
Oedipus: Merope, old man. The wife of Polybus.   1085
Messenger: The queen? What's there to fear in her?
Oedipus: A dreadful prophecy, stranger, sent by the gods.
Messenger: Tell me, could you? Unless it's forbidden
    other ears to hear.
Oedipus: Not at all.
    Apollo told me once—it is my fate—   1090
    I must make love with my own mother,
    shed my father's blood with my own hands.
    So for years I've given Corinth a wide berth,
    and it's been my good fortune too. But still,
    to see one's parents and look into their eyes   1095
    is the greatest joy I know.
Messenger: You're afraid of that?
    That kept you out of Corinth?
Oedipus: My *father*, old man—
    so I wouldn't kill my father.
Messenger: So that's it.
    Well then, seeing I came with such good will, my king,
    why don't I rid you of that old worry now?   1100
Oedipus: What a rich reward you'd have for that.
Messenger: What do you think I came for, majesty?
    So you'd come home and I'd be better off.
Oedipus: Never, I will never go near my parents.
Messenger: My boy, it's clear, you don't know what you're doing.   1105
Oedipus: What do you mean, old man? For god's sake, explain.
Messenger: If you ran from *them*, always dodging home . . .
Oedipus: Always, terrified Apollo's oracle might come true—
Messenger: And you'd be covered with guilt, from both your parents.
Oedipus: That's right, old man, that fear is always with me.   1110
Messenger: Don't you know? You've really nothing to fear.

Oedipus: But why? If I'm their son—Merope, Polybus?
Messenger: Polybus was nothing to you, that's why, not in blood.
Oedipus: What are you saying—Polybus was not my father?
Messenger: No more than I am. He and I are equals.
Oedipus: My father—   1115
    how can my father equal nothing? You're nothing to me!
Messenger: Neither was he, no more your father than I am.
Oedipus: Then why did he call me his son?
Messenger: You were a gift,
    years ago—know for a fact he took you
    from my hands.
Oedipus: No, from another's hands?   1120
    Then how could he love me so? He loved me, deeply . . .
Messenger: True, and his early years without a child
    made him love you all the more.
Oedipus: And you, did you . . .
    buy me? find me by accident?
Messenger: I stumbled on you,
    down the woody flanks of Mount Cithaeron.
Oedipus: So close,   1125
    what were you doing here, just passing through?
Messenger: Watching over my flocks, grazing them on the slopes.
Oedipus: A herdsman, were you? A vagabond, scraping for wages?
Messenger: Your savior too, my son, in your worst hour.
Oedipus: Oh—
    when you picked me up, was I in pain? What exactly?   1130
Messenger: Your ankles . . . they tell the story. Look at them.
Oedipus: Why remind me of that, that old affliction?
Messenger: Your ankles were pinned together; I set you free.
Oedipus: That dreadful mark—I've had it from the cradle.
Messenger: And you got your name from that misfortune too,   1135
    the name's still with you.
Oedipus: Dear god, who did it?—
    mother? father? Tell me.
Messenger: I don't know.
    The one who gave you to me, he'd know more.
Oedipus: What? You took me from someone else?
    You didn't find me yourself?
Messenger: No sir,   1140
    another shepherd passed you on to me.
Oedipus: Who? Do you know? Describe him.
Messenger: He called himself a servant of . . . .
    if I remember rightly—Laius.

    Jocasta turns sharply.

Oedipus: The king of the land who ruled here long ago?   1145
Messenger: That's the one. That herdsman was *his* man.
Oedipus: Is he still alive? Can I see him?
Messenger: They'd know best, the people of these parts.

    Oedipus and the Messenger turn to the Chorus.

Oedipus: Does anyone know that herdsman,
    the one he mentioned? Anyone seen him   1150
    in the fields, in town? Out with it!
    The time has come to reveal this once for all.
Leader: I think he's the very shepherd you wanted to see,
    a moment ago. But the queen, Jocasta,
    she's the one to say.
Oedipus: Jocasta,   1155
    you remember the man we just sent for?
    Is *that* the one he means?
Jocasta: That man . . .
    why ask? Old shepherd, talk, empty nonsense,
    don't give it another thought, don't even think —
Oedipus: What — give up now, with a clue like this?   1160
    Fail to solve the mystery of my birth?
    Not for all the world!
Jocasta: Stop — in the name of god,
    if you love your own life, call off this search!
    My suffering is enough.
Oedipus: Courage!
    Even if my mother turns out to be a slave,   1165
    and I a slave, three generations back,
    you would not seem common.
Jocasta: Oh no,
    listen to me, I beg you, don't do this.
Oedipus: Listen to you? No more. I must know it all,
    see the truth at last.
Jocasta: No, please —   1170
    for your sake — I want the best for you!
Oedipus: Your best is more than I can bear.
Jocasta: You're doomed —
    may you never fathom who you are!
Oedipus:

    To a servant.

    Hurry, fetch me the herdsman, now!
    Leave her to glory in her royal birth.   1175
Jocasta: Aieeeeee —
                man of agony —
    that is the only name I have for you,
    that, no other — ever, ever, ever!

    Flinging (herself) through the palace doors. A long, tense silence follows.

Leader: Where's she gone, Oedipus?
    Rushing off, such wild grief . . .   1180
    I'm afraid that from this silence
    something monstrous may come bursting forth.
Oedipus: Let it burst! Whatever will, whatever must!
    I must know my birth, no matter how common
    it may be — must see my origins face-to-face.   1185
    She perhaps, she with her woman's pride

may well be mortified by my birth,
but I, I count myself the son of Chance,
the great goddess, giver of all good things —
I'll never see myself disgraced. She is my mother!   1190
And the moons have marked me out, my blood-brothers,
one moon on the wane, the next moon great with power.
That is my blood, my nature — I will never betray it,
never fail to search and learn my birth!

Chorus: Yes — if I am a true prophet   1195
      if I can grasp the truth,
    by the boundless skies of Olympus,
at the full moon of tomorrow, Mount Cithaeron
you will know how Oedipus glories in you —
you, his birthplace, nurse, his mountain-mother!   1200
And we will sing you, dancing out your praise —
you lift our monarch's heart!
      Apollo, Apollo, god of the wild cry
        may our dancing please you!
                      Oedipus —
      son, dear child, who bore you?   1205
Who of the nymphs who seem to live forever
mated with Pan,° the mountain-striding Father?
Who was your mother? who, some bride of Apollo
the god who loves the pastures spreading toward the sun?
      Or was it Hermes, king of the lightning ridges?   1210
Or Dionysus, lord of frenzy, lord of the barren peaks —
did he seize you in his hands, dearest of all his lucky finds? —
      found by the nymphs, their warm eyes dancing, gift
to the lord who loves them dancing out his joy!

*Oedipus strains to see a figure coming from the distance. Attended by palace
guards, an old Shepherd enters slowly, reluctant to approach the king.*

Oedipus: I never met the man, my friends . . . still,   1215
if I had to guess, I'd say that's the shepherd,
the very one we've looked for all along.
Brothers in old age, two of a kind,
he and our guest here. At any rate
the ones who bring him in are my own men,   1220
I recognize them.

Turning to the Leader.

           But you know more than I,
you should, you've seen the man before.

Leader: I know him, definitely. One of Laius' men,
a trusty shepherd, if there ever was one.

Oedipus: You, I ask you first, stranger,   1225
      you from Corinth — is this the one you mean?

Messenger: You're looking at him. He's your man.

1207 *Pan:* God of shepherds, who was, like Hermes and Dionysus, associated with the
wilderness.

Oedipus:

> *To the Shepherd.*

> You, old man, come over here —
> look at me. Answer all my questions.
> Did you ever serve King Laius?

Shepherd: So I did . . .   1230
> a slave, not bought on the block though,
> born and reared in the palace.

Oedipus: Your duties, your kind of work?

Shepherd: Herding the flocks, the better part of my life.

Oedipus: Where, mostly? Where did you do your grazing?

Shepherd: Well,   1235
> Cithaeron sometimes, or the foothills round about.

Oedipus: This man — you know him? ever see him there?

Shepherd:

> *Confused, glancing from the Messenger to the King.*

> Doing what — what man do you mean?

Oedipus:

> *Pointing to the Messenger.*

> This one here — ever have dealings with him?

Shepherd: Not so I could say, but give me a chance,   1240
> my memory's bad . . .

Messenger: No wonder he doesn't know me, master.
> But let me refresh his memory for him.
> I'm sure he recalls old times we had
> on the slopes of Mount Cithaeron;   1245
> he and I, grazing our flocks, he with two
> and I with one — we both struck up together,
> three whole seasons, six months at a stretch
> from spring to the rising of Arcturus° in the fall,
> then with winter coming on I'd drive my herds   1250
> to my own pens, and back he'd go with his
> to Laius' folds.

> *To the Shepherd.*

>   Now that's how it was,
> wasn't it — yes or no?

Shepherd: Yes, I suppose . . .
> it's all so long ago.

Messenger: Come, tell me,
> you gave me a child back then, a boy, remember?   1255
> A little fellow to rear, my very own.

Shepherd: What? Why rake up that again?

Messenger: Look, here he is, my fine old friend —
> the same man who was just a baby then.

Shepherd: Damn you, shut your mouth — quiet!   1260

1249 *Arcturus:* A star whose rising marked the end of summer.

Oedipus: Don't lash out at him, old man —
  you need lashing more than he does.
Shepherd: Why,
  master, majesty — what have I done wrong?
Oedipus: You won't answer his question about the boy.
Shepherd: He's talking nonsense, wasting his breath.   1265
Oedipus: So, you won't talk willingly —
  then you'll talk with pain.

  The guards seize the Shepherd.

Shepherd: No, dear god, don't torture an old man!
Oedipus: Twist his arms back, quickly!
Shepherd: God help us, why? —
  what more do you need to know?   1270
Oedipus: Did you give him that child? He's asking.
Shepherd: I did . . . I wish to god I'd died that day.
Oedipus: You've got your wish if you don't tell the truth.
Shepherd: The more I tell, the worse the death I'll die.
Oedipus: Our friend here wants to stretch things out, does he?   1275

  Motioning to his men for torture.

Shepherd: No, no, I gave it to him — I just said so.
Oedipus: Where did you get it? Your house? Someone else's?
Shepherd: It wasn't mine, no, I got it from . . . someone.
Oedipus: Which one of them?

  Looking at the citizens.

                        Whose house?
Shepherd: No —
  god's sake, master, no more questions!   1280
Oedipus: You're a dead man if I have to ask again.
Shepherd: Then — the child came from the house . . .
  of Laius.
Oedipus: A slave? or born of his own blood?
Shepherd: Oh no,
  I'm right at the edge, the horrible truth — I've got to say it!
Oedipus: And I'm at the edge of hearing horrors, yes, but I must hear!   1285
Shepherd: All right! His son, they said it was — his son!
  But the one inside, your wife,
  she'd tell it best.
Oedipus: My wife —
  she gave it to you?   1290
Shepherd: Yes, yes, my king.
Oedipus: Why, what for?
Shepherd: To kill it.
Oedipus: Her own child,
  how could she?   1295
Shepherd: She was afraid —
  frightening prophecies.
Oedipus: What?

Shepherd: They said—
        he'd kill his parents.   1300
Oedipus: But you gave him to this old man—why?
Shepherd: I pitied the little baby, master,
        hoped he'd take him off to his own country,
        far away, but he saved him for this, this fate.
        If you are the man he says you are, believe me,   1305
        you were born for pain.
Oedipus: O god—
        all come true, all burst to light!
        O light—now let me look my last on you!
        I stand revealed at last—
        cursed in my birth, cursed in marriage,   1310
        cursed in the lives I cut down with these hands!

*Rushing through the doors with a great cry. The Corinthian Messenger, the
Shepherd, and attendants exit slowly to the side.*

Chorus: O the generations of men
        the dying generations—adding the total
        of all your lives I find they come to nothing . . .
                        does there exist, is there a man on earth   1315
        who seizes more joy than just a dream, a vision?
        And the vision no sooner dawns than dies
        blazing into oblivion.

        You are my great example, you, your life,
        your destiny, Oedipus, man of misery—   1320
        I count no man blest.

                        You outranged all men!
                Bending your bow to the breaking-point
        you captured priceless glory, O dear god,
        and the Sphinx came crashing down,
                        the virgin, claws hooked   1325
        like a bird of omen singing, shrieking death—
        like a fortress reared in the face of death
        you rose and saved our land.

        From that day on we called you king
        we crowned you with honors, Oedipus, towering over all—   1330
        mighty king of the seven gates of Thebes.

        But now to hear your story—is there a man more agonized?
        More wed to pain and frenzy? Not a man on earth,
        the joy of your life ground down to nothing
        O Oedipus, name for the ages—   1335
                one and the same wide harbor served you
                                son and father both
        son and father came to rest in the same bridal chamber.
        How, how could the furrows your father plowed
        bear you, your agony, harrowing on   1340
        in silence O so long?

But now for all your power
Time, all-seeing Time has dragged you to the light,
judged your marriage monstrous from the start —
the son and the father tangling, both one —
O child of Laius, would to god   1345
    I'd never seen you, never never!
        Now I weep like a man who wails the dead
and the dirge comes pouring forth with all my heart!
I tell you the truth, you gave me life
my breath leapt up in you   1350
and now you bring down night upon my eyes.

Enter a Messenger from the palace.

Messenger: Men of Thebes, always the first in honor,
    what horrors you will hear, what you will see,
    what a heavy weight of sorrow you will shoulder . . .
    if you are true to your birth, if you still have   1355
    some feeling for the royal house of Thebes.
    I tell you neither the waters of the Danube
    nor the Nile can wash this palace clean.
    Such things it hides, it soon will bring to light —
    terrible things, and none done blindly now,   1360
    all done with a will. The pains
    we inflict upon ourselves hurt most of all.
Leader: God knows we have pains enough already.
    What can you add to them?
Messenger: The queen is dead.
Leader: Poor lady — how?   1365
Messenger: By her own hand. But you are spared the worst,
    you never had to watch . . . I saw it all,
    and with all the memory that's in me
    you will learn what that poor woman suffered.

    Once she'd broken in through the gates,   1370
    dashing past us, frantic, whipped to fury,
    ripping her hair out with both hands —
    straight to her rooms she rushed, flinging herself
    across the bridal-bed, doors slamming behind her —
    once inside, she wailed for Laius, dead so long,   1375
    remembering how she bore his child long ago,
    the life that rose up to destroy him, leaving
    its mother to mother living creatures
    with the very son she'd borne.
    Oh how she wept, mourning the marriage-bed   1380
    where she let loose that double brood — monsters —
    husband by her husband, children by her child.
                    And then —
    but how she died is more than I can say. Suddenly
    Oedipus burst in, screaming, he stunned us so
    we couldn't watch her agony to the end,   1385
    our eyes were fixed on him. Circling

like a maddened beast, stalking, here, there
crying out to us —
                     Give him a sword! His wife,
no wife, his mother, where can he find the mother earth
that cropped two crops at once, himself and all his children?   1390
He was raging — one of the dark powers pointing the way,
none of us mortals crowding around him, no,
with a great shattering cry — someone, something leading him on —
he hurled at the twin doors and bending the bolts back
out of their sockets, crashed through the chamber.   1395
And there we saw the woman hanging by the neck,
cradled high in a woven noose, spinning,
swinging back and forth. And when he saw her,
giving a low, wrenching sob that broke our hearts,
slipping the halter from her throat, he eased her down,   1400
in a slow embrace he laid her down, poor thing . . .
then, what came next, what horror we beheld!

He rips off her brooches, the long gold pins
holding her robes — and lifting them high,
looking straight up into the points,   1405
he digs them down the sockets of his eyes, crying, "You,
you'll see no more the pain I suffered, all the pain I caused!
Too long you looked on the ones you never should have seen,
blind to the ones you longed to see, to know! Blind
from this hour on! Blind in the darkness — blind!"   1410
His voice like a dirge, rising, over and over
raising the pins, raking them down his eyes.
And at each stroke blood spurts from the roots,
splashing his beard, a swirl of it, nerves and clots —
black hail of blood pulsing, gushing down.   1415

These are the griefs that burst upon them both,
coupling man and woman. The joy they had so lately,
the fortune of their old ancestral house
was deep joy indeed. Now, in this one day,
wailing, madness and doom, death, disgrace,   1420
all the griefs in the world that you can name,
all are theirs forever.
Leader: Oh poor man, the misery —
has he any rest from pain now?

A voice within, in torment.

Messenger: He's shouting,
"Loose the bolts, someone, show me to all of Thebes!
My father's murderer, my mother's —"   1425
No, I can't repeat it, it's unholy.
Now he'll tear himself from his native earth,
not linger, curse the house with his own curse.
But he needs strength, and a guide to lead him on.
This is sickness more than he can bear.

The palace doors open.

Look, 1430
he'll show you himself. The great doors are opening —
you are about to see a sight, a horror
even his mortal enemy would pity.

Enter Oedipus, blinded, led by a boy. He stands at the palace steps, as if surveying his people once again.

Chorus: O the terror —
the suffering, for all the world to see,
the worst terror that ever met my eyes. 1435
What madness swept over you? What god,
what dark power leapt beyond all bounds,
beyond belief, to crush your wretched life? —
godforsaken, cursed by the gods!
I pity you but I can't bear to look. 1440
I've much to ask, so much to learn,
so much fascinates my eyes,
but you . . . I shudder at the sight.

Oedipus: Oh, Ohhh —
the agony! I am agony —
where am I going? where on earth? 1445
where does all this agony hurl me?
where's my voice? —
winging, swept away on a dark tide —
My destiny, my dark power, what a leap you made!

Chorus: To the depths of terror, too dark to hear, to see. 1450

Oedipus: Dark, horror of darkness
my darkness, drowning, swirling around me
crashing wave on wave — unspeakable, irresistible
headwind, fatal harbor! Oh again,
the misery, all at once, over and over 1455
the stabbing daggers, stab of memory
raking me insane.

Chorus: No wonder you suffer
twice over, the pain of your wounds,
the lasting grief of pain.

Oedipus: Dear friend, still here?
Standing by me, still with a care for me, 1460
the blind man? Such compassion,
loyal to the last. Oh it's you,
I know you're here, dark as it is
I'd know you anywhere, your voice —
it's yours, clearly yours.

Chorus: Dreadful, what you've done . . . 1465
how could you bear it, gouging out your eyes?
What superhuman power drove you on?

Oedipus: Apollo, friends, Apollo —
he ordained my agonies — these, my pains on pains!
But the hand that struck my eyes was mine, 1470

                    mine alone — no one else —
                              I did it all myself!
              What good were eyes to me?
              Nothing I could see could bring me joy.
Chorus: No, no, exactly as you say.
Oedipus: What can I ever see?   1475
              What love, what call of the heart
              can touch my ears with joy? Nothing, friends.
                  Take me away, far, far from Thebes,
                  quickly, cast me away, my friends —
          this great murderous ruin, this man cursed to heaven,   1480
              the man the deathless gods hate most of all!
Chorus: Pitiful, you suffer so, you understand so much . . .
              I wish you'd never known.
Oedipus: Die, die —
              whoever he was that day in the wilds
          who cut my ankles free of the ruthless pins,   1485
              he pulled me clear of death, he saved my life
              for this, this kindness —
                          Curse him, kill him!
              If I'd died then, I'd never have dragged myself,
              my loved ones through such hell.   1490
Chorus: Oh if only . . . would to god.
Oedipus: I'd never have come to this,
                  my father's murderer — never been branded
              mother's husband, all men see me now! Now,
                  loathed by the gods, son of the mother I defiled
                  coupling in my father's bed, spawning lives in the loins   1495
          that spawned my wretched life. What grief can crown this grief?
                          It's mine alone, my destiny — I am Oedipus!
Chorus: How can I say you've chosen for the best?
              Better to die than be alive and blind.
Oedipus: What I did was best — don't lecture me,   1500
              no more advice. I, with *my* eyes,
              how could I look my father in the eyes
              when I go down to death? Or mother, so abused . . .
              I've done such things to the two of them,
              crimes too huge for hanging.
                          Worse yet,   1505
              the sight of my children, born as they were born,
              how could I long to look into their eyes?
              No, not with these eyes of mine, never.
              Not this city either, her high towers,
              the sacred glittering images of her gods —   1510
              I am misery! I, her best son, reared
              as no other son of Thebes was ever reared,
              I've stripped myself, I gave the command myself.
              All men must cast away the great blasphemer,
              the curse now brought to light by the gods,   1515
              the son of Laius — I, my father's son!

Now I've exposed my guilt, horrendous guilt,
could I train a level glance on you, my countrymen?
Impossible! No, if I could just block off my ears,
the springs of hearing, I would stop at nothing — 1520
I'd wall up my loathsome body like a prison,
blind to the sound of life, not just the sight.
Oblivion — what a blessing . . .
for the mind to dwell a world away from pain.

O Cithaeron, why did you give me shelter? 1525
Why didn't you take me, crush my life out on the spot?
I'd never have revealed my birth to all mankind.

O Polybus, Corinth, the old house of my fathers,
so I believed — what a handsome prince you raised —
under the skin, what sickness to the core. 1530
Look at me! Born of outrage, outrage to the core.

O triple roads — it all comes back, the secret,
dark ravine, and the oaks closing in
where the three roads join . . .
You drank my father's blood, my own blood 1535
spilled by my own hands — you still remember me?
What things you saw me do? Then I came here
and did them all once more!

       Marriages! O marriage,
you gave me birth, and once you brought me into the world
you brought my sperm rising back, springing to light 1540
fathers, brothers, sons — one deadly breed —
brides, wives, mothers. The blackest things
a man can do, I have done them all!

        No more —
it's wrong to name what's wrong to do. Quickly,
for the love of god, hide me somewhere, 1545
kill me, hurl me into the sea
where you can never look on me again.

Beckoning to the Chorus as they shrink away.

        Closer,
it's all right. Touch the man of sorrow.
Do. Don't be afraid. My troubles are mine
and I am the only man alive who can sustain them. 1550

Enter Creon from the palace, attended by palace guards.

Leader: Put your requests to Creon. Here he is,
 just when we need him. He'll have a plan, he'll act.
 Now that he's the sole defense of the country
 in your place.
Oedipus: Oh no, what can I say to him?
 How can I ever hope to win his trust? 1555
 I wronged him so, just now, in every way.
 You must see that — I was so wrong, so wrong.

Creon: I haven't come to mock you, Oedipus,
or to criticize your former failings.

Turning to the guards.

                              You there,
have you lost all respect for human feeling?   1560
At least revere the Sun, the holy fire
that keeps us all alive. Never expose a thing
of guilt and holy dread so great it appalls
the earth, the rain from heaven, the light of day!
Get him into the halls — quickly as you can.   1565
Piety demands no less. Kindred alone
should see a kinsman's shame. This is obscene.

Oedipus: Please, in god's name . . . you wipe my fears away,
coming so generously to me, the worst of men.
Do one thing more, for your sake, not mine.   1570

Creon: What do you want? Why so insistent?

Oedipus: Drive me out of the land at once, far from sight,
where I can never hear a human voice.

Creon: I'd have done that already, I promise you.
First I wanted the god to clarify my duties.   1575

Oedipus: The god? His command was clear, every word:
death for the father-killer, the curse —
he said destroy me!

Creon: So he did. Still, in such a crisis
it's better to ask precisely what to do.   1580

Oedipus: You'd ask the oracle about a man like me?

Creon: By all means. And this time, I assume,
even you will obey the god's decrees.

Oedipus: I will,
I will. And you, I command you — I beg you . . .
the woman inside, bury her as you see fit.   1585
It's the only decent thing,
to give your own the last rites. As for me,
never condemn the city of my fathers
to house my body, not while I'm alive, no,
let me live on the mountains, on Cithaeron,   1590
my favorite haunt, I have made it famous.
Mother and father marked out that rock
to be my everlasting tomb — buried alive.
Let me die there, where they tried to kill me.
Oh but this I know: no sickness can destroy me,   1595
nothing can. I would never have been saved
from death — I have been saved
for something great and terrible, something strange.
Well let my destiny come and take me on its way!

About my children, Creon, the boys at least,   1600
don't burden yourself. They're men;
wherever they go, they'll find the means to live.
But my two daughters, my poor helpless girls,

clustering at our table, never without me
hovering near them . . . whatever I touched,   1605
they always had their share. Take care of them,
I beg you. Wait, better — permit me, would you?
Just to touch them with my hands and take
our fill of tears. Please . . . my king.
Grant it, with all your noble heart.   1610
If I could hold them, just once, I'd think
I had them with me, like the early days
when I could see their eyes.

Antigone and Ismene, two small children, are led in from the palace by a nurse.

                    What's that?
O god! Do I really hear you sobbing? —
my two children. Creon, you've pitied me?   1615
Sent me my darling girls, my own flesh and blood!
Am I right?
Creon: Yes, it's my doing.
I know the joy they gave you all these years,
the joy you must feel now.
Oedipus: Bless you, Creon!
May god watch over you for this kindness,   1620
better than he ever guarded me.
                              Children, where are you?
Here, come quickly —

*Groping for Antigone and Ismene, who approach their father cautiously, then
embrace him.*

                    Come to these hands of mine,
your brother's hands, your own father's hands
that served his once bright eyes so well —
that made them blind. Seeing nothing, children,   1625
knowing nothing, I became your father,
I fathered you in the soil that gave me life.

How I weep for you — I cannot see you now . . .
just thinking of all your days to come, the bitterness,
the life that rough mankind will thrust upon you.   1630
Where are the public gatherings you can join,
the banquets of the clans? Home you'll come,
in tears, cut off from the sight of it all,
the brilliant rites unfinished.
And when you reach perfection, ripe for marriage,   1635
who will he be, my dear ones? Risking all
to shoulder the curse that weighs down my parents,
yes and you too — that wounds us all together.
What more misery could you want?
Your father killed his father, sowed his mother,   1640
one, one and the selfsame womb sprang you —
he cropped the very roots of his existence.

Such disgrace, and you must bear it all!
Who will marry you then? Not a man on earth.
Your doom is clear: you'll wither away to nothing,   1645
single, without a child.

Turning to Creon.

                        Oh Creon,
you are the only father they have now . . .
we who brought them into the world
are gone, both gone at a stroke —
Don't let them go begging, abandoned,   1650
women without men. Your own flesh and blood!
Never bring them down to the level of my pains.
Pity them. Look at them, so young, so vulnerable,
shorn of everything — you're their only hope.
Promise me, noble Creon, touch my hand.   1655

Reaching toward Creon, who draws back.

You, little ones, if you were old enough
to understand, there is much I'd tell you.
Now, as it is, I'd have you say a prayer.
Pray for life, my children,
live where you are free to grow and season.   1660
Pray god you find a better life than mine,
the father who begot you.
Creon: Enough.
You've wept enough. Into the palace now.
Oedipus: I must, but I find it very hard.
Creon: Time is the great healer, you will see.   1665
Oedipus: I am going — you know on what condition?
Creon: Tell me. I'm listening.
Oedipus: Drive me out of Thebes, in exile.
Creon: Not I. Only the gods can give you that.
Oedipus: Surely the gods hate me so much —   1670
Creon: You'll get your wish at once.
Oedipus: You consent?
Creon: I try to say what I mean; it's my habit.
Oedipus: Then take me away. It's time.
Creon: Come along, let go of the children.
Oedipus: No —
don't take them away from me, not now! No no no!   1675

*Clutching his daughters as the guards wrench them loose and take them
through the palace doors.*

Creon: Still the king, the master of all things?
No more: here your power ends.
None of your power follows you through life.

*Exit Oedipus and Creon to the palace. The Chorus comes forward to address
the audience directly.*

Chorus: People of Thebes, my countrymen, look on Oedipus.
He solved the famous riddle with his brilliance, 1680
he rose to power, a man beyond all power.
Who could behold his greatness without envy?
Now what a black sea of terror has overwhelmed him.
Now as we keep our watch and wait the final day,
count no man happy till he dies, free of pain at last. 1685

Exit in procession.

CONSIDERATIONS FOR CRITICAL THINKING AND WRITING

1. **FIRST RESPONSE.** Is it possible for a twenty-first-century reader to identify with Oedipus's plight? What philosophic issues does he confront?

2. In the opening scene what does the priest's speech reveal about how Oedipus has been regarded as a ruler of Thebes?

3. What do Oedipus's confrontations with Tiresias and Creon indicate about his character?

4. Aristotle defined a tragic flaw as consisting of "error and frailties." What errors does Oedipus make? What are his frailties?

5. What causes Oedipus's downfall? Is he simply a pawn in a predetermined game played by the gods? Can he be regarded as responsible for the suffering and death in the play?

6. Locate instances of dramatic irony in the play. How do they serve as foreshadowings?

7. Describe the function of the Chorus. How does the Chorus's view of life and the gods differ from Jocasta's?

8. Trace the images of vision and blindness throughout the play. How are they related to the theme? Why does Oedipus blind himself instead of joining Jocasta in suicide?

9. What is your assessment of Oedipus at the end of the play? Was he foolish? Heroic? Fated? To what extent can your emotions concerning him be described as "pity and fear"?

10. **CRITICAL STRATEGIES.** Read the section on psychological criticism (pp. 2050–52) in Chapter 53, "Critical Strategies for Reading," and Sigmund Freud's "On the Oedipus Complex" (p. 1504). Given that the *Oedipus complex* is a well-known term used in psychoanalysis, what does it mean? Does the concept offer any insights into the conflicts dramatized in the play?

CONNECTIONS TO OTHER SELECTIONS

1. Consider the endings of *Oedipus the King* and Shakespeare's *Hamlet* (p. 1585). What feelings do you have about these endings? Are they irredeemably unhappy? Is there anything that suggests hope for the future at the ends of these plays?

2. Sophocles does not include violence in his plays; any bloodshed occurs offstage. Compare and contrast the effects of this strategy with the use of violence in *Hamlet*.

3. Write an essay explaining why *Oedipus the King* cannot be considered a realistic play in the way that Henrik Ibsen's *A Doll House* (p. 1709) can be.

Antigone

Antigone was actually written before Sophocles' other two plays about Oedipus and his family. *Oedipus the King* ends with Oedipus, the king of Thebes, blinding himself because he has unknowingly murdered his father and married his mother, Jocasta. Creon, his brother-in-law, becomes the ruler of Thebes and is entrusted with caring for Oedipus's two daughters, Antigone and Ismene. *Oedipus at Colonus* continues the story some twenty years later. Oedipus has been rejected by his two sons, Polynices and Eteocles, and wanders in exile, cared for by Antigone. Meanwhile, his sons struggle for power in Thebes. Polynices travels to Argos to gather a force to attack his brother as Oedipus arrives in Colonus, near Athens. There Oedipus curses his sons for their ruthless selfishness and predicts their violent deaths. Oedipus, however, dies in peace, with dignity, and bestows a blessing on Athens.

Antigone begins after the two brothers have killed each other in battle. The throne of Thebes subsequently returns to Creon, who decrees that Polynices was traitorous and therefore must not be buried. As the play opens, Antigone tells her sister that she will defy Creon's ruling, even though the penalty for disobedience is death.

Antigone's insistence on obeying the law of the gods instead of civil laws dramatizes a conflict that continues to move audiences and readers who ponder the relation of the individual's conscience to the demands of the state. One manifestation of this concern in the twentieth century was Jean Anouilh's 1944 production of *Antigone* in Paris, when that city was occupied by German troops during World War II. Anouilh's Antigone reflects the French resistance movement, and his Creon is a representative of German authority who must preserve order in the face of unyielding opposition. (A brief excerpt of this play appears on p. 1509.) Sophocles' play — as does Anouilh's — presents an agonizing dilemma. Neither Antigone nor Creon is wholly virtuous or blameless, so the complexities they embody remain a moral and intellectual challenge.

[Web] Explore contexts for Sophocles and approaches to this play at bedfordstmartins.com/meyerlit.

Sophocles (496?–406 B.C.)

Antigone   *c. 441 B.C.*

TRANSLATED BY ROBERT FAGLES

CHARACTERS

Antigone, daughter of Oedipus and Jocasta
Ismene, sister of Antigone
A *Chorus* of old Theban citizens and their *Leader*
Creon, king of Thebes, uncle of Antigone and
        Ismene

See Plays in Performance insert.

A Sentry
Haemon, son of Creon and Eurydice
Tiresias, a blind prophet
A Messenger
Eurydice, wife of Creon
Guards, attendants, and a boy

TIME AND SCENE: The royal house of Thebes. It is still night, and the invading armies of Argos have just been driven from the city. Fighting on opposite sides, the sons of Oedipus, Eteocles and Polynices, have killed each other in combat. Their uncle, Creon, is now king of Thebes.

Enter Antigone, slipping through the central doors of the palace. She motions to her sister, Ismene, who follows her cautiously toward an altar at the center of the stage.

Antigone: My own flesh and blood — dear sister, dear Ismene,
    how many griefs our father Oedipus handed down!
    Do you know one, I ask you, one grief
    that Zeus° will not perfect for the two of us
    while we still live and breathe? There's nothing,   5
    no pain — our lives are pain — no private shame,
    no public disgrace, nothing I haven't seen
    in your griefs and mine. And now this:
    an emergency decree, they say, the Commander
    has just declared for all of Thebes.   10
    What, haven't you heard? Don't you see?
    The doom reserved for enemies
    marches on the ones we love the most.
Ismene: Not I, I haven't heard a word, Antigone.
    Nothing of loved ones,   15
    no joy or pain has come my way, not since
    the two of us were robbed of our two brothers,
    both gone in a day, a double blow —
    not since the armies of Argos vanished,
    just this very night. I know nothing more,   20
    whether our luck's improved or ruin's still to come.
Antigone: I thought so. That's why I brought you out here,
    past the gates, so you could hear in private.
Ismene: What's the matter? Trouble, clearly . . .
    you sound so dark, so grim.   25
Antigone: Why not? Our own brothers' burial!
    Hasn't Creon graced one with all the rites,
    disgraced the other? Eteocles, they say,
    has been given full military honors,
    rightly so — Creon's laid him in the earth   30
    and he goes with glory down among the dead.
    But the body of Polynices, who died miserably —
    why, a city-wide proclamation, rumor has it,

4 *Zeus:* The highest Olympian deity.

forbids anyone to bury him, even mourn him.
He's to be left unwept, unburied, a lovely treasure   35
for birds that scan the field and feast to their heart's content.

Such, I hear, is the martial law our good Creon
lays down for you and me — yes, me, I tell you —
and he's coming here to alert the uninformed
in no uncertain terms,   40
and he won't treat the matter lightly. Whoever
disobeys in the least will die, his doom is sealed:
stoning to death inside the city walls!

There you have it. You'll soon show what you are,
worth your breeding, Ismene, or a coward —   45
for all your royal blood.
Ismene: My poor sister, if things have come to this,
who am I to make or mend them, tell me,
what good am I to you?
Antigone: Decide.
Will you share the labor, share the work?   50
Ismene: What work, what's the risk? What do you mean?
Antigone:

    Raising her hands.

Will you lift up his body with these bare hands
and lower it with me?
Ismene: What? You'd bury him —
when a law forbids the city?
Antigone: Yes!
He is my brother and — deny it as you will —   55
your brother too.
No one will ever convict me for a traitor.
Ismene: So desperate, and Creon has expressly —
Antigone: No,
he has no right to keep me from my own.
Ismene: Oh my sister, think —   60
think how our own father died, hated,
his reputation in ruins, driven on
by the crimes he brought to light himself
to gouge out his eyes with his own hands —
then mother . . . his mother and wife, both in one,   65
mutilating her life in the twisted noose —
and last, our two brothers dead in a single day,
both shedding their own blood, poor suffering boys,
battling out their common destiny hand-to-hand.

Now look at the two of us, left so alone . . .   70
think what a death we'll die, the worst of all
if we violate the laws and override
the fixed decree of the throne, its power —
we must be sensible. Remember we are women,

we're not born to contend with men. Then too,   75
we're underlings, ruled by much stronger hands,
so we must submit in this, and things still worse.

I, for one, I'll beg the dead to forgive me —
I'm forced, I have no choice — I must obey
the ones who stand in power. Why rush to extremes?   80
It's madness, madness.

Antigone: I won't insist,
no, even if you should have a change of heart,
I'd never welcome you in the labor, not with me.
So, do as you like, whatever suits you best —
I'll bury him myself.   85
And even if I die in the act, that death will be a glory.
I'll lie with the one I love and loved by him —
an outrage sacred to the gods! I have longer
to please the dead than please the living here:
in the kingdom down below I'll lie forever.   90
Do as you like, dishonor the laws
the gods hold in honor.

Ismene: I'd do them no dishonor . . .
but defy the city? I have no strength for that.

Antigone: You have your excuses. I am on my way,
I'll raise a mound for him, for my dear brother.   95

Ismene: Oh Antigone, you're so rash — I'm so afraid for you!

Antigone: Don't fear for me. Set your own life in order.

Ismene: Then don't, at least, blurt this out to anyone.
Keep it a secret. I'll join you in that, I promise.

Antigone: Dear god, shout it from the rooftops. I'll hate you   100
all the more for silence — tell the world!

Ismene: So fiery — and it ought to chill your heart.

Antigone: I know I please where I must please the most.

Ismene: Yes, if you can, but you're in love with impossibility.

Antigone: Very well then, once my strength gives out   105
I will be done at last.

Ismene: You're wrong from the start,
you're off on a hopeless quest.

Antigone: If you say so, you will make me hate you,
and the hatred of the dead, by all rights,
will haunt you night and day.   110
But leave me to my own absurdity, leave me
to suffer this — dreadful thing. I'll suffer
nothing as great as death without glory.

Exit to the side.

Ismene: Then go if you must, but rest assured,
wild, irrational as you are, my sister,   115
you are truly dear to the ones who love you.

*Withdrawing to the palace. Enter a Chorus, the old citizens of Thebes, chanting as
the sun begins to rise.*

Chorus: Glory! — great beam of sun, brightest of all
　　that ever rose on the seven gates of Thebes,
　　　　you burn through night at last!
　　　　　　　Great eye of the golden day, 　　　　　　　　120
　　mounting the Dirce's° banks you throw him back —
　　the enemy out of Argos, the white shield, the man of bronze —
　　he's flying headlong now
　　　　　　　the bridle of fate stampeding him with pain!

　　　　　And he had driven against our borders, 　　　　125
　　　　　launched by the warring claims of Polynices —
　　　　　like an eagle screaming, winging havoc
　　　　　over the land, wings of armor
　　　　　shielded white as snow,
　　　　　a huge army massing, 　　　　　　　　　　　130
　　　　　crested helmets bristling for assault.

He hovered above our roofs, his vast maw gaping
closing down around our seven gates,
　　　his spears thirsting for the kill
　　　　　　　but now he's gone, look, 　　　　　　　135
before he could glut his jaws with Theban blood
or the god of fire put our crown of towers to the torch.
He grappled the Dragon none can master — Thebes —
　　　the clang of our arms like thunder at his back!

　　　　　Zeus hates with a vengeance all bravado, 　　140
　　　　　the mighty boasts of men. He watched them
　　　　　coming on in a rising flood, the pride
　　　　　of their golden armor ringing shrill —
　　　　　and brandishing his lightning
　　　　　blasted the fighter just at the goal, 　　　　145
　　　　　rushing to shout his triumph from our walls.

Down from the heights he crashed, pounding down on the earth!
And a moment ago, blazing torch in hand —
　　　　　mad for attack, ecstatic
he breathed his rage, the storm 　　　　　　　　　150
　　of his fury hurling at our heads!
But now his high hopes have laid him low
and down the enemy ranks the iron god of war
　　　deals his rewards, his stunning blows — Ares°
　　　rapture of battle, our right arm in the crisis. 　　155

　　　　　Seven captains marshaled at seven gates
　　　　　seven against their equals, gave
　　　　　their brazen trophies up to Zeus,
　　　　　god of the breaking rout of battle,
　　　　　all but two: those blood brothers, 　　　　160
　　　　　one father, one mother — matched in rage,

121 *the Dirce:* A river near Thebes. 　　154 *Ares:* God of war.

        spears matched for the twin conquest —
        clashed and won the common prize of death.

    But now for Victory! Glorious in the morning,
    joy in her eyes to meet our joy   165
        she is winging down to Thebes,
    our fleets of chariots wheeling in her wake —
        Now let us win oblivion from the wars,
    thronging the temples of the gods
    in singing, dancing choirs through the night!   170
        Lord Dionysus,° god of the dance
        that shakes the land of Thebes, now lead the way!

Enter Creon from the palace, attended by his guard.

        But look, the king of the realm is coming,
        Creon, the new man for the new day,
        whatever the gods are sending now . . .   175
        what new plan will he launch?
        Why this, this special session?
        Why this sudden call to the old men
        summoned at one command?
Creon: My countrymen,
    the ship of state is safe. The gods who rocked her,   180
    after a long, merciless pounding in the storm,
    have righted her once more.
                            Out of the whole city
    I have called you here alone. Well I know,
    first, your undeviating respect
    for the throne and royal power of King Laius.   185
    Next, while Oedipus steered the land of Thebes,
    and even after he died, your loyalty was unshakable,
    you still stood by their children. Now then,
    since the two sons are dead — two blows of fate
    in the same day, cut down by each other's hands,   190
    both killers, both brothers stained with blood —
    as I am next in kin to the dead,
    I now possess the throne and all its powers.

    Of course you cannot know a man completely,
    his character, his principles, sense of judgment,   195
    not till he's shown his colors, ruling the people,
    making laws. Experience, there's the test.
    As I see it, whoever assumes the task,
    the awesome task of setting the city's course,
    and refuses to adopt the soundest policies   200
    but fearing someone, keeps his lips locked tight,
    he's utterly worthless. So I rate him now,
    I always have. And whoever places a friend

171 *Dionysus:* God of fertility and wine.

above the good of his own country, he is nothing:
I have no use for him. Zeus my witness,   205
Zeus who sees all things, always —
I could never stand by silent, watching destruction
march against our city, putting safety to rout,
nor could I ever make that man a friend of mine
who menaces our country. Remember this: 210
our country *is* our safety.
Only while she voyages true on course
can we establish friendships, truer than blood itself.
Such are my standards. They make our city great.

Closely akin to them I have proclaimed,   215
just now, the following decree to our people
concerning the two sons of Oedipus.
Eteocles, who died fighting for Thebes,
excelling all in arms: he shall be buried,
crowned with a hero's honors, the cups we pour   220
to soak the earth and reach the famous dead.

But as for his blood brother, Polynices,
who returned from exile, home to his father-city
and the gods of his race, consumed with one desire —
to burn them roof to roots — who thirsted to drink   225
his kinsmen's blood and sell the rest to slavery:
that man — a proclamation has forbidden the city
to dignify him with burial, mourn him at all.
No, he must be left unburied, his corpse
carrion for the birds and dogs to tear,   230
an obscenity for the citizens to behold!

These are my principles. Never at my hands
will the traitor be honored above the patriot.
But whoever proves his loyalty to the state:
I'll prize that man in death as well as life.   235
Leader: If this is your pleasure, Creon, treating
   our city's enemy and our friend this way . . .
   The power is yours, I suppose, to enforce it
   with the laws, both for the dead and all of us,
   the living.
Creon: Follow my orders closely then,   240
   be on your guard.
Leader: We're too old.
   Lay that burden on younger shoulders.
Creon: No, no,
   I don't mean the body — I've posted guards already.
Leader: What commands for us then? What other service?
Creon: See that you never side with those who break my orders.   245
Leader: Never. Only a fool could be in love with death.
Creon: Death is the price — you're right. But all too often
   the mere hope of money has ruined many men.

A Sentry enters from the side.

Sentry: My lord,
    I can't say I'm winded from running, or set out
    with any spring in my legs either—no sir,   250
    I was lost in thought, and it made me stop, often,
    dead in my tracks, wheeling, turning back,
    and all the time a voice inside me muttering,
    "Idiot, why? You're going straight to your death."
    Then muttering, "Stopped again, poor fool?   255
    If somebody gets the news to Creon first,
    what's to save your neck?"
                       And so,
    mulling it over, on I trudged, dragging my feet,
    you can make a short road take forever . . .
    but at last, look, common sense won out,   260
    I'm here, and I'm all yours,
    and even though I come empty-handed
    I'll tell my story just the same, because
    I've come with a good grip on one hope,
    what will come will come, whatever fate—   265

Creon: Come to the point!
    What's wrong—why so afraid?

Sentry: First, myself, I've got to tell you,
    I didn't do it, didn't see who did—
    Be fair, don't take it out on me.   270

Creon: You're playing it safe, soldier,
    barricading yourself from any trouble.
    It's obvious, you've something strange to tell.

Sentry: Dangerous too, and danger makes you delay
    for all you're worth.   275

Creon: Out with it—then dismiss!

Sentry: All right, here it comes. The body—
    someone's just buried it, then run off . . .
    sprinkled some dry dust on the flesh,
    given it proper rites.

Creon: What?   280
    What man alive would dare—

Sentry: I've no idea, I swear it.
    There was no mark of a spade, no pickaxe there,
    no earth turned up, the ground packed hard and dry,
    unbroken, no tracks, no wheelruts, nothing,
    the workman left no trace. Just at sunup   285
    the first watch of the day points it out—
    it was a wonder! We were stunned . . .
    a terrific burden too, for all of us, listen:
    you can't see the corpse, not that it's buried,
    really, just a light cover of road-dust on it,   290
    as if someone meant to lay the dead to rest
    and keep from getting cursed.

Not a sign in sight that dogs or wild beasts
had worried the body, even torn the skin.

But what came next! Rough talk flew thick and fast,   295
guard grilling guard—we'd have come to blows
at last, nothing to stop it; each man for himself
and each the culprit, no one caught red-handed,
all of us pleading ignorance, dodging the charges,
ready to take up red-hot iron in our fists,   300
go through fire, swear oaths to the gods—
"I didn't do it, I had no hand in it either,
not in the plotting, not in the work itself!"

Finally, after all this wrangling came to nothing,
one man spoke out and made us stare at the ground,   305
hanging our heads in fear. No way to counter him,
no way to take his advice and come through
safe and sound. Here's what he said:
"Look, we've got to report the facts to Creon,
we can't keep this hidden." Well, that won out,   310
and the lot fell on me, condemned me,
unlucky as ever, I got the prize. So here I am,
against my will and yours too, well I know—
no one wants the man who brings bad news.
Leader: My king,
ever since he began I've been debating in my mind,   315
could this possibly be the work of the gods?
Creon: Stop—
before you make me choke with anger—the gods!
You, you're senile, must you be insane?
You say—why it's intolerable—say the gods
could have the slightest concern for that corpse?   320
Tell me, was it for meritorious service
they proceeded to bury him, prized him so? The hero
who came to burn their temples ringed with pillars,
their golden treasures—scorch their hallowed earth
and fling their laws to the winds.   325
Exactly when did you last see the gods
celebrating traitors? Inconceivable!

No, from the first there were certain citizens
who could hardly stand the spirit of my regime,
grumbling against me in the dark, heads together,   330
tossing wildly, never keeping their necks beneath
the yoke, loyally submitting to their king.
These are the instigators, I'm convinced—
they've perverted my own guard, bribed them
to do their work.
                    Money! Nothing worse   335
in our lives, so current, rampant, so corrupting.
Money—you demolish cities, root men from their homes,

you train and twist good minds and set them on
to the most atrocious schemes. No limit,
you make them adept at every kind of outrage,   340
every godless crime — money!

                                Everyone —
the whole crew bribed to commit this crime,
they've made one thing sure at least:
sooner or later they will pay the price.

Wheeling on the Sentry.

You —   345
I swear to Zeus as I still believe in Zeus,
if you don't find the man who buried that corpse,
the very man, and produce him before my eyes,
simple death won't be enough for you,
not till we string you up alive   350
and wring the immorality out of you.
Then you can steal the rest of your days,
better informed about where to make a killing.
You'll have learned, at last, it doesn't pay
to itch for rewards from every hand that beckons.   355
Filthy profits wreck most men, you'll see —
they'll never save your life.

Sentry: Please,
    may I say a word or two, or just turn and go?
Creon: Can't you tell? Everything you say offends me.
Sentry: Where does it hurt you, in the ears or in the heart?   360
Creon: And who are you to pinpoint my displeasure?
Sentry: The culprit grates on your feelings,
    I just annoy your ears.
Creon: Still talking?
    You talk too much! A born nuisance —
Sentry: Maybe so,
    but I never did this thing, so help me!
Creon: Yes you did —   365
    what's more, you squandered your life for silver!
Sentry: Oh it's terrible when the one who does the judging
    judges things all wrong.
Creon: Well now,
    you just be clever about your judgments —
    if you fail to produce the criminals for me,   370
    you'll swear your dirty money brought you pain.

Turning sharply, reentering the palace.

Sentry: I hope he's found. Best thing by far.
    But caught or not, that's in the lap of fortune;
    I'll never come back, you've seen the last of me.
    I'm saved, even now, and I never thought,   375
    I never hoped —
    dear gods, I owe you all my thanks!

Rushing out.

Chorus: Numberless wonders
terrible wonders walk the world but none the match for man —
that great wonder crossing the heaving gray sea,
                    driven on by the blasts of winter   380
on through breakers crashing left and right,
      holds his steady course
and the oldest of the gods he wears away —
the Earth, the immortal, the inexhaustible —
as his plows go back and forth, year in, year out   385
      with the breed of stallions turning up the furrows.

And the blithe, lightheaded race of birds he snares,
the tribes of savage beasts, the life that swarms the depths —
                    with one fling of his nets
woven and coiled tight, he takes them all,   390
      man the skilled, the brilliant!
He conquers all, taming with his techniques
the prey that roams the cliffs and wild lairs,
training the stallion, clamping the yoke across
      his shaggy neck, and the tireless mountain bull.   395

And speech and thought, quick as the wind
and the mood and mind for law that rules the city —
      all these he has taught himself
and shelter from the arrows of the frost
when there's rough lodging under the cold clear sky   400
and the shafts of lashing rain —
            ready, resourceful man!
                    Never without resources
never an impasse as he marches on the future —
only Death, from Death alone he will find no rescue   405
but from desperate plagues he has plotted his escapes.

Man the master, ingenious past all measure
past all dreams, the skills within his grasp —
      he forges on, now to destruction
now again to greatness. When he weaves in   410
the laws of the land, and the justice of the gods
that binds his oaths together
            he and his city rise high —
                    but the city casts out
that man who weds himself to inhumanity   415
thanks to reckless daring. Never share my hearth
never think my thoughts, whoever does such things.

Enter Antigone from the side, accompanied by the Sentry.

      Here is a dark sign from the gods —
      what to make of this? I know her,

how can I deny it? That young girl's Antigone!   420
Wretched, child of a wretched father,
Oedipus. Look, is it possible?
They bring you in like a prisoner—
why? did you break the king's laws?
Did they take you in some act of mad defiance?   425

Sentry: She's the one, she did it single-handed—
we caught her burying the body. Where's Creon?

Enter Creon from the palace.

Leader: Back again, just in time when you need him.
Creon: In time for what? What is it?
Sentry: My king,
there's nothing you can swear you'll never do—   430
second thoughts make liars of us all.
I could have sworn I wouldn't hurry back
(what with your threats, the buffeting I just took),
but a stroke of luck beyond our wildest hopes,
what a joy, there's nothing like it. So,   435
back I've come, breaking my oath, who cares?
I'm bringing in our prisoner—this young girl—
we took her giving the dead the last rites.
But no casting lots this time; this is *my* luck,
my prize, no one else's.
                   Now, my lord,   440
here she is. Take her, question her,
cross-examine her to your heart's content.
But set me free, it's only right—
I'm rid of this dreadful business once for all.
Creon: Prisoner! Her? You took her—where, doing what?   445
Sentry: Burying the man. That's the whole story.
Creon: What?
You mean what you say, you're telling me the truth?
Sentry: She's the one. With my own eyes I saw her
bury the body, just what you've forbidden.
There. Is that plain and clear?   450
Creon: What did you see? Did you catch her in the act?
Sentry: Here's what happened. We went back to our post,
those threats of yours breathing down our necks—
we brushed the corpse clean of the dust that covered it,
stripped it bare . . . it was slimy, going soft,   455
and we took to high ground, backs to the wind
so the stink of him couldn't hit us;
jostling, baiting each other to keep awake,
shouting back and forth—no napping on the job,
not this time. And so the hours dragged by   460
until the sun stood dead above our heads,
a huge white ball in the noon sky, beating,
blazing down, and then it happened—
suddenly, a whirlwind!

Twisting a great dust-storm up from the earth,   465
a black plague of the heavens, filling the plain,
ripping the leaves off every tree in sight,
choking the air and sky. We squinted hard
and took our whipping from the gods.

And after the storm passed — it seemed endless —   470
there, we saw the girl!
And she cried out a sharp, piercing cry,
like a bird come back to an empty nest,
peering into its bed, and all the babies gone . . .
Just so, when she sees the corpse bare   475
she bursts into a long, shattering wail
and calls down withering curses on the heads
of all who did the work. And she scoops up dry dust,
handfuls, quickly, and lifting a fine bronze urn,
lifting it high and pouring, she crowns the dead   480
with three full libations.
                              Soon as we saw
we rushed her, closed on the kill like hunters,
and she, she didn't flinch. We interrogated her,
charging her with offenses past and present —
she stood up to it all, denied nothing. I tell you,   485
it made me ache and laugh in the same breath.
It's pure joy to escape the worst yourself,
it hurts a man to bring down his friends.
But all that, I'm afraid, means less to me
than my own skin. That's the way I'm made.
Creon:

  Wheeling on Antigone.

                                                    You,   490
with your eyes fixed on the ground — speak up.
Do you deny you did this, yes or no?
Antigone: I did it. I don't deny a thing.
Creon:

  To the Sentry.

You, get out, wherever you please —
you're clear of a very heavy charge.   495

  He leaves; Creon turns back to Antigone.

You, tell me briefly, no long speeches —
were you aware a decree had forbidden this?
Antigone: Well aware. How could I avoid it? It was public.
Creon: And still you had the gall to break this law?
Antigone: Of course I did. It wasn't Zeus, not in the least,   500
who made this proclamation — not to me.
Nor did that Justice, dwelling with the gods
beneath the earth, ordain such laws for men.

Nor did I think your edict had such force
that you, a mere mortal, could override the gods,   505
the great unwritten, unshakeable traditions.
They are alive, not just today or yesterday:
they live forever, from the first of time,
and no one knows when they first saw the light.

These laws — I was not about to break them,   510
not out of fear of some man's wounded pride,
and face the retribution of the gods.
Die I must, I've known it all my life —
how could I keep from knowing? — even without
your death-sentence ringing in my ears.   515
And if I am to die before my time
I consider that a gain. Who on earth,
alive in the midst of so much grief as I,
could fail to find his death a rich reward?
So for me, at least, to meet this doom of yours   520
is precious little pain. But if I had allowed
my own mother's son to rot, an unburied corpse —
that would have been an agony! This is nothing.
And if my present actions strike you as foolish,
let's just say I've been accused of folly   525
by a fool.
Leader: Like father like daughter,
passionate, wild . . .
she hasn't learned to bend before adversity.
Creon: No? Believe me, the stiffest stubborn wills
fall the hardest; the toughest iron,   530
tempered strong in the white-hot fire,
you'll see it crack and shatter first of all.
And I've known spirited horses you can break
with a light bit — proud, rebellious horses.
There's no room for pride, not in a slave,   535
not with the lord and master standing by.

This girl was an old hand at insolence
when she overrode the edicts we made public.
But once she'd done it — the insolence,
twice over — to glory in it, laughing,   540
mocking us to our face with what she'd done.
I'm not the man, not now: she is the man
if this victory goes to her and she goes free.

Never! Sister's child or closer in blood
than all my family clustered at my altar   545
worshiping Guardian Zeus — she'll never escape,
she and her blood sister, the most barbaric death.
Yes, I accuse her sister of an equal part
in scheming this, this burial.

To his attendants.

          Bring her here!
I just saw her inside, hysterical, gone to pieces.   550
It never fails: the mind convicts itself
in advance, when scoundrels are up to no good,
plotting in the dark. Oh but I hate it more
when a traitor, caught red-handed,
tries to glorify his crimes.   555
Antigone: Creon, what more do you want
  than my arrest and execution?
Creon: Nothing. Then I have it all.
Antigone: Then why delay? Your moralizing repels me,
  every word you say — pray god it always will.   560
  So naturally all I say repels you too.
              Enough.
Give me glory! What greater glory could I win
than to give my own brother decent burial?
These citizens here would all agree,

To the Chorus.

they'd praise me too   565
if their lips weren't locked in fear.

Pointing to Creon.

Lucky tyrants — the perquisites of power!
Ruthless power to do and say whatever pleases *them.*
Creon: You alone, of all the people in Thebes,
  see things that way.
Antigone: They see it just that way   570
  but defer to you and keep their tongues in leash.
Creon: And you, aren't you ashamed to differ so from them?
  So disloyal!
Antigone: Not ashamed for a moment,
  not to honor my brother, my own flesh and blood.
Creon: Wasn't Eteocles a brother too — cut down, facing him? 575
Antigone: Brother, yes, by the same mother, the same father.
Creon: Then how can you render his enemy such honors,
  such impieties in his eyes?
Antigone: He'll never testify to that,
  Eteocles dead and buried.
Creon: He will —   580
  if you honor the traitor just as much as him.
Antigone: But it was his brother, not some slave that died —
Creon: Ravaging our country! —
  but Eteocles died fighting in our behalf.
Antigone: No matter — Death longs for the same rites for all. 585
Creon: Never the same for the patriot and the traitor.
Antigone: Who, Creon, who on earth can say the ones below
  don't find this pure and uncorrupt?

Creon: Never. Once an enemy, never a friend,
not even after death.   590

Antigone: I was born to join in love, not hate —
that is my nature.

Creon: Go down below and love,
if love you must — love the dead! While I'm alive,
no woman is going to lord it over me.

Enter Ismene from the palace, under guard.

Chorus: Look,
Ismene's coming, weeping a sister's tears,   595
loving sister, under a cloud . . .
her face is flushed, her cheeks streaming.
Sorrow puts her lovely radiance in the dark.

Creon: You —
in my house, you viper, slinking undetected,
sucking my life-blood! I never knew   600
I was breeding twin disasters, the two of you
rising up against my throne. Come, tell me,
will you confess your part in the crime or not?
Answer me. Swear to me.

Ismene: I did it, yes —
if only she consents — I share the guilt,   605
the consequences too.

Antigone: No,
Justice will never suffer that — not you,
you were unwilling. I never brought you in.

Ismene: But now you face such dangers . . . I'm not ashamed
to sail through trouble with you,   610
make your troubles mine.

Antigone: Who did the work?
Let the dead and the god of death bear witness!
I've no love for a friend who loves in words alone.

Ismene: Oh no, my sister, don't reject me, please,
let me die beside you, consecrating   615
the dead together.

Antigone: Never share my dying,
don't lay claim to what you never touched.
My death will be enough.

Ismene: What do I care for life, cut off from you?

Antigone: Ask Creon. Your concern is all for him.   620

Ismene: Why abuse me so? It doesn't help you now.

Antigone: You're right —
if I mock you, I get no pleasure from it,
only pain.

Ismene: Tell me, dear one,
what can I do to help you, even now?

Antigone: Save yourself. I don't grudge you your survival.   625

Ismene: Oh no, no, denied my portion in your death?

Antigone: You chose to live, I chose to die.
Ismene: Not, at least,
    without every kind of caution I could voice.
Antigone: Your wisdom appealed to one world — mine, another.
Ismene: But look, we're both guilty, both condemned to death.   630
Antigone: Courage! Live your life. I gave myself to death,
    long ago, so I might serve the dead.
Creon: They're both mad, I tell you, the two of them.
    One's just shown it, the other's been that way
    since she was born.
Ismene: True, my king,   635
    the sense we were born with cannot last forever . . .
    commit cruelty on a person long enough
    and the mind begins to go.
Creon: Yours did,
    when you chose to commit your crimes with her.
Ismene: How can I live alone, without her?
Creon: Her?   640
    Don't even mention her — she no longer exists.
Ismene: What? You'd kill your own son's bride?
Creon: Absolutely:
    there are other fields for him to plow.
Ismene: Perhaps,
    but never as true, as close a bond as theirs.
Creon: A worthless woman for my son? It repels me.   645
Ismene: Dearest Haemon, your father wrongs you so!
Creon: Enough, enough — you and your talk of marriage!
Ismene: Creon — you're really going to rob your son of Antigone?
Creon: Death will do it for me — break their marriage off.
Leader: So, it's settled then? Antigone must die?   650
Creon: Settled, yes — we both know that.

    To the guards.

    Stop wasting time. Take them in.
    From now on they'll act like women.
    Tie them up, no more running loose;
    even the bravest will cut and run,   655
    once they see Death coming for their lives.

    *The guards escort Antigone and Ismene into the palace. Creon remains while
    the old citizens form their chorus.*

Chorus: Blest, they are the truly blest who all their lives
    have never tasted devastation. For others, once
    the gods have rocked a house to its foundations
        the ruin will never cease, cresting on and on   660
    from one generation on throughout the race —
    like a great mounting tide
    driven on by savage northern gales,
        surging over the dead black depths

roiling up from the bottom dark heaves of sand   665
and the headlands, taking the storm's onslaught full-force,
roar, and the low moaning
           echoes on and on
               and now
as in ancient times I see the sorrows of the house,
the living heirs of the old ancestral kings,
piling on the sorrows of the dead   670
     and one generation cannot free the next—
some god will bring them crashing down,
the race finds no release.
And now the light, the hope
        springing up from the late last root   675
in the house of Oedipus, that hope's cut down in turn
by the long, bloody knife swung by the gods of death
by a senseless word
        by fury at the heart.
                    Zeus,
yours is the power, Zeus, what man on earth
can override it, who can hold it back?   680
Power that neither Sleep, the all-ensnaring
    no, nor the tireless months of heaven
can ever overmaster—young through all time,
mighty lord of power, you hold fast
     the dazzling crystal mansions of Olympus.   685
And throughout the future, late and soon
as through the past, your law prevails:
no towering form of greatness
        enters into the lives of mortals
            free and clear of ruin.
                  True,   690
our dreams, our high hopes voyaging far and wide
bring sheer delight to many, to many others
    delusion, blithe, mindless lusts
and the fraud steals on one slowly . . . unaware
till he trips and puts his foot into the fire.   695
     He was a wise old man who coined
the famous saying: "Sooner or later
foul is fair, fair is foul
to the man the gods will ruin"—
     He goes his way for a moment only   700
        free of blinding ruin.

Enter Haemon from the palace.

    Here's Haemon now, the last of all your sons.
    Does he come in tears for his bride,
    his doomed bride, Antigone—
    bitter at being cheated of their marriage?   705
Creon: We'll soon know, better than seers could tell us.

Turning to Haemon.

Son, you've heard the final verdict on your bride?
Are you coming now, raving against your father?
Or do you love me, no matter what I do?
Haemon: Father, I'm your *son* . . . you in your wisdom   710
  set my bearings for me — I obey you.
  No marriage could ever mean more to me than you,
  whatever good direction you may offer.
Creon: Fine, Haemon.
  That's how you ought to feel within your heart,
  subordinate to your father's will in every way.   715
  That's what a man prays for: to produce good sons —
  households full of them, dutiful and attentive,
  so they can pay his enemy back with interest
  and match the respect their father shows his friend.
  But the man who rears a brood of useless children,   720
  what has he brought into the world, I ask you?
  Nothing but trouble for himself, and mockery
  from his enemies laughing in his face.
                           Oh Haemon,
  never lose your sense of judgment over a woman.
  The warmth, the rush of pleasure, it all goes cold   725
  in your arms, I warn you . . . a worthless woman
  in your house, a misery in your bed.
  What wound cuts deeper than a loved one
  turned against you? Spit her out,
  like a mortal enemy — let the girl go.   730
  Let her find a husband down among the dead.

  Imagine it: I caught her in naked rebellion,
  the traitor, the only one in the whole city.
  I'm not about to prove myself a liar,
  not to my people, no, I'm going to kill her!   735
  That's right — so let her cry for mercy, sing her hymns
  to Zeus who defends all bonds of kindred blood.
  Why, if I bring up my own kin to be rebels,
  think what I'd suffer from the world at large.
  Show me the man who rules his household well: 740
  I'll show you someone fit to rule the state.
  That good man, my son,
  I have every confidence he and he alone
  can give commands and take them too. Staunch
  in the storm of spears he'll stand his ground,   745
  a loyal, unflinching comrade at your side.

  But whoever steps out of line, violates the laws
  or presumes to hand out orders to his superiors,
  he'll win no praise from me. But that man
  the city places in authority, his orders   750

must be obeyed, large and small,
right and wrong.
                    Anarchy—
show me a greater crime in all the earth!
She, she destroys cities, rips up houses,
breaks the ranks of spearmen into headlong rout.   755
But the ones who last it out, the great mass of them
owe their lives to discipline. Therefore
we must defend the men who live by law,
never let some woman triumph over us.
Better to fall from power, if fall we must,   760
at the hands of a man—never be rated
inferior to a woman, never.

Leader: To us,
unless old age has robbed us of our wits,
you seem to say what you have to say with sense.

Haemon: Father, only the gods endow a man with reason, 765
the finest of all their gifts, a treasure.
Far be it from me—I haven't the skill,
and certainly no desire, to tell you when,
if ever, you make a slip in speech . . . though
someone else might have a good suggestion.   770

Of course it's not for you,
in the normal run of things, to watch
whatever men say or do, or find to criticize.
The man in the street, you know, dreads your glance,
he'd never say anything displeasing to your face.   775
But it's for me to catch the murmurs in the dark,
the way the city mourns for this young girl.
"No woman," they say, "ever deserved death less,
and such a brutal death for such a glorious action.
She, with her own dear brother lying in his blood—   780
she couldn't bear to leave him dead, unburied,
food for the wild dogs or wheeling vultures.
Death? She deserves a glowing crown of gold!"
So they say, and the rumor spreads in secret,
darkly . . .

                    I rejoice in your success, father—   785
nothing more precious to me in the world.
What medal of honor brighter to his children
than a father's growing glory? Or a child's
to his proud father? Now don't, please,
be quite so single-minded, self-involved,   790
or assume the world is wrong and you are right.
Whoever thinks that he alone possesses intelligence,
the gift of eloquence, he and no one else,
and character too . . . such men, I tell you,
spread them open—you will find them empty.

                                    No,   795

it's no disgrace for a man, even a wise man,
to learn many things and not to be too rigid.
You've seen trees by a raging winter torrent,
how many sway with the flood and salvage every twig,
but not the stubborn — they're ripped out, roots and all.   800
Bend or break. The same when a man is sailing:
haul your sheets too taut, never give an inch,
you'll capsize, go the rest of the voyage
keel up and the rowing-benches under.

Oh give way. Relax your anger — change!   805
I'm young, I know, but let me offer this:
it would be best by far, I admit,
if a man were born infallible, right by nature.
If not — and things don't often go that way,
it's best to learn from those with good advice.   810

Leader: You'd do well, my lord, if he's speaking to the point,
to learn from him,

Turning to Haemon.

> and you, my boy, from him.
You both are talking sense.
Creon: So,
men our age, we're to be lectured, are we? —
schooled by a boy his age?   815
Haemon: Only in what is right. But if I seem young,
look less to my years and more to what I do.
Creon: Do? Is admiring rebels an achievement?
Haemon: I'd never suggest that you admire treason.
Creon: Oh? —
isn't that just the sickness that's attacked her?   820
Haemon: The whole city of Thebes denies it, to a man.
Creon: And is Thebes about to tell me how to rule?
Haemon: Now, you see? Who's talking like a child?
Creon: Am I to rule this land for others — or myself?
Haemon: It's no city at all, owned by one man alone.   825
Creon: What? The city *is* the king's — that's the law!
Haemon: What a splendid king you'd make of a desert island —
you and you alone.
Creon:

To the Chorus.

> This boy, I do believe,
is fighting on her side, the woman's side.
Haemon: If you are a woman, yes;   830
my concern is all for you.
Creon: Why, you degenerate — bandying accusations,
threatening me with justice, your own father!
Haemon: I see my father offending justice — wrong.
Creon: Wrong?

To protect my royal rights?

Haemon: Protect your rights?   835
When you trample down the honors of the gods?

Creon: You, you soul of corruption, rotten through —
woman's accomplice!

Haemon: That may be,
but you'll never find me accomplice to a criminal.

Creon: That's what *she* is,   840
and every word you say is a blatant appeal for her —

Haemon: And you, and me, and the gods beneath the earth.

Creon: You'll never marry her, not while she's alive.

Haemon: Then she'll die . . . but her death will kill another.

Creon: What, brazen threats? You go too far!

Haemon: What threat?   845
Combating your empty, mindless judgments with a word?

Creon: You'll suffer for your sermons, you and your empty wisdom!

Haemon: If you weren't my father, I'd say you were insane.

Creon: Don't flatter me with Father — you woman's slave!

Haemon: You really expect to fling abuse at me   850
and not receive the same?

Creon: Is that so!
Now, by heaven, I promise you, you'll pay —
taunting, insulting me! Bring her out,
that hateful — she'll die now, here,
in front of his eyes, beside her groom!   855

Haemon: No, no, she will never die beside me —
don't delude yourself. And you will never
see me, never set eyes on my face again.
Rage your heart out, rage with friends
who can stand the sight of you.   860

    Rushing out.

Leader: Gone, my king, in a burst of anger.
A temper young as his . . . hurt him once,
he may do something violent.

Creon: Let him do —
dream up something desperate, past all human limit!
Good riddance. Rest assured,   865
he'll never save those two young girls from death.

Leader: Both of them, you really intend to kill them both?

Creon: No, not her, the one whose hands are clean;
you're quite right.

Leader: But Antigone —
what sort of death do you have in mind for her?   870

Creon: I'll take her down some wild, desolate path
never trod by men, and wall her up alive
in a rocky vault, and set out short rations,
just a gesture of piety
to keep the entire city free of defilement.   875
There let her pray to the one god she worships:

Death — who knows? — may just reprieve her from death.
Or she may learn at last, better late than never,
what a waste of breath it is to worship Death.

Exit to the palace.

Chorus: Love, never conquered in battle   880
Love the plunderer laying waste the rich!
Love standing the night-watch
                    guarding a girl's soft cheek,
you range the seas, the shepherds' steadings off in the wilds —
not even the deathless gods can flee your onset,   885
nothing human born for a day —
whoever feels your grip is driven mad.
                                                          Love
you wrench the minds of the righteous into outrage,
swerve them to their ruin — you have ignited this,
this kindred strife, father and son at war   890
                    and Love alone the victor —
warm glance of the bride triumphant, burning with desire!
Throned in power, side-by-side with the mighty laws!
Irresistible Aphrodite,° never conquered —
Love, you mock us for your sport.   895

Antigone is brought from the palace under guard.

But now, even I'd rebel against the king,
I'd break all bounds when I see this —
I fill with tears, can't hold them back,
not any more . . . I see Antigone make her way
to the bridal vault where all are laid to rest.   900
Antigone: Look at me, men of my fatherland,
          setting out on the last road
looking into the last light of day
the last I'll ever see . . .
the god of death who puts us all to bed   905
takes me down to the banks of Acheron° alive —
          denied my part in the wedding-songs,
no wedding-song in the dusk has crowned my marriage —
I go to wed the lord of the dark waters.
Chorus: Not crowned with glory, crowned with a dirge,   910
          you leave for the deep pit of the dead.
          No withering illness laid you low,
          no strokes of the sword — a law to yourself,
          alone, no mortal like you, ever, you go down
          to the halls of Death alive and breathing.   915
Antigone: But think of Niobe° — well I know her story —

---

894 *Aphrodite:* Goddess of love.   906 *Acheron:* A river in the underworld, to which the
dead go.   916 *Niobe:* A queen of Thebes who was punished by the gods for her pride and
was turned into stone.

think what a living death she died,
Tantalus' daughter, stranger queen from the east:
there on the mountain heights, growing stone
binding as ivy, slowly walled her round   920
and the rains will never cease, the legends say
the snows will never leave her . . .
    wasting away, under her brows the tears
showering down her breasting ridge and slopes —
a rocky death like hers puts me to sleep.   925

Chorus: But she was a god, born of gods,
    and we are only mortals born to die.
    And yet, of course, it's a great thing
    for a dying girl to hear, just hear
    she shares a destiny equal to the gods,   930
    during life and later, once she's dead.

Antigone: O you mock me!
Why, in the name of all my fathers' gods
why can't you wait till I am gone —
    must you abuse me to my face?
O my city, all your fine rich sons!   935
And you, you springs of the Dirce,
holy grove of Thebes where the chariots gather,
    you at least, you'll bear me witness, look,
unmourned by friends and forced by such crude laws
I go to my rockbound prison, strange new tomb —   940
    always a stranger, O dear god,
I have no home on earth and none below,
    not with the living, not with the breathless dead.

Chorus: You went too far, the last limits of daring —
    smashing against the high throne of Justice!   945
    Your life's in ruins, child — I wonder . . .
    do you pay for your father's terrible ordeal?

Antigone: There — at last you've touched it, the worst pain
the worst anguish! Raking up the grief for father
    three times over, for all the doom   950
that's struck us down, the brilliant house of Laius.
O mother, your marriage-bed
the coiling horrors, the coupling there —
    you with your own son, my father — doomstruck mother!
Such, such were my parents, and I their wretched child.   955
I go to them now, cursed, unwed, to share their home —
    I am a stranger! O dear brother, doomed
in your marriage — your marriage murders mine,
    your dying drags me down to death alive!

    Enter Creon.

Chorus: Reverence asks some reverence in return —   960
    but attacks on power never go unchecked,
    not by the man who holds the reins of power.
    Your own blind will, your passion has destroyed you.

Antigone:　No one to weep for me, my friends,
　　　　no wedding-song — they take me away　　　　　　　　965
　　　　in all my pain . . . the road lies open, waiting.
　　　　Never again, the law forbids me to see
　　　　the sacred eye of day. I am agony!
　　　　No tears for the destiny that's mine,
　　　　no loved one mourns my death.

Creon:　　　　　　　　　　　Can't you see?　　　　970
　　If a man could wail his own dirge *before* he dies,
　　he'd never finish.

　　To the guards.

　　　　　　　Take her away, quickly!
　　Wall her up in the tomb, you have your orders.
　　Abandon her there, alone, and let her choose —
　　death or a buried life with a good roof for shelter.　　975
　　As for myself, my hands are clean. This young girl —
　　dead or alive, she will be stripped of her rights,
　　her stranger's rights, here in the world above.

Antigone:　O tomb, my bridal-bed — my house, my prison
　　cut in the hollow rock, my everlasting watch!　　　　980
　　I'll soon be there, soon embrace my own,
　　the great growing family of our dead
　　Persephone° has received among her ghosts.
　　　　　　　　　　　　　　　　　I,
　　the last of them all, the most reviled by far,
　　go down before my destined time's run out.　　　　985
　　But still I go, cherishing one good hope:
　　my arrival may be dear to father,
　　dear to you, my mother,
　　dear to you, my loving brother, Eteocles —
　　When you died I washed you with my hands,　　　　990
　　I dressed you all, I poured the cups
　　across your tombs. But now, Polynices,
　　because I laid your body out as well,
　　this, this is my reward. Nevertheless
　　I honored you — the decent will admit it —　　　　995
　　well and wisely too.
　　　　　　　Never, I tell you,
　　if I had been the mother of children
　　or if my husband died, exposed and rotting —
　　I'd never have taken this ordeal upon myself,
　　never defied our people's will. What law,　　　　1000
　　you ask, do I satisfy with what I say?
　　A husband dead, there might have been another.
　　A child by another too, if I had lost the first.
　　But mother and father both lost in the halls of Death,
　　no brother could ever spring to light again.　　　　1005

---

983 *Persephone:* Queen of the underworld.

For this law alone I held you first in honor.
For this, Creon, the king, judges me a criminal
guilty of dreadful outrage, my dear brother!
And now he leads me off, a captive in his hands,
with no part in the bridal-song, the bridal-bed,   1010
denied all joy of marriage, raising children—
deserted so by loved ones, struck by fate,
I descend alive to the caverns of the dead.

What law of the mighty gods have I transgressed?
Why look to the heavens any more, tormented as I am?   1015
Whom to call, what comrades now? Just think,
my reverence only brands me for irreverence!
Very well: if this is the pleasure of the gods,
once I suffer I will know that I was wrong.
But if these men are wrong, let them suffer   1020
nothing worse than they mete out to me—
these masters of injustice!

Leader: Still the same rough winds, the wild passion
raging through the girl.

Creon:

  To the guards.

                    Take her away.
You're wasting time—you'll pay for it too.   1025

Antigone: Oh god, the voice of death. It's come, it's here.

Creon: True. Not a word of hope—your doom is sealed.

Antigone: Land of Thebes, city of all my fathers—
      O you gods, the first gods of the race!
      They drag me away, now, no more delay.   1030
      Look on me, you noble sons of Thebes—
      the last of a great line of kings,
      I alone, see what I suffer now
      at the hands of what breed of men—
      all for reverence, my reverence for the gods!   1035

  She leaves under guard; the Chorus gathers.

Chorus: Danaë, Danaë°—
      even she endured a fate like yours,
          in all her lovely strength she traded
      the light of day for the bolted brazen vault—
      buried within her tomb, her bridal-chamber,   1040
      wed to the yoke and broken.
          But she was of glorious birth
                      my child, my child
      and treasured the seed of Zeus within her womb,
      the cloudburst streaming gold!   1045
          The power of fate is a wonder,

1036 *Danaë:* Locked in a cell by her father because it was prophesied that her son would kill him, but visited by Zeus in the form of a shower of gold. Their son was Perseus.

dark, terrible wonder —
neither wealth nor armies
towered walls nor ships
black hulls lashed by the salt   1050
can save us from that force.

The yoke tamed him too
   young Lycurgus° flaming in anger
king of Edonia, all for his mad taunts
Dionysus clamped him down, encased   1055
in the chain-mail of rock
   and there his rage
         his terrible flowering rage burst —
sobbing, dying away . . . at last that madman
came to know his god —   1060
the power he mocked, the power
   he taunted in all his frenzy
   trying to stamp out
   the women strong with the god —
   the torch, the raving sacred cries —   1065
   enraging the Muses° who adore the flute.

And far north where the Black Rocks
   cut the sea in half
and murderous straits
split the coast of Thrace   1070
   a forbidding city stands
where once, hard by the walls
the savage Ares thrilled to watch
a king's new queen, a Fury rearing in rage
   against his two royal sons —   1075
      her bloody hands, her dagger-shuttle
stabbing out their eyes — cursed, blinding wounds —
their eyes blind sockets screaming for revenge!

They wailed in agony, cries echoing cries
   the princes doomed at birth . . .   1080
and their mother doomed to chains,
walled off in a tomb of stone —
   but she traced her own birth back
to a proud Athenian line and the high gods
and off in caverns half the world away,   1085
born of the wild North Wind
   she sprang on her father's gales,
      racing stallions up the leaping cliffs —
child of the heavens. But even on her the Fates
the gray everlasting Fates rode hard   1090
my child, my child.

1053 *Lycurgus:* Punished by Dionysus because he would not worship him.   1066 *Muses:* Goddesses of the arts.

Enter Tiresias, the blind prophet, led by a boy.

Tiresias: Lords of Thebes,
    I and the boy have come together,
    hand in hand. Two see with the eyes of one . . .
    so the blind must go, with a guide to lead the way.
Creon: What is it, old Tiresias? What news now?   1095
Tiresias: I will teach you. And you obey the seer.
Creon: I will,
    I've never wavered from your advice before.
Tiresias: And so you kept the city straight on course.
Creon: I owe you a great deal, I swear to that.
Tiresias: Then reflect, my son: you are poised,   1100
    once more, on the razor-edge of fate.
Creon: What is it? I shudder to hear you.
Tiresias: You will learn
    when you listen to the warnings of my craft.
    As I sat on the ancient seat of augury,°
    in the sanctuary where every bird I know   1105
    will hover at my hands — suddenly I heard it,
    a strange voice in the wingbeats, unintelligible,
    barbaric, a mad scream! Talons flashing, ripping,
    they were killing each other — that much I knew —
    the murderous fury whirring in those wings   1110
    made that much clear!
                    I was afraid,
    I turned quickly, tested the burnt-sacrifice,
    ignited the altar at all points — but no fire,
    the god in the fire never blazed.
    Not from those offerings . . . over the embers   1115
    slid a heavy ooze from the long thighbones,
    smoking, sputtering out, and the bladder
    puffed and burst — spraying gall into the air —
    and the fat wrapping the bones slithered off
    and left them glistening white. No fire!   1120
    The rites failed that might have blazed the future
    with a sign. So I learned from the boy here;
    he is my guide, as I am guide to others.
                    And it's you —
    your high resolve that sets this plague on Thebes.
    The public altars and sacred hearths are fouled,   1125
    one and all, by the birds and dogs with carrion
    torn from the corpse, the doomstruck son of Oedipus!
    And so the gods are deaf to our prayers, they spurn
    the offerings in our hands, the flame of holy flesh.
    No birds cry out an omen clear and true —   1130
    they're gorged with the murdered victim's blood and fat.
    Take these things to heart, my son, I warn you.

1104 *seat of augury:* Where Tiresias looked for omens among birds.

All men make mistakes, it is only human.
But once the wrong is done, a man
can turn his back on folly, misfortune too,   1135
if he tries to make amends, however low he's fallen,
and stops his bullnecked ways. Stubbornness
brands you for stupidity — pride is a crime.
No, yield to the dead!
Never stab the fighter when he's down.   1140
Where's the glory, killing the dead twice over?

I mean you well. I give you sound advice.
It's best to learn from a good adviser
when he speaks for your own good:
it's pure gain.

Creon: Old man — all of you! So,   1145
you shoot your arrows at my head like archers at the target —
I even have *him* loosed on me, this fortune-teller.
Oh his ilk has tried to sell me short
and ship me off for years. Well,
drive your bargains, traffic — much as you like —   1150
in the gold of India, silver-gold of Sardis.
You'll never bury that body in the grave,
not even if Zeus's eagles rip the corpse
and wing their rotten pickings off to the throne of god!
Never, not even in fear of such defilement   1155
will I tolerate his burial, that traitor.
Well I know, we can't defile the gods —
no mortal has the power.
                     No,
reverend old Tiresias, all men fall,
it's only human, but the wisest fall obscenely   1160
when they glorify obscene advice with rhetoric —
all for their own gain.

Tiresias: Oh god, is there a man alive
who knows, who actually believes . . .

Creon: What now?
What earth-shattering truth are you about to utter?   1165

Tiresias: . . . just how much a sense of judgment, wisdom
is the greatest gift we have?

Creon: Just as much, I'd say,
as a twisted mind is the worst affliction going.

Tiresias: You are the one who's sick, Creon, sick to death.

Creon: I am in no mood to trade insults with a seer.   1170

Tiresias: You have already, calling my prophecies a lie.

Creon: Why not?
You and the whole breed of seers are mad for money!

Tiresias: And the whole race of tyrants lusts to rake it in.

Creon: This slander of yours —
are you aware you're speaking to the king?   1175

Tiresias: Well aware. Who helped you save the city?

Creon: You—
    you have your skills, old seer, but you lust for injustice!
Tiresias: You will drive me to utter the dreadful secret in my heart.
Creon: Spit it out! Just don't speak it out for profit.
Tiresias: Profit? No, not a bit of profit, not for you.   1180
Creon: Know full well, you'll never buy off my resolve.
Tiresias: Then know this too, learn this by heart!
    The chariot of the sun will not race through
    so many circuits more, before you have surrendered
    one born of your own loins, your own flesh and blood,   1185
    a corpse for corpses given in return, since you have thrust
    to the world below a child sprung for the world above,
    ruthlessly lodged a living soul within the grave—
    then you've robbed the gods below the earth,
    keeping a dead body here in the bright air,   1190
    unburied, unsung, unhallowed by the rites.

    You, you have no business with the dead,
    nor do the gods above—this is violence
    you have forced upon the heavens.
    And so the avengers, the dark destroyers late   1195
    but true to the mark, now lie in wait for you,
    the Furies sent by the gods and the god of death
    to strike you down with the pains that you perfected!

    There. Reflect on that, tell me I've been bribed.
    The day comes soon, no long test of time, not now,   1200
    that wakes the wails for men and women in your halls.
    Great hatred rises against you—
    cities in tumult, all whose mutilated sons
    the dogs have graced with burial, or the wild beasts,
    some wheeling crow that wings the ungodly stench of carrion   1205
    back to each city, each warrior's hearth and home.

    These arrows for your heart! Since you've raked me
    I loose them like an archer in my anger,
    arrows deadly true. You'll never escape
    their burning, searing force.   1210

Motioning to his escort.

    Come, boy, take me home.
    So he can vent his rage on younger men,
    and learn to keep a gentler tongue in his head
    and better sense than what he carries now.

Exit to the side.

Leader: The old man's gone, my king—   1215
    terrible prophecies. Well I know,
    since the hair on this old head went gray,
    he's never lied to Thebes.

Creon: I know it myself — I'm shaken, torn.
    It's a dreadful thing to yield . . . but resist now?   1220
    Lay my pride bare to the blows of ruin?
    That's dreadful too.
Leader: But good advice,
    Creon, take it now, you must.
Creon: What should I do? Tell me . . . I'll obey.
Leader: Go! Free the girl from the rocky vault   1225
    and raise a mound for the body you exposed.
Creon: That's your advice? You think I should give in?
Leader: Yes, my king, quickly. Disasters sent by the gods
    cut short our follies in a flash.
Creon: Oh it's hard.
    giving up the heart's desire . . . but I will do it —   1230
    no more fighting a losing battle with necessity.
Leader: Do it now, go, don't leave it to others.
Creon: Now — I'm on my way! Come, each of you,
    take up axes, make for the high ground,
    over there, quickly! I and my better judgment   1235
    have come round to this — I shackled her,
    I'll set her free myself. I am afraid . . .
    it's best to keep the established laws
    to the very day we die.

    Rushing out, followed by his entourage. The Chorus clusters around the altar.

Chorus: God of a hundred names!
                    Great Dionysus —   1240
Son and glory of Semele! Pride of Thebes —
Child of Zeus whose thunder rocks the clouds —
Lord of the famous lands of evening —
King of the Mysteries!
              King of Eleusis, Demeter's plain°
her breasting hills that welcome in the world —   1245
Great Dionysus!
            Bacchus,° living in Thebes
the mother-city of all your frenzied women —
                           Bacchus
    living along the Ismenus'° rippling waters
standing over the field sown with the Dragon's teeth!

You — we have seen you through the flaring smoky fires,   1250
    your torches blazing over the twin peaks
where nymphs of the hallowed cave climb onward
              fired with you, your sacred rage —
we have seen you at Castalia's running spring°
and down from the heights of Nysa° crowned with ivy   1255

1244 *Demeter's plain:* The goddess of grain was worshiped at Eleusis, near Athens.
1246 *Bacchus:* Another name for Dionysus.   1248 *Ismenus:* A river near Thebes where the
founders of the city were said to have sprung from a dragon's teeth.   1254 *Castalia's running spring:* The sacred spring of Apollo's oracle at Delphi.   1255 *Nysa:* A mountain where
Dionysus was worshiped.

the greening shore rioting vines and grapes
   down you come in your storm of wild women
     ecstatic, mystic cries —
          Dionysus —
down to watch and ward the roads of Thebes!

First of all cities, Thebes you honor first   1260
you and your mother, bride of the lightning —
come, Dionysus! now your people lie
in the iron grip of plague,
come in your racing, healing stride
     down Parnassus'° slopes   1265
or across the moaning straits.
        Lord of the dancing —
dance, dance the constellations breathing fire!
Great master of the voices of the night!
Child of Zeus, God's offspring, come, come forth!
Lord, king, dance with your nymphs, swirling, raving 1270
arm-in-arm in frenzy through the night
   they dance you, Iacchus° —
       Dance, Dionysus
giver of all good things!

Enter a Messenger from the side.

Messenger: Neighbors,
friends of the house of Cadmus° and the kings,
there's not a thing in this life of ours   1275
I'd praise or blame as settled once for all.
Fortune lifts and Fortune fells the lucky
and unlucky every day. No prophet on earth
can tell a man his fate. Take Creon:
there was a man to rouse your envy once,   1280
as I see it. He saved the realm from enemies;
taking power, he alone, the lord of the fatherland,
he set us true on course — flourished like a tree
with the noble line of sons he bred and reared . . .
and now it's lost, all gone.
       Believe me,   1285
when a man has squandered his true joys,
he's good as dead, I tell you, a living corpse.
Pile up riches in your house, as much as you like —
live like a king with a huge show of pomp,
but if real delight is missing from the lot,   1290
I wouldn't give you a wisp of smoke for it,
not compared with joy.
Leader: What now?
What new grief do you bring the house of kings?
Messenger: Dead, dead — and the living are guilty of their death!
Leader: Who's the murderer? Who is dead? Tell us.   1295

1265 *Parnassus:* A mountain in Greece that was sacred to Dionysus as well as other gods and goddesses. 1272 *Iacchus:* Dionysus. 1274 *Cadmus:* The legendary founder of Thebes.

Messenger: Haemon's gone, his blood spilled by the very hand —
Leader: His father's or his own?
Messenger: His own . . .
    raging mad with his father for the death —
Leader: Oh great seer,
    you saw it all, you brought your word to birth!
Messenger: Those are the facts. Deal with them as you will.   1300

    As he turns to go, Eurydice enters from the palace.

Leader: Look, Eurydice. Poor woman, Creon's wife,
    so close at hand. By chance perhaps,
    unless she's heard the news about her son.
Eurydice: My countrymen,
    all of you — I caught the sound of your words
    as I was leaving to do my part,   1305
    to appeal to queen Athena° with my prayers.
    I was just loosing the bolts, opening the doors,
    when a voice filled with sorrow, family sorrow,
    struck my ears, and I fell back, terrified,
    into the women's arms — everything went black.   1310
    Tell me the news, again, whatever it is . . .
    sorrow and I are hardly strangers;
    I can bear the worst.
Messenger: I — dear lady,
    I'll speak as an eye-witness. I was there.
    And I won't pass over one word of the truth.   1315
    Why should I try to soothe you with a story,
    only to prove a liar in a moment?
    Truth is always best.
               So,
    I escorted your lord, I guided him
    to the edge of the plain where the body lay,   1320
    Polynices, torn by the dogs and still unmourned.
    And saying a prayer to Hecate of the Crossroads,
    Pluto° too, to hold their anger and be kind,
    we washed the dead in a bath of holy water
    and plucking some fresh branches, gathering . . .   1325
    what was left of him, we burned them all together
    and raised a high mound of native earth, and then
    we turned and made for that rocky vault of hers,
    the hollow, empty bed of the bride of Death.
    And far off, one of us heard a voice,   1330
    a long wail rising, echoing
    out of that unhallowed wedding-chamber;
    he ran to alert the master and Creon pressed on,
    closer — the strange, inscrutable cry came sharper,
    throbbing around him now, and he let loose   1335
    a cry of his own, enough to wrench the heart,
    "Oh god, am I the prophet now? going down

1306 *Athena:* Goddess of wisdom and protector of Greek cities.   1322–1323 *Hecate, Pluto:*
Gods of the underworld.

the darkest road I've ever gone? My son —
it's *his* dear voice, he greets me! Go, men,
closer, quickly! Go through the gap,   1340
the rocks are dragged back —
right to the tomb's very mouth — and look,
see if it's Haemon's voice I think I hear,
or the gods have robbed me of my senses."

The king was shattered. We took his orders,   1345
went and searched, and there in the deepest,
dark recesses of the tomb we found her . . .
hanged by the neck in a fine linen noose,
strangled in her veils — and the boy,
his arms flung around her waist,   1350
clinging to her, wailing for his bride,
dead and down below, for his father's crimes
and the bed of his marriage blighted by misfortune.
When Creon saw him, he gave a deep sob,
he ran in, shouting, crying out to him,   1355
"Oh my child — what have you done? what seized you,
what insanity? what disaster drove you mad?
Come out, my son! I beg you on my knees!"
But the boy gave him a wild burning glance,
spat in his face, not a word in reply,   1360
he drew his sword — his father rushed out,
running as Haemon lunged and missed! —
and then, doomed, desperate with himself,
suddenly leaning his full weight on the blade,
he buried it in his body, halfway to the hilt.   1365
And still in his senses, pouring his arms around her,
he embraced the girl and breathing hard,
released a quick rush of blood,
bright red on her cheek glistening white.
And there he lies, body enfolding body . . .   1370
he has won his bride at last, poor boy,
not here but in the houses of the dead.

Creon shows the world that of all the ills
afflicting men the worst is lack of judgment.

Eurydice turns and reenters the palace.

Leader: What do you make of that? The lady's gone,   1375
   without a word, good or bad.
Messenger: I'm alarmed too
  but here's my hope — faced with her son's death,
she finds it unbecoming to mourn in public.
Inside, under her roof, she'll set her women
to the task and wail the sorrow of the house.   1380
She's too discreet. She won't do something rash.
Leader: I'm not so sure. To me, at least,

a long heavy silence promises danger,
just as much as a lot of empty outcries.
Messenger: We'll see if she's holding something back,   1385
      hiding some passion in her heart.
      I'm going in. You may be right — who knows?
      Even too much silence has its dangers.

*Exit to the palace. Enter Creon from the side, escorted by attendants carrying
Haemon's body on a bier.*

Leader: The king himself ! Coming toward us,
            look, holding the boy's head in his hands.   1390
            Clear, damning proof, if it's right to say so —
            proof of his own madness, no one else's,
                no, his own blind wrongs.
Creon: Ohhh,
      so senseless, so insane . . . my crimes,
      my stubborn, deadly —   1395
      Look at us, the killer, the killed,
      father and son, the same blood — the misery!
      My plans, my mad fanatic heart,
      my son, cut off so young!
      Ai, dead, lost to the world,   1400
      not through your stupidity, no, my own.
Leader: Too late,
        too late, you see what justice means.
Creon: Oh I've learned
            through blood and tears! Then, it was then,
            when the god came down and struck me — a great weight
            shattering, driving me down that wild savage path,   1405
            ruining, trampling down my joy. Oh the agony,
                the heartbreaking agonies of our lives.

Enter the Messenger from the palace.

Messenger: Master,
        what a hoard of grief you have, and you'll have more.
        The grief that lies to hand you've brought yourself —

Pointing to Haemon's body.

        the rest, in the house, you'll see it all too soon.   1410
Creon: What now? What's worse than this?
Messenger: The queen is dead.
        The mother of this dead boy . . . mother to the end —
        poor thing, her wounds are fresh.
Creon: No, no,
            harbor of Death, so choked, so hard to cleanse! —
            why me? why are you killing me?   1415
            Herald of pain, more words, more grief?
            I died once, you kill me again and again!
            What's the report, boy . . . some news for me?

My wife dead? O dear god!
Slaughter heaped on slaughter?

The doors open; the body of Eurydice is brought out on her bier.

Messenger: See for yourself: 1420
now they bring her body from the palace.
Creon: Oh no,
another, a second loss to break the heart.
What next, what fate still waits for me?
I just held my son in my arms and now,
look, a new corpse rising before my eyes —   1425
wretched, helpless mother — O my son!
Messenger: She stabbed herself at the altar,
then her eyes went dark, after she'd raised
a cry for the noble fate of Megareus,° the hero
killed in the first assault, then for Haemon,   1430
then with her dying breath she called down
torments on your head — you killed her sons.
Creon: Oh the dread,
I shudder with dread! Why not kill me too? —
run me through with a good sharp sword?
Oh god, the misery, anguish —   1435
I, I'm churning with it, going under.
Messenger: Yes, and the dead, the woman lying there,
piles the guilt of all their deaths on you.
Creon: How did she end her life, what bloody stroke?
Messenger: She drove home to the heart with her own hand,   1440
once she learned her son was dead . . . that agony.
Creon: And the guilt is all mine —
can never be fixed on another man,
no escape for me. I killed you,
I, god help me, I admit it all!   1445

To his attendants.

Take me away, quickly, out of sight.
I don't even exist — I'm no one. Nothing.
Leader: Good advice, if there's any good in suffering.
Quickest is best when troubles block the way.
Creon:

Kneeling in prayer.

Come, let it come! — that best of fates for me   1450
that brings the final day, best fate of all.
Oh quickly, now —
so I never have to see another sunrise.
Leader: That will come when it comes;
we must deal with all that lies before us.   1455
The future rests with the ones who tend the future.

1429 *Megareus:* A son of Creon and Eurydice; he died when Thebes was attacked.

Creon: That prayer — I poured my heart into that prayer!
Leader: No more prayers now. For mortal men
    there is no escape from the doom we must endure.
Creon: Take me away, I beg you, out of sight.   1460
        A rash, indiscriminate fool!
        I murdered you, my son, against my will —
        you too, my wife . . .
                  Wailing wreck of a man,
        whom to look to? where to lean for support?

Desperately turning from Haemon to Eurydice on their biers.

        Whatever I touch goes wrong — once more   1465
        a crushing fate's come down upon my head.

The Messenger and attendants lead Creon into the palace.

Chorus: Wisdom is by far the greatest part of joy,
        and reverence toward the gods must be safeguarded.
        The mighty words of the proud are paid in full
        with mighty blows of fate, and at long last   1470
           those blows will teach us wisdom.

The old citizens exit to the side.

Considerations for Critical Thinking and Writing

1. **FIRST RESPONSE.** What are Creon's reasons for issuing the decree forbidding Polynices' burial? What are Antigone's reasons for rejecting Creon's order? Whose arguments are more convincing?

2. What is the Chorus's position on Creon's decree? Does the Chorus see the conflict between Antigone and Creon as simply a collision between two strong-willed individuals, or does it see a larger issue at stake?

3. How does Ismene serve as a foil to Antigone? Does Ismene seem weak, or is she reasonable? Why does Antigone reject her sister's offer to martyr herself?

4. How does Haemon serve as a foil to Creon? Is Haemon's decision to commit suicide plausible?

5. What is Creon's attitude toward women? How does this affect his reaction to Antigone's disobedience to the state?

6. Who is responsible for what happens? Does Sophocles suggest that the tragedy could have been avoided if Creon or Antigone had behaved differently? Do Creon and Antigone share any similar characteristics?

7. Describe what you think Sophocles' attitudes were concerning the competing claims for the authority of the state over the individual. Explain how those views are indicated in the play and whether you agree or disagree with them.

8. How might the emphasis of the play have been changed if Sophocles had included the scene in the tomb between Haemon and Antigone? Why do you think he left out such a potentially affecting scene?

9. **CREATIVE RESPONSE.** If you were to stage this play in a contemporary setting, describe what kinds of sets you would use and how you would costume the players.

CONNECTIONS TO OTHER SELECTIONS

1. How is Creon's reaction to Haemon's and Tiresias's pleas that he rescind the decree similar to Oedipus's reaction to Creon and Tiresias in *Oedipus the King*?

2. What similarities and differences are there in Sophocles' characterization of Creon in *Antigone* and in *Oedipus the King*?

3. Consider this assessment of Antigone by the leader of the Chorus (lines 526–528):

> Like father like daughter,
> passionate, wild . . .
> she hasn't learned to bend before adversity.

    Does this accurately characterize Antigone? What similarities are there between Oedipus and his daughter? Could these lines also be used to describe Haemon and Ismene?

Perspectives on Sophocles

ARISTOTLE (384–322 B.C.)

On Tragic Character

c. 340 B.C.

Now since in the finest kind of tragedy the structure should be complex and not simple, and since it should also be a representation of terrible and piteous events (that being the special mark of this type of imitation), in the first place, it is evident that good men ought not to be shown passing from happiness to misfortune, for this does not inspire either pity or fear, but only revulsion; nor evil men rising from ill fortune to prosperity, for this is the most untragic plot of all—it lacks every requirement, in that it neither elicits human sympathy nor stirs pity or fear. And again, neither should an extremely wicked man be seen falling from prosperity into misfortune, for a plot so constructed might indeed call forth human sympathy, but would not excite pity or fear, since the first is felt for a person whose misfortune is undeserved and the second for someone like ourselves—pity for the man suffering undeservedly, fear for the man like ourselves—and hence neither pity nor fear would be aroused in this case. We are left with the man whose place is between these extremes. Such is the man who on the one hand is not preeminent in virtue and justice, and yet on the other hand does not fall into misfortune through vice or depravity, but falls because of some mistake; one among the number of the highly renowned and prosperous, such as Oedipus . . . and other famous men from families like [his].

It follows that the plot which achieves excellence will necessarily be single in outcome and not, as some say, double, and will consist in a change of fortune, not to prosperity from misfortune, but the opposite, from prosperity to misfortune, occasioned not by depravity, but by some great mistake on the part of one who is either such as I have described or better than this rather than worse. What actually has taken place has confirmed this; for though at first the poets accepted whatever myths came to hand, today the finest tragedies are founded upon the stories of only a few houses . . . and such . . . as have chanced to suffer terrible things or to do them. So then, tragedy having this construction is the finest kind of tragedy from an artistic point of view. And consequently those persons fall into the same error who bring it as a charge against Euripides° that this is what he does in his tragedies and that most of his plays have unhappy endings. For this is in fact the right procedure, as I have said; and the best proof is that on the stage and in the dramatic contests, plays of this kind seem the most tragic, provided they are successfully worked out, and Euripides, even if in everything else his management is faulty, seems at any rate to be the most tragic of the poets.

Second to this is the kind of plot that some persons place first, that which like the *Odyssey*° has a double structure and ends in opposite ways for the better characters and the worse. If it seems to be first, that is attributable to the weakness of the audience, since the poets only follow their lead and compose the kind of plays the spectators want. The pleasure it gives, however, is not that which comes from tragedy, but is rather the pleasure proper to comedy; for in comedy those who in the legend are the worst of enemies . . . end by leaving the scene as friends, and nobody is killed by anybody. . . .

With regard to the characters there are four things to aim at. First and foremost is that the characters be good. The personages will have character if, as aforesaid, they reveal in speech or in action what their moral choices are, and a good character will be one whose choices are good. It is possible to portray goodness in every class of persons; a woman may be good and a slave may be good, though perhaps as a class women are inferior and slaves utterly base. The second requisite is to make the character appropriate. Thus it is possible to portray any character as manly, but inappropriate for a female character to be manly or formidable in the way I mean. Third is to make the characters lifelike, which is something different from making them good and appropriate as described above. Fourth is to make them consistent. Even if the person being imitated is inconsistent and this is what the character is supposed to be, he should nevertheless be portrayed as consistently inconsistent. . . .

In the characters and in the plot-construction alike, one must strive for that which is either necessary or probable, so that whatever a character of any kind says or does may be the sort of thing such a character will inevitably or probably say or do and the events of the plot may follow one after another either inevitably or with probability. (Obviously, then, the *dénouement* of the plot should arise from the plot itself and not be brought about "from the machine." . . . The machine is to be used for matters lying outside the drama, either antecedents of the action which a human being cannot know, or things subsequent to the action that have to be prophesied and announced; for we accept it that the gods see everything. Within the events of the plot itself, however, there should be nothing unreasonable, or if there is, it should be kept outside the play proper as is done in the *Oedipus* of Sophocles.)

Euripides: Fifth-century B.C. Greek playwright whose tragedies include *Electra, Medea,* and *Alcestis.* *Odyssey:* The epic by the ancient Greek poet Homer that chronicles the voyage home from the Trojan War of Odysseus (also known as Ulysses).

Inasmuch as tragedy is an imitation of persons who are better than the average, the example of good portrait-painters should be followed. These, while reproducing the distinctive appearance of their subjects in a recognizable likeness, make them handsomer in the picture than they are in reality. Similarly the poet when he comes to imitate men who are irascible or easygoing or have other defects of character should depict them as such and yet as good men at the same time.

From *Poetics,* translated by James Hutton

CONSIDERATIONS FOR CRITICAL THINKING AND WRITING

1. Why does Aristotle insist that both virtuous and depraved characters are unsuitable as tragic figures? What kind of person constitutes a tragic character according to him?

2. Aristotle argues that it is "inappropriate for a female character to be manly or formidable" (para. 4). Do you think Antigone fits this negative description? Does she seem "inferior" to the men in the play?

3. Aristotle says that characters should be "lifelike" (para. 4), but he also points out that characters should be made "handsomer . . . than they are in reality" (para. 6). Is this a contradiction? Explain why or why not.

SIGMUND FREUD (1856–1939)

On the Oedipus Complex 1900

If *Oedipus Rex* moves a modern audience no less than it did the contemporary Greek one, the explanation can only be that its effect does not lie in the contrast between destiny and human will, but is to be looked for in the particular nature of the material on which that contrast is exemplified. There must be something which makes a voice within us ready to recognize the compelling force of destiny in the *Oedipus.* . . . His destiny moves us only because it might have been ours — because the oracle laid the same curse upon us before our birth as upon him. It is the fate of all of us, perhaps, to direct our first sexual impulse toward our mother and our first hatred and our first murderous wish against our father. Our dreams convince us that this is so. King Oedipus, who slew his father Laïus and married his mother Jocasta, merely shows us the fulfillment of our own childhood wishes. But, more fortunate than he, we have meanwhile succeeded, in so far as we have not become psychoneurotics, in detaching our sexual impulses from our mothers and in forgetting our jealousy of our fathers. Here is one in whom these primeval wishes of our childhood have been fulfilled, and we shrink back from him with the whole force of the repression by which those wishes have since that time been held down within us. While the poet, as he unravels the past, brings to light the guilt of Oedipus, he is at the same time compelling us to recognize our own inner minds, in which those same impulses, though suppressed, are still to be found. The contrast with which the closing Chorus leaves us confronted —

> . . . Fix on Oedipus your eyes,
> Who resolved the dark enigma, noblest champion and most wise.
> Like a star his envied fortune mounted beaming far and wide:
> Now he sinks in seas of anguish, whelmed beneath a raging tide . . .[1]

—strikes as a warning at ourselves and our pride, at us who since our childhood have grown so wise and so mighty in our own eyes. Like Oedipus, we live in ignorance of these wishes, repugnant to morality, which have been forced upon us by Nature, and after their revelation we may all of us well seek to close our eyes to the scenes of our childhood.

There is an unmistakable indication in the text of Sophocles' tragedy itself that the legend of Oedipus sprang from some primeval dream material which had as its content the distressing disturbance of a child's relation to his parents owing to the first stirrings of sexuality. At a point when Oedipus, though he is not yet enlightened, has begun to feel troubled by his recollection of the oracle, Jocasta consoles him by referring to a dream which many people dream, though, as she thinks, it has no meaning:

> Many a man ere now in dreams hath lain
> With her who bare him. He hath least annoy
> Who with such omens troubleth not his mind.[2]

Today, just as then, many men dream of having sexual relations with their mothers, and speak of the fact with indignation and astonishment. It is clearly the key to the tragedy and the complement to the dream of the dreamer's father being dead. The story of Oedipus is the reaction of the imagination to these two typical dreams. And just as these dreams, when dreamt by adults, are accompanied by feelings of repulsion, so too the legend must include horror and self-punishment. Its further modification originates once again in a misconceived secondary revision of the material, which has sought to exploit it for theological purposes. . . . The attempt to harmonize divine omnipotence with human responsibility must naturally fail in connection with this subject matter just as with any other.

From *Interpretation of Dreams,* translated by James Strachey

[1] Lewis Campbell's translation, lines 1524ff. [in *The Bedford Introduction to Literature,* lines 1679–1683].

[2] Lewis Campbell's translation, lines 982ff. [in *The Bedford Introduction to Literature,* lines 1074–1076].

CONSIDERATIONS FOR CRITICAL THINKING AND WRITING

1. Read the section on psychological criticism in Chapter 53, "Critical Strategies for Reading" (pp. 2050–52), for additional information about Freud's theory concerning the Oedipus complex. Explain whether you agree or disagree that Freud's approach offers the "key to the tragedy" of *Oedipus the King.*

2. How does Freud's view of tragic character differ from Aristotle's?

SOPHOCLES (496?–406 B.C.)

Another Translation of a Scene from Oedipus the King   *1920*

TRANSLATED BY J. T. SHEPPARD

> *Enter Oedipus, blind.*

Chorus: O sight for all the world to see
          Most terrible! O suffering
     Of all mine eyes have seen most terrible!
     Alas! What Fury came on thee?
     What evil Spirit, from afar,
     O Oedipus! O Wretched!
          Leapt on thee, to destroy?
     I cannot even Alas! look
     Upon thy face, though much I have
     To ask of thee, and much to hear,
          Aye, and to see — I cannot!
          Such terror is in thee!

Oedipus: Alas! O Wretched! Whither go
          My steps? My voice? It seems to float
               Far, far away from me.
          Alas! Curse of my Life, how far
               Thy leap hath carried thee!

Chorus: To sorrows none can bear to see or hear.

Oedipus: Ah! The cloud!
     Visitor unspeakable! Darkness upon me horrible!
     Unconquerable! Cloud that may not ever pass away!
               Alas!
     And yet again, alas! How deep they stab —
     These throbbing pains, and all those memories.

Chorus: Where such afflictions are, I marvel not,
     If soul and body made one doubled woe.

Oedipus: Ah! My friend!
     Still remains thy friendship. Still thine is the help that comforts me,
     And kindness, that can look upon these dreadful eyes unchanged.
               Ah me!
     My friend, I feel thy presence. Though mine eyes
     Be darkened, yet I hear thy voice, and know.

Chorus: Oh, dreadful deed! How wert thou steeled to quench
     Thy vision thus? What Spirit came on thee?

Oedipus: Apollo! 'Twas Apollo, friends,
     Willed the evil, willed, and brought the agony to pass!
          And yet the hand that struck was mine, mine only, wretched.
          Why should I see, whose eyes
     Had no more any good to look upon?

Chorus: 'Twas even as thou sayest.

Oedipus: Aye. For me . . . Nothing is left for sight.
          Nor anything to love:
     Nor shall the sound of greetings any more

          Fall pleasant on my ear.
   Away! Away! Out of the land, away!
       Banishment, Banishment! Fatal am I, accursed,
       And the hate on me, as on no man else, of the gods!
Chorus: Unhappy in thy fortune and the wit
   That shows it thee. Would thou hadst never known.
Oedipus: A curse upon the hand that loosed
   In the wilderness the cruel fetters of my feet,
       Rescued me, gave me life! Ah! Cruel was his pity,
         Since, had I died, so much
    I had not harmed myself and all I love.
Chorus: Aye, even so 'twere better.
Oedipus: Aye, for life never had led me then
       To shed my father's blood;
       Men had not called me husband of the wife
       That bore me in the womb.
   But now — but now — Godless am I, the son
      Born of impurity, mate of my father's bed,
        And if worse there be, I am Oedipus! It is mine!
Chorus: In this I know not how to call thee wise,
   For better wert thou dead than living — blind.
Oedipus: Nay, give me no more counsel. Bid me not
   Believe my deed, thus done, is not well done.
   I know 'tis well. When I had passed the grave,
   How could those eyes have met my father's gaze,
   Or my unhappy mother's — since on both
   I have done wrongs beyond all other wrong?
   Or live and see my children? — Children born
   As they were born! What pleasure in that sight?
   None for these eyes of mine, for ever, none.
   Nor in the sight of Thebes, her castles, shrines
   And images of the gods, whereof, alas!
   I robbed myself — myself, I spoke that word,
   I that she bred and nurtured, I her prince,
   And bade her thrust the sinner out, the man
   Proved of the gods polluted — Laïus' son.
   When such a stain by my own evidence
   Was on me, could I raise my eyes to them?
   No! Had I means to stop my ears, and choke
   The wells of sound, I had not held my hand,
   But closed my body like a prison-house
   To hearing as to sight. Sweet for the mind
   To dwell withdrawn, where troubles could not come.
      Cithaeron! Ah, why didst thou welcome me?
   Why, when thou hadst me there, didst thou not kill,
   Never to show the world myself — my birth!
      O Polybus, and Corinth, and the home
   Men called my father's ancient house, what sores
   Festered beneath that beauty that ye reared,
   Discovered now, sin out of sin begot.

O ye three roads, O secret mountain-glen,
Trees, and a pathway narrowed to the place
Where met the three, do you remember me?
I gave you blood to drink, my father's blood,
And so my own! Do you remember that?
The deed I wrought for you? Then, how I passed
Hither to other deeds?
                 O Marriage-bed
That gave me birth, and, having borne me, gave
Fresh children to your seed, and showed the world
Father, son, brother, mingled and confused,
Bride, mother, wife in one, and all the shame
Of deeds the foulest ever known to man.
   No. Silence for a deed so ill to do
Is better. Therefore lead me hence, away!
To hide me or to kill. Or to the sea
Cast me, where you shall look on me no more.
Come! Deign to touch me, though I am a man
Accursèd. Yield! Fear nothing! Mine are woes
That no man else, but I alone, must bear.

CONSIDERATIONS FOR CRITICAL THINKING AND WRITING

1. This excerpt from Sheppard's translation corresponds to lines 1433–1550 in Robert Fagles's translation (pp. 1458–60). Examine both versions of the scene and describe the diction and tone of each. If you find one of the translations more effective than the other, indicate why.

2. Explain whether the different translations affect your understanding or interpretation of the scene.

MURIEL RUKEYSER (1913–1980)

On Oedipus the King
Myth
                                               1973

Long afterward, Oedipus, old and blinded, walked the
roads.   He smelled a familiar smell.   It was
the Sphinx.   Oedipus said, "I want to ask one question.
Why didn't I recognize my mother?"   "You gave the
wrong answer," said the Sphinx.   "But that was what   5
made everything possible," said Oedipus.   "No," she said.
"When I asked, What walks on four legs in the morning,
two at noon, and three in the evening, you answered,
Man.   You didn't say anything about woman."
"When you say Man," said Oedipus, "you include women   10
too. Everyone knows that."   She said, "That's what
you think."

CONSIDERATIONS FOR CRITICAL THINKING AND WRITING

1. What elements of the Oedipus story does Rukeyser allude to in the poem?

2. To what does the title of Rukeyser's poem, "Myth," refer? How does the word *myth* carry more than one meaning?

3. This poem is amusing, but its ironic ending points to a serious theme. What is it? Does Sophocles' play address any of the issues raised in the poem?

DAVID WILES

On Oedipus the King *as a Political Play*   2000

Oedipus becomes a political play when we focus on the interaction of actor and chorus, and see how the chorus form a democratic mass jury. Each sequence of dialogue takes the form of a contest for the chorus' sympathy, with Oedipus sliding from the role of prosecutor to that of defendant, and each choral dance offers a provisional verdict. After Oedipus' set-to with Teiresias the sooth-sayer, the chorus decide to trust Oedipus on the basis of his past record; after his argument with his brother-in-law Creon, the chorus show their distress and urge compromise. Once Oedipus has confessed to a killing and Jocasta has declared that oracles have no force, the chorus are forced to think about polit-ical tyranny, torn between respect for divine law and trust in their rulers. In the next dance they assume that the contradiction is resolved and Oedipus has turned out to be the son of a god. Finally a slave's evidence reveals that the man most honoured by society is in fact the least to be envied. The political implications are clear: there is no space in democratic society for such as Oedi-pus. Athenians, like the chorus of the play, must reject the temptation to believe one man can calculate the future.

                              From *Greek Theatre Performance: An Introduction*

CONSIDERATIONS FOR CRITICAL THINKING AND WRITING

1. Consider one of the scenes mentioned by Wiles and discuss in detail how "the chorus form a democratic mass jury" that judges Oedipus.

2. Discuss the "political implications" of the play that, according to Wiles, suggest "there is no space in democratic society for such as Oedipus."

JEAN ANOUILH (1910–1987)

A Scene from Antigone   1944

TRANSLATED BY LEWIS GALANTIÈRE

Creon: I shall save you yet. (*He goes below the table to the chair at end of table, takes off his coat, and places it on the chair.*) God knows, I have things enough to do today without wasting my time on an insect like you. There's plenty to do, I assure you, when you've just put down a revolution. But urgent things can wait. I am not going to let politics be the cause of your death. For it is a fact that this whole business is nothing but politics: the mournful shade of Polynices, the decomposing corpse, the sentimental weeping, and the hysteria that you mistake for heroism — nothing but politics.

Look here. I may not be soft, but I'm fastidious. I like things clean, ship-shape, well scrubbed. Don't think that I am not just as offended as you are by the thought of that meat rotting in the sun. In the evening, when the breeze comes in off the sea, you can smell it in the palace, and it nauseates me. But I refuse even to shut my window. It's vile; and I can tell you what I wouldn't tell anybody else: it's stupid, monstrously stupid. But the people of Thebes have got to have their noses rubbed into it a little longer. My God! If it was up to me, I should have had them bury your brother long ago as a mere matter of public hygiene. I admit that what I am doing is childish. But if the featherheaded rabble I govern are to understand what's what, that stench has got to fill the town for a month!

Antigone (turns to him): You are a loathsome man!

Creon: I agree. My trade forces me to be. We could argue whether I ought or ought not to follow my trade; but once I take on the job, I must do it properly.

Antigone: Why do you do it at all?

Creon: My dear, I woke up one morning and found myself King of Thebes. God knows, there were other things I loved in life more than power.

Antigone: Then you should have said no.

Creon: Yes, I could have done that. Only, I felt that it would have been cow-ardly. I should have been like a workman who turns down a job that has to be done. So I said yes.

Antigone: So much the worse for you, then. I didn't say yes. I can say no to any-thing I think vile, and I don't have to count the cost. But because you said yes, all that you can do, for all your crown and your trappings, and your guards — all that you can do is to have me killed.

Creon: Listen to me.

Antigone: If I want to. I don't have to listen to you if I don't want to. You've said your *yes.* There is nothing more you can tell me that I don't know. You stand there, drinking in my words. *(She moves behind chair.)* Why is it that you don't call your guards? I'll tell you why. You want to hear me out to the end; that's why.

Creon: You amuse me.

Antigone: Oh, no, I don't. I frighten you. That is why you talk about saving me. Everything would be so much easier if you had a docile, tongue-tied little Antigone living in the palace. I'll tell you something, Uncle Creon: I'll give you back one of your own words. You are too fastidious to make a good tyrant. But you are going to have to put me to death today, and you know it. And that's what frightens you. God! Is there anything uglier than a frightened man!

Creon: Very well. I am afraid, then. Does that satisfy you? I am afraid that if you insist upon it, I shall have to have you killed. And I don't want to.

Antigone: I don't have to do things that I think are wrong. If it comes to that, you didn't really want to leave my brother's body unburied, did you? Say it! Admit that you didn't.

Creon: I have said it already.

Antigone: But you did it just the same. And now, though you don't want to do it, you are going to have me killed. And you call that being a king!

Creon: Yes, I call that being a king.

Antigone: Poor Creon! My nails are broken, my fingers are bleeding, my arms are covered with the welts left by the paws of your guards—but I am a queen!

Creon: Then why not have pity on me, and live? Isn't your brother's corpse, rotting there under my windows, payment enough for peace and order in Thebes? My son loves you. Don't make me add your life to the payment. I've paid enough.

Antigone: No, Creon! You said yes, and made yourself king. Now you will never stop paying.

Creon: But God in heaven! Won't you try to understand me! I'm trying hard enough to understand you! There had to be one man who said yes. Somebody had to agree to captain the ship. She had sprung a hundred leaks; she was loaded to the water line with crime, ignorance, poverty. The wheel was swinging with the wind. The crew refused to work and were looting the cargo. The officers were building a raft, ready to slip overboard and desert the ship. The mast was splitting, the wind was howling, the sails were beginning to rip. Every man jack on board was about to drown—and only because the only thing they thought of was their own skins and their cheap little day-to-day traffic. Was that a time, do you think, for playing with words like yes and no? Was that a time for a man to be weighing the pros and cons, wondering if he wasn't going to pay too dearly later on; if he wasn't going to lose his life, or his family, or his touch with other men? You grab the wheel, you right the ship in the face of a mountain of water. You shout an order, and if one man refuses to obey, you shoot straight into the mob. Into the mob, I say! The beast as nameless as the wave that crashes down upon your deck; as nameless as the whipping wind. The thing that drops when you shoot may be someone who poured you a drink the night before; but it has no name. And you, braced at the wheel, you have no name, either. Nothing has a name—except the ship, and the storm. *(A pause as he looks at her.)* Now do you understand?

Antigone: I am not here to understand. That's all very well for you. I am here to say no to you, and die.

Creon: It is easy to say no.

Antigone: Not always.

Creon: It is easy to say no. To say yes, you have to sweat and roll up your sleeves and plunge both hands into life up to the elbows. It is easy to say no, even if saying no means death. All you have to do is to sit still and wait. Wait to go on living; wait to be killed. That is the coward's part. *No* is one of your man-made words. Can you imagine a world in which trees say *no* to the sap? In which beasts say *no* to hunger or to propagation? Animals are good, simple, tough. They move in droves, nudging one another onwards, all traveling the same road. Some of them keel over, but the rest go on; and no matter how many may fall by the wayside, there are always those few left that go on bringing their young into the world, traveling the same road with the same obstinate will, unchanged from those who went before.

Antigone: Animals, eh, Creon! What a king you could be if only men were animals!

CONSIDERATIONS FOR CRITICAL THINKING AND WRITING

1. What are Creon's reasons for not burying Polynices? How does he defend his actions as a ruler?

2. In what sense is Antigone correct when she describes Creon as "too fastidious to make a good tyrant"?

3. Do you agree with Creon that Antigone takes "the coward's part" by saying no rather than yes? With which character do you sympathize more? How might Creon's position be related to the fact that France was occupied by German troops during World War II, when Anouilh wrote this play?

4. How does Anouilh's treatment of Creon compare with Sophocles'?

MAURICE SAGOFF (1910–1998)

A Humorous Distillation of Antigone   1980

Tyrant Creon's stern advice is
"Do not bury Polynices!
Thebes' defenders had to squash him—
Now we'll let the buzzards nosh him!"
But Antigone, the brave,   5
Dared to dig her brother's grave:
"Man-made laws my soul defies—
Live by laws divine!" she cries.

Creon locks her up, the demon!
Though she's pledged to marry Haemon   10
(That's his son). Now comes a seer
Prophesying woes severe:
If her brother's not entombed
And she dies, then Haemon's doomed!

Creon seeing things go screwy,   15
Wilts, and tries to bang a U-ee,
But the Gods who drive the hearse
Seldom shove it in reverse . . .
Carnage follows, sure as Fate;
Here's the body-count to date—   20
1. Antigone   2. her brother
3. young Haemon   4. his mother
(If more bodies fail to fall,
It's because the cast is small).

Strung-out Creon takes the blame.   25
Exits, croaking "Rotten shame!"

From *Shrinklits: Seventy of the World's Towering Classics Cut Down to Size*

CONSIDERATIONS FOR CRITICAL THINKING AND WRITING

1. Sagoff writes in his tongue-in-cheek introduction to *Shrinklits* that "inside every fat book is a skinny book trying to get out, struggling to cut through the mummylike wrappings of long-winded descriptions, superfluous characters, endless conversations, and turgid style." How successful is this poem in summarizing the plot of *Antigone*? What is left out of Sagoff's account?

2. **CREATIVE RESPONSE.** Using Sagoff's version of *Antigone* as your inspiration, choose another play in the text and try writing a shrinklit that does it humorous justice.

Two Complementary Critical Readings

R. G. A. BUXTON (B. 1948)

The Major Critical Issue in Antigone   *1984*

It seems agreed that the main critical issue is: how do we evaluate the respective moral positions of Antigone and Creon. Provided this is not asked in order to achieve "that nice apportionment of blame to which critics are so much more prone than dramatists,"[1] but rather with the aim of teasing out just what is at stake between the two principal figures, the question is worthwhile.

Defenders of Creon appear from time to time. There is no doubt that some of the sentiments he expresses, particularly in his opening programmatic speech, are laudable in themselves; nor should there be any doubt that Creon receives some measure of sympathy as he carries his son's body on stage at the end. But is his original proclamation (it is not a law) morally acceptable? Tiresias' dire warnings strongly suggest it is not. There has been much argument about how Creon's edict related to Athenian law, but certain points are clear: although there was apparently nothing abnormal in the denial of burial in his homeland to a traitor, not only was there a custom, specifically associated with Athens, according to which one should not pass a corpse by without placing some dust upon it, but also, in forbidding Polynices burial *anywhere,* in actively ensuring that his body be torn apart by dogs and birds, Creon plainly went too far.

Most critics accept the moral impropriety of Creon's proclamation and disagree only in the degree (or absence) of qualification which they allow in their approval of Antigone. For some the approval is absolute; others, believing gray to be a more interesting color than black and white, stress problematic aspects of her behavior — harshness towards Ismene, relentless concern with honor, etc. A beneficial corollary of the latter approach is that, by emphasizing the particularity of Antigone's character, it makes us less likely to reduce the play to an opposition between principles — city *versus* kin-bond, state *versus* individual, or whatever. Neither Creon nor Antigone is the vehicle for a simple

---

[1] R. P. Winnington-Ingram, *Sophocles: An Interpretation* (Cambridge, England: Cambridge UP, 1980), 75.

idea: "the theme of . . . *Antigone* . . . [is] the tragedy of two human downfalls, separate in nature, . . . following one another as contrasting patterns."[2]

From *Sophocles*

[2] Reinhardt, *Sophocles* (Oxford, England: Oxford UP, 1979), 65. For *Antigone* as comprising two interdependent and equally important downfalls, see J. C. Hogan, "The Protagonists of the *Antigone*," *Arethusa* 5 (1972), 93–100.

CONSIDERATIONS FOR CRITICAL THINKING AND WRITING

1. How do you think "the particularity of Antigone's character . . . makes us less likely to reduce the play to an opposition between principles" (para. 3)? How does Sophocles' characterization of her make the play more complex?

2. Write an essay in which you agree or disagree that the theme of *Antigone* is "'the tragedy of two human downfalls, separate in nature, . . . following one another as contrasting patterns'" (para. 3). Do you think this theme is a means of resolving critical debate about the play or a way to evade having to choose between Antigone and Creon?

CYNTHIA P. GARDINER (B. 1942)
The Function of the Chorus in Antigone   1987

[*Antigone* is] concerned with the topic of political morality, with philosophies of governance and the conflict of religion and law. Yet despite the immensity of these abstractions, the immediate dramatic intent of the poet is not the subject of critical dispute, in that critics do not tend to hold violently contradictory opinions about the poet's own views. Nearly everyone agrees that Sophocles intended to portray Antigone's burial of Polynices as "right" — sanctioned by the gods according to Tiresias' revelations — and Creon's opposition to the burial as "wrong," insofar as his opposition arises from tyrannical behavior. It then becomes merely a question of the degree to which one condemns Creon or approves Antigone; the latter course usually involves an appraisal of Antigone's motives and of her behavior as a woman.

The lengthy and frequent lyrics have exerted considerable influence upon the interpretation of the play's symbolism and judgment. Some of the odes are apparently so loosely connected to the action that they can be readily lifted out of context to function as independent poems. Or, when left in the play, they seem sometimes so ambiguous that their relevance to the plot is perceptible only through the most detailed and subtle analysis. It is generally agreed nowadays that the most productive approach to interpreting the choral lyrics is to assume that they arise from a distinct and consistent persona. This being accepted, it is again a question of the degree to which one believes that the chorus support either Creon or Antigone. Some say that the chorus are utterly devoted to Creon throughout the play, or right up to the last possible moment at line 1272; some, that they begin by supporting the king but change their minds at one earlier point or another during the action. Others see the chorus as vacillating between viewpoints until a decision is forced upon them by Tiresias; still others see them as Antigone's partisans, though necessarily secret ones, from the very beginning.

From *The Sophoclean Chorus: A Study of Character and Function*

Considerations for Critical Thinking and Writing

1. Do you agree with Gardiner that Antigone was "right" and Creon "wrong" (para. 1)? Explain why. How is this issue made complicated by Antigone's character?

2. Of the various interpretations Gardiner summarizes concerning the chorus's loyalty to Creon or Antigone, which do you think is most accurate? In an essay explain why.

Suggested Topics for Longer Papers

1. In *Oedipus the King* and in *Antigone,* private and public worlds collide and produce overwhelming conflicts for the protagonists. In your essay, explore how the plays' conflicts can be framed by a consideration of the private and public identities of the major characters.

2. Individual responses to authority loom large in each play. Use the library to determine how Sophocles' contemporaries regarded individuals' responsibility to their kings and their kings' obligations to them. Given this context, how do you judge the behavior of Oedipus and Creon as kings in their respective societies?

48

A Study of
William Shakespeare

> All the world's a stage,
> And all the men and women
>   merely players:
> They have their exits and their
>   entrances;
> And one man in his time plays
>   many parts . . .
> —WILLIAM SHAKESPEARE

Shakespeare—the nearest thing in
incarnation to the eye of God.
—SIR LAURENCE OLIVIER

Although relatively little is known about William Shakespeare's life, his writings reveal him to have been an extraordinary man. His vitality, compassion, and insights are evident in his broad range of characters, who have fascinated generations of audiences, and his powerful use of the English language, which has been celebrated since his death nearly four centuries ago. Ben Jonson, his contemporary, rightly claimed that "he was not of an age, but for all time!" Shakespeare's plays have been produced so often and his writings read so widely that quotations from them have woven their way into our everyday conversations. If you have ever experienced "fear and trembling" because there was "something in the wind" or discovered that it

"First Folio" portrait (top). The image of William Shakespeare above is a portrait included on the *First Folio,* a collected edition of Shakespeare's plays published seven years after his death. **"Chandos" portrait** (middle). This is an image painted during Shakespeare's lifetime known as the "Chandos portrait," rumored to have been painted by Shakespeare's friend and fellow actor Richard Burbage. **Shakespeare's signature** (bottom). The signature shown here is one of the bard's six authenticated signatures in existence, and is from his last will and testament.

was "a foregone conclusion" that you would "make a virtue of necessity," then it wouldn't be quite accurate for you to say that Shakespeare "was Greek to me" because these phrases come, respectively, from his plays *Much Ado about Nothing, Comedy of Errors, Othello, The Two Gentlemen of Verona,* and *Julius Caesar.* Many more examples could be cited, but it is enough to say that Shakespeare's art endures. His words may give us only an oblique glimpse of his life, but they continue to give us back the experience of our own lives.

Shakespeare was born in Stratford-on-Avon on or about April 23, 1564. His father, an important citizen who held several town offices, married a woman from a prominent family; however, when their son was only a teenager, the family's financial situation became precarious. Shakespeare probably attended the Stratford grammar school, but no records of either his schooling or his early youth exist. As limited as his education was, it is clear that he was for his time a learned man. At the age of eighteen, he struck out on his own and married the twenty-six-year-old Anne Hathaway, who bore him a daughter in 1583 and twins, a boy and a girl, in 1585. Before he was twenty-one, Shakespeare had a wife and three children to support.

What his life was like for the next seven years is not known, but there is firm evidence that by 1592 he was in London enjoying some success as both an actor and a playwright. By 1594 he had also established himself as a poet with two lengthy poems, *Venus and Adonis* and *The Rape of Lucrece.* But it was in the theater that he made his living and his strongest reputation. He was well connected with a successful troupe first known as the Lord Chamberlain's Men; they built the famous Globe Theatre in 1599. Later this company, because of the patronage of King James, came to be known as the King's Men. Writing plays for this company throughout his career, Shakespeare also became one of its principal shareholders, an arrangement that allowed him to prosper in London as well as in his native Stratford, where in 1597 he bought a fine house called New Place. About 1611 he retired there with his family, although he continued writing plays. He died on April 23, 1616, and was buried at Holy Trinity Church in Stratford.

The documented details of Shakespeare's life provide barely enough information for a newspaper obituary. But if his activities remain largely unknown, his writings—among them thirty-seven plays and 154 sonnets—more than compensate for that loss. Plenty of authors have produced more work, but no writer has created so much literature that has been so universally admired. Within twenty-five years Shakespeare's dramatic works included *Hamlet, Macbeth, King Lear, Othello, Julius Caesar, Richard III, Henry IV, Romeo and Juliet, Love's Labour's Lost, A Midsummer Night's Dream, The Tempest, Twelfth Night,* and *Measure for Measure.* These plays represent a broad range of characters and actions conveyed in poetic language that reveals human nature as well as the author's genius.

Web Explore contexts for William Shakespeare at bedfordstmartins.com/meyerlit.

Chronology

1564	Born in April in Stratford-on-Avon. Shakespeare's birthday is traditionally observed on April 23.
1568	Shakespeare's father becomes bailiff (comparable to mayor).
1582	Marries Anne Hathaway.
1583	Daughter Susanna is born.
1585	Twins, Hamnet and Judith, are born.
1585–92	The "lost years." There are many myths about how Shakespeare spent this time before he became known as a playwright in London, but none can be proven and nothing definite is known.
1592	Works as an actor and playwright in London.
1592–93	Writes *Richard III,* among other plays.
1593	Narrative poem *Venus and Adonis* is published.
1594	Works as actor and playwright with the Lord Chamberlain's Company of players, a company that performs at the Globe Theatre.
c. 1594–96	Writes *Romeo and Juliet, Richard II,* and *A Midsummer Night's Dream,* among other plays.
1596	Hamnet (Shakespeare's son) dies.
1596–98	Writes *1 Henry IV* and *2 Henry IV.*
1599	Writes *Julius Caesar.*
c. 1600	Writes *Hamlet.*
1601	Shakespeare's father dies.
1603	Queen Elizabeth I of England dies.
1603–04	Writes *Othello.*
1604	King James I of England is coronated. (James patronizes Shakespeare's company, so they become known as the King's Men.)
1605–07	Writes *King Lear, Macbeth,* and *Antony and Cleopatra.*
c. 1610–11	Writes *The Tempest.*
1616	Dies on April 23.
1623	First Folio edition of Shakespeare's plays is published.

SHAKESPEARE'S THEATER

Drama languished in Europe after the fall of Rome during the fifth and sixth centuries. From about A.D. 400 to 900 almost no record of dramatic productions exists except for those of minstrels and other entertainers, such as acrobats and jugglers, who traveled through the countryside. The

Catholic church was instrumental in suppressing drama because the theater — represented by the excesses of Roman productions — was seen as subversive. No state-sponsored festivals brought people together in huge theaters the way they had in Greek and Roman times.

In the tenth century, however, the church helped revive theater by incorporating dialogues into the Mass as a means of dramatizing portions of the Gospels. These brief dialogues developed into more elaborate mystery plays, miracle plays, and morality plays, anonymous works that were created primarily to inculcate religious principles rather than to entertain. But these works also marked the reemergence of relatively large dramatic productions.

Mystery plays dramatize stories from the Bible, such as the Creation, the Fall of Adam and Eve, or the Crucifixion. The most highly regarded surviving example is *The Second Shepherd's Play* (c. 1400), which dramatizes Christ's nativity. *Miracle plays* are based on the lives of saints. An extant play of the late fifteenth century, for example, is titled *Saint Mary Magdalene*. *Morality plays* present allegorical stories in which virtues and vices are personified to teach humanity how to achieve salvation. *Everyman* (c. 1500), the most famous example, has as its central conflict every person's struggle to avoid the sins that lead to hell and practice the virtues that are rewarded in heaven.

The clergy who performed these plays gave way to trade guilds that presented them outside the church on stages featuring scenery and costumed characters. The plays' didactic content was gradually abandoned in favor of broad humor and worldly concerns. Thus by the sixteenth century religious drama had been replaced largely by secular drama.

Because theatrical productions were no longer sponsored and financed by the church or trade guilds during Shakespeare's lifetime, playwrights had to figure out ways to draw audiences willing to pay for entertainment. This necessitated some simple but important changes. Somehow, people had to be prevented from seeing a production unless they paid. Hence an enclosed space with controlled access was created. In addition, the plays had to change frequently enough to keep audiences returning, and this resulted in more experienced actors and playwrights sensitive to their audiences' tastes and interests. Plays compelling enough to attract audiences had to employ a powerful writing brought to life by convincing actors in entertaining productions. Shakespeare always wrote his dramas for the stage — for audiences who would see and hear the characters. The conventions of the theater for which he wrote are important, then, for appreciating and understanding his plays. Detailed information about Elizabethan theater (theater during the reign of Elizabeth I, from 1558 to 1603) is less than abundant, but historians have been able to piece together a good sense of what theaters were like from sources such as drawings, building contracts, and stage directions.

Early performances of various kinds took place in the courtyards of inns and taverns. These secular entertainments attracted people of all classes. To the dismay of London officials, such gatherings were also settings for the illegal activities of brawlers, thieves, and prostitutes. To avoid licensing regulations, some theaters were constructed outside the city's limits. The Globe, for instance, built by the Lord Chamberlain's Company, with which Shakespeare was closely associated, was located on the south bank of the Thames River. Regardless of the play, an Elizabethan theatergoer was likely to have an exciting time. Playwrights understood the varied nature of their audiences, so the plays appealed to a broad range of sensibilities and tastes. Philosophy and poetry rubbed shoulders with violence and sexual jokes, and somehow all were made compatible.

Physically, Elizabethan theaters resembled the courtyards where they originated, but the theaters could accommodate more people — perhaps as many as twenty-five hundred. The exterior of a theater building was many-sided or round and enclosed a yard that was only partially roofed over, to take advantage of natural light. The interior walls consisted of three galleries of seats looking onto a platform stage that extended from the rear wall. These seats were sheltered from the weather and more comfortable than the area in front of the stage, which was known as the *pit*. Here "groundlings" paid a penny to stand and watch the performance. Despite the large number of spectators, the theater created an intimate atmosphere because the audience closely surrounded the stage on three sides.

This arrangement produced two theatrical conventions: asides and soliloquies. An **aside** is a speech directed only to the audience. It makes the audience privy to a character's thoughts, allowing them to perceive ironies and intrigues that other characters know nothing about. In a large performing space, such as a Greek amphitheater, asides would be unconvincing because they would have to be declaimed loudly to be heard, but they were well suited to Elizabethan theaters. A **soliloquy** is a speech delivered while an actor is alone on the stage; like an aside, it reveals a character's state of mind. Hamlet's "To be or not to be" speech is the most famous example of a soliloquy.

The Elizabethan platform stage was large enough — approximately twenty-five feet deep and forty feet wide — to allow a wide variety of actions, ranging from festive banquets to bloody battles. Sections of the floor could be opened or removed to create, for instance, the gravediggers' scene in *Hamlet* or to allow characters to exit through trapdoors. At the rear of the platform an inner stage was covered by curtains that could be drawn to reveal an interior setting, such as a bedroom or tomb. The curtains were also a natural location for a character to hide in order to overhear conversations. On each side of the curtains were doors through which characters entered and exited. An upper stage could be used as a watchtower, a castle wall, or a balcony. Although most of the action occurred on the main platform stage, there were opportunities for fluid movements from one acting area to another, providing a variety of settings.

These settings were not, however, elaborately indicated by scenery or props. A scene might change when one group of characters left the stage and another entered. A table and some chairs could be carried on quickly

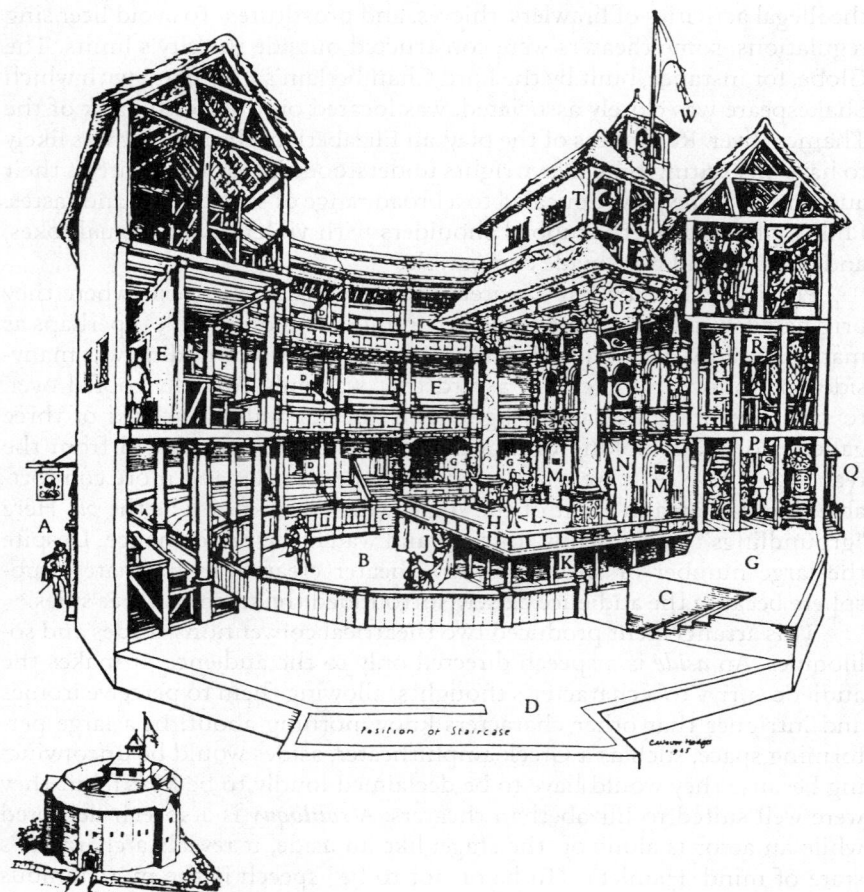

A	Main entrance
B	The yard
C	Entrances to lowest gallery
D	Position of entrances to staircase and upper galleries
E	Corridor serving the different sections of the middle gallery
F	Middle gallery ("Twopenny Rooms")
G	Position of "Gentlemen's Rooms" or "Lords' Rooms"
H	The stage
J	The hanging being put up round the stage
K	The "hell" under the stage

L	The stage trap leading down to the hell
M	Stage doors
N	Curtained "place behind the stage"
O	Gallery above the stage, used as required sometimes by musicians, sometimes by spectators, and often as part of the play
P	Backstage area (the tiring-house)
Q	Tiring-house door
R	Dressing-rooms
S	Wardrobe and storage
T	The hut housing the machine for lowering enthroned gods, etc., to the stage
U	The "heavens"
W	Hoisting the playhouse flag

A Conjectural Reconstruction of the Globe Theatre, 1599–1613. (Drawing by C. Walter Hodges from his *Globe Restored,* published by Oxford University Press © 1968 C. Walter Hodges. Reprinted with permission of Oxford University Press.)

to suggest a tavern. But the action was not interrupted for set changes. Instead, the characters' speeches often identify the location of a scene. (In modern editions of Shakespeare's plays, editors indicate in brackets the scene breaks, settings, and movements of actors not identified in the original manuscripts to help readers keep track of things.) Today's performances of the plays frequently use more elaborate settings and props. But Shakespeare's need to paint his scenery with words resulted in many poetic descriptions. Here is one of moonlight from *Merchant of Venice:*

> How sweet the moonlight sleeps upon this bank!
> Here will we sit and let the sounds of music
> Creep in our ears. Soft stillness and the night
> Become the touches of sweet harmony.

Although the settings were scant and the props mostly limited to what an actor carried onto the stage (a sword, a document, a shovel), Elizabethan costuming was an elaborate visual treat that identified the characters. Moreover, because women were not permitted to act in the theater, their roles were played by young boys dressed in female costumes. In addition, elaborate sound effects were used to create atmosphere. A flourish of trumpets might accompany the entrance of a king; small cannons might be heard during a battle; thunder might punctuate a storm. In short, Elizabethan theater was alive with sights and sounds, but at the center of the stage was the playwright's language; that's where the magic began.

THE RANGE OF SHAKESPEARE'S DRAMA: HISTORY, COMEDY, AND TRAGEDY

Shakespeare's plays fall into three basic categories: histories, comedies, and tragedies. Broadly speaking, a history play is any drama based on historical materials. In this case, Shakespeare's *Antony and Cleopatra* and *Julius Caesar* would fit the definition, since they feature historical figures. More specifically, though, a **history play** is a British play based primarily on Raphael Holinshed's *Chronicles of England, Scotland, and Ireland* (1578). This account of British history was popular toward the end of the sixteenth century because of the patriotic pride that was produced by the British defeat of the Spanish Armada in 1588, and it was an important source for a series of plays Shakespeare wrote treating the reigns of British kings from Richard II to Henry VIII. The political subject matter of these plays both entertained audiences and instructed them in virtues and vices involved in England's past efforts to overcome civil war and disorder. Ambition, deception, and treason were of more than historical interest. Shakespeare's audiences saw these plays about the fifteenth century as ways of sorting through the meanings of both the calamities of the past and the uncertainties of the present.

Although Shakespeare used Holinshed's *Chronicles* as a source, he did not hesitate to make changes for dramatic purposes. In *1 Henry IV,* for example, he ages Henry IV to contrast him with the youthful Prince Hal, and he makes Hotspur younger than he actually was to have him serve as a foil to the prince. The serious theme of Hal's growth into the kind of man who would make an ideal king is counterweighted by Shakespeare's comic creation of Falstaff, that good-humored "huge hill of flesh" filled with delightful contradictions. Falstaff had historic antecedents, but the true source of his identity is the imagination of Shakespeare, a writer who was, after all, a dramatist first.

Comedy is a strong element in *1 Henry IV,* but the play's overall tone is serious. Falstaff's behavior ultimately gives way to the measured march of English history. While Shakespeare encourages us to laugh at some of the participants, we are not invited to laugh at the history of English monarchies. Comedy even appears in Shakespeare's tragedies, as in Hamlet's jests with the gravediggers or in Emilia's biting remarks in *Othello.* This use of comedy is called **comic relief,** a humorous scene or incident that alleviates tension in an otherwise serious work. In many instances these moments enhance the thematic significance of the story in addition to providing laughter. When Hamlet jokes with the gravediggers, we laugh, but something hauntingly serious about the humor also intensifies our more serious emotions.

A true comedy, however, lacks a tragedy's sense that some great disaster will finally descend on the protagonist. There are conflicts and obstacles that must be confronted, but in comedy the characters delight us by overcoming whatever initially thwarts them. We can laugh at their misfortunes because we are confident that everything will turn out fine in the end. Shakespearean comedy tends to follow this general principle; it begins with problems and ends with their resolution.

Shakespeare's comedies are called **romantic comedies** because they typically involve lovers whose hearts are set on each other but whose lives are complicated by disapproving parents, deceptions, jealousies, illusions, confused identities, disguises, or other misunderstandings. Conflicts are present, but they are more amusing than threatening. This lightness is apparent in some of the comedies' titles: the conflict in a play such as *A Midsummer Night's Dream* is, in a sense, *Much Ado about Nothing—As You Like It* in a comedy. Shakespeare orchestrates the problems and confusion that typify the initial plotting of a romantic comedy into harmonious wedding arrangements in the final scenes. In these comedies life is a celebration, a feast that always satisfies, because the generosity of the humor leaves us with a revived appetite for life's surprising possibilities. Discord and misunderstanding give way to concord and love. Marriage symbolizes a pledge that life itself is renewable, so we are left with a sense of new beginnings.

Although a celebration of life, comedy is also frequently used as a vehicle for criticizing human affairs. **Satire** casts a critical eye on vices and follies by holding them up to ridicule — usually to point out an absurdity so that it can be avoided or corrected. In *Twelfth Night* Malvolio is satirized for his priggishness and pomposity. He thinks himself better than almost everyone around him, but Shakespeare reveals him to be comic as well as pathetic. We come to understand what Malvolio will apparently never comprehend: that no one can take him as seriously as he takes himself. Polonius is subjected to a similar kind of scrutiny in *Hamlet.*

Malvolio's ambitious efforts to attract Olivia's affections are rendered absurd by Shakespeare's use of both high and low comedy. **High comedy** consists of verbal wit, while **low comedy** is generally associated with physical action and is less intellectual. Through puns and witty exchanges, Shakespeare's high comedy displays Malvolio's inconsistencies of character. His self-importance is deflated by low comedy. We are treated to a **farce,** a form of humor based on exaggerated, improbable incongruities, when the staid Malvolio is tricked into wearing bizarre clothing and behaving like a fool to win Olivia. Our laughter is Malvolio's pain, but though he has been "notoriously abus'd" and he vows in the final scene to be "reveng'd on the whole pack" of laughing conspirators who have tricked him, the play ends on a light note. Indeed, it concludes with a song, the last line of which reminds us of the predominant tone of the play as well as the nature of comedy: "And we'll strive to please you every day."

Tragedy, in contrast, does not promise peace and contentment. The basic characteristics of tragedy have already been outlined in the context of Greek drama (see Chapter 47). Like Greek tragic heroes, Shakespeare's protagonists are exceptional human beings whose stature makes their misfortune all the more dramatic. These characters pay a high price for their actions. Oedipus's search for the killer of Laius, Antigone's and Creon's refusal to compromise their principles, Hamlet's agonized conviction that "The time is out of joint," and Othello's willingness to doubt his wife's fidelity all lead to irreversible results. Comic plots are largely free of this sense of inevitability. Instead of the festive mood that prevails once the characters in a comedy recognize their true connection to each other, tragedy gives us dark reflections that emanate from suffering. The laughter of comedy is a shared experience, a recognition of human likeness, but suffering estranges tragic heroes from the world around them.

Some of the wrenching differences between comedy and tragedy can be experienced in *Othello.* Although this play is a tragedy, Shakespeare includes in its plot many of the ingredients associated with comedy. For a time it seems possible that Othello and Desdemona will overcome the complications of a disapproving father, along with the seemingly minor deceptions, awkward misperceptions, and tender illusions that hover around them. But in *Othello* marriage is not a sign of concord displacing discord; instead, love and marriage mark the beginning of the tragic action.

Another important difference between tragedy and comedy is the way characters are presented. The tragic protagonist is portrayed as a remarkable individual whose unique qualities compel us with their power and complexity. Macbeth is not simply a murderer, nor is Othello merely a jealous husband. But despite their extreme passions, behavior, and even crimes, we identify with tragic heroes in ways that we do not with comic characters. We can laugh at pretentious fools, smug hypocrites, clumsy oafs, and thwarted lovers because we see them from a distance. They are amusing precisely because their problems are not ours; we recognize them as types instead of as ourselves (or so we think). No reader of *Twelfth Night* worries about Sir Toby Belch's excessive drinking; he is a cheerful "sot" whose passion for ale is cause for celebration rather than concern. Shakespeare's comedy is sometimes disturbing — Malvolio's character certainly is — but it is never devastating. Tragic heroes do confront devastation; they command our respect and compassion because they act in spite of terrifying risks. Their triumph is not measured by the attainment of what they seek but by the wisdom that defeat imposes on them.

A NOTE ON READING SHAKESPEARE

Readers who have had no previous experience with Shakespeare's language may find it initially daunting. They might well ask whether people ever talked the way, for example, Hamlet does in his most famous soliloquy:

> To be, or not to be: that is the question:
> Whether 'tis nobler in the mind to suffer
> The slings and arrows of outrageous fortune,
> Or to take arms against a sea of troubles,
> And by opposing end them?

People did not talk like this in Elizabethan times. Hamlet speaks poetry. Shakespeare might have had him say something like this: "The most important issue one must confront is whether the pain that life inevitably creates should be passively accepted or resisted." But Shakespeare chose poetry to reveal the depth and complexity of Hamlet's experience. This heightened language is used to clarify rather than obscure his characters' thoughts. Shakespeare has Hamlet, as well as many other characters, speak in prose too, but in general his plays are written in poetry. If you keep in mind that Shakespeare's dialogue is not typically intended to imitate everyday speech, it should be easier to understand that his language is more than simply a vehicle for expressing the action of the play.

Here are a few practical suggestions to enhance your understanding of and pleasure in reading Shakespeare's plays.

1. Keep track of the characters by referring to the *dramatis personae* (characters) listed and briefly described at the beginning of each play.
2. Remember that poetic language deserves to be read slowly and carefully.

A difficult passage can sometimes be better understood if it's read aloud. Don't worry if every line isn't absolutely clear to you.

3. Pay attention to the annotations, which explain unfamiliar words, phrases, and allusions in the text. These can be distracting, but they are sometimes necessary to determine the basic meaning of a passage.

4. As you read each scene, try to imagine how it would be played on a stage.

5. If you find the reading especially difficult, try listening to a recording of the play. (Most college libraries have records and tapes of Shakespeare's plays.) Allowing professional actors to do the reading aloud for you can enrich your imaginative reconstruction of the action and characters. Hearing a play can help you with subsequent readings of it.

6. After reading the play, view a film or videocassette recording of a performance. It is important to view the performance *after* your reading, though, so that your own mental re-creation of the play is not short-circuited by a director's production.

And finally, to quote Hamlet, "Be not too tame . . . let your own discretion be your tutor." Read Shakespeare's work as best you can; it warrants such careful attention not because the language and characters are difficult to understand but because they offer so much to enjoy.

A Midsummer Night's Dream

A Midsummer Night's Dream, one of Shakespeare's most popular plays with readers and audiences, is a romantic comedy about the complex nature of love and marriage. Though some serious points about law and social order are made along the way, the action is propelled by the powers of youth, romance, love, passion, and the hilarious pursuits of characters turned about by fairies, illusions, and their own misunderstandings.

Shakespeare uses several sets of couples to dramatize love's tribulations and triumphs. The play opens with Theseus, Duke of Athens, making arrangements to wed Hippolyta, queen of the Amazons. Once enemies, they now seek love and peace in the harmony of marriage. Their union represents the happy necessity of order in the state and suggests a model of behavior that the other characters struggle to achieve.

In contrast to the serene plans for the royal wedding is the conflict produced by four Athenian youths who are thwarted in love: Helena loves Demetrius, but Demetrius loves Hermia, who wants to marry Lysander. This collision of passions is further complicated by Hermia's father, who insists in the Duke's presence that if she doesn't marry Demetrius, she must die or spend her life in a nunnery. Much of the play's conflict concerns how these two young couples align their love for one another so that each desires and is desired by the right person. When Hermia defies her father and refuses to marry Demetrius, she flees to the woods, followed by Lysander and Demetrius as well as Helena, who is in pursuit of Demetrius.

Once in the woods, the lovers find themselves in a supernatural world, the unpredictable kingdom of Oberon and Titania, the king and queen of the fairies. The fourth couple creates even more confusion through Oberon's impatience with Titania. Their quarrel results in Oberon ordering his servant, Puck, to cast magical spells on the lovers as well as on Titania. This gives Puck the license to reveal their foolishness while eventually saving them from their own confused passions. Their reconciliations and reunions are not achieved, however, until Puck puts them through a series of comic encounters based on their illusions and vulnerabilities.

The final act includes the play within the play, "the most lamentable comedy" of two more lovers, Pyramus and Thisbe, who misunderstand one another. This travesty of a tragedy is put on by Athenian craftsmen — who are clearly better laborers than they are actors — at the Duke's request for a wedding entertainment. This play within the play reinforces the larger play's concerns about the nature of love and, indeed, of reality itself, because it raises questions about the fluid, complex relationship between art and reality. Ultimately, however, questions, issues, and conflicts give way to a generous sense of everything working out for the best as the play ends with Puck's warm assurances to the audience and his gentle urging to "Give me your hands."

WILLIAM SHAKESPEARE (1564–1616)
A Midsummer Night's Dream

c. 1595

[DRAMATIS PERSONAE

Theseus, Duke of Athens
Hippolyta, Queen of the Amazons, betrothed to Theseus
Philostrate, Master of the Revels
Egeus, father of Hermia

Hermia, daughter of Egeus, in love with Lysander
Lysander, in love with Hermia
Demetrius, in love with Hermia and favored by Egeus
Helena, in love with Demetrius

Oberon, King of the Fairies
Titania, Queen of the Fairies
Puck, or *Robin Goodfellow*
Peaseblossom,
Cobweb,
Mote, } fairies attending Titania
Mustardseed
Other Fairies attending

See Plays in Performance insert.

Peter Quince, a carpenter,
Nick Bottom, a weaver,
Francis Flute, a bellows mender,
Tom Snout, a tinker, } representing
Snug, a joiner,
Robin Starveling, a tailor,
Lords and Attendants on Theseus and Hippolyta

Prologue
Pyramus
Thisbe
Wall
Lion
Moonshine

SCENE: Athens, and a wood near it.]

[ACT I

SCENE I: *Athens. Theseus' court.*]

    Enter Theseus, Hippolyta, [and Philostrate,] with others.

Theseus: Now, fair Hippolyta, our nuptial hour
    Draws on apace. Four happy days bring in
    Another moon; but, O, methinks, how slow
    This old moon wanes! She lingers° my desires,
    Like to a stepdame° or a dowager°   5
    Long withering out° a young man's revenue.
Hippolyta: Four days will quickly steep themselves° in night;
    Four nights will quickly dream away the time;
    And then the moon, like to a silver bow
    New bent in heaven, shall behold the night   10
    Of our solemnities.°
Theseus: Go Philostrate,
    Stir up the Athenian youth to merriments.
    Awake the pert and nimble spirit of mirth.
    Turn melancholy forth to funerals;
    The pale companion° is not for our pomp.°   *[Exit Philostrate.]*   15
    Hippolyta, I wooed thee with my sword°
    And won thy love doing thee injuries;
    But I will wed thee in another key,
    With pomp, with triumph,° and with reveling.

    Enter Egeus and his daughter Hermia, and Lysander, and Demetrius.

Egeus: Happy be Theseus, our renownèd duke!   20
Theseus: Thanks, good Egeus. What's the news with thee?
Egeus: Full of vexation come I, with complaint

Act I, Scene I.   4 *lingers:* Postpones, delays the fulfillment of.   5 *stepdame:* Step-mother; *a dowager:* I.e., a widow (whose right of inheritance from her dead husband is eating into her son's estate).   6 *withering out:* Causing to dwindle.   7 *steep themselves:* Saturate themselves, to be absorbed in.   11 *solemnities:* Festive ceremonies of marriage.   15 *companion:* Fellow; *pomp:* Ceremonial magnificence.   16 *with my sword:* In a military engage-ment against the Amazons, when Hippolyta was taken captive.   19 *triumph:* Public festivity.

Against my child, my daughter Hermia. —
Stand forth, Demetrius. — My noble lord,
This man hath my consent to marry her. —   25
Stand forth, Lysander. — And, my gracious Duke,
This man hath bewitched the bosom of my child.
Thou, thou Lysander, thou hast given her rhymes
And interchanged love tokens with my child.
Thou hast by moonlight at her window sung   30
With feigning° voice verses of feigning° love,
And stol'n the impression of her fantasy°
With bracelets of thy hair, rings, gauds,° conceits,°
Knacks,° trifles, nosegays, sweetmeats — messengers
Of strong prevailment in° unhardened youth.   35
With cunning hast thou filched my daughter's heart,
Turned her obedience, which is due to me,
To stubborn harshness. And, my gracious Duke,
Be it so° she will not here before Your Grace
Consent to marry with Demetrius,   40
I beg the ancient privilege of Athens:
As she is mine, I may dispose of her,
Which shall be either to this gentleman
Or to her death, according to our law
Immediately° provided in that case.   45
Theseus: What say you, Hermia? Be advised, fair maid.
To you your father should be as a god —
One that composed your beauties, yea, and one
To whom you are but as a form in wax
By him imprinted, and within his power   50
To leave° the figure or disfigure° it.
Demetrius is a worthy gentleman.
Hermia: So is Lysander.
Theseus: In himself he is;
But in this kind,° wanting° your father's voice,°
The other must be held the worthier.   55
Hermia: I would my father looked but with my eyes.
Theseus: Rather your eyes must with his judgment look.
Hermia: I do entreat Your Grace to pardon me.
I know not by what power I am made bold,
Nor how it may concern° my modesty   60
In such a presence here to plead my thoughts;
But I beseech Your Grace that I may know
The worst that may befall me in this case
If I refuse to wed Demetrius.

---

31 *feigning:* (1) Counterfeiting (2) faining, desirous.   32 *And . . . fantasy:* And made her fall in love with you (imprinting your image on her imagination) by stealthy and dishonest means.   33 *gauds:* Playthings; *conceits:* Fanciful trifles.   34 *Knacks:* Knick-knacks.   35 *prevailment in:* Influence on.   39 *Be it so:* If.   45 *Immediately:* Directly, with nothing intervening.   51 *leave:* Leave unaltered; *disfigure:* Obliterate.   54 *kind:* Respect; *wanting:* Lacking; *voice:* Approval.   60 *concern:* Befit.

Theseus: Either to die the death° or to abjure   65
    Forever the society of men.
    Therefore, fair Hermia, question your desires,
    Know of your youth, examine well your blood,°
    Whether, if you yield not to your father's choice,
    You can endure the livery° of a nun,   70
    For aye° to be in shady cloister mewed,°
    To live a barren sister all your life,
    Chanting faint hymns to the cold fruitless moon.
    Thrice blessèd they that master so their blood
    To undergo such maiden pilgrimage;   75
    But earthlier happy° is the rose distilled°
    Than that which, withering on the virgin thorn,
    Grows, lives, and dies in single blessedness.
Hermia: So will I grow, so live, so die, my lord,
    Ere I will yield my virgin patent° up   80
    Unto his lordship, whose unwishèd yoke
    My soul consents not to give sovereignty.
Theseus: Take time to pause, and by the next new moon —
    The sealing day betwixt my love and me
    For everlasting bond of fellowship —   85
    Upon that day either prepare to die
    For disobedience to your father's will,
    Or° else to wed Demetrius, as he would,
    Or on Diana's altar to protest°
    For aye austerity and single life.   90
Demetrius: Relent, sweet Hermia, and, Lysander, yield
    Thy crazèd° title to my certain right.
Lysander: You have her father's love, Demetrius;
    Let me have Hermia's. Do you marry him.
Egeus: Scornful Lysander! True, he hath my love,   95
    And what is mine my love shall render him.
    And she is mine, and all my right of her
    I do estate unto° Demetrius.
Lysander: I am, my lord, as well derived° as he,
    As well possessed;° my love is more than his;   100
    My fortunes every way as fairly° ranked,
    If not with vantage,° as Demetrius';
    And, which is more than all these boasts can be,
    I am beloved of beauteous Hermia.
    Why should not I then prosecute my right?   105
    Demetrius, I'll avouch it to his head,°

---

65 *die the death:* Be executed by legal process.   68 *blood:* Passions.   70 *livery:* Habit, costume.   71 *aye:* Ever; *mewed:* Shut in (said of a hawk, poultry, etc.).   76 *earthlier happy:* Happier as respects this world; *distilled:* Separated to make perfume.   80 *patent:* Privilege.   88 *Or:* Either.   89 *protest:* Vow.   92 *crazèd:* Cracked, unsound.   98 *estate unto:* Settle or bestow upon.   99 *as well derived:* As well born and descended.   100 *possessed:* Endowed with wealth.   101 *fairly:* Handsomely.   102 *vantage:* Superiority.   106 *head:* I.e., face.

Made love to Nedar's daughter, Helena,
And won her soul; and she, sweet lady, dotes,
Devoutly dotes, dotes in idolatry
Upon this spotted° and inconstant man.   110
Theseus: I must confess that I have heard so much,
And with Demetrius thought to have spoke thereof;
But, being overfull of self-affairs,°
My mind did lose it. But, Demetrius, come,
And come, Egeus, you shall go with me;   115
I have some private schooling° for you both.
For you, fair Hermia, look you arm° yourself
To fit your fancies° to your father's will,
Or else the law of Athens yields you up —
Which by no means we may extenuate° —   120
To death or to a vow of single life.
Come, my Hippolyta. What cheer, my love?
Demetrius and Egeus, go° along.
I must employ you in some business
Against° our nuptial, and confer with you   125
Of something nearly that° concerns yourselves.
Egeus: With duty and desire we follow you.

                          Exeunt [all but Lysander and Hermia].
Lysander: How now, my love, why is your cheek so pale?
How chance the roses there do fade so fast?
Hermia: Belike° for want of rain, which I could well   130
Beteem° them from the tempest of my eyes.
Lysander: Ay me! For aught that I could ever read,
Could ever hear by tale or history,
The course of true love never did run smooth;
But either it was different in blood° —   135
Hermia: O cross!° Too high to be enthralled to low.
Lysander: Or else misgrafted° in respect of years —
Hermia: O spite! Too old to be engaged to young.
Lysander: Or else it stood upon the choice of friends° —
Hermia: O hell, to choose love by another's eyes!   140
Lysander: Or if there were a sympathy° in choice,
War, death, or sickness did lay siege to it,
Making it momentany° as a sound,
Swift as a shadow, short as any dream,
Brief as the lightning in the collied° night   145
That in a spleen° unfolds° both heaven and earth,

---

110 *spotted:* I.e., morally stained.   113 *self-affairs:* My own concerns.   116 *schooling:* Admonition.   117 *look you arm:* Take care you prepare.   118 *fancies:* Likings, thoughts of love.   120 *extenuate:* Mitigate, relax.   123 *go:* I.e., come.   125 *Against:* In preparation for.   126 *nearly that:* That closely.   130 *Belike:* Very likely.   131 *Beteem:* Grant, afford.   135 *blood:* Hereditary station.   136 *cross:* Vexation.   137 *misgrafted:* Ill-grafted, badly matched.   139 *friends:* Relatives.   141 *sympathy:* Agreement.   143 *momentany:* Lasting but a moment.   145 *collied:* Blackened (as with coal dust), darkened.   146 *in a spleen:* In a swift impulse, in a violent flash; *unfolds:* Reveals.

And ere a man hath power to say "Behold!"
The jaws of darkness do devour it up.
So quick° bright things come to confusion.°
Hermia: If then true lovers have been ever crossed,°   150
It stands as an edict in destiny.
Then let us teach our trial patience,°
Because it is a customary cross,
As due to love as thoughts, and dreams, and sighs,
Wishes, and tears, poor fancy's° followers.   155
Lysander: A good persuasion.° Therefore, hear me, Hermia:
I have a widow aunt, a dowager
Of great revenue, and she hath no child.
From Athens is her house remote seven leagues;
And she respects° me as her only son.   160
There, gentle Hermia, may I marry thee,
And to that place the sharp Athenian law
Cannot pursue us. If thou lovest me, then,
Steal forth thy father's house tomorrow night;
And in the wood, a league without° the town,   165
Where I did meet thee once with Helena
To do observance to a morn of May,°
There will I stay for thee.
Hermia: My good Lysander!
I swear to thee, by Cupid's strongest bow,
By his best arrow° with the golden head,   170
By the simplicity° of Venus' doves,°
By that which knitteth souls and prospers loves,
And by that fire which burned the Carthage queen°
When the false Trojan° under sail was seen,
By all the vows that ever men have broke,   175
In number more than ever women spoke,
In that same place thou hast appointed me
Tomorrow truly will I meet with thee.
Lysander: Keep promise, love. Look, here comes Helena.

Enter Helena.

Hermia: God speed, fair° Helena! Whither away?   180
Helena: Call you me fair? That "fair" again unsay.
Demetrius loves your fair.° O happy fair!°

---

149 *quick:* Quickly; also, living, alive; *confusion:* Ruin.   150 *ever crossed:* Always thwarted.
152 *teach . . . patience:* I.e., teach ourselves patience in this trial.   155 *fancy's:* Amorous passion's.   156 *persuasion:* Doctrine.   160 *respects:* Regards.   165 *without:* Outside.
167 *do . . . May:* Perform the ceremonies of May Day.   170 *best arrow:* Cupid's best gold-pointed arrows were supposed to induce love; his blunt leaden arrows, aversion.   171 *simplicity:* Innocence; *Venus' doves:* Doves that drew Venus's chariot.   173, 174 *Carthage queen, false Trojan:* (Dido, Queen of Carthage, immolated herself on a funeral pyre after having been deserted by the Trojan hero Aeneas.)   180 *fair:* Fair-complexioned (generally regarded by the Elizabethans as more beautiful than a dark complexion).   182 *your fair:* Your beauty (even though Hermia is dark-complexioned); *happy fair:* Lucky fair one.

Your eyes are lodestars,° and your tongue's sweet air°
More tunable° than lark to shepherd's ear
When wheat is green, when hawthorn buds appear.   185
Sickness is catching. O, were favor° so,
Yours would I catch, fair Hermia, ere I go;
My ear should catch your voice, my eye your eye,
My tongue should catch your tongue's sweet melody.
Were the world mine, Demetrius being bated,°   190
The rest I'd give to be to you translated.°
O, teach me how you look and with what art
You sway the motion° of Demetrius' heart.
Hermia: I frown upon him, yet he loves me still.
Helena: O, that your frowns would teach my smiles such skill!   195
Hermia: I give him curses, yet he gives me love.
Helena: O, that my prayers could such affection° move!°
Hermia: The more I hate, the more he follows me.
Helena: The more I love, the more he hateth me.
Hermia: His folly, Helena, is no fault of mine.   200
Helena: None, but your beauty. Would that fault were mine!
Hermia: Take comfort. He no more shall see my face.
     Lysander and myself will fly this place.
     Before the time I did Lysander see
     Seemed Athens as a paradise to me.°   205
     O, then, what graces in my love do dwell,
     That he hath turned a heaven unto a hell?
Lysander: Helen, to you our minds we will unfold.
     Tomorrow night, when Phoebe° doth behold
     Her silver visage in the watery glass,°   210
     Decking with liquid pearl the bladed grass,
     A time that lovers' flights doth still° conceal,
     Through Athens' gates have we devised to steal.
Hermia: And in the wood, where often you and I
     Upon faint° primrose beds were wont to lie,   215
     Emptying our bosoms of their counsel° sweet,
     There my Lysander and myself shall meet,
     And thence from Athens turn away our eyes
     To seek new friends and stranger companies.°
     Farewell, sweet playfellow. Pray thou for us,   220
     And good luck grant thee thy Demetrius!
     Keep word, Lysander. We must starve our sight
     From lovers' food till morrow deep midnight.

---

183 *lodestars:* Guiding stars; *air:* Music.   184 *tunable:* Tuneful, melodious.   186 *favor:* Appearance, looks.   190 *bated:* Excepted.   191 *translated:* Transformed.   193 *sway the motion:* Control the impulse.   197 *affection:* Passion; *move:* Arouse.   204–205 *Before . . . to me:* (Hermia seemingly means that love has led to complications and jealousies, making Athens hell for her.)   209 *Phoebe:* Diana, the moon.   210 *glass:* Mirror.   212 *still:* Always.   215 *faint:* Pale.   216 *counsel:* Secret thought.   219 *stranger companies:* The company of strangers.

Lysander: I will, my Hermia. *(Exit Hermia.)* Helena, adieu.
　　As you on him, Demetrius dote on you!　　　　　　*Exit Lysander.* 225
Helena: How happy some o'er other some can be!°
　　Through Athens I am thought as fair as she.
　　But what of that? Demetrius thinks not so;
　　He will not know what all but he do know.
　　And as he errs, doting on Hermia's eyes,　　　　　　　　　230
　　So I, admiring of° his qualities.
　　Things base and vile, holding no quantity,°
　　Love can transpose to form and dignity.
　　Love looks not with the eyes, but with the mind,
　　And therefore is winged Cupid painted blind.　　　　　　235
　　Nor hath Love's mind of any judgment taste;°
　　Wings and no eyes figure° unheedy haste.
　　And therefore is Love said to be a child,
　　Because in choice° he is so oft beguiled.°
　　As waggish° boys in game° themselves forswear,　　　　240
　　So the boy Love is perjured everywhere.
　　For ere Demetrius looked on Hermia's eyne,°
　　He hailed down oaths that he was only mine;
　　And when this hail some heat from Hermia felt,
　　So he dissolved, and showers of oaths did melt.　　　　245
　　I will go tell him of fair Hermia's flight.
　　Then to the wood will he tomorrow night
　　Pursue her; and for this intelligence°
　　If I have thanks, it is a dear expense.°
　　But herein mean I to enrich my pain,　　　　　　　　　250
　　To have his sight thither and back again.　　　　　　*Exit.*

[SCENE II: *Athens.*]

Enter Quince the carpenter, and Snug the joiner, and Bottom the weaver, and Flute the bellows mender, and Snout the tinker, and Starveling the tailor.

Quince: Is all our company here?
Bottom: You were best to call them generally,° man by man, according to
　　the scrip.°
Quince: Here is the scroll of every man's name which is thought fit,
　　through all Athens, to play in our interlude° before the Duke and the　　5
　　Duchess on his wedding day at night.

---

226 *o'er . . . can be:* Can be in comparison to some others.　　231 *admiring of:* Wondering at.
232 *holding no quantity:* I.e., unsubstantial, unshapely.　　236 *Nor . . . taste:* I.e., nor has Love,
which dwells in the fancy or imagination, any taste or least bit of judgment or reason.
237 *figure:* Are a symbol of.　　239 *in choice:* In choosing; *beguiled:* Self-deluded, making
unaccountable choices.　　240 *waggish:* Playful, mischievous; *game:* Sport, jest.　　242 *eyne:*
Eyes (old form of plural).　　248 *intelligence:* Information.　　249 *a dear expense:* I.e., a
trouble worth taking on my part, or a begrudging effort on his part; *dear:* Costly.
Scene II.　　2 *generally:* (Bottom's blunder for "individually.")　　3 *scrip:* Scrap (Bottom's
error for "script").　　5 *interlude:* Play.

Bottom: First, good Peter Quince, say what the play treats on, then read
   the names of the actors, and so grow to° a point.

Quince: Marry,° our play is "The most lamentable comedy and most cruel
   death of Pyramus and Thisbe."   10

Bottom: A very good piece of work, I assure you, and a merry. Now, good
   Peter Quince, call forth your actors by the scroll. Masters, spread
   yourselves.

Quince: Answer as I call you. Nick Bottom,° the weaver.

Bottom: Ready. Name what part I am for, and proceed.   15

Quince: You, Nick Bottom, are set down for Pyramus.

Bottom: What is Pyramus? A lover or a tyrant?

Quince: A lover, that kills himself most gallant for love.

Bottom: That will ask some tears in the true performing of it. If I do it, let
   the audience look to their eyes. I will move storms; I will condole° in   20
   some measure. To the rest—yet my chief humor° is for a tyrant. I
   could play Ercles° rarely, or a part to tear a cat° in, to make all split.°

     "The raging rocks
     And shivering shocks
     Shall break the locks   25
       Of prison gates;
     And Phibbus' car°
     Shall shine from far
     And make and mar
       The foolish Fates."   30

   This was lofty! Now name the rest of the players. This is Ercles' vein, a
   tyrant's vein. A lover is more condoling.

Quince: Francis Flute, the bellows mender.

Flute: Here, Peter Quince.

Quince: Flute, you must take Thisbe on you.   35

Flute: What is Thisbe? A wandering knight?

Quince: It is the lady that Pyramus must love.

Flute: Nay, faith, let not me play a woman. I have a beard coming.

Quince: That's all one.° You shall play it in a mask, and you may speak as
   small° as you will.   40

Bottom: An° I may hide my face, let me play Thisbe too. I'll speak in a monstrous little voice: "Thisne, Thisne!" "Ah, Pyramus, my lover dear! Thy
   Thisbe dear, and lady dear!"

Quince: No, no, you must play Pyramus, and Flute, you Thisbe.

Bottom: Well, proceed.   45

Quince: Robin Starveling, the tailor.

Starveling: Here, Peter Quince.

Quince: Robin Starveling, you must play Thisbe's mother. Tom Snout, the
   tinker.

---

8 *grow to:* Come to.   9 *Marry:* (A mild oath; originally the name of the Virgin Mary.)
14 *Bottom:* Object around which weavers wound thread.   20 *condole:* Lament, arouse pity.
21 *humor:* Inclination, whim.   22 *Ercles:* Hercules (the tradition of ranting came from
Seneca's *Hercules Furens*); *tear a cat:* I.e., rant; *make all split:* I.e., cause a stir, bring the house
down.   27 *Phibbus' car:* Phoebus's, the sun god's, chariot.   39 *That's all one:* It makes no
difference.   40 *small:* High-pitched.   41 *An:* If (also at line 59).

Snout: Here, Peter Quince.   50

Quince: You, Pyramus' father; myself, Thisbe's father; Snug, the joiner, you, the lion's part; and I hope here is a play fitted.

Snug: Have you the lion's part written? Pray you, if it be, give it me, for I am slow of study.

Quince: You may do it extempore, for it is nothing but roaring.   55

Bottom: Let me play the lion too. I will roar that I will do any man's heart good to hear me. I will roar that I will make the Duke say, "Let him roar again, let him roar again."

Quince: An you should do it too terribly, you would fright the Duchess and the ladies, that they would shriek; and that were enough to hang   60
us all.

All: That would hang us, every mother's son.

Bottom: I grant you, friends, if you should fright the ladies out of their wits, they would have no more discretion but to hang us; but I will aggravate° my voice so that I will roar you° as gently as any sucking   65
dove;° I will roar you an 'twere° any nightingale.

Quince: You can play no part but Pyramus; for Pyramus is a sweet-faced man, a proper° man as one shall see in a summer's day, a most lovely gentlemanlike man. Therefore you must needs play Pyramus.

Bottom: Well, I will undertake it. What beard were I best to play it in?   70

Quince: Why, what you will.

Bottom: I will discharge° it in either your° straw-color beard, your orange-tawny beard, your purple-in-grain° beard, or your French-crown-color° beard, your perfect yellow.

Quince: Some of your French crowns° have no hair at all, and then you   75
will play barefaced. But, masters, here are your parts. *[He distributes parts.]* And I am to entreat you, request you, and desire you to con° them by tomorrow night, and meet me in the palace wood, a mile without the town, by moonlight. There will we rehearse; for if we meet in the city, we shall be dogged with company, and our devices°   80
known. In the meantime I will draw a bill° of properties, such as our play wants. I pray you, fail me not.

Bottom: We will meet, and there we may rehearse most obscenely° and courageously. Take pains, be perfect.° Adieu.

Quince: At the Duke's oak we meet.   85

Bottom: Enough. Hold, or cut bowstrings.°   *Exeunt.*

---

65 *aggravate:* (Bottom's blunder for "moderate."); *roar you:* I.e., roar for you.   66 *sucking dove:* (Bottom conflates *sitting dove* and *sucking lamb,* two proverbial images of innocence.); *an 'twere:* As if it were.   68 *proper:* Handsome.   72 *discharge:* Perform; *your:* I.e., you know the kind I mean.   73 *purple-in-grain:* Dyed a very deep red (from *grain,* the name applied to the dried insect used to make the dye).   74 *French-crown-color:* I.e., color of a French crown, a gold coin.   75 *crowns:* Heads bald from syphilis, the "French disease."   77 *con:* Learn by heart.   80 *devices:* Plans.   81 *draw a bill:* Draw up a list. 83 *obscenely:* (An unintentionally funny blunder, whatever Bottom meant to say.)   84 *perfect:* I.e., letter-perfect in memorizing your parts.   86 *Hold . . . bowstrings:* (An archer's expression, not definitely explained, but probably meaning here "keep your promises, or give up the play.")

[ACT II

SCENE I: *A wood near Athens.*]

> *Enter a Fairy at one door, and Robin Goodfellow [Puck] at another.*

Puck: How now, spirit, whither wander you?
Fairy: Over hill, over dale,
    Thorough° bush, thorough brier,
  Over park, over pale,°
    Thorough flood, thorough fire,   5
  I do wander everywhere,
  Swifter than the moon's sphere;°
  And I serve the Fairy Queen,
  To dew° her orbs° upon the green.
  The cowslips tall her pensioners° be.   10
  In their gold coats spots you see;
  Those be rubies, fairy favors;°
  In those freckles live their savors.°
  I must go seek some dewdrops here
  And hang a pearl in every cowslip's ear.   15
  Farewell, thou lob° of spirits; I'll be gone.
  Our Queen and all her elves come here anon.°
Puck: The King doth keep his revels here tonight.
  Take heed the Queen come not within his sight.
  For Oberon is passing fell° and wrath,°   20
  Because that she as her attendant hath
  A lovely boy, stolen from an Indian king;
  She ne'er had so sweet a changeling.°
  And jealous Oberon would have the child
  Knight of his train, to trace° the forests wild.   25
  But she perforce° withholds the lovèd boy,
  Crowns him with flowers, and makes him all her joy.
  And now they never meet in grove or green,
  By fountain° clear, or spangled starlight sheen,°
  But they do square,° that all their elves for fear   30
  Creep into acorn cups and hide them there.
Fairy: Either I mistake your shape and making quite,
  Or else you are that shrewd° and knavish sprite°
  Called Robin Goodfellow. Are not you he
  That frights the maidens of the villagery,°   35

Act II, Scene I.   3 *Thorough:* Through.   4 *pale:* Enclosure.   7 *sphere:* Orbit.   9 *dew:* Sprinkle with dew; *orbs:* Circles, i.e., fairy rings (circular bands of grass, darker than the surrounding area, caused by fungi enriching the soil).   10 *pensioners:* Retainers, members of the royal bodyguard.   12 *favors:* Love tokens.   13 *savors:* Sweet smells. 16 *lob:* Country bumpkin.   17 *anon:* At once.   20 *passing fell:* Exceedingly angry; *wrath:* Wrathful.   23 *changeling:* Child exchanged for another by the fairies.   25 *trace:* Range through.   26 *perforce:* Forcibly.   29 *fountain:* Spring; *starlight sheen:* Shining starlight.   30 *square:* Quarrel.   33 *shrewd:* Mischievous; *sprite:* Spirit.   35 *villagery:* Village population.

    Skim milk,° and sometimes labor in the quern,°
    And bootless° make the breathless huswife° churn,
    And sometimes make the drink to bear no barm,°
    Mislead night wanderers,° laughing at their harm?
    Those that "Hobgoblin" call you, and "Sweet Puck,"°   40
    You do their work, and they shall have good luck.
    Are you not he?
Puck: Thou speakest aright;
    I am that merry wanderer of the night.
    I jest to Oberon and make him smile
    When I a fat and bean-fed° horse beguile,   45
    Neighing in likeness of a filly foal;
    And sometimes lurk I in a gossip's° bowl
    In very likeness of a roasted crab,°
    And when she drinks, against her lips I bob
    And on her withered dewlap° pour the ale.   50
    The wisest aunt,° telling the saddest° tale,
    Sometimes for three-foot stool mistaketh me;
    Then slip I from her bum, down topples she,
    And "Tailor"° cries, and falls into a cough;
    And then the whole choir° hold their hips and laugh,   55
    And waxen° in their mirth, and neeze,° and swear
    A merrier hour was never wasted° there.
    But, room,° fairy! Here comes Oberon.
Fairy: And here my mistress. Would that he were gone!

    Enter [Oberon] the King of Fairies at one door, with his train, and [Titania] the
    Queen at another, with hers.

Oberon: Ill met by moonlight, proud Titania.   60
Titania: What, jealous Oberon? Fairies, skip hence.
    I have forsworn his bed and company.
Oberon: Tarry, rash wanton.° Am not I thy lord?
Titania: Then I must be thy lady; but I know
    When thou hast stolen away from Fairyland   65
    And in the shape of Corin° sat all day,
    Playing on the pipes of corn° and versing love
    To amorous Phillida.° Why art thou here

---

36 *Skim milk:* I.e., steal the cream; *quern:* Hand mill (where Puck presumably hampers the grinding of grain).   37 *bootless:* In vain (Puck prevents the cream from turning to butter); *huswife:* Housewife.   38 *barm:* Head on the ale (Puck prevents the barm or yeast from producing fermentation).   39 *Mislead night wanderers:* I.e., mislead with false fire those who walk abroad at night (hence earning Puck his other names of Jack o' Lantern and Will o' the Wisp).   40 *Those . . . Puck:* I.e., those who call you by the names you favor rather than those denoting the mischief you do.   45 *bean-fed:* Well fed on field beans.   47 *gossip's:* Old woman's.   48 *crab:* Crab apple.   50 *dewlap:* Loose skin on neck.   51 *aunt:* Old woman; *saddest:* Most serious.   54 *Tailor:* (Possibly because she ends up sitting cross-legged on the floor, looking like a tailor, or else referring to the *tail* or buttocks.)   55 *choir:* Company.   56 *waxen:* Increase; *neeze:* Sneeze.   57 *wasted:* Spent.   58 *room:* Stand aside, make room.   63 *wanton:* Headstrong creature.   66, 68 *Corin, Phillida:* (Conventional names of pastoral lovers.)   67 *corn:* (Here, oat stalks.)

Come from the farthest step° of India,
But that, forsooth, the bouncing Amazon,   70
Your buskined° mistress and your warrior love,
To Theseus must be wedded, and you come
To give their bed joy and prosperity.

Oberon: How canst thou thus for shame, Titania,
Glance at my credit with Hippolyta,°   75
Knowing I know thy love to Theseus?
Didst not thou lead him through the glimmering night
From Perigenia,° whom he ravishèd?
And make him with fair Aegles° break his faith,
With Ariadne° and Antiopa?°   80

Titania: These are the forgeries of jealousy;
And never, since the middle summer's spring,°
Met we on hill, in dale, forest, or mead,°
By pavèd° fountain or by rushy° brook,
Or in° the beachèd margent° of the sea,   85
To dance our ringlets to° the whistling wind,
But with thy brawls thou hast disturbed our sport.
Therefore the winds, piping to us in vain,
As in revenge, have sucked up from the sea
Contagious° fogs which, falling in the land,   90
Hath every pelting° river made so proud
That they have overborne their continents.°
The ox hath therefore stretched his yoke° in vain,
The plowman lost his sweat, and the green corn°
Hath rotted ere his youth attained a beard;   95
The fold° stands empty in the drownèd field,
And crows are fatted with the murrain° flock;
The nine-men's morris° is filled up with mud,
And the quaint mazes° in the wanton° green
For lack of tread are indistinguishable.   100

---

69 *step:* Farthest limit of travel, or, perhaps, *steep,* "mountain range."   71 *buskined:* Wearing half-boots called buskins.   75 *Glance . . . Hippolyta:* Make insinuations about my favored relationship with Hippolyta.   78 *Perigenia:* I.e., Perigouna, one of Theseus's conquests. (She and the following women are named in Thomas North's translation of Plutarch's "Life of Theseus.")   79 *Aegles:* I.e., Aegle, for whom Theseus deserted Ariadne according to some accounts.   80 *Ariadne:* The daughter of Minos, King of Crete, who helped Theseus to escape the labyrinth after killing the Minotaur; later she was abandoned by Theseus; *Antiopa:* Queen of the Amazons and wife of Theseus, elsewhere identified with Hippolyta, but here thought of as a separate woman.   82 *middle summer's spring:* Beginning of midsummer.   83 *mead:* Meadow.   84 *pavèd:* With pebbled bottom; *rushy:* Bordered with rushes.   85 *in:* On; *margent:* Edge, border.   86 *ringlets to:* Dances in a ring (see *orbs* in II.i.9) to the sound of.   90 *Contagious:* Noxious.   91 *pelting:* Paltry.   92 *continents:* Banks that contain them.   93 *stretched his yoke:* I.e., pulled at his yoke in plowing.   94 *corn:* Grain of any kind.   96 *fold:* Pen for sheep or cattle.   97 *murrain:* Having died of the plague.   98 *nine-men's morris:* I.e., portion of the village green marked out in a square for a game played with nine pebbles or pegs.   99 *quaint mazes:* I.e., intricate paths marked out on the village green to be followed rapidly on foot as a kind of contest; *wanton:* Luxuriant.

The human mortals want° their winter° here;
No night is now with hymn or carol blessed.
Therefore° the moon, the governess of floods,
Pale in her anger, washes° all the air,
That rheumatic diseases° do abound.   105
And thorough this distemperature° we see
The seasons alter: hoary-headed frosts
Fall in the fresh lap of the crimson rose,
And on old Hiems'° thin and icy crown
An odorous chaplet of sweet summer buds   110
Is, as in mockery, set. The spring, the summer,
The childing° autumn, angry winter, change
Their wonted liveries,° and the mazèd° world
By their increase° now knows not which is which.
And this same progeny of evils comes   115
From our debate,° from our dissension.
We are their parents and original.°
Oberon: Do you amend it, then. It lies in you.
Why should Titania cross her Oberon?
I do but beg a little changeling boy   120
To be my henchman.°
Titania: Set your heart at rest.
The fairy land buys not the child of me.
His mother was a vot'ress of my order,°
And in the spicèd Indian air by night
Full often hath she gossiped by my side   125
And sat with me on Neptune's yellow sands,
Marking th' embarkèd traders° on the flood,°
When we have laughed to see the sails conceive
And grow big-bellied with the wanton° wind;
Which she, with pretty and with swimming° gait,   130
Following — her womb then rich with my young squire —
Would imitate, and sail upon the land
To fetch me trifles, and return again
As from a voyage, rich with merchandise.
But she, being mortal, of that boy did die;   135
And for her sake do I rear up her boy,
And for her sake I will not part with him.
Oberon: How long within this wood intend you stay?

---

101 *want:* Lack; *winter:* I.e., regular winter season; or, proper observances of winter, such as the *hymn* or *carol* in the next line (?).   103 *Therefore:* I.e., as a result of our quarrel. 104 *washes:* Saturates with moisture.   105 *rheumatic diseases:* Colds, flu, and other respiratory infections.   106 *distemperature:* Disturbance in nature.   109 *Hiems':* The winter god's.   112 *childing:* Fruitful, pregnant.   113 *wonted liveries:* Usual apparel; *mazèd:* Bewildered.   114 *their increase:* Their yield, what they produce.   116 *debate:* Quarrel. 117 *original:* Origin.   121 *henchman:* Attendant, page.   123 *was ... order:* Had taken a vow to serve me.   127 *traders:* Trading vessels; *flood:* Flood tide.   129 *wanton:* (1) Playful (2) amorous.   130 *swimming:* Smooth, gliding.

Titania: Perchance till after Theseus' wedding day.
    If you will patiently dance in our round°   140
    And see our moonlight revels, go with us;
    If not, shun me, and I will spare° your haunts.
Oberon: Give me that boy, and I will go with thee.
Titania: Not for thy fairy kingdom. Fairies, away!
    We shall chide downright, if I longer stay.   145
                  Exeunt [Titania with her train].
Oberon: Well, go thy way. Thou shalt not from° this grove
    Till I torment thee for this injury.
    My gentle Puck, come hither. Thou rememb'rest
    Since° once I sat upon a promontory,
    And heard a mermaid on a dolphin's back   150
    Uttering such dulcet° and harmonious breath°
    That the rude° sea grew civil at her song,
    And certain stars shot madly from their spheres
    To hear the sea-maid's music?
Puck: I remember.
Oberon: That very time I saw, but thou couldst not,   155
    Flying between the cold moon and the earth
    Cupid, all° armed. A certain° aim he took
    At a fair vestal° thronèd by° the west,
    And loosed° his love shaft smartly from his bow
    As° it should pierce a hundred thousand hearts;   160
    But I might° see young Cupid's fiery shaft
    Quenched in the chaste beams of the watery moon,
    And the imperial vot'ress passèd on,
    In maiden meditation, fancy-free.°
    Yet marked I where the bolt° of Cupid fell: 165
    It fell upon a little western flower,
    Before milk-white, now purple with love's wound,
    And maidens call it love-in-idleness.°
    Fetch me that flower; the herb I showed thee once.
    The juice of it on sleeping eyelids laid   170
    Will make or man or° woman madly dote
    Upon the next live creature that it sees.
    Fetch me this herb, and be thou here again
    Ere the leviathan° can swim a league.
Puck: I'll put a girdle round about the earth   175
    In forty° minutes.   *[Exit.]*
Oberon: Having once this juice,

---

140 *round:* Circular dance.   142 *spare:* Shun.   146 *from:* Go from.   149 *Since:* When.
151 *dulcet:* Sweet; *breath:* Voice, song.   152 *rude:* Rough.   157 *all:* Fully; *certain:* Sure.
158 *vestal:* Vestal virgin (contains a complimentary allusion to Queen Elizabeth as a vota-ress of Diana and probably refers to an actual entertainment in her honor at Elvetham in 1591); *by:* In the region of.   159 *loosed:* Released.   160 *As:* As if.   161 *might:* Could.
164 *fancy-free:* Free of love's spell.   165 *bolt:* Arrow.   168 *love-in-idleness:* Pansy, hearts-ease.   171 *or . . . or:* Either . . . or.   174 *leviathan:* Sea monster, whale.   176 *forty:* (Used indefinitely.)

I'll watch Titania when she is asleep
And drop the liquor of it in her eyes.
The next thing then she waking looks upon,
Be it on lion, bear, or wolf, or bull,   180
On meddling monkey, or on busy ape,
She shall pursue it with the soul of love.
And ere I take this charm from off her sight,
As I can take it with another herb,
I'll make her render up her page to me.   185
But who comes here? I am invisible,
And I will overhear their conference.

Enter Demetrius, Helena following him.

Demetrius: I love thee not; therefore pursue me not.
Where is Lysander and fair Hermia?
The one I'll slay; the other slayeth me.   190
Thou toldst me they were stol'n unto this wood;
And here am I, and wood° within this wood
Because I cannot meet my Hermia.
Hence, get thee gone, and follow me no more.
Helena: You draw me, you hardhearted adamant!°   195
But yet you draw not iron, for my heart
Is true as steel. Leave you° your power to draw,
And I shall have no power to follow you.
Demetrius: Do I entice you? Do I speak you fair?°
Or rather do I not in plainest truth   200
Tell you I do not nor I cannot love you?
Helena: And even for that do I love you the more.
I am your spaniel; and, Demetrius,
The more you beat me I will fawn on you.
Use me but as your spaniel, spurn me, strike me,   205
Neglect me, lose me; only give me leave,
Unworthy as I am, to follow you.
What worser place can I beg in your love —
And yet a place of high respect with me —
Than to be usèd as you use your dog?   210
Demetrius: Tempt not too much the hatred of my spirit,
For I am sick when I do look on thee.
Helena: And I am sick when I look not on you.
Demetrius: You do impeach° your modesty too much
To leave° the city and commit yourself   215
Into the hands of one that loves you not,
To trust the opportunity of night

---

192 *and wood:* And mad, frantic (with an obvious wordplay on *wood,* meaning "woods").
195 *adamant:* Lodestone, magnet (with pun on *hardhearted,* since adamant was also thought
to be the hardest of all stones and was confused with the diamond).   197 *Leave you:* Give
up.   199 *speak you fair:* Speak courteously to you.   214 *impeach:* Call into question.
215 *To leave:* By leaving.

And the ill counsel of a desert° place
With the rich worth of your virginity.
Helena: Your virtue° is my privilege.° For that°   220
It is not night when I do see your face,
Therefore I think I am not in the night;
Nor doth this wood lack worlds of company,
For you, in my respect,° are all the world.
Then how can it be said I am alone   225
When all the world is here to look on me?
Demetrius: I'll run from thee and hide me in the brakes,°
And leave thee to the mercy of wild beasts.
Helena: The wildest hath not such a heart as you.
Run when you will. The story shall be changed: 230
Apollo flies and Daphne holds the chase,°
The dove pursues the griffin,° the mild hind°
Makes speed to catch the tiger — bootless° speed,
When cowardice pursues and valor flies!
Demetrius: I will not stay thy questions.° Let me go!   235
Or if thou follow me, do not believe
But I shall do thee mischief in the wood.
Helena: Ay, in the temple, in the town, the field,
You do me mischief. Fie, Demetrius!
Your wrongs do set a scandal on my sex.°   240
We cannot fight for love, as men may do;
We should be wooed and were not made to woo.   *[Exit Demetrius.]*
I'll follow thee and make a heaven of hell,
To die upon° the hand I love so well.   *[Exit.]*
Oberon: Fare thee well, nymph. Ere he do leave this grove   245
Thou shalt fly him, and he shall seek thy love.

Enter Puck.

Has thou the flower there? Welcome, wanderer.
Puck: Aye, there it is.   *[He offers the flower.]*
Oberon: I pray thee, give it to me.
I know a bank where the wild thyme blows,°
Where oxlips° and the nodding violet grows,   250
Quite overcanopied with luscious woodbine,°
With sweet muskroses° and with eglantine.°
There sleeps Titania sometime of° the night,

---

218 *desert:* Deserted.   220 *virtue:* Goodness or power to attract; *privilege:* Safeguard, warrant; *For that:* Because.   224 *in my respect:* As far as I am concerned, in my esteem. 227 *brakes:* Thickets.   231 *Apollo . . . chase:* (In the ancient myth, Daphne fled from Apollo and was saved from rape by being transformed into a laurel tree; here it is the female who *holds the chase,* or pursues, instead of the male.)   232 *griffin:* A fabulous monster with the head and wings of an eagle and the body of a lion; *hind:* Female deer.   233 *bootless:* Fruit-less.   235 *stay thy questions:* Wait for or put up with your talk or argument.   240 *Your . . . sex:* I.e., the wrongs that you do me cause me to act in a manner that disgraces my sex. 244 *upon:* By.   249 *blows:* Blooms.   250 *oxlips:* Flowers resembling cowslip and prim-rose.   251 *woodbine:* Honeysuckle.   252 *muskroses:* A kind of large, sweet-scented rose; *eglantine:* Sweetbrier, another kind of rose.   253 *sometime of:* For part of.

Lulled in these flowers with dances and delight;
And there the snake throws° her enameled skin,   255
Weed° wide enough to wrap a fairy in.
And with the juice of this I'll streak° her eyes
And make her full of hateful fantasies.
Take thou some of it, and seek through this grove.
                                    [He gives some love juice.]
A sweet Athenian lady is in love   260
With a disdainful youth. Anoint his eyes,
But do it when the next thing he espies
May be the lady. Thou shalt know the man
By the Athenian garments he hath on.
Effect it with some care, that he may prove   265
More fond on° her than she upon her love;
And look thou meet me ere the first cock crow.

Puck: Fear not, my lord, your servant shall do so.   *Exeunt [separately].*

[SCENE II: *The wood.*]

Enter Titania, Queen of Fairies, with her train.

Titania: Come, now a roundel° and a fairy song;
Then, for the third part of a minute,° hence —
Some to kill cankers° in the muskrose buds,
Some war with reremice° for their leathern wings
To make my small elves coats, and some keep back   5
The clamorous owl, that nightly hoots and wonders
At our quaint° spirits. Sing me now asleep.
Then to your offices, and let me rest.

Fairies sing.

First Fairy: You spotted snakes with double° tongue,
                Thorny hedgehogs, be not seen;   10
            Newts° and blindworms,° do no wrong;
                Come not near our Fairy Queen.

Chorus [dancing]: Philomel,° with melody
                Sing in our sweet lullaby;
            Lulla, lulla, lullaby, lulla, lulla, lullaby.   15
                Never harm
                Nor spell nor charm
            Come our lovely lady nigh.
            So good night, with lullaby.

255 *throws:* Sloughs off, sheds.   256 *Weed:* Garment.   257 *streak:* Anoint, touch gently.
266 *fond on:* Doting on.   **Scene II.**   1 *roundel:* Dance in a ring.   2 *the third . . . minute:*
(Indicative of the fairies' quickness.)   3 *cankers:* Cankerworms (i.e., caterpillars or grubs).
4 *reremice:* Bats.   7 *quaint:* Dainty.   9 *double:* Forked.   11 *Newts:* Water lizards considered poisonous, as were *blindworms* — small snakes with tiny eyes — and spiders.
13 *Philomel:* The nightingale. (Philomela, daughter of King Pandion, was transformed into a
nightingale, according to Ovid's *Metamorphoses* 6, after she had been raped by her sister
Procne's husband, Tereus.)

First Fairy: Weaving spiders, come not here;   20
          Hence, you long-legged spinners, hence!
     Beetles black, approach not near;
          Worm nor snail, do no offense.°
Chorus [dancing]: Philomel, with melody
          Sing in our sweet lullaby;   25
     Lulla, lulla, lullaby, lulla, lulla, lullaby.
          Never harm
          Nor spell nor charm
     Come our lovely lady nigh.
     So good night, with lullaby.   *[Titania sleeps.]*   30
Second Fairy: Hence, away! Now all is well.
     One aloof stand sentinel.°   *[Exeunt Fairies, leaving one sentinel.]*

Enter Oberon [and squeezes the flower on Titania's eyelids].

Oberon: What thou seest when thou dost wake,
     Do it for thy true love take;
     Love and languish for his sake.   35
     Be it ounce,° or cat, or bear,
     Pard,° or boar with bristled hair,
     In thy eye that shall appear
     When thou wak'st, it is thy dear.
     Wake when some vile thing is near.   *[Exit.]*   40

Enter Lysander and Hermia.

Lysander: Fair love, you faint with wandering in the wood;
          And to speak truth, I have forgot our way.
     We'll rest us, Hermia, if you think it good,
          And tarry for the comfort of the day.
Hermia: Be it so, Lysander. Find you out a bed,   45
     For I upon this bank will rest my head.
Lysander: One turf shall serve as pillow for us both;
     One heart, one bed, two bosoms, and one troth.°
Hermia: Nay, good Lysander, for my sake, my dear,
     Lie further off yet. Do not lie so near.   50
Lysander: O, take the sense, sweet, of my innocence!°
     Love takes the meaning in love's conference.°
     I mean that my heart unto yours is knit,
     So that but one heart we can make of it;
     Two bosoms interchainèd with an oath —   55
     So then two bosoms and a single troth.
     Then by your side no bed-room me deny,
     For lying so, Hermia, I do not lie.°

---

23 *offense:* Harm.   32 *sentinel:* (Presumably Oberon is able to outwit or intimidate this guard.)   36 *ounce:* Lynx.   37 *Pard:* Leopard.   48 *troth:* Faith, trothplight.   51 *take . . . innocence:* I.e., interpret my intention as innocent.   52 *Love . . . conference:* I.e., when lovers confer, love teaches each lover to interpret the other's meaning lovingly.   58 *lie:* Tell a falsehood (with a riddling pun on *lie,* "recline").

Hermia: Lysander riddles very prettily.
  Now much beshrew° my manners and my pride   60
  If Hermia meant to say Lysander lied.
  But, gentle friend, for love and courtesy
  Lie further off, in human° modesty.
  Such separation as may well be said
  Becomes a virtuous bachelor and a maid,   65
  So far be distant; and, good night, sweet friend.
  Thy love ne'er alter till thy sweet life end!
Lysander: Amen, amen, to that fair prayer, say I,
  And then end life when I end loyalty!
  Here is my bed. Sleep give thee all his rest!   70
Hermia: With half that wish the wisher's eyes be pressed!°
           [They sleep, separated by a short distance.]

  Enter Puck.

Puck: Through the forest have I gone,
  But Athenian found I none
  On whose eyes I might approve°
  This flower's force in stirring love.   75
  Night and silence. — Who is here?
  Weeds of Athens he doth wear.
  This is he, my master said,
  Despisèd the Athenian maid;
  And here the maiden, sleeping sound,   80
  On the dank and dirty ground.
  Pretty soul, she durst not lie
  Near this lack-love, this kill-courtesy.
  Churl, upon thy eyes I throw
  All the power this charm doth owe.° *[He applies the love juice.]* 85
  When thou wak'st, let love forbid
  Sleep his seat on thy eyelid.
  So awake when I am gone,
  For I must now to Oberon.   *Exit.*

  Enter Demetrius and Helena, running.

Helena: Stay, though thou kill me, sweet Demetrius!   90
Demetrius: I charge thee, hence, and do not haunt me thus.
Helena: O, wilt thou darkling° leave me? Do not so.
Demetrius: Stay, on thy peril!° I alone will go.   *[Exit.]*
Helena: O, I am out of breath in this fond° chase!
  The more my prayer, the lesser is my grace.°   95
  Happy is Hermia, wheresoe'er she lies,°

---

60 *beshrew:* Curse (but mildly meant).   63 *human:* Courteous (and perhaps suggesting "humane").   71 *With . . . pressed:* I.e., may we share your wish, so that your eyes too are *pressed,* closed, in sleep.   74 *approve:* Test.   85 *owe:* Own.   92 *darkling:* In the dark. 93 *on thy peril:* I.e., on pain of danger to you if you don't obey me and stay.   94 *fond:* Doting.   95 *my grace:* The favor I obtain.   96 *lies:* Dwells.

For she hath blessèd and attractive eyes.
How came her eyes so bright? Not with salt tears;
If so, my eyes are oftener washed than hers.
No, no, I am as ugly as a bear,   100
For beasts that meet me run away for fear.
Therefore no marvel though Demetrius
Do, as a monster, fly my presence thus.°
What wicked and dissembling glass of mine
Made me compare° with Hermia's sphery eyne?°   105
But who is here? Lysander, on the ground?
Dead, or asleep? I see no blood, no wound.
Lysander, if you live, good sir, awake.

Lysander [awaking]: And run through fire I will for thy sweet sake.
Transparent° Helena! Nature shows art,°   110
That through thy bosom makes me see thy heart.
Where is Demetrius? O, how fit a word
Is that vile name to perish on my sword!

Helena: Do not say so, Lysander; say not so.
What though he love your Hermia? Lord, what though?   115
Yet Hermia still loves you. Then be content.

Lysander: Content with Hermia? No! I do repent
The tedious minutes I with her have spent.
Not Hermia but Helena I love.
Who will not change a raven for a dove?   120
The will° of man is by his reason swayed,
And reason says you are the worthier maid.
Things growing are not ripe until their season;
So I, being young, till now ripe not° to reason.
And, touching° now the point° of human skill,°   125
Reason becomes the marshal to my will
And leads me to your eyes, where I o'erlook°
Love's stories written in love's richest book.

Helena: Wherefore° was I to this keen mockery born?
When at your hands did I deserve this scorn?   130
Is't not enough, is't not enough, young man,
That I did never — no, nor never can —
Deserve a sweet look from Demetrius' eye,
But you must flout my insufficiency?
Good troth,° you do me wrong, good sooth,° you do,   135
In such disdainful manner me to woo.
But fare you well. Perforce I must confess
I thought you lord of° more true gentleness.°

102–103 *no marvel . . . thus:* I.e., no wonder that Demetrius flies from me as from a monster.
105 *compare:* Vie; *sphery eyne:* Eyes as bright as stars in their spheres.   110 *Transparent:*
(1) Radiant (2) able to be seen through, lacking in deceit; *art:* Skill, magic power.   121 *will:*
Desire.   124 *ripe not:* (Am) not ripened.   125 *touching:* Reaching; *point:* Summit; *skill:*
Judgment.   127 *o'erlook:* Read.   129 *Wherefore:* Why.   135 *Good troth, good sooth:* I.e.,
indeed, truly.   138 *lord of:* I.e., possessor of; *gentleness:* Courtesy.

O, that a lady, of° one man refused,
Should of another therefore be abused!°   *Exit.* 140
Lysander: She sees not Hermia. Hermia, sleep thou there,
     And never mayst thou come Lysander near!
     For as a surfeit of the sweetest things
     The deepest loathing to the stomach brings,
     Or as the heresies that men do leave   145
     Are hated most of those they did deceive,°
     So thou, my surfeit and my heresy,
     Of all be hated, but the most of° me!
     And, all my powers, address° your love and might
     To honor Helen and to be her knight!   *Exit.* 150
Hermia [awaking]: Help me, Lysander, help me! Do thy best
     To pluck this crawling serpent from my breast!
     Ay me, for pity! What a dream was here!
     Lysander, look how I do quake with fear.
     Methought a serpent ate my heart away,   155
     And you sat smiling at his cruel prey.°
     Lysander! What, removed? Lysander! Lord!
     What, out of hearing? Gone? No sound, no word?
     Alack, where are you? Speak, an if° you hear;
     Speak, of all loves!° I swoon almost with fear.   160
     No? Then I well perceive you are not nigh.
     Either death, or you, I'll find immediately.
                              Exit. [The sleeping Titania remains.]

[ACT III

SCENE I: *The wood.*]

     Enter the clowns° *[Quince, Snug, Bottom, Flute, Snout, and Starveling].*

Bottom: Are we all met?
Quince: Pat, pat,° and here's a marvelous convenient place for our re-
     hearsal. This green plot shall be our stage, this hawthorn brake° our
     tiring-house,° and we will do it in action as we will do it before
     the Duke.   5
Bottom: Peter Quince?
Quince: What sayest thou, bully° Bottom?
Bottom: There are things in this comedy of Pyramus and Thisbe that will

---

139 *of:* By.   140 *abused:* Ill treated.   145–146 *as . . . deceive:* As renounced heresies are
hated most by those persons who formerly were deceived by them.   148 *Of . . . of:* By . . .
by.   149 *address:* Direct, apply.   156 *prey:* Act of preying.   159 *an if:* If.   160 *of all
loves:* For love's sake.   **Act III, Scene I.**   *clowns:* Rustics.   2 *Pat:* On the dot, punctually.   3 *brake:* Thicket.   4 *tiring-house:* Attiring area, hence backstage.   7 *bully:* I.e.,
worthy, jolly, fine fellow.

never please. First, Pyramus must draw a sword to kill himself, which
the ladies cannot abide. How answer you that?   10

Snout: By 'r lakin,° a parlous° fear.

Starveling: I believe we must leave the killing out, when all is done.°

Bottom: Not a whit. I have a device to make all well. Write me° a prologue,
and let the prologue seem to say, we will do no harm with our swords,
and that Pyramus is not killed indeed; and for the more better   15
assurance, tell them that I, Pyramus, am not Pyramus but Bottom the
weaver. This will put them out of fear.

Quince: Well, we will have such a prologue, and it shall be written in eight
and six.°

Bottom: No, make it two more: let it be written in eight and eight.   20

Snout: Will not the ladies be afeard of the lion?

Starveling: I fear it, I promise you.

Bottom: Masters, you ought to consider with yourself, to bring in — God
shield us! — a lion among ladies° is a most dreadful thing. For there is
not a more fearful° wildfowl than your lion living, and we ought to   25
look to 't.

Snout: Therefore another prologue must tell he is not a lion.

Bottom: Nay, you must name his name, and half his face must be seen
through the lion's neck, and he himself must speak through, saying
thus or to the same defect:° "Ladies," or "Fair ladies, I would wish   30
you," or "I would request you," or "I would entreat you, not to fear,
not to tremble; my life for yours.° If you think I come hither as a lion,
it were pity of my life.° No, I am no such thing; I am a man as other
men are." And there indeed let him name his name, and tell them
plainly he is Snug the joiner.   35

Quince: Well, it shall be so. But there is two hard things: that is, to bring
the moonlight into a chamber; for, you know, Pyramus and Thisbe
meet by moonlight.

Snout: Doth the moon shine that night we play our play?

Bottom: A calendar, a calendar! Look in the almanac. Find out moon-   40
shine, find out moonshine.   *[They consult an almanac.]*

Quince: Yes, it doth shine that night.

Bottom: Why then may you leave a casement of the great chamber window
where we play open, and the moon may shine in at the casement.

Quince: Ay; or else one must come in with a bush of thorns° and a lantern   45

---

11 *By 'r lakin:* By our ladykin, i.e., the Virgin Mary; *parlous:* Perilous, alarming.   12 *when all is done:* I.e., when all is said and done.   13 *Write me:* I.e., write at my suggestion (*me* is used colloquially).   19 *eight and six:* Alternate lines of eight and six syllables, a common ballad measure.   24 *lion among ladies:* (A contemporary pamphlet tells how, at the christening in 1594 of Prince Henry, eldest son of King James VI of Scotland, later James I of England, a "blackamoor" instead of a lion drew the triumphal chariot, since the lion's presence might have "brought some fear to the nearest.")   25 *fearful:* Fear-inspiring.   30 *defect:* (Bottom's blunder for "effect.")   32 *my life for yours:* I.e., I pledge my life to make your lives safe.   33 *it were . . . life:* I.e., I should be sorry, by my life; or, my life would be endangered.   45 *bush of thorns:* Bundle of thornbush fagots (part of the accoutrements of the man in the moon, according to the popular notions of the time, along with his lantern and his dog).

and say he comes to disfigure,° or to present,° the person of Moonshine. Then there is another thing: we must have a wall in the great chamber; for Pyramus and Thisbe, says the story, did talk through the chink of a wall.

Snout: You can never bring in a wall. What say you, Bottom?   50

Bottom: Some man or other must present Wall. And let him have some plaster, or some loam, or some roughcast° about him, to signify wall; or let him hold his fingers thus, and through that cranny shall Pyramus and Thisbe whisper.

Quince: If that may be, then all is well. Come, sit down, every mother's   55
son, and rehearse your parts. Pyramus, you begin. When you have spoken your speech, enter into that brake, and so everyone according to his cue.

Enter Robin [Puck].

Puck [aside]: What hempen homespuns° have we swaggering here
                    So near the cradle° of the Fairy Queen?   60
                    What, a play toward?° I'll be an auditor;
                    An actor, too, perhaps, if I see cause.

Quince: Speak, Pyramus. Thisbe, stand forth.

Bottom [as Pyramus]: "Thisbe, the flowers of odious savors sweet —"

Quince: Odors, odors.   65

Bottom: "— Odors savors sweet;
                 So hath thy breath, my dearest Thisbe dear.
                 But hark, a voice! Stay thou but here awhile,
                 And by and by I will to thee appear."   *Exit.*

Puck: A stranger Pyramus than e'er played here.°   *[Exit.]*   70

Flute: Must I speak now?

Quince: Ay, marry, must you; for you must understand he goes but to see a noise that he heard, and is to come again.

Flute [as Thisbe]: "Most radiant Pyramus, most lily-white of hue,
                        Of color like the red rose on triumphant° brier,   75
                        Most brisky juvenal° and eke° most lovely Jew,°
                        As true as truest horse that yet would never tire.
                        I'll meet thee, Pyramus, at Ninny's tomb."

Quince: "Ninus'° tomb," man. Why, you must not speak that yet. That you answer to Pyramus. You speak all your part° at once, cues and all.   80
Pyramus, enter. Your cue is past; it is "never tire."

---

46 *disfigure:* (Quince's blunder for "figure"); *present:* Represent.   52 *roughcast:* A mixture of lime and gravel used to plaster the outside of buildings.   59 *hempen homespuns:* I.e., rustics dressed in clothes woven of coarse, homespun fabric made from hemp.   60 *cradle:* I.e., Titania's bower.   61 *toward:* About to take place.   70 *A stranger...here:* (Either Puck refers to an earlier dramatic version played in the same theater, or he has conceived of a plan to present a "stranger" Pyramus than ever seen before.)   75 *triumphant:* Magnificent. 76 *brisky juvenal:* Lively youth; *eke:* Also; *Jew:* (An absurd repetition of the first syllable of *juvenal* and an indication of how desperately Quince searches for his rhymes.)   79 *Ninus':* Mythical founder of Nineveh (whose wife, Semiramis, was supposed to have built the walls of Babylon where the story of Pyramus and Thisbe takes place).   80 *part:* (An actor's *part* was a script consisting only of his speeches and their cues.)

Flute: O — "As true as truest horse, that yet would never tire."

[Enter Puck, and Bottom as Pyramus with the ass head.°]

Bottom: "If I were fair,° Thisbe, I were° only thine."

Quince: O, monstrous! O, strange! We are haunted. Pray, masters! Fly, masters! Help! *[Exeunt Quince, Snug, Flute, Snout, and Starveling.]* 85

Puck: I'll follow you, I'll lead you about a round,°
    Thorough bog, thorough bush, thorough brake, thorough brier.
Sometimes a horse I'll be, sometimes a hound,
    A hog, a headless bear, sometimes a fire;°
And neigh, and bark, and grunt, and roar, and burn, 90
Like horse, hound, hog, bear, fire, at every turn. *Exit.*

Bottom: Why do they run away? This is a knavery of them to make me afeard.

Enter Snout.

Snout: O Bottom, thou art changed! What do I see on thee?

Bottom: What do you see? You see an ass head of your own, do you? 95
[Exit Snout.]

Enter Quince.

Quince: Bless thee, Bottom, bless thee! Thou art translated.° *Exit.*

Bottom: I see their knavery. This is to make an ass of me, to fright me, if they could. But I will not stir from this place, do what they can. I will walk up and down here, and will sing, that they shall hear I am not afraid. *[He sings.]* 100
    The ouzel cock° so black of hue,
      With orange-tawny bill,
    The throstle° with his note so true,
      The wren with little quill° —

Titania [awaking]: What angel wakes me from my flowery bed? 105
Bottom [sings]:
    The finch, the sparrow, and the lark,
      The plainsong° cuckoo gray,
    Whose note full many a man doth mark,
      And dares not answer nay° —
For indeed, who would set his wit to° so foolish a bird? Who would 110
give a bird the lie,° though he cry "cuckoo" never so?°

Titania: I pray thee, gentle mortal, sing again.
    Mine ear is much enamored of thy note;
    So is mine eye enthrallèd to thy shape;
    And thy fair virtue's force° perforce doth move me 115
    On the first view to say, to swear, I love thee.

---

with the ass head: (This stage direction presumably refers to a standard stage property.) 83 *fair:* Handsome; *were:* Would be. 86 *about a round:* Roundabout. 89 *fire:* Will-o'-the-wisp. 96 *translated:* Transformed. 101 *ouzel cock:* Male blackbird. 103 *throstle:* Song thrush. 104 *quill:* (Literally, a reed pipe; hence, the bird's piping song.) 107 *plainsong:* Singing a melody without variations. 109 *dares . . . nay:* I.e., cannot deny that he is a cuckold. 110 *set his wit to:* Employ his intelligence to answer. 111 *give . . . lie:* Call the bird a liar; *never so:* Ever so much. 115 *thy . . . force:* The power of your unblemished excellence.

Bottom: Methinks, mistress, you should have little reason for that. And
    yet, to say the truth, reason and love keep little company together
    nowadays — the more the pity that some honest neighbors will not
    make them friends. Nay, I can gleek° upon occasion.   120
Titania: Thou art as wise as thou art beautiful.
Bottom: Not so, neither. But if I had wit enough to get out of this wood,
    I have enough to serve mine own turn.°
Titania: Out of this wood do not desire to go.
    Thou shalt remain here, whether thou wilt or no.   125
    I am a spirit of no common rate.°
    The summer still doth tend upon my state,°
    And I do love thee. Therefore, go with me.
    I'll give thee fairies to attend on thee,
    And they shall fetch thee jewels from the deep,   130
    And sing while thou on pressèd flowers dost sleep.
    And I will purge thy mortal grossness° so
    That thou shalt like an airy spirit go.
    Peaseblossom, Cobweb, Mote,° and Mustardseed!

    Enter four Fairies [Peaseblossom, Cobweb, Mote, and Mustardseed].

Peaseblossom: Ready.   135
Cobweb: And I.
Mote: And I.
Mustardseed: And I.
All: Where shall we go?
Titania: Be kind and courteous to this gentleman.
    Hop in his walks and gambol in his eyes;°
    Feed him with apricots and dewberries,°
    With purple grapes, green figs, and mulberries;   140
    The honey bags steal from the humble-bees,
    And for night tapers crop their waxen thighs
    And light them at the fiery glowworms' eyes,
    To have my love to bed and to arise;
    And pluck the wings from painted butterflies   145
    To fan the moonbeams from his sleeping eyes.
    Nod to him, elves, and do him courtesies.
Peaseblossom: Hail, mortal!
Cobweb: Hail!
Mote: Hail!   150
Mustardseed: Hail!
Bottom: I cry your worships mercy,° heartily. I beseech your worship's name.
Cobweb: Cobweb.

---

120 *gleek:* Jest.   123 *serve ... turn:* Answer my purpose.   126 *rate:* Rank, value.   127 *still
... state:* Always waits upon me as a part of my royal retinue.   132 *mortal grossness:* Materi-
ality (i.e., the corporeal nature of a mortal being).   134 *Mote:* I.e., speck. (The two words
moth and *mote* were pronounced alike, and both meanings may be present.)   138 *in his eyes:*
In his sight (i.e., before him).   139 *dewberries:* Blackberries.   152 *I cry ... mercy:* I beg
pardon of your worships (for presuming to ask a question).

Bottom: I shall desire you of more acquaintance,° good Master Cobweb.
　　If I cut my finger, I shall make bold with you.°—Your name, honest   155
　　gentleman?
Peaseblossom: Peaseblossom.
Bottom: I pray you, commend me to Mistress Squash,° your mother,
　　and to Master Peascod,° your father. Good Master Peaseblossom, I
　　shall desire you of more acquaintance too.—Your name, I beseech   160
　　you, sir?
Mustardseed: Mustardseed.
Bottom: Good Master Mustardseed, I know your patience° well. That same
　　cowardly, giantlike ox-beef hath devoured many a gentleman of your
　　house. I promise you, your kindred hath made my eyes water° ere now.   165
　　I desire you of more acquaintance, good Master Mustardseed.
Titania: Come wait upon him; lead him to my bower.
　　　　The moon methinks looks with a watery eye;
　　And when she weeps,° weeps every little flower,
　　　　Lamenting some enforcèd° chastity.   170
　　Tie up my lover's tongue;° bring him silently.   *Exeunt.*

[SCENE II: The wood.]

　　Enter [Oberon,] King of Fairies.

Oberon: I wonder if Titania be awaked;
　　Then, what it was that next came in her eye,
　　Which she must dote on in extremity.

　　[Enter] Robin Goodfellow [Puck].

　　Here comes my messenger. How now, mad spirit?
　　What night-rule° now about this haunted° grove?   5
Puck: My mistress with a monster is in love.
　　Near to her close° and consecrated bower,
　　While she was in her dull° and sleeping hour,
　　A crew of patches,° rude mechanicals,°
　　That work for bread upon Athenian stalls,°   10
　　Were met together to rehearse a play
　　Intended for great Theseus' nuptial day.
　　The shallowest thickskin of that barren sort,°
　　Who Pyramus presented,° in their sport
　　Forsook his scene° and entered in a brake.   15
　　When I did him at this advantage take,

---

154 *I . . . acquaintance:* I crave to be better acquainted with you.   154–155 *If . . . you:* (Cobwebs were used to stanch bleeding.)   159 *Squash:* Unripe pea pod.   159 *Peascod:* Ripe pea pod.   163 *your patience:* What you have endured (mustard is eaten with beef).   165 *water:* (1) Weep for sympathy (2) smart, sting.   169 *she weeps:* I.e., she causes dew.   170 *enforcèd:* Forced, violated; or, possibly, constrained (since Titania at this moment is hardly concerned about chastity).   171 *Tie . . . tongue:* (Presumably Bottom is braying like an ass.)
Scene II.   5 *night-rule:* Diversion or misrule for the night; *haunted:* Much frequented.   7 *close:* Secret, private.   8 *dull:* Drowsy.   9 *patches:* Clowns, fools; *rude mechanicals:* Ignorant artisans.   10 *stalls:* Market booths.   13 *barren sort:* Stupid company or crew.   14 *presented:* Acted.   15 *scene:* Playing area.

An ass's noll° I fixèd on his head.
Anon his Thisbe must be answerèd,
And forth my mimic° comes. When they him spy,
As wild geese that the creeping fowler° eye,   20
Or russet-pated choughs,° many in sort,°
Rising and cawing at the gun's report,
Sever° themselves and madly sweep the sky,
So, at his sight, away his fellows fly;
And, at our stamp, here o'er and o'er one falls;   25
He "Murder!" cries and help from Athens calls.
Their sense thus weak, lost with their fears thus strong,
Made senseless things begin to do them wrong,
For briers and thorns at their apparel snatch;
Some, sleeves — some, hats; from yielders all things catch.°   30
I led them on in this distracted fear
And left sweet Pyramus translated there,
When in that moment, so it came to pass,
Titania waked and straightway loved an ass.
Oberon: This falls out better than I could devise.   35
But hast thou yet latched° the Athenian's eyes
With the love juice, as I did bid thee do?
Puck: I took him sleeping — that is finished too —
And the Athenian woman by his side,
That, when he waked, of force° she must be eyed.   40

Enter Demetrius and Hermia.

Oberon: Stand close. This is the same Athenian.
Puck: This is the woman, but not this the man.   *[They stand aside.]*
Demetrius: O, why rebuke you him that loves you so?
Lay breath so bitter on your bitter foe.
Hermia: Now I but chide; but I should use thee worse,   45
For thou, I fear, hast given me cause to curse.
If thou hast slain Lysander in his sleep,
Being o'er shoes° in blood, plunge in the deep,
And kill me too.
The sun was not so true unto the day   50
As he to me. Would he have stolen away
From sleeping Hermia? I'll believe as soon
This whole° earth may be bored, and that the moon
May through the center creep, and so displease
Her brother's° noontide with th' Antipodes.°   55
It cannot be but thou hast murdered him;
So should a murderer look, so dead,° so grim.

---

17 *noll:* Noddle, head.   19 *mimic:* Burlesque actor.   20 *fowler:* Hunter of game birds.
21 *russet-pated choughs:* Reddish brown or gray-headed jackdaws; *in sort:* In a flock.
23 *Sever:* I.e., scatter.   30 *from . . . catch:* I.e., everything preys on those who yield to fear.
36 *latched:* Fastened, snared.   40 *of force:* Perforce.   48 *Being o'er shoes:* Having waded
in so far.   53 *whole:* Solid.   55 *Her brother's:* I.e., the sun's; *th' Antipodes:* The people on
the opposite side of the earth (where the moon is imagined bringing night to noontime).
57 *dead:* Deadly, or deathly pale.

Demetrius: So should the murdered look, and so should I,
 Pierced through the heart with your stern cruelty.
 Yet you, the murderer, look as bright, as clear   60
 As yonder Venus in her glimmering sphere.
Hermia: What's this to° my Lysander? Where is he?
 Ah, good Demetrius, wilt thou give him me?
Demetrius: I had rather give his carcass to my hounds.
Hermia: Out, dog! Out, cur! Thou driv'st me past the bounds 65
 Of maiden's patience. Hast thou slain him, then?
 Henceforth be never numbered among men.
 O, once° tell true, tell true, even for my sake:
 Durst thou have looked upon him being awake?
 And hast thou killed him sleeping? O brave touch!° 70
 Could not a worm,° an adder, do so much?
 An adder did it; for with doubler° tongue
 Than thine, thou serpent, never adder stung.
Demetrius: You spend your passion° on a misprised mood.°
 I am not guilty of Lysander's blood,   75
 Nor is he dead, for aught that I can tell.
Hermia: I pray thee, tell me then that he is well.
Demetrius: And if I could, what should I get therefor?°
Hermia: A privilege never to see me more.
 And from thy hated presence part I so.   80
 See me no more, whether he be dead or no. *Exit.*
Demetrius: There is no following her in this fierce vein.
 Here therefore for a while I will remain.
 So sorrow's heaviness doth heavier° grow
 For debt that bankrupt° sleep doth sorrow owe, 85
 Which now in some slight measure it will pay,
 If for his tender here I make some stay.° *[He] lie[s] down [and sleeps].*
Oberon: What hast thou done? Thou hast mistaken quite
 And laid the love juice on some true love's sight.
 Of thy misprision° must perforce ensue 90
 Some true love turned, and not a false turned true.
Puck: Then fate o'errules, that, one man holding troth,°
 A million fail, confounding oath on oath.°
Oberon: About the wood go swifter than the wind,
 And Helena of Athens look° thou find. 95
 All fancy-sick° she is and pale of cheer°
 With sighs of love, that cost the fresh blood° dear.

---

62 *to:* To do with. 68 *once:* Once and for all. 70 *brave touch!:* Fine stroke! (said ironically). 71 *worm:* Serpent. 72 *doubler:* (1) More forked (2) more deceitful. 74 *passion:* Violent feelings; *misprised mood:* Anger based on misconception. 78 *therefor:* In return for that. 84 *heavier:* (1) Harder to bear (2) more drowsy. 85 *bankrupt:* (Demetrius is saying that his sleepiness adds to the weariness caused by sorrow.) 86–87 *Which . . . stay:* I.e., to a small extent, I will be able to "pay back" and hence find some relief from sorrow, if I pause here awhile (*make some stay*) while sleep "tenders" or offers itself by way of paying the debt owed to sorrow. 90 *misprision:* Mistake. 92 *that . . . troth:* In that, for each man keeping true faith in love. 93 *confounding . . . oath:* I.e., breaking oath after oath. 95 *look:* I.e., be sure. 96 *fancy-sick:* Lovesick; *cheer:* Face. 97 *sighs . . . blood:* (An allusion to the physiological theory that each sigh costs the heart a drop of blood.)

By some illusion see thou bring her here.
I'll charm his eyes against she do appear.°
Puck: I go, I go, look how I go,   100
    Swifter than arrow from the Tartar's bow.°   *[Exit.]*
Oberon [applying love juice to Demetrius' eyes]: Flower of this purple dye,
        Hit with Cupid's archery,
        Sink in apple° of his eye.
        When his love he doth espy,   105
        Let her shine as gloriously
        As the Venus of the sky.
        When thou wak'st, if she be by,
        Beg of her for remedy.

    Enter Puck.

Puck: Captain of our fairy band,   110
        Helena is here at hand,
        And the youth, mistook by me,
        Pleading for a lover's fee.°
        Shall we their fond pageant° see?
        Lord, what fools these mortals be!   115
Oberon: Stand aside. The noise they make
        Will cause Demetrius to awake.
Puck: Then will two at once woo one;
        That must needs be sport alone.°
        And those things do best please me   120
        That befall preposterously.°   *[They stand aside.]*

    Enter Lysander and Helena.

Lysander: Why should you think that I should woo in scorn?
        Scorn and derision never come in tears.
        Look when° I vow, I weep; and vows so born,
        In their nativity all truth appears.°   125
        How can these things in me seem scorn to you,
        Bearing the badge° of faith to prove them true?
Helena: You do advance° your cunning more and more.
        When truth kills truth,° O, devilish-holy fray!
        These vows are Hermia's. Will you give her o'er?   130
        Weigh oath with oath, and you will nothing weigh.
        Your vows to her and me, put in two scales,
        Will even weigh, and both as light as tales.°
Lysander: I had no judgment when to her I swore.
Helena: Nor none, in my mind, now you give her o'er.   135
Lysander: Demetrius loves her, and he loves not you.

---

99 *against . . . appear:* In anticipation of her coming.   101 *Tartar's bow:* (Tartars were famed
for their skill with the bow.)   104 *apple:* Pupil.   113 *fee:* Privilege, reward.   114 *fond
pageant:* Foolish spectacle.   119 *alone:* Unequaled.   121 *preposterously:* Out of the natural order.   124 *Look when:* Whenever.   124–125 *vows . . . appears:* I.e., vows made by one
who is weeping give evidence thereby of their sincerity.   127 *badge:* Identifying device
such as that worn on the servants' livery (here, his tears).   128 *advance:* Carry forward,
display.   129 *truth kills truth:* I.e., one of Lysander's vows must invalidate the other.
133 *tales:* Lies.

Demetrius [awaking]: O Helen, goddess, nymph, perfect, divine!
　　To what, my love, shall I compare thine eyne?
　　Crystal is muddy. O, how ripe in show°
　　Thy lips, those kissing cherries, tempting grow!　　　　　　　140
　　That pure congealèd white, high Taurus'° snow,
　　Fanned with the eastern wind, turns to a crow°
　　When thou hold'st up thy hand. O, let me kiss
　　This princess of pure white, this seal° of bliss!
Helena: O spite! O hell! I see you all are bent　　　　　　　145
　　To set against° me for your merriment.
　　If you were civil and knew courtesy,
　　You would not do me thus much injury.
　　Can you not hate me, as I know you do,
　　But you must join in souls° to mock me too?　　　　　　　150
　　If you were men, as men you are in show,
　　You would not use a gentle lady so —
　　To vow, and swear, and superpraise° my parts,°
　　When I am sure you hate me with your hearts.
　　You both are rivals, and love Hermia,　　　　　　　155
　　And now both rivals to mock Helena.
　　A trim° exploit, a manly enterprise,
　　To conjure tears up in a poor maid's eyes
　　With your derision! None of noble sort°
　　Would so offend a virgin and extort°　　　　　　　160
　　A poor soul's patience, all to make you sport.
Lysander: You are unkind, Demetrius. Be not so.
　　For you love Hermia; this you know I know.
　　And here, with all good will, with all my heart,
　　In Hermia's love I yield you up my part;　　　　　　　165
　　And yours of Helena to me bequeath,
　　Whom I do love, and will do till my death.
Helena: Never did mockers waste more idle breath.
Demetrius: Lysander, keep thy Hermia; I will none.°
　　If e'er I loved her, all that love is gone.　　　　　　　170
　　My heart to her but as guestwise sojourned,°
　　And now to Helen is it home returned,
　　There to remain.
Lysander:　　　　　　　Helen, it is not so.
Demetrius: Disparage not the faith thou dost not know,
　　Lest, to thy peril, thou aby° it dear.　　　　　　　175
　　Look where thy love comes; yonder is thy dear.

　　Enter Hermia.

Hermia: Dark night, that from the eye his° function takes,

---

139 *show:* Appearance.　　141 *Taurus:* A lofty mountain range in Asia Minor.　　142 *turns to a crow:* I.e., seems black by contrast.　　144 *seal:* Pledge.　　146 *set against:* Attack. 150 *in souls:* I.e., heart and soul.　　153 *superpraise:* Overpraise; *parts:* Qualities.　　157 *trim:* Pretty, fine (said ironically).　　159 *sort:* Character, quality.　　160 *extort:* Twist, torture. 169 *will none:* I.e., want no part of her.　　171 *to . . . sojourned:* Only visited with her. 175 *aby:* Pay for.　　177 *his:* Its.

The ear more quick of apprehension makes;
Wherein it doth impair the seeing sense,
It pays the hearing double recompense.   180
Thou art not by mine eye, Lysander, found;
Mine ear, I thank it, brought me to thy sound.
But why unkindly didst thou leave me so?

Lysander: Why should he stay, whom love doth press to go?

Hermia: What love could press Lysander from my side?   185

Lysander: Lysander's love, that would not let him bide —
Fair Helena, who more engilds° the night
Than all yon fiery oes° and eyes of light.
Why seek'st thou me? Could not this make thee know
The hate I bear thee made me leave thee so?   190

Hermia: You speak not as you think. It cannot be.

Helena: Lo, she is one of this confederacy!
Now I perceive they have conjoined all three
To fashion this false sport, in spite of me.°
Injurious Hermia, most ungrateful maid!   195
Have you conspired, have you with these contrived°
To bait° me with this foul derision?
Is all the counsel° that we two have shared —
The sisters' vows, the hours that we have spent
When we have chid the hasty-footed time   200
For parting us — O, is all forgot?
All schooldays' friendship, childhood innocence?
We, Hermia, like two artificial° gods
Have with our needles created both one flower,
Both on one sampler, sitting on one cushion,   205
Both warbling of one song, both in one key,
As if our hands, our sides, voices, and minds
Had been incorporate.° So we grew together,
Like to a double cherry, seeming parted,
But yet an union in partition,   210
Two lovely° berries molded on one stem;
So, with two seeming bodies but one heart,
Two of the first, like coats in heraldry,
Due but to one and crownèd with one crest.°
And will you rend our ancient love asunder,   215
To join with men in scorning your poor friend?
It is not friendly, 'tis not maidenly.
Our sex, as well as I, may chide you for it,
Though I alone do feel the injury.

Hermia: I am amazèd at your passionate words.   220
I scorn you not. It seems that you scorn me.

---

187 *engilds:* Gilds, brightens with a golden light.   188 *oes:* Spangles (here, stars).   194 *in spite of me:* To vex me.   196 *contrived:* Plotted.   197 *bait:* Torment, as one sets on dogs to bait a bear.   198 *counsel:* Confidential talk.   203 *artificial:* Skilled in art or creation. 208 *incorporate:* Of one body.   211 *lovely:* Loving.   213–214 *Two . . . crest:* I.e., we have two separate bodies, just as a coat of arms in heraldry can be represented twice on a shield but surmounted by a single crest.

Helena: Have you not set Lysander, as in scorn,
To follow me and praise my eyes and face?
And made your other love, Demetrius,
Who even but now did spurn me with his foot,   225
To call me goddess, nymph, divine, and rare,
Precious, celestial? Wherefore speaks he this
To her he hates? And wherefore doth Lysander
Deny your love, so rich within his soul,
And tender° me, forsooth, affection,   230
But by your setting on, by your consent?
What though I be not so in grace° as you,
So hung upon with love, so fortunate,
But miserable most, to love unloved?
This you should pity rather than despise.   235
Hermia: I understand not what you mean by this.
Helena: Ay, do! Persever, counterfeit sad° looks,
Make mouths° upon° me when I turn my back,
Wink each at other, hold the sweet jest up.°
This sport, well carried,° shall be chronicled.   240
If you have any pity, grace, or manners,
You would not make me such an argument.°
But fare ye well. 'Tis partly my own fault,
Which death, or absence, soon shall remedy.
Lysander: Stay, gentle Helena; hear my excuse,   245
My love, my life, my soul, fair Helena!
Helena: O excellent!
Hermia [to Lysander]: Sweet, do not scorn her so.
Demetrius [to Lysander]: If she cannot entreat,° I can compel.
Lysander: Thou canst compel no more than she entreat.   250
Thy threats have no more strength than her weak prayers.
Helen, I love thee, by my life, I do!
I swear by that which I will lose for thee,
To prove him false that says I love thee not.
Demetrius [to Helena]: I say I love thee more than he can do.   255
Lysander: If thou say so, withdraw, and prove it too.°
Demetrius: Quick, come!
Hermia: Lysander, whereto tends all this?
Lysander: Away, you Ethiope!°   *[He tries to break away from Hermia.]*
Demetrius: No, no; he'll
Seem to break loose; take on as° you would follow,
But yet come not. You are a tame man. Go!   260
Lysander [to Hermia]: Hang off,° thou cat, thou burr! Vile thing, let loose,
Or I will shake thee from me like a serpent!
Hermia: Why are you grown so rude? What change is this,
Sweet love?

---

230 *tender:* Offer.   232 *grace:* Favor.   237 *sad:* Grave, serious.   238 *mouths:* I.e., mows, faces, grimaces; *upon:* At.   239 *hold...up:* Keep up the joke.   240 *carried:* Managed. 242 *argument:* Subject for a jest.   249 *entreat:* I.e., succeed by entreaty.   256 *withdraw... too:* I.e., withdraw with me and prove your claim in a duel (the two gentlemen are armed). 258 *Ethiope:* (Referring to Hermia's relatively dark hair and complexion; see also *tawny Tartar* six lines later.)   259 *take on as:* Act as if, make a fuss as if.   261 *Hang off:* Let go.

Lysander: Thy love? Out, tawny Tartar, out!
     Out, loathèd med'cine!° O hated potion, hence!   265
Hermia: Do you not jest?
Helena: Yes, sooth,° and so do you.
Lysander: Demetrius, I will keep my word with thee.
Demetrius: I would I had your bond, for I perceive
     A weak bond° holds you. I'll not trust your word.
Lysander: What, should I hurt her, strike her, kill her dead?   270
     Although I hate her, I'll not harm her so.
Hermia: What, can you do me greater harm than hate?
     Hate me? Wherefore? O me, what news,° my love?
     Am not I Hermia? Are not you Lysander?
     I am as fair now as I was erewhile.°   275
     Since night you loved me; yet since night you left me.
     Why, then you left me — O, the gods forbid! —
     In earnest, shall I say?
Lysander: Ay, by my life!
     And never did desire to see thee more.
     Therefore be out of hope, of question, of doubt;   280
     Be certain, nothing truer. 'Tis no jest
     That I do hate thee and love Helena.
Hermia [to Helena]: O me! You juggler! You cankerblossom!°
     You thief of love! What, have you come by night
     And stol'n my love's heart from him?
Helena: Fine, i' faith!   285
     Have you no modesty, no maiden shame,
     No touch of bashfulness? What, will you tear
     Impatient answers from my gentle tongue?
     Fie, fie! You counterfeit, you puppet,° you!
Hermia: "Puppet"? Why, so!° Ay, that way goes the game.   290
     Now I perceive that she hath made compare
     Between our statures; she hath urged her height,
     And with her personage, her tall personage,
     Her height, forsooth, she hath prevailed with him.
     And are you grown so high in his esteem   295
     Because I am so dwarfish and so low?
     How low am I, thou painted maypole? Speak!
     How low am I? I am not yet so low
     But that my nails can reach unto thine eyes.
               [She flails at Helena but is restrained.]
Helena: I pray you, though you mock me, gentlemen,   300
     Let her not hurt me. I was never curst;°
     I have no gift at all in shrewishness;
     I am a right° maid for my cowardice.
     Let her not strike me. You perhaps may think,

---

265 *med'cine:* I.e., poison.   266 *sooth:* Truly.   269 *weak bond:* I.e., Hermia's arm (with a
pun on *bond,* "oath," in the previous line).   273 *what news:* What is the matter?   275 *ere-
while:* Just now.   283 *cankerblossom:* Worm that destroys the flower bud, or wild rose.
289 *puppet:* (1) Counterfeit (2) dwarfish woman (in reference to Hermia's smaller stature).
290 *Why, so:* I.e., Oh, so that's how it is.   301 *curst:* Shrewish.   303 *right:* True.

Because she is something° lower than myself, 305
That I can match her.
Hermia: Lower? Hark, again!
Helena: Good Hermia, do not be so bitter with me.
I evermore did love you, Hermia,
Did ever keep your counsels, never wronged you,
Save that, in love unto Demetrius, 310
I told him of your stealth° unto this wood.
He followed you; for love I followed him.
But he hath chid me hence° and threatened me
To strike me, spurn me, nay, to kill me too.
And now, so° you will let me quiet go, 315
To Athens will I bear my folly back
And follow you no further. Let me go.
You see how simple and how fond° I am.
Hermia: Why, get you gone. Who is't that hinders you?
Helena: A foolish heart, that I leave here behind. 320
Hermia: What, with Lysander?
Helena: With Demetrius.
Lysander: Be not afraid; she shall not harm thee, Helena.
Demetrius: No, sir, she shall not, though you take her part.
Helena: O, when she is angry, she is keen° and shrewd.°
She was a vixen when she went to school; 325
And though she be but little, she is fierce.
Hermia: "Little" again? Nothing but "low" and "little"?
Why will you suffer her to flout me thus?
Let me come to her.
Lysander: Get you gone, you dwarf!
You minimus,° of hindering knotgrass° made! 330
You bead, you acorn!
Demetrius: You are too officious
In her behalf that scorns your services.
Let her alone. Speak not of Helena;
Take not her part. For, if thou dost intend°
Never so little show of love to her, 335
Thou shalt aby° it.
Lysander: Now she holds me not.
Now follow, if thou dar'st, to try whose right,
Of thine or mine, is most in Helena.   *[Exit.]*
Demetrius: Follow? Nay, I'll go with thee, cheek by jowl.°
                    [Exit, following Lysander.]
Hermia: You, mistress, all this coil° is 'long of° you. 340
Nay, go not back.°
Helena: I will not trust you, I,

---

305 *something:* Somewhat.   311 *stealth:* Stealing away.   313 *chid me hence:* Driven me
away with his scolding.   315 *so:* If only.   318 *fond:* Foolish.   324 *keen:* Fierce, cruel;
shrewd: Shrewish.   330 *minimus:* Diminutive creature; *knotgrass:* A weed, an infusion of
which was thought to stunt the growth.   334 *intend:* Give sign of.   336 *aby:* Pay for.
339 *cheek by jowl:* I.e., side by side.   340 *coil:* Turmoil, dissension; *'long of:* On account of.
341 *go not back:* I.e., don't retreat (Hermia is again proposing a fight).

Nor longer stay in your curst company.
Your hands than mine are quicker for a fray;
My legs are longer, though, to run away.   *[Exit.]*
Hermia: I am amazed and know not what to say.   *Exit.* 345

[Oberon and Puck come forward.]

Oberon: This is thy negligence. Still thou mistak'st,
    Or else committ'st thy knaveries willfully.
Puck: Believe me, king of shadows, I mistook.
    Did not you tell me I should know the man
    By the Athenian garments he had on?   350
    And so far blameless proves my enterprise
    That I have 'nointed an Athenian's eyes;
    And so far° am I glad it so did sort,°
    As° this their jangling I esteem a sport.
Oberon: Thou seest these lovers seek a place to fight.   355
    Hie° therefore, Robin, overcast the night;
    The starry welkin° cover thou anon
    With drooping fog as black as Acheron,°
    And lead these testy rivals so astray
    As° one come not within another's way.   360
    Like to Lysander sometimes frame thy tongue,
    Then stir Demetrius up with bitter wrong;°
    And sometimes rail thou like Demetrius.
    And from each other look thou lead them thus,
    Till o'er their brows death-counterfeiting sleep   365
    With leaden legs and batty° wings doth creep.
    Then crush this herb° into Lysander's eye,   *[giving herb]*
    Whose liquor hath this virtuous° property,
    To take from thence all error with his° might
    And make his eyeballs roll with wonted° sight.   370
    When they next wake, all this derision°
    Shall seem a dream and fruitless vision,
    And back to Athens shall the lovers wend
    With league whose date° till death shall never end.
    Whiles I in this affair do thee employ,   375
    I'll to my queen and beg her Indian boy;
    And then I will her charmèd eye release
    From monster's view, and all things shall be peace.
Puck: My fairy lord, this must be done with haste,
    For night's swift dragons° cut the clouds full fast,   380
    And yonder shines Aurora's harbinger,°
    At whose approach ghosts, wand'ring here and there,
    Troop home to churchyards. Damnèd spirits all,

---

353 *so far:* At least to this extent; *sort:* Turn out.   354 *As:* In that.   356 *Hie:* Hasten.
357 *welkin:* Sky.   358 *Acheron:* River of Hades (here representing Hades itself).   360 *As:*
That.   362 *wrong:* Insults.   366 *batty:* Batlike.   367 *this herb:* I.e., the antidote
(mentioned in II.i.184) to love-in-idleness.   368 *virtuous:* Efficacious.   369 *his:* Its.
370 *wonted:* Accustomed.   371 *derision:* Laughable business.   374 *date:* Term of existence.   380 *dragons:* (Supposed by Shakespeare to be yoked to the car of the goddess of
night or the moon.)   381 *Aurora's harbinger:* The morning star, precursor of dawn.

That in crossways and floods have burial,°
Already to their wormy beds are gone.   385
For fear lest day should look their shames upon,
They willfully themselves exile from light
And must for aye° consort with black-browed night.
Oberon: But we are spirits of another sort.
    I with the Morning's love° have oft made sport,   390
    And, like a forester,° the groves may tread
    Even till the eastern gate, all fiery red,
    Opening on Neptune with fair blessèd beams,
    Turns into yellow gold his salt green streams.
    But notwithstanding, haste, make no delay.   395
    We may effect this business yet ere day.   *[Exit.]*
Puck: Up and down, up and down,
    I will lead them up and down.
    I am feared in field and town.
    Goblin,° lead them up and down.   400
    Here comes one.

    Enter Lysander.

Lysander: Where art thou, proud Demetrius? Speak thou now.
Puck [mimicking Demetrius]: Here, villain, drawn° and ready. Where art
    thou?
Lysander: I will be with thee straight.°
Puck: Follow me, then,
    To plainer° ground.   *[Lysander wanders about,° following the voice.]*
    Enter Demetrius.

Demetrius: Lysander! Speak again!   405
    Thou runaway, thou coward, art thou fled?
    Speak! In some bush? Where dost thou hide thy head?
Puck [mimicking Lysander]: Thou coward, art thou bragging to the stars,
    Telling the bushes that thou look'st for wars,
    And wilt not come? Come, recreant;° come, thou child,   410
    I'll whip thee with a rod. He is defiled
    That draws a sword on thee.
Demetrius: Yea, art thou there?
Puck: Follow my voice. We'll try° no manhood here.   *Exeunt.*

    [Lysander returns.]

Lysander: He goes before me and still dares me on.
    When I come where he calls, then he is gone.   415

---

384 *crossways . . . burial:* (Those who had committed suicide were buried at crossways, with a
stake driven through them; those who intentionally or accidentally drowned [in *floods* or
deep water] would be condemned to wander disconsolately for lack of burial rights.)
388 *for aye:* Forever.   390 *the Morning's love:* Cephalus, a beautiful youth beloved by Aurora; or perhaps the goddess of the dawn herself.   391 *forester:* Keeper of a royal forest.
400 *Goblin:* Hobgoblin (Puck refers to himself).   403 *drawn:* With drawn sword.
404 *straight:* Immediately.   405 *plainer:* More open.   *Lysander wanders about:* (Lysander
may exit here, but perhaps not; neither exit nor reentrance is indicated in the early texts.)
410 *recreant:* Cowardly wretch.   413 *try:* Test.

    The villain is much lighter-heeled than I.
    I followed fast, but faster he did fly,
    That fallen am I in dark uneven way,
    And here will rest me. *[He lies down.]* Come, thou gentle day!
    For if but once thou show me thy gray light,   420
    I'll find Demetrius and revenge this spite. *[He sleeps.]*

    [Enter] Robin [Puck] and Demetrius.

Puck: Ho, ho, ho! Coward, why com'st thou not?
Demetrius: Abide° me, if thou dar'st; for well I wot°
    Thou runn'st before me, shifting every place,
    And dar'st not stand nor look me in the face.   425
    Where art thou now?
Puck: Come hither. I am here.
Demetrius: Nay, then, thou mock'st me. Thou shalt buy° this dear,°
    If ever I thy face by daylight see.
    Now go thy way. Faintness constraineth me
    To measure out my length on this cold bed.   430
    By day's approach look to be visited.   *[He lies down and sleeps.]*

    Enter Helena.

Helena: O weary night, O long and tedious night,
    Abate° thy hours! Shine comforts from the east,
    That I may back to Athens by daylight
    From these that my poor company detest;   435
    And sleep, that sometimes shuts up sorrow's eye,
    Steal me awhile from mine own company.   *[She lies down and] sleep[s].*
Puck: Yet but three? Come one more;
    Two of both kinds makes up four.
    Here she comes, curst° and sad.   440
    Cupid is a knavish lad,
    Thus to make poor females mad.

    [Enter Hermia.]

Hermia: Never so weary, never so in woe,
    Bedabbled with the dew and torn with briers,
    I can no further crawl, no further go;   445
    My legs can keep no pace with my desires.
    Here will I rest me till the break of day.
    Heavens shield Lysander, if they mean a fray! *[She lies down and sleeps.]*
Puck: On the ground
    Sleep sound.   450
    I'll apply
    To your eye,
    Gentle lover, remedy.   *[He squeezes the juice on Lysander's eyes.]*
    When thou wak'st,
    Thou tak'st   455
    True delight

---

423 *Abide:* Confront, face; *wot:* know.   427 *buy:* Aby, pay for; *dear:* Dearly.   433 *Abate:* Lessen, shorten.   440 *curst:* Ill-tempered.

In the sight
Of thy former lady's eye;
And the country proverb known,
That every man should take his own,   460
In your waking shall be shown:
   Jack shall have Jill;°
   Naught shall go ill;
The man shall have his mare again, and all shall be well.

[Exit. The four sleeping lovers remain.]

[ACT IV

SCENE I: *The wood. The lovers are still asleep onstage.]*

Enter [Titania,] Queen of Fairies, and [Bottom the] clown, and Fairies; and [Oberon,] the King, behind them.

Titania: Come, sit thee down upon this flowery bed,
   While I thy amiable° cheeks do coy,°
And stick muskroses in thy sleek smooth head,
   And kiss thy fair large ears, my gentle joy.   *[They recline.]*
Bottom: Where's Peaseblossom?   5
Peaseblossom: Ready.
Bottom: Scratch my head, Peaseblossom. Where's Monsieur Cobweb?
Cobweb: Ready.
Bottom: Monsieur Cobweb, good monsieur, get you your weapons in your
   hand, and kill me a red-hipped humble-bee on the top of a thistle;   10
   and, good monsieur, bring me the honey bag. Do not fret yourself too
   much in the action, monsieur; and, good monsieur, have a care the
   honey bag break not. I would be loath to have you overflown with a
   honey bag, signor. *[Exit Cobweb.]* Where's Monsieur Mustardseed?
Mustardseed: Ready.   15
Bottom: Give me your neaf,° Monsieur Mustardseed. Pray you, leave your
   courtesy,° good monsieur.
Mustardseed: What's your will?
Bottom: Nothing, good monsieur, but to help Cavalery° Cobweb° to
   scratch. I must to the barber's, monsieur, for methinks I am mar-   20
   velous hairy about the face; and I am such a tender ass, if my hair do
   but tickle me I must scratch.
Titania: What, wilt thou hear some music, my sweet love?
Bottom: I have a reasonable good ear in music. Let's have the tongs and
   the bones.°   *[Music: tongs, rural music.°]*   25

---

462 *Jack shall have Jill:* (Proverbial for "boy gets girl.")   **Act IV, Scene I.**   2 *amiable:*
Lovely; *coy:* Caress.   16 *neaf:* Fist.   16–17 *leave your courtesy:* I.e., stop bowing, or put on
your hat.   19 *Cavalery:* Cavalier (form of address for a gentleman); *Cobweb:* (Seemingly an
error, since Cobweb has been sent to bring honey, while Peaseblossom has been asked to
scratch.)   24–25 *tongs . . . bones:* Instruments for rustic music (the tongs were played like a
triangle, whereas the bones were held between the fingers and used as clappers).   *Music . . .
music:* (This stage direction is added from the Folio.)

Titania: Or say, sweet love, what thou desirest to eat.

Bottom: Truly, a peck of provender.° I could munch your good dry oats.
    Methinks I have a great desire to a bottle° of hay. Good hay, sweet hay,
    hath no fellow.°

Titania: I have a venturous fairy that shall seek   30
    The squirrel's hoard, and fetch thee new nuts.

Bottom: I had rather have a handful or two of dried peas. But, I pray you,
    let none of your people stir° me. I have an exposition of° sleep come
    upon me.

Titania: Sleep thou, and I will wind thee in my arms.   35
    Fairies, begone, and be all ways° away.   *[Exeunt Fairies.]*
    So doth the woodbine° the sweet honeysuckle
    Gently entwist; the female ivy so
    Enrings the barky fingers of the elm.
    O, how I love thee! How I dote on thee!   *[They sleep.]*   40

Enter Robin Goodfellow [Puck].

Oberon [coming forward]: Welcome, good Robin. Seest thou this sweet sight?
    Her dotage now I do begin to pity.
    For, meeting her of late behind the wood
    Seeking sweet favors° for this hateful fool,
    I did upbraid her and fall out with her.   45
    For she his hairy temples then had rounded
    With coronet of fresh and fragrant flowers;
    And that same dew, which sometime° on the buds
    Was wont to swell like round and orient pearls,°
    Stood now within the pretty flowerets' eyes   50
    Like tears that did their own disgrace bewail.
    When I had at my pleasure taunted her,
    And she in mild terms begged my patience,
    I then did ask of her her changeling child,
    Which straight she gave me, and her fairy sent   55
    To bear him to my bower in Fairyland.
    And, now I have the boy, I will undo
    This hateful imperfection of her eyes.
    And, gentle Puck, take this transformèd scalp
    From off the head of this Athenian swain,   60
    That he, awaking when the other° do,
    May all to Athens back again repair,°
    And think no more of this night's accidents
    But as the fierce vexation of a dream.
    But first I will release the Fairy Queen.   65
                                        [He squeezes an herb on her eyes.]

---

27 *peck of provender:* One-quarter bushel of grain.   28 *bottle:* Bundle.   29 *fellow:* Equal.
33 *stir:* Disturb; *exposition of:* (Bottom's phrase for "disposition to.")   36 *all ways:* In all
directions.   37 *woodbine:* Bindweed, a climbing plant that twines in the opposite direction from that of honeysuckle.   44 *favors:* I.e., gifts of flowers.   48 *sometime:* Formerly.
49 *orient pearls:* I.e., the most beautiful of all pearls, those coming from the Orient.
61 *other:* Others.   62 *repair:* Return.

Be as thou wast wont to be;
See as thou wast wont to see.
Dian's bud° o'er Cupid's flower
Hath such force and blessèd power.
    Now, my Titania, wake you, my sweet queen.   70
Titania [awaking]: My Oberon! What visions have I seen!
    Methought I was enamored of an ass.
Oberon: There lies your love.
Titania: How came these things to pass?
    O, how mine eyes do loathe his visage now!
Oberon: Silence awhile. Robin, take off this head.   75
    Titania, music call, and strike more dead
    Than common sleep of all these five° the sense.
Titania: Music, ho! Music, such as charmeth° sleep!   *[Music.]*
Puck [removing the ass head]: Now, when thou wak'st, with thine own fool's
    eyes peep.
Oberon: Sound, music! Come, my queen, take hands with me,   80
    And rock the ground whereon these sleepers be.   *[They dance.]*
    Now thou and I are new in amity,
    And will tomorrow midnight solemnly°
    Dance in Duke Theseus' house triumphantly,
    And bless it to all fair prosperity.   85
    There shall the pairs of faithful lovers be
    Wedded, with Theseus, all in jollity.
Puck: Fairy King, attend, and mark:
    I do hear the morning lark.
Oberon: Then, my queen, in silence sad,°   90
    Trip we after night's shade.
    We the globe can compass soon,
    Swifter than the wandering moon.
Titania: Come, my lord, and in our flight
    Tell me how it came this night   95
    That I sleeping here was found
    With these mortals on the ground.
                    Exeunt [Oberon, Titania, and Puck]. Wind horn [within].

    Enter Theseus and all his train; [Hippolyta, Egeus].

Theseus: Go, one of you, find out the forester,
    For now our observation° is performed;
    And since we have the vaward° of the day,   100
    My love shall hear the music of my hounds.
    Uncouple° in the western valley; let them go.
    Dispatch, I say, and find the forester.   *[Exit an Attendant.]*
    We will, fair queen, up to the mountain's top

---

68 *Dian's bud:* (Perhaps the flower of the *agnus castus* or chaste-tree, supposed to preserve chastity; or perhaps referring simply to Oberon's herb by which he can undo the effects of "Cupid's flower," the love-in-idleness of II.i.166–168.)   77 *these five:* I.e., the four lovers and Bottom.   78 *charmeth:* Brings about, as though by a charm.   83 *solemnly:* Ceremoniously.   90 *sad:* Sober.   99 *observation:* I.e., observance to a morn of May (I.i.167). 100 *vaward:* Vanguard, i.e., earliest part.   102 *Uncouple:* Set free for the hunt.

And mark the musical confusion   105
Of hounds and echo in conjunction.
Hippolyta: I was with Hercules and Cadmus° once
When in a wood of Crete they bayed° the bear
With hounds of Sparta.° Never did I hear
Such gallant chiding;° for, besides the groves,   110
The skies, the fountains, every region near
Seemed all one mutual cry. I never heard
So musical a discord, such sweet thunder.
Theseus: My hounds are bred out of the Spartan kind,°
So flewed,° so sanded,° and their heads are hung   115
With ears that sweep away the morning dew;
Crook-kneed, and dewlapped° like Thessalian bulls;
Slow in pursuit, but matched in mouth like bells,
Each under each.° A cry° more tunable°
Was never holloed to nor cheered° with horn   120
In Crete, in Sparta, nor in Thessaly.
Judge when you hear. *[He sees the sleepers.]* But soft!° What nymphs
   are these?
Egeus: My lord, this is my daughter here asleep,
And this Lysander; this Demetrius is;
This Helena, old Nedar's Helena.   125
I wonder of° their being here together.
Theseus: No doubt they rose up early to observe
The rite of May, and hearing our intent,
Came here in grace of our solemnity.°
But speak, Egeus. Is not this the day   130
That Hermia should give answer of her choice?
Egeus: It is, my lord.
Theseus: Go bid the huntsmen wake them with their horns.
                                                      [Exit an Attendant.]

   Shout within. Wind horns. They all start up.

Good morrow, friends. Saint Valentine° is past.
Begin these woodbirds but to couple now?   135
Lysander: Pardon, my lord.   *[They kneel.]*
Theseus: I pray you all, stand up.   *[They stand.]*
I know you two are rival enemies;
How comes this gentle concord in the world,
That hatred is so far from jealousy°
To sleep by hate and fear no enmity?   140

---

107 *Cadmus:* Mythical founder of Thebes. (This story about him is unknown.)   108 *bayed:*
Brought to bay.   109 *hounds of Sparta:* (A breed famous in antiquity for their hunting skill.)
110 *chiding:* I.e., yelping.   114 *kind:* Strain, breed.   115 *So flewed:* Similarly having large
hanging chaps or fleshy covering of the jaw; *sanded:* Of sandy color.   117 *dewlapped:* Having
pendulous folds of skin under the neck.   118–119 *matched . . . each:* I.e., harmoniously
matched in their various cries like a set of bells, from treble down to bass; *cry:* Pack of
hounds; *tunable:* Well tuned, melodious.   120 *cheered:* Encouraged.   122 *soft:* I.e.,
gently, wait a minute.   126 *wonder of:* Wonder at.   129 *in . . . solemnity:* In honor of our
wedding ceremony.   134 *Saint Valentine:* (Birds were supposed to choose their mates on
Saint Valentine's Day.)   139 *jealousy:* Suspicion.

Lysander: My lord, I shall reply amazedly,
    Half sleep, half waking; but as yet, I swear,
    I cannot truly say how I came here.
    But, as I think — for truly would I speak,
    And now I do bethink me, so it is —   145
    I came with Hermia hither. Our intent
    Was to be gone from Athens, where° we might,
    Without° the peril of the Athenian law —
Egeus: Enough, enough, my lord; you have enough.
    I beg the law, the law, upon his head.   150
    They would have stol'n away; they would, Demetrius,
    Thereby to have defeated° you and me,
    You of your wife and me of my consent,
    Of my consent that she should be your wife.
Demetrius: My lord, fair Helen told me of their stealth,   155
    Of this their purpose hither° to this wood,
    And I in fury hither followed them,
    Fair Helena in fancy° following me.
    But, my good lord, I wot not by what power —
    But by some power it is — my love to Hermia,   160
    Melted as the snow, seems to me now
    As the remembrance of an idle gaud°
    Which in my childhood I did dote upon;
    And all the faith, the virtue of my heart,
    The object and the pleasure of mine eye,   165
    Is only Helena. To her, my lord,
    Was I betrothed ere I saw Hermia,
    But like a sickness did I loathe this food;
    But, as in health, come to my natural taste,
    Now I do wish it, love it, long for it,   170
    And will forevermore be true to it.
Theseus: Fair lovers, you are fortunately met.
    Of this discourse we more will hear anon.
    Egeus, I will overbear your will;
    For in the temple, by and by, with us   175
    These couples shall eternally be knit.
    And, for° the morning now is something° worn,
    Our purposed hunting shall be set aside.
    Away with us to Athens. Three and three,
    We'll hold a feast in great solemnity.°   180
    Come Hippolyta.   *[Exeunt Theseus, Hippolyta, Egeus, and train.]*
Demetrius: These things seem small and undistinguishable,
    Like far-off mountains turnèd into clouds.
Hermia: Methinks I see these things with parted° eye,
    When everything seems double.

---

147 *where:* Wherever; or, to where.   148 *Without:* Outside of, beyond.   152 *defeated:* Defrauded.   156 *hither:* In coming hither.   158 *in fancy:* Driven by love.   162 *idle gaud:* Worthless trinket.   177 *for:* Since; *something:* Somewhat.   180 *in great solemnity:* With great ceremony.   184 *parted:* I.e., improperly focused.

Helena: So methinks;   185
   And I have found Demetrius like a jewel,
   Mine own, and not mine own.°
Demetrius: Are you sure
   That we are awake? It seems to me
   That yet we sleep, we dream. Do not you think
   The Duke was here, and bid us follow him?   190
Hermia: Yea, and my father.
Helena: And Hippolyta.
Lysander: And he did bid us follow to the temple.
Demetrius: Why, then, we are awake. Let's follow him,
   And by the way let us recount our dreams.   *[Exeunt the lovers.]*
Bottom [awaking]: When my cue comes, call me, and I will answer. My   195
   next is "Most fair Pyramus." Heigh-ho! Peter Quince! Flute, the bellows mender! Snout, the tinker! Starveling! God's° my life, stolen
   hence and left me asleep! I have had a most rare vision. I have had a
   dream, past the wit of man to say what dream it was. Man is but an ass
   if he go about° to expound this dream. Methought I was—there is no   200
   man can tell what. Methought I was—and methought I had—but
   man is but a patched° fool if he will offer° to say what methought I
   had. The eye of man hath not heard, the ear of man hath not seen,
   man's hand is not able to taste, his tongue to conceive, nor his heart
   to report° what my dream was. I will get Peter Quince to write a bal-   205
   lad° of this dream. It shall be called "Bottom's Dream," because it
   hath no bottom;° and I will sing it in the latter end of a play, before
   the Duke. Peradventure, to make it the more gracious, I shall sing it
   at her° death.   *[Exit.]*

[**SCENE II:** *Athens.*]

   Enter Quince, Flute, [Snout, and Starveling].

Quince: Have you sent to Bottom's house? Is he come home yet?
Starveling: He cannot be heard of. Out of doubt he is transported.°
Flute: If he come not, then the play is marred. It goes not forward. Doth it?
Quince: It is not possible. You have not a man in all Athens able to dis-
   charge° Pyramus but he.   5
Flute: No, he hath simply the best wit° of any handicraft man in Athens.
Quince: Yea, and the best person° too, and he is a very paramour for a
   sweet voice.
Flute: You must say "paragon." A paramour is, God bless us, a thing of
   naught.°   10

   Enter Snug the joiner.

186–187 *like . . . mine own:* I.e., like a jewel that one finds by chance and therefore possesses
but cannot certainly consider one's own property.   197 *God's:* May God save.   200 *go
about:* Attempt.   202 *patched:* Wearing motley, i.e., a dress of various colors; *offer:* Venture.
203–205 *The eye . . . report:* (Bottom garbles the terms of 1 Corinthians 2:9.)   206 *ballad:*
(The proper medium for relating sensational stories and preposterous events.)   207 *hath
no bottom:* Is unfathomable.   209 *her:* Thisbe's (?).   **Scene II.**   2 *transported:* Carried
off by fairies; or, possibly, transformed.   5 *discharge:* Perform.   6 *wit:* Intellect.   7 *person:* Appearance.   9–10 *a . . . naught:* A shameful thing.

Snug: Masters, the Duke is coming from the temple, and there is two or
three lords and ladies more married. If our sport had gone forward,
we had all been made men.°

Flute: O sweet bully Bottom! Thus hath he lost sixpence a day° during his
life; he could not have scaped sixpence a day. An the Duke had not   15
given him sixpence a day for playing Pyramus, I'll be hanged. He
would have deserved it. Sixpence a day in Pyramus, or nothing.

Enter Bottom.

Bottom: Where are these lads? Where are these hearts?°

Quince: Bottom! O most courageous day! O most happy hour!

Bottom: Masters, I am to discourse wonders.° But ask me not what; for if I   20
tell you, I am no true Athenian. I will tell you everything, right as it fell
out.

Quince: Let us hear, sweet Bottom.

Bottom: Not a word of° me. All that I will tell you is that the Duke hath
dined. Get your apparel together, good strings° to your beards, new   25
ribbons to your pumps;° meet presently° at the palace; every man
look o'er his part; for the short and the long is, our play is preferred.°
In any case, let Thisbe have clean linen; and let not him that plays the
lion pare his nails, for they shall hang out for the lion's claws. And,
most dear actors, eat no onions nor garlic, for we are to utter sweet   30
breath; and I do not doubt but to hear them say it is a sweet comedy.
No more words. Away! Go, away!   *[Exeunt.]*

[ACT V

SCENE I: *Athens. The palace of Theseus.*]

Enter Theseus, Hippolyta, and Philostrate, [lords, and attendants].

Hippolyta: 'Tis strange, my Theseus, that° these lovers speak of.

Theseus: More strange than true. I never may° believe
These antique° fables nor these fairy toys.°
Lovers and madmen have such seething brains,
Such shaping fantasies,° that apprehend°   5
More than cool reason ever comprehends.°
The lunatic, the lover, and the poet
Are of imagination all compact.°
One sees more devils than vast hell can hold;
That is the madman. The lover, all as frantic,   10

---

13 *we . . . men:* I.e., we would have had our fortunes made.   14 *sixpence a day:* I.e., as a royal
pension.   18 *hearts:* Good fellows.   20 *am . . . wonders:* Have wonders to relate.   24 *of:*
Out of.   25 *strings:* (To attach the beards.)   26 *pumps:* Light shoes or slippers; *presently:*
Immediately.   27 *preferred:* Selected for consideration.   **Act V, Scene I.**   1 *that:* That
which.   2 *may:* Can.   3 *antique:* Old-fashioned (punning, too, on *antic,* "strange,"
"grotesque"); *fairy toys:* Trifling stories about fairies.   5 *fantasies:* Imaginations; *apprehend:*
Conceive, imagine.   6 *comprehends:* Understands.   8 *compact:* Formed, composed.

Sees Helen's° beauty in a brow of Egypt.°
The poet's eye, in a fine frenzy rolling,
Doth glance from heaven to earth, from earth to heaven;
And as imagination bodies forth
The forms of things unknown, the poet's pen   15
Turns them to shapes and gives to airy nothing
A local habitation and a name.
Such tricks hath strong imagination
That, if it would but apprehend some joy,
It comprehends some bringer° of that joy;   20
Or in the night, imagining some fear,°
How easy is a bush supposed a bear!

Hippolyta: But all the story of the night told over,
And all their minds transfigured so together,
More witnesseth than fancy's images°   25
And grows to something of great constancy;°
But, howsoever,° strange and admirable.°

Enter lovers: Lysander, Demetrius, Hermia, and Helena.

Theseus: Here come the lovers, full of joy and mirth.
Joy, gentle friends! Joy and fresh days of love
Accompany your hearts!
Lysander: More than to us   30
Wait in your royal walks, your board, your bed!
Theseus: Come now, what masques,° what dances shall we have,
To wear away this long age of three hours
Between our after-supper and bedtime?
Where is our usual manager of mirth?   35
What revels are in hand? Is there no play
To ease the anguish of a torturing hour?
Call Philostrate.
Philostrate: Here, mighty Theseus.
Theseus: Say, what abridgment° have you for this evening?
What masque? What music? How shall we beguile   40
The lazy time, if not with some delight?
Philostrate [giving him a paper]: There is a brief° how many sports are ripe.
Make choice of which Your Highness will see first.
Theseus [reads.]: "The battle with the Centaurs,° to be sung
By an Athenian eunuch to the harp"?   45
We'll none of that. That have I told my love,
In glory of my kinsman° Hercules.

---

11 *Helen's:* I.e., of Helen of Troy, pattern of beauty; *brow of Egypt:* I.e., face of a gypsy.
20 *bringer:* I.e., source.   21 *fear:* Object of fear.   25 *More . . . images:* Testifies to something
more substantial than mere imaginings.   26 *constancy:* Certainty.   27 *howsoever:* In any
case; *admirable:* A source of wonder.   32 *masques:* Courtly entertainments.   39 *abridgment:* Pastime (to abridge or shorten the evening).   42 *brief:* Short written statement,
summary.   44 *battle . . . Centaurs:* (Probably refers to the battle of the Centaurs and the
Lapithae, when the Centaurs attempted to carry off Hippodamia, bride of Theseus' friend
Pirothous. The story is told in Ovid's *Metamorphoses* 12.)   47 *kinsman:* (Plutarch's "Life of
Theseus" states that Hercules and Theseus were near kinsmen. Theseus is referring to a version of the battle of the Centaurs in which Hercules was said to be present.)

[He reads.] "The riot of the tipsy Bacchanals,
Tearing the Thracian singer in their rage"?°
That is an old device;° and it was played   50
When I from Thebes came last a conqueror.
[He reads.] "The thrice three Muses mourning for the death
Of Learning, late deceased in beggary"?°
That is some satire, keen and critical,
Not sorting with° a nuptial ceremony.   55
[He reads.] "A tedious brief scene of young Pyramus
And his love Thisbe; very tragical mirth"?
Merry and tragical? Tedious and brief?
That is, hot ice and wondrous strange° snow.
How shall we find the concord of this discord?   60

Philostrate: A play there is, my lord, some ten words long,
Which is as brief as I have known a play;
But by ten words, my lord, it is too long,
Which makes it tedious. For in all the play
There is not one word apt, one player fitted.   65
And tragical, my noble lord, it is,
For Pyramus therein doth kill himself.
Which, when I saw rehearsed, I must confess,
Made mine eyes water; but more merry tears
The passion of loud laughter never shed.   70

Theseus: What are they that do play it?

Philostrate: Hardhanded men that work in Athens here,
Which never labored in their minds till now,
And now have toiled° their unbreathed° memories
With this same play, against° your nuptial.   75

Theseus: And we will hear it.

Philostrate: No, my noble lord,
It is not for you. I have heard it over,
And it is nothing, nothing in the world;
Unless you can find sport in their intents,
Extremely stretched° and conned° with cruel pain   80
To do you service.

Theseus: I will hear that play;
For never anything can be amiss
When simpleness° and duty tender it.
Go, bring them in; and take your places, ladies.

                        [Philostrate goes to summon the players.]

Hippolyta: I love not to see wretchedness o'ercharged,°   85
And duty in his service° perishing.

48–49 *The riot . . . rage:* (This was the story of the death of Orpheus, as told in *Metamorphoses* 11.)   50 *device:* Show, performance.   52–53 *The thrice . . . beggary:* (Possibly an allusion to Spenser's *Teares of the Muses,* 1591, though "satires" deploring the neglect of learning and the creative arts were commonplace.)   55 *sorting with:* Befitting.   59 *strange:* (Sometimes emended to an adjective that would contrast with *snow,* just as *hot* contrasts with *ice.*) 74 *toiled:* Taxed; *unbreathed:* Unexercised.   75 *against:* In preparation for.   80 *stretched:* Strained; *conned:* Memorized.   83 *simpleness:* Simplicity.   85 *wretchedness o'ercharged:* Social or intellectual inferiors overburdened.   86 *his service:* Its attempt to serve.

Theseus: Why, gentle sweet, you shall see no such thing.
Hippolyta: He says they can do nothing in this kind.°
Theseus: The kinder we, to give them thanks for nothing.
    Our sport shall be to take what they mistake;   90
    And what poor duty cannot do, noble respect°
    Takes it in might, not merit.°
    Where I have come, great clerks° have purposèd
    To greet me with premeditated welcomes;
    Where I have seen them shiver and look pale,   95
    Make periods in the midst of sentences,
    Throttle their practiced accent° in their fears,
    And in conclusion dumbly have broke off,
    Not paying me a welcome. Trust me, sweet,
    Out of this silence yet I picked a welcome;   100
    And in the modesty of fearful duty
    I read as much as from the rattling tongue
    Of saucy and audacious eloquence.
    Love, therefore, and tongue-tied simplicity
    In least° speak most, to my capacity.°   105

    [Philostrate returns.]

Philostrate: So please Your Grace, the Prologue° is addressed.°
Theseus: Let him approach.   *[A flourish of trumpets.]*

    Enter the Prologue [Quince].

Prologue: If we offend, it is with our good will.
    That you should think, we come not to offend,
    But with good will. To show our simple skill,   110
    That is the true beginning of our end.
    Consider, then, we come but in despite.
    We do not come, as minding° to content you,
    Our true intent is. All for your delight
    We are not here. That you should here repent you,   115
    The actors are at hand; and, by their show,
    You shall know all that you are like to know.
Theseus: This fellow doth not stand upon points.°
Lysander: He hath rid° his prologue like a rough° colt; he knows not the
    stop.° A good moral, my lord: it is not enough to speak, but to speak 120
    true.
Hippolyta: Indeed, he hath played on his prologue like a child on a
    recorder:° a sound, but not in government.°

---

88 *kind:* Kind of thing.   91 *respect:* Evaluation, consideration.   92 *Takes . . . merit:* Values it for the effort made rather than for the excellence achieved.   93 *clerks:* Learned men.
97 *practiced accent:* I.e., rehearsed speech; or, usual way of speaking.   105 *least:* I.e., saying least; *to my capacity:* In my judgment and understanding.   106 *Prologue:* Speaker of the prologue; *addressed:* Ready.   113 *minding:* Intending.   118 *stand upon points:* (1) Heed niceties or small points (2) pay attention to punctuation in his reading. (The humor of Quince's speech is in the blunders of its punctuation.)   119 *rid:* Ridden; *rough:* unbroken.
120 *stop:* (1) Stopping of a colt by reining it in (2) punctuation mark.   123 *recorder:* Wind instrument like a flute; *government:* Control.

Theseus: His speech was like a tangled chain: nothing° impaired, but all
    disordered. Who is next?   125

*Enter Pyramus [Bottom], and Thisbe [Flute], and Wall [Snout], and
Moonshine [Starveling], and Lion [Snug].*

Prologue: Gentles, perchance you wonder at this show;
    But wonder on, till truth make all things plain.
This man is Pyramus, if you would know;
    This beauteous lady Thisbe is, certain.
This man with lime and roughcast doth present   130
    Wall, that vile wall which did these lovers sunder;
And through Wall's chink, poor souls, they are content
    To whisper. At the which let no man wonder.
This man, with lantern, dog, and bush of thorn,
    Presenteth Moonshine; for, if you will know,   135
By moonshine did these lovers think no scorn°
    To meet at Ninus' tomb, there, there to woo.
This grisly beast, which Lion hight° by name,
    The trusty Thisbe coming first by night
Did scare away, or rather did affright;   140
And as she fled, her mantle she did fall,°
    Which Lion vile with bloody mouth did stain.
Anon comes Pyramus, sweet youth and tall,°
    And finds his trusty Thisbe's mantle slain;
Whereat, with blade, with bloody, blameful blade,   145
    He bravely broached° his boiling bloody breast.
And Thisbe, tarrying in mulberry shade,
    His dagger drew, and died. For all the rest,
Let Lion, Moonshine, Wall, and lovers twain
At large° discourse, while here they do remain.   150

                      Exeunt Lion, Thisbe, and Moonshine.

Theseus: I wonder if the lion be to speak.
Demetrius: No wonder, my lord. One lion may, when many asses do.
Wall: In this same interlude° it doth befall
    That I, one Snout by name, present a wall;
And such a wall as I would have you think   155
That had in it a crannied hole or chink,
Through which the lovers, Pyramus and Thisbe,
Did whisper often, very secretly.
This loam, this roughcast, and this stone doth show
That I am that same wall; the truth is so.   160
And this the cranny is, right and sinister,°
Through which the fearful lovers are to whisper.
Theseus: Would you desire lime and hair to speak better?
Demetrius: It is the wittiest partition° that ever I heard discourse, my lord.

    [Pyramus comes forward.]

---

124 *nothing:* Not at all.   136 *think no scorn:* Think it no disgraceful matter.   138 *hight:* Is
called.   141 *fall:* Let fall.   143 *tall:* Courageous.   146 *broached:* Stabbed.   150 *At large:*
In full, at length.   153 *interlude:* Play.   161 *right and sinister:* I.e., the right side of it and
the left; or, running from right to left, horizontally.   164 *partition:* (1) Wall (2) section of a
learned treatise or oration.

Theseus: Pyramus draws near the wall. Silence!   165
Pyramus: O grim-looked° night! O night with hue so black!
    O night, which ever art when day is not!
  O night, O night! Alack, alack, alack,
    I fear my Thisbe's promise is forgot.
  And thou, O wall, O sweet, O lovely wall,   170
    That stand'st between her father's ground and mine,
  Thou wall, O wall, O sweet and lovely wall,
    Show me thy chink, to blink through with mine eyne.
  Thanks, courteous wall. Jove shield thee well for this.
    But what see I? No Thisbe do I see.   175
  O wicked wall, through whom I see no bliss!
    Cursed be thy stones for thus deceiving me!
Theseus: The wall, methinks, being sensible,° should curse again.°
Pyramus: No, in truth, sir, he should not. "Deceiving me" is Thisbe's cue:
  she is to enter now, and I am to spy her through the wall. You shall see,   180
  it will fall pat° as I told you. Yonder she comes.

    Enter Thisbe.

Thisbe: O wall, full often hast thou heard my moans
    For parting my fair Pyramus and me.
  My cherry lips have often kissed thy stones,
    Thy stones with lime and hair knit up in thee.   185
Pyramus: I see a voice. Now will I to the chink,
    To spy an° I can hear my Thisbe's face.
  Thisbe!
Thisbe: My love! Thou art my love, I think.
Pyramus: Think what thou wilt, I am thy lover's grace,°   190
    And like Limander° am I trusty still.
Thisbe: And I like Helen,° till the Fates me kill.
Pyramus: Not Shafalus to Procrus° was so true.
Thisbe: As Shafalus to Procrus, I to you.
Pyramus: O, kiss me through the hole of this vile wall!   195
Thisbe: I kiss the wall's hole, not your lips at all.
Pyramus: Wilt thou at Ninny's tomb meet me straightway?
Thisbe: 'Tide life, 'tide° death, I come without delay.
                               [Exeunt Pyramus and Thisbe.]
Wall: Thus have I, Wall, my part dischargèd so;
    And, being done, thus Wall away doth go.   *[Exit.]*   200
Theseus: Now is the mural down between the two neighbors.
Demetrius: No remedy, my lord, when walls are so willful° to hear without
  warning.°
Hippolyta: This is the silliest stuff that ever I heard.

---

166 *grim-looked:* Grim-looking.   178 *sensible:* Capable of feeling; *again:* In return.   181 *pat:*
Exactly.   187 *an:* If.   190 *lover's grace:* I.e., gracious lover.   191–192 *Limander, Helen:*
(Blunders for "Leander" and "Hero.")   193 *Shafalus, Procrus:* (Blunders for "Cephalus"
and "Procris," also famous lovers.)   198 *'tide:* Betide, come.   202 *willful:* Willing.
202–203 *without warning:* I.e., without warning the parents. (Demetrius makes a joke on the
proverb "Walls have ears.")

Theseus: The best in this kind° are but shadows,° and the worst are no   205
  worse, if imagination amend them.
Hippolyta: It must be your imagination then, and not theirs.
Theseus: If we imagine no worse of them than they of themselves, they may
  pass for excellent men. Here come two noble beasts in, a man
  and a lion.   210

  Enter Lion and Moonshine.

Lion: You, ladies, you, whose gentle hearts do fear
     The smallest monstrous mouse that creeps on floor,
  May now perchance both quake and tremble here,
     When lion rough in wildest rage doth roar.
  Then know that I, as Snug the joiner, am   215
  A lion fell,° nor else no lion's dam;
  For, if I should as lion come in strife
  Into this place, 'twere pity on my life.
Theseus: A very gentle beast, and of a good conscience.
Demetrius: The very best at a beast, my lord, that e'er I saw.   220
Lysander: This lion is a very fox for his valor.°
Theseus: True; and a goose for his discretion.°
Demetrius: Not so, my lord, for his valor cannot carry his discretion, and
  the fox carries the goose.
Theseus: His discretion, I am sure, cannot carry his valor; for the goose car- 225
  ries not the fox. It is well. Leave it to his discretion, and let us listen
  to the moon.
Moon: This lanthorn° doth the hornèd moon present—
Demetrius: He should have worn the horns on his head.°
Theseus: He is no crescent,° and his horns are invisible within the cir- 230
  cumference.
Moon: This lanthorn doth the hornèd moon present;
  Myself the man i' the moon do seem to be.
Theseus: This is the greatest error of all the rest. The man should be put
  into the lanthorn. How is it else the man i' the moon?   235
Demetrius: He dares not come there for° the candle, for you see it is already
  in snuff.°
Hippolyta: I am weary of this moon. Would he would change!
Theseus: It appears, by his small light of discretion, that he is in the wane;
  but yet, in courtesy, in all reason, we must stay the time.   240
Lysander: Proceed, Moon.
Moon: All that I have to say is to tell you that the lanthorn is the moon, I,
  the man i' the moon, this thornbush my thornbush, and this dog my
  dog.

---

205 *in this kind:* Of this sort; *shadows:* Likenesses, representations.   216 *lion fell:* Fierce lion
(with a play on the idea of "lion skin").   221 *is . . . valor:* I.e., his valor consists of craftiness
and discretion.   222 *a goose . . . discretion:* I.e., as discreet as a goose, that is, more foolish
than discreet.   228 *lanthorn:* (This original spelling, *lanthorn,* may suggest a play on the
horn of which lanterns were made and also on a cuckold's horns; however, the spelling *lanthorn*
is not used consistently for comic effect in this play or elsewhere. At Act V, Scene I, line 134, for
example, the word is *lantern* in the original.)   229 *on his head:* (As a sign of cuckoldry.)
230 *crescent:* A waxing moon.   236 *for:* Because of, for fear of.   237 *in snuff:* (1) Offended
(2) in need of snuffing or trimming.

Demetrius: Why, all these should be in the lanthorn, for all these are in 245
    the moon. But silence! Here comes Thisbe.

    Enter Thisbe.

Thisbe: This is old Ninny's tomb. Where is my love?
Lion [roaring]: O!
Demetrius: Well roared, Lion.   *[Thisbe runs off, dropping her mantle.]*
Theseus: Well run, Thisbe.   250
Hippolyta: Well shone, Moon. Truly, the moon shines with a good grace.
                                  [The Lion worries Thisbe's mantle.]

Theseus: Well moused,° Lion.

    [Enter Pyramus; exit Lion.]

Demetrius: And then came Pyramus.
Lysander: And so the Lion vanished.
Pyramus: Sweet Moon, I thank thee for thy sunny beams;   255
    I thank thee, Moon, for shining now so bright;
  For, by thy gracious, golden, glittering gleams,
    I trust to take of truest Thisbe sight.
      But stay, O spite!
      But mark, poor knight,   260
  What dreadful dole° is here?
      Eyes, do you see?
      How can it be?
  O dainty duck! O dear!
      Thy mantle good,   265
      What, stained with blood?
  Approach, ye Furies° fell!°
      O Fates,° come, come,
      Cut thread and thrum;°
    Quail,° crush, conclude, and quell!°   270
Theseus: This passion, and the death of a dear friend, would go near to
    make a man look sad.°
Hippolyta: Beshrew my heart, but I pity the man.
Pyramus: O, wherefore, Nature, didst thou lions frame?
  Since lion vile hath here deflowered my dear,   275
  Which is — no, no, which was — the fairest dame
  That lived, that loved, that liked, that looked with cheer.°
      Come, tears, confound,
      Out, sword, and wound
    The pap° of Pyramus;   280
      Ay, that left pap,
      Where heart doth hop.   *[He stabs himself.]*
  Thus die I, thus, thus, thus.

---

252 *moused:* Shaken, torn, bitten.   261 *dole:* Grievous event.   267 *Furies:* Avenging goddesses of Greek myth; *fell:* Fierce.   268 *Fates:* The three goddesses (Clotho, Lachesis, Atro-
pos) of Greek myth who spun, drew, and cut the thread of human life.   269 *thread and
thrum:* I.e., everything — the good and bad alike; literally, the warp in weaving and the loose
end of the warp.   270 *Quail:* Overpower; *quell:* Kill, destroy.   271–272 *This . . . sad:* I.e., if
one had other reason to grieve, one might be sad, but not from this absurd portrayal of passion.   277 *cheer:* Countenance.   280 *pap:* Breast.

>   Now am I dead,
>   Now am I fled;
>   My soul is in the sky.
>   Tongue, lose thy light;
>   Moon, take thy flight.   *[Exit Moonshine.]*
>   Now die, die, die, die, die.   *[Pyramus dies.]* 285

Demetrius: No die, but an ace,° for him; for he is but one.°   290
Lysander: Less than an ace, man; for he is dead, he is nothing.
Theseus: With the help of a surgeon he might yet recover, and yet prove
   an ass.°
Hippolyta: How chance Moonshine is gone before Thisbe comes back and
   finds her lover?   295
Theseus: She will find him by starlight.

[Enter Thisbe.]

   Here she comes; and her passion ends the play.
Hippolyta: Methinks she should not use a long one for such a Pyramus. I
   hope she will be brief.
Demetrius: A mote° will turn the balance, which Pyramus, which° Thisbe,   300
   is the better: he for a man, God warrant us; she for a woman, God
   bless us.
Lysander: She hath spied him already with those sweet eyes.
Demetrius: And thus she means,° videlicet:°
Thisbe: Asleep, my love?   305

>   What, dead, my dove?
>   O Pyramus, arise!
>   Speak, speak. Quite dumb?
>   Dead, dead? A tomb
> Must cover thy sweet eyes.   310
>   These lily lips,
>   This cherry nose,
> These yellow cowslip cheeks,
>   Are gone, are gone!
>   Lovers, make moan.   315
> His eyes were green as leeks.
>   O Sisters Three,°
>   Come, come to me,
> With hands as pale as milk;
>   Lay them in gore,   320
>   Since you have shore°
> With shears his thread of silk.
>   Tongue, not a word.
>   Come, trusty sword,
> Come, blade, my breast imbrue!°   *[She stabs herself.]* 325

---

290 *ace:* The side of the die featuring the single pip, or spot (the pun is on *die* as a singular of
dice; Bottom's performance is not worth a whole *die* but rather one single face of it, one small
portion); *one:* (1) An individual person (2) unique.   293 *ass:* (With a pun on *ace.*)   300 *mote:*
Small particle; *which...which:* Whether...or.   304 *means:* Moans, laments (with a pun on
the meaning "lodge a formal complaint"); *videlicet:* To wit.   317 *Sisters Three:* The Fates.
321 *shore:* Shorn.   325 *imbrue:* Stain with blood.

       And farewell, friends.
       Thus Thisbe ends.
    Adieu, adieu, adieu.   *[She dies.]*

Theseus: Moonshine and Lion are left to bury the dead.

Demetrius: Ay, and Wall too.   330

Bottom [starting up, as Flute does also]: No, I assure you, the wall is down
    that parted their fathers. Will it please you to see the epilogue, or to
    hear a Bergomask dance° between two of our company?

    [The other players enter.]

Theseus: No epilogue, I pray you; for your play needs no excuse. Never
    excuse; for when the players are all dead, there need none to be   335
    blamed. Marry, if he that writ it had played Pyramus and hanged him-
    self in Thisbe's garter, it would have been a fine tragedy; and so it
    is, truly, and very notably discharged. But, come, your Bergomask.
    Let your epilogue alone.   *[A dance.]*
    The iron tongue° of midnight hath told° twelve.   340
    Lovers, to bed, 'tis almost fairy time.
    I fear we shall outsleep the coming morn
    As much as we this night have overwatched.°
    This palpable-gross° play hath well beguiled
    The heavy° gait of night. Sweet friends, to bed.   345
    A fortnight hold we this solemnity,
    In nightly revels and new jollity.   *Exeunt.*

    Enter Puck [carrying a broom].

Puck: Now the hungry lion roars,
       And the wolf behowls the moon,
    Whilst the heavy° plowman snores,   350
       All with weary task fordone.°
    Now the wasted brands° do glow,
       Whilst the screech owl, screeching loud,
    Puts the wretch that lies in woe
       In remembrance of a shroud.   355
    Now it is the time of night
       That the graves, all gaping wide,
    Every one lets forth his sprite,°
       In the church-way paths to glide.
    And we fairies, that do run   360
       By the triple Hecate's° team
    From the presence of the sun,
       Following darkness like a dream,
    Now are frolic.° Not a mouse

---

333 *Bergomask dance:* A rustic dance named from Bergamo, a province in the state of Venice.
340 *iron tongue:* Clapper of a bell; *told:* Counted, struck ("tolled").   343 *overwatched:* Stayed
up too late.   344 *palpable-gross:* Palpably gross, obviously crude.   345 *heavy:* Drowsy,
dull.   350 *heavy:* Tired.   351 *fordone:* Exhausted.   352 *wasted brands:* Burned-out logs.
358 *Every . . . sprite:* Every grave lets forth its ghost.   361 *triple Hecate's:* (Hecate ruled in
three capacities: as Luna or Cynthia in heaven, as Diana on earth, and as Proserpina in hell.)
364 *frolic:* Merry.

> Shall disturb this hallowed house.   365
> I am sent with broom before,
> To sweep the dust behind° the door.

Enter [Oberon and Titania,] King and Queen of Fairies, with all their train.

Oberon: Through the house give glimmering light,
>   By the dead and drowsy fire;
>   Every elf and fairy sprite   370
>   Hop as light as bird from brier;
>   And this ditty, after me,
>   Sing, and dance it trippingly.

Titania: First, rehearse° your song by rote,
>   To each word a warbling note.   375
>   Hand in hand, with fairy grace,
>   Will we sing, and bless this place.   *[Song and dance.]*

Oberon: Now, until the break of day,
>   Through this house each fairy stray.
>   To the best bride-bed will we,   380
>   Which by us shall blessèd be;
>   And the issue there create°
>   Ever shall be fortunate.
>   So shall all the couples three
>   Ever true in loving be;   385
>   And the blots of Nature's hand
>   Shall not in their issue stand;
>   Never mole, harelip, nor scar,
>   Nor mark prodigious,° such as are
>   Despisèd in nativity,   390
>   Shall upon their children be.
>   With this field dew consecrate,°
>   Every fairy take his gait,°
>   And each several° chamber bless,
>   Through this palace, with sweet peace;   395
>   And the owner of it blest
>   Ever shall in safety rest.
>   Trip away; make no stay;
>   Meet me all by break of day.   *Exeunt [Oberon, Titania, and train].*

Puck [to the audience]: If we shadows have offended,   400
>   Think but this, and all is mended,
>   That you have but slumbered here°
>   While these visions did appear.
>   And this weak and idle theme,
>   No more yielding but° a dream,   405
>   Gentles, do not reprehend.

---

367 *behind:* From behind, or else like sweeping the dirt under the carpet (Robin Goodfellow was a household spirit who helped good housemaids and punished lazy ones, but he could, of course, be mischievous).   374 *rehearse:* Recite.   382 *create:* Created.   389 *prodigious:* Monstrous, unnatural.   392 *consecrate:* Consecrated.   393 *take his gait:* Go his way. 394 *several:* Separate.   402 *That … here:* I.e., that it is a "midsummer night's dream." 405 *No … but:* Yielding no more than.

If you pardon, we will mend.°
And, as I am an honest Puck,
If we have unearnèd luck
Now to scape the serpent's tongue,°   410
We will make amends ere long;
Else the Puck a liar call.
So, good night unto you all.
Give me your hands,° if we be friends,
And Robin shall restore amends.°   [*Exit.*] 415

407 *mend:* Improve.   410 *serpent's tongue:* I.e., hissing.   414 *Give . . . hands:* Applaud.
415 *restore amends:* Give satisfaction in return.

Considerations for Critical Thinking and Writing

1. **First Response.** Discuss the significance of the play's title. What expectations does it create for you?

2. Describe how the two settings, Athens and the nearby woods, reflect different social and physical environments as well as different types of behavior among the characters.

3. What is the symbolic function of the marriage of Theseus and Hippolyta? How is that function revealed in the scenes in which they appear?

4. Characterize the four young lovers. How individualized are their personalities? How does the extent of their characterizations suggest their function in the play?

5. What makes Bottom such a comic figure? How does his behavior shed light on the behavior of the other characters?

6. Consider how women — Hippolyta, Titania, Hermia, and Helena — are presented in the play. What characteristics do they have in common? How do they relate to the men in their lives?

7. Why does Puck describe "mortals" as "fools" (III.ii.115)? To what degree does this description fit the fairies as well?

8. How might Puck be regarded as the play's director as well as a central character?

9. How does the plot bring together the four groups of characters — Theseus and Hippolyta, the four lovers, the craftsmen, and the fairies — into a unified whole? Write a plot summary of the play that connects these four groups of characters. How does this summary resemble popular situation comedies that you've seen on television?

10. Choose a scene that you find particularly funny, and analyze how the humor is created. Describe how the scene contributes to the rest of the play.

11. What is the relationship between the play within the play, "Pyramus and Thisbe," and *A Midsummer Night's Dream*? How do the plot and theme of each serve as commentaries on each other?

12. Despite its comic scenes and happy ending, at various moments this play does raise the specter of potential tragedy. How seriously do you think we are meant to worry about the characters? What are your emotions about the young lovers as they struggle to sort things out in the woods? Discuss how this play might be transformed into a tragedy.

CONNECTIONS TO OTHER SELECTIONS

1. Discuss Shakespeare's use of the play within the play in both *A Midsummer Night's Dream* and *Hamlet* (below). What emotions does each produce? What conflicts and themes do they emphasize? What attitudes do they suggest about the nature of drama?

2. In an essay discuss the significance of marriage in *A Midsummer Night's Dream* and Henrik Ibsen's *A Doll House* (p. 1709).

3. Write an essay that explores the difficulty of distinguishing between reality and illusion in *A Midsummer Night's Dream* and a very different work, Tim O'Brien's short story "How to Tell a True War Story" (p. 346). What are the similarities and differences in their perspectives on the actual and imaginary?

Hamlet, Prince of Denmark

Hamlet, the most famous play in English literature, continues to fascinate and challenge both readers and audiences. Interpretations of Hamlet's character and actions abound, because the play has produced so many intense and varied responses. No small indication of the tragedy's power is that actors long to play its title role.

A brief summary can suggest the movement of the plot but not the depth of Hamlet's character. After learning of his father's death, Prince Hamlet returns to the Danish court from his university studies to find Claudius, the dead king's brother, ruling Denmark and married to Hamlet's mother, Gertrude. Her remarriage within two months of his father's death has left Hamlet disillusioned, confused, and suspicious of Claudius. When his father's ghost appears before Hamlet to reveal that Claudius murdered the king, Hamlet is confronted with having to avenge his father's death.

Hamlet's efforts to carry out this obligation would have been a familiar kind of plot to Elizabethan audiences. **Revenge tragedy** was a well-established type of drama that traced its antecedents to Greek and Roman plays, particularly through the Roman playwright Seneca (c. 3 B.C.–A.D. 65), whose plays were translated and produced in English in the late sixteenth century. Shakespeare's audiences knew its conventions, particularly from Thomas Kyd's popular *Spanish Tragedy* (c. 1587). Basically, this type of play consists of a murder that has to be avenged by a relative of the victim. Typically, the victim's ghost appears to demand revenge, and invariably madness of some sort is worked into subsequent events, which ultimately result in the deaths of the murderer, the avenger, and a number of other characters. Crime, madness, ghostly anguish, poison, overheard conversations, conspiracies, and a final scene littered with corpses: *Hamlet* subscribes to the basic ingredients of the formula, but it also transcends the conventions of revenge tragedy because Hamlet contemplates not merely revenge but suicide and the meaning of life itself.

Hamlet must face not only a diseased social order but also conflicts within himself when his indecisiveness becomes as agonizing as the corruption surrounding him. However, Hamlet is also a forceful and attractive character. His intelligence is repeatedly revealed in his penetrating use of language; through images and metaphors he creates a perspective on his world that is at once satiric and profoundly painful. His astonishing and sometimes shocking wit is leveled at his mother, his beloved Ophelia, and Claudius as well as himself. Nothing escapes his critical eye and divided imagination. Hamlet, no less than the people around him, is perplexed by his alienation from life.

Web) Explore contexts for William Shakespeare and approaches to this play at bedfordstmartins.com/meyerlit.

Hamlet's limitations as well as his virtues make him one of Shakespeare's most complex characters. His keen self-awareness is both agonizing and liberating. Although he struggles throughout the play with painful issues ranging from family loyalties to matters of state, he retains his dignity as a tragic hero, whom generations of audiences have found compelling.

1585 – 1590

WILLIAM SHAKESPEARE (1564–1616)
Hamlet, Prince of Denmark

1600

[DRAMATIS PERSONAE

Claudius, King of Denmark
Hamlet, son to the late and nephew to the
   present king
Polonius, lord chamberlain
Horatio, friend to Hamlet
Laertes, son to Polonius
Voltimand
Cornelius
Rosencrantz   } courtiers
Guildenstern
Osric
A Gentleman
A Priest
Marcellus } officers
Bernardo
Francisco, a soldier
Reynaldo, servant to Polonius
Players
Two Clowns, grave-diggers
Fortinbras, Prince of Norway
A Captain
English Ambassadors

See Plays in Performance insert.

"He's, like, 'To be or not to be,' and I'm, like, 'Get a life.'"

See Encountering Drama,
pages 1698–1703.

Gertrude, Queen of Denmark, and mother to Hamlet
Ophelia, daughter to Polonius
Lords, Ladies, Officers, Soldiers, Sailors, Messengers, and other Attendants
Ghost of Hamlet's Father

SCENE: Denmark.]

[ACT I

SCENE I: *Elsinore. A platform° before the castle.*]

Enter Bernardo and Francisco, two sentinels.

Bernardo: Who's there?
Francisco: Nay, answer me:° stand, and unfold yourself.
Bernardo: Long live the king!°
Francisco: Bernardo?
Bernardo: He.
Francisco: You come most carefully upon your hour.   5
Bernardo: 'Tis now struck twelve; get thee to bed, Francisco.
Francisco: For this relief much thanks: 'tis bitter cold,
       And I am sick at heart.
Bernardo: Have you had quiet guard?
Francisco: Not a mouse stirring.   10
Bernardo: Well, good night.
       If you do meet Horatio and Marcellus,
       The rivals° of my watch, bid them make haste.

Enter Horatio and Marcellus.

Francisco: I think I hear them. Stand, ho! Who is there?
Horatio: Friends to this ground.
Marcellus: And liegemen to the Dane.   15
Francisco: Give you° good night.
Marcellus: O, farewell, honest soldier:
       Who hath reliev'd you?
Francisco: Bernardo hath my place.
       Give you good night.   *Exit Francisco.*
Marcellus: Holla! Bernardo!
Bernardo: Say,
       What, is Horatio there?
Horatio: A piece of him.
Bernardo: Welcome, Horatio: welcome, good Marcellus.   20
Marcellus: What, has this thing appear'd again to-night?
Bernardo: I have seen nothing.
Marcellus: Horatio says 'tis but our fantasy,

Act I, Scene I.   *platform:* A level space on the battlements of the royal castle at Elsinore, a
Danish seaport; now Helsingör.   2 *me:* This is emphatic, since Francisco is the sentry.
3 *Long live the king:* Either a password or greeting; Horatio and Marcellus use a different one
in line 15.   13 *rivals:* Partners.   16 *Give you:* God give you.

And will not let belief take hold of him
Touching this dreaded sight, twice seen of us: 25
Therefore I have entreated him along
With us to watch the minutes of this night;
That if again this apparition come,
He may approve° our eyes and speak to it.

Horatio: Tush, tush, 'twill not appear.
Bernardo: Sit down awhile;   30
  And let us once again assail your ears,
  That are so fortified against our story
  What we have two nights seen.
Horatio: Well, sit we down,
  And let us hear Bernardo speak of this.
Bernardo: Last night of all,   35
  When yond same star that's westward from the pole°
  Had made his course t' illume that part of heaven
  Where now it burns, Marcellus and myself,
  The bell then beating one, —

    Enter Ghost.

Marcellus: Peace, break thee off; look, where it comes again!   40
Bernardo: In the same figure, like the king that's dead.
Marcellus: Thou art a scholar;° speak to it, Horatio.
Bernardo: Looks 'a not like the king? mark it, Horatio.
Horatio: Most like: it harrows° me with fear and wonder.
Bernardo: It would be spoke to.°
Marcellus: Speak to it, Horatio.   45
Horatio: What art thou that usurp'st this time of night,
  Together with that fair and warlike form
  In which the majesty of buried Denmark°
  Did sometimes march? by heaven I charge thee, speak!
Marcellus: It is offended.
Bernardo: See it stalks away!   50
Horatio: Stay! speak, speak! I charge thee, speak!   *Exit Ghost.*
Marcellus: 'Tis gone, and will not answer.
Bernardo: How now, Horatio! you tremble and look pale:
  Is not this something more than fantasy?
  What think you on 't?   55
Horatio: Before my God, I might not this believe
  Without the sensible and true avouch
  Of mine own eyes.
Marcellus: Is it not like the king?
Horatio: As thou art to thyself:
  Such was the very armour he had on   60
  When he the ambitious Norway combated;

---

29 *approve:* Corroborate.   36 *pole:* Polestar.   42 *scholar:* Exorcisms were performed in Latin, which Horatio as an educated man would be able to speak.   44 *harrows:* Lacerates the feelings.   45 *It . . . to:* A ghost could not speak until spoken to.   48 *buried Denmark:* The buried king of Denmark.

So frown'd he once, when, in an angry parle,
He smote° the sledded Polacks° on the ice.
'Tis strange.
Marcellus: Thus twice before, and jump° at this dead hour,   65
With martial stalk hath he gone by our watch.
Horatio: In what particular thought to work I know not;
But in the gross and scope° of my opinion,
This bodes some strange eruption to our state.
Marcellus: Good now,° sit down, and tell me, he that knows,   70
Why this same strict and most observant watch
So nightly toils° the subject° of the land,
And why such daily cast° of brazen cannon,
And foreign mart° for implements of war;
Why such impress° of shipwrights, whose sore task   75
Does not divide the Sunday from the week;
What might be toward, that this sweaty haste
Doth make the night joint-labourer with the day:
Who is't that can inform me?
Horatio: That can I;
At least, the whisper goes so. Our last king,   80
Whose image even but now appear'd to us,
Was, as you know, by Fortinbras of Norway,
Thereto prick'd on° by a most emulate° pride,
Dar'd to the combat; in which our valiant Hamlet —
For so this side of our known world esteem'd him —   85
Did slay this Fortinbras; who, by a seal'd compact,
Well ratified by law and heraldry,°
Did forfeit, with his life, all those his lands
Which he stood seiz'd° of, to the conqueror:
Against the which, a moiety competent°   90
Was gaged by our king; which had return'd
To the inheritance of Fortinbras,
Had he been vanquisher; as, by the same comart,°
And carriage° of the article design'd,
His fell to Hamlet. Now, sir, young Fortinbras,   95
Of unimproved° mettle hot and full,°
Hath in the skirts of Norway here and there
Shark'd up° a list of lawless resolutes,°
For food and diet,° to some enterprise
That hath a stomach in't; which is no other —   100
As it doth well appear unto our state —

---

63 *smote:* Defeated; *sledded Polacks:* Polanders using sledges.   65 *jump:* Exactly.   68 *gross and scope:* General drift.   70 *Good now:* An expression denoting entreaty or expostulation. 72 *toils:* Causes or makes to toil; *subject:* People, subjects.   73 *cast:* Casting, founding. 74 *mart:* Buying and selling, traffic.   75 *impress:* Impressment.   83 *prick'd on:* Incited; *emulate:* Rivaling.   87 *law and heraldry:* Heraldic law, governing combat.   89 *seiz'd:* Possessed.   90 *moiety competent:* Adequate or sufficient portion.   93 *comart:* Joint bargain.   94 *carriage:* Import, bearing.   96 *unimproved:* Not turned to account; *hot and full:* Full of fight.   98 *Shark'd up:* Got together in haphazard fashion; *resolutes:* Desperadoes.   99 *food and diet:* No pay but their keep.

But to recover of us, by strong hand
And terms compulsatory, those foresaid lands
So by his father lost: and this, I take it,
Is the main motive of our preparations,   105
The source of this our watch and the chief head
Of this post-haste and romage° in the land.
Bernardo: I think it be no other but e'en so:
Well may it sort° that this portentous figure
Comes armed through our watch; so like the king   110
That was and is the question of these wars.
Horatio: A mote° it is to trouble the mind's eye.
In the most high and palmy state° of Rome,
A little ere the mightiest Julius fell,
The graves stood tenantless and the sheeted dead   115
Did squeak and gibber in the Roman streets:
As stars with trains of fire° and dews of blood,
Disasters° in the sun; and the moist star°
Upon whose influence Neptune's empire° stands
Was sick almost to doomsday with eclipse: 120
And even the like precurse° of fear'd events,
As harbingers preceding still the fates
And prologue to the omen coming on,
Have heaven and earth together demonstrated
Unto our climatures and countrymen. —   125

Enter Ghost.

But soft, behold! lo, where it comes again!
I'll cross° it, though it blast me. Stay, illusion!
If thou hast any sound, or use of voice,
Speak to me!   *It° spreads his arms.*
If there be any good thing to be done,   130
That may to thee do ease and grace to me,
Speak to me!
If thou art privy to thy country's fate,
Which, happily, foreknowing may avoid,
O, speak!   135
Or if thou hast uphoarded in thy life
Extorted treasure in the womb of earth,
For which, they say, you spirits oft walk in death,   *The cock crows.*
Speak of it:° stay, and speak! Stop it, Marcellus.
Marcellus: Shall I strike at it with my partisan?°   140
Horatio: Do, if it will not stand.
Bernardo: 'Tis here!

---

107 *romage:* Bustle, commotion.   109 *sort:* Suit.   112 *mote:* Speck of dust.   113 *palmy state:* Triumphant sovereignty.   117 *stars . . . fire:* I.e., comets.   118 *Disasters:* Unfavorable aspects; *moist star:* The moon, governing tides.   119 *Neptune's empire:* The sea. 121 *precurse:* Heralding.   127 *cross:* Meet, face, thus bringing down the evil influence on the person who crosses it.   129 *It:* The Ghost, or perhaps Horatio.   133-139 *If . . . it:* Horatio recites the traditional reasons why ghosts might walk.   140 *partisan:* Long-handled spear with a blade having lateral projections.

Horatio: 'Tis here!

Marcellus: 'Tis gone!   *[Exit Ghost.]*
> We do it wrong, being so majestical,
> To offer it the show of violence;
> For it is, as the air, invulnerable,   145
> And our vain blows malicious mockery.

Bernardo: It was about to speak, when the cock crew.°

Horatio: And then it started like a guilty thing
> Upon a fearful summons. I have heard,
> The cock, that is the trumpet to the morn,   150
> Doth with his lofty and shrill-sounding throat
> Awake the god of day; and, at his warning,
> Whether in sea or fire, in earth or air,
> Th' extravagant and erring° spirit hies
> To his confine:° and of the truth herein   155
> This present object made probation.°

Marcellus: It faded on the crowing of the cock.
> Some say that ever 'gainst° that season comes
> Wherein our Saviour's birth is celebrated,
> The bird of dawning singeth all night long: 160
> And then, they say, no spirit dare stir abroad;
> The nights are wholesome; then no planets strike,°
> No fairy takes, nor witch hath power to charm,
> So hallow'd and so gracious° is that time.

Horatio: So have I heard and do in part believe it.   165
> But, look, the morn, in russet mantle clad,
> Walks o'er the dew of yon high eastward hill:
> Break we our watch up; and by my advice,
> Let us impart what we have seen to-night
> Unto young Hamlet; for, upon my life,   170
> This spirit, dumb to us, will speak to him.
> Do you consent we shall acquaint him with it,
> As needful in our loves, fitting our duty?

Marcellus: Let's do 't, I pray; and I this morning know
> Where we shall find him most conveniently.   *Exeunt.*   175

[SCENE II: *A room of state in the castle.*]

Flourish. Enter Claudius, King of Denmark, Gertrude the Queen, Councilors,
Polonius and his Son Laertes, Hamlet, cum aliis° [including Voltimand and
Cornelius].

King: Though yet of Hamlet our dear brother's death
> The memory be green, and that it us befitted
> To bear our hearts in grief and our whole kingdom

---

147 *cock crew:* According to traditional ghost lore, spirits returned to their confines at cockcrow.   154 *extravagant and erring:* Wandering. Both words mean the same thing.
155 *confine:* Place of confinement.   156 *probation:* Proof, trial.   158 *'gainst:* Just before.
162 *planets strike:* It was thought that planets were malignant and might strike travelers by night.   164 *gracious:* Full of goodness.   **Scene II.**   *cum aliis:* With others.

To be contracted in one brow of woe,
Yet so far hath discretion fought with nature   5
That we with wisest sorrow think on him,
Together with remembrance of ourselves.
Therefore our sometime sister, now our queen,
Th' imperial jointress° to this warlike state,
Have we, as 'twere with a defeated joy, —   10
With an auspicious and a dropping eye,
With mirth in funeral and with dirge in marriage,
In equal scale weighing delight and dole, —
Taken to wife: nor have we herein barr'd
Your better wisdoms, which have freely gone   15
With this affair along. For all, our thanks.
Now follows, that° you know, young Fortinbras,
Holding a weak supposal° of our worth,
Or thinking by our late dear brother's death
Our state to be disjoint° and out of frame,°   20
Colleagued° with this dream of his advantage,°
He hath not fail'd to pester us with message,
Importing° the surrender of those lands
Lost by his father, with all bands of law,
To our most valiant brother. So much for him.   25
Now for ourself and for this time of meeting:
Thus much the business is: we have here writ
To Norway, uncle of young Fortinbras, —
Who, impotent and bed-rid, scarcely hears
Of this his nephew's purpose, — to suppress   30
His further gait° herein; in that the levies,
The lists and full proportions, are all made
Out of his subject:° and we here dispatch
You, good Cornelius, and you, Voltimand,
For bearers of this greeting to old Norway;   35
Giving to you no further personal power
To business with the king, more than the scope
Of these delated° articles allow.
Farewell, and let your haste commend your duty.

Cornelius: ⎫
Voltimand: ⎬   In that and all things will we show our duty.   40
            ⎭
King: We doubt it nothing: heartily farewell.
                                        [Exeunt Voltimand and Cornelius.]
And now, Laertes, what's the news with you?
You told us of some suit; what is't, Laertes?
You cannot speak of reason to the Dane,°
And lose your voice:° what wouldst thou beg, Laertes,   45

---

9 *jointress:* Woman possessed of a jointure, or, joint tenancy of an estate.   17 *that:* That
which.   18 *weak supposal:* Low estimate.   20 *disjoint:* Distracted, out of joint; *frame:*
Order.   21 *Colleagued:* Added to; *dream . . . advantage:* Visionary hope of success.   23 *Importing:* Purporting, pertaining to.   31 *gait:* Proceeding.   33 *Out of his subject:* At the expense of Norway's subjects (collectively).   38 *delated:* Expressly stated.   44 *the Dane:*
Danish king.   45 *lose your voice:* Speak in vain.

That shall not be my offer, not thy asking?
The head is not more native° to the heart,
The hand more instrumental° to the mouth,
Than is the throne of Denmark to thy father.
What wouldst thou have, Laertes?

Laertes: My dread lord,   50
Your leave and favour to return to France;
From whence though willingly I came to Denmark,
To show my duty in your coronation,
Yet now, I must confess, that duty done,
My thoughts and wishes bend again toward France   55
And bow them to your gracious leave and pardon.°

King: Have you your father's leave? What says Polonius?

Polonius: He hath, my lord, wrung from me my slow leave
By laboursome petition, and at last
Upon his will I seal'd my hard consent: 60
I do beseech you, give him leave to go.

King: Take thy fair hour, Laertes; time be thine,
And thy best graces spend it at thy will!
But now, my cousin° Hamlet, and my son,—

Hamlet [aside]: A little more than kin, and less than kind!°   65

King: How is it that the clouds still hang on you?

Hamlet: Not so, my lord; I am too much in the sun.°

Queen: Good Hamlet, cast thy nighted colour off,
And let thine eye look like a friend on Denmark.
Do not for ever with thy vailed lids   70
Seek for thy noble father in the dust:
Thou know'st 'tis common; all that lives must die,
Passing through nature to eternity.

Hamlet: Ay, madam, it is common.°

Queen: If it be,
Why seems it so particular with thee?   75

Hamlet: Seems, madam! nay, it is; I know not "seems."
'Tis not alone my inky cloak, good mother,
Nor customary suits° of solemn black,
Nor windy suspiration° of forc'd breath,
No, nor the fruitful river in the eye,   80
Nor the dejected 'haviour of the visage,
Together with all forms, moods, shapes of grief,
That can denote me truly: these indeed seem,
For they are actions that a man might play:

---

47 *native:* Closely connected, related.   48 *instrumental:* Serviceable.   56 *leave and pardon:* Permission to depart.   64 *cousin:* Any kin not of the immediate family.   65 *A little . . . kind:* My relation to you has become more than kinship warrants; it has also become unnatural.   67 *I am . . . sun:* (1) I am too much out of doors (2) I am too much in the sun of your grace (ironical) (3) I am too much of a son to you. Possibly an allusion to the proverb "Out of heaven's blessing into the warm sun"; i.e., Hamlet is out of house and home in being deprived of the kingship.   74 *Ay . . . common:* It is common, but it hurts nevertheless; possibly a reference to the commonplace quality of the queen's remark.   78 *customary suits:* Suits prescribed by custom for mourning.   79 *windy suspiration:* Heavy sighing.

But I have that within which passeth show;   85
These but the trappings and the suits of woe.
King: 'Tis sweet and commendable in your nature, Hamlet,
    To give these mourning duties to your father:
    But, you must know, your father lost a father;
    That father lost, lost his, and the survivor bound   90
    In filial obligation for some term
    To do obsequious° sorrow: but to persever
    In obstinate condolement° is a course
    Of impious stubbornness; 'tis unmanly grief;
    It shows a will most incorrect° to heaven,   95
    A heart unfortified, a mind impatient,
    An understanding simple and unschool'd:
    For what we know must be and is as common
    As any the most vulgar thing° to sense,
    Why should we in our peevish opposition   100
    Take it to heart? Fie! 'tis a fault to heaven,
    A fault against the dead, a fault to nature,
    To reason most absurd; whose common theme
    Is death of fathers, and who still hath cried,
    From the first corse till he that died to-day,   105
    "This must be so." We pray you, throw to earth
    This unprevailing° woe, and think of us
    As of a father: for let the world take note,
    You are the most immediate° to our throne;
    And with no less nobility° of love   110
    Than that which dearest father bears his son,
    Do I impart° toward you. For your intent
    In going back to school in Wittenberg,°
    It is most retrograde° to our desire:
    And we beseech you, bend you° to remain   115
    Here, in the cheer and comfort of our eye,
    Our chiefest courtier, cousin, and our son.
Queen: Let not thy mother lose her prayers, Hamlet:
    I pray thee, stay with us; go not to Wittenberg.
Hamlet: I shall in all my best obey you, madam.   120
King: Why, 'tis a loving and a fair reply:
    Be as ourself in Denmark. Madam, come;
    This gentle and unforc'd accord of Hamlet
    Sits smiling to my heart: in grace whereof,
    No jocund health that Denmark drinks to-day,   125
    But the great cannon to the clouds shall tell,
    And the king's rouse° the heaven shall bruit again,°
    Re-speaking earthly thunder. Come away.

---

92 *obsequious:* Dutiful.   93 *condolement:* Sorrowing.   95 *incorrect:* Untrained, uncor-
rected.   99 *vulgar thing:* Common experience.   107 *unprevailing:* Unavailing.   109 *most
immediate:* Next in succession.   110 *nobility:* High degree.   112 *impart:* The object is
apparently *love* (l. 110).   113 *Wittenberg:* Famous German university founded in 1502.
114 *retrograde:* Contrary.   115 *bend you:* Incline yourself (imperative).   127 *rouse:* Draft
of liquor; *bruit again:* Echo.

Flourish. Exeunt all but Hamlet.

Hamlet: O, that this too too sullied flesh would melt,
        Thaw and resolve itself into a dew!   130
        Or that the Everlasting had not fix'd
        His canon 'gainst self-slaughter! O God! God!
        How weary, stale, flat and unprofitable,
        Seem to me all the uses of this world!
        Fie on't! ah fie! 'tis an unweeded garden,   135
        That grows to seed; things rank and gross in nature
        Possess it merely.° That it should come to this!
        But two months dead: nay, not so much, not two:
        So excellent a king; that was, to this,
        Hyperion° to a satyr; so loving to my mother   140
        That he might not beteem° the winds of heaven
        Visit her face too roughly. Heaven and earth!
        Must I remember? why, she would hang on him,
        As if increase of appetite had grown
        By what it fed on: and yet, within a month —   145
        Let me not think on't — Frailty, thy name is woman! —
        A little month, or ere those shoes were old
        With which she followed my poor father's body,
        Like Niobe,° all tears: — why she, even she —
        O God! a beast, that wants discourse of reason,°   150
        Would have mourn'd longer — married with my uncle,
        My father's brother, but no more like my father
        Than I to Hercules: within a month:
        Ere yet the salt of most unrighteous tears
        Had left the flushing in her galled° eyes,   155
        She married. O, most wicked speed, to post
        With such dexterity° to incestuous sheets!
        It is not nor it cannot come to good:
        But break, my heart; for I must hold my tongue.

        Enter Horatio, Marcellus, and Bernardo.

Horatio: Hail to your lordship!
Hamlet: I am glad to see you well: 160
        Horatio! — or I do forget myself.
Horatio: The same, my lord, and your poor servant ever.
Hamlet: Sir, my good friend; I'll change that name with you:°
        And what make you from Wittenberg, Horatio?
        Marcellus?   165
Marcellus: My good lord —
Hamlet: I am very glad to see you. Good even, sir.
        But what, in faith, make you from Wittenberg?

---

137 *merely:* Completely, entirely.   140 *Hyperion:* God of the sun in the older regime of
ancient gods.   141 *beteem:* Allow.   149 *Niobe:* Tantalus's daughter, who boasted that she
had more sons and daughters than Leto; for this Apollo and Artemis slew her children. She
was turned into stone by Zeus on Mount Sipylus.   150 *discourse of reason:* Process or faculty
of reason.   155 *galled:* Irritated.   157 *dexterity:* Facility.   163 *I'll . . . you:* I'll be your servant, you shall be my friend; also explained as "I'll exchange the name of friend with you."

Horatio: A truant disposition, good my lord.
Hamlet: I would not hear your enemy say so,   170
    Nor shall you do my ear that violence,
    To make it truster of your own report
    Against yourself: I know you are no truant.
    But what is your affair in Elsinore?
    We'll teach you to drink deep ere you depart.   175
Horatio: My lord, I came to see your father's funeral.
Hamlet: I prithee, do not mock me, fellow-student;
    I think it was to see my mother's wedding.
Horatio: Indeed, my lord, it follow'd hard° upon.
Hamlet: Thrift, thrift, Horatio! the funeral bak'd meats°   180
    Did coldly furnish forth the marriage tables.
    Would I had met my dearest° foe in heaven
    Or ever I had seen that day, Horatio!
    My father! — methinks I see my father.
Horatio: Where, my lord!
Hamlet: In my mind's eye, Horatio.   185
Horatio: I saw him once; 'a° was a goodly king.
Hamlet: 'A was a man, take him for all in all,
    I shall not look upon his like again.
Horatio: My lord, I think I saw him yesternight.
Hamlet: Saw? who?   190
Horatio: My lord, the king your father.
Hamlet: The king my father!
Horatio: Season your admiration° for a while
    With an attent ear, till I may deliver,
    Upon the witness of these gentlemen,
    This marvel to you.
Hamlet: For God's love, let me hear.   195
Horatio: Two nights together had these gentlemen,
    Marcellus and Bernardo, on their watch,
    In the dead waste and middle of the night,
    Been thus encount'red. A figure like your father,
    Armed at point exactly, cap-a-pe,°   200
    Appears before them, and with solemn march
    Goes slow and stately by them: thrice he walk'd
    By their oppress'd° and fear-surprised eyes,
    Within his truncheon's° length; whilst they, distill'd°
    Almost to jelly with the act° of fear,   205
    Stand dumb and speak not to him. This to me
    In dreadful secrecy impart they did;
    And I with them the third night kept the watch:
    Where, as they had deliver'd, both in time,
    Form of the thing, each word made true and good,   210

---

179 *hard:* Close.   180 *bak'd meats:* Meat pies.   182 *dearest:* Direst. The adjective *dear* in Shakespeare has two different origins: O.E. *deore,* "beloved," and O.E. *deor,* "fierce." *Dearest* is the superlative of the second.   186 *'a:* He.   192 *Season your admiration:* Restrain your astonishment.   200 *cap-a-pe:* From head to foot.   203 *oppress'd:* Distressed.   204 *truncheon:* Officer's staff; *distill'd:* Softened, weakened.   205 *act:* Action.

The apparition comes: I knew your father;
These hands are not more like.
Hamlet: But where was this?
Marcellus: My lord, upon the platform where we watch'd.
Hamlet: Did you not speak to it?
Horatio: My lord, I did;
But answer made it none: yet once methought   215
It lifted up it° head and did address
Itself to motion, like as it would speak;
But even then the morning cock crew loud,
And at the sound it shrunk in haste away,
And vanish'd from our sight.
Hamlet: 'Tis very strange.   220
Horatio: As I do live, my honour'd lord, 'tis true;
And we did think it writ down in our duty
To let you know of it.
Hamlet: Indeed, indeed, sirs, but this troubles me.
Hold you the watch to-night?
Marcellus: ⎤
Bernardo: ⎦   We do, my lord.   225
Hamlet: Arm'd, say you?
Marcellus: ⎤
Bernardo: ⎦   Arm'd, my lord.
Hamlet: From top to toe?
Marcellus: ⎤
Bernardo: ⎦   My lord, from head to foot.
Hamlet: Then saw you not his face?
Horatio: O, yes, my lord; he wore his beaver° up.
Hamlet: What, look'd he frowningly?
Horatio: A countenance more   230
In sorrow than in anger.
Hamlet: Pale or red?
Horatio: Nay, very pale.
Hamlet: And fix'd his eyes upon you?
Horatio: Most constantly.
Hamlet: I would I had been there.
Horatio: It would have much amaz'd you.
Hamlet: Very like, very like. Stay'd it long?   235
Horatio: While one with moderate haste might tell a hundred.
Marcellus: ⎤
Bernardo: ⎦   Longer, longer.
Horatio: Not when I saw't.
Hamlet: His beard was grizzled, — no?
Horatio: It was, as I have seen it in his life,
A sable° silver'd.
Hamlet: I will watch to-night;   240
Perchance 'twill walk again.
Horatio: I warr'nt it will.

---

216 *it:* Its.   229 *beaver:* Visor on the helmet.   240 *sable:* Black color.

Hamlet: If it assume my noble father's person,
    I'll speak to it, though hell itself should gape
    And bid me hold my peace. I pray you all,
    If you have hitherto conceal'd this sight,   245
    Let it be tenable in your silence still;
    And whatsoever else shall hap to-night,
    Give it an understanding, but no tongue:
    I will requite your loves. So, fare you well:
    Upon the platform, 'twixt eleven and twelve,   250
    I'll visit you.
All: Our duty to your honour.
Hamlet: Your loves, as mine to you: farewell.   *Exeunt [all but Hamlet].*
    My father's spirit in arms! all is not well;
    I doubt° some foul play: would the night were come!
    Till then sit still, my soul: foul deeds will rise,   255
    Though all the earth o'erwhelm them, to men's eyes.   *Exit.*

[SCENE III: *A room in Polonius's house.*]

    Enter Laertes and Ophelia, his Sister.

Laertes: My necessaries are embark'd: farewell:
    And, sister, as the winds give benefit
    And convoy is assistant,° do not sleep,
    But let me hear from you.
Ophelia: Do you doubt that?
Laertes: For Hamlet and the trifling of his favour,   5
    Hold it a fashion° and a toy in blood,°
    A violet in the youth of primy° nature,
    Forward,° not permanent, sweet, not lasting,
    The perfume and suppliance of a minute;°
    No more.
Ophelia: No more but so?
Laertes: Think it no more: 10
    For nature, crescent,° does not grow alone
    In thews° and bulk, but, as this temple° waxes,
    The inward service of the mind and soul
    Grows wide withal. Perhaps he loves you now,
    And now no soil° nor cautel° doth besmirch   15
    The virtue of his will: but you must fear,
    His greatness weigh'd,° his will is not his own;
    For he himself is subject to his birth:
    He may not, as unvalued persons do,
    Carve for himself; for on his choice depends   20

---

254 *doubt:* Fear.   **Scene III.**   3 *convoy is assistant:* Means of conveyance are available.
6 *fashion:* Custom, prevailing usage; *toy in blood:* Passing amorous fancy.   7 *primy:* In its
prime.   8 *Forward:* Precocious.   9 *suppliance of a minute:* Diversion to fill up a minute.
11 *crescent:* Growing, waxing.   12 *thews:* Bodily strength; *temple:* Body.   15 *soil:* Blemish; *cautel:* Crafty device.   17 *greatness weigh'd:* High position considered.

The safety and health of this whole state;
And therefore must his choice be circumscrib'd
Unto the voice and yielding° of that body
Whereof he is the head. Then if he says he loves you,
It fits your wisdom so far to believe it   25
As he in his particular act and place
May give his saying deed;° which is no further
Than the main voice of Denmark goes withal.
Then weigh what loss your honour may sustain,
If with too credent° ear you list his songs,   30
Or lose your heart, or your chaste treasure open
To his unmast'red° importunity.
Fear it, Ophelia, fear it, my dear sister,
And keep you in the rear of your affection,
Out of the shot and danger of desire.   35
The chariest° maid is prodigal enough,
If she unmask her beauty to the moon:
Virtue itself 'scapes not calumnious strokes:
The canker galls the infants of the spring,°
Too oft before their buttons° be disclos'd,°   40
And in the morn and liquid dew° of youth
Contagious blastments° are most imminent.
Be wary then; best safety lies in fear:
Youth to itself rebels, though none else near.
Ophelia: I shall the effect of this good lesson keep,   45
As watchman to my heart. But, good my brother,
Do not, as some ungracious° pastors do,
Show me the steep and thorny way to heaven;
Whiles, like a puff'd° and reckless libertine,
Himself the primrose path of dalliance treads,   50
And recks° not his own rede.°

Enter Polonius.

Laertes: O, fear me not.
I stay too long: but here my father comes.
A double° blessing is a double grace;
Occasion° smiles upon a second leave.
Polonius: Yet here, Laertes? aboard, aboard, for shame!   55
The wind sits in the shoulder of your sail,
And you are stay'd for. There; my blessing with thee!
And these few precepts° in thy memory
Look thou character.° Give thy thoughts no tongue,

---

23 *voice and yielding:* Assent, approval.   27 *deed:* Effect.   30 *credent:* Credulous.   32 *unmast'red:* Unrestrained.   36 *chariest:* Most scrupulously modest.   39 *The canker...spring:* The cankerworm destroys the young plants of spring.   40 *buttons:* Buds; *disclos'd:* Opened.   41 *liquid dew:* I.e., time when dew is fresh.   42 *blastments:* Blights.   47 *ungracious:* Graceless.   49 *puff'd:* Bloated.   51 *recks:* Heeds; *rede:* Counsel.   53 *double:* I.e., Laertes has already bade his father good-by.   54 *Occasion:* Opportunity.   58 *precepts:* Many parallels have been found to the series of maxims which follows, one of the closer being that in Lyly's *Euphues.*   59 *character:* Inscribe.

Nor any unproportion'd° thought his act.   60
Be thou familiar, but by no means vulgar.°
Those friends thou hast, and their adoption tried,
Grapple them to thy soul with hoops of steel;
But do not dull thy palm with entertainment
Of each new-hatch'd, unfledg'd° comrade. Beware   65
Of entrance to a quarrel, but being in,
Bear't that th' opposed may beware of thee.
Give every man thy ear, but few thy voice;
Take each man's censure, but reserve thy judgement.
Costly thy habit as thy purse can buy,   70
But not express'd in fancy;° rich, not gaudy;
For the apparel oft proclaims the man,
And they in France of the best rank and station
Are of a most select and generous chief in that.°
Neither a borrower nor a lender be;   75
For loan oft loses both itself and friend,
And borrowing dulleth edge of husbandry.°
This above all: to thine own self be true,
And it must follow, as the night the day,
Thou canst not then be false to any man.   80
Farewell: my blessing season° this in thee!
Laertes: Most humbly do I take my leave, my lord.
Polonius: The time invites you; go; your servants tend.
Laertes: Farewell, Ophelia; and remember well
     What I have said to you.
Ophelia: 'Tis in my memory lock'd,   85
     And you yourself shall keep the key of it.
Laertes: Farewell.   *Exit Laertes.*
Polonius: What is 't, Ophelia, he hath said to you?
Ophelia: So please you, something touching the Lord Hamlet.
Polonius: Marry, well bethought: 90
     'Tis told me, he hath very oft of late
     Given private time to you; and you yourself
     Have of your audience been most free and bounteous:
     If it be so, as so't is put on° me,
     And that in way of caution, I must tell you,   95
     You do not understand yourself so clearly
     As it behooves my daughter and your honour.
     What is between you? give me up the truth.
Ophelia: He hath, my lord, of late made many tenders°
     Of his affection to me.   100
Polonius: Affection! pooh! you speak like a green girl,
     Unsifted° in such perilous circumstance.
     Do you believe his tenders,° as you call them?

---

60 *unproportion'd:* Inordinate.   61 *vulgar:* Common.   65 *unfledg'd:* Immature.
71 *express'd in fancy:* Fantastical in design.   74 *Are . . . that: Chief* is usually taken as a
substantive meaning "head," "eminence."   77 *husbandry:* Thrift.   81 *season:* Mature.
94 *put on:* Impressed on.   99, 103 *tenders:* Offers.   102 *Unsifted:* Untried.

Ophelia: I do not know, my lord, what I should think.
Polonius: Marry, I will teach you: think yourself a baby;   105
    That you have ta'en these tenders° for true pay,
    Which are not sterling.° Tender° yourself more dearly;
    Or — not to crack the wind° of the poor phrase,
    Running it thus — you'll tender me a fool.°
Ophelia: My lord, he hath importun'd me with love   110
    In honourable fashion.
Polonius: Ay, fashion° you may call it; go to, go to.
Ophelia: And hath given countenance° to his speech, my lord,
    With almost all the holy vows of heaven.
Polonius: Ay, springes° to catch woodcocks.° I do know,   115
    When the blood burns, how prodigal the soul
    Lends the tongue vows: these blazes, daughter,
    Giving more light than heat, extinct in both,
    Even in their promise, as it is a-making,
    You must not take for fire. From this time   120
    Be somewhat scanter of your maiden presence;
    Set your entreatments° at a higher rate
    Than a command to parley.° For Lord Hamlet,
    Believe so much in him,° that he is young,
    And with a larger tether may he walk   125
    Than may be given you: in few,° Ophelia,
    Do not believe his vows; for they are brokers;°
    Not of that dye° which their investments° show,
    But mere implorators of° unholy suits,
    Breathing° like sanctified and pious bawds,   130
    The better to beguile. This is for all:
    I would not, in plain terms, from this time forth,
    Have you so slander° any moment leisure,
    As to give words or talk with the Lord Hamlet.
    Look to 't, I charge you: come your ways.   135
Ophelia: I shall obey, my lord.   *Exeunt.*

[SCENE IV: *The platform.*]

   Enter Hamlet, Horatio, and Marcellus.

Hamlet: The air bites shrewdly; it is very cold.
Horatio: It is a nipping and an eager air.
Hamlet: What hour now?
Horatio: I think it lacks of twelve.
Marcellus: No, it is struck.

---

106 *tenders:* Promises to pay.   107 *sterling:* Legal currency; *Tender:* Hold.   108 *crack the wind:* I.e., run it until it is broken-winded.   109 *tender . . . fool:* Show me a fool (for a daughter).   112 *fashion:* Mere form, pretense.   113 *countenance:* Credit, support.   115 *springes:* Snares; *woodcocks:* Birds easily caught, type of stupidity.   122 *entreatments:* Conversations, interviews.   123 *command to parley:* Mere invitation to talk.   124 *so . . . him:* This much concerning him.   126 *in few:* Briefly.   127 *brokers:* Go-betweens, procurers.   128 *dye:* Color or sort; *investments:* Clothes.   129 *implorators of:* Solicitors of.   130 *Breathing:* Speaking.   133 *slander:* Bring disgrace or reproach upon.

Horatio: Indeed? I heard it not: then it draws near the season   5
     Wherein the spirit held his wont to walk.

     A flourish of trumpets, and two pieces go off.

     What does this mean, my lord?
Hamlet: The king doth wake° to-night and takes his rouse,°
     Keeps wassail,° and the swagg'ring up-spring° reels;°
     And, as he drains his draughts of Rhenish° down,   10
     The kettle-drum and trumpet thus bray out
     The triumph of his pledge.°
Horatio: Is it a custom?
Hamlet: Ay, marry, is 't:
     But to my mind, though I am native here
     And to the manner born,° it is a custom   15
     More honour'd in the breach than the observance.
     This heavy-headed revel east and west
     Makes us traduc'd and tax'd of other nations:
     They clepe° us drunkards, and with swinish phrase°
     Soil our addition;° and indeed it takes   20
     From our achievements, though perform'd at height,
     The pith and marrow of our attribute.°
     So, oft it chances in particular men,
     That for some vicious mole of nature° in them,
     As, in their birth — wherein they are not guilty,   25
     Since nature cannot choose his origin —
     By the o'ergrowth of some complexion,
     Oft breaking down the pales° and forts of reason,
     Or by some habit that too much o'er-leavens°
     The form of plausive° manners, that these men,   30
     Carrying, I say, the stamp of one defect,
     Being nature's livery,° or fortune's star,° —
     Their virtues else — be they as pure as grace,
     As infinite as man may undergo —
     Shall in the general censure take corruption   35
     From that particular fault: the dram of eale°
     Doth all the noble substance of a doubt
     To his own scandal.°

     Enter Ghost.

Horatio: Look, my lord, it comes!

Scene IV.   8 *wake:* Stay awake, hold revel; *rouse:* Carouse, drinking bout.   9 *wassail:* Carousal; *up-spring:* Last and wildest dance at German merry-makings; *reels:* Reels through. 10 *Rhenish:* Rhine wine.   12 *triumph . . . pledge:* His glorious achievement as a drinker. 15 *to . . . born:* Destined by birth to be subject to the custom in question.   19 *clepe:* Call; *with swinish phrase:* By calling us swine.   20 *addition:* Reputation.   22 *attribute:* Reputation.   24 *mole of nature:* Natural blemish in one's constitution.   28 *pales:* Palings (as of a fortification).   29 *o'er-leavens:* Induces a change throughout (as yeast works in bread). 30 *plausive:* Pleasing.   32 *nature's livery:* Endowment from nature; *fortune's star:* The position in which one is placed by fortune, a reference to astrology. The two phrases are aspects of the same thing.   36–38 *the dram . . . scandal:* A famous crux: *dram of eale* has had various interpretations, the preferred one being probably "a dram of evil."

Hamlet: Angels and ministers of grace° defend us!
　　　Be thou a spirit of health or goblin damn'd,　　　　　　　　　40
　　　Bring with thee airs from heaven or blasts from hell,
　　　Be thy intents wicked or charitable,
　　　Thou com'st in such a questionable° shape
　　　That I will speak to thee: I'll call thee Hamlet,
　　　King, father, royal Dane: O, answer me!　　　　　　　　　　45
　　　Let me not burst in ignorance; but tell
　　　Why thy canoniz'd° bones, hearsed° in death,
　　　Have burst their cerements;° why the sepulchre,
　　　Wherein we saw thee quietly interr'd,
　　　Hath op'd his ponderous and marble jaws,　　　　　　　　　50
　　　To cast thee up again. What may this mean,
　　　That thou, dead corse, again in complete steel
　　　Revisits thus the glimpses of the moon,°
　　　Making night hideous; and we fools of nature°
　　　So horridly to shake our disposition　　　　　　　　　　　55
　　　With thoughts beyond the reaches of our souls?
　　　Say, why is this? wherefore? what should we do?

[Ghost] beckons [Hamlet].

Horatio: It beckons you to go away with it,
　　　As if it some impartment° did desire
　　　To you alone.
Marcellus:　　　Look, with what courteous action　　　　60
　　　It waves you to a more removed° ground:
　　　But do not go with it.
Horatio:　　　　　　　　No, by no means.
Hamlet: It will not speak; then I will follow it.
Horatio: Do not, my lord!
Hamlet:　　　　　　　Why, what should be the fear?
　　　I do not set my life at a pin's fee;　　　　　　　　　　65
　　　And for my soul, what can it do to that,
　　　Being a thing immortal as itself?
　　　It waves me forth again: I'll follow it.
Horatio: What if it tempt you toward the flood, my lord,
　　　Or to the dreadful summit of the cliff　　　　　　　　　70
　　　That beetles o'er° his base into the sea,
　　　And there assume some other horrible form,
　　　Which might deprive your sovereignty of reason°
　　　And draw you into madness? think of it:
　　　The very place puts toys of desperation,°　　　　　　　　75

---

39 *ministers of grace:* Messengers of God.　　43 *questionable:* Inviting question or conversation.　　47 *canoniz'd:* Buried according to the canons of the church; *hearsed:* Coffined.
48 *cerements:* Grave-clothes.　　53 *glimpses of the moon:* The earth by night.　　54 *fools of nature:* Mere men, limited to natural knowledge.　　59 *impartment:* Communication.
61 *removed:* Remote.　　71 *beetles o'er:* Overhangs threateningly.　　73 *deprive ... reason:* Take away the sovereignty of your reason. It was thought that evil spirits would sometimes assume the form of departed spirits in order to work madness in a human creature.
75 *toys of desperation:* Freakish notions of suicide.

Without more motive, into every brain
That looks so many fathoms to the sea
And hears it roar beneath.
Hamlet: It waves me still.
    Go on; I'll follow thee.
Marcellus: You shall not go, my lord.
Hamlet: Hold off your hands!   80
Horatio: Be rul'd; you shall not go.
Hamlet: My fate cries out,
    And makes each petty artere° in this body
    As hardy as the Nemean lion's° nerve.°
    Still am I call'd. Unhand me, gentlemen.
    By heaven, I'll make a ghost of him that lets° me!   85
    I say, away! Go on; I'll follow thee.   *Exeunt Ghost and Hamlet.*
Horatio: He waxes desperate with imagination.
Marcellus: Let's follow; 'tis not fit thus to obey him.
Horatio: Have after. To what issue° will this come?
Marcellus: Something is rotten in the state of Denmark.   90
Horatio: Heaven will direct it.°
Marcellus: Nay, let's follow him.   *Exeunt.*

[SCENE V: *Another part of the platform.*]

    Enter Ghost and Hamlet.

Hamlet: Whither wilt thou lead me? speak; I'll go no further.
Ghost: Mark me.
Hamlet: I will.
Ghost: My hour is almost come,
    When I to sulphurous and tormenting flames
    Must render up myself.
Hamlet: Alas, poor ghost!
Ghost: Pity me not, but lend thy serious hearing   5
    To what I shall unfold.
Hamlet: Speak; I am bound to hear.
Ghost: So art thou to revenge, when thou shalt hear.
Hamlet: What?
Ghost: I am thy father's spirit,
    Doom'd for a certain term to walk the night,   10
    And for the day confin'd to fast° in fires,
    Till the foul crimes done in my days of nature
    Are burnt and purg'd away. But that I am forbid
    To tell the secrets of my prison-house,
    I could a tale unfold whose lightest word   15

---

82 *artere:* Artery.   83 *Nemean lion's:* The Nemean lion was one of the monsters slain by Hercules; *nerve:* Sinew, tendon. The point is that the arteries which were carrying the spirits out into the body were functioning and were as stiff and hard as the sinews of the lion.   85 *lets:* Hinders.   89 *issue:* Outcome.   91 *it:* I.e., the outcome.   **Scene V.** 11 *fast:* Probably, do without food. It has been sometimes taken in the sense of doing general penance.

Would harrow up thy soul, freeze thy young blood,
Make thy two eyes, like stars, start from their spheres,°
Thy knotted° and combined° locks to part
And each particular hair to stand an end,
Like quills upon the fretful porpentine:° 20
But this eternal blazon° must not be
To ears of flesh and blood. List, list, O, list!
If thou didst ever thy dear father love —

Hamlet: O God!

Ghost: Revenge his foul and most unnatural° murder. 25

Hamlet: Murder!

Ghost: Murder most foul, as in the best it is;
But this most foul, strange and unnatural.

Hamlet: Haste me to know't, that I, with wings as swift
As meditation or the thoughts of love, 30
May sweep to my revenge.

Ghost: I find thee apt;
And duller shouldst thou be than the fat weed°
That roots itself in ease on Lethe wharf,°
Wouldst thou not stir in this. Now, Hamlet, hear:
'Tis given out that, sleeping in my orchard, 35
A serpent stung me; so the whole ear of Denmark
Is by a forged process of my death
Rankly abus'd: but know, thou noble youth,
The serpent that did sting thy father's life
Now wears his crown.

Hamlet: O my prophetic soul! 40
My uncle!

Ghost: Ay, that incestuous, that adulterate° beast,
With witchcraft of his wit, with traitorous gifts, —
O wicked wit and gifts, that have the power
So to seduce! — won to his shameful lust 45
The will of my most seeming-virtuous queen:
O Hamlet, what a falling-off was there!
From me, whose love was of that dignity
That it went hand in hand even with the vow
I made to her in marriage, and to decline 50
Upon a wretch whose natural gifts were poor
To those of mine!
But virtue, as it never will be moved,
Though lewdness court it in a shape of heaven,
So lust, though to a radiant angel link'd, 55
Will sate itself in a celestial bed,
And prey on garbage.

---

17 *spheres:* Orbits.   18 *knotted:* Perhaps intricately arranged; *combined:* Tied, bound.
20 *porpentine:* Porcupine.   21 *eternal blazon:* Promulgation or proclamation of eternity,
revelation of the hereafter.   25 *unnatural:* I.e., pertaining to fratricide.   32 *fat weed:*
Many suggestions have been offered as to the particular plant intended, including asphodel;
probably a general figure for plants growing along rotting wharves and piles.   33 *Lethe*
wharf: Bank of the river of forgetfulness in Hades.   42 *adulterate:* Adulterous.

But, soft! methinks I scent the morning air;
Brief let me be. Sleeping within my orchard,
My custom always of the afternoon,   60
Upon my secure° hour thy uncle stole,
With juice of cursed hebona° in a vial,
And in the porches of my ears did pour
The leperous° distilment; whose effect
Holds such an enmity with blood of man   65
That swift as quicksilver it courses through
The natural gates and alleys of the body,
And with a sudden vigour it doth posset°
And curd, like eager° droppings into milk,
The thin and wholesome blood: so did it mine;   70
And a most instant tetter bark'd about,
Most lazar-like,° with vile and loathsome crust,
All my smooth body.
Thus was I, sleeping, by a brother's hand
Of life, of crown, of queen, at once dispatch'd:°   75
Cut off even in the blossoms of my sin,
Unhous'led,° disappointed,° unanel'd,°
No reck'ning made, but sent to my account
With all my imperfections on my head:
O, horrible! O, horrible! most horrible!°   80
If thou hast nature in thee, bear it not;
Let not the royal bed of Denmark be
A couch for luxury° and damned incest.
But, howsomever thou pursues this act,
Taint not thy mind,° nor let thy soul contrive   85
Against thy mother aught: leave her to heaven
And to those thorns that in her bosom lodge,
To prick and sting her. Fare thee well at once!
The glow-worm shows the matin° to be near,
And 'gins to pale his uneffectual fire:°   90
Adieu, adieu, adieu! remember me.   *[Exit.]*
Hamlet: O all you host of heaven! O earth! what else?
And shall I couple° hell? O, fie! Hold, hold, my heart;
And you, my sinews, grow not instant old,
But bear me stiffly up. Remember thee!   95
Ay, thou poor ghost, whiles memory holds a seat
In this distracted globe.° Remember thee!

---

61 *secure:* Confident, unsuspicious.   62 *hebona:* Generally supposed to mean "henbane," conjectured *hemlock; ebenus,* meaning "yew."   64 *leperous:* Causing leprosy.   68 *posset:* Coagulate, curdle.   69 *eager:* Sour, acid.   72 *lazar-like:* Leperlike.   75 *dispatch'd:* Suddenly bereft.   77 *Unhous'led:* Without having received the sacrament; *disappointed:* Unready, without equipment for the last journey; *unanel'd:* Without having received extreme unction.   80 *O . . . horrible:* Many editors give this line to Hamlet; Garrick and Sir Henry Irving spoke it in that part.   83 *luxury:* Lechery.   85 *Taint . . . mind:* Probably, deprave not thy character, do nothing except in the pursuit of a natural revenge.   89 *matin:* Morning.   90 *uneffectual fire:* Cold light.   93 *couple:* Add.   97 *distracted globe:* Confused head.

Yea, from the table of my memory
I'll wipe away all trivial fond records,
All saws° of books, all forms, all pressures° past,   100
That youth and observation copied there;
And thy commandment all alone shall live
Within the book and volume of my brain,
Unmix'd with baser matter: yes, by heaven!
O most pernicious woman!   105
O villain, villain, smiling, damned villain!
My tables,° — meet it is I set it down,
That one may smile, and smile, and be a villain;
At least I am sure it may be so in Denmark: *[Writing.]*
So, uncle, there you are. Now to my word;°   110
It is "Adieu, adieu! remember me,"
I have sworn't.

    Enter Horatio and Marcellus.

Horatio: My lord, my lord —
Marcellus: Lord Hamlet, —
Horatio: Heavens secure him!
Hamlet: So be it!
Marcellus: Hillo, ho, ho,° my lord!   115
Hamlet: Hillo, ho, ho, boy! come, bird, come.
Marcellus: How is't, my noble lord?
Horatio: What news, my lord?
Hamlet: O, wonderful!
Horatio: Good my lord, tell it.
Hamlet: No; you will reveal it.
Horatio: Not I, my lord, by heaven.
Marcellus: Nor I, my lord.   120
Hamlet: How say you, then; would heart of man once think it?
    But you'll be secret?
Horatio: }
Marcellus: }   Ay, by heaven, my lord.
Hamlet: There's ne'er a villain dwelling in all Denmark
    But he's an arrant° knave.
Horatio: There needs no ghost, my lord, come from the grave 125
    To tell us this.
Hamlet: Why, right; you are in the right;
    And so, without more circumstance at all,
    I hold it fit that we shake hands and part:
    You, as your business and desire shall point you;
    For every man has business and desire,   130
    Such as it is; and for my own poor part,
    Look you, I'll go pray.
Horatio: These are but wild and whirling words, my lord.
Hamlet: I am sorry they offend you, heartily;
    Yes, 'faith, heartily.

---

100 *saws:* Wise sayings; *pressures:* Impressions stamped. 107 *tables:* Probably a small portable writing-tablet carried at the belt. 110 *word:* Watchword. 115 *Hillo, ho, ho:* A falconer's call to a hawk in air. 124 *arrant:* Thoroughgoing.

Horatio: There's no offence, my lord.   135
Hamlet: Yes, by Saint Patrick,° but there is, Horatio,
 And much offence too. Touching this vision here,
 It is an honest° ghost, that let me tell you:
 For your desire to know what is between us,
 O'ermaster 't as you may. And now, good friends,   140
 As you are friends, scholars and soldiers,
 Give me one poor request.
Horatio: What is 't, my lord? we will.
Hamlet: Never make known what you have seen to-night.
Horatio: ⎫
Marcellus: ⎬ My lord, we will not.
    ⎭
Hamlet: Nay, but swear 't.
Horatio: In faith,   145
 My lord, not I.
Marcellus: Nor I, my lord, in faith.
Hamlet: Upon my sword.°
Marcellus: We have sworn, my lord, already.
Hamlet: Indeed, upon my sword, indeed.   *Ghost cries under the stage.*
Ghost: Swear.
Hamlet: Ah, ha, boy! say'st thou so? art thou there, truepenny?°   150
 Come on — you hear this fellow in the cellarage —
 Consent to swear.
Horatio: Propose the oath, my lord.
Hamlet: Never to speak of this that you have seen,
 Swear by my sword.
Ghost [beneath]: Swear.   155
Hamlet: Hic et ubique?° then we'll shift our ground.
 Come hither, gentlemen,
 And lay your hands again upon my sword:
 Swear by my sword,
 Never to speak of this that you have heard.   160
Ghost [beneath]: Swear by his sword.
Hamlet: Well said, old mole! canst work i' th' earth so fast?
 A worthy pioner!° Once more remove, good friends.
Horatio: O day and night, but this is wondrous strange!
Hamlet: And therefore as a stranger give it welcome.   165
 There are more things in heaven and earth, Horatio,
 Than are dreamt of in your philosophy.
 But come;
 Here, as before, never, so help you mercy,
 How strange or odd soe'er I bear myself,   170
 As I perchance hereafter shall think meet
 To put an antic° disposition on,
 That you, at such times seeing me, never shall,
 With arms encumb'red° thus, or this head-shake,

---

136 *Saint Patrick:* St. Patrick was keeper of Purgatory and patron saint of all blunders and confusion.   138 *honest:* I.e., a real ghost and not an evil spirit.   147 *sword:* I.e., the hilt in the form of a cross.   150 *truepenny:* Good old boy, or the like.   156 *Hic et ubique?:* Here and everywhere?   163 *pioner:* Digger, miner.   172 *antic:* Fantastic.   174 *encumb'red:* Folded or entwined.

Or by pronouncing of some doubtful phrase,   175
As "Well, well, we know," or "We could, an if we would,"
Or "If we list to speak," or "There be, an if they might,"
Or such ambiguous giving out,° to note°
That you know aught of me: this not to do,
So grace and mercy at your most need help you,   180
Swear.
Ghost [beneath]: Swear.
Hamlet: Rest, rest, perturbed spirit! *[They swear.]* So, gentlemen,
With all my love I do commend me to you:
And what so poor a man as Hamlet is   185
May do, t' express his love and friending° to you,
God willing, shall not lack. Let us go in together;
And still your fingers on your lips, I pray.
The time is out of joint: O cursed spite,
That ever I was born to set it right!   190
Nay, come, let's go together.   *Exeunt.*

[ACT II

SCENE I: *A room in Polonius's house.*]

Enter old Polonius with his man [Reynaldo].

Polonius: Give him this money and these notes, Reynaldo.
Reynaldo: I will, my lord.
Polonius: You shall do marvellous wisely, good Reynaldo,
Before you visit him, to make inquire
Of his behaviour.
Reynaldo: My lord, I did intend it.   5
Polonius: Marry, well said; very well said. Look you, sir,
Inquire me first what Danskers° are in Paris;
And how, and who, what means, and where they keep,°
What company, at what expense; and finding
By this encompassment° and drift° of question   10
That they do know my son, come you more nearer
Than your particular demands will touch it:°
Take° you as 'twere, some distant knowledge of him;
As thus, "I know his father and his friends,
And in part him": do you mark this, Reynaldo?   15
Reynaldo: Ay, very well, my lord.
Polonius: "And in part him; but" you may say "not well:
But, if 't be he I mean, he's very wild;
Addicted so and so": and there put on° him

---

178 *giving out:* Profession of knowledge; *to note:* To give a sign.   186 *friending:* Friend-
liness.   **Act II, Scene I.**   7 *Danskers:* Danke was a common variant for "Denmark";
hence "Dane."   8 *keep:* Dwell.   10 *encompassment:* Roundabout talking; *drift:* Gradual
approach or course.   11–12 *come . . . it:* I.e., you will find out more this way than by asking
pointed questions.   13 *Take:* Assume, pretend.   19 *put on:* Impute to.

What forgeries° you please; marry, none so rank   20
As may dishonour him; take heed of that;
But, sir, such wanton,° wild and usual slips
As are companions noted and most known
To youth and liberty.
Reynaldo: As gaming, my lord.
Polonius: Ay, or drinking, fencing,° swearing, quarrelling,   25
   Drabbing;° you may go so far.
Reynaldo: My lord, that would dishonour him.
Polonius: 'Faith, no; as you may season it in the charge.
   You must not put another scandal on him,
   That he is open to incontinency;°   30
   That's not my meaning: but breathe his faults so quaintly°
   That they may seem the taints of liberty,°
   The flash and outbreak of a fiery mind,
   A savageness in unreclaimed° blood,
   Of general assault.°
Reynaldo: But, my good lord,—   35
Polonius: Wherefore should you do this?
Reynaldo: Ay, my lord,
   I would know that.
Polonius: Marry, sir, here's my drift;
   And, I believe, it is a fetch of wit:°
   You laying these slight sullies on my son,
   As 'twere a thing a little soil'd i' th' working,   40
   Mark you,
   Your party in converse, him you would sound,
   Having ever° seen in the prenominate° crimes
   The youth you breathe of guilty, be assur'd
   He closes with you in this consequence;°   45
   "Good sir," or so, or "friend," or "gentleman,"
   According to the phrase or the addition
   Of man and country.
Reynaldo: Very good, my lord.
Polonius: And then, sir, does 'a this—'a does—what was I about to say? By
   the mass, I was about to say something: where did I leave?   50
Reynaldo: At "closes in the consequence," at "friend or so," and "gentle-
   man."
Polonius: At "closes in the consequence," ay, marry;
   He closes thus: "I know the gentleman;
   I saw him yesterday, or t' other day,   55
   Or then, or then; with such, or such; and, as you say,

---

20 *forgeries:* Invented tales.   22 *wanton:* Sportive, unrestrained.   25 *fencing:* Indicative
of the ill repute of professional fencers and fencing schools in Elizabethan times.
26 *Drabbing:* Associating with immoral women.   30 *incontinency:* Habitual loose behavior.   31 *quaintly:* Delicately, ingeniously.   32 *taints of liberty:* Blemishes due to freedom.
34 *unreclaimed:* Untamed.   35 *general assault:* Tendency that assails all untrained youth.
38 *fetch of wit:* Clever trick.   43 *ever:* At any time; *prenominate:* Before-mentioned.
45 *closes . . . consequence:* Agrees with you in this conclusion.

There was 'a gaming; there o'ertook in 's rouse;°
There falling out at tennis": or perchance,
"I saw him enter such a house of sale,"
Videlicet,° a brothel, or so forth.   60
See you now;
Your bait of falsehood takes this carp of truth:
And thus do we of wisdom and of reach,°
With windlasses° and with assays of bias,°
By indirections° find directions° out: 65
So by my former lecture° and advice,
Shall you my son. You have me, have you not?
Reynaldo: My lord, I have.
Polonius: God bye ye;° fare ye well.
Reynaldo: Good my lord!
Polonius: Observe his inclination in yourself.°   70
Reynaldo: I shall, my lord.
Polonius: And let him ply his music.°
Reynaldo: Well, my lord.
Polonius: Farewell!   *Exit Reynaldo.*

    Enter Ophelia.

                How now, Ophelia! what's the matter?
Ophelia: O, my lord, my lord, I have been so affrighted!
Polonius: With what, i' th' name of God?   75
Ophelia: My lord, as I was sewing in my closet,°
    Lord Hamlet, with his doublet° all unbrac'd;°
    No hat upon his head; his stockings foul'd,
    Ungart'red, and down-gyved° to his ankle;
    Pale as his shirt; his knees knocking each other;   80
    And with a look so piteous in purport
    As if he had been loosed out of hell
    To speak of horrors, — he comes before me.
Polonius: Mad for thy love?
Ophelia: My lord, I do not know;
    But truly, I do fear it.
Polonius: What said he?   85
Ophelia: He took me by the wrist and held me hard;
    Then goes he to the length of all his arm;
    And, with his other hand thus o'er his brow,
    He falls to such perusal of my face
    As 'a would draw it. Long stay'd he so;   90
    At last, a little shaking of mine arm

---

57 *o'ertook in 's rouse:* Overcome by drink.   60 *Videlicet:* Namely.   63 *reach:* Capacity,
ability.   64 *windlasses:* I.e., circuitous paths; *assays of bias:* Attempts that resemble the
course of the bowl, which, being weighted on one side, has a curving motion.   65 *indirec-*
tions: Devious courses; *directions:* Straight courses, i.e., the truth.   66 *lecture:* Admonition.
68 *bye ye:* Be with you.   70 *Observe . . . yourself:* In your own person, not by spies; or conform your own conduct to his inclination; or test him by studying yourself.   72 *ply his*
music: Probably to be taken literally.   76 *closet:* Private chamber.   77 *doublet:* Close-
fitting coat; *unbrac'd:* Unfastened.   79 *down-gyved:* Fallen to the ankles (like gyves or
fetters).

And thrice his head thus waving up and down,
He rais'd a sigh so piteous and profound
As it did seem to shatter all his bulk°
And end his being: that done, he lets me go:　　　　　95
And, with his head over his shoulder turn'd,
He seem'd to find his way without his eyes;
For out o' doors he went without their helps,
And, to the last, bended their light on me.

Polonius: Come, go with me: I will go seek the king.　　　　　100
This is the very ecstasy of love,
Whose violent property° fordoes° itself
And leads the will to desperate undertakings
As oft as any passion under heaven
That does afflict our natures. I am sorry.　　　　　105
What, have you given him any hard words of late?

Ophelia: No, my good lord, but, as you did command,
I did repel his letters and denied
His access to me.

Polonius:　　　　　That hath made him mad.
I am sorry that with better heed and judgement　　　　　110
I had not quoted° him: I fear'd he did but trifle,
And meant to wrack thee; but, beshrew my jealousy!°
By heaven, it is as proper to our age
To cast beyond° ourselves in our opinions
As it is common for the younger sort　　　　　115
To lack discretion. Come, go we to the king:
This must be known; which, being kept close, might move
More grief to hide than hate to utter love.°
Come.　　　　　　　　　　　　　　　*Exeunt.*

[Scene II: *A room in the castle.*]

Flourish. Enter King and Queen, Rosencrantz, and Guildenstern [with others].

King: Welcome, dear Rosencrantz and Guildenstern!
Moreover that° we much did long to see you,
The need we have to use you did provoke
Our hasty sending. Something have you heard
Of Hamlet's transformation; so call it,　　　　　5
Sith° nor th' exterior nor the inward man
Resembles that it was. What it should be,
More than his father's death, that thus hath put him
So much from th' understanding of himself,
I cannot dream of: I entreat you both,　　　　　10
That, being of so young days° brought up with him,

---

94 *bulk:* Body.　102 *property:* Nature; *fordoes:* Destroys.　111 *quoted:* Observed.　112 *beshrew my jealousy:* Curse my suspicions.　114 *cast beyond:* Overshoot, miscalculate.　117–118 *might... love:* I.e., I might cause more grief to others by hiding the knowledge of Hamlet's love to Ophelia than hatred to me and mine by telling of it.　**Scene II.**　2 *Moreover that:* Besides the fact that.　6 *Sith:* Since.　11 *of...days:* From such early youth.

And sith so neighbour'd to his youth and haviour,
That you vouchsafe your rest° here in our court
Some little time: so by your companies
To draw him on to pleasures, and to gather,   15
So much as from occasion you may glean,
Whether aught, to us unknown, afflicts him thus,
That, open'd, lies within our remedy.

Queen: Good gentlemen, he hath much talk'd of you;
And sure I am two men there are not living   20
To whom he more adheres. If it will please you
To show us so much gentry° and good will
As to expend your time with us awhile,
For the supply and profit° of our hope,
Your visitation shall receive such thanks   25
As fits a king's remembrance.

Rosencrantz: Both your majesties
Might, by the sovereign power you have of us,
Put your dread pleasures more into command
Than to entreaty.

Guildenstern: But we both obey,
And here give up ourselves, in the full bent°   30
To lay our service freely at your feet,
To be commanded.

King: Thanks, Rosencrantz and gentle Guildenstern.

Queen: Thanks, Guildenstern and gentle Rosencrantz:
And I beseech you instantly to visit   35
My too much changed son. Go, some of you,
And bring these gentlemen where Hamlet is.

Guildenstern: Heavens make our presence and our practices
Pleasant and helpful to him!

Queen: Ay, amen!

Exeunt Rosencrantz and Guildenstern [with some Attendants].

Enter Polonius.

Polonius: Th' ambassadors from Norway, my good lord,   40
Are joyfully return'd.

King: Thou still hast been the father of good news.

Polonius: Have I, my lord? I assure my good liege,
I hold my duty, as I hold my soul,
Both to my God and to my gracious king:
And I do think, or else this brain of mine   45
Hunts not the trail of policy so sure
As it hath us'd to do, that I have found
The very cause of Hamlet's lunacy.

King: O, speak of that; that do I long to hear.   50

Polonius: Give first admittance to th' ambassadors;
My news shall be the fruit to that great feast.

King: Thyself do grace to them, and bring them in.   *[Exit Polonius.]*

---

13 *vouchsafe your rest:* Please to stay.   22 *gentry:* Courtesy.   24 *supply and profit:* Aid and
successful outcome.   30 *in . . . bent:* To the utmost degree of our mental capacity.

He tells me, my dear Gertrude, he hath found
The head and source of all your son's distemper.   55
Queen: I doubt° it is no other but the main;°
    His father's death, and our o'erhasty marriage.
King: Well, we shall sift him.

        Enter Ambassadors [Voltimand and Cornelius, with Polonius.]
                            Welcome, my good friends!
    Say, Voltimand, what from our brother Norway?
Voltimand: Most fair return of greetings and desires.   60
    Upon our first, he sent out to suppress
    His nephew's levies; which to him appear'd
    To be a preparation 'gainst the Polack;
    But, better look'd into, he truly found
    It was against your highness: whereat griev'd,   65
    That so his sickness, age and impotence
    Was falsely borne in hand,° sends out arrests
    On Fortinbras; which he, in brief, obeys;
    Receives rebuke from Norway, and in fine°
    Makes vow before his uncle never more   70
    To give th' assay° of arms against your majesty.
    Whereon old Norway, overcome with joy,
    Gives him three score thousand crowns in annual fee,
    And his commission to employ those soldiers,
    So levied as before, against the Polack: 75
    With an entreaty, herein further shown,   *[Giving a paper.]*
    That it might please you to give quiet pass
    Through your dominions for this enterprise,
    On such regards of safety and allowance°
    As therein are set down.
King: It likes° us well;   80
    And at our more consider'd° time we'll read,
    Answer, and think upon this business.
    Meantime we thank you for your well-took labour:
    Go to your rest; at night we'll feast together:
    Most welcome home!   *Exeunt Ambassadors.*
Polonius: This business is well ended.   85
    My liege, and madam, to expostulate
    What majesty should be, what duty is,
    Why day is day, night night, and time is time,
    Were nothing but to waste night, day and time.
    Therefore, since brevity is the soul of wit,°   90
    And tediousness the limbs and outward flourishes,°
    I will be brief: your noble son is mad:
    Mad call I it; for, to define true madness

---

56 *doubt:* Fear; *main:* Chief point, principal concern.   67 *borne in hand:* Deluded.
69 *in fine:* In the end.   71 *assay:* Assault, trial (of arms).   79 *safety and allowance:*
Pledges of safety to the country and terms of permission for the troops to pass.   80 *likes:*
Pleases.   81 *consider'd:* Suitable for deliberation.   90 *wit:* Sound sense or judgment.
91 *flourishes:* Ostentation, embellishments.

What is 't but to be nothing else but mad?
But let that go.
Queen: More matter, with less art. 95
Polonius: Madam, I swear I use no art at all.
That he is mad, 'tis true: 'tis true 'tis pity;
And pity 'tis 'tis true: a foolish figure;°
But farewell it, for I will use no art.
Mad let us grant him, then: and now remains 100
That we find out the cause of this effect,
Or rather say, the cause of this defect,
For this effect defective comes by cause:
Thus it remains, and the remainder thus.
Perpend.° 105
I have a daughter—have while she is mine—
Who, in her duty and obedience, mark,
Hath given me this: now gather, and surmise. *[Reads the letter.]* "To the
celestial and my soul's idol,
the most beautified Ophelia,"— 110
That's an ill phrase, a vile phrase; "beautified" is a vile phrase: but you
shall hear. Thus: *[Reads.]*
"In her excellent white bosom, these, & c."
Queen: Came this from Hamlet to her?
Polonius: Good madam, stay awhile; I will be faithful. *[Reads.]* 115
        "Doubt thou the stars are fire;
            Doubt that the sun doth move;
            Doubt truth to be a liar;
            But never doubt I love.
"O dear Ophelia, I am ill at these numbers;° I have not art to reckon° 120
my groans: but that I love thee best, O most best, believe it. Adieu.
    "Thine evermore, most dear lady, whilst this machine° is to him,
                                                    HAMLET."

This, in obedience, hath my daughter shown me,
And more above,° hath his solicitings, 125
As they fell out° by time, by means° and place,
All given to mine ear.
King: But how hath she
Receiv'd his love?
Polonius: What do you think of me?
King: As of a man faithful and honourable.
Polonius: I would fain prove so. But what might you think, 130
When I had seen this hot love on the wing—
As I perceiv'd it, I must tell you that,
Before my daughter told me—what might you,
Or my dear majesty your queen here, think,
If I had play'd the desk or table-book,° 135
Or given my heart a winking,° mute and dumb,

---

98 *figure:* Figure of speech. 105 *Perpend:* Consider. 120 *ill . . . numbers:* Unskilled at writing verses; *reckon:* Number metrically, scan. 122 *machine:* Bodily frame. 125 *more above:* Moreover. 126 *fell out:* Occurred; *means:* Opportunities (of access). 135 *play'd . . . table-book:* I.e., remained shut up, concealed this information. 136 *given . . . winking:* Given my heart a signal to keep silent.

Or look'd upon this love with idle sight;
What might you think? No, I went round to work,
And my young mistress thus I did bespeak:°
"Lord Hamlet is a prince, out of thy star;°   140
This must not be": and then I prescripts gave her,
That she should lock herself from his resort,
Admit no messengers, receive no tokens.
Which done, she took the fruits of my advice;
And he, repelled—a short tale to make—   145
Fell into a sadness, then into a fast,
Thence to a watch,° thence into a weakness,
Thence to a lightness,° and, by this declension,°
Into the madness wherein now he raves,
And all we mourn for.

King: Do you think 'tis this?   150
Queen: It may be, very like.
Polonius: Hath there been such a time—I would fain know that—
   That I have positively said " 'Tis so,"
   When it prov'd otherwise?
King: Not that I know.
Polonius [pointing to his head and shoulder]: Take this from this, if this be
      otherwise: 155
   If circumstances lead me, I will find
   Where truth is hid, though it were hid indeed
   Within the centre.°
King: How may we try it further?
Polonius: You know, sometimes he walks four hours together
   Here in the lobby.
Queen: So he does indeed.   160
Polonius: At such a time I'll loose my daughter to him:
   Be you and I behind an arras° then;
   Mark the encounter: if he love her not
   And be not from his reason fall'n thereon,°
   Let me be no assistant for a state,   165
   But keep a farm and carters.
King: We will try it.

   Enter Hamlet [reading on a book].

Queen: But, look, where sadly the poor wretch comes reading.
Polonius: Away, I do beseech you both, away:
                      Exeunt King and Queen [with Attendants].
   I'll board° him presently. O, give me leave.
   How does my good Lord Hamlet?   170
Hamlet: Well, God-a-mercy.
Polonius: Do you know me, my lord?
Hamlet: Excellent well; you are a fishmonger.°
Polonius: Not I, my lord.

---

139 *bespeak:* Address.   140 *out...star:* Above thee in position.   147 *watch:* State of sleep-
lessness.   148 *lightness:* Lightheadedness; *declension:* Decline, deterioration.   158 *centre:*
Middle point of the earth.   162 *arras:* Hanging, tapestry.   164 *thereon:* On that account.
169 *board:* Accost.   173 *fishmonger:* An opprobrious expression meaning "bawd," "procurer."

Hamlet: Then I would you were so honest a man. 175
Polonius: Honest, my lord!
Hamlet: Ay, sir; to be honest, as this world goes, is to be one man picked out of ten thousand.
Polonius: That's very true, my lord.
Hamlet: For if the sun breed maggots in a dead dog, being a good kissing 180 carrion,° — Have you a daughter?
Polonius: I have, my lord.
Hamlet: Let her not walk i' the sun:° conception° is a blessing: but as your daughter may conceive — Friend, look to 't.
Polonius [aside]: How say you by° that? Still harping on my daughter: yet 185 he knew me not at first; 'a said I was a fishmonger: 'a is far gone, far gone: and truly in my youth I suffered much extremity for love; very near this. I'll speak to him again. What do you read, my lord?
Hamlet: Words, words, words.
Polonius: What is the matter,° my lord? 190
Hamlet: Between who?°
Polonius: I mean, the matter that you read, my lord.
Hamlet: Slanders, sir: for the satirical rogue says here that old men have grey beards, that their faces are wrinkled, their eyes purging° thick amber and plum-tree gum and that they have a plentiful lack of wit, 195 together with most weak hams: all which, sir, though I most power-fully and potently believe, yet I hold it not honesty° to have it thus set down, for yourself, sir, should be old as I am, if like a crab you could go backward.
Polonius [aside]: Though this be madness, yet there is method in 't. — Will 200 you walk out of the air, my lord?
Hamlet: Into my grave.
Polonius: Indeed, that's out of the air. *(Aside.)* How pregnant sometimes his replies are! a happiness° that often madness hits on, which reason and sanity could not so prosperously° be delivered of. I will leave 205 him, and suddenly contrive the means of meeting between him and my daughter. — My honourable lord, I will most humbly take my leave of you.
Hamlet: You cannot, sir, take from me any thing that I will more willingly part withal: except my life, except my life, except my life. 210

Enter Guildenstern and Rosencrantz.

Polonius: Fare you well, my lord.
Hamlet: These tedious old fools!
Polonius: You go to seek the Lord Hamlet; there he is.
Rosencrantz [to Polonius]: God save you, sir! [*Exit Polonius.*]
Guildenstern: My honoured lord! 215
Rosencrantz: My most dear lord!
Hamlet: My excellent good friends! How dost thou, Guildenstern? Ah, Rosencrantz! Good lads, how do ye both?

180-181 *good kissing carrion:* I.e., a good piece of flesh for kissing (?). 183 *i' the sun:* In the sunshine of princely favors; *conception:* Quibble on "understanding" and "pregnancy." 185 *by:* Concerning. 190 *matter:* Substance. 191 *Between who:* Hamlet deliberately takes *matter* as meaning "basis of dispute." 194 *purging:* discharging. 197 *honesty:* Decency. 204 *happiness:* Felicity of expression. 205 *prosperously:* Successfully.

Rosencrantz: As the indifferent° children of the earth.

Guildenstern: Happy, in that we are not over-happy;   220
On Fortune's cap we are not the very button.

Hamlet: Nor the soles of her shoe?

Rosencrantz: Neither, my lord.

Hamlet: Then you live about her waist, or in the middle of her favours?

Guildenstern: 'Faith, her privates° we.   225

Hamlet: In the secret parts of Fortune? O, most true; she is a strumpet. What's the news?

Rosencrantz: None, my lord, but that the world's grown honest.

Hamlet: Then is doomsday near: but your news is not true. Let me question more in particular: what have you, my good friends, deserved at   230 the hands of Fortune, that she sends you to prison hither?

Guildenstern: Prison, my lord!

Hamlet: Denmark's a prison.

Rosencrantz: Then is the world one.

Hamlet: A goodly one; in which there are many confines,° wards and   235 dungeons, Denmark being one o' the worst.

Rosencrantz: We think not so, my lord.

Hamlet: Why, then, 'tis none to you; for there is nothing either good or bad, but thinking makes it so: to me it is a prison.

Rosencrantz: Why then, your ambition makes it one; 'tis too narrow for   240 your mind.

Hamlet: O God, I could be bounded in a nutshell and count myself a king of infinite space, were it not that I have bad dreams.

Guildenstern: Which dreams indeed are ambition, for the very substance of the ambitious° is merely the shadow of a dream.   245

Hamlet: A dream itself is but a shadow.

Rosencrantz: Truly, and I hold ambition of so airy and light a quality that it is but a shadow's shadow.

Hamlet: Then are our beggars bodies, and our monarchs and outstretched heroes the beggars' shadows. Shall we to the court? for, by   250 my fay,° I cannot reason.°

Rosencrantz: ⎫
Guildenstern: ⎬ We'll wait upon you.°

Hamlet: No such matter: I will not sort° you with the rest of my servants, for, to speak to you like an honest man, I am most dreadfully attended.° But, in the beaten way of friendship,° what make you at   255 Elsinore?

Rosencrantz: To visit you, my lord: no other occasion.

Hamlet: Beggar that I am, I am ever poor in thanks; but I thank you: and sure, dear friends, my thanks are too dear a° halfpenny. Were you not sent for? Is it your own inclining? Is it a free visitation? Come, come,   260 deal justly with me: come, come; nay, speak.

Guildenstern: What should we say, my lord?

---

219 *indifferent:* Ordinary.   225 *privates:* I.e., ordinary men (sexual pun on *private parts*).
235 *confines:* Places of confinement.   244–245 *very . . . ambitious:* That seemingly most
substantial thing which the ambitious pursue.   251 *fay:* Faith; *reason:* Argue.   252 *wait
upon:* Accompany.   253 *sort:* Class.   254–255 *dreadfully attended:* Poorly provided with
servants.   255 *in the . . . friendship:* As a matter of course among friends.   259 *a:* I.e., at a.

Hamlet: Why, any thing, but to the purpose. You were sent for; and there is a kind of confession in your looks which your modesties have not craft enough to colour: I know the good king and queen have sent for you. 265

Rosencrantz: To what end, my lord?

Hamlet: That you must teach me. But let me conjure° you, by the rights of our fellowship, by the consonancy of our youth,° by the obligation of our ever-preserved love, and by what more dear a better proposer° could charge you withal, be even and direct with me, whether you were sent for, or no? 270

Rosencrantz [aside to Guildenstern]: What say you?

Hamlet [aside]: Nay, then, I have an eye of you. — If you love me, hold not off. 275

Guildenstern: My lord, we were sent for.

Hamlet: I will tell you why; so shall my anticipation prevent your discovery,° and your secrecy to the king and queen moult no feather. I have of late — but wherefore I know not — lost all my mirth, forgone all custom of exercises; and indeed it goes so heavily with my disposition that this goodly frame, the earth, seems to me a sterile promontory, this most excellent canopy, the air, look you, this brave o'erhanging firmament, this majestical roof fretted° with golden fire, why, it appeareth nothing to me but a foul and pestilent congregation of vapours. What a piece of work is a man! how noble in reason! how infinite in faculties!° in form and moving how express° and admirable! in action how like an angel! in apprehension° how like a god! the beauty of the world! the paragon of animals! And yet, to me, what is this quintessence° of dust? man delights not me: no, nor woman neither, though by your smiling you seem to say so. 280 285 290

Rosencrantz: My lord, there was no such stuff in my thoughts.

Hamlet: Why did you laugh then, when I said "man delights not me"?

Rosencrantz: To think, my lord, if you delight not in man, what lenten° entertainment the players shall receive from you: we coted° them on the way; and hither are they coming, to offer you service. 295

Hamlet: He that plays the king shall be welcome; his majesty shall have tribute of me; the adventurous knight shall use his foil and target;° the lover shall not sigh gratis; the humorous man° shall end his part in peace; the clown shall make those laugh whose lungs are tickle o' the sere;° and the lady shall say her mind freely, or the blank verse shall halt for 't.° What players are they? 300

Rosencrantz: Even those you were wont to take delight in, the tragedians of the city.

---

268 *conjure:* Adjure, entreat.   269 *consonancy of our youth:* The fact that we are of the same age.   270 *better proposer:* One more skillful in finding proposals.   277-278 *prevent your discovery:* Forestall your disclosure.   283 *fretted:* Adorned.   286 *faculties:* Capacity; *express:* Well-framed (?), exact (?).   287 *apprehension:* Understanding.   289 *quintessence:* The fifth essence of ancient philosophy, supposed to be the substance of the heavenly bodies and to be latent in all things.   293 *lenten:* Meager.   294 *coted:* Overtook and passed beyond.   297 *foil and target:* Sword and shield.   298 *humorous man:* Actor who takes the part of the humor characters.   299-300 *tickle o' the sere:* Easy on the trigger.   300-301 *the lady . . . for 't:* The lady (fond of talking) shall have opportunity to talk, blank verse or no blank verse.

Hamlet: How chances it they travel? their residence,° both in reputation
and profit, was better both ways.   305

Rosencrantz: I think their inhibition° comes by the means of the late
innovation.°

Hamlet: Do they hold the same estimation they did when I was in the city?
are they so followed?

Rosencrantz: No, indeed, are they not.   310

Hamlet: How° comes it? do they grow rusty?

Rosencrantz: Nay, their endeavour keeps in the wonted pace: but there is,
sir, an aery° of children, little eyases,° that cry out on the top of question,° and are most tyrannically° clapped for 't: these are now the
fashion, and so berattle° the common stages° — so they call them —   315
that many wearing rapiers° are afraid of goose-quills° and dare scarce
come thither.

Hamlet: What, are they children? who maintains 'em? how are they escoted?° Will they pursue the quality° no longer than they can sing?°
will they not say afterwards, if they should grow themselves to com-   320
mon° players — as it is most like, if their means are no better — their
writers do them wrong, to make them exclaim against their own
succession?°

Rosencrantz: 'Faith, there has been much to do on both sides; and the nation holds it no sin to tarre° them to controversy: there was, for a   325
while, no money bid for argument,° unless the poet and the player
went to cuffs° in the question.°

Hamlet: Is't possible?

Guildenstern: O, there has been much throwing about of brains.

Hamlet: Do the boys carry it away?°   330

Rosencrantz: Ay, that they do, my lord; Hercules and his load° too.

Hamlet: It is not very strange; for my uncle is king of Denmark, and those
that would make mows° at him while my father lived, give twenty,
forty, fifty, a hundred ducats° a-piece for his picture in little.° 'Sblood,
there is something in this more than natural, if philosophy could find   335
it out.   *A flourish [of trumpets within].*

Guildenstern: There are the players.

---

304 *residence:* Remaining in one place.   306 *inhibition:* Formal prohibition (from acting
plays in the city or, possibly, at court).   307 *innovation:* The new fashion in satirical plays
performed by boy actors in the "private" theaters.   311–331 *How . . . load:* The passage is
the famous one dealing with the War of the Theatres (1599–1602); namely, the rivalry between
the children's companies and the adult actors.   313 *aery:* Nest; *eyases:* Young hawks.
313–314 *cry . . . question:* Speak in a high key dominating conversation; clamor forth the
height of controversy; probably "excel"; perhaps intended to decry leaders of the dramatic
profession.   314 *tyrannically:* Outrageously.   315 *berattle:* Berate; *common stages:* Public
theaters.   316 *many wearing rapiers:* Many men of fashion, who were afraid to patronize the
common players for fear of being satirized by the poets who wrote for the children; *goose-quills:*
I.e., pens of satirists.   318–319 *escoted:* Maintained.   319 *quality:* Acting profession; *no
longer . . . sing:* I.e., until their voices change.   320–321 *common:* Regular, adult.   323 *succession:* Future careers.   325 *tarre:* Set on (as dogs).   326 *argument:* Probably, plot for a play.
327 *went to cuffs:* Came to blows; *question:* Controversy.   330 *carry it away:* Win the day.
331 *Hercules . . . load:* Regarded as an allusion to the sign of the Globe Theatre, which was Hercules bearing the world on his shoulder.   333 *mows:* Grimaces.   334 *ducats:* Gold coins
worth 9s. 4d; *in little:* In miniature.

Hamlet: Gentlemen, you are welcome to Elsinore. Your hands, come then:
    the appurtenance of welcome is fashion and ceremony: let me com-
    ply° with you in this garb,° lest my extent° to the players, which, I tell   340
    you, must show fairly outwards, should more appear like entertain-
    ment than yours. You are welcome: but my uncle-father and aunt-
    mother are deceived.

Guildenstern: In what, my dear lord?

Hamlet: I am but mad north-north-west:° when the wind is southerly I   345
    know a hawk from a handsaw.°

    Enter Polonius.

Polonius: Well be with you, gentlemen!

Hamlet: Hark you, Guildenstern; and you too: at each ear a hearer: that
    great baby you see there is not yet out of his swaddling-clouts.°

Rosencrantz: Happily he is the second time come to them; for they say an   350
    old man is twice a child.

Hamlet: I will prophesy he comes to tell me of the players; mark it. — You
    say right, sir: o' Monday morning;° 'twas then indeed.

Polonius: My lord, I have news to tell you.

Hamlet: My lord, I have news to tell you. When Roscius° was an actor in   355
    Rome, —

Polonius: The actors are come hither, my lord.

Hamlet: Buz, buz!°

Polonius: Upon my honour, —

Hamlet: Then came each actor on his ass, —   360

Polonius: The best actors in the world, either for tragedy, comedy,
    history, pastoral, pastoral-comical, historical-pastoral, tragical-
    historical, tragical-comical-historical-pastoral, scene individable,° or
    poem unlimited:° Seneca° cannot be too heavy, nor Plautus° too light.
    For the law of writ and the liberty,° these are the only men.   365

Hamlet: O Jephthah, judge of Israel,° what a treasure hadst thou!

Polonius: What a treasure had he, my lord?

Hamlet: Why,
    "One fair daughter, and no more,
        The which he loved passing well."   370

Polonius [aside]: Still on my daughter.

Hamlet: Am I not i' the right, old Jephthah?

339–340 *comply:* Observe the formalities of courtesy.   340 *garb:* Manner; *extent:* Showing
of kindness.   345 *I am . . . north-north-west:* I am only partly mad, i.e., in only one point of
the compass.   346 *handsaw:* A proposed reading of *hernshaw* would mean "heron"; *handsaw*
may be an early corruption of *hernshaw.* Another view regards *hawk* as the variant of *hack,* a
tool of the pickax type, and *handsaw* as a saw operated by hand.   349 *swaddling-clouts:*
Cloths in which to wrap a newborn baby.   353 *o' Monday morning:* Said to mislead Polonius.   355 *Roscius:* A famous Roman actor.   358 *Buz, buz:* An interjection used at
Oxford to denote stale news.   363 *scene individable:* A play observing the unity of place.
364 *poem unlimited:* A play disregarding the unities of time and place; *Seneca:* Writer of Latin
tragedies, model of early Elizabethan writers of tragedy; *Plautus:* Writer of Latin comedy.
365 *law . . . liberty:* Pieces written according to rules and without rules, i.e., "classical" and
"romantic" dramas.   366 *Jephthah . . . Israel:* Jephthah had to sacrifice his daughter; see
Judges 11.

Polonius: If you call me Jephthah, my lord, I have a daughter that I love
    passing° well.
Hamlet: Nay, that follows not.   375
Polonius: What follows, then, my lord?
Hamlet: Why,
        "As by lot, God wot,"
and then, you know,
        "It came to pass, as most like° it was," —   380
the first row° of the pious chanson° will show you more; for look,
where my abridgement comes.°

Enter the Players.

You are welcome, masters; welcome, all. I am glad to see thee well.
Welcome, good friends. O, old friend! why, thy face is valanced° since
I saw thee last: comest thou to beard me in Denmark? What, my 385
young lady and mistress! By'r lady, your ladyship is nearer to heaven
than when I saw you last, by the altitude of a chopine.° Pray God,
your voice, like a piece of uncurrent° gold, be not cracked within the
ring.° Masters, you are all welcome. We'll e'en to 't like French falcon-
ers, fly at any thing we see: we'll have a speech straight: come, give us 390
a taste of your quality; come, a passionate speech.
First Player: What speech, my good lord?
Hamlet: I heard thee speak me a speech once, but it was never acted; or, if
it was, not above once; for the play, I remember, pleased not the million; 'twas caviary to the general:° but it was — as I received it, and 395
others, whose judgements in such matters cried in the top of°
mine — an excellent play, well digested in the scenes, set down with as
much modesty as cunning.° I remember, one said there were no sal-
lets° in the lines to make the matter savoury, nor no matter in the
phrase that might indict° the author of affectation; but called it an 400
honest method, as wholesome as sweet, and by very much more handsome than fine.° One speech in 't I chiefly loved: 'twas Æneas' tale to
Dido;° and thereabout of it especially, where he speaks of Priam's
slaughter: if it live in your memory, begin at this line: let me
see, let me see —   405
    "The rugged Pyrrhus,° like th' Hyrcanian beast,"° —
'tis not so: — it begins with Pyrrhus: —

---

374 *passing:* Surpassingly.   380 *like:* Probable.   381 *row:* Stanza; *chanson:* Ballad.
382 *abridgement comes:* Opportunity comes for cutting short the conversation.   384 *valanced:*
Fringed (with a beard).   387 *chopine:* Kind of shoe raised by the thickness of the heel;
worn in Italy, particularly at Venice.   388 *uncurrent:* Not passable as lawful coinage.
388–389 *cracked within the ring:* In the center of coins were rings enclosing the sovereign's
head; if the coin was cracked within this ring, it was unfit for currency.   395 *caviary to the
general:* Not relished by the multitude.   396 *cried in the top of:* Spoke with greater authority
than.   398 *cunning:* Skill.   398–399 *sallets:* Salads: here, spicy improprieties.   400 *indict:*
Convict.   401–402 *as wholesome . . . fine:* Its beauty was not that of elaborate ornament, but
that of order and proportion.   402–403 *Æneas' tale to Dido:* The lines recited by the player
are imitated from Marlowe and Nashe's *Dido Queen of Carthage* (II.i.214 ff.). They are written
in such a way that the conventionality of the play within a play is raised above that of ordinary drama.   406 *Pyrrhus:* A Greek hero in the Trojan War; *Hyrcanian beast:* The tiger; see
Virgil, *Aeneid,* IV.266.

"The rugged Pyrrhus, he whose sable arms,
Black as his purpose, did the night resemble
When he lay couched in the ominous horse,° 410
Hath now this dread and black complexion smear'd
With heraldry more dismal; head to foot
Now is he total gules;° horridly trick'd°
With blood of fathers, mothers, daughters, sons,
Bak'd and impasted° with the parching streets, 415
That lend a tyrannous and a damned light
To their lord's murder: roasted in wrath and fire,
And thus o'er-sized° with coagulate gore,
With eyes like carbuncles, the hellish Pyrrhus
Old grandsire Priam seeks." 420
So, proceed you.

Polonius: 'Fore God, my lord, well spoken, with good accent and good
discretion.

First Player: "Anon he finds him
Striking too short at Greeks; his antique sword, 425
Rebellious to his arm, lies where it falls,
Repugnant° to command: unequal match'd,
Pyrrhus at Priam drives; in rage strikes wide;
But with the whiff and wind of his fell sword
Th' unnerved father falls. Then senseless Ilium,° 430
Seeming to feel this blow, with flaming top
Stoops to his base, and with a hideous crash
Takes prisoner Pyrrhus' ear: for, lo! his sword
Which was declining on the milky head
Of reverend Priam, seem'd i' th' air to stick: 435
So, as a painted tyrant,° Pyrrhus stood,
And like a neutral to his will and matter,°
Did nothing.
But, as we often see, against° some storm,
A silence in the heavens, the rack° stand still, 440
The bold winds speechless and the orb below
As hush as death, anon the dreadful thunder
Doth rend the region,° so, after Pyrrhus' pause,
Aroused vengeance sets him new a-work;
And never did the Cyclops' hammers fall 445
On Mars's armour forg'd for proof eterne°
With less remorse than Pyrrhus' bleeding sword
Now falls on Priam.
Out, out, thou strumpet, Fortune! All you gods,
In general synod,° take away her power; 450
Break all the spokes and fellies° from her wheel,

---

410 *ominous horse:* Trojan horse.   413 *gules:* Red, a heraldic term; *trick'd:* Spotted,
smeared.   415 *impasted:* Made into a paste.   418 *o'er-sized:* Covered as with size or glue.
427 *Repugnant:* Disobedient.   430 *Then senseless Ilium:* Insensate Troy.   436 *painted
tyrant:* Tyrant in a picture.   437 *matter:* Task.   439 *against:* Before.   440 *rack:* Mass
of clouds.   443 *region:* Assembly.   446 *proof eterne:* External resistance to assault.
450 *synod:* Assembly.   451 *fellies:* Pieces of wood forming the rim of a wheel.

> And bowl the round nave° down the hill of heaven,
>   As low as to the fiends!"

Polonius: This is too long.

Hamlet: It shall to the barber's, with your beard. Prithee, say on: he's for a   455
    jig° or a tale of bawdry,° or he sleeps: say on: come to Hecuba.°

First Player: "But who, ah woe! had seen the mobled° queen —"

Hamlet: "The mobled queen?"

Polonius: That's good; "mobled queen" is good.

First Player: "Run barefoot up and down, threat'ning the flames   460
>   With bisson rheum;° a clout° upon that head
>   Where late the diadem stood, and for a robe,
>   About her lank and all o'er-teemed° loins,
>   A blanket, in the alarm of fear caught up;
>   Who this had seen, with tongue in venom steep'd,   465
>   'Gainst Fortune's state would treason have pronounc'd:°
>   But if the gods themselves did see her then
>   When she saw Pyrrhus make malicious sport
>   In mincing with his sword her husband's limbs,
>   The instant burst of clamour that she made,   470
>   Unless things mortal move them not at all,
>   Would have made milch° the burning eyes of heaven,
>   And passion in the gods."

Polonius: Look, whe'r he has not turned° his colour and has tears in 's
    eyes. Prithee, no more.   475

Hamlet: 'Tis well; I'll have thee speak out the rest soon. Good my lord, will
    you see the players well bestowed? Do you hear, let them be well used;
    for they are the abstract° and brief chronicles of the time: after
    your death you were better have a bad epitaph than their ill report
    while you live.   480

Polonius: My lord, I will use them according to their desert.

Hamlet: God's bodykins,° man, much better: use every man after his
    desert, and who shall 'scape whipping? Use them after your own hon-
    our and dignity: the less they deserve, the more merit is in your
    bounty. Take them in.   485

Polonius: Come, sirs.

Hamlet: Follow him, friends: we'll hear a play tomorrow. *[Aside to First
    Player.]* Dost thou hear me, old friend; can you play the Murder of
    Gonzago?

First Player: Ay, my lord.   490

Hamlet: We'll ha 't to-morrow night. You could, for a need, study a speech
    of some dozen or sixteen lines,° which I would set down and insert
    in 't, could you not?

First Player: Ay, my lord.

---

452 *nave:* Hub.   456 *jig:* Comic performance given at the end or in an interval of a play;
bawdry: Indecency; *Hecuba:* Wife of Priam, king of Troy.   457 *mobled:* Muffled.   461 *bis-
son rheum:* Blinding tears; *clout:* Piece of cloth.   463 *o'er-teemed:* Worn out with bearing
children.   466 *pronounc'd:* Proclaimed.   472 *milch:* Moist with tears.   474 *turned:*
Changed.   478 *abstract:* Summary account.   482 *bodykins:* Diminutive form of the
oath "by God's body."   492 *dozen or sixteen lines:* Critics have amused themselves by trying
to locate Hamlet's lines. Lucianus's speech III.ii.229–234 is the best guess.

Hamlet: Very well. Follow that lord; and look you mock him not. — My 495
  good friends, I'll leave you till night: you are welcome to Elsinore.
                              Exeunt Polonius and Players.
Rosencrantz: Good my lord!   *Exeunt [Rosencrantz and Guildenstern.]*
Hamlet: Ay, so, God bye to you. — Now I am alone.
      O, what a rogue and peasant° slave am I!
      Is it not monstrous that this player here,   500
      But in a fiction, in a dream of passion,
      Could force his soul so to his own conceit
      That from her working all his visage wann'd,°
      Tears in his eyes, distraction in 's aspect,
      A broken voice, and his whole function suiting   505
      With forms to his conceit?° and all for nothing!
      For Hecuba!
      What's Hecuba to him, or he to Hecuba,
      That he should weep for her? What would he do,
      Had he the motive and the cue for passion   510
      That I have? He would drown the stage with tears
      And cleave the general ear with horrid speech,
      Make mad the guilty and appall the free,
      Confound the ignorant, and amaze indeed
      The very faculties of eyes and ears.   515
      Yet I,
      A dull and muddy-mettled° rascal, peak,°
      Like John-a-dreams,° unpregnant of° my cause,
      And can say nothing; no, not for a king.
      Upon whose property° and most dear life   520
      A damn'd defeat was made. Am I a coward?
      Who calls me villain? breaks my pate across?
      Plucks off my beard, and blows it in my face?
      Tweaks me by the nose? gives me the lie i' th' throat,
      As deep as to the lungs? who does me this?   525
      Ha!
      'Swounds, I should take it: for it cannot be
      But I am pigeon-liver'd° and lack gall
      To make oppression bitter, or ere this
      I should have fatted all the region kites°   530
      With this slave's offal: bloody, bawdy villain!
      Remorseless, treacherous, lecherous, kindless° villain!
      O, vengeance!
      Why, what an ass am I! This is most brave,
      That I, the son of a dear father murder'd,   535

---

499 *peasant:* Base.   503 *wann'd:* Grew pale.   505–506 *his whole . . . conceit:* His whole being responded with forms to suit his thought.   517 *muddy-mettled:* Dull-spirited; *peak:* Mope, pine.   518 *John-a-dreams:* An expression occurring elsewhere in Elizabethan literature to indicate a dreamer; *unpregnant of:* Not quickened by.   520 *property:* Proprietorship (of crown and life).   528 *pigeon-liver'd:* The pigeon was supposed to secrete no gall; if Hamlet, so he says, had had gall, he would have felt the bitterness of oppression, and avenged it.   530 *region kites:* Kites of the air.   532 *kindless:* Unnatural.

Prompted to my revenge by heaven and hell,
Must, like a whore, unpack my heart with words,
And fall a-cursing, like a very drab,°
A stallion!°
Fie upon 't! foh! About,° my brains! Hum, I have heard   540
That guilty creatures sitting at a play
Have by the very cunning of the scene
Been struck so to the soul that presently
They have proclaim'd their malefactions;
For murder, though it have no tongue, will speak   545
With most miraculous organ. I'll have these players
Play something like the murder of my father
Before mine uncle: I'll observe his looks:
I'll tent° him to the quick: if 'a do blench,°
I know my course. The spirit that I have seen   550
May be the devil:° and the devil hath power
T' assume a pleasing shape; yea, and perhaps
Out of my weakness and my melancholy,
As he is very potent with such spirits,°
Abuses me to damn me: I'll have grounds   555
More relative° than this:° the play's the thing
Wherein I'll catch the conscience of the king.   *Exit.*

[ACT III

SCENE I: *A room in the castle.*]

Enter King, Queen, Polonius, Ophelia, Rosencrantz, Guildenstern, Lords.

King: And can you, by no drift of conference,°
     Get from him why he puts on this confusion,
     Grating so harshly all his days of quiet
     With turbulent and dangerous lunacy?
Rosencrantz: He does confess he feels himself distracted;   5
     But from what cause 'a will by no means speak.
Guildenstern: Nor do we find him forward° to be sounded,
     But, with a crafty madness, keeps aloof,
     When we would bring him on to some confession
     Of his true state.
Queen: Did he receive you well?   10
Rosencrantz: Most like a gentleman.
Guildenstern: But with much forcing of his disposition.°

---

538 *drab:* Prostitute.   539 *stallion:* Prostitute (male or female).   540 *About:* About it, or turn thou right about.   549 *tent:* Probe; *blench:* Quail, flinch.   551 *May be the devil:* Hamlet's suspicion is properly grounded in the belief of the time.   554 *spirits:* Humors.   556 *relative:* Closely related, definite; *this:* I.e., the ghost's story.   **Act III, Scene I.**   1 *drift of conference:* Device of conversation.   7 *forward:* Willing.   12 *forcing of his disposition:* I.e., against his will.

Rosencrantz: Niggard of question;° but, of our demands,
    Most free in his reply.
Queen: Did you assay° him
    To any pastime?   15
Rosencrantz: Madam, it so fell out, that certain players
    We o'er-raught° on the way: of these we told him;
    And there did seem in him a kind of joy
    To hear of it: they are here about the court,
    And, as I think, they have already order   20
    This night to play before him.
Polonius: 'Tis most true:
    And he beseech'd me to entreat your majesties
    To hear and see the matter.
King: With all my heart; and it doth much content me
    To hear him so inclin'd.   25
    Good gentlemen, give him a further edge,°
    And drive his purpose into these delights.
Rosencrantz: We shall, my lord.   *Exeunt Rosencrantz and Guildenstern.*
King: Sweet Gertrude, leave us too;
    For we have closely° sent for Hamlet hither,
    That he, as 'twere by accident, may here   30
    Affront° Ophelia:
    Her father and myself, lawful espials,°
    Will so bestow ourselves that, seeing, unseen,
    We may of their encounter frankly judge,
    And gather by him, as he is behav'd,   35
    If 't be th' affliction of his love or no
    That thus he suffers for.
Queen: I shall obey you.
    And for your part, Ophelia, I do wish
    That your good beauties be the happy cause
    Of Hamlet's wildness:° so shall I hope your virtues   40
    Will bring him to his wonted way again,
    To both your honours.
Ophelia: Madam, I wish it may.   *[Exit Queen.]*
Polonius: Ophelia, walk you here. Gracious,° so please you,
    We will bestow ourselves. *[To Ophelia.]* Read on this book;
    That show of such an exercise° may colour°   45
    Your loneliness. We are oft to blame in this, —
    'Tis too much prov'd — that with devotion's visage
    And pious action we do sugar o'er
    The devil himself.
King: *[aside]* O, 'tis too true!
    How smart a lash that speech doth give my conscience!   50

---

13 *Niggard of question:* Sparing of conversation.   14 *assay:* Try to win.   17 *o'er-raught:* Overtook.   26 *edge:* Incitement.   29 *closely:* Secretly.   31 *Affront:* Confront.   32 *lawful espials:* Legitimate spies.   40 *wildness:* Madness.   43 *Gracious:* Your grace (addressed to the king).   45 *exercise:* Act of devotion (the book she reads is one of devotion); *colour:* Give a plausible appearance to.

> The harlot's cheek, beautied with plast'ring art,
> Is not more ugly to° the thing° that helps it
> Than is my deed to my most painted word:
> O heavy burthen!

Polonius: I hear him coming: let's withdraw, my lord.   55

[Exeunt King and Polonius.]

Enter Hamlet.

Hamlet: To be, or not to be: that is the question:
> Whether 'tis nobler in the mind to suffer
> The slings and arrows of outrageous fortune,
> Or to take arms against a sea° of troubles,
> And by opposing end them? To die, to sleep;   60
> No more; and by a sleep to say we end
> The heart-ache and the thousand natural shocks
> That flesh is heir to, 'tis a consummation
> Devoutly to be wish'd. To die, to sleep;
> To sleep: perchance to dream: ay, there's the rub;   65
> For in that sleep of death what dreams may come
> When we have shuffled° off this mortal coil,°
> Must give us pause: there's the respect°
> That makes calamity of so long life;°
> For who would bear the whips and scorns of time,°   70
> Th' oppressor's wrong, the proud man's contumely,
> The pangs of despis'd° love, the law's delay,
> The insolence of office° and the spurns°
> That patient merit of th' unworthy takes,
> When he himself might his quietus° make   75
> With a bare bodkin?° who would fardels° bear,
> To grunt and sweat under a weary life,
> But that the dread of something after death,
> The undiscover'd country from whose bourn°
> No traveller returns, puzzles the will   80
> And makes us rather bear those ills we have
> Than fly to others that we know not of?
> Thus conscience° does make cowards of us all;
> And thus the native hue° of resolution
> Is sicklied o'er° with the pale cast° of thought,   85
> And enterprises of great pitch° and moment°

---

52 *to:* Compared to; *thing:* I.e., the cosmetic.   59 *sea:* The mixed metaphor of this speech has often been commented on; a later emendation *siege* has sometimes been spoken on the stage.   67 *shuffled:* Sloughed, cast; *coil:* Usually means "turmoil"; here, possibly "body" (conceived of as wound about the soul like rope); *clay, soil, veil,* have been suggested as emendations.   68 *respect:* Consideration.   69 *of . . . life:* So long-lived.   70 *time:* The world.   72 *despis'd:* Rejected.   73 *office:* Office-holders; *spurns:* Insults.   75 *quietus:* Acquittance; here, death.   76 *bare bodkin:* Mere dagger; *bare* is sometimes understood as "unsheathed"; *fardels:* Burdens.   79 *bourn:* Boundary.   83 *conscience:* Probably, inhibition by the faculty of reason restraining the will from doing wrong.   84 *native hue:* Natural color; metaphor derived from the color of the face.   85 *sicklied o'er:* Given a sickly tinge; *cast:* Shade of color.   86 *pitch:* Height (as of a falcon's flight); *moment:* Importance.

With this regard° their currents° turn awry,
And lose the name of action — Soft you now!
The fair Ophelia! Nymph, in thy orisons°
Be all my sins rememb'red.

Ophelia: Good my lord,   90
How does your honour for this many a day?

Hamlet: I humbly thank you; well, well, well.

Ophelia: My lord, I have remembrances of yours,
That I have longed long to re-deliver;
I pray you, now receive them.

Hamlet: No, not I;   95
I never gave you aught.

Ophelia: My honour'd lord, you know right well you did;
And, with them, words of so sweet breath compos'd
As made the things more rich: their perfume lost,
Take these again; for to the noble mind   100
Rich gifts wax poor when givers prove unkind.
There, my lord.

Hamlet: Ha, ha! are you honest?°

Ophelia: My lord?

Hamlet: Are you fair?   105

Ophelia: What means your lordship?

Hamlet: That if you be honest and fair, your honesty° should admit no
discourse to° your beauty.

Ophelia: Could beauty, my lord, have better commerce° than with honesty?

Hamlet: Ay, truly; for the power of beauty will sooner transform honesty   110
from what it is to a bawd than the force of honesty can translate beauty into his likeness: this was sometime a paradox, but now
the time° gives it proof. I did love you once.

Ophelia: Indeed, my lord, you made me believe so.

Hamlet: You should not have believed me; for virtue cannot so inoculate°   115
our old stock but we shall relish of it:° I loved you not.

Ophelia: I was the more deceived.

Hamlet: Get thee to a nunnery: why wouldst thou be a breeder of sinners?
I am myself indifferent honest;° but yet I could accuse me of such
things that it were better my mother had not borne me: I am very   120
proud, revengeful, ambitious, with more offences at my beck° than I
have thoughts to put them in, imagination to give them shape, or
time to act them in. What should such fellows as I do crawling
between earth and heaven? We are arrant knaves, all; believe none of us.
Go thy ways to a nunnery. Where's your father?   125

---

87 *regard:* Respect, consideration; *currents:* Courses.   89 *orisons:* Prayers.   103–108 *are you honest . . . beauty: Honest* meaning "truthful" and "chaste" and *fair* meaning "just, honorable" (line 105) and "beautiful" (line 107) are not mere quibbles; the speech has the irony of a *double entendre.*   107 *your honesty:* Your chastity.   108 *discourse to:* Familiar intercourse with.   109 *commerce:* Intercourse.   113 *the time:* The present age.   115 *inoculate:* Graft (metaphorical).   116 *but . . . it:* I.e., that we do not still have about us a taste of the old stock; i.e., retain our sinfulness.   119 *indifferent honest:* Moderately virtuous.   121 *beck:* Command.

Ophelia: At home, my lord.

Hamlet: Let the doors be shut upon him, that he may play the fool no
where but in 's own house. Farewell.

Ophelia: O, help him, you sweet heavens!

Hamlet: If thou dost marry, I'll give thee this plague for thy dowry: be　130
thou as chaste as ice, as pure as snow, thou shalt not escape calumny.
Get thee to a nunnery, go: farewell. Or, if thou wilt needs marry, marry
a fool; for wise men know well enough what monsters° you
make of them. To a nunnery, go, and quickly too. Farewell.

Ophelia: O heavenly powers, restore him!　　　　　　　　　　　　135

Hamlet: I have heard of your° paintings too, well enough; God hath given
you one face, and you make yourselves another: you jig,° you amble,
and you lisp; you nick-name God's creatures, and make your wantonness your ignorance.° Go to, I'll no more on 't; it hath made me mad. I
say, we will have no more marriage: those that are married already, all　140
but one,° shall live; the rest shall keep as they are. To a nunnery, go.

　　　　　　　　　　　　　　　　　　　　　　　　　　　Exit.

Ophelia: O, what a noble mind is here o'er-thrown!
　　The courtier's, soldier's, scholar's, eye, tongue, sword;
　　Th' expectancy and rose° of the fair state,
　　The glass of fashion and the mould of form,°　　　　　　　　145
　　Th' observ'd of all observers,° quite, quite down!
　　And I, of ladies most deject and wretched,
　　That suck'd the honey of his music vows,
　　Now see that noble and most sovereign reason,
　　Like sweet bells jangled, out of time and harsh;　　　　　　150
　　That unmatch'd form and feature of blown° youth
　　Blasted with ecstasy:° O, woe is me,
　　T' have seen what I have seen, see what I see!

　　Enter King and Polonius.

King: Love! his affections do not that way tend;
　　Nor what he spake, though it lack'd form a little,　　　　　155
　　Was not like madness. There's something in his soul,
　　O'er which his melancholy sits on brood;
　　And I do doubt° the hatch and the disclose°
　　Will be some danger: which for to prevent,
　　I have in quick determination　　　　　　　　　　　　　160
　　Thus set it down: he shall with speed to England,
　　For the demand of our neglected tribute:
　　Haply the seas and countries different
　　With variable° objects shall expel

---

133 *monsters:* An allusion to the horns of a cuckold.　136 *your:* Indefinite use.　137 *jig:*
Move with jerky motion; probably allusion to the *jig,* or song and dance, of the current stage.
138–139 *make . . . ignorance:* I.e., excuse your wantonness on the ground of your ignorance.
141 *one:* I.e., the king.　144 *expectancy and rose:* Source of hope.　145 *The glass . . . form:*
The mirror of fashion and the pattern of courtly behavior.　146 *observ'd . . . observers:* I.e.,
the center of attention in the court.　151 *blown:* Blooming.　152 *ecstasy:* Madness.
158 *doubt:* Fear; *disclose:* Disclosure or revelation (by chipping of the shell).　164 *variable:*
Various.

This something-settled° matter in his heart,   165
Whereon his brains still beating puts him thus
From fashion of himself.° What think you on 't?
Polonius: It shall do well: but yet do I believe
The origin and commencement of his grief
Sprung from neglected love. How now, Ophelia!   170
You need not tell us what Lord Hamlet said;
We heard it all. My lord, do as you please;
But, if you hold it fit, after the play
Let his queen mother all alone entreat him
To show his grief: let her be round° with him;   175
And I'll be plac'd, so please you, in the ear
Of all their conference. If she find him not,
To England send him, or confine him where
Your wisdom best shall think.
King: It shall be so: 180
Madness in great ones must not unwatch'd go.   *Exeunt.*

[SCENE II: *A hall in the castle.*]

Enter Hamlet and three of the Players.

Hamlet: Speak the speech, I pray you, as I pronounced it to you, trip-
pingly on the tongue: but if you mouth it, as many of your° players do, I had as lief the town-crier spoke my lines. Nor do not saw the
air too much with your hand, thus, but use all gently; for in the very
torrent, tempest, and, as I may say, whirlwind of your passion, you   5
must acquire and beget a temperance that may give it smoothness.
O, it offends me to the soul to hear a robustious° periwig-pated° fellow tear a passion to tatters, to very rags, to split the ears of the
groundlings,° who for the most part are capable of° nothing but
inexplicable° dumb-shows and noise: I would have such a fellow   10
whipped for o'er-doing Termagant;° it out-herods Herod:° pray you,
avoid it.
First Player: I warrant your honour.
Hamlet: Be not too tame neither, but let your own discretion be your
tutor: suit the action to the word, the word to the action; with this   15
special observance, that you o'er-step not the modesty of nature: for
any thing so overdone is from the purpose of playing, whose end,
both at the first and now, was and is, to hold, as 't were, the mirror up
to nature; to show virtue her own feature, scorn her own image, and
the very age and body of the time his form and pressure.° Now this   20

---

165 *something-settled:* Somewhat settled.   167 *From . . . himself:* Out of his natural manner.
175 *round:* Blunt.   **Scene II.**   2 *your:* Indefinite use.   7 *robustious:* Violent, boisterous; *periwig-pated:* Wearing a wig.   9 *groundlings:* Those who stood in the yard of the theater; *capable of:* Susceptible of being influenced by.   10 *inexplicable:* Of no significance
worth explaining.   11 *Termagant:* A god of the Saracens; a character in the St. Nicholas
play, where one of his worshipers, leaving him in charge of goods, returns to find them
stolen; whereupon he beats the god (or idol), which howls vociferously; *Herod:* Herod of
Jewry; a character in *The Slaughter of the Innocents* and other cycle plays. The part was played
with great noise and fury.   20 *pressure:* Stamp, impressed character.

overdone, or come tardy off,° though it make the unskilful laugh,
cannot but make the judicious grieve; the censure of the which one°
must in your allowance o'erweigh a whole theatre of others. O, there
be players that I have seen play, and heard others praise, and that
highly, not to speak it profanely, that, neither having the accent of   25
Christians nor the gait of Christian, pagan, nor man, have so
strutted and bellowed that I have thought some of nature's journey-
men° had made men and not made them well, they imitated humanity so abominably.

First Player: I hope we have reformed that indifferently° with us, sir.   30

Hamlet: O, reform it altogether. And let those that play your clowns speak
no more than is set down for them; for there be of° them that will
themselves laugh, to set on some quantity of barren° spectators to
laugh too; though, in the mean time, some necessary question of the
play be then to be considered: that's villanous, and shows a most   35
pitiful ambition in the fool that uses it. Go, make you ready.

                                                 [Exeunt Players.]

Enter Polonius, Guildenstern, and Rosencrantz.

     How now, my lord! will the king hear this piece of work?

Polonius: And the queen too, and that presently.

Hamlet: Bid the players make haste.   *[Exit Polonius.]*

     Will you two help to hasten them?   40

Rosencrantz: ⎫
Guildenstern: ⎬ We will, my lord.   *Exeunt they two.*
              ⎭

Hamlet: What ho! Horatio!

Enter Horatio.

Horatio: Here, sweet lord, at your service.

Hamlet: Horatio, thou art e'en as just° a man
     As e'er my conversation cop'd withal.

Horatio: O, my dear lord, —

Hamlet: Nay, do not think I flatter;   45
     For what advancement may I hope from thee
     That no revenue hast but thy good spirits,
     To feed and clothe thee? Why should the poor be flatter'd?
     No, let the candied tongue lick absurd pomp,
     And crook the pregnant° hinges of the knee   50
     Where thrift° may follow fawning. Dost thou hear?
     Since my dear soul was mistress of her choice
     And could of men distinguish her election,
     S' hath seal'd thee for herself; for thou hast been
     As one, in suff'ring all, that suffers nothing,   55
     A man that fortune's buffets and rewards
     Hast ta'en with equal thanks: and blest are those
     Whose blood and judgement are so well commeddled,

---

21 *come tardy off:* Inadequately done.   22 *the censure . . . one:* The judgment of even one of
whom.   27 *journeymen:* Laborers not yet masters in their trade.   30 *indifferently:* Fairly,
tolerably.   32 *of:* I.e., some among them.   33 *barren:* I.e., of wit.   43 *just:* Honest,
honorable.   50 *pregnant:* Pliant.   51 *thrift:* Profit.

That they are not a pipe for fortune's finger
To sound what stop° she please. Give me that man   60
That is not passion's slave, and I will wear him
In my heart's core, ay, in my heart of heart,
As I do thee. — Something too much of this. —
There is a play to-night before the king;
One scene of it comes near the circumstance   65
Which I have told thee of my father's death:
I prithee, when thou seest that act afoot,
Even with the very comment of thy soul°
Observe my uncle: if his occulted° guilt
Do not itself unkennel in one speech,   70
It is a damned° ghost that we have seen,
And my imaginations are as foul
As Vulcan's stithy.° Give him heedful note;
For I mine eyes will rivet to his face,
And after we will both our judgements join   75
In censure of his seeming.°

Horatio: Well, my lord:
If 'a steal aught the whilst this play is playing,
And 'scape detecting, I will pay the theft.

Enter trumpets and kettledrums, King, Queen, Polonius, Ophelia,
[Rosencrantz, Guildenstern, and others].

Hamlet: They are coming to the play; I must be idle:° Get you a place.
King: How fares our cousin Hamlet?   80
Hamlet: Excellent, i' faith; of the chameleon's dish:° I eat the air, promise-
crammed: you cannot feed capons so.
King: I have nothing with° this answer, Hamlet; these words are not
mine.°
Hamlet: No, nor mine now. *[To Polonius.]* My lord, you played once i' the   85
university, you say?
Polonius: That did I, my lord; and was accounted a good actor.
Hamlet: What did you enact?
Polonius: I did enact Julius Cæsar: I was killed i' the Capitol; Brutus
killed me.   90
Hamlet: It was a brute part of him to kill so capital a calf there. Be the
players ready?
Rosencrantz: Ay, my lord; they stay upon your patience.
Queen: Come hither, my dear Hamlet, sit by me.
Hamlet: No, good mother, here's metal more attractive.   95
Polonius [to the king]: O, ho! do you mark that?
Hamlet: Lady, shall I lie in your lap?   *[Lying down at Ophelia's feet.]*

---

60 *stop:* Hole in a wind instrument for controlling the sound.   68 *very . . . soul:* Inward
and sagacious criticism.   69 *occulted:* Hidden.   71 *damned:* In league with Satan.
73 *stithy:* Smithy, place of *stiths* (anvils).   76 *censure . . . seeming:* Judgment of his appearance or behavior.   79 *idle:* Crazy, or not attending to anything serious.   81 *chameleon's
dish:* Chameleons were supposed to feed on air. (Hamlet deliberately misinterprets the king's
"fares" as "feeds.")   83 *have . . . with:* Make nothing of.   83–84 *are not mine:* Do not
respond to what I ask.

Ophelia: No, my lord.

Hamlet: I mean, my head upon your lap?

Ophelia: Ay, my lord.   100

Hamlet: Do you think I meant country° matters?

Ophelia: I think nothing, my lord.

Hamlet: That's a fair thought to lie between maids' legs.

Ophelia: What is, my lord?

Hamlet: Nothing.   105

Ophelia: You are merry, my lord.

Hamlet: Who, I?

Ophelia: Ay, my lord.

Hamlet: O God, your only° jig-maker.° What should a man do but be merry? for, look you, how cheerfully my mother looks, and my father   110 died within's two hours.

Ophelia: Nay, 'tis twice two months, my lord.

Hamlet: So long? Nay then, let the devil wear black, for I'll have a suit of sables.° O heavens! die two months ago, and not forgotten yet? Then there's hope a great man's memory may outlive his life half a year: 115 but, by 'r lady, 'a must build churches, then; or else shall 'a suffer not thinking on,° with the hobbyhorse, whose epitaph is "For, O, for, O, the hobbyhorse is forgot."°

The trumpets sound. Dumb show follows.

Enter a King and a Queen [very lovingly]; the Queen embracing him, and he her. [She kneels, and makes show of protestation unto him.] He takes her up, and declines his head upon her neck: he lies him down upon a bank of flowers: she, seeing him asleep, leaves him. Anon comes in another man, takes off his crown, kisses it, pours poison in the sleeper's ears, and leaves him. The Queen returns; finds the King dead, makes passionate action. The Poisoner, with some three or four come in again, seem to condole with her. The dead body is carried away. The Poisoner woos the Queen with gifts: she seems harsh awhile, but in the end accepts love. [Exeunt.]

Ophelia: What means this, my lord?

Hamlet: Marry, this is miching mallecho;° it means mischief.   120

Ophelia: Belike this show imports the argument of the play.

Enter Prologue.

Hamlet: We shall know by this fellow: the players cannot keep counsel; they'll tell all.

Ophelia: Will 'a tell us what this show meant?

Hamlet: Ay, or any show that you'll show him: be not you ashamed to   125 show, he'll not shame to tell you what it means.

Ophelia: You are naught, you are naught:° I'll mark the play.

Prologue: For us, and for our tragedy,

---

101 *country:* With a bawdy pun.   109 *your only:* Only your; *jig-maker:* Composer of jigs (song and dance).   113–114 *suit of sables:* Garments trimmed with the fur of the sable, with a quibble on *sable* meaning "black."   116–117 *suffer...on:* Undergo oblivion. 117–118 *"For...forgot":* Verse of a song occurring also in *Love's Labour's Lost,* III.i.30. The hobbyhorse was a character in the Morris Dance.   120 *miching mallecho:* Sneaking mischief.   127 *naught:* Indecent.

         Here stooping° to your clemency,
         We beg your hearing patiently.   *[Exit.]*   130
Hamlet: Is this a prologue, or the posy° of a ring?
Ophelia: 'Tis brief, my lord.
Hamlet: As woman's love.

    Enter [two Players as] King and Queen.

Player King: Full thirty times hath Phoebus' cart gone round
         Neptune's salt wash° and Tellus'° orbed ground,   135
         And thirty dozen moons with borrowed° sheen
         About the world have times twelve thirties been,
         Since love our hearts and Hymen° did our hands
         Unite commutual° in most sacred bands.
Player Queen: So many journeys may the sun and moon   140
         Make us again count o'er ere love be done!
         But, woe is me, you are so sick of late,
         So far from cheer and from your former state,
         That I distrust° you. Yet, though I distrust,
         Discomfort you, my lord, it nothing must: 145
         For women's fear and love holds quantity;°
         In neither aught, or in extremity.
         Now, what my love is, proof hath made you know;
         And as my love is siz'd, my fear is so:
         Where love is great, the littlest doubts are fear;   150
         Where little fears grow great, great love grows there.
Player King: 'Faith, I must leave thee, love, and shortly too;
         My operant° powers their functions leave° to do:
         And thou shalt live in this fair world behind,
         Honour'd, belov'd; and haply one as kind   155
         For husband shalt thou —
Player Queen: O, confound the rest!
         Such love must needs be treason in my breast:
         In second husband let me be accurst!
         None wed the second but who kill'd the first.
Hamlet (aside): Wormwood, wormwood.   160
Player Queen: The instances that second marriage move
         Are base respects of thrift, but none of love:
         A second time I kill my husband dead,
         When second husband kisses me in bed.
Player King: I do believe you think what now you speak;   165
         But what we do determine oft we break.
         Purpose is but the slave to memory,
         Of violent birth, but poor validity:
         Which now, like fruit unripe, sticks on the tree;
         But fall, unshaken, when they mellow be.   170
         Most necessary 'tis that we forget
         To pay ourselves what to ourselves is debt:

---

129 *stooping:* Bowing.   131 *posy:* Motto.   135 *salt wash:* The sea; *Tellus:* Goddess of the earth (*orbed ground*).   136 *borrowed:* I.e., reflected.   138 *Hymen:* God of matrimony. 139 *commutual:* Mutually.   144 *distrust:* Am anxious about.   146 *holds quantity:* Keeps proportion between.   153 *operant:* Active; *leave:* Cease.

What to ourselves in passion we propose,
The passion ending, doth the purpose lose.
The violence of either grief or joy　　　　　　　　　　　　175
Their own enactures° with themselves destroy:
Where joy most revels, grief doth most lament;
Grief joys, joy grieves, on slender accident.
This world is not for aye,° nor 'tis not strange
That even our loves should with our fortunes change;　　　180
For 'tis a question left us yet to prove,
Whether love lead fortune, or else fortune love.
The great man down, you mark his favourite flies;
The poor advanc'd makes friends of enemies.
And hitherto doth love on fortune tend;　　　　　　　　185
For who° not needs shall never lack a friend,
And who in want a hollow friend doth try,
Directly seasons° him his enemy.
But, orderly to end where I begun,
Our wills and fates do so contrary run　　　　　　　　　190
That our devices still are overthrown;
Our thoughts are ours, their ends° none of our own:
So think thou wilt no second husband wed;
But die thy thoughts when thy first lord is dead.
Player Queen: Nor earth to me give food, nor heaven light!　　195
Sport and repose lock from me day and night!
To desperation turn my trust and hope!
An anchor's° cheer° in prison be my scope!
Each opposite° that blanks° the face of joy
Meet what I would have well and it destroy!　　　　　　200
Both here and hence pursue me lasting strife,
If, once a widow, ever I be wife!
Hamlet: If she should break it now!
Player King: 'Tis deeply sworn. Sweet, leave me here awhile;
My spirits grow dull, and fain I would beguile　　　　　　205
The tedious day with sleep.　　　　　　　　　　　*[Sleeps.]*
Player Queen:　　　　　　　　Sleep rock thy brain;
And never come mischance between us twain!　　　　　*Exit.*
Hamlet: Madam, how like you this play?
Queen: The lady doth protest too much, methinks.
Hamlet: O, but she'll keep her word.　　　　　　　　　　210
King: Have you heard the argument? Is there no offence in 't?
Hamlet: No, no, they do but jest, poison in jest; no offence i' the world.
King: What do you call the play?
Hamlet: The Mouse-trap. Marry, how? Tropically.° This play is the image
of a murder done in Vienna: Gonzago° is the duke's name; his wife,　215
Baptista: you shall see anon; 't is a knavish piece of work: but what o'

---

176 *enactures:* Fulfillments.　　179 *aye:* Ever.　　186 *who:* Whoever.　　188 *seasons:* Matures,
ripens.　　192 *ends:* Results.　　198 *An anchor's:* An anchorite's; *cheer:* Fare; sometimes printed
as *chair.*　　199 *opposite:* Adverse thing; *blanks:* Causes to *blanch* or grow pale.　　214 *Tropi-*
cally: Figuratively, *trapically* suggests a pun on *trap* in *Mouse-trap* (l. 214).　　215 *Gonzago:* In
1538 Luigi Gonzago murdered the Duke of Urbano by pouring poisoned lotion in his ears.

that? your majesty and we that have free souls, it touches us not: let
the galled jade° winch,° our withers° are unwrung.°

Enter Lucianus.

This is one Lucianus, nephew to the king.

Ophelia: You are as good as a chorus,° my lord.   220

Hamlet: I could interpret between you and your love, if I could see the
puppets dallying.°

Ophelia: You are keen, my lord, you are keen.

Hamlet: It would cost you a groaning to take off my edge.

Ophelia: Still better, and worse.°   225

Hamlet: So you mistake° your husbands. Begin, murderer; pox,° leave thy
damnable faces, and begin. Come: the croaking raven doth bellow for
revenge.

Lucianus: Thoughts black, hands apt, drugs fit, and time agreeing;
Confederate° season, else no creature seeing;   230
Thou mixture rank, of midnight weeds collected,
With Hecate's° ban° thrice blasted, thrice infected,
Thy natural magic and dire property,
On wholesome life usurp immediately.

            [Pours the poison into the sleeper's ears.]

Hamlet: 'A poisons him i' the garden for his estate. His name's Gonzago: 235
the story is extant, and written in very choice Italian: you shall see
anon how the murderer gets the love of Gonzago's wife.

Ophelia: The king rises.

Hamlet: What, frighted with false fire!°

Queen: How fares my lord?   240

Polonius: Give o'er the play.

King: Give me some light: away!

Polonius: Lights, lights, lights!   *Exeunt all but Hamlet and Horatio.*

Hamlet: Why, let the strucken deer go weep,
     The hart ungalled play;
For some must watch, while some must sleep: 245
     Thus runs the world away.°
Would not this,° sir, and a forest of feathers° — if the rest of my fortunes turn Turk with° me — with two Provincial roses° on my razed°
shoes, get me a fellowship in a cry° of players,° sir?   250

---

218 *galled jade:* Horse whose hide is rubbed by saddle or harness; *winch:* Wince; *withers:* The
part between the horse's shoulder blades; *unwrung:* Not wrung or twisted.   220 *chorus:* In
many Elizabethan plays the action was explained by an actor known as the "chorus"; at a puppet show the actor who explained the action was known as an "interpreter," as indicated by
the lines following.   222 *dallying:* With sexual suggestion, continued in *keen* (sexually
aroused), *groaning* (i.e., in pregnancy), and *edge* (i.e., sexual desire or impetuosity).
225 *Still...worse:* More keen, less decorous.   226 *mistake:* Err in taking; *pox:* An impreca-
tion.   230 *Confederate:* Conspiring (to assist the murderer).   232 *Hecate:* The goddess of
witchcraft; *ban:* Curse.   239 *false fire:* Fireworks, or a blank discharge.   244–247 *Why...
away:* Probably from an old ballad, with allusion to the popular belief that a wounded deer
retires to weep and die. Cf. *As You Like It,* II.i.66.   248 *this:* I.e., the play; *feathers:* Allusion to
the plumes which Elizabethan actors were fond of wearing.   249 *turn Turk with:* Go back
on; *two Provincial roses:* Rosettes of ribbon like the roses of Provins near Paris, or else the
roses of Provence; *razed:* Cut, slashed (by way of ornament).   250 *cry:* Pack (as of
hounds); *fellowship...players:* Partnership in a theatrical company.

Horatio: Half a share.°
Hamlet: A whole one, I.
    For thou dost know, O Damon dear,
      This realm dismantled° was
    Of Jove himself; and now reigns here   255
      A very, very° — pajock.°
Horatio: You might have rhymed.
Hamlet: O good Horatio, I'll take the ghost's word for a thousand pound.
    Didst perceive?
Horatio: Very well, my lord.   260
Hamlet: Upon the talk of the poisoning?
Horatio: I did very well note him.
Hamlet: Ah, ha! Come, some music! come, the recorders!°
    For if the king like not the comedy,
    Why then, belike, he likes it not, perdy.°   265
    Come, some music!

    Enter Rosencrantz and Guildenstern.

Guildenstern: Good my lord, vouchsafe me a word with you.
Hamlet: Sir, a whole history.
Guildenstern: The king, sir, —
Hamlet: Ay, sir, what of him?   270
Guildenstern: Is in his retirement marvellous distempered.
Hamlet: With drink, sir?
Guildenstern: No, my lord, rather with choler.°
Hamlet: Your wisdom should show itself more richer to signify this to
    his doctor; for, for me to put him to his purgation would perhaps 275
    plunge him into far more choler.
Guildenstern: Good my lord, put your discourse into some frame° and
    start not so wildly from my affair.
Hamlet: I am tame, sir: pronounce.
Guildenstern: The queen, your mother, in most great affliction of spirit, 280
    hath sent me to you.
Hamlet: You are welcome.
Guildenstern: Nay, good my lord, this courtesy is not of the right breed. If
    it shall please you to make me a wholesome° answer, I will do your
    mother's commandment; if not, your pardon and my return shall be 285
    the end of my business.
Hamlet: Sir, I cannot.
Guildenstern: What, my lord?
Hamlet: Make you a wholesome answer; my wit's diseased: but, sir, such
    answer as I can make, you shall command; or, rather, as you say, my 290
    mother: therefore no more, but to the matter:° my mother, you say, —

---

251 *Half a share:* Allusion to the custom in dramatic companies of dividing the ownership into a number of shares among the householders.   254 *dismantled:* Stripped, divested. 253–256 *For . . . very:* Probably from an old ballad having to do with Damon and Pythias. 256 *pajock:* Peacock (a bird with a bad reputation). Possibly the word was *patchock,* diminutive of *patch,* clown.   263 *recorders:* Wind instruments of the flute kind.   265 *perdy:* Corruption of *par dieu.*   273 *choler:* Bilious disorder, with quibble on the sense "anger." 277 *frame:* Order.   284 *wholesome:* Sensible.   291 *matter:* Matter in hand.

Rosencrantz: Then thus she says; your behaviour hath struck her into amazement and admiration.

Hamlet: O wonderful son, that can so 'stonish a mother! But is there no sequel at the heels of this mother's admiration? Impart. 295

Rosencrantz: She desires to speak with you in her closet, ere you go to bed.

Hamlet: We shall obey, were she ten times our mother. Have you any further trade with us?

Rosencrantz: My lord, you once did love me.

Hamlet: And do still, by these pickers and stealers.° 300

Rosencrantz: Good my lord, what is your cause of distemper? you do, surely, bar the door upon your own liberty, if you deny your griefs to your friend.

Hamlet: Sir, I lack advancement.

Rosencrantz: How can that be, when you have the voice° of the king himself for your succession in Denmark? 305

Hamlet: Ay, sir, but "While the grass grows,"° — the proverb is something musty.

Enter the Players with recorders.

O, the recorders! let me see one. To withdraw° with you: — why do you go about to recover the wind° of me, as if you would drive me into a toil?° 310

Guildenstern: O, my lord, if my duty be too bold, my love is too unmannerly.°

Hamlet: I do not well understand that. Will you play upon this pipe?

Guildenstern: My lord, I cannot. 315

Hamlet: I pray you.

Guildenstern: Believe me, I cannot.

Hamlet: I beseech you.

Guildenstern: I know no touch of it, my lord.

Hamlet: 'Tis as easy as lying: govern these ventages° with your fingers and thumb, give it breath with your mouth, and it will discourse most eloquent music. Look you, these are the stops. 320

Guildenstern: But these cannot I command to any utterance of harmony; I have not the skill.

Hamlet: Why, look you now, how unworthy a thing you make of me! You would play upon me; you would seem to know my stops; you would pluck out the heart of my mystery; you would sound me from my lowest note to the top of my compass:° and there is much music, excellent voice, in this little organ;° yet cannot you make it speak. 'Sblood, do you think I am easier to be played on than a pipe? Call me what instrument you will, though you can fret° me, you cannot play upon me. 325 330

300 *pickers and stealers:* Hands, so called from the catechism "to keep my hands from picking and stealing." 305 *voice:* Support. 307 *"While . . . grows":* The rest of the proverb is "the silly horse starves." Hamlet may be destroyed while he is waiting for the succession to the kingdom. 309 *withdraw:* Speak in private. 310 *recover the wind:* Get to the windward side. 311 *toil:* Snare. 312–313 *if . . . unmannerly:* If I am using an unmannerly boldness, it is my love which occasions it. 320 *ventages:* Stops of the recorders. 328 *compass:* Range of voice. 329 *organ:* Musical instrument, i.e., the pipe. 331 *fret:* Quibble on meaning "irritate" and the piece of wood, gut, or metal which regulates the fingering.

Enter Polonius.

God bless you, sir!
Polonius: My lord, the queen would speak with you, and presently.
Hamlet: Do you see yonder cloud that's almost in shape of a camel?   335
Polonius: By the mass, and 'tis like a camel, indeed.
Hamlet: Methinks it is like a weasel.
Polonius: It is backed like a weasel.
Hamlet: Or like a whale?
Polonius: Very like a whale.   340
Hamlet: Then I will come to my mother by and by. *[Aside.]* They fool me to
the top of my bent.° — I will come by and by.°
Polonius: I will say so.   *[Exit.]*
Hamlet: By and by is easily said.
Leave me, friends.   *[Exeunt all but Hamlet.]* 345
'Tis now the very witching time° of night,
When churchyards yawn and hell itself breathes out
Contagion to this world: now could I drink hot blood,
And do such bitter business as the day
Would quake to look on. Soft! now to my mother.   350
O heart, lose not thy nature; let not ever
The soul of Nero° enter this firm bosom:
Let me be cruel, not unnatural:
I will speak daggers to her, but use none;
My tongue and soul in this be hypocrites;   355
How in my words somever she be shent,°
To give them seals° never, my soul, consent!   *Exit.*

[SCENE III: *A room in the castle.*]

Enter King, Rosencrantz, and Guildenstern.

King: I like him not, nor stands it safe with us
To let his madness range. Therefore prepare you;
I your commission will forthwith dispatch,°
And he to England shall along with you:
The terms° of our estate° may not endure   5
Hazard so near us as doth hourly grow
Out of his brows.°
Guildenstern: We will ourselves provide:
Most holy and religious fear it is
To keep those many many bodies safe
That live and feed upon your majesty.   10
Rosencrantz: The single and peculiar° life is bound,
With all the strength and armour of the mind,

---

342 *top of my bent:* Limit of endurance, i.e., extent to which a bow may be bent; *by and by:* Immediately.   346 *witching time:* I.e., time when spells are cast.   352 *Nero:* Murderer of his mother, Agrippina.   356 *shent:* Rebuked.   357 *give them seals:* Confirm with deeds.   **Scene III.**   3 *dispatch:* Prepare.   5 *terms:* Condition, circumstances; *estate:* State.   7 *brows:* Effronteries.   11 *single and peculiar:* Individual and private.

To keep itself from noyance;° but much more
That spirit upon whose weal depend and rest
The lives of many. The cess° of majesty   15
Dies not alone; but, like a gulf,° doth draw
What's near it with it: it is a massy wheel,
Fix'd on the summit of the highest mount,
To whose huge spokes ten thousand lesser things
Are mortis'd and adjoin'd; which, when it falls,   20
Each small annexment, petty consequence,
Attends° the boist'rous ruin. Never alone
Did the king sigh, but with a general groan.

King: Arm° you, I pray you, to this speedy voyage;
For we will fetters put about this fear,   25
Which now goes too free-footed.

Rosencrantz: We will haste us.

          Exeunt Gentlemen [Rosencrantz and Guildenstern].

    Enter Polonius.

Polonius: My lord, he's going to his mother's closet:
Behind the arras° I'll convey° myself,
To hear the process;° I'll warrant she'll tax him home:°
And, as you said, and wisely was it said,   30
'Tis meet that some more audience than a mother,
Since nature makes them partial, should o'erhear
The speech, of vantage.° Fare you well, my liege:
I'll call upon you ere you go to bed,
And tell you what I know.

King: Thanks, dear my lord.   *Exit [Polonius].*   35
O, my offence is rank, it smells to heaven;
It hath the primal eldest curse° upon't,
A brother's murder. Pray can I not,
Though inclination be as sharp as will:°
My stronger guilt defeats my strong intent;   40
And, like a man to double business bound,
I stand in pause where I shall first begin,
And both neglect. What if this cursed hand
Were thicker than itself with brother's blood,
Is there not rain enough in the sweet heavens
To wash it white as snow? Whereto serves mercy   45
But to confront° the visage of offence?
And what's in prayer but this two-fold force,
To be forestalled° ere we come to fall,
Or pardon'd being down? Then I'll look up;   50

---

13 *noyance:* Harm.   15 *cess:* Decease.   16 *gulf:* Whirlpool.   22 *Attends:* Participates in.   24 *Arm:* Prepare.   28 *arras:* Screen of tapestry placed around the walls of household apartments; *convey:* Implication of secrecy, *convey* was often used to mean "steal."   29 *process:* Proceedings; *tax him home:* Reprove him severely.   33 *of vantage:* From an advantageous place.   37 *primal eldest curse:* The curse of Cain, the first to kill his brother.   39 *sharp as will:* I.e., his desire is as strong as his determination.   47 *confront:* Oppose directly.   49 *forestalled:* Prevented.

My fault is past. But, O, what form of prayer
Can serve my turn? "Forgive me my foul murder"?
That cannot be: since I am still possess'd
Of those effects for which I did the murder,
My crown, mine own ambition° and my queen.   55
May one be pardon'd and retain th' offence?°
In the corrupted currents° of this world
Offence's gilded hand° may shove by justice,
And oft 'tis seen the wicked prize° itself
Buys out the law: but 'tis not so above;   60
There is no shuffling,° there the action lies°
In his true nature; and we ourselves compell'd,
Even to the teeth and forehead° of our faults,
To give in evidence. What then? what rests?°
Try what repentance can: what can it not?   65
Yet what can it when one can not repent?
O wretched state! O bosom black as death!
O limed° soul, that, struggling to be free,
Art more engag'd!° Help, angels! Make assay!°
Bow, stubborn knees; and, heart with strings of steel,   70
Be soft as sinews of the new-born babe!
All may be well.   *[He kneels.]*

    Enter Hamlet.

Hamlet: Now might I do it pat,° now he is praying;
    And now I'll do't. And so 'a goes to heaven;
    And so am I reveng'd. That would be scann'd:°   75
    A villain kills my father; and for that,
    I, his sole son, do this same villain send
    To heaven.
    Why, this is hire and salary, not revenge.
    'A took my father grossly, full of bread;°   80
    With all his crimes broad blown,° as flush° as May;
    And how his audit stands who knows save heaven?
    But in our circumstance and course° of thought,
    'Tis heavy with him: and am I then reveng'd,
    To take him in the purging of his soul,   85
    When he is fit and season'd for his passage?°
    No!
    Up, sword; and know thou a more horrid hent:°
    When he is drunk asleep,° or in his rage,
    Or in th' incestuous pleasure of his bed;   90

---

55 *ambition:* I.e., realization of ambition.   56 *offence:* Benefit accruing from offense.
57 *currents:* Courses.   58 *gilded hand:* Hand offering gold as a bribe.   59 *wicked prize:*
Prize won by wickedness.   61 *shuffling:* Escape by trickery; *lies:* Is sustainable.   63 *teeth
and forehead:* Very face.   64 *rests:* Remains.   68 *limed:* Caught as with birdlime.
69 *engag'd:* Embedded; *assay:* Trial.   73 *pat:* Opportunely.   75 *would be scann'd:* Needs
to be looked into.   80 *full of bread:* Enjoying his worldly pleasures (see Ezekiel 16:49).
81 *broad blown:* In full bloom; *flush:* Lusty.   83 *in . . . course:* As we see it in our mortal situation.   86 *fit . . . passage:* I.e., reconciled to heaven by forgiveness of his sins.   88 *hent:*
Seizing; or more probably, occasion of seizure.   89 *drunk asleep:* In a drunken sleep.

At game, a-swearing, or about some act
That has no relish of salvation in't;
Then trip him, that his heels may kick at heaven,
And that his soul may be as damn'd and black
As hell, whereto it goes. My mother stays: 95
This physic° but prolongs thy sickly days.   *Exit.*

King: [Rising] My words fly up, my thoughts remain below:
Words without thoughts never to heaven go.   *Exit.*

[SCENE IV: *The Queen's closet.*]

Enter [Queen] Gertrude and Polonius.

Polonius: 'A will come straight. Look you lay° home to him:
Tell him his pranks have been too broad° to bear with,
And that your grace hath screen'd and stood between
Much heat° and him. I'll sconce° me even here.
Pray you, be round° with him.   5

Hamlet (within): Mother, mother, mother!

Queen: I'll warrant you,
Fear me not: withdraw, I hear him coming.

                                      [Polonius hides behind the arras.]

Enter Hamlet.

Hamlet: Now, mother, what's the matter?

Queen: Hamlet, thou hast thy father much offended.

Hamlet: Mother, you have my father° much offended.   10

Queen: Come, come, you answer with an idle tongue.

Hamlet: Go, go, you question with a wicked tongue.

Queen: Why, how now, Hamlet!

Hamlet: What's the matter now?

Queen: Have you forgot me?

Hamlet: No, by the rood,° not so:
You are the queen, your husband's brother's wife;
And — would it were not so! — you are my mother.   15

Queen: Nay, then, I'll set those to you that can speak.

Hamlet: Come, come, and sit you down; you shall not budge;
You go not till I set you up a glass
Where you may see the inmost part of you.   20

Queen: What wilt thou do? thou wilt not murder me?
Help, help, ho!

Polonius [behind]: What, ho! help, help; help!

Hamlet [drawing]: How now! a rat? Dead, for a ducat, dead!

                                      [Makes a pass through the arras.]

Polonius [behind]: O, I am slain!   *[Falls and dies.]*   25

Queen: O me, what hast thou done?

---

96 *physic:* Purging (by prayer).   **Scene IV.**   1 *lay:* Thrust.   2 *broad:* Unrestrained.
4 *Much heat:* I.e., the king's anger; *sconce:* Hide.   5 *round:* Blunt.   9–10 *thy father, my
father:* I.e., Claudius, the elder Hamlet.   14 *rood:* Cross.

Hamlet: Nay, I know not:
   Is it the king?
Queen: O, what a rash and bloody deed is this!
Hamlet: A bloody deed! almost as bad, good mother,
   As kill a king, and marry with his brother.   30
Queen: As kill a king!
Hamlet: Ay, lady, it was my word.
                [Lifts up the arras and discovers Polonius.]
   Thou wretched, rash, intruding fool, farewell!
   I took thee for thy better: take thy fortune;
   Thou find'st to be too busy is some danger.
   Leave wringing of your hands: peace! sit you down,   35
   And let me wring your heart; for so I shall,
   If it be made of penetrable stuff,
   If damned custom have not braz'd° it so
   That it be proof and bulwark against sense.
Queen: What have I done, that thou dar'st wag thy tongue   40
   In noise so rude against me?
Hamlet: Such an act
   That blurs the grace and blush of modesty,
   Calls virtue hypocrite, takes off the rose
   From the fair forehead of an innocent love
   And sets a blister° there, makes marriage-vows   45
   As false as dicers' oaths: O, such a deed
   As from the body of contraction° plucks
   The very soul, and sweet religion° makes
   A rhapsody° of words: heaven's face does glow
   O'er this solidity and compound mass   50
   With heated visage, as against the doom
   Is thought-sick at the act.°
Queen: Ay me, what act,
   That roars so loud, and thunders in the index?°
Hamlet: Look here, upon this picture, and on this.
   The counterfeit presentment° of two brothers.   55
   See, what a grace was seated on this brow;
   Hyperion's° curls; the front° of Jove himself;
   An eye like Mars, to threaten and command;
   A station° like the herald Mercury
   New-lighted on a heaven-kissing hill;   60
   A combination and a form indeed,
   Where every god did seem to set his seal,
   To give the world assurance° of a man:
   This was your husband. Look you now, what follows:

38 *braz'd:* Brazened, hardened.   45 *sets a blister:* Brands as a harlot.   47 *contraction:*
The marriage contract.   48 *religion:* Religious vows.   49 *rhapsody:* Senseless string.
49–52 *heaven's . . . act:* Heaven's face blushes to look down on this world, and Gertrude's
marriage makes heaven feel as sick as though the day of doom were near.   53 *index:* Prelude or preface.   55 *counterfeit presentment:* Portrayed representation.   57 *Hyperion's:*
The sun god's; *front:* Brow.   59 *station:* Manner of standing.   63 *assurance:* Pledge,
guarantee.

Here is your husband; like a mildew'd ear,° 65
Blasting his wholesome brother. Have you eyes?
Could you on this fair mountain leave to feed,
And batten° on this moor?° Ha! have you eyes?
You cannot call it love; for at your age
The hey-day° in the blood is tame, it's humble, 70
And waits upon the judgement: and what judgement
Would step from this to this? Sense, sure, you have,
Else could you not have motion;° but sure, that sense
Is apoplex'd;° for madness would not err,
Nor sense to ecstasy was ne'er so thrall'd° 75
But it reserv'd some quantity of choice,°
To serve in such a difference. What devil was't
That thus hath cozen'd° you at hoodman-blind?°
Eyes without feeling, feeling without sight,
Ears without hands or eyes, smelling sans° all, 80
Or but a sickly part of one true sense
Could not so mope.°
O shame! where is thy blush? Rebellious hell,
If thou canst mutine° in a matron's bones,
To flaming youth let virtue be as wax, 85
And melt in her own fire: proclaim no shame
When the compulsive ardour gives the charge,°
Since frost itself as actively doth burn
And reason panders will.°

Queen: O Hamlet, speak no more:
Thou turn'st mine eyes into my very soul; 90
And there I see such black and grained° spots
As will not leave their tinct.

Hamlet: Nay, but to live
In the rank sweat of an enseamed° bed,
Stew'd in corruption, honeying and making love
Over the nasty sty,—

Queen: O, speak to me no more; 95
These words, like daggers, enter in mine ears;
No more, sweet Hamlet!

Hamlet: A murderer and a villain;
A slave that is not twentieth part the tithe
Of your precedent lord;° a vice of kings;°

---

65 *mildew'd ear:* See Genesis 41:5-7.   68 *batten:* Grow fat; *moor:* Barren upland.   70 *hey-day:* State of excitement.   72-73 *Sense ... motion:* Sense and motion are functions of the middle or sensible soul, the possession of sense being the basis of motion.   74 *apoplex'd:* Paralyzed. Mental derangement was thus of three sorts: apoplexy, ecstasy, and diabolic possession.   75 *thrall'd:* Enslaved.   76 *quantity of choice:* Fragment of the power to choose.   78 *cozen'd:* Tricked, cheated; *hoodman-blind:* Blindman's buff.   80 *sans:* Without.   82 *mope:* Be in a depressed, spiritless state, act aimlessly.   84 *mutine:* Mutiny, rebel.   87 *gives the charge:* Delivers the attack.   89 *reason panders will:* The normal and proper situation was one in which reason guided the will in the direction of good; here, reason is perverted and leads in the direction of evil.   91 *grained:* Dyed in grain.   93 *enseamed:* Loaded with grease, greased.   99 *precedent lord:* I.e., the elder Hamlet; *vice of kings:* Buffoon of kings; a reference to the Vice, or clown, of the morality plays and interludes.

100

A cutpurse of the empire and the rule,
That from a shelf the precious diadem stole,
And put it in his pocket!

Queen: No more!

Enter Ghost.

Hamlet: A king of shreds and patches,°—
Save me, and hover o'er me with your wings,
You heavenly guards! What would your gracious figure?   105

Queen: Alas, he's mad!

Hamlet: Do you not come your tardy son to chide,
That, laps'd in time and passion,° lets go by
Th' important° acting of your dread command?
O, say!   110

Ghost: Do not forget: this visitation
Is but to whet thy almost blunted purpose.
But, look, amazement° on thy mother sits:
O, step between her and her fighting soul:
Conceit in weakest bodies strongest works: 115
Speak to her, Hamlet.

Hamlet: How is it with you, lady?

Queen: Alas, how is 't with you,
That you do bend your eye on vacancy
And with th' incorporal° air do hold discourse?
Forth at your eyes your spirits wildly peep;   120
And, as the sleeping soldiers in th' alarm,
Your bedded° hair, like life in excrements,°
Start up, and stand an° end. O gentle son,
Upon the heat and flame of thy distemper
Sprinkle cool patience. Whereon do you look?   125

Hamlet: On him, on him! Look you, how pale he glares!
His form and cause conjoin'd,° preaching to stones,
Would make them capable.—Do not look upon me;
Lest with this piteous action you convert
My stern effects:° then what I have to do   130
Will want true colour;° tears perchance for blood.

Queen: To whom do you speak this?

Hamlet: Do you see nothing there?

Queen: Nothing at all; yet all that is I see.

Hamlet: Nor did you nothing hear?

Queen: No, nothing but ourselves.

Hamlet: Why, look you there! look, how it steals away!   135

103 *shreds and patches:* I.e., motley, the traditional costume of the Vice.   108 *laps'd . . . passion:* Having suffered time to slip and passion to cool; also explained as "engrossed in casual events and lapsed into mere fruitless passion, so that he no longer entertains a rational purpose." 109 *important:* Urgent.   113 *amazement:* Frenzy, distraction.   119 *incorporal:* Immaterial. 122 *bedded:* Laid in smooth layers; *excrements:* The hair was considered an excrement or voided part of the body.   123 *an:* On.   127 *conjoin'd:* United.   129–130 *convert . . . effects:* Divert me from my stern duty. For *effects,* possibly *affects* (affections of the mind).   131 *want true colour:* Lack good reason so that (with a play on the normal sense of *colour*) I shall shed tears instead of blood.

My father, in his habit as he liv'd!
Look, where he goes, even now, out at the portal!   *Exit Ghost.*
Queen: This is the very coinage of your brain:
     This bodiless creation ecstasy
     Is very cunning in.
Hamlet: Ecstasy!   140
     My pulse, as yours, doth temperately keep time,
     And makes as healthful music: it is not madness
     That I have utt'red: bring me to the test,
     And I the matter will re-word,° which madness
     Would gambol° from. Mother, for love of grace,   145
     Lay not that flattering unction° to your soul,
     That not your trespass, but my madness speaks:
     It will but skin and film the ulcerous place,
     Whiles rank corruption, mining° all within,
     Infects unseen. Confess yourself to heaven;   150
     Repent what's past; avoid what is to come;°
     And do not spread the compost° on the weeds,
     To make them ranker. Forgive me this my virtue;°
     For in the fatness° of these pursy° times
     Virtue itself of vice must pardon beg,   155
     Yea, curb° and woo for leave to do him good.
Queen: O Hamlet, thou hast cleft my heart in twain.
Hamlet: O, throw away the worser part of it,
     And live the purer with the other half.
     Good night: but go not to my uncle's bed;   160
     Assume a virtue, if you have it not.
     That monster, custom, who all sense doth eat,
     Of habits devil, is angel yet in this,
     That to the use of actions fair and good
     He likewise gives a frock or livery,   165
     That aptly is put on. Refrain to-night,
     And that shall lend a kind of easiness
     To the next abstinence: the next more easy;
     For use almost can change the stamp of nature,
     And either . . . the devil, or throw him out°   170
     With wondrous potency. Once more, good night:
     And when you are desirous to be bless'd,°
     I'll blessing beg of you. For this same lord,   *[Pointing to Polonius.]*
     I do repent: but heaven hath pleas'd it so,
     To punish me with this and this with me,   175
     That I must be their scourge and minister.
     I will bestow him, and will answer well

---

144 *re-word:* Repeat in words.   145 *gambol:* Skip away.   146 *unction:* Ointment used medicinally or as a rite; suggestion that forgiveness for sin may not be so easily achieved. 149 *mining:* Working under the surface.   151 *what is to come:* I.e., the sins of the future. 152 *compost:* Manure.   153 *this my virtue:* My virtuous talk in reproving you.   154 *fatness:* Grossness; *pursy:* Short-winded, corpulent.   156 *curb:* Bow, bend the knee.   170 Defective line usually emended by inserting *master* after *either.*   172 *be bless'd:* Become blessed, i.e., repentant.

The death I gave him. So, again, good night.	
I must be cruel, only to be kind:	
Thus bad begins and worse remains behind.	180
One word more, good lady.	

Queen: What shall I do?
Hamlet: Not this, by no means, that I bid you do:
    Let the bloat° king tempt you again to bed;
    Pinch wanton on your cheek; call you his mouse;
    And let him, for a pair of reechy° kisses,   185
    Or paddling in your neck with his damn'd fingers,
    Make you to ravel all this matter out,
    That I essentially° am not in madness,
    But mad in craft. 'Twere good you let him know;
    For who, that's but a queen, fair, sober, wise,   190
    Would from a paddock,° from a bat, a gib,°
    Such dear concernings° hide? who would do so?
    No, in despite of sense and secrecy,
    Unpeg the basket on the house's top,
    Let the birds fly, and, like the famous ape,°   195
    To try conclusions,° in the basket creep,
    And break your own neck down.
Queen: Be thou assur'd, if words be made of breath,
    And breath of life, I have no life to breathe
    What thou hast said to me.   200
Hamlet: I must to England; you know that?
Queen: Alack,
    I had forgot: 'tis so concluded on.
Hamlet: There's letters seal'd: and my two schoolfellows,
    Whom I will trust as I will adders fang'd,
    They bear the mandate; they must sweep my way,°   205
    And marshal me to knavery. Let it work;
    For 'tis the sport to have the enginer°
    Hoist° with his own petar:° and 't shall go hard
    But I will delve one yard below their mines,
    And blow them at the moon: O, 'tis most sweet,   210
    When in one line two crafts° directly meet.
    This man shall set me packing:°
    I'll lug the guts into the neighbour room.
    Mother, good night. Indeed this counsellor
    Is now most still, most secret and most grave,   215

---

183 *bloat:* Bloated.   185 *reechy:* Dirty, filthy.   188 *essentially:* In my essential nature. 191 *paddock:* Toad; *gib:* Tomcat.   192 *dear concernings:* Important affairs.   195 *the famous ape:* A letter from Sir John Suckling seems to supply other details of the story, otherwise not identified: "It is the story of the jackanapes and the partridges; thou starest after a beauty till it be lost to thee, then let'st out another, and starest after that till it is gone too." 196 *conclusions:* Experiments.   205 *sweep my way:* Clear my path.   207 *enginer:* Constructor of military works, or possibly, artilleryman.   208 *Hoist:* Blown up; *petar:* Defined as a small engine of war used to blow in a door or make a breach, and as a case filled with explosive materials.   211 *two crafts:* Two acts of guile, with quibble on the sense of "two ships."   212 *set me packing:* Set me to making schemes, and set me to lugging (him), and, also, send me off in a hurry.

Who was in life a foolish prating knave.
Come, sir, to draw° toward an end with you.
Good night, mother.   *Exeunt [severally; Hamlet dragging in Polonius.]*

[ACT IV

SCENE I: *A room in the castle.]*

Enter King and Queen, with Rosencrantz and Guildenstern.

King: There's matter in these sighs, these profound heaves:
You must translate: 'tis fit we understand them.
Where is your son?
Queen: Bestow this place on us a little while.
                                        [Exeunt Rosencrantz and Guildenstern.]
Ah, mine own lord, what have I seen to-night!   5
King: What, Gertrude? How does Hamlet?
Queen: Mad as the sea and wind, when both contend
Which is the mightier: in his lawless fit,
Behind the arras hearing something stir,
Whips out his rapier, cries, "A rat, a rat!"   10
And, in this brainish° apprehension,° kills
The unseen good old man.
King: O heavy deed!
It had been so with us, had we been there:
His liberty is full of threats to all;
To you yourself, to us, to every one.   15
Alas, how shall this bloody deed be answer'd?
It will be laid to us, whose providence°
Should have kept short,° restrain'd and out of haunt,°
This mad young man: but so much was our love,
We would not understand what was most fit;   20
But, like the owner of a foul disease,
To keep it from divulging,° let it feed
Even on the pith of life. Where is he gone?
Queen: To draw apart the body he hath kill'd:
O'er whom his very madness, like some ore   25
Among a mineral° of metals base,
Shows itself pure; 'a weeps for what is done.
King: O Gertrude, come away!
The sun no sooner shall the mountains touch,
But we will ship him hence: and this vile deed   30
We must, with all our majesty and skill,
Both countenance and excuse. Ho, Guildenstern!

---

217 *draw:* Come, with quibble on literal sense.   **Act IV, Scene I.**   11 *brainish:* Head-strong, passionate; *apprehension:* Conception, imagination.   17 *providence:* Foresight.
18 *short:* I.e., on a short tether; *out of haunt:* Secluded.   22 *divulging:* Becoming evident.
26 *mineral:* Mine.

Enter Rosencrantz and Guildenstern.

Friends both, go join you with some further aid:
Hamlet in madness hath Polonius slain,
And from his mother's closet hath he dragg'd him: 35
Go seek him out; speak fair, and bring the body
Into the chapel. I pray you, haste in this.
                     [Exeunt Rosencrantz and Guildenstern.]
Come, Gertrude, we'll call up our wisest friends;
And let them know, both what we mean to do,
And what's untimely done . . .°   40
Whose whisper o'er the world's diameter,°
As level° as the cannon to his blank,°
Transports his pois'ned shot, may miss our name,
And hit the woundless° air. O, come away!
My soul is full of discord and dismay.   *Exeunt.*   45

[SCENE II: *Another room in the castle.*]

Enter Hamlet.

Hamlet: Safely stowed.
Rosencrantz: ⎫
Guildenstern: ⎬ *(within)* Hamlet! Lord Hamlet!
Hamlet: But soft, what noise? who calls on Hamlet? O, here they come.

Enter Rosencrantz and Guildenstern.

Rosencrantz: What have you done, my lord, with the dead body?
Hamlet: Compounded it with dust, whereto 'tis kin.
Rosencrantz: Tell us where 'tis, that we may take it thence   5
    And bear it to the chapel.
Hamlet: Do not believe it.
Rosencrantz: Believe what?
Hamlet: That I can keep your counsel° and not mine own. Besides, to be
    demanded of a sponge! what replication° should be made by the son   10
    of a king?
Rosencrantz: Take you me for a sponge, my lord?
Hamlet: Ay, sir, that soaks up the king's countenance, his rewards, his
    authorities.° But such officers do the king best service in the end: he
    keeps them, like an ape an apple, in the corner of his jaw; first   15
    mouthed, to be last swallowed: when he needs what you have gleaned,
    it is but squeezing you, and, sponge, you shall be dry again.
Rosencrantz: I understand you not, my lord.
Hamlet: I am glad of it: a knavish speech sleeps in a foolish ear.
Rosencrantz: My lord, you must tell us where the body is, and go with us   20
    to the king.

---

40 Defective line; some editors add: *so, haply, slander;* others add: *for, haply, slander;* other
conjectures.   41 *diameter:* Extent from side to side.   42 *level:* Straight; *blank:* White
spot in the center of a target.   44 *woundless:* Invulnerable.   **Scene II.**   9 *keep your
counsel:* Hamlet is aware of their treachery but says nothing about it.   10 *replication:*
Reply.   14 *authorities:* Authoritative backing.

Hamlet: The body is with the king, but the king is not with the body.° The
    king is a thing—
Guildenstern: A thing, my lord!
Hamlet: Of nothing: bring me to him. Hide fox, and all after.°   *Exeunt.*   25

[SCENE III: *Another room in the castle.*]

    Enter King, and two or three.

King: I have sent to seek him, and to find the body.
    How dangerous is it that this man goes loose!
    Yet must not we put the strong law on him:
    He's lov'd of the distracted° multitude,
    Who like not in their judgement, but their eyes;   5
    And where 'tis so, th' offender's scourge° is weigh'd,°
    But never the offence. To bear all smooth and even,
    This sudden sending him away must seem
    Deliberate pause:° diseases desperate grown
    By desperate appliance are reliev'd,   10
    Or not at all.

    Enter Rosencrantz, [Guildenstern,] and all the rest.

        How now! what hath befall'n?
Rosencrantz: Where the dead body is bestow'd, my lord,
    We cannot get from him.
King: But where is he?
Rosencrantz: Without, my lord; guarded, to know your pleasure.
King: Bring him before us.   15
Rosencrantz: Ho! bring in the lord.

    They enter [with Hamlet].

King: Now, Hamlet, where's Polonius?
Hamlet: At supper.
King: At supper! where?
Hamlet: Not where he eats, but where 'a is eaten: a certain convocation of   20
    politic° worms° are e'en at him. Your worm is your only emperor for
    diet: we fat all creatures else to fat us, and we fat ourselves for mag-
    gots: your fat king and your lean beggar is but variable service,° two
    dishes, but to one table: that's the end.
King: Alas, alas!   25

---

22 *The body . . . body:* There are many interpretations; possibly, "The body lies in death with
the king, my father; but my father walks disembodied"; or "Claudius has the bodily possession of kingship, but kingliness, or justice of inheritance, is not with him."   25 *Hide . . .
after:* An old signal cry in the game of hide-and-seek.   **Scene III.**   4 *distracted:* I.e., without power of forming logical judgments.   6 *scourge:* Punishment; *weigh'd:* Taken into
consideration.   9 *Deliberate pause:* Considered action.   20–21 *convocation . . . worms:* Allusion to the Diet of Worms (1521).   21 *politic:* Crafty.   23 *variable service:* A variety of
dishes.

Hamlet: A man may fish with the worm that hath eat of a king, and eat of
  the fish that hath fed of that worm.
King: What dost thou mean by this?
Hamlet: Nothing but to show you how a king may go a progress° through
  the guts of a beggar.   30
King: Where is Polonius?
Hamlet: In heaven; send thither to see: if your messenger find him not
  there, seek him i' the other place yourself. But if indeed you find him
  not within this month, you shall nose him as you go up the stairs
  into the lobby.   35
King [to some Attendants]: Go seek him there.
Hamlet: 'A will stay till you come.   *[Exeunt Attendants.]*
King: Hamlet, this deed, for thine especial safety, —
  Which we do tender,° as we dearly grieve
  For that which thou hast done, — must send thee hence   40
  With fiery quickness: therefore prepare thyself;
  The bark is ready, and the wind at help,
  Th' associates tend, and everything is bent
  For England.
Hamlet: For England!
King: Ay, Hamlet.
Hamlet: Good.
King: So is it, if thou knew'st our purposes.   45
Hamlet: I see a cherub° that sees them. But, come; for England! Farewell,
  dear mother.
King: Thy loving father, Hamlet.
Hamlet: My mother: father and mother is man and wife; man and wife is
  one flesh; and so, my mother. Come, for England!   *Exit.*   50
King: Follow him at foot;° tempt him with speed aboard;
  Delay it not; I'll have him hence to-night:
  Away! for every thing is seal'd and done
  That else leans on th' affair: pray you, make haste.
                                          [Exeunt all but the King.]
  And, England, if my love thou hold'st at aught —   55
  As my great power thereof may give thee sense,
  Since yet thy cicatrice° looks raw and red
  After the Danish sword, and thy free awe°
  Pays homage to us — thou mayst not coldly set
  Our sovereign process; which imports at full,   60
  By letters congruing to that effect,
  The present death of Hamlet. Do it, England;
  For like the hectic° in my blood he rages,
  And thou must cure me: till I know 'tis done,
  Howe'er my haps,° my joys were ne'er begun.   *Exit.*   65

---

29 *progress:* Royal journey of state.   39 *tender:* Regard, hold dear.   46 *cherub:* Cheru-
bim are angels of knowledge.   51 *at foot:* Close behind, at heel.   57 *cicatrice:* Scar.
58 *free awe:* Voluntary show of respect.   63 *hectic:* Fever.   65 *haps:* Fortunes.

[SCENE IV: *A plain in Denmark.*]

Enter Fortinbras with his Army over the stage.

Fortinbras: Go, captain, from me greet the Danish king;
Tell him that, by his license,° Fortinbras
Craves the conveyance° of a promis'd march
Over his kingdom. You know the rendezvous.
If that his majesty would aught with us,   5
We shall express our duty in his eye;°
And let him know so.
Captain: I will do't, my lord.
Fortinbras: Go softly° on.   *[Exeunt all but Captain.]*

Enter Hamlet, Rosencrantz, [Guildenstern,] &c.

Hamlet: Good sir, whose powers are these?
Captain: They are of Norway, sir.
Hamlet: How purpos'd, sir, I pray you?   10
Captain: Against some part of Poland.
Hamlet: Who commands them, sir?
Captain: The nephew to old Norway, Fortinbras.
Hamlet: Goes it against the main° of Poland, sir,   15
Or for some frontier?
Captain: Truly to speak, and with no addition,
We go to gain a little patch of ground
That hath in it no profit but the name.
To pay five ducats, five, I would not farm it;°   20
Nor will it yield to Norway or the Pole
A ranker rate, should it be sold in fee.°
Hamlet: Why, then the Polack never will defend it.
Captain: Yes, it is already garrison'd.
Hamlet: Two thousand souls and twenty thousand ducats   25
Will not debate the question of this straw:°
This is th' imposthume° of much wealth and peace,
That inward breaks, and shows no cause without
Why the man dies. I humbly thank you, sir.
Captain: God be wi' you, sir.   *[Exit.]*
Rosencrantz: Will 't please you go, my lord?   30
Hamlet: I'll be with you straight. Go a little before.
                                            [Exeunt all except Hamlet.]
How all occasions° do inform against° me,
And spur my dull revenge! What is a man,
If his chief good and market of his time°

Scene IV.   2 *license:* Leave.   3 *conveyance:* Escort, convoy.   6 *in his eye:* In his presence.   8 *softly:* Slowly.   15 *main:* Country itself.   20 *farm it:* Take a lease of it.
22 *fee:* Fee simple.   26 *debate . . . straw:* Settle this trifling matter.   27 *imposthume:*
Purulent abscess or swelling.   32 *occasions:* Incidents, events; *inform against:* Generally
defined as "show," "betray" (i.e., his tardiness); more probably *inform* means "take shape," as
in *Macbeth,* II.i.48.   34 *market of his time:* The best use he makes of his time, or, that for
which he sells his time.

Be but to sleep and feed? a beast, no more. 35
Sure, he that made us with such large discourse,
Looking before and after, gave us not
That capability and god-like reason
To fust° in us unus'd. Now, whether it be
Bestial oblivion, or some craven scruple 40
Of thinking too precisely on th' event,
A thought which, quarter'd, hath but one part wisdom
And ever three parts coward, I do not know
Why yet I live to say "This thing 's to do";
Sith I have cause and will and strength and means 45
To do 't. Examples gross as earth exhort me:
Witness this army of such mass and charge
Led by a delicate and tender prince,
Whose spirit with divine ambition puff'd
Makes mouths at the invisible event, 50
Exposing what is mortal and unsure
To all that fortune, death and danger dare,
Even for an egg-shell. Rightly to be great
Is not to stir without great argument,
But greatly to find quarrel in a straw 55
When honour's at the stake. How stand I then,
That have a father kill'd, a mother stain'd,
Excitements of° my reason and my blood,
And let all sleep? while, to my shame, I see
The imminent death of twenty thousand men, 60
That, for a fantasy and trick° of fame,
Go to their graves like beds, fight for a plot°
Whereon the numbers cannot try the cause,
Which is not tomb enough and continent
To hide the slain? O, from this time forth, 65
My thoughts be bloody, or be nothing worth!　　　　　　*Exit.*

[SCENE V: *Elsinore. A room in the castle.*]

Enter Horatio, [Queen] Gertrude, and a Gentleman.

Queen:　I will not speak with her.
Gentleman:　She is importunate, indeed distract:
　Her mood will needs be pitied.
Queen:　　　　　　　　　　What would she have?
Gentleman:　She speaks much of her father; says she hears
　There's tricks° i' th' world; and hems, and beats her heart;° 5
　Spurns enviously at straws;° speaks things in doubt,
　That carry but half sense: her speech is nothing,
　Yet the unshaped° use of it doth move

---

39 *fust:* Grow moldy.　　58 *Excitements of:* Incentives to.　　61 *trick:* Toy, trifle.　　62 *plot:* Piece of ground.　　**Scene V.**　　5 *tricks:* Deceptions; *heart:* I.e., breast.　　6 *Spurns . . . straws:* Kicks spitefully at small objects in her path.　　8 *unshaped:* Unformed, artless.

The hearers to collection;° they yawn° at it,
And botch° the words up fit to their own thoughts;   10
Which, as her winks, and nods, and gestures yield° them,
Indeed would make one think there might be thought,
Though nothing sure, yet much unhappily.°
Horatio: 'Twere good she were spoken with: for she may strew
Dangerous conjectures in ill-breeding minds.°   15
Queen: Let her come in.   *[Exit Gentleman.]*
      [Aside.] To my sick soul, as sin's true nature is,
Each toy seems prologue to some great amiss:°
So full of artless jealousy is guilt,
It spills itself in fearing to be spilt.°   20

      Enter Ophelia [distracted].

Ophelia: Where is the beauteous majesty of Denmark?
Queen: How now, Ophelia!
Ophelia (she sings): How should I your true love know
      From another one?
By his cockle hat° and staff,   25
      And his sandal shoon.°
Queen: Alas, sweet lady, what imports this song?
Ophelia: Say you? nay, pray you mark.
      (Song) He is dead and gone, lady,
          He is dead and gone;   30
At his head a grass-green turf,
      At his heels a stone.
      O, ho!
Queen: Nay, but, Ophelia —
Ophelia: Pray you, mark   35
      [Sings.] White his shroud as the mountain snow, —

      Enter King.

Queen: Alas, look here, my lord.
Ophelia (Song): Larded° all with flowers;
      Which bewept to the grave did not go
          With true-love showers.
King: How do you, pretty lady?   40
Ophelia: Well, God 'ild° you! They say the owl° was a baker's daughter.
      Lord, we know what we are, but know not what we may be. God be at
      your table!
King: Conceit upon her father.   45

---

9 *collection:* Inference, a guess at some sort of meaning; *yawn:* Wonder.   10 *botch:* Patch.
11 *yield:* Deliver, bring forth (her words).   13 *much unhappily:* Expressive of much unhappiness.   15 *ill-breeding minds:* Minds bent on mischief.   18 *great amiss:* Calamity, disaster.   19–20 *So . . . spilt:* Guilt is so full of suspicion that it unskillfully betrays itself in
fearing to be betrayed.   25 *cockle hat:* Hat with cockleshell stuck in it as a sign that the
wearer has been a pilgrim to the shrine of St. James of Compostella. The pilgrim's garb was a
conventional disguise for lovers.   26 *shoon:* Shoes.   38 *Larded:* Decorated.   42 *God
'ild:* God yield or reward; *owl:* Reference to a monkish legend that a baker's daughter was
turned into an owl for refusing bread to the Savior.

Ophelia: Pray let's have no words of this; but when they ask you what it
　　means, say you this:
　　　(Song) To-morrow is Saint Valentine's day,
　　　　All in the morning betime,
　　　And I a maid at your window,　　　　　　　　　　　　　　　　50
　　　　To be your Valentine.°
　　　Then up he rose, and donn'd his clothes,
　　　　And dupp'd° the chamber-door;
　　　Let in the maid, that out a maid
　　　　Never departed more.　　　　　　　　　　　　　　　　　55
King: Pretty Ophelia!
Ophelia: Indeed, la, without an oath, I'll make an end on 't:
　　　[Sings.] By Gis° and by Saint Charity,
　　　　Alack, and fie for shame!
　　　Young men will do 't, if they come to 't;　　　　　　　　　　60
　　　　By cock,° they are to blame.
　　　Quoth she, before you tumbled me,
　　　　You promis'd me to wed.
　　　So would I ha' done, by yonder sun,
　　　　An thou hadst not come to my bed.　　　　　　　　　　　65
King: How long hath she been thus?
Ophelia: I hope all will be well. We must be patient: but I cannot choose
　　but weep, to think they would lay him i' the cold ground. My brother
　　shall know of it: and so I thank you for your good counsel. Come, my
　　coach! Good night, ladies; good night, sweet ladies; good night, good　70
　　night.　　　　　　　　　　　　　　　　　　　　　　*[Exit.]*
King: Follow her close; give her good watch, I pray you.　　*[Exit Horatio.]*
　　O, this is the poison of deep grief; it springs
　　All from her father's death. O Gertrude, Gertrude,
　　When sorrows come, they come not single spies,　　　　　　75
　　But in battalions. First, her father slain:
　　Next your son gone; and he most violent author
　　Of his own just remove: the people muddied,
　　Thick and unwholesome in their thoughts and whispers,
　　For good Polonius' death; and we have done but greenly,°　　80
　　In hugger-mugger° to inter him: poor Ophelia
　　Divided from herself and her fair judgement,
　　Without the which we are pictures, or mere beasts:
　　Last, and as much containing as all these,
　　Her brother is in secret come from France;　　　　　　　　85
　　Feeds on his wonder, keeps himself in clouds,°
　　And wants not buzzers° to infect his ear
　　With pestilent speeches of his father's death;
　　Wherein necessity, of matter beggar'd,°
　　Will nothing stick° our person to arraign　　　　　　　　　90

51 *Valentine:* This song alludes to the belief that the first girl seen by a man on the morning of this day was his valentine or true love.　53 *dupp'd:* Opened.　58 *Gis:* Jesus.
61 *cock:* Perversion of "God" in oaths.　80 *greenly:* Foolishly.　81 *hugger-mugger:* Secret
haste.　86 *in clouds:* Invisible.　87 *buzzers:* Gossipers.　89 *of matter beggar'd:* Unprovided with facts.　90 *nothing stick:* Not hesitate.

In ear and ear.° O my dear Gertrude, this,
Like to a murd'ring-piece,° in many places
Gives me superfluous death. *A noise within.*
Queen: Alack, what noise is this?
King: Where are my Switzers?° Let them guard the door.

Enter a Messenger.

What is the matter?
Messenger: Save yourself, my lord: 95
The ocean, overpeering° of his list,°
Eats not the flats with more impiteous haste
Than young Laertes, in a riotous head,
O'erbears your officers. The rabble call him lord;
And, as the world were now but to begin, 100
Antiquity forgot, custom not known,
The ratifiers and props of every word,°
They cry "Choose we: Laertes shall be king":
Caps, hands, and tongues, applaud it to the clouds:
"Laertes shall be king, Laertes king!" *A noise within.* 105
Queen: How cheerfully on the false trail they cry!
O, this is counter,° you false Danish dogs!
King: The doors are broke.

Enter Laertes with others.

Laertes: Where is this king? Sirs, stand you all without.
Danes: No, let's come in.
Laertes: I pray you, give me leave. 110
Danes: We will, we will. *[They retire without the door.]*
Laertes: I thank you: keep the door. O thou vile king,
Give me my father!
Queen: Calmly, good Laertes.
Laertes: That drop of blood that's calm proclaims me bastard,
Cries cuckold to my father, brands the harlot 115
Even here, between the chaste unsmirched brow
Of my true mother.
King: What is the cause, Laertes,
That thy rebellion looks so giant-like?
Let him go, Gertrude; do not fear our person:
There's such divinity doth hedge a king, 120
That treason can but peep to° what it would,°
Acts little of his will. Tell me, Laertes,
Why thou art thus incens'd. Let him go, Gertrude.
Speak, man.
Laertes: Where is my father?
King: Dead.
Queen: But not by him. 125

---

91 *In ear and ear:* In everybody's ears. 92 *murd'ring-piece:* Small cannon or mortar; suggestion of numerous missiles fired. 94 *Switzers:* Swiss guards, mercenaries. 96 *overpeering:* Overflowing; *list:* Shore. 102 *word:* Promise. 107 *counter:* A hunting term meaning to follow the trail in a direction opposite to that which the game has taken. 121 *peep to:* I.e., look at from afar off; *would:* Wishes to do.

King: Let him demand his fill.

Laertes: How came he dead? I'll not be juggled with:

    To hell, allegiance! vows, to the blackest devil!

    Conscience and grace, to the profoundest pit!

    I dare damnation. To this point I stand,   130

    That both the worlds I give to negligence,°

    Let come what comes; only I'll be reveng'd

    Most throughly° for my father.

King: Who shall stay you?

Laertes: My will,° not all the world's:

    And for my means, I'll husband them so well,   135

    They shall go far with little.

King: Good Laertes,

    If you desire to know the certainty

    Of your dear father, is 't writ in your revenge,

    That, swoopstake,° you will draw both friend and foe,

    Winner and loser?   140

Laertes: None but his enemies.

King: Will you know them then?

Laertes: To his good friends thus wide I'll ope my arms;

    And like the kind life-rend'ring pelican,°

    Repast° them with my blood.

King: Why, now you speak

    Like a good child and a true gentleman.   145

    That I am guiltless of your father's death,

    And am most sensibly in grief for it,

    It shall as level to your judgement 'pear

    As day does to your eye.   *A noise within: "Let her come in."*

Laertes: How now! what noise is that?   150

    Enter Ophelia.

    O heat,° dry up my brains! tears seven times salt,

    Burn out the sense and virtue of mine eye!

    By heaven, thy madness shall be paid with weight,

    Till our scale turn the beam. O rose of May!

    Dear maid, kind sister, sweet Ophelia!   155

    O heavens! is 't possible, a young maid's wits

    Should be as mortal as an old man's life?

    Nature is fine in love, and where 'tis fine,

    It sends some precious instance of itself

    After the thing it loves.   160

Ophelia (Song): They bore him barefac'd on the bier;

    Hey non nonny, nonny, hey nonny;

    And in his grave rain'd many a tear: —

    Fare you well, my dove!

---

131 *give to negligence:* He despises both the here and the hereafter.   133 *throughly:* thoroughly.   134 *My will:* He will not be stopped except by his own will.   139 *swoopstake:* Literally, drawing the whole stake at once, i.e., indiscriminately.   143 *pelican:* Reference to the belief that the pelican feeds its young with its own blood.   144 *Repast:* Feed.   151 *heat:* Probably the heat generated by the passion of grief.

Laertes: Hadst thou thy wits, and didst persuade revenge,   165
     It could not move thus.
Ophelia [sings]: You must sing a-down a-down,
         An you call him a-down-a.
     O, how the wheel° becomes it! It is the false steward,° that stole his
     master's daughter.   170
Laertes: This nothing's more than matter.
Ophelia: There's rosemary,° that's for remembrance; pray you, love,
     remember: and there is pansies,° that's for thoughts.
Laertes: A document° in madness, thoughts and remembrance fitted.
Ophelia: There's fennel° for you, and columbines:° there's rue° for you;   175
     and here's some for me: we may call it herb of grace° o' Sundays: O,
     you must wear your rue with a difference. There's a daisy:° I would
     give you some violets,° but they withered all when my father died:
     they say 'a made a good end, —
     [Sings.] For bonny sweet Robin is all my joy.°   180
Laertes: Thought° and affliction, passion, hell itself,
     She turns to favour and to prettiness.
Ophelia (Song): And will 'a not come again?°
     And will 'a not come again?
         No, no, he is dead: 185
         Go to thy death-bed:
     He never will come again.

     His beard was as white as snow,
     All flaxen was his poll:°
         He is gone, he is gone,
         And we cast away° moan: 190
     God ha' mercy on his soul!
     And of all Christian souls, I pray God. God be wi' you.   *[Exit.]*
Laertes: Do you see this, O God?
King: Laertes, I must commune with your grief,   195
     Or you deny me right.° Go but apart,
     Make choice of whom your wisest friends you will,
     And they shall hear and judge 'twixt you and me:
     If by direct or by collateral° hand
     They find us touch'd,° we will our kingdom give,   200
     Our crown, our life, and all that we call ours,
     To you in satisfaction; but if not,

---

169 *wheel:* Spinning wheel as accompaniment to the song refrain; *false steward:* The story is unknown.   172 *rosemary:* Used as a symbol of remembrance both at weddings and at funerals.   173 *pansies:* Emblems of love and courtship (from the French *pensée*).   174 *document:* Piece of instruction or lesson.   175, 176 *fennel:* Emblem of flattery; *columbines:* Emblem of unchastity (?) or ingratitude (?); *rue:* Emblem of repentance. It was usually mingled with holy water and then known as *herb of grace*. Ophelia is probably playing on the two meanings of *rue*, "repentant" and "even for ruth (pity)"; the former signification is for the queen, the latter for herself.   177 *daisy:* Emblem of dissembling, faithlessness.   178 *violets:* Emblems of faithfulness.   180 *For . . . joy:* Probably a line from a Robin Hood ballad.   181 *Thought:* Melancholy thought.   183 *And . . . again:* This song appeared in the songbooks as "The Merry Milkmaids' Dumps."   189 *poll:* Head.   191 *cast away:* Shipwrecked.   196 *right:* My rights.   199 *collateral:* Indirect.   200 *touch'd:* Implicated.

Be you content to lend your patience to us,
And we shall jointly labour with your soul
To give it due content.
Laertes: Let this be so;   205
His means of death, his obscure funeral —
No trophy, sword, nor hatchment° o'er his bones,
No noble rite nor formal ostentation —
Cry to be heard, as 'twere from heaven to earth,
That I must call 't in question.
King: So you shall;   210
And where th' offence is let the great axe fall.
I pray you, go with me.   *Exeunt.*

[SCENE VI: *Another room in the castle.*]

Enter Horatio and others.

Horatio: What are they that would speak with me?
Gentleman: Sea-faring men, sir: they say they have letters for you.
Horatio: Let them come in.   *[Exit Gentleman.]*
I do not know from what part of the world
I should be greeted, if not from lord Hamlet.   5

Enter Sailors.

First Sailor: God bless you, sir.
Horatio: Let him bless thee too.
First Sailor: 'A shall sir, an 't please him. There's a letter for you, sir; it
comes from the ambassador that was bound for England; if your
name be Horatio, as I am let to know it is.   10
Horatio [reads]: "Horatio, when thou shalt have overlooked this, give
these fellows some means° to the king: they have letters for him. Ere
we were two days old at sea, a pirate of very warlike appointment gave
us chase. Finding ourselves too slow of sail, we put on a compelled
valour, and in the grapple I boarded them: on the instant they got   15
clear of our ship; so I alone became their prisoner. They have dealt
with me like thieves of mercy:° but they knew what they did; I am to
do a good turn for them. Let the king have the letters I have sent; and
repair thou to me with as much speed as thou wouldest fly death. I
have words to speak in thine ear will make thee dumb; yet are they   20
much too light for the bore° of the matter. These good fellows will
bring thee where I am. Rosencrantz and Guildenstern hold their
course for England: of them I have much to tell thee. Farewell.
                              "He that thou knowest thine, HAMLET."
Come, I will give you way for these your letters;   25
And do 't the speedier, that you may direct me
To him from whom you brought them.   *Exeunt.*

---

207 *hatchment:* Tablet displaying the armorial bearings of a deceased person.   **Scene VI.**
12 *means:* Means of access.   17 *thieves of mercy:* Merciful thieves.   21 *bore:* Caliber, importance.

[SCENE VII: *Another room in the castle.*]

Enter King and Laertes.

King: Now must your conscience° my acquittance seal,
        And you must put me in your heart for friend,
        Sith you have heard, and with a knowing ear,
        That he which hath your noble father slain
        Pursued my life.
Laertes: It well appears: but tell me   5
        Why you proceeded not against these feats,
        So criminal and so capital° in nature,
        As by your safety, wisdom, all things else,
        You mainly° were stirr'd up.
King: O, for two special reasons;
        Which may to you, perhaps, seem much unsinew'd,°   10
        But yet to me th' are strong. The queen his mother
        Lives almost by his looks; and for myself—
        My virtue or my plague, be it either which—
        She's so conjunctive° to my life and soul,
        That, as the star moves not but in his sphere,°   15
        I could not but by her. The other motive,
        Why to a public count° I might not go,
        Is the great love the general gender° bear him;
        Who, dipping all his faults in their affection,
        Would, like the spring° that turneth wood to stone,   20
        Convert his gyves° to graces; so that my arrows,
        Too slightly timber'd° for so loud° a wind,
        Would have reverted to my bow again,
        And not where I had aim'd them.
Laertes: And so have I a noble father lost;   25
        A sister driven into desp'rate terms,°
        Whose worth, if praises may go back° again,
        Stood challenger on mount° of all the age°
        For her perfections: but my revenge will come.
King: Break not your sleeps for that: you must not think   30
        That we are made of stuff so flat and dull
        That we can let our beard be shook with danger
        And think it pastime. You shortly shall hear more:
        I lov'd your father, and we love ourself;
        And that, I hope, will teach you to imagine—   35

Scene VII.   1 *conscience:* Knowledge that this is true.   7 *capital:* Punishable by death.
9 *mainly:* Greatly.   10 *unsinew'd:* Weak.   14 *conjunctive:* Conformable (the next line suggesting planetary conjunction).   15 *sphere:* The hollow sphere in which, according to Ptolemaic astronomy, the planets were supposed to move.   17 *count:* Account, reckoning.
18 *general gender:* Common people.   20 *spring:* I.e., one heavily charged with lime.
21 *gyves:* Fetters; here, faults, or possibly, punishments inflicted (on him).   22 *slightly timber'd:* Light; *loud:* Strong.   26 *terms:* State, condition.   27 *go back:* Return to Ophelia's
former virtues.   28 *on mount:* Set up on high, *mounted* (on horseback); *of all the age:* Qualifies *challenger* and not *mount.*

Enter a Messenger with letters.

How now! what news?

Messenger: Letters, my lord, from Hamlet:
These to your majesty; this to the queen.°

King: From Hamlet! who brought them?

Messenger: Sailors, my lord, they say; I saw them not:
They were given me by Claudio;° he receiv'd them   40
Of him that brought them.

King: Laertes, you shall hear them.
Leave us.   *[Exit Messenger.]*
[Reads.] "High and mighty, You shall know I am set naked° on your
kingdom. To-morrow shall I beg leave to see your kingly eyes: when I
shall, first asking your pardon thereunto, recount the occasion of my   45
sudden and more strange return."   "HAMLET."
What should this mean? Are all the rest come back?
Or is it some abuse, and no such thing?

Laertes: Know you the hand?

King: 'Tis Hamlet's character. "Naked!"
And in a postscript here, he says "alone."   50
Can you devise° me?

Laertes: I'm lost in it, my lord. But let him come;
It warms the very sickness in my heart,
That I shall live and tell him to his teeth,
"Thus didst thou."

King: If it be so, Laertes —   55
As how should it be so? how otherwise?°—
Will you be rul'd by me?

Laertes: Ay, my lord;
So you will not o'errule me to a peace.

King: To thine own peace. If he be now return'd,
As checking at° his voyage, and that he means   60
No more to undertake it, I will work him
To an exploit, now ripe in my device,
Under the which he shall not choose but fall:
And for his death no wind of blame shall breathe,
But even his mother shall uncharge the practice°   65
And call it accident.

Laertes: My lord, I will be rul'd;
The rather, if you could devise it so
That I might be the organ.°

King: It falls right.
You have been talk'd of since your travel much,

---

37 *to the queen:* One hears no more of the letter to the queen.   40 *Claudio:* This character
does not appear in the play.   43 *naked:* Unprovided (with retinue).   51 *devise:* Explain
to.   56 *As ... otherwise?* How can this (Hamlet's return) be true? (yet) how otherwise than
true (since we have the evidence of his letter)? Some editors read *How should it not be so,* etc.,
making the words refer to Laertes's desire to meet with Hamlet.   60 *checking at:* Used in
falconry of a hawk's leaving the quarry to fly at a chance bird; turn aside.   65 *uncharge the
practice:* Acquit the stratagem of being a plot.   68 *organ:* Agent, instrument.

And that in Hamlet's hearing, for a quality 70
Wherein, they say, you shine: your sum of parts
Did not together pluck such envy from him
As did that one, and that, in my regard,
Of the unworthiest siege.°
Laertes: What part is that, my lord?
King: A very riband in the cap of youth, 75
   Yet needful too; for youth no less becomes
   The light and careless livery that it wears
   Than settled age his sables° and his weeds,
   Importing health and graveness. Two months since,
   Here was a gentleman of Normandy: — 80
   I have seen myself, and serv'd against, the French,
   And they can well° on horseback: but this gallant
   Had witchcraft in 't; he grew unto his seat;
   And to such wondrous doing brought his horse,
   As had he been incorps'd and demi-natur'd° 85
   With the brave beast: so far he topp'd° my thought,
   That I, in forgery° of shapes and tricks,
   Come short of what he did.
Laertes: A Norman was 't?
King: A Norman.
Laertes: Upon my life, Lamord.°
King: The very same. 90
Laertes: I know him well: he is the brooch indeed
   And gem of all the nation.
King: He made confession° of you,
   And gave you such a masterly report
   For art and exercise° in your defence° 95
   And for your rapier most especial,
   That he cried out, 'twould be a sight indeed,
   If one could match you: the scrimers° of their nation,
   He swore, had neither motion, guard, nor eye,
   If you oppos'd them. Sir, this report of his 100
   Did Hamlet so envenom with his envy
   That he could nothing do but wish and beg
   Your sudden coming o'er, to play° with you.
   Now, out of this, —
Laertes: What out of this, my lord?
King: Laertes, was your father dear to you? 105
   Or are you like the painting of a sorrow,
   A face without a heart?

---

74 *siege:* Rank.   78 *sables:* Rich garments.   82 *can well:* Are skilled.   85 *incorps'd and demi-natur'd:* Of one body and nearly of one nature (like the centaur).   86 *topp'd:* Surpassed. 87 *forgery:* Invention.   90 *Lamord:* This refers possibly to Pietro Monte, instructor to Louis XII's master of the horse.   93 *confession:* Grudging admission of superiority.   95 *art and exercise:* Skillful exercise; *defence:* Science of defense in sword practice.   98 *scrimers:* Fencers. 103 *play:* Fence.

Laertes: Why ask you this?
King: Not that I think you did not love your father;
      But that I know love is begun by time;
      And that I see, in passages of proof,°   110
      Time qualifies the spark and fire of it.
      There lives within the very flame of love
      A kind of wick or snuff that will abate it;
      And nothing is at a like goodness still;
      For goodness, growing to a plurisy,°   115
      Dies in his own too much:° that we would do,
      We should do when we would; for this "would" changes
      And hath abatements° and delays as many
      As there are tongues, are hands, are accidents;°
      And then this "should" is like a spendthrift° sigh,   120
      That hurts by easing. But, to the quick o' th' ulcer:°—
      Hamlet comes back: what would you undertake,
      To show yourself your father's son in deed
      More than in words?
Laertes: To cut his throat i' th' church.
King: No place, indeed, should murder sanctuarize;°   125
      Revenge should have no bounds. But, good Laertes,
      Will you do this, keep close within your chamber.
      Hamlet return'd shall know you are come home:
      We'll put on those shall praise your excellence
      And set a double varnish on the fame   130
      The Frenchman gave you, bring you in fine together
      And wager on your heads: he, being remiss,
      Most generous and free from all contriving,
      Will not peruse the foils; so that, with ease,
      Or with a little shuffling, you may choose   135
      A sword unbated,° and in a pass of practice°
      Requite him for your father.
Laertes: I will do 't:
      And, for that purpose, I'll anoint my sword.
      I bought an unction of a mountebank,°
      So mortal that, but dip a knife in it,   140
      Where it draws blood no cataplasm° so rare,
      Collected from all simples° that have virtue
      Under the moon,° can save the thing from death
      That is but scratch'd withal: I'll touch my point

---

110 *passages of proof:* Proved instances.   115 *plurisy:* Excess, plethora.   116 *in his own too much:* Of its own excess.   118 *abatements:* Diminutions.   119 *accidents:* Occurrences, incidents.   120 *spendthrift:* An allusion to the belief that each sigh cost the heart a drop of blood.   121 *quick o' th' ulcer:* Heart of the difficulty.   125 *sanctuarize:* Protect from punishment; allusion to the right of sanctuary with which certain religious places were invested. 136 *unbated:* Not blunted, having no button; *pass of practice:* Treacherous thrust. 139 *mountebank:* Quack doctor.   141 *cataplasm:* Plaster or poultice.   142 *simples:* Herbs.   143 *Under the moon:* I.e., when collected by moonlight to add to their medicinal value.

With this contagion, that, if I gall° him slightly,   145
    It may be death.
King: Let's further think of this;
    Weigh what convenience both of time and means
    May fit us to our shape:° if this should fail,
    And that our drift look through our bad performance,°
    'Twere better not assay'd: therefore this project   150
    Should have a back or second, that might hold,
    If this should blast in proof.° Soft! let me see:
    We'll make a solemn wager on your cunnings:°
    I ha 't:
    When in your motion you are hot and dry—   155
    As make your bouts more violent to that end—
    And that he calls for drink, I'll have prepar'd him
    A chalice° for the nonce, whereon but sipping,
    If he by chance escape your venom'd stuck,°
    Our purpose may hold there. But stay, what noise?   160

    Enter Queen.

Queen: One woe doth tread upon another's heel,
    So fast they follow: your sister's drown'd, Laertes.
Laertes: Drown'd! O, where?
Queen: There is a willow° grows askant° the brook,
    That shows his hoar° leaves in the glassy stream;   165
    There with fantastic garlands did she make
    Of crow-flowers,° nettles, daisies, and long purples°
    That liberal° shepherds give a grosser name,
    But our cold maids do dead men's fingers call them:
    There, on the pendent boughs her crownet° weeds   170
    Clamb'ring to hang, an envious sliver° broke;
    When down her weedy° trophies and herself
    Fell in the weeping brook. Her clothes spread wide;
    And, mermaid-like, awhile they bore her up:
    Which time she chanted snatches of old lauds;°   175
    As one incapable° of her own distress,
    Or like a creature native and indued°
    Upon that element: but long it could not be
    Till that her garments, heavy with their drink,
    Pull'd the poor wretch from her melodious lay   180
    To muddy death.
Laertes: Alas, then, she is drown'd?
Queen: Drown'd, drown'd.

---

145 *gall:* Graze, wound.   148 *shape:* Part we propose to act.   149 *drift . . . performance:* Intention be disclosed by our bungling.   152 *blast in proof:* Burst in the test (like a cannon). 153 *cunnings:* Skills.   158 *chalice:* Cup.   159 *stuck:* Thrust (from *stoccado*).   164 *willow:* For its significance of forsaken love; *askant:* Aslant.   165 *hoar:* White (i.e., on the underside).   167 *crow-flowers:* Buttercups; *long purples:* Early purple orchids.   168 *liberal:* Probably, free-spoken.   170 *crownet:* Coronet; made into a chaplet.   171 *sliver:* Branch. 172 *weedy:* I.e., of plants.   175 *lauds:* Hymns.   176 *incapable:* Lacking capacity to apprehend.   177 *indued:* Endowed with qualities fitting her for living in water.

Laertes: Too much of water hast thou, poor Ophelia,
    And therefore I forbid my tears: but yet
    It is our trick;° nature her custom holds,   185
    Let shame say what it will: when these are gone,
    The woman will be out.° Adieu, my lord:
    I have a speech of fire, that fain would blaze,
    But that this folly drowns it.   *Exit.*
King: Let's follow, Gertrude:
    How much I had to do to calm his rage!   190
    Now fear I this will give it start again;
    Therefore let 's follow.   *Exeunt.*

[ACT V

SCENE I: *A churchyard.*]

Enter two Clowns° [with spades, &c.].

First Clown: Is she to be buried in Christian burial when she wilfully seeks
    her own salvation?
Second Clown: I tell thee she is; therefore make her grave straight:° the
    crowner° hath sat on her, and finds it Christian burial.
First Clown: How can that be, unless she drowned herself in her own   5
    defence?
Second Clown: Why, 'tis found so.
First Clown: It must be "se offendendo";° it cannot be else. For here lies
    the point: if I drown myself wittingly,° it argues an act: and an act
    hath three branches;° it is, to act, to do, and to perform: argal,° she   10
    drowned herself wittingly.
Second Clown: Nay, but hear you, goodman delver,° —
First Clown: Give me leave. Here lies the water; good: here stands the man;
    good: if the man go to this water, and drown himself, it is, will he,
    nill he, he goes, — mark you that; but if the water come to him and   15
    drown him, he drowns not himself: argal, he that is not guilty of his
    own death shortens not his own life.
Second Clown: But is this law?
First Clown: Ay, marry, is 't; crowner's quest° law.
Second Clown: Will you ha' the truth on 't? If this had not been a gentle-   20
    woman, she should have been buried out o' Christian burial.
First Clown: Why, there thou say'st:° and the more pity that great folk
    should have countenance° in this world to drown or hang themselves,

185 *trick:* Way.   186–187 *when . . . out:* When my tears are all shed, the woman in me will be
satisfied.   **Act V, Scene I.**   *Clowns:* The word *clown* was used to denote peasants as well
as humorous characters; here applied to the rustic type of clown.   3 *straight:* Straightway,
immediately; some interpret "from east to west in a direct line, parallel with the church."
4 *crowner:* Coroner.   8 *"se offendendo":* For *se defendendo,* term used in verdicts of justifiable homicide.   9 *wittingly:* Intentionally.   10 *three branches:* Parody of legal phrase-
ology; *argal:* Corruption of *ergo,* therefore.   12 *delver:* Digger.   19 *quest:* Inquest.
22 *there thou say'st:* That's right.   23 *countenance:* Privilege.

more than their even° Christian. Come, my spade. There is no ancient
gentlemen but gardeners, ditchers, and grave-makers: they hold up°   25
Adam's profession.

Second Clown: Was he a gentleman?

First Clown: 'A was the first that ever bore arms.

Second Clown: Why, he had none.

First Clown: What, art a heathen? How dost thou understand the Scrip-   30
ture? The Scripture says "Adam digged": could he dig without arms?
I'll put another question to thee: if thou answerest me not to the
purpose, confess thyself° —

Second Clown: Go to.°

First Clown: What is he that builds stronger than either the mason, the   35
shipwright, or the carpenter?

Second Clown: The gallows-maker; for that frame outlives a thousand
tenants.

First Clown: I like thy wit well, in good faith: the gallows does well; but
how does it well? it does well to those that do ill: now thou dost ill to   40
say the gallows is built stronger than the church: argal, the gallows
may do well to thee. To 't again, come.

Second Clown: "Who builds stronger than a mason, a shipwright, or a carpenter?"

First Clown: Ay, tell me that, and unyoke.°   45

Second Clown: Marry, now I can tell.

First Clown: To 't.

Second Clown: Mass,° I cannot tell.

Enter Hamlet and Horatio [at a distance].

First Clown: Cudgel thy brains no more about it, for your dull ass will not
mend his pace with beating; and, when you are asked this question   50
next, say "a grave-maker": the houses he makes lasts till doomsday.
Go, get thee in, and fetch me a stoup° of liquor.
                                        [Exit Second Clown.] Song. [He digs.]
In youth, when I did love, did love,
    Methought it was very sweet,
To contract — O — the time, for — a — my behove,°   55
    O, methought, there — a — was nothing — a — meet.

Hamlet: Has this fellow no feeling of his business, that 'a sings at grave-
making?

Horatio: Custom hath made it in him a property of easiness.°

Hamlet: 'Tis e'en so: the hand of little employment hath the daintier   60
sense.

First Clown: *(Song.)* But age, with his stealing steps,
    Hath claw'd me in his clutch,
And hath shipped me into the land
    As if I had never been such.   *[Throws up a skull.]*   65

---

24 *even:* Fellow.   25 *hold up:* Maintain, continue.   33 *confess thyself:* "And be hanged"
completes the proverb.   34 *Go to:* Perhaps, "begin," or some other form of concession.
45 *unyoke:* After this great effort you may unharness the team of your wits.   48 *Mass:* By
the Mass.   52 *stoup:* Two-quart measure.   55 *behove:* Benefit.   59 *property of easiness:*
A peculiarity that now is easy.

Hamlet: That skull had a tongue in it, and could sing once: how the knave
    jowls° it to the ground, as if 'twere Cain's jaw-bone,° that did the first
    murder! This might be the pate of a politician,° which this ass now
    o'er-reaches;° one that would circumvent God, might it not?

Horatio: It might, my lord. 70

Hamlet: Or of a courtier; which could say "Good morrow, sweet lord! How
    dost thou, sweet lord?" This might be my lord such-a-one, that
    praised my lord such-a-one's horse, when he meant to beg it; might it
    not?

Horatio: Ay, my lord. 75

Hamlet: Why, e'en so: and now my Lady Worm's; chapless,° and knocked
    about the mazzard° with a sexton's spade: here's fine revolution, an
    we had the trick to see 't. Did these bones cost no more the breeding,
    but to play at loggats° with 'em? mine ache to think on 't.

First Clown: (*Song.*) A pick-axe, and a spade, a spade, 80
        For and° a shrouding sheet:
    O, a pit of clay for to be made
        For such a guest is meet.   *[Throws up another skull.]*

Hamlet: There's another: why may not that be the skull of a lawyer?
    Where be his quiddities° now, his quillities,° his cases, his tenures,° 85
    and his tricks? why does he suffer this mad knave now to knock him
    about the sconce° with a dirty shovel, and will not tell him of his ac-
    tion of battery? Hum! This fellow might be in 's time a great buyer
    of land, with his statutes, his recognizances,° his fines, his double
    vouchers,° his recoveries:° is this the fine° of his fines, and the re- 90
    covery of his recoveries, to have his fine pate full of fine dirt? will
    his vouchers vouch him no more of his purchases, and double ones
    too, than the length and breadth of a pair of indentures?° The very
    conveyances of his lands will scarcely lie in this box; and must the
    inheritor° himself have no more, ha? 95

Horatio: Not a jot more, my lord.

Hamlet: Is not parchment made of sheep-skins?

Horatio: Ay, my lord, and of calf-skins° too.

Hamlet: They are sheep and calves which seek out assurance in that.°
    I will speak to this fellow. Whose grave's this, sirrah? 100

First Clown: Mine, sir.
    [Sings.] O, a pit of clay for to be made
        For such a guest is meet.

Hamlet: I think it be thine, indeed; for thou liest in 't.

---

67 *jowls:* Dashes; *Cain's jaw-bone:* Allusion to the old tradition that Cain slew Abel with the
jawbone of an ass.   68 *politician:* Schemer, plotter.   69 *o'er-reaches:* Quibble on the literal sense and the sense "circumvent."   76 *chapless:* Having no lower jaw.   77 *mazzard:*
Head.   79 *loggats:* A game in which six sticks are thrown to lie as near as possible to a stake
fixed in the ground, or block of wood on a floor.   81 *For and:* And moreover.   85 *quiddi-
ties:* Subtleties, quibbles; *quillities:* Verbal niceties, subtle distinctions; *tenures:* The holding of
a piece of property or office or the conditions or period of such holding.   87 *sconce:* Head.
89 *statutes, recognizances:* Legal terms connected with the transfer of land.   90 *vouchers:*
Persons called on to warrant a tenant's title; *recoveries:* Process for transfer of entailed estate;
fine: The four uses of this word are as follows: (1) end, (2) legal process, (3) elegant, (4) small.
93 *indentures:* Conveyances or contracts.   95 *inheritor:* Possessor, owner.   98 *calf-skins:*
Parchments.   99 *assurance in that:* Safety in legal parchments.

First Clown: You lie out on 't, sir, and therefore 't is not yours: for my part,   105
    I do not lie in 't, yet it is mine.

Hamlet: Thou dost lie in 't, to be in 't and say it is thine: 'tis for the dead,
    not for the quick; therefore thou liest.

First Clown: 'Tis a quick lie, sir; 'twill away again, from me to you.

Hamlet: What man dost thou dig it for?   110

First Clown: For no man, sir.

Hamlet: What woman, then?

First Clown: For none, neither.

Hamlet: Who is to be buried in 't?

First Clown: One that was a woman, sir; but, rest her soul, she's dead.   115

Hamlet: How absolute° the knave is! we must speak by the card,° or
    equivocation° will undo us. By the Lord, Horatio, these three years I
    have taken note of it; the age is grown so picked° that the toe of the
    peasant comes so near the heel of the courtier, he galls° his kibe.°
    How long hast thou been a grave-maker?   120

First Clown: Of all the day i' the year, I came to 't that day that our last king
    Hamlet overcame Fortinbras.

Hamlet: How long is that since?

First Clown: Cannot you tell that? every fool can tell that: it was the very
    day that young Hamlet was born; he that is mad, and sent into   125
    England.

Hamlet: Ay, marry, why was he sent into England?

First Clown: Why, because 'a was mad: 'a shall recover his wits there; or, if 'a
    do not, 'tis no great matter there.

Hamlet: Why?   130

First Clown: 'Twill not be seen in him there; there the men are as mad
    as he.

Hamlet: How came he mad?

First Clown: Very strangely, they say.

Hamlet: How strangely?   135

First Clown: Faith, e'en with losing his wits.

Hamlet: Upon what ground?

First Clown: Why, here in Denmark: I have been sexton here, man and boy,
    thirty years.°

Hamlet: How long will a man lie i' the earth ere he rot?   140

First Clown: Faith, if 'a be not rotten before 'a die — as we have many
    pocky° corses now-a-days, that will scarce hold the laying in — 'a will
    last you some eight year or nine year: a tanner will last you nine year.

Hamlet: Why he more than another?

First Clown: Why, sir, his hide is so tanned with his trade, that 'a will keep   145
    out water a great while; and your water is a sore decayer of your
    whoreson dead body. Here's a skull now hath lain you i' th' earth
    three and twenty years.

Hamlet: Whose was it?

---

116 *absolute:* Positive, decided; *by the card:* With precision, i.e., by the mariner's card on
which the points of the compass were marked.   117 *equivocation:* Ambiguity in the use of
terms.   118 *picked:* Refined, fastidious.   119 *galls:* Chafes; *kibe:* Chilblain.   139 *thirty
years:* This statement with that in line 125 shows Hamlet's age to be thirty years.
142 *pocky:* Rotten, diseased.

First Clown: A whoreson mad fellow's it was: whose do you think it was?   150
Hamlet: Nay, I know not.
First Clown: A pestilence on him for a mad rogue! 'a poured a flagon of
    Rhenish on my head once. This same skull, sir, was Yorick's skull, the
    king's jester.
Hamlet: This?   155
First Clown: E'en that.
Hamlet: Let me see. *[Takes the skull.]* Alas, poor Yorick! I knew him, Hora-
    tio: a fellow of infinite jest, of most excellent fancy: he hath borne me
    on his back a thousand times; and now, how abhorred in my imagi-
    nation it is! my gorge rises at it. Here hung those lips that I have   160
    kissed I know not how oft. Where be your gibes now? your gam-
    bols? your songs? your flashes of merriment, that were wont to set the
    table on a roar? Not one now, to mock your own grinning? quite
    chap-fallen? Now get you to my lady's chamber, and tell her, let her
    paint an inch thick, to this favour she must come; make her laugh at   165
    that. Prithee, Horatio, tell me one thing.
Horatio: What's that, my lord?
Hamlet: Dost thou think Alexander looked o' this fashion i' the earth?
Horatio: E'en so.
Hamlet: And smelt so? pah!   *[Puts down the skull.]*   170
Horatio: E'en so, my lord.
Hamlet: To what base uses we may return, Horatio! Why may not imagi-
    nation trace the noble dust of Alexander, till 'a find it stopping a
    bung-hole?
Horatio: 'Twere to consider too curiously,° to consider so.   175
Hamlet: No, faith, not a jot; but to follow him thither with modesty
    enough, and likelihood to lead it: as thus: Alexander died, Alexander
    was buried, Alexander returneth into dust; the dust is earth; of earth
    we make loam;° and why of that loam, whereto he was converted,
    might they not stop a beer-barrel?   180
        Imperious° Cæsar, dead and turn'd to clay,
        Might stop a hole to keep the wind away:
        O, that that earth, which kept the world in awe,
        Should patch a wall t'expel the winter's flaw!°
    But soft! but soft awhile! here comes the king,   185

*Enter King, Queen, Laertes, and the Corse of [Ophelia, in procession, with
Priest, Lords, etc.].*

    The queen, the courtiers: who is this they follow?
    And with such maimed rites? This doth betoken
    The corse they follow did with desp'rate hand
    Fordo° it° own life: 'twas of some estate.
    Couch° we awhile, and mark.   *[Retiring with Horatio.]*   190
Laertes: What ceremony else?
Hamlet: That is Laertes,
    A very noble youth: mark.

---

175 *curiously:* Minutely.   179 *loam:* Clay paste for brickmaking.   181 *Imperious:* Imperial.   184 *flaw:* Gust of wind.   189 *Fordo:* Destroy; *it:* Its.   190 *Couch:* Hide, lurk.

Laertes: What ceremony else?
First Priest: Her obsequies have been as far enlarg'd°
　　As we have warranty: her death was doubtful; 195
　　And, but that great command o'ersways the order,
　　She should in ground unsanctified have lodg'd
　　Till the last trumpet; for charitable prayers,
　　Shards,° flints and pebbles should be thrown on her:
　　Yet here she is allow'd her virgin crants,° 200
　　Her maiden strewments° and the bringing home
　　Of bell and burial.°
Laertes: Must there no more be done?
First Priest: 　　　　　　　　　No more be done:
　　We should profane the service of the dead
　　To sing a requiem and such rest to her 205
　　As to peace-parted° souls.
Laertes: 　　　　　　　　Lay her i' th' earth:
　　And from her fair and unpolluted flesh
　　May violets spring! I tell thee, churlish priest,
　　A minist'ring angel shall my sister be,
　　When thou liest howling.°
Hamlet: 　　　　　　　　What, the fair Ophelia! 210
Queen: Sweets to the sweet: farewell! 　　　　*[Scattering flowers.]*
　　I hop'd thou shouldst have been my Hamlet's wife;
　　I thought thy bride-bed to have deck'd, sweet maid,
　　And not have strew'd thy grave.
Laertes: 　　　　　　　　O, treble woe
　　Fall ten times treble on that cursed head, 215
　　Whose wicked deed thy most ingenious sense°
　　Depriv'd thee of! Hold off the earth awhile,
　　Till I have caught her once more in mine arms:　*[Leaps into the grave.]*
　　Now pile your dust upon the quick and dead,
　　Till of this flat a mountain you have made, 220
　　T' o'ertop old Pelion,° or the skyish head
　　Of blue Olympus.
Hamlet: 　　　　　　*[Advancing]* What is he whose grief
　　Bears such an emphasis? whose phrase of sorrow
　　Conjures the wand'ring stars,° and makes them stand
　　Like wonder-wounded hearers? This is I, 225
　　Hamlet the Dane. 　　　　　　　　　*[Leaps into the grave.]*
Laertes: 　　　　　　The devil take thy soul! 　　*[Grappling with him.]*
Hamlet: Thou pray'st not well.
　　I prithee, take thy fingers from my throat;

---

194 *enlarg'd:* Extended, referring to the fact that suicides are not given full burial rites.
199 *Shards:* Broken bits of pottery. 　　200 *crants:* Garlands customarily hung upon the biers
of unmarried women. 　　201 *strewments:* Traditional strewing of flowers. 　　201-202 *bringing...burial:* The laying to rest of the body, to the sound of the bell. 　　206 *peace-
parted:* Allusion to the text "Lord, now lettest thou thy servant depart in peace." 　210 *howling:*
I.e., in hell. 　　216 *ingenious sense:* Mind endowed with finest qualities. 　221 *Pelion:* Olympus, Pelion, and Ossa are mountains in the north of Thessaly. 　224 *wand'ring stars:*
Planets.

For, though I am not splenitive° and rash,
Yet have I in me something dangerous,   230
Which let thy wisdom fear: hold off thy hand.
King: Pluck them asunder.
Queen: Hamlet, Hamlet!
All: Gentlemen, —
Horatio: Good my lord, be quiet.

   [The Attendants part them, and they come out of the grave.]

Hamlet: Why, I will fight with him upon this theme
Until my eyelids will no longer wag.°   235
Queen: O my son, what theme?
Hamlet: I lov'd Ophelia: forty thousand brothers
Could not, with all their quantity° of love,
Make up my sum. What wilt thou do for her?
King: O, he is mad, Laertes.   240
Queen: For love of God, forbear° him.
Hamlet: 'Swounds,° show me what thou 'lt do:
Woo 't° weep? woo 't fight? woo 't fast? woo 't tear thyself?
Woo 't drink up eisel?° eat a crocodile?
I'll do 't. Dost thou come here to whine?   245
To outface me with leaping in her grave?
Be buried quick with her, and so will I:
And, if thou prate of mountains, let them throw
Millions of acres on us, till our ground,
Singeing his pate against the burning zone,°   250
Make Ossa like a wart! Nay, an thou 'lt mouth,
I'll rant as well as thou.
Queen: This is mere madness:
And thus awhile the fit will work on him;
Anon, as patient as the female dove.
When that her golden couplets° are disclos'd,   255
His silence will sit drooping.
Hamlet: Hear you, sir;
What is the reason that you use me thus?
I lov'd you ever: but it is no matter;
Let Hercules himself do what he may,
The cat will mew and dog will have his day.   260
King: I pray thee, good Horatio, wait upon him.   *Exit Hamlet and Horatio.*
   [To Laertes.] Strengthen your patience in° our last night's speech;
We'll put the matter to the present push.°
Good Gertrude, set some watch over your son.

---

229 *splenitive:* Quick-tempered.   235 *wag:* Move (not used ludicrously).   238 *quantity:* Some suggest that the word is used in a deprecatory sense (little bits, fragments).   241 *forbear:* Leave alone.   242 *'Swounds:* Oath, "God's wounds."   243 *Woo 't:* Wilt thou. 244 *eisel:* Vinegar. Some editors have taken this to be the name of a river, such as the Yssel, the Weissel, and the Nile.   250 *burning zone:* Sun's orbit.   255 *golden couplets:* The pigeon lays two eggs; the young when hatched are covered with golden down.   262 *in:* By recalling.   263 *present push:* Immediate test.

> This grave shall have a living° monument: 265
> An hour of quiet shortly shall we see;
> Till then, in patience our proceeding be.   *Exeunt.*

[SCENE II: *A hall in the castle.*]

Enter Hamlet and Horatio.

Hamlet: So much for this, sir: now shall you see the other;
> You do remember all the circumstance?
Horatio: Remember it, my lord!
Hamlet: Sir, in my heart there was a kind of fighting,
> That would not let me sleep: methought I lay   5
> Worse than the mutines in the bilboes.° Rashly,°
> And prais'd be rashness for it, let us know,
> Our indiscretion sometime serves us well,
> When our deep plots do pall:° and that should learn us
> There's a divinity that shapes our ends,   10
> Rough-hew° them how we will, —
Horatio: That is most certain.
Hamlet: Up from my cabin,
> My sea-gown° scarf'd about me, in the dark
> Grop'd I to find out them; had my desire,
> Finger'd° their packet, and in fine° withdrew   15
> To mine own room again; making so bold,
> My fears forgetting manners, to unseal
> Their grand commission; where I found, Horatio, —
> O royal knavery! — an exact command,
> Larded° with many several sorts of reasons   20
> Importing Denmark's health and England's too,
> With, ho! such bugs° and goblins in my life,°
> That, on the supervise,° no leisure bated,°
> No, not to stay the grinding of the axe,
> My head should be struck off.
Horatio: Is 't possible?   25
Hamlet: Here's the commission: read it at more leisure.
> But wilt thou hear me how I did proceed?
Horatio: I beseech you.
Hamlet: Being thus be-netted round with villanies, —
> Ere I could make a prologue to my brains,
> They had begun the play° — I sat me down,   30

---

265 *living:* Lasting; also refers (for Laertes's benefit) to the plot against Hamlet.   **Scene II.**
6 *mutines in the bilboes:* Mutineers in shackles; *Rashly:* Goes with line 12.   9 *pall:* Fail.
11 *Rough-hew:* Shape roughly; it may mean "bungle."   13 *sea-gown:* "A sea-gown, or a coarse, high-collered, and short-sleeved gowne, reaching down to the mid-leg, and used most by seamen and saylors" (Cotgrave, quoted by Singer).   15 *Finger'd:* Pilfered, filched; *in fine:* Finally.   20 *Larded:* Enriched.   22 *bugs:* Bugbears; *such . . . life:* Such imaginary dangers if I were allowed to live.   23 *supervise:* Perusal; *leisure bated:* Delay allowed.   30–31 *prologue . . . play:* I.e., before I could begin to think, my mind had made its decision.

Devis'd a new commission, wrote it fair:
I once did hold it, as our statists° do,
A baseness to write fair° and labour'd much
How to forget that learning, but, sir, now   35
It did me yeoman's° service: wilt thou know
Th' effect of what I wrote?
Horatio: Ay, good my lord.
Hamlet: An earnest conjuration from the king,
As England was his faithful tributary,
As love between them like the palm might flourish,   40
As peace should still her wheaten garland° wear
And stand a comma° 'tween their amities,
And many such-like 'As'es° of great charge,°
That, on the view and knowing of these contents,
Without debatement further, more or less,   45
He should the bearers put to sudden death,
Not shriving-time° allow'd.
Horatio: How was this seal'd?
Hamlet: Why, even in that was heaven ordinant.°
I had my father's signet in my purse,
Which was the model of that Danish seal;   50
Folded the writ up in the form of th' other,
Subscrib'd it, gave 't th' impression, plac'd it safely,
The changeling never known. Now, the next day
Was our sea-fight; and what to this was sequent°
Thou know'st already.   55
Horatio: So Guildenstern and Rosencrantz go to 't.
Hamlet: Why, man, they did make love to this employment;
They are not near my conscience; their defeat
Does by their own insinuation° grow:
'Tis dangerous when the baser nature comes   60
Between the pass° and fell incensed° points
Of mighty opposites.
Horatio: Why, what a king is this!
Hamlet: Does it not, think thee, stand° me now upon —
He that hath kill'd my king and whor'd my mother,
Popp'd in between th' election° and my hopes,   65
Thrown out his angle° for my proper life,
And with such coz'nage° — is 't not perfect conscience,
To quit° him with this arm? and is 't not to be damn'd,

---

33 *statists:* Statesmen.   34 *fair:* In a clear hand.   36 *yeoman's:* I.e., faithful.   41 *wheaten garland:* Symbol of peace.   42 *comma:* Smallest break or separation. Here *amity* begins and *amity* ends the period, and *peace* stands between like a dependent clause. The comma indicates continuity, link.   43 *'As'es:* The "whereases" of a formal document, with play on the word *ass; charge:* Import, and burden.   47 *shriving-time:* Time for absolution.   48 *ordinant:* Directing.   54 *sequent:* Subsequent.   59 *insinuation:* Interference.   61 *pass:* Thrust; *fell incensed:* Fiercely angered.   63 *stand:* Become incumbent.   65 *election:* The Danish throne was filled by election.   66 *angle:* Fishing line.   67 *coz'nage:* Trickery.   68 *quit:* Repay.

To let this canker° of our nature come
  In further evil?   70
Horatio: It must be shortly known to him from England
  What is the issue of the business there.
Hamlet: It will be short: the interim is mine;
  And a man's life's no more than to say "One."
  But I am very sorry, good Horatio,   75
  That to Laertes I forgot myself;
  For, by the image of my cause, I see
  The portraiture of his: I'll court his favours:
  But, sure, the bravery° of his grief did put me
  Into a tow'ring passion.
Horatio: Peace! who comes here?   80

  Enter a Courtier [Osric].

Osric: Your lordship is right welcome back to Denmark.
Hamlet: I humbly thank you, sir. *[To Horatio.]* Dost know this water-fly?°
Horatio: No, my good lord.
Hamlet: Thy state is the more gracious; for 'tis a vice to know him. He
  hath much land, and fertile: let a beast be lord of beasts,° and his crib   85
  shall stand at the king's mess:° 'tis a chough;° but, as I say, spacious
  in the possession of dirt.
Osric: Sweet lord, if your lordship were at leisure, I should impart a thing
  to you from his majesty.
Hamlet: I will receive it, sir, with all diligence of spirit. Put your bonnet to   90
  his right use; 'tis for the head.
Osric: I thank your lordship, it is very hot.
Hamlet: No, believe me, 'tis very cold; the wind is northerly.
Osric: It is indifferent° cold, my lord, indeed.
Hamlet: But yet methinks it is very sultry and hot for my complexion.   95
Osric: Exceedingly, my lord; it is very sultry,—as 'twere,—I cannot tell
  how. But, my lord, his majesty bade me signify to you that 'a has laid a
  great wager on your head: sir, this is the matter,—
Hamlet: I beseech you, remember°—

  [Hamlet moves him to put on his hat.]

Osric: Nay, good my lord; for mine ease,° in good faith. Sir, here is newly   100
  come to court Laertes; believe me, an absolute gentleman, full of
  most excellent differences, of very soft° society and great showing:°
  indeed, to speak feelingly° of him, he is the card° or calendar of gentry,° for you shall find in him the continent of what part a gentleman
  would see.   105

---

69 *canker:* Ulcer, or possibly the worm which destroys buds and leaves.   79 *bravery:*
Bravado.   82 *water-fly:* Vain or busily idle person.   85 *lord of beasts:* See Genesis 1:26, 28.
85–86 *his crib . . . mess:* He shall eat at the king's table and be one of the group of persons
(usually four) constituting a *mess* at a banquet.   86 *chough:* Probably, chattering jackdaw;
also explained as *chuff,* provincial boor or churl.   94 *indifferent:* Somewhat.   99 *remem-*
ber: I.e., remember thy courtesy; conventional phrase for "Be covered."   100 *mine ease:*
Conventional reply declining the invitation of "Remember thy courtesy."   102 *soft:*
Gentle; *showing:* Distinguished appearance.   103 *feelingly:* With just perception; *card:*
Chart, map.   103–104 *gentry:* Good breeding.

Hamlet: Sir, his definement° suffers no perdition° in you; though, I know, to divide him inventorially° would dozy° the arithmetic of memory, and yet but yaw° neither, in respect of his quick sail. But, in the verity of extolment, I take him to be a soul of great article;° and his infu-sion° of such dearth and rareness,° as, to make true diction of him,   110 his semblable° is his mirror; and who else would trace° him, his um-brage,° nothing more.

Osric: Your lordship speaks most infallibly of him.

Hamlet: The concernancy,° sir? why do we wrap the gentleman in our more rawer breath?°   115

Osric: Sir?

Horatio [aside to Hamlet]: Is 't not possible to understand in another tongue?° You will do 't, sir, really.

Hamlet: What imports the nomination° of this gentleman?

Osric: Of Laertes?   120

Horatio [aside to Hamlet]: His purse is empty already; all 's golden words are spent.

Hamlet: Of him, sir.

Osric: I know you are not ignorant —

Hamlet: I would you did, sir; yet, in faith, if you did, it would not much   125 approve° me. Well, sir?

Osric: You are not ignorant of what excellence Laertes is —

Hamlet: I dare not confess that, lest I should compare with him in excel-lence; but, to know a man well, were to know himself.°

Osric: I mean, sir, for his weapon; but in the imputation° laid on him by   130 them, in his meed° he's unfellowed.

Hamlet: What's his weapon?

Osric: Rapier and dagger.

Hamlet: That's two of his weapons: but, well.

Osric: The king, sir, hath wagered with him six Barbary horses: against   135 the which he has impawned,° as I take it, six French rapiers and poniards, with their assigns, as girdle, hangers,° and so: three of the carriages, in faith, are very dear to fancy,° very responsive° to the hilts, most delicate° carriages, and of very liberal conceit.°

Hamlet: What call you the carriages?   140

Horatio [aside to Hamlet]: I knew you must be edified by the margent° ere you had done.

Osric: The carriages, sir, are the hangers.

---

106 *definement:* Definition; *perdition:* Loss, diminution.   107 *divide him inventorially:* I.e., enumerate his graces; *dozy:* Dizzy.   108 *yaw:* To move unsteadily (of a ship).   109 *article:* Moment or importance.   109–110 *infusion:* Infused temperament, character imparted by nature.   110 *dearth and rareness:* Rarity.   111 *semblable:* True likeness; *trace:* Follow. 111–112 *umbrage:* Shadow.   114 *concernancy:* Import.   115 *breath:* Speech.   117–118 *Is 't . . . tongue?:* I.e., can one converse with Osric only in this outlandish jargon?   119 *nomi-nation:* Naming.   126 *approve:* Command.   129 *but . . . himself:* But to know a man as excellent were to know Laertes.   130 *imputation:* Reputation.   131 *meed:* Merit.   136 *he has impawned:* He has wagered.   137 *hangers:* Straps on the sword belt from which the sword hung.   138 *dear to fancy:* Fancifully made; *responsive:* Probably, well balanced, cor-responding closely.   139 *delicate:* Fine in workmanship; *liberal conceit:* Elaborate design. 141 *margent:* Margin of a book, place for explanatory notes.

Hamlet: The phrase would be more german° to the matter, if we could carry cannon by our sides: I would it might be hangers till then. But, 145 on: six Barbary horses against six French swords, their assigns, and three liberal-conceited carriages; that's the French bet against the Danish. Why is this "impawned," as you call it?

Osric: The king, sir, hath laid, that in a dozen passes between yourself and him, he shall not exceed you three hits: he hath laid on twelve for 150 nine; and it would come to immediate trial, if your lordship would vouchsafe the answer.

Hamlet: How if I answer "no"?

Osric: I mean, my lord, the opposition of your person in trial.

Hamlet: Sir, I will walk here in the hall: if it please his majesty, it is the 155 breathing time° of day with me; let the foils be brought, the gentleman willing, and the king hold his purpose, I will win for him as I can; if not, I will gain nothing but my shame and the odd hits.

Osric: Shall I re-deliver you e'en so?

Hamlet: To this effect, sir; after what flourish your nature will. 160

Osric: I commend my duty to your lordship.

Hamlet: Yours, yours. *[Exit Osric.]* He does well to commend it himself; there are no tongues else for 's turn.

Horatio: This lapwing° runs away with the shell on his head.

Hamlet: 'A did comply, sir, with his dug,° before 'a sucked it. Thus has 165 he—and many more of the same breed that I know the drossy° age dotes on—only got the tune° of the time and out of an habit of encounter;° a kind of yesty° collection, which carries them through and through the most fann'd and winnowed° opinions; and do but blow them to their trial, the bubbles are out.° 170

Enter a Lord.

Lord: My lord, his majesty commended him to you by young Osric, who brings back to him, that you attend him in the hall: he sends to know if your pleasure hold to play with Laertes, or that you will take longer time.

Hamlet: I am constant to my purposes; they follow the king's pleasure: if 175 his fitness speaks, mine is ready; now or whensoever, provided I be so able as now.

Lord: The king and queen and all are coming down.

Hamlet: In happy time.°

Lord: The queen desires you to use some gentle entertainment to Laertes 180 before you fall to play.

Hamlet: She well instructs me. *[Exit Lord.]*

Horatio: You will lose this wager, my lord.

---

144 *german:* Germane, appropriate.   156 *breathing time:* Exercise period.   164 *lapwing:* Peewit; noted for its wiliness in drawing a visitor away from its nest and its supposed habit of running about when newly hatched with its head in the shell; possibly an allusion to Osric's hat.   165 *did comply...dug:* Paid compliments to his mother's breast.   166 *drossy:* Frivolous.   167 *tune:* Temper, mood.   167-168 *habit of encounter:* Demeanor of social intercourse.   168 *yesty:* Frothy.   169 *fann'd and winnowed:* Select and refined.   170 *blow... out:* I.e., put them to the test, and their ignorance is exposed.   179 *In happy time:* A phrase of courtesy.

Hamlet: I do not think so; since he went into France, I have been in continual practice; I shall win at the odds. But thou wouldst not think 185
how ill all 's here about my heart: but it is no matter.

Horatio: Nay, good my lord, —

Hamlet: It is but foolery; but it is such a kind of gain-giving,° as would
perhaps trouble a woman.

Horatio: If your mind dislike any thing, obey it: I will forestall their repair 190
hither, and say you are not fit.

Hamlet: Not a whit, we defy augury: there's a special providence in the
fall of a sparrow. If it be now, 'tis not to come; if it be not to come,
it will be now; if it be not now, yet it will come: the readiness is all:°
since no man of aught he leaves knows, what is 't to leave betimes? 195
Let be.

*A table prepared. [Enter] Trumpets, Drums, and Officers with cushions; King,
Queen, [Osric,] and all the State; foils, daggers, [and wine borne in;] and Laertes.*

King: Come, Hamlet, come, and take this hand from me.

[The King puts Laertes's hand into Hamlet's.]

Hamlet: Give me your pardon, sir: I have done you wrong;
But pardon 't as you are a gentleman.
This presence° knows, 200
And you must needs have heard, how I am punish'd
With a sore distraction. What I have done,
That might your nature, honour and exception°
Roughly awake, I here proclaim was madness.
Was 't Hamlet wrong'd Laertes? Never Hamlet: 205
If Hamlet from himself be ta'en away,
And when he's not himself does wrong Laertes,
Then Hamlet does it not, Hamlet denies it.
Who does it, then? His madness: if 't be so,
Hamlet is of the faction that is wrong'd; 210
His madness is poor Hamlet's enemy.
Sir, in this audience,
Let my disclaiming from a purpos'd evil
Free me so far in your most generous thoughts,
That I have shot mine arrow o'er the house, 215
And hurt my brother.

Laertes: I am satisfied in nature,°
Whose motive, in this case, should stir me most
To my revenge: but in my terms of honour
I stand aloof; and will no reconcilement,
Till by some elder masters, of known honour, 220
I have a voice° and precedent of peace,
To keep my name ungor'd. But till that time,
I do receive your offer'd love like love,
And will not wrong it.

---

188 *gain-giving:* Misgiving.   194 *all:* All that matters.   200 *presence:* Royal assembly.
203 *exception:* Disapproval.   216 *nature:* I.e., he is personally satisfied, but his honor must
be satisfied by the rules of the code of honor.   221 *voice:* Authoritative pronouncement.

Hamlet: I embrace it freely;
    And will this brother's wager frankly play.   225
    Give us the foils. Come on.
Laertes: Come, one for me.
Hamlet: I'll be your foil,° Laertes: in mine ignorance
    Your skill shall, like a star i' th' darkest night,
    Stick fiery off° indeed.
Laertes: You mock me, sir.
Hamlet: No, by this hand.   230
King: Give them the foils, young Osric. Cousin Hamlet,
    You know the wager?
Hamlet: Very well, my lord;
    Your grace has laid the odds o' th' weaker side.
King: I do not fear it; I have seen you both:
    But since he is better'd, we have therefore odds.   235
Laertes: This is too heavy, let me see another.
Hamlet: This likes me well. These foils have all a length?

    [They prepare to play.]

Osric: Ay, my good lord.
King: Set me the stoups of wine upon that table.
    If Hamlet give the first or second hit,   240
    Or quit in answer of the third exchange,
    Let all the battlements their ordnance fire;
    The king shall drink to Hamlet's better breath;
    And in the cup an union° shall he throw,
    Richer than that which four successive kings   245
    In Denmark's crown have worn. Give me the cups;
    And let the kettle° to the trumpet speak,
    The trumpet to the cannoneer without,
    The cannons to the heavens, the heavens to earth,
    "Now the king drinks to Hamlet." Come begin: *Trumpets the while.* 250
    And you, the judges, bear a wary eye.
Hamlet: Come on, sir.
Laertes: Come, my lord.   *[They play.]*
Hamlet: One.
Laertes: No.
Hamlet: Judgement.
Osric: A hit, a very palpable hit.

    Drum, trumpets, and shot. Flourish. A piece goes off.

Laertes: Well; again.
King: Stay; give me drink. Hamlet, this pearl° is thine;
    Here's to thy health. Give him the cup.   255
Hamlet: I'll play this bout first; set it by awhile.
    Come. *[They play.]* Another hit; what say you?
Laertes: A touch, a touch, I do confess 't.

---

227 *foil:* Quibble on the two senses: "background which sets something off," and
"blunted rapier for fencing."   229 *Stick fiery off:* Stand out brilliantly.   244 *union:* Pearl.
247 *kettle:* Kettledrum.   254 *pearl:* I.e., the poison.

King: Our son shall win.
Queen: He's fat,° and scant of breath.
     Here, Hamlet, take my napkin, rub thy brows: 260
     The queen carouses° to thy fortune, Hamlet.
Hamlet: Good madam!
King: Gertrude, do not drink.
Queen: I will, my lord; I pray you, pardon me.   *[Drinks.]*
King [aside]: It is the poison'd cup: it is too late.
Hamlet: I dare not drink yet, madam; by and by.   265
Queen: Come, let me wipe thy face.
Laertes: My lord, I'll hit him now.
King: I do not think 't.
Laertes [aside]: And yet 'tis almost 'gainst my conscience.
Hamlet: Come, for the third, Laertes: you but dally;
     I pray you, pass with your best violence;   270
     I am afeard you make a wanton° of me.
Laertes: Say you so? come on.   *[They play.]*
Osric: Nothing, neither way.
Laertes: Have at you now!

     [Laertes wounds Hamlet; then, in scuffling, they change rapiers,° and Hamlet
     wounds Laertes.]

King: Part them; they are incens'd.
Hamlet: Nay, come again.   *[The Queen falls.]*
Osric: Look to the queen there, ho!   275
Horatio: They bleed on both sides. How is it, my lord?
Osric: How is 't, Laertes?
Laertes: Why, as a woodcock° to mine own springe,° Osric;
     I am justly kill'd with mine own treachery.
Hamlet: How does the queen?
King: She swounds° to see them bleed.   280
Queen: No, no, the drink, the drink, — O my dear Hamlet, —
     The drink, the drink! I am poison'd.   *[Dies.]*
Hamlet: O villany! Ho! let the door be lock'd:
     Treachery! Seek it out.   *[Laertes falls.]*
Laertes: It is here, Hamlet: Hamlet, thou art slain;   285
     No med'cine in the world can do thee good;
     In thee there is not half an hour of life;
     The treacherous instrument is in thy hand,
     Unbated° and envenom'd: the foul practice
     Hath turn'd itself on me; lo, here I lie,   290
     Never to rise again: thy mother's poison'd:
     I can no more: the king, the king's to blame.

---

259 *fat:* Not physically fit, out of training. Some earlier editors speculated that the term applied to the corpulence of Richard Burbage, who originally played the part, but the allusion now appears unlikely. *Fat* may also suggest "sweaty."   261 *carouses:* Drinks a toast.
271 *wanton:* Spoiled child.   *in scuffling, they change rapiers:* According to a widespread stage tradition, Hamlet receives a scratch, realizes that Laertes's sword is unbated, and accordingly forces an exchange.   278 *woodcock:* As type of stupidity or as decoy; *springe:* Trap, snare.
280 *swounds:* Swoons.   289 *Unbated:* Not blunted with a button.

Hamlet: The point envenom'd too!
　　Then, venom, to thy work. [*Stabs the King.*]
All: Treason! treason! 295
King: O, yet defend me, friends; I am but hurt.
Hamlet: Here, thou incestuous, murd'rous, damned Dane,
　　Drink off this potion. Is thy union here?
　　Follow my mother. [*King dies.*]
Laertes: 　　　　　　He is justly serv'd;
　　It is a poison temper'd° by himself. 300
　　Exchange forgiveness with me, noble Hamlet:
　　Mine and my father's death come not upon thee,
　　Nor thine on me! [*Dies.*]
Hamlet: Heaven make thee free of it! I follow thee.
　　I am dead, Horatio. Wretched queen, adieu! 305
　　You that look pale and tremble at this chance,
　　That are but mutes° or audience to this act,
　　Had I but time — as this fell sergeant,° Death,
　　Is strict in his arrest — O, I could tell you —
　　But let it be. Horatio, I am dead; 310
　　Thou livest; report me and my cause aright
　　To the unsatisfied.
Horatio: 　　　　　　Never believe it:
　　I am more an antique Roman° than a Dane:
　　Here's yet some liquor left.
Hamlet: 　　　　　　As th' art a man,
　　Give me the cup: let go, by heaven, I'll ha 't. 315
　　O God! Horatio, what a wounded name,
　　Things standing thus unknown, shall live behind me!
　　If thou didst ever hold me in thy heart,
　　Absent thee from felicity awhile,
　　And in this harsh world draw thy breath in pain, 320
　　To tell my story. *A march afar off.*
　　　　　　What warlike noise is this?
Osric: Young Fortinbras, with conquest come from Poland,
　　To the ambassadors of England gives
　　This warlike volley.
Hamlet: 　　　　　　O, I die, Horatio;
　　The potent poison quite o'er-crows° my spirit: 325
　　I cannot live to hear the news from England;
　　But I do prophesy th' election lights
　　On Fortinbras: he has my dying voice;
　　So tell him, with th' occurrents,° more and less,
　　Which have solicited.° The rest is silence. [*Dies.*] 330
Horatio: Now cracks a noble heart. Good night, sweet prince;
　　And flights of angels sing thee to thy rest!
　　Why does the drum come hither? [*March within.*]

300 *temper'd:* Mixed.　307 *mutes:* Performers in a play who speak no words.　308 *sergeant:* Sheriff's officer.　313 *Roman:* It was the Roman custom to follow masters in death. 325 *o'er-crows:* Triumphs over.　329 *occurrents:* Events, incidents.　330 *solicited:* Moved, urged.

Enter Fortinbras, with the [English] Ambassadors [and others].

Fortinbras: Where is this sight?
Horatio: What is it you would see?
   If aught of woe or wonder, cease your search.   335
Fortinbras: This quarry° cries on havoc.° O proud Death,
   What feast is toward in thine eternal cell,
   That thou so many princes at a shot
   So bloodily hast struck?
First Ambassador: The sight is dismal;
   And our affairs from England come too late: 340
   The ears are senseless that should give us hearing,
   To tell him his commandment is fulfill'd,
   That Rosencrantz and Guildenstern are dead:
   Where should we have our thanks?
Horatio: Not from his mouth,°
   Had it th' ability of life to thank you: 345
   He never gave commandment for their death.
   But since, so jump° upon this bloody question,°
   You from the Polack wars, and you from England,
   Are here arriv'd, give order that these bodies
   High on a stage° be placed to the view;   350
   And let me speak to th' yet unknowing world
   How these things came about: so shall you hear
   Of carnal, bloody, and unnatural acts,
   Of accidental judgements, casual slaughters,
   Of deaths put on by cunning and forc'd cause,   355
   And, in this upshot, purposes mistook
   Fall'n on th' inventors' heads: all this can I
   Truly deliver.
Fortinbras: Let us haste to hear it,
   And call the noblest to the audience.
   For me, with sorrow I embrace my fortune: 360
   I have some rights of memory° in this kingdom,
   Which now to claim my vantage doth invite me.
Horatio: Of that I shall have also cause to speak,
   And from his mouth whose voice will draw on more:°
   But let this same be presently perform'd,   365
   Even while men's minds are wild; lest more mischance,
   On° plots and errors, happen.
Fortinbras: Let four captains
   Bear Hamlet, like a soldier, to the stage;
   For he was likely, had he been put on,
   To have prov'd most royal: and, for his passage,°   370
   The soldiers' music and the rites of war
   Speak loudly for him.

---

336 *quarry:* Heap of dead; *cries on havoc:* Proclaims a general slaughter.   344 *his mouth:*
I.e., the king's.   347 *jump:* Precisely; *question:* Dispute.   350 *stage:* Platform.   361 *of*
memory: Traditional, remembered.   364 *voice . . . more:* Vote will influence still others.
367 *On:* On account of, or possibly, on top of, in addition to.   370 *passage:* Death.

Take up the bodies: such a sight as this
Becomes the field,° but here shows much amiss.
Go, bid the soldiers shoot.　　　　　　　　　　　　375

Exeunt [marching, bearing off the dead bodies; after which a peal of ordnance is shot off].

374 *field:* I.e., of battle.

Considerations for Critical Thinking and Writing

1. **FIRST RESPONSE.** Why does Hamlet find avenging his father's death so difficult? Why doesn't he take decisive action as soon as he seems convinced of Claudius's guilt?

2. Claudius urges Hamlet to leave behind his "obstinate condolement" and give up grieving for his dead father because it represents "impious stubbornness" (I.ii.93–94). Consider Claudius's advice in this speech (lines 87–117). Is it sensible? Why won't Hamlet heed this advice?

3. Are Polonius's admonitions to Laertes and Ophelia good advice (I.iii.55–81, 115–135)? What does his advice suggest about life at court, given that he is the chief counselor to the king?

4. When the ghost tells Hamlet that Claudius murdered him, Hamlet cries out, "O my prophetic soul!" (I.v.40). Why? What does the ghost demand of Hamlet?

5. What is known about the kind of person Hamlet was before his father's death? Does he have the stature of a tragic hero such as Oedipus? How does news of the murder and his mother's remarriage affect his behavior and view of life? Is he mad, as Polonius assumes, or is he pretending to be mad? Is there a "method in 't" (II.ii.200)? What do we learn from Hamlet's soliloquies?

6. What is the purpose of the play within the play? How does it provide a commentary on the action of the larger play?

7. Is Ophelia connected in any way with the crime Hamlet seeks to avenge? Why is he so brutal to Ophelia in Act III, Scene i? Why does she go mad?

8. Does Hamlet think Gertrude is as guilty as Claudius? Why is Hamlet so thoroughly disgusted by her in Act III, Scene iv?

9. Why doesn't Hamlet kill Claudius as he prays (III.iii)? Do you feel any sympathy for Claudius in this scene, or is he presented as a callous murderer?

10. If Hamlet had killed Claudius in Act III and the play had ended there, what would be missing in Hamlet's perceptions of himself and the world? How does his character develop in Acts IV and V? What softens our realization that Hamlet is in various degrees responsible for the deaths of Polonius, Ophelia, Laertes, Rosencrantz, Guildenstern, Claudius, and Gertrude?

11. What purpose does Fortinbras serve in the action? Would anything be lost if he were edited out of the play?

12. Despite its tragic dimensions, *Hamlet* includes humorous scenes and many witty lines delivered by the title character himself. Locate those scenes and lines, and then determine the tone and purpose of the play's humor.

13. **CRITICAL STRATEGIES.** Read the section on formalist criticism (pp. 2046–48) in Chapter 53, "Critical Strategies for Reading." Choose a soliloquy by

Hamlet and write an analysis of its images so that you reveal some significant portion of his character.

CONNECTIONS TO OTHER SELECTIONS

1. Compare in an essay Hamlet's attitudes about revenge with Matt Fowler's in Andre Dubus's short story "Killings" (p. 103).

2. What kind of king is Claudius? How does he compare with Creon in Sophocles' *Antigone* (p. 1465)? How are matters of state and the political atmosphere in the world of each play affected by the rules of Claudius and Creon?

3. Here's a long reach but a potentially interesting one: write an essay that considers Gertrude as a wife and mother alongside Nora in Henrik Ibsen's *A Doll House* (p. 1709). How responsible are they to themselves and to others? Can they be discussed in the same breath, or are they from such different worlds that nothing useful can be said about comparing them? Either way, explain your response.

Perspectives on Shakespeare

THE MAYOR OF LONDON (1597)

Objections to the Elizabethan Theater   1597

The inconueniences that grow by Stage playes abowt the Citie of London.

1. They are a speaciall cause of corrupting their Youth, conteninge nothinge but vnchast matters, lascivious devices, shiftes of Coozenage,° & other lewd & vngodly practizes, being so as that they impresse the very qualitie & corruption of manners which they represent, Contrary to the rules & art prescribed for the makinge of Comedies eaven amonge the Heathen, who vsd them seldom & at certen sett tymes, and not all the year longe as our manner is. Whearby such as frequent them, beinge of the base & refuze sort of people or such young gentlemen as have small regard of credit or conscience, drawe the same into imitacion and not to the avoidinge the like vices which they represent.

2. They are the ordinary places for vagrant persons, Maisterles men, thieves, horse stealers, whoremongers, Coozeners, Conycatchers,° contrivers of treason, and other idele and daungerous persons to meet together & to make theire matches to the great displeasure of Almightie God & the hurt & annoyance of her Maiesties people, which cannot be prevented nor discovered by the Gouernours of the Citie for that they are owt of the Citiees iurisdiction.

3. They maintaine idlenes in such persons as haue no vocation & draw apprentices and other seruantes from theire ordinary workes and all sortes of people from the resort vnto sermons and other Christian exercises, to the great hinderance of traides & prophanation of religion established by her highnes within this Realm.

---

shiftes of Coozenage: Perverse behavior.   *Conycatchers:* Tricksters.

4. In the time of sickness it is fownd by experience, that many hauing sores and yet not hart sicke take occasion hearby to walk abroad & to recreat themselves by heareinge a play Whearby others are infected, and them selves also many things miscarry.

From Edmund K. Chambers, *The Elizabethan Stage*

CONSIDERATIONS FOR CRITICAL THINKING AND WRITING

1. Summarize the mayor's objections to the theater. Do any of his reasons for protesting theatrical productions seem reasonable to you? Why or why not?

2. Are any of these concerns reflected in attitudes about the theater today? Why or why not?

3. How would you defend *Hamlet* or *A Midsummer Night's Dream* against charges that they draw some people into "imitacion and not to the avoidinge the like vices which they represent"?

LISA JARDINE (B. 1944)
On Boy Actors in Female Roles   1989

Every schoolchild knows that there were no women actors on the Elizabethan stage; the female parts were taken by young male actors. But every schoolchild also learns that this fact is of little consequence for the twentieth-century reader of Shakespeare's plays. Because the taking of female parts by boys was universal and commonplace, we are told, it was accepted as "verisimilitude" by the Elizabethan audience, who simply disregarded it, as we would disregard the creaking of stage scenery and accept the backcloth forest as "real" for the duration of the play.

Conventional or not, the taking of female parts by boy players actually occasioned a good deal of contemporary comment and created considerable moral uneasiness, even amongst those who patronized and supported the the-aters. Amongst those who opposed them, transvestism on stage was a main plank in the anti-stage polemic. "The appareil of wemen is a great provocation of men to lust and leacherie," wrote Dr. John Rainoldes, a leading Oxford divine (quoting the Bishop of Paris), in *Th' Overthrow of Stage-Playes* (Middleburgh, 1599). And he continues with an unhealthy interest which infuses the entire pamphlet: "A womans garment beeing put on a man doeth vehemently touch and moue him with the remembrance and imagination of a woman; and the imagination of a thing desirable doth stirr up the desire."

According to Rainoldes, and the authorities with whose independent testimony he lards his polemic, the wearing of female dress by boy players "is an occasion of wantonnes and lust." Sexuality, misdirected toward the boy masquerading in female dress, is "stirred" by attire and gesture; male prostitu-tion and perverted sexual activity is the inevitable accompaniment of female impersonation.

From *Still Harping on Daughters,* Second Edition

CONSIDERATIONS FOR CRITICAL THINKING AND WRITING

1. How does Jardine complicate the Elizabethan convention of boy actors assuming female roles? To what extent does it add to the representation of Elizabethan theater put forward by the mayor of London?

2. What do you think would be your own response to a boy actor playing a female role? Consider, for example, Hippolyta in *A Midsummer Night's Dream* or Ophelia in *Hamlet*.

SAMUEL JOHNSON (1709–1784)

On Shakespeare's Characters   1765

Shakespeare is above all writers, at least above all modern writers, the poet of nature: the poet that holds up to his readers a faithful mirror of manners and life. His characters are not modified by the customs of particular places, unpracticed by the rest of the world; by the peculiarities of studies or professions, which can operate but upon small numbers; or by the accidents of transient fashions or temporary opinions: they are the genuine progeny of common humanity, such as the world will always supply, and observation will always find. His persons act and speak by the influence of those general passions and principles by which all minds are agitated, and the whole system of life is continued in motion. In the writings of other poets a character is too often an individual; in those of Shakespeare it is commonly a species.

From the preface to Johnson's edition of Shakespeare's works

CONSIDERATIONS FOR CRITICAL THINKING AND WRITING

1. Johnson made this famous assessment of Shakespeare's ability to portray "common humanity" in the eighteenth century. As a twenty-first-century reader, explain why you agree or disagree with Johnson's view that Shakespeare's characters have universal appeal.

2. Write an essay discussing whether you think it is desirable or necessary for characters to be "a faithful mirror of manners and life." Along the way consider whether you encountered any characters in *Hamlet* or *A Midsummer Night's Dream* that do not provide what you consider to be an accurate mirror of human life.

SIGMUND FREUD (1856–1939)

On Repression in Hamlet   1900

Another of the great creations of tragic poetry, Shakespeare's *Hamlet,* has its roots in the same soil as *Oedipus Rex.* But the changed treatment of the same material reveals the whole difference in the mental life of these two widely separated epochs of civilization: the secular advance of repression in the emotional life of mankind. In the *Oedipus* the child's wishful fantasy that underlies it is brought into the open and realized as it would be in a dream. In *Hamlet* it remains repressed; and — just as in the case of a neurosis — we only learn of its existence from its inhibiting consequences. Strangely enough, the overwhelming effect produced by the more modern tragedy has turned out to be compatible with the fact that people have remained completely in the dark as to the hero's character. The play is built up on Hamlet's hesitations over fulfilling the task of revenge that is assigned to him; but its text offers no reasons or motives for these hesitations and an immense variety of attempts at interpreting them have failed to produce a result. According to the view which was originated by Goethe and is still the prevailing one today, Hamlet represents the type of man whose power of direct action is paralyzed by an excessive development of his intellect. (He is "sicklied o'er with the pale cast of thought.") According to another view, the dramatist has tried to portray a pathologically irresolute character which might be classed as neurasthenic. The plot of the drama shows us, however, that Hamlet is far from being represented as a person incapable of taking any action. We see him doing so on two occasions: first in a sudden outburst of temper, when he runs his sword through the eavesdropper behind the arras, and secondly, in a premeditated and even crafty fashion, when, with all the callousness of a Renaissance prince, he sends the two courtiers to the death that had been planned for himself. What is it, then, that inhibits him in fulfilling the task set him by his father's ghost? The answer, once again, is that it is the peculiar nature of the task. Hamlet is able to do anything — except take vengeance on the man who did away with his father and took that father's place with his mother, the man who shows him the repressed wishes of his own childhood realized. Thus the loathing which should drive him on to revenge is replaced in him by self-reproaches, by scruples of conscience, which remind him that he himself is literally no better than the sinner whom he is to punish. Here I have translated into conscious terms what was bound to remain unconscious in Hamlet's mind; and if anyone is inclined to call him a hysteric, I can only accept the fact as one that is implied by my interpretation. The distaste for sexuality expressed by Hamlet in his conversation with Ophelia fits in very well with this: the same distaste which was destined to take possession of the poet's mind more and more during the years that followed, and which reached its extreme expression in *Timon of Athens*. For it can of course only be the poet's own mind which confronts us in Hamlet. I observe in a book on Shakespeare by Georg Brandes (1896) a statement that *Hamlet* was written immediately after the death of Shakespeare's father (in 1601), that is, under the immediate impact of his bereavement and, as we may well assume, while his childhood feelings about his father had been freshly revived. It is known, too, that Shakespeare's own son who died at an early age bore the name "Hamnet," which is identical with "Hamlet." Just as *Hamlet* deals with the relation of a son to his parents, so *Macbeth* (written at approximately the same period) is concerned with the subject of childlessness. But just as all neurotic symptoms, and, for that matter, dreams, are capable of being "overinterpreted" and indeed need to be, if they are to be fully understood, so all genuinely creative writings are the product of more than a single motive and more than a single impulse in the poet's mind, and are open to more than a single interpretation. In what I have written I have only attempted to interpret the deepest layer of impulses in the mind of the creative writer.

From *The Interpretation of Dreams,* translated by James Strachey

CONSIDERATIONS FOR CRITICAL THINKING AND WRITING

1. What reason does Freud offer for Hamlet's inability to avenge his father's death? Explain whether you find Freud's reasoning convincing.

2. Read the section on psychological criticism (pp. 2050–52) in Chapter 53, "Critical Strategies for Reading," and then discuss Freud's assertion that "it can of course only be the poet's own mind which confronts us in Hamlet." Explain why you agree or disagree.

3. Write an essay discussing whether you think Freud's approach to Hamlet opens up perspectives on the play or narrowly limits them.

JAN KOTT (1914–2001)

On Producing Hamlet   1964

No Dane of flesh and blood has been written about so extensively as Hamlet. Shakespeare's prince is certainly the best known representative of his nation. Innumerable glossaries and commentaries have grown round Hamlet, and he is one of the few literary heroes who live apart from the text, apart from the theater. His name means something even to those who have never seen or read Shakespeare's play. In this respect he is rather like Leonardo's Mona Lisa. We know she is smiling even before we have seen the picture, as it were. It contains not only what Leonardo expressed in it but also everything that has been written about it. Too many people — girls, women, poets, painters — have tried to solve the mystery of that smile. It is not just Mona Lisa that is smiling at us now, but all those who have tried to analyze, or imitate, that smile.

This is also the case with *Hamlet,* or rather — with *Hamlet* in the theater. For we have been separated from the text not only by Hamlet's "independent life" in our culture, but simply by the size of the play. *Hamlet* cannot be performed in its entirety, because the performance would last nearly six hours. One has to select, curtail, and cut. One can perform only one of several *Hamlet*s potentially existing in this arch-play. It will always be a poorer *Hamlet* than Shakespeare's *Hamlet* is; but it may also be a *Hamlet* enriched by being of our time. It may, but I would rather say — it must be so.

For *Hamlet* cannot be played simply. This may be the reason why it is so tempting to producers and actors. Many generations have seen their own reflections in this play. The genius of *Hamlet* consists, perhaps, in the fact that the play can serve as a mirror. An ideal *Hamlet* would be one most true to Shakespeare and most modern at the same time. Is this possible? I do not know. But we can only appraise any Shakespearean production by asking how much there is of Shakespeare in it, and how much of us.

What I have in mind is not a forced topicality, a *Hamlet* that would be set in a cellar of young existentialists. *Hamlet* has been performed for that matter in evening dress and in circus tights; in medieval armor and in Renaissance costume. Costumes do not matter. What matters is that through Shakespeare's text we ought to get at our modern experience, anxiety, and sensibility.

There are many subjects in *Hamlet.* There is politics, force opposed to morality; there is discussion of the divergence between the theory and practice, of the ultimate purpose of life; there is tragedy of love, as well as family drama, political, eschatological, and metaphysical problems are considered. There is everything you want, including deep psychological analysis, a bloody story, a duel, and general slaughter. One can select at will. But one must know what one selects, and why.

From "*Hamlet* of the Mid-Century" in *Shakespeare Our Contemporary*, translated by Boleslaw Taborski

CONSIDERATIONS FOR CRITICAL THINKING AND WRITING

1. "Many generations have seen their own reflections in this play." Use this statement as a basis for researching productions of *Hamlet*. How have events contemporary to the play's performances influenced the ways it has been presented?

2. Explain why you think it is good or bad for a producer to interpret a play in light of events contemporary to it.

3. If you were to produce *Hamlet* today, what would you emphasize? Consider how you would handle the setting, costuming, casting, and theme.

4. What do you think a reader-response critic would have to say about Kott's comments on producing *Hamlet*? Base your answer on the discussion of reader-response criticism (pp. 2060–62) in Chapter 53, "Critical Strategies for Reading."

RUSSELL JACKSON (B. 1949)

A Film Diary of the Shooting of Kenneth Branagh's Hamlet   1996

Wednesday 3 January
Rehearsals Begin

First morning in Shepperton. This may be one of the major British studios but it's not, on first sight, impressive. Located in a semi-suburban hinterland southwest of London, it seems at first like an industrial estate, a jumble of sheds, hangars, workshops, and what look like builders' yards, with a mansion trapped in the middle of it all like a genteel hostage from Edwardian England. . . .

We're in the elegant boardroom of the old house, round a long green-baize covered table. First session is with Derek Jacobi (Claudius) and Julie Christie (Gertrude), plus Ken [Branagh], Orlando Seale (his "acting double"), Annie Wotton (Script Supervisor), Simon Mosley (First A.D.), and Hugh Cruttwell.

Ken distributes phials [vials] of a herbal "Rescue Remedy" (only half a joke, admitting nervous apprehension). Everyone has read the screenplay, and the actors have already had some discussion of their roles with Ken, but these days of rehearsal before we begin shooting will give everyone time for reappraisal, adjustments, and (most important) finding out how the story will be told by *this* company of actors, in *these* circumstances. We won't start with a read-through: better to edge toward the play. We discuss royal families (including the current one), privacy, politics, and draw toward a reading of the scenes when Claudius and Gertrude are together. There's talk about the issue of complicity between them (not at all, so far as murder is concerned) and the "essential" Claudius, which she took (and part of him still takes) as loving, kind, a "good" man. Derek goes along with this, though he and Hugh Cruttwell remind us of Hamlet's very different point of view. Gertrude and Claudius feel responsible for Hamlet but Claudius has another agenda she knows nothing about — concerning the potential threat posed by her son.

After lunch the Polonius family join us, with Horatio. By now we feel able to discuss frankly and simply (and off the record) our own experiences of family, bereavement, grief. (This is not just to canvass ideas about the emotions of the play to draw on them in performance: it also establishes common ground among us.) Then we try to imagine an "ideal" family, successful and well-balanced according to current middle-class notions, professional but not competitive, materially well-off but not showy — which (we agree) turns out quite repulsive. Then on to the Polonius family.

Polonius (Richard Briers) was promoted by new king. Laertes (Michael Maloney) is in Paris getting the gentlemanly accomplishments (N.B. not at Wittenberg). Ophelia (Kate Winslett) and Hamlet have been having an affair (yes, they have been to bed together, because we want this relationship to be as serious as possible) since the death of Hamlet senior. (Effect of a surge of feeling in time of bereavement and crisis?)

Thursday 4–Monday 8 January

We work through scenes, trying various approaches, finding snags, problems, opportunities. Ophelia's motivations in returning Hamlet's love tokens are considered: she is going further than Polonius suggested in any instructions we have heard, and whatever her father and the king expect from this confrontation, she has her own agenda (perhaps to find out why Hamlet is behaving this way to her, to put him on the spot?). The kinder and more circumspect Polonius seems, the harder it will be for her to betray him — hence her lying to Hamlet ("Where's your father? — At home, my lord"). In "To be or not to be" Ken wants to show Hamlet alone with his mirror image(s) in the vast space of the mirrored hall. He has to be careful not to give the soliloquy an energy or momentum that it does not need — those qualities are coming soon enough in what follows when he encounters Ophelia. Ken steers Derek toward seeming even more vulnerable as Claudius, "quietly anxious" about Hamlet after "nunnery" scene, rarely openly angry, even when Rosencrantz and Guildenstern have screwed up. So, when he does flare up, becomes desperate, it will be more shocking.

On 8 January we go over each actor's list of their character's priorities. Claudius has specific aims: inspiring confidence and trust in himself; loving Gertrude; making Hamlet look indulgent and neurotic (and thus defusing him); creating a new, strong, triumphalist Denmark (a military regime). Gertrude's aims are more general: decorum, sense of behaving properly in public; *noblesse oblige*, etiquette; sense of culture, confidence; loving Hamlet. Old Hamlet (Brian Blessed) points out that when he was alive he never let Claudius see how little he mattered — there has to be an underlying bitterness in what Claudius has done to get the crown as well as intense love for Gertrude. We consider different ways of showing these relationships in a short flashback — perhaps Old Hamlet and his son playing chess while Gertrude and Claudius watch, or some other activity (perhaps outdoors) that will focus their various feelings for each other.

From *Hamlet*. Screenplay and Introduction by
Kenneth Branagh. Film diary by Russell Jackson.

CONSIDERATIONS FOR CRITICAL THINKING AND WRITING

1. In what sense can the actors' discussions of character motivation and background be considered an interpretation of *Hamlet*? Why do you suppose the actors find these kinds of discussions useful?

2. Create a list of "priorities" for characters *not* already discussed by the actors on Branagh's set. Consider, for example, Horatio, Laertes, Rosencrantz, Guildenstern, Marcellus, or Bernardo.

3. How does Jackson's comment that it was essential for the actors to determine "how the story will be told by *this* company of actors, in *these* circumstances" compare with Jan Kott's observations on producing *Hamlet* (p. 1687)?

4. Rent a videotape of Branagh's *Hamlet* and write an essay that focuses on a single character or scene that you find especially effective (or not).

LINDA BAMBER (B. 1945)

Feminine Rebellion and Masculine Authority in A Midsummer Night's Dream

1981

In the comedies, the feminine challenges the status quo either overtly or through its command of socially subversive forces like sexuality, romantic passion, household revels, and so forth.

The best example of the relationship between male dominance and the status quo comes in *A Midsummer Night's Dream,* which begins with a rebellion of the feminine against the power of masculine authority. Hermia refuses the man both Aegeus and Theseus order her to marry; her refusal sends us off into the forest, beyond the power of the father and the masculine state. Once in the forest, of course, we find the social situation metaphorically repeated in this world of imagination and nature. The fairy king, Oberon, rules the forest. His rule, too, is troubled by the rebellion of the feminine. Titania has refused to give him her page, the child of a human friend who died in childbirth. But by the end of the story Titania is conquered, the child relinquished, and order restored. Even here the comic upheavals, whether we see them as May games or bad dreams, are associated with an uprising of women. David P. Young has pointed out how firmly this play connects order with masculine dominance and the disruption of order with the rebellion of the feminine:

> It is appropriate that Theseus, as representative of daylight and right reason, should have subdued his bride-to-be to the rule of his masculine will. That is the natural order of things. It is equally appropriate that Oberon, as king of darkness and fantasy, should have lost control of his wife, and that the corresponding natural disorder described by Titania should ensue.[1]

---

[1] David P. Young, *Something of Great Constancy* (New Haven, CT: Yale UP, 1966), 183.

The natural order, the status quo, is for men to rule women. When they fail to do so, we have the exceptional situation, the festive, disruptive, disorderly moment of comedy.

A Midsummer Night's Dream is actually an anomaly among the festive comedies. It is unusual for the forces of the green world to be directed, as they are here, by a masculine figure. Because the green world here is a partial reproduction of the social world, the feminine is reduced to a kind of first cause of the action while a masculine power directs it. In the other festive comedies the feminine Other presides. She does not *command* the forces of the alternative world, as Oberon does, but since she acts in harmony with these forces her will and desire often prevail.

Where are we to bestow our sympathies? On the forces that make for the disruption of the status quo and therefore for the plot? Or on the force that asserts itself against the disruption and reestablishes a workable social order? Of course we cannot choose. We can only say that in comedy we owe our holiday to such forces as the tendency of the feminine to rebel, whereas to the successful reassertion of masculine power we owe our everyday order. Shakespearean comedy endorses both sides. Holiday is, of course, the subject and the analogue of each play; but the plays always end in a return to everyday life. The optimistic reading of Shakespearean comedy says that everyday life is clarified and enriched by our holiday from it; according to the pessimistic reading the temporary subversion of the social order has revealed how much that order excludes, how high a price we pay for it. But whether our return to everyday life is a comfortable one or not, the return itself is the inevitable conclusion to the journey out.

> From *Comic Women, Tragic Men:*
> *A Study of Gender and Genre in Shakespeare*

CONSIDERATIONS FOR CRITICAL THINKING AND WRITING

1. What distinctions does Bamber make between the "optimistic" and "pessimistic" readings of Shakespearean comedy? In an essay explain how you would categorize your own reading of *A Midsummer Night's Dream*.

2. Compare Bamber's view of the "disruptive, disorderly moment of comedy" with James Kincaid's view of comedy (p. 1693). How do Bamber and Kincaid define the comic?

LOUIS ADRIAN MONTROSE (B. 1946)

On Amazonian Mythology
in A Midsummer Night's Dream   *1983*

The beginning of *A Midsummer Night's Dream* coincides with the end of a struggle in which Theseus has been victorious over the Amazon warrior:

> Hippolyta, I woo'd thee with my sword,
> And won thy love doing thee injuries;
> But I will wed thee in another key,
> With pomp, with triumph, and with revelling.
>
> (I.i.16–19)

Descriptions of the Amazons are ubiquitous in Elizabethan texts. . . .

Sixteenth-century travel narratives often recreate the ancient Amazons of Scythia in South America or in Africa. Invariably, the Amazons are relocated just beyond the receding boundary of *terra incognita*.° Thus, in Sierra Leone in 1582, the chaplain of an English expedition to the Spice Islands recorded the report of a Portuguese trader that "near the mountains of the moon there is a queen, empress of all these Amazons, a witch and a cannibal who daily feeds on the flesh of boys. She ever remains unmarried, but she has intercourse with a great number of men by whom she begets offspring. The kingdom, however, remains hereditary to the daughters, not to the sons."[1] This cultural fantasy assimilates Amazonian myth, witchcraft, and cannibalism into an anticulture which precisely inverts European norms of political authority, sexual license, marriage practices, and inheritance rules.[2] The attitude toward the Amazons expressed in such Renaissance texts is a mixture of fascination and horror. Amazonian mythology seems symbolically to embody and to control a collective anxiety about the power of the female not only to dominate or reject the male but to create and destroy him. It is an ironic acknowledgment by an androcentric° culture of the degree to which men are in fact dependent upon women: upon mothers and nurses, for their birth and nurture; upon mistresses and wives, for the validation of their manhood.

Shakespeare engages his wedding play in a dialectic with this mythological formation. The Amazons have been defeated before the play begins; and nuptial rites are to be celebrated when it ends. *A Midsummer Night's Dream* focuses upon different crucial transitions in the male and female life cycles: the fairy plot, upon taking "a little changeling boy" from childhood into youth, from the world of the mother into the world of the father; the Athenian plot, upon taking a maiden from youth into maturity, from the world of the father into the world of the husband. The pairing of the four Athenian lovers is made possible by the magical powers of Oberon and made lawful by the political authority of Theseus. Each of these rulers is preoccupied with the fulfillment of his own desires in the possession or repossession of a wife. Only after Hippolyta has been mastered by Theseus may marriage seal them "in everlasting bond of fellowship" (I.i.85). And only after "proud Titania" has been degraded by "jealous Oberon" (II.i.60, 61), has "in mild terms begg'd" (IV.i.53) his patience, and has readily yielded the changeling boy to him, may they be "new in amity" (IV.i.82).

---

terra incognita: Unknown land.   *androcentric*: Male-centered.

[1] *An Elizabethan in 1582: The Diary of Richard Madox, Fellow of All Souls,* ed. Elizabeth Story Donno, Hakluyt Society, second ser., no. 47 (London, 1977), p. 183. I owe this reference to Stephen Greenblatt, *Renaissance Self-Fashioning: From More to Shakespeare* (Chicago, 1980), p. 181.
[2] The linkage of Amazon, witch, and cannibal exemplifies a logic of inversion ingrained in European categories of thought. It has been suggested recently that sixteenth- and seventeenth-century witchcraft beliefs were a coherent, meaningful, and indeed necessary component of a larger intellectual system based upon principles of hierarchy, opposition, and inversion. This system linked together demonism, political sedition and rebellion, and female misrule as inversions of the divinely sanctioned order in the cosmos, state, and family. See Stuart Clark, "Inversion, Misrule and the Meaning of Witchcraft," *Past & Present* no. 87 (May 1980), 98–127. . . .

The . . . structure of *A Midsummer Night's Dream* eventually restores the inverted Amazonian system of gender and nurture to a patriarchal norm.

From " 'Shaping Fantasies': Figurations of Gender and Power
in Elizabethan Culture," *Representations,* Spring 1983

CONSIDERATIONS FOR CRITICAL THINKING AND WRITING

1. How does Montrose use "Amazonian mythology" to account for the plot elements in the play?

2. In an essay use the insights provided in Montrose's perspective to explore how order is associated with masculinity and rebellion is associated with femininity in *A Midsummer Night's Dream.*

JAMES KINCAID (B. 1937)
On the Value of Comedy in the Face of Tragedy   *1991*

[O]ur current hierarchical arrangement (tragedy high — comedy low) betrays an acquiescence in the most smothering of political conservatisms. Put another way, by coupling tragedy with the sublime, the ineffable, the metaphysical and by aligning comedy with the mundane, the quotidian, and the material we manage to muffle, even to erase, the most powerful narratives of illumination and liberation we have. . . .

The point is comic relief, the *concept* of comic relief and who it relieves. Now we usually refer to comic relief in the same tone we use for academic deans, other people's children, Melanie Griffith, the new criticism, jogging, Big Macs, the *New York Times Book Review,* leisure suits, people who go on cruises, realtors, and the MLA: bemused contempt. (Which is what we think about comic relief.) Comedy is that which attends on, offers relaxation from, prepares us for more of — something else, something serious and demanding. Comedy is not demanding — it does not demand or take, it gives. And we know that any agency which gives cannot be worth much. Tragedy's seriousness is guaranteed by its bullying greed, its insistence on having things its own way and pulling from us not only our tears, which we value little, but our attention, which we hate to give. Comedy, on the other hand, doesn't care if we attend closely. Tragedy is sleek and single-minded, comedy rumpled and hospitable to any idea or agency. Tragedy stares us out of countenance; comedy winks and leers and drools. Tragedy is all dressed up; comedy is always taking things off, mooning us. We find it inevitable that we associate tragedy with the high, comedy with the low. What is at issue here is the nature of that inevitability, our willingness to conspire in a discourse which pays homage to tragic grandeur and reduces comedy to release, authorized license, periodic relief — like a sneeze or yawn or belch. By allowing such discourse to flow through us, we add our bit of cement to the cultural edifice that sits on top of comedy, mashes it down into a mere adjunct to tragedy, its reverse and inferior half, its silly little carnival. By cooperating in this move, we relieve orthodox and conservative power structures of any pressure that might be exercised against them. Comic relief relieves the status quo, in other words, contains the power of comedy. . . .

Let's put it this way, comedy is not a mode that stands in opposition to tragedy. Comedy is the *whole* story, the narrative which refuses to leave things out. Tragedy insists on a formal structure that is unified and coherent, formally balanced and elegantly tight. Only that which is coordinate is allowed to adorn the tragic body. With comedy, nothing is sacrificed, nothing lost; the discoordinate and the discontinuous are especially welcome. Tragedy protects itself by its linearity, its tight conclusiveness; comedy's generosity and ability never to end make it gloriously vulnerable. Pitting tragedy against comedy is running up algebra against recess. . . .

From a paper read at the 1991 meeting of the Modern Language Association, "Who Is Relieved by the Idea of Comic Relief?"

Considerations for Critical Thinking and Writing

1. What distinctions does Kincaid make between comedy and tragedy? How does his description of tragedy compare with Aristotle's (see p. 1502)?

2. How does Kincaid's description of comedy fit *A Midsummer Night's Dream*?

3. According to Kincaid, why is the denigration of comedy a conservative impulse? In an essay explain why you agree or disagree with the argument.

Two Complementary Critical Readings

Joan Montgomery Byles (b. 1939)
Ophelia's Desperation   1989

Critics from Bradley on have been perplexed by Ophelia. Bradley found "slight psychological incongruity" in Hamlet's treatment of Ophelia as a wanton, for "there is nothing in the least wanton about Ophelia." Traversi saw Hamlet as "shattering Ophelia's spirit." Dover Wilson thought Hamlet's attitude towards Ophelia the "greatest puzzle" in the play, and Wilson-Knight saw Ophelia as Hamlet's "only hope." Francis Fergusson viewed Ophelia's death as a "maimed rite" where instead of a marriage we have a funeral. Linda Bamber suggests that Ophelia has no choices in the play, and as a consequence we are not very interested in her. Leverenz suggests that rather than "get mad, Ophelia goes mad."[1]

Ophelia is anxious; her alertness to disapproval encourages her to be uncertain in expression. At four different times she says, "I do not know what to think, my lord," twice to her father and twice to Hamlet. Ophelia is frightened

---

[1] A. C. Bradley, *Shakespearean Tragedy* (London: Macmillan, 1960); Derek Traversi, *An Approach to Shakespeare* (New York: Doubleday, 1956); J. Dover Wilson, *What Happens in Hamlet* (Cambridge, England: Cambridge UP, 1956); G. Wilson-Knight, *The Imperial Theme* (London: Methuen, 1970); Francis Fergusson, *The Idea of a Theater* (New York: Doubleday, 1972); Linda Bamber, *Comic Women, Tragic Men* (Stanford: U of California, 1982); David Leverenz, "The Woman in Hamlet: An Interpersonal View," in *Representing Shakespeare: New Psychoanalytic Essays,* ed. Murray M. Schwartz and Coppélia Kahn (Baltimore: Johns Hopkins UP, 1980).

of her father and dare not disobey him. She is not allowed to have, much less declare an emotional world of her own. Her sense of self seems very much defined and controlled by the men in her life: her father, her brother, and her lover. She exists in a world created by their need, in which she is an object at all times conformable to their egos — at least until she goes mad. . . .

Ophelia has been unable to establish a real dialogue with anyone in the play, now she establishes one with herself but — the listeners, who really listen to her for the first time, are no longer necessary. She needs no reply. She has discovered her own voice, her inner self. Her speech confers a spoken meaning on her frustration and suffering, her uncertain sense of self, her anger and dismay, and gives her an impressive independence for the first and last time in the play. Her death is the ultimate expression of her repressed anger and aggression turned inwards. Unable not to love, cruelly denied her desperate need to be loved, unable to displace her repressed anger and aggression directly onto Hamlet, her father, or her brother, she turns it against herself. Whose fault is this? Hers? Her father's? Hamlet's? Where does the problem in Ophelia's subjective identity and its inability to adequately express itself come from? Why is her only way out of her predicament madness and suicide? Shakespeare shows that Ophelia's destiny is the result of her position within her family circle, which is embedded in Elizabethan sexist society. The structure of Elizabethan family life, the objective conditions of women, and the role men played as fathers, brothers, and lovers, caused many women to live attached, dependent lives, with weak self-images. Shakespeare is well aware that his society and audience is a sexist one. Only exceptional women were educated sufficiently to be independent, socially, economically, and intellectually. There were precious few divorces and such divorces could leave a woman in a penurious or "beggarly" condition. . . . For some women one sort of release from the stranglehold family life could have on them was madness and even suicide.

From "The Problem of the Self and the Other in the Language of Ophelia, Desdemona and Cordelia," *American Imago*, Spring 1989

CONSIDERATIONS FOR CRITICAL THINKING AND WRITING

1. Of the competing readings of Ophelia cited by Byles in her first paragraph, which do you find most compelling?
2. How is Ophelia's "sense of self . . . defined and controlled by the men in her life" (para. 2)? What kind of evidence does Byles use to support this claim?
3. Explain why you agree or disagree that Ophelia's final speech "gives her an impressive independence for the first and last time in the play" (para. 3).

SANDRA K. FISCHER (B. 1950)

Ophelia's Mad Speeches

1990

Critical opinion about the function of Ophelia's mad rhetoric differs widely. Placing Ophelia in a dramatic context of madwomen and their talk, the Charneys find that "Madness enables her to assert her being; she is no longer enforced to keep silent" and that through madness she can "suddenly make a forceful assertion of . . . being. The lyric form and broken syntax and unbridled imagination all show ways of breaking through unbearable social restraints."[1] Certainly Ophelia's mad speeches rivet the attention, but they seem to point to a loss rather than an assertion of self: a theme of the songs is the inability to choose among a socially-circumscribed series of insufficient options. The voice of madness is indeed louder than her earlier rhetoric, yet it fails to break through or change the constraints. It manages to articulate them only indirectly, and her meaning remains unheard. R. S. White makes her allusiveness more mystical than insane: "By a kind of sympathetic magic, the conditions which face Ophelia find their way into her songs, in oblique and confused fashion."[2] David Leverenz, in applying gender theory to both Hamlet and Ophelia and their language, offers a perceptive summary of the pastiche of meanings embedded in Ophelia's final appearance:

> . . . contemporary work with schizophrenics reveals the tragic variety of people whose voices are only amalgams of other people's voices, with caustic self-observation or a still more terrifying vacuum as their incessant inward reality. This is Hamlet to a degree, as it is Ophelia completely. . . . [T]here are many voices in Ophelia's madness speaking through her, all making sense, and none of them her own. She becomes the mirror for a madness-inducing world. . . . Through her impossible attempt to obey contradictory voices, Ophelia mirrors in her madness the tensions that Hamlet perceives. . . . Her history is another instance of how someone can be driven mad by having her inner feelings misrepresented, not responded to, or acknowledged only through chastisement and repression.[3]

The ambiguity of the voices in Ophelia's songs and mad commentary is complex and fascinating. Nearly every reference has multiple signification, as if she attempts to squeeze and condense all the censored feelings and observations of the play into a compact logic of expression — hence, her admonitions to "mark," that is, to hear and understand. For example, "He is dead and gone" is actually the center of the play, referring to Hamlet, Sr., Polonius, and, if Claudius's order were carried out, to Hamlet himself. As Hamlet must try to connect past, present, and future, so Ophelia becomes a repository of memory, of events unconnected but through destiny linked in fatal concatenation.

From "Hearing Ophelia: Gender and Tragic Discourse in *Hamlet*,"
From *Renaissance and Reformation*, Winter 1990

[1]Maurice Charney and Hanna Charney, "The Language of Madwomen in Shakespeare and His Fellow Dramatists," *Signs* 3 (1977): 456, 459.

[2]"The Tragedy of Ophelia," *Ariel* 9, 2 (1978): 49.

[3]David Leverenz, "The Woman in Hamlet: An Interpersonal View," in *Representing Shakespeare: New Psychoanalytic Essays*, ed. Murray M. Schwartz and Coppélia Kahn (Baltimore: Johns Hopkins UP, 1980), 112, 117.

CONSIDERATIONS FOR CRITICAL THINKING AND WRITING

1. Do you think Ophelia finds herself or loses herself in her speeches? Explain.
2. Discuss Leverenz's observation that "Ophelia mirrors in her madness the tensions that Hamlet perceives."

3. Compare Fischer's view of Ophelia's madness with Byles's treatment in the preceding Perspective. Explain why you think they complement or contradict one another.

SUGGESTED TOPICS FOR LONGER PAPERS

1. Discuss Shakespeare's use of humor in *A Midsummer Night's Dream* and in *Hamlet*. Focus on at least one humorous scene in each play as the basis of your discussion and characterize the tone of the humor. What generalizations can you make about the tone and purpose of the humor in the plays?

2. Research how marriage was regarded in Elizabethan times and compare those attitudes and values with the treatment of marriage in *A Midsummer Night's Dream* or *Hamlet*.

ENCOUNTERING DRAMA: A VISUAL PORTFOLIO
HAMLET IN POPULAR CULTURE AND PERFORMANCE

Although William Shakespeare wrote *Hamlet* more than four hundred years ago, its impact on contemporary life — on literature, visual art, theater and film, and even everyday language — is wide-reaching and profound. *Hamlet* is the most famous play written in the English language, and its timeless themes and memorable characters continue to make it the subject of fine art, popular art, and numerous adaptations on stage and on film. This port-folio, which features multiple portrayals of the characters of Hamlet and Ophelia, offers a sense of *Hamlet*'s cultural presence and significance. In the following images, the character Hamlet is represented in fine art and in multiple performances — from Sarah Bernhardt to Ethan Hawke — and the character Ophelia is represented in nineteenth-century paintings, a con-temporary performance, and a cartoon from *The New Yorker*. How do these portrayals compare with your reading of the play and its characters?

Hamlet and Horatio in the Cemetery (1839). Inspired by a 1927 English production of *Hamlet* in Paris, the French Romantic painter Eugène Delacroix (1798–1863) rendered a series of images from the play, including this painting of the graveyard scene (Act V, Scene i). Here, under a brooding sky, a gravedigger hands Hamlet the skull of Yorick. "Alas, poor Yorick!" says Hamlet, "I knew him, Horatio: a fellow of infinite jest. . . ." (See also Delacroix's *The Death of Ophelia,* page 1703.)

CONSIDERATIONS AND CONNECTIONS

1. Given your own reading of the character Hamlet, how does the portrayal of Hamlet by Delacroix compare with how you imagine him?

2. Discuss the representations of death in this painting and in Delacroix's treatment of Ophelia (p. 1703). How does Delacroix's depiction of death compare with Shakespeare's?

Sarah Bernhardt as Hamlet (1900). In his book *Shakespeare in the Movies,* the film critic Douglas Brode writes, "[Shakespeare's plays] aren't plays at all; rather, they are screenplays, written, ironically, three centuries before the birth of cinema." The first film version of the play was a bold interpretation titled *Le Duel d'Hamlet,* produced for the Paris Exhibition of 1900. Playing the lead was Sarah Bernhardt (known as "The Divine Sarah"), the most famous, or at least most scandalous, actress of the nineteenth century. One of the earliest films with sound, the dialogue of *Le Duel* was dubbed (in French), and sound effects for swordfighting were made by clacking knives behind the screen.

© Bettmann/CORBIS.

CONSIDERATIONS AND CONNECTIONS

1. What advantages and/or disadvantages do you think there are when the role of Hamlet is played by a woman?

2. Comment on Bernhardt's costuming and that of Ethan Hawke (p. 1700). What are the effects of each costume upon your perception of Hamlet's character? Which do you prefer? Explain why.

Laurence Olivier as Hamlet
(1948). Since the first staging of *Hamlet* by Shakespeare's acting troupe (probably between 1600 and 1601, before the Quarto was first published in 1603), the role of the Prince of Denmark has been interpreted by countless performers. Sir Laurence Olivier, who directed, produced, and played the lead in this famous film version, called *Hamlet* "the tragedy of a man who couldn't make up his mind."
© Bettmann/CORBIS.

CONSIDERATIONS AND CONNECTIONS

1. How does this scene of Hamlet (Laurence Olivier) with Yorick's skull compare with Delacroix's (p. 1698)? Which scene emphasizes more the grim reality of death to you? Explain why.

2. How old is Hamlet in the play? Compare this image of Olivier with that of Ethan Hawke (above). Explain why you would choose one or the other actor as closer to your own sense of Hamlet's age.

Ethan Hawke as Hamlet (1999). Directed by Michael Almeryeda, this contemporary vision of *Hamlet* sets the tragedy in New York City, in the context of corporate America. Ethan Hawke (left) portrays Hamlet as a young filmmaker struggling to gain control over his deceased father's business. Hawke comments: "I always thought that in a modern sense Hamlet was mostly a kind of Holden Caulfield or Kurt Cobain, and I wanted to evoke that spirit. . . . Many of his dilemmas are a young man's dilemmas. He's concerned about his relationship with his father and his mother. He doesn't really know who he is or what he's about. He's got this girlfriend situation. These are all a young man's issues . . . seeking meaning and being confused and overwhelmed by events you don't feel you control."

CONSIDERATIONS AND CONNECTIONS

1. How accurately do you think Hawke's comments about Hamlet's dilemmas sum up his character? Explain why you think a contemporary treatment of the play enhances or damages it.

2. Except to identify Hawke as Hamlet, the caption does not indicate who the other three figures are. Who do you think those actors portray? Explain why.

Ophelia: Here Is Rosemary ▶

(mid- to late nineteenth century). Undone by the death of her father and abandonment by Hamlet, Ophelia's behavior becomes increasingly erratic. In Act IV, Scene v, she offers the grieving Laertes a sprig of rosemary: "There's rosemary, that's for remembrance; pray you, love, remember: and there is pansies, that's for thoughts." Laertes calls her speech "a document in madness," and the King, earlier in the scene, asks the Queen to "follow her close; give her good watch," as Ophelia is "divided from herself and her fair judgement." Ophelia's madness and sexuality were popular subjects among artists of the nineteenth century, and this painting by William Gorman Wills (Ireland, 1828–91), offers an especially provocative reading of Ophelia and her relationship to Laertes. (See also "Ophelia's Mad Speeches," page 1695.)

CONSIDERATIONS AND CONNECTIONS

1. Discuss the manner in which Ophelia and Laertes are posed together in this painting. What do you think Wills is suggesting about the nature of the connection between them? Does the play's text support that depiction of them?

2. Of the three images of Ophelia—Wills's, Delacroix's (p. 1703), and Winslet's (p. 1702)—which do you find to be the most in line with your reading of the character? Explain why.

"He's, like, 'To be or not to be,' and I'm, like, 'Get a life.'"

Ophelia cartoon from *The New Yorker* (Lee Lorenz, 1995). In "Reading Ophelia's Madness" Gabrielle Dane writes: "Ophelia has been shaped to conform to external demands, to reflect others' desires . . . she appears condemned to martyrdom on the altar of male fantasies and priorities." In the play, the character Ophelia is manipulated by those closest to her — by her father Polonius, her brother Laertes, and her beloved Hamlet. Not so the Ophelia of this *New Yorker* cartoon — here we see a rebellious and sassy version of the character, one who is fed up with Hamlet's turmoil and dramatic speeches, and far from mad.

CONSIDERATIONS AND CONNECTIONS

1. Are there any passages in the play that warrant Lorenz's cartoon representation of Ophelia? Why or why not?
2. Try creating your own cartoon of another character in Hamlet that captures some of the contemporary humorous tone that Lorenz evokes.

Kate Winslet as Ophelia (1996). Set in the late nineteenth century, with Victorian-inspired costumes and sets, Kenneth Branagh's epic film version of *Hamlet* intensifies the relationship between Hamlet and Ophelia by including an explicit sex scene. Ophelia (played by Kate Winslet) flashes back to this encounter when her father asks her about Hamlet: "Do you believe his tenders, as you call them?" She answers: "I do not know, my lord, what I should think." (Act I, Scene iii). Another twist is Ophelia's mad scene — Winslet performs it bound in a straitjacket (Act IV, Scene v). "Winslet plays Ophelia like Laura from *The Glass Menagerie*," wrote the film critic Chris Hewitt; "she's a delicate piece of glass, slowly breaking into a million pieces." (See also "A Film Diary of the Shooting of Kenneth Branagh's *Hamlet*," page 1688.)

1. Name at least two other contemporary actors that you think could effectively play the role of Ophelia and explain your choices.
2. View Kenneth Branagh's version of *Hamlet* and write a review that assesses Winslet's role as Ophelia.

The Death of Ophelia (1853, by Eugène Delacroix). There is much scholarly debate about the nature of Ophelia's death—was it an accident? a suicide? perhaps a murder by the queen? In Delacroix's vision of Ophelia's final moments, a passive figure, bathed in light and loosely clad, is both etherealized and eroticized. The image is, arguably, a departure from the "muddy death" described by Queen Gertrude (Act IV, Scene vii). (See also *Hamlet and Horatio in the Cemetery,* page 1698.)

The Art Archive / Musée du Louvre, Paris / Dagli Orti.

CONSIDERATIONS AND CONNECTIONS

1. Explain why you think Delacroix's image of Ophelia's death points to suicide, an accident, or ambiguity.
2. Compare the Queen's description of Ophelia's drowning (Act IV, Scene vii, lines 164–81) with the visual details of this painting. What important similarities and differences do you find in each rendering?

49

Modern Drama

A play should give you something to think about. When I see a play and understand it the first time, then I know it can't be much good.

—T. S. ELIOT

REALISM

Realism is a literary technique that attempts to create the appearance of life as it is actually experienced. Characters in modern realistic plays (written during and after the last quarter of the nineteenth century) speak dialogue that we might hear in our daily lives. These characters are not larger than life but representative of it; they seem to speak the way we do rather than in highly poetic language, formal declarations, asides, or soliloquies. It is impossible to imagine a heroic figure such as Oedipus inhabiting a comfortably furnished living room and chatting about his wife's household budget the way Torvald Helmer does in Henrik Ibsen's *A Doll House*. Realism brings into focus commonplace, everyday life rather than the extraordinary kinds of events that make up Sophocles' *Oedipus the King* or Shakespeare's *Hamlet*.

Realistic characters can certainly be heroic, but like Nora Helmer, they find that their strength and courage are tested in the context of events ordinary people might experience. Work, love, marriage, children, and death are often the focus of realistic dramas. These subjects can also constitute much of the material in nonrealistic plays, but modern realistic dramas present such material in the realm of the probable. Conflicts in realistic plays are likely to reflect problems in our own lives. Hence, making ends meet takes precedence over saving a kingdom; middle- and lower-class individuals take center stage as primary characters in main plots rather than being secondary characters in subplots. Thus we can see why the nineteenth-century movement toward realism paralleled the rise of a middle class eagerly seeking representations of its concerns in the theater.

Before the end of the nineteenth century, however, few attempts were made in the theater to present life as it is actually lived. The chorus's role in Sophocles' *Oedipus the King*, the allegorical figures in morality plays, the remarkable mistaken identities in Shakespeare's comedies, or the rhymed couplets spoken in seventeenth-century plays such as Molière's *Tartuffe* represent theatrical conventions rather than life. Theatergoers have understood and appreciated these conventions for centuries — and still do — but in the nineteenth century social, political, and industrial revolutions helped create an atmosphere in which some playwrights found it necessary to create works that more directly reflected their audiences' lives.

Playwrights such as Henrik Ibsen and Anton Chekhov refused to join the ranks of their romantic contemporaries, who they felt falsely idealized life. The most popular plays immediately preceding the works of these realistic writers consisted primarily of love stories and action-packed plots. Such **melodramas** offer audiences thrills and chills as well as happy endings. They typically include a virtuous individual struggling under the tyranny of a wicked oppressor, who is defeated only at the last moment. Suspense is reinforced by a series of pursuits, captures, and escapes that move the plot quickly and de-emphasize character or theme. These representations of extreme conflicts enjoyed wide popularity in the nineteenth century — indeed, they still do — because their formula was varied enough to be entertaining yet their outcomes were always comforting to the audience's sense of justice. From the realists' perspective, melodramas were merely escape fantasies that distorted life by refusing to examine the real world closely and objectively. But an indication of the popularity of such happy endings can be seen in Chekhov's farcical comedies, such as *The Proposal*, a one-act play filled with exaggerated characters and action. Despite his realist's values, Chekhov was also sometimes eager to please audiences.

Realists attempted to open their audiences' eyes; to their minds, the only genuine comfort was in knowing the truth. Many of their plays concern controversial issues of the day and focus on people who fall prey to indifferent societal institutions. English dramatist John Galsworthy (1867–1933) examined social values in *Strife* (1909) and *Justice* (1910), two plays whose titles broadly suggest the nature of his concerns. British playwright George Bernard Shaw (1856–1950) often used comedy and irony as means of awakening his audiences to contemporary problems: *Arms and the Man* (1894) satirizes romantic attitudes toward war, and *Mrs. Warren's Profession* (1898) indicts a social and economic system that drives a woman to prostitution. Chekhov's major plays are populated by characters frustrated by their social situations and their own sensibilities; they are ordinary people who long for happiness but become entangled in everyday circumstances that limit their lives. Ibsen also took a close look at his characters' daily lives. His plays attack social conventions and challenge popular attitudes toward marriage; he stunned audiences by dramatizing the suffering of a man dying of syphilis.

With these kinds of materials, Ibsen and his contemporaries popularized the **problem play,** a drama that represents a social issue in order to awaken the audience to it. These plays usually reject romantic plots in favor of holding up a mirror that reflects not simply what audiences want to see but what the playwright sees in them. Nineteenth-century realistic theater was no refuge from the social, economic, and psychological problems that melodrama ignored or sentimentalized.

NATURALISM

Related to realism is another movement, called **naturalism.** Essentially more of a philosophical attitude than a literary technique, naturalism derives its name from the idea that human beings are part of nature and subject to its laws. According to naturalists, heredity and environment shape and control people's lives; their behavior is determined more by instinct than by reason. This deterministic view argues that human beings have no transcendent identity because there is no soul or spiritual world that ultimately distinguishes humanity from any other form of life. Characters in naturalistic plays are generally portrayed as victims overwhelmed by internal and external forces. Thus literary naturalism tends to include not only the commonplace but the sordid, destructive, and chaotic aspects of life. Naturalism, then, is an extreme form of realism.

The earliest and most articulate voice of naturalism was that of French author Émile Zola (1840–1902), who urged artists to draw their characters from life and present their histories as faithfully as scientists report laboratory findings. Zola's best-known naturalistic play, *Thérèse Raquin* (1873), is a dramatization of an earlier novel involving a woman whose passion causes her to take a lover and plot with him to kill her husband. In his preface to the novel, Zola explains that his purpose is to take "a strong man and unsatisfied woman," "throw them into a violent drama and note scrupulously the sensations and acts of these creatures." The diction of Zola's statement reveals his nearly clinical approach, which becomes even more explicit when Zola likens his method of revealing character to that of an autopsy: "I have simply done on two living bodies the work which surgeons do on corpses."

Although some naturalistic plays have been successfully produced and admired (notably Maxim Gorky's *The Lower Depths* [1902], set in a grim board-inghouse occupied by characters who suffer poverty, crime, betrayal, disease, and suicide), few important dramatists fully subscribed to naturalism's extreme methods and values. Nevertheless, the movement significantly influenced playwrights. Because of its insistence on the necessity of closely observing characters' environment, playwrights placed a new emphasis on detailed settings and natural acting. This verisimilitude became a significant feature of realistic drama.

THEATRICAL CONVENTIONS OF MODERN DRAMA

The picture-frame stage that is often used for realistic plays typically repro-duces the setting of a room in some detail. Within the stage, framed by a proscenium arch (from which the curtain hangs), scenery and props are used to create an illusion of reality. Whether the "small bookcase with richly bound books" described in the opening scene of Ibsen's *A Doll House* is only painted scenery or an actual case with books, it will probably look real to the audience. Removing the fourth wall of a room so that an audi-ence can look in fosters the illusion that the actions onstage are real events happening before unseen spectators. The texture of Nora's life is commu-nicated by the set as well as by what she says and does. That doesn't happen in a play like Sophocles' *Oedipus the King*. Technical effects can make us believe there is wood burning in a fireplace or snow falling outside a win-dow. Outdoor settings are made similarly realistic by props and painted sets. In one of Chekhov's full-length plays, for example, the second act opens in a meadow with the faint outline of a city on the horizon.

In addition to lifelike sets, a particular method of acting is used to create a realistic atmosphere. Actors address each other instead of directing formal speeches toward the audience; they act within the setting, not merely before it. At the beginning of the twentieth century Konstantin Stanislavsky (1863–1938), a Russian director, teacher, and actor, developed a system of acting that was an important influence in realistic theater. He trained actors to identify with the inner emotions of the characters they played. They were encouraged to recall from their own lives emotional responses similar to those they were portraying. The goal was to present a role truthfully by first feeling and then projecting the character's situation. Among Stanislavsky's early successes in this method were the plays of Chekhov.

There are, however, degrees of realism on the stage. Tennessee Williams's *The Glass Menagerie* (1945), for example, is a partially realistic portrayal of characters whose fragile lives are founded on illusions. Williams's dialogue rings true, and individual scenes resemble the kind of real-life action we would imagine such vulnerable characters engaging in, but other elements of the play are nonrealistic. For instance, Williams uses Tom as a major character in the play as well as narrator and stage manager. Here is part of Williams's stage directions: "The narrator is an undisguised convention of the play. He takes whatever license with dramatic convention as is convenient to his purposes." Although this play can be accurately described as including realistic elements, Williams, like many other contemporary playwrights, does not attempt an absolute fidelity to reality. He uses flashbacks — as does Arthur Miller in *Death of a Salesman* (p. 1869) — to present incidents that occurred before the opening scene because the past impinges so heavily on the present. Most playwrights don't attempt to duplicate reality, since that can now be done so well by motion pictures.

Realism needn't lock a playwright into a futile attempt to make everything appear as it is in life. There is no way to avoid theatrical conventions: actors impersonate characters in a setting that is, after all, a stage. Indeed, even the dialogue in a realistic play is quite different from the pauses, sentence fragments, repetitions, silences, and incoherencies that characterize the way people usually speak. Realistic dialogue may seem like ordinary speech, but it, like Shakespeare's poetic language, is constructed. If we remember that realistic drama represents only the appearance of reality and that what we read on a page or see and hear onstage is the result of careful selecting, editing, and even distortion, then we are more likely to appreciate the playwright's art.

A Doll House

Henrik Ibsen was born in Skien, Norway, to wealthy parents, who lost their money while he was a young boy. His early experiences with small-town life and genteel poverty sensitized him to the problems that he subsequently dramatized in a number of his plays. At age sixteen he was apprenticed to a druggist; he later thought about studying medicine, but by his early twenties he was earning a living writing and directing plays in various Norwegian cities. By the time of his death he enjoyed an international reputation for his treatment of social issues related to middle-class life.

Time Life Pictures/Mansell/Getty Images.

Ibsen's earliest dramatic works were historical and romantic plays, some in verse. His first truly realistic work was *The Pillars of Society* (1877), whose title ironically hints at the corruption and hypocrisy exposed in it. The realistic social-problem plays for which he is best known followed. These dramas at once fascinated and shocked international audiences.

Among his most produced and admired works are *A Doll House* (1879), *Ghosts* (1881), *An Enemy of the People* (1882), *The Wild Duck* (1884), and *Hedda Gabler* (1890). The common denominator in many of Ibsen's dramas is his interest in individuals struggling for an authentic identity in the face of tyrannical social conventions. This conflict often results in his characters' being divided between a sense of duty to themselves and their responsibility to others.

Ibsen used such external and internal conflicts to propel his plays' action. Like many of his contemporaries who wrote realistic plays, he adopted the form of the ***well-made play.*** A dramatic structure popularized in France by Eugène Scribe (1791–1861) and Victorien Sardou (1831–1908), the well-made play employs conventions including plenty of suspense created by meticulous plotting. Extensive exposition explains past events that ultimately lead to an inevitable climax. Tension is released when a secret that reverses the protagonist's fortunes is revealed. Ibsen, having directed a number of Scribe's plays in Norway, knew their cause-to-effect plot arrangements and used them for his own purposes in his problem plays.

A Doll House dramatizes the tensions of a nineteenth-century middle-class marriage in which a wife struggles to step beyond the limited identity imposed on her by her husband and society. Although the Helmers' pleasant apartment seems an unlikely setting for the fierce conflicts that develop, the issues raised in the play are unmistakably real. *A Doll House* affirms the necessity to reject hypocrisy, complacency, cowardice, and stifling conventions if life is to have dignity and meaning. Several critical approaches to the play can be found in Chapter 50, "A Critical Case Study: Henrik Ibsen's *A Doll House.*"

HENRIK IBSEN (1828–1906)

A Doll House   *1879*

TRANSLATED BY ROLF FJELDE

THE CHARACTERS

Torvald Helmer, a lawyer
Nora, his wife
Dr. Rank
Mrs. Linde
Nils Krogstad, a bank clerk
The Helmers' three small children
Anne-Marie, their nurse
Helene, a maid
A Delivery Boy

See Plays in Performance insert.

SCENE: The action takes place in Helmer's residence.

ACT I

A comfortable room, tastefully but not expensively furnished. A door to the right in the back wall leads to the entryway; another to the left leads to Helmer's study. Between these doors, a piano. Midway in the left-hand wall a door, and further back a window. Near the window a round table with an armchair and a small sofa. In the right-hand wall, toward the rear, a door, and nearer the foreground a porcelain stove with two armchairs and a rocking chair beside it. Between the stove and the side door, a small table. Engravings on the walls. An etagère with china figures and other small art objects; a small bookcase with richly bound books; the floor carpeted; a fire burning in the stove. It is a winter day.

A bell rings in the entryway; shortly after we hear the door being unlocked. Nora comes into the room, humming happily to herself; she is wearing street clothes and carries an armload of packages, which she puts down on the table to the right. She has left the hall door open; and through it a Delivery Boy is seen, holding a Christmas tree and a basket, which he gives to the Maid who let them in.

Nora: Hide the tree well, Helene. The children mustn't get a glimpse of it till this evening, after it's trimmed. *(To the Delivery Boy, taking out her purse.)* How much?

Delivery Boy: Fifty, ma'am.

Nora: There's a crown. No, keep the change. *(The Boy thanks her and leaves. Nora shuts the door. She laughs softly to herself while taking off her street things. Drawing a bag of macaroons from her pocket, she eats a couple, then steals over and listens at her husband's study door.)* Yes, he's home. *(Hums again as she moves to the table right.)*

Helmer (from the study): Is that my little lark twittering out there?

Nora (busy opening some packages): Yes, it is.

Helmer: Is that my squirrel rummaging around?

Nora: Yes!

Helmer: When did my squirrel get in?

Nora: Just now. *(Putting the macaroon bag in her pocket and wiping her mouth.)* Do come in, Torvald, and see what I've bought.

Helmer: Can't be disturbed. *(After a moment he opens the door and peers in, pen in hand.)* Bought, you say? All that there? Has the little spendthrift been out throwing money around again?

Nora: Oh, but Torvald, this year we really should let ourselves go a bit. It's the first Christmas we haven't had to economize.

Helmer: But you know we can't go squandering.

Nora: Oh yes, Torvald, we can squander a little now. Can't we? Just a tiny, wee bit. Now that you've got a big salary and are going to make piles and piles of money.

Helmer: Yes — starting New Year's. But then it's a full three months till the raise comes through.

Nora: Pooh! We can borrow that long.

Helmer: Nora! *(Goes over and playfully takes her by the ear.)* Are your scatter-brains off again? What if today I borrowed a thousand crowns, and you squandered them over Christmas week, and then on New Year's Eve a roof tile fell on my head and I lay there —

Nora (putting her hand on his mouth): Oh! Don't say such things!

Helmer: Yes, but what if it happened — then what?

Nora: If anything so awful happened, then it just wouldn't matter if I had debts or not.

Helmer: Well, but the people I'd borrowed from?

Nora: Them? Who cares about them! They're strangers.

Helmer: Nora, Nora, how like a woman! No, but seriously, Nora, you know what I think about that. No debts! Never borrow! Something of freedom's lost — and something of beauty, too — from a home that's founded on borrowing and debt. We've made a brave stand up to now, the two of us; and we'll go right on like that the little while we have to.

Nora (going toward the stove): Yes, whatever you say, Torvald.

Helmer (following her): Now, now, the little lark's wings mustn't droop. Come on, don't be a sulky squirrel. *(Taking out his wallet.)* Nora, guess what I have here.

Nora (turning quickly): Money!

Helmer: There, see. *(Hands her some notes.)* Good grief, I know how costs go up in a house at Christmastime.

Nora: Ten — twenty — thirty — forty. Oh, thank you, Torvald; I can manage no end on this.

Helmer: You really will have to.

Nora: Oh yes, I promise I will! But come here so I can show you everything I bought. And so cheap! Look, new clothes for Ivar here — and a sword. Here a horse and a trumpet for Bob. And a doll and a doll's bed here for Emmy; they're nothing much, but she'll tear them to bits in no time anyway. And here I have dress material and handkerchiefs for the maids. Old Anne-Marie really deserves something more.

Helmer: And what's in that package there?

Nora (with a cry): Torvald, no! You can't see that till tonight!

Helmer: I see. But tell me now, you little prodigal, what have you thought of for yourself?

Nora: For myself? Oh, I don't want anything at all.

Helmer: Of course you do. Tell me just what — within reason — you'd most like to have.

Nora: I honestly don't know. Oh, listen, Torvald —

Helmer: Well?

Nora (fumbling at his coat buttons, without looking at him): If you want to give me something, then maybe you could — you could —

Helmer: Come on, out with it.

Nora (hurriedly): You could give me money, Torvald. No more than you think you can spare; then one of these days I'll buy something with it.

Helmer: But Nora —

Nora: Oh please, Torvald darling, do that! I beg you, please. Then I could hang the bills in pretty gilt paper on the Christmas tree. Wouldn't that be fun?

Helmer: What are those little birds called that always fly through their fortunes?

Nora: Oh yes, spendthrifts: I know all that. But let's do as I say, Torvald; then I'll have time to decide what I really need most. That's very sensible, isn't it?

Helmer (smiling): Yes, very — that is, if you actually hung onto the money I give you, and you actually used it to buy yourself something. But it goes for the house and for all sorts of foolish things, and then I only have to lay out some more.

Nora: Oh, but Torvald —

Helmer: Don't deny it, my dear little Nora. *(Putting his arm around her waist.)* Spendthrifts are sweet, but they use up a frightful amount of money. It's incredible what it costs a man to feed such birds.

Nora: Oh, how can you say that! Really, I save everything I can.

Helmer (laughing): Yes, that's the truth. Everything you can. But that's nothing at all.

Nora (humming, with a smile of quiet satisfaction): Hm, if you only knew what expenses we larks and squirrels have, Torvald.

Helmer: You're an odd little one. Exactly the way your father was. You're never at a loss for scaring up money; but the moment you have it, it runs right out through your fingers; you never know what you've done with it. Well, one takes you as you are. It's deep in your blood. Yes, these things are hereditary, Nora.

Nora: Ah, I could wish I'd inherited many of Papa's qualities.

Helmer: And I couldn't wish you anything but just what you are, my sweet little lark. But wait; it seems to me you have a very — what should I call it? — a very suspicious look today —

Nora: I do?

Helmer: You certainly do. Look me straight in the eye.

Nora (looking at him): Well?

Helmer (shaking an admonitory finger): Surely my sweet tooth hasn't been running riot in town today, has she?

Nora: No. Why do you imagine that?

Helmer: My sweet tooth really didn't make a little detour through the confectioner's?

Nora: No, I assure you, Torvald —

Helmer: Hasn't nibbled some pastry?

Nora: No, not at all.

Helmer: Not even munched a macaroon or two?

Nora: No, Torvald, I assure you, really —

Helmer: There, there now. Of course I'm only joking.

Nora (going to the table, right): You know I could never think of going against you.

Helmer: No, I understand that; and you *have* given me your word. *(Going over to her.)* Well, you keep your little Christmas secrets to yourself, Nora darling. I expect they'll come to light this evening, when the tree is lit.

Nora: Did you remember to ask Dr. Rank?

Helmer: No. But there's no need for that: it's assumed he'll be dining with us. All the same, I'll ask him when he stops by here this morning. I've ordered some fine wine. Nora, you can't imagine how I'm looking forward to this evening.

Nora: So am I. And what fun for the children, Torvald!

Helmer: Ah, it's so gratifying to know that one's gotten a safe, secure job, and with a comfortable salary. It's a great satisfaction, isn't it?

Nora: Oh, it's wonderful!

Helmer: Remember last Christmas? Three whole weeks before, you shut yourself in every evening till long after midnight, making flowers for the

Christmas tree, and all the other decorations to surprise us. Ugh, that was the dullest time I've ever lived through.

Nora: It wasn't at all dull for me.

Helmer (smiling): But the outcome *was* pretty sorry, Nora.

Nora: Oh, don't tease me with that again. How could I help it that the cat came in and tore everything to shreds.

Helmer: No, poor thing, you certainly couldn't. You wanted so much to please us all, and that's what counts. But it's just as well that the hard times are past.

Nora: Yes, it's really wonderful.

Helmer: Now I don't have to sit here alone, boring myself, and you don't have to tire your precious eyes and your fair little delicate hands —

Nora (clapping her hands): No, is it really true, Torvald, I don't have to? Oh, how wonderfully lovely to hear! *(Taking his arm.)* Now I'll tell you just how I've thought we should plan things. Right after Christmas — *(The doorbell rings.)* Oh, the bell. *(Straightening the room up a bit.)* Somebody would have to come. What a bore!

Helmer: I'm not home to visitors, don't forget.

Maid (from the hall doorway): Ma'am, a lady to see you —

Nora: All right, let her come in.

Maid (to Helmer): And the doctor's just come too.

Helmer: Did he go right to my study?

Maid: Yes, he did.

> *Helmer goes into his room. The Maid shows in Mrs. Linde, dressed in traveling clothes, and shuts the door after her.*

Mrs. Linde (in a dispirited and somewhat hesitant voice): Hello, Nora.

Nora (uncertain): Hello —

Mrs. Linde: You don't recognize me.

Nora: No, I don't know — but wait, I think — *(Exclaiming.)* What! Kristine! Is it really you?

Mrs. Linde: Yes, it's me.

Nora: Kristine! To think I didn't recognize you. But then, how could I? *(More quietly.)* How you've changed, Kristine!

Mrs. Linde: Yes, no doubt I have. In nine — ten long years.

Nora: Is it so long since we met? Yes, it's all of that. Oh, these last eight years have been a happy time, believe me. And so now you've come in to town, too. Made the long trip in the winter. That took courage.

Mrs. Linde: I just got here by ship this morning.

Nora: To enjoy yourself over Christmas, of course. Oh, how lovely! Yes, enjoy ourselves, we'll do that. But take your coat off. You're not still cold? *(Helping her.)* There now, let's get cozy here by the stove. No, the easy chair there! I'll take the rocker here. *(Seizing her hands.)* Yes, now you have your old look again; it was only in that first moment. You're a bit more pale, Kristine — and maybe a bit thinner.

Mrs. Linde: And much, much older, Nora.

Nora: Yes, perhaps a bit older: a tiny, tiny bit; not much at all. *(Stopping short; suddenly serious.)* Oh, but thoughtless me, to sit here, chattering away. Sweet, good Kristine, can you forgive me?

Mrs. Linde: What do you mean, Nora?

Nora (softly): Poor Kristine, you've become a widow.

Mrs. Linde: Yes, three years ago.

Nora: Oh, I knew it, of course: I read it in the papers. Oh, Kristine, you must believe me; I often thought of writing you then, but I kept postponing it, and something always interfered.

Mrs. Linde: Nora dear, I understand completely.

Nora: No, it was awful of me, Kristine. You poor thing, how much you must have gone through. And he left you nothing?

Mrs. Linde: No.

Nora: And no children?

Mrs. Linde: No.

Nora: Nothing at all, then?

Mrs. Linde: Not even a sense of loss to feed on.

Nora (looking incredulously at her): But Kristine, how could that be?

Mrs. Linde (smiling wearily and smoothing her hair): Oh, sometimes it happens, Nora.

Nora: So completely alone. How terribly hard that must be for you. I have three lovely children. You can't see them now; they're out with the maid. But now you must tell me everything—

Mrs. Linde: No, no, no, tell me about yourself.

Nora: No, you begin. Today I don't want to be selfish. I want to think only of you today. But there *is* something I must tell you. Did you hear of the wonderful luck we had recently?

Mrs. Linde: No, what's that?

Nora: My husband's been made manager in the bank, just think!

Mrs. Linde: Your husband? How marvelous!

Nora: Isn't it? Being a lawyer is such an uncertain living, you know, especially if one won't touch any cases that aren't clean and decent. And of course Torvald would never do that, and I'm with him completely there. Oh, we're simply delighted, believe me! He'll join the bank right after New Year's and start getting a huge salary and lots of commissions. From now on we can live quite differently—just as we want. Oh, Kristine, I feel so light and happy! Won't it be lovely to have stacks of money and not a care in the world?

Mrs. Linde: Well, anyway, it would be lovely to have enough for necessities.

Nora: No, not just for necessities, but stacks and stacks of money!

Mrs. Linde (smiling): Nora, Nora, aren't you sensible yet? Back in school you were such a free spender.

Nora (with a quiet laugh): Yes, that's what Torvald still says. *(Shaking her finger.)* But "Nora, Nora" isn't as silly as you all think. Really, we've been in no position for me to go squandering. We've had to work, both of us.

Mrs. Linde: You too?

Nora: Yes, at odd jobs—needlework, crocheting, embroidery, and such—*(Casually.)* and other things too. You remember that Torvald left the department when we were married? There was no chance of promotion in his office, and of course he needed to earn more money. But that first year he drove himself terribly. He took on all kinds of extra work that kept him going morning and night. It wore him down, and then he fell deathly ill. The doctors said it was essential for him to travel south.

Mrs. Linde: Yes, didn't you spend a whole year in Italy?

Nora: That's right. It wasn't easy to get away, you know. Ivar had just been born. But of course we had to go. Oh, that was a beautiful trip, and it saved Torvald's life. But it cost a frightful sum, Kristine.

Mrs. Linde: I can well imagine.

Nora: Four thousand, eight hundred crowns it cost. That's really a lot of money.

Mrs. Linde: But it's lucky you had it when you needed it.

Nora: Well, as it was, we got it from Papa.

Mrs. Linde: I see. It was just about the time your father died.

Nora: Yes, just about then. And, you know, I couldn't make that trip out to nurse him. I had to stay here, expecting Ivar any moment, and with my poor sick Torvald to care for. Dearest Papa, I never saw him again, Kristine. Oh, that was the worst time I've known in all my marriage.

Mrs. Linde: I know how you loved him. And then you went off to Italy?

Nora: Yes. We had the means now, and the doctors urged us. So we left a month after.

Mrs. Linde: And your husband came back completely cured?

Nora: Sound as a drum!

Mrs. Linde: But — the doctor?

Nora: Who?

Mrs. Linde: I thought the maid said he was a doctor, the man who came in with me.

Nora: Yes, that was Dr. Rank — but he's not making a sick call. He's our closest friend, and he stops by at least once a day. No, Torvald hasn't had a sick moment since, and the children are fit and strong, and I am, too. *(Jumping up and clapping her hands.)* Oh, dear God, Kristine, what a lovely thing to live and be happy! But how disgusting of me — I'm talking of nothing but my own affairs. *(Sits on a stool close by Kristine, arms resting across her knees.)* Oh, don't be angry with me! Tell me, is it really true that you weren't in love with your husband? Why did you marry him, then?

Mrs. Linde: My mother was still alive, but bedridden and helpless — and I had my two younger brothers to look after. In all conscience, I didn't think I could turn him down.

Nora: No, you were right there. But was he rich at the time?

Mrs. Linde: He was very well off, I'd say. But the business was shaky, Nora. When he died, it all fell apart, and nothing was left.

Nora: And then — ?

Mrs. Linde: Yes, so I had to scrape up a living with a little shop and a little teaching and whatever else I could find. The last three years have been like one endless workday without a rest for me. Now it's over, Nora. My poor mother doesn't need me, for she's passed on. Nor the boys, either; they're working now and can take care of themselves.

Nora: How free you must feel —

Mrs. Linde: No — only unspeakably empty. Nothing to live for now. *(Standing up anxiously.)* That's why I couldn't take it any longer out in that desolate hole. Maybe here it'll be easier to find something to do and keep my mind occupied. If I could only be lucky enough to get a steady job, some office work —

Nora: Oh, but Kristine, that's so dreadfully tiring, and you already look so tired. It would be much better for you if you could go off to a bathing resort.

Mrs. Linde (going toward the window): I have no father to give me travel money, Nora.

Nora (rising): Oh, don't be angry with me.

Mrs. Linde (going to her): Nora dear, don't you be angry with me. The worst of my kind of situation is all the bitterness that's stored away. No one to work for, and yet you're always having to snap up your opportunities. You have to live; and so you grow selfish. When you told me the happy change in your lot, do you know I was delighted less for your sakes than for mine?

Nora: How so? Oh, I see. You think maybe Torvald could do something for you.

Mrs. Linde: Yes, that's what I thought.

Nora: And he will, Kristine! Just leave it to me; I'll bring it up so delicately — find something attractive to humor him with. Oh, I'm so eager to help you.

Mrs. Linde: How very kind of you, Nora, to be so concerned over me — doubly kind, considering you really know so little of life's burdens yourself.

Nora: I — ? I know so little — ?

Mrs. Linde (smiling): Well, my heavens — a little needlework and such — Nora, you're just a child.

Nora (tossing her head and pacing the floor): You don't have to act so superior.

Mrs. Linde: Oh?

Nora: You're just like the others. You all think I'm incapable of anything serious —

Mrs. Linde: Come now —

Nora: That I've never had to face the raw world.

Mrs. Linde: Nora dear, you've just been telling me all your troubles.

Nora: Hm! Trivia! *(Quietly.)* I haven't told you the big thing.

Mrs. Linde: Big thing? What do you mean?

Nora: You look down on me so, Kristine, but you shouldn't. You're proud that you worked so long and hard for your mother.

Mrs. Linde: I don't look down on a soul. But it *is* true: I'm proud — and happy, too — to think it was given to me to make my mother's last days almost free of care.

Nora: And you're also proud thinking of what you've done for your brothers.

Mrs. Linde: I feel I've a right to be.

Nora: I agree. But listen to this, Kristine — I've also got something to be proud and happy for.

Mrs. Linde: I don't doubt it. But whatever do you mean?

Nora: Not so loud. What if Torvald heard! He mustn't, not for anything in the world. Nobody must know, Kristine. No one but you.

Mrs. Linde: But what is it, then?

Nora: Come here. *(Drawing her down beside her on the sofa.)* It's true — I've also got something to be proud and happy for. I'm the one who saved Torvald's life.

Mrs. Linde: Saved — ? Saved how?

Nora: I told you about the trip to Italy. Torvald never would have lived if he hadn't gone south —

Mrs. Linde: Of course; your father gave you the means —

Nora (smiling): That's what Torvald and all the rest think, but —

Mrs. Linde: But — ?

Nora: Papa didn't give us a pin. I was the one who raised the money.

Mrs. Linde: You? That whole amount?

Nora: Four thousand, eight hundred crowns. What do you say to that?

Mrs. Linde: But Nora, how was it possible? Did you win the lottery?

Nora (disdainfully): The lottery? Pooh! No art to that.

Mrs. Linde: But where did you get it from then?

Nora (humming, with a mysterious smile): Hmm, tra-la-la-la.

Mrs. Linde: Because you couldn't have borrowed it.

Nora: No? Why not?

Mrs. Linde: A wife can't borrow without her husband's consent.

Nora (tossing her head): Oh, but a wife with a little business sense, a wife who knows how to manage —

Mrs. Linde: Nora, I simply don't understand —

Nora: You don't have to. Whoever said I *borrowed* the money? I could have gotten it other ways. *(Throwing herself back on the sofa.)* I could have gotten it from some admirer or other. After all, a girl with my ravishing appeal —

Mrs. Linde: You lunatic.

Nora: I'll bet you're eaten up with curiosity, Kristine.

Mrs. Linde: Now listen here, Nora — you haven't done something indiscreet?

Nora (sitting up again): Is it indiscreet to save your husband's life?

Mrs. Linde: I think it's indiscreet that without his knowledge you —

Nora: But that's the point: he mustn't know! My Lord, can't you understand? He mustn't ever know the close call he had. It was to *me* the doctors came to say his life was in danger — that nothing could save him but a stay in the south. Didn't I try strategy then! I began talking about how lovely it would be for me to travel abroad like other young wives; I begged and I cried; I told him please to remember my condition, to be kind and indulge me; and then I dropped a hint that he could easily take out a loan. But at that, Kristine, he nearly exploded. He said I was frivolous, and it was his duty as man of the house not to indulge me in whims and fancies — as I think he called them. Aha, I thought, now you'll just have to be saved — and that's when I saw my chance.

Mrs. Linde: And your father never told Torvald the money wasn't from him?

Nora: No, never. Papa died right about then. I'd considered bringing him into my secret and begging him never to tell. But he was too sick at the time — and then, sadly, it didn't matter.

Mrs. Linde: And you've never confided in your husband since?

Nora: For heaven's sake, no! Are you serious? He's so strict on that subject. Besides — Torvald, with all his masculine pride — how painfully humiliating for him if he ever found out he was in debt to me. That would just ruin our relationship. Our beautiful, happy home would never be the same.

Mrs. Linde: Won't you ever tell him?

Nora (thoughtfully, half smiling): Yes — maybe sometime, years from now, when I'm no longer so attractive. Don't laugh! I only mean when Torvald loves me less than now, when he stops enjoying my dancing and dressing up and reciting for him. Then it might be wise to have something in reserve — *(Breaking off.)* How ridiculous! That'll never happen — Well, Kristine, what do you think of my big secret? I'm capable of something too, hm? You can imagine, of course, how this thing hangs over me. It really hasn't been easy meeting the payments on time. In the business world there's what they call quarterly interest and what they call amortization, and these are always so terribly hard to manage. I've had to skimp a little here and there, wherever I could, you know. I could hardly spare anything from my house allowance, because Torvald has to live well. I couldn't let the children go poorly dressed; whatever I got for them, I felt I had to use up completely — the darlings!

Mrs. Linde: Poor Nora, so it had to come out of your own budget, then?

Nora: Yes, of course. But I was the one most responsible, too. Every time Torvald gave me money for new clothes and such, I never used more than half; always bought the simplest, cheapest outfits. It was a godsend that everything looks so well on me that Torvald never noticed. But it did weigh me down at times, Kristine. It *is* such a joy to wear fine things. You understand.

Mrs. Linde: Oh, of course.

Nora: And then I found other ways of making money. Last winter I was lucky enough to get a lot of copying to do. I locked myself in and sat writing every evening till late in the night. Ah, I was tired so often, dead tired. But still it was wonderful fun, sitting and working like that, earning money. It was almost like being a man.

Mrs. Linde: But how much have you paid off this way so far?

Nora: That's hard to say, exactly. These accounts, you know, aren't easy to figure. I only know that I've paid out all I could scrape together. Time and again I haven't known where to turn. *(Smiling.)* Then I'd sit here dreaming of a rich old gentleman who had fallen in love with me —

Mrs. Linde: What! Who is he?

Nora: Oh, really! And that he'd died, and when his will was opened, there in big letters it said, "All my fortune shall be paid over in cash, immediately, to that enchanting Mrs. Nora Helmer."

Mrs. Linde: But Nora dear — who *was* this gentleman?

Nora: Good grief, can't you understand? The old man never existed; that was only something I'd dream up time and again whenever I was at my wits' end for money. But it makes no difference now; the old fossil can go where he pleases for all I care; I don't need him or his will — because now I'm free. *(Jumping up.)* Oh, how lovely to think of that, Kristine! Carefree! To know you're carefree, utterly carefree; to be able to romp and play with the children, and to keep up a beautiful, charming home — everything just the way Torvald likes it! And think, spring is coming, with big blue skies. Maybe we can travel a little then. Maybe I'll see the ocean again. Oh yes, it *is* so marvelous to live and be happy!

The front doorbell rings.

Mrs. Linde (rising): There's the bell. It's probably best that I go.

Nora: No, stay. No one's expected. It must be for Torvald.

Maid (from the hall doorway): Excuse me, ma'am — there's a gentleman here to see Mr. Helmer, but I didn't know — since the doctor's with him —

Nora: Who is the gentleman?

Krogstad (from the doorway): It's me, Mrs. Helmer.

Mrs. Linde starts and turns away toward the window.

Nora (stepping toward him, tense, her voice a whisper): You? What is it? Why do you want to speak to my husband?

Krogstad: Bank business — after a fashion. I have a small job in the investment bank, and I hear now your husband is going to be our chief —

Nora: In other words, it's —

Krogstad: Just dry business, Mrs. Helmer. Nothing but that.

Nora: Yes, then please be good enough to step into the study. *(She nods indifferently as she sees him out by the hall door, then returns and begins stirring up the stove.)*

Mrs. Linde: Nora — who was that man?

Nora: That was a Mr. Krogstad — a lawyer.

Mrs. Linde: Then it really was him.

Nora: Do you know that person?

Mrs. Linde: I did once — many years ago. For a time he was a law clerk in our town.

Nora: Yes, he's been that.

Mrs. Linde: How he's changed.

Nora: I understand he had a very unhappy marriage.

Mrs. Linde: He's a widower now.

Nora: With a number of children. There now, it's burning. *(She closes the stove door and moves the rocker a bit to one side.)*

Mrs. Linde: They say he has a hand in all kinds of business.

Nora: Oh? That may be true; I wouldn't know. But let's not think about business. It's so dull.

Dr. Rank enters from Helmer's study.

Rank (still in the doorway): No, no really — I don't want to intrude, I'd just as soon talk a little while with your wife. *(Shuts the door, then notices Mrs. Linde.)* Oh, beg pardon. I'm intruding here too.

Nora: No, not at all. *(Introducing him.)* Dr. Rank, Mrs. Linde.

Rank: Well now, that's a name much heard in this house. I believe I passed the lady on the stairs as I came.

Mrs. Linde: Yes, I take the stairs very slowly. They're rather hard on me.

Rank: Uh-hm, some touch of internal weakness?

Mrs. Linde: More overexertion, I'd say.

Rank: Nothing else? Then you're probably here in town to rest up in a round of parties?

Mrs. Linde: I'm here to look for work.

Rank: Is that the best cure for overexertion?

Mrs. Linde: One has to live, Doctor.

Rank: Yes, there's a common prejudice to that effect.

Nora: Oh, come on, Dr. Rank — you really do want to live yourself.

Rank: Yes, I really do. Wretched as I am, I'll gladly prolong my torment indefinitely. All my patients feel like that. And it's quite the same, too, with the morally sick. Right at this moment there's one of those moral invalids in there with Helmer —

Mrs. Linde (softly): Ah!

Nora: Who do you mean?

Rank: Oh, it's a lawyer, Krogstad, a type you wouldn't know. His character is rotten to the root — but even he began chattering all-importantly about how he had to *live*.

Nora: Oh? What did he want to talk to Torvald about?

Rank: I really don't know. I only heard something about the bank.

Nora: I didn't know that Krog—that this man Krogstad had anything to do with the bank.

Rank: Yes, he's gotten some kind of berth down there. *(To Mrs. Linde.)* I don't know if you also have, in your neck of the woods, a type of person who scuttles about breathlessly, sniffing out hints of moral corruption, and then maneuvers his victim into some sort of key position where he can keep an eye on him. It's the healthy these days that are out in the cold.

Mrs. Linde: All the same, it's the sick who most need to be taken in.

Rank (with a shrug): Yes, there we have it. That's the concept that's turning society into a sanatorium.

Nora, lost in her thoughts, breaks out into quiet laughter and claps her hands.

Rank: Why do you laugh at that? Do you have any real idea of what society is?

Nora: What do I care about dreary old society? I was laughing at something quite different—something terribly funny. Tell me, Doctor—is everyone who works in the bank dependent now on Torvald?

Rank: Is that what you find so terribly funny?

Nora (smiling and humming): Never mind, never mind! *(Pacing the floor.)* Yes, that's really immensely amusing: that we—that Torvald has so much power now over all those people. *(Taking the bag out of her pocket.)* Dr. Rank, a little macaroon on that?

Rank: See here, macaroons! I thought they were contraband here.

Nora: Yes, but these are some that Kristine gave me.

Mrs. Linde: What? I—?

Nora: Now, now, don't be afraid. You couldn't possibly know that Torvald had forbidden them. You see, he's worried they'll ruin my teeth. But hmp! Just this once! Isn't that so, Dr. Rank? Help yourself! *(Puts a macaroon in his mouth.)* And you too, Kristine. And I'll also have one, only a little one—or two, at the most. *(Walking about again.)* Now I'm really tremendously happy. Now there's just one last thing in the world that I have an enormous desire to do.

Rank: Well! And what's that?

Nora: It's something I have such a consuming desire to say so Torvald could hear.

Rank: And why can't you say it?

Nora: I don't dare. It's quite shocking.

Mrs. Linde: Shocking?

Rank: Well, then it isn't advisable. But in front of us you certainly can. What do you have such a desire to say so Torvald could hear?

Nora: I have such a huge desire to say—to hell and be damned!

Rank: Are you crazy?

Mrs. Linde: My goodness, Nora!

Rank: Go on, say it. Here he is.

Nora (hiding the macaroon bag): Shh, shh, shh!

Helmer comes in from his study, hat in hand, overcoat over his arm.

Nora (going toward him): Well, Torvald dear, are you through with him?

Helmer: Yes, he just left.

Nora: Let me introduce you—this is Kristine, who's arrived here in town.

Helmer: Kristine — ? I'm sorry, but I don't know —

Nora: Mrs. Linde, Torvald dear. Mrs. Kristine Linde.

Helmer: Of course. A childhood friend of my wife's, no doubt?

Mrs. Linde: Yes, we knew each other in those days.

Nora: And just think, she made the long trip down here in order to talk with you.

Helmer: What's this?

Mrs. Linde: Well, not exactly —

Nora: You see, Kristine is remarkably clever in office work, and so she's terribly eager to come under a capable man's supervision and add more to what she already knows —

Helmer: Very wise, Mrs. Linde.

Nora: And then when she heard that you'd become a bank manager — the story was wired out to the papers — then she came in as fast as she could and — Really, Torvald, for my sake you can do a little something for Kristine, can't you?

Helmer: Yes, it's not at all impossible. Mrs. Linde, I suppose you're a widow?

Mrs. Linde: Yes.

Helmer: Any experience in office work?

Mrs. Linde: Yes, a good deal.

Helmer: Well, it's quite likely that I can make an opening for you —

Nora (clapping her hands): You see, you see!

Helmer: You've come at a lucky moment, Mrs. Linde.

Mrs. Linde: Oh, how can I thank you?

Helmer: Not necessary. *(Putting his overcoat on.)* But today you'll have to excuse me —

Rank: Wait, I'll go with you. *(He fetches his coat from the hall and warms it at the stove.)*

Nora: Don't stay out long, dear.

Helmer: An hour; no more.

Nora: Are you going too, Kristine?

Mrs. Linde (putting on her winter garments): Yes, I have to see about a room now.

Helmer: Then perhaps we can all walk together.

Nora (helping her): What a shame we're so cramped here, but it's quite impossible for us to —

Mrs. Linde: Oh, don't even think of it! Good-bye, Nora dear, and thanks for everything.

Nora: Good-bye for now. Of course you'll be back this evening. And you too, Dr. Rank. What? If you're well enough? Oh, you've got to be! Wrap up tight now.

In a ripple of small talk the company moves out into the hall; children's voices are heard outside on the steps.

Nora: There they are! There they are! *(She runs to open the door. The children come in with their nurse, Anne-Marie.)* Come in, come in! *(Bends down and kisses them.)* Oh, you darlings — ! Look at them, Kristine. Aren't they lovely!

Rank: No loitering in the draft here.

Helmer: Come, Mrs. Linde — this place is unbearable now for anyone but mothers.

Dr. Rank, Helmer, and Mrs. Linde go down the stairs. Anne-Marie goes into the living room with the children. Nora follows, after closing the hall door.

Nora: How fresh and strong you look. Oh, such red cheeks you have! Like apples and roses. *(The children interrupt her throughout the following.)* And it was so much fun? That's wonderful. Really? You pulled both Emmy and Bob on the sled? Imagine, all together! Yes, you're a clever boy, Ivar. Oh, let me hold her a bit, Anne-Marie. My sweet little doll baby! *(Takes the smallest from the nurse and dances with her.)* Yes, yes, Mama will dance with Bob as well. What? Did you throw snowballs? Oh, if I'd only been there! No, don't bother, Anne-Marie — I'll undress them myself. Oh yes, let me. It's such fun. Go in and rest; you look half frozen. There's hot coffee waiting for you on the stove. *(The nurse goes into the room to the left. Nora takes the children's winter things off, throwing them about, while the children talk to her all at once.)* Is that so? A big dog chased you? But it didn't bite? No, dogs never bite little, lovely doll babies. Don't peek in the packages, Ivar! What is it? Yes, wouldn't you like to know. No, no, it's an ugly something. Well? Shall we play? What shall we play? Hide-and-seek? Yes, let's play hide-and-seek. Bob must hide first. I must? Yes, let me hide first. *(Laughing and shouting, she and the children play in and out of the living room and the adjoining room to the right. At last Nora hides under the table. The children come storming in, search, but cannot find her, then hear her muffled laughter, dash over to the table, lift the cloth up and find her. Wild shouting. She creeps forward as if to scare them. More shouts. Meanwhile, a knock at the hall door; no one has noticed it. Now the door half opens, and Krogstad appears. He waits a moment; the game goes on.)*

Krogstad: Beg pardon, Mrs. Helmer —

Nora (with a strangled cry, turning and scrambling to her knees): Oh! What do you want?

Krogstad: Excuse me. The outer door was ajar; it must be someone forgot to shut it —

Nora (rising): My husband isn't home, Mr. Krogstad.

Krogstad: I know that.

Nora: Yes — then what do you want here?

Krogstad: A word with you.

Nora: With — ? *(To the children, quietly.)* Go in to Anne-Marie. What? No, the strange man won't hurt Mama. When he's gone, we'll play some more. *(She leads the children into the room to the left and shuts the door after them. Then, tense and nervous:)* You want to speak to me?

Krogstad: Yes, I want to.

Nora: Today? But it's not yet the first of the month —

Krogstad: No, it's Christmas Eve. It's going to be up to you how merry a Christmas you have.

Nora: What is it you want? Today I absolutely can't —

Krogstad: We won't talk about that till later. This is something else. You do have a moment to spare, I suppose?

Nora: Oh yes, of course — I do, except —

Krogstad: Good. I was sitting over at Olsen's Restaurant when I saw your husband go down the street —

Nora: Yes?

Krogstad: With a lady.

Nora: Yes. So?

Krogstad: If you'll pardon my asking: wasn't that lady a Mrs. Linde?

Nora: Yes.

Krogstad: Just now come into town?

Nora: Yes, today.

Krogstad: She's a good friend of yours?

Nora: Yes, she is. But I don't see —

Krogstad: I also knew her once.

Nora: I'm aware of that.

Krogstad: Oh? You know all about it. I thought so. Well, then let me ask you short and sweet: is Mrs. Linde getting a job in the bank?

Nora: What makes you think you can cross-examine me, Mr. Krogstad — you, one of my husband's employees? But since you ask, you might as well know — yes, Mrs. Linde's going to be taken on at the bank. And I'm the one who spoke for her, Mr. Krogstad. Now you know.

Krogstad: So I guessed right.

Nora (pacing up and down): Oh, one does have a tiny bit of influence, I should hope. Just because I am a woman, don't think it means that — When one has a subordinate position, Mr. Krogstad, one really ought to be careful about pushing somebody who — hm —

Krogstad: Who has influence?

Nora: That's right.

Krogstad (in a different tone): Mrs. Helmer, would you be good enough to use your influence on my behalf?

Nora: What? What do you mean?

Krogstad: Would you please make sure that I keep my subordinate position in the bank?

Nora: What does that mean? Who's thinking of taking away your position?

Krogstad: Oh, don't play the innocent with me. I'm quite aware that your friend would hardly relish the chance of running into me again; and I'm also aware now whom I can thank for being turned out.

Nora: But I promise you —

Krogstad: Yes, yes, yes, to the point: there's still time, and I'm advising you to use your influence to prevent it.

Nora: But Mr. Krogstad, I have absolutely no influence.

Krogstad: You haven't? I thought you were just saying —

Nora: You shouldn't take me so literally. I! How can you believe that I have any such influence over my husband?

Krogstad: Oh, I've known your husband from our student days. I don't think the great bank manager's more steadfast than any other married man.

Nora: You speak insolently about my husband, and I'll show you the door.

Krogstad: The lady has spirit.

Nora: I'm not afraid of you any longer. After New Year's, I'll soon be done with the whole business.

Krogstad (restraining himself): Now listen to me, Mrs. Helmer. If necessary, I'll fight for my little job in the bank as if it were life itself.

Nora: Yes, so it seems.

Krogstad: It's not just a matter of income; that's the least of it. It's something else — All right, out with it! Look, this is the thing. You know, just like all the others, of course, that once, a good many years ago, I did something rather rash.

Nora: I've heard rumors to that effect.

Krogstad: The case never got into court; but all the same, every door was closed in my face from then on. So I took up those various activities you know about. I had to grab hold somewhere; and I dare say I haven't been among the worst. But now I want to drop all that. My boys are growing up. For their sakes, I'll have to win back as much respect as possible here in town. That job in the bank was like the first rung in my ladder. And now your husband wants to kick me right back down in the mud again.

Nora: But for heaven's sake, Mr. Krogstad, it's simply not in my power to help you.

Krogstad: That's because you haven't the will to — but I have the means to make you.

Nora: You certainly won't tell my husband that I owe you money?

Krogstad: Hm — what if I told him that?

Nora: That would be shameful of you. *(Nearly in tears.)* This secret — my joy and my pride — that he should learn it in such a crude and disgusting way — learn it from you. You'd expose me to the most horrible unpleasantness —

Krogstad: Only unpleasantness?

Nora (vehemently): But go on and try. It'll turn out the worse for you, because then my husband will really see what a crook you are, and then you'll *never* be able to hold your job.

Krogstad: I asked if it was just domestic unpleasantness you were afraid of?

Nora: If my husband finds out, then of course he'll pay what I owe at once, and then we'd be through with you for good.

Krogstad (a step closer): Listen, Mrs. Helmer — you've either got a very bad memory, or else no head at all for business. I'd better put you a little more in touch with the facts.

Nora: What do you mean?

Krogstad: When your husband was sick, you came to me for a loan of four thousand, eight hundred crowns.

Nora: Where else could I go?

Krogstad: I promised to get you that sum —

Nora: And you got it.

Krogstad: I promised to get you that sum, on certain conditions. You were so involved in your husband's illness, and so eager to finance your trip, that I guess you didn't think out all the details. It might just be a good idea to remind you. I promised you the money on the strength of a note I drew up.

Nora: Yes, and that I signed.

Krogstad: Right. But at the bottom I added some lines for your father to guarantee the loan. He was supposed to sign down there.

Nora: Supposed to? He did sign.

Krogstad: I left the date blank. In other words, your father would have dated his signature himself. Do you remember that?

Nora: Yes, I think —

Krogstad: Then I gave you the note for you to mail to your father. Isn't that so?

Nora: Yes.

Krogstad: And naturally you sent it at once — because only some five, six days later you brought me the note, properly signed. And with that, the money was yours.

Nora: Well, then; I've made my payments regularly, haven't I?

Krogstad: More or less. But — getting back to the point — those were hard times for you then, Mrs. Helmer.

Nora: Yes, they were.

Krogstad: Your father was very ill, I believe.

Nora: He was near the end.

Krogstad: He died soon after?

Nora: Yes.

Krogstad: Tell me, Mrs. Helmer, do you happen to recall the date of your father's death? The day of the month, I mean.

Nora: Papa died the twenty-ninth of September.

Krogstad: That's quite correct; I've already looked into that. And now we come to a curious thing — *(Taking out a paper.)* which I simply cannot comprehend.

Nora: Curious thing? I don't know —

Krogstad: This is the curious thing: that your father co-signed the note for your loan three days after his death.

Nora: How — ? I don't understand.

Krogstad: Your father died the twenty-ninth of September. But look. Here your father dated his signature October second. Isn't that curious, Mrs. Helmer? *(Nora is silent.)* Can you explain it to me? *(Nora remains silent.)* It's also remarkable that the words "October second" and the year aren't written in your father's hand, but rather in one that I think I know. Well, it's easy to understand. Your father forgot perhaps to date his signature, and then someone or other added it, a bit sloppily, before anyone knew of his death. There's nothing wrong in that. It all comes down to the signature. And there's no question about *that*, Mrs. Helmer. It really *was* your father who signed his own name here, wasn't it?

Nora (after a short silence, throwing her head back and looking squarely at him): No, it wasn't. *I* signed Papa's name.

Krogstad: Wait, now — are you fully aware that this is a dangerous confession?

Nora: Why? You'll soon get your money.

Krogstad: Let me ask you a question — why didn't you send the paper to your father?

Nora: That was impossible. Papa was so sick. If I'd asked him for his signature, I also would have had to tell him what the money was for. But I couldn't tell him, sick as he was, that my husband's life was in danger. That was just impossible.

Krogstad: Then it would have been better if you'd given up the trip abroad.

Nora: I couldn't possibly. The trip was to save my husband's life. I couldn't give that up.

Krogstad: But didn't you ever consider that this was a fraud against me?

Nora: I couldn't let myself be bothered by that. You weren't any concern of mine. I couldn't stand you, with all those cold complications you made, even though you knew how badly off my husband was.

Krogstad: Mrs. Helmer, obviously you haven't the vaguest idea of what you've involved yourself in. But I can tell you this: it was nothing more and nothing worse that I once did — and it wrecked my whole reputation.

Nora: You? Do you expect me to believe that you ever acted bravely to save your wife's life?

Krogstad: Laws don't inquire into motives.

Nora: Then they must be very poor laws.

Krogstad: Poor or not — if I introduce this paper in court, you'll be judged according to law.

Nora: This I refuse to believe. A daughter hasn't a right to protect her dying father from anxiety and care? A wife hasn't a right to save her husband's life? I don't know much about laws, but I'm sure that somewhere in the books these things are allowed. And you don't know anything about it — you who practice the law? You must be an awful lawyer, Mr. Krogstad.

Krogstad: Could be. But business — the kind of business we two are mixed up in — don't you think I know about that? All right. Do what you want now. But I'm telling you *this:* if I get shoved down a second time, you're going to keep me company. *(He bows and goes out through the hall.)*

Nora (pensive for a moment, then tossing her head): Oh, really! Trying to frighten me! I'm not so silly as all that. *(Begins gathering up the children's clothes, but soon stops.)* But — ? No, but that's impossible! I did it out of love.

The Children (in the doorway, left): Mama, that strange man's gone out the door.

Nora: Yes, yes, I know it. But don't tell anyone about the strange man. Do you hear? Not even Papa!

The Children: No, Mama. But now will you play again?

Nora: No, not now.

The Children: Oh, but Mama, you promised.

Nora: Yes, but I can't now. Go inside; I have too much to do. Go in, go in, my sweet darlings. *(She herds them gently back in the room and shuts the door after them. Settling on the sofa, she takes up a piece of embroidery and makes some stitches, but soon stops abruptly.)* No! *(Throws the work aside, rises, goes to the hall door and calls out.)* Helene! Let me have the tree in here. *(Goes to the table, left, opens the table drawer, and stops again.)* No, but that's utterly impossible!

Maid (with the Christmas tree): Where should I put it, ma'am?

Nora: There. The middle of the floor.

Maid: Should I bring anything else?

Nora: No, thanks. I have what I need.

The Maid, who has set the tree down, goes out.

Nora (absorbed in trimming the tree): Candles here — and flowers here. That terrible creature! Talk, talk, talk! There's nothing to it at all. The tree's going to be lovely. I'll do anything to please you, Torvald. I'll sing for you, dance for you —

Helmer comes in from the hall, with a sheaf of papers under his arm.

Nora: Oh! You're back so soon?

Helmer: Yes. Has anyone been here?

Nora: Here? No.

Helmer: That's odd. I saw Krogstad leaving the front door.

Nora: So? Oh yes, that's true. Krogstad was here a moment.

Helmer: Nora, I can see by your face that he's been here, begging you to put in a good word for him.

Nora: Yes.

Helmer: And it was supposed to seem like your own idea? You were to hide it from me that he'd been here. He asked you that, too, didn't he?

Nora: Yes, Torvald, but —

Helmer: Nora, Nora, and you could fall for that? Talk with that sort of person and promise him anything? And then in the bargain, tell me an untruth.

Nora: An untruth —?

Helmer: Didn't you say that no one had been here? *(Wagging his finger.)* My little songbird must never do that again. A songbird needs a clean beak to warble with. No false notes. *(Putting his arm about her waist.)* That's the way it should be, isn't it? Yes, I'm sure of it. *(Releasing her.)* And so, enough of that. *(Sitting by the stove.)* Ah, how snug and cozy it is here. *(Leafing among his papers.)*

Nora (busy with the tree, after a short pause): Torvald!

Helmer: Yes.

Nora: I'm so much looking forward to the Stenborgs' costume party, day after tomorrow.

Helmer: And I can't wait to see what you'll surprise me with.

Nora: Oh, that stupid business!

Helmer: What?

Nora: I can't find anything that's right. Everything seems so ridiculous, so inane.

Helmer: So my little Nora's come to *that* recognition?

Nora (going behind his chair, her arms resting on its back): Are you very busy, Torvald?

Helmer: Oh —

Nora: What papers are those?

Helmer: Bank matters.

Nora: Already?

Helmer: I've gotten full authority from the retiring management to make all necessary changes in personnel and procedure. I'll need Christmas week for that. I want to have everything in order by New Year's.

Nora: So that was the reason this poor Krogstad —

Helmer: Hm.

Nora (still leaning on the chair and slowly stroking the nape of his neck): If you weren't so very busy, I would have asked you an enormous favor, Torvald.

Helmer: Let's hear. What is it?

Nora: You know, there isn't anyone who has your good taste — and I want so much to look well at the costume party. Torvald, couldn't you take over and decide what I should be and plan my costume?

Helmer: Ah, is my stubborn little creature calling for a lifeguard?

Nora: Yes, Torvald, I can't get anywhere without your help.

Helmer: All right — I'll think it over. We'll hit on something.

Nora: Oh, how sweet of you. *(Goes to the tree again. Pause.)* Aren't the red flowers pretty —? But tell me, was it really such a crime that this Krogstad committed?

Helmer: Forgery. Do you have any idea what that means?

Nora: Couldn't he have done it out of need?

Helmer: Yes, or thoughtlessness, like so many others. I'm not so heartless that I'd condemn a man categorically for just one mistake.

Nora: No, of course not, Torvald!

Helmer: Plenty of men have redeemed themselves by openly confessing their crimes and taking their punishment.

Nora: Punishment —?

Helmer: But now Krogstad didn't go that way. He got himself out by sharp practices, and that's the real cause of his moral breakdown.

Nora: Do you really think that would —?

Helmer: Just imagine how a man with that sort of guilt in him has to lie and cheat and deceive on all sides, has to wear a mask even with the nearest and dearest he has, even with his own wife and children. And with the children, Nora — that's where it's most horrible.

Nora: Why?

Helmer: Because that kind of atmosphere of lies infects the whole life of a home. Every breath the children take in is filled with the germs of something degenerate.

Nora (coming closer behind him): Are you sure of that?

Helmer: Oh, I've seen it often enough as a lawyer. Almost everyone who goes bad early in life has a mother who's a chronic liar.

Nora: Why just — the mother?

Helmer: It's usually the mother's influence that's dominant, but the father's works in the same way, of course. Every lawyer is quite familiar with it. And still this Krogstad's been going home year in, year out, poisoning his own children with lies and pretense; that's why I call him morally lost. *(Reaching his hands out toward her.)* So my sweet little Nora must promise me never to plead his cause. Your hand on it. Come, come, what's this? Give me your hand. There, now. All settled. I can tell you it'd be impossible for me to work alongside of him. I literally feel physically revolted when I'm anywhere near such a person.

Nora (withdraws her hand and goes to the other side of the Christmas tree): How hot it is here! And I've got so much to do.

Helmer (getting up and gathering his papers): Yes, and I have to think about getting some of these read through before dinner. I'll think about your costume, too. And something to hang on the tree in gilt paper, I may even see about that. *(Putting his hand on her head.)* Oh you, my darling little songbird. *(He goes into his study and closes the door after him.)*

Nora (softly, after a silence): Oh, really! It isn't so. It's impossible. It must be impossible.

Anne-Marie (in the doorway, left): The children are begging so hard to come in to Mama.

Nora: No, no, no, don't let them in to me! You stay with them, Anne-Marie.

Anne-Marie: Of course, ma'am. *(Closes the door.)*

Nora (pale with terror): Hurt my children —! Poison my home? *(A moment's pause; then she tosses her head.)* That's not true. Never. Never in all the world.

ACT II

Same room. Beside the piano the Christmas tree now stands stripped of ornament, burned-down candle stubs on its ragged branches. Nora's street clothes lie on the sofa. Nora, alone in the room, moves restlessly about; at last she stops at the sofa and picks up her coat.

Nora (dropping the coat again): Someone's coming! *(Goes toward the door, listens.)* No — there's no one. Of course — nobody's coming today, Christmas Day — or tomorrow, either. But maybe — *(Opens the door and looks out.)* No, nothing in the mailbox. Quite empty. *(Coming forward.)* What nonsense! He won't do anything serious. Nothing terrible could happen. It's impossible. Why, I have three small children.

> *Anne-Marie, with a large carton, comes in from the room to the left.*

Anne-Marie: Well, at last I found the box with the masquerade clothes.

Nora: Thanks. Put it on the table.

Anne-Marie (does so): But they're all pretty much of a mess.

Nora: Ahh! I'd love to rip them in a million pieces!

Anne-Marie: Oh, mercy, they can be fixed right up. Just a little patience.

Nora: Yes, I'll go get Mrs. Linde to help me.

Anne-Marie: Out again now? In this nasty weather? Miss Nora will catch cold — get sick.

Nora: Oh, worse things could happen. How are the children?

Anne-Marie: The poor mites are playing with their Christmas presents, but —

Nora: Do they ask for me much?

Anne-Marie: They're so used to having Mama around, you know.

Nora: Yes, but Anne-Marie, I *can't* be together with them as much as I was.

Anne-Marie: Well, small children get used to anything.

Nora: You think so? Do you think they'd forget their mother if she was gone for good?

Anne-Marie: Oh, mercy — gone for good!

Nora: Wait, tell me, Anne-Marie — I've wondered so often — how could you ever have the heart to give your child over to strangers?

Anne-Marie: But I had to, you know, to become little Nora's nurse.

Nora: Yes, but how could you *do* it?

Anne-Marie: When I could get such a good place? A girl who's poor and who's gotten in trouble is glad enough for that. Because that slippery fish, he didn't do a thing for me, you know.

Nora: But your daughter's surely forgotten you.

Anne-Marie: Oh, she certainly has not. She's written to me, both when she was confirmed and when she was married.

Nora (clasping her about the neck): You old Anne-Marie, you were a good mother for me when I was little.

Anne-Marie: Poor little Nora, with no other mother but me.

Nora: And if the babies didn't have one, then I know that you'd — What silly talk! *(Opening the carton.)* Go in to them. Now I'll have to — Tomorrow you can see how lovely I'll look.

Anne-Marie: Oh, there won't be anyone at the party as lovely as Miss Nora. *(She goes off into the room, left.)*

Nora (begins unpacking the box, but soon throws it aside): Oh, if I dared to go out. If only nobody would come. If only nothing would happen here while I'm out. What craziness — nobody's coming. Just don't think. This muff — needs a brushing. Beautiful gloves, beautiful gloves. Let it go. Let it go! One, two, three, four, five, six — *(With a cry.)* Oh, there they are! *(Poises to move toward the door, but remains irresolutely standing. Mrs. Linde enters from the hall, where she has removed her street clothes.)*

Nora: Oh, it's you, Kristine. There's no one else out there? How good that you've come.

Mrs. Linde: I hear you were up asking for me.

Nora: Yes, I just stopped by. There's something you really can help me with. Let's get settled on the sofa. Look, there's going to be a costume party to-morrow evening at the Stenborgs' right above us, and now Torvald wants me to go as a Neapolitan peasant girl and dance the tarantella that I learned in Capri.

Mrs. Linde: Really, are you giving a whole performance?

Nora: Torvald says yes, I should. See, here's the dress. Torvald had it made for me down there; but now it's all so tattered that I just don't know —

Mrs. Linde: Oh, we'll fix that up in no time. It's nothing more than the trim-mings — they're a bit loose here and there. Needle and thread? Good, now we have what we need.

Nora: Oh, how sweet of you!

Mrs. Linde (sewing): So you'll be in disguise tomorrow, Nora. You know what? I'll stop by then for a moment and have a look at you all dressed up. But listen, I've absolutely forgotten to thank you for that pleasant evening yesterday.

Nora (getting up and walking about): I don't think it was as pleasant as usual yes-terday. You should have come to town a bit sooner, Kristine — Yes, Torvald really knows how to give a home elegance and charm.

Mrs. Linde: And you do, too, if you ask me. You're not your father's daughter for nothing. But tell me, is Dr. Rank always so down in the mouth as yes-terday?

Nora: No, that was quite an exception. But he goes around critically ill all the time — tuberculosis of the spine, poor man. You know, his father was a dis-gusting thing who kept mistresses and so on — and that's why the son's been sickly from birth.

Mrs. Linde (lets her sewing fall to her lap): But my dearest Nora, how do you know about such things?

Nora (walking more jauntily): Hmp! When you've had three children, then you've had a few visits from — from women who know something of medi-cine, and they tell you this and that.

Mrs. Linde (resumes sewing; a short pause): Does Dr. Rank come here every day?

Nora: Every blessed day. He's Torvald's best friend from childhood, and *my* good friend, too. Dr. Rank almost belongs to this house.

Mrs. Linde: But tell me — is he quite sincere? I mean, doesn't he rather enjoy flattering people?

Nora: Just the opposite. Why do you think that?

Mrs. Linde: When you introduced us yesterday, he was proclaiming that he'd often heard my name in this house; but later I noticed that your husband hadn't the slightest idea who I really was. So how could Dr. Rank —?

Nora: But it's all true, Kristine. You see, Torvald loves me beyond words, and, as he puts it, he'd like to keep me all to himself. For a long time he'd almost be jealous if I even mentioned any of my old friends back home. So of course I dropped that. But with Dr. Rank I talk a lot about such things, because he likes hearing about them.

Mrs. Linde: Now listen, Nora; in many ways you're still like a child. I'm a good deal older than you, with a little more experience. I'll tell you something: you ought to put an end to all this with Dr. Rank.

Nora: What should I put an end to?

Mrs. Linde: Both parts of it, I think. Yesterday you said something about a rich admirer who'd provide you with money—

Nora: Yes, one who doesn't exist—worse luck. So?

Mrs. Linde: Is Dr. Rank well off?

Nora: Yes, he is.

Mrs. Linde: With no dependents?

Nora: No, no one. But—

Mrs. Linde: And he's over here every day?

Nora: Yes, I told you that.

Mrs. Linde: How can a man of such refinement be so grasping?

Nora: I don't follow you at all.

Mrs. Linde: Now don't try to hide it, Nora. You think I can't guess who loaned you the forty-eight hundred crowns?

Nora: Are you out of your mind? How could you think such a thing! A friend of ours, who comes here every single day. What an intolerable situation that would have been!

Mrs. Linde: Then it really wasn't him.

Nora: No, absolutely not. It never even crossed my mind for a moment—And he had nothing to lend in those days; his inheritance came later.

Mrs. Linde: Well, I think that was a stroke of luck for you, Nora dear.

Nora: No, it never would have occurred to me to ask Dr. Rank—Still, I'm quite sure that if I had asked him—

Mrs. Linde: Which you won't, of course.

Nora: No, of course not. I can't see that I'd ever need to. But I'm quite positive that if I talked to Dr. Rank—

Mrs. Linde: Behind your husband's back?

Nora: I've got to clear up this other thing; *that's* also behind his back. I've *got* to clear it all up.

Mrs. Linde: Yes, I was saying that yesterday, but—

Nora (pacing up and down): A man handles these problems so much better than a woman—

Mrs. Linde: One's husband does, yes.

Nora: Nonsense. *(Stopping.)* When you pay everything you owe, then you get your note back, right?

Mrs. Linde: Yes, naturally.

Nora: And can rip it into a million pieces and burn it up—that filthy scrap of paper!

Mrs. Linde (looking hard at her, laying her sewing aside, and rising slowly): Nora, you're hiding something from me.

Nora: You can see it in my face?

Mrs. Linde: Something's happened to you since yesterday morning. Nora, what is it?

Nora (hurrying toward her): Kristine! *(Listening.)* Shh! Torvald's home. Look, go in with the children a while. Torvald can't bear all this snipping and stitching. Let Anne-Marie help you.

Mrs. Linde (gathering up some of the things): All right, but I'm not leaving here until we've talked this out. *(She disappears into the room, left, as Torvald enters from the hall.)*

Nora: Oh, how I've been waiting for you, Torvald dear.

Helmer: Was that the dressmaker?

Nora: No, that was Kristine. She's helping me fix up my costume. You know, it's going to be quite attractive.

Helmer: Yes, wasn't that a bright idea I had?

Nora: Brilliant! But then wasn't I good as well to give in to you?

Helmer: Good—because you give in to your husband's judgment? All right, you little goose, I know you didn't mean it like that. But I won't disturb you. You'll want to have a fitting, I suppose.

Nora: And you'll be working?

Helmer: Yes. *(Indicating a bundle of papers.)* See. I've been down to the bank. *(Starts toward his study.)*

Nora: Torvald.

Helmer (stops): Yes.

Nora: If your little squirrel begged you, with all her heart and soul, for something—?

Helmer: What's that?

Nora: Then would you do it?

Helmer: First, naturally, I'd have to know what it was.

Nora: Your squirrel would scamper about and do tricks, if you'd only be sweet and give in.

Helmer: Out with it.

Nora: Your lark would be singing high and low in every room—

Helmer: Come on, she does that anyway.

Nora: I'd be a wood nymph and dance for you in the moonlight.

Helmer: Nora—don't tell me it's that same business from this morning?

Nora (coming closer): Yes, Torvald, I beg you, please!

Helmer: And you actually have the nerve to drag that up again?

Nora: Yes, yes, you've got to give in to me; you *have* to let Krogstad keep his job in the bank.

Helmer: My dear Nora, I've slated his job for Mrs. Linde.

Nora: That's awfully kind of you. But you could just fire another clerk instead of Krogstad.

Helmer: This is the most incredible stubbornness! Because you go and give an impulsive promise to speak up for him, I'm expected to—

Nora: That's not the reason, Torvald. It's for your own sake. That man does writing for the worst papers; you said it yourself. He could do you any amount of harm. I'm scared to death of him—

Helmer: Ah, I understand. It's the old memories haunting you.

Nora: What do you mean by that?

Helmer: Of course, you're thinking about your father.

Nora: Yes, all right. Just remember how those nasty gossips wrote in the papers about Papa and slandered him so cruelly. I think they'd have had him dismissed if the department hadn't sent you up to investigate, and if you hadn't been so kind and open-minded toward him.

Helmer: My dear Nora, there's a notable difference between your father and me. Your father's official career was hardly above reproach. But mine is; and I hope it'll stay that way as long as I hold my position.

Nora: Oh, who can ever tell what vicious minds can invent? We could be so snug and happy now in our quiet, carefree home—you and I and the children, Torvald! That's why I'm pleading with you so—

Helmer: And just by pleading for him you make it impossible for me to keep
  him on. It's already known at the bank that I'm firing Krogstad. What if
  it's rumored around now that the new bank manager was vetoed by his
  wife —
Nora: Yes, what then — ?
Helmer: Oh yes — as long as our little bundle of stubbornness gets her way — !
  I should go and make myself ridiculous in front of the whole office —
  give people the idea I can be swayed by all kinds of outside pressure. Oh,
  you can bet I'd feel the effects of that soon enough! Besides — there's
  something that rules Krogstad right out at the bank as long as I'm the
  manager.
Nora: What's that?
Helmer: His moral failings I could maybe overlook if I had to —
Nora: Yes, Torvald, why not?
Helmer: And I hear he's quite efficient on the job. But he was a crony of mine
  back in my teens — one of those rash friendships that crop up again and
  again to embarrass you later in life. Well, I might as well say it straight out:
  we're on a first-name basis. And that tactless fool makes no effort at all to
  hide it in front of others. Quite the contrary — he thinks that entitles him to
  take a familiar air around me, and so every other second he comes booming
  out with his "Yes, Torvald!" and "Sure thing, Torvald!" I tell you, it's been excruciating for me. He's out to make my place in the bank unbearable.
Nora: Torvald, you can't be serious about all this.
Helmer: Oh no? Why not?
Nora: Because these are such petty considerations.
Helmer: What are you saying? Petty? You think I'm petty!
Nora: No, just the opposite, Torvald dear. That's exactly why —
Helmer: Never mind. You call my motives petty; then I might as well be just
  that. Petty! All right! We'll put a stop to this for good. *(Goes to the hall door
  and calls.)* Helene!
Nora: What do you want?
Helmer (searching among his papers): A decision. *(The maid comes in.)* Look here;
  take this letter; go out with it at once. Get hold of a messenger and have
  him deliver it. Quick now. It's already addressed. Wait, here's some money.
Maid: Yes, sir. *(She leaves with the letter.)*
Helmer (straightening his papers): There, now, little Miss Willful.
Nora (breathlessly): Torvald, what was that letter?
Helmer: Krogstad's notice.
Nora: Call it back, Torvald! There's still time. Oh, Torvald, call it back! Do it
  for my sake — for your sake, for the children's sake! Do you hear, Torvald;
  do it! You don't know how this can harm us.
Helmer: Too late.
Nora: Yes, too late.
Helmer: Nora dear, I can forgive you this panic, even though basically you're
  insulting me. Yes, you are! Or isn't it an insult to think that *I* should be
  afraid of a courtroom hack's revenge? But I forgive you anyway, because
  this shows so beautifully how much you love me. *(Takes her in his arms.)*
  This is the way it should be, my darling Nora. Whatever comes, you'll see;
  when it really counts, I have strength and courage enough as a man to take
  on the whole weight myself.

Nora (terrified): What do you mean by that?

Helmer: The whole weight, I said.

Nora (resolutely): No, never in all the world.

Helmer: Good. So we'll share it, Nora, as man and wife. That's as it should be. *(Fondling her.)* Are you happy now? There, there, there — not these frightened dove's eyes. It's nothing at all but empty fantasies — Now you should run through your tarantella and practice your tambourine. I'll go to the inner office and shut both doors, so I won't hear a thing; you can make all the noise you like. *(Turning in the doorway.)* And when Rank comes, just tell him where he can find me. *(He nods to her and goes with his papers into the study, closing the door.)*

Nora (standing as though rooted, dazed with fright, in a whisper): He really could do it. He will do it. He'll do it in spite of everything. No, not that, never, never! Anything but that! Escape! A way out — *(The doorbell rings.)* Dr. Rank! Anything but that! *Anything*, whatever it is! *(Her hands pass over her face, smoothing it; she pulls herself together, goes over and opens the hall door. Dr. Rank stands outside, hanging his fur coat up. During the following scene, it begins getting dark.)*

Nora: Hello, Dr. Rank. I recognized your ring. But you mustn't go in to Torvald yet; I believe he's working.

Rank: And you?

Nora: For you, I always have an hour to spare — you know that. *(He has entered, and she shuts the door after him.)*

Rank: Many thanks. I'll make use of these hours while I can.

Nora: What do you mean by that? While you can?

Rank: Does that disturb you?

Nora: Well, it's such an odd phrase. Is anything going to happen?

Rank: What's going to happen is what I've been expecting so long — but I honestly didn't think it would come so soon.

Nora (gripping his arm): What is it you've found out? Dr. Rank, you have to tell me!

Rank (sitting by the stove): It's all over for me. There's nothing to be done about it.

Nora (breathing easier): Is it you — then — ?

Rank: Who else? There's no point in lying to one's self. I'm the most miserable of all my patients, Mrs. Helmer. These past few days I've been auditing my internal accounts. Bankrupt! Within a month I'll probably be laid out and rotting in the churchyard.

Nora: Oh, what a horrible thing to say.

Rank: The thing itself is horrible. But the worst of it is all the other horror before it's over. There's only one final examination left; when I'm finished with that, I'll know about when my disintegration will begin. There's something I want to say. Helmer with his sensitivity has such a sharp distaste for anything ugly. I don't want him near my sickroom.

Nora: Oh, but Dr. Rank —

Rank: I won't have him in there. Under no condition. I'll lock my door to him — As soon as I'm completely sure of the worst, I'll send you my calling card marked with a black cross, and you'll know then the wreck has started to come apart.

Nora: No, today you're completely unreasonable. And I wanted you so much to be in a really good humor.

Rank: With death up my sleeve? And then to suffer this way for somebody else's sins. Is there any justice in that? And in every single family, in some way or another, this inevitable retribution of nature goes on —

Nora (her hands pressed over her ears): Oh, stuff! Cheer up! Please — be gay!

Rank: Yes, I'd just as soon laugh at it all. My poor, innocent spine, serving time for my father's gay army days.

Nora (by the table, left): He was so infatuated with asparagus tips and pâté de foie gras, wasn't that it?

Rank: Yes — and with truffles.

Nora: Truffles, yes. And then with oysters, I suppose?

Rank: Yes, tons of oysters, naturally.

Nora: And then the port and champagne to go with it. It's so sad that all these delectable things have to strike at our bones.

Rank: Especially when they strike at the unhappy bones that never shared in the fun.

Nora: Ah, that's the saddest of all.

Rank (looks searchingly at her): Hm.

Nora (after a moment): Why did you smile?

Rank: No, it was you who laughed.

Nora: No, it was you who smiled, Dr. Rank!

Rank (getting up): You're even a bigger tease than I'd thought.

Nora: I'm full of wild ideas today.

Rank: That's obvious.

Nora (putting both hands on his shoulders): Dear, dear Dr. Rank, you'll never die for Torvald and me.

Rank: Oh, that loss you'll easily get over. Those who go away are soon forgotten.

Nora (looks fearfully at him): You believe that?

Rank: One makes new connections, and then —

Nora: Who makes new connections?

Rank: Both you and Torvald will when I'm gone. I'd say you're well under way already. What was that Mrs. Linde doing here last evening?

Nora: Oh, come — you can't be jealous of poor Kristine?

Rank: Oh yes, I am. She'll be my successor here in the house. When I'm down under, that woman will probably —

Nora: Shh! Not so loud. She's right in there.

Rank: Today as well. So you see.

Nora: Only to sew on my dress. Good gracious, how unreasonable you are. (*Sitting on the sofa.*) Be nice now, Dr. Rank. Tomorrow you'll see how beautifully I'll dance; and you can imagine then that I'm dancing only for you — yes, and of course for Torvald, too — that's understood. (*Takes various items out of the carton.*) Dr. Rank, sit over here and I'll show you something.

Rank (sitting): What's that?

Nora: Look here. Look.

Rank: Silk stockings.

Nora: Flesh-colored. Aren't they lovely? Now it's so dark here, but tomorrow — No, no, no, just look at the feet. Oh well, you might as well look at the rest.

Rank: Hm —

Nora: Why do you look so critical? Don't you believe they'll fit?

Rank: I've never had any chance to form an opinion on that.

Nora (glancing at him a moment): Shame on you. *(Hits him lightly on the ear with the stockings.)* That's for you. *(Puts them away again.)*

Rank: And what other splendors am I going to see now?

Nora: Not the least bit more, because you've been naughty. *(She hums a little and rummages among her things.)*

Rank (after a short silence): When I sit here together with you like this, completely easy and open, then I don't know — I simply can't imagine — whatever would have become of me if I'd never come into this house.

Nora (smiling): Yes, I really think you feel completely at ease with us.

Rank (more quietly, staring straight ahead): And then to have to go away from it all —

Nora: Nonsense, you're not going away.

Rank (his voice unchanged): — and not even be able to leave some poor show of gratitude behind, scarcely a fleeting regret — no more than a vacant place that anyone can fill.

Nora: And if I asked you now for — ? No —

Rank: For what?

Nora: For a great proof of your friendship —

Rank: Yes, yes?

Nora: No, I mean — for an exceptionally big favor —

Rank: Would you really, for once, make me so happy?

Nora: Oh, you haven't the vaguest idea what it is.

Rank: All right, then tell me.

Nora: No, but I can't, Dr. Rank — it's all out of reason. It's advice and help, too — and a favor —

Rank: So much the better. I can't fathom what you're hinting at. Just speak out. Don't you trust me?

Nora: Of course. More than anyone else. You're my best and truest friend, I'm sure. That's why I want to talk to you. All right, then, Dr. Rank: there's something you can help me prevent. You know how deeply, how inexpressibly dearly Torvald loves me; he'd never hesitate a second to give up his life for me.

Rank (leaning close to her): Nora — do you think he's the only one —

Nora (with a slight start): Who — ?

Rank: Who'd gladly give up his life for you.

Nora (heavily): I see.

Rank: I swore to myself you should know this before I'm gone. I'll never find a better chance. Yes, Nora, now you know. And also you know now that you can trust me beyond anyone else.

Nora (rising, natural and calm): Let me by.

Rank (making room for her, but still sitting): Nora —

Nora (in the hall doorway): Helene, bring the lamp in. *(Goes over to the stove.)* Ah, dear Dr. Rank, that was really mean of you.

Rank (getting up): That I've loved you just as deeply as somebody else? Was *that* mean?

Nora: No, but that you came out and told me. That was quite unnecessary —

Rank: What do you mean? Have you known — ?

The Maid comes in with the lamp, sets it on the table, and goes out again.

Rank: Nora — Mrs. Helmer — I'm asking you: have you known about it?

Nora: Oh, how can I tell what I know or don't know? Really, I don't know what to say—Why did you have to be so clumsy, Dr. Rank! Everything was so good.

Rank: Well, in any case, you now have the knowledge that my body and soul are at your command. So won't you speak out?

Nora (looking at him): After that?

Rank: Please, just let me know what it is.

Nora: You can't know anything now.

Rank: I have to. You mustn't punish me like this. Give me the chance to do whatever is humanly possible for you.

Nora: Now there's nothing you can do for me. Besides, actually, I don't need any help. You'll see—it's only my fantasies. That's what it is. Of course! *(Sits in the rocker, looks at him, and smiles.)* What a nice one you are, Dr. Rank. Aren't you a little bit ashamed, now that the lamp is here?

Rank: No, not exactly. But perhaps I'd better go—for good?

Nora: No, you certainly can't do that. You must come here just as you always have. You know Torvald can't do without you.

Rank: Yes, but *you?*

Nora: You know how much I enjoy it when you're here.

Rank: That's precisely what threw me off. You're a mystery to me. So many times I've felt you'd almost rather be with me than with Helmer.

Nora: Yes—you see, there are some people that one loves most and other people that one would almost prefer being with.

Rank: Yes, there's something to that.

Nora: When I was back home, of course I loved Papa most. But I always thought it was so much fun when I could sneak down to the maids' quarters, because they never tried to improve me, and it was always so amusing, the way they talked to each other.

Rank: Aha, so it's *their* place that I've filled.

Nora (jumping up and going to him): Oh, dear, sweet Dr. Rank, that's not what I meant at all. But you can understand that with Torvald it's just the same as with Papa—

The Maid enters from the hall.

Maid: Ma'am—please! *(She whispers to Nora and hands her a calling card.)*

Nora (glancing at the card): Ah! *(Slips it into her pocket.)*

Rank: Anything wrong?

Nora: No, no, not at all. It's only some—it's my new dress—

Rank: Really? But—there's your dress.

Nora: Oh, that. But this is another one—I ordered it—Torvald mustn't know—

Rank: Ah, now we have the big secret.

Nora: That's right. Just go in with him—he's back in the inner study. Keep him there as long as—

Rank: Don't worry. He won't get away. *(Goes into the study.)*

Nora (to the Maid): And he's standing waiting in the kitchen?

Maid: Yes, he came up by the back stairs.

Nora: But didn't you tell him somebody was here?

Maid: Yes, but that didn't do any good.

Nora: He won't leave?

Maid: No, he won't go till he's talked with you, ma'am.

Nora: Let him come in, then — but quietly. Helene, don't breathe a word about this. It's a surprise for my husband.

Maid: Yes, yes, I understand — *(Goes out.)*

Nora: This horror — it's going to happen. No, no, no, it can't happen, it mustn't. *(She goes and bolts Helmer's door. The Maid opens the hall door for Krogstad and shuts it behind him. He is dressed for travel in a fur coat, boots, and a fur cap.)*

Nora (going toward him): Talk softly. My husband's home.

Krogstad: Well, good for him.

Nora: What do you want?

Krogstad: Some information.

Nora: Hurry up, then. What is it?

Krogstad: You know, of course, that I got my notice.

Nora: I couldn't prevent it, Mr. Krogstad. I fought for you to the bitter end, but nothing worked.

Krogstad: Does your husband's love for you run so thin? He knows everything I can expose you to, and all the same he dares to —

Nora: How can you imagine he knows anything about this?

Krogstad: Ah, no — I can't imagine it either, now. It's not at all like my fine Torvald Helmer to have so much guts —

Nora: Mr. Krogstad, I demand respect for my husband!

Krogstad: Why, of course — all due respect. But since the lady's keeping it so carefully hidden, may I presume to ask if you're also a bit better informed than yesterday about what you've actually done?

Nora: More than you could ever teach me.

Krogstad: Yes, I *am* such an awful lawyer.

Nora: What is it you want from me?

Krogstad: Just a glimpse of how you are, Mrs. Helmer. I've been thinking about you all day long. A cashier, a night-court scribbler, a — well, a type like me also has a little of what they call a heart, you know.

Nora: Then show it. Think of my children.

Krogstad: Did you or your husband ever think of mine? But never mind. I simply wanted to tell you that you don't need to take this thing too seriously. For the present, I'm not proceeding with any action.

Nora: Oh no, really! Well — I knew that.

Krogstad: Everything can be settled in a friendly spirit. It doesn't have to get around town at all; it can stay just among us three.

Nora: My husband must never know anything of this.

Krogstad: How can you manage that? Perhaps you can pay me the balance?

Nora: No, not right now.

Krogstad: Or you know some way of raising the money in a day or two?

Nora: No way that I'm willing to use.

Krogstad: Well, it wouldn't have done you any good, anyway. If you stood in front of me with a fistful of bills, you still couldn't buy your signature back.

Nora: Then tell me what you're going to do with it.

Krogstad: I'll just hold onto it — keep it on file. There's no outsider who'll even get wind of it. So if you've been thinking of taking some desperate step —

Nora: I have.

Krogstad: Been thinking of running away from home —
Nora: I have!
Krogstad: Or even of something worse —
Nora: How could you guess that?
Krogstad: You can drop those thoughts.
Nora: How could you guess I was thinking of *that*?
Krogstad: Most of us think about *that* at first. I thought about it too, but I discovered I hadn't the courage —
Nora (lifelessly): I don't either.
Krogstad (relieved): That's true, you haven't the courage? You too?
Nora: I don't have it — I don't have it.
Krogstad: It would be terribly stupid, anyway. After that first storm at home blows out, why, then — I have here in my pocket a letter for your husband —
Nora: Telling everything?
Krogstad: As charitably as possible.
Nora (quickly): He mustn't ever get that letter. Tear it up. I'll find some way to get money.
Krogstad: Beg pardon, Mrs. Helmer, but I think I just told you —
Nora: Oh, I don't mean the money I owe you. Let me know how much you want from my husband, and I'll manage it.
Krogstad: I don't want money from your husband.
Nora: What do you want, then?
Krogstad: I'll tell you what. I want to recoup, Mrs. Helmer; I want to get on in the world — and there's where your husband can help me. For a year and a half I've kept myself clean of anything disreputable — all that time struggling with the worst conditions; but I was satisfied, working my way up step by step. Now I've been written right off, and I'm just not in the mood to come crawling back. I tell you, I want to move on. I want to get back in the bank — in a better position. Your husband can set up a job for me —
Nora: He'll never do that!
Krogstad: He'll do it. I know him. He won't dare breathe a word of protest. And once I'm in there together with him, you just wait and see! Inside of a year, I'll be the manager's right-hand man. It'll be Nils Krogstad, not Torvald Helmer, who runs the bank.
Nora: You'll never see the day!
Krogstad: Maybe you think you can —
Nora: I have the courage now — for *that*.
Krogstad: Oh, you don't scare me. A smart, spoiled lady like you —
Nora: You'll see; you'll see!
Krogstad: Under the ice, maybe? Down in the freezing coal-black water? There, till you float up in the spring, ugly, unrecognizable, with your hair falling out —
Nora: You don't frighten me.
Krogstad: Nor do you frighten me. One doesn't do these things, Mrs. Helmer. Besides, what good would it be? I'd still have him safe in my pocket.
Nora: Afterwards? When I'm no longer — ?
Krogstad: Are you forgetting that *I'll* be in control then over your final reputation? *(Nora stands speechless, staring at him.)* Good; now I've warned you. Don't do anything stupid. When Helmer's read my letter, I'll be waiting

for his reply. And bear in mind that it's your husband himself who's forced me back to my old ways. I'll never forgive him for that. Good-bye, Mrs. Helmer. (*He goes out through the hall.*)

Nora (*goes to the hall door, opens it a crack, and listens*): He's gone. Didn't leave the letter. Oh no, no, that's impossible too! (*Opening the door more and more.*) What's that? He's standing outside — not going downstairs. He's thinking it over? Maybe he'll — ? (*A letter falls in the mailbox; then Krogstad's footsteps are heard, dying away down a flight of stairs. Nora gives a muffled cry and runs over toward the sofa table. A short pause.*) In the mailbox. (*Slips warily over to the hall door.*) It's lying there. Torvald, Torvald — now we're lost!

Mrs. Linde (*entering with costume from the room, left*): There now, I can't see anything else to mend. Perhaps you'd like to try —

Nora (*in a hoarse whisper*): Kristine, come here.

Mrs. Linde (*tossing the dress on the sofa*): What's wrong? You look upset.

Nora: Come here. See that letter? *There!* Look — through the glass in the mailbox.

Mrs. Linde: Yes, yes, I see it.

Nora: That letter's from Krogstad —

Mrs. Linde: Nora — it's Krogstad who loaned you the money!

Nora: Yes, and now Torvald will find out everything.

Mrs. Linde: Believe me, Nora, it's best for both of you.

Nora: There's more you don't know. I forged a name.

Mrs. Linde: But for heaven's sake — ?

Nora: I only want to tell you that, Kristine, so that you can be my witness.

Mrs. Linde: Witness? Why should I — ?

Nora: If I should go out of my mind — it could easily happen —

Mrs. Linde: Nora!

Nora: Or anything else occurred — so I couldn't be present here —

Mrs. Linde: Nora, Nora, you aren't yourself at all!

Nora: And someone should try to take on the whole weight, all of the guilt, you follow me —

Mrs. Linde: Yes, of course, but why do you think — ?

Nora: Then you're the witness that it isn't true, Kristine. I'm very much myself; my mind right now is perfectly clear; and I'm telling you: nobody else has known about this; I alone did everything. Remember that.

Mrs. Linde: I will. But I don't understand all this.

Nora: Oh, how could you ever understand it? It's the miracle now that's going to take place.

Mrs. Linde: The miracle?

Nora: Yes, the miracle. But it's so awful, Kristine. It mustn't take place, not for anything in the world.

Mrs. Linde: I'm going right over and talk with Krogstad.

Nora: Don't go near him; he'll do you some terrible harm!

Mrs. Linde: There was a time once when he'd gladly have done anything for me.

Nora: He?

Mrs. Linde: Where does he live?

Nora: Oh, how do I know? Yes. (*Searches in her pocket.*) Here's his card. But the letter, the letter — !

Helmer (*from the study, knocking on the door*): Nora!

Nora (with a cry of fear): Oh! What is it? What do you want?

Helmer: Now, now, don't be so frightened. We're not coming in. You locked the door — are you trying on the dress?

Nora: Yes, I'm trying it. I'll look just beautiful, Torvald.

Mrs. Linde (who has read the card): He's living right around the corner.

Nora: Yes, but what's the use? We're lost. The letter's in the box.

Mrs. Linde: And your husband has the key?

Nora: Yes, always.

Mrs. Linde: Krogstad can ask for his letter back unread; he can find some excuse —

Nora: But it's just this time that Torvald usually —

Mrs. Linde: Stall him. Keep him in there. I'll be back as quick as I can. *(She hurries out through the hall entrance.)*

Nora (goes to Helmer's door, opens it, and peers in): Torvald!

Helmer (from the inner study): Well — does one dare set foot in one's own living room at last? Come on, Rank, now we'll get a look — *(In the doorway.)* But what's this?

Nora: What, Torvald dear?

Helmer: Rank had me expecting some grand masquerade.

Rank (in the doorway): That was my impression, but I must have been wrong.

Nora: No one can admire me in my splendor — not till tomorrow.

Helmer: But Nora dear, you look so exhausted. Have you practiced too hard?

Nora: No, I haven't practiced at all yet.

Helmer: You know, it's necessary —

Nora: Oh, it's absolutely necessary, Torvald. But I can't get anywhere without your help. I've forgotten the whole thing completely.

Helmer: Ah, we'll soon take care of that.

Nora: Yes, take care of me, Torvald, please! Promise me that? Oh, I'm so nervous. That big party — You must give up everything this evening for me. No business — don't even touch your pen. Yes? Dear Torvald, promise?

Helmer: It's a promise. Tonight I'm totally at your service — you little helpless thing. Hm — but first there's one thing I want to — *(Goes toward the hall door.)*

Nora: What are you looking for?

Helmer: Just to see if there's any mail.

Nora: No, no, don't do that, Torvald!

Helmer: Now what?

Nora: Torvald, please. There isn't any.

Helmer: Let me look, though. *(Starts out. Nora, at the piano, strikes the first notes of the tarantella. Helmer, at the door, stops.)* Aha!

Nora: I can't dance tomorrow if I don't practice with you.

Helmer (going over to her): Nora dear, are you really so frightened?

Nora: Yes, so terribly frightened. Let me practice right now; there's still time before dinner. Oh, sit down and play for me, Torvald. Direct me. Teach me, the way you always have.

Helmer: Gladly, if it's what you want. *(Sits at the piano.)*

Nora (snatches the tambourine up from the box, then a long, varicolored shawl, which she throws around herself, whereupon she springs forward and cries out): Play for me now! Now I'll dance!

Helmer plays and Nora dances. Rank stands behind Helmer at the piano and looks on.

Helmer (as he plays): Slower. Slow down.

Nora: Can't change it.

Helmer: Not so violent, Nora!

Nora: Has to be just like this.

Helmer (stopping): No, no, that won't do at all.

Nora (laughing and swinging her tambourine): Isn't that what I told you?

Rank: Let me play for her.

Helmer (getting up): Yes, go on. I can teach her more easily then.

Rank sits at the piano and plays; Nora dances more and more wildly. Helmer has stationed himself by the stove and repeatedly gives her directions; she seems not to hear them; her hair loosens and falls over her shoulders; she does not notice, but goes on dancing. Mrs. Linde enters.

Mrs. Linde (standing dumbfounded at the door): Ah —!

Nora (still dancing): See what fun, Kristine!

Helmer: But Nora darling, you dance as if your life were at stake.

Nora: And it is.

Helmer: Rank, stop! This is pure madness. Stop it, I say!

Rank breaks off playing, and Nora halts abruptly.

Helmer (going over to her): I never would have believed it. You've forgotten everything I taught you.

Nora (throwing away the tambourine): You see for yourself.

Helmer: Well, there's certainly room for instruction here.

Nora: Yes, you see how important it is. You've got to teach me to the very last minute. Promise me that, Torvald?

Helmer: You can bet on it.

Nora: You mustn't, either today or tomorrow, think about anything else but me; you mustn't open any letters — or the mailbox —

Helmer: Ah, it's still the fear of that man —

Nora: Oh yes, yes, that too.

Helmer: Nora, it's written all over you — there's already a letter from him out there.

Nora: I don't know. I guess so. But you mustn't read such things now; there mustn't be anything ugly between us before it's all over.

Rank (quietly to Helmer): You shouldn't deny her.

Helmer (putting his arms around her): The child can have her way. But tomorrow night, after you've danced —

Nora: Then you'll be free.

Maid (in the doorway, right): Ma'am, dinner is served.

Nora: We'll be wanting champagne, Helene.

Maid: Very good, ma'am. (Goes out.)

Helmer: So — a regular banquet, hm?

Nora: Yes, a banquet — champagne till daybreak! (Calling out.) And some macaroons, Helene. Heaps of them — just this once.

Helmer (taking her hands): Now, now, now — no hysterics. Be my own little lark again.

Nora: Oh, I will soon enough. But go on in — and you, Dr. Rank. Kristine, help me put up my hair.

Rank (whispering, as they go): There's nothing wrong — really wrong, is there?

Helmer: Oh, of course not. It's nothing more than this childish anxiety I was telling you about. *(They go out, right.)*

Nora: Well?

Mrs. Linde: Left town.

Nora: I could see by your face.

Mrs. Linde: He'll be home tomorrow evening. I wrote him a note.

Nora: You shouldn't have. Don't try to stop anything now. After all, it's a wonderful joy, this waiting here for the miracle.

Mrs. Linde: What is it you're waiting for?

Nora: Oh, you can't understand that. Go in to them; I'll be along in a moment.

> *Mrs. Linde goes into the dining room. Nora stands a short while as if composing herself, then she looks at her watch.*

Nora: Five. Seven hours to midnight. Twenty-four hours to the midnight after, and then the tarantella's done. Seven and twenty-four? Thirty-one hours to live.

Helmer (in the doorway, right): What's become of the little lark?

Nora (going toward him with open arms): Here's your lark!

ACT III

> *Same scene. The table, with chairs around it, has been moved to the center of the room. A lamp on the table is lit. The hall door stands open. Dance music drifts down from the floor above. Mrs. Linde sits at the table, absently paging through a book, trying to read, but apparently unable to focus her thoughts. Once or twice she pauses, tensely listening for a sound at the outer entrance.*

Mrs. Linde (glancing at her watch): Not yet — and there's hardly any time left. If only he's not — *(Listening again.)* Ah, there he is. *(She goes out in the hall and cautiously opens the outer door. Quiet footsteps are heard on the stairs. She whispers:)* Come in. Nobody's here.

Krogstad (in the doorway): I found a note from you at home. What's back of all this?

Mrs. Linde: I just *had* to talk to you.

Krogstad: Oh? And it just *had* to be here in this house?

Mrs. Linde: At my place it was impossible; my room hasn't a private entrance. Come in; we're all alone. The maid's asleep, and the Helmers are at the dance upstairs.

Krogstad (entering the room): Well, well, the Helmers are dancing tonight? Really?

Mrs. Linde: Yes, why not?

Krogstad: How true — why not?

Mrs. Linde: All right, Krogstad, let's talk.

Krogstad: Do we two have anything more to talk about?

Mrs. Linde: We have a great deal to talk about.

Krogstad: I wouldn't have thought so.

Mrs. Linde: No, because you've never understood me, really.

Krogstad: Was there anything more to understand—except what's all too common in life? A calculating woman throws over a man the moment a better catch comes by.

Mrs. Linde: You think I'm so thoroughly calculating? You think I broke it off lightly?

Krogstad: Didn't you?

Mrs. Linde: Nils—is that what you really thought?

Krogstad: If you cared, then why did you write me the way you did?

Mrs. Linde: What else could I do? If I had to break off with you, then it was my job as well to root out everything you felt for me.

Krogstad (wringing his hands): So that was it. And this—all this, simply for money!

Mrs. Linde: Don't forget I had a helpless mother and two small brothers. We couldn't wait for you, Nils; you had such a long road ahead of you then.

Krogstad: That may be; but you still hadn't the right to abandon me for somebody else's sake.

Mrs. Linde: Yes—I don't know. So many, many times I've asked myself if I did have that right.

Krogstad (more softly): When I lost you, it was as if all the solid ground dissolved from under my feet. Look at me; I'm a half-drowned man now, hanging onto a wreck.

Mrs. Linde: Help may be near.

Krogstad: It was near—but then you came and blocked it off.

Mrs. Linde: Without my knowing it, Nils. Today for the first time I learned that it's you I'm replacing at the bank.

Krogstad: All right—I believe you. But now that you know, will you step aside?

Mrs. Linde: No, because that wouldn't benefit you in the slightest.

Krogstad: Not "benefit" me, hm! I'd step aside anyway.

Mrs. Linde: I've learned to be realistic. Life and hard, bitter necessity have taught me that.

Krogstad: And life's taught me never to trust fine phrases.

Mrs. Linde: Then life's taught you a very sound thing. But you do have to trust in actions, don't you?

Krogstad: What does that mean?

Mrs. Linde: You said you were hanging on like a half-drowned man to a wreck.

Krogstad: I've good reason to say that.

Mrs. Linde: I'm also like a half-drowned woman on a wreck. No one to suffer with; no one to care for.

Krogstad: You made your choice.

Mrs. Linde: There wasn't any choice then.

Krogstad: So—what of it?

Mrs. Linde: Nils, if only we two shipwrecked people could reach across to each other.

Krogstad: What are you saying?

Mrs. Linde: Two on one wreck are at least better off than each on his own.

Krogstad: Kristine!

Mrs. Linde: Why do you think I came into town?

Krogstad: Did you really have some thought of me?

Mrs. Linde: I have to work to go on living. All my born days, as long as I can remember, I've worked, and it's been my best and my only joy. But now I'm completely alone in the world; it frightens me to be so empty and lost. To work for yourself — there's no joy in that. Nils, give me something — someone to work for.

Krogstad: I don't believe all this. It's just some hysterical feminine urge to go out and make a noble sacrifice.

Mrs. Linde: Have you ever found me to be hysterical?

Krogstad: Can you honestly mean this? Tell me — do you know everything about my past?

Mrs. Linde: Yes.

Krogstad: And you know what they think I'm worth around here.

Mrs. Linde: From what you were saying before, it would seem that with me you could have been another person.

Krogstad: I'm positive of that.

Mrs. Linde: Couldn't it happen still?

Krogstad: Kristine — you're saying this in all seriousness? Yes, you are! I can see it in you. And do you really have the courage, then — ?

Mrs. Linde: I need to have someone to care for; and your children need a mother. We both need each other. Nils, I have faith that you're good at heart — I'll risk everything together with you.

Krogstad (gripping her hands): Kristine, thank you, thank you — Now I know I can win back a place in their eyes. Yes — but I forgot —

Mrs. Linde (listening): Shh! The tarantella. Go now! Go on!

Krogstad: Why? What is it?

Mrs. Linde: Hear the dance up there? When that's over, they'll be coming down.

Krogstad: Oh, then I'll go. But — it's all pointless. Of course, you don't know the move I made against the Helmers.

Mrs. Linde: Yes, Nils, I know.

Krogstad: And all the same, you have the courage to — ?

Mrs. Linde: I know how far despair can drive a man like you.

Krogstad: Oh, if I only could take it all back.

Mrs. Linde: You easily could — your letter's still lying in the mailbox.

Krogstad: Are you sure of that?

Mrs. Linde: Positive. But —

Krogstad (looks at her searchingly): Is that the meaning of it, then? You'll save your friend at any price. Tell me straight out. Is that it?

Mrs. Linde: Nils — anyone who's sold herself for somebody else once isn't going to do it again.

Krogstad: I'll demand my letter back.

Mrs. Linde: No, no.

Krogstad: Yes, of course. I'll stay here till Helmer comes down; I'll tell him to give me my letter again — that it only involves my dismissal — that he shouldn't read it —

Mrs. Linde: No, Nils, don't call the letter back.

Krogstad: But wasn't that exactly why you wrote me to come here?

Mrs. Linde: Yes, in that first panic. But it's been a whole day and night since then, and in that time I've seen such incredible things in this house.

Helmer's got to learn everything; this dreadful secret has to be aired; those
two have to come to a full understanding; all these lies and evasions can't
go on.

Krogstad: Well, then, if you want to chance it. But at least there's one thing I
can do, and do right away—

Mrs. Linde (listening): Go now, go quick! The dance is over. We're not safe another
second.

Krogstad: I'll wait for you downstairs.

Mrs. Linde: Yes, please do; take me home.

Krogstad: I can't believe it; I've never been so happy. (*He leaves by way of the outer
door; the door between the room and the hall stays open.*)

Mrs. Linde (straightening up a bit and getting together her street clothes): How different
now! How different! Someone to work for, to live for—a home to build.
Well, it is worth the try! Oh, if they'd only come! (*Listening.*) Ah, there they
are. Bundle up. (*She picks up her hat and coat. Nora's and Helmer's voices can be
heard outside; a key turns in the lock, and Helmer brings Nora into the hall almost
by force. She is wearing the Italian costume with a large black shawl about her; he
has on evening dress, with a black domino open over it.*)

Nora (struggling in the doorway): No, no, no, not inside! I'm going up again. I
don't want to leave so soon.

Helmer: But Nora dear—

Nora: Oh, I beg you, please, Torvald. From the bottom of my heart, *please*—
only an hour more!

Helmer: Not a single minute, Nora darling. You know our agreement. Come
on, in we go; you'll catch cold out here. (*In spite of her resistance, he gently
draws her into the room.*)

Mrs. Linde: Good evening.

Nora: Kristine!

Helmer: Why, Mrs. Linde—are you here so late?

Mrs. Linde: Yes, I'm sorry, but I did want to see Nora in costume.

Nora: Have you been sitting here, waiting for me?

Mrs. Linde: Yes. I didn't come early enough; you were all upstairs; and then I
thought I really couldn't leave without seeing you.

Helmer (removing Nora's shawl): Yes, take a good look. She's worth looking at, I
can tell you that, Mrs. Linde. Isn't she lovely?

Mrs. Linde: Yes, I should say—

Helmer: A dream of loveliness, isn't she? That's what everyone thought at the
party, too. But she's horribly stubborn—this sweet little thing. What's to
be done with her? Can you imagine, I almost had to use force to pry her
away.

Nora: Oh, Torvald, you're going to regret you didn't indulge me, even for just a
half hour more.

Helmer: There, you see. She danced her tarantella and got a tumultuous hand—
which was well earned, although the performance may have been a bit too
naturalistic—I mean it rather overstepped the proprieties of art. But never
mind—what's important is, she made a success, an overwhelming success.
You think I could let her stay on after that and spoil the effect? Oh no; I took
my lovely little Capri girl—my capricious little Capri girl, I should say—
took her under my arm; one quick tour of the ballroom, a curtsy to every
side, and then—as they say in novels—the beautiful vision disappeared.

An exit should always be effective, Mrs. Linde, but that's what I can't get Nora to grasp. Phew, it's hot in here. *(Flings the domino on a chair and opens the door to his room.)* Why's it dark in here? Oh yes, of course. Excuse me. *(He goes in and lights a couple of candles.)*

Nora (in a sharp, breathless whisper): So?

Mrs. Linde (quietly): I talked with him.

Nora: And—?

Mrs. Linde: Nora—you must tell your husband everything.

Nora (dully): I knew it.

Mrs. Linde: You've got nothing to fear from Krogstad, but you have to speak out.

Nora: I won't tell.

Mrs. Linde: Then the letter will.

Nora: Thanks, Kristine. I know now what's to be done. Shh!

Helmer (reentering): Well, then, Mrs. Linde—have you admired her?

Mrs. Linde: Yes, and now I'll say good night.

Helmer: Oh, come, so soon? Is this yours, this knitting?

Mrs. Linde: Yes, thanks. I nearly forgot it.

Helmer: Do you knit, then?

Mrs. Linde: Oh yes.

Helmer: You know what? You should embroider instead.

Mrs. Linde: Really? Why?

Helmer: Yes, because it's a lot prettier. See here, one holds the embroidery so, in the left hand, and then one guides the needle with the right—so—in an easy, sweeping curve—right?

Mrs. Linde: Yes, I guess that's—

Helmer: But, on the other hand, knitting—it can never be anything but ugly. Look, see here, the arms tucked in, the knitting needles going up and down—there's something Chinese about it. Ah, that was really a glorious champagne they served.

Mrs. Linde: Yes, good night, Nora, and don't be stubborn anymore.

Helmer: Well put, Mrs. Linde!

Mrs. Linde: Good night, Mr. Helmer.

Helmer (accompanying her to the door): Good night, good night. I hope you get home all right. I'd be very happy to—but you don't have far to go. Good night, good night. *(She leaves. He shuts the door after her and returns.)* There, now, at last we got her out the door. She's a deadly bore, that creature.

Nora: Aren't you pretty tired, Torvald?

Helmer: No, not a bit.

Nora: You're not sleepy?

Helmer: Not at all. On the contrary, I'm feeling quite exhilarated. But you? Yes, you really look tired and sleepy.

Nora: Yes, I'm very tired. Soon now I'll sleep.

Helmer: See! You see! I was right all along that we shouldn't stay longer.

Nora: Whatever you do is always right.

Helmer (kissing her brow): Now my little lark talks sense. Say, did you notice what a time Rank was having tonight?

Nora: Oh, was he? I didn't get to speak with him.

Helmer: I scarcely did either, but it's a long time since I've seen him in such high spirits. *(Gazes at her a moment, then comes nearer her.)* Hm—it's marvelous, though, to be back home again — to be completely alone with you. Oh, you bewitchingly lovely young woman!

Nora: Torvald, don't look at me like that!

Helmer: Can't I look at my richest treasure? At all that beauty that's mine, mine alone — completely and utterly.

Nora (moving around to the other side of the table): You mustn't talk to me that way tonight.

Helmer (following her): The tarantella is still in your blood, I can see — and it makes you even more enticing. Listen. The guests are beginning to go. *(Dropping his voice.)* Nora — it'll soon be quiet through this whole house.

Nora: Yes, I hope so.

Helmer: You do, don't you, my love? Do you realize — when I'm out at a party like this with you — do you know why I talk to you so little, and keep such a distance away; just send you a stolen look now and then — you know why I do it? It's because I'm imagining then that you're my secret darling, my secret bride-to-be, and that no one suspects there's anything between us.

Nora: Yes, yes; oh, yes, I know you're always thinking of me.

Helmer: And then when we leave and I place the shawl over those fine young rounded shoulders — over that wonderful curving neck — then I pretend that you're my young bride, that we're just coming from the wedding, that for the first time I'm bringing you into my house — that for the first time I'm alone with you — completely alone with you, your trembling young beauty! All this evening I've longed for nothing but you. When I saw you turn and sway in the tarantella — my blood was pounding till I couldn't stand it — that's why I brought you down here so early —

Nora: Go away, Torvald! Leave me alone. I don't want all this.

Helmer: What do you mean? Nora, you're teasing me. You will, won't you? Aren't I your husband — ?

A knock at the outside door.

Nora (startled): What's that?

Helmer (going toward the hall): Who is it?

Rank (outside): It's me. May I come in a moment?

Helmer (with quiet irritation): Oh, what does he want now? *(Aloud.)* Hold on. *(Goes and opens the door.)* Oh, how nice that you didn't just pass us by!

Rank: I thought I heard your voice, and then I wanted so badly to have a look in. *(Lightly glancing about.)* Ah, me, these old familiar haunts. You have it snug and cozy in here, you two.

Helmer: You seemed to be having it pretty cozy upstairs, too.

Rank: Absolutely. Why shouldn't I? Why not take in everything in life? As much as you can, anyway, and as long as you can. The wine was superb —

Helmer: The champagne especially.

Rank: You noticed that too? It's amazing how much I could guzzle down.

Nora: Torvald also drank a lot of champagne this evening.

Rank: Oh?

Nora: Yes, and that always makes him so entertaining.

Rank: Well, why shouldn't one have a pleasant evening after a well-spent day?

Helmer: Well spent? I'm afraid I can't claim that.

Rank (slapping him on the back): But I can, you see!

Nora: Dr. Rank, you must have done some scientific research today.

Rank: Quite so.

Helmer: Come now — little Nora talking about scientific research!

Nora: And can I congratulate you on the results?

Rank: Indeed you may.

Nora: Then they were good?

Rank: The best possible for both doctor and patient — certainty.

Nora (quickly and searchingly): Certainty?

Rank: Complete certainty. So don't I owe myself a gay evening afterwards?

Nora: Yes, you're right, Dr. Rank.

Helmer: I'm with you — just so long as you don't have to suffer for it in the morning.

Rank: Well, one never gets something for nothing in life.

Nora: Dr. Rank — are you very fond of masquerade parties?

Rank: Yes, if there's a good array of odd disguises —

Nora: Tell me, what should we two go as at the next masquerade?

Helmer: You little featherhead — already thinking of the next!

Rank: We two? I'll tell you what: you must go as Charmed Life —

Helmer: Yes, but find a costume for *that*!

Rank: Your wife can appear just as she looks every day.

Helmer: That was nicely put. But don't you know what you're going to be?

Rank: Yes, Helmer, I've made up my mind.

Helmer: Well?

Rank: At the next masquerade I'm going to be invisible.

Helmer: That's a funny idea.

Rank: They say there's a hat — black, huge — have you never heard of the hat that makes you invisible? You put it on, and then no one on earth can see you.

Helmer (suppressing a smile): Ah, of course.

Rank: But I'm quite forgetting what I came for. Helmer, give me a cigar, one of the dark Havanas.

Helmer: With the greatest pleasure. *(Holds out his case.)*

Rank: Thanks. *(Takes one and cuts off the tip.)*

Nora (striking a match): Let me give you a light.

Rank: Thank you. *(She holds the match for him; he lights the cigar.)* And now good-bye.

Helmer: Good-bye, good-bye, old friend.

Nora: Sleep well, Doctor.

Rank: Thanks for that wish.

Nora: Wish me the same.

Rank: You? All right, if you like — Sleep well. And thanks for the light. *(He nods to them both and leaves.)*

Helmer (his voice subdued): He's been drinking heavily.

Nora (absently): Could be. *(Helmer takes his keys from his pocket and goes out in the hall.)* Torvald — what are you after?

Helmer: Got to empty the mailbox; it's nearly full. There won't be room for the morning papers.

Nora: Are you working tonight?

Helmer: You know I'm not. Why — what's this? Someone's been at the lock.

Nora: At the lock — ?

Helmer: Yes, I'm positive. What do you suppose — ? I can't imagine one of the maids — ? Here's a broken hairpin. Nora, it's yours —

Nora (quickly): Then it must be the children —

Helmer: You'd better break them of that. Hm, hm — well, opened it after all. *(Takes the contents out and calls into the kitchen.)* Helene! Helene, would you put out the lamp in the hall. *(He returns to the room shutting the hall door, then displays the handful of mail.)* Look how it's piled up. *(Sorting through them.)* Now what's this?

Nora (at the window): The letter! Oh, Torvald, no!

Helmer: Two calling cards — from Rank.

Nora: From Dr. Rank?

Helmer (examining them): "Dr. Rank, Consulting Physician." They were on top. He must have dropped them in as he left.

Nora: Is there anything on them?

Helmer: There's a black cross over the name. See? That's a gruesome notion. He could almost be announcing his own death.

Nora: That's just what he's doing.

Helmer: What! You've heard something? Something he's told you?

Nora: Yes. That when those cards came, he'd be taking his leave of us. He'll shut himself in now and die.

Helmer: Ah, my poor friend! Of course I knew he wouldn't be here much longer. But so soon — And then to hide himself away like a wounded animal.

Nora: If it has to happen, then it's best it happens in silence — don't you think so, Torvald?

Helmer (pacing up and down): He'd grown right into our lives. I simply can't imagine him gone. He with his suffering and loneliness — like a dark cloud setting off our sunlit happiness. Well, maybe it's best this way. For him, at least. *(Standing still.)* And maybe for us too, Nora. Now we're thrown back on each other, completely. *(Embracing her.)* Oh you, my darling wife, how can I hold you close enough? You know what, Nora — time and again I've wished you were in some terrible danger, just so I could stake my life and soul and everything, for your sake.

Nora (tearing herself away, her voice firm and decisive): Now you must read your mail, Torvald.

Helmer: No, no, not tonight. I want to stay with you, dearest.

Nora: With a dying friend on your mind?

Helmer: You're right. We've both had a shock. There's ugliness between us — these thoughts of death and corruption. We'll have to get free of them first. Until then — we'll stay apart.

Nora (clinging about his neck): Torvald — good night! Good night!

Helmer (kissing her on the cheek): Good night, little songbird. Sleep well, Nora. I'll be reading my mail now. *(He takes the letters into his room and shuts the door after him.)*

Nora (with bewildered glances, groping about, seizing Helmer's domino, throwing it around her, and speaking in short, hoarse, broken whispers): Never see him again. Never, never. *(Putting her shawl over her head.)* Never see the children either — them, too. Never, never. Oh, the freezing black water! The depths — down — Oh,

I wish it were over—He has it now; he's reading it—now. Oh no, no, not yet. Torvald, good-bye, you and the children— (*She starts for the hall; as she does, Helmer throws open his door and stands with an open letter in his hand.*)

Helmer: Nora!

Nora (screams): Oh—!

Helmer: What is this? You know what's in this letter?

Nora: Yes, I know. Let me go! Let me out!

Helmer (holding her back): Where are you going?

Nora (struggling to break loose): You can't save me, Torvald!

Helmer (slumping back): True! Then it's true what he writes? How horrible! No, no, it's impossible—it can't be true.

Nora: It *is* true. I've loved you more than all this world.

Helmer: Ah, none of your slippery tricks.

Nora (taking one step toward him): Torvald—!

Helmer: What *is* this you've blundered into!

Nora: Just let me loose. You're not going to suffer for my sake. You're not going to take on my guilt.

Helmer: No more play-acting. (*Locks the hall door.*) You stay right here and give me a reckoning. You understand what you've done? Answer! You understand?

Nora (looking squarely at him, her face hardening): Yes. I'm beginning to understand everything now.

Helmer (striding about): Oh, what an awful awakening! In all these eight years— she who was my pride and joy—a hypocrite, a liar—worse, worse—a criminal! How infinitely disgusting it all is! The shame! (*Nora says nothing and goes on looking straight at him. He stops in front of her.*) I should have suspected something of the kind. I should have known. All your father's flimsy values—Be still! All your father's flimsy values have come out in you. No religion, no morals, no sense of duty—Oh, how I'm punished for letting him off! I did it for your sake, and you repay me like this.

Nora: Yes, like this.

Helmer: Now you've wrecked all my happiness—ruined my whole future. Oh, it's awful to think of. I'm in a cheap little grafter's hands; he can do anything he wants with me, ask for anything, play with me like a puppet—and I can't breathe a word. I'll be swept down miserably into the depths on account of a featherbrained woman.

Nora: When I'm gone from this world, you'll be free.

Helmer: Oh, quit posing. Your father had a mess of those speeches too. What good would that ever do me if you were gone from this world, as you say? Not the slightest. He can still make the whole thing known; and if he does, I could be falsely suspected as your accomplice. They might even think that I was behind it—that I put you up to it. And all that I can thank you for—you that I've coddled the whole of our marriage. Can you see now what you've done to me?

Nora (icily calm): Yes.

Helmer: It's so incredible, I just can't grasp it. But we'll have to patch up whatever we can. Take off the shawl. I said, take it off! I've got to appease him somehow or other. The thing has to be hushed up at any cost. And as for you and me, it's got to seem like everything between us is just as it was—to the outside world, that is. You'll go right on living in this house, of course.

But you can't be allowed to bring up the children; I don't dare trust you with them — Oh, to have to say this to someone I've loved so much! Well, that's done with. From now on happiness doesn't matter; all that matters is saving the bits and pieces, the appearance — *(The doorbell rings. Helmer starts.)* What's that? And so late. Maybe the worst —? You think he'd —? Hide, Nora! Say you're sick. *(Nora remains standing motionless. Helmer goes and opens the door.)*

Maid (half dressed, in the hall): A letter for Mrs. Helmer.

Helmer: I'll take it. *(Snatches the letter and shuts the door.)* Yes, it's from him. You don't get it; I'm reading it myself.

Nora: Then read it.

Helmer (by the lamp): I hardly dare. We may be ruined, you and I. But — I've got to know. *(Rips open the letter, skims through a few lines, glances at an enclosure, then cries out joyfully.)* Nora! *(Nora looks inquiringly at him.)* Nora! Wait — better check it again — Yes, yes, it's true. I'm saved. Nora, I'm saved!

Nora: And I?

Helmer: You too, of course. We're both saved, both of us. Look. He's sent back your note. He says he's sorry and ashamed — that a happy development in his life — oh, who cares what he says! Nora, we're saved! No one can hurt you. Oh, Nora, Nora — but first, this ugliness all has to go. Let me see — *(Takes a look at the note.)* No, I don't want to see it; I want the whole thing to fade like a dream. *(Tears the note and both letters to pieces, throws them into the stove and watches them burn.)* There — now there's nothing left — He wrote that since Christmas Eve you — Oh, they must have been three terrible days for you, Nora.

Nora: I fought a hard fight.

Helmer: And suffered pain and saw no escape but — No, we're not going to dwell on anything unpleasant. We'll just be grateful and keep on repeating: it's over now, it's over! You hear me, Nora? You don't seem to realize — it's over. What's it mean — that frozen look? Oh, poor little Nora, I understand. You can't believe I've forgiven you. But I have, Nora; I swear I have. I know that what you did, you did out of love for me.

Nora: That's true.

Helmer: You loved me the way a wife ought to love her husband. It's simply the means that you couldn't judge. But you think I love you any the less for not knowing how to handle your affairs? No, no — just lean on me; I'll guide you and teach you. I wouldn't be a man if this feminine helplessness didn't make you twice as attractive to me. You mustn't mind those sharp words I said — that was all in the first confusion of thinking my world had collapsed. I've forgiven you, Nora; I swear I've forgiven you.

Nora: My thanks for your forgiveness. *(She goes out through the door, right.)*

Helmer: No, wait — *(Peers in.)* What are you doing in there?

Nora (inside): Getting out of my costume.

Helmer (by the open door): Yes, do that. Try to calm yourself and collect your thoughts again, my frightened little songbird. You can rest easy now; I've got wide wings to shelter you with. *(Walking about close by the door.)* How snug and nice our home is, Nora. You're safe here; I'll keep you like a hunted dove I've rescued out of a hawk's claws. I'll bring peace to your poor, shuddering heart. Gradually it'll happen, Nora; you'll see. Tomorrow all this will look different to you; then everything will be as it was. I won't have to go on repeating I forgive you; you'll feel it for yourself. How can you imagine I'd ever conceivably want to disown you — or even blame you in any way? Ah, you don't know a man's heart, Nora. For a man there's something indescribably sweet and satisfying in knowing he's forgiven his wife — and forgiven her out of a full and open heart. It's as if she belongs to him in two ways now: in a sense he's given her fresh into the world again, and she's become his wife and his child as well. From now on that's what you'll be to me — you little, bewildered, helpless thing. Don't be afraid of anything, Nora; just open your heart to me, and I'll be conscience and will to you both — *(Nora enters in her regular clothes.)* What's this? Not in bed? You've changed your dress?

Nora: Yes, Torvald, I've changed my dress.

Helmer: But why now, so late?

Nora: Tonight I'm not sleeping.

Helmer: But Nora dear —

Nora (looking at her watch): It's still not so very late. Sit down, Torvald; we have a lot to talk over. *(She sits at one side of the table.)*

Helmer: Nora — what is this? That hard expression —

Nora: Sit down. This'll take some time. I have a lot to say.

Helmer (sitting at the table directly opposite her): You worry me, Nora. And I don't understand you.

Nora: No, that's exactly it. You don't understand me. And I've never understood you either — until tonight. No, don't interrupt. You can just listen to what I say. We're closing out accounts, Torvald.

Helmer: How do you mean that?

Nora (after a short pause): Doesn't anything strike you about our sitting here like this?

Helmer: What's that?

Nora: We've been married now eight years. Doesn't it occur to you that this is the first time we two, you and I, man and wife, have ever talked seriously together?

Helmer: What do you mean — seriously?

Nora: In eight whole years — longer even — right from our first acquaintance, we've never exchanged a serious word on any serious thing.

Helmer: You mean I should constantly go and involve you in problems you couldn't possibly help me with?

Nora: I'm not talking of problems. I'm saying that we've never sat down seriously together and tried to get to the bottom of anything.

Helmer: But dearest, what good would that ever do you?

Nora: That's the point right there: you've never understood me. I've been wronged greatly, Torvald — first by Papa, and then by you.

Helmer: What! By us — the two people who've loved you more than anyone else?

Nora (shaking her head): You never loved me. You've thought it fun to be in love with me, that's all.

Helmer: Nora, what a thing to say!

Nora: Yes, it's true now, Torvald. When I lived at home with Papa, he told me all his opinions, so I had the same ones too; or if they were different I hid them, since he wouldn't have cared for that. He used to call me his doll-child, and he played with me the way I played with my dolls. Then I came into your house —

Helmer: How can you speak of our marriage like that?

Nora (unperturbed): I mean, then I went from Papa's hands into yours. You arranged everything to your own taste, and so I got the same taste as you — or I pretended to; I can't remember. I guess a little of both, first one, then the other. Now when I look back, it seems as if I'd lived here like a beggar — just from hand to mouth. I've lived by doing tricks for you, Torvald. But that's the way you wanted it. It's a great sin what you and Papa did to me. You're to blame that nothing's become of me.

Helmer: Nora, how unfair and ungrateful you are! Haven't you been happy here?

Nora: No, never. I thought so — but I never have.

Helmer: Not — not happy!

Nora: No, only lighthearted. And you've always been so kind to me. But our home's been nothing but a playpen. I've been your doll-wife here, just as at home I was Papa's doll-child. And in turn the children have been my dolls. I thought it was fun when you played with me, just as they thought it fun when I played with them. That's been our marriage, Torvald.

Helmer: There's some truth in what you're saying — under all the raving exaggeration. But it'll all be different after this. Playtime's over; now for the schooling.

Nora: Whose schooling — mine or the children's?

Helmer: Both yours and the children's, dearest.

Nora: Oh, Torvald, you're not the man to teach me to be a good wife to you.

Helmer: And you can say that?

Nora: And I — how am I equipped to bring up children?

Helmer: Nora!

Nora: Didn't you say a moment ago that that was no job to trust me with?

Helmer: In a flare of temper! Why fasten on that?

Nora: Yes, but you were so very right. I'm not up to the job. There's another job I have to do first. I have to try to educate myself. You can't help me with that. I've got to do it alone. And that's why I'm leaving you now.

Helmer (jumping up): What's that?

Nora: I have to stand completely alone, if I'm ever going to discover myself and the world out there. So I can't go on living with you.

Helmer: Nora, Nora!

Nora: I want to leave right away. Kristine should put me up for the night —

Helmer: You're insane! You've no right! I forbid you!

Nora: From here on, there's no use forbidding me anything. I'll take with me whatever is mine. I don't want a thing from you, either now or later.

Helmer: What kind of madness is this!

Nora: Tomorrow I'm going home — I mean, home where I came from. It'll be easier up there to find something to do.

Helmer: Oh, you blind, incompetent child!

Nora: I must learn to be competent, Torvald.

Helmer: Abandon your home, your husband, your children! And you're not even thinking what people will say.

Nora: I can't be concerned about that. I only know how essential this is.

Helmer: Oh, it's outrageous. So you'll run out like this on your most sacred
   vows.

Nora: What do you think are my most sacred vows?

Helmer: And I have to tell you that! Aren't they your duties to your husband
   and children?

Nora: I have other duties equally sacred.

Helmer: That isn't true. What duties are they?

Nora: Duties to myself.

Helmer: Before all else, you're a wife and mother.

Nora: I don't believe in that anymore. I believe that, before all else, I'm a
   human being, no less than you — or anyway, I ought to try to become one.
   I know the majority thinks you're right, Torvald, and plenty of books
   agree with you, too. But I can't go on believing what the majority says, or
   what's written in books. I have to think over these things myself and try to
   understand them.

Helmer: Why can't you understand your place in your own home? On a point
   like that, isn't there one everlasting guide you can turn to? Where's your
   religion?

Nora: Oh, Torvald, I'm really not sure what religion is.

Helmer: What — ?

Nora: I only know what the minister said when I was confirmed. He told me
   religion was this thing and that. When I get clear and away by myself, I'll
   go into that problem too. I'll see if what the minister said was right, or, in
   any case, if it's right for me.

Helmer: A young woman your age shouldn't talk like that. If religion can't
   move you, I can try to rouse your conscience. You do have some moral feeling? Or, tell me — has that gone too?

Nora: It's not easy to answer that, Torvald. I simply don't know. I'm all confused about these things. I just know I see them so differently from you. I
   find out, for one thing, that the law's not at all what I'd thought — but I
   can't get it through my head that the law is fair. A woman hasn't a right to
   protect her dying father or save her husband's life! I can't believe that.

Helmer: You talk like a child. You don't know anything of the world you live in.

Nora: No, I don't. But now I'll begin to learn for myself. I'll try to discover
   who's right, the world or I.

Helmer: Nora, you're sick; you've got a fever. I almost think you're out of your
   head.

Nora: I've never felt more clearheaded and sure in my life.

Helmer: And — clearheaded and sure — you're leaving your husband and children?

Nora: Yes.

Helmer: Then there's only one possible reason.

Nora: What?

Helmer: You no longer love me.

Nora: No. That's exactly it.

Helmer: Nora! You can't be serious!

Nora: Oh, this is so hard, Torvald — you've been so kind to me always. But I
   can't help it. I don't love you anymore.

Helmer (struggling for composure): Are you also clearheaded and sure about that?

Nora: Yes, completely. That's why I can't go on staying here.

Helmer: Can you tell me what I did to lose your love?

Nora: Yes, I can tell you. It was this evening when the miraculous thing didn't come — then I knew you weren't the man I'd imagined.

Helmer: Be more explicit; I don't follow you.

Nora: I've waited now so patiently eight long years — for, my Lord, I know miracles don't come every day. Then this crisis broke over me, and such a certainty filled me: *now* the miraculous event would occur. While Krogstad's letter was lying out there, I never for an instant dreamed that you could give in to his terms. I was so utterly sure you'd say to him: go on, tell your tale to the whole wide world. And when he'd done that —

Helmer: Yes, what then? When I'd delivered my own wife into shame and disgrace —

Nora: When he'd done that, I was so utterly sure that you'd step forward, take the blame on yourself and say: I am the guilty one.

Helmer: Nora — !

Nora: You're thinking I'd never accept such a sacrifice from you? No, of course not. But what good would my protests be against you? That was the miracle I was waiting for, in terror and hope. And to stave that off, I would have taken my life.

Helmer: I'd gladly work for you day and night, Nora — and take on pain and deprivation. But there's no one who gives up honor for love.

Nora: Millions of women have done just that.

Helmer: Oh, you think and talk like a silly child.

Nora: Perhaps. But you neither think nor talk like the man I could join myself to. When your big fright was over — and it wasn't from any threat against me, only for what might damage you — when all the danger was past, for you it was just as if nothing had happened. I was exactly the same, your little lark, your doll, that you'd have to handle with double care now that I'd turned out so brittle and frail. *(Gets up.)* Torvald — in that instant it dawned on me that for eight years I've been living here with a stranger, and that I've even conceived three children — oh, I can't stand the thought of it! I could tear myself to bits.

Helmer (heavily): I see. There's a gulf that's opened between us — that's clear. Oh, but Nora, can't we bridge it somehow?

Nora: The way I am now, I'm no wife for you.

Helmer: I have the strength to make myself over.

Nora: Maybe — if your doll gets taken away.

Helmer: But to part! To part from you! No, Nora no — I can't imagine it.

Nora (going out, right): All the more reason why it has to be. *(She reenters with her coat and a small overnight bag, which she puts on a chair by the table.)*

Helmer: Nora, Nora, not now! Wait till tomorrow.

Nora: I can't spend the night in a strange man's room.

Helmer: But couldn't we live here like brother and sister —

Nora: You know very well how long that would last. *(Throws her shawl about her.)* Good-bye, Torvald. I won't look in on the children. I know they're in better hands than mine. The way I am now, I'm no use to them.

Helmer: But someday, Nora — someday — ?

Nora: How can I tell? I haven't the least idea what'll become of me.

Helmer: But you're my wife, now and wherever you go.

Nora: Listen, Torvald — I've heard that when a wife deserts her husband's house just as I'm doing, then the law frees him from all responsibility. In any case, I'm freeing you from being responsible. Don't feel yourself bound, any more than I will. There has to be absolute freedom for us both. Here, take your ring back. Give me mine.

Helmer: That too?

Nora: That too.

Helmer: There it is.

Nora: Good. Well, now it's all over. I'm putting the keys here. The maids know all about keeping up the house — better than I do. Tomorrow, after I've left town, Kristine will stop by to pack up everything that's mine from home. I'd like those things shipped up to me.

Helmer: Over! All over! Nora, won't you ever think about me?

Nora: I'm sure I'll think of you often, and about the children and the house here.

Helmer: May I write you?

Nora: No — never. You're not to do that.

Helmer: Oh, but let me send you —

Nora: Nothing. Nothing.

Helmer: Or help you if you need it.

Nora: No. I accept nothing from strangers.

Helmer: Nora — can I never be more than a stranger to you?

Nora (picking up her overnight bag): Ah, Torvald — it would take the greatest miracle of all —

Helmer: Tell me the greatest miracle!

Nora: You and I both would have to transform ourselves to the point that — Oh, Torvald, I've stopped believing in miracles.

Helmer: But I'll believe. Tell me! Transform ourselves to the point that — ?

Nora: That our living together could be a true marriage. *(She goes out down the hall.)*

Helmer (sinks down on a chair by the door, face buried in his hands): Nora! Nora! *(Looking about and rising.)* Empty. She's gone. *(A sudden hope leaps in him.)* The greatest miracle — ?

From below, the sound of a door slamming shut.

CONSIDERATIONS FOR CRITICAL THINKING AND WRITING

1. **FIRST RESPONSE.** What is the significance of the play's title?

2. Nora lies several times during the play. What kinds of lies are they? Do her lies indicate that she is not to be trusted, or are they a sign of something else about her personality?

3. What kind of wife does Helmer want Nora to be? He affectionately calls her names such as "lark" and "squirrel." What does this reveal about his attitude toward her?

4. Why is Nora "pale with terror" at the end of Act I? What is the significance of the description of the Christmas tree now "stripped of ornament, [with] burned-down candle stubs on its ragged branches" that opens Act II? What other symbols are used in the play?

5. What is Dr. Rank's purpose in the play?

6. How does the relationship between Krogstad and Mrs. Linde serve to emphasize certain qualities in the Helmers' marriage?

7. Is Krogstad's decision not to expose Nora's secret convincing? Does his shift from villainy to generosity seem adequately motivated?

8. Why does Nora reject Helmer's efforts to smooth things over between them and start again? Do you have any sympathy for Helmer?

9. Would you describe the ending as essentially happy or unhappy? Is the play more like a comedy or a tragedy?

10. Ibsen believed that a "dramatist's business is not to answer questions, but only to ask them." What questions are raised in the play? Does Ibsen propose any specific answers?

11. What makes this play a work of realism? Are there any elements that seem not to be realistic?

12. **CRITICAL STRATEGIES.** Read the section on new historicist criticism (pp. 2054–55) in Chapter 53, "Critical Strategies for Reading," and consider the following: Ibsen once wrote a different ending for the play to head off producers who might have been tempted to change the final scene to placate the public's sense of morality. In the second conclusion, Helmer forces Nora to look in on their sleeping children. This causes her to realize that she cannot leave her family even though it means sacrificing herself. Ibsen called this version of the ending a "barbaric outrage" and didn't use it. How do you think the play reflects or refutes social values contemporary to it?

CONNECTIONS TO OTHER SELECTIONS

1. What does Nora have in common with the protagonist in Gail Godwin's "A Sorrowful Woman" (p. 39)? What significant differences are there between them?

2. Explain how Torvald's attitude toward Nora is similar to the men's attitudes toward women in Susan Glaspell's *Trifles* (p. 1366). Write an essay exploring how the assumptions the men make about women in both plays contribute to the plays' conflicts.

3. Write an essay that compares and contrasts Nora's response to the social and legal expectations of her society with Antigone's in Sophocles' play (p. 1465). To what values does each character pledge her allegiance?

Perspective

HENRIK IBSEN (1828–1906)

Notes for A Doll House   *1878*

There are two kinds of spiritual law, two kinds of conscience, one in man and another, altogether different, in woman. They do not understand each other; but in practical life the woman is judged by man's law, as though she were not a woman but a man.

The wife in the play ends by having no idea of what is right or wrong; natural feeling on the one hand and belief in authority on the other have altogether bewildered her.

A woman cannot be herself in the society of the present day, which is an exclusively masculine society, with laws framed by men and with a judicial system that judges feminine conduct from a masculine point of view.

She has committed forgery, and she is proud of it; for she did it out of love for her husband, to save his life. But this husband with his commonplace principles of honor is on the side of the law and looks at the question from the masculine point of view.

Spiritual conflicts. Oppressed and bewildered by the belief in authority, she loses faith in her moral right and ability to bring up her children. Bitterness. A mother in modern society, like certain insects who go away and die when she has done her duty in the propagation of the race. Love of life, of home, of husband and children and family. Now and then a womanly shaking off of her thoughts. Sudden return of anxiety and terror. She must bear it all alone. The catastrophe approaches, inexorably, inevitably. Despair, conflict, and destruction.

From *From Ibsen's Workshop,* translated by A. G. Chater

CONSIDERATIONS FOR CRITICAL THINKING AND WRITING

1. Given the ending of *A Doll House,* what do you think of Ibsen's early view in his notes that "the wife in the play ends by having no idea of what is right or wrong" (para. 2)? Would you describe Nora as "altogether bewildered" (para. 2)? Why or why not?

2. "A woman cannot be herself in the society of the present day, which is an exclusively masculine society" (para. 3). Why is this statement true of Nora? Explain why you agree or disagree that this observation is accurate today.

3. How does oppressive "authority" (para. 5) loom large for Nora? What kind of authority creates "spiritual conflicts" for her?

More perspectives appear in the next chapter, "A Critical Case Study: Henrik Ibsen's *A Doll House,*" page 1764.

BEYOND REALISM

Realistic drama remained popular throughout the twentieth century, but from its beginnings it has been continually challenged by nonrealistic modes of theater. By the end of the nineteenth century, playwrights reacting against realism began to develop a variety of new approaches to setting, action, and character. Instead of creating a slice of life onstage, modern experimental playwrights drew on purely theatrical devices, ranging from stark sets and ritualistic actions to symbolic characterizations and audience participation. In general, such devices were designed to jar audiences' expectations and to heighten their awareness that what appeared before them was indeed a theatrical production. A glimpse of some of the nonrealistic movements in drama suggests how the possibilities for affecting audiences have been broadened by experimental theater.

Symbolist drama rejected the realists' assumption that life can be understood objectively and scientifically. The symbolists emphasized a subjective, emotional response to life because they believed that ultimate realities can be recognized only intuitively. Since absolute truth cannot be directly perceived, symbolists such as the Belgian playwright Maurice Maeterlinck (1862–1949) sought to express spiritual truth through settings, characters, and actions that suggest a transcendent reality. Maeterlinck's most famous symbolist play, *Pelléas and Mélisande* (1892), is a story of love and vengeance that includes mysterious forebodings, symbolic objects, and unexplained powerful forces. The elements of the play make no attempt to create the texture of ordinary life.

Other playwrights — such as William Butler Yeats (1865–1939) in Ireland, Paul Claudel (1868–1955) in France, Leonid Andreyev (1871–1919) in Russia, and Federico García Lorca (1898–1936) in Spain — also used some of the techniques associated with symbolist plays, but the movement never enjoyed wide popularity because audiences often found the plays' action too vague and their language too cryptic. Nevertheless, symbolist drama had an important influence on the work of subsequent playwrights, such as Tennessee Williams's *The Glass Menagerie* and Arthur Miller's *Death of a Salesman* (p. 1869); these dramatists effectively used symbols in plays that contain both realistic and nonrealistic qualities.

Another nonrealistic movement, known as **expressionism,** was popular from the end of World War I until the mid-1920s. Expressionist playwrights emphasized the internal lives of their characters and deliberately distorted reality by creating an outward manifestation of an inner state of being. The late plays of Swedish dramatist August Strindberg (1849–1912) anticipate expressionistic techniques. Strindberg's preface to *A Dream Play* (1902) reflects the impact that Freudian psychology would eventually have on the theater:

> The author has tried to imitate the disconnected but seemingly logical form of the dream. Anything may happen; everything is possible and probable. Time and space do not exist. On an insignificant background of reality, imagination designs and embroiders novel patterns: a medley of memories, experiences, free fancies, absurdities, and improvisations.

In such nonrealistic drama the action does not have to proceed chronologically because the playwright dramatizes the emotional life of the characters, which blends the past with the present rather than moving in a fixed, linear way. This fluidity of development can be seen in the **flashbacks** of Williams's *The Glass Menagerie* and Miller's *Death of a Salesman*.

The **epic theater** of Bertolt Brecht (1898–1956) is, like symbolism and expressionism, a long way from the realistic elements in Ibsen's *A Doll House*. Brecht kept a distance between his characters and the audience. This strategy of alienation was designed to alert audiences to important social problems that might be overlooked if an individual's struggles became too emotionally absorbing. Brecht's drama, by casting new light on chronic human problems such as poverty, injustice, and war, was a means to convey hope and evidence that society could be changed for the better. Brecht called his drama "epic" to distinguish it from Aristotle's notion of drama. The episodic structure was designed to prevent the audience from being swept up in the action or losing themselves in an inevitable tragedy. Instead, Brecht wanted the audience to analyze the action and realize that certain consequences weren't inevitable but could be avoided. This distancing, the dramatization of societal issues, and the use of loosely connected scenes sometimes narrated by a kind of stage manager are the hallmarks of epic drama.

Epic theater revels in stylized theatricality. The major action in *The Caucasian Chalk Circle,* for example, consists of a play within a play. Brecht's dramas use suggestive rather than detailed settings, and their scenery and props are frequently changed as the audience watches. His actors make clear that they are pretending to be characters. They may speak or sing in verse, address the audience, or comment on issues with other characters who are not participants in the immediate action. In brief, Brecht's theater is keenly conscious of itself as theater.

In contrast to this didactic theater, the ***theater of the absurd*** was a response to the twentieth century's loss of faith in reason, religion, and life itself. These doubts produced an approach to drama that emphasizes chaotic, irrational forces and portrays human beings as more the victims than the makers of their world.

Absurdists such as Samuel Beckett (1906–1989), French dramatist Eugène Ionesco (1912–1994), English playwright Harold Pinter (1930–2008), and American writer Edward Albee (b. 1928) employ a variety of approaches to drama, but they share some assumptions about what subjects are important. Absurdism challenges the belief that life is ordered and meaningful. Instead of positing traditional values that give human beings a sense of purpose in life, absurdists dramatize our inability to comprehend fully our identities and destinies. Unlike heroic characters such as Oedipus or Hamlet, who retain their dignity despite their defeats, the characters in absurdist dramas frequently seem pathetically comic as they drift from one destructive moment to the next. These ***antiheroes*** are often bewildered, ineffectual, deluded, and lost. If they learn anything, it is that the world isolates them in an existence devoid of God and absolute values.

The basic premise of absurdism — that life is meaningless — is often presented in a nonrealistic manner to disrupt our expectations. In a realistic play such as Ibsen's *A Doll House,* characters act pretty much the way we believe people behave. The motivation of these characters and the plausibility of their actions are comprehensible, but in an absurdist drama we are confronted with characters who appear in a series of disconnected incidents that lead to deeper confusion. What would we make of Nora if Ibsen had her appear in the final act costumed as a doll? This would be not only bizarre but unacceptable in a realistic play. However, it could make dramatic sense in an absurdist adaptation that sought to dramatize Nora's loss of identity and dehumanization as a result of her marriage.

Nora's appearance as a doll would, of course, be laughably inconsistent with what we judge to be real or reasonable. And yet we might find ourselves sympathizing with her situation. Suppose that instead of slamming the door and leaving her husband in the final scene, Nora moved stiffly about the room costumed as a doll while Helmer complacently sipped sherry and read the evening paper. Such an ending would suggest that she had been defeated by the circumstances in her life. Her condition — being nothing more than someone's toy — would be both absurd and pathetic. If we laughed at this scene, we would do so because Nora's situation is grotesquely humorous, a parody of her assumptions, hopes, and expectations. This is the world of **tragicomedy,** where laughter and pain coexist and where there is neither the happy resolution that typifies comic plots nor the transformational suffering that brings clarification to the tragic hero. It is the world dramatized, for example, in the opening scene of Harold Pinter's *The Dumb Waiter* when Ben tells Gus about an item he's read in the paper.

> *Ben:* A man of eighty-seven wanted to cross the road. But there was a lot of traffic, see? He couldn't see how he was going to squeeze through. So he crawled under a lorry [truck].
> *Gus:* He what?
> *Ben:* He crawled under a lorry. A stationary lorry.
> *Gus:* No?
> *Ben:* The lorry started and ran over him.
> *Gus:* Go on!
> *Ben:* That's what it says here.
> *Gus:* Get away.
> *Ben:* It's enough to make you want to puke, isn't it?
> *Gus:* Who advised him to do a thing like that?
> *Ben:* A man of eighty-seven crawling under a lorry!
> *Gus:* It's unbelievable.
> *Ben:* It's down here in black and white.
> *Gus:* Incredible.

As much as Gus finds the story difficult to believe and Ben is sickened by it, it is a fact that the old man was crushed under ridiculous circumstances. His death is unexpected, accidental, incomprehensible, and meaningless — except that what happened to the old man is, from an absurdist's perspective, really no different from what life has in store for all of us one way or the other.

An absurdist playwright may, as Pinter does, employ realistic settings and speech, but he or she goes beyond realistic conventions to challenge the rational assumptions we make about our lives. Pinter insists that "a play is not an essay." Background information, character motivation, action — nothing presented on an absurdist's stage is governed by the conventions of realism. The absurdists typically refuse to create the illusion of reality because there is, finally, no reality to imitate. If conversations in their plays are sometimes fragmented and seemingly inconsequential, the reason is that absurdists dramatize people's combined inability and unwillingness to communicate with one another. Indeed, Samuel Beckett's *Act without Words* contains no dialogue, and in his *Krapp's Last Tape* a single character addresses only his own tape-recorded voice. To some extent we must suspend common sense and logic if we are to appreciate the visions and voices in an absurdist play.

Although many other nonrealistic movements developed in the twentieth century, these four — symbolism, expressionism, epic theater, and the theater of the absurd — embrace the major differences between nonrealistic and realistic drama. The theater continually tests its own possibilities. In the 1960s and 1970s, for example, some acting companies in New York completely collapsed the usual distinctions between audience and actors. The Living Theater went even further by moving into the streets, where the actors and audiences engaged in dramatic political statements aimed at raising the social consciousness of people wherever they were. Some critics argued that this was not really theater but merely an exuberant kind of political rally. However, proponents of these productions — known as **guerrilla theater** — argued that protest drama is both politically and artistically valid. In any case, although today's playwrights seem considerably less inclined to take to the streets, there is a tolerance for a wide range of possible relationships between actors and audiences. Audiences (and readers) can expect symbolic characters, expressionistic settings, poetic language, monologues, and extreme actions in productions that also contain realistic elements. In *Route 1 & 9* (1981), a piece created by an experimental theater company called The Wooster Group, for example, audiences found themselves confronted with passages from Thornton Wilder's idealized version of America in *Our Town* that were coupled with a pornographic film and a black vaudeville act. This unlikely combination was used to comment on Wilder's conception of America in which issues of sex and race are largely ignored. Increasingly, experimental theater has cultivated an eclectic approach to drama, using a variety of media, cultures, playwrights, and even languages to enrich an audience's experience. Parts of Robert Wilson's *CIVIL warS* (1984) — a work never staged in its entirety in any one place — were performed in several countries, including France, Italy, and the United States, and drew on different languages as well as cultures to evoke a wide range of experiences from history, literature, myths, and even dreams. Chapter 51, "A Thematic Case Study: An Album of Contemporary Humor and Satire," attests to the traditions and innovations that contemporary dramatists have incorporated into their dramatic art.

50

A CRITICAL CASE STUDY

Henrik Ibsen's
A Doll House

Spiritual conflicts. Oppressed and bewildered by the belief in authority, she loses faith in her moral right and ability to bring up her children. Bitterness . . . Now and then a womanly shaking off of her thoughts. Sudden return of anxiety and terror. She must bear it all alone. The catastrophe approaches, inexorably, inevitably. Despair, conflict, and destruction.

— HENRIK IBSEN, from his notes for
   A Doll House

This chapter provides several critical approaches to Henrik Ibsen's *A Doll House,* which appears in Chapter 49, page 1709. There have been numerous critical approaches to this play because it raises so many issues relating to matters such as relationships between men and women, history, and biography, as well as imagery, symbolism, and irony. The following critical excerpts offer a small and partial sample of the possible biographical, historical, mythological, psychological, sociological, and other perspectives that have attempted to shed light on the play (see Chapter 53, "Critical Strategies for Reading," for a discussion of a variety of critical methods). They should help you to enjoy the play more by raising questions, providing insights, and inviting you to delve further into the text.

The following letter offers a revealing vignette of the historical contexts for *A Doll House.* Professor Richard Panofsky of the University of Massachusetts–Dartmouth has provided the letter and this background information: "The translated letter was written in 1844 by Marcus (1807–1865) to his wife Ulrike (1816–1888), after six children had been born. This upper-middle-class Jewish family lived in Hamburg, Germany, where Marcus was a doctor. As the letter implies, Ulrike had left home and children: the letter establishes conditions for her to return. A woman in upper-class society of the time had few choices in an unhappy marriage. Divorce or separation meant ostracism; as Marcus writes, 'your husband, children, and the entire city threaten indifference or even contempt.' And she could not take a job, as she would have no profession to step into. In any case, Ulrike did return home. Between 1846 and 1857 the marriage produced eight more children. Beyond what the letter shows, we do not know the reasons for the separation or what the later marriage relationship was like."

Perspectives

A Nineteenth-Century Husband's Letter to His Wife　　　1844

Dear Wife,　　　　　　　　　　　　　　　　　　　　　　　　June 23, 1844

You have sinned greatly — and maybe I too; but this much is certain: Adam sinned after Eve had already sinned. So it is with us; you, alone, carry the guilt of all the misfortune which, however, I helped to enlarge later by my behavior. Listen now, since I still believe certain things to be necessary in order that we may have a peaceful life. If we want not only to be content for a day but forever, you will have to follow my wishes. So examine yourself and determine if you are strong enough to conquer your false ambitions and your stubbornness to submit to all the conditions, the fulfillment of which I cannot ignore. Every sensible person will tell you that all I ask of you is what is easily understood. If you insist on remaining stubborn, then do not return to my house, for you will never be happy with me; your husband, children, and the entire city threaten indifference or even contempt.

But if you decide to act *sensibly* and *correctly,* that is *justly* and *kindly,* then be certain that many in the world will envy you.

I am including here the paper which I read to you in front of the rabbi; ask anyone in your residence if the wishes expressed by me are not quite reasonable, and are of a kind to which every wife can agree for the welfare of domestic happiness. In any case, act in a way you think best.

When you decide to return, write to tell me on which day and hour you depart from Berlin and give me your itinerary whether by way of Kuestrin and Pinne or by way of Wollstein. I will then meet you at Wollstein or Pinne. I expect you will bring Solomon with you.

Don't travel unprepared. If you need money, ask your father.

May God enlighten your heart and mind

　　　　　　　　　　　　　　　I remain your so far unhappy,　　　　[Marcus]

Greetings to my parents, brothers, and sisters; also your brother. Show them what you wish, this letter, the enclosure, whatever you want. The children are fortunately healthy.

If you want to return with joy and peace, write me by return mail. In that case, I would rather send you a carriage. Maybe Madam Fraenkel will come along. . . .

[Enclosure]

My wife promises — for which every wife is obligated to her husband — to follow my wishes in everything and to strictly obey my orders. It is already self-evident that our marital relations have often been disturbed by the fact that my wife does not follow my wishes but believes herself to be entitled to act on her own, even if this is totally against my orders. In order not to have to remind my wife every second what my wishes are regarding homemaking and public conduct — wishes which I have often expressed — I want to make here a few rules which shall serve as a code of conduct. A home is best run if the work for each hour is planned ahead of time, if possible.

Servants get up no later than 5:00 A.M. in summer and 6:00 A.M. in winter, the children an hour later. The cook prepares breakfast. The nursemaid puts out clothes for every child, prepares water and sponge, cleans the combs, etc. The cook should stay in the kitchen unless there is time to clean the rooms. At least once a week the rooms should be cleaned whenever possible, but not all on the same day.

Every Wednesday, the people in the house should do a laundry. Every last Wednesday in the month, there shall be a large laundry with an outside washerwoman. At least every Monday, the seamstress shall come into the house to fix what is necessary.

Every Thursday or Friday, bread is baked for the week; I think it is best to buy grain and have it ground, but to knead it at home.

Every Friday special bread (Barches) should be bought for the evening meal.

The kitchen list will be prepared and discussed every Thursday evening, jointly, by me and my wife; but my wish is to be decisive.

After this, provisions are to be bought every Friday at the market. For this purpose, my wife, herself, will go to the market on Fridays, accompanied by a servant; she can substitute a special woman who does errands (*Faktorfrau*) if she wishes, but not a servant.

All expenditures have to be written down daily and punctually.

The children receive a bath every Thursday evening. The children's clothes must be kept in a specially appointed chest, with a separate compartment for each child with the child's name upon it. The boys' suits and girls' dresses are to be kept separately. To keep used laundry, there must be a hamper easily accessible. Equally important is the food storage box in which provisions are kept in order, locked and safe from vermin.

The kitchen should be kept in order. Once a week all woodwork and copper must be scoured. The lights and lamps have to be cleaned daily. Toward servants, one has to be strict and just. Therefore, one should not call them names which aren't suitable for a decent wife. One should give them enough nourishing food. Disobedience and obstinacy are to be referred to me.

My wife will never make visits in my absence. However, she should visit the synagogue every Saturday—at least once a month; also she should go for a walk with the children at least once a week.

CONSIDERATIONS FOR CRITICAL THINKING AND WRITING

1. Describe the tone of Marcus's letter to his wife. To what extent does he accept responsibility for their separation? What significant similarities and differences do you find between Marcus and Torvald Helmer?

2. Read the discussion on historical criticism in Chapter 53, "Critical Strategies for Reading" (p. 2052). How do you think a new historicist would use this letter to shed light on *A Doll House*?

3. Write a response to the letter from what you imagine the wife's point of view to be.

4. No information is available about this couple's marriage after Ulrike returned home. In an essay, speculate on what you think their relationship was like later in their marriage.

BARRY WITHAM (B. 1939) AND
JOHN LUTTERBIE (B. 1948)

Witham and Lutterbie describe how they use a Marxist approach to teach *A Doll House* in their drama class, in which they teach plays from a variety of critical perspectives.

A Marxist Approach to A Doll House   1985

A principal tenet of Marxist criticism is that human consciousness is a product of social conditions and that human relationships are often subverted by and through economic considerations. Mrs. Linde has sacrificed a genuine love to provide for her brothers, and Krogstad has committed a crime to support his children. Anne-Marie, the maid, has also been the victim of her economic background. Because she's "a girl who's poor and gotten in trouble," her relationship with her child has been interrupted and virtually destroyed. In each instance the need for money is linked with the ability to exist. But while the characters accept the social realities of their misfortunes, they do not appear to question how their human attitudes have been thoroughly shaped by socioeconomic considerations.

Once students begin to perceive how consciousness is affected by economics, a Marxist reading of Ibsen's play can illuminate a number of areas. Krogstad, for example, becomes less of a traditional villain when we realize that he is fighting for his job at the bank "as if it were life itself." And his realization of the senselessness of their lives is poignantly revealed when he reflects on Mrs. Linde's past, "all this simply for money." Even Dr. Rank speaks about his failing health and imminent death in entirely financial terms. "These past few days I've been auditing my internal accounts. Bankrupt! Within a month I'll probably be laid out and rotting in the churchyard."

All these characters, however, serve as foils for the central struggle between Nora and Torvald and highlight the pilgrimage that Nora makes in the play. At the outset two things are clear: (1) Nora is enslaved by Torvald in economic terms, and (2) she equates personal freedom with the acquisition of wealth. The play begins joyfully not only because it is the holiday season but also because Torvald's promotion to bank manager will ensure "a safe, secure job with a comfortable salary." Nora is happy because she sees the future in wholly economic terms. "Won't it be lovely to have stacks of money and not a care in the world?"

What she learns, however, is that financial enslavement is symptomatic of other forms of enslavement — master-slave, male-female, sexual objectification, all of which characterize her relationship with Torvald — and that money is no guarantee of happiness. At the end of the play she renounces not only her marital vows but also her financial dependence because she has discovered that personal and human freedom are not measured in economic terms.

This discovery also prompts her to reexamine the society of which she is a part and leads us into a consideration of the ideology in the play. In what sense has Nora committed a criminal offense in forging her father's name? Is it indeed just that she should be punished for an altruistic act, one that cost her dearly both in terms of self-denial and the destruction of her family? Ibsen's defense of Nora is clear, of course, and his implicit indictment of a society that encourages this kind of injustice stimulates a discussion of the assumptions that created the law.

One of the striking things about *A Doll House* is how Anne-Marie accepts her alienation from her child as if it were natural, given the circumstances of class and money. It does not occur to her that laws were framed by other people and thus are capable of imperfection and susceptible to change. Nora broke a law that not only tries to stop thievery (the appropriation of capital) by outlawing forgery but also discriminates against anyone deemed a bad risk. Question leads to question as the class investigates why women were bad risks and why they had difficulty finding employment. It becomes obvious that the function of women in this society was not "natural" but artificial, a role created by their relationship to the family and by their subservience to men. In the marketplace they were a labor force expecting subsistence wages and providing an income to supplement that earned by their husbands or fathers.

An even clearer picture of Nora's society emerges when the Marxist critic examines those features or elements that are not in the play. These "absences" become valuable clues in understanding the ideology in the text. In the words of Fredric Jameson, absences are

> terms or nodal points implicit in the ideological system which have, however, remained unrealized in the surface of the text, which have failed to become manifest in the logic of the narrative, and which we can therefore read as what the text represses.[1]

The notion of absences is particularly intriguing for students, who learn quickly to apply it to such popular media as films and television (what can we

---

[1] Fredric Jameson, *The Political Unconscious: Narrative as a Socially Symbolic Act* (Ithaca: Cornell UP, 1981), p. 48.

learn about the experience of urban black Americans from sitcoms like *Julia* and *The Jeffersons?*). Absent from *A Doll House* is Nora's mother, an omission that ties her more firmly to a male-dominated world and the bank owners who promoted Torvald. These absences shape our view because they form a layer of reality that is repressed in the play. And an examination of this "repressed" material leads us to our final topic of discussion: What is the relation between this play and the society in which it was created and produced?

Most Marxist critics believe that there are only three possible answers: the play supports the status quo, argues for reforms in an essentially sound system, or advocates a radical restructuring. Though these options are seemingly reductive, discussion reveals the complexities of reaching any unanimous agreement, and students frequently disagree about Ibsen's intentions regarding reform or revolution. Nora's leaving is obviously a call for change, but many students are not sure whether this leave-taking is a way forward or a cul-de-sac for a system that is thoroughly controlled by the prevailing power structure. . . .

Viewing the play through the lens of Marxist atheists does make one thing clear. Nora's departure had ramifications for her society that went beyond the marriage bed. By studying the play within the context of its socioeconomic structure, we can see how the ideology in the text affects the characters and how they perpetuate the ideology. The conclusion of *A Doll House* was a challenge to the economic superstructures that had controlled and excluded the Noras of the world by manipulating their economic status and, by extension, their conscious estimation of themselves and their place in society.

From "A Marxist Approach to *A Doll House*"
in *Approaches to Teaching Ibsen's* A Doll House

CONSIDERATIONS FOR CRITICAL THINKING AND WRITING

1. To what extent do you agree or disagree with the Marxist "tenet" (para. 1) that "consciousness is affected by economics" (2)?

2. Do you think that Nora's "leave-taking is a way forward or a cul-de-sac for a system that is thoroughly controlled by the prevailing power structure" (para. 8)? Explain your response.

3. Consider whether "A Nineteenth-Century Husband's Letter to His Wife" supports or challenges Witham and Lutterbie's Marxist reading of *A Doll House*.

CAROL STRONGIN TUFTS (B. 1947)

A Psychoanalytic Reading of Nora 1986

I am not a member of the Women's Rights League. Whatever I have written has been without any conscious thought of making propaganda. I have been more the poet and less the social philosopher than people generally seem inclined to believe. . . . To me it has seemed a problem of mankind in general. And if you read my books carefully you will understand this. . . . My task has been the *description of humanity*. To be sure, whenever such a description is felt to be reasonably true, the reader will read his own feelings and sentiments into the work of the poet. These are then attributed to the poet; but incorrectly so. Every reader remolds the work beautifully and neatly, each according to his own personality. Not only those who write but also those who read are poets. They are collaborators.[1]

To look again at Ibsen's famous and often-quoted words—his assertion that *A Doll House* was not intended as propaganda to promote the cause of women's rights—is to realize the sarcasm aimed by the playwright at those nineteenth-century "collaborators" who insisted on viewing his play as a treatise and Nora, his heroine, as the romantic standard-bearer for the feminist cause. Yet there is also a certain irony implicit in such a realization, for directors, actors, audiences, and critics turning to this play a little over one hundred years after its first performance bring with them the historical, cultural, and psychological experience which itself places them in the role of Ibsen's collaborators. Because it is a theatrical inevitability that each dramatic work which survives its time and place of first performance does so to be recast in productions mounted in succeeding times and different places, *A Doll House* can never so much be simply reproduced as it must always be re-envisioned. And if the spectacle of a woman walking out on her husband and children in order to fulfill her "duties to (her)self" is no longer the shock for us today that it was for audiences at the end of the nineteenth century, a production of *A Doll House* which resonates with as much immediacy and power for us as it did for its first audiences may do so through the discovery within Ibsen's text of something of our own time and place. For in *A Doll House,* as Rolf Fjelde has written, "(i)t is the entire house . . . which is on trial, the total complex of relationships, including husband, wife, children, servants, upstairs and downstairs, that is tested by the visitors that come and go, embodying aspects of the inescapable reality outside."[2] And a production which approaches that reality through the experience of Western culture in the last quarter of the twentieth century may not only discover how uneasy was Ibsen's relationship to certain aspects of the forces of Romanticism at work in his own society, but, in so doing, may also come to fashion *A Doll House* which shifts emphasis away from the celebration of the Romantic belief in the sovereignty of the individual to the revelation of an isolating narcissism—a narcissism that has become all too familiar to us today.[3]

The characters of *A Doll House* are, to be sure, not alone in dramatic literature in being self-preoccupied, for self-preoccupation is a quality shared by characters from Oedipus to Hamlet and on into modern drama. Yet if a contemporary

---

[1] Speech delivered at the Banquet of the Norwegian League for Women's Rights, Christiana, 26 May 1898, in *Ibsen: Letters and Speeches,* ed. Evert Sprinchorn (New York: Hill and Wang, 1964), p. 337.

[2] Rolf Fjelde, Introduction to *A Doll House,* in Henrik Ibsen, *The Complete Major Prose Plays* (New York: Farrar, Straus, Giroux, 1978), p. 121.

[3] For studies of the prevalence of the narcissistic personality disorder in contemporary psychoanalytic literature, see Otto F. Kernberg, *Borderline Conditions and Pathological Narcissism* (New York: J. Aronson, 1975); Heinz Kohut, *The Analysis of the Self* (New York: International Universities Press, 1971); and Peter L. Giovachinni, *Psychoanalysis of Character Disorders* (New York: J. Aronson, 1975). See also Christopher Lasch, *The Culture of Narcissism* (New York: Norton, 1979), for a discussion of narcissism as the defining characteristic of contemporary American society.

production is to suggest the narcissistic self-absorption of Ibsen's characters, it must do so in such a way as to imply motivations for their actions and delineate their relationships with one another. Thus it is important to establish a conceptual framework which will provide a degree of precision for the use of the term "narcissism" in this discussion so as to distinguish it from the kind of self-absorption which is an inherent quality necessarily shared by all dramatic characters. For that purpose, it is useful to turn to the criteria established by the Task Force on Nomenclature and Statistics of the American Psychiatric Association for diagnosing the narcissistic personality:

A. Grandiose sense of self-importance and uniqueness, e.g., exaggerates achievements and talents, focuses on how special one's problems are.
B. Preoccupation with fantasies of unlimited success, power, brilliance, beauty, or ideal love.
C. Exhibitionistic: requires constant attention and admiration.
D. Responds to criticism, indifference of others, or defeat with either cool indifference, or with marked feelings of rage, inferiority, shame, humiliation, or emptiness.
E. At least two of the following are characteristics of disturbances in interpersonal relationships:
   1. Lack of empathy: inability to recognize how others feel, e.g., unable to appreciate the distress of someone who is seriously ill.
   2. Entitlement: expectation of special favors without assuming reciprocal responsibilities, e.g., surprise and anger that people won't do what he wants.
   3. Interpersonal exploitiveness: takes advantage of others to indulge own desires for self-aggrandizement, with disregard for the personal integrity and rights of others.
   4. Relationships characteristically vacillate between the extremes of over-idealization and devaluation.[4]

These criteria, as they provide a background against which to consider Nora's relationship with both Kristine Linde and Dr. Rank, will serve to illuminate not only those relationships themselves, but also the relationship of Nora and her husband which is at the center of the play. Moreover, if these criteria are viewed as outlines for characterization—but not as reductive psychoanalytic constructs leading to "case studies"—it becomes possible to discover a Nora of greater complexity than the totally sympathetic victim turned romantic heroine who has inhabited most productions of the play. And, most important of all, as Nora and her relationships within the walls of her "doll house" come to imply a paradigm of the dilemma of all human relationships in the greater society outside, the famous sound of the slamming door may come to resonate even more loudly for us than it did for the audiences of the nineteenth century with a profound and immediate sense of irony and ambiguity, an irony and ambiguity which could not have escaped Ibsen himself.

From "Recasting *A Doll House:* Narcissism as Character Motivation
in Ibsen's Play," *Comparative Drama,* Summer 1986

---

[4] Task Force on Nomenclature and Statistics, American Psychiatric Association, *DSM-III: Diagnostic Criteria Draft* (New York, 1978), pp. 103–04.

CONSIDERATIONS FOR CRITICAL THINKING AND WRITING

1. What is Tufts's purpose in arguing that Nora be seen as narcissistic?

2. Using the criteria of the American Psychiatric Association, consider Nora's personality. Write an essay either refuting the assertion that she has a narcissistic personality or supporting it.

3. How does Tufts's reading compare with Joan Templeton's feminist reading of Nora in the Perspective that follows? Which do you find more convincing? Why?

JOAN TEMPLETON (B. 1940)

This feminist perspective summarizes the arguments against reading the play as a dramatization of a feminist heroine.

Is A Doll House *a Feminist Text?*   1989

A Doll House is no more about women's rights than Shakespeare's Richard II *is about the divine right of kings, or* Ghosts *about syphilis.... Its theme is the need of every individual to find out the kind of person he or she is and to strive to become that person.*[1]

Ibsen has been resoundingly saved from feminism, or, as it was called in his day, "the woman question." His rescuers customarily cite a statement the dramatist made on 26 May 1898 at a seventieth-birthday banquet given in his honor by the Norwegian Women's Rights League:

> I thank you for the toast, but must disclaim the honor of having consciously worked for the women's rights movement.... True enough, it is desirable to solve the woman problem, along with all the others; but that has not been the whole purpose. My task has been the description of humanity.[2]

Ibsen's champions like to take this disavowal as a precise reference to his purpose in writing *A Doll House* twenty years earlier, his "original intention," according to Maurice Valency.[3] Ibsen's biographer Michael Meyer urges all reviewers of *A Doll House* revivals to learn Ibsen's speech by heart,[4] and James McFarlane, editor of *The Oxford Ibsen,* includes it in his explanatory material on *A Doll House,* under "Some Pronouncements of the Author," as though Ibsen had been speaking of the play.[5] Whatever propaganda feminists may have made of *A Doll House,* Ibsen, it is argued, never meant to write a play about the

---

[1] Michael Meyer, *Ibsen* (Garden City: Doubleday, 1971), 457. [This is not the Michael Meyer who is editor of *The Bedford Introduction to Literature.*]

[2] Henrik Ibsen, *Letters and Speeches,* ed. and trans. Evert Sprinchorn (New York: Hill, 1964), 337.

[3] Maurice Valency, *The Flower and the Castle: An Introduction to Modern Drama* (New York: Schocken, 1982), 151.

[4] Meyer, 774.

[5] James McFarlane, *"A Doll's House:* Commentary" in *The Oxford Ibsen,* ed. McFarlane (Oxford UP, 1961), V, 456.

highly topical subject of women's rights; Nora's conflict represents something other than, or something more than, woman's. In an article commemorating the half century of Ibsen's death, R. M. Adams explains, "*A Doll House* represents a woman imbued with the idea of becoming a person, but it proposes nothing categorical about women becoming people; in fact, its real theme has nothing to do with the sexes."[6] Over twenty years later, after feminism had resurfaced as an international movement, Einar Haugen, the doyen of American Scandinavian studies, insisted that "Ibsen's Nora is not just a woman arguing for female liberation; she is much more. She embodies the comedy as well as the tragedy of modern life."[7] In the Modern Language Association's *Approaches to Teaching* A Doll House, the editor speaks disparagingly of "reductionist views of *(A Doll House)* as a feminist drama." Summarizing a "major theme" in the volume as "the need for a broad view of the play and a condemnation of a static approach," she warns that discussions of the play's "connection with feminism" have value only if they are monitored, "properly channeled and kept firmly linked to Ibsen's text."[8]

Removing the woman question from *A Doll House* is presented as part of a corrective effort to free Ibsen from his erroneous reputation as a writer of thesis plays, a wrongheaded notion usually blamed on Shaw, who, it is claimed, mistakenly saw Ibsen as the nineteenth century's greatest iconoclast and offered that misreading to the public as *The Quintessence of Ibsenism*. Ibsen, it is now de rigueur to explain, did not stoop to "issues." He was a poet of the truth of the human soul. That Nora's exit from her dollhouse has long been the principal international symbol for women's issues, including many that far exceed the confines of her small world, is irrelevant to the essential meaning of *A Doll House,* a play, in Richard Gilman's phrase, "pitched beyond sexual difference."[9] Ibsen, explains Robert Brustein, "was completely indifferent to (the woman question) except as a metaphor for individual freedom."[10] Discussing the relation of *A Doll House* to feminism, Halvdan Koht, author of the definitive Norwegian Ibsen life, says in summary, "Little by little the topical controversy died away; what remained was the work of art, with its demand for truth in every human relation."[11]

Thus, it turns out, the *Uncle Tom's Cabin* of the women's rights movement is not really about women at all. "Fiddle-faddle," pronounced R. M. Adams, dismissing feminist claims for the play.[12] Like angels, Nora has no sex. Ibsen meant her to be Everyman.

From "The Doll House Backlash: Criticism, Feminism, and Ibsen,"
PMLA, January 1989

---

[6] R. M. Adams, "The Fifty-First Anniversary," *Hudson Review* 10 (1957): 416.
[7] Einar Haugen, *Ibsen's Drama: Author to Audience* (Minneapolis: U of Minnesota P, 1979), vii.
[8] Yvonne Shafer, ed., *Approaches to Teaching Ibsen's* A Doll House (New York: MLA, 1985), 32.
[9] Richard Gilman, *The Making of Modern Drama* (New York: Farrar, 1972), 65.
[10] Robert Brustein, *The Theatre of Revolt* (New York: Little, 1962), 105.
[11] Halvdan Koht, *Life of Ibsen* (New York: Blom, 1971), 323.
[12] Adams, 416.

CONSIDERATIONS FOR CRITICAL THINKING AND WRITING

1. According to Templeton, what kinds of arguments are used to reject *A Doll House* as a feminist text?

2. From the tone of the summaries provided, what would you say is Templeton's attitude toward these arguments?

3. Read the section on feminist criticism in Chapter 53, "Critical Strategies for Reading" (pp. 2056–57), and write an essay addressing the summarized arguments as you think a feminist critic might respond.

Questions for Writing

APPLYING A CRITICAL STRATEGY

This section offers advice about developing an argument that draws on the different strategies, or schools of literary theory, covered in Chapter 53. The following list of questions and suggestions will help you to apply one or more of these critical strategies to a work in order to shed light on it. Following the questions is a sample paper based on *A Doll House* (p. 1709).

There are many possible lenses through which to read a literary work. The Perspectives, Complementary Critical Readings, and Critical Case Studies in this anthology suggest a variety of approaches — including formalist, biographical, psychological, Marxist, new historicist, feminist, mythological, reader-response, and deconstructionist strategies — that can be used to explore the effects, meanings, and significances of a poem, short story, or play (see Chapter 53 for a discussion of these strategies).

Once you have generated a central idea about a work, you will need to choose the critical approach(es) that will allow you to develop your argument. In the following sample paper, the writer chose a new historicist approach because she was interested in speculating about what Nora faced after she left her husband on the other side of the slammed door in *A Doll House*. By using evidence external to the play, from a letter written by a nineteenth-century husband to his wife, the writer was able to recreate some of the historical context for *A Doll House* in order to argue that Nora's leaving home is a more risky, problematic action than her simple declaration of freedom from her husband. This historical approach allowed the writer to offer a substantive argument about what Nora might have faced beyond the slammed door.

Regardless of the approach — or combination of approaches — you find helpful, it is essential that you be thoroughly familiar with the text of the literary work before examining it through the lens of a particular critical strategy. Without a strong familiarity with the literary work you will not be able to judge the accuracy and validity of a critic's arguments, and you might find your own insights immediately superseded by those of the first critic you read. For additional advice on how to incorporate material from critical essays into your writing without losing track of your own argument about a work, see Questions for Writing: Incorporating the Critics (p. 523).

1. Which of the critical strategies discussed in Chapter 53 seems the most appropriate to the literary work under consideration? Why do you prefer one particular approach over another? Do any critical strategies seem especially inappropriate? Why?

2. Does the historical context of a literary work suggest that certain critical strategies, such as Marxism or feminism, might be particularly productive?

3. Does the literary work reflect or challenge the cultural assumptions contemporary to it in such a way as to suggest a critical approach for your paper?

4. Does the author comment on his or her own literary work in letters, interviews, or lectures? If so, how might these comments help you to develop an approach for your paper?

5. Are you able to formulate an interpretation of the work you want to discuss before reading the critics extensively? If so, how might the critics' discussions help you to develop, enhance, or qualify your argument about how to interpret the work?

6. If you haven't developed an argument before reading the critics, how might some exploratory reading lead you into significant questions and controversial issues that would offer topics that could be developed into a thesis?

7. If you are drawing on the work of a number of critics, how are their critical strategies — whether formalist, biographical, psychological, historical, or other — relevant to your own? How can you use their insights to support your own argument?

8. Is it possible and desirable to combine approaches — such as psychological and historical or biographical and feminist — so that multiple perspectives can be used to support your argument?

9. If the strategies or approaches the critics use to interpret the literary work tend to be similar, are there questions and issues that have been neglected or ignored that can become the focus of your argument about the literary work?

10. If the critics' approaches are very different from one another, is there a way to use those differences to argue your own critical approach that allows you to support one critic rather than another or to resolve a controversy among the critics?

11. Is your argument adequately supported with specific evidence from the literary text? Have you been careful not to avoid discussing parts of the text that do not seem to support your argument?

12. Is your own discussion of the literary text free of simple plot summary? Does each paragraph include a thesis statement that advances your argument rather than merely consisting of facts and plot summary?

13. Have you accurately and fairly represented the critics' arguments?

14. Have you made your own contributions, qualifications, or disagreements with the critics clear to your reader?

A SAMPLE STUDENT PAPER

On the Other Side of the Slammed Door in A Doll House

The following sample paper focuses on the magnitude of Nora Helmer's decision to leave her husband in *A Doll House*. Kathy Atner uses a new historicist perspective to show just how difficult Nora's decision would have been in the context of nineteenth-century attitudes toward marriage and women. The paper develops an argument primarily from evidence supplied by "A Nineteenth-Century Husband's Letter to His Wife" (p. 1765). By drawing on a source that ordinarily might have been ignored by literary critics, Atner is able to suggest how difficult Nora's life would have been after abandoning her husband and family. This historical strategy is combined with a feminist perspective that gives the modern reader a greater understanding of the issues Nora must inevitably confront once she slams the door shut on her conventional and accepted life as devoted wife and mother. By using both new historicist and feminist perspectives, Atner suggests that contemporary readers should be sensitive to the tragic as well as the heroic dimension of Nora's life.

Atner 1

Kathy Atner

Professor Porter

English 216

April 6, 2009

On the Other Side of the Slammed Door

in *A Doll House*

Nora Helmer's decision to leave her family in Henrik Ibsen's 1879 play *A Doll House* reflects the dilemma faced by many nineteenth-century women who were forced either to conform to highly restrictive gender roles or to abandon these roles in order to realize their value as individuals. Although Ibsen brings his audience to the moment that Nora chooses to disregard her social role and opt for her "freedom," his play does not clearly reveal the true fate of women who followed Nora's path in the nineteenth century. Historically, most women who chose not to acquiesce to the socially prescribed roles of marriage were treated as unnatural creatures and shunned by the respectable public. An actual letter, written in 1844 by a man named Marcus

Thesis placing play in historical context

to his estranged wife, Ulrike, reveals the effects of this severe social condemnation (1765). His letter implies the desperate fate that inevitably befalls women who reject their prescribed duties as wives and mothers. Through Marcus's letter to his wife, the painful ramifications of Nora's decision to accommodate her own personal desires instead of those of her family become even more poignant, courageous, and tragic.

> Argument supported by a historical document (letter to Ulrike)

In the nineteenth century, women had few alternatives to marriage, and women who "failed" at marriage were thought to have failed in their most important duty. In his letter, Marcus articulates society's deep disgust for women who reject what it believes is the sacred female role of home-maker. His letter, while on one level an angry condemnation of his wife's "stubbornness" (1765) and a cruelly condescending list of conditions to be met on her return, is on another level a plea for her to accept again the role that society has assigned her. He is clearly shaken by his wife's abandonment and interprets it as a betrayal of a social "law" or tradition, which, to Marcus's mind, ought to be carved in stone. He responds to this betrayal by demanding complete obedience from his wife in the form of a promise "to follow my wishes in everything and to strictly obey my orders" (1766). Only when she acquiesces to his conditions and returns to her role as docile and obedient wife will Marcus in turn be able to resume the comfortably familiar, socially sanctioned role of dominant, morally superior husband.

> Analysis of historical document

Like Ulrike, Nora decides to leave the security and comfort of her restrictive domestic life to try to become a human being. Ibsen neglects, however, to show his audience the actual result of that decision. At the conclusion of *A Doll House,* Nora slams the door on her past life, hoping to begin a new life that will somehow be more satisfying. Yet the modern audience has no genuine sense of what she may have found beyond that door, and perhaps neither did Nora. Through Ulrike's story, however, the reader understands the historical truth that the world awaiting Nora was hostile and unsympathetic. Marcus warns his wife that "your husband, children, and the entire city threaten indifference or even contempt" (1765) if she refuses to return immediately to her socially acceptable domestic role. This pressure to conform, combined with the bleak prospects of a single woman, results in

> Discussion of Nora's plight in relation to that of Ulrike

Ulrike's ultimate choice to keep up "appearances" rather than further subject herself to a contemptuous world that neither wants nor understands her. Although we cannot know Nora's fate after she leaves Torvald, we may assume that her future would be as bleak as Ulrike's and that the pressure to return to her domestic life would be equally strong.

When *A Doll House* was first produced in 1879, audiences had no more sympathy for Nora's predicament than they did for the real-life stories of women such as Ulrike. As Errol Durbach points out, in the nineteenth century, Ibsen's play "did not precipitate heated debate about feminism, women's rights, or male domination. The sound and the fury were addressed to the very question . . . What credible wife and mother would ever walk out this way on her family?" (14). A great many readers and audience members tended to side with Torvald, who seemed, to them, the innocent victim of Nora's consuming selfishness. The audience's repulsion toward Nora's apparently "unnatural" action of abandoning her family mirrors the responses of Marcus and Torvald Helmer, the bereft, perplexed, and angry husbands. Nora and Ulrike radically disrupt their husbands' perceptions of family relationships by walking out of their lives, preferring to recognize their own needs before any others. These women suggest that Torvald's claim that "Before all else, you're a wife and mother" (1755) may not necessarily be true for all women, but their brave rejections of domestic life cannot force society to condone their behavior.

Ibsen maintains that *A Doll House* is not about women's rights specifically but encompasses a more universal "description of humanity" (*Letters* 337). In showing a human being trying to create a new identity for herself, however, Ibsen reveals the extent to which people are trapped in societal norms and expectations. Nora's acknowledgment that she "can't go on believing what the majority says, or what's written in books" (1755) suggests a profound social upheaval that has the potential to subvert long-established gender roles. If Nora and Ulrike relinquish the role of the subservient and helpless wife, then Torvald and Marcus can no longer play the role of the dominating, protective husband. Without this role, the men are as helpless as they want their wives to be, and the traditional gender expectations

Marginal notes:

Analysis of status of women and audience of the 19th century

Analysis of play in context of 19th-century reality

Atner 4

are no longer beyond question. Yet the historical reality is that in spite of
Nora's daring escape from her oppressive family, the world was not ready to
accommodate women who rejected their feminine duties. Ulrike was thwarted
in her attempt to free herself from her family; history suggests that Nora may
have met a similar fate.

Modern audiences tend to see Nora as a strong, admirable woman who
is courageous enough to sacrifice everything in order to fulfill her own needs
as an individual and as a woman. She shatters gender stereotypes through
her defiant disregard for all that society demands of her. Yet, taken in the
context of nineteenth-century life, perhaps Nora's story is more tragic than
we might initially like to believe. Ulrike's story, told through her husband's
letter, suggests that in a time of turbulent social upheaval, what was interpreted as a collapse of what we now call "family values" was shocking,
scandalous, and deeply frightening to many. In the nineteenth century, Nora
was not the sympathetic character that she is today; instead, she symbolized
many negative attributes—what Marcus calls "false ambitions" and "stubbornness" (1765)—that were often ascribed to women. Ulrike's forced return to
her role as dutiful wife and mother suggests that society was quick to punish
disobedient women and that the slamming door at the end of *A Doll House*
was not necessarily the sound of freedom for Nora.

> Concluding historical analysis of play as tragedy

Atner 5

Works Cited

Durbach, Errol. *A Doll's House: Ibsen's Myth of Transformation*. Boston:
      Twayne, 1991. Print.

Ibsen, Henrik. *A Doll House*. Trans. Rolf Fjelde. Meyer 1709–57. Print.

---. *Letters and Speeches*. Ed. and trans. Evert Sprinchorn. New York: Hill,
      1964. 337. Print.

Meyer, Michael, ed. *The Bedford Introduction to Literature*. 9th ed. Boston:
      Bedford/St. Martin's, 2011. Print.

"A Nineteenth-Century Husband's Letter to His Wife." Meyer 1765–67. Print.

SUGGESTED TOPICS FOR LONGER PAPERS

1. In an essay, discuss whether you think *A Doll House* challenges or affirms the social order it describes. Pay particular attention to the ending of the play by providing a close reading of it.

2. Research marriage laws in the United States for the late nineteenth century. To what extent is Ibsen's 1879 Norwegian play relevant to American laws and attitudes toward marriage? Do you think any significant changes would have had to be made if the play had been set in the United States rather than Norway? Explain why or why not.

51

A THEMATIC CASE STUDY

An Album of Contemporary Humor and Satire

I'm very suspicious of theories. I tend to hate any sentence that starts "all comedy contains the element of [blank] in it."
— CHRISTOPHER DURANG

In contrast to the darkness and suffering that surrounds, for example, Hamlet's tragedy, comedy typically works out in the end: the hero triumphs; a sense of renewal flourishes; life is better, yielding to human hopes and aspirations; the implausible is happily possible and characters find freedom, acceptance, and love. Life in a comedy is, as Shakespeare would have it, a midsummer night's dream. Comedy does not mean, however, that there isn't trouble along the way. Humor in comedy can embody anger, criticism, and indignation in its response to life's absurdities and pretentiousness. Toothy wide grins can also produce biting satire.

You'll find the two coupled in the café provided by Joan Ackermann's play, *Quiet Torrential Sound* (p. 1807). Similarly, humor, satire, and social commentary ride together in Jane Martin's *Rodeo* (p. 1804), a rich monologue that reveals a powerful woman's character as well as the corrosive commercialization of a genuinely American sport. In Jane Anderson's *The Reprimand* (p. 1783), a short play in which humor serves as a corrective, two women engage in a strained phone conversation over an offhanded remark about one's body weight. Their subsequent dialogue is spiced with acid reflux and carefully measured pretenses that leave a bad aftertaste. These satiric plays make moral, social, and political points through humor, but they do not harangue or lecture audiences. There are no seats available for the presumptuous and the pretentious in comedy's theater.

Comedy is sometimes associated with another kind of bad taste. The essential differences between comedy and tragedy can be clearly discerned in the plot, characters, and themes of two plays like *A Midsummer Night's Dream* and *Hamlet,* but there are also important differences in style. James Kincaid neatly summarizes a crucial difference in his discussion of "Who Is Relieved by the Idea of Comic Relief?" (an excerpt from this essay appears on p. 1693). He shrewdly distinguishes between them: "Tragedy is sleek and single-minded, comedy rumpled and hospitable to any idea or agency. Tragedy stares us out of countenance; comedy winks and leers and drools. Tragedy is all dressed up; comedy is always taking things off, mooning us." Kincaid deftly puts his finger on the unruly nature of comedy without pointing his finger at it. Comedy celebrates the messy, untidy, confused disarrangements that life presents to us as it does in Christopher Durang's *Wanda's Visit* (p. 1785). Rich Orloff even makes fun of playwriting in his *Playwriting 101: The Rooftop Lesson* (p. 1814). This is not to say that satirizing one's own satire renders everything meaningless but rather to acknowledge that everything is fair game for comedy. As you'll see, even tragedy is figuratively mooned by comedy in David Ives's *Moby-Dude, Or: The Three-Minute Whale* (p. 1801). Bon voyage.

The Reprimand

Writer and director Jane Anderson started her career as an actor. She left college at the age of nineteen to pursue acting and was cast in the David Mamet hit play *Sexual Perversity in Chicago.* The experience familiarized Anderson with scriptwriting, and eventually she founded a writing group called New York Writers' Block. She later wrote and performed in a number of one-woman comedic plays, whose success afforded her the opportunity to write for the television sitcoms *The Facts of Life* and *The Wonder Years.*

"When you create drama," Jane Anderson writes, "you look for the best conflict."

Photo by permission of Jilly Wendell.

In 1986, Anderson wrote the play *Defying Gravity,* a composite of monologues about the space shuttle *Challenger* explosion. Her first screenplay, *The Positively True Adventures of the Alleged Texas*

Cheerleader-Murdering Mom, was a satirical look at the true story of a Texas mother who tried to hire a contract killer to murder her daughter's rival (and her mother) for the junior high school cheerleading squad. The HBO movie starred Holly Hunter and gave Anderson instant notoriety as a screenwriter. She has written the screenplays for a number of movies since, including *The Baby Dance,* starring Jody Foster, and *When Billie Beat Bobby,* the story of tennis champion Billie Jean King beating an aging Bobby Riggs. In 2009 she was nominated for the Writer's Guild of America Award for Best Dramatic Series for her writing on the second season of the television series *Mad Men.*

 The Reprimand was one of five "phone plays" that premiered in February 2000 at the annual Humana Festival of New American Plays held at Actors Theatre in Louisville, Kentucky. The phone call is a traditional stage convention that consists of an actor providing one side of a conversation, but for the Humana Festival performances, the actors conversed offstage and the audience heard both sides of the three-minute conversation. In *The Reprimand,* the overheard conversation reveals a complicated power struggle between two women.

JANE ANDERSON (B. 1954)
The Reprimand

2000

CHARACTERS

Rhona
Mim

Rhona: . . . we need to talk about what you did in the meeting this morning.
Mim: My God, what?
Rhona: That reference you made about my weight.
Mim: What reference?
Rhona: When we came into the room and Jim was making the introductions, you said, "Oh Rhona, why don't you take the bigger chair."
Mim: But that was — I thought since this was your project that you should sit in the better chair.
Rhona: But you didn't say better, you said bigger.
Mim: I did? Honest to God, that isn't what I meant. I'm so sorry if it hurt your feelings.
Rhona: You didn't hurt my feelings. This has nothing to do with my feelings. What concerns me — and concerns Jim by the way — is how this could have undermined the project.
Mim: Jim said something about it?
Rhona: Yes.
Mim: What did he say?
Rhona: He thought your comment was inappropriate.

Mim: Really? How? I was talking about a chair.

Rhona: Mim, do you honestly think anyone in that room was really listening to what I had to say after you made that comment?

Mim: I thought they were very interested in what you had to say.

Rhona: Honey, there was a reason why Dick and Danny asked you all the follow-up questions.

Mim: But that's because I hadn't said anything up to that point. Look, I'm a little confused about Jim's reaction, because after the meeting he said he liked what I did with the follow-up.

Rhona: He should acknowledge what you do. And I know the reason why he's finally said something is because I've been telling him that you deserve more credit.

Mim: Oh, thank you. But I think Jim already respects what I do.

Rhona: He should respect you. But from what I've observed, I think — because you're an attractive woman — that he still uses you for window dressing. Especially when you're working with me. You know what I'm saying?

Mim: Well, if that's the case, Jim is a jerk.

Rhona: I know that. And I know you know that. But I think you still have a lot of anger about the situation and sometimes it really shows.

Mim: I don't mean it to show.

Rhona: I know that. Look, I consider you — regardless of what Jim thinks — I think you're really talented and I really love working with you.

Mim: And I enjoy working with you.

Rhona: Thank you. And that's why I want to keep things clear between us. Especially when we're working for men like Jim.

Mim: No, I agree, absolutely.

Rhona: *(To someone off-phone.)* Tell him I'll be right there. *(Back to Mim.)* Mim, sorry — I have Danny on the phone.

Mim: Oh — do you want to conference me in?

Rhona: I can handle it, but thank you. Mim, I'm so glad we had this talk.

Mim: Well, thank you for being so honest with me.

Rhona: And thank you for hearing me. I really appreciate it. Let's talk later?

Mim: Sure. *(Rhona hangs up. A beat.) (Mumbling.)* Fat pig. *(Hangs up.)*

CONSIDERATIONS FOR CRITICAL THINKING AND WRITING

1. **FIRST RESPONSE.** Do you identify with one character more than the other? Consider whether Rhona or Mim is more sympathetic.

2. What is humorous about the nature of the conflict? Is there a resolution to the conflict?

3. How is the exposition presented? What does it reveal? How does Anderson's choice not to dramatize events onstage help to determine the focus of the play?

4. What can be said about the setting? Explain whether or not you think setting has any role in this play.

5. Discuss the significance of the title. To whom does it apply?

6. **CREATIVE RESPONSE.** Write a three-minute phone conversation (or instant e-mail message) between a student and professor that captures some dramatic tension in their relationship.

1. Compare the power relationship that exists between Rhona and Mim and that of Mrs. Peters and Mrs. Hale in Susan Glaspell's *Trifles* (p. 1366).
2. Discuss the ways in which hostility is manifested in characters' dialogue in *The Reprimand* and in Michael Hollinger's *Naked Lunch* (p. 1385).

Wanda's Visit

Born in Montclair, New Jersey, Christopher Durang graduated from Harvard College with a B.A. in English and from Yale Drama School with an M.F.A. in playwriting. As an actor, playwright, and screenwriter, he is especially known for his comedies and satires. Among his best-known works are *A History of the American Film* (1976), *The Actor's Nightmare* (1981), *Sister Ignatius Explains It All for You* (1980), *Baby with the Bathwater* (1983), *Laughing Wild* (1987), *Durang/Durang* (1994, a collection of short plays that includes *Wanda's Visit*), *Betty's Summer Vacation* (1999), and *Why Torture Is Wrong, and the People Who Love Them* (2009). He has published two collections of plays: *Christopher Durang: 27 Short Plays* (1995) and *Christopher Durang: Complete Full-Length Plays (1975–1995)* (1997). Since 1994, Durang has co-chaired the playwriting program at the Julliard School in Manhattan.

Chris Barth/Star Ledger/CORBIS.

Wanda's Visit begins with an old high school girlfriend showing up in the predictable domestic lives of a not too happily married couple, producing unpredictable results.

CHRISTOPHER DURANG (B. 1949)
Wanda's Visit

1994

CHARACTERS

Jim
Marsha, his wife
Wanda
Waiter
Two Men

SCENE: A comfortable home in Connecticut. Not realistically designed, though — different areas represent different rooms: the living room, the dining room, the bathroom, the kitchen. The dining room table later doubles as a table in a restaurant. The furniture and the colors are tastefully chosen. A "country" feel.

At Manhattan Theatre Club the setting was very simple: a round table and three chairs. When the chairs were one way, it was the living room. When the chairs were around the table, it was the dining room. For the bedroom, two chairs were put together and the actors sat on them and spread a comforter over themselves. The bathroom was defined by a square of light.

This is the home of Jim and Marsha. They enter and come to speak to the audience.

They are attractive, in their mid- to late thirties. He's in somewhat preppy relaxed clothes — khaki pants, a button-down shirt. She's in a comfortable skirt and blouse, with warm but pale colors. Her hair may be pulled back.

Their manner in talking to the audience is that of telling a story, but also, perhaps, of explaining themselves to a marriage counselor.

Jim: Our lives had been seeming dull for a while. You know, nothing major, just sometimes being quiet at dinner.

Marsha: After thirteen years, you run out of things to say, I guess. Or else it's a phase.

Jim: I think it's a phase.

Marsha: Me too. It'll pass.

Jim: We've been married for thirteen years.

Marsha: Our anniversary was in March.

Jim: So in March we went to dinner and tried to get drunk, but we just got sleepy.

Marsha: We didn't try to get drunk.

Jim: I did.

Marsha: We had a very nice time, but the wine made us sleepy.

Jim: We were in bed at ten thirty. Asleep in bed.

Marsha: Well, we were tired.

Jim: And then the next week I got this letter from this old classmate of mine.

Marsha: Wanda. He'd never mentioned her.

Jim: Well, she was just some girlfriend. You know. High school.

Marsha: Wanda.

Jim: And Wanda wrote me, saying she'd like to visit. And I asked Marsha if she'd mind.

Marsha: I have trouble saying no, most women do, I think. It's not pleasing or something. Anyway, Jim got this letter . . .

Jim: . . . and Wanda said she was going to be in our neck of the woods . . .

Marsha: . . . and I hate the phrase "neck of the woods" . . .

Jim: And I asked you if you'd mind, and you said, it would be fine.

Marsha: Well, I have trouble saying no. You know that. You should have said, "Are you sure?" or "Really?" or something.

Jim: (*Stymied, out to audience.*) Well, I didn't. I thought it would be fun. You know, to mull over the old high school days — the prom, the high school paper — I was editor . . .

Marsha: And really, what a ball for me . . .

Jim: And Marsha didn't seem to mind. I mean I can't be a mind reader. So I wrote Wanda back, and told her we'd love to have her visit. I mean, really it might have been fun. In high school Wanda had been quite a looker.

Marsha: And, of course, what an enticement for me. To meet an old high school fantasy. Lucky me.

Jim: So we set a date, and Marsha cleaned the house and baked a chicken.

Marsha: Jim refuses to cook or clean.

Jim: I mow the lawn, you make the chicken.

Marsha: We're old-fashioned. I guess.

Jim: And so we waited for her visit.

> *(Lights change. Sound of a car driving up, stopping, and a door slamming.)*

Jim: Oh, I'll go, honey. It must be Wanda.

> *(Jim goes off to greet Wanda. Marsha straightens up things one last time.*
> *Offstage we hear great whooping and enthusiastic cries of "Jim! Jim!"*
> *Marsha looks startled, curious.*
> *Wanda and Jim come into the room. Wanda is also late thirties, early forties, but unlike Jim and Marsha, she is not in as good shape. Her clothes are a little gaudy, her hair looks odd or messy, and she carries a sense of emotional disarray with her. But she also looks kind of fun and colorful.)*

Wanda: *(With longing.)* Jim!!!

> *(Wanda throws her arms around Jim with great abandon, and then holds this embrace as if her life depended on it.*
> *Marsha goes closer to them and waits patiently for the appropriate moment to be introduced.)*

Wanda: *(Still embracing him.)* Jim. Jim. Oh, Jim, Jim.

Marsha: *(Since the embrace doesn't seem to be ending.)* Hello. I'm Marsha, Jim's wife.

Wanda: *(Breaking from the embrace.)* Oh, hello. Nice to see you. I was just so excited at seeing this guy. Hey, guy. Hey. How ya doin'?

Jim: I'm fine. *(A little uncertain he recognizes her.)* Wanda?

Wanda: Are you expecting someone else?

Jim: No, it's just — well, didn't you used to be blond?

Wanda: Yeah, and I didn't used to be fat either — although I'm not really fat, my woman's group doesn't let me say that, I just have a food problem and some of it shows. But really. I just lost twenty pounds. You should have seen me last month.

Jim: You seem quite thin.

Wanda: Oh, you're sweet. I may look thin, but I'm really fat. *(To Marsha.)* Do you have anything I can eat?

Marsha: Well . . .

Wanda: No, I'm just kidding, it was a joke, it seemed like this setup, you know, I talk about my weight, and then I say, can I have some food?

Marsha: But if you're hungry . . .

Wanda: I am not hungry. *(Glares at Marsha; then becomes friendly again; to Jim.)* Say, Jim, I love your wife. She reminds me of my mother. *(To Marsha.)* No, no, the positive side of my mother. Really. I like both of you.

Marsha: *(Innocently.)* Thank you. I like both of you.

Wanda: What?

Marsha: *(Trying to fix what she said.)* I like you, and I like Jim.

Wanda: You better, you're married to Jim, you lucky dog, you. Oh, give me another hug, guy.

> *(Wanda gives Jim another bear hug.)*

Wanda: Hrrrrrrrrrrrrr.

Jim: Why don't we go in the living room?

> *(Wanda careens into the living room area, looks around her. They follow.)*

Wanda: Oh, I love this room. It's so "country." Did you do it, Marsha?

Marsha: Well, we bought the furniture. I never thought of it as "doing it," actually.

Wanda: Oh, it's wonderful. And I should know, because I have terrible taste.

Marsha: What?

Wanda: I mean I can evaluate good taste in others because I have such bad taste in all my own choices. For instance, my house looks like the interior of a Baskin-Robbins. Everything is plastic, and there are all these bright yellows and dark chocolates. Really, the only thing worse than being married to me is to have me decorate your house.

Jim: Well, I'm sure you underestimate yourself, Wanda.

Wanda: Isn't he a dreamboat? You're a dreamboat, dreamboat. Well, say thank you!

Jim: *(Embarrassed.)* Thank you.

Wanda: *(To Marsha; with sudden focus.)* Do you have anything to eat? Pretzels or something?

Marsha: Well, dinner should be ready soon.

Wanda: Oh, Lord, I don't want dinner yet. Just some pretzels would be good. Something to munch on.

Marsha: Would you like some pâté?

Wanda: Pâté? *(To Jim.)* Where'd you get her, honey, the back of *The New Yorker*? *(To Marsha.)* Sure, honey, I can eat pâté as long as you have crackers with it. And maybe some pretzels.

Marsha: Fine. I'll be right back. *(Exits to kitchen area.)*

Wanda: Oh, Jimbo, she's a jewel. An absolute jewel. *(Wanda sits next to Jim.)*

Jim: Thank you. We've been married thirteen years.

Wanda: Oh. An unlucky number. But she's a jewel. I hope she's not hard like a jewel — just precious.

Jim: Yes, she's very precious.

Wanda: Good.

Jim: You know, I hate to say this, but I don't recognize your face actually.

Wanda: That's very perceptive, Jim. I've had plastic surgery. But it wasn't the fancy-schmancy kind to make your face look better, it was so they couldn't find me.

Jim: Who couldn't find you?

Wanda: I don't want to talk about it. Not on the first night, at least.

Jim: Now you've piqued my interest.

Wanda: Oh, you men are always so impatient.

(Wanda squeezes his knee. Marsha comes in with the pâté, and notices the knee-squeezing. Marsha sits down with the pâté. Wanda is seated between Jim and Marsha.)

Marsha: Here is the pâté.

Wanda: Thanks, honey, I'll just have the crackers. *(Munches enthusiastically on a cracker.)* Stoned wheat thins, I love this. *(To Jim.)* She's a jewel, Jim.

Jim: *(Rather miserably.)* I know. You're a jewel, Marsha.

Marsha: Thank you. *(To Wanda.)* Would you like a drink?

(Wanda pauses for a moment, and then begins to sob, very genuinely.)

Marsha: *(At a loss what to say.)* Don't feel you have to have a drink.

Jim: Wanda, what's the matter?

Wanda: *(Through sobs.)* Oh, I don't want to burden you. Or your wife.

Marsha: That's all right, I'm sure we'd love to be burdened. I mean, if it would help you.

Jim: Yes. Tell us what's the matter.

Wanda: I don't know where to begin. I'm just so unhappy!

Jim: Gosh, Wanda. What is it?

(Wanda pulls herself together, and tries to explain why she felt so upset.)

Wanda: Well it all started the summer after high school graduation. *(To Marsha.)* Jim and I had gone to the prom together, and though of course nothing had been said, everyone just kind of presumed he and I would get married.

Jim: Really? Who presumed this?

Wanda: Well, everyone. My mother, my father, me, everyone.

Jim: Gosh. I mean, I knew we dated.

Wanda: Dated, Jimbo, we were inseparable. From about February of senior year to June senior year, we spent every spare moment together. You gave me your class ring. Look, I have it right here. *(Looks through her purse.)* No, I can't find it. *(Keeps looking.)*

Marsha: Jim gave me the nicest engagement ring.

Wanda: Uh-huh. Now, where is it? *(Wanda dumps out the messy contents of her purse; looks through the mess.)* No. No. Here's the prescription for Seconal I always carry with me in case I feel suicidal.

Marsha: I don't think any of the pharmacies are open this late.

(Wanda stares at Marsha for a moment, like a child who's crying and has suddenly been distracted. Before she can go any further comprehending whatever Marsha said, Jim speaks up.)

Jim: Forget about the ring, Wanda. Tell us why you cried a few minutes ago.

Wanda: Isn't it obvious?

Jim: Isn't what obvious?

Wanda: Seeing the path not taken. I could have had a happy life if I married you. Excuse me for talking this way, Marsha, I just want you to know how lucky you are.

Marsha: Oh, that's fine. Whatever.

Wanda: No, not whatever. Jimbo. *(Kisses him; looks at Marsha, speaks to Jim.)* You see, I do that in front of Marsha so she knows how lucky she is.

Marsha: Thank you. I feel lucky.

Wanda: Well, don't you forget it. Are you listening to me?

Marsha: No one else is speaking.

Wanda: (*Genuinely laughs.*) Oh I love her sense of humor. So anyway, after the prom, Jimbo went away for the whole summer, and he didn't write me . . .

Jim: I didn't know you wanted me to.

Wanda: And then you and I went to different colleges, and *then* when you didn't write me, I was heartbroken.

Jim: Really? I'm terribly sorry . . . I thought we were kind of casual. I mean, we were seventeen.

Wanda: I was eighteen. They held me back in third grade.

Jim: Wanda, if you felt this way, why didn't you tell me at the time? You haven't said anything in twenty years.

Wanda: Well, I've been very busy, and it's hard to be open about emotions, especially painful ones. (*Chomps on a cracker.*) So then I went to Ann Arbor, and oh, Jim and Marsha, I'm so ashamed to tell you this — I was promiscuous.

Marsha: Really?

Wanda: Yes. (*Emphatic, cranky.*) Gosh, these crackers are sure making me thirsty. When you offered me something to drink, I didn't think it was going to be my one chance.

Marsha: (*Startled, disoriented.*) I'm sorry. Would you like something to drink?

Wanda: (*Sweetly.*) Yes, thank you, Marsha. Anything at all. Preferably with vodka.

(*Marsha exits off to kitchen.*)

Wanda: She really is a jewel. She really is. Now where was I?

Jim: You were saying you had been promiscuous.

Wanda: It was awful. I became a campus joke. But it was because I was drowning my sorrow, you see — in flesh.

Jim: In flesh. Ah. Well, that's too bad.

Wanda: There was this one night a whole bunch of guys from the football team stood outside my window and they chanted my name.

Jim: Oh. Well, at least you made an impression.

Wanda: Yeah, but it was because I was missing a certain somebody. And also I liked sex.

(*Marsha comes in, just in time to hear this last remark.*)

Jim: (*Startled.*) Oh, Marsha's here. Hello, Marsha. We missed you.

Marsha: (*A bit of an edge.*) Here's your drink. I hope you like Kool-Aid.

Wanda: Oh, I love it! (*Gulps her entire drink.*) Mmmm, delicious.

(*Marsha looks disappointed.*)

Wanda: So anyway, the campus minister once had to give a whole sermon against me, which made me feel just awful. (*To Jim.*) And all because I was pining for you.

Marsha: I wonder if I should check on the chicken.

Jim: Please don't go just now. (*Jim gets up, to stand by Marsha.*)

Wanda: And, of course, I was raised Catholic, so I knew what I was doing was very, very wrong, but I was so unhappy . . . (*Weeps copiously.*)

(*Jim and Marsha stare at her for a little while.*)

Jim: (*Without too much enthusiasm.*) There, there, Wanda.

Marsha: Yes. There, there.

Wanda: And then my second husband gave me herpes, and every time the first one would call to threaten my life, it would trigger an outbreak . . .

(*Marsha sits back down in a chair, Jim sits on the arm.*)

Wanda: . . . herpes is often set off by emotional turmoil, you know.

Jim: (*Forcing interest.*) Oh, yes, I've read that.

Wanda: And then I thought to hell with men, maybe I should become a lesbian. And I tried that, but the problem was I just wasn't attracted to women, so the whole experiment was a dismal failure.

Marsha: Doesn't anyone want dinner yet?

Wanda: (*Suddenly switching moods.*) Marsha sounds hungry. Sure, honey, let's go eat.

(*Wanda bounds up and moves to the dining room table. Jim and Marsha follow.
  The dinner is not realistically done. It may be mimed with plates and
  silverware already set on the table.*)

Wanda: Oh, the dinner looks beautiful. Marsha, you're so talented as a homemaker. Now where was I?

Jim: Something about you were promiscuous.

Wanda: Well, I don't like to use that word. I slept around uncontrollably, that's what I prefer to say. Did you ever do that, Marsha?

Marsha: No, I didn't. I was a late bloomer.

Wanda: Uh-huh. So then there was that guy from prison. And then there was his father, Fred. Did I tell you about Fred? Well, Fred said to me, I married you because I thought you would be my anchor in the port of life, but now I think you're stark raving mad . . .

Marsha: Could I have the salt, please?

(*Jim passes Marsha the salt.*)

Wanda: . . . and I said, you think I'm crazy, who's the one who has hallucinations, and thinks that shoes go on the hands instead of the feet? Not me, buddy boy.

Jim: (*To Wanda.*) Did he take drugs or something?

Marsha: Please don't ask her questions.

Wanda: What?

Marsha: (*To Wanda.*) Well, I mean I want you to tell the story your own way.

Wanda: Thank you, Marsha. You know, Jim. I really feel close to Marsha.

Jim: I'm glad. (*To Marsha.*) Could I have the salt, please?

Wanda: (*Responding to him.*) Sure, honey. (*Passes him the salt; to Marsha.*) Don't you just love him? (*Continues on with story.*) So one day the washing machine blew up, and Fred said to me, you did that, everything about you is chaos, I'm leaving and I'm taking Tranquility with me.

Jim: He actually said "tranquility"?

Marsha: (*Muttered.*) Don't ask her questions.

Wanda: (*Explaining.*) Tranquility was our dog. And I said, I'm the one who fed Tranquility, and walked her and took care of her worms, and she used to throw up on the rug, and, of course, you can't just leave it there . . .

Marsha: Excuse me, I'll be right back.

Jim: Marsha, are you all right?

Marsha: I'm fine.

Wanda: I hope my talking about vomit didn't make you feel sick.

Marsha: *(Nearly out of the room.)* No, it's fine.

> *(Marsha has left the dining area and gotten to the bathroom area. She holds her head in pain, or leans on a wall for a support. She just couldn't stand to be at the table for a minute longer.)*

Wanda: She's a little hard to talk to.

Jim: I think she had a hard day.

Wanda: Really? What did she do? Spend it making up the guest room for me?

Jim: Oh.

Wanda: Really, I can sleep anywhere. I think I'm being evicted tomorrow anyway, so I'd prefer not to be there.

Jim: That's too bad.

Wanda: I roll with the punches. I enjoy the little things in life. I enjoy colors. I like textures, I like silk and cotton, I don't like corduroy, I don't like ridges . . .

Jim: *(On his way to find Marsha.)* Uh-huh. Hold on to the thought. I'll be right back.

> *(Jim exits and goes to the bathroom area, where he finds Marsha still crouched or leaning.)*

Jim: Why are you hiding in the bathroom?

Marsha: I needed aspirin. Then I just couldn't go downstairs again. When is she leaving?

Jim: I think she's staying overnight.

Marsha: What?

Jim: I think she's staying ov . . .

Marsha: Did she say that or did you say that?

> *(Wanda, bored alone, bounds into the bathroom area with them. The area is small, and they're all crowded together.)*

Wanda: What are you two talking about?

Jim: Oh, nothing. Marsha was just brushing her teeth.

Wanda: It's so intimate brushing your teeth, isn't it? When you live with someone, you don't have any secrets. I remember David said to me, why didn't you tell me you had herpes, and I said, I forgot, okay? People forget things, all right? And he said, not all right, I'm going to have this for life, and I said so what, you have your nose for life, is that *my* fault?

Marsha: *(Tired, but sort of annoyed by the logic.)* Yes, but his nose wasn't your fault, while . . .

Wanda: What?

Marsha: Nothing. I see your point.

Wanda: So then I thought I'd stay out of relationships for a while, and I went to work for this lawyer, only he wasn't a regular lawyer, he was a kingpin.

Jim: Kingpin?

Wanda: Of crime. He was a kingpin of crime, only I didn't realize it. Eventually, of course, I had to get my face redone so they couldn't find me. But I better not say anything more about this right now.

Marsha: *(Trying to tell her no.)* Jim says you were expecting to stay overnight . . .

Wanda: Thank you, I'd love to! I feel I'm just starting to scratch the surface with old Jimbo here. Jimbo, do you remember that girl with the teeth who won Homecoming Queen, what was her name?

Jim: I don't remember. She had teeth?

Wanda: Big teeth.

Marsha: I would like to leave the bathroom now.

Wanda: What?

Marsha: Well, we need to make your room up for you. I didn't know you were . . . well, we need to make it up.

Wanda: *(A little girl.)* I hope there's a quilt. I love quilts.

Marsha: I'll look for one.

> *(Wanda stares at her, happy, but doesn't get out of the way.)*

Marsha: You have to move or I can't get out of the bathroom.

Wanda: *(Serious.)* I'm holding you hostage.

Marsha: What?

Wanda: *(Shifting, cheerful.)* Isn't it awful the way they take hostages now? *(Cheerfully leaves the bathroom, talking away.)* It reminds me of my life with Augie. He was really violent, but he was really little, so I was able to push him down the stairs.

> *(Jim and Marsha look at one another, a little alarmed by the "hostage" exchange. Lights change. The prominent sound of a clock ticking. Time is passing.*
> *Wanda, Jim, and Marsha standing in a "hallway" area, about to make their good nights.)*

Wanda: *(Happy.)* Oh, you guys, it's been a great evening. I can't believe we played games for four hours!

Marsha: I'm really sorry I shouted at you during Monopoly.

Wanda: That's okay. I know somebody who got killed playing Monopoly.

Jim: But you were really good at charades.

Wanda: Thanks, but I'm sorry I broke the lamp.

Marsha: It's perfectly all right. Now the guest room is right down this hall.

Wanda: Well, good night, you two. See you in the morning.

Marsha: Good night.

> *(Wanda exits off to the guest room.*
> *Jim and Marsha go to their bedroom, or rearrange the set to stand in for a bedroom — move two chairs together into a "bed," put a comforter over themselves.*
> *They're too tired to talk. They kiss each other briefly and close their eyes to sleep.*
> *Wanda enters, wrapped up in a quilt.)*

Wanda: Oh, is this your bedroom? Oh, it's so pretty.

> *(Jim and Marsha open their eyes, very startled.)*

Marsha: Is something wrong with your room?

Wanda: No, it's lovely. Although not as nice as here. But then this is the master bedroom, isn't it?

Marsha: Can I get you a pill?

Wanda: No, thanks. Marsha, I love this bedroom. I feel very "enveloped" here. It makes me never want to leave. *(Wanda pulls up a chair right next to their bed.*

Keeps wrapped in her quilt.) I just love New England. I worked in Hartford for three weeks once as a receptionist in a sperm bank.

Marsha: Wanda, I'm sorry. I really think I need to sleep.

Wanda: You can sleep, I won't be offended. So I got fired from the sperm bank, and then I went to Santa Fe, 'cause I heard the furniture was nice there.

(Clock ticks. Time passes. Jim and Marsha change positions in bed.)

Wanda: And then Arthur's ex-wife kept making threatening phone calls to me.

(Clock ticks. Jim and Marsha change positions, now look more uncomfortable.)

Wanda: (Coquettish.) And I said, "Billy, why didn't you tell me you were sixteen?"

(Clock ticks.)

Wanda: (Chatty voice, just telling the facts.) And then the policeman said, let me see your pussy, and I thought, hey, maybe this way I won't get a ticket.

(Clock ticks.)

Wanda: (Teary voice, telling a tragic turning point.) And Leonard said, Wanda, you are a worthless piece of trash. And I said, don't you think I know that? Do you think this is news?

(Clock ticks.)

Wanda: (Energized, telling a fascinating story.) And Howard said he wanted me to kill his mother, and I said, "Are you crazy? I've never even *met* your mother." And he said, "All right, I'll introduce you."

(Jim and Marsha have closed their eyes, either asleep or pretending to be. Wanda looks over at them, suspicious.)

Wanda: Are you asleep? Jim? Marsha?

(Wanda looks to see if they're asleep. She shakes their shoulders a bit, to see if she can wake them.)

Wanda: Jim? Marsha? You're not pretending to be asleep, are you? Jim? Marsha?

(Wanda opens Marsha's eyelid with her finger.)

Marsha: Yes?

Wanda: I was just checking if you were asleep.

Marsha: Yes, I am. Good night. Sleep well.

Wanda: Good night.

(Wanda takes her comforter and curls up at the bottom of their bed. Then she pulls their blanket off them and onto her. Jim doesn't notice, he's asleep for real. Marsha is startled. But gives up, what to do. Lights dim.
Clock ticks.
Lights up for the morning. Wanda sound asleep. Jim and Marsha wake up, and abruptly leave the bedroom for the dining room area.)

Marsha: You know, she doesn't snore. I'm really surprised.

Jim: Want some coffee?

Marsha: I think I'd like some heroin.

Jim: Maybe Wanda has some connections.

Marsha: I'm sure she does. Oh God, why did she sleep on our bed? She seemed like some insane nightmare Golden Retriever.

Jim: Now I feel sorry for her.

Marsha: Well, good for you. Was she always this way?

Jim: Well, she was always vivacious.

Marsha: I see. High school prom queen. Girl Most Likely to Get Herpes.

Jim: Lots of people get herpes.

Marsha: Yes, but they don't talk about it for three hours.

Jim: Why are you so hostile to her? *(Not meaning to say this.)* Is it because she's attracted to me?

Marsha: *(Not expecting to hear that.)* Yes. *(Marsha goes off to the kitchen.)*

Jim: Are you getting coffee?

(Marsha reenters with two coffee mugs, one of which she kind of shoves at Jim.)

Marsha: And are you attracted to her?

Jim: Now come on, Marsha, she's an emotional mess.

Marsha: You're putting up with it very patiently. Why is that?

Jim: Well, that's because . . . I feel sympathy for her. She's someone I knew once who had a life, and look what's happened to her.

Marsha: She's attracted to you.

Jim: Now don't make a big thing out of it. It's just slightly interesting for me, that's all.

Marsha: Well, fine. I understand. I think I'll make a trip to the nearest loony bin and find some mental patient who finds *me* attractive. Then I'll bring him home and make you suffer through a forty-eight-hour visit while he drools on the carpet.

Jim: Oh, come on, stop making such a big deal about all this. It's no big deal . . . it's just . . . well, haven't you ever found it kind of exciting if someone finds you attractive?

Marsha: I've forgotten. *(Starts to leave.)* I'm going to the A&P. I have to get out of here. *(Marsha grabs a purse and exits.)*

Jim: Don't be mad.

(Jim sighs. With his coffee he walks after her, but Wanda, stirring on the bed, hears him.)

Wanda: Is that life out there?

Jim: You awake? *(Jim comes back into the bedroom area, holding his coffee mug.)*

Wanda: Do I smell coffee? Oh, thanks, Jimbo. *(Wanda takes Jim's coffee, thinking it's for her.)* Uh, I love this. You're like a little house slave. I knew I should've married you. Where's Marsha? Did she wake up dead or anything?

Jim: No, she went to the A&P.

Wanda: That's terrible of me to say. I don't want her dead. I'm just teasing 'cause I'm jealous of what she has.

Jim: Oh, I'm not so special.

Wanda: Oh, Jimbo, you are. *(Wanda starts to get up, then shows a grimace of pain. A bit flirtatious.)* Uh. I've slept wrong on my back, I think. You know, a tense muscle or something.

Jim: *(Thinking to himself, is this code?)* Oh. Your back is sore? Um, I'm not a professional masseur, but do you want me to rub it?

Wanda: Oh, would you?

(*Wanda pretty much flops over in delight. Jim starts to massage her back, sort of in the center.*)

Wanda: It's the lower back, Jimbo.
Jim: Oh. Okay. (*He starts to massage her lower back.*)
Wanda: Uh. Yes. Oh, yes. Oh, yes. Ohhhhhhh. Uhhhhhhhh.

(*Marsha comes back in the house, holding the purse and car keys. She stops and hears Wanda's moaning. She marches into the bedroom, finds Jim and Wanda in the midst of their orgasmic back rub.*)

Marsha: I'm back, if anybody cares.
Jim: (*Really jumps.*) Oh, Marsha. I didn't hear the car.
Marsha: I don't blame you. It was very noisy here.
Jim: I'm . . . giving Wanda . . . that is, her back hurts.
Wanda: He gives the most wonderful back rub.
Marsha: I'm so pleased to hear it. Do you need the number of a back specialist, perhaps? I could call my doctor. If you can't walk, we can arrange for an ambulance to take you there.
Jim: Now, Marsha, please, it's really quite innocent.
Wanda: Hey, Marsha, really—I know he's your guy. (*To Jim.*) You're her guy, Jimbo. (*To Marsha.*) It's just my back hurt.
Marsha: Yes, I follow what you say. Probably tension in the lower back. I have a tension headache in the back of my head today, it feels like it might split open. I think I'll go lie down. In the guest room that you never got to. (*Starts to leave.*) Jimbo, when you finish with her back, the car has a flat tire on the corner of Pleasantview and Maple. I thought you might do something about that.
Jim: Oh, I'll go now.
Marsha: No, finish the back rub. You've convinced me it's innocent, so finish it.

(*Marsha walks out. Jim and Wanda look at each other uncomfortably.*)

Wanda: Well, she said to finish it.
Jim: I don't feel comfortable with her in the house.
Wanda: Look, she said it was fine, let's take her at her word.

(*Jim looks dubious and touches her back lightly. At the merest touch, Wanda starts to moan loudly again.*)

Jim: (*Stopping the back rub.*) Can't you be more quiet?
Wanda: It feels so good.
Jim: Look, that's enough. I'm gonna go deal with the flat tire.
Wanda: Can I come?
Jim: Why don't you . . . soak in the bathtub for your back?
Wanda: All right. Thank you for the back rub, Jimbo. (*Gets up; calls after where Marsha went.*) Marsha? Do you have any bubble bath?

(*Marsha comes back.*)

Marsha: What?
Wanda: Do you have any bubble bath? Jim won't continue with the back rub, and I need to relax.
Marsha: The back rub . . . I . . . what was the question?
Jim: Bubble bath. Do we have some?

Marsha: Yes, I'm sure we do. Maybe Jim would like to pour it on you in the bathtub.

Jim: Marsha. Please.

Wanda: Oooh, kinky. (*Loudly.*) Hey! I have an idea! Why don't I cook dinner for you guys tonight? Do you like octopus?

Marsha: Thank you, Wanda, no. I thought we'd go to a restaurant tonight. The walls in this house are starting to vibrate.

Wanda: They are?

Marsha: Yes. So we'll go to a nice, soothing restaurant where they will take care of us. All right?

Wanda: Sure! Fine by me.

> (*Lights change. Maybe lovely classical music to change the mood. Jim, Marsha, and Wanda sit at the table.*
> *The Waiter comes out and puts a tasteful flower arrangement on the table, turning it into the restaurant.*)

Wanda: This is such a pretty restaurant. The music is so classical.

Waiter: Enjoy your meal.

Jim: Thank you.

> (*Waiter exits. Wanda and Jim mime eating from their plates.*)

Wanda: Ohhh, I think I know someone. (*Waves, calls out to imaginary table.*) Hi, there! Oh, no, I don't know them. (*Calls out again.*) Never mind! I thought you were my gynecologist.

Marsha: You thought he'd be up here?

Wanda: Well, he travels a lot. He also sells encyclopedias.

> (*Waiter reenters with a tray of wineglasses. He gives each person a wineglass, Wanda last.*)

Waiter: And here is your wine.

Wanda: They didn't have Kool-Aid?

Waiter: White Zinfandel was the closest we could get, madam.

Wanda: Well, all right. (*To Marsha and Jim.*) Here's mud in your eye.

> (*Everyone drinks. All of them finish their drinks in several quick gulps. The Waiter starts to leave.*)

Jim: Waiter! (*Signals to Waiter for another round. The Waiter nods and exits.*)

Wanda: I can't believe they didn't have octopus. It's a delicacy.

Jim: (*Referring to their plates.*) Well, the trout's pretty good.

Wanda: Yeah, but they put nuts on it or something.

Jim: Well, eat around them maybe.

Wanda: You know, Jim, tomorrow we should get out the old yearbook. You know, Marsha, you wouldn't believe how dashing he was back then. (*To Jim.*) Not that you're not now, of course.

Jim: You're sure a shot for my ego.

Marsha: I'd like to shoot your ego.

Jim: What?

Marsha: Nothing. Go back to talking about high school. I'll try to achieve a Zen state. (*Closes her eyes, puts her arms loose by her side, tries to relax her body.*)

Jim: I . . . I wonder where the waiter is with the drinks.

Marsha: (*With eyes closed; chant-like.*) I am sitting by a tree, and there's a lovely breeze.

Wanda: This restaurant is so adorable. This whole town. You know what I'm thinking? I'm thinking of maybe moving up here to the country with you all, finding a little house to rent. Nothing's happening in my life right now; this might be just the change I might need.

(*The Waiter arrives with three more glasses of wine, which he passes out to them. Marsha's eyes are open again; Wanda's comments above pretty much blew her attempt at a Zen state.*)

Wanda: I'm almost through with my facial surgery. I've had everything done on my face except my nose. I kept that the same.

Jim: You're right. I recognize your nose now. Yes.

Waiter: Will there be anything else?

Wanda: What? Done to my face?

Waiter: Anything else I can do for you at the restaurant?

Jim: We wanted three more glasses of wine.

Waiter: I just brought them.

Jim: Oh. So you did. Well, thank you.

(*The Waiter leaves. Wanda starts to eat her fish.*)

Marsha: So you're going to move up here, are you? Going to sweep up and stick your feet in the ground and root yourself in our "little neck of the woods," are you?

Jim: Marsha, we don't own this area.

Marsha: I feel differently. (*To Wanda.*) I don't want you moving here, is that clear? I don't want you invading my life with your endless ravings anymore, is that clear?

(*The Waiter returns. Wanda keeps eating, seemingly just listening to what's being said, finding it interesting rather than upsetting.*)

Waiter: Is everything all right?

Marsha: No, everything is not all right, this woman is trying to invade my life, and this man is too stupid to see it and hide from her. (*To Jim.*) Don't you realize she's insane?

Jim: Marsha, could we just finish dinner, please?

Marsha: No, I'd like the check.

Waiter: Are you unhappy with your fish?

Marsha: I'm very unhappy with it. It has too many bones in it.

(*Almost on cue, Wanda starts choking on a bone. She gasps and chokes. Jim, Marsha, and the Waiter look at her, shocked for a moment.*)

Jim: Shouldn't one of us do the Heimlich maneuver?

Marsha: I don't want to do it, I don't like her.

(*Wanda looks startled, even in the midst of her choking. She keeps choking and pointing to her throat.*)

Jim: Marsha! (*To Waiter.*) Can you do it?

Waiter: I don't know how to do it yet. It's my first day. Can't you do it?

Jim: Oh, very well.

(*Jim gets up and gets the choking Wanda to stand. He stands behind her and then, not sure what to do, puts his arms under her arms, and locks his hands behind her* neck: *That is, he puts her in a half nelson, and keeps jerking her head forward with his hands, hopefully, as if this should fix her choking.*)

Marsha: (*After a second.*) Oh, for God's sake.

(*Marsha gets up, pushes Jim away. She stands behind Wanda, puts her arms around Wanda's lower stomach and then rather violently and suddenly pulls her hands into Wanda's lower stomach. This does the trick. Wanda spits out the bit of fish and bone, and starts to breathe again.*
Wanda sits back down, exhausted.)

Wanda: Oh, thank God, I thought I was a goner.

(*Suddenly into the restaurant burst Two Men with handkerchiefs tied around their mouths, and carrying guns. They aim their guns at everyone but make straight for Wanda.*)

Man: There she is!

Wanda: Oh my God, they've found me!

(*The Men grab her and, pointing the guns at everyone else, drag Wanda out of the restaurant.*)

Wanda: (*Being dragged or carried out.*) Oh, God, it's the kingpin. Help me! Jim! Jim!

(*All this happens very fast and very suddenly. And now Wanda is gone. Jim, Marsha, and the Waiter seem stunned for a moment.*
A "talking-to-the-audience" light comes up, and the Waiter crosses down into it and addresses the audience.)

Waiter: The next day at the restaurant was considerably less intense, and eventually as time went on, I was made headwaiter. For a while I liked the added responsibility and the additional money, but after a while, I realized I wasn't doing what I wanted to do with my life. I wanted to be an actor. But then the story isn't really about me.

(*Humbly, the Waiter exits.*
Jim and Marsha look confused by the Waiter's behavior, and now address the audience themselves again.
They also straighten the set a bit while they talk, so that it resembles their house as it was at the beginning of the play.)

Jim: (*To audience.*) Well, all that happened a few weeks ago. Wanda hasn't been found yet, but she's probably fine.

Marsha: I feel guilty about what happened. I wasn't a good hostess.

Jim: Now, honey, she's probably fine. Wanda's sort of like a bacteria—wherever she is, she seems to grow and go on and on just fine, so you shouldn't feel bad.

Marsha: Yes, but right before Wanda started to choke on the fish bone, I had this momentary, stray thought of wishing she would choke on a fish bone. And then suddenly she did. I know it's not logical, but on some level, I feel I tried to kill her. And then thugs came and carried her away. I mean, in a way, it's just what I wanted.

Jim: Now, Marsha, you're not responsible for what happened.

Marsha: I chose the restaurant.

Jim: Now, Marsha. You're not omnipotent. Besides, awful things are always happening to Wanda. She's like a magnet for trouble.

Marsha: (*To the audience.*) Well, it was just the most awful two days. Three days, counting meeting with the police.

Jim: But some good came out of it.

Marsha: Yes. We had a big argument, and that was good.

Jim: It cleared the air.

Marsha: I said what I was feeling, and it was mostly negative, but it was good to say it.

Jim: It cleared the air.

Marsha: And one of the things I said was that we don't feel joy enough. Or hardly at all.

Jim: Right. We don't feel joy much. So we joined an aerobics class . . .

Marsha: To get the blood moving . . . When you move around, you tend to feel better . . .

Jim: And we're going to a marriage counselor who specializes in breaking down fear of intimacy in people who've known one another for over ten years . . .

Marsha: And, of course, we fit that. And all told, I guess Wanda's visit helped to stir us up in a good way, all told.

Jim: Right.

Marsha: Blessings come in unexpected ways.

Jim: Right.

Marsha: Now if only we were happy.

Jim: Right.

(*They look at each other. Then they look out at the audience. Some friendly, possibly optimistic music plays. Lights dim on Jim and Marsha.*)

CONSIDERATIONS FOR CRITICAL THINKING AND WRITING

1. **FIRST RESPONSE.** How does Durang's use of humor redeem what might otherwise be a depressingly grim set of characters and circumstances? If the humor doesn't work for you, explain why.

2. Who do you think is the protagonist? Who (or what) is the antagonist?

3. What is the major conflict? Where is the climax? Is the conflict resolved?

4. What do you think is the purpose of the waiter at the end of the play?

5. Why would it be inaccurate to describe this play as a work of realism (an attempt to create the appearance of life as it is actually lived)? Describe the techniques that Durang uses in the play that go beyond realism.

6. Is the theme stated directly, or is it developed implicitly through the action, dialogue, or plot?

7. **CRITICAL STRATEGIES.** Read the section on cultural criticism (pp. 2055–56) in Chapter 53, "Critical Strategies for Reading," and discuss how the play reflects the values of the society in which it is set. Explain why you think the play affirms or challenges contemporary American values.

CONNECTION TO ANOTHER SELECTION

1. **CREATIVE RESPONSE.** Rewrite a scene of your choice from either Susan Glaspell's *Trifles* (p. 1366) or Henrik Ibsen's *A Doll House* (p. 1709) as you think Durang would write it.

Moby-Dude, Or: The Three-Minute Whale

© Martha Ives.

Born in Chicago and educated at Northwestern University and the Yale School of Drama, David Ives writes for television, film, and opera. A recipient of a Guggenheim Fellowship in playwriting, he has created a number of one-act plays for the annual comedy festival called Manhattan Punch Line. Many of his one-act plays are available in *All in the Timing* (1994), *Lives of the Saints* (2000), and *Time Flies and Other Plays* (2001); his full-length plays are collected in *Polish Joke and Other Plays* (2004). *Moby-Dude, Or: The Three-Minute Whale* is a very brief play about a student trying to convince his teacher that he actually completed reading a very long novel. In the introduction to *Talk to Me: Monologue Plays*, from which *Moby-Dude* is reprinted, the editors, Nina Shengold and Eric Lane, offer a valuable perspective on the nature of monologue plays by describing them as a "modern form of that most ancient of human entertainments, storytelling. Our paleolithic ancestors listened to hunters enacting their sagas in front of a campfire, and members of every human community since have stood up in front of their peers and performed their trades." Here's Ives's updated version of classic storytelling.

DAVID IVES (B. 1950)

Moby-Dude, Or: The Three-Minute Whale   2004

SFX: sound of waves and gulls. Distant ship's bell.
Our Narrator is a stoned-out surfer of seventeen.

Our Narrator: Call me Ishmael, dude. Yes, Mrs. Podgorski, I *did* read *Moby-Dick* over the summer like I was supposed to. It was bohdacious. Actually, y'know, it's "Moby-*hyphen*-Dick." The title's got a little hyphen before the "Dick." And what is the meaning of this dash before the "Dick"? WHOAAA! Another mystery in this awesome American masterpiece, a peerless allegorical saga of mortal courage, metaphysical ambiguity and maniacal obsession! *What*, Mrs. Podgorski? You don't believe I really *read* Herman Melville's *Moby-Dick Or The Whale*? Five hundred sixty-two pages, fourteen ounces, published 1851, totally tanked its first weekend, rereleased in the 1920s as one of the world's gnarliest works of Art? You think I copped all this like off the back of the tome or by watching the crappy 1956 film starring Gregory Peck? Mrs. P., you been chasing my tail since middle school, do *I* get all testy? Do *I* say, what is the plot in under two minutes—besides a whale and a hyphen? *Moby-Dick* in two minutes, huh? Okay, kyool. Let's rip.

(SFX: ship's bell, close up and sharp, to signal the start and a ticking watch, underneath. Very fast.)

Fade in the boonies of Massachusetts, eighteen-something. Young dude possibly named Ishmael, like the Bible, meets-cute with, TAA-DAA!, *Quee-queg*, a South Sea cannibal with a heart of gold.

(SFX: cutesy voice going, "Awwww.")

Maybe they're gay.

(SFX: tongue slurp.)

Or maybe they represent some east-west, pagan-Christian duality action. Anyway, the two newfound bros go to Mass and hear a sermon about Jonah . . .

(SFX: one second of church organ.)

Biblical tie-in, then ship out on Christmas Day *(could be symbolical!)* aboard the USS *Pequod* with its mysterious wacko Captain Ahab . . .

(SFX: madman laughter.)

. . . who—*backstory*—is goofyfoot because the equally mysterious mom-boosaloid white whale Moby-like-the-singer Dick bit his leg off.

(SFX: chomp.)

Freudian castration action. I mean he's big and he's got sperm and his last name is "Dick," right? Moby is also a metaphor for God, Nature, Truth, obsessisical love, the world, the past, and white people. Check out Pip the Negro cabin boy who by a *fluke* . . .

(SFX: rimshot.)

. . . goes wacko too. Ahab says,

(SFX: echo effect.)

"Bring me the head of the Great White Whale and you win this prize!"

(SFX: echo effect out, cash register sound.)

The crew is stoked, by *NOT* first-mate like-the-coffee-Starbuck. Ahab wants the big one, Starbuck wants the whale juice. Idealism versus capitalism.

(SFX: an impressed "Whoo.")

Radical. Queequeg tells the carpenter to build him a coffin shaped like a canoe.

(SFX: theremin.)

Foreshadowing! Then lots of chapters everybody skips about the scientology of whales.

(SFX: yawn.)

Cut to . . .

(SFX: trumpet fanfare.)

Page 523, the Pacific Ocean. *"Surf's up!"* Ahab sights the Dick. He's totally amped. The boards hit the waves, the crew snakes the Dick for three whole days, bottom of the third Ahab is ten-toes-on-the-nose, he's aggro, Moby goes aerial, Ahab's in the zone, he fires his choicest harpoon, the rope does a 360 round his neck, Ahab crushes out, Moby totals the *Pequod,* everybody eats it 'cept our faithful narrator Ishmael who boogies to safety on Quee-queg's coffin . . .

(SFX: resounding echo effect, deeper voice.)

"AND I ONLY AM ESCAPED ALONE TO TELL THEE!"

(Resume normal voice.)

Roll final credits. The End.

(SFX: ship's bell to signal end of fight. End ticking watch.)

So what do you say, Mrs. Podgorski? You want to like hang and catch a cup of Starbucks sometime . . . ? — *Tubular!*

End of play

CONSIDERATIONS FOR CRITICAL THINKING AND WRITING

1. **FIRST RESPONSE.** Discuss whether you think it is necessary to have read Melville's *Moby-Dick* in order to appreciate the narrator's monologue.

2. How do the narrator's diction and style contribute to the play's humor?

3. In what sense is Mrs. Podgorski the antagonist?

4. Comment on the appropriateness of the sound effects.

5. **CREATIVE RESPONSE.** Write a monologue in which Mrs. Podgorski responds to the student.

CONNECTION TO ANOTHER SELECTION

1. How are the narrators' sensibilities revealed by their respective monologues in *Moby-Dude* and Jane Martin's *Rodeo* (p. 1804)?

2. Compare the tone of the narrator's monologue with that of Jane Martin's *Rodeo* (p. 1804).

Rodeo

Jane Martin is a pseudonym. The author's identity is known only to a handful of administrators at the Actors Theatre of Louisville who handle permissions for productions and reprints of the play. *Rodeo* is one of eleven monologues in *Talking With.* . . . Martin has also published other plays conveniently grouped in two volumes: *Jane Martin: Collected Plays 1980–1995* (1996) and *Jane Martin: Collected Plays 1996–2001* (2001).

Although only one character appears in *Rodeo,* the monologue is surprisingly moving as she describes what the rodeo once was, how it has changed, and what it means to her. At first glance the subject matter may not seem very promising for drama, but the character's energy, forthrightness, and colorful language transform seemingly trivial details into significant meanings.

JANE MARTIN
Rodeo   1981

A young woman in her late twenties sits working on a piece of tack. Beside her is a Lone Star beer in the can. As the lights come up we hear the last verse of a Tanya Tucker song or some other female country-western vocalist. She is wearing old worn jeans and boots plus a long-sleeved workshirt with the sleeves rolled up. She works until the song is over and then speaks.

See Plays in Performance insert.

Big Eight: Shoot — Rodeo's just goin' to hell in a handbasket. Rodeo used to be somethin'. I loved it. I did. Once Daddy an' a bunch of 'em was foolin' around with some old bronc over to our place and this ol' red nose named Cinch got bucked off and my Daddy hooted and said he had him a nine-year-old girl, namely me, wouldn't have no damn trouble cowboyin' that horse. Well, he put me on up there, stuck that ridin' rein in my hand, gimme a kiss, and said, "Now there's only one thing t' remember Honey Love, if ya fall off you jest don't come home." Well I stayed up. You gotta stay on a bronc eight seconds. Otherwise the ride don't count. So from that day on my daddy called me Big Eight. Heck! That's all the name I got anymore . . . Big Eight.

Used to be fer cowboys, the rodeo did. Do it in some open field, folks would pull their cars and pick-ups round it, sit on the hoods, some ranch hand'd bulldog him some rank steer and everybody'd wave their hats and call him by name. Ride us some buckin' stock, rope a few calves, git throwed off a bull, and then we'd jest git us to a bar and tell each other lies about how good we were.

Used to be a family thing. Wooly Billy Tilson and Tammy Lee had them five kids on the circuit. Three boys, two girls and Wooly and Tammy. Wasn't no two-beer rodeo in Oklahoma didn't have a Tilson entered. Used to call the oldest girl Tits. Tits Tilson. Never seen a girl that top-heavy could ride so well. Said she only fell off when the gravity got her. Cowboys used to say if she landed face down you could plant two young trees in the holes she'd leave. Ha! Tits Tilson.

Used to be people came to a rodeo had a horse of their own back home. Farm people, ranch people — lord, they *knew* what they were lookin' at. Knew a good ride from a bad ride, knew hard from easy. You broke some bones er spent the day eatin' dirt, at least ya got appreciated.

Now they bought the rodeo. Them. Coca-Cola, Pepsi Cola, Marlboro damn cigarettes. You know the ones I mean. Them. Hire some New York faggot t' sit on some ol' stuffed horse in front of a sagebrush photo n' smoke that junk. Hell, tobacco wasn't made to smoke, honey, it was made to chew. Lord wanted ya filled up with smoke he would've set ya on fire. Damn it gets me!

There's some guy in a banker's suit runs the rodeo now. Got him a pinky ring and a digital watch, honey. Told us we oughta have a watcha-macallit, choriographus or somethin', some ol' ballbuster used to be with the Ice damn Capades. Wants us to ride around dressed up like Mickey Mouse, Pluto, crap like that. Told me I had to haul my butt through the barrel race done up like Minnie damn Mouse in a tu-tu. Huh uh, honey! Them people is so screwed-up they probably eat what they run over in the road.

Listen, they got the clowns wearin' Astronaut suits! I ain't lyin'. You know what a rodeo clown does! You go down, fall off whatever — the clown runs in front of the bull so's ya don't git stomped. Pin-stripes, he got 'em in space suits tellin' jokes on a microphone. First horse see 'em, done up like the Star Wars went crazy. Best buckin' horse on the circuit, name of Piss 'N' Vinegar, took one look at them clowns, had him a heart attack and died. Cowboy was ridin' him got hisself squashed. Twelve hundred pounds of coronary arrest jes fell right through 'em. Blam! Vio con dios. Crowd thought that was funnier than the astronauts. I swear it won't be long before they're strappin' ice-skates on the ponies. Big crowds now. Ain't hardly no ranch people, no farm people, nobody I know. Buncha disco babies and dee-vorce lawyers — designer jeans and day-glo Stetsons. Hell, the whole bunch of 'em wears French perfume. Oh it smells like money now! Got it on the cable T and V — hey, you know what, when ya rodeo yer just bound to kick yerself up some dust — well now, seems like that fogs up the ol' TV camera, so they told us a while back that from now on we was gonna ride on some new stuff called Astro-dirt. Dust free. Artificial damn dirt, honey. Lord have mercy.

Banker Suit called me in the other day said "Lurlene . . ." "Hold it," I said, "Who's this Lurlene? Round here they call me Big Eight." "Well, Big Eight," he said, "My name's Wallace." "Well that's a real surprise t' me," I said, "Cause aroun' here everybody jes calls you Dumb-ass." My, he laughed real big, slapped his big ol' desk, an' then he said I wasn't suitable for the rodeo no more. Said they was lookin' fer another type, somethin' a little more in the showgirl line, like the Dallas Cowgirls maybe. Said the ridin' and ropin' wasn't the thing no more. Talked on about floats, cos-tumes, dancin' choreog-aphy. If I was a man I woulda pissed on his shoe. Said he'd give me a lifetime pass though. Said I could come to his rodeo any time I wanted.

Rodeo used to be people ridin' horses for the pleasure of people who rode horses — made you feel good about what you could do. Rodeo wasn't worth no money to nobody. Money didn't have nothing to do with it! Used to be seven Tilsons riding in the rodeo. Wouldn't none of 'em dress up like Donald damn Duck so they quit. That there's the law of gravity!

There's a bunch of assholes in this country sneak around until they see ya havin' fun and then they buy the fun and start in sellin' it. See, they figure if ya love it, they can sell it. Well you look out, honey! They want to make them a dollar out of what you love. Dress *you* up like Minnie Mouse. Sell your rodeo. Turn *yer* pleasure into Ice damn Capades. You hear what I'm sayin'? You're jus' merchandise to them, sweetie. You're jus' merchandise to them.

Blackout.

Considerations for Critical Thinking and Writing

1. **First response.** Big Eight is presented as an old-fashioned rodeo type. What associations or stereotypes do you have about such people? What assumptions do you make about them? How does the author use those expectations to heighten your understanding of Big Eight's character?

2. How has the rodeo changed from how it "used to be"? How do you account for those changes?

3. Comment on Big Eight's use of language. Why is it appropriate for her character?

4. How would you describe Big Eight's brand of humor? How does it affect your understanding of her?

5. How do your feelings about Big Eight develop during the course of the monologue?

6. What does the rodeo mean to Big Eight?

Connections to Other Selections

1. Compare and contrast a Shakespeare monologue from either *Hamlet* (p. 1585) or *A Midsummer Night's Dream* (p. 1528) with the style and content of *Rodeo*.

2. In an essay discuss the nostalgic tone in *Rodeo* and Stephen Crane's short story "The Bride Comes to Yellow Sky" (p. 298). In your response consider each work's treatment of the West.

3. Compare the attitudes expressed about merchandising in *Rodeo* with those expressed in Arthur Miller's *Death of a Salesman* (p. 1869).

Quiet Torrential Sound

A successful playwright, screenwriter, journalist, and actress, Joan Ackermann is also co-founder and Artistic Director of the twenty-five-year-old Mixed Company Theater in Great Barrington, Massachusetts. She has published and produced more than a dozen of her plays around the country in such venues as the Guthrie Theater, Circle Rep, Cleveland Playhouse, Shakespeare & Company, and the Atlantic Theatre Company. Her plays include *Off the Map* (1994), which was adapted and released as a motion picture at the Sundance Film Festival in 2003; *The Batting Cage* (1996); *Marcus Is Walking* (1999); and *Ice Glen* (2005). Ackermann was also a longtime writer and producer of the television series **Arli$$**. In addition to writing articles for *The Atlantic, Esquire,* and *Time,* her journalist writing included a seven-year stint as a special contributor to *Sports Illustrated. Quiet Torrential Sound* is set in the Berkshires, where Ackermann resides and takes pleasure in being a part-time hiking guide and leading audiences on dramatic adventures.

JOAN ACKERMANN (B. 1951)

Quiet Torrential Sound

1995

CHARACTERS

Monica, late thirties
Claire, early thirties
Waiter

TIME & PLACE: The Present. Cafe table with two chairs.

> *Monica and Claire enter, dressed up, from a concert.*

Monica: Well, isn't this charming.

Claire: Mmm.

Monica: How about this cute little table right here? My. Aren't these flowers delightful.

Claire: Mmm.

Monica: A little past their prime but . . . such a precious little vase.

Claire: Mmmm.

Monica: *(Sighs.)* Beethoven. Beethoven. I feel so . . . renewed, don't you? That was the greatest classical experience of my life.

Claire: Mm-mm.

Monica: Claire, I believe I've expressed this to you before. I wish you would make more of an effort to expand your vocabulary. No one would ever think that you're a junior college graduate if all you do is go around hmmmming things. *(Beat.)* And another thing. I wouldn't tell you this if we weren't sisters and the best of friends, but quite frankly, that blouse does very little for you. Blue is your color, Claire. Keep away from the pastels. They tend to wash you out. You don't have very strong features so you need more vibrancy of color to perk you up. Do you feel a draft?

Claire: I like this blouse.

Monica: It's not a question of liking it or not. As far as blouses go that one is perfectly acceptable. It's just pointless to wear something that does absolutely nothing for you. Clothes should make us appear as attractive as possible. Like wrapping paper. *(Waiter enters.)* Would you rather receive a gift in a plain brown paper bag or in nice cheerful paper with a bright colorful bow?

Waiter: Hi, my name is Nathan. Can I help you?

Monica: Nathan. At long last. Where have you been? I would like a cup of decaf, please, Nathan. Your freshest pot. With some Sweet and Low.

Waiter: Right-y-o. Anything to eat?

Monica: We've just been to the outdoor concert at Tanglewood. Beethoven's Seventh Symphony. So lovely, sitting out on the lawn.

Waiter: That's nice. Do you want something to eat?

Monica: I'm only telling you because I'm sure we smell of Avon Skin So Soft. For the bugs. It's an excellent bug repellent. Not completely effective, but . . . can you smell it?

Waiter: I smell something.

Monica: Avon Skin So Soft. Do you ever go to Tanglewood, Nathan? To hear the classical concerts?

Waiter: No.

Monica: I thought not. Pardon me for asking, but is your decaf truly decaf?

Waiter: Yes, we brew our own.

Monica: I'm so glad. I have ordered decaf before and received real coffee instead. The effects are not pleasant. My digestive system; I won't go into detail. Is there a fan on in here?

Waiter: No.

Monica: Could you turn it off, please?

Waiter: Sure.

Claire: I'd like a Coke and a hot fudge sundae.

Monica: Claire, dear. Really. A Coke and a hot fudge sundae? We were only just moments ago discussing your figure in the car.

Claire: Oh. Well, make it Diet Coke.

Waiter: Right-y-o. *(Starts to leave.)*

Monica: You're sure now about that decaf?

Waiter: Yes, m'am.

Monica: Thank you so very much. I appreciate your courtesy. *(Waiter exits.)* What a charming waiter. Doesn't seem to have been to the dentist recently but I'm sure he has a heart of gold. My, we are having a splendid little vacation aren't we, Claire? I never dreamed that the Berkshires held so many cultural attractions. I am so looking forward to the Norman Rockwell Museum this afternoon, aren't you?

Claire: Mmm. *(Then quickly:)* Yes, I am. Monica. I am. Looking forward.

Monica: I really should get subscription tickets to the Boston Symphony. I've been telling myself that for years. When I get home I will, I will, I'm going to, I'm making myself a promise right now, you're a witness. There's something about classical music, especially live classical music . . . something so pure, so humane, so . . . *honest.* There's no such thing as dishonest classical music — Claire, please don't pick at your face — it simply doesn't exist. You can see why it takes a certain intellect, a certain upbringing to appreciate it. An uncultivated mind could never appreciate classical music. Couldn't. Our waiter, for instance, Nathan. Classical music would just wash right over Nathan. Like rain on a duck. So. Do you have any observations from this morning you'd care to share with me?

Claire: Oh. I enjoyed the concert.

Monica: Yes?

Claire: Huh-huh. Yes. I did.

Monica: And what about it did you enjoy in particular?

Claire: Uh . . .

Monica: Was it the lovely outdoor setting? The view of distant rolling hills? The harmonious marriage between the natural beauty and Beethoven's Seventh Symphony? Was it the thrilling final movement?

Claire: I thought the conductor was exceptional.

Monica: Exceptional? Interesting choice of words. You're picking at your face again. Perhaps if you used a different moisturizer it wouldn't break out so. I'll give you some of mine when we get back to the hotel. In what way exceptional?

Claire: In the way he conducted. *(Clears throat.)* His musicians.

Monica: Ah . . . how astute of you, Claire. You know I think your hair is due for a trim. You're looking rather mousey of late, though you do have a strange glow about you I can't quite figure. *(Waiter enters.)* Maybe after the museum we can find a beauty shop.

Waiter: Here you go. *(Serves both and exits.)*

Monica: Why thank you so much, Nathan. *(Eyeing Claire's sundae.)* Oh my. I'm not saying a word. *(Takes Sweet and Low, shakes it hard, pours and watches it settle.)* Ah, it is decaf, I can tell by the way the Sweet and Low penetrates. Real coffee offers more resistance.

Claire: Monica . . .

Monica: You know what I find hard to believe, Claire, what I'll never understand, is how it could be, how it could come to pass that a man like Beethoven, a man blessed with such extraordinary gifts, such a superhuman capacity to paint with sound, paint giant murals of sound, how such a genius could actually become deaf. Did you know he became deaf in later years? He did. Such a tragedy. My coffee tastes like Avon Skin So Soft.

(Claire is eating an enormous hot fudge sundae.)

Claire: Monica . . .

Monica: It's hard to imagine what it would be like to be deaf and be Beethoven. To only listen in your mind. Actually, you would be listening in your mind, *to* your mind, to what your mind remembered. Sound was. Just imagine being Beethoven, deaf; listening to all that quiet sound, that quiet torrential sound. Is that real whipped cream? No, honey, I'm counting calories. But you enjoy it. Funny that his ears — of all parts of Beethoven's body — his ears should be the ones to break down. You use a certain part of your body so much, you just plum wear it out. Like a painter going blind. Like Renoir, for instance, going blind. Or Matisse, or Manet, or Monet, or Van Gogh, or Jackson Pollack, or Leonardo da Vinci. Or any of the great impressionists. Going blind. From overuse. The opposite of vestigial. Classical music is so stimulating, isn't it? My brain is full of thoughts.

Claire: Monica . . .

Monica: What?

Claire: *(Eating her sundae.)* You know that workshop on "Human Intimacy" that you suggested I go to a couple months ago?

Monica: No.

Claire: Remember? You gave me this brochure with workshops . . . the Adult Education Center. You had several circled, with an eyebrow pencil?

Monica: Mmm.

Claire: Well, I took one.

Monica: Good for you. *(Wanting more coffee.)* Where is our waiter? Where is Mr. Right-y-o? Imagine, a grown man speaking like that.

Claire: Remember too how we once talked about orgasms and how neither of us had ever had one? *(Pause.)* Remember? That night we got a little tipsy on peach wine coolers at Rose's?

Monica: We are sisters, Claire. We've shared many secrets with each other over the years. Such confidences are quite natural.

Claire: Well, I learned a couple of things at that workshop that really . . . helped.

Monica: I'm so glad. I was thinking of taking a music appreciation class there over the winter session. It's given by a Harvard professor and it's supposed to be excellent.

Claire: Mmm. My teacher was excellent.

Monica: Was he from Harvard?

Claire: No.

Monica: Oh.

Claire: Have you ever heard of multiple orgasms?

Monica: I'm an educated woman, Claire, and an avid magazine reader. I've heard about just about everything under the sun from multiple orgasms to multiple sclerosis. Just because I have experienced neither does not mean I am poorly informed on either topic.

Claire: Well, I'm having them.

Monica: Right now?

Claire: No, not right now.

Monica: *(Pause.)* Truly?

Claire: *(Eating ice cream.)* Huh-huh.

Monica: Well. Bless your heart.

Claire: Lots of them.

Monica: I'm very happy for you, dear. Now. Would you care to hear about the Norman Rockwell Museum? This guide book has been most informative.

Claire: First I figured out how to have them by myself. In the bathtub? Then I started seeing this guy, Jim, I call him Jimbo, sometimes Jumbo, inside joke, he helped me with my tax returns, he works for H&R Block? Monica . . . I can't tell you how wonderful it's been.

Monica: Then don't. Listen to this. "The Corner House in Stockbridge has the largest collection of Rockwell originals in the world, over four hundred. The museum changes its exhibit twice a year with a few exceptional paintings remaining on permanent display (for example, 'Stockbridge at Christmas'). There are six galleries within this beautifully restored 18th-century house, and the tour is a delight. All sorts of colorful information is passed along (such as pointers about the portraits of Grandma Moses and Rockwell's family contained within one painting). Helpful hints are given about how to appreciate Rockwell's attention to detail: 'Notice the ring finger on the old woman's hand; it's been indented by many years of wear . . .'"

(While Monica reads, Claire speaks.)

Claire: I'm thirty-three years old, Monica, and I've finally gotten in touch with my own body.

(Monica continues reading.)

Claire: It's like I've been walking around all these years with this hidden sunken treasure. It was there the whole time! What a feeling, I am telling you. Woo!

(Monica reads louder.)

Claire: I could have died and never even known, Monica, I could have gone my whole life and never known. I mean, I could have been in a car accident last year, I could easily have died in a car accident without ever knowing. What a crying shame that would have been.

(Monica reads louder.)

Claire: And to share that feeling with someone else. Monica. There's just nothing like it. Nothing. Not distant rolling hills. Not Beethoven's Seventh Symphony. *(Monica stops.)* Not even the thrilling final movement. Talk about thrilling final movements!

Monica: SHUT UP!

(Pause.)

Claire: Jimbo likes this blouse, Monica. He likes what's inside it no matter how it's packaged. He thinks it's vibrant.

(Pause. Waiter enters.)

Waiter: Did you call? Did you need something?

Monica: Yes, I need something, I need you to know that I know that that was not decaffeinated coffee, young man, it was not decaffeinated coffee you gave me, there was caffeine in it you assured me there wouldn't be but there was. Caffeine. Am I right, am I? I am. Do you know how many times that happens to me, how many times waiters and waitresses love to intentionally do that to me, just love to intentionally give me straight black coffee all the while smirking inside, insisting oh yes it's decaffeinated? Smirking, do you know? And do you know that as a result I'll be awake all night tonight, I'll be awake with a splitting headache and severe stomach cramps, awake all by myself alone in my bed. Tell me, Nathan, is that a cheerful picture? Is that a cheerful Norman Rockwell Saturday Evening Post cover, a woman alone in bed with a splitting headache and stomach cramps? Jaws clenched?

(Pause.)

Waiter: I'm sorry. I didn't think you would notice.

Monica: You know, Nathan, if you were the sort of person who went to classical concerts, the sort of person who was capable of enjoying classical concerts, capable of sitting there, quietly listening, appreciating, you would not be so cruel. So cruel. It's because I'm a cultured woman, isn't it? That's why, because I'm cultured.

(Silence. He exits.)

Claire: I don't think you were very nice to Nathan.

Monica: Nathan who did not turn off that fan, did willfully not turn off that fan on purpose when I asked him, asked him very cordially, I'll most likely end up with an earache from the draft; lying alone tonight in my bed with an earache and stomach cramps and a headache while my baby sister lies in the next bed . . . glowing. *(Takes a breath.)* Are you ready to leave, Claire? I was planning to have a dish of frozen light yogurt after sitting here watching you eat that Mt. Vesuvius of a hot fudge sundae but quite frankly, the unexpected turn in our conversation has left a disagreeable note in the atmosphere.

Claire: I'm ready to go. *(Looks at bill, opens purse, puts down money.)*

Monica: *(Stands.)* They have tours at the museum every twenty minutes. I plan to buy several postcards and perhaps a poster, if they are reasonably priced. *(Takes another breath.)* I think, Claire, that Stockbridge will be one of the highlights of our trip.

Claire: Mmm.

Monica: And far be it from me to be the one to suggest that there is ample room for you to show a little more appreciation for the fact that I have organized this vacation, this entire vacation, entirely by myself and by a little more appreciation I mean any at all.

Claire: I do. Appreciate.

Monica: How anyone could fathom why you would feel moved to share that kind of information with me at this point in time, at the very peak of our vacation.

Claire: That's why. You were in such a good mood. You just had the greatest classical experience of your life. The information was pretty . . . upbeat. I thought.

Monica: Upbeat.

Claire: I thought it was perfect vacation information. To share with my only living sister.

Monica: *(Starts walking out, turns back.)* Claire?

Claire: Mmm?

Monica: I apologize for my choice of words just then.

Claire: When?

Monica: Back then.

Claire: You mean when you said shut up?

Monica: Mm.

Claire: It's okay.

Monica: It was inappropriate. Uncalled for. The caffeine . . .

Claire: It's all right. Really.

Monica: *(Takes one step and turns back again.)* Claire?

Claire: Yes, Monica.

Monica: If you received any pertinent literature in your workshop—books, pamphlets, diagrams, whatever—I'd venture to say that I'd be willing to peruse whatever material you had.

Claire: All right. *(Smiles.)*

Monica: All right. *(She goes back and puts a bill on the table.)*

Claire: Ten dollars? Geez Louise.

Monica: Claire, don't say "geez Louise." It doesn't become a woman of your age. *(Starts to exit.)*

Claire: Okay.
Monica: (*Sarcastic.*) Or breadth of experience.

> (*Claire follows Monica off.*)

The end

CONSIDERATIONS FOR CRITICAL THINKING AND WRITING

1. **FIRST RESPONSE.** Analyze how Monica's opening conversation with Claire — before Nathan appears — serves to establish her character.
2. Discuss the significance of what the sisters order from Nathan in the café. What do their respective appetites reveal about them?
3. Describe the conflict that exists between Monica and Claire.
4. How is Monica's discussion of Beethoven relevant to the conflict in the play?
5. Comment on Ackermann's strategies for working humor and irony into the dialogue.
6. Consider the play's final scene. How would you characterize the tone of the ending and the sisters' future relationship?

CONNECTIONS TO OTHER SELECTIONS

1. Discuss the ways in which this play and Michael Hollinger's *Naked Lunch* (p. 1385) are stories about power in relationships.
2. Compare the themes of *Quiet Torrential Sound* and Xu Xi's short story "Famine" (p. 657).

Playwriting 101: The Rooftop Lesson

Photo by Rick Tormone.

Born in Chicago, Rich Orloff graduated from Oberlin College in 1973 and has built a successful career as a comedic playwright. He has written some ten full-length plays, more than a dozen one-act plays, and over fifty short plays, four of which have appeared in *Best American Short Plays*. His works are produced throughout the United States and have won a number of awards including the 2002–03 Dramatists Guild Playwriting Fellowship. On his Web site <www.richorloff.com> Orloff explains what prompted him to write *Playwriting 101: The Rooftop Lesson:* "The play was originally produced as part of a series of short plays produced on an actual rooftop in Manhattan. When I was invited to submit to the festival, every idea I came up with seemed completely clichéd. So I gathered the clichés into one story and satirized them. Voila, an original play!"

RICH ORLOFF (B. 1951)

Playwriting 101: The Rooftop Lesson

2000

See Plays in Performance insert.

NOTE: The characters [the Teacher, the Jumper, and the Good Samaritan] can be of either sex, but the Jumper and Good Samaritan should be of the same sex. References are written as if the characters are male, but that can be changed.

TIME: The present.

PLACE: The rooftop of a large urban building.

> *(As the play begins, The Jumper is on the ledge of the roof and is about to jump.)*

The Jumper: I'm going to jump, and nobody can stop me!

> *(The Good Samaritan enters quickly.)*

The Good Samaritan: Don't!!!!!

> *(The Teacher enters and stands to the side. The Teacher points a clicker at the others and clicks, freezing the action.)*

The Teacher *(addressing the audience):* A typical dramatic scenario: Two people in conflict — at least one in deep inner conflict — with high stakes, suspense, and affordable cast size. How will this situation play out? That depends, of course, on the level of craft and creativity in that remarkable art form known as playwriting. Let's rewind from the start — *(The Teacher clicks, and The Jumper and Good Samaritan return to their places at the top of the play, quickly reversing their initial movements.)* And see what happens.

> *(The Teacher clicks again to resume the action. The Jumper is on the ledge of the roof and is about to jump.)*

The Jumper: I'm going to jump, and nobody can stop me!

> *(The Good Samaritan enters quickly.)*

The Good Samaritan: Don't!!!!!
The Jumper: Okay.

> *(The Teacher clicks to freeze the action.)*

The Teacher: Not very satisfying, is it? Where's the suspense? Where's the tension? And what audience member will want to pay today's ticket prices for a play whose conflict resolves in forty-five seconds? But most importantly, where can you go from here?

> *(The Teacher clicks to unfreeze the action.)*

The Good Samaritan: Gee, you could've hurt yourself.
The Jumper: Gosh, you're right.
The Good Samaritan: Want to grab a brew?
The Jumper: Sure.

> *(The Teacher clicks to freeze the action.)*

The Teacher: Without intense oppositional desires, more commonly known as "conflict," there is no play. When Nora leaves in *A Doll's House,* nobody wants her husband to reply—*(upbeat)* "Call when you get work!" So let's start this scene over—*(The Teacher clicks. The Jumper and Good Samaritan rewind to their initial places.)* maintaining conflict.

(The Teacher clicks again.)

The Jumper: I'm going to jump, and nobody can stop me!

(The Good Samaritan enters quickly.)

The Good Samaritan: Don't!!!!!
The Jumper: Fuck you!
The Good Samaritan (giving an obscene gesture): No, you asshole, fuck you!

(The Teacher clicks and freezes the action.)

The Teacher: Let's rise above profanity, shall we? It alienates conservatives and makes liberals think you're second-rate David Mamet. *(Clicks.)* Rewind . . . And again: *(Clicks.)*
The Jumper: I'm going to jump, and nobody can stop me!

(The Good Samaritan enters quickly.)

The Good Samaritan: Don't!!!!!
The Jumper: Why not?!!!

(The Teacher clicks.)

The Teacher: Oooo, you can just feel the suspense rising now, can't you?

(The Teacher clicks again.)

The Good Samaritan: Because suicide is a sin!

(The Teacher clicks.)

The Teacher: Big deal. Theatre is written by sinners about sinners for sinners. Nobody goes to *Othello* to hear, "Iago, you're so naughty!" Always let the audience form their own judgments. Rewind a bit. *(Clicks.)* Now let's try a different tack. *(Clicks.)*
The Jumper: Why not?!
The Good Samaritan: Because I love you.
The Jumper: I didn't know!

(The Teacher clicks.)

The Teacher: I don't care! Let's see if we can find something less clichéd.

(The Teacher clicks again.)

The Jumper: Why not?!
The Good Samaritan: Because if you jump there, you'll land on my little girl's lemonade stand. And my little girl!

(The Jumper looks over the ledge and moves over two feet.)

The Jumper: Is this better?

(The Teacher clicks.)

The Teacher: Now what have we gained? Be wary of minor obstacles. Unless, of course, you need to fill time. Again.

(The Teacher clicks again.)

The Jumper: Why not?!

The Good Samaritan: Because life is worth living.

The Jumper: Mine isn't!

(*The Teacher clicks.*)

The Teacher: Excellent. We don't just have a plot anymore, we have a theme. Theme, the difference between entertainment and art. No theme, add a car chase and sell it to the movies. But with theme, you have the potential to create something meaningful, something memorable, something college students can write term papers about. So let's rewind a bit and see where this thematically rich drama goes now.

(*The Teacher clicks to rewind and clicks again to resume.*)

The Good Samaritan: Because life is worth living!

The Jumper: Mine isn't!

The Good Samaritan: Gosh. Tell me all about it.

(*The Teacher clicks.*)

The Teacher: Some expositional subtlety, please.

(*The Teacher clicks again.*)

The Good Samaritan: Because life is worth living!

The Jumper: Mine isn't!

The Good Samaritan: Are you sure?

(*The Teacher clicks.*)

The Teacher: Better.

(*The Teacher clicks again.*)

The Jumper: Yes, I'm sure. I'm broke, I have no friends, and I see no reason to continue.

The Good Samaritan: Look, so you're broke and friendless. All experiences are transient. Detach, as the Buddha once did.

(*The Teacher clicks.*)

The Teacher: Of all the world's great religions, Buddhism is the least entertaining. Let's try again.

(*The Teacher clicks again.*)

The Good Samaritan: So you're broke and you're friendless. Why not try Prozac?

(*The Teacher clicks.*)

The Teacher: The popularity and effectiveness of modern antidepressants is one of the great challenges of contemporary dramaturgy. We no more want Willy Loman to solve his problems with Prozac than we want Stanley and Stella Kowalski to get air-conditioning. How can today's playwright deal with today's medicinal deus ex machinas? Let's see.

(*The Teacher clicks again.*)

The Jumper: I tried Prozac once, and it made my mouth really dry.

(*The Teacher clicks.*)

The Teacher: Not great, but we'll let it slide.

> (*The Teacher clicks again.*)

The Good Samaritan: Let me help you.
The Jumper: It's too late.
The Good Samaritan: No, it's not.
The Jumper: You don't understand. I haven't told you the worst.

> (*The Teacher clicks.*)

The Teacher: Fictional characters are rarely straightforward.

> (*The Teacher clicks again.*)

The Jumper: You see, until a few weeks ago, I was in love. Deep love. True love. I was involved with two of the most wonderful gals in the world. One was sexy, rich, generous and caring. The other was streetwise, daring and even sexier. Between the two of them, I had everything. Then they found out about each other, and they both dumped me. Not just one, but both.

> (*The Teacher clicks.*)

The Teacher: Excellent playwriting. Here's a heartbreaking situation with which we can all identify. Maybe not in the specifics, but in the universal experience of rejection.

> (*The Teacher clicks again.*)

The Good Samaritan: At least you've had two exciting affairs. I haven't gotten laid in a year.

> (*The Teacher clicks.*)

The Teacher: A superb response. Another situation with which, um, well, we've all had friends who've had that problem.

> (*The Teacher clicks again.*)

The Jumper: So what are you telling me? That life can get *worse*? That's supposed to get me off this ledge?
The Good Samaritan: Hey, I'm just trying to help!
The Jumper: Well, you're doing a lousy job.
The Good Samaritan: At least I've got some money in the bank!
The Jumper: You've also got rocks in your head!

> (*The Teacher clicks.*)

The Teacher: A common beginner's mistake. Two characters in hostile disagreement isn't conflict, it's just bickering. We don't go to the theatre to hear petty, puerile antagonism; that's why we have families. Let's hope this goes somewhere interesting, or I'll have to rewind.

> (*The Teacher clicks again.*)

The Jumper: You've only got money in the bank because you're cheap.
The Good Samaritan: I am not.
The Jumper: Well, you certainly dress like you are.
The Teacher: Now this is really degenerating.

> (*The Teacher clicks, but the action continues.*)

The Good Samaritan: Listen, you stupid twerp —
The Jumper: At least I'm a twerp with a decent sex life.
The Good Samaritan: And if it was decent for *them,* maybe you'd still have a sex life.

(*The Teacher continues to click, but the action continues.*)

The Teacher (as the action continues): Now stop it . . . Stop it! . . . Stop it!! *(Etc.)*

(*Shouting above The Teacher's "Stop it"s, which they ignore:*)

The Jumper: Loser!
The Good Samaritan: Pervert!
The Jumper: Cheapskate!
The Good Samaritan: Cretin!
The Jumper: Asshole!
The Good Samaritan: Imbecile!
The Jumper: Shithead!
The Teacher (clicking in vain): Stop it!!!!

(*The Good Samaritan takes out a clicker and freezes The Teacher.*)

The Good Samaritan: Notice how organically the teacher's frustration has increased. What began as a minor irritation became unbearable when the human desire to control was thwarted.

(*The Good Samaritan clicks again.*)

The Teacher: What are you doing?! I hold the clicker around here. How dare —

(*The Good Samaritan clicks. The Teacher freezes.*)

The Good Samaritan: See how frustration becomes "anger"? Although the real life stakes are minor, the character's emotional investment is intense. That's good playwriting.

(*The Good Samaritan clicks again.*)

The Teacher: Stop that. What do you think this is, a Pirandello° play?
The Good Samaritan: Well, how do you think *we* feel? We can't say more than two lines without being interrupted by your self-important pronouncements. How'd you like it if I did that to you?
The Teacher: You have no dra—(*The Good Samaritan clicks and stops/starts The Teacher during the following:*) matically vi—able rea—son to inter—rupt me. Damn it, will you get back in the play?
The Good Samaritan: No, and you can't make me!

(*The Good Samaritan clicks at The Teacher, who dodges the clicker.*)

The Teacher: Aha, missed. You superficial stereotype!

(*The Teacher clicks at The Good Samaritan and vice versa during the following, both successfully dodging the other.*)

The Good Samaritan: Control freak!
The Teacher: Cliché!

Luigi Pirandello (1867–1936): Italian playwright famous for exploring illusion and reality in his plays.

The Good Samaritan: Semi-intellectual!

The Teacher: Contrivance!

The Good Samaritan: Academic tapeworm!

The Teacher: First draft mistake!

(*The Jumper, who has been watching this, takes out a gun and shoots it into the air.*)

The Jumper: Hey!!! I'm the one with the problem. This play's supposed to be about me.

The Good Samaritan: Tough. The well-made play died with Ibsen.

The Teacher (to The Good Samaritan): Damn it, get back into the play!

The Good Samaritan: Don't tell me what to do. Ever since I was a kid, everyone's told me how I'm supposed to behave. When I was five, my mom sent me to my room (*The Teacher starts clicking manically at The Good Samaritan.*) four thousand times because I wouldn't be the kid she wanted me —

The Teacher: This monologue is not justified!

The Good Samaritan: Tough shit, it's my life!

The Teacher: It's bad drama!

The Good Samaritan: I'll show you bad drama!

(*The Good Samaritan and The Teacher begin to fight.*)

The Jumper: Stop it! Come on, stop it, you're pulling focus.

The Teacher: Butt out!

(*The Jumper tries to break up the fight.*)

The Jumper: Come on, guys, cool it!

The Good Samaritan: Get away from us!

The Jumper: Just stop it!

The Good Samaritan: Leave us alone!

(*The three of them are in a tight cluster. We hear a gunshot. The Teacher pulls away. There's blood on The Teacher's chest.*)

The Teacher: I just got tenure.

(*The Teacher collapses.*)

The Good Samaritan: Oh my God.

The Jumper: He's dead.

(*The Good Samaritan looks at The Jumper.*)

The Good Samaritan: How horrible. Is that good playwriting or bad playwriting?

The Jumper: I, I don't know. It just happened.

(*The Good Samaritan and The Jumper look at The Teacher.*)

The Jumper and The Good Samaritan (simultaneously): Hmmmmmmm.

(*The Good Samaritan and The Jumper begin to exit.*)

The Good Samaritan: Gee, you could've hurt yourself.

The Jumper: Gosh, you're right.

The Good Samaritan: Want to grab a brew?

The Jumper: Sure.

(*The Teacher comes to life for a moment, clicks into the air and: Blackout.*)

CONSIDERATIONS FOR CRITICAL THINKING AND WRITING

1. FIRST RESPONSE. Comment on Orloff's statement that his purpose in *Playwriting 101* was to satirize dramatic clichés to make an "original play." Explain why you think he was or was not successful.

2. Why do you think the stage directions call for the Jumper and Good Samaritan to be of the same sex?

3. What do you learn from the Teacher about developing conflict and suspense?

4. What is the conflict in the play? Is there a resolution?

5. Describe the theme. Is it implicit or explicitly stated?

6. The Good Samaritan asks at the end, "Is that good playwriting or bad playwriting?" (p. 1819). What do you think?

CONNECTIONS TO OTHER SELECTIONS

1. Discuss *Playwriting 101* and Christopher Durang's *Wanda's Visit* (p. 1785) as metaplays, or plays about plays.

2. The Teacher claims that "When [Ibsen's] Nora leaves in *A Doll's House* [p. 1709], nobody wants her husband to reply — *(upbeat)* 'Call when you get work!'" Why not?

A Collection
of Plays

52

Plays for Further Reading

My plays are about love, honor, duty, betrayal — things humans have written about since the beginning of time.
— AUGUST WILSON

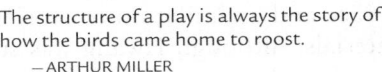

The structure of a play is always the story of how the birds came home to roost.
— ARTHUR MILLER

Trying to Find Chinatown

Born in Los Angeles, David Henry Hwang is the son of immigrant Chinese American parents; his father worked as a banker, and his mother was a professor of piano. Educated at Stanford University, from which he earned his B.A. in English in 1979, he became interested in theater after attending plays at the American Conservatory in San Francisco. His marginal interest in a law career quickly gave way to his involvement in the engaging world of live theater. By his senior year, he had written and produced his first play, *FOB* (an acronym for "fresh off the boat"), which marked the beginning of a meteoric rise as a playwright. After a brief stint as a writing teacher at a Menlo Park high school, Hwang attended the Yale University School of Drama from 1980 to 1981. Although he didn't stay to complete a degree, he studied theater history before leaving for New York City, where he thought the professional theater would provide a richer education than the student workshops at Yale.

© Michal Daniel.

In New York Hwang's work received a warm reception. In 1980 an off-Broadway production of *FOB* won an Obie Award for the best new play of the season. The play incorporates many of Hwang's characteristic concerns as a playwright. Growing up in California as a Chinese American made him politically conscious during his college years in the late 1970s; this interest in his Chinese roots is evident in the central conflicts of *FOB*, which focuses on a Chinese immigrant's relationship with two Chinese American students he meets in Los Angeles. The immigrant quickly learns that he is expected to abandon much of his Chinese identity if he is to fit into mainstream American culture. Chinese American life is also the focus of *The Dance and the Railroad* and *Family Devotions,* both produced off-Broadway in 1981. Hwang's early plays are populated with Chinese Americans attempting to find the center of their own lives as they seesaw between the conventions, traditions, and values of East and West.

Hwang's next two dramas, produced in 1983, consist of two one-act plays set in Japan. Together they are titled *Sound and Beauty,* but each has its own title—*The House of Sleeping Beauties* and *The Sound of a Voice.* In these plays Hwang moves away from tales of Chinese American immigrants and themes of race and assimilation to stories about tragic love based on Japanese materials. Although Hwang was successful in having additional plays produced in the mid-1980s and won prestigious fellowships from the Guggenheim Foundation and the National Endowment for the Arts, it was not until 1988, when *M. Butterfly*—a complex treatment of social, political, racial, cultural, and sexual issues—was produced on Broadway, that he achieved astonishing commercial success as well as widespread acclaim. His awards for this play include the Outer Critics Circle Award for best Broadway play, the Drama Desk Award for best new play, the John Gassner Award for best American play, and the Tony Award for best play of the year. By the end of 1988, Hwang was regarded by many critics as the most talented young playwright in the United States. *Trying to Find Chinatown* is a brief but complicated confrontation between two young men who argue about racial identity in unexpected ways. Hwang's strategy is to challenge the polemical stereotyping that often passes for discussions of ethnic and cultural heritage in the United States.

DAVID HENRY HWANG (B. 1957)
Trying to Find Chinatown   *1996*

CHARACTERS

Benjamin, Caucasian male, early twenties.
Ronnie, Asian-American male, mid-twenties.

TIME AND PLACE   A street corner on the Lower East Side, New York City. The present.
NOTE ON MUSIC   Obviously, it would be foolish to require that the actor portraying Ronnie perform the specified violin music live. The score of this play can be played on tape over the house speakers, and the actor can feign playing the violin using a bow treated with soap. However, in order to effect a convincing illusion, it is desirable that the actor possess some familiarity with the violin or another stringed instrument.

> *Darkness. Over the house speakers, sound fades in: Hendrix-like virtuoso rock 'n' roll riffs — heavy feedback, distortion, phase shifting, wah-wah — amplified over a tiny Fender pug-nose.*

> *Lights fade up to reveal that the music's being played over a solid-body electric violin by Ronnie, a Chinese-American male in his mid-twenties; he is dressed in retro-'60s clothing and has a few requisite '90s body mutilations. He's playing on a sidewalk for money, his violin case open before him; change and a few stray bills have been left by previous passersby.*
> *Benjamin enters; he's in his early twenties, blond, blue-eyed, a Midwestern tourist in the big city. He holds a scrap of paper in his hands, scanning street signs for an address. He pauses before Ronnie, listens for a while. With a truly bravura run, Ronnie concludes the number and falls to his knees, gasping. Benjamin applauds.*

Benjamin: Good. That was really great. *(Pause)* I didn't . . . I mean, a fiddle . . . I mean, I'd heard them at square dances, on country stations and all, but I never . . . wow, this must really be New York City!

> *(Benjamin applauds, starts to walk on. Still on his knees, Ronnie clears his throat loudly.)*

Oh, I . . . you're not just doing this for your health, right?

> *(Benjamin reaches in his pocket, pulls out a couple of coins. Ronnie clears his throat again.)*

Look, I'm not a millionaire, I'm just . . .

> *(Benjamin pulls out his wallet, removes a dollar bill. Ronnie nods his head and gestures toward the violin case as he takes out a pack of cigarettes, lights one.)*

Ronnie: And don't call it a "fiddle," OK?
Benjamin: Oh. Well, I didn't mean to —
Ronnie: You sound like a wuss. A hick. A dipshit.
Benjamin: It just slipped out. I didn't really —
Ronnie: If this was a fiddle, I'd be sitting here with a cob pipe, stomping my cowboy boots and kicking up hay. Then I'd go home and fuck my cousin.
Benjamin: Oh! Well, I don't really think —

Ronnie: Do you see a cob pipe? Am I fucking my cousin?

Benjamin: Well, no, not at the moment, but—

Ronnie: All right. Then this is a violin, now you give me your money, and I ignore the insult. Herein endeth the lesson.

(*Pause.*)

Benjamin: Look, a dollar's more than I've ever given to a . . . to someone asking for money.

Ronnie: Yeah, well, this is New York. Welcome to the cost of living.

Benjamin: What I mean is, maybe in exchange, you could help me—?

Ronnie: Jesus Christ! Do you see a sign around my neck reading "Big Apple Fucking Tourist Bureau"?

Benjamin: I'm just looking for an address, I don't think it's far from here, maybe you could . . . ?

(*Benjamin holds out his scrap of paper, Ronnie snatches it away.*)

Ronnie: You're lucky I'm such a goddamn softy. (*He looks at the paper*) Oh, fuck you. Just suck my dick, you and the cousin you rode in on.

Benjamin: I don't get it! What are you—?

Ronnie: Eat me. You know exactly what I—

Benjamin: I'm just asking for a little—

Ronnie: "13 Doyers Street"? Like you don't know where that is?

Benjamin: Of course I don't know! That's why I'm asking—

Ronnie: C'mon, you trailer-park refugee. You don't know that's Chinatown?

Benjamin: Sure I know that's Chinatown.

Ronnie: I know you know that's Chinatown.

Benjamin: So? That doesn't mean I know where Chinatown—

Ronnie: So why is it that you picked *me*, of all the street musicians in the city—to point you in the direction of Chinatown? Lemme guess—is it the earring? No, I don't think so. The Hendrix riffs? Guess again, you fucking moron.

Benjamin: Now, wait a minute. I see what you're—

Ronnie: What are you gonna ask me next? Where you can find the best dim sum in the city? Whether I can direct you to a genuine opium den? Or do I happen to know how you can meet Miss Saigon for a night of nookie-nookie followed by a good old-fashioned ritual suicide? Now, get your white ass off my sidewalk. One dollar doesn't even begin to make up for all this aggravation. Why don't you go back home and race bullfrogs, or whatever it is you do for—?

Benjamin: Brother, I can absolutely relate to your anger. Righteous rage, I suppose, would be a more appropriate term. To be marginalized, as we are, by a white racist patriarchy, to the point where the accomplishments of our people are obliterated from the history books, this is cultural genocide of the first order, leading to the fact that you must do battle with all of Euro-America's emasculating and brutal stereotypes of Asians—the opium den, the sexual objectification of the Asian female, the exoticized image of a tourist's Chinatown which ignores the exploitation of workers, the failure to unionize, the high rate of mental illness and tuberculosis—against these, each day, you rage, no, not as a victim, but as a survivor, yes, brother, a glorious warrior survivor!

(*Silence.*)

Ronnie: Say what?

Benjamin: So, I hope you can see that my request is not—

Ronnie: Wait, wait.

Benjamin: —motivated by the sorts of racist assumptions—

Ronnie: But, but where . . . how did you learn all that?

Benjamin: All what?

Ronnie: All that—you know—oppression stuff—tuberculosis . . .

Benjamin: It's statistically irrefutable. TB occurs in the community at a rate—

Ronnie: Where did *you* learn it?

Benjamin: I took Asian-American studies. In college.

Ronnie: Where did you go to college?

Benjamin: University of Wisconsin. Madison.

Ronnie: Madison, Wisconsin?

Benjamin: That's not where the bridges are, by the way.

Ronnie: Huh? Oh, right . . .

Benjamin: You wouldn't believe the number of people who—

Ronnie: They have Asian-American studies in Madison, Wisconsin? Since when?

Benjamin: Since the last Third World Unity hunger strike. *(Pause)* Why do you look so surprised? We're down.

Ronnie: I dunno. It just never occurred to me, the idea of Asian students in the Midwest going on a hunger strike.

Benjamin: Well, a lot of them had midterms that week, so they fasted in shifts. *(Pause)* The administration never figured it out. The Asian students put that "They all look alike" stereotype to good use.

Ronnie: OK, so they got Asian-American studies. That still doesn't explain—

Benjamin: What?

Ronnie: Well . . . what *you* were doing taking it?

Benjamin: Just like everyone else. I wanted to explore my roots. And, you know, the history of oppression which is my legacy. After a lifetime of assimilation, I wanted to find out who I really am.

(*Pause.*)

Ronnie: And did you?

Benjamin: Sure. I learned to take pride in my ancestors who built the railroads, my Popo who would make me a hot bowl of jok with thousand-day-old eggs when the white kids chased me home yelling, "Gook! Chink! Slant-eyes!"

Ronnie: OK, OK, that's enough!

Benjamin: Painful to listen to, isn't it?

Ronnie: I don't know what kind of bullshit ethnic studies program they're running over in Wuss-consin, but did they bother to teach you that in order to find your Asian "roots," it's a good idea to first be Asian?

(*Pause.*)

Benjamin: Are you speaking metaphorically?

Ronnie: No! Literally! Look at your skin!

Benjamin: You know, it's very stereotypical to think that all Asian skin tones conform to a single hue.

Ronnie: You're white! Is this some kind of redneck joke or something? Am I the first person in the world to tell you this?

Benjamin: Oh! Oh! Oh!

Ronnie: I know real Asians are scarce in the Midwest, but . . . Jesus!

Benjamin: No, of course, I . . . I see where your misunderstanding arises.

Ronnie: Yeah. It's called, "You white."

Benjamin: It's just that—in my hometown of Tribune, Kansas, and then at school—see, everyone knows me—so this sort of thing never comes up. *(He offers his hand)* Benjamin Wong. I forget that a society wedded to racial constructs constantly forces me to explain my very existence.

Ronnie: Ronnie Chang. Otherwise known as "The Bow Man."

Benjamin: You see, I was adopted by Chinese-American parents at birth. So, clearly, I'm an Asian-American—

Ronnie: Even though you're blond and blue-eyed.

Benjamin: Well, you can't judge my race by my genetic heritage alone.

Ronnie: If genes don't determine race, what does?

Benjamin: Perhaps you'd prefer that I continue in denial, masquerading as a white man?

Ronnie: You can't just wake up and say, "Gee, I *feel* black today."

Benjamin: Brother, I'm just trying to find what you've already got.

Ronnie: What do I got?

Benjamin: A home. With your people. Picketing with the laundry workers. Taking refuge from the daily slights against your masculinity in the noble image of Gwan Gung.

Ronnie: Gwan who?

Benjamin: C'mon—the Chinese god of warriors and—what do you take me for? There're altars to him up all over the community.

Ronnie: I dunno what community you're talking about, but it's sure as hell not mine.

(Pause.)

Benjamin: What do you mean?

Ronnie: I mean, if you wanna call Chinatown *your* community, OK, knock yourself out, learn to use chopsticks, big deal. Go ahead, try and find your "roots" in some dim sum parlor with headless ducks hanging in the window. Those places don't tell you a thing about who *I* am.

Benjamin: Oh, I get it.

Ronnie: You get what?

Benjamin: You're one of those self-hating, *assimilated* Chinese-Americans, aren't you?

Ronnie: Oh, Jesus.

Benjamin: You probably call yourself "Oriental," huh? Look, maybe I can help you. I have some books I can—

Ronnie: Hey, I read all those Asian identity books when you were still slathering on industrial-strength sunblock. *(Pause)* Sure, I'm Chinese. But folks like you act like that means something. Like, all of a sudden, you know who I am. You think identity's that simple? That you can wrap it all up in a neat package and say, "I have ethnicity, therefore I am"? All you fucking ethnic fundamentalists. Always settling for easy answers. You say you're looking for identity, but you can't begin to face the real mysteries of the search. So instead, you go skin-deep, and call it a day. *(Pause. He turns away from Benjamin and starts to play his violin—slow and bluesy.)*

Benjamin: So what are you? "Just a human being"? That's like saying you *have* no identity. If you asked me to describe my dog, I'd say more than, "He's just a dog."

Ronnie: What—you think if I deny the importance of my race, I'm nobody? There're worlds out there, worlds you haven't even begun to understand. Open your eyes. Hear with your ears.

(Ronnie holds his violin at chest level, but does not attempt to play during the following monologue. As he speaks, rock and jazz violin tracks fade in and out over the house speakers, bringing to life the styles of music he describes.)

I concede—it was called a fiddle long ago—but that was even before the birth of jazz. When the hollering in the fields, the rank injustice of human bondage, the struggle of God's children against the plagues of the devil's white man, when all these boiled up into that bittersweet brew, called by later generations, the blues. That's when fiddlers like Son Sims held their chin rests at their chests, and sawed away like the hillbillies still do today. And with the coming of ragtime appeared the pioneer Stuff Smith, who sang as he stroked the catgut, with his raspy, Louis Armstrong-voice—gruff and sweet like the timber of horsehair riding south below the fingerboard—and who finally sailed for Europe to find ears that would hear. Europe—where Stephane Grappelli initiated a magical French violin, to be passed from generation to generation—first he, to Jean-Luc Ponty, then Ponty to Didier Lockwood. Listening to Grappelli play "A Nightingale Sang in Berkeley Square" is to understand not only the song of birds, but also how they learn to fly, fall in love on the wing, and finally falter one day, to wait for darkness beneath a London street lamp. And Ponty—he showed how the modern violin man can accompany the shadow of his own lead lines, which cascade, one over another, into some nether world beyond the range of human hearing. Joe Venuti. Noel Pointer. Sven Asmussen. Even the Kronos Quartet, with their arrangement of "Purple Haze." Now, tell me, could any legacy be more rich, more crowded with mythology and heroes to inspire pride? What can I say if the banging of a gong or the clinking of a pickax on the Transcontinental Railroad fails to move me even as much as one note, played through a violin MIDI controller by Michael Urbaniak? *(He puts his violin to his chin, begins to play a jazz composition of his own invention)* Does it have to sound like Chinese opera before people like you decide I know who I am?

(Benjamin stands for a long moment, listening to Ronnie play. Then, he drops his dollar into the case, turns and exits right. Ronnie continues to play a long moment. Then Benjamin enters downstage left, illuminated in his own spotlight. He sits on the floor of the stage, his feet dangling off the lip. As he speaks, Ronnie continues playing his tune, which becomes underscoring for Benjamin's monologue. As the music continues, does it slowly begin to reflect the influence of Chinese music?)

Benjamin: When I finally found Doyers Street, I scanned the buildings for Number 13. Walking down an alley where the scent of freshly steamed char siu bao lingered in the air, I felt immediately that I had entered a world where all things were finally familiar. *(Pause)* An old woman bumped me with her shopping bag—screaming to her friend in Cantonese, though they walked no more than a few inches apart. Another man—shouting to a vendor in Sze-Yup. A youth, in white undershirt, perhaps a recent newcomer, bargaining with a grocer in Hokkien. I walked through this ocean of dialects, breathing in the richness with deep gulps, exhilarated by the energy this symphony brought to my step. And when I finally saw the number 13, I nearly wept at my good fortune. An old tenement, paint peeling, inside walls no doubt thick with a century of grease and broken dreams—and yet, to me, a temple—the house where my father was born. I suddenly saw it all: Gung Gung, coming home from his sixteen-hour days pressing shirts he could never afford to own, bringing with him candies for my father, each sweet wrapped in the hope of a better life. When my father left the ghetto, he swore he would never return. But he had, this day, in the thoughts and memories of his son, just six months after his death. And as I sat on the stoop, I pulled a hua-moi° from my pocket, sucked on it, and felt his spirit returning. To this place where his ghost, and the dutiful hearts of all his descendants, would always call home. *(He listens for a long moment)* And I felt an ache in my heart for all those lost souls, denied this most important of revelations: to know who they truly are.

(Benjamin sucks his salted plum and listens to the sounds around him. Ronnie continues to play. The two remain oblivious of one another. Lights fade slowly to black.)

End of play

Hua-moi: A dry, sour plum that is a Cantonese specialty food.

CONNECTIONS TO OTHER SELECTIONS

1. How do you think Ronnie in *Trying to Find Chinatown* would assess August Wilson's treatment of race in *Fences* (p. 1988)?
2. Discuss the perspective offered on white attitudes toward race in Hwang's play and in Nilaja Sun's *No Child . . .* (p. 1969).

Real Women Have Curves

Born in San Potosi, Mexico, Josefina Lopez's family moved to East Los Angeles when she was five years old, where they lived as undocumented immigrants. Her experiences as an undocumented Latina living close to Hollywood up through her late teens led her to write her first play, *Simply Maria, Or, the American Dream,* at the age of seventeen. Within two years she completed *Real Women Have Curves,* which describes her work in a sewing factory alongside women coping with their immigration status, romances, marriage, ambitions, and pleasure in each

Chelsea Lauren/WireImage.

other's company. Five years later, Lopez co-authored a screenplay version that was honored at the 2002 Sundance Film Festival and became a widely released popular film. Her own early ambitions were realized when she achieved residence status and graduated from UCLA with an M.F.A. Since then she has written a number of plays and screenplays. Lopez's most recent work is *Hungry Woman of Paris* (2009), a novel about a Mexican American journalist living on her own in Paris.

Real Women Have Curves features five full-figured women whose financial circumstances are meager but who share a hearty appetite for life and laughter.

Josefina Lopez (b. 1969)

Real Women Have Curves   *1988*

Playwright's Notes

When I was very young my best friend and I were walking to the corner store. My parents had warned me not to tell anyone I didn't have "papers" and to be careful walking the streets. On the way to the store we saw **"la migra"** (INS/immigration/Border Patrol). I quickly turned to my friend and tried to "act white." I spoke in English and talked about Jordache jeans and Barbie dolls hoping no one would suspect us. When I finally got my legal residence card, I remembered this incident knowing that I would never have to hide and be afraid again. I also laughed at my *naivete* and fear because what I had thought was **la migra** was only the L.A. Police Meter Maid.

In 1987 the Simpson-Rodino Amnesty Law, designed to stop the influx of undocumented people entering the country, granted thousands of undocumented people living in the U.S. since 1982 legal residency. This was an opportunity of a lifetime. However, thousands, not trusting the government, hesitated to apply, fearing this was a scheme to deport them. They, like me, couldn't believe that after hiding and being persecuted for so long they were finally going to have the freedom to live and work in this country.

I got my residence card soon after I graduated from high school and was then able to apply to college. I had been accepted to New York University, but I had to wait a year to be eligible for financial aid. During this year I worked at McDonald's, but I hated it. Then, desperate for a new job, I asked my sister to let me work at her tiny sewing factory. I worked there for five months and my experiences at the factory served as inspiration for *Real Women Have Curves*. At the factory there were a few Latina women, all older than me. They liked working for my sister because she wasn't stingy. We spent so much time together working, sweating and laughing, that we bonded. I remember feeling blessed that I was a woman because male bonding could never compare with what happens when women work together. We had something special and I wanted to show the world.

In the U.S. undocumented people are referred to as "illegal aliens" which conjures up in our minds the image of extraterrestrial beings who are not human, who do not bleed when they're cut, who do not cry when they feel pain, who do not have fears, dreams and hopes . . . Undocumented people have been used as scapegoats for so many of the problems in the U.S., from drugs and violence, to the economy. I hope that someday this country recognizes the very important contributions of undocumented people and remembers that they too came to this country in search of a better life.

Josefina Lopez

Los Angeles

March, 1992

CHARACTERS

Ana, 18, plump and pretty, sister of Estela, daughter of Carmen. She is a recent high school graduate and a young feminist

Estela, 24, plump, plain-looking, owner of the "Garcia Sewing Factory"

Carmen, 48, a short, large woman, mother of Ana and Estela. She has a talent for storytelling

Pancha, 32, a huge woman who is very mellow in her ways, but quick with her tongue

Rosalí, 29, only a bit plump in comparison to the rest of the women. She is sweet and easygoing

SETTING: A tiny sewing factory in East Los Angeles.

TIME: The first week of September 1987.

NOTE: *Words in Spanish are in* **bold** *print. You will find a glossary and Spanish terms in the back of the play.*

SYNOPSIS OF SCENES

ACT ONE

Scene 1: Monday morning, September 7, 1987, about 7:00 A.M.

Scene 2: A few hours later, about 11:30 A.M.

Scene 3: A few hours later, about 3:45 P.M.

Scene 4: The following day, about 7:10 A.M.

Scene 5: Later the same day. Late afternoon.

ACT TWO

Scene 1: Wednesday, September 9th, about 8:15 A.M.

Scene 2: Thursday, September 10th, about 2:00 A.M.

Scene 3: Same day, about 2:00 P.M.

Scene 4: Friday, September 11th, about 2:25 P.M.

ACT ONE

SCENE ONE

AT RISE: The stage becomes visible. The clock on the wall shows it is 6:59 A.M. Keys are heard outside the door. The door opens. Ana and Carmen enter. Ana drags herself in, goes directly to the electricity box and switches it on. Automatically all the machines "hummmm" loudly. The lights turn on at different times. The radio also blasts on with a song in Spanish. Carmen quickly turns off the radio. She puts her lunch on the table. Ana slumps on a machine. Carmen then gets a broom and uses it to get a mousetrap from underneath the table. She prays that today will be the day she caught the mouse. She sees the mousetrap empty and is very disappointed.

Carmen: **¡Pinche rata!** I'll get you. (*Carmen returns the broom. She takes two dollars from her purse, approaches Ana and presents them to her.*) **Ten.** Go to the bakery.

Ana: No. I want to go back to sleep!

Carmen: **¡Huevona!** If we don't help your sister who else is going to? She already works all hours of the night trying to finish the dresses. **Por fin** she's doing something productive with her life.

Ana: I know I'm trying to be supportive, **ayy!** I don't want to go to the bakery. I don't want any bread.

Carmen: That's good, at least you won't get fatter.

Ana: **¡Amá!**

Carmen: I only tell you for your own good. **Bueno,** I'll go get the bread myself, but you better not get any when I bring it. (*Carmen walks to the door.*) Ana don't forget to close the doors. This street is full of winos and drug addicts. And don't you open the door to any strangers!

Ana: Yeah, yeah, I know! I'm not a kid. (*Ana locks both doors with a key. She goes toward the toilet and turns on the water in the sink. Ana splashes water on her face to awaken. She sticks her hand behind the toilet seat and gets out a notebook and a pen. Spotlight on Ana. She sits and writes the following:*) Monday, September 7, 1987 . . . I don't want to be here! I only come because my mother practically drags me out of bed and into the car and into the factory. She pounds on the . . . No . . . (*Scratches "pounds."*) She knocks on . . . No . . . (*She scratches "knocks."*) She pounds on the garage wall, and since I think it's an earthquake, I run out. Then she catches me and I become her prisoner . . . Is it selfish of me not to want to wake up every morning at 6:30 A.M., Saturdays included, to come work here for 67 dollars a week? Oh, but such is the life of a Chicana in the garment industry. Cheap labor . . . I've been trying to hint to my sister for a raise, but she says I don't work fast enough for her to pay me minimum wage . . . The weeks get longer and I can't believe I've ended up here. I just graduated from high school . . . Most of my friends are in college . . . It's as if I'm going backwards. I'm doing the work that mostly illegal aliens do . . . (*Scratches "illegal aliens."*) No, "undocumented workers" . . . or else it sounds like these people come from Mars . . . Soon I will have my "Temporary Residence Card," then after two years, my green card . . . I'm happy to finally be legal, but I thought things would be different . . . What I really want to do is write . . .

Carmen (off, interrupting): Ana, open the door! (*Carmen pounds on the door outside. Ana quickly puts her writing away and goes to open the door.*) Hurry up! There's a wino following me! (*Ana gets the keys and unlocks both doors.*) Hurry! He's been following me from the bakery.

(*Ana opens the first door. Carmen is behind the bar door and is impatiently waiting for Ana to open it. Ana opens the door. Carmen hurries in nervously. Ana quickly shuts the doors. Ana looks out the window.*)

Ana: **Amá,** that's not a wino, it's an "Alelullah"!

Carmen: But he was following me!

Ana: I know, those witnesses don't give up. *(Carmen puts the bag of bread on the table. She fills a small pot with water and puts it on the little hot plate to boil the water for coffee.)*

Carmen: **Pos yo ya no veo.** I can't see a thing. *(Carmen goes to her purse and takes out her glasses. She puts them on. She looks out the window and sees no one.)* I should retire and be an **abuelita** by now, taking care of grandchildren . . . I don't know why I work, I have arthritis in my hands, I'm losing my sight from all this sewing, and this arm, I can hardly move it anymore . . . *(Ana does not pay attention as usual.)*

Ana (unsympathetically): Yeah, **Amá.**

Carmen: I wonder where's Estela. She should have been here by now.

Ana: I thought she left the house early.

(Pancha appears behind the bar door.)

Pancha: I don't know why you bother, all he cares about is his car.

Carmen: **Vénganse,** I think the water is ready. *(The women gather around the table for coffee. Pancha and Carmen grab bread. Estela goes to the bathroom and brushes her hair, puts on lipstick, then she puts on a girdle under her skirt, which she has great trouble getting on, but she is determined. She grabs a deodorant stick and applies it. She also gets a bottle of perfume and sprays it accordingly.)*

Estela: **Aquí por si me abraza.** *(She sprays her wrist.)*

Ana (mocks Estela in front of the women): Here in case he hugs me.

Estela: **Aquí por si me besa.** *(She sprays her neck.)*

Ana: Here in case he kisses me.

Estela: **Y aquí por si se pasa.** *(She sprays under her skirt.)*

Ana: And here in case he . . . you know what. *(The women are by the door and windows looking out. Estela comes out of the bathroom.)*

Rosalí: He's gone.

Carmen: **Sí, ya se fue.**

Estela: No! Are you sure? *(Estela goes toward the door, before she reaches it Carmen shuts the door.)*

Carmen (scared): **¡Dios mio!** *(Carmen quickly takes a drink of her coffee and can hardly breathe afterwards.)*

Estela: **¿Qué? ¿Amá, qué pasa?**

Carmen: I saw a van!

Rosalí: What van?

Carmen: **¡La migra!** *(All the women scatter and hide waiting to be discovered. Then after a few seconds Pancha makes a realization.)*

Pancha: **Pero,** why are we hiding? We're all legal now.

Pancha: **Buenos días, Doña** Carmen. Can you open the door?

Carmen: **Buenos días,** Pancha. **¿Cómo está?**

Pancha: Not too bad.

Carmen: **Que bien.** I brought my **mole** today for all of us.

Pancha: You're so generous, **Doña** Carmen.

Carmen: It was in the 'frigerator for three days, and I thought it was turning green, so I brought it. Why let it go to waste?

Pancha: Is it still good?

Carmen: Of course, I make great **mole.**

(Rosalí appears behind the bar door.)

Rosalí: **Doña** Carmen, the door.

Carmen: It's open, Rosalí. **Buenos días.** How are you?

Rosalí (entering): Okay, like always, **Doña** Carmen.

Carmen: I brought my **mole** for all of us.

Rosalí: Did you? **Ayy, gracias,** but remember I'm on a diet.

Carmen: Just try a small taco, **no te va hacer daño.** Try it.

Rosalí: I'm sure it's delicious, but I'm this close to being a size seven.

Carmen: **Sí.** You're looking thinner now. How are you doing it?

Rosalí: I'm on a secret diet . . . It's from the Orient.

Carmen: A-ha . . . It's true, those Japanese women are always skinny. **Pues,** give
me your secret, Rosalí. Maybe this way I can lose this ball of fat! *(She
squeezes her stomach.)* **No mas mira que paresco.** You can't even see my
waist anymore. But you know what it really is. It's just water. After having
so many babies I just stopped getting rid of the water. It's as if I'm clogged.
(Rosalí and Ana laugh.)

Rosalí: **Sí, Doña** Carmen.

Ana: Yeah, sure, **Amá!**

Carmen: **¿Y tu?** Why do you laugh? You're getting there yourself. When I was
your age I wasn't as fat as you. And look at your **chichis.**

Ana: **¡Amá!**

Carmen (grabs Ana's breasts as if weighing them): They must weigh five pounds each.

Ana: **Amá,** don't touch me like that!

Rosalí: Where's Estela?

Carmen: We don't know. Ana, I think you better call home now and check if
she's there.

Rosalí: Because her torment is outside washing his car.

All: He is?

*(From under a large blanket on the floor Estela jumps out. The women are startled
and scream, but they quickly join her as she runs to the window to spy on her
Tormento.)*

Estela: **¡Ayy que buenote!** He's so cute.

Ana: Don't exaggerate.

Estela: **¡Mi Tormento! ¡O mi Tormento!**

Carmen: We thought you left home early.

Estela: No, I worked so late last night I decided to sleep here.

Carmen: Then why didn't you tell us when—

Estela: I heard you come in, but I wanted to listen in on your **chisme** about
me, **Amá.**

Carmen: Me? I don't gossip!

Estela: Sure, **Amá** . . . I'm going to the store. *(Estela runs to the mirror.)*

Carmen: **¡Ayy, de veras!** I forget! All those years of being an **ilegal,** I still can't
get used to it.

Pancha: Me too! *(She picks up a piece of bread.)* I think I just lost my appetite.

Rosalí: I'm not scared of it! I used to work in factories and whenever they did a
raid, I'd always sneak out through the bathroom window, **y ya.**

Ana: Last night I heard on the news that **la migra** patrol is planning to raid a
lot of places.

Pancha: They're going to get mean trying to enforce that Amnesty law.

Ana: Thank God, I'm legal. I will never have to lie on applications anymore, except maybe about my weight . . .

Rosalí: **¿Saben qué?** Yesterday I got my first credit card.

Carmen: **¿Pos cómo le hiciste?** How?

Rosalí: I lied on the application and I got an **Americana** Express.

Ana: And now you have two green cards and you never leave home without them. *(Ana laughs her head off, but none of the women get the joke. Ana slowly shuts up.)*

Pancha: **Doña** Carmen, let those men in their van come! Who cares? We're all legal now! *(Pancha goes to the door and opens it all the way. They all smile in relief and pride, then Estela, who has been stuffing her face, finally speaks up.)*

Estela: I'm not. *(Pancha slams the door shut.)*

Everyone: You're not?!!!

Ana: But you went with me to get the fingerprints and the medical examination.

Estela: I didn't send them in.

Rosalí: But you qualify.

Estela: I have a criminal record.

Everyone: No!

Estela: So I won't apply until I clear it.

Carmen: Estela, what did you do?

Pancha: **¿Qué hiciste?**

Estela: Well, actually, I did two things.

Carmen: Two? **¿Y por qué no me habias dicho?** Why is the mother always the last one to know?

Estela: Because one is very embarrassing—

Carmen: **Aver dime, condenada!** What have you done?

Estela: I was arrested for illegal possession of—

Rosalí: Marijuana?!

Pancha: A gun?!

Estela: A lobster.

Everyone: No!

Estela: Out of season!

Carmen: **¡Mentirosa!**

Women: You're kidding!

Estela: A-ha! I'm not lying! I almost got handcuffed and taken to jail. Trying to "abduct" a lobster is taken very seriously in Santa Monica Beach. They wanted me to appear in court and I never did.

Pancha: That's not a serious crime; **¿de qué te apuras?** Why worry?

Carmen (not amused): That was the first crime? You mentioned two.

Estela: I'm being sued for not keeping up with my payments on the machines.

Ana: **Y los** eight thousand dollars you got from your accident settlement weren't enough?

Carmen: But I thought that everything was paid for.

Estela: I used most of it for a down-payment, but I still needed a new steam iron, the over-lock . . . I thought I could make the monthly payments if everything went as planned.

Carmen: **¿Pos qué paso?**

Pancha: What happened?

Estela: You know that we never finish on time. So the Glitz company doesn't pay me until we do.

Rosalí: **Pero** the orders are too big. We need at least two more seamstresses.

Estela: **Pues sí.** But the money they pay me is not enough to hire any more help. So because we get behind, they don't pay, I can't pay you, and I can't pay those pigs that sold me those machines.

Carmen: **Ayyy,** Estela, how much do you owe?

Estela: Two thousand dollars . . .

Carmen: **¡Hora si que estamos bien jodidas!** *(The women sigh hopelessly.)*

Estela: . . . I tried. I sent some money and explained the situation to them two weeks ago, but I got a letter from their lawyer. They're taking me to court . . .

Pancha: So you had money two weeks ago? Hey, hey, you told us you couldn't pay us because you didn't have any money. You had money! Here we are **bien pobres,** I can't even pay for the bus sometimes, and you care more about your machines than us.

Estela: They're going to take everything!

Rosalí: **¡¿Qué?!**

Estela: They're going to reposess everything if I don't pay them. And if I appear in court they'll find out that I don't have any papers.

Ana: Then why don't you apply for Amnesty?

Estela: Because I won't get it if they find out about my lawsuit.

Ana: You don't know that. Estela, you should talk to this lawyer I know.

Estela: Ana, you know I can't afford a lawyer!

Carmen: **Ayy,** Estela, **¡ya ni la friegas!** *(Estela fights the urge to cry.)*

Rosalí: If I had money I'd lend it to you.

Pancha (aside): I wouldn't.

Rosalí (kindly): But I don't have any money because you haven't paid me.

Estela: **Miren,** the Glitz company has promised to pay me for the last two weeks and this week if we get the order in by Friday.

Ana: How much of the order is left?

Estela: About 100 dresses.

Pancha: **N'ombre.** By this Friday? What do they think we are? Machines?

Estela: But they're not that difficult! **Amá,** you're so fast. This would be a cinch for you. All you have to do are the **blusas** on the dresses. Rosalí, the over-lock work is simple. It's a lot, but you're the best at it. And, Pancha, all you have to do is sew the skirts. The skirts are the easiest to sew. Now, Ana, with you doing all the ironing, we'll get it done by Friday. You see if we do little by little at what we do best . . . **¡Andenle!** We can do it. **¿Verá que sí,** Ana?

Ana (uncertain): Sure we can.

Estela: **¿Vera que sí, Amá?**

Carmen: **Pos** we can try.

Rosalí: Estela, we can do it. *(Estela looks to Pancha. Pancha remains quiet. Carmen breaks their stare.)*

Carmen: Wouldn't it be funny if the **migra** came and instead of taking the employees like they usually do, they take the **patrona.** *(The women laugh at the thought.)*

Estela: Don't laugh! It could happen. *(The women become silent.)*

Carmen: **Ayy,** Estela, I'm just kidding. I'm just trying to make you feel better. *(Beat.)*

Rosalí: **Bueno,** let's try to be serious . . . I'll do the zippers.

Estela: Yes, **por favor.** And, Pancha, please do the hems on the skirts.

Pancha: The machine is not working.

Estela: Not again! *(Estela goes to the machine. She fusses around with it trying to make it work. With confidence.)* There. It should be ready. Try it. *(Pancha sits down on a chair and tries the machine. She steps on the pedal and the machine makes an awful noise. Then it shoots off electric sparks and explodes. Pancha quickly gets away from the machine. The women hide under the machines.)*

Women: **¡Ay, ay, ay!**

Estela: Augghh! All this equipment is junk! *(Estela throws a thread spool at the machine and it explodes again.)* I was so stupid to buy this factory! *(Estela fights the urge to cry in frustration. The women stare at her helplessly.)*

Carmen: **Pos no nos queda otra.** Pancha, can you do the hems by hand?

Pancha: **Bueno,** I guess I have to.

Estela: **Gracias** . . . Ana, turn on the iron, I'm going to need you to do the ironing all this week . . . Tell me when the iron gets hot and I'll show you what you have to do.

Carmen: I'll help Rosalí with the zippers.

Estela: No . . . I need you to do the **blusas** on size 7/8.

Carmen: Didn't I already do them?

Estela: No.

Carmen: I guess it was size 13/14 then.

Estela: You couldn't have, because there is no size 13/14 for this dress style, **Amá.**

Carmen: No? . . . **Hoye** did you get any more pink thread from the Glitz?

Estela: Oh, no. I forgot . . . Go ahead and use the over-lock machine. That is already set up with thread.

Ana: What does the over-lock do?

Rosalí: It's what keeps the material from coming apart. *(Rosalí shows Ana.)*

Carmen: Why don't you give me the pink thread from the over-lock machine, then when you get the thread you can set it up again?

Estela: No. I don't know how to set it up on that new machine.

Carmen: Rosalí can do that later. She knows how to do it; **qué no,** Rosalí?

Rosalí: **Sí, Doña** Carmen.

Estela: Why don't you just do what I'm asking you to do?

Carmen: Estela, **no seas terca.** I know what I'm telling you.

Estela: So do I. I want to do things differently. I want us to work like an assembly line.

Carmen: Leave that to the big factories. I've been working long enough to know—

Estela: I haven't been working long enough, but I'm intelligent enough to—

Carmen: Estela, my way is better!

Estela: Why do you think your way is better? All my life your way has been better. Maybe that's why my life is so screwed up!

Carmen: **¡Desgraciada!** I'm only doing it to help you!

Estela: Because you know I won't be getting married any time soon so you want to make sure I'm doing something productive with my life so I can support myself. I don't need your help! *(Beat.)*

Carmen: Where did all that come from? I thought we were arguing about the thread.

Estela: You know what I mean. You know I'm right!

Carmen: All right. If you want me to do the over-lock work I'll do it . . . I have to remember I work for you now.

Estela: **Amá,** don't give me that!

Carmen: What?

Estela: Guilt!

Carmen: Well, it's true! It's not usual that a mother works for her daughter. So I have to stop being your mother and just be a regular employee that you can boss around and tell what to do.

Estela: ¡Ayy, **Amá, parele!** You are my mother, but sometimes you get out of line. How can I tell Rosalí and Pancha to stop gossiping when it's you who initiates the **chisme?** You're a bad example!

Carmen: Ay, sí. Blame me! ¡**Echame la culpa!** You gossip too when it's convenient.

Estela: Look, **Amá,** I don't want to argue with you anymore. I'm frustrated enough by the thought that I might get deported, at the sight of that machine, and at the thought that I am the biggest fool for buying all this junk. So I don't need my mother to make my life any worse! *(Beat.)*

Carmen: So what are we going to do about the thread?

Estela: ¡**Oiiiii!** And we're back to the same thing! *(She goes to the over-lock machine and angrily tears a thread spool from the machine and throws it at Carmen.)* Here! ¡**Tenga!** *(The thread spool misses Carmen by a hair.)*

Carmen (dramatically): ¡**Pegame, pegame!** Go ahead! Hit me! God's gonna punish you for **enojona!**

Ana: Estela, the iron is ready.

Estela: **Amá,** give me a finished dress from the box.

Carmen: Where are they?

Estela: Right next to you by the pile.

Carmen: **Qué** size?

Estela: For the mannequin.

Carmen: What size is it?

Rosalí: It's a size seven, **Doña** Carmen.

Carmen (sarcastically): Thank you, Rosalí. *(Carmen digs into the box and gets a dress. She gives it to Estela who begins to iron the dress carefully.)*

Estela (to Ana): Pay close attention to how I'm ironing this dress. Always, always use the steam. And don't burn the **tul, por favor.** On the skirt just a couple of strokes to make it look decent. It's real easy, just don't burn the **tul,** okay?

Ana: Okay.

Estela: Check the water, and when it gets low . . . Tell me so I can send you to buy some more water for it.

Ana: Why do you have to buy the water?

Estela: Because regular water is too dirty, it needs distilled water for clean steam. *(Estela finishes ironing the dress. She shakes it a bit then puts it on the mannequin. All the women stare at the dress.)*

Rosalí: **Que bonito.** How I would like to wear a dress like that.

Pancha: But first you have to turn into a stick to wear something like that.

Rosalí: Yeah, but they're worth it.

Ana: How much do they pay us for making these dresses?

Rosalí: Estela, we get thirteen dollars for these, no?

Ana: Oh, yeah? How much do they sell them for at the stores?

Estela: They tell me they sell them at Bloomingdale's for about two hundred dollars.

Women: ¡¡¿Qué?!!

Ana: Dang!! *(Lights fade.)*

SCENE TWO

AT RISE: Lights come on. The women are busy working. The **"Cucaracha"** is played on the horn by the lunch mobile outside announcing its arrival.

Ana: Okay, there's the **lonchera.** Anybody want anything for lunch?

Carmen: The **lonchera** is here already?

Estela: Ana, just hurry back.

Rosalí: Can you get me something to drink? How much are those tomato juices?

Ana: A V-8?

Rosalí: **Sí, eso.**

Ana: I think they're 80 cents. You want anything else?

Rosalí: No, no, I'm not hungry.

Estela: Ana, lend me a dollar.

Ana: What do you think I am? A bank? This is the third time. One can only go so far on 67 dollars a week.

Estela: Ana, if you are not happy here go back to working at McDonald's.

Ana: I would . . . *(Carmen stares at Ana.)* . . . But . . . You still want to borrow the dollar?

Estela: Are you going to charge me interest?

Ana: Of course. What do you want me to buy you?

Estela: A burrito **de chicharrón.**

Ana: Pancha, do you want anything?

Pancha: Sí. Bring me four tacos.

Carmen: Pancha, aren't you going to want some of my **mole?**

Pancha: Ana, bring me three tacos, **no más.** *(Pancha gives Ana money.)*

Estela: Ana, if you have money left, could you buy some distilled water at the corner store?

Ana: Anything else, boss? *(Ana leaves to buy the food. Carmen waits until Estela shuts the door.)*

Carmen: **Bueno,** if we are already going to hell for being a bunch of **chismosas,** there's no use in hiding it any longer. *(Carmen digs into a pile of dresses and takes out a book. She shows it to Pancha and Rosalí Carmen whispers.)* **¡Miren!** *(Rosalí quickly sees the illustrations on the front cover and is shocked.)*

Rosalí: **Doña** Carmen!

Carmen: I was cleaning the garage and I found a whole pile of dirty books. I think they belong to my oldest son.

Pancha: What's the book called?

Rosalí (reading title): Two Hundred Sexual Positions Illustrated.

Pancha: I didn't know there were so many. *(Rosalí and Pancha gather around Carmen to look at the book. Estela has not noticed them. Instead she notices a letter being dropped in the mail slot. Estela reads the letter.)*

Rosalí (shocked): **Ay, Dios,** how can these women do this?

Pancha: They're probably gymnasts.

Carmen: The photographer must have used a special lens on this picture.

Pancha: Which picture?

Carmen: The one on page 69.

Rosalí: I didn't know people could do that.

Pancha: **¡Híjole!** Imagine if you had married this man, and you had never seen him until your wedding night.

Carmen: **¡N'ombre, ni lo mande dios!** How it hurt with a regular one.

Pancha: **Mire, Doña** Carmen. This woman looks like you, but that doesn't stop her.

Carmen: Ahh. She's so big. **No le da verguenza.**

Rosalí: I didn't know they had large women in porno books.

Pancha: I guess some men enjoy watching big women.

Estela (sees them looking at the book): What are you looking at? You're suppose to be working! The food has not gotten here yet.

Pancha: Estela, come look. It's a dirty book.

Estela: Why are you looking at that?

Carmen: Estela, **no mas ven a ver.** *(Estela hesitates, but is curious and gives in. She sees the pictures of the large women and is shocked.)*

Estela: People this fat shouldn't be having sex! Ichhh!

Rosalí: Look, Estela, there's a guy in here that looks like your **"Tormento."**

Estela: Where?!! *(Rosalí shows her, then suddenly the door is kicked open.)* Aughhhhhh!!!!!

(Ana enters with her hands full of food.)

Pancha: Estela, calm down.

Estela: I thought it was **la migra**!

Ana: Sorry! I kicked the door open because my hands are full . . .

Estela: From now on these doors are to remain closed and locked at all times, okay? If you go outside, you knock on the door like this . . . *(She knocks in code rhythm)* . . . so we know it's just one of us. Don't ever kick the door again.

Ana: Isn't that going a bit to extremes?

Pancha: **Vamos a estar como gallinas enjauladas.**

Estela: No. We just have to be careful.

Rosalí: So how do you do the knock?

Estela (exemplifies): Knock once. Pause. Then knock twice. Then repeat.

Ana: Well, if it makes you feel better . . .

Estela: Yes, it would.

Ana: All right. Here's the food. *(Ana places the food on the table.)*

Estela: Did you remember the water?

Ana: Yeah, I brought the water! *(Ana gives the bottle of water to Estela and distributes the food. To the women:)* What were you doing?

All (hiding the book): Nothin'.

Ana: What are you hiding?

All: Nothin'. *(Pause.)*

Pancha: We don't want to pervert you.

Ana: You don't want to pervert me more than I've already perverted you?

Rosalí: It's a dirty book.

Ana: Let me see it.

Carmen: No! You're too young to be looking at these things.

Ana: Fine. You've seen them once, you've seen it all.

Pancha: Ana!

Carmen: ¿**Qué?** Repeat what you just said. Don't tell me you've been "messing around."

Ana: No. It's just that I probably know more than most of you and you're thinking that you can pervert me. Stuuuuupiiid!!

Carmen: And how is it that you know so much if you haven't done it?

Ana: . . . I read a lot.

Pancha: But not because you read a lot means you know what's what.

Ana: Go ahead. Ask me anything you always wanted to know about sex but were afraid to ask. I'll tell you. *(All the women are tempted.)*

Rosalí: How do you masturbate . . . ? *(Pancha, Carmen, and Estela stare at Rosalí in shock.)*

Ana: What?

Carmen: ¡**Híjole!** If your **Apá** were to hear you . . . ¡**Híjole!**

Ana: I wouldn't be talking like this in front of my father.

Carmen: Can you believe her? Girls nowadays think they know so much that's why they end up **panzonas.**

Ana: No. They end up pregnant because they don't use contraceptives.

Pancha: Are you sure all you do is read a lot?

Carmen: Your husband's not going to like you knowing so much.

Pancha: A girl shouldn't know so much.

Ana: I'm not a girl, I'm a woman.

Pancha: **Uuy, uy, la** Miss Know-it-all.

Carmen: In my day, a girl became a woman when she lost her virginity.

Ana: That was then. I read somewhere that calling someone a "girl" is just as bad as when white men used to call black men —

Carmen (starts to laugh uncontrollably): I . . . I . . . remember . . .

Estela: **Amá,** it's 12:20, no more stories. If we gossip people are gonna hear everything outside and even if we close the doors they'll know it's a sewing factory because only women talking **chisme** can sound like chickens cackling.

Carmen: But it's what I know how to do best, my reason for living.

Estela: I'm begging you. *(Carmen remains quiet for a few seconds then she begins to laugh uncontrollably again.)*

Pancha: Why are you laughing? *(Carmen continues laughing, unable to speak.)*

Ana: ¿**Amá, qué le píco?** *(The laughter is contagious.)*

Carmen: I just got a back flash of when I lost my virginity.

Ana: That bad, huh?

Carmen: The night I eloped with your father on the bike . . .

Estela: **Bueno,** if the **migra** deports me we know whose fault it is. **Amá,** no work, no money, no factory! Is that clear enough?!

Carmen: **Pero,** don't get upset. Estela, it's lunch time.

Pancha: **Pues sí.**

Estela: It gets me so annoyed to hear her talk and talk . . . And with all the work we have! Just promise me that you'll finish, all right? I'll stop bothering you if you can do that.

Women (look to each other): **Pues bueno.** We promise.

Estela: If not you'll go to hell?!

Women (look to each other again and think about it): **Pues bueno.**

Carmen: **Sí, sí, sí,** we'll go to hell. Can I continue? Okay, **pues** after riding on his bike for so long, I had to pee so bad! So we stopped in the mountains somewhere. I ran behind a tree, squatted, and just peed. That night, after we got settled, I didn't know what was going to happen. After we did it, I started itching and scratching down there 'til my **cuchupeta** got so red. I thought something was wrong, but I asked him and he said it was suppose to hurt and bleed. Then I found out it wasn't him. I had peed on poison ivy. And how it hurt! *(The women laugh sympathetically and slowly gather around the table to eat.)* Panchita, try some of my **mole.**

Pancha (looking at **mole***):* But, **Doña** Carmen, it's green.

Carmen: It's green **mole** . . . Ana, you didn't try some **mole.** It's real good.

Ana: No way! It looks like . . . yukkkk!

Carmen: **Aver,** Rosalí, come try some. There's plenty.

Rosalí: Thank you, **pero,** I'm not hungry.

Carmen: But you haven't eaten anything.

Rosalí: I drink eight glasses of water a day and I don't feel hungry. Water gets rid of the fat.

Carmen: Ana, you should be drinking eight waters.

Ana: And you should too . . . Oh no, you get clogged.

Estela: **Amá,** just be very careful with the **mole.** I don't want any of the dresses getting stained. *(Pancha scoops some* **mole** *with a piece of tortilla. She eats the scoop.)*

Carmen: You like it, Pancha?

Pancha (lying): Yeah, it's real good, **Doña** Carmen . . . *(Rosalí carefully strays away from the table and drinks her V-8. Rosalí swallows a pill. She goes to the window and peeks out through the curtain. She spots* **el Tormento** *outside.)*

Rosalí: **¡Míralo!** There's Andrés! Estela, come to the window! Your **Tormento** is outside! *(Pancha, Carmen, and Ana run to the window, beating Estela.)*

Estela: No, don't go to the window! Get away from the window!

Ana: No one can see us!

Estela: Get down! Make some room for me!

Carmen: I don't see what you could possibly see in him.

Estela: He's cute and he likes me.

Carmen: He doesn't even have good **nalgas.** They're this small. *(She exemplifies with her hands.)*

Ana: **Amá,** why are you so preoccupied with the size of a man's butt?

Rosalí: That's not what counts.

Carmen: Because your father doesn't have any. *(Estela goes to the door and opens it. She fixes herself a bit and stands in front of the door.)*

Pancha: Estela, I thought you said that door was going to remain closed.

Rosalí: Estela, get away from the door, because if the van passes they'll just see the **nopal** on your forehead and take you away.

Estela: But he wants to talk to me. He sent me a letter. *(Estela leaves, closing the door. Carmen and Pancha are still eating their tacos. They stick to the window like flies.)*

Carmen: What could he be telling her? She's laughing her head off.

Rosalí: **¡Miren cómo coquetea!** What a flirt. You never suspected she had it in her.

Pancha: She's worse than Ana.

Ana: What's that suppose to mean? *(Carmen holds her taco carelessly and the* **mole** *spills out onto some dresses.)*

Pancha: **¡Mire, Doña** Carmen! You're spilling the **mole**!

Ana: **Amá,** Estela is going to kill you!

Carmen: **¡Ayy, no!** *(Carmen quickly puts the taco on the table. She grabs a cloth and tries to clean the dresses.)*

Pancha: **¡Aguas!** Here she comes!

Carmen: What am I going to do?

Ana (runs to the door and locks it): Quick, **Amá.** Hide the dresses! We'll clean them later.

Carmen: **¿Dónde los escondo?**

Rosalí: Anywhere! *(Estela tries to open the door. While the women run around hysterically trying to find the best place to hide the dresses.)*

Estela: Let me in.

Ana: Who is it?

Estela: You know who it is!

Ana: I don't know who. *(She gestures to the women to hurry.)* You think we should open the door? What if it's **la migra**?

Estela: Ana, open the door! *(She pounds on the door.)*

Ana: How do we know it's you?

(Estela finally knocks the secret code and Ana lets her in.)

Estela: When the cat is away the mice come out to play. What were you doing?

Women: Nothing!

Carmen: **Ahora sí.** Show us the letter first, and tell us what you talked about.

Estela: It's private.

Rosalí: Come on, Estela, **no te hagas de rogar,** you know you want to show it to us.

Estela: **¡Que metiches!** This letter is for me. He only intended for me to read it . . . All right, I'll read it out loud. *(The women pull our their chairs and get comfortable. Estela clears her throat and reads the letter dramatically.)* "Dear Estela . . ." *(The women get excited after the first "Dear.")* "Dear Estela . . . How I dig you. Let me count the waves."

Rosalí: Ahhh, it's a poem.

Estela: "Wave one: 'cause you look real nice when you pass by me and say, 'Hi.' Wave two: 'cause you seem real smart. Wave three: 'cause your eyes are like **fresas.** And your lips are like mangos, juicy and delicious, **listos para chupar.**"

Pancha: Maybe he works at the supermarket in the fruit section.

Estela (continues): "So how about it? You wanna go cruising down Whittier Boulevard, see a movie, or anything else you wanna do?" I told him I liked the letter a lot. So we're going to the movies tonight.

Rosalí: To the movies? It sounds serious. But be careful with those wandering hands.

Estela: He's not that kind of guy.

Carmen: So what are you going to wear? Don't go dressing up like a scarecrow now.

Estela: I don't dress like that.

Carmen: That's why you scare them away.

Estela: **Como es, Amá.** He likes me for me. Didn't you hear? He said I'm intelligent. He doesn't care how I dress.

Carmen: Estela, let me make you a dress, **horitita te lo coso.**

Estela: No. I can dress myself. And anyway, what are we doing sitting around. Lunch is over. Let's get to work. **¡A trabajar!** *(Lights fade out.)*

Scene Three

AT RISE: Lights fade in. The women are busy working in their designated working areas. Pancha is by the racks attaching strings to hang the dresses.

Ana: Estela, there are no more dresses to iron. What else should I do?

Estela: Ah . . . Pancha, can you show Ana what you are doing? *(Ana goes to the racks. Rosalí turns on the radio.)*

Pancha (showing Ana): **Así hazlo.** This way. *(Ana quickly understands what she has to do and begins her work. The phone rings. Estela picks it up. On the radio we hear the following:)*

Radio (voice-over): It's 3:45 and another hot, beautiful day in L.A. This is KLOVE — **Radio Amor** . . . Now back to our talk show, "Esperanza."

Esperanza (voice-over): For those of you who just joined us today we are discussing abusive spouses. We have our last caller on the line. Caller, are you there?

Caller (voice-over): Hi. I'm not going to give you my name because my husband listens to this station. I wanted to know what I can do to . . . Well, I want to know how I can talk to my husband when he gets angry.

Esperanza (voice-over): How long has he been abusive?

Caller (voice-over): Ah . . . Well, he wasn't like this when we got married . . . He was always sweet. So I don't know what has happened to him. He tells me if I did whatever he asked he wouldn't have to hit me. But I do what he says and it's still not good enough. Last time he hit me because . . .

Pancha (switches the dial on the radio): Isn't there anything else?

Carmen: **Pobre mujer,** I'm lucky **mi viejo** doesn't hit me.

Ana: Lucky? Why lucky? It should be expected that he doesn't. That woman should leave her husband. Women have the right to say "no."

Pancha: You think it's that easy?

Ana: No, she's probably dependent on him financially, or the church tells her to endure, or she's doing it for the children.

Pancha: You're so young. Did it ever occur to you that maybe she loves him?

Ana: I'm sure she does. But we can't allow ourselves to be abused anymore. We have to assert ourselves. We have to realize that we have rights! We have the right to control our bodies. The right to exercise our sexuality. And the right to take control of our destiny. But it all begins when we start saying . . . *(Ana quickly climbs on top of a sewing machine to continue preaching.)* . . . **¡Ya basta!** No more! We should learn how to say no! Come on, **Amá,** say it! Say it!

Carmen: What?

Ana: Say it! "No!"

Carmen: Okay, I won't.

Ana: **Amá,** say "No!"

Carmen (as in she won't): No.

Ana: Good! Rosalí, say it.

Rosalí (casually): **¿Pues por qué no?** No.

Ana: Pancha, say it. No! *(Pancha stares at Ana, she won't say it.)*

Estela: **Ya, ya,** Norma Rae, get off and get back to work!

Pancha: Why don't you run for office? **Tan pequeña** and she thinks and acts like she knows everything.

Ana: I don't know everything, but I know a lot. I read a lot. But it just amazes me to hear you talk the way you do. A women's liberation movement happened 20 years ago, and you act like it hasn't even happened.

Pancha: **Mira,** all those **gringas** shouting about liberation hasn't done a thing for me . . . And if you were married you would realize it. **Bueno,** and if you know so much how come you're not in college?

Ana: Because I don't have the money. I have to wait a year to be eligible for financial aid.

Pancha: I always thought that if you were smart enough a college would give you a scholarship. Maybe you should read some more and get one so you don't have to be here making 67 dollars a week and hearing us talk the way we do. *(A car honking is heard outside.)*

Carmen: **Ya llegó mi viejo.** Ana, get ready. **¡Vámonos!**

Ana: **No, Amá,** you go. I'll take the bus . . . I want to finish this last pile.

Carmen: You do? Ah, I know why you want to stay, **metiche. Bueno. Adiós.**

Women: **Adiós.** *(Carmen leaves. Pancha collects her belongings. A car honking is heard outside.)*

Pancha: I'm leaving too.

Rosalí: Pancha, do you want a ride?

Pancha: **Sí, sí.** *(They get ready to leave.)*

Rosalí: **Adiós,** Estela. Good luck on your date with your **Tormento.** Well, not too good. I hope you won't need to go to confession tomorrow. *(Rosalí and Estela giggle.)* **Hasta mañana.** *(They leave. Soon after Estela hangs up the phone.)*

Ana: So who was that?

Estela: María . . . She called to wish me a happy birthday.

Ana: Isn't it this Friday?

Estela: Yes, but she couldn't wait to tell me that she's getting married in three months. She wants me to make her wedding dress. *(They continue working.)* Ana, before **el Tormento** gets here you have to leave.

Ana: Why?

Estela: Because I don't want you writing about it. I know what you do in the bathroom.

Ana: Come on, Estela, where else can I write? I come here and all it is, is "work, work, work" from you and **Amá.** I go home and then she still wants me to help her cook, and clean . . .

Estela: So what are you writing?

Ana: I'm keeping a journal so when I become "rich and famous" I can write my autobiography.

Estela: Ana, who do you think you are? "Rich and famous."

Ana: I'm not going to be stuck here forever.

Estela: And I am?

Ana: No . . . I didn't say that. **Amá y Apá,** always said that you wouldn't do anything with your life, but you're proving them wrong. It takes a lot of guts and courage to do what you're doing. And even if you're in a mess, you have your own business, at 24! I'm very proud of you.

Estela (a little embarrassed): All right, Ana, you can stay.

Ana: So when is **el Tormento** picking you up?

Estela: In a few minutes. I won't even have a chance to freshen up. *(Estela goes to the sink and washes her face. She stares at herself in the mirror.)* Ana, do you have any makeup?

Ana: Not with me.

Estela (continues to stare at herself with an excited face): I don't have anything to wear! *(Estela runs to look for clothes to wear. Ana goes to the bathroom and sits on the toilet and begins to write. Spotlight on Ana.)*

Ana: Another day and we're in deep . . . trouble . . . I keep having arguments with Pancha, and even though she doesn't like me, I feel sort of sorry for her. I wish I could tell her what to do, but she won't listen to me. Like the rest of the women, she won't take me seriously. They make fun of me . . . So why do I stay? . . . It's true. I stay. Because no matter how much my mother could try and force me to come, I could decide not to come back. But I do . . . Why? *(Fade out.)*

*(Lights come on. Estela is holding the pink dress. She looks to the bathroom to see if Ana is watching. She then holds the dress to her body as if wearing it. She dances slowly with it, imagining herself dancing with **el Tormento.** Lights slowly fade.)*

SCENE FOUR

AT RISE: Lights come on after a brief pause. On the calendar it is Tuesday, September 8, 1987. On the clock it is 7:10 A.M. Before the lights are fully on, Estela's crying is heard. The women are gathered around her.

Ana: So what happened?!

Estela: He . . . He . . .

Pancha: What did he do?

Estela: He . . . He . . .

Rosalí & Ana: What?!!

Estela: I don't want to talk about it! *(She pulls herself together.)* Let's forget about it and get started on the work . . . **Amá,** you said you were going to the bakery.

Carmen: Ah, **sí, sí.**

Estela: Rosalí, how are you doing with the zippers?

Rosalí: I'm halfway done.

Estela: Ana, turn on the iron. There are a lot more dresses that need ironing. Pancha, are you almost done with the skirts for size 3/4?

Pancha: No. I just started that lot a few minutes before I left yesterday.

Carmen: Does anybody want anything from the bakery?

Estela: I want a juice . . . Ana, could you . . . ? *(Estela decides to look in her purse instead. She takes out all of her pennies and gives them to Carmen.)*

Carmen: Estela, you can tell me. What could he have possibly done to get you this upset?

Estela: You're so stubborn, **Amá**! I said nothing happened. I'm just over-reacting.

Carmen: Just remember, I'm your mother. If you can't trust your mother, who can you trust? *(The women agree with Carmen, but Estela does not give in. Carmen leaves. Quickly after, before Ana has a chance to lock the door, Carmen runs back in and leans on the door to close it with her body. She is breathing heavily.)* It's out there again! Like a vulture!

Pancha: What?

All: **¡La migra!** *(They gasp. They all close the curtains and bolt the doors.)*

Rosalí: Was it going by slow or was it going by fast?

Carmen: It was going slow like it was going to turn at the corner and circle around the block and come back!

Ana: You don't know that for sure!

Carmen: Estela, it just occurred to me. Why don't you go home and work in the garage on our old sewing machine?

Estela: I could do that. But I can't. I don't trust you.

Rosalí: We'll work. Just go! **¡Rápido!**

Estela: And you'll work?

All: Yes!!

Estela: What should I take with me to work on?

Rosalí: Just go! I'll get my Jaime to take you the work. Go!

Estela: Okay! *(Estela begins to leave. She opens the door.)* He's out there! *(Estela runs to the bathroom.)*

Ana: Who? The man in the van?

Pancha: No. **¡El Tormento!**

Rosalí: Estela, come out of there! Go before they come. **¡Por favor!**

Carmen: Estela, get out of there right now! **¡No seas mensa!** Men are not worth crying over. And they're certainly not worth you getting deported. *(Carmen waits for Estela to come out.)* **Vas a verlo. ¡Entonces a la fuerza!** *(Carmen pulls on the curtain and tries to drag Estela out. Estela wraps herself with the curtain and Carmen is unable to get her out.)*

Estela: No! Leave me alone! I'm not coming out!

Ana: Estela, who's that **gringa** he's kissing? *(The curtain flies open and Estela races to the door.)*

Estela: Who?!! Where?!!

Ana: I lied. Now go home! *(Ana pushes Estela out the door and locks it. Beat.)*

Rosalí (looking out of the window): I don't think they're coming.

Pancha: Are you sure you saw it, **Doña** Carmen?

Ana: They would have been here by now. **¿Qué no?**

Carmen: I guess so . . . I don't understand. *(They sigh in relief.)*

Estela (offstage, knocking on the door): Ana, let me in.

(Estela knocks on the door and Ana finally lets her in.)

Estela: I'm going to stay.

Carmen: All right. *(Estela closes the door, locks it. The women begin working; machines roar.)*

Ana: Shit! I wish we had a fan here. *(Ana turns on the radio.)*

Estela: I don't want the dresses getting dirty with the dust. *(Lights fade.)*

SCENE FIVE

AT RISE: Lights come on. The women are busy working. Ana goes to the bathroom. She sits on the toilet and starts writing in her journal. Spotlight on Ana.

Ana: It feels just as bad as when I was doing the fries at McDonald's. Pouring frozen sticks of potatoes into boiling lard and the steam hitting my face for $3.35 an hour . . . This place stinks! I hate going to the store and having to climb over the winos, and ignore the catcalls of the sexist dope addicts and the smell of urine and marijuana on the street, and . . . I went to the store today and I saw an old friend. She's pregnant, again. She says she's happy and she doesn't care if she's on welfare. When she was still in high school she told me she knew I was going to do something with my life. I don't want her to know I work here.

(Lights come back on. The women shift in their chairs, uncomfortable with the heat in their buttocks. Rosalí fans herself and notices that Carmen has an odd facial expression.)

Rosalí: **Doña** Carmen, why do you have that strange look on your face?

Carmen: I reached over to get the next dress and I felt something moving inside. I think I'm pregnant.

Pancha: Don't say that, **Doña** Carmen, or I'll lose faith in God. You're almost 50 and already have eight children, I'm barely 32 and can't have any.

Carmen: Isn't that odd, I'm suppose to be an **abuelita** by now. **Pero no puede ser,** it can't be.

Estela: **Amá,** don't tell me you still have sex? At your age and in your physical condition?

Ana: **Cállense,** I heard something on the news about a raid. *(The women listen to the radio.)*

Radio (voice-over): KNXW News all the time . . . The time now is 2:35 P.M. Twenty illegal aliens were captured today at the Goodnight pillow factory . . .

Pancha: That's only a few blocks away!

Radio (voice-over): The INS was given a tip by anonymous sources yesterday of the factory's illegal hiring of aliens. The owner was fined up to 2,000 dollars per alien . . . *(Pancha, Carmen, and Rosalí do the sign of the holy cross.)*

Carmen: Estela, why don't you call the Glitz company and ask them, no, demand that they pay you for the past order of dresses. Even if they were late, they still have to pay us. You have to get the money. *(The radio is still on.)*

Estela: I don't want to be too pushy. They're the only company that has been willing to give us a contract.

Carmen: Then do it for Pancha and Rosalí. You haven't paid them and **las pobrecitas** can't even buy groceries.

Rosalí (lying): I'm all right, don't worry about me.

Ana: Well, I'm not. Estela, just call. *(Estela thinks about it, then she decides to do it.)*

Estela: Here I go. *(Ana turns off the radio. Estela dials the number on the phone and waits.)*

Pancha: **¿Saben qué?** My neighbor who works at the Del Monte canning factory is missing. I have a feeling they deported her. I'm so scared that I'll be waiting for the bus one day and they'll take me.

Carmen: But you're legal.

Pancha (realizing): **Ayy,** I keep forgetting.

Estela: Hello . . . Can I speak to Mrs. Glitz? . . . Hello, this is Estela. Estela Garcia . . . No, but we're almost finished . . . I know we agreed that you would pay me for the last two weeks this Friday, but I was wondering,

maybe, if it isn't too much trouble, if I could get an advance check . . .
today . . . I know . . . I know . . . You're right, Mrs. Glitz . . . Ah . . . But my
workers . . . I know, but I've got a lawyer working on that . . . I'll get it to you
by next week . . . No, I mean it this time. Next week . . . Okay, Mrs. Glitz . . .
I'm sorry . . . Yes, I'll see you on Friday. *(Estela hangs up. Her face expresses
worry and fear.)*

Carmen: **¿Qué te dijo la vieja?**

Pancha: What did she tell you?

Estela: She asked about my proof of employment papers again. Then she
warned me that if **la migra** shuts us down, she won't pay us for all the
work we've done.

Carmen: **¡Mendiga vieja!**

Ana: Do you think she would really do that? *(Carmen and Estela talk among
themselves.)*

Estela: **Amá,** why is this happening to me? I'm going to get deported, aren't I,
Amá?

Carmen: **Mira,** supposing you do get deported, we'll get a **coyote** to smuggle
you back in. Somehow we'll find the money.

Estela: But I would have let you and everybody down. I'll lose everything that
I've worked for, the factory, and my self-respect. And I don't know if I can
start again.

Carmen: Estela, your **Apá** was thrown back to Mexico four times, but he kept
coming back. If you did it once, you can do it again.

Estela: I hope so. *(Estela pulls herself together and continues working. She picks up a
bundle of sewn skirts and looks at them. She discovers that they have been sewn
wrong.)* Pancha, do you realize you sewed all of the size 3/4 skirts backwards?

Pancha: I did? No, I didn't!

Estela: Look! This is the outside of the material and this is the inside. Have
you been doing all the lots this way?

Pancha: I think so.

Estela: **¡Ay, no!** More repairs! Pancha, please do them again.

Pancha: No! It's so hot. I don't even feel like working. How do you expect us to
work with this heat?

Estela: Pancha, I'll help you take them apart.

Ana: Couldn't you open the door?

Estela: No!

Pancha: I can't work like this.

Estela: We're going to have to. *(Pancha grabs the skirt and begins to take them apart.
Estela is looking at another lot and discovers the stained dresses that Carmen hid.)*
¡Amá! What did I tell you about the **mole?!** *(Estela shoves a dress in Car-
men's face.)*

Carmen: The stains are not so obvious. I was going to clean them, I swear. I
didn't want you to see them and get worried.

Estela: It's going to be hell trying to take the stains out! *(Estela catches Ana acci-
dently burning the **tul.**)* Not so close! You're burning the **tul!** Pay close attention to your work or don't do it. Have you been burning it on the other
dresses too?! *(Estela quickly looks at the dresses on the racks and those that Ana
has finished ironing.)*

Ana: I thought if I did it this way it would be okay and save us time. I can't
stand the heat and the steam.

Estela: Can't any of you do anything right? Do I have to do everything myself so that these dresses get finished? *(Pancha gets busy pulling on the two pieces of material on the skirt instead of cutting the sewn thread one stitch at a time.)* Pancha, don't pull on them or you'll tear them. I said I was going to help you do the repairs.

Pancha: I want to get out of here and go home.

Estela: You have to finish this work.

Pancha: Not in this heat!

Ana: Estela, please open the door!

Estela: For the last time, I won't!

Pancha: Then I'll open it. *(Pancha walks determinedly towards the door. Estela stands in her way.)* We're all burning in here. I'm getting dizzy.

Estela: I'm sorry it's so hot, but the van may be out there and I don't want them to see anything.

Pancha: It's so selfish of you to keep the door closed when we are all burning!

Estela: I'm burning too!

Pancha: But you're the one with the criminal record! It's not fair that we are all paying for your fault. We are all legal now!

Estela: Then go! Open the door, then leave.

Pancha: All right! I'll leave, but with my work. *(Pancha grabs the skirts, begins pulling on them, tearing the material.)* Let's see what else I've done. *(Pancha continues tearing. Estela tries to stop her by holding Pancha's hands. Pancha and Estela begin to get physical, almost ready to strike each other. Rosalí quickly steps between them to prevent them from hitting each other.)*

Carmen: Estela, **¡párale!**

Rosalí: **¡Basta! ¡No se peleén!** *(Rosalí faints and falls to the floor. Estela and Pancha stop fighting.)*

Carmen: Rosalí!

Ana: Rosalí, are you all right?

Carmen: What could be wrong with her?

Pancha: It's this **pinche** heat! It's your fault, Estela. Here you have us all locked up! See what happened?!

Estela (shakes Rosalí, who does not respond): Rosalí, please wake up!

Pancha: Let's take her to the hospital!

Carmen: **¡¿Pero que locura?!** The hospital is three blocks away. We can't carry her, **la migra** is going to see us.

Pancha: **Ayy si, ¿entonces qué quiere?** You want her to die?

Carmen: She's not going to die!

Pancha: And how do you know?

Carmen: Don't exaggerate! *(While Pancha and Carmen argue, Ana thinks quickly of what to do. She searches around the bathroom for something. She finds Estela's perfume and grabs some tissue. Ana uses it to wake up Rosalí. Rosalí becomes conscious and Pancha and Carmen finally stop arguing.)*

Rosalí: Ah . . .

Pancha: Rosalí, you want to go to the hospital?

Rosalí: **¿Qué páso?**

Carmen: **M'ija,** you fainted.

Ana: Are you okay?

Rosalí: **Sí . . . Sí . . .** I'm okay.

Pancha: I'm gonna take you home.

Rosalí: I'll just rest a little . . . I'll feel better . . .

Pancha: You can't continue working like this. I'll take you home. It's no bother, because I'm going home myself. *(Carmen gets a glass of water and an aspirin.)*

Carmen: **Pobrecita,** here, drink this.

Estela: Rosalí, I'm sorry.

Pancha (helps Rosalí up): Where's your bag? *(Rosalí points to it. Pancha gets the bag.)* Let's go. *(Pancha leaves with Rosalí without hesitation or saying good-bye. Estela fights the urge to cry.)*

Estela (to herself): I'm sorry, Rosalí.

Carmen: Don't blame yourself. Something like this was going to happen.

Ana: Isn't Rosalí the only one who knows how to set up the over-lock machine? *(Ana and Carmen look at each other worried. Estela has an expression of hopelessness. Lights slowly fade out.)*

End of Act One

ACT TWO

SCENE ONE

AT RISE: Carmen and Estela are the only ones present, working silently. On the clock it is 8:15 A.M. On the calendar it is Wednesday, September 9, 1987.

Carmen: I don't think Pancha's coming back.

Estela: She's only an hour late. Maybe she went to visit Rosalí at her house.

Carmen: Pancha is never late. *(Footsteps are heard outside. Then the code knock is heard. Estela smiles and goes to open the doors.)*

Estela: See, **Amá**! I knew she would come. *(Estela rushes to open the door. Ana is at the door.)* Oh, it's just you.

(Ana quickly comes in carrying a brown paper bag with detergent which she puts on the table.)

Ana: ¡**Miren!** Come look out the window. There's this strange homeless person outside. *(They go look.)*

Carmen: What's so strange about him?

Ana: I don't recognize him.

Estela: So?

Ana: I think he's just disguised. He doesn't look desperate enough.

Carmen: I've never seen him before.

Ana: I think he's a spy?

Estela: A spy?

Ana: Look! There's Pancha!

Estela: God! Thank you! She's come back!

Carmen: But look, he's talking to her and she's pointing this way! *(They drop to the floor. A few seconds later they go back to looking.)* I wonder what he's asking her?

Estela: I wonder what she's telling him?

Ana: ¡**Aguas!** Here she comes.

(They scatter. Ana takes out the stain remover from the bag. Carmen goes back to sewing. The code knock is heard and Estela opens the door. Pancha comes in.)

Estela: Pancha, what did the bum ask you?

Pancha: The bum? Ooo. He asked me where your **Tormento** lives.

Ana: I guess he wasn't a spy after all.

Pancha: **¡N'ombre!** He's just another one of his **vago** friends.

Carmen: **¡Bola de viejos cochinos!** No good drug addicts!

Estela: Ya! Stop talking about him!

Carmen: Are you defending him? After what he did?

Ana (aside): **Amá,** Estela finally told you?

Carmen: No. I'm trying to get it out of her.

Estela: Forget it! I'll never tell you what happened on the date.

Ana: Okay, Estela. Be like that. I'll never tell you anything either. *(Estela doesn't budge. Ana and Carmen give up.)*

Carmen: Panchita, we were afraid you wouldn't come back.

Pancha: Why?

Carmen: Well, after what happened yesterday.

Pancha: I have to come to work even if I don't want to . . . I went to visit Rosalí this morning.

Ana: How is she doing?

Pancha: She's doing better.

Estela: Is there any chance of her coming back this week?

Pancha: **No se.** She looks pale. This heat will be bad for her. I'm surprised I didn't faint myself.

Estela: Maybe I will get a fan.

Pancha: Estela, what do you want me to work on?

Estela: I don't know how we are going to manage without her. Pancha, please finish the zippers that Rosalí was working on.

Carmen: Estela, give me the manual for the over-lock machine. I'm going to try and set it up myself.

Estela: **Alli esta en el cajon.** We'll just have to go on without her. Ana, did you get the stain remover?

Ana: It's on the table. How many dresses need washing?

Estela: Twelve. I should put my mother to wash them, but since she'll be busy with the over-lock I guess I'll do them.

Ana: How many dresses have we finished?

Estela: They're on the racks. And there are a couple in that box that just need ironing.

Ana (looking at the racks): That's all?

Estela: I found ten dresses with the **tul** burnt in them. Those were almost finished, but now the **tul** has to be replaced.

Ana: I guess I'll do that.

Estela: **Amá,** can you stay late today?

Carmen: **Pues sí.**

Estela: Ana, will you stay late too?

Ana: Stay late? . . . Sure. *(Ana irons a dress carefully and slowly. Estela observes Ana for a few seconds.)*

Estela: Ana, can you iron faster? Just make them look decent. *(Ana frowns at her suggestion and looks to Pancha who is attaching hanging strings on the dresses next to her.)*

Ana (to Pancha): It's not that I don't iron fast enough, it's that whenever I finish ironing a dress I stop for a minute to really look at it. I never realized just how much work, **puro lomo,** as my mother would say, went into making it. Then I imagine the dress at Bloomingdale's and I see a tall and skinny woman looking at it. She instantly gets it and with no second thoughts she says "charge it!" She doesn't think of the life of the dress before the rack, of the labor put into it. I shake the dress a little and try to forget it's not for me. I place a plastic bag over it then I put it on the rack and push it away. It happens to me with every dress.

Pancha: What an imagination. So what are you gonna study when you go to college next year? Where are you going?

Ana: To New York University. I'm going to study writing.

Carmen: **Así es que** you better be quiet, don't tell her any **chisme** or one day you're gonna read about it.

Pancha: And you think you'll make it?

Ana: I think so.

Pancha: **Pos,** I do think you're a bit **loquita,** but if that's what you need. I think you'll make it.

Ana: **Gracias,** Pancha. *(Pancha smiles at Ana seeing her differently for the first time. Meanwhile, Carmen is frustrated with the over-lock machine.)*

Carmen: **¡Ayy no! ¡No puedo!** I try and I try and I can't! **¡Esta cochinada no sirve!**

Estela: But what can we do? Who else could do it? Can you do it, Pancha?

Pancha: I don't know anything about those new machines.

Estela: **Amá,** give me the manual. *(Estela grabs the manual and begins to work on the machine. Talking to the machine:)* Please, **maquinita.** If you behave I'll put on you all the oil you want. **Maquinita,** if you love me, help me.

Carmen (touching her stomach): Ana, come here, quick. Feel my stomach. *(Ana puts her hand over Carmen's stomach.)* Can you feel the baby kicking?

Ana: No . . . **Amá,** are you sure you're pregnant?

Carmen: I think so. **Aver,** Pancha, tell me if you feel anything.

Pancha: I'm busy, **Doña** Carmen.

Carmen: Just come quick, Panchita. Ana doesn't believe me. *(Pancha gets up from her chair and goes over to Carmen. She places her hand on Carmen's stomach.)*

Pancha: I don't feel anything. I think the heat is getting to you too.

Carmen: **¿Cómo puede ser?** I can feel it! *(Pancha nods her head and walks away fanning herself. She heads to the bathroom.)*

Ana: How many months should you be pregnant by now? I haven't noticed you getting any bigger.

Carmen: I don't know. I've always been fat. I haven't noticed either.

Ana: Have you the symptoms?

Carmen: Not all of them, but I've been pregnant enough times to know.

Ana: Are you going to keep it?

Carmen: What do you mean?

Ana: You don't have to have it.

Carmen: Ana, I don't want to talk about this.

(Spotlight on Pancha. Pancha stands on the toilet in front of the small window. She opens the window and bathes her face with the breeze. Pancha begins to cry.)

Pancha: **Que bonito viento.** Wind, that's what I am. *(Touching her stomach.)* Empty, like an old rag . . . *(Praying.)* **Diosito,** why don't you make me a real woman? If I can't have children, why did you make me a woman? *(Pancha wipes her tears.)*

(Lights come on.)

Estela (talking to the machine): **Maquinita,** I'm going to set you up even if it's the last thing I do in this country. *(She holds the manual and follows directions.)* All right. Five threads. They all start from their spools onto the holes, then straight down, into the loops. Then they turn, go in between more loops underneath, then they all go into their needles. Then the electricity comes on . . . *(She turns on the machine.)* . . . I insert a piece of material, step on the pedal and . . . Ta-da! A chain of interwoven threads! I did it!

Carmen: You fixed it? **¿Pero cómo?**

Estela: I persisted and I did it!

Carmen: **¡Mira que inteligente!**

Ana: That's great, Estela! Now we don't have to worry about it anymore. *(They hear footsteps outside. They instantly freeze and become silent. They look to each other then Carmen, Ana, and Pancha quickly go to their purses. Someone is heard outside, then letters are slipped in through the mail slot. The women relax.)* Just the mailman . . .

(The women suddenly realize that it probably means bad news for Estela. Estela picks up an envelope and reads it. No one asks what it says out of respect for her, but they all know it's another letter from the lawyer. Estela opens it and is about to read it when they hear footsteps outside. They grab their "Temporary Employment" cards from their purses. Estela hides behind Carmen. Then the code knock is heard. The women rush to the door. Estela opens the door and Rosalí is behind the bar door.)

Everyone: What are you doing here?!

Estela: Aren't you suppose to be resting?

Rosalí: I was in bed and I kept imagining Estela getting deported. So I had to come back. I know how badly you must need the over-lock machine.

Estela: I fixed it!

Rosalí (disappointed): You did? Well, where are the zippers so I can get started now?

Pancha: I finished all the zippers.

Rosalí: You did?

Estela: Rosalí, I'd rather you go back and get well.

Rosalí: No, Estela, I'm fine. I can help.

Estela: It's not worth it if we're fighting and getting sick because of this heat.

Rosalí: It wasn't just the heat . . . I hadn't eaten and that's why I fainted. I didn't want you to think it was your fault.

Pancha: But why do you need to lose weight? **'Tas flaca.** *(Rosalí smiles, but doesn't believe Pancha.)*

Carmen: Have you eaten already, you still look pale?

Rosalí: No, I'm not hungry, **Doña** Carmen.

Carmen: But that's what you have been saying and look what happened. Come on, eat something.

Rosalí: I am not hungry.

Ana: Rosalí, you can't see yourself the way we see you and that's why you think you're fat.

Carmen: Rosalí, you need to eat something.

Rosalí: I'm not hungry!

Carmen: You need to eat something! *(Rosalí looks at each of them and finally reveals the truth.)*

Rosalí: I'm not hungry because I've been living on diet pills.

Carmen: So that's the secret diet? **Ayy,** Rosalí, don't you know those **cochinadas** are no good?

Ana: They're real bad for you because I read they're addictive.

Rosalí: I know. When I fainted I saw my body lying there, I thought I was going to die. I couldn't feel my body. And I just kept seeing Estela being deported. Estela, I want to come back to work. This is more important to me than being a size seven.

Estela (embraces Rosalí): **Gracias** . . . Can you work late?

Rosalí: **Claro.**

Estela: And you too, Pancha?

Pancha: **Pos bueno.**

Carmen: **Entonces todas a trabajar!** *(The women go to their sewing stations. Estela takes out her notebook and dictates the work.)*

Estela: **Amá,** let Rosalí do the over-lock work, she's faster. I want you to do lots size two through six. Pancha, you do lots size seven through twelve. Ana, you know what to do. *(Estela takes control and the women are determined to finish. The machines roar like race cars taking off. Lights slowly fade.)*

SCENE TWO

AT RISE: Lights come on. It is 2:00 A.M. and street sounds are heard outside. Rosalí looks around and then stares at her stomach.

Rosalí: Did you hear that?

Ana: No, what?

Rosalí: A stomach growling. Whose stomach was it?

Estela: I don't know, but I'm hungry.

Ana: Me too. **Amá,** is there any rice left?

Rosalí: Did you hear it again?

Pancha: Rosalí, it's your **panza.**

Rosalí: Yeah, it's me! I haven't heard my stomach growling in so long.

Estela: What's there to eat?

Carmen: I might have something in my purse. Why don't we make something?

Pancha: All this noise is driving me crazy. I'm going deaf. *(Pancha turns on the radio. Carmen gets up, looks around the table then in the refrigerator. All the women search in their purses for food.)*

Carmen: **Aaaa,** I found something. Tortillas and . . . the **mole**!

All: Not the **mole**!

Pancha: I've got something. *(Pancha takes out a large amount of food from her purse. The women are surprised with every item she takes out: a box of fried chicken, a hamburger, a bag of chips, a bag of cookies, and a Diet Coke.)* I'm on a diet!

Carmen (aside): **Se ve.** *(On the radio a "cumbia" has just finished. Then a Disc Jockey with a very mellow voice comes on the air.)*

Disc Jockey (voice-over): It's 2:25 A.M. on an early Thursday morning . . . I'm falling asleep here to pay my bills. And if you're listening now, you probably are too. So this is for you night owls! The ones that do the night shifts no one wants to do! *(The song "Tequila" blasts on the radio. The women are so sleepy, they jump around to the music trying to awaken. They eat and shake at the same time. Lights slowly fade.)*

SCENE THREE

AT RISE: Lights come on. It is Thursday, September 10, 1987. On the clock it is 2 P.M. The women are wearing the same clothes as the day before. As usual, it is extremely hot.

Carmen (smelling her armpits): Phueeehh! **¡Fuchi!** I stink. **Aquí huele a pura cuchupeta y pedo.** Phuehhh! Who farted?

Estela: **Amá,** it's probably you who did it. Like they say, the one who smells it first is the one who has it underneath her skirt.

Ana: **¡Que calor!** It feels like we're in hell!

Pancha: How many more dresses to finish, Estela?

Estela: Fifteen.

Rosalí: Only fifteen?!

Carmen: **Dios mio, ya mero acabamos.**

Estela (counting dresses on rack): 184, 185, 186. No, we only need 14!

Ana: What a relief! We're almost finished. *(Ana decides to take off her blouse, leaving on her sweaty bra.)*

Carmen (shocked at Ana's actions): Ana, what are you doing?!

Ana: All this steam has me sweating like a pig.

Carmen: We're sweating too, but we don't go taking our clothes off!

Ana: So why don't you? We're all women. We all have the same.

Carmen: Not really. You have bigger **chichis.**

Ana: And you have a bigger **panza**!

Carmen: That's because I'm pregnant!

Estela: You mean we're definitely going to have another baby brat to take care of?

Ana: **Amá,** do you really want to have it?

Pancha: **Doña** Carmen, give it to me if you don't want it.

Carmen: I can't just get rid of it, either way . . . But I don't want to have it.

Pancha: But you're lucky, **Doña** Carmen.

Carmen: No. It seems all I do is have children. One after another. I'm tired of this! I can't have this baby. I'll die. Last time I was pregnant the doctor said I almost didn't make it.

Ana: **Amá,** I didn't know that happened.

Carmen: Every time your **Apá** touches me, the next day I'm pregnant. When he would leave me in Mexico to go to **el norte,** he would leave me pregnant so no man would look at me and desire me. I was very beautiful.

Ana: You still are, **Amá.**

Carmen: I was always scared of him. And I let myself get fat after you were born hoping he would be disgusted by me and not touch me anymore.

Ana: Why didn't you just say "No"?

Carmen: Because, **M'ija,** I was never taught how to say no.

Pancha (comes forward and confesses): It's easy, **Doña** Carmen. You tell him "No!" and you get out from the bed.

Ana (realizing what Pancha is saying): Pancha?

Pancha: And then you take the blanket. *(Ana embraces Pancha as the women laugh.)*

Ana (to the women): Aren't you hot in those clothes? I feel sticky. I'm going to take off my pants. *(Ana takes off her pants. She is left wearing her bra and panties.)*

Carmen: Ana, aren't you embarrassed?

Ana: Why? You already think I'm fat.

Carmen: You know, Ana, you're not bad looking. If you lost 20 pounds you would be very beautiful.

Ana: Story of my life . . . Go ahead. Pick on me.

Carmen: Why don't you lose weight? Last time you lost weight you were so thin and beatifuller.

Ana: I like myself. Why should I?

Pancha: **Doña** Carmen, Ana is very pretty. She looks good the way she is.

Ana: Thank you, Pancha.

Carmen: It's because she's young. At this age young girls should try to make themselves as attractive as possible.

Ana: Why? Why not always? You're overweight too.

Carmen: But I'm already married.

Ana: Is that it? Make myself attractive so that I can catch a man?

Estela (sarcastically): Ana, listen to them, learn now, "or you'll end up like Estela."

Ana: **Amá,** I do want to lose weight. But part of me doesn't because my weight says to everyone, "Fuck you!"

Carmen: **¡Ave Maria Purissima!**

Ana: It says, "How dare you try to define me and tell me what I have to be and look like!" So I keep it on. I don't want to be a sex object.

Estela: Me neither.

Carmen: **¡Otra!**

Rosalí: What's wrong with being a sex object? What's wrong with wanting to be thin and sexy?

Estela: Because I want to be taken seriously, to be considered a person . . . You know with Andrés, on our date . . .

Carmen: **¡Aver cuentanos!** What happened on that infamous date?

Estela: On our date I got all fixed up . . . Then he showed up with jeans and a t-shirt and he smelled like he had been drinking . . . He wanted to take me to the drive-in and when I asked, "Why the drive-in?" He said because there he could kiss me and give me what I wanted . . . He said, "I don't care if you're fat. I like you even better; more to grab." That got me so angry! I thought he was interested in me because he was impressed that I owned this factory, my "intelligence," that I . . . "I'm smart" . . . When am I going to meet that man who will see the real me?

Carmen: So that's what happened.

Rosalí: **Pues** if he has a brother, tell him about me. I think I'm going to die a virgin.

Ana: You're still a virgin?! Dang!

Pancha: **¿Pero tu Jaime?** Nothing?

Rosalí: Nothing. I've felt fat ever since I can remember and I didn't want anybody to touch me until I got thin.

Ana: Is that why you were starving yourself?

Rosalí: That's part of it.

Estela: Rosalí, you're not fat.

Rosalí: Of course I am. Look at my **nalgas** . . . And my hips! **Paresen de elefante.**

Ana: No they don't!

Rosalí: I look like a cow.

Carmen: You look like a cow? Where does that leave us?

Pancha: Rosalí, you're so skinny in comparison to all of us.

Rosalí: No I'm not. Here, look at my fat hips. (*Rosalí pulls down her pants and shows them her hips.*)

Estela: That's nothing. **¡Mira!** (*Estela pulls down her pants and shows Rosalí her hips.*)

Carmen (to Rosalí): At least you have a waist! (*Carmen pulls down her skirt and shows Rosalí her stomach.*)

Pancha: **¡Uuuu!** That's nothing, **Doña** Carmen! (*Pancha raises her skirt and shows them her stomach.*)

Rosalí: But you don't understand. I've got all these stretch marks on my arms . . . (*Rosalí opens her blouse and shows them the stretch marks close to her breasts.*)

Estela: They're small. I have stretch marks that run from my hips to my knees. (*Estela takes off her pants to show them.*)

Carmen: Stretch marks?! Stretch marks!! You want to see stretch marks? (*Carmen lifts her blouse and exposes her stretch marks and scars.*) Stretch marks!!! (*Ana sits back as she watches the women slowly undressing. They continue to compare body parts ad libbing. Finally they are all in their underwear and they stop to notice Carmen's stretch marks.*)

Ana: **Amá,** what's that scar you have on your stomach?

Carmen: This one? That was Estela.

Ana: It's such a big scar.

Carmen: Estela was a big baby.

Estela: I gave you the most trouble, didn't I?

Carmen: A-ha. But that's okay. I've heard Elizabeth Potaylor has one just like it.

Pancha (suddenly realizing): Look how we are? What if somebody came in and saw us like this?

Carmen (fanning her breasts): **Pero que bien se siente.** It feels so good to be rid of these clothes and let it all hang out.

Ana: **Pues sí.** Nobody is watching us. Who cares how we look.

Estela: So this is how we look without clothes?

Carmen: Just as fat and beautiful . . . (*They all hug in a semicircle laughing triumphantly.*)

Ana: We can finally relax.

Estela: We're not finished yet.

Rosalí: Estela, all we need are 14 dresses.

Pancha: Those we can finish tomorrow for sure.

Carmen: So what are we going to do to celebrate?

Estela: To celebrate what? Finishing on time for the first time?

Pancha: No. All of us, most of us, finally being legal.

Carmen: It's true. And once you get the card you can do anything you want. **Tengo fe** . . . Estela, I've been thinking . . . You know what we could do? We could copy the patterns for these dresses, make the dresses ourselves, and have a fashion show. Maybe we could model them ourselves. *(The women laugh at the thought.)*

Ana: No, that's a great idea! Why don't we make them in larger sizes too?

Pancha: **Está loquita,** but sometimes she makes sense. We could probably sell more if we made them in larger sizes.

Rosalí: You know what we could also do? Jaime could sell them in the flea market. If they sell, little by little we could grow . . .

Estela (jumping in): And from there, if we make a lot of money, more money than what we're making now, maybe we can rent a place downtown on Broadway and start a boutique!!

Ana: But we'll need a name.

Rosalí: Well, why not just Estela Garcia?

Ana: I was thinking of something more French.

Carmen: No. A French name would make it sound **chafas.** No, Estela Garcia sounds fine.

Pancha: Estela, maybe you could go to school and study fashion design and design our dresses.

Estela: Yeah. I could do that. *(They all stop to imagine the possibilities.)*

Carmen: So what are we doing to celebrate?

Estela: First let's finish, then we can talk about celebrating. *(They go back to work. Carmen takes off her glasses as she fans her face.)*

Carmen: **Que calor.** I'll be glad when all of this is over.

Ana: Estela, can we please open the door?

Pancha: Open the door? **¿Pa qué?** So people that pass by can see us like this?

Rosalí: But it's so hot!

Ana: I don't think they're coming. Besides we're almost finished. *(The women look to Estela for a decision.)*

Estela: Okay . . . **Amá,** open the door. *(Carmen goes to open the door. She turns back to Estela as if to make sure. Carmen opens the door and fans herself with it. Beat. Carmen holds the door wide open and walks outside. The women can't believe their eyes. A few seconds later Carmen runs back in screaming.)*

Carmen: Estela! It's out there! **¡La Migra!** They're coming!! *(Carmen shuts the door. All the women immediately get dressed.)*

Estela: No! It's not fair! We were almost finished!! *(The women dig into their purses for their cards. Estela can only cry in desperation. She cannot find her clothes and has to head for the door in her slip. Rosalí and Ana peek through the curtains and quickly make a realization.)*

Rosalí: **Doña** Carmen, that's not **la migra**!

Ana: It's the police!

Carmen: The police? *(She peeks through the curtain.)* **¡¿Cómo?!**

Ana: That's the guy I thought was a spy. He's an undercover cop!

Rosalí: Like in the movies.

Ana: It's a drug bust!

Estela: Where?

Rosalí: I think it's **el Tormento's** house. *(Estela moves for the door.)*

Ana: **¡Sí, el Tormento!** They're taking him away. *(Estela and Ana jump up in excitement.)*

Carmen: That's what he deserves! *(The police are heard driving away.)*

Pancha: That's good they're taking him away in the van. **¡Bola de viejos cochinos!** *(The women laugh together. Then Ana stops laughing.)*

Ana: **Amá,** was that the same van you saw Monday?

Carmen (nodding her head hesitantly): I think so.

Ana: On Tuesday?

Carmen: I think so.

Ana: On Wednesday?

Carmen (sheepishly): **Pos sí.** *(She puts on her glasses.)*

Ana: **Amá,** that wasn't **la migra.** Everyone knows the vans are green!

Carmen: I didn't.

Estela: How could you not know?

Carmen: **Pos no se;** all those years of being undocumented I always imagined they were black.

Pancha & Rosalí: **Ayy, Doña** Carmen!!!

Carmen: Phueehhh! **Tanto pedo y para nada.**

Estela: Thank God! **¡Que susto!**

Carmen: It's time to retire! *(They laugh in relief then they become silent.)*

Ana: Well, it's over . . . for now. *(Beat.)*

Estela: If you want to take the rest of the day off . . . We'll finish tomorrow.

Pancha: We can go?

Estela: Yes. I know how tired you must be. Go ahead. I'll stay and continue working.

Rosalí: I can't wait to go home and take a shower.

Carmen: **Si, por favor, bañate** . . . Tomorrow, I'm going to make a fresh batch of **mole.**

Pancha (scared for her life): **Doña** Carmen, why don't you make some rice? *(Ana, Pancha, and Rosalí immediately run out.)*

Carmen (muttering to them): Ingrates! *(To Estela.)* Are you sure you won't need us anymore?

Estela: No. Now go! Before I change my mind. Don't you want to go outside? *(They gather their bags and quickly leave. Estela is left alone. Lights fade a little. She turns on the radio to a mellow jazz station. She goes around doing a final clean up, turning off lights and machines. She stops, recalling the five of them in their underwear, fantasizing about their own boutique. She grins to herself. She whispers.)* Large sizes? *(Estela shakes her head, dismissing the idea, but then stops and runs to a pile of stocked material. She eagerly searches and finds a roll of red fabric. Estela excitedly runs to a station and begins taking her measurements. As the lights slowly fade, we see Estela measuring herself with pride and pleasure, half laughing to herself, half defiantly . . . about to design and make her first dress. Lights slowly fade to black.)*

SCENE FOUR

AT RISE: Lights come on. There are no more dresses on the racks. It is Friday, on the clock it is 2:25 P.M. Ana and Pancha are busy blowing up balloons. Rosalí is cleaning up. There is a birthday cake with a large candle of the number "25." A large sign reads: *"Happy Birthday Estela."* Footsteps are heard outside. Ana runs to turn off the electricity, the women hide . . . The door opens.

Women: Surprise!!!!! *(Rosalí takes a picture. Carmen stands motionless holding a pot.)*
Ana: **Amá,** we thought you were . . .
Rosalí: **Doña** Carmen, what's wrong?
Carmen: I just got back from the doctor.
Pancha: What did she tell you?
Ana: **¿Amá?**
Carmen: She says I'm not pregnant.
Ana: Then why are you sad?
Carmen: She says, "it's only menopause." When you reach menopause it's over. You're no longer a woman. **Se te seca allí abajo.**
Ana: **Amá,** you are a real woman.
Carmen: What I should be is a grandmother by now, but the way you and Estela are going, I won't be one for a long time . . . **¿Y Estela?**
Rosalí: She hasn't returned from delivering the dresses. She should be coming soon.
Carmen: Here. *(Gives Rosalí the pot.)* I made rice.

(They hear footsteps outside. Ana turns off the lights. The door opens.)

Women: Surprise!!! *(Rosalí takes another picture. Lights come on. Estela stands shocked in her new dress.)*
Estela: You remembered?
Rosalí (gives Estela a gift): Happy twenty-fifth birthday, you old maid!
Carmen (referring to her dress): Estela, did you make it? **Que bonita te ves,** very nice. You see you're not ugly, you just didn't know how to dress.
Estela (hugs Rosalí): I brought a gift for all of you. *(Estela goes outside and brings in a large fan.)*
Pancha: Now the boss treats us pretty good.
Estela: Because now I have money.
Carmen: Did Mrs. Glitz finally pay you?
Estela: Yes, she paid me, but she kept threatening me . . . I've written out all the checks. *(Estela pulls out the checks from her bag. She distributes them, the first check going to Pancha.)*
Pancha (looking at her check): This is the biggest check I've ever gotten. *(Estela gives Rosalí her check.)*
Rosalí: Too bad I've already spent it on the **Americana** Express.
Carmen: **¡Válgame!** I didn't realize how much money you owed me.
Ana (looks at her check, disappointed): Estela, come here. *(Ana and Estela talk among themselves.)* Estela, how come I only get this much?
Estela: I took out for taxes.
Ana: Taxes? But you're not reporting . . .
Carmen: How much do you have left?
Estela: About six hundred. I'll send the lawyer some more money today. Maybe they won't take me to court.
Pancha: But if they deport you and take everything, we won't be able to work towards the boutique.
Rosalí: We're also going to have to look for another job. *(The women stare at the floor.)*

Ana: Back to McDonald's. *(Beat.)*

Pancha: Estela, I know my husband isn't going to like it, but here. *(Pancha extends her check to Estela.)* Take it. Pay me back when you can.

Estela: Pancha, are you sure?

Pancha: No, **pero,** take it before I change my mind.

Estela: **Muchas gracias** . . . *(They try hugging, but they find it difficult, it's awkward. To herself.)* Let's see. How much more do I need? *(Carmen stares at her check for a few more seconds and slowly says good-bye to it.)*

Carmen: **Ten, ten.** Take mine too. What kind of mother would I be if I didn't give it back?

Estela (hugs Carmen): **¡Que buena es!**

Carmen: You see, **¿No que no te quiero?** It's because I love you that I make your life so miserable.

Estela: Don't love me so much. *(Rosalí thinks about it too.)*

Rosalí: I guess the **Americana** Express can wait . . . Here is my check too. *(Estela hugs Rosalí. Now they all look to Ana. Ana holds her check tightly.)*

Ana: No, not me . . . I'm going to buy a typewriter . . . I can't. *(The women don't say anything, but continue staring at Ana.)* I really need this typewriter. I have this essay I have to type up for a contest . . . All right . . . Take half of it. *(Estela semi-hugs Ana.)*

Estela: Excuse me for just a minute. I have to make a phone call. *(Estela picks up the phone and dials.)* Hello . . . May I speak to Mrs. Glitz? This is Estela Garcia. I'm just calling to thank you for keeping your word and finally paying us today. I also wanted to tell you that you are a mean, wicked, bitter, unsympathetic, greedy, rude, awful . . .

Ana: Capitalist!

Estela: Capitalist! . . . No! We quit . . . Yeah, well I'll see you in hell. *(The women are shocked, incredulous of her actions.)*

Carmen: **¡Maldita!** What have you done?

Pancha: You got us fired, didn't you?

Estela: No, we quit. *(Estela laughs excitedly.)* . . . Don't worry about the work. I got us a contract with **Señor** Vasquez!

Everyone: **Señor** Vasquez!!!

Carmen: How did you convince him?

Estela: I just told him that we are the most hardworking women he could ever ask for. I know, I lied, but I got it.

Everyone: **¡Ayy!** *(All the women embrace excitedly. Rosalí brings out the birthday cake. They sing "Happy Birthday" not realizing that Rosalí is holding the cake backwards and it reads 52 instead of 25. They stop halfway through and turn it.)*

Estela: Fifty two?! *(They continue singing.)*

Rosalí: Ana, light up the candle so I can take a picture . . . *(Ana lights up the candle.)* Okay, Estela, blow out the candle. *(Estela stops to make a wish then blows it out. Rosalí takes a picture of her.)*

Ana: What did you wish for?

Estela: Maybe when you get back from New York you'll see. *(Ana and Pancha give their gift to Estela.)*

Rosalí: Ana, here, take a picture of us to remember this week . . . *(Rosalí gives Ana the camera. The women gather for the photo.)*

Ana: Okay! Ready? . . . One . . . two . . . three! *(The women suddenly hold up their "Temporary Residence Cards.")*

Women: Green!!! *(The women freeze in a pool of light. Ana steps out and turns to the audience. The women exit backstage. Spotlight on Ana.)*

Ana: I always took their work for granted, to be simple and unimportant. I was not proud to be working there at the beginning. I was only glad to know that because I was educated, I wasn't going to end up like them. I was going to be better than them. And I wanted to show them how much smarter and liberated I was. I was going to teach them about the women's liberation movement, about sexual liberation and all the things a so-called educated American woman knows. But in their subtle ways they taught me about resistance. About a battle no one was fighting for them except themselves. About the loneliness of being women in a country that looks down on us for being mothers and submissive wives. With their work that seems simple and unimportant, they are fighting . . . Perhaps the greatest thing I learned from them is that women are powerful, especially when working together . . . As for me, well, I settled for a secondhand typewriter and I wrote an essay on my experience and I was awarded a fellowship. So I went to New York and was a starving writer for some time before I went to New York University. When I came back the plans for making the boutique were no longer a dream, but a reality. *(Ana picks up a beautiful designer jacket and puts it on.)* Because I now wear original designs from Estela Garcia's boutique, "Real Women Have Curves."

(The lights come on and all the women enter the door wearing new evening gowns and accessories designed by Estela. The Women parade down the theater aisles voguing in a fashion-show style. They take their bows, continue voguing, and slowly exit. Lights slowly fade out.)

The End

GLOSSARY / SPANISH

A trabajar — To work it is
Abraza(r) — to hug
Abuelita — grandmother, granny
Adiós — good-bye
Aguas — look out
Ahora sí — okay, now
Alli esta en el cajon — It's there in the drawer
Amá — mama
¡Andenle! — Come on!
Apá — papa
Aquí huele a pura cuchupeta y a pedo — It smells like pussy and fart
Así es que — therefore/so
Así hazlo — Do it this way
¡Ave Maria Purissima! — Oh holy Mary of God!
Aver — Let's see, to have
Aver cuentanos — Come on tell us
¡Aver dime, condenada! — Damn you, tell me!
¡Ayy! — Ahh!, Oh!
¡Ayy que buenote! — He's so fine

Bañate — take a shower

Barrio — neighborhood

Basta — enough

Besa(r) — to kiss

Blusas — blouses

Bola de viejos cochinos — bunch of dirty old men

Bueno — well, good

Buenos días — good morning

Cállense — be quiet

Chafas — tacky

Chicharrón — pork rinds

Chichis — boobs, titties

Chisme — to gossip

Chismosa — gossip monger

Claro — of course

Cochinadas — junk

Como es — see how you are

¿Cómo estas? — How are you?

¿Cómo puede ser? — How can it be?

Corazón — heart

Coyote — someone who brings people across the border illegally for a price

Cumbia — Latin music from the Caribbean

¿De qué te apuras? — Why worry?

Desgraciada — ungrateful

Dios mio, ya mero acabamos — Oh, God, we're almost finished.

Diosito — God

Doña — a term of respect, literally meaning "old mother"; usually applied to the oldest woman present

¿Dónde los escondo? — Where shall I hide them?

¡Echame la culpa! — Blame me!

El Tormento — the heartthrob, or "crush"; or tormentor

Enojona — grouch

Entonces a la fuerza — then by force

¿Entonces qué quiere? — Then what do you want?

¡Entonces todas a trabajar! — Then to work it is!

¡Esa perra! — That bitch!

Eso — that

¡Esta cochinada no sirve! — This piece of junk doesn't work!

Está loquita — she's a little crazy

Estamos odidas — We are screwed

Fresas — strawberries, snooty upper class people in Mexico

Gringa — non Latinas (Anglos)

Hasta mañana — until tomorrow

Híjole — short for son of a bitch

¡Hora si que estamos bien jodidas! — Now we're really messed up!

Horita te lo coso — I'll sew it for you right now

Hoye — listen

Huevona — lazy, good for nothing

La migra — US Immigration and Naturalization Service officials, border patrol

Las pobrecitas — the poor women

Listos para chupar — delicious enough to suck
Lonchera — the lunch mobile
Loquita — a little crazy
Maldita — goddamned woman
Maquinita — little sewing machine
¡Mendiga vieja! — Damn witch!
¡Mentirosa! — Liars!
Metiche — nosy
Mi viejo — my husband, my old man
M'ija — my daughter
Mira(r) — to look, Look!
Mira que inteligente — look how smart
Mira que paresco — see what I look like
¡Miren! — Look!
¡Miren cómo coquetea! — Look how she flirts!
Mole — a sauce made of chocolate and chili
Nada — nothing
Nalgas — buttocks
Ni lo mande dios — god forbid
No le da verguenza — she's not ashamed
No mas mira que paresco — Just look what I look like
No mas ven a ver — Just come take a look
¡No puedo! — I can't
No que no te quiero — And you say I don't love you
No se — I don't know
¡No se peleen! — don't fight
No seas mensa — don't be dumb
No seas terca — don't be stubborn
No te hagas de rogar — don't make us beg
No te va hacer daño — It won't do you any harm
N'ombre — no way
Nopal — cactus
¡Otra! — Another one!
¿Pa qué? — For what?
Panza — stomach, belly
Panzonas — pregnant
Párele — stop it
Paresen de elefante — they look like they belong on an elephant
Patrona — boss
Pegame — hit me
Pero — but
¿Pero cómo? — But how?
Pero no puede ser — but it can't be
Pero que bien se siente — but it feels so good
Pero que loqura — what insanity
Pero tu — but you
Pinche — damn
¡Pinche rata! — Damn rat!
Pobre — poor
Pobre mujer — poor woman

Pobrecita — poor baby
Por favor — please
Por fin — finally
¿Pos cómo le hiciste? — Well, how did you do it?
Pos no nos queda otra — well we have no choice
Pos no se — Well, I don't know
¿Pos qué paso? — Well, what happened?
Pos yo ya no veo — I can't see a thing
Pues — Well
Pues por qué no — well why not
Puro lomo — all back
Que bonita, te ves — How pretty you look
Que bonito — how pretty
Que bonito viento — what beautiful wind
¡Que buena es! — How good you are!
¡Que calor! — It's so hot!
¿Qué hiciste? — What did you do?
¿Qué le píco? — What bit you?
Que locura — What madness
Que metiches — how nosey
¿Qué páso? — What happened?
¡Que susto! — What scare!
¿Qué te dijo la vieja? — What did the old hag tell you?
Rápido — quickly
¿Saben qué? — You know what?
"Se prohibe chismear!" — "Gossiping is Prohibited!"
Se te seca allí abajo — it gets dried down there
Se ve — It shows
Señor — mister, Mr., Sir
Sí, ya se fue — Yes, he's already left.
Tambien — also
Tan pequeña — so young
Tanto pedo y para nada — all this fuss/worrying and for nothing
'Tas flaca — You're skinny
Ten — Take it
Tengo fe — I have faith
Tul — tul, a synthetic material
Vago — loser, lazy, good for nothing
Válgame — oh my
Vámonos — let's go
Vamos a estar como gallinas enjauladas — we're going to be like caged chickens
Vas a verlo — you'll see
Vénganse — Come you all
¿Verá que sí? — Isn't it true?
Y los . . . — And the . . .
¿Y por qué no me habias dicho? — Why hadn't you told me?
¿Y tu? — And you?
Ya basta — enough already
Ya llego mi viejo — my husband is here
¡Ya ni la friegas! — You blew it

CONNECTIONS TO OTHER SELECTIONS

1. Discuss the thematic significance of issues associated with women's weight in Lopez's play and in Jane Anderson's *The Reprimand* (p. 1783).

2. Compare attitudes toward immigration law and the border patrol in *Real Women Have Curves* and in Gary Soto's poem "Mexicans Begin Jogging" (p. 1255).

Death of a Salesman

© CORBIS.

Arthur Miller was born in New York City to middle-class Jewish parents. His mother was a teacher and his father a clothing manufacturer. In 1938 he graduated from the University of Michigan, where he had begun writing plays. Six years later his first Broadway play, *The Man Who Had All the Luck,* closed after only a few performances, but *All My Sons* (1947) earned the admiration of both critics and audiences. This drama of family life launched his career, and his next play was even more successful. *Death of a Salesman* (1949) won a Pulitzer Prize and established his international reputation so that Miller, along with Tennessee Williams, became one of the most successful American playwrights of the 1940s and 1950s. During this period, his plays included an adaptation of Henrik Ibsen's *Enemy of the People* (1951), *The Crucible* (1953), and *A View from the Bridge* (1955). Among his later works are *The Misfits* (1961, a screenplay), *After the Fall* (1964), *Incident at Vichy* (1964), *The Price* (1968), *The Creation of the World and Other Business* (1972), *The Archbishop's Ceiling* (1976), *The American Clock* (1980), *Time Bends* (1987, essays), *The Ride Down Mt. Morgan* (1991), and *Broken Glass* (1994).

In *Death of a Salesman* Miller's concerns and techniques are similar to those of social realism. His characters' dialogue sounds much like ordinary speech and deals with recognizable family problems ranging from feelings about one another to personal aspirations. Like Ibsen and Chekhov, Miller places his characters in a social context so that their behavior within the family suggests larger implications: the death of this salesman raises issues concerning the significance and value of the American dream of success.

Although such qualities resemble some of the techniques and concerns of realistic drama, Miller also uses other techniques to express Willy Loman's thoughts. In a sense, the play allows the audience to observe what goes on inside the protagonist's head. (At one point Miller was going to title the play *The Inside of His Head.*) When Willy thinks of the past, we see those events reenacted on stage in the midst of present events. This reenactment is achieved through the use of symbolic nonrealistic sets that appear or disappear as the stage lighting changes to reveal Willy's state of mind.

Willy Loman is in many ways an ordinary human being—indeed, painfully so. He is neither brilliant nor heroic, and his life is made up of unfulfilled dreams and self-deceptions. Yet Miller conceived of him as a tragic figure because, as he wrote in "Tragedy and the Common Man" (see p. 1934), "the common man is as apt a subject for tragedy . . . as kings." Willy's circumstances are radically different from those of Oedipus or Hamlet, but Miller manages to create a character whose human dignity evokes tragic feelings for many readers and viewers.

ARTHUR MILLER (1915–2005)
Death of a Salesman   *1949*

Certain Private Conversations in Two Acts and a Requiem

CAST

Willy Loman	*Uncle Ben*
Linda	*Howard Wagner*
Biff	*Jenny*
Happy	*Stanley*
Bernard	*Miss Forsythe*
The Woman	*Letta*
Charley	

See Plays in Performance insert.

SCENE: The action takes place in Willy Loman's house and yard and in various places he visits in the New York and Boston of today.

Throughout the play, in the stage directions, left and right mean stage left and stage right.

ACT I

A melody is heard, played upon a flute. It is small and fine, telling of grass and trees and the horizon. The curtain rises.

Before us is the Salesman's house. We are aware of towering, angular shapes behind it, surrounding it on all sides. Only the blue light of the sky falls upon the house and forestage; the surrounding area shows an angry glow of orange. As more light appears, we see a solid vault of apartment houses around the small, fragile-seeming home. An air of the dream clings to the place, a dream rising out of reality. The kitchen at center seems actual enough, for there is a kitchen table with three chairs, and a refrigerator. But no other fixtures are seen. At the back of the kitchen there is a draped entrance, which leads to the living-room. To the right of the kitchen, on a level raised two feet, is a bedroom furnished only with a brass bedstead and a straight chair. On a shelf over the bed a silver athletic trophy stands. A window opens onto the apartment house at the side.

Behind the kitchen, on a level raised six and a half feet, is the boys' bedroom, at present barely visible. Two beds are dimly seen, and at the back of the room a dormer window. (This bedroom is above the unseen living-room.) At the left a stairway curves up to it from the kitchen.

The entire setting is wholly or, in some places, partially transparent. The roof-line of the house is one-dimensional; under and over it we see the apartment buildings. Before the house lies an apron, curving beyond the forestage into the orchestra. This forward area serves as the back yard as well as the locale of all Willy's imaginings and of his city scenes. Whenever the action is in the present the actors observe the imaginary wall-lines, entering the house only through its door at the left. But in the scenes of the past these boundaries are broken, and characters enter or leave a room by stepping "through" a wall onto the forestage.

From the right, Willy Loman, the Salesman, enters, carrying two large sample cases. The flute plays on. He hears but is not aware of it. He is past sixty years of age, dressed quietly. Even as he crosses the stage to the doorway of the house, his exhaustion is apparent. He unlocks the door, comes into the kitchen, and thankfully lets his burden down, feeling the soreness of his palms. A word-sigh escapes his lips— it might be "Oh, boy, oh, boy." He closes the door, then carries his cases out into the living-room, through the draped kitchen doorway.

Linda, his wife, has stirred in her bed at the right. She gets out and puts on a robe, listening. Most often jovial, she has developed an iron repression of her exceptions to Willy's behavior—she more than loves him, she admires him, as though his mercurial nature, his temper, his massive dreams and little cruelties, served her only as sharp reminders of the turbulent longings within him, longings which she shares but lacks the temperament to utter and follow to their end.

Linda (*hearing Willy outside the bedroom, calls with some trepidation*): Willy!

Willy: It's all right. I came back.

Linda: Why? What happened? (*Slight pause.*) Did something happen, Willy?

Willy: No, nothing happened.

Linda: You didn't smash the car, did you?

Willy (*with casual irritation*): I said nothing happened. Didn't you hear me?

Linda: Don't you feel well?

Willy: I'm tired to the death. (*The flute has faded away. He sits on the bed beside her, a little numb.*) I couldn't make it. I just couldn't make it, Linda.

Linda (*very carefully, delicately*): Where were you all day? You look terrible.

Willy: I got as far as a little above Yonkers. I stopped for a cup of coffee. Maybe it was the coffee.

Linda: What?

Willy (*after a pause*): I suddenly couldn't drive any more. The car kept going off onto the shoulder, y'know?

Linda (*helpfully*): Oh. Maybe it was the steering again. I don't think Angelo knows the Studebaker.

Willy: No, it's me, it's me. Suddenly I realize I'm goin' sixty miles an hour and I don't remember the last five minutes. I'm—I can't seem to—keep my mind to it.

Linda: Maybe it's your glasses. You never went for your new glasses.

Willy: No, I see everything. I came back ten miles an hour. It took me nearly four hours from Yonkers.

Linda (resigned): Well, you'll just have to take a rest, Willy, you can't continue this way.

Willy: I just got back from Florida.

Linda: But you didn't rest your mind. Your mind is overactive, and the mind is what counts, dear.

Willy: I'll start out in the morning. Maybe I'll feel better in the morning. *(She is taking off his shoes.)* These goddam arch supports are killing me.

Linda: Take an aspirin. Should I get you an aspirin? It'll soothe you.

Willy (with wonder): I was driving along, you understand? And I was fine. I was even observing the scenery. You can imagine, me looking at scenery, on the road every week of my life. But it's so beautiful up there, Linda, the trees are so thick, and the sun is warm. I opened the windshield and just let the warm air bathe over me. And then all of a sudden I'm goin' off the road! I'm tellin' ya, I absolutely forgot I was driving. If I'd've gone the other way over the white line I might've killed somebody. So I went on again — and five minutes later I'm dreamin' again, and I nearly — *(He presses two fingers against his eyes.)* I have such thoughts, I have such strange thoughts.

Linda: Willy, dear. Talk to them again. There's no reason why you can't work in New York.

Willy: They don't need me in New York. I'm the New England man. I'm vital in New England.

Linda: But you're sixty years old. They can't expect you to keep traveling every week.

Willy: I'll have to send a wire to Portland. I'm supposed to see Brown and Morrison tomorrow morning at ten o'clock to show the line. Goddammit, I could sell them! *(He starts putting on his jacket.)*

Linda (taking the jacket from him): Why don't you go down to the place tomorrow and tell Howard you've simply got to work in New York? You're too accommodating, dear.

Willy: If old man Wagner was alive I'd a been in charge of New York now! That man was a prince, he was a masterful man. But that boy of his, that Howard, he don't appreciate. When I went north the first time, the Wagner Company didn't know where New England was!

Linda: Why don't you tell those things to Howard, dear?

Willy (encouraged): I will, I definitely will. Is there any cheese?

Linda: I'll make you a sandwich.

Willy: No, go to sleep. I'll take some milk. I'll be up right away. The boys in?

Linda: They're sleeping. Happy took Biff on a date tonight.

Willy (interested): That so?

Linda: It was so nice to see them shaving together, one behind the other, in the bathroom. And going out together. You notice? The whole house smells of shaving lotion.

Willy: Figure it out. Work a lifetime to pay off a house. You finally own it, and there's nobody to live in it.

Linda: Well, dear, life is a casting off. It's always that way.

Willy: No, no, some people — some people accomplish something. Did Biff say anything after I went this morning?

Linda: You shouldn't have criticized him, Willy, especially after he just got off the train. You mustn't lose your temper with him.

Willy: When the hell did I lose my temper? I simply asked him if he was making any money. Is that a criticism?

Linda: But, dear, how could he make any money?

Willy (worried and angered): There's such an undercurrent in him. He became a moody man. Did he apologize when I left this morning?

Linda: He was crestfallen, Willy. You know how he admires you. I think if he finds himself, then you'll both be happier and not fight any more.

Willy: How can he find himself on a farm? Is that a life? A farmhand? In the beginning, when he was young, I thought, well, a young man, it's good for him to tramp around, take a lot of different jobs. But it's more than ten years now and he has yet to make thirty-five dollars a week!

Linda: He's finding himself, Willy.

Willy: Not finding yourself at the age of thirty-four is a disgrace!

Linda: Shh!

Willy: The trouble is he's lazy, goddammit!

Linda: Willy, please!

Willy: Biff is a lazy bum!

Linda: They're sleeping. Get something to eat. Go on down.

Willy: Why did he come home? I would like to know what brought him home.

Linda: I don't know. I think he's still lost, Willy. I think he's very lost.

Willy: Biff Loman is lost. In the greatest country in the world a young man with such—personal attractiveness, gets lost. And such a hard worker. There's one thing about Biff—he's not lazy.

Linda: Never.

Willy (with pity and resolve): I'll see him in the morning; I'll have a nice talk with him. I'll get him a job selling. He could be big in no time. My God! Remember how they used to follow him around in high school? When he smiled at one of them their faces lit up. When he walked down the street . . . *(He loses himself in reminiscences.)*

Linda (trying to bring him out of it): Willy, dear, I got a new kind of American-type cheese today. It's whipped.

Willy: Why do you get American when I like Swiss?

Linda: I just thought you'd like a change—

Willy: I don't want a change! I want Swiss cheese. Why am I always being contradicted?

Linda (with a covering laugh): I thought it would be a surprise.

Willy: Why don't you open a window in here, for God's sake?

Linda (with infinite patience): They're all open, dear.

Willy: The way they boxed us in here. Bricks and windows, windows and bricks.

Linda: We should've bought the land next door.

Willy: The street is lined with cars. There's not a breath of fresh air in the neighborhood. The grass don't grow any more, you can't raise a carrot in the back yard. They should've had a law against apartment houses. Remember those two beautiful elm trees out there? When I and Biff hung the swing between them?

Linda: Yeah, like being a million miles from the city.

Willy: They should've arrested the builder for cutting those down. They massacred the neighborhood. *(Lost.)* More and more I think of those days,

Linda. This time of year it was lilac and wisteria. And then the peonies would come out, and the daffodils. What fragrance in this room!

Linda: Well, after all, people had to move somewhere.

Willy: No, there's more people now.

Linda: I don't think there's more people. I think—

Willy: There's more people! That's what's ruining this country! Population is getting out of control. The competition is maddening! Smell the stink from that apartment house! And another one on the other side . . . How can they whip cheese?

On Willy's last line, Biff and Happy raise themselves up in their beds, listening.

Linda: Go down, try it. And be quiet.

Willy (turning to Linda, guiltily): You're not worried about me, are you, sweetheart?

Biff: What's the matter?

Happy: Listen!

Linda: You've got too much on the ball to worry about.

Willy: You're my foundation and my support, Linda.

Linda: Just try to relax, dear. You make mountains out of molehills.

Willy: I won't fight with him any more. If he wants to go back to Texas, let him go.

Linda: He'll find his way.

Willy: Sure. Certain men just don't get started till later in life. Like Thomas Edison, I think. Or B. F. Goodrich. One of them was deaf. *(He starts for the bedroom doorway.)* I'll put my money on Biff.

Linda: And Willy—if it's warm Sunday we'll drive in the country. And we'll open the windshield, and take lunch.

Willy: No, the windshields don't open on the new cars.

Linda: But you opened it today.

Willy: Me? I didn't. *(He stops.)* Now isn't that peculiar! Isn't that a remarkable— *(He breaks off in amazement and fright as the flute is heard distantly.)*

Linda: What, darling?

Willy: That is the most remarkable thing.

Linda: What, dear?

Willy: I was thinking of the Chevy. *(Slight pause.)* Nineteen twenty-eight . . . when I had that red Chevy— *(Breaks off.)* That funny? I coulda sworn I was driving that Chevy today.

Linda: Well, that's nothing. Something must've reminded you.

Willy: Remarkable. Ts. Remember those days? The way Biff used to simonize that car? The dealer refused to believe there was eighty thousand miles on it. *(He shakes his head.)* Heh! *(To Linda.)* Close your eyes, I'll be right up. *(He walks out of the bedroom.)*

Happy (to Biff): Jesus, maybe he smashed up the car again!

Linda (calling after Willy): Be careful on the stairs, dear! The cheese is on the middle shelf! *(She turns, goes over to the bed, takes his jacket, and goes out of the bedroom.)*

Light has risen on the boys' room. Unseen, Willy is heard talking to himself, "Eighty thousand miles," and a little laugh. Biff gets out of bed, comes downstage a bit, and stands attentively. Biff is two years older than his brother Happy, well built, but in these days bears a worn air and seems less self-assured. He has succeeded less, and his dreams are stronger and less acceptable than Happy's. Happy is tall, powerfully made. Sexuality is like a visible color on him, or a scent that many women have discovered. He, like his brother, is lost, but in a different way, for he has never allowed himself to turn his face toward defeat and is thus more confused and hard-skinned, although seemingly more content.

Happy (getting out of bed): He's going to get his license taken away if he keeps that up. I'm getting nervous about him, y'know, Biff?

Biff: His eyes are going.

Happy: No, I've driven with him. He sees all right. He just doesn't keep his mind on it. I drove into the city with him last week. He stops at a green light and then it turns red and he goes. *(He laughs.)*

Biff: Maybe he's color-blind.

Happy: Pop? Why he's got the finest eye for color in the business. You know that.

Biff (sitting down on his bed): I'm going to sleep.

Happy: You're not still sour on Dad, are you, Biff?

Biff: He's all right, I guess.

Willy (underneath them, in the living-room): Yes, sir, eighty thousand miles—eighty-two thousand!

Biff: You smoking?

Happy (holding out a pack of cigarettes): Want one?

Biff (taking a cigarette): I can never sleep when I smell it.

Willy: What a simonizing job, heh!

Happy (with deep sentiment): Funny, Biff, y'know? Us sleeping in here again? The old beds. *(He pats his bed affectionately.)* All the talk that went across those two beds, huh? Our whole lives.

Biff: Yeah. Lotta dreams and plans.

Happy (with a deep and masculine laugh): About five hundred women would like to know what was said in this room.

They share a soft laugh.

Biff: Remember that big Betsy something—what the hell was her name—over on Bushwick Avenue?

Happy (combing his hair): With the collie dog!

Biff: That's the one. I got you in there, remember?

Happy: Yeah, that was my first time—I think. Boy, there was a pig! *(They laugh, almost crudely.)* You taught me everything I know about women. Don't forget that.

Biff: I bet you forgot how bashful you used to be. Especially with girls.

Happy: Oh, I still am, Biff.

Biff: Oh, go on.

Happy: I just control it, that's all. I think I got less bashful and you got more so. What happened, Biff? Where's the old humor, the old confidence? *(He shakes Biff's knee. Biff gets up and moves restlessly about the room.)* What's the matter?

Biff: Why does Dad mock me all the time?

Happy: He's not mocking you, he—

Biff: Everything I say there's a twist of mockery on his face. I can't get near him.

Happy: He just wants you to make good, that's all. I wanted to talk to you about Dad for a long time, Biff. Something's—happening to him. He—talks to himself.

Biff: I noticed that this morning. But he always mumbled.

Happy: But not so noticeable. It got so embarrassing I sent him to Florida. And you know something? Most of the time he's talking to you.

Biff: What's he say about me?

Happy: I can't make it out.

Biff: What's he say about me?

Happy: I think the fact that you're not settled, that you're still kind of up in the air . . .

Biff: There's one or two other things depressing him, Happy.

Happy: What do you mean?

Biff: Never mind. Just don't lay it all to me.

Happy: But I think if you just got started—I mean—is there any future for you out there?

Biff: I tell ya, Hap, I don't know what the future is. I don't know—what I'm supposed to want.

Happy: What do you mean?

Biff: Well, I spent six or seven years after high school trying to work myself up. Shipping clerk, salesman, business of one kind or another. And it's a measly manner of existence. To get on that subway on the hot mornings in summer. To devote your whole life to keeping stock, or making phone calls, or selling or buying. To suffer fifty weeks of the year for the sake of a two-week vacation, when all you really desire is to be outdoors, with your shirt off. And always to have to get ahead of the next fella. And still—that's how you build a future.

Happy: Well, you really enjoy it on a farm? Are you content out there?

Biff (with rising agitation): Hap, I've had twenty or thirty different kinds of jobs since I left home before the war, and it always turns out the same. I just realized it lately. In Nebraska when I herded cattle, and the Dakotas, and Arizona, and now in Texas. It's why I came home now, I guess, because I realized it. This farm I work on, it's spring there now, see? And they've got about fifteen new colts. There's nothing more inspiring or—beautiful than the sight of a mare and a new colt. And it's cool there now, see? Texas is cool now, and it's spring. And whenever spring comes to where I am, I suddenly get the feeling, my God, I'm not gettin' anywhere! What the hell am I doing, playing around with horses, twenty-eight dollars a week! I'm thirty-four years old, I oughta be makin' my future. That's when I come running home. And now, I get here, and I don't know what to do with myself. *(After a pause.)* I've always made a point of not wasting my life, and everytime I come back here I know that all I've done is to waste my life.

Happy: You're a poet, you know that, Biff? You're a—you're an idealist!

Biff: No, I'm mixed up very bad. Maybe I oughta get married. Maybe I oughta get stuck into something. Maybe that's my trouble. I'm like a boy. I'm not married. I'm not in business, I just—I'm like a boy. Are you content, Hap? You're a success, aren't you? Are you content?

Happy: Hell, no!

Biff: Why? You're making money, aren't you?

Happy (moving about with energy, expressiveness): All I can do now is wait for the merchandise manager to die. And suppose I get to be merchandise manager? He's a good friend of mine, and he just built a terrific estate on Long

Island. And he lived there about two months and sold it, and now he's building another one. He can't enjoy it once it's finished. And I know that's just what I would do. I don't know what the hell I'm workin' for. Sometimes I sit in my apartment—all alone. And I think of the rent I'm paying. And it's crazy. But then, it's what I always wanted. My own apartment, a car, and plenty of women. And still, goddammit, I'm lonely.

Biff (with enthusiasm): Listen, why don't you come out West with me?

Happy: You and I, heh?

Biff: Sure, maybe we could buy a ranch. Raise cattle, use our muscles. Men built like we are should be working out in the open.

Happy (avidly): The Loman Brothers, heh?

Biff (with vast affection): Sure, we'd be known all over the counties!

Happy (enthralled): That's what I dream about, Biff. Sometimes I want to just rip my clothes off in the middle of the store and outbox that goddam merchandise manager. I mean I can outbox, outrun, and outlift anybody in that store, and I have to take orders from those common, petty sons-of-bitches till I can't stand it any more.

Biff: I'm tellin' you, kid, if you were with me I'd be happy out there.

Happy (enthused): See, Biff, everybody around me is so false that I'm constantly lowering my ideals . . .

Biff: Baby, together we'd stand up for one another, we'd have someone to trust.

Happy: If I were around you—

Biff: Hap, the trouble is we weren't brought up to grub for money. I don't know how to do it.

Happy: Neither can I!

Biff: Then let's go!

Happy: The only thing is—what can you make out there?

Biff: But look at your friend. Builds an estate and then hasn't the peace of mind to live in it.

Happy: Yeah, but when he walks into the store the waves part in front of him. That's fifty-two thousand dollars a year coming through the revolving door, and I got more in my pinky finger than he's got in his head.

Biff: Yeah, but you just said—

Happy: I gotta show some of those pompous, self-important executives over there that Hap Loman can make the grade. I want to walk into the store the way he walks in. Then I'll go with you, Biff. We'll be together yet, I swear. But take those two we had tonight. Now weren't they gorgeous creatures?

Biff: Yeah, yeah, most gorgeous I've had in years.

Happy: I get that any time I want, Biff. Whenever I feel disgusted. The trouble is, it gets like bowling or something. I just keep knockin' them over and it doesn't mean anything. You still run around a lot?

Biff: Naa. I'd like to find a girl—steady, somebody with substance.

Happy: That's what I long for.

Biff: Go on! You'd never come home.

Happy: I would! Somebody with character, with resistance! Like Mom, y'know? You're gonna call me a bastard when I tell you this. That girl Charlotte I was with tonight is engaged to be married in five weeks. *(He tries on his new hat.)*

Biff: No kiddin'!

Happy: Sure, the guy's in line for the vice-presidency of the store. I don't
know what gets into me, maybe I just have an overdeveloped sense of
competition or something, but I went and ruined her, and furthermore I
can't get rid of her. And he's the third executive I've done that to. Isn't that
a crummy characteristic? And to top it all, I go to their weddings! *(Indignantly, but laughing.)* Like I'm not supposed to take bribes. Manufacturers
offer me a hundred-dollar bill now and then to throw an order their way.
You know how honest I am, but it's like this girl, see. I hate myself for it.
Because I don't want the girl, and, still, I take it and — I love it!

Biff: Let's go to sleep.

Happy: I guess we didn't settle anything, heh?

Biff: I just got one idea that I think I'm going to try.

Happy: What's that?

Biff: Remember Bill Oliver?

Happy: Sure, Oliver is very big now. You want to work for him again?

Biff: No, but when I quit he said something to me. He put his arm on my
shoulder, and he said, "Biff, if you ever need anything, come to me."

Happy: I remember that. That sounds good.

Biff: I think I'll go to see him. If I could get ten thousand or even seven or eight
thousand dollars I could buy a beautiful ranch.

Happy: I bet he'd back you. 'Cause he thought highly of you, Biff. I mean,
they all do. You're well liked, Biff. That's why I say to come back here,
and we both have the apartment. And I'm tellin' you, Biff, any babe you
want . . .

Biff: No, with a ranch I could do the work I like and still be something. I just
wonder though. I wonder if Oliver still thinks I stole that carton of basket-
balls.

Happy: Oh, he probably forgot that long ago. It's almost ten years. You're too
sensitive. Anyway, he didn't really fire you.

Biff: Well, I think he was going to. I think that's why I quit. I was never sure
whether he knew or not. I know he thought the world of me, though. I was
the only one he'd let lock up the place.

Willy (below): You gonna wash the engine, Biff?

Happy: Shh!

Biff looks at Happy, who is gazing down, listening. Willy is mumbling in the parlor.

Happy: You hear that?

They listen. Willy laughs warmly.

Biff (growing angry): Doesn't he know Mom can hear that?

Willy: Don't get your sweater dirty, Biff!

A look of pain crosses Biff's face.

Happy: Isn't that terrible? Don't leave again, will you? You'll find a job here.
You gotta stick around. I don't know what to do about him, it's getting
embarrassing.

Willy: What a simonizing job!

Biff: Mom's hearing that!

Willy: No kiddin', Biff, you got a date? Wonderful!

Happy: Go on to sleep. But talk to him in the morning, will you?

Biff (reluctantly getting into bed): With her in the house. Brother!
Happy (getting into bed): I wish you'd have a good talk with him.

> The light on their room begins to fade.

Biff (to himself in bed): That selfish, stupid . . .
Happy: Sh . . . Sleep, Biff.

> Their light is out. Well before they have finished speaking, Willy's form is dimly seen
> below in the darkened kitchen. He opens the refrigerator, searches in there, and
> takes out a bottle of milk. The apartment houses are fading out, and the entire
> house and surroundings become covered with leaves. Music insinuates itself as the
> leaves appear.

Willy: Just wanna be careful with those girls, Biff, that's all. Don't make any
promises. No promises of any kind. Because a girl, y'know, they always believe what you tell 'em, and you're very young, Biff, you're too young to be
talking seriously to girls.

> Light rises on the kitchen. Willy, talking, shuts the refrigerator door and comes
> downstage to the kitchen table. He pours milk into a glass. He is totally immersed
> in himself, smiling faintly.

Willy: Too young entirely, Biff. You want to watch your schooling first. Then
when you're all set, there'll be plenty of girls for a boy like you. *(He smiles
broadly at a kitchen chair.)* That so? The girls pay for you? *(He laughs.)* Boy,
you must really be makin' a hit.

> Willy is gradually addressing—physically—a point offstage, speaking through the
> wall of the kitchen, and his voice has been rising in volume to that of a normal
> conversation.

Willy: I been wondering why you polish the car so careful. Ha! Don't leave the
hubcaps, boys. Get the chamois to the hubcaps. Happy, use newspaper on
the windows, it's the easiest thing. Show him how to do it, Biff! You see,
Happy? Pad it up, use it like a pad. That's it, that's it, good work. You're
doin' all right, Hap. *(He pauses, then nods in approbation for a few seconds, then
looks upward.)* Biff, first thing we gotta do when we get time is clip that big
branch over the house. Afraid it's gonna fall in a storm and hit the roof.
Tell you what. We get a rope and sling her around, and then we climb up
there with a couple of saws and take her down. Soon as you finish the car,
boys, I wanna see ya. I got a surprise for you, boys.
Biff (offstage): Whatta ya got, Dad?
Willy: No, you finish first. Never leave a job till you're finished—remember
that. *(Looking toward the "big trees.")* Biff, up in Albany I saw a beautiful
hammock. I think I'll buy it next trip, and we'll hang it right between
those two elms. Wouldn't that be something? Just swingin' there under
those branches. Boy, that would be . . .

> Young Biff and Young Happy appear from the direction Willy was addressing.
> Happy carries rags and a pail of water. Biff, wearing a sweater with a block "S,"
> carries a football.

Biff (pointing in the direction of the car offstage): How's that, Pop, professional?
Willy: Terrific. Terrific job, boys. Good work, Biff.

Happy: Where's the surprise, Pop?

Willy: In the back seat of the car.

Happy: Boy! *(He runs off.)*

Biff: What is it, Dad? Tell me, what'd you buy?

Willy (laughing, cuffs him): Never mind, something I want you to have.

Biff (turns and starts off): What is it, Hap?

Happy (offstage): It's a punching bag!

Biff: Oh, Pop!

Willy: It's got Gene Tunney's signature on it!

     Happy runs onstage with a punching bag.

Biff: Gee, how'd you know we wanted a punching bag?

Willy: Well, it's the finest thing for the timing.

Happy (lies down on his back and pedals with his feet): I'm losing weight, you notice, Pop?

Willy (to Happy): Jumping rope is good too.

Biff: Did you see the new football I got?

Willy (examining the ball): Where'd you get a new ball?

Biff: The coach told me to practice my passing.

Willy: That so? And he gave you the ball, heh?

Biff: Well, I borrowed it from the locker room. *(He laughs confidentially.)*

Willy (laughing with him at the theft): I want you to return that.

Happy: I told you he wouldn't like it!

Biff (angrily): Well, I'm bringing it back!

Willy (stopping the incipient argument, to Happy): Sure, he's gotta practice with a regulation ball, doesn't he? *(To Biff.)* Coach'll probably congratulate you on your initiative!

Biff: Oh, he keeps congratulating my initiative all the time, Pop.

Willy: That's because he likes you. If somebody else took that ball there'd be an uproar. So what's the report, boys, what's the report?

Biff: Where'd you go this time, Dad? Gee we were lonesome for you.

Willy (pleased, puts an arm around each boy and they come down to the apron): Lonesome, heh?

Biff: Missed you every minute.

Willy: Don't say? Tell you a secret, boys. Don't breathe it to a soul. Someday I'll have my own business, and I'll never have to leave home any more.

Happy: Like Uncle Charley, heh?

Willy: Bigger than Uncle Charley! Because Charley is not—liked. He's liked, but he's not—well liked.

Biff: Where'd you go this time, Dad?

Willy: Well, I got on the road, and I went north to Providence. Met the Mayor.

Biff: The Mayor of Providence!

Willy: He was sitting in the hotel lobby.

Biff: What'd he say?

Willy: He said, "Morning!" And I said, "You got a fine city here, Mayor." And then he had coffee with me. And then I went to Waterbury. Waterbury is a fine city. Big clock city, the famous Waterbury clock. Sold a nice bill there. And then Boston—Boston is the cradle of the Revolution. A fine city. And a couple of other towns in Mass., and on to Portland and Bangor and straight home!

Biff: Gee, I'd love to go with you sometime, Dad.

Willy: Soon as summer comes.

Happy: Promise?

Willy: You and Hap and I, and I'll show you all the towns. America is full of beautiful towns and fine, upstanding people. And they know me, boys, they know me up and down New England. The finest people. And when I bring you fellas up, there'll be open sesame for all of us, 'cause one thing, boys: I have friends. I can park my car in any street in New England, and the cops protect it like their own. This summer, heh?

Biff and Happy (together): Yeah! You bet!

Willy: We'll take our bathing suits.

Happy: We'll carry your bags, Pop!

Willy: Oh, won't that be something! Me comin' into the Boston stores with you boys carryin' my bags. What a sensation!

Biff is prancing around, practicing passing the ball.

Willy: You nervous, Biff, about the game?

Biff: Not if you're gonna be there.

Willy: What do they say about you in school, now that they made you captain?

Happy: There's a crowd of girls behind him everytime the classes change.

Biff (taking Willy's hand): This Saturday, Pop, this Saturday—just for you, I'm going to break through for a touchdown.

Happy: You're supposed to pass.

Biff: I'm takin' one play for Pop. You watch me, Pop, and when I take off my helmet, that means I'm breakin' out. Then you watch me crash through that line!

Willy (kisses Biff): Oh, wait'll I tell this in Boston!

Bernard enters in knickers. He is younger than Biff, earnest and loyal, a worried boy.

Bernard: Biff, where are you? You're supposed to study with me today.

Willy: Hey, looka Bernard. What're you lookin' so anemic about, Bernard?

Bernard: He's gotta study, Uncle Willy. He's got Regents next week.

Happy (tauntingly, spinning Bernard around): Let's box, Bernard!

Bernard: Biff! *(He gets away from Happy.)* Listen, Biff, I heard Mr. Birnbaum say that if you don't start studyin' math, he's gonna flunk you, and you won't graduate. I heard him!

Willy: You better study with him, Biff. Go ahead now.

Bernard: I heard him!

Biff: Oh, Pop, you didn't see my sneakers! *(He holds up a foot for Willy to look at.)*

Willy: Hey, that's a beautiful job of printing!

Bernard (wiping his glasses): Just because he printed University of Virginia on his sneakers doesn't mean they've got to graduate him, Uncle Willy!

Willy (angrily): What're you talking about? With scholarships to three universities they're gonna flunk him?

Bernard: But I heard Mr. Birnbaum say—

Willy: Don't be a pest, Bernard! *(To his boys.)* What an anemic!

Bernard: Okay, I'm waiting for you in my house, Biff.

Bernard goes off. The Lomans laugh.

Willy: Bernard is not well liked, is he?

Biff: He's liked, but he's not well liked.

Happy: That's right, Pop.

Willy: That's just what I mean. Bernard can get the best marks in school, y'understand, but when he gets out in the business world, y'understand, you are going to be five times ahead of him. That's why I thank Almighty God you're both built like Adonises.° Because the man who makes an appearance in the business world, the man who creates personal interest, is the man who gets ahead. Be liked and you will never want. You take me, for instance. I never have to wait in line to see a buyer. "Willy Loman is here!" That's all they have to know, and I go right through.

Biff: Did you knock them dead, Pop?

Willy: Knocked 'em cold in Providence, slaughtered 'em in Boston.

Happy (on his back, pedaling again): I'm losing weight, you notice, Pop?

> *Linda enters, as of old, a ribbon in her hair, carrying a basket of washing.*

Linda (with youthful energy): Hello, dear!

Willy: Sweetheart!

Linda: How'd the Chevy run?

Willy: Chevrolet, Linda, is the greatest car ever built. *(To the boys.)* Since when do you let your mother carry wash up the stairs?

Biff: Grab hold there, boy!

Happy: Where to, Mom?

Linda: Hang them up on the line. And you better go down to your friends, Biff. The cellar is full of boys. They don't know what to do with themselves.

Biff: Ah, when Pop comes home they can wait!

Willy (laughs appreciatively): You better go down and tell them what to do, Biff.

Biff: I think I'll have them sweep out the furnace room.

Willy: Good work, Biff.

Biff (goes through wall-line of kitchen to doorway at back and calls down): Fellas! Everybody sweep out the furnace room! I'll be right down!

Voices: All right! Okay, Biff.

Biff: George and Sam and Frank, come out back! We're hangin' up the wash! Come on, Hap, on the double! *(He and Happy carry out the basket.)*

Linda: The way they obey him!

Willy: Well, that's training, the training. I'm tellin' you, I was sellin' thousands and thousands, but I had to come home.

Linda: Oh, the whole block'll be at that game. Did you sell anything?

Willy: I did five hundred gross in Providence and seven hundred gross in Boston.

Linda: No! Wait a minute, I've got a pencil. *(She pulls pencil and paper out of her apron pocket.)* That makes your commission . . . Two hundred — my God! Two hundred and twelve dollars!

Willy: Well, I didn't figure it yet, but . . .

Linda: How much did you do?

Willy: Well, I—I did—about a hundred and eighty gross in Providence. Well, no—it came to—roughly two hundred gross on the whole trip.

Adonis: In Greek mythology, a young man known for his good looks and favored by Aphrodite, goddess of love and beauty.

Linda (without hesitation): Two hundred gross. That's . . . *(She figures.)*

Willy: The trouble was that three of the stores were half closed for inventory in Boston. Otherwise I woulda broke records.

Linda: Well, it makes seventy dollars and some pennies. That's very good.

Willy: What do we owe?

Linda: Well, on the first there's sixteen dollars on the refrigerator —

Willy: Why sixteen?

Linda: Well, the fan belt broke, so it was a dollar eighty.

Willy: But it's brand new.

Linda: Well, the man said that's the way it is. Till they work themselves in, y'know.

> *They move through the wall-line into the kitchen.*

Willy: I hope we didn't get stuck on that machine.

Linda: They got the biggest ads of any of them!

Willy: I know, it's a fine machine. What else?

Linda: Well, there's nine-sixty for the washing machine. And for the vacuum cleaner there's three and a half due on the fifteenth. Then the roof, you got twenty-one dollars remaining.

Willy: It don't leak, does it?

Linda: No, they did a wonderful job. Then you owe Frank for the carburetor.

Willy: I'm not going to pay that man! That goddam Chevrolet, they ought to prohibit the manufacture of that car!

Linda: Well, you owe him three and a half. And odds and ends, comes to around a hundred and twenty dollars by the fifteenth.

Willy: A hundred and twenty dollars! My God, if business don't pick up I don't know what I'm gonna do!

Linda: Well, next week you'll do better.

Willy: Oh, I'll knock 'em dead next week. I'll go to Hartford. I'm very well liked in Hartford. You know, the trouble is, Linda, people don't seem to take to me.

> *They move onto the forestage.*

Linda: Oh, don't be foolish.

Willy: I know it when I walk in. They seem to laugh at me.

Linda: Why? Why would they laugh at you? Don't talk that way, Willy.

> *Willy moves to the edge of the stage. Linda goes into the kitchen and starts to darn stockings.*

Willy: I don't know the reason for it, but they just pass me by. I'm not noticed.

Linda: But you're doing wonderful, dear. You're making seventy to a hundred dollars a week.

Willy: But I gotta be at it ten, twelve hours a day. Other men — I don't know — they do it easier. I don't know why — I can't stop myself — I talk too much. A man oughta come in with a few words. One thing about Charley. He's a man of few words, and they respect him.

Linda: You don't talk too much, you're just lively.

Willy (smiling): Well, I figure, what the hell, life is short, a couple of jokes. *(To himself.)* I joke too much! *(The smile goes.)*

Linda: Why? You're —

Willy: I'm fat. I'm very — foolish to look at, Linda. I didn't tell you, but Christmas time I happened to be calling on F. H. Stewarts, and a salesman

I know, as I was going in to see the buyer I heard him say something about—walrus. And I—I cracked him right across the face. I won't take that. I simply will not take that. But they do laugh at me. I know that.

Linda: Darling . . .

Willy: I gotta overcome it. I know I gotta overcome it. I'm not dressing to advantage, maybe.

Linda: Willy, darling, you're the handsomest man in the world—

Willy: Oh, no, Linda.

Linda: To me you are. *(Slight pause.)* The handsomest.

From the darkness is heard the laughter of a woman. Willy doesn't turn to it, but it continues through Linda's lines.

Linda: And the boys, Willy. Few men are idolized by their children the way you are.

Music is heard as behind a scrim, to the left of the house, The Woman, dimly seen, is dressing.

Willy (with great feeling): You're the best there is, Linda, you're a pal, you know that? On the road—on the road I want to grab you sometimes and just kiss the life outa you.

The laughter is loud now, and he moves into a brightening area at the left, where The Woman has come from behind the scrim and is standing, putting on her hat, looking into a "mirror" and laughing.

Willy: 'Cause I get so lonely—especially when business is bad and there's nobody to talk to. I get the feeling that I'll never sell anything again, that I won't make a living for you, or a business, a business for the boys. *(He talks through The Woman's subsiding laughter; The Woman primps at the "mirror.")* There's so much I want to make for—

The Woman: Me? You didn't make me, Willy. I picked you.

Willy (pleased): You picked me?

The Woman (who is quite proper-looking, Willy's age): I did. I've been sitting at that desk watching all the salesmen go by, day in, day out. But you've got such a sense of humor, and we do have such a good time together, don't we?

Willy: Sure, sure. *(He takes her in his arms.)* Why do you have to go now?

The Woman: It's two o'clock . . .

Willy: No, come on in! *(He pulls her.)*

The Woman: . . . my sisters'll be scandalized. When'll you be back?

Willy: Oh, two weeks about. Will you come up again?

The Woman: Sure thing. You do make me laugh. It's good for me. *(She squeezes his arm, kisses him.)* And I think you're a wonderful man.

Willy: You picked me, heh?

The Woman: Sure. Because you're so sweet. And such a kidder.

Willy: Well, I'll see you next time I'm in Boston.

The Woman: I'll put you right through to the buyers.

Willy (slapping her bottom): Right. Well, bottoms up!

The Woman (slaps him gently and laughs): You just kill me, Willy. *(He suddenly grabs her and kisses her roughly.)* You kill me. And thanks for the stockings. I love a lot of stockings. Well, good night.

Willy: Good night. And keep your pores open!

The Woman: Oh, Willy!

The Woman bursts out laughing, and Linda's laughter blends in. The Woman disappears into the dark. Now the area at the kitchen table brightens. Linda is sitting where she was at the kitchen table, but now is mending a pair of her silk stockings.

Linda: You are, Willy. The handsomest man. You've got no reason to feel that—

Willy (coming out of The Woman's dimming area and going over to Linda): I'll make it all up to you, Linda, I'll—

Linda: There's nothing to make up, dear. You're doing fine, better than—

Willy (noticing her mending): What's that?

Linda: Just mending my stockings. They're so expensive—

Willy (angrily, taking them from her): I won't have you mending stockings in this house! Now throw them out!

Linda puts the stockings in her pocket.

Bernard (entering on the run): Where is he? If he doesn't study!

Willy (moving to the forestage, with great agitation): You'll give him the answers!

Bernard: I do, but I can't on a Regents! That's a state exam! They're liable to arrest me!

Willy: Where is he? I'll whip him, I'll whip him!

Linda: And he'd better give back that football, Willy, it's not nice.

Willy: Biff! Where is he? Why is he taking everything?

Linda: He's too rough with the girls, Willy. All the mothers are afraid of him!

Willy: I'll whip him!

Bernard: He's driving the car without a license!

The Woman's laugh is heard.

Willy: Shut up!

Linda: All the mothers—

Willy: Shut up!

Bernard (backing quietly away and out): Mr. Birnbaum says he's stuck up.

Willy: Get outa here!

Bernard: If he doesn't buckle down he'll flunk math! *(He goes off.)*

Linda: He's right, Willy, you've gotta—

Willy (exploding at her): There's nothing the matter with him! You want him to be a worm like Bernard? He's got spirit, personality . . .

As he speaks, Linda, almost in tears, exits into the living-room. Willy is alone in the kitchen, wilting and staring. The leaves are gone. It is night again, and the apartment houses look down from behind.

Willy: Loaded with it. Loaded! What is he stealing? He's giving it back, isn't he? Why is he stealing? What did I tell him? I never in my life told him anything but decent things.

Happy in pajamas has come down the stairs; Willy suddenly becomes aware of Happy's presence.

Happy: Let's go now, come on.

Willy (sitting down at the kitchen table): Huh! Why did she have to wax the floors herself? Everytime she waxes the floors she keels over. She knows that!

Happy: Shh! Take it easy. What brought you back tonight?

Willy: I got an awful scare. Nearly hit a kid in Yonkers. God! Why didn't I go to Alaska with my brother Ben that time! Ben! That man was a genius, that man was success incarnate! What a mistake! He begged me to go.

Happy: Well, there's no use in —

Willy: You guys! There was a man started with the clothes on his back and ended up with diamond mines!

Happy: Boy, someday I'd like to know how he did it.

Willy: What's the mystery? The man knew what he wanted and went out and got it! Walked into a jungle, and comes out, the age of twenty-one, and he's rich! The world is an oyster, but you don't crack it open on a mattress!

Happy: Pop, I told you I'm gonna retire you for life.

Willy: You'll retire me for life on seventy goddam dollars a week? And your women and your car and your apartment, and you'll retire me for life! Christ's sake, I couldn't get past Yonkers today! Where are you guys, where are you? The woods are burning! I can't drive a car!

Charley has appeared in the doorway. He is a large man, slow of speech, laconic, immovable. In all he says, despite what he says, there is pity, and, now, trepidation. He has a robe over pajamas, slippers on his feet. He enters the kitchen.

Charley: Everything all right?

Happy: Yeah, Charley, everything's . . .

Willy: What's the matter?

Charley: I heard some noise. I thought something happened. Can't we do something about the walls? You sneeze in here, and in my house hats blow off.

Happy: Let's go to bed, Dad. Come on.

Charley signals to Happy to go.

Willy: You go ahead, I'm not tired at the moment.

Happy (to Willy): Take it easy, huh? *(He exits.)*

Willy: What're you doin' up?

Charley (sitting down at the kitchen table opposite Willy): Couldn't sleep good. I had a heartburn.

Willy: Well, you don't know how to eat.

Charley: I eat with my mouth.

Willy: No, you're ignorant. You gotta know about vitamins and things like that.

Charley: Come on, let's shoot. Tire you out a little.

Willy (hesitantly): All right. You got cards?

Charley (taking a deck from his pocket): Yeah, I got them. Someplace. What is it with those vitamins?

Willy (dealing): They build up your bones. Chemistry.

Charley: Yeah, but there's no bones in a heartburn.

Willy: What are you talkin' about? Do you know the first thing about it?

Charley: Don't get insulted.

Willy: Don't talk about something you don't know anything about.

They are playing. Pause.

Charley: What're you doin' home?

Willy: A little trouble with the car.

Charley: Oh. *(Pause.)* I'd like to take a trip to California.

Willy: Don't say.

Charley: You want a job?

Willy: I got a job, I told you that. *(After a slight pause.)* What the hell are you offering me a job for?

Charley: Don't get insulted.

Willy: Don't insult me.

Charley: I don't see no sense in it. You don't have to go on this way.

Willy: I got a good job. *(Slight pause.)* What do you keep comin' in here for?

Charley: You want me to go?

Willy (after a pause, withering): I can't understand it. He's going back to Texas again. What the hell is that?

Charley: Let him go.

Willy: I got nothin' to give him, Charley, I'm clean, I'm clean.

Charley: He won't starve. None a them starve. Forget about him.

Willy: Then what have I got to remember?

Charley: You take it too hard. To hell with it. When a deposit bottle is broken you don't get your nickel back.

Willy: That's easy enough for you to say.

Charley: That ain't easy for me to say.

Willy: Did you see the ceiling I put up in the living-room?

Charley: Yeah, that's a piece of work. To put up a ceiling is a mystery to me. How do you do it?

Willy: What's the difference?

Charley: Well, talk about it.

Willy: You gonna put up a ceiling?

Charley: How could I put up a ceiling?

Willy: Then what the hell are you bothering me for?

Charley: You're insulted again.

Willy: A man who can't handle tools is not a man. You're disgusting.

Charley: Don't call me disgusting, Willy.

> *Uncle Ben, carrying a valise and an umbrella, enters the forestage from around the right corner of the house. He is a stolid man, in his sixties, with a mustache and an authoritative air. He is utterly certain of his destiny, and there is an aura of far places about him. He enters exactly as Willy speaks.*

Willy: I'm getting awfully tired, Ben.

> *Ben's music is heard. Ben looks around at everything.*

Charley: Good, keep playing; you'll sleep better. Did you call me Ben?

> *Ben looks at his watch.*

Willy: That's funny. For a second there you reminded me of my brother Ben.

Ben: I only have a few minutes. *(He strolls, inspecting the place. Willy and Charley continue playing.)*

Charley: You never heard from him again, heh? Since that time?

Willy: Didn't Linda tell you? Couple of weeks ago we got a letter from his wife in Africa. He died.

Charley: That so.

Ben (chuckling): So this is Brooklyn, eh?

Charley: Maybe you're in for some of his money.

Willy: Naa, he had seven sons. There's just one opportunity I had with that man . . .

Ben: I must make a train, William. There are several properties I'm looking at in Alaska.

Willy: Sure, sure! If I'd gone with him to Alaska that time, everything would've been totally different.

Charley: Go on, you'd froze to death up there.

Willy: What're you talking about?

Ben: Opportunity is tremendous in Alaska, William. Surprised you're not up there.

Willy: Sure, tremendous.

Charley: Heh?

Willy: There was the only man I ever met who knew the answers.

Charley: Who?

Ben: How are you all?

Willy (taking a pot, smiling): Fine, fine.

Charley: Pretty sharp tonight.

Ben: Is Mother living with you?

Willy: No, she died a long time ago.

Charley: Who?

Ben: That's too bad. Fine specimen of a lady, Mother.

Willy (to Charley): Heh?

Ben: I'd hoped to see the old girl.

Charley: Who died?

Ben: Heard anything from Father, have you?

Willy (unnerved): What do you mean, who died?

Charley (taking a pot): What're you talkin' about?

Ben (looking at his watch): William, it's half-past eight!

Willy (as though to dispel his confusion he angrily stops Charley's hand): That's my build!

Charley: I put the ace—

Willy: If you don't know how to play the game I'm not gonna throw my money away on you!

Charley (rising): It was my ace, for God's sake!

Willy: I'm through, I'm through!

Ben: When did Mother die?

Willy: Long ago. Since the beginning you never knew how to play cards.

Charley (picks up the cards and goes to the door): All right! Next time I'll bring a deck with five aces.

Willy: I don't play that kind of game!

Charley (turning to him): You ought to be ashamed of yourself!

Willy: Yeah?

Charley: Yeah! *(He goes out.)*

Willy (slamming the door after him): Ignoramus!

Ben (as Willy comes toward him through the wall-line of the kitchen): So you're William.

Willy (shaking Ben's hand): Ben! I've been waiting for you so long! What's the answer? How did you do it?

Ben: Oh, there's a story in that.

Linda enters the forestage, as of old, carrying the wash basket.

Linda: Is this Ben?

Ben (gallantly): How do you do, my dear.

Linda: Where've you been all these years? Willy's always wondered why you—

Willy (pulling Ben away from her impatiently): Where is Dad? Didn't you follow
   him? How did you get started?

Ben: Well, I don't know how much you remember.

Willy: Well, I was just a baby, of course, only three or four years old—

Ben: Three years and eleven months.

Willy: What a memory, Ben!

Ben: I have many enterprises, William, and I have never kept books.

Willy: I remember I was sitting under the wagon in—was it Nebraska?

Ben: It was South Dakota, and I gave you a bunch of wild flowers.

Willy: I remember you walking away down some open road.

Ben (laughing): I was going to find Father in Alaska.

Willy: Where is he?

Ben: At that age I had a very faulty view of geography, William. I discovered
   after a few days that I was heading due south, so instead of Alaska, I ended
   up in Africa.

Linda: Africa!

Willy: The Gold Coast!

Ben: Principally diamond mines.

Linda: Diamond mines!

Ben: Yes, my dear. But I've only a few minutes—

Willy: No! Boys! Boys! *(Young Biff and Happy appear.)* Listen to this. This is your
   Uncle Ben, a great man! Tell my boys, Ben!

Ben: Why, boys, when I was seventeen I walked into the jungle, and when I was
   twenty-one I walked out. *(He laughs.)* And by God I was rich.

Willy (to the boys): You see what I been talking about? The greatest things can
   happen!

Ben (glancing at his watch): I have an appointment in Ketchikan Tuesday next
   week.

Willy: No, Ben! Please tell about Dad. I want my boys to hear. I want them to
   know the kind of stock they spring from. All I remember is a man with a
   big beard, and I was in Mamma's lap, sitting around a fire, and some kind
   of high music.

Ben: His flute. He played the flute.

Willy: Sure, the flute, that's right!

New music is heard, a high, rollicking tune.

Ben: Father was a very great and a very wild-hearted man. We would start in
   Boston, and he'd toss the whole family into the wagon, and then he'd drive
   the team right across the country; through Ohio, and Indiana, Michigan,
   Illinois, and all the Western states. And we'd stop in the towns and sell the
   flutes that he'd made on the way. Great inventor, Father. With one gadget
   he made more in a week than a man like you could make in a lifetime.

Willy: That's just the way I'm bringing them up, Ben—rugged, well liked, all-
   around.

Ben: Yeah? *(To Biff.)* Hit that, boy—hard as you can. *(He pounds his stomach.)*

Biff: Oh, no, sir!

Ben (taking boxing stance): Come on, get to me. *(He laughs.)*

Willy: Go to it, Biff! Go ahead, show him!

Biff: Okay! *(He cocks his fists and starts in.)*

Linda (to Willy): Why must he fight, dear?

Ben (sparring with Biff): Good boy! Good boy!

Willy: How's that, Ben, heh?

Happy: Give him the left, Biff!

Linda: Why are you fighting?

Ben: Good boy! *(Suddenly comes in, trips Biff, and stands over him, the point of his umbrella poised over Biff's eye.)*

Linda: Look out, Biff!

Biff: Gee!

Ben (patting Biff's knee): Never fight fair with a stranger, boy. You'll never get out of the jungle that way. *(Taking Linda's hand and bowing):* It was an honor and a pleasure to meet you, Linda.

Linda (withdrawing her hand coldly, frightened): Have a nice—trip.

Ben (to Willy): And good luck with your—what do you do?

Willy: Selling.

Ben: Yes. Well . . . *(He raises his hand in farewell to all.)*

Willy: No, Ben, I don't want you to think . . . *(He takes Ben's arm to show him.)* It's Brooklyn, I know, but we hunt too.

Ben: Really, now.

Willy: Oh, sure, there's snakes and rabbits and—that's why I moved out here. Why, Biff can fell any one of these trees in no time! Boys! Go right over to where they're building the apartment house and get some sand. We're gonna rebuild the entire front stoop now! Watch this, Ben!

Biff: Yes, sir! On the double, Hap!

Happy (as he and Biff run off): I lost weight, Pop, you notice?

Charley enters in knickers, even before the boys are gone.

Charley: Listen, if they steal any more from that building the watchman'll put the cops on them!

Linda (to Willy): Don't let Biff . . .

Ben laughs lustily.

Willy: You shoulda seen the lumber they brought home last week. At least a dozen six-by-tens worth all kinds a money.

Charley: Listen, if that watchman—

Willy: I gave them hell, understand. But I got a couple of fearless characters there.

Charley: Willy, the jails are full of fearless characters.

Ben (clapping Willy on the back, with a laugh at Charley): And the stock exchange, friend!

Willy (joining in Ben's laughter): Where are the rest of your pants?

Charley: My wife bought them.

Willy: Now all you need is a golf club and you can go upstairs and go to sleep. *(To Ben).* Great athlete! Between him and his son Bernard they can't hammer a nail!

Bernard (rushing in): The watchman's chasing Biff!

Willy (angrily): Shut up! He's not stealing anything!

Linda (alarmed, hurrying off left): Where is he? Biff, dear! *(She exits.)*

Willy (moving toward the left, away from Ben): There's nothing wrong. What's the matter with you?

Ben: Nervy boy. Good!

Willy (laughing): Oh, nerves of iron, that Biff!

Charley: Don't know what it is. My New England man comes back and he's bleedin', they murdered him up there.

Willy: It's contacts, Charley, I got important contacts!

Charley (sarcastically): Glad to hear it, Willy. Come in later, we'll shoot a little casino. I'll take some of your Portland money. *(He laughs at Willy and exits.)*

Willy (turning to Ben): Business is bad, it's murderous. But not for me, of course.

Ben: I'll stop by on my way back to Africa.

Willy (longingly): Can't you stay a few days? You're just what I need, Ben, because I—I have a fine position here, but I—well, Dad left when I was such a baby and I never had a chance to talk to him and I still feel—kind of temporary about myself.

Ben: I'll be late for my train.

They are at opposite ends of the stage.

Willy: Ben, my boys—can't we talk? They'd go into the jaws of hell for me, see, but I—

Ben: William, you're being first-rate with your boys. Outstanding, manly chaps!

Willy (hanging on to his words): Oh, Ben, that's good to hear! Because sometimes I'm afraid that I'm not teaching them the right kind of—Ben, how should I teach them?

Ben (giving great weight to each word, and with a certain vicious audacity): William, when I walked into the jungle, I was seventeen. When I walked out I was twenty-one. And, by God, I was rich! *(He goes off into darkness around the right corner of the house.)*

Willy: . . . was rich! That's just the spirit I want to imbue them with! To walk into a jungle! I was right! I was right! I was right!

Ben is gone, but Willy is still speaking to him as Linda, in nightgown and robe, enters the kitchen, glances around for Willy, then goes to the door of the house, looks out, and sees him. Comes down to his left. He looks at her.

Linda: Willy, dear? Willy?

Willy: I was right!

Linda: Did you have some cheese? *(He can't answer.)* It's very late, darling. Come to bed, heh?

Willy (looking straight up): Gotta break your neck to see a star in this yard.

Linda: You coming in?

Willy: Whatever happened to that diamond watch fob? Remember? When Ben came from Africa that time? Didn't he give me a watch fob with a diamond in it?

Linda: You pawned it, dear. Twelve, thirteen years ago. For Biff's radio correspondence course.

Willy: Gee, that was a beautiful thing. I'll take a walk.

Linda: But you're in your slippers.

Willy (starting to go around the house at the left): I was right! I was! *(Half to Linda, as he goes, shaking his head.)* What a man! There was a man worth talking to. I was right!

Linda (calling after Willy): But in your slippers, Willy!

Willy is almost gone when Biff, in his pajamas, comes down the stairs and enters the kitchen.

Biff: What is he doing out there?

Linda: Sh!

Biff: God Almighty, Mom, how long has he been doing this?

Linda: Don't, he'll hear you.

Biff: What the hell is the matter with him?

Linda: It'll pass by morning.

Biff: Shouldn't we do anything?

Linda: Oh, my dear, you should do a lot of things, but there's nothing to do, so go to sleep.

Happy comes down the stairs and sits on the steps.

Happy: I never heard him so loud, Mom.

Linda: Well, come around more often; you'll hear him. *(She sits down at the table and mends the lining of Willy's jacket.)*

Biff: Why didn't you ever write me about this, Mom?

Linda: How would I write to you? For over three months you had no address.

Biff: I was on the move. But you know I thought of you all the time. You know that, don't you, pal?

Linda: I know, dear, I know. But he likes to have a letter. Just to know that there's still a possibility for better things.

Biff: He's not like this all the time, is he?

Linda: It's when you come home he's always the worst.

Biff: When I come home?

Linda: When you write you're coming, he's all smiles, and talks about the future, and—he's just wonderful. And then the closer you seem to come, the more shaky he gets, and then, by the time you get here, he's arguing, and he seems angry at you. I think it's just that maybe he can't bring himself to—to open up to you. Why are you so hateful to each other? Why is that?

Biff (evasively): I'm not hateful, Mom.

Linda: But you no sooner come in the door than you're fighting!

Biff: I don't know why. I mean to change. I'm tryin', Mom, you understand?

Linda: Are you home to stay now?

Biff: I don't know. I want to look around, see what's doin'.

Linda: Biff, you can't look around all your life, can you?

Biff: I just can't take hold, Mom. I can't take hold of some kind of a life.

Linda: Biff, a man is not a bird, to come and go with the springtime.

Biff: Your hair . . . *(He touches her hair.)* Your hair got so gray.

Linda: Oh, it's been gray since you were in high school. I just stopped dyeing it, that's all.

Biff: Dye it again, will ya? I don't want my pal looking old. *(He smiles.)*

Linda: You're such a boy! You think you can go away for a year and . . . You've got to get it into your head now that one day you'll knock on this door and there'll be strange people here—

Biff: What are you talking about? You're not even sixty, Mom.

Linda: But what about your father?

Biff (lamely): Well, I meant him too.

Happy: He admires Pop.

Linda: Biff, dear, if you don't have any feeling for him, then you can't have any feeling for me.

Biff: Sure I can, Mom.

Linda: No. You can't just come to see me, because I love him. *(With a threat, but only a threat, of tears.)* He's the dearest man in the world to me, and I won't have anyone making him feel unwanted and low and blue. You've got to make up your mind now, darling, there's no leeway any more. Either he's your father and you pay him that respect, or else you're not to come here. I know he's not easy to get along with—nobody knows that better than me—but . . .

Willy (from the left, with a laugh): Hey, hey, Biffo!

Biff (starting to go out after Willy): What the hell is the matter with him? *(Happy stops him.)*

Linda: Don't—don't go near him!

Biff: Stop making excuses for him! He always, always wiped the floor with you. Never had an ounce of respect for you.

Happy: He's always had respect for—

Biff: What the hell do you know about it?

Happy (surlily): Just don't call him crazy!

Biff: He's got no character—Charley wouldn't do this. Not in his own house—spewing out that vomit from his mind.

Happy: Charley never had to cope with what he's got to.

Biff: People are worse off than Willy Loman. Believe me, I've seen them!

Linda: Then make Charley your father, Biff. You can't do that, can you? I don't say he's a great man. Willy Loman never made a lot of money. His name was never in the paper. He's not the finest character that ever lived. But he's a human being, and a terrible thing is happening to him. So attention must be paid. He's not to be allowed to fall into his grave like an old dog. Attention, attention must be finally paid to such a person. You called him crazy—

Biff: I didn't mean—

Linda: No, a lot of people think he's lost his—balance. But you don't have to be very smart to know what his trouble is. The man is exhausted.

Happy: Sure!

Linda: A small man can be just as exhausted as a great man. He works for a company thirty-six years this March, opens up unheard-of territories to their trademark, and now in his old age they take his salary away.

Happy (indignantly): I didn't know that, Mom.

Linda: You never asked, my dear! Now that you get your spending money someplace else you don't trouble your mind with him.

Happy: But I gave you money last—

Linda: Christmas time, fifty dollars! To fix the hot water it cost ninety-seven fifty! For five weeks he's been on straight commission, like a beginner, an unknown!

Biff: Those ungrateful bastards!

Linda: Are they any worse than his sons? When he brought them business, when he was young, they were glad to see him. But now his old friends, the old buyers that loved him so and always found some order to hand him in a pinch—they're all dead, retired. He used to be able to make six, seven calls a day in Boston. Now he takes his valises out of the car and puts them back and takes them out again and he's exhausted. Instead of walking he talks now. He drives seven hundred miles, and when he gets there no one knows him any more, no one welcomes him. And what goes through a man's mind, driving seven hundred miles home without having earned a cent? Why shouldn't he talk to himself? Why? When he has to go to Charley and borrow fifty dollars a week and pretend to me that it's his pay? How long can that go on? How long? You see what I'm sitting here and waiting for? And you tell me he has no character? The man who never worked a day but for your benefit? When does he get the medal for that? Is this his reward—to turn around at the age of sixty-three and find his sons, who he loved better than his life, one a philandering bum—

Happy: Mom!

Linda: That's all you are, my baby! *(To Biff.)* And you! What happened to the love you had for him? You were such pals! How you used to talk to him on the phone every night! How lonely he was till he could come home to you!

Biff: All right, Mom. I'll live here in my room, and I'll get a job. I'll keep away from him, that's all.

Linda: No, Biff. You can't stay here and fight all the time.

Biff: He threw me out of this house, remember that.

Linda: Why did he do that? I never knew why.

Biff: Because I know he's a fake and he doesn't like anybody around who knows!

Linda: Why a fake? In what way? What do you mean?

Biff: Just don't lay it all at my feet. It's between me and him—that's all I have to say. I'll chip in from now on. He'll settle for half my pay check. He'll be all right. I'm going to bed. *(He starts for the stairs.)*

Linda: He won't be all right.

Biff (turning on the stairs, furiously): I hate this city and I'll stay here. Now what do you want?

Linda: He's dying, Biff.

Happy turns quickly to her, shocked.

Biff (after a pause): Why is he dying?

Linda: He's been trying to kill himself.

Biff (with great horror): How?

Linda: I live from day to day.

Biff: What're you talking about?

Linda: Remember I wrote you that he smashed up the car again? In February?

Biff: Well?

Linda: The insurance inspector came. He said that they have evidence. That all these accidents in the last year—weren't—weren't—accidents.

Happy: How can they tell that? That's a lie.

Linda: It seems there's a woman . . . *(She takes a breath as):*

> *Biff (sharply but contained):* What woman?
>
> *Linda (simultaneously):* . . . and this woman . . .

Linda: What?

Biff: Nothing. Go ahead.

Linda: What did you say?

Biff: Nothing. I just said what woman?

Happy: What about her?

Linda: Well, it seems she was walking down the road and saw his car. She says that he wasn't driving fast at all, and that he didn't skid. She says he came to that little bridge, and then deliberately smashed into the railing, and it was only the shallowness of the water that saved him.

Biff: Oh, no, he probably just fell asleep again.

Linda: I don't think he fell asleep.

Biff: Why not?

Linda: Last month . . . *(With great difficulty.)* Oh, boys, it's so hard to say a thing like this! He's just a big stupid man to you, but I tell you there's more good in him than in many other people. *(She chokes, wipes her eyes.)* I was looking for a fuse. The lights blew out, and I went down the cellar. And behind the fuse box—it happened to fall out—was a length of rubber pipe—just short.

Happy: No kidding?

Linda: There's a little attachment on the end of it. I knew right away. And sure enough, on the bottom of the water heater there's a new little nipple on the gas pipe.

Happy (angrily): That—jerk.

Biff: Did you have it taken off?

Linda: I'm—I'm ashamed to. How can I mention it to him? Every day I go down and take away that little rubber pipe. But, when he comes home, I put it back where it was. How can I insult him that way? I don't know what to do. I live from day to day, boys. I tell you, I know every thought in his mind. It sounds so old-fashioned and silly, but I tell you he put his whole life into you and you've turned your backs on him. *(She is bent over in chair, weeping, her face in her hands.)* Biff, I swear to God! Biff, his life is in your hands!

Happy (to Biff): How do you like that damned fool!

Biff (kissing her): All right, pal, all right. It's all settled now. I've been remiss. I know that, Mom. But now I'll stay, and I swear to you, I'll apply myself. *(Kneeling in front of her, in a fever of self-reproach.)* It's just—you see, Mom, I don't fit in business. Not that I won't try. I'll try, and I'll make good.

Happy: Sure you will. The trouble with you in business was you never tried to please people.

Biff: I know, I—

Happy: Like when you worked for Harrison's. Bob Harrison said you were tops, and then you go and do some damn fool thing like whistling whole songs in the elevator like a comedian.

Biff (against Happy): So what? I like to whistle sometimes.

Happy: You don't raise a guy to a responsible job who whistles in the elevator!

Linda: Well, don't argue about it now.

Happy: Like when you'd go off and swim in the middle of the day instead of taking the line around.

Biff (his resentment rising): Well, don't you run off? You take off sometimes, don't you? On a nice summer day?

Happy: Yeah, but I cover myself!

Linda: Boys!

Happy: If I'm going to take a fade the boss can call any number where I'm supposed to be and they'll swear to him that I just left. I'll tell you something that I hate to say, Biff, but in the business world some of them think you're crazy.

Biff (angered): Screw the business world!

Happy: All right, screw it! Great, but cover yourself!

Linda: Hap, Hap!

Biff: I don't care what they think! They've laughed at Dad for years, and you know why? Because we don't belong in this nuthouse of a city! We should be mixing cement on some open plain, or—or carpenters. A carpenter is allowed to whistle!

Willy walks in from the entrance of the house, at left.

Willy: Even your grandfather was better than a carpenter. *(Pause. They watch him.)* You never grew up. Bernard does not whistle in the elevator, I assure you.

Biff (as though to laugh Willy out of it): Yeah, but you do, Pop.

Willy: I never in my life whistled in an elevator! And who in the business world thinks I'm crazy?

Biff: I didn't mean it like that, Pop. Now don't make a whole thing out of it, will ya?

Willy: Go back to the West! Be a carpenter, a cowboy, enjoy yourself!

Linda: Willy, he was just saying—

Willy: I heard what he said!

Happy (trying to quiet Willy): Hey, Pop, come on now . . .

Willy (continuing over Happy's line): They laugh at me, heh? Go to Filene's, go to the Hub, go to Slattery's, Boston. Call out the name Willy Loman and see what happens! Big shot!

Biff: All right, Pop.

Willy: Big!

Biff: All right!

Willy: Why do you always insult me?

Biff: I didn't say a word. *(To Linda.)* Did I say a word?

Linda: He didn't say anything, Willy.

Willy (going to the doorway of the living-room): All right, good night, good night.

Linda: Willy, dear, he just decided . . .

Willy (to Biff): If you get tired hanging around tomorrow, paint the ceiling I put up in the living-room.

Biff: I'm leaving early tomorrow.

Happy: He's going to see Bill Oliver, Pop.

Willy (interestedly): Oliver? For what?

Biff (with reserve, but trying, trying): He always said he'd stake me. I'd like to go into business, so maybe I can take him up on it.

Linda: Isn't that wonderful?

Willy: Don't interrupt. What's wonderful about it? There's fifty men in the City of New York who'd stake him. *(To Biff.)* Sporting goods?

Biff: I guess so. I know something about it and—

Willy: He knows something about it! You know sporting goods better than Spalding, for God's sake! How much is he giving you?

Biff: I don't know, I didn't even see him yet, but—

Willy: Then what're you talkin' about?

Biff (getting angry): Well, all I said was I'm gonna see him, that's all!

Willy (turning away): Ah, you're counting your chickens again.

Biff (starting left for the stairs): Oh, Jesus, I'm going to sleep!

Willy (calling after him): Don't curse in this house!

Biff (turning): Since when did you get so clean?

Happy (trying to stop them): Wait a . . .

Willy: Don't use that language to me! I won't have it!

Happy (grabbing Biff, shouts): Wait a minute! I got an idea. I got a feasible idea. Come here, Biff, let's talk this over now, let's talk some sense here. When I was down in Florida last time, I thought of a great idea to sell sporting goods. It just came back to me. You and I, Biff—we have a line, the Loman Line. We train a couple of weeks, and put on a couple of exhibitions, see?

Willy: That's an idea!

Happy: Wait! We form two basketball teams, see? Two water-polo teams. We play each other. It's a million dollars' worth of publicity. Two brothers, see? The Loman Brothers. Displays in the Royal Palms—all the hotels. And banners over the ring and the basketball court: "Loman Brothers." Baby, we could sell sporting goods!

Willy: That is a one-million-dollar idea!

Linda: Marvelous!

Biff: I'm in great shape as far as that's concerned.

Happy: And the beauty of it is, Biff, it wouldn't be like a business. We'd be out playin' ball again . . .

Biff (enthused): Yeah, that's . . .

Willy: Million-dollar . . .

Happy: And you wouldn't get fed up with it, Biff. It'd be the family again. There'd be the old honor, and comradeship, and if you wanted to go off for a swim or somethin'—well, you'd do it! Without some smart cooky gettin' up ahead of you!

Willy: Lick the world! You guys together could absolutely lick the civilized world.

Biff: I'll see Oliver tomorrow. Hap, if we could work that out . . .

Linda: Maybe things are beginning to—

Willy (wildly enthused, to Linda): Stop interrupting! *(To Biff.)* But don't wear sport jacket and slacks when you see Oliver.

Biff: No, I'll—

Willy: A business suit, and talk as little as possible, and don't crack any jokes.

Biff: He did like me. Always liked me.

Linda: He loved you!

Willy (to Linda): Will you stop! *(To Biff.)* Walk in very serious. You are not applying for a boy's job. Money is to pass. Be quiet, fine, and serious. Everybody likes a kidder, but nobody lends him money.

Happy: I'll try to get some myself, Biff. I'm sure I can.

Willy: I see great things for you kids, I think your troubles are over. But remember, start big and you'll end big. Ask for fifteen. How much you gonna ask for?

Biff: Gee, I don't know—

Willy: And don't say "Gee." "Gee" is a boy's word. A man walking in for fifteen thousand dollars does not say "Gee!"

Biff: Ten, I think, would be top though.

Willy: Don't be so modest. You always started too low. Walk in with a big laugh. Don't look worried. Start off with a couple of your good stories to lighten things up. It's not what you say, it's how you say it—because personality always wins the day.

Linda: Oliver always thought the highest of him—

Willy: Will you let me talk?

Biff: Don't yell at her, Pop, will ya?

Willy (angrily): I was talking, wasn't I?

Biff: I don't like you yelling at her all the time, and I'm tellin' you, that's all.

Willy: What're you, takin' over this house?

Linda: Willy—

Willy (turning on her): Don't take his side all the time, goddammit!

Biff (furiously): Stop yelling at her!

Willy (suddenly pulling on his cheek, beaten down, guilt ridden): Give my best to Bill Oliver—he may remember me. *(He exits through the living-room doorway.)*

Linda (her voice subdued): What'd you have to start that for? *(Biff turns away.)* You see how sweet he was as soon as you talked hopefully? *(She goes over to Biff.)* Come up and say good night to him. Don't let him go to bed that way.

Happy: Come on, Biff, let's buck him up.

Linda: Please, dear. Just say good night. It takes so little to make him happy. Come. *(She goes through the living-room doorway, calling upstairs from within the living-room.)* Your pajamas are hanging in the bathroom, Willy!

Happy (looking toward where Linda went out): What a woman! They broke the mold when they made her. You know that, Biff?

Biff: He's off salary. My God, working on commission!

Happy: Well, let's face it: he's no hot-shot selling man. Except that sometimes, you have to admit, he's a sweet personality.

Biff (deciding): Lend me ten bucks, will ya? I want to buy some new ties.

Happy: I'll take you to a place I know. Beautiful stuff. Wear one of my striped shirts tomorrow.

Biff: She got gray. Mom got awful old. Gee, I'm gonna go in to Oliver tomorrow and knock him for a—

Happy: Come on up. Tell that to Dad. Let's give him a whirl. Come on.

Biff (steamed up): You know, with ten thousand bucks, boy!

Happy (as they go into the living-room): That's the talk, Biff, that's the first time I've heard the old confidence out of you! *(From within the living-room, fading off.)* You're gonna live with me, kid, and any babe you want just say the word . . . (The last lines are hardly heard. They are mounting the stairs to their parents' bedroom.)*

Linda (entering her bedroom and addressing Willy, who is in the bathroom. She is straightening the bed for him): Can you do anything about the shower? It drips.

Willy (from the bathroom): All of a sudden everything falls to pieces! Goddam plumbing, oughta be sued, those people. I hardly finished putting it in and the thing . . . *(His words rumble off.)*

Linda: I'm just wondering if Oliver will remember him. You think he might?

Willy (coming out of the bathroom in his pajamas): Remember him? What's the matter with you, you crazy? If he'd've stayed with Oliver he'd be on top by now! Wait'll Oliver gets a look at him. You don't know the average caliber any more. The average young man today—(he is getting into bed)—is got a caliber of zero. Greatest thing in the world for him was to bum around.

Biff and Happy enter the bedroom. Slight pause.

Willy (stops short, looking at Biff): Glad to hear it, boy.

Happy: He wanted to say good night to you, sport.

Willy (to Biff): Yeah. Knock him dead, boy. What'd you want to tell me?

Biff: Just take it easy, Pop. Good night. *(He turns to go.)*

Willy (unable to resist): And if anything falls off the desk while you're talking to him—like a package or something—don't you pick it up. They have office boys for that.

Linda: I'll make a big breakfast—

Willy: Will you let me finish? *(To Biff.)* Tell him you were in the business in the West. Not farm work.

Biff: All right, Dad.

Linda: I think everything—

Willy (going right through her speech): And don't undersell yourself. No less than fifteen thousand dollars.

Biff (unable to bear him): Okay. Good night, Mom. *(He starts moving.)*

Willy: Because you got a greatness in you, Biff, remember that. You got all kinds a greatness . . . *(He lies back, exhausted. Biff walks out.)*

Linda (calling after Biff): Sleep well, darling!

Happy: I'm gonna get married, Mom. I wanted to tell you.

Linda: Go to sleep, dear.

Happy (going): I just wanted to tell you.

Willy: Keep up the good work. *(Happy exits.)* God . . . remember that Ebbets Field game? The championship of the city?

Linda: Just rest. Should I sing to you?

Willy: Yeah. Sing to me. *(Linda hums a soft lullaby.)* When that team came out— he was the tallest, remember?

Linda: Oh, yes. And in gold.

> *Biff enters the darkened kitchen, takes a cigarette, and leaves the house. He comes downstage into a golden pool of light. He smokes, staring at the night.*

Willy: Like a young god. Hercules—something like that. And the sun, the sun all around him. Remember how he waved to me? Right up from the field, with the representatives of three colleges standing by? And the buyers I brought, and the cheers when he came out—Loman, Loman, Loman! God Almighty, he'll be great yet. A star like that, magnificent, can never really fade away!

> *The light on Willy is fading. The gas heater begins to glow through the kitchen wall, near the stairs, a blue flame beneath red coils.*

Linda (timidly): Willy dear, what has he got against you?

Willy: I'm so tired. Don't talk any more.

> *Biff slowly returns to the kitchen. He stops, stares toward the heater.*

Linda: Will you ask Howard to let you work in New York?

Willy: First thing in the morning. Everything'll be all right.

> *Biff reaches behind the heater and draws out a length of rubber tubing. He is horrified and turns his head toward Willy's room, still dimly lit, from which the strains of Linda's desperate but monotonous humming rise.*

Willy (staring through the window into the moonlight): Gee, look at the moon moving between the buildings!

> *Biff wraps the tubing around his hand and quickly goes up the stairs.*

Curtain.

ACT II

Music is heard, gay and bright. The curtain rises as the music fades away. Willy, in shirt sleeves, is sitting at the kitchen table, sipping coffee, his hat in his lap. Linda is filling his cup when she can.

Willy: Wonderful coffee. Meal in itself.

Linda: Can I make you some eggs?

Willy: No. Take a breath.

Linda: You look so rested, dear.

Willy: I slept like a dead one. First time in months. Imagine, sleeping till ten on a Tuesday morning. Boys left nice and early, heh?

Linda: They were out of here by eight o'clock.

Willy: Good work!

Linda: It was so thrilling to see them leaving together. I can't get over the shaving lotion in this house!

Willy (smiling): Mmm—

Linda: Biff was very changed this morning. His whole attitude seemed to be hopeful. He couldn't wait to get downtown to see Oliver.

Willy: He's heading for a change. There's no question, there simply are certain men that take longer to get—solidified. How did he dress?

Linda: His blue suit. He's so handsome in that suit. He could be a—anything in that suit!

Willy gets up from the table. Linda holds his jacket for him.

Willy: There's no question, no question at all. Gee, on the way home tonight I'd like to buy some seeds.

Linda (laughing): That'd be wonderful. But not enough sun gets back there. Nothing'll grow any more.

Willy: You wait, kid, before it's all over we're gonna get a little place out in the country, and I'll raise some vegetables, a couple of chickens . . .

Linda: You'll do it yet, dear.

Willy walks out of his jacket. Linda follows him.

Willy: And they'll get married, and come for a weekend. I'd build a little guest house. 'Cause I got so many fine tools, all I'd need would be a little lumber and some peace of mind.

Linda (joyfully): I sewed the lining . . .

Willy: I could build two guest houses, so they'd both come. Did he decide how much he's going to ask Oliver for?

Linda (getting him into the jacket): He didn't mention it, but I imagine ten or fifteen thousand. You going to talk to Howard today?

Willy: Yeah. I'll put it to him straight and simple. He'll just have to take me off the road.

Linda: And Willy, don't forget to ask for a little advance, because we've got the insurance premium. It's the grace period now.

Willy: That's a hundred . . . ?

Linda: A hundred and eight, sixty-eight. Because we're a little short again.

Willy: Why are we short?

Linda: Well, you had the motor job on the car . . .

Willy: That goddam Studebaker!

Linda: And you got one more payment on the refrigerator . . .

Willy: But it just broke again!

Linda: Well, it's old, dear.

Willy: I told you we should've bought a well-advertised machine. Charley bought a General Electric and it's twenty years old and it's still good, that son-of-a-bitch.

Linda: But, Willy—

Willy: Whoever heard of a Hastings refrigerator? Once in my life I would like to own something outright before it's broken! I'm always in a race with the junkyard! I just finished paying for the car and it's on its last legs. The refrigerator consumes belts like a goddam maniac. They time those things. They time them so when you finally paid for them, they're used up.

Linda (buttoning up his jacket as he unbuttons it): All told, about two hundred dollars would carry us, dear. But that includes the last payment on the mortgage. After this payment, Willy, the house belongs to us.

Willy: It's twenty-five years!

Linda: Biff was nine years old when we bought it.

Willy: Well, that's a great thing. To weather a twenty-five-year mortgage is—

Linda: It's an accomplishment.

Willy: All the cement, the lumber, the reconstruction I put in this house! There ain't a crack to be found in it any more.

Linda: Well, it served its purpose.

Willy: What purpose? Some stranger'll come along, move in, and that's that. If only Biff would take this house, and raise a family . . . *(He starts to go.)* Good-by, I'm late.

Linda (suddenly remembering): Oh, I forgot! You're supposed to meet them for dinner.

Willy: Me?

Linda: At Frank's Chop House on Forty-eighth near Sixth Avenue.

Willy: Is that so! How about you?

Linda: No, just the three of you. They're gonna blow you to a big meal!

Willy: Don't say! Who thought of that?

Linda: Biff came to me this morning, Willy, and he said, "Tell Dad, we want to blow him to a big meal." Be there six o'clock. You and your two boys are going to have dinner.

Willy: Gee whiz! That's really somethin'. I'm gonna knock Howard for a loop, kid. I'll get an advance, and I'll come home with a New York job. Goddammit, now I'm gonna do it!

Linda: Oh, that's the spirit, Willy!

Willy: I will never get behind a wheel the rest of my life!

Linda: It's changing, Willy, I can feel it changing!

Willy: Beyond a question. G'by, I'm late. *(He starts to go again.)*

Linda (calling after him as she runs to the kitchen table for a handkerchief): You got your glasses?

Willy (feels for them, then comes back in): Yeah, yeah, got my glasses.

Linda (giving him the handkerchief): And a handkerchief.

Willy: Yeah, handkerchief.

Linda: And your saccharine?

Willy: Yeah, my saccharine.

Linda: Be careful on the subway stairs.

She kisses him, and a silk stocking is seen hanging from her hand. Willy notices it.

Willy: Will you stop mending stockings? At least while I'm in the house. It gets me nervous. I can't tell you. Please.

Linda hides the stocking in her hand as she follows Willy across the forestage in front of the house.

Linda: Remember, Frank's Chop House.

Willy (passing the apron): Maybe beets would grow out there.

Linda (laughing): But you tried so many times.

Willy: Yeah. Well, don't work hard today. (*He disappears around the right corner of the house.*)

Linda: Be careful!

As Willy vanishes, Linda waves to him. Suddenly the phone rings. She runs across the stage and into the kitchen and lifts it.

Linda: Hello? Oh, Biff! I'm so glad you called, I just . . . Yes, sure, I just told him. Yes, he'll be there for dinner at six o'clock, I didn't forget. Listen, I was just dying to tell you. You know that little rubber pipe I told you about? That he connected to the gas heater? I finally decided to go down the cellar this morning and take it away and destroy it. But it's gone! Imagine? He took it away himself, it isn't there! (*She listens.*) When? Oh, then you took it. Oh—nothing, it's just that I'd hoped he'd taken it away himself. Oh, I'm not worried, darling, because this morning he left in such high spirits, it was like the old days! I'm not afraid any more. Did Mr. Oliver see you? . . . Well, you wait there then. And make a nice impression on him, darling. Just don't perspire too much before you see him. And have a nice time with Dad. He may have big news too! . . . That's right, a New York job. And be sweet to him tonight, dear. Be loving to him. Because he's only a little boat looking for a harbor. (*She is trembling with sorrow and joy.*) Oh, that's wonderful, Biff, you'll save his life. Thanks, darling. Just put your arm around him when he comes into the restaurant. Give him a smile. That's the boy . . . Good-by, dear. . . . You got your comb? . . . That's fine. Good-by, Biff dear.

In the middle of her speech, Howard Wagner, thirty-six, wheels in a small typewriter table on which is a wire-recording machine and proceeds to plug it in. This is on the left forestage. Light slowly fades on Linda as it rises on Howard. Howard is intent on threading the machine and only glances over his shoulder as Willy appears.

Willy: Pst! Pst!

Howard: Hello, Willy, come in.

Willy: Like to have a little talk with you, Howard.

Howard: Sorry to keep you waiting. I'll be with you in a minute.

Willy: What's that, Howard?

Howard: Didn't you ever see one of these? Wire recorder.

Willy: Oh. Can we talk a minute?

Howard: Records things. Just got delivery yesterday. Been driving me crazy, the most terrific machine I ever saw in my life. I was up all night with it.

Willy: What do you do with it?

Howard: I bought it for dictation, but you can do anything with it. Listen to this. I had it home last night. Listen to what I picked up. The first one is my daughter. Get this. *(He flicks the switch and "Roll Out the Barrel" is heard being whistled.)* Listen to that kid whistle.

Willy: That is lifelike, isn't it?

Howard: Seven years old. Get that tone.

Willy: Ts, ts. Like to ask a little favor if you . . .

> *The whistling breaks off, and the voice of Howard's daughter is heard.*

His Daughter: "Now you, Daddy."

Howard: She's crazy for me! *(Again the same song is whistled.)* That's me! Ha! *(He winks.)*

Willy: You're very good!

> *The whistling breaks off again. The machine runs silent for a moment.*

Howard: Sh! Get this now, this is my son.

His Son: "The capital of Alabama is Montgomery; the capital of Arizona is Phoenix; the capital of Arkansas is Little Rock; the capital of California is Sacramento . . ." *(and on, and on).*

Howard (holding up five fingers): Five years old, Willy!

Willy: He'll make an announcer some day!

His Son (continuing): "The capital . . ."

Howard: Get that—alphabetical order! *(The machine breaks off suddenly.)* Wait a minute. The maid kicked the plug out.

Willy: It certainly is a—

Howard: Sh, for God's sake!

His Son: "It's nine o'clock, Bulova watch time. So I have to go to sleep."

Willy: That really is—

Howard: Wait a minute! The next is my wife.

> *They wait.*

Howard's Voice: "Go on, say something." *(Pause.)* "Well, you gonna talk?"

His Wife: "I can't think of anything."

Howard's Voice: "Well, talk—it's turning."

His Wife (shyly, beaten): "Hello." *(Silence.)* "Oh, Howard, I can't talk into this . . ."

Howard (snapping the machine off): That was my wife.

Willy: That is a wonderful machine. Can we—

Howard: I tell you, Willy, I'm gonna take my camera, and my bandsaw, and all my hobbies, and out they go. This is the most fascinating relaxation I ever found.

Willy: I think I'll get one myself.

Howard: Sure, they're only a hundred and a half. You can't do without it. Supposing you wanna hear Jack Benny, see? But you can't be at home at that hour. So you tell the maid to turn the radio on when Jack Benny comes on, and this automatically goes on with the radio . . .

Willy: And when you come home you . . .

Howard: You can come home twelve o'clock, one o'clock, any time you like, and you get yourself a Coke and sit yourself down, throw the switch, and there's Jack Benny's program in the middle of the night!

Willy: I'm definitely going to get one. Because lots of time I'm on the road, and I think to myself, what I must be missing on the radio!

Howard: Don't you have a radio in the car?

Willy: Well, yeah, but who ever thinks of turning it on?

Howard: Say, aren't you supposed to be in Boston?

Willy: That's what I want to talk to you about, Howard. You got a minute? *(He draws a chair in from the wing.)*

Howard: What happened? What're you doing here?

Willy: Well . . .

Howard: You didn't crack up again, did you?

Willy: Oh, no. No . . .

Howard: Geez, you had me worried there for a minute. What's the trouble?

Willy: Well, tell you the truth, Howard. I've come to the decision that I'd rather not travel any more.

Howard: Not travel! Well, what'll you do?

Willy: Remember, Christmas time, when you had the party here? You said you'd try to think of some spot for me here in town.

Howard: With us?

Willy: Well, sure.

Howard: Oh, yeah, yeah. I remember. Well, I couldn't think of anything for you, Willy.

Willy: I tell ya, Howard. The kids are all grown up, y'know. I don't need much any more. If I could take home — well, sixty-five dollars a week, I could swing it.

Howard: Yeah, but Willy, see I —

Willy: I tell ya why, Howard. Speaking frankly and between the two of us, y'know — I'm just a little tired.

Howard: Oh, I could understand that, Willy. But you're a road man, Willy, and we do a road business. We've only got a half-dozen salesmen on the floor here.

Willy: God knows, Howard, I never asked a favor of any man. But I was with the firm when your father used to carry you in here in his arms.

Howard: I know that, Willy, but —

Willy: Your father came to me the day you were born and asked me what I thought of the name of Howard, may he rest in peace.

Howard: I appreciate that, Willy, but there just is no spot here for you. If I had a spot I'd slam you right in, but I just don't have a single solitary spot.

He looks for his lighter. Willy has picked it up and gives it to him. Pause.

Willy (with increasing anger): Howard, all I need to set my table is fifty dollars a week.

Howard: But where am I going to put you, kid?

Willy: Look, it isn't a question of whether I can sell merchandise, is it?

Howard: No, but it's a business, kid, and everybody's gotta pull his own weight.

Willy (desperately): Just let me tell you a story, Howard —

Howard: 'Cause you gotta admit, business is business.

Willy (angrily): Business is definitely business, but just listen for a minute. You don't understand this. When I was a boy — eighteen, nineteen — I was already on the road. And there was a question in my mind as to whether selling had a future for me. Because in those days I had a yearning to go to Alaska. See, there were three gold strikes in one month in Alaska, and I felt like going out. Just for the ride, you might say.

Howard (barely interested): Don't say.

Willy: Oh, yeah, my father lived many years in Alaska. He was an adventurous man. We've got quite a little streak of self-reliance in our family. I thought I'd go out with my older brother and try to locate him, and maybe settle in the North with the old man. And I was almost decided to go, when I met a salesman in the Parker House. His name was Dave Singleman. And he was eighty-four years old, and he'd drummed merchandise in thirty-one states. And old Dave, he'd go up to his room, y'understand, put on his green velvet slippers — I'll never forget — and pick up his phone and call the buyers, and without ever leaving his room, at the age of eighty-four, he made his living. And when I saw that, I realized that selling was the great-est career a man could want. 'Cause what could be more satisfying than to be able to go, at the age of eighty-four, into twenty or thirty different cities, and pick up a phone, and be remembered and loved and helped by so many different people? Do you know? when he died — and by the way he died the <u>death of a salesman,</u> in his green velvet slippers in the smoker of the New York, New Haven, and Hartford, going into Boston — when he died, hundreds of salesmen and buyers were at his funeral. Things were sad on a lotta trains for months after that. *(He stands up. Howard has not looked at him.)* In those days there was personality in it, Howard. There was respect, and comradeship, and gratitude in it. Today, it's all cut and dried, and there's no chance for bringing friendship to bear — or personality. You see what I mean? They don't know me any more.

Howard (moving away, to the right): That's just the thing, Willy.

Willy: If I had forty dollars a week — that's all I'd need. Forty dollars, Howard.

Howard: Kid, I can't take blood from a stone, I—

Willy (desperation is on him now): Howard, the year Al Smith° was nominated, your father came to me and—

Howard (starting to go off): I've got to see some people, kid.

Willy (stopping him): I'm talking about your father! There were promises made across this desk! You mustn't tell me you've got people to see — I put thirty-four years into this firm, Howard, and now I can't pay my insur-ance! You can't eat the orange and throw the peel away — a man is not a piece of fruit! *(After a pause.)* Now pay attention. Your father — in 1928 I had a big year. I averaged a hundred and seventy dollars a week in commissions.

Howard (impatiently): Now, Willy, you never averaged—

Willy (banging his hand on the desk): I averaged a hundred and seventy dollars a week in the year of 1928! And your father came to me — or rather, I was in the office here — it was right over this desk — and he put his hand on my shoulder—

Howard (getting up): You'll have to excuse me, Willy, I gotta see some people. Pull yourself together. *(Going out.)* I'll be back in a little while.

On Howard's exit, the light on his chair grows very bright and strange.

Willy: Pull myself together! What the hell did I say to him? My God, I was yelling at him! How could I! *(Willy breaks off, staring at the light, which occupies*

Al Smith: Democratic candidate for president of the United States in 1928 who lost the elec-tion to Herbert Hoover.

the chair, animating it. He approaches this chair, standing across the desk from it.)
Frank, Frank, don't you remember what you told me that time? How you
put your hand on my shoulder, and Frank . . . *(He leans on the desk and as he
speaks the dead man's name he accidentally switches on the recorder, and instantly:)*

Howard's Son: " . . . of New York is Albany. The capital of Ohio is Cincinnati,
the capital of Rhode Island is . . . " *(The recitation continues.)*

Willy (leaping away with fright, shouting): Ha! Howard! Howard! Howard!

Howard (rushing in): What happened?

*Willy (pointing at the machine, which continues nasally, childishly, with the capital
cities):* Shut it off! Shut it off!

Howard (pulling the plug out): Look, Willy . . .

Willy (pressing his hands to his eyes): I gotta get myself some coffee. I'll get some
coffee . . .

Willy starts to walk out. Howard stops him.

Howard (rolling up the cord): Willy, look . . .

Willy: I'll go to Boston.

Howard: Willy, you can't go to Boston for us.

Willy: Why can't I go?

Howard: I don't want you to represent us. I've been meaning to tell you for a
long time now.

Willy: Howard, are you firing me?

Howard: I think you need a good long rest, Willy.

Willy: Howard—

Howard: And when you feel better, come back, and we'll see if we can work
something out.

Willy: But I gotta earn money, Howard. I'm in no position to—

Howard: Where are your sons? Why don't your sons give you a hand?

Willy: They're working on a very big deal.

Howard: This is no time for false pride, Willy. You go to your sons and you tell
them that you're tired. You've got two great boys, haven't you?

Willy: Oh, no question, no question, but in the meantime . . .

Howard: Then that's that, heh?

Willy: All right, I'll go to Boston tomorrow.

Howard: No, no.

Willy: I can't throw myself on my sons. I'm not a cripple!

Howard: Look, kid, I'm busy this morning.

Willy (grasping Howard's arm): Howard, you've got to let me go to Boston!

Howard (hard, keeping himself under control): I've got a line of people to see this
morning. Sit down, take five minutes, and pull yourself together, and then
go home, will ya? I need the office, Willy. *(He starts to go, turns, remembering
the recorder, starts to push off the table holding the recorder.)* Oh, yeah. Whenever
you can this week, stop by and drop off the samples. You'll feel better,
Willy, and then come back and we'll talk. Pull yourself together, kid,
there's people outside.

*Howard exits, pushing the table off left. Willy stares into space, exhausted. Now the
music is heard—Ben's music—first distantly, then closer, closer. As Willy speaks,
Ben enters from the right. He carries valise and umbrella.*

Willy: Oh, Ben, how did you do it? What is the answer? Did you wind up the
Alaska deal already?

Ben: Doesn't take much time if you know what you're doing. Just a short business trip. Boarding ship in an hour. Wanted to say good-by.

Willy: Ben, I've got to talk to you.

Ben (glancing at his watch): Haven't the time, William.

Willy (crossing the apron to Ben): Ben, nothing's working out. I don't know what to do.

Ben: Now, look here, William. I've bought timberland in Alaska and I need a man to look after things for me.

Willy: God, timberland! Me and my boys in those grand outdoors!

Ben: You've a new continent at your doorstep, William. Get out of these cities, they're full of talk and time payments and courts of law. Screw on your fists and you can fight for a fortune up there.

Willy: Yes, yes! Linda, Linda!

Linda enters as of old, with the wash.

Linda: Oh, you're back?

Ben: I haven't much time.

Willy: No, wait! Linda, he's got a proposition for me in Alaska.

Linda: But you've got— *(To Ben.)* He's got a beautiful job here.

Willy: But in Alaska, kid, I could—

Linda: You're doing well enough, Willy!

Ben (to Linda): Enough for what, my dear?

Linda (frightened of Ben and angry at him): Don't say those things to him! Enough to be happy right here, right now. *(To Willy, while Ben laughs.)* Why must everybody conquer the world? You're well liked, and the boys love you, and someday— *(to Ben)*—why, old man Wagner told him just the other day that if he keeps it up he'll be a member of the firm, didn't he, Willy?

Willy: Sure, sure. I am building something with this firm, Ben, and if a man is building something he must be on the right track, mustn't he?

Ben: What are you building? Lay your hand on it. Where is it?

Willy (hesitantly): That's true, Linda, there's nothing.

Linda: Why? *(To Ben.)* There's a man eighty-four years old—

Willy: That's right, Ben, that's right. When I look at that man I say, what is there to worry about?

Ben: Bah!

Willy: It's true, Ben. All he has to do is go into any city, pick up the phone, and he's making his living and you know why?

Ben (picking up his valise): I've got to go.

Willy (holding Ben back): Look at this boy!

Biff, in his high school sweater, enters carrying suitcase. Happy carries Biff's shoulder guards, gold helmet, and football pants.

Willy: Without a penny to his name, three great universities are begging for him, and from there the sky's the limit, because it's not what you do, Ben. It's who you know and the smile on your face! It's contacts, Ben, contacts! The whole wealth of Alaska passes over the lunch table at the Commodore Hotel, and that's the wonder, the wonder of this country, that a man can end with diamonds here on the basis of being liked! *(He turns to Biff.)* And that's why when you get out on that field today it's important. Because thousands of people will be rooting for you and loving you. *(To Ben, who has again begun to leave.)* And Ben! when he walks into a business office his name will sound out like a bell and all the doors will open to him! I've seen it, Ben, I've seen it a thousand times! You can't feel it with your hand like timber, but it's there!

Ben: Good-by, William.

Willy: Ben, am I right? Don't you think I'm right? I value your advice.

Ben: There's a new continent at your doorstep, William. You could walk out rich. Rich! *(He is gone.)*

Willy: We'll do it here, Ben! You hear me? We're gonna do it here!

> *Young Bernard rushes in. The gay music of the Boys is heard.*

Bernard: Oh, gee, I was afraid you left already!

Willy: Why? What time is it?

Bernard: It's half-past one!

Willy: Well, come on, everybody! Ebbets Field next stop! Where's the pennants? *(He rushes through the wall-line of the kitchen and out into the living-room.)*

Linda (to Biff): Did you pack fresh underwear?

Biff (who has been limbering up): I want to go!

Bernard: Biff, I'm carrying your helmet, ain't I?

Happy: I'm carrying the helmet.

Bernard: How am I going to get in the locker room?

Linda: Let him carry the shoulder guards. *(She puts her coat and hat on in the kitchen.)*

Bernard: Can I, Biff? 'Cause I told everybody I'm going to be in the locker room.

Happy: In Ebbets Field it's the clubhouse.

Bernard: I meant the clubhouse. Biff!

Happy: Biff!

Biff (grandly, after a slight pause): Let him carry the shoulder guards.

Happy (as he gives Bernard the shoulder guards): Stay close to us now.

> *Willy rushes in with the pennants.*

Willy (handing them out): Everybody wave when Biff comes out on the field. *(Happy and Bernard run off.)* You set now, boy?

> *The music has died away.*

Biff: Ready to go, Pop. Every muscle is ready.

Willy (at the edge of the apron): You realize what this means?

Biff: That's right, Pop.

Willy (feeling Biff's muscles): You're comin' home this afternoon captain of the All-Scholastic Championship Team of the City of New York.

Biff: I got it, Pop. And remember, pal, when I take off my helmet, that touchdown is for you.

Willy: Let's go! *(He is starting out, with his arm around Biff, when Charley enters, as of old, in knickers.)* I got no room for you, Charley.

Charley: Room? For what?

Willy: In the car.

Charley: You goin' for a ride? I wanted to shoot some casino.

Willy (furiously): Casino! *(Incredulously.)* Don't you realize what today is?

Linda: Oh, he knows, Willy. He's just kidding you.

Willy: That's nothing to kid about!

Charley: No, Linda, what's goin' on?

Linda: He's playing in Ebbets Field.

Charley: Baseball in this weather?

Willy: Don't talk to him. Come on, come on! *(He is pushing them out.)*

Charley: Wait a minute, didn't you hear the news?

Willy: What?

Charley: Don't you listen to the radio? Ebbets Field just blew up.

Willy: You go to hell! *(Charley laughs. Pushing them out.)* Come on, come on! We're late.

Charley (as they go): Knock a homer, Biff, knock a homer!

Willy (the last to leave, turning to Charley): I don't think that was funny, Charley. This is the greatest day of his life.

Charley: Willy, when are you going to grow up?

Willy: Yeah, heh? When this game is over, Charley, you'll be laughing out of the other side of your face. They'll be calling him another Red Grange. Twenty-five thousand a year.

Charley (kidding): Is that so?

Willy: Yeah, that's so.

Charley: Well, then, I'm sorry, Willy. But tell me something.

Willy: What?

Charley: Who is Red Grange?

Willy: Put up your hands. Goddam you, put up your hands!

Charley, chuckling, shakes his head and walks away, around the left corner of the stage. Willy follows him. The music rises to a mocking frenzy.

Willy: Who the hell do you think you are, better than everybody else? You don't know everything, you big, ignorant, stupid . . . Put up your hands!

Light rises, on the right side of the forestage, on a small table in the reception room of Charley's office. Traffic sounds are heard. Bernard, now mature, sits whistling to himself. A pair of tennis rackets and an overnight bag are on the floor beside him.

Willy (offstage): What are you walking away for? Don't walk away! If you're going to say something say it to my face! I know you laugh at me behind my back. You'll laugh out of the other side of your goddam face after this game. Touchdown! Touchdown! Eighty thousand people! Touchdown! Right between the goal posts.

Bernard is a quiet, earnest, but self-assured young man. Willy's voice is coming from right upstage now. Bernard lowers his feet off the table and listens. Jenny, his father's secretary, enters.

Jenny (distressed): Say, Bernard, will you go out in the hall?

Bernard: What is that noise? Who is it?

Jenny: Mr. Loman. He just got off the elevator.

Bernard (getting up): Who's he arguing with?

Jenny: Nobody. There's nobody with him. I can't deal with him any more, and your father gets all upset everytime he comes. I've got a lot of typing to do, and your father's waiting to sign it. Will you see him?

Willy (entering): Touchdown! Touch— *(He sees Jenny.)* Jenny, Jenny, good to see you. How're ya? Workin'? Or still honest?

Jenny: Fine. How've you been feeling?

Willy: Not much any more, Jenny. Ha, ha! *(He is surprised to see the rackets.)*

Bernard: Hello, Uncle Willy.

Willy (almost shocked): Bernard! Well, look who's here! *(He comes quickly, guiltily, to Bernard and warmly shakes his hand.)*

Bernard: How are you? Good to see you.

Willy: What are you doing here?

Bernard: Oh, just stopped by to see Pop. Get off my feet till my train leaves. I'm going to Washington in a few minutes.

Willy: Is he in?

Bernard: Yes, he's in his office with the accountant. Sit down.

Willy (sitting down): What're you going to do in Washington?

Bernard: Oh, just a case I've got there, Willy.

Willy: That so? *(Indicating the rackets.)* You going to play tennis there?

Bernard: I'm staying with a friend who's got a court.

Willy: Don't say. His own tennis court. Must be fine people, I bet.

Bernard: They are, very nice. Dad tells me Biff's in town.

Willy (with a big smile): Yeah, Biff's in. Working on a very big deal, Bernard.

Bernard: What's Biff doing?

Willy: Well, he's been doing very big things in the West. But he decided to establish himself here. Very big. We're having dinner. Did I hear your wife had a boy?

Bernard: That's right. Our second.

Willy: Two boys! What do you know!

Bernard: What kind of a deal has Biff got?

Willy: Well, Bill Oliver—very big sporting-goods man—he wants Biff very badly. Called him in from the West. Long distance, carte blanche, special deliveries. Your friends have their own private tennis court?

Bernard: You still with the old firm, Willy?

Willy (after a pause): I'm—I'm overjoyed to see how you made the grade, Bernard, overjoyed. It's an encouraging thing to see a young man really—really—Looks very good for Biff—very—*(He breaks off, then.)* Bernard—*(He is so full of emotion, he breaks off again.)*

Bernard: What is it, Willy?

Willy (small and alone): What—what's the secret?

Bernard: What secret?

Willy: How—how did you? Why didn't he ever catch on?

Bernard: I wouldn't know that, Willy.

Willy (confidentially, desperately): You were his friend, his boyhood friend. There's something I don't understand about it. His life ended after that Ebbets Field game. From the age of seventeen nothing good ever happened to him.

Bernard: He never trained himself for anything.

Willy: But he did, he did. After high school he took so many correspondence courses. Radio mechanics; television; God knows what, and never made the slightest mark.

Bernard (taking off his glasses): Willy, do you want to talk candidly?

Willy (rising, faces Bernard): I regard you as a very brilliant man, Bernard. I value your advice.

Bernard: Oh, the hell with the advice, Willy. I couldn't advise you. There's just one thing I've always wanted to ask you. When he was supposed to graduate, and the math teacher flunked him—

Willy: Oh, that son-of-a-bitch ruined his life.

Bernard: Yeah, but, Willy, all he had to do was go to summer school and make up that subject.

Willy: That's right, that's right.

Bernard: Did you tell him not to go to summer school?

Willy: Me? I begged him to go. I ordered him to go!

Bernard: Then why wouldn't he go?

Willy: Why? Why! Bernard, that question has been trailing me like a ghost for the last fifteen years. He flunked the subject, and laid down and died like a hammer hit him!

Bernard: Take it easy, kid.

Willy: Let me talk to you—I got nobody to talk to. Bernard, Bernard, was it my fault? Y'see? It keeps going around in my mind, maybe I did something to him. I got nothing to give him.

Bernard: Don't take it so hard.

Willy: Why did he lay down? What is the story there? You were his friend!

Bernard: Willy, I remember, it was June, and our grades came out. And he'd flunked math.

Willy: That son-of-a-bitch!

Bernard: No, it wasn't right then. Biff just got very angry, I remember, and he was ready to enroll in summer school.

Willy (surprised): He was?

Bernard: He wasn't beaten by it at all. But then, Willy, he disappeared from the block for almost a month. And I got the idea that he'd gone up to New England to see you. Did he have a talk with you then?

Willy stares in silence.

Bernard: Willy?

Willy (with a strong edge of resentment in his voice): Yeah, he came to Boston. What about it?

Bernard: Well, just that when he came back—I'll never forget this, it always mystifies me. Because I'd thought so well of Biff, even though he'd always taken advantage of me. I loved him, Willy, y'know? And he came back after that month and took his sneakers—remember those sneakers with "University of Virginia" printed on them? He was so proud of those, wore them every day. And he took them down in the cellar, and burned them up in the furnace. We had a fist fight. It lasted at least half an hour. Just the two of us, punching each other down the cellar, and crying right through it. I've often thought of how strange it was that I knew he'd given up his life. What happened in Boston, Willy?

Willy looks at him as at an intruder.

Bernard: I just bring it up because you asked me.

Willy (angrily): Nothing. What do you mean, "What happened?" What's that got to do with anything?

Bernard: Well, don't get sore.

Willy: What are you trying to do, blame it on me? If a boy lays down is that my fault?

Bernard: Now, Willy, don't get—

Willy: Well, don't—don't talk to me that way! What does that mean, "What happened?"

Charley enters. He is in his vest, and he carries a bottle of bourbon.

Charley: Hey, you're going to miss that train. *(He waves the bottle.)*

Bernard: Yeah, I'm going. *(He takes the bottle.)* Thanks, Pop. *(He picks up his rack-ets and bag.)* Good-by, Willy, and don't worry about it. You know. "If at first you don't succeed . . ."

Willy: Yes, I believe in that.

Bernard: But sometimes, Willy, it's better for a man just to walk away.

Willy: Walk away?

Bernard: That's right.

Willy: But if you can't walk away?

Bernard (after a slight pause): I guess that's when it's tough. *(Extending his hand.)* Good-by, Willy.

Willy (shaking Bernard's hand): Good-by, boy.

Charley (an arm on Bernard's shoulder): How do you like this kid? Gonna argue a case in front of the Supreme Court.

Bernard (protesting): Pop!

Willy (genuinely shocked, pained, and happy): No! The Supreme Court!

Bernard: I gotta run. 'By, Dad!

Charley: Knock 'em dead, Bernard!

Bernard goes off.

Willy (as Charley takes out his wallet): The Supreme Court! And he didn't even mention it!

Charley (counting out money on the desk): He don't have to—he's gonna do it.

Willy: And you never told him what to do, did you? You never took any interest in him.

Charley: My salvation is that I never took any interest in any thing. There's some money—fifty dollars. I got an accountant inside.

Willy: Charley, look . . . *(With difficulty.)* I got my insurance to pay. If you can manage it—I need a hundred and ten dollars.

Charley doesn't reply for a moment; merely stops moving.

Willy: I'd draw it from my bank but Linda would know, and I . . .

Charley: Sit down, Willy.

Willy (moving toward the chair): I'm keeping an account of everything, remem-ber. I'll pay every penny back. *(He sits.)*

Charley: Now listen to me, Willy.

Willy: I want you to know I appreciate . . .

Charley (sitting down on the table): Willy, what're you doin'? What the hell is goin' on in your head?

Willy: Why? I'm simply . . .

Charley: I offered you a job. You can make fifty dollars a week. And I won't send you on the road.

Willy: I've got a job.

Charley: Without pay? What kind of a job is a job without pay? *(He rises.)* Now, look, kid, enough is enough. I'm no genius but I know when I'm being insulted.

Willy: Insulted!

Charley: Why don't you want to work for me?

Willy: What's the matter with you? I've got a job.

Charley: Then what're you walkin' in here every week for?

Willy (getting up): Well, if you don't want me to walk in here—

Charley: I am offering you a job.

Willy: I don't want your goddam job!

Charley: When the hell are you going to grow up?

Willy (furiously): You big ignoramus, if you say that to me again I'll rap you one! I don't care how big you are! *(He's ready to fight.)*

Pause.

Charley (kindly, going to him): How much do you need, Willy?

Willy: Charley, I'm strapped. I'm strapped. I don't know what to do. I was just fired.

Charley: Howard fired you?

Willy: That snotnose. Imagine that? I named him. I named him Howard.

Charley: Willy, when're you gonna realize that them things don't mean anything? You named him Howard, but you can't sell that. The only thing you got in this world is what you can sell. And the funny thing is that you're a salesman, and you don't know that.

Willy: I've always tried to think otherwise, I guess. I always felt that if a man was impressive, and well liked, that nothing—

Charley: Why must everybody like you? Who liked J. P. Morgan? Was he impressive? In a Turkish bath he'd look like a butcher. But with his pockets on he was very well liked. Now listen, Willy, I know you don't like me, and nobody can say I'm in love with you, but I'll give you a job because—just for the hell of it, put it that way. Now what do you say?

Willy: I—I just can't work for you, Charley.

Charley: What're you, jealous of me?

Willy: I can't work for you, that's all, don't ask me why.

Charley (angered, takes out more bills): You been jealous of me all your life, you damned fool! Here, pay your insurance. *(He puts the money in Willy's hand.)*

Willy: I'm keeping strict accounts.

Charley: I've got some work to do. Take care of yourself. And pay your insurance.

Willy (moving to the right): Funny, y'know? After all the highways, and the trains, and the appointments, and the years, you end up worth more dead than alive.

Charley: Willy, nobody's worth nothin' dead. *(After a slight pause.)* Did you hear what I said?

Willy stands still, dreaming.

Charley: Willy!

Willy: Apologize to Bernard for me when you see him. I didn't mean to argue with him. He's a fine boy. They're all fine boys, and they'll end up big—all of them. Someday they'll all play tennis together. Wish me luck, Charley. He saw Bill Oliver today.

Charley: Good luck.

Willy (on the verge of tears): Charley, you're the only friend I got. Isn't that a remarkable thing? *(He goes out.)*

Charley: Jesus!

Charley stares after him a moment and follows. All light blacks out. Suddenly raucous music is heard, and a red glow rises behind the screen at right. Stanley, a young waiter, appears, carrying a table, followed by Happy, who is carrying two chairs.

Stanley (putting the table down): That's all right, Mr. Loman, I can handle it my-self. *(He turns and takes the chairs from Happy and places them at the table.)*

Happy (glancing around): Oh, this is better.

Stanley: Sure, in the front there you're in the middle of all kinds a noise. Whenever you got a party, Mr. Loman, you just tell me and I'll put you back here. Y'know, there's a lotta people they don't like it private, because when they go out they like to see a lotta action around them because they're sick and tired to stay in the house by theirself. But I know you, you ain't from Hackensack. You know what I mean?

Happy (sitting down): So how's it coming, Stanley?

Stanley: Ah, it's a dog's life. I only wish during the war they'd a took me in the Army. I coulda been dead by now.

Happy: My brother's back, Stanley.

Stanley: Oh, he come back, heh? From the Far West.

Happy: Yeah, big cattle man, my brother, so treat him right. And my father's coming too.

Stanley: Oh, your father too!

Happy: You got a couple of nice lobsters?

Stanley: Hundred per cent, big.

Happy: I want them with the claws.

Stanley: Don't worry, I don't give you no mice. *(Happy laughs.)* How about some wine? It'll put a head on the meal.

Happy: No. You remember, Stanley, that recipe I brought you from overseas? With the champagne in it?

Stanley: Oh, yeah, sure. I still got it tacked up yet in the kitchen. But that'll have to cost a buck apiece anyways.

Happy: That's all right.

Stanley: What'd you, hit a number or somethin'?

Happy: No, it's a little celebration. My brother is—I think he pulled off a big deal today. I think we're going into business together.

Stanley: Great! That's the best for you. Because a family business, you know what I mean?—that's the best.

Happy: That's what I think.

Stanley: 'Cause what's the difference? Somebody steals? It's in the family. Know what I mean? *(Sotto voce.°)* Like this bartender here. The boss is goin' crazy what kinda leak he's got in the cash register. You put it in but it don't come out.

Happy (raising his head): Sh!

Stanley: What?

Happy: You notice I wasn't lookin' right or left, was I?

Stanley: No.

Happy: And my eyes are closed.

Stanley: So what's the—?

Happy: Strudel's comin'.

Sotto voce: Softly, "under the breath" (Italian).

Stanley (catching on, looks around): Ah, no, there's no—

> *He breaks off as a furred, lavishly dressed girl enters and sits at the next table. Both follow her with their eyes.*

Stanley: Geez, how'd ya know?

Happy: I got radar or something. *(Staring directly at her profile.)* Oooooooo . . . Stanley.

Stanley: I think that's for you, Mr. Loman.

Happy: Look at that mouth. Oh, God. And the binoculars.

Stanley: Geez, you got a life, Mr. Loman.

Happy: Wait on her.

Stanley (going to the girl's table): Would you like a menu, ma'am?

Girl: I'm expecting someone, but I'd like a—

Happy: Why don't you bring her—excuse me, miss, do you mind? I sell champagne, and I'd like you to try my brand. Bring her a champagne, Stanley.

Girl: That's awfully nice of you.

Happy: Don't mention it. It's all company money. *(He laughs.)*

Girl: That's a charming product to be selling, isn't it?

Happy: Oh, gets to be like everything else. Selling is selling, y'know.

Girl: I suppose.

Happy: You don't happen to sell, do you?

Girl: No, I don't sell.

Happy: Would you object to a compliment from a stranger? You ought to be on a magazine cover.

Girl (looking at him a little archly): I have been.

> *Stanley comes in with a glass of champagne.*

Happy: What'd I say before, Stanley? You see? She's a cover girl.

Stanley: Oh, I could see, I could see.

Happy (to the Girl): What magazine?

Girl: Oh, a lot of them. *(She takes the drink.)* Thank you.

Happy: You know what they say in France, don't you? "Champagne is the drink of the complexion"—Hya, Biff!

> *Biff has entered and sits with Happy.*

Biff: Hello, kid. Sorry I'm late.

Happy: I just got here. Uh, Miss—?

Girl: Forsythe.

Happy: Miss Forsythe, this is my brother.

Biff: Is Dad here?

Happy: His name is Biff. You might've heard of him. Great football player.

Girl: Really? What team?

Happy: Are you familiar with football?

Girl: No, I'm afraid I'm not.

Happy: Biff is quarterback with the New York Giants.

Girl: Well, that is nice, isn't it? *(She drinks.)*

Happy: Good health.

Girl: I'm happy to meet you.

Happy: That's my name. Hap. It's really Harold, but at West Point they called me Happy.

Girl (now really impressed): Oh, I see. How do you do? *(She turns her profile.)*

Biff: Isn't Dad coming?

Happy: You want her?

Biff: Oh, I could never make that.

Happy: I remember the time that idea would never come into your head. Where's the old confidence, Biff?

Biff: I just saw Oliver—

Happy: Wait a minute. I've got to see that old confidence again. Do you want her? She's on call.

Biff: Oh, no. *(He turns to look at the Girl.)*

Happy: I'm telling you. Watch this. *(Turning to the Girl.)* Honey? *(She turns to him.)* Are you busy?

Girl: Well, I am . . . but I could make a phone call.

Happy: Do that, will you, honey? And see if you can get a friend. We'll be here for a while. Biff is one of the greatest football players in the country.

Girl (standing up): Well, I'm certainly happy to meet you.

Happy: Come back soon.

Girl: I'll try.

Happy: Don't try, honey, try hard.

> *The Girl exits. Stanley follows, shaking his head in bewildered admiration.*

Happy: Isn't that a shame now? A beautiful girl like that? That's why I can't get married. There's not a good woman in a thousand. New York is loaded with them, kid!

Biff: Hap, look—

Happy: I told you she was on call!

Biff (strangely unnerved): Cut it out, will ya? I want to say something to you.

Happy: Did you see Oliver?

Biff: I saw him all right. Now look, I want to tell Dad a couple of things and I want you to help me.

Happy: What? Is he going to back you?

Biff: Are you crazy? You're out of your goddam head, you know that?

Happy: Why? What happened?

Biff (breathlessly): I did a terrible thing today, Hap. It's been the strangest day I ever went through. I'm all numb, I swear.

Happy: You mean he wouldn't see you?

Biff: Well, I waited six hours for him, see? All day. Kept sending my name in. Even tried to date his secretary so she'd get me to him, but no soap.

Happy: Because you're not showin' the old confidence, Biff. He remembered you, didn't he?

Biff (stopping Happy with a gesture): Finally, about five o'clock, he comes out. Didn't remember who I was or anything. I felt like such an idiot, Hap.

Happy: Did you tell him my Florida idea?

Biff: He walked away. I saw him for one minute. I got so mad I could've torn the walls down! How the hell did I ever get the idea I was a salesman there? I even believed myself that I'd been a salesman for him! And then he gave me one look and—I realized what a ridiculous lie my whole life has been! We've been talking in a dream for fifteen years. I was a shipping clerk.

Happy: What'd you do?

Biff (with great tension and wonder): Well, he left, see. And the secretary went out. I was all alone in the waiting-room. I don't know what came over me,

Hap. The next thing I know I'm in his office — paneled walls, everything. I can't explain it. I — Hap, I took his fountain pen.

Happy: Geez, did he catch you?

Biff: I ran out. I ran down all eleven flights. I ran and ran and ran.

Happy: That was an awful dumb — what'd you do that for?

Biff (agonized): I don't know, I just — wanted to take something, I don't know. You gotta help me, Hap, I'm gonna tell Pop.

Happy: You crazy? What for?

Biff: Hap, he's got to understand that I'm not the man somebody lends that kind of money to. He thinks I've been spiting him all these years and it's eating him up.

Happy: That's just it. You tell him something nice.

Biff: I can't.

Happy: Say you got a lunch date with Oliver tomorrow.

Biff: So what do I do tomorrow?

Happy: You leave the house tomorrow and come back at night and say Oliver is thinking it over. And he thinks it over for a couple of weeks, and gradually it fades away and nobody's the worse.

Biff: But it'll go on forever!

Happy: Dad is never so happy as when he's looking forward to something!

> *Willy enters.*

Happy: Hello, scout!

Willy: Gee, I haven't been here in years!

> *Stanley has followed Willy in and sets a chair for him. Stanley starts off but Happy stops him.*

Happy: Stanley!

> *Stanley stands by, waiting for an order.*

Biff (going to Willy with guilt, as to an invalid): Sit down, Pop. You want a drink?

Willy: Sure, I don't mind.

Biff: Let's get a load on.

Willy: You look worried.

Biff: N-no. *(To Stanley.)* Scotch all around. Make it doubles.

Stanley: Doubles, right. *(He goes.)*

Willy: You had a couple already, didn't you?

Biff: Just a couple, yeah.

Willy: Well, what happened, boy? *(Nodding affirmatively, with a smile.)* Everything go all right?

Biff (takes a breath, then reaches out and grasps Willy's hand): Pal . . . *(He is smiling bravely, and Willy is smiling too.)* I had an experience today.

Happy: Terrific, Pop.

Willy: That so? What happened?

Biff (high, slightly alcoholic, above the earth): I'm going to tell you everything from first to last. It's been a strange day. *(Silence. He looks around, composes himself as best he can, but his breath keeps breaking the rhythm of his voice.)* I had to wait quite a while for him, and —

Willy: Oliver.

Biff: Yeah, Oliver. All day, as a matter of cold fact. And a lot of—instances—facts, Pop, facts about my life came back to me. Who was it, Pop? Who ever said I was a salesman with Oliver?

Willy: Well, you were.

Biff: No, Dad, I was a shipping clerk.

Willy: But you were practically—

Biff (with determination): Dad, I don't know who said it first, but I was never a salesman for Bill Oliver.

Willy: What're you talking about?

Biff: Let's hold on to the facts tonight, Pop. We're not going to get anywhere bullin' around. I was a shipping clerk.

Willy (angrily): All right, now listen to me—

Biff: Why don't you let me finish?

Willy: I'm not interested in stories about the past or any crap of that kind because the woods are burning, boys, you understand? There's a big blaze going on all around. I was fired today.

Biff (shocked): How could you be?

Willy: I was fired, and I'm looking for a little good news to tell your mother, because the woman has waited and the woman has suffered. The gist of it is that I haven't got a story left in my head, Biff. So don't give me a lecture about facts and aspects. I am not interested. Now what've you got to say to me?

Stanley enters with three drinks. They wait until he leaves.

Willy: Did you see Oliver?

Biff: Jesus, Dad!

Willy: You mean you didn't go up there?

Happy: Sure he went up there.

Biff: I did. I—saw him. How could they fire you?

Willy (on the edge of his chair): What kind of a welcome did he give you?

Biff: He won't even let you work on commission?

Willy: I'm out! (Driving.) So tell me, he gave you a warm welcome?

Happy: Sure, Pop, sure!

Biff (driven): Well, it was kind of—

Willy: I was wondering if he'd remember you. (To Happy.) Imagine, man doesn't see him for ten, twelve years and gives him that kind of a welcome!

Happy: Damn right!

Biff (trying to return to the offensive): Pop, look—

Willy: You know why he remembered you, don't you? Because you impressed him in those days.

Biff: Let's talk quietly and get this down to the facts, huh?

Willy (as though Biff had been interrupting): Well, what happened? It's great news, Biff. Did he take you into his office or'd you talk in the waiting-room?

Biff: Well, he came in, see, and—

Willy (with a big smile): What'd he say? Betcha he threw his arm around you.

Biff: Well, he kinda—

Willy: He's a fine man. (To Happy.) Very hard man to see, y'know.

Happy (agreeing): Oh, I know.

Willy (to Biff): Is that where you had the drinks?

Biff: Yeah, he gave me a couple of—no, no!

Happy (cutting in):   He told him my Florida idea.

Willy: Don't interrupt. *(To Biff.)* How'd he react to the Florida idea?

Biff: Dad, will you give me a minute to explain?

Willy: I've been waiting for you to explain since I sat down here! What happened? He took you into his office and what?

Biff: Well—I talked. And—and he listened, see.

Willy: Famous for the way he listens, y'know. What was his answer?

Biff: His answer was—*(He breaks off, suddenly angry.)* Dad, you're not letting me tell you what I want to tell you!

Willy (accusing, angered):   You didn't see him, did you?

Biff: I did see him!

Willy: What'd you insult him or something? You insulted him, didn't you?

Biff: Listen, will you let me out of it, will you just let me out of it!

Happy: What the hell!

Willy: Tell me what happened!

Biff (to Happy):   I can't talk to him!

> *A single trumpet note jars the ear. The light of green leaves stains the house, which holds the air of night and a dream. Young Bernard enters and knocks on the door of the house.*

Young Bernard (frantically):   Mrs. Loman, Mrs. Loman!

Happy: Tell him what happened!

Biff (to Happy):   Shut up and leave me alone!

Willy: No, no! You had to go and flunk math!

Biff: What math? What're you talking about?

Young Bernard: Mrs. Loman, Mrs. Loman!

> *Linda appears in the house, as of old.*

Willy (wildly):   Math, math, math!

Biff: Take it easy, Pop!

Young Bernard: Mrs. Loman!

Willy (furiously):   If you hadn't flunked you'd've been set by now!

Biff: Now, look, I'm gonna tell you what happened, and you're going to listen to me.

Young Bernard: Mrs. Loman!

Biff: I waited six hours—

Happy: What the hell are you saying?

Biff: I kept sending in my name but he wouldn't see me. So finally he . . . *(He continues unheard as light fades low on the restaurant.)*

Young Bernard: Biff flunked math!

Linda: No!

Young Bernard: Birnbaum flunked him! They won't graduate him!

Linda: But they have to. He's gotta go to the university. Where is he? Biff! Biff!

Young Bernard: No, he left. He went to Grand Central.

Linda: Grand—You mean he went to Boston!

Young Bernard: Is Uncle Willy in Boston?

Linda: Oh, maybe Willy can talk to the teacher. Oh, the poor, poor boy!

> *Light on house area snaps out.*

Biff (at the table, now audible, holding up a gold fountain pen):   . . . so I'm washed up with Oliver, you understand? Are you listening to me?

Willy (at a loss): Yeah, sure. If you hadn't flunked —

Biff: Flunked what? What're you talking about?

Willy: Don't blame everything on me! I didn't flunk math — you did! What pen?

Happy: That was awful dumb, Biff, a pen like that is worth —

Willy (seeing the pen for the first time): You took Oliver's pen?

Biff (weakening): Dad, I just explained it to you.

Willy: You stole Bill Oliver's fountain pen!

Biff: I didn't exactly steal it! That's just what I've been explaining to you!

Happy: He had it in his hand and just then Oliver walked in, so he got nervous and stuck it in his pocket!

Willy: My God, Biff!

Biff: I never intended to do it, Dad!

Operator's Voice: Standish Arms, good evening!

Willy (shouting): I'm not in my room!

Biff (frightened): Dad, what's the matter? *(He and Happy stand up.)*

Operator: Ringing Mr. Loman for you!

Willy: I'm not there, stop it!

Biff (horrified, gets down on one knee before Willy): Dad, I'll make good, I'll make good. *(Willy tries to get to his feet. Biff holds him down.)* Sit down now.

Willy: No, you're no good, you're no good for anything.

Biff: I am, Dad, I'll find something else, you understand? Now don't worry about anything. *(He holds up Willy's face.)* Talk to me, Dad.

Operator: Mr. Loman does not answer. Shall I page him?

Willy (attempting to stand, as though to rush and silence the Operator): No, no, no!

Happy: He'll strike something, Pop.

Willy: No, no . . .

Biff (desperately, standing over Willy): Pop, listen! Listen to me! I'm telling you something good. Oliver talked to his partner about the Florida idea. You listening? He — he talked to his partner, and he came to me . . . I'm going to be all right, you hear? Dad, listen to me, he said it was just a question of the amount!

Willy: Then you . . . got it?

Happy: He's gonna be terrific, Pop!

Willy (trying to stand): Then you got it, haven't you? You got it! You got it!

Biff (agonized, holds Willy down): No, no. Look, Pop. I'm supposed to have lunch with them tomorrow. I'm just telling you this so you'll know that I can still make an impression, Pop. And I'll make good somewhere, but I can't go tomorrow, see?

Willy: Why not? You simply —

Biff: But the pen, Pop!

Willy: You give it to him and tell him it was an oversight!

Happy: Sure, have lunch tomorrow!

Biff: I can't say that —

Willy: You were doing a crossword puzzle and accidentally used his pen!

Biff: Listen, kid, I took those balls years ago, now I walk in with his fountain pen? That clinches it, don't you see? I can't face him like that! I'll try elsewhere.

Page's Voice: Paging Mr. Loman!

Willy: Don't you want to be anything?

Biff: Pop, how can I go back?

Willy: You don't want to be anything, is that what's behind it?

Biff (now angry at Willy for not crediting his sympathy): Don't take it that way! You think it was easy walking into that office after what I'd done to him? A team of horses couldn't have dragged me back to Bill Oliver!

Willy: Then why'd you go?

Biff: Why did I go? Why did I go! Look at you! Look at what's become of you!

> *Off left, The Woman laughs.*

Willy: Biff, you're going to lunch tomorrow, or—

Biff: I can't go. I've got no appointment!

Happy: Biff, for . . . !

Willy: Are you spiting me?

Biff: Don't take it that way! Goddammit!

Willy (strikes Biff and falters away from the table): You rotten little louse! Are you spiting me?

The Woman: Someone's at the door, Willy!

Biff: I'm no good, can't you see what I am?

Happy (separating them): Hey, you're in a restaurant! Now cut it out, both of you! *(The girls enter.)* Hello, girls, sit down.

> *The Woman laughs, off left.*

Miss Forsythe: I guess we might as well. This is Letta.

The Woman: Willy, are you going to wake up?

Biff (ignoring Willy): How're ya, miss, sit down. What do you drink?

Miss Forsythe: Letta might not be able to stay long.

Letta: I gotta get up very early tomorrow. I got jury duty. I'm so excited! Were you fellows ever on a jury?

Biff: No, but I been in front of them! *(The girls laugh.)* This is my father.

Letta: Isn't he cute? Sit down with us, Pop.

Happy: Sit him down, Biff!

Biff (going to him): Come on, slugger, drink us under the table. To hell with it! Come on, sit down, pal.

> *On Biff's last insistence, Willy is about to sit.*

The Woman (now urgently): Willy, are you going to answer the door!

> *The Woman's call pulls Willy back. He starts right, befuddled.*

Biff: Hey, where are you going?

Willy: Open the door.

Biff: The door?

Willy: The washroom . . . the door . . . where's the door?

Biff (leading Willy to the left): Just go straight down.

> *Willy moves left.*

The Woman: Willy, Willy, are you going to get up, get up, get up, get up?

> *Willy exits left.*

Letta: I think it's sweet you bring your daddy along.

Miss Forsythe: Oh, he isn't really your father!

Biff (at left, turning to her resentfully): Miss Forsythe, you've just seen a prince walk by. A fine, troubled prince. A hard-working, unappreciated prince. A pal, you understand? A good companion. Always for his boys.

Letta: That's so sweet.

Happy: Well, girls, what's the program? We're wasting time. Come on, Biff. Gather round. Where would you like to go?

Biff: Why don't you do something for him?

Happy: Me!

Biff: Don't you give a damn for him, Hap?

Happy: What're you talking about? I'm the one who—

Biff: I sense it, you don't give a good goddamn about him. (*He takes the rolled-up hose from his pocket and puts it on the table in front of Happy.*) Look what I found in the cellar, for Christ's sake. How can you bear to let it go on?

Happy: Me? Who goes away? Who runs off and—

Biff: Yeah, but he doesn't mean anything to you. You could help him—I can't! Don't you understand what I'm talking about? He's going to kill himself, don't you know that?

Happy: Don't I know it! Me!

Biff: Hap, help him! Jesus . . . help him . . . Help me, help me, I can't bear to look at his face! (*Ready to weep, he hurries out, up right.*)

Happy (starting after him): Where are you going?

Miss Forsythe: What's he so mad about?

Happy: Come on, girls, we'll catch up with him.

Miss Forsythe (as Happy pushes her out): Say, I don't like that temper of his!

Happy: He's just a little overstrung, he'll be all right!

Willy (off left, as The Woman laughs): Don't answer! Don't answer!

Letta: Don't you want to tell your father—

Happy: No, that's not my father. He's just a guy. Come on, we'll catch Biff, and, honey, we're going to paint this town! Stanley, where's the check! Hey, Stanley!

> They exit. Stanley looks toward left.

Stanley (calling to Happy indignantly): Mr. Loman! Mr. Loman!

> Stanley picks up a chair and follows them off. Knocking is heard off left. The Woman enters, laughing. Willy follows her. She is in a black slip; he is buttoning his shirt. Raw, sensuous music accompanies their speech.

Willy: Will you stop laughing? Will you stop?

The Woman: Aren't you going to answer the door? He'll wake the whole hotel.

Willy: I'm not expecting anybody.

The Woman: Whyn't you have another drink, honey, and stop being so damn self-centered?

Willy: I'm so lonely.

The Woman: You know you ruined me, Willy? From now on, whenever you come to the office, I'll see that you go right through to the buyers. No waiting at my desk any more, Willy. You ruined me.

Willy: That's nice of you to say that.

The Woman: Gee, you are self-centered! Why so sad? You are the saddest, self-centeredest soul I ever did see-saw. (*She laughs. He kisses her.*) Come on inside, drummer boy. It's silly to be dressing in the middle of the night. (*As knocking is heard.*) Aren't you going to answer the door?

Willy: They're knocking on the wrong door.

The Woman: But I felt the knocking. And he heard us talking in here. Maybe the hotel's on fire!

Willy (his terror rising): It's a mistake.

The Woman: Then tell him to go away!

Willy: There's nobody there.

The Woman: It's getting on my nerves, Willy. There's somebody standing out there and it's getting on my nerves!

Willy (pushing her away from him): All right, stay in the bathroom here, and don't come out. I think there's a law in Massachusetts about it, so don't come out. It may be that new room clerk. He looked very mean. So don't come out. It's a mistake, there's no fire.

The knocking is heard again. He takes a few steps away from her, and she vanishes into the wing. The light follows him, and now he is facing Young Biff, who carries a suitcase. Biff steps toward him. The music is gone.

Biff: Why didn't you answer?

Willy: Biff! What are you doing in Boston?

Biff: Why didn't you answer? I've been knocking for five minutes, I called you on the phone—

Willy: I just heard you. I was in the bathroom and had the door shut. Did anything happen home?

Biff: Dad—I let you down.

Willy: What do you mean?

Biff: Dad . . .

Willy: Biffo, what's this about? *(Putting his arm around Biff.)* Come on, let's go downstairs and get you a malted.

Biff: Dad, I flunked math.

Willy: Not for the term?

Biff: The term. I haven't got enough credits to graduate.

Willy: You mean to say Bernard wouldn't give you the answers?

Biff: He did, he tried, but I only got a sixty-one.

Willy: And they wouldn't give you four points?

Biff: Birnbaum refused absolutely. I begged him, Pop, but he won't give me those points. You gotta talk to him before they close the school. Because if he saw the kind of man you are, and you just talked to him in your way, I'm sure he'd come through for me. The class came right before practice, see, and I didn't go enough. Would you talk to him? He'd like you, Pop. You know the way you could talk.

Willy: You're on. We'll drive right back.

Biff: Oh, Dad, good work! I'm sure he'll change it for you!

Willy: Go downstairs and tell the clerk I'm checkin' out. Go right down.

Biff: Yes, sir! See, the reason he hates me, Pop—one day he was late for class so I got up at the blackboard and imitated him. I crossed my eyes and talked with a lithp.

Willy (laughing): You did? The kids like it?

Biff: They nearly died laughing!

Willy: Yeah? What'd you do?

Biff: The thquare root of thixthy twee is . . . *(Willy bursts out laughing; Biff joins him.)* And in the middle of it he walked in!

Willy laughs and The Woman joins in offstage.

Willy (without hesitation): Hurry downstairs and—

Biff: Somebody in there?

Willy: No, that was next door.

   The Woman laughs offstage.

Biff: Somebody got in your bathroom!

Willy: No, it's the next room, there's a party—

The Woman (enters, laughing. She lisps this): Can I come in? There's something in the bathtub, Willy, and it's moving!

   Willy looks at Biff, who is staring open-mouthed and horrified at The Woman.

Willy: Ah—you better go back to your room. They must be finished painting by now. They're painting her room so I let her take a shower here. Go back, go back . . . *(He pushes her.)*

The Woman (resisting): But I've got to get dressed, Willy, I can't—

Willy: Get out of here! Go back, go back . . . *(Suddenly striving for the ordinary):* This is Miss Francis, Biff, she's a buyer. They're painting her room. Go back, Miss Francis, go back . . .

The Woman: But my clothes, I can't go out naked in the hall!

Willy (pushing her offstage): Get outa here! Go back, go back!

   Biff slowly sits down on his suitcase as the argument continues offstage.

The Woman: Where's my stockings? You promised me stockings, Willy!

Willy: I have no stockings here!

The Woman: You had two boxes of size nine sheers for me, and I want them!

Willy: Here, for God's sake, will you get outa here!

The Woman (enters holding a box of stockings): I just hope there's nobody in the hall. That's all I hope. *(To Biff.)* Are you football or baseball?

Biff: Football.

The Woman (angry, humiliated): That's me too. G'night. *(She snatches her clothes from Willy, and walks out.)*

Willy (after a pause): Well, better get going. I want to get to the school first thing in the morning. Get my suits out of the closet. I'll get my valise. *(Biff doesn't move.)* What's the matter? *(Biff remains motionless, tears falling.)* She's a buyer. Buys for J. H. Simmons. She lives down the hall—they're painting. You don't imagine—*(He breaks off. After a pause.)* Now listen, pal, she's just a buyer. She sees merchandise in her room and they have to keep it looking just so . . . *(Pause. Assuming command.)* All right, get my suits. *(Biff doesn't move.)* Now stop crying and do as I say. I gave you an order. Biff, I gave you an order! Is that what you do when I give you an order? How dare you cry! *(Putting his arm around Biff.)* Now look, Biff, when you grow up you'll understand about these things. You mustn't—you mustn't overemphasize a thing like this. I'll see Birnbaum first thing in the morning.

Biff: Never mind.

Willy (getting down beside Biff): Never mind! He's going to give you those points. I'll see to it.

Biff: He wouldn't listen to you.

Willy: He certainly will listen to me. You need those points for the U. of Virginia.

Biff: I'm not going there.

Willy: Heh? If I can't get him to change that mark you'll make it up in summer school. You've got all summer to—

Biff (his weeping breaking from him): Dad . . .

Willy (infected by it): Oh, my boy . . .

Biff: Dad . . .

Willy: She's nothing to me, Biff. I was lonely, I was terribly lonely.

Biff: You—you gave her Mama's stockings! *(His tears break through and he rises to go.)*

Willy (grabbing for Biff): I gave you an order!

Biff: Don't touch me, you—liar!

Willy: Apologize for that!

Biff: You fake! You phony little fake! You fake! *(Overcome, he turns quickly and weeping fully goes out with his suitcase. Willy is left on the floor on his knees.)*

Willy: I gave you an order! Biff, come back here or I'll beat you! Come back here! I'll whip you!

Stanley comes quickly in from the right and stands in front of Willy.

Willy (shouts at Stanley): I gave you an order . . .

Stanley: Hey, let's pick it up, pick it up, Mr. Loman. *(He helps Willy to his feet.)* Your boys left with the chippies. They said they'll see you home.

A second waiter watches some distance away.

Willy: But we were supposed to have dinner together.

Music is heard, Willy's theme.

Stanley: Can you make it?

Willy: I'll—sure, I can make it. *(Suddenly concerned about his clothes.)* Do I—I look all right?

Stanley: Sure, you look all right. *(He flicks a speck off Willy's lapel.)*

Willy: Here—here's a dollar.

Stanley: Oh, your son paid me. It's all right.

Willy (putting it in Stanley's hand): No, take it. You're a good boy.

Stanley: Oh, no, you don't have to . . .

Willy: Here—here's some more, I don't need it any more. *(After a slight pause.)* Tell me—is there a seed store in the neighborhood?

Stanley: Seeds? You mean like to plant?

As Willy turns, Stanley slips the money back into his jacket pocket.

Willy: Yes. Carrots, peas . . .

Stanley: Well, there's hardware stores on Sixth Avenue, but it may be too late now.

Willy (anxiously): Oh, I'd better hurry. I've got to get some seeds. *(He starts off to the right.)* I've got to get some seeds, right away. Nothing's planted. I don't have a thing in the ground.

Willy hurries out as the light goes down. Stanley moves over to the right after him, watches him off. The other waiter has been staring at Willy.

Stanley (to the waiter): Well, whatta you looking at?

The waiter picks up the chairs and moves off right. Stanley takes the table and follows him. The light fades on this area. There is a long pause, the sound of the flute coming over. The light gradually rises on the kitchen, which is empty. Happy appears at the door of the house, followed by Biff. Happy is carrying a large bunch of long-stemmed roses. He enters the kitchen, looks around for Linda. Not seeing her, he turns to Biff, who is just outside the house door, and makes a gesture with his hands, indicating "Not here, I guess." He looks into the living-room and freezes. Inside, Linda, unseen, is seated, Willy's coat on her lap. She rises ominously and quietly and moves toward Happy, who backs up into the kitchen, afraid.

Happy: Hey, what're you doing up? *(Linda says nothing but moves toward him implacably.)* Where's Pop? *(He keeps backing to the right, and now Linda is in full view in the doorway to the living-room.)* Is he sleeping?

Linda: Where were you?

Happy (trying to laugh it off): We met two girls, Mom, very fine types. Here, we brought you some flowers. *(Offering them to her.)* Put them in your room, Ma.

She knocks them to the floor at Biff's feet. He has now come inside and closed the door behind him. She stares at Biff, silent.

Happy: Now what'd you do that for? Mom, I want you to have some flowers—

Linda (cutting Happy off, violently to Biff): Don't you care whether he lives or dies?

Happy (going to the stairs): Come upstairs, Biff.

Biff (with a flare of disgust, to Happy): Go away from me! *(To Linda.)* What do you mean, lives or dies? Nobody's dying around here, pal.

Linda: Get out of my sight! Get out of here!

Biff: I wanna see the boss.

Linda: You're not going near him!

Biff: Where is he? *(He moves into the living-room and Linda follows.)*

Linda (shouting after Biff): You invite him for dinner. He looks forward to it all day — *(Biff appears in his parents' bedroom, looks around, and exits.)* — and then you desert him there. There's no stranger you'd do that to!

Happy: Why? He had a swell time with us. Listen, when I—*(Linda comes back into the kitchen)* — desert him I hope I don't outlive the day!

Linda: Get out of here!

Happy: Now look, Mom . . .

Linda: Did you have to go to women tonight? You and your lousy rotten whores!

Biff re-enters the kitchen.

Happy: Mom, all we did was follow Biff around trying to cheer him up! *(To Biff.)* Boy, what a night you gave me!

Linda: Get out of here, both of you, and don't come back! I don't want you tormenting him any more. Go on now, get your things together! *(To Biff.)* You can sleep in his apartment. *(She starts to pick up the flowers and stops herself.)* Pick up this stuff, I'm not your maid any more. Pick it up, you bum, you!

Happy turns his back to her in refusal. Biff slowly moves over and gets down on his knees, picking up the flowers.

Linda: You're a pair of animals! Not one, not another living soul would have had the cruelty to walk out on that man in a restaurant!

Biff (not looking at her): Is that what he said?

Linda: He didn't have to say anything. He was so humiliated he nearly limped when he came in.

Happy: But, Mom, he had a great time with us—

Biff (cutting him off violently): Shut up!

Without another word, Happy goes upstairs.

Linda: You! You didn't even go in to see if he was all right!

Biff (still on the floor in front of Linda, the flowers in his hand; with self-loathing): No. Didn't. Didn't do a damned thing. How do you like that, heh? Left him babbling in a toilet.

Linda: You louse. You . . .

Biff: Now you hit it on the nose! *(He gets up, throws the flowers in the wastebasket.)* The scum of the earth, and you're looking at him!

Linda: Get out of here!

Biff: I gotta talk to the boss, Mom. Where is he?

Linda: You're not going near him. Get out of this house!

Biff (with absolute assurance, determination): No. We're gonna have an abrupt conversation, him and me.

Linda: You're not talking to him!

Hammering is heard from outside the house, off right. Biff turns toward the noise.

Linda (suddenly pleading): Will you please leave him alone?

Biff: What's he doing out there?

Linda: He's planting the garden!

Biff (quietly): Now? Oh, my God!

Biff moves outside, Linda following. The light dies down on them and comes up on the center of the apron as Willy walks into it. He is carrying a flashlight, a hoe, and handful of seed packets. He raps the top of the hoe sharply to fix it firmly, and then moves to the left, measuring off the distance with his foot. He holds the flashlight to look at the seed packets, reading off the instructions. He is in the blue of night.

Willy: Carrots . . . quarter-inch apart. Rows . . . one-foot rows. *(He measures it off.)* One foot. *(He puts down a package and measures off.)* Beets. *(He puts down another package and measures again.)* Lettuce. *(He reads the package, puts it down.)* One foot — *(He breaks off as Ben appears at the right and moves slowly down to him.)* What a proposition, ts, ts. Terrific, terrific. 'Cause she's suffered, Ben, the woman has suffered. You understand me? A man can't go out the way he came in, Ben, a man has got to add up to something. You can't, you can't — *(Ben moves toward him as though to interrupt.)* You gotta consider, now. Don't answer so quick. Remember, it's a guaranteed twenty-thousand-dollar proposition. Now look, Ben, I want you to go through the ins and outs of this thing with me. I've got nobody to talk to, Ben, and the woman has suffered, you hear me?

Ben (standing still, considering): What's the proposition?

Willy: It's twenty thousand dollars on the barrelhead. Guaranteed, gilt-edged, you understand?

Ben: You don't want to make a fool of yourself. They might not honor the policy.

Willy: How can they dare refuse? Didn't I work like a coolie to meet every premium on the nose? And now they don't pay off? Impossible!

Ben: It's called a cowardly thing, William.

Willy: Why? Does it take more guts to stand here the rest of my life ringing up a zero?

Ben (yielding): That's a point, William. *(He moves, thinking, turns.)* And twenty thousand — that *is* something one can feel with the hand, it is there.

Willy (now assured, with rising power): Oh, Ben, that's the whole beauty of it! I
see it like a diamond, shining in the dark, hard and rough, that I can pick
up and touch in my hand. Not like — like an appointment! This would not
be another damned-fool appointment, Ben, and it changes all the aspects.
Because he thinks I'm nothing, see, and so he spites me. But the funeral —
(Straightening up.) Ben, that funeral will be massive! They'll come from
Maine, Massachusetts, Vermont, New Hampshire! All the old-timers with
the strange license plates — that boy will be thunder-struck, Ben, because
he never realized — I am known! Rhode Island, New York, New Jersey — I
am known, Ben, and he'll see it with his eyes once and for all. He'll see
what I am, Ben! He's in for a shock, that boy!

Ben (coming to the edge of the garden): He'll call you a coward.

Willy (suddenly fearful): No, that would be terrible.

Ben: Yes. And a damned fool.

Willy: No, no, he mustn't, I won't have that! *(He is broken and desperate.)*

Ben: He'll hate you William.

> *The gay music of the Boys is heard.*

Willy: Oh, Ben, how do we get back to all the great times? Used to be so full of
light, and comradeship, the sleigh-riding in winter, and the ruddiness on
his cheeks. And always some kind of good news coming up, always something nice coming up ahead. And never even let me carry the valises in the
house, and simonizing, simonizing that little red car! Why, why can't I
give him something and not have him hate me?

Ben: Let me think about it. *(He glances at his watch.)* I still have a little time. Remarkable proposition, but you've got to be sure you're not making a fool
of yourself.

> *Ben drifts off upstage and goes out of sight. Biff comes down from the left.*

*Willy (suddenly conscious of Biff, turns and looks up at him, then begins picking up the
packages of seeds in confusion):* Where the hell is that seed? *(Indignantly.)* You
can't see nothing out here! They boxed in the whole goddamn neighborhood!

Biff: There are people all around here. Don't you realize that?

Willy: I'm busy. Don't bother me.

Biff (taking the hoe from Willy): I'm saying good-by to you, Pop. *(Willy looks at
him, silent, unable to move.)* I'm not coming back any more.

Willy: You're not going to see Oliver tomorrow?

Biff: I've got no appointment, Dad.

Willy: He put his arm around you, and you've got no appointment?

Biff: Pop, get this now, will you? Everytime I've left it's been a fight that sent
me out of here. Today I realized something about myself and I tried to explain it to you and I — I think I'm just not smart enough to make any sense
out of it for you. To hell with whose fault it is or anything like that. *(He
takes Willy's arm.)* Let's just wrap it up, heh? Come on in, we'll tell Mom.
(He gently tries to pull Willy to left.)

Willy (frozen, immobile, with guilt in his voice): No, I don't want to see her.

Biff: Come on! *(He pulls again, and Willy tries to pull away.)*

Willy (highly nervous): No, no, I don't want to see her.

Biff (tries to look into Willy's face, as if to find the answer there): Why don't you want to see her?

Willy (more harshly now): Don't bother me, will you?

Biff: What do you mean, you don't want to see her? You don't want them calling you yellow, do you? This isn't your fault; it's me, I'm a bum. Now come inside! *(Willy strains to get away.)* Did you hear what I said to you?

Willy pulls away and quickly goes by himself into the house. Biff follows.

Linda (to Willy): Did you plant, dear?

Biff (at the door, to Linda): All right, we had it out. I'm going and I'm not writing any more.

Linda (going to Willy in the kitchen): I think that's the best way, dear. 'Cause there's no use drawing it out, you'll just never get along.

Willy doesn't respond.

Biff: People ask where I am and what I'm doing, you don't know, and you don't care. That way it'll be off your mind and you can start brightening up again. All right? That clears it, doesn't it? *(Willy is silent, and Biff goes to him.)* You gonna wish me luck, scout? *(He extends his hand.)* What do you say?

Linda: Shake his hand, Willy.

Willy (turning to her, seething with hurt): There's no necessity to mention the pen at all, y'know.

Biff (gently): I've got no appointment, Dad.

Willy (erupting fiercely): He put his arm around . . . ?

Biff: Dad, you're never going to see what I am, so what's the use of arguing? If I strike oil I'll send you a check. Meantime forget I'm alive.

Willy (to Linda): Spite, see?

Biff: Shake hands, Dad.

Willy: Not my hand.

Biff: I was hoping not to go this way.

Willy: Well, this is the way you're going. Good-by.

Biff looks at him a moment, then turns sharply and goes to the stairs.

Willy (stops him with): May you rot in hell if you leave this house!

Biff (turning): Exactly what is it that you want from me?

Willy: I want you to know, on the train, in the mountains, in the valleys, wherever you go, that you cut down your life for spite!

Biff: No, no.

Willy: Spite, spite, is the word of your undoing! And when you're down and out, remember what did it. When you're rotting somewhere beside the railroad tracks, remember, and don't you dare blame it on me!

Biff: I'm not blaming it on you!

Willy: I won't take the rap for this, you hear?

Happy comes down the stairs and stands on the bottom step, watching.

Biff: That's just what I'm telling you!

Willy (sinking into a chair at the table, with full accusation): You're trying to put a knife in me—don't think I don't know what you're doing!

Biff: All right, phony! Then let's lay it on the line. *(He whips the rubber tube out of his pocket and puts it on the table.)*

Happy: You crazy —

Linda: Biff! *(She moves to grab the hose, but Biff holds it down with his hand.)*

Biff: Leave it there! Don't move it!

Willy (not looking at it): What is that?

Biff: You know goddam well what that is.

Willy (caged, wanting to escape): I never saw that.

Biff: You saw it. The mice didn't bring it into the cellar! What is this supposed to do, make a hero out of you? This supposed to make me sorry for you?

Willy: Never heard of it.

Biff: There'll be no pity for you, you hear it? No pity!

Willy (to Linda): You hear the spite!

Biff: No, you're going to hear the truth — what you are and what I am!

Linda: Stop it!

Willy: Spite!

Happy (coming down toward Biff): You cut it now!

Biff (to Happy): The man don't know who we are! The man is gonna know! *(To Willy.)* We never told the truth for ten minutes in this house!

Happy: We always told the truth!

Biff (turning on him): You big blow, are you the assistant buyer? You're one of the two assistants to the assistant, aren't you?

Happy: Well, I'm practically —

Biff: You're practically full of it! We all are! And I'm through with it. *(To Willy.)* Now hear this, Willy, this is me.

Willy: I know you!

Biff: You know why I had no address for three months? I stole a suit in Kansas City and I was in jail. *(To Linda, who is sobbing.)* Stop crying. I'm through with it.

Linda turns away from them, her hands covering her face.

Willy: I suppose that's my fault!

Biff: I stole myself out of every good job since high school!

Willy: And whose fault is that?

Biff: And I never got anywhere because you blew me so full of hot air I could never stand taking orders from anybody! That's whose fault it is!

Willy: I hear that!

Linda: Don't, Biff!

Biff: It's goddam time you heard that! I had to be boss big shot in two weeks, and I'm through with it!

Willy: Then hang yourself! For spite, hang yourself!

Biff: No! Nobody's hanging himself, Willy! I ran down eleven flights with a pen in my hand today. And suddenly I stopped, you hear me? And in the middle of that office building, do you hear this? I stopped in the middle of that building and I saw — the sky. I saw the things that I love in this world. The work and the food and time to sit and smoke. And I looked at the pen and said to myself, what the hell am I grabbing this for? Why am I trying to become what I don't want to be? What am I doing in an office, making a contemptuous, begging fool of myself, when all I want is out there, waiting for me the minute I say I know who I am! Why can't I say that, Willy? *(He tries to make Willy face him, but Willy pulls away and moves to the left.)*

Willy (with hatred, threateningly): The door of your life is wide open!

Biff: Pop! I'm a dime a dozen, and so are you!

Willy (turning on him now in an uncontrolled outburst): I am not a dime a dozen! I am Willy Loman, and you are Biff Loman!

Biff starts for Willy, but is blocked by Happy. In his fury, Biff seems on the verge of attacking his father.

Biff: I am not a leader of men, Willy, and neither are you. You were never anything but a hard-working drummer who landed in the ash can like all the rest of them! I'm one dollar an hour, Willy! I tried seven states and couldn't raise it. A buck an hour! Do you gather my meaning? I'm not bringing home any prizes any more, and you're going to stop waiting for me to bring them home!

Willy (directly to Biff): You vengeful, spiteful mutt!

Biff breaks from Happy. Willy, in fright, starts up the stairs. Biff grabs him.

Biff (at the peak of his fury): Pop, I'm nothing! I'm nothing, Pop. Can't you understand that? There's no spite in it any more. I'm just what I am, that's all.

Biff's fury has spent itself, and he breaks down, sobbing, holding on to Willy, who dumbly fumbles for Biff's face.

Willy (astonished): What're you doing? What're you doing? *(To Linda.)* Why is he crying?

Biff (crying, broken): Will you let me go, for Christ's sake? Will you take that phony dream and burn it before something happens? *(Struggling to contain himself, he pulls away and moves to the stairs.)* I'll go in the morning. Put him—put him to bed. *(Exhausted, Biff moves up the stairs to his room.)*

Willy (after a long pause, astonished, elevated): Isn't that—isn't that remarkable? Biff—he likes me!

Linda: He loves you, Willy!

Happy (deeply moved): Always did, Pop.

Willy: Oh, Biff! *(Staring wildly.)* He cried! Cried to me. *(He is choking with his love, and now cries out his promise.)* That boy—that boy is going to be magnificent!

Ben appears in the light just outside the kitchen.

Ben: Yes, outstanding, with twenty thousand behind him.

Linda (sensing the racing of his mind, fearfully, carefully): Now come to bed, Willy. It's all settled now.

Willy (finding it difficult not to rush out of the house): Yes, we'll sleep. Come on. Go to sleep, Hap.

Ben: And it does take a great kind of a man to crack the jungle.

In accents of dread, Ben's idyllic music starts up.

Happy (his arm around Linda): I'm getting married, Pop, don't forget it. I'm changing everything. I'm gonna run that department before the year is up. You'll see, Mom. *(He kisses her.)*

Ben: The jungle is dark but full of diamonds, Willy.

Willy turns, moves, listening to Ben.

Linda: Be good. You're both good boys, just act that way, that's all.

Happy: 'Night, Pop. *(He goes upstairs.)*

Linda (to Willy): Come, dear.

Ben (with greater force): One must go in to fetch a diamond out.

Willy (to Linda, as he moves slowly along the edge of the kitchen, toward the door): I just want to get settled down, Linda. Let me sit alone for a little.

Linda (almost uttering her fear): I want you upstairs.

Willy (taking her in his arms): In a few minutes, Linda. I couldn't sleep right now. Go on, you look awful tired. *(He kisses her.)*

Ben: Not like an appointment at all. A diamond is rough and hard to the touch.

Willy: Go on now. I'll be right up.

Linda: I think this is the only way, Willy.

Willy: Sure, it's the best thing.

Ben: Best thing!

Willy: The only way. Everything is gonna be — go on, kid, get to bed. You look so tired.

Linda: Come right up.

Willy: Two minutes.

> *Linda goes into the living-room, then reappears in her bedroom. Willy moves just outside the kitchen door.*

Willy: Loves me. *(Wonderingly.)* Always loved me. Isn't that a remarkable thing? Ben, he'll worship me for it!

Ben (with promise): It's dark there, but full of diamonds.

Willy: Can you imagine that magnificence with twenty thousand dollars in his pocket?

Linda (calling from her room): Willy! Come up!

Willy (calling into the kitchen): Yes! Yes. Coming! It's very smart, you realize that, don't you, sweetheart? Even Ben sees it. I gotta go, baby. 'By! 'By! *(Going over to Ben, almost dancing.)* Imagine? When the mail comes he'll be ahead of Bernard again!

Ben: A perfect proposition all around.

Willy: Did you see how he cried to me? Oh, if I could kiss him, Ben!

Ben: Time, William, time!

Willy: Oh, Ben, I always knew one way or another we were gonna make it, Biff and I!

Ben (looking at his watch): The boat. We'll be late. *(He moves slowly off into the darkness.)*

Willy (elegiacally, turning to the house): Now when you kick off, boy, I want a seventy-yard boot, and get right down the field under the ball, and when you hit, hit low and hit hard, because it's important, boy. *(He swings around and faces the audience.)* There's all kinds of important people in the stands, and the first thing you know . . . *(Suddenly realizing he is alone.)* Ben! Ben, where do I . . . ? *(He makes a sudden movement of search.)* Ben, how do I . . . ?

Linda (calling): Willy, you coming up?

Willy (uttering a gasp of fear, whirling about as if to quiet her): Sh! *(He turns around as if to find his way; sounds, faces, voices, seem to be swarming in upon him and he flicks at them, crying.)* Sh! Sh! *(Suddenly music, faint and high, stops him. It rises in intensity, almost to an unbearable scream. He goes up and down on his toes, and rushes off around the house.)* Shhh!

Linda: Willy?

> *There is no answer. Linda waits. Biff gets up off his bed. He is still in his clothes. Happy sits up. Biff stands listening.*

Linda (with real fear): Willy, answer me! Willy!

> *There is the sound of a car starting and moving away at full speed.*

Linda: No!

Biff (rushing down the stairs): Pop!

> *As the car speeds off, the music crashes down in a frenzy of sound, which becomes the soft pulsation of a single cello string. Biff slowly returns to his bedroom. He and Happy gravely don their jackets. Linda slowly walks out of her room. The music has developed into a dead march. The leaves of day are appearing over everything. Charley and Bernard, somberly dressed, appear and knock on the kitchen door. Biff and Happy slowly descend the stairs to the kitchen as Charley and Bernard enter. All stop a moment when Linda, in clothes of mourning, bearing a little bunch of roses, comes through the draped doorway into the kitchen. She goes to Charley and takes his arm. Now all move toward the audience, through the wall-line of the kitchen. At the limit of the apron, Linda lays down the flowers, kneels, and sits back on her heels. All stare down at the grave.*

REQUIEM

Charley: It's getting dark, Linda.

> *Linda doesn't react. She stares at the grave.*

Biff: How about it, Mom? Better get some rest, heh? They'll be closing the gate soon.

> *Linda makes no move. Pause.*

Happy (deeply angered): He had no right to do that. There was no necessity for it. We would've helped him.

Charley (grunting): Hmmm.

Biff: Come along, Mom.

Linda: Why didn't anybody come?

Charley: It was a very nice funeral.

Linda: But where are all the people he knew? Maybe they blame him.

Charley: Naa. It's a rough world, Linda. They wouldn't blame him.

Linda: I can't understand it. At this time especially. First time in thirty-five years we were just about free and clear. He only needed a little salary. He was even finished with the dentist.

Charley: No man only needs a little salary.

Linda: I can't understand it.

Biff: There were a lot of nice days. When he'd come home from a trip; or on Sundays, making the stoop; finishing the cellar; putting on the new porch; when he built the extra bathroom; and put up the garage. You know something, Charley, there's more of him in that front stoop than in all the sales he ever made.

Charley: Yeah. He was a happy man with a batch of cement.

Linda: He was so wonderful with his hands.

Biff: He had the wrong dreams. All, all, wrong.

Happy (almost ready to fight Biff): Don't say that!

Biff: He never knew who he was.

Charley (stopping Happy's movement and reply. To Biff): Nobody dast blame this man. You don't understand: Willy was a salesman. And for a salesman, there is no rock bottom to the life. He don't put a bolt to a nut, he don't tell you the law or give you medicine. He's a man way out there in the blue, riding on a smile and a shoeshine. And when they start not smiling back — that's an earthquake. And then you get yourself a couple of spots on your hat, and you're finished. Nobody dast blame this man. A salesman is got to dream, boy. It comes with the territory.

Biff: Charley, the man didn't know who he was.

Happy (infuriated): Don't say that!

Biff: Why don't you come with me, Happy?

Happy: I'm not licked that easily. I'm staying right in this city, and I'm gonna beat this racket! *(He looks at Biff, his chin set.)* The Loman Brothers!

Biff: I know who I am, kid.

Happy: All right, boy. I'm gonna show you and everybody else that Willy Loman did not die in vain. He had a good dream. It's the only dream you can have — to come out number-one man. He fought it out here, and this is where I'm gonna win it for him.

Biff (with a hopeless glance at Happy, bends toward his mother): Let's go, Mom.

Linda: I'll be with you in a minute. Go on, Charley. *(He hesitates.)* I want to, just for a minute. I never had a chance to say good-by.

Charley moves away, followed by Happy. Biff remains a slight distance up and left of Linda. She sits there, summoning herself. The flute begins, not far away, playing behind her speech.

Linda: Forgive me, dear. I can't cry. I don't know what it is, but I can't cry. I don't understand it. Why did you ever do that? Help me, Willy, I can't cry. It seems to me that you're just on another trip. I keep expecting you. Willy, dear, I can't cry. Why did you do it? I search and search and I search, and I can't understand it, Willy. I made the last payment on the house today. Today, dear. And there'll be nobody home. *(A sob rises in her throat.)* We're free and clear. *(Sobbing more fully, released.)* We're free. *(Biff comes slowly toward her.)* We're free . . . We're free . . .

Biff lifts her to her feet and moves out up right with her in his arms. Linda sobs quietly. Bernard and Charley come together and follow them, followed by Happy. Only the music of the flute is left on the darkening stage as over the house the hard towers of the apartment buildings rise into sharp focus, and

The Curtain Falls.

CONNECTIONS TO OTHER SELECTIONS

1. Compare and contrast Willy Loman with Polonius in Shakespeare's *Hamlet* (p. 1585). To what extent is each character wise, foolish, deluded, and hypocritical? Explain why Loman can be seen as a tragic character while Polonius cannot be.

2. Read Tato Laviera's poem "AmeRícan" (p. 1020), and compare its treatment of the American dream with the one in *Death of a Salesman*. How do the tones of the two works differ?

3. What similarities do you find between the endings of *Death of a Salesman* and August Wilson's *Fences* (p. 1988)? Are the endings happy, unhappy, or something else?

Perspectives

ARTHUR MILLER (1915–2005)
Tragedy and the Common Man   *1949*

In this age few tragedies are written. It has often been held that the lack is due to a paucity of heroes among us, or else that modern man has had the blood drawn out of his organs of belief by the skepticism of science, and the heroic attack on life cannot feed on an attitude of reserve and circumspection. For one reason or another, we are often held to be below tragedy — or tragedy above us. The inevitable conclusion is, of course, that the tragic mode is archaic, fit only for the very highly placed, the kings or the kingly, and where this admission is not made in so many words it is most often implied.

I believe that the common man is as apt a subject for tragedy in its highest sense as kings were. On the face of it this ought to be obvious in the light of modern psychiatry, which bases its analysis upon classic formulations, such as the Oedipus and Orestes complexes, for instance, which were enacted by royal beings, but which apply to everyone in similar emotional situations.

More simply, when the question of tragedy in art is not at issue, we never hesitate to attribute to the well-placed and the exalted the very same mental processes as the lowly. And finally, if the exaltation of tragic action were truly a property of the high-bred character alone, it is inconceivable that the mass of mankind should cherish tragedy above all other forms, let alone be capable of understanding it.

As a general rule, to which there may be exceptions unknown to me, I think the tragic feeling is evoked in us when we are in the presence of a character who is ready to lay down his life, if need be, to secure one thing — his sense of personal dignity. From Orestes to Hamlet, Medea to Macbeth, the underlying struggle is that of the individual attempting to gain his "rightful" position in his society.

Sometimes he is one who has been displaced from it, sometimes one who seeks to attain it for the first time, but the fateful wound from which the inevitable events spiral is the wound of indignity, and its dominant force is indignation. Tragedy, then, is the consequence of a man's total compulsion to evaluate himself justly.

In the sense of having been initiated by the hero himself, the tale always reveals what has been called his "tragic flaw," a failing that is not peculiar to grand or elevated characters. Nor is it necessarily a weakness. The flaw, or crack in the character, is really nothing — and need be nothing — but his inherent unwillingness to remain passive in the face of what he conceives to be a challenge to his dignity, his image of his rightful status. Only the passive, only those who accept their lot without active retaliation, are "flawless." Most of us are in that category.

But there are among us today, as there always have been, those who act against the scheme of things that degrades them, and in the process of action, everything we have accepted out of fear or insensitivity or ignorance is shaken before us and examined, and from this total onslaught by an individual against the seemingly stable cosmos surrounding us — from this total examination of the "unchangeable" environment — comes the terror and the fear that is classically associated with tragedy.

More important, from this total questioning of what has been previously unquestioned, we learn. And such a process is not beyond the common man. In revolutions around the world, these past thirty years, he has demonstrated again and again this inner dynamic of all tragedy.

Insistence upon the rank of the tragic hero, or the so-called nobility of his character, is really but a clinging to the outward forms of tragedy. If rank or nobility of character was indispensable, then it would follow that the problems of those with rank were the particular problems of tragedy. But surely the right of one monarch to capture the domain from another no longer raises our passions, nor are our concepts of justice what they were to the mind of an Elizabethan king.

The quality in such plays that does shake us, however, derives from the underlying fear of being displaced, the disaster inherent in being torn away from our chosen image of what and who we are in this world. Among us today this fear is as strong, and perhaps stronger, than it ever was. In fact, it is the common man who knows this fear best.

Now, if it is true that tragedy is the consequence of a man's total compulsion to evaluate himself justly, his destruction in the attempt posits a wrong or an evil in his environment. And this is precisely the morality of tragedy and its lesson. The discovery of the moral law, which is what the enlightenment of tragedy consists of, is not the discovery of some abstract or metaphysical quantity.

The tragic right is a condition of life, a condition in which the human personality is able to flower and realize itself. The wrong is the condition which suppresses man, perverts the flowing out of his love and creative instinct. Tragedy enlightens — and it must, in that it points the heroic finger at the enemy of man's freedom. The thrust for freedom is the quality in tragedy which exalts. The revolutionary questioning of the stable environment is what terrifies. In no way is the common man debarred from such thoughts or such actions.

Seen in this light, our lack of tragedy may be partially accounted for by the turn which modern literature has taken toward the purely psychiatric view of life, or the purely sociological. If all our miseries, our indignities, are born and bred within our minds, then all action, let alone the heroic action, is obviously impossible.

And if society alone is responsible for the cramping of our lives, then the protagonist must needs be so pure and faultless as to force us to deny his validity as a character. From neither of these views can tragedy derive, simply because neither represents a balanced concept of life. Above all else, tragedy requires the finest appreciation by the writer of cause and effect.

No tragedy can therefore come about when its author fears to question absolutely everything, when he regards any institution, habit, or custom as being either everlasting, immutable, or inevitable. In the tragic view the need of man to wholly realize himself is the only fixed star, and whatever it is that hedges his nature and lowers it is ripe for attack and examination. Which is not to say that tragedy must preach revolution.

The Greeks could probe the very heavenly origin of their ways and return to confirm the rightness of laws. And Job could face God in anger, demanding his right, and end in submission. But for a moment everything is in suspension, nothing is accepted, and in this stretching and tearing apart of the cosmos, in the very action of so doing, the character gains "size," the tragic stature which is spuriously attached to the royal or the high born in our minds. The commonest of men may take on that stature to the extent of his willingness to throw all he has into the contest, the battle to secure his rightful place in his world.

17   There is a misconception of tragedy with which I have been struck in review after review, and in many conversations with writers and readers alike. It is the idea that tragedy is of necessity allied to pessimism. Even the dictionary says nothing more about the word than that it means a story with a sad or unhappy ending. This impression is so firmly fixed that I almost hesitate to claim that in truth tragedy implies more optimism in its author than does comedy, and that its final result ought to be the reinforcement of the onlooker's brightest opinions of the human animal.

✓ 18   For, if it is true to say that in essence the tragic hero is intent upon claiming his whole due as a personality, and if this struggle must be total and without reservation, then it automatically demonstrates the indestructible will of man to achieve his humanity.

19   The possibility of victory must be there in tragedy. Where pathos rules, where pathos is finally derived, a character has fought a battle he could not possibly have won. The pathetic is achieved when the protagonist is, by virtue of his witlessness, his insensitivity, or the very air he gives off, incapable of grappling with a much superior force.

20   Pathos truly is the mode for the pessimist. But tragedy requires a nicer balance between what is possible and what is impossible. And it is curious, although edifying, that the plays we revere, century after century, are the tragedies. In them, and in them alone, lies the belief—optimistic, if you will— in the perfectibility of man.

✓ 21   It is time, I think, that we who are without kings, took up this bright thread of our history and followed it to the only place it can possibly lead in our time—the heart and spirit of the average man.

From *Theater Essays of Arthur Miller*

CONSIDERATIONS FOR CRITICAL THINKING AND WRITING

1. According to Miller, why is there a "lack" (para. 1) of tragedy in modern literature? Why do psychological and sociological accounts of human behavior limit the possibilities for tragedy?

2. Why is the "common man" (para. 2) a suitable subject for tragedy? How does Miller's view of tragedy compare with Aristotle's (p. 1502)?

3. What distinction does Miller make between tragedy and pathos? Which term best characterizes Willy Loman in *Death of a Salesman*? Explain why.

ARTHUR MILLER (1915–2005)

On Biff and Willy Loman   1950

A serious theme is entertaining to the extent that it is not trifled with, not cleverly angled, but met in head-on collision. [The audience] will not consent to suffer while the creators stand by with tongue in cheek. They have a way of knowing. Nobody can blame them.

And there have been certain disappointments, one above all. I am sorry the self-realization of the older son, Biff, is not a weightier counterbalance to Willy's disaster in the audience's mind.

And certain things are more clearly known, or so it seems now. We want to give of ourselves, and yet all we train for is to take, as though nothing less will keep the world at a safe distance. Every day we contradict our will to create, which is to give. The end of man is not security, but without security we are without the elementary condition of humaneness.

To me the tragedy of Willy Loman is that he gave his life, or sold it, in order to justify the waste of it. It is the tragedy of a man who did believe that he alone was not meeting the qualifications laid down for mankind by those clean-shaven frontiersmen who inhabit the peaks of broadcasting and advertising offices. From those forests of canned goods high up near the sky, he heard the thundering command to succeed as it ricocheted down the newspaper-lined canyons of his city, heard not a human voice, but a wind of a voice to which no human can reply in kind, except to stare into the mirror at a failure.

From the *New York Times,* February 5, 1950

CONSIDERATIONS FOR CRITICAL THINKING AND WRITING

1. Discuss what you think Miller has in mind when he refers to Biff's "self-realization" (para. 2).
2. According to Miller, what influences Willy to make him feel like a failure?
3. How is Miller's description of "the tragedy of Willy Loman" (para. 4) dramatized in the play?

Doubt: A Parable

A playwright, screenwriter, and director, John Patrick Shanley was born the son of an Irish immigrant meatpacker and raised in the east Bronx, where he attended St. Anthony's Grammar School, was expelled from Cardinal Spellman High School, and subsequently graduated from Thomas More Preparatory School in New Hampshire. Shanley's life and writing has been steeped in the tumultuous blue-collar world of his Bronx youth. A former marine, he has  worked, among other jobs, as a bartender,

WWD/Condé Nast/CORBIS.

locksmith, house painter, and elevator operator; in 1977 he graduated from New York University as valedictorian. He has written more than two dozen plays, including *Women of Manhattan* (1986) and *Dirty Story* (2003), as well as a number of successful film and television screenplays. His breakthrough screenplay, *Moonstruck* (1987), won the Academy Award for Best Original Screenplay and the Writers Guild of America Award for Best Screenplay Written Directly for the Screen.

In *Doubt: A Parable,* all of Shanley's talents are apparent in an absorbing drama that he wrote for the stage, adapted as a screenplay, and then directed as a film starring Meryl Streep and Philip Seymour Hoffman. The play and film have been showered with recognition, including the Obie Award for Playwriting (2005), the Drama Critics' Circle Award (2005), the Tony Award for Best Play (2005), the Pulitzer Prize for Drama (2005), and the Academy Award for Best Adapted Screenplay (2008). Set in a 1964 Bronx Catholic school, the play is about a stern nun's suspicions concerning a popular liberal priest's relationship with a new young black student. Shanley substitutes our preconceptions about what we think we know about these characters with ambiguities and uncertainties so that what seems predictable becomes equivocal. Shanley has explained in a number of interviews that he likes to attack the notion that plays and films must affirm certainties or validate what audiences already believe. That's not what his work sets out to do: "The theme should arise like smoke off a play. It shouldn't be stated, or if it is, it should go by just like another line."

John Patrick Shanley (b. 1950)

Doubt : A Parable   *2005*

CHARACTERS

Father Brendan Flynn, late thirties
Sister Aloysius Beauvier, fifties/sixties
Sister James, twenties
Mrs. Muller, around thirty-eight

SETTING: St. Nicholas, a Catholic church and school in the Bronx, New York, 1964

The bad sleep well.
— *Title of Kurosawa film*

In much wisdom is much grief:
and he that increaseth knowledge increaseth sorrow.
                                   — *Ecclesiastes*

Everything that is hard to attain
is easily assailed by the mob.
                      — *Ptolemy*

I

A Priest, Father Flynn, in his late thirties, in green and gold vestments, gives a sermon. He is working class, from the Northeast.

Flynn: What do you do when you're not sure? That's the topic of my sermon today. You look for God's direction and can't find it. Last year when President Kennedy was assassinated, who among us did not experience the most profound disorientation. Despair. "What now? Which way? What do I say to my kids? What do I tell myself?" It was a time of people sitting together, bound together by a common feeling of hopelessness. But think of that! Your *bond* with your fellow beings was your *despair.* It was a public experience, shared by everyone in our society. It was awful, but we were in it together! How much worse is it then for the lone man, the lone woman, stricken by a private calamity? "No one knows I'm sick. No one knows I've lost my last real friend. No one knows I've done something wrong." Imagine the isolation. You see the world as through a window. On the one side of the glass: happy, untroubled people. On the other side: you. Something has happened, you have to carry it, and it's incommunicable. For those so afflicted, only God knows their pain. Their secret. The secret of their alienating sorrow. And when such a person, as they must, howls to the sky, to God: "Help me!" What if no answer comes? Silence. I want to tell you a story. A cargo ship sank and all her crew was drowned. Only this one sailor survived. He made a raft of some spars and, being of a nautical discipline, turned his eyes to the Heavens and read the stars. He set a course for his home, and, exhausted, fell asleep. Clouds rolled in and blanketed the sky. For the next twenty nights, as he floated on the vast ocean, he could no longer see the stars. He thought he was on course but there was no way to be certain. As the days rolled on, and he wasted away with fevers, thirst and starvation, he began to have doubts. Had he set his course right? Was he still going on towards his home? Or was he horribly lost and doomed to a terrible death? No way to know. The message of the constellations — had he imagined it because of his desperate circumstance? Or had he seen Truth once, and now had to hold on to it without further reassurance? That was his dilemma on a voyage without apparent end. There are those of you in church today who know exactly the crisis of faith I describe. I want to say to you: Doubt can be a bond as powerful and sustaining as certainty. When you are lost, you are not alone. In the name of the Father, the Son, and the Holy Ghost. Amen.

(He exits.)

II

The lights crossfade to a corner office in a Catholic school in the Bronx. The principal, Sister Aloysius Beauvier, sits at her desk, writing in a ledger with a fountain pen. She is in her fifties or sixties. She is watchful, reserved, unsentimental. She is of the order of the Sisters of Charity. She wears a black bonnet and floor-length black habit, rimless glasses. A knock at the door.

Sister Aloysius: Come in.

(Sister James, also of the Sisters of Charity, pokes her head in. She is in her twenties. There's a bit of sunshine in her heart, though she's reserved as well.)

Sister James: Have you a moment, Sister Aloysius?

Sister Aloysius: Come in, Sister James.

(She enters.)

Who's watching your class?

Sister James: They're having Art.

Sister Aloysius: Art. Waste of time.

Sister James: It's only an hour a week.

Sister Aloysius: Much can be accomplished in sixty minutes.

Sister James: Yes, Sister Aloysius. I wondered if I might know what you did about William London?

Sister Aloysius: I sent him home.

Sister James: Oh dear. So he's still bleeding?

Sister Aloysius: Oh yes.

Sister James: His nose just let loose and started gushing during The Pledge of Allegiance.

Sister Aloysius: Was it spontaneous?

Sister James: What else would it be?

Sister Aloysius: Self-induced.

Sister James: You mean, you think he might've intentionally given himself a nosebleed?

Sister Aloysius: Exactly.

Sister James: No!

Sister Aloysius: You are a very innocent person, Sister James. William London is a fidgety boy and if you do not keep right on him, he will do anything to escape his chair. He would set his foot on fire for half a day out of school.

Sister James: But why?

Sister Aloysius: He has a restless mind.

Sister James: But that's good.

Sister Aloysius: No, it's not. His father's a policeman and the last thing he wants is a rowdy boy. William London is headed for trouble. Puberty has got hold of him. He will be imagining all the wrong things, and I strongly suspect he will not graduate high school. But that's beyond our jurisdiction. We simply have to get him through, out the door, and then he's somebody else's project. Ordinarily, I assign my most experienced sisters to eighth grade but I'm working within constraints. Are you in control of your class?

Sister James: I think so.

Sister Aloysius: Usually more children are sent down to me.

Sister James: I try to take care of things myself.

Sister Aloysius: That can be an error. You are answerable to me, I to the monsignor, he to the bishop, and so on up to the Holy Father. There's a chain of discipline. Make use of it.

Sister James: Yes, Sister.

Sister Aloysius: How's Donald Muller doing?

Sister James: Steady.

Sister Aloysius: Good. Has anyone hit him?

Sister James: No.

Sister Aloysius: Good. That girl Linda Conte, have you seated her away from the boys?

Sister James: As far as space permits. It doesn't do much good.
Sister Aloysius: Just get her through. Intact.

(*Pause. Sister Aloysius is staring absently at Sister James. A silence falls.*)

Sister James: So. Should I go? (*No answer*) Is something the matter?
Sister Aloysius: No. Why? Is something the matter?
Sister James: I don't think so.
Sister Aloysius: Then nothing's the matter then.
Sister James: Well. Thank you, Sister. I just wanted to check on William's nose.

(*She starts to go.*)

Sister Aloysius: He had a ballpoint pen.
Sister James: Excuse me, Sister?
Sister Aloysius: William London had a ballpoint pen. He was fiddling with it while he waited for his mother. He's not using it for assignments, I hope.
Sister James: No, of course not.
Sister Aloysius: I'm sorry I allowed even cartridge pens into the school. The students really should only be learning script with true fountain pens. Always the easy way out these days. What does that teach? Every easy choice today will have its consequence tomorrow. Mark my words.
Sister James: Yes, Sister.
Sister Aloysius: Ballpoints make them press down, and when they press down, they write like monkeys.
Sister James: I don't allow them ballpoint pens.
Sister Aloysius: Good. Penmanship is dying all across the country. You have some time. Sit down.

(*Sister James hesitates and sits down.*)

We might as well have a talk. I've been meaning to talk to you. I observed your lesson on the New Deal at the beginning of the term. Not bad. But I caution you. Do not idealize Franklin Delano Roosevelt. He was a good president, but he did attempt to pack the Supreme Court. I do not approve of making heroes of lay historical figures. If you want to talk about saints, do it in Religion.
Sister James: Yes, Sister.
Sister Aloysius: Also. I question your enthusiasm for History.
Sister James: But I love History!
Sister Aloysius: That is exactly my meaning. You favor History and risk swaying the children to value it over their other subjects. I think this is a mistake.
Sister James: I never thought of that. I'll try to treat my other lessons with more enthusiasm.
Sister Aloysius: No. Give them their History without putting sugar all over it. That's the point. Now. Tell me about your class. How would you characterize the condition of 8-B?
Sister James: I don't know where to begin. What do you want to know?
Sister Aloysius: Let's begin with Stephen Inzio.
Sister James: Stephen Inzio has the highest marks in the class.
Sister Aloysius: Noreen Horan?
Sister James: Second highest marks.
Sister Aloysius: Brenda McNulty?
Sister James: Third highest.

Sister Aloysius: You see I am making a point, Sister James. I know that Stephen Inzio, Noreen Horan and Brenda McNulty are one, two and three in your class. School-wide, there are forty-eight such students each grade period. I make it my business to know all forty-eight of their names. I do not say this to aggrandize myself, but to illustrate the importance of paying attention. You must pay attention as well.

Sister James: Yes, Sister Aloysius.

Sister Aloysius: I cannot be everywhere.

Sister James: Am I falling short, Sister?

Sister Aloysius: These three students with the highest marks. Are they the most intelligent children in your class?

Sister James: No, I wouldn't say they are. But they work the hardest.

Sister Aloysius: Very good! That's right! That's the ethic. What good's a gift if it's left in the box? What good is a high IQ if you're staring out the window with your mouth agape? Be hard on the bright ones, Sister James. Don't be charmed by cleverness. Not theirs. And not yours. I think you are a competent teacher, Sister James, but maybe not our best teacher. The best teachers do not perform, they cause the students to perform.

Sister James: Do I perform?

Sister Aloysius: As if on a Broadway stage.

Sister James: Oh dear. I had no conception!

Sister Aloysius: You're showing off. You like to see yourself ten feet tall in their eyes. Another thing occurs to me. Where were you before?

Sister James: Mount St. Margaret's.

Sister Aloysius: All girls.

Sister James: Yes.

Sister Aloysius: I feel I must remind you. Boys are made of gravel, soot and tar paper. Boys are a different breed.

Sister James: I feel I know how to handle them.

Sister Aloysius: But perhaps you are wrong. And perhaps you are not working hard enough.

Sister James: Oh.

(*Sister James cries a little.*)

Sister Aloysius: No tears.

Sister James: I thought you were satisfied with me.

Sister Aloysius: Satisfaction is a vice. Do you have a handkerchief?

Sister James: Yes.

Sister Aloysius: Use it. Do you think that Socrates was satisfied? Good teachers are never content. We have some three hundred and seventy-two students in this school. It is a society which requires constant educational, spiritual and human vigilance. I cannot afford an excessively innocent instructor in my eighth grade class. It's self-indulgent. Innocence is a form of laziness. Innocent teachers are easily duped. You must be canny, Sister James.

Sister James: Yes, Sister.

Sister Aloysius: When William London gets a nosebleed, be skeptical. Don't let a little blood fuddle your judgment. God gave you a brain and a heart. The heart is warm, but your wits must be cold. Liars should be frightened to lie to you. They should be uncomfortable in your presence. I doubt they are.

Sister James: I don't know. I've never thought about it.

Sister Aloysius: The children should think you see right through them.

Sister James: Wouldn't that be a little frightening?

Sister Aloysius: Only to the ones that are up to no good.

Sister James: But I want my students to feel they can talk to me.

Sister Aloysius: They're children. They can talk to each other. It's more important they have a fierce moral guardian. You stand at the door, Sister. You are the gatekeeper. If you are vigilant, they will not need to be.

Sister James: I'm not sure what you want me to do.

Sister Aloysius: And if things occur in your classroom which you sense require understanding, but you don't understand, come to me.

Sister James: Yes, Sister.

Sister Aloysius: That's why I'm here. That's why I'm the principal of this school. Do you stay when the specialty instructors come in?

Sister James: Yes.

Sister Aloysius: But you're here now while the Art class is going on.

Sister James: I was a little concerned about William's nose.

Sister Aloysius: Right. So you have Art in class.

Sister James: She comes in. Mrs. Bell. Yes.

Sister Aloysius: And you take them down to the basement for Dance with Mrs. Shields.

Sister James: On Thursdays.

Sister Aloysius: Another waste of time.

Sister James: Oh, but everyone loves the Christmas pageant.

Sister Aloysius: I don't love it. Frankly it offends me. Last year the girl playing Our Lady was wearing lipstick. I was waiting in the wings for that little jade.

Sister James: Then there's Music.

Sister Aloysius: That strange woman with the portable piano. What's wrong with her neck?

Sister James: Some kind of goiter. Poor woman.

Sister Aloysius: Yes. Mrs. Carolyn.

Sister James: That's right.

Sister Aloysius: We used to have a Sister teaching that. Not enough Sisters. What else?

Sister James: Physical Education and Religion.

Sister Aloysius: And for that we have Father Flynn. Two hours a week. And you stay for those?

Sister James: Mostly. Unless I have reports to fill out or . . .

Sister Aloysius: What do you think of Father Flynn?

Sister James: Oh, he's a brilliant man. What a speaker!

Sister Aloysius: Yes. His sermon this past Sunday was poetic.

Sister James: He's actually very good, too, at teaching basketball. I was surprised. I wouldn't think a man of the cloth the personality type for basketball, but he has a way he has, very natural with dribbling and shooting.

Sister Aloysius: What do you think that sermon was about?

Sister James: What?

Sister Aloysius: This past Sunday. What was he talking about?

Sister James: Well, Doubt. He was talking about Doubt.

Sister Aloysius: Why?

Sister James: Excuse me, Sister?

Sister Aloysius: Well, sermons come from somewhere, don't they? Is Father Flynn in Doubt, is he concerned that someone else is in Doubt?

Sister James: I suppose you'd have to ask him.

Sister Aloysius: No. That would not be appropriate. He is my superior. And if he were troubled, he should confess it to a fellow priest, or the monsignor. We do not share intimate information with priests.

(A pause.)

Sister James: I'm a little concerned.

(Sister Aloysius leans forward.)

Sister Aloysius: About what?

Sister James: The time. Art class will be over in a few minutes. I should go up.

Sister Aloysius: Have you noticed anything, Sister James?

Sister James: About what?

Sister Aloysius: I want you to be alert.

Sister James: I don't believe I'm following you, Sister.

Sister Aloysius: I'm sorry I'm not more forthright, but I must be careful not to create something by saying it. I can only say I am concerned, perhaps needlessly, about matters in St. Nicholas School.

Sister James: Academically?

Sister Aloysius: I wasn't inviting a guessing game. I want you to pay attention to your class.

Sister James: Well, of course I'll pay attention to my class, Sister. And I'll try not to perform. And I'll try to be less innocent. I'm sorry you're disappointed in me. Please know that I will try my best. Honestly.

Sister Aloysius: Look at you. You'd trade anything for a warm look. I'm telling you here and now, I want to see the starch in your character cultivated. If you are looking for reassurance, you can be fooled. If you forget yourself and study others, you will not be fooled. It's important. One final matter and then you really must get back. Sister Veronica is going blind.

Sister James: Oh how horrible!

Sister Aloysius: This is not generally known and I don't want it known. If they find out in the rectory, she'll be gone. I cannot afford to lose her. But now if you see her making her way down those stone stairs into the courtyard, for the love of Heaven, lightly take her hand as if in fellowship and see that she doesn't destroy herself. All right, go.

III

The lights crossfade to Father Flynn, whistle around his neck, in a sweatshirt and pants, holding a basketball.

Flynn: All right, settle down, boys. Now the thing about shooting from the foul line: It's psychological. The rest of the game you're cooperating with your teammates, you're competing against the other team. But at the foul line, it's you against yourself. And the danger is: You start to think. When you think, you stop breathing. Your body locks up. So you have to remember to relax. Take a breath, unlock your knees — this is something for you to watch, Jimmy. You stand like a parking meter. Come up with a routine of what you do. Shift your weight, move your hips . . . You think that's funny, Ralph? What's funny is you never getting a foul shot. Don't worry if you look silly. They won't think you're silly if you get the basket. Come up with a routine, concentrate on the routine, and you'll forget to get tensed up. Now on another matter, I've noticed several of you guys have dirty nails. I don't want to see that. I'm not talking about the length of your nails, I'm talking about cleanliness. See? Look at my nails. They're long, I like them a little long, but look at how clean they are. That makes it okay. There was a kid I grew up with, Timmy Mathisson, never had clean nails, and he'd stick his fingers up his nose, in his mouth. — This is a true story, learn to listen! He got spinal meningitis and died a horrible death. Sometimes it's the little things that get you. You try to talk to a girl with those filthy paws, Mr. Conroy, she's gonna take off like she's being chased by the Red Chinese! *(Reacting genially to laughter)* All right, all right. You guys, what am I gonna do with you? Get dressed, come on over to the rectory, have some Kool-Aid and cookies, we'll have a bull session. *(Blows his whistle)* Go!

IV

Crossfade to a bit of garden, a bench, brick walls. Sister Aloysius, in full habit and a black shawl, is wrapping a pruned rosebush in burlap. Sister James enters.

Sister James: Good afternoon, Sister.
Sister Aloysius: Good afternoon, Sister James. Mr. McGinn pruned this bush, which was the right thing to do, but he neglected to protect it from the frost.
Sister James: Have we had a frost?
Sister Aloysius: When it comes, it's too late.
Sister James: You know about gardening?
Sister Aloysius: A little. Where is your class?
Sister James: The girls are having Music.
Sister Aloysius: And the boys?
Sister James: They're in the rectory.

(*Sister James indicates the rectory, which is out of view, just on the other side of the garden.*)

Sister Aloysius: With Father Flynn.
Sister James: Yes. He's giving them a talk.
Sister Aloysius: On what subject?
Sister James: How to be a man.
Sister Aloysius: Well, if Sisters were permitted in the rectory, I would be interested to hear that talk. I don't know how to be a man. I would like to know what's involved. Have you ever given the girls a talk on how to be a woman?
Sister James: No. I wouldn't be competent.
Sister Aloysius: Why not?
Sister James: I just don't think I would. I took my vows at the beginning . . . Before . . . At the beginning.
Sister Aloysius: The founder of our order, The Blessed Mother Seton, was married and had five children before embarking on her vows.

Sister James: I've often wondered how she managed so much in one life.

Sister Aloysius: Life perhaps is longer than you think and the dictates of the soul more numerous. I was married.

Sister James: You were!

(*Sister Aloysius smiles for the first time.*)

Sister Aloysius: You could at least hide your astonishment.

Sister James: I . . . didn't know.

Sister Aloysius: When one takes on the habit, one must close the door on secular things. My husband died in the war against Adolph Hitler.

Sister James: Really! Excuse me, Sister.

Sister Aloysius: But I'm like you. I'm not sure I would feel competent to lecture tittering girls on the subject of womanhood. I don't come into this garden often. What is it, forty feet across? The convent here, the rectory there. We might as well be separated by the Atlantic Ocean. I used to potter around out here, but Monsignor Benedict does his reverie at quixotic times and we are rightly discouraged from crossing paths with priests unattended. He is seventy-nine, but nevertheless.

Sister James: The monsignor is very good, isn't he?

Sister Aloysius: Yes. But he is oblivious.

Sister James: To what?

Sister Aloysius: I don't believe he knows who's President of the United States. I mean him no disrespect of course. It's just that he's otherworldly in the extreme.

Sister James: Is it that he's innocent, Sister Aloysius?

Sister Aloysius: You have a slyness at work, Sister James. Be careful of it. How is your class? How is Donald Muller?

Sister James: He is thirteenth in class.

Sister Aloysius: I know. That's sufficient. Is he being accepted?

Sister James: He has no friends.

Sister Aloysius: That would be a lot to expect after only two months. Has anyone hit him?

Sister James: No.

Sister Aloysius: Someone will. And when it happens, send them right down to me.

Sister James: I'm not so sure anyone will.

Sister Aloysius: There is a statue of St. Patrick on one side of the church altar and a statue of St. Anthony on the other. This parish serves Irish and Italian families. Someone will hit Donald Muller.

Sister James: He has a protector.

Sister Aloysius: Who?

Sister James: Father Flynn.

(*Sister Aloysius, who has been fussing with mulch, is suddenly rigid. She rises.*)

Sister Aloysius: What?

Sister James: He's taken an interest. Since Donald went on the altar boys. (*Pause*) I thought I should tell you.

Sister Aloysius: I told you to come to me, but I hoped you never would.

Sister James: Maybe I shouldn't have.

Sister Aloysius: I knew once you did, something would be set in motion. So it's happened.

Sister James: What?! I'm not telling you that! I'm not even certain what you mean.

Sister Aloysius: Yes, you are.

Sister James: I've been trying to become more cold in my thinking as you suggested . . . I feel as if I've lost my way a little, Sister Aloysius. I had the most terrible dream last night. I want to be guided by you and responsible to the children, but I want my peace of mind. I must tell you I have been longing for the return of my peace of mind.

Sister Aloysius: You may not have it. It is not your place to be complacent. That's for the children. That's what we give them.

Sister James: I think I'm starting to understand you a little. But it's so unsettling to look at things and people with suspicion. It feels as if I'm less close to God.

Sister Aloysius: When you take a step to address wrongdoing, you are taking a step away from God, but in His service. Dealing with such matters is hard and thankless work.

Sister James: I've become more reserved in class. I feel separated from the children.

Sister Aloysius: That's as it should be.

Sister James: But I feel. Wrong. And about this other matter, I don't have any evidence. I'm not at all certain that anything's happened.

Sister Aloysius: We can't wait for that.

Sister James: But what if it's nothing?

Sister Aloysius: Then it's nothing. I wouldn't mind being wrong. But I doubt I am.

Sister James: Then what's to be done?

Sister Aloysius: I don't know.

Sister James: You'll know what to do.

Sister Aloysius: I don't know what to do. There are parameters which protect him and hinder me.

Sister James: But he can't be safe if it's established. I doubt he could recover from the shame.

Sister Aloysius: What have you seen?

Sister James: I don't know.

Sister Aloysius: What have you seen?

Sister James: He took Donald to the rectory.

Sister Aloysius: What for?

Sister James: A talk.

Sister Aloysius: Alone?

Sister James: Yes.

Sister Aloysius: When?

Sister James: A week ago.

Sister Aloysius: Why didn't you tell me?

Sister James: I didn't think there was anything wrong with it. It never came into my mind that he . . . that there could be anything wrong.

Sister Aloysius: Of all the children. Donald Muller. I suppose it makes sense.

Sister James: How does it make sense?

Sister Aloysius: He's isolated. The little sheep lagging behind is the one the wolf goes for.

Sister James: I don't know that anything's wrong!

Sister Aloysius: Our first Negro student. I thought there'd be fighting, a parent or two to deal with . . . I should've foreseen this possibility.

Sister James: How could you imagine it?

Sister Aloysius: It is my job to outshine the fox in cleverness! That's my job!

Sister James: But maybe it's nothing!

Sister Aloysius: Then why do you look like you've seen the Devil?

Sister James: It's just the way the boy acted when he came back to class.

Sister Aloysius: He said something?

Sister James: No. It was his expression. He looked frightened and . . . he put his head on the desk in the most peculiar way. *(Struggles)* And one other thing. I think there was alcohol on his breath. There was alcohol on his breath.

(Sister Aloysius looks toward the rectory.)

Sister Aloysius: Eight years ago at St. Boniface we had a priest who had to be stopped. But I had Monsignor Scully then . . . who I could rely on. Here, there's no man I can go to, and men run everything. We are going to have to stop him ourselves.

Sister James: Can't you just . . . report your suspicions?

Sister Aloysius: To Monsignor Benedict? The man's guileless! He would just ask Father Flynn!

Sister James: Well, would that be such a bad idea?

Sister Aloysius: And he would believe whatever Father Flynn told him. He would think the matter settled.

Sister James: But maybe that is all that needs to be done. If it's true. If I had done something awful, and I was confronted with it, I'd be so repentant.

Sister Aloysius: Sister James, my dear, you must try to imagine a very different kind of person than yourself. A man who would do this has already denied a great deal. If I tell the monsignor and he is satisfied with Father Flynn's rebuttal, the matter is suppressed.

Sister James: Well then tell the bishop.

Sister Aloysius: The hierarchy of the Church does not permit my going to the bishop. No. Once I tell the monsignor, it's out of my hands, I'm helpless. I'm going to have to come up with a pretext, get Father Flynn into my office. Try to force it. You'll have to be there.

Sister James: Me? No! Why? Oh no, Sister! I couldn't!

Sister Aloysius: I can't be closeted alone with a priest. Another Sister must be in attendance and it has to be you. The circle of confidence mustn't be made any wider. Think of the boy if this gets out.

Sister James: I can't do it!

Sister Aloysius: Why not? You're squeamish?

Sister James: I'm not equipped! It's . . . I would be embarrassed. I couldn't possibly be present if the topic were spoken of!

Sister Aloysius: Please, Sister, do not indulge yourself in witless adolescent scruples. I assure you I would prefer a more seasoned confederate. But you are the one who came to me.

Sister James: You told me to!

Sister Aloysius: Would you rather leave the boy to be exploited? And don't think this will be the only story. If you close your eyes, you will be a party to all that comes after.

Sister James: You're supposed to tell the monsignor!

Sister Aloysius: That you saw a look in a boy's eye? That *perhaps* you smelled something on his breath? Monsignor Benedict thinks the sun rises and sets on Father Flynn. You'd be branded an hysteric and transferred.

Sister James: We can ask him.

Sister Aloysius: Who?

Sister James: The boy. Donald Muller.

Sister Aloysius: He'll deny it.

Sister James: Why?

Sister Aloysius: Shame.

Sister James: You can't know that.

Sister Aloysius: And if he does point the finger, how do you think that will be received in this community? A black child. *(No answer)* I am going to think this through. Then I'm going to invite Father Flynn to my office on an unrelated matter. You will be there.

Sister James: But what good can I do?

Sister Aloysius: Aside from the unacceptability of a priest and nun being alone, I need a witness.

Sister James: To what?

Sister Aloysius: He may tell the truth and lie afterwards.

(Sister James looks toward the rectory.)

Sister James: The boys are coming out of the rectory. They look happy enough.

Sister Aloysius: They look smug. Like they have a secret.

Sister James: There he is.

Sister Aloysius: If I could, Sister James, I would certainly choose to live in innocence. But innocence can only be wisdom in a world without evil. Situations arise and we are confronted with wrongdoing and the need to act.

Sister James: I have to take the boys up to class.

Sister Aloysius: Go on, then. Take them. I will be talking to you.

(The sound of wind. Sister Aloysius pulls her shawl tightly about her and goes. After a moment, Sister James goes as well.)

V

The principal's office. A phone rings. Sister Aloysius enters with a pot of tea, walking quickly to answer the phone.

Sister Aloysius: Hello, St. Nicholas School? Oh yes, Mr. McGinn. Thank you for calling back. That was quite a windstorm we had last night. No, I didn't know there was a Great Wind in Ireland and you were there for it. That's fascinating. Yes. I was wondering if you would be so kind as to remove a tree limb that's fallen in the courtyard of the church. Sister Veronica tripped on it this morning and fell on her face. I think she's all right. She doesn't look any worse, Mr. McGinn. Thank you, Mr. McGinn.

(She hangs up the phone and looks at her watch, a bit anxious. A knock at the door.)

Come in.

(The door opens. Father Flynn is standing there in his black cassock. He doesn't come in.)

Flynn: Good morning, Sister Aloysius! How are you today?

Sister Aloysius: Good morning, Father Flynn. Very well. Good of you to come by.

(Father Flynn takes a step into the office.)

Flynn: Are we ready for the meeting?

Sister Aloysius: We're just short Sister James. *(Father Flynn steps back into the door-way)* Did you hear that wind last night?

Flynn: I certainly did. Imagine what it must've been like in the frontier days when a man alone in the woods sat by a fire in his buckskins and listened to a sound like that. Imagine the loneliness! The immense darkness press-ing in! How frightening it must've been!

Sister Aloysius: If one lacked faith in God's protection, I suppose it would be frightening.

Flynn: Did I hear Sister Veronica had an accident?

Sister Aloysius: Yes. Sister Veronica fell on a piece of wood this morning and practically killed herself.

Flynn: Is she all right?

Sister Aloysius: Oh, she's fine.

Flynn: Her sight isn't good, is it?

Sister Aloysius: Her sight is fine. Nuns fall, you know.

Flynn: No, I didn't know that.

Sister Aloysius: It's the habit. It catches us up more often than not. What with our being in black and white, and so prone to falling, we're more like dominos than anything else.

(Sister James appears at the door, breathless.)

Sister James: Am I past the time?

(Father Flynn takes a step into the office.)

Flynn: Not at all. Sister Aloysius and I were just having a nice chat.

Sister James: Good morning, Father Flynn. Good morning, Sister. I'm sorry I was delayed. Mr. McGinn has closed the courtyard to fix something so I had to go back through the convent and out the side door and then I ran into Sister Veronica.

Flynn: How is she?

Sister James: She has a bit of a bloody nose.

Sister Aloysius: I'm beginning to think you're punching people.

Sister James: Sister?

Sister Aloysius: Well, after the incident with . . . Never mind. Well, come in, please. Sit down.

(They come in and sit down. Father Flynn takes Sister Aloysius's chair. He's sitting at her desk. She reacts, but says nothing.)

I actually have a hot pot of tea. *(Closes the door but for an inch)* And close this but not quite for form's sake. Would you have a cup of tea, Father?

Flynn: I would love a cup of tea.

Sister Aloysius: Perhaps you could serve him, Sister?

Sister James: Of course.

Sister Aloysius: And yourself of course.

Sister James: Would you like tea, Sister Aloysius?

Sister Aloysius: I've already had my cup.

Flynn: Is there sugar?

Sister Aloysius: Sugar? Yes! *(Rummages in her desk)* It's here somewhere. I put it in the drawer for Lent last year and never remembered to take it out.

Flynn: It mustn't have been much to give up then.

Sister Aloysius: No, I'm sure you're right. Here it is. I'll serve you, though for want of practice, I'm . . . *(Clumsy)*

(She's got the sugar bowl and is poised to serve him a lump of sugar with a small pair of tongs when she sees his nails.)

Your fingernails.

Flynn: I wear them a little long. The sugar?

Sister Aloysius: Oh yes. One?

Flynn: Three.

Sister Aloysius: Three.

(She's appalled but tries to hide it.)

Flynn: Sweet tooth.

Sister Aloysius: One, two, three. Sister, do you take sugar?

(Sister Aloysius looks at Sister James.)

Sister James (To Sister Aloysius): Never! *(To Father Flynn)* Not that there's anything wrong with sugar. *(To Sister Aloysius again)* Thank you.

(Sister Aloysius puts the sugar away in her desk.)

Sister Aloysius: Well, thank you, Father, for making the time for us. We're at our wit's end.

Flynn: I think it's an excellent idea to rethink the Christmas pageant. Last year's effort was a little woebegone.

Sister James: No! I loved it! *(Becomes self-conscious)* But I love all Christmas pageants. I just love the Nativity. The birth of the Savior. And the hymns of course. "O Little Town of Bethlehem," "O Come, O Come Emmanuel" . . .

Sister Aloysius: Thank you, Sister James. Sister James will be co-directing the pageant with Mrs. Shields this year. So what do you think, Father Flynn? Is there something new we could do?

Flynn: Well, we all love the Christmas hymns, but it might be jolly to include a secular song.

Sister Aloysius: Secular.

Flynn: Yes. "It's Beginning to Look a Lot Like Christmas." Something like that.

Sister Aloysius: What would be the point of performing a secular song?

Flynn: Fun.

Sister James: Or "Frosty the Snowman."

Flynn: That's a good one. We could have one of the boys dress as a snowman and dance around.

Sister Aloysius: Which boy?

Flynn: We'd do tryouts.

Sister Aloysius: "Frosty the Snowman" espouses a pagan belief in magic. The snowman comes to life when an enchanted hat is put on his head. If the music were more somber, people would realize the images are disturbing and the song heretical.

(Sister James and Father Flynn exchange a look.)

Sister James: I've never thought about "Frosty the Snowman" like that.

Sister Aloysius: It should be banned from the airwaves.

Flynn: So. Not "Frosty the Snowman."

(Father Flynn writes something in a small notebook.)

Sister Aloysius: I don't think so. "It's Beginning to Look a Lot Like Christmas" would be fine I suppose. The parents would like it. May I ask what you wrote down? With that ballpoint pen.

Flynn: Oh. Nothing. An idea for a sermon.

Sister Aloysius: You had one just now?

Flynn: I get them all the time.

Sister Aloysius: How fortunate.

Flynn: I forget them so I write them down.

Sister Aloysius: What is the idea?

Flynn: Intolerance.

(Sister James tries to break a bit of tension.)

Sister James: Would you like a little more tea, Father?

Flynn: Not yet. I think a message of the Second Ecumenical Council was that the Church needs to take on a more familiar face. Reflect the local community. We should sing a song from the radio now and then. Take the kids out for ice cream.

Sister Aloysius: Ice cream.

Flynn: Maybe take the boys on a camping trip. We should be friendlier. The children and the parents should see us as members of their family rather than emissaries from Rome. I think the pageant should be charming, like a community theatre doing a show.

Sister Aloysius: But we are not members of their family. We're different.

Flynn: Why? Because of our vows?

Sister Aloysius: Precisely.

Flynn: I don't think we're so different. *(To Sister James)* You know, I would take some more tea, Sister. Thank you.

Sister Aloysius: And they think we're different. The working-class people of this parish trust us to be different.

Flynn: I think we're getting off the subject.

Sister Aloysius: Yes, you're right, back to it. The Christmas pageant. We must be careful how Donald Muller is used in the pageant.

(Sister James shakes as she pours the tea.)

Flynn: Easy there, Sister, you don't spill.

Sister James: Oh, uh, yes, Father.

Flynn: What about Donald Muller?

Sister Aloysius: We must be careful, in the pageant, that we neither hide Donald Muller nor put him forward.

Flynn: Because of the color of his skin.

Sister Aloysius: That's right.

Flynn: Why?

Sister Aloysius: Come, Father. You're being disingenuous.

Flynn: I think he should be treated like every other boy.

Sister Aloysius: You yourself singled the boy out for special attention. You held a private meeting with him at the rectory. *(Turning to Sister James)* A week ago?

Sister James: Yes.

(He realizes something's up.)

Flynn: What are we talking about?

Sister James: Donald Muller?

Sister Aloysius: The boy acted strangely when he returned to class.

(*Father Flynn turns to Sister James.*)

Flynn: He did?

Sister James: When he returned from the rectory. A little odd, yes.

Sister Aloysius: Can you tell us why?

Flynn: How did he act strangely?

Sister James: I'm not sure how to explain it. He laid his head on the desk . . .

Flynn: You mean you had some impression?

Sister James: Yes.

Flynn: And he'd come from the rectory so you're asking me if I know anything about it?

Sister James: That's it.

Flynn: Hmmm. Did you want to discuss the pageant, is that why I'm here, or is this what you wanted to discuss?

Sister Aloysius: This.

Flynn: Well. I feel a little uncomfortable.

Sister Aloysius: Why?

Flynn: Why do you think? Something about your tone.

Sister Aloysius: I would prefer a discussion of fact rather than tone.

Flynn: Well. If I had judged my conversation with Donald Muller to be of concern to you, Sister, I would have sat you down and talked to you about it. But I did not judge it to be of concern to you.

Sister Aloysius: Perhaps you are mistaken in your understanding of what concerns me. The boy is in my school and his well-being is my responsibility.

Flynn: His well-being is not at issue.

Sister Aloysius: I am not satisfied that that is true. He was upset when he returned to class.

Flynn: Did he say something?

Sister James: No.

Sister Aloysius: What happened in the rectory?

Flynn: Happened? Nothing happened. I had a talk with a boy.

Sister Aloysius: What about?

Flynn: It was a private matter.

Sister Aloysius: He's twelve years old. What could be private?

Flynn: I'll say it again, Sister. I object to your tone.

Sister Aloysius: This is not about my tone or your tone, Father Flynn. It's about arriving at the truth.

Flynn: Of what?

Sister Aloysius: You know what I'm talking about. Don't you? You're controlling the expression on your face right now. Aren't you?

Flynn: My face? You said you wanted to talk about the pageant, Sister. That's why I'm here. Am I to understand that you brought me into your office to confront me in some way? It's outrageous. I'm not answerable to you. What exactly are you accusing me of?

Sister Aloysius: I am not accusing you of anything, Father Flynn. I am asking you to tell me what happened in the rectory.

(*Father Flynn stands.*)

Flynn: I don't wish to continue this conversation at all further. And if you are dissatisfied with that, I suggest you speak to Monsignor Benedict. I can only imagine that your unfortunate behavior this morning is the result of overwork. Perhaps you need a leave of absence. I may suggest it. Have a good morning. *(To Sister James)* Sister?

Sister James: Good morning, Father.

(Sister Aloysius's next words stop him.)

Sister Aloysius: There was alcohol on his breath. *(He turns)* When he returned from his meeting with you.

(He comes back and sits down. He rubs his eyes.)

Flynn: Alcohol.

Sister James: I did smell it on his breath.

Sister Aloysius: Well?

Flynn: Can't you let this alone?

Sister Aloysius: No.

Flynn: I see there's no way out of this.

Sister James: Take your time, Father. Would you like some more tea?

Flynn: You should've let it alone.

Sister Aloysius: Not possible.

Flynn: Donald Muller served as altar boy last Tuesday morning. After Mass, Mr. McGinn caught him in the sacristy drinking altar wine. When I found out, I sent for him. There were tears. He begged not to be removed from the altar boys. And I took pity on him. I told him if no one else found out, I would let him stay on.

(Sister James is overjoyed. Sister Aloysius is unmoved.)

Sister James: Oh, what a relief! That explains everything! Thanks be to God! Oh, Sister, look, it's all a mistake!

Sister Aloysius: And if I talk to Mr. McGinn?

Flynn: Talk to Mr. McGinn by all means. But now that the boy's secret's out, I'm going to have to remove him from the altar boys. Which I think is too bad. That's what I was trying to avoid.

Sister James: You were trying to protect the boy!

Flynn: That's right.

Sister James: I might've done the same thing! *(To Sister Aloysius)* Is there a way Donald could stay on the altar boys?

Sister Aloysius: No. If the boy drank altar wine, he cannot continue as an altar boy.

Flynn: Of course you're right. I'm just not the disciplinarian you are, Sister. And he is the only Negro in the school. That did affect my thinking on the matter. It will be commented on that he's no longer serving at Mass. It's a public thing. A certain ignorant element in the parish will be confirmed in their beliefs.

Sister Aloysius: He must be held to the same standard as the others.

Flynn: Of course. Do we need to discuss the pageant or was that just . . .

Sister Aloysius: No, this was the issue.

Flynn: Are you satisfied?

Sister Aloysius: Yes.

Flynn: Then I'll be going. I have some writing to do.

Sister Aloysius: Intolerance.

Flynn: That's right.

> *(He goes, then stops at the door.)*

I'm not pleased with how you handled this, Sister. Next time you are troubled by dark ideas, I suggest you speak to the monsignor.

> *(He goes. After a moment, Sister James weakly launches into optimism.)*

Sister James: Well. What a relief! He cleared it all up.

Sister Aloysius: You believe him?

Sister James: Of course.

Sister Aloysius: Isn't it more that it's easier to believe him?

Sister James: But we can corroborate his story with Mr. McGinn!

Sister Aloysius: Yes. These types of people are clever. They're not so easily undone.

Sister James: Well, I'm convinced!

Sister Aloysius: You're not. You just want things to be resolved so you can have simplicity back.

Sister James: I want no further part of this.

Sister Aloysius: I'll bring him down. With or without your help.

Sister James: How can you be so sure he's lying?

Sister Aloysius: Experience.

Sister James: You just don't like him! You don't like it that he uses a ballpoint pen. You don't like it that he takes three lumps of sugar in his tea. You don't like it that he likes "Frosty the Snowman." And you're letting that convince you of something terrible, just terrible! Well, I like "Frosty the Snowman"! And it would be nice if this school weren't run like a prison! And I think it's a good thing that I love to teach History and that I might inspire my students to love it, too! And if you judge that to mean I'm not fit to be a teacher, then so be it!

Sister Aloysius: Sit down. *(Sister James does)* In ancient Sparta, important matters were decided by who shouted loudest. Fortunately, we are not in ancient Sparta. Now. Do you honestly find the students in this school to be treated like inmates in a prison?

Sister James (Relenting): No, I don't. Actually, by and large, they seem to be fairly happy. But they're all uniformly terrified of you!

Sister Aloysius: Yes. That's how it works. Sit there.

> *(Sister Aloysius looks in a notebook, picks up the phone, dials.)*

Hello, this is Sister Aloysius Beauvier, the principal of St. Nicholas. Is this Mrs. Muller? I'm calling about your son, Donald. I would like you and your husband to come down here for a talk. When would be convenient?

> *(Lights fade.)*

VI

Father Flynn, in blue and white vestments, is at the pulpit.

Flynn: A woman was gossiping with a friend about a man she hardly knew—I know none of you have ever done this—and that night she had a dream. A great hand appeared over her and pointed down at her. She was immediately seized with an overwhelming sense of guilt. The next day she went to confession. She got the old parish priest, Father O'Rouke, and she told him the whole thing. "Is gossiping a sin?" she asked the old man. "Was that the Hand of God Almighty pointing a finger at me? Should I be asking your absolution? Father, tell me, have I done something wrong?" *(Irish brogue)* "Yes!" Father O'Rouke answered her. "Yes, you ignorant, badly brought-up female! You have borne false witness against your neighbor, you have played fast and loose with his reputation, and you should be heartily ashamed!" So the woman said she was sorry and asked forgiveness. "Not so fast!" says O'Rouke. "I want you to go home, take a pillow up on your roof, cut it open with a knife, and return here to me!" So she went home, took the pillow off her bed, a knife from the drawer, went up the fire escape to the roof, and stabbed the pillow. Then she went back to the old priest as instructed. "Did you gut the pillow with the knife?" he says. "Yes, Father." "And what was the result?" "Feathers," she said. "Feathers"? he repeated. "Feathers everywhere, Father!" "Now I want you to go back and gather up every last feather that flew out on the wind!" "Well," she says, "it can't be done. I don't know where they went. The wind took them all over." "And that," said Father O'Rouke, "is *gossip*!" In the name of the Father, Son, and the Holy Ghost, Amen.

VII

The lights crossfade to the garden. A crow caws. Sister James sits on the bench, deep in thought. Father Flynn enters.

Flynn: Good afternoon, Sister James.

Sister James: Good afternoon, Father.

Flynn: What is that bird complaining about? What kind of bird is that? A starling? A grackle?

Sister James: A crow?

Flynn: Of course it is. Are you praying? I didn't mean to interrupt.

Sister James: I'm not praying, no.

Flynn: You seem subdued.

Sister James: Oh. I can't sleep.

Flynn: Why not?

Sister James: Bad dreams. Actually one bad dream, and then I haven't slept right since.

Flynn: What about?

Sister James: I looked in a mirror and there was a darkness where my face should be. It frightened me.

Flynn: I can't sleep on occasion.

Sister James: No? Do you see that big hand pointing a finger at you?

Flynn: Yes. Sometimes.

Sister James: Was your sermon directed at anyone in particular?

Flynn: What do you think?

Sister James: Did you make up that story about the pillow?

Flynn: Yes. You make up little stories to illustrate. In the tradition of the parable.

Sister James: Aren't the things that actually happen in life more worthy of interpretation than a made-up story?

Flynn: No. What actually happens in life is beyond interpretation. The truth makes for a bad sermon. It tends to be confusing and have no clear conclusion.

Sister James: I received a letter from my brother in Maryland yesterday. He's very sick.

Flynn: Maybe you should go and see him.

Sister James: I can't leave my class.

Flynn: How's Donald Muller doing?

Sister James: I don't know.

Flynn: You don't see him?

Sister James: I see him every day, but I don't know how he's doing. I don't know how to judge these things. Now.

Flynn: I stopped speaking to him for fear of it being misunderstood. Isn't that a shame? I actually avoided him the other day when I might've passed him in the hall. He doesn't understand why. I noticed you didn't come to me for confession.

Sister James: No. I went to Monsignor Benedict. He's very kind.

Flynn: I wasn't?

Sister James: It wasn't that. As you know. You know why.

Flynn: You're against me?

Sister James: No.

Flynn: You're not convinced?

Sister James: It's not for me to be convinced, one way or the other. It's Sister Aloysius.

Flynn: Are you just an extension of her?

Sister James: She's my superior.

Flynn: But what about you?

Sister James: I wish I knew nothing whatever about it. I wish the idea had never entered my mind.

Flynn: How did it enter your mind?

Sister James: Sister Aloysius.

Flynn: I feel as if my reputation has been damaged through no fault of my own. But I'm reluctant to take the steps necessary to repair it for fear of doing further harm. It's frustrating, I can tell you that.

Sister James: Is it true?

Flynn: What?

Sister James: You know what I'm asking.

Flynn: No, it's not true.

Sister James: Oh, I don't know what to believe.

Flynn: How can you take sides against me?

Sister James: It doesn't matter.

Flynn: It does matter! I've done nothing. There's no substance to any of this. The most innocent actions can appear sinister to the poisoned mind. I had to throw that poor boy off the altar. He's devastated. The only reason I haven't gone to the monsignor is I don't want to tear apart the school. Sister Aloysius would most certainly lose her position as principal if I made her accusations known. Since they're baseless. You might lose your place as well.

Sister James: Are you threatening me?

Flynn: What do you take me for? No.

Sister James: I want to believe you.

Flynn: Then do. It's as simple as that.

Sister James: It's not me that has to be convinced.

Flynn: I don't have to prove anything to her.

Sister James: She's determined.

Flynn: To what?

Sister James: Protect the boy.

Flynn: It's me that cares about that boy, not her. Has she ever reached out a hand to that child or any child in this school? She's like a block of ice! Children need warmth, kindness, understanding! What does she give them? Rules. That black boy needs a helping hand or he's not going to make it here! But if she has her way, he'll be left to his own undoing. Why do you think he was in the sacristy drinking wine that day? He's in trouble! She sees me talk in a human way to these children and she immediately assumes there must be something wrong with it. Something dirty. Well, I'm not going to let her keep this parish in the Dark Ages! And I'm not going to let her destroy my spirit of compassion!

Sister James: I'm sure that's not her intent.

Flynn: I care about this congregation!

Sister James: I know you do.

Flynn: Like you care about your class! You love them, don't you?

Sister James: Yes.

Flynn: That's natural. How else would you relate to children? I can look at your face and know your philosophy: kindness.

Sister James: I don't know. I mean, of course.

Flynn: What is Sister Aloysius's philosophy do you suppose?

(*A pause.*)

Sister James: I don't have to suppose. She's told me. She discourages . . . warmth. She's suggested I be more . . . formal.

Flynn: There are people who go after your humanity, Sister James, who tell you the light in your heart is a weakness. That your soft feelings betray you. I don't believe that. It's an old tactic of cruel people to kill kindness in the name of virtue. Don't believe it. There's nothing wrong with love.

Sister James: Of course not, but . . .

Flynn: Have you forgotten that was the message of the Savior to us all. Love. Not suspicion, disapproval and judgment. Love of people. Have you found Sister Aloysius a positive inspiration?

Sister James: I don't want to misspeak, but no. She's taken away my joy of teaching. And I loved teaching more than anything. (*She cries a little. He pats her uneasily, looking around*)

Flynn: It's all right. You're going to be all right.

Sister James: I feel as if everything is upside down.

Flynn: It isn't though. There are just times in life when we feel lost. You're not alone with it. It happens to many of us.

Sister James: A bond. (*Becomes self-conscious*) I'd better go in.

Flynn: I'm sorry your brother is ill.

Sister James: Thank you, Father. (*Starts to go, stops*) I don't believe it!

Flynn: You don't?

Sister James: No.

Flynn: Thank you, Sister. That's a great relief to me. Thank you very much.

(*She goes. He takes out his little black book and writes in it. The crow caws. He yells at it:*)

Oh, be quiet.

(*Then he opens a prayer book and walks away.*)

VIII

Crossfade to the principal's office. Sister Aloysius is sitting looking out the window, very still. A knock at the door. She doesn't react. A second knock, louder. She pulls a small earplug out of her ear and scurries to the door. She opens it. There stands Mrs. Muller, a black woman of about thirty-eight, in her Sunday best, dressed for church. She's on red alert.

Sister Aloysius: Mrs. Muller?
Mrs. Muller: Yes.
Sister Aloysius: Come in.

(*Sister Aloysius closes the door.*)

Please have a seat.
Mrs. Muller: I thought I might a had the wrong day when you didn't answer the door.
Sister Aloysius: Oh. Yes. Well, just between us, I was listening to a transistor radio with an earpiece.

(*She shows Mrs. Muller a very small transistor radio.*)

Look at how tiny they're making them now. I confiscated it from one of the students and now I can't stop using it.
Mrs. Muller: You like music?
Sister Aloysius: Not really. News reports. Years ago I used to listen to all the news reports because my husband was in Italy in the war. When I came into possession of this little radio, I found myself doing it again. Though there is no war and the voices have changed.
Mrs. Muller: You were a married woman?
Sister Aloysius: Yes. But then he was killed. Is your husband coming?
Mrs. Muller: Couldn't get off work.
Sister Aloysius: I see. Of course. It was a lot to ask.
Mrs. Muller: How's Donald doing?
Sister Aloysius: He's passing his subjects. He has average grades.
Mrs. Muller: Oh. Good. He was upset about getting taken off the altar boys.
Sister Aloysius: Did he explain why?
Mrs. Muller: He said he was caught drinking wine.
Sister Aloysius: That is the reason.
Mrs. Muller: Well, that seems fair. But he's a good boy, Sister. He fell down there, but he's a good boy pretty much down the line. And he knows what an opportunity he has here. I think the whole thing was just a bit much for him.
Sister Aloysius: What do you mean, the whole thing?
Mrs. Muller: He's the only colored here. He's the first in this school. That'd be a lot for a boy.

Sister Aloysius: I suppose it is. But he has to do the work of course.

Mrs. Muller: He is doing it though, right?

Sister Aloysius: Yes. He's getting by. He's getting through. How is he at home?

Mrs. Muller: His father beat the hell out of him over that wine.

Sister Aloysius: He shouldn't do that.

Mrs. Muller: You don't tell my husband what to do. You just stand back. He didn't want Donald to come here.

Sister Aloysius: Why not?

Mrs. Muller: Thought he'd have a lot of trouble with the other boys. But that hasn't really happened as far as I can make out.

Sister Aloysius: Good.

Mrs. Muller: That priest, Father Flynn, been watching out for him.

Sister Aloysius: Yes. Have you met Father Flynn?

Mrs. Muller: Not exactly, no. I seen him on the altar, but I haven't met him face to face. No. Just, you know, heard from Donald.

Sister Aloysius: What does he say?

Mrs. Muller: You know, Father Flynn, Father Flynn. He looks up to him. The man gives him his time, which is what the boy needs. He needs that.

Sister Aloysius: Mrs. Muller, we may have a problem.

Mrs. Muller: Well, I thought you must a had a reason for asking me to come in. Principal's a big job. If you stop your day to talk to me, must be something. I just want to say though, it's just till June.

Sister Aloysius: Excuse me?

Mrs. Muller: Whatever the problem is, Donald just has to make it here till June. Then he's off into high school.

Sister Aloysius: Right.

Mrs. Muller: If Donald can graduate from here, he has a better chance of getting into a good high school. And that would mean an opportunity at college. I believe he has the intelligence. And he wants it, too.

Sister Aloysius: I don't see anything at this time standing in the way of his graduating with his class.

Mrs. Muller: Well, that's all I care about. Anything else is all right with me.

Sister Aloysius: I doubt that.

Mrs. Muller: Try me.

Sister Aloysius: I'm concerned about the relationship between Father Flynn and your son.

Mrs. Muller: You don't say. Concerned. What do you mean, concerned?

Sister Aloysius: That it may not be right.

Mrs. Muller: Uh-huh. Well, there's something wrong with everybody, isn't that so? Got to be forgiving.

Sister Aloysius: I'm concerned, to be frank, that Father Flynn may have made advances on your son.

Mrs. Muller: *May* have made.

Sister Aloysius: I can't be certain.

Mrs. Muller: No evidence?

Sister Aloysius: No.

Mrs. Muller: Then maybe there's nothing to it?

Sister Aloysius: I think there is something to it.

Mrs. Muller: Well, I would prefer not to see it that way if you don't mind.

Sister Aloysius: I can understand that this is hard to hear. I think Father Flynn gave Donald that altar wine.

Mrs. Muller: Why would he do that?

Sister Aloysius: Has Donald been acting strangely?

Mrs. Muller: No.

Sister Aloysius: Nothing out of the ordinary?

Mrs. Muller: He's been himself.

Sister Aloysius: All right.

Mrs. Muller: Look, Sister, I don't want any trouble, and I feel like you're on the march somehow.

Sister Aloysius: I'm not sure you completely understand.

Mrs. Muller: I think I understand the kind of thing you're talking about. But I don't want to get into it.

Sister Aloysius: What's that?

Mrs. Muller: Not to be disagreeing with you, but if we're talking about something floating around between this priest and my son, that ain't my son's fault.

Sister Aloysius: I'm not suggesting it is.

Mrs. Muller: He's just a boy.

Sister Aloysius: I know.

Mrs. Muller: Twelve years old. If somebody should be taking blame for anything, it should be the man, not the boy.

Sister Aloysius: I agree with you completely.

Mrs. Muller: You're agreeing with me but I'm sitting in the principal's office talking about my son. Why isn't the priest in the principal's office, if you know what I'm saying and you'll excuse my bringing it up.

Sister Aloysius: You're here because I'm concerned about Donald's welfare.

Mrs. Muller: You think I'm not?

Sister Aloysius: Of course you are.

Mrs. Muller: Let me ask you something. You honestly think that priest gave Donald that wine to drink?

Sister Aloysius: Yes, I do.

Mrs. Muller: Then how come my son got kicked off the altar boys if it was the man that gave it to him?

Sister Aloysius: The boy got caught, the man didn't.

Mrs. Muller: How come the priest didn't get kicked off the priesthood?

Sister Aloysius: He's a grown man, educated. And he knows what's at stake. It's not so easy to pin someone like that down.

Mrs. Muller: So you give my son the whole blame. No problem my son getting blamed and punished. That's easy. You know why that is?

Sister Aloysius: Perhaps you should let me talk. I think you're getting upset.

Mrs. Muller: That's because that's the way it is. You're just finding out about it, but that's the way it is and the way it's been, Sister. You're not going against no *man* in a *robe* and win, Sister. He's got the position.

Sister Aloysius: And he's got your son.

Mrs. Muller: Let him have 'im then.

Sister Aloysius: What?

Mrs. Muller: It's just till June.

Sister Aloysius: Do you know what you're saying?

Mrs. Muller: Know more about it than you.

Sister Aloysius: I believe this man is creating or has already brought about an improper relationship with your son.

Mrs. Muller: I don't know.

Sister Aloysius: I know I'm right.

Mrs. Muller: Why you need to know something like that for sure when you don't? Please, Sister. You got some kind a righteous cause going with this priest and now you want to drag my boy into it. My son doesn't need additional difficulties. Let him take the good and leave the rest when he leaves this place in June. He knows how to do that. I taught him how to do that.

Sister Aloysius: What kind of mother are you?

Mrs. Muller: Excuse me, but you don't know enough about life to say a thing like that, Sister.

Sister Aloysius: I know enough.

Mrs. Muller: You know the rules maybe, but that don't cover it.

Sister Aloysius: I know what I won't accept!

Mrs. Muller: You accept what you gotta accept and you work with it. That's the truth I know. Sorry to be so sharp, but you're in here in this room . . .

Sister Aloysius: This man is in my school.

Mrs. Muller: Well, he's gotta be somewhere and maybe he's doing some good too. You ever think of that?

Sister Aloysius: He's after the boys.

Mrs. Muller: Well, maybe some of them boys want to get caught. Maybe what you don't know maybe is my son is . . . that way. That's why his father beat him up. Not the wine. He beat Donald for being what he is.

Sister Aloysius: What are you telling me?

Mrs. Muller: I'm his mother. I'm talking about his nature now, not anything he's done. But you can't hold a child responsible for what God gave him to be.

Sister Aloysius: Listen to me with care, Mrs. Muller. I'm only interested in actions. It's hopeless to discuss a child's possible inclination. I'm finding it difficult enough to address a man's deeds. This isn't about what the boy may be, but what the man is. It's about the man.

Mrs. Muller: But there's the boy's nature.

Sister Aloysius: Let's leave that out of it.

Mrs. Muller: Forget it then. You're the one forcing people to say these things out loud. Things are in the air and you leave them alone if you can. That's what I know. My boy came to this school 'cause they were gonna kill him at the public school. So we were lucky enough to get him in here for his last year. Good. His father don't like him. He comes here, the kids don't like him. One man is good to him. This priest. Puts out a hand to the boy. Does the man have his reasons? Yes. Everybody has their reasons. *You* have your reasons. But do I ask the man why he's good to my son? No. I don't care why. My son needs some man to care about him and see him through to where he wants to go. And thank God, this educated man with some kindness in him wants to do just that.

Sister Aloysius: This will not do.

Mrs. Muller: It's just till June. Sometimes things aren't black and white.

Sister Aloysius: And sometimes they are. I'll throw your son out of this school. Make no mistake.

Mrs. Muller: But why would you do that? If nothing started with him?

Sister Aloysius: Because I will stop this whatever way I must.

Mrs. Muller: You'd hurt my son to get your way?

Sister Aloysius: It won't end with your son. There will be others, if there aren't already.

Mrs. Muller: Throw the priest out then.

Sister Aloysius: I'm trying to do just that.

Mrs. Muller: Well, what do you want from me?

(A pause.)

Sister Aloysius: Nothing. As it turns out. I was hoping you might know something that would help me, but it seems you don't.

Mrs. Muller: Please leave my son out of this. My husband would kill that child over a thing like this.

Sister Aloysius: I'll try.

(Mrs. Muller stands up.)

Mrs. Muller: I don't know, Sister. You may think you're doing good, but the world's a hard place. I don't know that you and me are on the same side. I'll be standing with my son and those who are good with my son. It'd be nice to see you there. Nice talking with you, Sister. Good morning.

(She goes, leaving the door open behind her. Sister Aloysius is shaken. After a moment, Father Flynn appears at the door. He's in a controlled fury.)

Flynn: May I come in?

Sister Aloysius: We would require a third party.

Flynn: What was Donald's mother doing here?

Sister Aloysius: We were having a chat.

Flynn: About what?

Sister Aloysius: A third party is truly required, Father.

Flynn: No, Sister. No third party. You and me are due for a talk.

(He comes in and slams the door behind him. They face each other.)

You have to stop this campaign against me!

Sister Aloysius: You can stop it at any time.

Flynn: How?

Sister Aloysius: Confess and resign.

Flynn: You are attempting to destroy my reputation! But the result of all this is going to be your removal, not mine!

Sister Aloysius: What are you doing in this school?

Flynn: I am trying to do good!

Sister Aloysius: Or even more to the point, what are you doing in the priest-hood?

Flynn: You are single-handedly holding this school and this parish back!

Sister Aloysius: From what?

Flynn: Progressive education and a welcoming church.

Sister Aloysius: You can't distract me, Father Flynn. This isn't about my behavior, it's about yours.

Flynn: It's about your unfounded suspicions.

Sister Aloysius: That's right. I have suspicions.

Flynn: You know what I haven't understood through all this? *Why* do you suspect me? What have I done?

Sister Aloysius: You gave that boy wine to drink. And you let him take the blame.

Flynn: That's completely untrue! Did you talk to Mr. McGinn?

Sister Aloysius: All McGinn knows is the boy drank wine. He doesn't how he came to drink it.

Flynn: Did his mother have something to add to that?

Sister Aloysius: No.

Flynn: So that's it. There's nothing there.

Sister Aloysius: I'm not satisfied.

Flynn: Well, if you're not satisfied, ask the boy then!

Sister Aloysius: No, he'd protect you. That's what he's been doing.

Flynn: Oh, and why would he do that?

Sister Aloysius: Because you have seduced him.

Flynn: You're insane! You've got it in your head that I've corrupted this child after giving him wine, and nothing I say will change that.

Sister Aloysius: That's right.

Flynn: But correct me if I'm wrong. This has nothing to do with the wine, not really. You had a fundamental mistrust of me before this incident! It was you that warned Sister James to be on the lookout, wasn't it?

Sister Aloysius: That's true.

Flynn: So you admit it!

Sister Aloysius: Certainly.

Flynn: Why?

Sister Aloysius: I know people.

Flynn: That's not good enough!

Sister Aloysius: It won't have to be.

Flynn: How's that?

Sister Aloysius: You will tell me what you've done.

Flynn: Oh I will?

Sister Aloysius: Yes.

Flynn: I'm not one of your truant boys, you know. Sister James is convinced I'm innocent.

Sister Aloysius: So you talked to Sister James? Well, of course you talked to Sister James.

Flynn: Did you know that Donald's father beats him?

Sister Aloysius: Yes.

Flynn: And might that not account for the odd behavior Sister James noticed in the boy?

Sister Aloysius: It might.

Flynn: Then what is it? What? What did you hear, what did you see that convinced you so thoroughly?

Sister Aloysius: What does it matter?

Flynn: I want to know.

Sister Aloysius: On the first day of the school year, I saw you touch William London's wrist. And I saw him pull away.

Flynn: That's all?

Sister Aloysius: That was all.

Flynn: But that's nothing.

(*He writes in his book.*)

Sister Aloysius: What are you writing now?

Flynn: You leave me no choice. I'm writing down what you say. I tend to get too flustered to remember the details of an upsetting conversation, and this may be important. When I talk to the monsignor and explain why you have to be removed as the principal of this school.

Sister Aloysius: This morning, before I spoke with Mrs. Muller, I took the precaution of calling the last parish to which you were assigned.

Flynn: What did he say?

Sister Aloysius: Who?

Flynn: The pastor?

Sister Aloysius: I did not speak to the pastor. I spoke to one of the nuns.

Flynn: You should've spoken to the pastor.

Sister Aloysius: I spoke to a nun.

Flynn: That's not the proper route for you to have taken, Sister! The Church is very clear. You're supposed to go through the pastor.

Sister Aloysius: Why? Do you have an understanding, you and he? Father Flynn, you have a history.

Flynn: You have no right to go rummaging through my past!

Sister Aloysius: This is your third parish in five years.

Flynn: Call the pastor and ask him why I left! It was perfectly innocent.

Sister Aloysius: I'm not calling the pastor.

Flynn: I am a good priest! And there is nothing in my record to suggest otherwise.

Sister Aloysius: You will go after another child and another, until you are stopped.

Flynn: What nun did you speak to?

Sister Aloysius: I won't say.

Flynn: I've not touched a child.

Sister Aloysius: You have.

Flynn: You have not the slightest proof of anything.

Sister Aloysius: But I have my certainty, and armed with that, I will go to your last parish, and the one before that if necessary. I will find a parent, Father Flynn! Trust me I will. A parent who probably doesn't know that you are *still working with children*! And once I do that, you will be exposed. You may even be attacked, metaphorically or otherwise.

Flynn: You have no right to act on your own! You are a member of a religious order. You have taken vows, obedience being one! You answer to us! You have no right to step outside the Church!

Sister Aloysius: I will step outside the Church if that's what needs to be done, though the door should shut behind me! I will do what needs to be done, Father, if it means I'm damned to Hell! You should understand that, or you will mistake me. Now, did you give Donald Muller wine to drink?

Flynn: Have you never done anything wrong?

Sister Aloysius: I have.

Flynn: Mortal sin?

Sister Aloysius: Yes.

Flynn: And?

Sister Aloysius: I confessed it! Did you give Donald Muller wine to drink?

Flynn: Whatever I have done, I have left in the healing hands of my confessor. As have you! We are the same!

Sister Aloysius: We are not the same! A dog that bites is a dog that bites! I do not justify what I do wrong and go on. I admit it, desist, and take my medicine. Did you give Donald Muller wine to drink?

Flynn: No.

Sister Aloysius: Mental reservation?

Flynn: No.

Sister Aloysius: You lie. Very well then. If you won't leave my office, I will. And once I go, I will not stop.

(*She goes to the door. Suddenly, a new tone comes into his voice.*)

Flynn: Wait!

Sister Aloysius: You will request a transfer from this parish. You will take a leave of absence until it is granted.

Flynn: And do what for the love of God? My life is here.

Sister Aloysius: Don't.

Flynn: Please! Are we people? Am I a person flesh and blood like you? Or are we just ideas and convictions. I can't say everything. Do you understand? There are things I can't say. Even if you can't imagine the explanation, Sister, remember that there are circumstances beyond your knowledge. Even if you feel certainty, it is an emotion and not a fact. In the spirit of charity, I appeal to you. On behalf of my life's work. You have to behave responsibly. I put myself in your hands.

Sister Aloysius: I don't want you.

Flynn: My reputation is at stake.

Sister Aloysius: You can preserve your reputation.

Flynn: If you say these things, I won't be able to do my work in the community.

Sister Aloysius: Your work in the community should be discontinued.

Flynn: You'd leave me with nothing.

Sister Aloysius: That's not true. It's Donald Muller who has nothing, and you took full advantage of that.

Flynn: I have not done anything wrong. I care about that boy very much.

Sister Aloysius: Because you smile at him and sympathize with him, and talk to him as if you were the same?

Flynn: That child needed a friend!

Sister Aloysius: You are a cheat. The warm feeling you experienced when that boy looked at you with trust was not the sensation of virtue. It can be got by a drunkard from his tot of rum. You're a disgrace to the collar. The only reason you haven't been thrown out of the Church is the decline in vocations.

Flynn: I can fight you.

Sister Aloysius: You will lose.

Flynn: You can't know that.

Sister Aloysius: I know.

Flynn: Where's your compassion?

Sister Aloysius: Nowhere you can get at it. Stay here. Compose yourself. Use the phone if you like. Good day, Father. I have no sympathy for you. I know you're invulnerable to true regret. (*Starts to go. Pause*) And cut your nails.

(*She goes, closing the door behind her. After a moment, he goes to the phone and dials.*)

Flynn: Yes. This is Father Brendan Flynn of St. Nicholas parish. I need to make an appointment to see the bishop.

(Lights fade.)

IX

The lights crossfade to Sister Aloysius walking into the garden. It's a sunny day. She sits on the bench. Sister James enters.

Sister Aloysius: How's your brother?

Sister James: Better. Much better.

Sister Aloysius: I'm very glad. I prayed for him.

Sister James: It was good to get away. I needed to see my family. It had been too long.

Sister Aloysius: Then I'm glad you did it.

Sister James: And Father Flynn is gone.

Sister Aloysius: Yes.

Sister James: Where?

Sister Aloysius: St. Jerome's.

Sister James: So you did it. You got him out.

Sister Aloysius: Yes.

Sister James: Donald Muller is heartbroken that he's gone.

Sister Aloysius: Can't be helped. It's just till June.

Sister James: I don't think Father Flynn did anything wrong.

Sister Aloysius: No? He convinced you?

Sister James: Yes, he did.

Sister Aloysius: Hmmm.

Sister James: Did you ever prove it?

Sister Aloysius: What?

Sister James: That he interfered with Donald Muller?

Sister Aloysius: Did I ever prove it to whom?

Sister James: Anyone but yourself?

Sister Aloysius: No.

Sister James: But you were sure.

Sister Aloysius: Yes.

Sister James: I wish I could be like you.

Sister Aloysius: Why?

Sister James: Because I can't sleep at night anymore. Everything seems uncertain to me.

Sister Aloysius: Maybe we're not supposed to sleep so well. They've made Father Flynn the pastor of St. Jerome.

Sister James: Who?

Sister Aloysius: The bishop appointed Father Flynn the pastor of St. Jerome Church and School. It's a promotion.

Sister James: You didn't tell them?

Sister Aloysius: I told our good Monsignor Benedict. I crossed the garden and told him. He did not believe it to be true.

Sister James: Then why did Father Flynn leave? What did you say to him to make him go?

Sister Aloysius: That I had called a nun in his previous parish. That I had found out his prior history of infringements.

Sister James: So you did prove it!

Sister Aloysius: I was lying. I made no such call.

Sister James: You lied?

Sister Aloysius: Yes. But if he had no such history, the lie wouldn't have worked. His resignation was his confession. He was what I thought he was. And he's gone.

Sister James: I can't believe you lied.

Sister Aloysius: In the pursuit of wrongdoing, one steps away from God. Of course there's a price.

Sister James: I see. So now he's in another school.

Sister Aloysius: Yes. Oh, Sister James!

Sister James: What is it, Sister?

Sister Aloysius: I have doubts! I have such doubts!

(Sister Aloysius is bent with emotion. Sister James comforts her. Lights fade.)

End of play

Connections to Other Selections

1. Discuss the ways in which ambiguity is used to complicate the plot and the theme of *Doubt: A Parable* and Nathaniel Hawthorne's "Young Goodman Brown" (p. 402).

2. Compare the school settings created in Shanley's play and in Nilaja Sun's *No Child . . .* (p. 1969). How are the assumptions, values, and characteristic experiences associated with these settings crucial to the tone of each play?

No Child . . .

Raised in the multicultural Lower East Side of Manhattan, Nilaja Sun has always been at home with the energy, variety, and ethnic richness that New York City has to offer. A graduate of Franklin and Marshall College, she has appeared in a number of New York plays and in television shows such as *30 Rock* and *Law and Order: SVU*. She has worked as a teaching artist in New York City's Epic Theatre Company's "Journeys" program, which introduces theater to city students through the study and production of a single play in their school. Written and first produced when she was only twenty-six years old, *No Child . . .* reflects some of Sun's experience as a teaching artist and has won a number of prizes, including an Outer Critics Circle Award,

Thos Robinson/Stringer/Getty Images.

an Obie Award, a John Gassner Award, and a San Francisco Bay Area Theatre Critics Circle Award.

The raucous class depicted in this play is both a challenge and
an eye-opener into the comic and chaotic lives of students that Sun
takes seriously. She manages to teach—and learn—from an unlikely,
unpromising group of kids who take for granted that they will be left
behind.

NILAJA SUN (B. 1974)

No Child...

2007

NOTES: *This play may be performed with one actor or with as many as sixteen actors.
The play takes place in several locations but is best staged in a fluid style with lights and
sounds suggesting scene changes.*

CHARACTERS

(In order of appearance:)
Janitor Baron, eighties, Narrator
Ms. Sun, thirties, teaching artist
Ms. Tam, twenties, teacher
Coca, sixteen, student
Jerome, eighteen, student
Brian, sixteen, student
Shondrika, sixteen, student
Xiomara, sixteen, student
Jose, seventeen, student
Chris, fifteen, student
Mrs. Kennedy, school principal
Security Guard, any age
Phillip, sixteen, student
Mrs. Projensky, substitute teacher
Mr. Johnson, Teacher
Doña Guzman, seventies, grandmother to Jose Guzman

TIME: Now

PLACE: New York

SCENE I

School. Morning. Janitor enters, mopping floor as he sings.

Janitor: Trouble in mind.
    I'm Blue.
    But I won't be blue always.

Cuz the sun's gonna shine
In my back door someday.
(To audience.)

Hear that? Silence. Beautiful silence, pure silence. The kind of silence that only comes from spending years in the back woods. We ain't in the back woods (though I'm thinking 'bout retirin' there). It's 8:04 AM—five minutes before the start of the day. And, we on the second floor of Malcolm X High School in the Bronx, U.S.A. Right over there is my Janitor's closet, just right of the girls' bathroom where the smell of makeup, hair pomade, and gossip fills the air in the morning light. There's Mrs. Kennedy's room—she the principal. For seventeen years, been leading this group of delinquents—Oh I'm sorry, academically and emotionally challenged youth. She got a lot to work with! Seventeen feet below my very own, lay one hundred-thousand-dollar worth of a security system. This include two metal-detecting machines, seven metal-detecting wands, five school guards, and three N.Y.C. police officers. All armed. Guess all we missing is a bomb-sniffing dog. Right over there's Ms. Tam's class, she one of them new teachers. Worked as an associate in the biggest investment firm in New York then coming home from a long dreary day at work, read an ad on the subway—ya'll know the ones that offer you a lifetime of glorious purpose and meaning if you just become a New York City teacher. Uh-huh—the devil's lair on the IRT. I adore Ms. Tam, she kind, docile, but I don't think she know what she got herself into. See, I been working here since 1958 and I done seen some teachers come and go, I said I seen teachers come and go. Ah! One more time for good luck, I seen teachers come and go and I do believe it is one of the hardest jobs in the whole wide world. Shoot, I don't gotta tell you that, y'all look like smart folk! The most underpaid, underappreciated, *underpaid* job in this crazy universe. But for some miracle, every year God creates people that grow up knowing that's what they gonna do for the rest of they life. God, ain't He sometin'! Now, you might say to me, "Jackson Baron Copeford the Third. Boy, what you doin' up dere on dat stage? You ain't no actor." That I know and neither are these kids you about to meet. *(He clears his throat.)* What you about to see is a story about a play within a play within a play. And a teacher (or as she likes to call herself—a teaching artist—just so as people know she do somethin' else on her free time). The kids call her Ms. Sun and in two minutes from now she gonna walk up them stairs towards the janitor's room and stop right at Ms. Tam's class. She gonna be something they done never seen before. Now I know what you're thinking: "Oh, Baron. I know about the public schools. I watch Eyewitness News." What I got to say to that? HUSH! You don't know unless you been in the schools on a day-to-day basis. HUSH! You don't know unless you been a teacher, administrator, student, or custodial staff. HUSH! Cuz you could learn a little sometin'. Here's lesson number one: Taking the 6 train, in eighteen minutes, you can go from Fifty-ninth Street, one of the richest congressional districts in the nation, all the way up to Brook Ave. in the Bronx, where Malcolm X High is, the poorest congressional district in the nation. In only eighteen minutes. HUSH!

SCENE 2

Before class.

Ms. Sun (On the phone in the hallway.): Mr. Pulaski! Hi, it's Nilaja Sun from Bergen Street. 280 Bergen. Apartment four? Hey! Mr. Pulaski, thanks for being so patient, I know how late my rent is . . . By the way, how's your wife Margaret? Cool. And your son Josh? Long Island University. That's serious. Oh he's gonna love it and he'll be close to home. But yes, I apologize for not getting you last month's rent on time, but see the IRS put a levy on my bank account and I just can't retrieve any money from it right now. Well, it should be cleared by Tuesday but the real reason why I called was to say I'm startin' a new teaching program up here in the Bronx and it's a six-week-long workshop and they're paying me exactly what I owe you so . . . what's that? Theater. I'm teaching theater. A play actually. It's called *Our Country's Good* . . . Have you heard of it? Well it's about a group of convicts that put on a play . . . So the kids are actually gonna be doing a play within a play within . . . What's that? Ah, yes, kids today need more discipline and less self-expression. Less "lulalula" and more daily structure like Catholic school during Pope Pious the Twelfth. On the flip side of the matter, having gone to Catholic school for thirteen years, I didn't even know I was black until college. *(She roars her laughter.)* Sir? Sir, are you still there? *(Bell rings.)* I gotta go teach, sir. Are we cool with getting you that money by the twenty-fifth? How about the thirtieth? Thirty-first? I know, don't push it. You rock. Yes, I'm still an actor. No, not in anything right now. But soon. Yes, sir, happy Lent to you too, sir.

SCENE 3

Classroom.

Ms. Tam: Ms. Sun? Come on in. I'm Cindy Tam and I'm so excited to have your program here in our English class. Sorry we weren't able to meet the last four times you set up a planning meeting but so much has been going on in my life. Is it true you've been a teaching artist for seven years? In New York City? Wow. That's amazing. I'm a new teacher. They don't know that. It's a *challenge*. The kids are really *spirited*. Kaswan, where are you going? Well, we're going to be starting in a few minutes and I would strongly suggest you not leave. *(Listens.)* OK, but be back in five minutes, um, Veronica, stop hitting Chris and calling him a motherfucker. I'm sorry, please stop hitting Chris and calling him a motherfucker. Thanks, Veronica. Sorry, like I said, very excited you're here. Where is everyone? The kids usually come in twenty to thirty minutes late because it's so early. I know it's only a forty-one-minute class but I've been installing harsher penalties for anyone who comes in after fifteen. After five? OK, we'll try that. Well, what we *can* do today is start the program in ten minutes and wait for the bulk of them to come in, eat their breakfast, and . . . You wanna start now? But there are only seven kids here. The rest of them will ask what's going on and what am I gonna say to each late student? *(Scared out of her wits.)* OK. Then, we'll start. Now. Class! Please welcome Ms. Sun. She's going to be teaching you a play, and teaching you about acting, and how to act and we're gonna do a play and it's gonna be fun.

Coca: Fun? This is stupid already. I don't wanna act. I wanna do vocabulary.

Jerome: Vocab? Hello, Ms. Sun. Thank you for starting the class on time. Since we usually be the only ones on time.

Brian: Niggah, you ain't never on time.

Jerome: Shut up, bitch motherfucker.

Ms. Tam: Jerome, Brian? What did I tell you about the offensive language?

Jerome: Yo, yo. We know. Pork-fried rice wonton coming up.

Ms. Tam: I heard that, Jerome.

Jerome: Sorry, Ms. Tam.

Brian: (Accent.) Solly, Ms. Tam.

Ms. Tam: Go on, Ms. Sun! *(Beat.)*

Ms. Sun: Ah, well, I'm Ms. Sun and I will be with you all for the next six weeks and by the end of those glorious weeks, you would have read a play, analyzed the play, been cast in it, rehearsed it and lastly performed it. It's gonna be a whirlwind spectacle that I want you to start inviting your parents and friends and loved ones to come see . . . What's that? No, it's not *Raisin in the Sun* . . . No, not *West Side Story*. It's a play called *Our Country's Good*.

Coca: Ew. This is some patrionism?

Ms. Sun: Patriotism? No. It's a play based in Australia in 1788 and it's written by a woman named Timberlake Wertenbaker.

Brian: Yo, Justin Timberlake done wrote himself a play. "Gonna rock yo' body. Today. Dance with me."

Ms. Tam: Brian, focus?

Brian: "People say she a gold digga, but she don't mess with no broke niggas."

Ms. Tam: Brian!!! Put down the Red Bull.

Brian: Beef-fried rice.

Ms. Tam: Brian.

Brian: Vegetable-fried rice.

Jerome: Ay yo! This some white shit. Ain't this illegal to teach this white shit no mo'?

Ms. Sun: Are you done?

Jerome: Huh?

Ms. Sun: Are you done?

Jerome: What?

Ms. Sun: With your spiel? With your little spiel?

Jerome: Yeah.

Ms. Sun: Because I'm trying to tell you what the play is about and I can't when you keep on interrupting.

Jerome: Oh my bad. Damn. She got attitude. I like that.

Shondrika: I don't. What's this play about anyway?

Ms. Sun: Well, what's your name?

Shondrika: Shondrika.

Ms. Sun: Well, Shondrika . . .

Shondrika: Shondrika!

Ms. Sun: Shondrika?

Shondrika: Shondrika!!!

Ms. Sun: Shondrika!!!

Shondrika: Close enough.

Ms. Sun: Ah-hah . . . *Our Country's Good* is about a group of convicts.

Xiomara: What are convicts?

Jerome: Jailbirds, you dumb in a can. Get it? *(Laugh/clap.)* Dominican! Dominican!

Ms. Sun: . . . And they put on a play called *The Recruiting Officer.* You'll be reading . . .

Coca: We gotta read?

Jerome: Aw hell no.

Ms. Tam: Yes, you'll be reading, but you're also gonna be creating a community.

Jerome: Ay yo! Last time I created a community the cops came. *(Latecomers enter.)*

Ms. Tam: Kaswan, Jose, Jennifer, Malika, Talifa, Poughkeepsie, come on in, you're late. What's your excuse this time, Jose?

Jose: Sorry, Miss. But that faggot Mr. Smith was yelling at us to stop running to class. Fucking faggot.

Ms. Sun: ENOUGH!

Jose: Who? Who this?

Ms. Sun: Hi. I'm Ms. Sun. Take your seats *now.* And as of today and for the next six weeks, when I'm in this classroom, you will not be using the word *faggot* or *bitch* or *nigga* or *motherfucker* or *motherfuckerniggabitchfaggot.* Anymore. Dominicans shall not be called and will not call each other dumb in a cans or platanos.

Coca: Ah, y pero quien e heta? Esa prieta?

Ms. Sun: La prieta soy yo, senorita. *(Coca is speechless.)*

Brian: Shwimp fwy why! Shwimp fwy why!

Ms. Sun: We will respect our teacher's ethnicity.

Brian: Shwimp fwy why??? *(No one else laughs.)*

Ms. Sun: Ladies will not call each other heifers or hos.

Shondrika: Shoot! That's what I'm talkin' about.

Ms. Sun: We will start class on time. We will eat our breakfast beforehand. And from now on we are nothing but thespians.

Xiomara: Lesbians? I ain't no Rosie O'Donnell.

Ms. Sun: No, no! Thespian! It means actor, citizen, lover of all things great.

Xiomara: I love that hard cash that bling-bling.

Ms. Sun: Say it with me, class, thespian.

Xiomara: *(Bored.)* Thespian.

Ms. Sun: Thespian!

Jerome: *(Bored.)* Thespian.

Ms. Sun: Thespian!

Coca: Thespian, already, damn!

Ms. Sun: Now, let's get up and form a circle.

Shondrika: Get up? Aw hell no!

Jose: Miss, we not supposed to do exercises this early.

Ms. Tam: Come on guys, stand up. Stand up.

Coca: Miss, this is mad boring.

Ms. Sun: Boredom, my love, usually comes from boring people.

Brian: OOOOOOOOOOOOOH!

Coca: *(Dissed.)* What's that supposed to mean?

Brian: That's O.D., yo! Oh she played you, yo!

Jerome: Ay yo, shut yo trap! Miss, I could be the lovable and charming leading man that gets all the honies' numbers?

Ms. Sun: We'll see.

Jerome: Miss, can I get your number? *(Beat.)* Nah, I'm just playing. Let's do this, yo. Get up. *(They get up.)*

Ms. Sun: OK, thank you . . .

Jerome: Jerome!

Ms. Sun: Jerome. Great circle! Let's take a deep breath in and out. In . . .

Brian: Ohm! Nah! I'm just playing. Keep going. Keep going. Keep going. Keep going.

Ms. Sun: . . . and out . . . In . . .

Coca: I'm hungry. What time it is?

Ms. Sun: . . . and out . . . stretch with me, will you? Now, who here has ever seen a play? *(No one raises their hand . . . but Chris.)* Really? Which show?

Chris: *Star Wars.* It was a live reenactment.

Ms. Sun: Was it in a theater?

Chris: Yeah. We all wore outfits and costumes and acted alongside the movie.

Jerome: Damn, Chris, you like SupaDupaJamaicanNerdNegro.

Chris: And for that, I zap you. *(To Ms. Sun.)* You really gonna make us act onstage?

Ms. Sun: Yup.

Chris: I'm scared.

Ms. Sun: Yeah, well guess what? Before I walked in here, even with all my acting and teaching experience, I was scared and nervous too, but you get over it once you get a feel for the audience and you see all of your parents and your friends and your teachers smiling at you. Did you guys know that public speaking is the number one fear for all humans — even greater than death?

Jerome: What? They ain't never lived in the hood.

Jose: But, Miss, you should be scared of this class, cuz we supposed to be the worst class in the school.

Ms. Tam: It's true. They are.

Ms. Sun: Really, well, in the past thirty-five minutes, I've met some pretty amazing young adults, thinkers, debaters, thespians . . .

Brian: Lesbians.

Ms. Sun: Keep breathing! *(Bell rings.)* Oh no, listen, read scenes one through five for the next time. Thanks guys, you are great.

Ms. Tam: Wow. That was amazing. You're really great with the kids. *(Beat.)* Just to let you know. They're probably not going to read the play and they are probably going to lose the handout and probably start to cut your class and their parents probably won't come to the show. Probably. OK, bye.

Ms. Sun: Bye. *(She watches her leave.)* For all our sake, Ms. Tam, I hope you're probably wrong.

SCENE 4

School hallway.

Mrs. Kennedy: Ms. Sun, hi, Mrs. Kennedy — the principal, so glad to meet you. Sorry about the attendance, Ms. Tam is a new teacher and we need all these kids to pass five Regents exams in the next two months. The pressure's on. Let me know when you'll be needing the auditorium. There are four schools in this building and it's like fighting diseased lions to book a night in it. But, you're priority. We've given you one of the most challenging classes. But I believe in them. I believe in you. Tyesha, can I have a word? *(She walks off. Security guard stops Sun.)*

Security Guard: Y'ave pass ta leave. I said do you have a pass to leave? Oh, you a teaching artist? Oh. Cuz you look like one a them. Well, excuse me for livin'! *(To other guards.)* Just trying to do mi job. I don't know the difference 'tween the teachers, teaching artists, parents, Board of Ed people, and these animals comin' in here. I don' know da difference. Just tryin' to do mi job. *(To student.)* Girl, girl! Whatcha t'ink dis is? You can't go in wifoot goin' tru da detector. I don care if you just walked out and now you come back in. Rules are rules. Put ya bag in and yo wallet and your selfish phone. *(Beep.)* Go back. Ya belt.
(Beep.) Go back. Ya earrings.
(Beep.) Go back. Ya shoes. Don't sass me!
(Beep.) Go back. Ya hair . . . t'ings.
(Beep.) Go back. Ya jewelry. Oh, oh I don' have time for your attitude. Open your arms, spread your legs. Oh, oh I don' care about your science class. Should know betta' than to just waltz in 'ere ten minutes 'fore class. Got ta give it one whole hour. Lemme see yo I.D. Don' have? Can't come in. Excuse?!!! What ya name is? Shondrika Jones! I don' care about ya Regents. Go, Go, Go back home. Next time don' bring all dat bling and don' bring all dat belt and don' bring all dat sass. Who ya t'ink ya is? The mayor of New York City? Slut! *(To another student.)* Boy, boy, don't you pass me! *(Light shift.)*

Janitor: *(To audience.)* Your tax dollars at work! As Ms. Sun makes her way back home on the train, she thinks to herself.

Scene 5

Subway car.

Ms. Sun: What will these six weeks bring? How will I persuade them to act onstage? *(Beat.)* Why did I choose a play about convicts? These kids aren't convicts. The kids in Rikers are convicts. These kids are just in tenth grade. They've got the world telling them they are going to end up in jail. Why would I choose a play about convicts? Why couldn't I choose a play about kings and queens in Africa or the triumphs of the Taino Indian? This totally wouldn't jive if I were white and trying to do this. How dare I! Why would I choose to do a play about convicts?

Scene 6

Classroom.

Jerome: Because we treated like convicts every day.
Ms. Tam: Jerome, raise your hand.
Jerome: *(Raises hand.)* We treated like convicts every day.

Ms. Sun: How do you mean?

Shondrika: First, we wake up to bars on our windows.

Coca: Then, our moms and dads.

Shondrika: You got a dad?

Coca: Yeah . . . so? Then our mom tells us where to go, what to do, and blah, blah, blah.

Jerome: Then, we walk in a uniformed line towards the subways, cramming into a ten-by-forty-foot cell *(Laughs.)* checking out the fly honies.

Brian: But there ain't no honies in jail, know what I'm saying?

Jerome: Unless, you there long enough, what, what!

Ms. Sun: Then, class, you'll walk into another line at the bodega at the corner store, to get what?

Xiomara: Breakfast.

Ms. Sun: And what's for breakfast?

Xiomara: Welch's Orange and a Debbie snack cake.

Ms. Sun: Exactly, then what?

Shondrika: Then, we go to school.

Chris: . . . Where a cool electronic object points out our every metal flaw.

Jerome: Damn, Chris, you read way too much sci-fi!

Shondrika: Then we go to a class they tell us we gotta go to, with a teacher we gotta learn from and a play we gotta do.

Ms. Sun: And now that you feel like prisoners . . . open to page twenty-seven. Phillip says, "Watkin: Man is born free, and everywhere he is in chains." What *don't* people expect from prisoners?

Jose: For them to succeed in life . . .

Ms. Sun: But, in the play . . .

Coca: They succeed by doing the exact opposite of what people expect.

Ms. Sun: And so . . . how does that relate to your lives?

Shondrika: Shoot, don't nobody expect us to do nothing but drop out, get pregnant, go to jail . . .

Brian: . . . or work for the MTA.

Xiomara: My mom works for the MTA, nigga. Sorry, Miss . . . NEGRO.

Shondrika: So, dese characters is kinda going through what we kinda going through right now.

Ms. Sun: Kinda, yeah. And so . . . Brian . . .

Brian: By us doing the show, see what I'm saying, we could prove something to ourselves and our moms and her dad and Mrs. Kennedy and Ms. Tam that we is the shi . . . shining stars of the school, see what I'm saying?

Ms. Sun: Great, turn to Act One, Scene Six. Can I have a volunteer to read? *(Sun looks around.)*

Shondrika: Shoot, I'll read, give me this: "We are talking about criminals, often hardened criminals. They have a habit of vice and crime. Habits . . ."

Jose: Damn, Ma, put some feeling into that!

Shondrika: I don't see you up here reading, Jose.

Jose: Cuz you the actress of the class.

Shondrika: (Realizing she is the "actress" of the class.) "Habits are difficult to BREAK! And it can be more than habit, an I-nate —"

Ms. Tam: (Correcting.) Innate . . .

Shondrika: See, Ms. Tam why you had to mess up my flow? Now I gotta start from the beginning since you done messed up my flow. *(Class sighs.)*

Brian: Aw. Come on!!!

Ms. Tam: Sorry, Shondrika.

Shondrika: Right. "Habits are difficult to break. And it can be more than habit, an innate tendency. Many criminals seem to have been born that way. It is in their nature." Thank you. *(Applause.)*

Ms. Sun: Beautiful, Shondrika. And is it in your nature to live like you're a convict?

Shondrika: No!

Ms. Sun: Well, what is in your nature? Coca?

Coca: Love.

Ms. Sun: What else? Chris?

Chris: Success. And real estate.

Ms. Sun: Jose, how about you?

Jose: Family. Yo. My brother and my *buela*.°

Ms. Sun: Brian?

Brian: And above all, money, see what I'm sayin', know what I mean, see what I'm saying?

Ms. Sun: Yes, Brian, we see what you're saying . . . and now that you know that you actually *can* succeed, let's get up and stretch!

Coca: Get up? Aw — hell no!

Jose: This is mad boring.

Xiomara: I just ate. I hate this part.

Jerome: Can I go to the bathroom? *(Bell rings. Lights shift.)*

Janitor: Not so bad for a second class. Although, due to discipline issues, attention problems, lateness and resistance to the project on the whole, Ms. Sun is already behind in her teaching lesson. And, the show is only four weeks away. Let's watch as Ms. Sun enters her third week of classes. The show must go on! (I'm good at this. I am!)

Scene 7

Classroom.

Coca: Miss. Did you hear? Most of our class is gone for the day . . . They went on an important school trip. To the UniverSoul Circus. There's only five of us here.

Ms. Sun: That's OK, Coca. We'll make due with the five of us, including Ms. Tam.

Ms. Tam: *(Tired.)* Ewww . . .

Ms. Sun: So, we will start the rehearsal section for *Our Country's Good.* We have the lovely Xiomara as Mary Brenham.

Xiomara: *(Deep voice.)* I don't want to be Mary Brenham, I want to be Liz . . . the pretty one.

Ms. Sun: I think I can make that happen. Chris as the Aborigine.

Chris: It's good.

Ms. Sun: And Phillip as . . . Phillip as . . . Ralph! Phillip, do me a favor, go to page thirty-one and read your big monologue about the presence of women on the stage.

---

buela: Short for the Spanish word *abuela* (grandmother).

Phillip: *(Inaudibly.)* "In my own small way in just a few hours I have seen something change. I asked some of the convict women to read me some lines, these women who behave often no better than animals." *(Pause.)*

Ms. Sun: Good, Phillip, good. Do me a favor and read the first line again but pretend that you are speaking to a group of a hundred people.

Phillip: *(Inaudibly.)* "In my own small way in just a few hours I have seen something change."

Ms. Sun: Thank you, Phillip. You can sit down now. *(She goes to work on another student.)* No, Phillip, get back up. Someone is stealing your brand new . . . what kind of car do you like, Phillip?

Phillip: *(Inaudibly.)* Mercedes LX 100, Limited edition.

Ms. Sun: That! And, you have to, with that line there, stop him from taking your prized possession. Read it again.

Phillip: *(Inaudibly.)* "In my own small way I have seen something change."

Ms. Sun: Now open your mouth . . .

Phillip: *(Inaudibly but with mouth wide.)* "In my own small way . . ."

Ms. Sun: Your tongue, your tongue is a living breathing animal thrashing about in your mouth—it's not just lying there on the bottom near your jaw—it's got a life of its own, man. Give it life.

Phillip: *(Full on.)* "In my own small way I have seen something change!" *(The bell rings.)*

Ms. Sun: That's it. That's it. Right there . . . *(She is alone now.)* God, I need a Vicodin.

Scene 8

School. Night.

Janitor: It may not look it, but this school has gone through many transformations. When I first arrived at its pristine steps, I marveled at the architecture . . . like a castle. Believe it or not, there were nothin' but Italian kids here and it was called Robert Moses High back then. Humph! See, I was the first Negro janitor here and ooh that made them other custodians upset. But I did my job, kept my courtesies intact. Them janitors all gone now . . . and I'm still here. Then came the 60s, civil rights, the assassination of President Kennedy right there on the TV, Vietnam. Those were some hot times. Italians started moving out and Blacks and Puerto Ricans moved right on in. Back then, landlords was burning up they own buildings just so as to collect they insurance. And, the Black Panthers had a breakfast program—would say "Brotha Baron! How you gonna fight the MAN today?" I say "With my broom and my grade D ammonia, ya dig?" They'd laugh. They all gone, I'm still here. Then came the 70s when they renamed the school Malcolm X after our great revolutionary. I say, "Alright, here we go. True change has got to begin now." Lesson number two: Revolution has its upside and its downside. Try not to stick around for the downside. Eighties brought Reagan, that goddamn crack ('scuse my cussin') and hip-hop. Ain't nothing like my Joe King Oliver's Creole Jazz Band but what you gonna do. And here we come to today. Building fallin' apart, paint chipping, water damage, kids running around here talking loud like crazy folk, half of them is raising themselves. Let me tell ya, I don't know nothing about no No Child, Yes Child, Who Child What

Child. I do know there's a hole in the fourth-floor ceiling ain't been fixed since '87, all the bathrooms on the third floor, they all broke. Now, who's accountable for dat? Heck, they even asked me to give up my closet, make it into some science lab class cuz ain't got no room. I say, "This my sanctuary. You can't take away my zen. Shoot, I read *O* magazine." They complied for now. Phew! Everything's falling apart . . . But these floors, these windows, these chalkboards — they clean . . . why? Cuz I'm still here!

SCENE 9

Classroom.

Coca: Miss, did you hear? Someone stole Ms. Tam's bag and she quit for good. We got some Russian teacher now.

Mrs. Projensky: Quiet Quiet Quiet Quiet Quiet Quiet Quiet. Quiet!

Ms. Sun: Miss, Miss, Miss. I'm the teaching artist for . . .

Mrs. Projensky: Sit down, you.

Shondrika: Aw, snap, she told her.

Mrs. Projensky: Sit down, quiet. Quiet, sit down.

Ms. Sun: No, I'm the teaching artist for this period. Maybe Miss Tam or Mrs. Kennedy told you something about me?

Jerome: (Shadowboxes.) Ah, hah, you being replaced, Russian lady.

Ms. Sun: Jerome, you're not helping right now.

Jerome: What?! You don't gotta tell me jack. We ain't got a teacher no more or haven't you heard? *(He flings a chair.)* We are the worst class in school.

Mrs. Projensky: Sit down! Sit down!

Ms. Sun: Guys, quiet down and focus. We have a show to do in a few weeks.

Coca: Ooee, I don't wanna do this no more. It's stupid.

Chris: I still want to do it.

Jerome: Shut the fuck up, Chris.

Jose: Yo man, she's right. This shit is mad fucking boring yo.

Coca: Yeah!

Xiomara: Yeah!

Brian: Yeah!

Shondrika: Yeah!

Coca: Mad boring.

Jerome: Fuckin' stupid.

Mrs. Projensky: Quiet! Quiet! Quiet!

Ms. Sun: What has gotten into all you? The first two classes were amazing, you guys were analyzing the play, making parallels to your lives. So, we missed a week when you went to go see, uh . . .

Shondrika: UniverSoul Circus.

Ms. Sun: Right! But, just because we missed a week doesn't mean we have to start from square one. Does it? Jerome, Jerome! where are you going?

Mrs. Projensky: Sit down, sit down, you! Sit down!

Jerome: I don't gotta listen to none of y'all. *(He flings another chair.)* I'm eighteen years old.

Brian: Yeah, and still in the tenth grade, nigga. *(Brian flings a chair.)*

Ms. Sun: Brian!

Jerome: I most definitely ain't gonna do no stupid-ass motha fuckin' Australian play from the goddamn seventeen-hundreds!

Ms. Sun: Fine, Jerome. You don't wanna be a part of something really special? There are others here who do.

Jerome: Who? Who in here want to do this show, memorize your lines, look like stupid fucking dicks on the stage for the whole school to laugh at us like they always do anyhow when can't none of us speak no goddamn English.

Ms. Sun: Jerome, that's not fair, no one is saying you don't speak English. You all invited your parents . . .

Coca: Ooee, my moms can't come to this. She gotta work. Plus the Metrocard ends at seven.

Xiomara: My mom ain't never even been to this school.

Jerome: That's what I'm sayin'! Who the fuck wanna do this? Who the fuck wanna do this?

Ms. Sun: I'll take the vote, Jerome, if you sit down. Everyone sit down.

Mrs. Projensky: Sit down!

Ms. Sun: Thank you, ma'am. OK, so, who, after all the hard work we've done so far building a team, analyzing the play in your own words (that is not easy, I know), developing self-esteem *y coraje* as great thespians . . .

Brian: Lesbians.

Ms. Sun: Who wants to quit . . . after all this? *(She looks around as they all raise their hands . . . except for Chris.)* I see.

Chris: Miss. No. I still wanna do the show.

Jerome: That's cuz you gay, Chris. Yo, I'm out! One. Niggas. *(Pause. Ms. Sun is hurt.)*

Ms. Sun: OK . . . Well . . . Ms.?

Mrs. Projensky: Projensky.

Ms. Sun: Ms. Projensky.

Mrs. Projensky: Projensky!

Ms. Sun: Projensky.

Mrs. Projensky: Projensky!!!

Ms. Sun: Projensky!!!

Mrs. Projensky: Is close.

Ms. Sun: Do they have any sample Regents to take?

Mrs. Projensky: Yes, they do.

Ms. Sun: Great. I'll alert Mrs. Kennedy of your vote.

Phillip: *(Audibly.)* Ms. Sun?

Ms. Sun: Yes, Phillip, what is it?

Phillip: Can I still do the show? *(Beat.)*

SCENE 10

Principal's office.

Mrs. Kennedy: So they voted you out? Well, Malcolm X Vocational High School did not get an eight-thousand-dollar grant from the Department of Education of the City of New York for these students to choose democracy now. They will do the show. Because I will tell them so tomorrow. If they do not do the show, each student in 10F will be suspended and *not* be able to join their friends in their beloved Great Adventures trip in May. The horror. Look, I understand that they consider themselves the worst class in school. News flash—They're not even close. I know that they've had five different teachers in the course of seven months. I also can wrap my brain around the fact that seventy-nine percent of those kids in there have been physically, emotionally, and sexually abused in their tender little sixteen-year-old lives. But that does not give them the right to disrespect someone who is stretching them to give them something beautiful. Something challenging. Something Jay-Z and P Diddly only *wish* they could offer them. Now, I will call all their parents this weekend and notify them of their intolerable behavior as well as invite them to *Our Country's Good.* Done. See you next Wednesday, Ms. Sun?

Ms. Sun: Yes, yes. Thanks! Yes! . . . Uh, no, Mrs. Kennedy. You won't be seeing me next Wednesday. I quit. I came to teaching to touch lives and educate and be this enchanting artist in the classroom and I have done nothing but lose ten pounds in a month and develop a disgusting smoking habit. Those kids in there? They need something much greater than anything I can give them—*they need a miracle* . . . and they need a miracle like every day. Sometimes, I dream of going to Connecticut and teaching the rich white kids there. All I'd have to battle against is soccer moms, bulimia, and everyone asking me how I wash my hair. But, I chose to teach in my city, this city that raised me . . . and I'm tired, and I'm not even considered a "real" teacher. I don't know how I would survive as a real teacher. But they do . . . on what, God knows. And, the worst thing, the worst thing is that all those kids in there are *me.* Brown skin, brown eyes, stuck. I can't even help my own people. Really revolutionary, huh?

   It seems to me that this whole school system, not just here but the whole system is falling apart from under us and then there are these testing and accountability laws that have nothing to do with any real solutions and if we expect to stay some sort of grand nation for the next fifty years, we got another thing coming. *Because we're not teaching these kids how to be leaders.* We're getting them ready for jail! Take off your belt, take off your shoes, go back, go back, go back. We're totally abandoning these kids and we have been for thirty years and then we get annoyed when they're running around in the subway calling themselves bitches and niggas, we get annoyed when their math scores don't pair up to a five-year-old's in China, we get annoyed when they don't graduate in time. It's because we've abandoned them. And, I'm no different, I'm abandoning them too. *(Beat.)* I just need a break to be an actor, get health insurance, go on auditions, pay the fucking IRS. Sorry. Look, I'm sorry about the big grant from the Department of Ed. but perhaps we could make it up somehow next year. I can't continue this program any longer, even if it is for our country's good. Bye! *(Light shift.)*

Janitor: (Sings.)
   I'm gonna lay. Lay my head
   On some lonesome railroad line.
   Let that 2:19 train—

SCENE 11

Outside of school.

Ms. Sun: (Sings.)
   Ease my troubled mind—
Jerome: Ms. Sun?

Ms. Sun: Hi. Jerome.

Jerome: You singing? *(Beat.)* We were talking about you in the cafeteria. Had a power lunch. *(He laughs.)* Most of us were being assholes . . . sorry . . . bad thespians when we did that to you.

Ms. Sun: You were the leader, do you know that, Jerome? Do you know that we teachers, we have feelings. And we try our best not to break in front of you all?

Jerome: Yeah, I know, my mom tells me that all the time.

Ms. Sun: Listen to her, sweetheart, she's right. *(Beat.)* Look, the show is off. I'll be here next year, and we'll start again on another more tangible play, maybe even *Raisin in the Sun.* Now, if you'll excuse me, I have an audition to prepare for. *(She turns to leave.)*

Jerome: Ms. Sun, "The theater is an expression of civilization . . ."

Ms. Sun: What?

Jerome: I said, "The theater is an expression of civilization. We belong to a great country which has spawned great playwrights: Shakespeare, Marlowe, Jonson, and even in our own time, Sheridan. The convicts will be speaking a refined, literate language and expressing sentiments of a delicacy they are not used to. It will remind them that there is more to life than crime, punishment. And we, this colony of a few hundred, will be watching this together. For a few hours we will no longer be despised prisoners and hated gaolers. We will laugh, we may be moved. We may even think a little. Can you suggest something else that would provide such an evening, Watkin?" *(Beat.)* Thank you.

Ms. Sun: Jerome, I didn't know . . .

Jerome: . . . that I had the part of Second Lieutenant Ralph Clark memorized. I do my thang. Guess I won't be doing it this year though. Shoot, every teacher we have runs away. *(Beat.)*

Ms. Sun: Listen, Jerome, you tell all your cafeteria buddies in there, OK, to have all their lines memorized from Acts One and Two and be completely focused when I walk into that room next week—that means no talking, no hidden conversations and blurting out random nonsense, no gum, and for crying out loud, no one should be drinking Red Bull.

Jerome: Aight. So you back?

Ms. Sun: . . . Yeah, and I'm bad. *(She does some Michael Jackson moves.)*

Jerome: Miss, you really do need an acting job soon. *(Light shift.)*

Janitor: Things are looking up for our little teaching artist. She got a new lease on life. Got on a payment plan with the IRS. Stopped smoking, ate a good breakfast, even took the early train to school this mornin'.

SCENE 12

Classroom.

Coca: Miss, did you hear? We got a new teacher permanently. He's kinda . . . good!

Mr. Johnson: What do we say when Ms. Sun walks in?

Shondrika: Good morning, Ms. Sun.

Mr. Johnson: Hat off, Jerome.

Jerome: Damn, he got attitude! *(Beat.)* I like that!

Ms. Sun: Wow, wow. You guys are lookin' really, really good.

Mr. Johnson: Alright, let's get in the formation that we created. First, the tableau.

Ms. Sun: (Intimate.) Tableau, you got them to do a tableau.

Mr. Johnson: (Intimate.) I figured you'd want to see them in a frozen non-speaking state for a while. Oh, Kaswan, Xiomara, and Brian are in the auditorium building the set.

Ms. Sun: (Intimate.) Wow. This is amazing. Thank you.

Mr. Johnson: Don't thank me. Thank Mrs. Kennedy, thank yourself, thank these kids. *(To class.)* And we're starting from the top, top, top. Only one more week left. Shondrika, let's see those fliers you're working on.

Shondrika: I been done. "Come see *Our Country's Good* cuz it's for your *own* good."

Ms. Sun: Beautiful, Shondrika. Let's start from the top. *(Sound of noise.)* What's all that noise out in the hallway?

Brian: Ay, yo. Janitor Baron had a heart attack in his closet last night. He died there.

Coca: What? He was our favorite . . .

Jerome: How old was he, like a hundred or something?

Shondrika: I just saw him yesterday. He told me he would come to the show. He died all alone, ya'll. *(Long pause.)*

Ms. Sun: Thespians, I can give you some time . . .

Jerome: Nah, nah we done wasted enough time. Let's rehearse. Do the show. Dedicate it to Janitor Baron, our pops, may you rest in peace.

Ms. Sun: Alright, then, we're taking it from the top. Chris, that's you, sweetheart.

Chris: "A giant canoe drifts onto the sea, clouds billowing from upright oars. This is a dream that has lost its way. Best to leave it alone." *(Light shift.)*

Janitor: My, My, My . . . them kids banded together over me. Memorized, rehearsed, added costumes, a small set, even added a rap or two at the end — don't tell the playwright! And, I didn't even think they knew my name. Ain't that something? I think I know what you saying to yourselves: I see dead people. Shoot, this is a good story, I wanna finish telling it! Plus, my new friend up here, Arthur Miller, tells me ain't no rules say a dead man can't make a fine narrator. Say he wish he thought of it himself. Meanwhile, like most teachers, even after-hours, Ms. Sun's life just ain't her own.

Scene 13

Sun's apartment. Night.

Ms. Sun: (On phone.) Hi. This is Ms. Sun from Malcolm X High. I'm looking for Jose Guzman. He's a lead actor in *Our Country's Good* but I haven't seen him in class or after-school rehearsals since last week. My number is . . . *(Light shift. On phone:)* Hi. This is Ms. Sun again from Malcolm X High. I know it's probably dinner time but I'm still trying to reach Jose or his grandmother, Doña Guzman . . . *(Light shift. On phone:)* Hi. Ms. Sun here. Sorry, I know it's early and Mrs. Kennedy called last night, but the show is in less than two days . . . *(Light shift. On phone:)* Hi. It's midnight. You can probably imagine who this is. Does anyone answer this phone? Why have a machine, I mean really . . . Hello, hello, yes. This is Ms. Sun from Malcolm X High, oh . . . Puedo hablar con Doña Guzman. Ah Hah! Finally. Doña Guzman, ah ha, bueno, Ingles, OK. I've been working with your grandson now for six weeks on a play that you might have heard of. *(Beat.)* Un espectaculo . . . ah ha, pero Ingles, OK. I haven't seen him in a week and the show is in twenty-four hours Mañana actually . . . Como? His brother was killed. Ave Maria, Lo siento, señora . . . How? Gangs . . . no, no, olvidate, forget about it. I'll send out prayers to you y tu familia. Buenas. *(She hangs up. Light shift.)*

Janitor: Chin up now!

SCENE 14

School auditorium.

Janitor: Cuz, it's opening night in the auditorium . . . I'm not even gonna talk about the logistics behind booking a high school auditorium for a night. Poor Mrs. Kennedy became a dictator.

Mrs. Kennedy: I booked this auditorium for the night and no one shall take it from me!!!

Janitor: The stage is ablaze with fear, apprehension, doubt, nervousness, and, well, drama.

Mr. Johnson: Anyone seen Jerome?

Ms. Sun: Anyone seen Jerome?

Coca: His mom called him at four. Told him he had to babysit for the night.

Ms. Sun: But, he's got a show tonight. Couldn't they find someone else? Couldn't he just bring the brats? Sorry.

Mr. Johnson: What are we going to do now? His part is enormous.

Phillip: Ms. Sun?

Ms. Sun: What, Phillip?

Phillip: . . . I could do his part.

Ms. Sun: *(With apprehension.)* OK, Phillip. You're on. Just remember . . .

Phillip: I know . . . someone is stealing my Mercedes LX one hundred Limited Edition.

Ms. Sun: And . . . ?

Phillip: . . . Let my tongue be alive!

Doña Guzman: Doña Guzman, buenas. Buenas. Doña Guzman. The abuela de Jose.

Ms. Sun: Jose, you made it. I'm so sorry about your brother.

Jose: Yeah, I know. Where's my costume at? Buela, no ta allí.

Doña Guzman: Mira pa ya, muchacho. We had very long week pero he love this class. He beg me "mami, mami, mami, Our Country Goo, Our Country Goo, Our Country Goo." What can I do? I say yes. What I can do, you know.

Ms. Sun: Oh señora. It's parents like you . . . thank you. Muchissima gracias por todo. Sit, sit in the audience por favor.

Mrs. Kennedy: Ms. Sun, everyone is in place, there are about seventy-five people in that audience, including some parents I desperately need to speak to. We're glad you're back. Good luck!

Shondrika: Miss, you want me to get the kids together before we start?

Ms. Sun: Yeah, Shondrika, would you?

Shondrika: Uh huh.

Janitor: Now, here's a teacher's moment of truth. The last speech before the kids go on!

Ms. Sun: Alright. This is it. We're here. We have done the work. We have lived this play inside and out. I officially have a hernia.

Coca: (Laughing.) She so stupid. I like her.

Ms. Sun: We are a success . . . no matter what happens on this stage tonight. No matter which actors are missing or if your parents couldn't make it. I see before me twenty-seven amazingly talented young men and women. And I never thought I'd say this but I'm gonna miss you all.

Shondrika: Ooh, she gonna make me cry!

Ms. Sun: Tonight is your night.

Coca: Ooee, I'm nervous.

Phillip: Me too.

Ms. Sun: I am too. That just means you care. Now let's take a deep breath in and out. In . . .

Brian: OHM! Nah, I'm just kiddin'. Keep going. Focus Focus.

Ms. Sun: . . . and out. In and out.

Shondrika: Miss, let's do this for Jose's brother and Janitor Baron.

Ms. Sun: Oh, Shondrika, that's beautiful. OK, gentlemen, be with us tonight! PLACES. *(Light shift.)*

Chris: A giant canoe drifts out onto the sea, best to leave it alone.

Coca: This hateful hary-scary, topsy-turvy outpost. This is not a civilization.

Xiomara: It's two hours, possibly of amusement, possibly of boredom. It's a waste, an unnecessary waste.

Phillip: The convicts will feel nothing has changed and will go back to their old ways.

Jose: You have to be careful OH DAMN. *(Nervously, he regains his thought.)* You have to be careful with words that begin with IN. It can turn everything upside down. INjustice, most of that word is taken up with justice, but the IN turns it inside out making it the ugliest word in the English language.

Shondrika: Citizens must be taught to obey the law of their own will. I want to rule over responsible human beings.

Phillip: Unexpected situations are often matched by unexpected virtues in people. Are they not?

Brian: A play should make you understand something new.

Shondrika: Human beings —

Xiomara: — have an intelligence —

Brian: — that has nothing to do —

Jose: — with the circumstances —

Coca: — into which they were born.

Chris: THE END. *(Raucous applause. Light shift.)*

Janitor: And the show did go on. A show that sparked a mini-revolution in the hearts of everyone in that auditorium. Sure, some crucial lines were fumbled, and some entrances missed and three cell phones went off in the audience. But, my God, if those kids weren't a success.

Scene 15

Backstage.

Coca: Miss, I did good, right? I did good? I did good. I did my lines right. I did my motivations right. I did good, right. I did good? I did good? I did good? *(Assured.)* I did good. I did good. I did good. Oh, Miss. I been wantin' to tell you. You know I'm pregnant right? . . . Oh don't cry . . . Damn. Why do everyone cry when I say that? No, I wanted to tell you because my baby will not live like a prisoner, like a convict. I mean we still gotta put the baby-proof bars on the windows but that's state law. But that's it. We gonna travel, explore, see somethin' new for a change. I mean I love the Bronx but there's more to life right? You taught me that. "Man is born free" right . . . I mean, even though it's gonna be a girl. *(Beat.)* I know we was mad hard so thank you.

Jose: Ms.? I don't know but, that class was still mad boring to me.

Phillip: *(Audibly.)* Ms. Sun?! I wanna be an actor now!

Security Guard: O, O! We gotta clear out the auditorium. You can't be lolly-gagging in here. Clear it out. Clear it out. Clear it out! By the way, I never done seen dem kids shine like they did tonight. They did good. You did good. Now, you got ta clear it out!

Ms. Sun: *(To herself.)* Jerome . . . Jerome. *(Beat.)* "And we, this colony of a few hundred, will be watching this together, and we will no longer be despised prisoners and hated gaolers. We will laugh, we may be moved. We may . . ."

Jerome: *(Gasping.)* ". . . even think a little!"

Ms. Sun: Jerome? What are you doing here?

Jerome: *(Panting.)* Mom came home early. Told me to run over here fast as I could . . . *(He realizes.)* I missed it. I missed it all. And I worked *hard* to learn my lines.

Ms. Sun: Yes, you did Jerome. You worked very hard. *(Long beat.)*

Jerome: You gonna be teaching here again next year?

Ms. Sun: That's the plan. But, only tenth-graders again. Sorry.

Jerome: Oh no worries. I'm definitely gonna get left back for you. Psyche . . . Lemme go shout out to all them other thespians. You gonna be around?

Ms. Sun: No, actually I have a commercial shoot early tomorrow morning.

Jerome: Really, for what?

Ms. Sun: *(Slurring.)* It's nothing . . .

Jerome: Aw, come on you could tell me.

Ms. Sun: Really, it's nothing.

Jerome: Lemme know. Lemme know. Come on lemme know.

Ms. Sun: It's for Red Bull, damn it. Red Bull.

Jerome: Aight! Ms. Sun's finally getting paid. *(Light shift.)*

SCENE 16

Janitor: And on to our third and final lesson of the evening: Something inter-esting happens when you die. You still care about the ones you left behind and wanna see how life ended up for them. Ms. Tam went back to the firm and wound up investing 2.3 million dollars towards arts in education with a strong emphasis on cultural diversity. Phillip proudly works as a conduc-tor for the MTA. Shondrika Jones graduated *summa cum laude* from Har-vard University and became the first black woman mayor of New York City. Alright now. Jose Guzman lost his life a week after the show when he decided to take vengeance on the Blood that killed his brother. Jerome. I might be omnipresent but I sure as heck ain't omniscient. Some of the brightest just slip through the cracks sometime. Do me a favor—you ever see him around town, tell him we thinkin' about him. And Ms. Sun. Well,

she went on to win an NAACP Award, a Hispanic Heritage Award, a Tony Award, and an Academy Award. She was also in charge of restructuring of the nation's No Child Left Behind law *and* lives happily with her husband, Denzel Washington. His first wife never had a chance, poor thang. She still comes back every year to teach at Malcolm X High; oh, oh, oh, recently renamed Saint Tupac Shakur Preparatory. Times—they are a-changin'! *(He grabs his broom and sings. Lights shift as he walks toward a bright light offstage.)*
Trouble in mind
It's true
I had almost lost my way
(Offstage light brightens as if the heavens await. He knows to walk "into" it.)
But, the sun's gonna shine
In my back door someday
That's alright, Lord. That's alright!

End of play

CONNECTIONS TO OTHER SELECTIONS

1. Discuss the purpose of the play within the play in *No Child* ... and in Shakespeare's *Hamlet* (p. 1585). Why do you think this device has been a favorite strategy of playwrights over the years?

2. Comment on the effects of having characters address the audience directly in *No Child* ... and in Christopher Durang's *Wanda's Visit* (p. 1785). Does this add to or diminish your enjoyment of the play? Explain why or why not.

Fences

August Wilson, who, as a young poet, "wanted to be Dylan Thomas," went on to become a major force in the American theater. Between the 1980s and 2005, Wilson wrote a sequence of ten plays that chronicled the black experience in the United States in each decade of the twentieth century. *Ma Rainey's Black Bottom,* the first of these to be completed, premiered at the Yale Repertory Theatre in 1984, went to Broadway shortly thereafter, and eventually won the New York Drama Critics' Circle Award. Other plays in the sequence include *Joe Turner's Come and Gone* (1986), *The Piano Lesson* (1987), *Two Trains Running* (1989), and Wilson's last play, *Radio Golf* (2005).

© Joan Marcus.

Born in Pittsburgh, Pennsylvania, Wilson grew up in the Hill, a black neighborhood to which his mother had come from North Carolina. His white father never lived with the family. Wilson quit school at sixteen and worked in a variety of menial jobs, meanwhile submitting poetry to a number of local publications. He didn't begin to find his writing voice, however, until he moved to Minneapolis–St. Paul, where he founded the Black Horizons Theatre Company in 1968 and later started the Playwrights Center. He supported himself during part of this time by writing skits for the Science Museum of Minnesota.

Fences offers a complex look at the internal and external pressures on a black tenement family living in Pittsburgh during the 1950s.

AUGUST WILSON (1945–2005)

Fences   1985

CHARACTERS

Troy Maxson
Jim Bono, Troy's friend
Rose, Troy's wife
Lyons, Troy's oldest son by previous marriage
Gabriel, Troy's brother
Cory, Troy and Rose's son
Raynell, Troy's daughter

SETTING: The setting is the yard which fronts the only entrance to the Maxson household, an ancient two-story brick house set back off a small alley in a big-city neighborhood. The entrance to the house is gained by two or three steps leading to a wooden porch badly in need of paint.

A relatively recent addition to the house and running its full width, the porch lacks congruence. It is a sturdy porch with a flat roof. One or two chairs of dubious value sit at one end where the kitchen window opens onto the porch. An old-fashioned icebox stands silent guard at the opposite end.

The yard is a small dirt yard, partially fenced, except for the last scene, with a wooden sawhorse, a pile of lumber, and other fence-building equipment set off to the side. Opposite is a tree from which hangs a ball made of rags. A baseball bat leans against the tree. Two oil drums serve as garbage receptacles and sit near the house at right to complete the setting.

THE PLAY: Near the turn of the century, the destitute of Europe sprang on the city with tenacious claws and an honest and solid dream. The city devoured them. They swelled its belly until it burst into a thousand furnaces and sewing machines, a thousand butcher shops and bakers' ovens, a thousand churches and hospitals and funeral parlors and money-lenders. The city grew. It nourished itself and offered each man a partnership limited only by his talent, his guile, and his willingness and capacity for hard work. For the immigrants of Europe, a dream dared and won true.

The descendants of African slaves were offered no such welcome or participation. They came from places called the Carolinas and the Virginias, Georgia,

Alabama, Mississippi, and Tennessee. They came strong, eager, searching. The city rejected them and they fled and settled along the riverbanks and under bridges in shallow, ramshackle houses made of sticks and tarpaper. They collected rags and wood. They sold the use of their muscles and their bodies. They cleaned houses and washed clothes, they shined shoes, and in quiet desperation and vengeful pride, they stole, and lived in pursuit of their own dream. That they could breathe free, finally, and stand to meet life with the force of dignity and whatever eloquence the heart could call upon.

By 1957, the hard-won victories of the European immigrants had solidified the industrial might of America. War had been confronted and won with new energies that used loyalty and patriotism as its fuel. Life was rich, full, and flourishing. The Milwaukee Braves won the World Series, and the hot winds of change that would make the sixties a turbulent, racing, dangerous, and provocative decade had not yet begun to blow full.

ACT I

SCENE I

> *It is 1957. Troy and Bono enter the yard, engaged in conversation. Troy is fifty-three years old, a large man with thick, heavy hands; it is this largeness that he strives to fill out and make an accommodation with. Together with his blackness, his largeness informs his sensibilities and the choices he has made in his life.*
>
> *Of the two men, Bono is obviously the follower. His commitment to their friendship of thirty-odd years is rooted in his admiration of Troy's honesty, capacity for hard work, and his strength, which Bono seeks to emulate.*
>
> *It is Friday night, payday, and the one night of the week the two men engage in a ritual of talk and drink. Troy is usually the most talkative and at times he can be crude and almost vulgar, though he is capable of rising to profound heights of expression. The men carry lunch buckets and wear or carry burlap aprons and are dressed in clothes suitable to their jobs as garbage collectors.*

Bono: Troy, you ought to stop that lying!

Troy: I ain't lying! The nigger had a watermelon this big. *(He indicates with his hands.)* Talking about . . . "What watermelon, Mr. Rand?" I liked to fell out! "What watermelon, Mr. Rand?" . . . And it sitting there big as life.

Bono: What did Mr. Rand say?

Troy: Ain't said nothing. Figure if the nigger too dumb to know he carrying a watermelon, he wasn't gonna get much sense out of him. Trying to hide that great big old watermelon under his coat. Afraid to let the white man see him carry it home.

Bono: I'm like you . . . I ain't got no time for them kind of people.

Troy: Now what he look like getting mad cause he see the man from the union talking to Mr. Rand?

Bono: He come to me talking about . . . "Maxson gonna get us fired." I told him to get away from me with that. He walked away from me calling you a troublemaker. What Mr. Rand say?

Troy: Ain't said nothing. He told me to go down the Commissioner's office next Friday. They called me down there to see them.

Bono: Well, as long as you got your complaint filed, they can't fire you. That's what one of them white fellows tell me.

Troy: I ain't worried about them firing me. They gonna fire me cause I asked a question? That's all I did. I went to Mr. Rand and asked him, "Why? Why you got the white mens driving and the colored lifting?" Told him, "what's the matter, don't I count? You think only white fellows got sense enough to drive a truck. That ain't no paper job! Hell, anybody can drive a truck. How come you got all whites driving and the colored lifting?" He told me "take it to the union." Well, hell, that's what I done! Now they wanna come up with this pack of lies.

Bono: I told Brownie if the man come and ask him any questions . . . just tell the truth! It ain't nothing but something they done trumped up on you cause you filed a complaint on them.

Troy: Brownie don't understand nothing. All I want them to do is change the job description. Give everybody a chance to drive the truck. Brownie can't see that. He ain't got that much sense.

Bono: How you figure he be making out with that gal be up at Taylors' all the time . . . that Alberta gal?

Troy: Same as you and me. Getting just as much as we is. Which is to say nothing.

Bono: It is, huh? I figure you doing a little better than me . . . and I ain't saying what I'm doing.

Troy: Aw, nigger, look here . . . I know you. If you had got anywhere near that gal, twenty minutes later you be looking to tell somebody. And the first one you gonna tell . . . that you gonna want to brag to . . . is me.

Bono: I ain't saying that. I see where you be eyeing her.

Troy: I eye all the women. I don't miss nothing. Don't never let nobody tell you Troy Maxson don't eye the women.

Bono: You been doing more than eyeing her. You done bought her a drink or two.

Troy: Hell yeah, I bought her a drink! What that mean? I bought you one, too. What that mean cause I buy her a drink? I'm just being polite.

Bono: It's all right to buy her one drink. That's what you call being polite. But when you wanna be buying two or three . . . that's what you call eyeing her.

Troy: Look here, as long as you known me . . . you ever known me to chase after women?

Bono: Hell yeah! Long as I done known you. You forgetting I knew you when.

Troy: Naw, I'm talking about since I been married to Rose?

Bono: Oh, not since you been married to Rose. Now, that's the truth, there. I can say that.

Troy: All right then! Case closed.

Bono: I see you be walking up around Alberta's house. You supposed to be at Taylors' and you be walking up around there.

Troy: What you watching where I'm walking for? I ain't watching after you.

Bono: I seen you walking around there more than once.

Troy: Hell, you liable to see me walking anywhere! That don't mean nothing cause you see me walking around there.

Bono: Where she come from anyway? She just kinda showed up one day.

Troy: Tallahassee. You can look at her and tell she one of them Florida gals. They got some big healthy women down there. Grow them right up out the ground. Got a little bit of Indian in her. Most of them niggers down in Florida got some Indian in them.

Bono: I don't know about that Indian part. But she damn sure big and healthy. Woman wear some big stockings. Got them great big old legs and hips as wide as the Mississippi River.

Troy: Legs don't mean nothing. You don't do nothing but push them out of the way. But them hips cushion the ride!

Bono: Troy, you ain't got no sense.

Troy: It's the truth! Like you riding on Goodyears!

> *Rose enters from the house. She is ten years younger than Troy, her devotion to him stems from her recognition of the possibilities of her life without him: a succession of abusive men and their babies, a life of partying and running the streets, the Church, or aloneness with its attendant pain and frustration. She recognizes Troy's spirit as a fine and illuminating one and she either ignores or forgives his faults, only some of which she recognizes. Though she doesn't drink, her presence is an integral part of the Friday night rituals. She alternates between the porch and the kitchen, where supper preparations are under way.*

Rose: What you all out here getting into?

Troy: What you worried about what we getting into for? This is men talk, woman.

Rose: What I care what you all talking about? Bono, you gonna stay for supper?

Bono: No, I thank you, Rose. But Lucille say she cooking up a pot of pigfeet.

Troy: Pigfeet! Hell, I'm going home with you! Might even stay the night if you got some pigfeet. You got something in there to top them pigfeet, Rose?

Rose: I'm cooking up some chicken. I got some chicken and collard greens.

Troy: Well, go on back in the house and let me and Bono finish what we was talking about. This is men talk. I got some talk for you later. You know what kind of talk I mean. You go on and powder it up.

Rose: Troy Maxson, don't you start that now!

Troy (puts his arm around her): Aw, woman . . . come here. Look here, Bono . . . when I met this woman . . . I got out that place, say, "Hitch up my pony, saddle up my mare . . . there's a woman out there for me somewhere. I looked here. Looked there. Saw Rose and latched on to her." I latched on to her and told her—I'm gonna tell you the truth—I told her, "Baby, I don't wanna marry, I just wanna be your man." Rose told me . . . tell him what you told me, Rose.

Rose: I told him if he wasn't the marrying kind, then move out the way so the marrying kind could find me.

Troy: That's what she told me. "Nigger, you in my way. You blocking the view! Move out the way so I can find me a husband." I thought it over two or three days. Come back—

Rose: Ain't no two or three days nothing. You was back the same night.

Troy: Come back, told her . . . "Okay, baby . . . but I'm gonna buy me a banty rooster and put him out there in the backyard . . . and when he see a stranger come, he'll flap his wings and crow . . ." Look here, Bono, I could watch the front door by myself . . . it was that back door I was worried about.

Rose: Troy, you ought not talk like that. Troy ain't doing nothing but telling a lie.

Troy: Only thing is . . . when we first got married . . . forget the rooster . . . we ain't had no yard!

Bono: I hear you tell it. Me and Lucille was staying down there on Logan Street. Had two rooms with the outhouse in the back. I ain't mind the outhouse none. But when that goddamn wind blow through there in the winter . . . that's what I'm talking about! To this day I wonder why in the hell I ever stayed down there for six long years. But see, I didn't know I could do no better. I thought only white folks had inside toilets and things.

Rose: There's a lot of people don't know they can do no better than they doing now. That's just something you got to learn. A lot of folks still shop at Bella's.

Troy: Ain't nothing wrong with shopping at Bella's. She got fresh food.

Rose: I ain't said nothing about if she got fresh food. I'm talking about what she charge. She charge ten cents more than the A&P.

Troy: The A&P ain't never done nothing for me. I spends my money where I'm treated right. I go down to Bella, say, "I need a loaf of bread, I'll pay you Friday." She give it to me. What sense that make when I got money to go and spend it somewhere else and ignore the person who done right by me? That ain't in the Bible.

Rose: We ain't talking about what's in the Bible. What sense it make to shop there when she overcharge?

Troy: You shop where you want to. I'll do my shopping where the people been good to me.

Rose: Well, I don't think it's right for her to overcharge. That's all I was saying.

Bono: Look here . . . I got to get on. Lucille going be raising all kind of hell.

Troy: Where you going, nigger? We ain't finished this pint. Come here, finish this pint.

Bono: Well, hell, I am . . . if you ever turn the bottle loose.

Troy (hands him the bottle): The only thing I say about the A&P is I'm glad Cory got that job down there. Help him take care of his school clothes and things. Gabe done moved out and things getting tight around here. He got that job. . . . He can start to look out for himself.

Rose: Cory done went and got recruited by a college football team.

Troy: I told that boy about that football stuff. The white man ain't gonna let him get nowhere with that football. I told him when he first come to me with it. Now you come telling me he done went and got more tied up in it. He ought to go and get recruited in how to fix cars or something where he can make a living.

Rose: He ain't talking about making no living playing football. It's just something the boys in school do. They gonna send a recruiter by to talk to you. He'll tell you he ain't talking about making no living playing football. It's a honor to be recruited.

Troy: It ain't gonna get him nowhere. Bono'll tell you that.

Bono: If he be like you in the sports . . . he's gonna be all right. Ain't but two men ever played baseball as good as you. That's Babe Ruth° and Josh Gibson.° Them's the only two men ever hit more home runs than you.

Babe Ruth (1895–1948): One of the greatest American baseball players.   *Josh Gibson* (1911–1947): Powerful baseball player known in the 1930s as the Babe Ruth of the Negro leagues.

Troy: What it ever get me? Ain't got a pot to piss in or a window to throw it out of.

Rose: Times have changed since you was playing baseball, Troy. That was before the war. Times have changed a lot since then.

Troy: How in hell they done changed?

Rose: They got lots of colored boys playing ball now. Baseball and football.

Bono: You right about that, Rose. Times have changed, Troy. You just come along too early.

Troy: There ought not never have been no time called too early! Now you take that fellow . . . what's that fellow they had playing right field for the Yankees back then? You know who I'm talking about, Bono. Used to play right field for the Yankees.

Rose: Selkirk?

Troy: Selkirk! That's it! Man batting .269, understand? .269. What kind of sense that make? I was hitting .432 with thirty-seven home runs! Man batting .269 and playing right field for the Yankees! I saw Josh Gibson's daughter yesterday. She walking around with raggedy shoes on her feet. Now I bet you Selkirk's daughter ain't walking around with raggedy shoes on her feet! I bet you that!

Rose: They got a lot of colored baseball players now. Jackie Robinson° was the first. Folks had to wait for Jackie Robinson.

Troy: I done seen a hundred niggers play baseball better than Jackie Robinson. Hell, I know some teams Jackie Robinson couldn't even make! What you talking about Jackie Robinson. Jackie Robinson wasn't nobody. I'm talking about if you could play ball then they ought to have let you play. Don't care what color you were. Come telling me I come along too early. If you could play . . . then they ought to have let you play.

Troy takes a long drink from the bottle.

Rose: You gonna drink yourself to death. You don't need to be drinking like that.

Troy: Death ain't nothing. I done seen him. Done wrassled with him. You can't tell me nothing about death. Death ain't nothing but a fastball on the outside corner. And you know what I'll do to that! Lookee here, Bono . . . am I lying? You get one of them fastballs, about waist high, over the outside corner of the plate where you can get the meat of the bat on it . . . and good god! You can kiss it goodbye. Now, am I lying?

Bono: Naw, you telling the truth there. I seen you do it.

Troy: If I'm lying . . . that 450 feet worth of lying! *(Pause.)* That's all death is to me. A fastball on the outside corner.

Rose: I don't know why you want to get on talking about death.

Troy: Ain't nothing wrong with talking about death. That's part of life. Everybody gonna die. You gonna die, I'm gonna die. Bono's gonna die. Hell, we all gonna die.

Rose: But you ain't got to talk about it. I don't like to talk about it.

Troy: You the one brought it up. Me and Bono was talking about baseball . . . you tell me I'm gonna drink myself to death. Ain't that right, Bono? You

---

Jackie Robinson (1919–1972): The first black baseball player in the major leagues (1947).

know I don't drink this but one night out of the week. That's Friday night. I'm gonna drink just enough to where I can handle it. Then I cuts it loose. I leave it alone. So don't you worry about me drinking myself to death. 'Cause I ain't worried about Death. I done seen him. I done wrestled with him.

Look here, Bono . . . I looked up one day and Death was marching straight at me. Like Soldiers on Parade! The Army of Death was marching straight at me. The middle of July, 1941. It got real cold just like it be winter. It seem like Death himself reached out and touched me on the shoulder. He touch me just like I touch you. I got cold as ice and Death standing there grinning at me.

Rose: Troy, why don't you hush that talk.

Troy: I say . . . what you want, Mr. Death? You be wanting me? You done brought your army to be getting me? I looked him dead in the eye. I wasn't fearing nothing. I was ready to tangle. Just like I'm ready to tangle now. The Bible say be ever vigilant. That's why I don't get but so drunk. I got to keep watch.

Rose: Troy was right down there in Mercy Hospital. You remember he had pneumonia? Laying there with a fever talking plumb out of his head.

Troy: Death standing there staring at me . . . carrying that sickle in his hand. Finally he say, "You want bound over for another year?" See, just like that . . . "You want bound over for another year?" I told him, "Bound over hell! Let's settle this now!"

It seem like he kinda fell back when I said that, and all the cold went out of me. I reached down and grabbed that sickle and threw it just as far as I could throw it . . . and me and him commenced to wrestling.

We wrestled for three days and three nights. I can't say where I found the strength from. Every time it seemed like he was gonna get the best of me, I'd reach way down deep inside myself and find the strength to do him one better.

Rose: Every time Troy tell that story he find different ways to tell it. Different things to make up about it.

Troy: I ain't making up nothing. I'm telling you the facts of what happened. I wrestled with Death for three days and three nights and I'm standing here to tell you about it. *(Pause.)* All right. At the end of the third night we done weakened each other to where we can't hardly move. Death stood up, throwed on his robe . . . had him a white robe with a hood on it. He throwed on that robe and went off to look for his sickle. Say, "I'll be back." Just like that. "I'll be back." I told him, say, "Yeah, but . . . you gonna have to find me!" I wasn't no fool. I wan't going looking for him. Death ain't nothing to play with. And I know he's gonna get me. I know I got to join his army . . . his camp followers. But as long as I keep my strength and see him coming . . . as long as I keep up my vigilance . . . he's gonna have to fight to get me. I ain't going easy.

Bono: Well, look here, since you got to keep up your vigilance . . . let me have the bottle.

Troy: Aw hell, I shouldn't have told you that part. I should have left out that part.

Rose: Troy be talking that stuff and half the time don't even know what he be talking about.

Troy: Bono know me better than that.

Bono: That's right. I know you. I know you got some Uncle Remus° in your blood. You got more stories than the devil got sinners.

Troy: Aw hell, I done seen him too! Done talked with the devil.

Rose: Troy, don't nobody wanna be hearing all that stuff.

> *Lyons enters the yard from the street. Thirty-four years old, Troy's son by a previous marriage, he sports a neatly trimmed goatee, sport coat, white shirt, tieless and buttoned at the collar. Though he fancies himself a musician, he is more caught up in the rituals and "idea" of being a musician than in the actual practice of the music. He has come to borrow money from Troy, and while he knows he will be successful, he is uncertain as to what extent his lifestyle will be held up to scrutiny and ridicule.*

Lyons: Hey, Pop.

Troy: What you come "Hey, Popping" me for?

Lyons: How you doing, Rose? *(He kisses her.)* Mr. Bono. How you doing?

Bono: Hey, Lyons . . . how you been?

Troy: He must have been doing all right. I ain't seen him around here last week.

Rose: Troy, leave your boy alone. He come by to see you and you wanna start all that nonsense.

Troy: I ain't bothering Lyons. *(Offers him the bottle.)* Here . . . get you a drink. We got an understanding. I know why he come by to see me and he know I know.

Lyons: Come on, Pop . . . I just stopped by to say hi . . . see how you was doing.

Troy: You ain't stopped by yesterday.

Rose: You gonna stay for supper, Lyons? I got some chicken cooking in the oven.

Lyons: No, Rose . . . thanks. I was just in the neighborhood and thought I'd stop by for a minute.

Troy: You was in the neighborhood all right, nigger. You telling the truth there. You was in the neighborhood cause it's my payday.

Lyons: Well, hell, since you mentioned it . . . let me have ten dollars.

Troy: I'll be damned! I'll die and go to hell and play blackjack with the devil before I give you ten dollars.

Bono: That's what I wanna know about . . . that devil you done seen.

Lyons: What . . . Pop done seen the devil? You too much, Pops.

Troy: Yeah, I done seen him. Talked to him too!

Rose: You ain't seen no devil. I done told you that man ain't had nothing to do with the devil. Anything you can't understand, you want to call it the devil.

Troy: Look here, Bono . . . I went down to see Hertzberger about some furniture. Got three rooms for two-ninety-eight. That what it say on the radio. "Three rooms . . . two-ninety-eight." Even made up a little song about it. Go down there . . . man tell me I can't get no credit. I'm working every day and can't get no credit. What to do? I got an empty house with some raggedy furniture in it. Cory ain't got no bed. He's sleeping on a pile of

---

Uncle Remus: Black storyteller who recounts traditional black tales in the book by Joel Chandler Harris.

rags on the floor. Working every day and can't get no credit. Come back here—Rose'll tell you—madder than hell. Sit down . . . try to figure what I'm gonna do. Come a knock on the door. Ain't been living here but three days. Who know I'm here? Open the door . . . devil standing there bigger than life. White fellow . . . white fellow . . . got on good clothes and everything. Standing there with a clipboard in his hand. I ain't had to say nothing. First words come out of his mouth was . . . "I understand you need some furniture and can't get no credit." I liked to fell over. He say, "I'll give you all the credit you want, but you got to pay the interest on it." I told him, "Give me three rooms worth and charge whatever you want." Next day a truck pulled up here and two men unloaded them three rooms. Man what drove the truck give me a book. Say send ten dollars, first of every month to the address in the book and everything will be all right. Say if I miss a payment the devil was coming back and it'll be hell to pay. That was fifteen years ago. To this day . . . the first of the month I send my ten dollars, Rose'll tell you.

Rose: Troy lying.

Troy: I ain't never seen that man since. Now you tell me who else that could have been but the devil? I ain't sold my soul or nothing like that, you understand. Naw, I wouldn't have truck with the devil about nothing like that. I got my furniture and pays my ten dollars the first of the month just like clockwork.

Bono: How long you say you been paying this ten dollars a month?

Troy: Fifteen years!

Bono: Hell, ain't you finished paying for it yet? How much the man done charged you?

Troy: Ah hell, I done paid for it. I done paid for it ten times over! The fact is I'm scared to stop paying it.

Rose: Troy lying. We got that furniture from Mr. Glickman. He ain't paying no ten dollars a month to nobody.

Troy: Aw hell, woman. Bono know I ain't that big a fool.

Lyons: I was just getting ready to say . . . I know where there's a bridge for sale.

Troy: Look here, I'll tell you this . . . it don't matter to me if he was the devil. It don't matter if the devil give credit. Somebody has got to give it.

Rose: It ought to matter. You going around talking about having truck with the devil . . . God's the one you gonna have to answer to. He's the one gonna be at the Judgment.

Lyons: Yeah, well, look here, Pop . . . let me have that ten dollars. I'll give it back to you. Bonnie got a job working at the hospital.

Troy: What I tell you, Bono? The only time I see this nigger is when he wants something. That's the only time I see him.

Lyons: Come on, Pop, Mr. Bono don't want to hear all that. Let me have the ten dollars. I told you Bonnie working.

Troy: What that mean to me? "Bonnie working." I don't care if she working. Go ask her for the ten dollars if she working. Talking about "Bonnie working." Why ain't you working?

Lyons: Aw, Pop, you know I can't find no decent job. Where am I gonna get a job at? You know I can't get no job.

Troy: I told you I know some people down there. I can get you on the rubbish if you want to work. I told you that the last time you came by here asking me for something.

Lyons: Naw, Pop . . . thanks. That ain't for me. I don't wanna be carrying nobody's rubbish. I don't wanna be punching nobody's time clock.

Troy: What's the matter, you too good to carry people's rubbish? Where you think that ten dollars you talking about come from? I'm just supposed to haul people's rubbish and give my money to you cause you too lazy to work. You too lazy to work and wanna know why you ain't got what I got.

Rose: What hospital Bonnie working at? Mercy?

Lyons: She's down at Passavant working in the laundry.

Troy: I ain't got nothing as it is. I give you that ten dollars and I got to eat beans the rest of the week. Naw . . . you ain't getting no ten dollars here.

Lyons: You ain't got to be eating no beans. I don't know why you wanna say that.

Troy: I ain't got no extra money. Gabe done moved over to Miss Pearl's paying her the rent and things done got tight around here. I can't afford to be giving you every payday.

Lyons: I ain't asked you to give me nothing. I asked you to loan me ten dollars. I know you got ten dollars.

Troy: Yeah, I got it. You know why I got it? Cause I don't throw my money away out there in the streets. You living the fast life . . . wanna be a musician . . . running around in them clubs and things . . . then, you learn to take care of yourself. You ain't gonna find me going and asking nobody for nothing. I done spent too many years without.

Lyons: You and me is two different people, Pop.

Troy: I done learned my mistake and learned to do what's right by it. You still trying to get something for nothing. Life don't owe you nothing. You owe it to yourself. Ask Bono. He'll tell you I'm right.

Lyons: You got your way of dealing with the world . . . I got mine. The only thing that matters to me is the music.

Troy: Yeah, I can see that! It don't matter how you gonna eat . . . where your next dollar is coming from. You telling the truth there.

Lyons: I know I got to eat. But I got to live too. I need something that gonna help me to get out of the bed in the morning. Make me feel like I belong in the world. I don't bother nobody. I just stay with the music cause that's the only way I can find to live in the world. Otherwise there ain't no telling what I might do. Now I don't come criticizing you and how you live. I just come by to ask you for ten dollars. I don't wanna hear all that about how I live.

Troy: Boy, your mamma did a hell of a job raising you.

Lyons: You can't change me, Pop. I'm thirty-four years old. If you wanted to change me, you should have been there when I was growing up. I come by to see you . . . ask for ten dollars and you want to talk about how I was raised. You don't know nothing about how I was raised.

Rose: Let the boy have ten dollars, Troy.

Troy (to Lyons): What the hell you looking at me for? I ain't got no ten dollars. You know what I do with my money. *(To Rose.)* Give him ten dollars if you want him to have it.

Rose: I will. Just as soon as you turn it loose.

Troy (handing Rose the money): There it is. Seventy-six dollars and forty-two cents. You see this, Bono? Now, I ain't gonna get but six of that back.

Rose: You ought to stop telling that lie. Here, Lyons. *(She hands him the money.)*

Lyons: Thanks, Rose. Look . . . I got to run . . . I'll see you later.

Troy: Wait a minute. You gonna say, "thanks, Rose" and ain't gonna look to see where she got that ten dollars from? See how they do me, Bono?

Lyons: I know she got it from you, Pop. Thanks. I'll give it back to you.

Troy: There he go telling another lie. Time I see that ten dollars . . . he'll be owing me thirty more.

Lyons: See you, Mr. Bono.

Bono: Take care, Lyons!

Lyons: Thanks, Pop. I'll see you again.

Lyons exits the yard.

Troy: I don't know why he don't go and get him a decent job and take care of that woman he got.

Bono: He'll be all right, Troy. The boy is still young.

Troy: The *boy* is thirty-four years old.

Rose: Let's not get off into all that.

Bono: Look here . . . I got to be going. I got to be getting on. Lucille gonna be waiting.

Troy (puts his arm around Rose): See this woman, Bono? I love this woman. I love this woman so much it hurts. I love her so much . . . I done run out of ways of loving her. So I got to go back to basics. Don't you come by my house Monday morning talking about time to go to work . . . 'cause I'm still gonna be stroking!

Rose: Troy! Stop it now!

Bono: I ain't paying him no mind, Rose. That ain't nothing but gin-talk. Go on, Troy. I'll see you Monday.

Troy: Don't you come by my house, nigger! I done told you what I'm gonna be doing.

The lights go down to black.

SCENE II

The lights come up on Rose hanging up clothes. She hums and sings softly to herself. It is the following morning.

Rose (sings): Jesus, be a fence all around me every day
Jesus, I want you to protect me as I travel on my way.
Jesus, be a fence all around me every day.

Troy enters from the house.

Jesus, I want you to protect me
As I travel on my way.
(*To Troy.*) 'Morning. You ready for breakfast? I can fix it soon as I finish hanging up these clothes?

Troy: I got the coffee on. That'll be all right. I'll just drink some of that this morning.

Rose: That 651 hit yesterday. That's the second time this month. Miss Pearl hit for a dollar . . . seem like those that need the least always get lucky. Poor folks can't get nothing.

Troy: Them numbers don't know nobody. I don't know why you fool with them. You and Lyons both.

Rose: It's something to do.

Troy: You ain't doing nothing but throwing your money away.

Rose: Troy, you know I don't play foolishly. I just play a nickel here and a nickel there.

Troy: That's two nickels you done thrown away.

Rose: Now I hit sometimes . . . that makes up for it. It always comes in handy when I do hit. I don't hear you complaining then.

Troy: I ain't complaining now. I just say it's foolish. Trying to guess out of six hundred ways which way the number gonna come. If I had all the money niggers, these Negroes, throw away on numbers for one week—just one week—I'd be a rich man.

Rose: Well, you wishing and calling it foolish ain't gonna stop folks from playing numbers. That's one thing for sure. Besides . . . some good things come from playing numbers. Look where Pope done bought him that restaurant off of numbers.

Troy: I can't stand niggers like that. Man ain't had two dimes to rub together. He walking around with his shoes all run over bumming money for cigarettes. All right. Got lucky there and hit the numbers . . .

Rose: Troy, I know all about it.

Troy: Had good sense, I'll say that for him. He ain't throwed his money away. I seen niggers hit the numbers and go through two thousand dollars in four days. Man bought him that restaurant down there . . . fixed it up real nice . . . and then didn't want nobody to come in it! A Negro go in there and can't get no kind of service. I seen a white fellow come in there and order a bowl of stew. Pope picked all the meat out the pot for him. Man ain't had nothing but a bowl of meat! Negro come behind him and ain't got nothing but the potatoes and carrots. Talking about what numbers do for people, you picked a wrong example. Ain't done nothing but make a worser fool out of him than he was before.

Rose: Troy, you ought to stop worrying about what happened at work yesterday.

Troy: I ain't worried. Just told me to be down there at the Commissioner's office on Friday. Everybody think they gonna fire me. I ain't worried about them firing me. You ain't got to worry about that. *(Pause.)* Where's Cory? Cory in the house? *(Calls.)* Cory?

Rose: He gone out.

Troy: Out, huh? He gone out 'cause he know I want him to help me with this fence. I know how he is. That boy scared of work.

Gabriel enters. He comes halfway down the alley and, hearing Troy's voice, stops.

Troy (continues): He ain't done a lick of work in his life.

Rose: He had to go to football practice. Coach wanted them to get in a little extra practice before the season start.

Troy: I got his practice . . . running out of here before he get his chores done.

Rose: Troy, what is wrong with you this morning? Don't nothing set right with you. Go on back in there and go to bed . . . get up on the other side.

Troy: Why something got to be wrong with me? I ain't said nothing wrong with me.

Rose: You got something to say about everything. First it's the numbers . . . then it's the way the man runs his restaurant . . . then you done got on

Cory. What's it gonna be next? Take a look up there and see if the weather suits you . . . or is it gonna be how you gonna put up the fence with the clothes hanging in the yard.

Troy: You hit the nail on the head then.

Rose: I know you like I know the back of my hand. Go on in there and get you some coffee . . . see if that straighten you up. 'Cause you ain't right this morning.

Troy starts into the house and sees Gabriel. Gabriel starts singing. Troy's brother, he is seven years younger than Troy. Injured in World War II, he has a metal plate in his head. He carries an old trumpet tied around his waist and believes with every fiber of his being that he is the Archangel Gabriel.° He carries a chipped basket with an assortment of discarded fruits and vegetables he has picked up in the strip district and which he attempts to sell.

Gabriel (singing): Yes, ma am, I got plums
You ask me how I sell them
Oh ten cents apiece
Three for a quarter
Come and buy now
'Cause I'm here today
And tomorrow I'll be gone

Gabriel enters.

Hey, Rose!

Rose: How you doing, Gabe?

Gabriel: There's Troy . . . Hey, Troy!

Troy: Hey, Gabe.

Exit into kitchen.

Rose (to Gabriel): What you got there?

Gabriel: You know what I got, Rose. I got fruits and vegetables.

Rose (looking in basket): Where's all these plums you talking about?

Gabriel: I ain't got no plums today, Rose. I was just singing that. Have some tomorrow. Put me in a big order for plums. Have enough plums tomorrow for St. Peter and everybody.

Troy reenters from kitchen, crosses to steps.

(To Rose.) Troy's mad at me.

Troy: I ain't mad at you. What I got to be mad at you about? You ain't done nothing to me.

Gabriel: I just moved over to Miss Pearl's to keep out from in your way. I ain't mean no harm by it.

Troy: Who said anything about that? I ain't said anything about that.

Gabriel: You ain't mad at me, is you?

Troy: Naw . . . I ain't mad at you, Gabe. If I was mad at you I'd tell you about it.

Gabriel: Got me two rooms. In the basement. Got my own door too. Wanna see my key? *(He holds up a key.)* That's my own key! Ain't nobody else got a key like that. That's my key! My two rooms!

Troy: Well, that's good, Gabe. You got your own key . . . that's good.

Archangel Gabriel: Considered one of God's primary messengers in the Old and New Testaments.

Rose: You hungry, Gabe? I was just fixing to cook Troy his breakfast.

Gabriel: I'll take some biscuits. You got some biscuits? Did you know when I was in heaven . . . every morning me and St. Peter° would sit down by the gate and eat some big fat biscuits? Oh, yeah! We had us a good time. We'd sit there and eat us them biscuits and then St. Peter would go off to sleep and tell me to wake him up when it's time to open the gates for the judgment.

Rose: Well, come on . . . I'll make up a batch of biscuits.

Rose exits into the house.

Gabriel: Troy . . . St. Peter got your name in the book. I seen it. It say . . . Troy Maxson. I say . . . I know him! He got the same name like what I got. That's my brother!

Troy: How many times you gonna tell me that, Gabe?

Gabriel: Ain't got my name in the book. Don't have to have my name. I done died and went to heaven. He got your name though. One morning St. Peter was looking at his book . . . marking it up for the judgment . . . and he let me see your name. Got it in there under M. Got Rose's name . . . I ain't seen it like I seen yours . . . but I know it's in there. He got a great big book. Got everybody's name what was ever been born. That's what he told me. But I seen your name. Seen it with my own eyes.

Troy: Go on in the house there. Rose going to fix you something to eat.

Gabriel: Oh, I ain't hungry. I done had breakfast with Aunt Jemimah. She come by and cooked me up a whole mess of flapjacks. Remember how we used to eat them flapjacks?

Troy: Go on in the house and get you something to eat now.

Gabriel: I got to sell my plums. I done sold some tomatoes. Got me two quarters. Wanna see? *(He shows Troy his quarters.)* I'm gonna save them and buy me a new horn so St. Peter can hear me when it's time to open the gates. *(Gabriel stops suddenly. Listens.)* Hear that? That's the hellhounds. I got to chase them out of here. Go on get out of here! Get out!

Gabriel exits singing.

Better get ready for the judgment
Better get ready for the judgment
My Lord is coming down

Rose enters from the house.

Troy: He's gone off somewhere.

Gabriel (offstage): Better get ready for the judgment
Better get ready for the judgment morning
Better get ready for the judgment
My God is coming down

Rose: He ain't eating right. Miss Pearl say she can't get him to eat nothing.

Troy: What you want me to do about it, Rose? I done did everything I can for the man. I can't make him get well. Man got half his head blown away . . . what you expect?

Rose: Seem like something ought to be done to help him.

Troy: Man don't bother nobody. He just mixed up from that metal plate he got in his head. Ain't no sense for him to go back into the hospital.

St. Peter: One of Jesus's disciples, believed to be the keeper of the gates of Heaven.

Rose: Least he be eating right. They can help him take care of himself.

Troy: Don't nobody wanna be locked up, Rose. What you wanna lock him up for? Man go over there and fight the war . . . messin' around with them Japs, get half his head blown off . . . and they give him a lousy three thousand dollars. And I had to swoop down on that.

Rose: Is you fixing to go into that again?

Troy: That's the only way I got a roof over my head . . . cause of that metal plate.

Rose: Ain't no sense you blaming yourself for nothing. Gabe wasn't in no condition to manage that money. You done what was right by him. Can't nobody say you ain't done what was right by him. Look how long you took care of him . . . till he wanted to have his own place and moved over there with Miss Pearl.

Troy: That ain't what I'm saying, woman! I'm just stating the facts. If my brother didn't have that metal plate in his head . . . I wouldn't have a pot to piss in or a window to throw it out of. And I'm fifty-three years old. Now see if you can understand that!

Troy gets up from the porch and starts to exit the yard.

Rose: Where you going off to? You been running out of here every Saturday for weeks. I thought you was gonna work on this fence?

Troy: I'm gonna walk down to Taylors'. Listen to the ball game. I'll be back in a bit. I'll work on it when I get back.

He exits the yard. The lights go to black.

SCENE III

The lights come up on the yard. It is four hours later. Rose is taking down the clothes from the line. Cory enters carrying his football equipment.

Rose: Your daddy like to had a fit with you running out of here this morning without doing your chores.

Cory: I told you I had to go to practice.

Rose: He say you were supposed to help him with this fence.

Cory: He been saying that the last four or five Saturdays, and then he don't never do nothing, but go down to Taylors. Did you tell him about the recruiter?

Rose: Yeah, I told him.

Cory: What he say?

Rose: He ain't said nothing too much. You get in there and get started on your chores before he gets back. Go on and scrub down them steps before he gets back here hollering and carrying on.

Cory: I'm hungry. What you got to eat, Mama?

Rose: Go on and get started on your chores. I got some meat loaf in there. Go on and make you a sandwich . . . and don't leave no mess in there.

Cory exits into the house. Rose continues to take down the clothes. Troy enters the yard and sneaks up and grabs her from behind.

Troy! Go on, now. You liked to scared me to death. What was the score of the game? Lucille had me on the phone and I couldn't keep up with it.

Troy: What I care about the game? Come here, woman. *(He tries to kiss her.)*

Rose: I thought you went down Taylors' to listen to the game. Go on, Troy! You supposed to be putting up this fence.

Troy (attempting to kiss her again): I'll put it up when I finish with what is at hand.

Rose: Go on, Troy. I ain't studying you.

Troy (chasing after her): I'm studying you . . . fixing to do my homework!

Rose: Troy, you better leave me alone.

Troy: Where's Cory? That boy brought his butt home yet?

Rose: He's in the house doing his chores.

Troy (calling): Cory! Get your butt out here, boy!

> *Rose exits into the house with the laundry. Troy goes over to the pile of wood, picks up a board, and starts sawing. Cory enters from the house.*

Troy: You just now coming in here from leaving this morning?

Cory: Yeah, I had to go to football practice.

Troy: Yeah, what?

Cory: Yessir.

Troy: I ain't but two seconds off you noway. The garbage sitting in there over-flowing . . . you ain't done none of your chores . . . and you come in here talking about "Yeah."

Cory: I was just getting ready to do my chores now, Pop . . .

Troy: Your first chore is to help me with this fence on Saturday. Everything else come after that. Now get that saw and cut them boards.

> *Cory takes the saw and begins cutting the boards. Troy continues working. There is a long pause.*

Cory: Hey, Pop . . . why don't you buy a TV?

Troy: What I want with a TV? What I want one of them for?

Cory: Everybody got one. Earl, Ba Bra . . . Jesse!

Troy: I ain't asked you who had one. I say what I want with one?

Cory: So you can watch it. They got lots of things on TV. Baseball games and everything. We could watch the World Series.

Troy: Yeah . . . and how much this TV cost?

Cory: I don't know. They got them on sale for around two hundred dollars.

Troy: Two hundred dollars, huh?

Cory: That ain't that much, Pop.

Troy: Naw, it's just two hundred dollars. See that roof you got over your head at night? Let me tell you something about that roof. It's been over ten years since that roof was last tarred. See now . . . the snow come this winter and sit up there on that roof like it is . . . and it's gonna seep inside. It's just gonna be a little bit . . . ain't gonna hardly notice it. Then the next thing you know, it's gonna be leaking all over the house. Then the wood rot from all that water and you gonna need a whole new roof. Now, how much you think it cost to get that roof tarred?

Cory: I don't know.

Troy: Two hundred and sixty-four dollars . . . cash money. While you thinking about a TV, I got to be thinking about the roof . . . and whatever else go wrong here. Now if you had two hundred dollars, what would you do . . . fix the roof or buy a TV?

Cory: I'd buy a TV. Then when the roof started to leak . . . when it needed fixing . . . I'd fix it.

Troy: Where you gonna get the money from? You done spent it for a TV. You gonna sit up and watch the water run all over your brand new TV.

Cory: Aw, Pop. You got money. I know you do.

Troy: Where I got it at, huh?

Cory: You got it in the bank.

Troy: You wanna see my bankbook? You wanna see that seventy-three dollars and twenty-two cents I got sitting up in there.

Cory: You ain't got to pay for it all at one time. You can put a down payment on it and carry it on home with you.

Troy: Not me. I ain't gonna owe nobody nothing if I can help it. Miss a payment and they come and snatch it right out your house. Then what you got? Now, soon as I get two hundred dollars clear, then I'll buy a TV. Right now, as soon as I get two hundred and sixty-four dollars, I'm gonna have this roof tarred.

Cory: Aw . . . Pop!

Troy: You go on and get you two hundred dollars and buy one if ya want it. I got better things to do with my money.

Cory: I can't get no two hundred dollars. I ain't never seen two hundred dollars.

Troy: I'll tell you what . . . you get you a hundred dollars and I'll put the other hundred with it.

Cory: All right, I'm gonna show you.

Troy: You gonna show me how you can cut them boards right now.

Cory begins to cut the boards. There is a long pause.

Cory: The Pirates won today. That makes five in a row.

Troy: I ain't thinking about the Pirates. Got an all-white team. Got that boy . . . that Puerto Rican boy . . . Clemente. Don't even half-play him. That boy could be something if they give him a chance. Play him one day and sit him on the bench the next.

Cory: He gets a lot of chances to play.

Troy: I'm talking about playing regular. Playing every day so you can get your timing. That's what I'm talking about.

Cory: They got some white guys on the team that don't play every day. You can't play everybody at the same time.

Troy: If they got a white fellow sitting on the bench . . . you can bet your last dollar he can't play! The colored guy got to be twice as good before he get on the team. That's why I don't want you to get all tied up in them sports. Man on the team and what it get him? They got colored on the team and don't use them. Same as not having them. All them teams the same.

Cory: The Braves got Hank Aaron and Wes Covington. Hank Aaron hit two home runs today. That makes forty-three.

Troy: Hank Aaron ain't nobody. That what you supposed to do. That's how you supposed to play the game. Ain't nothing to it. It's just a matter of timing . . . getting the right follow-through. Hell, I can hit forty-three home runs right now!

Cory: Not off no major-league pitching, you couldn't.

Troy: We had better pitching in the Negro leagues. I hit seven home runs off of Satchel Paige.° You can't get no better than that!

Cory: Sandy Koufax. He's leading the league in strikeouts.

Satchel Paige (1906?–1982): Legendary black pitcher in the Negro leagues.

Troy: I ain't thinking of no Sandy Koufax.

Cory: You got Warren Spahn and Lew Burdette. I bet you couldn't hit no home runs off of Warren Spahn.

Troy: I'm through with it now. You go on and cut them boards. *(Pause.)* Your mama tell me you done got recruited by a college football team? Is that right?

Cory: Yeah. Coach Zellman say the recruiter gonna be coming by to talk to you. Get you to sign the permission papers.

Troy: I thought you supposed to be working down there at the A&P. Ain't you suppose to be working down there after school?

Cory: Mr. Stawicki say he gonna hold my job for me until after the football season. Say starting next week I can work weekends.

Troy: I thought we had an understanding about this football stuff? You suppose to keep up with your chores and hold that job down at the A&P. Ain't been around here all day on a Saturday. Ain't none of your chores done . . . and now you telling me you done quit your job.

Cory: I'm going to be working weekends.

Troy: You damn right you are! And ain't no need for nobody coming around here to talk to me about signing nothing.

Cory: Hey, Pop . . . you can't do that. He's coming all the way from North Carolina.

Troy: I don't care where he coming from. The white man ain't gonna let you get nowhere with that football noway. You go on and get your booklearning so you can work yourself up in that A&P or learn how to fix cars or build houses or something, get you a trade. That way you have something can't nobody take away from you. You go on and learn how to put your hands to some good use. Besides hauling people's garbage.

Cory: I get good grades, Pop. That's why the recruiter wants to talk with you. You got to keep up your grades to get recruited. This way I'll be going to college. I'll get a chance . . .

Troy: First you gonna get your butt down there to the A&P and get your job back.

Cory: Mr. Stawicki done already hired somebody else 'cause I told him I was playing football.

Troy: You a bigger fool than I thought . . . to let somebody take away your job so you can play some football. Where you gonna get your money to take out your girlfriend and whatnot? What kind of foolishness is that to let somebody take away your job?

Cory: I'm still gonna be working weekends.

Troy: Naw . . . naw. You getting your butt out of here and finding you another job.

Cory: Come on, Pop! I got to practice. I can't work after school and play football too. The team needs me. That's what Coach Zellman say . . .

Troy: I don't care what nobody else say. I'm the boss . . . you understand? I'm the boss around here. I do the only saying what counts.

Cory: Come on, Pop!

Troy: I asked you . . . did you understand?

Cory: Yeah . . .

Troy: What?!

Cory: Yessir.

Troy: You go on down there to that A&P and see if you can get your job back. If you can't do both . . . then you quit the football team. You've got to take the crookeds with the straights.

Cory: Yessir. *(Pause.)* Can I ask you a question?

Troy: What the hell you wanna ask me? Mr. Stawicki the one you got the questions for.

Cory: How come you ain't never liked me?

Troy: Liked you? Who the hell say I got to like you? What law is there say I got to like you? Wanna stand up in my face and ask a damn fool-ass question like that. Talking about liking somebody. Come here, boy, when I talk to you.

> *Cory comes over to where Troy is working. He stands slouched over and Troy shoves him on his shoulder.*

Straighten up, goddammit! I asked you a question . . . what law is there say I got to like you?

Cory: None.

Troy: Well, all right then! Don't you eat every day? *(Pause.)* Answer me when I talk to you! Don't you eat every day?

Cory: Yeah.

Troy: Nigger, as long as you in my house, you put that sir on the end of it when you talk to me!

Cory: Yes . . . sir.

Troy: You eat every day.

Cory: Yessir!

Troy: Got a roof over your head.

Cory: Yessir!

Troy: Got clothes on your back.

Cory: Yessir.

Troy: Why you think that is?

Cory: Cause of you.

Troy: Ah, hell I know it's cause of me . . . but why do you think that is?

Cory (hesitant): Cause you like me.

Troy: Like you? I go out of here every morning . . . bust my butt . . . putting up with them crackers° every day . . . cause I like you? You are the biggest fool I ever saw. *(Pause.)* It's my job. It's my responsibility! You understand that? A man got to take care of his family. You live in my house . . . sleep you behind on my bedclothes . . . fill you belly up with my food . . . cause you my son. You my flesh and blood. Not cause I like you! Cause it's my duty to take care of you. I owe a responsibility to you! Let's get this straight right here . . . before it go along any further . . . I ain't got to like you. Mr. Rand don't give me my money come payday cause he likes me. He give me cause he owe me. I done give you everything I had to give you. I gave you your life! Me and your mama worked that out between us. And liking your black ass wasn't part of the bargain. Don't you try and go through life worrying about if somebody like you or not. You best be making sure they doing right by you. You understand what I'm saying, boy?

Cory: Yessir.

Troy: Then get the hell out of my face, and get on down to that A&P.

---

crackers: White people, often used to refer disparagingly to poor whites.

Rose has been standing behind the screen door for much of the scene. She enters as Cory exits.

Rose: Why don't you let the boy go ahead and play football, Troy? Ain't no harm in that. He's just trying to be like you with the sports.

Troy: I don't want him to be like me! I want him to move as far away from my life as he can get. You the only decent thing that ever happened to me. I wish him that. But I don't wish him a thing else from my life. I decided seventeen years ago that boy wasn't getting involved in no sports. Not after what they did to me in the sports.

Rose: Troy, why don't you admit you was too old to play in the major leagues? For once . . . why don't you admit that?

Troy: What do you mean too old? Don't come telling me I was too old. I just wasn't the right color. Hell, I'm fifty-three years old and can do better than Selkirk's .269 right now!

Rose: How's was you gonna play ball when you were over forty? Sometimes I can't get no sense out of you.

Troy: I got good sense, woman. I got sense enough not to let my boy get hurt over playing no sports. You been mothering that boy too much. Worried about if people like him.

Rose: Everything that boy do . . . he do for you. He wants you to say "Good job, son." That's all.

Troy: Rose, I ain't got time for that. He's alive. He's healthy. He's got to make his own way. I made mine. Ain't nobody gonna hold his hand when he get out there in that world.

Rose: Times have changed from when you was young, Troy. People change. The world's changing around you and you can't even see it.

Troy (slow, methodical): Woman . . . I do the best I can do. I come in here every Friday. I carry a sack of potatoes and a bucket of lard. You all line up at the door with your hands out. I give you the lint from my pockets. I give you my sweat and my blood. I ain't got no tears. I done spent them. We go upstairs in that room at night . . . and I fall down on you and try to blast a hole into forever. I get up Monday morning . . . find my lunch on the table. I go out. Make my way. Find my strength to carry me through to the next Friday. (Pause.) That's all I got, Rose. That's all I got to give. I can't give nothing else.

Troy exits into the house. The lights go down to black.

Scene IV

It is Friday. Two weeks later. Cory starts out of the house with his football equipment. The phone rings.

Cory (calling): I got it! (He answers the phone and stands in the screen door talking.) Hello? Hey, Jesse. Naw . . . I was just getting ready to leave now.

Rose (calling): Cory!

Cory: I told you, man, them spikes is all tore up. You can use them if you want, but they ain't no good. Earl got some spikes.

Rose (calling): Cory!

Cory (calling to Rose): Mam? I'm talking to Jesse. (Into phone.) When she say that? (Pause.) Aw, you lying, man. I'm gonna tell her you said that.

Rose (calling): Cory, don't you go nowhere!

Cory: I got to go to the game, Ma! *(Into the phone.)* Yeah, hey, look, I'll talk to you later. Yeah, I'll meet you over Earl's house. Later. Bye, Ma.

Cory exits the house and starts out the yard.

Rose: Cory, where you going off to? You got that stuff all pulled out and thrown all over your room.

Cory (in the yard): I was looking for my spikes. Jesse wanted to borrow my spikes.

Rose: Get up there and get that cleaned up before your daddy get back in here.

Cory: I got to go to the game! I'll clean it up *when I get back.*

Cory exits.

Rose: That's all he need to do is see that room all messed up.

Rose exits into the house. Troy and Bono enter the yard. Troy is dressed in clothes other than his work clothes.

Bono: He told him the same thing he told you. Take it to the union.

Troy: Brownie ain't got that much sense. Man wasn't thinking about nothing. He wait until I confront them on it . . . then he wanna come crying seniority. *(Calls.)* Hey, Rose!

Bono: I wish I could have seen Mr. Rand's face when he told you.

Troy: He couldn't get it out of his mouth! Liked to bit his tongue! When they called me down there to the Commissioner's office . . . he thought they was gonna fire me. Like everybody else.

Bono: I didn't think they was gonna fire you. I thought they was gonna put you on the warning paper.

Troy: Hey, Rose! *(To Bono.)* Yeah, Mr. Rand like to bit his tongue.

Troy breaks the seal on the bottle, takes a drink, and hands it to Bono.

Bono: I see you run right down to Taylors' and told that Alberta gal.

Troy (calling): Hey Rose! *(To Bono.)* I told everybody. Hey, Rose! I went down there to cash my check.

Rose (entering from the house): Hush all that hollering, man! I know you out here. What they say down there at the Commissioner's office?

Troy: You supposed to come when I call you, woman. Bono'll tell you that. *(To Bono.)* Don't Lucille come when you call her?

Rose: Man, hush your mouth. I ain't no dog . . . talk about "come when you call me."

Troy (puts his arm around Rose): You hear this, Bono? I had me an old dog used to get uppity like that. You say, "C'mere, Blue!" . . . and he just lay there and look at you. End up getting a stick and chasing him away trying to make him come.

Rose: I ain't studying you and your dog. I remember you used to sing that old song.

Troy (he sings): Hear it ring! Hear it ring! I had a dog his name was Blue.

Rose: Don't nobody wanna hear you sing that old song.

Troy (sings): You know Blue was mighty true.

Rose: Used to have Cory running around here singing that song.

Bono: Hell, I remember that song myself.

Troy (sings): You know Blue was a good old dog.
  Blue treed a possum in a hollow log.
  That was my daddy's song. My daddy made up that song.
Rose: I don't care who made it up. Don't nobody wanna hear you sing it.
Troy (makes a song like calling a dog): Come here, woman.
Rose: You come in here carrying on, I reckon they ain't fired you. What they say
  down there at the Commissioner's office?
Troy: Look here, Rose . . . Mr. Rand called me into his office today when I got
  back from talking to them people down there . . . it come from up top . . .
  he called me in and told me they was making me a driver.
Rose: Troy, you kidding!
Troy: No I ain't. Ask Bono.
Rose: Well, that's great, Troy. Now you don't have to hassle them people no
  more.

  Lyons enters from the street.

Troy: Aw hell, I wasn't looking to see you today. I thought you was in jail. Got
  it all over the front page of the *Courier* about them raiding Sefus's
  place . . . where you be hanging out with all them thugs.
Lyons: Hey, Pop . . . that ain't got nothing to do with me. I don't go down
  there gambling. I go down there to sit in with the band. I ain't got noth-
  ing to do with the gambling part. They got some good music down
  there.
Troy: They got some rogues . . . is what they got.
Lyons: How you been, Mr. Bono? Hi, Rose.
Bono: I see where you playing down at the Crawford Grill tonight.
Rose: How come you ain't brought Bonnie like I told you? You should have
  brought Bonnie with you, she ain't been over in a month of Sundays.
Lyons: I was just in the neighborhood . . . thought I'd stop by.
Troy: Here he come . . .
Bono: Your daddy got a promotion on the rubbish. He's gonna be the first col-
  ored driver. Ain't got to do nothing but sit up there and read the paper like
  them white fellows.
Lyons: Hey, Pop . . . if you knew how to read you'd be all right.
Bono: Naw . . . naw . . . you mean if the nigger knew how to *drive* he'd be all
  right. Been fighting with them people about driving and ain't even got a license. Mr. Rand know you ain't got no driver's license?
Troy: Driving ain't nothing. All you do is point the truck where you want it to
  go. Driving ain't nothing.
Bono: Do Mr. Rand know you ain't got no driver's license? That's what I'm
  talking about. I ain't asked if driving was easy. I asked if Mr. Rand know
  you ain't got no driver's license.
Troy: He ain't got to know. The man ain't got to know my business. Time he
  find out, I have two or three driver's licenses.
Lyons (going into his pocket): Say, look here, Pop . . .
Troy: I knew it was coming. Didn't I tell you, Bono? I know what kind of "Look
  here, Pop" that was. The nigger fixing to ask me for some money. It's Friday night. It's my payday. All them rogues down there on the avenue . . .
  the ones that ain't in jail . . . and Lyons is hopping in his shoes to get
  down there with them.

Lyons: See, Pop . . . if you give somebody else a chance to talk sometimes, you'd see that I was fixing to pay you back your ten dollars like I told you. Here . . . I told you I'd pay you when Bonnie got paid.

Troy: Naw . . . you go ahead and keep that ten dollars. Put it in the bank. The next time you feel like you wanna come by here and ask me for something . . . you go on down there and get that.

Lyons: Here's your ten dollars, Pop. I told you I don't want you to give me nothing. I just wanted to borrow ten dollars.

Troy: Naw . . . you go on and keep that for the next time you want to ask me.

Lyons: Come on, Pop . . . here go your ten dollars.

Rose: Why don't you go on and let the boy pay you back, Troy?

Lyons: Here you go, Rose. If you don't take it I'm gonna have to hear about it for the next six months. *(He hands her the money.)*

Rose: You can hand yours over here too, Troy.

Troy: You see this, Bono. You see how they do me.

Bono: Yeah, Lucille do me the same way.

> *Gabriel is heard singing offstage. He enters.*

Gabriel: Better get ready for the Judgment! Better get ready for . . . Hey! . . . Hey! . . . There's Troy's boy!

Lyons: How are you doing, Uncle Gabe?

Gabriel: Lyons . . . The King of the Jungle! Rose . . . hey, Rose. Got a flower for you. *(He takes a rose from his pocket.)* Picked it myself. That's the same rose like you is!

Rose: That's right nice of you, Gabe.

Lyons: What you been doing, Uncle Gabe?

Gabriel: Oh, I been chasing hellhounds and waiting on the time to tell St. Peter to open the gates.

Lyons: You been chasing hellhounds, huh? Well . . . you doing the right thing, Uncle Gabe. Somebody got to chase them.

Gabriel: Oh, yeah . . . I know it. The devil's strong. The devil ain't no pushover. Hellhounds snipping at everybody's heels. But I got my trumpet waiting on the judgment time.

Lyons: Waiting on the Battle of Armageddon, huh?

Gabriel: Ain't gonna be too much of a battle when God get to waving that Judgment sword. But the people's gonna have a hell of a time trying to get into heaven if them gates ain't open.

Lyons (putting his arm around Gabriel): You hear this, Pop. Uncle Gabe, you all right!

Gabriel (laughing with Lyons): Lyons! King of the Jungle.

Rose: You gonna stay for supper, Gabe? Want me to fix you a plate?

Gabriel: I'll take a sandwich, Rose. Don't want no plate. Just wanna eat with my hands. I'll take a sandwich.

Rose: How about you, Lyons? You staying? Got some short ribs cooking.

Lyons: Naw, I won't eat nothing till after we finished playing. *(Pause.)* You ought to come down and listen to me play Pop.

Troy: I don't like that Chinese music. All that noise.

Rose: Go on in the house and wash up, Gabe . . . I'll fix you a sandwich.

Gabriel (to Lyons, as he exits): Troy's mad at me.

Lyons: What you mad at Uncle Gabe for, Pop?

Rose: He thinks Troy's mad at him cause he moved over to Miss Pearl's.

Troy: I ain't mad at the man. He can live where he want to live at.

Lyons: What he move over there for? Miss Pearl don't like nobody.

Rose: She don't mind him none. She treats him real nice. She just don't allow all that singing.

Troy: She don't mind that rent he be paying . . . that's what she don't mind.

Rose: Troy, I ain't going through that with you no more. He's over there cause he want to have his own place. He can come and go as he please.

Troy: Hell, he could come and go as he please here. I wasn't stopping him. I ain't put no rules on him.

Rose: It ain't the same thing, Troy. And you know it.

Gabriel comes to the door.

Now, that's the last I wanna hear about that. I don't wanna hear nothing else about Gabe and Miss Pearl. And next week . . .

Gabriel: I'm ready for my sandwich, Rose.

Rose: And next week . . . when that recruiter come from that school . . . I want you to sign that paper and go on and let Cory play football. Then that'll be the last I have to hear about that.

Troy (to Rose as she exits into the house): I ain't thinking about Cory nothing.

Lyons: What . . . Cory got recruited? What school he going to?

Troy: That boy walking around here smelling his piss . . . thinking he's grown. Thinking he's gonna do what he want, irrespective of what I say. Look here, Bono . . . I left the Commissioner's office and went down to the A&P . . . that boy ain't working down there. He lying to me. Telling me he got his job back . . . telling me he working weekends . . . telling me he working after school . . . Mr. Stawicki tell me he ain't working down there at all!

Lyons: Cory just growing up. He's just busting at the seams trying to fill out your shoes.

Troy: I don't care what he's doing. When he get to the point where he wanna disobey me . . . then it's time for him to move on. Bono'll tell you that. I bet he ain't never disobeyed his daddy without paying the consequences.

Bono: I ain't never had a chance. My daddy came on through . . . but I ain't never knew him to see him . . . or what he had on his mind or where he went. Just moving on through. Searching out the New Land. That's what the old folks used to call it. See a fellow moving around from place to place . . . woman to woman . . . called it searching out the New Land. I can't say if he ever found it. I come along, didn't want no kids. Didn't know if I was gonna be in one place long enough to fix on them right as their daddy. I figured I was going searching too. As it turned out I been hooked up with Lucille near about as long as your daddy been with Rose. Going on sixteen years.

Troy: Sometimes I wish I hadn't known my daddy. He ain't cared nothing about no kids. A kid to him wasn't nothing. All he wanted was for you to learn how to walk so he could start you to working. When it come time for eating . . . he ate first. If there was anything left over, that's what you got. Man would sit down and eat two chickens and give you the wing.

Lyons: You ought to stop that, Pop. Everybody feed their kids. No matter how hard times is . . . everybody care about their kids. Make sure they have something to eat.

Troy: The only thing my daddy cared about was getting them bales of cotton in to Mr. Lubin. That's the only thing that mattered to him. Sometimes I used to wonder why he was living. Wonder why the devil hadn't come and got him. "Get them bales of cotton in to Mr. Lubin" and find out he owe him money . . .

Lyons: He should have just went on and left when he saw he couldn't get nowhere. That's what I would have done.

Troy: How he gonna leave with eleven kids? And where he gonna go? He ain't knew how to do nothing but farm. No, he was trapped and I think he knew it. But I'll say this for him . . . he felt a responsibility toward us. Maybe he ain't treated us the way I felt he should have . . . but without that responsibility he could have walked off and left us . . . made his own way.

Bono: A lot of them did. Back in those days what you talking about . . . they walk out their front door and just take on down one road or another and keep on walking.

Lyons: There you go! That's what I'm talking about.

Bono: Just keep on walking till you come to something else. Ain't you never heard of nobody having the walking blues? Well, that's what you call it when you just take off like that.

Troy: My daddy ain't had them walking blues! What you talking about? He stayed right there with his family. But he was just as evil as he could be. My mama couldn't stand him. Couldn't stand that evilness. She run off when I was about eight. She sneaked off one night after he had gone to sleep. Told me she was coming back for me. I ain't never seen her no more. All his women run off and left him. He wasn't good for nobody.

When my turn come to head out, I was fourteen and got to sniffing around Joe Canewell's daughter. Had us an old mule we called Greyboy. My daddy sent me out to do some plowing and I tied up Greyboy and went to fooling around with Joe Canewell's daughter. We done found us a nice little spot, got real cozy with each other. She about thirteen and we done figured we was grown anyway . . . so we down there enjoying ourselves . . . ain't thinking about nothing. We didn't know Greyboy had got loose and wandered back to the house and my daddy was looking for me. We down there by the creek enjoying ourselves when my daddy come up on us. Surprised us. He had them leather straps off the mule and commenced to whupping me like there was no tomorrow. I jumped up, mad and embarrassed. I was scared of my daddy. When he commenced to whupping on me . . . quite naturally I run to get out of the way. *(Pause.)* Now I thought he was mad cause I ain't done my work. But I see where he was chasing me off so he could have the gal for himself. When I see what the matter of it was, I lost all fear of my daddy. Right there is where I become a man . . . at fourteen years of age. *(Pause.)* Now it was my turn to run him off. I picked up them same reins that he had used on me. I picked up them reins and commenced to whupping on him. The gal jumped up and run off . . . and when my daddy turned to face me, I could see why the devil had never come to get him . . . cause he was the devil himself. I don't know what happened. When I woke up, I was laying right there by the creek, and Blue . . . this old dog we had . . . was licking my face. I thought I was blind. I couldn't see nothing. Both my eyes were swollen shut. I laid there and cried. I didn't know what I was gonna do. The only thing I knew was the time had come for me to leave my daddy's house. And right there the world suddenly got big. And it was a long time before I could cut it down to where I could handle it.

   Part of that cutting down was when I got to the place where I could feel him kicking in my blood and knew that the only thing that separated us was the matter of a few years.

Gabriel enters from the house with a sandwich.

Lyons: What you got there, Uncle Gabe?

Gabriel: Got me a ham sandwich. Rose gave me a ham sandwich.

Troy: I don't know what happened to him. I done lost touch with everybody except Gabriel. But I hope he's dead. I hope he found some peace.

Lyons: That's a heavy story, Pop. I didn't know you left home when you was fourteen.

Troy: And didn't know nothing. The only part of the world I knew was the forty-two acres of Mr. Lubin's land. That's all I knew about life.

Lyons: Fourteen's kinda young to be out on your own. *(Phone rings.)* I don't even think I was ready to be out on my own at fourteen. I don't know what I would have done.

Troy: I got up from the creek and walked on down to Mobile. I was through with farming. Figured I could do better in the city. So I walked the two hundred miles to Mobile.

Lyons: Wait a minute . . . you ain't walked no two hundred miles, Pop. Ain't nobody gonna walk no two hundred miles. You talking about some walking there.

Bono: That's the only way you got anywhere back in them days.

Lyons: Shhh. Damn if I wouldn't have hitched a ride with somebody!

Troy: Who you gonna hitch it with? They ain't had no cars and things like they got now. We talking about 1918.

Rose (entering): What you all out here getting into?

Troy (to Rose): I'm telling Lyons how good he got it. He don't know nothing about this I'm talking.

Rose: Lyons, that was Bonnie on the phone. She say you supposed to pick her up.

Lyons: Yeah, okay, Rose.

Troy: I walked on down to Mobile and hitched up with some of them fellows that was heading this way. Got up here and found out . . . not only couldn't you get a job . . . you couldn't find no place to live. I thought I was in freedom. Shhh. Colored folks living down there on the riverbanks in whatever kind of shelter they could find for themselves. Right down there under the Brady Street Bridge. Living in shacks made of sticks and tarpaper. Messed around there and went from bad to worse. Started stealing. First it was food. Then I figured, hell, if I steal money I can buy me some food. Buy me some shoes too! One thing led to another. Met your mama. I was young and anxious to be a man. Met your mama and had you. What I do that for? Now I got to worry about feeding you and her. Got to steal three times as much. Went out one day looking for somebody to rob . . . that's what I was, a robber. I'll tell you the truth. I'm ashamed of it today. But it's the truth. Went to rob this fellow . . . pulled out my knife . . . and he pulled out a gun. Shot me in the chest. I felt just like somebody had taken a hot branding iron and laid it on me. When he shot me I jumped at him with my knife. They told me I killed him and they put me in the penitentiary and locked me up for fifteen years. That's where I met Bono. That's where I learned how to play baseball. Got out that place and your mama had taken you and went on to make life without me. Fifteen years was a long time for her to wait. But that fifteen years cured me of that robbing stuff. Rose'll tell you. She asked me when I met her if I had gotten all that foolishness out of my system. And I told her, "Baby, it's you and baseball all what count with me." You hear me, Bono? I meant it too. She say, "Which one comes first?" I told her, "Baby, ain't no doubt it's baseball . . . but you stick and get old with me and we'll both outlive this baseball." Am I right, Rose? And it's true.

Rose: Man, hush your mouth. You ain't said no such thing. Talking about, "Baby, you know you'll always be number one with me." That's what you was talking.

Troy: You hear that, Bono. That's why I love her.

Bono: Rose'll keep you straight. You get off the track, she'll straighten you up.

Rose: Lyons, you better get on up and get Bonnie. She waiting on you.

Lyons (gets up to go): Hey, Pop, why don't you come on down to the Grill and hear me play?

Troy: I ain't going down there. I'm too old to be sitting around in them clubs.

Bono: You got to be good to play down at the Grill.

Lyons: Come on, Pop . . .

Troy: I got to get up in the morning.

Lyons: You ain't got to stay long.

Troy: Naw, I'm gonna get my supper and go on to bed.

Lyons: Well, I got to go. I'll see you again.

Troy: Don't you come around my house on my payday.

Rose: Pick up the phone and let somebody know you coming. And bring Bonnie with you. You know I'm always glad to see her.

Lyons: Yeah, I'll do that, Rose. You take care now. See you, Pop. See you, Mr. Bono. See you, Uncle Gabe.

Gabriel: Lyons! King of the Jungle!

Lyons exits.

Troy: Is supper ready, woman? Me and you got some business to take care of. I'm gonna tear it up too.

Rose: Troy, I done told you now!

Troy (puts his arm around Bono): Aw hell, woman . . . this is Bono. Bono like family. I done known this nigger since . . . how long I done know you?

Bono: It's been a long time.

Troy: I done know this nigger since Skippy was a pup. Me and him done been through some times.

Bono: You sure right about that.

Troy: Hell, I done know him longer than I known you. And we still standing shoulder to shoulder. Hey, look here, Bono . . . a man can't ask for no more than that. *(Drinks to him.)* I love you, nigger.

Bono: Hell, I love you too . . . I got to get home see my woman. You got yours in hand. I got to go get mine.

> *Bono starts to exit as Cory enters the yard, dressed in his football uniform. He gives Troy a hard, uncompromising look.*

Cory: What you do that for, Pop?

> *He throws his helmet down in the direction of Troy.*

Rose: What's the matter? Cory . . . what's the matter?

Cory: Papa done went up to the school and told Coach Zellman I can't play football no more. Wouldn't even let me play the game. Told him to tell the recruiter not to come.

Rose: Troy . . .

Troy: What you Troying me for. Yeah, I did it. And the boy know why I did it.

Cory: Why you wanna do that to me? That was the one chance I had.

Rose: Ain't nothing wrong with Cory playing football, Troy.

Troy: The boy lied to me. I told the nigger if he wanna play football . . . to keep up his chores and hold down that job at the A&P. That was the conditions. Stopped down there to see Mr. Stawicki . . .

Cory: I can't work after school during the football season, Pop! I tried to tell you that Mr. Stawicki's holding my job for me. You don't never want to listen to nobody. And then you wanna go and do this to me!

Troy: I ain't done nothing to you. You done it to yourself.

Cory: Just cause you didn't have a chance! You just scared I'm gonna be better than you, that's all.

Troy: Come here.

Rose: Troy . . .

> *Cory reluctantly crosses over to Troy.*

Troy: All right! See. You done made a mistake.

Cory: I didn't even do nothing!

Troy: I'm gonna tell you what your mistake was. See . . . you swung at the ball and didn't hit it. That's strike one. See, you in the batter's box now. You swung and you missed. That's strike one. Don't you strike out!

> *Lights fade to black.*

ACT II

SCENE I

> *The following morning. Cory is at the tree hitting the ball with the bat. He tries to mimic Troy, but his swing is awkward, less sure. Rose enters from the house.*

Rose: Cory, I want you to help me with this cupboard.

Cory: I ain't quitting the team. I don't care what Poppa say.

Rose: I'll talk to him when he gets back. He had to go see about your Uncle Gabe. The police done arrested him. Say he was disturbing the peace. He'll be back directly. Come on in here and help me clean out the top of this cupboard.

Cory exits into the house. Rose sees Troy and Bono coming down the alley.

Troy . . . what they say down there?

Troy: Ain't said nothing. I give them fifty dollars and they let him go. I'll talk to you about it. Where's Cory?

Rose: He's in there helping me clean out these cupboards.

Troy: Tell him to get his butt out here.

Troy and Bono go over to the pile of wood. Bono picks up the saw and begins sawing.

Troy (to Bono): All they want is the money. That makes six or seven times I done went down there and got him. See me coming they stick out their hands.

Bono: Yeah. I know what you mean. That's all they care about . . . that money. They don't care about what's right. *(Pause.)* Nigger, why you got to go and get some hard wood? You ain't doing nothing but building a little old fence. Get you some soft pine wood. That's all you need.

Troy: I know what I'm doing. This is outside wood. You put pine wood inside the house. Pine wood is inside wood. This here is outside wood. Now you tell me where the fence is gonna be?

Bono: You don't need this wood. You can put it up with pine wood and it'll stand as long as you gonna be here looking at it.

Troy: How you know how long I'm gonna be here, nigger? Hell, I might just live forever. Live longer than old man Horsely.

Bono: That's what Magee used to say.

Troy: Magee's a damn fool. Now you tell me who you ever heard of gonna pull their own teeth with a pair of rusty pliers.

Bono: The old folks . . . my granddaddy used to pull his teeth with pliers. They ain't had no dentists for the colored folks back then.

Troy: Get clean pliers! You understand? Clean pliers! Sterilize them! Besides we ain't living back then. All Magee had to do was walk over to Doc Goldblum's.

Bono: I see where you and that Tallahassee gal . . . that Alberta . . . I see where you all done got tight.

Troy: What you mean "got tight"?

Bono: I see where you be laughing and joking with her all the time.

Troy: I laughs and jokes with all of them, Bono. You know me.

Bono: That ain't the kind of laughing and joking I'm talking about.

Cory enters from the house.

Cory: How you doing, Mr. Bono?

Troy: Cory? Get that saw from Bono and cut some wood. He talking about the wood's too hard to cut. Stand back there, Jim, and let that young boy show you how it's done.

Bono: He's sure welcome to it.

Cory takes the saw and begins to cut the wood.

Whew-e-e! Look at that. Big old strong boy. Look like Joe Louis.° Hell, must be getting old the way I'm watching that boy whip through that wood.

Joe Louis (1914–1981): Black American boxer who held the world heavyweight championship title.

Cory: I don't see why Mama want a fence around the yard noways.

Troy: Damn if I know either. What the hell she keeping out with it? She ain't got nothing nobody want.

Bono: Some people build fences to keep people out . . . and other people build fences to keep people in. Rose wants to hold on to you all. She loves you.

Troy: Hell, nigger, I don't need nobody to tell me my wife loves me. Cory . . . go on in the house and see if you can find that other saw.

Cory: Where's it at?

Troy: I said find it! Look for it till you find it!

Cory exits into the house.

What's that supposed to mean? Wanna keep us in?

Bono: Troy . . . I done known you seem like damn near my whole life. You and Rose both. I done know both of you all for a long time. I remember when you met Rose. When you was hitting them baseball out the park. A lot of them old gals was after you then. You had the pick of the litter. When you picked Rose, I was happy for you. That was the first time I knew you had any sense. I said . . . My man Troy knows what he's doing . . . I'm gonna follow this nigger . . . he might take me somewhere. I been following you too. I done learned a whole heap of things about life watching you. I done learned how to tell where the shit lies. How to tell it from the alfalfa. You done learned me a lot of things. You showed me how to not make the same mistakes . . . to take life as it comes along and keep putting one foot in front of the other. *(Pause.)* Rose a good woman, Troy.

Troy: Hell, nigger, I know she a good woman. I been married to her for eighteen years. What you got on your mind, Bono?

Bono: I just say she a good woman. Just like I say anything. I ain't got to have nothing on my mind.

Troy: You just gonna say she a good woman and leave it hanging out there like that? Why you telling me she a good woman?

Bono: She loves you, Troy. Rose loves you.

Troy: You saying I don't measure up. That's what you trying to say. I don't measure up cause I'm seeing this other gal. I know what you trying to say.

Bono: I know what Rose means to you, Troy. I'm just trying to say I don't want to see you mess up.

Troy: Yeah, I appreciate that, Bono. If you was messing around on Lucille I'd be telling you the same thing.

Bono: Well, that's all I got to say. I just say that because I love you both.

Troy: Hell, you know me . . . I wasn't out there looking for nothing. You can't find a better woman than Rose. I know that. But seems like this woman just stuck onto me where I can't shake her loose. I done wrestled with it, tried to throw her off me . . . but she just stuck on tighter. Now she's stuck on for good.

Bono: You's in control . . . that's what you tell me all the time. You responsible for what you do.

Troy: I ain't ducking the responsibility of it. As long as it sets right in my heart . . . then I'm okay. Cause that's all I listen to. It'll tell me right from wrong every time. And I ain't talking about doing Rose no bad turn. I love Rose. She done carried me a long ways and I love and respect her for that.

Bono: I know you do. That's why I don't want to see you hurt her. But what you gonna do when she find out? What you got then? If you try and juggle both of them . . . sooner or later you gonna drop one of them. That's common sense.

Troy: Yeah, I hear what you saying, Bono. I been trying to figure a way to work it out.

Bono: Work it out right, Troy. I don't want to be getting all up between you and Rose's business . . . but work it so it come out right.

Troy: Ah hell, I get all up between you and Lucille's business. When you gonna get that woman that refrigerator she been wanting? Don't tell me you ain't got no money now. I know who your banker is. Mellon don't need that money bad as Lucille want that refrigerator. I'll tell you that.

Bono: Tell you what I'll do . . . when you finish building this fence for Rose . . . I'll buy Lucille that refrigerator.

Troy: You done stuck your foot in your mouth now!

Troy grabs up a board and begins to saw. Bono starts to walk out the yard.

Hey, nigger . . . where you going?

Bono: I'm going home. I know you don't expect me to help you now. I'm protecting my money. I wanna see you put that fence up by yourself. That's what I want to see. You'll be here another six months without me.

Troy: Nigger, you ain't right.

Bono: When it comes to my money . . . I'm right as fireworks on the Fourth of July.

Troy: All right, we gonna see now. You better get out your bankbook.

Bono exits, and Troy continues to work. Rose enters from the house.

Rose: What they say down there? What's happening with Gabe?

Troy: I went down there and got him out. Cost me fifty dollars. Say he was disturbing the peace. Judge set up a hearing for him in three weeks. Say to show cause why he shouldn't be recommitted.

Rose: What was he doing that cause them to arrest him?

Troy: Some kids was teasing him and he run them off home. Say he was howling and carrying on. Some folks seen him and called the police. That's all it was.

Rose: Well, what's you say? What'd you tell the judge?

Troy: Told him I'd look after him. It didn't make no sense to recommit the man. He stuck out his big greasy palm and told me to give him fifty dollars and take him on home.

Rose: Where's he at now? Where'd he go off to?

Troy: He's gone about his business. He don't need nobody to hold his hand.

Rose: Well, I don't know. Seem like that would be the best place for him if they did put him into the hospital. I know what you're gonna say. But that's what I think would be best.

Troy: The man done had his life ruined fighting for what? And they wanna take and lock him up. Let him be free. He don't bother nobody.

Rose: Well, everybody got their own way of looking at it I guess. Come on and get your lunch. I got a bowl of lima beans and some cornbread in the oven. Come and get something to eat. Ain't no sense you fretting over Gabe.

Rose turns to go into the house.

Troy: Rose . . . got something to tell you.

Rose: Well, come on . . . wait till I get this food on the table.

Troy: Rose!

> *She stops and turns around.*

I don't know how to say this. *(Pause.)* I can't explain it none. It just sort of grows on you till it gets out of hand. It starts out like a little bush . . . and the next thing you know it's a whole forest.

Rose: Troy . . . what is you talking about?

Troy: I'm talking, woman, let me talk. I'm trying to find a way to tell you . . . I'm gonna be a daddy. I'm gonna be somebody's daddy.

Rose: Troy . . . you're not telling me this? You're gonna be . . . what?

Troy: Rose . . . now . . . see . . .

Rose: You telling me you gonna be somebody's daddy? You telling your *wife* this?

> *Gabriel enters from the street. He carries a rose in his hand.*

Gabriel: Hey, Troy! Hey, Rose!

Rose: I have to wait eighteen years to hear something like this.

Gabriel: Hey, Rose . . . I got a flower for you. *(He hands it to her.)* That's a rose. Same rose like you is.

Rose: Thanks, Gabe.

Gabriel: Troy, you ain't mad at me is you? Them bad mens come and put me away. You ain't mad at me is you?

Troy: Naw, Gabe, I ain't mad at you.

Rose: Eighteen years and you wanna come with this.

Gabriel (takes a quarter out of his pocket): See what I got? Got a brand new quarter.

Troy: Rose . . . it's just . . .

Rose: Ain't nothing you can say, Troy. Ain't no way of explaining that.

Gabriel: Fellow that give me this quarter had a whole mess of them. I'm gonna keep this quarter till it stop shining.

Rose: Gabe, go on in the house there. I got some watermelon in the Frigidaire. Go on and get you a piece.

Gabriel: Say, Rose . . . you know I was chasing hellhounds and them bad mens come and get me and take me away. Troy helped me. He come down there and told them they better let me go before he beat them up. Yeah, he did!

Rose: You go on and get you a piece of watermelon, Gabe. Them bad mens is gone now.

Gabriel: Okay, Rose . . . gonna get me some watermelon. The kind with the stripes on it.

> *Gabriel exits into the house.*

Rose: Why, Troy? Why? After all these years to come dragging this in to me now. It don't make no sense at your age. I could have expected this ten or fifteen years ago, but not now.

Troy: Age ain't got nothing to do with it, Rose.

Rose: I done tried to be everything a wife should be. Everything a wife could be. Been married eighteen years and I got to live to see the day you tell me you been seeing another woman and done fathered a child by her. And you know I ain't never wanted no half nothing in my family. My whole family is half. Everybody got different fathers and mothers . . . my two sisters and my brother. Can't hardly tell who's who. Can't never sit down and talk about Papa and Mama. It's your papa and your mama and my papa and my mama . . .

Troy: Rose . . . stop it now.

Rose: I ain't never wanted that for none of my children. And now you wanna drag your behind in here and tell me something like this.

Troy: You ought to know. It's time for you to know.

Rose: Well, I don't want to know, goddamn it!

Troy: I can't just make it go away. It's done now. I can't wish the circumstance of the thing away.

Rose: And you don't want to either. Maybe you want to wish me and my boy away. Maybe that's what you want? Well, you can't wish us away. I've got eighteen years of my life invested in you. You ought to have stayed upstairs in my bed where you belong.

Troy: Rose . . . now listen to me . . . we can get a handle on this thing. We can talk this out . . . come to an understanding.

Rose: All of a sudden it's "we." Where was "we" at when you was down there rolling around with some godforsaken woman? "We" should have come to an understanding before you started making a damn fool of yourself. You're a day late and a dollar short when it comes to an understanding with me.

Troy: It's just . . . She gives me a different idea . . . a different understanding about myself. I can step out of this house and get away from the pressures and problems . . . be a different man. I ain't got to wonder how I'm gonna pay the bills or get the roof fixed. I can just be a part of myself that I ain't never been.

Rose: What I want to know . . . is do you plan to continue seeing her. That's all you can say to me.

Troy: I can sit up in her house and laugh. Do you understand what I'm saying. I can laugh out loud . . . and it feels good. It reaches all the way down to the bottom of my shoes. *(Pause.)* Rose, I can't give that up.

Rose: Maybe you ought to go on and stay down there with her . . . if she's a better woman than me.

Troy: It ain't about nobody being a better woman or nothing. Rose, you ain't the blame. A man couldn't ask for no woman to be a better wife than you've been. I'm responsible for it. I done locked myself into a pattern trying to take care of you all that I forgot about myself.

Rose: What the hell was I there for? That was my job, not somebody else's.

Troy: Rose, I done tried all my life to live decent . . . to live a clean . . . hard . . . useful life. I tried to be a good husband to you. In every way I knew how. Maybe I come into the world backwards, I don't know. But . . . you born with two strikes on you before you come to the plate. You got to guard it closely . . . always looking for the curve ball on the inside corner. You can't afford to let none get past you. You can't afford a call strike. If you going down . . . you going down swinging. Everything lined up against you. What you gonna do. I fooled them, Rose. I bunted. When I found you and Cory and a halfway decent job . . . I was safe. Couldn't nothing touch me. I wasn't gonna strike out no more. I wasn't going back to the penitentiary. I wasn't gonna lay in the streets with a bottle of wine. I was safe. I had me a family. A job. I wasn't gonna get that last strike. I was on first looking for one of them boys to knock me in. To get me home.

Rose: You should have stayed in my bed, Troy.

Troy: Then when I saw that gal . . . she firmed up my backbone. And I got to thinking that if I tried . . . I just might be able to steal second. Do you understand after eighteen years I wanted to steal second.

Rose: You should have held me tight. You should have grabbed me and held on.

Troy: I stood on first base for eighteen years and I thought . . . well, goddamn it . . . go on for it!

Rose: We're not talking about baseball! We're talking about you going off to lay in bed with another woman . . . and then bring it home to me. That's what we're talking about. We ain't talking about no baseball.

Troy: Rose, you're not listening to me. I'm trying the best I can to explain it to you. It's not easy for me to admit that I been standing in the same place for eighteen years.

Rose: I been standing with you! I been right here with you, Troy. I got a life too. I gave eighteen years of my life to stand in the same spot with you. Don't you think I ever wanted other things? Don't you think I had dreams and hopes? What about my life? What about me. Don't you think it ever crossed my mind to want to know other men? That I wanted to lay up somewhere and forget about my responsibilities? That I wanted someone to make me laugh so I could feel good? You not the only one who's got wants and needs. But I held on to you, Troy. I took all my feelings, my wants and needs, my dreams . . . and I buried them inside you. I planted a seed and watched and prayed over it. I planted myself inside you and waited to bloom. And it didn't take me no eighteen years to find out the soil was hard and rocky and it wasn't never gonna bloom.

But I held on to you, Troy. I held you tighter. You was my husband. I owed you everything I had. Every part of me I could find to give you. And upstairs in that room . . . with the darkness falling in on me . . . I gave everything I had to try and erase the doubt that you wasn't the finest man in the world. And wherever you was going . . . I wanted to be there with you. Cause you was my husband. Cause that's the only way I was gonna survive as your wife. You always talking about what you give . . . and what you don't have to give. But you take too. You take . . . and don't even know nobody's giving!

Rose turns to exit into the house; Troy grabs her arm.

Troy: You say I take and don't give!

Rose: Troy! You're hurting me!

Troy: You say I take and don't give!

Rose: Troy . . . you're hurting my arm! Let go!

Troy: I done give you everything I got. Don't you tell that lie on me.

Rose: Troy!

Troy: Don't you tell that lie on me!

Cory enters from the house.

Cory: Mama!

Rose: Troy. You're hurting me.

Troy: Don't you tell me about no taking and giving.

Cory comes up behind Troy and grabs him. Troy, surprised, is thrown off balance just as Cory throws a glancing blow that catches him on the chest and knocks him down. Troy is stunned, as is Cory.

Rose: Troy. Troy. No!

Troy gets to his feet and starts at Cory.

Troy . . . no. Please! Troy!

Rose pulls on Troy to hold him back. Troy stops himself.

Troy (to Cory): All right. That's strike two. You stay away from around me, boy. Don't you strike out. You living with a full count. Don't you strike out.

Troy exits out the yard as the lights go down.

Scene II

It is six months later, early afternoon. Troy enters from the house and starts to exit the yard. Rose enters from the house.

Rose: Troy, I want to talk to you.

Troy: All of a sudden, after all this time, you want to talk to me, huh? You ain't wanted to talk to me for months. You ain't wanted to talk to me last night. You ain't wanted no part of me then. What you wanna talk to me about now?

Rose: Tomorrow's Friday.

Troy: I know what day tomorrow is. You think I don't know tomorrow's Friday? My whole life I ain't done nothing but look to see Friday coming and you got to tell me it's Friday.

Rose: I want to know if you're coming home.

Troy: I always come home, Rose. You know that. There ain't never been a night I ain't come home.

Rose: That ain't what I mean . . . and you know it. I want to know if you're coming straight home after work.

Troy: I figure I'd cash my check . . . hang out at Taylors' with the boys . . . maybe play a game of checkers . . .

Rose: Troy, I can't live like this. I won't live like this. You livin' on borrowed time with me. It's been going on six months now you ain't been coming home.

Troy: I be here every night. Every night of the year. That's 365 days.

Rose: I want you to come home tomorrow after work.

Troy: Rose . . . I don't mess up my pay. You know that now. I take my pay and I give it to you. I don't have no money but what you give me back. I just want to have a little time to myself . . . a little time to enjoy life.

Rose: What about me? When's my time to enjoy life?

Troy: I don't know what to tell you, Rose. I'm doing the best I can.

Rose: You ain't been home from work but time enough to change your clothes and run out . . . and you wanna call that the best you can do?

Troy: I'm going over to the hospital to see Alberta. She went into the hospital this afternoon. Look like she might have the baby early. I won't be gone long.

Rose: Well, you ought to know. They went over to Miss Pearl's and got Gabe today. She said you told them to go ahead and lock him up.

Troy: I ain't said no such thing. Whoever told you that is telling a lie. Pearl ain't doing nothing but telling a big fat lie.

Rose: She ain't had to tell me. I read it on the papers.

Troy: I ain't told them nothing of the kind.

Rose: I saw it right there on the papers.

Troy: What it say, huh?

Rose: It said you told them to take him.

Troy: Then they screwed that up, just the way they screw up everything. I ain't worried about what they got on the paper.

Rose: Say the government send part of his check to the hospital and the other part to you.

Troy: I ain't got nothing to do with that if that's the way it works. I ain't made up the rules about how it work.

Rose: You did Gabe just like you did Cory. You wouldn't sign the paper for Cory . . . but you signed for Gabe. You signed that paper.

The telephone is heard ringing inside the house.

Troy: I told you I ain't signed nothing, woman! The only thing I signed was the release form. Hell, I can't read, I don't know what they had on that paper! I ain't signed nothing about sending Gabe away.

Rose: I said send him to the hospital . . . you said let him be free . . . now you done went down there and signed him to the hospital for half his money. You went back on yourself, Troy. You gonna have to answer for that.

Troy: See now . . . you been over there talking to Miss Pearl. She done got mad cause she ain't getting Gabe's rent money. That's all it is. She's liable to say anything.

Rose: Troy, I seen where you signed the paper.

Troy: You ain't seen nothing I signed. What she doing got papers on my brother anyway? Miss Pearl telling a big fat lie. And I'm gonna tell her about it too! You ain't seen nothing I signed. Say . . . you ain't seen nothing I signed.

Rose exits into the house to answer the telephone. Presently she returns.

Rose: Troy . . . that was the hospital. Alberta had the baby.

Troy: What she have? What is it?

Rose: It's a girl.

Troy: I better get on down to the hospital to see her.

Rose: Troy . . .

Troy: Rose . . . I got to go see her now. That's only right . . . what's the matter . . . the baby's all right, ain't it?

Rose: Alberta died having the baby.

Troy: Died . . . you say she's dead? Alberta's dead?

Rose: They said they done all they could. They couldn't do nothing for her.

Troy: The baby? How's the baby?

Rose: They say it's healthy. I wonder who's gonna bury her.

Troy: She had family, Rose. She wasn't living in the world by herself.

Rose: I know she wasn't living in the world by herself.

Troy: Next thing you gonna want to know if she had any insurance.

Rose: Troy, you ain't got to talk like that.

Troy: That's the first thing that jumped out your mouth. "Who's gonna bury her?" Like I'm fixing to take on that task for myself.

Rose: I am your wife. Don't push me away.

Troy: I ain't pushing nobody away. Just give me some space. That's all. Just give me some room to breathe.

Rose exits into the house. Troy walks about the yard.

Troy (with a quiet rage that threatens to consume him): All right . . . Mr. Death. See now . . . I'm gonna tell you what I'm gonna do. I'm gonna take and build me a fence around this yard. See? I'm gonna build me a fence around what belongs to me. And then I want you to stay on the other side. See? You stay over there until you're ready for me. Then you come on. Bring your army. Bring your sickle. Bring your wrestling clothes. I ain't gonna fall down on my vigilance this time. You ain't gonna sneak up on me no more. When you ready for me . . . when the top of your list say Troy Maxson . . . that's when you come around here. You come up and knock on the front door. Ain't nobody else got nothing to do with this. This is between you and me. Man to man. You stay on the other side of that fence until you ready for me. Then you come up and knock on the front door. Anytime you want. I'll be ready for you.

The lights go down to black.

SCENE III

The lights come up on the porch. It is late evening three days later. Rose sits listening to the ball game waiting for Troy. The final out of the game is made and Rose switches off the radio. Troy enters the yard carrying an infant wrapped in blankets. He stands back from the house and calls.

    Rose enters and stands on the porch. There is a long, awkward silence, the weight of which grows heavier with each passing second.

Troy: Rose . . . I'm standing here with my daughter in my arms. She ain't but a wee bittie little old thing. She don't know nothing about grownups' business. She innocent . . . and she ain't got no mama.

Rose: What you telling me for, Troy?

She turns and exits into the house.

Troy: Well . . . I guess we'll just sit out here on the porch.

He sits down on the porch. There is an awkward indelicateness about the way he handles the baby. His largeness engulfs and seems to swallow it. He speaks loud enough for Rose to hear.

A man's got to do what's right for him. I ain't sorry for nothing I done. It felt right in my heart. *(To the baby.)* What you smiling at? Your daddy's a big man. Got these great big old hands. But sometimes he's scared. And right now your daddy's scared cause we sitting out here and ain't got no home. Oh, I been homeless before. I ain't had no little baby with me. But I been homeless. You just be out on the road by your lonesome and you see one of them trains coming and you just kinda go like this . . .

He sings as a lullaby.

Please, Mr. Engineer let a man ride the line
Please, Mr. Engineer let a man ride the line
I ain't got no ticket please let me ride the blinds

Rose enters from the house. Troy, hearing her steps behind him, stands and faces her.

She's my daughter, Rose. My own flesh and blood. I can't deny her no more than I can deny them boys. *(Pause.)* You and them boys is my family. You and them and this child is all I got in the world. So I guess what I'm saying is . . . I'd appreciate it if you'd help me take care of her.

Rose: Okay, Troy . . . you're right. I'll take care of your baby for you . . . cause . . . like you say . . . she's innocent . . . and you can't visit the sins of the father upon the child. A motherless child has got a hard time. *(She takes the baby from him.)* From right now . . . this child got a mother. But you a womanless man.

Rose turns and exits into the house with the baby. Lights go down to black.

Scene IV

It is two months later. Lyons enters from the street. He knocks on the door and calls.

Lyons: Hey, Rose! *(Pause.)* Rose!

Rose (from inside the house): Stop that yelling. You gonna wake up Raynell. I just got her to sleep.

Lyons: I just stopped by to pay Papa this twenty dollars I owe him. Where's Papa at?

Rose: He should be here in a minute. I'm getting ready to go down to the church. Sit down and wait on him.

Lyons: I got to go pick up Bonnie over her mother's house.

Rose: Well, sit it down there on the table. He'll get it.

Lyons (enters the house and sets the money on the table): Tell Papa I said thanks. I'll see you again.

Rose: All right, Lyons. We'll see you.

Lyons starts to exit as Cory enters.

Cory: Hey, Lyons.

Lyons: What's happening, Cory? Say man, I'm sorry I missed your graduation. You know I had a gig and couldn't get away. Otherwise, I would have been there, man. So what you doing?

Cory: I'm trying to find a job.

Lyons: Yeah I know how that go, man. It's rough out here. Jobs are scarce.

Cory: Yeah, I know.

Lyons: Look here, I got to run. Talk to Papa . . . he know some people. He'll be able to help get you a job. Talk to him . . . see what he say.

Cory: Yeah . . . all right, Lyons.

Lyons: You take care. I'll talk to you soon. We'll find some time to talk.

Lyons exits the yard. Cory wanders over to the tree, picks up the bat, and assumes a batting stance. He studies an imaginary pitcher and swings. Dissatisfied with the result, he tries again. Troy enters. They eye each other for a beat. Cory puts the bat down and exits the yard. Troy starts into the house as Rose exits with Raynell. She is carrying a cake.

Troy: I'm coming in and everybody's going out.

Rose: I'm taking this cake down to the church for the bake sale. Lyons was by to see you. He stopped by to pay you your twenty dollars. It's laying in there on the table.

Troy (going into his pocket): Well . . . here go this money.

Rose: Put it in there on the table, Troy. I'll get it.

Troy: What time you coming back?

Rose: Ain't no use in you studying me. It don't matter what time I come back.

Troy: I just asked you a question, woman. What's the matter . . . can't I ask you a question?

Rose: Troy, I don't want to go into it. Your dinner's in there on the stove. All you got to do is heat it up. And don't you be eating the rest of them cakes in there. I'm coming back for them. We having a bake sale at the church tomorrow.

Rose exits the yard. Troy sits down on the steps, takes a pint bottle from his pocket, opens it, and drinks. He begins to sing.

Troy: Hear it ring! Hear it ring!
Had an old dog his name was Blue
You know Blue was mighty true
You know Blue was a good old dog
Blue trees a possum in a hollow log
You know from that he was a good old dog

Bono enters the yard.

Bono: Hey, Troy.

Troy: Hey, what's happening, Bono?

Bono: I just thought I'd stop by to see you.

Troy: What you stop by and see me for? You ain't stopped by in a month of Sundays. Hell, I must owe you money or something.

Bono: Since you got your promotion I can't keep up with you. Used to see you every day. Now I don't even know what route you working.

Troy: They keep switching me around. Got me out in Greentree now . . . hauling white folks' garbage.

Bono: Greentree, huh? You lucky, at least you ain't got to be lifting them barrels. Damn if they ain't getting heavier. I'm gonna put in my two years and call it quits.

Troy: I'm thinking about retiring myself.

Bono: You got it easy. You can *drive* for another five years.

Troy: It ain't the same, Bono. It ain't like working the back of the truck. Ain't got nobody to talk to . . . feel like you working by yourself. Naw, I'm thinking about retiring. How's Lucille?

Bono: She all right. Her arthritis get to acting up on her sometime. Saw Rose on my way in. She going down to the church, huh?

Troy: Yeah, she took up going down there. All them preachers looking for somebody to fatten their pockets. *(Pause.)* Got some gin here.

Bono: Naw, thanks. I just stopped by to say hello.

Troy: Hell, nigger . . . you can take a drink. I ain't never known you to say no to a drink. You ain't got to work tomorrow.

Bono: I just stopped by. I'm fixing to go over to Skinner's. We got us a domino game going over his house every Friday.

Troy: Nigger, you can't play no dominoes. I used to whup you four games out of five.

Bono: Well, that learned me. I'm getting better.

Troy: Yeah? Well, that's all right.

Bono: Look here . . . I got to be getting on. Stop by sometime, huh?

Troy: Yeah, I'll do that, Bono. Lucille told Rose you bought her a new refrigerator.

Bono: Yeah, Rose told Lucille you had finally built your fence . . . so I figured we'd call it even.

Troy: I knew you would.

Bono: Yeah . . . okay. I'll be talking to you.

Troy: Yeah, take care, Bono. Good to see you. I'm gonna stop over.

Bono: Yeah. Okay, Troy.

> *Bono exits. Troy drinks from the bottle.*

Troy: Old Blue died and I dig his grave
Let him down with a golden chain
Every night when I hear old Blue bark
I know Blue treed a possum in Noah's Ark.
Hear it ring! Hear it ring!

> *Cory enters the yard. They eye each other for a beat. Troy is sitting in the middle of the steps. Cory walks over.*

Cory: I got to get by.

Troy: Say what? What's you say?

Cory: You in my way. I got to get by.

Troy: You got to get by where? This is my house. Bought and paid for. In full. Took me fifteen years. And if you wanna go in my house and I'm sitting on the steps . . . you say excuse me. Like your mama taught you.

Cory: Come on, Pop . . . I got to get by.

> *Cory starts to maneuver his way past Troy. Troy grabs his leg and shoves him back.*

Troy: You just gonna walk over top of me?

Cory: I live here too!

Troy (advancing toward him): You just gonna walk over top of me in my own house?

Cory: I ain't scared of you.

Troy: I ain't asked if you was scared of me. I asked you if you was fixing to walk over top of me in my own house? That's the question. You ain't gonna say excuse me? You just gonna walk over top of me?

Cory: If you wanna put it like that.

Troy: How else am I gonna put it?

Cory: I was walking by you to go into the house cause you sitting on the steps drunk, singing to yourself. You can put it like that.

Troy: Without saying excuse me???

> *Cory doesn't respond.*

I asked you a question. Without saying excuse me???

Cory: I ain't got to say excuse me to you. You don't count around here no more.

Troy: Oh, I see . . . I don't count around here no more. You ain't got to say excuse me to your daddy. All of a sudden you done got so grown that your daddy don't count around here no more . . . Around here in his own house and yard that he done paid for with the sweat of his brow. You done got so grown to where you gonna take over. You gonna take over my house. Is that right? You gonna wear my pants. You gonna go in there and stretch out on my bed. You ain't got to say excuse me cause I don't count around here no more. Is that right?

Cory: That's right. You always talking this dumb stuff. Now, why don't you just get out my way?

Troy: I guess you got someplace to sleep and something to put in your belly. You got that, huh? You got that? That's what you need. You got that, huh?

Cory: You don't know what I got. You ain't got to worry about what I got.

Troy: You right! You one hundred percent right! I done spent the last seventeen years worrying about what you got. Now it's your turn, see? I'll tell you what to do. You grown . . . we done established that. You a man. Now, let's see you act like one. Turn your behind around and walk out this yard. And when you get out there in the alley . . . you can forget about this house. See? Cause this is my house. You go on and be a man and get your own house. You can forget about this. Cause this is mine. You go on and get yours cause I'm through with doing for you.

Cory: You talking about what you did for me . . . what'd you ever give me?

Troy: Them feet and bones! That pumping heart, nigger! I give you more than anybody else is ever gonna give you.

Cory: You ain't never gave me nothing! You ain't never done nothing but hold me back. Afraid I was gonna be better than you. All you ever did was try and make me scared of you. I used to tremble every time you called my name. Every time I heard your footsteps in the house. Wondering all the time . . . what's Papa gonna say if I do this? . . . What's he gonna say if I do that? . . . What's Papa gonna say if I turn on the radio? And Mama, too . . . she tries . . . but she's scared of you.

Troy: You leave your mama out of this. She ain't got nothing to do with this.

Cory: I don't know how she stand you . . . after what you did to her.

Troy: I told you to leave your mama out of this!

He advances toward Cory.

Cory: What you gonna do . . . give me a whupping? You can't whup me no more. You're too old. You just an old man.

Troy (shoves him on his shoulder): Nigger! That's what you are. You just another nigger on the street to me!

Cory: You crazy! You know that?

Troy: Go on now! You got the devil in you. Get on away from me!

Cory: You just a crazy old man . . . talking about I got the devil in me.

Troy: Yeah, I'm crazy! If you don't get on the other side of that yard . . . I'm gonna show you how crazy I am! Go on . . . get the hell out of my yard.

Cory: It ain't your yard. You took Uncle Gabe's money he got from the army to buy this house and then you put him out.

Troy (advances on Cory): Get your black ass out of my yard!

Troy's advance backs Cory up against the tree. Cory grabs up the bat.

Cory: I ain't going nowhere! Come on . . . put me out! I ain't scared of you.
Troy: That's my bat!
Cory: Come on!
Troy: Put my bat down!
Cory: Come on, put me out.

Cory swings at Troy, who backs across the yard.

What's the matter? You so bad . . . put me out!

Troy advances toward Cory.

Cory (*backing up*): Come on! Come on!
Troy: You're gonna have to use it! You wanna draw that bat back on me . . .
you're gonna have to use it.
Cory: Come on! . . . Come on!

*Cory swings the bat at Troy a second time. He misses. Troy continues to advance
toward him.*

Troy: You're gonna have to kill me! You wanna draw that bat back on me.
You're gonna have to kill me.

*Cory, backed up against the tree, can go no farther. Troy taunts him. He sticks out
his head and offers him a target.*

Come on! Come on!

Cory is unable to swing the bat. Troy grabs it.

Troy: Then I'll show you.

*Cory and Troy struggle over the bat. The struggle is fierce and fully engaged. Troy
ultimately is the stronger and takes the bat from Cory and stands over him ready
to swing. He stops himself.*

Go on and get away from around my house.

*Cory, stung by his defeat, picks himself up, walks slowly out of the yard and up the
alley.*

Cory: Tell Mama I'll be back for my things.
Troy: They'll be on the other side of that fence.

Cory exits.

Troy: I can't taste nothing. Helluljah! I can't taste nothing no more. (*Troy assumes a batting posture and begins to taunt Death, the fastball on the outside corner.*) Come on! It's between you and me now! Come on! Anytime you
want! Come on! I be ready for you . . . but I ain't gonna be easy.

The lights go down on the scene.

Scene V

*The time is 1965. The lights come up in the yard. It is the morning of Troy's funeral.
A funeral plaque with a light hangs beside the door. There is a small garden plot off
to the side. There is noise and activity in the house as Rose, Gabriel, and Bono have
gathered. The door opens and Raynell, seven years old, enters dressed in a flannel*

nightgown. She crosses to the garden and pokes around with a stick. Rose calls from the house.

Rose: Raynell!
Raynell: Mam?
Rose: What you doing out there?
Raynell: Nothing.

    Rose comes to the door.

Rose: Girl, get in here and get dressed. What you doing?
Raynell: Seeing if my garden growed.
Rose: I told you it ain't gonna grow overnight. You got to wait.
Raynell: It don't look like it never gonna grow. Dag!
Rose: I told you a watched pot never boils. Get in here and get dressed.
Raynell: This ain't even no pot, Mama.
Rose: You just have to give it a chance. It'll grow. Now you come on and do what I told you. We got to be getting ready. This ain't no morning to be playing around. You hear me?
Raynell: Yes, mam.

    Rose exits into the house. Raynell continues to poke at her garden with a stick. Cory enters. He is dressed in a Marine corporal's uniform, and carries a duffel bag. His posture is that of a military man, and his speech has a clipped sternness.

Cory (to Raynell): Hi. *(Pause.)* I bet your name is Raynell.
Raynell: Uh huh.
Cory: Is your mama home?

    Raynell runs up on the porch and calls through the screen door.

Raynell: Mama . . . there's some man out here. Mama?

    Rose comes to the door.

Rose: Cory? Lord have mercy! Look here, you all!

    Rose and Cory embrace in a tearful reunion as Bono and Lyons enter from the house dressed in funeral clothes.

Bono: Aw, looka here . . .
Rose: Done got all grown up!
Cory: Don't cry, Mama. What you crying about?
Rose: I'm just so glad you made it.
Cory: Hey Lyons. How you doing, Mr. Bono.

    Lyons goes to embrace Cory.

Lyons: Look at you, man. Look at you. Don't he look good, Rose. Got them Corporal stripes.
Rose: What took you so long?
Cory: You know how the Marines are, Mama. They got to get all their paperwork straight before they let you do anything.
Rose: Well, I'm sure glad you made it. They let Lyons come. Your Uncle Gabe's still in the hospital. They don't know if they gonna let him out or not. I just talked to them a little while ago.

Lyons: A Corporal in the United States Marines.

Bono: Your daddy knew you had it in you. He used to tell me all the time.

Lyons: Don't he look good, Mr. Bono?

Bono: Yeah, he remind me of Troy when I first met him. *(Pause.)* Say, Rose, Lucille's down at the church with the choir. I'm gonna go down and get the pallbearers lined up. I'll be back to get you all.

Rose: Thanks, Jim.

Cory: See you, Mr. Bono.

Lyons (with his arm around Raynell): Cory . . . look at Raynell. Ain't she precious? She gonna break a whole lot of hearts.

Rose: Raynell, come and say hello to your brother. This is your brother, Cory. You remember Cory.

Raynell: No, Mam.

Cory: She don't remember me, Mama.

Rose: Well, we talk about you. She heard us talk about you. *(To Raynell.)* This is your brother, Cory. Come on and say hello.

Raynell: Hi.

Cory: Hi. So you're Raynell. Mama told me a lot about you.

Rose: You all come on into the house and let me fix you some breakfast. Keep up your strength.

Cory: I ain't hungry, Mama.

Lyons: You can fix me something, Rose. I'll be in there in a minute.

Rose: Cory, you sure you don't want nothing? I know they ain't feeding you right.

Cory: No, Mama . . . thanks. I don't feel like eating. I'll get something later.

Rose: Raynell . . . get on upstairs and get that dress on like I told you.

    Rose and Raynell exit into the house.

Lyons: So . . . I hear you thinking about getting married.

Cory: Yeah, I done found the right one, Lyons. It's about time.

Lyons: Me and Bonnie been split up about four years now. About the time Papa retired. I guess she just got tired of all them changes I was putting her through. *(Pause.)* I always knew you was gonna make something out yourself. Your head was always in the right direction. So . . . you gonna stay in . . . make it a career . . . put in your twenty years?

Cory: I don't know. I got six already, I think that's enough.

Lyons: Stick with Uncle Sam and retire early. Ain't nothing out here. I guess Rose told you what happened with me. They got me down the workhouse. I thought I was being slick cashing other people's checks.

Cory: How much time you doing?

Lyons: They give me three years. I got that beat now. I ain't got but nine more months. It ain't so bad. You learn to deal with it like anything else. You got to take the crookeds with the straights. That's what Papa used to say. He used to say that when he struck out. I seen him strike out three times in a row . . . and the next time up he hit the ball over the grandstand. Right out there in Homestead Field. He wasn't satisfied hitting in the seats . . . he want to hit it over everything! After the game he had two hundred people standing around waiting to shake his hand. You got to take the crookeds with the straights. Yeah, Papa was something else.

Cory: You still playing?

Lyons: Cory . . . you know I'm gonna do that. There's some fellows down there we got us a band . . . we gonna try and stay together when we get out . . . but yeah, I'm still playing. It still helps me to get out of bed in the morning. As long as it do that I'm gonna be right there playing and trying to make some sense out of it.

Rose (calling): Lyons, I got these eggs in the pan.

Lyons: Let me go on and get these eggs, man. Get ready to go bury Papa. *(Pause.)* How you doing? You doing all right?

Cory nods. Lyons touches him on the shoulder and they share a moment of silent grief. Lyons exits into the house. Cory wanders about the yard. Raynell enters.

Raynell: Hi.

Cory: Hi.

Raynell: Did you used to sleep in my room?

Cory: Yeah . . . that used to be my room.

Raynell: That's what Papa call it. "Cory's room." It got your football in the closet.

Rose comes to the door.

Rose: Raynell, get in there and get them good shoes on.

Raynell: Mama, can't I wear these? Them other one hurt my feet.

Rose: Well, they just gonna have to hurt your feet for a while. You ain't said they hurt your feet when you went down to the store and got them.

Raynell: They didn't hurt then. My feet done got bigger.

Rose: Don't you give me no backtalk now. You get in there and get them shoes on.

Raynell exits into the house.

Ain't too much changed. He still got that piece of rag tied to that tree. He was out here swinging that bat. I was just ready to go back in the house. He swung that bat and then he just fell over. Seem like he swung it and stood there with this grin on his face . . . and then he just fell over. They carried him on down to the hospital, but I knew there wasn't no need . . . why don't you come on in the house?

Cory: Mama . . . I got something to tell you. I don't know how to tell you this . . . but I've got to tell you . . . I'm not going to Papa's funeral.

Rose: Boy, hush your mouth. That's your daddy you talking about. I don't want hear that kind of talk this morning. I done raised you to come to this? You standing there all healthy and grown talking about you ain't going to your daddy's funeral?

Cory: Mama . . . listen . . .

Rose: I don't want to hear it, Cory. You just get that thought out of your head.

Cory: I can't drag Papa with me everywhere I go. I've got to say no to him. One time in my life I've got to say no.

Rose: Don't nobody have to listen to nothing like that. I know you and your daddy ain't seen eye to eye, but I ain't got to listen to that kind of talk this morning. Whatever was between you and your daddy . . . the time has come to put it aside. Just take it and set it over there on the shelf and forget about it. Disrespecting your daddy ain't gonna make you a man, Cory.

You got to find a way to come to that on your own. Not going to your daddy's funeral ain't gonna make you a man.

Cory: The whole time I was growing up . . . living in his house . . . Papa was like a shadow that followed you everywhere. It weighed on you and sunk into your flesh. It would wrap around you and lay there until you couldn't tell which one was you anymore. That shadow digging in your flesh. Trying to crawl in. Trying to live through you. Everywhere I looked, Troy Maxson was staring back at me . . . hiding under the bed . . . in the closet. I'm just saying I've got to find a way to get rid of that shadow, Mama.

Rose: You just like him. You got him in you good.

Cory: Don't tell me that, Mama.

Rose: You Troy Maxson all over again.

Cory: I don't want to be Troy Maxson. I want to be me.

Rose: You can't be nobody but who you are, Cory. That shadow wasn't nothing but you growing into yourself. You either got to grow into it or cut it down to fit you. But that's all you got to make life with. That's all you got to measure yourself against that world out there. Your daddy wanted you to be everything he wasn't . . . and at the same time he tried to make you into everything he was. I don't know if he was right or wrong . . . but I do know he meant to do more good than he meant to do harm. He wasn't always right. Sometimes when he touched he bruised. And sometimes when he took me in his arms he cut.

When I first met your daddy I thought . . . Here is a man I can lay down with and make a baby. That's the first thing I thought when I seen him. I was thirty years old and had done seen my share of men. But when he walked up to me and said, "I can dance a waltz that'll make you dizzy," I thought, Rose Lee, here is a man that you can open yourself up to and be filled to bursting. Here is a man that can fill all them empty spaces you been tipping around the edges of. One of them empty spaces was being somebody's mother.

I married your daddy and settled down to cooking his supper and keeping clean sheets on the bed. When your daddy walked through the house he was so big he filled it up. That was my first mistake. Not to make him leave some room for me. For my part in the matter. But at that time I wanted that. I wanted a house that I could sing in. And that's what your daddy gave me. I didn't know to keep up his strength I had to give up little pieces of mine. I did that. I took on his life as mine and mixed up the pieces so that you couldn't hardly tell which was which anymore. It was my choice. It was my life and I didn't have to live it like that. But that's what life offered me in the way of being a woman and I took it. I grabbed hold of it with both hands.

By the time Raynell came into the house, me and your daddy had done lost touch with one another. I didn't want to make my blessing off of nobody's misfortune . . . but I took on to Raynell like she was all them babies I had wanted and never had.

The phone rings.

Like I'd been blessed to relive a part of my life. And if the Lord see fit to keep up my strength . . . I'm gonna do her just like your daddy did you . . . I'm gonna give her the best of what's in me.

Raynell (entering, still with her old shoes): Mama . . . Reverend Tollivier on the phone.

> *Rose exits into the house.*

Raynell: Hi.

Cory: Hi.

Raynell: You in the Army or the Marines?

Cory: Marines.

Raynell: Papa said it was the Army. Did you know Blue?

Cory: Blue? Who's Blue?

Raynell: Papa's dog what he sing about all the time.

Cory (singing): Hear it ring! Hear it ring!
> I had a dog his name was Blue
> You know Blue was mighty true
> You know Blue was a good old dog
> Blue treed a possum in a hollow log
> You know from that he was a good old dog.
> Hear it ring! Hear it ring!

> *Raynell joins in singing.*

Cory and Raynell: Blue treed a possum out on a limb
> Blue looked at me and I looked at him
> Grabbed that possum and put him in a sack
> Blue stayed there till I came back
> Old Blue's feets was big and round
> Never allowed a possum to touch the ground.

> Old Blue died and I dug his grave
> I dug his grave with a silver spade
> Let him down with a golden chain
> And every night I call his name
> Go on Blue, you good dog you
> Go on Blue, you good dog you

Raynell: Blue laid down and died like a man
> Blue laid down and died . . .

Both: Blue laid down and died like a man
> Now he's treeing possums in the Promised Land
> I'm gonna tell you this to let you know
> Blue's gone where the good dogs go
> When I hear old Blue bark
> When I hear old Blue bark
> Blue treed a possum in Noah's Ark
> Blue treed a possum in Noah's Ark.

> *Rose comes to the screen door.*

Rose: Cory, we gonna be ready to go in a minute.

Cory (to Raynell): You go on in the house and change them shoes like Mama told you so we can go to Papa's funeral.

Raynell: Okay, I'll be back.

> *Raynell exits into the house. Cory gets up and crosses over to the tree. Rose stands in the screen door watching him. Gabriel enters from the alley.*

Gabriel (calling): Hey, Rose!

Rose: Gabe?

Gabriel: I'm here, Rose. Hey Rose, I'm here!

    Rose enters from the house.

Rose: Lord . . . Look here, Lyons!

Lyons: See, I told you, Rose . . . I told you they'd let him come.

Cory: How you doing, Uncle Gabe?

Lyons: How you doing, Uncle Gabe?

Gabriel: Hey, Rose. It's time. It's time to tell St. Peter to open the gates. Troy, you ready? You ready, Troy. I'm gonna tell St. Peter to open the gates. You get ready now.

Gabriel, with great fanfare, braces himself to blow. The trumpet is without a mouthpiece. He puts the end of it into his mouth and blows with great force, like a man who has been waiting some twenty-odd years for this single moment. No sound comes out of the trumpet. He braces himself and blows again with the same result. A third time he blows. There is a weight of impossible description that falls away and leaves him bare and exposed to a frightful realization. It is a trauma that a sane and normal mind would be unable to withstand. He begins to dance. A slow, strange dance, eerie and life-giving. A dance of atavistic signature and ritual. Lyons attempts to embrace him. Gabriel pushes Lyons away. He begins to howl in what is an attempt at song, or perhaps a song turning back into itself in an attempt at speech. He finishes his dance and the gates of heaven stand open as wide as God's closet.

That's the way that go!

CONNECTIONS TO OTHER SELECTIONS

1. Compare and contrast Troy Maxson with Willy Loman in Miller's *Death of a Salesman* (p. 1869). How do these protagonists relate to their sons?

2. How might the narrator's experiences in Ralph Ellison's short story "Battle Royal" (p. 277) be used to shed light on Troy's conflicts in *Fences*?

Perspective

DAVID SAVRAN (B. 1950)

An Interview with August Wilson   1987

Savran: In reading *Fences,* I came to view Troy more and more critically as the play progressed, sharing Rose's point of view. We see that Troy has been crippled by his father. That's being replayed in Troy's relationship with Cory. Do you think there's a way out of that cycle?

    Wilson: Surely. First of all, we're all like our parents. The things we are taught early in life, how to respond to the world, our sense of morality — everything, we get from them. Now you can take that legacy and do with it anything you want to do. It's in your hands. Cory is Troy's son. How can he be Troy's son without sharing Troy's values? I was trying to get at why Troy made the choices he made, how they have influenced his values, and how he attempts to pass those along to his son. Each generation gives the succeeding generation what they think they need. One question in the play is "Are the tools we are given sufficient to compete in a world that is different from the one our parents knew?" I think they are—it's just that we have to do different things with the tools. That's all Troy has to give. Troy's flaw is that he does not recognize that the world was changing. That's because he spent fifteen years in a penitentiary.

As African-Americans, we should demand to participate in society as Africans. That's the way out of the vicious cycle of poverty and neglect that exists in 1987 in America, where you have a huge percentage of blacks living in the equivalent of South African townships, in housing projects. No one is inviting these people to participate in society. Look at the poverty levels—$8,500 for a family of four, if you have $8,501 you're not counted. Those statistics would go up enormously if we had an honest assessment of the cost of living in America. I don't know how anybody can support a family of four on $8,500. What I'm saying is that 85 or 90 percent of blacks in America are living in abject poverty and, for the most part, are crowded into what amount to concentration camps. The situation for blacks in America is worse than it was forty years ago. Some sociologists will tell you about the tremendous progress we've made. They didn't put me out when I walked in the door. And you can always point to someone who works on Wall Street, or is a doctor. But they don't count in the larger scheme of things.

Savran: Do you have any idea how these political changes could take place?

Wilson: I'm not sure. I know that blacks must be allowed their cultural differences. I think the process of assimilation to white American society was a big mistake. We don't want to be like you. Blacks living in housing projects are isolated from the society, for the most part—living as they choose, as Africans. Only they don't realize the value in what they're doing because they have accepted their victimization. They've marked themselves as victims. Once they recognize that, they can begin to move through society in a different manner, from a stronger position, and claim what is theirs.

Savran: A project of yours is to point up what happens when oppression is internalized.

Wilson: Yes, transfer of aggression to the wrong target. I think it's interesting that the two roads open to blacks for "full participation" are entertainment and sports. *Ma Rainey* and *Fences,* and I didn't plan it that way. I don't think that they're the correct roads. I think Troy's right. Now with the benefit of historical perspective, I can say that the athletic scholarship was actually a way of exploiting. Now you've got two million kids who think they're going to play in the NBA. In the sixties the universities made a lot of money off of athletics. You had kids playing for free who, by and large, were not getting educated, were taking courses in basketweaving. Some of them could barely read.

Savran: Troy may be right about that issue, but it seems that he has passed on certain destructive traits in spite of himself. Take the hostility between father and son.

Wilson: I think every generation says to the previous generation: you're in my way, I've got to get by. The father-son conflict is actually a normal generational conflict that happens all the time.

Savran: So it's a healthy and a good thing?

Wilson: Oh, sure. Troy is seeing this boy walk around, smelling his piss. Two men cannot live in the same household. Troy would have been tremendously disappointed if Cory had not challenged him. Troy knows that this boy has to go out and do battle with that world: "So I had best prepare him because I know that's a harsh, cruel place out there. But that's going to be easy compared to what he's getting here. Ain't nobody gonna whip your ass like I'm gonna whip it." He has a tremendous love for the kid. But he's not going to say, "I love you," he's going to demonstrate it. He's carrying garbage for seventeen years just for the kid. The only world Troy knows is the one that he made. Cory's going to go on to find another one, he's going to arrive at the same place as Troy. I think one of the most important lines in the play is when Troy is talking about his father: "I got to the place where I could feel him kicking in my blood and knew that the only thing that separated us was the matter of a few years."

Hopefully, Cory will do things a bit differently with his son. For Troy, sports was not the way to go, the white man wouldn't let him get away with that. "Get you a job, with your hands, something that nobody can take away from you." The idea of school—he doesn't know what that is. That's for white folks. Very few blacks had paperwork jobs. But if you knew how to fix cars, you could always make some money. That's what Troy wants for Cory. There aren't many people who ever jumped up in Troy's face. So he's proud of the kid at the same time that he expresses a hurt that all men feel. You got to cut your kid loose at some point. There's that sense of loss and separation. You find out how Troy left his father's house and you see how Cory leaves his house. I suspect with Cory it will repeat with some differences and maybe, after five or six generations, they'll find a different way to do it.

Savran: Where Cory ends up is very ambiguous, as a marine in 1965.

Wilson: Yes. For the average black kid on the street, that was an alternative. You went into the army because you could learn how to do something. I can remember my parents talking about the son of some friends: "He's in the navy. He *did* something"—as opposed to standing on the street corner, shooting drugs, drinking wine, and robbing stores. Lyons says to Cory, "I always knew you were going to make something out of yourself." It really wounds me. He's a corporal in the marines. For blacks, that is a sense of accomplishment. Therein lies one of the tragedies of blacks in America. Cory says, "I don't know. I put in six years. That's enough." Anyone who goes into the army and makes a career out of it is a loser. They sit there and are nurtured by the army and they don't have to confront life. Then they get out of the army and find there's nothing to do. They didn't learn any skills. And if they did, they can't find a job. Four months later, they're shooting dope. In the sixties a whole bunch of blacks went over, fought, and died in the Vietnam War. The survivors came back to the same street corners and found out nothing had changed. They still couldn't get a job.

At the end of *Fences* every person, with the exception of Raynell, is institutionalized. Rose is in a church. Lyons is in a penitentiary. Gabriel's in a mental hospital, and Cory's in the marines. The only free person is the girl, Troy's daughter, the hope for the future. That was conscious on my part because in '57 that's what I saw. Blacks have relied on institutions which are really foreign — except for the black church, which has been our saving grace. I have some problems with it but I recognize it as a central social organization and sometimes an economic organization for the black community. I would like to see blacks develop their own institutions that respond to their needs.

From *In Their Own Voices*

CONSIDERATIONS FOR CRITICAL THINKING AND WRITING

1. Wilson describes Troy's "flaw" as an inability to "recognize that the world was changing" (para. 2). Discuss how completely this assessment describes Troy.

2. Write an essay discussing how Wilson uses the hostility between father and son in *Fences* as a means of treating larger social issues for blacks in America.

3. Read the section on historical criticism (pp. 2052–53) in Chapter 53, "Critical Strategies for Reading." Discuss how useful and accurate you think *Fences* is in depicting black life in America for the past several decades.

CRITICAL
THINKING
AND WRITING

53

Critical Strategies
for Reading

Great literature is simply language
charged with meaning to the utmost
possible degree.
— EZRA POUND

The answers you get from literature
depend upon the questions you pose.
— MARGARET ATWOOD

CRITICAL THINKING

Maybe this has happened to you: the assignment is to write an analysis of
some aspect of a work — let's say, Nathaniel Hawthorne's *The Scarlet Letter* —
that interests you and takes into account critical sources
that comment on and interpret the work. You cheerfully begin research in the library but quickly find yourself bewildered by several seemingly unrelated articles.
The first traces the thematic significance of images of
light and darkness in the novel; the second makes a case for Hester Prynne
as a liberated woman; the third argues that Arthur Dimmesdale's guilt is a

Web Explore
the critical approaches
in this chapter at
bedfordstmartins.com/
meyerlit.

projection of Hawthorne's own emotions; and the fourth analyzes the introduction, "The Custom-House," as an attack on bourgeois values. These disparate treatments may seem random and capricious — a confirmation of your worst suspicions that interpretations of literature are hit-or-miss excursions into areas that you know little about or didn't know even existed. But if you understand that the four articles are written from four different perspectives — formalist, feminist, psychological, and Marxist — and that the purpose of each is to enhance your understanding of the novel by discussing a particular element of it, then you can see that the articles' varying strategies represent potentially interesting ways of opening up the text that might otherwise never have occurred to you. There are many ways to approach a text, and a useful first step is to develop a sense of direction, an understanding of how a perspective — your own or a critic's — shapes a discussion of a text.

This chapter offers an introduction to critical approaches to literature by outlining a variety of strategies for reading fiction, poetry, or drama. These strategies include approaches that have long been practiced by readers who have used, for example, the insights gleaned from biography and history to illuminate literary works as well as more recent approaches, such as those used by gender, reader-response, and deconstructionist critics. Each of these perspectives is sensitive to point of view, symbol, tone, irony, and other literary elements that you have been studying, but each also casts those elements in a special light. The formalist approach emphasizes how the elements within a work achieve their effects, whereas biographical and psychological approaches lead outward from the work to consider the author's life and other writings. Even broader approaches, such as historical and cultural perspectives, connect the work to historic, social, and economic forces. Mythological readings represent the broadest approach because they discuss the cultural and universal responses readers have to a work.

Any given strategy raises its own types of questions and issues while seeking particular kinds of evidence to support itself. An awareness of the assumptions and methods that inform an approach can help you to understand better the validity and value of a given critic's strategy for making sense of a work. More important, such an understanding can widen and deepen the responses of your own reading.

The critical thinking that goes into understanding a professional critic's approach to a work is not foreign to you because you have already used essentially the same kind of thinking to understand the work itself. You have developed skills to produce a literary *analysis* that, for example, describes how a character, symbol, or rhyme scheme supports a theme. These same skills are also useful for reading literary criticism because they allow you to keep track of how the parts of a critical approach create a particular reading of a literary work. When you analyze a story, poem, or play by closely examining how its various elements relate to the whole, your *interpretation* — your articulation of what the work means to you as sup-ported by an analysis of its elements — necessarily involves choosing what you focus on in the work. The same is true of professional critics.

Critical readings presuppose choices in the kinds of materials that are discussed. An analysis of the setting of John Updike's "A & P" (p. 733) would probably focus on the oppressive environment the protagonist asso-ciates with the store rather than, say, the economic history of that super-market chain. (For a student's analysis of the setting in "A & P," see p. 2089.) The economic history of a supermarket chain might be useful to a Marxist critic concerned with how class relations are revealed in "A & P," but for a formalist critic interested in identifying the unifying structures of the story, such information would be irrelevant.

The Perspectives, Complementary Critical Readings, and Critical Case Studies in this anthology offer opportunities to read critics using a wide variety of approaches to analyze and interpret texts. In the Critical Case Study on Ibsen's *A Doll House* (Chapter 50), for instance, Carol Strongin Tufts (p. 1769) offers a psychoanalytic reading of Nora that characterizes her as a narcissistic personality rather than as a feminist heroine. The crite-ria she uses to evaluate Nora's behavior are drawn from the language used by the American Psychiatric Association. In contrast, Joan Templeton (p. 1772) places Nora in the context of women's rights issues to argue that Nora must be read from a feminist perspective if the essential meaning of the play is to be understood. Each of these critics raises different questions, examines different evidence, and employs different assumptions to inter-pret Nora's character. Being aware of those differences — teasing them out so that you can see how they lead to competing conclusions — is a useful way to analyze the analysis itself. What is left out of an interpretation is sometimes as significant as what is included. As you read the critics, it's worth reminding yourself that your own critical thinking skills can help you to determine the usefulness of a particular approach.

The following overview of critical strategies for reading is neither exhaustive in the types of critical approaches covered nor complete in its presentation of the complexities inherent in them, but it should help you to develop an appreciation of the intriguing possibilities that attend liter-ary interpretation. The emphasis in this chapter is on ways of thinking about literature rather than on daunting lists of terms, names, and move-ments. Although a working knowledge of critical schools may be valuable and necessary for a fully informed use of a given critical approach, the aim here is more modest and practical. This chapter is no substitute for the shelves of literary criticism that can be found in your library, but it does suggest how readers using different perspectives organize their responses to texts.

The summaries of critical approaches that follow are descriptive, not evaluative. Each approach has its advantages and limitations. In practice, many critical approaches overlap and complement each other, but those matters are best left to further study. Like literary artists, critics have their personal values, tastes, and styles. The appropriateness of a specific critical approach will depend, at least in part, on the nature of the literary work under discussion as well as on your own sensibilities and experience. However, any approach, if it is to enhance understanding, requires sensitivity, tact, and an awareness of the various literary elements of the text, including, of course, its use of language.

Successful critical approaches avoid eccentric decodings that reveal so-called hidden meanings that are not only hidden but totally absent from the text. For a parody of this sort of critical excess, see "A Parodic Interpretation of 'Stopping by Woods on a Snowy Evening' " (p. 1121), in which Herbert R. Coursen Jr. has some fun with a Robert Frost poem and Santa Claus while making a serious point about the dangers of overly ingenious readings. Literary criticism attempts, like any valid hypothesis, to account for phenomena — the text — without distorting or misrepresenting what it describes.

THE LITERARY CANON: DIVERSITY AND CONTROVERSY

Before looking at the various critical approaches discussed in this chapter, it makes sense to consider first which literature has been traditionally considered worthy of such analysis. The discussion in the introduction called The Changing Literary Canon (p. 6) may have already alerted you to the fact that in recent years many more works by women, minorities, and writers from around the world have been considered by scholars, critics, and teachers to merit serious study and inclusion in what is known as the literary canon. This increasing diversity has been celebrated by those who believe that multiculturalism taps new sources for the discovery of great literature while raising significant questions about language, culture, and society. At the same time, others have perceived this diversity as a threat to the established, traditional canon of Western culture.

The debates concerning who should be read, taught, and written about have sometimes been acrimonious as well as lively and challenging. Bitter arguments have been waged on campuses and in the press over what has come to be called *political correctness*. Two main camps have formed around these debates — liberals and conservatives (the appropriateness of these terms is debatable, but the oppositional positioning is unmistakable). The liberals are said to insist on encouraging tolerant attitudes about race, class, gender, and sexual orientation, and opening up the curriculum to multicultural texts from Asia, Africa, Latin America, and elsewhere. These revisionists, seeking a change in traditional attitudes, are sometimes accused of trying to substitute ideological dogma for reason and truth and to intimidate opposing colleagues and students into silence and acceptance of their politically correct views. The conservatives are also portrayed as ideologues; in their efforts to preserve what they regard as the best from the past, they fail to acknowledge that Western classics, mostly written by white male Europeans, represent only a portion of human experience. These traditionalists are seen as advocating values that are neither universal nor eternal but merely privileged and entrenched. Conservatives are charged with ignoring the political agenda that their values represent and that is implicit in their preference for the works of canonical authors such as Homer, Virgil, Shakespeare, Milton, Tolstoy, and Faulkner. The reductive and contradictory nature of this national debate between liberals and conservatives has been neatly summed up by Katha Pollitt: "Read the conservatives' list and produce a nation of sexists and racists — or a nation of philosopher kings. Read the liberals' list and produce a nation of spiritual relativists — or a nation of open-minded world citizens" ("Canon to the Right of Me . . . ," *The Nation,* Sept. 23, 1991, p. 330).

These troubling and extreme alternatives can be avoided, of course, if the issues are not approached from such absolutist positions. Solutions to these issues cannot be suggested in this limited space, and, no doubt, solutions will evolve over time, but we can at least provide a perspective. Books — regardless of what list they are on — are not likely to unite a fragmented nation or to disunite a unified one. It is perhaps more useful and accurate to see issues of canonicity as reflecting political changes rather than being the primary causes of them. This is not to say that books don't have an impact on readers — that *Uncle Tom's Cabin,* for instance, did not galvanize antislavery sentiments in nineteenth-century America — but that book lists do not by themselves preserve or destroy the status quo.

It's worth noting that the curricula of American universities have always undergone significant and, some would say, wrenching changes. Only a little more than one hundred years ago there was strong opposition to teaching English, as well as other modern languages, alongside programs dominated by Greek and Latin. Only since the 1920s has American literature been made a part of the curriculum, and just five decades ago including twentieth-century writers such as James Joyce, Virginia Woolf, Franz Kafka, and Ernest Hemingway in the curriculum was regarded with raised eyebrows. New voices do not drown out the past; they build on it and eventually become part of the past as newer writers take their place beside them. Neither resistance to change nor a denial of the past will have its way with the canon. Though both impulses are widespread, neither is likely to dominate the other because there are too many reasonable, practical readers and teachers who instead of replacing Shakespeare, Melville, and other canonical writers have supplemented them with neglected writers from Western and other cultures. These readers experience the current debates about the canon not as a binary opposition but as an opportunity to explore important questions about continuity and change in our literature, culture, and society.

FORMALIST STRATEGIES

Formalist critics focus on the formal elements of a work — its language, structure, and tone. A formalist reads literature as an independent work of art rather than as a reflection of the author's state of mind or as a representation of a moment in history. Historic influences on a work, an author's intentions, or anything else outside the work are generally not treated by formalists (this is particularly true of the most famous modern formalists, known as the ***New Critics,*** who dominated American criticism from the 1940s through the 1960s). Instead, formalists offer intense examinations of the relationship between form and meaning within a work, emphasizing the subtle complexity of how a work is arranged. This kind of close reading pays special attention to what are often described as *intrinsic* matters in a literary work, such as diction, irony, paradox, metaphor, and symbol, as well as larger elements, such as plot, characterization, and narrative technique. Formalists examine how these elements work together to give a coherent shape to a work while contributing to its meaning. The answers to the questions formalists raise about how the shape and effect of a work are related come from the work itself. Other kinds of information that go beyond the text — biography, history, politics, economics, and so on — are typically regarded by formalists as *extrinsic* matters, which are considerably less important than what goes on within the autonomous text.

Poetry especially lends itself to close readings because a poem's relative brevity allows for detailed analyses of nearly all its words and how they achieve their effects. For a student's formalist reading of how a pervasive sense of death is worked into a poem, see "A Reading of Dickinson's 'There's a certain Slant of light'" (p. 2084).

Formalist strategies are also useful for analyzing drama and fiction. In his well-known essay "The World of *Hamlet*," Maynard Mack explores Hamlet's character and predicament by paying close attention to the words and images that Shakespeare uses to build a world in which appearances mask reality and mystery is embedded in scene after scene. Mack points to recurring terms, such as *apparition, seems, assume,* and *put on,* as well as repeated images of acting, clothing, disease, and painting, to indicate the treacherous surface world Hamlet must penetrate to get to the truth. This pattern of deception provides an organizing principle around which Mack offers a reading of the entire play:

> Hamlet's problem, in its crudest form, is simply the problem of the avenger: he must carry out the injunction of the ghost and kill the king. But this problem . . . is presented in terms of a certain kind of world. The ghost's injunction to act becomes so inextricably bound up for Hamlet with the character of the world in which the action must be taken — its mysteriousness, its baffling appearances, its deep consciousness of infection, frailty, and loss — that he cannot come to terms with either without coming to terms with both.

Although Mack places *Hamlet* in the tradition of revenge tragedy, his reading of the play emphasizes Shakespeare's arrangement of language rather than literary history as a means of providing an interpretation that accounts for various elements of the play. Mack's formalist strategy explores how diction reveals meaning and how repeated words and images evoke and reinforce important thematic significances.

For an example of a work in which the shape of the plot serves as the major organizing principle, let's examine Kate Chopin's "The Story of an Hour" (p. 15), a two-page short story that takes only a few minutes to read. With the story fresh in your mind, consider how you might approach it from a formalist perspective. A first reading probably results in surprise at the story's ending: a grieving wife "afflicted with a heart trouble" suddenly dies of a heart attack, not because she's learned that her kind and loving husband has been killed in a terrible train accident but because she discovers that he is very much alive. Clearly, we are faced with an ironic situation since there is such a powerful incongruity between what is expected to happen and what actually happens. A likely formalist strategy for analyzing this story would be to raise questions about the ironic ending. Is this merely a trick ending, or is it a carefully wrought culmination of other elements in the story so that in addition to creating surprise the ending snaps the story shut on an interesting and challenging theme? Formalists value such complexities over simple surprise effects.

A second, closer reading indicates that Chopin's third-person narrator presents the story in a manner similar to Josephine's gentle attempts to break the news about Brently Mallard's death. The story is told in "veiled hints that [reveal] in half concealing." But unlike Josephine, who tries to protect her sister's fragile heart from stress, the narrator seeks to reveal Mrs. Mallard's complex heart. A formalist would look back over the story for signs of the ending in the imagery. Although Mrs. Mallard grieves immediately and unreservedly when she hears about the train disaster, she soon begins to feel a different emotion as she looks out the window at "the tops of trees . . . all aquiver with the new spring life." This symbolic evocation of renewal and rebirth — along with "the delicious breath of rain," the sounds of life in the street, and the birds singing — causes her to feel, in spite of her own efforts to repress her thoughts and emotions, "free, free, free!" She feels alive with a sense of possibility, with a "clear and exalted perception" that she "would live for herself" instead of for and through her husband.

It is ironic that this ecstatic "self-assertion" is interpreted by Josephine as grief, but the crowning irony for this "goddess of Victory" is the doctors' assumption that she dies of joy rather than of the shock of having to abandon her newly discovered self once she realizes her husband is still alive. In the course of an hour, Mrs. Mallard's life is irretrievably changed: her husband's assumed accidental death frees her, but the fact that he lives and all the expectations imposed on her by his continued life kill her. She does, indeed, die of a broken heart, but only Chopin's readers know the real ironic meaning of that explanation.

Although this brief discussion of some of the formal elements of Chopin's story does not describe all there is to say about how they produce an effect and create meaning, it does suggest the kinds of questions, issues, and evidence that a formalist strategy might raise in providing a close reading of the text itself.

BIOGRAPHICAL STRATEGIES

A knowledge of an author's life can help readers understand his or her work more fully. Events in a work might follow actual events in a writer's life just as characters might be based on people known by the author. Ernest Hemingway's "Soldier's Home" (p. 187) is a story about the difficulties of a World War I veteran named Krebs returning to his small hometown in Oklahoma, where he cannot adjust to the pious assumptions of his family and neighbors. He refuses to accept their innocent blindness to the horrors he has witnessed during the war. They have no sense of the brutality of modern life; instead they insist he resume his life as if nothing has happened. There is plenty of biographical evidence to indicate that Krebs's unwillingness to lie about his war experiences reflects Hemingway's own responses on his return to Oak Park, Illinois, in 1919. Krebs, like Hemingway, finds he has to leave the sentimentality, repressiveness, and smug complacency that threaten to render his experiences unreal: "the world they were in was not the world he was in."

An awareness of Hemingway's own war experiences and subsequent disillusionment with his hometown can be readily developed through available biographies, letters, and other works he wrote. Consider, for example, this passage from *By Force of Will: The Life and Art of Ernest Hemingway*, in which Scott Donaldson describes Hemingway's response to World War I:

> In poems, as in [*A Farewell to Arms*], Hemingway expressed his distaste for the first war. The men who had to fight the war did not die well:
>
> > Soldiers pitch and cough and twitch —
> >   All the world roars red and black;
> > Soldiers smother in a ditch,
> >   Choking through the whole attack.
>
> And what did they die for? They were "sucked in" by empty words and phrases —
>
> > King and country,
> > Christ Almighty,
> > And the rest,
> > Patriotism,

Democracy,
Honor —

which spelled death. The bitterness of these outbursts derived from the distinction Hemingway drew between the men on the line and those who started the wars that others had to fight.

This kind of information can help to deepen our understanding of just how empathetically Krebs is presented in the story. Relevant facts about Hemingway's life will not make "Soldier's Home" a better written story than it is, but such information can make clearer the source of Hemingway's convictions and how his own experiences inform his major concerns as a storyteller.

Some formalist critics — some New Critics, for example — argue that interpretation should be based exclusively on internal evidence rather than on any biographical information outside the work. They argue that it is not possible to determine an author's intention and that the work must stand by itself. Although this is a useful caveat for keeping the work in focus, a reader who finds biography relevant would argue that biography can at the very least serve as a control on interpretation. A reader who, for example, finds Krebs at fault for not subscribing to the values of his hometown would be misreading the story, given both its tone and the biographical information available about the author. Although the narrator never *tells* the reader that Krebs is right or wrong for leaving town, the story's tone sides with his view of things. If, however, someone were to argue otherwise, insisting that the tone is not decisive and that Krebs's position is problematic, a reader familiar with Hemingway's own reactions could refute that argument with a powerful confirmation of Krebs's instincts to withdraw. Hence, many readers find biography useful for interpretation.

However, it is also worth noting that biographical information can complicate a work. Chopin's "The Story of an Hour" presents a repressed wife's momentary discovery of what freedom from her husband might mean to her. She awakens to a new sense of herself when she learns of her husband's death, only to collapse of a heart attack when she sees that he is alive. Readers might be tempted to interpret this story as Chopin's fictionalized commentary about her own marriage because her husband died twelve years before she wrote the story and seven years before she began writing fiction seriously. Biographers seem to agree, however, that Chopin's marriage was evidently satisfying to her and that she was not oppressed by her husband and did not feel oppressed.

Moreover, consider this diary entry from only one month after Chopin wrote the story (quoted by Per Seyersted in *Kate Chopin: A Critical Biography*):

> If it were possible for my husband and my mother to come back to earth, I feel that I would unhesitatingly give up everything that has come into my life since they left it and join my existence again with theirs. To do that, I would have to forget the past ten years of my growth — my real growth. But I would take back a little wisdom with me; it would be the spirit of perfect acquiescence.

This passage raises provocative questions instead of resolving them. How does that "spirit of perfect acquiescence" relate to Mrs. Mallard's insistence that she "would live for herself"? Why would Chopin be willing to "forget the past ten years of . . . growth" given her protagonist's desire for "self-assertion"? Although these and other questions raised by the diary entry cannot be answered here, this kind of biographical perspective certainly adds to the possibilities of interpretation.

Sometimes biographical information does not change our understanding so much as it enriches our appreciation of a work. It matters, for instance, that much of John Milton's poetry, so rich in visual imagery, was written after he became blind; and it is just as significant — to shift to a musical example — that a number of Ludwig van Beethoven's greatest works, including the Ninth Symphony, were composed after he succumbed to total deafness.

PSYCHOLOGICAL STRATEGIES

Given the enormous influence that Sigmund Freud's psychoanalytic theories have had on twentieth-century interpretations of human behavior, it is nearly inevitable that most people have some familiarity with his ideas concerning dreams, unconscious desires, and sexual repression, as well as his terms for different aspects of the psyche — the id, ego, and superego. Psychological approaches to literature draw on Freud's theories and other psychoanalytic theories to understand more fully the text, the writer, and the reader. Critics use such approaches to explore the motivations of characters and the symbolic meanings of events, while biographers speculate about a writer's own motivations — conscious or unconscious — in a literary work. Psychological approaches are also used to describe and analyze the reader's personal responses to a text.

Although it is not feasible to explain psychoanalytic terms and concepts in so brief a space as this, it is possible to suggest the nature of a psychological approach. It is a strategy based heavily on the idea of the existence of a human unconscious — those impulses, desires, and feelings that a person is unaware of but that influence emotions and behavior.

Central to a number of psychoanalytic critical readings is Freud's concept of what he called the **Oedipus complex,** a term derived from Sophocles' tragedy *Oedipus the King* (p. 1422). This complex is predicated on a boy's unconscious rivalry with his father for his mother's love and his desire to eliminate his father in order to take his father's place with his mother. The female version of the psychological conflict is known as the **Electra complex,** a term used to describe a daughter's unconscious rivalry for her father. The name comes from a Greek legend about Electra, who avenged the death of her father, Agamemnon, by plotting the death of her mother. In *The Interpretation of Dreams,* Freud explains why *Oedipus the King* "moves a modern audience no less than it did the contemporary Greek one." What unites their powerful attraction to the play is an unconscious response:

> There must be something which makes a voice within us ready to recognize the compelling force of destiny in the *Oedipus*. . . . His destiny moves us only because it might have been ours — because the oracle laid the same curse upon us before our birth as upon him. It is the fate of all of us, perhaps, to direct our first sexual impulse towards our mother and our first hatred and our first murderous wish against our father. Our dreams convince us that this is so. King Oedipus, who slew his father Laius and married his mother Jocasta, merely shows us the fulfillment of our own childhood wishes . . . and we shrink back from him with the whole force of the repression by which those wishes have since that time been held down within us.

In this passage Freud interprets the unconscious motives of Sophocles in writing the play, Oedipus in acting within it, and the audience in responding to it.

A further application of the Oedipus complex can be observed in a classic interpretation of *Hamlet* by Ernest Jones, who used this concept to explain why Hamlet delays in avenging his father's death. This reading has been tightly summarized by Norman Holland, a psychoanalytic critic, in *The Shakespearean Imagination*. Holland shapes the issues into four major components:

> One, people over the centuries have been unable to say why Hamlet delays in killing the man who murdered his father and married his mother. Two, psychoanalytic experience shows that every child wants to do just exactly that. Three, Hamlet delays because he cannot punish Claudius for doing what he himself wished to do as a child and, unconsciously, still wishes to do: he would be punishing himself. Four, the fact that this wish is unconscious explains why people could not explain Hamlet's delay.

Although the Oedipus complex is, of course, not relevant to all psychological interpretations of literature, interpretations involving this complex do offer a useful example of how psychoanalytic critics tend to approach a text. (For Freud's discussion of *Hamlet*, see p. 1685.)

The situation in which Mrs. Mallard finds herself in Chopin's "The Story of an Hour" is not related to an Oedipus complex, but it is clear that news of her husband's death has released powerful unconscious desires for freedom that she had previously suppressed. As she grieved, "something" was "coming to her and she was waiting for it, fearfully." What comes to her is what she senses about the life outside her window; that's the stimulus, but the true source of what was to "possess her," which she strove to "beat . . . back with her [conscious] will," is her desperate desire for the autonomy and fulfillment she had been unable to admit did not exist in her marriage. A psychological approach to her story amounts to a case study in the destructive nature of self-repression. Moreover, the story might reflect Chopin's own views of her marriage — despite her conscious statements about her loving husband. And what about the reader's response? How might a psychological approach account for different responses in female and male readers to Mrs. Mallard's death? One needn't be versed in psychoanalytic terms to entertain this question.

HISTORICAL STRATEGIES

Historians sometimes use literature as a window onto the past because literature frequently provides the nuances of a historic period that cannot be readily perceived through other sources. The characters in Harriet Beecher Stowe's *Uncle Tom's Cabin* (1852) display, for example, a complex set of white attitudes toward blacks in mid-nineteenth-century America that is absent from more traditional historic documents, such as census statistics or state laws. Another way of approaching the relationship between literature and history, however, is to use history as a means of understanding a literary work more clearly. The plot pattern of pursuit, escape, and capture in nineteenth-century slave narratives had a significant influence on Stowe's plotting of action in *Uncle Tom's Cabin*. This relationship demonstrates that the writing contemporary to an author is an important element of the history that helps to shape a work. There are many ways to talk about the historical and cultural dimensions of a work. Such readings treat a literary text as a document reflecting, producing, or being produced by the social conditions of its time, giving equal focus to the social milieu and the work itself. Four historical strategies that have been especially influential are literary history criticism, Marxist criticism, new historicist criticism, and cultural criticism.

Literary History Criticism

Literary historians shift the emphasis from the period to the work. Hence a literary historian might also examine mid-nineteenth-century abolitionist attitudes toward blacks to determine whether Stowe's novel is representative of those views or significantly to the right or left of them. Such a study might even indicate how closely the book reflects racial attitudes of twentieth-century readers. A work of literature may transcend time to the extent that it addresses the concerns of readers over a span of decades or centuries, but it remains for the literary historian a part of the past in which it was composed, a past that can reveal more fully a work's language, ideas, and purposes.

Literary historians move beyond both the facts of an author's personal life and the text itself to the social and intellectual currents in which the author composed the work. They place the work in the context of its time (as do many critical biographers, who write "life and times" studies), and sometimes they make connections with other literary works that may have influenced the author. The basic strategy of literary historians is to illuminate the historic background in order to shed light on some aspect of the work itself.

In Hemingway's "Soldier's Home" we learn that Krebs had been at Belleau Wood, Soissons, the Champagne, St. Mihiel, and the Argonne. Although nothing is said of these battles in the story, they were among the bloodiest of the war; the wholesale butchery and staggering casualties incurred by both sides make credible the way Krebs's unstated but lingering memories have turned him into a psychological prisoner of war. Knowing something about the ferocity of those battles helps us account for Krebs's response in the story. Moreover, we can more fully appreciate Hemingway's refusal to have Krebs lie about the realities of war for the folks back home if we are aware of the numerous poems, stories, and plays published during World War I that presented war as a glorious, manly, transcendent sacrifice for God and country. Juxtaposing those works with "Soldier's Home" brings the differences into sharp focus.

Similarly, a reading of William Blake's poem "London" (p. 850) is less complete if we do not know of the horrific social conditions — the poverty, disease, exploitation, and hypocrisy — that characterized the city Blake laments in the late eighteenth century.

One last example: the repression expressed in the lines on Mrs. Mallard's face is more distinctly seen if Chopin's "The Story of an Hour" is placed in the context of "the women's question" as it continued to develop in the 1890s. Mrs. Mallard's impulse toward "self-assertion" runs parallel with a growing women's movement away from the role of long-suffering housewife. This desire was widely regarded by traditionalists as a form of dangerous selfishness that was considered as unnatural as it was immoral. It is no wonder that Chopin raises the question of whether Mrs. Mallard's sense of freedom owing to her husband's death isn't a selfish, "monstrous joy." Mrs. Mallard, however, dismisses this question as "trivial" in the face of her new perception of life, a dismissal that Chopin endorses by way of the story's ironic ending. The larger social context of this story would have been more apparent to Chopin's readers in 1894 than it is to readers in the 2000s. That is why a historical reconstruction of the limitations placed on married women helps to explain the pressures, tensions, and momentary — only momentary — release that Mrs. Mallard experiences.

Marxist Criticism

Marxist readings developed from the heightened interest in radical reform during the 1930s, when many critics looked to literature as a means of furthering proletarian social and economic goals, based largely on the writings of Karl Marx. **Marxist critics** focus on the ideological content of a work — its explicit and implicit assumptions and values about matters such as culture, race, class, and power. Marxist studies typically aim at revealing and clarifying ideological issues and also correcting social injustices. Some Marxist critics have used literature to describe the competing socioeconomic interests that too often advance capitalist money and power rather than socialist morality and justice. They argue that criticism, like literature, is essentially political because it either challenges or supports economic oppression. Even if criticism attempts to ignore class conflicts, it is politicized, according to Marxists, because it supports the status quo.

It is not surprising that Marxist critics pay more attention to the content and themes of literature than to its form. A Marxist critic would more likely be concerned with the exploitive economic forces that cause Willy Loman to feel trapped in Miller's *Death of a Salesman* (p. 1869) than with the playwright's use of nonrealistic dramatic techniques to reveal Loman's inner thoughts. Similarly, a Marxist reading of Chopin's "The Story of an Hour" might draw on the evidence made available in a book published only a few years after the story by Charlotte Perkins Gilman titled *Women and Economics: A Study of the Economic Relation between Men and Women as a Factor in Social Evolution* (1898). An examination of this study could help explain how some of the "repression" Mrs. Mallard experiences was generated by the socioeconomic structure contemporary to her and how Chopin challenges the validity of that structure by having Mrs. Mallard resist it with her very life. A Marxist reading would see the protagonist's conflict as not only an individual issue but part of a larger class struggle.

New Historicist Criticism

Since the 1960s a development in historical approaches to literature known as **new historicism** has emphasized the interaction between the historic context of a work and a modern reader's understanding and interpretation of the work. In contrast to many traditional literary historians, however, new historicists attempt to describe the culture of a period by reading many different kinds of texts that traditional literary historians might have previously left for economists, sociologists, and anthropologists. New historicists attempt to read a period in all its dimensions, including political, economic, social, and aesthetic concerns. These considerations could be used to explain the pressures that destroy Mrs. Mallard. A new historicist might examine the story and the public attitudes toward women contemporary to "The Story of an Hour" as well as documents such as suffragist tracts and medical diagnoses to explore how the same forces—expectations about how women are supposed to feel, think, and behave—shape different kinds of texts and how these texts influence each other. A new historicist might, for example, examine medical records for evidence of "nervousness" and "hysteria" as common diagnoses for women who led lives regarded as too independent by their contemporaries.

Without an awareness of just how selfish and self-destructive Mrs. Mallard's impulses would have been in the eyes of her contemporaries, readers in the twenty-first century might miss the pervasive pressures embedded not only in her marriage but in the social fabric surrounding her. Her death is made more understandable by such an awareness. The doctors who diagnose her as suffering from "the joy that kills" are not merely insensitive or stupid; they represent a contrasting set of assumptions and values that are as historic and real as Mrs. Mallard's yearnings.

New historicist criticism acknowledges more fully than traditional historical approaches the competing nature of readings of the past and thereby tends to offer new emphases and perspectives. New historicism reminds us that there is not only one historic context for "The Story of an Hour." Those doctors reveal additional dimensions of late-nineteenth-century social attitudes that warrant our attention, whether we agree with them or not. By emphasizing that historical perceptions are governed, at least in part, by our own concerns and preoccupations, new historicists sensitize us to the fact that the history on which we choose to focus is colored by being reconstructed from our own present moment. This reconstructed history affects our reading of texts.

Cultural Criticism

Cultural critics, like new historicists, focus on the historical contexts of a literary work, but they pay particular attention to popular manifestations of social, political, and economic contexts. Popular culture — mass-produced and consumed cultural artifacts, today ranging from advertising to popular fiction to television to rock music — and "high" culture are given equal emphasis. A cultural critic might be interested in looking at how Baz Luhrmann's movie version of *Romeo + Juliet* (1996) was influenced by the fragmentary nature of MTV videos. Adding the "low" art of everyday life to "high" art opens up previously unexpected and unexplored areas of criticism. Cultural critics use widely eclectic strategies drawn from new historicism, psychology, gender studies, and deconstructionism (to name only a handful of approaches) to analyze not only literary texts but radio talk shows, comic strips, calendar art, commercials, travel guides, and baseball cards. Because all human activity falls within the ken of cultural criticism, nothing is too minor or major, obscure or pervasive, to escape the range of its analytic vision.

Cultural criticism also includes ***postcolonial criticism,*** the study of cultural behavior and expression in relationship to the formerly colonized world. Postcolonial criticism refers to the analysis of literary works written by writers from countries and cultures that at one time were controlled by colonizing powers — such as Indian writers during or after British colonial rule. The term also refers to the analysis of literary works written about colonial cultures by writers from the colonizing country. Many of these kinds of analyses point out how writers from colonial powers sometimes misrepresent colonized cultures by reflecting more their own values: Joseph Conrad's *Heart of Darkness* (published in 1899) represents African culture differently than Chinua Achebe's *Things Fall Apart* does, for example. Cultural criticism and postcolonial criticism represent a broad range of approaches to examining race, gender, and class in historical contexts in a variety of cultures.

A cultural critic's approach to Chopin's "The Story of an Hour" might emphasize how the story reflects the potential dangers and horrors of train travel in the 1890s or it might examine how heart disease was often misdiagnosed by physicians or used as a metaphor in Mrs. Mallard's culture for a variety of emotional conditions. Each of these perspectives can serve to create a wider and more informed understanding of the story. For a sense of the range of documents used by cultural critics to shed light on literary works and the historical contexts in which they are written and read, see the Cultural Case Study on James Joyce's short story "Eveline" (p. 536).

GENDER STRATEGIES

Gender critics explore how ideas about men and women — what is masculine and feminine — can be regarded as socially constructed by particular cultures. According to some critics, sex is determined by simple biological and anatomical categories of male or female, and gender is determined by a culture's values. Thus, ideas about gender and what constitutes masculine and feminine behavior are created by cultural institutions and conditioning. A gender critic might, for example, focus on Chopin's characterization of an emotionally sensitive Mrs. Mallard and a rational, composed husband in "The Story of an Hour" as a manifestation of socially constructed gender identity in the 1890s. *Gender criticism* expands categories and definitions of what is masculine or feminine and tends to regard sexuality as more complex than merely masculine or feminine, heterosexual or homosexual. Gender criticism, therefore, has come to include gay and lesbian criticism as well as feminist criticism. Although there are complex and sometimes problematic relationships among these approaches because some critics argue that heterosexuals and homosexuals are profoundly biologically different, gay and lesbian criticism, like feminist criticism, can be usefully regarded as a subset of gender criticism.

Feminist Criticism

Like Marxist critics, *feminist critics* reading "The Story of an Hour" would also be interested in Charlotte Perkins Gilman's *Women and Economics: A Study of the Economic Relation between Men and Women as a Factor in Social Evolution* (1898) because they seek to correct or supplement what they regard as a predominantly male-dominated critical perspective with a feminist consciousness. Like other forms of sociological criticism, feminist criticism places literature in a social context, and, like those of Marxist criticism, its analyses often have sociopolitical purposes — explaining, for example, how images of women in literature reflect the patriarchal social forces that have impeded women's efforts to achieve full equality with men.

Feminists have analyzed literature by both men and women in an effort to understand literary representations of women as well as the writers and cultures that create them. Related to concerns about how gender affects the way men and women write about each other is an interest in whether women use language differently from the way men do. Consequently, feminist critics' approach to literature is characterized by the use of a broad range of disciplines, including history, sociology, psychology, and linguistics, to provide a perspective sensitive to feminist issues.

A feminist approach to Chopin's "The Story of an Hour" might explore the psychological stress created by the expectations that marriage imposes on Mrs. Mallard, expectations that literally and figuratively break her heart. Given that her husband is kind and loving, the issue is not her being married to Brently but her being married at all. Chopin presents marriage as an institution that creates in both men and women the assumed "right to impose a private will upon a fellow-creature." That "right," however, is seen, especially from a feminist perspective, as primarily imposed on women by men. A feminist critic might note, for instance, that the protagonist is introduced as "Mrs. Mallard" (we learn that her first name is Louise only later); she is defined by her marital status and her husband's name, a name whose origin from the Old French is related to the word *masle,* which means "male." The appropriateness of her name points up the fact that her emotions and the cause of her death are interpreted in male terms by the doctors. The value of a feminist perspective on this work can be readily discerned if a reader imagines Mrs. Mallard's story being told from the point of view of one of the doctors who diagnoses the cause of her death as a weak heart rather than as a fierce struggle.

Gay and Lesbian Criticism

Gay and lesbian critics focus on a variety of issues, including how homosexuals are represented in literature, how they read literature, and whether sexuality and gender are culturally constructed or innate. Gay critics have produced new readings of works by and discovered homosexual concerns in writers such as Herman Melville and Henry James, while lesbian critics have done the same for the works of writers such as Emily Dickinson and Toni Morrison. A lesbian reading of "The Story of an Hour," for example, might consider whether Mrs. Mallard's ecstatic feeling of relief — produced by the belief that her marriage is over owing to the presumed death of her husband — isn't also a rejection of her heterosexual identity. Perhaps her glimpse of future freedom, evoked by feminine images of a newly discovered nature "all aquiver with the new spring of life," embraces a repressed new sexual identity that "was too subtle and elusive to name" but that was "approaching to possess her" no matter how much she "was striving to beat it back with her will." Although gay and lesbian readings often raise significant interpretive controversies among critics, they have opened up provocative discussions of seemingly familiar texts.

MYTHOLOGICAL STRATEGIES

Mythological approaches to literature attempt to identify what in a work creates deep universal responses in readers. Whereas psychological critics interpret the symbolic meanings of characters and actions in order to understand more fully the unconscious dimensions of an author's mind, a character's motivation, or a reader's response, *mythological critics* (also frequently referred to as *archetypal critics*) interpret the hopes, fears, and expectations of entire cultures.

In this context myth is not to be understood simply as referring to stories about imaginary gods who perform astonishing feats in the causes of love, jealousy, or hatred. Nor are myths to be judged as merely erroneous, primitive accounts of how nature runs its course and humanity its affairs. Instead, literary critics use myths as a strategy for understanding how human beings try to account for their lives symbolically. Myths can be a window into a culture's deepest perceptions about itself because myths attempt to explain what otherwise seems unexplainable: a people's origin, purpose, and destiny.

All human beings have a need to make sense of their lives, whether they are concerned about their natural surroundings, the seasons, sexuality, birth, death, or the very meaning of existence. Myths help people organize their experiences; these systems of belief (less formally held than religious or political tenets but no less important) embody a culture's assumptions and values. What is important to the mythological critic is not the validity or truth of those assumptions and values; what matters is that they reveal common human concerns.

It is not surprising that although the details of mythic stories vary enormously, the essential patterns are often similar because these myths attempt to explain universal experiences. There are, for example, numerous myths that redeem humanity from permanent death through a hero's resurrection and rebirth. The resurrection of Jesus symbolizes for Christians the ultimate defeat of death and coincides with the rebirth of nature's fertility in spring. Features of this rebirth parallel the Greek myths of Adonis and Hyacinth, who die but are subsequently transformed into living flowers; there are also similarities that connect these stories to the reincarnation of the Indian Buddha or the rebirth of the Egyptian Osiris. Important differences exist among these stories, but each reflects a basic human need to limit the power of death and to hope for eternal life.

Mythological critics look for underlying, recurrent patterns in literature that reveal universal meanings and basic human experiences for readers regardless of when or where they live. The characters, images, and themes that symbolically embody these meanings and experiences are called *archetypes.* This term designates universal symbols that evoke deep and perhaps unconscious responses in a reader because archetypes bring with them our hopes and fears since the beginning of human time. Surely one of the most powerfully compelling archetypes is the death and rebirth theme that relates the human life cycle to the cycle of the seasons. Many others could be cited and would be exhausted only after all human concerns were cataloged, but a few examples can suggest some of the range of plots, images, and characters addressed.

Among the most common literary archetypes are stories of quests, initiations, scapegoats, meditative withdrawals, descents to the underworld, and heavenly ascents. These stories are often filled with archetypal images — bodies of water that may symbolize the unconscious or eternity or baptismal rebirth; rising suns, suggesting reawakening and enlightenment; setting suns, pointing toward death; colors such as green, evocative of growth and fertility, or black, indicating chaos, evil, and death. Along the way are earth mothers, fatal women, wise old men, desert places, and paradisal gardens. No doubt your own reading has introduced you to any number of archetypal plots, images, and characters.

Mythological critics attempt to explain how archetypes are embodied in literary works. Employing various disciplines, these critics articulate the power a literary work has over us. Some critics are deeply grounded in classical literature, whereas others are more conversant with philology, anthropology, psychology, or cultural history. Whatever their emphases, however, mythological critics examine the elements of a work in order to make larger connections that explain the work's lasting appeal.

A mythological reading of Sophocles' *Oedipus the King,* for example, might focus on the relationship between Oedipus's role as a scapegoat and the plague and drought that threaten to destroy Thebes. The city is saved and the fertility of its fields restored only after the corruption is located in Oedipus. His subsequent atonement symbolically provides a kind of rebirth for the city. Thus, the plot recapitulates ancient rites in which the well-being of a king was directly linked to the welfare of his people. If a leader was sick or corrupt, he had to be replaced in order to guarantee the health of the community.

A similar pattern can be seen in the rottenness that Shakespeare exposes in Hamlet's Denmark. *Hamlet* reveals an archetypal pattern similar to that of *Oedipus the King:* not until the hero sorts out the corruption in his world and in himself can vitality and health be restored in his world. Hamlet avenges his father's death and becomes a scapegoat in the process. When he fully accepts his responsibility to set things right, he is swept away along with the tide of intrigue and corruption that has polluted life in Denmark. The new order — established by Fortinbras at the play's end — is achieved precisely because Hamlet is willing and finally able to sacrifice himself in a necessary purgation of the diseased state.

These kinds of archetypal patterns exist potentially in any literary period. Consider how in Chopin's "The Story of an Hour" Mrs. Mallard's life parallels the end of winter and the earth's renewal in spring. When she feels a surge of new life after grieving over her husband's death, her own sensibilities are closely aligned with the "new spring life" that is "all aquiver" outside her window. Although she initially tries to resist that renewal by "beat[ing] it back with her will," she cannot control the life force that surges within her and all around her. When she finally gives herself to the energy and life she experiences, she feels triumphant — like a "goddess of Victory." But this victory is short lived when she learns that her husband is still alive and with him all the obligations that made her marriage feel like a wasteland. Her death is an ironic version of a rebirth ritual. The coming of spring is an ironic contrast to her own discovery that she can no longer live a repressed, circumscribed life with her husband. Death turns out to be preferable to the living death that her marriage means to her. Although spring will go on, this "goddess of Victory" is defeated by a devastating social contract. The old, corrupt order continues, and that for Chopin is a cruel irony that mythological critics would see as an unnatural disruption of the nature of things.

READER-RESPONSE STRATEGIES

Reader-response criticism, as its name implies, focuses its attention on the reader rather than the work itself. This approach to literature describes what goes on in the reader's mind during the process of reading a text. In a sense, all critical approaches (especially psychological and mythological criticism) concern themselves with a reader's response to literature, but there is a stronger emphasis in reader-response criticism on the reader's active construction of the text. Although many critical theories inform reader-response criticism, all *reader-response critics* aim to describe the reader's experience of a work: in effect we get a reading of the reader, who comes to the work with certain expectations and assumptions, which are either met or not met. Hence the consciousness of the reader — produced by reading the work — is the subject matter of reader-response critics. Just as writing is a creative act, reading is, since it also produces a text.

Reader-response critics do not assume that a literary work is a finished product with fixed formal properties, as, for example, formalist critics do. Instead, the literary work is seen as an evolving creation of the reader as he or she processes characters, plots, images, and other elements while reading. Some reader-response critics argue that this act of creative reading is, to a degree, controlled by the text, but it can produce many interpretations of the same text by different readers. There is no single definitive reading of a work, because the crucial assumption is that readers create rather than discover meanings in texts. Readers who have gone back to works they had read earlier in their lives often find that a later reading draws very different responses from them. What earlier seemed unimportant is now crucial; what at first seemed central is now barely worth noting. The reason, put simply, is that two different people have read the same text. Reader-response critics are not after the "correct" reading of the text or what the author presumably intended; instead they are interested in the reader's experience with the text.

These experiences change with readers; although the text remains the same, the readers do not. Social and cultural values influence readings, so that, for example, an avowed Marxist would be likely to come away from Miller's *Death of a Salesman* with a very different view of American capitalism than that of, say, a successful sales representative, who might attribute Willy Loman's fall more to his character than to the American economic system. Moreover, readers from different time periods respond differently to texts. An Elizabethan — concerned perhaps with the stability of monarchical rule — might respond differently to Hamlet's problems than would a twenty-first-century reader well versed in psychology and concepts of what Freud called the Oedipus complex. This is not to say that anything goes, that Miller's play can be read as an amoral defense of cheating and rapacious business practices or that *Hamlet* is about the dangers of living away from home. The text does, after all, establish some limits that allow us to reject certain readings as erroneous. But reader-response critics do reject formalist approaches that describe a literary work as a self-contained object, the meaning of which can be determined without reference to any extrinsic matters, such as the social and cultural values assumed by either the author or the reader.

Reader-response criticism calls attention to how we read and what influences our readings. It does not attempt to define what a literary work means on the page but rather what it does to an informed reader, a reader who understands the language and conventions used in a given work. Reader-response criticism is not a rationale for mistaken or bizarre readings of works but an exploration of the possibilities for a plurality of readings shaped by readers' experiences with the text. This kind of strategy can help us understand how our responses are shaped by both the text and ourselves.

Chopin's "The Story of an Hour" illustrates how reader-response critical strategies read the reader. Chopin doesn't say that Mrs. Mallard's marriage is repressive; instead, that troubling fact dawns on the reader at the same time that the recognition forces its way into Mrs. Mallard's consciousness. Her surprise is also the reader's because although she remains in the midst of intense grief, she is on the threshold of a startling discovery about the new possibilities life offers. How the reader responds to that discovery, however, is not entirely controlled by Chopin. One reader, perhaps someone who has recently lost a spouse, might find Mrs. Mallard's "joy" indeed "monstrous" and selfish. Certainly that's how Mrs. Mallard's doctors — the seemingly authoritative diagnosticians in the story — would very

likely read her. But for other readers — especially twenty-first-century readers steeped in feminist values — Mrs. Mallard's feelings require no justification. Such readers might find Chopin's ending to the story more ironic
than she seems to have intended because Mrs. Mallard's death could be
read as Chopin's inability to envision a protagonist who has the strength
of her convictions. In contrast, a reader in 1894 might have seen the ending
as Mrs. Mallard's only escape from the repressive marriage her husband's
assumed death suddenly allowed her to see. A reader in our times probably
would argue that it was the marriage that should have died rather than
Mrs. Mallard, that she had other alternatives, not just obligations (as the
doctors would have insisted), to consider.

By imagining different readers, we can imagine a variety of responses
to the story that are influenced by the readers' own impressions, memories,
or experiences with marriage. Such imagining suggests the ways in which
reader-response criticism opens up texts to a number of interpretations. As
one final example, consider how readers' responses to "The Story of an
Hour" would be affected if it were printed in two different magazines, read
in the context of either *Ms.* or *Good Housekeeping.* What assumptions and
beliefs would each magazine's readership be likely to bring to the story?
How do you think the respective experiences and values of each magazine's
readers would influence their readings? For a sample reader-response student paper on "The Story of an Hour," see page 19.

DECONSTRUCTIONIST STRATEGIES

Deconstructionist critics insist that literary works do not yield fixed, single
meanings. They argue that there can be no absolute knowledge about anything because language can never say what we intend it to mean. Anything
we write conveys meanings we did not intend, so the deconstructionist
argument goes. Language is not a precise instrument but a power whose
meanings are caught in an endless web of possibilities that cannot be
untangled. Accordingly, any idea or statement that insists on being understood separately can ultimately be "deconstructed" to reveal its relations
and connections to contradictory and opposite meanings.

Unlike other forms of criticism, **deconstructionism** seeks to destabilize
meanings instead of establishing them. In contrast to formalists such as
the New Critics, who closely examine a work in order to call attention to
how its various components interact to establish a unified whole, deconstructionists try to show how a close examination of the language in a text
inevitably reveals conflicting, contradictory impulses that "deconstruct" or
break down its apparent unity.

Although deconstructionists and New Critics both examine the language of a text closely, deconstructionists focus on the gaps and ambiguities that reveal a text's instability and indeterminacy, whereas New Critics

look for patterns that explain how the text's fixed meaning is structured. Deconstructionists painstakingly examine the competing meanings within the text rather than attempting to resolve them into a unified whole.

The questions deconstructionists ask are aimed at discovering and describing how a variety of possible readings are generated by the elements of a text. In contrast to a New Critic's concerns about the ultimate meaning of a work, a deconstructionist is primarily interested in how the use of language — diction, tone, metaphor, symbol, and so on — yields only provisional, not definitive, meanings. Consider, for example, the following excerpt from an American Puritan poet, Anne Bradstreet. The excerpt is from "The Flesh and the Spirit" (1678), which consists of an allegorical debate between two sisters, the body and the soul. During the course of the debate, Flesh, a consummate materialist, insists that Spirit values ideas that do not exist and that her faith in idealism is both unwarranted and insubstantial in the face of the material values that earth has to offer — riches, fame, and physical pleasure. Spirit, however, rejects the materialistic worldly argument that the only ultimate reality is physical reality and pledges her faith in God:

> Mine eye doth pierce the heavens and see
> What is invisible to thee.
> My garments are not silk nor gold,
> Nor such like trash which earth doth hold,
> But royal robes I shall have on,
> More glorious than the glist'ning sun;
> My crown not diamonds, pearls, and gold,
> But such as angels' heads enfold
> The city where I hope to dwell,
> There's none on earth can parallel;
> The stately walls both high and strong,
> Are made of precious jasper stone;
> The gates of pearl, both rich and clear,
> And angels are for porters there;
> The streets thereof transparent gold,
> Such as no eye did e'er behold;
> A crystal river there doth run,
> Which doth proceed from the Lamb's throne.

A deconstructionist would point out that Spirit's language — her use of material images such as jasper stone, pearl, gold, and crystal — cancels the explicit meaning of the passage by offering a supermaterialistic reward to the spiritually faithful. Her language, in short, deconstructs her intended meaning by employing the same images that Flesh would use to describe the rewards of the physical world. A deconstructionist reading, then, reveals the impossibility of talking about the invisible and spiritual worlds without using materialistic (that is, metaphoric) language. Thus Spirit's very language demonstrates a contradiction and conflict in her conviction that the world of here and now must be rejected for the hereafter. Her language deconstructs her meaning.

Deconstructionists look for ways to question and extend the meanings of a text. A deconstructionist might find, for example, the ironic ending of Chopin's "The Story of an Hour" less tidy and conclusive than would a New Critic, who might attribute Mrs. Mallard's death to her sense of lost personal freedom. A deconstructionist might use the story's ending to suggest that the narrative shares the doctors' inability to imagine a life for Mrs. Mallard apart from her husband. As difficult as it is controversial, deconstructionism is not easily summarized or paraphrased.

54

Reading and the Writing Process

I can't write five words but that I change seven.

— DOROTHY PARKER

© Mary Evans Picture Library/Alamy.

THE PURPOSE AND VALUE OF WRITING ABOUT LITERATURE

Introductory literature courses typically include three components — reading, discussion, and writing. Students usually find the readings a pleasure, the class discussions a revelation, and the writing assignments — at least initially — a little intimidating. Writing an analysis of Melville's use of walls in "Bartleby, the Scrivener" (p. 142), for example, may seem considerably more daunting than making a case for animal rights or analyzing a campus newspaper editorial that calls for grade reforms. Like Bartleby, you might want to respond with "I would prefer not to." Literary topics are not, however, all that different from the kinds of papers assigned in English composition courses; many of the same skills are required for both. Regardless of the type of paper, you must develop a thesis and support it with evidence in language that is clear and persuasive.

Whether the subject matter is a marketing survey, a political issue, or a literary work, writing is a method of communicating information and perceptions. Writing teaches. But before writing becomes an instrument for informing the reader, it serves as a means of learning for the writer. An essay is a process of discovery as well as a record of what has been discovered. One of the chief benefits of writing is that we frequently realize what we want to say only after trying out ideas on a page and seeing our thoughts take shape in language.

More specifically, writing about a literary work encourages us to be better readers because it requires a close examination of the elements of a short story, poem, or play. To determine how plot, character, setting, point of view, style, tone, irony, or any number of other literary elements function in a work, we must study them in relation to one another as well as separately. Speed-reading won't do. To read a text accurately and validly — neither ignoring nor distorting significant details — we must return to the work repeatedly to test our responses and interpretations. By paying attention to details and being sensitive to the author's use of language, we develop a clearer understanding of how the work conveys its effects and meanings.

Nevertheless, students sometimes ask why it is necessary or desirable to write about a literary work. Why not allow stories, poems, and plays to speak for themselves? Isn't it presumptuous to interpret Hemingway, Dickinson, or Shakespeare? These writers do, of course, speak for themselves, but they do so indirectly. Literary criticism seeks not to replace the text by explaining it but to enhance our readings of works by calling attention to elements that we might have overlooked or only vaguely sensed.

Another misunderstanding about the purpose of literary criticism is that it crankily restricts itself to finding faults in a work. Critical essays are sometimes mistakenly equated with newspaper and magazine reviews of recently published works. Reviews typically include summaries and evaluations to inform readers about a work's nature and quality, but critical essays assume that readers are already familiar with a work. Although a critical essay may point out limitations and flaws, most criticism — and certainly the kind of essay usually written in an introductory literature course — is designed to explain, analyze, and reveal the complexities of a work. Such sensitive consideration increases our appreciation of the writer's achievement and significantly adds to our enjoyment of a short story, poem, or play. In short, the purpose and value of writing about literature are that doing so leads to greater understanding and pleasure.

READING THE WORK CLOSELY

Know the piece of literature you are writing about before you begin your essay. Think about how the work makes you feel and how it is put together. The more familiar you are with how the various elements of the text convey effects and meanings, the more confident you will be explaining whatever perspective on it you ultimately choose. Do not insist that everything make sense on a first reading. Relax and enjoy yourself; you can be attentive and still allow the author's words to work their magic on you. With subsequent readings, however, go more slowly and analytically as you try to establish relations between characters, actions, images, or whatever else seems important. Ask yourself why you respond as you do. Think as you read, and notice how the parts of a work contribute to its overall nature. Whether the work is a short story, poem, or play, you will read relevant portions of it over and over, and you will very likely find more to discuss in each review if the work is rich.

It's best to avoid reading other critical discussions of a work before you are thoroughly familiar with it. There are several good reasons for following this advice. By reading interpretations before you know a work, you deny yourself the pleasure of discovery. That is a bit like starting with the last chapter in a mystery novel. But perhaps even more important than protecting the surprise and delight that a work might offer is that a premature reading of a critical discussion will probably short-circuit your own responses. You will see the work through the critic's eyes and have to struggle with someone else's perceptions and ideas before you can develop your own.

Reading criticism can be useful, but not until you have thought through your own impressions of the text. A guide should not be permitted to become a tyrant. This does not mean, however, that you should avoid background information about a work — for example, that Joyce Carol Oates's story "The Lady with the Pet Dog" (p. 237) was based on a similar story by Anton Chekhov (p. 223). Knowing something about the author as well as historic and literary contexts can help to create expectations that enhance your reading.

ANNOTATING THE TEXT AND JOURNAL NOTE TAKING

As you read, get in the habit of annotating your texts. Whether you write marginal notes, highlight, underline, or draw boxes and circles around important words and phrases, you'll eventually develop a system that allows you to retrieve significant ideas and elements from the text. Another way to record your impressions of a work — as with any other experience — is to keep a journal. By writing down your reactions to characters, images, language, actions, and other matters in a reading journal, you can often determine why you like or dislike a work or feel sympathetic or antagonistic to an author or discover paths into a work that might have eluded you if you hadn't preserved your impressions. Your journal notes and annotations may take whatever form you find useful; full sentences and grammatical correctness are not essential (unless they are to be handed in and your instructor requires that), though they might allow you to make better sense of your own reflections days later. The point is simply to put in writing thoughts that you can retrieve when you need them for class discussion or a writing assignment. Consider the following student annotation of the first twenty-four lines of Andrew Marvell's "To His Coy Mistress" (p. 812) and the journal entry that follows it:

Annotated Text

If we had time . . .

> Had we but world enough, and time,   *Waste life and you*
> This coyness, lady, were no crime.   *steal from yourself.*
> We would sit down, and think which way
> To walk, and pass our long love's day.
> Thou by the Indian Ganges' side   5
> Shouldst rubies find; I by the tide
> Of Humber would complain.° I would   *Measurements*   *write love songs*
> Love you ten years before the Flood,   *of time*
> And you should, if you please, refuse
> Till the conversion of the Jews.   10
> My vegetable love should grow,°   *slow, unconscious growth*
> Vaster than empires, and more slow;
> An hundred years should go to praise
> Thine eyes and on thy forehead gaze,
> Two hundred to adore each breast,   15
> But thirty thousand to the rest:
> An age at least to every part,
> And the last age should show your heart.
> For, lady, you deserve this state,
> Nor would I love at lower rate.   20

contrast river and desert images

> But at my back I always hear   *Lines move faster here—*
> Time's wingèd chariot hurrying near;   *tone changes.*
> And yonder all before us lie
> Deserts of vast eternity.   *This eternity rushes in.*

Journal Note

He'd be patient and wait for his "mistress" if they had the time—sing songs, praise her, adore her, etc. But they don't have that much time according to him. He *seems* to be patient but he actually begins by calling patience—her coyness—a "crime." Looks to me like he's got his mind made up from the beginning of the poem. Where's her response? I'm not sure about him.

This journal note responds to some of the effects noted in the annotations of the poem; it's an excellent beginning for making sense of the speaker's argument in the poem.

Taking notes will preserve your initial reactions to the work. Many times first impressions are the best. Your response to a peculiar character in a story, a striking phrase in a poem, or a subtle bit of stage business in a play might lead to larger perceptions. The student paper on John Updike's "A & P" (p. 2089), for example, began with the student writing "how come?" next to the story's title in her textbook. She thought it strange that the title didn't refer to a character or the story's conflict. That annotated response eventually led her to examine the significance of the setting, which became the central idea of her paper.

You should take detailed notes only after you've read through the work. If you write too many notes during the first reading, you're likely to disrupt your response. Moreover, until you have a sense of the entire work, it will be difficult to determine how connections can be made among its various elements. In addition to recording your first impressions and noting significant passages, characters, actions, and so on, you should consult the Questions for Responsive Reading and Writing about fiction (p. 53), poetry (p. 791), and drama (p. 1408). These questions can assist you in getting inside a work as well as organizing your notes.

Inevitably, you will take more notes than you finally use in the paper. Note taking is a form of thinking aloud, but because your ideas are on paper you don't have to worry about forgetting them. As you develop a better sense of a potential topic, your notes will become more focused and detailed.

CHOOSING A TOPIC

If your instructor assigns a topic or offers a choice from among an approved list of topics, some of your work is already completed. Instead of being asked to come up with a topic about *Antigone,* you may be asked to write a three-page essay that specifically discusses "Antigone's decision to defy Creon." You also have the assurance that a specified topic will be manageable within the suggested number of pages. Unless you ask your instructor for permission to write on a different or related topic, be certain to address yourself to the assignment. An essay that does not discuss Antigone's decision but instead describes her relationship with her sister would be missing the point. Notice too that there is room even in an assigned topic to develop your own approach. One question that immediately comes to mind is whether Antigone is justified in defying Creon's authority. Assigned topics do not relieve you of thinking about an aspect of a work, but they do focus your thinking.

At some point during the course, you may have to begin an essay from scratch. You might, for example, be asked to write about a short story that somehow impressed you or that seemed particularly well written or filled with insights. Before you start considering a topic, you should have a sense of how long the paper will be because the assigned length can help to determine the extent to which you should develop your topic. Ideally, the paper's length should be based on how much space you deem necessary to present your discussion clearly and convincingly, but if you have any doubts and no specific guidelines have been indicated, ask. The question is important; a topic that might be appropriate for a three-page paper could be too narrow for ten pages. Three pages would probably be adequate for a discussion of why Emily murders Homer in Faulkner's "A Rose for Emily." Conversely, it would be futile to try to summarize Faulkner's use of the South in his fiction in even ten pages; this would have to be narrowed to something like "Images of the South in 'A Rose for Emily.'" Be sure that the topic you choose can be adequately covered in the assigned number of pages.

Once you have a firm sense of how much you are expected to write, you can begin to decide on your topic. If you are to choose what work to write about, select one that genuinely interests you. Too often students pick a story, poem, or play because it is mercifully short or seems simple. Such works can certainly be the subjects of fine essays, but simplicity should not be the major reason for selecting them. Choose a work that has moved you so that you have something to say about it. The student who wrote about "A & P" was initially attracted to the story's title because she had once worked in a similar store. After reading the story, she became fascinated with its setting because Updike's descriptions seemed so accurate. Her paper then grew out of her curiosity about the setting's purpose. When a writer is engaged in a topic, the paper has a better chance of being interesting to a reader.

After you have settled on a particular work, your notes and annotations of the text should prove useful for generating a topic. The paper on "The A & P as a State of Mind" developed naturally from the notes (p. 2089) that the student jotted down about the setting and antagonist. If you think with a pen in your hand, you are likely to find when you review your notes that your thoughts have clustered into one or more topics. Perhaps there are patterns of imagery that seem to make a point about life. There may be scenes that are ironically paired or secondary characters who reveal certain qualities about the protagonist. Your notes and annotations on such aspects can lead you to a particular effect or impression. Having chuckled your way through "A & P," you may discover that your notations about the story's humor point to a serious satire of society's values.

DEVELOPING A THESIS

When you are satisfied that you have something interesting to say about a work and that your notes have led you to a focused topic, you can formulate a **thesis,** the central idea of the paper. Whereas the topic indicates what the paper focuses on (the setting in "A & P"), the thesis explains what you have to say about the topic (because the intolerant setting of "A & P" is the antagonist in the story, it is crucial to our understanding of Sammy's decision to quit his job). The thesis should be a complete sentence (though sometimes it may require more than one sentence) that establishes your topic in clear, unambiguous language. The thesis may be revised as you get further into the topic and discover what you want to say about it, but once the thesis is firmly established, it will serve as a guide for you and your reader because all the information and observations in your essay should be related to the thesis.

One student on an initial reading of Andrew Marvell's "To His Coy Mistress" saw that the male speaker of the poem urges a woman to love now before time runs out for them. This reading gave him the impression that the poem is a simple celebration of the pleasures of the flesh, but on subsequent readings he underlined or noted these images: "Time's wingèd chariot hurrying near"; "Deserts of vast eternity"; "marble vault"; "worms"; "dust"; "ashes"; and these two lines: "The grave's a fine and private place, / But none, I think, do there embrace."

By listing these images associated with time and death, he established an inventory that could be separated from the rest of his notes on point of view, character, sounds, and other subjects. Inventorying notes allows patterns to emerge that you might have only vaguely perceived otherwise. Once these images are grouped, they call attention to something darker and more complex in Marvell's poem than a first impression might suggest.

These images may create a different feeling about the poem, but they still don't explain very much. One simple way to generate a thesis about a literary work is to ask the question "why?" Why do these images appear in the poem? Why does Hamlet hesitate to avenge his father's death? Why does Hemingway choose the Midwest as the setting of "Soldier's Home"? Your responses to these kinds of questions can lead to a thesis.

Writers sometimes use freewriting to help themselves explore possible answers to such questions. It can be an effective way of generating ideas. Freewriting is exactly that: the technique calls for nonstop writing without concern for mechanics or editing of any kind. Freewriting for ten minutes or so on a question will result in fragments and repetitions, but it can also produce some ideas. Here's an example of a student's response to the question about the images in "To His Coy Mistress":

He wants her to make love. Love poem. There's little time. Her crime. He exaggerates. Sincere? Sly? What's he want? She says nothing—he says it all. What about deserts, ashes, graves, and worms? Some love poem. Sounds like an old Vincent Price movie. Full of sweetness but death creeps in. Death—hurry hurry! Tear pleasures. What passion! Where's death in this? How can a love poem be so ghoulish? She does nothing. Maybe frightened? Convinced? Why death? Love and death—time—death.

This freewriting contains several ideas; it begins by alluding to the poem's plot and speaker, but the central idea seems to be death. This emphasis led the student to five potential thesis statements for his essay about the poem:

1. "To His Coy Mistress" is a difficult poem.

2. Death in "To His Coy Mistress."

3. There are many images of death in "To His Coy Mistress."

4. "To His Coy Mistress" celebrates the pleasures of the flesh, but it also recognizes the power of death to end that pleasure.

5. On the surface, "To His Coy Mistress" is a celebration of the pleasures of the flesh, but this witty seduction is tempered by a chilling recognition of the reality of death.

The first statement is too vague to be useful. In what sense is the poem difficult? A more precise phrasing, indicating the nature of the difficulty, is needed. The second statement is a topic rather than a thesis. Because it is not a sentence, it does not express a complete idea about how the poem treats death. Although this could be an appropriate title, it is inadequate as a thesis statement. The third statement, like the first one, identifies the topic, but even though it is a sentence, it is not a complete idea that tells us anything significant beyond the fact it states. After these preliminary attempts to develop a thesis, the student remembered his first impression of the poem and incorporated it into his thesis statement. The fourth thesis is a useful approach to the poem because it limits the topic and indicates how it will be treated in the paper: the writer will begin with an initial impression of the poem and then go on to qualify it. However, the fifth thesis is better than the fourth because it indicates a shift in tone produced by the ironic relationship between death and flesh. An effective thesis, like this one, makes a clear statement about a manageable topic and provides a firm sense of direction for the paper.

Most writing assignments in a literature course require you to persuade readers that your thesis is reasonable and supported with evidence. Papers that report information without comment or evaluation are simply summaries. A plot summary of Shakespeare's *The Tempest*, for example, would have no thesis, but a paper that discussed how Prospero's oppression of Caliban represents European imperialism and colonialism would argue a thesis. Similarly, a paper that merely pointed out the death images in "To His Coy Mistress" would not contain a thesis, but a paper that attempted to make a case for the death imagery as a grim reminder of how vulnerable flesh is would involve persuasion. In developing a thesis, remember that you are expected not merely to present information but to argue a point.

ARGUING ABOUT LITERATURE

An argumentative essay is designed to make persuasive your interpretation of a work. Arguing about literature doesn't mean that you're engaged in an angry, antagonistic dispute (though controversial topics do sometimes engender heated debates; see, for example, Joan Templeton's comments in the Critical Case Study on Ibsen's *A Doll House* [p. 1772]). Instead, argumentation requires that you present your interpretation of a work (or a portion of it) by supporting your discussion with clearly defined terms, ample evidence, and a detailed analysis of relevant portions of the text.

If you have a choice, it's generally best to write about a topic that you feel strongly about. If you're not fascinated by Bartleby the Scrivener's haunting presence in Melville's short story, then perhaps you'll find chilling Emily Grierson's behavior in Faulkner's "A Rose for Emily," or maybe you can explain why Bartleby's character is so excruciatingly boring to you. If your essay is to be interesting and convincing, what is important is that it be written from a strong point of view that persuasively argues your evaluation, analysis, and interpretation of a work. It is not enough to say that you like or dislike a work; instead you must give your reader some ideas and evidence that can be accepted or rejected based on the quality of the answers to the questions you raise.

One way to come up with persuasive answers is to generate good questions that will lead you further into the text and to critical issues related to it. Notice how the Perspectives, Complementary Critical Readings, Critical Case Studies, and Cultural Case Studies in this anthology raise significant questions and issues about texts from a variety of points of view. Moreover, the Critical Strategies for Reading summarized in Chapter 53 can be a resource for raising questions that can be shaped into an argument, and the Questions for Writing: Incorporating the Critics (p. 523) can help you to incorporate a critic's perspective into your own argument. The following lists of questions for the critical approaches covered in Chapter 53 should be useful for discovering arguments you might make about a short story, poem, or play. The page number that follows each heading refers to the discussion in the anthology for that particular approach.

Questions for Arguing about Literature

FORMALIST QUESTIONS (P. 2046)

1. How do various elements of the work — plot, character, point of view, setting, tone, diction, images, symbol, and so on — reinforce its meanings?
2. How are the elements related to the whole?

(continued)

3. What is the work's major organizing principle? How is its structure unified?

4. What issues does the work raise? How does the work's structure resolve those issues?

BIOGRAPHICAL QUESTIONS (P. 2048)

1. Are facts about the writer's life relevant to your understanding of the work?

2. Are characters and incidents in the work versions of the writer's own experiences? Are they treated factually or imaginatively?

3. How do you think the writer's values are reflected in the work?

PSYCHOLOGICAL QUESTIONS (P. 2050)

1. How does the work reflect the author's personal psychology?

2. What do the characters' emotions and behavior reveal about their psychological states? What types of personalities are they?

3. Are psychological matters such as repression, dreams, and desire presented consciously or unconsciously by the author?

HISTORICAL QUESTIONS (P. 2052)

1. How does the work reflect the period in which it is written?

2. What literary or historical influences helped to shape the form and content of the work?

3. How important is the historical context to interpreting the work?

MARXIST QUESTIONS (P. 2053)

1. How are class differences presented in the work? Are characters aware or unaware of the economic and social forces that affect their lives?

2. How do economic conditions determine the characters' lives?

3. What ideological values are explicit or implicit?

4. Does the work challenge or affirm the social order it describes?

NEW HISTORICIST QUESTIONS (P. 2054)

1. What kinds of documents outside the work seem especially relevant for shedding light on the work?

2. How are social values contemporary to the work reflected or refuted in the work?

3. How does your own historical moment affect your reading of the work and its historical reconstruction?

CULTURAL STUDIES QUESTIONS (P. 2055)

1. What does the work reveal about the cultural behavior contemporary to it?

2. How does popular culture contemporary to the work reflect or challenge the values implicit or explicit in the work?

3. What kinds of cultural documents contemporary to the work add to your reading of it?

4. How do your own cultural assumptions affect your reading of the work and the culture contemporary to it?

GENDER STUDIES QUESTIONS (P. 2056)

1. How are the lives of men and women portrayed in the work? Do the men and women in the work accept or reject these roles?

2. Is the form and content of the work influenced by the author's gender?

3. What attitudes are explicit or implicit concerning heterosexual, homosexual, or lesbian relationships? Are these relationships sources of conflict? Do they provide resolutions to conflicts?

4. Does the work challenge or affirm traditional ideas about men and women and same-sex relationships?

MYTHOLOGICAL QUESTIONS (P. 2058)

1. How does the story resemble other stories in plot, character, setting, or use of symbols?

2. Are archetypes presented, such as quests, initiations, scapegoats, or withdrawals and returns?

3. Does the protagonist undergo any kind of transformation such as a movement from innocence to experience that seems archetypal?

4. Do any specific allusions to myths shed light on the text?

READER-RESPONSE QUESTIONS (P. 2060)

1. How do you respond to the work?

2. How do your own experiences and expectations affect your reading and interpretation?

3. What is the work's original or intended audience? To what extent are you similar to or different from that audience?

4. Do you respond in the same way to the work after more than one reading?

DECONSTRUCTIONIST QUESTIONS (P. 2062)

1. How are contradictory and opposing meanings expressed in the work?

2. How does meaning break down or deconstruct itself in the language of the text?

3. Would you say that ultimate definitive meanings are impossible to determine and establish in the text? Why? How does that affect your interpretation?

4. How are implicit ideological values revealed in the work?

(continued)

These questions will not apply to all texts; and they are not mutually exclusive. They can be combined to explore a text from several critical perspectives simultaneously. A feminist approach to Kate Chopin's "The Story of an Hour" could also use Marxist concerns about class to make observations about the oppression of women's lives in the historical context of the nineteenth century. Your use of these questions should allow you to discover significant issues from which you can develop an argumentative essay that is organized around clearly defined terms, relevant evidence, and a persuasive analysis.

ORGANIZING A PAPER

After you have chosen a manageable topic and developed a thesis, a central idea about it, you can begin to organize your paper. Your thesis, even if it is still somewhat tentative, should help you decide what information will need to be included and provide you with a sense of direction.

Consider again the sample thesis in the section on developing a thesis:

On the surface, "To His Coy Mistress" is a celebration of the pleasures of the flesh, but this witty seduction is tempered by a chilling recognition of the reality of death.

This thesis indicates that the paper can be divided into two parts — the pleasures of the flesh and the reality of death. It also indicates an order: because the central point is to show that the poem is more than a simple celebration, the pleasures of the flesh should be discussed first so that another, more complex, reading of the poem can follow. If the paper began with the reality of death, its point would be anticlimactic.

Having established such a broad and informal outline, you can draw on your underlinings, margin notations, and note cards for the subheadings and evidence required to explain the major sections of your paper. This next level of detail would look like the following:

1. Pleasures of the flesh

   Part of the traditional tone of love poetry

2. Recognition of death

   Ironic treatment of love

   Diction

   Images

   Figures of speech

   Symbols

   Tone

This list was initially a jumble of terms, but the student arranged the items so that each of the two major sections leads to a discussion of tone. (The student also found it necessary to drop some biographical information from his notes because it was irrelevant to the thesis.) The list indicates that the first part of the paper will establish the traditional tone of love poetry that celebrates the pleasures of the flesh, while the second part will present a more detailed discussion about the ironic recognition of death. The emphasis is on the latter because that is the point to be argued in the paper. Hence, the thesis has helped to organize the parts of the paper, establish an order, and indicate the paper's proper proportions.

The next step is to fill in the subheadings with information from your notes. Many experienced writers find that making lists of information to be included under each subheading is an efficient way to develop paragraphs. For a longer paper (perhaps a research paper), you should be able to develop a paragraph or more on each subheading. On the other hand, a shorter paper may require that you combine several subheadings in a paragraph. You may also discover that while an informal list is adequate for a brief paper, a ten-page assignment could require a more detailed outline. Use the method that is most productive for you. Whatever the length of the essay, your presentation must be in a coherent and logical order that allows your reader to follow the argument and evaluate the evidence. The quality of your reading can be demonstrated only by the quality of your writing.

WRITING A DRAFT

The time for sharpening pencils, arranging your desk, and doing almost anything else instead of writing has ended. The first draft will appear on the page only if you stop avoiding the inevitable and sit, stand up, or lie down to write. It makes no difference how you write, just so you do. Now that you have developed a topic into a tentative thesis, you can assemble your notes and begin to flesh out whatever outline you have made.

Be flexible. Your outline should smoothly conduct you from one point to the next, but do not permit it to railroad you. If a relevant and important idea occurs to you now, work it into the draft. By using the first draft as a means of thinking about what you want to say, you will very likely discover more than your notes originally suggested. Plenty of good writers don't use outlines at all but discover ordering principles as they write. Do not attempt to compose a perfectly correct draft the first time around. Grammar, punctuation, and spelling can wait until you revise. Concentrate on what you are saying. Good writing most often occurs when you are in hot pursuit of an idea rather than in a nervous search for errors.

To make revising easier, leave wide margins and extra space between lines so that you can easily add words, sentences, and corrections. Write on only one side of the paper. Your pages will be easier to keep track of that way, and, if you have to clip a paragraph to place it elsewhere, you will not lose any writing on the other side.

If you are working on a word processor, you can take advantage of its capacity to make additions and deletions as well as move entire paragraphs by making just a few simple keyboard commands. Some software programs can also check spelling and certain grammatical elements in your writing. It's worth remembering, however, that though a clean copy fresh off a printer may look terrific, it will read only as well as the thinking and writing that have gone into it. Many writers prudently store their data on disks and print their pages each time they finish a draft to avoid losing any material because of power failures or other problems. These printouts are also easier to read than the screen when you work on revisions.

Once you have a first draft on paper, you can delete material that is unrelated to your thesis and add material necessary to illustrate your points and make your paper convincing. The student who wrote "The A & P as a State of Mind" wisely dropped a paragraph that questioned whether Sammy displays chauvinistic attitudes toward women. Although this is an interesting issue, it has nothing to do with the thesis, which explains how the setting influences Sammy's decision to quit his job. Instead of including that paragraph, she added one that described Lengel's crabbed response to the girls so that she could lead up to the A & P "policy" he enforces.

Remember that your initial draft is only that. You should go through the paper many times — and then again — working to substantiate and clarify your ideas. You may even end up with several entire versions of the paper. Rewrite. The sentences within each paragraph should be related to a single topic. Transitions should connect one paragraph to the next so that there are no abrupt or confusing shifts. Awkward or wordy phrasing or unclear sentences and paragraphs should be mercilessly poked and prodded into shape.

Writing the Introduction and Conclusion

After you have clearly and adequately developed the body of your paper, pay particular attention to the introductory and concluding paragraphs. It's probably best to write the introduction — at least the final version of it — last, after you know precisely what you are introducing. Because this paragraph is crucial for generating interest in the topic, it should engage the reader and provide a sense of what the paper is about. There is no formula for writing effective introductory paragraphs because each writing situation is different — depending on the audience, topic, and approach — but if you pay attention to the introductions of the essays you read, you will notice a variety of possibilities. The introductory paragraph to "The A & P as a State of Mind," for example, is a straightforward explanation of why the story's setting is important for understanding Updike's treatment of the antagonist. The rest of the paper then offers evidence to support this point.

Concluding paragraphs demand equal attention because they leave the reader with a final impression. The conclusion should provide a sense of closure instead of starting a new topic or ending abruptly. In the final paragraph about the significance of the setting in "A & P," the student brings together the reasons Sammy quit his job by referring to his refusal to accept Lengel's store policies. At the same time she makes this point, she also explains the significance of Sammy ringing up the "No Sale" mentioned in her introductory paragraph. Thus, we are brought back to where we began, but we now have a greater understanding of why Sammy quits his job. Of course, the body of your paper is the most important part of your presentation, but do remember that first and last impressions have a powerful impact on readers.

Using Quotations

Quotations can be a valuable means of marshaling evidence to illustrate and support your ideas. A judicious use of quoted material will make your points clearer and more convincing. Here are some guidelines that should help you use quotations effectively.

1. Brief quotations (four lines or fewer of prose or three lines or fewer of poetry) should be carefully introduced and integrated into the text of your paper with quotation marks around them:

According to the narrator, Bertha "had a reputation for strictness." He tells us that she always "wore dark clothes, dressed her hair simply, and expected contrition and obedience from her pupils."

For brief poetry quotations, use a slash to indicate a division between lines:

The concluding lines of Blake's "The Tyger" pose a disturbing question: "What immortal hand or eye / Dare frame thy fearful symmetry?"

Lengthy quotations should be separated from the text of your paper. More than three lines of poetry should be double spaced and centered on the page. More than four lines of prose should be double spaced and indented one inch from the left margin, with the right margin the same as for the text. Do *not* use quotation marks for the passage; the indentation indicates that the passage is a quotation. Lengthy quotations should not be used in place of your own writing. Use them only if they are absolutely necessary.

2. If any words are added to a quotation, use brackets to distinguish your addition from the original source:

"He [Young Goodman Brown] is portrayed as self-righteous and disillusioned."

Any words inside quotation marks and not in brackets must be precisely those of the author. Brackets can also be used to change the grammatical structure of a quotation so that it fits into your sentence:

Smith argues that Chekhov "present[s] the narrator in an ambivalent light."

If you drop any words from the source, use ellipses to indicate the omission:

"Early to bed . . . makes a man healthy, wealthy, and wise."

Use ellipses following a period to indicate an omission at the end of a sentence:

"Early to bed and early to rise makes a man healthy. . . ."

Use a single line of spaced periods to indicate the omission of a line or more of poetry or more than one paragraph of prose:

Nothing would sleep in that cellar, dank as a ditch,
Bulbs broke out of boxes hunting for chinks in the dark,

. . . .

Nothing would give up life:
Even the dirt kept breathing a small breath.

3. You will be able to punctuate quoted material accurately and confidently if you observe these conventions.

Place commas and periods inside quotation marks:

"Even the dirt," Roethke insists, "kept breathing a small breath."

Even though a comma does not appear after "dirt" in the original quotation, it is placed inside the quotation mark. The exception to this rule occurs when a parenthetical reference to a source follows the quotation:

"Even the dirt," Roethke insists, "kept breathing a small breath" (11).

Punctuation marks other than commas or periods go outside the quotation marks unless they are part of the material quoted:

What does Roethke mean when he writes that "the dirt kept breathing a small breath"?

Yeats asked, "How can we know the dancer from the dance?"

REVISING AND EDITING

Put some distance—a day or so if you can—between yourself and each draft of your paper. The phrase that seemed just right on Wednesday may be revealed as all wrong on Friday. You'll have a better chance of detecting lumbering sentences and thin paragraphs if you plan ahead and give yourself the time to read your paper from a fresh perspective. Through the process of revision, you can transform a competent paper into an excellent one.

Begin by asking yourself if your approach to the topic requires any rethinking. Is the argument carefully thought out and logically presented? Are there any gaps in the presentation? How well is the paper organized? Do the paragraphs lead into one another? Does the body of the paper deliver what the thesis promises? Is the interpretation sound? Are any relevant and important elements of the work ignored or distorted to advance the thesis? Are the points supported with evidence? These large questions should be addressed before you focus on more detailed matters. If you uncover serious problems as a result of considering these questions, you'll probably have quite a lot of rewriting to do, but at least you will have the opportunity to correct the problems—even if doing so takes several drafts.

A useful technique for spotting awkward or unclear moments in the paper is to read it aloud. You might also try having a friend read it aloud to you. If your handwriting is legible, your friend's reading—perhaps accompanied by hesitations and puzzled expressions—could alert you to passages that need reworking. Having identified problems, you can readily correct them on a word processor or on the draft, provided you've skipped lines and used wide margins. The final draft you hand in should be neat and carefully proofread for any inadvertent errors.

The following checklist offers questions to ask about your paper as you revise and edit it. Most of these questions will be familiar to you; however, if you need help with any of them, ask your instructor or review the appropriate section in a composition handbook.

Questions for Writing: A Revision Checklist

1. Is the topic manageable? Is it too narrow or too broad?
2. Is the thesis clear? Is it based on a careful reading of the work?
3. Is the paper logically organized? Does it have a firm sense of direction?
4. Is your argument persuasive?
5. Should any material be deleted? Do any important points require further illustration or evidence?

(continued)

6. Does the opening paragraph introduce the topic in an interesting manner?

7. Are the paragraphs developed, unified, and coherent? Are any too short or long?

8. Are there transitions linking the paragraphs?

9. Does the concluding paragraph provide a sense of closure?

10. Is the tone appropriate? Is it unduly flippant or pretentious?

11. Is the title engaging and suggestive?

12. Are the sentences clear, concise, and complete?

13. Are simple, complex, and compound sentences used for variety?

14. Have technical terms been used correctly? Are you certain of the meanings of all the words in the paper? Are they spelled correctly?

15. Have you documented any information borrowed from books, articles, or other sources? Have you quoted too much instead of summarizing or paraphrasing secondary material?

16. Have you used a standard format for citing sources (see p. 2106)?

17. Have you followed your instructor's guidelines for the manuscript format of the final draft?

18. Have you carefully proofread the final draft?

When you proofread your final draft, you may find a few typographical errors that must be corrected but do not warrant reprinting an entire paper. Provided there are not more than a handful of such errors throughout the paper, they can be corrected as shown in the following passage. This example condenses a short paper's worth of errors; no single passage should be this shabby in your essay:

To add a letter or word, use a caret on the line where the addition *is* needed. To delete a word draw a single line through ~~through~~ it. Run-on words are separated by a vertical line, and inadvertent spaces are closed like this. Transposed letters are indicated this way. New paragraphs are noted with the sign ¶ in front of where the next paragraph is to begin. Unless you . . .

These sorts of errors can be minimized by proofreading on the screen and simply entering corrections as you go along.

MANUSCRIPT FORM

The novelist and poet Peter De Vries once observed that he very much enjoyed writing but that he couldn't bear the "paper work." Behind this playful pun is a half-serious impatience with the mechanics of it all. You may feel some of that too, but don't let your thoughtful, carefully revised paper trip over minor details. The final draft you hand in to your instructor should not only read well but look neat. If your instructor does not provide specific instructions concerning the format for the paper, follow these guidelines:

1. Papers (particularly long ones) should be typed on 8-1/2 by 11-inch paper in double space. Avoid transparent paper such as onionskin; it is difficult to read and write comments on. If you compose on a word processor, be certain that the print is legible. If your instructor accepts handwritten papers, write legibly in ink on only one side of a wide-lined page.

2. Use a one-inch margin at the top, bottom, and sides of each page. Unless you are instructed to include a separate title page, type your name, instructor's name, course number and section, and date on separate lines one inch below the upper-left corner of the first page. Double space between these lines and then center the title two spaces below the date. Do not underline or put quotation marks around your paper's title, but do use quotation marks around the titles of poems, short stories, or other brief works, and italicize the titles of books and plays (for instance, Racial Stereotypes in "Battle Royal" and *No Child . . .*). Begin the text of your paper two spaces below the title. If you have used secondary sources, list them on a separate page at the end of the paper. Center the heading "Notes" or "Works Cited" one inch from the top of the page and then double space between it and the entries.

3. Number each page consecutively, beginning with page 1, a half inch from the top of the page in the upper-right corner.

4. Gather the pages with a paper clip rather than staples, folders, or some other device. That will make it easier for your instructor to handle the paper.

TYPES OF WRITING ASSIGNMENTS

The types of papers most frequently assigned in literature classes are explication, analysis, and comparison and contrast. Most writing about literature involves some combination of these skills. This section includes a sample explication, an analysis, and a comparison and contrast paper. For a sample research paper that demonstrates a variety of strategies for documenting outside sources, see page 2113. For genre-based assignments, see the sample papers for writing about fiction (p. 19), poetry (p. 795), and drama (p. 1410).

Explication

The purpose of this approach to a literary work is to make the implicit explicit. *Explication* is a detailed explanation of a passage of poetry or prose. Because explication is an intensive examination of a text line by line, it is mostly used to interpret a short poem in its entirety or a brief passage from a long poem, short story, or play. Explication can be used in any kind of paper when you want to be specific about how a writer achieves a certain effect. An explication pays careful attention to language — the connotations of words, allusions, figurative language, irony, symbol, rhythm, sound, and so on. These elements are examined in relation to one another and to the overall effect and meaning of the work.

The simplest way to organize an explication is to move through the passage line by line, explaining whatever seems significant. It is wise to avoid, however, an assembly-line approach that begins each sentence with "In line one (two, three) . . ." Instead, organize your paper in whatever way best serves your thesis. You might find that the right place to start is with the final lines, working your way back to the beginning of the poem or passage. The following sample explication on Dickinson's "There's a certain Slant of light" does just that. The student's opening paragraph refers to the final line of the poem in order to present her thesis. She explains that though the poem begins with an image of light, it is not a bright or cheery poem but one concerned with "the look of Death." Since the last line prompted her thesis, that is where she begins the explication.

You might also find it useful to structure a paper by discussing various elements of literature, so that you have a paragraph on connotative words followed by one on figurative language and so on. However your paper is organized, keep in mind that the aim of an explication is not simply to summarize the passage but to comment on the effects and meanings produced by the author's use of language in it. An effective explication (the Latin word *explicare* means "to unfold") displays a text to reveal how it works and what it signifies. Although writing an explication requires some patience and sensitivity, it is an excellent method for coming to understand and appreciate the elements and qualities that constitute literary art.

A SAMPLE STUDENT EXPLICATION

A Reading of Dickinson's "There's a certain Slant of light"

The sample paper by Bonnie Katz is the result of an assignment calling for an explication of about 750 words on any poem by Emily Dickinson. Katz selected "There's a certain Slant of light."

EMILY DICKINSON (1830–1886)

There's a certain Slant of light

c. 1861

There's a certain Slant of light,
Winter Afternoons —
That oppresses, like the Heft
Of Cathedral Tunes —

Heavenly Hurt, it gives us —   5
We can find no scar,
But internal difference,
Where the Meanings, are —

None may teach it — Any —
'Tis the Seal Despair —   10
An imperial affliction
Sent us of the Air —

When it comes, the Landscape listens —
Shadows — hold their breath —
When it goes, 'tis like the Distance   15
On the look of Death —

This essay comments on every line of the poem and provides a coher-ent reading that relates each line to the speaker's intense awareness of death. Although the essay discusses each stanza in the order that it ap-pears, the introductory paragraph provides a brief overview explaining how the poem's images contribute to its total meaning. In addition, the student does not hesitate to discuss a line out of sequence when it can be usefully connected to another phrase. This is especially apparent in the third paragraph, in her discussion of stanzas 2 and 3. The final paragraph describes some of the formal elements of the poem. It might be argued that this discussion could have been integrated into the previous para-graphs rather than placed at the end, but the student does make a connec-tion in her concluding sentence between the pattern of language and its meaning.

Several other matters are worth noticing. The student works quota-tions into her own sentences to support her points. She quotes exactly as the words appear in the poem, even Dickinson's irregular use of capital let-ters. When something is added to a quotation to clarify it, it is enclosed in brackets so that the essayist's words will not be mistaken for the poet's: "Seal [of] Despair." A slash is used to indicate line divisions as in "imperial affliction / Sent us of the Air."

Bonnie Katz

Professor Quiello

English 109-2

January 26, 2010

A Reading of Emily Dickinson's

"There's a certain Slant of light"

Because Emily Dickinson did not provide titles for her poetry, editors follow the customary practice of using the first line of a poem as its title. However, a more appropriate title for "There's a certain Slant of light," one that suggests what the speaker in the poem is most concerned about, can be drawn from the poem's last line, which ends with "the look of Death" (line 16). Although the first line begins with an image of light, nothing bright, carefree, or cheerful appears in the poem. Instead, the predominant mood and images are darkened by a sense of despair resulting from the speaker's awareness of death.

In the first stanza, the "certain Slant of light" is associated with "Winter Afternoons" (2), a phrase that connotes the end of a day, a season, and even life itself. Such light is hardly warm or comforting. Not a ray or beam, this slanting light suggests something unusual or distorted and creates in the speaker a certain slant on life that is consistent with the cold, dark mood that winter afternoons can produce. Like the speaker, most of us have seen and felt this sort of light: it "oppresses" (3) and pervades our sense of things when we encounter it. Dickinson uses the senses of hearing and touch as well as sight to describe the overwhelming oppressiveness that the speaker experiences. The light is transformed into sound by a simile that tells us it is "like the Heft / Of Cathedral Tunes" (3–4). Moreover, the "Heft" of that sound—the slow, solemn measures of tolling church bells and organ music— weighs heavily on our spirits. Through the use of shifting imagery, Dickinson evokes a kind of spiritual numbness that we keenly feel and perceive through our senses.

By associating the winter light with "Cathedral Tunes," Dickinson lets us know that the speaker is concerned about more than the weather. Whatever it is that "oppresses" is related by connotation to faith, mortality, and God. The second and third stanzas offer several suggestions about this connection. The pain caused by the light is a "Heavenly Hurt" (5). This "imperial affliction / Sent us of the Air" (11–12) apparently comes from God above, and yet it seems to be part of the very nature of life. The oppressiveness we feel is in the air, and it can neither be specifically identified at this point in the poem nor be eliminated, for "None may teach it—Any" (9). All we know is that existence itself seems depressing under the weight of this "Seal [of] Despair" (10). The impression left by this "Seal" is stamped within the mind or soul rather than externally. "We can find no scar" (6), but once experienced this oppressiveness challenges our faith in life and its "Meanings" (8).

> Explication of second, third, and fourth stanzas, focusing on connotations of words and imagery in relation to mood and meaning of poem as a whole. Supported with references to the text

The final stanza does not explain what those "Meanings" are, but it does make clear that the speaker is acutely aware of death. As the winter daylight fades, Dickinson projects the speaker's anxiety onto the surrounding landscape and shadows, which will soon be engulfed by the darkness that follows this light: "the Landscape listens— / Shadows—hold their breath" (13–14). This image firmly aligns the winter light in the first stanza with darkness. Paradoxically, the light in this poem illuminates the nature of darkness. Tension is released when the light is completely gone, but what remains is the despair that the "imperial affliction" has imprinted on the speaker's sensibilities, for it is "like the Distance / On the look of Death—" (15–16). There can be no relief from what that "certain Slant of light" has revealed because what has been experienced is permanent—like the fixed stare in the eyes of someone who is dead.

The speaker's awareness of death is conveyed in a thoughtful, hushed tone. The lines are filled with fluid *l* and smooth *s* sounds that are appropriate for the quiet, meditative voice in the poem. The voice sounds tentative and uncertain—perhaps a little frightened. This seems to be reflected in the slightly irregular meter of the lines. The stanzas are trochaic with the second and fourth lines of each stanza having five syllables, but no stanza is identical because each works a slight variation on the first stanza's seven syllables in the first and third lines. The rhymes also combine exact patterns with variations. The first and third lines of each stanza are not exact rhymes, but the second and fourth lines are exact so that the paired words are more closely related: *Afternoons, Tunes; scar, are; Despair, Air;* and *breath, Death.*

> Explication of the elements of rhythm and sound throughout poem

> Conclusion tying explication of rhythm and sound with explication of words and imagery in previous paragraphs

There is a pattern to the poem, but it is unobtrusively woven into the speaker's voice in much the same way that "the look of Death" (16) is subtly present in the images and language of the poem.

Work Cited

Dickinson, Emily. "There's a certain Slant of light." *The Bedford Introduction to Literature*. Ed. Michael Meyer. 9th ed. Boston: Bedford/St. Martin's, 2011. 2085. Print.

Analysis

The preceding sample essay shows how an explication examines in detail the important elements in a work and relates them to the whole. An analysis, however, usually examines only a single element — such as plot, character, point of view, symbol, tone, or irony — and relates it to the entire work. An analytic topic separates the work into parts and focuses on a specific one; you might consider "Point of View in 'A Rose for Emily,'" "Patterns of Rhythm in Browning's 'My Last Duchess,'" or "The Significance of Fortinbras in *Hamlet*." The specific element must be related to the work as a whole or it will appear irrelevant. It is not enough to point out that there are many death images in Marvell's "To His Coy Mistress"; the images must somehow be connected to the poem's overall effect.

Whether an analytic paper is just a few pages or many, it cannot attempt to discuss everything about the work it is considering. Only those elements that are relevant to the topic can be treated. This kind of focusing makes the topic manageable; this is why most papers that you write will probably be some form of analysis. Explications are useful for a short passage, but a line-by-line commentary on a story, play, or long poem simply isn't practical. Because analysis allows you to consider the central effect or meaning of an entire work by studying a single important element, it is a useful and common approach to longer works.

A SAMPLE STUDENT ANALYSIS

The A & P as a State of Mind

Nancy Lager's paper analyzes the setting in John Updike's "A & P" (the entire story appears on p. 733). The assignment simply asked for an essay of approximately 750 words on a short story written in the twentieth century. The approach was left to the student.

The idea for this essay began with Lager asking herself why Updike used "A & P" as the title. The initial answer to the question was that "the setting is important in this story." This answer was the rough beginning of a tentative thesis. What still had to be explained, though, was how the setting is important. To determine the significance of the setting, Lager jotted down some notes based on her underlinings and marginal notations:

A & P

"usual traffic"

lights and tile

"electric eye"

shoppers like "sheep," "houseslaves," "pigs"

"Alexandrov and Petrooshki" — Russia

New England Town	*Lengel*
typical: bank, church, etc.	"manager"
traditional	"doesn't miss that much"
conservative	(like lady shopper)
proper	Sunday school
near Salem — witch trials	"It's our policy"
puritanical	spokesman for A & P values
intolerant	

From these notes Lager saw that Lengel serves as the voice of the A & P. He is, in a sense, a personification of the intolerant atmosphere of the setting. This insight led to another version of her thesis statement: "The setting of 'A & P' is the antagonist of the story." That explained at least some of the setting's importance. By seeing Lengel as a spokesman for "A & P" policies, Lager could view him as a voice that articulates the morally smug atmosphere created by the setting. Finally, she considered why it is significant that the setting is the antagonist, and this generated her last thesis: "Because the intolerant setting of 'A & P' is the antagonist in the story, it is crucial to our understanding of Sammy's decision to quit his job." This thesis sentence does not appear precisely in these words in the essay, but it is the backbone of the introductory paragraph.

The remaining paragraphs consist of details that describe the A & P in the second paragraph, the New England town in the third, Lengel in the fourth, and Sammy's reasons for quitting in the concluding paragraph. Paragraphs 2, 3, and 4 are largely based on Lager's notes, which she used as an outline once her thesis was established. The essay is sharply focused, well organized, and generally well written. In addition, it suggests a number of useful guidelines for analytic papers:

1. Only the points related to the thesis are included. In another type of paper the role of the girls in the bathing suits, for example, might have been considerably more prominent.

2. The analysis keeps the setting in focus while at the same time indicating how it is significant in the major incident in the story—Sammy's quitting.

3. The title is a useful lead into the paper; it provides a sense of what the topic is. In addition, the title is drawn from a sentence (the final one of the first paragraph) that clearly explains its meaning.

4. The introductory paragraph is direct and clearly indicates the paper will argue that the setting serves as the antagonist of the story.

5. Brief quotations are deftly incorporated into the text of the paper to illustrate points. We are told what we need to know about the story as evidence is provided to support ideas. There is no unnecessary plot summary. Even though "A & P" is only a few pages in length and is an assigned topic, page numbers are included after quoted phrases. If the story were longer, page numbers would be especially helpful for the reader.

6. The paragraphs are well developed, unified, and coherent. They flow naturally from one to another. Notice, for example, the smooth transition worked into the final sentence of the third paragraph and the first sentence of the fourth paragraph.

7. Lager makes excellent use of her careful reading and notes by finding revealing connections among the details she has observed. The store's "electric eye," for instance, is related to the woman's and Lengel's watchfulness.

8. As events are described, the present tense is used. This avoids awkward tense shifts and lends an immediacy to the discussion.

9. The concluding paragraph establishes the significance of why the setting should be seen as the antagonist and provides a sense of closure by referring again to Sammy's "No Sale," which has been mentioned at the end of the first paragraph.

10. In short, Lager has demonstrated that she has read the work closely, has understood the relation of the setting to the major action, and has argued her thesis convincingly by using evidence from the story.

Nancy Lager
Professor Taylor
English 102-12
February 2, 2010

The A & P as a State of Mind

The setting of John Updike's "A & P" is crucial to our understanding of Sammy's decision to quit his job. Although Sammy is the central character in the story and we learn that he is a principled, good-natured nineteen-year-old with a sense of humor, Updike seems to invest as much effort in describing the setting as he does in Sammy. The setting is the antagonist and plays a role that is as important as Sammy's. The title, after all, is not "Youthful Rebellion" or "Sammy Quits" but "A & P." Even though Sammy knows that his quitting will make life more difficult for him, he instinctively insists on rejecting what the A & P comes to represent in the story. When he rings up a "No Sale" and "saunter[s]" (737) out of the store, he leaves behind not only a job but the rigid state of mind associated with the A & P.

Sammy's descriptions of the A & P present a setting that is ugly, monotonous, and rigidly regulated. The fluorescent light is as blandly cool as the "checkerboard green-and-cream rubber-tile floor" (735). We can see the uniformity Sammy describes because we have all been in chain stores. The "usual traffic" moves in one direction (except for the swimsuited girls, who move against it), and everything is neatly ordered and categorized in tidy aisles. The dehumanizing routine of this environment is suggested by Sammy's offhand references to the typical shoppers as "sheep" (735), "houseslaves" (735) and "pigs" (737). They seem to pace through the store in a stupor; as Sammy tells us, not even dynamite could move them.

The A & P is appropriately located "right in the middle" (735) of a proper, conservative, traditional New England town north of Boston. This location, coupled with the fact that the town is only five miles from Salem, the site of the famous seventeenth-century witch trials, suggests a narrow, intolerant social atmosphere in which there is no room for stepping beyond the boundaries of what is regarded as normal and proper. The importance of this setting can be appreciated even more if we imagine the action taking place in, say, a mellow suburb of southern California. In this prim New England setting, the girls in their bathing suits are bound to offend somebody's sense of propriety.

As soon as Lengel sees the girls, the inevitable conflict begins. He embodies the dull conformity represented by the A & P. As "manager" (736), he is both the guardian and enforcer of "policy" (737). When he gives the girls "that sad Sunday-school-superintendent stare" (736), we know we are in the presence of the A & P version of a dreary bureaucrat who "doesn't miss that much" (736). He is as unsympathetic and unpleasant as the woman "with rouge on her cheeks and no eyebrows" (734) who pounces on Sammy for ringing up her "HiHo crackers" twice. Like the "electric eye" (737) in the doorway, her vigilant eyes allow nothing to escape their notice. For Sammy the logical extension of Lengel's "policy" is the half-serious notion that one day the A & P might be known as the "Great Alexandrov and Petrooshki Tea Company" (735). Sammy's connection between what he regards as mindless "policy" (737) and Soviet oppression is obviously an exaggeration, but the reader is invited to entertain the similarities anyway.

The reason Sammy quits his job has less to do with defending the girls than with his own sense of what it means to be a decent human being. His decision is not an easy one. He doesn't want to make trouble or disappoint his parents, and he knows his independence and self-reliance (the other side of New England tradition) will make life more complex for him. In spite of his own hesitations, he finds himself blurting out "Fiddle-de-doo" (737) to Lengel's policies and in doing so knows that his grandmother "would have been pleased" (737). Sammy's "No Sale" rejects the crabbed perspective on life that Lengel represents as manager of the A & P. This gesture is more than just a negative, however, for as he punches in that last entry on the cash register, "the machine whirs 'pee-pul'" (737). His decision to quit his job at the A & P is an expression of his refusal to regard policies as more important than people.

Work Cited

Updike, John. "A & P." *The Bedford Introduction to Literature*. Ed. Michael
   Meyer. 9th ed. Boston: Bedford/St. Martin's, 2011. 733–38. Print.

Comparison and Contrast

Another essay assignment in literature courses often combined with analytic topics is the type that requires you to write about similarities and differences between or within works. You might be asked to discuss "How
Sounds Express Meanings in May Swenson's 'A Nosty Fright' and Lewis
Carroll's 'Jabberwocky,' " or "Sammy's and Stokesie's Attitudes about Conformity in Updike's 'A & P.' " A *comparison* of either topic would emphasize
their similarities, while a *contrast* would stress their differences. It is possible, of course, to include both perspectives in a paper if you find significant likenesses and differences. A comparison of Andrew Marvell's "To His
Coy Mistress" and Richard Wilbur's "A Late Aubade" would, for example,
yield similarities because each poem describes a man urging his lover to
make the most of their precious time together; however, important differences also exist in the tone and theme of each poem that would constitute
a contrast. (You should, incidentally, be aware that the term *comparison* is
sometimes used inclusively to refer to both similarities and differences. If
you are assigned a comparison of two works, be sure that you understand
what your instructor's expectations are; you may be required to include
both approaches in the essay.)

   When you choose your own topic, the paper will be more successful —
more manageable — if you write on works that can be meaningfully related
to each other. Although Robert Herrick's "To the Virgins, to Make Much
of Time" and Shakespeare's *Hamlet* both have something to do with hesitation, the likelihood of anyone making a connection between the two that
reveals something interesting and important is remote — though perhaps
not impossible if the topic were conceived imaginatively and tactfully.
That is not to say that comparisons of works from different genres should
be avoided, but the relation between them should be strong, as would a
treatment of African American identity in M. Carl Holman's "Mr. Z" and
August Wilson's *Fences*. Choose a topic that encourages you to ask significant questions about each work; the purpose of a comparison or contrast
is to understand the works more clearly for having examined them together.

Despite the obvious differences between Henrik Ibsen's *A Doll House* and Gail Godwin's "A Sorrowful Woman," the two are closely related if we ask why the wife in each work withdraws from her family.

Choose works to compare or contrast that intersect with each other in some significant way. They may, for example, be written by the same author, in the same genre, or about the same subject. Perhaps you can compare their use of some technique, such as irony or point of view. Regardless of the specific topic, be sure to have a thesis that allows you to organize your paper around a central idea that argues a point about the two works. If you merely draw up a list of similarities or differences without a thesis in mind, your paper will be little more than a series of observations with no apparent purpose. Keep in the foreground of your thinking what the comparison or contrast reveals about the works.

There is no single way to organize comparative papers since each topic is likely to have its own particular issues to resolve, but it is useful to be aware of two basic patterns that can be helpful with a comparison, a contrast, or a combination of both. One method that can be effective for relatively short papers consists of dividing the paper in half, first discussing one work and then the other. Here, for example, is a partial informal outline for a discussion of Sophocles' *Oedipus the King* and Shakespeare's *Hamlet;* the topic is a comparison and contrast: "Oedipus and Hamlet as Tragic Figures."

1. Oedipus
   a. The nature of the conflict
   b. Strengths and stature
   c. Weaknesses and mistakes
   d. What is learned
2. Hamlet
   a. The nature of the conflict
   b. Strengths and stature
   c. Weaknesses and mistakes
   d. What is learned

This organizational strategy can be effective provided that the second part of the paper combines the discussion of Hamlet with references to Oedipus so that the thesis is made clear and the paper unified without being repetitive. If the two characters were treated entirely separately, then the discussion would be merely parallel rather than integrated. In a lengthy paper, this organization probably would not work well because a reader would have difficulty remembering the points made in the first half as he or she reads on.

Thus, for a longer paper it is usually better to create a more integrated structure that discusses both works as you take up each item in your outline. Here is the second basic pattern using the elements in the partial outline just cited:

1. The nature of the conflict
   a. Oedipus
   b. Hamlet
2. Strengths and stature
   a. Oedipus
   b. Hamlet
3. Weaknesses and mistakes
   a. Oedipus
   b. Hamlet
4. What is learned
   a. Oedipus
   b. Hamlet

This pattern allows you to discuss any number of topics without requiring that your reader recall what you first said about the conflict Oedipus confronts before you discuss Hamlet's conflicts fifteen pages later. However you structure your comparison or contrast paper, make certain that a reader can follow its elements and keep track of its thesis.

A SAMPLE STUDENT COMPARISON

The Struggle for Women's Self-Definition in A Doll House *and "Eveline"*

The following paper was written in response to an assignment that required a comparison and contrast — about 750 words — of two works of literature. The student chose to write an analysis of how the women in each work respond to being defined by men.

Monica Casis

Professor Matthews

English 105-4

February 4, 2010

The Struggle for Women's Self-Definition

in *A Doll House* and "Eveline"

Although Henrik Ibsen's *A Doll House* (1879) and James Joyce's "Eveline" (1914) were written more than thirty years apart and portray radically different characters and circumstances, both works raise similar questions about the role of women and how they are defined in their respective worlds. Each work presents a woman who conforms to society's ideas of gender in an effort to be accepted and loved. While both Ibsen's Nora Helmer and Joyce's Eveline are intelligent and resourceful, Nora is able to break free of society's hold; Eveline cannot. Nevertheless, these narratives show the emergence of each woman's identity—Nora's refusal to be a submissive and belittled housewife and Eveline's awareness of the constraints placed upon her by her father and community. From the beginning, these women are more intelligent and self-aware than the people who oppress them; unfortunately, that does not necessarily lead to complete autonomy.

In *A Doll House*, Nora is treated as her father's, then her husband's, doll. She is called "squirrel," "spendthrift," and "lark" and is admonished for such things as eating sweets or asking her husband to take her ideas into consideration (1710). Torvald's concept of the ideal woman is a showpiece who can dress up, recite, and dance. As a mother, Nora only plays with her children; it is Anne Marie who takes care of them. As a housewife, she has no control over the household finances; her husband gives her an allowance.

Although Nora continually conforms to her husband's expectations, she has the strength and courage to borrow money for a trip to Italy to save his life and does odd jobs to pay the debt that she has committed forgery to secure. She is proud of her sacrifice for her family. At the same time, she plays the role of a frivolous, helpless, dependent woman in order to coax her husband into giving her money and to keep him away from Krogstad's incriminating letter; she lies in order to keep him happy. Though Nora appears to be a woman trapped within her husband's expectations of her, she does have a will of her own. Once she sees and understands Torvald's superficiality and selfishness—that he is concerned only with what threatens him—Nora realizes she must abandon him and the role he has defined for her. Eveline, who submits to her overbearing father for most of Joyce's story, ultimately sees the need for change—the need to break out of her current life. However, unlike Nora, Eveline does not imagine an independent life; she sees marriage to Frank as her only way out. It is marriage that she believes will bring respect, happiness, and a kind of freedom: "People would treat her with respect then. She would not be treated as her mother had been" (536).

The turning points in *A Doll House* and in "Eveline" occur when the women protagonists are faced with the choice of whether to leave the men in their lives. Nora is convinced that she will corrupt her children and home with the guilt she bears—for being with a man whom she no longer respects. When Torvald learns the truth from Krogstad, he regards her as a liar, hypocrite, and criminal and therefore repudiates her. Once Nora realizes the selfishness of her husband, she knows she cannot stay with him. She must leave him and her children in order to search for her own identity.

Eveline's turning point, on the other hand, results in inaction. She cannot bring herself to leave her home or her father, however unpleasant her daily life. The reasons are not entirely clear, but we can assume that her reluctance stems from the fear of such overwhelming change. Leaving her home and the people she has known her entire life is understandably daunting, especially for such a young person. However, there is also the possibility that Eveline recognizes the problem with her plan. Relocating and marrying Frank will only substitute one dependence with another. Leaving would force her to, once again, rely on the male presence in her life. As a married woman she would never truly gain her own identity.

When Nora and Eveline come to terms with themselves, their situations are no less problematic than when they falsely fulfilled the expectations imposed on them by the men in their lives. Nora leaves to pursue what may seem to be selfish desires, yet this bold move is necessary to gain independence and self-reliance. Eveline, however, cannot free herself from her

Casis 3

father's control or leave Dublin with Frank, because her fear and guilt entrap her "like a helpless animal" (538). She lacks Nora's strength and determination to embark on a new life of risky possibilities; instead, Eveline remains passive and unable to choose a different life for herself.

At the end of each work, both women face the struggles that will inform the rest of their lives, but whereas Nora's circumstances might be understood as potentially hopeful, Eveline's condition almost certainly must be considered as hopeless.

Casis 4

Works Cited

Ibsen, Henrik, *A Doll House. The Bedford Introduction to Literature*. Ed. Michael Meyer. 9th ed. Boston: Bedford/St. Martin's, 2011. 1709–56. Print.

Joyce, James, "Eveline." *The Bedford Introduction to Literature*. Ed. Michael Meyer. 9th ed. Boston: Bedford/St. Martin's, 2011. 536–38. Print.

55

The Literary
Research Paper

Does anyone know a good poet who's a
vegetarian?
— DONALD HALL

© Nancy Crampton.

A close reading of a primary source such as a short story, poem, or play can
give insights into a work's themes and effects, but sometimes you will want
to know more. A published commentary by a critic who knows the work
well and is familiar with the author's life and times can provide insights
that otherwise may not be available. Such comments and interpretations —
known as *secondary sources* — are, of course, not a substitute for the work
itself, but they often can take you into a work further than if you made the
journey by yourself.

After imagination, good sense, and energy, perhaps the next most important quality for writing a research paper is the ability to organize material. A research paper on a literary topic requires a writer to take account
of quite a lot at once: the text, ideas, sources, and documentation techniques all make demands on one's efforts to present a topic clearly and
convincingly.

The following list should give you a sense of what goes into creating a research paper. Although some steps on the list can be folded into one another, they offer an overview of the work that will involve you:

1. Choosing a topic
2. Finding sources
3. Evaluating sources
4. Taking notes
5. Developing a thesis
6. Organizing an outline
7. Writing drafts
8. Revising
9. Documenting sources
10. Preparing the final draft and proofreading

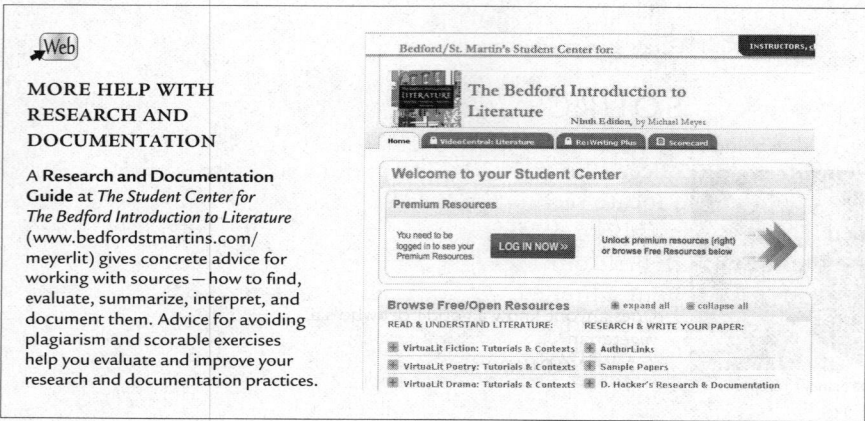

Web

MORE HELP WITH RESEARCH AND DOCUMENTATION

A **Research and Documentation Guide** at *The Student Center for The Bedford Introduction to Literature* (www.bedfordstmartins.com/ meyerlit) gives concrete advice for working with sources — how to find, evaluate, summarize, interpret, and document them. Advice for avoiding plagiarism and scorable exercises help you evaluate and improve your research and documentation practices.

Even if you have never written a research paper, you most likely have already had experience choosing a topic, developing a thesis, organizing an outline, and writing a draft that you then revised, proofread, and handed in. Those skills represent six of the ten items on the list. This chapter briefly reviews some of these steps and focuses on the remaining tasks, unique to research paper assignments.

CHOOSING A TOPIC

Chapter 54 discussed the importance of reading a work closely and taking careful notes as a means of generating topics for writing about literature. If you know a work well and record your understanding of it in notes, you'll have impressions and ideas to choose from for potential topics. You may find it useful to review the information on pages 2041–64 before reading the advice about putting together a research paper in this chapter.

The student author of the sample research paper "How the Narrator Cultivates a Rose for Emily" (p. 2113) was asked to write a five-page paper that demonstrated some familiarity with published critical perspectives on a Faulkner story of his choice. Before looking into critical discussions of the story, he read "A Rose for Emily" several times, taking notes and making comments in the margin of his textbook on each reading.

What prompted his choice of "A Rose for Emily" was a class discussion in which many of his classmates found the story's title inappropriate or misleading because they could not understand how and why the story constituted a tribute to Emily given that she murdered a man and slept with his dead body over many years. The gruesome surprise ending revealing Emily as a murderer and necrophiliac hardly seemed to warrant a rose and a tribute for the central character. Why did Faulkner use such a title? Only after having thoroughly examined the story did the student go to the library to see what professional critics had to say about this question.

FINDING SOURCES

Whether your college library is large or small, its reference librarians can usually help you locate secondary sources about a particular work or author. Unless you choose a very recently published story, poem, play, or essay about which little or nothing has been written, you should be able to find out more about a literary work efficiently and quickly. Even if a work has been published recently, you can probably find relevant information on the Internet (see Electronic Sources, below).

Electronic Sources

Researchers can locate materials in a variety of sources, including card catalogs, specialized encyclopedias, bibliographies, and indexes to periodicals. Libraries also provide online databases that you can access from home. This can be an efficient way to establish a bibliography on a specific topic. Consult a reference librarian about how to use your library's online resources and to determine how they will help you research your topic.

In addition to the many electronic databases ranging from your library's computerized holdings to the many specialized CD-ROMs available, such as *MLA International Bibliography* (a major source for articles and books on literary topics), the Internet also connects millions of sites with primary sources (the full texts of stories, poems, plays, and essays) and secondary sources (biography or criticism). If you have not had practice with research on the Web, it is a good idea to get guidance from your instructor or a librarian, and by using your library's home page as a starting point. Browsing on the Internet can be absorbing as well as informative, but unless you have plenty of time to spare, don't wait until the last minute to locate your electronic sources. You might find yourself trying to find reliable, professional sources among thousands of sites if you enter an unqualified entry such as "Charles Dickens." Here are several especially useful electronic databases that will provide you with bibliographic information in literature studies. Your school's English Department home page may offer online support as well.

Internet Public Library Online Criticism. <http://www.ipl.org/div/litcrit>. Maintained by the University of Michigan, this site provides links to literary criticism by author, work, country, or period.

JSTOR. An index that also offers abstracts of journal articles on language and literature.

A Literary Index. <http://www.vanderbilt.edu/AnS/english/flackcj/LitIndex .html>. An extensive list of Internet literary resources for students and scholars.

MLA International Bibliography. This is a standard resource for articles and books on literary subjects that allows topical and keyword searches.

Voice of the Shuttle. <http://vos.ucsb.edu>. Maintained by the University of California, this site is a wide-ranging resource for British and American literary studies.

Do remember that your own college library offers a broad range of electronic sources. If you're feeling uncertain, intimidated, and profoundly unplugged, your reference librarians are there to help you to get started.

EVALUATING SOURCES AND TAKING NOTES

Evaluate your sources for their reliability and the quality of their evidence. Check to see whether an article or book has been superseded by later studies; try to use up-to-date sources. A popular magazine article will probably not be as authoritative as an article in a scholarly journal. Sources that are well documented with primary and secondary materials usually indicate that the author has done his or her homework. Books printed by university presses and established trade presses are preferable to books privately printed. But there are always exceptions. If you are uncertain about how to assess a book, try to find out something about the author. Are there any other books listed in the card catalog that indicate the author's expertise? What do book reviews say about the work? Three valuable indexes to book reviews of literary studies are *Book Review Digest, Book Review Index,* and *Index to Book Reviews in the Humanities.* Your reference librarian can show you how to use these important tools for evaluating books. Reviews can be a quick means to gain a broad perspective on writers and their works because reviewers often survey previous approaches to the topic under discussion.

A cautionary note: assessing online sources can be more problematic than evaluating print sources because anyone with a computer and online access can publish on the Internet. Be sure to determine the nature of your sources and their authority. Is the site the work of a professional or an amateur? Is the information likely to be reliable? Is it documented? Before placing your trust in an Internet source, make sure that it warrants your confidence.

As you prepare a list of reliable sources relevant to your topic, record the necessary bibliographic information so that it will be available when you make up the list of works cited for your paper. For a book, include the author, complete title, place of publication, publisher, and date. For an article, include author, complete title, name of periodical, volume number, date of issue, and page numbers. For an Internet source, include the author, complete title, database title, periodical or site name, date of posting of the site (or last update), name of the institution or organization, and date when you accessed the source.

Once you have assembled a tentative bibliography, you will need to take notes on your readings. Be sure to keep track of where the information comes from by writing the author's name and page number. If you use more than one work by the same author, include a brief title as well as the author's name.

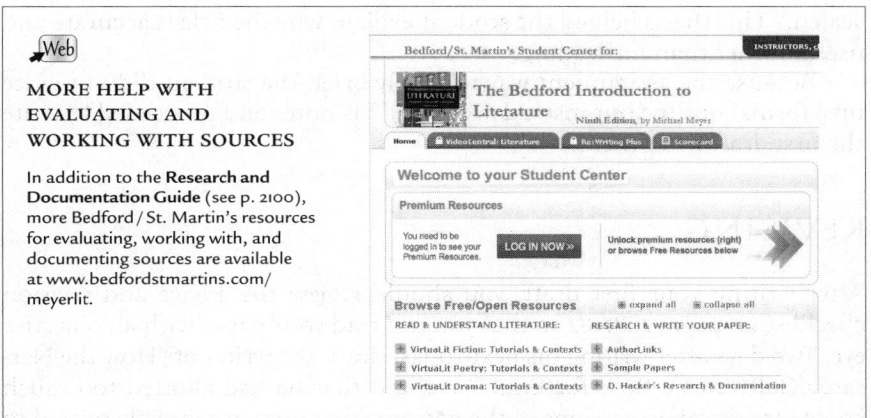

⬅Web

MORE HELP WITH EVALUATING AND WORKING WITH SOURCES

In addition to the **Research and Documentation Guide** (see p. 2100), more Bedford / St. Martin's resources for evaluating, working with, and documenting sources are available at www.bedfordstmartins.com/ meyerlit.

Bedford/St. Martin's Student Center for:

INSTRUCTORS,

The Bedford Introduction to Literature

Ninth Edition, by Michael Meyer

Home | Video Central: Literature | Re: Writing Plus | Scorecard

Welcome to your Student Center

Premium Resources

You need to be logged in to see your Premium Resources. | **LOG IN NOW »** | Unlock premium resources (right) or browse Free Resources below

Browse Free/Open Resources ⬜ expand all ⬜ collapse all

READ & UNDERSTAND LITERATURE: | RESEARCH & WRITE YOUR PAPER:

VirtualLit Fiction: Tutorials & Contexts | AuthorLinks

VirtualLit Poetry: Tutorials & Contexts | Sample Papers

VirtualLit Drama: Tutorials & Contexts | D. Hacker's Research & Documentation

DEVELOPING A THESIS AND ORGANIZING THE PAPER

As the notes on "A Rose for Emily" accumulated, the student sorted them into topics:

1. Publication history of the story
2. Faulkner on the title of "A Rose for Emily"
3. Is Emily simply insane?
4. The purpose of Emily's servant
5. The narrator
6. The townspeople's view of Emily
7. The surprise ending
8. Emily's admirable qualities
9. Homer's character

The student quickly saw that items 1, 4, and 9 were not directly related to his topic concerning the significance of the story's title. The remaining numbers (2, 3, 5, 6, 7, 8) are the topics taken up in the paper. The student had begun his reading of secondary sources with a tentative thesis that stemmed from his question about the appropriateness of the title. That "why" shaped itself into the expectation that he would have a thesis something like this: "The title justifies Emily's murder of Homer because . . ."

The assumption was that he would find information that indicated some specific reason. But the more he read, the more he discovered that it was possible to speak only about how the narrator prevents the reader from making a premature judgment about Emily rather than justifying her actions. Hence, he wisely changed his tentative thesis to this final thesis: "The narrator describes incidents and withholds information in such a way as to cause the reader to sympathize with Emily before her crime is revealed." This thesis helped the student explain why the title is accurate and useful rather than misleading.

Because the assignment was relatively brief, the student did not write up a formal outline but instead organized his notes and proceeded to write the first draft from them.

REVISING

After writing your first draft, you should review the advice and revision checklist on pages 2081–82 so that you can read your paper with an objective eye. Two days after writing his next-to-last draft, the writer of "How the Narrator Cultivates a Rose for Emily" realized that he had allotted too much space for critical discussions of the narrator that were not directly related to his approach. He wanted to demonstrate a familiarity with these studies, but it was not essential that he summarize or discuss them. He corrected this by consolidating parenthetical references: "Though a number of studies discuss the story's narrator (see, for example, Curry; Kempton; Sullivan; and Watkins). . . ." His earlier draft had included summaries of these studies that were tangential to his argument. The point is that he saw this himself after he took some time to approach the paper from a fresh perspective.

DOCUMENTING SOURCES AND AVOIDING PLAGIARISM

You must acknowledge the use of a source when you (1) quote someone's exact words, (2) summarize or borrow someone's opinions or ideas, or (3) use information and facts that are not considered to be common knowledge. The purpose of this documentation is to acknowledge your sources, to demonstrate that you are familiar with what others have thought about the topic, and to provide your reader access to the same sources. If your paper is not adequately documented, it will be vulnerable to a charge of *plagiarism* — the presentation of someone else's work as your own. Conscious plagiarism is easy to avoid; honesty takes care of that for most people. However, there is a more problematic form of plagiarism that is often inadvertent. Whether inadequate documentation is conscious or not, plagiarism is a serious matter and must be avoided. Papers can be evaluated only by what is on the page, not by their writers' intentions.

Let's look more closely at what constitutes plagiarism. Consider the following passage quoted from John Gassner's introduction to *Four Great Plays by Henrik Ibsen* (New York: Bantam, 1959), p. viii:

Today it seems incredible that *A Doll's House*° should have created the furor it did. In exploding Victorian ideals of feminine dependency the play seemed revolutionary in 1879. When its heroine Nora left her home in search of self-development it seemed as if the sanctity of marriage had been flouted by a playwright treading the stage with cloven-feet.

Now read this plagiarized version:

A Doll's House created a furor in 1879 by blowing up Victorian ideals about a woman's place in the world. Nora's search for self-fulfillment outside her home appeared to be an attack on the sanctity of marriage by a cloven-footed playwright.

Though the writer has shortened the passage and made some changes in the wording, this paragraph is basically the same as Gassner's. Indeed, several of his phrases are lifted almost intact. Even if a parenthetical reference had been included at the end of the passage and the source included in "Works Cited," the language of this passage would still be plagiarism because it is presented as the writer's own. Both language and ideas must be acknowledged.

Here is an adequately documented version of the passage:

John Gassner has observed how difficult it is for today's readers to comprehend the intense reaction against *A Doll's House* in 1879. When Victorian audiences watched Nora walk out of her stifling marriage, they assumed that Ibsen was expressing a devilish contempt for the "sanctity of marriage" (viii).

This passage makes absolutely clear that the observation is Gassner's, and it is written in the student's own language with the exception of one quoted phrase. Had Gassner not been named in the passage, the parenthetical reference would have included his name: (Gassner viii).

Some mention should be made of the notion of common knowledge before we turn to the standard format for documenting sources. Observations and facts that are widely known and routinely included in many of

---

Rolf Fjelde, whose translation is included in Chapter 49, renders the title as *A Doll House* in order to emphasize that the whole household, including Torvald as well as Nora, lives an unreal, doll-like existence.

your sources do not require documentation. It is not necessary to cite a source for the fact that Alfred, Lord Tennyson, was born in 1809 or that Ernest Hemingway loved to fish and hunt. Sometimes it will be difficult for you to determine what common knowledge is for a topic that you know little about. If you are in doubt, the best strategy is to supply a reference.

There are two basic ways to document sources. Traditionally, sources have been cited in footnotes at the bottom of each page or in endnotes grouped together at the end of the paper. Here is how a portion of the sample paper would look if footnotes were used instead of parenthetical documentation:

As Heller points out, before we learn of Emily's bizarre behavior we see her as a sympathetic—if antiquated—figure in a town whose life and concerns have passed her by; hence, "we are disposed to see Emily as victimized."[1]

[1] Terry Heller, "The Telltale Hair: A Critical Study of William Faulkner's 'A Rose for Emily,'" *Arizona Quarterly* 28.4 (1972): 306. Print.

Unlike endnotes, which are double spaced throughout under the title of "Notes" on separate pages at the end of the paper, footnotes appear four spaces below the text. They are single spaced with double spaces between notes.

No doubt you will have encountered these documentation methods in your reading. A different style is recommended, however, in the Modern Language Association's *MLA Handbook for Writers of Research Papers,* 7th ed. (2009). This style employs parenthetical references within the text of the paper; these are keyed to an alphabetical list of works cited at the end of the paper. This method is designed to be less distracting for the reader. Unless you are instructed to follow the footnote or endnote style for documentation, use the parenthetical method explained in the next section.

The List of Works Cited

Items in the list of works cited are arranged alphabetically according to the author's last name and indented a half inch after the first line. This allows the reader to locate quickly the complete bibliographic information for the author's name cited within the parenthetical reference in the text. The following are common entries for literature papers and should be used as models. If some of your sources are of a different nature, consult the *MLA Handbook for Writers of Research Papers,* 7th ed. (New York: MLA, 2009); or, for the latest updates, check MLA's Web site at mlahandbook.org.

The following entries include examples to follow when citing electronic sources. For electronic sources, include as many of the following elements as apply and as are available:

- Author's name
- Title of work (if it's a book, italicized; if it's a short work, such as an article or poem, use quotation marks)

- Title of the site (or of the publication, if you're citing an online periodical, for example), italicized
- Sponsor or publisher of the site (if not named as the author)
- Date of publication or last update
- Medium of publication
- Date you accessed the source

A BOOK BY ONE AUTHOR

Hendrickson, Robert. *The Literary Life and Other Curiosities*. New York: Viking, 1981. Print.

AN ONLINE BOOK

Frost, Robert. *A Boy's Will*. New York: Holt, 1915. *Bartleby.com: Great Books Online*. Web.

    11 May 2009.

PART OF AN ONLINE BOOK

Frost, Robert. "Into My Own." *A Boy's Will*. New York: Holt, 1915. N. pag. *Bartleby.com:*

    Great Books Online. Web. 11 May 2009.

Notice that the author's name is in reverse order. This information, along with the full title, place of publication, publisher, and date, should be taken from the title and copyright pages of the book. The title is italicized and is also followed by a period. If the city of publication is well known, it is unnecessary to include the state. Use the publication date on the title page; if none appears there, use the copyright date (after ©) on the back of the title page. Include the medium of publication.

A BOOK BY TWO AUTHORS

Horton, Rod W., and Herbert W. Edwards. *Backgrounds of American Literary Thought*. 3rd

    ed. Englewood Cliffs: Prentice, 1974. Print.

Only the first author's name is given in reverse order. The edition number appears after the title.

A BOOK WITH MORE THAN THREE AUTHORS

Gates, Henry Louis, Jr., et al., eds. *The Norton Anthology of African American Literature*.

    New York: Norton, 1997. Print.

(Note: The abbreviation *et al.* means "and others.")

A WORK IN A COLLECTION BY THE SAME AUTHOR

O'Connor, Flannery. "Greenleaf." *The Complete Stories*. By O'Connor. New York: Farrar,
    1971. 311–34. Print.

Page numbers are given because the reference is to only a single story in the collection.

A WORK IN A COLLECTION BY DIFFERENT WRITERS

Frost, Robert. "Design." *The Bedford Introduction to Literature*. Ed. Michael Meyer. 9th ed.
    Boston: Bedford/St. Martin's, 2011. 1116. Print.

Sun, Nilaja. *No Child. . . . The Bedford Introduction to Literature*. Ed. Michael Meyer. 9th
    ed. Boston: Bedford/St. Martin's, 2011. 1969–87. Print.

The titles of poems and short stories are enclosed in quotation marks; plays and novels are italicized.

CROSS-REFERENCE TO A COLLECTION

Frost, Robert. "Design." Meyer. 1116.

Sun, Nilaja. *No Child. . . .* Meyer. 1969–87.

Meyer, Michael, ed. *The Bedford Introduction to Literature*. 9th ed. Boston: Bedford/
    St. Martin's, 2011. Print.

O'Connor, Flannery. "Revelation." Meyer. 474–88.

When citing more than one work from the same collection, use a cross-reference to avoid repeating the same bibliographic information that appears in the main entry for the collection.

A TRANSLATED BOOK

Grass, Günter. *The Tin Drum*. Trans. Ralph Manheim. New York: Vintage-Random, 1962. Print.

AN INTRODUCTION, PREFACE, FOREWORD, OR AFTERWORD

Johnson, Thomas H. Introduction. *Final Harvest: Emily Dickinson's Poems*. By Emily
    Dickinson. Boston: Little, Brown, 1961. vii–xiv. Print.

This cites the introduction by Johnson. Notice that a colon is used between the book's main title and subtitle. To cite a poem in this book, use this method:

Dickinson, Emily. "A Tooth upon Our Peace." *Final Harvest: Emily Dickinson's Poems.*
    Ed. Thomas H. Johnson. Boston: Little, Brown, 1961. 110. Print.

AN ENTRY IN AN ENCYCLOPEDIA

"Wordsworth, William." *The New Encyclopedia Britannica.* 1984 ed. Print.

Because this encyclopedia is organized alphabetically, no page number or
other information is given, only the edition number (if available) and date.

AN ARTICLE IN A MAGAZINE

Morrow, Lance. "Scribble, Scribble, Eh, Mr. Toad." *Time* 24 Feb. 1986: 84. Print.

AN ARTICLE FROM AN ONLINE MAGAZINE

Wasserman, Elizabeth. "The Byron Complex." *Atlantic Online.* The Atlantic Monthly Group,
    22 Sept. 2002. Web. 4 Feb. 2004.

The citation for an unsigned article would begin with the title and be al-
phabetized by the first word of the title other than "a," "an," or "the."

AN ARTICLE IN A SCHOLARLY JOURNAL WITH CONTINUOUS PAGINATION BEYOND A SINGLE ISSUE

Mahar, William J. "Black English in Early Blackface Minstrelsy: A New Interpretation of
    the Sources of Minstrel Show Dialect." *American Quarterly* 37.2 (1985): 260–85.
    Print.

Regardless of whether the journal uses continuous pagination or separate
pagination for each issue, it is necessary to include the volume number and
the issue number for every entry (for example, "11.5" indicates volume 11,
issue 5). If a journal does not offer an issue number, use only the volume
number, as in the next entry. If a journal uses *only* issue numbers, use that
in place of the volume number.

AN ARTICLE IN A SCHOLARLY JOURNAL WITH SEPARATE PAGINATION FOR EACH ISSUE

Updike, John. "The Cultural Situation of the American Writer." *American Studies
    International* 15 (1977): 19–28. Print.

In the following citation, noting the winter issue helps a reader find the correct article among all of the articles published by the online journal in 2004.

AN ARTICLE FROM AN ONLINE SCHOLARLY JOURNAL

Mamet, David. "Secret Names." *The Threepenny Review* 96 (Winter 2004): n. pag. Web.
4 Feb. 2004.

The following citation indicates that the article appears on page 1 of section 7 and continues onto another page.

AN ARTICLE IN A NEWSPAPER

Ziegler, Philip. "The Lure of Gossip, the Rules of History." *New York Times* 23 Feb. 1986:
sec. 7: 1+. Print.

AN ARTICLE FROM AN ONLINE NEWSPAPER

Brantley, Ben. "Souls Lost and Doomed Enliven London Stages." *New York Times*. New York
Times, 4 Feb. 2004. Web. 5 Feb. 2004.

A LECTURE

Tilton, Robert. "The Beginnings of American Studies." English 270 class lecture.
University of Connecticut, Storrs. 12 Mar. 2004. Lecture.

LETTER, E-MAIL, OR INTERVIEW

Vellenga, Carolyn. Letter to the author. 9 Oct. 1997.

Harter, Stephen P. E-mail to the author. 28 Dec. 1997.

McConagha, Bill. Personal interview. 9 May 2009.

Following are additional examples for citing electronic sources.

WORK FROM A SUBSCRIPTION SERVICE

Libraries pay for access to databases such as *Lexis-Nexis, ProQuest Direct,* and
Expanded Academic ASAP. When you retrieve an article or other work from a
subscription database, cite your source based on this model:

Vendler, Helen Hennessey. "The Passion of Emily Dickinson." *New Republic* 3 Aug. 1992:
34-38. *Expanded Academic ASAP*. Web. 4 Feb. 2004.

A DOCUMENT FROM A WEB SITE

When citing sources from the Internet, include as much publication information as possible (see guidelines on pp. 2106–7). In some cases, as in the
following example, a date of publication for the document "Dickens in
America" is not available. The entry provides the author, title of document,
title of site, sponsor of the site, medium, and access date:

Perdue, David. "Dickens in America." *David Perdue's Charles Dickens Page*. David A.

Perdue, 1 Apr. 2009. Web. 13 Apr. 2009.

AN ENTIRE WEB SITE

Perdue, David. *David Perdue's Charles Dickens Page*. David A. Perdue, 1 Apr. 2009. Web.

13 Apr. 2009.

Treat a CD-ROM as you would any other source, but name the medium at
the end of the entry.

A WORK FROM A CD-ROM

Aaron, Belèn V. "The Death of Theory." *Scholarly Book Reviews* 4.3 (1997): 146–47.

CD-ROM. *ERIC*. SilverPlatter. Dec. 1997.

AN ONLINE POSTING

Shuck, John. "Hamlet." *PBS Discussions*. PBS, 16 May 2005. Web. 13 Apr. 2009.

Parenthetical References

A list of works cited is not an adequate indication of how you have used
sources in your paper. You must also provide the precise location of quotations and other information by using parenthetical references within the
text of the paper. You do this by citing the author's name (or the source's
title if the work is anonymous) and the page number:

Collins points out that "Nabokov was misunderstood by early reviewers of his work" (28).

or

Nabokov's first critics misinterpreted his stories (Collins 28).

Either way a reader will find the complete bibliographic entry in the list of
works cited under Collins's name and know that the information cited in
the paper appears on page 28. Notice that the end punctuation comes after
the parentheses.

If you have listed more than one work by the same author, you would add a brief title to the parenthetical reference to distinguish between them. You could also include the full title in your text:

Nabokov's first critics misinterpreted his stories (Collins, "Early Reviews" 28).

or

Collins points out in "Early Reviews of Nabokov's Fiction" that Nabokov's early work was misinterpreted by reviewers (28).

For electronic sources, provide the author's name. Unless your online source is a stable, paginated document (such as a pdf file), do not include page numbers in your parenthetical references. The following example shows an in-text citation to William Faulkner's acceptance speech for the Nobel Prize in Literature, found at the Nobel Web site.

William Faulkner believed that it was his duty as a writer to "help man endure by lifting his heart" (Faulkner).

This reference would appear in the works cited list as follows:

Faulkner, William. "Banquet Speech: The Nobel Prize in Literature." *The Nobel E-Museum.* The Nobel Foundation, 10 Dec. 1950. Web. 4 Feb. 2009.

There can be many variations on what is included in a parenthetical reference, depending on the nature of the entry in the list of works cited. But the general principle is simple enough: provide enough parenthetical information for a reader to find the work in "Works Cited." Examine the sample research paper for more examples of works cited and strategies for including parenthetical references. If you are puzzled by a given situation, refer to the *MLA Handbook.*

A SAMPLE STUDENT RESEARCH PAPER

How the Narrator Cultivates a Rose for Emily

The following research paper by Tony Groulx follows the format described in the *MLA Handbook for Writers of Research Papers,* 7th ed. (2009). This format is discussed in the preceding section on documentation and in Chapter 54 in the section on manuscript form (p. 2083). Though the sample paper is short, it illustrates many of the techniques and strategies useful for writing an essay that includes secondary sources. (Faulkner's "A Rose for Emily" is reprinted on p. 91.)

Groulx 1

Tony Groulx

Professor Hugo

English 109-3

February 4, 2010

How the Narrator Cultivates a Rose for Emily

William Faulkner's "A Rose for Emily" is an absorbing mystery story whose chilling ending contains a gruesome surprise. When we discover, along with the narrator and townspeople, what was left of Homer Barron's body, we may be surprised or not, depending on how carefully we have been reading the story and keeping track of details such as Emily Grierson's purchase of rat poison and Homer's disappearance. Probably most readers anticipate finding Homer's body at the end of the story because Faulkner carefully prepares the groundwork for the discovery as the townspeople force their way into that mysterious upstairs room where a "thin, acrid pall as of the tomb seemed to lie everywhere" (96). But very few readers, if any, are prepared for the story's final paragraph, when we realize that the strand of "iron-gray hair" (the last three words of the story) on the second pillow indicates that Emily has slept with Homer since she murdered him. This last paragraph produces the real horror in the story and an extraordinary revelation about Emily's character.

The final paragraph seems like the right place to begin a discussion of this story because the surprise ending not only creates a powerful emotional effect in us but also raises an important question about what we are to think of Emily. Is this isolated, eccentric woman simply mad? All the circumstantial evidence indicates that she is a murderer and necrophiliac, and yet Faulkner titles the story "A Rose for Emily," as if she is due some kind of tribute. The title somehow qualifies the gasp of horror that the story leads up to in the final paragraph. Why would anyone offer this woman a "rose"? What's behind the title?

Faulkner was once directly asked the meaning of the title and replied:

> Oh it's simply the poor woman had had no life at all. Her father had kept her more or less locked up and then she had a lover who was about to quit her, she had to murder him. It was just "A Rose for Emily"—that's all. (qtd. in Gwynn and Blotner 87-88)

This reply explains some of Emily's motivation for murdering Homer, but it doesn't actually address the purpose and meaning of the title. If Emily killed

Reference to text of the story

Reference to secondary source (Gwynn and Blotner)

Homer out of a kind of emotional necessity—out of a fear of abandonment—how does that explain the fact that the title seems to suggest that the story is a way of paying respect to Emily? The question remains.

Whatever respect the story creates for Emily cannot be the result of her actions. Surely there can be no convincing excuse made for murder and necrophilia; there is nothing to praise about what she does. Instead, the tribute comes in the form of how her story is told rather than what we are told about her. To do this Faulkner uses a narrator who tells Emily's story in such a way as to maximize our sympathy for her. The grim information about Emily's "iron-gray hair" on the pillow is withheld until the very end and not only to produce a surprise but to permit the reader to develop a sympathetic understanding of her before we are shocked and disgusted by her necrophilia.

Significantly, the narrator begins the story with Emily's death rather than Homer's. Though a number of studies discuss the story's narrator (see, for example, Curry; Kempton; Sullivan; and Watkins), Terry Heller's is one of the most comprehensive in its focus on the narrator's effects on the readers' response to Emily. As Heller points out, before we learn of Emily's bizarre behavior we see her as a sympathetic—if antiquated—figure in a town whose life and concerns have passed her by; hence, "we are disposed to see Emily as victimized" (306). Her refusal to pay her taxes is an index to her isolation and eccentricity, but this incident also suggests a degree of dignity and power lacking in the town officials who fail to collect her taxes. Her encounters with the officials of Jefferson—whether in the form of the sneaking aldermen who try to cover up the smell around her house or the druggist who unsuccessfully tries to get her to conform to the law when she buys arsenic—place her in an admirable light because her willfulness is based on her personal strength. Moreover, it is relatively easy to side with Emily when the townspeople are described as taking pleasure in her being reduced to poverty as a result of her father's death because "now she too would know the old thrill and the old despair of a penny more or less" (Faulkner 93). The narrator's account of their pettiness, jealousy, and inability to make sense of Emily causes the reader to sympathize with Emily's eccentricities before we must judge her murderous behavior. We admire her for taking life on her own terms, and the narrator makes sure this response is in place prior to our realization that she also takes life.

Reference to secondary sources (Curry; Kempton; Sullivan; Watkins) with signal phrase for Heller

Reference to secondary source (Heller) with signal phrase ("As Heller points out . . .")

Reference to text of the story

Groulx 3

We don't really know much about Emily because the narrator arranges the details of her life so that it's difficult to know what she's been up to. We learn, for example, about the smell around the house before she buys the poison and Homer disappears, so that the cause-and-effect relationship among these events is a bit slippery (for a detailed reconstruction of the chronology, see McGlynn and Nebecker's revision of McGlynn's work), but the effect is to suspend judgment of Emily. By the time we realize what she has done, we are already inclined to see her as outside community values almost out of necessity. That's not to say that the murdering of Homer is justified by the narrator, but it is to say that her life maintains its private—though no longer secret—dignity. Despite the final revelation, Emily remains "dear, inescapable, impervious, tranquil, and perverse" (Faulkner 96).

> Reference to secondary sources (McGlynn and Nebecker)

> References to text of the story

The narrator's "rose" to Emily is his recognition that Emily is all these things—including "perverse." She evokes "a sort of respectful affection for a fallen monument" (Faulkner 91). She is, to be sure, "fallen," but she is also somehow central—a "monument"—to the life of the community. Faulkner does not offer a definitive reading of Emily, but he does have the narrator pay tribute to her by attempting to provide a complex set of contexts for her actions—contexts that include a repressive father, resistance to a changing South and impinging North, the passage of time and its influence on the present, and relations between men and women as well as relations between generations. Robert Crosman discusses the narrator's efforts to understand Emily:

> The narrator is himself a "reader" of Emily's story, trying to put together from fragments a complete picture, trying to find the meaning of her life in its impact upon an audience, the citizens of Jefferson, of which he is a member. (212)

> Reference to secondary source (Crosman)

The narrator refuses to dismiss Emily as simply mad or to treat her life as merely a grotesque, sensational horror story. Instead, his narrative method brings us into her life before we too hastily reject her, and in doing so it offers us a complex imaginative treatment of fierce determination and strength coupled with illusions and shocking eccentricities. The narrator's rose for Emily is paying her the tribute of placing that "long strand of iron-gray hair" in the context of her entire life.

Works Cited

Crosman, Robert. "How Readers Make Meaning." *College Literature* 9.3 (1982): 207–15. Print.

Curry, Renee R. "Gender and Authorial Limitation in Faulkner's 'A Rose for Emily.'" *The Mississippi Quarterly* 47.3 (1994): 391–402. *Expanded Academic ASAP*. Web. 4 Feb. 2004.

Faulkner, William. "A Rose for Emily." *The Bedford Introduction to Literature*. Ed. Michael Meyer. 9th ed. Boston: Bedford/St. Martin's, 2011. 91–97. Print.

Gwynn, Frederick, and Joseph Blotner, eds. *Faulkner in the University: Class Conferences at the University of Virginia, 1957-58*. Charlottesville: U of Virginia P, 1959. Print.

Heller, Terry. "The Telltale Hair: A Critical Study of William Faulkner's 'A Rose for Emily.'" *Arizona Quarterly* 28.4 (1972): 301–18. Print.

Kempton, K. P. *The Short Story*. Cambridge: Harvard UP, 1954. 104-06. Print.

McGlynn, Paul D. "The Chronology of 'A Rose for Emily.'" *Studies in Short Fiction* 6.4 (1969): 461–62. Print.

Nebecker, Helen E. "Chronology Revised." *Studies in Short Fiction* 8.4 (1971): 471–73. Print.

Sullivan, Ruth. "The Narrator in 'A Rose for Emily.'" *Journal of Narrative Technique* 1.3 (1971): 159–78. Print.

Watkins, F. C. "The Structure of 'A Rose for Emily.'" *Modern Language Notes* 69.6 (1954): 508–10. Print.

56

Taking Essay
Examinations

It is the function of the liberal arts
education not to give right answers, but
to ask right questions.
— CYNTHIA OZICK

By permission of Alfred
A. Knopf, Inc.

PREPARING FOR AN ESSAY EXAM

Keep Up with the Reading

The best way to prepare for an examination is to keep up with the reading. If you begin the course with a commitment to completing the reading assignments on time, you will not have to read in a frenzy and cram just days before the test. The readings will be a pleasure, not a frantic ordeal. Moreover, you will find that your instructor's comments and class discussion will make more sense to you and that you'll be able to participate in class discussion. As you prepare for the exam, you should be rereading texts rather than reading for the first time. It may not be possible to reread everything, but you'll at least be able to scan a familiar text and reread passages that are particularly important.

Take Notes and Annotate the Text

Don't rely exclusively on your memory. The typical literature class includes a hefty amount of reading, so unless you take notes, annotate the text with your own comments, and underline important passages, you're likely to forget material that could be useful for responding to an examination question (see pp. 2067–69 for a discussion of these matters). The more you can retrieve from your reading, the more prepared you'll be for reviewing significant material for the exam. These notes can be used to illustrate points that were made in class. By briefly quoting an important phrase or line from the text, you can provide supporting evidence that will make your argument convincing. Consider, for example, the difference between writing that "Marvell's speaker in 'To His Coy Mistress' says that they won't be able to love after they die" and writing that "the speaker intones that 'The grave's a fine and private place / But none, I think, do there embrace.'" No one expects you to memorize the entire poem, but recalling a few lines here and there can transform a sleepy generality into an illustrative, persuasive argument.

Anticipate Questions

As you review the readings, keep in mind the class discussions and the focus provided by your instructor. Class discussions and the instructor's emphasis often become the basis for essay questions. You may not see the exact same topics on the exam, but you might find that the matters you've discussed in class will serve as a means of responding to an essay question. If, for example, class discussion of John Updike's "A & P" (see p. 733) centered on the story's small-town New England setting, you could use that conservative, traditional, puritanical setting to answer a question such as "Discuss how the conflicts that Sammy encounters in 'A & P' are related to the story's theme." A discussion of the intolerant rigidity of this New England town could be connected to A & P "policy" and the crabbed values associated with Lengel that lead to Sammy's quitting his job in protest of such policies. The point is that you'll be well prepared for an essay exam when you can shape the material you've studied so that it is responsive to whatever kinds of reasonable questions you encounter on the exam. Reasonable questions? Yes, your instructor is more likely to offer you an opportunity to demonstrate your familiarity with and understanding of the text than to set a trap that, for instance, demands you discuss how Updike's work experience as an adolescent informs the story when no mention was ever made of that in class or in your reading.

You can also anticipate questions by considering the generic Questions for Responsive Reading and Writing about fiction (p. 53), poetry (p. 791), and drama (p. 1408) and the Questions for Arguing about Literature (p. 2073), along with the Questions for Writing about an Author in Depth (p. 1082). Not all of these questions will necessarily be relevant to every work that you read, but they cover a wide range of concerns that should allow you to organize your reading, note taking, and reviewing so that you're not taken by surprise during the exam.

Studying with a classmate or a small group from class can be a stimulating and fruitful means of discovering and organizing the major topics and themes of the course. This method of brainstorming can be useful not only for studying for exams but throughout the semester for understanding and reviewing course readings. And, finally, you needn't be shy about asking your instructor what types of questions might appear on the exam and how best to study for them. You may not get a very specific reply, but almost any information is more useful than none.

TYPES OF EXAMS

Closed-Book versus Open-Book Exams

Closed-book exams require more memorization and recall than open-book exams, which permit you to use your text and perhaps even your notes to answer questions. Dates, names, definitions, and other details play less of a role in an open-book exam. An open-book exam requires no less preparation, however, because you'll need to be intimately familiar with the texts and the major ideas, themes, and issues that you've studied in order to quickly and efficiently support your points with relevant, specific evidence. Since every student has the same advantage of having access to the text, preparation remains the key to answering the questions. Some students find open-book exams more difficult than closed-book tests because they risk spending too much time reading, scanning, and searching for material and not enough time writing a response that draws on the knowledge and understanding that their reading and studying has provided them. It's best to limit the time you allow yourself to review the text and notes so that you devote an adequate amount of time to getting your ideas on paper.

Essay Questions

Essay questions generally fall within one of the following categories. If you can recognize quickly what is being asked of you, you will be able to respond to them more efficiently.

1. **Explication** Explication calls for a line-by-line explanation of a passage of poetry or prose that considers, for example, diction, figures of speech, symbolism, sound, form, and theme in an effort to describe how language creates meaning. (For a more detailed discussion of explication, see p. 2084.)

2. **Definition** Defining a term and then applying it to a writer or work is a frequent exam exercise. Consider: "Define *romanticism*. To what extent can Hawthorne's *The Scarlet Letter* be regarded as a romantic story?" This sort of question requires that you first describe what constitutes a romantic literary work and then explain how *The Scarlet Letter* does (and doesn't) fit the bill.

3. **Analysis** An analytical question focuses on a particular part of a literary work. You might be asked, for example, to analyze the significance of

images in John Keats's poem "Ode on a Grecian Urn" (p. 825). This sort of question requires you to discuss a specific element of the poem and also to explain how that element contributes to the poem's overall effect. (For a more detailed discussion of analysis, see p. 2088.)

4. **Comparison and Contrast** Comparison and contrast calls for a discussion of the similarities and/or differences between writers, works, or elements of works—for example, "Compare and contrast Lengel's sensibilities in John Updike's 'A & P' (p. 733) with John Wright's in Susan Glaspell's *Trifles* (p. 1366)." Despite the obvious differences in age and circumstances between these characters, a discussion of their responses to people—particularly to women—reveals some intriguing similarities. (For a more detailed discussion of comparison and contrast, see pp. 2093–95.)

5. **Discussion of a Critical Perspective** A brief quotation by a critic about a work is usually designed to stimulate a response that requires you to agree with, disagree with, or qualify a critic's perspective. Usually it is not important whether you agree or disagree with the critic; what matters is the quality of your argument. Think about how you might wrestle with this assessment of Robert Frost written by Lionel Trilling: "The manifest America of Mr. Frost's poems may be pastoral; the actual America is tragic." With some qualifications (surely not all of Frost's poems are "tragic") this could provide a useful way of talking about a poem such as "Mending Wall" (p. 1100).

6. **Imaginative Questions** To a degree every question requires imagination regardless of whether it's being asked or answered. However, some questions require more imaginative leaps to arrive at the center of an issue than others do. Consider, for example, the intellectual agility needed to respond to this question: "How do you think Dickens's Mr. Gradgrind from *Hard Times* and the narrator of Frost's 'Mending Wall' would respond to Sammy's character in Updike's 'A & P'?" As tricky as this triangulation of topics may seem, there is plenty to discuss concerning Gradgrind's literal-mindedness, the narrator's imagination, and Sammy's rejection of "policy." Or try a simpler but no less interesting version: "How do you think Frost would review Marvell's 'To His Coy Mistress' and Keats's 'Ode on a Grecian Urn'?" Such questions certainly require detailed, reasoned responses, but they also leave room for creativity and even wit.

STRATEGIES FOR WRITING ESSAY EXAMS

Your hands may be sweaty and your heart pounding as you begin the exam, but as long as you're prepared and you keep in mind some basic strategies for writing essay exams, you should be able to respond to questions with confidence and a genuine sense of accomplishment.

1. Before you begin writing, read through the entire exam. If there are choices to be made, make certain you know how many questions must be

answered (only one out of four, not two). Note how many points each question is worth; spend more time on the two worth forty points each, and perhaps leave the twenty-point question for last.

2. Budget your time. If there are short-answer questions, do not allow them to absorb you so that you cannot do justice to the longer essay questions. Follow the suggested time limit for each question; if none is offered, then create your own schedule in proportion to the points allotted for each question.

3. Depending on your own sensibilities, you may want to begin with the easiest or hardest questions. It doesn't really matter which you begin with as long as you pace yourself to avoid running out of time.

4. Be sure that you understand the question. Does it ask you to compare and/or contrast, define, analyze, explicate, or use some other approach? Determine how many elements there are to the question so that you don't inadvertently miss part of the question. Do not spend time copying the question.

5. Make some brief notes about how you plan to answer the question; even a simple list of what you'll need to cover can serve as a useful outline.

6. Address the question; avoid unnecessary summaries or irrelevant asides. Focus on the particular elements enumerated or implied by the question.

7. After beginning the essay, write a clear thesis that describes the major topics you will discuss: "*The Scarlet Letter* is typical of Hawthorne's concerns as a writer owing to its treatment of sin, guilt, isolation, and secrecy."

8. Support and illustrate your answer with specific, relevant references to the text. The more specificity — the more you demonstrate a familiarity with the text (rather than simply provide a plot summary) — the better the answer.

9. Don't overlap and repeat responses to questions; your instructor will recognize such padding. If two different questions are about the same work or writer, demonstrate the breadth and depth of your knowledge of the subject.

10. Allow time to proofread and to qualify and to add more supporting material if necessary. At this final stage, too, it's worth remembering that Mark Twain liked to remind his readers that the difference between the right word and the almost right word is the difference between lightning and a lightning bug.

Glossary of Literary Terms

Accent The emphasis, or STRESS, given a syllable in pronunciation. We say "*syllable*" not "syl*lable*," "*emphasis*" not "em*phasis*." Accents can also be used to emphasize a particular word in a sentence: *Is* she con*tent* with the *contents* of the *yellow package*? See also METER.

Act A major division in the action of a play. The ends of acts are typically indicated by lowering the curtain or turning up the houselights. Playwrights frequently employ acts to accommodate changes in time, setting, characters onstage, or mood. In many full-length plays, acts are further divided into scenes, which often mark a point in the action when the location changes or when a new character enters. See also SCENE.

Allegory A narration or description usually restricted to a single meaning because its events, actions, characters, settings, and objects represent specific abstractions or ideas. Although the elements in an allegory may be interesting in themselves, the emphasis tends to be on what they ultimately mean. Characters may be given names such as Hope, Pride, Youth, and Charity; they have few if any personal qualities beyond their abstract meanings. These personifications are not symbols because, for instance, the meaning of a character named Charity is precisely that virtue. See also SYMBOL.

Alliteration The repetition of the same consonant sounds in a sequence of words, usually at the beginning of a word or stressed syllable: "*descending dew drops*"; "*luscious lemons*." Alliteration is based on the sounds of letters, rather than the spelling of words; for example, "*keen*" and "*car*" alliterate, but "*car*" and "*cite*" do not. Used sparingly, alliteration can intensify ideas by emphasizing key words, but when used too self-consciously, it can be distracting, even ridiculous, rather than effective. See also ASSONANCE, CONSONANCE.

Allusion A brief reference to a person, place, thing, event, or idea in history or literature. Allusions conjure up biblical authority, scenes from Shakespeare's plays, historic figures, wars, great love stories, and anything else that might enrich an author's work. Allusions imply reading and cultural experiences shared by the writer and reader, functioning as a kind of shorthand whereby the recalling of something outside the work supplies an emotional or intellectual context, such as a poem about current racial struggles calling up the memory of Abraham Lincoln.

Ambiguity Allows for two or more simultaneous interpretations of a word, phrase, action, or situation, all of which can be supported by the context of a work. Deliberate ambiguity can contribute to the effectiveness and richness of a work, for example, in the open-ended conclusion to Hawthorne's "Young Goodman Brown." However, unintentional ambiguity obscures meaning and can confuse readers.

Anagram A word or phrase made from the letters of another word or phrase, as "heart" is an anagram of "earth." Anagrams have often been considered merely an exercise of one's ingenuity, but sometimes writers use anagrams to conceal proper names or veiled messages, or to suggest important connections between words, as in "hated" and "death."

Anapestic meter See FOOT.

Antagonist The character, force, or collection of forces in fiction or drama that opposes the PROTAGONIST and gives rise to the conflict of the story; an opponent of the protagonist, such as Claudius in Shakespeare's play *Hamlet*. See also CHARACTER, CONFLICT.

Antihero A protagonist who has the opposite of most of the traditional attributes of a hero. He or she may be bewildered, ineffectual, deluded, or merely pathetic. Often what antiheroes learn, if they learn anything at all, is that the world isolates them in an existence devoid of God and absolute values. Yossarian from Joseph Heller's *Catch-22* is an example of an antihero. See also CHARACTER.

Apostrophe An address, either to someone who is absent and therefore cannot hear the speaker or to something nonhuman that cannot comprehend. Apostrophe often provides a speaker the opportunity to think aloud.

Approximate rhyme See RHYME.

Archetype A term used to describe universal symbols that evoke deep and sometimes unconscious responses in a reader. In literature, characters, images, and themes that symbolically embody universal meanings and basic human experiences, regardless of when or where they live, are considered archetypes. Common literary archetypes include stories of quests, initiations, scapegoats, descents to the underworld, and ascents to heaven. See also MYTHOLOGICAL CRITICISM.

Aside In drama, a speech directed to the audience that supposedly is not audible to the other characters onstage at the time. When Hamlet first appears onstage, for example, his aside "A little more than kin, and less than kind!" gives the audience a strong sense of his alienation from King Claudius. See also SOLILOQUY.

Assonance The repetition of internal vowel sounds in nearby words that do not end the same, for example, "asleep under a tree," or "each evening." Similar endings result in rhyme, as in "asleep in the deep." Assonance is a strong means of emphasizing important words in a line. See also ALLITERATION, CONSONANCE.

Ballad Traditionally, a ballad is a song, transmitted orally from generation to generation, that tells a story and that eventually is written down. As such, ballads usually cannot be traced to a particular author or group of authors.

Typically, ballads are dramatic, condensed, and impersonal narratives, such as "Bonny Barbara Allan." A **literary ballad** is a narrative poem that is written in deliberate imitation of the language, form, and spirit of the traditional ballad, such as Keats's "La Belle Dame sans Merci." See also BALLAD STANZA, QUATRAIN.

Ballad stanza A four-line stanza, known as a QUATRAIN, consisting of alternating eight- and six-syllable lines. Usually only the second and fourth lines rhyme (an *abcb* pattern). Coleridge adopted the ballad stanza in "The Rime of the Ancient Mariner."

All in a hot and copper sky
The bloody Sun, at noon,
Right up above the mast did stand,
No bigger than the Moon.

See also BALLAD, QUATRAIN.

Biographical criticism An approach to literature that suggests that knowledge of the author's life experiences can aid in the understanding of his or her work. While biographical information can sometimes complicate one's interpretation of a work, and some formalist critics (such as the New Critics) disparage the use of the author's biography as a tool for textual interpretation, learning about the life of the author can often enrich a reader's appreciation for that author's work. See also CULTURAL CRITICISM, FORMALIST CRITICISM, NEW CRITICISM.

Blank verse Unrhymed iambic pentameter. Blank verse is the English verse form closest to the natural rhythms of English speech and therefore is the most common pattern found in traditional English narrative and dramatic poetry from Shakespeare to the early twentieth century. Shakespeare's plays use blank verse extensively. See also IAMBIC PENTAMETER.

Cacophony Language that is discordant and difficult to pronounce, such as this line from John Updike's "Player Piano": "never my numb plunker fumbles." Cacophony ("bad sound") may be unintentional in the writer's sense of music, or it may be used consciously for deliberate dramatic effect. See also EUPHONY.

Caesura A pause within a line of poetry that contributes to the rhythm of the line. A caesura can occur anywhere within a line and need not be indicated by punctuation. In scanning a line, caesuras are indicated by a double vertical line (||). See also METER, RHYTHM, SCANSION.

Canon Those works generally considered by scholars, critics, and teachers to be the most important to read and study, which collectively constitute the "masterpieces" of literature. Since the 1960s, the traditional English and American literary canon, consisting mostly of works by white male writers, has been rapidly expanding to include many female writers and writers of varying ethnic backgrounds.

Carpe diem The Latin phrase meaning "seize the day." This is a very common literary theme, especially in lyric poetry, which emphasizes that life is short, time is fleeting, and that one should make the most of present pleasures. Robert Herrick's poem "To the Virgins, to Make Much of Time" employs the *carpe diem* theme.

Catharsis Meaning "purgation," *catharsis* describes the release of the emotions of pity and fear by the audience at the end of a tragedy. In his *Poetics,* Aristotle discusses the importance of catharsis. The audience faces the misfortunes of the protagonist, which elicit pity and compassion. Simultaneously, the audience also confronts the failure of the protagonist, thus receiving a frightening reminder of human limitations and frailties. Ultimately, however, both these negative emotions are purged, because the tragic protagonist's suffering is an affirmation of human values rather than a despairing denial of them. See also TRAGEDY.

Character, characterization A character is a person presented in a dramatic or narrative work, and characterization is the process by which a writer makes that character seem real to the reader. A **hero** or **heroine,** often called the PROTAGONIST, is the central character who engages the reader's interest and empathy. The ANTAGONIST is the character, force, or collection of forces that stands directly opposed to the protagonist and gives rise to the conflict of the story. A **static character** does not change throughout the work, and the reader's knowledge of that character does not grow, whereas a **dynamic character** undergoes some kind of change because of the action in the plot. A **flat character** embodies one or two qualities, ideas, or traits that can be readily described in a brief summary. They are not psychologically complex characters and therefore are readily accessible to readers. Some flat characters are recognized as **stock characters;** they embody stereotypes such as the "dumb blonde" or the "mean stepfather." They become types rather than individuals. **Round characters** are more complex than flat or stock characters, and often display the inconsistencies and internal conflicts found in most real people. They are more fully developed, and therefore are harder to summarize. Authors have two major methods of presenting characters: **showing** and **telling. Showing** allows the author to present a character talking and acting, and lets the reader infer what kind of person the character is. In **telling,** the author intervenes to describe and sometimes evaluate the character for the reader. Characters can be convincing whether they are presented by showing or by telling, as long as their actions are motivated. **Motivated action** by the characters occurs when the reader or audience is offered reasons for how the characters behave, what they say, and the decisions they make. **Plausible action** is action by a character in a story that seems reasonable, given the motivations presented. See also PLOT.

Chorus In Greek tragedies (especially those of Aeschylus and Sophocles), a group of people who serve mainly as commentators on the characters and events. They add to the audience's understanding of the play by expressing traditional moral, religious, and social attitudes. The role of the chorus in dramatic works evolved through the sixteenth century, and the chorus occasionally is still used by modern playwrights such as T. S. Eliot in *Murder in the Cathedral.* See also DRAMA.

Cliché An idea or expression that has become tired and trite from overuse, its freshness and clarity having worn off. Clichés often anesthetize readers, and are usually a sign of weak writing. See also SENTIMENTALITY, STOCK RESPONSES.

Climax See PLOT.

Closet drama A play that is written to be read rather than performed on-stage. In this kind of drama, literary art outweighs all other considerations. See also DRAMA.

Colloquial Refers to a type of informal diction that reflects casual, conversational language and often includes slang expressions. See also DICTION.

Comedy A work intended to interest, involve, and amuse the reader or audience, in which no terrible disaster occurs and that ends happily for the main characters. **High comedy** refers to verbal wit, such as puns, whereas **low comedy** is generally associated with physical action and is less intellectual. **Romantic comedy** involves a love affair that meets with various obstacles (like disapproving parents, mistaken identities, deceptions, or other sorts of misunderstandings) but overcomes them to end in a blissful union. Shakespeare's comedies, such as *A Midsummer Night's Dream,* are considered romantic comedies.

Comic relief A humorous scene or incident that alleviates tension in an otherwise serious work. In many instances these moments enhance the thematic significance of the story in addition to providing laughter. When Hamlet jokes with the gravediggers we laugh, but something hauntingly serious about the humor also intensifies our more serious emotions.

Conflict The struggle within the plot between opposing forces. The PROTAGO-NIST engages in the conflict with the ANTAGONIST, which may take the form of a character, society, nature, or an aspect of the protagonist's personality. See also CHARACTER, PLOT.

Connotation Associations and implications that go beyond the literal meaning of a word, which derive from how the word has been commonly used and the associations people make with it. For example, the word *eagle* connotes ideas of liberty and freedom that have little to do with the word's literal meaning. See also DENOTATION.

Consonance A common type of near rhyme that consists of identical consonant sounds preceded by different vowel sounds: *home, same; worth, breath.* See also RHYME.

Contextual symbol See SYMBOL.

Controlling metaphor See METAPHOR.

Convention A characteristic of a literary genre (often unrealistic) that is understood and accepted by audiences because it has come, through usage and time, to be recognized as a familiar technique. For example, the division of a play into acts and scenes is a dramatic convention, as are soliloquies and asides. FLASHBACKS and FORESHADOWING are examples of literary conventions.

Conventional symbol See SYMBOL.

Cosmic irony See IRONY.

Couplet Two consecutive lines of poetry that usually rhyme and have the same meter. A **heroic couplet** is a couplet written in rhymed iambic pentameter.

Crisis A turning point in the action of a story that has a powerful effect on the protagonist. Opposing forces come together decisively to lead to the climax of the plot. See also PLOT.

Cultural criticism An approach to literature that focuses on the historical as well as social, political, and economic contexts of a work. Popular culture — mass produced and consumed cultural artifacts ranging from advertising to popular fiction to television to rock music — is given equal emphasis with "high culture." **Cultural critics** use widely eclectic strategies such as new historicism, psychology, gender studies, and deconstructionism to analyze not only literary texts but everything from radio talk shows, comic strips, calendar art, and commercials, to travel guides and baseball cards. See also HISTORICAL CRITICISM, MARXIST CRITICISM, POSTCOLONIAL CRITICISM.

Dactylic meter See FOOT.

Deconstructionism An approach to literature which suggests that literary works do not yield fixed, single meanings, because language can never say exactly what we intend it to mean. Deconstructionism seeks to destabilize meaning by examining the gaps and ambiguities of the language of a text. Deconstructionists pay close attention to language in order to discover and describe how a variety of possible readings are generated by the elements of a text. See also NEW CRITICISM.

Denotation The dictionary meaning of a word. See also CONNOTATION.

Dénouement A French term meaning "unraveling" or "unknotting," used to describe the resolution of the plot following the climax. See also PLOT, RESOLUTION.

Dialect A type of informational diction. Dialects are spoken by definable groups of people from a particular geographic region, economic group, or social class. Writers use dialect to contrast and express differences in educational, class, social, and regional backgrounds of their characters. See also DICTION.

Dialogue The verbal exchanges between characters. Dialogue makes the characters seem real to the reader or audience by revealing firsthand their thoughts, responses, and emotional states. See also DICTION.

Diction A writer's choice of words, phrases, sentence structures, and figurative language, which combine to help create meaning. **Formal diction** consists of a dignified, impersonal, and elevated use of language; it follows the rules of syntax exactly and is often characterized by complex words and lofty tone. **Middle diction** maintains correct language usage, but is less elevated than formal diction; it reflects the way most educated people speak. **Informal diction** represents the plain language of everyday use, and often includes idiomatic expressions, slang, contractions, and many simple, common words. **Poetic diction** refers to the way poets sometimes employ an elevated diction that deviates significantly from the common speech and writing of their time, choosing words for their supposedly inherent poetic qualities. Since the eighteenth century, however, poets have been incorporating all kinds of diction in their work and so there is no longer an automatic distinction between the language of a poet and the language of everyday speech. See also DIALECT.

Didactic poetry Poetry designed to teach an ethical, moral, or religious lesson. Michael Wigglesworth's Puritan poem *Day of Doom* is an example of didactic poetry.

Doggerel A derogatory term used to describe poetry whose subject is trite and whose rhythm and sounds are monotonously heavy-handed.

Drama Derived from the Greek word *dram,* meaning "to do" or "to perform," the term *drama* may refer to a single play, a group of plays ("Jacobean drama"), or to all plays ("world drama"). Drama is designed for performance in a theater; actors take on the roles of characters, perform indicated actions, and speak the dialogue written in the script. **Play** is a general term for a work of dramatic literature, and a **playwright** is a writer who makes plays.

Dramatic irony See IRONY.

Dramatic monologue A type of lyric poem in which a character (the speaker) addresses a distinct but silent audience imagined to be present in the poem in such a way as to reveal a dramatic situation and, often unintentionally, some aspect of his or her temperament or personality. See also LYRIC.

Dynamic character See CHARACTER.

Editorial omniscience See NARRATOR.

Electra complex The female version of the Oedipus complex. *Electra complex* is a term used to describe the psychological conflict of a daughter's unconscious rivalry with her mother for her father's attention. The name comes from the Greek legend of Electra, who avenged the death of her father, Agamemnon, by plotting the death of her mother. See also OEDIPUS COMPLEX, PSYCHOLOGICAL CRITICISM.

Elegy A mournful, contemplative lyric poem written to commemorate someone who is dead, often ending in a consolation. Tennyson's *In Memoriam,* written on the death of Arthur Hallam, is an elegy. *Elegy* may also refer to a serious meditative poem produced to express the speaker's melancholy thoughts. See also LYRIC.

End rhyme See RHYME.

End-stopped line A poetic line that has a pause at the end. End-stopped lines reflect normal speech patterns and are often marked by punctuation. The first line of Keats's "Endymion" is an example of an end-stopped line; the natural pause coincides with the end of the line, and is marked by a period:

A thing of beauty is a joy forever.

English sonnet See SONNET.

Enjambment In poetry, when one line ends without a pause and continues into the next line for its meaning. This is also called a **run-on line.** The transition between the first two lines of Wordsworth's poem "My Heart Leaps Up" demonstrates enjambment:

My heart leaps up when I behold
  A rainbow in the sky:

Envoy See SESTINA.

Epic A long narrative poem, told in a formal, elevated style, that focuses on a serious subject and chronicles heroic deeds and events important to a culture or nation. Milton's *Paradise Lost,* which attempts to "justify the ways of God to man," is an epic. See also NARRATIVE POEM.

Epigram A brief, pointed, and witty poem that usually makes a satiric or humorous point. Epigrams are most often written in couplets, but take no prescribed form.

Epiphany In fiction, when a character suddenly experiences a deep realization about himself or herself; a truth that is grasped in an ordinary rather than a melodramatic moment.

Escape literature See FORMULA FICTION.

Euphony *Euphony* ("good sound") refers to language that is smooth and musically pleasant to the ear. See also CACOPHONY.

Exact rhyme See RHYME.

Exposition A narrative device, often used at the beginning of a work, that provides necessary background information about the characters and their circumstances. Exposition explains what has gone on before, the relationships between characters, the development of a theme, and the introduction of a conflict. See also FLASHBACK.

Extended metaphor See METAPHOR.

Eye rhyme See RHYME.

Falling action See PLOT.

Falling meter See METER.

Farce A form of humor based on exaggerated, improbable incongruities. Farce involves rapid shifts in action and emotion, as well as slapstick comedy and extravagant dialogue. Malvolio, in Shakespeare's *Twelfth Night,* is a farcical character.

Feminine rhyme See RHYME.

Feminist criticism An approach to literature that seeks to correct or supplement what may be regarded as a predominantly male-dominated critical perspective with a feminist consciousness. Feminist criticism places literature in a social context and uses a broad range of disciplines, including history, sociology, psychology, and linguistics, to provide a perspective sensitive to feminist issues. Feminist theories also attempt to understand representation from a woman's point of view and to explain women's writing strategies as specific to their social conditions. See also GAY AND LESBIAN CRITICISM, GENDER CRITICISM, SOCIOLOGICAL CRITICISM.

Figures of speech Ways of using language that deviate from the literal, denotative meanings of words in order to suggest additional meanings or effects. Figures of speech say one thing in terms of something else, such as when an eager funeral director is described as a vulture. See also METAPHOR, SIMILE.

First-person narrator See NARRATOR.

Fixed form A poem that may be categorized by the pattern of its lines, meter, rhythm, or stanzas. A sonnet is a fixed form of poetry because by definition it must have fourteen lines. Other fixed forms include LIMERICK, SESTINA, and VILLANELLE. However, poems written in a fixed form may not always fit into categories precisely, because writers sometimes vary traditional forms to create innovative effects. See also OPEN FORM.

Flashback A narrated scene that marks a break in the narrative in order to inform the reader or audience member about events that took place before the opening scene of a work. See also EXPOSITION.

Flat character See CHARACTER.

Foil A character in a work whose behavior and values contrast with those of another character in order to highlight the distinctive temperament of that character (usually the protagonist). In Shakespeare's *Hamlet,* Laertes acts as a foil to Hamlet, because his willingness to act underscores Hamlet's inability to do so.

Foot The metrical unit by which a line of poetry is measured. A foot usually consists of one stressed and one or two unstressed syllables. An *iambic foot,* which consists of one unstressed syllable followed by one stressed syllable ("away"), is the most common metrical foot in English poetry. A *trochaic foot* consists of one stressed syllable followed by an unstressed syllable ("lovely"). An *anapestic foot* is two unstressed syllables followed by one stressed one ("understand"). A *dactylic foot* is one stressed syllable followed by two unstressed ones ("desperate"). A *spondee* is a foot consisting of two stressed syllables ("dead set"), but is not a sustained metrical foot and is used mainly for variety or emphasis. See also IAMBIC PENTAMETER, LINE, METER.

Foreshadowing The introduction early in a story of verbal and dramatic hints that suggest what is to come later.

Form The overall structure or shape of a work, which frequently follows an established design. Forms may refer to a literary type (narrative form, short story form) or to patterns of meter, lines, and rhymes (stanza form, verse form). See also FIXED FORM, OPEN FORM.

Formal diction See DICTION.

Formalist criticism An approach to literature that focuses on the formal elements of a work, such as its language, structure, and tone. Formalist critics offer intense examinations of the relationship between form and meaning in a work, emphasizing the subtle complexity in how a work is arranged. Formalists pay special attention to diction, irony, paradox, metaphor, and symbol, as well as larger elements such as plot, characterization, and narrative technique. Formalist critics read literature as an independent work of art rather than as a reflection of the author's state of mind or as a representation of a moment in history. Therefore, anything outside of the work, including historical influences and authorial intent, is generally not examined by formalist critics. See also NEW CRITICISM.

Formula fiction Often characterized as "escape literature," formula fiction follows a pattern of conventional reader expectations. Romance novels, westerns, science fiction, and detective stories are all examples of formula fiction; while the details of individual stories vary, the basic ingredients of each kind of story are the same. Formula fiction offers happy endings (the hero "gets the girl," the detective cracks the case), entertains wide audiences, and sells tremendously well.

Found poem An unintentional poem discovered in a nonpoetic context, such as a conversation, news story, or advertisement. Found poems serve as reminders that everyday language often contains what can be considered poetry, or that poetry is definable as any text read as a poem.

Free verse Also called OPEN FORM poetry, *free verse* refers to poems characterized by their nonconformity to established patterns of meter, rhyme, and stanza. Free verse uses elements such as speech patterns, grammar, emphasis, and breath pauses to decide line breaks, and usually does not rhyme. See OPEN FORM.

Gay and lesbian criticism An approach to literature that focuses on how homosexuals are represented in literature, how they read literature, and whether sexuality, as well as gender, is culturally constructed or innate. See also FEMINIST CRITICISM, GENDER CRITICISM.

Gender criticism An approach to literature that explores how ideas about men and women — what is masculine and feminine — can be regarded as socially constructed by particular cultures. Gender criticism expands categories and definitions of what is masculine or feminine and tends to regard sexuality as more complex than merely masculine or feminine, heterosexual or homosexual. See also FEMINIST CRITICISM, GAY AND LESBIAN CRITICISM.

Genre A French word meaning kind or type. The major genres in literature are poetry, fiction, drama, and essays. Genre can also refer to more specific types of literature such as comedy, tragedy, epic poetry, or science fiction.

Haiku A style of lyric poetry borrowed from the Japanese that typically presents an intense emotion or vivid image of nature, which, traditionally, is designed to lead to a spiritual insight. Haiku is a fixed poetic form, consisting of seventeen syllables organized into three unrhymed lines of five, seven, and five syllables. Today, however, many poets vary the syllabic count in their haiku. See also FIXED FORM.

Hamartia A term coined by Aristotle to describe "some error or frailty" that brings about misfortune for a tragic hero. The concept of *hamartia* is closely related to that of the tragic flaw: both lead to the downfall of the protagonist in a tragedy. *Hamartia* may be interpreted as an internal weakness in a character (like greed or passion or HUBRIS); however, it may also refer to a mistake that a character makes that is based not on a personal failure, but on circumstances outside the protagonist's personality and control. See also TRAGEDY.

Hero, heroine See CHARACTER.

Heroic couplet See COUPLET.

High comedy See COMEDY.

Historical criticism An approach to literature that uses history as a means of understanding a literary work more clearly. Such criticism moves beyond both the facts of an author's personal life and the text itself in order to examine the social and intellectual currents in which the author composed the work. See also CULTURAL CRITICISM, MARXIST CRITICISM, NEW HISTORICISM, POSTCOLONIAL CRITICISM.

Hubris or Hybris Excessive pride or self-confidence that leads a protagonist to disregard a divine warning or to violate an important moral law. In tragedies, hubris is a very common form of *hamartia*. See also HAMARTIA, TRAGEDY.

Hyperbole A boldly exaggerated statement that adds emphasis without intending to be literally true, as in the statement "He ate everything in the house." Hyperbole (also called **overstatement**) may be used for serious, comic, or ironic effect. See also FIGURES OF SPEECH.

Iambic meter See FOOT.

Iambic pentameter A metrical pattern in poetry which consists of five iambic feet per line. (An iamb, or iambic foot, consists of one unstressed syllable followed by a stressed syllable.) See also FOOT, METER.

Image A word, phrase, or figure of speech (especially a SIMILE or a METAPHOR) that addresses the senses, suggesting mental pictures of sights, sounds, smells, tastes, feelings, or actions. Images offer sensory impressions to the reader and also convey emotions and moods through their verbal pictures. See also FIGURES OF SPEECH.

Implied metaphor See METAPHOR.

In medias res See PLOT.

Informal diction See DICTION.

Internal rhyme See RHYME.

Irony A literary device that uses contradictory statements or situations to reveal a reality different from what appears to be true. It is ironic for a firehouse to burn down, or for a police station to be burglarized. **Verbal irony** is a figure of speech that occurs when a person says one thing but means the opposite. **Sarcasm** is a strong form of verbal irony that is calculated to hurt someone through, for example, false praise. **Dramatic irony** creates a discrepancy between what a character believes or says and what the reader or audience member knows to be true. **Tragic irony** is a form of dramatic irony found in tragedies such as *Oedipus the King,* in which Oedipus searches for the person responsible for the plague that ravishes his city and ironically ends up hunting himself. **Situational irony** exists when there is an incongruity between what is expected to happen and what actually happens due to forces beyond human comprehension or control. The suicide of the seemingly successful main character in Edwin Arlington Robinson's poem "Richard Cory" is an example of situational irony. **Cosmic irony** occurs when a writer uses God, destiny, or fate to dash the hopes and expectations of a character or of humankind in general. In cosmic irony, a discrepancy exists between what a character aspires to and what universal forces provide. Stephen Crane's poem "A Man Said to the Universe" is a good example of cosmic irony, because the universe acknowledges no obligation to the man's assertion of his own existence.

Italian sonnet See SONNET.

Limerick A light, humorous style of fixed form poetry. Its usual form consists of five lines with the rhyme scheme *aabba;* lines 1, 2, and 5 contain three feet, while lines 3 and 4 usually contain two feet. Limericks range in subject matter from the silly to the obscene, and since Edward Lear popularized them in the nineteenth century, children and adults have enjoyed these comic poems. See also FIXED FORM.

Limited omniscient narrator See NARRATOR.

Line A sequence of words printed as a separate entity on the page. In poetry, lines are usually measured by the number of feet they contain. The names for various line lengths are as follows:

monometer: one foot	pentameter: five feet
dimeter: two feet	hexameter: six feet
trimeter: three feet	heptameter: seven feet
tetrameter: four feet	octameter: eight feet

The number of feet in a line, coupled with the name of the foot, describes the metrical qualities of that line. See also END-STOPPED LINE, ENJAMBMENT, FOOT, METER.

Literary ballad See BALLAD.

Literary symbol See SYMBOL.

Low comedy See COMEDY.

Lyric A type of brief poem that expresses the personal emotions and thoughts of a single speaker. It is important to realize, however, that although the lyric is uttered in the first person, the speaker is not necessarily the poet. There are many varieties of lyric poetry, including the DRAMATIC MONOLOGUE, ELEGY, HAIKU, ODE, and SONNET forms.

Marxist criticism An approach to literature that focuses on the ideological content of a work — its explicit and implicit assumptions and values about matters such as culture, race, class, and power. Marxist criticism, based largely on the writings of Karl Marx, typically aims at not only revealing and clarifying ideological issues but also correcting social injustices. Some Marxist critics use literature to describe the competing socioeconomic interests that too often advance capitalist interests such as money and power rather than socialist interests such as morality and justice. They argue that literature and literary criticism are essentially political because they either challenge or support economic oppression. Because of this strong emphasis on the political aspects of texts, Marxist criticism focuses more on the content and themes of literature than on its form. See also CULTURAL CRITICISM, HISTORICAL CRITICISM, SOCIOLOGICAL CRITICISM.

Masculine rhyme See RHYME.

Melodrama A term applied to any literary work that relies on implausible events and sensational action for its effect. The conflicts in melodramas typically arise out of plot rather than characterization; often a virtuous individual must somehow confront and overcome a wicked oppressor. Usually, a melodramatic story ends happily, with the protagonist defeating the antagonist at the last possible moment. Thus, melodramas entertain the reader or audience with exciting action while still conforming to a traditional sense of justice. See also SENTIMENTALITY.

Metafiction The literary term used to describe a work that explores the nature, structure, logic, status, and function of storytelling.

Metaphor A metaphor is a figure of speech that makes a comparison between two unlike things, without using the word *like* or *as*. Metaphors assert the identity of dissimilar things, as when Macbeth asserts that life *is* a "brief candle." Metaphors can be subtle and powerful, and can transform people, places, objects, and ideas into whatever the writer imagines them to be. An **implied metaphor** is a more subtle comparison; the terms being compared are not so specifically explained. For example, to describe a stubborn man unwilling to leave, one could say that he was "a mule standing his ground." This is a fairly explicit metaphor; the man is being compared to a mule. But to say that the man "brayed his refusal to leave" is to create an implied metaphor, because the subject (the man) is never overtly identified as a mule. Braying is associated with the mule, a notoriously stubborn creature, and so the comparison between the stubborn man and the mule is sustained. Implied metaphors can slip by inattentive readers who are not sensitive to such carefully chosen, highly concentrated language. An **extended metaphor** is a sustained comparison in which part or all of a poem consists of a series of related metaphors. Robert Francis's poem "Catch" relies on an extended metaphor that compares poetry to playing catch. A **controlling metaphor** runs through an entire work and determines the form or nature of that work. The controlling metaphor in Anne Bradstreet's poem "The Author to Her Book" likens her book to a child. **Synecdoche** is a kind of metaphor in which a part of something is used to signify the whole, as when a gossip is called a "wagging tongue," or when ten ships are called "ten sails." Sometimes, synecdoche refers to the whole being used to signify the part, as in the phrase "Boston won the baseball game." Clearly, the entire city of Boston did not participate in the game; the whole of Boston is being used to signify the individuals who played and won the game. **Metonymy** is a type of metaphor in which something closely associated with a subject is substituted for it. In this way, we speak of the "silver screen" to mean motion pictures, "the crown" to stand for the king, "the White House" to stand for the activities of the president. See also FIGURES OF SPEECH, PERSONIFICATION, SIMILE.

Meter When a rhythmic pattern of stresses recurs in a poem, it is called *meter.* Metrical patterns are determined by the type and number of feet in a line of verse; combining the name of a line length with the name of a foot concisely describes the meter of the line. **Rising meter** refers to metrical feet which move from unstressed to stressed sounds, such as the iambic foot and the anapestic foot. **Falling meter** refers to metrical feet that move from stressed to unstressed sounds, such as the trochaic foot and the dactylic foot. See also ACCENT, FOOT, IAMBIC PENTAMETER, LINE.

Metonymy See METAPHOR.

Middle diction See DICTION.

Motivated action See CHARACTER.

Mythological criticism An approach to literature that seeks to identify what in a work creates deep universal responses in readers, by paying close attention to the hopes, fears, and expectations of entire cultures. Mythological critics (sometimes called *archetypal critics*) look for underlying, recurrent patterns in literature that reveal universal meanings and basic human experiences for readers regardless of when and where they live. These critics attempt to explain how archetypes (the characters, images, and themes that symbolically embody universal meanings and experiences) are embodied in literary works in order to make larger connections that explain a particular work's lasting appeal. Mythological critics may specialize in areas such as classical literature, philology, anthropology, psychology, and cultural history, but they all emphasize the assumptions and values of various cultures. See also ARCHETYPE.

Naive narrator See NARRATOR.

Narrative poem A poem that tells a story. A narrative poem may be short or long, and the story it relates may be simple or complex. See also BALLAD, EPIC.

Narrator The voice of the person telling the story, not to be confused with the author's voice. With a **first-person narrator,** the *I* in the story presents the point of view of only one character. The reader is restricted to the perceptions, thoughts, and feelings of that single character. For example, in Melville's "Bartleby, the Scrivener," the lawyer is the first-person narrator of the story. First-person narrators can play either a major or a minor role in the story they are telling. An **unreliable narrator** reveals an interpretation of events that is somehow different from the author's own interpretation of those events. Often, the unreliable narrator's perception of plot, characters, and setting becomes the actual subject of the story, as in Melville's "Bartleby, the Scrivener." Narrators can be unreliable for a number of reasons: they might lack self-knowledge (like Melville's lawyer), they might be inexperienced, they might even be insane. **Naive narrators** are usually characterized by youthful innocence, such as Mark Twain's Huck Finn or J. D. Salinger's Holden Caulfield. An **omniscient narrator** is an all-knowing narrator who is not a character in the story and who can move from place to place and pass back and forth through time, slipping into and out of characters as no human being possibly could in real life. Omniscient narrators can report the thoughts and feelings of the characters, as well as their words and actions. The narrator of *The Scarlet Letter* is an omniscient narrator. **Editorial omniscience** refers to an intrusion by the narrator in order to evaluate a character for a reader, as when the narrator of *The Scarlet Letter* describes Hester's relationship to the Puritan community. Narration that allows the characters' actions and thoughts to speak for themselves is called **neutral omniscience.** Most modern writers use neutral omniscience so that readers can reach their own conclusions. **Limited omniscience** occurs when an author restricts a narrator to the single perspective of either a major or minor character. The way people, places, and events appear to that character is the way they appear to the reader. Sometimes a limited omniscient narrator can see into more than one character, particularly in a work that focuses on two characters alternately from one chapter to the next. Short stories, however, are frequently limited to a single character's point of view. See also PERSONA, POINT OF VIEW, STREAM-OF-CONSCIOUSNESS TECHNIQUE.

Near rhyme See RHYME.

Neutral omniscience See NARRATOR.

New Criticism An approach to literature made popular between the 1940s and the 1960s that evolved out of formalist criticism. New Critics suggest that detailed analysis of the language of a literary text can uncover important layers of meaning in that work. New Criticism consciously downplays the historical influences, authorial intentions, and social contexts that surround texts in order to focus on explication — extremely close textual analysis. Critics such as John Crowe Ransom, I. A. Richards, and Robert Penn Warren are commonly associated with New Criticism. See also FORMALIST CRITICISM.

New historicism An approach to literature that emphasizes the interaction between the historic context of the work and a modern reader's understanding and interpretation of the work. New historicists attempt to describe the culture of a period by reading many different kinds of texts and paying close attention to many different dimensions of a culture, including political, economic, social, and aesthetic concerns. They regard texts not simply as a reflection of the culture that produced them but also as productive of that culture playing an active role in the social and political conflicts of an age. New historicism acknowledges and then explores various versions of "history," sensitizing us to the fact that the history on which we choose to focus is colored by being reconstructed from our present circumstances. See also HISTORICAL CRITICISM.

Objective point of view See POINT OF VIEW.

Octave A poetic stanza of eight lines, usually forming one part of a sonnet. See also SONNET, STANZA.

Ode A relatively lengthy lyric poem that often expresses lofty emotions in a dignified style. Odes are characterized by a serious topic, such as truth, art, freedom, justice, or the meaning of life; their tone tends to be formal. There is no prescribed pattern that defines an ode; some odes repeat the same pattern in each stanza, while others introduce a new pattern in each stanza. See also LYRIC.

Oedipus complex A Freudian term derived from Sophocles' tragedy *Oedipus the King.* It describes a psychological complex that is predicated on a boy's unconscious rivalry with his father for his mother's love and his desire to eliminate his father in order to take his father's place with his mother. The female equivalent of this complex is called the **Electra complex.** See also ELECTRA COMPLEX, PSYCHOLOGICAL CRITICISM.

Off rhyme See RHYME.

Omniscient narrator See NARRATOR.

One-act play A play that takes place in a single location and unfolds as one continuous action. The characters in a one-act play are presented economically and the action is sharply focused. See also DRAMA.

Onomatopoeia A term referring to the use of a word that resembles the sound it denotes. *Buzz, rattle, bang,* and *sizzle* all reflect onomatopoeia. Onomatopoeia can also consist of more than one word; writers sometimes create lines or whole passages in which the sound of the words helps to convey their meanings.

Open form Sometimes called **free verse,** open form poetry does not conform to established patterns of METER, RHYME, and STANZA. Such poetry derives its rhythmic qualities from the repetition of words, phrases, or grammatical structures, the arrangement of words on the printed page, or by some other means. The poet E. E. Cummings wrote open form poetry; his poems do not have measurable meters, but they do have rhythm. See also FIXED FORM.

Organic form Refers to works whose formal characteristics are not rigidly predetermined but follow the movement of thought or emotion being expressed. Such works are said to grow like living organisms, following their own individual patterns rather than external fixed rules that govern, for example, the form of a SONNET.

Overstatement See HYPERBOLE.

Oxymoron A condensed form of paradox in which two contradictory words are used together, as in "sweet sorrow" or "original copy." See also PARADOX.

Paradox A statement that initially appears to be contradictory but then, on closer inspection, turns out to make sense. For example, John Donne ends his sonnet "Death, Be Not Proud" with the paradoxical statement "Death, thou shalt die." To solve the paradox, it is necessary to discover the sense that underlies the statement. Paradox is useful in poetry because it arrests a reader's attention by its seemingly stubborn refusal to make sense.

Paraphrase A prose restatement of the central ideas of a poem, in your own language.

Parody A humorous imitation of another, usually serious, work. It can take any fixed or open form, because parodists imitate the tone, language, and shape of the original in order to deflate the subject matter, making the original work seem absurd. Anthony Hecht's poem "Dover Bitch" is a famous parody of Matthew Arnold's well-known "Dover Beach." Parody may also be used as a form of literary criticism to expose the defects in a work. But sometimes parody becomes an affectionate acknowledgment that a well-known work has become both institutionalized in our culture and fair game for some fun. For example, Peter De Vries's "To His Importunate Mistress" gently mocks Andrew Marvell's "To His Coy Mistress."

Persona Literally, a *persona* is a mask. In literature, a *persona* is a speaker created by a writer to tell a story or to speak in a poem. A persona is not a character in a story or narrative, nor does a persona necessarily directly reflect the author's personal voice. A persona is a separate self, created by and distinct from the author, through which he or she speaks. See also NARRATOR.

Personification A form of metaphor in which human characteristics are attributed to nonhuman things. Personification offers the writer a way to give the world life and motion by assigning familiar human behaviors and emotions to animals, inanimate objects, and abstract ideas. For example, in Keats's "Ode on a Grecian Urn," the speaker refers to the urn as an "unravished bride of quietness." See also METAPHOR.

Petrarchan sonnet See SONNET.

Picture poem A type of open form poetry in which the poet arranges the lines of the poem so as to create a particular shape on the page. The shape of the poem embodies its subject; the poem becomes a picture of what the poem is describing. Michael McFee's "In Medias Res" is an example of a picture poem. See also OPEN FORM.

Plausible action See CHARACTER.

Play See DRAMA.

Playwright See DRAMA.

Plot An author's selection and arrangement of incidents in a story to shape the action and give the story a particular focus. Discussions of plot include not just what happens, but also how and why things happen the way they do. Stories that are written in a **pyramidal pattern** divide the plot into three essential parts. The first part is the **rising action,** in which complication creates some sort of conflict for the protagonist. The second part is the **climax,** the moment of greatest emotional tension in a narrative, usually marking a turning point in the plot at which the rising action reverses to become the falling action. The third part, the **falling action** (or RESOLUTION), is characterized by diminishing tensions and the resolution of the plot's conflicts and complications. *In medias res* is a term used to describe the common strategy of beginning a story in the middle of the action. In this type of plot, we enter the story on the verge of some important moment. See also CHARACTER, CRISIS, RESOLUTION, SUBPLOT.

Poetic diction See DICTION.

Point of view Refers to who tells us a story and how it is told. What we know and how we feel about the events in a work are shaped by the author's choice of point of view. The teller of the story, the narrator, inevitably affects our understanding of the characters' actions by filtering what is told through his or her own perspective. The various points of view that writers draw upon can be grouped into two broad categories: (1) the third-person narrator uses *he, she,* or *they* to tell the story and does not participate in the action; and (2) the first-person narrator uses *I* and is a major or minor participant in the action. In addition, a second-person narrator, *you,* is also possible, but is rarely used because of the awkwardness of thrusting the reader into the story, as in "You are minding your own business on a park bench when a drunk steps out and demands your lunch bag." An **objective point of view** employs a third-person narrator who does not see into the mind of any character. From this detached and impersonal perspective, the narrator reports action and dialogue without telling us directly what the characters think and feel. Since no analysis or interpretation is provided by the narrator, this point of view places a premium on dialogue, actions, and details to reveal character to the reader. See also NARRATOR, STREAM-OF-CONSCIOUSNESS TECHNIQUE.

Postcolonial criticism An approach to literature that focuses on the study of cultural behavior and expression in relationship to the colonized world. Postcolonial criticism refers to the analysis of literary works written by writers from countries and cultures that at one time have been controlled by colonizing powers — such as Indian writers during or after British colonial rule. Postcolonial criticism also refers to the analysis of literary works written about colonial cultures by writers from the colonizing country. Many of these kinds of analyses point out how writers from colonial powers sometimes misrepresent colonized cultures by reflecting more their own values. See also CULTURAL CRITICISM, HISTORICAL CRITICISM, MARXIST CRITICISM.

Problem play Popularized by Henrik Ibsen, a problem play is a type of drama that presents a social issue in order to awaken the audience to it. These plays usually reject romantic plots in favor of holding up a mirror that reflects not simply what the audience wants to see but what the playwright sees in them. Often, a problem play will propose a solution to the problem that does not coincide with prevailing opinion. The term is also used to refer to certain Shakespeare plays that do not fit the categories of tragedy, comedy, or romance. See also DRAMA.

Prologue The opening speech or dialogue of a play, especially a classic Greek play, that usually gives the exposition necessary to follow the subsequent action. Today the term also refers to the introduction to any literary work. See also DRAMA, EXPOSITION.

Prose poem A kind of open form poetry that is printed as prose and represents the most clear opposite of fixed form poetry. Prose poems are densely compact and often make use of striking imagery and figures of speech. See also FIXED FORM, OPEN FORM.

Prosody The overall metrical structure of a poem. See also METER.

Protagonist The main character of a narrative; its central character who engages the reader's interest and empathy. See also CHARACTER.

Psychological criticism An approach to literature that draws upon psycho-analytic theories, especially those of Sigmund Freud or Jacques Lacan, to understand more fully the text, the writer, and the reader. The basis of this approach is the idea of the existence of a human unconscious—those impulses, desires, and feelings about which a person is unaware but which influence emotions and behavior. Critics use psychological approaches to explore the motivations of characters and the symbolic meanings of events, while biographers speculate about a writer's own motivations—conscious or unconscious—in a literary work. Psychological approaches are also used to describe and analyze the reader's personal responses to a text.

Pun A play on words that relies on a word's having more than one meaning or sounding like another word. Shakespeare and other writers use puns extensively, for serious and comic purposes; in *Romeo and Juliet* (III.i.101), the dying Mercutio puns, "Ask for me tomorrow and you shall find me a grave man." Puns have serious literary uses, but since the eighteenth century, puns have been used almost purely for humorous effect. See also COMEDY.

Pyramidal pattern See PLOT.

Quatrain A four-line stanza. Quatrains are the most common stanzaic form in the English language; they can have various meters and rhyme schemes. See also METER, RHYME, STANZA.

Reader-response criticism An approach to literature that focuses on the reader rather than the work itself, by attempting to describe what goes on in the reader's mind during the reading of a text. Hence, the consciousness of the reader—produced by reading the work—is the actual subject of reader-response criticism. These critics are not after a "correct" reading of the text or what the author presumably intended; instead, they are interested in the reader's individual experience with the text. Thus, there is no single definitive reading of a work, because readers create rather than discover absolute meanings in texts. However, this approach is not a rationale for mistaken or bizarre readings, but an exploration of the possibilities for a plurality of readings. This kind of strategy calls attention to how we read and what influences our readings, and what that reveals about ourselves.

Recognition The moment in a story when previously unknown or withheld information is revealed to the protagonist, resulting in the discovery of the truth of his or her situation and, usually, a decisive change in course for that character. In *Oedipus the King*, the moment of recognition comes when Oedipus finally realizes that he has killed his father and married his mother.

Resolution The conclusion of a plot's conflicts and complications. The resolution, also known as the **falling action,** follows the climax in the plot. See also DÉNOUEMENT, PLOT.

Revenge tragedy See TRAGEDY.

Reversal The point in a story when the protagonist's fortunes turn in an unexpected direction. See also PLOT.

Rhyme The repetition of identical or similar concluding syllables in different words, most often at the ends of lines. Rhyme is predominantly a function of sound rather than spelling; thus, words that end with the same vowel sounds rhyme, for instance, *day, prey, bouquet, weigh,* and words with the same consonant ending rhyme, for instance *vain, feign, rein, lane.* Words do not have to be spelled the same way or look alike to rhyme. In fact, words may look alike but not rhyme at all. This is called **eye rhyme,** as with *bough* and *cough,* or *brow* and *blow.*

End rhyme is the most common form of rhyme in poetry; the rhyme comes at the end of the lines:

> It runs through the reeds
>> And away it proceeds,
> Through meadow and glade,
>> In sun and in shade.

The **rhyme scheme** of a poem describes the pattern of end rhymes. Rhyme schemes are mapped out by noting patterns of rhyme with small letters: the first rhyme sound is designated *a,* the second becomes *b,* the third *c,* and so on. Thus, the rhyme scheme of the stanza above is *aabb.* **Internal rhyme** places at least one of the rhymed words within the line, as in "Dividing and gliding and sliding" or "In mist or cloud, on mast or shroud." **Masculine rhyme** describes the rhyming of single-syllable words, such as *grade* or *shade.* Masculine rhyme also occurs when rhyming words of more than one syllable, when the same sound occurs in a final stressed syllable, as in *defend* and *contend, betray* and *away.* **Feminine rhyme** consists of a rhymed stressed syllable followed by one or more identical unstressed syllables, as in *butter, clutter; gratitude, attitude; quivering, shivering.* All the examples so far have illustrated **exact rhymes,** because they share the same stressed vowel sounds as well as sharing sounds that follow the vowel. In **near rhyme** (also called **off rhyme, slant rhyme,** and **approximate rhyme**), the sounds are almost but not exactly alike. A common form of near rhyme is CONSONANCE, which consists of identical consonant sounds preceded by different vowel sounds: *home, same; worth, breath.*

Rhyme scheme   See RHYME.

Rhythm   A term used to refer to the recurrence of stressed and unstressed sounds in poetry. Depending on how sounds are arranged, the rhythm of a poem may be fast or slow, choppy or smooth. Poets use rhythm to create pleasurable sound patterns and to reinforce meanings. Rhythm in prose arises from pattern repetitions of sounds and pauses that create looser rhythmic effects. See also METER.

Rising action   See PLOT.

Rising meter   See METER.

Romantic comedy   See COMEDY.

Round character   See CHARACTER.

Run-on line   See ENJAMBMENT.

Sarcasm   See IRONY.

Satire   The literary art of ridiculing a folly or vice in order to expose or correct it. The object of satire is usually some human frailty; people, institutions, ideas, and things are all fair game for satirists. Satire evokes attitudes of amusement, contempt, scorn, or indignation toward its faulty subject in the hope of somehow improving it. See also IRONY, PARODY.

Scansion   The process of measuring the stresses in a line of verse in order to determine the metrical pattern of the line. See also LINE, METER.

Scene   In drama, a scene is a subdivision of an ACT. In modern plays, scenes usually consist of units of action in which there are no changes in the setting or breaks in the continuity of time. According to traditional conventions, a scene changes when the location of the action shifts or when a new character enters. See also ACT, CONVENTION, DRAMA.

Script   The written text of a play, which includes the dialogue between characters, stage directions, and often other expository information. See also DRAMA, EXPOSITION, PROLOGUE, STAGE DIRECTIONS.

Sentimentality   A pejorative term used to describe the effort by an author to induce emotional responses in the reader that exceed what the situation warrants. Sentimentality especially pertains to such emotions as pathos and sympathy; it cons readers into falling for the mass murderer who is devoted to stray cats, and it requires that readers do not examine such illogical responses. Clichés and stock responses are the key ingredients of sentimentality in literature. See also CLICHÉ, STOCK RESPONSES.

Sestet   A stanza consisting of exactly six lines. See also STANZA.

Sestina   A type of fixed form poetry consisting of thirty-six lines of any length divided into six sestets and a three-line concluding stanza called an ENVOY. The six words at the end of the first sestet's lines must also appear at the ends of the other five sestets, in varying order. These six words must also appear in the envoy, where they often resonate important themes. An example of this highly demanding form of poetry is Elizabeth Bishop's "Sestina." See also SESTET.

Setting   The physical and social context in which the action of a story occurs. The major elements of setting are the time, the place, and the social environment that frames the characters. Setting can be used to evoke a mood or atmosphere that will prepare the reader for what is to come, as in Nathaniel Hawthorne's short story "Young Goodman Brown." Sometimes, writers choose a particular setting because of traditional associations with that setting that are closely related to the action of a story. For example, stories filled with adventure or romance often take place in exotic locales.

Shakespearean sonnet See SONNET.

Showing See CHARACTER.

Simile A common figure of speech that makes an explicit comparison between two things by using words such as *like, as, than, appears,* and *seems:* "A sip of Mrs. Cook's coffee is like a punch in the stomach." The effectiveness of this simile is created by the differences between the two things compared. There would be no simile if the comparison were stated this way: "Mrs. Cook's coffee is as strong as the cafeteria's coffee." This is a literal translation because Mrs. Cook's coffee is compared with something like it — another kind of coffee. See also FIGURES OF SPEECH, METAPHOR.

Situational irony See IRONY.

Slant rhyme See RHYME.

Sociological criticism An approach to literature that examines social groups, relationships, and values as they are manifested in literature. Sociological approaches emphasize the nature and effect of the social forces that shape power relationships between groups or classes of people. Such readings treat literature as either a document reflecting social conditions or a product of those conditions. The former view brings into focus the social milieu; the latter emphasizes the work. Two important forms of sociological criticism are Marxist and feminist approaches. See also FEMINIST CRITICISM, MARXIST CRITICISM.

Soliloquy A dramatic convention by means of which a character, alone onstage, utters his or her thoughts aloud. Playwrights use soliloquies as a convenient way to inform the audience about a character's motivations and state of mind. Shakespeare's Hamlet delivers perhaps the best known of all soliloquies, which begins: "To be or not to be." See also ASIDE, CONVENTION.

Sonnet A fixed form of lyric poetry that consists of fourteen lines, usually written in iambic pentameter. There are two basic types of sonnets, the Italian and the English. The **Italian sonnet,** also known as the **Petrarchan sonnet,** is divided into an octave, which typically rhymes *abbaabba,* and a sestet, which may have varying rhyme schemes. Common rhyme patterns in the sestet are *cdecde, cdcdcd,* and *cdccdc.* Very often the octave presents a situation, attitude, or problem that the sestet comments upon or resolves, as in John Keats's "On First Looking into Chapman's Homer." The **English sonnet,** also known as the **Shakespearean sonnet,** is organized into three quatrains and a couplet, which typically rhyme *abab cdcd efef gg.* This rhyme scheme is more suited to English poetry because English has fewer rhyming words than Italian. English sonnets, because of their four-part organization, also have more flexibility with respect to where thematic breaks can occur. Frequently, however, the most pronounced break or turn comes with the concluding couplet, as in Shakespeare's "Shall I compare thee to a summer's day?" See also COUPLET, IAMBIC PENTAMETER, LINE, OCTAVE, QUATRAIN, SESTET.

Speaker The voice used by an author to tell a story or speak a poem. The speaker is often a created identity, and should not automatically be equated with the author's self. See also NARRATOR, PERSONA, POINT OF VIEW.

Spondee See FOOT.

Stage directions A playwright's written instructions about how the actors are to move and behave in a play. They explain in which direction characters should move, what facial expressions they should assume, and so on. See also DRAMA, SCRIPT.

Stanza In poetry, *stanza* refers to a grouping of lines, set off by a space, that usually has a set pattern of meter and rhyme. See also LINE, METER, RHYME.

Static character See CHARACTER.

Stock character See CHARACTER.

Stock responses Predictable, conventional reactions to language, characters, symbols, or situations. The flag, motherhood, puppies, God, and peace are common objects used to elicit stock responses from unsophisticated audiences. See also CLICHÉ, SENTIMENTALITY.

Stream-of-consciousness technique The most intense use of a central consciousness in narration. The stream-of-consciousness technique takes a reader inside a character's mind to reveal perceptions, thoughts, and feelings on a conscious or unconscious level. This technique suggests the flow of thought as well as its content; hence, complete sentences may give way to fragments as the character's mind makes rapid associations free of conventional logic or transitions. James Joyce's novel *Ulysses* makes extensive use of this narrative technique. See also NARRATOR, POINT OF VIEW.

Stress The emphasis, or accent, given a syllable in pronunciation. See also ACCENT.

Style The distinctive and unique manner in which a writer arranges words to achieve particular effects. Style essentially combines the idea to be expressed with the individuality of the author. These arrangements include individual word choices as well as matters such as the length of sentences, their structure, tone, and use of irony. See also DICTION, IRONY, TONE.

Subplot The secondary action of a story, complete and interesting in its own right, that reinforces or contrasts with the main plot. There may be more than one subplot, and sometimes as many as three, four, or even more, running through a piece of fiction. Subplots are generally either analogous to the main plot, thereby enhancing our understanding of it, or extraneous to the main plot, to provide relief from it. See also PLOT.

Suspense The anxious anticipation of a reader or an audience as to the outcome of a story, especially concerning the character or characters with whom sympathetic attachments are formed. Suspense helps to secure and sustain the interest of the reader or audience throughout a work.

Symbol A person, object, image, word, or event that evokes a range of additional meaning beyond and usually more abstract than its literal significance. Symbols are educational devices for evoking complex ideas without having to resort to painstaking explanations that would make a story more like an essay than an experience. **Conventional symbols** have meanings that are widely recognized by a society or culture. Some conventional symbols are the Christian cross, the Star of David, a swastika, or a nation's flag. Writers use conventional symbols to reinforce meanings. Kate Chopin, for example, emphasizes the spring setting in "The Story of an Hour" as a way of suggesting the renewed sense of life that Mrs. Mallard feels when she thinks herself free from her husband. A **literary** or **contextual symbol** can be a setting, character, action, object, name, or anything else in a work that maintains its literal significance while suggesting other meanings. Such symbols go beyond conventional symbols; they gain their symbolic meaning within the context of a specific story. For example, the white whale in Melville's *Moby-Dick* takes on multiple symbolic meanings in the work, but these meanings do not automatically carry over into other stories about whales. The meanings suggested by Melville's whale are specific to that text; therefore, it becomes a contextual symbol. See also ALLEGORY.

Synecdoche See METAPHOR.

Syntax The ordering of words into meaningful verbal patterns such as phrases, clauses, and sentences. Poets often manipulate syntax, changing conventional word order, to place certain emphasis on particular words. Emily Dickinson, for instance, writes about being surprised by a snake in her poem "A narrow Fellow in the Grass," and includes this line: "His notice sudden is." In addition to the alliterative hissing *s*-sounds here, Dickinson also effectively manipulates the line's syntax so that the verb *is* appears unexpectedly at the end, making the snake's hissing presence all the more "sudden."

Telling See CHARACTER.

Tercet A three-line stanza. See also STANZA, TRIPLET.

Terza rima An interlocking three-line rhyme scheme: *aba, bcb, cdc, ded,* and so on. Dante's *The Divine Comedy* and Frost's "Acquainted with the Night" are written in *terza rima.* See also RHYME, TERCET.

Theme The central meaning or dominant idea in a literary work. A theme provides a unifying point around which the plot, characters, setting, point of view, symbols, and other elements of a work are organized. It is important not to mistake the theme for the actual subject of the work; the theme refers to the abstract concept that is made concrete through the images, characterization, and action of the text. In nonfiction, however, the theme generally refers to the main topic of the discourse.

Thesis The central idea of an essay. The thesis is a complete sentence (although sometimes it may require more than one sentence) that establishes the topic of the essay in clear, unambiguous language.

Tone The author's implicit attitude toward the reader or the people, places, and events in a work as revealed by the elements of the author's style. Tone may be characterized as serious or ironic, sad or happy, private or public, angry or affectionate, bitter or nostalgic, or any other attitudes and feelings that human beings experience. See also STYLE.

Tragedy A story that presents courageous individuals who confront powerful forces within or outside themselves with a dignity that reveals the breadth and depth of the human spirit in the face of failure, defeat, and even death.

Tragedies recount an individual's downfall; they usually begin high and end low. Shakespeare is known for his tragedies, including *Macbeth, King Lear, Othello,* and *Hamlet.* The **revenge tragedy** is a well-established type of drama that can be traced back to Greek and Roman plays, particularly through the Roman playwright Seneca (c. 3 B.C.–A.D. 63). Revenge tragedies basically consist of a murder that has to be avenged by a relative of the victim. Typically, the victim's ghost appears to demand revenge, and invariably madness of some sort is worked into subsequent events, which ultimately end in the deaths of the murderer, the avenger, and a number of other characters. Shakespeare's *Hamlet* subscribes to the basic ingredients of revenge tragedy, but it also transcends these conventions because Hamlet contemplates not merely revenge but suicide and the meaning of life itself. A **tragic flaw** is an error or defect in the tragic hero that leads to his downfall, such as greed, pride, or ambition. This flaw may be a result of bad character, bad judgment, an inherited weakness, or any other defect of character. **Tragic irony** is a form of dramatic irony found in tragedies such as *Oedipus the King,* in which Oedipus ironically ends up hunting himself. See also COMEDY, DRAMA.

Tragic flaw See TRAGEDY.

Tragic irony See IRONY, TRAGEDY.

Tragicomedy A type of drama that combines certain elements of both tragedy and comedy. The play's plot tends to be serious, leading to a terrible catastrophe, until an unexpected turn in events leads to a reversal of circumstance, and the story ends happily. Tragicomedy often employs a romantic, fast-moving plot dealing with love, jealousy, disguises, treachery, intrigue, and surprises, all moving toward a melodramatic resolution. Shakespeare's *Merchant of Venice* is a tragicomedy. See also COMEDY, DRAMA, MELODRAMA, TRAGEDY.

Triplet A tercet in which all three lines rhyme. See also TERCET.

Trochaic meter See FOOT.

Understatement The opposite of hyperbole, understatement (or litotes) refers to a figure of speech that says less than is intended. Understatement usually has an ironic effect, and sometimes may be used for comic purposes, as in Mark Twain's statement, "The reports of my death are greatly exaggerated." See also HYPERBOLE, IRONY.

Unreliable narrator See NARRATOR.

Verbal irony See IRONY.

Verse A generic term used to describe poetic lines composed in a measured rhythmical pattern that are often, but not necessarily, rhymed. See also LINE, METER, RHYME, RHYTHM.

Villanelle A type of fixed form poetry consisting of nineteen lines of any length divided into six stanzas: five tercets and a concluding quatrain. The first and third lines of the initial tercet rhyme; these rhymes are repeated in each subsequent tercet (*aba*) and in the final two lines of the quatrain (*abaa*). Line 1 appears in its entirety as lines 6, 12, and 18, while line 3 reappears as lines 9, 15, and 19. Dylan Thomas's "Do not go gentle into that good night" is a villanelle. See also FIXED FORM, QUATRAIN, RHYME, TERCET.

Well-made play A realistic style of play that employs conventions including plenty of suspense created by meticulous plotting. Well-made plays are tightly and logically constructed, and lead to a logical resolution that is favorable to the protagonist. This dramatic structure was popularized in France by Eugène Scribe (1791–1861) and Victorien Sardou (1831–1908) and was adopted by Henrik Ibsen. See also CHARACTER, PLOT.

Acknowledgments (continued from p. iv)

Romare Bearden. *Watching the Good Trains Go By*, 1964. 34.9 × 42.9 (13 ¾ × 16 ⅛), collage of various papers on cardboard. © Romare Bearden Foundation/Licensed by VAGA, New York, NY.

Amy Bloom. "By-and-By" from *Where the God of Love Hangs Out* by Amy Bloom. Copyright © 2010 by Amy Bloom. Used by permission of Random House, Inc.

T. Coraghessan Boyle. "Carnal Knowledge" from *Without a Hero* by T. Coraghessan Boyle. Copyright © 1994 by T. Coraghessan Boyle. Used by permission of Viking Penguin, a division of Penguin Group (USA) Inc.

Matthew C. Brennan. "Point of View and Plotting in Chekhov's and Oates's 'The Lady with the Pet Dog'" excerpted from "Plotting against Chekhov: Joyce Carol Oates and 'The Lady with the Pet Dog,'" *Notes on Modern American Literature* (Winter 1985). Reprinted by permission of the author.

Gaylord Brewer. "The Joys of Secret Sin" from *The Martini Diet* (Dream Horse Press, 2008). Copyright © 2008 by Gaylord Brewer. Reprinted with the permission of the author.

Robert Olen Butler. "Jealous Husband Returns in Form of Parrot" from *Tabloid Dreams* by Robert Olen Butler. Copyright © 1996 by Robert Olen Butler. First appeared in *The New Yorker*, May 22, 1995. Reprinted by arrangement with Henry Holt and Company, LLC.

Ron Carlson. "Max" from *A Kind of Flying: Selected Stories* by Ron Carlson. Copyright © 2003, 1997, 1992, 1987 by Ron Carlson. Used by permission of W. W. Norton & Company, Inc.

Raymond Carver. "Popular Mechanics" from *What We Talk about When We Talk about Love* by Raymond Carver. Copyright © 1981 by Raymond Carver. Used by permission of Alfred A. Knopf, a division of Random House, Inc.

W. J. Cash. "The Old and the New South" excerpted from *The Mind of the South* by W. J. Cash. Copyright © 1941 by Alfred A. Knopf, Inc., and renewed 1969 by Mary R. Maury. Used by permission of Alfred A. Knopf, a division of Random House, Inc.

May-lee Chai. "Saving Sourdi," *ZYZZYVA*, no. 3 (Winter 2001), pp. 139–58. Copyright © 2001 by May-lee Chai. Used by permission of the author.

Anton Chekhov. "A Lady with a Dog" (excerpt), from *The Oxford Chekhov*, translated and edited by Ronald Hingley, Vol. IX (1975). By permission of Oxford University Press. "The Lady with the Pet Dog," translated by Avrahm Yarmolinsky, from *The Portable Chekhov* by Anton Chekhov, edited by Avrahm Yarmolinsky. Copyright 1947, © 1968 by Viking Penguin, Inc., renewed © 1975 by Avrahm Yarmolinsky. Used by permission of Viking Penguin, a division of Penguin Group (USA) Inc.

Sandra Cisneros. "Eleven" from *Woman Hollering Creek and Other Stories* by Sandra Cisneros. Copyright © 1991 by Sandra Cisneros. Reprinted by permission of Susan Bergholz Literary Services, New York, NY, and Lamy, NM. All rights reserved.

Colette. "The Hand" from *The Collected Stories of Colette*, edited by Robert Phelps and translated by Matthew Ward. Translation copyright © 1983 by Farrar, Straus & Giroux, Inc. Reprinted by permission of Farrar, Straus & Giroux, LLC.

A. R. Coulthard. "On the Visionary Ending of 'Revelation'" from "From Sermon to Parable: Four Conversion Stories by Flannery O'Connor," *American Literature* 55.1 (March 1983), pp. 55–71. Copyright 1983, Duke University Press. All rights reserved. Used by permission of the publisher.

Lydia Davis. "Letter to a Funeral Parlor" from *Samuel Johnson Is Indignant* by Lydia Davis. Copyright © 2001 by Lydia Davis. Reprinted by permission of Farrar, Straus & Giroux, LLC.

Benjamin DeMott. "Abner Snopes as a Victim of Class" from *Close Imaginings: An Introduction to Literature* by Benjamin DeMott, copyright © 1988. Reprinted by permission of Margaret DeMott.

Junot Díaz. "Fiesta, 1980" from *Drown* by Junot Díaz. Copyright © 1996 by Junot Díaz. Used by permission of Riverhead Books, an imprint of Penguin Group (USA) Inc.

Chitra Banerjee Divakaruni. "Clothes" from *Arranged Marriage* by Chitra Divakaruni. Copyright © 1995 by Chitra Divakaruni. Used by permission of Doubleday, a division of Random House, Inc.

Andre Dubus. "Killings" from *Finding a Girl in America* by Andre Dubus. Copyright © 1980 by Andre Dubus. Reprinted by permission of David R. Godine, Publisher, Inc.

Ralph Ellison. "Battle Royal" from *Invisible Man* by Ralph Ellison. Copyright © 1948 by Ralph Ellison. Used by permission of Random House, Inc.

William Faulkner. "Barn Burning" from *Collected Stories of William Faulkner* by William Faulkner. Copyright 1950 by Random House, Inc. Copyright renewed 1977 by Jill Faulkner Summers. Used by permission of Random House, Inc. "A Rose for Emily" from *Collected Stories of William Faulkner* by William Faulkner. Copyright 1930 and renewed 1958 by William Faulkner. Used by permission of Random House, Inc. "On 'A Rose for Emily'" from *Faulkner in the University*, edited by Frederick L. Gwynn and Joseph L. Blotner. Copyright © 1995 by the Rector and Visitors of the University of Virginia. Reprinted by permission of the University of Virginia Press.

James Ferguson. "Narrative Strategy in 'Barn Burning'" from *Faulkner's Short Fiction* by James Ferguson, copyright © 1991. Used by permission of the University of Tennessee Press.

Judith Fetterley. "A Feminist Reading of 'The Birthmark'" from *The Resisting Reader: A Feminist Approach to American Fiction* by Judith Fetterley. Copyright © 1978. Reprinted by permission of Indiana University Press.

Marshall Bruce Gentry. "On the Revised Ending of 'Revelation'" from *Flannery O'Connor's Religion of the Grotesque*. Copyright © 1986. Reprinted by permission of the University Press of Mississippi.

Dagoberto Gilb. "Love in L.A." from *The Magic of Blood* by Dagoberto Gilb. Copyright © 1993 by the University of New Mexico Press. Story originally published in *Buffalo*. Reprinted by permission.

Gail Godwin. "A Sorrowful Woman," published in 1971 by *Esquire* Magazine. Copyright © 1971 by Gail Godwin. Reprinted by permission of John Hawkins & Associates, Inc.

Mark Halliday. "Young Man on Sixth Avenue" from *The Pushcart Prize XXI: 1997 Best of the Small Presses* (Pushcart Press, 1996), pp. 358–60. Originally appeared in *Chicago Review* 1995. Copyright © 1995 by Mark Halliday. Reprinted by permission of the author.

Ron Hansen. "My Kid's Dog" from *Harper's*, March 2003. Copyright © 2003 by Ron Hansen. Reprinted by permission of the author.

Bessie Head. "The Prisoner Who Wore Glasses" from *Tales of Tenderness and Power*, 1989. Copyright © the Estate of Bessie Head. Reprinted with the permission of Johnson and Alcock Ltd.

Ernest Hemingway. "Soldier's Home" from *In Our Time* by Ernest Hemingway. Copyright © 1925 by Charles Scribner's Sons. Copyright renewed 1953 by Ernest Hemingway. Reprinted with the permission of Scribner, a division of Simon & Schuster, Inc. All rights reserved.

Jane Hiles. "Blood Ties in 'Barn Burning'" from "Kinship and Heredity in Faulkner's 'Barn Burning,'" *Mississippi Quarterly* 38, no. 3 (Summer 1985), pp. 329–37. Copyright © 1985 Mississippi State University, Mississippi State, Mississippi. Reprinted by permission of *Mississippi Quarterly: The Journal of Southern Culture*.

Irving Howe. "The Southern Myth," excerpted from "The Southern Myth and William Faulkner," *American Quarterly* 3, no. 4 (Winter 1951). Reprinted by permission of the University of Pennsylvania Press.

James Joyce. Photograph of James Joyce on page 529 courtesy of the Poetry/Rare Books Collection, UB Libraries, State University of New York at Buffalo.

Claire Katz. "The Function of Violence in O'Connor's Fiction" from "Flannery O'Connor's Rage of Vision," *American Literature* 46.1 (March 1974), pp. 545–67. Copyright 1974, Duke University Press. All rights reserved. Used by permission of the publisher.

Jamaica Kincaid. "Girl" from *At the Bottom of the River* by Jamaica Kincaid. Copyright © 1983 by Jamaica Kincaid. Reprinted by permission of Farrar, Straus & Giroux, LLC.

Jhumpa Lahiri. "Hell–Heaven" from *Unaccustomed Earth* by Jhumpa Lahiri. Copyright © 2008 by Jhumpa Lahiri. Used by permission of Alfred A. Knopf, a division of Random House, Inc., and Random House of Canada Limited.

Andrea N. Lee. "Anthropology" from *Interesting Women* by Andrea N. Lee. Copyright © 2002 by Andrea N. Lee. Used by permission of Random House, Inc.

"A Letter Home from an Irish Emigrant in Australia," from *Oceans of Consolation: Personal Accounts of Irish Migration to Australia* by David Fitzpatrick (Cornell UP, 1994). Reprinted by permission of David Fitzpatrick.

Dan McCall. "On the Lawyer's Character in 'Bartleby the Scrivener'" from *The Silence of Bartleby* by Dan McCall. Copyright © 1989 Cornell University. Used by permission of the publisher, Cornell University Press.

Naguib Mahfouz. "The Answer Is No" from *The Time and the Place & Other Stories* by Naguib Mahfouz. Copyright © 1991 by the American University in Cairo Press. Used by permission of Doubleday, a division of Random House, Inc.

Mordecai Marcus. "What Is an Initiation Story?" from *The Journal of Aesthetics and Art Criticism* 19.2 (Winter 1960), pp. 222–23. Copyright © 1960. Reprinted with permission of Blackwell Publishing Ltd.

Gabriel García Márquez. "One of These Days" from *No One Writes to the Colonel and Other Stories* by Gabriel García Márquez and translated by J. S. Bernstein. Copyright © 1968 in the English translation by Harper & Row, Publishers, Inc. Reprinted by permission of HarperCollins Publishers, Inc.

Peter Meinke. "The Cranes." Copyright © 1999 by Peter Meinke. Reprinted by permission of the author.

Susan Minot. "Lust" from *Lust and Other Stories* by Susan Minot. Copyright © 1989 by Susan Minot. Reprinted by permission of Houghton Mifflin Harcourt Publishing Company. All rights reserved.

Rick Moody. "Boys" from *Demonology* by Rick Moody. Copyright © 2001 by Rick Moody. By permission of Little, Brown & Company.

Kay Mussell. "Are Feminism and Romance Novels Mutually Exclusive?" from "All about Romance: The Back-Fence for Lovers of Romance Novels" at <http://www.likesbooks.com/mussell.html>. Kay Mussell is Professor of Literature and Interim Senior Vice Provost and Dean of Academic Affairs at American University in Washington, D.C.

Donald R. Noble. "The Future of Southern Writing" excerpted from *The History of Southern Literature,* edited by Louis D. Rubin et al. Copyright © 1985. Reprinted by permission of Louisiana State University Press.

Joyce Carol Oates. "Hi Howya Doin" from *Ploughshares* 32.1 (Spring 2007). Copyright © 2007 by Ontario Review. "The Lady with the Pet Dog" from *Marriages and Infidelities* by Joyce Carol Oates (Vanguard Press, 1972). Copyright © 1972 by Ontario Review. "Three Girls," published in *The Georgia Review* 56, no. 3 (Fall 2002). Copyright © 2002 by Ontario Review. All selections reprinted by permission of John Hawkins & Associates, Inc.

Tim O'Brien. "How to Tell a True War Story." Copyright © 1987 by Tim O'Brien. Originally published in *Esquire* Magazine. Reprinted by permission of the author.

Flannery O'Connor. "A Good Man Is Hard to Find," copyright © 1953 by Flannery O'Connor and renewed 1981 by Regina O'Connor, and "Good Country People," copyright © 1955 by Flannery O'Connor and renewed 1983 by Regina O'Connor, from *A Good Man Is Hard to Find and Other Stories.* Reprinted by permission of Houghton Mifflin Harcourt Publishing Company. "Revelation" from *The Complete Stories* by Flannery O'Connor. Copyright © 1971 by the Estate of Mary Flannery O'Connor. Reprinted by permission of Farrar, Straus & Giroux, LLC. "On Faith" excerpted from letter to "A", 20 July 1955, from *The Habit of Being: Letters of Flannery O'Connor,* edited by Sally Fitzgerald. Copyright © 1979 by Regina O'Connor. Reprinted by permission of Farrar, Straus & Giroux, LLC. "On the Materials of Fiction," "The Regional Writer," "On Theme and Symbol," and "On the Use of Exaggeration and Distortion" in *Mystery and Manners* by Flannery O'Connor. Copyright © 1969 by the Estate of Mary Flannery O'Connor. Reprinted by permission of Farrar, Straus & Giroux, LLC.

Michael Oppenheimer. "The Paring Knife." First published in *Sundog* 4.1 (1982). Reprinted by permission of the author.

POETRY

Yehuda Amichai. "Jerusalem, 1985" from *The Selected Poetry of Yehuda Amichai,* translated and edited by Chana Bloch and Stephen Mitchell. Copyright © 1996 by the Regents of the University of California. Reprinted by permission of the Regents of the University of California and the publisher, the University of California Press.

A. R. Ammons. "Coward" from *Diversifications* by A. R. Ammons. Copyright © 1975 by A. R. Ammons. Used by permission of W. W. Norton & Company, Inc.

Charles R. Anderson. "Eroticism in 'Wild Nights — Wild Nights!' " from *Emily Dickinson's Poetry: Stairway of Surprise* (Holt, Rinehart, and Winston, 1960). Reprinted by permission.

Richard Armour. "Going to Extremes" from *Light Armour* by Richard Armour. Permission to reprint this material is given courtesy of the family of Richard Armour.

Margaret Atwood. "A Holiday" from *Interlunar* by Margaret Atwood. Originally published by Oxford University Press. Copyright © 1984 by Margaret Atwood. Reprinted by permission of the author. "February" from *Morning in the Burned House: New Poems* by Margaret Atwood. Copyright © 1995 by Margaret Atwood. Reprinted by permission of Houghton Mifflin Harcourt Publishing Company and McClelland & Stewart, Ltd. All rights reserved. "you fit into me" from *Power Politics* by Margaret Atwood. Copyright © 1971, 1996 by Margaret Atwood. Reprinted by permission of House of Anansi Press, Toronto.

Jimmy Santiago Baca. "Green Chile" from *Black Mesa Poems* by Jimmy Santiago Baca. Copyright © 1989 by Jimmy Santiago Baca. Reprinted by permission of New Directions Publishing Corp.

Mary Barnard. "Prayer to my lady of Paphos" (Fragment #38) from *Sappho: A New Translation* by Mary Barnard. Copyright © 1958 by the Regents of the University of California, renewed © 1986 by Mary Barnard. Reprinted by permission of the Regents of the University of California and the publisher, the University of California Press.

Jeannette Barnes. "Battle-Piece." Reprinted from *Shenandoah: The Washington and Lee University Review,* with the permission of the editor and the author.

Regina Barreca. "Nighttime Fires" from *The Minnesota Review* (Fall 1986). Reprinted by permission of the author.

Matsuo Bashō. "Under cherry trees" from *Japanese Haiku,* trans. by Peter Beilenson, Series I, © 1955-56, Peter Beilenson, Editor. Reprinted by permission of Peter Pauper Press.

Michael L. Baumann. "The 'Overwhelming Question' for Prufrock" excerpted from "Let Us Ask 'What Is It?' " *Arizona Quarterly* 37 (Spring 1981): 47–58. Reprinted by permission of Friederike Baumann.

Jan Beatty. "My Father Teaches Me To Dream" from *Boneshaker* by Jan Beatty. First published in *Witness* Vol. 10, no. 2 (1996). Copyright © 2002. Reprinted by permission of the University of Pittsburgh Press.

Marvin Bell. "The Uniform" from *Nightworks: Poems 1962–2000.* Copyright © 1994, 2000 by Marvin Bell. Reprinted with the permission of Copper Canyon Press, www.coppercanyonpress.org.

Paula Bennett. "On 'I heard a Fly buzz — when I died —' " excerpted from *Emily Dickinson: Woman Poet* by Paula Bennett (University of Iowa Press, 1991). Copyright © 1991 by Paula Bennett. Reprinted by permission of the author.

Elizabeth Bishop. "The Fish" and "Manners" from *The Complete Poems, 1927–1979* by Elizabeth Bishop. Copyright © 1979, 1983 by Alice Helen Methfessel. Reprinted by permission of Farrar, Straus and Giroux, LLC.

Michelle Boisseau. "Self-Pity's Closet" from *Trembling Air.* Copyright © 2003 by Michelle Boisseau. Reprinted with the permission of the University of Arkansas Press, www.uapress.com. The poem first appeared in *The Yale Review* 89, no. 3 (July 2001).

Christian Bök. "Vowels" from *Eunoia* by Christian Bök (Toronto: Coach House Books, 2001). Copyright © 2001. Reprinted by permission.

Billie Bolton. "Memorandum." Copyright © 2006 by Billie Bolton. Reprinted by permission of the author.

Todd Boss. "Advance" from *Yellowrocket* by Todd Boss. Copyright © 2008 by Todd Boss. Used by permission of W. W. Norton & Company, Inc.

Allen Braden. "Sweethearts" from *Poetry Northwest* 41, no. 4 (2001). Copyright © 2001 by Allen Braden. Reprinted by permission of the author.

Gwendolyn Brooks. "We Real Cool" from *Blacks* by Gwendolyn Brooks. Copyright © 1991 by Gwendolyn Brooks. Reprinted by consent of Brooks Permissions.

Charles Bukowski. Photograph of Charles Bukowski on page 1245. © The Yale Collection of American Literature, Beinecke Rare Book and Manuscript Library, Yale University.

Anne Carson. "Father's Old Blue Cardigan" from *Men in the Off Hours* by Anne Carson. Copyright © 2000 by Anne Carson. Used by permission of Alfred A. Knopf, a division of Random House, Inc.

Keith Casto. "She Don't Bop," from *Light Year '87,* Robert Wallace, ed. Bits Press, Cleveland, 1986. Copyright © 1986 by Keith Casto. Reprinted by permission of the author.

Helen Chasin. "The Word Plum" from *Coming Close and Other Poems* by Helen Chasin. Copyright © 1968 by Yale University Press. Reprinted by permission of Yale University Press.

Kelly Cherry. "Alzheimer's" from *Death and Transfiguration* by Kelly Cherry. Copyright © 1997 by Kelly Cherry. Reprinted by permission of Louisiana State University Press.

David Chinitz. "The Romanticization of Africa in the 1920s" from "Rejuvenation through Joy: Langston Hughes, Primitivism, and Jazz," *American Literary History* 9, no. 1 (Spring 1997), pp. 60–78. Reprinted by permission of the author and Oxford University Press.

John Ciardi. "Suburban" from *For Instance* by John Ciardi. Copyright © 1979 by John Ciardi. Used by permission of W. W. Norton & Company, Inc.

Lucille Clifton. "this morning (for the girls of eastern high school)" from *Good Woman: Poems and a Memoir 1969–1980.* Copyright © 1987 by Lucille Clifton. Reprinted with the permission of BOA Editions, Ltd., www.boaeditions.org.

Judith Ortiz Cofer. "Common Ground" is reprinted with permission from the publisher of *Silent Dancing: A Partial Remembrance of a Puerto Rican Childhood* by Judith Ortiz Cofer (© 1990 Arte Público Press–University of Houston).

Billy Collins. "Building with Its Face Blown Off" from *The Trouble with Poetry and Other Poems* by Billy Collins. Copyright © 2005 by Billy Collins. Reprinted by permission of SLL/Sterling Lord Literistic, Inc. "On Writing 'Building with Its Face Blown Off,'" by Billy Collins. Printed by permission of Billy Collins and SLL/Sterling Lord Literistic, Inc. © 2008. "Introduction to Poetry" from *The Apple That Astonished Paris*. Copyright © 1988, 1996 by Billy Collins. Reprinted with the permission of the University of Arkansas Press, www.uapress.com. "Litany" from *Nine Horses* by Billy Collins. Copyright © 2002 by Billy Collins. Reprinted by permission of SLL/Sterling Lord Literistic, Inc. "On Writing 'Litany,'" by Billy Collins. Printed by permission of Billy Collins and SLL/Sterling Lord Literistic, Inc. © 2008. "Marginalia" from *Picnic, Lightning* by Billy Collins. Copyright © 1998. Reprinted by permission of the University of Pittsburgh Press. "Nostalgia" and "Questions About Angels" from *Questions About Angels* by Billy Collins. Copyright © 1991. Reprinted by permission of the University of Pittsburgh Press. "On Writing 'Nostalgia'" and "On Writing 'Questions About Angels,'" by Billy Collins. Printed by permission of Billy Collins and SLL/Sterling Lord Literistic, Inc. © 2008. "Osso Buco" from *The Art of Drowning* by Billy Collins. Copyright © 1995. Reprinted by permission of the University of Pittsburgh Press. "On Writing 'Osso Buco,'" by Billy Collins. Printed by permission of Billy Collins and SLL/Sterling Lord Literistic, Inc. © 2008.

Edmund Conti. "Pragmatist" from *Light Year '86*. Reprinted by permission of the author.

Wyn Cooper. "Puritan Impulse" from *The Way Back* (White Pine Press, 2000). Copyright © 2000 by Wyn Cooper. Reprinted with the permission of White Pine Press, www.whitepine.org. Originally appeared in the Winter 1999–2000 issue of *Ploughshares*.

Wendy Cope. "Lonely Hearts" from *Making Cocoa for Kingsley Amis* by Wendy Cope. Copyright © 1986 by Wendy Cope. Reprinted by permission of Faber and Faber Ltd. and by permission of United Agents on behalf of Wendy Cope.

Sally Croft. "Home-Baked Bread" from *Light Year '86*. Reprinted by permission of Bruce Croft.

Barbara Crooker. "On the Edge of Adolescence, My Middle Daughter Learns to Play the Saxophone" from *Line Dance* (Word Press, 2008). Copyright © 2008 by Barbara Crooker. Reprinted by permission of the author.

E. E. Cummings. "Buffalo Bill's" and "in Just-," copyright © 1923, 1951, 1991 by the Trustees for the E. E. Cummings Trust, copyright © 1976 by George James Firmage. "l(a," copyright © 1958, 1986, 1991 by the Trustees for the E. E. Cummings Trust. "next to of course god america i" and "since feeling is first," copyright © 1926, 1954, 1991 by the Trustees for the E. E. Cummings Trust, copyright © 1985 by George James Firmage. From *Complete Poems: 1904–1962* by E. E. Cummings, edited by George J. Firmage. Used by permission of Liveright Publishing Corporation.

Fazil Hüsnü Dağlarca. "Dead" from *The New Renaissance* 6, no. 1 (1984). Translated by Talât Sait Halman. Translation copyright © 1984 by Talât Sait Halman. Reprinted by permission of the translator.

Mahmoud Darwish. "Identity Card" from *The Music of Human Flesh,* translated by Denys Johnson-Davies (Three Continents Press, 1980). Copyright © 1980 by Denys Johnson-Davies. Reprinted by permission of Denys Johnson-Davies.

Joanne Diaz. "On My Father's Loss of Hearing," *The Southern Review* 42, no. 3 (Summer 2006). Copyright © 2006 by Joanne Diaz. Reprinted by permission of the author.

Emily Dickinson. "A Bird came down the Walk—," "After great pain, a formal feeling comes—," "A Light exists in Spring," "A narrow Fellow in the grass," "Because I could not stop for Death—," "Fame is the one that does not stay—," "'Heaven'—is what I cannot reach!," "'Hope' is the thing with feathers—," "I dwell in Possibility—," "I felt a Cleaving in my Mind—," "If I shouldn't be alive," "I heard a Fly buzz—when I died—," "I like a look of Agony," "I never saw a Moor—," "Much Madness is divinest Sense—," "One need not be a Chamber—to be Haunted—," "Pain—has an Element of Blank—," "Safe in their Alabaster Chambers—," "Some things that fly there be—," "Success is counted sweetest," "Tell all the Truth but tell it slant—," "The Morning after Wo—," "There is no Frigate like a Book," "There's a certain Slant of light," "The Robin's my Criterion for Tune—," "The Soul selects her own Society—," "They dropped like Flakes—," and "What Soft—Cherubic Creatures—." Reprinted by permission of the publishers and the Trustees of Amherst College from *The Poems of Emily Dickinson,* Thomas H. Johnson, ed., Cambridge, Mass.: The Belknap Press of Harvard University Press. Copyright © 1951, 1955, 1979, 1983 by the President and Fellows of Harvard College.

Tom Disch. "Birdsong Interpreted" from *About the Size of It* by Tom Disch. Copyright © 2007 by Tom Disch. Reprinted by permission of Anvil Press Poetry.

Chitra Banerjee Divakaruni. "Indian Movie, New Jersey" from the *Indiana Review,* 1990. Copyright © by Chitra Banerjee Divakaruni. Reprinted by permission of the author. Photograph on pages 275 and Crossing Boundaries insert, page A copyright © by Chitra Banerjee Divakaruni. Photo by Anand Divakaruni. Reprinted by permission of the author and the Sandra Dijkstra Literary Agency.

Mark Doty. "The Embrace" from *Sweet Machine* by Mark Doty. Copyright © 1998 by Mark Doty. "Tunnel Music" from *Atlantis* by Mark Doty. Copyright © 1995 by Mark Doty. Reprinted by permission of HarperCollins Publishers.

Rita Dove. "Fox Trot Fridays," from *American Smooth: Poems* by Rita Dove. Copyright © 2004 by Rita Dove. Used by permission of W. W. Norton & Company, Inc.

Denise Duhamel. "Language Police Report" from *Ka-Ching!* by Denise Duhamel. First published in *Sentence: A Journal of Prose Poetics* No. 4 (2006). Copyright © 2009. Reprinted by permission of the University of Pittsburgh Press.

James A. Emanuel. "Hughes's Attitudes toward Religion" from "Christ in Alabama: Religion in the Poetry of Langston Hughes" in *Modern Black Poets*, ed. Donald B. Gibson. Reprinted by permission of the author.

Martín Espada. "Bully" and "Latin Night at the Pawnshop" from *Rebellion Is the Circle of a Lover's Hands / Rebelión es el giro de manos del amante* by Martín Espada. Curbstone Press, 1990. Copyright © 1990 by Martín Espada. Reprinted with permission of Curbstone Press. Distributed by Consortium. "The Community College Revises Its Curriculum in Response to Changing Demographics" from *A Mayan Astronomer in Hell's Kitchen* by Martín Espada. Copyright © 2000 by Martín Espada. Used by permission of W. W. Norton & Company, Inc.

Ruth Fainlight. "The Clarinettist." Reprinted by permission from *The Hudson Review* Vol. LV, No. 1 (Spring 2002). Copyright © 2002 by Ruth Fainlight. "Crocuses" from *Moon Wheels* by Ruth Fainlight (Bloodaxe Books, 2006). Copyright © 2006 by Ruth Fainlight. Reprinted by permission of Bloodaxe Books Ltd.

Blanche Farley. "The Lover Not Taken" from *Light Year '86*. Reprinted by permission of the author.

Kenneth Fearing. "AD" from *Kenneth Fearing Complete Poems*, ed. by Robert Ryely (Orono, ME: National Poetry Foundation, 1997). Copyright © 1938 by Kenneth Fearing, renewed in 1966 by the Estate of Kenneth Fearing. Reprinted by the permission of Russell & Volkening as agents for the author.

Karen Jackson Ford. "Hughes's Aesthetics of Simplicity," from "Do Right to Write Right: Langston Hughes's Aesthetics of Simplicity," *Twentieth Century Literature* 38, no. 4 (Winter 1992). Reprinted by permission.

Katie Ford. "Ark" from *Colosseum*. Copyright © 2008 by Katie Ford. Reprinted with the permission of Graywolf Press, Saint Paul, Minnesota, www.graywolfpress.org.

Robert Francis. "Catch" and "The Pitcher" from *The Orb Weaver*. Copyright © 1960 by Robert Francis. Reprinted by permission of Wesleyan University Press, www.wesleyan.edu/wespress. "On 'Hard' Poetry" reprinted from *The Satirical Rogue on Poetry* by Robert Francis (Amherst: University of Massachusetts Press, 1968), copyright © 1968 by Robert Francis. Used by permission.

Daisy Fried. "Wit's End" from *She Didn't Mean to Do It* by Daisy Fried. Copyright © 2001. Reprinted by permission of the University of Pittsburgh Press.

Robert Frost. "Acquainted with the Night," "Design," "Fire and Ice," "Neither Out Far nor In Deep," "Nothing Gold Can Stay," "Stopping by Woods on a Snowy Evening," and "Unharvested," from *The Poetry of Robert Frost,* edited by Edward Connery Lathem. Copyright © 1923, 1928, 1936, 1969 by Henry Holt and Company, copyright © 1936, 1951, 1956 by Robert Frost, copyright © 1964 by Lesley Frost Ballantine. Reprinted by arrangement with Henry Holt and Company, LLC. "On the Figure a Poem Makes" from *The Selected Prose of Robert Frost,* edited by Hyde Cox and Edward Connery Lathem, copyright 1939, 1967 by Henry Holt and Company. Reprinted by permission of Henry Holt and Company. "On the Way to Read a Poem" from "Poetry and School" by Robert Frost in *The Atlantic Monthly,* June, 1951. Reprinted by permission of the Estate of Robert Frost. Robert Frost's signature on page 1089 copyright © Robert Lee Frost Copyright Trust.

Brendan Galvin. "An Evel Knievel Elegy" from *Shenandoah* 58.2 (2008), p. 6. Copyright © 2008. Reprinted by permission of the author.

Sandra M. Gilbert. "Chairlift" from *Belongings: Poems* by Sandra Gilbert. Copyright © 2005 by Sandra M. Gilbert. Used by permission of W. W. Norton & Company, Inc. "How We Didn't Tell Her" from *Southwest Review* 93, no. 4 (2008). Copyright © 2008 by Sandra M. Gilbert. Reprinted by permission of the author. "Mafioso" from *Kissing the Bread: New and Selected Poems, 1969–1999* by Sandra M. Gilbert. Copyright © 1979 by Sandra M. Gilbert. Reprinted by permission of the author.

Sandra M. Gilbert and Susan Gubar. "On Dickinson's White Dress" excerpted from *The Madwoman in the Attic,* Yale University Press, 1979. Reprinted by permission of Yale University Press.

Gary Gildner. "First Practice" from *Blue Like the Heavens: New and Selected Poems* by Gary Gildner. Copyright © 1984. Reprinted by permission of the University of Pittsburgh Press.

Louise Glück. "March" from *A Village Life* by Louise Glück. Copyright © 2009 by Louise Glück. Reprinted by permission of Farrar, Straus and Giroux, LLC.

Eamon Grennan. "Herringbone." Reprinted by permission from *The Hudson Review* Vol. LIX, No. 4 (Winter 2007). Copyright © 2007 by Eamon Grennan.

H.D. (Hilda Doolittle). "Heat" from *Collected Poems, 1912–1944*. Copyright 1982 by The Estate of Hilda Doolittle. Reprinted by permission of New Directions Publishing Corp.

Rachel Hadas. "The Compact" from *Laws* by Rachel Hadas (Zoo Press, 2004). Copyright © 2004 by Rachel Hadas. Reprinted by permission of the author. "The Red Hat" from *Halfway Down the Hall*. Copyright © 1998 by Rachel Hadas. Reprinted by permission of Wesleyan University Press, www.wesleyan.edu/wespress.

Richard Hague. "Directions for Resisting the SAT" from *Ohio Teachers Write* (Ohio Council of Teachers of English, 1996). Copyright © 1996 by Richard Hague. Reprinted by permission of the author.

Mark Halliday. "Graded Paper," *The Michigan Quarterly Review*. Reprinted by permission of the author.

Barbara Hamby. "Ode to American English" from *Babel* by Barbara Hamby. Copyright © 2004. Reprinted by permission of the University of Pittsburgh Press.

Mary Stewart Hammond. "The Big Fish Story." First published in *The New Yorker,* April 17, 2006. Copyright © 2006 by Mary Stewart Hammond. "High Ground." First published in *Shenandoah* 58, no. 1 (Spring/Summer 2008). Copyright © 2008 by Mary Stewart Hammond. Reprinted by permission of the author.

Jeffrey Harrison. "The Names of Things" from *Incomplete Knowledge*. Copyright © 2006 by Jeffrey Harrison. Reprinted with the permission of Four Way Books, www.fourwaybooks.com.

Robert Hass. "A Story about the Body" from *Human Wishes* by Robert Hass. Copyright © 1989 by Robert Hass. Reprinted by permission of HarperCollins Publishers.

William Hathaway. "Oh, Oh" from *Light Year '86*. This poem was originally published in *The Cincinnati Poetry Review*. Reprinted by permission of the author.

Robert Hayden. "Those Winter Sundays," copyright © 1966 by Robert Hayden, from *Collected Poems of Robert Hayden* by Robert Hayden, edited by Frederick Glaysher. Used by permission of Liveright Publishing Corporation.

Judy Page Heitzman. "The Schoolroom on the Second Floor of the Knitting Mill." Copyright © 1991 by Judy Page Heitzman. Originally appeared in *The New Yorker,* December 2, 1992, p. 102. Reprinted by permission of the author.

William Heyen. "The Trains" from *The Host: Selected Poems 1965–1990* by William Heyen. Copyright © 1994 by Time Being Press. Reprinted by permission of Time Being Books. All rights reserved.

Bob Hicok. "Making it in poetry," copyright © 2004 by Bob Hicok. "Making it in poetry" first appeared in the *Georgia Review* 58, no. 2 (Summer 2004). "Spam leaves an aftertaste," copyright © 2002 by Bob Hicok. "Spam leaves an aftertaste" first appeared in the *Gettysburg Review* 15, no. 1 (Spring 2002). Both poems are reprinted here with the acknowledgment of the editors and the permission of the author.

Edward Hirsch. "First Snowfall: Intimations" from *Earthly Measures* by Edward Hirsch. Copyright © 1994 by Edward Hirsch. Used by permission of Alfred A. Knopf, a division of Random House, Inc.

Jane Hirshfield. "Happiness" from *The October Palace* by Jane Hirshfield. Copyright © 1994 by Jane Hirshfield. Reprinted by permission of HarperCollins Publishers.

Tony Hoagland. "America," from *What Narcissism Means to Me.* Copyright © 1993 by Tony Hoagland. Reprinted with the permission of Graywolf Press, Saint Paul, Minnesota, www.graywolfpress.org.

M. Carl Holman. "Mr. Z." Reprinted by permission of the Estate of M. Carl Holman.

Andrew Hudgins. "The Cadillac in the Attic" from *Ecstatic in the Poison: New Poems.* Copyright © 2003 by Andrew Hudgins. Reprinted by permission of the Overlook Press, New York, NY. "The Cow." First published in *Poetry,* vol. 188 (July/August 2006). Copyright © 2006 by Andrew Hudgins. Reprinted with the permission of the author. "Elegy for My Father, Who Is Not Dead" from *The Glass Hammer: A Southern Childhood* by Andrew Hudgins. Copyright © 1994 by Andrew Hudgins. Reprinted by permission of Houghton Mifflin Harcourt Publishing Company. All rights reserved.

Langston Hughes. "125th Street," "50-50," "Ballad of the Landlord," "Cross," "Danse Africaine," "Dinner Guest: Me," "Dream Boogie," "Dream Variations," "Esthete in Harlem," "Formula," "Frederick Douglass: 1817–1895," "Harlem," "Harlem Sweeties," "High to Low," "I, Too," "Jazzonia," "Ku Klux," "Lenox Avenue: Midnight," "Motto," "Negro," "The Negro Speaks of Rivers," "Old Walt," "Red Silk Stockings," "Rent-Party Shout: For a Lady Dancer," "Song for a Dark Girl," "Un-American Investigators," and "The Weary Blues," from *The Collected Poems of Langston Hughes* by Langston Hughes, edited by Arnold Rampersad with David Roessel, Associate Editor. Copyright © 1994 by the Estate of Langston Hughes. Used by permission of Alfred A. Knopf, a division of Random House, Inc. "On Harlem Rent Parties," excerpted from "When the Negro Was in Vogue" from *The Big Sea* by Langston Hughes. Copyright © 1940 by Langston Hughes. Copyright renewed © 1968 by Arna Bontemps and George Houston Bass. Reprinted by permission of Hill and Wang, a division of Farrar, Straus and Giroux, LLC. Langston Hughes's signature on page 1129 reprinted by permission of Harold Ober Associates, Incorporated.

Paul Humphrey. "Blow" from *Light Year '86.* Reprinted with the permission of Eleanor Humphrey.

Colette Inez. "Back When All Was Continuous Chuckles." Reprinted by permission from *The Hudson Review* Vol. LVII, No. 3 (Autumn 2004). Copyright © 2004 by Colette Inez.

Mark Jarman. "Unholy Sonnet" from *Questions for Ecclesiastes* by Mark Jarman (Story Line Press, 1997). Copyright © 1997 by Mark Jarman. Reprinted with permission of the author.

Randall Jarrell. "The Death of the Ball Turret Gunner" from *The Complete Poems* by Randall Jarrell. Copyright © 1969, renewed 1997 by Mary von S. Jarrell. Reprinted by permission of Farrar, Straus and Giroux, LLC.

Kelli Lyon Johnson. "Mapping an Identity" excerpted from *Julia Alvarez: Writing a New Place on the Map* by Kelli Lyon Johnson. Copyright © 2005 University of New Mexico Press. Reprinted by permission of the author and University of New Mexico Press.

Alice Jones. "The Foot" and "The Larynx" from *Anatomy* by Alice Jones (San Francisco: Bullnettle Press, 1997). Copyright © 1997 by Alice Jones. Reprinted by permission of the author.

Donald Justice. "Order in the Streets" from *Losers Weepers: Poems Found Practically Everywhere,* edited by George Hitchcock. Reprinted by permission of the Estate of Donald Justice.

Katherine Kearns, "On the Symbolic Setting of 'Home Burial,'" excerpted from "The Place Is the Asylum: Women and Nature in Robert Frost's Poetry" in *American Literature* 59:2 (May 1987), pp. 190–210. Copyright © 1987 by Duke University Press. All rights reserved. Used by permission of the publisher.

X. J. Kennedy. "On a Young Man's Remaining an Undergraduate for Twelve Years." First published in the *Sewanee Review* 114, no. 1 (Winter 2006). Copyright © 2006 by X. J. Kennedy. Reprinted with the permission of the editor and the author. "The Purpose of Time Is to Prevent Everything from Happening at Once" from *The Lords of Misrule,* p. 5. Copyright © 2002 by X. J. Kennedy. Reprinted with permission of The Johns Hopkins University Press.

Jane Kenyon. "The Blue Bowl" and "Surprise," copyright © 2005 by the Estate of Jane Kenyon. Reprinted from *Collected Poems* with the permission of Graywolf Press, Saint Paul, Minnesota, www.graywolfpress.org.

Marne L. Kilates. "Python in the Mall" from *Poems en Route* by Marne L. Kilates (University of Santo Tomas Publishing House, 1998). Copyright © 1998 by Marne L. Kilates. Reprinted with the permission of the author.

Galway Kinnell. "After Making Love We Hear Footsteps" and "Blackberry Eating" from *Three Books* by Galway Kinnell. Copyright © 1993 by Galway Kinnell. Reprinted by permission of Houghton Mifflin Harcourt Publishing Company. All rights reserved.

Carolyn Kizer. "After Bashō" from *Cool, Calm & Collected: Poems 1960–2000.* Copyright © 2001 by Carolyn Kizer. Reprinted with the permission of Copper Canyon Press, www.coppercanyonpress.org.

Trevor West Knapp. "Touch" from *Poetry* vol. 178 (August 2001), p. 268. Copyright © 2001 by Trevor West Knapp. Reprinted with the permission of the author.

Yusef Komunyakaa. "Slam, Dunk, & Hook" from *Magic City.* Copyright © 1992 by Yusef Komunyakaa. Reprinted by permission of Wesleyan University Press, www.wesleyan.edu/wespress.

Maxine Kumin. "Though He Tarry" from *Still to Mow: Poems* by Maxine Kumin. Copyright © 2007 by Maxine Kumin. Used by permission of W. W. Norton & Company, Inc.

Philip Larkin. "A Study of Reading Habits" from *Collected Poems* by Philip Larkin. Copyright © 1988, 1989 by the Estate of Philip Larkin. Reprinted by permission of Farrar, Straus and Giroux, LLC. Also from *The Whitsun Weddings.* Copyright © 1964 by Philip Larkin. Reprinted by permission of Faber and Faber Ltd.

Ann Lauinger. "Marvell Noir." First appeared in *Parnassus: Poetry in Review* 28, no. 1 & 2 (2005). Copyright © 2005 by Ann Lauinger. Reprinted by permission of the author.

Tato Laviera. "AmeRícan" is reprinted with permission from the publisher of *AmeRícan* by Tato Laviera (© 2003 Arte Público Press–University of Houston).

David Lenson. "On the Contemporary Use of Rhyme" from "The Battle Is Joined: Formalists Take On Defenders of Free Verse," *The Chronicle of Higher Education* (February 24, 1988). Reprinted by permission of the author.

Phillis Levin. "May Day" from *May Day* by Phillis Levin. Copyright © 2008 by Phillis Marna Levin. Used by permission of Penguin, a division of Penguin Group (USA) Inc.

J. Patrick Lewis. "The Unkindest Cut" from *Light 5* (Spring 1993). Reprinted with the permission of the author.

Li Ho. "A Beautiful Girl Combs Her Hair," translated by David Young, from *Five T'ang Poets*. Copyright © 1990 by Oberlin College. Reprinted with the permission of Oberlin College Press, www.oberlin.edu/ocpress/.

Rachel Loden. "Locked Ward, Newtown, Connecticut." Copyright © 2005 by Rachel Loden. Reprinted by permission of the author.

Herbert Lomas. "The Fly's Poem about Emily." Reprinted by permission from *The Hudson Review* Vol. LXI, No. 1 (Spring 2008). Copyright © 2008 by Herbert Lomas.

Dave Lucas. "November," originally appeared in *Shenandoah* 57.1 (Spring 2007). Copyright © 2007 by Dave Lucas. Reprinted by permission of the author.

Thomas Lux. "Commercial Leech Farming Today" and "Onomatopoeia" from *New and Selected Poems, 1975–1995* by Thomas Lux. Copyright © 1997 by Thomas Lux. Reprinted by permission of Houghton Mifflin Harcourt Publishing Company. All rights reserved.

Thomas Lynch. "Liberty" from *Still Life in Milford* by Thomas Lynch. Copyright © 1998 by Thomas Lynch. Used by permission of W. W. Norton & Company, Inc.

Katharyn Howd Machan. "Hazel Tells LaVerne" from *Light Year '85*. Reprinted by permission of the author.

Haki R. Madhubuti. "The B Network" from *HeartLove: Wedding and Love Poems* by Haki R. Madhubuti. Copyright © 1998 by Haki R. Madhubuti. Reprinted by permission of Third World Press Inc., Chicago, Illinois.

Elaine Magarrell. "The Joy of Cooking" from *Sometime the Cow Kick Your Head, Light Year 88/89*. Reprinted with the permission of the author.

Julio Marzán. "Ethnic Poetry." Originally appeared in *Parnassus: Poetry in Review*. Reprinted by permission of the author. "The Translator at the Reception for Latin American Writers." Reprinted by permission of the author.

Donna Masini. "Slowly" from *Turning to Fiction: Poems* by Donna Masini. Copyright © 2004 by Donna Masini. Used by permission of W. W. Norton & Company, Inc.

Florence Cassen Mayers. "All-American Sestina," © 1996 Florence Cassen Mayers, as first published in *The Atlantic Monthly*. Reprinted with permission of the author.

David McCord. "Epitaph on a Waiter" from *Odds Without Ends*, copyright © 1954 by David T. W. McCord. Reprinted by permission of Arthur B. Page, executor of the estate of David McCord.

Walt McDonald. "Coming Across It" from *Embers* 13, no. 1 (1988), p. 17. Copyright © 1988 by Walt McDonald. Reprinted with the permission of the author.

Michael McFee. "In Medias Res" from *Colander* by Michael McFee. Copyright © 1996 by Michael McFee. Reprinted by permission of the author.

Peter Meinke. "The ABC of Aerobics" from *Night Watch on the Chesapeake* by Peter Meinke. Copyright © 1987. "Unnatural Light" from *Scars* by Peter Meinke. Copyright © 1996. "(Untitled)" ["This is a poem to my son Peter"] from *Liquid Paper: New and Selected Poems* by Peter Meinke. Copyright © 1991. All poems reprinted by permission of the University of Pittsburgh Press.

James Merrill. "Casual Wear" from *Selected Poems, 1946–1985* by James Merrill. Copyright © 1992 by James Merrill. Used by permission of Alfred A. Knopf, a division of Random House, Inc.

Edna St. Vincent Millay. "I will put Chaos into fourteen lines" from *Collected Poems*, HarperCollins. Copyright © 1954, 1982 by Norma Millay Ellis. All rights reserved. Reprinted by permission of Elizabeth Barnett, literary executor.

Susan Minot. "My Husband's Back." Copyright © 2005 by Susan Minot. Originally appeared in *The New Yorker* (August 22, 2005). Reprinted by permission of Georges Borchardt, Inc., on behalf of the author.

Janice Mirikitani. "Recipe," reprinted with permission from *Shedding Silence* by Janice Mirikitani. Copyright © 1987 by Janice Mirikitani, Celestial Arts, Berkeley, CA, www.tenspeed.com.

Elaine Mitchell. "Form" from *Light 9* (Spring 1994). Reprinted by permission of the author.

Janice Townley Moore. "To a Wasp" first appeared in *Light Year*, Bits Press. Reprinted by permission of the author.

Pat Mora. "Legal Alien" is reprinted with permission from the publisher of *Chants* by Pat Mora (© 1986 Arte Público Press–University of Houston).

Robert Morgan. "Fever Wit" from *Topsoil Road: Poems* by Robert Morgan. Copyright © 2000 by Robert Morgan. Reprinted by permission of Louisiana State University Press. "Mountain Graveyard" and "Overalls" from *Sigodlin*. Copyright © 1990 by Robert Morgan. Reprinted by permission of Wesleyan University Press, www.wesleyan.edu/wespress.

Thylias Moss. "Tornados" from *Rainbow Remnants in Rock Bottom Ghetto Sky* by Thylias Moss. Copyright © 1991 by Thylias Moss. Reprinted by permission of Persea Books, Inc. (New York).

Harryette Mullen. "Blah-Blah" from *Sleeping with the Dictionary* by Harryette Mullen. Copyright © 2002 by Harryette Mullen. Reprinted by permission of the Regents of the University of California and the publisher, the University of California Press.

Joan Murray. "Play-By-Play." Reprinted by permission from *The Hudson Review* Vol. XLIX, no. 4 (Winter 1997). Copyright © 1997 by Joan Murray. "We Old Dudes," copyright © 2006 by Joan Murray. First appeared in the July/August 2006 issue of *Poetry* magazine. Reprinted by permission of the author.

Taslima Nasrin. "At the Back of Progress . . . ," translated by Carolyne Wright and Mohammad Nurul Huda, from *The Game in Reverse: Poems* by Taslima Nasrin. Copyright © 1995 by Taslima Nasrin. English translation © 1995 by Carolyne Wright. Reprinted with the permission of George Braziller, Inc.

Marilyn Nelson. "Emily Dickinson's Defunct" from *For the Body: Poems* by Marilyn Nelson Waniek. Copyright © 1978 by Marilyn Nelson Waniek. Reprinted by permission of the author and Louisiana State University Press. "How I Discovered Poetry" from *The Fields of Praise: New and Selected Poems* by Marilyn Nelson. Copyright © 1997 by Marilyn Nelson. Reprinted by permission of the author and Louisiana State University Press.

Howard Nemerov. "Because You Asked about the Line between Prose and Poetry" from *Sentences* by Howard Nemerov. Copyright © 1980. "Walking the Dog" from *Trying Conclusions: New and Selected Poems 1961–1991.* Copyright © 1991. Reprinted by permission.

Pablo Neruda. "The United Fruit Co." from *Neruda & Vallejo: Selected Poems,* ed. and translated by Robert Bly. Reprinted with the permission of Robert Bly. "Verbo," poem from the work *Las Manos del Dia.* © Fundación Pablo Neruda, 1968. Reprinted by permission of Carmen Balcells Literary Agency, Barcelona, Spain, on behalf of the Pablo Neruda Foundation of Chile. "Word" ("Verbo" in English) from *Five Decades: Poems, 1925–1970* by Pablo Neruda, translated by Ben Belitt. Copyright © 1974 by Grove Press, Inc. Translation copyright © 1974 by Ben Belitt. Used by permission of Grove/Atlantic, Inc. "Word," translation by Kristin Linklater and Gilda Orlandi-Sanchez, from *Freeing Shakespeare's Voice: The Actor's Guide to Talking the Text* by Kristin Linklater. Copyright © 1992. Used by permission.

John Frederick Nims. "Love Poem" from *Selected Poems.* Copyright © 1982 by the University of Chicago. Reprinted by permission of the University of Chicago Press.

Alden Nowlan. "The Bull Moose" from *Alden Nowlan: Selected Poems* by Alden Nowlan. Copyight © 1967. Reprinted by permission of House of Anansi Press, Toronto.

Adrian Oktenberg. "Memory in 'The Negro Speaks of Rivers,' " excerpted from "From the Bottom Up: Three Radicals of the Thirties" in *A Gift of Tongues: Critical Challenges in Contemporary American Poetry,* ed. Marie Harris and Kathleen Aguero. Copyright © 1987. Reprinted by permission of the University of Georgia Press. [pp. 95–96]

Sharon Olds. "Last Night" from *The Wellspring* by Sharon Olds. Copyright © 1996 by Sharon Olds. Used by permission of Alfred A. Knopf, a division of Random House, Inc. "Rite of Passage" from *The Dead and the Living* by Sharon Olds. Copyright © 1987 by Sharon Olds. Used by permission of Alfred A. Knopf, a division of Random House, Inc.

Mary Oliver. "Oxygen" and "The Poet with His Face in His Hands" from *New and Selected Poems, Volume Two,* by Mary Oliver. Copyright © 2005 by Mary Oliver. Reprinted by permission of Beacon Press, Boston.

Lisa Parker. "Snapping Beans," from *Parnassus* 23, no. 2 (1998). Reprinted by permission of the author.

Linda Pastan. "Jump Cabling" from *Light Year: The Quarterly of Light Verse.* Copyright © 1984 by Linda Pastan. Reprinted by permission of Jean V. Naggar Literary Agency, Inc. "Marks" from *PM/AM: New and Selected Poems* by Linda Pastan. Copyright © 1978 by Linda Pastan. Used by permission of W. W. Norton & Company, Inc. "Pass/Fail" from *Aspects of Eve* by Linda Pastan. Copyright © 1970, 1971, 1972, 1973, 1974, 1975 by Linda Pastan. Used by permission of Liveright Publishing Corporation. "To a Daughter Leaving Home" from *Carnival Evening: New and Selected Poems 1968–1998* by Linda Pastan. Copyright © 1998 by Linda Pastan. Used by permission of W. W. Norton & Company, Inc.

Octavio Paz. "The Street" from *Early Poems 1935–1955.* Reprinted with permission of Indiana University Press.

Molly Peacock. "Desire" from *Cornucopia: New and Selected Poems* by Molly Peacock. Copyright © 2002 by Molly Peacock. Used by permission of W. W. Norton & Company, Inc. "Of Night" from *The Second Blush: Poems* by Molly Peacock. Copyright © 2008 by Molly Peacock. Used by permission of W. W. Norton & Company, Inc., and McClelland & Stewart Ltd.

Peter Pereira. "Anagrammer" from *What's Written on the Body.* Copyright © 2007 by Peter Pereira. Reprinted with the permission of Copper Canyon Press, www.coppercanyonpress.org.

Laurence Perrine. "The limerick's never averse." Reprinted by permission of Douglas Perrine.

Kevin Pierce. "Proof of Origin" from *Light* 50 (Autumn 2005). Copyright © 2005 by Kevin Pierce. Reprinted with the permission of the author.

Marge Piercy. "The Secretary Chant" from *Circles on the Water* by Marge Piercy. Copyright © 1982 by Marge Piercy. Used by permission of Alfred A. Knopf, a division of Random House, Inc.

Sylvia Plath. "Mirror" from *Crossing the Water* by Sylvia Plath. Copyright © 1963 by Ted Hughes. Originally appeared in *The New Yorker.* Reprinted by permission of HarperCollins Publishers. Also from *Collected Poems* by Sylvia Plath, ed. Ted Hughes, reprinted by permission of Faber and Faber, Ltd.

Peter D. Poland. "On 'Neither Out Far nor In Deep,' " from *The Explicator* 52, no. 2 (Winter 1994). Reprinted with permission of the Helen Dwight Reid Educational Foundation. Published by Heldref Publications, 1319 Eighteenth Street, NW, Washington, DC, 20036-1802. Copyright © 1994.

Ezra Pound. "In a Station of the Metro" from *Personae.* Copyright © 1926 by Ezra Pound. Reprinted by permission of New Directions Publishing Corp. Photograph of Ezra Pound on page 2041: National Portrait Gallery, London.

Arnold Rampersad. "On the Persona in 'The Negro Speaks of Rivers' " from "The Origins of Poetry in Langston Hughes," *Southern Review* 21, no. 3 (1985), pp. 703–4. Copyright © 1985 by Arnold Rampersad. Reprinted by permission of the author.

Henry Reed. "Lessons of the War" (1. Naming of Parts) from *Henry Reed: Collected Poems,* ed. Jon Stallworthy. Copyright © 1946, 1947, 1970, 1991, 2007 by the Executor of Henry Reed's Estate. Reprinted by permission of Carcanet Press Ltd.

Marny Requa. "From an Interview with Julia Alvarez" excerpted from "The Politics of Fiction," *Frontera* 5 (1997). 29 January 1997, http://www.fronteramag.com/issue5/Alvarez/index.htm. Reprinted with the permission of Marny Requa.

David S. Reynolds. "Popular Literature and 'Wild Nights — Wild Nights!' " excerpted from *Beneath the American Renaissance* by David S. Reynolds. Copyright © 1988 by David S. Reynolds. Used by permission of Alfred A. Knopf, a division of Random House, Inc.

Rainer Maria Rilke. "The Panther" from *The Selected Poetry of Rainer Maria Rilke* by Rainer Maria Rilke, translated by Stephen Mitchell. Copyright © 1982 by Stephen Mitchell. Used by permission of Random House, Inc.

Alberto Ríos. "Northern Desert Towns in the Turn of the Old Century" from *Theater of Night.* Copyright © 2006 by Alberto Ríos. Reprinted with the permission of Copper Canyon Press, www.coppercanyonpress.org. "The Gathering Evening" from *The Smallest Muscle in the Human Body.* Copyright © 2002 by Alberto Ríos. Reprinted with the permission of Copper Canyon Press, www.coppercanyonpress.org. "Seniors" from *Five Indiscretions.* Copyright © 1985 by Alberto Ríos. Reprinted by permission of the author.

Theodore Roethke. "Elegy for Jane," copyright © 1950 by Theodore Roethke, "My Papa's Waltz," copyright 1942 by Hearst Magazines, Inc., "Root Cellar," copyright 1943 by Modern Poetry Association, Inc., from *Collected Poems of Theodore Roethke* by Theodore Roethke. Used by permission of Doubleday, a division of Random House, Inc.

Jay Rogoff. "Death's Theater." First published in the *Sewanee Review* 114, no. 4 (Fall 2006). Copyright © 2006 by Jay Rogoff. Reprinted with the permission of the editor and the author.

Frederik L. Rusch. "Society and Character in 'The Love Song of J. Alfred Prufrock'" from "Approaching Literature through the Social Psychology of Erich Fromm" in *Psychological Perspectives on Literature: Freudian Dissidents and Non-Freudians,* edited by Joseph Natoli. Copyright © 1984. Reprinted by permission of the author.

Kay Ryan. "Hailstorm" from *The Niagara River* by Kay Ryan. Copyright © 2005 by Kay Ryan. Used by permission of Grove/Atlantic, Inc.

Michael Ryan. "Bunny" from *New and Selected Poems* by Michael Ryan. Copyright © 2004 by Michael Ryan. Reprinted by permission of Houghton Mifflin Harcourt Publishing Company. All rights reserved.

Yousif al-Sa'igh. "An Iraqi Evening," translated by Saadi A. Simawe, Ralph Savarese, and Chuck Miller, from *Iraqi Poetry Today,* ed. Saadi Simawe (Modern Poetry in Translation, 2003). Copyright © 2003 by Modern Poetry in Translation. Reprinted by permission of Modern Poetry in Translation.

Sonia Sanchez. "c'mon man hold me" from *Like the Singing Coming Off the Drums: Love Poems* by Sonia Sanchez. Copyright © 1998 by Sonia Sanchez. Reprinted by permission of Beacon Press, Boston. "Summer Words of a Sistuh Addict" from *We a BaddDDD People* by Sonia Sanchez, copyright © 1970 by Sonia Sanchez and published by the Broadside Press. Reprinted by permission of the author.

Peter Schmitt. "Friends with Numbers" from *Hazard Duty.* Copyright © 1995 by Peter Schmitt. Used by permission of Copper Beech Press.

Elisabeth Schneider. "Hints of Eliot in Prufrock." Reprinted by permission of the Modern Language Association of America from "Prufrock and After: The Theme of Change," *PMLA* 87 (1982): 1103–1117.

S. Pearl Sharp. "It's the Law: A Rap Poem" from *Typing in the Dark* (Writers and Readers Publishing, Inc., 1991). Reprinted in *African American Literature* 1998. Used by permission of the author.

Shu Ting. "O Motherland, Dear Motherland" (translated by Fang Dai, Dennis Ding, and Edward Morin) from *The Red Azalea: Chinese Poetry Since the Cultural Revolution,* ed. Edward Morin (Honolulu: U Hawai'i Press, 1990). Reprinted by permission of the University of Hawai'i Press.

Leslie Marmon Silko. "Love Poem." Copyright © 1970 by Leslie Marmon Silko. Reprinted with permission of The Wylie Agency LLC.

Charles Simic. "In the Library" from *The Book of Gods and Devils.* Copyright © 1990 by Charles Simic. Reprinted by permission of Houghton Mifflin Harcourt Publishing Company. "The Storm" from *The Virginia Quarterly Review* 84, no. 2 (Spring 2008), p. 92. Copyright © 2008 by Charles Simic. Reprinted by permission of the author.

Louis Simpson. "In the Suburbs" from *At the End of the Open Road* by Louis Simpson. Wesleyan University Press, 1963. Reprinted by permission of the author.

Floyd Skloot. "Winter Solstice" from *Approximately Paradise* by Floyd Skloot, published by Tupelo Press. Copyright © 2005 by Floyd Skloot. All rights reserved. Reproduced by permission of Tupelo Press.

David R. Slavitt. "Titanic" from *Change of Address: Poems New and Selected* by David R. Slavitt. Copyright © 2005 by David R. Slavitt. Reprinted by permission of Louisiana State University Press.

Ernest Slyman. "Lightning Bugs" from *Sometime the Cow Kick Your Head, Light Year 88/89.* Reprinted by permission of the author.

Patricia Smith. "What It's Like to Be a Black Girl (for Those of You Who Aren't)" from *Life According to Motown* by Patricia Smith. Copyright © 1991 by Patricia Smith. Reprinted by permission of the author.

Gary Snyder. "How Poetry Comes to Me" from *No Nature* by Gary Snyder. Copyright © 1992 by Gary Snyder. Used by permission of Pantheon Books, a division of Random House, Inc.

David Solway. "Windsurfing." Reprinted by permission of the author.

Cathy Song. "A Poet in the House" from *The Land of Bliss* by Cathy Song. Copyright © 2001. Reprinted by permission of the University of Pittsburgh Press. "The White Porch" and "The Youngest Daughter" from *Picture Bride.* Copyright © 1983 by Yale University Press. Reprinted by permission of Yale University Press. Photograph of Cathy Song on pages 739 and 1297 from School Figures, by Cathy Song, © 1994. Reprinted by permission of the University of Pittsburgh Press.

Gary Soto. "Behind Grandma's House" and "Mexicans Begin Jogging" from *New and Selected Poems* by Gary Soto. Copyright © 1995. Used with permission of Chronicle Books, LLC, San Francisco. Visit ChronicleBooks.com.

Bruce Springsteen. "You're Missing." Copyright © 2002 by Bruce Springsteen (ASCAP). Reprinted by permission. International copyright secured. All rights reserved.

William Stafford. "Traveling through the Dark," from *The Way It Is: New & Selected Poems.* Copyright © 1962, 1998 by the Estate of William Stafford. Reprinted with the permission of Graywolf Press, Saint Paul, Minnesota, www.graywolfpress.org.

Timothy Steele. "Waiting for the Storm" from *Sapphics and Uncertainties: Poems, 1970–1986.* Copyright © 1986, 1995 by Timothy Steele. Reprinted with the permission of the University of Arkansas Press, www.uapress.com.

Jim Stevens. "Schizophrenia." Originally appeared in *Light: The Quarterly of Light Verse* (Spring 1992). Copyright © 1992 by Jim Stevens. Reprinted by permission.

Wallace Stevens. "Anecdote of the Jar" from *The Collected Poems of Wallace Stevens* by Wallace Stevens. Copyright © 1954 by Wallace Stevens and renewed 1982 by Holly Stevens. Used by permission of Alfred A. Knopf, a division of Random House, Inc.

Robert Sward. "A Personal Analysis of 'The Love Song of J. Alfred Prufrock'" from *Touchstones: American Poets on a Favorite Poem,* ed. Robert Pack and Jay Parini, Middlebury College Press, published by UP New England. Copyright © 1995, 1997, 2000 by Robert Sward. Reprinted by permission of the author.

May Swenson. "All That Time" from *The Complete Love Poems of May Swenson.* Copyright © 1991, 2003 by the Literary Estate of May Swenson. Reprinted by permission of Houghton Mifflin Harcourt Publishing Company. All rights reserved. "A Nosty Fright" from *In Other Words* by May Swenson, 1987. Copyright © 1984 by May Swenson. Used with permission of the Literary Estate of May Swenson.

Dylan Thomas. "Do Not Go Gentle into That Good Night," copyright © 1952 by Dylan Thomas. Reprinted by permission of New Directions Publishing Corp. "The Hand That Signed the Paper," copyright © 1939 by New Directions Publishing Corporation, from *The Poems of Dylan Thomas.* Reprinted by permission of New Directions Publishing Corp.

Mabel Loomis Todd. "The Character of Amherst" from *The Years and Hours of Emily Dickinson,* volume 2, by Jay Leyda. Copyright © 1960 by Yale University Press. Reprinted by permission of Yale University Press.

Tomas Tranströmer. "April and Silence," trans. Robin Fulton, from *New Collected Poems* (Bloodaxe Books, 1997). Copyright © 1997 by Robin Fulton and Bloodaxe Books. Reprinted by permission of Bloodaxe Books Ltd.

Natasha Trethewey. "On Captivity." First published in *Five Points: A Journal of Literature and Art* vol. 11, no. 3 (2007). Copyright © 2007 by Natasha Trethewey. Reprinted by permission of the author.

Mark Turpin. "Sledgehammer's Song" from *Hammer: Poems.* Copyright © 2003 by Mark Turpin. Reprinted with the permission of Sarabande Books, www.sarabandebooks.org.

John Updike. "Dog's Death" from *Midpoint and Other Poems* by John Updike. Copyright © 1969 and renewed 1997 by John Updike. Used by permission of Alfred A. Knopf, a division of Random House, Inc. "Player Piano" from *Collected Poems, 1953–1993* by John Updike. Copyright © 1993 by John Updike. Used by permission of Alfred A. Knopf, a division of Random House, Inc.

Lee Upton. "Dyserotica" from *Undid in the Land of the Undone* by Lee Upton. Copyright © 2007. Reprinted by permission of New Issues Press.

Richard Wakefield. "The Bell Rope" from *East of Early Winters: Poems* by Richard Wakefield (University of Evansville Press, 2006). Copyright © 2006 by Richard Wakefield. Reprinted with permission from the author. "In a Poetry Workshop," *Light* (Winter 1999). Reprinted with permission from the author.

Derek Walcott. Excerpt from "The Road Taken" from *Homage to Robert Frost* by Joseph Brodsky, Seamus Heaney, and Derek Walcott. Copyright © 1996 by the Estate of Joseph Brodsky, Seamus Heaney, and Derek Walcott. Reprinted by permission of Farrar, Straus & Giroux, LLC.

Ronald Wallace. "Building an Outhouse" from *Makings of Happiness* by Ronald Wallace. Copyright © 1991. Reprinted by permission of the University of Pittsburgh Press. "In a Rut" from *The Best American Poetry 2003,* ed. Yusef Komunyakaa. Originally published in *Poetry Northwest.* Copyright © 2003. Reprinted by permission of the author. "Miss Goff" from the poem sequence "Teachers: A Primer," from *Time's Fancy* by Ronald Wallace. Copyright © 1994. Reprinted by permission of the University of Pittsburgh Press.

Bruce Weigl. "Snowy Egret" from *The Monkey Wars* by Bruce Weigl. Copyright © 1985. Reprinted by permission of the University of Georgia Press.

Gail White. "Dead Armadillos." Copyright © 2000 by Gail White. Reprinted by permission of the author.

C. K. Williams. "Shock" from *Repair* by C. K. Williams. Copyright © 1999 by C. K. Williams. Reprinted by permission of Farrar, Straus & Giroux, LLC. "The United States," *The New Yorker,* April 16, 2007. Copyright © 2007 by C. K. Williams. Reprinted by permission of the author.

Miller Williams. "Thinking about Bill, Dead of AIDS" from *Living on the Surface: New and Selected Poems* by Miller Williams. Copyright © 1972, 1975, 1976, 1979, 1980, 1987, 1988, 1989 by Miller Williams. Reprinted by permission of the author.

William Carlos Williams. "Poem," copyright © 1953 by William Carlos Williams, "The Red Wheelbarrow," copyright © 1938 by New Directions Publishing Corp., "Spring and All," copyright © 1938 by New Directions Publishing Corp, "This Is Just to Say," copyright © 1938 by New Directions Publishing Corp., from *Collected Poems: 1909–1939,* Volume I. Reprinted by permission of New Directions Publishing Corp.

Cynthia Griffin Wolff. "On the Many Voices in Dickinson's Poetry" excerpted from *Emily Dickinson* by Cynthia Griffin Wolff. Copyright © 1986 by Cynthia Griffin Wolff. Used by permission of Alfred A. Knopf, a division of Random House, Inc.

Baron Wormser. "Labor" from *Scattered Chapters: New and Selected Poems.* Copyright © 2008 by Baron Wormser. "Shoplifting" from *When.* Copyright © 1997 by Baron Wormser. Both poems reprinted with the permission of Sarabande Books, www.sarabandebooks.org.

William Butler Yeats. "Crazy Jane Talks with the Bishop." Reprinted with the permission of Scribner, a division of Simon & Schuster, Inc., from *The Collected Works of W. B. Yeats, Volume I: The Poems, Revised,* ed. Richard J. Finneran. Copyright © 1933 by the Macmillan Company. Copyright renewed © 1961 by Bertha Georgie Yeats. All rights reserved. "Leda and the Swan." Reprinted with the permission of Scribner, a division of Simon & Schuster, Inc., from *The Collected Works of W. B. Yeats, Volume I: The Poems, Revised,* ed. Richard J. Finneran. Copyright © 1928 by the Macmillan Company. Copyright renewed © 1956 by Bertha Georgie Yeats. All rights reserved. "Sailing to Byzantium." Reprinted with the permission of Scribner, a division of Simon & Schuster, Inc., from *The Collected Works of W. B. Yeats, Volume I: The Poems, Revised,* ed. Richard J. Finneran. Copyright © 1928 by the Macmillan

DRAMA

Thematic Contents

Love and Longing

Teaching and Learning

Humor and Satire

Culture and Identity

Home and Family

Nature

Animals

Language and Literature

Grief and Loss

Place

Ethics

Violence, War, and Peace

Race and Stereotypes

Travel

Gender

Sexuality

Index of First Lines

Index of Authors and Titles

Index of Terms

Boldface numbers refer to the Glossary of Literary Terms

"This is the best anthology of literature for an introductory course. No other text comes close."
— S. Elaine Craghead, *Massachusetts Maritime Academy*

"*The Bedford Introduction to Literature* is the most comprehensive and flexible text I have ever used. It lends itself to a wide variety of approaches without sacrificing quality. Meyer's tone is accessible to students at the same time that it challenges them to engage in a higher level of academic debate and discussion."
— Cathy Henrichs, *Pikes Peak Community College, Colorado*

"This is the only book an instructor needs to introduce students to the world of knowledge and pleasure that literature can offer."
— Gregory J. Underwood, *Pearl River Community College, Mississippi*

"*The Bedford Introduction to Literature* sets the standard in its field."
— Ronald Dotterer, *Salisbury University, Maryland*